SWEDISH-ENGLISH

DICTIONARY

PRISMA'S

SWEDISH

ENGLISH
D I C T I O N A R Y

UNIVERSITY OF MINNESOTA PRESS, MINNEAPOLIS AND LONDON
BOKFÖRLAGET PRISMA STOCKHOLM

Published by the University of Minnesota Press
2037 University Avenue Southeast,
Minneapolis MN 55414, U.S.A.
and Bokförlaget Prisma, Kungsgatan 44, Box 3192
103 63 Stockholm, Sweden
Printed in the United States of America on acid-free paper.

Library of Congress Cataloging in Publication Data
ISBN 0-8166-1732-5
Catalog Card Number 89-51075

The University of Minnesota
is an equal-opportunity
educator and employer.

FOREWORD

This dictionary has been compiled by Bokförlaget Prisma's Dictionary Editorial Office by Eva Gomer and Mona Morris-Nygren in collaboration with Erik Durrant, Michael Knight, Hans Nygren, Michael Phillips, Sture Sundell, and Gösta Åberg. The lexicographic advisor was Bertil Molde. The reworking of the fourth edition was the responsibility of Sture Sundell, Bengt Ellenberger, Hans Lindquist, and Birgit Örsmark. It contains approximately 54,000 headwords and 15,000 phrases, expressions, and other language constructions.

The selection of headwords reflects modern language usage. Technical terms within different fields, everyday usage, and slang expressions are abundantly represented. Even certain registered trademarks have been included. The fourth edition has been enlarged by over 2,000 new headwords.

For the benefit of non-Swedish readers in particular the book includes pronunciation and stress for the Swedish headwords as well as information about inflections of nouns, verbs, and adjectives. The principles employed are explained in the Notes on the Use of the Dictionary.

The grammatical apparatus is the simplest possible. Self-explanatory expressions rather than grammatical terminology have been used whenever possible.

All important available dictionaries and reference works have been consulted in the compiling of this dictionary. Those extensively consulted include *Collins Dictionary of the English Language*, *Collins Cobuild English Language Dictionary*, *The Concise Oxford Dictionary*, *The Advanced Learner's Dictionary of Current English*, *The American Heritage Dictionary*, *Svartvik-Sager Engelsk universitetsgrammatik*, *Illustrerad svensk ordbok*, *Svensk ordbok*, *Svensk Handordbok*, and *Nyrod i svenskan från 40-tal till 80-tal*.

BOKFÖRLAGET PRISMA
DICTIONARY EDITORIAL OFFICE

NOTES ON THE USE
OF THE DICTIONARY

General

The Swedish headwords are arranged in strict alphabetical order, e.g. **bildäck, bildöverföring, bilersättning**. Field labels appear in italics before the English translation, e.g. *tekn., mil., sport.* (see list of abbreviations, p. 15). American alternatives of the English translations are marked *AE*.

Symbols

If a headword has more than one meaning, each different part of speech is indicated by means of a roman numeral. Entirely different meanings within each part of speech are indicated by arabic numerals, smaller differences in meaning are indicated by a semi-colon.

| | stands after the part of a headword that reappears in one or more successive entries. It is also sometimes used for the sake of clarity to show how a word is made up, e.g. **bil|drulle**

- indicates the part of the entry separated by |, or (in compounds and derivatives) the entire preceding entry, e.g. **berör|a, -ing** (= **beröra, beröring**), **fasad, -klättrare** (= **fasad, fasadklättrare**).

-- indicates that the following word element is preceded by a hyphen. Note the difference, in the article on **svensk/amerikan** and its compounds, between **-amerikansk** (= **svenskamerikansk**) and **--engelsk** (= **svensk-engelsk**).

~ within the article indicates the entire headword, e.g. **arm** *gå ~ i ~, med ~arna i kors.*

( ) is used for complementary explanations, e.g. **hösäck** (*tom*) haysack; (*full*) sack of hay, and for alternative words and phrases, e.g. *ta ett hinder* (*sport.*) jump (take, clear) a hurdle (fence).

[ ] is used round the phonetic transcription and round a word or part of a word that can be omitted, e.g. **fönsterlucka** [window]shutter.

Spelling

With a very few exceptions British spelling has been used throughout the dictionary. The most important differences in spelling between British and

American English are listed below.

British usage	American usage	
travelling, waggon	traveling, wagon	A double consonant is sometimes written as a single consonant.
colour, neighbour	color, neighbor	The ending -our is written as -or.
metre, theatre	meter, theater	-re at the end of a word is usually written as -er.
cheque, plough, cata-logue, programme	check, plow, catalog, program	Letter combinations de-noting a single sound are sometimes simplified.
defence	defense	-ce at the end of a word is sometimes written as -se.

Abbreviations *see* p. 15.

Irregular verbs

The past participle and the supine of irregular Swedish verbs are given as headwords with a reference to the infinitive.

PRONUNCIATION OF
THE SWEDISH WORDS

Tone and stress

There are two kinds of tone in Swedish: the acute accent, or singletone, and the grave accent, or double-tone. The acute accent is a falling tone, as in English beggar, calendar. It occurs in words of one syllable and in a few words of two or more syllables. In this dictionary the acute accent in words of two or more syllables with the stress on the first syllable is always indicated in the phonetic transcription. The grave accent, which is characteristic of the Swedish language, occurs in words of two or more syllables. It is also a falling tone, but the second syllable begins on a higher pitch than the first. The main stress usually lies on the first syllable and there is a strong secondary stress on the second syllable.

Most Swedish words of two or more syllables have the stress on the first syllable and the grave accent.

Words with the following endings have the stress on the last syllable:

**-ang, -ant, -at, -ent, -eri, -ess, -ion, -ism,
-ist, -log, -nom, -tet, -tris, -ur, -ör, -ös**

Words with the following endings have the stress on the penultimate syllable:

-era, -inna, -issa

In words that are not pronounced in accordance with these rules, the stress is marked. When only the stress is indicated, this is done by means of a dot under the vowel of the stressed syllable in the headword. The stress may also be indicated in the phonetic transcription, where one is given (see below).

Pronunciation

The first column contains the Swedish letters and the second column the phonetic symbols used in this dictionary.

Vowels

a [aː] as in father. E.g. *far* [faːr].
[a] similar to the first element in the English diphthong in time, the French a in la, the German a in kann. E.g. *hatt* [hatt].

e [eː] has no exact English equivalent, is pronounced as in French les, German mehr. E.g. *leta* [ˣleːta], *se* [seː].
[e] as in let. E.g. *detta* [ˣdetta].

i [iː] as in three. E.g. *lida* [ˣliːda].
[i] similar to the i in fit. E.g. *sitta* [ˣsitta].

o [ɔː] similar to the vowel in too. E.g. *ropa* [ˣrɔːpa].
[ɔ] similar to the vowel in put. E.g. *hon* [hɔnn].

u [uː] has no English equivalent. Tongue position as for [eː] above, but lips rounded. E.g. *luta* [ˣluːta], *hus* [huːs].
[u] similar to English [ə] in letter, but lips rounded. E.g. *kulle* [ˣkulle].

y [yː] similar to the French u in rue, the German ü in früh, but lips more protruded and rounded. E.g. *gryta* [ˣgryːta], *sy* [syː].
[y] short [yː], compare French lune, German müssen. E.g. *syster* [ˣsysster], *hylla* [ˣhylla].

å [åː] similar to the vowel in saw. E.g. *båt* [båːt].
[å] as in long. E.g. *lång* [låŋ].

ä [äː] before r similar to the first element in the diphthong in bear. E.g. *bära* [ˣbäːra]. In other cases less open as in French chaise. E.g. *träd* [träːd], *läsa* [ˣläːsa], *säl* [säːl].
[ä] before r as in carry. E.g. *värre* [ˣvärre], *ärta* [ˣärrta]. In other cases similar to e in set. E.g. *mätt* [mätt].

ö [öː] before r similar to the vowel in bird. E.g. *höra* [ˣhöːra]. In other cases the sound is similar to the vowel in French deux, German Öl.
[ö] before r similar to the vowel in English cup, but lips rounded. E.g. *dörr* [dörr]. In other cases similar to the final vowel in English better. E.g. *höst* [hösst].

Consonants

b [b] as English b.

c [s] as in sea. E.g. *cykel* ['sykkel].

ch [ʃ] as in shall. E.g. *choklad* [ʃɔk'la:d].

ck [k] as English k.

d [d] as English d, but pronounced with the tongue against the back of the upper teeth.

f [f] as English f.

g [g] as English g in great, good, before a, o, u, å or unstressed -e. E.g. *god* [gɔ:d], *gul* [gu:l], *fågel* ['få:gel].

    [j] as English y in yes, before e, i, y, ä, ö and after l and r. E.g. *ge* [je:], *gynna* [ˣjynna], *göra* [ˣjö:ra], *arg* [arj].

    [k] as English k, before t. E.g. *sagt* [sakt].

gj [j] as English y in yes. E.g. *gjort* [jɔ:rt].

gn [ŋn] E.g. *regn* [reŋn].

h [h] as English h.

j [j] as English y in yes. E.g. *ja* [ja:].

k [k] as English k, before a, o, u, å. E.g. *kall* [kall], *kål* [kå:l].

    [ç] similar to the initial sound in child, but without the beginning t-sound, compare German ich. Comes before e, i, y, ä, ö. E.g. *kela* [ˣçe:la], *kyla* [ˣçy:la], *kött* [çött].

l [l] as English *l*.

m [m] as English *m*.

n [n] as English *n*.

ng [ŋ] as in song. E.g. *mangel* ['maŋel]. Note no g-sound should be heard after the ŋ-sound as it is in English.

p [p] as English *p*.

q [k] as English *k*.

r [r] similar to English r but rolled.

rd [rd] similar to rd, rt in ford, cart in British pronounciation. In the

rt [rt] phonetic transcription written rd, rt. E.g. *bord* [bɔ:rd], *sort* [sårrt].

rs [rs] pronounced as sh in shall. In the phonetic transcription written rs. E.g. *brorson* [ˣbrɔ:rså:n].

s [s] as English s in see (voiceless).

sch [ʃ] similar to sh in she. E.g. *marsh* [marʃ], *dimension* [dimen'ʃɔ:n],

si(on) *själv* [ʃällv], skjuta [ˣʃu:ta], *stjärna* [ˣʃä:rna]. (Most Swedes use a

sj different sound, which is, however, difficult for foreigners to

skj produce.)

stj

t [t] as English t, but pronounced with the tongue against the back of the upper teeth.

ti(on) [ʃ] see sch etc. above.

tj [ç] similar to the initial sound in child, but without the initial t-sound, compare German ich. E.g. *tjänst* [çänst], *tjuv* [çu:v].

v, w [v] as English v.

x [ks] never pronounced gs, as in example.

z [s] pronounced as English s in see (voiceless).

11

In addition to the phonetic symbols given after the Swedish letters above, the following symbols are used:

′ indicates acute accent. E.g. *allting* [′alltiŋ].
ˣ indicates grave accent. E.g. *arton* [ˣa:rtån].
: indicates long vowel. E.g. *adjö* [a′jö:].
- is used when only part of the word is transcribed. E.g. *alligator* [-ˣa:tår].

A consonant following a short, stressed vowel is written twice. E.g. *banjo* [′bann-].

It has not been considered necessary to give the pronounciation of ch, sch, stj where they are pronounced [ʃ], of -sion, -tion where they are pronounced [ʃo:n], of ng where it is pronounced [ŋ] or of c where it is pronounced [s].

No pronounciation is given for compounds. The reader is referred to the separate words which make up the compound. Within an article containing several headwords the first word normally gives the stress and pronounciation of the following words, but not the accent. For practical reasons only one pronounciation has often been given for words which have two or more possible pronounciations.

INFLECTION OF NOUNS, ADJECTIVES, AND VERBS

The following codes are used:

Nouns

The forms given are: sg indefinite – sg definite – pl indefinite.

s1	flicka – flickan – flickor
	toffel – toffeln – tofflor
	ros – rosen – rosor
s2	pojke – pojken – pojkar
	dag – dagen – dagar
	dager – dagern – dagrar
	dagg – daggen – no pl
	sky – skyn – skyar
	mun – munnen – munnar
	lämmel – lämmeln – lämlar
	kam – kammen – kammar
s3	rad – raden – rader
	doktor – doktorn – doktorer [-'to:-]
	filosofi – filosofin – filosofier
	djungel – djungeln – djungler

12

kollega – kollega*n* – kolleg*er*
pilgrim – pilgrim*en* – pilgrim*er*
konsul – konsul*n* – konsul*er* [-'su:]
parallellogram – parallellogramm*en* – parallellogramm*er*

s4   bryggeri – bryggeri*et* – bryggeri*er*
     fängelse – fängels*et* – fängels*er*
     studium – studi*et* – studi*er*
     drama – dramat – dram*er*

s5   sko – sko*n* – sko*r*
     hustru – hustru*n* – hustru*r*

s6   äpple – äpple*t* – äpple*n*
     schema – schema*t* – schema*n*

s7   *träd – trädet –* träd
     damm – damm*et* – no pl
     garage – garag*et* – garage
     fönster – fönstr*et* – fönster
     kummel – kuml*et* – kummel
     kapitel – kapitl*et* – kapitel
     gram – gramm*et* – gram

s8   faktum – faktum[et] – fakta or faktum
     centrum – centret or centrum[et] – centra or centrum
     natrium – natrium[et] or natriet – no pl

s9   studerande – studerand*en* – studerande
     hänsyn – hänsyn*en* – hänsyn

The same codes are used for nouns which have no plural form. For nouns with the following common endings no code is given in the entry.

-ang	*-en -er*
-ant	*-en -er*
-are	*-n =*
-at	*-en -er*
-else	*-n -r*
-ent	*-en -er*
-er	*-n =*
-eri	*-[e]t -er*
-ersk|a	*-an -or*
-ess	*-en -er*
-het	*-en -er*
-ing	*-en -ar*
-inn|a [-ˣinna]	*-an -or*
-ion	*-en -er*
-ism	*-en no pl*
-iss|a] [-ˣissa]	*-an -or*
-ist	*-en -er*
-log [-ˊlå:g]	*-en -er*
-ning	*-en -ar*
-nom [-ˊnå:m]	*-en -er*
-sk|a	*-an -or*
-tet	*-en no pl*
-tris	*-en -er*
-ur	*-en -er*
-ôr	*-en -er*
-ôs	*-en -er*

Indeclinable nouns are marked *n* (neuter) or *r* (common gender). For irregular nouns which do not fit the above paradigms the inflected forms are given in full, together with the gender if this is not evident from the forms.

Adjectives

The forms given are: positive – neuter positive – comparative – superlative.

al   stark – stark*t* – stark*are* – stark*ast*
      stilig – stilig*t* – stilig*are* – stilig*ast*
      lätt – lätt – lätt*are* – lätt*ast*
      röd – rött – röd*are* – röd*ast*
      fri – fri*tt* – fri*are* – fri*ast*
      vit – vi*tt* – vit*are* – vit*ast*
      blond – blon*t* – blond*are* – blond*ast*
      tunn – tun*t* – tunn*are* – tunn*ast*
      följsam – följsam*t* – följsamm*are* – följsamm*ast*
      allmän – allmän*t* – allmänn*are* – allmänn*ast*

a2   ädel – ädel*t* – ädl*are* – ädl*ast*
      vacker – vacker*t* – vackr*are* – vackr*ast*

a3   rutten – rutte*t* – ruttn*are* – ruttn*ast*
      trogen – troge*t* – trogn*are* – trogn*ast*
      försigkommen – försigkomme*t* – försigkomn*are* – försigkomn*ast*

a4   gängse – gängse – *mera* gängse – *mest* gängse
      defekt – defekt – *mera* defekt – *mest* defekt

a5   begåvad – begåva*t* – *mera* begåvad – *mest* begåvad
      komisk – komisk*t* – *mera* komisk – *mest* komisk
      prydd – prytt – *mera* prydd – *mest* prydd
      svulten – svulte*t* – *mera* svulten – *mest* svulten

The comparison of adjectives which do not fit these paradigms is indicated in full in the entry.

Verbs

Conjugations (infinitive, present tense, past tense, supine, past participle):

v1   kalla – kallar – kallade – kallat – kallad
      dagas – dagas – dagades – dagats

v2   böja – böjer – böjt – böjd
      breda – breder – bredde – brett – bredd
      skilja – skiljer – skilde – skilt – skild
      blygas – blyg(e)s – blygdes – blygts
      brännas – bränn(e)s – brändes – bränts
      klämma – klämmer – klämde – klämt – klämd
      tända – tänder – tände – tänt – tänd

v3   köpa – köper – köpte – köpt – köpt
      mista – mister – miste – mist – mist
      lyfta – lyfter – lyfte – lyft – lyft
      skvätta – skvätter – skvätte – skvätt – skvätt
      begynna – begynner – begynte – begynt – begynt
      hjälpas – hjälp(e)s – hjälptes – hjälpts

v4   tro – tror – trodde – trott – trodd

As a rule verbs belonging to *v1* are not marked. The past tense and the supine of *irregular verbs* are written out.

Förkortningar   Abbreviations

a adjektiv adjective
absol. absolut absolute[ly]
abstr. abstrakt abstract
adj. adjektiv[isk], adjective, adjectival
adv adverb adverb
AE. amerikansk engelska American English; [in] U.S.
akad. akademi academy
allm. allmän[t] general[ly]
anat. anatomi anatomy
a p. a person
arkeol. arkeologi archaeology
arkit. arkitektur architecture
astr. astronomi astronomy

bank. bankväsen banking
bergv. bergväsen mining
best. bestämd definite
beton. betonad (-t) stressed
bibl. bibliskt biblical
bildl. bildlig[t] figurative[ly]
biol. biologi biology
bokb. bokbinderi bookbinding
bokför. bokföring book-keeping
boktr. boktryckeri printing
bot. botanik botany
byggn. byggnadskonst building

data. databehandling data processing
demonstr. demonstrativ[t] demonstrative
dep deponens deponent
determ. determinativ[t] determinative
dial. dialektal[t] dialectal[ly]
dipl. diplomatterm diplomacy

eg. egentlig[en] literal[ly]
ekon. ekonomi economy
elektr. elektrisk, elektroteknisk electrical, electrotechnical
elektron. elektronisk, electronik electronic, electronics

fack. fackspråk technical term
fem. femininum feminine
film. filmterm cinema
filos. filosofi philosophy
fisk fiskeriterm fishing
flyg. flygväsen aviation
fonet. fonetik phonetics
foto. fotografikonst photography
fys. fysik physics
fysiol. fysiologi physiology
fäkt. fäktterm fencing
fören. förenad (-t) adjectival form
förh. förhållande relation[ship]
förk. förkortning abbreviation
försäkr. försäkringsväsen insurance

gen. genitiv genitive
geogr. geografi geography
geol. geologi geology
geom. geometri geometry
gjut. gjuteriterm foundry term

graf. grafisk term printing
gruv. gruvterm mining term
gymn. gymnastik gymnastics

hand. handelsterm commercial term
her. heraldik heraldry
hist. historisk[t] historical[ly]
hopskr. hopskrivs, hopskrivet written as one word
högt. högtidlig[t] formal[ly]

ibl. ibland sometimes
imperf. imperfektum past tense
indef. indefinit indefinite
inf. infinitiv infinitive
interj interjektion interjection
interr. interrogativ[t] interrogative
iron. ironisk[t] ironic[ally]
i sht i synnerhet particularly

jakt. jaktterm hunting
jfr jämför compare
jordbr. jordbruk agriculture
jur. juridik law
järnv. järnvägsväsen railway term

kat. katolsk Catholic
kem. kemi chemistry
kir. kirurgisk term surgery
kokk. kokkonst cookery
koll. kollektiv collective[ly]
komp. komparativ comparative
konj konjunktion conjunction
konkr. konkret concrete
konst. konstterm art
konstr. konstruktion construction
kortsp. kortspel card game
kyrkl. kyrklig term ecclesiastical

lantbr. lantbruk agriculture
lantm. lantmäteri land-surveying
litt. litterär[t], litteratur literary, literature
log. logik logic

mat. matematik mathematics
med. medicin medicine
meteor. meteorologi meteorology
mil. militärterm military term
miner. mineralogi mineralogy
mots. motsats opposite
mus. musik music
myt. mytologi mythology
mål. målarterm painting

n neutrum neuter
neds. nedsättande derogatory
neg. negation negative
ngn någon somebody
ngt något something

o. och and
obest. obestämd indefinite
obeton. obetonad (-t) unstressed

15

opers. opersonlig impersonal
opt. optik optics
ordspr. ordspråk proverb
o.s. oneself

parl. parlamentarisk term parliamentary term
pass. passiv, passivum passive
perf. part. perfekt particip, past principle
pers. person[lig] person[al]
pl pluralis plural
poet. poetisk[t] poetical[ly]
polit. politik politics
poss. possessiv[t] possessive
post. postterm postal term
predik. predikat, predikativ[t] predicate, predicative[ly]
prep preposition preposition
pres. presens present [tense]
pron pronomen pronoun
psykol. psykologi psychology

r reale common gender
radar. radarteknik radar
radio. radioteknik radio engineering
rel. relativ[t] relative
relig. religion religion
ret. retorisk[t] rhetoric[ally]
rfl reflexiv[t] reflexive
ridk. ridkonst equestrian term
rumsbet. rumsbetydelse spatial sense
räkn räkneord numeral

s substantiv substantive
s.b. somebody
schack. schackterm chess
sg singularis singular
självst. självständig[t] pronoun
sjö. sjöterm nautical term
skeppsb. skeppsbyggeri shipbuilding
skol. skolväsen education
skämts. skämtsam[t] jocular[ly]
sl. slang slang
slaktar. slaktarterm butchering term
sms. sammansättning[ar] compound[s]
snick. snickarterm joinery

s.o. someone
spel. spelterm game
sport. sportterm sporting term
spr. språk language
språkv. språkvetenskap linguistics
ss. såsom as
stat. statistik statistics
s.th. something
subj. subjekt subject
sup. supinum supine
superl. superlativ superlative
särskr. särskrivs, särskrivet written as two words
sömn. sömnad sewing

t. till to
tandläk. tandläkarterm dentistry
teat. teaterterm theatre
tekn. teknologi, teknisk technology, technical
tel. telefon telephone
teol. teologi theology
text. textilterm textiles
tidsbet. tidsbetydelse temporal sense
trädg. trädgårdsskötsel gardening
tullv. tullväsen customs
TV. television television

ung. ungefär approximately
univ. universitetsterm university
uttr. uttryck[ande] expression expressing

v verb verb
vanl. vanlig[en] usual[ly]
vard. vardagligt colloquial[ly]
versl. verslära prosody, metrics term
vetensk. vetenskaplig scientific
veter. veterinärväsen veterinary term
väv. vävnadsteknisk term weaving

zool. zoologi zoology

åld. ålderdomlig[t], föråldrad (-t) archaic

äv. även also

A

1 a [a:] *s6* a; ~ *och o* alpha and omega; *har man sagt* ~ *får man säga b* in for a penny, in for a pound
2 a *prep, se a conto, a dato, a priori*
à 1 of, containing; *5 påsar* ~ *20 gram* 5 bags of 20 grammes [each] **2** *2 biljetter* ~ *1 pund* 2 tickets at £1 each **3** or; *3* ~ *4 dagar* 3 or 4 days; *det tar 2* ~ *3 veckor* it takes from 2 to 3 weeks
AB (*förk. för aktiebolag*) Ltd.; *AE.* Inc.
abakus [ˈabba-] *s2* (*räkneram, arkit.*) abacus
abandon [abaŋˈdåŋ] *s3* abandon
abbé *s3* abbé **abbedissa** abbess
abborr|e [-å-] *s2* perch **-grund** *s7, ung.* perch angling shallow **-pinne** small perch
abbot [-ått] *s2* abbot
abbots|döme *s6*, **-värdighet** abbacy
abc [abeˈse:] *s6* ABC **-bok** ABC-book, primer
ABC-stridsmedel ABC weapons
abderitisk [-ˈri:-] *a5* Gothamite
abdik|ation abdication **-era** abdicate
abdom|en [-då:-] *n el. r, best. form -en, pl -en, äv. -ina* abdomen **-inal** *a5* abdominal
aber [ˈa:-] *n* but, drawback, catch; snag
aberration aberration; *kromatisk* ~ chromatic aberration; *sfärisk* ~ spherical aberration
Abessinien [-ˈsi:-] *n* Abyssinia **abessin|ier** [-ˈsi:-] *s9*, **-[i]sk** [-ˈsi:-] *a5* Abyssinian
abiturient matriculation candidate; *numera ung.* General Certificate of Education [A-level] candidate
ablation *jack.* ablation
ablativ *s3* ablative
ablution *kyrkl.* ablution
abnorm [-ˈnårm] *a1* abnormal **-itet** abnormity, abnormality; malformation, deformity
abolition abolition **-ism** abolitionism **-ist** abolitionist
abonnemang *s7* subscription (*på* to, for)
abonnemangs|avgift subscription [rate (fee, price)]; *tel.* telephone rental **-biljett** season ticket (*på* for) **-föreställning** performance for season-ticket holders
abonn|ent subscriber; (*konsert-, teater- etc.*) season-ticket (seat, box) holder **-era** subscribe (*på* to, for), contract (*på* for); ~*d buss* hired (private) bus; ~*d föreställning* closed (private) performance
abort [-ˈårt] *s3* abortion; *spontan* ~ miscarriage; *göra* ~ terminate pregnancy **-era** abort, miscarry
abortiv abortive **-medel** abortifacient
abort|lag law on abortion **-sökande** applicant for abortion **-ör** abortionist
abradera *geol.* abrade
abrakadabra [-ˣda:bra] *s7* abracadabra
abrasion *geol.* abrasion
abrupt *a1* abrupt, sudden
abscess [-ˈsess] *s3* abscess
absid *s3* apse, apsis

absint *s3* absinth[e]
abskissa [-ˣskissa] *s1* abscissa
absolut I *a1* absolute; *en* ~ *omöjlighet* an utter impossibility **II** *adv* absolutely, utterly, certainly, definitely; ~ *inte* definitely not, by no means, not at all; *den* ~ *bästa* by far the best; *han vill* ~ *gå* he insists on going **-belopp** absolute value
absolution absolution
absolut|ism 1 absolutism **2** (*helnykterhet*) teetotalism, total abstinence **-ist 1** absolutist **2** (*helnykterist*) teetotaller, total abstainer
absolvera [-å-] **1** absolve (*från* from) **2** finish, complete; ~ *en examen* pass an examination
absorb|ator [-ˣa:tår] *s3* (*i solfångare*) absorber **-era** [-å-] *d dos* absorbed dose
absorption [-pˈʃɔ:n] absorption
absorptions|förmåga power of absorption **-kylskåp** absorption[-type] refrigerator **-kärl** absorption drum **-medel** absorbent, absorber
abstinens abstinence **-symtom** withdrawal symptom
abstrahera abstract; ~ *från* disregard
abstrak|t I *a1* abstract **II** *adv* abstractly, in the abstract **-tion** [-kˈʃɔ:n] abstraction
abstraktionsförmåga ability to think in abstract terms
abstrus *a1* abstruse
absurd [-ˈurd *el.* -ˈu:rd] *a1* absurd, preposterous **-itet** *s3* absurdity, absurdness
a cappella [kaˈpella] *mus.* a cappella
accelerando [akseleˈrandå] *adv o. s6* accelerando
acceleration [aks-] acceleration; ~ *vid fritt fall* acceleration of free fall, acceleration due to (of) gravity
accelerations|fil [aks-] acceleration lane **-förmåga** acceleration capacity
acceler|ator [akseleˣra:tår] *s3* accelerator **-era** accelerate, speed up **-ometer** [-ˈme:-] *s2* accelerometer
accent [aks-] accent; (*tonvikt*) stress **-tecken** accent
accentuer|a [aks-] accentuate, stress **-ing** accentuation
accept [aks-] *s3* **1** (*växel*) acceptance, accepted bill; *dokument mot* ~ documents against acceptance **2** (*-ering*) acceptance **-abel** [-ˈa:bel] *a2* acceptable; passable **-ans** *s3* acceptance **-ant** acceptor **-era** accept; *vard.* buy **-vägran** nonacceptance
accession [akseˈʃɔ:n] acquisition; acquest **accessionskatalog** acquisition catalogue
accessoarer [aksesoˈa:rer] accessories
accesstid [akˣsess-] *data.* access time
accidenstryck [aks-] job-printing, job[bing] work **-eri** jobbing printer
accis [akˈsi:s] *s3* excise [tax, duty], inland duty **-fri** exempt from excise [duty] **-pliktig** liable to excise [duty]
acetat [-s-] *s7, s4* acetate **-silke** acetate [rayon]
aceton [asseˈtå:n] *s4* acetone
acetylen [-s-] *s3, s4* acetylene, ethyne **-gas** acetylene [gas] **-lampa** acetylene lamp **-svetsning** oxyacetylene welding
acetylsalicylsyra [-s-] acetylsalicylic acid
aciditet [-s-] acidity **acidos** [-ˈå:s] *s3, med.* aci-

dosis
ack oh [dear]!; *högt.* alas!; ~, *om han vore här!*
oh, if only he were here!
ackja *s1* Lapp sledge
acklamation acclamation; unanimous vote; *väljas med* ~ be voted by (with) acclamation
acklimatiser|a acclimatize; ~ *sig* become acclimatized, begin to feel at home **-ing** acclimatization, acclimation
ackommodation accommodation
ackommodations|förmåga accommodation **-växel** *hand.* accommodation bill
ackommodera accommodate
ackompanjatris, ackompanjatör [-å-] accompanist
ackompanj|emąng *s7* accompaniment; *till* ~ *av* to the accompaniment of **-era** accompany
ackord [-'å:rd] *s7* **1** *mus.* chord **2** (*arbete*) piecework [contract], piece rate; *arbeta på* ~ work at piece rates (by contract), do piecework **3** *jur.* agreement, composition [with one's creditors] **-era** (*köpslå*) negotiate (*om* about, for), bargain (*om* for)
ackords|arbete piecework **-lön** piece rate **-pris** piece price, piecework price **-sättning** rate fixing
ackrediter|a 1 *dipl.* accredit (*hos, vid* to), furnish with credentials **2** *hand.* open a credit for [a certain amount] (*hos en bank* at a bank); *bank. äv.* authorize **3** *väl* ~*d hos ngn* in a p.'s good books **-ing** accreditation
ackumul|ation accumulation **-atjv** *a5* accumulative **-ator** [-'×a:tår] *s3* accumulator, [storage] battery **-era** accumulate; ~*d ränta* accrued (accumulated) interest
ackurąt *al* accurate **-ess** accuracy, exactitude, precision; *med all* ~ adroitly, expertly
ackusativ *s3* accusative; *i* ~ in the accusative **-objekt** direct object
ackuschörska [-'×ʃö:r-] *s1* midwife
ackvirera procure
ackvisi|tion 1 (*förvärv*) acquisition **2** *hand.* canvassing **-tör** canvasser; *försäkr.* insurance agent
acne *se akne*
a conto [a 'kånto] on account **--betalning** payment on account
acyklisk [a'syck-] *a5* acyclic
adagio [a'da:dʒå] *s6 o. adv* adagio
Adam och Eva *bot.* elder-flowered orchid
adams|dräkt *i* ~ in one's birthday suit **-äpple** Adam's apple
adap|tation adaptation, adjustment **-tera** adapt, adjust **-tion** [-p'ʃo:n] *se adaptation*
a dato [a '×da:to] from date **--växel** time (term) bill, time draft (note)
ADB (*förk. för automatisk databehandling*) A.D.P. (automatic data processing)
add|ęnd *s3* addend **-era** add up (together), cast [up]; *absol. äv.* do sums **-ering** [-'de:-], **-ition** addition
addi|tionsmaskin adding machine **-tjv** *s7 o. al* additive
adekvąt *al* adequate, equivalent; apt
adel ['a:-] *s2* **1** (*härkomst*) noble birth **2** (*samhällsklass*) nobility; *i Storbritannien äv.* peerage **3** (*ädelhet*) nobility

adels|brev patent of nobility **-dam** noblewoman, titled lady **-kalender** peerage [book]
adelskap *s7* knighthood; baronetcy; peerage
adels|man nobleman, titled gentleman **-märke** mark of nobility **-privilegium** privilege of the nobility **-stånd** nobility **-titel** title **-välde** aristocracy
adenoid [-o'i:d] *a5, n sg obest. form undviks* adenoid; ~*a vegetationer* adenoids
adępt *s3* pupil, beginner, novice
aderton [×a:rtån] eighteen **-de** eighteenth **-[de] del** eighteenth [part]
adertonhundra eighteen hundred **-femtio** eighteen [hundred and] fifty **-nittiotalet** *på* ~ in the [eighteen] nineties **-talet** *på* ~ in the nineteenth century
aderton|tiden *vid* ~ about 6 p.m., about six o'clock in the evening **-årig** *al* eighteen-year-old; ~*vänskap* a friendship of eighteen years' standing; *en* ~ *pojke* a boy of eighteen **-åring** a boy (girl *etc.*) of eighteen, an eighteen-year-old boy (*etc.*) **-årsåldern** *i* ~ about eighteen [years of age]
adhe|sion [ade-] adhesion **-sionskraft** adhesive power **-sjv** *a5 o. s7* adhesive
ad hoc-grupp ad hoc committee
adiantum [-'×ann-] *s3, bot.* maidenhair [fern]
adjektiv *s7* adjective **-isk** *a5* adjectival
adjungera [-juŋg-] call in; co-opt; ~*d ledamot* co-opted member; ~*d professor* visiting professor
adjunkt [-'juŋkt] *s3* assistant master [at a secondary school]; *jfr kyrko-, pastorats-*
adjutant aide[-de-camp] (*hos* to)
adjö [a'jö:] **I** *interj* goodbye; *högt.* farewell; *äv.* good day (morning *etc.*); ~ *så länge* goodbye for now, so long **II** *n* farewell, adieu; *säga* ~ *till ngn* say goodbye to s.b., bid s.b. goodbye
adla [×a:d-] **1** (*i Storbritannien*) raise to the peerage; (*om eng. lågadel*) knight, make a baronet, confer a knighthood (*etc.*) on **2** *i sht bildl.* ennoble **adlig** *al* noble, aristocratic, of noble family; ~ *krona* nobleman's coronet; *upphöja i* ~*t stånd* raise to the nobility
administration administration, management
administrations|apparat administrative machinery **-kostnader** management (administrative, general) costs
administr|atjv *al* administrative; *på* ~ *väg* by administrative means, departmentally **-atör** administrator **-era** administrate, manage
admittans [-'ans *el.* -'aŋs] *s3, elektr.* admittance
admonition admonition
ad notam [add ×no:tamm] *ta* ~ pay attention to, obey, heed
adolescens [-'ʃens *el.* -'sens] *s3* adolescence
adonis [-'do:-] *s2* Adonis
adop|tera [-å-] adopt **-tion** [-p'ʃo:n] adoption
adoptiv|barn [-×ti:v-] adopted child **-föräldrar** adoptive parents **-hem** adoptive home, home of adoption
adrenaljn *s4* adrenaline **-avsöndring** adrenaline secretion
adręss 1 (*bostadsuppgift*) address; *utan* ~ (*om brev etc.*) unaddressed, undirected; *ändra* ~ change one's address; *han sade det med* ~ *till mig*

his remark was meant for me; *paketet har inte kommit fram till sin* ~ the parcel has not reached its destination **2** (*lyckönskningsskrivelse o.d.*) [illuminated] address **adress|at** addressee; (*på postanvisning e.d.*) payee; (*på paket e.d.*) consignee **-debatt** *parl.* debate on the address **adresser|a** address, send, direct; (*om varor*) consign **-ing 1** (*-ande*) addressing **2** (*adress*) address **adresseringsmaskin** addressing machine **adress|förändring** change of address **-kalender** [street] directory **-kort** dispatch note, address form **-land** [country of] destination **-lapp** [address] label (tag) **-ort** [place of] destination **-plåt** address plate **-postanstalt** post office of destination, receiving post office **-register** register of addresses **-ändring** *se adressförändring* **Adriatiska havet** [-i'a:tis-] the Adriatic [Sea] **adsor|bera** [-å-] adsorb **-ption** [-p'ʃɔ:n] adsorption **adstringerande** [-ŋ'ge:-] *a4* astringent (*äv. ~ medel*) **aducera** anneal **aducerings|järn** malleable [cast] iron **-verk** malleable iron foundry **A-dur** A major **advent** *s7* Advent; *första* [*söndagen i*] ~ Advent Sunday **-ist** Adventist **advents|kalender** Advent calendar **-tid** [the season of] Advent **adverb** *s7* adverb **-ial** *s7* adverbial [modifier] **-iell** *a5* adverbial **adversativ** [ˣadd- *el.* -'ti:v] *a5* adversative **advocera** plead (*för* for; *mot* against); quibble **advokat** lawyer, (*juridiskt ombud*) solicitor, (*sakförare vid domstol*) barrister[-at-law], (*pläderande*) counsel; (*i Skottland*) advocate; *AE.* attorney[-at-law], counselor[-at-law] **-arvode** attorney's (solicitor's) fee (charge) **-byrå** lawservice office **-firma** [firm of] solicitors, solicitor's firm, law office **-fiskal** *ung.* prosecuting counsel, prosecutor **-knep** legal quibble **-kontor** *se -byrå* **advokat|orisk** [-'tɔ:-] *a5* quibbling, pettifogging **-päron** *se avokado* **-samfund** bar association; *utesluta ur ~et* disbar; *Sveriges A*~ [the] Swedish Bar Association **advokat|yr** *s3* quibbling, casuistry **-yrke** legal profession; *avstänga från utövande av* ~*t* disbench; *slå sig på* ~*t* enter the legal profession **aerob** [aä'rå:b] **l** *s3* aerobe, aerobium (*pl* aerobia) **ll** *a5* aerobic **aero|biologi** [ˣaärå-, ˣaärɔ-] aerobiology **-drom** [-'drå:m] *s3* aerodrome **-dynamik** [*äv.* ˣaä-] aerodynamics (*pl, behandlas som sg*) **-dynamisk** [-'na:-, *äv.* ˣaä-] aerodynamic **-gram** [-'gramm] *s7* aerogram[me], air letter **-logi** *s3* aerology **-logisk** [-'lå:-] *a5* aerologic[al] **-naut** *s3* aeronaut **-nautik** *s2* aeronautics (*pl, behandlas som sg*) **-plan** aeroplane, aircraft; *AE. äv.* airplane **-sol** [-'såll] *s3* aerosol **-stat** *s3* aerostat **-statik** aerostatics (*pl, behandlas som sg*) **afa|si** *s3, med.* aphasia **-sisk** [-'fa:-] *a5,* **-tiker** [-'fa:-] *s9,* **-tisk** [-'fa:-] *a5* aphasic **affekt** *s3* [state of] emotion **-betonad** *a5* emo-

tional, agitated **-erad** [-'te:-] *a5* affected; mannered, theatrical; *vard.* la-di-da **-fri** unemotional, dispassionate, impassive **affektionsvärde** [-kˣʃɔ:ns-] sentimental value **affinitet** affinity **affisch** [a'fiʃ] *s3* poster, bill, placard; *sätta upp en* ~ post (stick) a bill **affischer|a** post (stick) bills, post **-ing** bill-posting; ~ *förbjuden* stick no bills, billposting prohibited **affisch|klistrare** *se affischör* **-pelare** poster (advertising) pillar **-tavla** hoarding; *AE.* billboard **affischör** bill|poster, -sticker **affär** *s3* **1** (*firma*) business, [business] firm, concern, establishment, enterprise **2** (*transaktion*) transaction, deal, operation; ~*er* business; *en dålig* ~ a bad bargain; *en fin* ~ a good stroke of business, a bargain; *bortrest i* ~*er* away on business; *göra* ~*er* i do business in; *göra stora* ~*er på Sydamerika* do a lot of business with South America; *ha* ~*er med* do business with; *inlåta sig på en* ~ enter into a business transaction; *prata* ~*er* talk business; *slutföra en* ~ close a deal; *hur går* ~*erna?* how is business? **3** (*butik*) shop; *särsk. AE.* store; *inneha en* ~ keep (own) a shop; *stå i* ~ be a shop assistant; *öppna en* ~ start a business, open a shop (store) **4** (*angelägenhet*) affair, matter, concern; *göra stor* ~ *av ngt* make a great fuss about s.th.; *ordna sina* ~*er* settle one's affairs; *sköt dina egna* ~*er* mind your own business **5** (*rättsfall*) case **6** (*spekulation*) venture **affärs|angelägenhet** business matter; *i* ~*er* on business **-anställd** shop employee (assistant, worker); *AE. äv.* store clerk **-bana** *gå* ~*n* go into business **-bank** commercial bank **-begåvning** gift for business **-besök** business call **-biträde** shop assistant; salesman, *fem.* saleswoman; *AE.* [sales]clerk **-bokföring** financial accounting **-brev** business letter **-byggnad** shop building **-centrum** shopping centre (precinct) **-drivande** *a5, statens* ~ *verk* government-owned enterprises and public utilities **-folk** businessmen, business people **-förbindelse** business connection; *stå i* ~ *med* have business relations with **-föreståndare** shopkeeper, storekeeper **-företag** business firm (enterprise), company; *AE . äv.* corporation **-gata** shopping street **-handling** business document; ~*ar* (*post.*) printed matter (*sg*), commercial papers **-hemlighet** trade secret **-hus 1** (*byggnad*) business (commercial) property **2** (*företag*) business firm (company, house) **-händelse** *bokför.* business transaction **-idkare** businessman, *fem.* businesswoman, tradesman, *fem.* tradeswoman **-innehavare** shopkeeper, storekeeper **-inredning** shop fittings (*pl*) **-jurist** solicitor; company lawyer, legal adviser (advisor) [of a company]; *AE. äv.* attorney **-knep** business trick **-korrespondens** commercial correspondence **-kretsar** business circles **-kutym** *se -sed* **-kvarter** shopping (business) area **-kvinna** businesswoman **-liv** business [life], trade; *inom* ~*et* in business **-lokal** business premises (*pl*), shop **-läge 1** (*lokalitet*) business site, store location **2** (*konjunktur*) business conditions (*pl*), state of business (the market) **-man** businessman **-meddelande** business communication **-medhjälpare** *se -biträde* **-metoder** business methods **-moral** business ethics (*pl*) **-mässig** *al* businesslike **-resa** business trip **-rörelse** business **-sed** commercial (business, trade) practice (custom) **-sinne** business sense, nose (flair) for business **-ställning** business position (standing) **-tid** business hours (*pl*) **-transaktion** business deal (transaction) **-uppgörelse** business transaction, closing of a deal **-vana** business experience **-verk** *se under affärsdrivande* **-verksamhet** business [activity] **-vän** business friend **-värde** good will **-världen** the business (commercial) world, business life

afghan [af'ga:n] *s3*, **-[i]sk** *a5* Afghan[i] **Afghanistan** *n* Afghanistan

aflatoxin aflatoxin

aforis|m aphorism **-tisk** *a5* aphoristic

Afrika ['a:-] *n* Africa

afrikaans [-'ka:ns] *r* Afrikaans

afrik|an *s3* African **-and** *s3* Afrikaner **-ansk** [-'ka:nsk] *a5* African

afro|-amerikansk Afro-American **-asiatisk** Afro-Asian

afrodisiakum [-'si:a-] *s8* aphrodisiac

afrofrisyr Afro

afton [-ån] **-en** *aftnar* evening; *i ~* this evening; *i går ~* yesterday evening; *i fredags ~* last Friday evening; *om ~en* in the evening; *sent på ~en* late in the evening; *det lider mot ~* the day is drawing to a close **-andakt** evening prayers (*pl*) **-bön** evening prayers (*pl*); *läsa ~* (*äv.*) say one's prayers [at bedtime] **-dräkt** evening dress **-gudstjänst** evening service **-klänning** evening gown **-kurs** evening classes (*pl*) **-kvist** *på ~en* in the early evening **-måltid** evening meal, supper **-psalm** evening hymn **-rodnad** sunset glow; afterglow **-skola** evening (night) school **-sol** evening sun **-stjärna** evening star **-stund** *ung.* twilight hour **-sång** evensong; vespers (*pl*) **-tidning** evening paper **-underhållning** evening entertainment **-vind** evening breeze

1 aga *s1* (*turkisk titel*) ag[h]a

2 aga I *s2* flogging, caning **II** *v1* flog, cane; *den man älskar den ~r man* (*ung.*) the ones we love, we chasten

agar[-agar] *s3* agar[-agar]

agat agate

agave [a'ga:ve] *s5* agave; (*hundraårsväxt*) century plant, American aloe

agenda [a*genda] *s1* **1** (*föredragningslista*) agenda **2** *parl.* order paper

agens ['a:-] *s3, kem.* agent

agent agent (*äv. språkv.*), representative; (*handelsresande*) travelling salesman, [commercial] traveller; *hemlig ~* secret agent **-provision** [agent's] commission

agentur agency; representation **-affär** agency [business] **-avtal** agency agreement **-firma** agency [firm]

agera act; *de ~nde* the performers, the actors, *koll.* the cast (*sg*)

agg *s7* grudge, rancour; *bära* (*hysa*) *~ mot ngn* have a grudge against s.b.

agglomera|t *s7* agglomerate **-tion** agglomeration

agglomerer|a agglomerate **-ing** agglomeration, sintering

agglutin|ation agglutination **-era** agglutinate; *~nde språk* agglutinative language

aggregat *s7* unit (set) [of machinery], plant, installation

aggregationstillstånd [-*ʃɔ:ns-] state of aggregation

aggression [-e'ʃɔ:n] aggression

aggressiv *al* aggressive **-itet** aggressiveness

agio ['a:giɔ] *s6* agio

agitation agitation, campaign **agitationsmöte** propaganda meeting

agit|ator [-*a:tår] *s3* agitator, propagandist **-atorisk** [-'to:-] *a5* agitatorial, agitational **-era** agitate (*för* for); (*vid val*) canvass, do canvassing; *~ upp en opinion* stir up [an] opinion

1 agn [aŋn] *s2* **1** (*blomfjäll*) palea (*pl* paleae) **2** (*på säd*) husk; *~ar* husks, chaff (*sg*); *skilja ~arna från vetet* separate the wheat from the chaff; *som ~ar för vinden* as chaff before the wind

2 agn [aŋn] *s7* (*vid fiske*) bait, gudgeon **agna** [*aŋna] bait

agnat [aɡ'na:t] agnate **-isk** *a5* agnatic; *~ tronföljd* agnatic succession

agnost|icism [aɡnås-] agnosticism **-iker** [aɡ'nåss-] *s9*, **-isk** [aɡ'nåss-] *a5* agnostic

agoni *s3* agony

agorafobi *s3* agoraphobia

agraff *s3* agraffe, clasp, buckle

agrar *s3* agrarian **-förbund** agrarian league **-parti** agrarian party

agremang [-'maŋ] *s7* agrément, approbation **-er** [-'maŋ-] *pl* **1** (*nöjen, behag*) amenities **2** (*bekvämligheter*) material comforts **3** (*prydnader*) ornaments

agrikultur agriculture **-ell** agricultural

agro|nom agronomist **-nomi** *s3* agronomy **-nomisk** [-'nå:-] *a5* agronomic[al]

ah oh **aha** aha, oho

air [ä:r] *s3* air

Aisopos ['aisåpås] Aesop

aiss [ajs] *s7* A sharp

aj [ajj] oh, ow; (*starkare*) ouch

à jour [a'ʃo:r] *a4, föra ~* keep up to date; *hålla ngn ~ med* keep s.b. informed on (as to), keep s.b. posted on

ajourner|a [aʃor-] adjourn; *parl.* prorogue, recess; *~ på obestämd tid* recess **-ing** adjournment, prorogation

akacia *s1* acacia

akademi *s3* **1** (*konst- etc.*) academy **2** *univ.* university, institution **3** (*vetenskaplig*) society, association **-elev** academy student

akademiker [-'de:-] **1** (*med akademisk examen*) university graduate **2** (*medlem av akademi*) academician

akademi|ledamot, -medlem member (fellow) of an academy (a society), academician

akadem|isk [-'de:-] *a5* academic; *~ avhandling* doctoral dissertation, thesis; *~ kvart* (*ung.*) quarter of an hour's allowance; *avlägga ~ examen* take a university degree, graduate **-iskt** *adv* academically; *~ bildad* with a university education

akantus *s2, bot., arkit.* acanthus

akilles|häl [a*kill-] Achilles heel **-sena** Achilles

tendon
akleja [-ˣlejja] *s1* columbine, aquilegia
akne *s5* acne
akribj *s3* accuracy
akrobat acrobat **-ik** *s3* acrobatics (*sg o. pl*) **-isk** [-ˈba:-] *a5* acrobatic
akrofobj *s3* acrophobia
akromat achromat, achromatic lens **-isk** [-ˈma:-] *a5* achromatic
akronym *s3* acronym
akropol [-ˈpå:l] *s3* acropolis
akrostik|on [aˈkråstikån] *-onet, pl -on el. -er* acrostic
akryl *s3* acrylic fabric **-at** *s7, s3* acrylate **-fiber** acrylic fibre **-harts** acrylic resin **-syra** acrylic acid
1 akt *s3* **1** (*handling*) act **2** (*ceremoni*) ceremony, act **3** (*avdelning av skådespel*) act **4** (*handling, dokument m.m.*) document, deed, record, file **5** *konst.* nude
2 akt *oböjligt s, förklara i* ~ proscribe, outlaw
3 akt *oböjligt s* (*uppmärksamhet, avsikt*) attention; *i* ~ *och mening* with intent, on purpose (*att* to); *ge* ~ *på* pay attention to; *giv* ~*!* attention!; *stå i giv* ~ stand at attention; *ta sig i* ~ be on one's guard (*för* against); *ta tillfället i* ~ seize the opportunity
akta 1 (*vara aktsam om, vårda*) be careful with, take care of; (*skydda*) guard, protect (*för* from); (*vara aktsam med*) be careful with; (*se upp för*) mind, look out for; ~ *huvudet* mind your head; ~*s för stötar* fragile, handle with care; ~*s för väta* keep dry, to be kept dry **2** *rfl* take care (*för att göra* not to do), be on one's guard (*för* against), look out (*för* for); ~ *er!* look out!, take care!; *han* ~*de sig noga för att komma i närheten av mig* he gave me a wide berth **3** (*ge akt på, lägga märke till*) take notice of **4** (*värdera, skatta*) esteem, respect **5** *han* ~*r inte för rov att stjäla* he thinks nothing of stealing **aktad** *a5* respected, esteemed
akter [ˈakt-] **I** *s2* stern; *från för till* ~ from stem to stern **II** *adv* aft; ~ *ifrån* from the stern; ~ *om* abaft; ~ *ut* (*över*) astern, aft **-däck** quarterdeck, afterdeck **-kant** aft side **-kastell** stern castle **-lanterna** stern light **-lastad** [down] by the stern, stern-heavy
akterlig *a1* abaft
akter|salong aftersaloon **-segel** aftersail **-seglad** *a5* left behind **-skepp** stern **-snurra** [boat with] outboard motor **-spegel** stern
akterst [ˈakt-] *adv* furthest astern **aktersta** [ˈakt-] *a i superl.* the sternmost (aft[er]most)
akter|städerska saloon stewardess **-stäv** sternpost
aktie [ˈaktsie] *s5* share; ~*r* (*koll.*) stock (*sg*); *en* ~ *på nominellt 100 kronor* a share of a par value of 100 kronor; *bunden* ~ restricted share; *ha* ~*r i ett bolag* hold shares in a company; *teckna* ~*r* subscribe to (for) shares
aktie|bolag joint-stock (limited) company; *AE.* stock (incorporated) company **-bolagslag** *BE.* Companies Act; *AE.* General Corporation Act **-brev** share (*AE.* stock) certificate **-börs** stock exchange (market) **-delning** stock split **-emission** share (*AE.* stock) issue **-innehav** holding of shares (*AE.* stock), shareholding, *AE.* stock-

holding **-kapital** joint stock, share capital; *AE.* capital stock **-kupong** [share] coupon **-kurs** price of shares **-majoritet** share majority; (*friare*) controlling interest **-mantel** share (*AE.* stock) certificate **-marknad** share (*AE.* stock) market **-portfölj** shares held, share portfolio **-post** block of shares; shareholding **-sparare** small investor **-sparklubb** investors' club **-stock** share capital **-teckning** subscription for shares; *AE.* capital stock subscription **-utdelning** dividend **-ägare** shareholder; *AE.* stockholder
aktin|jd *s3, kem.* actinide; ~*er* actinide series **-isk** [-ˈti:-] *a5* actinic **-ium** [-ˈti:-] *s8* actinium
aktion [akˈʃo:n] action
aktions|basis basis of action **-grupp** action group **-radie** range (radius) of action; cruising range
aktiv [ˈakt-] *a1* active, brisk, lively, busy; ~*t avfall* hot waste; ~*t kol* activated carbon (charcoal), active carbon
aktiva [ˈakt-] *pl* assets; ~ *och passiva* assets and liabilities
aktivator [-ˣa:tår] *s3* sensitizer; activator
aktiver|a activate, make [more] active **-ing** stimulation, activation, boost; *elektron.* sensitization; activation
aktiv|isera *se aktivera* **-ism** activism **-ist** activist **-itet** activity, activeness
aktivum [ˈakt-] *s4, språkv.* active [voice]
aktning 1 (*respekt*) respect (*för* for) **2** (*uppskattning*) esteem **3** (*hänsyn*) regard (*för* for), deference (*för* to); *av* ~ *för* out of consideration for, in deference to; *med all* ~ *för* with all deference to; *hysa* ~ *för* have respect for; *stiga i ngns* ~ rise in a p.'s esteem; *vinna allmän* ~ make o.s. generally respected
aktnings|bevis token of esteem **-bjudande** *a4* **1** commanding respect, imposing **2** (*ansenlig*) considerable **-full** respectful **-värd** *a1* entitled to (worthy of) respect; ~*a försök* creditable attempts
aktra, aktre *a4* after
aktris actress
aktsam *a1* careful (*med, om* with, of); prudent **-het** care[fulness], prudence
akt|samling file, dossier **-studie** nude **-stycke** [official] document
aktuali|sera 1 (*föra på tal*) bring to the fore; *frågan har* ~*ts* the question has arisen **2** (*modernisera*) bring up to date **-tet** topicality, topic of interest, news [value]
aktualitetsvärde topicality value
aktuarie [-ˈa:-] *s5* **1** (*vid ämbetsverk, ung.*) registrar, recording clerk **2** *försäkr.* actuary
aktuell *a1* [of] current [interest], topical, timely; ~ *fråga* burning (topical) question; *de* ~*a varorna* the goods in question; *det är mycket* ~*t just nu* it's very much in the news these days; *jag har inte siffran* ~ *just nu* I can't remember the exact figure just now
aktör actor
akupunktur acupuncture
akust|ik *s2* acoustics (*pl, behandlas som sg*) **-iker** [aˈkuss-] acoustician
akustikplatta sound-insulating board

akustisk [a'kuss-] *a5* acoustic; ~ *gitarr* acoustic guitar

akut *a1* acute; urgent; ~ *accent* acute accent; ~ *smärta* (*äv.*) sharp pain -**mottagning** casualty department -**sjukvård** emergency treatment

akvamarin *s3* aquamarine

akvarell *s3*, -**färg** watercolour -**ist** watercolourist

akvarie|fisk [-'va:-] aquarium fish -**växt** aquarium (aquatic) plant

akvarium [-'va:-] *s4* aquarium

akvatint *s3*, -**gravyr** aquatint

akvatisk [-'va:-] *a5*, ~ *energi* aquatic energy

akvavit *s3* aquavit; schnap[p]s (*pl* schnap[p]s)

akvedukt *s3* aqueduct

al *s2* alder

alabaster [-'bass-] *s2* alabaster

à la carte [alla'kart] à la carte

aladåb *s3* aspic (*på* of)

A-lag first team (string); *bildl.* topnotchers (*pl*)

alarm *s7* alarm; *falskt* ~ false alarm; *slå* ~ sound (beat) the alarm -**anordning** alarm device -**beredskap** state of emergency

alarmer|a alarm, sound the alarm -**ing** raising the alarm

alarm|klocka alarm bell -**signal** alarm signal; *flyg.* air-raid warning -**system** alarm system

Alaska [aˣlaska] *n* Alaska

alba *s1* alb

alban *s3* Albanian **Albanien** [-'ba:-] *n* Albania

albansk [-'ba:nsk] *a5* Albanian **albanska 1** (*språk*) Albanian **2** (*kvinna*) Albanian woman

albatross [-'tråss, *äv.* ˣalba-] *s3*, *zool.*, *golf.* albatross

albigens [-g-] *s3* Albigensian; ~*er* (*äv.*) Albigenses

albinism albinism **albino** [-'bi:-] -*n*, *pl albiner* albino

Albion ['albiån] *n* Albion

album ['all-] *s7* album

albumin *s4*, *s3* albumin, albumen -**uri** *s3* albuminuria

aldehyd *s3* aldehyde

aldrig 1 never; ~ *i livet!* not for the life of me!, *vard.* not on your life!; ~ *mera* never again, nevermore; ~ *någonsin* never once; *nästan* ~ hardly ever; *bättre sent än* ~ better late than never; *du kan* ~ *tro hur roligt vi har haft* you'll never guess what fun we had; *du är väl* ~ *sjuk?* you're not ill, are you?; *man skall* ~ *säga* ~ never say never **2** (*i koncessiva förbindelser*) *som* ~ *det* like anything; ~ *så litet* the least little bit; *du kan göra* ~ *så många invändningar* no matter how much you object; *om man också är* ~ *så försiktig* however careful you are

alert [a'lärt] **I** *a1* alert, watchful; lively **II** *s2*, *på* ~*en* on the alert

Aleuterna [-'levv-] *pl* the Aleutian Islands

alexandrin *s3* Alexandrine [verse]

alf *s3* elf

alfa *s6* alpha -**aktivitet** alpha rhythm (wave)

alfabet [ˣalfa- *el.* -'e:t] *s7* alphabet

alfabetiser|a teach how to read -**ingskampanj** literacy campaign

alfabetisk [-'be:- *el.* ˣalfa-] *a5* alphabetic[al]; ~ *ordning* alphabetical order

alfa|numerisk [-'me:-] alphanumeric, alphameric -**partikel** alpha particle -**strålar** alpha rays -**strålning** alpha ray

alfresko [-'fress-] *adv*, -**målning** fresco

al|fågel old squaw, oldwife -**förrädare** Steller's eider

alg [-j] *s3* alga (*pl* algae)

algebra ['alje-] *s1* algebra -**isk** [-'bra:-] *a5* algebraic[al]

Alger [-'ʃe:r] *n* Algiers **algerier** [-'ʃe:-] Algerian, Algerine **Algeriet** [-'ʃe'ri:-] Algeria **algerisk** [-'ʃe:-] *a5* Algerian, Algerine

algo|log algology -**logj** *s3* algological

algoritm *s3* algorithm, algorism

alhidad *s3* alidad[e]

alias ['a:-] alias

alibi ['a:li- *el.* ˣa:li-] *s6* alibi; *bevisa sitt* ~ prove an alibi; *han hade vattentätt* ~ he had a cast-iron alibi

alien|ation alienation -**era** alienate

alifatisk [-'fa:-] *a5* aliphatic

alika ['ali- *el.* ˣali-] *s1* jackdaw; *full som en* ~ drunk as a fish, dead drunk

alisarin *s4*, *s3* alizarin

alka *s1* auk

alkali ['all- *el.* -'ka:-] *s4* alkali -**beständig** alkaliproof -**metall** alkali metal

alkal|isera alkalize -**isk** [-'ka:-] *a5* alkaline; ~ *jordartsmetall* alkaline earth [metal]; ~ *reaktion* alkaline reaction -**iskt** [-'ka:-] *adv*, *reagera* ~ have an alkaline reaction

alkaloid [-o'i:d] *s3* alkaloid

aikan *s3* alkane, paraffin

alkekung little auk, dovekie

alkem|i [-çe-] *s3* alchemy -**ist** alchemist

alken [-k-] *s3* alkene, olefine

alkis [ˣallkis] *s2* dipso

alkohol [ˣall- *el.* -'hå:l] *s3* alcohol; spirit -**begär** craving for drink -**fri** nonalcoholic; ~ *dryck* soft drink -**förgiftning** alcoholic poisoning -**halt** alcoholic strenght -**haltig** *a1* alcoholic; ~*a drycker* alcoholic beverages, *AE.* alcoholic (hard) liquors

alkohol|iserad [-'se:-] alcoholized -**isk** [-'hå:-] *a5* alcoholic -**ism** alcoholism, dipsomania

alkoholist alcoholic, dipsomaniac, habitual drunkard -**anstalt** alcoholism treatment unit -**vård** treatment of alcoholics

alkohol|missbruk abuse of alcohol -**prov** sobriety test -**påverkad** *a5* under the influence of drink -**sjukdom** alcoholic disease -**skadad** *a5* alcoholic -**stark** strong, high-proof -**svag** low-proof -**test** alcohol test; (*vid trafikkontroll*) breath test, breathalyser test

alkotest *se* alkoholtest

alkov [-'kå:v] *s3* alcove; recess [in a wall]

alkyd|harts [-ˣky-d-] alkyd resin -**lack** alkyd varnish

alkyl [-'ky:l] *s3* alkyl

all I *pron* **1** *fören.* all; (*varje*) every; ~*e man på däck* all hands on deck; ~*a tiders* (*vard.*) great, super, swell, smashing; *av* ~*a krafter* with all one's energy, with might and main; *av* ~*t hjärta* with all one's heart; *för* ~ *del!* not at all!, don't mention it!, you're welcome!; *för* ~ *framtid* permanently; *en gång för* ~*a* once and for all; *i* ~ *enkelhet* in all simplicity, quite informally; *i* ~ *evighet* for ever and ever, ad infinitum; *i* ~*a fall* nevertheless, all the same; *i ~ hast* hurriedly, (*i brev*) in haste; *i ~ tysthet* very quietly, in strict secrecy; *med ~ aktning för* with due respect to; *mot ~t förnuft* absurd, absolutely senseless; *på ~a fyra* on all fours; *på ~t sätt* in every way; *till ~ lycka* fortunately enough; *under ~ kritik* beneath [all] criticism, miserable; *utan ~ anledning* for no reason at all, without any reason [whatever]; *utom ~ fara* out of danger, completely safe, past the crisis; *utom ~t tvivel* without any (beyond all) doubt; *gå ~ världens väg* go the way of all flesh; *ha ~ anledning till missnöje* have every reason to be dissatisfied; *~a barn i början* you must learn to creep before you run; *~a goda ting är tre* all good things are three in number; *~ vår början bliver svår* all things are difficult before they are easy; *han har ~a utsikter att lyckas* he has every chance of succeeding; *vad i ~ sin dar (i ~ världen) säger du?* what on earth are you saying? **2** *självst.* all; *~a* all, (*varenda en*) everybody, everyone; *~as krig mot ~a* (*skämts.*) free for all; *~as vår vän* our mutual friend; *~t eller intet* all or nothing; *~t som* all told, all in all; *trots ~t* after all; *ngns ~t i ~o* a p.'s factotum; *500 kronor i ett för ~t* a lump sum of 500 kronor; *en för ~a och ~a för en* one for all and all for one; *av ~t att döma* as far as can be judged; *sätta ~t på ett kort* stake everything on one card, put all one's eggs in one basket; *det är ej ~om givet* it is not given to everybody; *det är inte guld ~t som glimmar* all is not gold that glitters; *fartyget förliste med man och ~t* the ship went down with all hands; *han var ~t annat än glad* he was anything but happy; *när ~t kommer omkring* after all is said and done; *plikten framför ~t* duty first **II** *a* (*slut*) over; *hennes saga var ~* that was the end of her

alla *se all*

allaktivitetshus multi-activity centre

allaredan [-ˣre:-] already

all|bekant wellknown **-daglig** everyday; commonplace, ordinary

alldeles quite; altogether; absolutely, entirely, completely, all; exactly; *~ häpen* completely taken aback; *~ mörkt* pitch-dark, pitch-black; *~ nyss* just now; *~ omöjligt* utterly impossible; *~ rätt* perfectly right; *~ säkert* absolutely certain; *~ för tidigt* far too early, all too soon; *det gör mig ~ detsamma* it is all the same (all one) to me; *det är ~ i sin ordning* it is quite in order (quite all right); *kjolen är ~ för lång* the skirt is much too long

alldenstund inasmuch as; because, since; *jur.* whereas

allé *s3* avenue; walk

allegat *s7* voucher

allegor|i *s3* allegory **-isera** allegorize **-isk** [-ˈgo:-] *a5* allegoric[al]

allegretto [-ˈgrettɔ] *s6 o. adv* allegretto

allegro [-ˈle:grɔ] *s6 o. adv* allegro

allehanda I *oböjligt a* all sorts of, of all sorts, miscellaneous **II** *oböjligt s* all sorts of things, sundries

allemansrätt *ung.* right of common

allena [-ˣle:- *el.* -ˈle:-] *oböjligt a o. adv* alone **-rådande** *a4* in sole control; universally prevailing

allenast [-ˣle:- *el.* -ˈle:-] only; *endast och ~* [only and] solely, exclusively

allergen [-j-] *s7, s4* allergen

allerg|i [-ˈgi:] *s3* allergy **-iker** [-ˈlärr-] allergic person **-isk** [-ˈlärr-] *a5* allergic (*mot* to)

allergitest allergy (scratch) test **allergolog** [-goˈlå:g] allergist

allernådigst [-ˣnå:-] Most Gracious

alle|sammans all of them (*etc.*); *adjö ~!* goodbye everybody! **-städes** everywhere; *~ närvarande* omnipresent, ubiquitous

all|farväg highroad; *vid sidan av ~en* off the beaten track **-god** all-bountiful **-helgonadag [en]** [-ˣhell-] All Saints' Day

allians [-ˈaŋs] *s3* alliance **-fri** nonaligned; *~ politik* policy of non-alignment **-fördrag** treaty of alliance **-ring** eternity ring

alliera *rfl* ally o.s. (*med* to) **allierad** *a5* allied (*med* to); (*friare*) connected (*med* with); *de ~e* the allies

alligator [-ˣa:tår] *s3* alligator

allihop all [of us *etc.*]

allitter|ation alliteration **-era** alliterate

allmakt omnipotence

allmoge *s2* peasantry, country people (folk) **-dräkt** peasant costume **-konst** folk art **-stil** rustic style

allmos|a *s1* alms (*pl*); *-or* alms; *leva av -or* live on charity

allmoseutdel|are almsgiver; (*katolsk präst*) almoner **-ning** almsgiving

allmän *al* (*vanlig*) common, ordinary; (*gemensam el.* tillgänglig *för alla*) general; (*som gäller för alla*) universal; (*som står i samband med stat, kommun el. regering*) public; (*gängse*) current, prevalent; *~t bifall* universal approval; *~t bruk* (*sedvänja*) prevalent custom, (*användning*) general use; *~ idrott* athletics (*pl*); *~ landsväg* public highway; *~na meningen* public opinion; *~ rösträtt* universal suffrage; *det ~na* the community, the [general] public; *det ~na bästa* the public (common, general) good (weal); *i ~t bruk* in general use; *i ~na handeln* in general commerce, on the market; *i ~na ordalag* in general terms, (*fritt*) vaguely; *på ~ bekostnad* at public expense; *tallen är ~ i dessa trakter* the pine is common in these parts

allmän|belysning general lighting **-bildad** *ung.* well-informed, well-read **-bildande** *ung.* generally instructive **-bildning** all-round education; general knowledge **-farlig** *~ brottsling* dangerous criminal **-giltig** generally applicable, of universal application **-giltighet** universal applicability **-gods** commonplace things

allmänhet 1 *~en* the public; *den stora ~en* the general public, the man in the street; *i ~ens intresse* in the interest[s] of the public; *~en äger tillträde* open to the public **2** *i ~* in general, as a rule; *i största ~* very generally, in very broad terms

allmän|medicinare *se allmänpraktiker* **-mänsklig** human; universal; broadly humane

allmännelig [ˣall- *el.* -ˈmänne-] *a5* catholic; universal; *en helig ~ kyrka* the Holy Catholic Church

allmänning common [land]

allmän|nytta public good (utility) **-nyttig** for the public good (weal), for the commonweal; *~t företag* public utility company; *för ~t ändamål* for the use of the public, for purposes of public utility **-orientering** *en ~ i ämnet* a general introduction to the subject **-politisk** *~ debatt* general political debate **-praktik** general practice **-praktiker** general practitioner **-praktiserande** *~ läkare* general practitioner **-preventiv** *~a åtgärder* public-preventive measures

allmänt *adv* commonly, generally, universally; *~ bekant* generally known; *en ~ hållen redogörelse* a general account; *det talas ~ om henne* she is the talk of the town; *det är ~ känt* it is common knowledge

allmäntillstånd *med.* general condition
allo *se all I 2*
alloker|a allocate **-ing** allocation
allom [-âmm] *se all I 2*
allomfattande all-embracing, comprehensive, general
allonge [a'lånʃ] *s5 (på växel)* allonge, rider **-peruk** full-bottomed wig
allo|pat allopath[ist] **-pati** *s3* allopathy
allra of all; very; *~ först (sist)* first (last) of all; *~ helst* most of all, above all; *~ högst* at the very most; *~ överst* topmost; *de ~ flesta* the vast majority; *det ~ heligaste* the holy of holies, *(friare)* the sanctuary; *av ~ bästa kvalitet* of the very best quality; *i ~ högsta grad* in (to) the highest possible degree; *med ~ största nöje* with the greatest pleasure; *göra sitt ~ bästa (äv.)* do one's level best; *den kostar ~ minst 20 kronor* it costs 20 kronor at the very least; *han är ~ högst 40 år* he is 40 at the very most; *jag kommer med det ~ första* I shall come at the earliest possible opportunity
allra|högst *den ~e* the Most High **-käraste** [-ˣçä:-], **-käresta** *s9* most beloved, dearest of all
all|rengöringsmedel all-purpose cleaner **-riskförsäkring** comprehensive insurance
all round, allround *oböjligt a, se allsidig*
allrum multipurpose room
alls at all; *ingenting ~* nothing whatever (at all); *inget besvär ~* no trouble whatever (at all); *inte ~ trött* not at all (a bit) tired
all|seende *a4* all-seeing **-sidig** *al* all-round, comprehensive; *skänka en fråga ~ belysning* shed light on all aspects of a question **-sköns** [-ʃ-] *oböjligt a, i ~ ro* completely undisturbed, at peace with the world
allsmäktig [ˣalls- *el.* -'mäktig] almighty, omnipotent; *Gud ~* Almighty God
allström universal current
allströms|motor universal motor **-mottagare** universal receiver
allsång community singing, singsong
allt I *pron, se all* **II** *s7, se världsalltet* **III** *adv, ~ framgent* from now on, from this time forward, henceforth, henceforward[s]; *~ som oftast* fairly often; *i ~ större utsträckning* to an ever increasing extent; *du hade ~ rätt ändå* you were right after all; *hon blir ~ bättre* she is gradually improving, she is getting better and better
allt|efter according to **-eftersom** as **-emellanåt** from time to time, every now and then **-fort** still **-för** too, quite (altogether, all, only, far) too; *~ liten* far too small; *~ mycket av det goda* too much of a good thing; *det är ~ vänligt av er* it is too kind of you; *det gör jag blott ~ gärna* I shall be only too happy to do it

alltiallo [-ˣallo] *n el. r* right-hand man; maid-of-all-work; factotum
alltid always, ever; *för ~* for ever (good), forever; *det blir väl ~ någon råd* something is sure to turn up; *du kan ju ~ fråga honom* you can always ask him, why don't you ask him?
allt|ifrån ever since **-igenom** through and through, throughout; thoroughly; *en ~ lyckad fest* a very successful party; *han är ~ ärlig* he is thoroughly honest **-ihop[a]** all [of it], the whole lot
allting [ˣall-] everything
alltinget [ˣall-] *(på Island)* the Althing
allt|jämt still **-mer[a]** increasingly, more and more **-nog** in short, anyhow **-omfattande** all-embracing **-samman[s]** all [of it (them *etc.*)], the whole lot [of it *etc.*] **-sedan** *~ dess* ever since then **-så** so then; *(följaktligen)* accordingly, consequently, thus **-uppslukande** *bildl.* all-absorbing
allu|dera allude *(på to)* **-sion** allusion
alluv|ial *a5* alluvial **-ium** [-'lu:-] *s8* alluvium
allvar *s7* earnestness, seriousness; gravity; *på fullt ~* seriously, in real earnest; *på fullaste ~* in all seriousness; *göra ~ av ett löfte* fulfill a promise; *ta ngn på ~* take s.b. seriously; *är det ditt ~?* are you serious?, do you really mean that?; *detta är mitt fulla ~* I am quite serious; *jag menar ~* I am serious, I really mean it, *vard.* I mean business; *stundens ~ kräver* the gravity of the situation demands, in this hour of crisis we must; *vintern har kommit på ~* winter has come to stay
allvarlig *al* serious, grave; earnest; *~a avsikter* serious intentions; *~ fara* grave danger; *~a förmaningar* serious admonitions; *se ~ ut* look serious (grave); *ta en ~ vändning* take a turn for the worse **allvarligt** *adv* seriously; *~ sinnad* serious-minded; *~ talat (äv.)* joking apart
allvarsam *a5* serious, grave; *en ~ min* a serious (grave) expression; *hålla sig ~* keep serious, *(för skratt)* keep a straight face
allvars|diger fraught with gravity **-ord** serious word
all|vetande *a4* all-knowing, omniscient **-vetare** person with a vast fund of general knowledge; *iron.* oracle, know-all **-vis** all-wise **-ätare** omnivore
alm *s2* wych-elm, witch-elm
almanacka *s1* almanac, calendar; *(fick-)* diary
aln [a:ln] *s2, ung.* ell (= *45 eng. tum*)
aloe *s5* aloe **-hampa** aloe fibre
alp *s3* alp
alpacka [-ˣpacka] *s1* **1** *(lama)* alpaca **2** *(tyg)* alpaca **3** *miner.* nickel (German) silver
alpbestig|are alpine climber **-ning** alpine climbing
Alperna ['alp-] *pl* the Alps
alp|flora alpine flora **-glöd** alpenglow **-hydda** [alpine] chalet
alpin *a5* alpine **-ism** alpinism **-ist** alpinist
alp|jägare *mil.* alpine rifleman **-landskap** alpine landscape **-ros** rhododendron **-stav** alpenstock **-viol** cyclamen
alruna [ˣa:l-] *s1* mandrake, mandragora
alsikeklöver alsike [clover]
alster ['als-] *s7* product, production; *koll. äv.* pro-

duce, (*böcker*) works (*pl*)
alstr|a produce, manufacture; *elektr.* generate; *bildl.* engender **-ing** production, manufacture; generation; procreation **alstrings|drift** generative instinct **-duglig** *biol.* reproductive **-förmåga, -kraft** generative power; productivity **-linje** *se generatris*

alt *s2, mus.* (*manlig*) alto (*pl* altos), countertenor; (*kvinnlig*) alto, contralto

altan *s3* [roof] balcony; terrace

altar|bord communion table, altar **-duk** altar cloth

altare *s6* altar; ~*ts sakrament* the Eucharist

altar|kläde antependium **-kärl** sacred vessel **-ljus** altar candle **-ring** altar rails (*pl*) **-skrud** vestment **-skåp** triptych, reredos **-tavla** altarpiece **-tjänst** altar service, liturgy **-uppsats** retable

alteration agitation, anxiety

alter ego [ˈalter ˈeːgɔ] alter ego

altererad [-ˈreː-] *a5* flurried, excited

altern|ativ I *s7* alternative **II** [*äv.* ˈalt-] *a5* alternative **-era** alternate

alt|fiol viola **-horn** althorn

altityd *s3* altitude

alt|klarinett alto clarinet **-klav** alto (viola) clef

alto|cumulus [-ˈkuː-] *meteor.* altocumulus **-stratus** [-ˈstraː-] *meteor.* altostratus

altru|ism altruism **-ist** altruist **-istisk** [-ˈiss-] *a5* altruistic

alt|röst [contr]alto [voice] **-saxofon** alto saxophone **-stämma** [contr]alto voice; [contr]alto part **-violin** viola

aluminera aluminize

aluminium [-ˈmiː-] *s8* aluminium; *AE.* aluminum **-brons** aluminium bronze **-folie** aluminium foil **-kastrull** aluminium saucepan **-legering** aluminium alloy **-oxid** aluminium oxide, alumina **-plåt** sheet aluminium

alumn *s3* alumnus (*pl* alumni), *fem.* alumna (*pl* alumnae)

alun *s7* [potash] alum **-skiffer** alum shale **-stift** stick of alum; styptic pencil

alv *s2, geol.* subsoil, undersoil

alveol [-ˈåːl] *s3* alveolus (*pl* alveoli)

amalgam *s7, s4* amalgam **-era** amalgamate **-fyllning** amalgam stopping (filling)

amanuens *s3* assistant university teacher (librarian, archivist *etc.*), assistant, amanuensis; (*vid ämbetsverk*) chief (principal) clerk; (*vid kansli*) third secretary

amaryllis [-ˈryll-] *-en amaryller* amaryllis

amason [-ˈsåːn] *s3* Amazon **-drottning** Amazon queen

Amasonfloden the Amazon

amatör amateur (*på* of, at) **-bestämmelser** amateur rules (regulations) **-boxning** amateur boxing **-brottning** amateur wrestling **-foto** amateur snapshot **-fotograf** amateur photographer **-idrott** amateur athletics (*pl*) (sport) **-mässig** *a1* amateurish **-regler** amateur rules **-skap** *s7, hans* ~ his amateur status **-skådespelare** amateur actor **-spelare** amateur player **-sändare** amateur transmitter **-teater** amateur theatricals (*pl*) **-tävling** (*fri idrott*) amateur meeting

ambassad *s3* embassy **ambassadrjs** *s3* ambassadress

ambassad|råd [embassy] counsellor **-sekreterare** *förste* (*andre, tredje*) ~ first (second, third) secretary [of (to, at) an embassy] **-ör** ambassador

ambi|tion ambition **-tiös** [-ˈʃöːs] *a1* zealous, aspiring, pushing; (*plikttrogen*) conscientious

ambival|ens *s3* ambivalence **-ent** *a4* ambivalent

ambra *s2* ambergris

ambros|ia [-ˈbrɔ:-] *s1* ambrosia **-isk** *a5* ambrosial, ambrosian

ambulans [-ˈans *el.* -ˈaŋs] *s3* ambulance **-flygplan** ambulance (hospital) plane, air ambulance **-förare** ambulance driver

ambulatorisk [-ˈtoː-] *a5* ambulatory

ambuler|a *ung.* move (travel) [from place to place] **-ande** *a4* itinerant, travelling

amen [ˣamm- *el.* ˈamm-] amen; *säga ja och* ~ *till allt* (*ung.*) agree to anything; *så säkert som* ~ *i kyrkan* as sure as fate

americium [-ˈriː-] *s8* americium

Amerika [aˈmeː-] *n* America; ~*s förenta stater* the United States of America

amerika|arv *ung.* dollar inheritance **-brev** letter from America **-feber** America fever

amerikan *s3,* **-are** [-ˣkaː-] *s9* American **-isera** Americanize **-isering** [-ˈseː-] Americanization **-ism** *s3* Americanism **-ist** Americanist

amerikan|sk [-ˈkaːnsk] *a5* American **-ska 1** (*språk*) American **2** (*kvinna*) American woman

amerika|resa trip (journey) to America **-svensk** Swedish-American

ametist amethyst

amfetamin *s3, s4* amphetamine

amfibie [-ˈfiː-] *s5* amphibian **-artad** [-aːr-] *a5* amphibious **-båt** amphibious craft **-fordon** tracked landing craft **-plan** amphibian [plane] **-stridsvagn** amphibious tank

amfibisk [-ˈfiː-] *a5* amphibious

amfiteat|er [ˣamfi- *el.* -ˣfiː-] amphitheatre **-ralisk** [ˈraː-] *a5* amphitheatric[al]

amfora [ˈamfåra] *s1* amphora

amj *s3* muffler; comforter

amidplast [ˣmiːd-] polyamide

amjn *s3, s4* amine **-harts** aminoplastic [resin]

aminosyra [-ˣmiː-] amino acid

amiral *s3* **1** *mil.* admiral **2** *zool.* red admiral **-itet** *s7* admiralty; ~*et* (*Storbritannien*) the Admiralty Board, *AE.* Navy Department

amirals|flagg admiral's flag **-person** flag officer, admiral **-skepp** flagship, admiral's ship

amma I *s1* wet nurse **II** *v1* nurse, suckle, breast-feed; *hon* ~*r barnet själv* she feeds the baby herself, she breast-feeds the baby

ammoniak [-ˈmɔ:-] *s2* ammonia

ammonjt *s3* ammonite

ammonium [-ˈmɔ:-] *s8* ammonium **-karbonat** ammonium carbonate

ammunition *s3* ammunition; munitions (*pl*); *lös* ~ practice ammunition; blank cartridge *skarp* ~ live ammunition

ammunitions|depå ammunition dump **-fabrik** munitions factory **-fartyg** ammunition ship **-förråd** ammunition supply (stores) **-gördel** cartridge belt; bandoleer **-väska** ammunition pocket

amnesi *s3* amnesia
amnesti *s3* amnesty; *få ~* obtain [an] amnesty; *bevilja ngn ~* grant s.b. an amnesty **-kungörelse** act of indemnity
amning breast-feeding, nursing, suckling
amok [a'måck] *oböjligt s* amuck, amok; *löpa ~* run amuck
a-moll A minor
amoral|isk [-'ra:-] *a5* amoral **-itet** amorality
amorbåge Cupid's bow
amorf [-'årf] *al* amorphous
amorin *s3* cupid
amorter|a [-å-] amortize, pay off by instalments; *~ ett lån* pay off a loan **-ing** repayment by instalments, amortization
amorterings|belopp amortization [amount (payment)] **-fri** *~tt lån* straight loan, loan payable in full at maturity **-lån** instalment credit (loan); sinking-fund loan **-plan** amortization schedule **-tid** period of amortization **-villkor** terms of amortization (repayment)
amorös *a5* amorous
1 ampel [ˣamp-] *s2 (för växter)* hanging flowerpot; *(hänglampa)* hanging lamp
2 ampel ['amp-] *a2, ampla lovord* unstinted praise *(sg)*
amper ['amp-] *a2* pungent, sharp; biting, stinging
ampere [-'pä:r] *s9, s5* ampere **-meter** *s2*, **-mätare** ammeter **-timme** ampere-hour
ampersand *s3* ampersand
amplifiera amplify
amplitud *s3* amplitude **-modulering** amplitude modulation
ampull *s3* ampoule, ampul[e]; *Storbritannien äv.* ampulla
amput|ation amputation **-era** amputate
amsaga [ˣamm-] tall story, old wives' tale
amt *s7, ung.* shire, county
amulett *s3* amulet
amygdalin *s3, s4* amygdalin
amylacetat [-ˣmy:l-] amyl acetate
amöba [-ˣmö:-] *s1* amoeba
1 an [ann] *hand.* to
2 an [ann] *av och ~* up and down, to and fro; *gå av och ~ i rummet (äv.)* pace the room
ana have a feeling (presentiment); *~ oråd* suspect mischief; *intet ont ~nde* unsuspecting; *~ sig till ngns tankar* divine a p.'s thoughts; *det lät ~ it* hinted at (gave an inkling of); *du kan inte ~ hur glad jag blev* you have no idea how glad (happy) I was; *vem kunde ~ det* who would have suspected that; *det ante mig* I suspected as much
anabapt|ism Anabaptism **-ist** Anabaptist
anabol [-'bå:l] *al* anabolic; *~ steroid* anabolic steroid **-ism** anabolism
anacka [ˣnacka] *se anagga*
anaerob [anaä'rå:b] **I** *s3* anaerobe, anaerobium *(pl* anaerobia) **II** *a5* anaerobic
anagga [aˣnagga] dash it!, dang it!
anagram [-'gramm] *s7* anagram
anakolut *s3* anacoluthon *(pl* anacolutha)
anakonda [-ˣkånda] *s1* anaconda
anakoret *s3* anchorite
anakronis|m anachronism **-tisk** *a5* anachronistic
analfabet *s3*, **-isk** *a5* illiterate **-ism** illiteracy

analfena anal fin
analgetikum [-'ge:-] *s8* analgesic
analog [-'lå:g] *al* analogous *(med* to); *~ klocka* analog[ue] watch
analogi *s3* analogy; *i ~ med* on the analogy of **-bevis** analogical evidence **-bildning** analogical formation, analogy **-maskin** analog computer
analogisk [-'lå:-] *a5* analogic[al] **analogislut** analogism
analys *s3* analysis *(pl* analyses) **-era** analyse
analyt|iker [-'ly:-] analyst **-isk** *a5* analytic[al]
analöppning anus
anamm|a [a'namma] **1** receive, accept; *~ nattvarden* partake of the Holy Communion **2** *(tillägna sig)* appropriate, seize **3** *fan ~!* damn [it]!, damn and blast!, hell! **-ande** *s6* acceptance
anamnes *s3* anamnesis *(pl* anamneses)
ananas [ˣa:- *el.* ˣann-] *s9* pineapple
anapest *s3* anap[a]est
anark|i *s3* anarchy **-isk** [a'narr-] *a5* anarchic[al] **-ism** anarchism **-ist** anarchist **-istisk** [-'kiss-] *a5* anarchistic
anarkosyndikalism anarchosyndicalism
anastigmat anastigmat
anatema [-ˣte:- *el.* -'te:-] *s6* anathema
ana|tom [-'tå:m] *s3* anatomist **-tomi** *s3* anatomy **-tomisal** dissecting-room **-tomisk** [-'tå:-] *a5* anatomical
anbefall|a 1 *(ålägga, påbjuda)* enjoin, charge; *~ ngn tystnad* enjoin silence upon a p.; *läkaren -de honom vila* the doctor ordered him to rest **2** *(förorda, rekommendera)* recommend, advocate; *~ på det varmaste* sincerely recommend **3** *(anförtro, överlämna)* entrust command, commend; *~ sin själ i Guds hand* commend one's soul to God
anbelanga *vad mig ~r* as far as I am concerned
anblick sight; appearance, aspect; *en ståtlig ~* an imposing appearance; *vid ~en av* at the sight of; *vid första ~en* at first sight
anbring|a *(sätta, ställa)* place, put; *(sätta på etc.)* mount, affix, fit, apply **-ande** *s6* placing, mounting *etc.*
anbud *(köp-)* bid; *(sälj-)* offer; *(pris)* quotation; *lämna ~ på* send in a tender for; *~ infordras härmed på* tenders are invited for
anbuds|formulär tender form **-givare** tenderer, bidder **-givning** [-'ji:v-] tendering, bidding **-kartell** tendering cartel
anciennitet seniority; *efter ~* by seniority
and *-en änder* wild duck; *jfr gräs-*
anda *s2* **1** *(andedräkt, andhämtning)* breath; *med ~n i halsen* out of breath, *(med spänning)* with bated breath; *ge upp ~n* give up the ghost, expire; *hålla ~n* hold one's breath; *hämta ~n* catch one's breath; *kippa efter ~n* gasp for breath; *tappa ~n* lose one's breath; *allt som liv och ~ har* everything that lives and breathes **2** *(stämning)* spirit; *i en ~ av samförstånd* in a spirit of understanding; *i samma ~* in the same spirit; *samma ~s barn* kindred spirits; *tidens ~* the spirit of the age; *när ~n faller på* when the spirit moves him *(etc.)*, *vard.* when he *(etc.)* is in the mood **3** *(mod, disciplin)* morale
andakt *s3* devotion; *med ~* in a devotional spirit; *förrätta sin ~* perform one's devotions

andakts|bok devotional manual **-full** devotional; devout **-stund** devotional hour **-övningar** devotions, devotional exercises
Andalusien [-'lu:-] *n* Andalusia
andanom [-åmm] *se ande 1*
andante [-ˣdann-] *s6 o. adv* andante
andas *dep* breathe, respire; ~ *in* breathe in, inhale; ~ *ut* breathe out, exhale, *bildl.* breathe freely; ~ *djupt* take a deep breath, breathe deeply
ande *s2* **1** (*själ*) spirit; (*intelligens*) mind, intellect; *i ~ns rike* in the spiritual (intellectual) world; *i andanom* in the spirit, in one's mind's eye; *~n är villig, men köttet är svagt* the spirit is willing, but the flesh is weak; *de i ~n fattiga* the poor in spirit **2** (*övernaturligt väsen*) spirit, ghost; *Den helige ~* the Holy Ghost (Spirit); *ngns onda ~* a p.'s evil spirit; *tjänande ~* ministering spirit; *de avlidnas andar* the spirits of the dead **3** (*personlighet, natur*) spirit, mind; *en stor ~* a spiritual giant; *besläktade andar* kindred spirits **-besvärjare** raiser of spirits, exorcist **-besvärjelse** raising of spirits, exorcism **-drag** *se andetag* **-dräkt** breath; *dålig ~* bad breath **-fattig** (*om pers.*) dull, vacuous, inane; (*om sak*) uninspired
andel share (*i* of); *ha ~ i ett företag* have an interest in a business
andels|bevis scrip [certificate] **-förening** coop [erative] [society], co-op **-företag** coop[erative] undertaking **-lägenhet** time-share apartment (flat); *AE.* condominium **-mejeri** coop[erative] dairy **-slakteri** coop[erative] slaughterhouse
andemening spirit, inward sense
Anderna ['and-] *pl* the Andes
ande|skådare seer [of visions], visionary **-skådning** [-å:-] preternatural insight, second sight **-tag** breath; *i ett ~* [all] in one breath; *till sista ~et* to one's last breath; *ta ett djupt ~* take a deep breath **-viskning** ghostly whisper **-värld** spirit[ual] world **-väsen** spirit[ual being]
and|fådd *a1* out of breath, breathless; *vard.* winded, puffed **-fåddhet** breathlessness, shortness of breath **-hämtning** breathing, respiration **-hämtningspaus** breathing space
andjakt duck shooting
andlig *a1* **1** (*själslig*) spiritual; (*psykisk, förstånds-*) intellectual, mental; *~t liv* intellectual life; *~ odling* cultural life; *~a värden* spiritual values; *barnets ~a utveckling* the child's mental development **2** (*gudfruktig*) spiritual, sacred, religious; (*kyrklig*) ecclesiastical; (*prästerlig*) clerical; *~ makt* spiritual power; *~ orden* religious order; *~t stånd* clerical order; *~a sånger* sacred songs; *~t ämbete* ecclesiastical appointment; *inträda i det ~a ståndet* take [holy] orders **andligen** mentally, intellectually, spiritually
andlös breathless; *~ tystnad* dead silence
andmat *bot.* duckweed
andning breathing, respiration; *konstgjord ~* artificial respiration; *andra ~en* second wind
andnings|apparat breathing apparatus; respirator **-organ** respiratory organ **-paus** breathing space (spell) **-svårigheter** *se andnöd* **-vägar** respiratory system (*sg*)
andnöd difficulty in breathing, respiratory distress

1 andra [-a:] *se andraga*
2 andr|a [-a] *-e* I *pron, se annan* II *räkn* second; *A~ Mosebok* Exodus; *~ våningen* (*i bet. 1 trappa upp*) first (*AE.* second) floor; *ett ~ klassens hotell* (*neds.*) a second-rate hotel; *för det ~* in the second place, secondly; *-e opponent, se andreopponent; -e styrman* second mate; *den ~ maj* the second of May, (*i brev*) 2nd May (May 2); *göra ett ~ försök* make a second attempt, *vard.* have another go; *ha en uppgift ur ~ hand* have information second-hand; *köpa i ~ hand* buy second-hand; *det får komma i ~ hand* it will have to come second (later)
andrag|a state; advance, put forward, mention, set forth; ~ *till sitt försvar* plead in one's defence **-ande** *s6* statement; advancing *etc.*
andragradsekvation equation of the second degree
andrahands|- second-hand **-pris** resale price **-uppgift** second-hand information **-värde** trade-in value
andrakammarval elections to the Second Chamber [of the Swedish Riksdag]
andraklass|are second-form boy (girl) **-biljett** second-class ticket **-kupé** second-class compartment **-vagn** second-class carriage (coach; *AE.* car)
andra|placering *han fick en ~* he came second **-plansfigur** insignificant person
andre *se 2 andra*
andreaskors [-ˣdre:as-] *konst.* St. Andrew's cross, saltire
andre|maskinist second engineer **-opponent** opponent appointed by candidate for a doctorate **-pilot** copilot, second pilot **-styrman** second mate
androgen [-'je:n] I *a5* androgenic II *s7, s4* androgen
andrum room to breathe; *bildl.* breathing space
and|truten *a3* out of breath, breathless; winded **-täppa** *s1* shortness of breath **-täppt** *a4* short of breath; *vard.* winded, short-winded
andäktig *a1* devout; attentive **-het** devoutness; attentiveness
andäktigt *adv* devoutly; attentively; *lyssna ~ på ngn* hang on a p.'s words
anekdot [-'då:t] *s3* [humorous] anecdote, amusing story **-isk** *a5* anecdotal, anecdotic
anem|i *s3* anaemia **-isk** [-'ne:-] *a5* anaemic
anemometer [-'me:-] *s2* anemometer; (*vindmätare äv.*) wind gauge
anemon [-'å:n *el.* -'o:n] *s3* anemone
aneroidbarometer [-ɔˣi:d-] aneroid barometer
anestesi *s3* anaesthesia
anestesio|log anaesthetist; *AE.* anesthesiologist **-logi** *s3* anaesthetics (*pl, behandlas som sg*); *AE.* anesthesiology
anestet|ikum [-'te:-] *s8*, **-isk** [-'te:-] *a5* anaesthetic
anfader [ˣa:n-] ancestor
anfall attack; *i sht mil.* assault, charge; (*sjukdoms- etc.*) fit; *ett hysteriskt ~* a fit of hysteria; *i ett ~ av vrede* in a fit of anger; *gå till ~* attack, charge; *rikta ett ~ mot* direct an attack against
anfalla attack; assail, assault
anfalls|krig aggressive war **-mål** objective

-plan plan of attack **-robot** offensive missile **-spelare** attacker, forward **-vapen** offensive weapon **-vinkel** angle of attack

anfang [-'faŋ] *s3, boktr.* initial [letter]

an|flygning [ˣann-] approach [path]; homing **-fordran** demand; *att betalas vid ~* payable on demand **-frätning** corrosion; pitting **-frätt** *a4* corroded; *~a tänder* decayed teeth; *~ av rost* rusty

anfäkt|a harass; haunt; assail; *~s av tvivel* be haunted by doubts **-else** tribulation [of spirit], vexation; obsession

anför|a 1 (*leda*) lead, command, be in command of; *~ en orkester* conduct an orchestra **2** (*andraga, framhålla*) state, say; *~ besvär* complain (*över* of); *~ besvär mot ett beslut* appeal against a decision; *~ som bevis* bring (enter) as evidence; *~ som skäl* give as reason; *~ till sitt försvar* plead in one's defence **3** (*citera*) quote, cite; *på det -da stället* in the passage cited **-ande** *s6* **1** lead[ership], command[ing]; *mus.* conductorship **2** (*yttrande*) statement; speech, address; *hålla ett ~* give an address, make a speech **-are** commander, leader; *mus.* conductor **-ing** *direkt ~* direct speech; *indirekt ~* indirect (reported) speech, *AE.* indirect discourse

anförings|sats inserted clause **-tecken** quotation mark, inverted (turned) comma **-verb** leading verb

anförtro *~ ngn ngt* entrust s.th. to s.b., entrust s.b. with s.th.; *~ ngn en hemlighet* confide a secret to s.b.; *hon ~dde mig att* she confided to me the fact that; *~ sig åt* entrust o.s. to, (*ge sitt förtroende*) confide in

anförvant relation, relative, [family] connection

ange 1 (*upplysa om, uppge*) inform, state, mention; *~ noga* specify, detail; *~ skälet till* state the reason for; *det angivna skälet* the reason given; *det på fakturan angivna priset* the invoice[d] price **2** (*anmäla för myndighet*) report, inform against, denounce; *~ ngn för polisen* inform against s.b., report s.b. [to the police]; *~ sig själv* give o.s. up (in charge) **3** *~ takten* (*mus.*) indicate tempo, *bildl.* set the pace; *~ tonen* set the tone

angelsaxare [aŋel-] *se anglosaxare*

angelägen [ˣanje-] *a3* (*om sak*) urgent, pressing, important; (*om pers.*) anxious (*om* for); *~ om att göra* anxious to do, desirous of doing (to do); *~ om att vara till lags* anxious to please; *visa sig mycket ~* (*äv.*) be overanxious **-het 1** (*sak, ärende*) matter, affair, concern; *inre ~er* internal affairs; *sköta sina egna ~er* mind one's own business **2** (*betydelse, vikt*) urgency

angelägenhetsgrad degree of priority (urgency)

angenäm [ˣanje-] *a1* pleasant, agreeable; *det var ~t att träffas* it was a pleasure to meet you

angina [aŋˣgi:-] *s1* angina; *~ pectoris* angina pectoris

angiv|a [ˣanji:-] *se ange* **-are** informer **-else** information, denunciation, accusation; (*tull- etc.*) declaration **-eri** informing

angler ['aŋ(g)-] *s9* Angle

angli|cism [aŋ(g)li-] *s3* Anglicism **-kansk** [-'ka:nsk] *a5* Anglican; *~a kyrkan* Anglican Church, (*statskyrkan i England*) Church of England **-sera** anglicize

anglo|amerikansk ['aŋ(g)lo-] Anglo-American **-fil** *s3* Anglophil[e]

anglosax|are [aŋ(g)loˣsakks-] *s9*, **-isk** [-'sakks-] *a5*, **-iska** [-'sacks-] (*språk*) Anglo-Saxon

Angola [aŋˣgå:la] *n* Angola

angol|an *s3*, **-ansk** [-'a:nsk] *a5* Angolan

angora|garn [aŋˣgå:ra-] angora [wool] **-get** Angora goat **-kanin** Angora rabbit **-katt** Angora cat **-ull** (*från -get*) mohair; (*från -kanin*) angora [wool]

angostura [aŋgåˣstu:ra] *s2* angostura; (*smakessens vanl.*) angostura bitters (*pl*)

angrepp attack (*mot, på* on)

angrepps|punkt point of attack (application) **-vapen** offensive weapon

angripa attack, assault, assail; (*inverka skadligt på*) affect; (*skada*) injure; (*fräta på*) attack, corrode, rust; *~ ett problem* tackle (approach) a problem

angrip|are assailant, aggressor **-en** *a5*, *~ av röta* damaged by rot; *~ av sjukdom* diseased, struck down by illness; *metallen är ~ av rost* the metal has gone rusty

angränsande *a4* adjacent, adjoining, next

angå concern; (*avse, beträffa*) have reference to; *saken ~r dig inte* it is no concern of yours, *vard.* it's none of your business; *vad mig ~r* as far as I am concerned **-ende** regarding, concerning, as regards, as to, as for

angöra 1 *~ hamn* make port; *~ land* make land **2** (*fastgöra*) make fast

angörings|hamn [-j-] port of call **-plats** lay-by

anhalt *s3* halt; *AE.* way station

anhang *s7* following; (*patrask*) rabble; (*hejdukar*) tools (*pl*), hirelings (*pl*); *vard.* crew, gang; *hans ~* his likes (*pl*)

anhop|a heap (pile) up, amass; *~ sig* accumulate **-ning** piling up; accumulation; *~ av trupper* troop concentration

anhydrid *s3* anhydride

anhåll|a 1 (*fängsla, arrestera*) apprehend, arrest, take into custody **2** (*begära*) ask (*om* for), apply (*om* for), request, demand; *~ hos ngn om ngt* apply to s.b. for s.th.; *~ om en flickas hand* ask for a girl's hand [in marriage]; *~ om snar betalning* request [an] early settlement; *om svar -es* (*o.s.a.*) an answer will oblige (R.S.V.P.) **-an** *r*, *pl saknas* request, demand (*om* for); *enträgen ~* entreaty, solicitation; *ödmjuk ~* supplication **-ande** *s6* (*arrestering*) arrest; (*häktning*) apprehension

anhängare follower, adherent (*av, till* of); (*av idé*) supporter, advocate

anhängiggöra [ˣanhäŋigjö:ra] *~ vid domstol* bring into court; *~ ett mål vid domstol* bring an action before a court of law; *~ rättegång mot* take legal proceedings against

anhörig *subst. a* relative; *mina ~a* my family; *närmaste ~a* [av] next of kin

anilin *s2*, *s7* aniline **-färg** aniline dye **-förgiftning** aniline poisoning **-penna** indelible pencil, copying pencil

animal *a5*, **-isk** *a5* animal

animer|a animate; *stämningen var mycket ~d* there was a gay atmosphere **-ad** *a5* animate; *~*

A

film animated cartoon
animis|m animism **-tisk** *a5* animistic
animositet animosity
aning *s2* **1** (*förkänsla*) presentiment (*om* of; *om att* that); foreboding; hunch; *ond* ~ misgiving **2** (*föreställning*) notion, idea, feeling; *jag hade ingen* ~ *om* (*äv.*) I never suspected **3** (*smula, något litet*) *en* ~ a little, a trace, *vard.* a touch, a tiny (wee) bit, *kokk.* a dash, a sprinkle
anings|full apprehensive; expectant **-lös** unsuspecting
anis *s2* (*växt*) anise; (*krydda*) aniseed **-ett** *s3* anisette
anjon [ˣann-] *s3* anion
anka *s1* **1** [tame] duck **2** (*tidnings-*) hoax, canard
1 ankare *s6, s9* (*laggkärl*) *ung.* anker, firkin
2 ankare *s6* **1** *sjö. o. bildl.* anchor; *kasta ankar* cast (come to, drop) anchor; *lätta ankar* weigh anchor; *ligga för ankar* ride at anchor **2** *elektr.* armature **3** *byggn.* brace, cramp [iron] **4** (*i ur*) lever escapement
ankar|fly *s6* fluke, flue **-fäste** hold[ing-ground] **-klys** hawse[pipe] **-kätting** anchor chain **-plats** anchorage **-spel** anchor gear, capstan **-spole** armature coil **-stock** anchor stock **-tross** mooring (anchor) cable **-ur** lever watch
ank|bonde drake **-damm** duck pond
ankel *s2* ankle[bone] **-led** ankle joint **-lång** ankle-length **-socka** ankle sock; *AE.* anklet
anklaga ~ *ngn för ngt* accuse s.b. of s.th., charge s.b. with s.th.; *den* ~*des* the accused; *med* ~*nde miner* accusingly; *sitta på de* ~*des bänk* stand in the dock, *bildl.* stand accused, be under fire
anklagelse accusation, charge (*för* of); *rikta en* ~ *mot ngn* make an accusation against s.b.; *ömsesidiga* ~*r* cross accusations **-akt** bill of indictment **-punkt** count **-skrift** [written] indictment
anklang approval; *vinna* ~ meet with (win) approval; *väcka* ~ *hos ngn* appeal to s.b.
anknyt|a attach, join, unite (*till* to); connect, join (link) up (*till* with); *bibanan -er till stambanan vid C.* the branch line connects up with the main line at C.; *berättelsen -er till verkliga händelser* the story is based on real events **-ning** connection, attachment, link; *tekn.* extension
anknytningsapparat extension telephone
ankomm|a 1 (*anlända*) arrive (*till* at, in); ~*nde post* incoming (inward) mail; ~*nde tåg* (*i tidtabell o.d.*) [train] arrivals **2** (*bero*) depend (*på* on); *vad på mig -er* as far as I am concerned; *det -er på henne att se till det* it is up to her to see to that **-en** *a5* **1** (*anländ*) arrived **2** (*ngt skämd*) *-et kött* tainted meat; ~ *fisk* (*frukt*) fish (fruit) going bad **3** (*ngt berusad*) tipsy, merry
ankomst [-å-] *s3* arrival; *vid* ~*en till stationen* on my (*etc.*) arrival at the station **-datum** date of arrival **-hall** arrival hall **-tid** time of arrival
ankr|a anchor **-ing** anchoring, anchorage
ankrings|förbud anchoring prohibition **-plats** anchorage
anlag *s7* **1** *biol.* rudiment, germ, embryo (*till* of) **2** (*medfött*) talent, gift, aptitude (*för* for); *med.* tendency (*för* to), disposition (*för* towards); ~ *för fetma* tendency to put on weight; *musikaliska* ~ a gift for music; *ärftliga* ~ hereditary disposition (*sg*); *ha goda* ~ have a gift, be gifted, have good

mental powers
anlagd *a5* **1** *se anlägga* **2** *praktiskt* ~ of a practical turn; ~ *på förtjänst* planned (set up) on a profit basis
anlags|bärare *med.* carrier **-prov** aptitude test **-prövning** aptitude testing **-test** aptitude test
anledning (*skäl*) reason (*till* for, of); (*orsak*) cause, occasion (*till* for, of); *av vilken* ~? for what reason?, on what account?; *med* (*i*) ~ *av* on account of, owing to, in view of, because of; *med* ~ *härav* in view of this fact, for this reason, such being the case; *utan all* ~ without any (for no) reason; *vid minsta* ~ on the slightest provocation; *ge* ~ *till* give occasion to, cause; *ha* ~ *till missnöje* have cause for dissatisfaction; *det fanns ingen* ~ *till oro* there was no cause for alarm; *han hade all* ~ *att resa* he had every reason to leave; *på förekommen* ~ *får vi meddela* we find it necessary to point out
anlete *s6* visage, countenance, face; *i sitt* ~*s svett* by the sweat of one's brow **anletsdrag** feature, lineament
anligg|a ~ *mot* bear on **-ningsyta** contact surface
anlit|a 1 (*vända sig t.*) apply (turn) to (*ngn för a p.* for); ~ *advokat* engage (go to) a lawyer; ~ *läkare* call in a doctor; *vara mycket* ~*d* be in great demand, be successful (popular) **2** (*tillgripa*) have recourse to, resort to; ~ *lexikon* use (make use of) a dictionary; ~ *telefonen* use the telephone; ~ *vapenmakt* resort to arms; *en ofta* ~*d utväg* an expedient often resorted to **-ande** *s6, med* ~ *av* use being made of, with the aid of
anlopp 1 (*ansats*) run-up **2** (*rusning*) rush **3** (*anfall*) assault, attack (*mot* upon)
anlupen *a3* tarnished, discoloured; ~ *av fukt* tarnished by damp
anlägg|a 1 (*bygga*) build, construct, erect; (*grunda*) found, set up; ~ *en park* lay out a park **2** (*planera*) plan, design; ~ *mordbrand* commit arson **3** (*börja bära, lägga sig t. med*) take to, begin to wear, put on; ~ *skägg* grow a beard, let one's beard grow; ~ *sorg* put on mourning; ~ *kritiska synpunkter på* adopt a critical attitude towards **4** (*anbringa*) ~ *förband på ett sår* dress a wound, apply a bandage to a wound; *se äv. anlagd* **-are** builder, constructor; founder; designer **-ning 1** *abstr.* foundation; erection, construction **2** *konkr.* establishment; (*fabrik*) works (*pl*), plant, factory premises (*pl*); (*byggnad*) building, structure
anläggnings|arbetare construction worker **-kapital** fixed capital **-tillgångar** fixed (capital) assets
anlända arrive (*till* at, in); ~ *till* (*äv.*) reach
an|löpa 1 *sjö.,* ~ *en hamn* call at (touch) a port, put into a port **2** *tekn.* temper, anneal **-löpning** *tekn.* tempering, annealing **-löpningshamn** port of call
anman|a demand, request, urge (*ngn att s.b.* to); ~ *ngn att betala* demand payment from s.b. **-ing** request; *utan* ~ without reminder; *vid* ~ on demand
anmarsch advance
anmod|a request, call upon; (*enträget*) urge; instruct; demand **-an** *r* request; *på* ~ *av mig* at my

request
anmäl|a v2 **1** (*tillkännage, meddela*) announce, report; ~ *en besökande* announce a visitor; ~ *flyttning* give notice of changed address (residence); ~ *förhinder* send word to say one is prevented from coming; ~ *ngt för polisen* report s.th. to the police; ~ *sig för tjänstgöring* report for duty; ~ *sig som sökande till* put in an application for, apply for; ~ *sig till en examen* enter for an examination; ~ *sitt utträde ur en förening* withdraw one's membership from a club, resign from a club **2** (*recensera*) review **-an** r **1** announcement, notification (*om* of); report **2** (*recension*) review **3** (*tull-*) declaration **-are 1** (*angivare*) informer **2** (*recensent*) reviewer
anmälnings|avgift [-ä:-] registration fee; (*t. tävling etc.*) entry fee (money) **-blankett** registration (application) form **-lista** list of applicants (entrants) **-plikt** obligation to report [regularly] to police *etc.* **-tid** period of notification; (*idrott*) entry time
anmärk|a 1 (*påpeka, yttra*) remark, observe **2** (*klandra, ogilla*) find fault (*på* with); ~ *på* criticize; *han hade ingenting att* ~ *på* he found no fault with **-ning 1** (*yttrande, påpekande*) comment, remark, observation **2** (*förklaring*) remark, comment, observation, annotation; (*i bok*) note, footnote **3** (*klander*) objection, criticism, complaint **4** *skol.* bad [conduct] mark; *få* ~ be given a bad mark
anmärknings|bok conduct book; report card **-värd** a1 **1** (*märklig*) remarkable **2** (*beaktansvärd*) notable, noteworthy; (*märkbar*) noticeable
ann *se annan 1*
annaler [-'na:-] *pl* annals, records
annalkande I s6 approach[ing]; *vara i* ~ be approaching **II** a4 approaching; ~ *fara* imminent danger; *ett* ~ *oväder* a gathering storm
anna|n -*t andra* **1** other; (*efter självst. pron*) else; *en* ~ another, (*självst. äv.*) somebody (someone, anybody, anyone) else; *ingen* ~ nobody else; *ingen* ~ *än* no other than; *ingen* ~ *än du* no one [else] but you; *någon* ~ somebody (anybody) else; *en och* ~ *gång* occasionally, once in a while; *gång efter* ~ time and again, time after time; *tid efter* ~ from time to time; *av en eller* ~ *anledning* for some reason or other; *jag är av* ~ *mening* I am of another opinion, I don't agree; *en* ~ *gång är en skälm* tomorrow never comes; *bland annat, se under bland*; *på ett eller -t sätt* somehow or other; *ha -t att göra* (*vard.*) have other fish to fry; *lova är ett och hålla ett -t* it is one thing to make a promise and another thing to keep it; *säga ett och mena ett -t* speak with [one's] tongue in [one's] cheek; *hon är allt -t än vacker* she is anything but beautiful; *vi talade om ett och -t* we talked about one thing and another, we chatted; *inte -t än jag vet* as far as I know; *hon gör inte -t än gråter* she does nothing but cry; *hon kunde inte -t än skratta* she could not help laughing, she could not but laugh; *alla andra* all the others, (*om pers. ofta*) everybody else; *alla de andra* all the others (the rest); *en ann är så god som en ann* one man is as good as another **2** (*ej lik*) different; *det är en* ~ *historia* that's a different (another) story; *något helt -t än* something quite different from (to)

annan|dag ~ *jul* the day after Christmas Day, (*i Storbritannien*) Boxing Day; ~ *pingst* Whit Monday; ~ *påsk* Easter Monday **-stans** elsewhere; *ingen* ~ nowhere else
annars 1 (*i annat fall*) otherwise, or [else], else **2** (*för övrigt*) otherwise, else; *var det* ~ *något?* was there anything else? **3** (*i vanliga fall*) usually; *mera trött än* ~ more tired than usual
annat *se annan*
annekter|a annex **-ing** annexation
annex s7 annex[e] **-byggnad** annex[e], wing
annex|ion [-k'ʃɔ:n] annexation **-sjukhus** branch hospital
annihil|ationsstrålning annihilation radiation **-era** annihilate
anno [*anno el. 'anno] in [the year]; *från* ~ *dazumal* (*ung.*) ancient, *skämts.* antediluvian, as old as the hills
annons [-'åns el. -'åŋs] s3 advertisement, *vard.* ad[vert] (*om* about); (*födelse- etc.*) announcement; *enligt* ~ according to your advertisement, as advertised; *sätta in en* ~ *i en tidning* put an advertisement in a paper, advertise in a paper **-ackvisitör** advertising agent **-bilaga** advertisement supplement (section) **-byrå** advertising agency
annonser|a 1 (*tillkännage, söka etc. genom annons*) advertise (*efter* for; *om ngt* s.th.) **2** (*tillkännage*) announce **-ing** advertising
annons|kampanj advertising campaign **-organ** advertising medium **-pelare** advertising pillar; *AE.* billboard **-plats** advertisement space **-pris** advertising charge **-sida** advertisement page **-spalt** advertisement column **-tavla** advertisement board; *AE.* billboard **-taxa** advertisement rate **-text** copy
annonsör advertiser, space buyer
annor|ledes, -lunda otherwise, differently; *såvida ej* ~ *föreskrivs* unless otherwise prescribed; *han har blivit helt -lunda* he has changed completely, he is quite a different man **-städes** elsewhere, somewhere else
annotation note **annotationsblock** [scribbling] pad; *AE.* memo pad **annotera** note (take) down, make a note of
annuell a1 annual **annuitet** s3 **1** (*på lån*) annual instalment **2** (*livränta*) annuity, life interest **annuitetslån** instalment credit; annuity loan
annullation *försäkr.* cancellation
annuller|a cancel, withdraw, annul; (*kontrakt, äv.*) nullify; vitiate **-ing** cancellation, withdrawal, annulment, revocation, nullification
annulleringsklausul cancellation clause
anod s3 anode **-batteri** anode battery **-spänning** anode voltage
anomal|i a1 anomalous **-li** s3 anomaly **-listisk** [-'liss-] a5 anomalistic
anomi s3 anomie, anomy
anonym a1 anonymous **-itet** anonymity
anor *pl* ancestry (*sg*), ancestors; lineage (*sg*); *bildl.* progenitors, traditions; *ha gamla* ~ be of ancient lineage, *bildl.* have a long history, be a time-honoured tradition (custom); *det har* ~ *från antiken* it dates back to classical times
anorak [-'rack] s3 anorak; windcheater
anord|na (*bring into*) arrange, put in (bring into) order, set

up, organize; ~ *lekar* get up games **-ning** arrangement, preparation, setup; *(apparat)* apparatus, device; *(utrustning)* outfit; ~*ar (hjälpmedel o.d.)* facilities

anorexi *s3* anorexia

anpart [ˣann-] share, portion

anpass|a adapt, suit, adjust *(efter* to), bring in line with **-bar** *a5* adaptable **-ling** turncoat, yes man; *(medlöpare)* fellow traveller, camp follower **-ning** adap[ta]tion, adjustment, accommodation

anpassnings|förmåga adaptability **-svårigheter** adjustment problems; *han har* ~ he finds it difficult to adapt himself (fit in)

anrik [ˣa:n-] of ancient lineage

anrik|a [ˣann-] concentrate, enrich, dress; ~*t kärnbränsle* enriched nuclear fuel **-ning** concentration, enrichment

anrikningsverk dressing plant; *(för stenkol)* washing plant

anrop call; *mil.* challenge; *sjö.* hail **anropa** call [out to]; *mil.* challenge; *sjö.* hail; ~ *Gud om hjälp* invoke God's help

anropssignal call sign (signal)

anryck|a *v2,* **-ning** *s* advance

anrätt|a prepare, cook, dress **-ning 1** *(anrättande)* preparation, cooking **2** *(rätt)* dish; *(måltid)* meal; *göra heder åt* ~*arna* do justice to the meal, *vard.* tuck in[to], eat with gusto

ans *s2* care, tending; *(av jord)* dressing; *(av häst)* grooming **ansa** tend, see to; cultivate

ansaml|a collect, gather; ~ *sig (om t.ex. damm)* settle **-ing** collection; *(av vatten)* pool [of water] ; *(av skräp)* heap [of rubbish]

ansats 1 *(sats)* run-up; *mil.* bound, rush; *höjdhopp utan* ~ standing high jump; *framryckning i* ~*er* advance by rushes **2** *(början)* start; *(försök)* attempt; *(impuls)* impulse *(till* to); *(tecken)* sign *(till* of); *visa* ~*er till förbättring* show signs of improvement **3** *mus.* striking of a note **4** *tekn.* shoulder, projection

ansatt *a4* afflicted *(av* with); *hårt* ~ hard pressed, in a tight corner

an|se 1 *(mena)* think, consider, be of the opinion; *man* ~*r allmänt* it is generally considered; *han* ~*r sig orättvist behandlad* he considers himself unjustly treated **2** *(betrakta)* consider, regard, look upon; *jag* ~*r det som min plikt* I consider it my duty; *det* ~*s sannolikt* it is considered likely; *han* ~*s som vår största expert* he is regarded as our leading expert **-sedd** *a5 (aktad)* respected, esteemed, distinguished; *(om firma etc.)* reputable; *väl* ~ of good repute **-seende** *s6* **1** *(gott rykte)* reputation, standing, prestige **2** *(aktning)* esteem, respect **3** *utan* ~ *till person* without respect of persons; *i* ~ *till* considering **-senlig** [-e:-] *a1* considerable, large

ansikte *s6* face, countenance; *ett slag i* ~*t (bildl., vard.)* a smack in the eye; *det är ett slag i* ~*t på alla musikälskare* it is an insult to all music lovers; *han blev lång i* ~*t* his face fell; *kasta en anklagelse i* ~*t på ngn* throw an accusation in a p.'s face; *skratta ngn rätt upp i* ~*t* laugh in a p.'s face; *stå* ~ *mot* ~ *med* stand face to face with; *säga ngn ngt rakt i* ~*t* tell s.b. s.th. [straight] to his face; *tvätta sig i* ~*t* wash one's face; *vara lång i* ~*t* have a face

as long as a fiddle

ansikts|behandling facial [treatment] **-drag** features *(pl)* **-form** shape of a p.'s face **-färg** colouring, complexion **-kräm** face cream **-lyftning** face-lift *(äv. bildl.)* **-mask** face pack, mask **-servett** face tissue **-skydd** face protection; *(andnings-)* **-uttryck** [facial] expression **-vatten** skin tonic (lotion)

ansjovis [-ˈʃʊ:-] *s2* anchovy **-burk** tin of anchovies

anskaff|a procure, obtain, buy, acquire; provide **-ning** procurement, acquisition, purchase; provision

anskaffnings|kostnad acquisition (initial) cost; *sälja till* ~ sell at cost price **-pris** initial (purchase) price **-provision** new business commission **-värde** purchase (initial) value

anskri outcry, scream

anskriven *a5, väl (illa)* ~ *hos ngn* in (out of) favour with s.b., in a p.'s good (bad) books

anskrämlig [-ä:-] *a1* hideous, ugly, forbidding

anslag 1 *(kungörelse)* notice, placard, bill; *sätta upp ett* ~ stick up a bill **2** *(penningmedel)* provision; grant; subsidy; *(stats-)* appropriation; *bevilja ett* ~ make a grant **3** *(komplott)* design, plot **4** *mus.* touch **5** *filmens* ~ *är glatt* (ung.) the film strikes a happy note **6** *(projektils etc.)* impact

anslags|beviljande *a4,* ~ *myndighet* [appropriation] granting authority **-bevillning** voting of supplies **-kraft** force of impact **-tavla** notice *(AE.* bulletin) board **-äskande** budget estimate

ansluta connect *(till* with); ~ *sig till ett avtal* accede to (enter into) an agreement; ~ *sig till ett parti* join a party; ~ *sig till ngns åsikt* agree with a p.['s opinion]; *nära* ~ *sig till* be on much the same lines as

anslut|en *a5* connected *(till* with); associated *(till* with), affiliated *(till* to) **-ning 1** *(förbindelse)* connection *(till* with); *tel.* extension **2** *(stöd)* support; *(uppmuntran)* support, patronage; *i* ~ *till* in connection with; with (in) reference to; *i* ~ *till vårt brev* further to our letter; *vinna allmän* ~ gain general support

anslutnings|avgift connection charge **-flyg** connecting airline; air connection **-linje** *järnv.* branch line **-trafik** connecting traffic

anslå 1 *(kungöra)* ~ *en kungörelse* put up a notice; ~ *en tjänst ledig* advertise a post as vacant **2** *(anvisa)* assign, set aside, earmark *(till* for); *(pengar)* grant, allocate, allow **3** *(uppskatta)* estimate, rate, value **4** *mus.* strike; *jfr äv. slå an* **-ende** *a4* pleasing, attractive; *en* ~ *predikan* an impressive sermon

anspann *s7* team

anspel|a allude *(på* to), hint *(på* at) **-ning** allusion *(på* to)

anspråk claim, demand; pretention; *avstå från* ~ *på* waive a claim; *göra* ~ *på* lay claim to; *göra* ~ *på ersättning* claim compensation; *motsvara ngns* ~ satisfy (meet) a p.'s demands; *ta i* ~ claim, demand, make use of; *ta ngns tid i* ~ take up a p.'s time

anspråks|full pretentious, assuming; *(fordrande)* exacting **-fullhet** pretentiousness, exactingness **-lös** unpretentious, unassuming, modest, quiet, moderate **-löshet** unpretentiousness, modesty; *i all* ~ in all modesty, in a very modest way

anspänn|a 1 (*häst*) harness **2** *bildl.* strain, brace **-ing** *bildl.* exertion, strain, tension

anstalt *s3* **1** (*institution*) institution, establishment, home **2** (*anordning*) arrangement, preparation; step; *vidtaga ~er för* take steps to, make arrangements for

anstalts|behandling institutional treatment **-vård** institutional care

anstift|a cause, provoke; ~ *en sammansvärjning* hatch a plot; ~ *mordbrand* commit arson **-an** *r*, *på* ~ *av* at the instigation of **-are** instigator (*av* of), inciter (*av* to)

anstolt [ˣaːn-] proud of one's descent (pedigree)

anstorm|a, -ning assault

anstryk|a (*grundmåla*) prime; paint **-ning 1** (*målning*) coating, priming **2** (*skiftning*) tinge, shade, colour **3** (*tycke, prägel*) touch, trace, suggestion; *utan minsta* ~ *av förakt* without the slightest trace of contempt

ansträng|a *v2* strain; (*vara påkostande för*) try, tax; ~ *sig* exert o.s., endeavour; ~ *sig till det yttersta* do one's very utmost, make every possible effort; *läsning -er ögonen* reading is a strain on one's eyes; *-d* strained, (*om skratt e.d.*) forced **-ande** *a4* strenuous, trying, taxing; ~ *arbete* hard work **-ning** effort, exertion, strain, endeavour; *med gemensamma ~ar* by united efforts; *utan minsta* ~ without the slightest effort

ansträngt *adv* in a forced manner; *han log* ~ he gave a forced smile

anstucken *a5* infected, tainted (*av* with)

anstå 1 (*passa, vara värdig*) become, befit; be becoming (befitting) for; *det ~r inte mig att* it is not for me to **2** (*uppskjutas*) wait, be deferred (put off, postponed); *låta ngt* ~ let s.th. wait, postpone s.th. **anstånd** *s7* delay, respite, grace; *begära en veckas* ~ *med betalning* request a week's respite for payment

anställ|a 1 (*i tjänst*) employ, engage, hire, appoint; *fast -d* [permanently] employed; on the [permanent] staff; *vara -d* be employed (*hos ngn* by s.b., *vid* at, in) **2** (*anordna*) bring about, cause; ~ *blodbad* start a massacre; ~ *ett gästabud* give a banquet; ~ *skada* cause damage **3** (*företaga*) make; ~ *betraktelser över* contemplate; ~ *efterforskningar* institute inquiries; ~ *examen* hold an examination; ~ *förhör* subject [s.b.] to interrogation

anställ|d *subst. a* employee **-ning** employment, situation, job, position, post; (*tillfällig*) [temporary] engagement

anställnings|betyg testimonial, reference; *mil.* service record **-förmån** fringe benefit; perquisite, *vard.* perk **-intervju** interview **-kontrakt** contract of employment, service contract **-skydd** job security **-tid** period of employment, length of service **-trygghet** job security **-villkor** terms of employment

anständig *al* respectable, decent, decorous; (*passande*) proper; (*hygglig*) decent **-het** respectability; propriety; decency

anständighetskänsla sense of propriety **anständigtvis** in common decency, for decency's sake

anstöt *s2* offence; *ta* ~ *av* take offence at, be offended at; *väcka* ~ give offence, offend **-lig** *al* offensive (*för* to); objectionable

ansvar *s7* responsibility; (*ansvarsskyldighet*) liability; *på eget* ~ on one's own responsibility, at one's own risk; *vid laga* ~ under penalty of law; *bära ~et för* be responsible for; *ikläda sig ~et för* take the responsibility for; *ställa ngn till* ~ *för* hold s.b. responsible for; *yrka* ~ *på ngn* prefer a charge (accusation) against s.b., demand a p.'s conviction

ansvara be responsible (*för* for), answer (*för* for); ~ *för en förlust* be liable for a loss; *jag ~r inte för hur det går* I assume no responsibility for the consequences

ansvarig *a5* responsible, answerable, liable; *göras* ~ be made (held) responsible; ~ *utgivare* [legally responsible] publisher **-het** responsibility, liability; *begränsad* ~ limited liability; *bolag med begränsad* ~ limited [liability] company

ansvarighetsförsäkring [third party] liability insurance

ansvars|befrielse discharge [from liability] **-fri** free of responsibility **-frihet** freedom from responsibility; *bevilja* ~ grant discharge; *bevilja styrelse* ~ adopt the report [and accounts] **-full** responsible **-förbindelse** contingent liability **-försäkring** *se* ansvarighetsförsäkring **-kännande** *se -medveten* **-känsla** sense of responsibility **-lös** irresponsible **-löshet** irresponsibility **-medveten** responsible, conscious of one's responsibility **-påföljd** legal penalty **-yrkande** ~ *mot ngn* demand for a p.'s conviction

ansvällning swelling; enlargement

ansätta press, attack, beset, harass; *jfr ansatt*

ansök|a ~ *om* apply for **-an** *r*, *som pl används pl av ansökning* application (*om* for); *avslå en* ~ refuse (reject, deny) an application; *inlämna en* ~ make an application **-ning** application; petition; *inkomna ~ar* lodged applications

ansöknings|blankett application form **-förfarande** application procedure **-handling** application [paper, document] **-skrivelse** letter of application **-tid** period of application; *~en utgår den* applications must be sent in by the

anta *se antaga*

antabus [ˈanta-] *r* Antabuse **-kur** Antabuse treatment

antag|a 1 (*mottaga*) take, accept; ~ *en plats* take (accept) a post; ~ *en utmaning* accept a challenge; ~ *som elev* admit as a pupil **2** (*godkänna*) accept, consent to, approve; ~ *en lag* pass a law **3** (*göra t. sin, övergå t.*) adopt, assume, embrace; ~ *fast form* (*bildl.*) take definite shape, *fys.* solidify; ~ *kristendomen* adopt Christianity; ~ *namnet* take the name of; *under -et namn* under an assumed name **4** (*anlägga*) put on, assume; ~ *en dyster min* put on a gloomy expression, *vard.* look miserable **5** (*anställa*) engage, appoint **6** (*förmoda*) assume, suppose, presume; *AE. äv.* guess; *antag att* suppose (supposing) that; *jag antar att vi skall vänta här* I take it [that] we are to wait here

antag|ande *s6* **1** (*jfr antaga 1–5*) acceptance; adoption, assumption; engagement, appointment **2** (*förmodan*) assumption, supposition, presumption, guess **-bar** *a5* acceptable; reasonable **-lig** *al* **1** (*rimlig*) reasonable, plausible; (*sannolik*) probable, likely **2** (*antagbar*) acceptable; admissible; eligible **-ligen** probably, very likely, presumably **-ning** admission

antagnings|byrå *Centrala ~n* Central Student Admissions Office; (*i Storbritannien*) Universities Central Council on Admissions **-nämnd** admissions board

antagon|ism antagonism **-ist** antagonist, adversary **-istisk** [-'iss-] *a5* antagonistic

antal *s7* number, amount, quantity; *ett stort ~ böcker* a great number of books; *minsta ~ besökare* the fewest visitors; *i stort ~* in great numbers; *sex till ~et* six in number; *höra till de levandes ~* be numbered among the living

Antarktis [-'ark-] *n* the Antarctic [Zone]

antarktisk [-'ark-] *a5* Antarctic

antast|a 1 (*ofreda*) molest; ~ *kvinnor på gatan* accost women in the street **2** (*klandra*) ~ *ngns heder* throw doubt on a p.'s honour, discredit s.b. **-lig** *al* assailable; challengeable

antavla [ˣa:n-] genealogical table; (*friare*) family tree

anteceden|tia, -tier [-'dentsia, -er] antecedents

antecip|ation anticipation, forestalling **-ativ** *a5, jur.* anticipatory **-era** anticipate, forestall

anteckn|a note, make a note of, write down; (*uppteckna*) record; ~ *till protokollet* enter in the minutes, record; ~ *sig* put one's name down (*för* for, *som* as) **-ing** note, annotation, memorandum

anteckning|block notepad, writing pad **-bok** notebook, memo book

ante|datera antedate **-diluviansk** [-'a:-] *a5* antediluvian

antenn *s3* **1** *radio.* aerial, antenna; *radar.* scanner **2** *zool.* antenna (*pl* antennae); feeler

ante|pendium [-'penn-] *s4* antependium **-penultima** [-'ulti-] *s1* antepenult

anti|biotikum [-'å:-] *s8*, **-biotisk** [-'å:-] *a5* antibiotic **-chambrera** [-ʃam-] *ung.* wait for an audience **-cyklon** anticyclone, high **-fonj** *s3* antiphony **-frysvätska** antifreeze [fluid] **-gen** [-'je:n] *s7, s4* antigen **ll** *a5* antigenic **-histamjn** *s4* antihistamine **-hjälte** antihero

antjk l *al* antique, old[-fashioned] **ll** *r*, ~*en* classical antiquity; ~*ens historia* ancient history **-behandling** antique finish, antiquing **-handel** *se antikvitetshandel* **-isera** classicize; imitate classic style

anti|klerikal anticlerical **-kljmax** anticlimax **-konceptionell** *a5* contraceptive **-krjst** *s3* Antichrist **-kropp** *med.* antibody

antikva [-ˣti:k-] *s1, boktr.* roman [type]

antikv|ariat *s7* second-hand bookshop **-arie** [-'a:rie] *s5* antiquary **-arisk** [-'a:risk] *a5* antiquarian; ~ *böcker* second-hand books **-erad** [-'e:rad] *a5* antiquated, outmoded **-itet** antique

antikvitets|handel antique shop; curio shop **-handlare** antique dealer **-samlare** collector of antiques **-värde** antique value

Antillerna [-'till-] *pl* the Antilles

antilogaritm antilogarithm

antilop *s3* antelope

anti|makass *s3* antimacassar **-materia** [ˣanti-]

antimatter

antimilitar|ism antimilitarism **-ist** antimilitarist **-istisk** [-'iss-] *a5* antimilitaristic

antimon [-'å:n, *äv.* -'o:n] *s7, s3* antimony

antingen [-ŋ-] **1** (*ettdera*) either; ~ *skall han lämna rummet eller också gör jag det* either he leaves the room or I do **2** (*vare sig*) whether; ~ *du vill eller inte* whether you like it or not

antipartikel antiparticle

anti|patj *s3* antipathy (*mot* to) **-patisk** [-'pa:-] *a5* antipathetic[al] **-pod** [-'po:d *el.* -'på:d] *s3* **1** (*rak motsats*) antipode **2** ~*er* (*folk, plats*) antipodes **-podisk** [-'po:-] *a5* antipodal **-robot** antimissile **-robotvapen** antimissile weapon

antisemjt *s3* anti-Semite **-isk** *a5* anti-Semitic **-ism** anti-Semitism

antisept|ik *s3* antisepsis **-ikum** [-'sept-] *s8*, **-isk** [-'sept-] *a5* antiseptic

antision|ism anti-Zionism **-ist** *s3*, **-istisk** [-'iss-] *a5* anti-Zionist

anti|statisk [-'sta:-] *a5* antistatic **-statmedel** [-ˣsta:t-] antistatic agent **-tes** *s3* antithesis (*pl* antitheses) **-tetisk** [-'te:-] *a5* antithetic[al] **-toxjn** antitoxin **-ubåtsvapen** antisubmarine weapon

antivivisektion|ism antivivisectionism **-ist** antivivisectionist

antologj *s3* anthology

antonym *s3* antonym

antracjt *s3* anthracite, hard coal

antrakos [-'kå:s] *s3, med.* anthracosis

antropo|log anthropologist **-logj** *s3* anthropology **-logisk** [-'lå:-] *a5* anthropological **-morf** [-ˣmårf] *a5* anthropomorphic **-morfism** [-å-] anthropomorphism **-morfistisk** [-'fiss-] *a5* anthropomorphic **-sof** [-'så:f] *s3* anthroposophist **-sofj** *s3* anthroposophy

anträda set out (set off, embark) [up]on; begin

anträff|a find, meet with **-bar** *al* in; at home; available

Antwerpen *n* Antwerp

antyd|a 1 (*flyktigt omnämna*) suggest, hint at **2** (*låta förstå*) intimate (*för* to), imply, give [s.b.] to understand; (*ge en vink om*) hint [to s.b.] **3** (*tyda på*) indicate; *av -d art* of the kind indicated; *som titeln -er* as the title implies

antyd|an *r*, *som pl används pl av antydning* **1** (*vink*) intimation (*om* of), hint **2** (*ansats, första början*) suggestion (*till* of) **-ning** (*i förtäckta ordalag*) insinuation; (*vink*) hint; (*spår*) trace **-ningsvis** roughly, in rough outline

antågande *s6* advancing, advance, approach [ing]; *vara i ~* be approaching, be on the way

antänd|a set fire to, set...fire, ignite, light **-lig** *al* inflammable **-ning** ignition

anus ['a:-] *s2* anus

anvis|a 1 (*visa, utpeka*) show, indicate, point out; ~ *ngn en plats* show s.b. to a seat **2** (*tilldela*) allot, assign; *han ~des ett rum på baksidan [av huset]* he was given a room at the back **3** (*utanordna*) allot, assign **-ning 1** (*upplysning, instruktion*) direction, instruction; *få ~ på* be directed (referred) to; *ge ngn ~ på* direct (refer) s.b. to **2** (*utanordning*) assignment, remittance

anvisningsprovision arranger's fee

använd|a 1 (*begagna, bruka*) use (*till* for), make use of; ~ *tid* (*pengar*) *på* spend time (money) on (in); ~ *glasögon* wear glasses; ~ *käpp* carry (use) a stick; ~ *socker* take sugar; ~ *väl* make good use of; *färdig att ~s* ready for use **2** (*ägna, nedlägga*) devote; ~ *mycken energi på att* (*äv.*) put a great deal of effort into; *väl -a pengar* well-spent money **3** (*tillämpa*) apply (*om regel*), adopt (*om metod*) **-bar** *al* fit for use; (*nyttig*) useful (*till* for); serviceable (*om kläder*), practicable (*om metod*); *föga ~* of little use **-ning** use; (*av regel*) application; (*av pers.*) employment; *jag har ingen ~ för den* it is of no use to me; *komma till ~* be used, prove useful

användnings|område [field of] application, area of use **-sätt** mode of application; (*tryckt instruktion*) directions for use

aorta [a ˣårta] *s1* aorta

apa I *s1* monkey; (*svanslös*) ape; simian; *neds.* cat, cow, bitch **II** *v1,* ~ *efter* ape, mimic

apache [a'paʃ] *s5* apache

apanage [-'na:ʃ] *s7* ap[p]anage

apart [-'a:rt, *äv.* -'art] *a4* striking, remarkable, distinctive

apartheidpolitik [a'pa:rt-] apartheid [policy]

apat|i *s3* apathy **-isk** [-'pa:-] *a5* apathetic

apatit *s3* apatite

apbrödsträd baobab, monkey bread tree

apekatt (*upptågsmakare*) monkey, clown; (*efterhärmare*) mimic, parrot

apel ['a:-] *s2* apple [tree] **-kastad** *a5* dapple-grey

apelsin *s3* orange **-juice** orange juice **-marmelad** [orange] marmalade **-saft** (*pressad o.d.*) orange juice; (*koncentrerad*) orange squash **-skal** orange peel **-träd** [sweet] orange [tree]

Apenninerna [-'ni:-] *pl* the Apennines

aperitif [-'tiff] *s3* apéritif

apertur aperture

apex ['a:-] *s3, astr.* [solar] apex

AP-fonden *se* pensionsfond

aphelium [ap'he:-] *s4* aphelion (*pl* aphelia)

aphus monkey house

aplanat aplanatic lens

aplik simian, simious

aplomb [a'plåmb] *s3* (*säkerhet*) equanimity, self--confidence, self-possession; (*eftertryck*) emphasis, stress

apmänniska apeman

apné *s3* apnoea

apogeum [-'ge:-] *s4* apogee

apo|kalyps *s3* apocalypse **-kalyptisk** [-'lypt-] *a5* apocalyptic **-kromat** apochromat, apochromatic lens **-kryfisk** [-'kry:-] *a5* apocryphal; *de ~a böckerna* the Apocrypha

apollofjäril [aˣpållo-] apollo

apolog|et [-g-] *s3* apologist **-ik** *s3* apologetics (*pl, behandlas som sg*) **-isk** [-'ge:-] *a5* apologetic

apologi [-'gi] *s3* apologia, apology

apople|ktisk [-'pleck-] *a5* apoplectic **-xi** *s3* apoplexy

apostel [-'påss-] *s2* apostle

a posteriori [-ˣɔ:ri *el.* -ˣå:ri] a posteriori; empirical

Apostlagärningarna the Acts [of the Apostles]

apost|lahästar *använda ~na* use shanks's pony (*AE.* shanks's mare) **-olisk** [-'ɔ:-] *a5* apostolic [al]; *den ~a trosbekännelsen* the Apostles' Creed

apostrof [-'strå:f] *s3* apostrophe **-era** apostro-

phize

apotek *s7* pharmacy; dispensary; chemist's [shop]; *särsk. AE.* drugstore **-are** [-ˣte:-] pharmacist, *i Storbritannien* [dispensing] chemist; *AE.* druggist

apoteks|biträde dispenser **-vara** pharmaceutical preparation

apoteos [-'å:s] *s3* apotheosis (*pl* apotheoses)

apparat apparatus; *vard.* gadget, contrivance; (*anordning*) device, appliance; *sätta igång en stor ~* (*bildl.*) make extensive preparations

apparatur equipment; apparatus

apparition appearance

appell *s3* call; *mil.* roll call, muster; *jur.* appeal **appellation** *jur.* appeal **appellationsdomstol** court of appeal

appellativ *s7, s4* appellative, common noun

appellera appeal

append|icit *s3* appendicitis **-ix** [-'pend-] *s7* appendix; *anat.* [vermiform] appendix

applicer|a apply (*på* to) **-ing** application

applikation *sömn.* appliqué

applåd *s3* applause; *kraftiga ~er* enthusiastic (loud) applause (*sg*), *AE. o. vard.* a big hand; *hon hälsades med en ~* she was greeted with applause **-era** applaud; cheer, clap **-åska** storm of applause

apport [-'årt] *interj* retrieve; fetch it **-era** fetch; *jakt.* retrieve

apposition apposition

apprecier|a appreciate, revalue **-ing** appreciation, revaluation

appr|etera finish, dress **-etyr, -etyr** *s3* finishing, dressing

approxim|ation [-rå-] approximation **-atjv** *a5,* **-era** approximate

aprikos *s3* apricot [tree]

april [-'ill, *äv.* -'i:l] *r* April; *narra ⸜ngn* ~ make an April fool of s.b.; ~ ~! April fool! **-skämt** April fools' joke **-väder** April weather

a priori [-ˣɔ:- *el.* -ˣå:-] a priori

à-pris price per unit, unit price

apropå I *adv* by the bye (way); *helt ~* incidentally; casually; quite unexpectedly **II** *prep* apropos of, with regard to **III** *s6, s4, som ett ~ till detta* in this connection, as an illustration of this

apter|a adapt (*till* to; *för* for); (*anpassa*) adjust **-ing** adaptation; adjustment

aptit *s3* appetite; *ha ~ på livet* have an appetite for life; *ha god ~* have a hearty appetite; *~en kommer medan man äter* appetite comes with eating

aptit|lig [-'ti:t-] *a1* appetizing; savoury (*ej om söta rätter*); (*lockande*) inviting; (*smaklig*) tasty; (*läcker*) delicious; (*för ögat*) dainty **-lös** *vard.* off one's feed **-retande** *a4* appetizing, tempting; *vard. äv.* mouthwatering **-retare** apéritif, appetizer

ar *s9, s7* are; *1 ~* (*ung.*) 119.6 square yards

ara *s1, zool.* macaw

arab *s3* Arab, Arabian **-esk** *s3* arabesque

Arabien [a'ra:-] *n* Arabia

arab|isk [a'ra:-] *a5* Arabian, Arabic; Arab **-iska** *s1* **1** (*språk*) Arabic **2** Arab[ian] woman **-stat** Arab state **-världen** the Arab world

Aragonien [-'gɔ:-] *n* Aragon

aragon|ier [-'gɔ:-] *s9*, **-isk** [-'gɔ:-] *a5* Aragonese
aralia [a'ra:-] *s1, bot.* aralia
arame|isk [-'me:-] *a5* Aramaic; Aram[a]ean
-iska *s1* Aramaic
arbeta work, be at work (*med* with); (*tungt*) labour; (*mödosamt*) toil; (*fungera*) operate, work; ~ *bort* get rid of, eliminate; ~ *ihjäl sig* work o.s. to death; ~ *på att* strive to; ~ *på ngt* work at s.th.; ~ *upp en affär* work up a business; ~ *upp sig* improve [in one's work]; ~ *ut sig* wear o.s. out; ~ *över* be on (work) overtime; ~ *sig trött* tire o.s. out with work; ~ *sig upp* work one's way up, make one's way [in the world]; *tiden ~r för oss* time is on our side; *det ~s för att få honom fri* forces are at work to release him (get him aquitted)
arbetad *a5* manufactured, worked; (*om yta*) finished; (*om metall*) wrought
arbetarbostäder workmen's dwellings
arbetar|e worker; labourer; (*i motsats t. arbetsgivare*) employee; *se äv. diverse-, fabriks-, kropps-, verkstadsarbetare* **-klass** working class **-kommun** labour union **-parti** Labour Party **-regering** Labour Government **-rörelse** labour movement **-skydd** industrial welfare
arbetarskydds|fond *~en* [the Swedish] work environment fund **-lag** labour welfare act; (*i Storbritannien*) Factory Acts (*pl*) **-nämnd** labour welfare council **-styrelse** *~n* [the Swedish] national board of occupational safety and health
arbete *s6* work; *abstr. äv.* labour; (*sysselsättning*) employment, job; (*möda*) toil; *~n i äkta silver* real silver handicraft products; *ett ansträngande ~* hard work; *ett fint ~* fine workmanship; *offentliga ~n* public works; *med sina händers ~* by the labour of one's hands; *ha ~ hos* be employed by; *mista sitt ~* lose one's job; *nedlägga ~t* stop work, go on strike, strike, down tools; *sätta i ~* put to work; *vara under ~* be in preparation, be under construction; *vara utan ~* be out of work (unemployed)
arbeterska working woman, woman worker
arbetsam *a1* industrious, hard-working; (*mödosam*) laborious
arbets|analys work analysis **-avtal** labour contract (agreement) **-bas** *s2* foreman, *fem.* forewoman; *vard.* boss **-beskrivning** working instructions; operational directions **-besparande** *a4* labour-saving **-besparing** saving of labour **-bi** worker [bee] **-bord** worktable; desk **-bänk** [work]bench **-börda** workload, amount of work to be done **-dag** working day, *i sht AE.* workday **-domstol** labour (industrial) court, (*i Storbritannien*) Central Arbitration Committee; *~en* [the Swedish] labour court **-duglig** able to work, fit for work; able-bodied **-fred** industrial peace **-fri** ~ *inkomst* unearned income **-fysiologi** industrial physiology **-fält** sphere (field) of activity **-för** *a5* fit for work, able-bodied; ~ *ålder* working age; *partiellt ~* physically handicapped **-fördelning** *ekon.* division of labour; *~en* the distribution of the work **-förhållanden** working conditions **-förmedling** employment office, jobcentre; *~en* (*i Storbritannien*) the Employment Service Agency **-förmåga** capacity for work **-förtjänst** earnings (*pl*), pay

arbetsgivaravgift general payroll tax
arbetsgivar|e employer; master **-förening** employers' association; *Svenska ~en* [the] Swedish Employers' Confederation **-parten** the employers **-uppgift** particulars supplied by employer [regarding salaries *etc.*] **-verk** *Statens ~* [the Swedish] national agency for government employers
arbets|glädje pleasure in one's work **-grupp** [working] team **-handskar** protective gloves **-hygien** industrial (occupational) hygiene **-hypotes** working hypothesis (theory) **-häst** carthorse **-inkomst** wage earnings (*pl*), income from work **-inrättning** workhouse institution **-insats** work done; work effort, performance **-inställelse** stoppage of work, strike; lockout **-intensitet** rate of working **-intensiv** labour-intensive **-kamrat** workmate **-kapacitet** working capacity **-karl** workman **-kläder** working clothes; dungarees (*pl*) **-konflikt** labour dispute (conflict) **-kraft** labour, manpower; *en bra ~* a good worker **-kraftsreserv** manpower reserve **-lag** gang [of workmen], team **-lagstiftning** protective labour legislation, protective legislation for the workers **-ledare** foreman (*fem.* forewoman), supervisor **-ledning** [labour] management **-liv** working life **-livscentrum** centre for working life **-livserfarenhet** [professional] experience **-lokal** workroom; factory premises (*pl*) **-lust** zeal, zest **-läger** work camp **-lön** wages (*pl*), pay
arbetslös unemployed, out of work; *en ~* an unemployed person; *de ~a* the unemployed **-het** unemployment
arbetslöshets|försäkring unemployment insurance **-kassa** unemployment fund **-understöd** unemployment benefit (*AE.* compensation); *vard.* dole
arbetsmarknad labour market
arbetsmarknads|departement ministry of labour; *AE.* department of labor **-konflikt** *se arbetskonflikt* **-minister** minister of labour; *AE.* secretary of labor **-nämnd** *Statens a~* [the Swedish] national board for government employees **-politik** labour market policy **-styrelse** *~n* [the Swedish] national labour market board; (*i Storbritannien*) the Manpower Services Commission **-utbildning** vocational advancement **-utskott** *~et* [the Swedish parliamentary] standing committee on the labour market
arbets|material working material **-medicin** industrial (occupational) medicine **-metod** method of work[ing] **-miljö** work environment **-moment** suboperation, work operation **-myra** working-ant; *bildl.* busy bee **-människa** hard worker **-namn** [tentative] working title **-narkoman** workaholic **-nedläggelse** [work] stoppage, strike **-oduglig** unfit for work **-oförmåga** incapacity for work; disablement **-oförmögen** unable to work, incapacitated; (*varaktigt*) disabled, invalid **-ordning** work[ing] plan; programme **-ovillig** *se -skygg* **-pass** shift, working period **-plats** place of work; *byggn. äv.* [working] site; (*lokal*) [factory] premises (*pl*), office **-plikt** obligation to work **-prestation** output of work, performance **-program** working

programme **-projektor** overhead projector **-psykologi** occupational psychology **-ritning** workshop drawing **-ro** quiet (peace of mind) essential for work; good working atmosphere **-rock** work-coat; smock **-rum** workroom, study **-rätt** *jur.* labour law **-skygg** workshy **-studieingenjör** work-study engineer **-studieman** time and motion study man **-studier** time and motion study (*sg*) **-stycke** workpiece, piece to be machined **-styrka** labour force, number of hands **-sökande** job-seeker **-tag** *vara i ~en* be hard at work **-tagare** employee; (*arbetare*) wage earner (*AE.* worker); (*tjänsteman*) salaried employee **-takt** working pace; (*i motor*) power stroke; *han har en hög ~* he works quickly **-tempo** *se -takt* **-terapeut** occupational therapist **-terapi** occupational therapy **-tid** working hours, hours of work (*pl*); *efter ~ens slut* after hours **-tidsförkortning** reduction in working hours **-tillfälle** vacant job, job opportunity **-tillstånd** work permit **-uppgift** task, assignment **-utskott** working committee (party) **-vecka** working week, *i sht AE.* work week **-villkor** working conditions **-värdering** job evaluation **-växling** job rotation

arbitrage [-'a:ʃ] *s7* **1** *hand.* arbitrage, foreign exchange dealings (*pl*) **2** *jur.* arbitration, arbitral award **-affärer** *pl, se arbitrage 1*

arbiträr *a5* arbitrary

ardennerhäst [-ˣdenner-] Ardennes carthorse

Ardennerna [-'denn-] *pl* the Ardennes

area ['a:-] *s1* area **areal** *s3* area, space; (*jordegendoms*) acreage

arekapalm [aˣre:-] betel palm, areca

arena [aˣre:na] *s1* arena; *bildl.* scene of action **-teater** theatre-in-the-round, arena theatre

areometer [-'me:-] *s2* hydrometer

arg [-j] *a1* (*vred*) angry (*på ngn* with s.b.; *på ngt* at s.th.); *AE. o. vard.* mad; (*illvillig*) malicious, ill-natured; (*ilsken*) savage; *~ fiende* bitter enemy; *en ~ hund* a savage (vicious) dog; *~a konkurrenter* keen competitors, (*starkare*) ruthless rivals; *ana ~an list* suspect mischief, *vard.* smell a rat; *bli ~* get angry (*på ngn* with s.b.); *~a katter får rivet skinn* quarrelsome dogs get dirty coats (come limping home) **-bigga** *s1* shrew, vixen

Argentina [-ˣti:-] *n* Argentina, the Argentine **argent|inare** [-ˣti:-] *s9*, **-insk** [-'ti:-] *a5* Argentine, Argentinean

argon [-'å:n *el.* 'arg-] *s4* argon

argsint [ˣarj-] *a1* ill-tempered, irascible

argument *s7* argument **argumentation** argumentation; arguing **argumentationsanalys** argument analysis

argumenter|a argue **-ing** *se argumentation*

argusögon *med ~* Argus-eyed, vigilant

aria ['a:-] *s1* aria

arier ['a:-] *s9*, **arisk** ['a:-] *a5* Aryan, Arian

aristo|krat aristocrat **-krati** *s3* aristocracy **-kratisk** [-'kra:-] *a5* aristocratic

aritmet|ik *s3* arithmetic **-isk** [-'me:-] *a5* arithmetic[al]; *~t medium* arithmetic mean; *~ serie* arithmetic progression, (*summa*) arithmetic series

1 ark *s2* ark; *förbundets ~* the Ark of Covenant;

Noas ~ Noah's Ark

2 ark *s7* sheet [of paper]; (*del av bok*) sheet, section; *falsade ~* folded sheets

arkad *s3* arcade

Arkadien [-'ka:-] *n* Arcady, Arcadia

arkadisk [-'ka:-] *a5* Arcadian

arka|iserande [-'se:-] *a4* archaizing **-isk** [-'ka:-] *a5* archaic **-ism** *s3* archaism

Arkangelsk [-'kaŋ-] *n* Archangel

arkebuser|a [-k-] shoot **-ing** execution by a firing squad

arkeo|log arch[a]eologist **-logi** *s3* arch[a]eology **-logisk** [-'lå:-] *a5* arch[a]elogical

arkipelag [-k-] *s3* archipelago

arkitekt [-ki- *el.* -çi-] *s3* architect **-kontor** architect's office

arkitektonisk [-ki-, -çi-, -'tɔ:-] *a5* architectural, architectonic **arkitektur** architecture

arkiv [-k-] *s7* archives (*pl*); (*dokumentsamling äv.*) records (*pl*); (*bild- o.d.*) library; (*ämbetsverk*) record office **-alier** [-'va:-] *pl* records; rolls **-arie** [-'va:-] *s5* archivist; keeper of public records; *förste ~* senior archivist

arkiver|a file **-ing** filing

arkiv|exemplar (*lagstadgat*) statutory copy; (*hand.*) voucher copy; (*kontorsterm*) file copy **-forskning** archival research work **-skåp** filing cabinet

Arktis ['ark-] *n* the Arctic [zone]

arktisk ['ark-] *a5* Arctic

arla [ˣa:r-] early [in the morning]

1 arm *a1* (*stackars, fattig*) poor; (*utblottad*) destitute; (*usel*) wretched, miserable

2 arm *s2* arm; (*av flod, ljusstake etc.*) branch; *lagens ~* the arm of the law; *med ~arna i kors* with folded arms; *med öppna ~ar* with open arms; *på rak ~* (*bildl.*) offhand, straight; *bjuda ngn ~en* offer a p. one's arm; *gå ~ i ~* walk arm in arm; *hålla ngn under ~arna* (*bildl.*) back up (support) s.b.; *slå ~arna om halsen på ngn* fling one's arms [a]round a p.'s neck

armada [-ˣma:-] *s1* armada

armatur 1 *elektr.* [electric] fittings (*pl*); (*ljus-*) lighting fitting **2** *tekn.* (*tillbehör*) accessories (*pl*); (*ankare*) armature

arm|band bracelet **-bandsur** wristwatch **-bindel** armlet, armband; *med.* sling **-borst** crossbow **-brott** fractured (broken) arm

arm|båge *~ sig fram* elbow o.s. along **-båge** elbow

armbågs|led elbow joint **-rum** elbowroom **-veck** crook of the arm

armé *s3* army **-attaché** army attaché **-chef** commander in chief of the army **-förband** army troops (*pl*), army unit **-fördelning** [army] division **-förvaltning** army administration **-gevär** service (army) rifle **-kår** army corps **-ledning** army headquarters (*pl*) **-lotta** member of the Women's Royal Army Corps (W.R.A.C.); *AE.* member of the Women's Army Corps (WAC); *vard.* Wrac, *AE.* Wac **-museum** army museum

Armenien [-'me:-] *n* Armenia **armen|ier** [-'me:-] *s9*, **-isk** *a5* Armenian **-iska 1** (*språk*) Armenian **2** (*kvinna*) Armenian woman

armer|a (*beväpna*) arm; (*förstärka*) reinforce; *~d*

betong reinforced concrete **-ing** (*beväpning*) armament; (*förstärkning*) reinforcement
armeringsjärn reinforcing bar (iron)
arméstab army staff
arm|foting *zool.* brachiopod, lamp shell **-gång** travelling along the [horizontal] bar **-håla** armpit **-krok** arm in arm; *gå* ~ walk arm in arm
armod *s7* poverty, destitution
armring bangle, bracelet
armslängd *på* ~*s avstånd* at arm's lenght
arm|styrka strengt of [one's] arm **-stöd** elbow rest; (*på stol*) arm [of a chair] **-svett** underarm perspiration
arom [a'rå:m] *s3* aroma, flavour **-atisk** [-'ma:-] *a5* aromatic; ~ *förening* aromatic compound; ~*t kolväte* aromatic hydrocarbon **-glas** brandy (balloon) glass
arrak ['arrack] *s2* arrack, arak
arrang|emang [-ŋʃe- *el.* -nʃe-] *s7, s4* arrangement; organization **-era** arrange; organize; (*iscensätta*) stage
arrangör [-ŋ'ʃö:r *el.* -n'ʃö:r] arranger; organizer
arrendator [-ˣa:tår] *s3* tenant [farmer], leaseholder; lessee
arrende [aˣrende *el.* a'rende] *s6* (*-förhållande*) lease, tenancy; (*-tid*) lease; (*-avgift*) rent[al]; *betala* (*få*) *1 000 pund i* ~ pay (get, receive) a rent of 1,000 pounds **-avgift** rent[al] **-gård** leasehold [property], tenant holding **-kontrakt** lease, tenancy agreement **-nämnd** regional tenancies tribunal
arrende|ra lease, rent, take on lease; ~ *ut* let out on lease, lease out **-tid** lease
arrest *s3* custody, detention; *mil.* arrest; (*lokal*) jail, gaol, *mil.* guardroom; *A.E.* brig (*särsk. i fartyg*); *mörk* ~ confinement in a dark cell; *sträng* ~ close arrest; *sitta i* ~ be [kept] in custody; *sätta i* ~ place under arrest
arrester|a arrest, take into custody **-ing** arrest [ing] **-ingsorder** warrant [of arrest]
arriärgarde [-ˣä:r-] rearguard
arrog|ans [-'ans *el.* -'aŋs] *s3* arrogance, haughtiness **-ant** [-'ant *el.* -'aŋt] *al* arrogant, haughty; *vard.* high and mighty
arrowrot ['ärråo-] arrowroot
arsel *s7* arse, bum, backside; *A.E.* ass
arsenal *s3* arsenal (*äv. bildl.*), armoury
arsenik *s3* arsenic **-förgiftning** arsenic poisoning **-haltig** *al* arsenical
arsin *s3* arsine
art [a:rt] *s3* **1** (*sort*) kind, sort **2** (*natur*) nature, character **3** *biol.* species
arta [ˣa:rta] *rfl* shape; ~ *sig väl* shape well; *vädret tycks* ~ *sig* the weather is looking up
artefakt *s3* artefact; *A.E.* artifact
arteriell *al* arterial
arterioskleros [-'å:s] *s3* arteriosclerosis
artesisk [-'te:-] *a5*, ~ *brunn* artesian well
artfrämmande foreign to the species; extraneous
artificiell *al* artificial; (*konstlad*) sham; ~ *insemination* artificial insemination; ~ *intelligens* artificial intelligence
artig [ˣa:r-] *al* polite, courteous (*mot* to); (*svagare*) civil (*mot* to); (*uppmärksam*) attentive (*mot* to) **-het** politeness, courtesy; attention; *av*

~ *out* of politeness; *säga ngn en* ~ pay s.b. a compliment, flatter s.b.
artighets|betygelse mark of courtesy **-fras** polite phrase **-visit** courtesy call
artikel [-'tick-] *s2* article **-serie** series of articles
artikul|ation articulation **-era** articulate
artilleri artillery, ordnance **-eld** artillery fire, gunfire **-förband** artillery unit **-kår** artillery corps **-pjäs** gun, piece of ordnance **-regemente** artillery regiment; *A.E.* artillery group
artillerist artilleryman, gunner
artist (*målare etc.*) artist; (*om skådespelare, musiker e.d.*) artiste **-eri** artistry **-isk** *a5* artistic **-namn** (*skådespelares*) stage name
artnamn specific name
arton [ˣa:r-] *se aderton*
artrik rich in species
artrit *s3* arthritis
artros [-'å:s] *s3* arthrosis
art|skild specifically distinct **-skillnad** specific difference, differentia
artär *s3* artery
arv *s7* inheritance, (*testamenterad egendom*) legacy; *biol.* inheritance; (*andligt*) heritage; *få ett stort* ~ come into a fortune; *få i* ~ inherit; *gå i* ~ be handed down; *lämna ngt i* ~ *åt ngn* leave s.th. [as a legacy] to s.b.; *skifta* ~ divide an inheritance, distribute an estate (the estate of a deceased person); *den är ett* ~ *efter min mor* my mother left it to me; *rött hår är ett* ~ *i släkten* red hair runs in the family
arve|del share of an inheritance **-gods** hereditary (family) estate; inheritance
arv|fiende hereditary foe **-furste** hereditary prince **-följd** succession **-gods** *se arvegods*
arving|e *s2* heir, *fem.* heiress; *utan -ar* without issue, heirless
arvlös disinherited; *göra* ~ disinherit, cut out of a will
arvod|e *s6* remuneration; (*t. läkare etc.*) fee **-era** pay by fee
arv|prins hereditary prince **-rike** hereditary kingdom
arvs|anlag gene **-anspråk** claim to an inheritance (the succession) **-berättigad** entitled to an inheritance
arvskifte distribution of an estate; division of an inheritance
arvs|lott share (portion, part) of an inheritance **-massa** germ plasm; hereditary factors (*pl*) **-rätt** *jur.* law of succession (inheritance) **-skatt** death (succession) duty, inheritance tax **-tvist** dispute about an inheritance
arv|synd original sin **-tagare** *se arvinge* **-tant** wealthy aunt [who may leave me (*etc.*) money]
1 as *s7* (*djurlik*) carcass, carrion
2 as *s2, myt.* As (*pl* Æsir) **asalära** Æsir cult
asbest ['ass-] *s2* asbestos **-os** [-'å:s] *s3* asbestosis **-platta** asbestos mat (plate)
asch [aʃ] pooh!
asept|ik *s3* asepsis **-isk** [a'sepp-] *a5* aseptic
asfalt [ˣass-, 'ass-] *s3* asphalt, bitumen **-beläggning** asphalt surface; tarmac; (*i motsats t. grusväg ofta*) road metal **-era** asphalt, coat with asphalt
asfalt|kokare tar boiler **-läggare** asphalter

-papp asphalt roofing felt **-tjära** mineral tar
asfull *vard.* tight, canned, smashed, dead drunk
asiat *s3*, **-isk** *a5* Asian **Asien** ['a:-] *n* Asia;
Främre ~ the Middle East; *Mindre* ~ Asia Minor
asimut [*äv.* 'a:-] *s3* azimuth
1 ask *s2*, *bot.* ash [tree]; *av* ~ (*äv.*) ash[en]
2 ask *s2* box; (*bleck-*) tin [box]; *en* ~ *cigaretter* a
packet of cigarettes
aska l *s2* ashes (*pl*); (*av visst slag*) ash; *ur* ~*n i elden* out of the frying pan into the fire **ll** *v*, ~ [*av*]
knock the ash off
A-skatt *ung.* pay-as-you-earn (P.A.Y.E.)
askblond ash blond
ask|es [-k-] *s3* asceticism **-et** *s3* ascetic **-etisk**
[-'ke:-] *a5* ascetic[al] **-etism** asceticism
ask|fat ashtray **-grå** ashen, ashgrey **-kopp** *se
askfat* **-onsdag** Ash Wednesday
askorbinsyra [-*bi:n-] ascorbic acid
askregn shower of ashes
Askungen Cinderella
askurna cinerary urn
asocial *a1* antisocial, asocial **-itet** social malad-
justment
1 asp *s2*, *zool.* rapacious carp
2 asp *s2*, *bot.* aspen; *av* ~ (*äv.*) aspen
aspekt *s3* aspect
aspir|ant applicant, candidate (*till* for); trainee;
bildl. aspirant (*på, till* to); *mil.* cadet **-ation** aspiration **-era 1** *språkv.* aspirate **2** ~ *på* aspire to,
aim at
aspirin *s4* aspirin
asp|löv aspen leaf **-virke** aspen [wood]
1 ass *s7*, *se assurera*
2 ass *s7*, *mus.* A flat
Ass-dur A flat major
assegaj *s3* assegai, assagai
assemblage [-'a:ʃ] *s7* assemblage
assembler|are [-*ble:-] *data.* assembler
-ingsspråk assembly (assembler) language
assessor [a*sessår] *s3* assessor; deputy judge
assiett [a'ʃett] *s3* (*tallrik*) small plate; (*maträtt*)
hors d'œuvre dish
assimil|ation assimilation **-era** assimilate
assist|ans [-'ans *el.* -'aŋs] *s3* assistance **-ent** as-
sistant; (*tjänstetitel*) clerical officer **-era l** (*hjälpa
till*) assist; act as assistant **ll** (*hjälpa*) assist, help
associa|tion association **-tionsförmåga** abil-
ity to form associations **-tiv** *a5* associative
associer|a associate; ~ *sig med* associate with
-ing association
assonans [-'aŋs] *s3* assonance
assuradör insurer; (*sjöförsäkr. äv.*) underwriter;
(*livförsäkr. äv.*) assurer
assurans [-'ans *el.* -'aŋs] *s3* insurance **-belopp**
insured value
assurer|a insure; ~*t brev* insured letter **-ing** in-
surance
Assyrien [a'sy:-] *n* Assyria **assyr|ier** [a'sy:-] *s9*,
-isk [a'sy:-] *a5* Assyrian **-iska 1** (*språk*) Assyrian **2** (*kvinna*) Assyrian woman
astat astatine
asten|i *s3* asthenia, astheny **-iker** [-'te:-] *s9*, **-isk**
[-'te:-] *a5* asthenic
aster ['ass-] *s2*, *bot.* aster
asterisk *s3* asterisk
asteroid [-o'i:d] *s3* asteroid, minor planet

astigmat|iker [-'ma:-] *s9*, **-isk** [-'ma:-] *a5* astig-
matic **-ism** astigmatism, astigmia
astma *s1* asthma **-anfall** attack of asthma
astmat|iker [-'ma:-] *s9*, **-isk** [-'ma:-] *a5* asth-
matic
astrakan *s3* (*skinn*) astrakhan
astral *a1* astral **-kropp** astral body
astro|biologi astrobiology **-fysik** astrophysics
(*pl, behandlas som sg*) **-geologi** astrogeology
-kemi astrochemistry **-log** astrologer, astrolo-
gist **-logi** *s3* astrology **-logisk** [-'lå:-] *a5*
astrological **-metri** *s3* astrometry **-naut** *s3* astronaut **-nautik** astronautics (*pl, behandlas som sg*)
-nom astronomer **-nomi** *s3* astronomy **-no-
misk** [-'nå:-] *a5* astronomic[al]; ~ *enhet* astro-
nomical unit; ~ *navigation* celestial navigation,
astronavigation
asur *se azur*
asyl *s3* asylum, [place of] refuge; (*fristad*) sanctuary **-rätt** right of asylum
asymmetr|i *s3* asymmetry **-isk** [-'me:-] *a5*
asymmetric[al]
asymptot [-'tå:t] *s3* asymptote
asynkron [-'å:n] asynchronous
atavis|m *s3* atavism **-tisk** *a5* atavistic, atavic
ate|ism atheism **-ist** atheist **-istisk** [-'iss-] *a5*
atheistic[al]
ateljé *s3* studio; (*sy- etc.*) workroom
Aten *n* Athens
atenare [-*te:-] *s9*, **atensk** [-'te:nsk] *a5* Atheni-
an
aterman *a5* athermanous
atlantdeklarationen [-*lant-] the Atlantic
Charter
Atlanten [-'lann-] *n* the Atlantic [Ocean]
atlant|fartyg [-*lant-] transatlantic liner **-pak-
ten** the North Atlantic Treaty **-paktsorgani-
sationen** the North Atlantic Treaty Organization (NATO) **-ångare** *se atlantfartyg*
1 atlas ['att-] *s3* (*tyg*) satin
2 atlas ['att-] *s3* (*kartbok*) atlas (*över* of); (*kota*)
atlas
Atlasbergen [*att-] *pl* the Atlas Mountains
atlet *s3* athlete; (*stark man*) strong man, Hercules
-isk *a5* athletic
atmosfär *s3* atmosphere **-isk** atmospheric[al];
~*a störningar* atmospherics; *radio. äv.* [radio]
interference **-tryck** atmospheric pressure
atoll [-å-] *s3* atoll
atom [a'tå:m] *s3* atom **-bomb** atom[ic] bomb, A-
-bomb, fission bomb **-drift** atomic propulsion
(operation) **-driven** nuclear-powered, atomic-
-powered **-energi** *se kärnenergi* **-forskare** nuclear scientist **-forskning** nuclear research **-fy-
sik** nuclear physics **-klocka** atomic clock **-kraft**
se kärnkraft **-kärna** [atomic] nucleus **-massa**
atomic mass; *relativ* ~ relative atomic mass
-masseenhet [unified] atomic mass unit, dalton **-mila** nuclear reactor; (*äldre namn*) atomic
pile **-nummer** atomic (proton) number **-reak-
tor** nuclear reactor **-sopor** nuclear waste (*sg*)
-sprängning nuclear fission **-teori** atomic
theory **-ubåt** nuclear[-powered] submarine **-ur**
se -klocka **-vapen** nuclear (atomic) weapon
-vikt atomic weight **-värde** valency, *särsk. AE.*
valence **-åldern** the atomic age

atomär *a5* atomic
atonal *a5* atonal
ATP [ate'pe:] *r* (*förk. för allmän tilläggspensionering*) *se tilläggspensionering*
atrium ['a:-] *s4* atrium **-hus** atrium house; courtyard house
atrof|i *s3*, **-iera[s]** *vl* atrophy **-isk** *a5* atrophic
atropin *s7, s3* atropin[e]
att I *infinitivmärke* to; ~ *vara eller inte vara* to be or not to be; ~ *åka skidor är roligt* skiing is fun; *genom* ~ *arbeta* by working; *av utseendet* ~ *döma* judging (to judge) by appearances; *envisas med* ~ *göra ngt* persist in doing s.th.; *efter* ~ *ha misslyckats* having failed; *vanan* ~ *röka* the habit of smoking; *skicklig i* ~ *sy* good at sewing; *sanningen* ~ *säga* to tell the truth; *han lämnade landet för* ~ *aldrig återvända* he left the country never to return; *han var rädd* ~ *störa henne* he was afraid of disturbing her; *han är inte* ~ *leka med* he is not [a man] to be trifled with, he is not one to stand any nonsense; *jag kunde inte låta bli* ~ *skratta* I could not help laughing; *vad hindrar honom från* ~ *resa* what prevents him from going **II** *konj* that; *på det* ~, *så* ~ [in order] that, so that; *under det* ~ while; whereas; *vänta på* ~ *ngn skall komma* wait for s.b. to come; *förlåt* ~ *jag stör* excuse my (me) disturbing you; ~ *du inte skäms!* you ought to be ashamed of yourself!; ~ *jag inte tänkte på det!* why didn't I think of that!; *utan* ~ *ngn såg honom* without anyone seeing him; *frånsett* ~ *han inte tycker om musik* apart from the fact that he does not like music; *jag litar på* ~ *du gör det* I rely on your doing it, I am relying on you to do it; *jag trodde* ~ *han skulle komma* I thought [that] he would come; *jag är glad* ~ *det är över* I am glad [that] it is over; *så dumt* ~ *jag inte kom ihåg det* how stupid of me not to remember it; *säg till honom* ~ *han gör det* tell him to do it
attaché [-'ʃe:] *s3* attaché **-väska** attaché case
attack *s3* attack (*mot, på* on); (*sjukdoms-*) attack, fit **-era** attack **-plan** fighter [aircraft] **-robot** air-to-surface missile
attent|at *s7* attempt (*mot ngn* on a p.'s life), attempted assassination; (*friare*) outrage (*mot* on) **-ator** [-ˣa:tår] *s3* would-be assassin; perpetrator of an (the) outrage
attest *s3* attestation (*på* to); certificate, testimonial **-era** attest, certify
attiralj *s3* apparatus; paraphernalia (*pl*)
attisk ['att-] *a5* Attic; ~*t salt* Attic salt (wit)
attityd *s3* attitude; posture, pose
atto- atto-
attrahera attract
attrak|tion [-k'ʃo:n] attraction, appeal **-tionsförmåga** [power of] attraction **-tiv** *al* attractive, appealing **-tivitet** attractiveness, attractivity, attraction
attrapp *s3* dummy
attri|buera *vl*, **-but** *s7* attribute **-butiv** *al* attributive
att-sats that-clause
aubergine [åbär'ʃinn] *s5* aubergine; *AE.* eggplant
audiens [au-] *s3* audience; *få* ~ *hos* obtain an audience of (with); *mottaga ngn i* ~ receive s.b. [in audience]; *söka* ~ *hos* seek an audience with

audio|gram [audio'gramm] *s7* audiogram **-logi** *s3* audiology **-meter** [-'me:-] *s2* audiometer **-metri** *s3* audiometry **-visuell** *se audivisuell*
audi|tiv [au-] *a5* auditory **-torium** [-'to:-] *s4* (*sal*) auditorium; (*åhörare*) audience **-tör** judicial adviser (advisor) [to a regiment]; (*vid krigsrätt*) judge advocate
audivisuell [au-] *al* audiovisual; ~*a hjälpmedel* audiovisual aids
augiasstall [ˣaugias-, *äv.* -ˣgi:as-] Augean stables (*pl*)
augur [au-] augur; soothsayer **-leende** *ung.* conspiratorial smile
augusti [au'gusti] *r* August
augustiner [augus'ti:-] *s9* Augustine friar
augustin[er]|munk Augustine friar **-orden** Order of St. Augustine
Augustinus [augus'ti:-] St. Augustine
auktion [auk'ʃo:n] [sale by] auction, [public] sale (*på* of); *exekutiv* ~ compulsory auction; *köpa på* ~ buy at an auction; *sälja på* ~ sell by auction **-era** ~ *bort* auction [off], auctioneer, sell by auction **-ist** *se auktions|förrättare, -utropare*
auktions|bridge auction bridge **-bud** bid at an auction **-förrättare** auctioneer **-kammare** auction rooms (*pl*) **-utropare** auctioneer, auctioneer's assistant
auktor ['auktår] *s3* author; (*sagesman*) authority, informant
auktoris|ation [au-] authorization **-era** authorize; ~*d revisor* chartered accountant **-ering** [-'se:-] *se auktorisation*
auktori|tativ [au-] *al* authoritative; *på* ~*t håll* in authoritative circles **-tet** authority **-tetstro** belief in authority **-tär** *a5* authoritarian
auktorskap *s7* authorship
auktorsrätt copyright
aula ['au-] *sl* assembly hall, lecture hall; *AE.* auditorium
aura ['au-] *sl* aura
aureomycin [au-] *s7* aureomycin
aurikel [au'rikkel] *s3, s2, bot.* auricula
auskult|ant [au-] **1** *skol., ung.* student teacher observing classroom methods **2** *med.* auscultator **-ation 1** *skol.* attending classes as an observer **2** *med.* auscultation, stethoscopy **-era 1** *skol.* attend classes as an observer **2** *med.* auscultate
auspicier [au'spi:-] *pl* auspices; *under ngns* ~ under the auspices of s.b.
Australien [au'stra:-] *n* Australia
austral|iensare [-ˣensa-] *s9*, **-ier** [-'stra:-] *s9*, **-isk** [-'stra:-] *a5* Australian **-neger** Australian aborigene, native Australian
autarki [au-] *s3* autarchy; (*självförsörjning*) autarky, autarchy
autent|icitet [au-] authenticity, genuineness **-isk** [-'tenn-] *a5* authentic
aut|ism [au-] autism **-ist** autistic person **-istisk** [-'tist-] *a5* autistic
autodafé [au-] *s3* auto-da-fé
autodidakt [au-] *s3* autodidact, self-taught person **-isk** *a5* autodidactic, self-taught
auto|gen [auto'je:n] *a5* autogenous **-giro** [-'ji:-] *el.* -'gi:-] *s5* autogiro, gyroplane
autograf [au-] *s3* autograph **-isk** *a5* autographic[al] **-jägare** autograph hunter

auto|klav [au-] *s3* autoclave; sterilizer **-krat** autocrat **-krati** *s3* autocracy **-kratisk** [-'kra:-] *a5* autocratic

automat [au-] automatic machine, automaton; (*varu-*) slot machine; vending machine, automat; (*person*) automaton **-gevär** automatic [rifle]

automa|tik [au-] *s3* automatism **-tion** automation

automatiser|a [au-] introduce automatic operation; automate; *tel.* automatize **-ing** automation, automatization

automat|isk [auto'ma:-] *a5* automatic; ~ *data-behandling* automatic data processing **-kanon** automatic gun **-låda** (*i bil*) *se* -*växel* **-pistol** automatic [pistol] **-svarv** automatic lathe **-telefon** dial (automatic) telephone **-vapen** automatic weapon **-växel** *tel.* automatic switchboard; (*i bil*) (-*växellåda*) automatic gearbox (transmission), (-*växling*) automatic gear-change

automobil [au-] *s3* [motor]car, automobile

auto|nom [au-] *a5* autonomous; ~*a nervsystemet* autonomic nervous system **-nomi** *s3* autonomy **-pilot** automatic pilot, autopilot

autopsi [au-] *s3* autopsy, postmortem examination

auto|strada [auto'stra:da] *s1*, *se motorväg* **-typi** *s3* halftone [plate]

av I *prep* **1** *vanl.* of; ~ *god familj* of good family; *född* ~ *fattiga föräldrar* born of poor parents; *en man* ~ *folket* a man of the people; *en man* ~ *heder* a man of honour; *drottningen* ~ *England* the queen of England; *ett tal* ~ *Churchill* a speech of Churchill's (*jfr 2*); *turkarnas erövring* ~ *Wien* the conquest of Vienna by the Turks; *ingen* ~ *dem* none of them; *ägaren* ~ *huset* the owner of the house; *hälften* ~ *boken* half [of] the book; *en klänning* ~ *siden* a dress of silk, a silk dress; *byggd* ~ *trä* built of wood; *till ett pris* ~ at a (the) price of; *en del* ~ *tiden* part of the time; *i två fall* ~ *tre* in two cases out of three; *ett avstånd* ~ *fem kilometer* a distance of five kilometres; *det var snällt* ~ *dig* it was kind of you; *vad har det blivit* ~ *henne?* what has become of her? **2** (*betecknande den handlande, medlet*) by; ~ *en händelse* by chance; ~ *misstag* by mistake; ~ *naturen* by nature; *ett tal* ~ *Churchill* a speech made by Churchill (*jfr 1*); *författad* ~ *Byron* written by Byron; *hatad* ~ *många* hated by many; *leva* ~ *sitt arbete* live by one's work **3** (*betecknande orsak*) *a*) (*t. ofrivillig handling el. tillstånd*) with, *ibl.* for, *b*) (*t. frivillig handling*) out of, *c*) (*i en del stående uttryck*) for, on; ~ *allt mitt hjärta* with all my heart; ~ *brist på* for want of; ~ *den anledningen* for that reason; ~ *fruktan för* for fear of; ~ *nyfikenhet* out of curiosity; ~ *olika orsaker* for various reasons; ~ *princip* on principle; *darra* ~ *köld* (*rädsla*) shiver with cold (fear); *gråta* ~ *glädje* (*rädsla*) shiver with cold (fear); *gråta* ~ *glädje* weep for joy; *leva* ~ *fisk* live on fish; *skrika* ~ *förtjusning* scream with delight; *utom sig* ~ *raseri* beside o.s. with rage **4** *göra ngt* ~ *sig själv* do s.th. by o.s. (of one's own accord); *det faller* ~ *sig själv* [*t*] it is a matter of course; *det går* ~ *sig själv*[*t*] it runs by (of) itself **5** (*från*) from; (*bort från*) off; ~ *egen erfarenhet* from [my own] experience; ~ *gammalt* from of old; ~ *gammal vana* from force of habit; *svart* ~ *sot* black from soot; *en present* ~

min mor a present from my mother; *få* (*köpa, låna, veta*) *ngt* ~ *ngn* get (buy, borrow, learn) s.th. from s.b.; *gnaga köttet* ~ *benen* gnaw the meat off the bones; *hoppa* ~ *cykeln* jump off one's bicycle; *stiga* ~ *tåget* get off the train; *ta* ~ [*sig*] *skorna* take one's shoes off; ~ *jord är du kommen* from dust art thou come; *det kommer sig* ~ *att jag har* it comes from my having; *vi ser* ~ *Ert brev* we see from your letter **6** (*oöversatt el. annan konstruktion*) ~ *bara tusan* like hell; *med utelämnande* ~ excluding; *rädd* ~ *sig* timid, timorous; *bryta nacken* ~ *sig* break one's neck; *njuta* ~ enjoy; *vara* ~ *samma färg* be the same colour **II** *adv* **1** ~ *och an* to and fro, up and down; ~ *och till* now and then, occasionally **2** (*bort*[*a*], *ner, i väg*) off; *ge sig* ~ start off; *ramla* ~ fall off (*hästen* the horse); *stiga* ~ *tåget* get off the train; *ta* ~ *till höger* turn [off to the] right; *torka* ~ *dammet* wipe off the dust **3** *borsta* ~ *en kappa* brush a coat, give a coat a brush; *diska* ~ *tallrikarna* wash up the plates; *klä* ~ *ngn* undress s.b.; *lasta* ~ unload; *rita* (*skriva*) ~ copy; *svimma* ~ faint away **4** (*itu*) in two; (*bruten*) broken; *benet är* ~ the leg is broken; *åran gick* ~ the oar snapped in two

aval *s3* bank guarantee for a bill

avancemang [-aŋse-] *s7* promotion **avance-mangsmöjlighet** promotion prospect[s *pl*], opportunity for promotion **avancera** advance; be promoted, rise; ~*d* advanced, progressive, (*djärv*) bold, daring

avannonsera (*t.ex. radioprogram*) sign off

avans [-'aŋs] *s3* profit, gains (*pl*)

avant|garde [a*x*vaŋt- *el.* a*x*vant-] van[guard]; *konst. o.d.* avant-garde **-gardism** avant-gardism **-gardist** avant-gardist **-scenloge** stage box

avart variety; (*oart*) degenerate species

avbalk|a partition off **-ning** partitioning off; *konkr.* partition

avbasning [-ba:s-] beating; (*upptuktelse*) scolding

avbeställ|a cancel **-ning** cancellation **-nings-avgift** cancellation fee

avbeta graze; crop

avbetal|a pay off, pay by instalments **-ning** (*belopp*) instalment; (*system*) hire-purchase plan, *A.E.* installment buying; *köpa på* ~ buy on the hire-purchase plan

avbetalnings|kontrakt hire-purchase contract **-köp** (*entaka*) hire-purchase transaction; *koll.* hire-purchase **-villkor** hire-purchase terms

avbetning [-e:-] grazing; cropping

av|bild representation; copy; *han är sin fars* ~ he is the very image of his father **-bilda** reproduce; draw, paint **-bildning** reproduction

avbitartång nippers (*pl*); *en* ~ a pair of nippers

avblås|a bring to an end; (*strid*) call off; *se äv. blåsa av* **-ning** *sport.* stoppage of game

avbländ|a shade; *foto.* stop down; *se äv. blända av* **-ning** shading *etc.*

avboka cancel

avbrott 1 (*uppehåll*) interruption, break; (*upp-hörande*) cessation, stop[page], intermission; (*i radioutsändning*) breakdown [in transmission]; *ett* ~ *i fientligheterna* a cessation of hostilities; *ett angenämt* ~ a pleasant break; *ett kort* ~ *i regnandet* a short break in the rain; *utan* ~ without stop-

ping, continuously, without a break **2** (*motsats*) contrast, change; *utgöra ett ~ mot* make a change in, break the monotony of
avbrottsförsäkring loss of profits insurance
avbruten broken
avbryta break off, interrupt; cut off; *~ ngn* (*vard.*) break (butt) in on s.b.; *~ en resa* break a journey; *~ ett samtal* cut short a conversation; *~ förhandlingar* break off negotiations; *~ sitt arbete* stop work, leave off working; *~ sig* check o.s., stop speaking; *se äv. bryta av*
av|bräck *s7* (*skada*) damage, injury; (*men*) disadvantage; *lida ~* suffer a setback **-bränning** *hand.* deduction [from profits], incidental expenses **-bröstning** *mil.* unlimbering **-bytare** replacement, relief, substitute; (*för chaufför*) driver's mate; (*vid motortävling*) co-driver **-böja** decline, refuse; *~ ett erbjudande* decline an offer; *~nde svar* refusal, answer in the negative **-böjning** *radar.* deflection **-bön** apology; *göra ~* apologize **-börda 1** (*samvete*) unburden **2** *rfl* free o.s. of; *~ sig en skuld* discharge a debt
av|dagataga [-ˣda:-] put to death **-damning** *ge ngt en ~* give s.th. a dust **-dankad** *a5* discharged, discarded
avdel|a (*uppdela*) divide [up] (*i* into), partition [off]; divide off; *mil.* detail, tell off **-ning** (*del*) part; (*avsnitt*) section; (*av skola, domstol*) division; (*av företag*) department, division; (*sjukhus-, fängelse-*) ward; (*i skåp*) compartment; *mil.* detachment, unit; (*av flotta, flyg*) division, squadron
avdelnings|chef (*i departement*) *ung.* undersecretary; (*i ämbetsverk*) head of a department; (*i affär*) departmental manager **-direktör** principal administrative officer **-kontor** branch [office]ʲ **-sköterska** ward sister, head-nurse
avdik|a (*mark*) drain; (*vatten*) drain off **-ning** [-i:-] draining, drainage
avdomna *se domna*
avdrag 1 deduction; (*beviljat*) allowance; (*rabatt äv.*) reduction; (*på skatt*) abatement, relief; *~ för inkomstens förvärvande* professional outlay (expenses *pl*); *efter ~ av omkostnaderna* expenses deducted; *med ~ för* after a deduction of; *göra ~ för* deduct; *yrka ~ med 1 000 pund* claim a deduction of 1,000 pounds **2** *boktr.* proof [sheet], pull, impression
avdraga 1 (*draga ifrån*) deduct, take **2** *boktr.* pull
avdragsgill deductible; *~t belopp* allowable deduction
av|dramatisera play down **-drift** *sjö.* drift; leeway; (*projektils*) deviation
avdunst|a evaporate; (*försvinna*) clear off (out) **-ning** evaporation
av|döda *~t vaccin* killed-virus vaccine **-döma** decide, judge
avel [ˈa:-] *s2* breeding, rearing
avels|djur breeder; *koll.* breeding-stock **-hingst** stallion, studhorse **-reaktor** breeder [reactor] **-sto** brood mare **-sugga** *ung.* prize sow **-tjur** breeding bull
avenbok [ˣa:-] *s2* hornbeam, ironwood
aveny *s3* avenue
aversion [-rˈʃɔ:n] aversion (*mot* to)

av|fall 1 (*avskräde*) waste, refuse; (*köks-*) garbage, rubbish; (*vid slakt*) offal; *radioaktivt ~* radioactive waste[s *pl*] **2** *bildl.* falling away, backsliding; (*från parti*) desertion, defection; (*från religion*) apostasy **-falla** fall away (*från* from); desert (*från* from), turn deserter (apostate), defect **-fallen 1** (*om frukt etc.*) fallen **2** (*mager*) thin, worn; *-fallna kinder* pinched cheeks
avfalls|kvarn [garbage] disposer **-kärl** dustbin; *AE.* garbage (trash) can **-produkt** waste product; *kem.* residual product
av|fart[sväg] slip road, turn-off; exit [road] **-fasa** bevel, slope, cant **-fasning** bevel **-fatta** word, indite; (*avtal*) draw up; (*lagförslag*) draft **-fattning** version; wording, draft **-fetta** defat, degrease **-flytta** move [away] **-flyttning** removal; *de är uppsagda till ~* they have been given notice to quit **-flöde** outflow, effluent
avfolk|a [-å-] depopulate **-ning** depopulation **-ningsbygd** depopulated region, depressed area
av|fordra *~ ngn ngt* demand s.th. from (of) s.b., call upon s.b. for s.th.; *~ ngn räkenskap* call s.b. to account (*över* for) **-frosta** [-å-] defrost **-frostning** [-å-] defrosting **-fuktning** dehumidification
avfyr|a fire [off], discharge **-[n]ing** firing [off], discharge **-[n]ingsramp** launch[ing] pad
av|fälling apostate, renegade, backslider **-färd** [-ä:-] departure, going away, start **-färda** [-ä:-] **1** (*skicka*) dispatch, send off **2** (*bli färdig med*) dismiss (finish with) (*ngn* s.b.); finish (*ngt* s.th.); *jag låter inte ~ mig så lätt* I am not going to be put off that easily **-färga 1** (*beröva färgen*) decolour, bleach, decolorize **2** *se färga* **-färgning** bleaching, discolouration **-föda** offspring, progeny, brood; *I huggormars ~* (*bibl.*) O, generation of vipers
avför|a 1 (*bortföra*) remove, carry off **2** (*utstryka*) cancel, cross out (*från* from); *~ från dagordningen* remove from the agenda; *~ ur ett register* strike off a register **-ing 1** removal, cancelling **2** *med.* evacuation [of the bowels], motion; *konkr.* motions (*pl*), faeces (*pl*) **-ingsmedel** laxative; purgative
avgas exhaust [gas] **-renare** exhaust purifier [device] **-rör** exhaust pipe **-ventil** exhaust valve
avge 1 (*ge ifrån sig, avsöndra*) emit, give off; yield **2** (*lämna, avlägga*) give; *~ ett omdöme om* give (deliver) an opinion on; *~ protest* make (lodge) a protest; *~ sin röst* vote, cast one's vote; *~ vittnesmål* give evidence, testify
avgift [-j-] *s3* charge; (*medlems- etc.*) fee, dues (*pl*); (*tull-*) duty; (*hamn-*) dues (*pl*); (*för färd*) fare; *extra ~* surcharge, additional charge; *för halv ~* at half price (fare, fee); *mot ~* at a fee; *utan ~* free of charge
avgifta [-j-] detoxify; detoxicate
avgifts|belagd *a5* subject to a charge **-belägga** put a charge on **-fri** free [of charge]
av|giva *se avge* **-gjord** decided; (*påtaglig*) distinct; definite; *-gjort!* done!, it's a bargain!; *en ~ förbättring* a marked improvement; *en ~ sak* a settled thing; *en på förhand ~ sak* a foregone conclusion
av|gjuta take a cast of **-gjutning** casting; *konkr.*

cast **-gnaga** gnaw off; ~ *ett ben* pick a bone **-grena** *rfl* branch off **-grening** branch; (*rör*) branch pipe

avgrund *s3* abyss, precipice; (*klyfta*) chasm; (*svalg*) gulf; *bildl.* pit; (*helvete*) hell **avgrunds|ande** infernal spirit, fiend **-djup I** *a5* abysmal, unfathomable **II** *s7* [abysmal] depths (*pl*), abyss **-kval** *pl* pains of hell **-lik** *a5* abysmal, hellish

avgräns|a demarcate, delimit; *klart* ~*d* clearly defined **-ning** demarcation, delimitation

av|gud idol, god **-guda** idolize, adore (*äv. bildl.*)

avguda|bild idol; image of a god **-dyrkan** idol worship, idolatry **-dyrkare** idol worshipper, idolater (*fem.* idolatress)

avguderi idolatry

avgå 1 leave, start, depart; (*om fartyg äv.*) sail (*till* for); ~*ende tåg* (*i tidtabell o.d.*) outgoing trains, departures [of trains] **2** (*avsändas*) be sent off (dispatched) (*till* to); ~*ende brev* outgoing letters; ~*ende gods* outward goods **3** *bildl.* retire, resign; ~ *med döden* decease; ~ *med seger* come off (emerge, be) victorious **4** (*vid räkning*) be deducted; *78 kr* ~*r för omkostnader* less 78 kronor for expenses **5** (*förflyktigas*) evaporate, vanish

avgång 1 departure, (*fartyg äv.*) sailing (*från* from; *till* to, for) **2** (*persons*) retirement, resignation; *naturlig* ~ natural wastage

avgångs|betyg leaving certificate **-examen** final (leaving) examination **-hall** departure hall **-hamn** port of departure **-signal** starting signal **-station** departure station **-tid** time of departure **-vederlag** severance pay; *vard.* golden handshake

avgäld rent [in kind]

avgäng|a thread off **-ning** threading off

avgör|a decide; (*bedöma*) determine (*huruvida* whether); (*slutgiltigt bestämma*) settle, conclude **-ande I** *a4*, ~ *beslut* final decision; ~ *betydelse* vital importance; ~ *faktor* determining factor; ~ *prov* crucial test; ~ *seger* (*steg*) decisive victory (step); ~ *skäl* conclusive argument; ~ *stöt* decisive blow; ~ *ögonblick* critical (crucial) moment **II** *s6* (*jfr avgöra*); deciding, decision; determination; settlement; conclusion; *i* ~*ts stund* in the hour of decision; *träffa ett* ~ make a decision

av|handla (*förhandla om*) discuss; (*behandla*) deal with, treat [of] **-handling** (*skrift*) treatise; (*akademisk*) thesis, dissertation; (*friare*) essay, paper (*över* on) **-hjälpa** (*fel*) remedy; (*missförhållande*) redress; (*nöd*) relieve; (*brist*) supply; (*skada*) repair; *skadan är lätt att* ~ the damage is easily repaired (put right) **-hopp** *polit.* defection **-hoppare** *polit.* person seeking political asylum, defector **-hugga** hew (lop) off; chop (cut) off; (*knut o.d.*) sever **-hysa** evict **-hysning** [-y:-] eviction **-hyvla** plane smooth; (*borttaga med hyvel*) plane off (away) **-hyvling** [-y:-] planing down (off, away); *bildl.* dressing down

avhåll|a 1 (*hindra*) keep, restrain, deter, prevent (*från* from) **2** (*möte o.d.*) hold **3** ~ *sig från a*) keep away from, *b*) (*nöjen o.d.*) abstain from, *c*) (*att uttala sin mening*) refrain from, *d*) (*undvika sällskap med*) shun, avoid; ~ *sig från att röka* abstain from smoking **-en** *a5* beloved, dear[ly loved], cherished; (*svagare*) popular **-sam** *a1*

temperate, abstemious **-samhet** temperance, abstemiousness; *fullständig* ~ total abstinence **av|hämta** fetch, call for, collect **-hämtning** collection; *till* ~ (*om paket*) to be called for **-hända** deprive [s.b.] of; ~ *sig* part with **-hängig** [-häŋig] dependent (*av* on) **-hängighet** [-häŋig-] dependence **-härda** soften, wet **-härdning** softening, wetting **-härdningsmedel** [water] softener **-höra** listen to; (*obemärkt*) overhear; (*förhöra*) examine

avj *s3* advice, notice; ~ *om försändelse* dispatch note

aviat|ik *s3* aviation **-iker** [-'a:ti-] aviator

avig *a1* **1** wrong; inside out; (*i stickning*) purl **2** (*om person*) awkward **avig|a** *s1*, **-sida** *s1* wrong side, back, reverse; *det har sina* -*sidor* it has its drawbacks **-vänd** *a5* turned inside (wrong side) out

1 avisa [a*vi:-] *s1* newspaper

2 avisa [*a:v-] *v1* de-ice

aviser|a advise, notify, inform **-ing** (*aviserande*) advising; (*av*) advice

avisoväxel [a*vi:-] bill payable at a fixed date after sight, after-sight bill

avista [a*vista] at sight, on demand **-växel** sight draft (bill)

av|jonisering deionization **-jämna** level, make even; (*kant*) trim; *bildl. se avrunda* **-kall** *n, ge* (*göra*) ~ *på* renounce, waive, resign **-kapa** cut off

avkast|a 1 throw off; ~ *oket* shake off the yoke **2** *ekon.* yield, bring in; (*om jord äv.*) produce, bear **-ning** proceeds (*pl*), return[s *pl*], yield; (*behållning*) takings (*pl*); (*vinst*) profit; (*gröda etc.*) produce; *årlig* ~ annual yield (returns *pl*); *ge god* ~ yield well

avkastnings|förmåga earning capacity **-grad** rate of return

av|klara clear, clarify; *se äv. klara av* **-klinga** wear off; *fys.* decay, disintegrate **-klingning** [radioactive] decay, disintegration **-klingningsbassäng** decay tank **-kläda** undress; divest (strip) of; *se äv. klä av* **-klädning** [-ä:-] undressing *etc.* **-klädningshytt** dressing cubicle; (*på badstrand*) bathing hut **-kok** decoction (*på* of) **-komling** [-å-] descendant; child **-komma** [-å-] *s1* offspring, progeny; *jur.* issue **-koppla** uncouple; disconnect; *se äv. koppla av* **-koppling** *tekn.* uncoupling, disconnection; (*avspänning*) relaxation **-korta** shorten, curtail; (*text*) abridge, abbreviate; (*minska*) reduce, diminish **-kortning** [-å-] shortening; abbreviation; reduction, diminution **-kriminalisera** decriminalize **-kristna** dechristianize **-kristning** dechristianization **-krok** out-of-the-way spot (corner); *han bor i en* ~ he lives at the back of beyond (*A E. vard.* the sticks) **-kräva** ~ *ngn ngt* demand s.th. from s.b. **-kunna** *v1* pronounce, deliver, pass; (*lysning*) publish; ~ *ett utslag* record a verdict **-kvista** trim [a felled tree] **-kyla** cool, refrigerate; *bildl.* cool down, dampen **-kylning** cooling, refrigeration, chilling **-köna** [-ç-] *en helt* ~*d varelse* a completely sexless creature

avla [*a:v-] beget; (*om djur o. bildl.*) breed, engender; ~ *av sig* multiply

av|lagd *a5*, ~*a kläder* discarded (cast-off) clothes

(clothing); *jfr avlägga* **-lagra** deposit in layers; ~ *sig* be deposited in layers **-lagring** deposit, stratum (*pl* strata), layer

avlast|a (*befria från last*) unload; (*varor*) discharge; unship; *bildl.* relieve **-are** shipper, consignor, sender **-ning** unloading; discharge; *fys.* stress-relieving, load-relieving; *bildl.* relief

avlat [ˣa:v-] *s3* indulgence

avlats|brev letter of indulgence **-krämare** seller of indulgences

avled|a carry off; (*vatten*) drain, draw off; (*friare*) turn away (off), divert; (*blixt*) conduct; *språkv.* derive; ~ *misstankarna från* turn away suspicion from; ~ *ngns uppmärksamhet* divert a p.'s attention **-are** conductor; *bildl.* diversion **-ning** conduction; diversion; *språkv.* derivative

avledningsändelse derivative ending (suffix)

avlelse [ˣa:v-] conception; *den obefläckade ~n* the Immaculate Conception

avleverera deliver [up]

av|lida die, expire, pass away (on, over) **-liden** *a5* deceased, dead; *den -lidne* the deceased, *AE.* the decedent; *den -lidne president R.* the late President R.

avling [ˣa:vliŋ] propagation, breeding **avlingsduglig** procreative, reproductive

av|liva put to death, kill; (*sjuka djur*) destroy; *bildl.* confute, scotch **-livning** [-i:v-] putting to death, killing *etc.* **-ljud** ablaut [vowel], gradation **-locka** ~ *ngn en bekännelse* draw a confession from s.b.; ~ *ngn en hemlighet* worm (lure) a secret out of s.b.; ~ *ngn ett löfte* extract a promise from s.b.; ~ *ngn ett skratt* make s.b. laugh; ~ *ngn upplysningar* elicit information from s.b.

avlopp [out]flow, outlet; sewer, drain; (*i badkar o.d.*) drain, plug-hole

avlopps|brunn cesspool, sink, sump; gully **-dike** drainage ditch **-ledning** drainpipe; sewer **-rör** discharge (waste) pipe, drainpipe, sewer; (*för ånga*) exhaust pipe **-trumma** drain, sewer **-vatten** waste water; sewage

av|lossa fire [off], discharge **-lossning** discharge **-lusa** delouse **-lusning** [-u:-] delousing **-lutning** alkali removing **-lyftning** lifting off, removal; relief **-lysa** suspend, cancel, call off **-lysning** suspending *etc.* **-lyssna** listen to; (*ofrivilligt*) overhear; ~ *telefonsamtal* tap [the wires] **-lyssning** (*av telefon*) wire-tapping **-lyssningsapparat** listening (bugging) device **-lång** oblong, oval, elliptical **-låta** (*utfärda*) issue; (*avsända*) dispatch, send off **-lägga 1** (*kläder*) leave off; lay aside (by) (*äv. bildl.*) **2** ~ *en bekännelse* make a confession; ~ *besök hos* pay a visit to, call upon; ~ *ed* take an oath, swear; ~ *examen* pass an examination; ~ *rapport om* report on; ~ *räkenskap för* render an account of, account for **-läggare** *bot.* shoot, layer; *bildl.* offshoot, branch

avlägs|en *a3* distant; remote; *-na släktingar* distant relatives; *i en ~ framtid* in the remote future; *inte ha den -naste aning om* not have the remotest (faintest) idea about **-et** *adv* remotely, distantly; ~ *liggande* (*äv.*) remote, out-of-the-way, far-off

avlägsna remove; (*avskeda*) dismiss; (*göra främmande*) estrange, alienate; ~ *sig [från]* go away, leave, retire, withdraw, (*för ögat*) recede

avlämn|a (*varor*) deliver; (*t. förvaring*) leave, give up; (*inlämna*) hand in; (*resande*) drop, set down **-ande** *s6* delivering *etc.*; *mot ~ av* against [the] delivery of **-ing** delivery

avlänka deflect, deviate

avläs|a read [off]; ~ *ngt i ngns ansikte* read s.th. on a p.'s face **-are** meter inspector **-bar** readable **-ning** reading

avlön|a pay, remunerate **-ing** pay, remuneration; (*arbetares*) wages (*pl*); (*tjänstemans*) salary; (*prästs*) stipend

avlönings|dag payday **-kuvert** pay packet **-lista** payroll

av|löpa (*sluta*) end; (*utfalla*) turn out; ~ *lyckligt* turn out well, end happily

avlös|a (*vakt*) relieve; (*följa efter*) succeed; (*ersätta*) replace, displace; *teol.* absolve **-are** relief (*äv. mil.*); successor **-ning** relieving *etc.*; *mil.* relief; *teol.* absolution

avlöva strip of [its] leaves, defoliate; *~d* leafless; *~s* (*äv.*) shed its leaves

avmagnetiser|a demagnetize; (*fartyg mot minor*) degauss **-ing** demagnetization; (*av fartyg*) degaussing

avmagring [-a:-] growing thin; loss of weight

avmagrings|kur reducing (slimming) cure **-medel** slimming (reducing) preparation

avmarsch march[ing] off, departure

1 avmaska (*vid stickning*) cast off

2 avmask|a (*befria från mask*) deworm **-ning** deworming

avmasta dismast

avmatt|a weaken, enfeeble; (*utmatta*) exhaust **-as** grow weak, languish, flag, lose strength **-ning** flagging, weakening, languor, relaxed vigour

avmattningstendens weakening trend

avmobiliser|a demobilize **-ing** demobilization

av|montera dismantle, dismount **-måla** paint; (*beskriva*) depict; *glädjen ~de sig i hans ansikte* joy was depicted in (on) his face **-mäta** measure; (*i lantmäteri*) trace out, measure up; (*straff o.d.*) mete out **-mätning** measuring *etc.*; measurement **-mätt** *a4* measured, deliberate; (*reserverad*) reserved, guarded

avmönstr|a 1 (*avlöna*) pay off, discharge **2** (*avgå från tjänstgöring*) sign off **-ing** paying-off *etc.*

av|navla [-na:v-] cut the umbilical cord **-njuta** enjoy **-nämare** buyer, purchaser, consumer, customer

avnöt|a wear off **-ning** wearing off; *geol.* abrasion, detrition

avog *a1* unkind **avoghet** averseness, aversion (*mot* to) **avogt** *adv* unkindly; ~ *stämd mot ngn* unfavourably disposed towards s.b.

avokado [-ˈka:-] *s5* **1** (*träd*) avocado **2** (*frukt*) avocado [pear], alligator pear

avpass|a fit (*efter* to); *bildl. äv.* adapt, adjust (*efter* to); ~ *tiden för* time, choose the right time for **-ning** fitting, adaption, adjustment

avpatruller|a patrol **-ing** patrolling

avplock|a (*frukt*) pick, gather; (*buske o. friare*) strip **-ning** picking *etc.*

avpolitisera make nonpolitical, unpoliticize

avpolletter|a *bildl.* dispose (get rid of) **-ing** dis-

missal
avporträtter|a portray **-ing** portrayal
avpressa ~ *ngn ngt* extort (extract) s.th. from
s.b.
avprick|a tick [off] **-ning** checking
avprickningslista check list
avprov|a test, try. give a trial; (*avsmaka*) taste,
sample **-ning** testing *etc.*
avprägla stamp; ~ *sig* stamp (imprint) itself (*i,
på* on)
avputs|a clean, finish, polish **-ning** cleaning *etc.*
av|raka shave [off] **-reagera** abreact; ~ *sig* work
off one's annoyance, vard. let off steam **-reda**
thicken **-redning** thickening
avregistrer|a strike off a register; (*fordon*)
deregister **-ing** deregistration
av|resa I *v3* depart, leave, set out, start (*till* for)
II *s1* departure, leaving, setting out (*till* for) **-re-
sedag** day of departure
avrevider|a *boktr.* revise **-ing** *boktr.* revising
av|rigga unrig, untackle **-ringning** ring[ing]-off
-rinna flow (drain) away (off); *låta* ~ drain,
stand to strain **-rinning** runoff, outflow **-riva**
tear off **-rivning** tearing off; *kall* ~ cold rub-
down **-romantisera** deglamorize **-rop** suborder **-ropa** suborder
avrund|a round [off]; *~d summa* round sum
-ning rounding [off]
avrust|a demobilize, disarm; *sjö.* lay up **-ning**
disarmament; *sjö.* laying up
av|rustningskonferens disarmament confer-
ence **-råda** ~ *ngn från ngt* advise (warn) s.b.
against s.th., dissuade s.b. from s.th.; ~ *ngn från
att komma* advise s.b. against coming (s.b. not to
come), dissuade s.b. from coming **-rådan** *r* dis-
suasion, discouragement **-räkna** deduct, discount; ~ *mot* apply against; *detta ~t* making
allowance for that **-räkning** deduction, discount; *hand.* settlement [of accounts]; *i* ~ *mot* in
settlement of, to be deducted from; *betala i* ~ pay
on account **-rätta** execute, put to death (*genom
by); ~ *genom hängning* hang; ~ *med elektricitet*
electrocute **-rättning** execution, putting to
death; electrocution **-rättningsplats** place of
execution **-röja** clear away **-röjning** clearing
away, removal **-rösa** demarcate, set landmarks
-rösning [-ö:-] demarcation **-rösningsjord**
uncultivated land
av|sadla unsaddle **-sadling** [-a:-] unsaddling
-saknad *r* want; *vara i* ~ *av* lack, be without
-salta desalinate, desalt **-salu** *oböjligt s, till* ~
for sale **-sats** *s3* ledge, shelf; (*trapp-*) landing
avse 1 (*hänsyfta på*) concern, bear upon, have
reference to, refer to **2** (*ha i sikte*) have in view,
aim at **3** (*ha för avsikt*) mean, intend; *~dd för*
intended (designed, meant) for; *~ende* concerning, bearing upon, referring to
avseende *s6* (*syftning*) reference; (*beaktande*)
consideration; (*hänseende*) respect, regard; *i alla
~n* in all respects, in every way; *i rättsligt* ~ from
a judicial point of view; *i varje* (*intet, detta*) ~ in
every (no, this) respect; *med* (*i*) ~ *på* with regard
(reference, respect) to, regarding, concerning;
utan ~ *på person* without respect of persons; *fästa
~ vid* take notice of, pay attention (heed, regard)
to; *förtjäna* ~ deserve consideration; *ha* ~ *på*

have reference to, refer to; *lämna utan* ~ pay no
regard to, take no notice of, disregard
av|segla sail, leave (*till* for) **-segling** sailing, de-
parture **-sela** unharness
avsevärd *al* considerable, appreciable; ~ *rabatt*
substantial discount
avsides aside; ~ *belägen* remote, out-of-the-
-way; *ligga* ~ lie apart **-replik** aside
avsigkommen [-å-] *a3* broken-down; *se* ~ *ut*
look shabby (seedy)
avsikt *s3* (*syfte*) intention; purpose; object, end;
(*uppsåt*) design, motive; *jur.* intent; *i* ~ *att* for the
purpose of; *i bästa* ~ with the best of intentions;
med ~ on purpose; *med* ~ *att* with the intention
of (+ *ing-form*), *jur.* with intent to; *utan* ~ unintentionally; *utan* ~ *att såra* without intending to
hurt; *utan ond* ~ without [an] evil intent; *ha för*
~ *att* have the intention to, intend to; *vad har hon
för* ~ *med det?* what is her purpose in doing that?
avsikt|lig *al* intentional; (*överlagd*) deliberate
-ligt intentionally, on purpose
av|sjunga sing **-skaffa** abolish, get rid of, do
away with; put an end to; (*upphäva*) repeal
-skaffande *s6* abolishing *etc.*; abolition; repeal
avsked [-ʃ-] **1** (*entledigande*) dismissal, discharge; (*tillbakaträdande*) retirement, resignation; *begära* ~ hand in one's resignation; *få* ~ be
dismissed; *få* ~ *med pension* retire on a pension;
få ~ *på grått papper* be dismissed forthwith, vard.
be turned off, be sacked; *ta* ~ *från* resign, leave
2 (*farväl*) parting, leave-taking, leave; farewell; *i
~ets stund* at the moment of parting; *ta* ~ *av* say
farewell to, take leave of **avskeda** dismiss, discharge, give notice to; vard. fire, sack
avskeds|ansökan resignation; *inlämna sin* ~
hand in one's resignation **-besök** farewell visit
-föreställning farewell performance **-häls-
ning** parting greeting **-kyss** parting kiss **-ord**
parting word **-tagande** *se avsked 2* **-tal** valedic-
tory (farewell) speech
avskepp|a ship [off] **-ning** shipping [off]; *klar
till* ~ ready for shipment **-ningshamn** port of
shipment
avskild secluded; isolated; *leva* ~ *från* live apart
from **-het** retirement, seclusion; isolation
avskilj|a separate, detach; (*avhugga*) sever, cut
off; (*avdela, t.ex. med skiljevägg*) partition [off]
-are separator
avskjut|a fire, discharge; (*raket*) launch **-ning**
firing, discharge; launching; (*av vilt*) shooting off
-ningsbas launching base **-ningsramp** launch
[ing] pad
av|skrap *s7* scrapings (*pl*), refuse; *bildl.* dregs
-skrapa scrape [off]
avskrift copy, transcript[ion]; *bevittnad* ~ attested copy; *~ens riktighet bekräftas* I (we) certify
this to be a true copy; *i* ~ in copy
avskriv|a 1 (*kopiera*) copy, transcribe; *rätt -et in-
tygas* true copy certified by **2** hand. write off;
depreciate **3** *jur.* remove from the cause list
-ning 1 hand. writing off; (*summa*) item written
off; *vara på* ~ (*bildl.*) fall (go, pass) out of use **2**
copying
avskräck|a *v3* frighten (*från att* from + *ing-
form*); (*förhindra*) deter; (*svagare*) discourage;
han låter inte ~ *sig* he is not to be intimidated

-ande *a4* (*om exempel*) warning; (*om straff*) exemplary; (*om verkan*) deterrent; *verka* ~ act as a deterrent

av|skräde *s6* refuse; (*efter slakt o.d.*) offal; (*friare*) rubbish **-skrädeshög** refuse (rubbish) heap

av|skum scum; skimmings (*pl*); *bildl. äv.* scum, dregs (*pl*) **-skuren** *a5* cut [off], severed; isolated

avsky [-ʃy] **I** *v4* detest, abhor, loathe **II** *s2* disgust (*för, över* at); abhorrence (*för* of); loathing (*för* for); *känna* ~ *för* feel a loathing for; *vända sig bort i* ~ turn away in disgust **-värd** *a1* abominable, detestable; *-värt brott* heinous crime

av|skära 1 *se skära av* **2** ~ *återtåget* intercept the retreat **-skärma** screen off; *radio.* shield **-skärmning** screening; *radio.* shielding **-skärning** cutting off; (*genomskärning*) section

avslag *s7* refusal, declining; (*på förslag*) rejection; *få* ~ *på* have turned down; *yrka* ~ move the rejection of the proposal **avslagen** *a5* rejected *etc.*, *se avslå*; (*om dryck*) stale, flat; dead **avslagsyrkande** motion for the rejection [of a proposal (bill)]

av|slappnad relaxed **-slappning** slackening, relaxation **-slipa** grind, polish [off]; (*om vatten*) wear away (down); (*juvel*) cut; *bildl.* rub off, polish **-slipning** grinding *etc.* **-slockna** die away; go out

avslut *hand.* contract, bargain, deal; (*bokslut*) balancing [of one's books]

avslut|a 1 (*göra färdig*) finish [off], complete; (*ge en avslutning*) conclude, bring to an end; (*göra slut på*) end, close; ~*s* be finished off; come to an end; *sammanträdet ~des* the meeting was closed **2** (*göra upp köp o.d.*) conclude; (*räkenskaper*) balance **-ning 1** (*avslutande*) finishing off, completion; conclusion, concluding **2** (*avslutande del*) conclusion, finish; (*slut*) end, termination; *skol.* break-up [ceremony]; speech day; *A E.* commencement

avslutningsvis by way of conclusion, in conclusion

av|slå 1 *se slå av* **2** (*vägra*) refuse, decline, reject **3** (*avvärja*) repulse **-slöja** unveil; *bildl.* expose, unmask, disclose **-slöjande** *s6* unveiling; *bildl.* disclosure, revelation

avsmak dislike, distaste; (*starkare*) aversion (*för* to), disgust (*för* with); *få* ~ *för* take a dislike to; *känna* ~ feel disgusted; *väcka* ~ arouse disgust

avsmak|a taste; (*prova*) sample **-ning** tasting **avsmaln|a** narrow [off]; (*långsamt*) taper **-ande** *a4* narrowing; tapering

av|sminka remove make-up **-smälta** (*om snö etc.*) melt away; (*om säkring*) fuse

av|snitt sector; (*av bok*) section, part; (*av följetong etc.*) instalment **-snöra** cut off **-snörning** cutting off **-somna** pass away; *de saligen ~de* the [dear] departed **-spark** *sport.* kickoff **-spegla** reflect, mirror; ~ *sig* be reflected **-spegling** reflection **-spela** play back **-spelning** playback; (*spelande*) playing back **-spisa** put off; *vard.* fob off **-spänd** relaxed **-spändhet** relaxation **-spänning** relaxation (slackening) [of tension], easing of **-spärra** bar, block; shut (cordon) off (*från* from); *mil.* blockade; (*med rep o.d.*) rope (rail, fence) off; (*avstänga*) close (*för* for)

-spärrning barring *etc.*; (*område*) rope-off area; (*polis-*) cordon

avstalinisering de-Stalinization

av|stamp take-off **-stanna** stop, come to a standstill, cease; (*om samtal o.d.*) die down **-stava** divide [into syllables] **-stavning** division into syllables, syllabi[fi]cation **-stavningsregel** syllabi[fi]cation rule **-steg** departure, deviation; ~ *från den rätta vägen* lapse from the right path **-stickare** (*utflykt*) detour, deviation; (*från ämnet*) digression **-stigning** alighting **-stjälpa** tip, dump **-stjälpning** tipping, dumping **-stjälpningsplats** tip, dumping-ground **-stressad** relaxed **-stressande** relaxing **-stycka** parcel out, divide **-styckning** parcelling out, division **-styra** prevent; avert, ward off **-styrka** discountenance, oppose; recommend the rejection of **-styrkande** *s6* disapproval; rejection

avstå give up, relinquish, cede (*till* to); ~ *från* give up, relinquish; (*avsäga sig*) renounce, waive; (*låta bli*) refrain from, pass up; (*undvara*) do without, dispense with **-ende** *s6* giving up *etc.* (*från* of)

avstånd *s7* distance; (*till målet*) range; *på* ~ at a distance, (*i fjärran*) in the distance; *på vederbörligt* ~ at a discreet distance; *på 6 m* ~ (*äv.*) six metres away; *hålla ngn på* ~ keep s.b. at a distance (at arm's length); *ta* ~ *från* dissociate o.s. from, (*avvisa*) repudiate, (*ogilla*) deprecate, take exception to; disclaim

avstånds|bedömning determination of distance[s *pl*] **-bestämning** range-finding **-inställning** *foto.* (*abstr.*) focusing; (*konkr.*) focusing lever **-mätare** rangefinder; *tekn.* telemeter **-tagande** *s6* dissociation, repudiation (*från* of); deprecation (*från* of); disclaiming (*från* of)

avstäm|ma *bokför.* tick (*A E.* check) [off]; *radio.* tune [in] **-ning** *bokför.* tick; *A E.* check; *radio.* tuning **-ningsindikator** tuning indicator, magic eye **-ningskrets** tuning circuit

avstämpl|a stamp; ~ *en aktie* have a share stamped **-ing** stamping

av|stämplingsdag *järnv. o.d.* day of issue; *post.* date of postmark **-stänga** shut off; (*inhägna*) fence in (off), enclose; close; (*avspärra*) bar, block; (*vatten o.d.*) turn off; (*elektrisk ström*) cut off; *bildl. äv.* exclude; *gatan avstängd* no thoroughfare **-stängning** shutting off *etc.*; (*område*) enclosure **-stängningsventil** stop valve **-stöta** reject **-stötning** rejection **-stötningsprocess** rejection process **-svalna** cool [down, off], grow cool; *bildl.* wane **-svalning** cooling **-svavla** [-a:v-] desulphurize **-svavling** sulphur removal, desulphurization **-svimmad** *a5* in a faint (swoon); *falla* ~ *till marken* fall fainting to the ground **-svärja** ~ [*sig*] abjure; forswear **-svärjning** abjuration; foreswearing **-syna** inspect and certify **-synare** inspector **-syning** official inspection **-syningsförrättning** inspection **-såga** saw [off]; ~*d* (*vard.*) finished, washed up **-säga** *rfl* resign, give up; (*avböja*) decline; (*frisäga sig från*) disclaim; renounce; ~ *sig kronan* abdicate; ~ *sig allt ansvar* renounce all responsibility **-sägelse** resignation; renunciation; abdication

avsänd|a send [off], dispatch; ship; post **-are** sender; (*av gods*) consignor, consigner, shipper; (*av postanvisning*) remitter, remittor **-ning** dispatch; shipment **-ningsavi** dispatch note; shipping bill

avsätt|a 1 (*ämbetsman*) remove, dismiss; (*regent*) depose, dethrone **2** (*varor*) sell, find a market for, dispose of **3** (*lägga undan*) set (put) aside, reserve **4** (*bottensats*) deposit **5** (*upprita*) set off; ~ *märken* leave marks (traces) **-bar** *a5* dismissable, removable; (*om vara*) marketable **-ning 1** (*ämbetsmans*) dismissal, removal; (*regents*) deposition, dethronement **2** (*varors*) sale, market; *finna god* ~ meet with a ready market, sell well **3** *bokför.* appropriation

avsättnings|möjligheter *pl* market potential (*sg*) **-område** market [area] **-svårigheter** *pl* marketing problems; ~ *för stål* a poor market for steel

avsök|a scan **-ning** scanning

avsöndr|a (*avskilja*) separate [off], sever, detach; (*utsöndra*) secrete; ~ *sig* isolate o.s.; ~*s* separate off, be secreted **-ing** separation, severance; secretion; isolation **-ingsorgan** secretory organ

avta *se ta av*

av|tacka thank s.b. for his (her) services **-tacklad** *a5* thin and worn, haggard

avtag|a 1 *se ta av* **2** (*försvagas, minska*) decrease, diminish; (*om månen*) wane; (*om storm o.d.*) abate, subside; (*om hälsa, anseende*) decline, fail, fall off **-ande** *s6* decrease, diminution; waning; abatement; decline; *vara i* ~ be on the decrease, grow less, (*om månen*) be on the wane **-bar** *a5* removable, detachable

avtagsväg turn[ing]

avtal *s7* agreement; contract; (*mellan stater*) treaty, agreement, convention; *enligt* ~ as agreed upon; *träffa* ~ *om* come to (make) an agreement about (concerning, for); **avtala 1** (*träffa avtal*) agree (*med* with; *om* about) **2** (*överenskomma om*) agree upon; (*tid*) fix, appoint; *ett* ~*t tecken* a prearranged sign; *på* ~*d plats* at the appointed place; *som* ~*t var* as arranged

avtals|brott breach of [an] agreement ([a] contract) **-brytare** violator of an agreement **-enlig** [-e:n-] *a5* as agreed [upon], as stipulated **-förhandlingar** *pl* wage negotiations, pay talks **-mässig** *a5* contractual **-rätt** law of contract **-rörelse** collective bargaining, wage negotiations (*pl*) **-stridig** contrary to agreement (contract)

av|tappa (*låta rinna ut*) draw [off], tap (*ur* from, out of); (*tömma*) draw **-tappning** drawing *etc.*; (*av valuta*) drain **-teckna** draw, sketch (*efter* from); ~ *sig* stand out, be outlined (*mot* against) **-tjäna** work off; ~ *fängelsestraff* serve a prison sentence **-tona** *konst.* shade off **-torka** wipe [off], wipe down, clean; (*tårar*) dry, wipe away **-torkning** wiping [off] *etc.* **-trappa** de-escalate **-trappning** de-escalation **-trubba** blunt, dull; *tekn.* bevel [down] **-trubbning** blunting

avtryck 1 imprint, impression; (*kopia*) print **2** *boktr.* proof [impression], print; (*omtryck*) reprint; *konst.* reproduction

avtryck|a impress, imprint; *boktr.* print [off],

copy [off]; (*omtrycka*) reprint **-are** (*på gevär*) trigger; *foto.* shutter lever

avträd|a give up, leave, surrender; (*landområde*) cede; (*avgå från*) retire, withdraw **-ande** *s6* giving up *etc.*; cession, retirement, withdrawal **avträde** *s6* **1** *jur.* compensation **2** (*hemlighus*) privy

av|tvagning [-a:g-] washing [away] **-tvinga** ~ *ngn ngt* extort s.th. from s.b., wring (force) s.th. out of s.b. **-två** wash [off]; *bildl.* wash away; (*beskyllning*) clear o.s. of **-tyna** languish; (*om pers. äv.*) pine away, decline **-tynande I** *s6* [gradual] decline **II** *a4* languishing **-tåg** *s7* departure, marching off; (*friare*) decampment; *fritt* ~ liberty to march off **-tåga** march off, decamp **-täcka** uncover; (*staty*) unveil **-täckning** uncovering *etc.* **-täckningsceremoni** unveiling ceremony **-tärd** worn, emaciated, gaunt

avund *s2* envy; *blek av* ~ pale with envy; *känna* ~ *mot* (*över*) feel envious of; *väcka* ~ arouse envy **avund|as** *dep* envy **-sam** *al* envious **-samhet** enviousness **-sjuk** envious, jealous (*på, över* of) **-sjuka** enviousness, envy

avunds|man *ung.* antagonist, enemy; *han har många -män* there are many who bear him a grudge **-värd** *al* enviable

avvakta (*svar, ankomst*) await; (*händelsernas utveckling*) wait and see; (*lura på, invänta*) wait (watch) for; ~ *lägligt tillfälle* wait for an opportunity, mark time; ~ *tiden* bide one's time; *förhålla sig* ~*nde* play a waiting game; *intaga en* ~*nde hållning* adopt a wait-and-see policy

avvaktan *r, i* ~ *på* while waiting for, pending, *hand.* awaiting, looking forward to

av|vand [-a:n-] *a5* (*om dibarn*) weaned **-vara** *endast i inf.* spare **-vattna** drain [off], dewater **-vattning** dewatering, drainage **-veckla** (*affär o.d.*) wind up; (*friare*) liquidate, settle **-veckling** winding up; liquidation; settlement **-verka** (*hugga*) fell; *AE.* cut, log; (*slutföra*) accomplish, finish **-verkning** (*huggning*) felling *etc.*

avvik|a 1 (*från regel*) diverge; (*från ämne*) digress; (*från kurs, sanning*) deviate, depart **2** (*vara olik*) differ **3** (*rymma*) abscond **-ande** *a4* divergent; deviating; (*mening*) dissentient **-are** deviant, deviate **-else 1** divergence; digression; deviation, departure **2** (*rymning*) absconding **3** (*kompassens*) deviation; *tekn.* aberration

av|vinna ~ *jorden sin bärgning* get a living from the soil; ~ *ett ämne nya synpunkter* evolve new aspects of a subject

avvis|a send (turn) away; (*ansökan*) dismiss; (*förslag, anbud*) reject; (*beskyllning*) repudiate; (*invändning*) overrule, meet; (*anfall*) repulse, repel; (*leverans*) refuse acceptance of; *bli* ~*d* be refused [entrance], meet with a rebuff; ~ *tanken på* reject the idea of **-ande I** *s6* sending away *etc.*; dismissal; rejection; repudiation, repulse **II** *a4* repudiating, deprecatory; *ställa sig* ~ *till* adopt a negative attitude towards, object to

av|vita *oböjligt a* **1** *jur.* insane **2** (*dåraktig*) preposterous, absurd **-vittra** erode **-vittring** erosion **-väg** (*biväg*) bypath; byroad, bylane; *komma på* ~*ar* go astray

avväg|a (*skäl o.d.*) weigh [in one's mind], balance [against each other]; (*i lantmäteri*) take the level of, level; *väl -d* well-balanced **-ning** weighing *etc.*

avvägnings|fråga question of priorities **-instrument** levelling instrument

av|vända (*misstanke*) divert; (*olycka*) avert; ~ *uppmärksamheten från* divert attention from **-vänja** (*dibarn*) wean; *jfr vänja av* **-vänjning** weaning **-vänjningskur** cure (*mot* for) **-väpna** disarm **-väpning** disarmament **-värja** ward (fend) off; parry; (*olycka*) avert **-värjning** warding off *etc.* **-yttra** dispose of, sell **-yttring** sale, disposal **-äta** eat; have; ~ *en finare middag* have a grand dinner

ax *s7* **1** *bot.* spike; (*sädes-*) ear; *gå i* ~ form ears, ear **2** (*nyckel-*) bit, web

1 axel ['aks-] *s2* **1** (*geom.; jord-; polit.*) axis (*pl* axes) **2** (*hjul-*) axle[tree]; (*maskin-*) shaft; arbor; spindle

2 axel ['aks-] *s2* (*skuldra*) shoulder; *rycka på axlarna* shrug one's shoulders; *på* ~ *gevär!* shoulder arms!, slope arms!; *se ngn över* ~*n* look down on s.b., look down one's nose at s.b.

axel|band shoulder strap; *utan* ~ (*om damkläder*) strapless **-bred** broad-shouldered **-bredd** width across the shoulders

axelbrott axle fracture

axelklaff shoulder strap

axelkoppling shaft coupling

axelled shoulder joint

axelmakterna *pl* the Axis powers

axel|rem carrying (shoulder, satchel) strap **-remsväska** satchel; *A.E.* shoulder bag **-ryckning** shrug [of the shoulders]

axeltryck axle load, shaft pressure

axel|vadd shoulder pad **-väska** *se axelremsväska*

axiał, axiełl *a5* axial

axiom [-'å:m] *s7* axiom **-atisk** [-'ma:-] *a5* axiomatic[al]

axla put on, shoulder; *bildl.* take over

axplock gleanings (*pl*); *några* ~ *från* a few examples (facts *etc.*) gleaned from

ayatoll|ah *-ahn -or* ayatollah

azalea [asaˣle:a] *s1* azalea

azimut *se asimut*

Azorerna [a'så:-] *pl* the Azores

aztek [as'te:k] *s3* Aztec **-isk** *a5* Aztec[an]

azur [ˣa:sur *el.* 'a:sur, *äv.* -'su:r] *s2* azure **-blå** azure-blue

B

b *s6* b; *mus.* (*ton*) B flat, (*tecken*) flat sign
babbel ['babb-] *s7*, **babbla** *v1* babble
babelstorn [Tower of] Babel
babian *s3* baboon

babord ['ba:-] *s*, *böjligt endast i genitiv* port; *ligga för* ~*s halsar* be (stand) on the port tack; *land om* ~ land to port; ~ *med rodret!* helm aport! **babordslanterna** port light

baby ['be(i)bi *el.* -y] *s2, s3* baby **-kläder** baby clothes **-lift** carrycot

Babylonien [-'lo:-] *n* Babylonia

babylon|ier [-'lo:-] Babylonian **-isk** *a5* Babylonian; ~ *förbistring* babel, confusion of tongues; ~*a fångenskapen* [the] Babylonian captivity (*äv. påvarnas*)

baby|säng cot **-utstyrsel** layette

bacill *s3* bacillus (*pl* bacilli); germ; *A E. vard.* bug **-bärare** *se smittbärare* **-fri** germ-free **-skräck** *ha* ~ have a horror of contagion

1 back *s2* **1** (*lådfack*) tray; (*öl-*) crate **2** *sjö.* (*kärl*) bowl, kid

2 back *s2* **1** *sjö.* forecastle,fo'c's'le

3 back *s2, tekn.* (*broms-*) shoe; (*gäng-*) die

4 back *s2* **1** *sport.* back, fullback **2** (*-växel*) reverse [gear]; *lägga i* ~*en* put the car in reverse

5 back *adv* back; *brassa* ~ brace aback; *gå* (*slå*) ~ back, go astern; *sakta* ~*!* (slow) easy astern!; *slå* ~ *i maskin* reverse [the engine]

backa back, reverse; (*om fartyg*) go astern; ~ *upp, se uppbacka*; ~ *ur* (*bildl.*) back out

backanal *s3* bacchanal **-isk** bacchanalian

backant bacchant, *fem.* bacchante

back|e *s2* **1** (*sluttning*) hill; slope, hillside; ~ *upp och* ~ *ner* up hill and down dale; *sakta i -arna!* easy does it!; *över berg och -ar* across [the] country, over hill and dale; *streta uppför en* ~ struggle (trudge) up a hill; *åka nerför* ~*n* go downhill **2** (*mark*) ground; *komma på bar* ~ be left penniless; *regnet står som spön i* ~*n* it is raining cats and dogs

backfisch ['back-] *s2* teenage girl, teenager

backhammer (*i brottning*) hammerlock

backhand *s2* backhand **backhandsslag** backhander

backhopp|are ski jumper **-ning** ski-jumping

backig *al* hilly; undulating

backkrön brow [of a hill]

back|ljus, -lykta reversing light **-ning** backing, reversing

backsippa pasqueflower

back|slag *sjö.* reversing gear **-slagstangent** backspace [key]

backsluttning slope [of a hill], hillside

backspegel rear-view mirror

back|stuga hut, cabin **-stugusittare** crofter **-svala** sand martin **-tävling** ski-jumping competition; (*för bil*) hill climb

backväxel reverse gear

1 bad *imperf. av* bedja

2 bad *s7* bath; (*utomhus*) bathe; *ligga i* ~*et* (*äv.*) soak in the bath; *ta sig ett* ~ have a bath (bathe)

bada 1 (*ta sig ett bad*) take (have) a bath; (*utomhus*) bathe, take a swim; ~ *i svett* be bathed in perspiration; ~ *naken* skinny-dip; *gå* (*åka*) *och* ~ go for a swim **2** (*tvätta*) bath (*ett barn* a child)

bad|balja bathtub **-bassäng** swimming pool; (*inomhus*) swimming bath **-borste** bath brush **-byxor** [swimming] trunks

badda bathe; ~ *en svullnad* sponge (dab) a swelling

baddare bouncer, corker; *en ~ till gädda* a whopper of a pike

baddning bathing; sponging

bad|dräkt swimming (bathing) costume, swimsuit; *AE. äv.* bathing suit **-erska** [female] bath attendant **-flicka** bathing beauty **-förbud** bathing ban; (*på skylt*) Bathing Prohibited! **-gäst** (*vid -ort*) visitor; (*vid -inrättning*) bather **-handduk** bath towel **-hotell** seaside hotel; (*vid kurort*) health-resort hotel **-hus** bathhouse, public baths (*pl*) **-hytt** bathing cubicle (hut) **-inrättning** *se* **-hus -kappa** bathrobe **-kar** bath[tub] **-klåda** swimmer's itch **-kur** course of baths; *genomgå en ~ i* take the baths at **-lakan** large bath towel

badminton ['bädd-, *äv.* 'badd-] *n* badminton **-boll** shuttle[cock] **-plan** badminton court **-racket** badminton racket **-spelare** badminton player

bad|mästare bath attendant **-mössa** bathing cap **-ort** seaside resort; (*hälsobrunn*) health resort, spa **-rock** *se badkappa* **-rum** bathroom **-rumsmatta** bath mat **-rumsvåg** bathroom scales (*pl*) **-saker** bathing gear **-salt** bath salts (*pl*) **-sejour** stay at a spa (health resort) **-sko** bathing shoe **-strand** [bathing] beach **-ställe** bathing place **-svamp** [bath] sponge **-säsong** bathing season **-termometer** bath thermometer **-tvål** bath soap **-vatten** bath water; *kasta ut barnet med -vattnet* throw the baby out with the bath water

bag [bägg *el.* bagg] *s2* bag

bagage [-'ga:ʃ] *s7* luggage; *AE. äv.* baggage **-hylla** luggage rack **-hållare** luggage carrier **-inlämning** left-luggage office, cloakroom; *AE.* checkroom **-kärra** [luggage] trolley **-lucka** (*utrymme*) boot; *AE.* trunk **-utlämning** luggage delivery [office]; (*på skylt*) claim baggage here

bagarbarn *bjuda ~ på bröd* (*ung.*) carry coals to Newcastle

bagar|e baker **-mössa** baker's cap

bagatell *s3* trifle; *det är en ren ~* it's a mere trifle **-artad** [-a:r-] *a5* petty, trivial

bagatelliser|a make light of; belittle; (*överskyla*) extenuate, palliate **-ing** making light of *etc.*

bageri bakery **-arbetare** baker

bagge *s2* ram

baguette [ba'gätt] *s5* baguet[te]

baham|an *s3*, **-ansk** [-'a:nsk] *a5* Bahamian

Bahamaöarna [-ˣha:-] [the] Bahamas, [the] Bahama Islands

Bahrein *n* Bahrain, Bahrein

bahrein|are [-ˣrei-] *s9*, **-sk** [-ˣrei-] *a5* Bahraini, Bahreini

bahytt *s3* bonnet

baisse [bä:s] *s5* decline, fall [in prices]; slump; bear market; *spekulera i ~* operate for a fall; *det är ~ på börsen* it is a bear market **-spekulation** bear operation

bajadär *s3* bayadere

Bajern ['bajj] *n* Bavaria **bajersk** ['bajj-] *a5* Bavarian

bajonett *s3* bayonet **-fattning** bayonet **-fäktning** bayonet drill **-koppling** bayonet **-stöt** bayonet thrust

bajrare Bavarian

bajs *s7* number two **bajsa** do a number two

1 bak *s2* (*rygg*) back; (*ända*) behind, backside

2 bak I *adv* behind, at the back; *~ i boken* at the end of the book; *~ och fram* the wrong way round, back to front; *kjolen knäpps ~* the skirt buttons at the back **II** *prep* behind

3 bak *s7* (*bakning*) baking; (*bakat bröd*) batch

baka bake; *~ ihop sig* cake; *~ in* (*bildl.*) include; *~ ut en deg* knead and shape dough [into buns (*etc.*)]

bak|axel rear axle **-ben** hind leg **-binda** pinion

bakbord breadboard

bak|danta *se baktala* **-dantare** *se baktalare* **-del** back, hinder (back) part; (*människas*) buttock[s *pl*]; (*kreaturs*) hindquarter[s *pl*] **-däck** rear tyre **-dörr** back door; (*bils*) rear door **-efter** behind

bakelit *s3* Bakelite (*varumärke*)

bakelse *s5* pastry, [fancy] cake

bakerst ['ba:k-] **I** *adv* furthest back **II** *superl. a* hind[er]most

bakficka hip pocket; (*restaurangs*) restaurant annexe [with cheaper menu]; *ha ngt i ~n* have s.th. up one's sleeve

bakform baking-tin, patty pan

bak|fot hind foot; *få ngt om ~en* get hold of the wrong end of the stick **-fram** back to front, [the] wrong way round (about) **-full** hung over, crapulous, under the weather; *vara ~* have a hangover; *AE. äv.* be hung over **-gata** backstreet **-grund** background, setting; *teat.* backcloth, backdrop; *mot ~[en] av* (*äv.*) in [the] light of

bakgrunds|figur background figure **-strålning** background radiation

bak|gård back yard **-hal** slippery, tending to slide backwards **-hasor** *i ~na* hot on the heels; *sätta sig på ~na* dig one's heels in, jib **-hjul** rear (back) wheel **-hjulsdrift** rear [wheel] drive **-huvud** back of the (one's) head **-håll** ambush; *ligga i ~ för ngn* lie in ambush for s.b., waylay s.b.

bak|i I *adv* at the back, behind **II** *prep* behind in, in the back of **-ifrån** from behind

bak|kappa counter **-kropp** (*hos insekt*) abdomen **-laddare** breechloader **-laddningsmekanism** breech mechanism **-land** *geogr.* hinterland **-lucka** (*i bil*) boot cover; *AE.* trunk cover; (*utrymme*) *se bagagelucka* **-lykta**, **-lyse** rear light (lamp); *AE.* taillight, tail lamp **-lås** *dörren har gått i ~* the lock [of the door] has jammed; *hela saken har gått i ~* the whole affair has reached a deadlock **-länges** backwards; *falla ~* fall on one's back; *åka ~* (*i tåg*) sit (travel) with one's back to the engine, (*i buss etc.*) sit (travel) with one's back to the front (driver, horses) **-läxa** *få ~* have to do s.th. (homework) [all] over again

bakning [ˣba:k-] baking

bakom [-å-] behind; *AE. äv.* [in] back of; *~ knuten* round the corner; *föra ngn ~ ljuset* hoodwink s.b.; *klia sig ~ örat* scratch one's ear; *känna sig ~* feel dull (stupid); *vara ~* [flötet] be soft [in the head]; *man förstår vad som ligger ~* one understands what is at the bottom of it [all] **-liggande** *a4* lying behind [it *etc.*], underlying

bak|plåt baking-sheet **-pulver** baking powder

bakpå I *adv* behind, at (on) the back **II** *prep* at (on) the back
bakre ['ba:k-] back; hind
bak|rus *gå i* ~ have a hangover **-ruta** rear window **-sida** back; (*på mynt o.d.*) reverse; *på* ~*n* on the back, overleaf; *medaljens* ~ (*bildl.*) the other side of the coin **-slag** rebound, rebuff; *biol.* atavism; *tekn.* backfire; *bildl.* reverse, setback, recession; *det blev ett* ~ it was a setback **-slug** underhand, sly, crafty **-slughet** slyness **-smälla** hangover **-strävare** reactionary **-sträveri** reaction **-ström** back (backward) current; backwater; (*elström*) reverse current **-stycke** back **-säte** back (rear) seat **-tala** slander, backbite **-talare** slanderer, backbiter **-tanke** secret (ulterior) motive; *utan -tankar* (*äv.*) unreservedly, straightforwardly; *ha en* ~ have an axe to grind **-tass** hind paw
baktericjd *s3* bactericide; germicide
bakterie [-'te:-] *s3* bacterium (*pl* bacteria), germ, microbe **-dödande** germicidal, bactericidal **-fri** germ-free **-härd** colony of bacteria **-krigföring** germ warfare **-kultur** culture [of bacteria] **-stam** strain [of bacteria]
bakterio|log bacteriologist **-logj** *s3* bacteriology **-logisk** [-'lå:-] *a5* bacteriological; *Statens* ~*a laboratorium* [the Swedish] national bacteriological laboratory **-stas** *s3* bacteriostasis
baktill behind, at the back
baktråg kneading trough
baktung heavy at the back
bakugn [baker's] oven
bakut backwards; behind; *slå* (*sparka*) ~ kick [out]; lash out (*äv. bildl.*)
bak|vagn back of a carriage (*etc.*) **-vatten** backwater; (*bakström*) eddy; *råka i* ~ (*bildl.*) get separated from the main stream [of life]
bakverk [piece of] pastry
bak|väg back way; *gå in* ~*en* go in the back way; *gå* ~*ar* use clandestine methods **-vänd** *a5* the wrong way round; (*befängd*) absurd, preposterous; (*förvrängd*) perverted; (*tafatt*) awkward **-vänt** *adv* the wrong way; *bära sig* ~ *åt* be clumsy, act clumsily
bakåt backward[s]; (*tillbaka*) back **-böjd** *a5* bent back **-böjning** backward bend **-kammad** *a5* combed back **-lutande** leaning (sloping) backward[s]; ~ *handstil* backhand [(hand)writing] **-riktad** *a5* pointing backward[s] **-strävande** reactionary **-strävare** *se baksträvare*
bakända *se bakdel*
1 bal *s2* (*packe*) bale; package
2 bal *s3* (*danstillställning*) ball; *gå på* ~ go to a ball; *öppna* ~*en* open the ball; ~*ens drottning* belle of the ball
balalajka [-'lajka] *s1* balalaika
balans [-'ans *el.* -'aŋs] *s3* **1** (*jämvikt*) balance, equilibrium **2** (*saldo*) balance; (*kassabrist*) deficit; *ingående* ~ balance brought forward; *utgående* ~ balans carried forward **3** *tekn.* beam; (*i ur*) balance [wheel]
balanser|a [-ans- *el.* -aŋs-] **1** (*hålla i jämvikt*) balance, poise **2** *hand.* balance **-ad** *a5* [well-]balanced; poised; self-controlled **-ing** balancing
balans|gång balancing; *gå* ~ balance [o.s.], walk a tightrope **-hjul** flywheel **-konto** balance

account **-organ** organ of equilibrium **-rubbning** disequilibrium **-räkning** balance sheet **-sinne** sense of balance, equilibrium sense **-våg** balance, beam scales
balata [-ˣla:-] *s1* balata
baldakjn *s3* canopy
baldersbrå *s5, s6* scentless mayweed
balett *s3* ballet; *dansa* ~ *a*) (*vara -dansör*) be a ballet dancer, *b*) (*ta -lektioner*) go to ballet classes **-dansör, -dansös** ballet dancer **-mästare** ballet master **-sko** blocked shoe
1 balja *s1* (*kärl*) tub; bowl
2 balja *s1* **1** *bot.* pod **2** (*fodral*) sheath, scabbard
balj|frukt podded fruit **-växt** leguminous plant
1 balk *s2, jur.* code, section
2 balk *s2, byggn.* beam; (*järn-*) girder
Balkan|halvön ['ball-] the Balkan Peninsula **-länderna** the Balkans, the Balkan States
balklänning ball dress
balkong [-'kåŋ] *s3* balcony **-dörr** balcony door **-låda** balcony flower box **-räcke** balcony parapet
ballad *s3* ballad, lay
ballast, ballasta *se barlast, barlasta*
ballerina [-ˣri:-] *s1* ballerina; *prima* ~ prima ballerina
ballist|jk *s3* ballistics (*pl, behandlas som sg*) **-isk** [-'liss-] *a5* ballistic; ~ *missil* ballistic missile
ballong [-'åŋ] *s3* balloon **-farare** balloonist **-försäljare** balloon seller **-spärr** balloon barrage **-uppstigning** balloon ascent
balloter|a [vote by] ballot **-ing** balloting
balsa *s1* balsa
balsal ballroom
balsam [ˣball-, *pl* -'sa:-] *s3* balsam; *bildl.* balm **-era** embalm **-ering** [-'me:-] embalming **-jn** *s3* balsam **-isk** [-'sa:-] *a5* balsamic **-poppel** balsam poplar
balsaträ balsa[wood]
balt *s3* Balt; *han är* ~ he is an Estonian (a Latvian, a Lithuanian) **Baltikum** ['ball-] *n* the Baltic States **baltisk** ['ball-] *a5* Baltic
balustrad *s3* balustrade
bambu ['bamm-] *s2* bamboo **-ridån** *polit.* the bamboo curtain **-rör** bamboo **-skott** *kokk.* bamboo shoots (*pl*)
bana I *s1* path; *astr.* orbit; (*projektils*) trajectory; (*lopp*) course; (*levnads-*) career; (*lärt yrke*) profession; (*järnväg*) line; *sport.* track, ground, rink; *i långa banor* quantities (lots, no end) of; *vid slutet av sin* ~ at the end of one's career; *välja den prästerliga* ~*n* enter the Church, take holy orders **II** *v1*, ~*d* väg beaten track; ~ *väg[en] för ngn* (*bildl.*) pave the way for s.b.; ~ *väg genom* make (clear) a path (way) through; ~ *sig väg* make one's way
banal *a1* banal, commonplace; ~*a fraser* hackneyed phrases **-isera** reduce to the commonplace **-itet** *s3* banality
banan *s3* banana **-fluga** drosophila (*pl äv.* drosophilae), fruit (vinegar) fly **-kontakt** banana plug **-plantage** banana plantation **-skal** banana skin **-stock** banana stem **-träd** banana
banbryt|ande *a4* pioneering, groundbreaking; ~ *arbete* pioneer[ing] work **-are** pioneer (*för* of)
1 band *imperf. av binda*

2 band *s7* **1** (*ngt som binder*) band; (*remsa, i sht som prydnad*) ribbon; (*linne-, bomulls-*) tape; (*som hopsnör*) tie, string[s *pl*]; (*bindel*) sling; *anat.* ligament; (*bok-*) binding, cover; (*volym*) volume; *tekn.* belt; (*inspelnings-*) tape; *halvfranskt* ~ half-binding; *löpande* ~ assembly line; *ha armen i* ~ have one's arm in a sling; *måla tavlor på löpande* ~ produce (turn out) paintings in a steady stream; *spela in på* ~ record on tape, make a tape recording; *bilen har just lämnat* ~*et* the car has just left the assembly line **2** (*ngt som sammanbinder*) tie, bond; (*boja*) bond; (*för hund*) leash, lead; (*tunn-*) hoop; (*tvång*) restraint; *enande* ~ unifying bond; *kärlekens* ~ the ties of love; *träldomens* ~ the bonds of slavery; *lossa tungans* ~ loosen a p.'s tongue; *lägga* ~ *på ngn* lay restraint upon s.b.; *lägga* ~ *på sig* restrain (control) o.s.; *hunden går i* ~ the dog is on the lead **3** (*följe, anhang*) band, gang **4** (*orkester*) band

banda *radio.* tape[-record], record

bandage [-'da:ʃ] *s7* bandage

banderoll [-'råll] *s3* banderol[e], banner, streamer

band|hund watchdog; *skälla som en* ~ (*bildl.*) swear the devil out of hell **-inspelning** tape recording

bandit *s3* bandit, brigand; *enarmad* ~ (*spelautomat*) one-armed bandit, slot machine **-hövding** brigand chief

band|järn hoop (strip, band) iron **-mask** tapeworm **-rosett** tuft of ribbons; favour **-spelare** tape recorder **-såg** band saw **-traktor** caterpillar [tractor] **-tång** *bot.* eelgrass **-upptagning** tape recording **-vagn** tracked vehicle

bandy ['bandy *el.* -i] *s2* bandy **-klubba** bandy [stick] **-lag** bandy team **-match** bandy match **-spelare** bandy player

1 bane *oböjligt s, bringa å* ~ bring up, set on foot

2 bane *oböjligt s* death; *få sin* ~ meet one's death, perish; *skottet blev hans* ~ the shot proved fatal [to him] **-man** slayer, assassin

baner *s7* banner, standard **-förare** standard-bearer

banesår mortal wound

bang *s2* (*överljudsknall*) sonic boom (bang)

Bangladesh [-'deʃ] *n* Bangladesh

bangladesh|are [-ˣdeʃ-] *s9*, **-isk** [-'deʃ-] *a5* Bangladeshi

bangård [railway, *AE.* railroad] yard

banjo ['bann-] *s5* banjo

1 bank *s2* (*undervattensgrund*) bank, bar; (*vall*) embankment, dyke; (*moln-*) [cloud]bank

2 bank *s3* (*penninginrättning*) bank; banking house; (*blod- etc.*) bank; *pengar på* ~*en* money in (at) the bank; *spränga* ~*en* (*spel.*) break the bank; *sätta in på* ~*en* deposit in the bank, bank; *ta ut från* ~*en* withdraw from the bank

1 banka *se bulta*

2 banka *flyg.* bank

bank|affärer bank[ing] business (transactions) **-automat** *se bankomat* **-bok** bankbook, passbook **-bud** bank messenger **-direktör** bank executive; bank manager

bankett *s3* banquet

bank|fack safe-deposit box **-filial** branch [of a bank] **-fridag** bank holiday **-förbindelse** bank [ing] connection; (*i brevhuvud*) bank[er] **-garanti** bank[er's] guarantee **-giro** bank giro service (account) **-inspektion** ~*en* [the Swedish] bank inspection board

bankir *s3* [private] banker **-firma** banking house, bankers (*pl*)

bank|kamrer *ung.* chief clerk of a bank department, bank accountant; (*vid filial*) branch manager **-kassör** bank cashier; *AE.* teller **-konto** bank account **-kontor** bank (banking, branch) office **-kort** banker's card, bank card **-kredit** bank credit **-lån** bank loan **-man** banker, bank official; bank clerk

bankofullmäktige the board of governors of the Riksbank (Bank of Sweden)

bankomat automatic cash dispensing machine, cash dispenser

bankrutt I *s3* bankruptcy, failure; *göra* ~ become bankrupt **II** *a4* bankrupt, ruined; *vara* (*bli*) ~ be (go) bankrupt **-era** become bankrupt; go bankrupt **-mässig** *a1, vara* ~ be insolvent, be on the verge of bankruptcy **-ör** bankrupt

bank|rån bank robbery **-rånare** bank robber **-räkning** bank account **-ränta** bank rate **-tillgodohavande** bank balance **-tjänsteman** bank clerk; *AE.* teller **-valv** strongroom; vault **-väsen** ~[*det*] banking

bann *s7* ban; anathema; *jfr bannlysning* **banna** scold

bann|bulla papal bull of excommunication **-lysa** excommunicate, put under a ban; (*friare*) ban, prohibit **-lysning** excommunication; banishment, ostracism **-or** *pl* scolding (*sg*); *få* ~ be scolded, get a scolding **-stråle** anathema; *utslunga en* ~ *mot* condemn vehemently, fulminate against

banrekord track record

banta slim; ~ *ner* reduce (*utgifterna* expenses)

bantamvikt bantamweight

bantlär *s3* bandoleer, shoulder belt

bantning slimming **bantningskur** [course of] slimming

bantu|neger Bantu **-språk** Bantu **-stan** Bantustan, homeland

ban|vagn *fritt å* ~ free on rail (*förk.* f.o.r.), *AE.* free on truck (*förk.* f.o.t.) **-vakt** lineman **-vaktsstuga** lineman's cottage **-vall** [railway] embankment, roadbed **-övergång** level (*AE.* grade) crossing

bapt|ism Baptist faith **-ist** *s3*, **-istisk** [-'ist-] *a5* Baptist

baptistsamfund Baptist Church

1 bar *s3* (*självservering*) snack bar, cafeteria; (*utskänkningsställe*) bar, cocktail lounge

2 bar *s9* (*måttenhet*) bar

3 bar *a1* bare; naked; (*blottad*) exposed; *inpå* ~*a kroppen* to the skin; *under* ~ *himmel* under the open sky; *be på sina* ~*a knän* pray on one's bended knees; *blomma på* ~ *kvist* blossom on a leafless (bare) twig; *ertappa ngn på* ~ *gärning* catch s.b. red-handed (in the act)

4 bar *imperf. av bära*

bara I *adv* only; merely; *i* ~ *skjortan* in one's shirt; *det fattas* ~ *det!* that would be the last straw!; *du skulle* ~ *våga!* just you dare!, do it, if you dare!;

gör ~ *som jag säger* you just do as I tell you; *hon är* ~ *barnet* she is a mere (just a) child; *vänta* ~*!* just you wait! **II** *konj* if only; *(för så vitt)* provided, so (as) long as

barack *s3* barracks *(ibl. äv.* barrack); *(skjul)* shed; *(bostad)* tenement [building]

bar|armad *a5* barearmed **-axlad** *a5* bareshouldered

barb *s3 (fisk)* barbel

barbacka [ˣbaːr-] bareback[ed]

barbar *s3* barbarian **barbari** *s4* barbarism, barbarity, barbarousness

barbar|isk [-ˈbaː-] *a5* barbarian, barbaric, barbarous **-iskhet** barbarity, barbarousness **-ism** barbarism

barbent [ˣbaːrbeːnt] *a4* barelegged

barberare [-ˣbeː-] barber

barbiturat *s7, s4* barbiturate

1 bard [-aː-] *s3 (hos val)* whalebone, baleen

2 bard [-aː-] *s3 (skald)* bard; minstrel

bardisan *s3* partisan

bardisk [ˣbaːr-] bar [counter]

bardun *s3, sjö.* backstay

bardval whalebone (baleen) whale

barett *s3* peakless cap; *(kantig)* biretta

barfota *adv o. oböjligt a* barefoot[ed] **-läkare** barefoot doctor

bar|huvad *a5* bareheaded **-hänt** *a4* barehanded

barium [ˈbaː-] *s8* barium **-gröt** barium meal

1 bark *s3, s2 (skepp)* barque, bark

2 bark *s2, s3 (på träd)* bark

3 bark *s2, s3, med.* cortex *(pl* cortices)

1 barka *(träd)* bark; *(hudar)* tan; *~de händer* horny hands

2 barka ~ *i väg* fly off; *det ~r åt skogen för honom* he's sunk

barkaroll [-ˈråll] *s3* barcarol[l]e

barkass *s3* launch; longboat

bark|borre *s2* bark beetle **-bröd** bark bread **-båt** bark boat **-ning** barking, removal of the bark

bar|last ballast; *bildl.* dead weight **-lasta** ballast

barm *s2* bosom, breast; *bildl. äv.* heart; *nära en orm vid sin* ~ nourish a viper in one's bosom

barmark [ˣbaːr-] bare (snowless) ground

barmhärtig [-ˈhärt-, *ibl.* ˣbarm-] *a1* merciful *(mot* to); *(välgörande)* charitable *(mot* to) **-het** mercy; *visa* ~ *mot* show mercy to

barmhärtighetsverk act of mercy (charity)

barmästare bartender

1 barn [-aː-] *r el. n, fys.* barn

2 barn [-aː-] *s7* child *(pl* children); *(späd-)* baby, infant; *ett stundens* ~ a creature of impulse; *samma andas* ~ birds of a feather; *med* ~ *och blomma* with the whole family, with kith and kin; *bli* ~ *på nytt* be in one's second childhood; *vara (bli) med* ~ be (become) pregnant; *han är som* ~ *i huset* he is like one of the family; *hon är bara* ~*et* she is a mere child; *hon är ett* ~ *av sin tid* she is a child of her age; *alla* ~ *i början* everyone is a fumbler at first; *av* ~*s och spenabarns mun* out of the mouths of babes and sucklings; *bränt* ~ *skyr elden* once bitten, twice shy; *kärt* ~ *har många namn* a pet child has many names; *lika* ~ *leka bäst* birds of a feather flock together

barna|dödlighet infant mortality **-fader** father [of an illegitimate child] **-föderska** woman in confinement

barnalstring procreation (begetting) of children

barna|mord infanticide **-mun** *i* ~ in the mouth of a child **-mördare** infanticide

barnarbete child labour

barna|rov kidnapping **-sinne** childlike mind; *det rätta* ~*t* true childlike piety; *ha sitt* ~ *kvar* be still young at heart **-skara** *se barnskara* **-tro** childlike faith

barnavdelning children's section; *(på sjukhus)* children's ward

barnavård child welfare (care)

barnavårds|central child welfare clinic; *AE.* well baby clinic **-man** child welfare officer **-nämnd** child welfare committee

barnaår childhood

barn|barn grandchild **-barnsbarn** great grandchild **-beck** *med.* meconium **-begränsning** birth control **-bespisning** meals for [poor] children; *skol.* provision of free meals for school children **-bidrag** [government] child benefit **-biljett** child's ticket **-bok** child's (children's) book **-bördshus** maternity (lying-in) hospital **-daghem** day nursery, crèche

barndom childhood; *(späd)* infancy *(äv. bildl.)*

barndoms|hem home of one's childhood **-minne** memory from one's childhood **-vän** friend of one's childhood

barn|dop christening **-familj** family with children **-film** children's film **-flicka** nurse[ry]maid, nurse **-förbjuden** for adults only; ~ *film* adult audience (A) film **-förlamning** polio[myelitis], infantile paralysis **-hage** playpen **-hem, -hus** orphanage **-husbarn** orphanage child **-jungfru** nurse[ry]maid, nurse, nanny **-kalas** children's party **-kammare** nursery **-kammarrim** nursery rhyme **-kläder** children's (baby) clothes **-koloni** [children's] holiday camp **-konfektion** children's wear **-krubba** crèche **-kär** fond of children **-lek** children's game; *bildl.* child's play **-läkare** children's specialist; paediatrician **-lös** childless **-mat** baby food **-misshandel** child abuse **-morska** *s1* midwife **-omsorg** child welfare **-parkering** crèche **-passning** child minding **-piga** *se -jungfru* **-program** children's programme **-psykiater** child psychiatrist **-psykiatri** child psychiatry **-psykolog** child psychologist **-psykologi** child psychology **-puder** baby powder **-radio** radio broadcast for children; children's programme **-rik** ~*a familjer* large families **-rumpa** *skämts.* baby, silly fool; *han är en riktig* ~ he is a real baby

barns|ben *från* ~ from early childhood **-börd** childbirth, confinement

barn|sjukdom children's disease (illness); ~*ar (bildl.)* teething troubles **-sjukhus** children's hospital **-skara** family of children **-sko** child's (baby) shoe; *ha trampat ur* ~*rna* be out of the cradle **-skrik** child's howling **-sköterska** [child's, children's] nurse

barnslig *a1* childlike; *(oförståndig)* childish **-het** childishness

barn|stuga child day-care centre **-säker** childproof **-säng 1** child's bed, cot **2** *med.* childbed, childbirth, confinement; *ligga i* ~ be lying-in; *dö* *i* ~ die in childbirth **-sängsfeber** childbed (puerperal) fever **-teater** children's theatre **-tillsyn** child minding **-tillåten** for children also; ~ *film* universal exhibition (U) film **-trädgård** nursery school, kindergarten **-unge** child, kid; (*neds.*) brat **-uppfostran** education (bringing up) of children **-vagn** perambulator, pram; *A E.* baby carriage **-vakt** baby-sitter; *sitta (vara)* ~ baby-sit **-visa** children's song **-vänlig** ~*t dörrhandtag* childadapted door handle; ~ *miljö* environment suitable for children

barock [-'råck] **I** *al* **1** *konst.* baroque **2** (*orimlig*) odd, absurd **II** *s2* baroque **-ornament** baroque ornament **-pärla** baroque (irregularly shaped) pearl **-stil** baroque

barograf *s3* barograph

barometer [-'me:-] *s2* barometer; *vard.* glass **-stånd** barometric pressure

baron *s3* baron; (*brittisk titel*) Lord; (*icke brittisk titel*) Baron **-essa** [-*ˣessa] *s1* baroness; (*brittisk titel*) Lady; (*icke brittisk titel*) Baroness

1 barr *s3* (*gymnastikredskap*) (*för herrar*) parallel bars (*pl*), (*för damer*) uneven [parallel] bars (*pl*)

2 barr *s7*, *bot.* needle **barra** shed its needles

barracuda [-*ˣku:-] *s1* barracuda

barrikad *s3*, **-era** *v1* barricade

barriär *s3* barrier

barr|skog coniferous forest (woodland) **-träd, -växt** conifer; fir

barservering snack bar, cafeteria

barsk *al* gruff, harsh, rough **-het** gruffness *etc.*

barskrap|a scrape bare **-ad** *a5*, *vard.* stony broke; *han är inte* ~ he is not badly off

bar|skåp cocktail cabinet **-stol** bar stool

bart [-a:-] *blott och* ~ merely, only

bartender *s2* bartender

bartolomeinatten [-*ˣme:i-] *hist.* St. Bartholomew's Day Massacre

barvinter snowless winter

baryon [-'å:n] *s3* baryon

barysfär *s3* barysphere

baryt *s3*, *miner.* barytes

baryton ['barrytån *el.* 'barri-] *s3* baritone

1 bas *s2*, *mus.* bass; bass voice

2 bas *s2* (*arbetsförman*) foreman, *fem.* forewoman; *vard.* boss

3 bas *s3*, *mat. o. kem.* base; (*utgångspunkt*) base

4 bas *s3* (*grund*) basis

1 basa (*aga*) whip, smack

2 basa (*ångbehandla*) steam

3 basa *vard.* (*vara ledare*) be the boss (*för* of)

basalt *s3* basalt

basar *s3* baza[a]r **-stånd** *s7* stall

basbelopp basic amount

baseball ['beisbå:l] *s2* baseball **-spelare** baseball player

Basedows sjukdom ['ba:-] Graves' disease

basera base; ~ *sig på* to be based upon; base one's statements upon

basfiol double bass; *vard.* bass [fiddle]

bashyra basic rent

basilika [-'si:- *el.* -*ˣsi:-] *s1* **1** (*byggnad*) basilica **2** (*kryddväxt*) [sweet] basil

basilisk *s3* basilisk; (*fabeldjur äv.*) cockatrice

basindustri basic industry

basis ['ba:-] *r* basis; *på* ~ *av* on the basis of

basisk ['ba:-] *a5* basic

basist double-bass player; bassist

bask *s3* Basque

basker ['bass-] *s2* beret

basketboll ['ba:sket-] basketball

bask|isk ['bask-] *a5* **-iska** *s1* (*språk*) Basque

bas|klav bass clef, F clef **-linje** baseline **-livsmedel** staple foods

basrelief *s3* bas-relief

basröst bass [voice]

basse *s2*, *vard.* lubber; *mil. ung.* private, Tommy

bassångare bass [singer]

bassäng *s3* basin; (*bad-*) pool

bast *s7* bast; (*fiber*) bast, bass; (*t. flätning etc.*) raffia

1 basta *och därmed* ~*!* and there's an end of it!, and that's that!

2 basta *vard.* (*bada bastu*) take a sauna

bastant *al* substantial, solid; (*tjock*) stout

bastard [-'a:rd] *s3* bastard; *naturv.* hybrid

bastfiber bast fibre

Bastiljen [-'tiljen] the Bastille

bastingering [-iŋ'ge:-] *sjö.* topgallant bulwark

bastion [basti'o:n] *s3* bastion

bast|matta bass (bast) mat **-omspunnen** *a5*, ~ *flaska* bast-encased bottle

baston [*ˣba:s-] bass note

bastonad *s3* bastinado, thrashing

bastrumma bass drum

bastu *s5* sauna; *bada* ~ take a sauna

bastuba bass tuba

basun *s3* trombone; (*friare*) trumpet; *stöta i* ~ *för sig* blow one's own trumpet **-era** ~ *ut* noise abroad (about) **-ist** trombonist **-stöt** trumpet blast

bas|vara staple commodity **-år** base year

batalj *s3* battle; (*tumult*) turmoil, tussle **-målning** painting of battle scene[s]; battlepiece

bataljon *s3* **1** *mil.* battalion **2** (*i kägelspel*) *slå* ~ make a strike, knock down all the pins

batat sweet potato, batata

batjk *s3* bat[t]ik

batist batiste, cambric, lawn

batong [-'tåŋ] *s3* truncheon; *AE. äv.* blackjack

batteri *s3*; *tekn. o. fys.* storage battery, accumulator; *mus.* rhythm section, drums **-driven** battery operated (powered) **-laddare** [battery] charger **-radio** battery receiver (set)

batterist drummer; timpanist

baty|sfär bathysphere **-skaf** *s3* bathyscaph[e]

baud *r* (*måttenhet*) baud

bautasten [*ˣbau-] *ung.* menhir, old Norse memorial stone

bauxit [bau'ksi:t] *s3* bauxite

B-avdrag leave on partial pay

baxa prise; *AE.* pry

baxna be astounded; *han ljuger så man* ~*r* his lies take one's breath away

BB *förk. för barnbördshus*

B-dur B flat major

be *bad bett* **1** (*anhålla*) ask (*ngn om ngt* s.b. for s.th.); (*hövligt*) request (*ngn att göra ngt* s.b. to do s.th.); (*enträget*) beg, implore, entreat, beseech; *får jag* ~ *om brödet?* may I trouble you for the bread?; *jag ber att få beklaga sorgen* may I express my deep sympathy; *jag ber om min hälsning* *till* my kind regards to, please remember me to; *jag ber om ursäkt* I beg your pardon; *litet gladare, om jag får* ~ do cheer up a little; *nu ber du för din sjuka mor* that's one for her *(etc.)* and two for yourself; *se bedjande på ngn* look imploringly at s.b.; *å jag ber!* don't mention it! **2** *(förrätta bön)* pray **3** *(inbjuda)* ask, invite

beakt|a [-'akta] pay attention to; notice, observe; *(fästa avseende vid)* pay regard to, heed; *(ta hänsyn t.)* consider, take into consideration; *att* ~ to be noted **-ande** *s6* consideration; *med* ~ *av* in (with) regard to, considering **-ansvärd** [-ˣakt-] *a1* worth (worthy of) attention, noteworthy; *(ansenlig)* considerable

bearbet|a [ˣbe:-] *(gruva o.d.)* work; *(jord)* cultivate; *kem.* treat, process; *tekn.* machine, *(med verktyg)* tool; *(bok)* revise; *(teaterpjäs)* adapt; *(vetenskapligt material, råmaterial)* work up; *mus.* arrange; *(bulta på)* pound; *bildl.* [try to] influence; *(väljare, kunder)* canvass **-ning** working *etc.*

béarnaisesås Béarnaise [sauce]

bebland|a [-'blanda] *rfl* **1** *(umgås)* associate, mix *(med* with) **2** have sexual intercourse *(med* with) **-else 1** association **2** sexual intercourse

bebǫ inhabit; *(hus)* occupy, live in **-elig** [-'bo:-] *a5* [in]habitable, fit to live in

bebygg|a [-'bygga] *(område)* build [up]on; *(befolka)* colonize, settle [down] in; *glest -da områden* thinly populated (rural) areas; *tätt -da områden* densely built-up areas **-else 1** *konkr.* buildings *(pl)*, houses *(pl)* **2** building up; colonization, settlement

bebåd|a [-'bå:-] *(tillkännage)* announce, proclaim; *(förebåda)* herald, betoken; *(ställa i utsikt)* foreshadow **-else** *bibl.* Annunciation **-elsedag** Marie ~ Lady (Annunciation) Day

béchamelsås [-ˣmell-] béchamel sauce

beck *s7* pitch

beckasjn *s3* snipe

beckbyxa *(sjöman)* Jack Tar

beck|lig pitchy **-mörk** pitch-dark **-mörker** pitch-darkness **-svart** pitch-black

becquerel [bek'räll] *r (måttenhet)* becquerel

be|dagad [-'da:-] *a5* passé; past one's prime **-darra** [-'darra] calm down, lull, abate

bedja [ˣbe:-] *se be*

be|drǫ**[ga]** deceive, impose upon; *vard.* dupe, trick; *(på pengar)* swindle, defraud; *(vara otrogen mot)* betray; *om inte mitt minne -drar mig* if [my] memory serves me right; *skenet -drar* appearances are deceptive; *snålheten -drar visheten* penny-wise and pound-foolish; *världen vill* ~*s* the world likes to be cheated; ~ *sig* be mistaken *(på ngn* in s.b.)

bedrag|are, -erska [-'dra:-] impostor, swindler; *vard.* fraud

be|drǫ**ft** *s3* exploit, achievement, feat **-driva** [-'dri:-] carry on, manage; *(studier)* pursue; *(sysselsättning)* prosecute; ~ *hotellrörelse* run a hotel

bedräg|leri *(brott)* fraud, imposture, swindle; *(bländverk)* illusion; *lögn och* ~ fraud and falsehood **-lig** [-'drä:g-] *a1 (om pers.)* false, deceitful; *(om sak)* deceptive, delusive, illusory, fraudulent; ~*t förfarande* fraudulent proceeding[s *pl*], deceit; *på* ~*t sätt* fraudulently, by fraud

bedröv|a [-'drö:-] distress, grieve; *det* ~*r mig djupt* it distresses me deeply **-ad** *a5* distressed, grieved *(över* at, about) **-else** distress, grief, sorrow, affliction; *efter sju sorger och åtta* ~*r* after countless troubles and tribulations **-lig** *a1* deplorable, lamentable; *(svagare)* regrettable, sad; *(usel)* miserable

beduin *s3* Bed[o]uin

bedyr|a [-'dy:-] protest *(inför* to; *vid* on); asseverate; ~ *sin oskuld* protest one's innocence; *edligen* ~ swear **-ande** *s6* protesting; protestation *(om* of), asseveration

bedår|a [-'då:-] infatuate, fascinate; enchant **-ande** *a4* infatuating *etc.*; charming

bedöm|a [-'dömma] judge, form an opinion of; *(uppskatta)* estimate; *(betygsätta)* mark; *(en bok)* review, criticize **-ande** *s6* judging, judg[e]ment; estimate; mark-setting; review, criticism; *efter eget* ~ at one's own discretion; *det undandrar sig mitt* ~ that is beyond my judgment **-are** judge **-ning** *se -ande* **-ningsfråga** matter of judgment

bedöv|a [-'dö:-] make (render) unconscious; stun, stupefy; *med.* anaesthetize **-ande** *a4* stunning, stupefying; *med.* anaesthetic; narcotic; *(öron-)* deafening **-ning** *(medvetslöshet)* unconsciousness; *(narkos)* anaesthesia **-ningsmedel** anaesthetic [agent]

beediga [-'e:di-] swear to, confirm by oath; ~*d* sworn [to]; ~*t intyg* sworn certificate

befall|a [-'falla] *v2* **1** *(kommendera)* order; *(högtidligt)* command; *(tillsäga)* tell; *(föreskriva)* prescribe, direct; *(an-)* commit, commend; *inte låta sig* ~*s av vem som helst* not take orders from just anybody; *vad* ~*s?* what do you choose (please); *vad* -*s?* I beg your pardon? **2** *(föra befälet)* [have, exercise] command; ~ *fram* call for; ~ *fram sina hästar* order one's horses; *ni har blott att* ~ you have only to say the word **-ande** *a4* commanding; imperative; imperious **-ning** order, command; *på ngns* ~ by the order of s.b.; *få* ~ *att* receive orders to, be ordered to; *ge* ~ *om ngt* issue orders about s.th. **-ningshavande** *s9, konungens* ~ *(ung.)* County Administration

1 befara [-'fa:-] *v1 (frukta)* fear; ~ *det värsta* expect the worst

2 befar|a [-'fa:-] *befor befarit (fara på el. över)* travel through, traverse; *(om fartyg)* navigate; ~ *en väg* use (frequent) a road **-en** *a5, sjö.* experienced

befatt|a [-'fatta] *rfl,* ~ *sig med* concern o.s. with, *vard.* go in for; *sådant* ~*r jag mig inte med* that is no business of mine **-ning 1** *(beröring)* dealing, connection; *ta* ~ *med* take notice of; *vi vill inte ha ngn* ~ *med den saken* we do not want to have anything to do with that **2** *(anställning)* post, appointment, position; office

befattnings|beskrivning job description **-havare** employee; *(ämbetsman)* official; *koll.* staff, *AE.* personnel

befinn|a [-'finna] *rfl (vara)* be; *(känna sig)* feel; *(upptäcka sig vara)* find o.s.; *hur -er ni er i dag?* how are you today? **-ande** *s6* [state of] health, condition **-as** prove (turn out) [to be]; *han befanns vara oskyldig* he turned out to be innocent; *vägd och befunnen för lätt* weighed in the balance and found wanting

befintlig [-'fint-] *a5* (*förefintlig*) existing; (*tillgänglig*) available; *i ~t skick* in [its] existing condition **-het** existence; presence

be|fjädrad [-'fjä:d-] *a5* feathered **-flita** [-'fli:-] *rfl*, *~ sig om* exert o.s. to maintain, strive after [to attain] **-fläcka** [-'fläcka] stain, defile

befogad [-'fo:-] *a5* (*om pers.*) authorized, entitled (*att* to); (*om sak*) justifiable, justified, legitimate; *det ~e i* the justness (legitimacy) of **befogenhet** [-'fo:-] authority, powers (*pl*), right; *sakna ~* lack competence; *överskrida sina ~er* exceed one's powers

befolk|a [-'fålka] populate, people; *glest* (*tätt*) *~d trakt* sparsely (densely) populated region **-ning** population

befolknings|explosion population explosion **-förhållanden** *pl* demographic (population) situation (*sg*) **-grupp** group of the population **-lager** stratum (*pl* strata) of the population **-lära** demography **-pyramid** population pyramid **-statistik** vital (population) statistics (*pl*) **-tillväxt** population growth **-täthet** population density **-överskott** surplus population

befordr|a [-'fo:rdra] **1** (*sända*) convey, transport, forward, send; (*skeppa*) ship; (*med post*) send by mail **2** (*upphöja*) promote; *~ ngn till kapten* promote s.b. captain **3** (*främja*) promote, further; *arbete ~r hälsa och välstånd* he that labours and thrives spins gold; *~ matsmältningen* aid digestion **-an** *r* **1** conveyance *etc.*; *för vidare ~* to be forwarded **2** promotion, advancement, furtherance **-ande** *a4* promotive (*för* of)

befordrings|avgift [-'fo:rd-] forwarding charge[s *pl*], postage, carriage **-gång** system of promotion **-medel** means of conveyance (transport), transportation **-möjligheter** chances of promotion **-sätt** mode of conveyance

befrakt|a [-'frakta] charter, freight **-are** charterer, freighter, shipper **-ning** chartering, freighting **-ningsavtal** freight contract; *sjö.* [time] charter

befri|a [-'fria] set free, liberate; (*från löfte o.d.*) release; (*frälsa*) deliver (*från* from; *ur* out of); (*från börda o.d.*) relieve; (*från bojor*) unchain; (*från ansvar o.d.*) exonerate; (*frikalla*) exempt; (*från examensprov*) excuse; (*undsätta*) relieve; *~d från* free (exempt) from; *~ träd från ohyra* rid trees of blight; *~ från rost* derust, clean of rust; *~ från straff* remit a penalty (punishment); *~ sig från* free o.s. from; *~ sig från ngt obehagligt* shake off s.th. unpleasant **-ande I** *a4* liberating *etc.*; *en ~ suck* a sigh of relief **II** *adv*, *verka ~* have a relieving effect, give relief **-are** liberator; deliverer; rescuer

befrielse [-'fri:-] **1** (*frigörelse*) freeing; liberation; release; *~ns timme* the hour of deliverance **2** (*frikallande*) exemption; *~ från avgift* exemption from duty **3** (*lättnad*) relief **-front** liberation front **-krig** war of liberation **-rörelse** liberation movement

befrukt|a [-'frukta] fertilize, fecundate; *bildl.* stimulate, inspire **-ning** fertilization, fecundation; *konstgjord ~* artificial insemination

befrynd|a [-'frynda] *rfl* ally o.s. (*med ngn* to s.b.) **-ad** *a5* related (*med* to); allied (*med* to, with) (*äv. bildl.*)

befrämj|a [-'främja] promote, further, stimulate; encourage **-ande I** *s6* furthering; promotion, furtherance; encouragement **II** *a4* promoting *etc.* **-are** promoter, supporter

befullmäktig|a [-ˣfull-] authorize, empower; *en ~d* an attorney, a proxy; *~t ombud* authorized representative, proxy **-ande** *s6* authorization

befäl *s7* **1** command; *föra ~ över* be in command of; *inneha högsta ~et* be first in command **2** *pers. koll.* [commissioned and noncommissioned] officers (*pl*) **-havande** *s9*, *~ officer* commanding officer, officer in command **-havare** commander (*över* of); *sjö.* master, captain (*på ett fartyg* of a ship)

befäls|föring the exercise of command **-person** *se befäl 2* **-post** command **-tecken** broad pennant

befängd [-'fäŋd] *al* preposterous, absurd, ridiculous; (*om pers.*) out of his (*etc.*) senses **-het** madness, absurdity

befäst|a [-'fästa] fortify; *bildl.* consolidate, confirm, strengthen; *~ sin ställning* consolidate one's position **-ning** fortification

befäst|ningskonst [science of] fortification **-ningsverk** fortifications (*pl*), defensive works (*pl*)

begabb|a [-'gabba] scoff [at], mock **-else** scoffing, mockery

begagn|a [-'gaŋna] use, make use of, employ; *~ sig av a*) (*använda*) make use of, employ, *b*) (*dra fördel av*) profit by, avail o.s. of; *~ sig av tillfället* seize the opportunity **-ad** *a5* used; (*om vara*) second-hand **-ande** *s6* use, employment

begapa [-'ga:pa] gape at

be|ge [-'je:] *rfl* go, proceed; *~ sig av* depart (*till* to, for), set out (off) (*till* for), start (*till* for); repair (*till* to); *~ sig på flykt* take to flight; *~ sig till sjöss* go (put out) to sea; *på den tiden det -gav sig* in the good old days; *det -gav sig inte bättre än att han* as ill-luck would have it, he

begeistr|ad [-'gei- *el.* -'gai-] *a5* enthusiastic **-ing** enthusiasm

begiva [-'ji:-] *se bege*

begiven [-'ji:-] *a3* given (*på* to), fond (*på* of), keen (*på* on) **-het** (*böjelse*) fondness (*på* for); (*händelse*) [great] event; (*attraktion*) highlight

begjuta [-'ju:-] pour upon; soak, water

begonia [-'gɔ:-] *s1* begonia

begrav|a [-'gra:-] *v2* bury; *död och -en* dead and buried; *~ i glömska* consign to oblivion; *här ligger en hund -en* I smell a rat **-ning** (*jordfästning*) burial; (*ceremoni*) funeral

begravnings|akt funeral ceremony **-byrå** firm of undertakers (*AE. äv.* morticians) **-entreprenör** undertaker; *AE. äv.* mortician **-hjälp** death grant **-kassa** funeral expenses fund **-marsch** dead march **-plats** (*äldre*) burial ground; (*modern*) cemetery **-procession** funeral procession

begrepp *s7* conception, notion, idea; *filos.* concept, idea; *göra sig* (*ge*) *ett ~ om* form (give) an idea of; *inte ha det ringaste ~ om* not have the slightest idea (notion) of, know nothing whatever about; *stå i ~ att* be on the point of, be about to

begrepps|analys concept analysis **-bestämning** concept definition **-förvirring** confusion of ideas **-vidrig** illogical

begrip|a [-'gri:p-] understand, comprehend; grasp; see; *få ngn att* ~ make clear to s.b.; ~ *sig på* understand **-lig** *a1* intelligible, comprehensible (*för* to); *av lätt ~a skäl* for obvious reasons; *göra ngt ~t för ngn* make s.th. clear to s.b.

begrundan [-'grund-] *r* meditation, reflection **begrundansvärd** [-ˣgrunn-] *a1* worth considering

begråta [-'grå:-] mourn, weep for, deplore, lament; (*högljutt*) bewail

begräns|a [-'gränsa] bound, border; *bildl.* define; (*inskränka*) limit, restrict, circumscribe; ~ *sig* limit (restrict, confine) o.s. (*till* to); *bolag med ~d ansvarighet* limited [liability] company; *ha ~de resurser* have limited resources (means) **-ning** boundary; *bildl.* limitation, restriction, restraint

begynn|a [-'jynna] *v3* begin **-else** beginning, outset

begynnelse|bokstav initial [letter]; *stor* ~ capital **-lön** commencing salary **-ord** initial (opening) word **-stadium** initial (first) stage (phase)

begå 1 (*göra sig skyldig t.*) commit; ~ *ett fel* make a mistake; ~ *självmord* (*ett brott*) commit suicide (a crime) **2** (*fira*) celebrate; ~ *nattvarden* go to Communion **-ende** *s6* **1** committing *etc.* **2** celebration

begåv|a [-'gå:-] endow **-ad** *a5* gifted, clever, talented; *klent* ~ untalented; *konstnärligt* ~ artistic; *han är konstnärligt* ~ (*äv.*) he has artistic gifts **-ning 1** (*anlag*) talent[s *pl*], gift[s *pl*] **2** *pers.* talented (gifted) person; *en av våra största ~ar* one of our best (most brilliant) minds

begåvnings|flykt brain drain **-reserv** unexploited talent

begär [-'jä:r] *s7* desire (*efter* for); (*starkare*) craving, longing (*efter* for); (*åtrå*) appetite, lust (*efter* for); *fatta* ~ *till* conceive a desire for; *hysa* ~ *efter* (*till*) feel a desire for, covet; *tygla sina* ~ restrain one's desires (passions)

begära [-'jä:-] *v2* ask [for], demand; (*anhålla om*) request; (*ansöka om*) apply for; (*fordra*) require; (*trakta efter*) covet; (*vänta sig*) expect; ~ *avsked* hand in one's resignation; ~ *ordet* ask permission to speak; *är det för mycket begärt?* is it too much to ask?

begär|an [-'jä:r-] *r* (*anhållan*) request (*om* for); (*anmodan*) demand (*om* for); (*ansökan*) application (*om* for); *på* ~ on request; *på egen* ~ at his (*etc.*) own request; *bifalla en* ~ grant a request; *skickas på* ~ will be sent on request (application) **-else** desire **-lig** *a5* (*eftersökt*) in demand, sought after; (*tilltalande*) attractive; (*lysten*) covetous **-ligt** *adv* covetously; ~ *gripa efter* reach greedily for

behag *s7* **1** (*belåtenhet*) pleasure, delight; (*tillfredsställelse*) satisfaction; (*tycke*) fancy; *fatta* ~ *till* take a fancy to; *finna* ~ *i* [take] pleasure in, delight in **2** (*gottfinnande*) pleasure, will; *efter* ~ at pleasure, at one's own discretion **3** (*behaglighet*) charm; amenity; *äga nyhetens* ~ have the charm of novelty; *det har sitt* ~ it has a charm of its own **4** (*behagfullhet*) grace, charm; *åldras med* ~ grow old gracefully **5** (*yttre företräden*) charms (*pl*), allurements (*pl*); *kvinnliga* ~ feminine charms

behag|a [-'ha:-] **1** (*tilltala*) please, appeal to; (*verka tilldragande*) attract; *gör som det ~r er!* do as you please! **2** (*önska, finna för gott*) like, choose, wish; *ni ~r skämta* you see fit to make jokes; *~s det te?* do you wish to have tea?; *vad ~s?* what would you like?; *som ni ~r* as you please **-full** graceful; charming **-lig** *a1* pleasant; (*tilltalande*) pleasing, attractive; (*starkare*) delightful; *en* ~ *röst* a pleasant voice; *~t sätt* engaging manners **-sjuk** coquettish **-sjuka** coquettishness, coquetry

behandl|a [-'hand-] treat; (*handskas med, avhandla, handla om*) deal with; (*dryfta*) discuss, consider; (*hantera*) handle, use, manipulate; (*sår*) dress; *tekn.* process, work; ~ *illa* ill-treat, treat badly; *~s varsamt* handle with care **-ing** treatment; dealing [with]; discussion; handling, usage; process; *parl.* reading, discussion; *jur.* conduct, hearing **-ingsmetod** method of treatment; procedure

behandskad [-'hand-] *a5* gloved

behaviorism [bihei-] behaviourism

be|hjälplig [-'jälp-] *a5, vara ngn* ~ *med* help s.b. (*att göra ngt* to do s.th., in doing s.th.) **-hjärtad** [-'järtad] *a5* brave, courageous **-hjärtansvärd** [-ˣjärt-] *a1* worth[y of] earnest consideration; *-hjärtansvärt ändamål* deserving cause **-hornad** [-'ho:r-] *a5* horned

behov *s7* **1** (*brist; krav*) want, need, lack; (*nödvändighet*) necessity; (*förråd*) requirement[s *pl*]; *allt efter* ~ as required; *av ~et påkallad* necessary, essential; *för framtida* ~ for future needs; *vid* ~ when necessary; *fylla ett länge känt* ~ supply a long-felt demand; *ha* ~ *av* need, have need of; *vara i* ~ *av* be in need of; *tobak är ett* ~ *för honom* tobacco is a necessity for him **2** (*naturbehov*) förrätta sina ~ relieve o.s.

behovsprövning means test

behå *s2* brassiere; *vard.* bra

behåll *n, i* ~ left intact; *i gott* ~ safe and sound; *undkomma med livet i* ~ escape alive

behåll|a [-'hålla] keep, retain; (*bi-*) preserve; (*fattningen*) keep one's head; ~ *ngt för sig själv* keep s.th. to o.s.; *inte få* ~ *maten* not be able to keep one's food down; *om jag får* ~ *hälsan* if I am allowed to keep my health **-are** container; (*vatten-*) tank, cistern; (*större*) reservoir **-en** *a5* remaining; (*om vinst*) clear, net **-ning** (*återstod*) remainder, rest, surplus; (*saldo*) balance; (*vinst*) [net] profit (proceeds [*pl*]), yield; (*i dödsbo*) residue; *bildl.* profit, benefit; *ha* ~ *av ngt* (*bildl.*) profit (benefit) by s.th.

behår|ad [-'hå:-] *a5* covered with hair **-ing** hair growth

be|häftad [-'häft-] *a5*, ~ *med* afflicted with; ~ *med brister* defective; ~ *med fel* marred by errors, defective; ~ *med skulder* in debt **-händig** [-'händ-] *a1* (*flink*) deft, dexterous; (*fyndig*) clever; (*lätthanterlig*) handy; (*näpen*) natty; *ett ~t litet barn* a sweet (*AE.* cute) little child **-hänga** [-'häŋa] hang all over

behärsk|a [-'härs-] **1** (*härska över*) rule over, control; (*vara herre över*) be master of; (*dominera*) command; (*vara förhärskande*) dominate; ~ *marknaden* (*havet*) control the market (the sea); ~ *situationen* be master of the situation **2**

(*tygla*) control; ~ *sina känslor* (*sig*) control one's feelings (o.s.) **3** (*vara hemma i*) ~ *franska fullständigt* have a complete mastery of French **-ad** *a5* [self-]controlled, [self-]restrained **-ning** control, [self-]restraint

behörig [-ˈhö:-] *a5* **1** (*vederbörlig*) proper, fitting, due; *i* ~ *ordning* in due course; *på* ~*t avstånd* at a safe distance **2** (*berättigad*) appropriate, competent, duly qualified; (*om lärare o.d.*) certificated; *icke* ~ unauthorized, incompetent; ~ *domstol* court of competent jurisdiction; ~ *ålder* required age **-en** properly, duly **-het** authority, competence; *domstols* ~ the jurisdiction of a court; *styrka sin* ~ prove one's authority

behöv|a [-ˈhö:-] *v2* **1** (*ha behov av*) need, be in need of, want, require; *jag -er det inte längre* I have no more use for it; *han -de bara visa sig på gatan för att* he only had to appear in the street to **2** (*vara tvungen*) need, have [got] to; *detta -er inte innebära* this does not necessarily imply (mean); *du hade inte -t komma* you need not have come; *jag har aldrig -t ångra detta* I have never had occasion to regret it **-ande** *a4* needy **-as** *v2*, *dep* be needed (necessary, wanted); *det -s inte* there's no need [for (of) it]; *om* (*när*) *så -s* if (when) necessary; *mer än som -s* more than enough, enough and to spare; *det -des bara att hon sade* all it needed was for her to say **-lig** *a1* necessary

beige [bä:ʃ] *oböjligt s o. a* beige

beivr|a [-ˈi:v-] denounce, protest against; *lagligen* ~ bring an action against, take legal action (steps) **-an** *r* denunciation

bej *s3* bey

bejak|a [-ˈja:-] (*fråga*) answer in the affirmative; (*anhållan*) assent to **-ande I** *s6* answering; affirmative answer; assent (*av* to) **II** *a4* affirmative, assenting

bekajad [-ˈkajj-] *a5* affected, afflicted (*med* with)

bekant I *a1* (*känd*) known; *som* ~ as you know, as is well known; *enligt vad jag har mig* ~ as far as I know, to the best of my knowledge; *det är allmänt* ~ it is generally known **2** (*allmänt känd*) well-known; (*omtalad*) noted (*för* for); (*ökänd*) notorious; ~ *för sin skönhet* famous (celebrated) for its (*etc.*) beauty **3** (*personligen* ~) acquainted; *nära* ~ intimate; *hur blev ni* ~*a?* how did you become acquainted? **4** (*förtrogen med*) familiar with, cognizant of; *han föreföll mig* ~ his face seemed familiar [to me] **II** *subst. a* acquaintance, friend

bekant|a [-ˈkanta] *rfl* get to know (*med ngn* s.b.), make acquaintance (*med* with) **-göra** [-ˈkant-] announce, proclaim, make known; (*i tidning*) publish, advertise **-skap** *s3* acquaintance; (*kännedom*) knowledge; *vid närmare* ~ on [closer] acquaintance; *göra* ~ *med* become acquainted with; *stifta* ~ *med ngn* make a p.'s acquaintance; *säga upp* ~*en med* cease to be friends with **-skapskrets** [circle of] acquaintances

bekika [-ˈçi:-] stare (gaze) at

beklag|a [-ˈkla:-] (*tycka synd om*) be sorry for; (*hysa medlidande med*) pity; (*vara ledsen över*) regret; (*känna ledsnad över*) deplore; (*ta avstånd från*) deprecate; ~ *sorgen* extend one's condolences; ~ *sig* complain (*över* of; *för, hos* to); *jag* ~*r att jag inte kan komma* I regret I cannot come;

jag ber att få ~ *sorgen* I am grieved to hear about your bereavement, please accept my deep sympathy **-ande I** *s6* [expression of] sorrow (regret); *det är med* ~ *jag måste meddela* I regret to inform you **II** *a4* regretful **-ansvärd** [-ˣkla:-] *a1* (*om sak*) regrettable, deplorable, sad; (*om pers.*) poor, pitiable, to be pitied, wretched **-lig** *a1* regrettable, deplorable, unfortunate; *det är* ~*t* it is to be deplored **-ligtvis** unfortunately, to my (*etc.*) regret, I (*etc.*) regret to say

bekläd|a [-ˈkla:-] **1** (*påkläda*) clothe **2** (*täcka*) cover, case; (*med bräder*) board [up]; (*med plattor*) tile [over]; (*invändigt*) line; (*utvändigt*) face **3** (*inneha*) fill, hold; ~ *ngn med ett ämbete* invest s.b. with an office **-nad** *s3* **1** (*beklädande*) clothing, covering **2** (*överdrag*) *tekn.* (*invändigt*) lining, (*utvändigt*) covering, *byggn.* (*utvändigt*) facing, revetment; (*trä-*) boarding, panelling **-nadsindustri** clothing industry

bekläm|d *a1* oppressed, depressed **-mande** *a4* depressing, distressing; *det är* ~ *att se* (*äv.*) it is a depressing sight **-ning** oppression, depression

bekomm|a [-ˈkåmma] **1** (*erhålla*) receive; *valuta -en* value received **2** ~ *ngn väl* (*illa*) agree (disagree) with s.b.; *do s.b. good* (harm); *väl -e!* (*välönskan*) (*ung.*) it's a pleasure!, *AE.* you're welcome [to it]!, *iron.* serve[s] you right! **3** (*göra intryck på*) concern; *det -er henne ingenting* it has no effect upon her; *utan att låta sig* ~ without taking any notice

bekost|a [-ˈkåsta] pay for, defray (cover) [the expenses of] **-nad** *r* expense, cost; *på allmän* ~ at the public expense; *på egen* ~ at one's own expense; *på ngns* ~ at a p.'s expense; *på* ~ *av* at the expense of

be|kransa [-ˈkransa] wreathe; (*friare*) festoon **-kriga** [-ˈkri:-] wage war [up]on, fight against

bekräft|a [-ˈkräfta] **1** (*bestyrka*) confirm, corroborate; (*intyga*) certify; (*erkänna*) acknowledge; (*säga ja*) affirm; ~ *en uppgift* confirm a statement, *jur.* corroborate evidence; ~ *riktigheten av* bear [s.b.] out; ~ *med ed* swear [to]; *undantaget som* ~*r regeln* the exception that proves the rule; ~ *mottagandet av* acknowledge receipt of **2** (*stadfästa*) ratify **-else** **1** (*bestyrkande*) confirmation, corroboration; (*intygande*) certification; (*erkännande*) acknowledg[e]ment **2** (*stadfästelse*) ratification, sanction

bekväm *a1* **1** (*angenäm*) comfortable; (*hemtrevlig*) cosy; (*läglig*) convenient, handy; *göra det* ~*t för sig* make o.s. comfortable **2** (*maklig*) easy-going, indolent; *vara* ~ [*av sig*] like to take things easy, be lazy **bekväma** [-ˈkvä:ma] *rfl*, ~ *sig till* be induced (bring o.s.) to [do s.th.] **bekvämlighet** [-ˈkvä:m-] **1** (*bekvämhet*) convenience; (*trevnad*) comfort; *till de resandes* ~ for the convenience of the passengers **2** (*maklighet*) love of ease **3** (*komfort*) convenience; *med alla moderna* ~*er* with every modern convenience

bekvämlighets|flagg flag of convenience **-hänsyn** *av* ~ for the sake of convenience **-inrättning** public convenience **-skäl** reasons of convenience

bekymmer [-ˈçymm-] *s7* (*oro*) anxiety, concern, worry; (*omsorg*) care; (*starkare*) trouble; *ha* ~ *för* be worried about; *ekonomiska* ~ economic

worries
bekymmer|fri [-ˣçymm-] free from care, care-
free, untroubled **-sam** *a1* anxious, troubled, full
of care, distressing; *det ser ~t ut för oss* things
look bad for us **-samt** *adv, ha det* ~ be having a
worrying time
bekymmerslös [-ˣçymm-] light-hearted; *(slarvig)* careless **-het** light-heartedness; carelessness
bekymr|a [-ˈçymra] trouble, worry; *det ~r mig
föga* that doesn't worry me much; *vad ~r det
henne* what does she care; ~ *sig om* trouble
(worry) o.s. about, *äv.* care about; ~ *sig för framtiden* worry about the future **-ad** *a5* distressed,
worried, troubled, concerned *(för, över* about)
bekyttad [-ˈcytt-] *a5* in a quandary
bekämp|a [-ˈçämpa] fight against, combat; *(i de-
batt)* oppose **-ande** *s6* combating **-ningsmedel**
[-ˣçämp-] means of control; ~ *för skadeinsekter*
insecticide; ~ *för ogräs* weedkiller
bekänn|a [-ˈçänna] *(erkänna)* confess; *(öppet* ~)
avow, profess; ~ *[sig skyldig]* confess, *jur. äv.*
plead guilty; ~ *sig till kristendomen* confess the
Christian faith; ~ *färg* follow suit, *bildl.* show
one's hand **-are** confessor **-else** confession; *(re-
ligionssamfund)* confession, creed, religion; *avlägga* ~ confess, make a confession; *Augsburgska
~n* the Confession of Augsburg
bel *r* bel
be|lacka [-ˈlacka] slander, backbite **-lackare**
[-ˈlack-] slanderer, backbiter **-lamra** [-ˈlamra]
encumber, clutter up; *(väg)* block up
belast|a [-ˈlasta] **1** load, charge, burden; *bildl.*
saddle **2** *hand.* charge, debit; *ärftligt ~d* with a
hereditary taint **-ning** load[ing], charge, stress,
pressure; *med.* affliction; *bildl.* strain, burden;
hand. charge, debit **-ningsprov** load (toler-
ance) test
beledsag|a [ˣbe:-, *äv.* -ˣle:d-] accompany; *(följa
efter)* follow; *(uppvakta)* attend **-are** companion
-ning *mus.* accompaniment
belevad [-ˈle:-] *a5* well-bred, polite, mannerly,
well-mannered
belgare [ˈbelg-] Belgian **Belgien** [ˈbelg-] *n* Bel-
gium **belg|ier** [ˈbelg-] *s9*, **-isk** *a5* Belgian
beljuga [-ˈju:ga] tell lies (a lie) about
belladonna [-ˈdånna, -ˣdånna] *s1, bot.* deadly
nightshade, belladonna, dwale; *med.* belladonna
bellis [ˈbell-] *s2* daisy
belopp [-å-] *s7* amount, sum [total]; *till ett* ~ *av*
amounting to, to the value of; *intill ett* ~ *av* not
exceeding; *överskjutande* ~ surplus [amount]
belys|a [-ˈly:-] light [up], illuminate; *bildl.* shed
light on, illuminate, illustrate **-ande** *a4*
illuminating; illustrative, characteristic; *ett* ~ *exempel* an illustrative example **-ning** lighting; illumination; *(dager)* light; *bildl.* light, illustration;
elektrisk ~ electric light; *i historisk* ~ in the light
of history; *i ~ av dessa omständigheter* in the light
of these circumstances
belysnings|anläggning lighting plant **-arma-
tur** *s3, ej pl* light fittings *(pl)*
belän|a [-ˈlå:-] **1** *(pantsätta)* pledge, pawn; *(upp-
taga lån på)* raise (borrow) money on; *(om fastighet)* mortgage; *fastigheten är högt ~d* the estate is
heavily mortgaged **2** *(ge lån på)* lend [money] on;
~ *en växel* discount a bill **-ing 1** *(upptagande av*

lån) raising a loan, borrowing [on] **2** *(beviljande
av lån)* lending **-ingsvärde** loan (collateral) value
belåten [-ˈlå:-] *a3* (*om pers.*) content[ed]; *(om
min o.d.)* satisfied, pleased **-het** contentment;
satisfaction; *till allmän* ~ to everybody's satisfaction; *utfalla till* ~ prove satisfactory; *vara till* ~
give satisfaction
belägen [-ˈlä:-] *a5* situated, located; *avsides* ~ remote, secluded **-het** situation, position, site, location; *bildl.* situation, state, position; *svår* ~
predicament, plight
be|lägg *s7* (*bevis)* proof, evidence *(för* of); *(citat)*
quotation **-lägga 1** *(täcka*) cover; *(med färg
o.d.)* coat; *(plats)* reserve, secure, occupy **2** *(ut-
fästa straff för)* impose upon; ~ *med böter* impose
a fine upon, make punishable by a fine; ~ *med
kvarstad* sequestrate, embargo **3** *(förse med)* put
on; ~ *med handbojor* handcuff; ~ *med stämpel*
stamp **4** ~ *ett hotell med gäster* accommodate
guests at a hotel **5** *(med exempel)* support [by ex-
amples]; *formen finns inte -lagd före 1500* there is
no instance of the form before 1500 **6** *stopp och
-lägg!* belay there! **-läggning** *(täckning)* cover
[ing]; *(färg- o.d.)* coat[ing]; *(av plats)* reservation; *(på sjukhus)* number of occupied beds; *(ga-
tu- o.d.)* paving, pavement; *(på tungan)* fur
belägr|a [-ˈlä:-] besiege **-ing** siege; *häva ~en*
raise the siege **-ingstillstånd** state of siege;
proklamera ~ proclaim martial law
be|läsenhet [-ˈlä:-] wide reading; book-learning
-läst [-ˈlä:st] *a4* well-read
beläte [ˣbe:-] *s6* **1** *(avbild)* image, likeness **2** *(av-
guda-)* idol
belön|a [-ˈlö:-] reward; *(vedergälla)* recompense;
(med pengar) remunerate **-ing** reward; recompense; remuneration; *(pris)* award, prize
belöpa [-ˈlö:-] *rfl,* ~ *sig till* amount (come) to
bemann|a [-ˈmanna] man; ~ *sig* nerve o.s., pull
o.s. together; ~ *sig med tålamod* summon up patience; ~ *sig mot* harden o.s. against **-ing** crew
bemedlad [-ˈme:d-] *a5, en ~ person* a well-to-do
person, a person of means; *mindre* ~ of small
means
bemyndig|a [-ˈmynn-] authorize, empower
-ande *s6* authorization; *(fullmakt)* authority,
power; *(av myndighet)* sanction, warrant
be|mäktiga [-ˈmäkt-] *rfl* take possession of,
seize; *vreden ~de sig henne* wrath took possession of her **-mälde** [-ˈmä:l-] *oböjligt a,* ~ *man* the
said man; *ovan ~ person* the aforesaid [person]
-mänga [-ˈmäŋa] *v2, -mängd med* mixed [up]
(mingled) with, *bildl. äv.* interlarded with
bemärk|a [-ˈmärka] observe, note **-else** sense; *i
ordets egentliga* ~ in the strict sense of the word
-elsedag red-letter (important) day
bemärkt *a4* (*uppmärksammad)* noted, well-
-known; *(framskjuten)* prominent; *göra sig* ~
make one's mark
be|mästra [-ˈmästra] master; get the better of,
overcome
bemöd|a [-ˈmö:da] ~ *sig* endeavour, strive; *ab-
sol.* try [hard], exert o.s.; ~ *sig om ett gott uppförande* try hard to behave well **-ande** *s6* (*ansträngning)* effort, exertion; *(strävan)* endeavour
bemöt|a [-ˈmö:ta] **1** *(besvara)* answer; *(tillbaka-*

visa) refute **2** (*behandla*) treat; (*mottaga*) receive; *bli väl bemött* be treated politely **-ande** *s6* **1** reply (*av* to); refutation (*av* of) **2** treatment; *vänligt* ~ kind treatment, a kind reception

ben *s7* **1** (*i kroppen*) bone; *bara skinn och* ~ only skin and bone; *få ett* ~ *i halsen* have a bone stick in one's throat; *gå genom märg och* ~ pierce to the marrow; *skinna inpå bara* ~*en* fleece to the very skin **2** (*lem*) leg; *inte veta på vilket* ~ *man skall stå* be at one's wit's end; *bryta* ~*et* [*av sig*] break one's leg; *dra* ~*en efter sig* loiter along, dawdle; *hela staden var på* ~*en* the whole town was astir; *komma på* ~*en* get on one's feet; *lägga* ~*en på ryggen* cut and run, make off; *rör på* ~*en!* stir your stumps!, get moving!; *sticka svansen mellan* ~*benen* droop away with one's tail between one's legs; *stå på egna* ~ stand on one's own feet; *ta till* ~*en* take to one's heels; *vara på* ~*en igen* be up and about again

1 bena l *v1* (*hår*) part **II** *s1* parting
2 bena *v1* (*fisk*) bone; ~ *upp* (*bildl.*) analyze
ben|aska bone ash **-brott** fracture **-byggnad** frame[work], skeleton
benediktjn[er]|munk Benedictine [monk] **-orden** the Order of St. Benedict, the Benedictine order
ben|fisk bony fish **-fri** off the bone; boneless
Bengalen [benn'ga:-] *n* Bengal **bengal|ier** [benn'ga:-] *s9*, **-isk** *a5* Bengali, Bengalese; ~ *eld* Bengal light
ben|get *hon är en sån* ~ she's as thin as a rake **-hinna** *med.* periosteum (*pl* periostea) **-hård** [as] hard as bone; *bildl.* rigid, adamant
benig *a1* **1** bony; full of bones **2** (*invecklad*) puzzling
benign [-'niŋn] *a5* benign
ben|kläder trousers; *AE.* pants; (*kalsonger*) pants, undershorts, *AE.* underpants; (*dambyxor*) panties **-knota** *s1* bone **-linda** *s1* puttee, putty **-mjöl** bone meal **-märg** bone marrow **-pipa** *anat.* shaft **-porslin** bone china **-rangel** [-'raŋel] *s7* skeleton **-röta** caries
bensaldehyd *s3* benzaldehyde
bensen *s3*, benzene
bensjn *s3*, *kem.* benzine; (*motorbränsle*) petrol, *AE.* gas[oline]; *fylla på* ~ fill up **-bolag** petroleum (*AE.* oil) company **-bomb** petrol bomb; *vard.* Molotov cocktail **-driven** petrol powered **-dunk** petrol can **-mack** *se -station* **-motor** petrol engine **-mätare** fuel (gas tank) gauge **-pump** petrol pump **-snål** petrol-saving **-station** filling (petrol) station; *AE. äv.* gas station **-tank** petrol tank
benskydd *sport.* shin guard, leg pad
bensoe ['bensåe] *s5* benzoin **-syra** benzoic acid
bensol [-'å:l] *s3* (*äldre namn på bensen*) benzol[e]
ben|stomme skeleton **-sår** varicose ulcer **-vit** ivory white **-vävnad** bone tissue
benåd|a [-'nå:da] pardon; (*dödsdömd*) reprieve **-ning** pardon[ing]; (*av dödsdömd*) reprieve
benäg|en [-'nä:-] *a3* **1** (*böjd*) inclined, willing; given; ~ *för att skämta* given (prone) to joking **2** (*välvillig*) kind, [well-]disposed; *med -et tillstånd* by kind permission; *till -et påseende* on approval; *vi emotser Ert -na svar* we await your kind reply **-enhet** inclination (*för* to, for), disposition (*för*

to, towards), preference (*för* for), tendency (*för* to, towards), propensity (*för* to, towards, for)
benämn|a [-'nämna] call, name; (*beteckna*) designate; *-da tal* denominate numbers **-ing** name, denomination (*på* for); designation, term
beordra [-'å:r-] order; direct; (*tillsäga äv.*) instruct
beostare hill myna, Indian grackle
be|pansra [-'pans-] armour **-prisa** [-'pri:-] praise, extol **-pryda** [-'pry:-] adorn **-prövad** [-'prö:-] *a5* [well-]tried, tested; (*om botemedel*) approved; *en* ~ *vän* a staunch friend **-pudra** [-'pu:d-] dust **-rama** [-'ra:-] plan, arrange
berber ['bärr-] Berber
berberis ['bärr-] *s2* barberry
bereda [-'re:-] **1** (*tillreda, för-*) prepare; (*bearbeta*) dress, process; (*hudar*) curry; (*tillverka*) make; (*skaffa*) furnish; (*förorsaka*) cause, give; ~ *ngn* an opportunity; ~ *ngn glädje* (*bekymmer*) cause s.b. joy (trouble); ~ *plats för ngn* make room for s.b. **2** *rfl* prepare o.s. (*på, till* for), get (make) ready (*för* for); (*skaffa sig*) find, furnish (give, cause, provide) o.s.; ~ *sig på avslag* be prepared for a refusal; ~ *sig tillträde till* effect (force) an entry to, gain access to
berędd prepared, ready (*på* for); *vara* ~ *på det värsta* be prepared for the worst
beredning [-'re:d-] (*bearbetning*) dressing; currying; (*tillverkning*) manufacture; (*förberedelse*) preparation **beredningsutskott** working committee
beredskap [-'re:d-] *s3* [military] preparedness; *i* ~ in readiness, ready, prepared; *ha ngt i* ~ have s.th. up one's sleeve; *hålla i* ~ hold in readiness (store)
beredskaps|arbete relief work **-tillstånd** state of emergency **-tjänst** emergency service
beredvillig [-ˣre:d-] ready, willing **-het** readiness, willingness
berest [-'re:st] *a4* travelled; *vara mycket* ~ have travelled a great deal
berg [bärj] *s7* mountain (*äv. bildl.*); (*vid egennamn ofta*) mount; (*klippa*) rock (*äv. geol.*); (*mindre*) hill; *det sitter som* ~ it won't budge
bergamott [bärga'mått] *s3* (*päron*) bergamot
berg|art rock **-bana** mountain railway **-bestigare** mountaineer, [mountain] climber **-bestigning** mountaineering; (*med pl*) [mountain] climb, ascent **-borr** jumper; (*maskin*) rock drill **-fast** [as] firm (solid) as a rock; ~ *tro* steadfast belief **-grund** bedrock **-häll** rock face; flat rock
bergig [ˣbärrjig] *a1* mountainous; rocky; hilly
berg|knalle rocky knoll, hillock **-kristall** [rock] crystal **-landskap** mountainous country; mountain scenery **-massiv** *s7* mountain massif **--och-dalbana** switchback; (*i nöjespark*) roller coaster, big dipper **-olja** rock oil, petroleum
bergs|bo highlander **-bruk** mining **-hantering** mining [industry] **-ingenjör** mining engineer **-kam** mountain crest **-kedja** mountain chain (range) **-knalle** *se bergknalle*
bergskreva crevice
bergslag *s3* mining district
bergsluttning mountain slope (side)
bergs|man occupier of a miner's homestead **-pass** mountain pass **-platå** mountain plateau

-predikan [the] Sermon on the Mount
bergsprängare rock blaster
bergs|rygg ridge **-topp** mountain peak **-trakt** mountainous district **-vetenskap** mining and metallurgy, metallurgy and materials technology
berg|säker dead certain **-tagen** *a5* spirited away [into the mountain] **-troll** mountain sprite **-uv** eagle owl **-verk** mining [industry], mine **-vägg** rock face
beriberi [-'be:ri] *s2* beriberi
berid|are [-'ri:-] horse-breaker; *mil. äv.* riding-master **-en** *a5* mounted
berika [-'ri:-] enrich
beriktig|a [-'rikti-] correct, rectify; adjust **-ande** *s6* correction, rectification; adjustment
berkelium [-'ke:-] *s8* berkelium
berlinare [bär*li:-] **1** inhabitant of Berlin, Berliner **2** (*vagn*) berlin **berlinerblått** Prussian blue
berlock [bär'låck] *s3* charm
bermudarigg [-ˣmu:-] Bermuda rig
Bermudasöarna [bärˣmu:-] the Bermudas, the Bermuda Islands
berọ *v4* **1** ~ *på* (*ha sin grund i*) be due (owing) to; (*komma an på*) depend on; *det ~r på* that depends, that's all according; *det ~r på tycke och smak* it is a question of taste; *det ~r på vad man menar med dyrt* it all depends on what you mean by expensive; *det ~dde på ett missförstånd* it was due to a misunderstanding **2** (*stå i beroende*) be dependent (*av* on) **3** *låta det ~ vid* be content with; *låta saken ~* let the matter rest **-ende I** *s6* dependence (*av* on) **II** *a4* dependent (*av* on); ~ *på* (*på grund av*) *ett misstag* owing to a mistake; ~ *på omständigheterna* depending on circumstances; *vara ~ av andra* be dependent on others
beroende|framkallande *a4* habit-forming **-ställning** dependence
berså [bär'så:] *s3* arbour, bower
berus|a [-'ru:-] intoxicate, inebriate; ~ *sig* intoxicate o.s., get drunk (*med* on); ~*d* intoxicated, drunk, *vard.* tipsy, tight; *smått* ~*d* a bit merry **-ande** *a4* intoxicating **-ning** intoxication, inebriation **-ningsmedel** intoxicant
beryktad [-'ryktad] *a5* notorious; *illa* ~ of bad repute, disreputable
beryll *s3* beryl **beryllium** [-'ryll-] *s8* beryllium
be|råd *n* **1** (*villrådighet*) hesitation; perplexity **2** *stå i* ~ *att* intend to **-rätt** *oböjligt a, med* ~ *mod* deliberately, in cold blood
beräkn|a [-'rä:kna] calculate, compute, reckon; (*noggrant*) determine; (*uppskatta*) estimate (*till* at); (*ta med i beräkningen*) take into account, count (reckon) on; (*debitera*) charge; ~ *en planets bana* determine the orbit of a planet; ~ *ränta* calculate interest; ~*d ankomsttid* scheduled time of arrival; ~*d kapacitet* rated capacity; *fartyget ~s kosta 5 miljoner kr att bygga* the cost of building the ship is estimated at 5 million kronor **-ande** *a4* calculating, scheming **-ing** calculation, computation, reckoning; estimate, estimation; *med* ~ with a shrewd eye [to the effect]; *ta med i* ~*en* allow for, take into consideration (account)
berätt|a tell, relate, narrate; *absol.* tell stories; ~*nde stil* narrative style; ~ *till slut* get to the end of one's story; *det ~s att* it is reported that; *jag har*

hört ~s I have been told **-are** storyteller
berättar|glädje *han visar stor* ~ he takes great pleasure in storytelling **-talang** gift for telling stories, narrative skill; *pers.* born storyteller **-teknik** narrative technique
berättelse [-'rätt-] tale, short story; narrative; (*redogörelse*) report (*om* about, on), account (*om* of)
berättig|a [-'rätt-] entitle, justify; (*kvalificera*) qualify; (*bemyndiga*) empower, authorize **-ad** *a5* entitled, authorized, justified; (*rättmätig*) just, legitimate; well-founded, well-grounded; ~*e tvivel* reasonable doubts **-ande** *s6* justification; authorization; *sakna allt* ~ be completely unjustified
beröm [-'römm] *s7* praise; (*heder*) credit; *få* ~ be praised; *eget* ~ *luktar illa* self-praise stinks in the nostrils; *med* [*utmärkt*] ~ *godkänd* passed with [great] distinction; *icke utan* ~ *godkänd* passed with credit **berömd** *a1* famous, well-known **berömdhet** [-'römd-] celebrity **berömlig** [-'römm-] *a1* praiseworthy, laudable; (*betyg*) excellent **berömma** [-'römma] *v2* praise, commend; (*starkare*) laud; ~ *sig av* boast of; *i* ~*nde ordalag* in eulogistic terms **berömmelse** [-'römm-] (*ryktbarhet*) fame, renown; (*anseende*) credit; *det länder honom inte till* ~ it reflects no credit on him; *vinna* ~ gain distinction **berömvärd** [-ˣrömm-] *a1* praiseworthy, commendable
berör|a [-'rö:ra] touch; (*omnämna*) touch upon; (*påverka*) affect; *ytterligheterna berör varandra* extremes meet; *illa* (*angenämt*) -*d* unpleasantly (agreeably) affected; *bagerierna -s inte av strejken* the bakeries are not affected by the strike; *nyss -da förhållanden* circumstances just mentioned **-ing** contact, touch; (*förbindelse*) connection; *komma i* ~ *med* get into touch with, come into contact with **-ingspunkt** point of contact; *bildl.* interest (point) in common
be|röva [-'rö:-] ~ *ngn ngt* deprive (rob) s.b. of s.th.; ~ *ngn friheten* deprive s.b. of his liberty; ~ *sig livet* take one's own life **-sanna** [-'sanna] verify; *drömmen ~des* the dream came true **-sạts** braiding; ornament
besạtt *a1* (*behärskad*) possessed, obsessed; (*förryckt*) absurd; ~ *av en idé* obsessed by an idea; ~ *av en demon* possessed by a demon; *skrika som en* ~ cry like one possessed **-het** possession; absurdity
be|se see, look at (over); ~ *Paris* see the sights of (*vard.* do) Paris **-segla** [-'se:g-] **1** sail, navigate **2** (*bekräfta*) seal; *hans öde var ~t* his fate was sealed
besegr|a [-'se:g-] beat, conquer, vanquish; (*fullständigt*) defeat; (*svårighet o.d.*) overcome, get the better of; *ve de ~de!* woe to the vanquished! **-are** conqueror, vanquisher
besiffr|a [-'siffra] *mus.* figure **-ing** *mus.* figure
besikt|iga [-'sikt-] inspect, survey, examine **-ning** inspection, survey, examination
besiktnings|instrument (*för motorfordon*) registration certificate (book) **-man** surveyor; (*för motorfordon*) motor vehicle examiner; (*för körkortsprov*) driving examiner
besinn|a [-'sinna] **1** consider, think of, bear in mind **2** *rfl* (*betänka sig*) consider, reflect, stop to

think; (*ändra mening*) change one's mind **-ande**
s6 consideration; *vid närmare* ~ on second
thoughts **-ing 1** *se -ande* **2** (*medvetande*) consciousness; *förlora* ~*en* lose one's head; *komma*
till ~ come to one's senses
besinnings|full calm, deliberate; (*klok*) dis-
creet **-lös** rash; (*hejdlös*) reckless
besitt|a [-'sitta] possess, have, own **-ning** posses-
sion; *franska* ~*ar* French possessions; *komma i* ~
av come into possession of; *ta i* ~ take possession
of, (*med våld*) seize
besittnings|havare possessor, occupant, own-
er **-rätt** possession, tenure, seisin (*AE.* seizin)
-skydd security of tenure **-tagare** possessor,
occupant, owner
be|sjunga [-'ʃuŋa] sing [of] **-själa** [-'ʃä:la] ani-
mate, inspire
besk I *a1* bitter; ~ *kritik* caustic criticism **II** *s2* bitters (*pl*)
beskaff|ad [-'skaffad] *a5* conditioned; constitut-
ed; *annorlunda* ~ of a different nature **-enhet**
nature, character; (*varas*) quality
beskatt|a [-'skatta] tax, impose taxes [up]on;
högt ~*d* heavily taxed **-ning** taxation, imposition
of taxes; (*skatt*) tax[es *pl*]; *progressiv* ~ progressive taxation
beskattnings|bar *a1* taxable (*inkomst* income)
-år fiscal year
beskęd [-ʃ-] *s7* answer, reply; (*upplysning*) information; (*bud*) message; (*order*) instructions (*pl*),
order; *ge* ~ give an answer, send word; *ge ngn*
rent ~ tell s.b. straight out; *veta* ~ *om* know
about; *med* ~ well and good, with a will, properly; *det regnar med* ~ it is raining in earnest; *det*
är aldrig ngt ~ *med honom* he doesn't know his
own mind
beskedlig [-'ʃe:d-] *a1* (*flat*) meek and mild, submissive; (*anspråkslös*) modest; (*snäll*) kind,
good[-natured]; ~*t våp* milksop **-het** submissiveness; modesty; kindness, good-naturedness
beskhet bitterness
beskickning [-'ʃick-] embassy, legation; diplomatic representation, mission
beskjut|a [-'ʃu:ta] fire at; shell, bombard **-ning**
firing; shelling, bombardment
beskriv|a [-'skri:-] describe, depict; *det kan inte*
~*s* it is indescribable (not to be described); *bollen*
beskrev en vid båge the ball described a wide
curve **-ande** *a4* descriptive **-ning** description,
account (*av, på* of); *ge en* ~ *av* describe, depict;
trotsa all ~ defy description
beskugga [-'skugga] shade
beskydd [-ʃ-] *s7* protection (*mot* from, against);
under kungligt ~ under royal patronage; *ställa sig*
under ngns ~ take refuge with s.b.
beskydd|a [-'ʃydda] protect, guard, shield (*för,*
mot from, against); patronize **-ande I** *s6* protection **II** *a4* protective; patronizing **-are** protector;
patron
beskyddarmin patronizing air
beskyll|a [-'ʃylla] accuse (*för* of), charge (*för*
with) **-ning** accusation, charge (*för* of)
beskåd|a [-'skå:-] look at **-ande** *s6* inspection;
utställd till allmänt ~ placed on [public] view
beskäftig [-'ʃäftig] *a1* meddlesome, fussy [self-]
important **-het** meddlesomeness, self-import-

ance
beskällare [-'ʃäll-] stallion, studhorse
beskänkt [-ʃ-] *a4* tipsy, the worse for drink
1 beskär|a [-'ʃä:-] *v2* (*ge*) vouchsafe (*ngn ngt* s.b.
s.th.), grant (*ngn ngt* s.th. to s.b.); *få sin -da del*
receive one's [allotted, due] share
2 beskära [-'ʃä:-] *beskar beskurit*, (*avskära*)
tekn. trim; (*träd*) prune; (*reducera*) cut [down],
reduce
be|skärma [-'ʃärma] *rfl* lament (*över* over),
complain (*över* of) **-skärning** [-'ʃä:r-] *tekn.*
trimming; (*av träd*) pruning; (*reducering*) cutting
beslag *s7* **1** (*metallskydd, prydnad*) fittings,
mountings (*pl*); *koll.* ironwork, furniture; (*på*
nyckelhål o.d.) escutcheon **2** (*kvarstad*) seizure,
confiscation; *lägga* ~ *på* requisition, seize, *vard.*
bag; *bildl.* secure; *lägga* ~ *på hela uppmärksam-*
heten monopolize everybody's attention **-ta[ga]**
confiscate, seize, requisition; commandeer
beslut *s7* decision; (*avgörande*) determination;
(*av möte*) resolution; (*av myndighet o. jur.*) decision, decree, judgment; *fatta* ~ make (come to) a
decision, make up one's mind, (*av möte*) pass a
resolution; *det är mitt fasta* ~ it is my firm resolve;
med ett raskt ~ without [a moment's] hesitation,
at once
besluta [-'slu:-] **1** (*bestämma*) decide (*om, över*
upon); (*föresätta sig*) resolve, determine **2** *rfl*
(*bestämma sig*) decide (*för* upon), make up one's
mind; (*föresätta sig*) resolve, determine (*för att*
to) **beslutanderätt** [-*slu:-] right of decision;
competence to pass a resolution **besluten**
[-'slu:-] *a5* resolved, determined; *fast* ~ firmly resolved **beslutför** [-*slu:t-] *se beslutsmässig*
beslutsam [-'slu:t-] *a1* resolute **-het** resolution
besluts|fattare decision-maker **-mässig** *a1,*
vara ~ form a quorum; ~*t antal* quorum **-pro-**
cess decision-making process
be|slå 1 (*förse med beslag*) fit with metal; mount;
(*överdraga*) cover, case; *sjö.* furl **2** (*ertappa*) ~
ngn med lögn catch s.b. lying **-släktad** [-'släkt-]
a5 related, akin (*med* to); (*om språk o.d.*) cognate; (*om folkslag, anda*) kindred; *andligen* ~
med spiritually allied to **-slöja** [-'slöjja] veil;
bildl. obscure; ~*d blick* veiled glance; ~*d röst*
husky voice
besman *s7* steelyard
besmitt|a [-'smitta] infect, taint; *bildl. äv.* con-
taminate **-else** infection, contagion; contamination
bespara [-'spa:ra] (*spara*) save; (*förskona*) spare;
det kunde du ha ~*t dig* you might have spared
yourself the trouble **besparing 1** saving; *göra*
~*ar* effect economies **2** *sömn.* yoke **bespa-**
ringsåtgärd economy measure
be|speja [-'spejja] spy upon, watch **-spetsa**
[-'spetsa] *rfl*, ~ *sig på* look forward to, set one's
heart on
bespis|a [-'spi:-] feed **-ning** *abstr.* feeding,
konkr. (*skol-*) dining-hall
bespott|a [-'spåtta] mock [at], scoff at, deride
-else mocking *etc.*
besprut|a [-'spru:-] sprinkle, spray **-ning** sprink-
ling, spraying **-ningsmedel** spray [disinfectant,
insecticide *etc.*]
bessarab Bessarabian **Bessarabien** [-'ra:-] *n*

Bessarabia **bessarabisk** [-'ra:-] *a5* Bessarabian
bessemer|process [*bess-] Bessemer process
-ugn Bessemer converter
besserwisser ['bess-] know-all, wiseacre
best *s2* beast, brute; monster **bestialisk** [-ti'a:-]
a5 bestial, beastly **bestialitet** [-sti-] *s3* bestiality, beastliness
bestick *s7* **1** (*rit- o.d.*) set of instruments; (*mat-*)
set of knife, spoon and fork, cutlery **2** *sjö*. [dead]
reckoning; *föra* ~ work out the [ship's] position
besticka [-'sticka] bribe; corrupt
bestickande [-'stick-] *a4* seductive, insidious;
låta ~ sound attractive enough
bestick|lig [-'stick-] *a1* open to bribes; corrup-
tible **-ning** bribery; corruption
bestickräkning dead reckoning
bestig|a [-'sti:-] (*tron*) ascend; (*berg*) climb;
(*häst; schavott; talarstol*) mount; *bildl.* scale
-ning climbing; ascent
bestorma [-'storma] attack, assault; *bildl.* assail,
overwhelm
bestraff|a [-'straffa] punish; (*med ord*) rebuke
-ning punishment; *jur.* penalty; (*i ord*) rebuke
1 bestrida [-'stri:-] (*opponera sig mot*) contest,
dispute; (*förneka*) deny; (*tillbakavisa*) repudiate;
(*förvägra*) contest, dispute, deny; *det kan inte ~s
att* it is incontestable that
2 bestrida [-'stri:-] **1** (*sköta*) fill; be responsible
for **2** (*betala*) defray, pay for
1 bestridande *s6* (*t. 1 bestrida*) contesting *etc.*;
denial; repudiation
2 bestridande *s6* (*t. 2 bestrida*) **1** filling **2** (*betalning*) payment; *till* ~ *av* in defrayment of
bestryka [-'stry:-] smear, daub; (*med färg o.d.*)
coat; (*beskjuta*) sweep, cover
bestrål|a [-'strå:-] irradiate (*äv. med.*), shine, il-
lumine **-ning** [ir]radiation, exposure to rays
beströ strew, sprinkle, dot; (*med pulver*) powder
bestseller ['best-] *s2*, *s9* best seller **-författare**
author of popular books, best seller
bestyck|a [-'stycka] arm **-ning** armament
bestyr *s7* **1** (*göromål*) work; (*uppdrag*) duty,
task; (*skötsel*) management **2** (*besvär*) cares (*pl*),
trouble
bestyra [-'sty:-] (*göra*) do; (*ordna*) manage, arrange; (*sköta*) see about, attend to; *ha mycket att*
~ have a great deal to do (attend to)
bestyrelse [-'sty:-] [organizing, managing] committee
bestyrka [-'styrka] (*bekräfta*) confirm, corrobo-
rate; (*intyga*) attest, certify; (*stödja*) bear out;
(*bevisa*) prove; ~ *riktigheten av en uppgift* au-
thenticate a statement; *bestyrkt avskrift* attested
(certified) copy
bestå 1 (*vara*) last, continue, remain; (*existera*)
exist, subsist **2** (*utgöras*) consist (*av* of; *i* in); *däri
~r just svårigheten* that just constitutes the difficulty; *svårigheten bestod i* the difficulty lay in **3**
(*genomgå*) go through, stand, endure; ~ *provet*
stand the test **4** (*bekosta*) pay for, defray; (*bjuda
på*) treat [s.b.] to, stand s.b.; (*skänka*) provide,
furnish, procure **-ende** *a4* **1** (*varaktig*) lasting,
abiding; *av* ~ *värde* of lasting value; *den* ~ *ordningen* the established order of things **2** (*existerande*) existing
bestånd 1 (*existens*) existence; persistence; du-

ration; *äga* ~ last **2** (*samling*) stock; *bot.* stand,
clump; (*antal*) number; *zool.* population; (*av
kreatur*) stock **beståndsdel** constituent, component, part; (*i matvaror*) ingredient
beställ|a [-'ställa] **1** (*tinga*) order (*av* off, from);
(*plats, biljett*) book, reserve; ~ *tid hos* make an
appointment with; *får jag* ~ please take my order; *komma som -d* come just when it (one *etc.*)
is wanted; *-da tyger* textiles on order **2** *det är illa
-t med henne* she is in a bad way; *ha mycket att*
~ have a great deal to do **-are** (*köpare*) buyer,
purchaser, orderer; (*kund*) customer, client
-ning 1 (*rekvisition*) order; *på* ~ [made] to order
2 (*befattning*) appointment
beställnings|blankett, -sedel order form
-skrädderi bespoke tailor's; *AE.* custom tailor
beställsam [-'ställ-] *a1* (*beskäftig*) fussy, officious
bestämbar [-*stämm-] *a1* determinable; defin-
able
bestämd *a1* (*besluten*) determined; (*beslutsam*)
resolute, determined; (*om tid, ort o.d.*) fixed, appointed, settled; (*viss*) definite; (*tydlig*) clear,
distinct; *språkv.* definite; (*avsedd*) meant,
intended (*för* for); *på det ~aste* most emphati-
cally **-het** definiteness; determination; *veta med*
~ know for certain
bestämma [-'stämma] **1** (*fastställa*) fix, settle,
determine; (*tid, plats*) appoint, set; ~ *tid* make an
appointment, fix a time **2** (*stadga*) decree; provide, lay down **3** (*avgöra*) decide [upon] **4** ~ *sig*
decide (*för* [up]on), make up one's mind (*för att*
to) **5** (*begränsa, fixera*) determine **6** (*ämna, avse*)
intend, mean **7** (*fastställa, konstatera*) establish;
(*klassificera*) classify, determine, define **8**
språkv. modify, qualify
bestämmande [-'stämm-] **I** *s6* fixing *etc.*; decision; determination; classification **II** *a4* determin-
ing, determinative; (*avgörande*) decisive **-rätt**
right to decide, right of determination; authority
bestämmelse [-'stämm-] **1** (*stadga*) provision,
regulation; (*i kontrakt*) stipulation, condition **2**
(*ändamål*) purpose; (*uppgift*) task, mission **-ort**
[place of] destination
bestämning [-'stämm-] **1** (*bestämmande*) determination **2** *språkv.* qualifying word, adjunct (*till*
of); (*friare*) attribute, qualification **bestäm-
ningsord** qualifier
bestämt *adv* **1** (*med visshet*) definitely; decid-
edly; resolutely; positively; *veta* ~ know for certain **2** (*högst sannolikt*) certainly; *du mår* ~ *inte
bra* you are surely not well; *närmare* ~ more exactly; *det blir* ~ *regn* it's sure to rain
beständig [-'stänn-] *a1* **1** (*stadig*) settled, steady;
(*ståndaktig*) constant, steadfast **2** (*oföränderlig*)
impervious, resistant **3** (*bestående*) perpetual,
continuous
bestänka [-'stänka] [be]sprinkle; (*med smuts,
färg o.d.*) splash
bestört *a4* dismayed, perplexed (*över* at) **-ning**
dismay, consternation; perplexity
be|sudla [-'su:d-] soil, stain; *bildl. äv.* sully, tar-
nish **-sutten** [-'sutt-] *a5* propertied, landed,
well-to-do
besvara [-'sva:-] **1** (*svara på*) answer, reply to **2**
(*återgälda*) return, reciprocate; (*vädjan o.d.*) re-

spond to; ~ *en skål* respond to a toast
besvik|else [-'svi:-] disappointment (*över* at);
vard. letdown **-en** *a5* disappointed (*på* in; *över*
at)
besvär *s7* **1** (*olägenhet*) trouble, inconvenience;
(*möda*) [hard] work, labour, pains (*pl*); *göra sig*
~et att komma hit take the trouble (make the effort) to come [here]; *gör dig inget ~!* don't bother!; *ha mycket ~ med ngn* have no end of trouble
with s.b., have a hard time with s.b.; *kärt ~ no*
trouble at all; *kärt ~ förgäves* love's labour's lost;
tack för ~et! thank you for all the trouble you
have taken; *vara* [*ngn*] *till ~* be a trouble to [s.b.];
inte vara rädd för ~ not mind taking trouble; *vålla*
[*ngn*] *~* cause s.b. trouble **2** (*klagan*) appeal; *anföra ~* complain [of]; *anföra ~ hos* appeal to
besvära [-'svä:-] **1** (*störa*) trouble, bother; *får jag*
~ er att komma den här vägen may I trouble you
to step this way; *får jag ~ om ett kvitto* may I trouble you for a receipt; *förlåt att jag ~r* excuse my
troubling you; *värmen ~r mig* I find the heat trying; *hon ~s av allergi* she suffers from an allergy
2 *rfl* (*göra sig omak*) trouble (bother) o.s.;
(*klaga*) complain (*över* of), protest (*över*
against); *jur.* appeal, lodge a protest
besvär|ad [-'svä:-] *a5* troubled, bothered (*av ngn*
by s.b.); *känna sig ~* feel embarrassed **-ande** *a4*
troublesome, annoying; embarrassing
besvärj|a [-'svärja] **1** (*frammana*) conjure up **2**
(*anropa*) beseech **3** (*gå ed på*) confirm by oath
-else conjuration, invocation; (*trolldom*) sor-
cery **-elseformel** spell, charm
besvärlig [-'svä:r-] *a1* troublesome, tiresome;
(*svår*) hard, difficult; (*ansträngande*) trying; (*mödosam*) laborious; *ett ~t barn* a difficult child; *en*
~ väg a tiresome road **-het** troublesomeness;
(*med pl*) trouble, hardship, difficulty
besvärs|instans board (court) of appeal **-rätt**
right of appeal **-skrift** petition [for a new trial],
complaint **-tid** term of appeal
besynnerlig [-'synn-] *a1* strange, odd, peculiar;
(*underlig*) queer; (*märkvärdig*) curious **-het**
strangeness *etc.*; (*med pl*) peculiarity, oddity
besynnerligt [-'synn-] *adv* strangely *etc.*; *~ nog*
strangely enough
beså *v4* sow
besätt|a [-'sätta] **1** (*förse*) set; (*med spik*) stud;
(*med spetsar*) trim **2** *mil.* occupy **3** (*upptaga,
förse med innehavare*) fill; *väl* (*glest*) *besatt* well
(sparsely) filled **-ning 1** *sjö.* crew; *mil.* garrison
2 (*kreatursbestånd*) stock, herd [of cows] **3** (*garnering*) trimming[s *pl*], braiding **-ningsman** one
(member) of the crew
besök *s7* visit (*hos, i* to); (*vistelse*) stay (*hos* with;
vid at); (*kortvarigt*) call (*hos* on); *avlägga ~ hos*
pay a visit to, call on; *få ~* have a visitor (caller);
komma på ~ come to see, visit; *tack för ~et* thank
you for calling (coming); *under ett ~ hos* while
staying with; *väl värd ett ~* well worth a visit;
vänta ~ expect visitors
besök|a [-'sö:-] visit, pay a visit to; (*hälsa på*) call
on, go to see; (*bevista*) attend; (*regelbundet*) resort to, frequent; *en mycket -t restaurang* a much
frequented restaurant **-ande** *s9*, **-are** *s9* visitor,
caller (*i, vid* to)
besöks|dag visitors' day **-frekvens** (*på möte*

etc.) attendance rate **-tid** visiting hours (*pl*)
besörja [-'sörja] *~* [*om*] attend to, deal with, take
care of
1 bet *imperf. av bita*
2 bet *s2* **1** (*straffinsats vid spel*) forfeit, loo;
(*mark*) counter **2** *gå* (*bli*) *~* (*spel.*) have to pay
the game, *bildl.* be stumped (nonplussed); *han*
gick ~ på uppgiften the task was too much for him
1 beta I *s1* (*munsbit*) bite, morsel; *efter den ~n*
after that experience **II** *v1* (*bryta i stycken*) break
2 beta *v1* (*om djur*) graze; *absol. äv.* browse; *~*
av graze, crop
3 beta I *v1* (*metaller*) pickle, bate; (*hudar*) soak;
(*textilier*) mordant; *biol.* disinfect **II** *s1, tekn.*
steep; (*färg*) mordant
4 beta *v1* (*agna*) bait
5 beta *s1, bot.* beet
6 beta *s6* (*bokstav*) beta
7 beta *se betaga*
betacka [-'tacka] *rfl, ~ sig* [*för*] decline; *jag ~r*
mig! no, thanks, not for me!
beta[ga] [-'ta:(ga)] **1** (*fråntaga*) *~ ngn ngt* deprive (rob) s.b. of s.th.; *det betog mig lusten att* it
robbed me of all desire to **2** (*överväldiga*) overwhelm, overcome **betagande** [-'ta:-] *a4* (*förtjusande*) charming, captivating **betagen** [-'ta:-] *a5*
overcome (*av* with); *~ i* charmed by, enamoured
of
betal|a [-'ta:-] pay; (*vara, arbete*) pay for; (*skuld*
äv.) pay off, settle; *~ av* pay off; *~ fiolerna* foot
the bill; *~ för sig* pay for one's keep; *~ kontant*
pay [in] cash; *~ sig* pay, be worth while; *~ tillbaka* pay back; *~t kvitteras* received with thanks;
~ ngn med samma mynt pay s.b. back in his own
coin; *få -t* be paid; *få bra -t* get a good price; *det*
här ska du få -t för! I'll pay you out for this!; *ge -t*
för gammal ost pay [s.b.] out, *AE.* get back at,
fix; *svar -t* reply prepaid; *vaktmästarn, får jag ~!*
Waiter! May I have the bill, please?
betalare [-'ta:-] payer
betal|bar [-ˣta:l-] *a5* payable **-kort** charge (deb-
it) card **-kurs** buying price
betalning [-'ta:l-] payment; (*lön*) pay; (*avgift*)
charge; (*ersättning*) compensation, remuneration; *förfalla till ~* be (become, fall) due; *inställa*
~arna stop (suspend) payment[s]; *mot kontant ~*
for ready money, against cash; *som ~* [*för*] in
payment [for]; *utan ~* free [of charge]; *verkställa*
~ar make payments; *vid kontant ~* on payment
of cash
betalnings|anstånd respite [for payment] **-an-
svar** payment liability **-balans** balance of payments **-beredskap** liquidity **-dag** date (day) of
payment; due date **-föreläggande** injunction
to pay **-förmåga** solvency, ability to pay **-in-
ställelse** suspension of payments **-medel**
means of payment; (*ett lands*) currency; *lagligt ~*
legal tender, *AE.* lawful money **-påminnelse**
collection letter **-skyldig** liable for payment
-svårigheter *pl* insolvency (*sg*); *ha ~* be insolvent **-termin** day (term) of payment **-villkor** *pl*
terms of payment
beta|partikel beta particle **-stråle** beta ray
-strålning beta radiation
betatron [-'trå:n] *s3* betatron
1 bete *s2* (*huggtand*) tusk

2 bete *s6, lantbr.* pasture; pasturage; *gå på* ~ be grazing; *saftigt* ~ verdant pasture[s *pl*]
3 bete *s6* (*agn*) bait
4 bete *v4, rfl* behave; (*bära sig åt äv.*) act
beteckna [-'teckna] (*symbolisera*) represent; (*utmärka*) indicate, designate; (*markera*) mark; label; (*betyda*) denote, signify, stand for; imply; (*karakterisera*) characterize, describe; *detta ~r höjdpunkten* this marks the peak (culmination); *x och y ~r obekanta storheter* x and y represent (stand for) unknown quantities
beteckn|ande [-'teck-] *a4* characteristic (*för* of); typical, significant (*för* of) **-ing** (*benämning*) designation; term, denomination; (*symbol*) symbol; (*angivelse*) indication **-ingssätt** method of notation
beteende [-'te:en-] *s6* behaviour **-forskare** behavioural scientist **-forskning** behavioural science **-mönster** pattern of behaviour **-rubbning** behavioural disturbance **-vetare** social scientist **-vetenskap** social science
betel ['be:-] *s2* betel **-blad** betel **-nöt** betel nut **-palm** betel palm **-tuggning** betel chewing
betes|hage enclosed grazing **-mark** pasture, grazing land **-vall** pasture[-land]
beting *s7* piecework; *på* ~ by contract
betinga [-'tiŋa] **1** (*kosta*) command, fetch; involve **2** (*utgöra förutsättning för*) presuppose; (*utgöra villkor för*) condition; *~d av* conditioned by, dependent on; *~d reflex* conditioned response (*särsk. förr* reflex) **3** ~ *sig* stipulate (bargain) for
beting|else [-'tiŋ-] condition; stipulation; (*förutsättning, om pers.*) qualification **-ning** conditioning
betitla [-'tittla] *se titulera; den ~de adeln* the titled nobility
betjän|a [-'çä:-] serve; (*passa upp*) attend [on]; (*vid bordet*) wait on; *tekn.* operate, work; ~ *sig av* make use of, avail o.s. of; *vara -t av* (*med*) have use for
betjäning [-'çä:-] service; attendance; waiting on; *tekn.* operation, working; (*tjänare*) attendants, servants (*pl*), staff **betjäningsavgift** tip, service [charge]
betjänt [-'çä:nt] *s3* man[servant], footman; *neds.* flunk[e]y
betmedel seed disinfectant (dressing)
betning [ˣbe:t-] grazing *etc.*, *se 2, 3 o. 4 beta*; (*av utsäde*) dressing **betningsmedel** seed disinfectant
betodl|are beet-grower **-ing** beet-growing
betona [-'to:-] emphasize, accentuate (*att* the fact that); *fonet.* stress; *kulturellt ~de kretsar* cultural circles
betong [-'tåŋ] *s3* concrete **-beläggning** concrete surface **-blandare** concrete mixer **-gjutning** concreting **-konstruktion** concrete structure **-vägg** concrete wall
betoning [-'to:-] emphasis, stress, accent[uation]
betrakt|a [-'trakta] **1** (*se på*) look at, watch, observe; (*ägna uppmärksamhet åt*) contemplate, consider **2** ~ *som* regard (look upon) as, consider **-ande** *s6* watching *etc.*; contemplation; *ta i ~* take into consideration; *i ~ av* considering,

in consideration of **-are** observer, onlooker
betraktelse [-'trakt-] reflection, meditation (*över* upon); (*anförande i religiöst ämne*) discourse; (*åskådande*) regarding; *försjunken i ~r* lost in contemplation; *anställa ~r över* meditate upon **-sätt** outlook, way of looking at things
be|tro ~ *ngn med ngt* entrust s.b. with s.th. **-trodd** trusted
betryck (*trångmål*) embarrassment; (*nöd*) distress **betryckt** *a4* oppressed; dejected
betrygg|ad [-'trygg-] *a5* secure, safe **-ande I** *a4* (*trygg*) reassuring; (*tillfredsställande*) satisfactory, adequate; *på ett fullt ~ sätt* in a way that ensures complete safety **II** *s6, till ~ av* for the safeguarding of
beträda [-'trä:-] set foot on; *bildl.* tread, enter upon; *förbjudet att ~ gräset* keep off the grass
beträff|a [-'träffa] *vad mig ~r* as far as I am concerned; *vad det ~r* as to that, for that matter **-ande** regarding, concerning, in (with) regard to; (*i brevrubrik*) re
beträngd *a5* hard pressed, distressed
1 bets [be:-] *imperf. av bitas*
2 bets *s3* (*för trä*) stain; (*för hudar*) lye **betsa** stain
bets|el ['bets-] *s7* bridle **-la** bridle **-ling** bridling
betsning staining; *konkr.* stain
betsocker beet sugar
1 bett *sup. av bedja*
2 bett *s7* **1** (*hugg, insekts-*) bite **2** (*på betsel*) bit **3** (*tandställning*) dentition, bite **4** (*egg*) edge
bettl|a beg **-are** beggar **-eri** begging
betung|a [-'tuŋa] burden; overload; *~s av* be oppressed by **-ande** *a4* burdensome; oppressive
betuttad [-'tuttad] *a5, vara ~ i* be sweet on, be enamoured of
betving|a [-'tviŋa] subdue; (*underkuva*) subjugate; *bildl.* overpower, overcome, repress, control; ~ *sig* control (check) o.s. **-are** subjugator; subduer
betvivla [-'tvi:v-] doubt, question, call in question
betyd|a [-'ty:-] **1** (*beteckna*) mean, signify, denote; imply, connote; *vad skall detta ~?* what is the meaning of this? **2** (*vara av vikt*) be of importance, matter, mean; *det -er ingenting* that doesn't matter, it makes no difference **-ande** *a4* (*betydelsefull*) important; (*ansenlig*) considerable, substantial, large; (*framstående*) notable, of mark; *en ~ man* a prominent man
betydelse [-'ty:-] **1** (*innebörd*) meaning, signification; (*ords äv.*) sense; *i bildlig ~* in a figurative sense **2** (*vikt*) importance, significance; *det har ingen ~* it is of no importance, it doesn't matter; *av föga ~* of little consequence **-full** significant; important, momentous **-lära** semantics (*pl, behandlas som sg*) **-lös** meaningless; insignificant, unimportant
betydenhet [-'ty:-] importance, consequence
betydlig [-'ty:d-] *a1* considerable, substantial; *en ~ skillnad* (*äv.*) a great [deal of] difference
betyg *s7* certificate, testimonial; (*arbets-*) character; (*termins-*) report, *AE.* report card; (*vitsord*) mark, *AE.* credit, grade; *univ.* class; *få fina ~* get high marks, do very well; *sätta ~* allot marks **betyga** [-'ty:-] **1** (*intyga*) certify; testify **2** (*bedyra*)

protest, profess, declare **3** (*uttrycka*) express; ~ ngn sin vördnad pay one's respect to s.b.

betygs|avskrift copy of testimonial (certificate) **-hets** examination fever **-poäng** credit total **-skala** scale of marks

betygsätt|a grade, mark; *bildl.* pass judgment on **-ning** grading, marking

betäck|a [-'täcka] cover (*äv. göra dräktig*); *mil. äv.* shelter **-ning** cover[ing]; *mil. äv.* shelter; (*eskort*) convoy, escort; *ta* ~ take cover

betänk|a [-'tänka] consider, think of, bear in mind; *när man -er saken* when you come to think of it; ~ *sig* think it over, (*tveka*) hesitate **-ande** *s6* **1** (*övervägande*) thought, reflection; (*tvekan*) hesitation, scruple[s *pl*]; *ta ngt i* ~ take s.th. into consideration; *utan* ~ without [any] hesitation **2** (*utlåtande*) report

betänketid [-ˣtänke-] time for consideration

betänklig [-'tänk-] *al* (*misstänkt*) questionable, dubious; (*oroande*) precarious; hazardous, dangerous; (*allvarlig*) serious, grave; (*vågad*) doubtful **-het** misgiving, doubt, apprehension, scruple; *hysa ~er* have (entertain) misgivings, hesitate; *uttala ~er* express doubts

betänksam [-'tänk-] *al* (*eftertänksam*) deliberate; (*försiktig*) cautious; (*tveksam*) hesitant **-het** wariness

betänkt *a4*, *vara ~ på att göra* think of doing, contemplate doing

beundr|a [-'und-] admire **-an** *r* admiration **-ansvärd** [-ˣund-] *al* admirable; (*friare*) wonderful

beundrar|e, -inna admirer **-post** fan mail

bevak|a [-'va:-] (*vakta*) guard; (*misstänksamt*) watch, spy upon; (*tillvarataga*) look after; ~*d järnvägsövergång* controlled level (*AE.* grade) crossing; ~ *sina intressen* look after one's interests; ~ *ett testamente* prove a will **-ning** guard; custody; *sträng* ~ close custody; *stå under* ~ be under guard

bevaknings|kedja cordon of patrols **-manskap** guard **-tjänst** guard-duty; *sjö.* patrol-duty

bevandrad [-'vand-] *a5* (*förtrogen*) acquainted, familiar (*i* with); (*skicklig*) versed, skilled (*i* in)

bevar|a [-'va:-] *vl* **1** (*skydda*) protect (*för, mot* from, against); *-e mig väl!* goodness gracious!; *Gud -e konungen* God save the King; *Herren välsigne dig och -e dig* the Lord bless thee and keep thee **2** (*bibehålla*) preserve; maintain; (*hålla fast vid*) retain; (*förvara, gömma*) keep; ~ *fattningen* retain one's self-possession, keep unruffled; ~ *i tacksamt minne* keep in thankful remembrance; ~ *åt eftervärlden* hand down to posterity **-ande** *s6* protection, preserving *etc.*; preservation, maintenance

bevars good heavens!, goodnes [, gracious] me!

bevattn|a [-'vatt-] water; (*med kanaler o.d.*) irrigate **-ning** watering; irrigation **-ningsanläggning, -ningssystem** irrigation system

bevek|a [-'ve:-] *v3* (*förmå*) induce; (*röra*) move; *låta sig ~s* [allow o.s. to] be persuaded **-ande** *a4* moving, persuasive; entreating **-elsegrund** motive, inducement

bevilja [-'vilja] *vl* grant, accord, allow; *parl.* vote

bevill|ning [-'vill-] appropriation, vote of supply, government grant **-ningsutskott** ~*et* (*i USA o. Storbritannien*) the Committee of Ways and

Means

bevingad [-'viŋad] *a5* winged; ~*e ord* familiar quotations

bevis *s7* proof (*på* of); (*skäl*) argument; (*vittnesmål*) evidence (*för* of); (*-föring*) demonstration; (*uttryck för känsla o.d.*) proof, evidence, demonstration (*på* of); (*intyg*) certificate; (*kvitto*) receipt; *bindande* ~ conclusive proof; *framlägga* ~ (*jur.*) introduce evidence, (*friare*) furnish proof of; *leda i* ~ prove, demonstrate; *vilket härmed till* ~ *meddelas* which is hereby certified; *frikänd i brist på* ~ acquitted in default of proof of guilt; ~ *på högaktning* mark (token) of esteem

bevis|a [-'vi:-] (*utgöra bevis på, ge prov på*) prove, demonstrate; (*ådagalägga*) show; ~ *riktigheten av* bear [s.b.] out; *vilket skulle ~s* which was to be proved **-ande** *a4* demonstrative; conclusive **-bar** *se bevislig*

bevis|börda burden of proof **-föring** argument [ation], demonstration; submission of evidence **-kraft** conclusive power

bevislig [-'vi:s-] *al* provable, demonstrable **-en** demonstrably

bevis|material evidence **-medel** [means of] evidence

bevisning [-'vi:s-] argumentation, demonstration; *det brister i ~en* there is a flaw in the argument

bevista [-'vista] attend

bevisvärde value as evidence

bevittn|a [-'vitt-] witness; (*intyga äv.*) attest, certify **-ning** witnessing

bevuxen [-'vuxen] *a3* overgrown, covered; ~ *med skog* wooded, woody

bevåg *n, endast i uttr.: på eget* ~ on one's own responsibility

bevågen [-'vå:-] *a3, vara ngn* ~ be kindly disposed towards s.b., favour s.b. **-het** favour, good will

bevänt *a, n sg, det är inte mycket* ~ *med honom* he is not up to much

beväpn|a [-'vä:p-] arm; *bildl.* fortify **-ing** arming; (*vapen*) armament, arms (*pl*)

bevärdiga [-'vä:r-] ~ *ngn med ett leende* condescend to smile at s.b.

beväring [-'vä:-] (*beväringsman*) conscript, recruit **beväringsmönstring** enrolment of conscripts

beväxt *a4, se bevuxen*

Bhutan Bhutan **bhutanes** *s3*, **-isk** *a5* Bhutanese

1 bi *adv* **1** *stå* ~ hold out, stand the test **2** *sjö., dreja* ~ heave to; *ligga* (*lägga*) ~ lie (lay) to

2 bi *s6, zool.* bee; *arg som ett* ~ [absolutely] furious, spluttering with rage

1 bi- (*bredvid, intill*) by-

2 bi- (*två-, dubbel-*) bi-

biaccent secondary accent (stress)

biavel beekeeping

bi|avsikt subsidiary purpose; (*baktanke*) ulterior motive **-bana** branch line

bibehåll|a keep; preserve; (*upprätthålla*) maintain, keep up; (*ha i behåll*) retain; ~ *gamla seder och bruk* keep up (preserve) old customs; ~ *sig* (*om kläder*) wear, (*om färg*) stand, (*om seder*) last; ~ *sin värdighet* maintain one's dignity; ~

sina själsförmögenheter retain one's faculties; ~ *sitt anseende som* keep up one's reputation for; *väl -en* well preserved; *en väl -en byggnad* a building in good repair; *han är väl -en* he is well kept **-ande** *s6* keeping *etc.*; preservation; maintenance; retention; *tjänstledighet med ~ av lönen* leave with full pay

bibel ['bi:-] *s2* bible; *~n* the [Holy] Bible **-citat** biblical quotation **-forskning** biblical research **-konkordans** concordance to the Bible **-kritik** biblical criticism **-kunskap** knowledge of the Bible **-ord** quotation from the Scriptures **-papper** bible (India) paper **-språk** *se -ställe* **-sprängd** *a5* versed in the Bible **-ställe** Bible passage **-tolkning** exegesis **-översättning** Bible translation

bibetydelse subordinate sense, secondary meaning

bibliofil *s3* bibliophil[e] **-upplaga** de luxe edition

biblio|graf *s3* bibliographer **-grafi** *s3* bibliography **-grafisk** [-'gra:-] *a5* bibliographical

bibliotek *s7* library **-arie** [-'a:rie] *s5* librarian

biblioteks|band library binding **-väsen** libraries [and library organization]

biblisk ['bi:-] *a5* biblical; *~a historien* biblical narratives, Bible stories (*pl*)

bibringa *~ ngn ngt* impart (convey) s.th. to s.b., imbue s.b. with s.th.; *~ ngn en åsikt* impress s.b. with an opinion

biceps ['bi:-] *s3* biceps

bida bide; await, wait for; *~ sin tid* bide one's time **bidan** *r* [time of] waiting

bidé *s3* bidet

bidevind *a5* close to (by) the wind; *segla ~* sail close-hauled **-seglare** *zool.* velella; Portuguese man-of-war

bidrag contribution; share; (*penning-*) allowance, benefit; (*stats-*) subsidy; *lämna ~* make a contribution **bidraga** contribute; (*samverka*) combine; *~ med* contribute; *~ till* aid, promote, help; *~ till att förklara* help to explain, be instrumental in explaining **bidragande** *a4* contributory, contributing

bidrags|förskott advance maintenance payment **-givare** contributor

bidrottning queen bee

biedermeierstil ['bidermaier-] Biedermeier style

biённ *bient, pl ~a* biennial **biennal** *s3* biennial

bifall (*samtycke*) assent, consent; (*godkännande*) sanction; (*medhåll*) approval, approbation; (*applåder*) applause, acclamation; *stormande ~* thunderous applause; *vinna ~* meet with approval; *yrka ~* support **bifalla** approve [of], assent to; (*godkänna*) sanction; (*bevilja*) grant; *~ en anhållan* grant a request; *begäran bifölls* the request was granted

bifalls|rop shout of approval **-storm** burst (storm) of applause **-yrkande** motion in favour [of the proposal] **-yttring** applause, acclamation

biff *s2* [beef]steak; *saken är ~* (*vard.*) everything is all right (okay, O.K.); *jag ska ordna ~en* (*vard.*) I'll swing it somehow **-kor** *pl* beef cattle, dual-purpose cattle (*sg*) **-stek** *se biff*

bi|figur subsidiary (minor) character **-flod** tribu-

tary, affluent

bifoga attach; (*närsluta*) enclose; (*tillägga vid slutet*) append, subjoin; *betygen skall ~s ansökan* testimonials (*etc.*) should be attached to the application, (*friare*) apply with full particulars; *~d blankett* accompanying form; *härmed ~s* enclosed please find; *med ~nde av* enclosing, appending; *~t översänder vi* we are enclosing; *vara ~d (till dokument o.d.)* be attached, (*i brev etc.*) be enclosed

bifokal *a5* bifocal **-glas** bifocals (*pl*)

bifurkation bifurcation

biförtjänst extra (additional) income; incidental earnings (*pl*)

biga crease, bow

bigam|i *s3* bigamy **-ist** bigamist

bigarrå *s3* white heart cherry, bigarreau

bigata side street

bigning [ˣbi:g-] crease, bow

bigott [-'gått] *a1* bigoted **-eri** bigotry

bigård apiary

bi|handling episode **-hang** *s7* appendage; (*i bok*) appendix (*pl* append|ixes *el.* -ices); *mask-formiga ~et* the [vermiform] appendix **-hustru** concubine **-håla** *med.* sinus **-håleinflammation** sinusitis **-hänsyn** secondary consideration **-inkomst** *se biförtjänst* **-intresse** sideline

bijouteri|er [biʃote'ri:-], **-varor** *pl* jewellery (*sg*), jewellery goods, trinkets

bjkarbonat [*äv.* -'a:t] bicarbonate [of soda]

bikini [-'ki:-] *s9, s3* bikini

bj|konkav [*äv.* -'ka:v] biconcave **-konvex** [*äv.* -'vex] biconvex

bikt *s3* confession **bikta** *~ [sig]* confess

bikt|barn confessant **-fader** confessor **-stol** confessional

bikupa *s1* beehive

bil *s2* [motor]car; *AE.* car, auto[mobile]; *köra ~* drive a car **1 bila** *v1* travel (go) by car, motor; go motoring **2 bila** *s1* broad-axe

bilaccis car tax

bilaga *s1* (*i brev*) enclosure; (*i bok, tidning*) appendix, supplement

biland dependency

bilateral *a1* bilateral

bil|besiktning (*ung.*) [annual] motor vehicle inspection **-buren** motorized **-bälte** (*safety*) belt **-chassi** [*motorcar*] chassis

bild *s3* picture; (*illustration*) illustration; (*avbildning, äv. bildl. o. opt.*) image; (*spegel-*) likeness, reflection; (*på mynt*) effigy; *språkv.* figure [of speech], metaphor; *ge ngn en ~ av situationen* put s.b. in the picture; *tala i ~er* speak figuratively (metaphorically)

bilda 1 (*åstadkomma, grunda, utgöra*) form (*äv. språkv.*), found establish **2** (*uppfostra, förädla*) educate; cultivate **3** *rfl* (*uppstå*) form, be formed; (*skaffa sig bildning*) educate (improve) o.s.; *~ sig en uppfattning om* form an idea of **bildad** *a5* cultivated; educated; refined, civilized; *akademiskt ~* with a university education; *bland ~e människor* in cultural (intellectual) circles; *en ~ uppfostran* a liberal education **bildande** *a4* educative, instructive; *~ konster* imitative arts

bild|arkiv photo archive **-band** film strip

bildbar *al* **1** (*formbar*) plastic **2** capable of being educated, educable
bild|erbok picture book **-galleri** [picture] gallery **-huggare** sculptor **-huggarkonst** sculpture **-hållning** *TV* frame hold; *A E.* vertical hold **-konst** visual arts
bild|lig *al* figurative, metaphorical **-material** illustrative material; illustrations (*pl*)
bildning 1 formation; (*form*) form, shape **2** (*odling*) culture; (*skol-*) education; (*själs-*) cultivation; (*levnadsvett*) breeding, refinement; *en man av* ~ a man of culture (refinement)
bildnings|förbund adult education institute **-grad** degree of culture **-törst** thirst for knowledge
bild|ordbok illustrated (pictorial) dictionary **-redaktör** illustrations editor **-rik 1** (*stil, språk*) picturesque, ornate, flowery **2** (*bok*) richly illustrated
bil|drulle road hog
bild|reportage picture story **-ruta** *film.* frame; *TV* [viewing] screen **-rör** *TV* television (picture) tube, [tele]tube **-serie** comic strip, strip cartoon; *särsk. A E.* comics (*pl*) **-sida** pictorial page; (*på mynt*) obverse, face **-skrift** picture writing, pictography; hieroglyphics (*pl, behandlas som sg*) **-skärm** screen **-skärpa** *foto.*, *TV* definition **-skön** pretty as a picture, of statuesque beauty, well-favoured **-språk** imagery; metaphorical language **-stod** statue **-stormare** iconoclast **-telefon** videophone **-telegrafi** phototelegraphy, telephotography **-text** [picture] caption **-tidning** pictorial, picture magazine **-verk** volume of pictures
bildäck 1 [motorcar] tyre; *A E.* [automobile] tire **2** *sjö.* car deck
bildöverföring transmission of visual matter, picture transmission
bil|ersättning mil[e]age [allowance] **-fabrik** motor works, car factory **-firma** car dealer **-fri** ~ *gata* pedestrian street; ~*tt område* pedestrian precinct **-färd** car drive (trip) **-färja** car ferry **-förare** driver **-försäkring** motorcar insurance **-försäljare** car salesman **-handlare** car dealer
bilharzios [-tsi'å:s] *s3, med.* schistosomiasis, bilharziasis, bilharziosis
bil|hjul car wheel **-industri** motor (*A E.* automotive*) industry
bil|ism motorism, motoring **-ist** motorist, driver
biljard [-'ja:rd] *s3, ej pl* billiards (*pl*) **-boll** billiard ball **-bord** billiard table **-kö** [billiard] cue **-salong** billiard room **-spelare** billiard player
biljett *s3* ticket; (*brev*) note; *enkel* ~ single (*A E.* one-way) ticket; *lösa* ~ *till* buy (get) a ticket for **-automat** ticket vending machine **-försäljare** booking (ticket) clerk; *A E.* ticket agent **-försäljning** sale of tickets **-häfte** book of coupons **-kontor** ticket office; *järnv.* booking office; *teat. o.d.* box office **-kontrollör** ticket collector (inspector) **-lucka** *järnv.* booking office; *teat. o.d.* box office [window] **-pris** price of admission; (*för resa*) fare
biljon *s3* (*1 miljon miljoner*) billion; *A E.* trillion
biljud intruding sound; *med.* accessory sound, (*vid andning*) rale
bil|karosseri car body **-karta** road map **-krock**

car crash **-kö** line of cars **-körning** [car] driving; motoring
bill *s2* (*plog*) [plough]share
billig *al* **1** cheap (*äv. bildl.*); inexpensive; (*om pris äv.*) low, moderate, reasonable **2** (*rättmätig*) fair, reasonable; *det är inte mer än rätt och* ~*t* it's only fair **-bok** low-price edition **-het 1** (*rättvisa*) justice, fairness **2** (*lågt pris*) cheapness *etc.* **-hetsupplaga** cheap edition
billigt *adv* cheaply; *köpa* (*sälja*) ~ buy (sell) cheap; *komma för* ~ *undan* be let off too cheaply; *mycket* ~ [at] a bargain [price]
billion *s3, se* biljon
bil|lots car pilot **-lån** car theft **-lånare** car thief, joy rider **-mekaniker, -montör** car mechanic (fitter) **-märke** make [of car] **-nyckel** car key **-olycka** motor accident **-park** car fleet **-parkering** car park; *A E.* parking lot **-provning** *A B Svensk B*~ Swedish Motor Vehicle Inspection Co. **-radio** car radio **-register** vehicle register **-reparationsverkstad** motorcar repair shop, garage **-reparatör** motor mechanic **-ring 1** *se bildäck* 2 *vard.* (*fettvalk*) spare tyre **-ruta** car window **-salong** *se* bilutställning **-sjuk** travelsick **-skatt** [motorcar] licence duty **-skola** driving school **-skollärare** driving instructor **-speditionsfirma** road haulage firm, haulier **-sport** motoring; car racing **-stöld** car theft **-tjuv** car thief
biltog *a5* outlawed; ~ *man* outlaw
bil|trafik motor traffic **-tur** [motor]drive, ride; (*längre*) motor trip, trip by car **-tvätt** (*anläggning*) car wash; (*-tvättning*) car washing **-tävling** car race **-uthyrning** car rental **-utställning** motor show **-verkstad** *se* bilreparationsverkstad **-vrak** car wreck **-väg** motor road; *A E.* motor highway **-ägare** car owner
bil|läger [royal, princely] nuptials (*pl*) **-lägga 1** *se* bifoga **2** (*åstadkomma förlikning*) settle, make up, reconcile **-läggande** *s6* settlement, adjustment
bimetall bimetal
binamn by-name
bind|a I *s1* roller [bandage]; *elastisk* ~ elastic bandage **II** *v, band bundit* **1** bind; (*knyta*) tie; (*fästa*) fasten (*vid* [on] to); (*hålla fästad vid*) confine; (*nät, kvastar o.d.*) make; ~ *fast* tie up (*vid* to); ~ *för ngns ögon* blindfold s.b.; ~ *ihop* tie up, bind together; ~ *in böcker* have books bound, bind books; ~ *om* tie up, (*böcker*) rebind; ~ *upp* tie up, *kokk.* truss; ~ *åt* tie; ~ *ngn till händer och fötter* bind s.b. hand and foot (*äv. bildl.*); ~ *ris åt egen rygg* make a rod for one's own back; *bunden vid sängen* bedridden, confined to bed **2** (*fästa, sammanhålla*) bind, hold; *limmet -er bra* the glue sticks well **3** *rfl* bind (pledge) o.s.; tie o.s. down (*vid, för* to) **-ande** *a4* binding; (*avgörande*) conclusive; ~ *bevis* conclusive proof; ~ *order* firm order
bindehinna *se* bindhinna
bindel *s2* bandage
binde|medel binder, fixing agent; (*lim o.d.*) adhesive **-ord** conjunction **-streck** hyphen
bind|galen stark [staring] mad **-garn** twine, packthread **-hinna** conjunctiva **-hinneinflammation** conjunctivitis

bindning binding; (*av bok*) binding; (*på skida*) [ski] binding; *språkv.* liaison; *mus.* slur[ring]
bindsle [ˣbinnsle] *s6* fastening; (*på skida*) [ski] binding
bind|sula insole **-väv** connective tissue
bingbång ding dong
binge [ˣbiŋe] *s2* bin
bingo [ˈbiŋ(g)ɔ] *s2* bingo
binjure adrenal (suprarenal) gland **-bark** cortex of the adrenal gland
binnikemask tapeworm
binom [-ˈnåːm] *s7* binomial
binomial|fördelning binomial distribution **-teorem** binomial theorem
binär *a1* binary, twofold; ~*a talsystemet* the binary notation (system)
binäring subsidiary (ancillary) industry (occupation)
bio [ˈbiːɔ] *s9* cinema, motion-picture theatre; *A.E.* movies, movie theater; *gå* (*vara*) *på* ~ go to (be at) the cinema (the pictures, *sl.* the flicks, *A.E.* the movies) **-besök** cinema visit **-besökare** cinemagoer **-biljett** cinema (*A.E.* movie) ticket
biobränsle [ˣbiːɔ-] biomass fuel, biofuel **biocid** *s3* biocide **biocykel** [ˣbiːɔ-] biocycle
biodl|are beekeeper **-ing** beekeeping, apiculture
bio|dynamik biodynamics (*pl, behandlas som sg*) **-dynamisk** [-ˈnaː-] biodynamic[al]
bio|ekologi bioecology
bio|fysik biophysics (*pl, behandlas som sg*) **-fysisk** [-ˈfyː-] biophysical
biogas biogas
bio|gen [-ˈjeːn] *a5* biogenetic[al], biogenous **-genes** [-j-] biogenesis **-genetisk** [-jeˈneː-] *se -gen*
biogeografi biogeography
biograf *s3* **1** (*levnadstecknare*) biographer **2** *se bio* **-byrå** *Statens* ~ [the Swedish] national board of film censors **-föreställning** cinema performance (show)
bio|grafi *s3* biography **-grafisk** [-ˈgraː-] *a5* biographical
biograf|publik cinema audience; filmgoers (*pl*); *A.E.* moviegoers (*pl*) **-vaktmästare** cinema attendant; (*dörrvaktmästare*) ticket collector
bio|kemi biochemistry **-kemisk** [-ˈçeː-] biochemical **-kemist** biochemist
bio|log biologist **-logi** *s3* biology **-logisk** [-ˈlåː-] *a5* biological; ~ *klocka* biological clock; ~ *krigföring* biological warfare; ~*t nedbrytbar* biodegradable
bio|massa biomass **-medicin** biomedicine **-metri** *s3* biometry, biometrics (*pl, behandlas som sg*)
biomständighet minor incident, incidental circumstance
bionik *s3* bionics (*pl, behandlas som sg*)
biopsi *s3* biopsy
biopublik *se biografpublik*
bi|orsak subsidiary reason, incidental cause **-person** *se bifigur*
bio|sfär biosphere **-syntes** biosynthesis **-teknik** biotechnology **-teknisk** biotechnological, biotech
bioteknologi ergonomics (*pl, behandlas som sg*); *A.E.* biotechnology

biotisk [biˈåː-] *a5* biotic
biotit *s3* biotite
bio|top [-ˈåːp] *s3* biotope **-typ** *s3* biotype
bi|plan biplane **-polär** bipolar **-produkt** by--product; (*avfall*) waste product
birfilare [ˣbiːr-] fiddler
bi|roll subordinate part, minor role **-sak** matter of secondary importance; side issue; *huvudsak och* ~ essentials and nonessentials (*pl*)
bisam [ˈbiː-] *s3* musquash (muskrat) fur
bisamhälle colony of bees
bisamrätta muskrat
bisarr *a1* bizarre, odd, fantastic
bisats subordinate clause
Biscayabukten [bisˣkajja-] Bay of Biscay
bisektris *s3* bisector
bisexuell bisexual
bisittare [legal] assessor, member of lower court
biskop [ˣbiskåp] *s2* bishop **-inna** bishop's wife **-lig** *a1* episcopal
biskops|döme *s6* bishopric, episcopate **-mössa 1** mitre **2** *se fingerborgsblomma* **-stav** pastoral [staff] **-stift** diocese, see **-stol** [bishop's] throne; *bildl.* see **-säte** see **-ämbete** episcopate, see, office of a bishop
biskvi *s3* macaroon, ratafia (ratafee) [biscuit]
bisköldkörtel parathyroid gland
biskötsel beekeeping
bismak [extraneous] flavour; smack; tang; *i sht bildl.* taint
bison [ˈbiːsån] *r* bison **-oxe** European bison, wisent; *amerikansk* ~ American bison, *A.E.* buffalo
bisp *s2, se biskop*
bispringa assist, succour; ~ *ngn med råd och dåd* support s.b. in word and deed (by word and act)
bisser|a give over again, repeat **-ing** encore
bist|er [ˈbiss-] *a2* grim, fierce, forbidding; (*sträng*) stern; (*om köld o.d.*) severe; *-ra tider* hard times
bisting bee sting
bisträck|a ~ *ngn med pengar* advance s.b. money **-ning** pecuniary assistance, financial help
bistå assist, help **bistånd** assistance, help, aid; *med benäget* ~ *av* kindly assisted by
biståndspakt pact of mutual assistance
bisvärm swarm of bees
bi|syfte *se biavsikt* **-syssla** spare-time occupation, sideline
bisätt|a remove to the mortuary; ~ *ngn* remove a p.'s remains to the mortuary **-ning** removal [of a p.'s remains] to the mortuary
bit *s2* piece, bit; (*socker-*) lump [of sugar]; (*fragment*) fragment; (*muns-*) mouthful, morsel; *data.* bit; *följa ngn en* ~ *på vägen* accompany s.b. part of the way; *inte en* ~ *bättre* not a bit (scrap) better; *äta en* ~ [*mat*] have [a little] s.th. to eat; *gå i* ~*ar* go to pieces; *gå i tusen* ~*ar* be smashed to smithereens
bit|a *bet bitit* **1** bite; ~ *huvudet av skammen* be past all sense of shame; ~ *i det sura äpplet* swallow the bitter pill; ~ *i gräset* bite (lick) the dust; ~ *på naglarna* bite one's nails; ~ *sig fast i* (*vid*) cling tight on to; ~ *sig i tungan* bite one's tongue **2** (*vara skarp*) bite; (*om ankare*) hold; (*om kniv*) cut; (*om köld*) nip, be sharp; ~ *av* bite off, (*en sup*) sip; ~ *ifrån sig* hit back, retort; ~ *ihjäl* bite

B

to death; ~ *ihop tänderna* clench one's teeth; ~ *sönder* bite to pieces; *ingenting -er på honom* nothing has any effect on him **-ande** *a4* biting; (*om vind äv.*) piercing; (*om köld*) intense; (*om svar äv.*) stinging, cutting, sharp; (*om smak, lukt*) pungent; (*om kritik äv.*) caustic

bitanke underlying thought; ulterior motive

bitas *bets bitits, dep* bite **bitit** *sup. av bita*

bi|testikel epididymis (*pl* epididymides) **-ton** *språkv.* secondary accent (stress); *mus.* secondary tone

bitring teething ring

bitryck *se biaccent*

biträd|a 1 (*hjälpa*) assist, help; ~ *ngn vid rättegång* appear (plead) for s.b. at trial **2** (*mening, förslag*) accede to, support, subscribe to; (*parti*) join **-ande** *a4* assistant, auxiliary **biträde** *s6* **1** (*medverkan*) assistance, help **2** (*medhjälpare*) assistant, hand; *rättsligt* ~ counsel

bitsk *a1* ill-tempered, savage

bitsocker lump (cube) sugar

bitter ['bitt-] *a2* bitter; (*om smak äv.*) acrid; (*plågsam*) acute, severe, sore; ~ *fiende* (*saknad*) bitter enemy (grief); ~ *nöd* dire want (distress); ~*t öde* harsh fate; *till det bittra slutet* to the bitter end **-het** bitterness; (*om smak*) acridity; (*sinnesstämning*) embitterment, bitter feeling **-ligen** bitterly **-ljuv** bittersweet **-mandel** bitter almond **-mandelolja** bitter-almond oil **-salt** Epsom salts (*pl*)

bittersta ['bitt-] *i uttr.: inte det* ~ not in the least, not at all

bittert *adv, det känns* ~ *att* it feels hard to

bitti[da] early; *i morgon* ~ [early] tomorrow morning

bitum|en [-'tu:-] *-en el. -inet, pl saknas* bitumen **-inös** *al* bituminous

bitvarg curmudgeon

bitvis bit by bit, piecemeal; here and there

biuppgift additional (subsidiary) task

bivack *s3,* **bivackera** *v1* bivouac

bivax beeswax

biverk|an, -ning side effect, secondary effect

bivråk honey buzzard

biväg byway, bypath

bjud|a *bjöd bjudit* **1** (*befalla*) bid, order, enjoin; ~ *och befalla* order and command; *anständigheten -er* decency dictates **2** (*säga, hälsa*) bid, say; ~ *farväl* bid farewell **3** (*erbjuda*) offer; (*ge bud på auktion*) [make a] bid; ~ *motstånd* offer resistance; ~ *ngn att sitta ner* ask s.b. to sit down; ~ *ngn spetsen* defy s.b. **4** (*undfägna med*) treat to; ~ *ngn på en god middag* treat s.b. to an excellent dinner; *vad får jag* ~ *dig på?* what may I offer you?; *staden har mycket att* ~ *på* the town has many attractions; *han bjöd alla på drinkar* all drinks were on him, he stood everybody drinks **5** (*inbjuda*) invite; ~ *ngn på lunch* invite s.b. to lunch; ~ *ngn på middag på restaurang* invite s.b. out for dinner, dine s.b. at a restaurant; *det -er mig emot att* it is repugnant to me to; ~ *hem ngn* ask (invite) s.b. home; ~ *igen* invite back; ~ *in* ask in; ~ *omkring* hand round; ~ *till* try; ~ *under* underbid; ~ *upp* ask for a dance; ~ *ut varor* offer goods for sale; ~ *över* outbid

bjud|it *sup. av bjuda* **-ning 1** (*kalas*) party **2** (*in-*

bjudan) invitation **-ningskort** invitation card

bjäbba (*om hund*) yelp; ~ *emot* answer back

bjäfs *s7* finery; trinkets (*pl*)

bjälk|e *s2* beam; (*stor*) ba[u]lk; (*bärande*) girder; (*stock*) log; ~*n i ditt eget öga* (*bibl.*) the beam that is in thine own eye **-lag** *s7* system of joists

bjäll|erklang jingle of sleigh bells **-ko** *se skällko* **-ra** *s1* bell, jingle

bjärt l*a1* gaudy, glaring **ll** *adv* glaringly; *sticka av* ~ *mot* be in glaring contrast to

bjässe *s2* colossal man; hefty chap; (*baddare äv.*) whopper

bjöd *imperf. av bjuda*

björk *s2* birch; *av* ~ (*äv.*) birch; *möbel av* ~ birchwood suite [of furniture]

björkna white (silver) bream

björk|ris birch twigs; (*t. aga*) birch[rod] **-skog** birch wood **-trast** fieldfare **-ved** birchwood

björn [-ö:-] *s2* **1** bear; *Stora* (*Lilla*) *Björn*[*en*] [the] Great (Little) Bear; *väck inte den* ~ *som sover* let sleeping dogs lie; *sälj inte skinnet innan* ~*en är skjuten* don't count your chickens before they are hatched **2** (*fordringsägare*) dun **-bär** blackberry, bramble **-hona** she-bear **-jägare** bear hunter **-kloört** *bot.* bear's-breech **-loka** *s1* cow parsnip, hogweed, keck **-mossa** hairy-cap moss **-ram** bear's paw **-skinn** bearskin **-skinnsmössa** bearskin **-tjänst** *göra ngn en* ~ do s.b. a disservice **-tråd** patent strong yarn **-unge** [bear] cub

bl.a. (*förk. för bland annat, bland andra*) *se under bland*

1 black *s2* fetter, iron; *vara en* ~ *om foten för* be a drag on

2 black I *al* (*smutsgul*) tawny, drab (*äv. bildl.*); (*grå*) gray, dingy; (*urb*[*l. kt*) faded **ll** *s2* cream-coloured horse, dun

blad *s7* (*löv, bok-*) leaf (*pl* leaves); (*kron-, blom-*) petal; (*ark*) sheet; (*tidning*) paper; (*kniv-, år-, propeller- o.d.*) blade; *oskrivet* ~ clean sheet, *bildl.* unknown quantity; ~*et har vänt sig* the tide has turned; *spela från* ~*et* play at sight; *ta* ~*et från munnen* speak out (one's mind)

blad|bagge gold beetle, goldbug **-fjäder** plate spring **-formig** leaf-shaped, foliate[d] **-grönt** chlorophyll **-guld** gold leaf, (*tjockare*) gold foil **-horning** [-ɔ:-] *zool.* dung beetle (chafer) **-lus** plant lo***[***ɹ]***.*** aphid, (*grön äv.*) greenfly **-mage** third stomach, psalterium, omasum, manyplies (*pl, behandlas som sg*) **-mossa** [leaf] moss **-mögel** leaf mould, rust [fungus] **-selleri** *se blekselleri* **-veck** axil

B-lag second team (eleven, *särsk. AE.* string); *bildl.* second-raters (*pl*)

blam|age [-'ma:ʃ] *s5* faux pas **-era** bring discredit on; ~ *sig* bring discredit on o.s., put one's foot in it

blanchera blanch

blancmangé [blaŋmaŋ'ʃe: *el.* blammaŋ'ʃe:] *s5* blancmange

blanco *se blanko*

bland among[st]; ~ *andra* among others; ~ *annat* among other things, for instance, inter alia; *programmet upptar* ~ *annat* the programme includes; ~ *det bästa jag vet* one of the best things I know; *en* ~ *tio* one in ten; *många* ~ *läsarna* many of the readers; *omtyckt* ~ *damerna* a favourite with the ladies

blanda mix; (~ *tillsammans*) blend; *bildl.* mingle; *kem.* compound; (*metaller*) alloy; (*kort*) shuffle, mix; ~ *vatten i mjölken* mix water with milk, adulterate milk with water; ~ *bort* muddle away; ~ *bort korten för ngn* confuse s.b., put s.b. out; ~ *ihop* mix up; ~ *in* (*tillsätta*) admix; ~ *in ngn i ngt* get s.b. mixed up in s.th.; ~ *till* mix; ~ *upp ngt med ngt* mix s.th. with s.th.; ~ *ut vin med vatten* dilute wine with water; ~ *sig* mix, mingle; ~ *sig i* meddle in, interfere with; ~ *sig med mängden* mingle in (mix with) the crowd

bland|ad *a5* mixed *etc.*; ~*e känslor* mixed feelings; ~ *kör* mixed choir; *-at sällskap* mixed company **-are** mixing machine, mixer

bland|ekonomi mixed economy **-ekonomisk** of (associated with) a mixed economy **-folk** mixed people (race)

blandning mixture; (*av olika kvaliteter el. sorter*) blend; (*legering*) alloy; (*korsning*) hybrid; *med en* ~ *av hopp och fruktan* with mixed hope and fear

bland|ras mixed breed **-skog** mixed forest **-språk** mixed language **-säd** mixed grain; (*växande*) mixed crops (*pl*) **-äktenskap** mixed (interracial) marriage

blank *a1* shiny, bright; ~ *sida* blank page; ~ *som en spegel* smooth as a mirror; *med* ~*a vapen* honourably, with clean hands; *mitt på* ~*a förmiddagen* right in the middle of the morning; ~*t game* (*i tennis*) love game; *ett* ~*t nej* a flat (curt) no

blanka polish; (*skor*) clean; black

blankett *s3* form; blank; *fylla i en* ~ fill in (up) a form **-raseri** mania for form-filling

blank|lax [Atlantic] salmon **-nött** shiny

blanko ['blann-] *se in blanko* **-check** blank cheque **-endossement** *se -överlåtelse* **-fullmakt** blank cheque **-växel** blank bill **-överlåtelse** blank endorsement, endorsement in blank

blank|polera polish **-skinn** patent leather **-slipa** polish, finish, smooth **-sliten** shiny **-svärta** blacking

blankt *adv* shinily *etc.*; *dra* ~ draw one's sword; *rösta* ~ return a blank vote; *säga* ~ *nej* flatly refuse; *strunta* ~ *i* not give a damn about

blankvers blank verse

blasé *oböjligt a*, **blaserad** [-'se:-] *a5* blasé

blasfem|i *s3* blasphemy **-isk** [-'fe:-] *a5* blasphemous

blask *s7* wash, dishwater; (*snö-*) slush

1 blaska *v1* splash

2 blaska *s1*, *neds.* rag

blaskig *a1* (*om potatis*) watery; (*om färg*) washy, washed out

blast *s3*, *ej pl* tops (*pl*)

blazer ['blä:- *el.* 'blei-] *s2* [sports] jacket; (*skol-, klubb-*) blazer

bleck *s7* **1** *se -plåt* **2** ~*et* (*mus.*) the brass **-blåsinstrument** brass instrument **-burk**, **-dosa** tin, (*särsk. AE.*) can **-plåt** [thin] sheet metal, sheet [iron]; tin plate; *av* ~ (*äv.*) tin **-slagare** tinsmith

blek *a1* pale; (*starkare*) pallid; (*svag*) faint; ~ *av fasa* pale with terror; ~ *av raseri* pallid with rage; ~ *om kinden* pale-cheeked; ~ *som ett lik* deathly pale; ~*a döden* pallid Death; ~*a vanvettet* utter

madness; ~*t ljus* faint light; *göra ett* ~*t intryck* make a lifeless (tame) impression; *inte ha den* ~*aste aning om* not have the faintest idea of

bleka *v3* bleach; (*färg*) fade; ~*s* become discoloured

blekansikte paleface

bleke *s6* (*stiltje*) calm

blek|fet pasty **-het** paleness, pallor **-lagd** *a5* pale-faced; (*sjukligt*) sallow **-medel** bleach[er]; bleaching agent

blekn|a [*ble:-] turn pale (*av* with); (*om färger, kinder, minnen o.d.*) fade, grow paler **-ing** bleaching

blek|nos washed-out little thing **-selleri** [blanched] celery **-siktig** *a1* chlorotic **-sot** chlorosis, greensickness

blemm|a *s1* pimple **-ig** *a1* pimpled, pimply

bless|era wound **-yr** *s3* wound

blev *imperf. av* **bli**

bli (bliva) *blev blivit* **I** *passivbildande hjälpv* be; *vard.* get; (*vid utdragen handling*) become **II** *självst. v* **1** be; ~ *överraskad* be surprised; *festen blev lyckad* the party was a success; (*innebärande förändring*) become; ~ *fattig* (*soldat*) become poor (a soldier); (*vard., med adjektivisk pred.fylln.*) get; (*långsamt*) grow, (*plötsligt*) fall, turn; ~ *arg* (*gift, våt*) get angry (married, wet); ~ *blek* (*katolik*) turn pale (Catholic); ~ *gammal* grow old; ~ *sjuk* (*kär*) fall ill (in love); ~ *skämd* (*tokig*) go bad (mad); *vi* ~*r fyra till bordet* there'll be four of us at table; *det skall* ~ *mig ett nöje* it'll be a pleasure; *hur mycket* ~*r notan på?* what does the bill come to? **2** (*förbli*) remain; ~ *sittande* remain seated; *det måste* ~ *oss emellan* this must be between ourselves; *skomakare,* ~*v vid din läst!* let the cobbler stick to his last **3** *det* ~*r tio pund* it makes ten pounds, (*vid betalning*) that'll be ten pounds; *han* ~ *r 20 år i morgon* he will be 20 [years old] tomorrow; *det* ~*r svårt* it will be difficult; *när* ~*r det?* when will it be?; *när jag* ~*r stor* when I grow up **4** *låt* ~*!* don't!; *låt* ~ *att skrika!* stop shouting!; *jag kunde inte låta* ~ *att skratta* I could not help laughing; *låt* ~ *mig!* leave me alone! **5** (*med betonad partikel*) ~ *av* take place, come about; ~*r det ngt av?* will it come to anything?; *festen* ~*r inte av* the party is off; *vad har det* ~*vit av henne?* what has become of her?; ~ *av med* (*bli kvitt*) get rid of, (*förlora*) lose, (*få sälja*) dispose of; ~ *borta* stay away, (*omkomma*) be lost (missing); ~ *efter* drop (lag) behind; ~ *ifrån sig* beside o.s.; ~ *kvar* (*stanna kvar*) remain, stay [behind], (~ *över*) be left [over]; ~ *till* come into existence; ~ *till sig* get excited; ~ *utan* get nothing; ~ *utan pengar* run out of money; ~ *utom sig* be beside o.s. (*av* with); ~ *över* be left [over]

blick *s2* **1** look; (*ihärdig*) gaze; (*hastig*) glance; *kasta en* ~ *på* look (glance) at **2** (*öga*) eye; *sänka* (*lyfta*) ~*en* lower (raise) one's eyes; *följa ngn med* ~*en* gaze after s.b.; *föremål för allas* ~*ar* focus of attention; *ha* ~ *för* have an eye for

blick|a look; gaze; glance **-fång** eye-catcher **-punkt** focus; *bildl.* limelight **-stilla** calm; [as] smooth as glass

blid *a1* mild; (*om röst o.d.*) soft; (*vänlig*) gentle, kind; *tre grader blitt* three degrees above freezing point **blidhet** [*bli:d-] mildness *etc.* **blidka**

[ˣblidd-] appease, conciliate, placate; *låta ~ sig* relent, give in **blidväder** mild weather; thaw **bliga** glare, stare *(på at)*

blimp *s2, film.* blimp

blind *a1* blind *(för* to); *(okritisk, obetingad)* implicit; *bli ~* go blind; *~ lydnad* implicit (passive) obedience; *~ på ena ögat* blind in one eye; *~a fläcken* the blind spot; *den ~e* the blind man; *en ~ höna hittar också ett korn* a fool's bolt may sometimes hit the mark; *stirra sig ~ på (bildl.)* let o.s. be hypnotized by, get stuck at **-bock** blind man's buff

blindering [-'de:-] blindage

blind|flygning instrument (blind) flying **-fönster** blind window **-gångare** dud, unexploded bomb **-het** blindness **-hund** guide dog **-institut** blind school, school for the blind

blindo *i uttr.:* *i ~* blindly, at random

blind|skola *se blindinstitut* **-skrift** Braille; *trycka i (skriva med) ~* Braille **-skär** sunken rock **-styre** blind buffer **-tarm** caecum **-tarmsinflammation** appendicitis

blinj *s3, ~er* blini[s] *(pl)*

blink *s2* **1** *(-ande)* twinkling **2** *(-ning)* wink; *i en ~* in a twinkling, in the twinkling of an eye

blinka *(med ögat)* blink, wink *(mot, åt* at); *(om ljus)* twinkle; *utan att ~* without batting an eyelid, unflinchingly

blink|er *s2* blinker, [flashing direction] indicator **-fyr** *se blänkfyr* **-hinna** nic[ti]tating membrane, third eyelid, haw **-ljus** flashing light **-ning** blinking *etc.*; wink

blint *adv* blindly *etc., se blind; gatan slutar ~* it is a blind alley

bliv|a *se bli* **-ande** *a4 (tillkommande)* future, ...to be; *(tilltänkt)* prospective; *~ mödrar* expectant mothers **-it** *sup. av* bliva

blixt I *s2* lightning; *(konstgjord o. bildl.)* flash; *en ~* a flash of lightning; *~en slog ner i huset* the house was struck by lightning; *som en oljad ~* like a streak of lightning; *som en ~ från klar himmel* like a bolt from the blue; *som träffad av ~en* thunderstruck; *hans ögon sköt ~ar* his eyes flashed **II** *adv, bli ~ kär* fall madly in love **-anfall** lightning attack (raid), *(särsk. om flyg)* blitz **-belysning** *i ~* in a flash **-fotografering** flash photography **-halka** extreme slipperiness **-krig** blitz, lightning warfare **-kub** *foto.* flash bulb; *(med fyra blixtar)* flash cube **-ljus** flashing light; *foto.* flashlight **-ljuslampa** flash bulb, photoflash **-lås** zip [fastener]; *AE.* zipper **-nedslag** stroke of lightning

blixt|ra lighten *(äv. ~ till); (friare)* flash, sparkle; *~nde ögon* flashing eyes; *~nde huvudvärk* splitting headache; *~nde kvickhet* sparkling wit **-snabb** [as] swift as a lightning **-visit** flying visit

block [-å-] *s7* block; *geol. äv.* boulder; *polit.* bloc; *(skriv-)* pad; *(hissanordning)* block; *(sko-)* shoetree **blocka** [-å-] *~ ut skor* tree shoes

blockad [-å-] *s3* blockade; *förklara i ~* impose a blockade; *häva (bryta) en ~* raise (run) a blockade **-brytare** blockade runner

block|bildning formation of blocs **-choklad** cooking chocolate

blocker|a [-å-] blockade; *(friare)* block **-ing** block

block|flöjt recorder **-hus** blockhouse **-ämne** subject block

blod *s7* blood; *levrat ~* clotted blood, gore; *gråta ~ (ung.)* cry one's eyes out; *med kallt ~* in cold blood; *~ är tjockare än vatten* blood is thicker than water; *~et steg mig åt huvudet* the blood went to my head; *det har gått dem i ~et* it has got into their blood; *det ligger i ~et* it runs in the blood; *prins av ~et* prince of the blood; *väcka ont ~* breed bad blood **bloda** *~ ner* stain with blood; *få ~d tand (bildl.)* acquire the taste

blod|apelsin blood orange **-bad** blood bath, massacre; *anstäla ~ på* butcher wholesale **-bana** blood vessel **-bank** blood bank **-befläckad** *a5* bloodstained **-bok** copper beech **-brist** anaemia **-cirkulation** circulation of the blood **-drypande** *a4* bloody; *~ historia* bloodcurdling story **-fattig** anaemic **-fläck** bloodstain **-flöde** flow of blood; haemorrhage **-full** full-blooded **-förgiftning** blood poisoning **-förlust** loss of blood **-givarcentral** blood donor centre **-givare** blood donor **-givning** donation of blood **-grupp** blood group (type) **-gruppsbestämning** blood-group determination **-hosta** *ha ~* cough blood **-hund** bloodhound

blodig *a1* bloody; bloodstained, gory, sanguinary; *(friare)* deadly; grievous; *~ biffsteak* underdone *(AE.* rare) steak; *det var inte så ~t (vard.)* this wasn't too stiff

blod|igel medicinal leech **-korv** black (blood) pudding *(AE.* sausage) **-kropp** blood cell (corpuscle); *röd ~* red blood cell, erythrocyte; *vit ~* white blood cell, leucocyte **-kräfta** leukaemia **-kärl** blood vessel **-lönn** apple (American) blight **-lönn** red maple **-omlopp** circulation of the blood **-plasma** blood plasma **-platta, -plätt** platelet, *(särsk. förr)* thrombocyte **-propp** thrombus **-proppsbildning** thrombosis **-prov** blood sample; *(-analys)* blood test **-pudding** black (blood) pudding **-röd** blood red; *bli ~ i ansiktet* turn crimson

blods|band *pl* ties of blood; *besläktad genom ~* related by blood **-drama** bloody drama **-droppe** drop of blood **-dåd** bloody deed **blod|serum** blood serum

blods|förvant kinsman **-hämnd** blood feud, vendetta

blod|sjukdom blood disease **-skam** incest **-skuld** blood guilt **-socker** blood sugar **-sprängd** bloodshot **-spår** track of blood; blood mark **-sten** haematite **-stillande** *a4* haemostatic, styptic; *~ medel* styptic **-stockning** congestion, engorgement **-störtning** haemorrhage of the lungs; haematemesis; violent haemoptysis **-sugare** bloodsucker; *bildl. äv.* vampire, extortioner

blodsutgjutelse bloodshed

blod|sänka [blood] sedimentation [rate] **-transfusion** [blood] transfusion **-tryck** blood pressure; *för högt ~* hypertension; *för lågt ~* hypotension **-törst** bloodthirstiness **-törstig** bloodthirsty **-utgjutning** extravasation [of blood] **-vallning** flush **-vite** *s6* blood wound **-värde** blood count **-åder** blood vessel, [blood] vein **-överföring** *se -transfusion*

blom [blomm] *s2* blossom; *koll. äv.* bloom; *slå ut*

_i_ ~ [come out in] blossom; _stå i_ ~ be in bloom (flower) **-axel** _bot._ receptacle, thalamus **-blad** petal **-bord** plant (flower) stand, flower box **-botten** _bot._, _se -axel_ **-bukett** bouquet, bunch of flowers **-doft** scent of flowers **-fat** flowerpot saucer **-foder** _bot._ calyx **-fäste** _bot._, _se -axel_ **-hylle** _bot._ floral envelope, perianth **-kalk** _bot._ flower cup **-knopp** [flower] bud **-korg** _se blomsterkorg_ **-krona** _bot._ corolla **-kruka** flowerpot **-kål** cauliflower **-kålshuvud** head of cauliflower **-kålsöra** cauliflower ear; boxer's ear **-låda** flower box **-lös** flowerless

blom|ma [*blomma] **I** _s1_ flower; _i ~n av sin ålder_ in one's prime **II** _v1_ flower, bloom, blossom; ~ _upp_ (_bildl._) take on a new lease of life; ~ _ut_ shed its blossoms **-mig** _a1_ flowery, flowered

blommografera [blommo-] send flowers by Interflora

blom|ning [*blomm-] flowering, blooming **-ningstid** flowering season

blomster ['blåmm-] _s7_ flower **-affär** florist's [shop] **-arrangemang** flower arrangement **-dekoration** floral decoration **-frö** flower seed **-förmedling** _B~en_ Interflora Flower Relay **-försäljare** flower seller **-försäljerska** flower girl **-girland** garland of flowers **-handel** _se -affär_ **-hyllning** floral tribute **-korg** flower basket **-krans** wreath [of flowers]; lei **-kvast** bunch of flowers **-lök** bulb **-odlare** floriculturist, flower grower **-odling** floriculture, flower growing **-prakt** floral splendour, floweriness **-prydd** _a5_ flowered, flowery **-rabatt** flowerbed **-skrud** flower array **-språk** language of flowers; _bildl._ flowery language **-säng** flowerbed **-uppsats** flower arrangement **-utställning** flower show; floricultural exposition **-vän** lover of flowers, flower fancier **-äng** flower field; _poet._ flowery mead

blomstr|a [*blåmm-] blossom, bloom; _bildl._ flourish, prosper **-ing** _bildl._ prosperity **-ingstid** _bildl._ era of prosperity; heyday

blom|ställning inflorescence **-vas** flower vase

blond [-ånd _el._ -ǎnd] _a1_ blond, _fem._ blonde; fair **-era** bleach **-jn** _s3_ blonde

bloss [-å-] _s7_ **1** (_fackla_) torch; (_fastsatt_) flare **2** (_på cigarett o.d._) puff, pull, whiff; _vard._ drag; _ta sig ett_ ~ have (take) a smoke **blossa** blaze, flare; _bildl. äv._ burn, flush [up]; ~ _upp_ (_om eld_) flare up; (_om pers._) flare up, kindle; ~_nde kinder_ burning cheeks; ~_nde röd_ crimson

blot _s7_ sacrificial feast **blota** _v1_ sacrifice

1 blott [-å-] **I** _adv_ only, but, merely; ~ _och bart_ only; _det vet jag_ ~ _alltför väl_ that I know only too well; _icke_ ~...utan även not only...but also; _det är ett minne_ ~ it is but a memory **II** _konj_ if only

2 blott [-å-] _a._ _mest i best. form_ mere; bare; _med_ ~_a ögat_ with the naked eye; ~_a tanken därpå_ the mere thought of it; _slippa undan med_ ~_a förskräckelsen_ get off with a fright [only]

blotta [-å-] **I** _s1_ gap; _bildl._ opening, weak spot **II** _v1_ **1** lay bare, expose; ~ _sitt huvud_ uncover [one's head]; _med_ ~_t huvud_ bareheaded; _med_ ~_t svärd_ with the sword drawn **2** (_röja_) disclose, unveil, expose; ~ _ngns brister_ expose a p.'s shortcomings; ~ _sin okunnighet_ expose one's ignorance; ~ _sig_ uncover, _bildl._ expose o.s.; ~_d på_

destitute (void) of **blottare** exhibitionist **blottställ|a** expose (_för_ to); ~ _sig_ expose o.s. (_för_ to); _familjen är alldeles -d_ the family is absolutely destitute

bluff _s2_ bluff **bluffa** bluff; ~ _sig till en plats_ bluff one's way to a job; ~ _sig fram_ make one's way by bluff **bluffare**, **bluffmakare** bluffer

blund _s3_, _inte få en_ ~ _i ögonen_ not get a wink of sleep; _ta sig en_ ~ take a nap (_vard._ shuteye); _John B~_ (_ung._) the sandman **blunda** shut one's eyes (_för_ to) **blunddocka** sleeping doll

blunder ['blunn-] _s2_ blunder; _vard._ boob

blus _s2_ blouse **-liv** [lady's] blouse

bly _s7_ lead; _av_ ~ (_äv._) lead[en] **-ackumulator** lead accumulator **-dagg** plummet, plumb bob **blyerts** [*bly:- _el._ 'bly:-] _s2_ **1** (_ämne_) black lead, graphite; (_i pennor_) lead **2** (_penna_) lead pencil; _skriva med_ ~ write in pencil **-penna** _se blyerts 2_ **-stift** lead **-teckning** pencil drawing

bly|fri lead-free **-förgiftad** [-j-] _a5_ lead poisoned **-förgiftning** lead poisoning

blyg _a1_ shy (_för_ of), bashful **-as** _v2_, _dep_ be ashamed (_för_ of); blush (_över_ at)

blygd _s3_, _ej pl_ private parts (_pl_) **-ben** pubic bone, pubis **-läppar** _pl_ labia [pudendi]

blyghet [*bly:g-] shyness, bashfulness

bly|glans galena, galenite **-glas** lead glass **-glete** _s7_, _s5_ lead monoxide, litharge **-grå** livid; leaden

blyg|sam [*bly:g-] _a1_ modest, unassuming **-samhet** modesty **-sel** ['blygg-] _s2_ shame; _känna_ ~ _över_ feel ashamed of; _rodna av_ ~ blush with shame

bly|hagel lead shot **-halt** lead content **-haltig** _a1_ lead-bearing, plumbiferous **-infattad** _a5_, ~_e rutor_ leaded panes **-infattning** lead mounting **-kula** lead bullet **-malm** lead ore **-mönja** red lead, minium; (_färg_) red-lead paint **-tung** [as] heavy as lead; (leaden) **-vitt** white lead, lead paint

blå _a1_ blue; _ett ~tt öga_ a black eye; _slå ngn gul och_ ~ beat s.b. black and blue; _i det_ ~ up in the clouds **-aktig** _a1_ blu[e]ish **-anlupen** blue-tempered **-bandist** blue-ribbonist **-blodig** blue-blooded **-byxor** _pl_ blue jeans **-bär** whortleberry, blaeberry; bilberry; _AE._ blueberry **-bärsris** whortleberry wire[s] **-bärssylt** bilberry jam **-dåre** madman **-eld** viper's bugloss; _AE._ blueweed **-else** blue, blu[e]ing **-fisk** bluefish, snapper **-frusen** blue with cold **-grå** bluish grey **-grön** bluish green, sea green; ~_a alger_ blue-green algae **-gul** blue and yellow **-hake** _zool._ bluethroat **-jacka** (_matros_) bluejacket **-klint** cornflower, bluebottle **-klocka** harebell, (_i Skottland_) bluebell **-klädd** dressed in blue **-kläder** _pl_ overalls; dungarees **-kopia** blueprint, cyanotype **-kopiering** blueprinting **-krage** _se -jacka_ **-kråka** European roller

Blåkulla _n_ the Brocken **-färd** witches' ride

blå|lera blue clay **-lusern** alfalfa, lucerne, purple medic **-mes** bluetit **-mussla** sea (edible) mussel **-märke** bruise

blåna become blue; ~_nde berg_ (_ung._) distant blue mountains **blånad** _s3_ bruise

blåneka flatly deny

blånor _pl_ tow, oakum (_sg_)

blå|penna blue pencil **-räv** blue fox **-röd** purple

1 blås|a *s1, med.* bladder; *(luft-, i glas o.d.)* bubble; *(hud-; i metall)* blister; *full av -or* bubbly; blistery; *med.* vesicular, vesiculate

2 blås|a *v3* blow; *det -er kallt* there is a cold wind blowing; *det -er nordlig vind* the wind is in the north; ~ *[nytt] liv i* infuse fresh life into; ~ *av* blow (call) off, *sport.* stop play; ~ *bort* blow away; ~ *in luft i* inflate [with air]; ~ *ner* blow down; ~ *omkull* blow over; ~ *upp en ballong* inflate (blow up) a balloon; *det -er upp* it is blowing up; *fönstret -te upp* the window blew open; ~ *upp sig* puff o.s. up; ~ *ut* blow out **-are** *(musiker)* player of a wind instrument; *-arna (koll. ung.)* the wind[s *pl*]

blåsbildning blistering, bubble formation

blåsbälg bellows *(behandlas som sg el. pl)*; *en* ~ a pair of bellows

blåshalskörtel prostate [gland]

1 blåsig *al (t 1 blåsa)* blistery

2 blåsig *al (t. 2 blåsa)* windy, breezy

blåsinstrument wind instrument

blåsippa hepatica

blåskatarr cystitis

Blåskägg *riddar* ~ Bluebeard

blåslagen *a3* black and blue

blås|lampa blowlamp; *AE.* blowtorch **-ljud** *med.* [heart] murmur **-ning** blowing; *åka på en* ~ be taken in **-orkester** *(mässingsorkester)* brass band

blåsprit methylated spirits

blåsrör blowpipe; *AE.* blowgun

1 blåst [-å:-] *s2* wind

2 blåst [-å:-] *oböjligt a, vard.* **1** *se korkad* **2** *(lurad)* bamboozled, taken in

blåstrumpa bluestocking

blåstång bladderwrack

blå|ställ *ung.* [blue] overalls *(pl)* **-svart** blue black

blåsväder windy weather

blåsyra prussic (hydrocyanic) acid

blått *s, best. form: det blåa* blue; *jfr blå*

blå|val blue whale **-vinge** *(scout)* Brownie [Guide] **-vit** bluish white **-ögd** *a5* blue-eyed; *(naiv)* dewy-eyed; ~ *optimism* starry-eyed optimism

bläck *s7* ink; *skriva med* ~ write in ink

1 bläcka *v1,* ~ *ner sig* ink one's fingers; get o.s. inky

2 bläcka *v1 (märka träd)* blaze

3 bläcka *s1, ta sig en* ~ get drunk, have a booze, go on a drinking bout

bläck|fisk cuttle[fish]; squid; *(åttaarmad)* octopus **-fläck** inkstain **-horn** inkpot, inkwell **-penna** pen; *(reservoarpenna)* fountain pen **-plump** blot [of ink] **-svamp** ink cap; *fjällig* ~ shaggy cap **-säck** ink sac

blädderblock flipover

bläddra turn over the leaves (pages) *(i en bok of* a book); ~ *igenom* skim [through], glance through; ~ *tillbaka* turn back a few pages

bländ|a blind, dazzle; *bildl. äv.* fascinate; ~ *av (bilstrålkastare)* dip [the headlights]; *foto.* stop down **-ande** *a4* blinding; dazzling, glaring

bländar|e *foto.* diaphragm, stop **-öppning** *foto.* aperture

blände *s6* blende

bländ|fri non-glare **-skydd** *foto.* lens hood; *(på bil)* sun visor (shield) **-verk** delusion, illusion **-vit** dazzlingly white

blänga *v2* glare, stare *(på at)*

blänk *s7, s2* **1** flash **2** *se blänke* **blänka** *v3* shine, gleam, glitter, glisten; ~ *till* flash, flare **blänkare** *(i tidning)* short notice

blänk|e *s6, (vid pimpelfiske)* lure, jig **-fyr** longflashing light **-ljus** long-flashing light

bläs *s2* blaze **-and** wi[d]geon

bläster ['bläss-] *s2* blast, blower **-smide** blastfurnace (osmund) iron **-ugn** blast furnace

blästr|a blast **-ing** blasting

blöda *v2* bleed *(äv. bildl.)*

blödar|e bleeder **-sjuka** haemophilia

blödig *al* soft, timid, chicken-hearted, chicken-livered **-het** softness *etc.*

blödning [ˣblö:d-] bleeding

blöj|a [ˣblöjja] *s1* nappy, napkin; *AE.* diaper **-byxor** [plastic] baby pants **-snibb** tie-on **-vadd** *se cellstoff*

blöt I *al* wet; *(vattnig)* watery, soggy; *bli* ~ get soaked **II** *oböjligt s, ligga i* ~ be in soak; *lägga i* ~ [put...to] soak, steep; *lägga sin näsa i* ~ poke one's nose into everything; *lägg inte näsan i* ~! mind your own business!

blöt|a *v3* soak, steep, wet; ~ *ner sig* get o.s. all wet; ~ *upp* soak, sop **-djur** mollusc **-lägga** *se blöt II* **-läggningsmedel** soaking agent **-snö** wet snow; *(sörja)* slush

b-moll B-flat minor

BNP *(förk. för bruttonationalprodukt)* GNP

bo I 1 *s5 (i sms.)* inhabitant; *moskva*~ inhabitant of Moscow, *äv.* Muscovite; *london*~ Londoner; *paris*~ Parisian; *newyork*~ New Yorker **2** *s6 (fågel-)* nest; *(däggdjurs)* den, lair **3** *s6 (kvarlåtenskap)* estate; *(bohag)* furniture; *sitta i orubbat* ~ retain undivided possession of the estate; *sätta* ~ settle, set up house; *hustrun medförde...i* ~*et* his wife brought...into the home **II** *v4* live; *(vanl. förnämt)* reside; *(tillfälligt)* stay; *(i högre stil)* dwell; ~ *billigt* pay a low rent; ~ *inackorderad hos* board and lodge with; ~ *kvar* stay on; ~ *trångt* have limited living space, be overcrowded; ~ *åt gatan* have rooms facing the street; *I can put you up; här* ~*r jag* this is where I live; *på Grönland* ~*r eskimåer* there are Eskimos living in Greenland

boa *s1* boa **-orm** boa constrictor

boaser|a panel, wainscot **-ing** panelling, wainscot, wainscot[t]ing

bobb [-å-] *s2* bobsleigh

1 bobba [-å-] *v1 (håret)* bob

2 bobba [-å-] *s1* **1** bug; *(kackerlacka)* cockroach **2** *(liten böld)* pimple

bobjn *s3* bobbin

1 bock [-å-] *s2* **1** *(djur)* he-goat, buck; *sätta* ~*en till trädgårdsmästare* set a thief to catch a thief **2** *(gymnastikredskap)* buck **3** *(stöd)* trestle **4** *hoppa* ~ play [at] leapfrog **5** *(fel)* [grammatical] fault (mistake); howler; *(tecken)* cross, tick; *sätta* ~ *för* mark as wrong

2 bock [-å-] *s2 (bugning)* bow

bocka [-å-] **1** *tekn.* bend **2** *(buga)* bow; ~ *sig för* bow to **3** ~ *för (markera)* tick

bockfot *där stack* ~*en fram!* the (your, his *etc.*)

cloven hoof is showing!
bockning [-å-] **1** *tekn.* bending **2** (*bugning*) bow
bock|skägg goat's beard; (*hakskägg*) goatee
-språng caper, gambol
bod *s2* **1** (*affär*) shop **2** (*uthus*) shed; storehouse
-betjänt, -biträde *se affärsbiträde*
bodega [-ˣde:-] *s1* bodega
bodelning (*vid skilsmässa*) partition (division)
of joint property [upon separation]; (*av dödsbo*)
partition (division) of the estate (inheritance)
Bodensjön [ˣbå:-] the Lake of Constance
bodknodd counter jumper
bodräkt *jur.* fraud on one's next of kin
boende *a4* living; resident; who lives **-form** type
of housing **-kostnad** housing costs (*pl*) **-stan-
dard** housing (living) conditions (*pl*)
boer [ˈbɔ:-] Boer **-kriget** [the] Boer War
boett *s3* watchcase
bofast resident, domiciled, settled
bofink *s2* chaffinch
bog *s2* **1** (*på djur*) shoulder **2** *sjö.* bow; *lägga om
på en ny ~* (*bildl.*) go off on a fresh tack; *slå in på
fel ~* (*bildl.*) take a wrong tack **-ankare** bower
-blad shoulder blade; *anat.* scapula
boggi [ˈbåggi] *s3* bogie, bogy; truck **-vagn** bogie
car[riage]
bogser|a tow, take in tow, tug **-bil** *se bärgnings-
bil* **-båt** tug[boat], towboat **-ing** towing, towage
-lina, -tross towrope, towline
bogspröt bowsprit
bohag *s7* household goods (*pl*) (furniture)
bohem *s3* Bohemian **-artad** [-a:r-] *a5* Bohemian
-eri *se bohemliv* **-isk** *a5* Bohemian **-liv** Bohemia, Bohemianism
1 boj [båjj] *s3* (*tyg*) baize
2 boj [båjj] *s2, sjö.* buoy; *förtöja vid ~* moor;
lägga ut en ~ put down a buoy
boj|a [båjja] *s1* fetter, shackle; *bildl.* bond; *slå
ngn i -or* put s.b. in irons
bojar [-å-] *s3* boyar
bojkott [ˣbåjj- el. -ˈkått] *s3*, **bojkotta** [ˣbåjj- el.
-ˈkåtta] *v1* boycott
1 bok *s2, bot.* beech[tree]; *av ~* (*äv.*) beech[en]
2 bok *-en böcker* **1** book; *häftad ~* paperback; *in-
bunden ~* hardback; *avsluta böckerna* close the
books; *föra böcker* keep books; *föra ~ över* keep
a record of; *hänga näsan över ~en* bury one's
nose in one's book; *tala som en ~* talk like a book
2 (*24 el. 25 ark papper*) quire
1 boka 1 *hand.,* se *bokföra* **2** (*beställa biljett
o.d.*) book, reserve
2 boka (*krossa malm*) stamp, pound
bok|anmälan book review **-anmälare** book re-
viewer, critic **-auktion** book auction **-band** (*del
av bokverk*) volume; (*pärmar etc.*) binding **-be-
stånd** stock of books **-bindare** bookbinder
-binderi bookbindery, bookbinder's [work-
shop] **-buss** mobile library; *AE.* bookmobile
-cirkel book circle **-flod** season's new books;
(*friare*) flood of fiction **-form** *i ~* in book form,
as a book
bokför|a book, enter [in the books]; *-t värde*
book value **-are** accountant, book-keeper; clerk
bokför|ing book-keeping, accounts; *dubbel* (*en-
kel*) ~ book-keeping by double (single) entry
-ingslag accounting act (law) **-ingsmaskin** ac-

counting (book-keeping) machine **-ingsplikt**
obligation (liability) to keep books
bok|förlag publishing company (house),
publishers (*pl*) **-förläggare** publisher **-handel**
bookshop, bookseller's [shop]; bookstore; *i
~handeln* (*abstr.*) in the book trade; *utgången ur
-handeln* out of print **-handlare** bookseller
-hylla bookcase; (*enstaka hylla*) bookshelf **-hål-
lare** accountant, book-keeper; *vanl.* clerk
-klubb book club
boklig [ˣbɔ:k-] *a1* literary, bookish; *~ bildning*
book-learning
bok|låda *se bokhandel* **-lärd** well-read; bookish;
scholarly **-mal** bookworm **-marknad** book market **-märke** bookmark[er]
bokning [ˣbɔ:k-] **1** (*bokföring*) posting [of
items]; (*av enskild post*) [book] entry **2** (*biljett-
beställning o.d.*) booking, reservation
bokollon beechnut; *koll.* beech mast
bok|omslag dust jacket (cover), [book] jacket,
wrapper **-pärm** book cover **-rygg** spine, back of
a book **-samlare** book collector, bibliophil[e]
-samling collection of books, library
bokskog beech woods (*pl*)
bok|skåp bookcase **-slut** balancing of the
books; *konkr.* final accounts; *göra ~* close (balance) the books, make up a balance sheet
bokstav *-en bokstäver* letter; character; *grekiska
bokstäver* Greek characters; *liten ~* small letter;
stor ~ capital [letter]; *efter ~en* literally; to the
letter **bokstavera** spell **bokstavlig** [-a:-] *a1*
literal **bokstavligen** [-a:-] *adv* literally; (*rent
av*) positively
bokstavs|följd alphabetical order **-gåta** ana-
gram; logograph **-lås** combination (letter) lock
-ordning *se -följd* **-trogen** true to the letter
bok|stöd book end **-synt** [-y:-] *a1* well-read
-synthet book knowledge **-titel** book title, title
of a book **-tryck** book printing; (*högtryck*) let-
terpress [printing] **-tryckare** printer **-tryckar-
konst** [art of] printing, typography **-tryckeri**
printing-house, printing-office **-verk** book
-ägarmärke bookplate, ex-libris **-älskare**
booklover, bibliophil[e]
bolag *s7* company; *AE.* corporation; *enkelt ~*
partnership; *ingå i ~ med* enter into partnership
with
bolags|beskattning company (corporate) tax-
ation **-man** partner **-ordning** articles of association (*pl*), corporate bylaws (*pl*) **-styrelse** board
of directors **-stämma** annual meeting of share-
holders, annual general meeting
bolero [bå'le:rå] *s5* bolero
bolid *s3* bolide, fireball
bolin *s3, sjö.* bowline; *låta allt gå för lösa ~er* let
things go as they please, allow things to slide
Bolivia [-ˈli:-] *n* Bolivia **bolivian** *s3*, **bolivi-
ansk** [-ˈa:-] *a5* Bolivian
boll [-å-] *s2* **1** ball; (*slag i tennis*) stroke; *kasta ~*
play catch; *sparka ~* play football; *en hård ~* a
hard stroke; *~en ligger hos dig* the ball is in your
court **2** *sl.* (*huvud*) nut, loaf; *AE.* bean; *vara tom
i ~en* be batty, be off one's nut
boll|a play ball; *~ med ord* play (juggle) with
words, split hairs **-kalle** *s2* ball boy **-kastning**
ball-throwing **-sinne** ball-sense **-spel** ball game

-spelare ballplayer **-sport** ball games (*pl*) **-trä** bat

bolma [-å-] (*om sak*) belch out smoke; (*om pers.*) puff; ~ *på en pipa* puff away at a pipe

bolmört [-å-] henbane

bolometer [-'me:-] *s2* bolometer

bolsjev|ik [bålʃe-] *s3* Bolshevik **-ism** Bolshevism **-istisk** [-'viss-] *a5* Bolshevist[ic]

bolster ['båll-] *s2, s7* soft mattress; feather bed **-var** *s7* tick; (*tyg*) ticking

1 bom [bɔmm] *s2* (*stång*) bar, *järnv.* level-crossing (*AE.* grade-crossing) gate; (*väg-*) barrier; (*gymnastikredskap*) [balance] beam; *sjö.* boom; (*last-*) derrick, jib; (*på vävstol*) beam; *inom lås och* ~ under lock and key

2 bom [bɔmm] **I** *s2* (*felskott*) miss, wide **II** *adv,* *skjuta* ~ miss [the mark] **III** *interj* boom

bomb [-å-] *s3* bomb; *fälla* ~*er* drop bombs, bomb; *slå ner som en* ~ (*bildl.*) come as a bombshell

bomb|a [-å-] bomb **-anfall** bombing attack **bombard|emang** [-'maŋ] *s7* bombardment **-era** bomb, bombard; batter; (*friare*) pelt

bombas|m [-å-] *s3* bombast **-tisk** *a5* bombastic

bomb|attentat bomb outrage (attempt) **-flyg** bombers; bomb command **-flygplan** bomber **-fällning** bomb dropping, release of bombs **-hot** bomb warning **-krater** bomb crater **-last** bombload **-matta** bomb carpet **-nedslag** impact of a bomb; *ett blont* ~ a blonde bombshell **-ning** bombing **-plan** *se -flygplan* **-rum** (*i flygplan*) bomb bay **-räd** bomb raid **-sikte** bombsight **-stopp** bomb[ing] halt **-säker** bombproof

1 bomma (*missa*) miss [the mark]; ~ *på* miss

2 bomma ~ *för* (*igen, till*) bar, lock up

3 bomma *sl.* (*låna*) cadge, scrounge; *AE.* bum, mooc

bomolja [ˣbomm-] industrial olive oil

bomsegel [ˣbomm-] boomsail

bomskott [ˣbomm-] *se 2 bom I*

bomull [ˣbomm-] cotton; (*förbands-*) cotton wool, purified (*AE.* absorbent) cotton; *av* ~ (*äv.*) cotton

bomulls|bal bale of cotton **-band** cotton tape **-buske** cotton shrub **-fabrik** cotton mill **-flanell** flannelette **-frö** cottonseed **-garn** cotton yarn **-klänning** cotton dress **-krut** guncotton **-odlare** cotton grower **-odling** cotton growing **-plantage** cotton plantation **-spinneri** cotton mill **-trikå** cotton stockinet **-tråd** cotton thread; *en rulle* ~ a reel of cotton **-tuss** piece of cotton-wool **-tyg** cotton fabric (cloth) **-vadd** cotton wool **-växt** cotton plant

bomärke [owner's] mark; (*på kreatur*) brand [mark]

1 bona (*polera*) wax, polish

2 bona ~ *om* wrap up well; *se äv. ombona*

bonad *s3* hanging [piece of] tapestry

bonapparat floor polisher

bonbonjär [båŋbåŋ'jä:r] *s3* sweetmeat dish, bonbonnière

bond|bröllop peasant wedding **-by** farming village **-böna** broad (horse) bean **-dräng** farm hand; ploughboy

bonde -*n bönder* **1** farmer; (*allmogeman*) peasant, countryman **2** (*schack-*) pawn **-befolkning** farming population; [the] farmers (*pl*) **-här** army

of peasants **-kultur** peasant culture **-praktika** *s1, ung.* farmers' almanac **-stånd** peasantry **-uppror** peasants' revolt

bond|flicka country girl **-folk** country people **-fångare** con[fidence] man, trickster **-fångeri** confidence trick (*AE.* game), con trick **-förnuft, -förstånd** common sense **-försök** *ung.* unblushing (cheeky) attempt; *vard.* try-on **-grann** gaudy, showy **-gubbe** old countryman **-gumma** old countrywoman **-gård** farm; (*boningshus*) farmhouse **-hund** mongrel **-jänta** country wench **-komik** burlesque; lowbrow comedy **-komiker** lowbrow comedian; (*dålig amatör*) ham actor **-kvinna** countrywoman **-land** ~*et, se bondvischan* **-lurk** *s2* yokel; *AE.* hick **-neka** stubbornly deny **-permission** French leave **-piga** farm maid; *neds.* country ninny **-pojke** country lad (boy)

bondsk *a1* peasantlike, rustic; boorish

bond|slug sly, shrewd **-spelman** village fiddler **-stuga** farmhouse **-tur** *rena* ~*en* a real fluke **-tölp** country bumpkin **-vatten** Adam's ale (wine), [drinking] water **-vischan** the backwoods (sticks) (*pl*); *AE.* Hicksville; *på* ~ in the sticks **-änger** [maudlin] self-reproach

bong [båŋ] *s2* voucher; (*på restaurang*) bill, *AE.* check; (*vid totalisator*) tote ticket **bonga** *ung.* register

bongotrumma [ˣbåŋgå-] bongo

1 boning (*t. 1 bona*) polishing

2 boning (*bostad*) dwelling [place], abode

bonings|hus dwelling house **-rum** living room

bonjour [båŋˈʃo:r *el.* -ˈʃu:r] *s3* frock coat

bonnett *s3* bonnet

bonus ['bo:-] *s2* bonus **-klass** bonus class

bonvax [ˣbo:n-] floor wax (polish)

bo|plats habitation, dwelling place; site **-pålar** *pl*, *slå ner sina* ~ settle down

bor [bå:r] *s2* boron **-at** [bo- *el.* bå-] *s4* borate **-ax** ['bo:- *el.* 'bå:-] *s2* borax; (*mineral äv.*) tincal

1 bord [-o:-] *s7* table; (*skriv-*) desk; *tekn.* platform; *duka* ~*et* lay the table; *gående* ~ buffet; *vi var tio till* ~*et* we were ten at table; *dricka ngn under* ~*et* drink s.b. under the table; *föra ngn till* ~*et* take s.b. in to dinner; *lägga korten på* ~*et* put one's cards on the table; *passa upp vid* ~*et* wait at (*AE.* on) table; *sitta* (*sätta sig*) *till* ~*s* sit at (sit down to) table

2 bord [-o:-] *s7, sjö.* board; (*i bordläggning*) plank; *kasta över* ~ jettison; throw overboard; *falla över* ~ fall overboard; *man över* ~! man overboard!; *se äv. ombord* **borda** board

bord|beställning table reservation **-dans** table-turning **-duk** tablecloth

borde [ˣbo:r-] *imperf. av böra*

bordeaux [bårˈdå:] *s3*, **bordeauxvin** [bårˣdå:-] Bordeaux; (*rött*) claret **bourdeauxvätska** [bårˣdå:-] Bordeaux mixture

bordell [-å-] *s3* brothel

1 bordlägga shelve; table; postpone

2 bordlägga *sjö.* plank; (*stålfartyg*) plate

1 bordläggning shelving; tabling; *parl.* first reading

2 bordläggning *sjö. (av trä)* [outside] planking; (*av plåt*) shell-plating

bordlöpare [table] runner

bords|bön grace; *läsa* ~ say grace **-dam** [lady] partner at table **-dekoration** table decoration; centrepiece **-duk** *se bordduk* **-granne** neighbour (partner) at table **-kavaljer** [gentleman] partner at table **-kniv** table knife **-lampa** table lamp **-låda** [table] drawer **-salt** table salt **-samtal** table talk **-servis** tableware **-silver** table silver **-skick** table manners (*pl*) **-skiva** tabletop **-tändare** tablelighter **-uppsats** centrepiece **-vatten** mineral water **-vin** table wine **-visa** drinking song **-ända** end of the table; *sitta vid övre* ~*n* sit at the top (head) of the table; *nedre* ~*n* the bottom (end, foot) of the table

bordtennis table tennis **-racket** bat

bordåvätska *se bordeauxvätska*

Bore Boreas

bor|en [ˣbå:-] *a5* born; *han är den -ne ledaren* he is a born leader

borg [bårj] *s2* castle; stronghold

borga [ˣbårja] buy (sell) on credit; ~ *för* guarantee, warrant, vouch for

borgarbracka [ˣbårjar-] *s1* narrow-minded bourgeois, Philistine; *AE.* Babbitt

borgar|e [ˣbårr-] citizen, townsman; commoner; *hist.* burgher; burgess; **-na** (*äv.*) the bourgeoisie (*sg*) **-klass** ~*en* the bourgeoisie, the middle classes (*pl*) **-press** Liberal and Conservative press **-råd** city commissioner **-stånd** ~*et* the burghers (*pl*); (*i Storbritannien*) the commons (*pl*)

borgen [ˈbårjen] *r* [personal] guarantee, security, warrant; *gå i* ~ *för* stand surety for, warrant, (*friare*) vouch for, stand (go) bail for; *ställa* ~ give surety; *teckna* ~ provide a personal guarantee; *frige mot* ~ release on bail; *den som går i* ~ *går i sorgen* go bail for a borrower and come home a sorrower

borgens|förbindelse personal guarantee, surety bond, security **-lån** loan against a [personal] guarantee **-man** guarantor; surety

borgenär [bårje-] *s3* creditor

borgerlig [ˣbårjer-] *a1* **1** civil; ~ *vigsel* civil marriage; ~*a rättigheter* civil rights; ~*t år* civil (calendar) year **2** (*av medelklass*) middle-class, bourgeois; ~*t yrke* ordinary occupation **3** *polit.*, *de* ~*a partierna* the Liberals and Conservatives **4** *neds.* Philistine, narrow-minded, square **-het** [middle--class] respectability

borgerskap [ˣbårjer-] *s7*, *ej pl* burghers (*pl*)

borg|fred party truce **-fru** chatelaine **-gård** castle courtyard

borgis [ˈbårgis *el.* -jis] *s2*, *boktr.* bourgeois

borgmästar|e (*kommunal-*) mayor, (*i Skottland*) provost, (*i större engelska städer*) lord mayor **-inna** [lord] mayoress

borgruin ruined castle

boricka [ˣbo:-] *s1* donkey

bornera [-å-] effervesce; (*om vin*) sparkle

bornerad [-år'ne:-] *a5* narrow-minded; Philistine

bornyr [-å-] *s3* head, froth; (*i vin*) sparkle

borr [-å-] *s2*, *s7* borer; (*drill-*) drill; (*navare*) auger; *tandläk.* dental drill, bur; (*liten hand-*) gimlet

borr|a (*i material*) bore, drill; (*brunn, gruva*) bore, sink; ~ *efter vatten* bore for water; ~ *hål i* (*äv.*) hole; ~ *igenom* (*äv.*) perforate; ~ *i sank*

sink; scuttle; ~ [*ner*] *huvudet i kudden* bury one's head in the pillow; ~ *upp* bore a hole in, drill; ~ *ögonen i ngn* give s.b. a piercing stare **-are** borer **-fluga** fruit fly **-hål** drill hole, bore[hole] **-krona** drill bit **-maskin** drilling (boring) machine **-ning** boring, drilling **-plattform** drilling platform **-stål** drill steel **-sväng** brace; ~ *med borr* brace and bit **-torn** derrick, drilling tower

borst [-å-] *s7* bristle; *resa* ~ bristle [up]; *försedd med* ~ bristled **borsta** brush; (*skor, tänder äv.*) clean

borst|bindare brushmaker; *svära som en* ~ swear like a trooper **-binderi** brush factory

borste [-å-] *s2* brush **-ig** *a1* bristly

borst|mask chaetopod **-nejlika** sweet william **-ning** brushing; cleaning

borsyr|a boric (orthoboric) acid **-esalva** boracic ointment

1 bort [-ɔ:-] *sup. av böra*

2 bort [-å-] away; *gå* ~ *a*) (*på kalas*) go [to a party], go out [to dinner], *b*) (*dö*) pass away; ~ *med er!* away with you!; ~ *med tassarna!* hands off!; *långt* ~ far away; *längst* ~ at the far end

borta [-å-] away; (*försvunnen*) gone; (*frånvarande*) absent; (*ej tillfinnandes*) missing, lost; (*ute*) out; *där* ~ over there; ~ *bra men hemma bäst* East or West, home is best; ~ *från skolan* absent from school; ~ *med vinden* gone with the wind; ~ *på kalas* [out] at a party; *känna sig alldeles* ~ feel completely lost (*förvirrad:* muddled)

bortackordera board out

borta|lag *sport.* away team **-match** *sport.* away game

bortanför *se bortom*

bortaplan *sport.* away ground

bort|arbeta eliminate [by hard work] **-arrendera** let out

bortaseger *sport.* away win

bort|auktionera sell at (by) auction, auction off **-bjuden** *a5* invited out (*på middag* to dinner) **-blåst** *a4*, *är som* ~ has vanished into thin air **-byting** changeling **-bytt** *a4*, *få sina galoscher* ~*a* get s.b. else's galoshes [by mistake]; *mina barn var som* ~*a* they did not seem like my children at all **-döende** *a4* dying away **-efter** along **-emot** (*i riktning mot*) in the direction of; (*nära*) nearly **-erst** [ˈbårt-] **I** *adv* farthest off **II** *a, superl.* farthest, farthermost **-fall** falling off; (*försvinnande*) disappearance **-falla** drop (fall) off; (*försvinna*) disappear, be dispensed with, be omitted **-forsla** carry away; (*med t.ex. kärra*) cart away; remove **-frakta 1** remove **2** ~ *ett fartyg* charter a ship, let a ship by charter party **-fraktare** (*rederi*) shipowner, charterer **-fraktning** removal **-färd 1** outward journey **2** departure **-förklara** explain away **-förklaring** prevarication; trumped-up excuse **-gift** *bli* ~ be given away in marriage; *få en dotter* ~ marry off a daughter **-glömd** *a5* forgotten **-gång** decease; departure (*ur tiden* from this life) **-gången** *a5* gone away; (*död*) deceased; *den -gångne* the deceased **-ifrån I** *prep* from [the direction of] **II** *adv, där* ~ from over there; *långt* ~ from far off (away) **-igenom** away through **-kastad** *a5* thrown away; wasted; ~ *möda* wasted effort **-klemad** *a5* coddled [and spoiled] **-kollrad** [-å-] *a5*, *bli alldeles* ~ have one's head quite turned **-kommen** [-å-] *a5* lost; (*om pers. äv.*) absent-minded, confused; *känna sig* ~ feel like a fish out of water **-lovad** [-å-] *a5* promised; (*tingad*) bespoken **-manövrera** eliminate by a [clever] manoeuvre **-om I** *prep* beyond; ~ *all ära och redlighet* beyond the pale [of civilization] **II** *adv, där* ~ beyond that **-operera** remove [by surgery]

bortovaro *s2* absence

bort|rationalisera make redundant by efficiency improvement

bortre ['bårt-] *a, komp.* further; *i* ~ *delen av* at the far end of; ~ *parkett* pit stalls

bort|resonera reason away, get over by argument[s *pl*] **-rest** [-e:-] *a4, han är* ~ he is (has gone) away **-ryckt** *a4* pulled out; (*av döden*) snatched away by death **-röva** kidnap, run away with; (*kvinna*) abduct **-se** ~ *från* disregard, leave out of account;; ~*tt från* apart from, irrespective of **-skriva** sign away **-skämd** *a1* spoilt (*med* by) **-slarvad** *a5* lost **-slumpa** sell off **-sprungen** *a5* strayed **-stött** *a4* expelled **-trängning** *psykol.* repression **-val** optional exclusion **-väg** *på* ~*en* on the way there **-vänd** *a5* turned away; *med -vänt ansikte* with averted face **-åt** ['bårt- *el.* -'å:t] **I** *adv* **1** *där* ~ somewhere in that direction; *en tid* ~ for some time **2** (*nästan*) nearly **II** *prep* towards, in the direction of; ~ *gatan* along the street; ~ *kyrkan* near the church; *hon är* ~ *femtio år* she is going on for fifty **-över** [-'ö:- *el.* 'bårt-] **I** *prep* away over **II** *adv, dit* ~ away over there

bosatt *a4* residing; resident; *vara* ~ *i* reside (live) in

bosch [-å-] *s7* bosh

boskap [ˣbɔ:-] *s2, ej pl* cattle (*behandlas som pl*), livestock (*behandlas som sg el. pl*)

boskaps|avel stockbreeding **-hjord** herd of cattle **-marknad** cattle market **-skötsel** cattlebreeding, cattleraising **-uppfödare** stockbreeder, cattlebreeder **-vagn** cattle truck; *AE.* stock car

bo|skifte *se bodelning* **-skillnad** judicial division of a joint estate

Bosnien ['båss-] *n* Bosnia **bosnier** ['båss-] *s9,* **bosnisk** ['båss-] *a5* Bosnian

boson [-'så:n] *s3* boson

Bosporen [bås'på:-] *n* the Bosporus

1 boss [-å-] *s2, polit.* [party] boss

2 boss [-å-] *s7* (*agnar*) chaff

bossa nova ['båssa 'nå:va] *r* bossa nova

bostad *-en bostäder* dwelling, habitation, housing [accommodation]; (*våning*) flat, *AE.* apartment; (*hyrda rum*) lodgings (*pl*), vard. digs (*pl*); (*hem*) home, house; *jur.* domicile; *fast* ~ permanent address (residence, home); *fri* ~ free housing (accommodation); *utan* ~ homeless; *olämplig som* ~ unfit for habitation

bostads|adress home (private) address; *jur.* domicile **-bidrag** housing allowance **-brist** housing shortage **-byggande** housing construction, house building **-departement** ministry of housing and physical planning **-domstol** ~*en* [the Swedish] rents and tenancies court of appeal **-fastighet** block of flats, residential property, dwelling house **-förening** *se -rättsförening* **-förmedling** housing agency, local housing author-

ity **-hus** *se -fastighet* **-kvarter** residential quarter **-kö** housing queue **-lån** housing loan **-lägenhet** flat; *AE. äv.* apartment **-lös** homeless **-marknad** housing market **-minister** minister of housing and physical planning **-område** residential area, housing estate (development) **-politik** housing policy **-problem** housing problem **-rättsförening** tenant-owners' society **-standard** housing standard **-styrelse** ~*n* [the Swedish] national housing board **-tillägg** housing allowance **-utskott** ~*et* [the Swedish parliamentary] standing committee on housing **-yta** dwelling space, floor space of a flat

boston|terrier Boston terrier (bull) **-vals** boston

boställe [official] residence

bosätt|a *rfl* settle [down], take up residence **-ning** (*handlingen att sätta bo*) setting up house, starting a home; (*anskaffande av husgeråd m.m.*) housefurnishing; (*bebyggande*) settlement; establishment

bosättnings|affär household equipment store **-lån** government loan for setting up house

bot *s3* **1** (*botemedel*) remedy; cure; *finna* ~ *för* find a cure for; *råda* ~ *för* (*på*) remedy, set right **2** (*gottgörelse*) penance; *göra* ~ *och bättring* do penance, turn over a new leaf **3** *jur.* penalty

bota 1 (*läka*) cure (*för* of) **2** (*avhjälpa*) remedy, set right

botan|ik *s3* botany **-iker** [-'ta:-] botanist **-isera** botanize **-isk** [-'ta:-] *a5* botanic[al]; ~ *exkursion* botanical excursion; ~ *geografi* botanic geography; ~ *trädgård* botanical garden **-ist** botanist

bot|dag day of penance **-emedel** remedy, cure **-färdig** penitent **-färdighet** penitence **-görare** [-j-] penitent **-göring** [-j-] penance **-predikan** penitential sermon

Botswana [båts'va:na] *n* Botswana

botten ['båtten] **I** *s2* bottom; (*mark*) soil; (*på tapet, tyg*) ground; *dricka i* ~ drain (empty) [one's glass]; ~ *opp!* bottoms up!, down the hatch!, no heeltaps!; *det finns ingen* ~ *i honom* there's no limit to his appetite; *gå till* ~ go to the bottom, sink, founder; *gå till* ~ *med ngt* (*bildl.*) get to the bottom of s.th.; *i grund och* ~ at heart (bottom), (*helt o. hållet*) thoroughly; *på nedre* ~ on the ground (*AE.* first) floor; *på svensk* ~ on Swedish soil **II** *obojligt a, vard.* lousy, rotten **-beskaffenhet** quality of the bottom **-frysa** freeze solid (to the bottom) **-färg** ground [colour]; (*grundningsfärg*) primer, priming; *sjö.* bottom coat

Bottenhavet [ˣbått-] the southern part of the Gulf of Bothnia

botten|hederlig *se -ärlig* **-inteckning** first mortgage **-kran** *sjö.* seacock **-kurs** bottom price (quotation) **-känning** grounding; *ha* ~ (*sjö.*) touch bottom (ground) **-lån** first mortgage loan **-läge** lowest point **-lös** bottomless; (*friare*) unfathomable, fathomless, immeasurable; ~*a vägar* roads deep in (impassable for) mud **-pris** rockbottom price **-rekord** [the] lowest level ever reached **-reva** *sjö.* close-reef; ~*d* close-reeved **-rik** made of (rolling in) money **-sats** sediment; (*i vin, kaffe o.d.*) dregs (*pl*); *bildl. o. kem.* deposit **-skikt** bottom layer; (*geol. o. befolknings-*) lower strata (*pl*); (*drägg*) residuum **-skrap** (*äv.*

bildl.) last scraps (*pl*) **-skrapa I** *s1* trawl, dredge **II** *v1* **1** scrape [a ship's bottom] **2** *bildl.*, ~ *sina tillgångar* exhaust one's funds **-skyla** [-ʃ-] *s1* enough to cover the bottom **-våning** ground (*A E.* first) floor **-ärlig** downright honest, honest to the core

bottjn [-å-] *s3* galosh (snow) boot

bottna [-å-] **1** (*nå botten*) reach (touch) the bottom **2** *det ~r i* it originates in, it springs from

Bottniska viken ['bått-] [the] Gulf of Bothnia

botulism botulism

botövning discipline, penance

boudoir *s3 se budoar*

bougie [boˈʃiː] *r* bougie

bouillabaisse [bojaˈbäːs] *s3* bouillabaisse

boulevard [boleˈvaːrd] *s3* boulevard; (*i Storbritannien*) avenue **-kafé** boulevard café

bouppteck|ning estate inventory; *förrätta ~* [make an estate] inventory **-ningsman** administrator; (*förordnad i testamente*) executor

bouquet [boˈkeː] *s3* flavour; (*t.ex. vin-*) bouquet

bourgeoisie [borʃoaˈsiː] *s3* bourgeoisie

bourgogne [borˈgånj] *s5*, **bourgognevin** [borˣgånj-] Burgundy

boutique [boˈtick] *s5* boutique

boutred|ning administration of the estate of a deceased **-ningsman** (*förordnad av domstol*) administrator; (*förordnad i testamente*) executor

bov *s2*, *eg.* crook; villain (*äv. teat.*); *skämts.* rascal, rogue; *~en i dramat* the villain of the piece **-aktig** *al* villainous; rascally, roguish **-aktighet** villainy; rascality

bovete buckwheat

bovfysionomi villainous countenance

bowl|a [ˣbåo- *el.* ˣbåvv-] bowl **-are** bowler **-ing** ['båo- *el.* 'båvv-] [tenpin] bowling; *A E.* tenpins **-bana**, **-hall** bowling alley **-klot** bowl **-kägla** [ten]pin

bovstreck [piece of] villainy; dirty trick

box [båcks] *s2* box, case; (*kol-*) bunker; (*kätte*) box, stall; (*post-*) [post-office] box

box|a [ˣbocksa] ~ *till ngn* give s.b. a punch (blow) **-are** boxer, pugilist **-as** *dep* box

boxer ['båckser] *s2* boxer

boxhandske [ˣbocks-] boxing glove

boxkalv [ˣbåcks-] box calf

boxning [ˣbocks-] boxing, pugilism

boxnings|match boxing match **-ring** boxing ring **-sporten** boxing, the noble art of self-defence

bra *bättre bäst* **I** *a* **1** good; (*starkare*) excellent; (*som det skall vara*) all right; ~ *karl reder sig själv* self-help is a primary virtue, an honest man does his own odd jobs; *blir det ~ så?* will that do?; *det är ~ (tillräckligt)* that'll do, that's enough; *det var ~!* that's good!; *det var ~ att du kom*[*mer*] it is a good thing (job) you came, I am glad you came; *allt skall nog bli ~ igen* I am sure everything will turn out for the best; *vad skall det vara ~ för?* what is the good (use) of that? **2** (*frisk*) well; *han är ~ igen* he is all right again; *har du blivit ~ från din förkylning?* have you recovered from your cold? **3** (*ganska lång*) good[ish], long[ish] **II** *adv* **1** well; *lukta* (*smaka*) ~ smell (taste) nice; *tack ~* very well, thank you; *jag mår inte riktigt ~* I am not feeling well, I am feeling a bit under the

weather; *ha det ~* be well off, (*trivas*) be happy, like it, feel at home; *se ~ ut* be good-looking; *tycka ~ om* like very much **2** (*mycket, ganska mycket*) very; *vard.* jolly; *få ~ betalt* be well paid, get a good price; *det var ~ synd att* what a pity that; *det dröjde ett ~ tag innan* it took quite a while before; *jag skulle ~ gärna vilja veta* I should very much like to know

bracka *s1*, **brackig** *al* Philistine **brackighet** Philistinism

brackvatten brackish water

bragd *s3* exploit, feat; achievement

bragelöfte boastful vow

bragt [brackt] *sup. av bringa* **bragte** [ˣbrack-] *imperf. av bringa*

brahman *se braman*

brailleskrift [ˣbrajj-] Braille

brak *s7* crash; (*om kanon*) boom; (*om åska*) peal **braka** crasch, crack; ~ *ihop* (*slåss*) come to blows; ~ *lös* break out, get going; ~ *ner* come crashing down; ~ *samman* collapse

brak|middag *en riktig ~* quite a banquet **-skit** *vard.* fart; loud one **-succé** smash-hit

brakteat *s3* bracteate

brakved *s2*, *bot.* alder buckthorn

brallis ['brall-] *s2*, *sl.*, *se brud 2*

brallor *pl*, *vard.* bags

bram|an *s3* Brahman **-anism** Brahmanism **-jn** *s3* Brahman, Brahmin

bramsegel [ˣbramm-] toppgallant sail

brand *-en bränder* **1** fire; (*större*) conflagration; (*brinnande trästycke*) [fire]brand; *råka i ~* catch fire; *stå i ~* be on fire; *sätta i ~* set fire to, set on fire, (*om känslor*) inflame **2** *med.* gangrene **3** *bot.* blight, mildew

brand|alarm fire alarm **-bil** fire engine **-bomb** firebomb, incendiary [bomb] **-chef** [department] chief, head of a fire brigade; *A E.* fire marshal **-damm** fire dam, emergency tank **-fackla** incendiary torch; *bildl.* firebrand **-fara** danger of fire **-fast** fireproof **-försvar** fire fighting, fire prevention; (*brandkår*) fire brigade; *A E.* fire department (company)

brandförsäkr|a insure against fire **-ing** fire insurance **-ingsbolag** fire company

brand|gata firebreak, fire line **-gavel** fireproof gable **-gul** orange, flame-coloured **-kår** fire brigade; *A E.* fire department **-larm** *se -alarm* **-lukt** smell of fire (burning) **-man** fireman **-mur** fire wall **-plats** place of fire **-post** fire hydrant; *A E.* fireplug **-redskap** fire-fighting equipment **-risk** fire hazard **-rök** smoke from a fire **-segel** jumping sheet **-skada** fire damage **-skadad** damaged by fire **-skadeersättning** fire indemnity **-skatta** extort contributions from; overtax; *bildl.* plunder, fleece **-skattning** [extortion of] contributions; *bildl.* plundering **-skydd** fire protection **-skåp** fire-alarm [box] **-slang** firehose **-släckare** fire-extinguisher **-släckning** fire fighting **-soldat** fireman **-spruta** fire-extinguisher **-station** fire station; *A E.* firehouse, station house **-stege** fire escape **-stodsbolag** fire-insurance company **-säker** fireproof, flameproof **-tal** inflammatory speech **-talare** fiery speaker **-vakt** fire watcher; *gå ~* (*bildl.*) be compelled to pace the streets all night **-väsen**

fire-fighting services (*pl*) **-övning** fire drill
brann *imperf. av brinna*
bransch *s3* line [of business], branch **-känne-dom** knowledge of a (the) trade **-man** expert (specialist) in a line of trade (business) **-organi-sation** trade association **-vana** experience of a line of business
brant I *s3* precipice; *på ruinens* ~ on the verge of ruin **II** *a1* steep, precipitous, sheer; ~ *udde* (*klippa, strandbank*) bluff **III** *adv* steeply *etc.*; *stupa* ~ *ner* (*äv.*) fall sheer away
brasa *s1* [log-]fire; *lägga in en* ~ lay a fire; *sitta vid* (*framför, kring*) ~*n* sit at (in front of, round) the fire; *tända en* ~ make (light) a fire; *göra en* ~ *av* make a bonfire of
brasilianare [-ˣa:n-] *s9*, **brasiliansk** [-'a:nsk] *a5* Brazilian **Brasilien** [-'si:-] *n* Brazil
braska (*bli kallt*) be frosty, freeze
braskande *a4* showy, ostentatious; ~ *annonser* ostentatious (showy, blazing) advertisements
brasklapp [ˣbrask-] *s2, ung.* mental reservation
bras|kudde hearth cushion **-redskap** fire irons
brass *s2, sjö.* brace
1 brassa *sjö.* brace; ~ *fullt* (*back*) brace full (aback)
2 brassa ~ *på* (*elda*) stoke up [the fire]; (*eldva-pen*) fire away
brasserie [brass'ri:] *s4* brasserie
brast *imperf. av brista*
braständare firelighter
Braunschweig [ˈbraɔnʃvajg] *n* Brunswick
bravad *s3* exploit; bravado **bravera** (*utmärka sig*) be brilliant; (*skryta*) boast (*med* of), brag (*med* about)
bravo [ˈbra:-] bravo!, well done! **-rop** cheer
bravur dash; valour; *mus.* bravura **-nummer** star turn
braxen [ˈbraksen] *best. form* =, *pl braxnar* bream **-panka** *s1* young bream
bre *se breda*
bred *a1* broad, wide; *på* ~ *front* on a broad front; *brett uttal* broad accent; *de* ~*a lagren* the masses; *göra sig* ~ assert o.s.; *på* ~ *bas* on a broad scale
breda *v2* spread; ~ *en smörgås* make a sandwich, butter a slice of bread; ~ *på* (*om smörgås*) spread, make, (*överdriva*) pile it on [thick], lay it on; ~ *ut* spread out; ~ *ut sig* spread, extend
bred|axlad *a5* broad-shouldered **-bar** *a1* easy-spreading, spreadable **-bent** [-be:nt] *a1* straddle-legged; *stå* ~ stand with one's legs wide apart **-brättig** *a1* wide-brimmed **-bröstad** *a5* broad-chested
bredd *s3* **1** breadth, width; *gå i* ~ walk side by side; *i* ~ *med* abreast of, (*i jämförelse med*) compared to; *på* ~*en* in breadth; *största* ~ (*sjö.*) overall width, beam **2** *geogr.* latitude
bredd|a broaden, make wider **-grad** [degree of] latitude; *på varmare* ~*er* in warmer climes **-ning** broadening, widening
bred|flikig *a1* broad-lobed **-näsapa** *zool.* New World monkey **-randig** *a1* broad-striped **-sida** broadside; *avfyra en* ~ fire a broadside **-spekt-rumantibiotikum** broad-spectrum antibiotic **-spårig** *järnv.* broad-gauge
bredvid [bre(d)'vi:d *el.* ˣbre:(d)vid] **I** *prep* beside, at (by) the side of, by; (*intill*) next to; ~ *var-*

andra side by side; *prata* ~ *munnen* give the game (show) away, blab; ~ *sin fru verkar han obetydlig* beside his wife he looks insignificant **II** *adv* close by; (*-liggande, -stående*) adjacent, adjoining; (*ex-tra*) in addition; *där* ~ close to it; *här* ~ close by here; *rummet* (*huset*) ~ the next (adjacent, adjoining) room (house), *äv.* next door; *halla* ~ miss the cup (glass *etc.*); *han tjänar en del* ~ he has some additional sources of income, he makes some extra cash in his spare time
breitschwanz [ˈbraitʃvants] *s2* (*pälsverk*) broadtail
bretagnare [-ˣtanjare] Breton **Bretagne** [-'tanj] *n* Brittany **bretagnisk** [-'tanjisk] *a5* Breton
breton *s3* Breton **bretonsk** [-'tɔ:nsk] *a5* Breton
brett *adv* broadly, widely; *tala vitt och* ~ talk at great length
brev *s7* letter; (*bibl. o. friare*) epistle; *vard.* line[s *pl*]; *komma som ett* ~ *på posten* [seem to] drop straight into one's lap **-befordran** transmission of letters **-bomb** letter bomb **-bärare** postman, *fem.* postwoman; *AE.* mailman **-bäring** mail-delivery service **-censur** postal censorship **-duva** carrier pigeon **-form** *i* ~ in the form of a letter **-hemlighet** secrecy of the mails **-huvud** letterhead
breviarium [-vi'a:-] *s4* breviary
brev|kopia carbon copy **-kort** postcard; ~ *med betalt svar* reply postcard **-ledes** by letter **-låda** letter box; *AE. äv.* mailbox; (*pelare, i Storbritan-nien*) pillar box, post; (*i dörr*) *AE.* [mail] drop **-papper** notepaper, writing paper; stationery; (*med tryck*) letterhead **-porto** [letter] postage **-press** letter-weight, paperweight **-pärm** [let-ter] file **-remissa** mail remittance **-skola** cor-respondence school **-skrivare** letter writer, cor-respondent **-skrivning** letter writing, corre-spondence **-ställare** guide to letter-writing **-te-legram** letter telegram **-våg** letter balance **-vän** pen pal (friend) **-växla** correspond **-växling** correspondence **-öppnare** letter opener
brick|a *s1* tray; (*för visitkort etc.*) salver; (*karott-underlägg*) [table]mat; (*plåt-*) plate; (*igenkän-ningstecken*) badge; (*spel-*) counter, piece; man; (*nummer-*) tab, check; *tekn.* washer; *en* ~ *i spelet* (*bildl.*) a pawn in the game **-duk** traycloth
bridge [briddʃ] *s2* bridge **-parti** game of bridge **-spelare** bridge player
bridreaktor [ˣbri:d-] breeder [reactor]
brigad *s3* brigade **-general** brigadier; *AE.* briga-dier general
brigg *s2* brig
brikett *s3* briquet[te]
briljans [-'ans *el.* -'aŋs] *s3* brilliance
briljant [-'ant *el.* -'aŋt] **I** *s3* brilliant [cut], diamond **II** *a1* brilliant, first-rate **-era** set with brilliants (diamonds), diamond **-in** [-an- *el.* -aŋ-] *s4, s3* brilliantine **-ring** brilliant (diamond) ring **-smycke** set of brilliants, diamond ornament
briljera shine, show off; ~ *med* show off
brillor *pl* specs, spectacles
1 bringa *s1* breast; *kokk.* brisket
2 bringa *bragte bragt el.* v1 bring; (*föra t. annan plats*) convey, conduct, carry; ~ *hjälp* render as-sistance; ~ *i dagen* bring to light; ~ *i oordning* put

out of order, make a mess of; ~ *i säkerhet* convey into safety; ~ *klarhet i* throw light upon, make clear; ~ *ngn lycka* bring s.b. happiness; ~ *ngn om livet* put s.b. to death, do s.b. in; ~ *ngn på fall* bring s.b. to ruin, cause a p.'s ruin; ~ *ngn sin hyllning* pay one's respect to s.b.; ~ *ngn till förtvivlan* reduce s.b. to despair; ~ *olycka över* bring disaster to, bring down ruin on; ~ *ordning i* put in order; ~ *på tal* bring up [for discussion], broach [a matter]; ~ *ur världen* dispose of; ~ *det därhän att man är* come (get) to the point of being

brink *s2* hill; (*älv-*) bank

brinn|a *brann brunnit* burn; be on fire; *det -er i spisen* there is a fire in the stove; *det -er i knutarna* the place is getting too hot [for me (*etc.*)]; *huset -er* the house is on fire; ~ *av iver* be full of enthusiasm; ~ *av nyfikenhet* (*otålighet*) be burning with curiosity (impatience); ~ *av* go off, explode; ~ *inne* be burnt to death; ~ *ner* burn down, (*om brasa*) burn low; ~ *upp* be destroyed by fire, be burnt out; ~ *ut* burn itself out, go out **brinnande** *a4* burning; ~ *bön* fervent prayer; ~ *kärlek* (*hängivenhet*) ardent love (affection); ~ *ljus* lighted candle; *springa för* ~ *livet* run for dear life; *mitt under* ~ *krig* while war is (was) raging (at his height)

brio ['briɔ] *s3* brio, vivacity; *med* ~ with zest (ardour)

bris *s2, s3* breeze; *lätt* ~ light breeze; *god* (*frisk*) ~ gentle (moderate) breeze; *styv* (*hård*) ~ fresh (strong) breeze

bris|ad *s3*, **brisera** *vl* burst

brist *s3* **1** (*otillräcklighet*) lack, want, shortage, scarcity; (*saknad*) want; (*fel*) defect, flaw, shortcoming; *biol.* deficiency; (*nackdel*) disadvantage, drawback; *lida* ~ *på* be short of, be in want of; *i* (*av*) ~ *på* for want of, failing, lacking; *i* ~ *på bättre* for want of s.th. better **2** (*underskott*) deficit, shortage

brist|a *brast brustit* **1** (*sprängas*) burst; (*gå av, gå sönder*) break, snap; (*ge vika*) give way; (*rämna*) split; ~ *i gråt* burst into tears; ~ *i sömmarna* burst at the seams; ~ *ut i skratt* burst out laughing; *brusten blick* shattered glance; *brusten blindtarm* perforated appendix; *brustna illusioner* shattered illusions; *det varken bär eller -er* the ice holds but won't carry; *det var som om hjärtat ville* ~ my heart was ready to break; *hennes tålamod brast* her patience gave way; *det må bära eller* ~ sink or swim **2** (*vara otillräcklig*) fall short, be lacking (wanting) (*i* in); ~ *i lydnad* be wanting in obedience

bristande *a4* (*otillräcklig*) deficient, inadequate, insufficient; (*bristfällig*) defective; ~ *betalning* default, nonpayment; ~ *kunskaper* inadequate knowledge; (*bristfällig*) disobedience; ~ *uppmärksamhet* inattention; *på grund av* ~ *bevis* in default of (for lack of) evidence

bristfällig *al* defective, imperfect, faulty **-het** defectiveness, imperfectness, imperfection, faultiness

brist|ning burst[ing], break[ing]; *med.* rupture **-ningsgräns** breaking-limit, breaking-point; *fylld till* ~*en* filled to the limit of its capacity, (*friare*) full to overflowing

brist|situation [state of] shortage **-sjukdom** deficiency disease

britanniametall [-'tannia-] Britannia metal **Britannien** [-'tann-] *n* Britain **britannisk** [-'tann-] *a5* Britannic

brits *s2* bunk

britt *s3* Briton; (*i sht AE.*) Britisher; ~*erna* the British **-isk** ['britt-] *a5* British; *B*~*a öarna* the British Isles

brittsommar Indian summer

bro *s2* bridge; *slå en* ~ *över* bridge, throw a bridge across **-avgift** bridge toll **-byggare** bridge-builder **-byggnad** bridge construction

broccoli ['brɔkːɔli] *s2* broccoli

brock *se* bråck

brockfågel [-å-] plover; (*ljungpipare*) golden plover

1 brodd [-å-] *s2, bot.* sprout, shoot

2 brodd [-å-] *s2,* (*järnpigg*) spike; (*i hästsko*) calk [in] **brodda** calk

broder *-n bröder, se* bror

brodera embroider

broderfolk sister nation

brodergarn [-ˣde:r-] embroidery thread

broderi embroidery

broder|lig *al* brotherly, fraternal **-mord, -mördare** fratricide **-skap** *s7* brotherhood, fraternity

broderskärlek brotherly love

brod|yr *s3* embroidered edging **-ös** embroiderer

bro|fäste [bridge] abutment **-förbindelse** connecting bridge **-huvud** bridgehead

broiler ['brɔi-] *s2, s9* broiler

brokad *s3* brocade

brokig *al* motley, multicoloured; variegated; (*grann*) gaudy, gay; *bildl. äv.* miscellaneous; ~ *samling* motley crowd **-het** variegation; diversity

brom [-å-] *s3* bromine **-id** *s3* bromide

1 broms [-å-] *s2, zool.* gadfly

2 broms [-å-] *s2, tekn.* brake; *bildl.* check

broms|a [-å-] brake; *bildl.* [put a] check [on] **-anordning** brake mechanism **-are** *järnv., AE.* brakeman **-back** brake shoe **-band** brake band **-belägg** brake lining **-fallskärm** brake parachute **-kloss** *se* -back **-ledning** brake line **-ljus** brake light, stoplight **-ning** braking **-olja** *se* -vätska **-pedal** brake pedal **-prov** brake test **-raket** retrorocket **-rör** *se* -ledning **-skiva** [brake] disc **-sko** drag, skid **-spår** skid mark **-sträcka** braking distance **-system** brake system **-trumma** brake drum **-vagn** *järnv.* brake van; *AE.* caboose **-vätska** brake fluid

bronker ['brɔŋker] *pl* bronchi (*sg* bronchus) **-jt** *s3* bronchitis

brons [-å-] *s3* bronze **-era** bronze **-medalj, -märke** bronze medal **-staty** bronze statue **-åldern** the Bronze Age

bropelare pier; pillar; tower; (*för hängbro*) pylon

bror *brodern bröder* brother; (*bibl. o. poet. pl ibl.* brethren); *Bröderna Grimm* the Brothers Grimm; *Bröderna A.* (*firma*) A. Brothers (*förk.* Bros.); *Bäste Bror* (*i brev*) Dear (My dear) (James *etc.*); *vara* [*du och*] ~ *med ngn* (*ung.*) be on familiar terms with s.b.

brors|barn brother's child **-dotter** niece

brorskål *dricka* ~ (*ung.*) drink to the use of Christian names

brorslott lion's share

brorson nephew
broräcke bridge railing (parapet)
brosch [-å:-] *s3* brooch; breastpin
broschyr [-å-] *s3* brochure, booklet, pamphlet, folder
brosk [-å-] *s7*, *anat.* cartilage; (*särsk. i kött*) gristle **-artad** *a5* cartilaginous; gristly **-fisk** cartilaginous fish
bro|slagning bridging **-spann** span of a bridge
brotsch [bråttʃ] *s2* reamer **-a** ream **-ning** reaming
brott [-å-] *s7* **1** (*brytande*) break, fracture; (*på rör äv.*) burst; leak; (*brutet ställe*) breach, break[age]; (*ben-*) fracture; (*sten-*) quarry; (*yta äv.*) fracture, break **2** (*straffbar gärning*) crime; (*mindre svårt*) offence; (*förseelse*) breach, infringement, violation; *begå ett* ~ commit a crime; *ett* ~ *mot reglerna* a violation of the rules (regulations)
brottanvisning *tekn.* stress raiser
brott|are [-å-] wrestler **-as** *dep* wrestle; grapple
brott|hållfasthet tensile strength **-mål** criminal case **-målsdomstol** criminal court
brottning [-å-] wrestling; (*friare äv.*) struggle
brottningsmatch wrestling match
brotts|balk criminal code (law) **-förebyggande** *a4*, ~ *rådet* [the Swedish] national council for crime prevention; ~ *åtgärder* crime-prevention measures
brottsjö breaker; heavy sea
brottslig [-å-] *al* criminal; (*skyldig t. brott*) guilty **-het** crime, criminality; guilt
brottsling [-å-] criminal; (*gärningsman*) culprit
brottsplats scene of [the] crime, venue **-undersökning** scene of crime investigation; on-the--spot crime investigation
brott|stycke fragment **-ställe** fracture **-yta** [area of] fracture
bro|valv bridge-arch **-öppning** (*om klaffbro*) raising of a bridge
brr *interj* brrh!, ugh!
brud *s2* **1** bride; *hemföra ngn som* [*sin*] ~ bring home one's bride; *stå* ~ be married **2** *sl.* (*flicka*) bird, chick; *AE.* broad; *en snygg* ~ a smasher **-bröd** *bot.* dropwort **-bukett** bridal bouquet **-följe** bridal train **-gum** *s2* bridegroom **-klänning** wedding dress **-krona** bridal crown **-näbb** (*flicka*) bridesmaid; (*pojke*) page **-par** bridal couple, bride and bridegroom; ~*et A.* (*i telegram*) Mr. and Mrs. A- **-rov** bride abduction **-slöja** bridal veil **-sporre** *bot.* fragrant gymnadenia **-stol** *gå* (*träda*) *i* ~ get married **-säng** marriage bed; *träda i* ~ enter into marriage **-tärna** bridesmaid
brugd *s3*, *zool.* basking shark
bruk *s7* **1** (*användning*) use, employment, usage; *för eget* ~ for personal (one's own) use; *ha* ~ *för* find a use for; *inte ha* ~ *för* have no use for; *komma i* ~ come into use; *komma ur* ~ fall into disuse, go out of use; *ta i* ~ begin using; *till utvärtes* ~ for external application (use) only; *vara i* ~ be used; *vid sina sinnens fulla* ~ in one's right mind **2** (*sed*) custom, usage, practice; ~*et att röka tobak* the habit (practice) of smoking tobacco; *seder och* ~ usages and customs **3** (*odling*) cultivation **4** (*fabrik*) factory, mill; works (*sg o. pl*) **5** (*mur-*) mortar; (*puts-*) grout, plaster

bruka 1 (*begagna*) use, make use of, employ; *han* ~*r sprit* he will take a drink [occasionally]; ~ *våld* use force **2** (*odla*) cultivate, till; (*gård*) farm **3** (*ha för vana*) be in the habit of; (*ofta omskrivning med adv såsom*) generally, usually; *jag* ~*r äta lunch kl. 12* I usually have lunch at twelve o'clock; (*endast i imperf.*) ~*de* used to **4** (*kunna, pres. o. imperf.*) will, would; *han* ~*de sitta i timmar utan att göra någonting* he would sit for hours doing nothing
brukas *dep, det* ~ *inte* it is not customary (the fashion)
brukbar [-u:-] *al* useful, fit for use; *i* ~*t skick* in working order, in serviceable condition; *försätta ur* ~*t skick* make useless, disable **-het** usefulness, fitness for use, serviceability, serviceableness
bruk|lig [-u:-] *al* customary, usual **-ning** tillage
bruks|anvisning directions for use (*pl*) **-artikel** utility article **-disponent** managing director, mill (works) manager **-föremål** *se -artikel* **-patron** *se -ägare* **-samhälle** industrial community **-vara** utility product **-värde** utility value **-ägare** foundry proprietor, mill owner
brulépudding *se brylépudding*
brum|björn [ˣbrumm-] *bildl.* growler, grumbler **-ma** growl; (*om insekt*) hum, buzz, drone **-ning** growl[ing], hum[ming], buzz[ing]
brun *al* brown; (*läderfärgad*) tan; ~ *bönor* (*maträtt*) brown beans **-aktig** *al* brownish, browny **-alger** *pl* brown algae **-and** pochard **-björn** brown bear **-bränd** *a5* singed, scorched; (*av solen*) bronzed, tanned
brunett *s3* brunette
brun|grön brownish green **-hyad** *a5* brown-complexioned **-hyllt** *a4* swarthy; tanned **-kol** lignite, brown coal
brunn *s2* well; (*hälso-*) [mineral] spring, spa
brunnen *a5* burnt; ~ *gödsel* decomposed manure; *jfr brinna* **brunnit** *sup. av brinna*
brunns|borrning well boring (drilling) **-gäst** health spa visitor **-kur** water cure **-ort** health resort, spa **-vatten** well-water
brunst *s3* (*honas*) heat; (*hanes*) rut **-ig** *al* in heat; ruttish **-tid** oestrus; heat
brunt [-u:-] *s, best. form det bruna* brown
brunte *s2* dobbin
brunögd *a5* brown-eyed
brus *s7* roar[ing]; (*vindens*) sough[ing]; (*vattnets äv.*) rush[ing], surge; *mus.* swell[ing]; *tekn.* noise
brus|a roar; sough; swell; *det* ~*r i mina öron* there's a buzzing in my ears; *det* ~*nde livet* (*ung.*) the hustle [and excitement] of life; ~ *upp* (*bildl.*) flare up, get into a heat; ~ *ut* (*bildl.*) fly out **-hane** ruff; (*hona*) reeve **-huvud** hotspur, hot-head
brusning [-u:-] *se brus*
brustablett effervescent tablet
brusten *a5*, *se brista* **brustit** *sup. av brista*
brutal *al* brutal **-isera** brutalize **-itet** *s3* brutality
brut|en *a5* broken; *en* ~ *man* a broken man; *-et tak* curb roof; mansard [roof]; *AE.* gambrel [roof]; *jfr bryta* **-it** *sup. av bryta*
brutto *s6* gross; ~ *för netto* gross for net **-belopp** gross amount **-inkomst** gross income **-nationalprodukt** gross national product (*förk.* GNP) **-pris** gross price **-prissättning** resale

price maintenance **-registerton, -ton** gross register ton **-vikt** gross weigh **-vinst** gross profit

bry *v4* **1** ~ *sin hjärna* (*sitt huvud*) puzzle one's head (*med* over; *med att* over + *ing-form*), cudgel (rack) one's brains (*med att* to + *inf.*) **2** ~ *ngn för ngn* (*ngt*) tease s.b. about s.b. (s.th.) **3** ~ *sig om* (*bekymra sig*) mind, (*tycka om*) care; ~ *dig inte om det* don't bother about it; *det är ingenting att ~ sig om* that's nothing to worry about; *vad ~r jag mig om det?* what do I care?; *jag ~r mig inte ett dugg om det* I don't care a hang about it; ~ *dig inte om vad han säger* take no notice of what he says; *hon ~r sig inte om honom* she gives him the cold shoulder, she cold-shoulders him

brydd *a1* puzzled (*för* about); embarrassed; confused; abashed

bryd|eri perplexity; embarrassment; *vara i ~ hur man skall göra* be puzzled what to do; *försätta ngn i ~* put s.b. in a quandary; *råka i ~* get embarrassed; *i ~ för pengar* hard up for money **-sam** *a1* awkward; embarrassing; perplexing

brygd *s3, abstr.* brewing; *konkr.* brew

1 brygga *s1* bridge; (*tilläggsplats*) landing stage; (*lastkaj*) wharf; *tandläk.* bridge[work]

2 brygga *v2* brew; (*kaffe*) percolate, make

brygg|are brewer **-arhäst** drayhorse **-eri** brewery **-erijäst** brewer's yeast **-hus** brewing-house; (*tvättstuga*) wash-house **-kaffe** drip-coffee, percolator coffee **-kar** brewer's vat **-mal|en** *-et kaffe* fine-ground coffee

brylépudding caramel custard

brylling third cousin

bryn *s7* edge, verge, fringe

1 bryn|a *v3* (*göra brun*) brown; *kokk.* brown, fry; *-t av solen* tanned

2 bryna *v3* (*vässa*) whet, sharpen

bryne *s6* whetstone

1 bryning browning *etc.*, *jfr 1 bryna*

2 bryning whetting *etc.*, *jfr 2 bryna*

brynja *s1* [coat of] mail, hauberk

brynsten whetstone

bryo|log bryologist **-logi** *s3* bryology

brysk *a1* brusque, curt

Bryssel ['bryssel] *n* Brussels

bryssel|kål Brussels sprout **-matta** Brussels carpet **-spets** Brussels lace

bryta *bröt brutit* **1** (*av-, komma att brista*) break; (*elektrisk ström*) break, switch off; (*malm o.d.*) mine, dig for; (*sten*) quarry; (*färg, smak*) modify, vary; (*ljusstråle*) refract; (*brev*) open; (*sigill*) break open; (*servett*) fold; (*telefonsamtal o.d.*) cut off, disconnect, interrupt; (*förlovning*) break [off]; ~ *en blockad* run a blockade; ~ *kön* (*vard.*) jump the queue **2** (*om vågor*) break; (*avtal, lag o.d. äv.*) infringe, violate, offend; (*begå brott*) offend (*mot* against); ~ *med ngn* break with s.b.; ~ *med en vana* give up a habit; ~ *mot lagen* infringe (violate, break) the law; ~ *på tyska* speak with a German accent **3** (*med betonad partikel*) ~ *av* break [off]; ~ *av mot* be in contrast to (with); ~ *fram* break out, (*om tand o.d.*) break through; ~ *in* (*om årstid, natt*) set in; ~ *in i ett land* invade a country; ~ *lös* break loose; *stormen bryter lös*[*t*] the storm breaks; ~ *samman* break down, collapse; ~ *upp* break up, make a move; *mil.* decamp; ~ *upp en dörr* (*ett lås*) break open (force)

a door (lock); ~ *ut* break out **4** *rfl* break; (*om ljuset*) be refracted; (*om meningar*) diverge

bryt|arspets contact-breaker point **-böna** French (dwarf, kidney) bean, haricot

brytning [-y:-] breaking *etc.*; (*av kol etc.*) mining; (*av sten*) quarrying; (*ljusets*) refraction; (*i uttal*) accent; *kokk.* relish; *bildl.* breach, break; (*åsikters*) divergence

brytnings|index refractive index **-tid** [period of] transition **-vinkel** [angle of] refraction **-ålder, -år** time of maturity; (*pubertet*) puberty, pubescence

brytärt pea

bräck *s7, med.* hernia, rupture **-band** truss

bråd *a1* hasty; sudden; (*om tid*) busy; *en ~ tid* a busy time; *ond, ~ död* violent and sudden death **-djup I** *s7* precipice **II** *a5* precipitous; *här är det ~t* it gets deep suddenly here **-mogen** *bildl.* precocious **-rasket** *i ~* all at once; *inte i ~* not at the drop of a hat, none too quickly

brådsk|a [×bråsska] **I** *s1* hurry; haste; *det är ingen ~* there is no hurry; *vi har ingen ~* we needn't hurry; *hon gör sig ingen ~* she takes her time, she is in no hurry (*med* about) **II** *v1* (*om pers.*) hurry; (*om sak*) be urgent; *det ~r inte med betalningen* there is no hurry about paying **-ande** *a4* urgent, pressing; hasty; *ett ~ arbete* a rush job

brådstörtad *a5* precipitate; headlong

1 bråk *s7, mat.* fraction; *allmänt ~* simple (common, vulgar) fraction; *egentligt* (*oegentligt*) ~ proper (improper) fraction

2 bråk *s7* **1** (*buller*) noise, disturbance, clamour; (*gräl*) row; (*oro*) fuss **2** (*besvär*) trouble, bother, difficulty; *ställa till ~* stir up trouble, make a [great] fuss (*för, om* about)

1 bråka 1 (*stoja*) be noisy (boisterous); (*ställa t. uppträde*) make a disturbance; (*kritisera*) crab, carp, nag **2** (*krångla*) make difficulties **3** *se bry 1*

2 bråka (*lin*) break, bruise

bråkdel fraction[al part]

bråkig *a1* (*bullersam*) noisy; (*stojande*) boisterous; (*oregerlig*) disorderly; (*om barn*) fidgety, restless; (*besvärlig*) troublesome, fussy; (*grälsjuk*) quarrelsome, cantankerous, contentious **-het** noisiness *etc.*

bråk|makare *s9, -stake* *s2* troublemaker; noisy person; (*orostiftare*) disturber of the peace

bråkstreck solidus (*pl* solidi), diagonal, separatrix (*pl* separatrices), shilling mark, stroke

brånad *s3* lust

brås *v4, dep,* ~ *på* take after

bråte *s2* **1** (*skräp*) rubbish, lumber **2** (*timmer-*) log jam

brått *n av bråd o. adv,* **bråttom** [×bråttåmm *el.* 'brått-] *adv, ha ~* be in a hurry (*med* for; *med att* to + *inf*); *det är mycket ~* it is very urgent, there is no time to lose; *det är ~ med leveransen* the delivery is urgent

1 bräcka *s1* flaw, crack, breach **II** *v3* **1** break, crack; (*övertrumfa*) outdo, surpass, trump; ~ *till* (*av*) snub, flatten **2** (*gry*) break

2 bräcka *v3, kokk.* fry

bräck|age [-'a:ʃ] *s7* breakage **-järn** crowbar

bräckkorv smoked sausage for frying

bräcklig *a1* fragile, brittle; (*om pers.*) frail, puny **-het** fragility, brittleness; frailness, puniness

bräckt *a4*, ~ *vatten* brackish water
bräda I *s1, se* **bräde II** *v1* (*slå ut rival*) cut out, supplant
brädd *s2* edge, brim; brink; *fylla ett glas till* ~*en* fill a glass to the brim; *floden stiger över sina* ~*ar* the river overflows [its banks]; *stå på gravens* ~ be on the brink of the grave, have one foot in the grave **bräddad** *a5*, **bräddfull** *a5* brimming, brimful
bräd|e *s7, s6* **1** board; *hyvlade* ~*r* planed boards, floorings; *slå ur* ~*t* cut out; *sätta allt på ett* ~ put all one's eggs in one basket **2** *se -spel* **-fodra** cover with boards, board, wainscot **-fodring** [-o:-] boarding, wainscot[t]ing **-golv** board[ed] floor **-gård** timberyard; *AE.* lumberyard **-skjul** wooden shed **-spel** backgammon **-stapel** pile of boards
bräk|a *v3* bleat, baa; *bildl.* bray **-ande** *a4* bleating *etc.*
bräken ['brä:-] *s2, bot.* bracken **-växt** fern
bräm *s4* **1** border, edging, edge; (*päls-*) fur trimming **2** *bot.* limb
bränna *v2* **1** burn; (*sveda*) scorch, singe; parch; (*rosta*) calcine; (*tegel*) bake; (*keramik*) fire; (*lik, värdepapper*) cremate; (*i bollspel*) hit out; ~ *hål på* burn a hole in (on); ~ *sina skepp* burn one's boats (bridges); ~ *sitt ljus i båda ändar* burn the candle at both ends; *brända mandlar* burnt almonds; *bränd lera* fired clay; *bränt barn skyr elden* a burnt child dreads the fire; ~ *av ett fyrverkeri* let off fireworks; ~ *upp* burn; ~ *vid* burn **2** (*smärta*) burn **3** *rfl* burn (*på vatten, ånga*: scald) *o.s.*; (*på nässlor*) get stung; ~ *sig på tungan* burn one's tongue; ~ *fingrarna* burn one's fingers (*äv. bildl.*)
brännande *a4* burning; (*om hetta*) scorching; (*om smärta*) lancinating, sharp; (*om törst*) parching, consuming; (*frätande*) caustic; *bildl.* burning, ardent, intense; (*fråga*) crucial, urgent, vital, burning **brännare** burner **brännas** *v2, dep* burn; *det bränns!* (*i lek*) you are getting warm!; *nässlor bränns* nettles sting
bränn|bar *a1* [in]flammable, combustible; *bildl.* risky, controversial, touchy **-blåsa** blister [from a burn] **-boll** *ung.* rounders (*pl*)
bränneri distillery
bränn|glas burning glass **-het** *a1* burning hot, scorching
1 bränning burning; (*av lik*) cremation
2 bränning (*våg*) breaker, surf
bränn|manet giant jellyfish **-märka** brand; *bildl. äv.* stigmatize **-märke** brand; *bildl. äv.* stigma **-nässla** (*hopskr. brännässla*) stinging nettle **-offer** burnt offering **-olja** fuel oil **-punkt** focus; focal point, principal focus **-skada, -sår** burn; ~ *av första (andra, tredje) graden* first-degree (second-degree, third-degree) burn **-tid** combustion time **-ugn** furnace, kiln **-vidd** focal length (distance) **-vin** *ung.* Scandinavian vodka; schnap[p]s
brännvins|advokat pettifogger **-bränneri** distillery **-glas** dram glass; shot
bränsle *s6* fuel; *fasta och flytande* ~*n* solid and liquid fuels **-behållare** fuel tank **-besparande** *a4* fuel-saving **-cell** fuel cell **-element** (*för kärnreaktor*) fuel element **-flis** fuel chips (*pl*) **-för-**

brukning fuel consumption **-insprutning** fuel injection **-mätare** fuel gauge **-påfyllning** fill-up, refuelling **-snål** fuel-saving **-tank** *se -behållare* **-tillförsel** (*i motor*) fuel feed **-tillägg** heating surcharge **-upparbetning** (*i kärnteknik*) fuel reprocessing
bräsch [-ä(:)-] *s3* breach; *gå* (*ställa sig*) *i* ~*en för* take up the cudgels for; *skjuta en* ~ breach, batter
bräsera braise
bräss *s2, anat.* thymus; *kokk.* sweetbread
brätte *s6* brim
bröa sprinkle with crumbs
bröd *s7* bread; *franskt* ~ (*långt*) French bread, (*litet*) roll; *hårt* ~ crispbread; *rostat* ~ toast; *förtjäna sitt* ~ earn one's living; *den enes* ~, *den andres död* one man's loss is another man's gain; *ta* ~*et ur munnen på ngn* take the bread out of a p.'s mouth **-bit** piece of bread; *jfr brödskiva* **-butik** bakery, baker's [shop] **-fat** bread dish (plate) **-frukt** breadfruit **-fruktträd** breadfruit [tree] **-föda** bread; *slita för* ~*n* struggle to make a living **-kaka** round loaf **-kant** crust [of bread] **-kavel** rolling pin **-korg** breadbasket **-lös** *bättre* ~ *än rådlös* better breadless than witless
brödra|folk [-ö:-] sister nations **-skap** *s7* brotherhood, fraternity, fellowship
bröd|rost *s2* toaster **-skiva** slice of bread **-skrin** breadbin, breadbox **-smula** crumb **-spade** peel **-stil** *boktr.* body (text) type **-säd** cereals (*pl*); (*spannmål*) corn, grain
bröllop [-åpp] *s7* wedding; *boktr.* (*dubbelsättning*) double[t]
bröllops|dag wedding day; (*årsdag*) wedding anniversary **-gåva** wedding present **-marsch** wedding (bridal) march **-middag** wedding feast (dinner, *i Storbritannien vanl.* breakfast) **-natt** wedding night **-resa** wedding trip, honeymoon **-tårta** *ung.* wedding cake **-vittne** marriage witness
bröst *s7* breast; (*-korg*) chest; (*barm*) bosom; *kokk.* breast, (*av fågel*) white meat; *ha klent* ~ have a weak chest; *ha ont i* ~*et* have a pain in one's chest; *förkylningen sitter i* ~*et* I (*etc.*) have a cold on my chest; *ge ett barn* ~*et* give a baby the breast; *kom till mitt* ~*!* come into my arms!; *slå sig för* ~*et* beat one's breast
brösta ~ *av* (*mil.*) unlimber; ~ *sig över* glory in, boast of (about)
bröst|arvinge direct heir, heir of the body, issue (*sg o. pl*) **-barn** breast-fed baby **-ben** breastbone; *anat.* sternum **-bild** half-length [portrait] **-böld** mammary abscess **-cancer** cancer of the breast, mammary cancer **-droppar** *pl* cough mixture (*sg*) **-fena** pectoral fin **-ficka** breastpocket **-gänges** [-jäŋes] *gå* ~ *till väga* act highhandedly, go at it full tilt **-håla** cavity of the chest, thoracic cavity **-hållare** brassiere, bra **-höjd** breast height **-karamell** cough drop **-korg** chest, thorax **-körtel** mammary gland **-ning** *byggn.* breast [wall] **-sim** breaststroke **-sjuk** consumptive **-sjukdom** lung disease, chest disease **-socker** sugar (rock) candy **-ton** chest voice (register); *ta till* ~*erna* beat the drum, speechify, spout **-vidd** chest measurement **-vårta** nipple, teat, mamilla **-värn** breastwork, parapet

1 bröt *s2* log jam

2 bröt *imperf. av bryta*

B-skatt business profit tax **B-språk** *skol.* second foreign language

bu *interj*, **bua** *v1* boo

bubbelkammare bubble chamber

bubbla *s1 o. v1* bubble

buckanjär *s3* buccaneer

buckl|a I *s1* **1** (*upphöjning*) boss, knob **2** (*inbuktning*) dent, dint; (*på bil*) bodywork damage **II** *v1* buckle; ~ *till* dent; batter **-ig** *a1* **1** embossed **2** dented

bud *s7* **1** (*befallning*) command, order; *tio Guds* ~ the Ten Commandments; *hederns* ~ the dictates of honour; *det är hårda* ~ that's a tall order **2** (*an-*) offer; (*på auktion*) bid; *kortsp.* call, bid; *ett* ~ *på 5 pund* an offer of 5 pounds; *vara många om* ~*et* be many bidders **3** (*underrättelse*) message; *skicka* ~ *efter* send for; *skicka* ~ *att* send word to say that; *få* ~ *om ngt* receive message about s.th. **4** (*-bärare*) messenger **5** *stå till* ~*s* be available (at hand); *med alla till* ~*s stående medel* with all available means

bud|a summon, call in, send for **-bärare** messenger

budd|ism Buddhism **-ist** *s3*, **-istisk** [-'diss-] *a5* Buddhist

budget ['buddjet] *s3, s2* budget; *balanserad* ~ balanced budget; *göra upp en* ~ budget, prepare (draw up) a budget **-chef** (*i finansdepartementet*) budget director **-era** *v1* budget **-ering** budgeting **-förslag, -proposition** budget [proposals *pl*] **-år** financial (*AE.* fiscal) year

budgivning [-ji:-] *kortsp.* bidding

budkavle *hist.* (*i Skottland*) fiery cross; ~*n går!* the fiery cross is out! **-tävling** *sport.* relay race

budning [ˣbu:d-] **1** summoning *etc.*, *se buda* **2** (*om tömning av latrinkärl*) notice to nightmen

budoar [budɔ'a:r] *s3* boudoir

bud|ord commandment **-skap** *s7* message, announcement; address **-skickning** [-ʃ-] messenger service

buffé *s3, se byffé*

buffel ['buff-] *s2* buffalo; *bildl.* boor, lout, churl **-aktig** *a1, bildl.* boorish, loutish, churlish **-hjord** buffalo herd **-hud** buffalo hide

buffert ['buff-] *s2* buffer **-lager** buffer stock **-stat** buffer state **-zon** buffer zone

bug|a ~ [*sig*] bow (*för to*) **-ning** [-u:-] bow

buk *s2* belly; *neds.* paunch; *anat.* abdomen

Bukarest ['bu:-] *n* Bucharest

bukett *s3* bouquet; (*mindre*) nosegay, posy; bunch (*äv. bildl.*)

buk|fena pelvic (ventral) fin **-fylla, -fyllnad** filling food **-hinna** peritoneum **-hinneinflammation** peritonitis **-håla** abdominal cavity

bukig *a1* bulging, bulged

bukland|a belly land **-ning** belly landing

bukolisk [-'kå-] *a5* bucolic

bukspott pancreatic juice **-körtel** pancreas

bukt *s3* **1** (*böjning*) bend, winding, turn **2** (*större vik*) bay, gulf; (*mindre*) cove, creek **3** (*slinga på tross e.d.*) bight, fake, coil **4** *få* ~ *med* (*på*) manage, master **bukta** *rfl* bend, curve, wind; ~ *sig utåt* bulge

buktalare ventriloquist

bukt|ig *a1* bending, curving, winding **-ning** bend, curve, turn, winding

bula *s1* bump, lump, swelling

bulb *s3* bulb **-är** *a1* bulbous, bulbaceous

bulevard *se boulevard*

bulgar *s3* Bulgarian **Bulgarien** [-'ga:-] *n* Bulgaria **bulgarisk** [-'ga:-] *a5* Bulgarian

bulimi *s3, med.* bulimia

buljong [-'jåŋ] *s3* bouillon, clear soup, meat broth (stock); (*för sjuka*) beef tea **-tärning** meat extract cube

bulk *s2* bulk **-last** bulk cargo

1 bulla *s1* (*påvlig*) bull

2 bulla *v1*, ~ *upp* make a spread

bull|dogg [-å-] *s2* bulldog **-dozer** *s9* bulldozer

bull|e *s2* bun, roll; *nu ska ni få se på andra* -*ar* you'll be seeing some changes around here

buller ['bull-] *s7* noise, sound, row, din; racket, clamour; (*dovt*) rumbling; *med* ~ *och bång* with a great hullabaloo **-bekämpning** noise [nuisance] control **-matta** noise strip **-mätning** noise measurement **-nivå** noise level **-sam** *a1* noisy **-skada** injury caused by noise **-skadad** suffering from noise-induced hearing impairment (loss) **-skydd** noise (sound) protection

bulletin *s3* bulletin

bullr|a make a noise; (*mullra*) rumble; (*dåna*) roar, thunder **-ande** *a4* noisy, boisterous **-ig** *a1* noisy

buln|a [ˣbu:l-] fester; gather **-ad** *s3* swelling; (*böld*) boil, furuncle

bult *s2* bolt; (*gängad äv.*) screw

bult|a **1** (*kött*) pound; beat; *med* ~*nde hjärta* with a pounding (palpitating) heart **2** (*knacka*) knock (*i, på* on, at); (*om puls*) throb; (*dunka*) thump; *det* ~*de på dörren* there was a knock at the door **-ning** pound, pounding; knock, knocking

bulvan *s3* decoy; *bildl. äv.* dummy; *köp genom* ~ acquisition via ostensible buyer

bumerang boomerang

bums right away, instantly, on the spot

bunden *a5* bound (*äv. om bok*); *bildl.* tied, fettered; (*fästad*) attached (*vid* to); ~ *aktie* restricted share; *bundet lån* fixed-term loan; ~ *stil* poetry; *bundet värme* latent heat **-het** confinement; (*stelhet*) constraint, stiffness

bundit *sup. av binda*

bundsförvant ally; confederate

bunke *s2* bowl; dish; (*av metall*) pan

bunker ['bunn-] *s2* **1** *sjö.* bunker **2** *mil.* concrete dugout, pillbox **3** bunker, (*särsk. AE.*) sand trap **bunkerkol** bunker coal **bunkra** bunker

bunsenbrännare Bunsen burner

bunt *s2* bundle, pack, truss; (*papper, hö*) sheaf; *hela* ~*en* the whole bunch (lot) **bunta** ~ [*ihop*] make up into bundles (packs)

buntmakare furrier

buntvis in bundles (packs)

bur *s2* cage; (*emballage*) crate; (*för transport av smådjur, höns-*) coop; (*fotbollsmål o.d.*) goal; (*vard. finka*) clink, cooler, jug, nick, stir; *känna sig som en fågel i* ~ feel cooped up (in) **bura** ~ *in* lock up

burdus I *adv* abruptly, slapdash **II** *a1* abrupt; *bildl.* blunt, bluff

burfågel cagebird, cageling

burgen [-j-] *a3* well-to-do, affluent; *han är en ~ man* he is very well-off (well-to-do) **-het** affluence

Burgund *n* Burgundy **burgunder** [-'gunn-] *s9*, **burgundisk** [-'gunn-] *a5* Burgundian

burit *sup. av bära*

burk *s2* pot; (*sylt-*) jar; (*bleck-*) tin, *AE.* can; (*apoteks-*) gallipot; *på ~* tinned, *AE.* canned **-mat** tinned (*AE.* canned) food **-öl** canned beer **-öppnare** tin (*AE.* can) opener

burlesk *a1 o. s3* burlesque, burlesk

Burma *n* Burma **burman** *s3* Burmese **burmansk** [-'ma:nsk] *a5* Burmese, Burman

burmes *s3, se burman* **-isk** *a5, se burmansk*

burnus *s2, s3* burnoose, burnous[e]

1 burr *se brr*

2 burr *s7* (*om hår*) frizz[le]

burra *~ upp* ruffle up; *fågeln ~de upp sig* the bird ruffled up its feathers **burrig** *a1* frizz[l]y, frizzled

burskap [*bu:r-] *s7* **1** *hist.* burghership **2** *vinna ~* be adopted (*i* into), become established, (*friare*) gain ground

burspråk [*bu:r-] *s7* oriel; (*utbyggt fönster*) bay window

bus *leva ~* make a nuisance of o.s., (*skämts.*) make mischief, be noisy **busa** make trouble; be noisy **busaktig** *a1* rowdy; mischievous, noisy

buschman Bushman

bus|e *s2* **1** *barnspr.* bogeyman, bogyman **2** (*ruskig karl*) ruffian, rowdy **-fasoner** *pl* rowdy behaviour (*sg*) **-frö** ragamuffin **-ig** *a1, se busaktig*

buskablyg bashful, timid

buskage [-'ka:ʃ] *s7* shrubbery; thicket; copse, coppice **buske** *s2* bush; (*liten, risig*) scrub; (*större*) shrub; *sticka huvudet i ~en* bury one's head in the sand **buskig** *a1* bushy; shrubby

buskis ['buss-] *s2, vard.* ham acting

busk|skvätta *s1* whinchat **-snär** thicket **-teater** *ung.* farcical open-air play

busliv rowdyness, rowdyism

1 buss 1 *s2* (*krigs-*) old campaigner; *~ar* warriors bold; *se äv. sjöbuss* **2** *oböjligt s o. a, vara ~ med ngn* be pals with s.b.

2 buss *s2* (*tugg-*) quid

3 buss *s2* (*fordon*) bus; (*turist-*) coach

4 buss *interj o. adv, ~ på honom!* at him!

bussa *~ hunden på ngn* set the dog on s.b.

bussarong [-'rån] *s3* [sailor's] jumper

buss|chaufför bus driver **-fil** bus lane **-förbindelse** bus connection **-hållplats** bus stop, (*med regnskydd*) bus shelter

bussig *a1* (*förträfflig*) capital; (*hygglig*) kind, good; *hon är en ~ flicka* she is a good sort

buss|konduktör [bus] conductor **-linje** bus service (line)

bussning *tekn.* bush; (*särsk. AE.*) bushing; sleeve

busstation (*särskr. buss-station*) *se bussterminal*

buss|terminal bus terminal; *AE.* depot **-trafik** bus service

bus|unge *vard.* little blighter (rascal, devil); urchin **-vissling** wolf whistle **-väder** foul (squally) weather

butadien *s3, s4* butadiene

butan *s4* butane

butelj *s3* bottle; *tappa på ~er* draw off into bottles, bottle **-axlar** champagne shoulders **-era** bottle **-grön** bottle green **-importerad** bottle imported

butik *s3* shop; *AE.* store; *slå igen* (*stänga*) *~en* shut [up] (close) the shop, (*upphöra med butiken*) shut up shop; *stå i ~* work (serve) in a shop **butiks|biträde** shop assistant; salesman, *fem.* saleswoman; *AE.* [sales]clerk **-centrum** shopping centre (precinct) **-föreståndare** shop manager, shopkeeper **-innehavare** shopkeeper, proprietor **-inredning** shop fittings (*pl*) **-kedja** chain, multiple stores (shops) (*pl*) **-rätta** shoplifter **-snatteri, -stöld** shoplifting

butter ['butt-] *a2* sullen, sulky, morose **-het** sullenness *etc.*

butyl *s3* butyl **-gummi** butyl rubber

buxbom *s2* box; (*träslag*) boxwood

1 by *s2* (*vindstöt*) squall, gust

2 by *s2* (*samhälle*) village; (*mindre*) hamlet

byalag [*by:a-] *s7* village community; (*i modern bet. ung.*) concerned citizens committee

byallmänning land owned in common by a village

byffé *s3* **1** (*för förfriskningar*) buffet, refreshment counter **2** (*skänk*) sideboard

by|fåne village idiot **-gata** village street

bygd *s3* (*nejd*) district, countryside; (*odlad*) settled country; *ute i ~erna* out in the country

bygde|gård community centre **-mål** dialect **-spelman** country fiddler; folk musician

bygel *s2 tekn.* loop, yoke; clamp; (*beslag*) mount [ing]; (*på handväska*) [hand]grip; (*på hänglås*) shackle; (*på sabel*) guard **-häst** (*gymnastikredskap*) pommel horse

bygga *v2* build, construct; (*uppföra*) erect; (*grunda*) base, found; *~ och bo* set up house, reside; *ingenting att ~ på* nothing to build [up]on, not to be relied on; *~ om* rebuild; *~ på* (*om hus*) add [a storey] to, (*öka*) add to, increase, enlarge; *~ till* enlarge; *~ upp* build up, erect

bygg|ande *s6* building; construction, erection **-branschen** the building trade

bygg|e *s6* building, construction **-element** building unit **-herre** commissioner of a building project; future owner **-kloss** brick, building block **-kostnader** *pl* building (construction) costs **-lekplats** adventure playground **-låda** box of bricks **-mästare** building contractor, builder

byggnad *s3* **1** *se byggande* **2** (*bildning, konstruktion*) construction, structure **3** (*hus*) building, edifice

byggnads|arbetare building worker **-entreprenör** building contractor **-firma** construction firm **-förbud** building ban **-komplex** block **-konst** structural engineering, architecture **-kreditiv** building credit (loan) **-lov** building permit **-lån** building loan **-material** building (construction) materials (*pl*) **-nämnd** local housing (building) committee **-reglering** building control **-stadga** building bylaws (*pl*) **-stil** architectural style **-styrelse** *~n* [the Swedish] national board of public building **-ställning** scaffold[ing] **-tillstånd** building licence (permit) **-uppvärmning** [domestic] space heating **-verk** structure **-verksamhet** construction (building) [activity]

byggnation construction work
bygg|sats building kit **-stopp** [temporary] prohibition of all building work
byig *a1* squally, gusty; *flyg.* bumpy
byk *s2* wash[ing]; *han har en trasa med i ~en* he has a finger in that pie **byka** *v3* wash
byke *s6* rabble, pack
bykkar [×by:k-] washtub
byling *vard.* cop[per]
bylta ~ *ihop* make into a bundle; ~ *på ngn* muffle s.b. up **bylte** *s6* bundle, pack
byracka *s1, vard.* mongrel, cur
byrętt *s3* buret[te]
1 byrå [×by:- *el.* 'by:-] *s2* (*möbel*) chest of drawers; *AE.* bureau
2 byrå [×by:- *el.* 'by:-] *s3* (*ämbetsverk etc.*) office, department, agency, bureau; division
byrå|assistent senior clerical officer **-chef** head of a division **-direktör** senior administrative officer **-ingenjör** technical officer; *förste ~* higher technical officer **-inspektör** executive officer (inspector, accountant *etc.*); *förste ~* higher executive officer *etc.*
byråkrat bureaucrat; *vard.* red-tapist, bigwig
byråkrat|i *s3* bureaucracy; *vard.* red tape **-isera** bureaucratize **-isering** [-'se:-] bureaucratization **-isk** [-'kra:-] *a5* bureaucratic; *vard.* red tape **-ism** bureaucratism
byrålåda drawer
byråsekreterare administrative officer; *förste ~* higher administrative officer
Bysans ['by:-] *n* Byzantium **bysantįn** *s3*, **bysantinsk** [-'ti:nsk] *a5* Byzantine
byst *s3* bust **-hållare** brassiere, bra
bysätt|a arrest for debt **-ningshäkte** debtor's prison
byta *v3* change; (*utbyta*) exchange; (*vid byteshandel*) barter; trade; (*utväxla*) interchange; *vard.* swap; ~ *buss* (*spårvagn etc.*) transfer; ~ *ord med ngn* bandy words with s.b.; ~ *plats a*) change places (*med ngn* with s.b.) *b*) (*ändra*) move *c*) (*byta tjänst*) get a new post; ~ *av ngn* relieve s.b.; ~ *bort* exchange (*mot* for); ~ *bort sin rock* take s.b. else's coat; ~ *in* (*t.ex. bil*) trade in; ~ *om* change [one's clothes]; ~ *till sig* get by exchange; ~ *ut* exchange (*mot* for)
byte *s6* **1** change, exchange; *förlora på ~t* lose by the exchange; *göra ett gott ~* (*vard.*) make a good swap, gain by the exchange **2** (*rov*) booty, spoils (*pl*); (*rovdjurs o. bildl.*) prey; (*jakt-*) game, quarry
bytes|affär barter transaction **-balans** balance of current payments **-handel** barter, exchange, trade **-rätt** right to exchange
byting tot, toddler, urchin
bytta *s1* firkin; (*smör-*) tub
byx|a [×bycksa] *s1, se byxor* **-bak** *s2* trouser seat **-ben** trouser leg **-dress** trouser suit **-ficka** trouser pocket **-gördel** panty girdle **-kjol** culottes (*pl*), divided skirt **-linning** trouser waistband
byxor [×bycksɔr] *pl* (*lång-*) trousers; *AE.* pants; (*korta*) shorts; (*golf-*) plus fours; (*knä-*) knickerbockers, knickers; (*lediga lång-*) slacks; (*damunder-*) pants, (*långa*) knickers, [under]drawers, (*korta*) panties, briefs
byxångest *vard.* blue funk

1 båda *v1* (*förebåda*) betoken, foreshadow; (*ngt ont*) [fore]bode, portend, presage; *det ~r inte gott* it is a bad omen, it bodes no good; ~ *upp, se uppbåda*
2 båda *pron* (*betonat*) both (*äv.*: ~ *två*); (*obetonat*) the two; *vi ~* we two (both), both of us; *mina ~ bröder* my two brothers; *av ~ könen* of either sex; *i ~ fallen* in both cases, in either case; *för ~s vår skull* for both our sakes; *~s föräldrar* the parents of both of them; *en vän till oss ~* a mutual friend
3 båda *s1, sjö.* shoal
bådadera both
både both; ~ *han och hon* (*äv.*) he as well as she
båg *s7* hoax, confidence trick (*AE.* game), *vard.* con trick; *det är rena ~et* it's all eyewash **båga** bluff, hoax, swindle, hoodwink
båg|e *s2* **1** (*vapen*) bow; *ha flera strängar på sin ~* have several strings to one's bow; *spänna en ~* draw a bow; *spänna ~n för högt* aim too high **2** (*linje*) curve; *mat.* arc **3** *mus.* slur; tie **4** *arkit.* arch **5** (*på glasögon*) frame, rim **6** (*sy-*) frame **-fil** hacksaw **-formig** [-å-] *a1* curved; arched **-fris** arched moulding **-fönster** arched window **-gång** *anat.* semicircular canal **-lampa** arc light (lamp) **-linje** curve, curvature **-ljus** arc light **-minut** minute [of arc] **-sekund** second [of arc]
bågna [×båggna *el.* ×båŋna] bend; sag, bulge
båg|skytt archer **-skytte** archery **-sträng** bowstring
båk *s2* **1** (*sjömärke*) [tower] beacon **2** (*fyrtorn*) lighthouse
1 bål *s2, anat.* trunk, torso; body
2 bål *s2* (*skål*) bowl; (*dryck*) punch
3 bål *s7* (*ved- o.d.*) bonfire; (*lik-*) [funeral] pyre; *brännas på ~* be burnt at the stake
båld [-å:-] *a1* dauntless, bold, doughty
bålgeting hornet
bålrullning (*kroppsövning*) trunk gyration
bålverk *s7* bulwark; *bildl. äv.* safeguard
bångstyrig *a1* refractory, rebellious, unruly; (*om häst, åsna*) stubborn
bår *s2* (*lik-*) bier; (*sjuk-*) stretcher; litter; *ligga på ~* be lying on one's bier **-bärare** (*lik|bår, -kista*) pallbearer; (*sjukbår*) stretcher-bearer
bård [-å:-] *s3* border; (*särsk. på tyg*) edging
bår|hus mortuary, morgue; funeral parlour (*AE.* home) **-täcke** pall
bås *s7* stall, crib, box; (*friare*) compartment, booth
båt *s2* boat; (*fartyg*) ship; (*mindre äv.*) skiff; *sitta i samma ~* (*bildl.*) be in the same boat; *gå i ~arna* take to the boats; *ge ngt på ~en* give s.th. up as a bad job, fling s.th. to the winds; *ge ngn på ~en* throw s.b. over, jilt s.b., *vard.* chuck s.b. [up (in)]
båta *det ~r föga att* it is no use (+ *ing*-form)
båt|ben *anat.* navicular[e] [bone] **-brygga** landing stage **-byggare** boatbuilder **-däck** (*på fartyg*) boat deck **-förbindelse** boat connection **-hus** boathouse **-last** shipload, cargo **-ledes** by boat **-lägenhet** *med första ~* by [the] first [available] ship **-motor** marine engine **-mössa** forage cap
båtnad [-å:-] *s3* advantage; *till ~ för* to the advantage of

båts|hake boathook **-man** boatswain, bosun, bo's'n **-mansstol** boatswain's chair
båtsport|kort yachting chart **-led** yachting course
båtvarv boatyard, boatbuilding yard
bä *interj* baa; bah
bäck *s2* brook, rill, rivulet; *AE.* creek; *många ~ar små gör en stor å* many a little makes a mickle; *det är bättre att stämma i ~en än i ån* a stitch in time saves nine
bäckebölja *s1* (*tyg*) cotton crepe
bäcken ['bäck-] *s7* **1** *anat.* pelvis **2** (*fat*) basin; (*säng-*) bedpan **3** *geol.* basin **4** *mus.* cymbal **-ben** pelvic girdle (arch)
bäckröding brook (speckled) trout
bädd *s2* bed; (*fundament*) foundation; (*maskin-*) bedplate
bädda make a (the, one's) bed; *det är ~t för* (*bildl.*) the ground is prepared for; *som man ~r får man ligga* as you make your bed, so you must lie on it; *~ ner* put to bed; *~ upp* make the (one's) bed
bädd|bar convertible into a bed **-jacka** bed jacket **-ning** bed-making **-soffa** sofa bed; day bed; studio couch
bädeker ['bä:-] *s2* Baedeker
bägare cup, mug; *kyrkl.* chalice
bägge *se 2* **båda**
bälg [-j] *s2* bellows (*pl*); *en ~* a pair of bellows
bälga [-j-] *~ i sig* gulp down **bälgkamera** folding camera
Bält *n, Stora* (*Lilla*) *~* Great (Little) Belt
bält|a *s1,* **-djur** armadillo
bältdäck radial [tyre]
bälte *s6* belt; (*gördel*) girdle; *ett slag under ~t* a blow below the belt **-spännare** *ung.* knife-wrestler
bältros shingles
bända *v2* prise; *AE.* pry (*loss* loose; *upp* open)
bändsel ['bänn-] *s2, sjö.* lashing; seizing
bändsla [ˣbänn-] *sjö.* lash; seize
bängel [ˣbäŋ-] *s2* (*drasut*) great lout; (*slyngel*) rascal
bänk *s2* seat; (*arbets- o. parl.*) bench; (*kyrk-*) pew; (*skol-*) desk; (*lång*) form; bench; *teat.* row; *sport.* bench
bänk|a *rfl* seat o.s. **-kamrat** *vi var ~er* we sat next to one another at school **-rad** row
bänsel *se* **bändsel**
bär *s7* berry; *plocka ~* pick (gather) berries, berry; *lika som ~* as like as two peas [in a pod]
bära *bar burit* **I 1** (*lyfta o. gå med*) carry; (*friare o. bildl.*) bear; (*kläder*) wear; (*stötta*) support; *~ ansvar för* be responsible for; *~ bud om* bring (take, carry) word (a message) about; *~ frukt* (*vittnesbörd*) bear fruit (witness); *~ hand på ngn* use violence on s.b.; *~ huvudet högt* carry one's head high; *~ sina år med heder* carry one's years well; *~ skulden för* be responsible for, be to blame for; *gå och ~ på ngt* have s.th. on one's mind, be suffering under s.th. **2** (*leda, föra*) lead **3** (*om is*) bear; *det må ~ eller brista* sink or swim **4** (*med betonad partikel*) *~ av* (*sjö.*) bear off; *när bär det av?* when are you going (leaving)?; *det bär* [*mig*] *emot* it goes against the grain [for me]; *bär hit böckerna* bring me the books; *han såg vart det*

bar *hän* he saw what it would lead to; *~ på sig* carry about [with] one, have on one; *han bär upp hela föreställningen* he is the backbone of the whole performance; *han kan ~ upp en frack* he can carry off a dress suit, he looks well in tails; *vägen bär uppför* (*utför*) the road goes uphill (downhill); *bär ut det!* take it out! **II** *rfl* **1** *det bar sig inte bättre än att han* as ill-luck would have it he **2** (*löna sig*) pay **3** *~ sig åt* behave; *~ sig illa åt* misbehave; *hur bar du dig åt för att* how did you manage to; *hur jag än bär mig åt* whatever I do
bär|ande *a4* carrying *etc.*; *den ~ tanken* the fundamental idea; *~ vägg* load-bearing wall **-are** bearer; (*stadsbud*) porter, *AE. äv.* redcap; (*av idé*) exponent **-bar** [-ä:-] *a1* portable
bär|buske berrybush **-fis** *s2* stink bug
bärga [-j-] **I 1** (*rädda*) save; (*bil o.d.*) tow; *sjö.* salvage **2** (*skörda*) harvest, reap **3** (*segel*) take in; furl **II** *rfl* **1** (*reda sig*) get along **2** (*behärska sig*) contain o.s.
bärgad [-j-] *a5* well-to-do, well-off
bärg|arlön salvage [money] **-ning 1** (*av bil etc.*) tow; *sjö.* salvage **2** (*av skörd*) harvest **3** (*av segel*) taking-in; furl **4** (*utkomst*) livelihood
bärgnings|bil breakdown van (truck); *AE.* wrecker, tow truck **-fartyg** salvage ship (vessel, boat)
bärig *a1, se* **bärkraftig -het 1** (*lastförmåga*) carrying capacity; (*flytförmåga*) buoyancy **2** (*räntabilitet*) profitability, earning capacity; *tekn.* ultimate bearing resistance
bäring *sjö.* bearing
bärkasse string bag; carrier bag
bärkorg berrybasket
bärkraft *tekn.* bearing capacity; *ekon.* financial strength; (*fartygs*) buoyancy **bärkraftig** strong; *ekon.* economically sound
bärnsten [-ä:-] amber **bärnstenssyra** succinic acid
bärplan *flyg.* aerofoil, plane, wing; *sjö.* hydrofoil
bärplansbåt hydrofoil [vessel]
bärplock|are berry picker **-ning** berry-picking, berry-gathering
bär|raket carrier rocket **-rem** strap **-stol** palanquin, palankeen; (*hist.*) sedan [chair]
bärsärk [ˣbä:r-] *s2* berserk[er]; *gå fram som en ~* go berserk, run amuck (amok)
bärvåg *radio.* carrier [wave]
bäst *superl. t.* **bra, god, väl I** *a* best; *de allra ~a* vänner the best of friends; *de här skorna har sett sina ~a dagar* these shoes are past praying for; *efter ~a förmåga* to the best of one's ability; *i ~a fall* at [the] best; *i ~a mening* in the best sense; *det var i ~a välmening* I (he, she *etc.*) only meant well; *i sina ~ år* in the prime of life; *med de ~a avsikter* with the best of intentions; *med ~a vilja i världen* with the best will in the world; *på ~ möjliga sätt* in the best way possible; *vid första ~a tillfälle* at the earliest opportunity; *det är ~ vi går* we had better go; *hon är ~ i engelska* she is best at English; *hoppas på det ~a* hope for the best; *~e bror!, se* **broder II** *adv* best; *vad tyckte du ~ om?* what did you like best?; *jag höll som ~ på med* I was in the middle of; *det vet jag ~ själv* I know best; *du får klara dig ~ du kan* you must manage as best you can; *du gör ~ i att* it would be

best for you to **III** *konj*, ~ [*som*] just as; ~ *som det var* all at once; ~ *som vi pratade* just as we were talking

bäst|a *s* good, benefit, welfare; *det allmänna* ~ the public good; *tänka på sitt eget* ~ think of one's own good; *få ngt till* ~ have some refreshments; *ta sig för mycket till* ~ take a drop too much; *förste -e* the first that comes; *det kan hända den -e* that (it) can happen to the best of us; *göra sitt* [*allra*] ~ do one's [very] best; *göra det* ~ *möjliga av situationen* make the best of a bad job

bästis ['bästis] *s2, vard.* chum, pal; *AE.* buddy

bättra improve [on]; ~ *på* touch (*vard.* brush) up; revamp; ~ *sig* mend, improve

bättre ['bätt-] *komp. t. bra, god, väl* **I** *a* better; *bli* ~ get better; *få* (*ha*) *det* ~ be better off; *han har sett* ~ *dagar* he has seen better days; ~ *mans barn* well-born child[ren]; ~ *kvalitet* superior quality (*än* to); *komma på* ~ *tankar* think better of it; *mot* ~ *vetande* against one's better judgement; *så mycket* ~ *för mig* so much better for me; ~ *upp* one better; *ju förr desto* ~ the sooner the better **II** *adv* better; *han förstår inte* ~ he doesn't know any better; *han borde veta* ~ *än att* he ought to know better than to; *det hände sig inte* ~ *än att han* as ill-luck would have it, he

bättring improvement; (*om hälsa*) recovery; *relig.* repentance **bättringsvägen** *vara på* ~ be on the road to recovery, *vard.* be on the mend

bäva tremble; (*darra*) quiver, shake; (*rysa*) shudder (*för* at) **bävan** *r* dread, fear

bäver ['bä:-] *s2* beaver **-råtta** coypu, nutria

böckling smoked Baltic herring

bödel ['bö:-] *s2* executioner, hangman; *bildl.* tormentor **bödelsyxa** executioner's axe

bög *s2, vard.* gay, queer, fairy

böhmare [ˣbö:mare] Bohemian **Böhmen** ['bö:-men] *n* Bohemia **böhmisk** ['bö:misk] *a5* Bohemian

böja [ˣböjja] *v2* **I 1** bend, curve; (*huvudet*) bow, incline; (*lemmarna äv.*) flex; ~ *knä inför* bend the knee to; *knäna böj!* knees bend!; *det skall* ~*s i tid som krokigt skall bli* best to bend while it is a twig; ~ *undan* turn aside, deflect **2** *språkv.* inflect, conjugate **II** *rfl* **1** bend (stoop) [down]; ~ *sig undan* turn aside; ~ *sig över* bend (lean) over **2** (*foga sig*) bow; ~ *sig för det oundvikliga* bow to the inevitable **3** (*ge efter*) yield (give in) (*för* to) **böjbar** *a1* bendy, bendable

böjd *a1* **1** bent, bowed; (*om hållning*) stooping; (*krökt*) curved; (*bågformig*) arched; ~ *av ålder* bent with age **2** *språkv.* inflected, conjugated **3** (*benägen*) inclined, disposed

böjelse [ˣböjj-] inclination, bent, proneness (*för* for, to[wards]); tendency (*för* to); (*öm känsla*) fancy, liking (*för* for)

böjhållfasthet bending strength

böjlig *a1* flexible; *bildl.* pliable, supple **-het** flexibility; *bildl.* pliability, suppleness

böjning bending; (*krökning*) flexure, curvature; *språkv.* inflection

böjnings|form inflected form **-mönster** paradigm **-ändelse** inflectional ending

bök|a root, grub **-ig** *a1, vard.* tiresome; awkward; messy

böl *s7* bellow **böla** bellow; (*råma*) low, moo

böld *s3* boil; *med.* furuncle; (*svårare*) abscess **-pest** bubonic plague

bölj|a **I** *s1* billow, wave; *bildl.* surge **II** *v1* undulate; (*om sädesfält*) billow **-ande** *a4* (*om hav*) billowy, rolling, swelling; (*om sädesfält*) billowing; (*om hår*) wavy, waving; (*om människomassa*) surging

bömare, bömisk *se* böhmare, böhmisk

bön *s3* **1** (*anhållan*) petition, request (*om* for); (*enträgen*) solicitation, supplication, plea, entreaty (*om* for) **2** *relig.* prayer; *Herrens* ~ the Lord's Prayer; *be en* ~ say a prayer; *förrätta* ~ offer [up] prayer

1 böna *v1, ung.* beseech, implore; ~ *för ngn* plead for a p., speak in favour of a p.

2 böna *s1* **1** bean **2** *sl.* (*flicka*) bird, chick; *AE.* broad

bön|bok prayer book **-dag** *ung.* intercession day **böne|hus** chapel; meeting house **-kvarn** prayer wheel **-man** beadsman; wooer's proxy **-matta** prayer rug (mat) **-möte** prayer meeting **-skrift** petition **-timme** hour of prayer

bönfalla plead (*om* for); implore (beseech, entreat) (*ngn om ngt* s.b. for s.th.)

bönhas [ˣbö:n-] *s2* interloper

bönhör|a ~ *ngn* hear a p.'s prayer; *han blev -d* his prayer was heard, (*friare*) his request was granted **-else** hearing (answering) of prayer

bön|syrsa [praying] mantis **-söndag** *B~en* Rogation Sunday

böra *borde bort* (*pres. o. imperf.*) ought to, should; (*inf. o. sup.* översätts genom omskrivning); *hon bör vara framme nu* she should be there by now; *jag anser mig* ~ *göra det* I think I ought to do it; *det borde vi ha tänkt på* we ought to have thought of that; *det är alldeles som sig bör* it is quite fitting; *man bör aldrig glömma* one should never forget (ought never to) forget

börd [-ö:-] *s3* birth; (*härkomst äv.*) ancestry, lineage, descent; *till* ~*en* by birth; *av ringa* ~ of lowly birth

börda [ˣbö:r-] *s1* burden; load; *digna under* ~*n* be borne down by (droop under) the load; *livet blev honom en* ~ life became a burden to him; *lägga sten på* ~ increase the burden, add insult to injury

1 bördig [ˣbö:r-] *a1* (*härstammande*) *hon är* ~ *från* she was born in, she is a native of

2 bördig [ˣbö:r-] *a1* (*fruktbar*) fertile **-het** fertility

börds|adel hereditary nobility **-stolt** proud of one's birth

börja begin; start; *vard.* kick off; (*mera högt.*) commence; (~ *på med*) set about, enter upon; *det* ~*r bli mörkt* it is getting dark; *till att* ~ *med* to begin (start) with; *nu* ~*s det* here we go, now we are in for it; ~ *i fel ände* put the cart before the horse; ~ *om* begin again; ~ *om från början* start afresh, make a fresh start

början *r* beginning; start; (*av brev*) opening; (*ursprung*) origin; *från första* ~ from the very beginning; *från* ~ *till slut* from beginning to end, from first to last; *i* (*från*) ~ at first; *i* ~ *av* at the beginning of; *i* ~ *av åttiotalet* in the early eighties; *till en* ~ to begin (start) with

börs 1 *s2* (*portmonnä*) purse **2** *s3* (*fond-*) exchange; *spela på* ~*en* speculate on the stock exchange (market) **-affärer** exchange business (dealings) **-hus** stock exchange **-jobbare** stockjobber **-kupp** stock exchange manoeuvre **-lista** [stock] exchange list; (*för aktier*) share (*A E.* stock) list **-mäklare** [stock]broker **-notera** list on the stock exchange **-noteringar** [stock] exchange quotations **-spekulant** speculator on the [stock] exchange; stockjobber **-spekulation** speculation on the [stock] exchange; stockjobbery, stockjobbing **-transaktion** stock exchange transaction

böss|a *s1* **1** (*gevär*) gun, rifle; (*hagel-*) shotgun **2** (*penningskrin*) moneybox **-håll** *inom* ~ within gunshot **-kolv** butt-end **-mynning** muzzle **-pipa** gun barrel **-skott** (*hopskr. bösskott*) gunshot

böta pay a fine; ~ *för* suffer (pay) for **böter** ['bö:-] *pl* fine (*sg*); *döma ngn till 10 punds* ~ fine s.b. 10 pounds; *belagd med* ~ liable to (punishable by) a fine

bötes|föreläggande order to pay fine[s] **-straff** fine, pecuniary penalty

bötfäll|a fine, mulct; *-d till* fined

bövel *s2* deuce, devil

C

ca *förk. för cirka*

cabotage [kabɔ'ta:ʃ] *s7* cabotage

cabriolet [kabriɔ'le: *el.* -'lä:] *s3* drophead coupé; convertible

café-au-lait [ka'fe: å 'lä:] coffee with milk

cafeteria [-'te:-] *s1* cafeteria

caffè espresso [ka'fä es'presså] *se espresso*

californium [-'få:r-] *s8* californium

calmettevaccination [kal'mett-] BCG vaccination

calvados [kalva'då:s] *s3* Calvados

calypso *s5* calypso

camembert [kamåŋ'bä:r] *s3* Camembert

camouflage [kamɔ'fla:ʃ] *s7* camouflage **-färg** camouflage colour

camouflera [kamɔ'fle:ra] camouflage

camp|a [ˣkamm-] camp **-are** camper

camping ['kamm-] camping **-plats** camp[ing] site, camping ground

Canada ['kann-] *n* Canada

canasta [ka'ˣnasta] *s1* canasta; (*bud äv.*) meld

cancan [ˣkaŋkaŋ] *r* cancan

cancer ['kanser] *s2* cancer **-cell** cancer cell **-forskning** cancer research **-framkallande** cancer-inducing, carcinogenic

cancer|ogen [kanserɔ'je:n] *a5* cancer-inducing, carcinogenic **-tumör** malignant tumour, cancer

candela [kan'de:la] *r* candela

cannabis ['kann-] *s3* cannabis, hemp

cape [keip *el.* kä:p] *s5* cape

capita ['ka:-] *per* ~ of (for) each person, per capita

cappuccino [kappɔ'tçi:nɔ] *s9* cappuccino

carci|nogen [karsinɔ'je:n] **I** *a5* carcinogenic **II** *s4* carcinogen **-nom** [-'nå:m] *s3* carcinoma

cardigan ['karr-] *s3* cardigan

carnet [kar'nä:] *s4* carnet

C-dur C major

ceder ['se:-] *s2* cedar

cedera cede

cederträ cedar [wood]

cedilj *s3* cedilla

cekal *a5, anat.* caecal

celeber [se'le:-] *a2* distinguished, famous **celebrera** celebrate **celebritet** *s3* celebrity

celest *a4* celestial; ~ *mekanik* celestial mechanics (*pl, behandlas som sg*)

celesta [se'ˣlesta] *s1* celesta, celeste

celiakj [s-] *s3, med.* sprue; (*hos barn*) coeliac disease

celibat *s7* celibacy

cell *s3* cell; *data.* location **-delning** cell division **-forskning** cytological research; cytology **-fånge** prisoner in solitary confinement **-gift** cytotoxin, cytotoxic drug

cellist cellist

cell|kärna nucleus (*pl äv.* nuclei) **-lära** *se cellära*

cello ['sellɔ] *-n celli* cello

cellofan *s3, s4* cellophane

cellskräck claustrophobia

cell|stoff cellulose wadding, cellucotton **-ull** rayon staple

cellular *a5* cellular

cellulit *s3* cellulitis

celluloid *s3* Celluloid

cellulosa [-ˣlo:sa] *s1* cellulose **-acetat** cellulose acetate **-fabrik** cellulose plant; pulp mill **-lack** cellulose lacquer (enamel) **-nitrat** *se nitrocellulosa* **-vadd** *se cellstoff*

cell|vägg cell wall **-vävnad** cellular tissue

cellära cytology

Celsius ['sell-] *r, fem grader* ~ five degrees Celsius (centigrade) **celsiustermometer** Celsius (centigrade) thermometer

cembalist [çemm-] harpsichordist; cembalist **cembalo** ['çemm-] *s5* harpsichord; cembalo

cement *s3, s4* cement **-blandare** cement mixer **cementer|a** cement **-ing** cementation **cementfabrik** cement works (*pl*)

cendré [saŋ'dre:] *oböjligt a* ash-coloured, ash-blond

censor [-år] *s3* censor; *skol.* [external] examiner

censur (*censurerande*) censoring; censorship; *sträng* ~ strict censorship; *öppnat av* ~*en* opened by censor **-era** censor **-ering** [-'re:-] censoring

census [ˣsenn-] *r* census

centaur [s-] *s3* centaur

center ['senn-] *s2, s4* centre; *AE.* center **-bord** *sjö.* centreboard; daggerboard **-forward** centre forward **-halv** centre half **-halvback** centre halfback

center|ism centrism **-ist** centrist

centerpart|i centre party **-ist** member of the

centre party

centi- centi- **centi|gram** [-'gramm] centigram [me] **-liter** [-'li:-] centilitre **-long[storlek]** children's size **-meter** [-'me:-] centimetre

centner ['sent-] *s9* centner, short hundredweight

centra (*i bollspel*) centre; *AE.* center

central I *a1* central; (*väsentlig*) essential **II** *s3* centre; *AE.* center; central office; (*huvudstation*) central station; *tel.* [telephone] exchange

Centralamerika *n* Central America

central|antenn communal aerial (antenna) **-bank** central bank **-dirigerad** *a5* centrally controlled **-dirigering** central[ized] control **-dispensär** mass radiography centre **-enhet** *data.* central processing unit **-figur** central figure **-förvaltning** central administration

centraliser|a centralize **-ing** centralization

central|kommitté *polit.* Central Committee **-lyrik** *ung.* lyrical poetry **-makterna** *pl, hist.* Central Powers **-postkontor** General Post Office **-station** central station **-stimulerande** stimulating the central nervous system **-uppvärmning, -värme** central heating

centrer|a centre; *AE.* center **-ing** centring; *AE.* centering

centrifug *s3* centrifuge; (*för tvätt*) spin-dryer

centrifugal *a1* centrifugal **-kraft** centrifugal force

centrifugera centrifuge; (*tvätt*) spin-dry

centripetal *a1* centripetal **-kraft** centripetal force

centrisk ['senn-] *a5* centric[al]

centrum ['senn-] *s8* centre; *AE.* center

cepheid [sefe'i:d] *s3, astr.* Cepheid variable

cerat *s7, s4* cerate

cerebral *a1* cerebral, of the brain; ~ *pares* cerebral palsy

cerebrospinal *a1* cerebrospinal **-vätska** cerebrospinal fluid

ceremoni *s3* ceremony; *AE. äv.* exercises (*pl*); *utan* ~*er* (*bildl.*) without ceremony **ceremoniel** *s7*, **ceremoniell** *s7 o. a1* ceremonial **ceremonimästare** master of ceremonies; *AE. äv.* emcee (M.C.) **ceremoniös** *a1* ceremonious

cerise [se'ri:s] *a5* cerise

cerium ['se:-] *s8* cerium

cerner|a *mil.* invest **-ing** *mil.* investment

certeparti *s4* charter party

certifikat *s7* certificate

cervelat *kokk.* cervelat

cesium ['se:-] *s8* caesium; *AE.* cesium

cession [se'ʃo:n] *s3* **1** *jur.* cession **2** (*konkurs*) bankruptcy

cesur caesura

cetan *s4, s3* cetane **-värde** cetane number (rating)

c & f *hand.* c & f (cost and freight)

cha-cha-cha cha-cha-cha, cha-cha

chagrin [ʃa'gräŋ] *s3, s4* shagreen

chalet [ʃa'lä:] *s3* chalet

champagne [ʃam'panj] *s5* champagne

champinjon [ʃampin'jo:n] *s3* champignon; (*ängs-*) meadow mushroom; (*snöbolls-*) horse mushroom

changera [ʃaŋ'ʃe:ra *el.* -'se:ra] lose colour, fade; (*om utseende*) deteriorate, go (run) to seed

chans [çaŋs *el.* ʃ-] *s3* chance, opportunity (*till* of); opening (*till* for)

chans|a [ˣçaŋsa *el.* ʃ-] chance, take a chance **-artad** [-a:r-] *a5* hazardous; *vard.* dicey **-lös** *han är* ~ he does not stand a chance **-ning** venture

chapeau-claque [ʃapå'klack] *s5* opera hat

charabang [ʃara'baŋ] *s3* charabanc

charad [ʃa'ra:d] *s3* charade; (*lek*) charades (*pl*)

chargé d'affaires [ʃar'ʒe: da'fä:r] *s3* chargé d'affaires

chargera [ʃar'ʃe:ra] exaggerate

charkuteri [ʃ-] *s4*, **charkuteriaffär** butcher; delicatessen [shop] **charkuterist** [ʃ-] butcher **charkuterivaror** [ʃ-] cured meats and provisions

charlatan [ʃ-] *s3* charlatan; quack **-eri** charlatanism, charlatanry; quackery

charm [ʃ-] *s3* charm; attractiveness **charma** [ʃ-] *vard.* charm **charmant** [ʃar'maŋt, äv.* -'mant] *a1* delightful, charming **charmera** [ʃ-] charm; ~*d av* charmed with **charmerande** [ʃar'me:-] *a4* charming

charmeuse [ʃar'mö:s] *s5* Charmeuse

charmfull [ʃ-] *a1*, **charmig** [ʃ-] *a1* charming **charmlös** [ʃ-] without charm, unattractive; dull **charmör** [ʃ-] charmer

charner [ʃ-] *s7, tekn.* hinge

charter|flyg [*svenskt uttal* 'ça:r-] air charter; charter flight **-resa** charter trip **chartr|a** [ˣça:rtra] charter **-ing** chartering; affreightment

chassi [ʃa'si:, äv.* 'ʃassi] *s4* chassis (*pl* chassis)

chateaubriand [ʃaˣtå:briaŋ *el.* -'aŋ] *s3* Chateaubriand

chaufför [ʃå'fö:r] driver; (*anställd*) chauffeur

chauvin|ism [ʃå-] chauvinism. jingoism **-ist** chauvinist, jingoist **-istisk** [-'istisk] *a5* chauvinistic, jingoistic

check [ç-] *s3, s2* cheque; *AE.* check; *en* ~ *på 100 pund* a cheque for 100 pounds; *korsad* ~ crossed cheque; *betala med* ~ pay by cheque; *utställa en* ~ draw a cheque; ~ *utan täckning* uncovered cheque

checka [ç-] *vard.* check; ~ *in* (*på flygplats, hotell o.d.*) check in; ~ *ut* (*från hotell, arbete*) check out

check|bedrägeri cheque forgery (fraud) **-blankett** cheque [form] **-häfte** cheque book **-konto** current (*AE.* checking) account

checklista [ç-] check list

check|lön [ç-] salary (wages) paid by cheque **-räkning** *se checkkonto*

chef [ʃe:f] *s3* head, principal, manager (*för* of); *vard.* boss, chief; (*för stab o.d.*) chief, director; (*för förband*) commanding officer **-konstruktör** chief designer, chief design engineer **-redaktör** editor in chief

chefs|befattning position as head, managerial post (position) **-egenskaper** *pl* executive talent (*sg*)

chefskap [ˣʃe:f-] *s7* headship, leadership

chefs|rådman senior judge **-åklagare** chief district prosecutor; *AE.* district attorney

chevaleresk [ʃ-] *a1* chivalrous

cheviot ['ʃe:viått] *s3* Cheviot; *blå* ~ (*äv.*) blue serge

chevreau [ʃev'rå:] *s3* kid[skin], chevrette

C

chianti [ki'anti] *s5* chianti
chic [ʃick] *a1* chic, stylish
chiffer ['ʃiff-] *s7*, *s3* **1** code, cipher; *forcera ett* ~ break a code **2** (*namn*-) monogram **-skrift** code, cipher **-telegram** code (cipher) telegram
chiffong [ʃi'fåŋ] *s3* chiffon
chiffonjé [ʃiffån'je:] *s3* chiffon[n]ier, bureau
chiffr|era [ʃ-] encode, encipher **-ering** [-'re:-] encoding, enciphering **-ör** encoder, encipherer
chikan *s3* **1** (*förolämpning*) affront, insult; (*vanheder*) ignominy **2** (*kortsp.*) chicane **-era** affront; offend, insult; humiliate
Chile [ˣçi:le] *n* Chile **chilen** [ç-] *s3*, **chilenare** [çiˣle:-] *s9*, **chilensk** [çi'le:nsk] *a5* Chilean **-salpeter** Chile saltpetre (nitre), soda nitre
chimär *s3* chim[a]era
chinchilla [çinˣçilla] *s1* chinchilla
chinjong [çin'jåŋ] *s3* chignon
chintz [çints] *s3* chintz
chips [çipps] *s7* **1** *kokk.* crisp; *AE.* chip **2** *data.* chip
chock [ʃåck] *s3* **1** (*anfall*) charge; *göra* ~ *mot* charge **2** *med.* shock **chocka** [ˣʃåcka] **1** *med.* shock **2** *vard.* (*chockera*) shock
chock|artad [-a:r-] *a5*, *en* ~ *upplevelse* a shock **-behandling** shock therapy (treatment)
chocker|a [ʃåck-] (*uppröra*) shock; (*väcka anstöt*) offend **-ande** *a4* (*upprörande*) shocking; (*stötande*) offensive
chock|skadad *a5*, *bli* ~ get a shock **-verkan** shock effect
choka [ˣçå:ka] *v1*, **choke** [çå:k] *s2* choke
choklad [ʃo-] *s3* chocolate; (*dryck*) cocoa **-ask** box of chocolates; (*i sht tom*) chocolate box **-bit** piece of chocolate; (*pralin*) chocolate [cream] **-brun** chocolate **-kaka** bar of chocolate **-pralin** chocolate cream **-pudding** chocolate pudding
chosa [ˣʃå:sa] *rfl* show off **choser** [ˣʃå:-] *pl* affectation (*sg*) **chosefri** [ˣʃå:-s] unaffected, natural **chosig** [ˣʃå:-] *a1* affected
chuck [ʃuck. çuck] *s2* chuck
cicero ['si:-] *s9* cicero
ciceron *s3* cicerone, guide
cider ['si:-] *s2* cider; (*alkoholhaltig*) hard cider
cif [siff] *hand.* cif, c.i.f. (cost, insurance, freight) **-pris** cif-price
cigarett *s3* cigarette, *vard.* cig[gy], *sl.* fag, *AE.* butt **-aska** cigarette ash **-etui** cigarette case **-fimp** *vard.* butt; cigarette end **-munstycke** cigarette holder **-märke** brand of cigarettes **-paket** pack[et] of cigarettes **-papper** cigarette paper **-rökning** cigarette smoking **-tändare** (*hopskr. cigarettändare*) [cigarette] lighter
cigarill *s3* cigarillo
cigarr *s3* cigar **-affär** tobacconist **-aska** cigar ash **-cigarett** *se cigarill*
cigarrett *se cigarett*
cigarr|handlare *se -affär* **-låda** cigar box **-snoppare** cigar cutter
cikada [-ˣka:-] *s1* cicada, cicala
cikoria [-ˣko:-] *s1* chicory, succory
cilie ['si:-] *s5* **1** (*flimmerhår*) cilium (*pl* cilia) **2** (*ögonhår*) cilium, eyelash
cimbrer ['simm-] *s9* Cimbrian
cineast *s3* cineaste
cinerarium [-'ra:-] *s4* cinerarium (*pl* cineraria)

cinnober [-'nå:- *el.* -'nɔ:-] *s9* cinnabar; (*färg äv.*) vermil[l]ion
cirka about, approximately, roughly **-pris** approximate (standard) price
cirkel *s2*, *geom.* circle (*äv. friare*); *rubba ngns cirklar* (*ung.*) upset a p.'s plans **-bevis** vicious circle; *göra ett* ~ reason in a circle **-båge** arc **-definition** vicious circle **-formig** *a1*, **-rund** *a1* circular **-segment** segment [of a circle] **-sektor** sector [of a circle] **-såg** circular saw **-yta** area [of a circle]
cirkla circle **cirklad** *a5* (*tillgjord*) affected; formal
cirkulation circulation
cirkulations|organ circulatory organ **-rubbning** circulatory disturbance
cirkulera circulate, go round; *låta* ~ circulate, send round
cirkulär I *s7* circular **II** *a5* circular; ~*t resonemang* vicious circle **-skrivelse** circular [letter]
cirkum|flex *s3* circumflex **-polär** *a5*, *astr.*, **-polär** *a5* circumpolar
cirkus ['sirr-] *s2* circus **-arena** ring **-artist** circus performer **-direktör** circus manager **-föreställning** circus [performance] **-ryttare** circus rider (equestrian); (*kvinnlig äv.*) equestrienne **-tält** circus marquee; *vard.* big top
cirrocumulusmoln [-'ku:-] *meteor.* cirrocumulus (*pl* cirrocumuli)
cirros [-'å:s] *s3* cirrhosis
cirrostratusmoln [-'stra:-] *meteor.* cirrostratus (*pl* cirrostrati)
cirrusmoln ['sirr-] *meteor.* cirrus (*pl* cirri)
cisalpinsk [-'pi:nsk] *a5* cisalpine
cisel|era chase **-ering** [-'le:-] chasing **-ör** chaser
ciss C sharp **Ciss-dur** C-sharp major **ciss-moll** C-sharp minor
cisterciens *s3*, **cistercienser** *s9* Cistercian, White Monk **-orden** Cistercian order
cistern [-'ä:rn] *s3* tank; (*särsk. för vatten*) cistern
citadell *s7* citadel
citat *s7* quotation **citationstecken** quotation mark; inverted (turned) comma **citera** quote; (*anföra som exempel*) cite
citrat *s7* citrate
citron *s3* lemon **-fjäril** brimstone **-fromage** lemon mousse **-gul** lemon [yellow] **-press** lemon squeezer **-saft** lemon juice **-skal** lemon peel **-syra** citric acid **-syracykeln** Krebs cycle, citric acid cycle **-träd** lemon [tree]
citrusfrukt [ˣsi:-] citrous (citrus) fruit
cittra *s1* zither
city ['sitti *el.* -y] *s6* city centre, business district; *AE.* downtown
civil *a1* civil[ian]; (*ej i uniform*) in plain clothes; (*motsats t. militär*) civil **-befolkning** civilian population **-befälhavare** director [regional civilian defence area] **-departement** ministry of public administration **-ekonom** graduate from a [Swedish] School of Economics; (*i Storbritannien ung.*) Bachelor of Economic Science; (*i USA ung.*) Master of Business Administration **-flyg** civil aviation **-flygare** civil pilot **-försvar** civil defence **-försvarsstyrelse** ~*n* [the Swedish] civil defence administration **-förvaltning** civil service **-ingenjör** graduate (university-

-trained) engineer
civilis|ation civilization **-era** civilize; ~*d* civilized
civilist civilian
civil|klädd in civilian clothes; in mufti; (*om polis etc.*) in plain clothes **-kurage** moral courage **-lista** civil list **-minister** minister of public administration **-motstånd** civil defence **-mål** civil case **-person** civilian **-rätt** civil law **-rättslig** [in] civil law **-stånd** civil status
c-klav *s3* C clef
clair|obscur *se* **klärobskyr** **-voyance** *se* klärvoajans
cleara [ˣkliːra] clear **clearing** [ˈkliː-] clearing **clearingavtal** clearing agreement
clementin *se* klementin
clips *se* klips
clitoris *se* klitoris
clou [kloː] *s2* highlight, star turn; showpiece
clown [klaon] *s3* clown **-eri** clownery, clowning
c-moll C minor
cocktail [ˈkåckteil] *s2* cocktail **-pinne** cocktail stick
coda [ˣkåː-] *s1* coda
colchicin [kålkiˈsiːn] *s4* colchicine
collage [kåˈlaːʃ] *s7* collage
collier [kålˈjeː] *s3* (*smycke*) necklace
Colombia [kåˈlåm-] *n* Colombia **colombian** *s3*, **colombiansk** [-ˈaːnsk] *a5* Colombian
columbarium *se* kolumbarium
commando|räd [kåˈmandåː-] commando raid **-trupp** commando unit, task force; *AE.* ranger [unit]
Comorerna *se* Komorerna
container *s2*, *s9* container **-fartyg** container ship **-hamn** container port
corps-de-logi [kårdöloˈʃiː] *s4* manor [house (seat)], hall
corps diplomatique [kåːr diplåmaˈtick] *r* diplomatic corps (body), corps diplomatique
cortes [ˈkårr-] *r* Cortes
cortison *se* kortison
cosinus [ˣkoː- *el.* ˈkoː-] *r*, *best. form* =, *mat.* cosine
Costa Rica [ˈkåsta ˈriːka] *n* Costa Rica **costarican** *s3*, **costaricansk** [-aː-] *a5* Costa Rican
cotangent *se* kotangent
coulomb [koˈlåmb] *s9* coulomb
courtage [kɔrˈtaːʃ] *s4* brokerage
cowboy [ˈkaobåi] *s3* cowboy **-film** cowboy film; Western
crawl [kråːl] *s3* crawl **-a** [ˣkråː-] crawl **-are** [ˣkråː-] crawler
crêpe 1 [kräːp] -*n*, *pl* -*s* (*pannkaka*) crepe; ~ *Suzette* crêpe suzette **2** *se* kräpp
crescendo [kreˈʃendå] *s6 o. adv* crescendo
croquis [kråˈkiː] *s3* sketch
croupier [krɔpˈjeː] *s3* croupier
C-språk *skol.* third foreign language
Cuba *n* Cuba **cuban** *s3*, **cubansk** *a5* Cuban
cumulonimbusmoln [-ˈnimm-] *meteor.* cumulonimbus (*pl äv.* cumulonimbi)
cumulusmoln [ˈkuː-] *meteor.* cumulus (*pl* cumuli)
cup [*svenskt uttal* kupp] *s3* cup **-final** cup final **-match** cup tie **-tävling** cup competition

curaçao [ˣkyrrasåː] *s3* Curaçao
curare [kuˣraː-] *s6* curare, curari
curium [ˈkuː-] *s8* curium
curling [ˈköliŋ] curling **-bana** curling rink **-sten** curling stone
curry [ˈkurry] *s2* curry powder
cyan *s3*, *s4* cyanogen
cyan|id *s3* cyanide **-kalium** potassium cyanide
cyano|s [-ˈåːs] *s3* cyanosis **-tisk** [-ˈnåː-] *a5* cyanotic
cyanväte hydrogen cyanide, hydrocyanic acid
cybernet|ik *s3* cybernetics (*pl, behandlas som sg*) **-iker** [-ˈneː-] cyberneticist **-isk** [-ˈneː-] *a5* cybernetic
cykel [ˈsyck-] **1** *s3*, *s2* (*serie, följd*) cycle **2** *s2* (*fordon*) bicycle, cycle; *vard.* bike; *åka* ~ ride a bicycle, [bi]cycle **-affär** bicycle dealer **-bana** cycle path (track); (*tävlingsbana*) bicycle-racing track, velodrome **-belysning** bicycle lights (*pl*) **-däck** bicycle tyre **-hjul** bicycle wheel **-kedja** bicycle chain **-klocka** bicycle bell **-klämma** bicycle clip **-korg** pannier, bicycle basket **-lopp** *se* -*tävling* **-lykta** bicycle lamp **-pump** bicycle pump **-ram** bicycle frame **-slang** bicycle [inner] tube **-sport** bicycling **-ställ** (*på cykel*) kickstand; (*för cyklar*) bicycle stand **-tur** bicycling tour; (*kortare*) bicycle ride **-tävling** bicycle race **-väska** carrier bag; (*för verktyg*) tool bag **-åkare** bicyclist, bicycler **-åkning** [-åːk-] bicycling
cykla bicycle; *vard.* ride a bike
cyklamat cyclamate
cyklamen [-ˈklaː-] *r* cyclamen
cykling *se* cykelåkning
cyklisk [ˈsyck-] *a5* cyclic
cyklist bicyclist, bicycler; cyclist; *AE.* cycler
cykloid I *a* (*i psykiatri*) cycloid **II** *s3*, geom. cycloid
cyklon [-ˈåːn] *s3*, *meteor. o. tekn.* cyclone
cyklop [-ˈåːp] *s3* Cyclops (*pl* Cyclop[s]es) **-öga** (*för sportdykare*) skin-diver's mask
cyklotron [-ˈtråːn] *s3* cyclotron
cylinder [-ˈlinn-] *s2* cylinder; *se äv.* -*hatt* **-diameter** bore **-formig** [-åː-] *a1* cylindrical **-hatt** top (high) hat; silk hat **-press** flat-bed (cylinder) press **-volym** cylinder capacity
cylindrisk [-ˈlind-] *a5* cylindrical
cymbal *s3* cymbal
cyn|iker [ˈsyː-] cynic **-isk** [ˈsyː-] *a5* cynical; (*oanständig*) indecent; (*rå*) coarse **-ism** *s3* cynicism; indecency; coarseness
Cypern [ˈsyː-] *n* Cyprus
cypress *s3* cypress **-lund** cypress grove
cyprier [ˈsyː-] *s9*, **cypriot** *s3*, **cypriotisk** [-ˈoː-] *a5* Cypriot[e]
cysta *s1* cyst **cystisk** [ˈsyss-] *a5* cystic **cystit** *s3* cystitis
cysto|skop *s7* cystoscope **-skopi** *s3* cystoscopy
cyto|log cytologist **-logi** *s3* cytology **-logisk** [-ˈlåː-] *a5* cytological

dabba *rfl* make a blunder

dada|ism Dada, Dadaism **-ist** Dadaist **-istisk** [-'ist-] *a5* Dadaist[ic]

dadda *s1* nanny; (*amma*) [wet] nurse

dadel ['dadd-] *s2* date **-palm** date palm

dag *s2* **1** day; ~ *efter annan* day after day; ~ *för* ~ day by day; ~ *ut och* ~ *in* day in, day out; day after day; ~*en därpå* (*förut*) the following (preceding) day; ~*en efter* the day after, the following day; *vara* ~*en efter* feel like the day after the night before; ~*en före anfallet* the day before (the eve of) the attack; ~*en lång* all day long; ~*ens rätt* today's special; *en* ~ one day (*om förfluten tid*), some day (*om framtid*); *endera* ~*en* one of these days; *god* ~*!, se god* [*dag*]; *samma* ~, *se samma*; *varannan* ~, *se varannan*; *bestämma* ~ name the day; *den* ~ *som i* ~ *är* this very day; *den* ~*en den sorgen* don't meet trouble halfway; *för* ~*en har vi inga bananer* we have no bananas today; *en fråga för* ~*en* a question of the day; *han har gått för* ~*en* he has gone for the day; *leva för* ~*en* live from hand to mouth (from day to day); *göra sig en glad* ~ make a day of it; *hela* ~*en* [*i ända*] all [the] day; *i* ~ today; *i* ~ *om ett år* a year today; *i* ~ [*om*] *åtta* ~*ar* this day week; *i* ~ *på morgonen* this morning; *i* ~ *röd, i morgon död* here today and gone tomorrow; *från och med i* ~ as from today; *vad är det för* ~ *i* ~? what day [of the week] is it?; *vad är det för väder i* ~? what sort of day is it?; *den skulle vara färdig till i* ~ it was to be ready [by] today; *just i* ~*arna* just recently (*om förfluten tid*), during the next few days (*om kommande tid*); *ännu i denna* ~ to this very day; *i forna* ~*ar* in the old[en] days; *i sin krafts* ~*ar* in the full vigour of life, in his (*etc.*) prime; *i morgon* ~ tomorrow; *i våra* ~*ar* in our days, nowadays; *i yngre* ~*ar* in his (*etc.*) earlier days (early life); *kors i all min dar!* well, I never!; *kommer* ~ *kommer råd* tomorrow is another day; *de närmaste* (*senaste*) ~*arna* the next (last) few days; *om* (*på*) ~*en* (~*arna*) in the daytime; *två gånger om* ~*en* twice a day; *om några* ~*ar* in a few days[' time]; *betala per* ~ pay by the day; *på* ~*en ett år sedan* a year ago to the day; *det var långt lidet på* ~*en* the day was far advanced; *senare på* ~*en* later in the day; *på gamla* ~*ar* in one's old age; *på mången god* ~ for many a [long] day; *sedan ett par* ~*ar* for some days past; *de sista* ~*arnas heliga* the Latter--Day Saints; *ta* ~*en som den kommer* take each day as it comes; *under* ~*ens lopp* during the course of the day; *en vacker* ~ *på sommaren* on a fine summer day; *en vacker* ~ *slår du dig* one fine day you will hurt yourself; *för var* ~ *som går* with every day that passes; *var* ~ *har nog av sin egen plåga* sufficient unto the day is the evil thereof (*bibl.*); *var fjortonde* ~ every fortnight; *våra* ~*ars Paris* present-day Paris **2** (*dagsljus*) daytime; daylight; *full* ~ broad daylight; *vacker som en* ~

a flame of loveliness; *det ligger i öppen* ~ it is obvious to everybody; *bringa* (*lägga*) *i* ~*en* reveal, show; *likna ngn upp i* ~*en* be the very image of s.b.; *mitt på ljusa* ~*en* in broad daylight; *klart som* ~*en* as clear as daylight; *se* ~*ens ljus* see the light [of day]; ~*sens sanning* gospel [truth]

daga *i uttr.: ta ngn av* ~ put s.b. to death

dagas *dep* dawn; *det* ~ day is dawning

dag|barn child in day care in private home **-blindhet** day blindness **-bok** diary; *bokför.* daybook, journal, book of account (original entry) **-boksanteckning** entry in a (one's) diary **-brott** opencast **-brytning** opencast (*särsk. AE.* strip) mining **-bräckning** *i* ~*en* at dawn (daybreak)

dagdriv|are idler, loafer **-eri** idleness, loafing

dagdröm daydream **-mare** daydreamer

dager ['da:-] *s2* [day]light; (*ljusning*) ray of light; *full* ~ full light; *framställa ngt i fördelaktig* ~ put s.th. in a favourable light; *framträda i sin rätta* ~ stand out in its right light; *skuggor och dagrar* light and shade

dagerro|typ *s3* daguerreotype **-typi** *s3* daguerreotypy

dagfjäril butterfly

1 dagg *s2* (*straffredskap*) cat-o'-nine-tails

2 dagg *s2* dew **-droppe** dewdrop

daggert ['dagg-] *s2* dagger

dagg|frisk fresh as dew **-ig** *a1* dewy **-kåpa** lady's mantle **-mask** earthworm **-punkt** dew point

dag|gryning dawn, daybreak; *i* ~*en* at dawn **-hem** day nursery, crèche; *AE.* care center **-jämning** equinox **-jämningspunkt** equinoctial point, equinox

daglig ['da:g-] *a1* daily; day-to-day; *fack.* diurnal; ~ *tidning* daily [paper]; ~*t tal* everyday (colloquial) speech (conversation) **-dags, -en** every day, daily **-varor** *pl* everyday commodities

dag|lönare day-labourer **-mamma** woman providing day-care for other's child[ren]

dagning ['da:g-] dawn, daybreak

dag|officer officer of the day, orderly officer **-order** order of the day **-ordning** (*föredragningslista*) agenda; *parl.* order paper; *stå på* ~*en* be on the agenda; *övergå till* ~*en* proceed to the business of the day, (*bildl.*) get down to business **-ort** gallery, adit **-rum** (*sällskapsrum*) day room

dags [dakks] *i vissa uttr.: hur* ~? [at] what time?; when?; *det är* ~ *nu* it is [about] time now; *det är så* ~ *nu!* (*iron.*) it is a bit late now!; *så här* ~ *på natten* at this time of [the] night; *till* ~ *dato* to date

dags|aktuell topical; of current interest **-behov** daily requirement **-bot** *-en dagsböter* fine assessed on the basis of one's daily income

dagsedel *vard.* biff, sock

dagsens ['dacks-] *se dag 2*

dags|förtjänst daily earnings (*pl*), daily pay **-kassa** daily takings (*pl*) **-kurs** *hand.* rate of the day, current price **-ljus** daylight; *vid* ~ by daylight **-läge** present-day situation

dagslända mayfly, dayfly

dags|marsch day's march **-meja** [-mejja] *s1* noonday thaw **-nyheter** *pl* (*i radio, TV*) today's news (*pl, behandlas som sg*) **-press** daily press; ~*en* the press **-pris** current price; *till gällande* ~ at the current price **-regn** continuous rain **-resa**

day's run (journey, voyage) -**temperatur** day temperature -**tidning** daily [paper] -**tur** day trip -**verke** s6 day's work; *göra* ~ work by the day

dag|teckna date -**tinga** (*kompromissa*) compromise; (*köpslå*) bargain -**tingan** compromise; bargain -**traktamente** daily allowance [for expenses]; *ha 20 pund i* ~ be allowed 20 pounds a day for expenses

dahlia ['da:lia] s1 dahlia
dajak s3 Dyak, Dayak
dakapo [-'ka:-] **I** adv da capo **II** s6 (*extranummer*) encore **III** interj encore
daktyl s3 dactyl[ic]
dal s2 valley; dale
dala decline, sink, go down; (*om snö*) fall gently
dalahäst painted wooden horse from Dalarna (Dalecarlia)
Dalarna n Dalarna, Dalecarlia
daler ['da:-] s9, *ung.* rix-dollar, rigsdaler
dalgång s2 glen, valley
dalj s7 thrashing, licking
dalkulla [ˣda:l-] Dalecarlian woman (girl)
dallr|a tremble, quiver; (*om ljud*) vibrate -**ing** tremble; vibration
dal|mas man from Dalarna (Dalecarlia), Dalecarlian
dalmatiner [-'ti:-] Dalmatian
dalmål Dalecarlian dialect
dal|ripa willow grouse -**sänka** depression [of the ground]
dalt s7 coddling **dalta** ~ *med ngn* coddle (pamper) s.b., (*kela*) fondle s.b.
daltonplanen *skol.* the Dalton plan (system)
1 dam s3 **1** lady; (*bords- etc.*) partner; *mina ~er och herrar* ladies and gentlemen; *hon är stora ~en nu* she is quite the young lady now **2** *spel.* queen
2 dam s3 (-*spel*) draughts (*pl, behandlas som sg*); *AE.* checkers (*pl, behandlas som sg*)
damask s3 gaiter; (*herr-*) spat
damask|enerstål [-ˣʃe:- el. -ˣske:-] Damascus (damask) steel -**era** damascene, damask
damast [ˣdamm- el. 'damm-, äv. -'mast] s3 damask
dam|avdelning ladies' department -**badhus** ladies' baths -**bekant** lady friend -**besök** *ha* ~ have a lady visitor -**binda** sanitary towel (*AE.* napkin) -**bjudning** ladies' party; *vard.* hen party -**byxor** (*med ben*) knickers, drawers; (*trosor*) panties, briefs -**cykel** lady's bicycle
damejeanne [damme'ʃann el. -'ʃa:n] s5 demijohn; (*för frätande vätskor*) carboy
damfris|ering ladies' hairdresser's -**ör**, -**örska** [ladies'] hairdresser
damgambit queen's gambit
dam|ig al ladylike -**kappa** lady's coat -**klocka** lady's watch -**kläder** pl women's wear (*sg*) -**konfektion** ladies' ready-made clothing -**kör** ladies' choir
1 damm s2 **1** (*vattensamling*) pond **2** (*fördämning*) dam; dyke (*AE.* dike); weir; barrage
2 damm s7 (*stoft*) dust
1 damma s2 **1** (*befria från damm*) dust **2** (*avge damm*) make (raise) a dust; *vägarna ~r* (*äv.*) the roads are dusty; ~ *av* dust [down], take the dust off; ~ *ner* make dusty, cover with dust

2 damma *vard.*, ~ *på* (*till*) ngn hit (clout) s.b.
dammanläggning dam, weir plant
dammborste dust[ing]-brush
dammbyggnad se *dammanläggning*
damm|fri dustless, free from dust -**handduk** se *dammtrasa*
damm|ig al dusty -**korn** grain of dust
dammlucka floodgate, head gate; sluice[gate]
damm|lunga *med.* pneumo[no]coniosis -**moln** (*hopskr. dammoln*) cloud of dust -**påse** dustbag -**suga** vacuum -**sugare** vacuum cleaner -**sugarpåse** dustbag -**sugning** vacuum cleaning -**torka** dust -**trasa** duster; *AE.* dust cloth -**vippa** feather-duster
damning [ˣdamm-] dusting
damoklessvärd [-ˣmåkles-] Sword of Damocles
damp imperf. av *dimpa*
dam|rum ladies' room, ladies (*pl, behandlas som sg*); *AE.* rest room -**sadel** side-saddle
damspel se *2 dam*
dam|sällskap i ~ with ladies (a lady) -**tidning** women's magazine -**toalett** ladies' cloakroom; powder room -**underkläder** pl ladies' underwear, lingerie -**väska** handbag, bag; *AE.* purse, pocketbook
dana fashion, shape, form (*till* into); (*karaktär*) mould; (*om skola*) educate, turn out; (*utbilda*) train
danaarv escheat
dandy [-y el. -i] s3 dandy, fop
1 dank s2 (*ljus*) [tallow] candle, dip
2 dank s, i uttr.: *slå* ~ idle, loaf [about]
Danmark ['dann-] n Denmark
dans s3 dance; (-*ande*, -*konst*) dancing; *damernas* ~ ladies' invitation (excuse-me) [dance]; *gå som en* ~ go like clockwork; *en* ~ *på rosor* a bed of roses; *middag med* ~ dinner and dancing; *bli bjuden på* ~ be invited to a dance; *bjuda upp ngn till* ~ ask (invite) s.b. to a dance, ask s.b. for a dance; *börja* ~ open the ball
dansa dance; ~ *bra* be a good dancer; ~ *efter ngns pipa* dance to a p.'s tune; ~ *omkull* go tumbling over; ~ *på lina* dance on the tightrope; ~ *sig varm* dance o.s. warm; ~ *ut a*) (*börja dansa*) dance out, *b*) (*sluta dansa*) stop dancing; ~ *ut julen* (*ung.*) wind up Christmas with a children's dance (party); ~ *vals* waltz; *gå och* ~ go dancing; *det ~des hela natten* the dance lasted all night; *när katten är borta ~r råttorna på bordet* when the cat's away, the mice will play
dans|ande a4 dancing; *de* ~ the dancers -**ant** [-'sant, äv. -'saŋt] al, *inte vara* ~ be no dancer -**are** dancer -**bana** open-air dance floor; (*med tak*) dance pavilion -**erska** dancer -**golv** dance floor -**högskola** ~n [the Swedish] national college of dance
dansk I al Danish; ~ *skalle* butt with the head **II** s2 Dane **danska** s1 **1** (*språk*) Danish **2** (*kvinna*) Danish woman **dansk-svensk** Dano-Swedish
dans|lek dance game -**lektion** dancing lesson -**lokal** dance hall, dancing rooms (*pl*) -**lysten** keen on dancing -**lärare** dancing instructor (*fem.* instructress) -**melodi** dance tune -**musik** dance music -**orkester** dance orchestra -**restaurang** dance restaurant -**sjuka** St. Vitus's dance -**skola** dancing school -**steg** dance step -**till-**

D

ställning dance **-visa** dancing song **-ör, -ös** dancer

Dardanellerna [-'nell-] *pl* the Dardanelles

darr *s7* tremble; *med* ~ *på rösten* with a quiver in the voice **darra** tremble; (*huttra*) shiver (*av köld* with cold); (*skälva*) quiver; (*skaka*) shake; (*om röst, ton*) quaver, tremble; ~ *i hela kroppen* tremble all over; *hon ~r på handen* her hands shake; *hon ~de på målet* her voice quavered (trembled)

darr|ande *a4* trembling *etc.*; (*om röst, handstil* *äv.*) tremulous **-gräs** quaking grass

darrhänt *a1, han är så* ~ his hands are so shaky **-het** tremor (shaking) of the hands

darr|ig *a1* trembling *etc.*; (*om pers. äv.*) doddering **-ning** trembling; tremulation, tremor; quiver [ing], shiver **-rocka** (*hopskr. darrocka*) electric ray **-ål** electric eel

darwin|ism Darwinism, Darwinian theory **-ist** Darwinist, Darwinite **-istisk** [-'ist-] *a5* Darwinistic

dask 1 *s7* (*stryk*) spanking **2** *s2* (*slag*) slap, spank **daska** spank, slap

dass *s7, vard.* lav, loo, bog

data *pl* (*årtal*) dates; (*fakta*) data (*vanl. sg*), particulars **-bank, -bas** data bank (base) **-behandla** computerize **-behandling** data processing **-bärare** data carrier; storage device **-central** data processing centre **-inspektion** ~*en* [the Swedish] data inspection board **-logi** computer science **-maskin** *se* dator **-medium** data medium **-program** [computer] program; software **-styrd** [-y:-] *a5* computer controlled **-sättning** *boktr.* computer (automatic) typesetting **-teknik** computer technology **-terminal** computer terminal **-ålder** computer age

dater|a date; ~ *sig från* date from (back to) **-bar** *a5* dat[e]able **-ing** dating

dativ *s3* dative; *i* ~ in the dative **-objekt** indirect object

dato *s6* date; *a* ~ from date; *till dags* ~ to date

dator *s3* computer

datoriser|a computerize **-ing** computerization

dator|språk computer language **-styrd** [-y:-] *a5* computer controlled **-system** computer system **-tomografi** computer tomography

datoväxel time bill (draft)

datt *se* 2 *ditt*

datum *s8* date; *poststämpelns* ~ date of postmark; *av gammalt* ~ of ancient date; *av senare* ~ of later date **-gräns, -linje** [international] date line **-märka** mark with date **-märkning** sell--by-date marking **-parkering** *ung.* night parking on alternate sides of the street according to even or odd date **-stämpel** date stamp; (*poststämpel*) postmark

davidsstjärna Star of David

D-dagen (*6 juni 1944*) D-day

D-dur D major

de I *best. art. pl* the; ~ *flesta människor* most people; *hon är över* ~ *femtio* she is over fifty; ~ *dansande* the dancers; ~ *närvarande* those present **II** *pron* **1** *pers.* they; ~ *själva* they themselves **2** *demonstr.*, ~ *där* those, ~ *här* these **3** *determ.* those, the ones (*som* who); *fören. äv.* the **4** *obest.* they, people; ~ *säger på stan* they say, I hear,

people are saying

deaktivera deactivate

debacle [-'backel] *s5, s7* debacle

debarker|a disembark **-ing** disembarkation, disembarkment

debatt *s3* debate, discussion; *livlig* ~ lively debate; *ställa* (*sätta*) *ngt under* ~ bring s.th. up for discussion **-era** debate, discuss **-inlägg** contribution to a debate **-ämne** subject of discussion (debate) **-ör** debater

debet ['de:-] *n* debit; ~ *och kredit* debit and credit; *få* ~ *och kredit att gå ihop* make both ends meet; *införa under* ~ enter on the debit side **-konto** debit account **-saldo** debit balance **-sedel** [income tax] demand note; *AE.* tax bill; ~ *å slutlig skatt* final tax demand note **-sida** debit side

debil *a1* mentally retarded **-itet** mental retardation

debiter|a debit (*ngn för* s.b. with); charge (*för* for); *kostnaderna skall ~s oss* the costs should be charged to our account **-ing** charge, debit; *för hög* ~ overcharge

debitor ['de:- *el.* 'de:-] *s3* debtor; ~*er* (*bokför.*) (*AE.*) account receivable

debut *s3* debut **-ant** singer *etc.* making his (*etc.*) debut; (*i societetslivet*) debutante **-bok** first book **-era** make one's debut

deceler|ation deceleration **-era** decelerate

december [-'semm-] *r* December

decennium [-'senn-] *s4* decade

decentraliser|a decentralize **-ing** decentralization

decharge [-'ʃarʃ] *s5*, ~ *beviljades* (*vägrades*) (*polit., ung.*) the vote of censure was defeated (passed) **-debatt** *ung.* vote of censure debate

dechiffrer|a decipher, decode **-ing** deciphering, decoding **-ör** decipherer, decoder

deci- deci-

decibel [-'bell] *r, pl* = decibel

deciderad [-'de:-] *a5* pronounced, decided

deci|gram [-'gramm] decigram[me] **-liter** [-'li:-] decilitre

decimal *s3* decimal **-bråk** decimal [fraction]; *periodiskt* ~ recurring (circulating, repeating) decimal **-komma** decimal point **-system** decimal system **-våg** decimal balance

decimer|a decimate; (*friare*) reduce [in number] **-ing** decimating; ~ *av personalen* depletion of the staff

decimeter [-'me:-] decimetre

deckar|e (*roman*) detective story, mystery; *vard.* whodun[n]it; (*person*) *vard.* sleuth; *jfr detektiv, detektivroman*

dedi|cera dedicate **-kation** dedication

dedikationsexemplar dedication (inscribed) copy

deducera deduce

deduk|tion [-duk'ʃɔ:n] deduction **-tiv** *a1* deductive

de facto ['faktɔ] de facto

defait|ism [-fä-] defeatism **-ist** *s3*, **-istisk** [-'ist-] *a5* defeatist

defekt I *s3* defect; deficiency **II** *a1* defective

defensiv *s3 o. a1* defensive; *hålla sig på* ~*en* be on the defensive

defibrillator [-ˣaːtår] *s3* defibrillator
deficit [ˈdeː-] *s7* deficit
defiler|a defile; ~ *förbi* march past **-ing** defiling; march past
definier|a define **-bar** [-ˣeːr-] *a1* definable
defini|tion definition **-tjv** [*äv.* 'deff-] *a1* definite, definitive, final; *~t beslut* final decision
deflagration deflagration
deflation deflation
deflor|ation defloration **-era** deflower
defoliant defoliant
deform|ation deformation, distortion **-era** deform, distort **-itet** *s3* deformity
defroster [-ˈfråss-] *s2, s3* defroster
deg *s2* dough; (*mör-, smör-*) paste
degel [ˣdeːg-] *s2* crucible, melting pot
degenera|tion [-j-] degeneration **-tjv** *a1* degenerative
degenerer|a [-j-] degenerate; *~d* degenerate **-ing** degeneration
deg|ig [ˣdeːg-] *a1* doughy; pasty **-klump** lump of dough
degrader|a degrade **-ing** degradation
degression [-greˈʃoːn] degression
degsporre pastry wheel
dehumanisera dehumanize
dehydr|ation dehydration **-era** dehydrate
de|ism deism **-ist** deist **-istisk** [-ˈist-] *a5* deist, deistic[al]
dejlig *a1* fair, lovely
deka ~ *ner sig* (*vard.*) go to the dogs
deka- deca-, deka-
dekad *s3* decade
dekadans [-ˈdans *el.* -ˈdaŋs] *s3* decadence, decline **-period** [period of] decadence
dekadent *a1* decadent
dekal *s3* decal **dekalkomanj** *s3* decalcomania
dekan *s3* dean
dekanter|a decant **-ing** decanting
dekanus [-ˈkaː-] *se* dekan
dekis [ˈdeːk-] *s, uttr. i uttr.*: *vara på* ~ be down on one's luck; *komma på* ~ go to the dogs **-figur** seedy-looking character
deklam|ation recitation; (*högtravande*) declamation **-atorisk** [-ˈtoː-] *a5* declamatory **-atör** reciter **-era** recite; (*tala högtravande*) declaim
deklar|ant person filing a tax return **-ation** declaration; (*själv-*) tax return
deklarations|blankett tax-return form **-skyl-dighet** obligation to file a tax return **-uppgift** income-tax statement
deklarera declare; (*förkunna*) proclaim; (*in-komst*) file one's tax return; *han ~r för 100 000* he has a taxable income of 100,000
deklasser|a bring down in the world **-ing** decline
deklin|ation *språkv.* declension; *fys.* declination **-era 1** *språkv.* decline **2** (*förfalla*) go off, deteriorate; (*mista sin skönhet*) fade
dekokt [-ˈkåkkt] *s3* decoction (*på* of)
dekollet|age [-kåll(e)ˈtaːʃ] *s4* décolletage **-erad** [-ˈteː-] *a5* décolleté, wearing a low-necked dress; (*om plagg*) low-necked
dekompression decompression **dekompres-sionskammare** decompression chamber
dekor [-ˈkåːr] *s3* décor, decor; scenery **-ation**

decoration; ornament **-atjv** *a1* decorative; ornamental **-atör** decorator; (*för skyltfönster*) window-dresser; *teat.* stage designer **-era** decorate (*äv. med orden*); ornament
dekorum [-ˣkåː- *el.* -ˣkoː-] *n* decorum; *iaktta* (*hålla på*) ~ observe the proprieties
dekret *s7* decree **-era** decree; dictate
del *s2* **1** part, portion; (*band*) volume; (*avsnitt*) section; *en* ~ *av eleverna* some of the pupils; *en* ~ *av sändningen* part of the consignment; *en hel* ~ *besvär* (*s utan pl*) a good deal of trouble; *en hel* ~ *kvinnor* (*s med pl*) a great (good) many women; *en hel* ~ *fel* quite a lot (a fair number) of mistakes; *större* (*största*) *~en av* most of; *för en* ~ *år sedan* a few years ago; *i en* ~ *fall* in some cases; *till* ~*s* partly; *till stor* ~ largely, to a large extent; *till större* (*största*) *~en* mostly, to a large extent **2** (*andel*) share, portion; (*lott*) lot; ~ *i kök* part-use of the kitchen; *få* ~ *av* be notified of; *få sin be-skärda* ~ receive one's due [share]; *för min* (*egen*) ~ for my [own] part; *ha* (*få*) ~ *i* have a share in; *komma ngn till* ~ accrue to s.b., fall to a p.'s lot; *ta* ~ *av* acquaint o.s. with, study **3** (*av-seende*) respect; (*punkt*) point; *för den ~en* as far as that goes; *till alla ~ar* in all respects **4** *för all* ~! (*avböjande*) don't mention it!; that's all right!; *ja, för all* ~! yes, to be sure!; *nej, för all* ~! certainly not!; *gör er för all* ~ *inget besvär* please don't go to any trouble!; *kom för all* ~ *inte hit!* whatever you do, don't come here!
dela 1 (*i delar*) divide [up], split up; ~ *i lika delar* divide into equal parts **2** (*sinsemellan*) share; (*in-stämma i*) share, participate in; ~ *lika* share evenly, divide fair[ly], *vard.* go shares; ~ *ngns uppfattning* share a p.'s opinion; ~ *rum med ngn* share a room with s.b.; ~ *med 52* divide by 52; ~ *52 med 13* divide 52 by 13, divide 13 into 52; ~ *av, se avdela*; ~ *med sig* share with others; share and share alike; ~ *ut a*) (*distribuera*) distribute, (*post*) deliver, *b*) (*order*) issue, *c*) (*nattvard*) administer **3** *rfl* divide [up], split up; (*gå isär*) part; *vägen ~r sig* the road forks
delad *a5* divided *etc.*; *~e meningar* divergent opinions; *det rådde ~e meningar om det* opinions were divided about it; ~ *glädje är dubbel glädje* a joy that's shared is a joy made double
delaktig *a1* participant (*av, i* in); concerned, involved (*av, i* in); *vara* ~ *i* participate in, (*förbry-telse o.d.*) be a party (an accessory) to **-het** participation, share; (*i förbrytelse*) complicity
del|bar *a1* divisible **-betalning** part payment **-betänkande** interim report
delcredere [-ˈkreː-] del credere, guarantor for; *stå* ~ work on a del credere basis
deleatur [-eˈaːtur] *n* dele
deleg|at delegate **-ation** delegation, mission **-era** [-g-] delegate; *en ~d* a delegate
delfjn *s3* dolphin
del|ge (*delgiva*) inform (*ngn ngt* s.b. of s.th.), communicate (*ngn ngt* s.th. to s.b.) **-givning** [-jiː-] communication; *jur.* service
delikat *a1* delicate; (*välsmakande*) delicious
delikatess delicacy; *~er* (*äv.*) delicatessen **-af-fär** delicatessen [shop]; *AE., vard.* deli
delinkvent criminal; culprit; delinquent
deliri|um [-ˈliː-] *s4* delirium; ~ *tremens* delirium

tremens **-ös** *al* delirious

delkredere *se delcredere*

del|leverans part delivery **-likvid** part payment

delning [ˣde:l-] (*uppdelning*) division, partition; (*i underavdelningar*) subdivision; (*sinsemellan*) sharing; *biol.* fission

delo *s, i uttr.*: *komma* (*råka*) *i ~ med* fall out with, quarrel with

delpension partial pension

dels [-e:-] *dels...dels...* partly...partly...; (*å ena sidan...å andra sidan*) on [the] one hand...on the other

del|stat federal (constituent) state **-sträcka** section; (*etapp*) stage; *sport.* leg

1 delta [ˣde:lta] *se deltaga*

2 delta [ˣdellta] *s6, geogr. o. bokstav* delta

deltaga 1 (*i handling*) take part, participate (*i in*); *~ i en expedition* be a member of an expedition; *~ i en kurs i franska* attend a course in French; *~ i konversationen* join in the conversation; *~ i luncheon* be present at the luncheon; *han deltog i första världskriget* he served in World War I **2** (*i känsla*) share, participate

deltagande I *a4* participant; *de ~* those taking part (*etc.*), (*i tävling o.d.*) the competitors **2** (*medkännande*) sympathizing, sympathetic **II** *s6* **1** participation, taking part; (*bevistande*) attendance (*i* at); (*medverkan*) cooperation **2** (*medkänsla*) sympathy; *känna* (*hysa*) *~ med* (*för*) *ngn* sympathize with s.b., feel sympathy for s.b.; *ert vänliga ~ i min sorg* your kind message of sympathy in my bereavement

deltagare participant, participator, sharer; (*i expedition*) member; (*i möte*) attender; (*i idrott*) participant, entrant, competitor

delta|muskel deltoid **-vinge** delta wing

deltid *arbeta på ~* work part time

deltidsanställ|d part-time employee **-ning** part-time employment

deltids|arbete part-time work (job) **-pension** part-time retirement pension

del|vis [ˣde:l-] **I** *adv* partially, partly, in part **II** *al* partial **-ägare** partner, joint owner; *passiv ~* sleeping (*AE.* silent) partner

dem [demm, *vard.* dåmm] *pron* (*objektsform av de*) **1** *pers.* them; *~ själva* themselves **2** *demonstr., determ.* those (*som* who, which)

dema|gog [-ˈgå:g] *s3* demagogue **-gogj** *s3* demagoguery, demagogy **-gogisk** [-ˈgå:-] *a5* demagogic[al]

demarkationslinje line of demarcation

demarsch *s3* démarche; approach, action

demaskera *~* [*sig*] unmask

demens *s3* dementia

dementera deny, contradict **dementj** *s3* denial, contradiction

demilitariser|a demilitarize **-ing** demilitarization

demimond [-ˈmåŋd] *s3* demimonde

demission resignation **-era** resign

demissionsansökan *inlämna sin ~* hand in one's resignation, resign

demobiliser|a demobilize **-ing** demobilization

demodul|ation demodulation **-ator** [-ˣa:tår] *s3* demodulator **-era** demodulate

demo|graf *s3* demographer, demographist

-grafj *s3* demography **-grafisk** [-ˈgra:-] *a5* demographic[al]

demokrat democrat

demokrat|i *s3* democracy **-isera** democratize **-isering** [-ˈse:-] democratization **-isk** [-ˈkra:-] *a5* democratic

demoler|a demolish, tear down **-ing** demolition

demon [-ˈmå:n] *s3* demon, fiend **-isk** [-ˈmå:-] *a5* demoniac[al], fiendish

demonstra|nt [-å-] demonstrator **-tion** demonstration

demonstrations|möte mass meeting **-tåg** demonstration; protest march

demonstra|tiv [-ˈti:v, -ˈmånn-, ˈde:-] demonstrative **-tris, -tör** demonstrator

demonstrera 1 (*förevisa*) demonstrate **2** (*tillkännage sin mening*) demonstrate, make a demonstration

demonter|a dismantle, dismount **-ing** dismantling, dismounting

demoraliser|a demoralize **-ande** *a4* demoralizing **-ing** demoralization

den [denn] *jfr det, de* **I** *best. art.* the **II** *pron* **1** *pers.* it; (*om djur äv.*) he, she; (*syftande på kollektiv äv.*) they **2** *demonstr.* that; *~ dåren!* that fool!; *~ där a*) from. that, *b*) *självst.* (*om sak*) that one, (*om pers.*) that man (woman *etc.*); *~ här a*) *fören.* this, *b*) *självst.* (*om sak*) this one, (*om pers.*) this man (woman *etc.*); *hör på ~ då!* just listen to him (her)! **3** *determ. a*) *fören.* the, *b*) *självst., ~ som* (*om sak*) the one that, (*om pers.*) the man (woman *etc.*) who, anyone who, whoever; *~ av som* the one of you that, whichever of you; *han är inte ~ som ger sig* he is not one (the man) to give in; *till ~ det vederbör* to whom it may concern; *~ som ändå vore rik!* would I were rich! **4** *obest., ~ eller ~* this or that person; *herr ~ och ~* Mr. So and So; *på ~ och ~ dagen* on such and such a day **5** *opers. det, se det II*

denaturalis|ation denaturalization **-era** denaturalize

denaturera denature; *~d sprit* methylated spirits, metho

dendro|kronologi dendrochronology **-log** dendrologist **-logj** *s3* dendrology **-logisk** [-ˈlå:-] *a5* dendrologic[al], dendrologous

denier [denˈje:] *r* denier

denitrifikation denitrification

denn|e *-a, pron* **1** *fören.* (*nära den talande*) this, (*längre bort*) that; *-a min uppfattning* this view of mine; *-a min kritik* (*tidigare gjord*) that criticism of mine **2** *självst.* (*om pers.*) he, she, this (that) man (woman *etc.*); (*om sak*) it; this [one]; (*den senare*) the latter; *förklaringen är -a* the explanation is this

dennes (*vid datum*) instant (*förk.* inst.)

denot|ation denotation **-era** denote

densamm|e [-ˈsamme] *-a* the same; (*den*) it

densitet *s3* density

dental *al o. s3* dental

dentist dental technician

denukleariser|a denuclearize **-ing** denuclearization

deodorant deodorant

departement *s7* department (*äv. franskt distrikt*); ministry, office, board

departements|chef head of a department; minister, secretary of state **-råd** assistant under-secretary **-sekreterare** senior administrative officer; principal administrative officer
depensera [-pen'se:- *el.* -paŋ'se:-] disburse
depesch *s3* dispatch **-byrå** news-office
depil|ation depilation **-era** depilate
deplacement *s7* displacement
deponens [-'på:-] *n* deponent
deponer|a deposit (*hos ngn* with s.b.; *i en bank* at a bank) **-ing** deposit; (*av avfall*) deposition, controlled tipping
deport|ation [-å-] deportation **-ationsort** penal colony **-era** deport
deposition deposit, deposition; depositing; (*nedfall av luftföroreningar*) [contaminant] fall-out
depositions|bevis (*värdehandling*) depositary receipt; (*pengar*) deposit receipt; (*kvitto*) deposit slip **-räkning** deposit account
depp|a *vard.* have the blues, be down in the dumps **-ig** *a1* down in the dumps
depravera deprave; ~*d* depraved
deprecier|a depreciate **-ing** depreciation
depress|ion [-e'ʃɑ:n] depression; *ekon. äv.* slump **-iv** *a1* depressive
deprimera depress; ~*d* depressed
deputation deputation **deputerad** [-'te:-] *-en, pl -e* deputy **deputeradekammare** chamber of deputies
depå *s3* depot **-fartyg** depot ship
derangera [-aŋ'ʃe:-] derange
deras *pron* **1** *poss., fören.* their; *självst.* theirs **2** *determ.*, ~ *åsikt som* the opinion of those who
derby [*svenskt uttal* 'därrby *el.* -i] *s6* Derby; (*lokal-*) local Derby
deriv|at *s7* derivative **-ata** [-ˣva:-] *s1, mat.* derivative **-era** derive
dermatit *s3* dermatitis
dermato|log dermatologist **-logi** *s3* dermatology **-logisk** [-'lå:-] *a5* dermatological
dervisch *s3* dervish; *dansande* ~*er* whirling dervishes
desamma [-'samma] the same; (*de*) they
desarmer|a disarm **-ing** disarming; disarmament
desavouer|a repudiate, disavow **-ing** repudiation, disavowal
desegregation desegregation
desensibiliser|a desensitize **-ing** desensitization
desert|era desert **-ering** [-'te:-] desertion **-ör** deserter
design [*svenskt uttal* di'sajn] *s3* design **-er** [*svenskt uttal* di'sajner] designer
designera [-iŋ'ne:- *el.* -in'je:-] designate, name; ~*d* designate[d]
desillusion disillusion **-erad** [-'e:rad] *a5* disillusioned
desinfek|tera disinfect **-tion** [-k'ʃɑ:n] disinfection **-tionsmedel** disinfectant
desinficer|a [-'se:-] disinfect **-ing** disinfection
desinformation disinformation
desintegrator [-ˣgra:tår] disintegrator
deskalera de-escalate
deskriptiv *a1* descriptive

desmanråtta [ˣdess-] Russian desman
desolat *a1* desolate
des|organisera disorganize **-orientera** disorientate; ~*d* disorientated; confused, at a loss
desper|ado [-'ra:-] *s5* desperado **-at** *a1* desperate **-ation** desperation
despot [-'på:t] *s3* despot
despot|i *s3* despotism **-isk** [-'på:-] *a5* despotic[al] **-ism** *se despoti* **-välde** tyrannic rule
1 dess *s7, mus.* D flat
2 dess I *pron* its; *om koll. äv.* their **II** *adv, innan* (*sedan, till*) ~ before (since, till) then; *till* ~ *att* until, till; *ju förr* ~ *bättre* the sooner the better; ~ *bättre* (*värre*) *vaknade jag* fortunately (unfortunately) I woke up
dessa (*de här*) these; (*de där*) those; (*de*) they; (*dem*) them
Dess-dur D-flat major
dessemellan [-ˣmell- *el.* 'dess-] in between; at intervals, every now and then
dessert [de'sä:r] *s3* dessert, sweet; *vid* ~*en* at dessert **-kniv** dessertknife **-sked** dessertspoon **-tallrik** dessertplate **-vin** dessertwine
dess|förinnan [-ˣinn- *el.* 'dess-] before then **-förutan** [-ˣu:tan *el.* 'dess-] without it
dessinatör pattern designer
dess|likes [-ˣli:-] likewise, also **-utom** [-ˣu:tåm *el.* 'dess-] besides, as well; (*vidare*) furthermore; (*ytterligare*) moreover, in addition
dessäng *s3* **1** (*avsikt*) plan; scheme **2** (*anvisning*) pointer; hint; wink **3** (*mönster*) design, pattern
destill|at *s7* distillate, distillation **-ation** distillation, distilling **-ationsapparat** still; distilling apparatus **-ator** [-ˣa:tår] *s3* distiller
destiller|a distil **-ing** *se destillation*
destin|ation destination **-ationsort** [place of] destination **-erad** [-'ne:-] *a5, sjö.* bound (*till* for); ~ *till hemorten* homeward bound
desto ['dess-] *icke* ~ *mindre* none the less, nevertheless; *ju förr* ~ *hellre* the sooner the better; ~ *bättre* all (so much) the better
destru|era destruct **-ktion** [-k'ʃɑ:n] destruction **-ktiv** *a1* destructive
det (*jfr den*) **I** *best. art.* the **II** *pers. pron* **1** it; (*om djur, barn äv.*) he, she; *betonat* that; ~ *har jag aldrig sagt* I never said that; ~ *var* ~, ~! that's that!; ~ *var snällt av dig!* that's very kind of you!; ~ *vill säga* that is; *är* ~ *så?* is that so?; *ja, så är* ~ yes, that's [how] it [is]; *är* ~ *där aprikoser? nej,* ~ *är persikor* are those apricots? no, they are peaches; *känner du den där pojken* (*de där pojkarna*)? ~ *är min bror* (*mina bröder*) do you know that boy (those boys)? he is my brother (they are my brothers) **2** (*i opers. uttr.*) *a*) (*som eg. subj.; som formellt subj. då det eg. subj. är en inf., ett pres. part. el. en hel sats*) it; *b*) (*som formellt subj. då det eg. subj. är ett subst. ord*) there; *c*) (*ibl.*) that, this; ~ *blir storm* there will be a storm; ~ *går tolv månader på ett år* there are twelve months in a year; ~ *regnar* (*snöar*) it is raining (snowing); ~ *ser ut att bli regn* it looks like rain; ~ *skulle dröja många år innan* it was to be many years before; ~ *står i tidningen att* it says in the paper that; ~ *tjänar ingenting till att försöka* it is no use trying; ~ *tjänar ingenting till att försöka göra* ~ there is no use in trying to do that; ~

var en gång en prins once upon a time there was a prince; ~ *var frost i natt* there was a frost last night; ~ *återstår inget annat att göra* there remains nothing to be done; ~ *är bra många år sedan jag* it is a good many years since I; ~ *är ~ jag vill* that is what I want; ~ *är fem grader kallt* it is five degrees below freezing point; ~ *är här jag bor* this is where I live; ~ *är ingen brådska* there is no hurry; ~ *är ingenting kvar* there is nothing left; ~ *är jag* it is I (*vard.* me); ~ *är långt till* it is a long way to; ~ *är lätt att säga* it is easy to say; ~ *är mycket folk här* there are a lof of people here; ~ *är synd att* it is a pity that; *när ~ gäller att arbeta* when it is a question of working; *så måste ~ ha varit* that must have been it; *vad är ~ du talar om?* what is it you are (what are you) talking about?; *vad är ~ för dag i dag?* what day is it today?; *vem är ~ som kommer?* who is [it (that)] coming?; *är ~ mig du söker?* is it me you want?, are you looking for me? **3** (*ibl. som pred.fylln. o. obj.*) so; ~ *tror jag*, ~*!* I should just think so!; *jag antar* (*tror*) ~ I suppose (think; *vard., särsk. AE.* guess) so; *och ~ är jag med* and so am I; *var ~ inte ~ jag sa!* I told you so! **4** (*översatt el. annan konstruktion*) ~ *drar här* there is a draught here; ~ *gör ont i fingret* my finger hurts; *och ~ gör inte jag heller* nor do I; ~ *knackar* there's a knock; ~ *luktar gott här* there is a nice smell here; ~ *lyckades mig att få* I succeeded in getting, I managed to get; ~ *pratades mycket litet* there was very little talk[ing]; ~ *talas mycket om* there is much talk about; ~ *var mycket varmt i rummet* the room was very hot; ~ *var roligt att höra* I am glad to hear it; ~ *vet jag inte* I don't know; ~ *är inte tillåtet att röka här* smoking is not allowed here; ~ *är mulet* the sky is overcast; *efter middagen dansades ~ litet* after dinner we danced a little; *i dag är ~ torsdag* today is Thursday; *jag kände ~ som om* I felt as if; *jag tror inte jag kan* (*vågar*) ~ I don't think I can (dare); *nej*, ~ *har jag inte* no, I haven't; *som ~ nu ser ut* as matters now stand; *som ~ sedan visade sig* as appeared later; *varför frågar du ~?* why do you ask?; *vore ~ inte bättre med...* wouldn't... be better **5** *subst.* it; *hon har ~* she has it **III** *demonstr. pron* that; ~ *där* (*här*) that (this); ~ *eller ~* this or that; ~ *har du rätt i* you are right there; ~ *har jag aldrig hört* I never heard that; ~ *är just likt henne* that's just like her; *med ~ och ~ namnet* with such and such a name; *så var ~ med ~* so much for that **IV** *determ. pron a*) *fören.* the, *betonat* that, *b*) *självst.* the person (*man etc.*), the one; ~ *som* that which, what; *allt ~ som* all (everything) that; *vi hade ~ gemensamt att* we had this in common that, one thing we had in common was that

detache|ment *s7* detachment **-era** detach

detal|j *s3* detail; particular; (*maskindel*) part, component; *i ~* in detail, minutely; *i ~ gående minute; *in i minsta* ~ in every detail; *gå in på ~er* enter (go) into details; *närmare ~er* further details; *sälja i ~* retail, sell [by] retail **-anmärkning** criticism in (on points of) detail **-arbete** detail work

detalj|erad [-'je:-] *a5* detailed, circumstantial **-granskning** detailed examination **-handel** retail trade; (*butik*) retail shop **-handelspris** re-

tail price **-handlare** retailer

detalj|ist retailer **-rik** full of details, very detailed, circumstantial **-rikedom** wealth of detail

detek|tera detect **-tion** [-k'ʃo:n] detection

detektiv *s3* detective, criminal investigator; ~*a polisen, se kriminalpolis* **-byrå** detective agency **-författare** author of detective stories, crime writer **-roman** detective story, mystery

detektor [-'tecktår] *s3* detector

detergent [-g-] detergent

determin|ativ [-'tärr- *el.* -'ti:v] *a1* determinative **-era** determine **-ism** determinism **-ist** determinist

deton|ation detonation **-ator** [-'a:tår] *s3* detonator **-era** detonate

detronisera dethrone

detsamma [-'samma] the same [thing]; (*det*) it; *det gör ~* it doesn't matter; *det gör mig alldeles ~* it is all the same to me; *i ~* at that very moment; *med ~* at once, right away; *tack*, ~*!* thanks, and the same to you!

detta this; ~ *mitt beslut* this decision of mine; ~ *om ~* so much for that; ~ *är mina systrar* these are my sisters; *före ~* (*f.d.*) former, late, ex-; *livet efter ~* the life to come

deuterium [dev'te:-] *s8* deuterium

devalver|a devalue **-ing** devaluation

devi|ation deviation **-era** deviate

devis *s3* device; motto

devot [-'vå:t] *a1* devout

dextrin *s4, s3* dextrin[e] **dextros** [-'å:s] *s3* dextrose, grape sugar

di *s2, ge* ~ give suck to, suckle; *få ~* be put to the breast

1 dia *v1* suck, suckle

2 dia *s1, se diapositiv*

diabas *s3* diabase

diabet|es [-'be:-] *s3* diabetes; (*sockersjuka*) diabetes [mellitus] **-iker** [-'be:-], **-isk** [-'be:-] *a5* diabetic

diabild slide, transparency

diabolisk [-'bå:-] *a5* diabolic

diadem *s7* diadem, tiara

diafragma [-'fragma] *s4, s1* diaphragm

diagnos [-'gnå:s] *s3* diagnosis (*pl* diagnoses); *ställa en ~* diagnose, make a diagnosis **-tjk** *s3* diagnostics (*pl, behandlas som sg*) **-tisera** diagnose **-tisk** [-'gnåss-] *a5* diagnostic

diagonal I *s3* diagonal; (*tyg*) diagonal [cloth] **II** *a1* diagonal **-däck** cross-ply tyre

diagram [-'gramm] *s7* diagram, chart, graph

diakon [-'kå:n] *s3* deacon; lay worker

diakoniss|a deaconess; lay worker **-anstalt** training school for deaconesses

diakritisk [-'kri:-] *a5* diacritical; ~*t tecken* diacritic, diacritical mark

dialekt *s3* dialect **-al** *a1* dialectal

dialekt|ik *s3* dialectics (*pl, behandlas som sg*) **-isk** [-'lekk-] *a5* dialectic[al]; ~ *materialism* dialectical materialism

dialog dialogue **-form** *i ~* in [the form of a] dialogue

dialy|s *s3* dialysis; *med.* [haemo]dialysis, extracorporeal dialysis **-sera** dialyse **-tisk** [-'ly:-] *a5* dialytical

diamagnetism diamagnetism

diamant diamond **-borr** diamond drill **-borrning** diamond drilling **-bröllop** diamond wedding **-gruva** diamond mine **-ring** diamond ring **-slipare** diamond cutter **-slipning** diamond cutting

diameter [-'me:-] *s2* diameter; *invändig (utvändig)* ~ inside (outside) diameter **diametral** *a1* diametrical **diametralt** [-'a:lt] *adv*, ~ *motsatt* diametrically opposed

diapositiv *s7* transparency, slide

diarieföra [di*x*a:rie-] enter in a journal, record **diarium** [di'a:-] *s4* [official] register; *(dagbok)* diary; *hand.* daybook

diarré *s3* diarrhoea

diatermi *s3* diathermy, diathermia

diatonisk [-'tɔ:-] *a5* diatonic

dibarn unweaned child; suckling

dibbla *(gruppså)* dibble

didaktik *s3* didactics *(pl, behandlas som sg)* **-isk** [-'dakk-] *a5* didactic

diesel|motor [*x*di:sel-] diesel engine (motor) **-olja** diesel oil (fuel)

diet *s3* diet; *hålla* ~ be on a diet, diet **dietetik** *s3* dietetics *(pl, behandlas som sg)* **dietetisk** [-'te:-] *a5* dietetic[al] **dietisk** [-'e:-] *a5, se dietetisk* **dietist** dietitian **dietmat** diet food

differens [-'ens *el.* -'aŋs] *s3* difference **differential** [-entsi'a:l] *s3* differential **-kalkyl** differential calculus **-växel** differential gear **differentier|a** [-tsi'e:ra] differentiate; diversify **-ing** differentiation; diversification

differera differ

diffraktion [-k'ʃɔ:n] diffraction

diffundera diffuse

diffus *a1* diffuse **diffusera** diffuse **diffusion** diffusion **diffusor** [di*x*fu:sår] *s3* diffuser

difteri *s3* diphtheria

diftong [-'tåŋ] *s3* diphthong **-era** [-åŋ'ge:ra] diphthongize **-ering** [-'e:-] diphthongization

dig [*vard.* dejj] *pron (objektsform av du)* you; *bibl. o. poet.* thee; *rfl* yourself; thyself

digel *s2* platen **-press** platen press

diger ['di:-] *a2* thick, bulky; *(om bok äv.)* voluminous **-döden** the Black Death

digestion [-ge'ʃɔ:n *el.* -je-] digestion

digga *vard.* dig

digital *a1* digital

digitalis [-gi*x*ta:- *el.* -gi'ta:-] *s2* **1** *bot., se fingerborgsblomma* **2** *med.* digitalis

digital|maskin digital computer **-ur** digital watch (clock)

digivning [-ji:-] suckling, breast-feeding

digna [*x*diŋna] sink down, succumb; collapse; ~ *under bördan* be borne down by (droop under) the load; *ett ~nde bord* a table loaded with food

digni|tet [diŋni-] *s3* **1** *(värdighet)* dignity **2** *mat.* power **-tär** *s3* dignitary

digression [-e'ʃɔ:n] digression

dika ditch, drain, trench **dike** *s6* ditch, drain, trench; *han körde i ~t* he drove into the ditch **dikes|kant, -ren** ditchside, ditchbank

dikning [*x*di:k-] draining, ditching

1 dikt *a4 o. adv, sjö.* close

2 dikt *s3* **1** *(skaldestycke)* poem; *koll.* poetry **2** *(osanning)* fiction, fabrication; invention

1 dikta *sjö.* caulk

2 dikta 1 *(författa)* write [poetry] **2** *(fabulera)* fabricate, invent

diktafon [-'få:n] *s3* dictaphone *(varumärke)*; [tape] recorder

dikta|men *-men -mina, n el. r* dictation

diktan *s, endast i uttr.*: ~ *och traktan* aim and endeavour

diktanalys analysis of poetry

dikt|arbegåvning poetic[al] talent **-are** poet, writer **-arskap** poetic calling **-art** type of composition (poetry)

diktcykel cycle of poems

diktera dictate *(för* to) **dikteringsmaskin** dictating machine, [tape] recorder

diktion [-k'ʃɔ:n] diction

dikt|konst [art of] poetry **-ning** writing; fiction; *(poesi)* poetry; *hans* ~ his literary production **-samling** collection of poems **-verk** poem; poetical work

dilemma [-*x*lemma] *s6* dilemma, quandary

dilettant dilettante; amateur **-isk** *a5, se -mässig* **-ism** dilettantism **-mässig** *a1* dilettantish; amateurish

diligens [-'aŋs] *s3* stagecoach

dill *s2* dill

dilla babble **dille** *s6* **1** *(delirium)* D.T.'s **2** *(mani)* craze *(på* for); *ha fått* ~ *på ngt* be crazy (mad, *sl.* nuts) about s.th.

dill|krona head of dill **-kött** boiled mutton (veal) with dill sauce

diluvial *a1* diluvial

dim|bank fog bank **-bildning** smoke screening **-bälte** belt of fog (mist)

dimension [-n'ʃɔ:n] dimension, size; *~er (äv.)* proportions **-era** dimension **-ering** [-'ne:-] dimensioning

dim|figur phantom, vague shape **-höljd** *a5* shrouded in mist (fog)

diminuendo [-u'endå] *s6 o. adv* diminuendo **diminutiv** *a1 o. s4, s7* diminutive **-form** diminutive form **-ändelse** diminutive affix

dim|kammare [Wilson] cloud chamber **-ljus** foglight

dimm|a *s1* mist; *(tjocka)* fog; *(dis)* haze **-ig** *a1* misty, foggy; *bildl.* hazy

dimpa *damp dumpit* fall, tumble *(i golvet* on to the floor), tumble *(i* in, into)

dimridå smoke screen *(äv. bildl.)*

din [dinn] *(ditt, dina) pron* **1** *fören.* your; *bibl. o. poet.* thy; ~ *toker!* you fool! **2** *självst.* yours; *bibl. o. poet.* thine; *de ~a* your people; *du och de ~a* you and yours

dinar *s3* dinar

diné *s3* dinner **dinera** dine

dinge *s2* ding[h]y

dingla dangle, swing; ~ *med benen* dangle one's legs

dinosaurie [-'sau-] *s5* dinosaur

diod [-'å:d] *s3* diode

dionysisk [-'ny:-] *a5* Dionysian

diop|tri *s3* dioptre **-trik** *s3* dioptrics *(pl, behandlas som sg)* **-trisk** [di'åpp-] *a5* dioptric[al]

diorama [-*x*ra:ma] *s6* diorama

dioxid dioxide

diplom [-'å:m] *s7* diploma, certificate **diplom|at** diplomat **-ati** *s3* diplomacy **-atisk**

[-'ma:-] *a5* diplomatic[al]; *på* ~ *väg* through diplomatic channels; ~*a kåren* the diplomatic corps (body); ~ *immunitet* diplomatic immunity
diplomerad [-'me:-] *a5* holding a diploma; *han är* ~ *(äv.)* he is a diplomate
dipolantenn [-ˣpɒ:l-] dipole [aerial]
dippa (*doppa i sås*) dip
direkt I *a1* direct; (*omedelbar*) immediate; (*rak*) straight; (*trafikterm*) through, nonstop; ~ *anföring* direct speech; ~ *skatt* direct tax; *den ~a orsaken* the immediate cause **II** *adv* (*om tid*) directly, immediately, at once; (*om riktning*) direct, straight; (*avgjort*) distinctly; ~ *från fabrik* direct from factory; *hon var* ~ *oförskämd* she was downright rude; *inte* ~ *utsvulten* not actually starved; *uppgiften är* ~ *felaktig* the information (statement) is quite wrong (incorrect)
direkt|flyg[ning] nonstop flight **-förbindelse** direct connection **-försäljning** direct sale[s *pl*] (selling) **-insprutning** direct injection
direktion [-k'ʃɔ:n] (*styrelse*) board [of directors], management; (*riktning*) direction
direktions|sammanträde management (managers') meeting **-sekreterare** secretary to management
direktiv *s7* directions, *ibl.* direction; terms of reference, directive; *ge ngn* ~ *(äv.)* instruct s.b.
direktreferat running commentary
direktris woman manager, manageress; (*mode-*) dress designer, stylist
direkt|sändning live broadcast **-trafik** through traffic
direktör director; (*affärschef*) manager; *AE.* vice president; *verkställande* ~ managing director, *AE.* president **direktörsassistent** assistant manager
dirigent [-'gent *el.* -'ʃent] conductor, (*äv., särsk. AE.*) director **-pult** conductor's platform, podium
diriger|a [-'ge:- *el.* -'ʃe:-] direct; *mus.* conduct, (*äv., särsk. AE.*) direct **-ing** control; direction; *mus.* conducting
dis *s7* haze
discipel [-'sipp, *äv.* -'ʃipp-] *s2* pupil
disciplin [dissi'pli:n] *s3* **1** (*läroämne*) branch of learning (instruction), discipline **2** (*lydnad*) discipline; *hålla* ~ maintain discipline, keep order **-brott** breach of discipline, [act of] insubordination **-era** discipline **-straff** disciplinary punishment **-är** *a1* disciplinary
disharmoni *s3* disharmony, discord **-era** discord; clash **-isk** [-'mo:-] *a5* disharmonious, discordant
disig *a1* hazy
disjunktiv [*el.* 'diss-] *a1* disjunctive
1 disk *s2* **1** (*butiks-*) counter; (*bar-*) bar **2** *anat.* disc
2 disk *s2* **1** *abstr.* washing-up **2** *konkr.* washing-up, dishes (*pl*); *torka ~en* dry the dishes
1 diska (*rengöra*) wash up; *AE.* wash the dishes
2 diska *sport.* disqualify
diskant treble **-klav** treble (G) clef
disk|balja washing-up bowl; *AE.* dishpan **-borste** dishbrush (washing-up) brush
diskbråck slipped disc
diskbänk [kitchen] sink

diskett *s3* flexible diskette, floppy disk
disk-jockey *s3* disc jockey
disk|maskin dishwasher **-medel** washing-up liquid (powder, detergent) **-ning 1** washing-up **2** *sport.* disqualification
diskofil *s3* discophil[e], gramophone-records collector
diskonter|a discount **-ing** (*transaktion*) discounting of a bill; (*rörelse*) discounting, discount[ing] business
diskontinuerlig [-'e:r-] *a1* discontinuous, intermittent
diskontnota [diss ˣkånt-] discount note
diskonto [-'kånto] *s6* official discount [rate]; *höja* (*sänka*) ~*t* raise (lower) the official discount rate **-höjning** increase in the official discount rate
diskont|ränta discount rate **-ör** discounter
diskomusik disco music **diskotek** *s7* **1** (*grammofonarkiv*) record library **2** (*danslokal*) discotheque, disco
diskplockare table clearer
diskreditera discredit; *~nde för* discreditable to
diskrepans [-'ans *el.* -'aŋs] *s3* discrepancy
diskret *a1* discreet, tactful; (*om färg*) quiet **diskretion** discretion
diskrimination discrimination **diskriminera** discriminate **diskriminering** discrimination
disk|ställ plate rack **-trasa** dishcloth; *ibl.* dish-clout
diskurs *s3* discourse
diskus ['diss-] *s2* discus **-kastare** discus thrower **-kastning** throwing the discus; (*idrottsgren*) the discus
diskussion [-u'ʃɔ:n] discussion, debate **diskussions|inlägg** contribution to a debate **-ämne** subject of (for) discussion
diskut|abel [-'ta:-] *a2* debatable **-era** discuss; debate; argue; *det skall vi inte* ~ *om* we won't argue the point; *det kan ju* ~*s* it is open to discussion
diskvalificera disqualify **diskvalificering, diskvalifikation** disqualification
diskvatten dishwater
disparat *a1* disparate
dispasch *s3, sjö.* average statement **-ör** average adjuster
dispens [-'ans] *s3* exemption; *kyrkl.* dispensation; *få* ~ be exempted **-era** [-paŋ'se:- *el.* -pen-] exempt **-är** [-aŋ'sä:r] *s3* tuberculosis clinic
dispersion dispersion
disponent [works (factory)] manager
disponera 1 ~ [*över*] (*förfoga över*) have at one's disposal (command) **2** (*ordna*) arrange, organize; (*göra mottaglig*) render liable (susceptible) to; ~ *en uppsats* plan (organize) an essay
disponerad *a5* disposed, inclined; ~ *för infektioner* susceptible to infection; *hon kände sig inte* ~ *att sjunga* she did not feel like singing
disponibel [-'ni:-] *a2* available, in hand, disposable **disponibilitet** availability; *i* ~ unattached; (*mil.*) on the inactive list; on half pay
disposition disposition; disposal; (*utkast*) outline; (*arrangemang*) arrangement; (*anlag o.d.*) tendency, predisposition; *ha ngt till sin* ~ have s.th. at one's disposal; *stå till ngns* ~ be at a p.'s

disposal (service); *ställa ngt till ngns* ~ place s.th. at a p.'s disposal; *vidtaga ~er* make dispositions **dispositions|fond** special reserve fund **-rätt** right of disposal

dispositiv [*el.* 'diss-] *a1* optional

disproportion disproportion

disput|ation disputation; *univ. äv.* oral defence of a [doctor's] thesis **-era** dispute, argue; *univ.* defend one's thesis; *han ~de på* his doctor's thesis was about (on)

dispyt *s3* dispute, controversy, argument; altercation; *råka i* ~ get involved in a dispute

diss *s7, mus.* D sharp

dissekera dissect **dissektion** [-k'ʃɔ:n] dissection

dissenter [-'senn-] dissenter, nonconformist

dissimil|ation dissimilation **-era** dissimilate

diss-moll D-sharp minor

dissoci|ation dissociation **-era** dissociate

dissonans [-'ans *el.* -'aŋs] *s3* dissonance

distans [-'ans *el.* -'aŋs] *s3* distance **-era** outdistance, leave behind; beat **-minut** [international] nautical mile

distingerad [-iŋ'ge:-] *a5* distinguished **distinkt** *a1* distinct **distinktion** [-k'ʃɔ:n] distinction

distorsion [-r'ʃɔ:n] distortion

distrahera ~ *ngn* distract a p.'s attention, disturb s.b.; *utan att låta sig ~s* without becoming confused **distraherad** *a5* distraught **distraktion** [-k'ʃɔ:n] distraction (*äv. förströelse*); (*tankspriddhet*) absent-mindedness

distribuer|a distribute **-ing** distribution

distribution distribution; *i* ~ (*om bok*) published (sold) for the author (*hos* by)

distributions|ekonomi marketing [efficiency] **-företag** distribution firm; distributors (*pl*) **-kostnad** distribution (marketing) cost

distribut|iv [*el.* 'diss-] *a1* distributive **-ör** distributor

distrikt *s7* district, region, area

distrikts|läkare district medical officer **-mästare** district champion **-mästerskap** district championship **-sköterska** district nurse **-åklagare** district prosecutor (*AE.* attorney)

distré *a1* absent-minded, distrait

disör diseur **disös** diseuse

dit *adv* **1** *demonstr.* there; ~ *bort* (*fram, in, ner, upp, ut, över*) away (up, in, down, up, out, over) there; ~ *hör även* to that category also belong[s] ; *det var* ~ *jag ville komma* that's what I was getting at; *hit och* ~ to and fro; (*högre stil*) hither and thither; *är det långt ~?* (*om plats*) is it a long way there?, (*om tid*) is it a long time ahead? **2** *rel.* where; (*varthelst*) wherever **-hän** *se därhän* **-hörande** *a4* belonging to it; (*t. saken*) relevant; *ej* ~ irrelevant **-intills** ['di:t- *el.* ˣdi:t-] till (up to) then

dito ['di:- *el.* ˣdi:-] **I** *oböjligt a* ditto (*förk.* do.) **II** *adv* likewise

ditresa journey (*etc.*) there

1 ditt *se din, sköt du* ~ mind your own business

2 ditt *i uttr.*: ~ *och datt* one thing and another, this and that; *tala om* ~ *och datt* talk about all sorts of things

dittills ['di:t-] till then **-varande** *a4, hans* ~ *arbete* his work till then, his previous work

dit|vägen *på* ~ on the way there **-åt** ['di:t-] in that direction, that way; *någonting* ~ something like that

diva *s1* diva **-later** *ung.* airs and graces

divan *s3* couch, divan

diverg|ens [-g-] *s3* divergence **-era** diverge; *~nde* divergent

diverse [-ˣvärse] **I** *oböjligt a* sundry, various; ~ *utgifter* incidental (sundry) expenses **II** *s pl* sundries, odds and ends; (*rubrik o.d.*) miscellaneous, sundries **-arbetare** odd-jobman, oddjobber; labourer **-handel** general shop (store) **-handlare** general dealer

diversifier|a diversify **-ing** diversification

divid|end *s3* dividend; *minsta gemensamma* ~ lowest (least) common multiple **-era 1** *mat.* divide (*med* by; *i* into) **2** (*resonera*) argue (*om* about)

divis *s3* hyphen

division division; *flyg.* squadron

divisions|chef divisional commander; *flyg.* squadron leader **-tecken** division sign

divisor [-ˣvi:sår] *s3* divisor

djonk [djånk] *s3* junk

djungel ['juŋel] *s3* jungle **-telegraf** bush telegraph; *vard.* grapevine [telegraph]

djup [ju:p] **I** *s7* depth; *bildl. äv.* profundity; *högt. äv.* depths (*pl*); *kaptenen följde fartyget i ~et* the captain went down with his ship; *gå på ~et med ngt* go to the bottom of s.th.; *på ringa* ~ at no great depth; *ur ~et av mitt hjärta* from the depths of my heart **II** *a1* deep; (*högre stil o. bildl.*) profound; (*fullständig*) complete; (*stor*) great; ~ *tystnad* profound silence; *~t ogillande* profound disapproval; *en* ~ *skog* a thick forest; *de ~a leden* the rank and file; *den ~aste orsaken till* the fundamental cause of; *i* ~*a tankar* deep in thought; *i ~aste hemlighet* with utmost secrecy; *mitt i ~aste skogen* in the very depths of the forest; *ge sig ut på ~t vatten* (*bildl.*) get out of one's depth

djup|blå deep blue **-borrning** deep-drilling **-dykning** deep-sea diving **-frys** deepfreeze **-frysa** deepfreeze **-frysning** deepfreezing **-fryst** ~ *mat* frozen food **-gående I** *a4* deep; *bildl.* profound, deep; *sjö.* deep-drawing **II** *s6, sjö.* draught **-hav** ocean **-havsfiske** deep-sea fishing **-havsforskning** oceanography

djup|ing [ˣju:-] *vard., en* ~ a deep one **-kurva** *sjö.* depth contour **-loda** strike deep-sea soundings

djup|na [ˣju:p-] get deeper; deepen **-psykologi** depth psychology **-rotad** *a5* deep-rooted, deepseated **-sinne** profundity, depth; profoundness **-sinnig** *a1* deep; profound; (*svårfattlig*) abstruse **-skärpa** *foto.* depth of field

djupt [ju:pt] *adv* deeply; profoundly; ~ *allvarlig* very serious (grave); ~ *liggande* (*bildl.*) deep-rooted, deep-seated; ~ *rörd* deeply (profoundly) moved; ~ *sårad* intensely hurt; *buga sig* ~ bow low; *sjunka* (*falla, gräva, ligga*) ~ sink (fall, dig, lie) deep; *känna sig* ~ *kränkt* feel deeply injured; *djupast sett* at bottom

djuptryck photogravure [printing], intaglio

djur [ju:r] *s7* animal; (*större; föraktfullt*) beast; (*boskaps-*) cattle (*behandlas som pl*); *slita som ett* ~ work like a horse; *vilda* ~ (*ej tama*) wild animals, (*farliga för människan*) wild beasts; *de oskäliga ~en* the dumb brutes; *reta inte ~en* do not tease dumb animals **-art** species (*pl* species) [of animal], animal species **-besättning** [animal] stock **-fabel** [beast] fable **-fabrik** factory farm **-fett** animal fat **-försök** animal experimentation

djur|isk ['ju:-] *a5* animal; (*bestialisk*) bestial; (*rå*) brutal; (*sinnlig*) carnal **-kretsen** the zodiac **-park** zoological garden, zoo **-plågare** tormentor of animals **-plågeri** cruelty to animals **-riket** the animal kingdom **-sjukhus** animal (veterinary) hospital **-skydd** protection of animals **-skyddsförening** society for the prevention of cruelty to animals **-skötare** *lantbr.* cattleman; (*-vårdare*) keeper **-tämjare** animal tamer **-uppfödning** [animal] breeding (farming) **-vårdare** keeper **-vän** *vara stor ~* be very fond of animals **-vänlig** kind to animals **-värld** animal world

djäkne [ˣjä:k-] *s2, ung.* upper-school scholar

djärv [järv] *a1* bold; (*oförvägen*) intrepid, audacious; (*dristig*) daring; (*vågad*) venturesome, venturous; *lyckan står den ~e bi* Fortune favours the brave **djärvas** [ˣjärr-] *v2, dep* dare, venture **djärvhet** [ˣjärv-] boldness; daring; intrepidity, audacity

djäv|la [ˣjä:vla] *oböjligt a* bloody; damn[ed]; *A E. äv.* goddam[n]; *din ~ drummel* you bloody fool **-las** *v1, dep* make hell (*med* for); provoke, incite to anger **-lig** *a1, se djävulsk* **-ligt** *adv, jag är ~ trött* I am devilish (desperately) tired; *en ~ bra pianist* a damn good pianist

djävul [ˣjä:-] *-en djävlar* devil; *djävlar, anamma!* damn [it]!; *jag ska djävlar anamma visa honom* I am bloody well going to show him **djävulsdyrkan** [ˣjä:-] devil-worship **djävulsk** [ˈjä:-] *a5* hellish, devilish; fiendish **djävulskap** [ˣjä:-] *s7* devilry **djävulsrocka** [ˣjä:-] manta [ray], devilfish, devil ray **djävulstyg** *s7* devilry

d-moll D minor

dobbel [ˈdåbb-] *s7* gambling **dobbla** [ˣdåbb-] gamble

docent reader, senior research fellow; *AE.* associate professor

docentur readership *etc.*

docer|a hold forth, pontificate, pontify **-ande** didactic, magisterial; *neds.* lecturing

dock [-å-] (*likväl*) yet, still; (*emellertid*) however; (*ändå*) for all that

1 docka [-å-] *sl* **1** (*leksak, äv. bildl.*) doll; (*marionett o. bildl.*) puppet **2** (*garn-*) skein

2 dock|a [-å-] **l** *sl, sjö.* dock **ll** *v1, sjö. o. rymdfart* dock **-ning** docking

dock|skåp doll's house **-teater** puppet theatre **-vagn** doll's pram

doft [-å-] *s3* scent, odour (*äv. bildl.*); fragrance

dofta [-å-] **1** smell; *det ~r rosor* there is a scent of roses; *vad det ~r härligt!* what a delicious scent! **2** (*beströ*) dust; *~ socker på en kaka* dust a cake with sugar

dog *imperf. av dö*

doge [då:ʃ *el.* ˈdå:dʒe] *s5* doge

dogg [-å-] *s2* bulldog; (*större*) mastiff

dogm [-å-] *s3* dogma **dogmatjk** *s3* dogmatics (*pl, behandlas som sg*), dogmatic (doctrinal) theology **dogmatiker** [-ˈma:-] dogmatist **dogma-**

tisera dogmatize **dogmatisk** [-ˈma:-] *a5* dogmatic[al] **dogmatism** dogmatism

doktor [ˣdåktår] *s3* doctor; (*läkare*) physician; *medicine ~* doctor of medicine

doktorand [-å-] *s3* candidate for the doctorate (doctor's degree) **-stipendium** postgraduate scholarship

doktor|era [-å-] work for a doctor's degree **-inna** *~n A.* Mrs A.

doktors|avhandling doctor's thesis (dissertation) **-disputation** oral defence (public examination) of a [doctor's] thesis **-grad** doctorate, doctor's degree **-hatt** doctor's hat **-promotion** conferring of doctor's degrees **-ring** doctor's ring **-värdighet** doctorate

doktrin [-å-] *s3* doctrine **-är** *a1* doctrinaire

dokument [-å-] *s7* document; *jur. äv.* deed, instrument **-arisk** [-ˈta:-] *a5* documentary **-ation** documentation

dokument|era [-å-] document, substantiate, prove; *~ sig som* establish o.s. as **-förstörare** paper shredder **-portfölj** document case, briefcase **-samling** file [of documents] **-skåp** filing cabinet

dokumentär [-å-] *a1* documentary **-film** documentary [film] **-roman** documentary novel

dold [-å:-] *a1* hidden, concealed; *~a reserver* hidden reserves (assets); *illa ~* ill-concealed, ill-disguised **dolde** [-å:-] *imperf. av dölja*

dolk [-å:-] *s2* dagger; (*kort*) poniard; *sticka ner ngn med ~* stab s.b. **-styng, -stöt** stab [with a dagger *etc.*], dagger-thrust

dollar [ˈdåll-] *s9* dollar; *AE. sl.* buck **-kurs** dollar rate [of exchange] **-prinsessa** dollar princess **-sedel** dollar note (*AE.* bill); *AE. sl.* greenback

dolma [ˣdåll-] *sl* (*plagg*) dolman; (*husars äv.*) dolman jacket

dolomjt *s3* dolomite **Dolomiterna** [-ˈmi:-] *pl* the Dolomites

dolsk [-å:-] *a1* (*lömsk*) insidious; (*bedräglig*) deceitful; (*lurande*) treacherous

dolt [-å:-] *sup. av dölja*

1 dom [då:m, *i sms.* dɔmm] *s3* (*kyrka*) cathedral

2 dom [dɔmm] *s2* (*utlåg*)[e]ment; (*utslag*) verdict; (*i sht i brottmål*) sentence; *~ens dag* Judgment Day, Day of Judgment; *fällande (friande) ~* sentence (verdict) of guilty (not guilty); *yttersta ~en* the Last Judgment; *fälla ~ över* pass sentence upon; *sitta till ~s över* sit in judgment upon; *sätta sig till ~s över* set o.s. up as a judge of

Domarboken [ˣdɔmmar-] [the Book of] Judges **domarbord** [ˣdɔmmar-] judge's (judges') table **domar|e** [ˣdɔmmare] judge; magistrate; (*i högre instans*) justice; (*friare o. bildl.*) arbiter; (*i sporttävling*) umpire; (*i fotboll m.m.*) referee **-ed** judicial oath **-kår** judiciary, bench

domdera [dåmm-] bluster

domedag [ˣdɔmme-] judgment day, doomsday; *till ~s otta* until kingdom come

domedags|basun last trump **-predikan** hellfire sermon

domes|ticera domesticate **-tjk** *s3* **1** (*fodertyg*) cotton lining, denim; (*underklädestyg*) calico **2** (*tjänare*) servant

domherre [ˣdɔmm-] bullfinch

domicjl *s4* domicil[e]

domin|ans [-'ans *el.* -'aŋs] *s3* domination; dominance **-ant** *s3 o. a1* dominant **-era** dominate; (*vara förhärskande*) be predominant, prevail; (*behärska, ha utsikt över*) dominate, command; (*tyrannisera*) domineer **-erande** [-'ne:-] *a4* dominating *etc.*, predominant; ~ *anlag* dominant

dominikan *s3* Dominican **-[er]orden** [the] Dominican Order

dominikansk [-'a:nsk] *a5* Dominican **Dominikanska republiken** Dominican Republic

domino ['dåmm- *el.* 'då:-] **1** *s5* (*dräkt*) domino **2** *s6* (*spelbricka*) domino; (*spel*) *se* **-spel**; **spela ~** play dominoes **-bricka** domino **-spel** dominoes (*pl, behandlas som sg*), game of dominoes **-teori** domino theory

domkapitel [ˣdomm-] [cathedral] chapter

domkraft [ˣdomm-] *s3* jack

domkyrka [ˣdomm-] cathedral; (*i Storbritannien äv.*) minster

domn|a [ˣdåmna] go numb (*äv. ~ av, bort*); *foten har ~t* my foot has gone to sleep **-ing** numbness

domprost [ˣdomm-] dean

dompt|era [-å-] tame [animals] **-ör** [animal] tamer

domsaga [ˣdomm-] *s1* judicial district

domsbasun *se* **domedagsbasun**

domslut judicial decision

domssöndagen the Sunday before Advent

domstol [ˣdomm-] court [of justice (law)]; tribunal (*äv. bildl.*); *vid ~* in the law court; *dra ngn inför ~* bring s.b. before the court; *dra ngt inför ~* go to court (law) about s.th.; *Högsta ~en, ung.* (*i England*) the Supreme Court of Judicature, (*i Skottland*) Court of Justiciary, (*i USA*) the Supreme Court, (*friare*) the supreme court

domstols|förhandlingar court proceedings **-verk** *~et* [the Swedish] national courts administration

domsöndagen *se* **domssöndagen**

dom|villa miscarriage of justice **-värjo** *r* jurisdiction; *lyda under ngns ~* fall under a p.'s jurisdiction

domän *s3* domain **-styrelse** national board of crown forests and lands **-verk** *~et* [the Swedish] forest service

don *s7* (*verktyg*) tool; implement; (*anordning*) device; (*grejor*) gear, tackle; *~ efter person* to every man his due **dona ~ med** (*vard.*) busy o.s. with

donation donation, legacy **donationsfond** donation fund **donator** [-'na:tår] *s3* donor

Donau ['då:nau] *r* the Danube

donera donate; *den ~e summan* the sum presented

doningar *pl, vard.* tools, gear (*sg*), tackle (*sg*)

donjuan [dånn'ju:-] *best. form =, äv. -en, pl -er* Don Juan

donkeypanna [ˣdåŋki-] *sjö.* donkey boiler

donna [-å-] *s1, sl.* (*särsk. AE.*) dame, broad

dop *s7* baptism; (*barn-, fartygs-*) christening; *bära ngn till ~et* present s.b. at the font

dopa dope

dop|attest certificate of baptism **-funt** baptismal (christening) font **-gåva** baptismal gift

doping *se* **dopning**

dop|klänning christening robe **-namn** Christian name

dopning [ˣdo:p-] doping

dopp [-å-] *s7* **1** (*-ning*) dip[ping]; *ta sig ett ~* take a swim **2** (*kaffebröd*) buns, cakes (*pl*) **doppa** dip; (*hastigt*) plunge; (*helt o. hållet*) immerse; (*ge ngn ett dopp*) duck; *~ i grytan* (*ung.*) soak bread in ham broth; *~ sig* have a dip (plunge) **dopparedagen** Christmas Eve

dopping [-å-] *zool.* grebe

dopplereffekt [ˣdåpp-] Doppler effect (shift)

doppning [-å-] dip, plunge; immersion

doppsko [ˣdåpp-] (*beslag*) ferrule

doppvärmare immersion heater

dor[i]er ['do:-] Dorian **dorisk** ['do:-] *a5* Doric, Dorian

dormitorium [dårmi'to:-] *s4* dormitory

dorn [-å:- *el.* -o:-] *s2* mandrel, arbor

dos *s3* dose; *dödlig ~* lethal dose; *för stor ~* overdose

dosa *s1* box; (*för te o.d.*) canister, (*mindre*) caddy

dosekvivalent dose equivalent

1 dosera *med.* dose

2 dosera (*slutta*) slope; *~ en kurva* superelevate (bank, camber) a curve

1 dosering *med.* dosage

2 dosering (*av kurva*) superelevation, bank, camber

dosimeter [-'me:-] *s2* dosimeter, dosemeter

dosis ['do:-] *s3, se* **dos**; *en rejäl ~* a good measure (share)

dosmätare *se* **dosimeter**

dosrat (*måttenhet*) dose rate

dossera *se* **2 dossera** **dossering** *se* **2 dossering**

dossié [dåssi'e:] *s3*, **dossier** [dåssi'e:] *s3* dossier, file

dotter [-å-] **-n** *döttrar* daughter **-bolag** affiliated company, affiliate; subsidiary [company] **-dotter** granddaughter **-lig** *a1* daughterly **-son** grandson **-svulst** metastasis

douglasgran Douglas fir (spruce, hemlock)

dov [-å:-] *a1* (*om ljud*) dull, hollow, muffled; (*om värk*) aching; (*halvkvävd*) stifled, suppressed

dovhjort fallow deer; (*hane*) buck

doyen [*svenskt uttal* doa'jäŋ] *s3* doyen

dra (*draga*) drog dragit **1 1** draw; (*kraftigare*) pull, tug; (*släpa*) drag, haul; *drag!* pull!; *~ en historia* reel off a story; *~ fullt hus* draw full houses; *~ ngn i håret* pull s.b. by the hair, pull a p.'s hair; *~ i* (*ur*) *led* set into (put out of) joint; *~ ngn inför rätta* bring s.b. before the court; *~ kniv* draw a knife (*mot* on); *~ en kopia* run off a copy; *~ ett kort* draw a card; *~ lakan* stretch (pull) sheets; *~ ett tungt lass* pull a heavy load; *~ lott* draw lots; *~ en lättnadens suck* breathe a sigh of relief; *~ olycka över ngn* bring disaster [up]on s.b.; *~ slutsatser om* draw conclusions on, conclude; *~ ett streck över* draw a line across, *bildl.* let bygones be bygones; *~ det kortaste strået* come off worst, get the worst of it; *~ sitt strå till stacken* do one's part (bit); *~ uppmärksamheten till* draw attention to; *komma ~gandes med* come along with; *~s* (*känna sig dragen*) *till ngn* feel drawn to (attracted by) s.b. **2** (*driva*) work (*en maskin* a machine); (*vrida*) turn (*veven* the crank) **3** (*subtrahera*) take [away], subtract; (*erfordra*) take; (*förbruka*) use [up]; *~ kostnader* involve cost (expenses) **4** (*om te o.d.*) draw **5** (*tåga*) march, go; *~ i fält* take the

D

field; ~ *i krig* go to the wars; ~ *sina färde* take one's departure; ~ *åt skogen* go to blazes; *gå och* ~ hang about (around) **6** ~ *efter andan* gasp for breath; ~ *på munnen* smile; *det ~r här* there is a draught here **II** *rfl* **1** *(förflytta sig)* move, pass; *(bege sig)* repair **2** *ligga och* ~ *sig (om morgnarna)* lie in; ~ *sig efter (om klocka)* lose, be losing; *klockan ~r sig tio minuter [efter] varje dag* the clock loses ten minutes every day; *klockan har ~git sig fem minuter [efter]* the clock is five minutes slow; ~ *sig före (om klocka)* gain, be gaining; *klockan ~r sig fem minuter före varje dag* the clock gains five minutes every day; *klockan har ~git sig fem minuter före* the clock is five minutes fast; ~ *sig fram* get on (along); ~ *sig för ngt (för att + inf.)* be afraid of s.th. (of + ing-form); *inte* ~ *sig för ngt (för att)* (äv.) not mind s.th. (not mind + ing-form); ~ *sig tillbaka* draw [o.s.] back, retire, *mil.* retreat; ~ *sig undan* move (draw) aside, withdraw; ~ *sig ur spelet* quit the game, *(friare)* back out, give up, *vard.* chuck [up] **III** *(med betonad partikel)* **1** ~ *av a)* *(klä av)* pull (take) off, *b)* *(dra ifrån)* deduct; ~ *av ringen från fingret* slip the ring from one's finger **2** ~ *bort a)* draw away, *(trupper e.d.)* withdraw, *b)* *(gå bort)* move off, go away, *(om trupper e.d.)* withdraw **3** ~ *fram a)* *(ta fram)* draw (pull) out, *(väg e.d.)* construct, *bildl.* bring up, produce, *b)* *(gå fram)* advance, march; ~ *fram stolen till bordet* draw up the chair to the table; ~ *fram genom (äv.)* traverse **4** ~ *för* pull *(gardinerna* the curtains) **5** ~ *förbi* go past, pass by **6** ~ *ifrån a)* draw (pull) back *(gardinerna* the curtains), *b)* *(ta bort)* take away, subtract, *c)* *sport.* draw away *(de andra* from the rest) **7** ~ *igen (dörr e.d.)* close, shut **8** ~ *igenom (band e.d.)* pull (draw) through; ~ *igenom boken* skim (through) the book **9** ~ *i gång ngt* set s.th. working; ~ *i gång med ngt* get s.th. going **10** ~ *ihop sig* contract, *(sluta sig)* close; *det ~r ihop sig till oväder* a storm is gathering; *det ~r ihop sig till regn* it looks like rain **11** ~ *in* draw in *(äv. bildl.)*, *(återtaga, återfordra)* withdraw, *(avskaffa)* abolish, do away with, *(konfiskera)* confiscate; *(underhåll o.d.)* stop, discontinue; *(tidning, körkort)* suspend; ~ *in ett körkort* take away *(på viss tid:* suspend) a driving licence; ~ *in ett flyg* cancel (call off) a flight; ~ *in magen* pull in one's stomach; ~ *in (installera) vatten* lay on water; ~ *in på (inskränka)* cut down **12** ~ *i väg* move off, march away **13** ~ *jämnt* get on (along) *(med ngn* with s.b.) **14** ~ *med* drag along; ~ *med sig a) eg.* take about with one, *b) bildl.* bring with it (them), *(innebära)* involve; ~ *med sig ngn i fallet* drag s.b. down with one **15** ~ *ner a)* pull down *(rullgardinen* the blind), *b)* *(smutsa ner)* make dirty **16** ~ *omkull* pull down, *(slå omkull)* knock down **17** ~ *på (starta)* start [up], *(öka farten)* speed up; ~ *på sig* pull (put) on, *(bildl.)* catch **18** ~ *till (hårdare)* pull tighter, tighten; ~ *till bromsen* apply the brake; ~ *till med en svordom* come out with an oath; ~ *till sig a) eg.* draw towards one, *b)* *(attrahera)* attract *(äv. bildl.)* **19** ~ *tillbaka* draw back, *(trupper äv.)* withdraw **20** ~ *undan* draw (pull) aside, withdraw, remove **21** ~ *upp* draw (pull) up, *(fisk äv.)* land, *(butelj)* uncork, *(klocka)* wind up; ~ *upp ankaret* weigh an-

chor; ~ *upp benen under sig* curl up one's legs; ~ *upp med roten* pull up by the roots **22** ~ *ur* draw (pull) out **23** ~ *ut a)* draw (pull) out, *(förlänga)* draw out, prolong, *(tänja ut)* stretch out, *b)* *(tåga ut)* go off *(i krig* to the wars), *c)* *(om rök e.d.)* find its way out; ~ *ut en tand* extract a tooth; *det ~r ut på tiden (tar lång tid)* it takes rather a long time, *(blir sent)* it is getting late; *det drog ut på tiden innan* it was a long time (a long time elapsed) before **24** ~ *vidare* move (march) on **25** ~ *åt* draw (pull) tight[er], tighten; ~ *åt svångremmen (bildl.)* tighten one's belt; ~ *åt sig (bildl.)* attract, *(absorbera)* absorb, suck up *(damm* dust) **26** ~ *över på ett konto* overdraw an account; ~ *över tiden* run over [the] time; ~ *över sig* pull over one

drabant 1 *(livvakt)* bodyguard; *(följeslagare)* henchman **2** *astr. o. bildl.* satellite **-stat** satellite state

drabba 1 *(träffa)* hit, strike; *(hända ngn)* happen to, *åld. o. litt.* befall; *(komma på ngns lott)* fall [up]on; *(beröra)* affect; *förlusten ~r honom ensam* he, alone, bears the loss, the loss falls upon him alone; ~*s av en olycka* meet with misfortune; ~*s av en svår förlust* suffer a heavy loss; ~*s av sjukdom* be stricken with illness **2** ~ *ihop (samman)* meet, have an encounter *(om trupper)*, come to blows *(om enskilda)*, *bildl.* [come into] conflict, clash **drabbning** battle; action; *(friare)* encounter

drack *imperf. av dricka*

drag *s7* **1** *(-ande)* pull, tug; *(med penna, stråke etc.)* stroke; *i några snabba* ~ with a few bold strokes **2** *(spel. o. friare)* move; *ett skickligt* ~ a clever move **3** *(luftström)* draught, *AE.* draft; *sitta i* ~ sit in a draught; *det är dåligt* ~ *i spisen* the stove is drawing badly **4** *(bloss)* puff, whiff; *njuta i fulla* ~ enjoy to the full **5** *(drickande)* draught; *tömma glaset i ett* ~ empty the glass at a gulp (draught) **6** *(anletsdrag)* feature; *(karaktärsdrag)* trait; *(anstrykning)* touch, strain; *ett utmärkande* ~ *för* a characteristic [feature] of **7** *(fiskredskap)* spoon[bait], spinner **8** *vard.*, *i det ~et* at this juncture

draga *se dra*

dragant *s3, s4* tragacanth

dragare *(lastdjur)* draught animal, beast of burden

dragas *se dras*

drag|band drawstring **-basun** slide trombone **-djur** *se dragare*

dragé [-ʃe:] *s3* dragée

dragen *a5 (lindrigt berusad)* tipsy

dragg *s2* drag, dragnet; *(litet ankare)* grapnel **dragga** drag *(efter* for); *(om båt)* drag anchor **draggning** dragging

drag|harmonika concertina **-hund** draught dog **-hållfasthet** tensile strength

drag|ig *a1* draughty **-it** *sup. av dra[ga]*

drag|kamp tug of war **-kedja** *se blixtlås* **-kraft** traction force; *(järnv. etc.* traction power **-kärra** handcart **-nagel** *vard.* dram, tot

dragning [-a:-] **1** draw *(äv. lott- o. bildl.)*; dragging; pull **2** *(böjelse)* tendency, inclination *(till* for); *(dragningskraft)* attraction **3** *(skiftning)* tinge *(åt gult* of yellow)

dragnings|kraft attraction; *(tyngdkraft)* gravity

-lista lottery prize list
dragoman s3 dragoman (pl äv. *dragomen*)
dragon s3 **1** (*ryttare*) dragoon **2** bot. tarragon, estragon
drag|plåster bildl. attraction, vard. draw; AE. äv. drawing card **-skåp** kem. fume cupboard **-snöre** se *dragband* **-spel** accordion; (*mindre*) concertina **-spänning** tension, tensile stress **-stift** drawing pen
drakblod dragon's blood (äv. *harts*) **drakblodsträd** dragon tree; (*släkte*) dracaena
drak|e s2 dragon (äv. bildl.); (*leksak o. meteor.*) kite; (*skepp*) Viking [dragon] ship **-flygning** kite flying
drakma ['drack-] s3 drachma
drakonisk [-'kɔ:-] a5 Draconian, Draconic
drak|skepp se *drake* **-sådd** en ~ a sowing of dragon's teeth
drama s4 drama
dramat|ik s3 drama, dramatics (*pl, behandlas vanl. som sg*) **-iker** [-'ma:-] dramatist, playwright **-isera** dramatize **-isering** [-'se:-] dramatization **-isk** [-'ma:-] a5 dramatic; *D~a institutet* University College of Film, Television, Radio and the Theatre; *Kungliga Dramatiska teatern* the Royal Dramatic Theatre **-urg** [-g] s3 dramaturge, dramaturgist
drank s3 slop[s]
drapa s1 [bardic] ode (*över* on)
drapera drape, hang **draperi** curtain, drapery, hangings (*pl*); AE. äv. drapes **drapering** draping, drapery
dras (*dragas*) drogs dragits, dep, ~ *med* a) (*sjukdom*) be afflicted with, suffer from, b) (*skulder, bekymmer*) be harassed by, c) (*utstå*) put up with
drastisk ['drass-] a5 drastic
drasut s3 tall ungainly fellow
drav s2, s4 draff; (*skräp*) rubbishy mess
dravel ['dravv-] s7 drivel, nonsense
dreg|el ['dre:-, äv. 'dregg-] s7, **dregla** [ˣdre:-, äv. ˣdregg-] drivel, slobber
drej|a [ˣdrejja] **1** tekn. turn **2** sjö.: ~ *bi* heave (lay) to **-skiva** potter's wheel
dress s3, s2 dress, attire; togs (*pl*)
dresser|a train (*till* for); (*friare*) drill; (*häst, hund* äv.) break **-ing** training etc.
dressin s3 trolley
dressing ['dress-] [salad] dressing
dressyr s3 (*animal*) training; (*häst-*) dressage; *i sht bildl.* drill **-ridning** dressage [riding]
dressör trainer [of animals]
1 drev s7 (*blånor o.d.*) oakum
2 drev s7 (*hjul*) [driving] pinion; (*växel*) gear [wheel]
3 drev s7, jakt. drive, beat
4 drev imperf. av *driva*
dreva (*t. 1 drev*) caulk
drev|jakt battue **-karl** beater, driver
dribbl|a dribble **-are** dribbler **-ing** dribbling, dribble
dricka I s7 (*läskedryck*) soft drink, lemonade; (*öl*) beer; ~*t* (= *sjön, havet*), vard. the drink **II** *drack druckit* drink; (*intaga*) have, take; ~ *brunn* take (drink) the waters; ~ *i botten* drain one's glass; ~ *kaffe* have coffee; ~ *ngns skål* drink a p.'s health, drink the health of a p.; ~ *ngn till* pledge

s.b.; ~ *ngn under bordet* drink s.b. under the table; ~ *ur kaffet* finish one's coffee; ~ *ur sitt glas* empty (drain) one's glass; ~ *sig full* get drunk (intoxicated); ~ *sig otörstig* quench one's thirst; *han har börjat* ~ he has taken to drinking
drickbar a1 drinkable, fit to drink
dricks s3 tip; *ge* ~ tip; *ge 1 pund i* ~ give a one-pound tip **-fontän** bubbler, drinking fountain **-glas** [drinking] glass; tumbler; *ett* ~... a glass [ful] of... **-pengar** tip (*sg*); gratuity (*sg*); service [charge] (*sg*) **-vatten** drinking water
drift s3 **1** (*drivande*) drifting; *råka (komma i)* ~ get adrift; *ungdom på* ~ youth (young people) adrift **2** (*skötsel*) management, administration, (*gång*) running, operation; *i (ur)* ~ in (out of) operation (service); *billig i* ~ economical; *stoppa* ~*en* stop production; *övergå till elektrisk* ~ change to electric power **3** (*trafik*) traffic **4** (*instinkt, böjelse*) instinct, urge; impulse; *göra ngt av egen* ~ do s.th. of one's own accord **5** (*gyckel*) joking
driftig a1 energetic, enterprising, pushing **-het** energy, enterprise, push
drift|kapital working capital **-kucku** s2 laughing stock **-liv** instincts (*pl*)
drifts|budget working budget **-ingenjör** production engineer **-inskränkning** production cutback **-inställelse** stoppage, close-down, shutdown **-kostnad** running costs (*pl*)
drift|stopp se *driftinställelse* **-störning** breakdown, stoppage **-säker** dependable, reliable
1 drill s2 (*exercis*) drill
2 drill s2 (*borr*) drill
3 drill s2, mus. trill, quaver; (*fåglars*) warble; *slå sina* ~*ar* warble
1 drilla (*exercera*) drill
2 drilla (*borra*) drill
3 drilla mus. trill, quaver; warble
drillande a4, mus. trilling etc.
drillborr [spiral] drill, wimble
drilling three-barrel gun
drillsnäppa common sandpiper
drink s2 drink **-are** drunkard
drista ~ *sig* [*till*] *att* be bold enough to, venture to **dristig** a1 bold, daring **dristighet** boldness, daring
drittel s2 cask, butter keg
driv|a I s1 [snow]drift; *snön låg i djupa* ~*or* the snow lay in huge drifts **II** *drev drivit* **1** drive; (*maskin*) work, operate; (*fram-*) propel; (*fabrik o.d.*) run, conduct **2** (*i drivbänk*) force **3** (*täta*) caulk **4** (*metall*) chase **5** (*bedriva*) carry on; (*politik*) pursue **6** (*tvinga*) drive, force **7** (*förmå*) impel, urge, prompt **8** ~ *ngn på flykten* rout s.b., put s.b. to flight; ~ *ngt i höjden* force (screw) s.th. up; ~ *saken för långt* push (carry) things too far **9** (*föras undan*) drive; (*sjö. o. om moln, snö e.d.*) drift; ~ *för ankar* drag anchor **10** *gå och* ~ walk aimlessly about, loaf [about] **11** ~ *med ngn* poke fun at s.b. **12** (*med betonad partikel*) ~ *igenom ett lagförslag* force (push) through a bill; ~ *sin vilja igenom* get one's own way; ~ *in* (*pengar, fordran*) collect, call in, jur. recover; ~ *omkring* drift (walk aimlessly) about; *fartyget drev omkring* the ship was adrift; ~ *på* urge on; ~ *samman boskapen* herd the cattle; ~ *tillbaka* drive back, repel; ~ *upp* (*i*

höjden) force up; *(damm e.d.)* raise; *(villebråd)* rouse, raise; *(affär)* work up; ~ *ut* drive (push) out, cast out

driv|ande *a4* driving *etc.*; *den* ~ *kraften* the driving force, *(om pers. äv.)* the prime mover; ~ *karl* pushing man; ~ *vrak* floating wreck **-ankare** sea (drift) anchor **-axel** [driving] shaft **-bänk** hotbed

driv|en *a3* **1** *(skicklig)* clever; *(erfaren)* skilful, skilled, practised; ~ *handstil (ung.)* flowing hand **2** *(ciselerad)* chased **-fjäder** mainspring; *bildl. äv.* incentive, motive **-garn** drift net **-hjul** driving wheel (gear) **-hus** greenhouse, hothouse **-huseffekt** greenhouse effect **-husplanta** hothouse plant **-is** drift ice

driv|it *sup. av driva* **-kraft** motive power; *(om pers. äv.)* prime mover; *tekn. äv.* propelling force **-medel** *(för fordon)* [motor] fuel; *(för projektil)* propulsive agent, propellant **-mina** floating (drifting) mine **-ning** [-i:-] driving; *(tätning)* caulking **-raket** booster [rocket], launching vehicle **-rem** driving (transmission) belt **-ved** driftwood

1 drog [-ɔ:-] *imperf. av dra[ga]*

2 drog [-å:-] *s3* drug

drog|a [-å:-] drug **-fri** drug free **-handel** drugstore **-handlare** druggist **-växt** medicinal plant

dromedar *s3* dromedary, Arabian camel

dropp [-å-] *s7* drip; *med. äv.* infusion

dropp|a [-å-] **1** *(falla i droppar)* drip, fall in drops **2** *(hälla droppvis)* drop *(i* into) **-avskiljare** droplet separator **-boll** *sport.* drop shot

dropp|e *s2* drop; globule; *(svett-)* bead; *en* ~ *i havet* a drop in the bucket (the ocean) **-flaska** drop bottle **-fri** nondrop **-infektion** droplet infection **-skål** *kokk.* drip[ping] pan **-sten** dripstone; *(nedhängande)* stalactite; *(upprättstående)* stalagmite **-torka** drip-dry **-vis** drop by drop

drosk|a [-å-] *s1* cab **-bil** cab, [taxi]cab **-chaufför, -förare** cab (taxi) driver, cabman **-kusk** cabman **-station** cab rank **-ägare** taxi owner (proprietor)

drossel ['dråss-] *s2, radio.* choke [coil]

drots [-å-] *s2, hist.* Lord High Steward

drott [-å-] *s2* king, ruler, sovereign, sire

drottning [-å-] queen; *(bi-)* queen [bee]; *balens* ~ belle of the ball; *göra en bonde till* ~ *(schack.)* queen [a pawn]

drucken *a3, predik.* drunk; intoxicated, tipsy **druckit** *sup. av dricka*

drulla ~ *omkull* sprawl, fall over; ~ *i vattnet* tumble into the water **drulle** *s2* oaf **drulleförsäkring** liability insurance **drullig** *a1* clumsy **drullighet** clumsiness

drumla *se drulla* **drumlig** *a1* clumsy, awkward; *(fumlig)* bungling **drummel** [ˣdrumm- *el.* ˈdrumm-] *s2* lout

drunkna be (get) drowned; *bildl.* be (get) swamped *(i* with); *en* ~*nde* a drowning man *(etc.)* **drunkning** drowning **drunkningsolycka** drowning accident

drupit *sup. av drypa*

druv|a *s1* grape **-blå** grape-purple **-hagel** grapeshot **-klase** bunch (cluster) of grapes **-saft** grape juice **-socker** grape sugar, dextrose

dryad *s3* dryad

dryck *s3* drink; beverage; *mat och* ~ meat and drink; *alkoholfri* ~ nonalcoholic beverage; *starka* ~*er* strong drinks, liquor *(sg)*

dryckenskap *s3* drunkenness, inebriation

dryckes|broder fellow toper; pot (boon) companion **-horn** drinking horn **-kanna** stoup **-kärl** drinking vessel **-lag** *s7* drinking bout, binge, spree, carousal **-varor** *pl* drinks, beverages **-visa** drinking song

dryckjom [-åmm] *n, r* **1** drinking, carousing **2** *se dryckesvaror*

dryfta discuss, talk over

dryg *a1* **1** *(som räcker länge)* lasting; *(som väl fyller måttet)* liberal, ample, large; *(rågad)* heaped; *en* ~ *mil* a good mile; ~*t mått* full measure; ~ *portion* large helping; ~ *timme* full (good) hour **2** *(mödosam)* hard; *(betungande)* heavy; ~*t arbete* hard work; ~*a böter* a heavy fine **3** *(högfärdig)* stuck-up, self-important **dryga** ~ *ut vin med vatten* add water to the wine **dryghet** self-importance **drygt** [-y:-] *adv*, ~ *hälften* a good half of it (them); *mäta* ~ give full measure; ~ *mätt* full measure

drypa *dröp drupit* **1** *(hälla droppvis)* drop, pour a few drops of *(på* on to; *i* into) **2** *(ge ifrån sig vätska)* drip; *(rinna ned)* trickle; *han dröp av svett* he was dripping with perspiration

dråp *s7* homicide; *jur.* manslaughter **-are** homicide **-lig** [-å:-] *a1* very funny, killing **-slag** deathblow; *bildl. äv.* staggering blow

dråsa come down in masses; ~ *ner* come tumbling down

drägel, drägla *se dregel, dregla*

drägg *s2, ej pl* dregs *(pl)*; *(slödder)* scum

dräglig [-ä:-] *a1* tolerable, endurable; fairly acceptable

dräkt *s3* dress; *(jacka o. kjol)* suit costume; *(national-)* costume; *(friare)* attire, garb

dräktig *a1* pregnant, big with young **-het 1** pregnancy **2** *sjö.* tonnage, capacity

dräll *s3* diaper

dräll|a *v2* **1** spill **2** *gå och* ~ hang about (around); *det -er av karlar* it's lousy with men

drämma *v2*, ~ *näven i bordet* bang one's fist on the table; ~ *till ngn* strike s.b., give s.b. a clout

drän *s3* drain *(äv. med.)* **-age** [-ˈa:ʃ] *s7, se drän* **-era** drain **-ering** [-ˈne:-] draining, drainage **-eringsrör** drainpipe

dräng *s2* farm hand; *själv är bästa* ~ if you want a thing well done, do it yourself; *sådan herre sådan* ~ like master like man **-kammare** farm-hand's room **-stuga** farm-hand's quarters *(pl)*

dränk|a *v3* drown; *(översvämma)* flood; ~ *in med olja* [impregnate with] oil; ~ *sig* drown o.s. **-ning** drowning

dräpa *v3* kill; *åld. o. litt.* slay; *du skall icke* ~ thou shalt not kill; ~*nde svar* crushing reply

drätsel|kammare, -nämnd [borough] finance department

dröglapp [-ö:-] *zool.* dewlap

dröj|a [ˣdröjja] *v2* **1** *(låta vänta på sig)* be late *(med att* in + *ing*-form); *(vara sen)* be long *(med ngt* about s.th.; *med att* about + *ing*-form); *du har -t länge* it has taken you a long time; *svaret -de* the answer was a long time in coming **2** *(låta anstå)* postpone, delay, put off; *(tveka)* hesitate; ~ *med* *svaret* (*att svara*) hesitate to answer, put off answering; ~ *på stegen* dawdle **3** (*vänta med*) wait **4** (*stanna kvar*) stop, stay; tarry, linger; *var god och dröj* (*tel.*) hold the line, please; ~ *kvar till slutet* stay on (remain) till the end; ~ *vid ngt* dwell [up]on **5** *opers., det -er länge innan* it will be a long time before; *det -de inte länge förrän* it was not long before; *det -de en evighet innan* it was ages before **-ande** *a4*, ~ *steg* dawdling footsteps; ~ *blick* lingering gaze; ~ *svar* hesitating answer

dröjs|mål *s7* delay; *utan* ~ without delay, immediately **-målsränta** penalty interest on arrears

dröm [-ömm] *s2* dream; *bildl. äv.* daydream, reverie, revery; *hon var vacker som en* ~ she looked a dream; ~*men slog in* the dream came true; *försjunken i* ~*mar* lost in a reverie (daydreams *pl*) **-bild** vision **-bok** book of dreams **-jobb** dream job **-lik** dreamlike; dreamy **-lös** dreamless

drömm|a *v2* dream; *bildl. äv.* muse; ~ *sig tillbaka till* carry o.s. back in imagination to **-ande** *a4* dreamy **-are** dreamer; visionary **-eri** dreaming; *ett* ~ a reverie

dröm|sk *a5* dreamy **-slott** *mitt* ~ the castle of my dreams **-sömn** REM (rapid eye movement) sleep **-tydning** interpretation of dreams (a dream) **-villa** dream house **-värld** dream world

drön|a drowse, idle **-are 1** (*bi*) drone [bee] **2** *pers.* sluggard, snail

dröp *imperf. av* drypa

dröppel ['dröpp-] *s2, se* gonorré

drös|a shower (tumble) down **-vis** *vard.* masses [of]

du you; *bibl., poet., dial.* thou; ~ *själv* you yourself; *hör* ~, *kan jag få låna...?* I say, can you lend me...?; *hör* ~, *det här går inte!* look here, this won't do!; *nej. vet* ~ [*vad*]! I never heard of such a thing!; *nej, vet* ~ *vad, nu gör vi ngt annat* look here (listen), let's do something else; *det skall* ~ *säga!* you've no room to talk!; *vi är* ~ *med varandra* we call each other by our Christian names; *bli* ~ *med* drop the formalities of address with

dua be on Christian name terms with

dual|ism dualism **-ist** dualist **-istisk** [-'liss-] *a5* dualistic

dubb *s2* stud (*äv. på t.ex. fotbollsskor*), knob; (*is-*) [ice] prod; (*däck-*) stud, (*för tävling*) spike **1 dubba** ~ *ngn till riddare* dub s.b. a knight **2 dubba** (*film e.d.*) dub **3 dubba|a** (*däck*) stud **-däck** studded tyre

dubbel ['dubb-] **1** *a2* double; ~ *bokföring* double-entry book-keeping; *ligga* ~ *av skratt* be doubled up with laughter; *vika* ~ [fold] double; *det dubbla* twice as much; *dubbla beloppet* twice the amount; *dubbla storleken* double the size **2** *s2* (*i tennis m.m.*) doubles (*pl*) **-agent** double agent **-arbetande** *a4* doing two jobs; ~ *kvinnor* housewives with a paid (an outside) job **-arbete** (*samma arbete*) duplication of work; (*två arbeten*) two jobs

dubbel-b *mus.* double flat

dubbel|beckasin great snipe **-beskattning** double taxation **-betydelse** *se* -mening **-bindning** *kem.* double bond **-bottnad** [-å-] *a5* (*om sko*) double-soled; *bildl.* ambiguous, with double meaning **-bröllop** double wedding **-bössa** double-barrelled gun **-däckare** double-decker

-dörr double door **-exponering** *foto.* double exposure **-fel** (*i tennis*) double fault, double **-fönster** double glazing **-gångare** double **-haka** double chin **-het** doubleness **-knäppt** *a4* double-breasted **-kommando** dual control **-kontakt** *elektr.* two-way plug **-kontroll** double check **-kontrollera** double-check **-kors** *mus.* double sharp **-liv** double life **-match** (*i tennis m.m.*) doubles (*pl*) **-mening** double meaning **-moral** double standard [of morality] **-mord** double murder **-myntfot** bimetallism, gold and silver standard **-namn** double-barrelled (hyphenated) name **-natur** split personality **-nelson** (*i brottning*) full nelson **-parkera** double-park **-pipig** *a1* double-barrelled **-riktad** *a5*, ~ *trafik* two-way traffic **-roll** dual role; *bildl.* double game **-rum** double room **-schack** double check **-seende** *s6* double vision **-seger** double win **-sidig** *a1* double-sided; ~ *lunginflammation* double pneumonia **-spel** *bildl.* double-dealing, double-cross; (*i tennis m.m.*) doubles (*pl*) **-spelare** (*i tennis m.m.*) doubles player **-spion** *se* -agent **-spår** double track **-spårig** *a1* double-track[ed] **-stjärna** double star; (*fysisk*) binary star; (*optisk*) optical double star **-säng** double bed

dubbel|t ['dubb-] *adv* doubly; (*två gånger*) twice (*så* as); ~ *försiktig* doubly careful; ~ *så gammal som jag* twice my age; *bjuda* ~ *upp* bid as much again; *se* ~ see double **-trampa** (*i bil*) double-declutch; *AE.* double-clutch **-trast** mistle (missel) thrush **-tydig** *a1, se* tvetydig **-verkande** *a4* double-acting **-vikt** [-i:-] *a4* doubled; ~ *av skratt* doubled up with laughter; ~ *krage* turndown collar **-yxa** two-edged axe **-örn** double eagle

dubbla double

dubblé *s3* **1** (*guldsmedsarbete*) gold (silver) plated metal **2** *jakt.* double hit **3** *spel.* cushion[ing]

dubbler|a 1 double **2** *sjö.* round **3** *teat.* understudy **-ing** doubling *etc.*

dubblett *s3* **1** (*kopia*) duplicate, copy, double **2** (*tvårumslägenhet*) two-roomed flat **3** (*ord-*) doublet **-exemplar** duplicate copy **-nyckel** duplicate key

1 dubbning (*av riddare*) dubbing, accolade

2 dubbning (*av film*) dubbing

dubi|er ['du:-] *pl, ha sina* ~ have one's doubts (*om* about) **-ös** *a1* dubious

ducka duck

duell *s3* duel (*på pistol* with pistols) **-ant** dueller, duellist **-era** duel

duenna [-ˣenna] *s1* duenna

duett *s3* duet[te], duo

duffel ['duff-] *s2* duffel coat **-knapp** toggle

dug|a *v2 el. dög dugt* do; be suitable (*till* for); (*komma t. pass*) serve; (*vara god nog*) be good enough (*åt* for); *det -er* that will do; *det -er inte att* it won't do to; *-er ingenting till* is no use (good); *det var en karl som hette* ~ that is what I call a man; *visa vad man -er till* show what one is worth; *han dög inte till lärare* he was no good as a teacher **-ande** *a4* efficient; competent; *en* ~ *kraft* a competent person; *se äv.* duglig

dugg *s7* **1** (*regn*) drizzle **2** *inte ett* ~ not a bit (scrap), not the least; *det är inte värt ett* ~ it is not worth a farthing (jot); *inte bry sig ett* ~ *om* not care a fig for; *hon gör aldrig ett* ~ she never does a thing

dugg|**a** drizzle; *det* ~*r* it is drizzling; *det* ~*de* [*med*] *ansökningar* applications came pouring in **-regn** drizzle **-regna** *se* dugga

duglig [ˣduːg-] *a1* able; capable (*till* of; *till att* of + *ing-form*); competent, qualified, efficient **-het** competence; capability; ability; efficiency

duk *s2* cloth; (*bord-*) tablecloth; (*målar- o. sjö.*) canvas; (*film-*) screen; (*flagga*) flag, bunting **1 duka** ~ [*bordet*] lay the table; *bordet var* ~*t för två* the table was laid for two; *ett* ~*t bord* a table ready laid; ~ *av* clear the table; ~ *fram* put on the table; ~ *upp en historia* cook up a story **2 duka** ~ *under* succumb (*för* to)

dukat ducat

dukning [-uː-] laying the (a) table

dukt *s3* strand

duktig *a1* **1** (*dugande*) able, capable, efficient (*i att* at + *ing-form*); (*skicklig*) clever, accomplished (*i ngt* at s.th.; *i att* at + *ing-form*) **2** (*käck*) brave **3** (*kraftig*) vigorous, powerful; (*frisk*) strong **4** *ett* ~*t mål mat* a substantial meal; *en* ~ *portion* a good-sized helping **5** *han fick en* ~ *skrapa* he got a good rating (telling-off); *det var* ~*t!* well done!

duktigt *adv* (*kraftigt*) powerfully; (*ihärdigt*) sturdily; (*med besked*) soundly, thoroughly; (*strängt*) hard; (*skickligt*) efficiently, cleverly; *han har arbetat* ~ he has worked hard; *han tjänar* ~ *med pengar* he earns plenty of money; *äta* ~ eat heartily; *få* ~ *med stryk* get a sound thrashing

dum [dumm] *a1* stupid; *AE.* dumb; (*obetänksam*) silly, foolish; *han är ingen* ~ *karl* he is no fool; *han är inte så* ~ *som han ser ut* he is not such a fool as he looks; *så* ~ *jag var!* what a fool I was!; *det var bra* ~*t av mig att* I was a fool to; *det vore inte så* ~*t att* it would not be a bad idea to **-bom** *s2* fool, ass, blockhead; *din* ~*!* you silly (stupid) [fool]! **-burk** *vard.* goggle box; *särsk. AE.* boob tube **-dristig** foolhardy, rash **-dryg** vain, pompous

dumdumkula dumdum [bullet]

dum|**het** stupidity, folly; silliness, foolishness; ~*er!* rubbish!, nonsense!; *göra en* ~ do a foolish thing, (*svagare*) make a blunder; *prata* ~*er* talk nonsense; *vad är det här för* ~*er?* what is all this nonsense? **-huvud** blockhead, dolt

dumma *rfl* make a fool of o.s.

dummerjöns tomfool

dummy [*svenskt uttal* ˈdummy] *s5* dummy

dump|**a 1** *hand.* dump; undersell **2** (*tippa*) dump **-er** *s2* dumper **-ing** *se* dumpning

dumpit *sup. av* dimpa

dumpning 1 dumping; underselling **2** (*tippning*) dumping

dum|**skalle, -snut** silly idiot

dumt *adv*, *bära sig* ~ *åt* be silly (stupid), act like a fool

dun *s7* down **-bolster** feather bed

dunder [ˈdunn-] *s7* thunder[ing], rumble; (*kanon-, åsk- äv.*) peal, boom; *väggen föll med* ~ *och brak* the wall came crashing down **dundra** thunder, rumble, boom; ~ *mot* thunder (fulminate) against; *åskan* ~*de* there was a clap of thunder **dundrande** *a4*, *en* ~ *succé* a roaring success; *ett*

~ *kalas* a terrific party; *sl.* a humdinger of a party

dunge *s2* grove; (*mindre*) clump of trees

dunig *a1* downy, fluffy

1 dunk *s2* (*behållare*) can

2 dunk 1 *s2* (*slag*) thump **2** *s7* (*dunkande*) thud, thudding **3** *leka* ~ play hide-and-seek (*AE.* hide-and-go-seek); ~ *för mig!* I'm in!

dunka thud; (*bulta*) throb, beat; ~ *ngn i ryggen* thump s.b. on the back; ~ *på piano* thump on the piano

dunkel [ˈdunn-] **I** *a2* dusky, dark; (*hemlighetsfull*) mysterious; (*svårbegriplig*) obscure, abstruse; (*obestämd*) vague; ~ *belysning* (*uppfattning*) dim light (idea); ~*t minne* dim (vague) recollection **II** *s7* dusk, shadow; gloom; dimness; *höljd i* ~ wrapped in obscurity; *skingra dunklet* clear up the mystery **-blå** dark (darkish) blue

dunkning thump[ing]; throbbing

dunkudde down cushion (pillow)

duns *s2* bump, thud **dunsa** ~ *ner* come down with a thud

dunst *s3* fume, vapour, exhalation; *slå blå* ~*er i ögonen på ngn* pull the wool over a p.'s eyes **dunsta 1** ~ *av* (*bort, ut*) evaporate **2** *vard.* (*ge sig iväg*) make o.s. scarce, clear off (out)

dun|**täcke** eiderdown **-unge** fledg[e]ling, (*om pers. äv.*) greenhorn

duo [ˈduːɔ] *s5* duet[te], duo

duodenjt *s3* duodenitis

duol [-ˈɔːl *el.* -ˈåːl] *s3, mus.* duplet

dupera dupe, bluff; *låta sig* ~*s* [allow o.s. to] be duped

duplett *s3, se* dubblett

duplicera duplicate **dupliceringsmaskin** duplicator **duplikat** *s7* duplicate **duplikation** duplication **duplikator** [-ˣaːtår] *s3* duplicator **duplo** [ˈduːplɔ] *in* ~ in duplicate

dur *s3* major; *gå i* ~ be in the major key

durabel [-ˈraː-] *a2* durable; (*präktig*) splendid

durackord major chord

duraluminium duralumin

duration duration

durk *s2, sjö.* floor; (*förvaringsrum*) storeroom; (*ammunitions-, krut-*) magazine

durka bolt, run away

durkdriven (*fullfjädrad*) thoroughpaced, thoroughgoing, cunning, crafty; (*skicklig*) practised

durkslag strainer, colander

duroplast thermosetting plastic

durra *s1, s4* durra, Guinea corn, Indian millet

dur|**skala** major scale **-tonart** major key

dus *n, se sus 2*

dusch *s2* shower [bath] **duscha** take (have) a shower; (*ge en dusch*) [give a] shower **duschrum** shower room

dusk *s7* drizzle **duska** drizzle **duskig** *a1* drizzly **duskväder** drizzly weather

duskål *dricka* ~ (*ung.*) drink to the use of Christian names

dussin *s7* dozen; *ett halvt* ~ half a dozen; *två* ~ *knivar* two dozen knives; *tretton på* ~*et* thirteen to the dozen **-människa** commonplace person **-roman** *vard.* potboiler, penny-dreadful; *AE.* pulp novel **-tal** *s7* dozen; *i* ~ by the dozen **-tals** [-aː-] dozens of **-vara** cheap-line article **-vis** by the dozen

dust *s3* (*strid*) tussle, clash, bout; *bildl. äv.* tilt; *ha en ~ med* have a tussle (bout) with; *det blir en hård ~* it will be a tough fight; *utstå många ~er* have many a tussle, take a lot of knocks

dusör gratuity, fee; (*dricks*) tip

duv|a *s1* pigeon; dove (*äv. bildl. o. poet.*); *-or och hökar* (*polit.*) doves and hawks **-blå** pigeon-blue

duven *a3* (*avslagen*) flat, insipid, vapid; (*dåsig*) drowsy

duv|grå dove-grey **-hök** goshawk **-kulla** *s1, se skogsstjärna*

duvning [-u:-] **1** (*avbasning*) upbraiding, dressing-down; (*handgriplig*) hiding **2** (*inpluggande*) coaching; *ge ngn en ~* coach a p.

duv|slag dovecot[e] **-unge** young pigeon; *hon är ingen ~* she is no chicken

dvala *s1* (*halvslummer*) doze, drowse; (*halv medvetslöshet*) trance, coma; *bildl. äv.* torpor, apathy; *ligga i ~* (*vintertid*) lie dormant, hibernate

dvaldes [-a:-] *imperf. av dväljas*

dvalliknande lethargic; torpid; trance-like

dvalts [-a:-] *sup. av dväljas*

dvs. (*förk. för det vill säga*) i.e.

dväljas *dvaldes dvalts el. v2, dep* dwell, abide, sojourn

dvärg [-j] *s2* dwarf, (*sagofigur äv.*) gnome; pygmy; (*på cirkus*) midget

dvärg|alåt whining **-björk** dwarf birch **-folk** pygmaean people; pygmies (*pl*) **-hund** miniature (toy) dog **-palm** dwarf fan palm, palmetto **-stjärna** dwarf star **-tall** *se martall* **-träd** dwarf tree **-växt 1** (*dvärgform av växt*) dwarf plant **2** (*förkrympt utveckling*) dwarfishness, dwarfism; *vara av ~* be dwarf-sized, be stunted

d.y. (*förk. för den yngre*) *se under yngre*

dy *s3* mud, sludge; *bildl.* mire, slough **-blöt** *se dyvåt*

dyckert ['dyck-] *s2* brad

dyft *endast i uttr.: inte ett ~, se dugg 2*

dygd *s3* virtue; (*kyskhet äv.*) chastity; *~ens väg* the path of virtue; *göra en ~ av nödvändigheten* make a virtue of necessity **dygdemönster** paragon of virtue **dygdig** *a1* virtuous

dygn [dyŋn] *s7* day [and night], twenty-four hours; *~et om* throughout the twenty-four hours, twice (all) round the clock; *en gång om ~et* once in twenty-four hours, once a day

dygns|gammal one-day-old **-lång** *en ~ färd* a twenty-four-hour trip **-rytm** daily rhythm

dyig *a1* muddy, sludgy, miry

dyk|a *v3 el. dök dykt* dive; (*hastigt*) duck [under the surface]; (*om flygplan äv.*) nose dive; *~ ner* dive down, plunge (*i* into); *~ upp* emerge (*ur* out of), *bildl.* crop (turn) up, (*om tanke e.d.*) suggest itself **-and** diving (sea) duck

dykardräkt diving suit (dress)

dykar|e 1 diver **2** *zool.* diving beetle **-glasögon** diving (scuba) mask **-hjälm** diver's helmet **-klocka** diving bell **-sjuka** decompression sickness (illness), *vard.* the bends **-utrustning** diving outfit (equipment)

dykdalb *s3* dolphin

dykläge (*om ubåt*) in the awash position; (*om flygplan*) ready for diving

dykning [-y:-] diving; *konkr.* dive, plunge; *flyg.*

nose dive; (*ubåts*) submergence, submersion, (*snabb*) crash dive

dylik *a5* of that kind (sort), like that, such, similar; *eller* (*och*) *~t* or (and) the like, et cetera; *ngt ~t* something of the sort

dymedelst by that (those) means

dymling dowel [pin]

dymmel|onsdag Wednesday in Holy Week **-vecka[n]** [the] Holy Week

dyn 1 *s3* (*sand-*) dune **2** *r* (*kraftenhet*) dyne

dyna *s1* cushion; pad (*äv. stämpel-*)

dynam|ik *s3* dynamics (*pl, behandlas som sg*) **-isk** [-'na:-] *a5* dynamic

dynamit *s3* dynamite **-and** [-'a:rd] *s3* dynamiter **-patron** stick of dynamite, dynamite cartridge

dynamo [*ˣ*dy:- *el.* 'dy:- *el.* -'na:-] *s5* dynamo **-meter** [-'me:-] *s2* dynamometer

dynasti *s3* dynasty

dyng|a dung, muck; (*gödsel*) manure **-bagge** dung beetle (chafer) **-grep[e]** *s2* muckrake **-hög** dunghill

dyning swell; *i sht bildl.* backwash

dynt *s2, s4* bladder worm

dypöl [mud] puddle

dyr *a1* **1** dear; (*kostsam*) expensive, costly; *det blir ~t i längden* it comes expensive in the long run; *det är ~t att leva här* living is expensive here; *det kommer att stå dig ~t* I'll make you pay for that **2** (*älskad*) dear; (*högtidlig*) solemn; *svära en ~ ed* swear a solemn oath **3** *nu var goda råd ~a* here was a dilemma, now we were in a pickle **-bar** *a1* **1** (*kostsam*) costly, expensive, dear **2** (*värdefull*) valuable; (*högt värderad*) precious **-barhet 1** *abstr.* costliness *etc.* **2** *konkr.* expensive article; *~er* valuables **-grip** *s2* treasure

dyrk *s2* skeleton key, passkey, picklock

1 dyrka *~ upp* (*lås*) pick

2 dyrka (*tillbedja*) worship; (*starkt beundra*) adore

dyrkan *r* worship; adoration **dyrkansvärd** *a1* adorable

dyrkfri burglar-proof

dyr|köpt [-çö:pt] *a4* dearly-bought; (*om seger o.d.*) hard-earned **-ort** cost-of-living index locality

dyrorts|grupp cost-of-living index region **-gruppering** regional division according to cost of living **-tillägg** area (local) allowance

dyrt [-y:-] *adv* **1** (*om kostnad*) dearly, expensively; *bo ~* pay a high rent; *köpa* (*sälja*) *~* buy (sell) dear; *han fick ~ betala sitt misstag* he paid heavily (dear) for his mistake; *stå ngn ~* cost s.b. dear; *sälja sitt liv ~* sell one's life dearly **2** (*högt*) dearly **3** (*högtidligt*) solemnly; *lova ~* promise solemnly, vow

dyrtid period of high prices **dyrtidstillägg** cost-of-living allowance

dys *s3*, **dysa** *s1* spray nozzle

dyscha *s1*, **dyschatell** *s3* couch

dysenteri *s3* dysentery

dys|funktion dysfunction **-lexi** *s3* dyslexia **-pepsi** *s3* dyspepsia

dysprosium ['pro:-] *s8* dysprosium

dyster ['dyss-] *a2* gloomy, dreary; (*till sinnes*) melancholy, sad; *~ färg* sombre colour **dysterhet** gloominess, dreariness; melancholy, sadness

dystra ~ *till* get down in the dumps
dyvelsträck asafoetida
dyvika *s1, sjö.* plug
dyvåt soaking wet, wet through
då I *adv* **1** demonstr. then; at that time, in those days; (*senast vid den tiden*) by then; (*i så fall*) then, in that case; ~ *och då* now and then, once in a while; *det var* ~ *det* things were different then; ~ *för tiden* at that time, in those days; *nå,* ~ *så!* well, then!; *vad nu* ~? what now?; *än sen* ~? what then (next)?, *vard.* so what?; (*har du läst brevet?*) *vilket* ~? which one?; (*sitt inte uppe för länge*) ~ *blir du för trött* or you will be too tired **2** *rel.* (*om tid*) when; (*i vilket fall*) in which case; *den tid kommer* ~ the time will come when; *nu* ~ *vi* now that we **II** *konj* **1** (*temporal*) when; (*med participialkonstruktion*) on; ~ *jag fick se honom tänkte jag* on seeing him I thought; *just* ~ just as **2** (*kausal*) as, since; ~ *så är förhållandet* that being the case; ~ *vädret nu är vackert* since the weather is fine now, the weather being fine now
dåd *s7* deed, act; (*bragd*) feat, exploit; *med råd och* ~ by word and act; *bistå ngn med råd och* ~ give s.b. advice and assistance **-kraftig** energetic, active **-lust** eagerness to achieve great things **-lysten** eager to achieve [great things] **-lös** inactive, inert
dåförtiden *då för tiden* at that time, in those days
dålig *-t sämre sämst* **1** bad; (*otillräcklig, skral*) poor; (*otillfredsställande*) unsatisfactory; (*sämre*) inferior; (*ond*) evil, wicked; (*usel*) mean, base; *en* ~ *affär* a bad bargain; ~ *andedräkt* bad breath; ~*t hjärta* a weak heart; *på* ~*t humör* in a bad temper; ~ *hörsel* bad hearing; ~ *kvalitet* poor (inferior, bad) quality; ~ *luft* bad air; *han är ingen* ~ *människa* there is no harm in him; ~*t rykte* (*samvete*) a bad reputation (conscience); ~ *sikt* poor visibility; ~ *smak* bad taste (*äv. bildl.*); *komma i* ~*t sällskap* get into bad company; ~*a tider* bad (hard) times; ~*a vanor* bad habits; *det var inte* ~*t!* that's not bad! **2** (*sjuk*) ill, not quite well; indisposed; poorly; *AE. äv.* mean; *känna sig* ~ feel out of sorts, feel bad (*AE. äv.* mean)
dålighet *vara ute på* ~*er* (*vard.*) be out on the spree, paint the town red
dåligt *adv* badly; poorly; *affärerna går* ~ business is bad; *höra* ~ hear badly; *ha det* ~ [*ställt*] be badly off; *det gick* ~ *för henne i franska* she did badly in French; *det är* ~ *med respekten* there is a lack of respect; *det blir* ~ *med päron i år* there will not be many pears this year; *se* ~ have poor sight (weak eyes); *äta* ~ have a poor appetite
1 dån *s3, bot.* hemp nettle
2 dån *s7* noise, roar[ing]; thunder; rumble
1 dåna (*dundra*) roar, boom; thunder; rumble
2 dåna (*svimma*) faint [away], swoon [away]
dåndimpen *s i uttr.: få* ~ have a fainting-fit
dår|a infatuate, bewitch **-aktig** *a1* foolish; (*starkare*) idiotic, insane, mad **-aktighet** foolishness; idiocy, madness; *en* ~ a [piece of] folly
dår|e *s2* madman (*fem.* madwoman), lunatic: (*friare*) fool **-fink** nut **-hus** lunatic asylum; *AE., vard.* booby-hatch; *ett rent* ~ bedlam **-skap** *s3* [piece of] folly; *rena* ~*en* sheer madness (folly)
dåsa doze, be drowsy **dåsig** *a1* drowsy, half asleep **dåsighet** drowsiness

dåtida *oböjligt a* the...of that time **dåtiden** *en-ligt* ~*s sed* according to the customs of the time (day)
dåvarande *a4* the...of that time, then; ~ *fröken A.* Miss A., as she was then; *i sakernas* ~ *läge* in the then [existing] state of affairs; *under* ~ *förhållanden* as things were then
d.ä. (*förk. för den äldre*) *se under* äldre
däck *s7* **1** (*fartygs-*) deck; *alle man på* ~! all hands on deck!; *under* ~ below deck; under hatches **2** (*bil-*) tyre; *AE.* tire; *slanglöst* ~ tubeless tyre
däcka *sjö.* deck **däckad** *a5* decked
däckel *s2, boktr.* tympan, packing; (*papperstillverkning*) deckle, deckel
däcks|befäl ship's officers (*pl*) **-hus** deckhouse **-last** deck cargo **-personal** deck staff **-stol** deck chair
dädan from there, thence
dägg|a suck[le] **-djur** mammal
däld *s3* dell, glen
dämma *v2* dam, bank up, stem, block; ~ *för* (*igen, till, upp*) dam up **dämmare** *mus.* damper
dämp|a moderate, check; (*starkare*) subdue; (*ljud*) muffle, hush; (*färg äv.*) tone down, soften; (*eld*) damp [down], extinguish; (*instrument*) mute; *bildl. äv.* damp, calm; (*vrede e.d.*) subdue, suppress; (*en boll*) trap; *med* ~*d röst* in a hushed (subdued) voice **-ning** moderation *etc.*
dän away; *gå* ~! go away!
däng *s7* walloping **dänga** *v2* **1** (*slå*) wallop; smack **2** ~ *iväg* rush off; ~ *till ngn* strike s.b.
där 1 *demonstr.* there; ~ *borta* (*framme, inne, nere, uppe, etc.*) over (on *el.* up, in, down, up *etc.*) there; ~ *hemma* at home; ~ *har vi det!* there you are!; ~ *sa du ett sant ord* you hit the nail on the head there; ~ *ser du* I told you so; *så* ~ like that, in that way; *vem* ~? who's there?; *det finns ingenting* ~ there is nothing there **2** *rel.* where; *ett hus* ~ *man* a house where (in which) you
där|an *vara illa* ~ be in a bad way; *vara nära* ~ *att* come near + ing-form **-av** of (by; from; off, out of; with) it (that, them); ~ *blev ingenting* nothing came of it; ~ *följer att* hence (from that) it follows that; ~ *kommer det sig att* that's [the reason] why; *fem barn,* ~ *tre pojkar* five children, three of them boys; *i anledning* (*till följd*) ~ on that account
där|efter after (for; about; according to by) that (it, them); (*om tid äv.*) afterwards; (*därnäst*) then; *ett par dagar* ~ a few days later; *först* ~ *känner man sig* not until after that will you feel; *resultatet blev* ~ the result was as might have been expected; *rätta sig* ~ conform to it (that) **-emellan** between them; (*om tid*) in between; (*stundtals*) at times **-emot 1** (*emot det*) against it **2** (*emellertid*) on the other hand; (*tvärtom*) on the contrary; *då* ~ whereas, while **-est** if; (*ifall*) in case; ~ *icke* unless
därför I *adv* for (to; of; before; on; in) it (that, them); *han kunde inte ange ngt skäl* ~ he could give no reason for this; *till stöd* ~ in support of it **II** *konj* therefore; (*i början av sats*) so, consequently, accordingly, for that reason, on that account; ~ *att* because; *det var* ~ *som* that is [the reason] why; *det var just* ~ *som* it was just on that account that

därhän 1 (*så långt*) so far, to that point; to such an extent; *det har gått ~ att* it has gone so far that **2** *lämna det* ~ leave it at that

däri in that (it, the matter, the letter *etc.*); (*i detta avseende*) in that respect; (*vari*) in which; ~ *ligger skillnaden* that is where the difference is; ~ *misslyckades han fullständigt* he failed completely there

där|ibland among them (others; other things); including **-ifrån** from there (it, the place *etc.*); ~ *och dit* from there to there; *borta* (*bort*) ~ away, gone; *jag reser* ~ *i morgon* I shall be leaving [there] tomorrow; *han bor inte långt* ~ he lives not so far away [from there]; *långt* ~ (*bildl.*) far from it **-igenom 1** (*från det*) through it (them, the room *etc.*) **2** (*med hjälp därav, medelst detta*) thereby; by that [means], by this, in this way; *redan* ~ *är mycket vunnet* even this is a step in the right direction

därjämte besides, in addition

därmed 1 (*med detta*) by (with) that (it, them, that remark *etc.*); *i enlighet* ~ accordingly; *i samband* ~ in this connection; ~ *gick han sin väg* with that (those words) he departed; ~ *var saken avgjord* that settled the matter; ~ *är inte sagt att* that is not to say that; ~ *är mycket vunnet* that helps a great deal; ~ *är vi inne på* that brings us to; *och* ~ *basta!* and that's that!; *och* ~ *jämförliga varor* and other similar goods **2** (*medelst detta*) by that (those) means **3** (*följaktligen*) so, consequently

därnäst next, in the next place; *den* ~ *följande* the one immediately following

därom 1 *rumsbet.* of it; *norr* (*till höger*) ~ to the north (to the right) of it **2** (*angående den saken*) about (concerning, as to) that (it, the matter *etc.*), on (to, in, of) that; ~ *tvista de lärde* on that point the scholars disagree; ~ *är vi eniga* we agree about that; *vittna* ~ bear witness to that

därpå 1 *rumsbet.* [up]on (in; to; at) it (them *etc.*) **2** *tidsbet.* after that; (*sedan äv.*) then, afterwards; (*därnäst*) next; *dagen* ~ the following (next) day; *strax* ~ immediately afterwards **3** *bildl.* [up]on (of, by, to) it (them *etc.*); *ett bevis* ~ *är* a proof of it (that) is; *ta miste* ~ mistake it

därstädes there

därtill 1 to (for; into; of; at; towards) it (that, them *etc.*); ~ *behövs pengar* for that money is required; ~ *bidrog också* a contributory factor was; ~ *hör också* to that category also belong; ~ *kommer* to that must be added, then there is; *anledningen* ~ *är okänd* the reason for that is unknown; *med* ~ *hörande* with the...belonging to it (relating thereto); *med allt vad* ~ *hör* with everything that goes with it; *med hänsyn* ~ in consideration of that **2** (*därutöver*) in addition, besides

därunder 1 *rumsbet.* under (beneath, below) it (that *etc.*) **2** (*om tid*) during the time; while it (*etc.*) lasts (lasted); meanwhile; ~ *fick han* while doing so he received **3** *barn på sex år och* ~ children of six and under; *äpplen till... och* ~ apples at...and less

däruppå *se* därpå

därur out of it

därutöver above [that]; *vad* ~ *är* the rest is; *önskas ngt* ~ should you require anything more; *jfr* däröver

därvarande *a4* local; residing (stationed) there

därvid 1 *rumsbet.* at (in; on; along; by; near; close to; beside; of; to; over) it (that, them *etc.*) **2** (*om tid*) at (during) it (the time *etc.*), on that occasion, then; in doing so, when that happens; ~ *bör man helst* when that happens it is best to; ~ *föll han och* in doing so he fell and; ~ *upptäckte man* then (on that being done) it was discovered; *och sade* ~ saying in doing so; (*ett sammanträde hölls*) *och* ~ *beslöts* during which it was decided **3** ~ *blev det* it was left at that; *fästa avseende* ~ pay attention to that

därvidlag in that respect; on that point (subject); ~ *måste man vara försiktig* great care must be taken in this respect

däråt at (to; in; [out] of; over) it (that *etc.*); *den kostade 15 pund eller någonting* ~ it cost 15 pounds or something like that

däröver over (above; across; of; at) it (that, them *etc.*); ~ *i USA* over there in the USA; *100 pund och* ~ 100 pounds and upwards; *jfr* därutöver

däst [-ä:-] *a1* (*tjock o. fet*) obese; (*övermätt*) full up, gorged

däven *a3* damp, moist

dävert ['dä:-] *s2, sjö.* davit

dö *dog dött* die; ~ *av skratt* die with laughter; ~ *av svält* (*törst, ålderdom*) die of starvation (thirst, old age); ~ *bort* die away; ~ *en naturlig död* die a natural death; ~ *för egen hand* die by one's own hand; ~ *för fosterlandet* die for one's country; ~ *i lunginflammation* die of pneumonia; ~ *ifrån hustru och barn* die leaving wife and children; ~ *ut* die out (off), (*om ätt äv.*) become extinct; *så nyfiken så jag kan* ~ I am dying of curiosity; *vinden mojnade och dog* the wind died down

döbattang folding door

död I *s2* death; (*frånfälle*) decease, demise; *~en i grytan* (*bibl.*) death in the pot, *vard.* a sure death; *~en inträdde efter några timmar* he (she) died after a few hours; *~en var ögonblicklig* death was instantaneous; *det blir min* ~ it will be the death of me; *du är ~ens om* you are a dead man (woman *etc.*) if; *ligga för ~en* be dying, be at death's door; *gå i ~en för* die for; *in i* (*intill*) *~en* unto death; *ta* ~ *på* kill [off], exterminate; *strid på liv och* ~ life and death struggle; *pina ngn till ~s* torture s.b. to death; *vara ~ens lammunge* be done for **II** *a1* dead; *den ~e* (*~a*) the dead man (woman *etc.*), the deceased; *de ~a* the dead; *~a* (*tidningsrubrik*) deaths; *~a, sårade och saknade* killed, wounded and missing; ~ *för världen* dead to the world; ~ *mans grepp* dead man's handle (pedal); ~ *punkt* (*tekn.*) dead centre (point), (*-läge*) deadlock, *bildl.* dull moment; ~ *vinkel* dead (blind) angle; *bollen är* ~ the ball is out of play; *falla* ~ *ner* fall down dead; *Döda havet* the Dead Sea; *dött kapital* (*språk*) dead capital (language); *dött lopp* dead heat

döda 1 kill (*äv. bildl.*) **2** (*växel, inteckning, motbok*) cancel; (*konto*) close; (*check äv.*) stop

Dödahavsrullarna the Dead Sea Scrolls

död|ande *I* *s6* killing *etc.* **II** *a4* killing; fatal; *ett* ~ *slag* a mortal blow **III** *adv,* ~ *tråkig* deadly dull **-dagar** *pl, till* ~ till death, to one's dying day **-dansare** bore; *vard.* spoilsport, wet blanket **-full** blind [drunk] **-född** *a5* stillborn; (*friare*) abortive; *-fött förslag* abortive project **-förklara** officially declare...dead **-förklaring** official declaration of death **-grävare 1** gravedigger, sexton **2** *zool.* burying beetle, sexton **-gång** *tekn.* backlash, play **-kött** proud flesh; *med.* granulation tissue

dödlig [ˣdö:d-] *a1* deadly; mortal, fatal, lethal; ~ *dos* lethal dose; *sjukdomen fick* ~ *utgång* the illness was fatal; *en vanlig* ~ an ordinary mortal **dödlighet** mortality **dödlighetsprocent** death (*särsk. AE.* mortality) rate

död|ligt [ˣdö:d-] *adv* mortally, fatally; *vara* ~ *kär* be madly in love **-läge** deadlock, stalemate **-period** slack period

döds|aning premonition of death **-annons** obituary [notice] **-attest**, **-bevis** death certificate **-blek** deadly pale, livid

dödsbo estate [of a deceased person] **-delägare** party to an estate; (*arvtagare äv.*) heir, inheritor **-förvaltare** estate administrator (executor), trustee

döds|bricka identification (identity) disc **-bringande** *a4* deadly **-bud** news of a p.'s death **-bädd** deathbed; *på* ~*en* on one's deathbed **-cell** death cell **-dag** *ngns* ~ day (anniversary) of a p.'s death **-dans** dance of death; danse macabre **-dom** death sentence **-dömd** *a5* sentenced to death; *bildl.* doomed; (*sjuk*) given up [by the doctors]; *hon är* ~ there is no hope for her **-fall** death; (*säljs*) *på grund av* ~ owing to decease of owner (*etc.*) **-fara** mortal danger **-fiende** mortal enemy; deadly foe **-fruktan** fear of death **-fälla** deathtrap **-förakt** contempt of death **-föraktande** *a4* intrepid **-förskräckt** *a4* terrified; *vara* ~ *för ngt* be frightened (scared) to death of s.th. **-hjälp** mercy killing; *med.* euthanasia

dödskalle death's-head, skull **-fjäril** death's--head moth

döds|kamp death struggle, agony **-körning** fatal car accident **-lik** deathlike, deathly **-mask** death mask **-märkt** *a4*, *vara* ~ be marked by death; fey **-mässa** Requiem **-offer** victim, fatal casualty; *olyckan krävde ett* ~ the accident claimed one victim **-olycka** fatal accident **-orsak** cause of death **-riket** the kingdom of the dead; Hades, hell **-rossling** death rattle **-runa** obituary [notice] **-ryckningar** *pl* death throes (*äv. bildl.*) **-siffra** death toll **-sjuk** dying, moribund **-skri** dying shriek **-skugga** shadow of death **-stilla** *a4* deathly still **-straff** capital punishment, death penalty; *förbjudet vid* ~ forbidden on pain of death **-stråle** death ray **-stöt** deathblow **-synd** mortal (deadly) sin **-trött** *a4* dog-tired, tired to death **-tyst** *a4* silent as the grave **-tystnad** dead silence **-ur** *zool.* death-watch beetle **-ångest** agony [of death]; *bildl.* mortal (deadly) fear **-år** *ngns* ~ the year of a p.'s death **-ängel** angel of death

död|säsong off-season (slack) period **-vatten** (*bildl.*) deadlock; *råka i* ~ reach a deadlock **-vikt** deadweight **-viktton** deadweight ton

döende dying, moribund

dög *imperf. av* duga

dök *imperf. av* dyka

dölja *dolde dolt* hide; conceal (*för* from); (*över- skyla*) disguise; *bakom signaturen...döljer sig*

...is the pen name of

döma [ˣdömma] *v2* **1** (*be-*) judge (*efter* by); ~ *andra efter sig själv* judge others by o.s.; ~ *ngn för hårt* be too severe in one's judgment of s.b. **2** (*avkunna dom över*) sentence, condemn; ~ *ngn till böter* fine s.b.; ~ *ngn till döden* sentence s.b. to death; *dömd att misslyckas* doomed to failure **3** (*fälla omdöme*) judge (*om, över* of); *av allt att* ~ to all appearances; *av* ~ *omständigheterna* (*utse- endet*) *att* ~ judging from circumstances (by appearances); *mänskligt att* ~ as far as one can judge; *döm om min förvåning* judge of (imagine) my surprise **4** (*avkunna dom*) pronounce sentence (*över* on); (*friare*) pronounce judgment (*över* on); (*i fotboll, boxning m.m.*) referee; (*i fri idrott*) judge; (*i kricket, baseball, tennis*) umpire

döp|a *v3* baptize; (*barn, fartyg*) christen; *han -tes till John* he was christened (given the name of) John **-are** baptizer, baptist; *Johannes D~n* John the Baptist **-else** baptism

dörj *s2* (*fiskredskap*) handline **dörja** fish by hand- line

dörr *s2* door; *följa ngn till* ~*en* see s.b. out; *gå från* ~ *till* ~ go from door to door; *inom lyckta* ~*ar* behind closed doors, in camera, *parl.* in a secret session; *stå för* ~*en* (*bildl.*) be imminent ([near] at hand); *visa ngn på* ~*en* turn s.b. out, show s.b. the door; *öppna* ~*ens politik* open-door policy **-handtag** [door]knob **-karm** doorframe, door- case **-klapp** knocker **-klocka** doorbell **-knac- kare** door-to-door salesman, hawker **-lås** [door] lock **-matta** doormat **-nyckel** latchkey, door- key **-post** doorjamb, doorpost **-spegel** door panel **-springa** chink of the door **-stopp[are]** doorstop **-stängare** door closer **-tröskel** door- sill; doorstep **-vakt** doorkeeper; (*t.ex. på hotell*) doorman **-vred** *se* **-handtag -öppning** doorway

dös *s2* dolmen

dösnack *s7, vard.* gibberish, chatter, twaddle **dösnacka** talk rubbish (rot), twaddle, chatter

dött *sup. av* dö

döv *a1* deaf (*för* to); ~ *på ena örat* deaf in one ear; *tala för* ~*a öron* talk to deaf ears

döv|a deafen; alleviate; *bildl.* stun, benumb; ~ *hungern* still one's hunger; ~ *sitt samvete* silence one's conscience; ~ *smärtorna* deaden the pains **-het** deafness **-lärare** teacher of the deaf **-skola** school for the deaf **-stum** deaf-and-dumb, deaf- -mute; *en* ~ a deaf-mute **-stumhet** deaf-mute- ness, deaf-mutism **-öra** *mest i uttr.: slå* ~*t till* turn a deaf ear (*för* to)

E

EAN *fork. för European Article Numbering*
eau-de-cologne [ådökå'lånj] *s5* cologne, Cologne water, eau de Cologne
eau-de-vie [ådö'vi:] *s5* brandy
ebb *s3*; ~ *och flod* ebb and flow; *det är* ~ it is low tide; *det är* ~ *i kassan* my (*etc.*) funds are low, I am (*etc.*) short of money **ebba** ~ *ut* ebb [away], peter out
ebenholts [-å-] *s3, s4* ebony **-svart** [as black as] ebony **-trä** ebony
ebonit *s3* vulcanite, ebonite; hard rubber
echaufferad [eʃå'fe:-] *a5* hot [and bothered]
ecklesiastik|departement ~*et* the [Swedish] ministry of education and ecclesiastical affairs, (*i Storbritannien, ung.*) the ministry of education **-minister** minister of education and ecclesiastical affairs, (*i Storbritannien, ung.*) minister of education
Ecuador [ekua'då:r] *n* Ecuador **ecuadorian** *s3,* **ecuadoriansk** [-'a:nsk] *a5* Ecuador[i]an
e.d. (*fork. för eller dylikt*) *se under dylik*
ed *s3* oath; *avlägga* ~ take an oath, swear; *gå* ~ *på* take one's oath upon, swear to; *gå* ~ *på att* swear that; *låta ngn gå* ~ *på* take a p.'s oath; *under* ~ on (upon, under) oath
edamerost [ˣe:dam-] Edam
EDB (*fork. för elektronisk databehandling*) E.D.P. (electronic data processing)
edda *s1* Edda; *äldre (poetiska) E*~*n* Elder (Poetic) Edda; *yngre (prosaiska) E*~*n* Younger (Prose) Edda **-diktning** Eddaic poetry **-kväde** Eddaic poem (song)
edelweiss [ˣe:delvais *el.* 'e:del-] *s3* edelweiss
Eden ['e:den] *n* Eden; ~*s lustgård* Garden of Eden
eder ['e:-] *se er*
edera edit
edgång swearing
edikt *s7* edict
edil *s3* aedile
edition edition
edlig [ˣe:d-] *a1* sworn; *under* ~ *förpliktelse* under oath
eds|avläggelse taking of an oath **-förbund** confederation
edsvuren *a5* sworn
E-dur E major
EEG (*fork. för elektroencefalogram*) EEG (electroencephalogram)
efedrin *s3, med.* ephedrin[e]
efemerid *s3 astr.* ephemeris **-sekund** ephemeris second **-tid** ephemeris time
efemär *a1* ephemeral
efes[i]er [e'fe:-] Ephesian **-brevet** Ephesians (*pl, behandlas som sg*); *eg.* the Epistle of Paul the Apostle to the Ephesians
effekt *s3* **1** (*verkan*) effect; *göra god (dålig)* ~ produce (make, have) a good (bad) effect **2** *tekn.*

power, efficiency; (*maskins*) output, capacity **3** (*föremål*) ~*er* goods [and chattels], effects; *kvarglömda* ~ lost property; *expedition för tillvaratagna* ~ lost property office; *jfr reseffekter* **-full** striking, effective **-förvaring** left-luggage office, cloakroom; *AE.* checkroom
effektiv *a1* effective, efficient, efficacious, effectual; (*verklig*) actual; ~ *arbetstid* actual working hours; ~ *avkastning* actual yield; ~ *hästkraft* brake horsepower; ~ *ränta* effective (actual) rate [of interest]; ~*t värmevärde* net calorific (*AE.* heating) value **-[is]era** make more effective (efficient), increase the capacity of **-itet** efficiency, effectiveness, capacity **-värde** *elektr.* root mean square value
effektsökeri straining (striving) after effect
effektuera execute, accomplish, fulfil, carry out
effeminerad [-'ne:-] *a5* effeminated
efor [e'få:-r] *s3* ephor
efter ['eff-] **I** *prep* **1** after; (*bakom äv.*) behind; [*omedelbart*] ~ on, immediately after; ~ *att ha sett pjäsen* after seeing (having seen) the play; ~ *avslutat arbete* when work is over; ~ *en timme* (*vanl.*) an hour later; ~ *Kristi födelse* (*e.Kr.*) anno Domini (A.D.); ~ *mottagandet av* on receipt of; *den ena* ~ *den andra* one after the other; *göra rent* ~ *sig* clean up after one; *stå* ~ *ngn i kön* stand behind s.b. in the queue (*AE.* line); *stå* ~ *ngn på listan* be after s.b. on the list; *vara* ~ *de andra* (*äv. bildl.*) be behind the others; *vara* ~ *sin tid* be behind the times; *han lämnade en väska* ~ *sig* he left a bag behind [him]; *hon heter Anna* ~ *sin mamma* she is called Anna after her mother, Anna is named after her mother; *hon är klen* ~ *sjukdomen* she is frail after her illness; *stäng dörren* ~ *dig!* shut the door after (behind) you! **2** (*utmed*) along; (*nedför*) down; (*uppför*) up; ~ *kanten* along the edge; *fukten rann* ~ *väggarna* the walls were glistening with moisture **3** (*betecknande mål el. syfte*) for; *annonsera* (*ringa, skicka, skriva*) ~ advertise (ring, send, write) for; *böja sig* ~ *ngt* stoop to pick up s.th.; *jaga* ~ *popularitet* run after popularity; *sökandet* ~ the search for; *polisen var* ~ *honom* the police were after him **4** (*från*) from; (*efterlämnad av*) of; *arvet* ~ *föräldrarna* the inheritance from one's parents; *märken* ~ *fingrarna* marks of the fingers; *spela* ~ *noter* play from music; *trött* ~ *resan* tired from the journey; *utplåna spåren* ~ obliterate the tracks of; *hon är änka* ~ *en kapten* she is the widow of a captain **5** (*enligt*) according to; (*med ledning av äv.*) by, from, on, to; (*efter förebild el. mönster av äv.*) after; ~ *bästa förmåga* to the best of one's ability; ~ *gällande priser* at present prices; ~ *min uppfattning* in (according to) my opinion; ~ *mått* to measure; ~ *vad de säger* according to them; ~ *vad du har gjort så skall du inte klaga* after what you have done, you shouldn't complain; ~ *vad jag har hört* from what I have heard; ~ *vad jag vet* as far as I know; *inga spår att gå* ~ no clues to go by; *gå* ~ *kompass* walk by the compass; *klädd* ~ *senaste modet* dressed after the latest fashion; *ordna* ~ *storlek* arrange according to size; *rätta sig* ~ conform to; *segla* ~ *stjärnorna* sail by the stars; *spela* ~ *gehör* play by ear; *ställa klockan* ~ *radion* set one's watch by the radio; *sälja ngt* ~

vikt sell s.th. by weight; *teckna* ~ *modell* draw from a model **6** ([*in*]*om*) in; (*alltsedan*) since; (*räknat från*) of; ~ *den dagen har jag varit* since that day I have been; ~ *några dagar* in (after) a few days (days' time); *inom ett år* ~ *giftermålet* within a year of the marriage **7** (*i riktning mot*) at; *slå* ~ aim a blow at **8** ~ *hand* (*så småningom*) gradually, little by little, by degrees, (*steg för steg*) step by step; ~ *hand som* [according] as **II** *adv* **1** (*om tid*) after; *dagen* ~ the day after, the following day; *min klocka går* ~ my watch is slow (losing); *kort* ~ shortly after[wards] **2** (*bakom, kvar*) behind; *vara* ~ *med* be behind (*om betalning*: in arrears) with **III** *konj* **1** *vard.* (*eftersom*) since **2** ~ [*det att*] after

efter|apa imitate, ape, mimic **-apning** [-a:-] imitation, mimicry (*äv. konkr.*); (*förfalskning*) counterfeit **-behandling** after-treatment, finishing; curing; follow-up **-besiktning** supplementary (final) inspection **-beskattning** additional (supplementary) taxation **-beställning** reorder, repeat (follow-up) order **-bild** after-image, aftersensation **-bilda** imitate, copy **-bildning** imitation, copy **-bliven** *a5* (*outvecklad*) backward; retarded; (*föråldrad*) old-fashioned, out of date **-blivenhet** backwardness **-blomstring** after-flowering **-brännkammare** afterburner **-börd** afterbirth **-börs** [exchange] dealings (*pl*) after trading hours **-dyningar** repercussions, consequences, aftereffects; aftermath (*sg*) **-forska** search for, investigate, inquire into (after) **-forskning** search (*efter* for), inquiry (*efter* about, *i* into), investigation (*i* into) **-fråga** inquire (ask) for; *mycket ~d* in great demand **-frågan** *r* **1** (*förfrågan*) inquiry **2** (*eftersökthet*) demand, request (*på* for); *livlig* (*dålig*) ~ brisk (slack) demand; *ha stor* ~ be in great demand; *tillgång och* ~ supply and demand **-följande** *a4* following, succeeding, subsequent **-följansvärd** *a5* worth following, worthy of imitation **-följare** **1** (*anhängare*) follower, adherent **2** (*efterträdare*) successor **-följd** *mana till* ~ be worth imitating **-gift** *s3* **1** (*medgivande*) concession **2** (*efterskänkande*) remission **-given** [-j-] *a5* compliant, indulgent, yielding (*mot* to) **-givenhet** [-j-] indulgence, compliance, compliancy (*mot* towards, to) **-gjord** *a5* imitated; (*förfalskad*) counterfeit **-granskning** final examination (scrutiny)

1 efterhand *s*, *komma i* ~ take second place; *sitta i* ~ be the last player

2 efterhand *adv, se under hand 1*

efter|hängsen *a3* importunate, persistent; *en ~ person* a hanger-on **-härma** imitate, copy; echo **-härmning** imitation, copy; echo **-kalkyl** cost account[ing] **-klang** lingering note, resonance; *bildl.* reminiscence; echo **-klok** *vara* ~ be wise after the event **-klokhet** hindsight **-komma** comply with, obey **-kommande II** *s pl* (*avkomlingar*) [one's] descendants **-kontroll** supervisory control **-krav** cash on delivery (*förk.* C.O.D.); *sända varor mot* ~ send goods C.O.D.; *uttaga genom* ~ cash (*A.E.* collect) on delivery, charge forward **-krigstid** postwar period **-kälke** *komma på ~n* get behind-hand, be outdistanced, (*med betalning*) be in ar-

rears **-känning** aftereffect; *ha ~ar av* suffer from the aftereffects of **-leva** (*rätta sig efter*) observe, obey, act up to **-levande I** *a4* surviving **II** *s9* survivor **-leverans** supplementary delivery **-levnad** observance (*av* of), obedience, adherence (*av* to) **-likna** imitate; (*tävla med*) emulate (*i* in) **-lysa** **1** (*person*) search for, notify as missing, send out (*i radio* broadcast) a p.'s description; post s.b. as wanted [by the police]; *vara -lyst av polisen* be wanted by the police; *-lysta arvingar* heirs sought for **2** (*sak*) advertise for, advertise as missing, search for **-lysning 1** (*av pers.*) notification of missing person, circulation (*i radio* broadcasting) of a p.'s description **2** (*av sak*) advertisement of the loss of, search for **-låten** *a5* lenient, indulgent (*mot* to, towards) **-lämna** leave [behind]; (*arv*) leave; ~ *skrifter* posthumous works, literary remains; *hans ~de förmögenhet* the fortune he left; *hans ~de maka, fru A.* Mrs. A., widow of the late Mr. A. **-längtad** *a5* [eagerly] longed for, eagerly awaited

efter|middag afternoon; *i* ~ this afternoon; *i går* (*i morgon*) ~ yesterday (tomorrow) afternoon; *på ~en* (*~arna*) in the afternoon (afternoons); *på lördag* ~ on Saturday afternoon **-middagskaffe** afternoon coffee **-mäle** *s6* posthumous reputation; *han har fått ett gott* ~ he has been judged favourably **-namn** surname; *AE. äv.* last name **-natt** later part of the night; *på ~en* late at night **-ord** (*i bok*) epilogue, afterword **-prövning** supplementary examination **-rationalisering** hindsight wisdom **-räkning 1** (*tilläggsräkning*) additional bill **2** (*obehaglig påföljd*) unpleasant consequence **-rätt** sweet, dessert; pudding; *vard.* afters (*sg el. pl*) **-rättelse** observance, example; *lända till* ~ serve as an example, be complied with **-satt** *a4* (*försummad*) neglected; *de ~a grupperna i samhället* the underprivileged [social] groups **-siktväxel** *se avisoväxel* **-sinna** think [over], meditate [on] **-sinnande I** *a4* thoughtful, contemplative, reflecting **II** *s6* consideration, reflection; *vid närmare* ~ on second thoughts **-skalv** aftershock **-skicka** send for; *komma som ~d* arrive at the right moment **-skott** [-å-] *s7, i* ~ in arrears; *betala i* ~ pay after (on) delivery **-skrift** appendix, supplement; (*t. brev*) postscript **-skänka** (*straff*) remit, pardon; (*skuld*) remit, release **-skänkning** [-ʃ-] remission **-skörd** aftermath (*äv. bildl.*); gleanings (*pl*) **-släckning** final extinction [of a fire]; *bildl.* day-after party **-släng** *en* ~ *av* another slight bout (attack) of **-släntrare** laggard, straggler; (*sölare*) latecomer, dawdler, lingerer **-släpning** [-ä:-] lag, delay **-smak** aftertaste **-snack** *vard.* postmortem [talk]

eftersom as, seeing [that], since; (*alldenstund*) inasmuch as; (*allteftersom*) [according] as

efter|spana search for; *~d av polisen* wanted by the police **-spaning** search, inquiry; *anställa ~ar* institute a search (*efter* for), make inquiries **-spel 1** *mus.* postlude **2** epilogue; *bildl.* sequel, consequences (*pl*); *saken kommer att få rättsligt* ~ the matter will have legal consequences **-sträva** aim at, strive to attain; *det ~de målet* the objective, the target aimed at **-strävansvärd** *al* worth striving for, desirable **-stygn** backstitch

-synkronisering playback **-sägare** repeater; echo **-sända 1** (*skicka efter*) send for **2** (*skicka vidare*) forward, send on; *-sändes* (*på brev*) please forward, to be forwarded (redirected) **-sätta** (*försumma*) neglect, disregard **-sätts- blad** *bokh.* [back] flyleaf (endpaper) **-sökt** *a4* (*begärlig*) in great demand, popular, sought af- ter; *vara mycket* ~ be in great demand **efter|tanke** reflection, consideration; *utan* ~ carelessly, thoughtlessly; *vid närmare* ~ on sec- ond thoughts, on further consideration; *~ns kranka blekhet* the pale cast of thought **-taxera** assess [for arrears] **-taxering** additional assess- ment [for arrears] **-trakta** *se eftersträva*; *~d* cov- eted **-trupp** rearguard **-tryck 1** (*kraft*) energy, vigour; *med* ~ energetically **2** (*betoning*) stress, emphasis; *ge* ~ *åt* lay stress on, emphasize; *med* ~ emphatically, with emphasis **3** (*avtryckt upplaga*) reprint; (*olovligt*) piracy; ~ *förbjudes* all rights reserved, copyright **-trycklig** *al* **1** (*om hand- ling*) energetic, vigorous **2** (*om yttrande*) emphatic **-träda** succeed; (*ersätta*) replace **-trä- dare** successor; *B:s* ~ (*förk. eftr.*) (*hand.*) Successor[s *pl*] (*förk.* Succ.) to B. **-tänksam** *al* thoughtful; (*förståndig*) prudent, circumspect **-verkan** aftereffect **-vård** aftercare **-värkar** af- terpains **-värld[en]** posterity; *gå till* ~*en* go (be handed) down to posterity, (*till historien*) go down in history

efteråt 1 (*senare*) afterwards, later **2** (*bakom*) behind, after

EG (*förk. för europeiska gemenskaperna*) EEC (European Economic Community)

egal *al*, *det är mig* ~*t* it is all one (all the same) to me **egalisera** make uniform; establish equality

Egeiska havet [e'ge:-] the Aegean Sea

eg|en *a3* **1** (*tillhörande ngn*) own (*föregånget av genitiv el. poss. pron*); *mina -na barn* my own children; *skolans -na elever* the school's own pu- pils; *bilda sig en* ~ *uppfattning om* form an opin- ion about; *ha* ~ *bil* have a car of one's own; *ha* ~ *ingång* have a private entrance; *vara sin* ~ be one's own master; *öppna -et* (~ *affär*) start a busi- ness of one's own; *av* ~ *erfarenhet* from one's own experience; *av* ~ *fri vilja* of one's own free will; *för* ~ *del* for my (*etc.*) own part, personally; *för -et bruk* for private (personal) use; *i* ~ *hög person* in person; *tala i* ~ *sak* plead one's own cause; *i* [*sitt*] *-et hem* in one's own home; *i sitt -et intresse* in one's own interest; *i -et namn* in one's own name; *med -na ord* in one's own words; *på* ~ *begäran* on his (her) request; *på* ~ *bekostnad* at one's own expense; *på* ~ *hand* by oneself; *på -et initiativ* on one's own initiative; *stå på -na ben* stand on one's own feet **2** (*karakteristisk*) pecu- liar (*för* to), characteristic (*för* of) **3** (*underlig*) odd, strange

egen|art distinctive character, individuality **-ar- tad** [-a:r-] *a5* (*säregen*) peculiar, odd **-dom** [-domm] *s2* **1** (*utan pl*) property; *enskild* ~ pri- vate property; *fast* ~ real property (estate); *lös* ~ personal property, personalty; (*ägodel[ar]*) possession[s] *pl* (*med pl, jordagods*) estate **egendomlig** [-domm-] *al* **1** (*besynnerlig*) pecu- liar, strange, odd, queer, singular **2** (*utmär- kande*) characteristic (*för* of), peculiar (*för* to)

-het 1 (*besynnerlighet*) peculiarity, strangeness, oddity, queerness, singularity **2** (*utmärkande drag*) characteristic [trait], peculiarity **egendoms|agent** estate (house) agent; *AE. äv.* realtor **-brott** crime involving property **-folk** ~*et* (*bibl.*) the peculiar people **-gemenskap** (*fleras*) community of property; (*allas*) public (common) ownership **-lös** unpropertied, without property

egen|het peculiarity; *han har sina* ~*er* he has his own little ways **-händig** in one's own hand[writ- ing], autograph; ~ *namnteckning* own (proper) signature, autograph **-händigt** *adv* with one's own hands; (*friare*) in person, oneself; ~ *bakade kakor* home-made cakes **-kär** conceited; [self-]- complacent **-kärlek** conceit; [self-]complacency **-mäktig** arbitrary, high-handed; ~*t förfarande* unlawful (unauthorized) interference **-namn** proper noun (name) **-nytta** selfishness, self- -interest **-nyttig** selfish, self-interested **-rätt- färdig** self-righteous **-rättfärdighet** self-right- eousness **-sinne** wilfulness, obstinacy **-sinnig** *al* wilful, obstinate, headstrong

egenskap *s3* **1** (*beskaffenhet*) quality; *besitta en* ~ possess a quality; *god* (*dålig*) ~ good (bad) quality **2** (*kännetecken*) attribute; (*kännemärke*) characteristic **3** (*särskild* ~) property; *järnets* ~*er* the properties of iron **4** (*erforderlig* ~) qualifica- tion **5** (*persons ställning, roll*) capacity, quality; *i min* ~ *av lärare* in my capacity of (as a) teacher **egentlig** [e'jent-] *al* **1** (*huvudsaklig, främst*) real; *det* ~*a syftet med* the chief (real) purpose of **2** (*verklig, sann*) real, true, intrinsic[al]; *i ordets* ~*a* (*motsats t. bildliga*) *betydelse* in the literal (strict, proper) sense of the word; ~*a England* England proper; ~*t bråk* (*mat.*) proper fraction **3** *fys.*, ~ *(specifik) vikt* specific gravity (weight) **egentligen** [e'jent-] (*i själva verket*) really, in fact; (*med rätta*) by right[s]; ~ *borde jag gå och lägga mig* I ought to go to bed, really; ~ *är hon ganska snäll* she is really quite nice **egenvärde** intrinsic value

egg *s2* edge

egg|a ~ [*upp*] egg on, incite; (*stimulera*) stimulate **-ande** *a4* inciting, incentive **-else** incitement, in- centive; stimulation

egg|vapen cutting weapon; side arms (*pl*) **-verktyg** sharp-edged tool

egid *s3* aegis

egnahem owner-occupied house **egnahems- lån** loan to build one's own home

ego [e'go] *n* ego, self **-centricitet** egocentricity **-centriker** [-'senn-] egocentric **-centrisk** [-'senn-] *a5* egocentric, self-centred **-ism** egoism **-ist** egoist **-istisk** [-'iss-] *a5* egoistic[al], selfish **-tism** egotism **-tripp** ego trip

Egypten [e'jypp-] *n* Egypt

egypt|i[e]r [e'jyppt(s)ier] Egyptian **-isk** *a5* Egyptian **-iska 1** (*språk*) Egyptian **2** (*kvinna*) Egyptian woman **-olog** Egyptologist **-ologi** *s3* Egyptology

ehọ *åld.* whosoever

ehuru [e*x*hu:-] [al]though, even if

einsteinium [ain'stain-] *s8* einsteinium

ej [ejj] *se inte*; ~ *heller* nor

eja [*x*ejja] ~ *vore vi där!* would we were there!

ejakul|at *s7* ejaculate, semen **-ation** ejaculation **-era** ejaculate

ejder ['ejj-] *s2* eider [duck] **-dun** eiderdown **-hane** eider drake, male eider **-hona** female eider

ejektor [e×jektår] *s3* ejector, jet

ek *s2* oak; (*virke*) oak [wood]; *av ~* (*äv.*) oak[en] **1 eka** *s1* skiff, punt **2 eka** *v1* echo; reverberate; resound (*äv. bildl.*)

eker ['e:-] *s2* spoke

EKG (*förk. för elektrokardiogram*) E.C.G. (electrocardiogram)

ekip|age [-'pa:ʃ] *s7* carriage [and horses], turnout; equipage **-era** equip, fit out **-ering** [-'pe:-] equipment, outfit; *se äv. herrekipering*

ekivok [-'vå:k] *a1* indelicate, indecent, suggestive; dubious

eklatant [-'ant *el.* -'aŋt] *a1* striking; brilliant, startling **eklatera** announce, make public **eklatt I** *a* official, public **II** *adv* officially, publicly

eklekt|icism eclecticism **-iker** [e'klekk-] *s9*, **-isk** [e'klekk-] *a5* eclectic

eklip|s *s3* eclipse **-tika** [e'klipp-] *s1* ecliptic

eklog [-'lå:g] *s3* eclogue

eklut [×e:k-] assay; *gå igenom ~en* (*bildl.*) go through the mill

eklärera illuminate, light up

eklöv oak leaf

eko ['e:kɔ] *s6* echo; *ge ~* [make an] echo

ekocjd *s3* ecocide

ekollon acorn

ekolod echo sounder, sonar, asdic **-ning** echo sounding

ekolog|i *s3* ecology **-isk** [-'lå:-] *a5* ecological

ekon|om economist **-ometri** *s3* econometrics (*pl, behandlas som sg*)

ekonomj *s3* economy; (*affärsställning*) financial position, finances (*pl*); (*vetenskap*) economics (*pl, behandlas som sg*); *han har god ~* his financial position is good **-avdelning** (*i företag*) economic department; (*på hotell o.d.*) catering department **-byggnad** (*på lantgård*) farm building, annex **-chef** financial manager, accountant **-departement** ministry of economics **-förpackning** economy pack (size) **-klass** economy (tourist) class **-minister** minister of economics (for economic affairs)

ekonomisera economize **ekonomisk** [-'nå:-] *a5* economic; (*penning-*) financial; (*sparsam*) economical; *~ fråga* economic question; *~ förening* incorporated (economic) association; *~ geografi* economic geography; *~ livslängd* economic life; *~ ställning* financial status (position); *~a svårigheter* financial difficulties; *~ utveckling* economic development; *~ i drift* economical in operation; *i ~t avseende* economically, financially **ekonomiskt** [-'nå:-] *adv* economically; *~ oberoende* financially independent; *~ sett* from an economic point of view

ekorr|e [red] squirrel **-hjul** treadwheel, treadmill (*äv. bildl.*)

eko|sfär ecosphere **-system** ecosystem **-typ** ecotype

ekoxe stag beetle

e.Kr. (*förk. för efter Kristus*) A.D. (anno Domini)

eksem *s7* eczema **-artad** [-a:r-] *a5* eczematous

ekstock 1 (*stock*) oak log **2** (*eka*) punt, skiff

ekumen|ik *s3* ecumenicalism, ecumenicism **-isk** [-'me:-] *a5* ecumenic[al]

ekvation equation

ekvations|lära theory of equations **-system** compound equation

ekvator [e×kva:tår] *s3* equator **-ial** *a5* equatorial

ekvecklare *zool.* green oak tortricid

ekvilibrist equilibrist **-isk** *a5* equilibristic

ekvival|ens *s3* equivalence, (*särsk. kem.*) equivalency **-ent** *s3 o. a1* equivalent

el- *se äv. elektricitets-, elektrisk*

elaffär electrical appliance shop (store)

elak [×e:lak] *a1* **1** (*ond, ondskefull*) evil, wicked, bad; (*stygg, bråkig*) naughty, mischievous; (*illvillig, illasinnad*) malicious, spiteful, malevolent, (*starkare*) malignant; (*giftig*) venomous; (*bitande*) cynical, caustic; (*t. karaktären*) ill-disposed (*mot* towards); ill-natured; (*ovänlig*) unkind, mean (*mot* to); (*grym*) cruel (*mot* to) **2** (*obehaglig, motbjudande*) nasty, horrid, bad; *~ lukt* (*smak*) nasty (bad) smell (taste); (*besvärlig*) troublesome; *en ~ hosta* a troublesome (nasty) cough **-artad** [-a:r-] *a5* (*om sjukdom o.d.*) malignant, virulent, pernicious; (*om olyckstillbud e.d.*) serious **-het** evilness *etc.*; malice, spitefulness, malevolence; malignancy; venom; evil disposition; unkindness, meanness; cruelty

elakt *adv* spitefully, ill-naturedly, unkindly *etc.*; *det var ~ gjort av honom* it was nasty (spiteful, horrid) of him to do that

elasticitet elasticity; resilience **elasticitetsmodul** modulus of elasticity, elastic modulus **elastisk** [e'lass-] *a5* elastic; resilient; *~ binda* elastic bandage

el|behandling electroconvulsive (electroshock) therapy **-belysning** electric lighting

eld *s2* **1** fire; *~en är lös!* fire!; *~ upphör!* cease fire!; *fatta (ta) ~* catch (take) fire; *ge ~* fire, begin firing; *göra upp ~* make a fire, light a (the fire); *koka vid sakta ~* boil over a slow fire; *sätta (tända) ~ på* set on fire, set fire to; *vara i ~en* be under fire; *öppna ~ mot* open fire on **2** (*för cigarett o.d.*) light; *stryka ~ på en tändsticka* strike a match; *vill du låna mig lite ~?* may I trouble you for a light? **3** *bildl.* fire, spirit; (*eldighet*) ardour, fervour; (*entusiasm*) enthusiasm; *gå genom ~ och vatten* go through fire and water; *leka med ~en* play with fire; *mellan två ~ar* between two fires; *vara ~ och lågor* be all aflame, be on fire

elda 1 (*göra upp eld*) light a fire; keep a fire burning; *~ med kol (ved)* burn coal (wood), use coal (wood) for heating; *~ ordentligt* make a good fire; *~ på* keep up a good fire; *vi måste ~ här* we must light a fire here **2** (*uppvärma*) heat; get hot; (*ångpanna e.d.*) fire; (*egga*) rouse, inspire; *pannan ~s med koks* the furnace is fired by coke; *~ upp a*) (*värma upp*) heat, *b*) (*i maskin e.d.*) get up the fire[s *pl*], *c*) (*förbruka*) burn up, consume; *~ upp sig* get excited

eld|are stoker, fireman **-begängelse** [-'jäŋ-] cremation **-dop** baptism of fire; *få sitt ~* (*äv.*) be put to the test for the first time **-fara** danger (risk) of fire, fire risk; *vid ~* in case of fire **-farlig** inflammable **-fast** fireproof; *~ form* ovenware,

casserole; ~ *glas* heat-resistant glass; ~ *lera* fire clay; ~ *tegel* firebrick **-fluga** firefly **-fängd** [-äŋd] *al* [in]flammable; *bildl. äv.* fiery **-gaffel** poker **-givning** [-ji:v-] firing **-handvapen** firearm **-hastighet** rate of fire **-hav** sea of fire **-hund** firedog, andiron **-härd** seat of the (a) fire **-härjad** *a5* fire ravaged
eldig *al* fiery, ardent, passionate
eldistribution distribution of electrical energy
eld|kastare flame-thrower **-klot** fireball **-kraft** *mil.* fire power **-kula** fireball; *astr. äv.* bolide **-kvast** puff of flame and smoke **-ledning** *mil.* fire control **-linje** *mil.* firing line
eldning firing, heating; lighting of fires; ~ *med ved* wood firing, *(på ångbåt)* stoking **eldnings-olja** [domestic] fuel oil, heating oil; *tjock* ~ *(tjockolja)* heavy fuel oil; *tunn* ~ *(villaolja)* light fuel oil
eldorado [-'ra:-] *s6* eldorado
eld|prov *(gudsdom)* ordeal by fire; *bildl.* ordeal **-röd** red as fire, flaming red **-rör 1** *(på kanon o.d.)* tube, barrel **2** *(i ångpanna)* fire-tube **-salamander** European fire salamander **-själ** dedicated person **-sken** firelight **-skrift** *i* ~ in letters of fire **-skärm** fire screen
Eldslandet Tierra del Fuego
eldsljus *vid* ~ by candlelight (artificial light)
eldslukare fire-eater
eldslåga flame of fire
eldsläck|are fire-extinguisher **-ning** fire fighting
eldsläcknings|apparat *se eldsläckare* **-manskap** fire brigade, firemen *(pl)*
eldsländare Fuegian
eldsmärke *med.* haemangioma
eld|sprutande *a4* fire-spitting; ~ *berg* volcano; ~ *drake* firedrake, firedragon **-stad** *-staden -städer* fireplace, hearth; *(kamin, kakelugn)* stove; *(på lok)* firebox; *(på ångbåt)* furnace **-stod** *bibl.* pillar of fire **-strid** gunfight **-stål** steel
eldsvåda *s1* fire; *(större)* conflagration; *vid* ~ in case of fire
eld|säker fireproof, flameproof **-tång** fire-tongs *(pl)* **-understöd** *mil.* fire support **-vapen** firearm, gun **-vatten** firewater **-verkan** *mil.* fire effect
elefant elephant **-bete** elephant's tusk **-gräs** elephant grass **-hane** bull elephant **-hona** cow elephant
elefantiasis [-ˣti:- *el.* -'ti:-] *r* elephantiasis
elefantunge calf elephant
eleg|ans [-'ans *el.* -'aŋs] *s3* elegance; *(stass)* finery; *(i uppträdande)* refinement, polish; *(smakfullhet)* style; *(prakt)* splendour **-ant** [-'ant *el.* -'aŋt] *al* *(om stil)* elegant; *(om kläder)* stylish, tasteful, fashionable, smart; *(om uppträdande)* refined
elegi [-'gi: *el.* -'ʃi:] *s3* elegy *(över* on) **elegisk** [-'le:-] *a5* elegiac
elektor [eˣlektår] *s3* elector **elektorskår** electorate
elektrakomplex Electra complex
elektricitet electricity
elektricitets|lära electricity **-mängd** [electric] charge
elektrifi|era electrify **-ering** electrification

elektriker [e'leck-] electrician
elektrisera electrify; *bildl.* enthuse
elektrisk [e'leck-] *a5* electric; *(friare o. bildl.)* electrical; ~ *affär (anläggning)* electric appliance shop (plant); ~ *belysning* electric light[ing]; ~ *energi* electrical energy; ~ *industri* electrical industry; ~ *laddning* [electric] charge; ~*a ledningar* electric wiring; ~ *motor (spis, uppvärmning)* electric motor (cooker *el.* stove, heating); ~*a stolen* the electric chair, *vard.* the chair; ~ *ström* [electric] current; ~ *urladdning* electric discharge; ~*t värmeelement* electric heater (heating element)
elektrod [-'å:d] *s3* electrode
elektro|dynamik electrodynamics *(pl, behandlas som sg)* **-dynamisk** electrodynamic[al] **-encefalogram** electroencephalogram **-filter** electrofilter; electrostatic filter (precipitator) **-fon** [-'få:n] *s3* electrophone **-for** [-'få:r] *s3* electrophorus **-fores** *s3* electrophoresis **-fysiologi** electrophysiology **-ingenjör** electrical engineer **-kardiogram** electrocardiogram **-kemi** electrochemistry **-kemisk** electrochemical **-kirurgi** electrosurgery
elektro|lys *s3* electrolysis **-lysera** electrolyse **-lyt** *s3* electrolyte **-lytisk** [-'ly:-] *a5* electrolytic[al]
elektro|magnet electromagnet **-magnetisk** electromagnetic; ~ *strålning* electromagnetic radiation **-magnetism** electromagnetism
elektro|mekanik electromechanics *(pl, behandlas som sg)* **-mekanisk** electromechanical **-metallurgi** electrometallurgy **-motorisk** electromotive *(kraft* force)
elektron [-'å:n] *s3* electron **-blixt** electronic flash **-fysik** electron physics **-hjärna** *vard.* electronic brain, computer
elektronjk *s3* electronics *(pl, behandlas som sg)* **elektronisk** [-'trå:-] *a5* electronic; ~ *databehandling* electronic data processing; ~ *musik* electronic music
elektron|kanon electron gun **-mikroskop** electron microscope **-negativitet** electronegativity **-optik** electron optics **-rör** electron tube; [electronic] valve, tube; *AE.* vacuum tube **-ugn** electron oven **-volt** electronvolt
elektro|skop electroscope **-statik** *s3* electrostatics *(pl, behandlas som sg)* **-statisk** electrostatic **-stål** electric steel
elektro|teknik *s3* electrotechnology, electrical engineering **-tekniker** electrical engineer **-teknisk** electrotechnical **-terapi** *(behandling)* electrotherapy; *(vetenskap)* electrotherapeutics *(pl, behandlas som sg)*
elelement [ˣe:l-] heating element, electric heater
element *s7* **1** element; *de fyra ~en* the four elements; *~ens raseri* the fury of the elements; *vara i sitt rätta* ~ be in one's element; *ljusskygga* ~ shady characters **2** *(första grund)* element, rudiment **3** *tekn.* cell; *galvaniskt* ~ galvanic cell (element); *byggn.* unit; *(värme-)* radiator; *(elektriskt)* heating element, electric heater
elementar|analys [-ˣta:r-] elementary analysis **-bok** primer *(i* of) **-partikel** elementary (fundamental) particle **-skola** secondary school

E

elementborste radiator brush
elementär *al* elementary, basic; ~ *kunskaper* elementary (fundamental) knowledge; (*enkel, ursprunglig*) simple; rudimentary
elenergi electrical energy
elev *s3* pupil; (*vid högskola, kurs o.d.*) student; (*praktikant*) learner, trainee; (*lärling*) apprentice; (*kontors-, bank-*) junior [clerk]; *en av mina f.d. ~er* one of my former pupils; *skolans f.d. ~er* the old boys (girls *etc.*); *AE.* the alumni (*sg* alumnus), *fem.* alumnae (*sg* alumna)
eleva|tion elevation **-tionsvinkel** angle of elevation
elevator [-ˣa:tår] *s3* elevator; (*för tungt gods*) hoist
elev|hem [college] hostel; *AE.* dormitory **-kår** body of pupils (students) **-organisation** student (pupil) organization **-råd** student (pupil) council **-skola** *teat.* drama[tic] school **-tid** period of training **-tjänstgöring** probationership; apprenticeship
elfenben ivory; *av ~* (*äv.*) ivory
Elfenbenskusten the Ivory Coast
elfenbens|torn ivory tower **-vit** ivory [white]
elfte eleventh; *Karl XI* Charles XI (the Eleventh); *i ~ timmen* at the eleventh hour **-del** eleventh [part]; *en ~* one-eleventh
el|förbrukning electricity consumption **-gitarr** electric guitar
Elia[s] [eˣli:-] (*profet*) Elijah; (*i Nya testamentet*) Elias
elidera elide
eliminer|a eliminate **-ing** elimination
elinstallatör electrician; (*firma*) electrical contractor
Elisabet [eˣli:-] Elizabeth **elisabetansk** [-'a:nsk] *a5* Elizabethan
elision elision
elit *s3* elite; pick; flower; choice; *en ~ av* a picked group of; *~en av* the pick (cream) of **-idrott** competitive sports **-ism** elitism **-ist** elitist
elit|kår corps d'élite **-trupp** picked troop **-tänkande** elitism
elixir *s7* elixir
eljes[t] *se* annars
elkraft electrical power **-försörjning** power supply **-station** [electrical] power plant **-verk** [electrical] power station
eller ['ell-] **1** or; ~ *dylikt* or something like that; ~ *hur, se* hur 2; ~ *också* or [else]; *antingen…~* either…or; *en ~ annan person* some person or other; *om en ~ annan timme* in an hour or two (so) **2** (*efter varken*) nor; *varken min bror ~ min syster* neither my brother nor my sister
ellips *s3* **1** *geom.* ellipse **2** *språkv.* ellipsis (*pl* ellipses) **-formig** *al* elliptic[al], oval
elliptisk [e'lipp-] *a5 geom., språkv.* elliptic[al]
el|lok electric locomotive **-motor** electric motor
elmseld Saint (St.) Elmo's fire, corposant
el|mängd [electric] charge **-mätare** electricity meter **-nät** electric mains (*pl*), electric supply network
eloge [e'lå:ʃ] *s5* commendation, praise, eulogy; *ge ngn en ~* congratulate s.b. (*för* on), pay a tribute to s.b.
elokvens *s3* eloquence

elorgel electric organ; electronic organ
eloxera anodize
el|panna electric boiler **-ransonering** electricity rationing **-reparatör** electrician
elritsa [ˣe:l-, *äv.* ˣell-] *s1* minnow
elräkning electricity bill
Elsass ['ell-] *n* Alsace **elsassare** [-ˣsass-] *s9*, **elsassisk** [-'sass-] *a5* Alsatian
elsevier *se* elzevier
el|spis electric cooker **-ström** [electric] current **-svetsning** arc (electric) welding **-taxa** electricity rate **-transmission** transmission of electrical energy
eludera elude
el|uppvärmning electric heating **-uttag** socket
elva eleven (*för sms. jfr fem-*) **-hundratalet** the twelfth century **-tiden** *vid ~* round (about) eleven **-tåget** the eleven o'clock train
el|verk electric (electricity) works **-visp** electric whisk **-värme** electric heating
elyseisk [-'se:-] *a5* Elysian; *E~a fälten* Elysian fields, Elysium
elzevier [-se'vi:r] *s3* Elzevir
elände [ˣe:- *el.* e'länn-] *s6* misery; (*nöd*) distress; (*missöde, otur*) misfortune, bad luck; (*obehag*) nuisance; *ett ~ till bil* a scrapheap of a car; *råka i ~* fall on evil days; *störta ngn i ~* reduce s.b. to misery; *vilket ~!* *a*) what misery!, *b*) what a misfortune!, *c*) what a nuisance! **eländig** [ˣe:- *el.* e'länn-] *al* miserable, wretched
e.m. (*förk. för eftermiddagen*) p.m., P.M. (post meridiem)
emalj *s3* enamel (*äv. tand-*) **-arbete** [a piece of] enamelwork **-era** enamel; *~de kärl* enamelware (*sg*) **-ering** enamelling **-öga** glass (artificial) eye **-ör** enameller, enamellist
emanation emanation
emancip|ation emancipation **-era** emancipate
emanera emanate
emball|age [emm- *el.* amm-, -'a:ʃ] *s7* packing, wrapping; ~ *återtages* empties (packing) returnable; *exklusive* (*inklusive*) ~ packing excluded (included) **-era** pack, wrap up **-ering** [-'le:-] packing, wrapping
embargo ['barr-] *s6* embargo; *lägga ~ på ett fartyg* lay (put) an embargo on a ship; *lägga ~ på* (*bildl.*) seize; *upphäva ett ~* raise (take off) an embargo
embarker|a [emm- *el.* amm-] embark **-ing** embarkation **-ingskort** *flyg.* boarding pass
emblem *s7* emblem; badge
embolj *s3* embolism
embonpoint [*svenskt uttal* aŋ- *el.* ambåŋpo'äŋ] *s3* plumpness, stoutness
embryo ['emm-] *s6* embryo (*pl* embryos) **-log** embryologist **-logj** *s3* embryology **-nål** *al* embryonic, embryonal
emedan [eˣme:-] (*därför att*) because; (*eftersom*) as, since, seeing [that]; ~ *jag var upptagen kunde jag inte komma* as I was (being) busy I could not come
emellan [eˣmell-] **I** *prep* (*jfr* mellan); (*om två*) between; (*om flera*) among; *man och man ~* as one man to another; *det stannar oss ~* it remains strictly between ourselves; *oss ~ sagt* between ourselves; *vänner ~* between friends **II** *adv* be-

tween; *trädgårdar med staket* ~ gardens with fences between; *ngt mitt* ~ something in between; *inte lägga fingrarna* ~ not spare s.b.; handle the matter without mittens; *ge 100 pund* ~ give 100 pounds in the bargain (to square the transaction) **-åt** [e^xmell-] occasionally, sometimes, at times; *allt* ~ from time to time, every now and then

emellertjd however

emerit|us [e'me:-] I *-us -i, r* emeritus (*pl* emeriti) II *oböjligt a* emeritus; *professor* ~ professor emeritus

emfa|s *s3* emphasis **-tisk** *a5* emphatic

emfysem *s7, med.* emphysema

emigr|ant emigrant **-ation** emigration **-era** emigrate

emin|ens *s3, Ers (Hans)* ~ Your (His) Eminence (Eminency) **-ent** *a1* eminent

emjr *s3* emir **emiret** *s7* emirate

emissarie [-'a:rie] *s5* emissary

emission [emi'ʃo:n] (*av värdepapper*) issue

emissions|bank investment bank **-kurs** price (rate) of issue

emittera issue

emk (*förk. för elektromotorisk kraft*) emf, EMF (electromotive force)

emma *s1,* **emmastol** easy chair

emmentalerost [-^xta:-] Emmenthal[er]

e-moll E minor

emot I *prep, se mot; mitt* ~ *ngn* opposite [to] s.b.; *alla var* ~ *honom* everybody was against him II *adv, mitt* ~ opposite; *för och* ~ for and against; *skäl för och* ~ (*äv.*) pros and cons; *det bär mig* ~ it goes against the grain; *inte mig* ~ I have no objection, it's O.K. by me

emotion emotion **emotionell** *a1* emotional

emotjv *a1* emotive

emot|se [^xe:mɔ:t- *äv.* e^xmɔ:t-], **-taga** *se motse, mottaga*

empatj *s3* empathy

empjr [emm- *el.* aŋ-] *s3, se empirstil* **-iker** empiricism **-isk** *a5* empirical **-ism** empiricism

empirstil [-^xpi:r-] Empire style

emsersalt Ems salt

emu ['e:-] *s3* emu

emulg|ator [-^xga:tår] *s3* emulsifier **-era** emulsify **-eringsmedel** emulsifier

emul|sion emulsion **-sionsfärg** emulsion paint

1 en [e:n] *s2* (*buske*) [common] juniper; (*trä*) juniper [wood]

2 en [enn] *adv* (*omkring*) about, some; *det var väl* ~ *fem sex personer* there were some five or six persons; *han gick för* ~ *tio minuter sedan* he left about ten minutes ago

3 en [enn] (*jfr ett*) I *räkn.* one; ~ *och* ~ one by one; ~ *gång* once; ~ *och samma* one and the same; ~ *till* another; ~ *åt gången* (*i taget*) one at a time; ~ *för alla och alla för* ~ one for all and all for one; *det är inte* ~*s fel att två träter* it takes two to make a quarrel; *ta* ~ *kaka till!* help yourself to another biscuit! II *obest. art* a, an; *ibl.* one; (*framför vissa, i sht abstr. substantiv*) a piece of; ~ *dag* one day; ~ *upplysning* (*oförskämdhet*) a piece of information (impudence) III *obest. pron* one; (*kasusform av man*) one, you, me; *mitt* ~*a öga* one of my eyes; ~*s egen* one's own; ~ *och annan*

besökare occasional visitors; ~ *av de bästa böcker jag läst* one of the best books I have read; *den* ~*e av pojkarna* one of the boys; *den* ~*e...den andre* [the] one...the other; *den* ~*a efter den andra* one after another; *det* ~*a med det andra gör att jag* what with one thing and another I; *från det* ~*a till det andra* from one thing to another; *vad är du för* ~*?* who are you[, my boy *etc.*]?; *ingen tycker om* ~ *om man är elak* nobody likes you if you are nasty; *du var just en snygg* ~*!* you are a nice chap, I must say!

ena [^xe:na] (*förena*) unite; (*foga samman*) unify; (*förlika*) conciliate; ~ *sig* (*bli enig*) come to an agreement (*om* as to), (*komma överens*) agree (*om* [up]on, about, as to), *A.E. äv.* get together

enahanda [^xe:na-] I *a4* (*alldeles likanande*) identical, same II *s7* (*enformighet*) monotony, sameness

enaktare one-act play

enande [^xe:n-] I *s6* unification, uniting II *a4* (*förenande*) uniting, unifying; (*förlikande*) conciliating

enarmad *a5* one-armed; ~ *bandit* one-armed bandit, slot machine

enastående [^xe:na-] I *a4* unique, unparalleled, exceptional; (*friare*) matchless, extraordinary II *adv* exceptionally, extremely

enbart [^xe:nba:rt] merely; (*uteslutande*) solely, exclusively

enbent *a4* one-legged

enbuske [^xe:n-] juniper [shrub]

enbyggare [^xe:n-] *bot.* mon[o]ecious plant

enbär ['e:n-] juniper berry **enbärsbrännvin** gin

encefaljt *s3* encephalitis

encefalogram [-'gramm] *s7* encephalogram

encellig *a1* unicellular

encykl|ika [-'sykk-] *s1* encyclical **-isk** *a5* encyclic[al]

encykloped|i [aŋ- *el.* enn-] *s3* encyclop[a]edia **-isk** [-'pe:-] *a5* encyclop[a]edic **-ist** encyclop[a]edist

encylindrig *a5* single-cylinder

end|a *pron* only, single, sole, one; *den* -*e* the only man; *det* ~ the only thing; *en* ~ *gång* just once; *denna* ~ *vän* this one friend; *ingen* ~ not a single one; *inte en* ~ *blomma* not a single flower; *hon är* ~ *barnet* she is an only child; *det blev en* ~ *röra* it turned into one big muddle

endast *adv* only, but; ~ *för vuxna* adults only **endaste** *pron* one single

endels in part

endemj *s3,* **endemisk** [-'de:-] *a5* endemic

endera ['enn-] I *pron* one [or the other] of the two; ~ *dagen* one of these days, some day or other; *i ettdera fallet* in either case II *konj, se antingen*

endjv *s3,* **endivsallad** (*grönsallad*) endive; *A.E.* chicory crown; (*handelsnamn på sallatcikoria*) chicory, succory

endo|ergisk [-'ärg-] *a5* endoergic **-gen** [-'je:n] *a5* endogenous

endokrjn *a5* endocrine; ~ *körtel* endocrine (ductless) gland **-ologj** endocrinology **-ologisk** [-'lå:-] *a5* endocrinologic[al]

endo|skop [-'skå:p] *s7* endoscope **-skopj** *s3* endoscopy

endossat [aŋ-, *äv.* enn-] endorsee; transferee

E

endoss|ement [aŋdåsse'maŋ] *el.* enn-] *s7* endorsement **-ent** endorser **-era** endorse **-ering** [-'se:-] endorsement

endotęrm[isk] *a5* endothermic, endothermal

endräkt [ˣe:n-] *s3* concord, harmony; (*enstämmighet*) unanimity

energi [-'ʃi:] *s3* energy; *elektrisk* ~ electrical energy **-analys** energy analysis **-användning** energy application **-balans** energy balance **-bärare** energy carrier **-distribution** energy distribution **-förbrukning** energy consumption; (*elförbrukning*) power consumption **-förlust** loss of energy **-försörjning** energy supply (supplies) **-gröda** energy crop **-hushållning** rational use of energy **-knippe** bundle of energy **-kris** energy crisis **-källa** source of energy **-lagring** energy storage **-omvandling** energy conversion (transformation)

energisk [e'närgisk] *a5* (*full av energi*) energetic (*i* in, at); (*kraftfull*) vigorous

energi|skatt energy tax **-skog** energy forest **-snål** power saving **-sparande** energy saving **-system** energy system **-tillgång** energy supply; (*eltillgång*) power supply **-täthet** volume energy, energy density **-utvinning** energy recovery **-verk** Statens ~ [the Swedish] national energy administration **-åtgång** energy consumption **-överföring** energy transfer

enerver|a enervate, unnerve **-ande** *a4* enervating, trying

en face [aŋ'fass] (*om porträtt*) fullface

enfald [ˣe:n-] *s3* silliness, foolishness; (*starkare*) stupidity; *heliga* ~ sancta simplicitas **-ig** *a1* silly, foolish; stupid

enfamiljshus [one-family] house

en famille [aŋfa'mij] with one's family; at home; (*utan formaliteter*) informally

en|fasmotor single-phase motor **-filig** *a5* single-file **-formig** [-å-] *a1* monotonous, tedious, dull **-formighet** [-å-] monotony, dullness **-färgad** one-coloured; plain; (*om ljus, målning*) monochromatic **-född** *relig.*, *den* ~*e sonen, Hans* ~*e son* the (His) only begotten Son

engag|emang [aŋgaʃe'maŋ] *s7* **1** (*anställning*) engagement, contract **2** *hand.* (*förpliktelse*) engagement, obligation, commitment; (*penningplacering*) investment **-era 1** (*anställa*) engage **2** (*förplikta*) engage, commit; *vara starkt* ~*d i* be deeply committed (engaged) in **3** *rfl*, ~ *sig i* engage (be engaged) in, concern o.s. with, (*intressera sig för*) interest o.s. in; ~ *sig för* stand up for

en garde [aŋ'gard] on guard

engelsk [ˣeŋ-] *a5* English; British; ~*t horn* cor anglais, English horn; *E*~*a kanalen* the [English] Channel; ~*a kyrkan* (*såsom institution*) the Church of England; ~ *mil* [English] mile; ~*a pund* pound sterling; ~*t salt* Epsom salts (*pl*); ~*a sjukan* [the] rickets, rachitis; ~*a språket* the English language, English

engelska [ˣeŋ-] **1** (*språk*) English; *på* ~ in English; *översätta till* ~ translate into English **2** (*kvinna*) Englishwoman, English lady

engelsk|fientlig anti-English, Anglophobe **-född** English-born, British-born **-språkig** *a5* English-speaking; (*om litteratur o.d.*) in English **--svensk** Anglo-Swedish; ~ *ordbok* English-

-Swedish dictionary **-talande** *a4* English-speaking, Anglophone **-vänlig** pro-English, pro-British, Anglophili[a]c

engels|man [ˣeŋ-] Englishman; -*männen a*) (*hela nationen*) the English, Englishmen, *b*) (*några engelsmän*) the Englishmen

engifte [ˣe:n-] monogamy; *leva i* ~ be monogamous

England ['eŋ-] *n* England; (*Storbritannien*) [Great] Britain; (*officiellt*) the United Kingdom [of Great Britain and Northern Ireland]

en gros [aŋ'grå:] wholesale

engros|firma [aŋ'grå:-] wholesaler **-handel** wholesale

engångs|belopp non-recurring (non-recurrent) amount **-bägare** (*dricks-*) disposable cup **-företeelse** non-recurrent phenomenon, isolated case **-förpackning** disposable packing (package) **-glas** nonreturnable bottle **-kostnad** non-recurrent charge, once-for-all cost **-lakan** disposable sheet **-servis** disposable tableware

enhet [ˣe:n-] (*enhetlighet*) unity; *mat.*, *mil.*, *sjö. m.m.* unit

enhetlig [ˣe:nhe:t-] *a1* (*om begrepp o.d.*) unitary; (*likartad*) uniform, homogeneous; (*om mode, typ o.d.*) standardized **-het** unity; uniformity, homogeneity; standardization

enhets|front united front **-pris** standard (uniform) price **-rörelse** *italienska* ~*n* the movement for Italian unity **-strävan** struggle for unity

en|hjärtbladig [ˣe:n-] *a5* monocotyledonous **-hällig** *a1* unanimous **-hänt** *a4* one-handed **-hörning** [-hö:r-] unicorn

enig *a1* (*om ena*) united, unanimous; (*ense*) of one opinion, agreed; *bli* ~[*a*] come to an agreement (*med* with; *om* as to) **-het** unity; unanimity; agreement; concord; ~ *ger styrka* unity is strength

enkammarsystem unicameral (single-chamber) system

enkannerligen [en'kann-] [more] particularly

enkel ['enn-] *a2* **1** (*motsats dubbel el. flerfaldig*) single; ~ *biljett* single (*AE.* one-way) ticket **2** (*motsats sammansatt, tillkrånglad o.d.*) simple; (*flärdlös äv.*) plain; *av* ~ *konstruktion* of simple construction; *en vanlig* ~ *människa* just an ordinary person; ~ *uppgift* easy task (job); *av det enkla skälet att* for the simple reason that, simply because; *ju enklare ju simplare* the simpler the easier; *ha enkla vanor* have simple habits; *får jag bjuda på en* ~ *middag?* may I invite you to a simple dinner?; *känna sig* ~ feel very small

enkel|beckasin common (Wilson's) snipe **-het** (*jfr enkel*) singleness; simplicity **-knäppt** *a4* single-breasted **-rikta** ~*d gata* (*trafik*) one-way street (traffic) **-rum** single room **-spårig** *a5* single-track, one-track (*äv. bildl.*); *vara* ~ (*bildl.*) have a one-track mind

enkel|t ['enn-] *adv* simply; *helt* ~ [quite] simply **-verkande** single-acting

enkilosburk [one-]kilo tin

enklav *s3* enclave; enclosure

enkom [ˣennkåm] purposely, expressly, especially; ~ *för att* for the sole purpose of (+ *ing-form*), solely to (+ *inf.*)

enkrona *en* ~ a one-krona [piece]

enkät [aŋ-, *äv.* enn-] *s3* inquiry, investigation **-undersökning** opinion poll
enkönad [-ç-] *a5* unisexual
enlever|a [aŋle-] run away with; abduct **-ing** abduction
enlighet [ˣe:n-] *i uttr.*: *i ~ med* in accordance (conformity) with, according to
enligt [ˣe:n-] according to; *hand. äv.* as per; *~ faktura* as per invoice; *~ kontrakt (lag)* by contract (law); *~ min uppfattning* in my opinion
enmans|hytt single cabin **-kanot** single[-seater] canoe **-teater** one-man show **-valkrets** single-member constituency
enmotorig *a5* single-engined
enorm [-ˈårm] *a1* enormous, immense
enpartivälde one-party rule
en passant [aŋpaˈsaŋ] *schack.* in passing
en|plansvilla one-storey house, bungalow **-procentig** *a5* one-percent **-pucklig** *a5* single--humped
enquete *se* enkät
enradig *a5* (*om kavaj*) single-breasted; (*om halsband*) single row
enris [ˣe:n-] *s7* juniper twigs (*pl*) **-rökt** *a4* smoked over a fire of juniper twigs
enroller|a [aŋ-] enrol, enlist **-ing** enrolment, enlistment
en|rum [ˣe:n-] *i ~* in private; *tala med ngn i ~* have a private interview with s.b. **-rummare, -rumslägenhet** one-room[ed] flatlet; bed-sitter
1 ens *oböjligt a, sjö.* in line with each other
2 ens *adv, inte ~* not even; *med ~* all at once; *utan att ~ säga* without even saying; *om ~ så mycket* if that much
ensak [ˣe:n-] *det är min ~* it is my [private] affair (my [own] business)
ensam *a1* **1** (*enda*) sole; *~ innehavare* sole proprietor **2** (*allena*) alone; lonely, lonesome; (*ensamstående*) solitary; *~ i sitt slag* unique of its kind; *känna sig ~* feel lonely; *leva ett ~t liv* live a secluded life; *vara (bli) ~* be (be left) alone; *vara ~ sökande* be the only applicant; *en olycka kommer sällan ~* misfortunes seldom come singly; *vi fick en ~ kupé* we had a compartment to (for) ourselves **-boende** *a4* living alone (on one's own) **-cell** solitary confinement **-försäljare** sole (exclusive) agent
ensamhet (*jfr* ensam) **1** solitariness **2** loneliness; *i ~en* in [one's] solitude; *i min ~* in my loneliness
ensamhetskänsla [feeling of] loneliness
ensam|jungfru maid-of-all-work, general [servant] **-rätt** sole (exclusive) right[s *pl*] **-stående** *a4* solitary, isolated; (*om person*) single, living alone; (*fristående*) detached; *~ förälder* single parent
ensartad *a5* similar, uniform
ense *bli ~ om* agree upon, come to an agreement (understanding) about; *vara ~* be agreed (*om* about), agree (*om att* that); *vi är fullständigt ~ med er* we are one (in complete agreement) with you
ensemble [aŋˈsambel] *s5* ensemble **-spel** ensemble playing
ensfyr *sjö.* range (leading) light
ensidig *a1* one-sided (*äv. bildl.*); (*partisk äv.*)

partial, prejudiced, biased; (*om avtal o.d.*) unilateral **-het** one-sidedness *etc.*; prejudice, bias
ensiffrig *a5* one-figure; *~t tal* digit, figure
ensilage [aŋsiˈla:ʃ *el.* enn-] *s7, lantbr.* ensilage
ensitsig *a1, ~t jaktplan* single-seater fighter
enskil|d [ˣe:nʃild] *a1* **1** (*privat*) private, personal; *-t rum* (*område*) private room (property, grounds); *inta (stå i) ~ ställning* come to (stand at) attention; *~ väg* private road **2** (*enstaka*) individual; (*särskild*) specific, particular; *i varje -t fall* in each specific case
enskildhet privacy; *gå in på ~er* enter into particulars (details)
ensl|ig [ˣe:ns-] *a1* solitary, lonely; *~t belägen* solitary, isolated **-ing** *se* enstöring
ens|linje [ˣe:ns-] *sjö.* range (leading) line **-märke** *sjö.* range target (marker)
en|språkig *a5* unilingual **-spännare** gig, trap, buggy
enstaka [ˣe:n-] *oböjligt a* (*enskild*) separate, detached; (*sporadisk*) occasional; (*sällsynt*) exceptional; *i ~ fall* in exceptional cases; *någon ~ gång* once in a while; *på ~ ställen* in certain places; *vid ~ tillfällen* very occasionally
en|stavig *a5* monosyllabic; *~t ord* monosyllable **-stämmig** *a5* unanimous; *mus.* unison **-stämmigt** unanimously; *mus.* in unison **-ständigt** persistently; urgently **-störing** solitary, recluse, hermit **-tal 1** *mat.* unit **2** *språkv.* singular
entent[e] [aŋˈtaŋt] *s3* [*s5*] entente
enterit *s3* enteritis
entita [ˣe:n-] *s1* marsh tit
entitet entity
entledig|a [-ˈle:-] dismiss, discharge **-ande** *s6* dismissal, discharge
entomo|log entomologist **-logi** *s3* entomology **-logisk** [-ˈlå:-] *a5* entomologic[al]
entonig *a5* monotonous; *mus.* monotone **-het** monotony; *mus.* monotone
entré [aŋˈtre:] *s3* **1** entrance; (*intåg*) entry; *göra sin ~* make one's appearance **2** *se -avgift; fri ~* admission free **-avgift** admission (entrance) fee; *~er* (*vid tävling m.m.*) gate money **-biljett** ticket [of admission]
entrecote [aŋtreˈkå:t] *s5* entrecôte
entrepren|ad [aŋtre- *el.* entre-] *s3* contract [by tender]; *ta på ~* sign a contract for; *utlämna ett arbete på ~* invite tenders for a job **-ör** contractor
entrérätt entrée, first course
entresol[l] [aŋter- *el.* aŋtreˈsåll] *s3*, **-våning** mezzanine [floor], entresol
entropi *s3* entropy
enträgen [ˣe:n-] *a3* urgent, pressing; earnest; (*efterhängsen*) importunate; (*envis*) insistent; *~ begäran* urgent request; *~ bön* earnest prayer
enträget [ˣe:n-] *adv* urgently *etc.*; *be ngn ~ att* implore (entreat) s.b. to
entusi|asm [aŋ- *el.* enn-] *s3* enthusiasm **-asmera** inspire with enthusiasm, make enthusiastic **-ast** *s3* enthusiast **-astisk** [-ˈass-] *a5* enthusiastic (*för* for), keen (*för* on)
en|tydig *a5* (*om ord o.d.*) univocal; (*otvetydig*) unequivocal, unambiguous; (*klar*) clear-cut, distinct **-var** everybody; *alla och ~* each and all **-veten** *a3, se* envis **-vig** [ˣe:nvi:g] *s7* duel, single

E

combat

environger [aŋvi'råŋer] *pl* environs

envis [ˣe:n-] *a1* stubborn, obstinate; *(ihärdig)* dogged; *(om pers. äv.)* pertinacious, headstrong; *(om sak äv.)* persistent; ~ *hosta* persistent cough; ~ *som synden* as obstinate as sin **envisas** *dep* be obstinate *etc.*; ~ [*med*] *att* persist in (+ *ing-form*) **envishet** stubbornness, obstinacy *etc.*

envoyé [aŋvɔa'je:] *s3* envoy

en|våldshärskare absolute ruler, dictator **-våningshus** one-storey house **-välde** [ˣe:n-] absolutism; dictatorship; autocracy **-väldig** [ˣe:n-] absolute; autocratic; sovereign **-värd[ig]** *a5* monovalent, univalent

enzym [-'(t)sy:m] *s4, s7* enzyme

enäggstvilling identical twin

enär *se eftersom, emedan*

enögd *a5* one-eyed

e.o. *(förk. för extra ordinarie)* pro tem (pro tempore)

eolsharpa [ˣe:åls-] aeolian (wind) harp

eon [e'å:n] *s3* aeon; *A.E.* eon

eosin *s4* eosin[e]

epicentrum [-'senn-] epicentre

epidemi *s3* epidemic **epidemiologi** *s3* epidemiology **epidemisjukhus** isolation hospital, infectious disease unit **epidemisk** [-'de:-] *a5* epidemic

epi|fyt *s7* epiphyte **-gon** [-'gå:n] *s3* poor imitator **-grafik** epigraphy **-gram** [-'gramm] *s7* epigram

epik *s3* epic poetry **epiker** ['e:-] epic poet

epikuré *s3* epicurean; *(goddagspilt)* epicure **epikureisk** [-'re:-] *a5* epicurean

epilation epilation

epilepsi *s3* epilepsy **epileptiker** [-'lepp-] *s9,* **epileptisk** [-'lepp-] *a5* epileptic **epileptoid** [-tɔ'i:d] *a5* epileptoid, epileptiform

epilera epilate

epilog epilogue

episk ['e:-] *a5* epic

episkopal *a5* episcopal **-kyrkan** *(anglikanska kyrkan)* Church of England

episod *s3* episode, incident

epistel [-'piss-] *s2* epistle

epitaf *s7, s4,* **epitafium** [-'ta:-] *s4* memorial tablet; *(inskrift)* epitaph

epitel *s7* epithelium **-cell** epithelial cell

epitet *s7* epithet

epizooti *s3* epizootic

epok [e'på:k] *s3* epoch; *bilda* ~ make [a new] epoch; be a turning point **-görande** [-j-] *a4* epoch-making

eponym *s3* eponym

epos ['e:pås] *s7* epos, epic

epoxi|harts [eˣpåcksi-] epoxy (epoxide) resin **-plast** epoxy plastic

epsilon ['epsilån] *s7* epsilon

epsomsalt [ˣepsåm-] Epsom salts *(pl)*

epålett *s4* epaulet[te]

er *pron* **1** *pers.* you; *rfl* yourself, *pl* yourselves **2** *poss.* a) *fören.* your b) *självst.* yours; *Ers Majestät* Your Majesty; ~*a dumbommar!* you fools!; *Er tillgivne (i brevslut)* Yours sincerely

era *s1* era

erbarmlig [-'barm-] *a1* *(ömkansvärd, ynklig)* pitiable; *(eländig)* wretched, woeful

erbium ['err-] *s4* erbium

erbjud|a [ˣe:r-] **1** *(med personsubj.)* offer; *(mera formellt)* proffer, tender; *jag blev -en att (äv.)* I was invited to **2** *(med saksubj.)* *(förete)* present; *(ge, lämna)* afford, provide; ~ *en ståtlig anblick* present an imposing sight; ~ *skydd mot* provide shelter from **3** *rfl (med personsubj.)* offer; volunteer; *(med saksubj.)* offer [itself]; present itself; occur, arise **erbjudan** *r* offer **erbjudande** *s6* *(anbud)* offer; *A.E.* proposition; *(pris-)* quotation, tender

erektion [-k'ʃo:n] erection

eremit *s3* hermit **-age** [-'a:ʃ] *s7* hermitage; *E~t (i Leningrad)* the Hermitage **-boning** hermitage **-kräfta** hermit crab

erfara [ˣe:r-] **1** *(få veta)* learn *(av* from); learn, get to know **2** *(röna)* experience, feel

erfaren [ˣe:r-] *a3* experienced, practised; *(kunnig)* skilled, versed *(i* in) **-het** experience; *bli en* ~ *rikare* gain by experience, be taught by an experience; *veta av egen* ~ know from [one's own] experience; *vis av* ~*en* wise by experience; *ha dåliga* ~*er av ngt* have negative experience of s.th., find s.th. unsatisfactory **-hetsmässig** *a1* acquired by experience

erforderlig [ˣe:rfo:r-] *a1* requisite, necessary **erfordra** require, need, want; demand, call for; *om så* ~*s* if required *(etc.)*, if necessary

erg *(enhet för energi)* erg

ergo|meter [-'me:-] *s2* ergometer **-nom** ergonomist; *A.E.* biotechnologist **-nomi** *s3* ergonomics *(pl, behandlas som sg)*; *A.E.* biotechnology **-nomisk** [-'nå:-] *a5* ergonomic; *A.E.* biotechnological

erhåll|a [ˣe:r-] *(få)* receive, get; *(bli tillerkänd äv.)* be awarded (granted); *(skaffa sig)* obtain, acquire, procure, secure; *vi har -it Ert brev* we are in receipt of your letter **-ande** *s6* receiving *etc.*, receipt; obtaining; *omedelbart efter* ~*t av* [immediately] on receipt of

erigera [-g-] erect

eriksgata [a Swedish] king's tour of the country

erinra 1 *(påminna)* remind *(ngn om ngt* s.b. of s.th.); ~ *sig* remember, recollect, recall; *hon* ~*r om sin mormor* she resembles her grandmother **2** *(invända)* jag har ingenting att ~ *mot* I have no objection to make to **erinran** *r* **1** *(påminnelse)* reminder *(om* of) **2** *(varning)* admonition *(om* as to) **3** *(invändning)* objection *(mot* to) **erinring 1** *se erinran* **2** *(hågkomst)* recollection, remembrance

erkänd [ˣe:r-] *a5* acknowledged, recognized, accepted

erkänn|a [ˣe:r-] acknowledge; *(medge äv.)* admit; *(godkänna)* recognize, accept; ~ *mottagandet av ett brev* acknowledge receipt of a letter; ~ *sig besegrad* acknowledge defeat; ~ *sig skyldig* confess o.s. [to be] guilty, *jur. äv.* plead guilty **-ande** *s6* acknowledg[e]ment; admission; recognition **-sam** *a1* appreciative; grateful *(mot* to)

erkänsla [ˣe:r-] *s1* gratitude *(mot* to); *mot kontant* ~ for a consideration; *som en* ~ *för* in recognition of

erlägg|a [ˣe:r-] pay; ~ *avgift för* make payment for, pay **-ande** *s6* paying, payment; *mot* ~ *av* on (against) payment of

ernå [ˣeːr-] attain, achieve **-ende** s6 attaining, achievement; *för* ~ *av* in order to attain
erodera erode
erogen [-ˈjeːn] a5 erogenous; ~*a zoner* erogenous zones [of the body]
erosion erosion
erot|ik s3 eroticism, erotism; sex **-isk** [-ˈrɑː- *el.* -ˈråː-] a5 erotic[al]
eroto|man s3 erotomaniac **-mani** s3 erotomania
ers [eːrs] *se er*
ersätt|a [ˣeːr-] **1** (*gottgöra*) ~ *ngn för ngt* compensate s.b. for s.th., make up to s.b. for s.th.; ~ *ngn för hans arbete* pay (recompense) s.b. for his work **2** (*träda i stället för, byta ut*) replace, take the place of; supersede **-are** substitute; proxy; (*efterträdare*) successor **-ning 1** compensation; (*skade-*) indemnity, damages (*pl*); (*betalning*) remuneration; ~ *för sveda och värk* damages (*pl*) for pain and suffering; *AE.* smart money **2** (*surrogat*) substitute
ersättnings|anspråk claim for compensation (damages, indemnity) **-belopp** [amount of] compensation (indemnity) **-medel** substitute **-skyldig** liable to pay damages **-skyldighet** liability
ertappa [ˣeːr-] catch; ~ *ngn i färd med att* catch s.b. (+ *ing-form*); ~ *sig med att sitta och stirra* catch o.s. staring; ~ *ngn på bar gärning* catch s.b. red-handed (in the act)
erupt|ion [-pˈʃoːn] eruption **-iv** eruptive
erövra [-öːv-] conquer; *bildl. äv.* vanquish; (*intaga*) capture; (*pris, mästerskap o.d.*) win **erövrare** conqueror **erövrarfolk** nation of conquerors **erövring** conquest; capture; *göra ~ar* (*äv. bildl.*) make conquests
erövrings|krig war of conquest (aggression) **-lust[a]** eagerness (thirst) for conquest **-politik** policy of aggrandizement **-tåg** military expedition
Esaias [eˈsai-] Isaiah; (*i Nya testamentet*) Esaias
eskader [-ˈkaː-] s2, *sjö.* squadron; *flyg.* group **-chef** *sjö.* commodore; *flyg.* group captain
eskal|ation escalation **-era** escalate
eskapad s3 escapade
eskap|ism escapism **-ist** s3, **-istisk** a5 escapist
eskarp s3 escarp
eskatolog|i [-låˈgiː] s3 eschatology **-isk** [-ˈlåːg-] a5 eschatological
eskimå s3 Eskimo **-isk** a5 Eskimo
eskort [-ˈårt] s3, **eskortera** escort **eskortfartyg** escort vessel
esomoftast [esåmˣåff-] (*då o. då*) every now and then; (*för det mesta*) mostly; (*allt som oftast*) very often
esoterisk [-ˈteː-] a5 esoteric
espadrill s3 espadrille
esparto [esˈpartå] s9, **-gräs** esparto [grass]
esperan|tist Esperantist **-to** [-ˈrantå] r Esperanto
esplanad s3 esplanade, avenue
espresso [-ˈpresså] s3 espresso
espri s3 **1** (*kvickhet*) esprit, wit **2** (*fjäderknippe*) osprey plume, aigret[te]
1 ess *kortsp., se äss*
2 ess s7, *mus.* E flat
essay *se essä*

Ess-dur E flat major
esse *n, vara i sitt* ~ be in one's element
essens [-ˈens *el.* -ˈaŋs] s3 essence
essentiell [-n(t)siˈell] a5 essential
esskornett cornet
essä s3 essay **-ist** essayist **-samling** collection of essays
est s3 Est[h]onian
ester [ˈess-] s2, *kem.* ester
estet s3 aesthete **esteticism** aestheticism **estetik** s3 aesthetics (*pl, behandlas som sg*) **estetiker** [-ˈteː-] aesthetician **estetisk** [-ˈteː-] a5 aesthetic[al] **estetsnobb** aesthete
estimera esteem; *stat.* estimate
Estland [ˈest-] *n* Est[h]onia **estländare** s9, **estländsk** a5 Est[h]onian **estländska 1** (*språk*) Est[h]onian **2** (*kvinna*) Est[h]onian woman
estnisk[a] [ˈest-] *se estländsk[a]*
estrad s3 platform, dais, rostrum; stand **-debatt** panel [discussion]
e-sträng *mus.* E string
estuarium [-ˈaː-] s4 estuary
etabler|a establish; ~ *sig* set up [in business] for o.s., (*bosätta sig*) settle down; ~ *sig som* set up as a **-ad** establishment **-ing** establishment
etablissemang s7 establishment; ~*et* (*det bestående samhället*) the Establishment
etage [eˈtaːʃ] s5 storey, floor **-lägenhet** maison-[n]ette; *AE.* duplex [apartment]
etan s4, s3 ethane **etanol** [-ˈnåːl] s3 ethanol, ethyl alcohol
etapp s3 **1** (*förråds- el. rastställe*) halting-place; (*vägsträcka*) day's march; (*friare*) stage, lap; *rycka fram i ~er* advance by stages (*mil., i ansatser* by bounds; *i omgångar* by echelon); *försiggå i ~er* take place in stages **2** (*förråd*) depot **-linje** *mil.* supply route, communication zone **-vis** by (in) stages, gradually
etcetera [-ˈsettra] et cetera (*förk.* etc., &c.)
eten s3,s4 ethylene, ethene
eter [ˈeː-] s2 ether, [di]ethyl ether, ethoxyethane; ~*n* (*rymden*) the ether **-isera** etherize **-isk** [eˈteː-] a5 ethereal; ~*a oljor* (*äv.*) essential oils
eternell s3 immortelle, everlasting [flower]
eter|rus ether intoxication **-våg** ether wave
etik s3 ethics (*pl, behandlas som sg i betydelsen vetenskap*) **etiker** [ˈeː-] moral philosopher, ethicist
etikett s3 **1** (*lapp*) label (*äv. bildl.*); *sätta* ~[*er*] *på* label **2** (*umgängesformer, regler*) etiquette **-era** label
etiketts|brott breach of etiquette **-fråga** question of etiquette
etiologi s3 aetiology
Etiopien [etiˈoː-] *n* Ethiopia **etiopier** [etiˈoː-] s9, **etiopisk** [etiˈoː-] a5 Ethiopian
etisk [ˈeː-] a5 ethical, moral
Etna [ˣeːt-] *n* [Mount] Etna
etnisk [ˈeː-] a5 ethnic[al]
etno|centrisk [-ˈsenn-] a5 ethnocentric **-centrism** ethnocentrism **-graf** s3 ethnographer **-grafi** s3 ethnography **-grafisk** [ˈgraː-] a5 ethnographical **-log** ethnologist **-logi** s3 ethnology **-logisk** [-ˈlåː-] a5 ethnological
eto|log ethologist **-logi** s3 ethology **-logisk** [-ˈlåː-] a5 ethological

E

Etrurien [-'tru:-] *n* Etruria
etrusk *s3*, **etrusker** [e'truss-] *s9*, **etruskisk**
[e'truss-] *a5* Etruscan, Etrurian
ets|a etch; ~ *sig in a*) eat its way (*i* into), *b*) *bildl.*
make an indelible impression, engrave itself (*i*
on) **-are** etcher **-medel** etchant **-ning** etching
-nål etching-needle **-plåt** etched plate
ett (*se 3 en*); ~, *tu, tre* all of a sudden; hey presto!;
~ *är nödvändigt* one thing is necessary; *vara* ~
med be at one with; *klockan är* ~ it is one o'clock;
i ~ continuously; *betalning i* ~ *för allt* composition (lump sum) payment; *hålla tre mot* ~ lay
three to one; *det kommer på* ~ *ut* it is all one, it's
as broad as it's long **etta** *s1* **1** one; *komma in som*
god ~ come in an easy first; ~*n*[*s växel*] [the] first
[gear] **2** *se enrumslägenhet* **ettdera** *se endera*
etter ['ett-] **I** *s7* poison, venom; *bildl.* virulence,
venom **II** *adv,* ~ *värre* worse and worse **-myra**
fire ant
etthundrafemtio one hundred and fifty
ettiden *vid* ~ about one o'clock
ettrig *a1* poisonous; *bildl. äv.* fiery, hot-tempered, irascible
ett|struken *a5, mus.* one-line; *-strukna C* middle
C **-tusen** (*hopskr. ettusen*) one (a) thousand **-tå-
get** (*hopskr. ettåget*) the one o'clock train **-årig**
a5 one year's, one-year; (*årsgammal*) one-year
old; (*som gäller för ett år*) annual **-åring** one-
-year old child (*etc.*), child of one (*etc.*); (*djur*
äv.) yearling **-öring** one-öre piece
etui *s4* case; étui
etyd *s3* étude; study
etyl *s3* ethyl **-alkohol** *se etanol*
etylen *se eten* **-glykol** ethanediol, [ethylene] glycol
etymo|log etymologist **-logi** *s3* etymology **-lo-
gisk** [-'lå:-] *a5* etymological
eufemis|m *s3* euphemism **-tisk** *a5* euphemistic
eufon|i [evfå'ni:] *s3* euphony **-isk** [-'få:-] *s5*
euphonic, euphonious
eufor|i [evfo'ri:] *s3* euphoria **-isk** [-'få:-] *a5*
euphoric
eugen|ik [evg- *el.* evj-] *s3* eugenics (*pl, behandlas*
som sg) **-isk** [-'ge:- *el.* -'je:-] *a5* eugenic
eukalyptus [evka'lypp-] *s2* eucalypt[us]
Euklides [-'kli:-] Euclid
eunuck [ev-] *s3* eunuch
Eurasien [-'a:-] *n* Eurasia
euro|dollar Eurodollar **-kommunism** Euro-
communism
Europa Europe **-marknaden** the European
Economic Community, the Common Market
europa|mästare European champion **-mäs-
terskap** European championship
Europarådet the Council of Europe
europaväg European highway
europé *s3* European
europe|isera Europeanize **-isk** [-'pe:isk *el.*
-'pejsk] *a5* European
europium [-'ro:-] *s8* europium
Eurovision Eurovision
eutanasj [ev-] *s3* euthanasia, mercy killing
Eva Eve
evad whatever; ~ *som* whatsoever
evakostym *i* ~ in the nude (the altogether, *vard.*
the raw); *vard.* in one's birthday suit

evakuer|a evacuate; *de* ~*de* the evacuees **-ing**
evacuation
evaluera evaluate
evalver|a (*värdera*) estimate, evaluate; (*om-
räkna*) convert **-ing** estimation, evaluation; conversion
evangel|isation [-j-] evangelization **-isera**
evangelize **-isk** [-'je:-] *a5* evangelical **-ist** evan-
gelist **-ium** [-'je:-] *s4* gospel
evar where[so]ever
evenemang *s7* [great] event; function
eventualitet *s3* eventuality, contingency; *för*
alla ~*er* against (for) an emergency
eventuell *a5* [if] any, possible, prospective; ~*a*
förbättringar emendations (improvements), if
any; ~*a kostnader* any expenses that may arise;
~*a köpare* prospective buyers **eventuellt** *adv*
possibly, perhaps; if necessary (required); *jag*
kommer ~ I may [possibly] come
evertebrat *zool.* invertebrate
evidens *s3, bevisa ngt till full* ~ prove conclu-
sively **evident** *al* evident, obvious
evig *al* eternal, everlasting; (*oavbruten*) perpetual; *den* ~*e* the Eternal one; *den* ~*a staden* (*Rom*)
the Eternal City; *det* ~*a livet* eternal (everlasting)
life; *var* ~*a dag* every single day; *en* ~ *lögn* a confounded lie; *detta* ~*a regnande* this perpetual
(everlasting) rain; ~ *snö* perpetual snow; *det tog*
en ~ *tid* it took ages **evighet** eternity; *i* [*all*] ~
for ever, in perpetuity; *för tid och* ~ now and for
evermore; *det är* ~*er sedan vi sågs* it's ages since
we met
evighets|blomma *se eternell* **-göra** never-end-
ing job **-låga** (*gas-*) pilot flame; *relig. e.d.* eternal
flame **-längtan** yearning for things eternal **-ma-
skin** perpetual motion machine **-tro** belief in
eternity
evigt *adv* eternally; *för* ~ for ever
evinnerlig [e'vinn-] *a5* eternal, everlasting, endless **-en** eternally; for ever
evolution evolution **-ist** evolutionist
evolutionsteori theory of evolution
evärdlig [e'vä:rd-] *a5* eternal; *för* ~*a tider* for
ever, for all time
exakt *al* exact; precise **-het** exactness; precision
exalt|ation exaltation **-erad** [-'te:-] *a5* exalted;
(*friare*) excited, agitated
exam|en *-en -ina, r* examination; *vard.* exam; *av-
lägga akademisk* ~ take a university degree,
graduate; *ta* ~ pass one's examination; *gå upp i* ~
present o.s. for one's examination
examens|betyg examination certificate **-bok**
ung. examination record book **-feber** exam
nerves (*pl*) **-fordringar** examination requirements **-förrättare** examiner **-läsning** reading
[up] for an examination **-nämnd** examining
board, board of examiners **-uppgift** examination paper **-ämne** examination subject
examin|and *s3* examinee **-ation** examination
-ator [-'a:tår] *s3* examiner -*era* examine, question; (*växt*) determine **-ering** (*av växt*) determination
excell|ens *s3* excellency; *Ers* ~ Your Excellency
-ent *al* excellent **-era** excel (*i* in, at)
excenter [ek'senn-] *s2* eccentric **-skiva** eccentric
disc (sheave)

excentr|icitet s3 eccentricity **-isk** [ek'senn-] a5 eccentric

exceptionell [eksepʃɔ-] exceptional

excerper|a [ekser-] excerpt, make excerpts **-ing** excerpting, excerption

excerpt [ek'särpt] s7, s3 excerpt

excess [ek'sess] s3 excess; ~er (utsvävningar) orgies

excitera excite (äv. fys.); ~d excited

exdrottning ex-queen

exe|ges [-g-] s3 exegesis **-get** [-g-] s3 exegete, exegetist **-getik** [-g-] s3 exegetics (pl, behandlas som sg) **-getisk** [-'ge:-] a5 exegetic[al]

exekution 1 (avrättning) execution **2** (utmätning) distraint, distress

exekutions|betjänt bailiff **-pluton** firing squad

exekutiv a5 o. s3 executive; ~ auktion compulsory auction **exekutor** [-ˣku:tår] s3 executor; executory officer **exekutör** executor

exekvera execute

exempel [eck'semm-] s7 example; (inträffat fall) instance; belysande (avskräckande) ~ illustrative (warning) example; belysa med ~ illustrate by examples, exemplify; föregå med gott ~ set an (a good) example; statuera ett ~ make an example; till ~ for instance, say, (vid uppräkning) e.g. **-lös** unprecedented, unparalleled; exceptional **-samling** collection of examples **-vis** for instance; by way of example

exemplar s7 copy; naturv. specimen; i två (tre) ~ in duplicate (triplicate); i fem ~ in five [identical] copies; renskrivet ~ fair copy **-isk** a5 exemplary; en ~ ung man a model (an exemplary) young man

exemplifi|era exemplify **-kation** exemplification

exercera drill, train; ~ beväring do one's military service; ~ med drill, work **exercis** s3 drill; military service **exercisfält** drill-ground

exergi [-'gi:] s3 exergy

exhibition|ism exhibitionism **-ist** exhibitionist **-istisk** a5 exhibitionistic

exil s3 exile **-regering** exile government

existens s3 **1** (tillvaro) existence, life; being; (utkomst) living, subsistence **2** (person) individual **-berättigande** raison d'être, right to exist **-minimum** subsistence level **-möjlighet** means of support, possibility of making a living **-villkor** pl conditions of existence

existential|ism [-(t)sia-] existentialism **-ist** s3, **-istisk** a5 existentialist

existera exist; live; subsist; ~r fortfarande is still in existence, is extant

exklamation exclamation

exklu|dera exclude, reject, expel **-siv** al exclusive **-sive** [-'si:-] excluding, exclusive of; ~ emballage excluding packing, packing excluded **-sivitet** exclusiveness, exclusivity

exkommuni|cera excommunicate **-kation** excommunication

exkonung ex-king

exkrementer [-'menn-] pl excrements, faeces

exkret s7 excreta (pl) **-tion** excretion

exkurs s3 excursus **-ion** [-r'ʃɔ:n] excursion; göra en ~ go on an excursion

exlibris [-'li:-] s7 ex-libris, bookplate

exo|biologi exobiology, astrobiology **-ergisk** [-'ärg-] a5 exoergic

ex officio [å'fi:siå] ex officio, by right of office (position)

exo|gen [-'je:n] a5 exogenous **-krin** a5 exocrine; ~ körtel exocrine gland

exorc|ism exorcism **-ist** exorcist

exosfär s3 exosphere

exo|terisk [-'te:-] a5 exoteric **-term[isk]** a5 exothermic, exothermal

exot|isk [eck'så:-] a5 exotic **-ism** exoticism

expander [-'pann-] s2 expander **expandera** expand **expanderbult** expansion bolt

expansion [-n'ʃɔ:n] expansion; stadd i ~ expanding **-ism** expansionism **-istisk** [-'niss-] a5 expansionistic

expansions|förmåga capacity of expansion **-kärl** expansion tank

expansiv al expansive

expatrier|a expatriate **-ing** expatriation

expedier|a 1 (sända) send, dispatch, forward; (per post) post, mail; (ombesörja) carry out, dispatch **2** (betjäna) attend to **3** (göra slut på) settle **-ing** (av kunder) attendance, serving; jfr äv. expedition

expedit s3 shop assistant; salesman, fem. saleswoman; AE. [sales]clerk

expedition 1 (avsändande) sending, dispatch, forwarding; (per post) posting, mailing; (ombesörjande) execution, carrying out **2** (betjänande) attendance, serving of customers **3** (lokal för expediering) office; department **4** (forsknings- o. mil.) expedition

expeditions|avgift service (dispatch) fee **-chef** permanent undersecretary **-ministär** caretaker government **-tid** office (business) hours (pl)

expeditör sender, forwarding agent

expenser [-'penn-] pl expenses; (småutgifter) petty expenditure (sg)

experiment s7 experiment; (prov) trial, test; jfr äv. försök **-ator** [-ˣa:tår] s3 experimenter **-djur** se försöksdjur **-ell** a5 experimental **-era** experiment (på on) **-stadium** experimental stage

expert s3 expert (på in); specialist (på on) **-expertis** s3 expertise, expertness; (sakkunniga) experts (pl)

expert|kommission commission of experts **-kommitté** committee of experts, advisory committee **-utlåtande** expert opinion, report of experts **-utredning** [findings of a] specialist investigation

explanativ a5 explanatory, explanative

explicit a4 explicit

explikation (tolkning) explication, explanation

exploat|era (bearbeta) exploit; (gruva äv.) work; (uppfinning äv.) develop; (utsuga) make money (capital) out of, tap **-ering** [-'te:-] exploitation: working **-ör** developer

explodera explode, blow up; (detonera) detonate; (om bildäck) burst

explor|ation exploration **-era** explore

explosion explosion; detonation; burst

explosions|artad [-a:r-] a5 explosive **-fri** explosion-proof **-motor** internal-combustion engine **-risk** danger of explosion **-ritning** exploded

E

view

explosiv *a1* explosive; *~a varor* explosives
exponen|t exponent (*för* of); *mat. äv.* power, index **-tiell** [-tsi'ell] exponential
exponer|a (*utställa*) exhibit, show; (*blottställa o. foto.*) expose; *~ sig* expose o.s. **-ing** *foto.* exposure
exponerings|mätare exposure (light) meter **-tid** [time of] exposure
export [-'pårt] *s3* (*utförsel*) export, export trade; exportation; (*varor*) exports (*pl*) **-affär** export business, exportation **-artikel** *se* -vara **-avgift** export duty
export|era export **-firma** export[ing] firm **-förbud** ban on export[s] **-förening** export[ers'] association; *Sveriges allmänna ~* [the] General Export Association of Sweden **-hamn** export port **-handel** export trade **-industri** export[ing] industry **-kreditnämnd** *~en* [the Swedish] export credits guarantee board **-licens** export licence **-marknad** export market **-råd** *Sveriges ~* [the] Swedish Trade Council **-tillstånd** export permit (licence) **-tull** export duty **-underskott** export deficit **-vara** export product; exports, export goods (*pl*); *AE äv.* exportation **-öl** export beer
export|ör exporter **-överskott** export surplus
expos|é *s3* survey; summary **-ition** exhibition
expresident ex-President, former P.

express I *s3, se expressbyrå, expresståg* **II** *adv* express; *sända ~* send by express (special delivery) **-brev** express (special delivery) letter **-bud** express (special) message **-byrå** (*åkeri*) transport firm (agency); (*budcentral*) parcel-delivery agency **-försändelse** (*paket*) express (special delivery) parcel; *se äv. -brev* **-gods** express goods (*pl*); *sända som ~* send by express, express
expression|ism [-preʃo-] expressionism **-ist** expressionist **-istisk** [-'ist-] *a5* expressionistic
expressiv *a1* expressive
expresståg express train
expropri|ation expropriation **-era** expropriate
exspir|ation [eksp-] expiration **-era** expire
exsudat *s7, med.* exudation, exudate
extas|s *s3* ecstasy; *råka i ~* (*bildl.*) go into ecstasies (raptures) **-tisk** *a5* ecstatic
extemporera extemporize
extensiv [*äv.* 'eks-] *a1* extensive
exteriör exterior
extern [-'tä:rn] **I** *s3* (*elev*) day scholar, extern **II** *a1* (*yttre*) external
exterritorialrätt [-ˣa:l-] extraterritorial rights (*pl*)
extra *oböjligt a o. adv* extra, additional; (*ovanlig*) extraordinary, special; (*biträdande äv.*) assistant; (*mycket fin*) superior; *~ avgift* surcharge; *~ billig* exceptionally cheap; *~ kontant* prompt cash; *~ tilldelning* supplementary allowance **-arbete** extra work; additional source of income **-förtjänst** extra income; *~er* extras
extrahera extract
extra|inkomst *se* extraförtjänst **-knäck** job on the side; *vard.* moonlighting; *jag tjänar några pund i veckan på ~* (*vard.*) I'm raking in a few quid every week on extra work **-knäcka** *vard.* moonlight
extrakt *s7, s4* extract; essence **extraktion**

[-k'ʃo:n] extraction **extraktor** [-ˣaktår] extractor
extra|lektion extra (private) lesson **-lärare** temporary master **-nummer 1** (*av tidning*) special issue, extra [edition] **2** (*utöver programmet*) extra performance, encore **-ordinarie** [-'na:-] **I** *oböjligt a* temporary-staff, pro tempore, pro tem. **II** *s5* temporary officer (official, clerk); *vara ~* be on the temporary staff **-ordinär** extraordinary **-personal** extras (*pl*), extra staff (personnel) **-polera** *mat.* extrapolate **-polering** *mat.* extrapolation **-pris** special offer **-säng** spare bed **-tur** special trip; extra service **-tåg** relief (special) [train] **-uppdrag** special assignment **-upplaga** special edition **-utgift** additional expense
extravag|ans [-'aŋs *el.* -'aŋs] *s3* extravagance **-ant** [-'ant *el.* -'aŋt] *a1* extravagant
extrem *a1 o. s7, s3* extreme **-ism** extremism **-ist** extremist **-istisk** *a5* extremist
extremitet *s3* extremity
extrovert [-'värt] *a4* extrovert, extravert

fabel ['fa:-] *s3* fable **-aktig** *a1* fabulous **-diktning** writing of fables **-djur** fabulous beast
fabla [ˣfa:-] *~ om* romance about, make up fantastic stories about
fabricera manufacture, make, produce; *bildl.* make up, fabricate
fabrik *s3* factory; works (*pl, behandlas vanl. som sg*); mill, workshop; *AE.* [manufacturing] plant; *fritt ~* ex works, free at mill **fabrikant** (*fabriksägare*) factory owner, manufacturer; (*tillverkare*) maker, manufacturer **fabrikat** *s7* (*vara*) manufacture, product; (*i sht textil-*) fabric; (*tillverkning*) make **fabrikation** manufacture, manufacturing, making, production
fabrikations|fel flaw, defect [in manufacture] **-hemlighet** trade secret
fabriks|anläggning *se* fabrik **-arbetare** factory worker (hand) **-byggnad** factory building **-gjord** *a5* factory-made **-idkare** manufacturer, factory owner **-kontor** factory office **-lokal** *~er* factory premises **-märke** trademark **-mässig** *a1* factory, large-scale **-mässigt** *adv* on an industrial basis **-ny** brandnew **-skorsten** factory chimney **-tillverkad** factory-made **-vara** factory-made article; *-varor* manufactured goods
fabrikör factory owner, manufacturer
fabuler|a fable; *~ om* romance (make up stories) about **-ing** fable-making **-ingsförmåga** *ha ~* have a fertile imagination
fabulös *a1* fabulous
facil *a1* (*om pris*) moderate, reasonable **-itet** *s3*

facility
facit ['fa:-] **1** *n* answer, result; *bildl.* result **2** *best.
form* = el. *-en*, *r* (*bok*) key
fack *s7* **1** (*förvaringsrum*) partition, box; (*del av
hylla e.d.*) compartment, pigeonhole **2** (*gren,
bransch*) department, line, branch; (*yrke*) profession, trade; *det hör inte till mitt* ~ it is not in
my line **-arbetare** skilled worker **-bok** book of
nonfiction; handbook, textbook
fackel|bärare torchbearer (*äv. bildl.*) **-tåg**
torchlight procession
fack|förbund federation [of trade unions] **-för-
ening** trade (*AE.* labor) union
fackförenings|medlem trade unionist, trade-
-union member **-pamp** union boss **-rörelse**
trade unionism, trade-union movement
fack|idiot narrow specialist **-kretsar** *pl* profes-
sional circles **-kunnig** experienced, skilled
-kunskap professional knowledge
fackla *s1* torch, flare
facklig *al* [trade-]union
fack|litteratur nonfiction **-lärare** teacher spe-
cializing in one subject (group of subjects) **-man**
professional [man]; specialist, expert; *han är inte
~ på området* he is not a specialist in the field
-mannahåll *i uttr.*: *på* ~ among experts; *på* ~
anser man experts agree **-mässig** *al* professional **-ord** *se -term* **-press** specialist (professional, technical) press **-skola** continuation
school **-språk** technical language **-studier** vocational studies; *bedriva* ~ *i* specialize in **-term**
technical term **-tidskrift** trade (professional,
technical, scientific) journal **-utbildning** professional (specialized) training **-uttryck** se *-term*
fack|verk framework **-verksbro** truss (lattice)
bridge
factoring ['fäktəriŋ] factoring **-bolag** factoring
company
fadd *al* flat, stale; *bildl.* vapid, insipid
fadder ['fadd-] *s2* godfather, godmother; (*friare*)
sponsor; *stå* ~ *för* be (act as) [a] godfather (*etc.*)
to, *bildl.* stand sponsor to **-barn** godchild; spon-
sored (adopted) child **-gåva** *i* ~ as a christening
gift
fader *-n fäder* (*jfr far*) father (*till* of); (*alstrare
äv.*) procreator; (*-djur*) sire; *Gud F~* God the
Father; *F~ vår, som är i himmelen* Our Father,
which art in Heaven; *stadens fäder* the city fathers; *han har samlats till sina fäder* he has been
gathered to this fathers **-lig** *al* fatherly, paternal
-lös fatherless **-mördare 1** parricide **2** (*slags
krage*) high starched collar, choker
fadersarv patrimony
fader|skap *s7* fatherhood; *i sht jur.* paternity
-skapsmål affiliation proceedings (*pl*); *AE.* pa-
ternity suit **-vår** *n* the Lord's Prayer; *läsa ett* ~
say the Lord's Prayer
fading ['fejdiŋ] *radio.* fading
fadäs *s3* foolishness, blunder; faux pas
fager ['fa:-] *a2* fair; (*om löften, ord*) fine; ~ *under
ögonen* good-looking, bonny
faggorna *best. form pl, vara i* ~ be imminent (in
the offing); *ha ngt i* ~ be in for, (*om sjukdom*)
have...coming on
fagocyt *s3* phagocyte
fagott [-'gått] *s3* bassoon **-ist** bassoonist

Fahrenheit ['fa:-] Fahrenheit
faiblesse *s5, se* **fäbless**
fajans [-'jans *el.* -'jaŋs] *s3* faïence, tin-glazed
earthenware
fajt *s3*, **fajtas** *v1* fight
fakir *s3* fakir
faksimil *s7* facsimile **-tryck** facsimile print **-ut-
gåva** facsimile edition
faktaspäckad crammed with (full of) facts, in-
formation-packed
faktisk ['fack-] *a5* real, actual, founded on facts;
det ~a förhållandet the facts (*pl*), the actual situation **faktiskt** ['fack-] *adv* really *etc.*; in fact;
(*bekräftande*) honestly
faktor [-år] *s3* **1** factor; *den mänskliga ~n* the human element **2** (*tryckeriföreståndare*) foreman,
overseer **-analys** factor analysis
faktori *s4* **1** (*varunederlag*) factory, trading settlement **2** (*fabrik*) [manu]factory
faktotum [-ˣto:-] *n* factotum, right-hand man
fakt|um *s8* fact; ~ *är* the fact is; *konstatera -a*
point out facts
faktura [-ˣtu:-] *s1* invoice, bill (*på ett belopp* for
an amount); *det på ~n angivna beloppet* the
invoice[d] amount; *enligt* ~ as per invoice **-be-
lopp** invoice amount
fakturer|a invoice, bill **-ing** invoicing, billing
-ingsmaskin billing machine
fakultativ [*äv.* 'fack-] *al* optional
fakultet *s3* faculty
fal *al* (*om sak*) for sale; (*om pers.*) mercenary, ve-
nal
falang phalanx; wing, group; *F~en* (*i Spanien*)
Falange **-ist** Falangist
falk *s2* falcon; *AE.* hawk
falk|a spy out (*efter* for); ~ *efter ngt* (*att bli ngt*)
have one's eye on s.th. (on becoming s.th.)
-blick *ha* ~ be eagle-eyed (hawk-eyed)
falk|enerare [-ˣne:-] falconer **-jakt** hawking;
(*som konst*) falconry
Falklandsöarna [ˣfå:k-] the Falkland Islands
falkög|a *ha -on, se* **falkblick**
fall *s7* **1** (*av falla*) fall; descent; (*lutning*) slope;
(*kläders o.d.*) hang; *bildl.* [down]fall, collapse;
(*pris- o.d.*) fall, decline; (*vatten-*) falls (*pl*), wa-
terfall; *platt* ~ (*brottn.*) [pin]fall, *bildl.* fiasco,
vard. flop; *hejda ngn i ~et* prevent s.b. from falling; *bringa ngn på* ~ cause a p.'s downfall;
komma på ~ come to ruin **2** (*händelse, tillfälle,
exempel o.d.*) case, instance, event; *ett typiskt* ~
a typical case; *från* ~ *till* ~ in each specific case; *i
alla* ~ *a*) eg. in all cases, *b*) (*i alla händelser*) in
any case, at all events, anyhow, anyway, at least;
i annat ~ [or] else, otherwise; *i bästa* ~ at best; *i
de* ~ *då* where, when; *i förekommande* ~ where
applicable; *i så* ~ in that case; *i varje* ~ in any
case; *i vilket* ~ *som helst* in any case, come what
may; *i värsta* ~ if the worst comes to the worst **3**
sjö. halyard
fall|a *föll fallit* **I** (*störta* [*ner*]) fall; (*om kläder
o.d.*) hang; (*om regering*) fall, be overthrown; ~
av hästen (*i vattnet*) fall off one's horse (into the
water); *låta* ~ let fall, (*släppa*) let go; *låta frågan*
~ drop the question; *hur föll hans ord?* what were
his actual words?; *det -er av sig självt* that is a matter of course; ~ *för frestelsen* yield to temptation;

~ *för ngn* fall for s.b.; ~ *i glömska* be forgotten, fall into oblivion; ~ *i god jord* fall on good ground; ~ *i händerna på ngn* fall into a p.'s hands; ~ *i pris* fall in price; ~ *i sömn* fall asleep; ~ *i ögonen* catch (strike) the eye; ~ *ngn i ryggen* attack s.b. from behind; ~ *ngn i smaken* be to a p.'s taste; ~ *ngn i talet* interrupt s.b.; ~ *ngn om halsen* fling one's arms around a p.'s neck; ~ *till föga* yield, give in; ~ *ur minnet* escape one's memory; ~ *ur rollen* act out of character **II** (*med betonad partikel*) **1** ~ *av* fall off, (*om frukt, löv*) come down, drop off, *bildl.* droop, be in the decline, *sjö.* fall off **2** ~ *ifrån* die, pass away **3** ~ *igen* fall (shut) to **4** ~ *igenom* (*i examen*) fail, *vard.* be ploughed, (*vid val*) be rejected, be defeated **5** ~ *ihop* (*om pers.*) collapse **6** ~ *in* fall in, *mus.* strike in, (*om ljus*) come in **7** ~ *ngn in* occur to s.b., enter a p.'s head; *det föll mig aldrig in* it never occurred to me; *det skulle aldrig ~ mig in att* I should never dream of (+ *ing-form*) **8** ~ *in i ledet* (*mil.*) fall in; get into line **9** ~ *isär, se ~ sönder* **10** ~ *ner* fall down (*död* dead, *för en trappa* a flight of stairs) **11** ~ *omkull* fall [over], tumble down **12** ~ *på* come on; *när andan -er på* when one is in the mood **13** ~ *sönder* fall to pieces **14** ~ *tillbaka* fall (drop, slip) back (*på* on), (*om beskyllning*) come home (*på* to), (*om sparkapital e.d.*) fall back (*på* on) **15** ~ *undan* fall away, *bildl.* give way (yield) (*för* to) **16** ~ *upp* (*om bok*) open [itself], fall open **17** ~ *ut* (*om flod o.d.*) fall (*i* into) **18** ~ *ut genom fönstret* fall out of the window **III** *rfl* chance, happen, fall out; *det föll sig naturligt att* it came natural to; *det föll sig så att* so happened that

fallande|sjuk epileptic **-sjuka** falling sickness (evil), epilepsy

fall|bila guillotine

fallen *a5* **1** fallen (*äv. bildl.*); *de fallna* the fallen (slain); *en ~ storhet* a fallen star; ~ *efter* (*om husdjur*) [bred] out of; *stå som ~ från skyarna* be struck all of a heap **2** ~ *för studier* have a gift for studying **-het** (*för ngt förmånligt*) gift (talent, aptitude) (*för* for); (*för ngt oförmånligt*) predisposition (*för* to, towards)

fallera *vard.* (*fattas*) lack, be short of; (*slå fel*) go wrong, miscarry

fall|frukt *koll.* windfall[s *pl*] **-färdig** tumble-down, ramshackle, dilapidated **-grop** pitfall (*äv. bildl.*) **-höjd** [height of] fall, drop

fallisk ['fall-] *a5* phallic

fallissemang *s7, s4* failure, collapse, crash

fallit *sup. av falla*

fallos ['fallås] *s2* phallus

fall|rep 1 *sjö.*, *se fallrepstrappa* **2** *vara på ~et* be at the end of one's tether, be on the brink of bankruptcy **-repstrappa** *sjö.* gangplan, gangway

fallskärm parachute; *hoppa i* ~ make a parachute jump; *landsätta med* ~ [drop by] parachute

fallskärms|hopp parachute jump (descent) **-hoppare** parachutist **-jägare** paratrooper; *koll.* paratroop[er]s, parachute troops **-trupper** parachute troops, paratroop[er]s

fallstudie case study

fallucka trap door

falna [ˣfa:l-] (*om glöd o.d.*) die down

fals *s2* **1** (*på bleckplåtar o.d.*) lap; (*på gryta o.d.*)

rim **2** *bokb.* guard **3** *snick.* (*löpränna*) groove **falsa 1** lap **2** fold **3** groove

falsarium [-'sa:-] *s4* forgery; falsification

falsett *s3, mus.* falsetto; *fonet.* head voice (register); *sjunga i* ~ sing falsetto; *tala i* ~ talk in a fluting voice **-röst** falsetto voice

falsifiera falsify **falsifikat** *s7* counterfeit, forgery **falsifikation** falsification

falsk *a1* false; (*oriktig*) wrong; (*bedräglig*) delusive; (*förfalskad*) forged; (*eftergjord*) fictitious, sham, counterfeit, bogus; (*låtsad*) feigned, pretended; ~*t alarm* a false alarm; ~ *blygsamhet* false modesty; ~*t pass* forged passport; ~*a pengar* counterfeit (bad) money; ~*a påståenden* incorrect (false) statements; ~*a pärlor* sham (imitation) pearls; *göra sig* ~*a föreställningar om ngt* fool o.s. about s.th.; *under* ~ *flagg* under false colours; *under* ~*t namn* under a false name **-deklarant** tax evader (dodger) **-deklaration** tax evasion (dodging)

falsk|eligen falsely *etc.*, *jfr falsk* **-het** falseness; (*hos pers. äv.*) duplicity, deceit; (*oäkthet*) spuriousness, fictitiousness **-myntare** counterfeiter, coiner **-skyltad** *a5* (*om bil*) provided with false [number, *AE.* license] plates **-spel** cheating (swindling) at cards (*etc.*); cardsharping **-spelare** cheat; cardsharp[er]

falskt *adv* falsely; *spela* ~ (*mus.*) play false notes (out of tune)

falukorv *ung.* lightly-smoked bologna (polony) sausage

familj *s3* family; ~*en B.* the B. family; *bilda* ~ raise a family, marry and have children; *av god* ~ of good family; *vara av god* ~ come of a good family

familje|angelägenheter *pl* family affairs (matters) **-bibel** family Bible **-bidrag** family allowance; *mil.* separation allowance **-bolag** family business **-daghem** registered child-minding home; pre-school play group **-drama** family tragedy **-far** father of a (the) family; family man **-flicka** girl of good family **-företag** *se -bolag* **-förhållanden** *pl* family circumstances **-förpackning** economy pack (size) **-försörjare** breadwinner, supporter of a (the) family **-grav** family grave (vault) **-hotell** *se kollektivhus* **-krets** family circle **-liv** family life **-medlem** member of a (the) family **-namn** family name, surname **-planering** family planning **-rådgivning** family guidance (counselling) **-rätt** family law **-skäl** *av* ~ for family reasons **-överhuvud** head of [the] family

familjär *a1* familiar; *alltför* ~ (*äv.*) too free [and easy] (*mot* with)

faml|a grope (*efter* for); ~ *i mörkret* grope about in the dark **-ande I** *s6* groping **II** *a4* groping; *bildl.* tentative

famn *s2* **1** (*ngns* a p.'s) arms (*pl*); (*fång*) armful; *ta ngn i* [*sin*] ~ embrace s.b.; *kom i min ~!* come into my arms! **2** (*längdmått*) fathom; (*rymdmått*) cord (*ved* of firewood) **famna** embrace; (*omsluta*) encompass, encircle **famntag** embrace; (*häftigt*) hug

famös *a1, iron.* [so] famous; (*illa beryktad*) notorious

1 fan *s7* (*på fjäder*) web, vane [of a feather]

2 fan *r* the devil, the deuce; ~ *heller!* hell, no!; *fy ~!* hell!, damn it all!; *åh ~!* well, I'll be damned!; *stackars ~! (om pers.)* poor devil!; *det vete ~* the devil only knows; *det ger jag ~ i* I don't care a damn; *ta mig ~, om* I'm damned if; *han är full i (av) ~* he is a cunning [old] devil; *har man tagit ~ i båten får man också ro honom i land* in for a penny, in for a pound

3 fan [fänn] *en fan, pl =, äv. -s (entusiast)* fan

fan|a *s1* banner, standard, flag *(äv. bildl.)*; mil. colours *(pl)*; *den blågula ~n* the Swedish colours; *med flygande -or och klingande spel* with flags flying and drums beating; *hålla konstens ~ högt* keep the banner of Art flying

fanat|iker [-'na:-] fanatic **-isk** *a5* fanatic[al] **-ism** fanaticism

fan|borg massed standards *(pl)* **-bärare** standard-bearer

fanders ['fann-] *oböjligt s, vard., åt ~ med...!* ...be hanged!; *dra åt ~!* go to the devil!, go to hell!, drop dead!

fanér *s7,* **fanera** *v1* veneer

fanerogam I *s3* phanerogam **II** *a5* phanerogamic, phanerogamous

fanerskiva veneer sheet

fanfar *s3* fanfare; *blåsa en ~* sound a fanfare

fanflykt desertion [from the colours] **-ing** deserter [from the colours]

fanjunkare *(vid armén, kustartilleriet)* warrant officer class 1 (class 2); *(vid flottan)* fleet chief petty officer; *(vid flygvapnet)* warrant officer; *AE. (vid armén, marinkåren)* master sergeant, *(vid flottan)* senior chief petty officer, *(vid flygvapnet)* senior master sergeant

fanken *r, ta mig ~* I'll be damned

fann *imperf. av finna*

fanskap [ˣfa:n-] *s7,* **fanstyg** [ˣfa:ns-] *s7* [piece of] devilry

fantasi *s3* **1** *(inbillningskraft, föreställningsförmåga)* imagination, imaginative power; *(djärvare)* fancy, fantasy; *livlig ~* vivid imagination; *ge ~n fritt spelrum* give free rein to one's imagination, let one's imagination run away with one **2** *(inbillningsprodukt)* fancy; imagination, fantasy; *~ och verklighet* dreams and reality; *fria ~er* pure fantasy (fabrications), wild imaginings; *försjunken i [sina] ~er* absorbed in reveries (daydreams) **3** *mus.* fantasia

fantasi|eggande stimulating to the imagination; *det är ~* it stirs the imagination **-foster** figment of the imagination **-full** imaginative **-lös** unimaginative **-pris** fancy price **-rik** highly imaginative **-rikedom** wealth of imagination **-värld** world of the imagination; *(barns)* make-believe world

fantasma [-'tass-] *s1* phantasm **-gori** *s3* phantasmagoria

fantast *s3* fantast, dreamer **-isk** *a5* fantastic[al]; fanciful

fantisera indulge in daydreams (reveries), dream; *(mus. o. friare)* improvise; *~ ihop* concoct, imagine

fantom [-'tå:m] *s7, s3* phantom **-smärta** phantom limb pain

fanvakt colour guard

far *fadern fäder (jfr fader); smeks.* dad[dy]; *bli ~* become a father; *han är ~ till* he is the father of

1 fara *s1* danger; *(stor)* peril; *(vågspel)* hazard; *(risk)* risk; *~n över! (signal)* all clear!; *ingen ~ [på taket]!* don't worry!, no harm done!; *med ~ för eget liv* at the risk of one's life; *med ~ att* at the risk of (+ *ing-form*); *utom all ~* [quite] out of danger; *sväva i ~* be in danger; *utsätta för ~* expose to danger; *det är ~ värt att* there is a risk that; *det är ingen ~ med honom* he's all right (out of danger)

2 fara *for farit* **1** go; *(färdas)* travel; *(i vagn)* drive; *(avresa)* leave *(till* for); *~ i luften (explodera)* blow up, *(bli rasande)* vard. fly off the handle; *~ illa* fare badly, be badly treated; *hatten far illa av att* it is bad for the hat to; *~ illa med* handle roughly, knock about; *~ med osanning* tell lies; *~ med tåg* go by rail (train); *~ sin väg* go away, depart, leave; *~ till a) (en pers.)* go to see, *b) (en plats)* go (travel, drive) to; *det är ett annat namn jag far efter* it is another name I am trying to get hold of **II** *(med betonad partikel)* **1** *~ bort* drive away, *(friare)* leave [home], go away [from home] **2** *~ efter ngn (hämta)* fetch s.b. **3** *~ fram (eg.)* drive up *(till* to); *~ varligt fram med* treat gently, go gently with; *~ fram som ett vilddjur* carry (go) on like a wild thing (a madman); *~ illa fram med* be rough in one's treatment of **4** *~ förbi* go (drive) past (by), pass **5** *~ före ngn* go on ahead of s.b. **6** *~ i; vad har farit i honom?* what has taken possession of him (got into him)? **7** *~ ifrån* go (drive) away from, depart from, leave **8** *~ igenom* travel (pass) through; *en tanke for igenom honom* a thought flashed through his mind; *jfr genomfara* **9** *~ in till staden* go (run) up to town; *~ in från landet* travel in from the country **10** *~ iväg* go off **11** *~ med a)* go too (with the others), *b) (ngn)* go *(ibl.* come) with s.b. **12** *~ omkring* travel about *(i* in); *~ omkring som ett torrt skinn* bustle about **13** *~ på* fly (rush) at *(ngn* s.b.) **14** *~ upp a) (om pers.)* spring (jump) to one's feet, *b) (öppna sig)* fly up, open **15** *~ ut på landet* go into the country; *~ ut mot ngn* let fly at s.b. **16** *~ vilse* lose one's way, go astray **17** *~ över ngt med handen* pass one's hand over (across) s.th.; *~ över med blicken* glance over

farad *s3, fys.* farad

farao *s3* Pharaoh

farbar [ˣfa:r-] *a1 (om väg)* passable, open to traffic, *sjö.* navigable

far|broderlig [ˣfarr-] *a1* avuncular; *(välvillig)* benevolent **-bror** [ˣfarr-] uncle; *eg.* father's brother; *(friare)* [kindly old] gentleman

far|far [ˣfarrfar] [paternal] grandfather, *vard.* grandpa[pa] **-farsfar** [-fa:r] great-grandfather **-föräldrar** [ˣfa:r-] [paternal] grandparents

fargalt [ˣfa:r-] *s2* boar

farhåg|a [ˣfa:r-] apprehension, fear, misgiving; *hysa -or* entertain (have) apprehensions *(för* about, as to); *mina -or besannades* my fears came true

farin *s4, s3,* **farinsocker** demerara (brown) sugar

faris|é *s3* Pharisee **-eisk** [-'se:-] *a5* Pharisaic[al] **-eism** Pharisaism, Phariseeism

farit *sup. av 2 fara*

far|kost [ˣfa:rkåst] *s3* vessel, boat, craft; *poet.*

barque **-led** channel, [navigable] course (passage), track, fairway

farlig [ˣfaːr-] *a1* **1** dangerous (*för* for); (*förenad med stor fara*) perilous; (*äventyrlig*) hazardous, risky; (*kritisk*) critical; ~ *för den allmänna säkerheten* a danger to the public; *det är inte så ~t med honom* there is not much wrong with him; *det är inte så ~t som det låter* it is not so bad as it seems **2** (*'förskräcklig'*) awful, dreadful **-het** dangerousness *etc.*

farm *s2, s3* farm

farmaceut [-ˈsevt] *s3* pharmac[eut]ist, dispenser **-isk** *a5* pharmaceutic[al], pharmacal

farmacj *s3* pharmacy, pharmaceutics (*pl, behandlas som sg*)

farmako|log pharmacologist **-logj** *s3* pharmacology **-logisk** [-ˈlåː-] *a5* pharmacological

farmakopé *s3* pharmacopoeia

farmare farmer

far|mor [ˣfarrmɔr] [paternal] grandmother, grandma[ma]; *smeks.* gran[ny] **-morsmor** great grandmother

faro|fylld *a5* fraught with danger **-zon** danger zone

fars *s3* farce

farsa *s1, vard.* dad; pop; *se äv. farsgubben*

farsartad [ˣfarsaːr-] *a5* farcical

fars|arv [ˣfaːrs-] patrimony **-gubben** vard. my (*etc.*) [old] dad; the old man, the governor, the guv

farsot [ˣfaːr-] *s3* epidemic; pestilence

farstu *s5, se förstuga*

fart [-aː-] *s3* **1** (*hastighet*) speed; (*i sht vetenskapligt*) velocity; (*takt, tempo*) pace; (*fartygs- o.d.*) headway; *med en ~ av* at a speed of; *i* (*med*) *full ~* at full speed; *i rasande ~* at breakneck speed; *alltid i ~en* always on the go; *komma i ~en* get into stride, get going; *medan man är i ~en* while one is at it; *minska ~en* slow down; *öka ~en* speed up; *sätta full ~* go full speed ahead; *det gick av bara ~en* it went automatically, it happened unintentionally **2** (*ansats*) start, run; *ta ~* get a start **3** (*livlighet, raskhet*) force, energy, activity; push; *komma riktigt i ~en* get into full swing; *sätta ~ på* speed up, get going; *det gick med ~ och fläkt* it went with a bang; *det är ingen ~ i honom* there is no go (*vard.* dash) about him **4** *sjö.* trade; *gå i utrikes ~* be in foreign trade

fart|begränsning speed limit **-blind** speed-blinded **-dåre** scorcher **-gräns** speed limit **-kontroll** speed trap **-vidunder** speedster

fartyg [ˣfaːr-] *s7* ship, vessel; (*mindre o. koll.*) craft; (*linje-*) liner; (*ångare*) steamer

fartygs|befäl ship's officers (*pl*) **-befälhavare** captain, [ship]master, shipman **-register** register of shipping

farvatten [ˣfaːr-] waters (*pl*), sea[s *pl*]; (*farled*) fairway (*se äv. farled*); *i egna ~* in home waters

farväl I *interj* farewell!, goodbye! **II** *s7* farewell; *säga ~ åt, ta ~ av* bid farewell (say goodbye) to

faryngjt *s3* pharyngitis

fas *s3* phase; *bildl. äv.* aspect, appearance; (*avsneddad kant*) bevel, cant; chamfer

1 fasa *v1, tekn.* bevel; chamfer

2 fas|a I *s1* horror; (*stark rädsla*) terror; (*bävan*) dread; *blek* (*stel*) *av ~* horrified, terrified; *krigets*

-or the horrors of war; *väcka ~ hos* horrify, terrify; *till min ~ fick jag se* to my horror I saw **II** *v1* shudder (*för, över* at); (*rygga tillbaka*) shrink back (*för* at, from); ~ *för tanken* shudder at the thought

fasąd *s3* face, front; *med ~en åt gatan* facing the street **-beklädnad** facing, cladding **-belysning** floodlighting **-klättrare** cat burglar **-krona** *tandläk.* artificial crown **-tegel** facing brick

fasąn *s3* pheasant **-höna** hen pheasant **-jakt** pheasant shooting

fasansfull horrible; terrible; awful; ghastly

fasantupp cock pheasant

fasaväckande *a4* horrifying, appalling

fascin|ation (*faʃi- el.* fassi-) fascination **-era** fascinate **-erande** [-ˈneː-] *a4* fascinating

fasc|ism [faˈʃism] fascism **-ist** fascist **-istisk** [-ˈiss-] *a5* fascist[ic]

fasętt *s3* facet **-era** facet **-erad** [-ˈteː-] *a5* faceted; (*friare*) many-sided **-ering** [-ˈteː-] faceting

fasett|slipning facet cut **-öga** compound eye

fasförskjutning phase shift (displacement)

fashionabel [-ˈʃoˈnaː-] *a2* fashionable

faskin [faˈʃiːn] *s3* fascine

faslig [ˣfaːs-] *a1* dreadful, frightful, terrible; (*förskräcklig*) awful; (*avskyvärd*) horrid; *ha ett ~t besvär* have no end of trouble; *ett ~t oväsen* a terrible row

fasning [ˣfaːs-] (*av kant*) bevelling; chamfering; *elektr.* paralleling, phasing

fasomvandling *kem.* phase transformation (change)

fasọn *s3* **1** (*form*) shape, form; *sätta ~ på* get into shape **2** (*sätt*) way; (*beteende*) manners (*pl*); *är det skick och ~?* do you call that good form?; *vad är det för ~er?* where are your manners?; *låta var och en bli salig på sin ~* live and let live **-era** shape, figure; *~d* ornamented, figured

1 fast *konj* though, although

2 fast *al* **1** (*motsats lös*) firm, solid, rigid; (*fastgjord, fastsatt*) fixed, attached; (*motsats flyttbar*) stationary, fixed; (*motsats flytande*) solid; (*tät*) compact, massive, dense; ~ *knut* tight knot; ~ *konduktör* stationary conductor **2** (*säker*) firm; (*jur., motsats t. lös*) real; (*bestämd*) fixed; (*varaktig*) permanent; (*fångad*) caught; ~ *beslut* (*grepp, övertygelse*) firm resolve (hold, conviction); ~ *bostad* permanent address; ~ *egendom* real property (estate); ~ *kapital* (*pris*) fixed capital (price); ~*a kostnader* fixed costs, overheads; ~ *kund* regular customer; ~ *ljus* (*sken*) fixed light; ~ *utgift* fixed charge; *ta ~ form* assume [a] definite shape; *få ~ fot* get a firm footing; *med ~ hand* with a firm hand; *känna ~ mark under fötterna* be on firm ground (*äv. bildl.*); *köpa* (*sälja*) *ngt i ~ räkning* give (receive) a firm order for s.th. **3** (*i förbindelse med verb*) *bli ~* be (get) caught; *frysa ~* freeze [in]; *göra ~* make fast (firm), fasten; *hålla ~* hold fast, keep [fast (firm) hold of]; *hålla ~ vid* maintain, stick (stand) to; *hänga ~ a*) (*fästa*) fasten (*vid* to), *b*) (*vara upphängd*) remain hanging (*vid* from); *klistra ~* (*på väggen*) paste (stick) up; *köra ~* get stuck, come to a standstill; *sitta ~* (*ha fastnat*) stick, adhere, (*om fordon, pers. o.d.*) be stuck, (*vara inklämd*) be jammed; *slå ~* hammer on (down), *bildl. se* *fastslå; spika* ~ nail [up, on]; *stå* ~ *a*) (*om pers.*) stand firm (steadfast), *b*) (*om anbud e.d.*) hold (stand) good; *stå* ~ *vid sitt löfte* abide by (keep) one's promise; *sätta* ~ fix, fasten, attach *(i, vid* to); *sätta* ~ *ngn (bildl.)* drive s.b. into a corner; *sätta sig* ~ (*om sak*) stick, (*friare*) establish o.s.; *ta* ~ catch, capture, seize; *ta* ~ *tjuven!* stop thief!

3 fast *adv* firmly; compactly; permanently; *vara* ~ *anställd* have a permanent appointment; *vara* ~ *besluten att* be firmly resolved (determined) to

1 fasta *oböjligt s, ta* ~ *på* bear in mind, seize upon

2 fasta I *s1* **1** (*fastande*) fasting **2** (*fastetid*) fast; ~*n* Lent **II** *v1* fast; *på* ~*nde mage* on an empty stomach

fastedag fast day; fasting day

faster [ˣfass- *el.* ˈfass-] *s2* [paternal] aunt

fastetid fast, time of fasting

fast|frusen frozen fast; ~ *kredit* frozen credit **-grodd** *a5, vara* ~ have taken root (*i* in) **-het** firmness *etc.*; solidity; stability; strength

fasthåll|a *se under 2 fast* **3 -ande** *s6* holding *etc.*; persistence (*vid* in); (*vid krav*) insistence on; ~*t vid principer* the adherence to principles

fastighet (*hus*) house [property]; (*jordagods*) landed property (estate); (*fast egendom*) real property (estate)

fastighets|förvaltare property manager **-marknad** property market **-mäklare** estate (house) agent; (*i Skottland*) house factor; *A.E.* realtor **-skatt** real-estate tax **-skötare** caretaker; *A.E.* janitor **-taxering** real-estate assessment **-ägare** house owner; property owner, estate owner

fast|kedja chain [up] (*vid* to) **-kila** wedge [fast, tight] **-klämd** *a5, sitta* ~ sit jammed in; *vara* ~ be squeezed tight in, be jammed **-knuten** *a5* firmly tied (*vid* to)

fastlagen Lent

fastlags|bulle *se semla* **-ris** twigs with coloured feathers affixed [used as decoration during Lent] **-söndagen** Quinquagesima [Sunday]

fastland *s7* continent; (*i motsats t. öar*) mainland **fastlandsklimat** continental climate

fastmer[a] [much] rather

fastna get caught; (*om sak*) catch; (*i ngt klibbigt samt om pers.*) stick, get stuck; (*i kläm*) get jammed; ~ *för* decide on, choose; ~ *i minnet* stick (remain) in the (one's) memory; ~ *på kroken* get hooked; *han* ~*de med handen i* his hand got caught in

fast|nagla nail [firmly] (*vid, på* to); *stå som* ~*d* stand riveted to the spot **-nitad** *a5* firmly riveted (*vid* to) **-rostad** *a5, är* ~ has got rusted in **-rotad** *a5* fixed (fastened) [on] (*vid* to) **-sittande** *a4* fixed, attached (*vid* to) **-skruvad** *a5* screwed tight (firmly) (*i* into; *vid* onto) **-slå** *bildl.* lay down; (*fastställa*) establish; (*bestämma*) settle, fix

fastställ|a (*bestämma*) fix, settle; determine, decide; (*stadfästa*) confirm, ratify, sanction; (*konstatera*) establish, ascertain; *-d i lag* prescribed (laid down) by law; *på de -da villkoren* on the terms approved **-else** fixing; determination; confirmation; establishment

fast|sättning fastening **-tagande** *s6* catching

etc.; se 2 fast **3 -vuxen** firmly rooted (*vid* to)

fastän [ˣfast-, *äv.* -ˈänn] although, [even] though

fat *s7* **1** (*för matvaror*) dish **2** (*te-, blom-*) saucer **3** (*bunke, tvätt- o.d.*) basin; bowl **4** (*tunna*) cask, barrel; (*kar*) vat; *öl från* ~ draught beer; *vin på* ~ wine from the wood **5** *ligga ngn i* ~*et* stand in a p.'s way

fatabur *se fatbur*

fatal *a1* (*ödesdiger*) fatal, disastrous; (*olycklig*) unfortunate; (*obehaglig*) awkward, annoying; ~ *situation* awkward situation; *det var* ~*t att låta honom undkomma* it was a bad mistake to let him escape

fatal|ism fatalism **-ist** fatalist **-istisk** [-ˈliss-] *a5* fatalistic **-itet** *s3* stroke of bad luck, misfortune

fatbur [ˣfaːt-] *s2* storeroom; *ur egen* ~ out of one's own head

1 fatt *oböjligt a, hur är det* ~? what's the matter?, what's up?

2 fatt *adv, få* (*ta*) ~ *i* (*på*) get (catch) hold of; *hinna* ~ *ngn* catch s.b. up

fatta 1 (*ta tag i*) grasp, seize; take hold of (*äv. fatta tag i*); ~ *pennan* (*glaset*) take up one's pen (glass) **2** ~ *posto* post o.s., take one's stand **3** (*börja hysa*) conceive (*avsky för* a hatred of; *avsmak för* a distaste for), take (*tycke för* a fancy to; *motvilja för* a dislike to), form (*agg mot* a grudge against); ~ *ett beslut* make (come to, arrive at) a decision; ~ *humör* flare up; ~ *kärlek till* fall in love with; ~ *misstankar* get suspicious, be seized with suspicion; ~ *mod* take (pick up) courage; ~ *motvilja mot ngn* take a dislike to s.b. **4** (*begripa*) understand, comprehend, grasp; ~ *galoppen* catch the drift; ~*r du inte vad jag menar?* don't you see (understand) what I mean?; *jag kan inte* ~ *att* it beats me how; *ha lätt* (*svårt*) [*för*] *att* ~ be quick (slow) on the uptake **5** ~ *sig kort* be brief, make a long story short

fattad *a5* (*lugn*) composed

fatta|s *dep* **1** (*föreligga brist på*) be wanting (short); (*saknas*) be missing; (*brista, med personobj.*) want, lack, be short of; *det* ~ *folk* we (they *etc.*) are short of people; *det* ~ *ett pund i kassan* there is one pound missing from the funds, *vard.* the kitty is a pound short; *det -des ingenting av livets nödtorft i det huset* that household was not wanting in the necessities of life; *det* ~ *bara* (*det skulle bara* ~) *att* we are only waiting for **2** (*felas*) *vad* ~ *dig?* what is the matter [with you]?

fattbar *a1* comprehensible (*för* to); conceivable

fattig 1 (*motsats rik*) poor; (*medellös*) penniless; (*utarmad*) impoverished, poverty-stricken; (*behövande*) needy, indigent; (*om jordmån o.d.*) meagre; ~*t folk*, ~*a* poor people; *de* ~*a* the poor; *de i anden* ~*a* the poor in spirit; *en* ~ *stackare* a poor wretch; ~*a riddare* (*kokk.*) bread fritters **2** (*friare*) poor; (*usel*) miserable; (*obetydlig*) paltry; *efter* ~ *förmåga* to the best of one's poor ability; *en enda* ~ *brödkant kvar* one miserable crust left

fattig|begravning pauper's funeral **-bössa** poor box

fattigdom *s2* poverty (*på* in, of); (*armod*) penury, indigence; (*nödställdhet*) destitution; (*torftighet*) poorness, meagreness (*på* in); (*social företeelse*) pauperism; (*brist*) deficiency (*på* in, of), lack (want) (*på* of) **fattigdomsbevis** *bildl.* confession of failure

fattig|hjon pauper **-hus** poorhouse; workhouse **-kvarter** slum **-lapp** *s2* pauper **-man** *~s barn* a poor man's child (*pl* poor people's children)

fattigt *adv, ha det ~* be badly (poorly) off; *~ klädd* dressed in poor clothes

fattigvård (*förr*) poor[-law] relief; *se äv. social-vård m.m.* **fattigvårdsunderstöd** (*förr*) poor relief

fattning 1 (*grepp*) hold, grip (*om* on, round) **2** (*för glödlampa*) socket **3** (*avfattning*) version **4** (*besinning*) self-possession, self-control; (*lugn*) composure; *bringa ngn ur ~en* discompose s.b.; *förlora ~en* lose one's head; *återvinna ~en* recover one's composure

fattningsförmåga ability to comprehend (understand); intelligence, capacity; *ha god ~* (*vard.*) be quick on the uptake

fatöl draught beer

faun *s3* faun

fauna ['fau-] *s1* fauna

favoriser|a favour, treat with special favour **-ing** favouring *etc.*

favorit *s3* favourite; pet; *hon är allas ~* she is a favourite with everybody **-författare** favourite writer **-system** favouritism

favör favour; (*förmån*) advantage; *till ngns ~* to a p.'s advantage

f.d. (*förk. för före detta*) *se detta*

F-dur F major

fe *s3* fairy; *god ~* fairy godmother

feber ['fe:-] *s2* fever; (*stegrad kroppstemperatur, vard.*) temperature; (*spänning*) excitement; (*nervös brådska*) flurry; *hög ~* a high fever; *ha ~* have a temperature, be feverish; *ligga i 40° (Celsius) ~* be in bed with a temperature of 104° (Fahrenheit) **-aktig** *a1* feverish (*äv. bildl.*); febrile **-anfall** attack of fever **-artad** [-a:r-] *a5, se -aktig* **-fantasier** *pl* delirium (*sg*) **-fri** free from fever; *vara ~* have no (a normal) temperature **-glänsande** *a4* bright with fever **-gummiträd** *se feberträd* **-het** *a1* very feverish **-kurva** temperature curve (chart) **-nedsättande** *a4*, antipyretic; *~ medel* antipyretic **-sjukdom** fever **-termometer** clinical thermometer **-träd** blue gum **-yrsel** feverish rambling, delirium

febrig ['*fe:-] *a1* feverish **febril** *a1* feverish, febrile

februari [-'a:ri] *r* February **-revolutionen** the February Revolution

federal *a5* federal **-ism** federalism **-ist** federalist **-istisk** ['-liss-] *a5* federalistic

feder|ation federation **-ativ** *a5* federative; federal **-erad** [-'re:-] *a5* [con]federate[d]

fedrottning fairy queen **feeri** fairy pageant; enchanting scenery

feg *a1* cowardly; (*räddhågad*) timorous, timid; *vard.* wet; *en ~ stackare* a coward; *visa sig ~* show (prove) o.s. a coward **feghet** cowardice, cowardliness *etc.* **fegis** *s2*, *vard.* funk, mouse; *AE.* milquetoast **fegt** [-e:-] *adv* in a cowardly fashion, timorously *etc.*

feja [*fejja] clean

fejd *s3* feud; (*friare*) strife; *bildl. äv.* quarrel, controversy; *ligga i ~ med* be at feud with; *litte-*

rära ~er literary controversies

fejka *vard.* fake

fejs *s7, vard.* face; *sl.* mug, kisser

fel I *s7* **1** (*mera stadigvarande*) fault; (*kroppsligt*) defect; (*moraliskt*) imperfection; (*brist*) shortcoming, failing; (*avigsida*) demerit, weak point; *avhjälpa ett ~* remedy a defect, put a fault right; *det är ~ på hissen* the lift is out of order; *det är ngt ~ med mitt hjärta* there is s.th. wrong with my heart **2** (*mera tillfälligt*) fault; error; (*misstag*) mistake; (*grovt fel*) blunder; (*förbiseende*) slip; (*försummelse*) omission; (*fabrikations- o.d.*) flaw (*hos, i, på* in); *begå ett ~* make a mistake, be at fault; *ha ~* be [in the] wrong; *hela ~et är att* the real trouble is that **3** (*skuld*) fault; *det är hans ~* he is to blame (*att* for + *ing-form*); *det är inte ens ~ att två träter* it takes two to make a quarrel; *vems är ~et?* whose fault is it? **II** *oböjligt a* wrong; *på ~ sida* on the wrong side **III** *adv, gissa ~* guess wrong; *~ underrättad* wrongly informed; *läsa* (*räkna, höra*) *~* misread (miscalculate, mishear); *klockan går ~* the clock (watch) is wrong; *slå ~ a*) *eg.* miss [the mark], *b*) (*misslyckas*) go wrong, fail, prove a failure, (*om plan o.d.*) miscarry; *det slår inte ~ att han* he cannot fail to; *ta ~* make a mistake (*på dag* in the day); *ta ~ på vägen* miss the way; *jag tog ~ på honom och hans bror* I mistook him for his brother; *om jag inte tar ~ så* if I am not mistaken

1 fela *v1* (*begå fel*) err; (*brista*) be wanting; (*göra orätt*) do wrong; *det är mänskligt att ~* to err is human

2 fela *s1, vard.* fiddle

feladressera misdirect

felaktig *a1* (*oriktig*) erroneous, wrong, mistaken; (*behäftad med fel*) incorrect, faulty; (*bristfällig*) defective, faulty; (*osann*) false, misleading **-het** (*utan pl*) faultiness, incorrectness, defect [iveness]; (*med pl*) fault, mistake, error

felande *a4* missing; *den ~ länken* the missing link

fel|as *dep, se fattas* **-bedöma** misjudge **-bedömning** misjudgment **-behandling** malpractice **-beräkning** miscalculation **-citera** misquote **-datera** misdate **-debitering** mischarge **-dosering** wrong dosage **-drag** wrong move **-expediering** incorrect dispatch; mistake [made by salesman *etc.*] **-fri** faultless, flawless; perfect, impeccable **-grepp** *mus.* false touch; *bildl.* mistake, blunder **-kalkyl** miscalculation **-konstruerad** wrongly constructed **-källa** source of error[s *pl*] **-läsning** (*i text*) misreading; (*vid uppläsning*) slip (fault) in reading **-manöver** mismanoeuvre **-marginal** margin of error **-orienterad** misorientated **-parkerad** wrongly parked **-parkering** (*förseelse*) parking offence **-placerad** *a5* misplaced **-planerad** *a5* miscalculated, wrongly planned **-procent** percentage of error **-räkning** miscalculation (*på* of); miscount **-skriven** *a5* wrongly written **-skrivning** miswriting; *genom ~* (*äv.*) by an error in writing **-slagen** *~ skörd* a failure of the crops; *-slagna förhoppningar* disappointed hopes **-slut** false (wrong) conclusion **-sortera** misfile **-spekulation** wrong (bad) speculation **-stava** misspell **-stavad** *a5* wrongly spelt, misspelt **-stavning** misspelling **-steg** false step, slip; *bildl. äv.* lapse

-syn erroneous point of view **-sägning** [-ä:-] slip of the tongue **-sökning** [-ö:-] fault localization, fault-detecting **-tolka** misinterpret; misconstrue **-tolkning** misinterpretation; misconstruction **-tryck** faulty print; (*frimärke*) printing error **-tända** *v2*, **-tändning** *s2* misfire **-underrättad** *a5* misinformed **-vänd** *a5* back--to-front, upside down; turned the wrong way **-översättning** mistranslation

fem [femm] five; *ha* (*kunna*) *ngt på sina ~ fingrar* have s.th. at one's fingertips; *en ~ sex stycken* five or six **-dagarsvecka** [a] five-day [working] week **-dubbel** fivefold **-etta** [-ˣetta] bull's-eye **-femma** *ung.* certified mental case; *förklara ngn som ~* certify a p. **-hundratalet** *på ~* in the sixth century **-hörning** [-ö:-] pentagon

feminin ['fe:- *el.* -'ni:n] *al* feminine **femininum** ['fe:-] *s4* **1** (*feminint ord*) feminine [noun] **2** (*honkön*) feminine [gender]

femin|isera feminize **-ism** feminism **-ist** *s3*, **-istisk** [-'niss-] *a5* feminist

fem|kamp pentathlon **-kampare** pentathlete **-krona** *en ~* a five-krona [piece] **-kronesedel** five-kronor note

femling quintuplet, *vard.* quin

femma *s1* (*siffra*) five; (*på tärning, spelkort äv.*) cinque; (*sedel*) fiver; *det var en annan ~* that is quite another story; *jfr äv. femkronesedel*

fem|mastare five-master **-siffrig** *a5* five-figure

femte fifth; *F~ Mosebok* Deuteronomy; *den ~ april* [on] the fifth of April, (*i början av brev o.d.*) April 5 (5th); *för det ~ in* the fifth place, fifthly; *vart ~ år* every five years; *~ hjulet under vagnen* the fifth wheel **-del** fifth [part] **-kolonn** fifth column **-kolonnare** fifth columnist

femti[o] fifty **-elfte** [-ˣelfte] *för ~ gången* for the umpteenth time **-elva** [-ˣelva] umpteen **-lapp** fifty-kronor note

femtion|de [-å-] fiftieth **-[de]del** fiftieth [part]

femti[o]|tal [(the) number] fifty; *ett ~* some (about) fifty; *på ~et* in the fifties **-åring** *a5* fifty--year-old **-årsdag** fiftieth anniversary (birthday) **-årsjubileum** fiftieth anniversary, jubilee **-årsålder** *i ~n* [aged] about fifty **-öring** *en ~* a fifty-öre [piece]

femto- femto-

femton [-ån] fifteen **-de** fifteenth **-hundratalet** *på ~* in the sixteenth century **-årig** *a5* fifteen--year-old **-åring** boy (*etc.*) of fifteen; *~ar* fifteen--year-olds

femuddig *a5*, *~ stjärna* pentacle, pentagram, pentangle

femår|ig *a5* **1** five-year-old **2** (*för fem år*) five--year **-ing** child of five, five-year-old

femårs|dag fifth anniversary (birthday) **-plan** five-year plan **-ålder** *i ~n* [aged] about five

femöring *en ~* a five-öre [piece]; *bildl., inte värd en ~* not worth a penny (cent)

fena *s1* fin; (*AE., på flygplan*) vertical stabilizer; *inte röra en ~* not move a muscle

fender[t] *s2, sjö.* fender

Fenicien [-'ni:-] *n* Phoenicia **fenicier** [-'ni:-] *s9*, **fenicisk** [-'ni:-] *a5* Phoenician

Fenix ['fe:-] [*Fågel*] *~* [the] Phoenix

fenköl fin keel

fenol [-'å:l] *s3* phenol, carbolic acid; *~er* phenols

fenolftalein phenolphthalein

fenolharts phenolic resin

fenologi *s3* phenology

fenomen *s7* phenomenon **-el** *al* phenomenal, extraordinary **-ologi** *s3* phenomenology

fenoxisyra [-ˣnåksi-] phenoxy acid

fenotyp *s3* phenotype

fenval finback

fenyl *s3* phenyl **-ketonuri** [-ˣtå:n-] *s3* phenylketonuria

feodal *a5* feudal **-herre** feudal lord **-ism, -väsen** feudalism, feudal system

ferie ['fe:-] *s5, mest i pl* holiday; *AE.* vacation **-arbete** holiday course (task) **-läsning** holiday studies (*pl*) **-skola** summer school

fermat *s3, s7, mus.* pause, fermata

ferment *s7, s4*, **fermentera** *v1* ferment

fermion [-'å:n] *s3* fermion

fermium ['ferr-] *s8* fermium

ferniss|a [-'nissa] *s1 o. v1* varnish **-ning** varnishing

feromon [-'må:n] *s7, s4* pheromone

ferri|förening [ˣfärri-] ferric compound **-magnetism** ferrimagnetism

ferrit *s3* ferrite **-antenn** ferrite-rod aerial

ferro|förening [ˣfärro-] ferrous compound **-magnetism** ferromagnetism

fertil *al* fertile **-itet** fertility

fes *imperf. av fisa*

fesaga fairy tale

fest *s3* festival; celebration; (*munter fest*) festivity, merrymaking; (*bjudning*) party, celebration; *en ~ för ögat* a feast for the eyes; *gå på ~* go [out] to a party; *ställa till ~* give (throw) a party **festa** feast; have a gay time; *~ på färsk potatis* feast on new potatoes; *~ av* throw a farewell party (*ngn for s.b.*); *~ upp* squander on a gay life **festande** *s6* feasting, merrymaking

fest|arrangör organizer of a festival (party) **-dag** festival day; *allmän ~* public holiday **-dräkt** festive attire; evening dress **-föremål** fêted guest, guest of honour **-föreställning** gala performance **-glädje** festivity

festiv|al *s3* festival **-itas** [-'ti:-] *r* [air of] festivity

fest|klädd dressed in evening dress, dressed for a party **-kommitté** [festival] committee

festlig *al* **1** festive, festival; (*storartad*) grand **2** *se lustig, komisk* **-het** festivity

festmåltid banquet, feast

feston[g] [-'ån] *s3* festoon

fest|prisse *s2* gay dog **-skrift** festschrift; *en ~ tillägnad* a publication (volume) dedicated to **-spel** dramatic (musical, opera) festival **-stämning** gay atmosphere, festive mood **-talare** *se högtidstalare* **-våning** reception room, banqueting rooms (*pl*); functions room

fet *al* fat; (*fetlagd*) stout; corpulent; (*fyllig*) plump; (*abnormt fet*) obese; (*om kött o. fläsk*) fatty; (*om mat utom kött o. fläsk; om jordmån*) rich; (*flottig*) oily, greasy; *bli ~ fat*[ten], (*äv.*) put on weight; *det blir han inte ~ på* he won't get much out of that; *de har det inte ~t* they are none too well off

fetisch *s3* fetish, fetich **-dyrkan, -ism** fetishism, fetichism **-ist** fetishist, fetichist

fet|knopp *bot.* stonecrop **-lagd** *a5* inclined to stoutness, [somewhat] stout; (*fyllig*) plump; (*om kvinna äv.*) buxom
fetma [ˣfett-] **I** *s1* fatness; (*i sht hos pers.*) stoutness, corpulence **II** *v1*, *se* [*bli*] *fet*
fets *se fez*
fet|sill fat herring **-stil** extra bold type
fett *s4* fat; (*för håret o.d.*) oil, grease; (*smörj-*) grease, lubricant; (*stek-*) dripping; (*späck*) lard; *kokk.* shortening **-bildande** *a4* fattening **-bildning** *konkr.* accumulation (layer) of fat; *sjuklig* ~ fatty degeneration **-emboli** *med.* fat embolus (embolism) **-fena** adipose fin **-fläck** grease spot **-fågel** oilbird **-halt** fat content **-haltig** *a1* fatty, containing fat **-hjärta** fatty heart
fettisdag [ˣfe:t-] *~en* Shrove Tuesday, Pancake Day **fettisdagsbulle** *se semla*
fett|klump lump of fat **-körtel** sebaceous gland **-lager** layer of fat **-lever** fatty liver **-löslig** fat--soluble **-sot** *med.* adiposity **-svansfår** fat--tailed sheep **-svulst** wen; *med.* lipoma **-syra** fatty acid **-valk** roll of fat **-vävnad** fatty tissue **-ämne** fatty substance
fetvadd unrefined cotton wool
fez [fetz *el.* fäss] *s3* fez; tarboosh
fia [ˣfi:a] *s1* ludo
fiasko [fiˈasskɔ] *s6* fiasco, failure; *göra* ~ be a fiasco, (*om tillställning*) fall flat
fiaspel *se fia*
fibbla *bot.* hawkweed
fiber [ˈfi:-] *s3* fibre **-kost** roughage **-optik** fibre optics **-platta** fibreboard **-rik** rich in fibres; ~ *kost* roughage **-växt** fibre plant
fibrig [ˣfi:-] *a1* fibred
fibrin *s7, s4* fibrin **fibrinogen** [−ˈje:n] *s7, s4* fibrinogen **fibrinös** *a5* fibrinous
fibrös *a5* fibrous
fick *imperf. av 2 få*
fick|a *s1* pocket; *tekn. äv.* bin, hopper **-almanacka** pocket almanac **-bok** pocket book **-dagbok** pocket diary **-flaska** [hip] flask **-format** pocket size; *i* ~ pocket-sized **-kniv** pocketknife **-lampa** torch; *A.E.* flashlight **-lock** pocket flap **-ordbok** pocket dictionary **-parkera** park between two cars **-pengar** pocket money (*sg*) **-plunta** *se -flaska* **-räknare** pocket calculator **-spegel** pocket mirror **-stöld** pocket picking **-tjuv** pickpocket **-ur** pocket watch
fideikommiss *s7* estate in tail, entail **-arie** [-ˈsa:rie] *s5* tenant in tail (*till* to, of), entailer
Fidji Fiji
fiende *s5* enemy (*till* of); *poet.* foe (*till* of); *skaffa sig ~r* make enemies **-hand** *falla för* ~ die at the hand of the enemy; *falla i* ~ fall into the hands of the enemy **-land** hostile country
fiendskap *s3* enmity; hostility (*mot* towards, to)
fientlig [-ˈent-] *a1* hostile, inimical (*mot* to, towards); *attr.* enemy; *stå på* ~ *fot med* be on bad terms with, be at enmity with **-het** hostility; *inställa ~erna* suspend hostilities
fientligt [-ˈent-] *adv* hostilely; *vara* ~ *stämd mot* be hostile (antagonistic) to (towards)
fiffa ~ *upp* smarten up
fiffel [ˈfiff-] *s7* crooked dealings (*pl*), tricks (*pl*), manipulations (*pl*)
fiffig *a1* smart; (*slug*) shrewd

fiffla cheat, wangle; ~ *med böckerna* cook the books
figur figure; (*i sht neds.*) individual, character; (*ritad*) diagram, design; *göra en slät* ~ cut a poor figure; *vad är det där för en* ~? who on earth (what sort of a specimen) is that?
figur|ant figurant **-ation** embellishment; ornamentation **-atjv** *a5* figurative **-era** (*förekomma*) figure; (*uppträda*) appear, pose
figurframställning figure painting
figurin *s3* figurine
figurlig [-ˈgu:r-] *a1* figurative; *i* ~ *betydelse* in a figurative sense
figur|målning figure painting **-nära** closely fitting; hugging the figure **-sydd** *a5* close-fitting; waisted
fik *s7, vard.* café
1 fika *vard.* (*dricka kaffe*) have coffee
2 fika hanker (*efter* after, for)
fikon [-ån] *s7* fig **-löv** fig leaf **-träd** fig tree
fiktion [-kˈʃo:n] fiction **fiktjv** *a1* fictitious, imaginary
fikus [ˈfi:-] *s2* **1** *bot.* rubber plant **2** (*homosexuell man*) pansy
1 fil *s3* **1** (*rad*) row; *rummen ligger i* ~ the rooms are in a suite **2** (*trafik-*) lane; (*fordons-*) line **3** *data.* file
2 fil *s2* (*verktyg*) file
3 fil *s3, se filmjölk*
fila file; *bildl. äv.* polish; ~ *på en fiol* scrape a fiddle
filan|trop [-ˈå:p] *s3* philanthropist, philanthrope **-tropj** *s3* philanthropy **-tropisk** *a5* [-ˈtrå:-] *a5* philanthropic[al]
filatel|j *s3* philately **-ist** philatelist **-istisk** [-ˈliss-] *a5* philatelic
filbunke [bowl of] processed sour whole milk; *lugn som en* ~ as cool as a cucumber
filé *s3* **1** *kokk.* fillet **2** (*spetsvävnad*) netting, fillet lace **filea** [-ˈle:a] *kokk.* fillet
filharmonisk [-ˈmo:-] *a5* philharmonic
filial *s3* branch [office]; (*-affär*) multiple store (shop) **-affär** multiple store (shop) **-avdelning** branch department **-kontor** branch [office]
filibuster *s2*, [-ˈbust-], **filibustra** *v1, AE.* filibuster
filigran *s7, s3* filigree **-arbete** [a piece of] filigree work
filipin *s3, spela* ~ *med ngn* play philippina (philippine) with s.b.
filipper [-ˈlipp-] Philippian **-brevet** Philippians (*pl, behandlas som sg*); *eg.* the Epistle of Paul the Apostle to the Philippians
filippik *s3* philippic
filippinare [-ˣpi:-] Filipino **Filippinerna** [-ˈpi:-] *pl* the Philippines **filippinsk** [-ˈpi:nsk] *a5* Philippine, Filipino
filisté *s3*, **filisteisk** [-ˈte:-] *a5*, **filister** [-ˈliss-] *s2*, **filiströs** *a1* Philistine
filkörning driving in lanes
film *s3* film; (*smal-*) cine (*A.E.* movie) film; (*spel-*) film; *A.E.* motion (moving) picture, *vard.* movie; *~en* (*-konsten*) the cinema; *gå in vid ~en* go on the films; *spela in en* ~ make a film, film; *sätta in en* ~ *i en kamera* load a camera
film|a [take (make) a] film, shoot; (*uppträda i*

film) act in a film; *(låtsas, vard.*) feign, simulate **-ateljé** film studio **filmatiser|a** adapt for the screen **-ing** adaptation for the screen; *(film)* screen version **film|atisk** [-'ma:-] *a5* filmic **-bolag** film company **-branschen** the movie business **-censur** film censorship **-festival** film festival **-fotograf** cameraman **-föreställning** cinema performance (show) **-hjälte** hero of the screen **-idol** movie idol **-industri** film industry; *~n* the screen (cinema) **-inspelning** filming, shooting **-institut** *Svenska F~et* [the] Swedish Film Institute

filmisk ['fill-] *a5* filmic

filmjölk *ung.* processed sour milk

film|kamera film camera, cine *(AE.* movie) camera **-kassett** film cassette **-komiker** screen comedian **-konst** *~en* [the] art of film, the cinema **-kännare** cineaste **-manuskript** [film]-script, screenplay

filmo|grafi *s3* filmography **-tek** *s7* film library

film|premiär first (opening) night [of a film] **-producent** film *(AE.* motion picture) producer **-regissör** film *(AE.* motion picture) director **-roll** [film] role (part) **-rulle** roll of film; *(kassett med film)* reel [of film] **-skådespelare** film actor **-skådespelerska** film actress **-stjärna** film star **-studio** film studio **-upptagning** filming, film shooting

filning [*'fi:l-*] filing; *bildl. äv.* polishing

filo|log philologist, philologer **-logi** *s3* philology **-logisk** [-'lå:-] *a5* philological

filosof [-'så:f] *s3* philosopher **-era** philosophize *(över* [up]on, about)

filosof|i *s3* philosophy; *~e doktor* Doctor of Philosophy; *~e kandidat (magister)* Bachelor (Master) of Arts (Science, Education) **-isk** [-'så:-] *a5* philosophic[al]; *~ fakultet* Faculty of Arts and Sciences

filspån filings *(pl)*

filt *s2* **1** *(material)* felt **2** *(säng-)* blanket; *(res-)* rug **filta** felt; *~ ihop sig* get matted **filtduk** felted cloth, felting

filter ['fill-] *s7, s4* filter **-cigarett** filter-tipped cigarette, filter tip

filt|hatt felt hat, trilby, fedora **-penna** felt tip marker (pen)

filtrat *s7* filtrate

filtrer|a filter, filtrate **-apparat** filtering apparatus **-ing** filtration **-papper** filter paper

filt|sula felt (hair) sole **-toffel** felt slipper **-underlägg** felt pad

filur sly dog

fimbulvinter a bitter winter

fimmelstång shaft, thill

fimp *s2, vard.* fag end, butt **fimpa** stub (put) out

fin *a1* **1** *(motsats grov)* fine; *(tunn, smal)* thin; *(spenslig)* slender, thin; *(späd)* tender; *(skör, ömtålig)* delicate; *(mjuk o. len)* soft; *(slät)* smooth; *~t damm* fine dust; *~ stil* small type (handwriting); *~ tråd* finespun thread **2** *(väl renad)* refined; *~t silver* refined silver **3** *(motsats enklare, sämre)* fine; *(prydlig)* neat, clean, tidy; *(elegant)* elegant; *(vacker)* handsome; *(utsökt)* choice, exquisite, select; *(läcker)* delicious; *(förnäm)* aristocratic, distinguished; *(belevad)* pol-

ished, well-bred; *(förfinad)* refined; *(värdig)* dignified; *(försynt)* tactful, considerate; *(omdömesgill)* fine, discriminating; *(känslig)* sensitive; *(skarp)* keen; *(förstklassig)* first-rate, first-class, superior, excellent; *iron.* fine, nice; *~ hörsel* acute hearing; *~ och behaglig* well-bred; charming; *en ~ affär* a bargain; *en ~ dam* an aristocratic lady; *en ~ flicka* a girl of good family; *en ~ herre* a gentleman; *en ~ och hygglig karl* a nice gentlemanly fellow; *en ~ vink* a delicate (gentle) hint; *extra ~* superfine; *klä sig ~* dress up [in one's best]; *göra ~t (städa)* tidy up, *(pryda)* make things look nice; *det anses inte ~t att* it is not good manners to; *i ~t sällskap* in polite society; *det ~a i* the best part (the point) of **4** *mus.* (hög, gäll) high[-pitched]

final *s3, mus.* finale; *sport.* final[s *pl*]; *gå till ~en* enter the finals **-ist** finalist

finans [-'ans *el.* -'aŋs] *s3* finance; *~en (finansmännen)* high finance; *~er* finances; *ha dåliga ~er (äv.)* be in financial difficulties **-departement** ministry of finance; *~et (i Storbritannien)* the Treasury, *(i USA)* department of the treasury **-expert** financial expert **-furste** financial magnate **-geni** financial genius

finansi|ell *a5* financial **-era** finance **-ering** [-i'e:-] financing **-är** *s3* financier

finans|man financier **-minister** minister of finance; *(i Storbritannien)* chancellor of the Exchequer; *(i USA)* secretary of the treasury **-politik** financial policy **-rätt** [public] finance **-tull** revenue duty **-utskott** *~et* [the Swedish parliamentary] standing committee on finance **-världen** the world of finance **-väsen** finance, public finance[s *pl*] **-år** financial *(AE.* fiscal) year

finbageri fancy bakery

finemang *vard.* great

finess finesse; tact; *~er* refinements; niceties; *bilen har många ~er* the car is fitted with a lot of gadgets

finfin splendid, tiptop; exquisite; *vard.* topnotch, crack

finfördel|a grind, pulverize; levigate; *(vätska)* atomize **-ning** grinding, pulverization; levigation; *(av vätska)* atomization

fing|er ['fiŋer] *s7, s2* finger; *ha ett ~ med i spelet* have a finger in the pie; *peka ~ åt* point one's finger at; *inte röra (lyfta) ett ~* not stir (lift, raise) a finger; *sätta -ret på den ömma punkten* put (lay) one's finger on the weak (sore) spot; *kunna ngt på sina fem -rar* have s.th. at one's fingers ends; *hålla -rarna borta från ngt (bildl.)* keep one's hands off s.th.; *det kliar i -rarna på mig att* my fingers are itching to; *inte lägga -rarna emellan* handle the matter without kid gloves; *räkna på -rarna* count on one's fingers; *se genom -rarna med ngt* turn a blind eye to s.th.; *slå ngn på -rarna (bildl.)* come down on s.b.

fingera [fiŋ'ge:-] feign, simulate; *~d* fictitious, imaginary; mock, sham; *~t namn* assumed (false) name

finger|avtryck fingerprint **-borg** thimble **-borgsblomma** foxglove

fingerfärdig nimble-fingered; dexterous **-het** dexterity, manual skill; *mus.* execution, technique

F

finger|hatt se fingerborgsblomma **-krok** i uttr.: dra ~ med (ung.) have a locked-fingers tug of war with **-skiva** [telephone] dial **-spets** fingertip **-språk** se handalfabet **-svamp** coral fungi **-sättning** mus. fingering **-topp** fingertip **-tuta** fingerstall, cot, fingertip **-vante** [woollen (cotton)] glove **-visning** hint, pointer **-övning** mus. five-finger exercise

fingra ~ på finger

fingransk|a scrutinize **-ning** scrutiny

fin|hacka chop finely **-het** fineness etc., jfr fin o. finess **-hyllt** a4 delicate-complexioned, delicate-hued

fininställ|a calibrate **-ning** precision (fine) adjustment

finjt a4, språkv. finite

finjustera (motor) tune up

fink s2 finch

finka I s1 **1** (polishäkte) sl. quod, jug; clink, nick **2** (godsvagn) covered wagon; [luggage] van; AE. boxcar; baggage car **II** v1, sl. nick

fin|kalibrig [-li:b-] a1 small-bore **-kamma** comb with a fine-tooth[ed] comb; bildl. comb out, examine thoroughly, go over (through) with a fine-tooth[ed] comb

finkel ['finn-] s2, se finkelolja; (dåligt brännvin, vard.) rotgut **-olja** fusel [oil]

fin|klippa cut up fine **-klädd** dressed up; well-dressed **-kornig** fine-grained; foto. fine-grain **-kultur** highbrow culture (ibl. neds.)

finkänslig delicate; tactful, discreet **-het** delicacy [of feeling]; tactfulness, discretion

Finland ['finn-] n Finland **finlandssvensk I** s2 Swedish Finn **II** a5 Finno-Swedish

finlemmad a5 slender-limbed

finländ|are Finn, Finlander **-sk** a5 Finnish

fin|mala grind fine (small) **-malen** a5 finely ground **-maskig** a5 fine-meshed **-mekaniker** precision-tool maker **-mekanisk** ~ verkstad precision-tool workshop

finn|a fann funnit **I 1** find; (upptäcka) discover, find out, perceive; (träffa på) come upon (across); (röna) meet with **2** (erfara) find, see, learn **3** (anse) think, consider; ~ för gott att think it best to; ~ lämpligt think fit; ~ på find out, invent; ~ på råd find a way; den står inte att ~ it is not to be found **II** rfl **1** (finna sig vara) find o.s.; (anse sig) consider (think) o.s. **2** (känna sig) feel **3** (nöja, foga sig) be content (i with); ~ sig i (äv.) put up with, submit to, stand **4** (ge rätta svaret e.d.) han -er sig alltid he is never at a loss; han fann sig snart he soon collected his wits

finn|ande i uttr.: vara till ~s be to be found, exist **-as** dep (vara) be; (stå att finna) to be found, exist; det -s gott om there is plenty of; han -s ej mer he is no longer; det -s inte att få it is not to be had; -s det äpplen? have you [got] any apples?; ~ kvar a) (återstå) be left, (i behåll) be extant, b) (finnas på samma plats) be still there; ~ till exist, be in existence

finnbygd Finnish settlement

1 finne s2 Finn

2 finne s2 (blemma) pimple

finnig a1 pimpled, pimply

finnmark (mynt) Finnish mark, markka

fin|polera high-polish; ~d highly polished **-putsa** byggn. plaster; (friare) put final touches to **-rum** ung. drawing room

finsk a1 Finnish; F~a viken the Gulf of Finland

finsk|a 1 (språk) Finnish **2** (kvinna) Finnish woman **-språkig** a5 Finnish-speaking **--ugrisk** [-u:g-] a5 Finno-Ugric

fin|skuren a5 **1** kokk. finely cut **2** (om tobak e.d.) fine-cut **3** bildl. finely chiselled **-slipa** polish smooth; bildl. put the finishing touches to; ~d polished, elegant **-smakare** epicure, gourmet **-smide** whitesmithery **-snickare** cabinet-maker **-stilt** [-i:lt] a4 in small type; det ~a (i kontrakt e.d.) the fine (small) print **-stämd** a1, bildl. delicate; moving **-stött** a4 pounded fine

1 fint s3 feint (äv. i boxning, fäktning o.d.); (knep) trick, dodge, stratagem

2 fint [-i:-] adv finely etc., jfr fin; ~ bildad [well] educated, cultured; ~ utarbetad elaborately worked out

fint|a feint; (i fotboll ung.) dribble (av past) **-lig** a1 ingenious, clever

fin|trådig fine-threaded **-tvätt** washing requiring careful handling

finurlig ['nu:r-] a1 (om pers.) shrewd, knowing; (om sak) ingenious, clever

fiol s3 violin; vard. fiddle; spela ~ play the violin; spela första (andra) ~[en] (eg.) play [the] first (second) violin, bildl. play first (second) fiddle **-byggare** violin maker **-låda** violin case **-spelare** violinist, fiddler **-sträng** violin string **-stämma** violin part

1 fira 1 (högtidlighålla) celebrate; (minne äv.) commemorate; (hedra) fête, honour; ~ gudstjänst hold divine service; var tänker du ~ jul? where are you going to spend Christmas? **2** (skolka från arbetet) absent o.s.

2 fira (släppa efter) ease [away]; (skot) slack, ease off; ~ ner lower

firma s1 [business] firm; ~ Jones & Co. Messrs. Jones & Co.; teckna ~n sign for the firm **-bil** company car

firmament s7, på ~et in the firmament

firma|märke trademark **-namn** name of a firm, trade name **-tecknare** person authorized to sign for a (the) firm **-teckning** signing for a (the) firm

firn s3 névé, firn

firning [*fi:r-] vard. (arbetsfrånvaro) absenteeism

fis s2, **fisa** fes fisit fart

fischy s3 fichu

fisit sup. av fisa

fisk s2 fish; en ful ~ (bildl.) an ugly customer; vara som en ~ i vattnet take like a fish to water, be in one's element; fånga några ~ar catch a few fish; våra vanligaste ~ar our commonest fishes; få sina ~ar varma be ticked off; i de lugnaste vattnen går de största ~arna still waters run deep **fiska** fish; ~ efter (bildl.) fish (angle) for; ~ upp (bildl.) fish out; ~ i grumligt vatten fish in troubled water; vara ute och ~ be out fishing

fiskaffär fishmonger

fiskafänge s6 (utan pl) fishing; (med pl) catch [of fish]; Petri ~ (bibl.) the miraculous draught of fishes

fiskal s3, ung. public prosecutor

fiskarbefolkning fishing population
fiskare fisherman
fisk|ben fishbone **-bensmönster** herringbone pattern **-blåsa** sound **-bulle** fishball; fish cake **-damm** fishpond
fiske s6 fishing; (näringsgren) fishery **-bank** fishing bank **-båt** fishing boat **-don** fishing tackle **-fartyg** fishing vessel **-flotta** fishing fleet **-fyr** fishing light **-garn** fishing net **-gräns** fishing--limits (pl), limit of the fishing zone **-hamn** fishing port (harbour) **-kort** fishing licence (permit) **-lycka** luck at fishing **-läge** fishing village **-plats** fishing ground, fishery
fiskeri fishery **-intendent** inspector of fisheries **-konsulent** fisheries expert **-näring** fishing industry **-styrelse** ~n [the Swedish] national board of fisheries
fiske|rätt piscary, fishery, fishing **-vatten** fishing ground, fishery
fisk|filé fillet of fish **-fjäll** fish scale **-färs** minced fish **-gjuse** [-ju:se] s2 osprey, fish eagle (AE. hawk) **-handlare** fishmonger; ('fiskgumma') fishwife **-konserv** tinned (AE. canned) fish **-leverolja** cod-liver oil **-lim** fish glue **-lir** s7, **-lira** v1 play for time **-mjöl** fish meal **-mås** common (mew) gull, [sea] mew **-nät** fish[ing] net **-odling** fishfarm **-pinne** fishfinger; AE. fish stick **-redskap** fishing tackle **-restaurang** fish restaurant **-rätt** fish course **-soppa** fish soup (AE. chowder) **-stim** shoal [of fish] **-stjärt** fishtail **-sump** corf; crawl **-trappa** fish ladder **-tärna** common tern **-yngel** spawn **-öga** fish eye; foto. fish-eye lens
fiss s7 F sharp
fissil a5 fissile, fissionable **fission** [fi'ʃɑ:n] fission
fissur anat., med. fissure
fistel s2, med. fistula
fitta s1, vard. cunt
fix a5 **1** (fast) fixed; ~ idé fixed idea, (friare) rooted idea, craze; ~t pris fixed price **2** ~ och färdig all ready **fixa** vard. fix up **fixare** vard. fixer
fixativ s7 fixative
fixer|a 1 (fastställa) fix (till at) **2** (se skarpt på) stare hard at; AE. fixate **3** foto., konst., med. fix **-bad** foto. fixer **-ing** fixing, fixation; (med blicken) stare, staring; foto. fixing
fixerings|bild puzzle picture **-vätska** foto. fixer, hypo; (för teckning o.d.) fixative
fixersalt fixing salt
fix|punkt fixed point **-stjärna** fixed star
fixtur fixture, fixing plate
fjant s2 busybody, officious blighter; twerp, jerk **fjanta** ~ för fawn [up]on; ~ omkring fuss around **fjantig** a1 fussy
fjol i uttr.: i ~ last year; i ~ vinter last winter; från i ~ last year's
fjoll|a [-å-] s1 foolish (silly) woman (girl) **-ig** a1 foolish, silly **-ighet** foolishness, silliness
fjol|år ~et last year **-årskalv** last year's calf
fjompig [-å-] a1 dumb, silly
fjor se fjol
fjord [-ɑ:- el. -å-] s2 (i Norge) fjord, fiord; (i Skottland) firth
fjorton [ˣfjɑ:rtɔn] fourteen; ~ dagar [a] fortnight; i dag ~ dagar today fortnight; i dag för ~

dagar sedan a fortnight ago today; med ~ dagars mellanrum at fortnightly intervals **-de** fourteenth; var ~ dag once a (every) fortnight, fortnightly **-[de]del** fourteenth [part] **-hundratalet** på ~ in the fifteenth century **-årig** etc., se femårig etc.
fjun s7 (dun) down; (på växt äv.) floss; (på persika) fur **-ig** a1 downy; flossy
1 fjäd|er ['fjä:-] s2 (på fågel) feather; bildl. äv. plume; en ~ i hatten a feather in one's cap; lysa med lånta -rar strut in borrowed plumes
2 fjäder ['fjä:-] s2, tekn. spring
fjäder|beklädd a5 feathered, plumy **-boll** shuttle[cock] **-buske** plume, panache **-dräkt** plumage, feathering, feathers
fjäderfä poultry **-avel** poultry breeding **-skötsel** poultry farming (keeping)
fjäder|gräs feather grass **-lätt** [as] light as a feather **-moln** cirrus
fjäderstål spring steel
fjädervikt featherweight
fjädervåg spring balance (AE. scale)
fjädr|a [-ä:-] be elastic, spring; ~ sig show off (för to), be cocky (över about) **-ande** a4 elastic; (om gång) springy **-ing** spring system; (fjädringsförmåga) spring, elasticity
1 fjäll s7 (berg) mountain; (i Skandinavien äv.) fjeld
2 fjäll s7 scale
fjälla 1 (fisk) scale [off] **2** (flagna av) peel; ~ av [sig] scale (peel) off
fjäll|bestigare mountaineer, alpinist **-bestigning** mountaineering; (med pl) [mountain (alpine)] climb **-boskap** mountain cattle
fjäll|ig a1 scaly, scaled **-ning** scaling; med. peeling
fjäll|pipare dott[e]rel **-ripa** ptarmigan **-räddning** mountain rescue [service] **-räv** arctic fox **-sippa** [mountain] avens (pl, behandlas som sg) **-sjö** tarn **-skivling** bot. parasol mushroom **-topp** summit, peak; mountain top **-vandring** mountain hike (tour) **-vidd** på ~erna (ung.) on the boundless hills **-vråk** rough-legged buzzard **-växt** alpine plant
fjällämmel (särskr. fjäll-lämmel) lemming
fjär a1 standoffish, distant
fjärd [-ä:-] s2, ung. bay
fjärde [-ä:-] fourth; F~ Mosebok Numbers **-del** fourth [part], quarter; tre ~ar three fourths (quarters) **-delsnot** crotchet; AE. quarter note
fjärding [-ä:-] (kärl o. mått) ung. firkin
fjärdings|man ung. country (parish) constable **-väg** pl =, en ~ a quarter of a [Swedish] mile
fjäril s2 butterfly; (natt-) moth
fjärils|hund papillon **-håv** butterfly net
fjärilsim butterfly [stroke]
fjärilslarv caterpillar
fjärma remove [far off]; bildl. estrange, alienate; ~ sig draw away (från from), remove o.s. **fjärmare** komp. t. fjärran farther (further) [off]
fjärran I adv afar, far [away, off]; från när och ~ from far and near; komma ~ ifrån come from far off; det vare mig ~ att far be it from me to **II** a, fjärmare fjärmast distant, remote, faraway, far[off]; F~ östern the Far East **III** obögligt n distance; i ~ in the distance, afar off; i ett avlägset ~ in the

[remote] distance
fjärr|kontroll remote control **-manövrera** operate by remote control **-manövrering** remote control **-skrivare** teleprinter **-skådande I** *s6* clairvoyance, second sight **II** *a4* **1** *eg.* far--seeing **2** clairvoyant, second-sighted **-skådare** clairvoyant, seer **-styrd** [-y:-] *a5* remote-controlled; ~ *raket* guided missile **-styrning** remote control **-trafik** long-distance traffic
fjärrvärme distant heating **-nät, -system** district heating system **-verk** district heating plant
fjärsing weever
fjärt *s2, vard.* fart
fjäsa ~ *för* make a fuss of; fawn on
fjäsk *s7* **1** (*brådska*) hurry, flurry; bustle **2** (*krus*) fuss (*för* of; *med* about) **fjäska 1** be in a hurry (*etc.*) **2** ~ *för* make a fuss of; fawn on **fjäskig** *al* fussy, bustling; (*krypande*) fawning
fjät *s7* footstep
fjättra fetter, shackle, bind, chain; ~*d till händer och fötter* bound hand and foot; ~*d vid sängen* (*äv.*) bedridden **fjättrar** *pl, litt.* fetters, shackles
fjöl *s2* closet seat
f-klav bass clef, F clef
f.Kr. (*förk. för före Kristus*) B.C.
flabb 1 *s7* (*skratt*) guffaw; vulgar laugh **2** *s2* (*pratmakare*) driveller **flabba** guffaw **flabbig** *al* drivelling
flack *al* **1** (*jämn o. öppen*) flat, level **2** (*ytlig*) superficial
flacka roam about (around)
flacktång flat pliers (*pl*)
fladder ['fladd-] *s7* flutter; *bildl.* levity; (*flärd*) empty show **-mus** bat
fladdr|a flutter; (*om fågel*) flit; (*om flagga*) strea.   .lap; (*om ljus, låga*) flicker **-ig** *al* **1** (*löst hängande*) flapping **2** *bildl.* (*ostadig*) volatile, fickle
flaga I *sl* flake **II** *vl* shed flakes (*äv.* ~ *av* [*sig*]); ~ *sig* flake, scale off
flagell|ant Flagellant **-at** *biol.* flagellate
flageolett [-ʃå'lätt] *s3* flageolet **-ton** (*hopskr. flageoletton*) flageolet tone, fluted note
flagg *s2* flag; colours (*pl*); *föra brittisk* ~ fly the British flag; *segla under falsk* (*främmande*) ~ sail under false colours (a foreign flag); *stryka* ~ strike one's colours
flagga I *sl* flag; *hala* ~*n* lower the flag; *hissa* ~*n på halv stång* fly the flag at half-mast **II** *vl* fly flags (the flag, one's flag); *det* ~*s för* the flags are (the flag is) flying for (in honour of)
flagg|adjutant flag lieutenant **-duk 1** (*tyg*) bunting **2** (*flagga*) flag **-lina** flag halyard **-man** flag officer **-ning** *allmän* ~ a general display of flags **-prydd** *a5* decorated with flags **-signalering** signalling with flags **-skepp** flagship **-spel** flagstaff, ensignstaff **-stång** flagpole, flagstaff
flag|ig *al* flaky, scaly **-na** [-a:g-] flake [off], scale off, peel
flagrant [-'ant *el.* -'aɳt] *al* flagrant
flak *s7* **1** *se isflak* **2** (*last-*) platform [body]
flakong [-'åɳ] *s3* flacon
flakvagn open-sided waggon
flambera flame
flamenco [-'menn-] *s5* flamenco
flamingo [-'miɳ(g)o] *s5* flamingo

flam|ländare Fleming; -*ländarna* (*koll.*) the Flemish **-ländsk** *a5* Flemish **-ländska 1** (*språk*) Flemish **2** (*kvinna*) Flemish woman
flamma I *sl* **1** flame (*äv. bildl.*); (*häftig äv.*) blaze, flare **2** (*svärmeri*) flame; *vard.* baby **II** *vl* flame, blaze, flash; ~ *för* (*vara entusiastisk*) be enthusiastic for, (*vara förälskad i*) be sweet on; ~ *upp* blaze up, flare up **flammig** *al* flamelike; (*fläckig*) patchy, blotchy **flamning** blaze, flare
flampunkt flash[ing] point
flams *s7* gabble; giggle; loud chatter **flamsa** fool, monkey about **flamsig** *al* silly; giggly
flamsk *a5, se flamländsk*
flam|säker flameproof **-ugn** reverberatory furnace
Flandern ['flann-] *n* Flanders **flandrisk** ['flann-] *a5, se flamländsk*
flanell *s3, s4* flannel **-byxor** *pl* flannel trousers, flannels
flanellograf *s3* flannel|board, -graph
flanera stroll
flank *s3* flank **-angrepp** flank attack, attack in the flank **-era** flank
flanör flâneur, idler, loafer, man about town
flarn [-a:-] *s7, driva som ett* ~ *på vattnet* drift along like a straw in the stream
flask|a *sl* bottle; (*fick-*) [hip] flask; (*av metall*) can; *ge ett barn* ~*n* give a baby its bottle; *tappa på* -*or* put in bottles, bottle; *öl på* -*or* bottled beer **-barn** bottle-fed baby **-borste** bottlebrush **-hals** bottleneck (*äv. bildl.*) **-post** message sent in a bottle [thrown into the sea] **-propp** stopper
flat *al* **1** *eg.* flat; ~ *tallrik* [shallow] plate; *med* ~*a handen* with the flat of the (one's) hand **2** (*förlägen*) aghast, dumbfounded, taken aback **3** (*släpphänt*) weak, indulgent (*mot* to)
flat|a *sl, se handflata* **-bottnad** [-å-] *a5* flat-bottomed **-het 1** *eg.* flatness **2** (*förlägenhet*) dumbfoundedness, blank amazement **3** (*släpphänthet*) weakness, indulgence **-lus** crab louse **-skratt** guffaw
flau *oböjligt a* dull, flat, depressed
flax *s2, vard.* [piece of good] luck; *ha* ~ be lucky (in luck)
flaxa flutter; ~ *med vingarna* flap (flutter) its (*etc.*) wings
flegma ['flegg-] *sl* phlegm; indifference **-tiker** [-'ma:-] phlegmatic person **-tisk** [-'ma:-] *a5* phlegmatic[al]; impassive
flekterande [-'te:-] *a4,* ~ *språk* (*pl*) inflectional languages
flektion *se flexion*
flenört common figwort
flera ['fle:-] *komp. t. många* **1** (*med jämförelse*) (*mera* [*än*]) more; (*talrikare*) more numerous; *allt* ~ *och* ~ more and more; *mycket* ~ *människor* many more people; *många* ~ many more; *vi blir inte* ~ there won't be any more of us **2** (*utan jämförelse*) many; (*talrika*) numerous; (*åtskilliga*) several; *med* ~ and others; ~ *gånger*, *vid* ~ *tillfällen* on several occasions, on more than one occasion; *det blir billigare om vi är* ~ the more we are, the cheaper it will be
fler|barnsfamilj large family **-dubbel** multiple, manifold **-dubbla** multiply **-faldig** *a5,* ~ *vinnare av* several times the winner of; *jfr mång-*

faldig **-faldiga** multiply; (*skrift o.d.*) reproduce **-falt** many times, [ever so] much **-familjshus** block of flats; *AE.* apartment building (house) **-filig** *a5* multiple-lane **-färgad** multicoloured **-färgstryck** multicolour process printing; *konkr.* multicolour print **-omättad** polyunsaturated **-sidig** *a5* polygonal **-siffrig** *a5* of several figures **-språkig** *a5* multilingual, polyglot **-stavig** *a5* polysyllabic **-stegsraket** multistage rocket **-städes** in several places **-stämmig** *a5* polyphonous; ~ *sång* part song **-stämmigt** *adv,* *sjunga* ~ sing in parts **-tal** *s7* **1** *språkv.* plural **2** (*större delen*) majority; ~*et människor* the [great] majority of people, most people; *i* ~*et fall* in most cases **3** *ett* ~ several, a number of **-värd** *kem.* polyvalent **-årig** *a5* of several years[' duration]; *bot.* perennial

flesta *best. superl. t. många, de* ~ *a*) *fören.* most, *b*) *självst.* (*om förut nämnda*) most of them; *de* ~ [*människor*] most people; *de* ~ *pojkarna* most of the boys; *av vilka de allra* ~ by far the greater number of whom (which)

flex|a be on flexitime **-ibel** [-'i:-] *a2* flexible **-ibilitet** flexibility

flexion [-k'ʃɑ:n] inflection

flex|skiva *data.* floppy disk, flexible diskette **-tid** flexitime, flexible working hours

1 flicka *v1* patch, cobble

2 flick|a *s1* girl; *-orna Jones* the Jones girls

flick|aktig *a1* girlish **-aktighet** girlishness **-bekant** girlfriend **-bok** book for girls; *-böcker* (*äv.*) girls' books **-ebarn** [baby] girl, girl-child **-jägare** skirtchaser **-namn** girl's name; (*frus*) maiden name **-pension** girls' boarding school **-scout** [Girl] Guide; *AE.* Girl Scout **-snärta** young thing **-tjusare** charmer **-tycke** *ha* ~ be a favourite with girls **-vän** girlfriend

flik *s2* (*på plagg, kuvert*) flap; (*snibb*) lappet; (*bit*) patch; (*yttersta kant*) edge, end; *bot.* lobe **-ig** *a1, bot.* lobate

flimmer ['flimm-] *s7* flicker **-hår** cilium (*pl* cilia), flagellum (*pl* flagella)

flimra quiver, shimmer, flicker; *det* ~*r för ögonen* my (*etc.*) eyes are dazzled

flin *s7* grin; (*hångrin*) sneer **flina** grin; sneer

flinga *s1* flake

flink *a1* (*kvick* [*av sig*]) quick, nimble (*i* at); (*färm*) prompt; (*driftig*) active; ~ *i fingrarna* nimble-fingered, deft

flint *s3, vard.* **1** (*panna*) *mitt i* ~*en* full in the (one's) face **2** [bald] crown of the head; *början till* ~ first signs of baldness

flint|a *s1* flint **-bössa** *se -låsgevär* **-glas** flint glass, [optical] flint **-kniv** flint knife **-låsgevär** flintlock, firelock **-porslin** flintware **-redskap** flint implement[s *pl*]

flintskall|e bald head; (*person*) baldhead **-ig** *a1* bald[headed]

flint|vapen flint weapon **-verktyg** *se flintredskap* **-yxa** flint axe

flipperspel pinball machine

flirt [flört] *se flört*

flis *s3* wood chips (*pl*)

flisa I *s1* (*skärva, trä-*) splinter; (*tunn bit*) flake **II** *v1,* ~ [*sig*] splinter

flis|are *s9,* **-hugg** *s7* chipper **-stack** chip pile

flit *s3* **1** diligence; (*arbetsiver*) industry; (*trägenhet*) assiduity **2** *med* ~ (*avsiktligt*) on purpose, purposely, deliberately **-ig** *a1* diligent; (*idog*) industrious; (*arbetsam*) hard-working; (*trägen*) assiduous; (*aldrig sysslolös*) busy; (*ofta återkommande, t.ex. om besök*) frequent; *en* ~ *kyrkobesökare* a habitual churchgoer; *F~a Lisa* busy Lizzie **-pengar** overtime allowance (*sg*)

1 flock [-å-] *s7* (*avfall av ull o.d.*) flock

2 flock [-å-] *s2* **1** (*av fåglar, får o.d.*) flock; (*av renar*) herd; (*av vargar*) pack; (*av fåglar äv.*) flight; (*av människor*) crowd, party **2** *bot.* umbel

flock|a *rfl* flock [together], cluster **-blommig, -blomstrig** [-å-] *a5* umbelliferous **-instinkt** herd instinct

flod *s3* **1** *eg.* river; *bildl.* flood, torrent **2** (*högvatten*) flood, tide **-arm** branch (arm) of a (the) river **-bank** river bank **-bädd** riverbed **-fåra** river channel **-häst** hippopotamus; *vard.* river horse **-mynning** river mouth; (*stor äv.*) estuary **-spruta** fireboat **-system** river system **-våg** tidal wave **-ångare** river steamer

flopp [-å-] *s2,* **floppa** [-å-] *v1* flop

1 flor *s7* (*tyg*) gauze; (*sorg-*) crape; (*slöja*) veil

2 flor *n, stå* (*vara*) *i* [*sitt fulla*] ~ be in full bloom

flora *s1* flora

Florens ['flå-] *n* Florence

florentin|are [-ˣti:-] *s9,* **-sk** *a5* Florentine

florer|a flourish, be at its (*etc.*) prime; *neds.* be rife (rampant) **-ande** *a4* widely prevalent

florett *s3* foil **-fäktare** foilsman **-fäktning** foil fencing

florin *s3* florin; *holländska* ~*er* [Dutch] guilders (*förr äv.* florins)

flors|huva [-ɔ:-] tipsiness **-tunn** thin as gauze; filmy

floskler ['flåsk-] *pl* empty phrases, balderdash (*sg*) **floskulös** *a1* inflated, bombastic

flossamatta pile rug (carpet)

1 flott [-å-] *a* oböjligt *a, sjö., komma* (*bli*) ~ get afloat

2 flott [-å-] *a1* (*elegant*) stylish, smart; (*frikostig*) generous; (*överdådig*) extravagant; *leva* ~ live in great style, lead a gay life

3 flott [-å-] *s4* grease; (*stek-*) dripping; (*ister-*) lard

1 flotta [-å-] *s1* (*örlogs-, handels-*) navy, fleet; (*fartygssamling*) fleet; *gå in vid* ~*n* join the Navy

2 flotta [-å-] *v1* float, drive, raft

3 flotta [-å-] *v1,* ~ *ner* make all greasy

flottare log-floater, log-driver

flottbas naval base

flottbro pontoon bridge

flotte *s2* raft

flottfläck grease spot

flotthet stylishness; generosity *etc.*

flottig *a1* greasy

flottilj [-å-] *s3, sjö.* flotilla; *flyg.* wing **-chef** *flyg.* wing commander; *AE.* lieutenant colonel **-enhet** *sjö.* naval unit

flottist [-å-] *s7* seaman, sailor

flottled floating channel, floatway

flottmanöver naval manoeuvres (*pl*)

flottning [-å-] *s7* floating, log-driving **flottningsränna** log flume (chute)

flottstyrka naval operating force

flottyr [-å-] *s3* frying-fat **-koka** deep-fry; *-kokt potatis* [potato] chips, French fried potatoes, *AE*. French fries **-kokning** deep-frying **-stekt** deep--fried

flottör float

flox [-å-] *s2* phlox

fluffig *al* fluffy

flug|**a** *s1* **1** fly; *slå två -or i en smäll* kill two birds with one stone **2** *(halsduk)* bow [tie] **3** *(vurm)* craze **-fiske** fly-fishing *(efter forell* for trout) **-fångare** flypaper; flytrap

flugig *al* cranky

flugit *sup. av flyga*

flug|**nät** fly net **-smuts** flyspeck **-smälla** fly swatter **-snappare** flycatcher; *grå (svart och vit)* ~ spotted (pied) flycatcher **-svamp** amanita; *(röd)* fly agaric; *(lömsk)* death cap (angel) **-vikt** flyweight **-viktare** flyweight [boxer *etc.*]

flujd *s3* fluid **-isera** fluidize **-isering** [-'se:-] fluidization **-istor** [-ˣistår] *s3* fludistor **-itet** fluidity, fluidness **-um** ['flu:i-] *s4* fluid, liquid

fluktu|**ation** fluctuation **-era** fluctuate

flum|**debatt** mixed-up debate **-mig** *al vard.* spaced out; mixed-up

flundra *s1* flounder, flatfish

fluor [-'å:r] *s3* fluorin[e] **-era** fluoridate **-ering** [-'re:-] fluoridation

fluoresc|**ens** [-e'sens *el.* -'ʃens] *s3* fluorescence **-ent** [-'sent *el.* -'ʃent] fluorescent **-era** [-'se:- *el.* -'ʃe:-] fluoresce **-erande** [-'se:- *el.* -'ʃe:-] fluorescent

fluorjd *s3* fluoride

fluorider|**a**, **-ing** *se fluorera, fluorering*

1 fluss *s3, med., se flytning, inflammation, katarr*

2 fluss *s3, kem.* flux[ing agent]

fluss|**glas** milk glass **-medel** *se 2 fluss* **-spat** *(hopskr. flusspat) s3* fluorspar, fluor; *AE.* fluorite

fluster ['fluss-] *s7* beehive entrance

flutit *sup. av flyta*

flux straight [away], all in a jiffy

1 fly *se ankarfly*

2 fly *se gungfly*

3 fly *s6, zool.* noctuid moth

4 fly *v4* **1** *(ta t. flykten)* fly, flee *(för fienden* before the enemy); *(rymma)* run away; *(undkomma)* escape; *(friare)* vanish, disappear; *~dda tider* bygone days; *livet hade ~tt* he *(etc.)* was dead; *bättre ~ än illa fäkta* discretion is the better part of valour **2** *(undfly)* flee from, escape; *(faran)* shun

5 fly *adv, bli ~ förbannad* fly into a rage, get absolutely furious

flyg *s7* **1** *se flygvapen* **2** *(-konst)* aviation **3** *(-plan)* aeroplane; *AE.* airplane; *med* ~ by air

flyga *flög flugit* fly; *(högt, uppåt)* soar *(mot höjden* aloft); *(ila, rusa)* dart, dash, rush; *~ i luften (explodera)* blow (go) up; *~ på ngn* fly at s.b.; *vad har det flugit i henne?* what [ever] can have possessed (got into) her?, what's bitten her?; *ordet flög ur honom* the word escaped him

flyg|**ande** *a4* flying; *~ besiktning (av bil etc.)* roadside inspection (safety check); *~ fästning (mil.)* flying fortress; *F~ holländaren* the Flying Dutchman; *~ hund* flying fox; *~ mara* flying mare; *~ start* flying start *(äv. bildl.)*; *~ tefat* flying

saucer; *i ~ fläng* in a terrific hurry, posthaste **-anfall** air raid (attack)

flygar|**e** flier, flyer, aviator, *mil.* airman; *(förare)* pilot **-sjuka** aeroembolism, decompression sickness (illness)

flyg|**aska** fly ash, flue dust **-attaché** air attaché **-bas** air base (station) **-bild** *se flygfoto* **-biljett** air ticket **-blad** leaflet, handbill; fly sheet **-bolag** airline [company] **-buren** *a3* airborne **-buss** airbus **-båt** *(flygplan)* flying boat; *(båt)* hydrofoil **-certifikat** pilot's certificate, flying licence **-duglig** airworthy **-däck** *(på hangarfartyg)* flight deck

flygel *s2* **1** wing; *(stänkskärm)* wing, *AE.* fender; *mil., polit., sport.* flank **2** *mus.* grand piano **-byggnad** wing **-karl** *mil.* pivot [man]

flyg|**eskader** group **-fisk** flying fish **-flottilj** wing **-foto** aerial photograph (view) **-fotografera** photograph from the air **-fotografering** aerial photography **-frakt** air freight **-fyr** aeronautical (air) light; *(radiofyr)* [radio] beacon **-fä** winged insect; *förbaskade ~n!* blasted flies! **-fält** airfield, landing field, *(mindre)* flying field; *jfr flygplats* **-färd** flight **-färdig** *(om flygare)* ready to fly; *(om fågelunge)* fully fledged, full-fledged **-förband** flying unit **-förbindelse** air service; plane connection

flygg *al, se flygfärdig*

flyg|**hamn** [marine] airport **-haveri** aircraft crash (accident) **-havre** wild oat **-industri** aircraft industry **-kapten** *(vid trafikflyget)* pilot **-korridor** air corridor, airway **-kropp** fuselage **-larm** air-raid alarm (warning) **-ledare** control officer **-ledartorn** [airport] control tower **-ledning** air-traffic control **-linje** airline, air route **-lotta** *ung. (i Storbritannien)* member of the Women's Auxiliary Air Force (W.A.A.F.); *vard.* Waaf *se flygplan* **-medicin** aviation medicine **-mekaniker** aircraft mechanic **-motor** aircraft (aero) engine **-myra** winged ant **flyg**|**ning** [-y:-] flying; aeronautics *(pl, behandlas som sg)*; *(-tur)* flight **-officer** air-force officer **-olycka** *se flyghaveri* **-parad** fly-past; *AE.* flyover **-plan** aircraft; aeroplane; *AE.* airplane

flygplans|**besättning** aircrew **-kapare** [aircraft] hijacker **-kapning** [aircraft] hijack

flyg|**plats** airport, *(mindre)* air station, aerodrome, *AE.* airdrome; *jfr flygfält* **-porto** airmail postage **-post** airmail **-resa** flight, [air] trip **-rutt** air route (service) **-räd** air raid **-rädd** afraid of flying **-sand** shifting sand **-simulator** flight simulator **-sinnad** *a5* air-minded **-sjuk** airsick **-sjuka** airsickness **-skydd** *mil.* shelter (support) **-spaning** air reconnaissance **-stab** air staff **-stridskrafter** air forces **-styrman** first officer **-säker** airworthy **-säkerhet** safety in flight **-säkerhetstjänst** air security service **-terminal** air terminal **-tidtabell** [air service] timetable (schedule) **-trafik** air traffic (service) **-transport** air transport (transportation) **-tur** flying trip, flight **-uppvisning** air show **-vapen** air force; *-vapnet (i Storbritannien)* the Royal Air Force (R.A.F., RAF), *(i USA)* United States Air Force (USAF, U.S.A.F.) **-värdinna** air hostess, stewardess **-ödla** pterosaur

flyhänt *al* deft; *bildl.* dext[e]rous, quick **-het**

deftness; *bildl.* dexterity, quickness
1 flykt *s3* (*t. flyga*) flight; *fälla en fågel i ~en* shoot a bird on the wing; *gripa tillfället i ~en* seize the opportunity
2 flykt *s3* (*t. fly*) flight; (*rymning*) escape; *vara på ~* be on the run; *~en från landsbygden* the flight from the land; *~en till Egypten* (*bibl.*) the flight into Egypt; *jaga på* (*ta till*) *~en* put (take) to flight
flyktförsök attempted escape
flykthastighet *rymdtekn.* escape velocity
flyktig *al* **1** (*övergående*) fleeting, passing, fugitive; *en ~ bekantskap* a slight acquaintance; *kasta en ~ blick på ngt* give s.th. a hasty (passing, cursory) glance; *~ genomläsning* cursory perusal **2** *kem. o.d.* volatile **3** (*ostadig*) fickle, flighty
flykting refugee; (*flyende*) fugitive **-hjälp** aid to refugees **-läger** refugee camp **-ström** stream of refugees
flyta *flöt flutit* **1** (*motsats sjunka*) float (*äv. bildl. och om valuta*); *~ i land* be washed ashore **2** (*rinna o.d.*) flow (*äv. bildl.*); (*om tårar, svett o.d.*) run; *~ med strömmen* float down with (be carried along by) the stream (current); *blod kommer att ~* blood will be shed **3** (*ha flytande konsistens*) be fluid; (*om bläck o.d.*) run **4** *~ ihop* (*om floder*) flow into each other, (*om färger*) run into each other; *~ upp* rise to the surface; *han vill gärna ~ ovanpå* he likes to be superior
flyt|ande *a4* **1** (*på vätska*) floating; (*om fartyg*) afloat; *hålla det hela ~* keep things going **2** (*rinnande*) flowing, running; *bildl. äv.* fluent (*franska* French); *tala engelska ~* speak English fluently **3** (*i vätskeform*) fluid, liquid; *~ bränsle* liquid fuel; *~ föda* liquid nourishment (food); *~ kristaller* (*t.ex. i fickräknare*) liquid crystal display; *~ luft* liquid air; *~ naturgas* liquefied natural gas; *~ syre* liquid oxygen; (*som raketbränsle äv.*) lox; *~ tvål* liquid soap; *~ valuta* floating currency **-docka** floating [dry] dock **-glas** floatglass **-kropp** float
flytning [-y:-] **1** floating **2** *med.* discharge, flux
flytta 1 (*ändra plats för*) move; remove (*äv. flytta bort*); (*i spel*) move; *bli ~d* (*skol., uppflyttad*) be moved up (*till* [in]to) **2** (*byta bostad*) move (*äv. flytta på* [*sig*]); (*lämna anställning*) leave (*från en plats* a place); (*från hotell etc.*) check out; (*om fåglar*) migrate; *~ fram klockan* put the clock on (forward); *~ fram resan* (*resa tidigare*) arrange an earlier date for the journey, advance the journey, (*uppskjuta*) postpone the journey; *~ fram trupperna* advance the troops; *~ ihop* move [closer] together; *~ ihop med ngn* go to live with s.b.; *~ om* shift, rearrange; *~ upp* (*i grad*) move up; *~ sig* move, change one's place
flytt|bar *a5* mov[e]able, portable **-block** *geol.* erratic [block] **-buss** removal van **-fågel** migratory bird **-fågelssträck** flight of migratory birds **-kalas** house-warming [party] **-karl** furniture remover **-lass** vanload of furniture
flyttning moving *etc.*, removal, transportation; move; (*fåglars, nomaders*) migration
flyttnings|anmälan notification of change of residence (abode) **-betyg** (*utfärdat på pastorsexpedition*) certificate of change of address
flyttsaker movables
flytväst life jacket; *AE.* life preserver

flå *v4* flay; (*om fisk*) skin
flås *s7, vard.* wind **-a** puff [and blow]; (*pusta o. flämta*) pant; *~nde av* breathless with **-ig** *al* wheezy **-patos** strained pathos
fläck *s2* **1** stain, mark, spot; (*av färg*) smudge; *bildl.* stain, blot, (*fel*) blemish; *sätta en ~ på duken* stain the tablecloth **2** (*på djurhud*) spot **3** (*ställe*) spot; *på ~en* (*genast*) on the spot, at once; *jag får den inte ur ~en* I cannot move it; *han rörde sig inte ur ~en* he did not move (budge); *vi kommer inte ur ~en* we are not getting anywhere (making any progress)
fläck|a spot, stain (*äv. bildl.*); (*smutsa*) [be]smear; (*söla ner*) soil; *~ ner sig* get o.s. (one's clothes) all stained (soiled) **-borttagning** spot (stain) removal **-borttagningsmedel** spot (stain) remover **-feber** spotted fever **-fri** stainless, spotless; unsoiled; *bildl. äv.* unspotted, blameless, immaculate
fläck|ig *al* **1** spotted; (*nedfläckad*) stained, soiled **2** (*om djur*) spotted **-vis** in spots (places)
fläder ['flä:-] *s2* elder[berry] **-buske** elder shrub
fläddermus *se fladdermus*
fläder|märg elder pith **-te** elder tea
fläka *v3* slit, split open
fläkt *s2* **1** (*vindpust*) breath [of air]; breeze; puff, blow; (*friare o. bildl.*) breath, waft; *en frisk ~* a breath of fresh air; *inte en ~ rörde sig* not a breath was stirring **2** (*apparat*) fan, ventilator, blower
fläkt|a fan; *~ med solfjädern* fan (fan) the air; *det ~r skönt* there is a nice breeze blowing **-rem** fan belt **-ventilation** mechanical ventilation
flämt|a 1 pant, puff **2** (*fladdra*) flicker **-ning 1** pant **2** flicker
fläng *s7* bustling; hurry; *i flygande ~* in a [flying] hurry **flänga** *v2* **1** (*rusa*) fling (*omkring i* round); *~ och fara* rush to and fro; *~ omkring* (*i väg*) dash about (away) **2** (*rycka*) strip (*av* off)
fläns *s2* flange **flänsa 1** *tekn.* flange **2** (*valar*) flense, flench
flärd [-ä:-] *s3* vanity; frivolity **-fri** unaffected, artless, simple; (*blygsam*) modest **-full** vain; frivolous
fläsk *s7* pork; (*sid-*) bacon; (*hull*) flesh; *magert* (*randigt*) *~* lean (streaky) bacon; *rökt* (*stekt*) *~* smoked (fried) bacon; *~ och bruna bönor* pork and beans; *ärter och ~* yellow pea soup and pork **-ben** ham bone **-filé** fillet of pork **-flott** pork dripping **-hare** *kokk.* boneless loin of pork
fläsk|ig *al* porky **-karré** loin of pork **-korv** pork sausage **-kotlett** pork chop **-lägg** hand (knuckle) of pork **-läpp** swollen lip **-pannkaka** pancake with diced pork **-svål** pork (bacon) rind (skin) **-änger** *s2* larder beetle
flät|a I *s1* plait; tress; (*nack-*) pigtail; (*bröd, tobaks-*) twist **II** *v1* plait; braid; (*krans o.d.*) twine, wreathe; *~ in* (*bildl.*) intertwine, intertwist; *~ in i* (*bildl.*) weave into; *~ sig* entwine itself (*omkring* round) **-ning** [-ä:-] plaiting *etc.* **-verk** plaited work
flöda flow; (*häftigt*) gush, pour, stream; *~ av* overflow with; *~ över* flow (run) over, *bildl.* brim over (*av* with); *champagnen ~de* the champagne flowed **flödande** *a4* flowing *etc.*; *bildl.* fluent; abounding, exuberant **flöde** *s6* flow; torrent, stream; *fys.* flux

flödes|diagram, -schema flow chart (sheet)
flög imperf. av flyga
flöjel [ˣflöjj-] s2 vane, weathercock
flöjt s3 flute **-blåsare, -ist** flute player, flautist; AE.
flutist **-lik** flutelike, fluty
flört s3 **1** (flörtande) flirtation **2** pers. flirt **flörta** flirt **flörtig** a1 flirtatious, flirty
flöt imperf. av flyta
flöte s6 float; vara bakom ~t be dull (stupid)
flöts s3, geol. seam
FM (förk. för frekvensmodulering) FM
f.m. (förk. för förmiddagen) a.m.
f-moll F minor
FN (förk. för Förenta nationerna) U.N.
f.n. (förk. för för närvarande) se under närvarande
fnas s7 husk, shuck **fnasa** husk **fnasig** a1 scaly; chapped
fnask s7 **1** (obetydlighet) trifle **2** (grand) jot, scrap **3** (prostituerad) tart **-er** ['fnass-] s2 (pojkvasker) shrimp [of a lad]
fnatt få ~, vard. blow one's top
FN-bataljon United Nations battalion
fnissa v1, **fnissning** s2 titter, giggle
fnitter ['fnitt-] s7, **fnittra** v1, se fnissning, fnissa **fnittrig** prone to giggle, giggly
FN-|kommission United Nations commission **-observatör** United Nations observer
fnoskig [-å-] a1 dotty, silly; (om person) barmy, AE. balmy, loco
FN-stadgan United Nations Charter
fnurra s1, det har kommit en ~ på tråden mellan dem they have fallen out
fnysa v3 el. fnös fnyst, **fnysning** [-y:-] s2 snort
fnös imperf. av fnysa
fnösk|e s6 tinder, touchwood; torr som ~ dry as tinder **-ticka** s1 tinder fungus
foajé s3 foyer
fob [fåbb] f.o.b. (free on board)
fobi s3 phobia
fob-pris f.o.b.-price
fock s2, sjö. foresail, forecourse; (på mindre båt) jib
focka [-å-] (avskeda) turn off, [give...the] sack
fock|mast foremast **-skot** foresheet **-stag** forestay
1 foder ['fo:-] s7 (kreatursföda) [cattle]food; forage; (kraft-) fodder, feed
2 foder ['fo:-] s7 (i kläder o.d.) lining; (hylsa o.d.) casing; (dörr-, fönster- o.d.) architrave; bot. calyx
foderbeta mangel[wurzel], mangold[wurzel]
foderblad bot. sepal
foder|kaka oil cake **-säd** fodder grain
foderväv lining material
foderväxt fodder (forage) plant
1 fodra [ˣfo:-] (t. 1 foder) [give...a (its etc.)] feed, fodder
2 fodra [ˣfo:-] (t. 2 foder) line
fodral s7 case; (låda äv.) box; (hölje) casing, cover
1 fodring [ˣfo:-] (t. 1 foder) feeding etc.
2 fodring [ˣfo:-] (t. 2 foder) lining
1 fog n (skäl) justice, [good] reason, justification, right; med [allt] ~ with good reason, reasonably; utan ringaste ~ without the slightest reason;

ha ~ för sig be reasonable; ha [fullt] ~ för have every reason for
2 fog s2 (skarv) joint; (söm) seam; med. suture
foga l 1 (förena) join (till, i to); bildl. add [to], attach [to], affix **2** (avpassa) suit, fit **3** (bestämma) ordain; ödet har ~t det så fate has so ordained (determined) **II** rfl **1** (ansluta) join [itself (etc.)] on (till to) **2** (falla sig) det har ~t sig så att things have so turned out that **3** (ge med sig) give in; ~ sig efter accommodate o.s. to; ~ sig i resign o.s. to
fogde [ˣfogg-] s2, ung. sheriff, bailiff; AE. marshal
foglig [ˣfo:g-] a1 accommodating, compliant; (medgörlig) amenable **-het** compliance, compliancy; amenability
fogning [ˣfo:g-] joining etc., jfr foga
fogsvans foxtail saw; handsaw
fokal a5 focal **-distans** focal length (distance) **-infektion** focal infection
fokus ['fo:-] -en el. =, pl -ar focus **-era** focus **-ering** [-'se:-] focusing
folder ['fåll-] s2, s9 folder
foliant [book in] folio [volume]
folie ['fo:-] s5 foil; (plast- äv.) film, sheet **folier|a 1** tekn. foliate, foil **2** hand. folio **-ing** tekn. o. hand. foliation
folio ['fo:-] folio **-band** folio volume **-format** folio size
folk [-å-] s7 **1** (folkslag, nation) people **2** (underlydande) servants (pl); mil, sjö. men **3** (människor) people (pl); vard. folks (pl); F~ets hus community centre, assembly hall; göra ~ av ngn teach s.b. manners; uppföra sig som ~ behave properly; som ~ är mest like the general run of people; se ut som ~ gör mest be ordinary looking; det var mycket ~ på gatan there were a lot of people in the street; det är skillnad på ~ och fä there are people and people; har du inte sett ~ förr? what are you standing there gaping for?
folkbildning (bildningsnivå) general level of education; (undervisning) adult education
folkbildnings|arbete adult educational activities **-förbund** adult education organization
folk|bok popular book **-bokföring** national registration
folk|dans folk dance
folkdemokrat|i people's democracy **-isk** of (belonging to) a people's democracy
folk|djup ur ~et from the masses **-domstol** people's court **-dräkt** national costume **folketymologi** folk (popular) etymology
folk|fattig sparsely populated **-fest** national holiday; (folklig fest) popular festivity **-front** popular front **-församling** national assembly **-försörjning** national food supply
folkgrupp polit. national group; (minoritet) minority
folk|hem ung. welfare state **-hjälte** national hero **-hop** crowd [of people]; neds. mob **-humor** popular (folk) humour **-hushållning** national economy **-hälsa** public health **-högskola** residential college for adult education
folkilsken vicious; savage
folk|kommissarie (i Sovjetunionen) People's Commissar **-kär** beloved by the people

folk|lager class [of society] **-ledare** popular leader **-lek** national game
folklig [-å-] *al* **1** (*tillhörande folket*) popular; democratic **2** (*i umgänge*) affable **-het 1** popularity **2** affability
folkliv 1 street life; crowds (*pl*) **2** (*allmogens liv*) life of the people; *svenskt* ~ the life and manners of the Swedish people
folklivs|forskning folklore research **-skildring** description of the life of the [common] people
folklor|[e] [-'lå:r] *s3* folklore **-ist** folklorist **-istik** *s3* folklore [research] **-istisk** [-'riss-] *a5* folkloristic
folklåt folk song
folk|massa *se folkhop* **-medicin** folk medicine **-minnesforskning** folklore research **-mord** genocide **-mun** *i* ~ in popular speech, colloquially **-musik** folk music **-mål** dialect **-mängd** population **-mängdsstatistik** population statistics (*pl, behandlas som sg*) **-möte** public (mass) meeting
folk|nykterhet national standard of temperance **-näring** *se folkförsörjning* **-nöje** popular entertainment
folk|omröstning popular vote; referendum; plebiscite **-opinion** public opinion
folk|park amusement park **-parti** liberal party
folkpension national old age pension **-ering** [-'ne:-] national old age pensions scheme **-är** old--age pensioner
folk|ras race **-representation** parliament, legislature **-republik** people's republic **-resning** insurrection, popular rising **-rik** populous **-räkning** census **-rätt** international law **-rättslig** of (in) international law **-rörelse** popular (national) movement
folk|saga folk tale (story) **-samling** gathering of people, crowd **-sjukdom** endemic disease **-skara** *se folkhop*
folkskola elementary school; *AE.* grade school
folkskole|seminarium [elementary-school teacher's] training college **-stadga** elementary--education statute
folkskollärar|e, **-inna** elementary school teacher
folk|skygg shy, retiring; (*om djur*) shy **-slag** nationality **-spillra** remnant of a nation **-stam** tribe **-storm** mass protest, general uproar **-styre** democracy, representative government **-sång 1** (*folkvisa*) folk song **2** (*nationalsång*) national anthem **-sångare** folk singer **-sägen** popular tradition (legend)
folk|talare popular speaker (orator) **-tandvård** national dental service **-tom** (*om gata o.d.*) deserted, empty; (*om land o.d.*) depopulated **-ton** *visa i* ~ song on a folk-song theme **-tribun** tribune **-tro** folklore, popular belief; lay opinion **-trängsel** crowd[s *pl*] [of people] **-tät** densely populated **-täthet** density of population
folk|upplaga popular edition **-upplopp** riot, tumult
folk|vald *a5* popularly elected **-vandring** migration **-vandringstiden** the time of the Great Migration **-vett** [good] manners (*pl*) **-vilja** will of the people **-vimmel** *i* -vimlet in the throng

(crowd, crush) [of people] **-visa** folk song **-välde** democracy **-vänlig** democratic (democratically) disposed **-ökning** increase of population, population growth
follik|el [-'likk-] *s2*, *anat.* follicle **-ulär** follicular, folliculate
fon [få:n] *s3* **1** *språkv.* phone **2** *fys.*, *se phon*
1 fond [fånd] *s3* (*bakgrund*) background; *teat.* back [of the stage] (*på scenen*), centre (*i salongen*); *första radens* ~ the dress-circle centre **2 fond** [fånd] *s3* (*kapital*) fund[s *pl*], capital; (*stiftelse o.d.*) foundation; (*förråd*) stock, store **-börs** stock exchange (market)
fonddekoration backcloth, backdrop
fond|emission bonus (scrip) issue; *AE.* stock dividend issue **-era** fund, consolidate **-kommissionär** member of the stock exchange, stockbroker
fondloge *första radens* ~ the dress-circle box
fondmäklare stockbroker
fondvägg *teat.* backscene
fondy [fåŋdy] *s3* fondue
fonem *s7* phoneme
fonet|ik *s3* phonetics (*pl, behandlas som sg*) **-iker** [-'ne:-] phonetician **-isk** [-'ne:-] *a5* phonetic
fonograf *s3* phonograph
font [-å-] *s3* fount, (*särsk. AE.*) font
fontanell [-å-] *s3* fontanel[le]
fontän [-å-] *s3* fountain; jet [of water]
for *imperf. av 2 fara*
fora *s1* (*lass*) [wag(g)on]load; (*vagn*) cart
force majeure [fårs ma'ʒö:r] force majeure
forcer|a [får'se:ra] **1** (*påskynda*) speed up, rush; (*intensifiera*) intensify **2** (*tilltvinga sig tillträde etc.*) force; (*chiffer*) break, cryptanalyse **-ad** *a5* forced, strained; *i* -at tempo at top speed **-ing** speeding up; forcing; (*kryptoanalys*) cryptanalysis
fordom[dags] [ˣfɔ:r-] formerly; in times past; in bygone days; *från* ~ from former times; *i* ~ *tid* in former times, in olden days
fordon [ˣfɔ:r-] *s7* vehicle; (*last-*) van, truck, cart
fordons|skatt vehicle licence duty **-våg** weighbridge
fordra [-ɔ:-] **1** (*med personsubj.*) demand (*ngt av ngn* s.th. of s.b.); *betalning* payment); (*bestämt yrka på*) insist upon; (*omilt kräva*) demand; (*göra anspråk på*) require (*att ngn skall veta* s.b. to know; *hövlighet av ngn* civlity of [*el.* from] s.b.); (*som sin rätt*) claim; ~ *räkenskap av ngn* call (bring) s.b. to account; ~ *skadeersättning* demand (claim) damages; *ha 10 pund att* ~ *av ngn* have a claim of 10 pounds on s.b. **2** (*med saksubj.*) *a*) (*erfordra*) require, want, call for, *b*) ([*på*]*bjuda*) prescribe, *c*) (*ta tid i anspråk*) take; *arbetet* ~*r stor noggrannhet* the work demands great care
fordr|an [ˣfɔ:r-] *r*, *i pl används fordringar* **1** demand (*på ngn* on s.b.); requirement (*på ngn* in s.b.) **2** (*penning-*) claim (*på ngn* on s.b.; *på 10 pund* of 10 pounds) **-ande** *a4* exacting **-as** *dep* be required (needed)
fordring [ˣfɔ:r-] *se fordran*; ~*ar a*) demands, (*förväntningar*) expectations, (*anspråk*) claims, *b*) (*tillgodohavanden*) claims, [*active*] debts;

osäkra ~ar doubtful claims, (*friare*) bad debts; *ha stora* ~ar *på livet* expect a lot of life; *ställa stora* ~ar *på* demand a great deal of, be exacting in one's demands on; *uppfylla* ~arna *för godkänd examen* satisfy the examiner[s *pl*] **fordringsägare** creditor

forell *s3* trout

form [-å-] **1** *s3* form; (*fason o.d.*) shape, cut; (*tillstånd*) state; *för* ~ens *skull* for form's sake, as a matter of form; *i* ~ *av a*) in [the] form of (*en roman* a novel), *b*) in the shape of (*en cirkel* a circle, *c*) in the state of (*is* ice); *i fast* (*flytande*) ~ in solid (fluid) form; *hålla mycket på* ~en stand on ceremony, be a stickler for etiquette; *i många* ~er *trivs det sköna* beauty appears in many guises **2** *s3, sport. o. bildl.* form; *inte vara i* ~ be out of form **3** *s2* (*gjut-*) mould; *kokk.* dish, tin

forma [-å-] form, mould (*äv. bildl.*); (*friare*) shape, model; ~ *en mening* frame a sentence

formaldehyd [ˣfårm-] *s3* formaldehyde

formalia [får'ma:-] *pl* formalitites

formalin [-å-] *s4, s3* formalin

formaliser|a [-å-] formalize **-ing** formalization

formal|ism [-å-] formalism **-ist** formalist **-istisk** [-'ist-] *a5* formalistic

formalitet [-å-] *s3* formality, matter of form; *utan* ~er without ceremony

forma|t [-å-] *s7* size, format; *bildl.* importance, weight **-tion** formation

formbar [-å-] *a1* formable; mouldable, plastic **-het** mouldability, plasticity, workability

formbröd tin [loaf]

formel ['fårr-] *s3* formula **formell** *a1* formal, conventional

formenlig [-e:-] *a5* correct [in form]

former|a [-å-] **1** *mil.*, ~ [*sig*] form **2** (*vässa*) sharpen **-are** sharpener **-ing** formation; (*vässning*) sharpening

form|fast non-deformable; ~*a jerseybyxor* jersey trousers that keep their shape **-fel** error in form **-fulländad** *a5* perfect in form **-fulländning** perfection of form **-förändring** modification of form; *konkr. äv.* deformation

formge design

formgiv|a *se formge* **-are** designer **-ning** [-ji:v-] designing, shaping; *konkr.* [creative] design

formgjut|a die-cast **-ning** die-casting

formidabel [fårmi'da:-] *a2* formidable

formligen [-å-] (*bokstavligen*) literally; (*rentav*) positively; (*helt enkelt*) simply

form|lära *språkv.* accidence **-lös** formless, shapeless; (*obestämd*) vague

form|ning [-å-] shaping, forming **-pressa** die--cast; press, mould **-pressning** die-casting; moulding **-rik** abundant in forms; (*om språk*) highly inflectional **-sak** matter of form, formality **-skön** beautiful in form, beautifully shaped **-sättning** *byggn.* casing, mould

formuler|a [-å-] formulate, word; ~ *frågor* frame questions **-ing** formulation; (*ordalydelse*) wording

formulär [-å-] *s7* form

forn [-o:-] *a5* former, earlier; (*-tida*) ancient **-borg** hillfort **-engelsk** Anglo-Saxon **-engelska** Old English, Anglo-Saxon **-forskare** archaeologist, antiquary **-forskning** archaeology,

archaeological research **-fynd** archaeological find **-grekisk, -grekiska** Ancient Greek **-historia** ancient history **-historisk** of ancient history **-högtysk, -högtyska** Old High German **-isländsk, -isländska** Old Icelandic **-kunskap** *se fornforskning* **-lämning** ancient monument; ~*ar* ancient remains **-minne** ancient monument, relic of antiquity **-minnesvård** preservation of ancient monuments **-nordisk, -nordiska** Old Norse **-sak** archaelogical relic **-svensk, -svenska** Old Swedish **-tid** prehistoric age (period); ~*en* antiquity; *i den grå* ~*en* in the dim and distant past **-tida** *oböjligt a* ancient

fors [-å-] *s2* **1** rapids (*pl*); cataract **2** (*friare o. bildl.*) stream, cascade, torrent **forsa** rush; (*friare*) gush; *en* ~*nde bäck* a torrent; *blodet* ~*de ur såret* the blood gushed from the wound; *regnet* ~*r ner* it rains cats and dogs **forsfarare** rapids shooter

forsk|a [-å-] search (*efter* for); *absol.* [carry out] research; ~ *i* (*undersöka*) inquire into, investigate **-ande** *a4* inquiring; (*prövande*) searching

forskar|begåvning gift for research; *pers.* gifted researcher **-bragd** triumph of research, scientific feat

forskar|e [-å-] [research] scientist, researcher; investigator (*i* of) **-flykt** brain drain **-grupp** group of researchers (research scientists) **-gärning** scientific achievement **-möda** painstaking research

forskning [-å-] research (*i* upon); (*naturvetenskap*) science; (*undersökning*) investigation (*i* into, on)

forsknings|anslag research grant **-anstalt** research institute **-arbete** research work **-centrum** research centre **-fält** field of research **-institut** *se -anstalt* **-resa** exploration expedition **-resande** explorer **-resultat** research findings (*pl*)

forsl|a [-å-] transport, convey, carry; ~ *bort* carry away, remove **-ing** carriage, transportation, conveyance

forst|mästare [-å-] [certified] forester, forest officer **-väsen** forestry organization

forsythia [får'sy:tia] *s1* forsythia

1 fort [-å-] *s7* (*fästning*) fort

2 fort [-o-] **I** *adv* (*i snabbt tempo*) fast; (*på kort tid, snabbt*) quickly, speedily; (*raskt*) rapidly; (*i* [*all*] *hast*) hastily; *det gick* ~ *för honom* it didn't take him long, he was quick about it, it was over quickly for him; *det går inte så* ~ *för mig att* I must take my time about (+ *ing-form*), I am rather slow at (+ *ing-form*); *han tröttnade* ~ he soon got tired, he tired easily; *gå lika* ~ *som ngn* keep pace with s.b.; *klockan går för* ~ the (my *etc.*) watch (clock) is fast **II** *interj* quick!, sharp!

forta [ˣforr-] *rfl* (*om klocka*) gain

fortbe|stå continue [to exist] **-stånd** continued existence

fortbild|a train (educate *etc.*) further; ~ *sig* continue one's training (education) **-ning** further training (education) **-ningskurs** extension (continuation) course

forte [ˣfårr-] *adv o. s6* forte **-piano** *adv o. s6* pianoforte]

fortfar|a continue, go on (*att sjunga* singing); (*hålla i*) keep on (*med* with); (*fortvara*) last **-ande** still

fortfärdig expeditious; nimble, quick

fortgå go on, proceed; (*fortsätta*) continue **-ende I** *s6* continuance **II** *a4* continued

fortifikation [-å-] fortification

fortifikations|förvaltning ~*en* [the Swedish] fortifications administration **-officer** military engineer

fortissimo [får'tiss-] *adv o. s6* fortissimo

fortkörning speeding [offence]

fort|leva live on; survive **-löpande** *a4* continuing, continuous; ~ *kommentar* running commentary

fortplant|a *v1* **1** (*om människor, djur, växter*) propagate, reproduce **2** (*friare o. bildl.*) transmit **3** *rfl* propagate [o.s., itself] (*äv. om ljud, ljus*); *eg. äv.* breed; (*om rykte*) spread; (*om sjukdom*) be transmitted, spread **-ning** propagation, breeding; transmission

fortplantnings|drift reproductive (propagative, procreative) instinct **-duglig** reproductive, procreative **-förmåga 1** procreative faculty **2** *fys.* power of transmission **-organ** reproductive organ

fortsatt *a4* continued; (*-löpande*) continuous; (*återupptagen*) resumed; (*ytterligare*) further

fortskaff|a transport, convey **-ningsmedel** means (*sg o. pl*) of conveyance (transport[ation])

fortskrida proceed; (*framskrida äv.*) advance

fortsätt|a 1 (*fortfara med*) continue; go on (proceed) with; (*efter uppehåll*) take up, resume; (*fortsätta o. fullfölja*) carry on **2** (*fortgå*) go on (continue) (*att spela* playing); (*efter uppehåll*) proceed; *fortsätt bara!* go ahead! **-ning** continuation; proceeding; ~ *följer* (*forts.*) to be continued; *i* ~*en* henceforth, from now on **-ningsvis** (*vidare*) further

fortuna [-ˣtu:-] *n*, **-spel** bagatelle

fort|vara continue [to exist] **-varo** *s5* continued existence

forum *s8* forum; quarter; *rätt* ~ *för* [the] proper authority for, the right place for

forwardskedja [ˣfå:rvards-] forward line

fosfat [-å-] *s7, s4* phosphate

fosfor [ˣfåssfår] *s2* phosphorus

fosforesc|ens [-'sens *el.* -'ʃens] *s3* phosphorescence **-ent** [-'sent *el.* -'ʃent] phosphorescent **-era** [-'se:- *el.* -'ʃe:-] phosphoresce **-erande** [-'se:- *el.* -'ʃe:-] phosphorescent

fosfor|förgiftning phosphorus poisoning **-syra** [orto]phosphoric acid **-tändsticka** phosphorus match

fosgen [fåss'je:n] *s3* phosgene

fossil [-å-] **I** *s7* fossil **II** *a5* fossil; ~*t bränsle* fossil fuel **-fynd** fossil find **-kraftverk** fossil-fuelled power station

fostbrödralag *s7* sworn brotherhood

foster ['fɔss-] *s7* fetus, foetus; *bildl.* offspring, product, creation

fosterbarn foster child

fosterfördriv|ande *a4* abortive, abortifacient **-are** abortionist **-ning** [criminal] abortion

foster|föräldrar foster parents **-hem** foster home **-hinna** fetal membrane **-jord** native soil **-land** [native] country

fosterlands|förrädare traitor [to one's country] **-förräderi** high treason **-kärlek** patriotism, love of one's country **-vän** patriot

fosterljud fetal heart sound

fosterländsk *a5* patriotic

foster|rörelse fetal movement **-utveckling** development (growth) of the fetus **-vatten** amniotic fluid

fostra bring up, rear; *bildl.* foster, breed **fostran** *r* bringing up *etc.*; (*upp-*) education; *fysisk* ~ physical training **fostrare** fosterer; (*friare*) trainer of the young

fot 1 *-en fötter* foot (*pl* feet); (*på glas*) stem; (*lamp-*) stand; *bildl.* footing, terms (*pl*), standing; ~*!* (*t. hund*) heel!; *lätt på* ~*en* light of foot, *bildl.* of easy virtue; *på resande* ~ on the move; *på stående* ~ instantly; *få fast* ~ get a footing; *försätta på fri* ~ set free; *gå till* ~*s* go on foot, walk; *leva på stor* ~ live in grand style, live it up; *stryka på* ~*en* give in (*för* to); *stå på god* ~ *med ngn* be on a friendly footing with s.b.; *inte veta på vilken* ~ *man skall stå* not know which leg to stand on; *han har inte satt sin* ~ *där* he has not set foot there, *neds.* he has not darkened the roof of that home (house *etc.*); *dra fötterna efter sig* drag one's feet (heels); *kasta sig för ngns fötter* fall down at a p.'s feet; *komma på fötter igen* get on to one's feet again, (*bli frisk*) be up and about again; *trampa under fötterna* trample underfoot; *vara kall om fötterna* have cold feet **2** *s9* (*längdmått*) foot

fota base; ~ *sig på* be based on

fotabjälle *s6*, *från hjässan till* ~*t* from top to toe (head to foot); cap-a-pie

fot|arbete *sport.* footwork **-bad** foot bath **-behandling** pedicure **-beklädnad** (*skor*) footwear, footgear **-boja** fetter, shackle; (*förr*) foot and chain **-boll** football; (*spelet*) [association] football, soccer; *vard.* footer; *AE.* soccer

fotbolls|domare referee **-fantast** football (*AE.* soccer) fan **-lag** football (*AE.* soccer) team **-förbund** football association; *AE.* soccer league **-match** football (*AE.* soccer) match **-plan** football (*AE.* soccer) ground **-spelare** football (*AE.* soccer) player, footballer **-tröja** *vard.* strip

fot|broms (*i bil*) foot (pedal) brake; brake pedal **-fel** foot fault **-folk** infantry **-fäste** foothold; (*insteg*) footing; *få* (*vinna*) ~ get (gain) a foothold (footing); *förlora* ~*t* lose one's foothold **-gavel** footboard **-gängare** [-jän-] pedestrian **-knöl** ankle **-kurtis** *vard.* footsie **-led** ankle joint **-not** footnote

foto *s6* photo (*pl* photos); *se fotografi* **-affär** camera shop; photographic dealer's **-album** *se fotografialbum* **-atelj é** photographic studio **-blixt** flashlight, flash **-cell** photocell, photoelectric cell **-elektricitet** photoelectricity **-elektrisk** [-'lekk-] photoelectric[al]

fotogen [-'ʃe:n] *s3, s4* paraffin[e] [oil]; *AE.* kerosene

fotogenisk [-'je:-] *a5* photogenic

fotogen|kök oil (paraffin, *AE.* kerosene) stove **-lampa** paraffin (*AE.* kerosene) lamp

fotograf *s3* photographer **-era** photograph; *absol. äv.* take photographs; ~ *sig* have one's photo (photograph) taken **-ering** [-'fe:-] photography; (*-erande*) photographing

fotografi *s4, s3* photograph, *vard.* photo; (*som konst*) photography **-album** photograph album

fotografisk [-'gra:-] *a5* photographic

fotogrammetr|i *s3* photogrammetry **-isk** [-'me:-] *a5* photogrammetric

fotogravyr photogravure

fotokem|i photochemistry **-isk** [-'çe:-] photochemical

fotokopi|a print; *se äv. fotostat*[*kopia*] **-era** photocopy **-ering** [-i'e:-] photocopying

fotolampa photoflood

fotoly|s *s3* photolysis **-tisk** *a5* photolytic

foto|meter [-'me:-] *s2* photometer **-metri** *s3* photometry **-metrisk** [-'me:-] *a5* photometric

foto|modell photographer's model **-montage** photomontage

foton [-'tå:n] *s3* photon

fotosfär photosphere

fotostat *s3*, **-kopia** photostat [copy], photocopy

foto|syntes photosynthesis **-sätta** filmset, photoset; *AE.* photocompose **-sättning** filmsetting; *AE.* photocomposition, phototypesetting **-terapi** phototherapy, phototherapeutics (*pl, behandlas som sg*) **-tropism** phototropism **-typi** (*metod*) photoengraving; (*kliché, tryck*) photoengraving, line block

fot|pall footstool, footrest **-riktig** ~*a skor* well-fitting shoes **-sack** *s2* foot muff

fotsdjup one foot deep

fot|sid reaching [down] to the (one's) feet **-soldat** foot soldier, infantryman **-spår** footprint, footmark; (*i sht bildl.*) footsteps (*pl*) **-steg** [foot]-step; (*på bil o.d.*) running board **-stöd** (*på t.ex. motorcykel*) footrest **-sula** sole [of a (the, one's) foot **-svamp** athlete's foot **-svett** *ha* ~ have sweaty feet (*pl*) **-valv** arch of the foot **-vandra** walk; hike **-vandring** walking tour; hike **-vård** pedicure **-vårta** verruca **-vänlig** ~*a skor* comfortable shoes **-ända** foot of the bed

fox|terrier [*fåkks-] fox terrier **-trot[t]** ['fåkks-] *s3* foxtrot

frack *s2* (*kostym*) dress suit; (*rock*) tail (dress) coat, tails (*pl*) **-skjorta** dress shirt **-skört** dress-coat tail

fradga I *s1* froth, foam; ~*n står om munnen på honom* he is frothing (foaming) at the mouth; *tugga* ~ foam with rage **II** *v1*, ~ [*sig*] foam, froth

fragil [-'ʃi:l *el.* -'gi:l] *a1* fragile

fragment *s7* fragment **-arisk** [-'ta:-] *a5* fragmentary, fragmental

frakt *s3* freight; (*t. lands*) goods (*pl*); (*skeppslast*) cargo, shipload, *äv.* freight; ~ *betald* freight (carriage) paid; ~[*en*] *betalas vid framkomsten* freight (carriage) forward **frakta** transport, convey; (*t. lands äv.*) carry; *AE. äv.* ship

frakt|avgift freight charge **-brev** *se fraktsedel* **-fart** carrying trade **-fartyg** freighter, cargo vessel **-flyg** cargo plane; air cargo service **-fritt** freight prepaid; *järnv.* carriage paid; ~ *London* freight (carriage) paid to London **-gods** goods (*pl*); *AE.* [regular] freight; (*motsats ilgods m.m.*) goods forwarded by goods train

fraktion [-k'ʃɒ:n] **1** (*grupp*) faction, group [of a party] **2** *kem.* fraction

fraktioner|a *kem.* fractionate; ~*d destillation* fractional distillation **-ing** fractioning **-ingskolonn** fractionating column

frakt|kostnad freight [charge, cost] **-sats** freight rate **-sedel** (*t. lands*) consignment note, waybill; (*t. sjöss*) bill of lading; *flyg.* air waybill (consignment note)

fraktur 1 *med.* fracture **2** *boktr.* Gothic, black letter **-stil** *se fraktur 2*

fram [-amm] *adv* **1** *rumsbet. a*) (*framåt, vidare*) on, along, forward, *b*) (*genom*) through, *c*) (*i dagen*) out, *d*) (*fram t. ngn, ngt*) up [to], *e*) (*t. målet*) there, *f*) (*framme*) further on, *g*) (*motsats bak*) in front; ~ *med det!* out with it!; *längre* ~ further on; *ända* ~ all the way there; *ända* ~ *till* right up to; *få sin vilja* ~ get one's own way; *gå* ~ *och tillbaka* go there and back, (*av o. an*) go to and fro; *gå rakt* ~ go (walk) straight on; *gå vägen* ~ walk on along the road; *hinna* ~ *i tid* get there in time; *om sanningen skall* ~ to tell the truth, to be quite honest; *stig* ~! come out (here)!; *solen tittar* ~ the sun peeps [out] **2** *tidsbet.* on; *litet längre* ~ a little later on; ~ *på dagen* later in the day; *till långt* ~ *på natten* until far into the night; *ända* ~ *till våra dagar* right up to the present day (to our own time); ~ *till 1990* up to 1990

fram|axel front axle **-ben** foreleg, front leg **-besvärja** conjure up **-bringa** bring forth; (*skapa*) create; (*ljud, säd etc.*) produce **-bära** take (*etc.*) [up] (*till* to); (*gåva o.d.*) present, offer; (*vad ngn sagt*) report, pass on; (*hälsning*) deliver, convey; (*lyckönskan, tacksägelse*) tender

fram|del forepart, front [part] **-deles** later on; (*i framtiden*) in the future **-driva** propel; *bildl.* urge on, drive **-drivning** propulsion

fram|emot [on] towards **-fall** *med.* prolapse **-faren** *a5* past; *i -farna dagar* in days gone by **-fart** (*friare*) rampaging[s *pl*], sweep; (*ödeläggelse*) ravaging[s *pl*]; (*körning*) reckless driving **-flytta** move forward; (*uppskjuta*) postpone, put off **-flyttning** postponement **-fot** forefoot; *visa -fötterna* show one's paces **-fusig** *a1* pushing, bumptious, forward **-fusighet** pushingness *etc.* **-föda** bring forth; give birth to

framför I *prep* **1** (*rumsbet., äv. bildl.*) before, in front of; (*framom*) ahead of; *mitt* ~ *näsan på ngn* straight in front of s.b., right under a p.'s nose **2** (*om företräde a*) (*i vikt, värde*) above, ahead of, *b*) (*hellre än*) preferably (in preference) to, rather than; ~ *allt* above all (everything); ~ *alla andra* of all others, above all the rest; ~ *allt gäller detta om* this applies particularly to; *fördra te* ~ *kaffe* prefer tea to coffee **II** *adv* in front; ahead

framför|a *se föra fram 2* (*uppföra, uppvisa*) present, produce **3** (*överbringa*) convey, deliver, give; (*anföra*) state, put forward **-ande** *s6* **1** (*av motorfordon*) conveyance **2** (*anförande*) delivery; (*av teaterpjäs o.d.*) performance

fram|gaffel (*på cykel*) front fork **-gent** [-je:-] henceforth, for (in) the future; *allt* ~ ever after

fram|gå *bildl.* be clear (evident); *härav* ~*r att* from this we conclude that, (*friare*) it appears from this that; *av vad han säger* ~*r* it appears from what he says; *av Ert brev* ~*r att* we see (understand) from your letter that; *det -gick tydligt att* it was made very clear that; **-gång** *s2* success; *med* ~ (*äv.*) successfully; *utan* ~ (*äv.*) unsuccessfully **-gångsrik** successful

fram|hjul front wheel **-hjulsdrift** front-wheel drive **-hjulsinställning** alignment of front wheels

fram|hålla (*framhäva*) give prominence (call attention) to; (*betona*) [lay] stress [on], emphasize; (*påpeka*) declare, say; ~ *nödvändighten av* emphasize the necessity of; *jfr framhäva* **-härda** persist, persevere **-häva** *bildl.* hold up, bring out; *jfr framhålla* **-hävande** *s6* holding up *etc.*; *med* ~ *av* [in] bringing out

fram|ifrån from the front; *ett hus sett* ~ the front view of a house **-ilande** *s6* rushing forwards

framkall|a 1 (*i minnet, för tanken*) recall **2** (*uppkalla t. försvar o.d.*) call up **3** *foto.* develop **4** *bildl.* (*frambringa*) call forth, provoke, evoke; (*förorsaka*) cause; (*åstadkomma*) bring about, give rise to; (*uppväcka*) arouse, raise **-ning** *foto.* developing, development **-ningsvätska** *foto.* developer

fram|kant front edge **-kasta** *bildl.* throw out; (*idé*) put forward, suggest; (*tanke*) bring up; (*omnämna*) mention; ~ *beskyllningar* bring forward (*starkare*: hurl) accusations; *ett löst* ~*t påstående* a haphazard statement

fram|komlig [-å-] *a1* (*om väg*) passable, trafficable; (*om vatten*) navigable; (*friare*) practicable; *bildl.* feasible **-komma 1** *se komma fram* **2** (*friare o. bildl.*) come out, appear; ~ *med* bring forward, produce; *det har -kommit önskemål om att* wishes have been expressed that **-komst** [-å-] *s3* **1** (*fortkomst*) advance, progress **2** (*ankomst*) arrival; *att betalas vid* ~*en* charges forward, cash on delivery

framkörning driving up

fram|laddare muzzle-loader **-leva** live; ~ *sina dagar* pass one's days **-liden** *a5* (*avliden*) past; *den -lidne...* the late... **-locka** bring (draw) forth; (*upplysningar, nyheter*) elicit **-lykta** headlight **-lägga** *bildl.* (*framkomma med*) put (bring) forward; (*anföra*) adduce; (*förete*) present; (*förslag*) table; ~ *bevis* produce evidence; ~ *för* produce before, submit to **-länges** [-län-] forwards; *åka* ~ (*i tåg*) sit (travel) facing the engine, (*i buss etc.*) sit (travel) facing forward (the front)

fram|mana *bildl.* call forth, evoke; (*frambesvärja*) conjure up **-marsch** advance; *bildl.* advancement, progress; *stadd på* ~ advancing, making headway **-matning** feed

framme 1 in front **2** (*vid målet*) at one's destination, there; *när vi var* ~ when we got there; *nu är vi* ~ here we are **3** (*framlagd o.d.*) out; on view; (*ej undanlagd*) about; *låta ngt ligga* ~ leave s.th. about; (*till hands*) ready, at hand; *har pojkarna varit* ~? is it the boys who have done it (been at work)?; *när olyckan är* ~ when things go wrong **4** *hålla sig* ~ push o.s. forward, keep o.s. to the fore

frammumla mutter, mumble

framom I *adv* ahead, in advance **II** *prep* before, ahead of, in advance of

fram|pressa *bildl.* extract (*ur* out of); (*tårar*) squeeze out; (*ljud*) utter, ejaculate **-provocera**

provoke **-på I** *prep* **1** (*om rum*) in front of, in (on) the front part of **2** (*om tid*) a little later; *till långt* ~ *natten* far into the night **II** *adv* in [the] front

fram|rusande *a4* (*om vatten*) gushing; (*framåtrusande*) onrushing **-ryckning** advance

fram|sida front; (*på check, sedel o.d.*) face; (*på mynt*) obverse **-skjutande** *a4* projecting, protruding; prominent **-skjuten** *a5* advanced; *bildl.* prominent **-skrida** (*om tid, arbete o.d.*) progress, advance **-skriden** *a5* advanced; *tiden är långt* ~ it is getting late **-skymta** *se skymta fram*; *låta* ~ give an intimation **-släpa** ~ *sitt liv* drag on one's existence **-smygande** *komma* ~ creep along **-springande** *se framskjutande*; *komma* ~ come running up **-stamma** stammer out (forth) **-steg** progress, advance[ment]; *göra* ~ make progress (headway)

framstegs|fientlig reactionary, anti-progressive **-man** progressive **-parti** progressive party **-vänlig** progressive

fram|stormande *se framrusande* **-stupa** flat, headlong, prostrate

framstå stand (come) out (*som* as); appear **-ende** prominent; (*högt ansedd*) eminent; (*förträfflig*) distinguished

framställa I 1 (*återge, visa*) represent; show; (*konstnärligt*) depict, represent, draw; (*på scen*) [im]personate **2** (*skildra*) describe; (*beteckna*) represent **3** (*framföra, komma fram med*) bring (put) forward; ~ *en fråga* put a question; ~ *klagomål* lodge complaints; ~ *krav* make demands; (*uttala, ge uttryck åt*) express, state; ~ *önskemål* express a wish, state requirements **4** (*tillverka*) produce, make; (*fabriksmässigt*) manufacture; (*utvinna*) extract; *börja* ~ put in hand **II** *rfl* represent o.s.; (*uppstå, yppa sig*) arise

framställan *r, se framställning*; *på* ~ *av* at the instance of

framställning 1 (*i bild*) representation, picture, depiction **2** (*skildring*) description, rendering; (*redogörelse*) account; (*muntlig*) narration **3** (*framställningssätt*) a) (*författares*) style b) (*talares*) delivery, c) (*talares, konstnärs*) presentation, presentment, d) *teat.* rendering, interpretation **4** (*förslag*) proposal, proposition; (*hemställan*) petition, request **5** (*tillverkning*) production; (*fabriksmässig*) manufacture; (*utvinning*) extraction

framställnings|förmåga descriptive power, power of [re]presentation **-kostnad** cost of production **-metod, -sätt** method of production, manufacturing process

fram|stöna (*utter*) groan[ingly] **-stöt** *mil. o. bildl.* drive, thrust; attack, assault **-synt** [-y:-] *a1* **1** (*förutseende*) far-seeing, far-sighted **2** (*klärvoajant*) gifted with second sight **-synthet** [-y:-] **1** foresight **2** [gift of] second sight **-säga 1** (*uttala, yttra*) articulate, pronounce **2** (*deklamera*) recite **-säte** front seat **-tand** front tooth **-tass** forepaw

framtid future; *för all* ~ for all time (evermore); *det får* ~*en utvisa* time will show; *för* ~*en måste jag* in (for the) future I shall have to; *ha* ~*en för sig* have the future before you; *saken får ställas på* ~*en* it must wait until later, the matter must be postponed; *tänka på sin* ~ think of one's [future] career **framtida** *oböjligt a* future **framtids|dröm** dream of the future **-forskare** futurologist **-forskning** futurology **-man** coming man **-mål** prospective aim, future goal **-plats** position (job) offering good (excellent) prospects **-studier** futurology **-tro** belief in the future **-utsikter** [future] prospects **-vision** vision of the future

framtill in front

framtoning image

framträd|a 1 *se träda fram* **2** (*uppträda*) appear (*inför offentligheten* before the public; *på scenen* upon the stage) **3** *bildl.* make one's appearance, appear; (*ur det fördolda*) come into sight (view); (*om anlag, egenskap o.d.*) assert (display) itself; (*avteckna sig*) stand out; *låta* ~ bring out (into relief) **-ande I** *s6* appearance **II** *a4* prominent, outstanding, salient

fram|tränga penetrate, force one's (its *etc.*) way **-tung** heavy forward (in front); *flyg.* nose-heavy **-tvinga** extort; [en]force; (*kräva*) necessitate **-vagn** front part of the chassis **-vagnsupphängning** front suspension **-visa** show [up]

framåt ['framm-] **I** *adv* **1** *rumsbet.* ahead; (*vidare framåt*) on[ward], onwards; forward[s]; *fortsätt* ~*!* keep straight on!; *gå* ~ *a*) (*promenera*) walk along (*emot* towards; *till* to), *b*) (*utvecklas*) go ahead, [make] progress; *se rakt* ~ look straight ahead **2** *tidsbet.* ahead, to come, into the future; *gå raskt* ~ make rapid strides; *komma* ~ *i världen* get on in the world **II** *prep* **1** (*i rummet*) [on] toward[s]; ([*fram*] *längs*) [on] along **2** (*i tiden*) [on] toward[s] **III** *interj* on!, onward!, forward!; *sjö.* ahead!

framåt|anda go-ahead spirit **-böjd** *a1*, **-lutad** *a5* bent forward[s]; *gå* ~ walk with a stoop **-skridande I** *s6* progress, advance **II** *a4* progressive **-strävande** *a4, bildl.* pushing, go-ahead

fram|ända front end **-över I** *prep* out (away) across **II** *adv* forwards; onwards, ahead

franc [fraŋ] *s9* franc

franciskan *s3*, **franciskaner** [-'ka:-] *s9* Franciscan [monk] **-orden** Franciscan Order

francium ['frans-] *s8* francium

1 frank *a1* frank, open, straightforward

2 frank *s3* Frank

Franken ['frann-] *n* Franconia

franker|a (*frimärka*) stamp **-ing** stamping **-ingsmaskin** franking machine

frankisk ['frann-] *a5* Frankish, Franconian

franko ['frann-] post-free, postpaid; *hand.* franco, free of charge (carriage) **-stämpel** postage impression **-tecken** postage stamp

Frankrike ['frank-] *n* France

frans *s2*, **fransa** *v1* fringe; ~ *sig* fray **fransad** *a5* fringed **fransig** *a1* (*trasig*) frayed

fransk *a1* French; ~*a fönster* French windows (*AE.* doors); ~ *lilja* (*her.*) fleur-de-lis, *äv.* lily of France **franska 1** (*språk*) French **2** (*bröd*) French roll; (*lång-*) French loaf

fransk|bröd *se franska 2* **—engelsk** Franco-British; French-English **-klassicism** French classicism **—svensk** Franco-Swedish; French-Swedish **-talande** French-speaking, Francophone **-vänlig** pro-French, Francophil[e]

fransman Frenchman; *-männen a*) (*hela nationen*) the French, *b*) (*några fransmän*) the Frenchmen **fransos** *s3*, *se fransman* **fransysk** *a5* French; ~ *visit* flying visit (call) **fransyska** [-ˣsyska] **1** (*kvinna*) Frenchwoman **2** *kokk.* rump-steak piece **fransäs** [fraŋ- *el.* frann-] *s3*

frapp|ant [-'ant *el.* -'aŋt] *al* striking **-era** strike; surprise **-erande** [-'pe:-] *a4* striking; surprising **1 fras** *s3* (*uttryck*) phrase (*äv. mus.*); *stående* ~ current phrase; *tomma* ~*er* empty phrases, mere twaddle, hollow words **2 fras** *s7* (*-ande*) rustle, rustling **frasa** rustle

fras|eologi *s3* phraseology **-era** phrase **-ering** [-'se:] phrasing **-fri** without circumlocution; straightforward; natural

frasig *al* crisp

fras|makare chatterbox; windbag **-radikal** high-flown (high-sounding) radical

frasvåffla crisp waffle

fraterniser|a fraternize **-ing** fraternization

fred *s3* peace; *hålla* (*sluta*) ~ keep the (conclude) peace; *leva i* ~ *med* live at peace with; *lämna ngn i* ~ leave s.b. alone; *jag får inte vara i* ~ *för honom* he never leaves me in peace

freda protect (*mot, för* from, against); ~ *sitt samvete* appease one's conscience; *med* ~*t samvete* with a clear conscience; ~ *sig för misstanken att* banish the suspicion from one's mind that

fredag ['fre:-] Friday; ~*en den 13 april* on Friday, April 13th, (*i början av brev o.d.*) Friday, April 13th; *om* ~*arna* on Fridays

fredlig [-e:-] *al* peaceful; (*fridsam*) gentle, inoffensive; *på* ~ *väg* in a peaceful way, by peaceful means **-het** peacefulness

fredlös outlawed; *en* ~ an outlaw

freds|anbud peace offer **-appell** call (appeal) for peace **-domare** justice of the peace **-duva** dove of peace **-forskare** peace researcher **-forskning** peace research **-fot** *ställa krigsmakten på* ~ restore armed forces to peacetime strength **-fördrag** peace treaty **-förhandlingar** peace negotiations **-konferens** peace conference **-kongress** peace congress **-kår** peace corps **-kårist** member of peace corps **-mäklare** peacemaker, mediator **-pipa** peace pipe, calumet **-plikt** peace obligation **-pris** peace prize **-rörelse** peace movement **-slut** conclusion of peace **-strävan[de]** effort to achieve peace **-tid** peacetime, time of peace **-traktat** peace treaty **-trevare** peace feeler **-underhandlingar** peace negotiations **-vilja** willingness to make peace **-villkor** peace terms **-älskande** peaceloving

fregatt *s3* frigate **-fågel** frigate bird, man-of-war bird

frejd *s3* character, reputation **-ad** *a5* renowned, celebrated

frejdig *al* spirited; (*oförskräckt*) bold, intrepid, plucky

frekvens *s3* frequency; (*av besökande etc.*) patronage **-modulering** frequency modulation **-undersökning** activity (work) sampling

frekvent *al* frequent, common **-era** patronize, frequent

frene|si *s3* frenzy **-tisk** [-'ne:-] *a5* frantic, frenzied; frenetic

freno|log phrenologist **-logi** *s3* phrenology

freon [-'å:n] *s4* freon

fresia *s1* freesia

fresk *s3* fresco **freskomålning** painting in fresco; *konkr. äv.* fresco

fresnellins [fre'nell-] Fresnel lens

frest|a 1 (*söka förleda*) tempt **2** (*pröva, försöka*) try; ~ *lyckan* try one's luck **3** (*utsätta för ansträngning*) try, strain; *tekn.* strain **-ande** *a4* tempting **-are** tempter **-else** temptation; *falla för ~n* give way (yield) to temptation **-erska** temptress

freudian *s3* Freudian

fri *a1* **1** free; (*oavhängig*) independent; (*öppen, oskymd*) open; (*i frihet*) at large; *på* ~ *hand* by hand, (*oförberett*) offhand[ed]; ~ *höjd* headroom, headway; ~ *idrott* athletics (*pl o. sg*); ~ *kost* free board; *i* ~*a luften* (*det fria*) in the open air; ~*tt val* option, free choice; *av* ~ *vilja* of one's own accord (will), voluntarily; *förklara ordet* ~*tt* declare the meeting open [for discussion]; *försätta på* ~ *fot* set free; *gå* ~ *a*) (*vara på fri fot*) be at large, *b*) (*bli frikänd*) be acquitted, *c*) (*undkomma*) escape, *d*) (*från obehag*) get off, dodge [trouble *etc.*]; *gå* ~ *för misstankar* be cleared of suspicion; *göra sig* ~ *från* rid o.s. of; *ha* ~ *tillgång till* have free access to; *lämna ngn* ~*tt spelrum* allow s.b. (let s.b. have) ample scope; *det står dig* ~*tt att* you are free (at liberty) to; *svära sig* ~ *från* swear o.s. out of (free from) **2** (*oupptagen*) vacant, unoccupied

1 fria 1 propose (*till* to) **2** ~ *till ngns gunst* court a p.'s favour, curry favour with

2 fria (*frikänna*) acquit; ~*nde dom* verdict of not guilty, acquittal; ~ *sig från misstankar* clear o.s. of suspicion; *hellre* ~ *än fälla* give s.b. the benefit of the doubt

friarbrev written proposal of marriage

friar|e suitor (*till* for the hand of); *ibl.* admirer **-strät** *vara på* ~ be courting

fri|biljett *järnv.* pass; *teat. o.d.* free ticket, complimentary ticket **-bord** freeboard **-boren** free born **-brev** *försäkr.* paid-up policy **-brottning** freestyle wrestling; catch-as-catch-can **-bytare** freebooter **-bärande** overhung

frid *s3* peace; (*lugn*) tranquillity, serenity; *allting är* ~ *och fröjd* everything is fine (all serene); *vad i* ~*ens namn nu då?* whatever's happening now?, what's up now?

fridag free day, day off; (*tjänstefolks*) day out

frid|full peaceful **-lysa** place under the protection of the law, protect by law **-lysning** protection by law **-sam** *a1* peaceable

fridsfurste *F—n* the Prince of Peace

fridstörare disturber of the peace; (*friare*) intruder

frielev nonpaying pupil

frieri proposal [of marriage]

fri|exemplar free (complimentary, presentation) copy **-flykt** *rymdtekn.* free flight

frige liberate, [set] free; release; (*upphäva ransonering*) deration; (*från beslag*) derequisition; (*slav*) emancipate; *frigivna varor* free-listed goods

frigid [-'gi:d] *a1*, *n* undviks frigid **-itet** frigidity

fri|giva *se frige* **-givning** [-ji:-] liberation, setting free, release; derationing; derequisition; emancipation

frigjord *a1* emancipated **-het** (*i sätt*) free and easy manners (*pl*); emancipation

frigång *tekn.*, *gå på* ~ freewheel

frigör|a liberate, set free (*äv. kem.*); free, release; (*göra disponibel*) make available; (*från slaveri*) emancipate; ~ *sig* free (*etc.*) o.s., *kem.* [be] disengage[d] **-else** liberation *etc.*; *kvinnans* ~ the emancipation of woman **-elsehastighet** *se flykthastighet*

fri|hamn free port **-handel** free trade **-handelsområde** free trade area **-handsteckning** freehand drawing

friherr|e baron; (*i Storbritannien som titel äv.*) lord **-inna** baroness; (*i Storbritannien som titel äv.*) lady **-lig** *a5* baronial

frihet 1 freedom (*motsats tvång, fångenskap*) liberty; (*från skyldighet*) exemption; (*oavhängighet*) independence; (*fritt spelrum*) scope, latitude; ~, *jämlikhet, broderskap* liberty, equality, fraternity; *poetisk* ~ poetic licence; *skänka ngn* ~*en* give s.b. his freedom; *återfå* ~*en* regain one's freedom (liberty) **2** (*privilegium*) privilege; (*självsvåld*) liberty; *fri- och rättigheter* rights and privileges; *ta sig* ~*er mot ngn* take liberties with s.b.; *ta sig* ~*en att* take the liberty of (+ *ing-form*) **frihets|hjälte** champion of liberty **-kamp** struggle for liberty **-krig** war of independence **-kämpe** fighter for freedom, patriot **-kärlek** love of liberty **-rörelse** liberty movement; (*motståndsrörelse*) resistance movement **-straff** imprisonment, detention, confinement **-strävan** effort to attain independence **-tiden** *hist.*, *ung.* the Period of Liberty, the period 1718-1772 **-älskande** freedom-loving, liberty-loving

fri|hjul freewheel **-hult** *s7, s2* fender **-idrott** athletics (*pl o. sg*)

frikadell *s3, kokk.* forcemeat ball, quenelle

frikall|a (*från plikt, ansvar*) exempt (*äv. mil.*); (*från löfte*) release **-else** exemption; release

frikassé *s3* fricassee (*på* of)

frikast *sport.* free throw

frikativa ['fricka-] *s1* fricative

frikoppl|a declutch **-ing** declutching, disengagement of the clutch; *konkr.* slipping clutch

frikostig [-å-] *a1* liberal, generous; (*om gåva äv.*) handsome **-het** liberality, generosity

friktion [-k'ʃo:n] friction

friktions|fri frictionless; *bildl.* smooth **-koefficient** friction coefficient **-koppling** friction clutch **-motstånd** frictional resistance

frikyrk|a Free Church; (*i Storbritannien äv.*) Nonconformist Church **-lig** Free-Church

frikyrko|församling Nonconformist Church **-predikant** Nonconformist (Free-Church) preacher **-präst** Nonconformist (Free-Church) minister

frikänn|a acquit (*från* of); find (pronounce) not quilty **-ande I** *s6* acquittal; *yrka* ~ plead not guilty **II** *a4*, ~ *dom* verdict of not guilty

frilans *s2* freelance[r] **-a** freelance **-are** freelance [r] **-basis** *på* ~ on a freelance basis

frilista *s1* free list

frilla *s1* paramour

frilufts|bad open-air pool; public beach **-guds-tjänst** open-air service **-liv** outdoor life **-människa** sportsman, lover of open-air life **-teater** open-air theatre

frilägga lay bare, uncover

frimodig frank, candid; (*modig*) fearless **-het** frankness *etc.*

fri|murare Freemason **-murarloge** *s3* Masonic lodge **-murarorden** Free and Accepted Masons; Masonic order **-mureri** Freemasonry; *bildl.* freemasonry

frimärk|a stamp **-e 1** *post.* [postage] stamp **2** *sjö.* clearing line

frimärks|album stamp album **-automat** stamp [-vending] machine **-häfte** book of stamps **-samlare** stamp collector **-samling** stamp collection

fri- och rättigheter rights and privileges

fri|passagerare stowaway; (*med fribiljett*) *vard.* deadhead **-plats** (*i skola*) free place; *teat. o.d.* free seat **-religiös** dissenting

1 fris *s3, byggn.* frieze

2 fris *s3* (*folkslag*) Fri[e]sian

frisbee ['frisbi:] *s3* Frisbee

frisedel *mil.* exemption warrant

friser|a *bildl.* doctor [up]; ~ *ngn* dress a p.'s hair **-ing** hairdressing **-salong** hairdresser's, hairdressing saloon

fri|sim freestyle swimming **-sinnad** *a5* liberal, broad-minded; *polit.* Liberal

frisisk ['fri:-] *a5* Fri[e]sian; *F~a öarna* Frisian Islands **frisiska** ['fri:-] **1** (*språk*) Fri[e]sian **2** (*kvinna*) Fri[e]sian woman

frisk *a1* **1** (*sund, felfri*) sound; (*ej sjuklig*) healthy; (*som pred.fylln.*: *ej sjuk*) well; ~ *och kry* hale and hearty; ~ *och stark* strong and well; ~ *som en nötkärna* [as] sound as a bell **2** (*ny, bibehållen*) fresh; (*kall*) cold; (*uppfriskande*) refreshing; (*bitande*) keen; ~*a krafter* renewed strength; *hämta* ~ *luft* get some [fresh] air; *bevara ngt i* ~*t minne* have a vivid recollection of s.th.; ~*t mod!* cheer up!; *med* ~*t mod* with a will; *vara vid* ~*t mod* be of good cheer; ~ *smak* a refreshing taste; ~*t vatten* cold water; *se* ~ *ut* look well

friska *vinden* ~*r* [*i*] the wind is freshening; ~ *upp minnet av* refresh one's memory of; ~ *upp sina kunskaper* brush up (refresh) one's knowledge

friskara *mil.* free company

frisk|förklara *se friskskriva* **-het** freshness *etc.* **-intyg** certificate of health

frisklufts|intag fresh-air intake **-ventil** fresh-air ventilator

frisk|na ~ *till* recover **-skriva** declare fit; *vard.* give a clean bill of health **-sportare** [-å-] fitness freak, health nut

friskt *adv* freshly *etc.*; *vard.* (*duktigt*) ever so [much], like anything; *det blåser* ~ there is a fresh (strong) breeze blowing

frisk|us [-friss-] *s2, han är en riktig* ~ he is always full of beans **-vård** prophylaxis

friskytt charmed-bullet marksman

fri|slag, **-spark** *sport.* free hit (kick)

frispråkig *a1* outspoken **-het** outspokenness

frist *s3* respite, grace; time limit, deadline

fri|stad [place of] refuge, sanctuary, asylum; resort (*för* of) **-stat** free state **-stund** spare (leisure) time **-stående** *a4* detached, standing alone; ~ *gymnastik* freestanding exercises (*pl*), Swedish drill (exercises *pl*, gymnastics *pl*)

friställ|a release; (*permittera*) lay off; *-d arbetskraft* released manpower, redundant labour **-ning** lay-off

frisyr *s3* (*dam-*) hairstyle, coiffure; *vard.* hairdo; (*herr-*) haircut **frisör** barber, hairdresser **frisörska** hairdresser

frita[ga] exempt, release; ~ *sig från ansvar* disclaim any responsibility

fritera deep-fry

fritid spare (leisure) time; *på* ~*en* in leisure hours **fritids|aktivitet** leisure-time activity **-båt** pleasure boat **-gård**, **-hem** youth recreation centre **-hus** leisure house (cottage), holiday cottage **-kläder** casual clothes, sportswear **-pedagog** youth worker **-problem** leisure problem **-sysselsättning** spare-time occupation, hobby

fritt *adv* freely; (*öppet*) openly; *tala* ~ speak openly (frankly); (*gratis*) free; ~ *banvagn* (*kaj, ombord*) free on rail (alongside [ship], on board); ~ *fabrik* ex works; ~ *förfoga över* have entirely at one's disposal; *huset ligger* ~ the house stands on open ground (commands a free view); *historien är* ~ *uppfunnen* the story is a pure invention

frityr *s3, se flottyr*

fri|tänkare freethinker **-vakt** *sjö.* off-duty watch; *ha* ~ be off duty **-vikt** *flyg.* free luggage allowance

frivillig voluntary, optional; *en* ~ (*mil.*) a volunteer **-het** voluntariness; (*fri vilja*) free will **-kår** volunteer corps

frivilligt *adv* voluntarily, of one's own free will; optionally

frivol [-'å:l] *a1* (*lättsinnig*) flippant; (*oanständig*) indecent **-itet** *s3* **1** flippancy; indecency **2** ~*er* (*ett slags spets*) tatting (*sg*); *slå* ~*er* do tatting

frivolt somersault

frivård noninstitutional care

frodas *dep* thrive, flourish; *bildl.* be rife, grow rampant

frodig *a1* (*om växt o. bildl.*) luxuriant; (*om pers. o. djur*) fat, plump **-het** luxuriance *etc.*

from [-omm] *a1* **1** (*gudfruktig*) pious; (*andäktig*) devout, religious; ~*ma önskningar* pious hopes, idle wishes **2** (*saktmodig*) quiet, gentle; (*om hund*) good-tempered; ~ *som ett lamm* [as] gentle as a lamb

fromage [-'ma:ʒ] *s5* mousse

fromhet 1 piety **2** quietness *etc.*

froml|a be sanctimonious **-eri** sanctimoniousness, hypocrisy

from|ma *oböjligt s, till* ~ *för* for the benefit of **-sint** *a1* gentle

fronder|a [frånd-] *polit.* oppose authority [of one's party]; rebel **-ing** faction politics; dissention

frondör [frånd-] rebel

front [frånt *el.* frånt] *s3* front; *göra* ~ *mot* face, *bildl.* stand up against

frontal *a5* frontal **-angrepp** frontal attack **-kollision**, **-krock** head-on collision

frontespis *s3, byggn.* front gable; frontispiece (*äv. boktr.*)

front|förändring change of front (*bildl.* tactics)
-linje front [line] **-matad** front-loading **-soldat**
combat soldier **-tjänst** active service (*särsk. AE.*
duty)

frosch [-å-] *s3* nut, frog (*särsk. AE.*)

1 frossa [-å-] *s1*, *med.* ague; (*malaria*) malaria;
ha ~ have the shivers

2 frossa [-å-] *v1* **1** *eg.* gormandize; gorge (*på* on)
2 *bildl.* revel (*i* in)

frossare [-å-] glutton (*på* of), gormandizer (*på*
on); reveller (*i* in)

frossbrytning fit of shivering (ague)

frosseri [-å-] gluttony; gormandizing *etc.*

frost [-å-] *s3* frost **frosta** *~ av* defrost

frost|bildning frost formation **-biten** *a5* frost-
bitten **-fjäril** winter moth **-fri** frostless **-härdig**
frost-resistant, frostproof

frost|ig *a1* frosty **-knöl** chilblain **-natt** frosty
night **-skada** frost injury **-skadad** *a5* damaged
by frost **-skyddsvätska** antifreeze

frotté *s3* towelling, terry cloth **-handduk** Turkish (terry) towel

frotter|a rub, chafe; *~ sig med ngn* hobnob with
s.b. **-ing** rubbing, chafing

fru *s2* (*gift kvinna*) married woman; (*hustru*) wife;
(*titel*) Mrs.; *~ Fortuna* Dame Fortune; *Vår ~* Our
Lady; *~n i huset* the lady of the house; *vad önskar
~n?* what would you like, Madam?, can I help
you, Madam?

fruga *s1*, *~n* the (*my etc.*) missis (missus), the
little woman

frugal *a1* frugal

frukost ['frukkåst] *s2* (*morgonmål*) breakfast;
(*lunch*) lunch; *äta* [*ägg till*] *~* have [eggs for]
breakfast **-bord** breakfast table **-bricka** breakfast tray **-dags** *adv*, *det är ~* it is time for breakfast; *vid ~* at breakfast time **-era** have breakfast
-middag brunch **-rast** *se lunchrast* **-rum** breakfast room

frukt *s3* **1** fruit (*äv. koll.*); (*jordbruksprodukter
äv.*) yield; *bära ~* (*äv. bildl.*) [bear] fruit, fructify;
sätta ~ (*äv. bildl.*) form fruit **2** *bildl.* fruit[s *pl*]
; (*resultat*) consequence, result; *njuta ~en av sin
möda* enjoy the fruits of one's labour

frukta fear; (*starkare*) dread; (*vara rädd för*) be
afraid of; *en ~d motståndare* a dreaded adversary; *~ för* (*hysa fruktan för*) fear, dread, (*dra sig
för*) be afraid of, shun; *man ~r för hans liv* they
fear for his life

fruktaffär fruit shop, fruiterer's [shop]

fruktan *r* fear (*för* of); (*starkare*) dread (*för* of);
(*skrämsel*) fright (*för* of); (*oro*) apprehension,
anxiety (*för* about); *av ~ för* for fear of; *hysa ~
för* be in fear of, (*hysa respekt*) stand in awe of;
injaga ~ hos ngn inspire s.b. with fear

fruktansvärd *a1* terrible, fearful; (*förfärlig*)
dreadful; (*svagare*) formidable; (*friare*) terrific

frukt|assiett fruit plate **-bar** *a1* fertile; *bildl. äv.*
fruitful; (*om jordmån*) productive, rich **-barhet**
fertility; fruitfulness; productivity **-barhetskult**
fertility cult **-bärande** fruit-bearing, fructifer-
ous; (*friare*) fruitful, advantageous **-fluga** *se
borrfluga* **-handlare** fruiterer

frukt|ig *a1* fruity **-kniv** fruit knife **-konserv**
tinned (*AE.* canned) fruit **-kött** pulp **-lös** fruitless; *bildl. äv.* unavailing, futile **-odlare** fruit

grower **-odling 1** *abstr.* fruit growing **2** *konkr.*
fruit farm

frukt|os [-'å:s] *s3* fructose, fruit sugar **-saft** fruit
juice **-sallad** fruit salad **-salt** fruit salts (*pl*)

fruktsam *a1* fruitful (*äv. bildl.*); (*om kvinna*) fertile; (*alstringsrik*) prolific, fecund **-het** fruitfulness; fertility; fecundity

frukt|skål fruit bowl **-socker** *se fruktos* **-träd**
fruit tree, fruiter **-trädgård** [fruit] orchard
-ämne *bot.* ovary

fruntimmer *s7* woman; *neds.* female

fruntimmers|karl ladies' (lady's) man, ladykill-
er **-veckan** *ung.* Ladies' Week, the period July
18-24

frusa gush forward (out)

frus|en *a3* **1** frozen; (*om växt, gröda o.d.*) blight-
ed by frost, frostbitten; *kokk.* chilled; *-et kött*
cold-storaged meat **2** (*kall*) cold; (*genomfrusen
äv.*) chilled; *vara ~ av sig* be sensitive to cold,
vard. be a chilly mortal **-it** *sup. av frysa*

frust|a snort **-ning** snort[ing]

frustr|ation frustration **-era** frustrate **-ering**
[-'re:-] *r* frustration

Frygien ['fry:g-] *n* Phrygia **fryg|ier** ['fry:g-] *s9*,
-isk ['fry:g-] *a5* Phrygian; *-isk mössa* Phrygian
cap

fryntlig *a1* genial; jovial

frys *s2*, *se frysbox, frysfack, frysskåp*

frys|a *frös frusit* (*i bet. frysa matvaror o. frysa till
is äv. v3*) freeze; (*känna kyla*) be (feel) cold;
(*skadas av frost*) get frostbitten; *~ till is* freeze [to
ice]; *~ öronen av sig* get one's ears frostbitten; *jag
-er* I am cold; *jag -er om fötterna* my feet are cold
(freezing); *det har frusit i natt* there was a frost
last night; *~ fast i* get frozen fast in; *~ ihjäl* get
frozen to death; *~ inne* be (get) icebound; *~ ner*
(*mat*) freeze; *~ sönder* be (get) split by the frost,
burst by the frost; *~ till* freeze (get frozen) over;
~ ut cold-shoulder, send to Coventry

frys|box deepfreeze, freezer **-disk** frozen-food
merchandiser (counter) **-eri** freezing plant **-fack**
freezing compartment **-hus** cold storage **-ning**
freezing; refrigeration **-punkt** freezing point
-skåp freezer **-torka** freeze-dry **-torkning**
freeze-drying

fråg|a I *s1* question; (*förfrågan*) inquiry; (*sak*)
question, matter, point; *en ~ om* a matter of; *i ~
om* as to, regarding, in the matter of; *saken i ~*
the matter in question (at issue); *dagens -or* current questions (issues); *göra ngn en ~* ask s.b. a
question; *komma i ~ som chef* be in the running
for manager's post; *sätta i ~* (*betvivla*) question,
call in question; *det blir en senare ~* that will be a
matter for later consideration; *det kommer aldrig
i ~* (*på ~n*) it is quite out of the question; *det är
en annan ~* that is another question (matter); *det
är inte ~[n] om det* that is not the point; *det är nog
~[n] om* you never can tell, *vard.* I wouldn't bank
on it; *~n är fri* anybody may ask a question; *there
is no harm in asking; *vad är det ~n om?* a) (*vad
står på*) what is the matter?, b) (*vad gäller frågan*)
what is it all about?, c) (*vad vill ni*) what do you
want? **II** *v1* ask (*ngn om ngt* s.b. about s.th.); inquire (*äv. fråga om, efter*); (*förhöra*) question
(*ngn om* s.b. about); *absol. äv.* ask questions; *~
efter ngn* ask (inquire) for s.b., (*bry sig om*) ask

after s.b.; ~ *om (igen)* ask again, repeat the (one's) question; ~ *ngn om lov att* ask a p.'s permission to; ~ *om (efter) priset på* ask (inquire) the price of; ~ *sig* ask o.s. [the question] (*om* whether); ~ *sig fram* ask one's way; ~ *sig för* make inquiries (*om* about, as to); ~ *ut ngn* question s.b. (*om* about), interrogate s.b. (*om* as to); *förlåt att jag ~r, men* excuse my asking, but

frågande *a4* inquiring; questioning; *se ~ ut* look puzzled (bewildered)

fråge|formulär questionnaire **-sats** interrogative clause **-spalt** questions and answers column **-sport** quiz **-stund** question time **-ställning** (*formulering av fråga*) framing of a (the) question; (*problem*) problem, question at issue **-tecken** question mark

frågvis [-å:-] *a1* inquisitive **-het** inquisitiveness

från I *prep* from; (*bort, ner från*) off; (*ända från*) [ever] since; ~ *och med nu* from now on; ~ *och med 1 april* as from April 1st; ~ *vettet* out of one's wits; *herr A. ~ N. mr. A. of N.; år ~ år* from year to year; *berättelser ~ hans barndom* stories of his childhood; *doften ~ en blomma* the scent of a flower; *för att börja ~ början* to begin at the beginning; *undantag ~ regeln* exceptions to the rule; *jag känner honom ~ Paris*[*tiden*] *a*) I got to know him in Paris, *b*) I have known him ever since we were in Paris together **II** *adv*, (*frånslagen*) off; ~ *och till a*) (*av o. till*) to and fro, *b*) (*då o. då*) off and on; *gå ~ och till* (*som hjälp*) come and go; *det gör varken ~ eller till* that is neither here nor there

från|döma ~ *ngn ngt* sentence s.b. to forfeit (lose) **-fälle** *s6* death, decease **-gå 1** (*avgå, avräknas*) to be deducted [from] **2** (*ändra, uppge*) relinquish (*ett tidigare beslut* a previous decision); abandon (*sin ståndpunkt* one's point of view) **-hända** *v2*, ~ *ngn ngt* deprive s.b. of s.th.; ~ *sig* part with, dispose of **-känna** ~ *ngn rätten att* deny s.b. the right to; ~ *ngn talang* deny a p.'s [possession of] talent **-landsvind** offshore wind **-lura** ~ *ngn ngt* wheedle s.th. out of s.b. **-rycka** ~ *ngn ngt* snatch s.th. from s.b. (out of a p.'s hands) **-se** disregard, leave out of account; ~*tt detta* (*att*) apart from that (the fact that) **-sida** back; (*på mynt o.d.*) reverse **-skild** (*om makar*) divorced **-skilja** detach, separate **-slagen** switched off **-stötande** repellent; (*starkare*) repulsive; (*om utseende*) unattractive **-säga** *rfl* (*avvisa*) decline, refuse; (*ansvar*) disclaim; (*nöje*) renounce **-ta[ga]** ~ *ngn ngt* deprive s.b. of s.th. **-träda** (*befattning*) retire from, resign; (*egendom*) surrender; (*arrende*) leave **-varande** *a4* absent; *bildl.* absent-minded, preoccupied; *de ~* those absent, (*vid möte o.d.*) the absentees **-varo** *s9* absence (*av* of; *från* from); (*brist, avsaknad*) lack, want; *lysa med sin ~* be conspicuous by one's absence

fräck *a1* impudent, insolent; (*oblyg, om pers.*) audacious; (*ogenerad*) cheeky, cool; *vard.* fresh; (*djärv*) daring; (*oanständig*) indecent **-het** impudence, audacity, audaciousness, insolence; *vard.* cheek, gall; *ha ~en att* have the impudence to

fräckis *s2, vard.* dirty story

fräken ['frä:-] *s2,* **-växt** *bot.* horsetail

fräkn|e [*fräː-] *s2* freckle **-ig** *a1* freckled, freckly

frälsa *v1 el. v3* save (*från* from); *relig. äv.* redeem; (*befria*) deliver; (*rädda äv.*) rescue; *fräls oss ifrån ondo* deliver us from evil; *han har blivit frälst* he has found salvation

frälsar|e saviour; *F-n, Vår F~* the (our) Saviour **-krans** life buoy

frälse I *s6* (*befrielse från skatt*) exemption from land dues to the Crown **2** (*adel ung.*) privileged classes (*pl*) **II** *oböjligt a,* ~ *och ofrälse* [*män*] noblemen and commoners **-hemman** farmstead exempt from land dues **-stånd** *se frälse I 2*

frälsning saving *etc.; relig. äv.* salvation; (*räddning*) deliverance

frälsnings|armé *F~n* the Salvation Army **-soldat** Salvationist

främj|a further; (*ngns intresse e.d.*) promote; (*uppmuntra*) encourage; (*understödja*) support **-ande** *s6* furtherance; promotion; encouragement; support; *till ~ av* for the furtherance (*etc.*) of, in order to promote **-are** supporter; promoter

främling stranger (*för* to); (*utlänning*) foreigner

främlingshat hatred of foreigners (strangers), xenophobia

främlingskap *s7* alienation; *bildl.* estrangement

främlings|legion foreign legion; [*franska*] *F~n* the Foreign Legion **-pass** alien's passport

främmande I 1 *s9* (*främling*) stranger; (*gäst*) guest; (*besökande*) visitor, caller **2** *s7, koll.* company; guests, visitors (*pl*); *vi skall ha ~ till middag* we are having company (guests) to dinner **II** *oböjligt a* (*utländsk*) foreign, alien; (*okänd*) strange, unknown (*för* to), unfamiliar (*för* with); (*ovidkommande*) extraneous; ~ *språk* foreign languages; *en ~ herre* an unknown gentleman, a stranger; *en vilt ~ människa* a complete stranger; *förhållande*[*t*] *till ~ makter* [our] relationship to foreign powers; *de är ~ för varandra* they are strangers to one another; *han är helt ~ för tanken* the idea is quite alien to him

främmandegöra alienate (*för* from), estrange (*för* from)

främre ['främm-] *a komp.* fore; front; *fack.* anterior; *F~ Asien* (*ung.*) southwest Asia; *F~ Orienten, se* Mellersta Östern

främst *adv* (*om rang, rum*) foremost; (*om ordning*) first; (*framför allt o.d.*) principally, especially; *först och ~* first and foremost, first of all; ~ *i boken* at the beginning of the book; ~ *i skaran* in the forefront of the crowd; *ligga ~* (*i tävling*) be ahead (leading); *sitta ~* sit right at the front, sit in the front row; *stå ~ på listan* stand first on the list

främst|a *a best. superl.* (*om rum, rang*) foremost; (*om ordning*) first; *i ~ rummet* in the first place, first of all; *vår -e kund* our biggest (most important) customer; *vår -e leverantör* our principal supplier

frän *a1* rank; (*om smak äv.*) acrid; *bildl.* acrimonious, caustic; (*högdragen*) arrogant; (*cynisk, rå*) coarse

fränd|e *s5* kinsman, *fem.* kinswoman, relative **-skap** *s3* kinship, relationship; *bildl.* affinity

fränhet [-å:-] rankness; acrimony; arrogance

fränka *s1* kinswoman

1 fräs *s7* **1** hissing; frying; *jfr 1 fräsa* **2** *för full ~* at top speed

2 fräs *s2, tekn.* milling machine, miller
1 fräsa *v3* **1** (*väsa*) hiss; (*stänka o. fräsa*) sp[l]utter; (*om katt*) spit; (*i stekpanna*) sizzle; *fräs!* (*snyt ut*) blow [your nose]! **2** (*hastigt steka upp*) *kokk.* fry, frizzle **3** ~ *fram* (*förbi*) zoom (rip) along (past)
2 fräsa *v3, tekn.* mill
fräsare milling-machine operator (worker)
fräsch [-ä:-] *a1* fresh[-looking]; (*obegagnad*) [quite] new; (*ny o. frisk*) fresh, clean
fräsch|a ~ *upp* freshen up **-het** *se fräschör* **-ör** freshness; newness
1 fräsning [-ä:-] *se 1 fräs*
2 fräsning [-ä:-] *tekn.* milling
frästorv milled peat
frät|a *v3* **1** (*om syror o.d.*) corrode; eat (*hål på a* hole in); ~ *bort* eat (corrode) away; erode; ~ *sig igenom* eat its way through **2** *bildl.* fret, gnaw (*äv. fräta på*) **-ning** corrosion; erosion **-sår** malignant ulcer; *bildl.* canker
frö *s6, pl hand. äv. -er* seed; *koll.* seed[s *pl*]; *bildl.* germ, embryo; *gå i* ~ go to seed
frö|a ~ *sig* go to seed; ~ [*av sig*] shed its seed **-handel** seed shop **-hus** seed capsule, seedcase, seed vessel, pericarp
fröjd *s3* joy, delight; *bordets ~er* the delights of the table; *i* ~ *och gamman* merrily **fröjda** delight, give joy to; ~ *sig* rejoice (*åt, över* at), delight (*åt, över* in) **fröjdefull** joyful, joyous
frö|kapsel *se fröhus* **-katalog** seed catalogue
frök|en ['frö:-] *-en -nar* unmarried woman, young lady; (*som civilstånd*) spinster; (*som titel*) Miss; (*lärarinna*) teacher; (*servitris*) waitress; *F~ Ur* speaking clock; *F~ Väder* telephone weather forecast
frö|kontroll seed testing **-mjöl** pollen **-odling** *abstr.* seed cultivation; *konkr.* seed-cultivation station
frös *imperf. av frysa*
frö|skal seed coat **-träd** seed tree **-vita** endosperm; perisperm **-växt** seed plant **-ämne** ovule
fuchsia ['fukksia] *s1* fuchsia
fuffens ['fuff-] *n* trick[s *pl*], dodge[s *pl*]; *koll. äv.* mischief; *ha* [*ngt*] ~ *för sig* be up to s.th. (mischief)
fuga *s1* fugue
fukt *s3* damp, moisture **fukta 1** (*väta*) moisten, damp[en]; (*med tårar*) wet **2** (*vara fuktig*) be (get) damp **fuktas** *dep* moisten
fukt|bevarare humectant **-drypande** *a4* wet with damp **-fläck** damp stain **-halt** moisture content
fuktig *a1* damp; (*genom-*) moist; (*om luft*) humid **-het** dampness; moisture; humidity
fukt|ighetsmätare hygrometer **-skada** damage caused by damp **-svabb** damp mop **-torka** damp wipe
ful *a1* ugly; *AE. äv.* homely; (*föga tilltalande*) unattractive; (*obehaglig för örat*) harsh; (*om väder*) bad; ~ *i mun[nen]* foul-mouthed; *~a ord* dirty words, bad (foul) language (*sg*); ~ *som stryk* [as] ugly as sin; *en ~ fisk* (*bildl.*) an ugly customer; *ett ~t spratt* a nasty (dirty) trick; *hon är inte* ~ she is not bad-looking **-ing** fright; (*om barn*) scamp, rascal
full *a1* **1** full (*av, med* of); filled (*av, med* with); ~

av idéer teeming with ideas; ~ *i* (*av*) *skratt* brimming over with laughter; *för ~a segel* in full sail; *ropa med* ~ *hals* roar; *spela för ~a hus* play to crowded houses; *det är ~t med människor på gatan* the street is crowded with people **2** (*hel, fullständig*) full (*fart* speed; *sysselsättning* employment; *verksamhet* activity); complete, whole; ~ *hand* (*kortsp.*) full house; ~ *sommar* full (the height of) summer; ~ *tid* (*sport.*) full time; ~ *tjänstgöring* full-time duty; *~a tre månader* fully three months, a full three months; *dussinet ~t* a full dozen; *med* ~ *rätt* quite rightly; *till* ~ *belåtenhet* to full satisfaction; *vara i sin ~a rätt* have every right **3** *till ~o* in full, fully **4** (*drucken*) drunk; *vard.* tight
full|belagd *a5*, *sjuksalen är* ~ the ward is full up **-blod** *s7* thoroughbred, full blood **-blodshäst** thoroughbred [horse], full blood **-bokad** *a5* booked up; fully booked
fullborda [-ɔ:-] complete, accomplish, finish; ~ *sin avsikt* fulfil one's intention; *ett ~t faktum* an accomplished fact; *det är ~t* (*bibl.*) it is finished **-an** **1** completion; accomplishment **2** (*uppfyllelse*) fulfilment; *i tidernas* ~ in the fullness of time; *nalkas* (*nå*) *sin* ~ be approaching (reach) its (*etc.*) completion
full|fjädrad [-ä:-] *a5* fully fledged, full-fledged; *bildl.* full-blown **-följa 1** (*slutföra*) complete; (*föresatser, planer*) carry out; (*fortsätta* [*med*]) continue, carry on, proceed; (*följa upp*) follow up **2** *jur.* prosecute; carry on **-gjord** *efter -gjort uppdrag* on the completion of a mission (an assignment) **-god** [perfectly] satisfactory, perfect, adequate; (*om mynt*) standard; ~ *säkerhet* full security **-gången** *a5* fully developed **-göra** (*utföra*) carry out; (*plikt*) perform; (*uppfylla*) fulfil; ~ *sin militärtjänst* do one's military service **-het** fullness *etc.*, *jfr full*
fullkomlig [-å-] *a1* perfect; (*fullständig*) complete, entire; (*absolut*) utter, absolute **-het** perfection
fullkom|ligt *adv* perfectly; completely *etc.*, *se fullkomlig* **-na** [make] perfect; (*fullborda*) accomplish, finish **-ning** perfection
fullkorns|bröd wholemeal bread **-mjöl** wholemeal
full|makt 1 (*bemyndigande*) power[s *pl*]; (*dokument*) power (letter) of attorney, warrant; (*vid röstning*) proxy; *enligt* ~ as per power of attorney, by proxy; *äga* ~ be authorized, to have authority **2** (*ämbetsmans*) letters (*pl*) of appointment; (*officers*) commission; (*riksdagsmans*) proxy **-måne** full moon **-mäktig** *-en -e* authorized representative, proxy, delegate
full|o *s3 full 3* **-proppad** [-å-] *a5* stuffed; crammed **-riggare** full-rigged vessel (*etc.*) **-satt** *a4* (*om lokal o.d.*) full, crowded, filled to capacity; (*översållad*) studded; ~ *till sista plats* full up, not a seat left **-skalig** *a1* full-scale **-skriven** *a5* filled with writing **-stoppad** [-å-] *a5* crammed full (*av, med* of), crammed (*av, med* with)
fullständig *a1* complete, entire; total; (*absolut o.d.*) utter, absolute; ~ *avhållsamhet* total abstinence; *med ~a rättigheter* (*spritservering*) fully licensed
fullständig|a make complete; complete **-ande**

s6 (*utan pl*) completing, completion; (*med pl*) supplement; *till ~ av* to supplement, as a supplement to **-het** completeness

fullständigt *adv* completely; entirely

fullt *adv* fully; (*alldeles*) quite; (*fullständigt*) completely; *inte ~ en timme* not quite an hour; *ha ~ upp med pengar* (*att göra*) have plenty of money (to do); *njuta ~ och helt av ngt* enjoy s.th. to the full; *tro ngt ~ och fast* have absolute faith in s.th., be firmly convinced of s.th.

full|talig *a1* [numerically] complete; full; *är vi ~a?* are we all here? **-teckna** (*lista*) fill with signatures; (*belopp*) subscribe in full; *lånet ~des snabbt* the loan was fully subscribed quickly **-träff** direct hit; *bildl.* [real] hit **-tränad** in peak condition **-vuxen** full-grown, fully grown; *en ~ a* grown-up [person], an adult **-värdig** (*om mynt, vikt*) standard; *bildl.* sound

fulländ|a complete (*jfr fullborda*); *~d* perfect, complete; *~d smak* consummate taste; *~ sig* perfect o.s. **-ning** completion; perfection

fullärd (*särskr.* full-lärd) *a5* fully trained (qualified); skilled

fullödig (*särskr.* full-lödig) *a1* standard; (*gedigen*) sterling; *bildl. äv.* thorough, genuine; *~t uttryck* fully adequate expression

fult [-u:-] *adv* in an unsightly (ugly) way; (*för örat*) harshly; (*obehagligt*) disagreeably; (*starkare*) nastily; *det var ~ gjort av dig* it was a nasty thing of you to do

fuml|a fumble (*med* with, at) **-ig** *a1* fumbling **-ighet** fumblingness

fundament *s7* foundation; (*för maskin*) bed, footing; (*sockel*) base **-al** *a1* fundamental, basic

funder|a (*grubbla*) ponder (*på* upon); muse, meditate (*på* upon, about); think; (*undra*) wonder; *~ hit och dit* turn the matter over in one's mind; *~ på att göra ngt* think of (consider) doing s.th.; *~ på saken* think the matter over; *~ ut* think (work) out **-are** *ta sig en ~* have a good think **-ing** *~ar* thoughts, reflections, speculations, (*idéer*) ideas, notions

fundersam [-'de:r-] *a1* (*tankfull*) thoughtful, contemplative, meditative; (*tveksam*) hesitative **-het** thoughtfulness *etc.*; hesitativeness

fungera [-ŋ'ge:-] (*om maskin e.d.*) work, function; (*om pers.*) officiate, serve, act

fungi|cid [-ŋgi-] *s3* fungicide **-stat** *s3* fungistat

funkis ['funnkis] *oböjligt s* functional style **-villa** functionalist (*friare* modern-looking) house

funktion [-ŋk'ʃo:n] function[ing]; (*plikt*) function, duty; *i* (*ur*) *~* in (out of) operation (order), (not) working; *försätta ngt ur ~* throw s.th. out of gear

funktional|ism [-ŋkʃo-] functionalism **-ist** *s3*, **-istisk** [-'liss-] *a5* functionalist

funktion|ell [-ŋkʃo-] *a1* functional **-era** *se fungera*

funktions|duglig serviceable; adequate; *i ~t skick* in working order **-duglighet** serviceability; adequacy **-oduglig** inadequate; out of order **-teori** *mat.* theory of functions

funktionär [-ŋkʃo-] *s3* functionary, official

funnit *sup. av finna*

funt *s2, se dopfunt*

funtad *a5, se beskaffad*

fur *s1* **1** (*träd*) *se fura* **2** (*trä*) *se furu*

fura *s1* pine

furag|e [-'ra:ʃ] *s7*, **-era** *v1, mil.* forage

furie ['fu:-] *s5* fury

furioso [-'å:så] *adv, mus.* furioso

furir *s3* corporal; (*vid flottan*) leading rating; *A E.* sergeant, (*vid flottan*) petty officer 2nd class, (*vid flygvapnet*) staff sergeant

furner|a furnish, supply **-ing** furnishing, supply

furnissör purveyor

furor [-'å:r] *r* furore; *göra ~* create a furore

furste *s2* prince **-hus** *se fursteätt*

furste|ndöme *s6* principality **-ätt** princely (royal) house

furst|inna princess **-lig** *a1* princely **-ligt** *adv* like a prince; *belöna ngn ~* give s.b. a princely reward

furu *oböjligt s* pine [wood] **-bräda** deal, fir board

furunkel [-'runn-] *s2* boil; *fack.* furuncle

furu|planka deal, fir board **-ved** pine firewood

fusion fusion; *hand. äv.* merger, amalgamation; *kärnfys.* [nuclear] fusion **-era** fuse, amalgamate

fusk *s7* **1** (*slarv*) scamping; (*illa gjort arbete*) botch **2** (*svek*) cheating; *skol. äv.* cribbing **fuska 1** (*med arbete o.d.*) scamp, botch; *~ i fotografyrket* dabble in photography; *~ med ngt* scamp (skimp) s.th. **2** *skol., spel., hand. o.d.* cheat (*i* at); *skol. äv.* crib

fusk|are 1 botcher; dabbler **2** cheat[er], crib[ber] **-bygge** jerry-building **-lapp** crib **-verk** *se fusk 1*

fustanella [-ˣnella] *s1* fustanella

futhark *s3* futhark

futil *a1* futile **-itet** *s3* futility

futtig *a1* paltry; (*småaktig, obetydlig*) petty **-het 1** (*utan pl*) paltriness **2** (*med pl*) pettiness

futur|al *a5* future **-ism** futurism **-ist** *s3*, **-istisk** [-'riss-] *a5* futurist

futuro|log futurologist **-logi** futurology

futur|um [-ˣtu:-] *s8, pl äv. -er* the future [tense]; *~ exactum* the future perfect

fux *s2* bay [horse]

fy ugh!, oh!, phew!; *~ sjutton!* confound it!; *~ skäms!* shame [on you]!

fylka *hist.* draw up in battle formation; (*friare*) array; *~ sig* (*fylkas*) draw together, (*friare*) flock (*kring* round), *bildl. äv.* rally (*kring ngn* round s.b., *to* s.b.)

fylke *s6, angl.* shire, county

fylking [-k-] *hist.* wedge-shaped battle formation

fylla I *s1* booze; *i ~n och villan* [when] in a drunken fit; *ta sig en ~* have a booze; *vara på ~n* (*vard.*) be on the booze **II** *v2* **1** fill; (*fullproppa o. kokk.*) stuff; (*utfylla*) fill up; (*behov, brist*) supply; *bildl.* fulfil, serve; *~ en ballong* inflate a balloon; *~ ett länge känt behov* supply a long-felt want; *~ sin uppgift* (*om sak*) fulfil (serve) its purpose; *~ vin i glasen* pour wine into the glasses **2** (*med betonad partikel*) *~ i a*) (*kärl e.d.*) fill up, (*blankett*) fill in (up), *b*) (*ngt som fattas*) fill in, *c*) (*vätska*) pour in; *~ igen* fill up (in); *~ på a*) (*kärl*) fill [up], replenish, *b*) (*vätska*) pour [out]; *~ upp* fill up; *~ ut* (*t.ex. en rad, kläder*) fill out, (*t.ex. program, brist, äv.*) fill up **3** *han fyller 25 år i morgon* he will be 25 tomorrow, tomorrow is his 25th birthday **4** (*berusa*) intoxicate, make drunk

fyllbult *s2* boozer

fylleri drunkenness, intoxication **-förseelse** offence of drunkenness

fyllerist drunkard, drunk

fyllest *till* ~ sufficiently; *vara till* ~ be sufficient (satisfactory)

fyll|hicka drunken hiccup **-hund** boozer

fyllig *a1* **1** (*om pers.*) plump **2** (*om ljud*) full, full-toned, rich, mellow; (*om vin*) full-bodied; (*om cigarr*) full-flavoured; (*detaljerad*) detailed **-het** fullness *etc.*; fullness of tone (flavour *etc.*)

fyllkaja boozer

fyllna ~ *till* get tipsy

fyllnad *s3* filling; (*tillägg*) supplement; (*ut- äv.*) complement

fyllnads|material filling [material] **-prövning** supplementary examination **-sten** *koll.* filling stone **-val** *polit.* (*i Storbritannien*) by-election

fyllning filling [material]; (*i tand*) filling, *vard.* stopping; *kokk.* stuffing

fyll|o ['fyllo] *s6* drunk **-sjuk** *vara* ~ be sick (ill) after drinking **-skiva** booze, boozing party **-tratt** boozer

fynd *s7* find; finding; (*upptäckt*) discovery; (*oväntad gåva*) godsend; (*lyckat påhitt*) stroke of genius; *göra ett* ~ make a [real] find; find a treasure, (*i affär etc.*) find a [real] bargain; *mannen är ett verkligt* ~ the man is a regular find

fynd|a bargain-hunt **-gruva** *bildl.* mine, treasure house **-jägare** bargain-hunter

fyndig *a1* **1** (*uppfinningsrik*) inventive; (*påhittig, förslagen*) resourceful, ingenious; (*rådig*) ready--witted; *ett* ~*t svar* a quick-witted reply, a repartee **2** *miner.* metalliferous **-het 1** ingenuity **2** *miner.* deposit, mining find

fynd|ort site [of a find]; *biol.* habitat **-pris** bargain price

1 fyr *oböjligt s,* *ha ngt* ~ *för sig* be up to s.th. (mischief)

2 fyr *s2* lad; *en glad* (*lustig*) ~ a gay spark; a cheerful chap

3 fyr *s2* **1** *mil.,* [*ge*] ~*!* fire! **2** (*eldstad*) stove **3** (*eld i spis e.d.*) fire **4** ~ *och flamma* all afire (a-flame)

4 fyr *s2,* *sjö.* light[house]; beacon

1 fyra *v1,* ~ *av se avfyra;* ~ *på a*) (*elda*) keep a fire burning, stoke, *b*) (*skjuta*) fire away

2 fyra I *räkn* (*för sms jfr fem-*) four; ~ *hundra* four hundred; *mellan* ~ *ögon* in private; *på alla* ~ on all fours **II** *s1* four; ~*n*[*s växel*] [the] fourth [gear]; *han går i* ~*n* he is in the fourth form (class)

fyra|hundratalet the fifth century **-rummare** four-room flat **-tiden** *vid* ~ [at] about four o'clock **-årig** *a1* **1** four-year-old **2** (*för fyra år*) four-year **-åring** child of four, four-year-old

fyrbent [-e:-] *a4* (*om djur*) four-footed, quadruped; (*om möbel o.d.*) four-legged

fyr|byggnad lighthouse **-båk** beacon

fyr|cylindrig *a5* four-cylinder **-dela** quarter **-dimensionell** *a5* four-dimensional **-dubbel** four-fold, quadruple **-dubbla** quadruple, multiply by four **-faldig** *a5* fourfold

fyrfat firepan

fyr|fota *a4,* **-fotadjur** quadruped **-färgstryck** four-colour print[ing] **-handsfattning** (*gullstol*) chair grip **-hjulig** *a5* four-wheel[ed] **-hjulsdrift** four-wheel drive **-händig** *a5* four-handed; ~*t pianostycke* duet **-hörning** [-ö:-] quadrangle **-kant** square; quadrangle; *fem yards i* ~ five yards square **-kantig** square; quadrangular **-klöver** four-leaf clover; *bildl.* quartet[te] **-ling** quadruplet, quad

fyrlista list of lights

fyr|motorig *a5* four-engined **-sidig** *a5* four-sided **-siding** quadrilateral **-siffrig** *a5* four-figure; *in the fourfigures* **-sitsig** *a5* four-seated; ~ *bil* four-seater

fyr|sken lighthouse beam, light **-skepp** lightship **-spann** four-in-hand; *köra* ~ drive a carriage and four **-språng** *i* ~ at a full gallop, (*friare*) at full speed **-stämmig** *a5* four-part **-taktsmotor** four-stroke (*AE.* four-cycle) engine **-tal** [the number] four; (*i poker*) four of a kind

fyrti[o] [ˣförti] forty

fyrtion|de [ˣförr-] fortieth **-[de]del** fortieth part

fyrti[o]|talist writer (author) of the forties **-årig** *etc., se femtioårig etc.* **-åttatimmarsvecka** forty-eight-hour week

fyr|torn lighthouse tower **-vaktare** lighthouse keeper

fyrverkeri fireworks (*pl*) **-pjäs** firework

fyr|väppling *se fyrklöver* **-värd** *kem., vara* ~ have a valency (*AE.* valence) of four, be tetravalent (quadrivalent)

fyrväsen lighthouse service

fysik *s3* **1** (*vetenskap*) physics (*pl, behandlas som sg*) **2** (*kroppsbeskaffenhet*) physique; constitution **-alisk** [-'ka:-] *a5* physical; ~ *behandling* physiotherapeutic treatment; ~ *kemi* physical chemistry

fysik|er ['fy:-] physicist **-laboratorium** physics laboratory **-lektion** physics lesson **-lärare** physics teacher

fysikum ['fy:-] *n* physics institution

fysiokrat|i *s3* physiocracy **-isk** [-'kra:-] *a5* physiocratic **-ism** physiocracy

fysio|log physiologist **-logi** *s3* physiology **-logisk** [-'lå:-] *a5* physiological **-nom** physiognomist **-nomi** *s3* physiognomy **-nomisk** [-'nå:-] *a5* physiognomic[al] **-terapeut** [-'pevt] physiotherapist **-terapi** physiotherapy, physical therapy; *AE. äv.* physiatrics (*pl, behandlas som sg* sg)

fysisk ['fy:-] *a5* physical; (*kroppslig äv.*) bodily; ~ *person* natural person; *en* ~ *omöjlighet* a sheer (downright) impossibility

fytotron [-'å:n] *s3* phytotron

1 få *pron* few; (*några få*) a few; *alltför* ~ all too few; *om några* ~ *dagar* in a few days

2 få *fick fått* **1 1** (*erhålla, mottaga*) receive, get; (*lyckas få, skaffa sig*) get, obtain; (*förvärva*) get, acquire; (*få o. behålla*) keep, have; ~ *arbete* get a job; ~ *barn* have a baby; ~ *betalt* be (get) paid; ~ *en fråga* be asked a question; ~ *en gåva* receive a present; ~ *huvudvärk* get a headache; ~ *ett namn* get (*om småbarn* be given) a name; ~ *ro* find peace; ~ *ett slut* come to an end; ~ *snuva* catch [a] cold; ~ *sitt straff* be punished; ~ *tid* get (find) [the] time; ~ *tillträde* be admitted, obtain admission; ~ *torra kläder på kroppen* get dry clothes on; ~ *ngt att tänka på* get s.th. to think about; ~ [*sig*] *en bit mat* get s.th. to eat; ~ *sig ett gott skratt* have a good laugh; *vad* ~*r vi till middag?* what are we having for dinner?; *vem har du*

~tt den av? who gave you that?; *har blommorna ~tt vatten?* have the flowers been watered?; *den ~r inte plats* there is no room for it; *den varan går inte att ~ längre* that article is no longer obtainable; *då skall du ~ med mig att göra!* then you'll catch it from me!; *det skall du ~ för!* I'll pay you out for that!; *där fick du!* serves you right!; *där fick han så han teg!* that shut him up! **2** *(lyckas göra el. bringa el. laga)* get, have; *~ ngt färdigt* get s.th. finished, finish s.th.; *~ kläderna förstörda* get one's clothes spoilt; *~ ett slut på* put an end to; *~ sin önskan uppfylld* get (have) one's wish; *de har ~tt det bra (ekonomiskt)* they are well off **3** *(förmå, bringa)* make, get, bring; *~ ngn att göra ngt (ngn till ngt)* get s.b. to do (make s.b. do) s.th.; *~ ngt till stånd* bring about s.th. **4** *(ha tillåtelse)* be allowed (permitted) to; *~r* may, can; *fick (i indirekt tal)* might, could; *~r (i indirekt tal: fick) inte* must not; *~ ej vidröras!* do not touch!; *jag ~r inte glömma* I must not forget; *jag ~r inte för min mamma* my mummy won't let me; *du ~r inte bli ond* you must not get angry; *~r jag följa med?* may I come too?; *~r jag komma in? Nej, det ~r du inte* may (can) I come in? No, you may not; *~r jag störa dig ett ögonblick?* could you spare me a minute?; *om jag ~r ge dig ett råd* if I might give you a piece of advice; *huset fick inte byggas* they were not allowed to build the house, permission was not given for the house to be built **5** *(i artighetsuttryck)* be att ~ tala med ask to speak to; *~r jag tala med* can (could) I speak to; *~r jag fråga* may (might) I ask; *låt mig ~ försöka* let me try; *~r jag be om litet ost? (vid bordet)* may I have some cheese?; *~r det vara en cigarett?* would you like a cigarette?; *vad ~r det lov att vara?* what can I do for you[, Sir (Madam)]?; *jag ~r tacka så mycket* [I should like to] thank you very much; *vi ~r härmed meddela att* we wish to inform you that; *det ~r jag verkligen hoppas* I should hope so **6** *(vara tvungen att, nödgas)* have to, *vard.* have got to; *det ~r duga* that will have to do; *jag ~r lov att gå nu* I must go now; *jag ~r väl försöka då* I shall have to try, then; *du ~r ursäkta mig* you must excuse me; *då ~r det vara* we'll leave it at that, then; *jag fick vänta* I had to wait, I was kept waiting **7** *(kunna, ha möjlighet att)* be able to; *~r can;* *~ höra (veta etc.) se under höra, veta etc.;* *vi ~r tala om det senare* we'll talk about that later; *vi ~r väl se* we'll see [about that] *; har du fått sova i natt?* were you able to sleep last night?; *jag fick göra som jag ville* I could do as I liked **II** *(med betonad partikel)* **1** *~ av* get off **2** *~ bort* remove **3** *~ fingrarna emellan* get one's fingers caught **4** *~ fram (ta fram)* get out, *(skaffa)* procure, *(framställa)* produce; *jag fick inte fram ett ord* I could not utter a word **5** *~ för sig (inbilla sig)* imagine, *(få ett infall)* get it into one's head **6** *~ i ngt* I get s.th. into; *~ i ngn ngt* get s.b. to take s.th.; *~ i sig (svälja)* swallow, *(tvinga i sig)* get down **7** *~ igen a) (återfå)* get back, *b) (stänga)* close; *det skall du ~ igen!* I'll pay you back for that, you'll see! **8** *~ igenom* get through **9** *~ ihop a)* *(stänga)* close, *b) (samla ihop)* get together, *(pengar)* collect **10** *~ in* get in, radio. collect; *~ in...i* get...into; *~ in pengar (samla ihop)* collect money, *(tjäna)* make money **11** *~ med [sig]* bring

[along]; *inte ~ med (lämna kvar)* leave behind, *(utelämna)* omit; *~ med sig (få på sin sida)* get over to one's side, *(få att följa med)* get to come along **12** *~ ner* get down **13** *~ på [sig]* get on **14** *~ tillbaka på 1 pund* get change for 1 pound **15** *~ undan* get out of the way **16** *~ upp (dörr e.d.)* get open, *(lock e.d.)* get off, *(kork e.d.)* get out, *(knut)* undo, untie, *(lyfta)* raise, lift, *(fisk)* land, *(kräkas upp)* bring up; *~ upp farten* pick up speed; *~ upp ögonen för* have one's eyes opened to, *(inse)* realize **17** *~ ur ngn ngt* get s.th. out of s.b. **18** *~ ut* get out, *(arv)* obtain; *~ ut lön* get one's pay, get paid; *jag kunde inte ~ ut ngt av honom* I could not get anything out of him **19** *~ över (kvar)* have left (over)

fåfäng *a1* **1** *(inbilsk)* conceited; *(ytlig)* vain **2** *(fruktlös)* vain, useless **3** *(sysslolös)* idle

fåfäng|a *s1* vanity; *(inbilskhet)* conceit[edness] **-lig** ['få:- *el.* -'fäŋ-] *a1* vain **-lighet** vanity

fågel ['få:-] *s2* bird; *(i sht höns-)* fowl, *koll.* poultry; *koll. jakt. o. kokk.* game birds *(pl);* *varken ~ eller fisk* neither fish, flesh, nor fowl; *bättre en ~ i handen än tio i skogen* a bird in the hand is worth two in the bush **-art** bird species **-bad** birdbath **-berg** bird cliff **-bo** bird's nest *(pl birds' nests)* **-bord** bird table **-bur** birdcage **-bär** sweet cherry **-bössa** fowling-piece **-fri** *se fredlös* **-frö** birdseed, canary seed **-fångare** bird catcher; fowler **-holk** birdhouse **-hund** pointer; setter; *AE. äv.* bird dog **-jakt** bird shooting **-kvitter** bird twitter (chirp) **-kännare** birdman, ornithologist **-näbb** beak, bill **-perspektiv** bird's-eye view; *Paris i ~* a bird's-eye view of Paris **-skrämma** *s1* scarecrow **-skytte** game-bird shooting **-skådare** bird-watcher **-skådning** [-å:-] bird-watching **-spindel** bird spider **-station** ornithological station **-sträck** flight of birds **-sång** [the] singing of [the] birds, bird song **-unge** young bird, nestling **-vägen** as the crow flies **-ägg** bird's egg *(pl birds' eggs)*

fåglalåt *se fågelsång*

fåkunnig *I al* ignorant **II** *s, en ~* an ignoramus **-het** ignorance

fåle *s2* colt; *poet.* steed

fåll *s2* hem

1 fålla *v1, sömn.* hem; *~ upp* hem up

2 fålla *s1* pen, fold

fållbänk *ung.* turn-up bedstead

fåll|ning hemming **-söm** hemstitching

få|mannavälde oligarchy **-mansbolag** close corporation **-mäld** [-ä:-] *a5, se fåordig*

fån *s7, se fåne* **fåna** *rfl* be silly (asinine); *(prata dumheter)* drivel **fåne** *s2* fool; *(starkare)* idiot

fång *s7* **1** armful; *ett ~ ved* an armful [of] wood **2** *jur.* acquisition; *laga ~* acquest

1 fånga *i uttr.: ta till ~* take prisoner[s *pl*], capture; *ta sitt förnuft till ~* listen to reason, be sensible

2 fånga *v1* catch, *(ta till fånga)* capture; *(med fälla)* trap

fångdräkt prison (convict's) dress

fånge *s2* prisoner, captive

fången *a5* imprisoned, captive; *ge sig ~* surrender; *hålla ~ a)* keep in prison, hold [a] captive (prisoner), *b) (om uppmärksamhet e.d.)* hold; *sitta ~* be kept in prison, be imprisoned **-skap** *s3* captivity; (*vistelse i fängelse*) imprisonment; *befria ngn ur ~en* release s.b. from captivity

fång|lina *sjö.* painter **-läger** (*för krigsfångar*) prisoner-of-war camp

fångrin [ˣfå:n-] stupid grin

fångst *s3* **1** (*fångande*) catching *etc.*, capture **2** (*byte*) catch (*äv. bildl.*); (*jakt- o. bildl.*) bag; (*fiskares*) draught, haul **-arm** *zool.* tentacle **-fartyg** fishing boat; (*val-*) whale catcher, whaler; (*säl-*) sealer **-redskap** *koll.* trapping tackle (gear); (*fisk- koll.*) fishing tackle (gear)

fång|vaktare warder, *fem.* wardress (*AE.* matron), jailer, gaoler **-vård** correctional treatment [of prisoners], prison welfare

fångvårds|anstalt prison, penal institution **-styrelse** *f~n, se kriminalvårdsstyrelsen*

fånig *a1* idiotic; (*friare*) silly, stupid **-het** silliness, stupidity; *~er* stupidities

fåntratt sap; silly idiot

fåordig [-ɔ:-] *a1* of few words; (*ordkarg*) taciturn, laconic[al], reticent **-het** taciturnity *etc.*

får *s7* sheep (*pl lika*); (*kött*) mutton; *skilja ~en från getterna* separate the sheep from the goats

fåra I *s1* furrow; (*rynka*) line; *bildl. äv.* groove **II** *v1* furrow; line

fåra|herde shepherd, *fem.* shepherdess **-kläder** *pl, en ulv i ~* a wolf in sheep's clothing

får|aktig *a1* (*enfaldig*) sheepish, sheeplike **-avel** sheep breeding **-fiol** leg of mutton **-hjord** flock of sheep **-hund** sheepdog **-klippning** sheepshearing **-kött** mutton **-lus** sheep ked (tick) **-sax** sheep shears (*pl*) **-skalle** *bildl.* num[b]-skull, goon **-skinn** fleece, sheepskin **-skinnspäls** sheepskin coat **-skock** flock of sheep **-skötsel** sheep farming **-stek** leg of mutton; (*tillagad*) roast mutton **-stuvning** mutton stew **-styng** [sheep] botfly **-ticka** *s1* sheep polyporus **-ull** sheep's wool

fåt *s3* mistake, error, blunder

fåtal *s7, ett ~ personer* a few people; *i ett ~ fall* in a minority of cases **-ig** *a1* few [in number]; *en ~ församling* a small assembly

fått *sup. av 2 få*

fåtölj *s3* armchair, easy chair

fåvitsk [ˈfå:-] *a5* foolish **fåvitsko** *s i uttr.: i ~* foolishly, witlessly

fåvälde oligarchy

fä *s6* beast; *koll.* cattle; (*bildl. om pers.*) dolt, blockhead; *både folk och ~* [both] man and beast **-aktig** *a1* caddish, doltish

fäbless weakness, partiality

fäbod *ung.* chalet **-vall** *ung.* mountain pasture (grazing)

fäderne *s7, på ~t* on the (one's) father's (the paternal) side **-arv** patrimony **-bygd** home of one's fathers, native place **-gård** family estate **-jord** *~en* one's native soil

fädernesland native country

fäderneärvd *a5* handed down from father to son, hereditary

fä|fluga horsefly **-fot** *ligga för ~* lie uncultivated; *bildl.* lie waste

fägna [ˣfäŋna] *det ~r mig* I am delighted; *~ sig* rejoice (*över* at) **fägnad** *s3* delight

fägring [-ä:-] beauty

fä|hund *bildl.* cad, blighter, heel, rat, rotter **-hus**
cattle shed

fäkta 1 fence (*med florett* with a foil); (*friare*) fight; *bildl.* tilt (*mot* at) **2** *~ med armarna* gesticulate wildly

fäkt|are fencer, swordsman **-mask** fencer's mask **-mästare** fencing master **-ning** fencing (*med, på* with); (*strid*) fight, encounter

fälb *s3* long pile plush

fälg [-j] *s2* rim

fäll *s2* fell; (*djurskinnstäcke*) skin rug **1 fälla** *s1* trap; *bildl.* pitfall; *gå i ~n* fall (walk) into the trap, get caught [in the trap]; *sätta ut en ~ för* set a trap for **2 fäll|a** *v1* (*nedhugga*) fell, cut [down]; (*slå omkull*) knock down; (*regering*) overthrow **2** (*döda*) kill, slay; *jakt.* bring down **3** (*sänka*) lower; (*låta falla*) drop; (*tårar*) shed; (*bajonett*) level; (*lans*) couch; (*ankare*) cast, drop; *bildl.* lose (*modet* courage) **4** (*tappa*) lose (*håret* one's hair); (*om djur, t.ex. horn*) shed; (*löv, blad*) shed; (*färga av sig*) bleed; *färgen -er* the colour runs **5** *kem.* deposit, precipitate **6** (*uttala, avge*) drop, let fall; *~ ett omdöme* express an opinion **7** (*döma*) condemn, convict, damn, (*avkunna*) pronounce (*dom* a verdict) **8** (*med betonad partikel*) *~ igen* shut [up]; *~ ihop* fold, (*kniv*) shut, clasp; *~ in a*) (*infoga*) let in, inlay, *b*) (*t.ex. landningsställ*) retract; *~ ner* let down, (*lock e.d.*) shut [down], (*krage*) turn down; *~ ut kem.*) precipitate

fällande I *s6* felling *etc.*; conviction, condemnation; pronouncement **II** *a4, ~ dom, se dom; ~ vittnesmål* incriminating evidence

fäll|bar *a5* collapsible, foldable, folding **-bord** drop-leaf table **-bro** bascule [bridge], drawbridge **-kniv** clasp knife **-ning 1** *abstr.* felling *etc.* **2** *konkr., kem.* precipitate; (*bottensats*) sediment; *geol.* deposit **-stol** folding chair; (*vilstol*) deck chair; (*på teater o.d.*) tip-up seat **-söm** lap (lapped) seam

fält *s7* field; *bildl. äv.* sphere, scope; (*dörr-*) panel; (*vägg-*) bay, panel; *i ~* (*mil.*) in the field; *dra i ~* take the field; *ha ~et fritt* have a free hand; *ligga i vida ~et* be far from being settled; *rymma ~et* quit the field; *över hela ~et* over the whole expanse **-arbete** field work **-artilleri** field artillery **-befästning** *mil.* fieldwork **-biologi** biology in the field **-flaska** canteen **-flygare** *ung.* sergeant pilot; *AE. ung.* second lieutenant **-grå** field-grey **-gudstjänst** field service **-hare** European hare **-herre** general, military commander **-herrebegåvning** strategic talent **-jägare** *ung.* rifleman **-kikare** field glasses (*pl*) **-kök** field kitchen **-lasarett** field hospital **-läkare** army surgeon **-marskalk** field marshal **-mässig** *a1* active-service; *AE.* active-duty **-mätning** [detail] surveying **-post** army postal service, field post (mail) **-präst** army chaplain **-rop** watchword, password **-skjutning** field shooting [practice] **-skär** *s3, hist., ung.* barber-surgeon **-slag** pitched battle **-spat** *s3* felspar; *AE.* feldspar **-säng** camp bed **-tecken** (*fana*) banner **-tjänst** field (active) service **-tjänstövning** manoeuvres (*pl*) **-tåg** campaign (*mot* against, *on*) **-tågsplan** plan of campaign **-undersökning** field survey **-uniform** battledress **-väbel** *ung.* sergeant major; *AE.* master sergeant

F

fänad s3 livestock
fängelse s4 **1** (byggnad) prison, jail, gaol; AE. äv. penitentiary; sitta i ~ be in prison; sätta ngn i ~ put s.b. in prison, imprison s.b. **2** (straff) imprisonment; livstids ~ imprisonment for life, life sentence; dömas till två månaders ~ be sentenced to two months' imprisonment, get a two months' sentence **-cell** prison cell **-direktör** prison governor; AE. warden **-håla** dungeon **-kund** jailbird, gaolbird, lag; vard. con **-präst** prison chaplain **-straff** imprisonment
fäng|hål touchhole **-krut** priming [powder]
fängsl|a 1 (fjättra) fetter, shackle **2** (sätta i fängelse) imprison, arrest **3** bildl. fascinate, captivate; (dra t. sig) attract **-ande** a4 fascinating; attractive **-ig** i uttr.: hålla i ~t förvar keep in custody
fänkål [ˣfäŋ-, äv. ˣfänn-] fennel
fänrik ['fänn-] s2 (vid armén, kustartilleriet) second lieutenant, (vid flottan) midshipman, (vid flygvapnet) pilot officer; AE. second lieutenant, (vid flottan) ensign
färd [-ä:-] s3 **1** journey; (t. sjöss) voyage; (turist-) trip, tour; (bil- etc.) ride; (flyg-) flight; (forsknings-) expedition; ställa ~en till make for **2** bildl., vara i ~ med att göra ngt be busy doing s.th.; ge sig i ~ med ngt (att) set about s.th. (+ ing-form) **3** dra sina ~e take one's departure; fara på ~e danger ahead; vad är på ~e? what is up (the matter)?
färd|as [-ä:-] dep travel **-bevis** travel document **-biljett** ticket **-broms** foot (pedal) brake
färde [-ä:-] se färd 3
färdhandling travel document
färdig [-ä:-] a5 **1** (fullbordad) finished, done; (avslutad) complete; (klar) ready **2** (om pers., beredd) ready (till for), prepared; (slut) done for, worn-out; bli ~ med ngt get through with s.th., get s.th. done; få ~ get done; göra ~ get ready, finish; vara ~ have done; vara ~ att be ready to; vara ~ med have done [with], have finished (got through); nu är det ~t! (vard.) now the fat's in the fire! **3** (nära att) on the point of **4** (ej ofärdig) sound
färdig|förpackad a5 prepacked; AE. prepackaged **-gjord** finished, complete; (om kläder) ready-made
färdig|het (kunnighet) skill, proficiency (i in, at); (händighet) dexterity (i in, at); (talang) accomplishment; övning ger ~ practice makes perfect **-klädd** a5 dressed; jag är inte ~ I have not finished dressing **-kokt** a4 cooked, boiled; är äggen ~a? are the eggs done? **-köpt** [-çö:pt] a4 bought ready-made **-lagad** a5 ready-to-eat; ~ mat, äv. convenience food **-ställa** get ready, finish, complete **-sydd** a5 ready-made **-utbildad** fully trained
färd|knäpp s2, vard. one for the road **-kost** ung. eatables (provisions) for the journey **-ledare** leader [of an expedition], guide **-medel** means of conveyance (transport) **-mekaniker** flyg. flight engineer **-riktning** direction of travel **-riktningsvisare** (visare) trafficator; (blinker) blinker, (direction) indicator **-skrivare** (i bil) tachograph; flyg. flight recorder, vard. black box **-sätt** method (means) of travel **-tjänst** taxi ser-

vice for the disabled **-väg** route
färg [-j] s3 **1** colour (äv. bildl.); (målar-) paint; (-ämne) dye; (nyans) shade, tone; (hy) complexion, colour; (klang-) timbre; boktr. ink; kortsp. suit; röd till ~en red in colour; gå i ~ med match in (for) colour; i vilken ~ skall den målas? what colour is it to be painted?
färg|a [-j-] colour (äv. bildl.); (textil o.d.) dye; (glas, trä o.d.) stain; (måla) paint; ~ av sig lose (give off) its colour **-ad** a5 coloured; socialistiskt ~ tinged with socialism **-are** dyer
färg|bad dyeing bath **-band** (för skrivmaskin) [typewriter] ribbon **-beständig** colourfast **-bild** se färgfoto **-blandning** konkr. colour blend **-blind** colour-blind **-blindhet** colour blindness **-borttagningsmedel** paint remover **-brytning** colour refraction **-dia[positiv]** colour transparency (slide) **-dyna** stamp pad
färg|eri [-j-] dye works **-film** colour film **-filter** colour filter **-foto** colour photo **-fotografering** colour photography **-fotografi** colour photograph **-glad** gay, gaily coloured **-glädje** gaiety of colour **-grann** neds. gaudy; se äv. -glad **-handel** paint (colourman's) shop **-klick** daub (splash) of colour (paint) **-kopp** colour well **-krita** (vax-) crayon **-känslig** colour-sensitive **-låda** paintbox, colourbox **-lägga** colour **-läggning** colouring **-lös** colourless (äv. bildl.) **-löshet** colourlessness; lack of colour
färg|ning [-j-] dyeing **-penna** coloured pencil **-plansch** (i bok) colour plate; coloured illustration **-prakt** display of colour **-prov** colour sample **-pyts** paint pot **-rik** profusely (richly) coloured; bildl. äv. vivid **-rikedom** richness (variety) of colour **-sinne** sense of colour **-skala** range of colours; konkr. colour chart (guide) **-skiftning 1** (nyans) hue, tint; tinge; (om pärlemor) iridescence **2** (-förändring) changing (change) of colour **-stark** highly coloured, colourful (äv. bildl.) **-sätta** decide on colours (a colour scheme) **-sättning** colouration, colouring; colour scheme **-television** colour television **-ton** colour shade, hue, tinge **-tryck** colour printing; konkr. colour print **-tub** paint tube **-TV** colour-TV set **-verkan** colour effect **-äkta** colourfast **-ämne** colouring agent, colorant; (lösligt) dye, dyestuff
färing se färöbo
färj|a s1 ferry[boat] **II** v1 ferry (över across) **-förbindelse** ferry service **-karl** ferryman **-läge** ferry berth
färla [-ä:-] s1 ferule
färm a1 prompt, expeditious **-itet** promptness
färnbock [-ä:-] brazil [wood]
färre ['färre] fewer; less numerous
färs s3, kokk. forcemeat, farce[meat] **-era** stuff
färsk a1 **1** (nyligen tillagad etc., ej gammal) new; (ej skämd, saltad, konserverad) fresh; (ej torkad) green; ~t bröd fresh bread; ~ frukt fresh fruit; ~a jordgubbar fresh strawberries; ~ potatis new potatoes; ~a ägg new-laid eggs **2** (som nyligen gjorts, inträffat etc.) fresh; av ~t datum of recent date; ~a spår fresh tracks; de ~aste nyheterna the latest news
färsk|a tekn. refine **-ning** oxidation, refining **-ningsprocess** refining process **-rökt** ~ lax

smoked salmon **-varor** perishable goods, perishables **-vatten** fresh water
Färöarna pl the Fa[e]roes, the Fa[e]roe Islands **färö|bo, -ing** Fa[e]roese (pl lika) **färöisk** a5 Fa[e]roese **färöiska** 1 (språk) Fa[e]roese 2 (kvinna) Fa[e]roese woman
fästa v3, v1 1 (fastgöra) fasten, fix, pin (vid to, on [to]); attach (vid to) 2 (friare o. bildl.) ~ blicken på fix one's eyes upon; ~ uppmärksamheten på call attention to; ~ vikt vid attach importance to 3 (anteckna, överföra) commit (på papperet to paper, to writing) 4 (fastna, häfta) affix, stick; (om spik e.d.) hold 5 rfl, ~ sig vid ngn become attached to s.b.; ~ sig vid ngt notice, pay attention to; inte ~ sig vid småsaker not bother about trifles; det är inget att ~ sig vid ignore it, don't take any notice of it, it is nothing to worry about
fäste s6 1 (fast stöd el. grund) hold; bildl. stronghold, foundation; (rot-) root; få ~ get a hold (grip), take root 2 (skaft, handtag) shaft, attachment; (hållare) holder; (svärd-) hilt 3 bot. receptacle 4 (himlavalv) firmament 5 (befästning) stronghold
fäst|ekvinna hans ~ his betrothed **-folk** engaged couple
fästing zool. tick
fäst|man fiancé; hennes ~ (äv.) her young man **-mö** fiancée; hans ~ (äv.) his young lady
fästning mil. fort[ress] **fästningsanläggning** fortification[s pl]
fästpunkt [point of] attachment
fäsör hack
föda I s1 food; (kost) diet; (näring) nourishment; (uppehälle) living; arbeta för ~n work for a living (one's bread); inte göra skäl för ~n not be worth one's keep **II** v2 1 (bringa t. världen) give birth to; bear; absol. bear children; ~s be born 2 bildl. bring forth; breed 3 (ge näring åt) feed (på on); nourish; (underhålla) maintain, support; ~ sig live, earn one's (a) living (av, på on; med by), (om djur) feed **födas** se föda II 1
född a5 born (av of); ~a (rubrik) births; fru Jones, ~ Smith Mrs. Jones, née (formerly) Smith; han är ~ den 1 maj he was born on the 1st of May; han är ~ engelsman he is an Englishman by birth; han är ~ till musiker he is a born musician
födelse birth; alltifrån ~n from [one's] birth **-annons** birth announcement **-attest** birth certificate **-dag** birthday; hjärtliga gratulationer på ~en! many happy returns [of the day]!
födelsedags|barn person celebrating a birthday **-kalas** birthday party (celebration) **-present** birthday present **-tårta** birthday cake
födelse|datum date of birth **-kontroll** birth control **-märke** birthmark **-nummer** birth registration number **-ort** birthplace; (i formulär e.d.) place of birth **-siffra, -tal** birth rate **-underskott** excess of deaths over births **-år** year of birth **-överskott** excess of births over deaths
föd|geni [an] eye to the main chance **-krok** means of livelihood
födo|ämne food[stuff]; ~n (äv.) comestibles, eatables, provisions **-ämneslära** dietetics (pl, behandlas som sg)
födsel ['född-] s2 1 (förlossning) childbirth; de-

livery 2 (födelse) birth
födslo|vånda travail **-värkar** labour pains
1 föga I n [very] little **II** oböjligt a [very (but)] little **III** adv [very (but)] little; (icke just) not exactly; (knappast) scarcely, hardly; ~ angenäm disagreeable; ~ givande hardly profitable, rather unprofitable (unfruitful); ~ uppbygglig unedifying
2 föga oböjligt s i uttr.: falla till ~ yield, submit (för for), give in
fögderi county administrative division; hist. bailiwick; bildl. domain
föhnvind föhn, foehn
föl s7 foal; (unghäst) colt; (sto-) filly **föla** foal
följ|a v2 1 (följa efter) follow 2 (ledsaga) accompany (äv. bildl.); go (come) with; ~ ngn till graven (äv.) pay one's last honours (respects) to s.b.; ~ ngn hem (äv.) see s.b. home 3 (efterträda) succeed 4 (förflytta, sträcka sig längs) follow 5 (iakttaga, studera, förstå) follow; (följa med blicken) watch; ~ föreläsningar attend lectures 6 (rätta sig efter) follow (modet the fashion; ngns exempel a p.'s example); obey; comply with; observe 7 (inträffa efter ngt annat) follow; (om tid äv.) ensue; brev -er letter to follow; brevet lyder som -er the letter runs as follows; fortsättning -er to be continued; härav -er hence it follows 8 (med betonad partikel) ~ efter follow [on behind]; ~ med a) (gå med) go (come) with s.b., go (come) too, b) (hålla jämna steg med) keep pace with, keep abreast of (sin tid the times), c) (vara uppmärksam) follow; ~ med [på utfärden] join the party; han har svårt att ~ med i engelska he has difficulty in keeping pace in English; ~ upp (driva vidare) follow up
följaktligen accordingly, consequently
följande a4 following, next; successive; (som konsekvens) consequent, resulting; ~ dag [on] the following (the next) day; i det ~ (nedan) below, (senare) in the sequel; med därav ~ consequently entailing; på ~ sätt in the following way, as follows; på varandra ~ successive; ett brev av ~ innehåll a letter to the following effect
följas v2, dep, ~ åt go together, bildl. run together, occur at the same time
följd s3 1 (verkan, konsekvens) consequence; result; ha till ~ att have the result that; till ~ av in consequence of 2 (räcka, serie) succession, line; series (pl lika); en lång ~ av år a long succession of years; i ~ running, in succession; i löpande ~ consecutively **-företeelse** consequence, sequel **-riktig** logical; (konsekvent) consistent **-sats** corollary **-sjukdom** complication **-verkan** resulting effect, aftereffect
följe s6 1 (svit, uppvaktning) suite, retinue; attendants (pl); (väpnat) escort; (pack) gang, crew 2 (sällskap) company; göra (slå) ~ med ngn accompany s.b. **-brev** covering (accompanying) letter **-sedel** delivery note **-slagare** companion; follower
följetong [-åŋ] s3 serial [story]
följsam a1 (med anpassningsförmåga) adaptable, accommodating; (smidig) flexible, pliant
föll imperf. av falla
föna blow-dry
fönst|er ['fönn-] s7 window; kasta ut genom -ret

F

throw out of the window; *sova för öppet* ~ sleep with one's (the) window open; *stå i -ret a) (om pers.)* stand at the window, *b) (om sak)* be in the window

fönster|bleck metal [window]sill **-bord** table by the window **-bräde** windowsill, window ledge **-båge** window frame; *(för skjutfönster)* sash **-bänk** window ledge **-glas** window glass **-hake** window catch; *jfr -krok* **-hållare** window stay; *jfr -hake* **-karm** window frame **-krok** window stay; *jfr -hake* **-kuvert** window envelope **-lucka** [window] shutter **-nisch** window bay (recess) **-plats** *(på buss, tåg e.d.)* window seat **-post** mullion **-putsare** window-cleaner **-putsning** window-cleaning **-ruta** windowpane; *jfr isolerruta* **-shoppa** [-ʃåppa] window-shop **-skyltning** window-dressing, window-display **-smyg** *s2* embrasure **-tittare** Peeping Tom

1 för *sjö.* I *s2* stem, prow; *från ~ till akter* from stem to stern; *i ~en* at the prow II *adv* fore; ~ *och akter* fore and aft; ~ *om masten* before the mast; ~ *ut (över)* ahead, *(inombords)* forward

2 för I *prep* **1** *(framför, inför)* before; *gardiner ~ fönstren* curtains before the windows; ~ *öppen ridå* with the curtain up, *bildl.* in public; *hålla handen ~ munnen* hold one's hand to one's mouth; *skjuta sig en kula ~ pannan* blow one's brains out; *sova ~ öppet fönster* sleep with one's window open; *stå ~ dörren (bildl.)* be at hand, be near **2** *(i tidsuttr.)* ~ *alltid* for ever; ~ *ett år sedan* one (a) year ago; ~ *lång tid framåt* for a long time to come; ~ *länge sedan* long ago; ~ *de närmaste tio åren* for the next ten years **3** *(i förhållande t., med hänsyn t., i stället för, i utbyte mot, på grund av, t. följd av, t. förmån el. skada för, avsedd för)* for; *en almanacka ~ 1960* an almanac for 1960; *en ~ alla och alla ~ en* one for all and all for one; *en gång ~ alla* once [and] for all; *känd ~* known for; ~ *våra förhållanden* by our standards; *öga ~ öga* an eye for an eye; *arbeta ~ ngt* work for s.th.; *göra ngt ~ ngn* do s.th. for s.b.; *ha öga ~* have an eye for; *köpa ~ 100 pund* buy for £100; *tala ~ ngn* speak for (on behalf of) s.b.; *äta ~ tre* eat for three; ~ *mig får du* as far as I am concerned you can; *vad tar ni ~...?* what do you charge for...?; *det har du ingenting ~* you won't gain anything by that; *det blir inte bättre ~ det* that won't make it any better; *det är bra ~ dig* it is good for you; *han är stor ~ sin ålder* he is tall for his age; *jag får inte ~ mamma* mother won't let me; *jag vill ~ mitt liv inte göra det* I don't want to do it for the life of me; *vi betalar var och en ~ sig* each of us will pay for himself **4** *(i dativkonstruktion o. liknande)* to; *en fara ~* a danger to; *blind ~ fördelarna* blind to the advantages; *svag ~ ngn* partial to s.b.; *det blev en besvikelse ~ henne* it was a disappointment to her; *det var nytt ~ mig* it was new to me; *tiden blev lång ~ henne* time seemed long to her **5** *(i genitivkonstruktion)* of; *chefen ~ armén* the commander in chief of the army; *dagen ~ avresan* the day of my *(etc.)* departure; *platsen ~ brottet* the scene of the crime; *priset ~* the price of; *tidningen ~ i dag* today's paper; *bli ett offer ~* be a victim of; *vara föremål ~* be the object of **6** *(mot, från, hos)* from; *dölja ngt ~ ngn* conceal s.th. from s.b.; *gå och dansa ~ ngn* take dancing les-

sons with (from) s.b.; *skydda ngn ~ ngt* protect s.b. from s.th.; *ta lektioner ~ ngn* take lessons with (from) s.b.; *vi har engelska ~ magister A.* we have Mr. A. in English **7** *(i fråga om)* about; *oroa sig ~* be anxious about **8** *(såsom)* as, for; ~ *det första* in the first place, firstly; *anse (förklara, kalla m.fl.) ngn ~ ngt* consider (declare, call) s.b. s.th.; *hålla ngt ~ troligt* regard s.th. as likely **9** *(t. ett pris av)* at; *köpa ngt ~ 2 kronor kilot* buy s.th. at 2 kronor a kilo **10** *(andra prep)* ~ *egna pengar* with one's own money; *dag ~ dag* day by day; *rädd ~* afraid of; *steg ~ steg* step by step; *utmärkande ~* characteristic of; *intressera sig ~* take an interest in; *skriva ~ hand* write by hand **11** *(utan prep)* *bli värre ~ varje dag (gång)* get worse every day (each time) **12** *bo ~ sig själv* live by oneself; *han går ofta ~ sig själv* he often walks alone (by himself); *le (tänka) ~ sig själv* smile (think) to o.s.; *den kan stå ~ sig själv* it can stand by itself II *konj* **1** *(ty)* for **2** ~ *att (därför att)* because; *nog ~ att det finns orsak att* to be sure (it is true) there is reason to; *inte ~ att jag bryr mig om det* not that I care [about it]; *jag är glad ~ att det är vackert väder* I am happy because the weather is fine **3** *den var för liten ~ att passa* it was too small to fit; *den var för tung ~ att jag skulle kunna bära den* it was too heavy for me to carry **4** ~ *att (uttr. avsikt) a) (före bisats)* so (in order) that, *b) (före inf.)* [in order] to (+ *inf.*), with the intention of (+ *ing-form); liksom ~ att* as if to; ~ *att inte tala om* not to mention, let alone; ~ *att säga som det är* to tell the truth; *hon har gått ut ~ att handla* she has gone out shopping; *han reste ~ att aldrig mer återvända* he left, never to return; *man måste stödja den ~ att den inte skall falla* one must support it so that it does not fall; *vi kom i tid ~ att se flygplanet lyfta* we arrived in time to see the plane take off **5** *vara misstänkt ~ att ha* be suspected of having; *jag skäms ~ att säga* I am ashamed to say; *han är duktig ~ att vara så liten* he's good for such a little boy **6** ~ *såvitt* provided [that]; ~ *såvitt inte* unless III *adv* **1** *(alltför)* too; *mycket ~ liten* much too small; *hon är ~ näpen!* she's just too sweet! **2** *stå ~ (dölja)* stand in front; *stå ~ ngn (skymma)* stand in a p.'s way; *gardinerna är ~* the curtains are drawn; *regeln är ~* the bolt is to **3** *(motsats emot)* for (och emot and against); *vara ~ ett förslag (äv.)* be in favour of a proposal

föra *v2* **1** *(förflytta)* convey; transport, remove; ~ *ett glas till läpparna* raise a glass to one's lips; ~ *handen över* pass one's hand over **2** *(ta med sig) a) (hit)* bring, *b) (dit)* take; *(bära)* carry *(äv. bildl.); (leda)* lead *(äv. bildl.); (ledsaga)* conduct; *(bil e.d.)* drive; *(fartyg)* navigate, sail; ~ *ngn bakom ljuset* hoodwink s.b.; ~ *ngn till bordet* take s.b. in to dinner; ~ *ngt på tal* broach a matter **3** *(ha t. salu)* stock, carry, run, keep *(en vara* a line of goods) **4** *(hantera, manövrera)* handle **5** *bildl. (hän-, räkna)* assign; ~ *krig (ett samtal)* carry on war (a conversation); ~ *oväsen* make a row; ~ *ett fritt språk* talk freely, be outspoken **6** *(skriva, uppgöra)* keep *(böcker* books; *räkenskaper* accounts) **7** *(om våg o.d.)* lead; *det skulle ~ alltför långt* it would take us too far **8** *(med betonad partikel)* ~ *bort* carry (take) away (off), remove; ~ *fram* bring up (forward); ~ *fram en kan-*

didat launch a candidate; ~ *ihop* bring (put) together; ~ *in a*) bring (take; *om pers.* el. *djur* lead) in (into a [*resp.* the] room *etc.*), *b*) (*i protokoll, räkenskaper o.d.*) enter; ~ *med sig a*) carry [along] with one (it *etc.*), *b*) (*ha t. följd*) involve, entail; ~ *ut* bring (take; *om pers.* el. *djur* lead) out (*på* into; *ur* of); ~ *vidare* (*skvaller o.d.*) pass on; ~ *över* convey (bring, carry *etc.*) across, (*varor äv.*) transport **9** *rfl* carry o.s.; *hon för sig väl* she carries herself well (has poise)

förakt *s7* contempt, scorn (*för* for, of); (*överlägset*) disdain (*för* of, for); (*ringaktning*) disregard (*för* of, for); *hysa ~ för* feel contempt for

förakt|a [-'akta] despise; scorn; (*försmå*) disdain **-full** contemptuous; disdainful, scornful **-lig** *al* contemptible; (*starkare*) despicable, mean

förandliga [-'and-] spiritualize

föraning premonition

förankr|a [-'ank-] anchor, moor; *bildl.* establish firmly; *fast ~d i* deeply rooted in **-ing 1** anchoring; *konkr.* anchorage **2** *byggn.* abutment

föran|leda *v2* give rise to, bring about, lead to, result in; *känna sig -ledd att* feel impelled (led) to **-låta** *se föranleda*; *se sig -låten att* feel called upon to, think fit to

föranstalt|a ~ [*om*] arrange, organize (*ngt* s.th.) **-ande** *s6* arranging; *på ~ av* thanks to, by direction of **-ning** arrangement; *vidtaga ~ar för ngt* make preparations (arrangements) for s.th.

för|arbeta prepare, work [up] (*till* into) **-arbete** preparatory (preliminary) work

förare (*vägvisare*) guide; (*av bil etc.*) driver; *flyg.* pilot

förarga [-'arja] annoy, provoke; (*reta äv.*) vex; *bli ~d,* ~ *sig* be annoyed (get angry, vexed) (*över* at); *det ~r mig mycket* it makes me so annoyed (*etc.*)

förargelse [-'arj-] annoyance; (*förtrytelse*) vexation; (*anstöt*) offence; (*bannor*) scolding **-klippa** stumbling block **-väckande I** *a4* offensive, intolerable; (*starkare*) scandalous; ~ *beteende* disorderly conduct [in a public place]; *disturbing the peace* **II** *adv,* *uppträda* ~ commit nuisance

förarglig [-'arj-] *al* **1** (*förtretlig*) provoking, annoying, vexing; (*brydsam*) awkward; *så ~t!* what a nuisance!, how annoying! **2** (*retsam*) irritating, aggravating

förar|hytt (*driver's*) cab; *flyg.* cockpit, (*större*) flight deck **-säte** driver's seat

förband *s7* **1** *med.* bandage, [surgical] dressing; *första* ~ first-aid bandage; *lägga* ~ apply a bandage (*på* to) **2** *mil.* unit; *flyg.* formation

förbands|artiklar first-aid supplies, dressing materials **-gas** surgical gauze **-låda** first-aid kit (box)

förbann|a [-'banna] curse, damn; *-e mig* I'm (I'll be) damned **-ad** *a5* cursed; (*svordom*) damned; (*svagare*) confounded; *bli* ~ *på ngn* get furious (mad) with s.b.; *det var då* [*alldeles*] *-at!* damn it [all]!; *är du* [*rent*] ~? are you quite crazy? **-else** curse; *fara ut i ~r mot* curse

förbarm|a [-'barma] *rfl* take pity (*över* on); *Herre,* ~ *dig över...!* Lord, have mercy on...! **-ande** *s6* compassion, pity; *bibl.* mercy

förbask|ad [-'bask-] *a5* confounded, blasted, ruddy; *-at också!* botheration!

förbehåll *s7* reserve, reservation; (*begränsning*) restriction; (*villkor*) condition; (*klausul*) proviso, [*saving*] clause; *med* ~ with reservations; *med* ~ *att* provided that; *med* ~ *för fel* with reservation for possible errors; *utan* ~ (*äv.*) unconditionally

förbehålla ~ *ngn ngt* (*ngn att*) reserve s.th. for s.b. (s.b. the right to); ~ *sig a*) (*betinga sig*) reserve for (to) o.s., *b*) (*kräva*) demand

förbehållsam *al* reserved, guarded **-het** reserve, reticence

förbehållslös unconditional; unreserved

förbena [-'be:-] *äv. förbenas,* ~ *sig* ossify

förbered|a 1 prepare (*för, på* for), make preparations for **2** *rfl* prepare [o.s.] (*för, på, till* for); (*göra sig redo*) get [o.s.] ready (*för, till* for); ~ *sig på ett tal* (*för en lektion*) prepare a speech (a lesson) **-ande** *a4* (*om skola*) preparatory; (*om möte, arbete, åtgärder*) preliminary **-else** preparation (*för, på, till* for)

förbj I *prep* past, by **II** *adv* **1** *eg.* past, by **2** (*t. ända*) over; (*borta*) gone; (*avslutad*) done; *min tid är* ~ my time is up (over) **3** (*uttröttad*) done in (up), all in

förbid|a [-'bi:-] wait upon (for) **-an** *i* (*under*) ~ *på* awaiting, while waiting for

förbi|farande [-ˣbi:-] *a4* passing **-fart** ['fö:r-] *i* *~en* in (when) passing **-fartsled** bypass

förbi|gå [ˣfö:r-] pass over (*med tystnad* in silence), ignore **-gående I** *s6,* *i* ~ (*flyktigt*) incidentally, by the way; *i ~ sagt* by the way; *med* ~ *av* passing over, omitting **II** *a4* passing; *en* (*de*) ~ a passer-by ([the] passers-by) **-gången** *bli* ~ be passed over; *känna sig* ~ feel left out

förbilliga [-'bill-] cheapen

förbimarsch *mil.* march past

1 förbinda [ˣfö:r-] *se binda för*

2 förbind|a [-'binda] **1** (*sår*) bandage, dress **2** (*förena*) join (*med* to); attach (*med* to); connect, combine (*med* with); (*associera*) associate, connect **3** (*förplikta*) bind over, pledge (*till* to) **4** *rfl* bind (pledge) o.s.; *vi -er oss att* we undertake to

förbindelse [-'bind-] **1** connection; (*mellan personer*) relations (*pl*), relationship; *stå i* ~ *med* be in communication (touch, contact) with; *sätta sig i* ~ *med* get in touch (contact) with, contact **2** (*samfärdsel*) communication (*äv. mil.*); (*trafiklinje*) service, line **3** ~*r* (*bekantskaper*) connections **4** (*förpliktelse*) obligation, engagement; (*skuldsedel e.d.*) bond; (*skuld*) liability, debt; *utan* ~ under no obligation, without engagement, (*om pris*) not binding **-gång** tunnel **-led** connecting link **-officer** liaison officer

förbindlig [-'bind-] *al* courteous, obliging; *~t leende* engaging smile **-het** courtesy

förbipasserande [ˣfö:r- el. -'bi:-] *a4* passing-by; *en* (*de*) ~ a passer-by ([the] passers-by)

förbise ['fö:r-] overlook; disregard **-ende** *s6* oversight; *av* [*rent*] ~ through an (a pure) oversight, [quite] inadvertently

förbistring [-'bist-] confusion

förbittr|a [-'bitt-] **1** (*göra bitter*) embitter **2** (*uppreta*) exasperate **-ad** *a5* bitter; (*uppretad*) exasperated (*på ngn* with s.b.; *över* at); (*våldsam*) enraged **-ing** bitterness; exasperation; (*starkare*) rage

förbjud|a [-'bju:-] forbid; ban (*kärnvapen* nuclear weapons); (*om myndighet o.d.*) prohibit **-en** *a5* forbidden (*frukt* fruit); prohibited; ~ *ingång* (*väg*) no admission (thoroughfare); *-et område* prohibited area, no trespassing; *parkering* ~ no parking; *rökning* ~ no smoking, smoking prohibited; *tillträde -et* no admittance

för|blanda [-'blanda] mix [up]; confuse **-blekna** [-'ble:k-] fade

förblind|a [-'blinda] blind; *bildl. äv.* infatuate; (*blända*) dazzle; ~*d* blind[ed] **-else** infatuation

förbli|va] remain; (*stanna kvar*) stay; *är och förblir* is and will remain; *den var och förblev borta* it was gone for good [and all]

förbluff|a [-'bluffa] amaze, astound; *vard.* flabbergast **-ande** amazing

förblöda [-'blö:-] bleed to death

förbomma bar [up], barricade

för|borga [-'bårja] conceal (*för* from); ~*d* hidden (*för* from) **-borgerliga** [-'bårj-] turn into bourgeois; ~*s* become bourgeois **-brinna** [-'brinna] burn; *bildl.* burn out, be consumed **-broskas** [-'bråsk-] turn into cartilage

förbruk|a [-'bru:ka] consume; use [up]; (*pengar, kraft*) spend **-are** consumer; user **-ning** consumption

förbruknings|artikel consumers' article, consumer goods (*pl*), article of consumption **-material** incidental material[s *pl*], expendable supplies (*pl*) **-ändamål** *för* ~ for consumption purposes, for use

förbruten [-'bru:-] *a5, se förverkad*

förbrylla [-'brylla] confuse, bewilder, perplex; ~*d, vard.* foxed

för|bryta [-'bry:-] *vanl. rfl* offend, trespass (*mot* against); *vad har han förbrutit?* what wrong has he done? **-brytarband** gang of criminals **-brytare** criminal; (*svagare*) offender; (*dömd fånge*) prisoner, convict **-brytarslang** lingo of the underworld; argot **-brytelse** crime; (*svagare*) offence

förbränn|a [-'bränna] burn [up]; *bildl.* blast; (*sveda*) scorch **-ing** burn[ing]; *fys.* combustion; *ofullständig* ~ incomplete combustion

förbrännings|kammare combustion chamber **-motor** internal-combustion engine **-produkt** product of combustion; metabolic waste product; slag

förbrödr|a [-'brö:d-] **1** (*förena*) unite in brotherhood **2** *rfl* fraternize **-ing** fraternization

förbyd *s7* prohibition (*mot* of), ban, embargo (*mot* on); *häva ett* ~ raise a ban, repeal a prohibition; *införa* ~ *för* lay an embargo on

förbuds|anhängare prohibitionist **-fråga** question of prohibition **-lagstiftning** restrictive legislation **-skylt** (*trafikmärke*) prohibition sign

förbynd *s7* **1** (*avtal om samverkan*) compact; *relig.* covenant; (*allians, förbindelse*) alliance, union; *sluta* ~ *med ngn* make an alliance with s.b.; *stå i* ~ *med* enter into an alliance with, be allied with **2** ([*sammanslutning av*] *förening[ar]*) federation, association; *polit.* confederation, league; *hemligt* ~ secret society; *Nationernas* ~ the League of Nations

1 förbund|en [ˣfö:r-] *a5, med -na ögon* [with] blindfold[ed eyes]

2 förbund|en [-'bunn-] *a5* **1** (*förenad*) connect-

ed (*med* with, to); communicating, in communication (*med* with); (*allierad*) allied (*med* to); *det är -et med stora risker* it involves considerable risks **2** (*förpliktad*) bound (*till* to); *vara ngn mycket* ~ be very much obliged to s.b. **3** *med.* dressed, bandaged

förbunds|dagen (*västty. riksdagen*) the Bundestag, the West German parliament **-kansler** federal chancellor **-kapten** *sport.* coach (trainer) of the national team **-nivå** *på* ~ at the national level **-president** (*i Västtyskland o. Österrike*) federal president **-regering** federal government; *den tyska* ~*en* the German federal government **-republik** federal republic; *F~n Tyskland* the Federal Republic of Germany, *vard.* West Germany **-råd** national council **-stat** federal state **-styrelse** national executive committee

förbusk|as [-'busk-] *dep, ängarna* ~ the meadows are becoming overgrown with bushes **-ning** ~*en av* the invasion of woodland into

förbygga [-'bygga] *rfl* overbuild; build beyond one's means

förbyt|a [-'by:-] **1** *se byta bort* **2** (*förvandla*) change, transform (*i, till* into); *han var som -t* he was changed beyond recognition **-as** *dep* change, be turned (*i, till* into)

förbält [-'å:lt] deuced, confounded[ly]

förbättr|a [-'bätt-] improve; ameliorate; (*rätta*) amend; (*moraliskt*) change for the better, reform; *det* ~*r inte saken* that does not mend matters; ~ *sig,* ~*s* improve **-ing** improvement; betterment, amelioration; (*av hälsan*) recovery

förbön intercession

fördatera predate, antedate

fördel *s2* advantage (*framför* over; *för* to; *med* of); (*fromma*) benefit; (*nytta*) good; (*vinst*) profit; *dra* ~ *av* benefit by, derive advantage from; *förändra sig till sin* ~ change for the better; *tala till ngns* ~ speak (be) in a p.'s favour; *vara till* ~ *för ngn* be to a p.'s advantage; *väga för- och nackdelar* weigh the pros and cons; *det kan med* ~ *göras nu* it may very well be done now

fördela [-'de:-] (*utdela*) distribute (*bland, emellan, på* among[st]); (*genom lottning*) allot; (*uppdela*) divide (*bland, emellan* among[st]; *i* into); (*allmosor*) dispense; (*skingra*) dissipate; ~ *på grupper* distribute on groups; ~ *rollerna* cast (distribute) the parts; ~ *sig* distribute themselves, be distributed

fördelaktig *a1* advantageous (*för* to, for); (*gynnsam*) favourable; (*inbringande*) profitable (*för* to, for); (*tilltalande*) attractive, prepossessing; *ett* ~*t yttre* a prepossessing appearance

fördelning 1 (*uppdelning*) distribution, division (*bland, emellan, på* among[st]); allotment; ~ *av exporten på varuslag* breakdown of exports by commodity **2** *mil.* division **fördelningspolitik** distribution policy

fördetting [-ˣdett-] has-been; (*gammalmodig*) back number

fördevind *adv, sjö.* before the wind; *vända* ~ veer

fördjup|a [-'ju:-] **1** deepen, make deeper **2** *rfl* (*i ett ämne*) enter deeply (*i* into); (*i studier, sysselsättning*) become (get) absorbed (engrossed) (*i* in) **-ad** a5 (om pers.) absorbed; (om studier) deeper **-ning** depression; (grop) cavity; (i marken äv.) hollow; (i vägg o.d.) recess, niche

fördold [-'då:ld] a5 hidden; secret

fördom s2 prejudice; full av ~ar, se fördomsfull **fördoms|fri** unprejudiced, unbias[s]ed; broad--minded; (skrupelfri) unscrupulous **-frihet** freedom from prejudice; broad-mindedness; (skrupelfrihet) unscrupulousness **-full** prejudiced **-fullhet** prejudice, bias

fördra se fördraga

fördrag s7 **1** (överenskommelse) treaty, pact; agreement; sluta ~ med conclude a treaty with **2** (tålamod) patience; forbearance

fördrag|a [-'dra:-] bear, stand; (tåla) put up with; (uthärda) endure **-sam** a1 tolerant, forbearing (mot to, towards) **-samhet** tolerance, forbearance

fördrags|brott breach of a treaty **-enlig** [-e:n-] a1 according to (in accordance with) a treaty; ~a förpliktelser treaty obligations

fördragsgardin [ˣfö:r-] curtain

fördragsstridig contrary to the terms of a treaty

fördriv|a [-'dri:-] **1** (driva bort) drive away (out); (driva i landsflykt) banish **2** ~ tiden while away the time, kill time **-ning** driving away (out); expulsion

fördröj|a [-'dröjja] delay; retard; (uppehålla) detain, keep; stall; **-d** utlösning delayed action; ~ sig be delayed **-ning** delay; retardation; detention

fördubbl|a [-'dubb-] double; bildl. redouble; ~ sig, se fördubblas **-as** dep [re]double

fördum|ma [-'dumma] make stupid; absol. blunt the intellect **-ning** dulling of the intellect

fördunkla [-'dunn-] darken; obscure (äv. bildl.); (ställa i skuggan) overshadow; (överträffa) eclipse

fördyr|a [-'dy:-] make dearer (more expensive), raise the price of **-ing** ~ av rise in the price[s pl] of

fördystra [-'dyst-] make gloomy; cast a gloom over; ~ stämningen spoil the [happy] atmosphere

fördäck foredeck

fördäm|ma [-'dämma] dam [up] **-ning** dam; embankment

för|därv s7 **1** (olycka) ruin; (undergång) destruction; störta ngn i ~et lead (drive) s.b. to destruction, bring s.b. to ruin **2** (moraliskt förfall) corruption, depravation; (tidens o.d.) depravity **-därva 1** (i grund) ruin; (tillintetgöra) destroy; (skada) damage; (skämma) spoil **2** (sedligt) corrupt, deprave; (försämra) blight (ngns utsikter a p.'s prospects) **-därvad** a5 **1** ruined etc.; skratta sig ~ die with laughter, burst one's sides with laughing **2** corrupt etc.

fördärv|as [-'därv-] dep be ruined; (skadas) get damaged **-bringande** a4 fatal, ruinous, destructive **-lig** a1 pernicious; (skadlig) injurious, deleterious, destructive

för|dölja se dölja **-döma** [-'dömma] condemn; (ogilla) blame; relig. damn

fördöm|d a5, relig. damned; ~t! hang it [all]! **-else** s5, relig. condemnation **-lig** a1 to be condemned, reprehensible

1 före s6 (på snö etc.) surface [for skiing etc.]

2 före I prep before; in front of; (framom) ahead (in advance) of (äv. bildl.); ~ detta, se under detta; ~ Kristi födelse (f.Kr.) before Christ (B.C.) **II** adv before; min klocka går ~ my watch is fast (gaining); ärendet skall ~ i morgon the matter is to come up tomorrow

förebild prototype (för, till of); (mönster) pattern, model; ha som ~ have as a pattern **-lig** a5 exemplary, ideal, model

förebringa produce, bring in

förebrå v4 reproach; (högtidligt) upbraid; (klandra) blame; ~ sig reproach o.s. (för with); han har ingenting att ~ sig he has nothing to reproach himself with **-else** reproach; få ~r be reproached **-ende** a4 reproaching, reproachful

förebud 1 poet. (föregångare) harbinger **2** (varsel) presage (till of); omen, portent (till of)

förebygg|a (förhindra) prevent; provide against; (förekomma) forestall **-ande I** s6 preventing etc.; prevention; till ~ av for the prevention of **II** a4 preventive

förebåda forebode; portend

förebär|a plead, allege **-ande** s6, under ~ av on the plea of

föredra 1 (framföra) deliver; (utantill) recite; (musikstycke) execute **2** (redogöra för) [present a] report **3** (ge företräde åt) prefer (framför to); det är att ~ it is preferable

föredrag s7 **1** discourse; (kåserande) talk; (föreläsning) lecture; (tal) address; hålla ~ give (deliver) a discourse (lecture), lecture **2** (framställningssätt) delivery; diction; mus. execution, interpretation

föredrag|a se föredra **-ande I** s9 person reporting on a case **II** a4, den ~ a) the reciter (singer etc.), b) se I **-ning** report, submission **-ningslista** agenda

föredragshållare lecturer

föredöm|e s6 example; (mönster) model, pattern **-lig** a5 (efterföljansvärd) worthy of imitation; (förebildlig) ideal, model; ~t uppförande exemplary conduct

före|falla 1 (inträffa) occur, pass **2** (tyckas) seem, appear (ngn to s.b.) **-finnas** dep exist; de -finns hos they are to be found in (at) **-fintlig** a5 existing; available

förege se föregiva

föregiv|a pretend, allege **-ande** s6, under ~ av under (on) the pretext of, pretending to **-en** a5 alleged

föregripa anticipate, forestall

före|gå 1 (inträffa tidigare) precede **2** ~ med gott exempel set an (a good) example **-gående I** a4 preceding, previous, former **II** s6 (tidigare liv) previous (former) life; antecedents (pl) **-gång-are** precursor, forerunner; (företrädare) predecessor

föregångs|land leading country **-kvinna, -man** pioneer

före|ha[va] have in (on) hand, be doing **-havande** s6, ngns ~n a p.'s doings

förehålla point out; ~ ngn ngt expostulate with s.b. on (for, about) s.th.

förekomm|a 1 (hinna före) be in advance of; (föregripa) anticipate, forestall; bättre ~ än ~s better to forestall than be forestalled **2** (hindra) prevent; (*omintetgöra*) frustrate **3** (*anträffas*) be found (met with) **4** (*hända*) occur; *på -en anledning får vi påpeka* it has been found necessary to point out **-ande** *a4* **1** occurring; *i ~ fall* whenever (wherever) applicable; *ofta* (*sällan*) ~ frequent (rare) **2** (*tillmötesgående*) obliging; (*artig*) courteous

förekomst [-å-] *s3* occurrence; presence (*i* in); (*fyndighet*) deposit

föreligg|a be before us (*etc.*); be to hand; (*finnas*) exist; (*finnas att tillgå*) be available; *inget bevis -er ännu* no evidence is as yet forthcoming; *här -er ett misstag* this is a mistake; *det -er risk för* there is a risk of **-ande** *a4* in question, before us; *i ~ fall* in the present case

förelägg|a 1 ~ *ngn ngt* place (put, lay) s.th. before s.b.; (*underställa*) submit (*ngn ngt* s.th. to s.b.) **2** (*föreskriva*) prescribe; (*ålägga*) enjoin upon; (*pålägga*) impose; (*befalla*) command, order **-ande** *s6* command, order, injunction (*äv. jur.*)

föreläs|a 1 (*uppläsa*) read (*för* to) **2** (*hålla föreläsningar*) lecture (*i, om, över* on; *vid* at) **-are 1** reader **2** lecturer **-ning 1** reading **2** lecture; *bevista* (*hålla*) *~ar* attend (give) lectures (*över* on)

föreläsnings|sal lecture room **-serie** series of lectures

föremål *s7* **1** (*ting*) object; article, thing **2** (*mål för tanke, känsla e.d.*) object; *vara ~ för ngns medlidande* be an object of pity to s.b. **3** (*ämne*) subject (*för* of); *han blev ~ för stark kritik* he was subjected to severe criticism; *den blev ~ för vårt intresse* it attracted our interest

för|ena [-'e:na] unite (*med* to; *till* into); (*förbinda*) join, connect; *i sht bildl.* associate; (*kem. o. friare*) combine; (*sammanföra*) bring together; (*förlika*) reconcile; *F~de Arabemiraten* the United Arab Emirates; *Förenta nationerna* (*staterna*) the United Nations (States [of America]) **2** *rfl* unite (*med* with); associate o.s. (*med* with); (*kem. o. friare*) combine (*med* with); ~ *sig med* (*äv.*) join (*ett parti* a party); *floderna ~r sig längre ner* the rivers join (meet) further down **-enad** *a5* united *etc.*; (*om arméer o.d.*) allied; (*om bolag*) associated; (*om stater*) federated; *med ~e krafter* with combined strength (united forces); *vara ~ med a*) eg. be bound up (associated) with, *b*) (*medföra, innebära*) involve, entail

förening 1 (*utan pl*) uniting *etc.* (*till* into); (*av pers., stater*) union, unification; (*friare*) association; *i ~ in* combination (*med* with), jointly **2** (*med pl*) (*förbund*) alliance, union, league, federation; (*samfund*) society; (*större*) association; (*mer intim*) club; *kem.* compound

förenings|band bond [of union]; (*friare*) tie **-liv** organizational activities (*pl*) **-medlem** member of a (the) society (an organization) **-rätt** *ung.* freedom (right) of association

förenkl|a [-'enk-] simplify **-ing** simplification

förenlig [-'e:n-] *a1* consistent, compatible; *är inte ~t med* is inconsistent with, does not accord (tally) with **-het** consistency, compatibility

förent [-'e:nt] *a4, se förena*

före|sats purpose, intention; (*beslut*) resolution; *goda ~er* good resolutions; *i den* [*fasta*] *~en att* with the [firm] purpose of (+ *ing-form*) **-skrift**

direction, instruction; (*läkares*) prescription, directions (*pl*); (*befallning*) order, command; *meddela ~er angående* issue directions (instructions) as to **-skriva** prescribe (*ngn vad han skall göra* what [s.b. is] to do); direct (*ngn att göra ngt* s.b. to do s.th.); ~ *ngn villkor* dictate terms to (lay down conditions for) s.b. **-slå** propose, suggest (*ngn ngt* s.th. to s.b.); *absol.* make a suggestion; (*rekommendera*) recommend; ~ *ngn som kandidat* nominate s.b. (*till* for)

förespegl|a ~ *ngn ngt* hold out the prospect (promise) of...to s.b.; ~ *sig* promise o.s. in advance **-ing** promise, prospect (*om* of); *falska ~ar* false (dazzling) promises

före|språkare 1 (*böneman*) intercessor, pleader (*för* for; *hos* with) **2** (*som förordar*) advocate (*för* of); spokesman (*för* for) **-spå** prophecy, predict **-stava 1** (*säga före*) dictate (*för* to); ~ *eden* administer the oath (*för ngn* to s.b.) **2** (*orsaka, föranleda*) prompt; induce

förestå 1 (*handha*) be [at the] head of; (*affär e.d.*) manage, supervise, conduct **2** (*stunda*) be at hand, be near, impend **-ende** *a4* approaching; imminent; *vara* [*nära*] ~ be approaching ([close] at hand, impending

föreståndar|e manager; principal, director, head; (*för institution*) superintendent; (*för skola*) headmaster, principal **-inna** manageress; principal; (*för anstalt*) matron; (*för skola*) headmistress, principal

föreställa I 1 (*framställa*) represent; (*spela ngns roll*) play the part of; *skall detta ~ konst?* is this supposed to be art? **2** (*presentera*) introduce (*för* to) **II** *rfl* **1** (*tänka sig*) imagine; fancy; envisage, visualize **2** (*presentera sig*) introduce o.s. (*för* to)

föreställning 1 (*framförande*) representation; *teat. o.d.* performance, show **2** (*begrepp*) conception, notion, idea (*om* of); *bilda sig en ~ om* form a conception (*etc.*) of **3** (*erinring, varning*) remonstrance, protest; *göra ngn ~ar* remonstrate (expostulate) with s.b.

föreställnings|ram conceptual framework **-värld** [personal] philosophy

före|sväva *det ~r mig att jag har* I seem to have a dim recollection of having; *det har aldrig ~t mig* such an idea never crossed my mind **-sätta** *rfl* set one's mind [up]on; ~ *sig en uppgift* set o.s. a task

företa *se företaga*

företag *s7* **1** (*förehavande, verk*) undertaking, enterprise; (*vågsamt*) venture; *mil.* operation; *det är ett helt ~ att* it is quite an undertaking to **2** (*affärs-*) company, [business] firm, business; *AE. äv.* corporation

företag|a 1 (*utföra*) undertake; get about; (*om t.ex. resa, undersökning*) make **2** *rfl* undertake (*att* to); (*göra*) do (*med* with) **-are** businessman; entrepreneur; *egen* ~ self-employed person **-sam** *a1* enterprising **-samhet** enterprise, initiative; *fri* ~ free enterprise

företags|demokrati industrial democracy **-ekonom** business economist **-ekonomi** business (industrial) economics (*pl, behandlas som sg*) **-ekonomisk** ~ *teori* theory of business economics; *från* ~ *synpunkt* from the point of view of business economics **-inteckning** floating charge **-jurist** company lawyer **-ledare**

manager; executive **-ledning** [company, business] management **-nedläggelse** close-down, shutdown **-nämnd** works council (committee) **-vinst** [company (*AE.* corporate)] profits (*pl*)
företal preface
förete 1 (*uppvisa*) show [up]; (*framtaga*) produce **2** (*förebringa*) present (*bevis* proof) **3** (*ådagalägga*) exhibit, show; ~ *tecken på utmattning* show signs of fatigue **-else** phenomenon (*pl* phenomena); (*friare*) fact; (*person*) apparition; *en vanlig* ~ a common occurrence **-ende** *s6* showing [up] (*etc.*); production; presentation; *vid* ~ *av* on the production of
företräd|a 1 (*gå före*) precede; ~ *ngn* be a p.'s predecessor **2** (*representera*) represent **-are** (*i ämbete o.d.*) predecessor; (*representant*) representative; (*för idé o.d.*) advocate, leader
företräde *s6* **1** (*audiens*) audience; *begära* ~ *hos ngn* request s.b. for an audience; *få* ~ *hos* obtain an audience of **2** (*förmån framför andra*) preference; (*i rang*) precedence; *ge* ~ *åt* give the preference to; *ha* ~ *framför* take precedence over **3** (*fördel*) advantage, merit (*framför* over); (*överlägsenhet*) superiority (*framför* to)
företrädes|rätt [right of] priority (precedence) **-vis** preferably; especially, particularly
förevarande *a4* present
föreviga [-'e:vi-] perpetuate (*i* in); immortalize
förevis|a show; (*för pengar äv.*) exhibit; *fack.* demonstrate **-ning** exhibition; demonstration; (*föreställning*) performance
förevändning pretext; (*ursäkt*) excuse; (*undanflykt*) evasion; *ta ngt till* ~ take s.th. as an excuse, use s.th. as a pretext
förfader forefather, ancestor
1 förfall (*förhinder*) excuse [for nonattendance], hindrance; *laga* ~ lawful excuse; *utan laga* ~ without due cause
2 förfall (*förstöring*) decay, ruin, decline; (*urartning*) degeneration; (*moraliskt*) decadence, degradation
förfalla [-'falla] **1** (*försämras*) [fall into] decay, deteriorate; (*om byggnad o.d.*) go to ruin, fall into disrepair, dilapidate; (*moraliskt*) go downhill, degenerate; ~ *till dryckenskap* take to drink [ing] **2** (*bli t. intet*) come to nothing; (*om patent, fordran*) lapse, expire; (*om förslag*) be dropped; (*bli ogiltig*) become invalid; ~ *till betalning* fall (be, become) due [for payment], be payable
förfallen [-'fall-] *a5* **1** decayed *etc.*; dilapidated (*äv. om pers.*); (*om byggnad äv.*) in disrepair, tumble-down **2** (*ogiltig*) invalid; (*om skuld*) due, payable, (*om premie*) outstanding; *jur.* forfeited, lapsed
förfallodag [-ˣfallɔ-] expiry (due) date, maturity
förfalsk|a [-'falska] (*räkenskaper o.d.*) falsify; (*dokument, namnteckning*) forge, counterfeit; (*pengar*) counterfeit; (*varor*) adulterate **-are** forger, counterfeiter **-ning** falsification; forgery; counterfeiting; adulteration; *konkr.* imitation, forgery, counterfeit, fake
förfar|a [-'fa:-] *förfor förfarit* proceed; act **-ande** *s6* procedure, proceeding[s *pl*]; *tekn.* process **-as** *förfors förfarits, dep* be wasted; go bad; *låta* ~ (*äv.*) waste **-en** *a3* experienced, skilled (*i* in)

förfaringssätt procedure, method of proceeding; *tekn.* process
förfasa [-'fa:-] *rfl* be horrified (*över* at)
författa [-'fatta] write; (*avfatta*) pen
författarbegåvning literary talent; *pers.* gifted (brilliant) author
författar|e [-'fatt-] author (*av, till* of); writer **-honorar** author's fee[s *pl*]; (*royalty*) royalty **-inna** authoress **-namn** (*antaget*) pen name **-rätt** copyright, author's rights **-skap** *s7* authorship; (*konkr. produktion*) writings (*pl*)
författning [-'fatt-] **1** (*stats-*) constitution; (*förordning*) statute; ordinance **2** (*tillstånd*) condition, state **3** *gå i* ~ *om* proceed (take steps) to (for + *ing-form*)
författnings|enlig [-e:-] *a1* constitutional; statutory **-reform** constitutional reform **-rätt** constitutional law **-samling** statute book; code **-stridig** unconstitutional
förfel|a [-'fe:-] miss; ~ *sin verkan* fail to produce the desired effect **-ad** *a5* ineffective; *ett -at liv* misspent life; *vara* ~ prove a failure
förfin|a [-'fi:-] refine; ~*de seder* polished manners; ~*d smak* cultivated taste **-ing** refinement; polish
förfjol *i* ~ [during, in] the year before last
förflack|a [-'flakka] make shallow, vulgarize **-ning** superficial|ity, -ness
för|flugen [-'flu:-] *a3* (*om plan, tanke*) wild, random; (*om ord*) idle; (*om kula*) stray **-fluten** [-'flu:-] *a5* past; (*förra*) last; *det -flutna* the past **-flyktigas** [-'flykt-] *dep* volatilize, vaporize; (*friare äv.*) evaporate **-flyta** [-'fly:-] pass; (*om tid äv.*) go by, elapse
förflytt|a [-'flytta] **1** [re]move, transport, transfer; (*befolkningsgrupp*) relocate; *bildl.* transplant **2** *rfl* move; *i sht bildl.* transport o.s. **-ning** removal, transfer; transplantation
förfoga [-'fɔ:-] **1** ~ *över* have at one's disposal, have recourse to **2** *rfl* repair (*till* to); ~ *sig bort* remove o.s.
förfogande [-'fɔ:-] *s6* disposal; *stå (ställa ngt till) ngns* ~ be (place s.th.) at a p.'s disposal **-rätt** right of disposition
förfrisk|a [-'friska] refresh **-ning** refreshment
förfrusen [-'fru:-] *a5* frostbitten; (*om växt*) blighted with frost
förfrys|a [-'fry:-] get frostbitten; (*om växt*) get blighted with frost; ~ *händerna* get one's hands frostbitten **-ning** frostbite
förfråg|a [-'frå:-] *rfl* inquire (make inquiries) (*hos ngn om ngt* of s.b. about s.th.) **-an** *r, som pl används då av förfrågning* **-ning** inquiry; *göra -ningar* make inquiries (*om* about; *efter* for)
för|fula [-'fu:-] make ugly **-fuska** [-'fuska] bungle, botch, spoil **-fång** *n* detriment; (*skada*) damage, injury; *till* ~ *för* to the prejudice (detriment) of; *vara ngn till* ~ be a hindrance to s.b. **-fäa** [-'fä:a] brutalize; (*förslöa*) stupefy
förfäder *pl* ancestors, forefathers
förfäkta [-'fäkta] defend, uphold; (*förespråka*) advocate; (*hävda*) maintain, assert; (*rättighet*) vindicate
förfär|a [-'fä:-] terrify (*med* with); appal **-an** *r* terror, horror **-ande** *a4*, *se förfärlig* **-as** *dep* be horror-struck; be appalled (shocked) (*över* at,

by)

förfärdiga [-'fä:r-] make (*av* [out] of); (*industriellt*) manufacture, produce; (*konstruera*) construct

förfärlig [-'fä:r-] *a1* terrible; frightful, dreadful; (*hemsk*) appalling; (*vard.* oerhörd) terrific, awful

förfölj|a [-'följa] pursue, chase; (*plåga*) persecute; -*d av otur* dogged by misfortune; *tanken -er mig* the idea haunts me **-are** pursuer; persecutor

förföljelse [-'följ-] pursuit; *bildl.* persecution (*mot* of) **-mani** persecution complex (mania), *vard.* paranoia

förför|a [-'fö:-] seduce; (*locka*) allure; (*t. ngt orätt*) corrupt, pervert **-are** seducer

förfördela wrong, injure

förförelse [-'fö:-] seduction; (*lockelse*) allurement; (*t. ngt orätt*) corruption **-konst** art of seduction; seductive trick

förförerska [-'fö:-] seductress; (*friare*) temptress

förförisk [-'fö:-] *a5* seductive; (*om kvinna*) bewitching, fascinating **-het** seductiveness; allurement; fascination

förgapa [-'ga:-] *rfl* go crazy (*i* about)

förgas|a [-'ga:-] gasify; ~*s* become gas **-are** carburettor **-ning** gasification; carburation

förgift|a [-'jifta] poison; (*förbittra*) infect, taint **-ning** poisoning; *bildl.* infection **-ningssymtom** toxic symptom

för|gjord *a5, det är som -gjort* everything is going wrong **-glömma** [-'glömma] forget

förgren|a [-'gre:-] *rfl*, **-as** *-dep* ramify, branch off; *-ad* ramified; branchy **-ing** ramification; fork

förgrip|a [-'gri:-] *rfl*, ~ *sig på* (*mot*) outrage, use violence against, violate **-lig** *a1* (*kränkande*) outrageous; (*brottslig*) criminal; (*förolämpande*) injurious

förgrova [-'grɔ:-] coarsen

förgrund *s3* foreground; *träda i* ~*en* (*bildl.*) come to the fore

förgrunds|figur, -gestalt prominent (outstanding) figure

förgrymm|ad [-'grymm-] *a5* incensed (*på* with; *över* at); (*ursinnig*) enraged (*på* with; *över* at) **-as** *dep* become incensed

för|gråten [-'grå:-] *a3* (*om ögon*) red (swollen) with weeping; *hon var alldeles* ~ she had been crying her eyes out **-grämd** [-'grä:md] *a1* grieved; (*om min e.d.*) woeful **-gubbning** [-'gubb-] ageing; (*befolkningens*) increasing proportion of old people

förgud|a [-'gu:-] (*avguda*) idolize; (*dyrka*) adore **-ning** idolization; adoration

förgyll|a [-'jylla] *v2* gild; *bildl.* äv. embellish; ~ *upp* (*bildl.*) touch up, embellish; -*d* gilt, gold-plated **-are** gilder **-ning** gilding

för|gå pass [away, by]; (*försvinna*) disappear, vanish; ~ *sig* forget o.s. (*mot* and insult) **-gången** [-'gången] *a5* past, bygone

förgår *se* förrgår

förgård forecourt; *helvetets* ~ limbo

för|gås *-gicks -gåtts, dep* (*gå förlorad*) be lost; (*försmäkta, dö*) perish, die (*av* with); [*vara nära att*] ~ *av nyfikenhet* be dying (consumed) with curiosity

förgäng|else [-'jäŋ-] decay, dissolution; *i sht bibl.* corruption **-lig** *al* perishable; corruptible; (*dödlig*) mortal; (*kortvarig*) fugitive, transient **-lighet** perishability; (*dödlighet*) mortality; (*kortvarighet*) transience

förgäta [-'jä:-] *förgat* (*åld.*) förgätit forget

förgätmigej *s3, s9* forget-me-not, scorpion grass

förgäves [-'jä:-] in vain

förgöra [-'jö:-] destroy, annihilate; (*bringa om livet*) put to death

förhal|a [-'ha:-] **1** *sjö.* warp **2** (*försena*) delay, retard; ~ *förhandlingarna* drag out the proceedings; ~ *tiden* spin out the time **-ning 1** *sjö.* warping **2** (*försening*) delay, retardation

förhalnings|politik policy of obstruction **-taktik** delaying tactics; *AE. polit.* filibuster[ing]

förhand 1 *kortsp.* elder hand; *ha* ~ have the lead **2** *på* ~ beforehand, in advance

förhandenvarande [-'*hann-] *a4, under* ~ *omständigheter* under [the] present circumstances

förhandl|a [-'hand-] negotiate (*med* with; *om* about); (*överlägga*) deliberate, discuss **-are** negotiator **-ing** (*överläggning*) deliberation; (*vid domstol, möte e.d.*) proceeding; (*underhandling*) negotiation; *avbryta* (*inleda*) ~*ar* suspend (start) negotiations

förhandlings|basis basis for (of) negotiations **-bord** negotiation table **-delegation** negotiation delegation **-läge** bargaining position **-part** negotiating party **-partner** counterpart in negotiations **-rätt** right to negotiate **-villig** willing to negotiate

förhands|anmälan advance registration **-avisera** preadvise **-besked** advance notice **-beställning** advance booking **-diskussion** preliminary discussion **-granskning** preliminary examination **-inställning** attitude taken in advance; prejudiced view; *om du redan har en* ~ *om* if you have already made up your mind about **-löfte** promise in advance **-meddelande** advance notice **-reklam** advance publicity **-rätt** prior right **-visa** preview **-visning** preview, trade show

förhast|a [-'hasta] *rfl* be rash (too hasty) **-ad** *a5* rash; *dra* ~*e slutsatser* jump to conclusions

förhatlig [-'ha:t-] *al* hateful, detestable, odious (*för* to)

förhind|er [-'hind-] *få* ~ be prevented [from] going (coming); *med* ~ with impediments; *i händelse av* ~ in case of impediment **-ra** prevent (*ngn från att* s.b. from + *ing-form*); (*stoppa*) stop

förhistor|ia 1 prehistory **2** background **-isk** prehistoric[al]

förhjälpa ~ *ngn till ngt* help (assist) s.b. to obtain s.th.

förhoppning [-'håpp-] hope; (*förväntning*) expectation; ~*ar* (*utsikter*) prospects; *göra sig* ~*ar* indulge in expectations; *hysa* ~*ar om* hope for; *inge ngn* ~*ar* inspire s.b. with hopes, give s.b. hope; *i* ~ *om* (*att*) hoping for (to)

förhoppnings|full hopeful; (*lovande*) promising **-vis** hopefully

förhud foreskin

förhyd|a [-'hy:-] *v2, sjö.* sheathe **-ning** *sjö.* sheathing

förhyra [-'hy:-] **1** (*hus o.d.*) rent **2** (*sjöman*) hire

förhåll|a [-'hålla] *rfl* **1** (*om pers.*) *a*) (*uppföra sig*) behave; (*handla*) act, *b*) (*förbli*) keep (*lugn* quiet), remain (*passiv* passive, *likgiltig* indifferent) **2** (*om sak*) *a*) (*kem. o.d.*) behave, *b*) (*mat. o. friare*) be; *hur -er det sig med...?* what is the position as regards...?, how are things with...?; *så -er sig saken* that is how matters stand; *bredden -er sig till längden som 1 till 3* the breadth is to the length as 1 to 3

förhållande [-'håll-] *s6* **1** (*tillstånd*) state of affairs (things), (*pl äv.*) conditions; (*omständigheter*) circumstances; *rätta ~t* the fact [of the matter]; *under alla ~n* in any case; *under inga ~n* under (in) no circumstances, in no case **2** (*inbördes ställning*) relations (*pl*), relationship; (*kärleks-*) intimacy, connection; *spänt ~* strained relations (*pl*), estrangement; *i ~ till* in relation to; *stå i vänskapligt ~ till* be on friendly terms with; *ha ett ~ med ngn* have an affair with s.b. **3** (*proportion*) proportion; *mat.* ratio; *i ~ till hans inkomster* in proportion to his income; *inte stå i ngt rimligt ~ till* be out of all proportion to; *i ~ till sin ålder är han* for his age he is **4** (*uppträdande*) behaviour, conduct **-vis** [-ˣhåll-] proportionately

förhållning [ˣfö:r- *el.* -'håll-] *mus.* suspension

förhållnings|order [-ˣhåll-] *pl* orders, instructions, directions **-regel** direction, rule of conduct

för|håna [-'hå:-] scoff at **-hårdnad** [-'hå:rd-] *s3* induration, callus, callosity

förhänge curtain

förhärd|a [-'hä:r-] harden; *~ sig* harden one's heart **-ad** *a5* hardened, obdurate; (*inbiten*) inveterate; *en ~ skurk* a double-dyed villain **-as** *dep* [become] harden[ed] **-else** obduracy, obdurateness

för|härja [-'härja] ravage, devastate, lay waste **-härliga** [-'hä:r-] *i sht bibl.* glorify; (*prisa*) extol, laud

förhärsk|a [ˣfö:r-, *äv.* -'härr-] predominate, prevail **-ande** *a4* predominant, prevailing; prevalent; *vara ~, se förhärska*

förhäv|a [-'hä:-] *rfl* pride o.s. (*över ngt* on s.th.); (*skryta*) boast (*över ngt* of s.th.) **-else** arrogance; boasting

förhäx|a [-'häxa] bewitch **-ning** bewitchment

förhöj|a [-'höjja] raise; (*friare*) increase; *bildl.* heighten, enhance **-ning** raising; (*mera konkr.*) increase, rise, *AE.* raise

för|hör *s7* examination; (*utfrågning*) interrogation; (*rättsligt*) inquest, hearing; *skol.* test, *AE.* quiz **-höra** [-'hö:-] examine; (*fråga ut*) interrogate; *skol.* question (*på* on), test; *AE.* quiz; *~ sig, se höra [sig för]*

förhörs|ledare interrogator **-protokoll** statement **-teknik** cross-examination technique

förhöst early autumn

förinta [-'inta] annihilate, destroy; *~nde blick* withering glance

förintelse [-'inn-] annihilation, destruction **-strålning** annihilation radiation **-vapen** weapon of extermination

för|irra [-'irra] *rfl* go astray, lose one's way; wander **-ivra** [-'i:v-] *rfl* get [too] excited; lose one's head (self-control) **-jaga** [-'ja:-] chase (drive) away, expel; *i sht bildl.* dispel

förkalk|a[s] [-'kall-] *fysiol.* calcify **-ning** calcification

förkalkyl preliminary calculation (estimate)

förkasta [-'kasta] **1** (*ogilla, avslå*) reject, repudiate; (*förslag äv.*) turn down, refuse **2** (*fördöma*) denounce; *en ~d människa* a rejected person, an outcast

förkastelse [-'kast-] rejection; repudiation **-dom** condemnation; *uttala en ~ över* pass a condemnation upon, denounce

förkast|lig [-'kast-] *a1* (*fördömlig*) to be condemned; (*friare*) unjustifiable; (*avskyvärd*) abominable **-ning** *geol.* fault **-ningsspricka** *geol.* fault fissure

förklara [-'kla:-] **1** explain; (*klargöra*) make clear, elucidate; (*tolka*) interpret; (*utlägga*) expound **2** (*tillkännage*) declare; (*uppge*) state; (*kungöra*) proclaim; *~ krig* declare war; *~ ngn för segrare* proclaim s.b. [the] victor; *~ ngn sin kärlek* declare one's love for s.b.; *han ~des skyldig till* he was found guilty of **3** (*förhärliga*) glorify **4** *rfl* explain o.s.; *~ sig för (mot)* declare for (against); *~ sig om (över) ngt* declare (state) one's opinion of s.th.

förklar|ad [-'kla:-] *a5* **1** (*avgjord*) declared, avowed **2** (*överjordisk*) glorified, transfigured **-ing 1** explanation (*av, på, till, över* of); elucidation; (*tolkning*) interpretation; *till ~* in (by way of) explanation; *utan ett ord till ~* without a word of explanation **2** (*tillkännagivande*) declaration; statement; *avge ~* make a declaration **-lig** *a1* explicable; (*lätt insedd*) comprehensible; *av lätt ~a skäl* for obvious reasons

för|klena [-'kle:-] disparage, depreciate; *i ~nde ordalag* in disparaging terms **-klinga** [-'kliŋa] die away; *~ ohörd* fall on deaf ears

förklä *s6, se förkläde*

förkläd|a [-'klä:-] disguise (*till* as); *-d till brevbärare* disguised as (in the disguise of) a postman

förkläde 1 apron; (*för barn*) pinafore **2** *bildl.* chaperon

för|klädnad [-'klä:d-] *s3* disguise; *skyddande ~* (*biol.*) mimicry **-knippa** [-'knippa] associate

förkol|a *rfl*, **-as** [-'kå:-] *dep* char **-na** char, carbonize; *bildl.* cool [down, off]

förkomm|a [-'kämma] get lost; (*om försändelse*) miscarry **-en** *a5* missing; (*förfallen*) lost

förkonstl|a [-'kånst-] artificialize; *~d* artificial; sophisticated **-ing** artificiality; sophistication

förkoppra [-'kåpp-] copper

förkort|a [-'kårta] shorten; (*ord e.d.*) abbreviate; (*bok e.d.*) abridge; (*tiden*) while away, beguile; *mat.* reduce, simplify **-ning** shortening; (*av ord e.d.*) abbreviation; (*av bok e.d.*) abridgment; *mat.* reduction

förkovr|a [-'kå:v-] **1** improve; (*öka*) increase **2** *rfl* improve; advance; *~ sig i engelska* improve one's English **-an** *r* improvement; (*framsteg*) advance

för|krigstiden *under ~* in the prewar period, *äv.* before the war **-kristen** pre-Christian

förkroma [-'krå:-] chrome

förkroppslig|a [-'krâpps-] embody, incarnate **-ande** *s6* embodiment, incarnation

förkross|a [-'kråssa] crush; overwhelm **-ad** *a5* brokenhearted; (*ångerfull*) contrite **-ande** *a4* crushing; heartbreaking; ~ *majoritet* overwhelming majority **-else** contrition; brokenheartedness

förkrympt *a4* stunted, dwarfed; *fysiol.* abortive

förkunn|a [-'kunna] *v1* announce *(för* to); *(utropa)* proclaim; *(predika)* preach; *(förebåda)* foretell, herald **-are** announcer, preacher; herald **-else** announcement, proclamation; preaching

förkunskaper *pl* previous knowledge *(sg)* (*i* of); *ha goda (dåliga)* ~ be well (poorly) grounded (*i* in)

förkväv|a [-'kvä:-] choke, stifle **-as** *dep* stifle

förkyl|a [-'çy:-] *rfl* catch [a] cold; *bli -d* catch [a] cold; *vara mycket -d* have a bad (severe) cold; *nu är det -t!* (*vard.*) that's torn it! **-ning** cold

för|kämpe champion *(för* of) **-känning,** **-känsla** presentiment, premonition, forewarning **-kärlek** predilection *(för* for), partiality *(för* for, to)

förkättrad [-'çätt-] *a5* decried, run (cried) down

förköp advance booking; *köpa i* ~ book in advance

förköpa [-'çö:-] *rfl* spend too much money

för|köpspris advance-booking price **-körsrätt** [-çö:rs-] right of way **-laddning** (*i äldre vapen*) wad[ding]; (*i sprängborrhål*) stemming

förlag *s7* (*bok-*) publishing house (company, firm), publishers (*pl*); *utgiven av A:s* ~ published by A; *utgiven på eget* ~ published by the author

förlaga [ˣfö:r-] *s1* (*original*) original; (*förebild*) model, pattern

förlags|beteckning [publisher's] imprint **-bevis** [subordinated] debenture **-man** sleeping partner, advancer of capital **-redaktör** editor [in a publishing house] **-rätt** publishing right[s *pl*], copyright **-verksamhet** publishing

förlam|a [-'la:-] paralyse (*äv. bildl.*); ~*d av* *skräck* paralysed with fright (horror) **-ning** paralysis

förled *språkv.* first element

förled|a [-'le:-] entice; seduce (*till* into) **-ande** *a4* enticing; seductive

förlegad [-'le:-] *a5* antiquated, out-of-date, old-fashioned, outmoded; ~ *kvickhet* stale joke

förlid|a [-'li:-] go by, pass **-en** *a5* past, over, spent; (*förra*) last

förlig [ˣfö:r-] *a1*, *sjö.* forward; ~ *vind* following (favourable) wind

förlik|a [-'li:-] *v3, v1* reconcile (*med* to); ~ *sig* become reconciled (*med* to, with) **-as** *v3, dep* be [come] reconciled; (*sämjas*) agree, get on **-ning** reconciliation; (*överenskommelse*) agreement, settlement; *avgöras genom* ~ be settled out of court; *träffa* ~ come to terms, settle out of court

förliknings|förslag mediation offer; offer of a compromise **-kommission** conciliation board **-man** [official] conciliator, arbitrator, mediator **-mannaexpedition** *Statens* ~ [the Swedish] national conciliators' office

förlis|a [-'li:-] *v3* be wrecked, sink, founder; (*om pers.*) be shipwrecked **-ning** loss, [ship]wreck

förlit|a [-'li:-] *rfl*, ~ *sig på a*) (*ngn*) trust in s.b., *b*) (*ngt*) trust to (rely on) s.th., *c*) (*att få*) rely on obtaining **-an** *r* confidence (*på* in); *i* ~ *på* trusting to, relying on

förljud|ande [-'ju:-] *s6* report; rumour, hearsay;

enligt ~ according to what one hears, from hearsay **-as** *förljöds förljudits, dep, det -es att* it is reported that

förljugen [-'ju:-] *a3* mendacious, false **-het** mendacity, inveterate falsity

för|ljuva [-'ju:-] gladden, sweeten **-lopp** [-'låpp] *s7* **1** (*utgång*) lapse; *efter* ~*et av ett år* after [the lapse of] a year **2** (*utveckling*) course; ~*et av händelsen var följande* the course of events was this

förlor|a [-'lo:-] lose; ~ *besinningen* lose one's head; ~ *i styrka* decrease in strength; ~ *i vikt* lose weight; ~ *på affären* lose on the transaction; ~ *på en vara* lose on an article; ~ *sitt hjärta till* lose one's heart to; ~ *sig* lose o.s. (be lost) (*i* in), (*om ljud*) die away **-ad** *a5* lost; (*borta*) missing; (*bortkastad, om möda o.d.*) wasted; *den* ~*e sonen* the Prodigal Son; ~ *ägg* poached eggs; *gå* ~ be lost (*för* to); *ge ngn* ~ (*ngt -at*) give s.b. (s.th.) up for lost **-are** loser

förloss|a [-'låssa] *relig.* redeem **-are** *relig.* redeemer **-ning 1** *relig.* redemption **2** *med.* delivery; childbirth

förlossnings|avdelning maternity ward **-konst** obstetrics (*pl, behandlas som sg*); midwifery **-kramp** eclampsia **-tång** [obstetric(al)] forceps (*sg o. pl*)

förlov [-'lå:v, *äv.* ˣfö:r-] *i uttr.: med* ~ *sagt* with your permission, if I may say so

förlov|a [-'lå:-] *åld.* betroth (*med* to); ~ *sig* become engaged (*med* to) **-ad** *a5* **1** *det* ~*e landet* the Promised Land; *ett -at land för* a promised land (paradise) for **2** engaged [to be married] (*med* to), *högt.* betrothed (*med* to) ; *de* ~*e* the engaged couple **-ning** engagement, *högt.* betrothal

förlovnings|annons announcement of an (the) engagement **-ring** engagement ring

förlupen [-'lu:-] *a5* runaway; ~ *kula* stray bullet

förlust *s3* loss (*av* of; *för* for; *på* on); ~*er* (*i fältslag*) casualties; *en ren* ~ a dead loss; *gå* (*sälja*) *med* ~ run (sell) at a loss; *göra* (*lida*) *stora* ~*er* sustain heavy (severe) losses; *företaget går med* ~ it is a losing concern

förlusta [-'lusta] divert (*sig o.s.*)

förlustbringande *a4* involving a loss, with a heavy loss (*för* to, for); *ett* ~ *företag* a company running at a loss; *vara* ~ be attended with losses

förlustelse [-'lust-] amusement, entertainment

förlust|ig [-'lust-] *a5, gå* ~ lose, be deprived of, forfeit **-konto** loss account **-lista** *mil.* casualty list **-sida** debit side; *uppföra på* ~*n* enter as a debit, *bildl.* write off as a loss

förlyfta [-'lyfta] *rfl*, ~ *sig på a*) *eg.* overstrain o.s. by lifting, *b*) *bildl.* fail to accomplish, overreach o.s. in

förlåt [ˣfö:r-] *s3* (*förhänge*) veil; *lyfta på* ~*en* unveil, uncover, disclose, allow s.b. to catch a glimpse

förlåta [-'lå:-] forgive (*ngn ngt* s.b. for s.th.); pardon; (*ursäkta*) excuse; *förlåt!* (*ursäkt*) [I am] sorry!; *förlåt att jag avbryter* excuse my interrupting; *förlåt, jag hörde inte* I beg your pardon, but I didn't catch what you said; *det tror jag inte, det får du* ~ *mig* I don't believe it, whatever you may say

förlåt|else [-'lå:-] forgiveness (*för* for); *syndernas* ~ remission of [one's] sins; *be [ngn] om* ~ ask (beg) a p.'s forgiveness; *få* ~ be pardoned (for-given) **-lig** *a1* pardonable, excusable, forgivable **förlägen** [-'lä:-] *a3* abashed; embarrassed (*över* at); (*blyg*) shy; (*brydd*) perplexed; (*förvirrad*) confused; *göra ngn* ~ embarrass (disconcert) s.b. **-het** embarrassment, confusion; shyness; (*trång-mål*) embarrassment, difficulty, trouble; *råka i* ~ *för pengar* get into financial difficulties, be hard up for money

förlägg|a [-'lägga] **1** (*slarva bort*) mislay **2** (*placera*) locate (*till* in); *mil.* station (*i, vid* in, at); (*inkvartera*) accommodate, billet; (*förflytta*) re-move, transfer (*till* to); (*t. annan tid*) assign, alter the time for; *handlingen är förlagd till medeltiden* the action (story) takes place in the Middle Ages **3** (*böcker o.d.*) publish **-are** (*bok-*) publisher **-ning** accommodation, location; *mil.* station, camp **-ningsort** *mil.* garrison [town]

förläggsgaffel [*fö:r-] serving fork

förläna [-'lä:-] **1** ~ *ngn ngt* grant s.b. s.th., confer s.th. on s.b., (*begåva*) endow s.b. with **2** *hist.*, ~ *ngn ngt* enfeoff s.b. with s.th.

förläng|a [-'läŋa] *v2* lengthen, extend; (*giltighet, i tid*) extend, prolong; ~ *ett bråk* (*mat.*) extend a fraction **-ning** lengthening, extension; (*av giltighet, i tid*) prolongation, extension **-ningssladd** extension flex (*AE.* cord)

för|läning [-'lä:-] (*gods*) fief, fee; (*utdelning av gods*) enfeoffment **-läsa** [-'lä:-] ~ *sig* overwork o.s. by reading; study too much **-läst** [-'lä:st] *a4* overworked (strained) by too much study; (*verklighetsfrämmande*) starry-eyed **-löjliga** [-'löjj-] [turn (hold up) to] ridicule

förlöp|a [-'lö:-] *v3 el. förlöpte förlupit* **1** (*förlida*) pass; (*avlöpa*) pass off; (*gå t. ända*) pass away **2** (*rymma från*) run away from; desert, abandon **3** *rfl* lose one's head **-ning** (*överilning*) indiscre-tion

förlös|a [-'lö:-] *med.* deliver **-ande** *a4, det* ~ *ordet* the right word at the right time; *ett* ~ *skratt* a laugh that relieves the tension

förmak [*fö:r-] *s7* **1** (*sällskapsrum*) drawing room **2** *anat.* auricle

förmal|a [-'ma:-] grind, mill **-ning** grinding, milling

förman foreman, supervisor; (*överordnad*) superior, *vard.* boss; *kvinnlig* ~ forewoman

förman|a [-'ma:-] (*råda o. varna*) warn; (*uppmana t.*) exhort; (*tillrättavisa*) admonish **-ing** warning; exhortation; admonition **-ingstal** admonitory address; (*friare*) mild lecture

för|mast foremast **-match** preliminary (opening) match

förmedelst [-'me:-] *se medelst*

förmedl|a [-'me:d-] mediate, act as [an] inter-mediary in; (*åstadkomma*) bring about; (*nyheter e.d.*) supply; (*telefonsamtal*) connect, put through; ~ *en affär* act as [an] intermediary in a transaction; ~ *trafiken mellan* ply between **-ande** *a4* intermediary **-are** intermediary, me-diator **-ing** mediation; supplying; (*kontor*) agency, office; *genom* ~ *av* through the agency of **förmedlings|länk** intermediary link, connec-tion **-provision** agent's commission; brokerage

1 förmena [-'me:-] *v1* (*hindra, neka*) deny (*ngn ngt* s.b. s.th.); (*förbjuda*) forbid

2 förmen|a [-'me:-] *v1 el. -ade -t* (*anse*) think, believe, be of opinion; ~ *sig ha rätt* consider that one is right

för|menande *s6, enligt mitt* ~ in my opinion **-ment** *a4* supposed

förmer[a] *oböjligt a* better (*än* than), superior (*än* to)

förmera [-'me:-] *se föröka*

förmiddag forenoon; *vanl.* morning; *kl. 8* ~*en* (*förk. f.m.*) at eight o'clock in the morning (*förk. at 8* [o'clock] a.m.); *i dag på* ~*en, i* ~*s* this morn-ing; *i morgon* ~ tomorrow morning; *på* (*om*) ~*arna* in the mornings

förmiddags|bröllop morning wedding **-dräkt** morning dress

förmildrande [-'mild-] *a4, * ~ *omständigheter* ex-tenuating circumstances

förminsk|a [-'minska] diminish, lessen, reduce; *foto.* reduce; *i* ~*d skala* on a reduced scale **-as** *dep* diminish, decrease **-ning** reduction, diminu-tion; *foto.* reduction

förmod|a [-'mo:-] suppose, imagine; *AE. äv.* guess; (*ta för givet*) assume; (*med stor säkerhet*) presume **-an** *r* supposition; *efter* ~ as supposed; *mot* [*all*] ~ contrary to [all] expectation **-ligen** presumably

förmultn|a [-'mult-] moulder [away]; decay **-ing** mouldering; decay **-ingsprocess** process of de-cay (mouldering away)

förmyndar|e [-'mynn-, *äv.* *fö:r-] guardian (*för* for, of); *stå under* ~ be under guardianship; *ställa under* ~ place under a guardian **-regering** re-gency

förmynderskap [-'mynn-, *äv.* *fö:r-] *s7* guardi-anship; *bildl.* authority

förmå *v4* **1** (*kunna, orka*) be able to (+ *inf.*), be capable of (+ *ing-form*); (*i pres.*) can; (*i imperf.*) could; *allt vad jag* ~*r* all that I can; *allt vad huset* ~*r* all I (we) can offer you; *jag* ~*r inte mer* I can do no more, (*orkar äta*) I can't eat any more, I'm quite satisfied, thank you **2** ~ *ngn* [*till*] *att* induce (prevail upon, get) s.b. to, (*övertala*) persuade s.b. to; *jag kan inte* ~ *mig* [*till*] *att* I can't induce (bring) myself to

förmåga [-'må:-] *s1* **1** (*kraft*) power[s *pl*] (*att* to); (*prestations-*) capacity (*att* for); (*medfödd fallen-het*) faculty (*att* for, of + *ing-form*); (*duglighet*) ability (*att* to); (*begåvning*) gift, talent; ~*n att tänka* the power of thought; *efter bästa* ~ to the best of one's ability; *uppbjuda all sin* ~ tax one's power to the utmost; *det går över min* ~ it surpasses (is beyond) my powers (capacity) **2** *pers.* man (woman) of ability (parts); (*talang*) talent, outstanding actor (singer *etc.*)

förmån [*fö:r-] *s3* advantage; privilege; (*gagn, nytta*) benefit; (*förmånsrätt*) *sociala* ~*er* social benefits; *till* ~ *för* to the benefit of, in favour of; *ha* ~*en att* have the privilege of; *detta talar till hans* ~ this weighs in his favour **-lig** [-'å:-] *a1* advantageous (*för* to); (*gynnsam*) favourable; (*vinstgivande*) profitable; (*välgörande*) beneficial

förmåns|erbjudande special offer, bargain **-rätt** priority [right]; *med* ~ preferential, privi-leged **-ställning** preferential (priority) position **-tagare** *försäkr. jur.* beneficiary

1 förmäl|a [-'mä:-] *v2, v3* (*omtala*) state, report,

tell; *ryktet -er att* it is rumoured that
2 förmäla [-'mä:-] *v2* (*bortgifta*) marry; ~ *sig med* wed, marry
förmälning [-'mä:l-] marriage
för|mänskliga [-'männ-] give human form to; (*personifiera*) personify **-märka** [-'märka] notice
förmäten [-'mä:-] *a3* presumptuous; (*djärv*) audacious, bold; *vara nog* ~ *att* make so bold as to **-het** presumption; arrogance
förmögen [-'mö:-] *a3* **1** (*i stånd*) capable (*att of* + *ing-form*) **2** (*välbärgad*) wealthy, well-to-do; (*predikativt*) well off; *en* ~ *man* (*äv.*) a man of means (property); *de förmögna klasserna* the propertied classes **-het 1** ~*er* (*andliga o. kroppsliga*) powers **2** (*rikedom*) fortune; (*samlad egendom*) property; (*kapital*) capital
förmögenhets|beskattning taxation of capital (property) **-brott** crime against property **-fördelning** distribution of wealth **-förhållanden** *pl* financial (economic) circumstances **-rätt** law of property **-skatt** capital levy
förmörk|a [-'mörka] darken; (*himlen o. bildl.*) cloud; (*skymma*) dim; *astr.* eclipse **-as** *dep* [be] darken[ed] **-else** *astr.* eclipse
förna [*ˣfö:r-] *s1, biol., geol.* litter
förnam *imperf. av* förnimma
för|namn Christian (first, given) name; *vad heter hon i* ~? what is her Christian name? **-natt** *på* ~*en* before midnight
förnedr|a [-'ne:-] **1** (*vanära*) degrade, disgrace, dishonour; *hur kan du* ~ *dig till sådant?* how can you stoop to that? **2** *bibl.* (*förringa*) abase, humble **-ing** degradation; humiliation **-ingstillstånd** state of humiliation (*etc.*)
förnek|a [-'ne:-] (*neka t.*) deny; (*bestrida*) dispute; (*t.ex. sitt barn*) disown; ~ *sin natur* abnegate (renounce) one's nature; *han* ~*r sig aldrig* he is always true to type, *iron.* trust him to do such a thing; *hans goda hjärta* ~*r sig aldrig* his kindness of heart never fails **-else** denial; repudiation; abnegation
förnickl|a [-'nick-] nickel **-ing** nickel plate, nickelling
förnimbar [-'nimm— *el.* -ˣnimm-] *a1* perceptible (*för* to), sensible (*för* to); (*synlig äv.*) perceivable; (*hörbar*) audible
för|nimma [-'nimma] *-nam -nummit* **1** (*uppfatta*) be sensible of; (*höra*) hear; (*se*) perceive; (*andligt*) apprehend **2** (*märka*) notice; (*få veta*) hear [of]
förnimmelse [-'nimm-] **1** (*uppfattning*) perception; apprehension **2** (*känsla*) sense, sensation; (*sinnesintryck o. friare*) impression **-förmåga** power of perception, perceptivity
förning [*ˣfö:r-] (guest's) contribution to a (the) meal (party); *ha* ~ *med sig* bring something to eat and drink
förnuft *s7* reason (*äv. förnuftet*); *sunt* ~ common sense; *ta sitt* ~ *till fånga* listen to reason; *tala* ~ *med* talk sense to
förnuftig [-'nuft-] *a1* reasonable; (*förståndig*) sensible **-het** reasonableness; rationality
förnufts|enlig [-e:-] *a1*, **-mässig** *a1* rational **-skäl** rational argument **-stridig, -vidrig** *a1* contrary to all reason; irrational; (*friare*) unreasonable

förnummit [-'numm-] *sup. av* förnimma
förnumst|ig [-'nums-] *a1* would-be-wise, sapient **-ighet** sapience **-igt** *adv* as one who knows (knew)
förny|a [-'ny:a] renew; (*upprepa*) repeat; (*återuppliva*) refresh; ~ *sig* renew o.s.; ~ *sitt lager* replenish one's stock **-are** renewer **-bar** *a5* renewable; ~ *energi* renewable energy
förnyelse [-'ny:-] renewal; (*upplivande*) revival, regeneration **-bar** *se* förnybar
förnäm *a1* noble, aristocratic, distinguished; (*högättad*) highborn; (*högdragen*) lofty, haughty, *vard.* high and mighty; (*värdig*) dignified; ~ *av sig* stately, proud; *med* ~ *min* with a stately air; ~*t folk* people of rank; *i* ~ *avskildhet* in splendid isolation; *det var värst vad hon är* ~ *av sig* she certainly puts on airs **-het 1** (*börd*) high breeding **2** (*högdragenhet*) superciliousness **-itet** *s3* **1** *se förnämhet* **2** (*förnäm pers.*) distinguished person, celebrity
förnämlig [-'nä:m-] *a1* distinguished; excellent **-ast** *adv* chiefly, principally
förnämst [-ä:-] **I** *a superl.* foremost, first; (*om pers.*) greatest, most distinguished **II** *adv, se* främst
förnär *se 2 när I*
för|närma [-'närma] offend; affront; insult; *känna sig* ~*d av* take offence at **-nödenheter** [-ˣnö:-] *pl* necessities, requirements; (*livs-*) necessities of life, *jur.* necessaries
förnöj|a [-'nöjja] *v2* (*roa*) gratify, please; *ombyte -er* variety is the spice of life
förnöj|d *a1* **1** (*tillfredsställd*) content, satisfied **2** (*glad*) pleased, delighted (*över* at) **-else** [-'nöjj-] (*förlustelse*) amusement, pleasure; *finna sin* ~ *i* delight in, find pleasure in
förnöjsam [-'nöjj-] *a1* contented **-het** contentedness
förnöta [-'nö:-] *bildl.* use up; ~ *tiden* waste one's time (*med att* in + *ing-form*)
förolyck|ad *a5* mortally wounded; (*t. sjöss*) wrecked; (*om flygplan*) crashed; *de* ~*e* the victims [of the accident], the casualties **-as** *dep* meet with an accident; (*t. sjöss*) be wrecked
förolämp|a insult, offend, affront; *känna sig* ~*d över* (*av*) feel very much offended at (by) **-ning** insult, offence, affront (*mot* to)
för|ord 1 (*företal*) preface, foreword **2** (*rekommendation*) [special] recommendation **-orda** recommend (*hos* to; *till* for); *livligt* ~ highly recommend
förordn|a [-'å:rd-] **1** (*påbjuda*) ordain, decree; (*testamentariskt*) provide (*om* for) **2** (*ordinera*) prescribe, order **3** (*utse*) appoint, nominate; (*bemyndiga*) authorize, commission **-ande** *s6* **1** (*föreskrift*) ordaining, ordination; (*testamentariskt*) provision **2** (*bemyndigande*) authorization, commission; (*tjänste-*) appointment; *hans* ~ *utgår* his commission (appointment) expires **-ing** ordinance, decree, order
föroren|a contaminate, defile, pollute **-ing** contamination, defilement, pollution; *konkr.* impurity, pollutant
för|orsaka cause, occasion **-ort** suburb
förorts|bo suburban[ite]; commuter **-område** suburban area

förorätta wrong, injure
förpack|a [-'pakka] pack (wrap) [up] **-ning**
abstr. packing, wrapping up; *konkr.* package,
packet; *(ask)* box; *(låda)* case; *(emballage)* packing, wrapping, package; *exklusive (inklusive)* ~
packing excluded (included)
förpacknings|dag packing date **-industri**
packaging industry **-teknik** packaging technique
för|paktare [-'pakt-] leaseholder; tenant **-panta**
[-'panta] pledge, pawn
förpassa [-'passa] *(befordra)* dispatch, send [off]
; ~ *till evigheten* dispatch into eternity; ~ *ur landet* deport; ~ *sig bort* take o.s. off
förpesta [-'pesta] poison, pollute, infect *(äv.
bildl.)*
förpik *sjö.* forepeak
förpinad [-'pi:-] *a5* harrowed; tortured
förplikt|a [-'plikta] ~ *ngn att* put (lay) s.b. under
an (the) obligation to, bind s.b. to; *rikedom ~r
wealth* entails responsibility; *adelskap ~r (äv.)*
noblesse oblige; ~ *sig* bind (engage) o.s.; *känna
sig ~d att* feel [in duty] bound to **-else** *(plikt)*
duty, obligation; *(förbindelse)* engagement, commitment, obligation; *ha ~r mot ngn* have obligations towards s.b.; *ikläda sig ~r* assume obligations **-iga** *se förplikta*
förpläg|a [-'plä:-] provide with food and drink,
treat *(med* to) **-nad** [-ä:-] *s3* fare, food **2** *(pro-
viantering)* provisioning **-nadstjänst** supply
service **-ning** [-ä:-] entertainment; *(utspisning
äv.)* feeding
förpost outpost *(mot* against) *(äv. bildl.)* **-fäkt-
ning** outpost skirmish
förprick|a tick [off], mark [off], check [off]
-ning marking (checking) off; tick
förprövning preliminary examination
förpupp|a *rfl,* **-as** [-'pupp-] *dep* change into a
chrysalis, pupate **-ning** pupation
förr 1 *(förut)* before; *(fordom)* formerly *(äv. förr
i tiden)*; ~ *och nu* then and now; ~ *låg det en lada
här* there used to be a barn here; ~ *trodde man
people* used to think **2** *(tidigare)* sooner, earlier;
ju ~ *dess bättre* the sooner the better **3** *(hellre)*
rather, sooner
förre *förra, a komp.* **1** *(förutvarande)* the former;
~ *ägaren* the former (late) owner; *([nyss] av-
gångne)* late; *(motsats senare)* early; *förra hälften
av 1800-talet* the first half of the 19th century **2**
(föregående, senaste) [the] last; *i förra månaden*
last month; *mitt förra brev* my last letter; *den
förra* the former *(...den senare* the latter)
förresten [-'ress-] *se rest 1*
förr|fjol *se förfjol* **-förra** last but one; ~ *veckan*
the week before last **-går** *i* ~ the day before yesterday
förridare outrider
för|ringa [-'riŋa] *vl* minimize, lessen; *(nedvär-
dera)* depreciate; *(ngns förtjänst o.d.)* belittle
-rinna [-'rinna] run (flow) away *(i* into); *i sht
bibl.* ebb away
förromant|iken pre-Romanticism **-isk**
[-'mann-] *a5* preromantic
förrum anteroom
förruttna [-'rutt-] rot, putrefy, decompose; decay
förruttnelse [-'rutt-] putrefaction, corruption;

decay **-bakterie** putrefactive bacteria
förrycka [-'rykka] distort; *(friare)* dislocate
förryckt *a4* distracted; mad; *är du [alldeles]* ~?
are you [quite] mad? **-het** madness
förrymd *a5* runaway; *(om fånge e.d.)* escaped
förrysk|a [-'ryss-] Russianize **-ning** Russianiza-
tion
förråa [-'rå:a] coarsen, brutalize; *verka ~nde*
have a brutalizing effect *(på* on)
förråd *s7, s4* store *(äv. bildl.)*; *(lager)* stock; *(tillgång)* supply; *(lokal)* storeroom, storage room;
lägga upp ett ~ *av* lay up a store of, store up
förråda [-'rå:-] betray *(åt* to); *(röja)* reveal *(för
to)*; ~ *sig* betray o.s., give o.s. away
förråds|arbetare store[house]man **-byggnad**
storehouse; warehouse **-fartyg** supply ship,
store carrier **-förman** storekeeper
förråd|are [-'rä:-] traitor *(mot* to); betrayer *(mot
of)* **-eri** treachery *(mot* to); *(lands-)* [an act of]
treason *(mot* to); *(friare)* betrayal *(mot* of) **-isk**
a5 treacherous
förrän [*förr-, 'förr-, *el.* -'änn, *vard.* förrn] before; *icke* ~ *a) (ej tidigare än)* not before, not earlier than, *b) (först)* not until (till); *det dröjde inte
länge* ~ it was not long before; *knappt hade de
kommit* ~ no sooner had they come than
förränt|a [-'ränta] *(placera mot ränta)* place at
interest, invest; ~ *sig [bra]* yield (bring in) [a
good] interest **-ning** yield; *dålig* ~ low yield (rate
of interest)
förrätt *kokk.* first course
förrätt|a [-'rätta] *(utföra)* perform; *(uträtta)* ac-
complish; *kyrkl.* officiate at, conduct; *(auktion
o.d.)* hold; *efter väl ~t värv* having accomplished
one's task successfully, one's duties done **-ning**
1 *(utan pl)* performing, execution, carrying out **2**
(med pl) function; duty; ceremony; *vara ute på
~ar* be out on official duties **-ningsman** executor, executive official
försagd *a1* timid, pusillanimous **-het** timidity,
pusillanimity
försak|a [-'sa:-] *(vara utan)* go without, give up;
(avsäga sig) renounce; *(avstå från)* deny o.s., do
without **-else** *(umbärande)* privation; *(frivillig)*
[act of] self-denial
församl|a [-'samla] **1** assemble, gather **2** *rfl, se
församlas* **-as** *dep* assemble; gather together;
meet **-ing 1** *(möte)* meeting; *(samling personer)*
assembly, convention, body **2** *(kyrka, kyrkosam-
fund)* church; *(menighet)* congregation; *(administrativ enhet)* parish
församlings|bo parishioner; *~rna (koll.)* the
parish **-bok** parish register **-hus** parish hall
-kyrka parish church **-liv** parish (congrega-
tional) life **-rätt** right of public assembly **-syster**
ung. deaconess
försats *språkv.* antecedent clause
för|se furnish, supply, provide; *(med utrustning)*
equip; ~ *med strängar (underskrift)* string (sign);
~ *sig* furnish *(etc.)* o.s., *(vid bordet)* help o.s.
(med to) **-sedd** *a5* furnished *(etc.) (med* with);
~ *med (äv.)* with; *väl* ~ *(om pers.)* well supplied
(etc.); *vara* ~ *med (äv.)* have
förseelse [-'se:-] offence, fault; *jur.* misde-
meanour
försegel headsail, foresail

försegl|a [-'se:-] seal [up]; *~de läppar* sealed lips; *med ~de order* under sealed orders **-ing** seal; sealing

försen|a [-'se:-] delay; retard; hold up; *10 minuter ~d* 10 minutes late; *vara ~d* be late (delayed) **-ing** delay **-ingsavgift** extra charge for overdue payment

försiggå take place; *(inträffa)* happen, come about; *(avlöpa)* pass *(vard.* come) off; *(pågå)* be going on; *handlingen ~r på (i)* the scene is laid at (in); *vad ~r här?* what is going on here?

försigkommen [-å-] *a3* advanced, forward; precocious; *de mest försigkomna eleverna* the most advanced pupils **-het** maturity; precociousness, precocity

försiktig [-'sikt-] *a1* cautious *(med* with); guarded; *(aktsam)* careful *(med* with, of); *var ~ med vad du säger* be careful of what you say, watch your words **-het** caution; guardedness; *(aktsamhet)* care

försiktighets|mått, -åtgärd precaution, precautionary measure; *vidtaga ~er* take precautions

försiktigtvis [-ˣsikt-] so as to be on the safe side

försilvr|a [-'silv-] silver, -silver-plate **-ing** silver-plating, silvering

för|sinka [-'sinka] *se försena* **-sitta** [-'sitta] *~ chansen* miss the chance; *~ tiden* [be in] default; *~ tillfället* lose the opportunity **-sjunka** [-'ʃunka] sink *(i* into); *bildl. äv.* fall *(i* into); *~ i tankar* be lost in thought; *~ i tystnad* fall silent **-skaffa** [-'skaffa] *(skaffa)* procure, obtain; *(skänka)* afford; *vad ~r mig äran av ert besök?* to what do I owe the honour of your visit?

förskans|a [-'skansa] entrench; *~ sig* entrench o.s., *bildl.* take shelter *(bakom* behind) **-ning** entrenchment

förskepp forebody; bow

förskingr|a [-'ʃiŋra] *(försnilla)* embezzle, defalcate; *(bortslösa)* dissipate, squander **-are** embezzler **-ing 1** *(försnillning)* embezzlement, defalcation **2** *svenskarna i ~en* the Swedes scattered abroad; *judarna i ~en* the [Jewish] Diaspora

förskinn leather apron

1 förskjut|a [ˣfö:r-] *se skjuta [för]; regeln är -en* the door is bolted

2 förskjut|a [-'ʃu:-] **1** *(stöta ifrån sig)* reject; cast [off]; *(barn)* disown **2** *(försträcka)* advance **3** *(rubba)* displace **4** *rfl, se förskjutas*

förskjut|as [-'ʃu:t-] *dep* get displaced, shift; *(om last)* shift **-ning** *(rubbning)* displacement, shifting; *(av last)* shifting; *geol.* fault; *(friare)* change

förskola nursery school; kindergarten

förskol[e]|barn preschool child **-lärare, -lärarinna** nursery school (kindergarten) teacher **-lärarlinje** nursery school teacher training centre

förskon|a [-'sko:-] *~ ngn för (från)* ngt spare s.b. s.th., preserve s.b. from s.th. **-ing** forbearance, mercy

förskott *s7* advance [payment], payment in advance; *~ på lön* advance on salary; *betala i ~* pay in advance **-era** [pay in] advance

förskotts|belopp advance amount **-likvid** payment in advance, advance [payment]

förskrift copy; *skriva efter ~* write (make) copies

förskriv|a [-'skri:-] **I 1** *(rekvirera)* order **2** *(över-*

låta) convey, assign *(till, åt* to) **II** *rfl* **1** *(härröra)* come, originate, derive [one's (its) origin] **2** *~ sig åt satan* sell one's soul to the devil **-ning 1** *(rekvisition)* order, request **2** *(skuldförbindelse)* certificate of debt, bond

förskräck|a [-'skräkka] *v3* frighten, scare, startle; *bli -t* be (get) frightened *(etc.)* *(för, över* at); *spåren -er* the footprints frighten me *(etc.)* **-as** *v3, dep* be frightened *(etc.)*, jfr *förskräcka* **-else** fright, alarm; consternation; *ta en ända med ~* come to a tragic end **-lig** *a1* dreadful, frightful; *(ohygglig)* horrible; *vard.* awful; *se ~ ut* look a fright

för|skrämd *a1* frightened, scared [out of one's wits]; *(skygg)* shy, subdued **-skyllan** [-'ʃyll-] *r, utan egen ~* through no fault of mine *(etc.)*; *utan egen ~ och värdighet* no thanks to me **-skämd** [-ʃ-] foul; *bildl. äv.* corrupt

förskärar|e, -kniv carving knife, carver

förskön|a [-'ʃö:-] embellish, beautify; *(med prydnader o. friare)* adorn **-ing** embellishment; adornment

1 förslag [ˣfö:r-] *mus.* grace [note]

2 förslag 1 proposal; *i sht AE.* proposition; *(anbud)* offer *(om, till* for); *(uppslag)* suggestion, recommendation; *parl.* motion, *(lag-)* bill; *på ~ av* at the suggestion of; *antaga (förkasta) ett ~* accept (reject) a proposal; *framlägga ett ~* submit (make) a proposal; *gå in på ett ~* agree to a proposal; *väcka ~ om* move **2** *(plan)* project, scheme *(till* for); *(utkast)* draft *(till* of); *(kostnads-)* estimate *[of cost(s)]* **3** *(vid besättande av tjänst)* nomination list

förslagen [-'sla:-] *a3* cunning, artful; *(fyndig)* smart

förslags|rum place on the nomination list; *komma i första ~met* be the leading candidate (frontrunner) **-ställare** proposer [of a motion], mover **-vis** as a suggestion, [let us] say

förslapp|a [-'slappa] weaken; *(t.ex. seder, disciplin)* relax **-as** *dep* be (become) relaxed **-ning** weakening; *(av moralen)* laxity

förslava [-'sla:-] enslave

förslit|a [-'sli:-] wear out **-ning** wear[ing out]; wear and tear

förslum|mas [-'slummas] *dep, området ~* the district is becoming (turning into) a slum **-ning** deterioration into slum

förslut|a [-'slu:-] *förslöt förslutit* close, lock; seal **-ning** *konkr.* locking (closing) device; seal

förslå suffice, be enough; *det ~r inte långt* that won't go far (last long); *dumt så [att] det ~r* as stupid as can be

förslö|a [-'slö:a] *bildl.* make apathetic, dull **-as** *dep* grow (get) apathetic (dull)

förslösa [-'slö:-] waste, squander *(på* on); *(friare)* dissipate, use up *(på* in)

försmak foretaste; *få en ~ av* have a foretaste of

försmå *v4* disdain; *(förakta)* despise; *~dd friare* rejected lover

försmäd|lig [-'smä:d-] *a1* *(hånfull)* sneering, scoffing; *(förtretlig)* annoying **-ligt** *adv* sneeringly *etc.*; *~ nog* provokingly enough

försmäkta [-'smäkta] *(i fängelse e.d.)* pine [away], languish; grow faint *(av törst* of thirst; *av värme* from heat)

försnill|a [-'snilla] embezzle [money] (*för ngn off s.b.*; *ur* from) **-ning** embezzlement
försockra [-'såkkra] saccharify, saccharize; (*söta*) sugar
försoff|a [-'såffa] *v1* dull, make apathetic; ~*d* dulled, apathetic **-ning** apathy; sloth[fulness]
försommar early summer
förson|a [-'sɔ:-] **1** (*blidka*) conciliate, propitiate **2** (*förlika*) reconcile (*med* to) **3** (*sona*) atone for; (*friare*) expiate, make amends for **4** *rfl* reconcile o.s. (*med* to); (*inbördes*) make it up, become reconciled **-as** *dep, se försona 4* **-ing** reconciliation; atonement, expiation (*äv. relig.*); *till ~ för sina synder* in expiation (atonement) of one's sins
försonings|dag *F~en* the Day of Atonement, Yom Kippur **-död** expiatory death **-fest** Feast of Expiation **-offer** propitiatory sacrifice **-politik** policy of reconciliation
försonlig [-'sɔ:n-] *a1* conciliatory, forgiving
för|sorg [-'sårj] *r* **1** *dra ~ om* provide for; take care of **2** *genom ngns ~* through (by) s.b. **-sova** [-'så:-] *rfl* oversleep [o.s.]
för|spann *s7* leading horses (*pl*) **-spel** prelude (*till* to, of); (*till sexuellt umgänge*) foreplay
förspilla [-'spilla] waste; throw away; (*förslösa*) squander; (*förverka*) forfeit
för|språng start, lead; *bildl. äv.* advantage; *få ~ före* get a start over; *ha en timmes ~* have an hour's start **-spänd** *a5* (*om häst*) in the shafts; *vagnen är ~* the carriage is ready **-spänt** *adv, ha det väl ~* have a good start in life, be well off (well-to-do)
först I *konj* when...first **II** *adv* first; (*inte förrän*) not until (till), only; (*i början*) at first; (*för det första*) in the first place; (*vid uppräkning*) first[ly] ; *~ nu* not until now, only now; *~ och främst* first of all; *den ~ anlände* the first arrival, the first to arrive; *lika väl ~ som sist* just as well now as later; *komma ~* be first; *komma ~ fram* get there first; *stå ~ på listan* [be at the] head [of] the list; *det är ~ nyligen som* it is only recently that; *jag hörde det ~ i går* I only heard it yesterday; *den som kommer ~ till kvarnen får ~ mala* first come, first served
förste *se förste*
förstad suburb
förstadags|kuvert first-day cover **-stämpel** first day of issue
förstadium preliminary stage
förstads|bo suburban[ite]; commuter **-område** suburban area
förstag *sjö.* forestay
förstagradsekvation equation of the first degree
förstagångs|förbrytare first offender **-väljare** new voter, s.b. voting for the first time
förstahandsuppgift first-hand information
förstaklass|are first-form boy (*etc.*) **-biljett** first-class ticket
förstamaj|blomma [-'majj-] May-Day flower, [artificial] buttonhole flower worn on May Day **-demonstration** May-Day manifestation (demonstration) **-firande** May-Day celebrations (*pl*)
förstaplacering *sport.* first place
förstatlig|a [-'sta:t-] nationalize; (*socialisera*)

socialize **-ande** *s6* nationalization; socialization
förstaupplaga first edition
för|stavelse prefix **-steg** precedence
först|e *-a, a superl.* [the] first; (*i tiden*) earliest; (*i rummet*) foremost; (*i betydenhet, värde e.d.*) principal, chief, head; (*ursprunglig*) original, primary; *-a avbetalning* initial payment; *~ bibliotekarie* principal librarian; *-a bästa* the first that comes; *-a hjälpen* first aid; *-a juni* [on] the first of June, (*i brev*) June 1st; *F-a Mosebok* Genesis; *-a raden* (*teat.*) dress circle, *AE.* balcony; *-a öppet vatten* (*hand.*) first open water (*förk.* f.o.w.); *från -a början* from the very beginning; *för det -a, i -a rummet* in the first place; *i -a hand* [at] first hand; *den ~ jag mötte* the first person I met; *det -a jag såg* the first thing I saw
förstelna [-'ste:l-] stiffen, become (get) quite stiff; *bildl.* numb; *fack.* fossilize, petrify
försten|a [-'ste:-] petrify (*äv. bildl.*) **-ing** petrifaction
först|född *a5* first-born; *vår ~e* our first-born (eldest) [child] **-föderska** primipara **-födslorätt** right of primogeniture; birthright; *sälja sin ~* sell one's birthright
förstklassig *a1* first-class, first-rate; crack
först|ling firstling **-lingsverk** first (maiden) work
först|nämnda, -nämnde *a5* the first-mentioned; (*den, det förra*) the former
förstock|ad [-'ståkk-] *a5* hardened, obdurate **-else** hardness of heart; obduracy
förstone *s, endast i uttr.: i ~* at first, to begin with
förstopp|a [-'ståppa] constipate **-ning** constipation
förstor|a [-'stɔ:-] enlarge (*äv. foto.*); *opt. o. bildl.* magnify; *starkt ~d* greatly enlarged, highly magnified **-ing** enlargement; magnification
förstorings|apparat enlarger **-glas** magnifying glass, magnifier
förstrykning mark, tick; (*understrykning*) underline, underscore
försträck|a [-'sträkka] **1** (*sträcka för mycket*) strain; *~ sig* strain o.s. (a limb) **2** (*låna*) advance **-ning 1** (*skada*) strain (*i* of) **2** (*lån*) advance
förströ divert; (*roa*) entertain, amuse; *~ sig* amuse (divert) o.s.
förströdd *a5* preoccupied **-het** preoccupation
förströelse [-'strö:-] diversion; recreation **-litteratur** light reading
förstubro porch step
förstucke|n [-'stukk-] *a5* concealed, hidden; *-t hot* veiled threat
för|studie pilot study **-studium** preparatory study
förstu|ga [entrance] hall; (*mindre*) passage **-kvist** porch
förstulen [-'stu:-] *a5* furtive, surreptitious
förstumm|a [-'stumma] silence **-as** *dep* become (fall) silent; be struck dumb
förstå 1 understand (*av* from, by; *med, på* by); (*begripa*) comprehend, grasp; *vard.* dig; (*inse*) see; (*få klart för sig*) realize; (*veta*) know; *~s* (*naturligtvis*) of course; *det ~s!* that is clear!; *~ mig rätt* don't misunderstand me; *låta ngn ~ att* give s.b. to understand that, (*antyda*) intimate (hint) to s.b. that; *åh, jag ~r!* oh, I see!; *~r du inte*

skämt? can't you see a joke?; *han ~r inte bättre* he doesn't know any better; *jag förstod på honom att han* he gave me to understand that he, I saw that he **2** *rfl,* ~ *sig på a)* understand, *b) (affärer)* be clever at (skilled in), *c) (konst, mat e.d.)* be a judge of; ~ *sig på att* know (understand) how to; *jag ~r mig inte på den flickan* I can't make that girl out

förstå|elig [-'stå:-] *a5* understandable, comprehensible, intelligible *(för* to) **-else** understanding, comprehension *(för* of); *finna ~ för* meet with understanding for **-ende** *a4* sympathetic

förstånd *s7* understanding, comprehension; *(tankeförmåga)* intellect; *(begåvning)* intelligence; *(sunt förnuft)* [common] sense; *(omdöme)* discretion, judg[e]ment; *vard.* brains; *efter bästa ~* to the best of one's ability; *förlora ~et* lose one's reason; *ha ~ om att göra ngt* have the sense to do s.th.; *tala ~ med* talk sense to; *han talar som han har ~ till* he speaks according to his lights; *mitt ~ står stilla* I am at my wit's end; *det övergår mitt ~* it is beyond me

förståndig [-'stånd-] *a1* intelligent; *(klok)* wise; prudent; *(förnuftig)* sensible

förstånds|gåvor intellectual powers **-handikappad** educationally subnormal **-mässig** *a1* rational

förstås [-'ståss] *se förstå 1*

förståsigpåare [-ˣpå:-] connoisseur, expert; *iron.* would-be authority

förställ|a [-'ställa] disguise *(rösten* one's voice); ~ *sig* dissimulate, dissemble; *-d* disguised, *(låtsad)* feigned **-ning** dissimulation

förstäm|d *a5* **1** *bildl.* out of (in low) spirits, disheartened **2** *(om trumma o.d.)* muffled **-ning** gloom; depression

förständiga [-'stänn-] ~ *ngn att [icke]* enjoin (order) s.b. [not] to

förstärk|a [-'stärka] strengthen; *bildl. äv.* fortify; *mil.* reinforce; *tekn.* reinforce; magnify; *elektron.* amplify **-are** *elektron.* amplifier; *tekn.* magnifier **-arrör** *elektron.* [pre]amplifier valve; *AE.* vacuum tube amplifier **-ning** strengthening; *i sht mil.* reinforcement; *elektron.* amplification

förstäv *sjö.* stem, prow

förstör|a [-'stö:-] *v2* **1** destroy *(äv. bildl.)*; *(ödelägga)* lay waste, devastate, *bildl. äv.* wreck, blast; *([allvarligt] skada)* damage, injure; *se -d ut* look a wreck **2** *([totalt] fördärva)* ruin *(äv. bildl.)*; *(förslösa)* waste, dissipate, squander **3** *(förta, skämma)* spoil **-as** *v2, dep* be destroyed *(etc.)*; decay; *(totalt)* perish

förstörelse [-'stö:-] destruction **-lusta** love of destruction, destructive urge **-vapen** weapon of [mass] destruction **-verk** work of destruction

förstöring [-'stö:-] *se förstörelse; Jerusalems ~* the Fall of Jerusalem

försum|bar [-ˣsumm- el. -'summ-] *a5* insignificant; trifling **-lig** *a1* negligent; dilatory; *(vårdslös)* neglectful, careless **-lighet** negligence

försumm|a [-'summa] *(underlåta)* neglect; *(utebli från)* miss, let slip; *(vansköta)* neglect, be careless of; ~ *att* fail to; ~ *tillfället* let the opportunity slip; *känna sig ~d* feel neglected (slighted); *ta igen det ~de* make up for lost ground (time) **-else** neglect, negligence; *(förbiseende)*

sight; *(underlåtenhet)* failure, omission

försump|a [-'sumpa] *bildl.* allow to stagnate **-as** *dep* **1** become waterlogged **2** *bildl.* get bogged down **-ning 1** waterlogging **2** *bildl.* stagnation

försupen [-'su:-] *a5* sottish; drunken

försur|a [-'su:-] acidify **-ning** acidification

försutten [-'sutt-] *a5* forfeited, lost

försvag|a [-'sva:-] weaken; enfeeble, debilitate; *(skada)* impair; *(mildra)* soften **-as** *dep* grow (become, get) weak[er], weaken **-ning** weakening; enfeeblement, debilitation

försvann *imperf. av försvinna*

försvar *s7* defence; *(berättigande)* justification *(av, för* of); *(beskydd)* protection *(för* of); *det svenska ~et* the Swedish national defence; *till ~ för* in defence of; *andraga ngt till sitt ~* say s.th. for (in justification of) o.s.; *ta ngn i ~* stand up for s.b.

försvar|a [-'sva:-] defend *(mot* from, against); *(rättfärdiga)* justify; *(i ord äv.)* advocate, stand up for **-are** defender; *offentlig ~* [court-appointed] counsel for the defence, *AE.* public defender **-bar** *a5, se försvarlig 1* **-lig** *a1* **1** *(försvarbar)* defensible; justifiable; *(ursäktlig)* excusable; *(hjälplig)* passable **2** *(ansenlig)* considerable; *(betydande)* respectable, *vard.* jolly big

försvars|advokat counsel for the defence **-allians** defensive alliance **-anläggning, -anordning** *~ar* defences **-attaché** defence attaché **-beredskap** defensive preparedness **-departement** ministry of defence; *AE.* department of defense **-duglig** *sätta i ~t skick* make capable of defence **-fientlig** opposed to national defence **-förbund** defensive alliance **-fördrag** defence treaty **-gren** arm, [fighting] service **-högskola** defence college; *F~n* [the Swedish] national defence college **-krig** defensive war **-linje** line of defence **-lös** defenceless **-löshet** defencelessness **-makt** defence force, national defence **-medel** means of defence **-mekanism** *psykol.* defence mechanism **-minister** minister of defence; *AE.* secretary of defense **-obligation** defence bond **-plan** plan of defence **-politik** defence policy **-skrift** apology **-stab** defence staff **-styrka** defence force (unit) **-ställning** defensive position **-tal** speech for the defence; *(friare)* apology **-talan** *jur.* plea for the defendant **-utgifter** *pl* defence spendings (expenditure *[sg]*) **-utskott** *~et* [the Swedish parliamentary] standing committee on defence **-vapen** defensive weapon **-vilja** will to defend o.s. **-vänlig** in favour of national defence **-åtgärd** defensive measure

försvensk|a [-'svens-] give a Swedish character, make Swedish; *(översätta)* turn into Swedish **-as** *dep* become Swedish **-ning** [the] changing (rendering) *(av of...)* into Swedish; [the] Swedish form

försvinn|a [-'svinna] *försvann försvunnit* disappear *(från, ur* from; *[in] i* into); *(plötsligt)* vanish [away]; *(förflyta)* pass [away]; *(ur sikte)* be lost; *(upphöra att finnas till)* cease to exist; ~ *i fjärran* disappear in (vanish into) the distance; *försvinn!* be off with you!, get lost!, clear out!, scram! **-ande I** *s6* disappearance **II** *adv* exceedingly; infinitesimal[ly]

försvunn|en [-'svunn-] *a5* vanished; gone; (*bortkommen*) missing **-it** *sup. av försvinna*

för|svåra [-'svå:-] make (render) [more] difficult; (*förvärra*) aggravate; (*lägga hinder i vägen för*) obstruct; (*trassla till*) complicate **-svär[j]a** [-'své(:)r-] forswear; ~ *sig* (*med ed binda sig vid*) commit o.s. (*åt, till* to); ~ *sig åt djävulen* sell one's soul to the devil

försyn *s3* **1** *relig.* providence; ~*en* Providence; *genom* ~*ens skickelse* by an act of providence; *låta det gå på Guds* ~ trust to luck, let matters take their own course **2** (*hänsyn*) consideration

försynd|a [-'synda] *rfl* sin (*mot* against) **-else** sin, offence (*mot* against); (*friare*) breach (*mot* of)

försynt [-'sy:nt] *a1* considerate, tactful; discreet **-het** considerateness; modesty, discretion

försåt *s7* (*bakhåll*) ambush; (*fälla*) trap; (*svek*) treachery; *ligga i* ~ lie in ambush; *lägga* ~ *för* lay an ambush (set snares) for **-lig** *a1* treacherous; ~*a frågor* tricky questions

för|såvida [-'vi:da], **-såvitt** *se såvida, såvitt*

försäga [-'säjja] *rfl* (*förråda ngt*) blab out a secret, let the cat out of the bag

försäkra [-'sä:k-] **I 1** (*betyga*) assure (*ngn om* s.b. of), aver; *jag kan* ~ *dig* [*om*] *att* I can assure you that, you can take my word for it that; *du kan vara* ~*d om att* you may rest assured that **2** (*assurera*) insure; (*om sjö- o. flygförsäkring äv.*) underwrite; *den* ~*de* the insured, the policyholder; *högt* ~*d* heavily insured; *för högt* ~*d* overinsured; *lågt* ~*d* insured for (at) a low figure **II** *rfl* **1** (*förvissa sig*) secure (*om ngt* s.th.), make sure(*om ngt* of s.th.) **2** (*ta en försäkring*) insure one's life (o.s.)

försäkr|an [-'sä:k-] *r, som pl används pl av försäkring* assurance, declaration; assertion; affirmation **-ing 1** *se försäkran* **2** (*brand-, liv-*) insurance; (*liv- äv.*) life assurance (insurance); (*sjö-*) underwriting; *teckna en* ~ take out (effect) an insurance

försäkrings|agent insurance agent **-avgift** insurance contribution (fee) **-avtal** insurance contract **-bar** *a5* insurable **-bedrägeri** insurance fraud **-belopp** sum insured **-besked** insurance statement **-bolag** insurance company **-brev** insurance policy **-domstol** *F~en, se Försäkringsöverdomstolen* **-givare** insurer; (*om brittisk livförsäkring*) assurer **-inspektion** ~*en* [the Swedish] private insurance supervisory service **-kassa** *allmän* ~ [local] social insurance office **-matematik** actuarial mathematics (*pl, behandlas som sg*) **-polis** *se -brev* **-premie** insurance premium **-rätt** (*domstol*) [regional] social insurance court **-summa** *se -belopp* **-tagare** [the] insured, policyholder **-tjänsteman** insurance officer **-villkor** insurance terms (conditions) **-värde** (*som kan försäkras*) insurable value; (*som är försäkrat*) insured value **-överdomstol** ~*en* [the Swedish] supreme social insurance court

försälj|a [-'sälja] sell **-are** salesman, seller, *fem.* saleswoman, salesgirl ~*ing* selling; sale[*s pl*]; *till* ~ for (on) sale; *utbjuda till* ~ offer for sale

försäljnings|bolag trading company; (*-ombud*) broker **-chef** sales manager **-distrikt** sales terri-

tory **-främjande** *a4*, ~ *åtgärder* sales promotion (*sg*) **-kostnad** sales (selling) cost **-omkostnad** selling expense **-organisation** marketing (sales) organization **-pris** sales (selling) price **-provision** commission on sales **-villkor** *pl* terms of sale

försämr|a [-'sämra] deteriorate; (*skada, förvärra*) impair, make worse **-as** *dep* deteriorate; get (grow) worse; (*moraliskt*) degenerate **-ing** deterioration, impairment (*i* in, of); (*moralisk*) degeneration (*i* in); (*av hälsotillstånd*) change for the worse

försändelse [-'sänd-] (*varu-*) consignment; (*kolli*) parcel; (*post-*) [postal] packet (package); *assurerad* ~ insured articles

försänk|a [-'sänka] **1** *tekn.* countersink **2** *bildl.* plunge (*i sorg* into grief); put (*i sömn* to sleep); reduce (*i fattigdom* to poverty) **-ning 1** *tekn.* countersink **2** ~*ar* (*bildl.*) influential friends; *ha goda* ~*ar* have good connections

försätta [-'sätta] **1** (*bringa*) set (*i rörelse* in motion; *på fri fot* free); put (*i raseri* in a rage); ~ *ngn i konkurs* adjudge (declare) s.b. bankrupt **2** *bibl.* remove (*berg* mountains)

försätts|blad *bokb.* [front] flyleaf (endpaper) **-lins** lens attachment

försök *s7* (*ansats*) attempt (*till* at); (*bemödande*) effort, endeavour (*till* at); (*prov*) trial, test (*med* with, of); (*experiment*) experiment (*med* with; *på* on); ~ *till brott* attempted crime; (*på* ~ *a*) by way of [an] experiment, just for a trial, on trial, *b*) (*på måfå*) at random, at a venture; *våga* ~*et* risk it, take one's chance [with it]; *det är värt ett* ~ it is worth trying

försöka [-'sö:-] *try; absol. äv.* have a try; (*bemöda sig*) endeavour, seek; (*pröva på*) attempt; ~ *duger* there's no harm in trying; ~ *sig på* try one's hand at, (*våga sig på*) venture on, have a go, *vard.* take a crack at; *försök bara! a*) (*uppmuntrande*) just try!, *b*) (*hotande*) just you try it on!; *försök inte!* don't try that on with me!, *AE.* you're kidding!

försöks|anläggning pilot (experimental) plant **-ballong** pilot balloon; *släppa upp en* ~ (*bildl.*) send up a kite **-djur** laboratory animal **-fel** error in [carrying out] an experiment **-heat** qualifying heat **-kanin** *bildl.* guinea pig **-ledare** experimenter; (*vid institut*) research officer **-metod** experimental method **-objekt** subject of experiments (an experiment) **-order** trial order **-person** test subject **-stadium** experimental stage; *på* ~*stadiet* at the experimental stage **-utskriva, -utskrivning** discharge on trial [from mental hospital] **-verksamhet** experimental work; research **-vis** experimentally; by way of experiment

försörj|a [-'sörja] (*underhålla*) support, keep; (*dra försorg om*) provide for; ~ *sig* earn a living (support o.s.) (*genom, med* by) **-are** supporter, breadwinner **-ning** providing *etc.*; support, maintenance; provision

försörjnings|balans balance of resources **-börda** maintenance burden **-inrättning** charitable institution **-plikt** maintenance liability (obligation); ~ *mot* liability for the maintenance of **-skyldig** bound (obliged) to maintain (support)

[s.b.]

förta[ga] 1 (*hindra*) take away (*verkan* the effect); (*dämpa*) deaden; (*fördunkla*) obscure **2** (*fråntaga*) deprive (*ngn ngt* s.b. of s.th.) **3** ~ *sig* overwork o.s.; *han förtar sig inte* he doesn't overwork himself

för|tal slander; (*starkare*) calumny (*mot* against, upon); *elakt* ~ foul slander, black calumny **-tala** [-'ta:-] slander; calumniate **-tappad** [-'tapp-] *a5* lost; *en* ~ *varelse* a lost soul

förtecken *mus.* key signature

förteckn|a [-'tekk-] note down; make a list of **-ing** (*lista*) list, catalogue (*över* of)

förtegen [-'te:-] uncommunicative, reticent **-het** reticence

förtenn|a [-'tenna] *v1* el. *förtennade förtent* tin, tin-plate **-ing** tinning

förti *se fyrti[o]*

förtid *i uttr.*: *i* ~ too early (soon), prematurely; *gammal i* ~ old before one's (its) time

förtidig (*skrivs äv. för tidig*) [*fö:r- el. -'ti:-] premature

förtidspension early retirement pension; (*invalidpension*) supplementary disability pension **-era** grant early retirement pension, pension off

för|tiga [-'ti:-] keep secret; (*förbigå med tystnad*) say nothing about **-tjockning** [-'çåkk-] thickening; (*utvidgning*) swelling

förtjus|a [-'çu:-] enchant, charm, fascinate **-ande** *a4* charming; delightful **-ning** (*hänryckning*) enchantment (*över* at); (*entusiasm*) enthusiasm (*över* about, at, over); (*glädje*) delight (*över* at, in); *jag kommer med* ~ I shall be delighted to come

förtjust [-'çu:st] *a4* (*intagen*) charmed *etc.* (*i* with); (*betagen, förälskad*) in love (*i* with), enamoured, fond (*i* of); (*mycket glad*) delighted, happy, pleased

förtjäna [-'çä:-] **1** (*förvärva*) earn; (*friare*) make; (*vinna*) gain, [make a] profit (*på en affär* by a bargain, *on* a transaction; *på en vara* on an article); ~ *en förmögenhet på* make a fortune out of (by); ~ *sitt uppehälle* earn one's living **2** (*vara värd[ig]*) deserve; (*vara saksubj. äv.*) be worth (*ett besök* a visit); *han* ~*r inte bättre* he deserves no better; *han fick vad han* ~*de* he got what he deserved; *det* ~*r att nämnas att* it is worth mentioning that

förtjänst *s3* **1** (*inkomst*) earnings (*pl*); (*vinst*) profit[s *pl*]; *ren* ~ clear profit; *gå med* ~ be run at a profit **2** (*merit*) merit; *utan egen* ~ without any merit of one's own; *behandla ngn efter* ~ treat s.b. according to his deserts; *det är min* ~ *att* it is thanks (due) to me that **-full** (*om pers.*) deserving; (*om handling*) meritorious **-tecken** badge of merit

förtjänt [-'çä:nt] *a4* (*värd*) deserved, merited; *göra sig* (*vara*) ~ *av* show o.s. (be) deserving of, deserve; *göra sig* ~ *om fosterlandet* deserve well of one's country

förton|a [-'to:-] (*förklinga*) die (fade) away; ~ *sig* stand out (*mot* against) **-ing** *sjö.* view **-ingspunkt** view point

förtork|a [-'tårka] dry [up], parch; (*vissna*) wither [away] **-ning** drying, parching, withering

förtrampa [-'trampa] trample [upon], tread down; ~*d* (*i sht bildl.*) downtrodden

förtret *s3* annoyance, vexation (*över* at); (*trassel*) trouble; (*grämelse*) chagrin; *till sin stora* ~ much to his chagrin; *svälja* ~*en* pocket one's pride; *vara till* ~ *för* be a nuisance to; *vålla ngn* ~ cause s.b. annoyance, give s.b. trouble

förtret|a [-'tre:-] annoy, vex; *med* ~*d min* with a look of annoyance **-lig** *a1* vexatious, annoying **-lighet** (*med pl*) vexation, annoyance

förtro confide (*ngn ngt* s.th. to s.b.); ~ *sig till* (*åt*) place confidence in

förtroende [-'tro:-] *s6* **1** (*tillit*) confidence; faith, trust; reliance; *i* ~ *sagt* confidentially speaking, between ourselves; *med* ~ confidently; *hysa* ~ *för* have confidence in; *inge* ~ inspire confidence; *mista* ~*t för* lose confidence (one's faith) in; *åtnjuta allmänt* ~ enjoy public confidence **2** (*förtroligt meddelande*) confidence; *utbyta* ~*n* exchange confidences **-fråga** *göra ngt till* ~ put s.th. to a vote of confidence **-full** trusting, trustful; confiding **-ingivande** *a4* (*om uppträdande*) reassuring; *vara* ~ inspire confidence **-klyfta** confidence gap **-kris** crisis of confidence **-man** fiduciary; (*ombud*) agent, representative; (*inom fackförening*) appointed representative **-post** position of trust **-uppdrag** commission of trust; *få* ~*et att* be entrusted with the task of (+ *ingform*) **-vald** *en* ~ an elected representative **-votum** vote of confidence **-väckande** *a4*, *se -ingivande*

förtrogen [-'tro:-] **I** *a3* **1** (*förtrolig*) confidential; (*intim*) intimate, close **2** (*hemmastadd med*) familiar with, cognizant of **II** *s* confidant[e *fem.*]; *göra ngn till sin förtrogne* take s.b. into one's confidence, make s.b. one's confidant[e] **-het** familiarity (*med* with), [intimate] knowledge (*med* of)

förtrolig [-'tro:-] *a1* (*intim*) intimate; close; (*familjär*) familiar; (*konfidentiell*) confidential; *stå på* ~ *fot med* be on an intimate footing (on familiar terms) with **-het** intimacy; familiarity

förtroll|a [-'trålla] enchant; bewitch (*äv. bildl.*) **-ande** *a4* enchanting, bewitching, fascinating **-ning** enchantment; bewitchment; spell; *bryta* ~*en* break the spell

förtrupp *mil.* advance guard; (*friare*) van[guard]

förtryck oppression; tyranny; *lida* ~ be oppressed

förtryck|a [-'trycka] oppress; tyrannize over **-are** oppressor

förtryt|a [-'try:-] provoke, annoy, vex **-else** displeasure, resentment (*över* at); (*starkare*) exasperation, indignation (*över* at) **-sam** *al* indignant, resentful

förträfflig [-'träff-] *a1* excellent, splendid **-het** excellence; splendid qualities (*pl*)

förträng|a [-'träŋa] (*göra trång*) narrow, constrict, contract; *psykol.* repress **-ning** narrowing, constriction, contraction; *psykol.*, *se bortträngning*

förtröst|a [-'trösta] trust (*på Gud* in God; *på försynen* to Providence) **-an** *r* trust; reliance; confidence (*på* in); *i* ~ *på* in reliance on

förtröttas [-'tröttas] *dep* tire, [grow] weary

förtull|a [-'tulla] (*låta tullbehandla*) clear, declare [in the customs]; (*betala tull för*) pay duty on (for); *har ni något att* ~? have you anything to declare? **-ning** (*tullbehandling*) [customs] clearance (examination)

förtullnings|avgift customs clearance fee **-kostnad** customs duty

förtunn|a [-'tunna] thin [down]; (gas) rarefy; (utspäda) dilute **-as** dep get thin[ner] **-ing 1** thinning; rarefaction; dilution **2** (förtunningsmedel) thinner

förtur, förtursrätt ha ~ have priority (right of precedence) (framför over)

förtvin|a [-'tvi:-] wither [away] (av with); bildl. äv. languish [away] **-ing** withering [away]; med. atrophy

förtvivl|a [-'tvi:v-] despair (om ngt of s.th.; om ngn about s.b.) **-ad** a5 (om pers.) in despair (över at); (desperat) desperate; ett -at läge a desperate situation; vara ~ be in despair (exceedingly sorry) (över att ha gjort det at having done it); det kan göra en ~ it is enough to drive one to despair **-an** r despair (över at); (desperation) desperation (över at); med ~s mod with the courage of despair

förtvålning [-'två:l-] saponification

förtvätt pre-wash **-medel** pre-washing detergent

för|ty therefore; icke ~ nevertheless, none the less **-tycka** [-'tykka] du får inte ~ om (att) jag you must not take it amiss if I

förtydlig|a [-'ty:d-] make clear[er]; bildl. äv. elucidate **-ande I** s6 elucidation **II** a4 elucidative

för|täckt a4 veiled, covert; i ~a ordalag circuitously, in a roundabout way **-tälja** [-'tälja] v2 tell; relate, narrate **-tänka** [-'tänka] inte ~ ngn att (om) han not blame (think ill of) s.b. for (+ ing-form)

förtänksam [ˣföː-] a1 prudent; (förutseende) far-sighted **-het** forethought, prudence; foresight

förtär|a [-'tä:-] eat; (göra slut på) eat up (äv. bildl.); (friare) consume; (starkare) devour; (fräta på) gnaw, wear away; Farligt att ~! Poison. Not to be taken!; aldrig ~ sprit never touch (take) spirits; ~s av svartsjuka be consumed by jealousy **-ing** consumption; konkr. food [and drink], refreshments (pl)

förtät|a [-'tä:-] condense (till into); (friare o. bildl.) concentrate (till into); ~d stämning tense atmosphere **-ning** condensation; concentration

förtöj|a [-ˣtöjja] moor, make fast (vid to) **-ning** mooring

förtöjnings|boj mooring buoy **-lina** mooring rope **-plats** moorage, tie-up wharf; berth **-ring** mooring ring

för|törna [-'tö:r-] provoke, anger; ~d provoked (angry) (på with; över at); ~s (bli förtörnad) över take offence at **-underlig** [-'under-] wondrous, marvellous; (underlig) strange

förundersök|a subject to a preliminary investigation **-ning** preliminary investigation (examination, study); jur. preliminary hearing[s pl]

förundr|a [-'und-] fill with wonder; astonish; ~d struck with wonder; ~ sig, se förundras **-an** r wonder (över at) **-ansvärd** [-ˣund-] a1 wondrous, marvellous; astonishing **-as** dep wonder, be astonished (över at)

förunna [-'unna] bibl. o.d. vouchsafe; (friare) grant; det är inte alla ~t att not everyone gets the

chance to

1 förut ['föː-] sjö., se 1 för II

2 förut ['föː-r- el. -'uːt] before, in advance; (om tid äv.) previously; (förr) formerly

förutan [-ˣuːtan] without

förutbeställ|a [ˣföː-r-] order in advance **-ning** advance order

förutbestämm|a [ˣföː-] settle beforehand; (predestinera) predestine, predestinate **-else** predestination

förutfattad [ˣföː-r-] a5 preconceived; ~ mening (äv.) prejudice; ha en ~ mening be prejudiced

förutom [-ˣuːtɔm] besides ([det] att han är his being)

förutsatt [ˣföː-r-] a i uttr.: ~ att provided [that]

förutse [ˣföː-r-] foresee; anticipate; efter vad man kan ~ as far as one can see **-bar** a5 foreseeable **-ende I** s6 foresight; (framsynthet) forethought **II** a4 foreseeing; provident

förut|skicka [ˣföː-r-] premise **-spå** predict

förutsäg|a [ˣföː-r-] predict, foretell; (förespå) prophesy; forecast **-else** prediction; forecast; prophecy

förutsätt|a [ˣföː-r-] (antaga) assume, presume, suppose; (ta för givet) take it for granted; log. postulate; (bygga på förutsättningen [att]) imply, presuppose **-ning** (antagande) assumption, presumption, supposition; log. postulation; (villkor) condition, prerequisite; (erforderlig egenskap) qualification; ekonomiska ~ar economic prerequisites; under ~ att on condition that; skapa ~ar för create the necessary conditions for; han har alla ~ar att lyckas he has every chance of succeeding **-ningslös** unprejudiced, impartial, unbias[s]ed

förutvarande [ˣföː-r-] a4 (förra) former; (föregående) previous

förvalt|a [-'valta] administer; manage; (ämbete) discharge, exercise; ~ sitt pund väl put one's gifts to good use **-are** administrator; (av lantgods) steward, bailiff; (av dödsbo) trustee; (konkurs-) receiver; mil., ung. sergeant major, **-arskap** s7 trusteeship **-ning** administration, management; (stats-) public (state) administration, government services (pl)

förvaltnings|apparat administrative organization **-berättelse** administration report; (styrelseberättelse) annual report **-bolag** holding company **-byggnad** administration building **-domstol** administrative court **-kostnad** administration cost **-område** administrative district (abstr. sphere) **-organ** administrative body (agency) **-utskott** executive committee **-år** financial year

förvandl|a [-'vand-] transform, turn, convert (till, i into); (förbyta) change (till, i into); (till ngt sämre) reduce (till into); jur. commute (till into); tekn. convert; teol. transsubstantiate **-as** dep be transformed (etc.); äv. turn, change (till, i into) **-ing** transformation; conversion; change; reduction; teol. transsubstantiation

förvandlings|konstnär quick-change artist **-nummer** quick-change act

förvansk|a [-'vans-] corrupt, distort; tamper with; misrepresent **-ning** corruption etc.

förvar s7 [safe]keeping, custody; charge; i säkert ~ in safe custody; lämna i ~ hos ngn commit to a p.'s charge (custody); *ta i* ~ take charge (custody) of; *se äv. under fängslig*

förvar|a [-'va:-] *vl* (*ha i förvar*) keep; (*deponera*) deposit; ~*s kallt* (*oåtkomligt för barn*) keep in a cool place (out of the reach of children) **-ing** keeping; charge, custody; ~ *på säkerhetsanstalt* preventive detention in prison; *inlämna till* ~ leave to be called for, *järnv.* put in the cloakroom; *AE. äv.* check; *mottaga till* ~ receive for safekeeping

förvarings|avgift storing (*bank. etc.* safekeeping) fee, *järnv.* cloakroom fee **-box** [storage] locker **-kärl** receptacle **-plats** repository, storeroom, storage space **-pärm** [letter] file **-skåp** filing cabinet **-utrymme** storage space

förvarn|a forewarn, warn in advance **-ing** [advance] notice, forewarning

förveckl|a [-'vekk-] complicate; entangle **-ing** complication; entanglement

förvedas [-'ve:-] *dep* become lignified, lignify

förveklig|a [-'ve:k-] emasculate **-as** *dep* become emasculate

förverka [-'verka] forfeit

förverklig|a [-'verk-] (*t.ex. förhoppningar*) realize; (*t.ex. plan, idé*) carry out **-ande** *s6* realization **-as** *dep* be realized; (*om dröm e.d.*) come true

förveten [-'ve:, ˣfö:r-] *a3* overcurious, nosy

förvild|ad [-'vill-] *a5* (*om djur, växt*) undomesticated, wild; (*vanskött*) that has run wild; ~*e seder* demoralized customs **-as** *dep* return to natural state; (*om människor*) become uncivilized; (*om barn*) be turned into young savages; (*om djur, växter*) run wild; (*om odlad mark*) go out of cultivation

förvill|a [-'villa] (*föra vilse*) lead astray (*äv. bildl.*); (*vilseleda*) mislead; (*förleda*) deceive; (*förvirra*) bewilder, confuse; ~*nde lik* confusingly like; ~*nde likhet* deceptive likeness; ~ *sig* lose one's way, *bildl.* get bewildered **-else** error, aberration; (*sedlig*) delinquency

förvinter early winter

förvirr|a [-'virra] confuse; (*förbrylla*) bewilder, perplex; (*svagare*) puzzle, embarrass; (*bringa ur fattningen*) disconcert; (*bringa i oordning*) derange, disorder; *tala* ~*t* talk incoherently **-ing** confusion; (*persons äv.*) perplexity, embarrassment, bewilderment; (*om sak äv.*) disorder[ed state]; *i första* ~*en* in the confusion of the moment

förvis|a [-'vi:-] banish, exile, send away (*ur* from, out of) (*äv. bildl.*); (*deportera*) deport; (*relegera*) expel **-ning** banishment, exile; deportation; expulsion **-ningsort** place of banishment (exile)

förvissa [-'vissa] ~ *ngn om ngt* (*om att*) assure s.b. of s.th. (that); *vara* ~*d* rest assured, (*övertygad*) be convinced; ~ *sig* make sure (*om* of; [*om*] *att* that)

1 förvissning [-'viss-] assurance; conviction; *i* ~ *om* in the assurance of

2 förvissning [-'viss-] (*förvissnande*) withering [away]

förvisso [-ˣvissɔ] (*utan tvivel*) for certain; (*visserligen*) certainly

förvittr|a [-'vitt-] (*på ytan*) weather; (*upplösas*) disintegrate; (*sönderfalla*) crumble, moulder

-ing weathering; erosion, disintegration; crumbling

förvittrings|process weathering process **-produkt** sedimentary material

förvrid|a [-'vri:-] distort, twist; ~ *huvudet på ngn* turn a p.'s head **-en** distorted

förvräng|a [-'vräŋa] distort; (*fakta äv.*) misrepresent **-ning** distortion; misrepresentation

för|vunnen [-'vunn-] (*överbevisad*) convicted (*till* of); (*förklarad skyldig*) found guilty (*till* of) **-vuxen** [-'vuxen] overgrown; (*missbildad*) deformed

förväll|an [-'våll-] *r, se följande* **-ande** *s6, genom eget* ~ through one's own negligence; *utan eget* ~ by no fault of one's own

förvån|a [-'vå:-] **1** surprise, astonish; ~*d* surprised *etc.* (*över* at); *det* ~*r mig* I am surprised (*etc.*) **2** *rfl* be surprised (*etc.*) (*över* at); *det är ingenting att* ~ *sig över* it is not to be wondered at **-ande** *a4*, **-ansvärd** *al* surprising, astonishing **-as** *dep, se förvåna* 2 **-ing** surprise, astonishment

förvår early spring

förväg *i uttr.*: *i* ~ in advance, ahead, before, beforehand

för|vägen [-'vä:-] *a3* overbold, rash **-vägra** [-'vä:g-] (*vägra*) refuse; (*neka*) deny; *han* ~*des rätten att träffa sina barn* he was denied the right to see his children

förväll|a [-'välla] parboil **-ning** parboiling

förvänd *al* disguised, distorted; (*dålig, syndig*) perverted

förvänd|a [-'vända] (*förvränga*) distort; disguise; ~ *synen på folk* throw dust in people's eyes **-het** perversity

förvänt|a [-'vänta] ~ [*sig*] expect; look forward to **-an** *r, som pl används pl av förväntning* expectation (*på* of); *efter* (*mot*) ~ according (contrary) to expectations; *över* ~ *bra* better than expected, unexpectedly good **-ansfull** expectant **-ning** expectation; *motsvara ngns* ~*ar* come up to a p.'s expectations

för|värkt *a4* crippled with rheumatism **-världsliga** [-'vä:rds-] secularize; ~*d* (*om pers. äv.*) worldly

förvärm|a preheat **-are** preheater **-ning** preheating

förvärr|a [-'värra] make worse, aggravate **-as** *dep* grow worse, become aggravated

för|värv *s7* **1** (*förvärvande*) acquisition **2** *ngt förvärvat*) acquisition; (*genom arbete*) earnings (*pl*) **-värva** [-'värva] acquire; (*förtjäna*) earn; (*komma över*) procure; (*vinna*) gain; ~ *vänner* make friends; *surt* ~*de slantar* hard-earned money

förvärvs|arbeta have gainful employment; (*om kvinna*) go out to work **-arbetande** *a4* wage-earning, gainfully employed; ~ *kvinnor* (*äv.*) women out at work **-arbete** gainful employment; *ha* ~ have a job **-avdrag** tax allowance on earnings **-begär** acquisitiveness **-källa** source of income **-liv** *träda ut i* ~*et* start working [for one's living] **-syfte** *i* ~ with a view to making money

förvätsk|a[s] [-'vätska(s)] liquefy **-ning** liquefaction

förväxl|a [-'växla] confuse, mix up **-ing** confusion; (*misstag*) mistake, mix-up

förväxt *a4, se förvuxen*
föryngr|a [-'yŋra] rejuvenate, make [look] younger; (*skog*) reafforest, *AE.* reforest **-as** *dep* grow young again **-ing** rejuvenation; (*av skog*) reafforestation, *AE.* reforestation
föryngrings|källa source of rejuvenation (fresh vitality) **-medel** rejuvenation tonic
förytliga [-'y:t-] superficialize
förzink|a [-'sinka] coat with zinc; *särsk. AE.* zinc; (*galvanisera*) galvanize **-ning** zinc-plating; galvanizing
föråldr|ad [-'åld-] antiquated, out of date; ~*e ord* obsolete words **-as** *dep* get (grow) old; become antiquated (*etc.*)
förädl|a [-'ä:d-] **1** ennoble **2** *biol.* breed, improve **3** (*bearbeta råvara*) refine, work up; ~*d smak* refined taste **-ing 1** ennoblement **2** breeding *etc.* **3** refinement, processing
förädlings|anstalt *lantbr.* breeding-centre **-industri** processing industry **-metod** processing technique
föräktenskaplig *a5* premarital; ~ *förbindelse* premarital intimacy
förälder [-'äld-] *s2* parent; *ensamstående* ~ single parent
föräldra|auktoritet parental authority **-förening** parents association **-försäkring** parental insurance **-hem** [parental] home **-ledig** on parental leave **-ledighet** parental leave **-lös** orphan; *hem för* ~*a barn* orphanage **-möte** parent--teacher association (P.T.A.) meeting **-penning** parent's allowance **-skap** *s7* parenthood
förälsk|a [-'älska] *rfl* fall in love (*i* with) **-ad** *a5* in love (*i* with); ~ *blick* amorous (loving) glance **-else** love (*i* for); (*kortvarig*) infatuation
föränderlig [-'änd-] *a1* variable; (*ombytlig*) changeable; *lyckan är* ~ fortune is fickle **-ra 1** (*ändra*) alter; (*byta* [*om*]) change (*till* into); *inte* ~ *en min* not move a muscle **2** *rfl, se* **-ras -ras** *dep* change, alter; *tiderna* ~ times change; *hon har* -*rats till oigenkännlighet* she has changed beyond recognition **-ring** change; alteration; *sjuklig* ~ pathological change
förär|a [-'ä:ra] ~ *ngn ngt* make s.b. a present of s.th. **-ing** present
föräta [-'ä:ta] *rfl* overeat [o.s.] (*på* on), eat too much (*på* of)
föröd|ande [-'ö:dan-] *a4* devastating, ravaging **-else** devastation; ~*ns styggelse* (*bibl.*) the abomination of desolation; *anställa stor* ~ make (play) havoc
förödmjuk|a humiliate (*sig* o.s.) **-else** humiliation
förök|a [-'ö:ka] (*utöka*) increase; (*mångfaldiga, fortplanta*) multiply; ~ *sig* increase, multiply **-ning 1** increase **2** (*fortplantning*) multiplication, propagation
föröv|a [-'ö:va] commit **-are** perpetrator; ~*n av brottet* the man guilty of the crime
föröver ['fö:r-] *se I för II*
förövning preliminary exercise
förövrigt [-'ö:v-] *se under övrig*
fösa *v3* drive, (*friare*) shove (*fram* along; *ihop* together)

G

gabardin *s3, s4* gaberdine
Gabon *n* Gabon **gabones** *s3*, **gabonsk** [-'bɔ:-] *a5* Gabonese
gadd *s2* sting; *ta* ~*en ur* (*av*) *ngn* take the sting out of s.b.
gadda ~ *ihop sig* gang together (up) (*mot* against); ~ *sig samman, se sammangadda sig*
gaddstekel *zool.* aculeate hymenopteran
gadolinium [-'li:-] *s8* gadolinium
gael [ga'e:l *el.* gä:l] *s3* Gael **-isk** *a5* Gaelic **-iska 1** (*språk*) Gaelic **2** (*kvinna*) Gaelic woman
gaff *s2* (*huggkrok*) gaff
gaffel [ˣgaff- *el.* 'gaff-] *s2* **1** fork; *kniv och* ~ a knife and fork; *jag har det på* ~*n* it's in the bag, it's all wrapped up **2** *sjö.* gaff **-antilop, -bock** pronghorn, American antelope **-segel** gaffsail **-truck** fork-lift truck
gaffla babble, jabber
gagat jet
gage [ga:ʃ] *s7, s4* (*sångares o.d.*) fee
gagg *s7 vard.* gag
gagg|a babble **-ig** *a1* gaga
gagn [gaŋn] *s7* (*nytta*) use; (*fördel*) advantage, benefit; *mera till namnet än till* ~*et* more for show than use; *vara till* ~ *för* be of advantage to
gagn|a [ˣgaŋna] be of use (advantage) to, benefit; (*ngns intressen*) serve; *det* ~*r föga* it is of little use (advantage); *vartill* ~*r det?* what is the use of that? **-elig** *a1* useful **-lös** useless, of no use; fruitless, unavailing **-virke** (*värt att förädlas*) merchantable wood **-växt** utility plant
gaj *s2, sjö.* guy
gala gol galit il. v2 crow; (*om gök*) call
2 gala *s1* gala; *i* [*full*] ~ in gala (full) dress
galaföreställning gala performance
galaktisk [-'lakt-] galactic
galaktometer [-'me:-] *s2* galactometer
galaktos [-'å:s] *s3* galactose
galamiddag gala banquet
galant [-'ant, -aŋt] **I** *a1* (*artig*) gallant **II** *adv, det gick* ~ it went off splendidly
galanteri gallantry **-varor** *pl* fancy goods
Galaterbrevet [-'la:-] [The Epistle of Paul the Apostle to the] Galatians
gala|uniform full-dress uniform **-vagn** state coach
galax *s3* galaxy
galeas *s3, ung.* ketch
galej [-'lejj] *s7* party, celebration; spree, fling; *gå på* ~ (*vard.*) paint the town red
galeja [-ˣlejja] *s1* galley
galen *a3* **1** mad; *vard.* crazy, (*oregerlig*) wild; (*överförtjust*) passionately fond (*i* of), crazy (*i* about); *skvatt* ~ stark mad, as mad as a hatter; *bli* ~ go mad (*etc.*); *det är så man kan bli* ~ it is enough to drive one mad **2** (*om sak: orätt*) wrong (*ända* end); (*dåraktig*) mad, wild; (*förryckt*) absurd; *hoppa i* ~ *tunna* make a blunder, get into

the wrong box; *det var inte så galet* [it's] not bad **-panna** madcap **-skap** *s3* **1** (*utan pl*) (*vansinne*) madness; (*dåraktighet*) folly **2** (*med pl*) act of folly; *hitta på ~er* (*tokerier*) play the giddy goat
galet *adv* wrong; *bära sig ~ åt a*) (*bakvänt*) be awkward, *b*) (*oriktigt*) go about in the wrong way; *det gick ~ för henne* things went wrong with her
galgbacke gallows hill
galge [ˣgalje] *s2* gallows (*sg*), gallow[s] tree; (*med en arm*) gibbet; (*klädhängare*) [coat] hanger; *sluta i ~n* come to the gallows
galgenfrist [ˣgalg-, *äv.* ˣgalj-] short respite
galg|fysionomi [-j-] (*gallows* (*hangdog*) look, sinister face **-fågel** gallows bird **-humor** gallows (grim) humour
galilé *s3* Galilean **Galiléen** [-'le:en] *n* Galilee
galileisk [-'le:-] *a5* Galilean
galit *sup. av 1 gala*
galjons|bild, -figur [-ˣjoːns-] figurehead (*äv. bildl.*)
gall *oböjligt a* barren
galla *s1* bile (*äv. bildl.*); *åld.* gall; *utgjuta sin ~ över* vent one's spleen upon
gallbildning gall
gallblåsa gall bladder
1 galler [ˣgall-] *s9* (*folkslag*) Gaul
2 galler [ˣgall-] *s7* (*skydds-*) grating, grate, grill [e]; (*fängelse- o.d.*) bars (*pl*), grating; (*spjälverk*) lattice[work], trellis; *radio.* grid; *sätta ~ för* lattice, grate
galler|fönster lattice window; (*med skyddsgaller*) barred window **-grind** wrought-iron gate
galleri gallery
gallerverk latticework
gall|feber *få ~* have (get) one's blood up; *reta ~ på ngn* infuriate s.b. **-gång** bile duct
gallicism *s3* Gallicism
Gallien [ˣgall-] *n* Gaul **gallier** [ˣgall-] *se 1 galler*
gallimatias [-ˣtiː-] *r* balderdash
gallion- *se galjon-*
gallisk [ˣgall-] *a5* Gallic
gallium [ˣgall-] *s8* gallium
gallko barren cow
gallmygga gall midge (gnat)
gallr|a (*plantor*) thin out; (*skog*) thin; *~ bort* (*ut*) (*ngt onyttigt o.d.*) sort (weed) out **-ing** thinning [out] *etc.*; sorting out
gall|skrik, -skrika yell, howl
gallsprängd *a5* with burst gall bladder; *bildl.* splenetic[al], choleric
gallstekel gallfly
gall|sten gallstone, bilestone **-stensanfall** biliary colic
gallupundersökning Gallup poll; public opinion poll
gallussyra gallic acid
gallväg *~ar* bile ducts
galläpple oakapple, gall
galn|as [ˣgaːl-] *dep* act (play) the fool **-ing** madman, *fem.* madwoman, lunatic, maniac; *som en ~* (*äv.*) like mad
1 galon *s4* (*plastväv*) PVC-coated fabric
2 galon *s3* (*uniformsband*) gold (silver) braid; galloon
galonerad [-'ne:-] *a5* braided, gallooned

galopp [-'åpp] *s3* **1** *ridk.* gallop; *i ~* at a gallop; *i full ~* [at] full gallop (*friare speed*); *kort ~* canter, hand gallop; *falla in i ~* break into a gallop; *fatta ~en* (*bildl.*) catch the drift **2** (*dans*) galop **3** *mus.* galop, gal[l]opade **-bana** racecourse; *särsk. AE.* racetrack **-era** gallop; *~nde lungsot* galloping consumption **-sport** horse racing
galosch [-'låʃ] *s3* galosh, *ibl.* golosh; *~er, AE. äv.* rubbers **-hylla** rack for galoshes
galt *s2* **1** *zool.* boar **2** (*tackjärn*) pig
galvaniser|a galvanize, electroplate **-ing** galvanization, electroplating
galvanisk [-'va:-] *a5* galvanic, voltaic; *~t element* primary cell, galvanic (voltaic) cell
galvano|meter [-'me:-] *s2* galvanometer **-plastjk** *s3* galvanoplastics (*pl, behandlas som sg*) **-skop** [-'skåp] *s7* galvanoscope
galär *s3* galley **-slav** galley slave
gam *s2* vulture (*äv. bildl.*)
Gambia [ˈgamm-] *n* [the] Gambia
gamb|ier [ˈgamm-] *s9*, **-isk** *a5* Gambian
gambit [ˈgamm-] *s2, schack.* gambit
gamling old man (woman); *~ar* old folks (people)
gamma [ˈgamma] *s6* gamma **-globulin** gamma globulin **-kamera** gamma camera
gammal *~t äldre äldst* old; (*forn[tida]*) ancient; (*antik*) antique; (*som varat länge*) long-established, of long standing; (*åldrig*) aged; (*ej färsk, om bröd o.d.*) stale; (*begagnad äv.*) second- -hand; *~t nummer* (*av tidning o.d.*) back issue; *~ nyhet* stale [piece of] news; *en fem år ~ pojke* a five-year old boy, a boy of (aged) five; *~ som gatan* as old as the hills; *av ~t* of old; *av ~ vana* from [long-accustomed] habit; *den gamle* (*gamla*) the old man (woman); *den gamla goda tiden* the good old days; *på gamla dagar* in one's old age; *känna ngn sedan ~t* know s.b. of old (for many years); *vara ~ och van* be an old campaigner (hand); *~ är äldst* old folks know best; *låta ngt bli vid det gamla* let s.th. remain as it is
gammal|dags *oböjligt a* old-fashioned **-dans** old-time dance; (*dansande*) old-time dancing **-modig** *a1, se gammaldags*; (*omodern äv.*) out of fashion, outmoded; (*uråldrig*) antiquated; *~ hat* old hat **-stavning** old spelling **-testament-lig** *a5* of the Old Testament **-vals** old-time waltz
gamman *oböjligt s, i* (*med*) *fröjd och ~* merrily
gammastrål|ar *pl* gamma rays **-ning** gamma radiation
gamäng *s3* gamin
ganglie [ˈgaŋ-] *s5* ganglion (*pl äv. ganglia*)
gangster [ˈgaŋ-] *s2* gangster; *AE. sl.* mobster **-band, -liga** gang; *AE. sl.* mob **-metoder** ruthless methods **-välde** gang (*AE. sl.* mob) rule
gans *s3* [fancy] braid
ganska (*mycket*) very; (*oftast i positiv betydelse*) quite (*roligt* fun); (*oftast i negativ betydelse*) rather (*tråkigt* boring); (*inte så litet*) pretty; (*tämligen*) fairly, tolerably; *~ mycket a*) (*som adjektiv*) a great (good) deal of, [rather] a large (quite a) number of (*folk* people), quite a lot of, *b*) (*som adv*) very much, a great (good) deal, quite a lot; *det var ~ mycket folk på teatern* there was quite a good audience at the theatre
gap *s7* mouth; (*djurs o. tekn.*) jaws (*pl*); *bildl.*

gape, jaws; *(öppning)* gap, opening **gapa 1** *(om pers. o. djur)* open one's mouth; hold one's mouth open; *(förvånat)* gape *(av* with); *(stirra)* stare; *(skrika)* bawl, yell; *den som ~r över mycket mister ofta hela stycket* grasp all, lose all **2** *(om avgrund o.d.)* yawn; *(stå öppen)* stand open **gap|ande** *a4* gaping *(folkhop* crowd; *sår* wound); wide-open *(mun* mouth) **-hals** *vard.* loudmouth; *(pratmakare)* chatterbox **-skratt** roar of laughter, guffaw; *ge till ett ~* burst out laughing **-skratta** roar with laughter, guffaw

garag|e [-'a:ʃ] *s7* garage **-era** put in a garage **garageinfart** garage entrance

garanti *s3* guarantee; *(ansvarighet)* responsibility; *(säkerhet)* security; *ställa ~[er] för ngt* give (furnish) a guarantee for s.th. **-belopp** guarantee amount **-sedel** certificate of guarantee

garçon [-'såŋ] *s3* waiter; *en glad ~* a merrymaker

gard *s3* **1** *sport.* guard; *ställa sig i ~* take one's guard **2** *kortsp.* guard; *ha ~* be guarded

garde ['garr-] *s6* guards *(pl)*; *[det] gamla ~t* the old guard

gardenia [-'de:-] *s1* gardenia

garder|a guard, safeguard, cover; *(i tips)* cover, allow [up to] **-ing** guard; *i tips, se hel- resp. halvgardering*

garderob [-'å:b] *s3* **1** *(skåp)* wardrobe; *(klädkammare)* clothes closet; *(i offentlig lokal)* cloakroom; *AE.* checkroom **2** *(kläder)* wardrobe, clothes *(pl)* **garderobié** [-åb'je:] *s3*, **garderobiär** [-åb'jä:r] *s3*, *se garderobsvakt*

garderobs|avgift cloakroom (*AE.* checkroom) fee **-sorg** *ha ~* have only one's Sunday best to wear **-vakt** cloakroom (*AE.* checkroom) attendant

gardin *s3* curtain; *(rull-)* [roller] blind; *dra för (ifrån) ~erna* pull (pull back) the curtains; *dra upp ~en* draw up the blind **-kappa** pelmet, valance **-stång** curtain rod *(av trä:* pole) **-uppsättning** curtain arrangement

gardist guardsman

garfågel [ˣga:r-] great auk, garefowl

garn [-a:-] *s7, s4* yarn; *(bomulls- äv.)* cotton; *(silkes- äv.)* silk; *(ull- äv.)* wool; *(fångst-)* net; *snärja ngn i sina ~* entangle (catch) s.b. in one's toils **-bod** shop selling yarn

garner|a *(kläder)* trim; *(mat)* garnish **-ing** trimming; garnish

garnison *s3* garrison; *ligga i ~* äv.) be garrisoned

garnisons|ort garrison station **-sjukhus** military hospital

garnityr *s7* garniture; *(sats, uppsättning)* set

garn|nystan ball of yarn *(etc.)* **-ända** end of yarn, thrum

garrottering [-'te:-] gar[r]otte

garv *s7, vard.* horse laugh

1 garva *vard. (skratta)* laugh; guffaw

2 garva tan *(äv. bildl.)*; dress, curry

garvad *bildl. (erfaren)* seasoned

garv|are tanner, leather dresser **-eri** tannery **-ning** tanning **-syra** tannin, tannic acid **-ämne** tanning agent

1 gas *s3* *(tyg)* gauze

2 gas *s3* gas; *ge ~* *(t. motor)* step on the gas, accelerate; *minska på ~en* *(t. motor)* slow down;

släcka (tända) ~en turn out (on) the gas **gas|a** gas; *~ på* step on the gas **-betong** porous concrete **-bildning** gas formation

gasbinda gauze bandage

gasbrännare gas burner

gascognare *se gaskonjare* **Gascogne** [-'kånj] *n* Gascony

gasell *s3* gazelle

gas|form *i ~* in the form of gas, in a gaseous state **-formig** [-å-] *a1* gaseous **-förgiftning** gas poisoning

gask *s2, s3 (fest)* spree, party **gaska** *~ upp sig* cheer up, buck up; *(rycka upp sig)* pull o.s. together

gas|kamin gas fire (stove) **-kammare** gas chamber (oven) **-klocka** gasholder, gasometer

gaskonjare [-ˣkånja-] Gascon

gas|krig gas war[fare] **-kromatografi** gas chromatography **-kök** gas ring **-lampa** gas lamp **-ledning** gas pipe; *(huvudledning)* gas main **-ljus** gaslight **-lykta** *se -lampa* **-låga** gas jet **-mask** gas mask; respirator **-mätare** gas meter **-ning** [-a:-] gassing

gasol [-'å:l] *s3* liquefied petroleum gas *(förk. LPG, LP gas)* **-driven** *a5* operated on liquefied petroleum gas **-kök** liquid-gas stove **-tub** bottle (cylinder) of liquefied petroleum gas

gas|pedal accelerator, throttle **-pollett** gas-meter disc **-reglage** throttle lever

gass *s7* heat, [full] blaze

gass|a be blazing [hot]; *~ sig i solen* bask in the sun **-ande** *s6*, **-ig** *a1* blazing, broiling

gas|spis gas cooker (range, stove) **-svetsning** gas welding; oxyacetylene welding

1 gast *s2 (matros)* ghost

2 gast *s2 (spöke)* ghost

gasta yell, howl

gastera appear as a visiting company (actor)

gastkram|a hug violently; *~d* ghostridden **-ande** *a4* hair-raising **-ning** iron grip; stranglehold

gastr|ektomi *s3* gastrectomy **-isk** ['gast-] *a5* gastric **-it** *s3* gastritis

gastro|enterit *s3* gastroenteritis **-enterologi** gastroenterology **-nom** gourmet; *äv.* gastronome[r], gastronomist **-nomi** *s3* gastronomy **-nomisk** [-'nå:-] *a5* gastronomic[al] **-skop** [-'skå:p] *s7* gastroscope **-skopi** *s3* gastroscopy **-stomi** *s3* gastrostomy

gas|turbin gas turbine **-tändare** gas lighter **-ugn** gas oven **-utveckling** gas generation, gasification **-verk** gasworks *(sg o. pl)*; gas company

gata *s1* street; *(körbana)* roadway; *~ upp och ~ ner* up and down the streets; *på ~n* in the street; *på sin mammas ~* on one's native heath; *gammal som ~n, se gammal*; *rum åt ~n* front room, room facing the street; *gå och driva på gatorna* walk the streets

gat|flicka streetwalker **-hus** part of house facing the street **-hörn** street corner **-lopp** *springa ~* run the gauntlet **-lykta** streetlamp, streetlight **-sopare** scavenger, street sweeper *(AE.* cleaner) **-sten** paving stone *(koll.* paving stones *pl)*

gatt *s7, sjö.* **1** *(hål)* hole **2** *(inlopp)* gut, narrow inlet

gatu|adress [street] address **-belysning** street lighting **-beläggning** street paving (surface) **-försäljare** street vendor, hawker **-korsning** intersection; crossing **-kök** *ung.* snack bar **-liv** street life **-namn** street name **-nät** street system **-plan** street level **-renhållning** street cleansing **-skylt** street sign **-strid** street fighting (*äv.* ~*er*) **-vimmel** *i gatuvimlet* in the throng of the streets
gaucho ['gaotʃå] *s5* gaucho
gav *imperf. av* ge (*giva*)
1 gavel ['ga:-] *i uttr.: på vid* ~ wide open
2 gavel ['ga:-] *s2* gable; (*på säng o.d.*) end; *ett rum på* ~*n* a room in the gable
gavelfönster gable window
gavial *s3* gavial, garial
gavott [-'vått] *s3* gavot[te]
g-dräkt *flyg.* G-suit, anti-G suit
G-dur G major
ge (*giva*) gav givit *el.* gett **I 1** (*skänka*) give; (*förära*) present (*ngn ngt* s.b. with s.th.), bestow (*ngn ngt* s.th. on s.b.); (*förläna äv.*) lend (*glans åt* splendour to); (*bevilja äv.*) grant (*tillåtelse* permission; *kredit* credit); (*bispringa med äv.*) render ([*ngn*] *hjälp* help (assistance) [to s.b.]); (*räcka äv.*) hand (*ngn ngt* s.b. s.th.); (*skicka* [*hit, dit*]) pass (*ngn brödet* s.b. the bread); ~ *dricks* tip; ~ *ngn sin hyllning* pay (do) one's homage to s.b.; *jag skall* ~ *dig!* I'll give it you!; *vad* ~*r du mig för det?* what do you say to that?; *Gud give att...!* God grant that...! **2** (*uppföra*) play, perform, give; *vad* ~*r dom i kväll?* what are they giving (what's on) tonight? **3** (*avkasta*) yield; give; ~ *ett gott resultat* yield (give) an excellent result **4** *kortsp.* deal **II** (*med betonad partikel*) **1** ~ *bort* give away **2** ~ *efter* yield, give way (*för* to) **3** ~ *emellan* give into the bargain **4** ~ *hit!* give me!; hand over! **5** ~ *ifrån sig a*) *fys.* emit, give off, *b*) (*ljud, tecken*) give, *c*) (*lämna ifrån sig*) give up, deliver **6** ~ *igen* give back, return, *bildl.* retaliate, pay back **7** ~ *med sig a*) (*ge efter*) yield, (*om pers. äv.*) give in, come [a]round, *b*) (*minska i styrka*) abate, subside, (*om sjukdom äv.*) yield to treatment; *inte* ~ *med sig* (*äv.*) stand firm, hold one's own **8** ~ *till ett skrik* give a cry, set up a yell **9** ~ *tillbaka a*) *se ge* II 6, *b*) (*vid växling*) give [s.b.] change (*för* for); *jag kan inte* ~ *tillbaka* I have no change **10** ~ *upp* give up (*äv. absol.*) **11** ~ *ut a*) (*pengar*) spend, *b*) (*publicera*) publish, *c*) (*utfärda*) issue, emit **III** *rfl* **1** give o.s. (take) (*tid* time) **2** (*ägna sig*) devote o.s. (*åt* to) **3** (*erkänna sig besegrad*) yield; *mil.* surrender; (*friare*) give in **4** (*om sak*) yield, give way (*för* to); (*töja sig*) stretch; (*slakna*) slacken **5** (*minska i styrka*) abate, subside **6** *det* ~*r sig* [*självt*] it goes without saying; *det* ~*r sig nog med tiden* things will come right in time **7** ~ *sig i kast med* grapple with, tackle; ~ *sig i samspråk med* enter into conversation with; ~ *sig i strid med* join battle with; tackle **8** (*med betonad partikel*) ~ *sig av a*) set out (start) (*på* on), *b*) (*bege sig i väg*) be off, take one's departure; ~ *sig in på* embark upon (*ett företag* an enterprise), enter into (*en diskussion* a discussion); ~ *sig in vid teatern* go on the stage; ~ *sig på a*) (*börja med*) set about, tackle, *b*) (*angripa*) fly at, attack (*ngn* s.b.); ~ *sig ut att skjuta* start (set about) shooting; ~ *sig ut a*) go out (*och fiska* fish-

ing), set out (start) (*på en resa* on a journey), *b*) (*våga sig ut*) venture out; ~ *sig ut för att vara* pretend (profess [o.s.]) to be
gebit [g- *el.* j-] *s7* domain, province
gecko ['geckɔ] *s5*, *s3*, **-ödla** gecko
gedige|n [je'di:-] *a3* **1** (*metall*) pure; (*massiv*) solid **2** *bildl.* solid, sterling; genuine; ~ *karaktär* sound character; *-t arbete* sterling piece of work, excellent workmanship
gegg|amoja [ˣgeggamåjja] *s1* mess **-ig** *a1* sticky, messy
gehenna [je ˣhenna] *s7* Gehenna
gehör [j-] *s7* **1** *mus. o. språkv.* ear; *absolut* ~ absolute (perfect) pitch; *spela efter* ~ play by ear **2** hearing; (*aktning*) respect; (*uppmärksamhet*) attention; *vinna* ~ meet with sympathy; find a ready listener (audience); *skaffa sig* ~ gain a hearing
geigermätare [ˣgajger-] Geiger (Geiger-Müller) counter
geisha [ˣgejʃa *el.* 'gejʃa] *s1* geisha
geist [gajst *el.* gejst] *s3* liveliness, spark; passion
gejd [g-] *s3*, *tekn.* guide; slide
gejser ['gejj-] *s2* geyser
gel [j-] *s4*, *kem.* gel
gelatin [ʃ-] *s4*, *s3* gelatin[e] **-artad** [-a:-] *a5* gelatinous
gelé *s4*, *s3* jelly **gelea** [ʃe'le:a] *rfl* jelly, jellify; congeal **geléartad** [-a:-] *a5* gelatinous
gelik|e [je'li:-] *s2* equal; *du och dina -ar* you and your likes; *hennes -ar* (*äv.*) the likes of her
1 gem [jemm *el.* g-] *s3* (*ädelsten*) engraved (inlaid) jewel
2 gem [ge:m] *s7* (*pappersklämma*) paperclip
gemak [j-] *s7* apartment, stateroom
gemen [j-] *a1* **1** (*nedrig*) low, mean; (*lågsinnad*) base; (*friare: otäck*) horrid; dirty **2** ~*e man a*) the man in the street, *b*) *mil.* the rank and file; *i* ~ in general **3** (*folklig*) friendly; sociable **4** *boktr.*, ~ *bokstav* lower case, lower-case letter
gemen|het [je'me:n-] (*egenskap*) lowness etc.; (*handling o.d.*) [act of] meanness; mean (*vard.* dirty) trick; (*starkare*) infamy **-ligen** commonly, in general
gemensam [je'me:n-] *a5* (*i sht för alla*) common (*för* to); (*i sht för två el. flera*) joint (*beslut* resolution); (*ömsesidig*) mutual (*vän* friend); *ett* ~*t intresse* an interest in common; *två våningar med* ~*t kök* two flats with shared kitchen; *med* ~*ma ansträngningar* by united effort; *göra* ~ *sak med* make common cause with; *ha ngt* ~*t* have s.th. in common **-het** community (*i* of)
gemensamhetskänsla sense of community
gemen|samt [je'me:n-] *adv* in common, jointly **-skap** *s3* community; fellowship; (*samfund*) communion; (*samband*) connection; *känna* ~ *med* have a fellow feeling for
gemmo|log [j- *el.* g-] gem[m]ologist **-logi** gem[m]ology
gems [g- *el.* j-] *s3* chamois
gemyt [j- *el.* g-] *s7* (*sinnelag*) disposition, temperament; (*godlynthet*) good nature **-lig** [-'my:t-] *a1* **1** (*om pers.*) good-natured, good-humoured, genial **2** (*om sak*) [nice and] cosy; comfortable **-lighet 1** good nature (humour), geniality **2** cosiness

gemål [j-] *s3* consort; spouse

1 gen [j-] *s3, biol.* gene

2 gen [j-] *a1* short, near, direct

gena take a short cut

genant [ʃe'naṇt *el.* -'ant] *a1* embarrassing, discomfiting, awkward

genast [ˣje:-] *adv* at once, immediately, straight away; (*om ett ögonblick*) directly; ~ *på morgonen* first thing in the morning

genbank *biol.* gene bank

gendarm [ʃaŋ-] *s3* gendarme **-eri** gendarmerie, gendarmery

gendriva [ˣje:-] disprove (*ett påstående* a statement); refute (*kritik* criticism)

genea|log [j-] genealogist **-logi** *s3* genealogy **-logisk** [-'lå:-] *a5* genealogic[al]

genera [ʃ-] (*besvära*) bother, trouble, inconvenience; be a nuisance to; (*göra förlägen*) be embarrassing to; *ljuset ~r mig* the light bothers me; *~r det om jag röker?* do you mind if I smoke?; *låt inte mig ~!* don't mind me!; *~ er inte för att säga mig sanningen* don't hesitate to tell me the truth; *det skulle inte ~ honom att* he would never hesitate to; *han ~r sig inte* he is not one to stand on ceremony

generad [ʃe'ne:-] *a5* embarrassed; self-conscious; *jag är ~ för honom* I feel embarrassed in his presence

general [j-] *s3* general, (*vid flygvapnet*) air chief marshal; *AE.* general **-agent** general agent **-agentur** general agency **-bas** *mus.* thorough bass, [basso] continuo **-direktör** director-general **-församling** general assembly **-guvernör** governor general

generaliser|a [ʃ-] generalize, make sweeping statements **-ing** generalization

general|konsul consul general **-löjtnant** (*vid armén, kustartilleriet*) lieutenant general, (*vid flygvapnet*) air marshal; *AE.* lieutenant general **-major** (*vid armén, kustartilleriet*) major general, (*vid flygvapnet*) air vice-marshal; *AE.* major general **-order** general order[s *pl*] **-paus** *mus.* general pause (*förk.* G.P.) **-plan** general plan **-repetition** dress rehearsal **-sekreterare** secretary-general **-stab** general staff

generalstabs|karta ordnance [survey] map **-officer** general-staff officer

general|strejk general strike **-tullstyrelse** ~*n* [the Swedish] board of customs

generation [j-] generation

generations|klyfta, -motsättning conflict between generations; generation gap **-växling** *biol.* alternation of generations, metagenesis

generativ [j-] *a5* generative

generator [jeneˣra:tår] *s3* generator **-gas** *se* gengas

generatris [j-] *s3* generatrix (*pl* generatrices)

gener|ell [ʃ-] *a1* general **-ellt** *adv*, ~ *sett* generally speaking, from a general point of view

generera [j-] generate

generisk [jeˣne:-] *a5* generic[al]

gener|ositet [ʃ-] generosity **-ös** *a1* generous (*mot* to)

genet|ik [j-] *s3* genetics (*pl, behandlas som sg*) **-iker** [-'ne:-] geneticist **-isk** [-'ne:-] *a5* genetic[al]; ~ *kod* genetic code

genętt [j-] *s3, se ginstkatt*

Genève [ʃöˈnä:v] *n* Geneva

genever [ʃöˈnä:-] *s9* hollands (*sg*)

Genèvesjön the Lake of Geneva

gengas [ˣje:n-] producer (air) gas **-aggregat** producer-gas unit

gen|gångare [ˣje:n-] ghost, spectre **-gåva** gift in return **-gäld** *i* ~ in return (*för* for) **-gälda** ~ *ngn ngt* pay s.b. back for s.th.; *jag kan aldrig ~ hans vänlighet* I shall never be able to repay his kindness

geni [ʃ-] *s4, s6* genius (*pl* geniuses)

genial [j-, *äv.* ʃ-] *a1*, **-isk** [-'a:-] *a5* brilliant; (*fyndig*) ingenious **-itet** brilliance; (*ngns äv.*) genius

genie [ʃe:-] *s5, se genius*

geniknöl bump of genius; *gnugga ~arna* cudgel one's brains

genital [j-] *a5* genital **-ier** *pl*, **-organ** genitals, genitalia

genitiv [ˈje:-] *s3* genitive; *i* ~ in the genitive

geni|us [ˈje:-] *-en -er* genius (*pl äv.* genii)

gen|klang [ˣje:n-] echo; *bildl. äv.* sympathy, approbation, response; *vinna* ~ meet with response **-ljud** echo, reverberation; *ge* ~ awake an echo **-ljuda** echo, reverberate (*av* with)

genmanipulation genetic manipulation

gen|mäla [ˣje:n-] *v2, v3* (*svara*) reply; (*starkare*) rejoin; (*invända*) object (*mot, på* to) **-mäle** *s6* reply; (*starkare*) retort; (*i tidning*) rejoinder)

genom [ˈje:nåm] **1** *rumsbet.* through; *fara hem* ~ go home by way of (via); *kasta ut* ~ *fönstret* throw out of the window; *komma in* ~ *dörren* (*fönstret*) come in at the door (window) **2** *tidsbet.* through; ~ *hela...* all through..., throughout... **3** (*angivande mellanhand*) through; (*angivande överbringare*) by; *jag fick veta det* ~ *henne* I got to know it through her; *skicka ett meddelande* ~ *ngn* send a message by s.b. **4** (*angivande medel*) by [means of]; ~ *enträgna böner* by means of persistent prayers **5** (*angivande orsak*) by, owing to, thanks to; ~ *drunkning* by drowning; ~ *hans hjälp* by (thanks to) his assistance; ~ *olyckshändelse* through (owing to) an accident **6** *mat.*, *12* ~ *4* 12 divided by 4

genom|andad *a5* penetrated, instinct (*av* with) **-andas** *dep* be penetrated (*etc.*) (*av* with) **-arbeta** deal with thoroughly, work through

genombläddr|a leaf (skim) through **-ing** cursory perusal

genom|blöt soaking wet **-blöta** soak, drench **-borra** (*med svärd o. bildl.*) pierce; (*med dolk*) stab; (*med blicken*) transfix **-brott** breakthrough, breaking through; *mil. o. bildl.* breakthrough, (*bildl. äv.*) triumph **-bruten** broken through; (*nätartad*) latticed, open-work **-bäva** ~*s av* be thrilled with, thrill with **-diskutera** thrash out **-driva** force through, get carried, carry; *AE. vard.* railroad **-dränka** soak (*med* in), saturate (*med* with) **-dålig** thoroughly bad **-fara** *se fara* [*igenom*]; ~*s av en rysning* experience a sudden thrill, (*av obehag*) shudder **-fart** way through; passage; *ej* ~ no thoroughfare

genomfarts|trafik through traffic **-väg** thoroughfare

genom|forska explore thoroughly **-frusen** chilled through (to the bone)

genomför|a carry through (out), realize; *(utföra)* accomplish, effect **-ande** *s6* carrying through, accomplishment, realization **-bar** *a5* feasible, practicable

genom|gjuten [-ju:-] *a5*, ~ *linoleum* inlaid linoleum **-gripande** *a4* thorough, exhaustive; ~ *förändringar* radical (sweeping) changes **-gräddad** *a5* well-baked

genomgå *se gå* [*igenom*]; *bildl.* go (pass) through; *(genomlida)* undergo, suffer; *(erfara)* experience; *(undersöka)* go through, examine **-ende I** *a4* [all-]pervading *(drag i* characteristic of); *(ständigt förekommande)* constant *(fel* error); *(grundlig)* thorough; *järnv.* through; ~ *trafik* through (transit) traffic **II** *adv* all through, throughout

genomgång *s2* going through *etc.*; *(väg o.d.)* passage, thoroughfare; *förbjuden* ~*!* no passage!

genomgångs|rum room giving access to another; in-between room **-trafik** through traffic

genom|hederlig downright (thoroughly) honest **-ila** *se ila* [*igenom*]; *bildl.* pass through; ~*s av skräck* shudder with fear, *vard.* be in a blue funk **-kokt** [-ɔ:-] *a4* thoroughly done; *ej* ~ not done **-korsa** cross [and recross] **-kämpa** fight through **-leta** search through, ransack **-leva** live through; *(uppleva)* experience **-lida** ~ *mycket* go through a great deal [of suffering]; ~ *en föreställning (skämts.)* endure a performance to the bitter end

genomlys|a *(med röntgenstrålar)* X-ray, x-ray; *-t av godhet* radiant with goodness **-ande** *a4* translucent **-ning** fluoroscopy

genomlysningsskärm fluorescent screen

genomläs|a read through, peruse **-ning** reading through, perusal

genom|löpa *v3, bildl. äv. -lopp -lupit* **1** *(tillryggalägga)* run through **2** *(genom|gå, -se)* pass through **3** *(genomleva)* live through **-musikalisk** exceedingly musical **-präktig** *en* ~ *flicka* an exceedingly fine girl **-pyrd** [-y:-] *a5* impregnated *(av, med* with); *bildl.* steeped *(av* in), brimming over *(av* with)

genom|resa I *s1* journey through, transit; *vara på* ~ *till* be passing through [the town *etc.*] on one's way to **II** *v3* travel (pass) through, traverse **-resetillstånd** transit permit

genom|rolig exceedingly (awfully) funny **-rutten** rotten all through (to the core)

genomse look through; *(granska)* revise

genomskinlig [-ʃi:-] *a1* transparent; diaphanous; *vard.* seethrough; *bildl. äv.* plain **-het** transparency

genom|skåda see through; *(hemlighet)* penetrate, find out; *(avslöja)* unmask **-skärning 1** *(avskärning)* intersection **2** *(tvärsnitt)* cross section **-slag 1** *se genomslagskopia* **2** *(projektils)* penetration **3** *elektr.* disruptive discharge

genomslags|kopia carbon copy **-kraft** penetration; *mil.* penetrative power

genomsläpplig *a5* pervious, permeable

genomsnitt 1 *(genomskärning)* cross section **2** *(medeltal)* average, mean; *i* ~ on [an] average; *under* ~*et* below average **-lig** *a5* average

genom|snitthastighet average speed **-stekt** well done **-stråla** irradiate

genomström|ma flow through; ~*s av floder* be traversed by rivers **-ning** flowing (running) through

genom|strÖva roam through **-svettig** wet through with perspiration **-syn** inspection, perusal **-syra** *bildl.* leaven [all through], permeate **-söka** *se genomleta* **-trevlig** delightful, very pleasing **-tryckt** *(om tyg)* printed right through **-tråkig** insufferably dull, very boring

genomträng|a *se tränga* [*igenom*]; *(genomborra)* pierce *(äv. bildl.)*; *(tränga in i)* penetrate *(äv. bildl.)*; *(sprida sig i)* permeate *(äv. bildl.)* **-ande** *a4 (om blåst, blick)* piercing; *(om lukt, röst)* penetrating **-lig** *a5* penetrable *(för* by), pervious *(för* to) **-ning** penetration

genom|trött tired out, *vard.* dog-tired **-tänka** meditate upon, think out; *väl -tänkt* well thought out; *ett väl -tänkt tal* a carefully prepared speech **-vakad** *a5*, ~ *natt* sleepless night **-våt** wet through; *(om kläder)* soaking wet **-vävd** *a5* interwoven; *-vävt tyg* double-faced cloth

genotyp [j-] *s3* genotype

genre [ˈʃaŋer] *s5* genre **-bild** genre picture **-målning** genre painting

genrep [ˣjeːn-] *s7* dress rehearsal

gensaga [ˣjeːn-] *s1* protest

gensare [ˣgenn-] guernsey

gen|skjuta [ˣjeːn-] *(hinna upp)* [take a short cut and] overtake; *(hejda)* intercept **-stridig** *a1*, **-strävig** *a1*, **-störtig** *a1 (motsträvig)* reluctant, refractory *(mot* to) **-svar** reply; *(genklang, sympati)* response **-sägelse** contradiction; *utan* ~ incontestably, indisputably

genteknologi [ˣjeːn-] genetic engineering

gentemot [j-] *prep (emot)* against; *(i jämförelse med)* in comparison to (with); *(i förhållande t.)* in relation to

gentiana [g- *el.* j-, -t(s)iˣaːna] *s1* gentian

gentjl [ʃaŋ-] *a1 (fin)* fine, stylish; *(frikostig)* generous, handsome

gentjänst [ˣjeːn-] service in return

gentle|man gentleman **-mannamässig** *a1* gentleman-like, gentlemanly

Genua [ˈjeː-] *n* Genoa **Genuabukten** the Gulf of Genoa

genuafock *sjö.* genoa [jib], *vard.* genny, jenny

genues [j-] *s3*, **-isk** *a5* Geno[v]ese

genujn [j-] *a1* genuine; *(utpräglad)* out-and-out; *en* ~ *snobb* a real snob

genus [ˈjeː-] *n, språkv.* gender

genväg [ˣjeːn-] short cut; ~*ar är senvägar* a short cut is often the longest way round

geocentrisk [jeɔˈsenn-] *a5* geocentric

geo|desj [j-] *s3* geodesy, geodetics *(pl, behandlas som sg)* **-det** *s3* geodesist **-detisk** [-ˈdeː-] *a5* geodetic[al]; ~ *linje* geodesic [line]

geofys|jk [j-] geophysics *(pl, behandlas som sg)* **-iker** [-ˈfyː-] geophysicist **-isk** [-ˈfyː-] *a5* geophysical

geo|graf [j-] *s3* geographer **-grafj** *s3* geography **-grafisk** [-ˈgraː-] *a5* geographic[al]; ~ *bredd* latitude; ~ *längd* longitude

geokem|j [j-] geochemistry **-isk** [-ˈçeː-] *a5* geochemical

geokronologj [j-] geochronology

geo|log [j-] geologist, geologer **-logj** *s3* geology

-logisk [-'lå:-] *a5* geologic[al]
geometr|i [j-] *s3* geometry; *analytisk* ~ analytical geometry **-iker** [-'me:-] geometer, geometrician **-isk** [-'me:-] *a5* geometric[al]; ~ *serie* geometric progression, (*summa*) geometric series; ~*t medium* geometric mean
geo|morfologi [j-] geomorphology **-politik** geopolitics (*sg o. pl*)
georgette [ʃår'ʃett] *s5* georgette [crepe]
Georgien [je'årgien *el.* -ji-] *n* Georgian Soviet Socialist Republic, *vard.* Georgia **georgier** [je'årgier *el.* -ji-] Georgian
geo|statik [j-] geostatics (*pl, behandlas som sg*) **-stationär** ~ *satellit* geostationary satellite
geoteknik [j-] geotechnics (*pl, behandlas som sg*) **-isk** [-'tekn-] *a5* geotechnical
geoterm|alvatten geothermal (hot) water **-isk** geothermal, geothermic; ~ *energi* geothermal energy
geovetenskap [ˣje:ɔ-] geoscience
gepard [je'pa:rd] *s3* cheetah
gepäck [g-, *äv.* j-] *s7* luggage
gerani|um [je'ra:-] *-en -er* geranium
geriatr|i[k] [g-] *s3* geriatrics (*pl, behandlas som sg*) **-iker** [-'a:-] geriatrician, geriatrist **-isk** [-'a:-] *a5* geriatric
gerilla [ge'rilla] *s1* guer[r]illa **-krig** guer[r]illa warfare **-rörelse** guer[r]illa movement
gering [ˣje:-] *fack.* mitre **geringslåda** mitre block (box)
german [j-] *s3* Teuton **-ism** *s3* Germanism **-ist** Germanic philologist
germanium [jer'ma:-] *s8* germanium
germansk [-'a:-] *a5* Germanic; Teutonic
geronto|log [g-] gerontologist **-logi** *s3* gerontology **-logisk** [-'lå:-] *a5* gerontological
gerundium [-'runn-] *s8* gerund
ges *gavs givits el. getts, dep, det* ~ (*finns*) there is (are)
geschäft [g- *el.* j-] *s7* business
gesims [j-, *äv.* g-] *s3* cornice, moulding
gess [j-, *äv.* g-] *s7* G flat **Gess-dur** G flat major
gest [ʃ-] *s3* gesture
gestalt [j-] *s3* figure; (*pers.*) character; (*avbildad* ~) image; (*form*) shape, form; *psykol.* gestalt; *ta* ~ take on (assume) shape; *i en tiggares* ~ in the guise (shape) of a beggar; *en av vår tids största* ~*er* one of the greatest figures (characters) of our time
gestalta [je'stalta] **1** shape, form, mould; ~ *en roll* (*äv.*) create a character **2** *rfl* (*utveckla sig*) turn out; (*arta sig*) shape; *hur framtiden än kommer att* ~ *sig* no matter what the future holds
gestalt|ning formation; (*form*) form; shape, configuration; (*av roll e.d.*) creation **-ningsförmåga** power of portrayal (creating) characters
gestaltpsykologi Gestalt psychology
gestikuler|a [ʃ-] gesticulate **-ing** gesticulation
gesäll [j-] *s3* journeyman **-brev** journeyman's certificate **-prov** apprentice's examination work
get [j-] *-en -ter* goat **getabock** [ˣje:-] he-goat, billy goat
geting [ˣje:-] wasp **-bo** wasp's nest; *röra om* (*sticka handen*) *i ett* ~ stir up a hornet's nest **-midja** wasp waist **-stick** wasp's sting
get|ost goat's-milk cheese **-ragg** goat's wool

-rams *s3, bot.* [angular] Solomon's seal **-skinn** goatskin, kid; (*getfäll*) goat-fell **-väppling** kidney vetch, ladies' fingers
gett [j-] *sup. av giva* (*ge*)
getto ['gettɔ] *s6* ghetto
getöga goat's eye; *kasta ett* ~ *på* take a quick look at
gevär [j-] *s7* (*räfflat*) rifle; (*friare*) gun; *för fot* ~*!* order arms!; *i* ~*!* to arms!; *på axel* ~*!* shoulder arms!; *sträcka* ~ lay down one's arms
gevärs|eld rifle fire **-exercis** rifle drill **-faktori** arms manufacturers (factory) **-kolv** [rifle] butt **-kula** [rifle] bullet **-mynning** muzzle **-pipa** [rifle] barrel **-skott** rifle shot **-skytt** rifleman **-stock** gunstock
Ghana [ˣga:-] *n* Ghana **ghan|an** *s3*, **-ansk** [-'a:-] *a5* Ghanaian
gibbon [-'å:n] *s3* gibbon
Gibraltar sund [ʃi'brall-] the Straits of Gibraltar
gick [jikk] *imperf. av gå*
gid [gidd] *s3* guide
giffel ['g- *el.* 'j-] *s2* croissant
1 gift [j-] *s4* poison (*äv. bildl.*); (*orm- o.d.*) venom (*äv. bildl.*); *fack.* toxin
2 gift [j-] *a4* married (*med* to)
gifta [ˣjifta] *gifte gift*; ~ *bort* marry off; give away in marriage; ~ *sig* marry (*äv.* ~ *sig med*) (*av kärlek* for love), get married; ~ *sig för pengar* marry for money; ~ *sig rikt* marry money; ~ *in sig i en familj* marry into a family; ~ *om sig* [*med*] remarry
giftas|lysten keen on getting married **-tankar** *gå i* ~ be thinking of getting married **-vuxen** old enough to get married, of marriageable age
gift|blandare, -blanderska poisoner **-blåsa** poison bag, venom sac; *bildl.* venomous person **-bägare** poison cup
gifte [j-] *s6* marriage; *barn i första* ~*t* children of the first marriage
giftermål [j-] marriage; match
giftermåls|anbud offer (proposal) of marriage **-annons** marriage advertisement **-balk** marriage act
gift|fri nonpoisonous, nontoxic **-gas** poison gas
giftig [j-] *a1* poisonous; venomous; toxic **-het** poisonousness; venomousness; toxicity; ~*er* (*bildl.*) venomous remarks
gift|mord murder by poison[ing] **-mördare** poisoner
giftoman [ˣjiftɔmann] *jur.* guardian
giftorm poisonous snake
giftorätt [j-] *jur.* widow's (widower's) right to property held jointly
giftorättsgods property held jointly by husband and wife, matrimonial property
gift|pil poisoned arrow **-skåp** poison cupboard **-stadga** poisons act **-tand** [poison] fang **-tecken** poison sign **-verkan** toxic effect
giga [j-] *s1* fiddle
gigant [g- *el.* j-] giant **-isk** *a5* gigantic
gigg [j-] *s2* gig (*äv. sjö.*)
gigolo ['ji:- *el.* 'jigg- *el.* 'ʃ-] *s5* gigolo
gikt [j-] *s3* gout **-bruten** gouty, gout-ridden
gilj|a [j-] woo; court **-are** wooer
giljar|färd, -stråt *dra på* ~ go wooing
giljotin [j-] *s3*, **-era** *v1* guillotine

gill [j-] *a5*, *gå sin ~a gång* be going on just as usual; *tredje gången ~t!* third time lucky!

gill|a (*godkänna*) approve of; *vard.* (*tycka om*) like, *AE.* dig; *det ~s inte!* (*vid lek*) [that's] not fair!, that doesn't count! **-ande** *s6* approval, approbation; *vinna ngns ~* meet with a p.'s approval

gille [j-] *s6* **1** (*gästabud*) banquet, feast; party **2** (*skrå*) guild; (*samfund*) guild, society

giller ['jill-] *s7* trap, gin; *bildl. äv.* snares (*pl*)

gille[s]stuga *ung.* informal [basement] lounge; *AE. äv.* rumpus room

gillra [j-] set (*en fälla* a trap)

giltig [j-] *a1* valid, effective; current; (*om dokument, överenskommelse*) effectual; (*om biljett äv.*) available; *bli ~* become valid (effective), come into force; *inget ~t skäl* no just cause **-het** validity; availability; *äga ~* be in force

giltighetstid period of validity; *förlängning av ~en* extension of the validity; *~ens utgång* expiry

gimmick ['gimm-] *s2* gimmick

1 gin [ji:n] *se 2 gen*

2 gin [jinn *el.* ji:n] *s3, s4* gin

ginnungagap [ˣjinn-] yawning gulf

ginseng ['ginn-] *s2* ginseng

ginst [g-] *s3, bot.* broom, genista

ginstkatt [g-] genet[te]

ginväg *se genväg*

gip[p] *s2, sjö.* gybe, jibe

1 gipa [j-] *s1, se mungipa*

2 gipa *el.* **gippa** [j-] *v1, sjö.* gybe, jibe

gips [j-] *s3* **1** (*mineral*) gypsum **2** (*gipsmassa*) plaster of Paris, *vard.* plaster

gips|a (*tak e.d.*) plaster; (*lägga förband [på]*) äv. put in plaster [of Paris] **-avgjutning** plaster cast **-figur** plaster figure **-förband** plaster[-of-Paris] cast (bandage) **-katt** plaster cat **-ning** plastering **-platta** plasterboard

gir [j-] *s2*, **gira** [j-] *v1, sjö.* sheer; (*friare*) turn, swerve

giraff [ʃ-] *s3* giraffe

girer|a [j-], **-ing** transfer

girig [j-] *a1* avaricious, miserly; (*lysten*) covetous, greedy (*efter* of); *den ~e* the miser **-buk** miser **-het** avariciousness *etc.*; avarice, greed; (*lystnad*) cupidity (*efter* for); (*vinstbegär*) avidity

girland [g- *el.* j-, -'and *el.* -'aŋ(d)] *s3* garland, festoon

giro ['ji:-] *s6* **1** *se girering* **2** (*jfr äv. postgiro*) *se -konto* **-konto** giro account

giss [j-] *s7* G sharp

gissa [j-] guess; (*förmoda*) conjecture; (*sluta sig t.*) divine; *rätt ~t!* you've got it!, right!; *~ sig till* guess, divine; *det kan man inte ~ sig till* that's impossible to guess

gissel ['jiss-] *s7* scourge; *satirens ~* the sting of the satire **-djur** flagellate **-slag** lash with a scourge

gissla [j-] scourge; *bildl. äv.* lash

gisslan [j-] *r* hostage[*s pl*]; *ta ~* seize hostages (a hostage)

gisslare [j-] scourger

gissning [j-] guess; conjecture, surmise; *bara ~ar* (*äv.*) pure guesswork (*sg*)

gissnings|tävlan guessing competition **-vis** at a guess

gisten [j-] *a3* (*om båt, laggkärl*) leaky, open at the joints; (*om golv*) gaping **gistna** become leaky; open at the joints; begin to gape

gitarr [j-] *s3* guitar; *akustisk ~* acoustic guitar; *elektrisk ~* electric guitar; *knäppa på ~* twang the guitar **-ackompanjemang** guitar accompaniment **-ist** guitarist

gitt|a [j-] *v1 el. gitte gittat* (*idas*) *bäst hon -er* as much as ever she likes, to her heart's content; *jag -er inte svara* I can't be bothered to answer

gitter ['g- *el.* 'j-] *s7* **1** *fys.* grating; *radio.* grid **2** *miner.* lattice

giv [j-] *s2* deal; *nya ~en* (*i USA*) the New Deal

giva [j-] *se ge*

givakt [j-] *n, se 3 akt*; *bildl., ett ~* a [word of] warning

giv|ande [j-] *a4* (*fruktbar*) fertile; *bildl. äv.* fruitful; (*lönande*) profitable, rewarding **-are, -arinna** [j-] giver, donor

givas [j-] *se ges*

giv|en [j-] *a3* given; (*avgjord*) clear, evident; *-na förutsättningar* understood prerequisites; *på ett -et tecken* at an agreed sign (signal); *ta för -et att* take it for granted that; *jag tar för -et att* I assume (take it) that; *det är -et!* of course!; *det är en ~ sak* it is a matter of course

giv|etvis [j-] of course, naturally **-it** *sup. av giva* (*ge*)

givmild [ˣji:v-] generous, open-handed **-het** generosity, open-handedness

1 gjord [jɔ:rd] *a5* done; made; (*jfr göra*); *historien verkar ~* the story seems to be made-up

2 gjord [jɔ:rd] *s2* girth

gjorde [ˣjɔ:r-] *imperf. av göra* **gjort** [jɔ:rt] *sup. av göra*

gjut|a [j-] *göt gjutit* **1** (*hälla*) pour **2** (*sprida, låta flöda*) shed **3** *tekn.* cast; (*metall o. glas äv.*) found; (*glas äv.*) press; (*friare*) mould; *rocken sitter som -en* the coat fits like a glove

gjut|are [j-] founder **-eri** [iron] foundry **-form** mould **-gods** *s7* castings (*pl*)

gjut|it [j-] *sup. av gjuta* **-järn** cast iron **-ning** casting *etc.* **-stål** cast steel

g-klav treble (G) clef

glacéhandske kid glove

glacial *a5* glacial **-period** glacial period (epoch), ice age

glacio|log glaciologist, glacialist **-logi** *s3* glaciology **-logisk** [-'lå:-] *a5* glaciologic[al]

glaciär *s3* glacier

glad *a1* (*gladlynt*) cheerful; (*upprymd*) merry, jolly, gay; (*lycklig*) happy; (*belåten*) delighted, pleased (*över* at); *~a färger* gay colours; *en ~ lax* (*bildl.*) a jolly chap; *~a nyheter* good news (*sg*); *~ påsk!* [A] Happy Easter!; *G~a änkan* the Merry Widow; *~ och munter* cheerful and gay; *glittrande ~* radiantly happy; *~ som en lärka* [as] happy as a lark; *med glatt hjärta* with a cheerful heart; *göra sig ~a dagar* make a day of it; *vara ~ i* (*t.ex. mat*) be fond of

glada *s1, zool.* [red] kite

gladde *imperf. av glädja*

gladeligen gladly; (*utan svårighet*) easily

gladiator [-ˣa:tår] *s3* gladiator **-spel** gladiatorial games

gladiol|us [-'di:-] *-usen -us, pl äv. -er* gladiolus (*pl äv.* gladioli, gladiolus), sword lily

gladlynt [ˣglaːd-] *a1* cheerful; (*glad t. sitt sinne*) good-humoured **-het** cheerfulness; good humour

glam [glamm] *s7* gaiety, merriment **-ma** talk merrily; (*stimma*) be noisy

glamo[u]r [glaˈmɔːr, *äv.* ˈglämmə] *s3* glamour **-isera** glamorize **-ös** *a5* glamo[u]rous

glans *s3* **1** (*glänsande yta*) lustre; (*tygs o.d. äv.*) gloss; (*guld-*) glitter; (*genom gnidning e.d.*) polish; (*sken*) brilliance, brightness; (*bländande*) glare; (*strål-*) radiance **2** (*härlighet, prakt*) magnificence, splendour; (*ära*) glory; *sprida ~ över* shed lustre over; *visa sig i all sin ~* appear (come out) in all its glory **3** *med ~* (*med bravur*) brilliantly, with flying colours, (*utan svårighet*) with great ease **-dagar** *pl* palmy days; heyday (*sg*) **-full** brilliant

glans|ig *a1* glossy; lustrous; (*om papper*) glazed **-[k]is** glassy ice **-lös** lustreless, lacklustre, dull **-nummer** (*persons*) showpiece; (*aftonens*) star turn **-papper** glazed paper **-period** heyday, golden age **-roll** brilliant (celebrated) role **-tid** *se -period*

glapp I *s7* backlash; play **II** *a1* loose; *vara ~ (äv.)* gape **glappa** be loose, gape; (*om skor o.d.*) fit loosely

glas *s7* **1** glass; (*mängd av en dryck äv.*) glassful; (*-varor*) glasswork; *ett ~ mjölk* a glass of milk; *ta ett ~ med ngn* have a jar with s.b.; *gärna ta sig ett ~* be fond of a drink; *han har tagit sig ett ~ för mycket* he has had a drop too much, *vard.* he has one over the eight; *sätta inom ~ och ram* frame [and glaze] **2** *sjö.* bell

glas|a glaze **-artad** [-aːr-] *a5* glassy, glasslike; *~ blick* a glassy look **-assiett** glass side plate **-berget** *sitta på ~* be left on the shelf **-bit** piece of glass **-björk** downy birch **-blåsare** glassblower **-bruk** glassworks (*pl, behandlas som sg*) **-burk** glass jar

glaser|a glaze; *kokk.* frost, ice **-ing** glazing; frosting, icing

glas|fiber glass fibre **-armerad** *a5* reinforced with glass fibre **-plast** glass-fibre plastic **-ull** glass wool **-väv** fibreglass [fabric]

glas|flaska glass bottle **-hal** slippery as glass **-hus** glasshouse; *man skall inte kasta sten när man sitter i ~* those who live in glasshouses should not throw stones **-klar** as clear as glass **-kropp** *anat.* vitreous body **-kupa** glass cover; bell jar (glass); (*på lampa*) glass shade **-massa** melted glass **-målning** *~ar* (*konkr.*) stained glass (*sg*); *fönster med ~ar* stained-glass window **-mästare** glazier **-mästeri** glaziery **-putsmedel** glass cleaner **-ruta** pane [of glass] **-rör** glass tube

glass *s3* ice cream **-bomb** bombe [glacée]

glas|skiva glass plate (sheet) **-skärva** glass splinter **-slipare** glass grinder (cutter)

glass|pinne ice [cream] **-strut** (*hopskr.* glasstrut) ice-cream cone (cornet) **-stånd** (*hopskr. glasstånd*) ice-cream stall

glas|ull glass wool **-varor** *pl* glasswork, glassware (*sg*) **-veranda** glassed-in veranda, sun lounge

glasyr *s3* glazing; (*på porslin*) glaze; *kokk.* frosting, icing

glasål glass eel

glasögon *pl* glasses, spectacles, *vard.* specs; *särsk. AE.* eyeglasses; (*stora*) goggles **-bågar** *pl* spectacle frame (*sg*) **-fodral** spectacle case **-orm** cobra

1 glatt *adv* gaily *etc.*; *bli ~ överraskad* be pleasantly surprised; *det gick ~ till* we (*etc.*) had a very gay time

2 glatt *a1* smooth; (*glänsande*) glossy, sleek; (*hal*) slippery; *~ muskel* smooth muscle; *springa för ~a livet* run for all one is worth

3 glatt *sup. av* glädja

glattmask oligochaete

glaubersalt Glauber['s]salt

glaukom [-ˈkåːm] *s4* glaucoma

gled *imperf. av* glida

gles *a1* (*ej tät, tätt bevuxen o.d.*) thin (*hårväxt* growth of hair; *fläck* spot); (*om vävnad o.d.*) loose; *~ befolkning* sparse population; *~ skog* open forest; *~a tänder* teeth with spaces in between **-befolkad** [-åː-] *a5* sparsely populated **-bevuxen** sparsely covered **-bygd** thinly populated area

glesna [ˣgleːs-] grow thin (*etc.*); (*om hår äv.*) get thin; become [more] open; *leden ~r* the ranks are thinning

gli *s6* **1** (*fiskyngel*) [small] fry (*pl*) **2** (*barnunge*) brat; *~n* small fry (*pl*)

glid *s7* **1** (*glidning*) glide, slide **2** (*glidförmåga, skidföre*) running **3** *på ~* on the glide, going astray

glida gled glidit glide; (*över ngt hårt*) slide; (*halka*) slip; *flyg.* sideslip; (*friare*) pass; *~ ifrån* glide away from; *~ isär* drift apart; *~ undan* slip away, (*slingra sig*) dodge, evade; *låta handen ~ över* pass one's hand over

glid|ande *a4* (*rörelse*) gliding; (*skala*) sliding **-bana** [sliding] chute, slide

glidflyg|are glider pilot **-ning** gliding, glide **-plan** glider

glid|flykt glide; gliding flight; *flyg.* volplane, volplaning; *gå ner i ~* volplane **-form** *byggn.* sliding form

glid|it *sup. av* glida **-lager** plain bearing **-ning** gliding, glide; sliding, slide

glimlampa [ˣglimm-] glow lamp **glimma** gleam; (*glittra*) glitter, glisten; *det är inte guld allt som ~r* all is not gold that glitters **glimmer** [ˈglimm-] **1** *s7* gleam[ing], glitter[ing] **2** *s2, miner.* mica **glimra** *se* glimma

glimt *s2* gleam (*äv. bildl.*); (*i ögat*) glint, twinkle; (*skymt*) glimpse; *en ~ i ögat* a glint (twinkle) in the eye; *få en ~ av* catch a glimpse of **glimt|a** glance, glimpse, glint **-vis** by glimpses (flashes)

glindra *se* glittra, glimma

glipa *s1* [narrow] gap

gliring gibe, jibe, sneer; dig; *få en ~* be gibed (sneered) at

glitter [ˈglitt-] *s7* **1** glitter, lustre; (*daggens etc.*) glistening; (*julgrans- e.d.*) tinsel; (*grannlåt*) gewgaws, baubles (*pl*) **2** *bildl.* (*tomt* empty) show **glittra** glitter, sparkle, shimmer; *~nde glad, se glad*

glo *v4* stare (*på* at); glare, goggle (*på* at)

glob *s3* globe; (*friare äv.*) ball

global *a5* global; worldwide **-avtal** global agreement

globin *s4* globin **globulin** *s4* globulin

glop *s2* whippersnapper, whipster, jackanapes; *vard.* puppy

glopp [-å-] *s7, se* snöglopp

gloria ['glo:-] *s1* (*strålkrans*) halo, glory; (*helgons äv.*) aureole, nimbus **2** *bildl.* nimbus

glori|fiera glorify **-fiering** glorifying, glorification **-ös** *a5* glorious

glos|a *s1* **1** word; vocable **2** (*glåpord*) gibe, jibe, sneer **-bok** vocabulary [notebook]; (*tryckt*) glossary, vocabulary

glossarium [glås'sa:-] *s4* glossary

glosögd *a5* popeyed, fisheyed

glottis ['glått-] *best. form* = glottis **-stöt** glottal stop

gloxinia [glå'xi:-] *s1* gloxinia

glufsa ~ *i sig* [*maten*] gobble up (down) [one's food]

glugg *s2* hole, aperture

glukagon [-'gå:n] *s4* glucagon

glukos [-'å:s] *s3* glucose **-id** *s3* glucoside

glunkas *det ~s* there is a rumour (*om* about; *om att* that)

glup|a *se* glufsa **-ande** *a4* ravenous (*aptit* appetite); voracious; ~ *ulvar* ravening wolves

glupsk *a1* greedy; (*omättlig*) voracious, ravenous, gluttonous **-het** greed[iness]; voracity, gluttony

glutamat *s4* glutamate

gluten ['glu:-] *best. form* = *el.* -*et* gluten

glutta peep, glance

glycer|id *s3* glyceride **-in** *s3, s4, se* glycerol

glycerol [-'å:l] *s3* glycerol, glycerin[e]

glykol [-'kå:l] *s3* ethanediol, [ethylene] glycol

glykos [-'kå:s] *s3, se* glukos **-id** *s3* glycoside

glytt *s2* lad

glåmig *a1* washed out; *blek och* ~ pale and washed out **-het** washed-out appearance; sallowness

glåpord taunt, scoff, jeer

gläd|ja [-ä:-] gladde glatt **1** give pleasure; make happy, please; (*starkare*) delight; ~ *ngn med ett besök* give s.b. pleasure by visiting him (*etc.*); *det -er mig* I am so glad [of that (to hear it)]; *om jag kan* ~ *dig därmed* if it will be any pleasure to you **2** *rfl* be glad (delighted) (*åt, över* at, about); rejoice (*åt, över* in, at); *kunna* ~ *sig åt ngt* (*åtnjuta*) enjoy s.th.; *jag -er mig mycket åt att få träffa dig* I am looking forward very much to seeing you **glädj|ande** [-ä:-] *a4* joyful, pleasant (*nyheter news* [*sg*]); (*tillfredsställande*) gratifying (*resultat* result); ~ *nog* fortunately enough; *en* ~ *tilldragelse i familjen* a happy event in the family **-as** *gladdes glatts, dep, se* glädja 2

glädje [-ä:-] *s3* joy (*över* at); (*nöje*) pleasure (*över* in); (*starkare*) delight (*över* at); ([*känsla av*] *lycka*) happiness; (*munterhet*) mirth; (*tillfredsställelse*) satisfaction; *i* ~ *och sorg* in joy and sorrow; *med* ~ (*äv.*) gladly; *till min stora* ~ to my great delight; *bereda ngn* ~ give s.b. happiness (*etc.*); *finna* ~ *i, ha* ~ *av* find (take) pleasure (*etc.*) in (*att göra* doing); *gråta av* ~ weep for joy; *känna* ~ *över* feel joy (rejoice) at; *vara till* ~ *för* be a joy (*etc.*) to; *vara utom sig av* ~ be beside o.s. with joy; ~*n stod högt i tak* [the] mirth ran

high; *det var en sann* ~ *att se* it was a real treat to see; *han har haft mycken* ~ *av sina barn* his children have been a great joy to him

glädje|bud[skap] good tidings (*pl*); *ett* ~ (*friare*) wonderful (a wonderful piece of) news **-dödare** kill-joy; *vard.* wet blanket **-fattig** *se* -*lös* **-flicka** prostitute **-hus** brothel **-källa** source of joy **-lös** joyless; cheerless **-rik** full of joy, joyful **-rop** cry (shout) of joy **-rus** transport of joy, rapture **-spridare** bringer of happiness; (*barn*) ray of sunshine **-språng** leap for joy, caper **-strålande** radiant (beaming) [with joy] **-tjut** shout of joy **-tårar** *pl* tears of joy **-yra** whirl of happiness **-yttring** manifestation of joy **-ämne** subject for (of) rejoicing

gläfs *s7* yelp, yap **gläfsa** *v3* yelp, yap (*på* at)

gläns|a *v3* shine (*av, med* with) (*äv. bildl.*); glitter; (*om tårar, ögon*) glisten; (*om siden e.d.*) be lustrous **-ande** *a4* shining *etc.*, shiny; (*om ögon*) lustrous; (*om siden e.d.*) glossy; *bildl.* brilliant, splendid

glänt, *s, i uttr.: stå på* ~ stand (be) ajar

glänta I *s1* (*skogs-*) glade **II** *v1,* ~ *på* open slightly

glätta smooth; (*papper*) glaze; (*läder*) sleek; (*polera*) polish

glättig *a1* gay; cheerful, light-hearted **-het** gaiety; cheerfulness *etc.*

glättning smoothing; glazing *etc.*

glöd *s7, s3* **1** (*glödande kol*) live coal; (*koll. ofta*) embers (*pl*) **2** (*glödande sken o. bildl.*) glow; (*hetta*) heat; (*lidelse*) passion; *bildl. äv.* ardour, fervour

glöd|a *v2* glow (*av* with); *i sht bildl.* be [all] aglow (*av* with); (*om järn o.d.*) be red-hot; (*brinna*) burn **-ande** *a4* glowing; (*om järn*) red-hot (*äv. bildl.*); (*häftig*) burning, ardent, fervent; ~ *hat* fiery hatred; *samla* ~ *kol på ngns huvud* heap coals of fire on a p.'s head

glödg|a [ˣglöddga] make red-hot; (*stål*) anneal; (*vin*) mull; (*göra glödande*) ignite **-ning** (*av järn o.d.*) [the] bringing of…to a red heat; (*av stål*) annealing

glöd|het red-hot, white-hot, glowing **-lampa** [light] bulb; *fack.* incandescent lamp **-steka** grill; fry on the embers **-strumpa** incandescent mantle **-ström** filament current **-tråd** filament **-tändning** ignition by incandescence

glögg *s2, ung.* mulled and spiced wine

glöm|ma *v2* forget; (*försumma*) neglect; (*kvarglömma*) leave [behind], forget; ~ *bort* forget; *man -mer så lätt* one is apt to forget; *jag har -t vad han heter* I forget his name; *jag hade alldeles -t* [*bort*] *det* (*äv.*) it had entirely escaped (slipped) my memory (mind); ~ *sig* (*förgå sig*) forget o.s.; ~ *sig själv* be forgetful of o.s. ; ~ *sig kvar* stay on **glöm|sk** *a5* forgetful; absent-minded; (*ej aktande på*) unmindful (*av sina plikter* of one's duties); oblivious (*av omgivningen* of one's surroundings); *vara* ~ [*av sig*] have a bad memory, be absent-minded **-ska** *s1* **1** forgetfulness; *av ren* ~ out of sheer forgetfulness **2** (*förgätenhet*) oblivion; *falla i* ~ be forgotten, fall into oblivion

g-moll G minor

gnabb *s7* bickering[s *pl*], wrangling[s *pl*], tiff; *AE.* spat **-as** *dep* bicker, wrangle

gnag|a *v2* gnaw (*på* at); (*knapra*) nibble; ~ *sig*

gnaw its (*etc.*) way (*igenom* through) **-ande** *a4* nagging (*oro* worry); *bildl. äv.* fretting, worrying **-are** *zool.* rodent

gnat *s7* nagging (*på* at; *över* about); cavilling (*på, över* at) **gnata** nag, cavil (*på* at) **gnatig** *a1* nagging; ~ *av sig* fretful, peevish

gned *imperf. av gnida*

gnejs *s3* gneiss

gnet *-en gnetter* (*lusägg*) nit

gnet|a write in a crabbed hand **-ig** *a1* (*om handstil*) crabbed

gnid|a *gned gnidit* rub; (*friare*) scrape (*äv.* ~ *på*); (*för att värma*) chafe; (*snåla*) pinch **-are** miser, skinflint **-ig** *a1* stingy, miserly, mean **-it** *sup. av gnida* **-ning** rubbing *etc.*; *fys.* friction

gnissel ['gniss-] *s7* **1** screech[ing] *etc.*, *se gnissla* **2** *bildl.* (*slitningar*) jars (*pl*); (*knot*) croak[ing] **gnissla** screech; (*om gångjärn e.d.*) creak; (*om hjul e.d.*) squeak; (*knorra*) croak; ~ [*med*] *tänder* [*na*] grind (gnash) one's teeth; *det* ~*r i maskineriet* (*bildl.*) things are not working smoothly

gnist|a *s1* **1** spark (*äv. bildl.*); (*genialitet*) spark of genius; *den tändande* ~*n* (*bildl.*) the igniting spark; *ha* ~*n* have the spark of genius; *spruta -or* give off sparks, *bildl.* flash **2** (*uns*) vestige, shade, particle; *en* ~ *hopp* a ray of hope; *en* ~ *sunt förnuft* a vestige of common sense **-bildning** formation of sparks, sparking **-galler** fireguard, fire screen **-gap** spark gap

gnist|ra emit sparks; (*blixtra*) sparkle; *i sht bildl.* flash (*av vrede* with rage); ~*nde kvickhet* sparkling wit; *få ett slag så det* ~*r för ögonen* get a blow that makes one see stars **-regn** shower of sparks

gno *v4* **1** (*gnugga*) rub **2** (*arbeta*) toil (work) [away] (*med* at) **3** (*springa*) run (*för brinnande livet* for dear life); ~ *på* a) (*arbeta*) work away, b) (*springa*) run hard[er], scurry

gnola hum; ~ *på en melodi* hum a tune

gnom [-å:-] *s3* gnome

gnost|icism [-å-] [G] Gnosticism **-iker** ['gnåss-] *s9*, **-isk** ['gnåss-] *a5* Gnostic

gnu *s3* gnu

gnugg|a rub (*sig i ögonen* one's eyes); (*plugga med*) *vard.* cram **-bild** transfer picture **-bokstav** transfer letter

gnugg|is *s2*, *se gnuggbild, gnuggbokstav* **-ning** rub[bing]

gnutta *s1* particle, tiny bit

gny I *s6* din; (*vapen-*) clatter; (*brus*) roar; *bildl.* cry-out, disturbance **II** *v4* **1** (*dåna*) roar; (*om vapen*) clatter; (*larma*) clamour **2** (*jämra sig*) whimper

gnägg *s7*, *vard.* (*skratt*) neigh, whinny **gnägga** neigh; (*lågt*) whinny (*äv. bildl.*) **gnäggning** neigh[ing]

gnäll *s7* **1** (*gnissel*) creak[ing], squeak[ing] **2** (*klagan*) whining, whine, whimper; (*småbarns*) puling; (*knot*) grumbling **gnälla** *v2* **1** (*om dörrar e.d.*) creak, squeak **2** (*klaga*) whine, whimper; (*om småbarn*) pule; (*yttra sitt missnöje med*) grumble (*över* about, at); (*gnata*) nag

gnäll|ig *a1* **1** (*gnisslande*) creaking *etc.*, creaky **2** (*klagande*) whining; (*om röst äv.*) strident, shrill; (*som yttrar sitt missnöje*) grumpy **-måns** *s2* croaker, whiner; (*barn*) crybaby

gnöla *vard.* grumble (*över* at)

gobeläng *s3* Gobelin [tapestry], tapestry

god *gott bättre bäst* (*jfr gott*) good (*mot* to); (*vänlig*) kind (*mot* to); (*välvillig*) kindly; (*utmärkt*) excellent, first-rate, (*i ledigare stil*) capital; (*tillfredsställande*) satisfactory; (*välsmakande o.d. äv.*) nice; ~ *dag!* good morning (afternoon, evening)!, (*vid första mötet med ngn*) how do you do!; ~ *morgon!* good morning!; ~ *natt!* good night!; ~ *man* (*boutredningsman*) executor, (*konkursförvaltare*) trustee, (*förordnad av domstol*) administrator, receiver; *en* ~ *vän* a good (great) friend; *denna världens* ~*a* the good things of this world; *av* ~ *familj* of a good family; *för den* ~*a sakens skull* for the good of the cause; *för mycket av det* ~*a* too much of a good thing; *i* ~*an ro* in peace and quiet; *på mången* ~ *dag* for many a long day; *på* ~*a grunder* for good (sound) reasons; *på* ~ *svenska* in good Swedish; *bli* ~ *två* come in a good second; *här finns* ~ *plats* there is plenty of room here; *gå i* ~ *för* vouch for; *ha* ~ *lust att* have a good mind to; *hålla* (*anse*) *sig för* ~ *att* consider it beneath one to; *lägga ett gott ord för* put in a [good] word for; *inte* ~ *att tas med* not easy to deal with; *var så* ~! a) (*när man ger ngt*) here you are [Madam (Sir)]!, b) (*ta för er*) help yourself, please!, c) (*ja, naturligtvis*) by all means!; *var så* ~ *och...*, *vill ni vara så* ~ *och...* please..., will you [kindly]...; *vara* ~ *för 5 000 pund* be good for 5,000 pounds; *vara på* ~ *väg att* be well on the way to; *vara vid gott mod* be of good courage; *han är inte* ~ *på dig* he's got it in for you; *det har det* ~*a med sig att man kan* the advantage of this is that

Godahoppsudden [-ˣhåpps-] the Cape of Good Hope

god|artad [-a:r-] *a5* (*lindrig, ej elakartad*) nonmalignant, benign **-bit** titbit (*äv. bildl.*), dainty morsel **-dag** *se god* [*dag*] **-dagspilt** [ˣgo:d-] bon vivant, easy-going chap **-het** goodness *etc.*, *jfr god; ha* ~*en att* be kind enough to **-hetsfullt** kindly **-hjärtad** [-j-] *a5* kind-hearted

godis ['gå:-] *oböjligt s*, *se godsaker*

god|känd *a5* approved (*som* as); *bli* ~ [*i examen*] pass [one's examination] **-känna** approve (*ngn som s.b.* as); (*förslag e.d.*) approve of, sanction; (*i examen*) pass; (*gå med på äv.*) agree to; accept (*en leverans* a delivery; *som bevis* as evidence; *en växel* a bill of exchange) **-kännande** *s6* approval, approbation; sanction; admission; acceptance

god|lynt *a4* good-humoured, good-tempered **-modig** good-natured **-morgon, -natt** *se god* [*morgon, natt*] **-nattkyss** good-night kiss

godo *i uttr.*: *i* ~ amicably, in a friendly spirit; *uppgörelse i* ~ amicable settlement, *jur.* settlement out of court; *mig till* ~ in my favour; *håll till* ~! a) (*ta för er*) please help yourself!, b) (*svar på tack*) you are welcome [to it]!; *hålla till* ~ *med* [have to] put up with; *komma ngn till* ~ be of use to s.b.; *räkna ngn ngt till* ~ (*äv. bildl.*) put s.th. down to a p.'s credit; *får jag ha det till* ~ *till en annan gång?* can I leave it standing over for some future occasion?, *AE.* can I take a raincheck?

gods [gåtts, *äv.* gådds] *s7* **1** (*egendom*) property; (*ägodelar*) possessions (*pl*); ~ *och guld* money

and possessions **2** (*varor*, *last*) goods (*pl*); *AE.* freight; *lättare* ~ (*bildl.*) light wares (*pl*) **3** (*material*) material **4** (*jorda-*) estate, manor **5** *sjö.*, *löpande* (*stående*) ~ running (standing) rigging
godsaker *pl* (*sötsaker*) sweets; *vard.* goodies; *AE.* candy (*sg*)
gods|befordran conveyance of goods, goods traffic **-expedition** goods (*AE.* freight) office **-finka** luggage van; goods waggon; *AE.* boxcar, freight car **-inlämning** goods [forwarding] office; *AE.* freight office **-magasin** goods depot, warehouse **-trafik** goods traffic; *AE.* freight traffic (service) **-tåg** goods (*AE.* freight) train **-vagn** *se godsfinka* **-ägare** estate owner, landed proprietor; ~*n* the landlord
god|ta[ga] accept, approve [of] **-tagande** *s6* acceptance, approval **-tagbar** [-a:g-] *a5* acceptable
godtemplar|e [ˣgɔ:d- *el.* -ˣtemm-] Good Templar **-loge** [-lå:ʃ] Good-Templar lodge **-orden** the [Independent] Order of Good Templars
godtrogen credulous, unsuspecting **-het** credulity
godtrosförvärv *jur.* acquisition made in good faith
godtyck|e 1 (*gottfinnande*) discretion, pleasure, will; *efter eget* ~ at one's own discretion **2** (*egenmäktighet*) arbitrariness; *rena* ~*t* pure arbitrariness **-lig** *a1* **1** (*vilken som helst*) just any, fortuitous **2** (*egenmäktig*) arbitrary; (*nyckfull*) capricious; (*utan grund*) gratuitous **-lighet 1** fortuitousness **2** arbitrariness *etc.*
godvil|lig voluntary **-ligt** *adv* voluntarily, of one's own free will
goffrer|a [-å-] *v1*, **-ing** *s2* goffer, gauffer
goja [ˣgåjja] *s1* **1** *se papegoja* **2** *vard.* rubbish, bosh; *prata* ~ talk through one's hat
gol *imperf. av 1 gala*
1 golf [-å-] *s3* (*havsvik*) gulf
2 golf [-å-] *s3* (*spel*) golf
golf|bana golf course (links *vanl. sg*) **-boll** golf ball **-byxor** *pl* plus fours **-klubb** golf club **-klubba** golf club **-spelare** golfer, golf player
Golfströmmen the Gulf Stream
Golgata [ˈgållgata] *n* Calvary; Golgotha
golv [-å-] *s7* floor; (*-beläggning*) flooring; *från* ~ *till tak* from floor to ceiling; *falla i* ~*et* fall to the floor
golv|a [-å-] *sport.* floor **-beläggning** flooring **-bonare** floor polisher **-borste** [floor] brush **-brunn** draining gutter **-bräda** floorboard **-drag** draught along (through) the floor **-lampa** floor lamp **-list** skirting board; *AE.* baseboard **-läggare** floor-layer, floorer **-mopp** [floor] mop **-raka** *s1* floor squeegee **-ur** grandfather (longcase) clock **-vård** floor care **-vårdsmaskin** floor-care machine **-växel** (*i bil*) floor-[-mounted] gearshift **-yta** floor area (space); surface of a floor
gom [gomm] *s2* palate **-segel** soft palate; velum **-spalt** cleft palate
gon [-å:-] *s3* (*nygrad*) grade
gona *rfl* relax to one's heart's content
gonad *s3*, *biol.* gonad
gondol [gån'då:l] *s3* **1** gondola **2** (*ballongkorg*) car **-jär** *s3* gondolier
gonggong [ˣgåŋgåŋ] *s3*, *s2* [dinner] gong; ~*en*

har gått the gong has gone; *räddad av* ~*en* saved by the bell
gonokock [-ˈkåkk] *s3* gonococcus (*pl* gonococci) **gonorré** *s3* gonorrhoea
gordisk [ˈgå:r-] *a5*, ~ *knut* Gordian knot
gorgonzola [gårgånˣså:la] *s1* Gorgonzola [cheese]
gorilla [-ˣilla] *s1* gorilla (*äv. bildl.*, *vard.*)
gorm|a [-å-] brawl; kick up a row (*för*, *om* about) **-ande** *s6* brawl, racket, row
gorän [ˣgɔ:-] *s7* wafer
gosa *v1*, ~ *med* cuddle
gossaktig [-å-] *a1* boyish
gosse [-å-] *s2* boy; lad; *mammas* ~ mother's boy; *gamle* ~*!* old boy (chap, fellow)! **-barn** boy child; [baby] boy **-lynne** youthful outlook, optimism
gosskör boys' choir
got [gɔ:t, *äv.* gå:t] *s3* Goth **-jk** *s3*, **-isk** [ˈgɔ:-, *äv.* 'gå:-] *a5*, **-iska** [ˈgɔ:-, *äv.* 'gå:-] *s2* Gothic
Gotland [ˈgått-] *n*, Got[h]land **gotländsk** [ˣgått-] *a5* Got[h]land
gott [-å-] (*jfr god*) **I** *s* (*sötsaker*) *se godsaker* **II** *a o. oböjligt s* **1** *varmt och* ~ nice and warm; ~ *och väl en vecka* at least a week; *det var inte* ~ *att veta* how could I (he *etc.*) know; *det vore lika* ~ *att* it would be just as well to; *det är* ~ *och väl*, men it's all very well, but **2** *göra mycket* ~ do a great deal of good; *ha* ~ *av* [derive] benefit from; *önska ngn allt* ~ wish s.b. every happiness **3** ~ *om a*) (*tillräckligt med*) plenty of, *b*) (*mycket*) a great many (deal of), *vard.* lots of; *på* ~ *och ont* that cuts both ways **III** *adv* well; (*starkare*) capitally, excellently; (*lätt*) easily, very well; (*medgivande*) very well; *kort och* ~ *a*) (*i korthet*) briefly, *b*) (*helt enkelt*) simply; *så* ~ *som* practically, almost, all but; *finna för* ~ think fit (proper); *göra så* ~ *man kan* do one's best; *komma* ~ *överens* get on well; *leva* ~ live well (sumptuously); *lukta* (*smaka*) ~ smell (taste) nice; *må så* ~*!* take care of yourself!; *skratta* ~ laugh heartily; *sova* ~ sleep soundly, (*som vana*) sleep well; *det kan* ~ *hända* it may very well happen
gott|a [-å-] *rfl* have a good time; ~ *sig åt* thoroughly enjoy **-er** *se godsaker* **-finnande** *s6*, *efter* [*eget*] ~ as one thinks best, according to one's own choice
gottgör|a 1 (*ersätta*) make good (*ngn ngt* to s.b. s.th.), make up (*ngn ngt* to s.b. for s.th.), recompense; (*för skada äv.*) indemnify, compensate **2** (*försona*) make good, make up for; (*reparera*) redress, repair; (*kreditera*) credit **3** *rfl* allow o.s. **-else** [-jö:-] (*ersättning*) compensation, indemnification, recompense; (*betalning*) remuneration, payment; (*skadestånd*) indemnity
gottis [-å-] *oböjligt s*, *se godsaker*
gottköps|affär bargain store, cut-price shop; *AE.* cut-rate store **-pris** *till* ~ at a bargain price **-varor** *pl* cheap-line goods
gottskriv|a credit; ~ *ngn ett belopp* credit s.b. with an amount **-ning** credit[ing]
gottsugen *a5*, *vara* ~ (*just nu*) feel like s.th. sweet to eat, (*alltid*) have a sweet tooth
gouache [goˈaʃ] *s5* gouache; (*tekniken äv.*) body colour
gour|mand [gɔrˈman(d)] *s3* go[u]rmand **-mé** *s3* gourmet

gouterad [goˈteː-] *a5* appreciated, acclaimed
grabb *s2* chap; *AE.* fellow
grabba ~ *tag i* grab [hold of], lay hands on; ~ *åt (för) sig* grab for o.s., appropriate; cop **-tag** *se* grabbtag
grabb|näve [big] fist[ful] **-tag** grab
grace [graːs] *s5* **1** (*behag*) grace[fulness], charm **2** (*gunst*) favour; *fördela sina* ~*r* spread one's favours **gracerna** [ˈgraːs-] *de tre* ~ the three Graces
grac|il [-s-] *a1* gracile, slender **-ös** *a1* graceful
1 grad *a, n sg obest. form saknas, tekn.* (*rak*) straight; (*jämn*) even
2 grad *s3, tekn.* burr
3 grad *s3* **1** degree; (*omfattning*) extent; *i hög* ~ to a great extent, highly, exceedingly (*intressant interesting*); *i högsta* ~ extremely, exceedingly; *till den* ~ *oförskämd* so terribly insolent **2** (*vinkelmått, temperaturenhet, mat.*) degree; *i 90* ~*ers vinkel* at an angle of 90 degrees; *på 90* ~*ers nordlig bredd* at 90 degrees North Latitude; *15* ~*er kallt* 15 degrees below freezing point (zero) **3** (*rang*) rank, grade; (*doktors-*) [doctor's] degree; *tjänsteman av lägre* ~ a minor official, a low-salaried worker; *stiga i* ~*erna* rise in the ranks
gradbeteckning badge of rank
grader|a *tekn.* graduate; calibrate; (*friare*) grade (*efter* according to) **-ing** *tekn.* graduation; calibration; (*friare*) gradation, grading
gradient *fys., mat.* gradient
grad|indelning division into degrees; graduation **-skillnad** difference of (in) degree **-skiva** protractor **-tal** *mat.* degree; *vid höga* ~ (*temperaturer*) at high temperature
gradual|avhandling doctor's dissertation **-psalm** gradual
gradvis I *adv* by degrees, gradually **II** *a5* gradual
graf *s3, mat.* graph
grafem *s7, språkv.* grapheme
graffit|o [-ˈfiːtå] **-on** *-i* graffito
graf|ik *s3, abstr.* graphic arts (*pl*); *konkr.* prints (*pl*) **-iker** [ˈgraː-] graphic artist, printmaker **-isk** [ˈgraː-] *a5* graphic[al]; ~ *framställning* graphic representation, (*kurva*) graph, diagram; ~ *industri* printing industry
grafit *s3* graphite
grafo|log graphologist **-logi** *s3* graphology **-logisk** [-ˈlåː-] *a5* graphologic[al]
grahamsmjöl graham flour
gram [-amm] *s7* gram[me] **-atom** gram atom, gramatomic weight **-kalori** [gram] calorie
grammat|ik *s3* grammar **-ikalisk** [-ˈkaː-] *a5* grammatical[ly correct] **-iker** [-ˈmatt-] grammarian **-isk** [-ˈmatt-] *a5* grammatical **-iskt** [-ˈmatt-] *adv, det är* ~ *fel* it is bad grammar
grammofon [-ˈfåːn] *s3* gramophone, record-player; *AE.* phonograph **-inspelning** recording; *konkr.* disc **-musik** gramophone music **-skiva** [gramophone] record, disc **-stift** gramophone needle
grammolekyl gram molecule, grammolecular weight
gramse *oböjligt a, vara* ~ *på ngn* bear s.b. a grudge
1 gran *s7* (*vikt*) grain
2 gran *s2* **1** (*träd*) fir; spruce; *vanlig* ~ Norway

spruce **2** (*virke*) fir; spruce
1 granat *bot.* pomegranate [shrub, tree]
2 granat (*ädelsten*) garnet
3 granat *mil.* shell; (*hand-*) [hand] grenade
granat|eld shellfire **-gevär** recoilless antitank rifle **-kastare** trench mortar(gun)
granatsmycke set of garnets
granatsplitter shell splinter
granatäpple pomegranate
granbarr fir (spruce) needle
1 grand *s7* **1** ~*et* mote and the beam **2** (*aning*) atom, whit; *litet* ~ just a little (wee bit); *inte göra ett skapande[s]* ~ not do a [single] mortal thing; *vänta litet* ~ wait a little (a minute)
2 grand *s3* (*titel*) grandee
grandezza [-ˈdessa] *s1* grandeur, dignity
grandios [-iˈåːs] *a1* grandiose
granit *s3* granite **-block** granite block **-klippa** granite rock
gran|kotte fir (spruce) cone **-kvist** fir (spruce) twig
1 grann *se 1 grand 2*
2 grann *a1* **1** (*brokig*) gaudy, gay; (*lysande*) brilliant; (*prålig*) gorgeous, showy **2** (*ståtlig*) fine[-looking], (*om väder*) magnificent **3** (*högtravande*) high-flown, high-sounding, fine
grann|e *s2* neighbour **-fru** neighbour['s wife] **-gård** neighbouring house (farm *etc.*); *i* ~*en* at the next house (*etc.*) [to ours]
grannlag|a *oböjligt a* (*finkänslig*) tactful; considerate; (*ömtålig*) delicate **-enhet** tactfulness *etc.*; discretion, delicacy
grannland neighbouring country; *vårt södra* ~ our neighbour-country to the south
grannlåt *s3* show, display; ~[*er*] gewgaws, (*floskler*) pretty phrases
grann|skap *s7* neighbourhood, vicinity **-sämja** neighbourliness, [good] neighbourship
granntyckt *a1* fastidious, overparticular (*i, på* in)
gran|ris fir (spruce) twigs (*pl*) **-ruska** fir (spruce) branch
gransk|a examine, scrutinize; scan; (*kontrollera*) check; (*recensera*) review; (*rätta*) correct; ~*nde blick* scrutinizing (critical) look **-are** examiner **-ning** examining *etc.*; examination, scrutiny; (*kontroll*) checkup **-ningsarvode** inspection (scrutiny) fee
granskog fir (spruce) forest
granul|at *s7* granulated (granular) material **-era** granulate (*fys.*) **-ering** [-ˈeː-] granulation
granvirke fir (spruce) timber; (*sågat*) white deal
grapefrukt [ˣgrejp-] grapefruit
grasser|a (*om sjukdom*) rage, be prevalent (rife); (*om missbruk o.d.*) run (be) rampant **-ande** *a4* rife, prevalent; rampant
gratierna [ˈgratsi-] *se gracerna*
gratifikation gratuity, bonus
gratin [-ˈtän] *s3, se gratäng* **-era** [-tiˈneː-] bake in a gratin dish; ~*d* au gratin
gratis [ˈgraː- el. ˣgraː-] *adv o. oböjligt a* free [of charge], gratuitous; ~ *och franko* delivered free, carriage (postage) paid **-aktie** bonus share **-biljett** complimentary ticket, free ticket (pass) **-emission** bonus issue **-erbjudande** free offer

G

-exemplar se friexemplar **-föreställning** free performance **-nöje** free entertainment **-prov** free sample, hand-ou' **-värme** incidental heat gain

grattis ['gratt-] interj, äv. s, vard. congratulations! (pl)

gratul|ant congratulator **-ation** congratulation; hjärtliga ~er på födelsedagen many happy returns [of the day] **-ationskort** greetings card **-era** congratulate (till on)

gratäng s3 gratin; ~ på fisk baked fish

1 grav s2 **1** grave; (murad e.d.) tomb; på ~ens brädd (bildl.) on the brink of the grave; tyst som i ~en [as] silent as the grave **2** (dike) trench (i sht mil.), ditch **3** (grop) pit, hole

2 grav a1 (svår) serious

3 grav a1, ~ accent grave accent

grava kokk. pickle raw

gravallvarlig very solemn

gravand zool. common shelduck (hane äv. sheldrake)

gravation encumbrance, mortgage

gravations|bevis abstract of the register of land charges; (i Storbritannien äv.) certificate of search **-fri** unencumbered, unmortgaged

1 gravera jur. encumber; ~nde omständigheter (friare) aggravating circumstances

2 gravera (inrista) engrave

graver|ing engraving **-nål** engraving needle

grav|fynd grave find **-fält** grave field **-häll** grave slab **-hög** barrow, mound

gravid a, n sg obest. form undviks pregnant **-itet** pregnancy **-itetstest** pregnancy test

gravita|tion gravitation, gravity **-tionslagen** the (Newton's) law of gravitation

gravite|ra gravitate (åt towards) **-tisk** a5 grave, solemn; (friare) pompous

grav|kammare sepulchral chamber, sepulchre **-kapell** mortuary chapel **-kor** s7 crypt **-kulle** grave, mound

gravlax kokk. raw spiced salmon

grav|lik a5 sepulchral; med ~ stämma in a sepulchral voice; ~ tystnad deathly quiet **-monument** monument; memorial **-plats** burial ground; [piece of ground for a] grave **-plundrare** grave robber **-plundring** grave robbery

gravrost deep-seated rust

grav|skick burial custom **-skrift 1** (inskrift) epitaph **2** (minnesord) memorial words (pl) **-skändning** grave desecration **-sten** gravestone, tombstone **-sänka** geol. rift valley **-sättning** interment **-urna** sepulchral urn **-valv** tomb; crypt **-vård** memorial stone, sepulchral monument; jfr -sten

gravyr s3 engraving

gravöl funeral feast

gravör engraver

gredelin a5 heliotrope, mauve, lilac

gregoriansk [-a:-] a5, ~a kalendern the Gregorian calendar; ~ sång Gregorian chant, plainsong, plainchant

grej [-ejj] s3 thing, article; ~or (vard.) paraphernalia, tackle (sg), gear (sg) **greja** (sg) grej fix, put right; ~ med bilen work on (tinker with) the car

grek s3 Greek **-cypriot** Greek Cypriot[e] **-inna** [-ˣinna] n Greek woman

grek|isk ['gre:-] a5 Greek; (antik äv.) Grecian **-iska 1** (språk) Greek **2** se grekinna

grekisk|-katolsk, --ortodox ~a kyrkan the Eastern Orthodox Church, the Greek [Orthodox] Church; en ~ trosbekännare a member of the Eastern Orthodox Church **--romersk** ~ brottning Greco-Roman wrestling

Grekland ['gre:k-] n Greece

gren s2 **1** branch (äv. bildl.); limb, bough; (av flod e.d.) arm **2** (förgrening) fork; (skrev) crotch, crutch **grena** rfl branch, fork

Grenada [-ˣna:-] n Grenada **grenadier** [-ˈna:-] s9 Grenadian

grenadjn 1 (fruktsaft) grenadine **2** (råsilke) grenadine

grenadisk [-ˈna:-] a5 Grenadian

grenadjär s3 grenadier

gren|ig a1 branched **-klyka** fork of a bough **-ljus** branched candle **-rör** branch pipe; manifold

grensla straddle, bestride **grensle** astride (över of); sitta ~ straddle

grenverk [network of] branches

grep imperf. av gripa

grep s2 pitchfork

1 grepe s2, se grep

2 grepe s2 (handtag) handle

grepp s7 grasp (i, om of); (vid brottning o. bildl.) grip (i, om of); (tag äv.) hold; mus. touch; nya ~ new methods, moves; få ~ på ett ämne grasp (get the hang of) a subject; ha ett gott ~ (bildl.) have the knack **-bräde** mus. fingerboard

greve s2 count; (i Storbritannien) earl; ~n (vid tilltal) Your Lordship, My Lord; i ~ns tid in the nick of time **-titel** title of count (earl) **-värdighet** countship, earldom

grev|inna countess; ~n (vid tilltal) Your Ladyship, My Lady **-lig** a5, ett ~t gods a count's (etc.) estate; upphöjas i ~t stånd be created (made) an earl **-skap** s7 **1** (område) county **2** se grevevärdighet

griffel s2 slate pencil **-tavla** slate

grift s3 tomb, grave

grifte|ro quiet of the tomb **-tal** funeral oration

griljera grill (roast, fry) after coating with egg and breadcrumbs

grill s2 grill, gridiron, vard. grid; (-rum) grill [room]; (på bil) grill[e]

grill|a grill **-bar** s3 rotisserie

griller ['grill-] pl fads, fancies, whims

grill|korv sausage for grilling **-panna** grill pan **-restaurang** grillroom **-spett** skewer, brochette

grimas s3 grimace; göra en ~ pull (make) a [wry] face **-era** pull (make) faces, grimace

grimma s1 halter

grin s7 **1** se grimas **2** (flin) grin; (hån-) leer **3** (gråt) whine **grina 1** se grimasera; ~ illa pull faces (åt at), bildl. sneer (åt at) **2** (gapa) gape; armodet ~de dem i ansiktet poverty stared them in the face **3** (flina) grin; leer **4** (gråta) whine, pule

grind s2 gate **-slant** gate money **-stolpe** gatepost **-stuga** [gatekeeper's] lodge **-vakt** gatekeeper; (i kricket) wicketkeeper

grindval pilot (black) whale, blackfish

grin|ig a1 **1** (som gråter) whining, puling **2** (missnöjd) complaining, fault-finding; (kinkig) peev-

ish **-olle** *s2* crybaby, whiner
grip *s2* griffin
gripa *grep gripit* **1** *(fatta tag i)* seize *(äv. bildl.*); *(tjuv e.d.)* catch, capture; *(fatta kraftigt tag i)* catch (take) hold of, clasp, clutch; ~ *tag i* get hold of; ~ *tillfället* seize the opportunity; ~ *tyglarna* catch hold of *(bildl.* take) the reins; ~ *ngn på bar gärning* catch s.b. red-handed (in the act); ~ *ngt ur luften* make s.th. up; ~*s av förtvivlan* be seized by despair **2** *(djupt röra)* affect, move **3** ~ *sig an med* set about, *(ett arbete* a job; *att arbeta* working); ~ *efter* catch (grasp) at; ~ *i varandra (i mekanism)* interlock, *(om kugghjul)* engage; ~ *in i* interfere with, intervene in; ~ *omkring sig* spread, gain ground
grip|ande *a4* touching, moving; pathetic **-arm 1** *zool.* prehensile arm **2** *tekn.* transferring arm **-bar** *a1 (fattbar)* comprehensible; *(påtaglig)* palpable, tangible; *(konkret)* concrete
gripen *a3* **1** seized *(av* with) **2** *(rörd)* touched, moved **-het** emotion
grip|it *sup. av gripa* **-klo** *zool.* prehensile claw **-tång** clutching-tongs *(pl)*
gris *s2* **1** pig; *(kött)* pork; *helstekt* ~ sucking pig roasted whole; *köpa* ~*en i säcken* buy a pig in a poke **2** *(om pers.)* pig
gris|a 1 *eg.* farrow **2** ~ *ner (till)* make a mess, muck up; ~ *ner sig* get o.s. in a mess **-aktig** *se grisig* **-eri, -farm** piggery **-fot** pig's foot; *-fötter (kokk.)* pig's trotters **-huvud** pig's head
gris|ig *a1* piggish; filthy **-kulting** sucking pig, piglet; *vard.* piggy **-mat** pig feed
grissla *s1* guillemot
grisslybjörn grizzly [bear]
grisöga pig's eye *(äv. bildl.)*
gro *v4* germinate, sprout; *(växa)* grow; *bildl.* rankle; ~ *igen* a) *(om jord)* grass over, b) *(om dike e.d.)* get filled up [with grass]; *det [ligger och]* ~*r i ngn* it rankles in a p.'s breast; *medan gräset* ~*r dör kon* while the grass grows the steed starves **-bar** *a5* germinable, germinative **-barhet** germinativeness; fertility
grobian *s3* boor, churl; *(starkare)* ruffian
groblad *bot.* [great] plantain
groda *s1* **1** *zool.* frog **2** *bildl.* blunder, howler
grodd *s2* germ, sprout; *koll.* sprouts *(pl)* **-blad** germ layer
grod|djur batrachian **-lår** frog's leg **-man** frogman **-mansutrustning** scuba gear; frogman's equipment; underwater diving kit **-perspektiv** *i* ~ *(bildl.)* from a worm's eye view **-rom** frogspawn **-spott** cuckoo (frog) spit, frog spittle **-yngel** tadpole; *koll.* tadpoles *(pl)*
grogg *[-å-] s2* grog; whisky (brandy) and soda; *AE.* highball
grogg|a *[-å-]* [drink] grog **-glas** *(hopskr. grogglas)* grog tumbler, whisky glass
grogrund *eg.* fertile soil; *bildl.* hotbed
groll *[-å-] s7* grudge; *gammalt* ~ long-standing grudge; *hysa* ~ *mot ngn* bear s.b. a grudge
groning germination, sprouting
grop *s2* pit; *(större)* hollow, cavity; *(i väg)* hole; *(i hakan, kinden)* dimple; *flyg.* bump, pocket; *den som gräver en* ~ *åt andra faller själv däri* he who diggeth a pit shall fall therein **-ig** *a1* **1** full of holes; *(om golv o.d.)* worn into holes; *(om väg)*

bumpy, uneven **2** *(om hav)* rough; *flyg.* bumpy
1 gross *[-å-] s7 (tolv dussin)* gross; *i* ~ by the gross
2 gross *[-å-] s i uttr.: i* ~ *(i parti)* wholesale
grossess pregnancy; *i* ~ pregnant, big with child
grosshandel wholesale trade
grosshandels|firma wholesale business (firm) **-pris** wholesale price
gross|handlare, -ist wholesale dealer, wholesaler **-istförbund** *Sveriges G*~ Federation of Swedish Wholesalers and Importers
grotesk I *a1* grotesque **II** *s3, boktr.* sans serif, sanserif, grotesque
grotta *[-å-] s1* cave; *(större)* cavern; *(konstgjord o. måleriskt)* grotto
grottekvarn *[-å-]* treadmill
grott|forskare cave explorer, speleologist **-forskning** speleology **-målning** cave painting **-människa** *förhist.* caveman, troglodyte
grov *-t grövre grövst* **1** *(motsats fin)* coarse; *(stor)* large; *(storväxt)* big; *(tjock)* thick; *(om röst)* rough, coarse; *(om yta)* rough; ~*t artilleri* heavy artillery; ~*t bröd (salt)* coarse bread (salt); ~ *sjö* rough sea **2** *bildl.* rough; *(nedsättande)* coarse, gross, crude; *(allvarlig)* grave; *(ohyfsad)* rude, rough; ~*t brott* heinous crime; ~ *förolämpning (okunnighet)* gross insult (ignorance); *i* ~*a drag* in rough outline *(sg)*; *tjäna* ~ *a pengar* make big money; *vara* ~ *i munnen* use foul language
grov|arbetare labourer, unskilled worker **-arbete** unskilled labour **-göra** heavy (rough) work; *AE. äv.* chore **-hacka** chop coarsely
grov|het *[-å:-]* coarseness *etc., jfr grov*; ~*er* foul language *(sg)* **-huggare** *se grobian* **-huggen** *a5* **1** *(om utseende)* rugged, coarsely chiselled **2** *se grovkornig* 2 **-hyvla** rough-plane **-kalibrig** *[-i:b-] a1* large-bore, large-calibred **-kornig 1** coarse-grained **2** *bildl.* coarse, gross, rude; ~*t skämt* broad joke **-lek** *s2* thickness **-lemmad** *a5* heavy-limbed **-mala** grind coarsely **-maskig** *a1* wide-meshed, coarse-meshed **-rengöringsmedel** heavy duty cleaner **-sortera** do the first sorting **-sortering** first sorting **-sysslor** *pl* rough jobs
grov|t *[-å:-] adv* coarsely *etc.*; *tjäna* ~ *på* make a pile of money on; *gissa* ~ make a rough guess; *ljuga* ~ tell barefaced lies **-tarm** colon
grubbel *['grubb-] s7 (funderande)* musing[s *pl*], rumination; *relig. äv.* obsession; *(sjukligt morbid)* brooding
grubbl|a *(ängsligt)* brood; *(fundera)* cogitate, muse, ruminate; puzzle [one's head]; ~ *sig fördärvad över* rack one's brains over **-are** brooder, cogitator; *(friare)* philosopher **-eri** *se grubbel*
gruff *s7* row, wrangle; *råka i* ~ *med* get at loggerheads with **gruffa** make *(vard.* kick up) a row, squabble *(för, om* about; *med* with)
grumla *eg.* make muddy, soil; *(friare, äv. bildl.)* cloud, dim; *(göra suddig)* blur; *(bildl. smutsa ner)* soil, tarnish; *(fördunkla)* obscure; ~ *själens lugn* disturb the peace of mind **grumlig** *al* muddy, turbid *(äv. bildl.*); *(virrig)* muddled, confused; *(dunkel)* obscure; *(om röst)* thick; *fiska i* ~*t vatten* fish in troubled water
grums *s7* grounds *(pl)*, dregs *(pl)*; *(i vatten)* sediment

G

grumsa grumble

1 grund *s7* (*grunt ställe*) shallow[s *pl*], shoal; (*sand- o.d.*) bank; (*klipp-*) sunken rock; *gå* (*stöta*) *på* ~ run aground; *komma av* ~*et* get afloat

2 grund *a1* (*föga djup*) shallow

3 grund *s3* **1** (*botten*) ground; (*mark äv.*) soil; *i* ~ [*och botten*] (*helt o. hållet*) completely, entirely; *i* ~ *och botten, i* ~*en* in reality, (*i själva verket*) at heart, basically, (*på det hela taget*) after all, essentially; *gå från gård och* ~ give up one's house [and lands]; *gå till* ~*en med* go to the bottom of **2** (*underlag*) foundation (*för, till* of); *bildl. äv.* basis; (*hus- äv.*) foundations (*pl*); *kemins* ~*er* the elements of chemistry; *tillbaka till* ~*erna* back to basics; *brinna ner till* ~*en* be burnt to the ground; *ligga till* ~ *för* be the basis (at the bottom) of; *lägga* ~*en till* lay the foundation[s *pl*] (*bildl.* basis) of; *lägga ngt till* ~ *för* make s.th. the basis of, base on s.th. **3** (*orsak*) cause; (*skäl*) reason; (*motiv*) motive, ground[s *pl*]; *på* ~ *av* on account of, because of, owing to; *på goda* ~*er* for excellent reasons; *på mycket lösa* ~*er* on very flimsy grounds; *ha sin* ~ *i* be due to, originate in; *sakna all* ~ be groundless (completely unfounded)

grund|a 1 (-*lägga*) found; establish, set up; start; (*friare*) lay the foundation of **2** (*stödja*) base (*ett påstående på* a statement on); ~ *sig på* be based on **3** (-*måla o. konst.*) ground, prime **-are** founder

grund|avgift basic charge (fee, rate) **-begrepp** fundamental principle **-betydelse** basic meaning (sense) **-bok** *bokför.* daybook **-drag 1** (*karakteristiskt drag*) fundamental feature, basic trait **2** (*huvuddrag*) ~*en* [*till*] the [main] outlines [of] **-element** essential (basic) element **-enhet** fundamental unit

grund|era *se* **grunda** 3 **-falsk** fundamentally wrong **-fel** fundamental fault (error) **-form** primary form; *gram.* common case **-forskning** basic research **-färg 1** *fys.* primary colour **2** (*huvudsaklig färg*) predominating colour **3** (*bottenfärg*) primer, first coat **-förutsättning** primary (fundamental) condition (prerequisite) **-hyra** basic rent **-kurs** basic course **-lag** fundamental law; (*författning*) constitution[al law]

grundlags|beredning working committee on the constitution (the fundamental laws) **-enlig** [-e:-] *a5* constitutional **-stridig** *a5* unconstitutional **-ändring** constitutional amendment

grundlig *a1* thorough; (*djup*) profound; (*ingående*) close; (*gedigen*) solid, sound; (*fundamental*) fundamental, radical **-het** thoroughness etc.

grund|linje base[line]; ~*rna till* (*bildl.*) the outlines of **-lurad** *a5* thoroughly (completely) taken in

grundlägg|a found, lay the foundation[s *pl*] (*bildl. äv.* basis) of **-ande** *a4* fundamental, basic **-are** founder **-ning** foundation

grund|lön basic salary (wages *pl*) **-lös** groundless; baseless; unfounded **-murad** *a5, bildl.* solidly established, firmly rooted

grund|ning (-*målning*) priming **-orsak** primary cause **-plåt** nucleus (*till* of); first contribution **-polish** sealer **-princip** fundamental (basic) principle **-regel** fundamental (basic) rule **-rit-**

ning ground plan (*äv. bildl.*) **-sats** principle **-skola** comprehensive (*AE.* elementary, grade) school **-skott** *bildl., ett* ~ *mot* a death blow to **-slag** (*i tennis*) ground stroke **-sten** foundation stone **-stomme** groundwork (*till* of); *bildl. äv.* nucleus (*till* of) **-stämning** keynote **-stöta** run aground **-stötning** grounding **-syn** basic view **-tal** cardinal number (numeral) **-tanke** fundamental (basic, leading) idea **-tema** main theme **-text** original [text] **-ton 1** *fys.* fundamental tone **2** *mus. o. bildl.* keynote **-tillstånd** *fys.* ground state (level) **-utbildning** basic education (training) **-val** *s2* foundation; *bildl. äv.* basis, groundwork; *på* ~ *av* on the basis of **-valla** (*för skidor*) tar primer **-vatten** subsoil water **-villkor** fundamental (basic) condition **-ämne** element

grunka *s1, se* **grej**

grunna cogitate, ponder; ~ *på* (*äv.*) turn over in one's mind; *sitta och* ~ sit musing, sit and think

grupp *s3* group; (*klunga*) cluster; *polit. o.d. äv.* section; *mil. äv.* squad, section; *flyg.* flight **-arbete** teamwork **-bild** group picture **-bildning** group formation; grouping **-biljett** party ticket **-chef** *mil.* squad commander (leader) **-dynamik** group dynamics (*pl, behandlas som sg*)

grupper|a group **-ing** grouping; *mil.* deployment

grupp|försäkring group [accident, life] insurance **-ledare** (*sport- e.d.*) group leader **-livförsäkring** group insurance **-resa** conducted tour **-samtal** *tel.* conference call **-sex** group sex **-terapi** group therapy **-vis** in (by) groups

grus *s7* gravel (*äv. med.*) **grusa 1** gravel **2** *bildl.* dash [to the ground], spoil; (*gäcka*) frustrate; ~*de förhoppningar* dashed hopes

grus|grop gravel pit **-gång** gravel walk **-hög** gravel heap; *bildl.* heap of ruins **-tag** *s7*, **-täkt** *s3* gravel pit

1 gruva *v1, rfl,* ~ *sig för* (*över*) dread

2 gruva *s1* mine; (*kol- äv.*) pit

gruv|arbetare miner; (*i kolgruva äv.*) collier, pitman **-arbete** mining; colliery **-brytning** *se* -drift **-distrikt** mining district **-drift** mining [operations *pl*] **-fält** mining area, (*kol-*) coalfield **-gas** firedamp **-gång** heading, gallery **-industri** mining industry **-ingenjör** mining engineer; (*i kolgruva*) colliery engineer **-lampa** miner's (safety, Davy) lamp

gruv|lig [-u:-] *a1* dreadful, horrible **-olycka** pit (mining) accident **-ras** *s7* caving-in of a mine, fall **-samhälle** mining community **-schakt** shaft **-stötta** *s1* pit prop **-öppning** mouth of a mine

1 gry *s7, det är gott* ~ *i honom* he has [got] grit

2 gry *v4* dawn (*äv. bildl.*); break; *dagen* ~*r* day is breaking

gryende *a4* dawning; ~ *anlag* (*äv.*) budding talents

grym [-ymm] *a1* cruel (*mot* to); (*bestialisk*) fierce, ferocious; *ett* ~*t öde* a cruel (harsh) fate **-het** cruelty (*mot* to); (*begången äv.*) atrocity

1 grymt *adv, bli* ~ *besviken* be terribly disappointed

2 grymt *s7* grunt

grymta grunt **grymtning** grunt[ing]

gryn *s7, s4* [hulled] grain; (*havre-, vete- äv.*)

groats (*pl*) **-ig** *al* grainy, granular

gryning dawn (*äv. bildl.*); daybreak; *i ~en* at dawn; *i första ~en* at first light

gryningsljus light of early dawn

grynmat farinaceous food

grynna *s1* sunken rock, reef

grynvälling *bildl.* mess of pottage

gryt *s7* **1** (*lya*) earth, burrow **2** (*stenrös*) pile of stones

gryt|a *s1* pot; (*med lock*) casserole; (*maträtt*) casserole; *små -or har också öron* little pitchers have long ears

grythund burrower

gryt|lapp saucepan (kettle) holder **-lock** casserole (pot) lid **-stek** pot roast; braised beef

grå *al* grey; *i sht AE.* gray; (*gråsprängd äv.*) grizzled; (*om väder*) overcast; (*dyster*) dull, drab, dreary, gloomy; ~ *eminens* grey eminence; ~ *marknad* grey market; *i den ~ forntiden* in the hoary past; *tillbaka till den ~ vardagen igen* back into harness again, back to the humdrum of every day **-aktig** *a5* greyish **-al** grey alder **-berg** granite **-blek** ashen grey **-blå** greyish blue **-bo** *bot.* mugwort **-broder** Grey Friar **-brödrakloster** Franciscan monastery **-dask** *s7* greyness **-daskig** *a5* dirty grey **-gam** black vulture **-gosse** elderly messenger **-gås** greylag [goose]; *AE.* graylag **-hårig** grey-haired; (*gråsprängd*) grizzled **-kall** bleak, chill, raw **-kråka** hooded (*i Skottland* hoodie) crow

grålle *s2* grey horse

grå|na turn grey; (*om pers.*) go (get) grey; ~*d* (*om hår*) grey, grizzled, (*åldrig*) grey-headed **-papper** (*för växtpressning*) pressing paper **-päron** butter-pear **-sej** [-sejj] *s2* coalfish, saithe, coley **-sparv** house (*AE.* English) sparrow **-sprängd** *a5* grizzled; (*om skägg äv.*) grizzly **-sten** granite **-sugga** woodlouse **-säl** grey seal

gråt *s3* crying, weeping; (*snyftande*) sobbing; *brista i ~* burst into tears; *ha ~en i halsen* be on the verge of tears, have a lump in one's throat; *kämpa med ~en* fight back tears

gråt|a *grät -it* **1** cry (*av glädje* for joy; *av ilska* with rage); weep (*av* for); ~ *ut* have a good cry; ~ *över spilld mjölk* cry over spilt milk; *det är ingenting att ~ för* (*över*) it is nothing to cry about; *det är så man kan ~* it is enough to make one cry; *hon har lätt för att ~* she cries easily **2** ~ *sina ögon röda* cry one's eyes red **3** *rfl* cry o.s. (*till sömns* to sleep) **-attack** fit of crying

gråt|erska [professional] mourner, weeper **-färdig** on the verge of tears, ready to cry

gråt|it *sup. av gråta* **-mild** tearful; (*sentimental*) maudlin

gråtrut herring gull

grått *s, best. form det grå[a]* grey

gråverk squirrel fur

gråväders|dag grey (*bildl.* cheerless) day **-stämning** gloom, gloomy atmosphere (mood)

1 grädda *v1* bake; (*uppe på spisen*) fry, make

2 grädda *s1*, ~*n av* the cream of (*societeten* society)

gräddbakelse cream cake, éclair

grädd|e *s2* cream; *vispad ~* whipped cream **-fil** *s3* sour[ed] cream **-glass** ice cream **-gul** cream-coloured, creamy **-kanna** cream jug; *AE.*

creamer **-kola** cream caramel

gräddning baking; frying

grädd|snipa, **-snäcka** *se gräddkanna* **-tårta** cream-layer cake **-visp** whisk, beater

gräl *s7* (*tvist*) quarrel; (*ordväxling äv.*) squabble, wrangle; *råka i ~* fall out, clash (*med ngn* with s.b.); *söka ~* pick a quarrel (*med ngn* with s.b.) **gräla** quarrel; squabble, wrangle; ~ *på ngn* scold s.b. (*för att han är* for being)

gräll *al* loud, glaring; garish

gräl|makare quarreller; squabbler, wrangler **-sjuk** quarrelsome, cantankerous; (*som bannar*) scolding

gräm|a *v2* grieve, vex; ~ *sig* grieve (*över* at, for), fret (*över* about); ~ *sig till döds* fret one's heart out **-else** grief; worry

gränd *s3* alley, [by-]lane; (*ruskig*) slum

gräns *s3* **1** (*-linje*) *geogr.* boundary; *polit.* frontier, *AE.* border; (*friare*) borderline; *dra ~en* (*polit.*) fix the boundary, *bildl.* draw the line; *stå på ~en till* (*bildl.*) be on the verge of **2** (*slutpunkt*) limit (*för* of); *bildl. äv.* bounds (*pl*); *inom vissa ~er* within certain limits;; *sätta en ~ för a*) (*begränsa*) set bounds (limits) to, *b*) (*stävja*) put an end (a stop) to; *det finns ingen ~ för hans fåfänga* his vanity knows no bounds; *det här går över alla ~er!* [no really,] that's the limit! **3** ([*område utmed*] *gränslinje*) confines (*pl*), border[s *pl*] ; *vid belgiska ~en* on the Belgian border

gräns|a ~ *till* border [up]on (*äv. bildl.*); (*om land, område*) be bounded (*till* by); (*om ägor*) adjoin, abut on; *med en till visshet ~nde sannolikhet* with a probability almost amounting to certainty; *det ~r till det otroliga* it borders on the incredible **-befolkning** border (frontier) population **-befästning** frontier fortification **-bevakning** frontier patrol[ling] **-bo** borderer **-bygd** border country **-dragning** delimitation **-fall** borderline case **-intäkt** marginal revenue **-kontroll** border checkpoint **-kostnad** marginal cost **-kränkning** violation of the frontier **-land** border country

gränsle *se grensle*

gräns|linje boundary line; *bildl.* borderline, dividing line **-lös** boundless, limitless; *bildl.* unbounded; (*ofantlig*) tremendous, immense **-märke** boundary mark; landmark **-nytta** marginal utility **-område** border district; *bildl.* borderland, confines (*pl*) **-oroligheter** *pl* border fighting (disturbances) **-postering** frontier outpost **-påle** boundary post **-station** frontier station **-trakt** *se -område* **-värde** limit

gräs *s7* grass; *i ~et a*) (*på gräset*) on the grass, *b*) (*bland gräset*) in the grass; *bita i ~et* lick the dust; *ha pengar som ~* have a mint of money **-and** mallard **-bevuxen** *a5* grass-grown, grassy **-frö** grass seed[s *pl*] **-grön** grass-green **-hoppa** grasshopper; locust **-klippare** lawn mower

gräslig [-ä:-] *al* atrocious, horrid (*mot* to); terrible, shocking; (*friare*) awful, frightful **-het** atrociousness *etc.*; ~*er* atrocities

gräs|lök chive; *kokk.* chives **-matta** lawn; grass; green **-rot** *bildl.* grass roots (*pl*) **-rotsdemokrati** grassroot democracy **-slätt** grassy plain; prairie **-strå** blade [of grass] **-stäpp** *se stäpp o.*

gräsmslätt -torv turf **-torva** sod, turf **-tuva** tuft

G

[of grass] **-växt** gramineous plant **-änka** grass widow **-änkling** grass widower **-ätare** graminivorous animal, grass-eater

grät imperf. av gråta

grätten a3 fastidious; squeamish

gräva v2 dig (efter for); (t.ex. kanal, tunnel) cut; (om djur) grub, burrow; (friare o. bildl.) delve (i en byrålåda in a drawer); (rota) rummage (i fickorna in one's pockets); ~ fram dig up, unearth; ~ igen fill up; ~ ner dig down (i into), bury (i in); ~ ner sig i dig (burrow) one's way down into, (begrava sig) bury o.s. in; ~ ut dig out, excavate

grävling [-ä:-] [Eurasian] badger

grävmaskin excavator, power shovel **-ist** excavator operator

gräv|ning [-ä:-] digging; fack. excavation **-skopa** bucket, dipper; jfr grävmaskin

gröda s1 (växande) crops (pl); (skörd) harvest, crop

grön a1 green (av with) (äv. bildl.); ~ våg (trafik) synchronized [green] traffic lights (pl); ~a ön (Irland) the Emerald Isle; i det ~a in the [green] fields (the country); i min ~ ungdom in my callow youth, vard. in my salad days; komma på ~ kvist be in clover, do well for o.s. **-aktig** a5 greenish **-alg** green alga (seaweed) **-bete** [grass] pasture; vara på ~ (bildl.) be in the country **-fink** greenfinch **-foder** green forage **-gräset** i ~ on the grass **-göling** [-j-] **1** zool. green woodpecker **2** bildl. greenhorn **-kål** kale, borecole

Grönköping n Little Puddleton **grönköpings-mässig** a1 Puddletonian; parochial

Grönland ['grö:n-] n Greenland; på ~ in Greenland

grönlandsval Greenland whale

grönländ|are Greenlander **-sk** a5 Greenlandic **-ska 1** (språk) Greenlandic **2** (kvinna) Greenland woman

grön|mögelost blue cheese **-område** green area **-peppar** green pepper **-sak** s3 vegetable

grönsaks|affär greengrocer's shop, greengrocery **-handlare** greengrocer **-land** vegetable patch **-soppa** vegetable soup

grön|sallad (växt) lettuce; (rätt) green salad **-siska** s1 siskin

grönska I s1 **1** (vårens) verdure; ängarnas ~ the green of the meadows **2** (trädens etc.) greenery, green foliage **II** v1 be (become) green

grönsåpa soft soap

grönt [-ö:-] s, best. form det gröna **1** green **2** (grönfoder, grönsaker) greenstuff **3** (prydnad) greenery

gröpa v3, ~ ur hollow out

gröpe s7 groats (pl); (mindre grovt) grits (pl)

gröt s2, kokk. porridge; (risgryns-) rice pudding; tekn. pulp, pap; (friare) mush; med. poultice; gå som katten kring het ~ beat about the bush; vara het på ~en be overeager **-ig** a1 porridge-like; pulpy; mushy; (om röst) thick **-myndig** pompous, high and mighty **-rim** doggerel [rhyme]

grövre ['grö:v-] komp. t. grov **grövst** [-ö:-] superl. t. grov

g-sträng G-string

guano [gu'a:nå] s2, s7 guano; bildl. rubbish, nonsense

Guatemala [-ˣma:-] n Guatemala **guatema-**

l|an s3, **-ansk** [-'a:nsk] a5 Guatemalan

gubbaktig a1 old-mannish, old man's...; senile **gubbe** s2 **1** old man; ~n A. old A.; min ~ lille! my lad! **2** (bild) picture; (grimas) face; ~ eller pil (på mynt) heads or tails; rita gubbar (klottra) doodle **3** (tabbe) blunder **4** den ~n går inte! that won't wash!, tell that to the marines!; för hundra gubbar! by all the saints!

gubb|lig a1, se gubbaktig **-strutt** s2 old buffer, dodderer

gubevars ['gu:-,-'vars] **I** interj goodness me! **II** adv of course, to be sure

guckusko s5 lady's-slipper

gud s2 god; G~ Fader God the Father; G~ bevare oss! God preserve us!; G~ nåde dig! God have mercy upon you!; G~ vet Heaven knows; om G~ vill God willing; ta G~ i hågen take one's courage in both hands; för G~s skull for the love of God, (utrop) for goodness' (God's, Heaven's) sake!; inte G~s bästa barn no angel; det vete ~arna! Heaven only knows!

guda|benådad a5 divinely gifted; en ~ konstnär a real artist **-bild** image of a god, idol **-dryck** drink of the gods, nectar **-god** divine **-gåva** godsend, gift of the gods **-lik** godlike **-lära** se mytologi **-saga** myth **-skymning** Twilight of the Gods, Ragnarök **-skön** divinely beautiful **-sänd** a5 god-sent **-väsen** god

gud|barn godchild **-dotter** goddaughter **-fa-[de]r** godfather **-fruktig** a1 god-fearing, devout; jfr gudlig

gudi i uttr.: en ~ behaglig gärning a pious deed; ~ lov God be praised; ha ~ nog av have enough and to spare of

guding eider drake, male eider

gud|inna goddess **-lig** [-u:-] a1 godly, pious; (gudsnådelig) goody-goody **-lös** godless; impious; (hädisk) blasphemous; ~t leverne wicked life; ~t tal profane language, blasphemy **-mo-[de]r** godmother

gudom [ˣgudomm] s2 divinity; ~en the Godhead **gudomlig** [-'domm-] a1 divine; (underbar) superb, magnificent **-het 1** (gudomlig natur) divineness etc. **2** (gud) divinity; god

guds|begrepp concept of God **-bevis** proof of God's existence **-dom** ordeal **-dyrkan** worship [of God], religion **-fruktan** piety, godliness **-förgäten** a5 **1** (om plats) godforsaken **2** se gudlös **-förnekare** atheist **-förnekelse** denial of God; atheism **-förtröstan** trust in God **-ge-menskap** communion with God

gudskelov [ˣguʃe-, 'guʃe- el. -'lå:v] thank goodness (Heaven)

guds|man man of God **-nåd[e]lig** [ˣgutts-, -ˣnå:- el. -'nå:-] a1 sanctimonious; (salvelsefull) unctuous

gudson godson

gudstjänst [divine] service; bevista ~en (äv.) attend church (chapel); förrätta ~ officiate [at the service], conduct [the] service; hålla ~ hold divine service **-förrättare** officiating clergyman **-ordning** order for divine service, liturgy

gudstro faith (belief) [in God]

guida [ˣgaj-] v1, **guide** [gajd] s5 guide

Guinea [giˣne:a] n Guinea **Guinea-Bissau** [bi-'sau] n Guinea-Bissau

guine|an [gine'a:n] *s3*, **-ansk** [-'a:nsk] *a5* Guinean

gul *a1* yellow; *slå ngn ~ och blå* beat s.b. black and blue; *~a febern* yellow fever; *~a pressen* the gutter (yellow) press

gul|a *s1* yolk **-aktig** *a5* yellowish

gulasch *s3* **1** *kokk.* [Hungarian] goulash **2** [war] profiteer; *vard.* spiv **-baron** *se gulasch 2*

gul|blek sallow **-brun** yellowish brown

guld *s7* gold; *trogen som ~* [as] true as steel; *gräva ~ dig* for gold; *lova ngn ~ och gröna skogar* promise s.b. the moon; *skära ~ med täljknivar* make a mint of (coin) money **-armband** gold bracelet **-brun** golden brown **-bröllop** golden wedding **-bågad** *a5 (om glasögon)* gold-rimmed **-dubblé** rolled (filled) gold; gold plate

guld|en ['guld-] *r*, *pl =*, guilder **-feber** gold fever **-fisk** goldfish **-fyndighet** gold deposit **-färgad** gold-coloured, golden **-förande** *a4* gold-bearing, auriferous **-galon** gold braid **-galonerad** *a5* gold-braided **-glans** gold *(bildl.* golden) lustre **-glänsande** shining like gold **-gruva** gold mine *(äv. bildl.)* **-grävare** gold-digger **-gul** golden **-halt** percentage of gold, gold content **-kalven** the golden calf **-kantad** *a5* gilt-edged; *(om servis e.d.)* gold-rimmed; *~e papper* gilt-edged securities **-klimp** gold nugget **-klocka** gold watch **-korn** grain of gold; *bildl.* pearl **-krog** *vard.* plush (posh) restaurant **-krona** gold[en] crown

Guldkusten *(förutvarande namn på Ghana)* the Gold Coast

guld|lamé *s3* gold lamé **-lock** *(blond pers.)* Goldilocks **-lockig** with golden curls **-makare** alchemist **-medalj** gold medal **-mynt** gold coin (piece) **-myntfot** gold standard **-plomb** gold filling **-ring** gold ring **-rush** *s3* gold rush **-skiva** *(grammofon-)* golden disc **-slagare** gold-beater **-smed** goldsmith; *(som butiksägare vanl.)* jeweller **-smedsaffär** jeweller's [shop]; *AE.* jewelry store **-smide** goldsmith's work **-snitt** *(på bok)* gilt edge[s *pl*] **-stämpel** hallmark **-tacka** gold ingot (bar) **-tand** gold tooth **-vaskning** gold washing, placer-mining **-våg** assay balance; *väga sina ord på ~* weigh one's words carefully **-åder** gold (auriferous) vein **-ålder** golden age

gul|filter yellow filter **-ing** *vard.* **1** *(mongol)* yellowman **2** *(strejkbrytare)* blackleg; *AE.* scab **-kroppen** *anat. (lat.)* corpus luteum

gull|gosse [spoilt] darling; blue-eyed (white-headed; *AE.* fair-haired) boy; *en lyckans ~* a lucky beggar (dog) **-höna** *se nyckelpiga*

gull|ig *a1* sweet; *AE.* cute **-regn** *bot.* laburnum **-ris** *bot.* goldenrod **-stol** *bära ngn i ~* chair s.b. **-viva** *s1* cowslip

gul|metall brass, yellow metal **-måra** *s1* lady's bedstraw

gul|na [-u:-] [turn (grow)] yellow **-sot** jaundice **-sparv** yellowhammer

gult [-u:-] *s*, *best. form det gula* yellow

gumaktig [ˣgumm-] *a1* old womanish, old woman's…; senile

gumma *s1* old woman; *min ~ (maka)* the wife, my old woman; *min ~ lilla!* my pet!

gummer|a gum, rubberize **-ing** gumming

gummi *s6* **1** *(växtämne)* rubber; gum **2** *(kaut-*

schuk) [India] rubber **3** *(preventivmedel)* French letter, rubber; *AE.* safe **-band** rubber (elastic) band **-boll** rubber ball **-båt** rubber boat **-gutta** [-ˣgutta, -'gutta] *s1* gamboge **-handske** rubber glove **-hjul** rubber-tyred wheel **-lacka** [-ˣlacka, -'lacka] *s1* lac **-lösning** rubber solution **-madrass** rubber mattress **-plantage** rubber plantation **-ring** rubber ring (tyre) **-sko** rubber shoe **-slang** rubber hose (tube, pipe) **-snodd** rubber band **-stövel** rubber boot; *-stövlar (äv.)* Wellington boots, gumboots **-sula** rubber sole **-träd 1** *(Eucalyptus)* gumtree **2** *(Ficus elastica)* rubber plant **-varor** *pl* rubber products (articles) **-verkstad** vulcanizing [work]shop

gump *s2, zool.* uropygium; *(friare)* rump

gumse *s2* ram

gung|a I *s1* swing **II** *v1* swing; *(på -bräde o. friare)* seesaw; *(i vagga, -stol; om vågor)* rock; *(ett barn på foten e.d.)* dandle; *~ på stolen* tilt the chair; *~ på vågorna* float up and down *(om pers.)* be tossed) on the waves; *marken ~de under deras fötter* the ground quaked (rocked) beneath their feet **-bräde** seesaw **-fly** *s6* quagmire *(äv. bildl.)* **-häst** rocking horse

gung|ning swinging etc.; *sätta ngt i ~ (bildl.)* set s.th. rocking, rock the boat **-stol** rocking chair; *AE. äv.* rocker

gun[n]rum wardroom, gun room

gunst *s3* favour; *stå [högt] i ~ hos ngn* be in high favour with s.b., be in a p.'s good books **-ig** *a1* **1** *(välvillig)* well-disposed, friendly *(mot* towards, to); *(om lyckan)* propitious; *(gynnsam)* favourable **2** *vard. vanl. oböjt: min ~ herre* my fine friend (fellow, Sir); *det passade inte ~ herrn* it didn't suit his lordship **-ling** favourite **-lingssystem** favouritism

gunås alas; worse luck

gupp *s7* **1** bump; *(grop)* hole, pit; *(i skidbacke)* jump **2** *(knyck)* jolt, jog **guppa** jolt, jog; *(om åkdon äv.)* bump; *(om flytande [mindre] föremål)* bob [up and down] **guppig** *a1* bumpy

guppy *s3, zool.* guppy

gurgel ['gurr-] *s7, vard.* row, squabble **-vatten** gargle, gargling fluid

gurgl|a *~ halsen* gargle, gargle one's throat; *~ sig [i halsen]* gargle [one's throat]; *ett ~nde ljud* a gurgling sound **-ing** gargling, gargle; *(om ljud)* gurgling

gurk|a *s1* cucumber; *(inläggnings-)* gherkin **-meja** [-ˣmejja, äv. ˣgurk-] *s1* curcuma, turmeric **-säng** cucumber bed

guru ['gu:-] *s3* guru

gustavi|an *s3*, **-ansk** [-'a:nsk] *a5* Gustavian

gut [gutt] *s3, s4 (till metrev)* gut

gute *s2* inhabitant of Gotland

guterad *se gouterad*

gutt *se gut*

guttaperka [-ˣperr-, -'perr-] *s1* gutta-percha

guttural *a5* guttural

gutår *åld., ung.* cheers!

guvernant [-'ant *el.* -'aŋt] governess *(för* to)

guvern|ement *s7* province; colony **-ör** governor

Guyana [gai'änna] *n* Guyana

guyan|an [gaiänn'a:n] *s3*, **-ansk** [-'a:nsk] *a5* Guyanese, Guyanan

gyckel ['jykk-] *s7 (skoj)* play, sport; *(skämt)* fun;

G

(upptåg) joking, jesting, larking, joke[s *pl*]; *bli föremål för ~* be made a laughing stock of; *driva ~ med ngn, se gyckla med ngn* **-makare** joker, jester, wag **-spel** *(-bild)* illusion; *(taskspeleri)* jugglery, hocus-pocus

gyckl|a [ˣjykk-] jest, joke *(med, över* at); *~ med ngn* make fun of (poke fun at) s.b. **-are** joker, jester, wag; *neds.* buffoon, clown

gylf [j-] *s2* fly [of the trousers]

gyllen|e [ˣjyll-] *oböjligt a* golden; *(av guld)* gold, golden; *G~ Horden* the Golden Horde; *~ snittet* the golden section (mean); *den ~ friheten* glorious liberty; *den ~ medelvägen* the golden mean, the happy medium **-blond** golden haired **-läder** gilt leather

gymnasie|elev [jymˈnaː-] *se gymnasist* **-ingenjör** *ung.* technical college graduate **-lärare** *ung.* upper secondary school teacher; *AE.* senior high school teacher **-skola** *ung.* upper secondary school; *AE.* senior high school

gymnas|ist [j-] *ung.* pupil of upper secondary school; *AE.* senior high school student **-ium** [ˈnaː-] *s4, ung.* upper secondary school; *AE.* senior high school

gymnast [j-] *s3* gymnast

gymnastj|k [j-] *s3* gymnastics *(pl, behandlas som sg); skol. äv.* physical training, drilling; *vard.* gym; *...är en bra ~ ...is* [an] excellent [form of] exercise **-direktör** certified physical training instructor **-dräkt** gymnasium *(vard.* gym) suit **-högskola** university college of gymnastics, physical training college; *Gymnastik- och idrottshögskolan i Stockholm* [the] Stockholm college of physical education **-lärare** physical training master (mistress) **-redskap** gymnastics apparatus *(koll.* appliances *pl)* **-sal** gymnasium; *vard.* gym **-sko** gym[nasium] shoe; *~r, AE. vard.* sneakers **-uppvisning** gymnastic display

gymnast|isera [j-] do gymnastics **-isk** [ˈnass-] *a5* gymnastic; *~a övningar* physical exercises

gyneko|log [j-, *äv.* g-] gynaecologist **-logj** *s3* gynaecology **-logisk** [ˈlåː-] *a5* gynaecologic[al]

gynn|a [j-] favour, *(bistå äv.)* support; *(främja äv.)* further, promote **-are** *l* favourer *etc.*; patron **2** *skämts.* fellow, chap, customer **-sam** favourable, advantageous *(för* to); *i ~maste fall* *(äv.)* at best; *ta en ~ vändning* take a favourable turn (a turn for the better)

gyro [ˈgyː- *el.* ˈjyːrå] *s6* gyro **-horisont** artificial (gyro) horizon **-kompass** gyrocompass **-skop** [ˈskåːp] *s7* gyroscope **-stabilisator** gyrostabilizer

gytter [ˈjytt-] *s7* conglomeration

gyttja [j-] *s1* mud; slough; *(blöt)* ooze; *(smörja)* mire, slush **gyttjebad** [j-] mud bath **gyttjig** [j-] *a1* muddy; oozy; miry, slushy

gyttr|a [j-] *~ ihop* [*sig*] cluster together **-ig** *a1* conglomerate[d], clustered together

gå *gick gått* **l** *eg. bet.* **1** *(motsats åka, stå e.d.)* walk; *(om t.ex. hund)* trot; *(om t.ex. anka)* waddle; *(stiga)* step *(åt sidan* to one side); *(med långa steg)* stride; *(gravitetiskt)* stalk; *~ rak* walk upright **2** *(motsats stanna kvar, stå stilla)* go; *(tyst e.d. äv.)* pass; *(röra sig äv.)* move; *(förfoga sig, komma)* get; *(bege sig av)* go away, leave, *absol.* be off; *~ hemifrån kl. 8* leave home at 8 o'clock;

~ ur fläcken move from the spot; *~ ur vägen för ngn* get out of a p.'s way; *~ och sätta sig (hämta)* go and sit down (to fetch); *jag måste ~ nu (äv.)* I must be off now; *vart skall du ~?* where are you going? **3** *(om sak)* go, pass; *(om t.ex. båt, flygplan tåg äv.)* travel; *(regelbundet)* run, ply; *(segla äv.)* sail; *~ med en hastighet av (om bil o.d.)* travel at a speed of; *bussar ~r varje timme* buses run every hour **4** *(avgå, avresa)* start *(till* for), leave *(äv.* gå från) **5** *(röra sig [på visst sätt]*, äv. om sjön, vågorna) run; *~ på hjul* run on wheels; *lådan ~r lätt* the drawer runs easily; *sjön ~r hög* the sea runs high **6** *(vara i gång)* go; *(om fabrik, maskin)* run, work; *~ med elektricitet* be worked by electricity; *~ varm* run hot; *klockan ~r fel* the clock is wrong **ll** *(friare o. bildl.)* **1** go; *~ i kyrkan* go to church; *~ [omkring] i trasor* go about in rags; *~ på föreläsningar* attend (go to) lectures; *~ och gifta sig* go and get married; *se vad ngn ~r för* put s.b. through his paces, see what sort of a fellow s.b. is; *får jag komma som jag ~r och står?* may I come as I am?; *jag har ~tt hos tandläkaren* I have been going to the dentist's; *det ~r inte* it won't work (is out of the question) **2** *(avgå, lämna sin tjänst)* retire; *(om regering)* resign **3** *(vara)* be *(i första klassen* in the first form); *(rymmas)* go *(i* into); *~ arbetslös* be out of work; *dansen ~r* the dancing is on; *påssjukan ~r* there is an outbreak of mumps; *(ta ~ två liter i flaskan* the bottle holds two liters; *det ~r 100 pence på ett pund* there are 100 pence in a pound **4** *(om tiden)* pass [away], go [by] **5** *(sträcka sig)* go, extend; *(nå)* reach; *(om flod, väg e.d.)* run; *(om väg äv.)* go, lead; *(om dörr, trappa e.d.)* lead **6** *(om varor)* sell, be sold, go **7** *(belöpa sig)* amount *(till* to); *det ~r till stora pengar* it runs into a lot of money **8** *(avlöpa)* turn out, go off; *hur det än ~r* whatever happens; *så ~r det när* that's what happens when; *hur ~r det med...?* what about...?, how is...going?; *hur ~r det för dig?* how are you getting on?; *hur ~r det för barnen om...?* what will happen to the children if...?; *det får ~ som det vill* let it ride; *det gick bra för honom* he got on well **lll** *rfl, ~ sig* trött tire o.s. out [with] walking **lV** *(med betonad partikel)* **1** *~ an (passa sig)* do, be all right; *det ~r inte an* it won't do; *det ~r väl an för dig som* it is all right for you who **2** *~ av a) (stiga av)* get out (off), *b) (nötas av)* wear through, break off, *(om färg e.d.)* wear off, *(brista)* break, *c) (om skott, vapen)* go off **3** *~ bort a) (gå ut)* go out *(på middag* to dinner), *b) (avlägsna sig)* go away, *c) (dö)* die, pass away, *c) (om fläck o.d.)* disappear, come out **4** *~ därifrån* leave [there, the place], go away [from there] **5** *~ efter a)* walk behind, *b) (om klocka)* be slow (behind [time]), *c) (hämta)* go and fetch, go for **6** *~ emot a) (möta)* go to meet, *b) (stöta emot)* go against, walk into, *c) (vara motigt)* go against, *d) (motsätta sig)* oppose; *allting ~r mig emot* everything goes wrong for me **7** *~ fram a)* go (walk) forward (on), *b) se konfirmeras; ~ fram med stor försiktighet* proceed with great care; *~ fram till* go up to **8** *~ framför a)* go (walk) in front [of], *b) (ha företräde framför)* rank before **9** *~ före a) se gå framför, b) (om klocka)* be fast **10** *~ för sig, se gå an* **11** *~ hem till ngn* go to a p.'s home, call on

s.b. at his home **12** ~ *i a*) go in[to], *b*) *se rymmas*; *det* ~ *inte i mig!* that won't go down with me! **13** ~ *ifrån* leave; *båten gick ifrån mig* I missed the boat **14** ~ *igen a*) *dörren* ~*r inte igen* the door doesn't (won't) shut [to], *b*) (*spöka*) haunt, *c*) (*upprepa sig*) reappear, recur **15** ~ *igenom a*) go (walk) through, *b*) (*utstå*) pass (go) through; *jfr genomgå, c*) (*om förslag o.d.*) be passed, (*efter omröstning*) be carried, *d*) (*om begäran*) be granted; ~ *igenom i examen* pass one's examination **16** ~ *ihop* (*mötas*) meet, (*förenas*) join, unite, *bildl.* agree, (*passa ihop*) correspond, match; *få debet och kredit att* ~ *ihop* make both ends meet; *det* ~*r inte ihop med* it doesn't tally (fit in) with **17** ~ *in* go in[side]; ~ *in för* go in for, set one's mind upon; ~ *in i a*) enter, *b*) (*förening e.d.*) join, become a member of; ~ *in på a*) (*ge sig in på*) enter upon, *b*) (*bifalla*) agree to, accept; ~ *in vid teatern* go on the stage **18** ~ *inåt* (*om fönster e.d.*) open inwards; ~ *inåt med tårna* be pigeon-toed, turn one's toes inward **19** ~ *isär* come apart, (*om åsikter e.d.*) diverge **20** ~ *löst på a*) (*anfalla*) go for, *b*) (*uppgå till*) run into (up to) **21** ~ *med a*) *se följa med*; *absol.* go (come) too (as well), *b*) (*vara med*) join in (*i, på* at); ~ *med på ett förslag* agree to a proposal **22** ~ *ner* go down, (*t. nedre våning*) go downstairs, (*om flygare, flygplan äv.*) descend, (*om ridå äv.*) fall, drop, (*om himlakropp äv.*) set; ~ *ner sig på isen* go through the ice **23** ~ *om* (*skolklass*) repeat a year, be kept down; ~ *om ngn* overtake s.b. [in walking], (*vid tävling*) pass s.b., get (go) ahead of s.b.; ~ *om varandra* (*om pers.*) pass each other, (*om brev*) cross in the post **24** ~ *omkring* (*hit o. dit*) walk about, go round; *jfr kringgå* **25** ~ *omkull* (*om företag*) go bankrupt, come to grief **26** ~ *sönder* be (get) broken (smashed), (*om maskin o.d.*) break down, have a breakdown **27** ~ *till a*) (*hända*) happen, come about, *b*) (*om sill e.d.*) come in; ~ *till och från* come in for a few hours; *hur gick det till?* how did it happen?, what happened?; *hur skall det* ~ *till?* how is that to be done?; *det gick livligt till* things were lively **28** ~ *tillbaka a*) go back, return, *b*) (*i tiden*) date back (*till* to), (*t. ursprunget*) originate (*till* in, from), have its origin (*till* in), *c*) (*avtaga*) recede, subside, abate, *d*) (*försämras*) deteriorate, *e*) (*om avtal*) be cancelled, be broken off **29** ~ *undan a*) (*ur vägen*) get out of the way, *b*) (*gå fort*) get on (progress) fast (rapidly) **30** ~ *under* (*om fartyg*) go down, be lost, (*om pers. o. friare*) be ruined **31** ~ *upp a*) go up, (*om pris, temperatur äv.*) rise, ascend, *b*) (*stiga upp*) rise, (*om pers. äv.*) get up, (*ur vattnet*) get (come) out, *c*) (*öppnas*) [come] open, (*om is*) break up, (*om knut*) come undone, (*om plagg i sömmarna*) give [way]; *det gick upp för mig att* it dawned upon me that; ~ *upp mot* come up (be equal) to; *ingenting* ~*r upp mot* there is nothing like (to compare with); ~ *upp i sitt arbete* be absorbed in one's work; ~ *upp i* (*om företag*) be (become) incorporated in; ~ *upp i ner* (*om priser*) fluctuate **32** ~ *ur a*) get out [of], (*klubb e.d.*) leave, (*tävling*) withdraw, *b*) (*om fläck*) come out, disappear, (*om knapp e.d.*) come (fall) out **33** ~ *ut och* ~ go for (take) a walk; ~ *ut och äta* eat out; ~ *ut på* (*avse*) be aimed at,

have as its aim, amount to; *låta sin vrede* ~ *ut över* vent one's anger upon **34** *hon* ~*r utanpå dem alla* she is superior to them all **35** ~ *utför* go downwards (downhill); *det* ~*r utför med dem* they are going downhill **36** ~ *utåt* (*om fönster e.d.*) open outwards; ~ *utåt med tårna* turn one's toes outward **37** ~ *vidare* go on; *låta ngt* ~ *vidare* pass s.th. on **38** ~ *åt a*) (*ta slut*) be consumed (used up), (*behövas*) be needed, (*finna åtgång*) sell, *b*) (*förgås*) perish, be dying (*av* with); *vad* ~*r åt dig?* what is the matter with you?; ~ *illa åt, se fara* [*illa med*]; *det* ~ *åt mycket tyg till den här klänningen* this dress takes a lot of material **39** ~ *över a*) (*walk*) over, cross [over], *b*) (*se igenom*) look through (over), (*maskin äv.*) overhaul, *c*) *se övergå*, *d*) (*om smärta*) pass [over], subside

gåborts|kläder [-ˣbårts-] *pl* party clothes **-kostym** best suit

gå|ende *a4 o. s6* walking, going *etc.*; *en* ~ a pedestrian; ~ *bord* buffet, stand-up meal **-gata** pedestrian street

1 gång *s3* **1** (*levande varelsers*) walking; (*sätt att gå*) gait, walk; (*hästs*) pace; *spänstig* ~ springy step (gait); *känna igen ngn på* ~*en* recognize s.b. by his walk (step) **2** (*rörelse*) going, moving; (*motors o.d.*) running, working, motion, action; (*lopp*) run; (*fortgång*) progress; (*förlopp*) course; *i full* ~ well under way, (*om arbete äv.*) in full swing; *under samtalets* ~ in the course of the conversation; *få i* ~ get going (started), start; *hålla i* ~ keep going; *komma i* ~ get started, (*om maskin*) begin running (working); *sätta i* ~ start (set) going (running), start; *vara i* ~ be running (working, going, in operation), (*om förhandlingar e.d.*) be in progress, be proceeding

2 gång *s2* **1** (*väg*) path[way], walk **2** (*korridor*) passage, corridor; (*i kyrka*) aisle; (*i teater, i buss*) gangway, *AE.* aisle; (*under gata*) subway **3** *anat.* duct, canal

3 gång *s3* **1** (*tillfälle*) time; *en* ~ *a*) once (*om dagen* a day), *b*) (*om framtid*) some time, some (one) day, *c*) (*ens*) even; *en* ~ *för alla* once and for all, for good; *en* ~ *är ingen* ~ once is no custom; *en* ~ *till* once more, [over] again; *en halv* ~ *till så mycket* half as much again; *en och annan* ~ once in a while, every now and then, occasionally; *en åt* ~*en* one at a time; *för en* ~*s skull* for once [in a while]; *bara för den här* ~*en* just [for] this once; *förra* ~*en* last time; *inte en* ~ *hans barn* not even his children; *med en* ~ all at once; *ngn* ~ some time, (*ibland äv.*) now and then, from time to time; *ngn enda* ~ very rarely, on some rare occasion; *nästa* ~ next time; ~ *på* ~ time and again, time after time, over and over [again]; *på en* ~ *a*) (*samtidigt*) at the same time, *b*) (*i en omgång*) in one go, *c*) (*plötsligt*) all at once, suddenly; *på en och samma* ~ at one and the same time; *det var en* ~ once upon a time there was; *det är nu en* ~ *så* the fact is that **2** *två* ~*er två är fyra* twice two is four; *tre* ~*er* three times; *ett par* ~*er* ~*er* two or three times; *rummet är tre* ~*er tre meter* the room is three by three metres (three metres square)

gång|are (*häst*) steed; *sport.* walker **-art** (*hästs*) pace **-avstånd** walking distance **-bana** pavement; *AE.* sidewalk **-bar** *a1* **1** (*om väg*) negoti-

G

able **2** (*gällande, gängse*) current **3** (*kurant*) saleable, marketable **-bro** footbridge
gång|en *a5* gone; (*förfluten*) gone by; *långt ~ far advanced* (*sjukdom* disease); *-na tider* the past, past time; *den -na veckan* the past week **-grift** chambered barrow **-järn** hinge **-kläder** *pl* wearing-apparel (*sg*), clothing (*sg*) **-låt** marching tune **-matta** runner **-sport** [long-distance] walking **-stig** footpath, footway **-trafik** pedestrian traffic **-trafikant** pedestrian **-tunnel** [pedestrian] subway **-väg** footpath
gåpåaraktig [-ˣpå:-] *a5* hustling, go-ahead
gåpåar|e [-ˣpå:-] pusher, go-getter **-fasoner** *pl* go-getting (*sg*)
går *i uttr.*: *i ~* yesterday; *i ~ kväll* yesterday evening, (*senare*) last night; *i ~ morse* yesterday morning; *i ~ för en vecka sedan* a week [ago] yesterday; *tidningen för i ~* yesterday's paper
gård [-å:-] *s2* **1** (*kringgärdad plats*) yard; (*bak-*) backyard; (*vid bondgård*) farmyard; (*framför herrgård o.d.*) courtyard; *rum åt ~en* back room; *två trappor upp åt ~en* on the second floor at the back **2** (*bond-*) farm; (*större*) estate; (*man-*) farmstead, homestead
går|dagen yesterday **-dagstidning[en]** yesterday's paper
gårdfarihand|el [-å:-] house-to-house peddling **-lare** [itinerant] pedlar, hawker
gårds|hus back-yard house **-karl** odd-jobman, odd-jobber; caretaker **-musikant** itinerant musician **-plan** courtyard **-sida** *åt ~n* at the back [of the house]
gårdvar [-å:-] *s2* watchdog
gås *-en gäss* goose (*pl* geese); *vitkindad ~* barnacle goose; *ha en ~ oplockad med ngn* have a bone to pick with s.b.; *det är som att hälla vatten på en ~* it's like [pouring] water on a duck's back; *det går vita gäss på havet* there are white horses on the sea **-hud** goose flesh (bumps *pl*, pimples *pl*, skin); *få ~* get goose pimples **-karl** gander **-lever** goose liver **-leverpastej** pâté de foie gras; goose-liver paste **-krås** goose giblets (*pl*) **-marsch** *i ~* in single file **-penna** quill **-ögon** (*citationstecken*) French quotation marks, guillemets **-ört** *bot.* silverweed
gåt|a *s1* riddle; (*friare*) enigma, puzzle, mystery **-full** mysterious, puzzling, enigmatic[al]
gått *sup. av* gå
gåva *s1* gift; present (*till* for, to); (*genom testamente*) bequest; *en man med stora gåvor* (*äv.*) a man of great parts
gåvo|brev deed of gift **-paket** gift parcel **-skatt** capital transfer (gift) tax
gäck [j-] **1** *s7, driva ~ med, se gäckas* [*med*] **2** *s2, slå ~en lös* let o.s. go **gäcka** (*svika*) baffle; disappoint; frustrate; *bli ~d i sina förhoppningar* have one's hopes dashed; *bli ~d i kärlek* be crossed in love **gäckande** *a4* roguish, elusive **gäckas** *dep, ~ med* mock (scoff) [at], deride; (*gyckla med*) make fun of, poke fun at **gäckeri** mocking, derision (*med* at)
gädd|a [j-] *s1* [northern] pike (*pl äv.* pike) **-drag** (*hopskr. gäddrag*) [trolling] spoon[bait]
gäl [j-] *s2* gill; *djur som andas med ~ar* gill-breathing animals
gälbgjutare [ˣjälb-] brazier

gäld [j-] *s3* debt[s *pl*] **gälda 1** (*betala*) pay; (*bestrida kostnad*) defray **2** (*försona*) atone for; (*återgälda*) requite
gäld|enär *s3* debtor **-ränta** debt interest **-stuga** debtor's prison
gäll [j-] *a1* shrill; (*genomträngande*) piercing
gäll|a [j-] *v2* **1** (*vara giltig*) be valid; (*om lag e.d.*) be in force, AE. be effective; (*om biljett äv.*) be available; (*om mynt*) be current; (*om påstående*) be true (*om* of; *ännu* still); (*äga tillämpning*) apply, be applicable (*för, på* to) **2** (*vara värd*) be worth **3** (*väga tungt*, *betyda*) have (carry) weight **4** (*anses*) pass (*för* for; *som* as); be looked (regarded) upon (*för, som* as) **5** (*avse*) be intended for; (*åsyfta*) have as its object; (*röra*) concern, have reference to; *vad -er saken?* what is it about?; *samma sak -er om* the same thing may be said of **6** *opers.*, *det -er livet* it is a question of life or death; *nu -er det att* now we have got to; *när det verkligen -er* when it really comes to the point (*att* of + *ing-form*); *han sprang som om det -de livet* he ran for dear life **-ande** *a4* **1** (*giltig*) valid (*för* for), in force, AE. effective; available; (*tilllämplig*) applicable; *~ priser* current (ruling) prices **2** *göra ~* (*påstå*) assert, maintain; *göra sina kunskaper ~* bring one's knowledge to bear; *göra sina anspråk ~* establish one's claims; *göra sitt inflytande ~* assert one's influence; *göra sig ~* (*om pers.*) assert o.s., (*om sak*) manifest itself, make itself felt
gällen [j-] *a5* on the turn
gällock gill cover (lid)
gäms *se gems*
gäng [j-] *s7* ([*arbets*]*lag*) gang; (*klick*) set
gäng|a [j-] **I** *s1* [screw] thread; *gå i de gamla -orna* be in the old groove; *komma ur -orna* get out of the gear; *vara ur -orna* be off colour, be under the weather **II** *v1* **1** thread **2** *sl.* (*ha samlag*) screw **3** *rfl, vard.* get spliced **-kloppa** [-å-] *s1* diestock **gänglig** [j-] *a1* lank[y] **-het** lank[i]ness
gängning [j-] [screw] threading
gängse [j-] *oböjligt a* current; (*rådande*) prevalent
gäng|snitt [j-] die **-tapp** tap
gärd [jä:rd] *s3* tribute; token (*av tacksamhet* of gratitude)
gärda [ˣjä:r-] fence
gärde [ˣjä:r-] *s6* (*fält*) field; *~t är upprivet* (*bildl.*) the game is lost
gärds|gård [*vard.* 'järs-] fence **-gårdsstör** hurdle pole
gärdsmyg [ˣjä:rd-] *s2, zool.* wren; AE. winter wren
gärna [ˣjä:r-] *hellre helst, adv* **1** (*med nöje*) gladly; (*villigt*) willingly; (*utan hinder*) easily, readily; *ja, ~* [*för mig*]*!* by all means!; *lika ~* just as well; *en ~ sedd gäst* an ever-welcome guest; *hur ~ jag än vill* though nothing can give me more pleasure; *jag erkänner ~ att* I am quite prepared (ready) to admit that; *jag kommer mer än ~* I shall be delighted to come; *jag skulle ~ vilja* I should be glad to; *jag skulle ~ vilja veta* I should like to know; *du får ~ stanna här* you are quite welcome to stay here; *du kan ~ läsa högt* you may just as well read aloud; *han talar ~ om* he likes (is fond of) talking of; *han kan inte ~ hinna fram i*

tid he will hardly get there in time **2** (*ofta*) often; *följden blir* ~ *den att* the result is liable to be that **gärning** [ˣjä:r-] **1** (*handling*) act, deed; *goda ~ar* good deeds, kind actions; *i ord och* ~ in word and deed; *tagen på bar* ~ caught red-handed (in the act) **2** (*syssla*) work

gärningsman criminal, culprit, pertetrator

gärs [j-] *s2, zool.* ruff[e], pope

gäsp|a [j-] yawn **-ning** yawning; *en* ~ a yawn

gässling [j-] gosling

gäst [j-] *s3* guest; (*besökande*) visitor; (*hotell-*) resident; (*restaurang-*) guest, patron

gästa [j-] ~ *ngn* be a p.'s guest; ~ *ngns hem* be a guest at a p.'s home **-bud** feast; banquet **-budssal** banqueting hall

gäst|bok guest book **-dirigent** visiting conductor **-fri** hospitable **-frihet** hospitality **-föreläsare** visiting lecturer

gästgiv|are [ˣjäst-, *vard.* ˣjäʃi-] innkeeper **-argård, -eri** inn, hostelry

gäst|hamn guest harbour **-handduk** guest towel **-rum** spare (guest) room **-spel** special performance **-spela** give a special performance **-vänlig** *se* gästfri

göd|a [j-] *v2* **1** (*djur*) fatten; (*människor äv.*) feed up; *slakta den -da kalven* kill the fatted calf **2** (*jord, växter*) fertilize **3** *rfl* feed (fatten) [o.s.] up **-boskap** beef (fat[tening]) cattle (*pl*) **-kalv** beef (fatted) calf, fatling; *kokk.* prime veal **-kyckling** broiler

gödning [ˣjö:d-] **1** fattening *etc.* **2** fertilizing, fertilization **gödningsmedel** fertilizer, fertilizing substance

gödsel [ˈjödd-] *s9* manure, dung, muck; (*konst-*) fertilizer[s *pl*] **-grep** muckrake **-spridare** manure spreader **-stack** dunghill

gödsl|a [j-] manure, dung; (*konst-*) fertilize **-ing** manuring; fertilizing

gödsvin [j-] fattening (fatted) pig

gök [j-] *s2* **1** *zool.* [European] cuckoo **2** *bildl. o. skämts.* fellow, chap **3** *vard., se* kaffekask **-blomster** ragged robbin, cuckooflower **-otta** *ung.* dawn picnic to hear first birdsong **-tyta** *s1* wryneck **-unge** young cuckoo **-ur** cuckoo clock **-ärt** bitter vetch

göl [j-] *s2* pool; (*mindre sjö äv.*) mere

gömfröig [ˣjömm-] *a5* angiospermous; ~ *växt* angiosperm

göm|ma [j-] **I** *s1* hiding place; place where one keeps things; *gravens tysta* ~ the silent harbourage of the grave; *leta i sina -mor* search in one's drawers (cupboards) **II** *v2* **1** (*dölja*) hide [away], conceal (*för* from); (*begrava*) bury (*ansiktet i händerna* one's face in one's hands) **2** (*förvara*) keep (*till, åt* for); save [up]; (*låta ligga*) keep back, put by; ~ *undan* put away; ~ *sig* hide, conceal o.s.

gömme [j-] *s6* **1** *se* gömma *I* **2** *bot.* pericarp

göm|sle *s6*, **-ställe** *s6* hiding place, hide-out, hideaway

1 göra [j-] *gjorde gjort* **I 1** (*syssla med, ombesörja*) do (*affärer med* business with; *ett gott arbete* good work; *sin plikt* one's duty; *ngn en tjänst* s.b. a favour); perform (*en uppgift* a task); (*utföra*) carry out, execute; *gör det själv* do it yourself **2** (*åstadkomma, avge o.d.*) make (*ngns be-*

kantskap a p.'s acquaintance; *intryck på* an impression upon; *ett misstag* a mistake; *slut på* an end of; *en uppfinning* an invention; *en överenskommelse* an agreement); (*åstadkomma*) bring about (*en förändring* a change); ~ *underverk* work wonders **3** (*obj. är ett neutralt pron el. a*) do; ~ *sitt bästa* do one's best; *sitta och* ~ *ingenting* sit doing nothing; *vad gör du i kväll?* what are you doing (going to do) this evening?; *vad är att* ~? what is to be done?; *det är inget att* ~ *åt saken* nothing can be done about it (in the matter), it cannot be helped **4** (*bereda*) give, afford, do (*ngn den glädjen att* s.b. the pleasure of + *ing-form*); (*tillfoga*) do, inflict upon; (*skapa, utgöra*) make; (*betyda*) be of importance, matter; (*företaga resa e.d.*) go; ~ *en resa* go on a journey; ~ *ngn skada* do s.b. harm; *det gör ingenting a*) (*har ingen betydelse*) it is of no importance, *b*) (*är alldeles detsamma*) it doesn't matter!, never mind!, *c*) (*avböjande ursäkt*) not at all!, don't mention it!; *det gör mig ont att höra* I am sorry to hear; *kläderna gör mannen* clothes make the man **5** (*tillverka*) make; (*konstnärligt äv.*) do; (*göra färdig*) do, finish **6** (*bese*) do; ~ *Paris* do Paris **7** (*i vissa förbindelser*) make (*ngn lycklig* s.b. happy; *ngn till kung* s.b. [a] king; *det klart för ngn att* it is clear to s.b. that; *saken värre* matters worse); do (*ngn gott, orätt* s.b. good, wrong); ~ *ngn tokig* drive s.b. crazy; ~ *det möjligt för ngn att* enable s.b. to; ~ *det till sin plikt* make it one's duty; *det gjorde att jag bestämde mig för* this made me decide to (+ *inf.*) **8** (*handla*) act; do; *inte veta hur man bör* ~ not know how to act; *gör som jag säger* do as I tell you **9** (*uppföra sig*) behave **II** (*i stället för tidigare nämnt verb*) do; be; shall; will; *han läser mer än jag gör* he reads more than I do; *han sprang, och det gjorde jag med* he ran, and so did I; *om du inte tar den gör jag det* if you don't take it I shall; *skiner solen? ja, det gör den* is the sun shining? yes, it is **III** (*med betonad partikel*) **1** ~ *av*; *var skall jag* ~ *av...?* where am I to put...?, what am I to do with...?; ~ *av med* (*mörda*) bump off; *AE. waste*; ~ *av med pengar* spend (run through) money; *inte veta var man skall* ~ *av sig* not know what to do with o.s. **2** ~ *bort sig* drop a brick **3** ~ *efter* imitate, copy **4** ~ *ngn emot* cross (thwart) s.b. **5** ~ *fast* make fast, fasten **6** ~ *färdig* get finished, finish, (*i ordning*) get ready **7** ~ *ifrån sig ett arbete* get a piece of work off one's hands; ~ *bra ifrån sig* give a good account of o.s. **8** ~ *om a*) (*på nytt*) do over again, *b*) (*upprepa*) repeat, *c*) (*ändra*) alter **9** ~ *rent efter sig* clean (*AE.* fix) up before leaving **10** ~ *till*; *om det kan* ~ *ngt till* if that can help matters at all; ~ *sitt till för att det skall lyckas* do one's part to make it a success; *det gör varken till eller från* it makes no difference **11** ~ *undan* get done (off one's hands) **12** ~ *upp a*) (*eld, planer o.d.*) make, *b*) (*förslag, program o.d.*) draw up, *c*) (*räkning*) settle, *d*) (*ha en uppgörelse*) agree, settle, come to terms (*med* with; *om* about) **13** ~ *ngt åt saken* do s.th. about it (the matter) **IV** *rfl* **1** make o.s. (*omtyckt* popular; *förtrogen med* acquainted with); (*låtsas vara*) make o.s. out (pretend) to be (*bättre än man är* better than one is) **2** (*ta sig ut*) look (come out) (*bra* well) **3** (*tillverka åt sig*) make o.s. (*en klänning* a dress); *(låta göra)* have made; *(förvärva)* make *(en förmögenhet* a fortune); *(bilda sig)* form *(ett begrepp om* a conception of) **4** ~ *sig av med* get rid of; ~ *sig till* be affected, give o.s. airs, *(förställa sig)* dissimulate, sham; ~ *sig till för* make up to

2 göra [j-] *s6 (arbete)* task, work; *(göromål)* business; *(besvär)* trouble

görande [j-] *s6, ~n och låtanden* doings

gördel [ˣjö:r-] *s2* girdle **-däck** radial [tyre]

gör|lig [ˣjö:r-] *a1* feasible, practicable; *(möjlig)* possible; *i ~aste mån* as far as possible **-ningen** *best. form i uttr.: ngt är i* ~ s.th. is brewing

göromål [j-] *s7 (arbete)* work, business; *(syssla)* occupation; *(åliggande)* duty

1 gös [j-] *s2 (fisk)* pikeperch

2 gös [j-] *s2, sjö.* jack

gösstake jack staff

1 göt [j-] *s2, s3 (om forntida svenskar)* Geat

2 göt [j-] *s7, tekn.* casting, billet, bloom, ingot

3 göt [j-] *imperf. av gjuta*

Göteborg [jöte'bårj] *n* Göteborg, Gothenburg

götisk ['jö:-] *a5* Geatish

göt|stål [j-] ingot (cast) steel **-valsverk** cogging *(AE.* blooming) mill

h *s6* **1** h; *stumt* ~ silent h; *utelämna* ~ drop one's h's (aitches) **2** *mus.* B [natural]

1 ha *interj* ha[h]!

2 ha *(hava)* hade haft **I** hjälpv have **II** huvudv **1** have; *(mera vard.)* have got; *(äga)* possess; *(få, erhålla)* get; ~ *det bra* be well off; ~ *ledigt* be free; ~ *roligt* have a good time [of it]; ~ *rätt* be right; ~ *stort behov av* be in great need of; ~ *svårt för ngt* find s.th. difficult; *här ~r ni!* here you are!; *här ~r ni mig!* here I am!; *nu ~r jag det!* now I've got it!; *var ~r vi söder?* where is [the] south?; *vad vill ni ~?* *a)* what do you want?, *b)* *(att förtära)* what would you like?, what will you take?, *c)* *(i betalning)* what do you want (is your charge)?; *allt vad jag äger och ~r* everything I possess; *hur ~r du det nu för tiden?* how are things [with you] nowadays?; *hur mycket pengar ~r du på dig?* how much money have you got [on you]?; *jag vet inte var jag ~r honom* I don't know where he stands **2** *(förmå, låta)* get, have, make; ~ *ngn att lyda* make (have) s.b. (get s.b. to) obey **III** *(med betonad partikel)* **1** ~ *bort a)* *(tappa)* lose, *(förlägga)* mislay, *b)* *(ta bort)* have removed, take away **2** ~ *emot, inte* ~ *ngt emot* have nothing against **3** ~ *för sig a)* *(ha framför sig)* have before one, *b)* *(vara sysselsatt med)* be doing (up to), *c)* *(före-*

ställa sig) be under the impression, have an idea **4** ~ *ngn hos sig (som gäst)* have s.b. staying with one **5** ~ *i* put in **6** ~ *inne (varor)* have in stock; ~ *åldern inne* have reached the right age **7** ~ *kvar a)* *(ha över)* have left, *b)* *(ha i behåll)* have still **8** ~ *med sig* have with one **9** ~ *på sig (kläder o.d.)* have on; ~ *hela dagen på sig* have the whole day before one; ~ *bara en timme på sig* have only one hour left (to spare) **10** ~ *sönder* break, *vard.* smash **11** ~ *över (ha kvar)* have left

Haag [ha:g] *n* the Hague

habegär acquisitiveness

habil *a1 (skicklig)* clever; *(smidig)* adroit; *(duglig)* able; *(förbindlig)* suave

habit *s3* attire

habitué *s3* habitué **-ell** *a5* habitual

habitus ['ha:-] *oböjligt s, r (hållning)* bearing

1 hack *i uttr.: följa ngn* ~ *i häl* follow hard on the heels of s.b.

2 hack *s7* **1** *(skåra)* jag[g], notch, hack **2** *(lätt hugg)* peck

1 hacka **1** *kortsp.* small (low) card **2** *(liten summa) en* ~ a little cash; *en rejäl* ~ a tidy sum **3** *han går inte av för hackor* he is not just a nobody, he's a competent chap

2 hacka I *s1* pick[axe]; *(bred)* mattock; *(för jordluckring)* hoe **II** *v1* **1** hoe **2** *kokk.* chop; *(fin-)* mince; *det är varken ~t eller malet* it is neither one thing nor the other **3** *(om fåglar)* peck *(på at)* **4** *han ~de tänder* his teeth were chattering **5** *(i bord, mark med t.ex. kniv)* hack, pick **6** *(klanka)* find fault *(på* with); *(gnata)* nag *(på* at) **7** *(tala med avbrott)* stammer, stutter

hackelse chopped (cut) straw, chaff **-maskin** chaff cutter

hackhosta hacking cough

hack|ig *a1 (full med hack)* jagged **2** *(stammande)* stuttering **-kyckling** *hon är deras* ~ they are always picking on her **-mat** *bildl.* mincemeat

hack|ning hoeing etc., se 2 hacka II **-spett** *s2* woodpecker

hade *imperf av ha[va]*

haffa nab, cop, nick, collar

hafnium ['haff-] *s8* hafnium

hafs *s7 (slarv)* slovenliness; *(brådska)* scramble

hafs|a do things in a hurry; ~ *ifrån sig* scramble through **-ig** *a1* slapdash, slovenly **-verk** scamped (slovenly) work

haft *sup av ha[va]*

hagalen [ˣha:-] avaricious

hage *s2* **1** *(betesmark)* enclosed pasture[-land]; *(lund)* grove **2** *(för småbarn)* [baby's] playpen **3** *hoppa* ~ play hopscotch

hagel ['ha:-] *s7* **1** *(iskorn, koll.)* hail *(sg)*; *ett* ~ a hailstone **2** *(blykula)* [small] shot *(sg o. pl)* **-by** hailstorm **-bössa** shotgun, fowling piece **-korn** hailstone **-patron** shot cartridge **-skott** shot from a shotgun **-skur** hailshower, hailstorm **-svärm** *jakt.* charge [of shot]

hagga *s1* hag

hagla [ˣha:g-] hail; *bildl. äv.* rain, come thick and fast

hagtorn [ˣhakk-] *s2* hawthorn, may [tree]

Haiti [ha'i:ti] *n* Haiti **haiti|an** *s3,* **-ansk** [-'a:nsk] *a5* Haitian, Haytian

haj [hajj] *s2* shark

haja [ˣhajja] (förstå) get, dig; ~ till give a start; be
startled (scared)
hajfena shark's fin
hajk s2 hike
hak s7 notch; hack, dent
1 haka v1 hook (i, vid to); ~ av unhook; ~ fast a)
hook [on], fasten, b) (fastna) get caught (i by,
on), catch (i in); ~ i, se haka fast b); ~ upp a)
(fästa upp) loop up, b) (öppna) unhook, unfasten; ~ upp sig a) get caught, b) bildl. get stuck; ~
upp sig på småsaker stick at (worry about) trifles;
~ sig get stuck; ~ sig fast (äv. bildl.) cling (vid to)
2 haka s1 chin; tappa ~n be taken aback; stå i vatten upp till ~n be in water up to one's chin
hakband string; (brett) cheek band
hake s2 1 hook; (fönster-) catch **2** det finns en ~
(bildl.) there is a snag in it; [för] tusan hakar! the
deuce! -**bössa** [h]arquebus, hackbut, hagbut
hak|formig [-å-] a5 hooked, hooklike -**kors**
swastika
haklapp bib, feeder
hakmask hookworm -**sjuka** hookworm disease
hak|rem chin strap -**spets** point of the chin
hal a1 slippery; bildl. äv. evasive; (glatt) oily,
sleek; ~ tunga smooth tongue; ~ som en ål [as]
slippery as an eel; på ~ is (bildl.) on treacherous
ground, on thin ice; sätta ngn på det ~a drive s.b.
into a corner; det är ~t på vägarna the roads are
slippery
hala 1 sjö. haul; pull, tug; ~ flaggan lower the
flag; hissa och ~ hoist and lower; ~ an haul (tally)
aft; ~ in haul in; ~ fram haul (friare draw, drag)
forwards **2** bildl., ~ ut på tiden drag out the time
3 rfl, ~ sig ner lower o.s., let o.s. down
halka I s1 slipperiness; svår ~ very slippery roads
(road surface) **II** v1 slip [and fall], slide, glide;
(slira) skid; ~ förbi (bildl.) skim past, skilfully
elude; ~ omkull slip over (down), slip and fall;
ordet ~de över mina läppar the word escaped me
(my lips)
halk|bana (för träningskörning) skidpan -**fri** se
-säker -**ig** a1 slippery -**säker** nonskid, nonslip
hall s2 hall; (förrum) lounge; (pelar-) colonnade
halleluja [-'ja:, äv. -ˣlu:-] hallelujah!
hallick ['hall-] s2 pimp, ponce
hallon [-ån] s7 raspberry -**buske** raspberry bush
(shrub); -buskar (äv.) raspberry canes -**saft**
raspberry juice (syrup) -**sylt** raspberry jam
-**änger** s2 raspberry fruitworm
hallstämpel hallmark
hallucin|ation hallucination -**atorisk** [-'tɔ:-] a5
hallucinatory -**era** be subject to hallucinations
-**ogen** [-'je:n] s3 hallucinogen
hallå I interj hello, hallo[o], hullo **II** s6 (oväsen)
hullabal[l]oo
hallå|a vard. **I** [-ˣlå:a] s1, se -kvinna **II** [-'lå:a] v1,
radio. announce -**kvinna** [woman] announcer
-**man** announcer
halm s3 straw; av ~ (äv.) straw
halma n halma; spela ~ play halma
halm|arbete article made of straw; abstr. o. koll.
straw work -**gul** straw[-coloured] -**hatt** straw
hat; (platt) boater -**kärve** sheaf -**madrass** straw
mattress (bed) -**stack** straw stack (rick) -**strå**
straw; gripa efter ett ~ (bildl.) catch at a straw
-**tak** thatched roof -**täckt** a4 straw-covered,

thatched
halo ['ha:-] s5, meteor. halo
halogen [-'je:n] s3 halogen -**lampa** halogen
lamp -**ljus** halogen light
hals s2 1 neck; (strupe o. tekn.) throat; ~ över
huvud head over heels; med (av) full ~ at the top
of one's voice; bryta ~en av sig break one's neck;
falla ngn om ~en fall on a p.'s neck; få ngn på ~en
get saddled with s.b.; få nya bekymmer på ~en be
saddled with new adversities; ge ~ a) (om hund)
give tongue, b) (om pers.) raise a cry; ha ont i ~en
have a sore throat; sitta ända upp till ~en i be im-
mersed up to the neck in; sätta ett ben i ~en have
a bone stick in one's throat; det står mig upp i ~en
it makes me sick, I am fed up with it; orden fast-
nade i ~en på mig the words stuck in my throat;
skjortan är trång i ~en the shirt is tight round the
neck **2** (på instrument) neck; (på nottecken) stem
3 sjö. tack; ligga för babords ~ar be (stand) on
the port tack
hals|a 1 (dricka) take a swig **2** sjö. wear, tack
-**band** necklace; (hund-) collar -**bloss** dra ~ inhale [the smoke] -**brytande** a4 breakneck
-**bränna** s1 heartburn -**böld** quinsy -**duk** scarf,
neckerchief; (tjock) muffler; (fischy) fichu; (kravatt) tie, AE. necktie; vit ~ a white tie -**fluss** s3
tonsillitis -**grop** ha hjärtat i ~en have one's heart
in one's mouth (throat) -**hugga** behead, decapi-
tate -**huggning** beheading, decapitation -**järn**
iron collar -**katarr** pharyngitis -**kedja** chain
[round the neck] -**kota** cervical vertebra -**krås**
ruff, frill -**linning** neckband -**mandlar** pl [pala-
tine] tonsils -**ont** sore throat -**pulsåder** carotid
[artery] -**smycke** necklace -**starrig** a1 stubborn, obstinate -**tablett** throat lozenge, cough
drop
halst|er ['hals-] s7 gridiron, grill -**ra** grill
1 halt s3 1 (proportion, kvantitet) content; (percentage; (i guldarbeten o. mynt) standard **2** bildl.
substance; worth, value
2 halt I s3 (uppehåll) halt **II** interj halt!; (stanna)
stop!
3 halt a1 lame (på ena benet in one leg)
halta limp (på ena foten with one foot); ~ iväg
limp along; jämförelsen ~r the comparison does
not hold good; versen ~r the [rhythm of the]
verse halts
halv a5 half; ~ biljett half fare; ~ lön half pay; ~a
året half the year; ett ~t dussin half a dozen; ett ~t
löfte a half-promise; en ~ gång till så stor half as
big again; en och en ~ månad six weeks; ett och
ett ~t år eighteen months; till ~a priset at half
price, half-price; hissa flaggan på ~ stång fly the
flag at half-mast, half-mast; mötas på ~a vägen
meet halfway; klockan är ~ ett it is half past
twelve
halv|a s1 **1** half; en ~ öl half a (a small) bottle of
beer; de tog var sin ~ they took one half each **2**
(andra sup) second glass -**annan** [-ˣann-] n =
halvtannat one and a half -**apa** zool. prosimian
-**automatisk** semiautomatic -**back** sport. halfback -**bildad** half-educated -**blod** s7 1 (människa) half-breed **2** (häst) half-blood -**bra** so-so; indifferent; middling -**bror** half-brother -**butelj**
half-bottle -**cirkel** semicircle -**cirkelformig**
semicircular -**dager** twilight -**dagsplats** part-

-time job **-dan[n]** *a5* mediocre, middling **-dunkel I** *s7* dusk, semi-darkness **II** *a5* dusky, dim **-dussin** half-dozen; *ett* ~ (*äv.*) half a dozen **-däck** half-deck; (*på örlogsfartyg*) quarter-deck **-död** half-dead **halver|a** halve, divide into halves; *geom.* bisect; *absol. äv.* go halves **-ing** halving *etc.* **halv|eringstid** *kärnfys.* half-life **-fabrikat** semi-manufacture, semi-manufactured product **-fet** low-fat (*ost* cheese); *boktr.* bold; ~ *stil* bold face **-figur** *porträtt i* ~ half-length [portrait] **-fransk** ~*t band* half-binding; *i* ~*t band* half-bound **-full** half full; (*om pers.*) tipsy **-färdig** half-finished; *vara* ~ be half ready (finished, done) **-gammal** no longer young **-gardering** (*i tips*) 2-ways [forecast] **-genomskinlig** semitransparent **-gräs** sedges (*pl*) **-gud** demigod; (*friare*) hero **halv|het** (*halvmesyr*) half measure; (*ljumhet*) half-heartedness **-hjärtad** [-j-] *a5* half-hearted **-hög** of medium height; *med* ~ *röst* in an undertone, in a low whisper **-klot** hemisphere **-klädd** *a5* half-dressed **-kokt** half boiled; underdone; *AE.* rare **-kombi** hatchback **-kväden** *i uttr.*: *förstå* ~ *visa* be able to take a hint **-kvävd** [-ä:-] *a5* half-choked **-ledare** *elektron.* semiconductor **-lek** *sport.* half; *under första* ~ during the first half **-ligga** recline **-liter** *en* ~ half a litre **-ljus I** *s7* half-light; (*på bilar*) dipped (*AE.* dimmed) headlights **II** *a5* semitransparent **-mesyr** *s3* half measure **-mil** *en* ~ half a [Swedish] mile; *den första* ~*en* the first half-mile **-måne** half-moon **-månformig** [-år-] *a5* shaped like a half-moon, semilunar **-mätt** half full **-mörker** semidarkness, half-light **-naken** half naked, seminude **-nelson** (*i brottning*) half-nelson **-not** minim; *AE.* half note **-officiell** semiofficial **-part** half share, half **-pension** half board, demi-pension **-professionell** semiprofessional **-profil** *i* ~ in semi-profile **-ras** half-breed **-rund** semicircular **-sanning** half-truth **-sekel** half-century **-sekelgammal** half-a-century (fifty-year) old **-sida** half-page **-skugga** half-shade **-slag** half-hitch; *dubbelt* ~ clove hitch **-slummer** drowse **-sluten** half-closed **-sova** doze, be half asleep **-statlig** partly owned by the state (government) **-stekt** [-e:-] half roasted; (*ej tillräckligt stekt*) underdone; *AE.* rare **-stor** medium-sized **-strumpa** sock **-sula** *s1 o. v1* [half-]sole **-sulning** [-u:-] soling **-syskon** half-brothers and half-sisters **-syster** half-sister **-söt** medium sweet **halv|t** *adv* half; ~ *om* ~ *lova* more or less promise **-tid** *sport.* half-time; *arbeta* ~ work half (part) time **halvtids|anställd** part-timer, part-time employee **-tjänst** part-time work **halv|timme** half-hour; *en* ~ half an hour; *en* ~*s resa* half an hour's (a half-hour's) journey; *om en* ~ in half an hour['s time]; *varje* ~ every half-hour, half-hourly **-timmeslång** *en* ~ a[n] ...of half an hour, a half-hour... **-ton** *mus.* semitone; *AE.* half step **-torr** (*om vin o.d.*) medium dry **-trappa** *en* ~ half a flight [of stairs] **-vaken** half-awake **-vild** (*om folkstam*) semibarbarian; (*om tillstånd*) half-wild **-vokal** semivowel

-vuxen (*om pers.*) half grown-up, adolescent; (*om djur, växt*) half-grown **-vägs** halfway **-år** six months, half-year; *ett* ~ [a] half-year, six months; *varje* ~ semiannually **-årig** *a5* half-year's, six months'; (*som återkommer varje halvår*) half-yearly, semiannual

halvårs|gammal six months old; of six months **-ränta** half-yearly interest **-vis** semiannually, every six months, half-yearly **halvädelsten** semiprecious stone **halv|ö** peninsula **-öppen** half-open, (*på glänt*) ajar; *med* ~ *mun* with lips parted **hambo** ['hamm-] *s5* Hambo; *dansa* ~ dance the Hambo **hamburger** hamburger **-erkött** smoked salt horseflesh **hamit** *s3* Hamite **-isk** *a5* Hamitic **hammar|e** hammer; mallet; *anat.* malleus; ~*n och skäran* the hammer and sickle **-haj** hammerhead **-skaft** hammer handle **-slag** hammer blow (stroke) **-tå** *med.* hammertoe **hammock** ['hammåkk] *s2* hammock settee **1 hamn** *s2* **1** (*skepnad*) guise **2** (*vålnad*) ghost, apparition **2 hamn** *s2* harbour; (*hamnstad, mål för sjöresa*) port; *bildl. o. poet.* haven; *inre* ~ inner harbour (port); *yttre* ~ outer basin (harbour); *anlöpa en* ~ call at a (make) port; *löpa in i en* ~ enter a port; *söka* ~ seek harbour; *äktenskapets lugna* ~ the haven of matrimony **hamn|a** land [up]; ~ *i en soffa* come to rest on (be placed on) a sofa; ~ *i galgen* end up on the gallows; ~*de i vattnet* landed in the water **-anläggning** harbour; docks (*pl*) **-arbetare** docker, stevedore; *AE.* longshoreman **-arbetarstrejk** dock strike **-avgifter** harbour dues, port charges **-bassäng** dock **-fyr** harbour light **-förvaltning** (*myndighet*) port authorities (*pl*) **-inlopp** harbour entrance **-kapten** harbour master **-kontor** port authority; harbour master's office **-kvarter** dock district; dockland **-område** dockyard **-plats** berth, wharf **-stad** port; seaport **1 hampa** *v1, det* ~*de sig så* it so turned out **2 hampa** *s1* hemp; *ta ngn i* ~*n* (*vard.*) collar s.b., *bildl.* take s.b. to task **hamp|frö** hempseed **-rep** hemp rope **hamr|a** hammer (*på* at); *tekn. äv.* forge, beat; (*friare o. bildl.*) drum (*på bordet* on the table); pound (*på piano* [on] the piano); (*om hårt föremål*) pound, beat **-ad** *a5* hammered; beaten **-ing** hammering *etc.* **hamster** ['hamm-] *s2* hamster **hamstr|a** hoard; pile up **-are** hoarder **-ing** hoarding **han** [hann] he; (*om djur, sak*) it, *äv.* he, she; ~ *som står där borta är* the man standing over there is

hanblomma [ˣha:n-] male flower **hand** -*en händer* **1** hand; ~*en på hjärtat!* cross your heart!; *ngns högra* ~ (*bildl.*) a p.'s right-hand man; *efter* ~ gradually, little by little; *efter* ~ *som* [according] as; *för* ~ by hand; *i första* ~ in the first place, first of all, above all, (*omedelbart*) immediately; *i andra* ~ [at] second-hand, in the second place; *köpare i andra* ~ second-hand buyer; *i sista* ~ in the last resort, in the end, finally; *med varm* ~ readily, gladly, of one's own free will; *på egen* ~ a) (*självständigt*) for o.s., b) (*utan hjälp*) by o.s.; *på fri* ~ a) (*utan hjälpmedel*) by hand, b) (*oförberett*) off-hand; *på tu man* ~ by ourselves (*etc.*); *under* ~ privately; *anhålla om ngns* ~ ask for a p.'s hand; *byta om* ~ change hands; *bära* ~ *på ngn* lay hands on s.b.; *bära ngn på sina händer* make life a bed of roses for s.b.; *börja med två tomma händer* start empty-handed; *dö för egen* ~ die by one's own hand; *få ngt ur händerna* get s.th. off one's hands; *ge ngn fria händer* give s.b. a free hand; *ge vid ~en* indicate, show, make it clear; *gå* ~ *i* ~ *med* go (walk) hand in hand with; *gå ur* ~ *i* ~ go from hand to hand; *ha* ~ *om* be in charge of; *ha* [*god*] ~ *med barn* be able to manage (have a way with) children; *ha ngn helt i sin* ~ have s.b. entirely in one's hands (pocket); *ha ngt helt i sin* ~ have complete control over s.th.; *ha ngt för händer* have s.th. on (in) hand; *ha ngt på* ~ have the option of s.th.; *hyra ut i andra* ~ (*äv.*) sublet; *hålla sin* ~ *över* hold a protecting hand over; *komma i orätta händer* get into the wrong hands; *kyssa ngn på ~en* kiss a p.'s hand; *leva ur* ~ *i mun* live from hand to mouth; *låta ngt gå sig ur händerna* let s.th. slip through one's fingers; *inte lyfta en* ~ *för att* not lift a hand to; *lägga sista ~en vid* put the finishing touches to; *räcka ngn* ~ *en* hold out one's hand to s.b.; *räcka ngn en hjälpande* ~ lend s.b. a [helping] hand; *sitta med händerna i kors* sit with [folded hands, sit idle; *skaka* ~ *med* shake hands with; *stå på händerna* do a handstand; *sätta händerna i sidan* put one's arms akimbo; *ta* ~ *om* take in hand, take charge of; *ta emot med uppräckta händer* be only too pleased to receive; *ta mig i* ~ *på* [give me] your hand on; *ta ngn i* ~ take a p.'s hand; (*hälsa*) shake hands with s.b., shake a p.'s hand; *ta sin* ~ *ifrån* (*bildl.*) withdraw one's support from, drop, abandon; *två sina händer* wash one's hands of it; *tvätta händerna* wash one's hands of; *upp med händerna!* hands up!, stick'em up!; *vara för ~en a*) (*finnas*) exist, b) (*vara nära*) be close at hand; *vinka med kalla ~en* turn s.th. down flat, refuse point-blank, blankly refuse; *äta ur ~en på ngn* (*bildl.*) eat out of a p.'s hands; *de kan ta varann i* ~ it's six of one and half a dozen of the other, it's six and two threes; *det var som att vända om en* ~ it was a complete right about face; *hon var som en omvänd* ~ she was quite a different person; *allt gick honom väl i händer* fortune smiled on him, everything he touched succeeded **2** (*sida*) hand, side; *på höger* ~ on the right (righthand) side **3** *till ~a* (*på brev*) to be delivered by hand; *gå ngn till ~a* assist (wait) on s.b.; *komma ngn till ~a* come to hand, reach s.b. **4** *till ~s* at hand; *ligga nära till ~s* be close (near) at hand, be handy; *nära till ~s liggande* (*om förklaring o.d.*) plausible, reasonable

hand|alfabet manual alphabet **-arbete** (*sömnad o.d.*) needlework; (*broderi*) embroidery; (*stickning*) knitting; (*motsats maskinarbete*) handwork; *ett* ~ a piece of needlework **-bagage** hand luggage (*AE.* baggage) **-boja** handcuff, manacle (*båda äv.* = *belägga med handbojor*) **-bok** handbook; (*lärobok äv.*) manual, guide

-boll handball **-brev** personal (private) letter **-broderad** *a5* hand-embroidered **-broms** handbrake **-diskmedel** manual dishwashing detergent **-duk** towel; (*köks-*) [tea] cloth **-dusch** hand shower

handel ['hann-] *s9* **1** trade; (*i stort, i sht internationell*) commerce; (*handlande*) trading, dealing; (*affärstransaktion*) transaction; (*köp*) bargain; (*bytes-*) barter; (*i sht olaglig*) traffic; (*butik*) shop; ~ *och industri* trade (commerce) and industry; ~*n med utlandet* foreign trade; *i* [*allmänna*] ~*n* on (in) the [open] market; *driva* (*idka*) ~ carry on trade (business); *driva* (*idka*) ~ *med a*) (*land, pers.*) trade with, carry on trade with, b) (*vara*) trade (deal) in **2** ~ *och vandel* dealings (*pl*), conduct

handeldvapen firearm; *pl äv.* small arms; *AE. äv.* handgun

handels|agent commercial (trade) agent **-anställd** commercial employee **-attaché** commercial attaché **-avtal** trade agreement **-balans** (*lands*) balance of trade; (*firmas*) trade balance **-balk** commercial code **-bod** shop; *särsk. AE.* store **-bolag** trading company **-bruk** trade (business) custom **-departement** ministry of commerce; ~*et* (*i Storbritannien*) the Department of Trade, (*i USA*) the Department of Commerce **-fartyg** merchant vessel (ship) **-flagga** merchant flag **-flotta** merchant navy (*i sht AE.* marine) **-förbindelser** *pl* trade relations; (*firmor*) business connections **-gymnasium** higher commercial (business) school **-hus** business house (firm) **-högskola** school of economics and business administration **-idkare** tradesman (*pl äv.* tradespeople, tradesfolk) **-institut** business institute, institute of commerce **-järn** commercial iron, ordinary steel **-kammare** chamber of commerce **-kontor** [Swedish] trade office **-korrespondens** commercial (business) correspondence **-lära** commercial science; (*lärobok*) textbook in commerce **-lärare** teacher of commerce **-man** shopkeeper, storekeeper **-minister** minister of commerce; (*i USA*) secretary of commerce **-politik** trade (commercial) policy **-politisk** of trade (commercial) policy **-resande** travelling salesman, commercial traveller (*för* representing; *i* in); *AE.* traveling salesman **-räkning** commercial arithmetic **-rätt** commercial law **-rättighet** trader's licence **-sekreterare** trade commissioner **-skola** business (commercial) school, school of commerce **-stad** commercial (trading) city (town) **-teknik** trading technique **-teknisk** commercial, business, trade **-trädgård** market garden; *AE.* truck farm **-utbildning** commercial (business) training **-utbyte** trade, exchange of commoditites **-vara** commodity; *pl äv.* merchandise (*sg*), goods **-vinst** trading (business) profit **-väg** trade route **hand|fallen** nonplussed, taken aback **-fast** sturdy, stalwart **-fat** washbasin, washbowl **-flata** palm, flat of the (one's) hand **-full** oböjligt *s, en* ~ a handful of, (*friare*) a few **-gemäng** [-j-] *s7*, *mil.* hand-to-hand fighting; (*friare*) scuffle, affray; *råka i* ~ (*mil.*) come to close quarters, (*friare*) come to blows **-gjord** handmade **-granat** hand grenade **-grepp** manipulation, grip; *mil.*

motion; *invanda* ~ practised manipulation[s *pl*]
handgriplig [-i:p-] *a1* **1** (*som utförs med händerna*) ett ~*t skämt* a practical joke; ~ *tillrättavis-
ning* corporal punishment **2** (*påtaglig*) obvious,
palpable, tangible; ~*t bevis* tangible proof **-en**
adv, gå ~ *till väga* use [physical] force **-heter** *pl*,
gå (komma) till ~ take (come) to blows
hand|gången *a5, ngns* -*gångne man* a p.'s
henchman **-ha** (*ha vård om*) have (be in) charge
of, be responsible for; (*ämbete*) administer; (*hantera*) handle **-havande** *s6* administration, management, handling
handikapp ['hand-] *s7*, **handikappa** *v1* handicap
handikapp|ad *a5* handicapped, disabled **-lä-
genhet** apartment designed for disabled person
-råd *Statens* ~ [the Swedish] national council for
the disabled **-tävling** handicap competition
hand|kammare still room, storeroom, pantry
-kanna water-jug; (*vattenkanna*) watering-can
-klappning clapping of hands; ~*ar* applause
(*sg*) **-klaver** accordion; concertina **-klove** *se
handboja* **-kraft** manual power; *drivas med* ~ be
worked by hand **-kyss** kiss on the (a p.'s) hand
-kärra handcart
handla 1 (*göra uppköp*) shop, do shopping,
make one's purchases; *gå ut och* ~ go shopping;
handla ~ buy milk **2** (*göra affärer*) trade, deal,
do business (*i, med* in; *med ngn* with s.b.) **3** (*bete
sig*) act (*efter sitt samvete* according to one's conscience; *i god tro* in good faith; *mot ngn* towards
s.b.); ~ *orätt* act wrongly, do wrong **4** (*vara verksam*) act; *tänk först och* ~ *sen!* think before you
act! **5** ~ *om a*) (*ha t. innehåll*) deal with, be
about, treat of, *b*) (*vara fråga om*) be a question
of
handlag *s7, ngns* ~ *med ngt* a p.'s way of doing
(handling) things; *det rätta* ~*et* the right knack;
ha gott ~ *med barn* have a good hand with (be
good at managing) children
handl|ande 1 *s6* acting *etc.* **2** *s9* (*handelsman*)
shopkeeper, storekeeper; (*köpman*) tradesman
(*pl äv.* tradespeople, tradesfolk), dealer **-are** *se
handlande 2*
handled *s3* wrist
handled|a *v2* (*i studier*) guide, tutor; (*vid upp-
fostran e.d.*) have oversight over, superintend;
(*undervisa*) instruct **-are** instructor, teacher, tu-
tor, supervisor; guide **-ning** supervision, guidance; (*lärobok*) guide; *ge ngn* ~ *i* give s.b. guidance in
handling 1 (*gärning*) action; (*bedrift*) act, deed;
en ~*ens man* a man of action; *goda* ~*ar* good
deeds; *gå från ord till* ~ translate words into
deeds **2** (*i roman o.d.*) action, scene; (*intrig*)
story, plot **3** (*dokument*) document, deed; *lägga
till* ~*arna* put aside
handlings|frihet freedom of action; *ha full* ~
(*äv.*) be a free agent **-kraft** energy, drive **-kraf-
tig** energetic, active **-människa** man (woman)
of action **-sätt** conduct, line of action; behaviour
hand|lov[e] *s2* wrist **-lån** temporary loan
handlägg|a deal with, handle; *jur.* hear **-ning**
dealing (*av* with), handling; *jur.* hearing; trial;
målets ~ the hearing of the case
hand|löst headlong, precipitately, violently

-målad *a5* hand-painted **-penning** down payment, deposit **-plocka** (*utvälja*) hand-pick **-på-
läggning** *relig.* imposition (laying on) of hands
-rengöringsmedel hand cleaner **-räckning 1**
assistance (*äv. jur.*); *ge ngn en* ~ give (lend) s.b.
a [helping] hand **2** *mil.* fatigue duty **-rörelse**
motion (movement) of the (one's) hand
handsbredd handbreadth
handsekreterare private secretary
handskaffär [˟hansk-] gloveshop, glover's shop
handskakning handshake
handskas [˟hanskas] *dep*, ~ *med a*) (*hantera*)
handle, *b*) (*behandla*) treat, deal with; ~ *varligt
med* (*äv.*) be careful about, handle with care
handskbeklädd [˟hansk-] *a5* gloved
handsk|e [˟hanske] *s2* glove; (*krag-*) gauntlet;
kasta ~*n åt ngn* (*bildl.*) throw down the gauntlet
to s.b.; *ta upp* [*den kastade*] ~*n* take up the gauntlet, accept the challenge **-fack** (*i bil*) glove compartment **-makare** glover
hand|skrift 1 (*stil*) hand[writing]; (*motsats ma-
skinskrift äv.*) [manu]script **2** (*manuskript*)
manuscript (*förk.* MS., *pl* MSS.) **-skriven** *a5*
written by hand, handwritten
handskskinn [˟hansk-] glove-leather
hand|slag handshake **-stickad** *a5* hand-knit-
[ted] **-stil** [hand]writing **-stöpt** [-ö:-] *a4*, ~ *ljus*
hand-dipped candle **-svett** excessive sweating of
the hands; *ha* ~ have clammy hands **-sydd** *a5*
hand-sewn; handmade **-såg** handsaw **-sättare**
boktr. hand-compositor **-sättning** *boktr.* hand-
-composition **-tag 1** (*fäste*) handle (*på, till* of);
(*på kniv etc. äv.*) haft; (*runt*) knob **2** (*tag med
handen*) grip, grasp, hold; *ge ngn ett* ~ give s.b. a
[helping] hand **-tryck** block printing, hand-
-printing; *konkr.* block-print **-tryckning 1** pressure (squeezing) of the hand **2** (*dusör*) tip; *ge ngn
en* ~ tip s.b., grease a p.'s palm **-uppräckning**
show of hands; *rösta genom* ~ vote by show of
hands **-vapen** hand weapon; *pl* (*eldvapen*) small
arms, firearms **-volt** handspring **-vändning** *i en*
~ in a twink[ling] (trice), in [next to] no time;
AE. äv. in short order **-väska** handbag, bag;
AE. äv. purse, pocketbook **-vävd** hand-woven
1 hane *s2* (*djur*) male; (*fågel- äv.*) cock
2 hane *s2* **1** (*tupp*) cock; *den röda* ~*n* the fire
fiend **2** (*på handeldvapen*) cock, hammer;
spänna ~*n på* cock
hanegäll [-j-] *s7, i* ~*et* at cockcrow
hangar [-ŋ'ga:r] *s3* hangar **-fartyg** aircraft carrier
hanhund [he-]dog
hank *s2, inom stadens* ~ *och stör* within the
bounds (confines) of the town
hanka *gå och* ~ be ailing (puling), go about
looking poorly; ~ *sig fram* manage to get along
somehow
hankatt tomcat
hankig *a1* ailing, off-colour
han|kön male sex **-lig** *a5* male
hann *imperf. av hinna*
hanne *se 1 hane*
hanrej [˟ha:n-] *s2, s3* cuckold
hans his; (*om djur*) its
Hansan *s, best. form* the Hanseatic League **han-
sestad** Hanseatic city (town)

hantel *s2* dumbbell
hanter|a handle; (*sköta*) manage; (*racket, svärd e.d.*) wield; (*använda*) use, make use of; (*behandla*) treat **-ing 1** (*hanterande*) handling *etc.* **2** (*näring*) trade, business; (*sysselsättning*) occupation **-lig** *a1* handy; manageable
hantlangare helper, assistant; (*murar-*) hodman; *neds.* henchman, tool
hantverk *s7* [handi]craft; trade **-are** craftsman, artisan; (*friare*) workman
hantverks|mässig *a1* manual; handicraft; (*schablonmässig*) mechanical **-produkt** handicraft product **-skicklighet** skill of craftsmanship
harakiri [-'ki:-] *s6, s7* harakiri
harang long speech; harangue; *hålla en lång ~ om* produce a long rigmarole about **-era** [-ŋg-] harangue
hare *s2* hare; (*vid hundkapplöpning*) electric hare; *bildl.* coward, *vard.* funk; *ingen vet var ~n har sin gång* (*ung.*) there's no knowing what the upshot will be
harem ['ha:-] *s7* harem **haremsdam** lady of a (the) harem
harhjärtad [-j-] *a5* chicken-hearted, chicken-livered
haricots verts [arrikå'vä:r] *pl* haricots, French beans
harig *a1* timid; *vard.* funky; (*försagd*) pusillanimous
harkl|a hawk; *~ sig* clear one's throat **-ing** hawk [ing]
harklöver *bot.* hare's-foot
harkrank [ˣha:r-] *s2* crane fly, daddy-longlegs
harlekin [ˣha:r-, *äv.* 'ha:r-] *s3* harlequin
harm *s3* indignation (*mot* against, with; *över* at); (*svagare*) resentment; (*förtret*) annoyance, vexation
harm|a vex, annoy, fill with indignation; *det ~r mig att han* (*äv.*) I am annoyed at his (+ *ingform*) **-as** *dep* get (be) annoyed (*över* at); feel indignant (*på* with; *över* at) **-lig** *a1* provoking, vexatious, annoying **-lös** (*oförarglig*) inoffensive; innocuous; (*ofarlig*) harmless **-löshet** inoffensiveness; innocence
harmonj *s3* harmony; (*samstämmighet*) concord **-era** harmonize; *~ med* (*äv.*) be in harmony with
harmon|ik *s3, se harmonilära* **-ika** [-'mɔ:-] *s1* harmonica
harmon|ilära theory of harmony; harmonics (*pl o. sg*) **-isera** harmonize **-isk** [-'mɔ:-] *a5* harmonious; *mat. o. mus.* harmonic; *~t medium* harmonic mean **-ium** [-'mɔ:-] *s4* harmonium
harmsen *a3* indignant, angry; vexed, annoyed (*på* with; *över* at)
harmynt [ˣha:r-] *a4* harelipped **-het** harelip
harnesk ['ha:r-] *s7* cuirass; armour (*äv. bildl.*); *bringa ngn i ~ mot* rouse s.b. to hostility against, set s.b. up against; *vara i ~ mot* be up in arms against
1 harpa *s1* **1** *mus.* harp **2** *vard.* (*om kvinna*) old hag, witch
2 harpa *s1, lantbr.* sifting machine; (*såll*) riddle
harpest rabbit fever, tularaemia
harpist harper, harpist **harpolekare** harp player, harper

harpun *s3* harpoon
harpuner|a harpoon **-are** [-ˣne:-] harpoone[e]r **-ing** harpooning
harpunkanon harpoon gun
harpya [-ˣpy:a *el.* -'py:a] *s1* **1** *zool.* harpy eagle **2** *myt.* Harpy
harr *s2, zool.* grayling
harskla *se harkla*
har|skramla beater's rattles (*pl*), harestop **-spår** hare's track, pricks (*pl*); *ett ~ a prick* **-syra** *bot.* [wood] sorrel
hart [-a:-] *adv, ~ när* well-nigh; almost; *~ när omöjligt* well-nigh impossible
hartass hare's foot; *stryka över med ~en* smooth it over, set things straight again
harts *s4* resin; (*renat, hårt*) rosin **hartsa** rosin; (*stråke äv.*) resin; (*flaska o.d. äv.*) seal up [with resin]
harv *s2,* **harva** *v1* harrow **harvning** harrowing
harvärja [ˣha:r-] *i uttr.: ta till ~n* take to one's heels
has *s1, s2* hock; ham; *dra ~orna efter sig* loiter along; *rör på ~orna!* stir your stumps! **hasa** shuffle, shamble; *~ ner* (*om strumpa e.d.*) slip down; *~ sig fram* shuffle (*etc.*) along; *~ sig nedför* slither (slide) down
hasard [-'a:rd] *s3* (*slump*) chance, luck; *se äv. hasardspel* **-artad** [-a:r-] *a5* accidental, chance **-era** hazard
hasardspel game of chance; (*~ande*) gambling; (*vågspel*) hazard; *ett ~ a gamble* **-are** gambler
hasch[isch] ['haʃ(iʃ)] *s2, s7* hashish, hasheesh **-rökning** hashish smoking
hasp *s2,* **haspa** *v1* hasp
haspel *s2* reel; spool; (*härvel*) coiler; *gruv.* [hauling] windlass **-fiske** fishing with spinning rod **-rulle** spinning reel **-spö** spinning rod
haspla reel, coil; *~ ur sig* (*bildl.*) reel off
hassel ['hass-] *s2* hazel, cob; *koll.* hazels, hazel trees (*pl*) **-buske** hazel shrub **-mus** dormouse **-nöt** hazelnut, filbert, cob[nut] **-snok** smooth snake
hassena [ˣha:s-] hamstring
hast *r* haste, hurry; *i* [*all*] *~ in a hurry, hastily,* (*plötsligt*) *all of a sudden; i största ~ in great haste, in a great hurry* **hasta** hasten, hurry; *saken ~r the matter is very urgent; tiden ~r time is short; det ~r inte med betalningen there is no hurry about the payment*
hastig *a1* (*snabb*) rapid, quick; (*påskyndad*) hurried; (*plötslig*) sudden; (*skyndsam, överilad*) hasty; *i ~t mod* unpremeditatedly, *jur.* without premeditation **-ast** *som ~ in a great hurry; titta in som ~ look* (*vard.* pop) *in for a moment* **-het 1** (*fart*) speed; rate; *fys.* velocity; *med en ~ av* at a rate (speed) of; *med hög ~ at a high* (great) *speed; högsta tillåtna ~ speed limit, maximum* [permitted] *speed; minska ~en* (*äv.*) *slow down, decelerate; öka ~en* (*äv.*) *speed up, accelerate* **2** (*snabbhet*) rapidity; quickness **3** (*brådska*) hurry, haste, hastiness; *i ~en glömde jag* in my hurry (haste) I forgot
hastighets|begränsning speed limit **-kontroll** speed check-up; (*plats*) speed trap **-minskning** deceleration, slowing down **-mätare** speedometer; *flyg. äv.* airspeed indicator **-re-**

kord speed record **-åkning** (*på skridskor*) speed-skating **-ökning** acceleration, speeding up **hast|igt** *adv* (*snabbt*) rapidly, quickly, fast; (*brådskande*) hastily; ~ *och lustigt* without more ado, straight away; ~ *verkande* of rapid effect; *helt* ~ all of a sudden, (*oväntat*) quite unexpectedly **-verk** *det är bara ett* ~ it's just been thrown together

hat *s7* hatred; *poet.* hate; (*agg*) spite; (*avsky*) detestation; *bära* ~ *mot* (*till*) *ngn* cherish hatred towards s.b., loathe s.b. **hata** hate; (*avsky*) detest, abhor, abominate; ~ *som pesten* hate like poison **hat|full** full of hatred (*mot* towards), spiteful (*mot* towards); ~ *blickar* malignant glances **-isk** ['ha:-] *a5, se hatfull o.* **hätsk** **-kärlek** love-hate relationship **-propaganda** propaganda of hatred

hatt *s2* hat; (*på svamp*) cap, pileus (*pl* pilei); *tekn.* cap, hood, top; *vara i* ~*en* (*vard.*) have had a drop too much; *vara karl för sin* ~ stand up for o.s., hold one's own **hatt|a** dilly-dally, shillyshally **-affär** hat shop, hatter's [shop] **-ask** hatbox; (*kartong*) bandbox **-brätte** hat brim **-hylla** hatrack **-kulle** crown of a hat **-makare** hatter, hat manufacturer **-nummer** size, head-fitting **-nål** hatpin **-skrålla** *s1* wreck of a hat **-stomme** hat shape, felt hood **-svamp** mushroom

haubits ['hau- *el.* -'bitts] *s3, s2* howitzer **hausse** [hå:s] *s5* rise, boom; bull market **-artad** [-a:r-] *a5* bullish, boom-like **-spekulant** bull [operator]

hautrelief [å:rel'jeff] *s3* high relief **hav** *s7* sea (*äv. bildl.*); (*världs-*) ocean; *till* ~*s a*) (*riktning*) to sea, *b*) (*befintlighet*) at sea; *vid* ~*et a*) (*vistas*) at the seaside, by the sea, *b*) (*vara belägen*) on the sea [coast]; *öppna* ~*et* the open sea, the high seas (*pl*); *höjd över* ~*et* altitude above sea level; *mitt ute på* ~*et* right out at sea, in the middle of the ocean; *som en droppe i* ~*et* like a drop in the ocean

hava *se 2 ha*

havande *a4* pregnant **-skap** *s7* pregnancy

havanna [-ˣvanna] *s1*, **-cigarr** Havana [cigar]

haverera be wrecked; *bildl. äv.* get (be) shipwrecked; (*om el. med flygplan*) crash, have a breakdown

haveri (*förlisning*) shipwreck, loss of ship; *flyg.* crash, breakdown; (*skada*) damage, loss; *jur.* average; *enskilt* ~ particular average; *gemensamt* ~ general average **-kommission** commission of inquiry; *Statens* ~ [the Swedish] board of accident investigation

haveri|st 1 (*fartyg*) disabled (shipwrecked) vessel; *flyg.* wrecked (crashed) aeroplane **2** (*pers.*) shipwrecked man; *flyg.* wrecked airman **-utredning** average statement (adjustment)

havre [ˣha:v-] *s2* (*växten*) oat; (*säd*) oats (*sg o. pl*); *av* ~ (*äv.*) oat **-gryn** *koll.* hulled oats, oatgroats (*pl*); *vanl.* rolled oats (*pl*) **-grynsgröt** oatmeal porridge **-mjöl** oatmeal

havs|anemon [ˣhaffs-] sea anemone **-arm** arm of the sea **-bad 1** [a] sea bathe **2** (*badort*) seaside resort, watering place **-band** *i* ~*et* on (among) the seaward skerries **-borstmask** polychaete **-botten** sea (ocean) bed; *på* -*bottnen* at (on) the

bottom of the sea **-bris** sea breeze **-djup** depth of the sea **-fisk** marine (sea) fish **-fiske** deep-sea fishing **-forskning** oceanography, marine research **-gud** sea god **-gudinna** sea goddess **-katt** *zool.* wolffish, catfish **-kryssare** cruising yacht, ocean racer **-kräfta** Norway lobster **-kust** seacoast, seashore; *särsk. AE.* seaboard **-orm** sea snake **-sköldpadda** sea turtle **-ström** ocean current **-sula** gannet **-trut** great black-backed gull **-tulpan** acorn barnacle (shell) **-vatten** sea water **-vik** (*bred*) bay; (*långsmal*) gulf; (*i Skottland*) loch, (*i Irland*) lough **-växt** seaweed **-yta** surface of the sea; *under* (*över*) ~*n* below (above) sea level **-ål** conger **-öring** sea trout **-örn** European sea eagle, white-tailed eagle

havtorn sea buckthorn

H-dur B major

hebré *s3* Hebrew

Hebreerbrevet [-ˣbre:er-] Hebrews (*pl, behandlas som g*)

hebre|isk [-'bre:-] *a5* Hebrew, Hebraic[al] **-iska** *s1* (*språk*) Hebrew; *det är rena* ~*n för mig* it's [all] Greek to me

Hebriderna [-'bri:-] *pl* the Hebrides

hed *s2* moor[land]; (*ljung- äv.*) heath; (*särsk. i södra England*) downs (*pl*), downland

heden *a5* heathen; (*från hednisk tid*) pagan **-dom** [-domm] *s2* (*hednatid*) heathendom; (*hednisk tro*) heathenism, heathenry; (*mångguderi o.d.*) paganism **-hös** *oböjligt s, från* ~ from time immemorial

heder ['he:-] *s2* honour; (*berömmelse äv.*) credit; (*oförvitlighet*) honesty; *på* ~ *och samvete* [up]on my (*etc.*) honour; *göra* ~ *åt anrättningarna* do justice to the meal, *vard.* eat with gusto; *komma till* ~*s igen* be restored to its place of honour; *lända ngn till* ~ do s.b. credit; *ta* ~ *och ära av ngn* calumniate (defame) s.b.; *den pojken har du all* ~ *av* that boy is a credit to you

hederlig [ˣhe:-] *a1* **1** honourable; (*ärlig*) honest; (*ärbar*) respectable **2** (*anständig*) decent; (*frikostig*) handsome; *få* ~*t betalt* be paid handsomely **-het** honourableness; honesty; respectability; decency; *han är* ~*en själv* he is honesty itself

hedersam *a1* honourable; flattering

heders|begrepp concept of honour **-betygelse** mark (token) of honour (respect); *under militära* ~*r* with full military honours **-bevisning** *se -betygelse* **-doktor** honorary doctor **-gåva** testimonial, token of respect **-gäst** guest of honour **-knyffel** *s2, en riktig* ~ a real brick, a card **-kodex** code of honour **-kompani** guard of honour **-känsla** sense of honour **-ledamot** honorary member **-legionen** the Legion of Honour **-man** *en* ~ an honest man, a man of honour **-omnämnande** honourable mention **-ord** word of honour; *frigiven på* ~ liberated on parole **-pascha** *se -knyffel* **-plats** place of honour; (*sitt-*) seat of honour **-prick** *se -knyffel* **-pris** special prize **-sak** point of honour **-skuld** debt of honour **-tecken** sign (mark) of distinction, badge of honour **-titel** honorary title **-uppdrag** honorary task **-vakt** guard of honour

hedervärd *a1* (*aktningsvärd*) estimable, creditable; (*redbar*) honourable, honest

hedlandskap moorland, heath country

hedna|folk [ˣheːd-] heathen people **-mission**
~**en** foreign missions (*pl*)
hed|ning [ˣheːd-] heathen; (*från förkristen tid*)
pagan; *bibl.* Gentile **-isk** *a5* heathen; pagan
hedr|a [ˣheːd-] honour; show honour to; (*göra
heder åt*) do honour (credit) to; ~ *sig* do o.s. honour (credit), (*utmärka sig*) distinguish o.s. **-ande**
a4, se hedersam; ~ *uppförande* honourable conduct
hegemonj *s3* hegemony
hej [hejj] hallo!; (*adjö*) cheerio!; *hej* [då]! bye-
-bye!, so long; ~ *hopp!* heigh-ho!; *man skall inte
ropa* ~ *förrän man är över bäcken* do not halloo
until you are out of the wood, don't crow too
soon
heja I ['hejja] *interj* hurrah!, *vard.* 'rah!; *sport.*
come on! **II** [ˣhejja] *v1*, ~ *på* cheer [on], (*hålla
på*) support, *AE. äv.* root [for]
1 hejare [ˣhejj-] *tekn.* drop forge (hammer);
(*pålkran*) pile-driver
2 hejare [ˣhejj-] *se baddare*
heja|rklack claque [of supporters]; cheer section
-rop cheer
hejarsmide drop forging
hejd *r, utan* ~ inordinately, *vard.* no end; *det är
ingen* ~ *på* there are no bounds to
hejd|a stop; (*ngt abstr. äv.*) put a stop to, check;
~ *sig* stop (check) o.s., (*om talare e.d.*) break off
-lös (*ohejdad*) uncontrollable; (*ohämmad*) violent; (*måttlös*) inordinate, excessive
hejduk [ˣhejj- *el.* 'hejj-] *s2* henchman; tool
hej|dundrande [-ˣdunn-] *a4* tremendous **-san**
['hejj-] *interj, se hej*
hekatomb [-'tåmb] *s3* hecatomb
hektar *s7, s9* hectare; *ett* ~ (*ung.*) two and a half
acres
hektisk ['hekk-] *a5* hectic
hekto ['hekk-] *s7* hectogram[me]; *ett* ~ (*ung.*)
three and a half ounces **-graf** *s3*, **-grafera** hec-
tograph **-gram** [-'gramm] *se hekto* **-liter** [-'liː-]
hectolitre; *en* ~ (*ung.*) twenty-two gallons
hel *a1* **1** (*odelad, total*) whole; entire; complete;
~*a dagen* all (the whole) day; ~*a namnet* (*äv.*) the
name in full; ~*a Sverige* (*landet*) the whole of
Sweden, (*folket*) all Sweden; ~*a tal* whole (integral) numbers; *en* ~ *del* a great deal of; *en* ~ *förmögenhet* quite a fortune; *tre* ~*a och en halv*
three wholes and a half; *det* ~*a a*) eg. the whole
(total), *b*) (*friare*) the whole matter (affair,
thing); *i det stora* ~*a* on the whole; *i* ~*a två veckor*
for a whole fortnight; *på det* ~*a taget* on the
whole, in general; *som en* ~ *karl* like a man; *varje
~ timme* every hour on the hour; ~*a Sverige*
throughout Sweden; *det blir aldrig något* ~*t med*
nothing satisfactory ever comes of; *det är inte så
~t med den saken* things are not all they should
be in that respect; *jag var vaken* ~*a natten* I was
awake all night **2** (*oskadad*) whole, unbroken;
(*om glas o.d. äv.*) uncracked; (*om plagg*) not in
holes, not worn through (out); *hålla barnen* ~*a
och rena* keep the children neat and clean
1 hela *s1* (*helbutelj*) whole (large) bottle; (*första
sup*) first dram; ~*n går!* (*ung.*) now for the first!
2 hela *v1* heal
hel|afton *göra sig en* ~ make a night of it **-ark**
folio **-automatisk** fully automatic

helbrägda [-j-, *äv.* -g-, *äv.* ˣhell-] *oböjligt a*
whole **-görare** [-j-] [faith-]healer **-görelse** [-j-]
[faith-]healing; ~ *genom tron* saved by faith
hel|butelj whole (large) bottle **-fet 1** full-cream
(*ost* cheese) **2** *boktr.* extra bold **-figur** full figure; *porträtt i* ~ full-length portrait **-flaska** *se
-butelj* **-försäkring** (*för motorfordon*) comprehensive motorcar insurance
helg [-j] *s3* (*kyrklig högtid*) festival; (*friare*)
holiday[s *pl*]; *i* ~ *och söcken* [on] high days and
working days alike
helga [-g-] sanctify; (*inviga*) consecrate, dedi-
cate; (*hålla helig*) keep holy, hallow; ~*t varde ditt
namn!* hallowed be thy name!; ~ *vilodagen*
(*bibl.*) remember the Sabbath day to keep it
holy; *ändamålet* ~*r medlen* the end justifies the
means
helgarder|ad *a5* fully covered **-ing** (*i tips*)
3-ways [forecast]
helgd [-j-] *s3* (*okränkbarhet*) sanctity; (*t.ex. löf-
tes, ställes*) sacredness; *hålla i* ~ hold sacred
helgdag holy day; (*ledighetsdag*) holiday; *allmän*
~ public (bank) holiday
helgdags|afton [the] day (evening) before a
public holiday **-kläder** *pl* holiday (best) clothes
helgedom [ˣhelgedomm] *s2* sanctuary; (*byggnad äv.*) sacred edifice, temple; (*relik*) sacred
thing
helgeflundra [ˣhellje-] *se hälleflundra*
helgelse [-g-] (*helgande*) sanctification
helg|erån [-g-, *äv.* -j-] sacrilege **-fri** [-j-] ~ *dag*
ordinary business (normal working) day
helgjuten [-j-] *a5, bildl.* [as if] cast in one piece,
sterling; (*harmonisk*) harmonious
helgmålsringning [the] ringing in of the (the)
Sabbath
Helgoland *n* Heligoland
helgon [-j-gån] *s7* saint **-dyrkan** saint worship
-förklarad *a5* canonized **-gloria** halo; aureole
-legend legend of saints (a saint) **-lik** *a5* saint-
like, saintly
helhet entirety, whole; completeness, whole-
ness; totality; *i sin* ~ a) in its entirety, as a whole,
b) (*helt o. hållet*) entirely
helhets|bild general picture **-intryck** general
impression **-syn** comprehensive view **-verkan**
total effect
helhjärtad [-j-] *a5* wholehearted
helig *a1* holy; (*-gjord*) sacred; (*högtidlig*) solemn
(*försäkran* assurance); ~*a alliansen* (*landet*) the
Holy Alliance (Land); ~*a tre konungar* (*bibl.*)
the three Magi; *ett* ~*t löfte* a sacred (solemn)
promise; *Erik den* ~*e* Saint Eric; *den* ~*a natten*
the Night of the Nativity; *den* ~*a staden* (*om Jerusalem*) the Holy City; *den* ~*a stolen* the Holy See;
det allra ~*aste* (*bibl.*) the holy of holies, (*friare*)
the inner sanctum; *svära vid allt vad* ~*t är* swear
by all that one holds sacred
helig|förklara canonize **-het** holiness; *Hans H*~
(*om påven*) His Holiness **-hålla** keep (hold) sacred
helikopter [-'kåpp-] *s2* helicopter; *vard.* chopper
-landningsplats heliport
helinackordering 1 full board and lodging **2**
pers. boarder; lodger
helio|centrisk [-'senn-] heliocentric **-graf** *s3* he-

liograph **-stat** s3 heliostat **-trop** [-'å:p] s3 helio-trope

helium ['he:-] s8 helium

helix ['he:-] s2 helix

hel|konserv fully-sterilized tinned goods **-kväll** se helafton

hell [all] hail!; ~ dig! hail to thee!

hellen s3 Hellene, Hellenian **-ism** Hellenism **-ist** Hellenist **-istisk** [-'iss-] a5 Hellenistic[al]

hellensk [-'e:nsk] a5 Hellenic

heller ['hell-] (efter negation) either; ej ~ nor, neither; och det hade inte jag ~ nor had I, and I hadn't either, neither had I; du är väl inte sjuk ~? you are not ill, are you?

hel|linne pure linen; (i sms.) all-linen **-ljus** (på bil) köra med ~ drive with headlights full on

hellre ['hell-] adv, komp. t. gärna rather; sooner; ju förr dess ~ the sooner the better; så mycket ~ som [all] the rather as; ~ dö än ge sig rather die than surrender; jag vill ~ I would rather; jag dricker ~ kaffe än te I prefer coffee to tea; jag önskar ingenting ~ I wish no better

hel|lång full-length **-not** semibreve; AE. whole note **-nykter** teetotal **-nykterist** teetotaller, total abstainer **-omvändning** about-turn; AE. about-face; i sht bildl. volte-face **-pension 1** se helinackordering **2** (skola) boarding school **-sida** full (whole) page **-siden** pure silk; (i sms.) all-silk **-sidesannons** full-page advertisement

helsike [*hell-] s6 hell; i ~ heller! hell, no!

hel|skinnad [-ʃ-] a5, komma ~ ifrån ngt get off scot-free, escape unhurt, vard. save one's bacon **-skägg** full beard **-spänn** i uttr.: på ~ a) (om gevär o.d.) at full cock, b) bildl. on tenterhooks; med alla sinnen på ~ with all one's senses at full stretch (on the qui vive)

helst I adv, superl. t. gärna preferably, by preference; hur som ~ a) (sak samma hur) anyhow, no matter how, b) (i varje fall) anyhow, in any case, c) (som svar) [just] as you like (please); när som ~ [at] any time, whenever you (etc.) like; vad som ~ anything [whatever]; vem som ~ anybody, anyone; hur liten som ~ no matter how small; hur länge som ~ any length of time, as long as you like; ingen som ~ risk no risk whatever; i vilket fall som ~ anyhow, in any case; allra ~ skulle jag vilja most (best) of all I should like; därmed må vara hur som ~ be that as it may, however that may be; jag kan betala hur mycket som ~ I can pay any amount (as much as you like) **II** konj especially (all the more) (som as; då when)

hel|stekt roasted whole; (om större djur äv.) barbecued **-svart** all black **-syskon** full brothers and sisters

helt [-e:-] adv entirely, wholly; completely, totally; (alldeles) altogether, quite; (ganska) quite, rather; ~ enkelt simply; ~ igenom all through; ~ och fullt to the full; ~ och hållet altogether, completely; ~ om! about turn! (AE. face!); ~ säkert quite sure, no doubt [about it]; en ~ liten quite a small; gå ~ upp i be completely engrossed (absorbed) in; göra ~ om a) mil. about-turn, AE. about-face, b) (friare o. bildl.) turn right about

hel|tal integer, whole number **-tid** adv full time; arbeta ~ work full time

heltids|anställd full-time employee **-arbete**

full-time job (work) **-tjänst** se -arbete

hel|ton whole tone (AE. step) **-täckande** a4, ~ matta wall-to-wall carpet **-täckningsmatta** (i metervara) broadloom carpet **-täckt** a4, ~ bil closed car **-veckad** a5, ~ kjol [knife-]pleated skirt

helvete [*hell-] s6 hell; (dödsrike[t]) Hell; ett riktigt ~ sheer hell; ett ~s oväsen a hell of a row, an infernal row; av bara ~ for very hell, like blazes; i ~ heller! hell, no!; dra åt ~! go to hell!, drop dead!

helvetes|hund hellhound **-maskin** infernal (clockwork) machine **-straff** eternal damnation

1 helvetisk [-'ve:-] a5 (schweizisk) Helvetic

2 helvetisk [-'ve:-] a5 (helvetes-) infernal, hellish

hel|ylle pure wool; (i sms.) all-wool **-år** whole year

helårs|prenumeration annual subscription **-vis** yearly, annually

helägd a5 wholly-owned

hem [hemm] **I** s7 home (äv. institution); (bostad äv.) house, place; i ~met in the (one's) home, at home; vid ~mets härd at the domestic hearth; lämna ~met leave home **II** adv home; bjuda ~ ngn invite s.b. to one's home; gå ~ (i spel) get home, (i bridge) make the contract; gå ~ och lägg dig! (vard.) make yourself scarce!; hälsa ~! remember me (kind regards) to your people!; låna ngt med sig ~ borrow s.th. and take it home [with one]; ta ~ ett spel win a game; det gick ~ the point (it) went home

hem|arbetande a4, ~ kvinna [a] woman working in the home **-arbete** homework; (hushållsarbete) housework **-bageri** small-scale bakery **-bakad** a5 home-made **-besök** home visit (call) **-biträde** [domestic] servant, maid **-bjuda 1** se hem II **2** jur. offer to those having the right of first refusal **-bränd** a5 home-distilled; (olagligt) illicitly distilled **-bränning** home-distilling; (olaglig) illicit distilling **-buren** a5, fritt ~ delivered free; få ngt -buret have s.th. delivered at one's home **-bygd** native place, home district

hembygds|gård folk museum **-kunskap** local geography and history **-museum** se -gård

hem|bära bildl. (framföra) present, offer; (vinna) carry off (ett pris a prize), win (segern the day) **-dragande** a4, komma ~ med a) (sak) come home lugging, b) pers. come home bringing (with) [...om i one's train] **-falla 1** (åter tillfalla) devolve (till upon), revert (till to) **2** (förfalla) yield, give way (åt dryckenskap to drinking); (hänge sig) give o.s. up; (drabbas) fall a victim (åt to) **-fallen** addicted (åt to) **-fridsbrott** unlawful entering of a p.'s residence (house) **-färd** homeward journey, journey home **-föra** take (hit bring) home; (gifta sig med) marry **-förhållanden** home background (sg) **-förlova** mil. disband, demobilize; parl. prorogue; adjourn; (skolungdom) dismiss **-försäkring** householder's comprehensive insurance **-försäljare** door-to-door salesman (saleswoman) **-försäljning** door-to-door sales (pl) **-gift** [-j-] s3 dowry **-gjord** home-made **-hjälp** domestic (home) help **-ifrån** from home **-inredning** home furnishing, interior decoration **-inredningsar-**

kitekt interior decorator (designer)
hemisfär hemisphere
hem|kalla summon home; *polit.* recall **-kommen** [-å-] *a5, nyligen* ~ just back [home] **-kommun** home municipality, *(friare)* city (town, borough) where s.b. is registered **-komst** [-å-] *s3* return [home], homecoming **-konsulent** domestic science adviser **-kunskap** domestic science **-känsla** homely atmosphere **-kär** home-loving **-körd** delivered **-körning** delivery **-lagad** *a5* home-cooked, home-made **-land** native country, country of birth; *(i Sydafrika)* homeland, Bantustan **-landstoner** *pl, det är verkligen* ~ this is quite like home
hemlig *a1* secret *(för* from); *(dold)* hidden, concealed *(för* from); *(motsats offentlig)* private; *(i smyg)* clandestine; ~ *agent* secret agent; ~*t förbehåll* mental (tacit) reservation; *strängt* ~ strictly confidential, top secret **-het 1** *(med pl)* secret; *offentlig* ~ open secret **2** *(utan pl)* secrecy, privacy; *i [all]* ~ in secret (private), secretly, *vard.* strictly on the q.t.
hemlighets|full mysterious; *(förtegen)* secretive **-makare** mystery maker **-makeri** mystery making, *vard.* hush-hush
hemlig|hus privy **-hålla** keep secret, conceal *(för* from) **-stämpla** stamp as secret, classify as strictly (top) secret; ~*d (äv.)* classified
hem|lik homelike **-liv** home life; domesticity **-lån** *(om bok)* for home reading **-längtan** homesickness, longing for home; *ha* ~ feel homesick **-läxa** homework **-lös** homeless **-löshet** homelessness
hemma at home; ~ *från skolan* away from school; ~ *hos mig* at my place (home); *höra* ~ *i (om sak)* belong to; *han hör* ~ *i Stockholm* his home is in Stockholm; *känna sig som* ~ feel at ease (home); *vara* ~ *i (kunnig)* be at home in (on, with) **-bruk** *för* ~ for domestic use **-dotter** daughter living at home **-front** home front **-fru** housewife **-hörande** *a4,* ~ *i a)* *(om pers.)* native of, domiciled in, with one's home in, *b) (om fartyg)* of, belonging to, hailing from **-kvinna** woman not working outside the home **-kväll** evening at home **-lag** home team **-man** house husband **-marknad** home (domestic) market **-match** *sport.* home game
hemman *s7* homestead; [freehold] farm
hemmansägare yeoman [farmer], freeholder; *vanl.* [small] farmer
hemma|plan home ground; *match på* ~ home game **-stadd** *a5* at home; *vara* ~ *i* be at home in (familiar with, versed in) **-varande** *a4,* ~ *barn* children [living] at home
hemmiljö home environment (atmosphere)
hemoglobin *s4* haemoglobin
hemorrojder [-'råjd-] *pl* haemorrhoids
hem|ort legal domicile, place of residence; *sjö.* home port, port of registry **-ortskommun** municipality of residence **-ortsrätt 1** *jur.* domiciliary rights **2** *bildl.,* *vinna* ~ *i* gain recognition in **-permanent** home perm **-permittera** grant home leave; ~*d* on home leave **-resa** *s1* journey (voyage, return) home, home[ward] journey; *på* ~*n* while going *(etc.)* home, on the way home **-samarit** health visitor; home help

hemsk *a1* **1** ghastly; *(skrämmande)* frightful, shocking; *(kuslig)* uncanny, weird, gruesome; *(hisklig)* grisly; *(dyster)* dismal, gloomy; *(olycksbådande)* sinister **2** *vard. (väldig)* awful, frightful, tremendous; *det var* ~*t!* how awful! **-het** ghastliness *etc.*
hemskillnad judicial separation
hemskt *adv (väldigt)* awfully, frightfully; ~ *mycket folk* an awful lot of people
hem|slöjd hand[i]craft; domestic (home) crafts (industries) *(pl)* **-språksundervisning** immigrant language teaching **-stad** home town; *(födelsestad)* native town **-ställa** *(föreslå)* propose, suggest; ~ *om* request (ask) for; ~ *till ngns prövning* submit to a p.'s consideration **-ställan** oböjligt *s* request, proposal, suggestion **-syster** trained home help, home aide **-sända** send home; *(varor äv.)* deliver; *(fångar äv.)* repatriate **-söka** *(om högre makter)* visit *(med krig* with war); *(om rövare, pest)* infest; *(om spöke)* haunt; *(om sjukdom)* attack, inflict **-sökelse** visitation; scourge; infliction **-sömmerska** home dressmaker **-tagningskostnader** delivery costs **-tam** domesticated **-trakt** home district; *i min* ~ *(äv.)* near my home **-trevlig** nice and comfortable (cosy), homelike **-trevnad** homelike atmosphere, domestic comfort **-vist** *s7, s9* residence, domicile address; *fack.* habitat; *bildl.* abode; *vara* ~ *för (äv.)* be a seat (centre) of **-vårdare** health visitor; home help **-väg** way home; *(-färd)* homeward journey; *bege sig på* ~ start for home; *vara på* ~ be on the way home, *(om fartyg)* be homeward bound **-värn** home defence; *konkr.* home guard[s *pl*] **-värnsman** home guard **-vävd** handwoven; *-vävt tyg (äv.)* homespun **-åt** homewards, towards home
henna *s9* henna
henne *pron (objektsform av hon) (om pers., fartyg)* her; *(om djur, sak)* it **hennes 1** *fören.* her; *(om djur, sak)* its, *ibl.* her **2** *självst.* hers
henry ['henn-] *r (måttenhet)* henry
hepa|rin *s4* heparin **-tjt** *s3, med.* hepatitis
herald|jk *s3* heraldry **-iker** [-'rall-] heraldist, herald **-isk** [-'rall-] *a5* heraldic
herbarium [-'ba:-] *s4* herbarium
herbicid [-s-] *s3* herbicide
herdabrev [ˣhe:r-] pastoral letter
herde [ˣhe:r-] *s2* shepherd; *bildl. o. poet. äv.* pastor **-diktning** pastoral poetry **-stund** amorous interlude
herdinna shepherdess
Herkules ['härr-] Hercules
herkul|esarbete [ˣhärr-] Herculean task **-isk** [-'ku:-] *a5* Herculean
hermafrodjt *s3* hermaphrodite
hermelin *s3* stoat; *(i vinterdräkt)* ermine
hermelinsmantel ermine cloak
hermet|isk [-'me:-] *a5* hermetic[al] **-iskt** *adv,* ~ *tillsluten* hermetically sealed
hero [-'rå:] *s3, el. heros,* *pl heroer* hero
Herodes [-'ro:-] Herod
heroin *s4* heroin **-ist** heroin addict
hero|isk [-'rå:-] *a5* heroic[al] **-ism** heroism
heros ['he:rås] *se hero*
herostratisk [-'stra:-] *a5,* ~ *ryktbarhet* notoriety
herpes *s2* herpes

herr [-ä-] **1** (framför namn) Mr. (pl Messrs.) (förk. för Mister, pl Messieurs); (på brev o.d., efter namnet, i Storbritannien) Esq. (förk. för Esquire); ~arna J. och R. Mason Messrs. J. and R. Mason, the Messrs. Mason; unge ~ Tom (vanl.) Master Tom; er ~ fader (ung.) your respected father **2** (framför titel) ~ professor (doktor) Jones Professor (Doctor) Jones **3** (vid tilltal) ~ domare! Your Honour!; ja, ~ general yes, General (Sir); ~ greve (baron)! Count! (Baron!), (i Storbritannien) Your Lordship!; ~ ordförande! Mr. Chairman!, Sir!

herradöme s6 dominion

Herran se herre 5

herr|avälde 1 (makt) domination (över over); (välde) dominion, supremacy (över over, of); (styrelse) rule, sway (över over, of) **2** (kontroll, övertag) control, mastery, command (över of); förlora ~t över lose control of; ha ~t till sjöss have the mastery of the seas, have supremacy at sea; vinna ~ över sig själv gain control of o.s., get o.s. under control **-bekant** gentleman friend **-betjänt** stand for men's clothes **-bjudning** men's (vard. stag) party **-cykel** man's bicycle

herr|e s2 **1** gentleman **2** (i tilltal) a) (framför namn, titel) se herr, b) (utan titel, namn) you; vad önskar ni? what do you want, sir?, may I help you, sir?; förlåt ~n, kan ni säga mig excuse me, sir, can you tell me **3** (förnäm, adlig) nobleman; i Storbritannien lord; andliga och världsliga -ar lords spiritual and temporal **4** (härskare) lord, ruler; (friare o. husbonde) master; min ~ och man my lord and master; situationens ~ master of the situation; bli ~ över gain the mastery of (over), get the better of; spela ~ lord it; vara ~ på täppan rule the roost; vara sin egen ~ be one's own master **5** H~n the Lord; ~ gud! Good heavens (God)!; i -ans namn (vard.) for goodness' sake; för många -ans år sedan years and years ago, ages ago; vilket -ans oväder! what awful weather!

herrefolk master race

herrekipering[saffär] [gentle]men's outfitter's, outfitter

herre|lös without a master; (om egendom) ownerless, abandoned; (om hund äv.) stray **-man** gentleman; (godsägare) country gentleman, squire **-säte** country seat, manor

herr|frisör barber **-gård** manor (country) house, mansion, estate, hall **-gårdsvagn** estate car; AE. station wagon **-kläder** pl [gentle]men's wear (sg) (clothes) **-konfektion** men's [ready--made] clothing **-kostym** [man's] suit **-middag** [gentle]men's dinner party **-mode** s6, s4 [gentle]men's fashion

herrnhutare pl Moravians, Moravian Brethren

herrskap s7 **1** (fin familj) gentleman's family; (herre o. fru) master and mistress; det höga ~et the august couple (om fler än två personages); det unga ~et the young couple; spela ~ play the gentlefolks; ~et är bortrest the family (Mr. and Mrs. Y.) are (have gone) away **2** (vid tilltal) mitt ~! ladies and gentlemen!; hos ~et Jones at the Jones's; skall ~et gå redan!? are you leaving already?

herrskaps|aktig a5 genteel **-folk** gentry; gentlefolk[s]

herr|sko man's shoe **-skräddare** [gentle]men's tailor **-skrädderi** gentlemen's tailor **-sällskap** i ~ in male company, (bland herrar) among gentlemen **-toalett** [gentle]men's lavatory; AE. men's room **-tycke** sex appeal

hertig s2 duke **-döme** s6 duchy, dukedom **-inna** duchess **-lig** a5 ducal **-titel** ducal title

hertz r hertz (pl hertz)

hes a1 hoarse; (om röst äv.) husky **-het** hoarseness; huskiness

het a1 hot; (om klimat äv.) torrid (zon zone); bildl. äv. ardent, fervent; (hetsig) heated, excited; ~a linjen the hot line; ~ potatis hot potato; kvävande ~ suffocatingly ~ (vard. stifling) hot; vara ~ på gröten be overeager; var inte så ~ på gröten hold your horses

het|a -te -at **1** (kallas) be called (named); allt vad böcker -er everything in the way of books; allt vad karlar -er anything that goes by the name of man, the whole tribe (race) of men; jag -er Kate my name is Kate; det var en yxa som -te duga that was a fine axe; vad -er det på tyska? what is the German for it (is it in German)?; vad -er det i pluralis? what is the plural of it?; vad -er hon i sig själv? what was her maiden name?; vad han nu -er whatever he's called **2** opers., som det -er på engelska as it is called (as one says) in English; det -er att it is said (people say) that; det -er att han he is said to

hetat sup av heta

hetero|dox [-'dåcks] a5 heterodox **-gen** [-'je:n] a1 heterogeneous **-nym I** s3 heteronym **II** a5 heteronymous

heterosexu|alitet heterosexuality **-ell** heterosexual

het|levrad [-e:v-] a5 hot-headed, hot-tempered; (kolerisk) choleric, irascible **-luft** hot air

hets s2 **1** (förföljelse) baiting, persecution (mot of) **2** (iver) bustle

hets|a 1 (förfölja) bait, worry (t. döds to death); (bussa) hound (på on to); (uppegga) incite (till to), egg on; ~ upp sig get excited **-ande** a4 inflammatory; (om dryck) fiery, heady; (om kryddor) fiery, hot **-hunger** bulimia

hetsig a1 hot, fiery; passionate, vehement; heated (diskussion discussion) **-het** hotness etc.; impetuosity, vehemence

hetsjakt hunt[ing], chasing (på of); (efter nöjen o.d.) chase (efter after), eager pursuit (efter of)

hetsporre hotspur

hets|propaganda inflammatory propaganda **-ätande** s6 compulsive eating

hett adv hotly etc., se het; ha det ~ om öronen be in hot water; det börjar osa ~ the place is getting too hot to hold me (etc.); det gick ~ till (blev slagsmål) it was a real roughhouse, (i diskussion etc.) feelings ran high; när striden stod som hetast in the very thick of the struggle (fight)

hetta I s1 heat; bildl. äv. ardour; passion; (häftighet) impetuosity; i stridens ~ in the heat of the struggle (bildl. debate) **II** v1 emit heat; ~ upp heat, make hot; det ~r om kinderna my cheeks are burning

hette imperf av heta

hetvatten high-temperature hot water

hetär s3 hetaera, hetaira; (friare) courtesan

heuristik *s3* heuristics (*pl, behandlas som sg*)
hexa|decimalsystem [-ˣma:l-] hexadecimal [notation] **-meter** [-ˣxa:- *el.* -ˈxa:-] *s2* hexameter
hibiskus [-ˈbiss-] *s2* hibiscus
hick|a I *s1* hiccup, hiccough; *ha* ~ have the hiccups **II** *v1* hiccup **-ning** hiccup; (*-ande*) hiccuping
hickory [ˈhikk-] *s9* hickory
hierark|i *s3* hierarchy **-isk** [-ˈrarr-] *a5* hierarchic [al]
hieroglyf *s3* hieroglyph[ic] **-isk** *a5* hieroglyphic [al]
hihi he, he!
hillebard [-ˈa:rd] *s3* halberd, halbert
Himalaya [-ˈma:-] *n* the Himalayas (*pl*)
himla I *v1*, *rfl* turn (roll) up one's eyes [to heaven] **II** *oböjligt a*, *vard.* awful **-kropp** heavenly (celestial) body; *särsk. poet.* orb **-päll** *se -valv* **-stormare** *se* himmelsstormare **-valv** ~*et* the vault (canopy) of heaven, the heavens (*pl*), the sky, *poet.* the welkin
him|mel *-meln, -len el. -melen, pl -lar* **1** sky; firmament; *under bar* ~ in the open [air]; *allt mellan* ~ *och jord* everything under the sun; *röra upp* ~ *och jord* move heaven and earth, (*friare*) make a tremendous to-do **2** (*Guds boning, paradis*) heaven, Heaven; *o, ~!* good heavens!; *i sjunde -len* in the seventh heaven; *uppstiga till -len* ascend into heaven
himmelrike heaven; ~*t* the kingdom of heaven; *ett* ~ *på jorden* a heaven on earth
himmels|blå sky blue, azure **-ekvator** celestial equator, equinoctial [circle] **-färd** *Kristi* ~ the Ascension **-färdsdag** *Kristi* ~ Ascension Day
himmelsk [ˈhimm-] *a5* heavenly; celestial (*sällhet* bliss); *bildl. äv.* divine; ~*t tålamod* angelic patience; *det* ~*a riket* (*Kina före republiken*) the Celestial Empire
himmels|pol celestial pole **-sfär** celestial sphere **-skriande** crying, glaring (*orättvisa* injustice); atrocious (*brott* crime) **-stormare** [-å-] heavenstormer, titan **-säng** canopied bed, four-poster [bed] **-vid** huge, immense, enormous; *en* ~ *skillnad* all the difference in the world
hin [hi:n, *äv.* hinn] the devil; Old Harry; ~ *håle* the Evil One; *han är ett hår av* ~ he is a devil of a man
hind *s2* hind
hinder [ˈhinn-] *s7* obstacle (*för, mot* to); impediment (*för* to); (*ngt som fördröjer o.d.*) hindrance; (*avsiktligt utsatt*) obstruction; *sport.* hurdle; fence; (*dike, grav*) ditch, bunker; (*spärr*) bar, barrier (*äv. bildl.*); *lägga* ~ *i vägen för ngn* place obstacles in a p.'s way, obstruct s.b.; *ta ett* ~ (*sport.*) jump (take, clear) a hurdle (fence); *vara till* ~*s för ngn* be in a p.'s way; *övervinna alla* ~ surmount every obstacle, overcome all difficulties; *det möter inga* ~ *från min sida* there is nothing to prevent it if as far as I am concerned, I have no objection to it **-bana** steeplechase course **-hoppning** *ridk.* hurdle-jumping **-löpning, -ritt** steeplechase **-sam** *a1, vara* ~ be a hindrance, (*besvärande*) be cumbersome
hindersprövning application for a marriage licence
hindra (*för-*) prevent (*ngn från att göra ngt* s.b. from doing s.th.); (*avhålla äv.*) deter, restrain,

keep, withhold; (*hejda*) stop; (*störa*) hinder; (*lägga hinder i vägen för*) impede, hamper, keep back, stand in the way of; (*trafik, utsikt*) obstruct, block; (*fördröja*) delay; *stå* ~*nde i vägen* be an obstacle (a hindrance), get in the way; *det* ~*r inte att du försöker* there's nothing to stop you trying; *han låter inte* ~ *sig* nothing can stop him
hindu *s3, -isk* *a5* Hindu **-ism** Hinduism **-stani** [-ˈsta:-] *r* Hindustani
hingst *s2* stallion
hink *s2* bucket; (*mjölk-, slask-*) pail
1 hinna *s1, biol.* membrane; (*friare*) coat; (*mycket tunn*) film
2 hinna *hann hunnit* **1** (*uppnå*) reach, get as far as; (*upp-*) catch up; (*komma*) get, (*mot den talande*) come; *hur långt har du hunnit?* how far have you got? **2** (*komma i tid*) be in time; (*ha el. få tid*) have (find) time; (*få färdig*) get done; *allt vad jag hinner* as fast as [ever] I can; *jag har inte hunnit hälften* I haven't got half of it done **3** (*med betonad partikel*) ~ *fatt* catch up with, (*pers. äv.*) catch up, overtake; ~ *fram* arrive (*till* at, in), absol. äv. reach one's (its) destination; ~ *fram i tid* arrive (get there) in time; ~ *förbi* manage to get past; ~ *med a*) (*följa med*) keep up (pace) with, *b*) (*tåget etc.*) [manage to] catch, *c*) (*hinna avsluta*) [manage to] finish (get done); *inte* ~ *med tåget* miss (not catch) the train
1 hipp *interj,* ~, ~, *hurra!* hip, hip, hurrah!
2 hipp *det är* ~ *som happ* it's neither here nor there, it amounts to the same thing
hippa *s1, vard.* party
hippodrom [-ˈå:m] *s3* hippodrome
hird [-i(:)-] *s3* housecarls **-man** housecarl
hirs *s3, bot.* millet
hisklig *a1* horrid, horrible; (*skräckinjagande*) terrifying; (*avskyvärd*) abominable; (*hemsk*) gruesome
hisna *se* hissna
hiss *s2* lift; *AE.* elevator; (*varu-*) hoist, *AE.* freight elevator
hiss|a hoist; (*pers.*) toss; ~ *en flagga* hoist (run up) a flag; ~ *segel* (*äv.*) set sail; ~ *upp* hoist (run) up **-konduktör** liftman, liftboy **-korg** lift cage (car)
hissna feel dizzy (giddy); ~*nde avgrund* appalling abyss; ~*nde höjd* dizzy height[s]; *en* ~*nde känsla* a feeling of dizziness (giddiness)
hisstrumma lift shaft (well)
histamin *s4* histamine
histo|gram [-ˈamm] *s7* histogram **-log** histologist **-logi** *s3* histology **-logisk** [-ˈlå:-] *a5* histologic[al]
histori|a [-ˈtɔ:-] *-en* (*i bet. 2 o. 3 vard. äv. -an*) *-er* **1** history; (*lärobok*) history book; ~ *med samhällslära* history and civics; *gamla* (*nyare*) *tidens* ~ ancient (modern) history; *gå till -en* become (go down in) history **2** (*berättelse*) story **3** (*sak, händelse*) story, thing, business, affair; *en ledsam* ~ a sad (unpleasant) business (affair); *en snygg* ~ a fine (pretty) business **-citet** historicity
historie|berättare storyteller **-bok** history book **-skrivning** (*som vetenskap*) historiography
histor|ik *s3* history **-iker** [-ˈtɔ:-] historian **-isk** [-ˈtɔ:-] *a5* historical; (*historiskt betydande*)

H

historic; *H~a museet* museum of national antiquities

hit here; ~ *och dit* here and there, hither and thither, to and fro; *ända* ~ as far as this; *fundera* ~ *och dit* cast about in one's mind; *prata* ~ *och dit* talk of one thing and another; *det hör inte* ~ that has nothing to do with this (is not relevant) **-hörande** *a4* in (of) this category, pertinent, relevant **-intills** *se hittills*

hitlista [ˣhitt-] hit list

hitom [on] this side [of]

hitta 1 (*finna*) find; (*påträffa*) come (light) [up] on; *det var som* ~*t* it was a real godsend (bargain) **2** (*hitta vägen*) find the (one's) way; (*känna vägen*) know the (one's) way **3** ~ *på* (*komma på*) hit upon, (*upptäcka*) find [out], discover, (*uppfinna*) invent, (*dikta upp*) make up; *vad skall vi* ~ *på* [*att göra*]*?* what shall we do?

hittebarn foundling

hittegods lost property **-magasin** lost property office

hittelön reward

hittills up to now, hitherto, till now; (*så här långt*) so far **-varande** *a4* hitherto (*etc.*) existing (*etc.*); (*nu avgående*) retiring, outgoing

hit|vägen *på* ~ on the (my *etc.*) way here **-åt** [ˈhiːt-, *äv.* -ˈåːt] in this direction, this way

hiva heave

hjon [joːn] *s7* (*tjänare*) servant; (*på inrättning*) inmate **hjonelag** *s7* connubial union

hjord [joːrd] *s2* herd; (*får- o. bildl.*) flock **-instinkt** herd instinct

hjort [joːrt] *s2* deer (*pl äv.* deer); *se äv. dovhjort, kronhjort* **-horn 1** antler **2** (*ämne*) hartshorn **-hornssalt** ammonium carbonate, sal volatile **-kalv** fawn

hjortron [ˣjoːrtrån *el.* ˣjɔrr-] *s7* cloudberry **-sylt** cloudberry jam

hjul [juːl] *s7* wheel; (*utan ekrar*) trundle; (*under möbel o.d.*) caster, castor; (*på -ångare*) paddle wheel **hjula** [ˣjuːla] turn cartwheels

hjul|axel axle[tree] **-bas** wheelbase **-bent** [-eː-] *a4* bow-legged, bandy-legged **-nav** hub **-spår** wheel track; (*djupare*) rut **-tryck** wheel pressure **-upphängning** wheel suspension **-ångare** paddle steamer

hjälm [j-] *s2* helmet **-buske** crest

hjälp [j-] *s3* **1** help; (*bistånd*) assistance, aid; (*undsättning*) rescue; (*understöd*) support; *första* ~*en* first aid; *med* ~ *av* with the help of; *få* ~ *av* be helped (assisted) by; *komma ngn till* ~ come to a p.'s assistance; *tack för* ~*en!* thanks for your [kind] help!; *ta ngt till* ~ make use of (have recourse to) s.th.; *vara ngn till stor* ~ be a great help to s.b. **2** (*biträde*) help, assistant **3** (*botemedel*) remedy (*mot* for) **4** *ridk.*, ~*er* aids

hjälp|a [j-] *v3* **1** help; (*bistå*) assist, aid; (*bota*) remedy; (*om läkemedel e.d.*) be effective; relieve, ease; (*rädda*) save, rescue; *Gud -e mig!* Goodness gracious!; *så sant mig Gud -e!* so help me God!; *det -er inte hur mycket jag än* it makes no difference however much I; *det -te inte* it had no effect (was of no avail); *hos honom -te inga böner* he turned a deaf ear to our (*etc.*) pleas; *jag kan inte* ~ *att* (*äv.*) it is not my fault that; *vad -er det att han* what is the use (good) of his (+ *ing-*

form); ~ *sig själv* help o.s., (*reda sig*) manage **2** (*med betonad partikel*) ~ *ngn av med kappan* help s.b. off with his (*etc.*) coat; ~ *fram ngn* help s.b. [to get] on (*etc.*); ~ *till* help (*med att göra ngt* to do s.th.), *absol. äv.* make o.s. useful; ~ *upp a*) (*ngn på fötterna*) help s.b. on to his feet (to get up, to rise), *b*) (*förbättra*) improve

hjälpaktion relief action

hjälp|ande [j-] *a4* helping *etc.*; *träda* ~ *emellan* come to the rescue **-are** helper *etc.*; supporter **-as** *v3, dep, det kan inte* ~ it can't be helped; ~ *åt* help each other (one another); *om vi -s åt* if we do it together (make a united effort)

hjälp|behövande *a4, de* ~ those requiring (in need of) help, the needy **-klass** class for backward children **-lig** *a1* passable, tolerable, moderate **-lös** helpless; (*tafatt äv.*) shiftless **-medel** aid, help, means (*sg o. pl*) [of assistance]; (*utväg*) expedient, shift; (*-källa*) resource, (*litterär*) work of reference **-motor** auxiliary engine (motor) **-präst** assistant priest; *i Storbritannien ung.* curate **-reda** *s1* **1** (*biträde*) helper, assistant **2** (*bok*) guide

hjälpsam [j-] *a1* helpful, ready (willing) to help **-het** helpfulness

hjälp|sökande I *s9* applicant [for assistance (relief)] **II** *a4* seeking relief **-trupp** auxiliary force; ~*er* auxiliary troops, auxiliaries **-verb** auxiliary verb

hjälte [j-] *s2* hero **-dikt** heroic poem **-dåd** heroic achievement (deed) **-död** heroic death; *dö* ~*en* die the death of a hero **-mod** valour, heroism **-modig** heroic **-tenor** Heldentenor

hjältinna [j-] heroine

hjärn|a [ˣjäːr-] *s1* brain; (*förstånd*) brains (*pl*); *lilla* ~*n* [the] cerebellum; *stora* ~*n* [the] cerebrum; *bry sin* ~ rack one's brains **-bark** cerebral cortex **-bihanget** *undre* ~, *se hypofysen*; *övre* ~, *se tallkottkörteln* **-blödning** cerebral haemorrhage **-död I** *s2* brain death **II** *a5* brain dead **-feber** *se -inflammation* **-flykt** *vard.* brain drain **-gymnastik** mental gymnastics **-hinna** cerebral membrane **-hinneinflammation** meningitis **-inflammation** inflammation of the brain **-kontor** *skämts.* upper storey **-skada** brain injury **-skakning** concussion [of the brain] **-skål** brainpan **-spöke** *det är bara* ~*n* they are idle imaginings **-stammen** the brain stem **-trust** brains trust **-tumör** brain tumour **-tvätt** brainwashing **-tvätta** brainwash

hjärta [ˣjärta] *s6* **1** heart; *ett gott* ~ a kind heart; *av allt* (*hela*) *mitt* ~ with all my heart, from [the bottom of] my heart; *i* ~*t av* in the heart (very centre) of (*staden* the town); *med glatt* (*tungt*) ~ with a light (heavy) heart; *given med gott* ~ given out of the goodness of one's heart, given gladly; *med sorg i* ~*t* with grief in one's heart; *lätt om* ~*t* light of heart; *ha ngt på* ~*t* have s.th. on one's mind; *ha* ~*t på rätta stället* have one's heart in the right place; *lätta sitt* ~ unburden o.s., get s.th. off one's chest; *rannsaka* ~*n och njurar* search the hearts and reins; *säga sitt* ~*s mening* speak one's mind; *tala fritt ur* ~*t* speak straight from the heart; *trycka ngn till sitt* ~ clasp s.b. to one's bosom; *det ligger mig varmt om* ~*t* it is very close to my heart; *det skär mig i* ~*t* it cuts me to the quick;

en sten föll från mitt ~ a weight was lifted off my mind; *hon hade inte* ~ [*till*] *att göra det* she hadn't [got] the heart for (to do) it; *jag känner mig varm om* ~*t* my heart is warmed **2** ~*ns gärna a*) with all my (*etc.*) heart, *b*) (*för all del*) by all means; *av* ~*ns lust* to one's heart's content **3** *kära* ~*n*[*d*]*es!* dear me!, well, I never!

hjärt|anskär sweetheart, truelove **-attack** heart attack **-besvär** heart trouble; cardiac complaint **-blad** *bot.* cotyledon; *vard.* seed leaf **-block** heart block **-död I** *s2* cardiac death **II** *a5* cardiac dead

hjärte|angelägenhet affair of the heart **-god** very kind-hearted **-krossare** [-å-] heartbreaker **-lag** *s7* disposition

hjärter ['järt-] *s9, kortsp., koll.* hearts (*pl*); *en* ~ a heart; ~ *ess* ace of hearts; ~ *fem* five of hearts; ~ *knekt* the jack of hearts

hjärte|rot *ända in i* ~*en* to the very marrow **-sak** *det är en* ~ *för honom* he has it very much at heart **-sorg** poignant (deep) grief; *dö av* ~ die of a broken heart **-vän** bosom (best) friend

hjärt|fel [organic] heart disease **-flimmer** fibrillation **-formig** [-å-] *a5* heart-shaped **-förlamning** heart failure **-förmak** auricle **-förstoring** cardiac enlargement, hypertrophy of the heart **-infarkt** myocardial infarction (*AE.* infarct) **-innerlig** [*mest* -'inn-] most fervent **-kammare** ventricle **-klaff** cardiac valve **-klappning** palpitation [of the heart]

hjärtlig [ˣjärr-] *a1* hearty; (*svagare*) cordial; (*friare*) kind, warm; ~*a hälsningar* kind regards; ~*a lyckönskningar* sincere congratulations, good wishes; ~*t tack* hearty thanks **-het** heartiness, cordiality

hjärt-lungmaskin heart-lung machine

hjärtlös heartless; unsympathetic, unfeeling **-het** heartlessness

hjärt|massage heart massage **-medicin** heart drug; (*stimulerande*) cardiac stimulating agent; (*lugnande*) cardiac depressant (depressive agent) **-mur** *byggn.* main partition-wall **-muskel** heart muscle **-nupen** *a3* sentimental; (*om pers. äv.*) tenderhearted **-punkt** *bildl.* centre, heart; core **-sjukdom** heart disease **-skärande** heart-rending; heartbreaking **-slag 1** (*pulsslag*) heartbeat, heart-throb **2** *se hjärtförlamning* **3** (*innanmäte*) pluck **-slitande** *a4, se -skärande* **-specialist** cardiologist **-stock** *sjö.* rudder|post, -stock **-svikt** heart failure **-säck** heart sac **-trakten** *i* ~ in the region of the heart **-transplantation** heart transplant **-verksamhet** action of the heart **-åkomma** heart trouble **-ängslig** nervous and frightened (*över* at)

hjäss|a [ˣjässa] *s1* crown; *kal* ~ (*äv.*) bald pate; *från* ~*n till fotabjället* from top to toe (head to foot); *cap-a-pie* **-ben** parietal bone

H.K.H. (*förk. för Hans* [*el. Hennes*] *Kunglig Höghet*) H.R.H.

hm hem!, h'm!

h-moll B minor

1 ho *interr. pron., åld.* who

2 ho *s2* trough

hobby ['håbbi *el.* -y] *s3* hobby **-arbete** hobby work **-rum** home workshop, hobby room **-verksamhet** hobby activity

---

hockey ['håkki *el.* -y] *s2* (*is*-) ice hockey; (*land*-) field hockey **-klubba** hockey stick

hoj [håjj] *s2, vard.* bike

hojta [ˣhåjj-] shout, yell (*till* to, at)

hokuspokus ['hoː-, -'poː-] **I** *n* hocus-pocus **II** *interj* hey presto!

holdingbolag holding company

holis|m holism **-tisk** *a5* holistic

holk [-å-] *s2* **1** (*fågel*-) birdhouse **2** *bot.* epicalyx, calycle **-fjäll** *bot.* bract

Holland ['håll-] *n* Holland

hollandaise [hållan'däːs] *s5*, **-sås** hollandaise sauce

holländare [ˣhåll-] Dutchman; *-arna* (*koll.*) the Dutch

holländ|sk [ˣhåll-] *a5* Dutch **-ska 1** (*språk*) Dutch **2** (*kvinna*) Dutchwoman

holm|e [ˣhåll-] *s2* islet, holm[e] **-gång** *s2, ung.* single combat

holmium ['håll-] *s8* holmium

holo|grafi *s3* holography **-gram** [-'amm] *s7* hologram **-kaust** ['hållo-] *s3* holocaust

homeo|pat hom[o]eopath[ist] **-pati** *s3* hom[o]eopathy **-patisk** [-'pa:-] *a5* hom[o]eopathic

homerisk [-'meː-] *a5* Homeric, Homerian

Homeros [-'meː-] Homer

hominid *s3* hominid

homofil *s3* homosexual

homogen [-'jeːn] *a1* homogen[e]ous **-isera** homogenize **-itet** homogeneity

homonym I *a1* homonymic, homonymous **II** *s3* homonym

homosexu|alitet homosexuality **-ell** homosexual; *en* ~ a homosexual

hon [honn] (*om pers.*) she; (*om djur, sak*) it, *ibl.* she; ~ *som sitter där borta är* the woman sitting over there is

hon|a *s1* female; *jfr björnhona etc.* **-blomma** female flower **-djur** female animal

hondur|en *s3*, **-ansk** [-'aːnsk] *a5* Honduran

Honduras [-'duː-] *n* Honduras

hon|katt she-cat **-kön** female sex **-lig** *a5* female

honnett *a1, åld.* honest, fair, straightforward

honnör 1 (*hälsning*) salute (*äv. göra honnör* [*för*]); (*hedersbevisning*) honours (*pl*) **2** (*erkännande*) honour **3** *kortsp.* honour

honnörs|bord table of honour **-ord** prestige word

honom [ˣhånnåm, *äv.* ˣhoː-] *pron* (*objektsform av han*) (*om pers.*) him; (*om djur*) it, *ibl.* him; (*om sak*) it

honorar *s7* fee, remuneration; (*författares äv.*) royalty

honor|atiores [-atsiˣåːres] *pl, stadens* ~ the notabilities of the town **-era** (*betala*) remunerate; (*skuld*) settle, pay off; ~ *en växel* take up (honour, pay) a bill **-är** *a1* honorary

honung [ˣhåː-] *s2* honey

honungs|bi honeybee, hive bee **-kaka** honeycomb **-len** honeyed, honied (*röst* voice) **-slungare** honey extractor

1 hop *adv, se ihop*

2 hop *s2* **1** (*hög*) heap (*med* of); (*uppstaplad*) pile (*med* of) **2** (*av människor*) crowd, multitude; *höja sig över* ~*en* rise above the common herd **3** (*mängd*) lot; heap, multitude

hopa heap (pile) up; (*friare o. bildl.*) accumulate; ~ *sig a*) (*om levande varelser*) crowd together, *b*) (*om saker*) accumulate, (*om snö*) drift
hop|biten *a5*, *med -bitna läppar* with compressed lips **-diktad** *a5* made-up, concocted **-fantisera** compose out of one's own imagination **-foga** join; (*med fog*) joint; *snick. äv.* splice **-fällbar** folding; collapsible, collapsable **-fälld** *a5* shut-up **-gyttra** conglomerate, cluster together **-klibbad** *a5*, stuck together **-klämd** *a5* squeezed together **-knycklad** *a5* crumpled up **-knäppt** *a4* buttoned up; (*om händer*) folded, clasped **-kok** hotchpotch **-kommen** [-å-] *a5, bra* ~ (*om bok o.d.*) well put together (composed) **-krupen** *a5*, **-kurad** *a5* hunched up; *sitta* ~ sit crouching (crouched up, huddled up) **-lagd** *a5* folded [up] **-lappad** *a5* pieced together, patched [up]

1 hopp [-å-] *s7* (*förhoppning*) hope (*om* of); *ha* (*hysa*) ~ *om* have (entertain) hopes of (*att kunna being able to*); *ha gott* ~ (*absol.*) be of good hope; *låta* ~*et fara* abandon hope; *sätta sitt* ~ *till* pin one's faith on; *uppge* ~*et* give up hope; *i* ~ *om att snart få höra från dig* hoping to hear from you soon; *det är föga* ~ *om hans tillfrisknande* there is little hope of his recovery

2 hopp [-å-] *s7* (*språng*) jump (*äv. bildl.*); (*djärvt*) leap; (*elastiskt*) spring; (*skutt*) bound; (*lekfullt*) skip; (*fågels, bolls etc.*) hop; (*sim-*) dive; (*stav-, gymnastik-*) vault

hoppa [-å-] jump; leap; spring; bound; skip; hop; dive; vault; *se 2 hopp*; ~ *med fallskärm* make a parachute jump (descent), bale (bail) out; ~ *och skutta* hop about, caper; ~ *av* jump off (out [of]), *polit.* seek (ask for) political asylum; defect; ~ *på a*) (*ta sig upp på*) jump on (on to, in, into), *b*) (*inlåta sig på*) seize upon, grasp at; ~ *till* give a start (jump); ~ *över* (*eg.*) jump over, *bildl.* skip (*några rader* a few lines)

hoppas [-å-] *dep* hope (*på* for); ~ *på ngn* be hoping in (pin hopes on) s.b.; *jag* ~ *det* I hope so; *det skall vi väl* ~ let us hope so; *bättre än man hade hoppats* better than expected

hoppbacke ski jump
hoppetossa [ˣhåppetåssa] *s1* flibbertigibbet
hopp|full hopeful; confident **-fullhet** hopefulness **-ingivande** [-j-] *a4* hopeful, promising
hoppjerk|a [-å-] *s1* rolling stone; **-or** (*äv.*) migratory workers
hoppla [ˈhåpp-] houp la!
hopplock [ˣhoꞏp-plåck] *s7* miscellany
hopplös hopeless; (*om pers. äv.*) devoid of hope; (*desperat*) desperate; *ett* ~*t företag* (*äv.*) a forlorn hope **-het** hopelessness
hopp|ning [-å-] jump[ing] **-rep** skipping-rope; *AE.* jump rope; *hoppa* ~ skip **-rätvinge** orthopteran, orthopteron
hoppsan [ˈhåpp-] upsy-daisy!, upsadaisy!, whoops!
hopp|ställning *sport.* take-off **-torn** *sport.* diving-tower **-tävling** jumping (diving) competition
hop|rafsad *a5* scrambled together **-rullad** *a5* rolled up; (*om rep, orm*) coiled up **-sjunken** *a5* shrunken **-skrynklad** *a5* creased, crumpled
hopslag|en *a5* **1** (*om bord e.d.*) folded-up; (*om bok*) shut-up, closed; (*om paraply*) rolled up **2**

(*hopspikad*) nailed (fastened) up together **3** (*sammanhålld*) poured together **4** *bildl.* combined, united; (*om bolag e.d.*) amalgamated **-ning** folding up etc.; (*av bolag e.d.*) amalgamation, fusion; (*av skolklasser*) uniting
hop|slingrad *a5* intertwined **-snörd** [-ö:-] *a5* **1** laced up **2** (*friare o. bildl.*) compressed, constricted **-sparad** *a5*, ~*e slantar* savings **-sättning** putting together; (*av maskin*) assembly, mounting **-tagning** [-a:-] (*vid stickning*) decreasing, narrowing **-trängd** *a5* crowded (packed, cramped) together; (*om handstil*) cramped **-vikbar** foldable, collapsible, collapsable **-vikt** [-i:-] *a4* folded up
hor *s7* adultery; (*otukt*) fornication; *bedriva* ~ commit adultery
hor|a *s1 o. v1* whore **-bock** *se horkarl*
hord [-å:-] *s3* horde
horhus whorehouse
horisont [-ånt] *s3* horizon; skyline; *från vår* ~ (*bildl.*) from our viewpoint; *vid* ~*en* on the horizon; *avteckna sig mot* ~*en* stand out against the horizon; *det går över min* ~ it is beyond me
horisontal *a5* horizontal **-plan** horizontal plane
horisontell *a5*, *se horisontal*
horkarl [ˣhoꞏrka:r] fornicator; whore|master, -monger
hormon [-å:n *el.* -ˈoꞏn] *s7, s4* hormone **-avsöndring** hormone secretion **-behandling** hormone treatment **-ell** *a5* hormonal
horn [-å:-] *s7* horn (*äv. ämne o. mus.*); (*på hjortdjur*) antler; (*jakt-*) [hunting] horn; (*signal-*) bugle; (*bil-*) car horn, hooter; *blåsa* (*stöta*) *i* ~ sound the bugle; *stånga* ~*en av sig* (*bildl.*) sow one's wild oats; *ha ett* ~ *i sidan till ngn* bear s.b. a grudge; *ta tjuren vid* ~*en* (*äv. bildl.*) take the bull by the horns **-artad** [-a:r] *a5* hornlike, horny **-blåsare** horn|player, -blower; *mil. äv.* bugler **-blände** *s6, miner.* hornblende **-boskap** horned cattle **-bågad** *a5*, ~*e glasögon* horn-rimmed spectacles **-hinna** cornea **-musik** horn (brass) music **-orkester** brass band **-stöt** *mus.* bugle blast **-uggla** long-eared owl **-ämne** horny substance, keratin
horoskop [-ˈå:p] *s7, ställa ngns* ~ cast a p.'s horoscope
horribel [-ˈri:-] *a2* horrible
horsgök [ˣhårs-] *zool.*, *se enkelbeckasin*
horst [-å-] *s2, geol.* horst
hortensia [-ˈtensia] *s1* hydrangea
hort|ikultur [-å-] horticulture **-onom** horticulturist
horunge 1 bastard **2** *boktr.* widow
hos 1 (*i ngns hus, hem o.d.*) at; with; ~ *juveleraren* at the jeweller's [shop]; *hemma* ~ *oss* in our home; *inne* ~ *mig* in my room; *bo* ~ *sin syster* live at one's sister's [place *etc.*] (with one's sister); *göra ett besök* ~ pay a visit to, call on **2** (*bredvid, intill*) by, beside, next to; *kom och sätt dig* ~ *mig* come and sit down by (beside) me **3** *adjutant* ~ *kungen* A.D.C. to the king; *anställd* ~ employed by; *arbeta* ~ *ngn* work for s.b.; *göra en beställning* ~ place an order with, order from; *han var* ~ *mig när he was with me when*; *jag har varit* ~ *henne med blommorna* I have been to her with the flowers; *jag har varit* ~ *tandläkaren* I have been to the

dentist **4** (*i uttr. som anger egenskap, utseende, känsla o.d.*) in; about; with; *en ovana ~ ngn* a bad habit with s.b.; *ett vackert drag ~ ngn* a fine trait in s.b.; *det finns ngt ~ dem som* there is s.th. about them that; *det finns ~ Shakespeare* it is in Shakespeare; *felet ligger ~ mig* the fault lies with me, the mistake is mine

hosianna [-'anna] *interj o.* s6 hosanna

hospital s7 [lunatic] asylum

host|a I s1 cough; *ha ~* have a cough **II** v1 cough; (*om motor*) splutter; *~ blod* cough up blood; *~ till* give a cough (hem) **-attack** attack of coughing

hostia ['håss-] s1 Host

host|ig a5 troubled with a cough; (*om motor*) spluttering **-medicin** cough mixture **-ning** cough; (-*ande*) coughing

hot s7 threat[s *pl*] (*mot* against; *om* of); (-*ande fara*) menace (*mot* to), threatening; [*ett*] *tomt ~* empty threats (*pl*)

hot|a threaten; (*i högre stil*) menace; (*vara överhängande äv.*) be impending, impend; *~ ngn till livet* threaten a p.'s life **-ande** a4 threatening *etc.*; (*överhängande äv.*) impending, imminent

hotchpotchsoppa ['håttʃpåttʃ-] hotchpotch [soup]

hotell [hå- *el.* hɔ-] s7 hotel; *H~ Baltic* the Baltic Hotel; *ta in på ~* put up at a hotel **-betjäning** hotel staff (attendants *pl*) **-gäst** resident **-reception** hotel reception desk **-rum** hotel room; *beställa ~* make a reservation (book a room) at a hotel **-räkning** hotel bill **-rörelse** hotel business **-ägare** hotel proprietor, hotelier

hotelse threat (*mot* against); menace (*mot* to); *sätta sin ~ i verket* carry out a (one's) threat; *utslunga ~r mot* utter threats against **-brev** threatening letter

hotfull menacing

hottentott [ˣhått- *el.* -'tått] s3 Hottentot

1 hov [-ɔ:-] s2 (*på djur*) hoof; *försedd med ~ar* (*äv.*) hoofed

2 hov [-å:-] s7 (*regerande furstes*) court; *vid ~et* at court; *vid ~et i* at the court in (of); *hålla ett lysande ~* keep court with great splendour

hovdam lady-in-waiting (*hos* to)

hovdjur [ˣhɔ:v-] *~en* the hoofed animals

hovdräkt [ˣhå:v-] court dress

hovera [-ɔ-] *rfl* swagger, strut about

hov|folk [ˣhå:v-] courtiers (*pl*) **-fotograf** photographer to H.M. the King (*etc.*) **-fröken** maid of honour **-funktionär** court functionary (official) **-kapell** *mus.* royal orchestra; *Kungl. ~et* the Royal Opera House Orchestra **-kapellmästare** *förste ~* master of the king's (*etc.*) music **-lakej** royal footman **-leverantör** purveyor to H.M. the King (*etc.*) **-man** courtier **-marskalk** marshal of the court; *i Storbritannien ung.* Lord Chamberlain [of the Household] **-mästare 1** (*på restaurang*) head waiter **2** (*i privathus*) butler **-narr** court jester **-nigning** reverence, court curts[e]y **-predikant** court chaplain

hovra [ˣhå:v- *el.* -ɔ:-] hover

hovrätt [ˣhå:v-] court of appeal

hovrätts|assessor associate judge of appeal **-fiskal** reporting clerk [to a (the) court of appeal] **-lagman** head of division [to a (the) court

of appeal] **-notarie** law clerk [of a (the) court of appeal] **-president** president [of a (the) court of appeal]; *i Storbritannien* Lord Chief Justice **-råd** judge of appeal

hovsam [ˣhɔ:v-] a1 moderate; *i ~ma ordalag* in measured terms

hovslagare [ˣhå:v-] farrier, blacksmith

hov|sorg [ˣhå:v-] court mourning **-stall** *~et* the royal stables (*pl*) **-stallmästare** crown equerry **-stat** *~en* the royal household **-sångare, -sångerska** court singer

hovtång [ˣhɔ:v-] [large (heavy)] pincers (*pl*); *en ~* a pair of [large (heavy)] pincers

hu ugh!, whew!; *~, så du skrämde mig!* oh, what a shock you gave me!

huckle s6 kerchief

hud s2 skin; (*av större djur*) hide; *anat.* (*överhud*) cuticle, epidermis; *~ar och skinn* hides and skins; *ge ngn på ~en* give s.b. a good hiding (rating) **-flänga** v2, *äv. bildl.* scourge, horsewhip **-färg 1** (*hudens färg*) colour of the skin; (*hy*) complexion **2** (*köttfärg*) flesh colour **-färgad** a5 flesh-coloured **-kräm** skin cream; face cream, cold cream **-sjukdom** skin disease **-specialist** dermatologist **-veck** fold of the skin **-transplantat** skin graft **-transplantation** skin grafting; *en ~* a skin graft

hugad a5, *~e spekulanter* prospective buyers

hugenott [-ge'nått] s3 Huguenot

hugfäst|a [ˣhu:g-] commemorate; celebrate (*minnet av* the memory of) **-else** *till ~ av* in commemoration of

hugg s7 **1** (*med vapen el. verktyg*) cut; (*vårdslöst*) slash; (*med spetsen av ngt*) stab (*äv. bildl.*); (*träff*) hit; (*slag*) blow, stroke; (*med tänder e.d.*) bite; *~ och slag* violent blows; *med kniven i högsta ~* with one's knife ready to strike; *ge ~ på sig* lay o.s. open to attack (criticism); *rikta ett ~ mot* aim a blow at **2** (*märke efter*) cut; (*häftig smärta*) spasm; twinge; (*håll*) stitch

hugga *högg huggit* **1** (*med vapen el. verktyg*) cut; (*vårdslöst*) slash; (*med spetsen av ngt*) stab; (*fälla*) cut down, fell; (*skog, sten*) hew; (*ved*) chop; (*om bildhuggare*) carve; *~ i sten* (*bildl.*) go wide of the mark; *det kan inte vara hugget som stucket* it doesn't make much difference **2** (*om djur*) (*med tänder*) bite, (*med klor e.d.*) grab, clutch, (*om orm*) sting **3** *bildl.* (*gripa*) seize (catch) [hold of] **4** (*med betonad partikel*) *~ för sig* help o.s. (*av* to), grab; *~ i* (*gripa sig an*) set to; *hugg i och dra!* pull away! (*med* at); *~ in på* å) *mil.* charge, b) (*mat e.d.*) fall to; *~ tag i* a) (*om pers.*) seize (catch) hold of, b) (*om sak*) catch [in]; *~ till* a) (*ge hugg*) strike, deal a blow, b) (*svara på måfå*) hazard, make a guess, c) (*ta betalt*) ask an exorbitant price

huggare 1 *pers., se skogs-, stenhuggare etc.* **2** (*vapen*) cutlass; *en ~ till karl* (*vard.*) a topper (corker, humdinger)

hugg|it *sup. av hugga* **-järn** chisel **-krok** gaff **-kubb[e]** chopping-block **-orm** adder; viper (*äv. bildl.*) **-sexa** grab-and-scramble meal **-tand** (*bete*) tusk; (*hos orm, rovdjur*) fang **-vapen** cutting-weapon **-värja** rapier

hugn|a [ˣhuŋna] favour; gladden **-ad** s3, *till ~ för* to the comfort of **-esam** a1 comforting

hug|skott [-u:-] passing fancy; (*nyck*) whim, caprice **-stor** (*om pers.*) magnanimous; (*om sak*) sublime **-svala** *vl* comfort; solace, soothe **-svalelse** comfort; solace; consolation

huj [hujj] *oböjligt s o. interj, i ett* ~ in a flash; ~, *vad det gick!* whew (oh), that was fast!

huk *oböjligt s, sitta på* ~ squat, sit on one's heels huka *rfl* crouch [down]

huld *al* (*ljuv*) fair; (*välvillig*) benignant, kindly; (*bevågen*) propitious (*mot* towards, to); (*nådig*) gracious; *om lyckan är mig* ~ if fortune smiles on me

huldra *sl* lady of the woods

hull *s7* flesh; *med* ~ *och hår* completely, bodily, (*svälja ngt* swallow s.th.) whole; *lägga på ~et* put on weight

huller om buller ['hull-, 'bull-] pell-mell, higgledy-piggledy

hulling barb; (*på harpun o.d.*) fluke

hum [humm] *oböjligt s, n el. r, ha litet* ~ *om* have some idea (notion) of

hum|an *al* (*människovänlig*) humane; (*friare*) kind, fair, considerate; ~*a priser* reasonable prices **-biologi** human biology

humaniora [-ˣå:ra] *oböjligt s, pl* [the] humanities, the arts

human|isera humanize **-ism** humanism **-ist** humanist; arts student (*etc.*) **-istisk** [-'ist-] *a5* humanistic; humane; ~ *fakultet* faculty of arts; ~*a vetenskaper* [the] humanities, the arts **-itet** humanity **-itär** humanitarian

humbug ['hummbugg] *s2* humbug; fraud (*äv. pers.*)

humla *sl* bumblebee

humle *s9, s7* (*planta*) hop; (*som handelsvara*) hops (*pl*) **-ranka** hopbine, hopbind **-stör** hoppole; *lång som en* ~ lanky as a beanpole

hummer ['humm-] *s2* lobster **-tina** lobster pot (trap)

humor ['hu:-] *s9* humour **-esk** *s3* humorous story (sketch) **-ist** humorist **-istisk** [-'ist-] *a5* humorous **-lös** devoid of humour

humus ['hu:-] *s2* humus **-syra** humic acid

humör *s7* temperament; (*lynne*) temper; (*sinnesstämning*) humour, mood, spirits (*pl*); *på dåligt* ~ in a bad humour (temper, mood), out of spirits; *på gott* ~ in a good temper (humour), in good spirits; *fatta* ~ flare up, take offence (*över* at); *hålla ~et uppe* keep up one's spirits; *tappa ~et* lose one's temper; *visa* ~ show bad temper; *är du på det ~et?* is that the mood you are in?

hund *s2* dog; (*jakt- äv.*) hound; *röda* ~ German measles; *frysa som en* ~ be chilled to the marrow; *leva som* ~ *och katt* lead a cat-and-dog life; *slita* ~ work like a horse, rough it; *inte döma ~en efter håren* not judge the dog by its coat; *här ligger en* ~ *begraven* I smell a rat here; *lära gamla ~ar sitta* teach an old dog new tricks **-aktig** *al* doglike; canine **-ben** dogbone **-biten** *a5* dog-bitten **-göra** [a piece of] drudgery **-halsband** dog collar **-huvud** *bära ~et för* be made the scapegoat for **-kapplöpning** greyhound racing **-kex** dog biscuit **-koja** kennel; *AE. äv.* doghouse **-koppel** leash, lead **-käx** *s3*, **-käxa** *sl*, *se -loka* **-liv** *leva ett* ~ lead a dog's life **-loka** *sl, bot.* cow parsley, keck **-lort** dog's dung **-mat** dog food

hundra ['hund-] hundred; *ett* ~ a (*betonat* one) hundred; *många* ~ many hundreds of; ~ *tusen* (one) hundred thousand

hundracka *sl* cur, mongrel

hundra|de I *s6* hundred; *i* ~*n* in hundreds II (*ordningstal*) hundredth **-[de]del** one hundredth part **-faldig** *a5*, **-falt** *adv* hundredfold **-kronesedel, -kronorssedel** hundred-kronor note **-lapp** *se -kronesedel* **-procentig** *a5* one-hundred per cent

hundras breed of dog

hundra|tal *tiotal och* ~ tens and hundreds; *ett* ~ a hundred or so, about a (some) hundred; *i* ~ in hundreds; *på ~et e.Kr.* in the second century A.D. **-tals** [-a:-] hundreds (*böcker of* books) **-tusentals** hundreds of thousands **-årig** *a5* a (one) hundred years old; one-hundred-year-old **-åring** centenarian

hundraårs|dag centennial day, centenary; hundredth anniversary **-jubileum, -minne** centenary

hundsfott [ˣhundsvått] *avdelat hunds-fott, sjö.* becket **-era** *avdelat hunds-fottera* bully

hund|skall barking of dogs (a dog); *jakt.* cry of hounds; *ett* ~ a dog bark **-skatt** dog licence **-skattemärke** dog-licence plate **-släde** dog sledge **-släkten** the canine genus **-spann** dog team **-utställning** dog show **-vakt** *sjö.* middle watch **-valp** pup[py] **-väder** vile (dirty) weather **-vän** dog lover (fancier) **-år** *pl* years of struggle (of hard life) **-ägare** dog owner **-öra** dog['s]-ear (*äv. bildl.*)

hunger ['huŋ-] *s2* hunger (*efter* for); (*svält*) starvation; *dö av* ~ die of hunger (starvation), starve to death; *lida ~ns kval* suffer from [the pangs of] hunger; *vara nära att dö av* ~ be [on the point of] starving; ~*n är den bästa kryddan* hunger is the best sauce

hungersnöd famine

hunger|strejk, -strejka hunger strike

hungr|a [ˣhuŋ-] be hungry (starving); *bildl.* hunger (*efter* for); ~ *ihjäl* starve to death **-ig** *al* hungry; (*svulten*) starving; ~ *som en varg* (*äv.*) ravenously hungry

hunner ['hunn-] Hun; ~*na* the Huns

hunnit *sup. av* hinna

hunsa bully; browbeat

hur 1 (*frågande*) how; what; ~ *sa?* what did you say?, I beg your pardon?; ~ *så?* why?; ~ *blir det med...?* (*äv.*) what about...?; ~ *mår du?* how are you?; ~ *menar du?* what do you mean?; ~ *ser han ut?* what does he look like? 2 *eller* ~? (*inte sant*) isn't that so?, don't you think?, am I not right?; *du tycker inte om det, eller* ~? you don't like it, do you?; *du kan simma, eller* ~? you can swim, can't you? 3 ~...*än* however; ~ *hon än gör* whatever she may do; ~ *mycket jag än arbetade* however [much] I worked, work as I might; ~ *trött han än är* however tired (tired as) he may be; ~ *det nu kom sig* whatever happened; ~ *det nu var* somehow or other; ~ *gärna jag än ville* however much I should like to 4 ~ *som helst, se helst*

hurdan ['hu:r-, -ˣda:n, -'dann] *a5*, ~ *är han som lärare?* what kind (sort) of a teacher is he?; ~*t vädret än blir* whatever (no matter what) the weather may be

hurra I [-'ra:] *interj* hurrah! **II** [ˣhurra] *s6, s7 o. v1* hurrah; ~ *för ngn* cheer s.b., give s.b. a cheer; *det är ingenting att* ~ *för* it is nothing to write home about **-rop** [ˣhurra-] cheer

hurr|il *s2,* **-ing** *s2* box [of the ear]

hurt|bulle *vard.* hearty **-frisk** hearty

hurtig *a1 (livlig)* brisk, keen; *(käck)* dashing; *(frimodig)* frank; *(rapp)* smart; *(spänstig)* alert **-het** briskness *etc.*; dash

hurts *s2* [drawer] pedestal

huru *se hur* **-dan** *se hurdan* **-ledes** how, in what way (manner) that **-vida** [-ˣvi:da] whether

hus *s7* house; *(byggnad)* building, block; *(familj)* house, family; ~ *och hem* house and home; *en vän i ~et* a friend of the family; *frun i ~et* the lady of the house; *habsburgska ~et* the House of Hapsburg; *föra stort* ~ keep [up] a large establishment; *gå man ur ~e* turn out to a man; *göra rent* ~ make a clean sweep; *spela för fullt* ~ play to a full house; *allt vad ~et förmår* all I (we) can offer you; *var har ni hållit* ~? where have you been?

hus|a *s1* housemaid; *(som passar upp vid bordet)* parlourmaid **-aga** domestic chastisement **-apotek** family medicine chest

husar *s3* hussar **-regemente** hussar regiment

hus|arrest house arrest **-behov** *till* ~ for household use; *kunna ngt till* ~ know s.th. just passably, have a rough knowledge of s.th. **-bil** caravanette, dormobile; *AE.* camper, winnebago, mobile home **-bock** *zool.* old house borer **-bonde** master; *~ns röst* his master's voice **-bondfolk** master and mistress **-bygge** house under construction **-djur** houseboat **-djur** domestic animal; *~en (på lantgård)* the livestock *(sg)* **-djursavel** livestock breeding

husera *(hålla till)* haunt; *(härja)* ravage, make havoc; *(fara fram)* carry on; *(fara vilt fram)* run riot; ~ *fritt* run riot

hus|esyn *förrätta* ~ *i* carry out the prescribed inspection of; *gå* ~ *i* make a tour of inspection of **-fader** father (head) of a (the) family **-fluga** housefly **-frid** domestic peace **-fru** mistress of a (the) household; *(på hotell)* [head] housekeeper, matron **-föreståndare, -föreståndarinna** housekeeper **-förhör** parish catechetical meeting **-geräd** [-j-] *s7* household utensils *(pl)* **-gud** *~ar* household gods; *bildl.* idol

hushåll *s7* **1** *(arbetet i ett hem)* housekeeping; *ha eget* ~ do one's own housekeeping; *sköta ~et åt ngn* do a p.'s housekeeping for him, keep house for s.b. **2** *(familj)* household, family; *ett fyra personers* ~ a household of four [persons]

hushåll|a *v1* **1** keep house **2** *(vara sparsam)* economize; ~ *med* be economical (careful) with **-erska** housekeeper **-ning 1** housekeeping **2** *(sparsamhet)* economizing; economy **3** *(förvaltning)* economic administration (management) **-ningssällskap** [county] agricultural society

hushålls|arbete housework **-göromål** *pl* household (domestic) duties, housework; *(skolämne)* household management, domestic science **-kassa** *se -pengar* **-lärare** domestic science teacher **-maskin** household appliance *(vanl. pl)* **-pengar** housekeeping [money (allowance)] **-rulle** kitchen roll **-skola** domestic science school

hus|katt domestic cat **-knut** corner of a (the) house **-kors** *skämts.* shrew **-kur** household remedy

huslig [ˣhu:s-] *a1* **1** *(familje-)* domestic, household; ~ *ekonomi* household economy; *~t arbete* domestic work, housework **2** *(intresserad av hushåll)* domesticated, house-proud **-het** domesticity

hus|läkare family doctor **-länga** *(rad av hus)* row of houses; *(långsträckt hus)* long low house, wing **-man** crofter **-manskost** homely fare, plain food **-moder** housewife; *(matmor)* mistress of a (the) household; *(på institution)* matron **-modersförening** housewives' association; *(i Storbritannien)* Women's Institute **-mor** *se -moder* **-mus** house mouse **-rannsakan** *se husundersökning* **-rum** accomodation, lodging; *(tak över huvudet)* shelter

husse *s2* master

hussjt *s3* Hussite

hus|svala house martin **-tomte** brownie

hustru *s5* wife **-byte** wife swapping **-misshandel** wife batting **-plågare** *han är en* ~ he is a torment (devil) to his wife

hus|tyrann family tyrant **-undersökning** domiciliary visit, search [of a house] **-vagn** caravan; *AE.* trailer **-vill** homeless **-värd** landlord **-ägare** house owner

hut I *interj,* ~ *människa!* how dare you! **II** *r, lära ngn veta* ~ teach s.b. manners; *vet ~!* none of your insolence!; *han har ingen* ~ *i kroppen* he has no sense of shame (no decency) **huta** ~ *åt ngn* tell s.b. to mind his manners, *(läxa upp)* snub s.b., take s.b. down a peg [or two]

hutch *se hurts*

hutlös shameless *(äv. om pris)*, impudent

hutt *s2* spot, snort[er]

huttel ['hutt-] *s7* shillyshallying **huttla** [ˣhutt-] *(tveka)* shillyshally; *(vara undfallande)* yield *(med* to); *(driva gäck)* trifle; *jag låter inte* ~ *med mig* I am not to be trifled with

huttra shiver *(av* with)

huv *s2* hood; cap; *(skrivmaskins- etc)* cover; *(motor-)* bonnet, *AE.* hood; *(rök-)* cowl; *(te-)* [tea] cosy; *(på reservoarpenna)* cap, top

huva *s1* hood; *('kråka' äv.)* bonnet

huvud *s7, pl äv. -en* head; *(förstånd äv.)* brains *(pl)*, intellect; *efter mitt* ~ my own way; *med ~et före* headfirst; *upp med ~et! (bildl.)* keep your chin up!; *över* ~ *taget* on the whole, *(alls)* at all; *bli ett* ~ *kortare (bildl.)* get one's head blown off; *få ngt i sitt* ~ get s.th. into one's head; *ha ~et fullt av* have one's head full of; *ha ~et på skaft* have a head on one's shoulders, be all there; *ha gott* ~ be clever (brainy); *hålla ~et kallt* keep cool, keep one's head; *köra ~et i väggen (bildl.)* bang one's head against a brick wall; *slå ~et på spiken* hit the nail on the head, strike home; *stiga ngn åt ~et* go to a p.'s head; *ställa allting på* ~ make everything topsy-turvy; *sätta sitt* ~ *i pant på* stake one's life on; *tappa ~et* lose one's head; *vara ~et högre än (bildl.)* be head and shoulders above; *växa ngn över ~et a) eg.* outgrow s.b., *b) bildl.* get beyond a p.'s control; *om vi slår våra kloka ~en ihop* if we put our heads together

huvud- (*i sms., bildl.*) (*förnämst*) principal, main, head, chief; (*ledande*) leading; (*i första hand*) primary **huvud|accent** primary accent (stress) **-ansvar** main responsibility **-bangård** central (main) station, main terminus **-beståndsdel** principal (main) ingredient **-bok** hand. [general] ledger **-bonad** headgear **-bry** s7, *göra sig mycket* ~ puzzle a great deal; *vålla ngn* ~ be a worry (puzzle) to s.b. **-byggnad** main (central) building **-del** main (greater) part, bulk **-drag** main (principal) feature; *~en av engelska historien* the main outlines of English history **-duk** kerchief, headscarf **-däck** main deck **-figur** se -person **-form 1** anat. shape of the head **2** (*-art*) principal (main) form **3** *språkv.* voice **-förhandling** jur. main session, trial, hearing **-förutsättning** first (principal) prerequisite **-gata** main street, thoroughfare **-gavel** headboard [of a bed] **-gärd** bed's head; (*kudde*) pillow **-ingång** main entrance **-innehåll** principal (main) contents (*pl*); *redogöra för ~et i* give a summary of **-intresse** principal (chief, main) interest **-intryck** principal (main) impression **-jägare** head-hunter **-kontor** head (main, central) office **-kudde** pillow **-led** (*väg*) major road **-ledning** (*för gas, vatten*) main [pipe]; *elektr.* main circuit **-lus** head louse **-lös** (*tanklös*) thoughtless; (*dåraktig*) foolish; (*dumdristig*) foolhardy **-man** (*för familj*) head (*för* of); (*uppdragsgivare*) principal, client; (*i sparbank o.d.*) trustee; (*ledare*) leader, head **-motiv** principal motive, main reason **-mål 1** se huvudsyfte **2** (*måltid*) principal meal **-nummer** principal item **-nyckel** master (pass) key **-näring 1** (*föda*) principal nutriment **2** (*yrkesgren*) principal (main, chief) industry **-ord 1** (*nyckelord*) key word **2** *språkv.* headword **-orsak** principal (main, chief) cause **-part** se -del **-person** principal (leading) figure; (*i roman o.d.*) principal (leading) character; protagonist **-post** main (general) post office **-princip** main principle **-punkt** main (principal) point; (*i anklagelse*) [principal] count **-redaktör** editor in chief **-regel** principal (chief) rule **-riktning** general direction **-roll** leading (principal) part **-rubrik** main heading **-räkning** mental arithmetic **-rätt** kokk. main course **-rörelse** movement of the head

huvudsak *~en* the main (principal) thing; *i ~* in the main, on the whole **-lig** al principal, main, chief, primary; (*väsentlig*) essential **-ligen** principally etc.; (*för det mesta*) mostly, for the most part

huvud|sanning primary (cardinal) truth **-sats 1** (*i logiken*) [the] main proposition **2** *språkv.* main clause **-skyddsombud** senior safety delegate **-skål** cranium **-stad** capital; (*stor o. bildl.*) metropolis **-stadsbo** inhabitant of the capital **-stupa** headfirst; (*friare*) headlong; (*brådstörtat*) precipitately **-styrka** mil. main body **-sväl** scalp **-syfte** main purpose (aim) **-synpunkt** main point of view **-sysselsättning** main (principal) occupation **-säte** centre; headquarters (*behandlas äv. som sg*) **-tanke** main (principal) idea **-tema** main theme **-tes** principal thesis **-titel** (*i riksstat*) ung. section (classification) of govern-

ment estimates (budget); *första ~n* the Royal Household and Establishment, (*i Storbritannien*) the Civil List **-ton 1** mus. keynote **2** språkv., se huvudaccent **-tonart** principal key **-uppgift** main task (function) **-verb** main verb **-vikt** lägga *~en vid* lay the main stress upon, attach primary importance to **-villkor** principal (essential) condition **-vittne** chief witness **-väg** trunk road **-värk** headache **-värkstablett** headache tablet **-ämne** chief (principal) subject; *univ.* major subject **-ändamål** main (chief) purpose

hux flux (*med detsamma*) straight away; (*plötsligt*) all of a sudden

hy s3 complexion; skin

hyacint s3, bot. o. miner. hyacinth

hybrid s3 o. al hybrid **-isera** hybridize

hybris ['hy:-] best. form =, äv. -en arrogance

hyckl|a (*ställa sig from*) play the hypocrite (*inför* before); (*förställa sig*) dissemble (*inför* to); (*låtsas*) simulate, feign **-ad** a5 (*låtsad*) mock, sham, pretended, simulated **-ande** a4 hypocritical **-are** hypocrite **-eri** hypocrisy; (*i tal*) cant[ing]

hydda s1 hut, cabin

hydra [ˣhy:-] s1 hydra (äv. bildl.)

hydrat s7, s4, **-isera** v1 hydrate

hydraul|ik s3 fluid mechanics, hydraulics (*pl, behandlas som sg*) **-isk** ['drau-] a5 hydraulic

hydrer|a hydrogenate, hydrogenize **-ing** hydrogenation, hydrogenization

hydrid s3 hydride

hydro|dynamik hydrokinetics, hydrodynamics (*pl, behandlas som sg*) **-dynamisk** [-'na:-] a5 hydrokinetic[al] **-fon** [-'få:n] s3 hydrophone **-for** [-'få:r] s3 pressure tank, air-loaded water storage **-graf** s3 hydrographer **-grafi** s3 hydrography **-grafisk** ['gra:-] a5 hydrographic[al] **-kinon** [-çi'nå:n] s3, s7 hydroquinone, hydroquinol **-kopter** [−'kåpp-] s2 airboat, swamp boat **-log** hydrologist **-logi** s3 hydrology **-logisk** ['lå:-] a5 hydrologic[al]; ~ *cykel* water (hydrologic) cycle **-lys** s3 hydrolysis **-mekanik** hydromechanics (*pl, behandlas som sg*) **-mekanisk** ['ka:-] a5 hydromechanical **-meter** [-'me:-] s2 hydrometer **-metri** s3 hydrometry **-metrisk** [-'me:-] a5 hydrometric[al]; (*pl*) äv. s7 seaplane **-sfär** hydrosphere **-statik** hydrostatics (*pl, behandlas som sg*) **-statisk** ['sta:-] a5 hydrostatic[al] **-teknik** hydrotechnology

hydrox|id s3 hydroxide **-yl** s3 hydroxyl

hyena [-ˣe:na] s1 hy[a]ena (äv. bildl.)

hyende [ˣhy:en-] s6 cushion; *lägga* ~ *under lasten* (*bildl.*) bolster up vice

hyfs r, se hyfsning; *sätta* ~ *på*, se hyfsa

hyfs|a 1 (*äv.* ~ *till*) trim (tidy) up, make tidy; *bildl.* teach manners; *~t uppträdande* proper behaviour; *en ~d ung man* a well-behaved (well-mannered) young man **2** mat. simplify, reduce **-ning** trimming up etc.; (*belevenhet*) good manners (*pl*)

hygge s6 cutting (felling) area

hygglig al **1** (*väluppfostrad*) well-behaved; (*vänlig*) kind, good, vard. decent; (*tilltalande*) nice; *en* ~ *karl* a nice (decent) fellow (chap) **2** (*anständig*) respectable **3** (*skälig*) decent; (*moderat*) fair, reasonable, moderate

hygien [-g-] s3 hygiene; *personlig* ~ personal hy-

giene **-iker** hygienist **-isk** a5 hygienic; sanitary
hygro|graf s3 hygrograph **-meter** [-'me:-] s2
hygrometer **-metrisk** [-'me:-] a5 hygrometric
-skop [-'skå:p] s7 hygroscope **-skopisk** [-'skå:-]
a5 hygroscopic **-stat** s3 humidistat, hygrostat
1 hylla s1 **1** shelf (pl shelves); (möbel) set of
shelves; (bagage-, sko-, tallriks- o.d.) rack; lägga
ngt på ~n (bildl.) put s.th. on the shelf, shelve
s.th. **2** teat., vard. (översta rad) ~n the gods (pl)
2 hylla v1 **1** (svära tro) swear allegiance to; (erkänna) acknowledge **2** (uppvakta, hedra) congratulate; pay (do) homage to; honour **3** (om-
fatta) embrace, favour **4** rfl, ~ sig till ngn attach
o.s. to s.b.
hylle s6, bot. involucre, perianth
hyllning congratulations (pl); homage; (ovation)
ovation; bringa ngn sin ~ pay (do) homage to s.b.
hyllningsdikt complimentary poem
hyll|papper shelf (lining) paper **-remsa** shelf-
edging, shelf-strip **-värmare** hand., vard.
sticker, drug [on the market]
hyls|a s1 case, casing; tekn. socket, sleeve; bot.
shell, hull **-nyckel** box spanner
hymen ['hy:-] r **1** myt. Hymen; knyta ~s band tie
the nuptial knot **2** anat. hymen
hymla vard. (hyckla) pretend; (smussla [med])
try to shuffle away
hymn s3 hymn; (friare) anthem **-diktning** hymn
writing, hymnody
hynda s1 bitch
hyperaktiv [ˣhy:-] hyperactive
hyperbel [-'pärr-] s3 hyperbola **-formig** [-å-] a5
hyperbolic[al]
hyper|bolisk [-'bå:-] a5 hyperbolic[al] **-boré** s3
Hyperborean
hyper|elegant [ˣhy:-] very stylish **-korrekt** me-
ticulously correct **-kritisk** hypercritical **-käns-
lig** hypersensitive **-modern** ultramodern **-ner-
vös** extremely nervous
hyperon [-'å:n] s3 hyperon
hyper|snabb high-velocity; high-speed **-venti-
lation** hyperventilation
hypnos [-'å:s] s3 hypnosis (pl hypnoses)
hypnot|isera hypnotize **-isk** [-'nå:-] a5 hypnotic
-ism hypnotism **-isör** hypnotist
hypofys s3 hypophysis (pl hypophyses), pituitary
gland (body)
hypoidväxel [-poˣi:d-] hypoid gear
hypokond|er [-'kånn-] s3 hypochondriac **-ri** s3
hypochondria **-risk** [-'kånn-] a5 hypochondriac
[al]
hypotek s7 mortgage; encumbrance; (säkerhet)
security
hypoteks|bank, -inrättning, -kassa mort-
gage bank (institution); building society; AE.
building and loan [association] **-lån** mortgage
loan
hypotenusa [-ˣnu:-] s1 hypotenuse
hypote|s s3 hypothesis (pl hypotheses) **-tisk** a5
hypothetic[al]; (tvivelaktig) doubtful
hyra I s1 rent; (för bil, båt e.d.) hire, rental; betala 50 pund i ~ pay a rent of 50 pounds **2** sjö.
(tjänst) berth; (lön) [seaman's] wages (pl); ta ~
ship (på on board, aboard) **II** v2 rent; (bil, båt
e.d.) hire, take on hire; att ~! to let!, AE. for
rent!, (om bil etc.) for hire; ~ av ngn rent from

s.b.; ~ in sig hos ngn take lodgings in a p.'s
house; ~ ut (rum) let, AE. äv. rent, (fastighet äv.)
lease, (bil etc.) hire out, let out on hire; ~ ut i
andra hand (äv.) sublet
hyrbil hire[d] car
hyres|bidrag rent allowance **-fri** bo ~tt live rent-
free **-förmedling** housing rental agency **-gäst**
tenant; (för kortare tid) lodger; AE. äv. roomer
-haj rack-renter **-hus** block of flats; AE. apartment house (building) **-kasern** tenement [build-
ing] **-kontrakt** lease, tenancy agreement; (för
lösöre) hire contract **-kontroll** rent control
-marknad housing market **-nämnd** [regional]
rent tribunal **-reglering** rent control **-värd**
landlord
hyr|kusk [hackney] coachman **-verk** car-hire
service; (för häst o. vagn) livery stable
hysa v3 **1** (bereda rum åt) house (äv. bildl.), accommodate; (pers. äv.) put up, take in; (in-
rymma) contain **2** (nära, bära) entertain, have;
~ betänkligheter have (entertain) misgivings,
hesitate; ~ förhoppningar om entertain (cherish)
hopes for, hope for; ~ förtroende för have confidence in; ~ illvilja mot ngn bear s.b. ill will, have
a grudge against s.b.
hyska s1 eye; ~ och hake hook and eye
hyss s7, ha ngt ~ för sig be up to [some] mischief
hyssj [hyʃ] hush!,shsh! **hyssja** [ˣhyʃa] cry hush
(på, åt to); ~ [på] hush
hysta ung. toss
hysterektomj s3 hysterectomy
hyster|i s3, s4 hysteria; med. äv. hysterics (pl)
-ika [-'te:-] s1 hysterical woman **-iker** [-'te:-] hysterical person, hysteric **-isk** [-'te:-] a5 hysteric[al]
; bli ~ go into hysterics; få ett ~t anfall have a fit
of hysterics
hytt s3, sjö. berth, cabin; (telefon- etc.) booth,
box
1 hytta v3, se höta
2 hytta s1, tekn. smeltery, foundry; (masugn)
blast furnace
hytt|plats sjö. berth **-ventil** porthole
hyvel s2 plane; (-maskin) planer **-bänk** carpenter's bench **-spån** koll. shavings (pl)
hyvl|a [ˣhy:v-] plane; (ost e.d.) slice; bildl. polish
up; ~t virke planed boards (pl); ~ av plane
smooth, smooth off **-ing** planing; (friare) slicing
hå oh!; ~ ~! oho!; ~ ~, ja ja! oh, dear, dear!
håg s3 **1** (sinne) mind; thoughts (pl); glad i ~en
gay at heart, carefree; slå ngt ur ~en dismiss s.th.
from one's mind, give up all idea of s.th.; ta Gud
i ~en trust to Providence (one's lucky star); det
leker honom i ~en his mind is set on it (att göra
on doing) **2** (lust) inclination; (fallenhet) bent,
liking; hans ~ står till he has an inclination towards
håg|ad a5 inclined; disposed; vara ~ att göra ngt
feel like doing s.th. **-komst** s3 remembrance, recollection **-lös** listless; (oföretagsam)
unenterprising; (loj) indolent **-löshet** listlessness; indolence
håkäring s2 Greenland shark
hål s7 hole; (öppning äv.) aperture, mouth;
(lucka) gap; (läcka) leak; (rivet) tear; tandläk.
cavity; nöta (bränna) ~ på wear (burn) a hole
(holes) in; ta ~ på make a hole in, (sticka hål äv.)

pierce, perforate, *med.* lance; *hon har ~ på arm-bågarna* her dress (*etc.*) is out at the elbows; *det har gått ~ på strumpan* there is a hole in the (my *etc.*) stocking
hål|a *s1* cave, cavern; (*vilda djurs o. bildl.*) den; (*rävs, grävlings o.d.*) earth; *anat.* cavity; (*landsorts-*) ward. hole **-fot** arch of the foot **-fotsin-lägg** arch support
hål|ig *a1* full of holes; (*ihålig, äv. bildl.*) hollow; (*pipig*) honeycombed **-ighet** hollow, cavity **-kort** punch[ed] card **-kortsmaskin** punched--card machine
håll *s7* **1** (*tag*) hold, grip; *få ~ på ngn* get a hold (grip) on s.b. **2** (*avstånd*) distance; *på långt ~* at a long distance, (*skjutning*) at a long range; *släkt på långt ~* distantly related; *på nära ~* close at hand, near by (at hand); *sedd på nära ~* seen at close quarters (range) **3** (*riktning*) direction; (*sida*) quarter, side; *från alla ~* [*och kanter*] from all directions (quarters); *från säkert ~* from a reliable quarter (source); *på annat ~* in another quarter, elsewhere; *på sina ~* in places; *åt andra ~et* the other way; *åt vilket ~?* which way?; *åt mitt ~* my way; *de gick åt var sitt ~* they went their separate ways **4** *jakt.* station; stand; (*skott-*) range, [rifle] shot **5** (*häftig smärta*) stitch
hålla *höll hållit* **I 1** (*ha tag i; fasthålla*) hold (*sin hand över* a protecting hand over; *ngn i handen* a p.'s hand; *andan* one's breath); *~ hårt om* hold tight; *~ ngn kär* hold s.b. dear; *~ stånd* hold out, keep one's ground, stand firm **2** (*bibehålla; hålla sig med*) keep (*dörren öppen* the door open; *maten varm* the dinner [*etc.*] hot; *ngt för sig själv* s.th. to o.s.; *hemligt* secret); (*upprätt-*) maintain; *~ ett löfte* keep a promise; *~ i minnet* keep (bear) in mind; *~ värmen* (*om kamin e.d.*) retain its heat; *~ öppet hus* (*två tjänare*) keep open house (two servants); *den håller vad den lovar* it fulfils its promise **3** (*förrätta*) hold (*auktion* an auction; *möte* a meeting) **4** (*debitera*) charge (*höga priser* high prices) **5** (*slå vad om*) bet, lay, wager, stake (*tio mot ett på att* ten to one that) **6** (*anse; hålla för*) consider, regard, look upon [as]; *~ ngt för troligt* think s.th. likely **7** (*rymma*) hold; (*inne-*) contain; *~ måttet* be full measure, come up [the] standard **II 1** (*ej gå sönder*) hold, not break; (*om kläder*) wear, last (*i evighet* for ever); (*om bro, is*) bear; *allt vad tygen håller* at [the] top [of one's] speed, (*springa*) for dear life **2** (*styra sina steg*) keep (*t. höger* to the right); (*sikta på*) aim, hold (*för högt* too high) **3** *~ på sin värdighet* stand on one's dignity; *~ styvt på sin mening* stick to one's opinion; *~ till godo, se godo*; *hon håller på sig* she stands by her virtue **4** (*stanna*) stop **III** (*med betonad partikel*) **1** *~ av a*) (*tycka om*) be fond of, *b*) (*väja*) turn [aside] **2** *~ efter* (*övervaka*) keep a close check (tight hand) on **3** *~ emot* (*ta spjärn*) put one's weight against, (*hindra att falla*) hold (bear) up, (*motarbeta*) resist, set o.s. against it **4** *~ i a*) hold [*vard.* on to], (*stödja*) hold on to, *b*) (*fortfara*) continue, go on, persist **5** *~ igen* (*bildl.*) act as a check **6** *~ igång* keep swinging, live it up **7** *~ ihop* hold (keep, *vard.* stick) together **8** *~ in a*) (*hålla indragen*) hold in, *b*) (*häst*) pull up, rein in **9** *~ med ngn a*) (*vara av samma mening*) agree with s.b., *b*) (*ställa sig på ngns sida*)

support s.b., back s.b. up, side with s.b. **10** *~ om ngn* hold one's arms round s.b. **11** *~ på a*) (*vara sysselsatt*) be busy (at work) (*med ngt* with s.th.), *b*) (*vara nära att*) be on the point of (*kvävas* choking); *vad håller du på med?* what are you doing [now]? **12** *~ till*; *var håller du till?* where are you [to be found]?, *vard.* where do you hang out?; (*om djur*) be found, have its (their) haunts **13** *~ tillbaka* keep back, withhold **14** *~ upp a*) (*hålla upplyft*) hold up, *b*) (*hålla öppen*) hold (keep) open, *c*) *sjö.* (*hålla upp i vinden*) go (sail) close to the wind, *d*) (*göra uppehåll*) [make a] pause (*med* in), stop, cease; *när det håller upp[e]* when it stops raining **15** *~ uppe a*) eg. hold upright, *b*) (*ovan vattenytan*) keep afloat (above water), *c*) *bildl.* keep up (*modet* one's courage) **16** *~ ut a*) hold out, *b*) (*ton*) sustain; *~ ut med* stand, put up with **IV** *rfl* **1** hold o.s. (*beredd* in readiness; *upprätt* upright); keep [o.s.] (*ren* clean; *vaken* awake); keep (*i sängen* in bed; *borta* away; *ur vägen* out of the way); *~ sig* (*i fråga om naturbehov*) hold o.s.; *~ sig väl med ngn* keep in with s.b.; *~ sig framme* keep to the fore; *~ sig hemma* stay at home; *~ sig kvar* keep (stick) (*i* to); *~ sig uppe* keep [o.s.] up, keep afloat **2** (*om pjäs*) retain its place (*på repertoaren* in the repertory) **3** (*om mat e.d.*) keep; *~ sig för skratt* keep o.s. from laughing; *jag kunde inte ~ mig för skratt* I couldn't help laughing **4** *~ sig för god att* consider o.s. above; *~ sig med bil* keep a car; *~ sig med tidning* take (have) a paper; *~ sig till a*) keep (*vard.* stick) to (*fakta* facts), *b*) (*ngn*) hold (*vard.* stick) to
håll|are holder; clip, cramp, hook, buckle **-as** *dep* **1** (*vistas*) be, spend one's time **2** *låt dem ~!* leave them alone!, let them have their way!
hållbar *al* **1** (*som kan hållas*) tenable; *mil. äv.* defensible; (*om argument o.d. äv.*) valid **2** (*varaktig*) durable, lasting; (*färg*) fast; (*om tyg o.d.*) that wears well (will wear); (*om födoämnen*) that keeps well (will keep) **-het 1** tenability; validity **2** durability, lastingness; wearing (keeping) qualities (*pl*)
håll|en *a5* (*skött*) kept; (*avfattad*) written; (*målad*) painted; *hel och ~* the whole [of], all over; *strängt ~* strictly brought up **-fasthet** strength, firmness, tenacity, solidity **-fasthetslära** *s1* mechanics (*pl, behandlas som sg*) of materials **-hake** check; hold (*på* on) **-igång** *s7* jamboree
håll|it *sup. av hålla* **-ning 1** (*kropps-*) carriage; (*uppträdande*) deportment; *militärisk ~* military deportment; *ha bra ~* (*äv.*) hold o.s. well **2** (*beteende*) attitude (*mot* towards); *intaga en avvaktande ~* take up a wait-and-see attitude; *intaga en fast ~* make a firm stand (*mot* against) **3** (*stadga*) firmness, backbone
hållningslös vacillating, vacillant; *vard.* wobbly, flabby; (*utan ryggrad*) spineless; unstable, unprincipled **-het** vacillation; spinelessness; instability
håll|plats stop, halt **-punkt** basis; grounds (*pl*)
hål|remsa paper (punch[ed]) tape **-rum** cavity **-slag** punch; perforator **-slagning** perforation **-slev** perforated ladle **-slå** punch; perforate **-stans** punch[ing machine] **-söm** drawn (drawnthread) work; *sy ~* hemstitch **-tegel** air-brick **-timme** *skol.* free period **-ven** vena cava

(*pl* venae cavae) **-väg** gorge, ravine **-ögd** *a5* hollow-eyed

hån *s7* scorn; (*spe*) derision, mockery; (*i ord äv.*) scoffing, taunting, sneering, jeering; *ett ~ mot* an insult to, a mockery of

hån|a (*förlöjliga*) deride, make fun of; (*föraktfullt*) put to scorn; (*i ord äv.*) scoff (sneer, jeer) at, mock, taunt **-flin** *se* hångrin **-full** scornful; scoffing *etc.*, derisive

hång|el ['håŋ-] *s7* petting; necking **-la** pet; neck **hån|grin** mocking grin **-grina** grin contemptuously **-le** smile scornfully, sneer, jeer (*åt* at) **-leende** scornful smile **-skratt** derisive (scornful, mocking) laugh[ter] **-skratta** laugh derisively (*etc.*), jeer (*åt* at)

hår *s7* hair; *kortklippt ~* short hair; *inte kröka ett ~ på ngns huvud* not touch (injure) a hair on a p.'s head; *skaffa ngn gråa ~* give s.b. grey hairs; *slita sitt ~ i förtvivlan* tear one's hair in despair; *~et reste sig på mitt huvud* my hair stood on end; *det var på ~et att jag* I was within a hair's-breadth (an ace) of (+ *ing-form*)

hår|a *~ av sig* shed (lose) its hair; *~ ner* cover with hair[s *pl*] **-band** fillet **-beklädnad** hairy coat; *zool.* pelage **-bevuxen** hairy **-borste** hairbrush **-borttagningsmedel** depilatory **-botten** capillary matrix; (*friare*) scalp

hård [-å:-] *a1* hard; (*fast äv.*) firm, solid; (*sträng, svår äv.*) severe (*mot* towards, to, on); (*bister*) stern; (*högljudd*) loud; (*om ljud, barsk*) harsh; (*påfrestande*) tough; *hårt klimat* severe climate; *~ konkurrens* keen (fierce) competition; *~ i magen* constipated; *ett hårt slag* a hard (severe, serious) blow; *~a tider a*) (*arbetsamma*) tough times, *b*) (*nödtider*) hard times, times of hardship; *~a villkor* severe conditions, tough terms; *sätta hårt mot hårt* give as good as one gets; *vara ~ mot ngn* be hard on s.b.; *det vore hårt för dem om* it would be hard on them, if

hård|arbetad *a5* hard to work (shape, mould); **-arbetat material** difficult material **-bränd** *a5* **1** (*svår att bränna*) difficult to burn **2** (*hårt bränd*) hard-burnt, hard-baked **-exploatera** exploit mercilessly **-fjällad** *a5, bildl.* hard-boiled; *en ~ brottsling* a hardened criminal; *en ~ fisk* a difficult fish to scale **-flörtad** *a5* standoffish **-frusen** frozen hard; hard-frozen (*is* ice) **-för** *a1* hardy, tough **-förhet** hardiness, toughness **-gummi** hard rubber; vulcanite, ebonite **-handskarna** *ta i med ~* take drastic action (a hard line) **-het** hardness *etc.*; severity **-hetsgrad** degree of hardness **-hjärtad** [-j-] *a5* hardhearted; (*känslolös*) callous **-hudad** *a5, bildl.* thick-skinned **-hänt I** *a1, bildl.* rough, heavy-handed (*mot* with); (*friare*) severe **II** *adv, gå ~ till väga* be rough (*med* with) **-hänthet** heavy-handedness; severity

hård|ing [-å:-] *s2, han är en riktig ~* he's as hard as nails **-knut** tight knot **-kokt** hard-boiled **-körning** *bildl.* tough programme

hård|na [-å:-] harden; become (get, grow) hard; (*bli okänslig*) get callous (hardened) **-nackad** *a5, bildl.* stubborn (*motstånd* resistance); obstinate (*nekande* denial) **-porr** hard-porn

hårdrag|a [ˣhå:r-] *bildl.* strain **-en** *a5, bildl.* forced, strained, far-fetched

hård|rock metal (hard) rock **-smält** *a1* **1** (*om föda*) difficult (hard) to digest; (*friare*) indigestible **2** (*om metall*) refractory **-träna** train hard **-valuta** hard currency (exchange) **-vara** hardware

hår|fin 1 (*om tråd o.d.*) [as] thin (fine) as a hair **2** *bildl.* exceedingly fine, subtle **-frisör** barber, hairdresser **-frisörska** hairdresser **-färg** colour of the hair; (*färgämne*) hair-dye **-fäste** edge of the scalp; *rodna upp till ~t* blush to the roots of one's hair

hår|ig *a1* hairy **-klippning** haircut[ting] **-klyveri** hairsplitting (*äv. ~er*) **-kors** cross wires (*AE.* hairs) **-lock** lock of hair; (*kvinnas äv.*) tress **-nål** hairpin **-nålskurva** hairpin bend **-nät** hairnet **-olja** hair oil **-piska** pigtail; (*stång-*) queue **-pomada** pomade [for the hair] **-resande** *a4* hair-raising, appalling, bloodcurdling, shocking; *en ~ historia* (*äv.*) a story to make one's hair stand on end **-rör** capillary tube **-rörskärl** capillary vessel **-slinga** strand of hair

hårsmån *r* hair's-breadth; (*friare*) trifle, shade **hår|sprej** *s3, s2* hairspray **-spänne** hair slide **-strå** hair **-svall** thick wavy hair **-säck** hair follicle

hårt [-å:-] *adv* hard; (*fast, tätt*) firm[ly], tight[ly]; (*högljutt*) loud; *bildl.* severely; *en ~ prövad man* a severely tried man; *arbeta ~* work hard; *fara ~ fram med* be rough with; *gå ~ åt* handle roughly, be hard on; *ta ngt ~* take s.th. very much to heart; *tala ~ till ngn* speak harshly to s.b.; *det känns ~ att* it feels hard to; *det satt ~ åt* it was a job

hår|test *s2* wisp of hair **-tork[ningsapparat]** hair dryer **-tuss** tuft of hair **-uppsättning** *konkr.* hairstyle, coiffure **-vatten** hair tonic (lotion) **-växt** growth of hair; *missprydande ~* superfluous hair

håv *s2* (*fiskares*) landing net; (*sänk-*) dip-net; (*insekts-*) butterfly net; (*kollekt-*) collection bag; *gå med ~en* (*bildl.*) fish [for compliments]; *~ in* gather (rake) in; *~ upp* land

håvor *pl* gifts, bounties; *jordens ~* the fruits of the earth

1 häck *s2* **1** hedge; *bilda ~* (*om människor*) form a lane **2** *sport.* hurdle; *110 m ~* 110 metres hurdle

2 häck *s2* **1** (*foder-*) hack, rack **2** (*vagns-*) rack **3** (*låda*) crate

3 häck *s2, vard.* bottom, behind, backside

häckl|a I *s1* (*lin*) heckle, heckle **II** *v1* **1** (*lin*) hackle, heckle **2** *bildl.* cavil (carp) at, find fault with **3** *polit.* heckle **-ing** *s* (*av lin*) hackling, heckling **2** *polit.* heckling

häcklöp|are hurdler **-ning** hurdle-racing, hurdle-race, hurdling

häckning breeding

häcknings|plats breeding ground (place) **-tid** breeding season

häda blaspheme (*äv. ~ Gud*)

hädan hence; *skiljas ~* depart this life; *vik ~!* get thee hence!, begone! **-efter** henceforth, from now on **-färd** passing, departure [from this life] **-gången** *a5, se avliden* **-kalla** (*om Gud*) call unto Himself

häd|are blasphemer **-else** blasphemy; *utslunga ~r* hurl blasphemies, blaspheme **-isk** ['hä:-] *a5* blasphemous; (*friare*) profane, impious; (*grovt* *respektlös*) irreverent

häfta I *s1, se häftplåster* **II** *v1* **1** *bokb.* sew, stitch; ~*d bok* sewn (stitched) book, paperback **2** (*hålla fäst*) fasten, fix (*blicken vid* one's gaze on) **3** (*fastna*) stick, adhere (*vid* to) **4** *misstanken* ~*r vid honom* suspicion attaches to him **5** ~ *i skuld till ngn* be in a p.'s debt

häftapparat stapler, stapling machine

häfte *s6* (*tryckalster*) folder, booklet, brochure, pamphlet; (*del av bok*) part, instalment; (*nummer av tidskrift*) number, issue; (*skrivbok*) exercise book

häftig *a1* **1** (*våldsam*) violent; (*obehärskad*) vehement; (*impulsiv*) impetuous (*människa* individual); (*hetsig*) heated (*diskussion* discussion); (*om smärta*) sharp, acute; *ett* ~*t regn* a heavy downpour; ~ *törst* violent thirst; *ett* ~*t uppträde* a scene **2** (*temperamentsfull*) impulsive, hasty; (*hetlevrad*) hot-headed, hot-tempered **3** (*förstärkande*) *vard.* hot, groovy

häftighet violence; vehemence; impetuosity; impulsiveness; hot-headedness *etc.*; irascibility; hot temper

häftigt *adv* violently *etc.*; *vard.* groovy; *andas* ~ breathe quickly, pant; *gräla* ~ quarrel violently; *koka* ~ boil fast; *hjärtat slog* ~ the (my *etc.*) heart beat excitedly

häft|klammer [paper] staple **-ning 1** *bokb.* sewing, stitching **2** (-*ande*) fastening, fixing; sticking, adherence; attaching **-plåster** [sticking] plaster; *A E.* adhesive tape **-stift** drawing pin; *A E.* thumbtack

häger [ˈhäː-] *s2* heron

hägg *s2* bird cherry

hägn [häŋn] *s7, i* ~ *av* under the cover of; *vara i ngns* ~ be under a p.'s protection (aegis) **hägna** [ˣhäŋna] protect, guard

hägr|a [ˣhäːg-] loom (*äv. bildl.*) **-ing** mirage; *bildl. äv.* illusion

häkta I *s1* hook **II** *v1* **1** (*fästa*) hook (*fast* [*vid*] on [to]); ~ *av* unhook; ~ *upp sig* catch, get caught up **2** (*arrestera*) arrest, take into custody; *den* ~*de* the man (*etc.*) under arrest, the prisoner; ~ *ngn i hans frånvaro* issue a warrant for s.b.'s arrest

häkt|e *s6* custody; jail, gaol **-ning** arrest

häktnings|förhandlingar court proceedings for issue of arrest warrant **-order** [arrest] warrant

häl *s2* heel; *följa ngn tätt i* ~*arna* follow close upon a p.'s heels

hälare receiver [of stolen goods], *vard.* fence

hälben heel bone

häleri receiving [of stolen goods]

hälft *s3* half; *äkta* ~ (*vard.*) better half; ~*en av månaden* half the month; ~*en så mycket* half as much; ~*en så stor* half as large (*som* as), half the size (*som* of); *på* ~*en så kort tid* in half the time; *till* ~*en dold* half hidden; *göra ngt till* ~*en* do s.th. by halves

hälftenbruk métayage

hälgångare *zool.* plantigrade

häll *s2* (*klippa*) flat rock; (*sten*) slab [of stone]; (*i öppen spis*) hearthstone

1 hälla *s1* (*under foten*) strap; (*för bälte o.d.*) loop

2 hälla *v2* pour; ~ *i* pour in (*el. upp* out); ~ *i ett glas vin* pour out a glass of wine; ~ *ur* pour out; ~*nde regn* pouring rain

hälle|berg [bed]rock, solid rock **-flundra** halibut

hällkista *arkeol.* cist

hällre *se hellre*

häll|regn pouring rain, downpour **-regna** pour [with rain]

hällristning rock-carving, petroglyph

1 hälsa *s1* health; *vid god* ~ in good health

2 hälsa *v1* **1** (*välkomna, mottaga*) greet; (*högtidligt*) salute; ~ *ngn välkommen* bid s.b. welcome, welcome s.b.; ~ *ngn som sin kung* salute s.b. as one's king **2** (*säga goddag e.d.*) say good morning (good afternoon, good evening, *vard.* hello) [to s.b.], (*ta i hand*) shake hands [with s.b.], (*buga*) bow [to s.b.], (*lyfta på hatten*) raise one's hat [to s.b.]; *mil.* salute (*på ngn* s.b.); ~ *god morgon på ngn* wish s.b. good morning **3** (*upptaga*) receive (*ett förslag med glädje* a proposition with delight) **4** (*framföra hälsning*) send (*ngn* s.b.) one's regards (compliments, respects, love); ~ *hem!* remember me to your people!; ~ *på* (*besöka*) go (come) and see; ~ *henne så hjärtligt!* give her my best regards (*etc.*)!; *låta* ~ send word; *nu kan vi* ~ *hem!* (*vard.*) now it's all up with us!; *jag kan* ~ [*dig*] *från* I can give you news from; *jag skulle* ~ *från fru A. att hon* Mrs. A. asked me to tell you that she; *vem får jag* ~ *ifrån?* what (may I have your) name, please?, (*i telefon*) who is speaking [, please]?

hälsena Achilles tendon, heel string

hälsning 1 greeting; (*högtidlig*) salutation **2** (*översänd e.d.*) compliments (*pl*); (*bud*) message, word; *hjärtliga* ~*ar* kind regards, love (*sg*); *byta om* ~ pass the time of day; *får jag be om min* ~ *till* please remember me to **3** (*bugning*) bow; (*honnör*) salute

hälsnings|anförande address of welcome, opening speech **-ord** *pl* words of welcome (greeting); *se äv. -anförande*

hälso|bringande *a4* healthy, health-giving **-brunn** spa **-farlig** injurious to one's health, unhealthy **-kontroll** [health] checkup **-kost** health food **-kostbutik** health [food] store **-källa** mineral spring **-lära** (*skolämne*) hygiene **-risk** health hazard **-sam** *a1* wholesome; (*om klimat*) salubrious, healthy; *bildl. äv.* salutary; (*välgörande*) beneficial **-skäl** *av* ~ for reasons of health **-tecken** healthy sign, sign of wellbeing **-tillstånd** state of health; *mitt* ~ [the state of] my health **-undersökning** medical examination **-vådlig** (*ohygienisk*) insanitary; (*om klimat*) unhealthy **-vård** (*enskild*) care of one's health; (*allmän*) public health, health service[s *pl*] **-vårdsinspektör** environmental health officer **-vårdsnämnd** public health committee **-vårdsstadga** public health act[s *pl*]

hälta *s1* [form of] lameness

hämm|a (*hejda*) check, curb, arrest, stop; (*blodflöde äv.*) sta[u]nch; (*hindra*) obstruct, block (*trafiken* the traffic); (*ngns rörelser*) impede, hamper; (*fördröja*) retard; *psykiskt* ~*d* inhibited; ~ *ngt i växten* stunt the growth of s.th. **-ande** *a4* checking *etc.*; *verka* ~ *på* have a checking (*etc.*)

effect on, act as a check on, curb, depress
hämn|a avenge, revenge; *slöseri ~r sig* waste
brings woe **-are** avenger, revenger **-as** *dep*
avenge (revenge) o.s., wreak one's vengeance
(*på* on), retaliate (~ *ngn* avenge s.b., take vengeance for s.b.
hämnd *s3* revenge; *högt.* vengeance; retaliation;
~en är ljuv revenge is sweet **-begär** desire for
vengeance
hämnd|eaktion reprisal **-girig** revengeful; vin-
dictive **-girighet** revengefulness; vindictiveness
-lysten *se -girig* **-lystnad** *se hämndbegär*
hämning 1 checking *etc., se hämma* **2** *psykol.* in-
hibition
hämningslös uninhibited; unrestrained
hämpling *zool.* linnet
hämsko drag (*äv. bildl.*)
hämta fetch; (*av-, komma o. hämta*) collect, call
for; (*ta, skaffa sig e.d.*) take, gather; (*ngt abstr.*)
draw, derive; ~ *ngn med bil* fetch s.b. by car; ~
frisk luft get fresh air; ~ *mod* (*styrka*) *från* draw
(derive) courage (strength) from; ~ *nya krafter*
recover (get up) one's strength; *låta* ~ send for;
uppgiften är ~d ur I have the information from;
~ *sig* recover (*efter, från* from); *jag har inte ~t*
mig än (*äv.*) I haven't got over it yet
hämtpris cash-and-carry price
hän away; ~ *mot* towards; *vart skall du ~?* where
are you going?
hända *v2* **1** happen; (*förekomma*) occur, take
place; ~ *sig* happen, chance, come about (to
pass); ~ *vad som* ~ *vill* happen what may; *det kan*
~ *att jag går ut i kväll* I may go out this evening;
det kan nog ~ that may be [so]; *det hände sig inte*
bättre än att jag as ill luck would have it I; *det må*
vara hänt it can't be helped
händelse 1 occurrence; (*betydelsefull*) event,
happening; (*episod*) incident **2** (*tillfällighet*) coincidence; (*slump*) chance; *av en ren* ~ quite by
chance, by a pure coincidence **3** (*fall*) case; *i* ~ *av*
in case of; *i alla* ~*r* at all events; *för den* ~ *att han*
skulle komma in case he comes, in the event of
his coming **-fattig** uneventful **-förlopp** course
of events **-lös** uneventful **-rik** eventful **-utveck-**
ling development of [the] events; trend of affairs
-vis by chance; accidentally; (*apropå*) casually;
du har ~ *inte en penna på dig?* you don't happen
to have a pencil [on you], do you?; *jag träffade*
henne ~ I just happened to meet her, I ran across
her
händig *al* handy, dext[e]rous (*med* with) **-het**
handiness, dexterity
hänföra 1 (*föra...till*) assign, refer, relate (*till*
to); (*räkna*) class[ify] (*till* among), range (*till* under) **2** (*tjusa*) carry away, transport; (*gripa äv.*)
thrill; *låta sig* ~*s av* allow o.s. to be carried away
by **3** *rfl* have reference (*till* to); (*datera sig*) date
back (*från* to)
hänför|ande *a4* ravishing; enchanting **-bar** *a5*
assignable (*till* to); classifiable (*till* as) **-else** rap-
ture; exultation; (*entusiasm*) enthusiasm **-lig** *a5,*
se -bar
hänga *v2* **1** (*uppfästa o.d.*) hang (*äv. avrätta*);
(*tvätt*) hang up; (*låta hänga*) droop; (*t.ex. tak-*
lampa) suspend; ~ *läpp* pout, sulk, be bad-tem-
pered; ~ *näsan över boken* pore over (bury one's

nose in) the book[s *pl*] **2** (*vara upphängd*) hang;
(*hänga fritt*) be suspended; (*om kjol*) hang down
(*bak* at the back); (*sväva*) hover; ~ *ngn i kjolarna*
cling to a p.'s skirt; ~ *ngn om halsen* cling round
a p.'s neck; ~ *och dingla* hang loose, dangle; *stå*
och ~ loiter about; *hela företaget hänger i luften*
the whole enterprise is hanging in the air; *slags-*
målet hänger i luften there's a fight in the air **3**
(*bero*) depend (*på* [up]on); (*komma sig*) be due
(owing) (*på* to) **4** (*med betonad partikel*) ~ *efter*
ngn run after (hang around) s.b.; ~ *fram* (*kläder*)
put out; ~ *för* hang in front; ~ *i* (*vard.*) keep at
it; ~ *ihop*; *jag hänger knappt ihop* I can scarcely
keep body and soul together; *så hänger det ihop*
that's how it is; ~ *med a*) keep up with (*i klassen*
the rest of the class), *b*) (*förstå*) follow, catch on,
c) (*följa med*) go along with; ~ *upp sig på* (*bildl.*)
take exception to **5** ~ *sig* hang o.s.; ~ *sig fast vid*
hang on firm to; ~ *sig på ngn* hang on (attach
o.s.) to s.b.
häng|ande *a4* hanging; (*fritt*) suspended (*i taket*
from the ceiling); *bli* ~ *i* get caught (hooked) on
-are (*krok*) hook; (*pinne*) peg; (*med flera kro-*
kar) rack; (*i kläder*) hanger, loop; (*galge*) [coat]
hanger **-björk** weeping birch **-bro** suspension
bridge
1 hänge [ˣhäŋe] *s6, bot.* catkin
2 hänge [ˣhä:nje:] *rfl* surrender o.s., give o.s. up
(*åt* to); (*ägna sig*) devote (apply) o.s. (*åt* to);
(*hemfalla*) abandon o.s. (give way) (*åt* to); (*för-*
sjunka) fall (*åt* into)
häng|färdig *se* ~ *ut* (*vard.*) look down in (at) the
mouth **-ig** *al* limp; out of sorts
hängiv|a *se* 2 *hänge* **-else** [the] surrendering of
o.s.
hängiven (*tillgiven*) devoted, affectionate **-het**
devotion, attachment (*för* to)
häng|lås padlock; *sätta* ~ *för* padlock **-mapp**
suspended pocket (file) **-matta** hammock **-ning**
hanging **-ränna** gutter
hängs|elstropp brace end **-le** *s6* brace; *ett par*
~n a pair of braces (*AE.* suspenders)
häng|smycke pendant **-torr** drip-dry **-växt**
hanging plant
hän|rycka ravish, enrapture **-ryckning** rapture
[*s pl*]; ecstasy **-ryckt** *a4* rapturous; *vara* ~ be in
raptures
hänseende *a6, i tekniskt* ~ from a technical point
of view; *i vissa ~n* in certain respects; *med* ~ *till*
in consideration of, with respect (regard) to
hän|skjuta refer, submit **-syfta** allude (*på* to);
(*mera förtäckt*) hint (*på* at) **-syftning** allusion
(*på* to); hint (*på* at)
hänsyn *s9* consideration; regard, respect; *av* ~
till out of consideration for; *med* ~ *till* with regard
(respect) to, as regards, (*i betraktande av*) in view
of, considering; *utan* ~ *till* without [any] consideration (regard) to, regardless of, disregarding;
låta alla ~ *fara* throw discretion to the winds; *ta*
~ *till* take into consideration, pay regard to
hänsynsfull considerate (*mot* to, towards) **-het**
considerateness; consideration
hänsynslös regardless of other people[s' feel-
ings]; inconsiderate; (*skoningslös*) ruthless; ~
framfart (*bildl.*) reckless impetuosity; ~ *upprik-*
tighet brutal frankness **-het** inconsiderateness,

lack of consideration; ruthlessness
häntyd|**a** ~ *på a*) (*tyda på*) suggest, indicate, *b*)
se hänsyfta **-ning** allusion (*på* to), hint (*på* at)
hänvis|**a** (*visa till*) direct; (*ge anvisning, referera*)
refer; (*åberopa*) point; *jur.* assign, allot; *vara* ~*d*
till be obliged to resort to, be reduced to (*att* +
ing-form); *vara* ~*d till sig själv* be thrown upon
one's own resources **-ning** reference; direction;
(*i ordbok e.d. äv.*) cross-reference **-ningston**
tel. special information tone
hänvänd|**a** *rfl* apply (*till* to) **-else** application;
(*vädjan*) appeal; *genom* ~ *till* by applying (making application) to
häpen *a3* amazed (*över* at); (*bestört*) startled
(*över* at) **-het** amazement; *i* ~*en över* in his (*etc.*)
amazement at; *i första* ~*en* in the confusion of the
moment
häpn|**a** [ˣhä:p-] be amazed (*inför, vid, över* at);
hör och ~! who'd have thought it! **-ad** *s3, se hä-
penhet*; *slå ngn med* ~ strike s.b. with amazement
-adsväckande *a4* amazing, astounding
1 här *s2* army; *bildl. äv.* host
2 här *adv* here; ~ *borta* (*nere, uppe*) over (down,
up) here; ~ *och där* here and there; ~ *och var* in
places; ~ *i staden* in this town; *så* ~ *års* at this
time of the year; ~ *bor jag* this is where I live; ~
har vi det! here we are!, here it is!; *nu är han* ~
igen! here he is again!
härad *s7, s4, s6, ung.* jurisdictional district; *hist.*
hundred
härads|**domare** *ung.* senior juryman, foreman
of a jury **-hövding** *ung.* circuit judge
härav ['hä:r-] from (by, of, out of) this; hence; ~
följer att [hence] it follows that, (*friare*) this
means that
härbre *s6, ung.* wooden storehouse
härbärg|**e** [-je] *s6* shelter, accommodation, lodg-
ing; (*för husvilla*) [common] lodging house;
(*Frälsningsarméns o.d.*) [night] refuge **-era**
lodge; put up
härd [-ä:-] *s2* **1** (*eldstad*) hearth (*äv. tekn.*); *hem-
mets* ~ the domestic hearth **2** *bildl.* seat, centre,
focus (*för* of); (*näste*) nest, hotbed
härd|**a** [-ä:-] **1** *tekn.* anneal, temper; (*plast*) set,
cure **2** (*göra motståndskraftigare*) harden (*mot*
against); *bildl. äv.* inure (*mot* to) **3** *rfl* harden
o.s.; inure o.s.; (*stålsätta sig*) steel o.s. (*mot*
against) **-are** hardener
härdig *a1* hardy; inured to hardship[s *pl*]; (*mot
frost äv.*) hardened **-het** hardiness
härd|**ning** hardening, tempering; (*av plast*) set-
ting, curing **-plast** thermosetting plastic
härdsmälta (*i kärnreaktor*) core meltdown
här|**efter** (*efter denna händelse, tidpunkt*) after
this; (*från denna tid*) from now (this date), hence;
(*hädanefter*) from now on, from this time forth
-emot against this (it)
härflyta spring, emanate (*ur, från, av* from); (*ha
sitt ursprung*) originate (*ur, från, av* from)
härfågel hoopoe
härförare army leader, general
härförleden [-'le:-] some time ago; (*nyligen*) recently
här|**i** in this (that); (*i detta avseende*) in this (that)
respect **-ibland** among these (those) **-ifrån**
from here; *bildl.* from this **-igenom** through

here; *bildl.* owing to this (that), on this (that) account; (*medelst detta*) by this (that, these, those)
means, in this (that) way
härj|**a 1** ravage (*i ett land* a country); (*ödelägga*)
devastate, lay waste; (*om skadedjur*) wreak havoc; ~ *svårt* make [great] havoc; *se* ~*d ut* look
worn and haggard **2** (*om sjukdom*) be rife (prevalent); rage **3** (*väsnas*) make a row, run riot **-ning**
ravaging, devastation, havoc; ~*ar* ravages
-ningståg ravaging expedition
härjämte in addition [to this]
härkomst [-å-] *s3* extraction, descent; (*ursprung*) origin; *av borgerlig* ~ of middle-class extraction (origin)
härled|**a** *v2* derive (*äv. språkv.*); (*sluta sig t.*) de-
duce; ~ *sig* be derived (*från, ur* from); **-d enhet**
derived unit
1 härledning språkv. derivation; deduction
2 härledning *mil.* [the] army command; *konkr.*
army staff
härlig [ˣhä:r-] *a1* glorious; (*präktig*) magnificent,
splendid; (*ljuvlig*) lovely; (*vacker*) fine (*äv.
iron.*); *så det står* ~*a till* like anything **-het** glory;
magnificence, splendour; *hela* ~*en* the whole
business
härma imitate; (*naturv.; förlöjliga*) mimic; (*efter-
apa*) copy
härmed with (by, at, to) this; *hand.* herewith,
hereby; *i enlighet* ~ accordingly; *i samband* ~ in
connection herewith; ~ *vill vi meddela* (*hand.*)
we wish to inform you; *vi sänder* ~ (*hand.*) we are
sending you enclosed, we enclose herewith
härm|**fågel** mockingbird **-ning** imitation; mim-
icry **-ningsdrift** mimicry instinct
härnad [ˣhä:r-] *s3, draga i* ~ *mot* take up arms
against **härnadståg** war[like] expedition
härnäst next; (*nästa gång*) next time
härold [-å-] *s3* herald
härom (*norr north*) from here; (*angående denna
sak*) about (concerning, as to this) **-dagen** the
other day **-kring** all round here, in this neighbourhood **-sistens** a little while ago; (*nyligen*)
recently **-året** a year or so (two) ago
härpå *rumsbet.* on this (that); *tidsbet.* after this
(that)
härröra ~ *från* (*av*) come (arise) from, originate
(in from)
härs ~ *och tvärs* to and fro, in all directions; hither and thither
härsk|**a 1** (*styra*) rule; (*regera*) reign **2** (*om sak*)
predominate; (*vara förhärskande*) prevail, be
prevalent **-ande** *a4* ruling; (*om parti*) dominat-
ing; (*gängse*) prevalent, prevailing
härskara host
härskar|**e** ruler; monarch, sovereign; (*herre*)
master (*över* of) **-inna** ruler *etc.*; (*som behärskar
ngn*) mistress **-natur** masterful character, domineering nature; *pers.* man (*etc.*) of despotic nature
härsken *a3* rancid
härsklyst|**en** with a thirst for power; domi-
neering, imperious **-nad** thirst for power; mas-
terfulness *etc.*
härskna go (become, turn, get) rancid; *bildl.*
sour
härskri war cry; (*friare*) outcry

härsmakt armed force, army; *med* ~ by force of arms

härstam|ma ~ *från* be descended from, (*om pers. o. sak*) derive one's (its) origin from, (*datera sig från*) date from **-ning** descent; (*ursprung*) origin; (*ords*) derivation

härstädes here, in this place

härtapp|ad *a5* bottled in this country (by the importers) **-ning** local bottling (*äv. konkr.*)

här|till to this (that, it); ~ *kommer att vi måste* besides (in addition to this) we must **-under** *rumsbet.* under this; *tidsbet.* during the time this was (is) going on (lasted; lasts) **-ur** out of this **-utav** *se härav* **-utinnan** in this (that) respect **-utöver** *bildl.* beyond this, in addition to this

härva *s1* skein; (*virrvarr*) tangle

här|varande *a4*, *en* ~ a[n]...of this place, a local **-vid** at (on, to) this **-vidlag** in this respect; (*i detta fall*) in this case **-åt 1** *rumsbet.*, *se hitåt* **2** (*åt den här saken e.d.*) at this

hässja [ˣhäʃa] **I** *s1* hay fence **II** *v1*, ~ *hö* pile hay on fences to dry

häst *s2* **1** horse; *sitta till* ~ be on horseback; *sätta sig på sina höga* ~*ar* ride the high horse; *man skall inte skåda given* ~ *i munnen!* don't look a gift-horse in the mouth! **2** *gymn.* [vaulting] horse, buck, (*bygel-*) pommel horse; *schack.* knight, *vard.* horse **-ansikte** *bildl.* horse-face **-avel** horse-breeding **-djur** *pl* [the] horses **-droska** horse-drawn cab **-fluga** horsefly **-gardist** trooper (*officer* officer) in the Horse Guards **-handlare** horse-dealer **-hov 1** horse's hoof **2** *bot.* coltsfoot **-kapplöpning** horse-racing; *en* ~ a horse-race **-kastanj[e]** horse chestnut **-kraft** (*beräknad, effektiv, bromsad* indicated, effective, brake) horsepower; *vard.* horse **-krake** hack, jade *bildl.* drastic cure **-kött** (*livsmedel*) horseflesh **-lass** cartload **-lort** horse dung **-längd** *sport.* [horse-]length **-minne** *vard.* phenomenal memory **-polo** polo **-ras** breed [of horses] **-rygg** horse's back; *sitta på* ~*en* be on horseback **-skjuts** horse-drawn conveyance **-sko** horseshoe **-skojare** horse-swindler, [horse-]coper **-skosöm** horseshoe nail **-skötare** groom **-spillning** horse dung **-sport** equestrian sport; ~*en* (*kapplöpningssporten*) horse-racing, the turf **-styng** botfly **-svans** horse's tail; (*frisyr*) ponytail **-tagel** horsehair **-täcke** horse-cloth **-väg** *det var något i* ~ that's really something

hätsk *al* rancorous, spiteful (*mot* towards); (*bitter*) bitter, fierce **-het** spitefulness; rancour

hätta *s1* hood; (*munk-*) cowl; (*barn-*) bonnet

häva *v2* **1** heave; (*kasta*) toss, chuck; *på tå häv!* on your toes!; ~ *sig* raise o.s., (*om bröst o.d.*) heave **2** (*undanröja*) remove; raise (*en belägring* a siege); (*bota*) cure; *jur.* cancel; (*bilägga*) settle **3** ~ *ur sig* come out with

häv|arm lever **-as** *v2, dep* heave

hävd *s3* **1** *jur.* prescription; (*besittningsrätt*) usage; *urminnes* ~ immemorial prescription **2** (*tradition*) tradition, custom **3** (*historia*) [chronicled] history; ~*er* (*äv.*) annals of the past; *gå till* ~*erna* go down in history **4** *lantbr.* (*gott tillstånd o.d.*) cultivation

hävda 1 (*försvara*) vindicate, maintain (*sina rät-*

tigheter one's rights); (*vidmakthålla*) maintain (*sin ställning* one's position), uphold (*sina intressen* one's interests) **2** (*påstå*) maintain, assert, state **3** *rfl* hold one's own, vindicate o.s. **-teckning** *se historieskrivning*

hävdvunnen time-honoured, established; *jur.* prescriptive

hävert ['hä:-] *s2* siphon

häv|ning [ˣhä:v-] heaving *etc.*, *se häva* **-stång** lever

häx|a [ˣhäksa] *s1* witch; (*ondskefull kvinna*) old hag **-brygd** witch-broth **-dans** witches' dance; *bildl.* welter **-eri** witchery, witchcraft; sorcery **-kittel** *bildl.* maelstrom **-mästare** wizzard; *eg. bet. äv.* sorcerer **-process** witch-trial **-ring** *bot.* fairy ring

hö *s4* hay **-bärgning** haymaking

1 höft *s, i uttr.*: *på en* ~ (*efter ögonmått*) roughly, approximately, (*på en slump*) at random

2 höft *s3* hip; ~*er fäst!* hands to hips!

höft|ben hipbone **-benskam** iliac crest **-hållare** girdle; foundation garment **-kam** *se -bens-kam* **-led** hip joint **-skynke** loincloth

1 hög *s2* **1** heap (*av, med* of); (*uppstaplad*) pile (*av, med* of); (*trave*) stack (*av, med* of); *samla* (*lägga*) *på* ~ pile (heap) up, accumulate; *ta ett exempel ur* ~*en* take an example at random; *kläderna låg i en* ~ the clothes were lying [all] in a heap **2** (*kulle*) hillock; mound (*äv. konstgjord*)

2 hög *-t -re -st* **1** high; (*reslig*) tall; (*högt liggande*) elevated; (*tung, svår*) heavy, severe; (*högt uppsatt*) exalted; (*om furstlig pers.*) august; (*-dragen*) haughty; ~[*a*] *och låg*[*a*] high and low, the exalted and the lowly; ~*a böter* a heavy fine; ~*t gräs* long grass; ~ *militär* high-ranking officer [in the army *etc.*], *vard.* brass hat; ~ *panna* high (lofty) forehead; *H*~*a Porten* the Sublime Porte; *i egen* ~ *person* in person; *vid* ~ *ålder* at an advanced age; *ha* ~*a tankar om* think highly of; *spela ett* ~*t spel* (*bildl.*) play a risky game; *det är* ~ *tid* it is high time; *diskussionens vågor gick* ~*a* the debate was heated **2** (*-ljudd*) loud; *mus.* high [-pitched]; *med* ~ *röst* in a loud voice **3** (*om luft*) clear **4** *skrika i* ~*an sky* scream to high heaven **5** (*upprymd; narkotikaberusad*) high

högad|el ~*n* the higher nobility, *vard.* the upper crust **-lig** belonging to the higher nobility

högaffel hayfork, pitchfork

högakt|a esteem; (*svagare*) respect; think highly of, value **-ning** esteem; respect; *med utmärkt* ~, *se högaktningsfullt*

högaktnings|full respectful **-fullt** *adv* (*i brev*) Yours faithfully, *AE.* Very truly yours

hög|aktuell of great current (immediate) interest; topical **-altare** high altar **-avlönad** highly paid **-barmad** *a5* full-bosomed, bosomy **-borg** *bildl.* stronghold **-borgerlig** upper middle class **-bröstad** *a5*, *se -barmad* **-buren** *a5 med -buret huvud* with one's head held high **-djur 1** *koll.* high game **2** *bildl.*, *sl.* bigwig, big shot, *vard.* V.I.P. (*förk. för* very important person) **-dragen** haughty, lofty, arrogant **-effektiv** (*om pers.*) very efficient; *en* ~ *maskin* a high-efficiency (high-production, high-capacity) machine

högeligen exceedingly; highly

höger ['hö:-] **I** *a, best. form högra* right; right-hand; *min högra hand* (*bildl.*) my right-hand man; *på min högra sida* on my right[-hand side] **II** *adv,* ~ *om!* right turn!; *göra* ~ *om* turn by the right **III** *s9* **1** right; *från* ~ from the right; *till* ~ *om* to the right of **2** *polit.,* ~*n* the Right, the Conservative Party, the Conservatives (*pl*) **3** *sport.,* *en rak* ~ a straight right **-back** *sport.* right [full] back **-extremist** right-wing extremist **-halvback** *sport.* right half[back] **-hand** right hand **-handske** right-hand glove **-hänt** *a4* right--handed; dextral **-inner** *sport.* inside right **-kurva** right-hand curve (bend) **-man** conservative **-parti** *se höger III 2* **-styrd** [-y:-] *a5* (*om bil*) right-hand driven **-sväng** right turn **-trafik** right-hand traffic **-vriden** *polit.* rightist **-vridning** *polit.* rightism **-ytter** *sport.* outside right

hög|fjäll high mountain; ~*en* the High Alps **-fjällshotell** mountain hotel **-form** *i* ~ in great form **-frekvens** high frequency **-frekvent** high-frequent; *bildl.* occurring often, of high frequency

högfärd [ˣhö:g- *el.* ˣhökk-] pride (*över* in); (*fåfänga*) vanity; (*inbilskhet*) [self-]conceit **-ig** proud (*över* of); cocky (*över* about); (*fåfäng*) vain; (*inbilsk*) [self-]conceited, *vard.* hoity-toity, stuck-up

högfärds|blåsa *vard.* swank[pot] **-galen** bursting with self-importance

högförräderi high treason

högg *imperf. av hugga*

hög|gradig *a5* (*av hög halt*) high-grade; (*ytterlig*) extreme; (*svår*) severe; (*intensiv*) intensive **-halsad** *a5* high-necked **-hastighetståg** high--speed train

höghet [ˣhö:g-] **1** (*upphöjdhet*) loftiness; sublimity; ([*världslig*] *storhet*) greatness **2** (*högdragenhet*) haughtiness, high-and-mightiness **3** (*titel*) highness; *Ers H*~ Your Highness

höghus high-rise [building], tower block; multistorey building **-bebyggelse** high-rise development **-område** high-rise area (development)

hög|inkomsttagare high-income earner **-intressant** highly interesting **-kant** *på* ~ on end **-klackad** *a5* high-heeled **-klassig** *a1* high-class **-konjunktur** [business, trade] boom; ~*en inom* the boom [period] in **-kultur** *lantbr.* high farming **-kvarter** headquarters (*pl*) **-kyrka** High Church **-kyrklig** High-Church **-land** upland; *Skotska -länderna* the Highlands

höglast high load

högljudd [-judd] *a1* loud; (*högröstad*) loud-voiced, vociferous; (*bullersam*) noisy **-het** loudness; vociferousness; noisiness

hög|ländare Highlander **-länt** *a1* upland; *ön är* ~ the island is elevated (lies high) **-läsning** reading aloud **-lönegrupp** high-income category (group) **-mod** pride; (*överlägsenhet*) haughtiness, loftiness, airs (*pl*); (*övermod*) arrogance; ~ *går före fall* pride goeth before destruction **-modern** absolutely up-to-date **-modig** proud; haughty, lofty; arrogant ¨**-målsbrott** [high] treason, lese-majesty **-mäld** [-ä:-] *a1, se högljudd* **-mält** *adv* in a loud voice **-mässa** morning service; *kat.* high mass **-nivåspråk** *data.* high-level language **-oktanig** *a5* high--octane **-platå** tableland **-prosa** literary prose

högre [ˈhö:g-] *komp. t. 2 hög* higher *etc.,* *se 2 hög*; *de* ~ *klasserna* the upper classes (*skol.* forms); *en* ~ *makt* a higher power; *den* ~ *matematiken* higher (advanced) mathematics (*pl*); *en* ~ *officer* a high-ranking officer; *den* ~ *skolan* the upper (*friare* advanced) school, *ridk.* the higher manège; *ett* ~ *väsen* a superior being; *i allt* ~ *grad* to an ever-increasing extent; *i den* ~ *stilen* in the lofty style (*iron.* sublime manners); *på* ~ *ort* in high quarters; *intet* ~ *önska än att* desire nothing better than to; *tala* ~ speak louder

hög|relief high relief **-renässans** ~*en* the Mid--Renaissance **-rest** [-e:-] *a4* tall **-röd** vermil[l]ion, scarlet, bright red **-röstad** *a5, se högljudd* **-sint** *a1* high-minded; (*storsint*) magnanimous **-sjöflotta** ocean-going fleet **-skola** university college; (*friare*) academy; *teknisk* ~ institute (college) of technology **-skoleutbildning** university (college) education **-slätt** tableland, plateau **-sommar** *på* ~*en* at the height of the summer **-spänd** *a5, elektr.* high-tension, high-voltage **-spänn** *i uttr.: på* ~ (*bildl.*) at high tension, agog **-spänning** high tension (voltage) **-spänningsledning** high-tension (high-voltage) [transmission] line

högst [hökst] **I** *superl. t. 2 hög* highest *etc., se 2 hög*; ~*a tillåtna hastighet* speed limit, maximum [permitted] speed; *H*~*a domstolen* [the] supreme court; *H*~*a sovjet* Supreme Soviet; *min* ~*a önskan* my most fervent wish; *i* ~*a laget* as high (*etc.*) as it ought to be, (*äv.*) a little too high (*etc.*) if anything; *på* ~*a ort* at top level; *när solen står som* ~ when the sun is at its height (highest [point]) **II** *adv* highest *etc.*; most highly; (*mest*) most; (*i* ~*a grad*) in the highest degree; (*ytterst*) exceedingly, extremely; (*mycket*) very (*avsevärd* considerable); (*på sin höjd*) at most, at the [ut]-most; *allra* ~ at the utmost (very most)

högstadium advanced (higher, senior) stage; (*i grundskola*) senior level

högstbjudande *a4, den* ~ the highest bidder

hög|stämd *bildl.* elevated, high-pitched, lofty **-säsong** height of the season, peak **-säte** high settle; (*förnämsta plats*) seat of honour

högt [hökt] *adv* high; highly; (*om ljud*) loud[ly]; (*motsats för sig själv*) aloud; (*högeligen*) highly; ~ *belägen* on high ground, (situated) high up; ~ *ställda fordringar* great (exacting) demands; ~ *uppsatt person* person of high station; ~ *älskad* dearly beloved; *lova* ~ *och dyrt* promise solemnly; *spela* ~ (*spel.*) play for high stakes; *stå* ~ *över* (*bildl.*) be far above, be far removed from

högtalare loudspeaker

högtflygande high-flying, high-soaring; ~ *planer* ambitious plans

högtid [ˣhökk-, *äv.* ˣhö:g-] *i sht bibl.* feast; *i sht kyrkl.* festival

högtidlig [ˣhökk-, *äv.* -ˈti:d-, *äv.* ˣhö:g-] *a1* solemn; (*ceremoniell*) ceremonious, ceremonial; *vid* ~*a tillfällen* on state (formal, ceremonious) occasions; *se* ~ *ut* look solemn; *ta det inte så* ~*t!* don't be so solemn about it! **-het 1** solemnity; (*ståt*) state, pomp **2** (*med pl*) ceremony; solemnity **-hålla** celebrate, commemorate **-hållande** *s6* celebrating; celebration

högtids|blåsa *vard.* Sunday best **-dag** festival

(commemoration) day; red-letter day **-dräkt** festival attire; (*frack*) evening dress **-firande I** a4 festive **II** s6 celebration, festival **-klädd** a5 in festival attire; (*i frack*) in full dress **-sal** ceremonial room (hall), stateroom **-stund** time of real enjoyment, precious moment; *en musikalisk* ~ a musical treat **-talare** the speaker at a function (ceremony, festival *etc.*)

hög|trafik heavy (peak) traffic **-travande** a4 bombastic, high-flown; (*om pers.*) grandiloquent, pompous **-tryck** high pressure; *boktr.* letterpress, relief printing

högtrycks|aggregat high-pressure unit **-område** area of high pressure **-rygg** ridge of high pressure **-tvättning** high-pressure (jet) cleaning

högt|stående a4, *kulturellt* ~ on a high level of culture **-svävande** high-soaring; (*om planer*) ambitious

hög|tyska High German **-vakt 1** (*manskap*) main guard **2** (*vakthållning*) main guard duty **-varv** s, *arbeta på* ~ work full out **-varvig** a5 high-speed **-vatten** high water; (*tidvatten*) high tide **-vilt** big game **-vinst** top lottery prize

högvis in heaps (piles, stacks); ~ *med* piles of

hög|välboren *Högvälborne Greve A.* The Right Honourable Earl A., *i Storbritannien* The Earl [of] A. **-växande** tall-growing **-växt** a4 tall **-vördighet** *hans* ~ *biskopen* the Right Reverend the Lord Bishop; *Ers* ~ *torde* you will..., My Lord **-ättad** a5 of noble lineage, highborn **-önsklig** *mest i uttr.: i* ~ *välmåga* in the best of health, *vard.* in the pink

höj|a [ˣhöjja] v2 raise; make higher, put up; (*för-*) heighten; (*förbättra*) improve; (*öka*) increase; ~ *priset på* raise (put up) the price of, mark up; ~ *ngn till skyarna* praise (exalt) s.b. [up] to the skies; ~ *upp* raise; ~ *sig* (*äv. bildl.*) rise above, raise o.s.; *-d över alla misstankar* above suspicion; *-d över allt tvivel* beyond all doubt; *det -des röster för* voices were raised in favour of **-bar** a5, *höj- och sänkbar* vertically adjustable

höjd s3 **1** (*kulle o.d.*) height; hill **2** height; (*högsta* ~) top, summit; (*nivå*) level; *fack.* altitude; *geogr.* latitude; *mus.* pitch; *fri* ~ [free] headroom, [overhead] clearance; *största* ~ maximum height; *vishetens* ~*er* the pinnacles of wisdom; ~*en av oförskämdhet* the height of impudence; *i* ~ *med* on a level with; *på sin* ~ at the [ut]most; *driva i* ~*en* intensify, force up, boost; *flyga på en* ~ *av* fly at an altitude (a height) of; *stå på* ~*en av sin bana* be at the height of one's career; *det är väl ändå* ~*en!* that's really the limit!

höjd|are sl. bigwig, big shot; *vard.* V.I.P. (*förk. för* very important person); *mil.* brass hat; *-arna* (*vard.*) the higher-ups **-hopp** high jump **-hoppare** high jumper **-led** *i* ~ vertically **-läge** *mus.* upper register **-mätare** altimeter **-punkt** highest point; peak; *bildl.* height, maximum; (*kulmen*) climax; ~*en i hans diktning* the height of his literary production **-roder** *flyg.* elevator **-skillnad** difference in altitude (height) **-vind** upper wind

höjning (*höjande*) raising; (*av pris*) rise, increase; (*av lön*) rise, AE. raise; ~ *och sänkning* raising and lowering, (*i pris äv.*) rise and fall, *geol.* elevation and depression

hök s2 hawk; *duvor och* ~*ar* (*polit.*) doves and hawks; ~ *och duva* (*lek*) tig

hökare *ung.* grocer

hö|lada hay barn **-lass** [cart]load of hay

hölj|a v2 cover; (*insvepa*) wrap [up], envelop; (*friare*) coat; *-d i dunkel* veiled (wrapped) in obscurity, nebulous; ~ *sig med ära* cover o.s. with glory

hölje s6 envelope; (*fodral*) case, casing

höll *imperf. av hålla*

hölster ['höll-] s7 **1** (*pistol-*) holster **2** *bot.* spathe

höna s1 **1** hen; *kokk.* chicken **2** (*våp*) goose

höns s7 **1** *pl* [domestic] fowls; (*hönor*) hens; *koll.* *äv.* poultry (*sg*); *springa omkring som yra* ~ rush around like a hen on a hot griddle; *vara högsta* ~*et* [*i korgen*] be cock of the roost, be top dog **2** *kokk.* chicken **-avel** poultry rearing **-buljong** chicken broth **-bur** hencoop **-bär** *bot.* dwarf cornel

höns|eri poultry (chicken) farm, hennery **-foder** chicken (poultry) feed **-fåglar** *pl* gallinaceous birds **-gård 1** poultry yard, hen (chicken) run **2** *se hönseri* **-hjärna** *bildl.* addle-pate (*äv. pers.*) **-hud** goose flesh (skin) **-hus** poultry house, henhouse **-minne** memory like a sieve **-nät** chicken wire **-skötsel** poultry keeping (farming) **-ägg** hen's egg

1 höra v2 (*räknas*) belong (*till* to); ~ *hemma* belong (*i* to); ~ *ihop* belong together; ~ *ihop med* be connected with, (*bero på*) be dependent on; *det hör till yrket* it is part of the profession (job); *han hör till familjen* (*äv.*) he is one of the family; *det hör inte hit* it has nothing to do with this; *det hör till att* it is the right and proper thing that (to + *inf.*)

2 höra v2 **1** (*uppfatta ljud*) hear; *han hör illa* (*äv.*) he is hard of hearing; *det hörs bra härifrån* you can hear well from here; *hör nu!* come now!; *hör du, kan du* I say (look here), can you; *han lät* ~ *en djup suck* he gave a deep sigh **2** (*erfara, få* ~) hear, learn; be told; (*fråga efter*) hear, inquire, ask, find out; *så snart han fick* ~ *om* directly he heard (was told) of; *jag har just fått* ~ *att* I have just heard that; *jag har hört sägas att* I have heard it said that; *jag vill inte* ~ *talas om det* I will not hear of it (such a thing); *gå och hör om han har rest* go and find out if he has gone; *har man hört på maken!* did you ever hear the like?; *låt* ~*!* out with it! **3** (*lyssna*) listen; (*åhöra*) hear (*en predikan* a sermon), attend (*en föreläsning* a lecture); ~ *ngns mening* ask a p.'s opinion; *jag vill* ~ *din mening om* I would like your opinion on (about); *han ville inte* ~ *på det örat* he just wouldn't listen **4** (*för-*) hear; (*vittne äv.*) examine **5** *rfl, det låter* ~ *sig!* that's s.th. like!; ~ *sig för* make inquiries (*om* about); ~ *sig för hos ngn* (*på en plats*) inquire of s.b. (at a place) **6** (*med betonad partikel*) ~ *av* hear from; *låta* ~ *av sig* send word; ~ *efter a*) (*lyssna till*) listen to, *b*) (*fråga efter*) inquire (*hos ngn* of s.b., *om ngt* for s.th., about s.th.), *c*) (*ta reda på*) hear, inquire, find out; ~ *fel* hear amiss, mishear; *hör in i morgon!* look in and inquire tomorrow!; ~ *på* listen; *hör upp ordentligt!* mind you pay proper attention!

hör|apparat hearing aid **-bar** a5 audible **-central** hearing-aids centre **-fel** (*missuppfattning*)

mishearing **-håll** i uttr.: inom (utom) ~ within
(out of) earshot **-lur 1** (för lomhörda) ear trumpet **2** (t. telefon) receiver, earpiece; (t. radioapparat) earphone; ~ar headphones, vard. cans
hörn [-ö:-] s7 corner; (vrå äv.) nook; (vinkel) angle; i ~et at (om inre hörn in) the corner; bo om ~et live round the corner; vara med på ett ~ join in; vika om ~et turn the corner
hörn|a s1 **1** vard., se hörn **2** sport. corner **-hus** corner house **-pelare** corner pillar; bildl. pillar of strength **-skåp** corner cupboard **-sten** cornerstone (äv. bildl.) **-tand** eyetooth, canine [tooth], dogtooth
hör|propp earphone **-sal** lecture hall, auditorium
hörsam [ˣhö:r-] a1 obedient **-ma** obey; (kallelse e.d.) respond to; (inbjudan) accept; (uppmaning) pay heed to
hörsel [ˈhörs-] s2 hearing **-ben** auditory bone (ossicle) **-gång** auditory canal (meatus) **-klinik** hearing clinic **-minne** auditive memory **-nerv** auditory nerve **-organ** organ of hearing **-sinne** [sense of] hearing, auditory sense **-skada** impairment of hearing **-skadad** a5 with impaired hearing **-skydd** ear protection (guard); (öronpropp) earplug
hör|spel radio play **-sägen** (enligt from) hearsay **-telefon** [telephone] receiver, earpiece
hö|räfsa hayrake **-skrinda** haycart **-skulle** haymow **-skörd** hayharvest; konkr. äv. haycrop **-snuva** hay fever
höst s2 autumn; AE. fall; i ~ a) (nu) this autumn, b) (nästkommande) next autumn; i ~as last autumn; om ~en (~arna) in the autumn; på ~en 1966 in the autumn of 1966
höstack haystack, hayrick
höst|dag autumn day, day in the autumn **-dagjämning** autumnal equinox **-kanten** i uttr.: på ~ around the beginning of the autumn **-lig** a5 autumnal **-löv** autumn leaf **-mörker** autumn darkness **-storm** autumn[al] gale **-säd** autumnsown grain **-säsong** autumn season **-termin** autumn term
hösäck (tom) haysack; (full) sack of hay
höta v3, ~ åt ngn (med näven) shake one's fist at s.b., (med käpp) brandish one's stick at s.b.
hö|tapp wisp of hay **-tjuga** [-çu:-] s1 hayfork, pitchfork **-torgskonst** ung. trashy art
hövan best. form sg i uttr.: över ~ beyond measure, excessively **hövas** v2, dep be befitting for
hövding chief[tain]
hövisk [ˈhö:-] a5 (anständig) decent, seemly; (ärbar) modest; (artig) courteous; (belevad) refined; (ridderlig) chivalrous **-het** decency, seemliness; modesty; courteousness, courtesy; refinement; chivalry
hövitsman captain; bibl. äv. centurion
hövlig [-ö:-] a1 civil, polite (mot to); (belevad) courteous; (aktningsfull) respectful (mot to) **-het** civility, politeness, courtesy; respect **-hetsvisit** courtesy (polite) call
hövligt [-ö:-] adv civilly etc.; bli ~ bemött be treated with civility; svara ~ give a polite reply (på to)
hövolm [-å-] s2 haycock

1 i s6 i; pricken över ~ the dot over the i, bildl. äv. the finishing touch
2 i prep **I** rumsbet. o. bildl. **1** (befintl.) in (världen the world; Sverige Sweden; London London); at (Cambridge Cambridge; skolan school); (vid genitivförhållande vanl.) of; (på ytan av) on (soffan the sofa); ~ en bank in (at) a bank; ~ brödbutiken at the baker's; ~ gräset on the grass, (bland grässtråna) in the grass; ~ trappan on the staircase; ~ ena änden av at one end of; freden ~ B. the peace of B.; högsta berget ~ the highest mountain in; professor ~ engelska professor of English; det roliga ~ historien the amusing part of the story; uttrycket ~ hans ansikte the expression on his face; han bor ~ Bath he lives at Bath; jag bor här ~ Bath I live here in Bath; pojken satt ~ trädet the boy is standing at the window **2** (friare) among (buskarna the bushes); over (högtalaren the loudspeaker); through (kikaren the binoculars); in (litteraturen literature); at (arbete work); ~ frihet udspeaker); through (kikaren the binoculars); in (litteraturen literature); at (arbete work); ~ frihet at liberty; ~ stor skala on a large scale; för trång ~ halsen too tight round the neck; blåsa ~ trumpet blow a trumpet; göra ett besök ~ pay a visit to; sitta ~ en styrelse be on a board; tala ~ näsan talk through one's nose; tala ~ radio (TV) speak on the radio (on TV); lampan hänger ~ taket the lamp is hanging from the ceiling; 6 går ~ 30 fem gånger 6 goes into 30 five times **3** (vid rörelse, förändring) into; in; dela ngt ~ fyra delar divide s.th. into four parts; falla ~ vattnet fall into the water; få ngt ~ sitt huvud (bildl.) get s.th. into one's head; klättra upp ~ ett träd climb up a tree; placera ngt ~ place s.th. in; resultera ~ result in; stoppa ngt ~ fickan put s.th. in[to] one's pocket; störta landet ~ krig plunge the country into war; titta ~ taket look up at the ceiling **4** (gjord av) of, in; (medelst) by (bil car); (om hastighet o.d.) at (full fart full speed); (i o. för) on; (i form av) in; (såsom) as; en kjol ~ bomull a skirt of cotton, a cotton skirt; gjuten ~ brons cast in bronze; ~ lag förbjudet forbidden by law; ~ regel as a rule; ~ stor utsträckning to a large extent; bortrest ~ affärer away on business; inte ~ min smak not to my taste; dra ngn ~ håret pull s.b. by the hair, pull a p.'s hair; dö ~ cancer die of cancer; få ~ present get as a present; gripa ngn ~ kragen seize s.b. by the collar; ligga ~ influensa be down with the flu; ta ngn ~ armen take s.b. by the arm; vad har du ~ lön? what wages (salary) do you get? **5** duktig (dålig) ~ good (bad) at; förtjust ~ fond of, delighted with; tokig ~ crazy about; ha ont ~ magen have a stomach ache; jag är trött ~ fötterna my feet are tired **II** tidsbet. **1** (tidpunkt) in (maj May; medelåldern the middle age); at (jul Christmas; början av the beginning of; solnedgången sunset); last (höstas autumn); next (vår spring); (före) to; ~ en ålder av at the age of; ~ natt a)

(*som är el. kommer*) tonight, *b*) (*som var*) last night; *förr* ~ *tiden* in earlier times, formerly; *en kvart* ~ *åtta* a quarter to eight **2** (*tidslängd*) for (*åratal brukas*); ~ *trettio år* (*de senaste trettio åren*) [for] the last thirty years, (*om framtid*) [for] the next thirty years; *vi stannade* ~ *två veckor* we stayed [for] two weeks **3** (*per*) a[n], per; *två gånger* ~ *månaden* twice a month; *60 miles* ~ *timmen* 60 miles per (an) hour **III** (*i adverbiella, prepositionella o. konjunktionella förbindelser*) ~ *och för utredning* for the purpose of investigation; ~ *och för sig* in itself; ~ *och med detta* with this; ~ *och med att han gick var han* in going he was;~ *det att* [just] as; ~ *det att han gick* as he went, in going; *han gjorde rätt* ~ *att komma* he was right in coming

3 i *adv, en skål med choklad* ~ a bowl with chocolate in it; *hoppa* ~ jump in; *hälla* ~ *kaffe åt ngn* pour [out] coffee for s.b.; *hälla* ~ *vatten i en vas* pour water into a vase

iaktta|ga] 1 (*observera*) observe; (*lägga märke t. äv.*) notice; (*uppmärksamt betrakta äv.*) watch **2** *bildl.* observe (*tystnad* silence); exercise (*största försiktighet* the greatest caution); (*fasthålla vid äv.*) adhere to, keep (*reglerna* the rules)

iakttag|ande *s6* observance, observation; *under* ~ *av* observing **-are** observer **-else** observation **-elseförmåga** powers of observation

I-balk I-beam

iber *s3*, **-isk** *a5* Iberian; *I~a halvön* Iberian Peninsula

ibis ['i:-] *s2* ibis

ibland I *prep, se bland; mitt* ~ amid[st], in the midst of **II** *adv* (*stundom*) sometimes; (*då o. då*) occasionally; (*vid vissa tillfällen äv.*) at times, now and then

icke not; no; none; ~ *desto mindre* nevertheless, nonetheless; *i* ~ *ringa grad* in no small degree

icke|- *i sms.* non- **-angreppspakt** nonaggression pact **-rökare** nonsmoker **-spridningsavtal** nonproliferation treaty **-våld** nonviolence **-våldsmetoder** passive resistance (*sg*)

1 id *s2 zool.* ide

2 id *s2* (*verksamhet*) occupation[s *pl*], pursuit[s *pl*]; (*flit*) industry

idag *se dag*

idas *iddes itts, dep* have enough energy (energy enough) (*göra ngt* to do s.th.); *han iddes inte ens svara* he couldn't even be bothered to answer

ide *s6* hibernating-den; winter quarters (*pl*), winter lair; *gå i* ~ go into hibernation, *bildl.* shut o.s. away (up in one's den); *ligga i* ~ (*äv.*) hibernate, lie dormant (*äv. bildl.*)

idé *s3* idea (*om* about, as to, of); *få en* ~ get (have) an idea; *det är ingen* ~ *att göra* it is no use (good) doing, there is no point in doing; *hur har du kommit på den* ~*n?* what put that idea into your head?; *han har sina* ~*er* he has some odd ideas

ideal *s7 o. a1* ideal (*av, för* of) **-bild** ideal image **-figur** ideal figure; (*-mått*) ideal measurements (*pl*) **-gestalt** ideal figure

ideal|ism idealism **-ist** idealist **-istisk** [-'ist-] *a5* idealistic **-itet** ideality

ideal|samhälle ideal society; Utopia **-tillstånd** ideal state; ideal existence

idé|association association of ideas **-drama** problem play; ideological drama

ideell *a1* idealistic; ~ *förening* non-profit-making association

idé|fattig unimaginative **-givare** inspirer; brain

idegran yew [tree]

idé|historia history of ideas **-historisk** ideo-historical, pertaining to the history of ideas **-innehåll** idea-content (*i* of)

idel ['i:-] *oböjligt a* (*uteslutande*) mere, nothing but; (*ren*) pure, sheer; *vara* ~ *öra* be all ears; ~ *glädje* pure joy; *han var* ~ *solsken* he was all sunshine

idelig *a5* perpetual; continual, incessant **-en** perpetually *etc.*; over and over again; *han frågar* ~ he keeps on asking

idélära (*Platons*) doctrine of ideas

identifi|era identify **-ering** [-'e:-], **-kation** identification

identi|sk [-'denn-] *a5* identical **-tet** *s3* identity; *fastställa ngns* ~ establish a p.'s identity; *styrka sin* ~ prove one's identity

identitets|bricka *mil.* identity disc **-kort** identity card

ideo|log ideologist, ideologue **-logi** *s3* ideology **-logisera** ideologize **-logisk** [-'lå:-] *a5* ideologic[al]

idé|rik full of ideas **-skiss** draft, rough sketch **-utbyte** exchange of ideas **-värld** [personal] philosophy

idiom [-'å:m] *s7* idiom **-atisk** [-'ma:-] *a5* idiomatic[al]

idiosynkra|si *s3* idiosyncrasy; (*motvilja*) aversion **-tisk** [-'kra:-] *a5* idiosyncratic

idiot *s3* idiot; (*svagare*) imbecile

idiot|i *s3* idiocy; imbecility **-isk** [-'ɔ:t-] *a5* idiotic **-säker** foolproof

idissl|a ruminate, chew the cud; *bildl.* repeat, harp on **-ande** *s6* rumination; repetition **-are** ruminant

idka carry on; (*yrke, idrott äv.*) practise; (*yrke äv.*) follow; ~ *familjeliv* devote o.s. to one's family; ~ *handel* carry on business

ID-kort ID card

idog *a1* industrious; laborious; (*trägen*) assiduous **-het** industriousness *etc.*; industry

idol [-'å:l] *s3* idol **-dyrkan** idol worship

idrott [-å-] *s3* sport; [athletic] sports (*pl*); *skol., univ.* games (*pl*); *allmän* (*fri*) ~ athletics (*pl o. sg*)

idrotta go in for sport; *skol. o.d. äv.* play games

idrotts|anläggning stadium, sports arena **-dag** sports day **-evenemang** sporting event **-förening** athletic (sports) club **-gren** branch of athletics (sport) **-intresse** sporting interest **-klubb** *se* -*förening* **-kvinna** woman athlete, sportswoman **-lig** *a5* athletic **-lov** *skol.* time off (holiday) for sports **-man** athlete, sportsman **-märke** athletics (sports) badge **-plats** sports ground (field), athletic ground[s *pl*] **-tävling** sports (athletics) meeting

ids [i:-, *vard.* iss] *se idas*

idyll *s3* idyll; (*plats*) idyllic spot **-iker** idyllist **-isk** *a5* idyllic

ifall 1 if, in case; (*förutsatt*) supposing (provided)

[that] **2** (*huruvida*) if, whether
ifatt *gå* (*köra, simma*) ~ *ngn* catch s.b. up
i|fjol *se fjol* **-frd** *se fred*
ifråga|komma [iˣfrå:-] *se fråga I*; ~ *vid en be-
fordran* be considered (a possible choice) for a
promotion; *brukar sådant* ~? do such things usually happen? **-sätta 1** (*föreslå*) propose, suggest
2 (*betvivla*) question, call in question **-varande**
a4 in question, at issue
ifrån I *prep, se från I*; *söder* ~ from the south;
vara ~ *sig* be beside o.s. **II** *adv, komma* ~ (*bli fri
el. ledig*) get off (away); *man kommer inte* ~ *att*
there is no getting away from the fact that
iföra *rfl, se ikläda*
igel *s2* leech
igelkott [-å-] *s2* hedgehog
igen [i'jenn] **1** (*ånyo*) again; *om* ~ over again; (*en
gång till*) once more **2** (*tillbaka*) back; *slå* ~ hit
back; *ta* ~ (*om tid*) make up for; *jag kommer
snart* ~ I shall (will) soon be back **3** (*kvar*) left **4**
(*tillsluten*) to; *dörren slog* ~ the door slammed to
5 *fylla* ~ fill in
igen|bommad *a5, huset var -bommat* the house
was barred (shut) up; *dörrarna är* ~*e* the doors
have been fastened **-grodd** *a5* choked up, (*om
stig e.d.*) overgrown (*av ogräs* with weeds) **-känd**
a5 recognized **-kännande** *s6* recognition **-kän-
ningstecken** distinctive (distinguishing) mark
-kännlig *a5* recognizable (*för* to; *på* by) **-mulen**
a5 overclouded, overcast, clouded over
igenom [i'je:-] *prep o. adv* through; *rakt* ~ right
(straight) through; *tvärs* ~ right across; *natten* ~
all through (throughout) the night, all night long;
hela livet ~ all (throughout) one's life; *han har
gått* ~ *mycket* he has suffered (gone through) a
great deal
igen|proppad [-å-] *a5* clogged up **-snöad** *a5*
(*om väg*) snowed-up; (*om spår*) obliterated by
snow **-stängd** *a5* shut up, closed **-växt** *a4* (*om
gångstig*) overgrown; (*om sjö o.d.*) choked-up
iglo[o] ['i:glo] *s5* igloo
ignor|ans [iŋnå'rans *el.* injå- *el.* -'aŋs] *s3* igno-
rance **-ant** ignorant person **-era** ignore, take no
notice of; disregard
igång *se 1 gång 2* **-sättning** starting, start **-sätt-
ningstillstånd** building start permit
igår *se går*
ihjäl [i'jä:l] to death; *skjuta* ~ *ngn* (*äv.*) shoot s.b.
dead; *slå* ~ kill; *slå* ~ *tiden* kill time; *svälta* ~
(*äv.*) die of hunger, starve to death; *arbeta* ~ *sig*
work o.s. to death; *skratta* ~ *sig* die of laughing;
slå ~ *sig* get (be) killed **-frusen** *a5* frozen to
death **-skjuten** [-ʃu:-] *a5* shot dead **-skrämd** *a5*
frightened (*etc.*) to death **-slagen** *a5* killed
-sparkad *a5* kicked to death **-trampad** *a5*
trampled to death
ihop 1 (*tillsammans*) together; *passa* ~ go well together, (*om pers.*) suit each other **2** *fälla* ~ shut
up; *krympa* ~ shrink [up]; *sätta* ~ *en historia*
make up a story
ihåg *komma* ~ remember, (*erinra sig äv.*) recollect, (*lägga på minnet*) bear (keep) in mind; *jag
kommer inte* ~ (*äv.*) I forget **-komma** *se ihåg*;
det bör ~*s att* it should be borne in mind that
ihålig *a1* hollow (*äv. bildl.*); (*tom*) empty **-het**
konkr. cavity; hole; hollow; *abstr.* hollowness,

emptiness
ihållande *a4* prolonged (*applåder* applause; *kyla*
frost); continuous, steady (*regn* rain)
ihärdig *a1* (*om pers.*) persevering; (*trägen*) assiduous, tenacious; (*om sak*) persistent; ~*t nekande*
persistent denial **-het** perseverance; assiduity,
tenacity; persistence
ikapp (*i tävlan*) in competition; *hinna* ~ *ngn* catch
s.b. up; *springa* ~ *med ngn* run a race with s.b.;
de rider ~ *med varandra* they are racing each other on horseback
ikläda dress in; clothe in (*äv. bildl.*); ~ *sig* (*på-
taga sig*) take upon o.s., assume, make o.s. responsible for
ikon [i'ka:n] *s3* icon **-ografi** *s3* iconography
ikraftträdande *a4* coming into force; ~ *av lag*
passing into law
ikring *se kring, omkring*
iktyo|log ichthyologist **-logi** *s3* ichthyology **-lo-
gisk** [-'lå:-] *a5* ichthyologic[al]
ikull *se omkull*
ikväll *se kväll*
1 il *s2* (*vind-*) gust [of wind]; squall
2 il *s7, se -gods, -samtal o.d.*; (*påskrift på telegram
o.d.*) urgent
1 ila *det* ~*r i tänderna på mig* I have a shooting
pain in my teeth
2 ila *litt.* speed; fly, dart, dash; (*mera vard.*)
hurry; *tiden* ~*r* time flies [apace]
i-land *se industriland*
ilast|a load **-ning** loading
il|bud urgent message (*efter* for); *pers.* express
messenger **-fart** *med* ~ at full (top) speed **-gods**
koll. express goods, goods sent by express train;
sända som ~ send by express **-godsförsän-
delse** express parcel
illa *komp. värre el. sämre, superl. värst el. sämst;
adv (dåligt)* badly; (*låta* sound) bad; (*klent*) poorly; (*på tok*) wrong; (*elakt, skadligt*) ill, evil;
(*svårt*) badly, severely; (*mycket*) very (*trött*
tired); ~ *behandlad* ill-treated; ~ *berörd* un-
pleasantly affected; ~ *dold avundsjuka* ill-concealed envy; ~ *kvickt* pretty (damn) quick; ~ *till
mods* sick at heart, downhearted; *behandla ngn*
~ treat s.b. badly; *göra ngn* ~ hurt s.b.; *göra sig*
~ *i foten* hurt one's foot; *må* ~ feel poorly (out
of sorts), (*vilja kräkas*) feel sick; *ta* ~ *upp* take
it amiss; *ta* ~ *vid sig* be very upset (grieved) (*av*
about); *tala* ~ *om ngn* run s.b. down, speak ill of
s.b.; *tycka* ~ *vara* take it amiss, mind; *det går* ~
för mig things are going badly (*på tok* wrong) for
me; *den* ~ *gör han* ~ *får sig* the evil does, he evil
fares; *man ligger* ~ *i den här sängen* this bed is
uncomfortable; *den luktar (smakar)* ~ it has a
nasty smell (taste); *hon ser* ~ her sight is bad; *hon
ser inte* ~ *ut* she is not bad-looking; *det var* ~*!*
that's a pity!; *det var inte* ~*!* that is not bad!, that
is pretty good!; *det var inte så* ~ *menat* no offence
was intended (meant); *är det så* ~? is it as bad as
all that?
illa|luktande *a4* nasty-smelling, evil-smelling
-mående *a4* poorly, out of sorts, unwell; indisposed; *känna sig* ~ (*ha kväljningar*) feel sick
illande *a4,* ~ *röd* flaming red
illa|sinnad *a5* ill-disposed; (*om handling*) mali-
cious **-sittande** badly fitting **-smakande** *a4*

with a nasty (disagreeable) taste; (*om mat äv.*) unsavoury **-varslande** *a4* evil-boding, ill-boding; ominous

illdåd wicked (evil) deed; outrage (*mot* on)

illeg|al *a1* illegal **-itim** *a5* illegitimate

iller ['ill-] *s2* polecat

ill|fundig *a1, se -listig* **-fänas** *dep* **1** (*väsnas*) pester **2** (*envisas*) bother (*med* with) **-gärning** malicious (evil, wicked) deed; outrage (*mot* on) **-gärningsman** evil-doer; malefactor **-listig** (*hopskr. illistig*) cunning, wily; insidious (*påhitt* device); (*listig äv.*) crafty **-listighet** (*hopskr. illistighet*) malicious cunning (craftiness)

illitterat *a1* illiterate, unlettered

illmarig *a1* sly, knowing; (*slug*) cunning; (*skälmsk*) arch

illojal *a1* disloyal; ~ *konkurrens* unfair competition **-itet** disloyalty

ill|röd glaring red **-tjut** piercing yell; *ge till ett* ~ make a hell of a row **-tjuta** scream

illudera produce an illusion of

illumin|ation illumination **-era** illuminate

illusion illusion; (*falsk föreställning*) delusion; *göra sig ~er om* cherish illusions about; *ta ngn ur hans ~er* disillusion s.b.

illusionist illusionist **-isk** *a5* illusionistic

illusions|fri, -lös free from all illusion[s *pl*]; absolutely disillusioned

illusorisk [-'sɔ:-] *a5* illusory; (*bedräglig*) illusive; (*inbillad*) imaginary

illust|er [-'lust-] *a2* illustrious **-ration** illustration **-rativ** *a5* illustrative; *boktr. äv.* illustrational **-ratör** illustrator **-rera** illustrate

ill|vilja (*ont uppsåt*) spite, ill will (*mot* towards); (*elakhet*) malevolence; (*djupt rotad*) malignity **-villig** spiteful, malicious, malevolent (*mot* towards) **-vrål** *se illtjut*

ilmarsch forced march

ilning ['i:l-] thrill (*av glädje* of joy); (*av smärta*) shooting pain

il|paket express parcel **-samtal** *tel.* express call

ilsk|a *s1* [hot] anger, [boiling] rage, [intense] fury (*över ngt* at s.th.); *i ~n* in his (*etc.*) anger, for very rage; *göra ngt i ~n* do s.th. in a fit of anger **-en** *a3* angry; (*ursinnig*) furious; (*om djur*) savage, ferocious; *bli* ~ get angry (*på ngn* with s.b.; *över ngt* at s.th) **-na** ~ *till* fly (*så småningom* work o.s.) into a rage (fury); ~ *till mer och mer* get angrier and angrier

iltelegram express telegram (wire, cable)

imaginär [-ʃi-] *a5* imaginary (*äv. mat.*); unreal, fancied

imam *s3* ima[u]m

imbecill *a5* imbecile **-itet** imbecility

imit|ation imitation **-ativ** *a5* imitative **-atör** imitator; (*varietéartist o.d.*) mimic **-era** imitate; copy; (*människor äv.*) take off, mimic; ~*t läder* imitation leather

imma I *s1* (*ånga*) mist, vapour; (*beläggning*) steam, moisture; *det är* ~ *på fönstret* the window is steamed (misted) over **II** *v1* get misted [over]

imman|ens *s3* immanence, immanency **-ent** *a4* immanent

immateriell *a5* immaterial

immatrikulera matriculate

immersion immersion

immig *a1* misty, steamy

immigr|ant immigrant **-ation** immigration **-era** immigrate (*till* into)

immun *a1* immune (*mot* against, from, to) **-globulin** immunoglobulin **-isera** immunize **-isering** [-'se:-] immunization **-itet** immunity

immuno|log immunologist **-logi** *s3* immunology **-logisk** [-'lå:-] *a5* immunologic[al]

immunserum serum

imorgon *se morgon* 2

impala[antilop] ['imp-] impala

impedans [*äv.* -'aŋs] *s3, elektr.* impedance

imperativ I *a5* (*i* in the) imperative **II** *a5* imperative **-isk** *a5* imperative

imperator [-*ˣ*a:tår] *s3* imperator **-isk** [-'tɔ:-] *a5* imperial; (*om gest o.d.*) imperious

imperfekt *s7, s4* **-um** *s4* imperfect; *i* ~ in the past tense

imperial|ism imperialism **-ist** imperialist **-istisk** [-'ist-] *a5* imperialist[ic]

imperium [-'pe:-] *s4* empire

impertin|ens *s3* impertinence **-ent** *a1* impertinent

implant|at *s7* implant **-ation** implantation **-era** implant

implic|era implicate **-it** *a4* implicit

implo|dera implode **-sion** implosion

imponer|a make an impression (*på* on); impress; *jag blev mycket ~d* I was very much impressed (*av* by) **-ande** *a4* impressive; imposing; *ett* ~ *antal* a striking[ly large] number of; *en* ~ *gestalt* an imposing figure; ~ *siffror* striking figures

impopul|aritet unpopularity **-är** *a1* unpopular (*bland, hos* with)

import [-å-] *s3* (*-erande*) import[ation]; (*varor*) imports (*pl*) **-avgift** import duty

import|era import (*till* [in]to); ~*de varor* (*äv.*) imports **-firma** import[ing] firm; importers (*pl*) **-förbud** import prohibition (ban) **-licens** import licence **-restriktioner** import restrictions **-tillstånd** import permit (licence) **-tull** import duty **-underskott** import deficit **-vara** imported article, import[ation]

import|ör importer **-överskott** import surplus

imposant [-'ant *el.* -'aŋt] *a1, se imponerande*; (*storslagen*) grand

impot|ens *s3* impotence, impotency **-ent** *a4* impotent

impregner|a [-eŋ'ne:- *el.* -en'je:-] impregnate; (*mot väta*) waterproof; (*trä*) creosote **-ing** impregnation; (*mot vatten*) waterproofing; (*av trä*) creosoting **-ingsmedel** impregnating agent

impressario [-'sa:-] *s2* impresario

impression|ism [-eʃɔ-] impressionism **-ist** impressionist **-istisk** [-'ist-] *a5* impressionist[ic]

improduktiv *a1* unproductive; (*oräntabel*) unprofitable **-itet** unproductiveness; unprofitability

impromptu [-'åmp-] *s6* impromptu

improvis|ation improvisation **-atör** improviser **-era** improvise; (*om talare äv.*) extemporize

impuls *s3* impulse; (*utifrån kommande äv.*) stimulus, incentive, spur, impetus (*till* to); *elektr.* excitation **-givare** *elektr.* exciter

impulsiv *a1* impulsive **-itet** impulsiveness

impulsköp (*-ande*) impulse buying; *ett* ~ a pur-

chase made on [the] impulse; *göra ett* ~ buy on [the] impulse
imrör vent
in [inn] in; (~ *i huset o.d.*) inside; *hit (dit)* ~ in here (there) ~ *i* into; ~ *till staden in (äv.* up) to town; *till långt* ~ *på natten* until far [on] into the night
inackorder|a [×inn-] board and lodge (*hos* with); *vara* ~*d* board and lodge, be a boarder; ~ *sig* arrange to board and lodge (*hos* with) **-ing 1** *abstr.* board [and lodging], board-and-lodging accommodation **2** *pers.* boarder; *ha* ~*ar* take in boarders **-ingsrum** rented room
inadekvat *a4* inadequate
inadvertens *s3* inadvertence
inaktiv [*el.* 'inn-] inactive; inert **-itet** inactivity
inaktuell (*förlegad*) out of date; *problemet är* ~*t* the problem does not arise (is not pertinent)
inalles [-'all-] in all, altogether
inand|as inhale; breathe in **-ning** inhalation
inarbeta 1 work in **2** (*förtjäna tillbaka*) work off (*en förlust* a loss) **3** (*skaffa avsättning för*) push [the sale of], find a market for; *en väl* ~*d firma* a well-established firm
inätt *se natt*
inaugurera inaugurate
in|avel inbreeding **-begripa** comprise, comprehend; (*innesluta*) include; (*medräkna*) take into account; ...*ej* -*begripen* not including...; -*begripen i samtal* engaged in conversation **-beräkna** include, take into account; *allt* ~*t* everything included **-berätta** report (*ngt för ngn s.th.* to s.b.) **-bespara** save **-besparing** saving **-betala** pay [in, up]; ~ *till en bank* (*på sitt konto*) pay into a bank (one's account); -*betalda avgifter* paid-up fees -' ـtalning paying [in, up], payment; *in- och utbetalningar* receipts and disbursements, in- and outgoing payments **-betalningskort** *post.* paying-in form
inbilla ~ *ngn ngt* make s.b. (get s.b. to) believe s.th.; ~*d* imagined, fancied, imaginary; *vem har* ~*t dig det?* whoever put that into your head?; *det kan du* ~ *andra!* tell that to the marines!; ~ *sig* imagine, fancy; ~ *sig vara* imagine that one is; ~ *sig vara ngt* think a great deal of o.s.
inbillning imagination; (*falsk föreställning*) fancy; *det är bara* ~[*ar*]*!* that is pure imagination (all fancy)!
inbillnings|foster figment of the imagination **-sjuk** *en* ~ an imaginary invalid, a hypochondriac; *vara* ~ suffer from an imagined complaint
inbilsk *a1* conceited **-het** conceit
in|binda (*böcker*) bind **-bindning** binding; *lämna till* ~ leave to be bound **-biten** *a5* confirmed (*ungkarl* bachelor); inveterate (*rökare* smoker)
inbjud|a invite; ~ *till kritik* invite criticism; ~ *till teckning av aktier* invite subscription[s] to a share issue; *har äran* ~ ... *till middag* request the pleasure of the company of...to dinner
inbjud|an *r, pl saknas* invitation **-ande** *a4* inviting; (*lockande*) tempting **-ning** invitation **-ningskort** invitation card
inbland|a *se blanda*; *bli* ~*d i ngt* become (get) involved (implicated, mixed up) in s.th. **-ning** *bildl.* interference, meddling; (*ingripande*) inter-

vention
in blanko ['blann-] in blank; in blanco
in|blick insight (*i* int); *få en* ~ *i (äv.*) catch a glimpse of **-boka** book **-bokning** booking; reservation **-bringa** yield, bring [in] **-bringande** *a4* profitable; lucrative **-bromsning** braking, application of the brake[s *pl*]
inbrott 1 (*början*) setting in; *vid dagens* ~ at the break of day, at daybreak (dawn); *vid nattens* ~ at nightfall; *vid mörkrets* ~ at the approach of darkness **2** (*under dagen*) housebreaking; (*under natten*) burglary; *göra* ~ *hos ngn* break into (commit a burglary at) a p.'s house
inbrotts|försäkring burglary insurance **-tjuv** (*under dagen*) housebreaker; (*under natten*) burglar
in|brytning *mil.* break-in (*i* in) **-buktning** inward bend **-bunden** *a3* **1** (*om bok*) bound **2** *bildl.* uncommunicative, reserved **-bundenhet** uncommunicativeness *etc.*; reserve **-burad** *a5* locked up **-byggare** (*bebyggare*) settler; *se äv.* invånare **-byggd** *a5* built in; *en* ~ *veranda* a closed-in veranda[h] **-byte** trading-in **-bytesbil** trade-in car; *vi använder vår gamla Morris som* ~ *när vi köper Buicken* we trade in our old Morris for the Buick **-bytesvärde** trade-in value **-bäddad** *a5* embedded
inbördes [-ö:-] **I** *adv* (*ömsesidigt*) mutually; reciprocally; (*med varandra*) with one another; (*inom sig själva*) among[st] themselves **II** *oböjligt a* mutual; reciprocal; *deras* ~ *avstånd* their relative distance; *sällskap för* ~ *beundran* mutual admiration society; ~ *testamente* mutual ([con]joint) will **-krig** civil war
incest *s3* incest
incheck|a *se checka in* **-ning** checking-in **-ningsdisk** check-in [counter]
incident *s3* incident
incitament *s7* incentive; incitement
indata *data.* input
indefinit [*äv.* 'inn-] *a4* indefinite
indel|a divide (*i* into); (*uppdela*) divide up (*i* into; *efter* according to); (*i klasser*) classify, group; (*i underavdelningar*) subdivide **-ning** dividing [up] ; division; classification, grouping; subdivision **-ningsgrund** principle (basis) of division (*etc.*)
indelt [-e:-] *a4, mil. ung.* tenement (*soldat* soldier)
index ['inn-] *s7, s9* index (*pl äv.* indices); *mat.* subscript **-reglerad** *a5* index-linked **-tal** index [number (figure)] **-tillägg** index increment
indian *s3* [American] Indian **-bok** Red-Indian storybook **-dräkt** Red-Indian costume **-hövding** [Red-]Indian chief **-krasse** *bot.* nasturtium, Indian cress
indian|sk [-a:-] *a5* [Red-]Indian **-ska** [Red-]Indian woman **-sommar** Indian summer **-stam** Indian tribe **-tjut** Indian war whoop
indicera *se indikera*
indici|ebevis [-×di:-] circumstantial evidence **-um** [-'di:-] *s4* indication (*på* of); *jur.* circumstantial evidence; *bildl.* criterion; *starka* -*er* weighty evidence; *döma ngn på* -*er* convict s.b. on circumstantial evidence
indiefarare person (ship) bound for (sailing from) India; (*fartyg äv.*) Indiaman

Indien ['inn-] India; *Bortre* ~ Farther India **indier** ['inn-] Indian

indifferens *s3* indifference **-ent** *a4* indifferent

indign|ation [-diŋna-, *äv.* -dinja-] indignation **-erad** [-'e:-] *a5* indignant (*över* of)

indigo ['inn-] *s5* (*växt*) indigo; (*färgämne*) indigo, indigotin **-blå** indigo [blue]

indikation indication

indikativ *s3 o. a1* indicative; *stå i* ~ be in the indicative

indikator [-ˣa:tår] *s3* indicator

indiker|a indicate **-ing** indication, indicating

indirekt ['inn-, *äv.* -'ekt] *a4* indirect; ~ *anföring* indirect (reported) speech, *AE.* indirect discourse; ~ *belysning* indirect (concealed) lighting; ~ *bevis* indirect proof; ~ *skatt* indirect tax; ~ *val* (*ung.*) election by ad hoc appointed electors

indi|sk ['inn-] *a5* Indian **-ska** Indian woman; *I~a oceanen* [the] Indian Ocean

indiskre|t *a1* indiscreet; tactless; (*lösmynt*) talkative **-tion** indiscretion

indis|ponerad [-'ne:-] *a5* indisposed, out of sorts; (*om sångare*) not in good voice **-ponibel** [-'ni:-] unavailable **-position** indisposition

indium ['inn-] *s8* indium

individ *s3* individual; (*om djur äv.*) specimen; (*neds. om pers. äv.*) specimen, character

individual|isera individualize **-ism** individualism **-ist** individualist **-istisk** [-'ist-] *a5* individualistic **-itet** individuality

individuell *a5* individual

indoeurop|é *s3,* **-eisk** [-'e:-] *a5* Indo-European

Indokina Indochina, Indo-China, Farther India

indoktriner|a indoctrinate **-ing** indoctrination

indol|ens *s3* indolence; idleness **-ent** *a1* indolent; idle, lazy

indo|log Indologist **-logi** *s3* Indology

indones *s3, se* indonesier

Indonesien [-'ne:-] *n* Indonesia

indones|ier [-'ne:-] *s9,* **-isk** *a5* Indonesian

indragtation, indent

indrag|a *se dra* [*in*]; (*friare*) draw in; (*inveckla*) involve, implicate (*i* in) **-ning** drawing in; involvement, implication; withdrawal; stoppage, discontinuation; confiscation; suspension

indriv|a (*inkassera*) collect, call in; (*på rättslig väg*) recover **-are** debt collector **-ning** collection; recovery

indräktig *a1* lucrative

indränka soak, saturate

inducera induce

induk|tans *s3* inductance **-tion** [-k'ʃo:n] induction

induktions|spole inductance coil **-ström** induction (induced) current

indunstning [concentration by] evaporation

industri *s3* industry; ~ *och hantverk* the crafts and industries

industrial|isera industrialize **-isering** [-'se:-] industrialization **-ism** industrialism

industri|arbetare industrial (factory) worker **-departement** ministry (*AE.* department) of industry

industri|ell *a5* industrial **-förbund** *Sveriges I~* [the] Federation of Swedish Industries **-företag** industrial enterprise (concern, company) **-gren**

[branch of] industry **-idkare** industrialist, manufacturer **-land** industrialized country **-man** industrialist **-minister** minister (*AE.* secretary) of industry **-mässa** industrial fair **-nedläggelse** close-down of a factory **-område** industrial region (area); (*planerat område*) industrial estate (*AE.* park) **-produktion** industrial production **-robot** industrial robot **-semester** general industrial holiday **-spionage** industrial espionage **-stad** industrial town **-varor** *pl* industrial goods (products), manufactured goods **-verk** *Statens I~* [the Swedish] National Industrial Board

ineffektiv *a1* ineffective; (*om pers. äv.*) inefficient **-itet** ineffectiveness; inefficiency

inemot ['inn-] (*om tid*) towards; (*om antal o.d.*) nearly, close on

inert *a1* inert

inexakt *a1* inexact, inaccurate **-het** inaccuracy; inexactitude

in extenso [-'tenn-] in full

in|fall *s7* **1** (*angrepp*) invasion (*i* of); incursion (*i* into) **2** (*påhitt*) idea, fancy; (*nyck*) whim; *jag fick ett* ~ I had a bright idea (a brain wave) **3** (*kvickhet*) sally **-falla 1** (*om vattendrag o.d.*) fall (*i* into) **2** ~ *i ett land* invade a country **3** (*inskjuta yttrande*) put in **4** (*inträffa*) fall (*på en söndag* on a Sunday) **-fallen** *a5, infallna kinder* sunken (hollow) cheeks

infallsvinkel angle of incidence (*bildl.* approach)

infam *a1* infamous; abominable; *vara* ~*t påpassad* be under close surveillance **infami** *s3* infamy

infanteri infantry **-avdelning, -förband** infantry unit **-regemente** infantry regiment

infanterist infantryman

infantil *a1* infantile **-ism** infantilism

infarkt *s3, med.* infarct[ion]; *AE.* infarct

infart [-a:-] *s3* approach (*äv. sjö.*); ~ *förbjuden!* No Entry!; *under* ~*en till* when approaching (entering)

infarts|led arterial road **-parkering** commuter parking **-väg** drive[way], approach

infatt|a (*kanta*) border; (*juveler e.d.*) set, mount; ~ *i ram* frame **-ning** (*kant*) border; edging; (*ram*) frame[work]; (*för juveler e.d.*) setting, mounting; (*t. glasögon e.d.*) rim; (*t. fönster e.d.*) trim

infek|tera infect **-tion** [-k'ʃo:n] infection

infektions|härd focus of infection **-sjukdom** infectious disease **-ämne** infectious organism; germ

infektiös [-k'ʃö:s] infectious; contagious

infernalisk [-'na:-] *a5* infernal

inferno [-'fä(:)rnå] *s6* inferno

infiltr|at *s7* infiltrate **-ation** infiltration **-atör** infiltrator **-era** infiltrate

infinit *a4* infinite

infinitiv *s3* (*i* in the) infinitive **-märke** sign of the infinitive, infinitive marker

infinna *rfl* appear, make one's appearance; put in an appearance; turn up; ~ *sig hos ngn* present o.s. (appear) before s.b.; ~ *sig vid en begravning* (*på sammanträdet*) attend a funeral (the meeting)

inflamm|ation inflammation (*i* in, of) **-atorisk** [-'to:-] *a5* inflammatory **-era** inflame

inflation inflation **-istisk** [-'ist-] *a5* inflationary

inflations|drivande inflationary **-fara** risk of inflation **-skydda** inflation-proof **-spiral** inflationary spiral
inflatorisk [-'tɔ:-] *a5* inflationary
infli[c]ka put in, interpose
influens *s3* influence
influensa [-ˣenn-] *s1* influenza, *vard.* flu **-epidemi** influenza epidemic **-virus** influenza virus
in|fluera ~ [*på*] influence **-flygning** (*mot flygplats*) approach **-flyta** (*om pengar*) come (be paid) in; (*publiceras*) appear, be inserted
inflyt|ande *s6* (*inverkan*) influence (*på ngn* with s.b.); (*om sak*) impact, effect, power; *göra sitt* ~ *gällande* make one's influence felt, use one's influence; *röna* ~ *av* be influenced by; *öva* ~ *på* exert influence on **-elserik** influential
inflytt|a (*invandra*) immigrate (*i* into) **-ning** moving in, taking possession; (*immigration*) immigration **-ningsklar** ready for occupation
in|fläta *se fläta II* **-flöde** influx, inflow (*i* into)
in|fo (*kortform för information*) *vard.* info **-foga** fit in; insert (*bildl.*) **-fordra** (*anmoda*) demand; *i sht hand.* solicit, request; (*återkräva*) demand back; (*lån*) call in; ~ *anbud* invite tenders (*på* for)
informa|nt [-å-] informant **-tik** informatics (*pl, behandlas som sg*) **-tion** information; (*underrättelse*) intelligence; *mil.* briefing
informations|behandling data processing **-möte** meeting to give information **-sekreterare** information officer **-teori** data processing theory
informat|iv *a5* informative **-or** [-ˣa:tår] *s3* [private] tutor **-ör** person who gives information, informant; (*angivare*) informer
inform|ell *a5* informal **-era** inform (*om* of); *mil.* brief; *hålla ngn ~d* keep s.b. posted
infra|grill infrared grill **-lampa** infrared lamp **-ljud** infra sound **-röd** infrared; ~ *strålning* infrared radiation **-struktur** infrastructure **-värme** infrared heating
in|fria 1 redeem; (*förbindelse äv.*) meet; (*skuld äv.*) discharge 2 (*uppfylla*) redeem, fulfil (*ett löfte* a promise) **-frusen** frozen in; *bildl.* frozen; ~ *i isen* icebound; *-frusna tillgodohavanden* frozen assets **-frysning** freezing; (*av matvaror äv.*) refrigeration
infusion infusion
infusionsdjur ciliate, infusorian
infånga catch; (*rymling o.d. äv.*) capture
infäll|a *tekn.* let into; *sömn.* insert; *boktr.* inset **-bar** *a5* retractable, retractile **-ning** letting into; *konkr. sömn.* inlay; *tekn.* insertion, inset
in|född native; *en ~ stockholmare* a native of Stockholm **-föding** native
inför ['inn-] 1 *rumsbet.* before; (*i närvaro av*) in the presence of; ~ *domstol* in court; *finna nåd* ~ *ngn* find favour with s.b.; *ställas* ~ *problem* be brought face to face (confronted) with problems 2 *tidsbet.* (*nära*) on the eve of; (*friare*) at (*underrättelsen om* the news of); ~ *julen* with Christmas [near] at hand
inför|a *se föra* [*in*]; (*importera*) import; (*friare o. bildl.*) introduce; (*annons*) insert; ~ *förbud för* lay embargo on, prohibit **-ing** introduction; (*i protokoll e.d.*) entry, entering; (*av annons*) insertion

införliv|a incorporate (*med* with, in[to]); ~ *en bok med sina samlingar* add a book to one's collection **-ande** *s6* incorporation
införsel *s2* 1 *se import o. sms.* 2 ~ *i lön* attachment of wages (*etc.*)
inför|skaffa procure (*upplysningar om* particulars about) **-stådd** *a5, vara ~ med* agree with, be in agreement with
inga [ˣiŋa] *se ingen* **-lunda** by no means; not at all
inge 1 (*inlämna*) send (hand) in **2** *bildl.* inspire (*ngn respekt* s.b. with respect)
ingefära [ˣiŋe-] *s1* ginger
ingefärs|dricka ginger ale; (*alkoholhaltig*) ginger beer **-päron** *pl* pear ginger (*sg*)
ingen [ˣiŋen] 1 *fören.* no (*lätt sak* easy matter); ~ *människa* (*vanl.*) nobody, (*starkare*) not a soul; *det var* ~ *dum ide!* that's not a bad idea! 2 *självst.* nobody, no one, none; ~ (*inga*) *av dem* none of them; *inga* none; ~ *alls* nobody (no one) at all, not a single person; ~ *mindre än* no less [a person] than; *nästan* ~ hardly any (*etc.*) **-dera** neither [of them (the two)]
ingenium [in'je:-] *s4* understanding; brains (*pl*); (*snille*) genius; wit
ingenjör [inʃen'jö:r] engineer
ingenjörs|firma engineering firm **-kår** *mil.* corps of engineers **-trupper** *pl* engineers, sappers; ~*na* (*i Storbritannien*) the Royal Engineers **-vetenskap** [science of] engineering **-vetenskapsakademi** *I~en* [the Swedish] Academy of Engineering Sciences
ingenmansland no-man's-land
ingen|stans, -städes nowhere; *AE. vard.* no place
ingenting nothing; *nästan* ~ hardly anything, next to nothing; *det blir* ~ *av med det!* that's off!, *vard.* there's nothing doing!; *det gör* ~ it does not matter; *det säger jag* ~ *om!* I have nothing to say to that!
ingenue [äŋʃe'ny:] *s3* ingénue
in|gift *a4, bli* ~ *i* marry into **-gifte** intermarriage
ingiv|a *se inge* **-else** inspiration; (*impuls*) idea, impulse; *stundens* ~ the spur of the moment
in|gjuta *bildl.* infuse (*nytt mod hos ngn* fresh courage into s.b.) **-gravera** engrave
ingrediens [ing-] *s3* ingredient; component
ingrepp 1 *kir.* [surgical] operation 2 *bildl.* interference; (*intrång*) encroachment, infringement 3 *tekn.* engagement; (*av kuggar*) mesh[ing]
ingress *s3* preamble, introduction
ingrip|a *bildl.* intervene; (*hjälpande*) step in, come to the rescue; (*göra intrång*) interfere **-ande I** *s6* intervening *etc.*; intervention; interference **II** *a4* far-reaching; radical, thorough; ~ *förändringar* radical changes
ingrodd *a5* 1 ingrained (*smuts* dirt) 2 (*inrotad*) inveterate (*ovana* bad habit); deep-rooted (*misstro* suspicion)
ingå 1 ~ *i eviga vilan* enter into the everlasting peace 2 (*om tid*) set in, come, begin; *dagen ingick strålande klar* the day dawned radiantly clear 3 (*inkomma*) arrive; (*om underrättelse*) come to hand; (*om pengar*) come in 4 (*inlåta sig*) enter (*på* into); (*utgöra del*) be (become) [an integral] part (*i* of); (*medräknas*) be included; ~ *i*

allmänna medvetandet become part of the public consciousness; *det ~r i hans skyldigheter* it is part (one) of his duties **5** (*avtal, förbund e.d.*) enter into; ~ *fördrag* conclude (make) a treaty; ~ *förlikning* come to terms, arrive at a compromise; ~ *ett vad* make a bet (wager); ~ *äktenskap* [*med*] marry

ingående I *a4* **1** (*ankommande*) arriving; (*om brev o.d.*) incoming; ~ *balans* balance brought forward **2** (*grundlig*) thorough, close (*granskning* scrutiny); ~ *kännedom om* intimate knowledge of; ~ *redogörelse för* detailed report of **II** *adv* thoroughly *etc.*; *diskutera* ~ discuss in detail; ~ *redogöra för* give a full and detailed account of **III** *s6* **1** *fartyget är på* ~ the vessel is inward bound **2** (*av fred o.d.*) conclusion; (*av äktenskap*) contraction

ingång 1 entrance; (*port äv.*) door, gate; *förbjuden ~!* No Admittance! **2** (*början*) commencement, beginning; (*gryning*) dawn

ingångs|psalm opening hymn **-värde** initial (opening) value

inhal|ation inhalation **-ator** [-ˣa:tår] inhalator **-era** inhale

in|handla buy **-hav** inland sea

inhemsk *a5* **1** (*motsats utländsk*) home, domestic; *äv.* English, Swedish (*etc.*) **2** *biol.* indigenous, native

inhiber|a inhibit; cancel, call off **-ing** inhibition; cancellation

inhopp *bildl.* sudden initiative

inhuman inhuman

in|hysa house; accommodate; *vara -hyst hos ngn* (*om sak*) be stored at a p.'s house **-hyseshjon** dependent tenant **-hägna** [-häŋna] enclose; ~ *med plank* (*staket*) board (fence) in **-hägnad** [-häŋnad] *s3* (*område*) enclosure; (*fålla*) fold, pen; (*staket*) fence

inhämta 1 (*skaffa sig*) gather, pick up; procure, secure; (*lära sig*) learn; ~ *kunskaper* acquire knowledge; ~ *ngns råd* ask a p.'s advice, consult s.b.; ~ *upplysningar* obtain information, make inquiries **2** (*nå fatt*) catch up; ~ *ett försprång* gain on, reduce a lead

inhöst|a *bildl.* reap; (*poäng*) score **-ande** *s6* reaping; scoring

ini *se inuti, inne i* **-från I** *adv* from within; from [the] inside **II** *prep* from the interior of; from inside (within)

initial [-tsi-] *s3* initial **-kostnad** initial cost **-ord** initialism **-skede** initial phase **-svårigheter** initial difficulties, teething troubles

initiativ [-tsia-] *s7* initiative; *på eget* ~ on one's own initiative; *ta* ~ *till ngt* take the initiative in doing s.th. **-förmåga** power of initiative **-rik** full of initiative, enterprising **-rikedom** abundance of initiative **-tagare** initiator, originator, promoter (*till* of)

initier|a [-tsi-] initiate **-ad** *a5* initiated (*i* into); well-informed (*i* on); *i* ~*e kretsar* in well-informed circles

injaga ~ *respekt hos ngn* command respect in s.b.; ~ *skräck hos ngn* strike terror into (intimidate) s.b.

injek|tera inject **-tion** [-kˈʃɑːn] injection; *vard.* shot

injektions|nål [hypodermic] needle **-spruta** hypodermic syringe; *vard.* needle

injic[i]era inject

injustering adjustment

inka *-n -s* Inca **-folket** the Incas

inkall|a call in; (*möte e.d.*) summon (*äv. jur.*), convoke, convene; *mil.* call up, *AE.* draft (*t. militärtjänst* for military service); *en* ~*d* (*mil.*) a conscript, *AE.* a draftee **-ande** *s6* calling in; summoning, convocation, convening

inkallelse summons; *mil.* call-up, *AE.* draft [call] **-order** calling-up papers (order), *AE.* induction papers

in|kapabel [-ˈpa:-] incapable

inkapsl|a enclose, encase **-ing** enclosure; encapsulation

inkariket the Inca Empire

inkarn|ation incarnation **-era** incarnate **-erad** [-ˈe:-] *a5* incarnate

inkasser|a [ˣinn-] collect, recover; *bildl.* receive **-are** collector **-ing** *se inkasso*

inkasso [-ˈkassɔ] *s6* collection [of debts], collecting, recovery **-avgift** collecting (collection) fee **-byrå** debt-collecting agency (firm) **-uppdrag** collection (encashment) order

in|kast 1 *sport.* throw-in **2** (*invändning*) objection, observation **-kilad** [-çi:-] *a5* wedged (*i* into; *mellan* in between)

inklarer|a [ˣinn-] (*fartyg*) clear (enter) inwards **-ing** clearance (entry) inwards

inklin|ation inclination; (*om magnetnål äv.*) dip **-era** incline; dip

inklu|dera include **-sive** [-ˈsi:-] included; including, inclusive of

inklämd *a5* squeezed (jammed) in; *med.* strangulated

inkognito [-ˈkåŋni-] *adv o. s6* incognito, *fem.* incognita

inkokning preserving; bottling; canning; *jfr koka* [*in*] **inkokt** *a4* preserved *etc.*; (*i socker*) candied; ~ *fisk* poached fish

inkomm|a ~ *med* (*anbud, redogörelse etc.*) hand in, submit; ~ *med klagomål* lodge complaints **-ande** *a4* incoming

inkommendera [ˣinn-] call up

inkommensurab|el [-ˈa:bel] *-la storheter* incommensurable quantities

inkompatib|el [-ˈti:-] incompatible **-ilitet** incompatibility

inkompet|ens incompetence; incapacity; disability **-ent** incompetent; (*om platssökande*) unqualified

inkomplett incomplete

inkomst [-å-] *s3* income; earnings (*pl*) (*av, på* from); (*stats-*) revenue[s *pl*]; (*avkastning*) yield, proceeds (*pl*); ~ *av arbete* earned income; ~ *av kapital* unearned income; *fast* ~ settled income; ~*er och utgifter* income and expenditure; *ha goda* ~*er* have a good income; *hur stora* ~*er har han?* what is his income?

inkomst|baserad earnings-related **-beskattning** income taxation **-bortfall** loss of income; income shortfall **-bringande** [-briŋ-] *a4* profitable, remunerative, rewarding **-fördelning** distribution of income **-klass** income bracket **-källa** source of income **-läge** income bracket

-politik incomes policy **-prövning** means test **-sida** *på* ~*n* on the income (credit) side **-skatt** income tax **-tagare** wage earner **-år** income year
inkongru|ens incongruity **-ent** incongruous; *geom. äv.* incongruent
inkonsekv|ens inconsistency **-ent** inconsistent
inkontin|ens *s3* incontinence **-ent** *a4* incontinent
inkonvertibel [-'i:bel] *a5* inconvertible
inkoppl|a 1 couple, connect; *elektr.* switch in (on), turn on **2** inform, advice, get in touch with; *polisen är* ~*d* the police have been called in **-ing** coupling, connection; *elektr.* switching in (on), turning on
inkorporer|a [-'e:ra *el.* ˣinn-] incorporate (*i, med* in[to]) **-ing** incorporation
in|korrekt *al* incorrect **-krupen** *a5, sitta* ~ *i* sit huddled-up in **-kräm** *s7* **1** (*av bröd*) crumb **2** (*av fågel o.d.*) entrails (*pl*)
inkräkt|a [-ˣkräkk-] encroach, trespass, intrude (*på* [up]on] **-are** trespasser, intruder; (*i ett land*) invader
inkrökt [-ö:-] *a4, bildl.* egotistic[al], egocentric
inkubationstid incubation period
inkunabel [-'na:-] *s3* incunabulum (*pl* incunabula)
inkurant *al* unsaleable, unmarketable
inkvarter|a [ˣinn-] *mil.* billet, quarter (*hos* on); (*friare*) accommodate **-ing 1** billeting; accommodation **2** (*plats*) quarters (*pl*), billet
inkvisi|tion ~*en* the Inquisition **-tionsdomstol** court of inquisition; ~*en* the Court of the Inquisition **-tor** [-ˣi:tår] *s3* inquisitor **-torisk** [-'tɔ:-] *a5* inquisitorial
inköp purchase; *göra* ~ (*i butik*) do shopping, shop; *den kostar...i* ~ the cost price is...
inköp|a buy, purchase **-are** buyer, purchaser
inköps|anmälan notification of purchase **-avdelning** buying department **-chef** chief (head) buyer **-lista** shopping list **-pris** cost price
inkör|d [-çö:-] *a5* (*om bil*) run-in; (*om häst*) broken[-in]; ~*a fraser* well-drilled phrases **-ning** (*av hö e.d.*) bringing in; (*av motor*) running-in; *bilen är under* ~ the car is being run (driven) in
inkörsport entrance [gate]; *bildl.* gateway
in|laga *sl* **1** (*skrift*) petition, address, memorial **2** (*i cigarr e.d.*) filler **3** (*boks inre*) body **-lagd** *a5* **1** (*i ättika*) pickled; (*i olja*) put down; (*i flaska*) bottled; (*i bleckburk*) tinned, canned **2** *-lagt arbete* inlaid work, inlay **-lagring** *geol.* inclusion **-land** interior, inland parts (*pl*); *i in- och utlandet* at home and abroad
inlands|is inland ice **-klimat** inland climate
inlast|a *sjö.* ship; *järnv.* load **-ning** shipping; loading
inleda *v2* **1** (*förbindelser, förhandlingar, möte, samtal*) open, enter into (upon); (*diskussion e.d.*) introduce, begin, start off; (*undersökning e.d.*) initiate, set on foot, institute; usher in, initiate (*en ny epok* a new epoch); ~ *en offensiv* launch an offensive **2** (*locka*) lead (*i frestelse* into temptation)
inled|ande *a4* introductory, opening (*anförande* address); (*förberedande*) preparatory, preliminary **-are** opening (first) speaker **-ning** introduction; (*friare*) opening, beginning

inlednings|anförande introductory address, opening speech **-skede** initial stage **-vis** by way of introduction; to start (begin) with
inlemma incorporate
inlevelse feeling insight, vivid realization (*i* of) **-förmåga** ability to enter into
in|leverera [ˣinn-] deliver, hand in (over) **-lopp 1** (*infartsled*) entrance, [sea] approach **2** (*inflöde*) inflow, inlet **3** *tekn.* inlet, intake
inlån borrowing; (*av ord äv.*) adoption **-ing** borrowing; (*i bank*) [bank] deposits (*pl*), receiving on deposit; *affärsbankernas* ~ the deposits of the commercial banks **-ingsränta** interest on deposit[s *pl*]; deposit rate
in|låta *rfl*, ~ *sig i* (*på*) enter into; ~ *sig i strid* engage (get involved) in a fight; ~ *sig med ngn* have dealings (take up) with s.b. **-lägg** *s7* **1** (*ngt inlagt*) inlay, inset; (*bilaga*) enclosure, insert; (*i sko*) insertion; *sömn.* tuck **2** (*i diskussion*) contribution (*i* to)
inlägg|a 1 *se lägga* [*in*] **2** *bildl.* put in (*ett gott ord för* a word for); (*infóra*) insert (*i* in); *jur.* enter, lodge; ~ *känsla i* put feeling into **3** *konst. o.d.* inlay **-ning 1** *abstr.* putting in; insertion; (*av grönsaker e.d.*) bottling, preserving, tinning, *AE.* canning; *konst.* inlaying **2** *konkr.* bottled (tinned) fruit (*etc.*); *konst.* inlay
inläggssula insole, inner sole
inläm|na hand (send) in; (*deponera*) leave, deposit; ~ *ansökan* make (lodge, hand in) an application **-ning 1** handing (sending) in; (*deponering*) leaving, depositing **2** (*inlämningsställe*) cloakroom **-ningskvitto** *post.* certificate of posting; (*for postanvisning*) certificate of issue; *järnv.* cloakroom receipt (ticket, check)
in|ländsk *a5* internal, domestic, home **-länka** insert
inlär|a learn; (*lära andra*) teach, instruct **-ning** learning; (*utantill*) memorizing; instruction
inlärnings|förmåga learning capacity **-kurva** learning curve **-maskin** teaching machine **-psykologi** psychology of learning **-studio** learning laboratory
inlöpa 1 *sjö.* put in; ~ *i hamn* put into (enter) port **2** (*om underrättelse o.d.*) come in (to hand), arrive
inlös|a (*betala*) pay; (*check e.d.*) cash; (*växel*) honour, take up; (*fastighet*) buy [in]; (*pant*) redeem **-en** *oböjligt s,* **-ning** *s2* payment; cashing; honouring, taking up; (*av lån, pant e.d.*) redemption; (*av sedlar*) withdrawal
in|malning mixing [of certain percentage] of home-grown with foreign grain in flour-milling **-marsch** march in, entry
inmat|a *tekn.* feed **-ning** *tekn.* feeding (*i* into); *data.* input
in|montera [ˣinn-] install, set up, put in **-mundiga** consume, eat, partake of
inmur|a (*i vägg e.d.*) wall (bond) in; (*inspärra*) immure (*i* in) **-ning** walling in *etc.*
inmut|a take out a mining concession for, [put in a] claim **-ning** *konkr.* mining concession (claim)
innan I *konj o. prep* before **II** *adv* **1** *utan och* ~ inside and out[side]; *känna ngn utan och* ~ know s.b. thoroughly (inside out) **2** *tidsbet.* before; *dagen* ~ the day before **-döme** *s6* inside, interior;

jordens ~ the bowels (*pl*) of the earth **-fönster** inner window **-för I** *prep* inside, within; (*bakom*) behind **II** *adv, den* ~ belägna... the...within (on the inside) **-hav** *se inhav* ~ *lår kokk.* (*av oxe o.d.*) thick flank; (*av kalv*) fillet **-läsning** reading [aloud] **-mäte** *s6* (*av djur*) entrails (*pl*), guts (*pl*), bowels (*pl*); (*av frukt e.d.*) pulp **-till** *läsa* ~ read from the book (*etc.*)

in natura [-ˣtu:-] in kind

inne 1 (*motsats ute*) inside; (*motsats utomhus*) indoors, in the house; (*hemma*) in **2** (*på lager*) in stock, on hand; (*i kassan*) in hand; *sport., kortsp.* in play; (*hemmastadd*) up, at home (*i* in); *vara* ~ (*insatt*) *i* be familiar with, be well versed in **3** *tiden är* ~ *att* the time has come to **4** (*på modet*) trendy, in

inne|bana *se inomhusbana* **-boende 1** *oböjligt s, alla i huset* ~ all the people living in the house; *en* ~ a lodger, *AE.* *äv.* a roomer; *vara* ~ *hos* lodge (live) with s.b. **2** *a4, bildl.* inherent (*anlag* talent); intrinsic (*värde* value) **-bruk** *för* ~ for indoor use **-bränd** *a5, bli* ~ be burnt to death in a house (*etc.*) **-bära** imply, mean, denote; (*föra med sig*) involve **-börd** signification, meaning; implication; *av* [*den*] ~*en att* to the effect that; *av följande* ~ of the following purport **-fatta** (*inbegripa*) include, comprise; (*omfatta*) embrace; (*bestå av*) consist of **-ha** (*äga*) be in possession of, have in one's possession; (*aktier, ämbete, titel*) hold

inne|hav *s7* possession; *konkr.* holding (*av guld* of gold) **-havare** possessor; owner; (*av firma e.d.*) proprietor; (*av värdepapper, ämbete*) holder; (*av prästämbete*) incumbent; ~ *av ett patent* patent owner (holder), patentee **-havarpapper** bearer bond

inne|håll *s7* contents (*pl*); *geom., filos. o.d.* content; (*ordalydelse äv.*) tenor; (*kontrakts o.d. äv.*) terms **-hålla 1** contain; (*rymma äv.*) hold; (*om tidning äv.*) carry **2** (*ej utbetala*) withhold, keep back, retain

innehålls|deklaration declaration of contents **-förteckning** table of contents, index **-lös** empty, inane **-mässigt** as regards contents; *AE.* contents-wise **-rik** containing a great deal; (*omfattande*) comprehensive; *en* ~ *dag* an eventful day; *ett* ~*t liv* a full life, a life rich in experience

inneliggande *a4* (*på lager*) in hand; (*bifogad*) enclosed; ~ *beställningar* orders on hand; ~ *varulager* (*äv.*) stock in trade

inner ['inn-] *-n inrar, sport.* inside forward **-bana** inside track **-belysning** (*i bil*) courtesy light **-dörr** inner door **-ficka** inside (inner) pocket **-fil** inside lane **-kurva** inside curve

inner|lig *a1* (*djupt känd*) ardent (*kärlek* love), fervent (*önskningar* desires); intimate (*vänskap* friendship); (*hjärtlig*) heartfelt; (*uppriktig*) sincere; *min* ~*aste önskan* (*äv.*) my dearest wish; *dikten har en* ~ *ton* the poem has a warm sincerity **-ligen, -ligt** ardently *etc.*; (*friare*) heartily, utterly (*trött på* tired of)

inner|sida inner side; (*handens äv.*) palm **-skär** *sport., åka* ~ do the inside edge **-slang** inner tube

inner|st ['inn-] *adv,* ~ [*inne*] farthest (furthest) in; ~ *inne* (*bildl.*) at heart **-sta I** *a, best. form*

---

superl. innermost, inmost (*tankar* thoughts), (*friare*) deepest **II** *n, i sitt* ~ in one's heart [of hearts] **inner|stad** city (town) centre; *AE.* downtown **-tak** ceiling

innerv|ation innervation **-era** innerve

inner|vägg interior (inside) wall; (*mellanvägg*) partition [wall] **-öra** internal (inner) ear, labyrinth

innesko indoor shoe

inneslut|a enclose; (*omge*) encompass, encircle, shut in; (*innefatta*) include **-ning** kärntekn. containment

inne|stående *a4* (*outtagen*) still due; (*i bank*) deposited, on deposit; ~ *fordringar* claims remaining to be drawn; ~ *lön* salary (wages) due **-ställe** in-place **-varande** *a4* present; ~ *år* this year; *den 6:e* ~ *månad* on the 6th inst. (of this month) **-vånare** *se invånare*

innov|ation innovation **-atör** innovator **-era** innovate

in|nästla *rfl* insinuate (wheedle) o.s. (*hos* into the confidence of) **-nöta** drum in

inofficiell unofficial; informal

inokulera inoculate

inom [ˣinnåm] *prep* **1** *rumsbet.* within; (*inuti*) in; ~ *sig* inwardly, in one's heart (mind); *vara* ~ *synhåll* keep within sight; ~ *sitt område är han* in his speciality (field) he is; *styrelsen utser* ~ *sig* the directors elect from among their number **2** (*om rörelse*) within, into; *komma* ~ *hörhåll* get within hearing **3** *tidsbet.* within; (*om*) in (*ett ögonblick* a moment); ~ *kort* shortly, before long; ~ *loppet av* [with]in the course of; ~ *den närmaste tiden* in the immediate future; ~ *mindre än en timme* in less than an hour

inombordare [-ɔ:r-] boat with inboard motor

inombords [-ɔ:r-] *sjö.* (*ombord*) on board, aboard; *bildl.* (*invärtes*) inside; *han har mycket* ~ he has got a lot in him **-motor** inboard motor

inomeuropeisk intra-European

inomhus indoors **-antenn** indoor aerial (antenna) **-bana** *sport.* covered (indoor) court; (*ishockey-*) indoor rink **-sport** indoor sports

inom|skärs [-ʃä:rs] in the skerries, inside the belt of skerries (islands) **-statlig** intrastate **-äktenskaplig** marital, matrimonial

inopportun *a5* inopportune

in|ordna range, arrange, adapt; ~ *i ett system* arrange according to a system, systematize; ~ *sig under* conform to **-packning 1** packing [up], wrapping **2** *med.* pack **-pass** *s7* interjection, remark; observation **-passa 1** fit in (into), adapt **2** (*inflicka*) put in

inpisk|ad *a5* thoroughpaced, out-and-out; *en* ~ *lögnare* a consummate liar; *en* ~ *skojare* an out-and-out rogue **-are** whip **-ning** whipping up

inplacer|a [ˣinn-] place **-ing** placing

in|planera [ˣinn-] schedule, plan the organization of **-planta** implant

inplanter|a [ˣinn-] **1** (*i krukor*) transplant **2** (*från annat land e.d.*) naturalize **-ing** (*av växter*) transplanting; (*av fiskyngel äv.*) introduction, putting out; (*av skog*) afforestation

inpricka dot, point

inprägl|a engrave (*ngt i sitt minne* s.th. on one's mind); impress (*i* on) **-ing** engraving *etc.*

in|pränta impress (*hos* on); bring home (*hos* to); *få ngt ~t i sig* have s.th. drummed into one **-pyrd** [-y:-] *a5* reeking, stuffy, choked; *bildl.* impregnated, steeped in

inpå I [*×*inn *el.* 'inn-] *prep* **1** *våt ~ bara kroppen* wet to the [very] skin; *för nära ~ varandra* too close to one another (together) **2** *till långt ~ natten* until far into the night **II** [-'på:] *adv, för nära ~* too close [to it, him *etc.*]

inram|a frame **-ning** framing; *konkr.* frame [work]; (*friare*) setting

in|rangera [*×*inn-] *se inordna* **-rapportera** report; (*friare*) give a report of

inre ['inn-] **I** *a, komp.* **1** inner; interior; internal; (*inom familj, hus, land äv.*) domestic, home; ~ *angelägenheter* domestic (home) affairs; ~ *diameter* inside (inner, internal) diameter; ~ *energi* internal energy; ~ *mission* home mission; ~ *organ* internal organ; ~ *oroligheter* civil (internal) disturbances; ~ *säkerhet* public safety **2** *bildl.* intrinsic (*värde* value); essential (*sanning* truth); innate (*egenskap* quality); (*andlig*) inner (*liv* life); ~ *öga* inward eye **II** *n* (*saks*) interior; inside; (*ngns*) inner man; *i sitt ~* inwardly, deep down; *det ~ av landet* the inland (upcountry); *hela mitt ~ är upprört över* my whole soul (being) is revolted at

inred|a fit up, equip (*till* as); (*med möbler*) furnish **-ning 1** fitting up *etc.*; equipment **2** *konkr.* fittings (*pl*), appointments (*pl*); interior decoration **-ningsarkitekt** interior decorator (designer)

inregistrer|a [*×*inn-] register; enter; *hand.* file, docket; (*friare*) score (*en framgång* a success) **-ing** registering *etc.*; registration; enrolment

inresa *s1* journey up (*till staden* [in]to town); (*t. annat land*) entry, arrival

inresekretorisk [-'tɔ:-] internal-secretion

inrese|tillstånd entry permit **-visum** entry visa

inrid|en *a5* broken[-in], broken to the saddle **-ning** breaking[-in]; horse-breaking

inrikes I *adv* [with]in the country **II** *oböjligt a* inland (*porto* postage); home (*angelägenheter* affairs); domestic, internal **-departement** ministry of the interior; (*i Storbritannien ung.*) Home Office; *AE. ung.* department of the interior **-flyg** domestic (inland) aviation; domestic airlines **-handel** domestic (home) trade **-minister** minister of the interior; (*i Storbritannien ung.*) Home Secretary; *AE. ung.* secretary of the interior **-nyheter** *pl* home news (*sg*) **-politik** domestic policy; ~[*en*] home (internal) politics **-politisk** [of] domestic [policy] **-porto** inland postage

inrikt|a put in position, adjust; (*vapen*) aim (*mot* at); *bildl.* direct (*mot, på* towards, *fientligt* against); ~ *sig på* direct one's energies towards, concentrate upon, (*sikta på*) aim at **-ning** putting in position, adjusting; (*av vapen*) aiming; *bildl.* [aim and] direction, concentration

in|rim assonance **-ringa** encircle, surround; *bildl. äv.* close (hedge) in **-ringning** encircling *etc.* **-rista** engrave; carve, cut **-ristning** engraving *etc.* **-rop** (*på auktion*) bid; *konkr.* [auction] purchase **-ropa 1** *teat.*, *bli ~d* be called before the curtain **2** (*på auktion*) buy [at an (the) auc-

tion] **-ropning** [-ɔ:-] curtain call **-rotad** *a5, bildl.* deep-rooted, deep-seated, inveterate, ingrained **-rusning** rushing in; inrush **-ruta** chequer [out], divide up into squares **-rutad** *a5, bildl.* regular, dictated by routine **-rutning** [-u:-] chequering *etc.* **-ryckning 1** *mil.* reporting for active service **2** *boktr.* indentation, inden[tion] **-rymma 1** (*rymma*) accommodate; (*innehålla*) contain; (*innefatta*) include **2** (*bevilja*) accord, grant

inrådan *r, på* (*mot*) *min ~* on (contrary to) my advice (recommendation)

inrätt|a 1 (*anlägga*) establish, set up; (*skola e.d.*) found; (*ämbete*) create; (*inreda*) equip **2** (*ordna*) arrange **3** *rfl* settle down (*bekvämt* comfortably); (*rätta sig*) adapt (accommodate) o.s. (*efter* to) **-ning 1** (*anstalt*) establishment; (*allmän, social äv.*) institution **2** (*anordning*) device, appliance, apparatus

insalta salt [down], cure; (*gurkor, sill*) pickle

insaml|a collect, gather **-ing** collection; (*av pengar äv.*) subscription; *starta en ~* start (get up) a subscription (*för* for, in aid of)

insamlings|aktion fundraising (collection) drive **-lista** subscription list

insats 1 *tekn.* lining, inset **2** (*i spel, företag o.d.*) stake[s *pl*]; (*i affär*) deposit; (*i bolag*) investment **3** (*prestation*) achievement, effort; (*bidrag*) contribution (*i* to; *för* towards); (*andel*) share, part; *göra en ~* make a contribution (an effort) **-lägenhet** owner (freehold) flat; *AE.* cooperative apartment

in|satt *a4, ~ i* initiated in, well-informed on, familiar with **-scenera** stage **-se** see, perceive; (*förstå*) realize; (*vara medveten om*) be aware of **-seende** *s6, ha ~ över* supervise, superintend **-segel** seal

insegl|ing *under ~ till* inward bound for; *under ~en till Stockholm* while sailing into Stockholm **-ingsränna** [navigable] channel, waterway

insekt *s3* insect; *AE. äv.* bug

insekticid *s3* insecticide

insekt[s]|art species of insect **-bett** insect bite **-forskare** entomologist **-larv** larva (*pl* larvae) **-medel** insect repellent; insecticide **-samling** entomological collection **-ätare** insect eater, insectivore

insemin|ation insemination **-era** inseminate

insida inside; inner side; (*hands äv.*) palm; (*friare o. bildl.*) interior

insignier [-'siɳni-] *pl* insignia

insikt *s3* **1** (*förståelse*) understanding (*i* of); (*inblick*) insight (*i* into); (*kännedom*) knowledge (*i, om* of); *komma till ~ om* realize, see, become aware of **2** (*kunskap*) *~er* knowledge (*sg*); *~er och färdigheter* knowledge and practical attainments

insiktsfull well-informed; (*sakkunnig*) competent

insinu|ant [-'ant *el.* -'aɳt] *a1* insinuating **-ation** insinuation **-era** insinuate

insistera insist (*på* on)

insjukna [-'ʃu:-] fall (be taken) ill (*i* with); *hon har ~t i mässlingen* she has caught the measles

insjung|en [-'ʃuɳ-] *a5* (*på grammofon, band*) recorded **-ning** recording

insjö lake **-fisk** freshwater fish
inskepp|a (varor) import by ship, ship; (pers., hästar e.d.) embark; ~ sig go on board, embark (på on; till for) **-ning** (av varor) importing by ship; (av pers. etc.) embarkation **-ningshamn** (för varor) port of shipment; (för pers. etc.) port of embarkation
in|skjuta 1 se inflicka **2** (föra) insert, interpolate **-skolningsperiod** period of adjustment to school **-skott** insertion
in|skrida intervene, step in (mot to prevent; t. förmån för on behalf of) **-skridande** s6 intervention, stepping in **-skrift** inscription; (på grav) epitaph; (på mynt) legend, inscription **-skription** [-p'ʃɔːn] inscription; legend
inskriv|a 1 enter; geom. o. bildl. inscribe; (pers.) enrol (äv. mil.); mil. enlist; jur. register **2** rfl, [låta] ~ sig enter one's name, enrol o.s.; univ. register **-ning** entering etc., entry; inscription; enrolment; enlistment; registration
inskrivnings|avgift admission fee **-bok** mil. enrolment book **-domare** ung. court registrar **-område** registration area
inskränk|a v3 (begränsa) restrict, confine; limit; (minska) reduce, cut down, curtail; ~ sig restrict o.s., economize, cut down one's expenses; ~ sig till confine o.s. to, (om sak) be confined (restricted) to, (ej överstiga) not exceed **-ning** restriction; limitation; reduction; curtailment; (förbehåll) qualification
inskränkt a1 **1** restricted etc.; i ~ bemärkelse in a restricted (limited) sense; ~ monarki constitutional (limited) monarchy **2** (trångsynt) stupid; narrow-minded **-het** (trångsynthet) stupidity; narrowness of outlook
inskärning konkr. incision; cut, notch; (i kust o.d. samt bot.) indentation
inskärp|a inculcate (hos in); (klargöra) bring home (hos to); (med eftertryck) enforce, enjoin, impress (hos upon) **-ning** inculcating etc., inculcation
inslag 1 (i väv) weft, filling, woof **2** bildl. element; feature; streak (av humor of humour), strain (av grymhet of cruelty) **-en** a5 (om paket) wrapped up; (om fönster) smashed, broken **-ning** (av paket) wrapping up; (av fönster) smashing, breaking; (av spik) knocking (driving) in
inslagsgarn weft thread (yarn)
insmickr|a rfl ingratiate o.s. (hos with) **-ande** a4 ingratiating
in|smord smeared **-smuggla** smuggle [into] **-smyga** rfl (om fel e.d.) creep (slip) in [unnoticed] **-smörjning** greasing [up], oiling **-snärja** entangle; ~ sig get [o.s.] entangled **-snöad** a5 **1** bli ~ get (be) snowed up, (blockeras) get (be) held up by snow **2** bildl., vard. narrow-minded
insolv|ens insolvency **-ent** insolvent
insomn|a go off to sleep; fall asleep; (avlida) pass away, die; djupt ~d fast asleep **-ande** s6 going off to sleep
insorter|a [ˣinn-] sort, assort **-ing** sorting, assortment
inspark sport. goal kick
in spe future, to be
inspek|tera inspect **-tion** [-k'ʃɔːn] inspection

-tionsresa tour of inspection **-tor** s3 **1** [-ˣspektår] inspector (för, över of); (för skola o. univ.) inspector **2** [-'tɔːr] lantbr. steward; bailiff **-tris** inspectress, woman inspector **-tör** inspector; surveyor, superintendent, supervisor
inspel|a (på band, skiva) record; (film) produce, shoot; ~t program recorded programme **-ning** recording; (grammofon- äv.) record; (film-) production; filmen är under ~ the film is being shot (is in production)
inspelnings|apparat recorder **-bil**, **-buss** outside broadcast car (unit)
inspicient teat. stage manager; film. studio manager
inspi|ration inspiration **-rationskälla** source of inspiration **-ratör** inspirer **-rera** inspire; ~d inspired; ~nde inspiring
insprut|a inject (i into) **-ning** injection **-ningsmotor** fuel-injection motor
insprängd a5 **1** blasted (i berget into the mountain) **2** (inblandad) disseminated; interspersed, intermixed
inspärr|a shut up: pers. äv. lock up **-ning** shutting up etc.; confinement, imprisonment
instabil unstable **-itet** instability
installation installation; univ. inauguration; (av präst) induction; (av biskop) enthronement
installations|firma electrical fitters (pl); (för värme o. sanitet) sanitary engineers (pl) **-föreläsning** inaugural (inauguration) lecture
install|atör electrician; installation engineer **-era 1** install: univ. äv. inaugurate; (präst) induct; (biskop) enthrone **2** tekn. install, fit [in], set up, mount **3** rfl install (establish, settle) o.s.
instans [-'ans el. -'aŋs] s3, jur. instance; (myndighet) authority [in charge]; högsta ~ final (highest) court of appeal; lägsta ~ court of first instance
insteg (få (vinna) ~ get (obtain, gain) a footing (i in; hos with); gain ground
instift|a institute (en orden an order); relig. äv. ordain; (grunda) found, establish **-are** founder; institutor **-else** institution; foundation
instinkt [ˣinn-, äv. -'inkt] s3 instinct **-iv** [äv. ˣinn-] a5 instinctive **-ivt** [-'iːvt, äv. ˣinn-] adv, instinctively, by instinct **-mässig** a5 instinctive; intuitive
institut s7 institute; institution (äv. jur.); (skola) school, college
institution institution, institute **-alisera** institutionalize **-ell** a5 institutional
instruera instruct; mil. brief
instruk|tion [-k'ʃɔːn] instruction; (föreskrift, äv. konkr) instructions (pl); mil. briefing **-tionsbok** instruction book, manual **-tiv** [äv. 'inn-] a1 instructive **-tör** instructor
instrument s7 instrument
instrumental a5 instrumental **-ist** instrumentalist **-musik** instrumental music
instrument|ation instrumentation, orchestration **-bräda**, **-bräde** se instrumentpanel
instrument|ell a5 instrumental **-era** orchestrate, instrument
instrument|flygning instrument flying **-landning** instrument landing **-makare** instrument maker **-panel** instrument panel (board); (i bil äv.) dashboard **-tavla** instrument board (panel);

switchboard

in|strödd *a5, bildl.* interspersed **-strömmande** *a4* inpouring

instuder|a [ˣinn-] study; rehearse **-ing** studying *etc.*; rehearsal

instundande *a4* coming, approaching (*måndag* Monday)

inställa 1 (*avpassa*) adjust, set; (*kamera, kikare e.d.*) focus; (*radio, TV*) tune in; (*rikta*) point, direct **2** (*upphöra med*) cancel, call off; (*arbete*) discontinue, cease, stop; (*betalningar*) suspend, stop; ~ *fientligheterna* suspend hostilities, cease fire; ~ *förhandlingarna* discontinue (suspend) negotiations **3** *rfl* (*infinna sig*) appear (*inför rätta* in court); *mil.* report [for duty]; (*vid möte*) put in an appearance, turn up; (*om sak*) make its appearance; (*om känsla*) make itself felt (*hos* in); (*uppenbara sig*) present itself; ~ *sig på* (*bereda sig på*) prepare o.s. for, (*räkna med*) count on

inställ|ande *s6* **1** adjustment *etc.* **2** (*inhibering*) cancellation, discontinuance, suspension **-bar** *a5* adjustable

inställd *a5* adjusted *etc.*; *fientligt* ~ inimically disposed; *vara* ~ *på* be prepared for; *vara* ~ *på att* intend to

inställelse *jur.* appearance (*inför* before) **-order** *mil.* calling-up papers (order)

inställ|ning 1 adjustment; setting; (*tids-*) timesetting, timing; *foto. äv.* focusing; *radio.* tuning in **2** *bildl.* attitude (*till* to, towards); outlook (*till* on) **-sam** *a1* ingratiating, cringing **-samhet** ingratiation

1 instämma *jur.* summon to appear; call (*som vittne* as a witness)

2 instämma *bildl.* agree (*i* with), concur (*i* in); ~ *med ngn* agree with s.b.

instämmande *s6* concurrence, agreement

instängd *a5* shut up; (*inlåst*) locked up; confined; (*unken*) stuffy, close **-het** (*unkenhet*) stuffiness; closeness

insubordina|tion insubordination **-tionsbrott** case of insubordination, breach of discipline

insufficiens *s3* insufficiency

insug|a suck in; (*inandas*) inhale; (*friare, om sak*) suck up, absorb, imbibe; *bildl.* drink in (*beröm* praise); (*tillägna sig*) acquire, pick up **-ning** sucking in *etc.*; absorption, imbibition; *tekn.* intake, suction

insugnings|rör (*i motor*) inlet pipe **-ventil** inlet valve

insulin *s4* insulin **-behandling** insulin treatment **-chock** insulin reaction (shock) **-koma** insulin coma

insulär *a5* insular

insupa (*frisk luft e.d.*) drink in, inhale; (*uppsuga*) absorb; *bildl.* imbibe

insurgent insurgent, rebel

insvepa envelop, enwrap; ~ *sig i* wrap o.s. up (envelop o.s.) in

insväng|d *a5* curved inwards; ~ *i midjan* shaped at the waist **-ning** curving inwards; *en* ~ an inward curve

in|sydd *a5, vard.* placed behind bars, doing time **-syltad** *a5, bildl.* involved, mixed up **-syn 1** observation; view; *skyddad mot* ~ protected from view **2** *bildl.* insight; public control (*i* of)

insändar|e 1 *pers.* sender[-in]; (*t. tidning*) correspondent **2** (*brev t. tidning*) letter to the editor **-spalt** letters-to-the-editor column

insätta put in; (*inbetala*) pay in; (*i bank*) deposit; (*i företag*) invest; (*förordna*) appoint, install; (*ngn i hans rättigheter*) establish; ~ *ngn som sin arvinge* make s.b. one's heir

insätt|are (*i bank*) depositor **-ning** putting in *etc.*; (*av pengar*) deposition, investment; *konkr.* deposit **-ningskvitto** deposit receipt (ticket)

insöndr|ing endocrine secretion **-ingsorgan** endocrine gland

insöva *bildl., se invagga*

inta *se intaga*

intag *tekn.* intake; *elektr.* lead-in; (*friare*) inlet

intaga 1 take in; (*förtära*) take; (*måltid*) eat, have; (*på sjukhus, i skola etc.*) admit; (*i tidning*) insert, publish **2** (*ta i besittning*) take; occupy (*äv. mil.*); (*upptaga*) take up, occupy; ~ *sin plats* take one's seat; ~ *en avvaktande hållning* take up a wait-and-see attitude; ~ *en framskjuten ställning* hold (occupy) a prominent position **3** (*betaga*) captivate

intag|ande *a4* attractive, charming **-ning** taking in *etc.*; taking; admission; insertion; *mil. äv.* capture

intagnings|nämnd admissions board **-poäng** admission credits

intakt *a4* intact, whole

intala 1 (*på band o.d.*) record **2** ~ *ngn ngt* put s.th. into a p.'s head; ~ *ngn att göra ngt* persuade s.b. to do (into doing) s.th.; ~ *ngn mod* inspire s.b. with courage; ~ *sig* persuade o.s.; ~ *sig mod* give o.s. courage

intarsia [-ˈtarsia] *s1* inlaid wood, intarsia

inte not; no; ~ *för* ~ not for nothing; ~ *en enda gång* (*äv.*) never once; ~ *mig emot* I have no objection, *vard.* OK by me; ~ *sant?* don't you think so?, isn't that so?; ~ *senare än* not (no) later than; ~ *för att jag klagar* not that I'm complaining; *jaså,* ~ *det?* oh, you don't (aren't *etc.*)?; *det var* ~ *för tidigt* that was none too early; *det är* ~ *utan att jag tycker* I must say I think

inteckn|a mortgage **-ing** mortgage; encumbrance, security; *ha en* ~ *i* have a mortgage on **-ingslån** mortgage loan

integral *s3* integral **-kalkyl** integral calculus **-tecken** [symbol denoting an] integral

integration integration

integrer|a integrate; ~*d krets* integrated circuit **-ande** *a4* integral, integrant; *utgöra en* ~ *del av* form an integral part of **-ing** integration

integritet integrity

intele|fonera [ˣinn-] dictate over a telephone, send in by telephone **-grafera** send in by telegram (wire, cable)

intellekt *s7* intellect; *ett rörligt* ~ a lively intellect **intellektu|alisera** intellectualize **-alism** intellectualism **-ell** *a5* intellectual

intelligens *s3* intelligence **-aristokrati** intellectual aristocracy **-fri** unintelligent, stupid **-kvot** intelligence quotient (*förk.* I.Q.) **-mätning** intelligence measurement **-prov** intelligence test **-snobb** intellectual snob **-test** intelligence test **-ålder** mental age

intelligent *a1* intelligent; (*starkare*) clever

intelligentia [-'gentsia] *s1* intelligentsia
intendent (*förståndare*) manager, superintendent; (*förvaltare*) steward; (*vid museum*) keeper, curator; (*i ämbetsverk*) comptroller, controller; (*polis*-) superintendent; *mil.* commissary, quartermaster, *AE.* quartermaster supply officer
intendentur *mil.* commissariat [service] **-förband** quartermaster unit **-kår** ~en (*i Storbritannien*) the Army Supply Corps, (*i USA*) the Quartermaster Corps
intensifier|a intensify **-ing** intensification
intensitet intensity
intensjv [*äv.* 'inn-] *a1* (*motsats extensiv*) intensive; (*stark, kraftig*) intense; (*ivrig*) keen, energetic **-kurs** crash course **-vård** intensive care **-vårdsavdelning** intensive care unit
intention intention
inter|agera [-a'ge:ra] interact **-aktion** [-ak'ʃɔ:n] interaction **-aktjv** interactive
interdjkt *s7* interdict; injunction
interdisciplinär interdisciplinary
interferens *s3* interference **-fenomen** interference phenomenon
interferera interfere
interferon [-'å:n] *s3* interferon
interfolier|a interleave; (*friare*) intersperse **-ing** interleaving *etc.*
inter|galaktisk [-'lakt-] *a5* intergalactic **-glacial** interglacial
interimistisk [-'mist-] *a5* provisional, temporary
interims|bevis [ˣ'inn-] scrip; *AE.* interim certificate **-regering** caretaker government **-styrelse** provisional (interim) board
interkontinental intercontinental **-robot** intercontinental ballistic missile (*förk.* ICBM)
inter|lokutör interlocutor **-ludium** [-'lu:-] *s4* interlude **-messo** [-'messɔ], **-mezzo** [-'metså] *s6* (*mus. o. friare*) intermezzo; (*uppträde*) interlude **-mittent** *a4* intermittent; ~ *ljus* (*i fyr*) occulting light
intern [-'tä:rn] **I** *s3* internee; (*i fängelse*) inmate **II** *a5* internal; domestic (*angelägenhet* matter) **-alisera** internalize
internat *s7, se internatskola*
international *s3* **1** *polit.* International **2** *I~en* The Internationale **-isera** internationalize **-isering** [-'se:-] internationalization **-ism** internationalism **-ist** internationalist **-istisk** [-'ist-] *a5* international
internationell international
internatskola boarding school; (*i Storbritannien*) public school
interner|a shut up, confine; (*krigsfånge e.d.*) intern, detain; *de ~de* the internees (inmates) **-ing** shutting up, confinement; internment, detention **-ingsläger** internment (detention) camp
internist internist
internordisk [-'nɔ:r-] inter-Nordic
intern|rekrytering internal (inside) recruitment **-TV** closed-circuit television (CCTV)
interpella|nt questioner, interpellator **-tion** question, interpellation; (*i Storbritannien vanl.*) question [in debate] **-tionsdebatt** debate on question raised in parliament
interpellera interpellate; (*i Storbritannien vanl.*)

ask a question, question
inter|planetarisk [-'ta:-] *a5* interplanetary **-polera** interpolate **-polering** interpolation **-pret** *s3* interpreter
interpunkt|era punctuate; point **-tion** [-k'ʃɔ:n] punctuation **-tionstecken** punctuation mark
inter|regnum [-ˣreŋn- *el.* -'reŋn-] *s7* interregnum **-rogativ** ['inn- *el.* -'i:v] *a5* interrogative
interurban *a5* interurban **-samtal** trunk call; *AE.* long-distance call
intervall *s3, s7* interval
interven|era intervene; (*medla*) mediate **-tion** intervention; mediation
intervju *s3* interview
intervju|a [-'vju:a] interview **-are** interviewer
intervju|objekt interviewee, person interviewed **-offer** *skämts.* interviewee **-undersökning** field survey (investigation) **-uttalande** statement made during an interview
intet I *pron, se ingen*; ~ *ont anande* unsuspecting, suspecting no mischief **II** *n* **1** nothing; *gå om* ~ come to naught (nothing), miscarry; *därav blev* ~ nothing came of it, it came to nothing **2** (*intighet*) (*tomma* empty) nothingness **-dera** *se ingendera* **-sägande** *a4* (*tom*) empty; (*obetydlig*) insignificant; (*uttryckslös*) vacant
intig *a5* (*tom*) empty; (*fåfänglig*) vain **-het** emptiness; vanity
intill I [ˣ'inn-, 'inn- *el.* -'till] *prep* **1** *rumsbet.* up to, to; next to; (*emot*) against; *nära* ~ close (near) to; *strax* ~ quite close to **2** *tidsbet.* until, up to **II** [-'till] *adv* adjacent, adjoining; *nära* ~ close (near) by **-liggande** [-ˣtill-] *a4* (*hopskr. intilliggande*) adjacent, adjoining
intjm *a1* intimate, close **-itet** intimacy
intjäna earn, make; ~*d lön* salary earned in advance
intoler|abel [-'a:bel] *a2* intolerable **-ans** [-'ans *el.* -'aŋs] intolerance **-ant** [-'ant *el.* -'aŋt] intolerant
inton|ation intonation **-era** intone
intramuskulär *a5* intramuscular
intransitiv [ˣ'inn- *el.* 'inn-] *a5* intransitive
intravenös *a5* intravenous
intressant [-'ant *el.* -'aŋt] *a1* interesting
intresse [-ˣ'tresse] *s6* interest; *av* ~ *för saken* out of interest in the matter; *fatta* ~ *för, finna* ~ *i* take an interest in; *tappa* ~*t för* lose interest in; *tillvarataga sina* ~*n* protect one's interests; *vara av* ~ be of interest (*för* to); *det ligger inte i hans* ~ it is not in his interests **-gemenskap** community of interests **-grupp** pressure group **-inriktning** main interest **-konflikt** conflict of interests **-lös** without interest; uninteresting (*äv. om pers.*) **-motsättning** conflict of interests
intressent interested party; participant; (*delägare*) partner
intresseområde *se intressesfär*
intressera interest; ~*de parter* interested parties, parties concerned; *musikaliskt* ~*d* with musical interests; ~*d av* (*för*) interested in; ~ *ngn för ngt* interest s.b. in s.th.; ~ *sig för* take [an] interest in, be interested in; *det* ~*r mig mycket* it is of great interest to me, I take [a] great interest in it
intresse|sfär sphere of interest **-väckande** *a4* interesting

I

intrig *s3* intrigue; *(stämpling äv.)* plot *(äv. i drama e.d.)*; *(friare)* scheme **-ant** [-'ant *el.* -'aŋt] *a1* intriguing; plotting; scheming **-era** intrigue, plot; scheme **-makare** intriguer; *(ränksmidare)* plotter, schemer **-spel** plotting, scheming; intrigues *(pl)* **-ör** *se -makare*
intrikat *a1* intricate, complicated
intrimma trim, run in
introducera introduce *(hos* to)
introduktion [-k'ʃɑ:n] introduction
introduktions|brev letter of introduction **-erbjudande** introductory offer **-kurs** introductory course
introduktör introducer
introspek|tion [-k'ʃɑ:n] introspection **-tiv** *a5* introspective
introvert *a4* introvert
intrumfa *se trumfa*
intryck 1 *(märke)* impress, mark *(efter* from, of) **2** *bildl.* impression; *mottaglig för* ~ susceptible to impressions, impressionable; *göra* ~ *av att vara* give the impression of being; *göra* ~ *på* make an impression on; *ta* ~ *av* be influenced by; *jag har det ~et att* I have the impression that
in|trång *s7* encroachment, trespass *(i, på* on); *göra* ~ *på* encroach (trespass) on **-träda 1** ~ [*i*] enter **2** *bildl. (om pers.)* step in *(i ngns ställe* to a p.'s place); *(om sak)* set in; *(börja)* begin, commence; *(följa)* ensue; *(uppstå)* arise **-träde** *s6* entrance *(i* into); *(i sht bildl.* entry *(i* into); admission, admittance; *(början)* commencement, setting in; *vid mitt* ~ *i rummet* on my entering the room; *göra sitt* ~ *i (vanl.)* enter; *söka* ~ apply for admission
inträdes|ansökan application for admission **-avgift** entrance (admission) fee **-biljett** admission (entrance) ticket *(till* for) **-fordringar** entrance requirements, qualifications for admission **-prov** entrance examination **-spärr** *(t. utbildning)* restricted admission **-sökande** *s9* applicant [for admission]
in|träffa 1 *(hända)* happen; occur, come about **2** *(-falla)* occur, fall *(i slutet av maj* at the end of May) **3** *(anlända)* arrive, turn up *(i* at, in) **-träna** drill
inträng|a penetrate; *(med våld)* intrude **-ande I** *s6* penetration; intrusion **II** *a4* penetrating; penetrative *(förstånd* intelligence) **-ing** intruder
intui|tion intuition **-tiv** *a5* intuitive
in|tvåla soap; *(haka äv.)* lather **-tyg** *s7 (i sht av myndighet)* certificate *(om* of); *(i sht av privatpers.)* testimonial *(om, på, över* respecting, as to); *jur.* affidavit **-tyga** *(skriftligen)* certify; *(bekräfta)* affirm; *härmed ~s att* this is to certify that; *rätt avskrivet ~r* true copy certified by **-tåg** entry *(i* into); march (marching) in; *hålla sitt* ~ make one's entry **-tåga** march in; ~ *i* march into **-täkt** *s3* **1** ~*er* income *(sg)*, receipts, *(statens, kommuners)* revenue *(sg)*, *(avkastning)* yield *(sg)*, *(biljett-)* takings, *vard.* take *(sg)* **2** *ta ngt till* ~ *för* use s.th. as a justification for **-under** [-'und-] underneath; *i våningen* ~ in the flat below **-uti** inside; within **-vadera** invade **-vagga** ~ *ngn i säkerhet* lull s.b. into a sense of security, throw s.b. off his guard; ~ *sig* lull o.s. *(i* into) **-val** *s7* election *(i* into)

invalid *s3* disabled person (soldier *etc.*); invalid **-bil, -fordon** invalid car
invalidi|sera disable **-tet** disability; *fullständig* ~ total disability (disablement)
invalid|itetsersättning disablement benefit **-pension** disability pension, disablement annuity **-vagn** invalid car
invand [-a:-] *a5* habitual; ~*a föreställningar* ingrained ideas (notions, opinions)
invandra immigrate *(till* into); *(om djur, växter)* find (make) its way in (into the country)
invandrar|e immigrant **-verk** *Statens* ~ [the] Swedish immigration board
invandring immigration
invandrings|förbud ban on immigration **-kvot** immigration quota **-tillstånd** immigration certificate (permit)
invasion invasion **invasionsarmé** army of invasion, invading army
inveckl|a involve; ~ *sig* get [o.s.] involved (entangled) *(i* in) **-ad** *a5* involved *(i* in); *(svårlöst)* complicated, intricate
invektiv *s7* invective
inventarie|bok inventory (stock) book **-förteckning** inventory **-konto** fittings and fixtures account
inventar|ium [-'ta:-] *s4* **1** *(förteckning)* inventory **2** *(fast)* fixture; *-ier* effects, movables, *(i hus, på kontor e.d.)* furniture (fittings) and fixtures, *(i fabrik e.d.)* equipment, *hand. o. lantbr.* stock *(sg)* **3** *pers.* fixture
inventer|a make an inventory of, inventory; *hand.* take stock of **-ing** inventory; *hand.* stock-taking
inven|tionssoffa [-n'ʃo:ns-] sofa bed **-tiös** [-'ʃö:s] *a1* ingenious; ingeniously planned
inverk|a have an effect (influence) *(på* on); ~ *på (äv.)* influence, affect **-an** influence, effect; *utsatt för luftens* ~ *(äv.)* exposed to the air; *röna* ~ *av* be influenced (affected) by; *utöva* ~ *på* influence, affect
inversion inversion
invertebrat invertebrate [animal]
invert|era invert **-socker** [-ˣvärt-] invert sugar
invester|a invest **-are** investor **-ing** investment
investerings|avgift investment tax (duty) **-bolag** investment company **-kostnad** investment cost **-objekt** investment object (project) **-volym** volume of investment
investitur investiture
investmentbolag investment trust company
invid I [ˣinn-, 'inn- *el.* -'vi:d] *prep* by; *(utefter)* alongside; *tätt* ~ *vägen* close to the road **II** [-'vi:d] *adv* close (near) by *(äv. tätt* ~)
invig|a 1 *(t.ex. kyrka, flagga, biskop)* consecrate; *(t.ex. skolhus, bro)* inaugurate, open; *(präst)* ordain; *(använda första gången)* put on (wear, use) for the first time **2** *(göra förtrogen med)* initiate *(i* into) **3** *(helga)* consecrate, dedicate **-ning 1** consecration; dedication; inauguration, opening; ordination **2** initiation
invignings|fest inaugural (opening) ceremony **-tal** inaugural (dedicatory) address (speech)
invikning [-vi:k-] turning (folding) in; *konkr.* inward fold
invit *s3 (inbjudan)* invitation; *(påstötning)* inti-

mation; (*vink*) hint **-ation** invitation **-era** invite
invokation invocation
involvera involve
invån|arantal number of inhabitants, [total] population **-are** inhabitant; (*i hus äv.*) inmate; (*i stadsdel o.d.*) resident; *per* ~ (*äv.*) per head (capita)
inväg|a weigh in **-ning** weighing in
invälja elect; return
invänd|a object, raise (make) objections (*mot* to, against); *jag har ingenting att* ~ [*mot det*] I have no objection; *har du ngt att* ~? have you any objection to make (anything to say against)?; *nej, -e hon* no, she protested (demurred) **-ig** *a5* internal, inside **-igt** *adv* internally; (*på insidan*) [on the] inside; (*i det inre*) in the interior **-ning** objection (*mot* to); *göra* ~*ar, se* invända **-vändningsfri** unobjectionable
invänta wait for; (*avvakta*) await
invärtes *oböjligt a* (*om sjukdom o.d.*) internal; inward (*suck* sigh); *för* ~ *bruk* for internal use; ~ *medicin* internal medicine
invävd *a5* woven in[to] (*äv. bildl.*)
inymp|a inoculate; *i sht bildl.* implant (*hos ngn in s.b.*) **-ning** inoculation; engraftment
inåt ['inn-] **I** *prep* towards the interior of; into; ~ *landet* up country **II** *adv* inwards; *gå längre* ~ go (move) further in; *dörren går* ~ the door opens inwards
inåt|buktad *a5,* **-böjd** *a5* bent inwards; in [ward]-bent **-gående** *I s6* (*om fartyg*) *på* ~ inward bound **II** *a4* (*om dörr e.d.*) *vara* ~ open inwards **-riktad** *a5* pointing (that points) inwards; *bildl. se följande* **-vänd** *a5* turned inwards; (*om blick, tanke e.d. äv.*) introverted, introspective; *psykol.* introvert **-vändhet** introspectiveness
inägor *pl* infields
inälvor *pl* bowels, intestines; (*hos djur*) viscera, entrails; *vard.* guts
inälvsparasit intestinal parasite
inöv|a practise; (*repetera*) rehearse; train **-ande** *s6* practising; rehearsal; training
iordning|gjord [i*x*å:rd-] *a5, är* ~ has been got ready **-ställa** put in order
Irak *n* Iraq **irak|ier** [i'ra:-] *s9,* **-isk** *a5* Iraqi
Iran *n* [Islamic Republic of] Iran **iran|ier** [i'ra:-] *s9,* **-sk** [i'ra:-] *a5* Iranian
irer ['i:-] Irish Celt, Gael
iridium [i'ri:-] *s8* iridium
iris ['i:-] *s2, anat. o. bot.* iris **-bländare** *foto.* iris diaphragm
irisk ['i:-] *a5* Irish **iriska** ['i:-] (*språk*) Irish Gaelic
Irland ['i:r-] *n* (*ön*) Ireland; (*republiken*) [Republic of] Ireland, Irish Republic, Southern Ireland
irländ|are [*x*i:r-] Irishman; *skämts.* Paddy; *-arna* (*äv.*) the Irish **-sk** *a5* Irish; *I~a fristaten* Irish Free State; *I~a republiken, se* Irland **-ska 1** (*språk*) Irish [Gaelic] **2** (*kvinna*) Irishwoman
iron|i *s3* irony **-iker** [i'ro:-] ironic[al] person **-isera** speak ironically (*över* of, about) **-isk** [i'ro:-] *a5* ironic[al]
irra ~ [*omkring*] wander (rove) about
irrationell *a1* irrational; ~*a tal* irrational numbers
irrbloss will-o'-the-wisp, friar's lantern, jack-o'-lantern

ir|reell unreal **-reguljär** irregular **-relevant** [-'ant *el.* -'aŋt] irrelevant **-religiös** [-'ʃö:s, -'jö:s, -gi'ö:s] irreligious **-reparabel** [-'a:bel] irreparable **-reversibel** [-'i:bel] irreversible
irr|färd roving (rambling) expedition; ~*er* wanderings [hither and thither] **-gång** maze; labyrinth
irrita|bel [-'a:bel] *a2* irritable **-ment** *s7* excitant; stimulus **-tion** irritation **-tionsmoment** source of irritation
irritera irritate; *bildl. äv.* annoy, harass
irrlära false doctrine, heresy
irrlärig *a5* heretical **-het** heresy
iråkad *a5, hans* ~*e svårigheter* the difficulties he has got into
is *s2* ice; *under* ~*en* (*bildl.*) (*moraliskt*) done for, (*ekonomiskt*) down on one's luck; *bryta* ~*en* (*bildl.*) break the ice; *frysa till* ~ freeze [in]to ice; *gå ner sig på* ~*en* go through the ice [and get drowned]; *ha* ~ *i magen* (*bildl.*) keep one's cool; *lägga på* ~ (*bildl.*) postpone, defer; ~*arna är osäkra* the ice on the lakes is not safe; ~*en har inte lagt sig än* the lake is not frozen yet; ~*en låg till in i april* the lake[s] remained frozen until April; *varning för svag* ~ (*på anslag, ung.*) Notice: Ice unsafe here
isa cover with ice; (*drycker*) ice, put in ice; (*mat*) store on ice
isabellafärgad [-*x*bella-] Isabella [coloured]
is|ande *a4, bildl.* icy; ~ *kyla a*) *eg.* biting (severe) frost, *b*) *bildl.* icy coldness **-as** *dep, blodet -ades i mina ådror* my blood ran cold
is|bana *sport.* ice track; (*skridskobana*) skating rink **-bark** coating of ice **-belagd** *a5,* icy, covered with ice **-berg** iceberg **-bergssallad** iceberg lettuce **-bildning** *abstr.* formation of ice, *konkr.* ice formation **-bill** *s2* ice pick, ice chisel **-bit** piece (lump) of ice **-björn** polar bear **-blomma** (*på fönster*) ice fern; *-blommor* frostwork **-blåsa** ice bag; (*omslag*) ice pack **-brytare** icebreaker **-brytning** icebreaking **-bälte** ice belt
iscensätt|a [i*x*se:n-] stage, produce; *bildl.* stage, engineer **-ning** staging (*äv. bildl.*), production
ischias [i*ʃ*-] *s3* sciatica **-nerv** sciatic nerve
is|dubb *s2* ice prod **-flak** ice floe **-fri** ice-free; (*om hamn äv.*) open **-gata** ice-coated (ice-glazed) road **-glass** water ice **-hav 1** *geogr., Norra (Södra) I~et* the Arctic (Antarctic) Ocean **2** *geol.* glacial sea **-hinder** ice obstacle (obstruction) **-hink** ice pail
ishockey ice hockey **-hjälm** ice-hockey helmet **-klubba** ice-hockey stick **-rink** ice-hockey rink **-rör** ice-hockey skate **-spelare** ice-hockey player
is|ig *a5* icy **-jakt** ice yacht **-kall** ice-cold, as cold as ice; (*friare*) icy cold; icy (*blick* gaze; *ton* tone of voice) **-kalott** icecap **-konvalj** [late-flowering] lily of the valley **-kristall** ice crystal **-kyld** ice-cold, iced
i|skänka fill the glasses **-slagen** *en snett* ~ *spik* a nail driven in askew; *kaffet är islaget* coffee has been poured out
islam *r* Islam **-isk** [-'la:-] *a5,* **-itisk** [-'i:t-] *a5* Islamic
Island ['i:s-] *n* Iceland

islands|lav Iceland moss **-sill** Iceland herring[s *pl*] **-tröja** Iceland sweater

is|lossning break-up of the ice, clearing of ice **-läggning** freeze-up

isländ|are Icelander **-sk** *a5* Icelandic **-ska 1** (*språk*) Icelandic **2** (*kvinna*) Icelandic woman

islänning *se isländare*

ism *s3* ism

isobar *s3* isobar

isolat *s7* isolate

isolation isolation; *tekn.* insulation **-ism** isolationism **-istisk** [-'ist-] *a5* isolationist

isolator [-ˣa:tår] *s3* insulator; (*ämne*) insulant, insulating material

isoler|a isolate; *tekn.* insulate; *bo ~t* live in a house isolated from others; *leva ~t* lead an isolated life, isolate o.s. from others **-band** insulating tape **-ing** isolation; *tekn.* insulation

isolerings|förmåga insulating capacity **-material** insulating (nonconducting) material

iso|mer I *s3* isomer **II** *a5* isomeric **-meri** *s3* isomerism

isometrisk [-'me:-] *a5*, *~ träning* isometrics (*pl, behandlas som sg*)

isomorf [-'årf] *a5* isomorphic, isomorphous **isomorfi** [-å-] *s3* isomorphism

isop [ˣisåp *el.* 'isåp] *s2*, *bot.* hyssop

iso|term *s3* isotherm **-top** [-'ta:p] *s3* isotope

is|period glacial period **-pigg** icicle **-pik** ice stick **-prinsessa** ice princess

Israel [ˣi:s-] *n* Israel

israel *s3*, **-ier** *s9*, **-isk** *a5* Israeli

israelit *s3* Israelite **-isk** *a5* Israelitic, Israelite

is|ranunkel glacier crowfoot **-rapport** ice report **-ränna** channel through the ice **-situation** ice situation **-skorpa** ice crust **-skruvning** [-u:-] [rotatory] ice pressure **-skåp** icebox **-stack** ice store **-sörja** (*på land*) ice slush; (*i vatten*) broken ice

istadig *a1* restive, refractory **-het** restiveness

istapp icicle

ister ['ist-] *s7* lard **-buk** potbelly **-flott** lard

istid glacial period; *~en* (*äv.*) the Great Ice Age

iståndsätt|a put in order; restore **-ning** refitting; restoration

istället *se ställe 2*

is|tärning ice cube **-vatten** icy water; (*kylt med is*) ice[d] water **-vidd** icy expanse

isänder *se sänder*

isär (*åtskils*) apart; (*från varandra*) away from each other **-tagbar** [-a:g-] *a5* dismountable

isättika glacial acetic acid

isätt|ning 1 (*-ande*) putting in (*etc.*) **2** *konkr.* insertion

italer [i'ta:-] *~na* the Itali **Italien** [i'ta:-] *n* Italy

italien|are [-ˣe:n-] *s9*, **-sk** *a5* Italian **-ska 1** (*språk*) Italian **2** (*kvinna*) Italian woman

iter|ation iteration **-atjv** *a5* iterative **-era** iterate

itu 1 in two; in half (halves); (*i bitar*) in pieces; *falla ~* fall to pieces; *gå ~* go to pieces **2** *ta ~ med ngn* take s.b. in hand; *ta ~ med ngt* set about (set to work at) s.th.

ituta *jag blev alltid ~d att* they always kept on at me about

ity *~ att* inasmuch as, since, as

iver ['i:-] *s2* eagerness; keenness; (*nit*) ardour, zeal; (*brinnande*) fervour, enthusiasm; *i ~n* (*hettan*) in one's ardour (enthusiasm); *med ~* (*äv.*) with great zest, with alacrity

ivra [ˣi:v-] *~ för ngt* be a zealous (keen) supporter (an ardent advocate) of s.th.; *~ för att* be eager (keen) on (*ngt görs s.th.* being done)

ivr|are [ˣi:v-] eager supporter, champion (*för* of) **-ig** *a1* eager; (*nitisk*) zealous; (*brinnande av iver*) ardent, fervent, avid; (*angelägen*) anxious; keen (*efter* on)

iögon[en]fallande [i ˣö:gån-] *a4* striking; conspicuous, noticeable; obvious

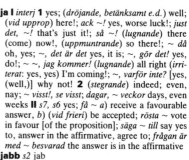

ja I *interj* **1** yes; (*dröjande, betänksamt e.d.*) well; (*vid upprop*) here!; *ack ~!* yes, worse luck!; *just det, ~!* that's just it!; *så ~!* (*lugnande*) there (come) now!, (*uppmuntrande*) so there!; *~ då* oh, yes; *~, det är det* yes, it is; *~, gör det!* yes, do!; *~ ~, jag kommer!* (*lugnande*) all right (*irriterat*: yes, yes) I'm coming!; *~, varför inte?* [yes, (well,)] why not! **2** (*stegrande*) indeed; even, nay; *~ visst!, se visst*; *dagar, ~ veckor* days, even weeks **II** *s7, s6* yes; *få ~ a*) receive a favourable answer, *b*) (*vid frieri*) be accepted; *rösta ~* vote in favour [of the proposition]; *säga ~ till* say yes to, answer in the affirmative, agree to; *frågan är med ~ besvarad* the answer is in the affirmative

jabb *s2* jab

1 jack *s7* (*hack*) gash, cut

2 jack *s2, tel.* jack

jacka *s1* (*dam-*) jacket; (*herr- äv.*) coat

jacketkrona jacket crown

jackett [ʃ-] *s3* (*mansrock*) morning coat

jackpott ['jakkpått] *s3* jackpot

jade [jeid, jä:d, *äv.* ja:d] *s5*, *miner.* jade

jag I [*vard.* ja] *pron* I; *~ själv* I myself; *det är ~* it is me **II** *s7,* self; *filos.* ego; *ngns bättre ~* a p.'s better self; *visa sitt rätta ~* show one's true colours

jag|a 1 hunt; (*hare, högvilt, fågel äv.*) shoot **2** (*förfölja*) chase, pursue; (*driva, fösa*) drive; *~ ngn på dörren* turn s.b. out; *~ ngn på flykten* put s.b. to flight; *~ livet ur ngn* worry the life out of s.b. **3** (*ila*) drive, chase; (*skynda*) hurry, dash **-are** *sjö.* **1** *mil.* destroyer **2** (*segel*) flying jib

jag|betonad *a5* egocentric **-form** *s3, i ~* in the I-form (the first person singular) **-medvetande** awareness of self, self-knowledge

jaguar *s3* jaguar

jaha well; (*jaså*) oh, I see

jaja well, well; *~ dig!* you just look out!, mind what you are doing!

jak *s2* yak

jak|a say 'yes' (*till* to), answer in the affirmative **-ande** *s6* affirmative; ~ *sats* affirmative clause; *svara* ~ answer in the affirmative

jakaranda [ʃ- *el.* j-, -ˣranda] *s1* (*trä*) jacaranda

jakob|in *s3* Jacobin **-insk** [-i:-] *a5* Jacobinic[al]

jakobsstege Jacob's ladder

1 jakt *s3, sjö.* yacht

2 jakt *s3* hunting; (*med gevär*) shooting; (-*tillfälle*) day's shooting; (*förföljande*) pursuit, chase; (*letande*) hunt (*efter* for); ~*en efter lyckan* the pursuit of happiness; *gå på* ~ go out hunting; *vara på* ~ *efter* be hunting (on the hunt) for (*äv. bildl.*) **jakt|bombplan** fighter-bomber **-byte** (*jägares*) bag; (*djurs*) prey, game; (*dagens äv.*) kill **-falk** *zool.* gyrfalcon, gerfalcon **-fasan** ring-necked pheasant **-flyg** fighter-aircraft; fighters (*pl*) **-flygare** fighter-pilot **-gevär** sporting gun **-horn** hunting horn **-hund** sporting (hunting, gun) dog; ~*arna* (*äv.*) the hounds **-kniv** hunting knife **-lag** *s2* game act **-licens** hunting licence **-lycka** the luck of the chase; *har* ~*n varit god?* have you had a good day's sport? **-mark** hunting (shooting) ground; (*inhägnad*) preserve; (*ej inhägnad*) chase; *de sälla* ~*erna* the happy hunting grounds **-plan** interceptor, fighter **-robot** *mil.* air-to-air missile; *målsökande* ~ homing missile **-rätt** shooting (hunting) rights (*pl*) **-slott** hunting seat **-stig** *ge sig ut på* ~*en* go out hunting **-stuga** shooting box (lodge), hunting lodge **-sällskap** *koll.* hunting (shooting) party; ~*et* (*äv.*) the hunt (field) **-säsong** hunting (shooting) season **-vapen** hunting (sporting) weapon **-vård** game management **-vårdare** gamekeeper; *AE.* game warden **-väska** game bag

jaly [ʃ-] *oböjligt a* jealous (*på* of)

jalusi [ʃ-] *s3* **1** (*svartsjuka*) jealousy **2** (*fönsterskärm*) jalousie; Venetian blind **3** (*på skrivbord o.d.*) roll-top; (*på skåp o.d.*) roll-front

jama mew, miaow; ~ *med* (*bildl.*) acquiesce [in everything]

Jamaica [-ˣmaika] *n* Jamaica **jamai|can, -kan** *s3,* **-cansk** [-a:-], **-kansk** [-a:-] *a5* Jamaican

jamande *s6* mew, miaow

jamb *s3* iamb[us] **-isk** ['jamm-] *a5* iambic

jams *s3* yam

jamsa drivel

jamsrot yam

janitsjar [-t'ʃa:r] *s3* janissary, janizary **-musik** Turkish music

januari [-'a:ri] *r* January

janusansikte Janus face

Japan ['ja:-] *n* Japan

japan *s3* Japanese; *vard.* Jap **-lack** [ˣja:-] japan **japan|sk** [-'pa:nsk] *a5* Japanese **-ska** *s1* **1** (*språk*) Japanese **2** (*kvinna*) Japanese woman

jardinjär [ʃ-] *s3* jardinière; flower stand

jargong [ʃar'gåŋ] *s3* lingo, jargon; slang; (*svada*) jabber; (*rotvälska*) gibberish

jarl [-a:-] *s2* jarl

ja|rop cry of 'yes' **-röst** vote in favour; aye

jasmin [ʃ-] *s3* jasmine, jessamine

jaspis ['jass-] *s2, miner.* jasper

jass *se jazz*

jaså [ˣjasså, 'jasså] oh!, indeed!, is that so?, really!; ~ *inte det!* no?, not?

jasägare yes man

Java *n* Java

javan *s3,* **-es** *s3,* **-esisk** [-'ne:-] *a5* Javan[ese]

javanesiska [-'ne:-] (*kvinna*) Javan[ese] woman

javan|sk [-'va:nsk] *a5* Javan[ese] **-ska** (*kvinna*) Javan[ese] woman

javisst *se* visst

jazz [jass] *s3* jazz

jazz|a dance [to jazz music], jazz **-balett** jazz (modern) ballet **-musik** jazz music **-orkester** jazz band

jeep [ji:p] *s2* jeep

jehu *i uttr.: som ett* ~ like a hurricane

Jemen ['je:-] *n* Yemen [Arab Republic]

jemenit *s3,* **-isk** [-'ni:-] *a5* Yemeni

Jeremia [-ˣmi:a] Jeremiah

jeremiad *s3* jeremiad, lamentation

Jeremias *se* Jeremia

Jeriko ['je:-] *n* Jericho

jersey ['jö:rsi] *textil.* jersey

Jesaja [-ˣsajja *el.* -'sajja] Isaiah

jesuit *s3* Jesuit **-isk** *a5* Jesuitic; *neds.* Jesuitical **-orden** the Society of Jesus

Jesus [ˣje:- *el.* 'je:-] Jesus **-barnet** the Infant Jesus, the Holy Child

1 jet [jett] *s3, miner.* jet

2 jet [jett] *s3, tekn.* jet

jet|aggregat jet propulsion unit **-bränsle** jet fuel **-drift** jet propulsion **-driven** *a5* jet-propelled **-flygplan** *se* jetplan **-motor** jet engine

jetong [ʃe'tåŋ] *s3* (*spelmark*) counter; (*belöning*) medal

jet|plan jet plane (aircraft) **-ström** jet stream **-åldern** the jet age

jiddisch ['jidd-] *s2* Yiddish

jigg *s2* (*dans o. tekn.*) jig

jippo ['jippo] *s6* [publicity] stunt

jiu-jitsu [-'jitsu] *s5* jujitsu, jujutsu

JK [ˣji:kå:] *förk. för justitiekanslern*

JO [ˣji:ɔ:] *förk. för justitieombudsmannen*

jo, oh yes, oh yes, why yes; (*eftertänksamt*) well, why; ~ *då* yes, to be sure; oh yes; ~ *visst vill jag det!* oh yes, certainly I will!, to be sure I will!

jobb [-å-] *s7* **1** work, job; (*knog*) job **2** *se jobberi* **jobb|a** [-å-] **1** work, be on the job; (*knoga*) go at it; (*syssla*) dabble (*med* in) **2** (*spekulera*) speculate, do jobbing **-are** **1** jobber, worker **2** (*som gör tvetydiga affärer*) profiteer **-eri** speculation; profiteering **-ig** *a1* (*mödosam*) laborious; (*besvärlig*) bothersome; *det är* ~*t* it's hard work

jobbspost [ˣjåbs-] *s3, en* ~ evil tidings (*pl*), [a piece of] bad news

jock|ej [ʃå'kej] *s3,* **-ey** ['djäcki] *s3* jockey

jod [jådd] *s3* iodine **jodda** [ˣjådda] iodize

joddel ['jådd-] *s7* yodel

joddl|a [ˣjådd-] yodel **-are** yodeller **-ing** yodelling

jod|haltig *a1* iodic **-sprit** tincture of iodine

jogg|a [-å-] jog **-are** jogger **-ning** jogging

Johannes [-'hann-] ~ *evangelium* the Gospel according to St. John, John; ~ *döparen* John the Baptist

johannes|bröd (*träd*) carob; (*frukt*) carob, St. John's bread **-ört** St. John's wort

johannit|orden [-ˣni:t-] Knights Hospitallers, Knights [of the Hospital] of St. John of Jerusalem **-riddare** Hospitaller

John Blund (*ung.*) the Sandman
joho oh yes, to be sure
jojk [-å-] *s2* Lappish song
1 jojo [ˣjɔjjɔ] *interj* why, yes to be sure!
2 jojo [ˣjɔjjɔ] *s5* yo-yo
joker [ˈjå:-] *s2* joker
jolle [-å-] *s2* ding[h]y, skiff; yawl
joller [ˈjåll-] *s7* babble; (*småbarns äv.*) crowing, prattle **jollra** [ˣjåll-] babble; crow, prattle
jolmig [ˣjåll-] *a1* mawkish, vapid; *vard.* wishy--washy
jolt [-å-] *s7* silly talk, twaddle
jon *s3* ion **-bytare** ion exchange [resin]
jongl|era [ˈjåŋ- *el.* ˈʃåŋ-] juggle (*äv. bildl.*) **-ering** [-ˈeːriŋ] juggling; jugglery **-ör** juggler
jonier [ˈjoː-] Ionian
jonisa|tion ionization **-tionskammare** ionization chamber
joniser|a ionize; ~*nde strålning* ionizing radiation **-ing** ionization
jonisk [ˈjoː-] *a5* Ionic; (*om invånare o.d.*) Ionian
jonkammare ionization (ion) chamber
jonosfär ionosphere
jord [-ɔ:-] *s2* **1** earth; (*värld*) world; *Moder J~* Mother Earth; *här på ~en* here on earth; *på hela ~en* in the whole world; *resa ~en runt* travel round the world **2** (*-yta*) ground; soil; earth; *ovan ~* above ground; *på svensk ~* on Swedish soil; *förbinda med ~* (*elektr.*) connect to earth (*särsk. AE.* ground), earth; *gå under ~en* go underground; *komma ner på ~en igen* come back (down) to earth; *sjunka genom ~en* (*bildl.*) sink into the ground **3** (*ämne, -art o.d.*) earth; (*mat-*) soil; (*stoft*) dust; *falla i god ~* fall into good ground **4** (*-område*) land; *odlad ~* cultivated land
jorda [ˣjɔ:r-] **1** (*begrava*) bury **2** *elektr.* earth
jorda|balk *s2* code of land laws, land law **-gods** landed estate (property)
jordande *s2* earth spirit
Jordanien [-ˈda:-] *n* Jordan **jordan|ier** [-ˈda:-] *s9*, **-sk** *a5* Jordanian
jord|art 1 *geol.* earth deposit **2** *lantbr.* soil **3** *kem.* earth **-artsmetall** earth metal **-axel** axis of the earth
jordbruk *s7* **1** *abstr.* farming, agriculture; *bedriva ~* do farming, farm, be a farmer **2** *konkr.* farm
jordbruk|arbefolkning agricultural population **-are** farmer, agriculturist
jordbruks|arbetare farm hand (worker) **-arbete** farming, agricultural work **-bygd** agricultural district **-departemente** ministry (*AE.* department) of agriculture **-fastighet** farm property **-maskin** agricultural machine **-minister** minister (*AE.* secretary) of agriculture **-nämnd** *Statens ~* [the Swedish] national agricultural market board **-näring** farming [industry], agriculture **-politik** agricultural policy **-produkt** agricultural product **-redskap** agricultural (farming) implement **-utskott** ~*et* [the Swedish parliamentary] standing committee on agriculture
jord|bunden *bildl.* earthbound, earthy **-bävning** [-ä:-] earthquake **-egendom** landed property
jordeliv life upon earth; ~*et* (*äv.*) this life

jordenrunt|farare [-ˣrunt-] globetrotter **-resa** round-the-world trip
jord|fräs rotary cultivator **-fästa** inter., read the burial service over **-fästning** burial (funeral) service **-förbättring** soil improvement **-geting** ground-dwelling wasp **-glob** globe **-golv** earthen floor **-gubbe** [garden] strawberry **-gubbssylt** strawberry jam **-håla** cave in the earth **-hög** earth mound, mound of earth **-höjd** earth-covered hill
jord|ig [ˣjɔ:r-] *a1* (*-aktig*) earthy; (*nersmutsad*) soiled with earth **-isk** [ˈjɔ:r-] *a5* earthly; terrestrial; (*världslig*) worldly; mundane; (*timlig*) temporal; ~*a kvarlevor* mortal remains; *lämna detta ~a* depart this life
jord|kabel underground cable **-klot** earth; ~*et* (*äv.*) the globe **-koka** *s1* clod [of earth] **-kula** den; (*djurs äv.*) cavern **-källare** underground storehouse, mattamore **-lager** earth layer; stratum [of earth] **-lapp** patch (plot) of ground **-ledning 1** *elektr.* earth (*särsk. AE.* ground) connection; *konkr.* earthing wire **2** (*underjordisk ledning*) underground conduit **-loppa** flea beetle **-lott** plot, allotment **-löpare** *zool.* ground beetle **-magnetism** terrestrial magnetism **-mån** *s3* soil (*äv. bildl.*)
jord|ning [ˣjɔ:rd-] *elektr.* earthing; *AE.* grounding **-nära** down-to-earth **-nöt** peanut, groundnut **-reform** land reform **-register** land register **-ränta** ground (land) rent **-satellit** earth satellite **-skalv** earthquake **-skorpa** [earth] crust; ~*n* the earth's crust **-skred** landslide (*äv. polit.*); landslip **-skredsseger** landslide [win] **-slå** earth up **-stöt** earthquake [shock] **-svin** aardvark **-värme** ground heat; geothermal energy **-yta** surface of the ground; (*ytområde*) area of ground; *på ~n* on the earth's surface, on the face of the earth **-ägare** landowner **-ärtskocka** [-å-] *s1* Jerusalem artichoke
jos *se* juice
jota 1 *s6* (*grekisk bokstav*) iota **2** *n, inte ett ~* not a jot (an iota)
joule [joːl] *s9, elektr.* joule
jour [ʃoːr] *s3* **1** *ha ~[en]* be on call (duty) **2** *hålla ngn à ~ med* keep s.b. informed on (as to); *hålla sig à ~ med* (*äv.*) keep [o.s.] abreast of (up to date on) **-havande** *a4*, ~ *läkare* doctor on duty (emergency call); ~ *officer* duty (orderly) officer, officer of the day **-läkare** doctor on duty
journal [ʃɔr-] *s3* **1** *bokför.* journal, diary; (*läkar-*) case book; (*sjukhus-*) case record; (*för enskild patient*) case sheet; *föra ~* keep a journal **2** *film.* newsreel **3** (*tidskrift*) journal, magazine **-film** newsreel **-föring** keeping a journal
journalism [ʃɔr-] journalism
journalist [ʃɔr-] journalist; newspaperman, *fem.* newspaperwoman; pressman **-högskola** college of journalism
journalist|ik [ʃɔr-] *s3* journalism **-isk** [-ˈist-] *a5* journalistic
jourtjänst on-call duty
jovial *a1*, **-isk** *a5* jovial **-itet** [-ˈteːt] joviality
jovisst *se under* jo
jox [jɔks] *s7* stuff, rubbish **joxa** [ˣjɔksa] peddle; ~ *ihop* (*mat e.d.*) concoct, (*trassla till*) muddle up; ~ *med ngt* mess about with s.th.

ju I *adv* why; (*som du vet*) you know (see); (*naturligtvis*) of course; (*visserligen*) it is true; (*som bekant*) as we [all] know; (*det förstås*) to be sure; *du vet ~ att* you know of course that; *där är du ~!* why, there you are!; *jag har ~ sagt det flera gånger* I have said (told you) so several times, haven't I?; *du kan ~ göra det a*) (*om du vill*) there's nothing to prevent you doing so, *b*) (*uppmanande*) you may [just] as well do it **II** *konj* the; *~ förr desto bättre* the sooner the better

jubel ['ju:-] *s7* (*hänförelse*) jubilation, rejoicing, exultation; (*glädjerop*) shout[s] of joy, enthusiastic cheering (cheers *pl*) (*över* at); (*bifall*) shouts of applause (*över* at); *allmänt ~* general rejoicing; *jublet brast löst* a storm of rejoicing broke out **-doktor** person who has held a doctorate for fifty years **-idiot** arch idiot **-rop** shout of joy **-år** [year of] jubilee

jubil|er *s3* person celebrating an anniversary **-era** celebrate

jubileum [-ˣle:-] *s4* jubilee

jubileums|fest anniversary celebration **-firande** celebration of a jubilee **-skrift** anniversary issue **-utställning** jubilee exhibition

jubl|a [ˣju:b-] shout for joy; (*inom sig*) rejoice, exult **-ande** *a4* shouting for joy; jubilant, exultant

jucka *vard.* bump

Juda Judah **juda|folket** the Jewish people; the Jews (*pl*) **-konung** *~en* the King of the Jews

Judas Judas **judaskyss** Judas (traitor's) kiss

jude *s2* Jew; Hebrew, Israelite; *vandrande ~n a*) (*Ahasverus*) the Wandering Jew, *b*) *bot.* spiderwort, tradescantia **-fientlig** anti-Jewish, anti--Semitic **-förföljelse** persecution of [the] Jews **-hat** hatred of the Jews; anti-Semitism **-kristen** Jewish Christian **-kvarter** Jewish quarter, ghetto **-körs** [-ç-] *s3* strawberry tomato, Cape gooseberry

juden|dom [-dɔmm] *s2* Judaism **-heten** the Jews, the Jewish people

judetyska Yiddish

judiciell *a5* judicial

jud|inna Jewish woman, Jewess **-isk** ['ju:-] *a5* Jewish

judo ['ju:-] *s5* judo

jujutsu *se jiujitsu*

jul *s2* Christmas (*förk.* Xmas); (*hednisk jul o. poet.*) Yule[tide]; *god ~!* A Merry Christmas!; *i ~* at (this) Christmas; *i ~as* last Christmas; *fira ~* [*en*] keep (spend) [one's] Christmas

jul|a *se* [*fira*] *jul* **-afton** Christmas Eve **-bock** Christmas goat **-boksfloden** the Christmas-book inundation **-bord** Christmas smorgasbord (buffet) **-brådska** *i ~n* in the Christmas rush **-bön** Christmas Eve service (evensong) **-dag** Christmas Day **-evangeliet** the Gospel for Christmas Day **-ferier** *pl* Christmas holidays (vacation *sg*) **-fest** Christmas party (celebration) **-firande** *s6* [the] keeping (celebration) of

Christmas **-glädje** Christmas cheer **-gran** Christmas tree

julgrans|belysning Christmas-tree illumination **-fot** Christmas-tree stand **-karamell** Christmas-tree decoration filled with sweets **-plundring** party when the Christmas tree is stripped of decorations

jul|gris Christmas pig **-gröt** boiled rice pudding **-gåva** Christmas gift **-handel** Christmas trade **-handla** do one's Christmas shopping **-helg** *under ~en* during Christmas (*ledighet* the Christmas holidays), at Christmas **-hälsning** Christmas greeting

juli ['ju:-] *r* July

juliansk [-ˈa:nsk] *a5* Julian

jul|kaktus Christmas (crab) cactus **-klapp** Christmas present; *önska sig i ~* want for Christmas **-klappsvers** rhymed inscription written on a Christmas present **-kort** [-ɔ:-] Christmas card **-krubba** [Christmas] crib

julle *s2, se jolle*

jul|lek Christmas game **-lik** *a5* Christmassy **-lov** Christmas holidays (*pl*) (vacation) **-natt** Christmas night **-otta** early service on Christmas Day

julp *s2, se gylf*

jul|prydnader *pl* Christmas decorations **-ros** Christmas (winter) rose, hellebore **-rush** Christmas rush **-skinka** Christmas ham **-stjärna 1** *hist.*, *~n* the Star of Bethlehem **2** (*i julgran*) Christmas-tree star **3** *bot.* poinsettia **-stämning** Christmas spirit (atmosphere) **-stök** preparations (*pl*) for Christmas **-sång** Christmas carol (song) **-tid** (*äv. ~en*) Christmas time, *poet. äv.* Yuletide **-tomte** Christmas gnome; *~n* Santa Claus, Father Christmas

Julön Christmas Island

jumbo ['jumm-] *s5, sport., komma ~* come last **-jet** *vard.* jumbo [jet] **-pris** booby prize

jumpa jump from one sheet of floating ice to another

jumper ['jump-] *s2* jumper **-set** twin-set

jungfru *s5* **1** (*ungmö*) virgin; maid[en]; *J~ Maria* the Virgin Mary, the Blessed Virgin, Our Lady; *J~n av Orléans* the Maid of Orléans **2** *se hembiträde* **3** (*för gatläggning*) [paving] beetle, punner; *sjö.* deadeye **-bur** maiden's (lady's) bower **-dom** [-dɔmm] *s2* virginity, maidenhood **-födsel** *teol.* Virgin Birth; *biol.* parthenogenesis, virgin birth **-kammare** servant's [bed]room

jungfrulig [ˣjuŋ-, *äv.* -ˈfru:-] *a1* maidenly, maidenlike, maiden; *bildl.* virgin (*mark* soil) **-het** maidenliness; virginity

jungfru|lin [common] milkwort **-resa** maiden voyage **-tal** maiden speech

jungman [ˣjuŋ- *el.* 'juŋ-] ordinary seaman; deck hand

juni ['ju:-] June

junior ['ju:niär, *sport.* -'å:r] *oböjligt a o. s3* junior; *univ. ung* undergraduate **-lag** junior team

junker ['junk-] *s2* **1** *hist.* (*titel ung.*) squire; (*tysk godsägare*) Junker **2** *gunstig ~* young gentleman

junonisk [-ˈnɔ:-] *a5* Junoesque; (*friare*) majestic

junta *s1* **1** *polit.* junta **2** (*klubb o.d.*) junta, junto; *AE. äv.* bee

jura *s1,* **-perioden** the Jurassic [period]

jurid|ik *s3* law; (*vetenskap äv.*) jurisprudence;

J

studera ~ study [the] law **-isk** [-'ri:-] *a5* **1** juridical; (*friare*) legal; *den ~a banan* the legal profession; ~ *fakultet* faculty of law; *~t ombud* legal representative; ~ *person* juridical (juristic) person; ~ *rådgivare* legal adviser; *~a uppdrag* legal (lawyer's, law) work **2** (*rättslig*) judicial; *~t förfarande* judicial procedure **3** (*om rättsvetenskap*) jurisprudential

juris ['ju:-] ~ *doktor* Doctor of Laws (*förk., efter namnet* LL.D.); ~ *kandidat* (*licentiat*) (*ung.*) Bachelor (Master) of Laws (*förk., efter namnet* LL.B., LL.M.) **-diktion** [-k'ʃɔ:n] jurisdiction **-prudens** *s3* jurisprudence

jurist lawyer; (*ngns äv.*) legal adviser; (*rättslärd*) jurist **-eri** lawyer's quibbling, juridical formalism

jury ['jurry, *äv.* -i] *s3* jury; *sitta i en* ~ be (serve) on a jury **-man, -medlem** juryman, juror

1 just *adv* just; (*precis äv.*) exactly, precisely; (*alldeles*) quite; (*egentligen*) really; ~ *det* [, *ja*]! that's exactly it!; ~ *ingenting* nothing in particular; ~ *så* [, *ja*]! exactly (precisely, quite)!; *ja*, ~ *han!* yes, the very man!, to be sure, he and no other!; *jag vet* ~ *inte det!* I am not so sure!; *det var* ~ *snyggt!* oh, very nice, I must say!; *det var* ~ *det jag trodde* that was (is) just (exactly) what I thought; *varför välja* ~ *mig?* why choose me of all people?

2 just [ʃyst] *a1* (*rättvis*) fair; (*oklanderlig*) correct, right; (*som sig bör*) seemly, *åld.* meet; (*noggrann*) exact, accurate; *vara* ~ *mot* (*äv.*) treat s.b. fairly (justly)

juster|a 1 (*inställa, korrigera*) adjust; (*avhjälpa fel*) correct; (*friare*) put right (to rights); (*instrument*) regulate, set right, rectify; (*mått o. vikt*) verify, inspect; (*granska o. godkänna*) revise; ~ *protokollet* sign the minutes [as correct] **2** *sport.* injure; *vard.* nobble **-are** adjuster; (*av mått o. vikt*) inspector [of weights and measures]; (*av instrument*) regulator **-bar** *a5* adjustable **-ing** adjustment; correction; regulation; inspection; revision

justerings|man person who checks minutes **-skruv** adjusting (adjustment) screw

justitie|departement [-ˣti:tsie-] ministry (*AE.* department) of justice; (*i England och Wales*) Lord Chancellor's Office **-kansler** chancellor of justice; *~n* (*ämbetet*) [the] office of the chancellor of justice **-minister** minister of justice; (*i England och Wales*) Lord Chancellor; (*i USA*) attorney general **-mord** judicial murder; miscarriage of justice **-ombudsman** [the Swedish] parliamentary ombudsman **-råd** justice of the supreme court; (*i Storbritannien*) Lord Justice of Appeal; (*i USA*) associate justice of the supreme court **-utskott** *~et* [the Swedish parliamentry] standing committee on justice

1 jute *s2* Jute; (*jyllänning*) Jutlander

2 jute *s2, s7* (*spånadsämne*) jute

juteväv jute cloth; *AE. äv.* gunny

juvel *s3* jewel (*äv. bildl.*); gem; *~er* (*koll.*) jewellery **-armband** jewelled bracelet **-besatt** *a4* jewelled

juvelerar|affär [-ˣle:-] jeweller's [shop] **-arbete** jeweller's work, jewellery

juvelerare [-ˣle:-] jeweller

juvel|prydd *a5* [be]jewelled **-skrin** jewel case

-smycke jewelled ornament

juvenjl *a1* juvenile

juver ['ju:-] *s7* udder

jycke *s2* dog; *neds.* cur; ("*kurre*") beggar, johnny

Jylland ['jyll-] *n*, **jylländsk** [ˣjyll-] *a5* Jutland

jädrans [ˣjä:d-] *oböjligt a* darned, confounded

jägar|e hunter, shooter; sportsman; *bildl.* huntsman, hunter; (*anställd*) huntsman; *mil.* commando [soldier], light infantryman, *AE.* ranger **-folk** nation of hunters **-hatt** huntsman's hat; (*mjuk mössa med brätte fram o. bak*) deerstalker **-horn** hunter's horn, hunting horn

jägmästare [ˣjä:g-] forester, forest officer (supervisor)

jäkel *s2* devil; *jäklar!* damn! **-skap** *s3, s4 på* ~ just for the hell of it

jäk|la [ˣjä:k-] *oböjligt a o. adv* blasted **-las** *dep*, ~ *med* be nasty to, provoke **-lig** *a1* rotten; damn [ed]

jäkt *s7* (*brådska*) hurry, haste; (*hets*) drive, hustle

jäkta 1 (*driva på* [*ngn*]) hurry on, keep [s.b.] on the drive (run) **2** (*hasta*) be constantly on the go (move), be in a hurry **jäktad** *a5* hurried, worried **jäktig** *a1* bustling, hectic **jäktigt** *adv, ha det* ~ have a hectic time of it

jäm|bredd *i uttr.: i* ~ *med* side by side with **-bördig** *eg.* equal in birth; *bildl.* equal [in merit] (*med* to), of equal merit (*med* with) **-fota** *hoppa* ~ jump with both feet together

jämför|a *v2* compare; ~ *med* compare with, (*likna vid*) compare to; *jämför* compare (*förk.* cp.), confer (*förk.* cf.); *~nde språkvetenskap* comparative philology **-bar** *a1* comparable; *fullt* ~ *med* (*hand.*) quite up to the standard of

jämförelse comparison; *göra ~r* make comparisons (*mellan* between); *det är ingen ~!* there is no comparison! **-material** comparison material **-vis** comparatively; relatively

jämförlig [-ö:-] *a1* comparable (to be compared) (*med* with, to); (*likvärdig*) equivalent (*med* to)

jämförpris unit price

jäm|gammal of the same age (*med* as) **-god** *se jämngod*

jämk|a (*flytta*) move, shift; *bildl.* adjust, adapt, modify; ~ *på* (*ändra*) modify, (*pruta på*) give way (in), (*pris*) knock off; ~ *ihop* (*bildl.*) adjust; ~ *ihop sig* move closer together **-ning** [re] adjustment, modification; (*kompromiss*) compromise; (*av skatt*) tax adjustment

jäm|lik *a5* equal (*med* to) **-like** equal **-likhet** equality **-likt** [-i:-] *adv* according to, in accordance with

jämmer ['jämm-] *s9* groaning; (*kvidande*) moaning; (*missnöje*) complaint; (*veklagan*) lamentation; (*elände*) misery **-dal** vale of tears **-lig** [ˣjämm-] *a1* miserable, deplorable; wretched; (*jämrande*) mournful, wailing **-rop** plaintive cry, cry of pain (distress)

jämn *a1* **1** (*om yta*) level, even; (*slät*) smooth **2** (*likformig*) uniform (*värme* heat); even; equable (*klimat* climate; *lynne* temperament); (*oavbruten*) continuous, steady; (*regelbunden*) regular; *med ~a mellanrum* at regular intervals; *hålla ~a steg med* keep in step with, *bildl.* keep pace with **3** (*motsats udda*) even; *~a hundratal kronor* even hundreds of kronor; *~a par* an equal number of men and women; ~*a pengar* even money, the exact sum; *en ~ summa (äv.)* a round sum

jämna level, make level (even, smooth), even out; (*klippa jämn*) trim; *bildl.* smooth; ~ *med marken* level with the ground; ~ *ut* level off; ~ *väg[en] för ngn* (*bildl.*) pave the way for s.b.; *det ~r ut sig* it evens itself out

jämn|an *i uttr.: för ~* for always **-god** *vara ~a* be equal to one another, be equals; ~ *med* equal to, as good as **-grå** of an even grayness; overcast **-het** levelness; evenness, smoothness; equality; uniformity **-hög** of [a] uniform height; *två ~a* two equally tall **-höjd** *i uttr.: i ~ med* on (at) a level with; *vara i ~ med* be of the same level as **-mod** equanimity, composure **-mulen** entirely overcast **-stor** of [a] uniform size; *vara ~a* be equal in size

jämnt [*vard.* jämt] **1** level; evenly *etc.*; even; (*lika*) equally; (*regelbundet*) regularly, steadily; *dra ~ med ngn* get on with s.b.; *väga ~* (*om t.ex. våg*) [just] balance, *bildl.* be even; *det är ~!* (*kan behållas som dricks*) keep the change!; *och därmed ~* and there's an end of it **2** (*exakt*) exactly; ~ *så mycket som* exactly (just) so (as) much as; *inte tro ngn mer än ~* only half believe s.b.; *3 går ~ upp i 9* nine is divisible by three

jämn|tjock of [a] uniform thickness, equally thick **-varm** ~*a djur* warm-blooded (*fack.* homoiothermic) animals **-årig** *a1* of the same age (*med* as); (*samtidig*) contemporary; *mina ~a* persons of my [own] age, my contemporaries

jämra *rfl* wail, moan; (*gnälla*) whine; (*klaga*) complain (*över* about); (*högljutt*) lament; (*stöna*) groan

jäms ~ *med* at the level of, level with; (*längs*) alongside [of]

jäm|sides side by side (*med* with), abreast (*med* of), (*vid tävling äv.*) neck and neck; alongside [of]; ~ *med sina studier* alongside [of] his studies; *fartygen ligger ~* the ships lie alongside each other **-spelt** [-e:-] *a1* evenly matched, even (*med* with) **-ställa** place side by side (on a level) (*med* with), juxtapose (*med* to); place on an equal footing (*med* with); (*jämföra*) draw a parallel between; *-ställd med* on a par (an equality) with **-ställdhet** equality, parity **-ställdhetsombudsman** equal opportunities ombudsman; *~nen* (*ämbetet*) [the] office of the equal opportunities ombudsman

jämt always; (*gång på gång*) constantly; (*oupphörligt*) incessantly, perpetually; ~ *och ständigt* (*samt*) always, for ever, everlastingly

jämte together with, in addition to; (*förutom*) besides; (*och även*) and [also]

jämvikt *s3* equilibrium (*äv. bildl.*); *fys.* equilibrium; *i ~* (*bildl.*) [well-]balanced; *förlora ~en* lose one's (its *etc.*) balance; *åstadkomma ~ mellan* establish equilibrium between, equipoise; *återställa ~en* restore equilibrium (the balance)

jämvikts|läge position (state) of equilibrium; balanced position **-organ** organ of balance (equilibrium) **-rubbning** disturbance of equilibrium; disequilibrium

jämväl [ˣjämm-, *äv.* -'vä:l] likewise; (*även*) also

jänkare *vard.* Yankee

jänta *s1* lass

järn [-ä:-] *s7* iron; *ge ~et* (*vard.*) go in for s.th., give one's all; *ha många ~ i elden* have several irons in the fire; *smida medan ~et är varmt* strike while the iron is hot; *ta sig ett ~* (*vard.*) take a schnapps **-affär** *se -handel* **-beslag** iron mounting **-beslagen** *a5* iron|sheathed, -bound **-brist** iron deficiency **-bro** iron bridge **-bruk** ironworks (*sg o. pl*); foundry **-ek** *bot.* holly **-fil** iron file **-filspån** iron filings (*pl*) **-fysik** *se -hälsa* **-förande** *a4* iron-bearing, ferriferous **-förening** *kem.* iron compound **-grepp** iron grip **-gruva** iron mine **-halt** iron content **-haltig** *a5* containing iron, ferriferous **-hand** *styra med ~* rule with an iron hand **-handel** *konkr.* ironmonger's [shop], ironmongery; *AE.* hardware store **-handlare** ironmonger; *AE.* hardware dealer **-hantering** iron industry (trade) **-hård** [as] hard as iron, iron-hard; *bildl.* iron[-hard]; ~ *disciplin* iron discipline **-hälsa** iron constitution **-industri** iron industry **-kamin** iron stove **-korset** (*orden*) the Order of the Iron Cross **-malm** iron ore **-malmsfält** iron-ore field **-manufaktur** hardware **-medicin** iron tonic **-natt** frosty night **-näve** *bildl.* iron fist **-oxid** (*med tvåvärt järn*) ferrous oxide; (*med trevärt järn*) ferric oxide **-plåt** sheet iron **-ridå** *teat.* safety curtain; *polit.* iron curtain **-skrot** scrap iron **-smide** hammered ironware **-spis** iron range **-stång** iron bar **-säng** iron bedstead **-tråd** [iron] wire **-varor** *pl* iron goods; ironware (*sg*); hardware (*sg*) **-verk** ironworks (*sg o. pl*) **-vilja** iron will **-väg** railway; *AE.* railroad; *Statens ~ar* (*SJ*) Swedish State Railways; *anställd vid ~en* employed on the railway; *fritt å ~* free on rail (*AE.* truck); *resa med ~* go by rail (train); *underjordisk ~* underground, tube, *AE.* subway

järnvägs|arbetare 1 (*-byggare*) navvy **2** (*vid färdig järnväg*) railway worker **-bank** [railway] embankment **-bro** railway bridge **-förbindelse** train service, railway connection **-karta** railway map **-knut** railway junction **-linje** railway line, track **-man** railwayman, railway employee **-nät** railway system (network) **-olycka** railway accident **-resa** railway journey (trip) **-restaurang** railway-station refreshment room, railway restaurant; (*mindre*) buffet **-skena** rail **-spår** railway (*AE.* railroad) track **-station** railway station; (*änd-*) terminus, *AE.* terminal **-trafik** railway traffic (service) **-tunnel** railway tunnel **-tåg** [railway] train **-vagn** railway carriage; *AE.* railroad car; (*godsvagn*) goods waggon, *AE.* freight car **-övergång** railway crossing; (*plankorsning*) level (*AE.* grade) crossing; *bevakad* (*obevakad*) ~ guarded (ungated) level crossing

järnåldern the Iron Age

järpe *s2* hazelhen

järtecken [ˣjä:r-] omen, portent, presage

järv *s2* wolverine

jäs|a *v3* ferment; (*om sylt o.d.*) go fermented; *bildl.* a) (*om missnöje o.d.*) ferment, b) (*vara uppblåst*) swell up; *låta degen ~* let the dough rise; ~ *upp* (*om deg*) ferment, rise; ~ *över* ferment and run over; *han -te av vrede* he boiled with fury; *det -te i sinnena* people's minds were in a ferment **-ning** fermentation; *bildl.* ferment;

bringa i ~ bring to fermentation, *bildl.* work up into a ferment
jäsnings|process fermentation (fermentative) process **-ämne** ferment
jäst *s3* yeast **-pulver** baking powder **-svamp** yeast [fungus]
jätte *s2* giant **-arbete** gigantic (herculean) [piece of] work **-bra** super, topnotch; *AE.* great **-fin** first-rate, terrific; *AE.* dandy **-format** gigantic size **-glad** pleased as punch **-gryta** *geol.* giant's kettle, pothole **-kvinna** giantess, female giant; (*storväxt kvinna*) enormous woman, (*på cirkus*) fat woman **-lik** *a5* gigantic; giant-like **-panda** [giant] panda **-planet** giant planet **-skön** very comfy (comfortable) **-steg** giant stride; *gå framåt med* ~ (*bildl.*) make tremendous progress, progress by leaps and bounds **-stjärna** giant star **-stor** gigantic, enormous, huge **-tanker** mammoth tanker, supertanker **-trevlig** awfully nice, delightful, charming **-ödla** great saurian, dinosaur
jättinna *se jättekvinna*
jäv *s7, jur.* challenge (*mot* to); *anmäla* ~ *mot* challenge, make (lodge) a challenge to; *laga* ~ lawful disqualification
jäva *1 jur.* take exception to; (*testamente e.d.*) challenge the validity of **2** (*bestrida*) belie
jävig *a5* (*om vittne*) challengeable, exceptionable; (*inkompetent, partisk*) disqualified, noncompetent **-het** challengeability; non-competence
jäv|la, -las, -lig, -ligt *se djävla, djävlas, djävlig, djävligt*
jökel ['jö:-] *s2* glacier **-älv** glacier stream
jöns *s2* johnny; ninny
jösse *s2, ung.* Jack hare
jösses good heavens!; *vad i jösse namn!* what on earth!

K

kabal *s3* cabal
kabaré *s3* cabaret **-artist** cabaret artiste
kabball|a ['kabb-] *s1* cab[b]ala **-ist** cab[b]alist **-istisk** [-'ist-] *a5* cab[b]alistic
kabb[e]leka *s1* marsh marigold
kabel ['ka:-] *s2* cable; *sjö. äv.* hawser **-bro** cable suspension bridge **-brott** cable breakdown
kabeljo [ˣkabb-] *s5* dried [cured] cod
kabel|ledning cable **-längd** cable, cable['s] length **-sko** *elektr.* [cable] socket **--TV** cable television, cablevision
kabin *s3* (*för passagerare*) cabin; (*för pilot äv.*) cockpit **-båt** cabin (family) cruiser

kabinett *s7, s4* cabinet (*äv. polit.*); (*budoar*) boudoir
kabinetts|fråga vote of confidence; *ställa* ~ demand a vote of confidence **-kammarherre** lord--in-waiting **-medlem** cabinet member, member of the cabinet **-sekreterare** undersecretary of state for foreign affairs
kabla [ˣka:-] cable
kabriolett *s3* cabriolet, convertible
kabyl *s3* Kabyle
kabyss *s3, sjö.* [cook's] galley, caboose
kackalorum [-ˣlo:-] *s7* to-do, hullabaloo
kackel ['kack-] *s7, se kacklande*
kackerlacka *s1* cockroach
kackl|a cackle; (*om höna äv.*) cluck **-ande** *a4 o. s6* cackling; cluck-clucking
kadaver [-'da:-] *s7* carcass; (*lik*) corpse **-disciplin** blind discipline
kadens [*el.* -'aŋs] *s3, mus.* (*slutfall*) cadence, fall; (*solo-*) cadenza
kader ['ka:-] *s2, s3, mil.* cadre
kadett *s3* cadet; *sjö.* [naval] cadet **-skola** military academy (school)
kadmium ['kadd-] *s8* cadmium
kadrilj *s3* (*dans*) quadrille
kafé *s4* café; coffee bar (shop, house); teashop, tearoom; *AE. äv.* cafeteria
kafeteria [-'te:-] *se cafeteria*
kaffe *s7* coffee; *koka* ~ make coffee; ~ *med grädde* (*mjölk*) white coffee; ~ *utan grädde* (*mjölk*) black coffee **-automat** coffee machine **-blandning** blend of coffee **-bricka** coffee tray **-bryggare** percolator, coffee maker (machine) **-bröd** *koll.* buns, cakes **-buske** coffee shrub (bush) **-böna** coffee bean **-dags** coffee time, time for coffee **-grädde** coffee cream **-gök** *se -kask* **-junta** coffee club (party) **-kanna** coffeepot **-kask** *s2* coffee laced with schnapps **-kokning** coffee-making **-kopp** coffee cup; (*mått*) coffee-cupful **-kvarn** coffe mill (grinder) **-panna** coffeepot **-paus** coffee break **-plantage** coffee plantation
kaffer ['kaff-] *s3, åld. el. neds.* Kaf[f]ir
kafferast coffee break
kafferbuffel African buffalo
kaffe|rep *s7* coffee party **-rosteri** coffee-roasting factory **-servering** *se kafé* **-servis** coffee set **-sked** coffee spoon **-sump** coffee grounds (*pl*) **-surrogat** coffee substitute, ersatz coffee **-träd** coffee tree **-tår** drop of coffee
kaftan *s3* (*prästrock*) cassock; (*österländsk*) kaftan, caftan
kagge *s2* keg, cask
kainsmärke [ˣka:ins-] mark (brand) of Cain
kaj [kajj] *s3* quay; wharf, dock, (*hamngata*) embankment; (*utskjutande*) jetty; *fritt vid* (*å*) ~ free at (on) quay
kaja [ˣkajja] *s1* jackdaw
kajak *s3* kayak
kajavgift quayage; wharfage; quay-dues (*pl*)
kajennpeppar [-ˣjenn-] cayenne [pepper]
kajka row around (mess about) in an old boat
kajman *s3* cayman
kajplats quay berth
kajuta [-ˣju:-] *s1* cabin; (*liten*) cuddy
kaka *s1* cake, pastry; (*små-*) biscuit, *AE.* cookie;

(av hårt bröd) round; ~ *söker maka* birds of a feather flock together

kakadu[a] [-'du:, -ˣdu:a] *s3* [*s1*] cockatoo

kakao *s9* cacao; *(dryck, pulver)* cocoa **-böna** cocoa bean **-fett** cocoa butter **-likör** crème de cacao

kakburk biscuit tin

kakel *s7* [Dutch, glazed] tile **-klädd** *a5* tiled **-platta** *se kakel* **-ugn** tiled stove

kak|fat cake dish **-form** baking tin

kaki ['ka:-] *s9* khaki **-färgad** khaki [coloured]

kak|mix [ready-made] cake mix **-mått** pastry cutter

kakofoni *s3* cacophony

kakskrin biscuit tin

kakt|é *s3* cactaceous plant **-us** ['kakk-] *s2* cactus

kaktång pastry tongs *(pl)*

kal *a1* bare; *(om kust)* naked; *(om gren)* leafless; *(om pers.)* bald

kalabalik *s3* uproar, fracas, tumult

kalamitet *(missöde)* mishap, *(starkare)* calamity; *(olycka)* misfortune

kalas *s7* party; feast; *(friare o. bildl.)* treat; *få betala* ~*et* have to pay for the whole show; *ställa till med stort* ~ *för* throw a big party for

kalas|a feast **-kula** paunch, potbelly **-mat** delicious food; a real delicacy

kalcedon [-se'då:n *el.* -'do:n] *s3* chalcedony

kalciner|a calcine **-ing** calcining; calcination **-ingsugn** kiln, calcining furnace

kalcium ['kall-] *s8* calcium **-fosfat** calcium phosphate **-hydroxid** calcium hydroxide **-karbid** [calcium] carbide **-karbonat** calcium carbonate **-klorid** calcium chloride **-oxid** calcium oxide

kaldé *s3* Chaldean **Kaldéen** [-'de:en] *n* Chaldea; *Ur i* ~ Ur of the Chaldees **kaldeisk** [-'de:-] *a5* Chaldean

kalebass *s3* calabash

kaledonisk [-'do:-] *a5* Caledonian; *K~a bergskedjan* the Caledonian folding

kalejdoskop [-'å:p] *s7* kaleidoscope **-isk** *a5* kaleidoscopic

kalendarium [-'da:-] *s4* calendar

kalender [-'lenn-] *s2* calendar; almanac; *(årsbok)* annual, yearbook **-bitare** *han är* ~ he is a who's-who specialist **-dag** calendar (civil) day **-månad** calendar month **-år** calendar (civil) year

kalesch [-'ä(:)ʃ] *s3* barouche; calash, calèche

kalfaktor [-ˣfakktår] *s3* batman, officer's servant

kalfatra [ˣkall- *el.* -'fa:-] **1** *sjö.* caulk **2** *bildl.* find fault with

kal|fjäll bare mountain **-hugga** deforest **-huggning** deforestation **-hygge** deforestation

kali ['ka:-] *s7* potash

kaliber [-'li:-] *s2*, *s3* calibre *(äv. bildl.)*

kalibrer|a calibrate **-ing** calibration

kalif *s3* caliph, calif **-at** *s7* caliphate

Kalifornien [-'få:r-] *n* California

kaligödsel potassic fertilizer

kalikå [ˣkall-, 'kall- *el.* -'kå:] *s3* calico

kali|lut lye **-salpeter** potassium nitrate, saltpetre

kalium ['ka:-] *s8* potassium **-cyanid** potassium cyanide **-hydroxid** potassium hydroxide, caustic potash **-karbonat** potassium carbonate, potash **-klorid** potassium chloride

---

1 kalk *s2* **1** *(bägare)* chalice; *bildl.* cup: *tömma den bittra* ~*en* drain the bitter cup **2** *bot.* perianth

2 kalk *s3* lime; *(bergart)* limestone; *osläckt* ~ quicklime, unslaked lime; *släckt* ~ slaked lime

kalk|a whitewash, limewash; *(göda)* lime **-avlagring** lime deposit

kalk|brott limestone quarry **-brist** *(i kost)* calcium deficiency **-bruk 1** *(-bränneri)* lime works *(sg o. pl)* **2** *(murbruk)* lime mortar

kalker|a trace; *bildl.* copy **-ing** tracing **-papper** tracing (carbon) paper

kalk|fattig lime-deficient; *(om kost)* deficient in calcium **-gruva** lime pit **-halt** lime content **-haltig** *a1* calcareous, calciferous; limy **-kväve** calcium cyanamide **-målning** fresco (mural) painting

kalkon *s3* turkey

kalk|salpeter nitrate of lime **-sten** limestone **-stensbrott** limestone quarry **-stryka** limewash **-tablett** calcium tablet

kalkyl *s3* calculation; *hand.* cost estimate; *mat.* calculus **-ator** [-ˣa:tår] *s3 (person)* cost accountant, calculator; *(maskin)* calculator, calculating machine

kalkyler|a calculate, estimate, work out **-ing** *(-ande)* calculating, estimating; *se äv. kalkyl* **-ingsmaskin** calculating machine; *(elektronisk)* [electronic] computer

1 kall *a1* cold *(äv. bildl.)*; *(om t.ex. zon)* frigid; *(kylig)* chilly; *(sval)* cool; *två grader* ~*t* two degrees below zero; *det* ~*a kriget* the cold war; *bli* ~ *om fötterna* get cold feet; *hålla huvudet* ~*t* keep cool; *han håller huvudet* ~*t* he has a cool head; *vinka med* ~*a handen* dismiss s.b. coldly; *jag blev alldeles* ~ *(av förskräckelse)* I went cold all over

2 kall *s7* calling, vocation; *(uppgift)* task, mission

1 kalla *s1, bot.* calla, calla (arum) lily

2 kalla call; name, designate; *(ropa [på], till-)* summon; *(utnämna)* appoint, nominate; ~ *på läkare* send for (call in) the doctor; *det kan man* ~ *tur!* that is what you may call luck!; ~ *sig* call o.s., *(antaga namnet)* take the name of

kallad *a5* called *etc.*; *så* ~ so-called; *även* ~ alias, otherwise called; *känna sig* ~ *till* feel fitted for (called upon to); *han blev* ~ *till president* he was called to be president (to the presidency)

kall|bad cold bath; *(ute-)* bathe **-blodig** cold-blooded; *bildl. äv.* cool; ~*a djur, se växelvarma djur* **-blodigt** *adv* coolly, in cold blood **-blodighet** cold-bloodedness **-brand** gangrene **-dragen** *a5, tekn.* cold-drawn **-dusch** cold shower (douche) *(äv. bildl.)*

Kalle Anka Donald Duck

kallelse 1 *(t. möte e.d.)* summons, notice; *univ.* call; *kyrkl.* invitation; *(utnämning)* nomination **2** *se 2 kall*

kall|front *meteor.* cold front **-garage** unheated garage **-grin** sneer **-grina** sneer [superciliously] *(åt* at) **-hamra** cold-hammer; ~*d (bildl.)* hard-boiled

kalli|graf *s3* calligrapher, calligraphist **-grafi** *s3* calligraphy **-grafisk** [-'gra:-] *a5* calligraphic

kall|jord *på* ~ in cold soil, outdoors **-lim** *(hopskr. kallim)* cold-water glue **-mangel** mangle

kall|na cool; *(om mat e.d.)* get cold **-prat** small talk **-prata** talk about trivialities **-sinnig** *a1* cold, cool; (*likgiltig*) indifferent **-sinnighet** coldness *etc.*; indifference **-skuret** *n*, *best. form*: *det -skurna, litet* ~ a few cold-buffet dishes **-skänk** *s2* cold buffet **-skänka** [-ʃ-] *sl* cold-buffet manageress **-start** cold start **-sup** involuntary gulp of cold water **-svett** cold sweat (perspiration) **-svettas** *dep* be in a cold sweat **-svettig** *vara* ~ be in a cold sweat

kallt *adv* coldly *etc*; *förvaras* ~ keep in a cool place; ~ *beräknande* coldly calculating; *ta saken* ~ take the matter coolly, keep cool about **-valsning** cold-rolling **-vatten** cold water **-vattenskran** cold-water tap

kalmuck *s3* **1** Kalmuck, Kalmyk **2** (*tyg*) kalmuck

kalops [-'åps] *s3, ung.* spiced beef stew

kalorj *s3* calorie **-behov** calorie requirement **-fattig** low calorie

kalorimet|er [-'me:-] *s2* calorimeter **-rj** *s3* calorimetry **-risk** [-'me:-] *a5* calorimetric[al]

kalorivärde calorific (calorie) value

kalott [-'ått] *s3* (*huvudbonad*) calotte, skullcap

kalsonger [-'såŋ-] *pl* (*korta*) underpants, undershorts; (*långa*) long underpants

kalufs *s3* forelock

kaluv *s3* **1** *se kalufs* **2** *på nykter* ~ (*bildl.*) in one's sober senses

kalv *s2* calf (*pl* calves); *kokk.* veal

kalv|a calve **-bräss** sweetbread **-dans** *kokk.* curds (*pl*) **-filé** fillet of veal **-frikassé** fricassee of veal **-färs** minced veal

kalvin|ism Calvinism **-ist** Calvinist **-istisk** [-'ist-] *a5* Calvinistic[al]

kalv|kotlett veal chop (cutlet) **-kätte** calf's crib (pen) **-kött** veal **-lever** calf's liver

kalv|ning calving **-skinn** *hand.* calfskin **-stek** *slaktar.* joint of veal; *kokk.* roast veal

kam [kamm] *s2* comb; (*berg-, tupp-, våg-*) crest; (*excenter-*) cam; *skära alla över en* ~ judge (treat) all alike

kamarilla [-ˣrilla, -'rilla] *sl* camarilla; clique

kamaxel camshaft

Kambodja [-ˣbådja] *n* Cambodia

kambrik ['kamm-] *s3* cambric

kambr|isk ['kamm-] *a5* Cambrian **-ium** *s8* Cambrian **-osilur** *s3* Cambro-Silurian

kamé *s3* cameo

kamel *s3* camel; *enpucklig* ~ dromedary **-drivare** camel driver

kameleont [-'ånt] *s3* chameleon **-isk** *a5* chameleonic

kamel|hår camel's hair, camelhair **-hårskappa** camelhair coat

kamelia [-'me:-] *sl* camellia

kamera ['ka:-] *sl* camera **-jakt** hunt for [sensational] photographs

kameral *a5* fiscal; financial

kameraman cameraman

Kamerun *n* Cameroon

kamfer ['kamm-] *s9* camphor **-liniment** camphor embrocation **-olja** camphorated oil **-sprit** camphorated spirits (*pl*)

kamgarn worsted [yarn]; (*tyg*) worsted [fabric]

kamjn *s3* [heating] stove; (*fotogen- e.d.*) heater; *elektrisk* ~ electric fire (heater)

kamkofta dressing jacket, peignoir

kamma comb; ~ *håret* comb (do) one's hair; ~

noll (*vard.*) draw a blank

kammar|e -[e]n *kamrar, äv. s9* room; *polit., tekn., biol.* chamber; (*hjärt-*) ventricle; (*i Storbritannien, polit.*) house; *första* ~n (*förr i riksdagen*) the First Chamber, (*i Storbritannien*) the House of Lords; *andra* ~n (*förr i riksdagen*) the Second Chamber, (*i Storbritannien*) the House of Commons

kammar|herre chamberlain (*hos* to) **-jungfru** lady's maid **-kollegiet** [the Swedish] national judicial board for public lands and funds **-lärd** *n* ~ a bookish person **-musik** chamber music **-opera** chamber opera **-orkester** chamber ensemble **-rätt** administrative court of appeal

kammarrätts|assessor associate judge [of the administrative court of appeal] **-fiskal** reporting clerk [of the administrative court of appeal] **-president** president [of the administrative court of appeal]

kammar|spel *teat.* chamber play **-tjänare** valet **-åklagare** district prosecutor

kam|mussla pecten **-ning** combing; (*frisyr*) coiffure, hairstyle

kamomjll *s3* wild (German) camomile **-te** camomile tea

kamouflage, kamouflera *se camouflage, camouflera*

1 kamp *s2* (*häst*) jade

2 kamp *s3* (*strid*) struggle (*om* for); fight, combat (*om* for) (*äv. bildl.*); (*drabbning*) battle (*äv. bildl.*); (*brottning*) wrestle, wrestling; ~*en för tillvaron* the struggle for existence; *en* ~ *på liv och död* a life-and-death struggle

kampa *se campa*

kampanda fighting spirit

kampanjl *s3* campanile

kampanj *s3* campaign; (*reklam- äv.*) drive

kamp|are *se campare* **-era** be (lie) encamped (in camp); ~ *ihop* (*tillsammans*) share the same tent (room *etc.*), be fellow workers **-ing** ['kamp-] *se camping*

kamp|lust fighting spirit **-sång** camp song **-vilja** will to fight

Kampuchea [-ˣtçe:a] *n* Kampuchea

kamrat comrade, fellow; (*vän*) friend; (*följeslagare*) companion; (*arbets-*) fellow worker; (*skol-*) schoolmate, schoolfellow; (*studie-*) fellow student; (*kollega*) colleague; *en god* ~ a good chap; *mina* ~*er på kontoret* my colleagues at the office; *vi är* ~*er från skoltiden* we are old schoolmates **-anda** comradeship, fellowship **-förening** society of fellow students (schoolmates *etc.*); *mil.* service club **-krets** *i* ~*en* among [one's] friends (*etc.*)

kamratlig [-'ra:t-] *al* friendly (*mot* towards) **-het** friendliness

kamrat|skap *s7* companionship, comradeship **-äktenskap** companionate marriage

kamrer *s3*, **-are** [-ˣre:-] *s9* accountant (*i, på* at, in)

1 kan [ka:n] *s3* khan

2 kan [kann] *pres av kunna*

kana *sl* slide; *åka* ~ slide, go sliding **II** *vl* slide, go sliding

Kanaan *n* Canaan

Kanada ['kann-] *n* Canada

kanadagås Canada goose
kanadens|are [-ˣdens-] Canadian (*äv. kanot*)
-isk [-'dens-] *a5* Canadian **-iska** [-'dens-] Canadian woman
kanąl *s3* (*naturlig*) channel (*äv. elektron. o. bildl.*); (*grävd samt anat. o. naturv.*) canal; *tekn.* channel, duct; *Engelska K~en* the [English] Channel **-avgift** canal dues (*pl*)
kanaliser|a canalize, channel (*äv. bildl.*) **-ing** canalization
kanalje [-'nalje] *s5* blackguard, villain; *din lille ~* you little rascal
kanal|system canal system, network of canals **-väljare** channel selector
Kanalöarna *n* the Channel Islands
kanané *s3* Canaanite **kananeisk** [-'ne:-] *a5* Canaanitic
kanapé *s3* **1** (*soffa*) settee, canapé **2** (*bakelse*) pig's ear [of puff pastry]
kanarie|fågel [-ˣna:-] canary **-gul** canary yellow
Kanarieöarna [-ˣna:-] the Canary Islands, the Canaries
kancer, kancerogen *se cancer, cancerogen*
kandelaber [-'la:-] *s2* candelabra
kander|a candy; *~d* candied, preserved in sugar **-ing** candying
kandidat **1** (*sökande*) candidate, applicant (*till for*) **2** *univ.* Bachelor; *filosofie ~* Bachelor of Arts (*förk.* B.A.); *medicine ~* graduate in medicine, medical student **-examen** *ta ~* take one's B.A. degree **-lista** list of candidates; *polit. äv.* nomination list; *AE. äv.* ticket **-nominering** nominations (*pl*) [of candidates]
kandid|atyr *s3* candidature **-era** set [o.s.] up as a candidate; *polit.* stand (*AE.* run) for
kandisocker sugar candy
kanęl *s3* cinnamon **-stång** bark cinnamon
kanfas ['kann-] *s3* canvas, duck
kanhända [-ˣhänn-] perhaps; *jfr kanske*
kanjk *s3* canon
kanjn *s3* rabbit **-avel** rabbit breeding **-bur** rabbit hutch **-hanne** buck rabbit **-hona** doe rabbit **-pest** myxomatosis **-skinn** *hand.* rabbit skin **-unge** young rabbit
kanister [-'nist-] *s2* canister, can, tin
kanjon ['kanjån] *s3* canyon
kanna *s1* (*kaffe- etc.*) pot; (*grädd-*) jug
kannel|era flute; *~d* fluted **-ering** [-'le:-] fluting **-yr** *s3* flute
kannibąl *s3* cannibal **-isk** *a5* cannibal[istic] **-ism** cannibalism
kannring *tekn.* piston ring
kannstöp|a talk politics without having any real knowledge **-are** armchair politician, political windbag **-eri** [airing of] uninformed political opinions
1 kanon ['ka:nån] *s3, s9* **1** (*rättesnöre o.d.*) canon **2** *mus.* canon, round
2 kanon [ka'no:n] *s3* (*artilleripjäs*) gun; (*äldre*) cannon; *som skjuten ur en ~* like a shot
kanon|ąd *s3* cannonade **-båt** gunboat **-dunder** thunder (roaring) of guns **-eld** gunfire **-form** *sport.* great form **-fotograf** street photographer **-gjuteri** cannon foundry
kanon|isation canonization **-isera** canonize **-isk** [-'no:-] *a5* canonical; *~a böcker* canon (*sg*);

~ rätt canon law
kanon|kula cannonball **-lavett** gun carriage **-lockar** cannon curls **-mat** *bildl.* cannon fodder **-mynning** gun muzzle **-port** gun port[hole] **-skott** gunshot **-torn** gun turret
kanọt *s3*, **kanota** [-'no:-] *vl* canoe
kanot|färd canoe trip **-ist** canoeist **-sport** canoeing
kanske [ˣkanʃe] perhaps; (*måhända*) maybe; *~, ~ inte* maybe, maybe not; *han kommer ~* he may (might) come; *du skulle ~ vilja hjälpa mig?* would you mind helping me?; *~ vi skulle gå ut?* what about going out?
kansler [ˣkann-, *äv.* 'kann-] *s3* chancellor
kanslersämbete chancellorship
kanslj *s4, s6* (*vid ämbetsverk o.d.*) secretariat, [secretary's] office; (*i Storbritannien äv.*) chancery; *AE. äv.* chancellery; *univ.* registrar's office; *teat.* general manager's office; *Kungl. Maj:ts ~* the Government Offices (*pl*) **-biträde** clerical officer **-chef** (*vid ambassad*) head of chancery; (*vid HD, regeringsrätten*) senior judge referee; (*vid riksdagens utskott*) secretary; (*vid kommun, landsting*) chief executive; (*vid nämnd m.m.*) administrative director **-råd** deputy assistant undersecretary **-sekreterare** administrative officer [second (third) secretary] **-skrivare** clerk **-språk** official (civil service) English (*etc.*); official jargon, officialese; *vard.* gobbledygook
kanslist clerical officer
kansli|stil, -svenska *se kanslispråk*
kant *s3* **1** edge; (*bård o.d.*) border; (*marginal*) margin; (*på kläder e.d.*) edging, selvage; (*på kärl*) rim, brim; (*på huvudbonad*) brim **2** (*bröd-*) crust; (*ost-*) rind **3** *hålla sig på sin ~* keep one's distance, hold aloof; *komma på ~ med ngn* get at cross-purposes with s.b., fall out with s.b.
kanta edge; (*omge*) border, line; (*kantskära*) trim
kantaręll *s3* chanterelle
kantat cantata
kantband edging, trimming
kantele [ˣkann-, 'kann-] *s5* kantele
kantig *al* angular; (*om anletsdrag o. bildl.*) rugged; (*till sättet äv.*) unpolished, abrupt **-het** angularity; ruggedness *etc.*
kantjn *s3* canteen
kantọn *s3* canton
kantor [ˣkann-, 'kanntår] *s3* cantor, precentor
kantr|a turn over, capsize, [be] upset; (*om vind o. bildl.*) veer [round] **-ing** capsizal, upset; veering [round]
kant|sten kerbstone; *AE.* curbstone **-ställd** placed on edge **-stött** chipped [at edge]; (*om anseende o.d.*) damaged
kantänka [-ˣtänn-] no doubt; of course; (*försmädligt*) if you please
kanyl *s3* cannula (*pl cannulae*)
kaolin *s4, s3* kaolin, china clay (*stone*)
kao|s ['ka:ås] *s7* chaos **-tisk** [ka'o:-] *a5* chaotic
1 kap *s7* (*udde*) cape
2 kap *s7* (*fångst*) capture; *ett gott ~* a fine haul
1 kapa (*uppbringa*) capture, take; (*flygplan*) hijack; skyjack
2 kapa *sjö.* cut away; (*lina äv.*) cut; (*timmer etc.*) crosscut; *~ av* cut off

kapabel [-'pa:-] *a2* capable
kapaci|tans *s3, elektr.* capacitance **-tet** capacity; (*pers. äv.*) able man
kapar|e privateer; (*flygplans-*) hijacker; skyjacker **-fartyg, -kapten** privateer
1 kapell *s7* (*överdrag*) cover, cap, hood
2 kapell *s7* **1** (*kyrkobyggnad*) chapel **2** *mus.* orchestra, band
kapellmästare conductor [of an orchestra]; bandmaster
kaperi privateering; piracy
kapillaritet capillarity
kapillär *s3 o. a5* capillary **-kraft** capillarity **-kärl** capillary **-rör** capillary tube
1 kapital *a1* downright; ~*t misstag* capital mistake, flagrant error
2 kapital *s7* capital; (*pengar äv.*) funds, money
kapital|behållning capital [in hand] **-bildning** capital accumulation (formation) **-brist** lack of capital **-budget** capital budget **-flykt** flight of capital **-försäkring** endowment assurance (insurance) **-intensiv** capital-intensive
kapitaliser|a capitalize **-ing** capitalization
kapital|ism capitalism **-ist** capitalist **-istisk** [-'ist-] *a5* capitalist[ic]; ~*t samhälle* capitalist society **-konto** capital account **-marknad** capital market **-placering** [capital] investment **-räkning** [long-term] deposit account **-samlingsräkning** [long-term] deposit account, capital accumulation account **-stark** financially strong
kapitalt [-'a:lt] *adv* downright, radically; (*fullständigt*) completely, totally
kapital|varor capital goods **-värde** capital value
kapitel [ka'pittel] *s7* chapter; *ett helt annat* ~ (*bildl.*) quite another story; *när man kommer in på kapitlet om* (*bildl.*) when you get on to the topic of **-indelning** division into chapters **-rubrik** chapter heading
kapitul|ation capitulation **-ationsvillkor** terms of surrender **-era** capitulate, surrender
kapitäl 1 *s7, s3, arkit.* capital **2** *s3, boktr.* small capital
kaplan *s3* chaplain
kapning [ˣka:p-] **1** (*uppbringande*) capture; (*av flygplan*) hijacking; skyjacking **2** *sjö.* cutting [away] **3** (*av timmer etc.*) crosscutting
kapock [-'påkk] *s3* kapok
kapp *se ikapp*
kapp|a *s1* **1** coat; cloak; (*akademisk, domares, prästs*) gown; *vända* ~*n efter vinden* trim one's sails according to the wind, veer with every wind **2** (*gardin-*) pelmet, valance; (*volang*) flounce **-affär** coat shop
kappas *dep* vie (compete) [with one another]
kappe *s2, ung.* half-peck
kappkörning racing; *en* ~ *a race*
kapplöp|ning racing (*efter* for); *en* ~ *a race* **-ningsbana** racetrack; (*häst-*) racecourse, *AE.* racetrack **-ningshäst** racehorse, racer
kapprak bolt upright
kapprodd boat-racing; *en* ~ *a boat race* **-are** member of a boat-race crew; single sculler
Kapprovinsen [ˣka:p-] *r* [the] Cape Province
kapprum cloakroom
kapprustning arms (armaments) race
kappsegl|a compete in sailing-races (yacht-races) **-ing** yacht-racing; *en* ~ *a sailing-match* (sailing-race), a yacht-race **-ingsbåt** racing-boat, racing-yacht, racer
kappsimning competition swimming; *en* ~ *a swimming-race* (swimming-competition)
kappsäck suitcase; portmanteau; (*mjuk*) bag
kapriciös [-si'ö:s] *a1* capricious
kaprifol *s3,* **kaprifoli|um** [-'fɔ:-] *-en -er, best. form äv.* *-er* honeysuckle
kapriol *s3* capriole
1 kapris *s3* (*nyck*) caprice, whim
2 kapris [ˈka:-] *s2* (*krydda*) capers (*pl*)
kapsejs|a [-'sejsa] capsize; (*om bil etc.*) turn over **-ning** capsizing
kaps|el *s2* capsule; *bot.* [seed] capsule, seedcase, pericarp **-la** *tekn.* enclose, encase
kapson *s3* cavesson
Kapstaden *r* Cape Town
kapsyl *s3* [bottle] cap, capsule; (*skruv-*) screw cap **-öppnare** bottle opener
kapsåg crosscut saw
kapten *s3* captain; *sjö. äv.* master, *vard.* skipper; (*vid flottan*) lieutenant; (*vid flyget*) flight lieutenant; *AE.* captain, (*vid flottan*) lieutenant
kapucin *s3* Capuchin
kapucin[er]|apa capuchin [monkey] **-munk** Capuchin [monk]
kapun *s3* capon
kapuschong [-'ʃåŋ] *s3* hood
kaputt *oböjligt a, vard.* done for
Kap Verde [ˈvärr-] *n* (*staten*) Cape Verde; (*ögruppen*) Cape Verde Islands
kar *s7* vat; (*bad-*) bathtub, bath
karabinjär *s3* car[a]bineer
karaff *s3* decanter; *hand. äv.* carafe; (*vatten-*) water bottle **karaffin** *s3* carafe
karakteriser|a characterize **-ing** characterizing; characterization
karakteristik *s3* characterization, descriptive account (*över* of)
karakterist|ika [-'riss-] *s1* index, characteristic **-ikon** *best. form* -ikon, *äv.* -ikonet, *pl* -ikon, *äv.* -ika characteristic [feature] **-isk** *a5* characteristic, typical (*för* of)
karaktär *s3* character; (*beskaffenhet, natur äv.*) quality, nature; (*karaktärsfasthet*) strength of character
karaktärs|danande *a4,* **-daning** *s2* character-building **-drag, -egenskap** characteristic [feature, trait]; trait of character **-fast** firm (steadfast) in character; *of* [a] firm character **-fasthet** firmness (strength) of character **-fel** flaw in character **-lös** lacking in character, unprincipled **-löshet** lack of character (principle) **-roll** character part **-skildring** portraiture of a cháracter (person) **-skådespelare** character actor **-studie** character study (*över* of) **-styrka** strength of character **-svag** weak [in character]; spineless **-svaghet** weakness [of character]; spinelessness **-teckning** character-drawing; characterization
karam|bolage [-'la:ʃ] *s7* (*slags biljardspel*) cannon; *särsk. AE.* carom **-boll** [-'båll] *s3, se karambolage*
karamell *s3* sweet, candy **-fabrik** confectionery, sweet factory **-färg** colouring essence **-påse** bag of sweets (*etc.*)

karantän *s3* quarantine; *ligga i* ~ be in quarantine

karantäns|flagga quarantine flag, yellow jack **-tid** quarantine period

karat *s9, s7* carat

karate [-ˣra:-] *s2* karate

karavan *s3* caravan **-seraj** *s3, s4* caravanserai **-väg** caravan route

karavel[l] *s3* caravel

karbad bath

karbamjd *s3* urea **-plast** urea-formaldehyde resin

karbas *s3* cane

karbjd *s3* [calcium] carbide **-lampa** carbide lamp

karbjn *s3* carbine **-hake** snap-hook, spring-hook

karbol [-ˈå:l] *s3, tidigare namn på fenol* **-kalk** carbolic lime **-syra** *se karbol*

karbon [-ˈå:n] *s3* carbon **-at** *s7, s4* carbonate **-isera** carbonize **-papper** carbon paper

karborundum [-ˣrund-] *s8* carborundum **-skiva** carborundum wheel

karbunkel [-ˈbunk-] *s2* carbuncle

karburator [-ˣa:tår] *s3* carburettor **-sprit** carburettor spirit

karcinogen, karcinom *se carcinogen, carcinom*

karda [ˣka:r-] **I** *s1* card[ing-brush] **II** *v1* card

kardan *s3* cardan **-axel** propeller (cardan) shaft **-knut** universal joint (coupling), cardan joint

kardansk [-ˈda:-] *a5*, ~ *upphängning, se kardanupphängning*

kardan|upphängning cardanic suspension **-växel** cardan drive

kardborr|e (*växt*) burdock; (*blomhuvud*) bur **-band** velcro closing

kardel *s3* strand

kardemumma [-ˣmumma] *s1* cardamom

kardigan *se cardigan*

kardinal *s3* cardinal

kardinalfel cardinal error

kardinal[s]|kollegium the Sacred College, the College of Cardinals **-rött** cardinal [red]

kardinal|streck cardinal point **-synd** *se dödssynd* **-system** *sjö.* cardinal marking system **-tal** cardinal number (numeral)

kardio|graf *s3* cardiograph **-grafj** *s3* cardiography **-gram** [-ˈgramm] *s7* [electro]cardiogram **-log** cardiologist **-logj** *s3* cardiology **-logisk** [-ˈlå:-] *a5* cardiological

kardning [ˣka:-] carding

kardus *s3* (*omhölje*) cartridge, cartouche **-papper** cartridge paper

Karelen [-ˈre:-] *n* Karelia

karens|dag [-ˣrens-] *försäkr.* day of qualifying period for benefit **-tid** qualifying (waiting) period

karess *s3* caress

karet *s3* coach; (*gammalmodig vagn*) shandrydan

karg [-j] *a1* **1** (*om pers.*) chary, sparing (*på* of) **2** (*om natur*) barren

Karibiska havet [-ˈri:-] *n* the Caribbean [Sea]

karibo [ˈka:-] *s5* caribou

karies [ˈka:-] *r* [dental] caries

karikatyr *s3* caricature; *polit. äv.* cartoon **-isk** *a5* caricatural **-tecknare** caricaturist; *polit. äv.* cartoonist

karikera caricature, make a caricature of; (*friare*) overdraw, burlesque

karisma [ˈka:-, *äv.* -ˈrisma] *s3* charisma **-tisk** [-ˈma:-] *a5* charismatic

Karl [-a:-] Charles; ~ *den store* Charlemagne, Charles the Great; ~ *XII* Charles XII (the Twelfth)

karl [ka:r] *s2* man; fellow; (*mansperson*) male; *vard.* chap, *AE.* guy; *som en hel* ~ like a man; *vara* ~ *för sin hatt* hold one's own; *han är stora* ~*en nu* he is quite the man now; *bra* ~ *reder sig själv* an honest man does his own odd jobs

karlakarl [ˣka:rakar] *en* ~ a man of men

karlaktig [ˣka:r-] *a1* manly; (*om kvinna*) mannish **-het** manliness *etc.*

karlatag [ˣka:ra-] *det var* ~*!* that was man-size effort!

Karlavagnen [ˣka:rla-] the Plough, Charles's Wain; *AE.* the Big Dipper

karl|avulen [ˣka:ra-] *a5* manly **-göra** *det är* ~ it is a man's job **-hatare** man-hater

karljohans|stil [-ˣjo:-] Swedish Empire style **-svamp** cep

karlsbadersalt [ˣka:rls-, *äv.* -ˣba:-] Carlsbad salts (*pl*)

karl|tokig [ˣka:r-] man-mad **-tycke** *ha* ~ be attractive to men, have sex appeal

karm *s2* (*armstöd*) arm; (*ram*) frame

karma [ˈkarr-] *s1* karma

karmeljt[er] *s3* [*s9*] Carmelite **-munk** Carmelite monk, white friar **-nunna** Carmelite nun **-orden** the Carmelite Order

karmjn *s4, s3* carmine **-röd** carmine[-red]

karmosjn *s4, s3* crimson **-röd** crimson[-red]

karmstol armchair

karnaubavax [-ˣnauba-] carnauba [wax]

karneol [-ˈo:l *el.* ˈ-å:l] *s3* carnelian

karneval *s3* carnival

karnevals|dräkt carnival costume **-upptåg** carnival escapade **-yra** riotous revelry [of the carnival]

karnjs *s3* cornice

karnivor [-ˈvå:r] *s3* carnivore

karolin *s3* soldier of Charles XII of Sweden

karolingisk [-ˈliŋ-] *a5* Carolingian, Carlovingian

kaross [-ˈråss] *s3* chariot **-eri** [car] body, coachwork

karoten *s4* carotene, carotin

1 karott [-ˈrått] *s3* (*morot*) carrot

2 karott [-ˈrått] *s3* deep dish, vegetable dish

karottunderlägg table mat

karp *s2* carp

Karpaterna [-ˈpa:-] *pl* the Carpathian Mountains, the Carpathians

karpdamm carp pond

karré *s3, fläskkarré*

karriär *s3* **1** *i full* ~ at (in) full career **2** (*levnadsbana*) career; *göra* ~ make a career for o.s., get on in the world **-ist** careerist, [social] climber

karsk *a1* plucky; bold; cocky

karsk|a ~ *upp sig* pluck up [one's] courage **-het** pluck; cocksureness

karstbildning karst formation

kart [-a:-] *s2, s9* green (unripe) fruit

karta [ˣka:r-] *s1* map (*över* of); *komma på överblivna* ~*n* be on the shelf, become an old maid

kartagisk [-'ta:-] *a5* Carthaginian
Kartago [-'ta:-] *n* Carthage
kart|blad map sheet **-bok** atlas
kartell *s3* cartel; (*val- o.d.*) [com]pact **-bildning** cartelization
kartera *se kartlägga*
kartesch [-'e(:)ʃ] *s3* cartouche, case shot
kartfodral map case (cover)
kartig [ˣka:r-] *a1* unripe, green
kartlagd mapped [out]
kartlägg|a map [out], chart, make a map of; delineate **-ning** mapping, survey
kart|läsare (*i bilsport*) codriver **-läsning** map reading **-mätare** cartometric wheel pen
kartnagel [ˣka:rt-] deformed nail
karto|graf *s3* cartographer **-grafi** *s3* cartography **-grafisk** [-'gra:-] *a5* cartographic[al] **-gram** [-'gramm] *s7* cartogram
kartong [-'åŋ] *s3* **1** (*styvt papper*) cardboard **2** (*pappask*) cardboard box, carton **3** *konst.* cartoon
kartonn|age [-'a:ʃ] *s7* (*papparbete*) cardboard article; (*pappband*) [binding in] paper boards **-era** bind in paper boards
kartotek *s7* card index (file); *föra ~ över* keep a file (card index) of
kartotekskort index card
kart|projektion [ˣka:-] map projection **-ritare** cartographer **-tecken** map symbol
kartusian *s3* Carthusian **-kloster** Carthusian monastery
kartverk [ˣka:-] **1** (*ämbetsverk*) map[-issuing] office **2** (*atlas*) atlas
karusell *s3* roundabout, merry-go-round; *AE. äv* car[r]ousel; *åka ~* ride on the roundabout (merry-go-round) **-svarv** vertical boring and turning mill
karva whittle, chip (*på* at); (*skära äv.*) cut (*äv. ~ i*)
karyatid *s3* caryatid
kaschmir ['kaʃ- *el.* -'i:r] *s3, s4* cashmere **-sjal** cashmere shawl **-ull** cashmere wool
kase *s2* beacon fire
kasein *s4* casein **-lim** casein glue
kasematt *s3* casemate
kasern [-'ä:rn] *s3* barracks (*pl*) **-förbud** confinement to barracks **-gård** barrack square (yard) **-liv** barrack life
kasino [-'si:-] *s6* casino
1 kask *se kaffekask*
2 kask *s2* casque, helmet
kaskad *s3* cascade; torrent
kaskelott [-'ått] *s3* cachalot, sperm whale
kaskett *s3* [brimmed] cap
kaskoförsäkring hull insurance; (*fordons-*) insurance against material damage to a motor vehicle
kasper ['kass-] *s9* Punch **-teater** Punch-and-Judy show
Kaspiska havet ['kass-] *n* the Caspian Sea
kass *a1 vard.* (*dålig*) poor, miserable, wretched; (*starkare*) lousy, rotten
kassa *s1* **1** (*penningförråd*) cash, purse; money; (*-låda*) cash box, till; (*intäkt*) takings (*pl*), receipts (*pl*); *per ~* (*hand.*) for cash; *brist i ~n* deficit in the cash [account]; *ha hand om ~n* keep the cash; *vara stadd vid ~* be in funds; *~n stämmer* the cash account balances; *min ~ tillåter inte* my purse will not allow **2** (*fond*) fund **3** (*-avdelning*) cashier's department; (*i butik*) cash (cashier's) desk, checkout; (*i bank*) cashier['s desk], *AE. äv.* teller['s desk]; (*teater-*) box office

kassa|apparat cash register **-behållning** cash balance, cash in hand **-bok** cash-book **-brist** deficit; (*förskingring*) defalcation **-fack** safe-deposit box **-förvaltare** cashier, treasurer **-kista** strongbox **-kladd** rough cash-book **-konto** cash account **-kontor** pay-office, cashier's office **-kvitto** sales slip, cash receipt **-kvot** cash ratio **-låda** cash box (drawer) **-pjäs** box-office play **-rabatt** cash discount; *minus 2 % ~* less 2 % discount [for cash] **-register** cash register **-skrin** cash box **-skåp** safe
kassations|domstol supreme court of appeal **-procent** rejection percentage
kassava [-ˣsa:-] *s9* cassava, manioc
kassavalv strongroom, safe-deposit vault
kasse *s2* string bag; (*pappers-*) paper carrier [bag]
kassera reject; (*förslag äv.*) turn down; (*utdöma*) condemn; (*kasta bort*) discard
kassett *s3, foto.* film holder, cartridge, cassette, magazine; (*bok-*) slipcase **-bandspelare** cassette [tape] recorder **-däck** cassette deck
kassler ['kass-] *s9* smoke-cured loin of pork
kassun *s3* caisson **-sjuka** decompression sickness, caisson disease
kassör cashier; (*AE. bank-*) teller; (*förenings-*) treasurer **-ska** [lady] cashier (*etc.*)
1 kast *s3, boktr.* case
2 kast *s3* (*klass*) caste
3 kast *s7* **1** throw; (*slungande*) fling, pitch, toss; (*häftigt*) jerk; (*med metspö e.d.*) cast; *stå sitt ~* put up with the consequences **2** (*hastig rörelse*) toss, jerk (*på huvudet* of the head); *tvära ~ i vinden* sudden [chops and] changes in (of) the wind **3** *ge sig i ~ med* grapple with, tackle
kasta I 1 throw; fling, pitch, toss; jerk; cast **2** *veter.* abort **3** (*sy*) overcast, whip[stitch] **4** (*om vind*) chop about, veer [round] **5** (*~ bort*) throw away; *kortsp.* discard; *~ pengarna i sjön* (*vard.*) throw (chuck) money down the drain **6** *rfl* throw (*etc.*) o.s.; *~ sig av och an i sängen* toss about in bed; *~ sig in i* fling o.s. (plunge) into; *~ sig om halsen på ngn* throw o.s. round s.b.'s neck; *~ sig upp i sadeln* fling o.s. into the saddle; *~ sig upp på cykeln* jump on to one's bicycle; *~ sig över* fling o.s. upon, fall upon **II** (*med betonad partikel*) **1** *~ av* throw off **2** *~ bort* throw away, (*slösa äv.*) waste, squander **3** *~ i sig maten* bolt one's food **4** *~ loss a*) (*lösgöra*) let go, *b*) (*lägga ut*) cast off, *bildl. äv.* cut adrift **5** *~ om a*) (*ändra om*) change [round], rearrange, *b*) (*en gång till*) throw again, *c*) (*om vind*) change [round] (*äv. bildl.*), veer [round] **6** *~ omkull* throw (knock) down (over); *bildl. se kullkasta* **7** *~ på sig* fling on (hurry into) (*kläderna* one's clothes) **8** *~ tillbaka a*) throw back, *mil. äv.* repulse, *b*) (*ljus*) reflect, (*ljud*) re-echo; *~ huvudet tillbaka* toss one's head back
kastanj[e] [-'anj(e)] *s3, s5* chestnut [tree]; *krafsa ~[e]rna ur elden åt ngn* be a p.'s cat's-paw **-brun**

chestnut [brown]
kastanjett *s3* castanet
kastby gust [of wind], squall
kastell *s7* citadel **-en** *s3* caretaker; *(förr)* castellan
kastfiske spinning; *AE.* baitcasting
kastili|an *s3*, **-ansk** [-'a:nsk] *a5* Castilian
Kastilien [-'ti:-] *n* Castile
kastlek throwing-game
kastlös outcaste; *de ~a (äv.)* the untouchables
kastmaskin 1 *mil.* catapult **2** *lantbr.* winnowing-machine, winnower
kastmärke caste mark
kastning 1 throwing *etc.* **2** *veter.* abortion
kastor [-'å:r] *s3* beaver
kastrat eunuch **-sångare** castrato
kastrer|a castrate; *(djur äv.)* geld **-ing** castration; gelding
kastrull *s3* saucepan
kast|sjuka *se kastning 2* **-spjut** javelin **-spö** casting rod; *(för flugfiske)* fly rod **-söm** overcasting; *(stygn)* whipstitch **-vapen** missile **-vind** *se kastby*
kastväsen caste system
kasuar *s3*, *zool.* cassowary
kasus ['ka:-] *n*, *best. form och pl =*, case **-form** case form **-ändelse** case ending
kata|bolism catabolism **-falk** *s3* catafalque **-komb** [-'åmb] *s3* catacomb
katal|an *s3*, **-ansk** [-'a:nsk] *a5* Catalan **-anska** [-'a:nska] **1** *(språk)* Catalan **2** *(kvinna)* Catalan woman
katalog catalogue
katalogiser|a catalogue **-ing** cataloguing
katalogpris list (catalogue) price
katalys *s3* catalysis *(pl catalyses)* **-ator** [-'a:tår] *s3* catalyst **-era** catalyse
katalytisk [-'ly:-] *a5* catalytic
katamaran *s3* catamaran
katapult *s3* catapult **-stol** ejection (ejector) seat
katarakt *(vattenfall o. med.)* cataract
katarr *s3* catarrh **-al** *a5* catarrhal, catarrhous
katastrof [-'å:f] *s3* catastrophe; *ekon. äv.* crash; *(olycka)* disaster **-al** *a5* catastrophic; disastrous **-fall** emergency case **-läge** emergency (catastrophic) situation **-situation** state of disaster
kateder [-'te:-] *s2*, *skol.* teacher's desk; *univ. o.d.* lecturer's desk, rostrum
katedral *s3* cathedral
kategori *s3* category; class, group; *alla ~er* all types (kinds) *(av* of) **-klyvning** classification by category, grouping
kategoriser|a categorize **-ing** categorization
kategor|isk [-'go:-] *a5* categoric[al]; *(obetingad)* unconditional; *~ vägran* categorical (flat) refusal **-iskt** *adv*, *neka ~ till ngt* flatly deny s.th.
katekes [-'çe:s] *s3* catechism
katek|et [-'ke:t, *äv.* -'çe:t] *s3* catechist **-isation** catechizing
katet *s3* cathetus *(pl catheti)*
katet|er [-'te:t-] *s2* catheter **-risera** catheterize
katgut *se kattgutt*
katjon [ˣkatt-] *s3* cation
katod [-'o:d *el.* -'å:d] *s3* cathode **-rör** cathode tube (valve) **-stråle** cathode ray **-strålerör** cathode-ray tube

katolicism [Roman] Catholicism
katolik *s3* [Roman] Catholic
katolsk [-'o:lsk] *a5* [Roman] Catholic; *~a kyrkan (vanl.)* the Roman Catholic Church
katrinplommon [-ˣtri:n-] *(torkat)* prune
katzenjammer [ˣkatt-] *s9* caterwauling
katt *s3* cat; *för ~en!* confound it!; *jag ger ~en i det!* I don't care a fig for that!; *jag kan ge mig ~en på* I'll swear; *arga ~er får rivet skinn* quarrelsome dogs come limping home; *i mörkret är alla ~er grå* all cats are grey in the dark; *när ~en är borta dansar råttorna på bordet* when the cat's away the mice will play
katt|a *s1* female cat, she-cat **-aktig** *a1* catlike, cattish; feline **-djur** feline **-fot** *bot.* cat's-foot **-guld** *miner.* yellow mica; *bildl.* glitter
kattgutt ['katt- *el.* ˣkatt-] *s3* catgut
katt|hane tom[cat] **-ost** *bot.* mallow **-rakande** *s6* hullabaloo **-skinn** catskin **-uggla** tawny owl
kattun [*el.* ˣkatt-] *s4*, *s3* printed calico
katt|unge kitten **-öga** *(reflexanordning)* cat's-eye *(äv. miner.)*, reflector
Kaukasien [-'ka:-] *n* Caucasia
kaukas|ier [-'kas:-] *s9*, **-isk** *a5* Caucasian
Kaukasus ['kau-] *n* the Caucasus
kaurisnäcka ['kauri-] cowry
kaus [-au-] *s3*, *sjö.* [stay] thimble, eyelet
kausal *a5* causal **-itet** causality **-sammanhang** causal nexus **-sats** causal clause
kausativ [ˣkau-, 'kau-, *äv.* -'i:v] *s7*, *s4 o. a5* causative
kaustik *a5* caustic
kautschuk ['kau-] *s2* caoutchouc, [India] rubber; *(radergummi)* eraser, rubber
kav *~ lugnt* absolutely (dead) calm
kavaj [-'ajj] *s3* jacket, coat; *(på bjudningskort)* informal dress **-kostym** lounge *(AE.* business) suit **-skutt** informal dance
kavalett *s3* revolving chassis
kavaljer *s3* cavalier; *(bords-, dans- e.d.)* partner; *(ledsagare)* escort
kavalkad *s3* cavalcade
kavalleri cavalry **-anfall** cavalry charge **-regemente** cavalry regiment
kavallerist cavalryman, trooper
kavat *a1* game, spirited; plucky
kavatina [-ˣi:na] *s1* cavatina *(pl cavatine)*
kavel *s2* roller; *(för bakning äv.)* rolling pin **-dun** *bot.* bulrush, reed mace
kavern [-'vä:rn] *s3* cavity
kaviar ['kavv- *el.* ˣkavv-] *s9* caviar[e]
kavi|tation cavitation **-tet** cavity
kavla [ˣka:v-] roll; *~ ner (äv.)* unroll; *~ upp (äv.)* tuck up *(ärmarna* one's sleeves); *~ ut* roll out *(degen* the dough)
kavle [ˣka:v-] *s2*, *se kavel*
kavring [ˣka:v-] *ung.* black rye bread
kax|e *s2* bigwig, big shot (gun) **-ig** *a1* cocky, high and mighty *(över* about); *(översittaraktig)* overbearing *(mot* to[wards])
kebab [-'babb] *s3* [shish] kebab
kedj|a [ˣçe:-] **I** *s1* chain; *sport.* forward line; *slå ngn i -or* put s.b. into chains, chain s.b. **II** *v1* chain *(vid* to); fasten with chains
kedje|brev chain letter **-bråk** continued fraction **-butik** multiple store (shop), chain store **-byte**

(*t.ex. om lägenhet*) multiple exchange **-driven** chain-driven **-hus** link house **-reaktion** chain reaction (*äv. bildl.*) **-röka** chain-smoke **-rökare** chain smoker **-rökning** chain-smoking **-skydd** chain guard **-såg** chain saw **-söm** chain-stitch embroidery

kejsardöme [ˣçejj-] *s6* empire

kejsar|e [ˣçejj-] emperor **-inna** empress **-krona 1** imperial crown **2** *bot.* crown imperial **-pingvin** emperor penguin **-snitt** Caesarean section **-tiden** *under* ~ under (in the time[s] of) the Emperors; ~*s romare* the Romans of the Empire **-värdighet** emperorship

kejserlig [ˣçejj-] *a5* imperial; *de* ~*a* the Imperialists

kel|a [ˣçe:-] pet; ~ *med* (*äv.*) fondle, dandle **-en** *a3, se* kelig **-gris** pet, favourite **-ig** *a1* loving **-sjuk** wanting to be cuddled

kelp [k-] *s3* kelp

kelt [k-] *s3* Celt **-isk** ['kelt-] *a5* Celtic

kelvin ['kelv-] *oböjligt s, fys.* kelvin

kemi [ç-] *s3* chemistry **-graf** *s3* photoengraver **-grafi** *s3* photoengraving

kemikal|ieaffär [-ˣka:-] paint and chemicals shop **-ier** [-'ka:-] *pl* chemicals, chemical preparations

kem|isk ['çe:-] *a5* chemical; ~ *förening* chemical compound; ~ *industri* chemical industry; ~ *reaktion* chemical reaction; ~ *tvätt, se* kemtvätt **-iskt** *adv* chemically; *tvätta* ~ dry-clean

kemisk-teknisk chemicotechnical, chemical; ~ *industri* chemical industry

kemist [ç-] *chemist*

kemoterapi [ç-] chemotherapy

kem|tvätt [ˣçe:-] dry-cleaning; (*lokal*) dry-cleaner's **-tvätta** dry-clean

kentaur [k-] *s3* centaur

Kenya ['ke:-] *n* Kenya

keny|an [k-] *s3,* **-ansk** [-'a:nsk] *a5* Kenyan

keps [k-] *s2* cap

keram|ik [ç-, *äv.* k-] *s3* ceramics (*pl, behandlas som sg*); (*artiklar*) pottery, ceramic ware **-iker** [-'ra:-] ceramist, potter **-isk** [-'ra:-] *a5* ceramic

kerrcell [k-] Kerr cell

kerub [ç-] *s3* cherub **-ansikte** cherubic face

kesa [ç-] (*om kreatur*) rush around

keso [k-] curd (cottage) cheese

ketch [k-] *s3* ketch

ketchup ['ketʃupp] *s3* [tomato] ketchup, catchup

keton [ke'tå:n] *s3* ketone

kex [k-, *äv.* ç-] *s7, s6* biscuit; cracker (*äv. AE.*)

KFUK [kåäffˣu:ká:] (*förk. för Kristliga Föreningen av Unga Kvinnor*) YWCA, *se under kristlig* **KFUM** [kåäffˣu:ämm] (*förk. för Kristliga Föreningen av Unga Män*) YMCA, *se under kristlig*

kibbutz [ki'bɒtts] *s3* kibbutz

1 kick [k-] *oböjligt s i uttr.: på ett litet* ~ in a tick

2 kick [k-] *s2* (*spark*) kick; *få* ~*en* (*vard.*) get the sack

1 kicka [k-] *s1* lassie, girlie

2 kick|a [k-] *v1* kick; ~ *boll* play football

kickstart kick-starter

kid [ç-] *s7* fawn

kidnapp|a [k-] kidnap **-are** kidnapper **-[n]ing** kidnapping

Kielkanalen [ˣki:l-] the Kiel Canal

kika [ç-] peep, peer (*på* at)

kikar|e [ˣçi:-] binoculars (*pl*); field glasses; (*större*) telescope; *ha ngt i* ~*n* have one's eye on s.th., have s.th. in view; *vad har du nu i* ~*n?* what are you up to now? **-sikte** telescopic sight

kikhosta [ˣçi:k-] whooping cough

kikkran [ˣçi:k-] [stop]cock, tap

kikna [ˣçi:k-] whoop; ~ *av skratt* choke with laughter

kikärt [ˣçi:k-] chickpea

kil [ç-] *s2* wedge; *sömn.* gusset, gore; (*på strumpa*) slipper heel

1 kila [ç-] (*springa*) scamper; ~ *stadigt* (*vard.*) go steady; *jag* ~*r nu!* now I'm off!

2 kila [ç-] (*med kil*) wedge

kil|ben sphenoid [bone] **-formig** [-å-] *a5* wedgeshaped, wedgelike

kiliasm [k-, *äv.* ç-] *s3* chiliasm, millenarianism

killa [k-] *se* kittla

kille [k-] *s2* boy; chap; *AE.* guy

killing [ç-] kid

kilo ['çi:- *el.* 'ki:-] *s7* kilo

kilogram [-'gramm] kilogram[me] **-kalori** kilogram calorie, kilocalorie, Calorie **-meter** kilogram metre

kilo|hertz kilohertz **-joule** [-'jɔ:l] kilojoule **-kalori** *se* kilogramkalori

kilometer [-'me:-] kilometre **-lång** a kilometre long

kilo|pond [-'pånd] *s7* kilopond **-pris** price per kilogram **-ton** [-'tånn] kiloton **-watt** kilowatt **-wattimme** *särskr. kilowatt-timme* kilowatt-hour **-vis** by the kilo[gram] **-volt** [-'vålt] kilovolt

kil|rem V-belt **-skrift** cuneiform [writing]

kilt [k-] *s2* kilt

kimbrer ['kimm-] *s9* Cimbrian

kimono ['kimm-] *s5* kimono

kimrök [ˣçimm-] carbon black; lampblack

Kina [ˣçi:-] *n* [People's Republic of] China

kina [ˣçi:-] *s9* quinine **-bark** cinchona bark

kind [ç-] *s3* cheek **-ben** cheekbone

kindergarten [ˣkinn-] *r* kindergarten, nursery school

kind|k[n]ota cheekbone **-påse** cheek pouch **-tand** molar

kinematograf [ç-, *äv.* k-] *s3* cinematograph

kines [ç-] *s3* Chinese; Chinaman; ~*erna* the Chinese

kines|a [çi'ne:-] *han* ~*de hos oss* we put him up for the night **-eri 1** (*pedanteri*) pedantry; red tape **2** *konst.* Chinese ornamentation, chinoiserie **-isk** *a5* Chinese; *K*~*a muren* Chinese wall **-iska** *s1* **1** (*språk*) Chinese **2** (*kvinna*) Chinese woman **-ögon** *pl* slanting eyes

kinet|ik [ç-] *s3* kinetics (*pl, behandlas som sg*) **-isk** [-'ne:-] *a5* kinetic; ~ *energi* kinetic energy

kinin [ç-] *s4, s3* quinine

1 kink [ç-] *s2* (*ögla*) kink, catch-fake

2 kink [ç-] *s7* (*gnäll*) petulance, fretfulness

kink|a [ç-] fret, whimper **-ig** *a1* petulant, fretful; (*fordrande*) particular, hard to please, exacting; (*om fråga o.d.*) delicate, ticklish, *vard.* tricky

kiosk [ki'åsk, *äv.* çi-, *vard.* çåsk] *s3* kiosk; (*tidnings-*) newsstand, bookstall, newspaper stall

1 kippa [ç-] ~ *efter andan* gasp (pant) for breath

2 kippa [ç-] *skon* ~*r* the shoe slips up and down
kippskodd [ç-] *a5*, *gå* ~ walk about in shoes
  without stockings on
kirgis [k-] *s3* Kirg[h]iz **-isk** *a5* Kirg[h]iz[ian]
Kiribati [k-, -'ba:-] *n* Kiribati
kiro|manti [ç-] *s3* palmistry, chiromancy **-prak-
  tiker** [-'prakt-] *s9*, **-praktor** [-ˣpraktår] *s3*
  chiropractor
kirra [k-] *vard.* fix
kirsch[wasser] [k-] *r* Kirsch[wasser]
kirurg [ç-] *s3* surgeon
kirurg|i *s3* surgery **-isk** [-'urg-] *a5* surgical
kis [ç-] *s3*, *miner.* pyrites (*pl*)
kisa [ç-] screw up one's eyes; ~ *mot solen* screw
  up one's eyes in the sun; ~*nde ögon* screwed up
  eyes
kisel ['çi:-] *s2*, *s7* silicon **-alg** diatom **-gur** *s3*
  kieselguhr **-haltig** *a5* siliceous, siliciferous
  -sten pebble
1 kiss [k-] *interj*, ~ ~*!* puss puss!
2 kiss [k-] *s7* wee, pee
kissa [k-] wee, pee
kisse|katt [k-] *s3*, **-mjss** *s2* pussy[cat]
kist|a [ç-] *s1* chest; (*penning-*) coffer; (*lik-*) coffin
  -botten *ha pengar på* ~ have money saved up
  -lock coffin lid
kitjn [ç-] *s4*, *s3* chitin
kitslig [ç-] *a1* (*snarstucken*) touchy; (*retsam*) annoying; (*småaktig*) petty; (*om sak*) *jfr besvärlig*,
  kinkig **-het** touchiness; annoyance; pettiness
kitt [ç-] *s7* cement; (*fönster-*) putty **kitta** cement;
  putty
kittel [ç-] *s2* boiling-pot; (*stor*) ca[u]ldron (*äv.
  bildl.*); (*fisk-, te-*) kettle (*äv. bildl.*); (*tvätt-*) copper **-dal** basin **-flickare** tinker
kittl|a [ç-] tickle; *det* ~*r i fingrarna på mig att*
  (*bildl.*) my fingers are itching (tingling) to **-as**
  dep tickle; ~ *inte!* don't tickle! **-ig** *al* ticklish **-ing**
  tickling; tickle
kiv [ç-] *s7* strife, contention; quarrelling **-as** *dep*
  contend [with each other] (*om* for); (*träta*) quarrel, wrangle (*om* about, as to)
kivi ['ki:-] *s5*, **-fågel** kiwi
kiwi ['ki:-] *s5*, **-frukt** kiwi, Chinese gooseberry
kjol [çо:l] *s2* skirt; *hänga ngn i* ~*arna* be tied to
  s.b.'s apron strings **-linning** waistband **-längd**
  skirt length **-regemente** petticoat government
  -tyg *vard.* skirt
kjortel [ˣçо:r-] *s2*, *se kjol*
1 klabb *s2* (*trästycke*) chunk of wood
2 klabb *s7* **1** (*snö-*) sticky snow **2** *hela* ~*et* the
  whole lot
klabb|a (*om snö*) cake **-ig** *al* sticky
1 klack *imperf. av 1 kläcka*
2 klack *s2*, *jfr hejarklack*
3 klack *s2* (*på sko etc.*) heel; *tekn.* boss; *slå ihop*
  ~*arna* click one's heels; *slå* ~*arna i taket* kick up
  one's heels; *snurra runt på* ~*en* turn on one's heel
klack|a heel **-bar** heel bar **-järn** heel iron **-ning**
  heeling **-ring** signet ring
1 kladd *s2* (*utkast*) rough copy
2 kladd *s7* (*klotter*) scribble
kladd|a mess about, dabble; (*med färg*) daub; ~
  ner sig mess o.s. up, get o.s. mucky (sticky) **-ig**
  al smeary; (*degig*) doughy; (*klibbig*) sticky
klaff *s2* flap; (*bords-*) drop leaf; (*på blåsinstru-

ment) key; *anat.* valve; *hålla* ~*en* shut up
klaffa (*gå ihop*) tally; *allting* ~*de* everything fitted in
klaff|bord gate-leg[ged] (drop-leaf) table **-bro**
  drawbridge; (*med rörlig sektion*) bascule [bridge]
  -fel (*hopskr. klaffel*) valvular disorder **-stol**
  folding chair
klafsa splash, squelch
klaga complain (*för* to; *över* about, of); *absol.*
  make complaints; (*jämra*) lament, wail; *gudi* ~*t*
  worse luck; *uppassningen var inte att* ~ *på* the service left no room for complaint
klag|an *r* complaint (*äv. jur.*); (*jämmer*) lament
  [ation], wail[ing] **-ande I** *s9*, *jur.*, ~*n* the com-
  plainant, the lodger of the complaint **II** *a4* complaining, plaintive; (*sorgsen*) mourning
klago|låt wailing, moaning, lamentation **-mur**
  wailing wall **-mål** complaint; *jur. äv.* protest; (*re-
  klamation*) claim; *anföra* ~ *mot* complain of; *inge*
  ~ *mot* (*hos*) lodge a complaint against (with)
  -skri wail; outcry **-skrift** written complaint
  (protest); *jur.* bill of protest **-tid** ~*en utgår i morgon* the time for appeal expires tomorrow **-visa**
  lamentation, jeremiad
klammer ['klamm-] *s9*, *pl äv. klamrar* [square]
  bracket; *sätta inom* ~ put in brackets
klammeri altercation, wrangle; *råka i* ~ *med* be
  at cross-purposes with; *råka i* ~ *med rättvisan* fall
  foul of the law
1 klamp *s2* (*trästycke*) block of wood
2 klamp *s7* (*-ande*) tramping, tramp
klampa tramp
1 klamra *rfl* cling (*intill* on to); ~ *sig fast vid*
  (*bildl.*) cling firmly to
2 klamra *bokb.* stitch
klan *s3* clan
klander ['klann-] *s7* blame; censure; (*kritik*) criticism (*mot* of); (*bestridande*) contesting, dispute
  -fri blameless, irreproachable, impeccable
  -värd blameworthy, reprehensible, censurable
klandr|a blame; censure, find fault with, criti-
  cize; (*bestrida*) contest, dispute **-ande** *a4* fault-
  -finding, censorious
klang *s3* ring; sound, clang; (*av glas*) clink; (*ton*)
  tone; *hans namn har god* ~ he has a good name;
  rösten har fyllig ~ it is a resonant voice **-full**
  sonorous; (*om röst äv.*) full, rich **-färg** timbre,
  quality **-lös** thin, flat **-tid** *klang- och jubeltid*
  time of glee and rejoicing
klank *s7*, **klanka** *v1* grumble (*på* at)
klant|a *rfl*, ~ *sig* put one's foot in it **-ig** *al*, *vard.*
  clumsy **-skalle** *vard.* clumsy clot
klapp *s2* tap; (*smeksam*) pat
klappa (*ge en klapp*) tap; pat; (*om hjärtat*) beat,
  (*häftigt*) palpitate, (*hårdare*) throb; ~ [*i*] *händerna* clap [one's hands]; ~ *ihop* (*vard.*) go to
  pieces
klapper ['klapp-] *s7* clattering *etc.*, *se klappra*
klappersten cobblestone
klappjakt battue; *bildl.* witch-hunt; *anställa* ~ *på*
  (*friare*) start a hue and cry after
klappmyts *s2*, *zool.* hooded seal, bladdernose
klappra clatter; rattle; (*om träskor e.d.*) clip-clop
klappträ beater, batlet
klar *al* clear; (*om färg, solsken*) bright; (*genomskinlig*) transparent; (*om vatten*) limpid; *bildl.*

K

clear, lucid, (*tydlig*) plain, (*bestämd*) definite, (*avgjord*) decided, distinct; (*färdig*) ready; *sjö.* clear, ready; ~*t besked* definite orders, [a] plain answer; ~*t väder* fair weather; ~*t till London!* (*tel.*) [you are] through to London!; *bilda sig en* ~ *uppfattning om* form a clear conception of; *bli* ~ *över* realize; *få* ~*t för sig* get a clear idea of; *göra* ~*t för ngn att* make it clear to s.b.; ~*t att* make it clear to s.b. that; *göra* ~*t skepp* clear the ship (decks) for action; *ha* ~*a papper* have one's paper in order; *komma på det* ~*a med* be clear on (about), see one's way clearly in; *den saken är* ~ *nu* that is settled now (cleared up)

klara 1 *i sht tekn.* clarify, clear (*äv. bildl.*); (*rösten*) clear; (*reda upp*) settle, clear up, solve; (*gå i land med*) manage, cope with, tackle successfully; ~ *begreppen* make things clearer; ~ *en examen* pass (get through) an exam[ination] **2** *rfl* get off, escape; (*reda sig*) manage, get on (along); ~ *sig undan* get off, escape; ~ *sig utan* do without; *han* ~*r sig alltid* he always falls on his feet; *han* ~*r sig nog* (*äv.*) he'll do all right **3** (*med betonad partikel*) ~ *av* clear off, (*skuld e.d. äv.*) settle [up]; ~ *upp* clear up, settle

klar|blå bright blue **-bär** sour cherry

klarer|a *sjö.* clear **-are** (*fartygs-*) shipping agent, shipbroker; *se äv.* tågklarerare **-ing** clearance, clearing

klargöra make clear, bring home (*för* to); (*förklara äv.*) explain

klarhet clearness *etc.*; clarity; *jfr klar*; (*upplysning*) enlightenment, light; *bringa* ~ *i ngt* throw (shed) light on s.th., elucidate s.th.; *gå från* ~ *till* ~ (*friare*) go from strength to strength; *komma till* ~ *om* (*i*) *ngt* get a clear idea of (understand) s.th.

klarinett *s3* clarinet **-ist** clarinet player, clarinet [t]ist

klarlägg|a make clear, explain; elucidate **-ande** *s6* elucidation

klarmedel clarifier

klar|na [ˣklaːr-] *tekn.* clarify; (*om kaffe äv.*) settle; (*om himlen*) [become] clear; (*om vädret äv.*) clear up; *bildl.* become clear[er]; (*ljusna*) brighten [up] **-signal** go-ahead signal; *få* ~ get the go-ahead **-språk** straight talking; *tala* ~ (*AE., vard.*) talk turkey **-syn** clear vision; sharp perception; (*klärvoajans*) clairvoyance **-synt** [-yː-] *a1* clear-sighted; (*skarp-*) perspicacious **-synthet** clear-sightedness, clarity of vision; (*skarp-*) perspicacity **-tecken** road (line) clear sign; *jfr -signal* **-text** text en clair; *bildl.* plain language **-tänkt** *a1* clear-headed, level-headed **-vaken** wide awake **-ögd** *a5* bright-eyed, clear-eyed

klase *s2* bunch (*druvor* of grapes); (*klunga*) cluster; *bot.* raceme

klass *s3* class; *skol. äv.* form, *AE.* grade; *den bildade* ~*en* the educated classes (*pl*); *tredje* ~*ens hotell* third-rate hotel; *indela i* ~*er* arrange in classes, classify; *stå i* ~ *med* be of the same class as, be classed with; *åka tredje* ~ travel third class

klass|a class, classify **-anda** class spirit **-delningstal** class division index, statutory maximum class size **-fest** class party **-föreståndare** form teacher; *AE.* homeroom teacher **-hat** class hatred

klassic|ism classicism **-ist** classicist **-istisk** [-'ist-] *a5* classicistic

klassifi|cera classify **-cering** [-'seː-], **-kation** classification; breakdown

klassiker [ˈklass-] classic; (*filolog*) classical philologist (scholar)

klassindelning (*klassificering*) classification; *skol.* division into forms (classes); (*social*) class division

klassisk [ˈklass-] *a5* classical; (*mönstergill*) classic; ~ *musik* classical music; ~*a språk* classical languages

klass|kamp class struggle **-kamrat** classmate, classfellow; *mina* ~*er* the fellows (boys *etc.*) in my form; *vi är gamla* ~*er* we were in the same form at school **-lärare** form master **-lös** classless **-medvetande** class-consciousness **-motsättning** ~*ar* differences between classes

klass|ning *sjö.* classification **-rum** classroom **-samhälle** (*hopskr. klassamhälle*) class society **-skillnad** (*hopskr. klasskillnad*) class distinction **-stämpel** (*hopskr. klasstämpel*) *polit.* class mark **-träff** class reunion **-utjämning** levelling out of classes **-vis** by (in) classes

klatsch I *interj* crack! **II** *s2* lash; crack, smack

klatscha 1 (*med piska*) give a crack (flick); (*om piska*) crack; (*klå upp*) smack **2** (*färg*) daub (*på* on to) **3** ~ *med ögonen åt* ogle, make eyes at **-ig** *a1* striking; (*schvungfull*) dashing; (*med kraftig färg*) bold

klaustrofobj *s3* claustrophobia

klausul *s3* clause

klav *s3* key; *mus. äv.* clef

klavbinda tie down; shackle

klave *s2, se krona 5*

klavecin *s3* harpsichord, clavecin

klaver *s7, mus.* keyboard instrument; *trampa i* ~*et* (*bildl.*) drop a brick, put one's foot in it **-tramp** blunder, faux pas

klaviatur keyboard

klema ~ *med* pamper, coddle

klematis [ˈkleː-, *äv.* -ˈmaː-] *s9* clematis

klementjn *s3* clementine

klemig *a1* pampered, coddled; effeminate, soft

klen *a1* (*svag, kraftlös*) feeble; delicate, frail, (*tillfälligt*) poorly, ailing; (*om muskelstyrka*) weak; (*tunn*) thin (*planka* plank); (*motsats dryg*) meagre (*bidrag* contribution); *bildl.* (*dålig*) poor; (*om resultat äv.*) meagre, slender; *en* ~ *ursäkt* a poor (feeble) excuse; ~ *till förståndet* of feeble intellect; ~ *till växten* (*om pers.*) of delicate frame

klen|het feebleness *etc.*; (*t. hälsan äv.*) delicacy, frailty **-mod** timidity, pusillanimity **-modig** timid, pusillanimous

klenod *s3* jewel; gem; (*friare*) treasure

klen|smed jobbing blacksmith, *äv.* village blacksmith **-smedja** small smithy

klent [-eː-] *adv* feebly *etc.*; ~ *begåvad* poorly gifted; *det är* ~ *beställt med* it is a poor lookout as regards..., ...leaves much to be desired

klentrogen incredulous, sceptical **-het** incredulity, scepticism; lack of faith

klenät *s3, ung.* cruller

klepto|man [-ˈaːn] *s3* kleptomaniac **-manj** *s3* kleptomania

klerikạl *a5* clerical
klerk *s3* cleric
klet *s7* daub **-a** daub, smear; scribble **-ig** *a1* messy, mucky
klev *imperf. av kliva*
kli *s7* bran
klia *(förorsaka klåda)* itch; *(riva)* scratch; *det ~r i fingrarna på mig att (bildl.)* my fingers itch to; *~ sig* scratch o.s.; *~ sig på benet* scratch one's leg
klibb|**a** *(vara klibbig)* be sticky (adhesive); *(fastna)* stick *(vid* [on] *to); ~ ihop* stick together **-al** *bot.* [common] alder **-ig** *a1* sticky *(av* with); adhesive; *(limaktig)* gluey
kliché *s3* cliché *(till* for); *boktr. äv.* block, cut, plate; *bildl.* cliché, stereotyped phrase, tag **-anstalt** process engraving works **-artad** [-a:r-] *a5* stereotype **-avdrag** block pull, engraver's proof
klicher|**a** stereotype, electrotype **-ing** stereotyping, electrotyping
1 klick *s2 (sluten krets)* clique, set; *polit.* faction
2 klick *s2 (klimp)* pat; *(mindre)* dab *(sylt* of jam); *(färg-)* daub, smear; *få en ~ på sig (bildl.)* get a blot on one's reputation, *vard.* blot one's copybook
3 klick I *interj* click!; *det sa ~ för oss* we clicked
II *s2 (av vapen)* misfire; *(kameras)* click
klicka *(om vapen)* misfire; *(mankera)* go wrong; be at fault
klickvälde clique rule
klient client **-ẹl** *s7, s9* clientele
klimakter|**isk** [-'te:-] *a5* climacteric **-ium** *s4* menopause, climacteric
klimạt *s7* climate **-bälte** climatic region (zone) **-isk** *a5* climatic **-kammare** grow chamber; *tekn.* phytotron
klimatolog|**i** *s3* climatology **-isk** [-'lå:-] *a5* climatologic[al]
klimat|**ombyte** change of climate **-område, -zon** se klimatbälte
klimax ['kli:-] *s2* climax
klimp *s2* lump; *kokk.* [small] dumpling
klimp|**a** *rfl* get (go) lumpy **-ig** *a1* lumpy
1 kling|**a** *s1* blade; *korsa sina -or* cross swords
2 klinga *v1* ring, have a ring; *(ljuda)* sound, resound; *(om mynt o.d.)* jingle, chink; *(om glas)* clink; *~ i glaset (för att begära tystnad)* tap one's glass
kling|**ande** *a4* ringing *(skratt* laughter); *på ~ latin* in high-sounding Latin; *~ mynt* hard cash **-eljng** *interj* jingle, jangle!
klin|**ik** *s3* clinic; [department of a] hospital; *(privat sjukhem)* nursing home **-iker** ['kli:-] clinical instructor; clinician **-isk** ['kli:-] *a5* clinical
klink *s7* *(dåligt spel)* strum[ming]
1 klinka *v1* strum *(på piano* [on] the piano)
2 klinka *s1 (dörr-)* latch
klinkbyggd *a5* clinker-built
klinker ['klinn-] *s9 (tegel)* clinker [brick]; *(slagg)* clinkers *(pl)* **-platta** clinker slab
klint *s2 (höjd)* hill; *(bergskrön)* brow of a (the) hill; *(bergstopp)* peak
klipp *s7* **1** clip, cut; *(tidningsurklipp)* cutting, clipping *(AE.) (ur* out of) **2** *göra ett ~ (en god affär)* make a killing
1 klipp|**a** *v3* cut; *(gräsmatta o.d.)* mow; *(naglar)* pare; *(får)* shear; *(biljett)* punch; *(häck, skägg)*

trim; *~ itu* cut in two (half); *~ kuponger* clip coupons; *~ med ögonen* blink (wink) *(mot ngn* at s.b.); *~ med öronen* twitch one's ears; *~ till* cut out; *~ till ngn (vard.)* land s.b. one; *som -t och skuren till* just cut out for; *~ sig* have one's hair cut
2 klipp|**a** *s1* rock *(äv. bildl.)*; *(hög, brant)* cliff
klipp|**avsats** ledge **-block** [piece of] rock, boulder
klippbok book for cuttings
klippbrant precipice
klippdocka cut-out doll
klippduva rock dove (pigeon)
klipper ['klipp-] *s2*, **-skepp** clipper [ship]
klippfisk split cod *(sg o. pl)*
klippfyr isophase light
klipp|**grav** rock tomb **-hylla** ledge **-ig** *a1* rocky; *K~a bergen* the Rocky Mountains, the Rockies
klipp|**ljus** isophase light **-ning** cutting *etc.*; *(hår-)* haircutting, [a] haircut; *(av film)* cutting, editing
klipp|**rev** ledge **-tempel** rock temple **-ö** rocky island
klips *s7* clip; *(öron-)* ear clip
klipsk *a1* shrewd; quick-witted
klirr *s7* jingling *etc.*, *se* klirra **klirra** jingle; *(om glas, is)* clink; *(om mynt)* chink; *(om porslin)* clatter
klister ['klist-] *s7* **1** paste **2** *råka i klistret* get into a scrape; *sitta i klistret* be in the soup **-burk** paste pot **-remsa** adhesive tape
klistr|**a** paste, cement, glue, stick *(fast vid* on to); *~ igen (till)* stick down; *~ upp (på väggen)* paste (stick) up; *~ upp på väv* mount on cloth **-ing** pasting
klitoris ['kli:-] *r* clitoris
klitter ['klitt-] *pl* dunes, sandhills
kliv *s7* stride; *med stora ~* in (with) long strides
kliva *klev klivit* stride, stalk; *(stiga)* step; *(klättra)* climb; *~ fram* step (walk) up *(till* to); *~ ner* step down, descend; *~ upp* climb up *(för trapporna* the stairs); *~ över (dike e.d.)* step across, *(gärdesgård e.d.)* climb over
klivit *sup. av kliva*
klo *s5* claw; *friare o. bildl. äv.* clutch; *(kräftdjurs)* pincers *(pl)*; *(på gaffel e.d.)* prong; *få ngn i sina ~r* get s.b. into one's clutches; *råka i ~rna på ngn* into the clutches of; *slå ~rna i* get one's claws into; *visa ~rna* be up in arms *(mot* against)
kloạk *s3* **1** *(avloppsledning)* sewer; drain **2** *zool.* cloaca *(pl* cloacae) **-brunn** cesspool, cesspit **-djur** monotreme **-ledning** [main] sewer, conduit **-rör** sewer **-system** sewage system **-vatten** sewage
1 klocka [-å-] *s1 (kyrk-, ring-)* bell
2 klocka [-å-] *s1 (vägg- o.d.)* clock; *(fick-)* watch; *hur mycket är ~n?* what time is it?, what is the time?; *~n är fem* it is five o'clock; *~n är halv sex* it is half past five, it is five thirty; *går den här ~n rätt?* is this clock (watch) right?; *~n är bara barnet (vard.)* it's early days yet, there's bags of time; *~n är mycket* it is getting late; *~n närmar sig åtta* it is getting near eight o'clock; *förstå vad ~n är slagen* understand the situation, know what to expect
3 klocka [-å-] *v1 (ge klockform åt kjol)* gore,

flare

4 klocka [-å-] *vl, sport. (ta tid på)* clock

klockar|e [-å-] parish clerk and organist; *(kyrkomusiker)* precentor **-katt** *kär som en ~* be madly in love **-kärlek** fondness, affection *(för* for)

klockarmband watchstrap; *AE.* watchband; *(av metall)* [watch] bracelet

klockboj bell buoy

klock|fjäder clock (watch) spring **-fodral** watchcase

klock|formad [-fårm-] *a5* bell-shaped **-gjutare** bell-founder

klockkedja watch chain

klock|kjol flared skirt **-klang** ringing of a bell (of bells) **-ljung** bell heather **-malm, -metall** bell metal

klockradio clock radio

klock|ren [as] clear as a bell-ringing (tolling) **-ringning** bell-ringing

klock|skojare clock-and-watch hawker **-slag** *på ~et* on the stroke [of the clock]; *på bestämt ~* at a definite time

klock|spel chime (peal) of bells, carillon **-stapel** detached bell tower, bell frame **-sträng** bell pull **-torn** bell tower, belfry

klok *al* **1** *(förståndig)* wise, judicious; *(intelligent)* intelligent, clever; *(förnuftig)* sensible; *(försiktig)* prudent, discreet; *(tillrådlig, lämplig)* advisable; *~ gubbe, se kvacksalvare; de slog sina ~a huvuden ihop* they put their heads together; *jag är lika ~ för det* I am none the wiser [for that]; *jag blir inte ~ på det* I cannot make it out, I can make neither head nor tail of it **2** *(vid sina sinnens fulla bruk)* sane, in one's senses; *inte riktigt ~* not in one's right senses, not all there, *AE.* nuts

klokhet [-o:-] wisdom, judiciousness, prudence, sagacity

klokoppling clutch coupling, jaw clutch

klokskap [-o:-] *s3* overwiseness; *(självklokhet)* self-sufficiency; *jfr äv. klokhet*

klokt [-o:-] *adv* wisely *etc.; det var ~ gjort* it was the sensible thing to do; *du gjorde ~ i att* you would be wise to

klon [-o:n] *s3* clone **klona** [ˣklo:-] clone **kloning** [ˣklo:-] cloning

klor [-å:r] *s3* chlorine **-amin** [ˣklå:r-, -ˈi:n] chloramine **-at** *s7, s4* chlorate **-era** chlorinate **-gas** chlorine [gas] **-haltig** *a5* chlorinous **-id** *s3* chloride **-kalk** chloride of lime, bleaching powder

kloroform [-ˈfårm] *s3,* **-era** *vl* chloroform

klor|ofyll *s4, s3* chlorophyll **-syra** chloric acid **-väte** hydrogen chloride **-vätesyra** hydrochloric acid

klosett *s3* closet; *(vatten-)* toilet, lavatory **-borste** lavatory brush

kloss [-å-] *s2* block; clump

kloster [ˈklåss-] *s7* abbey, priory; *(munk-)* monastery; *(nunne-)* convent, nunnery; *(franciskan-, dominikan-)* friary; *(mindre)* community; *gå i ~* enter a monastery **-arbete** *bildl.* [extremely] fine needlework **-broder** monk **-cell** monastery (convent *etc.*) cell **-löfte** *avlägga ~* take [the] vows **-regel** monastic (conventual) rule **-ruin** ruined abbey *(etc.)* **-skola** monastery (convent) school **-väsen** *~det* monasticism, the monastic system

1 klot *s7 (kula)* ball; *sport. äv.* bowl; *(jord-)* globe; *fack.* sphere

2 klot *s3 (t. foder)* sateen; *(t. bokband)* cloth, buckram

klotband cloth binding; *i ~* in cloth, clothbound

klot|blixt fireball **-formig** [-år-] *a5* ball-shaped; globular; spherical **-rund** round like a ball; *(om pers. äv.)* rotund, tubby

klots [-å-] *s2 (rit-)* model

klotter [ˈklått-] *s7* scrawl, scribble **-plank** [public] scribble board

klottr|a [-å-] scrawl, scribble **-ig** *a5* scrawling

klove *s2, tekn.* vice; *AE.* vise

klubb *s2* club

klubba I *sl* club; *sport. äv.* stick; *(krocket-)* mallet; *(ordförande-)* gavel, hammer; *(slickepinne)* lollipop; *föra ~n* hold the chair; *gå under ~n* go under the hammer **II** *vl* club; knock on the head; *~ ner (talare)* call to order; *boken ~des för 100 kronor (vid auktion)* the book was knocked down for 100 kronor

klubb|hus clubhouse **-jacka** blazer **-kamrat** fellow club member; *vi är ~er (äv.)* we belong to the same club **-lokal** club premises *(pl)* **-medlem** club member **-märke** club badge **-mästare 1** master of ceremonies; *AE.* emcee **2** *sport.* club champion **-rum** clubroom; *univ. ung.* common room

klubbslag stroke with a (the) club; *(vid auktion)* blow of the hammer; *sport.* shot; *bildl.* knockout blow

kluck *s7* cluck

kluck|a cluck; *(skvalpa)* gurgle **-ande** *a4* clucking *etc.; ett ~ skratt* a chuckle

kludd *s7,* **-a** *vl* daub **-ig** *al* dauby

klump *s2* lump; *(jord-; pers.)* clod; *i ~* in the lump, wholesale; *sitta som en ~ i bröstet* lie like a lump on the chest

klumpa *rfl, se klimpa sig*

klump|eduns *s2* clodhopper **-fot** club foot

klumpig *al (otymplig)* lumbering, unwieldy; *(tung)* heavy; *(ovig o. tafatt)* clumsy, awkward; *(ohyfsad)* churlish **-het** clumsiness

klump|summa lump sum **-vis** in clumps

klunga *sl* cluster; bunch; group; *(hop)* crowd

klunk *s2* draught, gulp *(vatten* of water); *(liten)* sip; *ta [sig] en ~* have (take) a swig **klunka** gulp

kluns *s2* lump **-ig** *al* lumpy

klurig *al* artful; ingenious

klusjl *s3, språkv.* plosive

klut *s2* patch; *(trasa)* rag; *sätta till alla ~ar* clap on all sail, *(friare)* do one's level best

kluv|en *a3* split (*i* into); *bot.* cleft; *(om läpp)* slit; *(om stjärt)* forked; *~ gom* cleft palate; *~ personlighet* split personality **-enhet** *bildl.* duality, dualism **-it** *sup av klyva*

klyfta *sl* **1** *(bergs-)* gorge; cleft; *(ravin)* ravine; *(rämna)* fissure, crevice; *bildl.* breach; gap, gulf **2** *(vitlöks-)* clove; *(apelsin-)* segment; *(äppel-, ägg-, tomat-)* wedge, slice

klyftig *al* shrewd, bright, clever; *inte så värst ~* not overbright **-het** shrewdness *etc.*

klyka *sl (träd- o.d.)* fork; *(år-)* rowlock, *AE.* oarlock; *(telefon-)* receiver rest, hook

klys *s7, sjö.* hawse[hole]

klyscha *sl* cliché, hackneyed phrase

klyva klöv kluvit split; (dela) divide, split up (i into); (ved) chop, cleave; fys. break up, split, disintegrate; ~ sig split

klyv|arbom jib boom **-are** sjö. jib **-bar** a5 cleavable; (del-) divisible; (kärnfys.) fissionable; ~t material (kärnfys.) fissile material **-frukt** schizocarp **-ning** splitting etc.; split; fissure; (kärn-) fission; fack. division, disintegration **-ningsprodukt** kärnfys. fission product

klå v4 **1** (ge stryk) thrash, beat; ~ upp ngn give s.b. a [good] thrashing **2** (pungslå) fleece, cheat

klåda s1 itch[ing]

klåfing|er pers. person who fingers everything **-rig** a5, vara ~ be unable to let things alone **-righet** inability to let things alone

klåpare bungler, botcher, fumbler (i at)

klä v4 **1** (förse med kläder) clothe; (iföra kläder) dress; (pryda) array, deck; som man är ~dd blir man hädd a man is measured by the cut of his coat **2** bildl. clothe; ~ sina tankar i ord clothe one's thoughts in words, put one's thoughts into words **3** (möbler) cover; (julgran) dress; (fodra) line **4** rfl dress [o.s.]; put on one's clothes; (om naturen) clothe itself; ~ sig fin dress up; ~ sig varmt put on warm clothes, wrap [o.s.] up well **5** (med betonad partikel) ~ av [sig] undress; ~ om (möbler) re-cover; ~ om sig change (till middagen for dinner); ~ på ngn help s.b. on with his (etc.) clothes; ~ på sig dress, put one's clothes on; ~ ut sig dress [o.s.] up (till as) **6** (passa) suit; become; be becoming; hon ~r i blått blue suits her, she looks well in blue

1 kläcka klack, opers. vard.: det klack till i mig när jag såg honom the sight of him gave me quite a start

2 kläcka v3 (ägg) hatch; ~ fram (bildl.) hatch, hit on; ~ ur sig en dumhet come out with a stupid remark

kläckning hatching

kläcknings|maskin [poultry] incubator, brooder **-tid** hatching (incubation) period

kläda v2, se klä

kläde s6 broadcloth **-dräkt** costume, dress

kläder ['klä:-] pl clothes; koll. clothing, apparel; bli varm i ~na (bildl.) [begin to] find one's feet; jag skulle inte vilja vara i dina ~ I wouldn't be in your shoes

klädes|borste clothes brush **-plagg** article of clothing, garment; pl äv. outfit (pl)

kläd|hängare coat hanger; (väggfast) clothes rail; (fristående) hat and coat stand **-kammare** clothes closet **-konto** clothing account **-korg** clothes basket **-loge** dressing room **-lus** body louse **-lyx** extravagance in dress **-mal** clothes moth **-medveten** clothes-conscious **-mod** fashion

kläd|nad [-ä:-] s3 **1** (utan pl) dress **2** (med pl) garment[s pl], vestment[s pl] **-nypa** clothes peg

kläd|sam [-ä:-] a1 becoming (för to) **-sel** ['klädd-] s2 **1** (utan pl) dressing, attiring **2** (dräkt) dress, attire **3** (möbels) covering, upholstery

kläd|skåp wardrobe **-snobb** dandy **-streck** clothesline **-sömnad** dressmaking **-visning** fashion show **-vård** [the] care of clothes **-väg** i ~ in the way of clothes

kläm [klämm] s2 **1** komma i ~ a) eg. get jammed,

b) bildl. get into a scrape; få foten i ~ get one's foot caught **2** (fart) go, dash, push, pep; (kraft) force, vigour; med fart och ~ with vigour and dash **3** (sammanfattning) [summarized] statement (declaration); (slut-) summing-up **4** få ~ på ngt get the hang of s.th.; ha ~ på ngt be well up in s.th. **-dag** working day between holidays

klämma I s1 **1** (knipa) pinch; straits (pl); komma i ~ get into a scrape (tight corner, fix) **2** (hår-, pappers- e.d.) clip; (fjädrad) spring-holder **II** v2 **1** squeeze; (trycka) press; (nypa, äv. om sko) pinch; (absol., om sko e.d.) be tight; ~ fingret (foten) get one's finger pinched (foot jammed) **2** rfl get pinched (squeezed) **3** (med betonad partikel) ~ fast fasten, squeeze together; ~ fram squeeze out; ~ fram med come out with; ~ i strike up (med en sång a song); ~ ihop squeeze up, jam; ~ sönder squeeze (crush) to pieces; ~ till (slå till) go at it, give a good one; ~ ur sig (vard.) bring out, come out with; ~ åt ngn clamp down on s.b., badger (pester) s.b.

kläm|mare clip **-mig** a1 (om t.ex. melodi) dashing; (stilig) tiptop **-skruv** clampscrew

klämt|a toll (i klockan the bell) **-ning** toll, tolling

klänga [ˣkläŋa] v2, ~ [sig] climb (uppför up); ~ sig fast vid cling on to

kläng|e [ˣkläŋe] s6, bot tendril **-ros** rambler [rose] **-växt** climbing plant, climber; creeper

klänning dress; frock; (gala- o.d.) gown

klänningstyg dress material

kläpp s2 **1** (klock-) clapper, tongue **2** (i ljuskrona) drop

klärobskyr [-ˈsky:r] s3 chiaroscuro

klärvoaj|ans [-ˈjans el. -ˈjaŋs] s3 clairvoyance **-ant** [-ˈjant el. -ˈjaŋt] a4 clairvoyant

klätter|fot zool. scansorial foot **-ställning** climbing frame **-växt** climbing plant, creeper

klättr|a climb (nedför down; uppför, upp [i] up); (klänga) scramble **-ing** climbing; en ~ a climb

klös|a v3 scratch; ~ ut ögonen på ngn scratch a p.'s eyes out **-as** v3, dep scratch

1 klöv imperf. av klyva

2 klöv s2, zool. hoof (pl hooves, cloven hoof (foot)

klöv|bärande a4 hoofed **-djur** cloven-hoofed (cloven-footed) animal

1 klöver ['klö:-] s9, kortsp., koll. clubs (pl); jfr hjärter

2 klöver ['klö:-] s9, bot. o. lantbr. clover; bot. äv. trefoil

klöver|blad cloverleaf; arkit. trefoil; (tre pers.) trio **-vall** field of clover

klövja [ˣklö:v-] transport on packhorses (a packhorse)

klövje|djur pack animal **-sadel** packsaddle

knacka (bulta) rap; (svagare) tap; (på dörren) knock; (sten) break; ~ bort rost från chip the rust off; ~ hål på ett ägg crack an egg; ~ ner ngt på skrivmaskin tap s.th. out on the typewriter; ~ på' knock [at the door]; ~ sönder knock to pieces; det ~r! there's a knock!

knack|ig a1, vard., ~ svenska poor Swedish **-igt** adv, vard., ha det ~t have a job to make ends meet **-ning** knock (äv. i motor); rap; tap

knagg|la ~ fram push on to; ~ sig fram (igenom) struggle along to (through) **-lig** a1 rough,

bumpy, uneven; (*om stil*) rugged, laboured; ~ *engelska* broken English **-ligt** *adv, det gick ~ för honom a*) (*i tentamen*) he didn't do too well, *b*) (*med studierna*) it was tough going for him
knak|a crack; creak (*i alla fogar* in every joint) **-ande** *a4* cracking *etc.*

knal *a1, det var ~t med maten* food was scarce
knall *s2* report; (*smäll*) crack, bang; (*vid explosion*) detonation; (*åsk-*) peal, clap; (*duns*) bang; ~ *och fall* on the spot, all of a sudden
1 knalla (*gå*) trot; ~ *vidare* (*äv.*) push on; ~ *sig iväg* trot off; *det ~r och går* I am (*etc.*) jogging along
2 knall|a (*explodera*) detonate; (*smälla*) bang, pop; (*om åskan*) crack
knallblå bright blue
knalle *s2* (*bergs-*) hill, hillock
knall|effekt sensational effect **-gas** oxyhydrogen gas **-hatt** percussion cap **-pulver** fulminating powder **-pulverpistol** toy pistol **-röd** scarlet
knalt [-a:-] *adv, ha det ~* be hard up
knap *s2, sjö.* cleat
knapadel petty nobility; (*i Storbritannien ung.*) baronetage
knapert ['kna:-] *adv, ha det ~* be badly off
1 knapp *s2* **1** button; (*lös skjort-*) stud; *försedd med ~ar* buttoned **2** (*på käpp, lock e.d.*) knob; (*prydnads- äv.*) boss; (*på svärd*) pommel
2 knapp *a1* scanty; (*knappt tillmätt äv.*) short; (*röstövervikt, utkomst e.d.*) bare; (*seger äv.*) narrow; (*om omständigheter e.d.*) reduced, straitened; (*ord-*) sparing, chary (*på* of); *~a tre veckor senare* barely three weeks later; *i ~aste laget* hardly sufficient; *på sin ~a lön* on his (*etc.*) meagre s. y; *ha det ~t* be poorly off (in straitened circumstances); *ha ~t om* be short of; *rädda sig med ~ nöd* narrowly escape, have a narrow escape; *tillgången på...är ~ ...*are in short supply
knapp|a ~ *av* (*in*) *på* reduce, cut down **-ast** scarcely, hardly **-het** scantiness *etc.*; scarcity (*på* of); shortage (*på* of)
knapphål buttonhole
knapphåls|blomma buttonhole; *AE.* boutonniere **-silke** buttonhole silk **-stygn** buttonhole stitch
knapphändig *a1* meagre; (*förklaring, ursäkt e.d. äv.*) curt, scantily worded
knappnål pin
knappnåls|brev sheet of pins **-dyna** pincushion **-huvud** pinhead **-stick** pinprick
knappologj *s3* trifle, pedantry
knapp|rad row of buttons **-slagning** [-a:g-] button-making
knappt *adv* **1** scantily *etc.*; *leva ~* live sparingly; *mäta ~* give short measure **2** *vinna ~* win by a narrow margin **3** (*nätt o. jämnt*) barely; *jfr äv. knappast*; *~...förrän* scarcely...before (when), no sooner...than
knapptelefon push-button telephone
knapr|a [ˣkna:-] nibble (*på* at); ~ *i sig* munch (chew) up; ~ *på en skorpa* crunch (munch) a rusk **-ig** *a1* crisp
knark *s7* dope; *AE. äv.* junk
knark|a use (take) dope **-are** dope [fiend]; (*särsk. marijuana*) pothead; *AE. äv.* junkie

knark|arkvart dope nest, pad **-langare** [dope] peddler (pusher)
knarr 1 *s7* (*-ande*) creak[ing]; (*i dörr etc.*) squeak **2** *s2, s7, ha ~ i skorna* have creaking (squeaky) shoes **3** *s2* (*knarrig människa*) old growler (croaker)
knarr|a (*om trappa, skor e.d.*) creak; (*om dörr, gångjärn e.d.*) squeak; (*om snö*) crunch **-ig** *a1* (*om pers.*) cross, morose; (*grinig*) peevish, grumpy
knasig *a1* (*tokig*) (*vard.*) daft
knast *s2* knot, knag
1 knaster ['knass-] *s9* (*tobak*) canaster
2 knaster ['knass-] *s7* crackling *etc.*; [a] crackle
knast|ertorr as dry as a stick **-ra** crackle; crepitate; (*krasa äv.*) [s]crunch; (*om tobak i pipa*) rustle; *~de mellan tänderna* grated between my (*etc.*) teeth; *gruset ~de under hans fötter* the gravel crunched under his feet
knata *vard.*, ~ *iväg* trot off
knatte *s2* nipper
knatter ['knatt-] *s7*, **knattra** [ˣknatt-] *v1* rattle, clatter
kneg|a toil; *vard.* slog **-are** *vard.* wage-slave
knekt *s2* (*soldat*) soldier; (*i Storbritannien ung.*) redcoat; (*bildl., 'verktyg'*) myrmidon; *kortsp.* jack, knave
1 knep *imperf. av 1 knipa II*
2 knep *s7* trick, device; (*list*) stratagem, ruse; (*fuffens*) dodge; (*konstgrepp*) artifice
knepig *a1* **1** (*listig*) artful, cunning; (*sinnrik*) ingenious, clever **2** (*svår*) hard, ticklish, tricky
knesset *r* Knesset[h]
knip *s7*, ~ *i magen* stomachache
1 knip|a 1 *s1, komma i en svår ~* get into a fix; *vara i ~* be in straits (in difficulties, in a tight place) **II** *knep knipit* **1** pinch; ~ *en applåd* elicit a cheer; ~ *ihop* pinch together; ~ *ihop läpparna* compress one's lips; ~ *ihop ögonen* screw up one's eyes **2** *om det -er* (*bildl.*) at a pinch, if need be; *det -er i magen på mig* I have [got] a griping pain in my stomach
2 knipa *s1* (*fågel*) goldeneye
knipit *sup. av 1 knipa II*
knippa *s1* bunch
knippe *s6* cluster, fascicle; bundle; *bot.* cyme
knipsa clip (*av* off)
knip|slug knowing, shrewd; (*listig*) sly **-tång** pincers (*pl*), nippers (*pl*) **-tångsmanöver** pincer movement
knirk *s7* grating (creaking) [sound] **knirka** grate; (*knarra*) creak, [s]crunch
knittelvers doggerel [verse]
kniv *s2* knife (*pl* knives); *med ~en på strupen* with the knife at one's throat; *strid på ~en* war to the knife; *dra ~* draw one's knife; *ränna ~en i* run one's knife into **-blad** knife blade, blade of a knife **-drama** knifing tragedy **-hugg** stab [with a knife] **-hugga** stab [with a knife]; *bli -huggen* be stabbed [with a knife]
kniv|ig *a1* (*om sak*) delicate, tricky; (*om pers.*) shrewd, crafty **-kastning** *bildl.* altercation
knivsegg knife edge
kniv|skaft knife handle **-skarp** [as] sharp as a razor **-skuren** *a5* knifed, gashed with a knife **-skära** knife **-spets** knife-point **-styng** stab

[with (of) a knife]
knivsudd knife-point; *en ~ salt* a pinch of salt
knix *s2* curts[e]y; *göra en ~ för* drop a curts[e]y
knixa bob, curts[e]y
knock|a [ˣnåcka] knock s.b. out **-out** [nåck'aot]
s3 knockout [blow]; *slå ngn ~* knock s.b. out;
vinna på ~ win by a knockout
knodd [-å-] *s2, vard.* bounder **-aktig** *a1* slick
knog *s7* work, toil; *vard.* fag **knoga** labour
(work, plod) (*med* at); *~ på' a*) trudge (plod)
along, *b*) *bildl.* peg away
knoge *s2* knuckle
knogig *a1* fagging, strenuous
knogjärn knuckle-duster
knollr|a [-å-] *rfl* curl **-ig** *a1* curly, frizzy
knop *s2* (*som hastighet s9*) sjö. knot; *med åtta ~*
at [a speed of] eight knots; *göra tolv ~* do twelve
knots
knopp [-å-] *s2* **1** *bot.* bud; *skjuta ~* bud **2** (*knapp*)
knob **3** (*huvud-*) nob, nut; *klar i ~en* clear-
-headed; *vara konstig i ~en* be a bit cracked **-as**
dep bud **-ning** budding
1 knorr [-å-] *s2* (*krökning*) curl; *ha ~ på svansen*
have a curly tail
2 knorr *s7, se 2 knot*
knorr|a *se 2 knota* **-hane** *zool.* grey gurnard
(gurnet)
1 knot *s2* (*fisk*) *se knorrhane*
2 knot *s7* (-*ande*) murmuring (*mot* against);
grumbling (*mot, över* at)
1 knota *s1, anat.* condyle; (*friare*) bone
2 knota *v1* murmur; grumble (*över* at)
knotig *a1* (*om träd*) knotty; (*om trädrot*) twisted;
(*om pers.*) bony, (*mager*) scraggy
knott [-å-] *s7, s9* black fly
knottr|a [-å-] **I** *s1* [goose] pimple **II** *v1, rfl* become
granulated **-ig** *a1* granular; (*om hud*) rough;
(*kinkig*) touchy; *jag blev alldeles ~* I got goose
flesh all over
knubb|ig *a1* plump; chubby **-säl** harbour seal
knuff *s2* push, shove; (*med armbågen*) elbowing,
nudge; (*i sidan*) poke, dig **knuffa** push, shove,
shoulder *etc.*; *~ omkull* push (shove, knock)
over, upset; *~ till* push (bump, knock) into; *~ undan* push (*etc.*) out of the way; *~ sig fram*
shoulder one's way along **knuffas** *dep, ~ inte!*
don't push (shove)!
knull *s7, vard.*, **knulla** *v1, vard.* fuck
knussel ['knuss-] *s7* niggardliness; (*svagare*) par-
simony; *utan ~* without stint
knuss|la be niggardly (*etc., se -lig*) (*med* with)
-lig *a1* niggardly, stingy, sparing; parsimonious,
mean
knut *s2* **1** (*hörn*) corner; *bakom ~en* round the
corner; *inpå ~arna* at our (*etc.*) very doors **2**
knot; (*hår- äv.*) bun; (*ögle-*) tie; *knyta* (*slå*) *en ~*
tie (make) a knot (*på* in); *~en har gått upp the
knot has come untied (undone); *det har blivit ~
på tråden* the thread has got into a knot **3** *bildl.*
point; *det var just ~en!* that's just the [crucial]
point! **4** *fack.* node
knut|a I *s1* (*förhårdnad i vävnad*) node **II** *v1, rfl*
snarl, become entangled (knotted) **-en** *a5* tied
(*äv. bildl.*), knotted; clenched (*näve* fist); *bildl.*
bound up (*vid* with); *vara ~ vid* (*till*) *a*) (*verksamhet*) be bound up (associated) with, *b*) (*lä-

---

roanstalt, tidning) be on the [permanent] staff of
-ig *a1* knotty **-it** *sup. av knyta* **-piska** knout
-punkt junction, intersection; (*friare*) centre
-timra *~d stuga* cabin built of logs dovetailed at
corners
knyck *s2* jerk; twitch
knyck|a *v3* **1** jerk, twitch (*på* at); *~ på nacken*
toss one's head, (*friare*) turn up one's nose (*åt* at)
2 (*stjäla*) pinch, bone **-ig** *a1* jerky
knyckla crease; *~ ihop* crumple up
knyppel|dyna lace-pillow **-pinne** lace-bobbin
knyppl|a make lace; *~d spets* pillow (bobbin)
lace **-erska** lacemaker **-ing** lacemaking
knyst *n* sound; *inte säga ett ~* not breathe a word
(*om* about)
knysta utter a sound; *utan att ~* without uttering
a sound, (*utan att mucka*) without murmuring
knyta *knöt knutit* **1** tie (*igen, till* up); (*fästa*) fasten; (*näven*) clench; *bildl.* attach; bind, unite (*vid*
to), connect (*till* to); *~ bekantskap med ngn* make
a p.'s acquaintance; *~ förbindelser* establish connections; *~ upp* untie, undo, (*öppna*) open, (*fästa upp*) tie up; *~ åt* tie tight **2** *rfl* knot, get knotted; (*om sallad o.d.*) head; (*gå t. sängs*) turn in;
~ sig i växten become stunted
knyt|e *s6* bundle (*med* of) **-kalas** Dutch treat
-näve fist **-nävsslag** punch **-nävsstor** as big as
a fist **-skärp** sash
knåd|a knead **-ning** kneading
knåp *s7, se knåpgöra*
knä *s6* **1** knee; *tekn. äv.* elbow; *~na böj!* knees
bend!; *byxor med* [*stora*] *~n* trousers with [great]
baggy knees; *på sina bara ~n* on one's bended
knees; *falla på ~ för* kneel [down] to, go down on
one's knees to; *ha ett barn i ~t* have a child on
one's knee[s] (on [in] one's lap); *ligga på ~ för*
kneel to; *tvinga ngn på ~* (*bildl.*) bring s.b. to his
knees **2** *bot.* articulation; (*krök*) bend, elbow
knä|a bend one's knees; *~ fram* walk with bended
knees **-byxor** *pl* short trousers; breeches **-böja**
bend the knee, kneel (*för* to; *inför* before, to);
relig. genuflect
1 knäck *s2, kokk.* toffee, butterscotch
2 knäck *s2* **1** (-*ning*) crack **2** (*nederlag*) blow; *ta
~en på* do for, ruin
knäck|a *v3* crack; (*bryta av*) break; (*gåta, prob-
lem*) scotch, floor; *en hård nöt att ~* a hard nut to
crack; *~ till* give a crack; *det -te honom* that broke
him
knäckebröd crispbread, hard bread
knäckform toffee cup
knä|fall kneeling, genuflection **-hund** lap dog
-höjd knee-height **-kort** *~ kjol* knee-length skirt
-led knee-joint **-liggande** *a4* kneeling
1 knäpp *s2* (-*ning*) click; (*finger-*) flip, flick **2**
s7 (*ljud*) sound
2 knäpp *a1, vard.* (*tokig*) daft, bananas
1 knäpp|a *v3* **1** *det -te i klockan* the clock gave a
click; *det -er i väggarna* there's a ticking in the
walls **2** (*fotografera*) snap; (*i sht film*) shoot **3**
(*med fingrarna*) flip, flick, snap; *~ ngn på näsan*
rebuke s.b. **4** *mus.*, *~* [*på*] twang, pluck (*på gi-
tarren* one's guitar) **5** *~ nötter* crack nuts
2 knäppa *v3* **1** button; (*spänne*) buckle, clasp; *~
av* (*upp*) unbutton; *~ igen* button [up]; *~ på
(elektr.*) switch on **2** *~ händerna* fold (clasp)

K

one's hands
knäppe *s6* clasp, snap
knäppinstrument plucked string instrument
knäpp|känga button boot **-ning** (*till 2 knäppa*) buttoning
knä|skydd kneepad **-skål** kneecap; *anat.* panatella **-strumpa** knee sock **-stående** *a4*, *sport.* crouching; ~ *ställning* kneeling position **-svag** weak in the knees **-sätta** adopt **-veck** hollow of the knee; *darra i* ~*en* tremble at the knees; *hänga i* ~*en* hang by the knees
knävelborr [-å-] *s2* military moustache (*sg*)
knöl *s2* **1** bump; (*upphöjning e.d.*) boss, knob, knot; (*utväxt*) tuber, protuberance; *fack.* node; *bot.* bulb **2** (*drummel*) swine, cad
knöl|a ~ *ihop* crumple up; ~ *till* batter, knock out of shape **-aktig** *a1* loutish; caddish **-begonia** tuberous begonia **-ig** *a1* **1** bumpy (*väg* road); (*om madrass e.d.*) lumpy; (*om träd e.d.*) knotty; (*om finger, frukt*) knobbly; *fack.* nodose, nodular **2** *se -aktig* **-påk** thick knotted stick; (*vapen*) cudgel **-ros** *med.* traumatic erysipelas **-svan** mute swan
knös *s2* swell, nob; *en rik* ~ a [rich] nabob
knöt *imperf. av knyta*
KO *se konsumentombudsman*
ko *s5* cow
koaff|era *se frisera* **-yr** *s3* coiffure **-ör** hairdresser
koagulation coagulation
koaguler|a coagulate, clot **-ing** coagulation
koala [-'a:la] *s1* koala [bear]
koalition coalition
koalitionsregering coalition government
koaxialkabel [-ˣa:l-] coaxial cable
kobbe [-å-] *s2* islet [rock], rock
kobbel ['kåbb-] *s2* cobbler
kobent [-e:-] *a1* knock-kneed
kobolt [-å-] *el.* 'kå:-] *s3* cobalt **-blå** cobalt blue **-bomb** cobalt bomb **-glans** cobaltite **-kanon** gammatron
kobra [ˣkå:-] *s1* cobra
1 kock [-å-] *s3* (*bakterie*) coccus (*pl* cocci)
2 kock [-å-] *s2* [male] cook; (*kökschef*) chef; *ju flera* ~*ar dess sämre soppa* too many cooks spoil the broth
kock|a [-å-] *s1* [female] cook **-mössa** chef's hat
kod [-å:-] *s3*, **koda** [-å:-] *v1* code **kodbeteckning** code notation
kodejn *s4, s3* [kå-] codeine
kod|ex ['kå:- *el.* 'kå:-] *s2* **1** (*handskrift*) codex (*pl äv.* codices) **2** (*lagsamling*) code **3** (*norm*) code
kodicill *s3* codicil
kodifier|a codify, code **-ing** codification
kod|meddelande code message **-ning** coding
koefficient coefficient
koexistens *s3* coexistence
koff [-å-] *s2, sjö.* koff
koffejn [-å-] *s4, s3* caffeine
kofferdikapten [-å-] captain in the merchant navy
kofferdist [-å-] **1** (*sjöman*) merchant seaman **2** (*fartyg*) merchantman, trader, trading vessel
koffert ['kåff-] *s2* trunk; (*på bil*) boot, *AE.* trunk
kofot (*bräckjärn*) crowbar; *vard.* jemmy, *AE.* jimmy
kofta [-å-] *s1* (*stickad*) cardigan
kofångare *se stötfångare*

koger ['ko:-] *s7* quiver
kognat [kåg'na:t *el.* kåŋ'na:t] cognate **-isk** *a5* cognate
kognitiv [*äv.* 'kåggn- *el.* 'kåŋn-] *a5* cognitive
kogubbe cowherd
kohandel *polit.* logrolling, party-bargaining, vote-bartering
kohe|rens *s3* coherence **-ent** *a4* coherent **-sion** cohesion
kohort [-'hårrt] *s3, hist.* cohort
koj [kåjj] *s3* (*häng-*) hammock; (*fast*) bunk; *gå* (*krypa*) *till* ~*s* turn in
1 koja [ˣkåjja] *s1* cabin, hut
2 koja [ˣkåjja] *v1, se under koj*
kojplats *sjö.* bunk, [sleeping] berth
kok *s7* boiling; *ett* ~ *stryk* a good hiding
1 kok|a *v1, v3* **1** (*bringa i -ning*) boil; (*tillreda mat*) cook; (*t.ex. gröt, kaffe, karameller*) make; ~ *ihop a*) (*koncentrera genom -ning*) boil down, *b*) *bildl.* concoct, make up, fabricate; ~ *in* (*frukt o.d.*) preserve; (*i glasflaska*) bottle; *jfr inkokt;* ~ *upp* bring to the boil **2** (*befinna sig i -ning*) boil, be boiling; ~ *upp* come to the boil; ~ *över* boil over; ~ *av vrede* foam with rage
2 koka *s1* clod
kokajn [-å-] *s3* cocaine **-ist** cocainist
kokard [-'a:rd] *s3* cockade
kokbok cookery book; *i sht AE.* cookbook
kokerska [female] cook
kokett I *a1* coquettish **II** *s3* coquette **-era** coquet (*för, med* with) **-eri** coquetry
kok|fru hired cook **-het** boiling (steaming) hot; -*hett vatten* (*vanl.*) boiling water
kokjll *s3* **1** (*gjutform*) chill [mould] **2** (*parerplåt*) coquille
kok|konst cookery, culinary art; (*ngns*) culinary skill **-kärl** cooking-vessel; *pl äv.* pots and pans; (*soldats*) mess kit (gear), billy[can] **-ning** boiling; cooking; making
kokong [-'kåŋ] *s3* cocoon
kokoppor *pl* cowpox
kokos ['ko:-] *s2* coconut **-fett** coconut butter (oil) **-fiber** coconut fibre, coir **-flingor** *pl* shredded coconut **-matta** coir mat **-mjölk** coconut milk **-nöt** coconut **-nötsolja** coconut oil **-palm** coconut palm (tree), coco palm
kokott [-'kått] *s3* cocotte; *vard.* demirep
kok|platta hotplate **-punkt** *på* ~*en* at boiling point (*äv. bildl.*)
koks [-å-] *s3*, **koksa** [-å-] *v1* coke
koksalt (*vanligt* common) salt **-lösning** salt solution
koks|ning [ˣkåks-] coking **-verk** coke-oven plant
kok|t [-o:-] *a4* boiled; *nu är det* ~*a fläsket stekt!* now the fat's in the fire! **-tid** *ngts* ~ the time required for boiling s.th. **-vagn** *mil.* field kitchen **-vrå** kitchenette
kol [-å:-] *s7, kem.* carbon; (*trä-, rit-*) charcoal; (*bränsle* coal; *utbrända* ~ cinders; *samla glödande* ~ *på ngns huvud* heap coals of fire on a p.'s head
1 kola [ˣkå:-] *s1* caramel, toffee
2 kola [ˣkå:-] *v1* **1** (*bränna* [*t.*] *kol*) make charcoal out of, burn to charcoal; *kem.* carbonize **2** (*ta in kol*) coal; *sjö.* bunker

3 kola [ˣkɔ:-] *v1* (*dö, vard.*) kick the bucket
kolar|e [ˣkå:-] charcoal-burner **-tro** implicit (blind) faith
kol|atom carbon atom **-box** coal box; *sjö.* [coal] bunker
kolchos [kåll'ʃå:s] *s3* kolkhoz, collective [farm]
kol|dammslunga *med.* anthracosis, coal-miner's lung **-dioxid** carbon dioxide **-distrikt** coal-mining district, coalfield **-disulfid** carbon disulphide **-eldad** *a5* coal-fired, coal-heated
kolera [ˣkɔ:-] *s9* [epidemic] cholera **-epidemi** cholera epidemic
koler|iker [-'le:-] choleric (irascible) person **-isk** *a5* choleric, irascible
kolesterin *s3, s4,* **kolesterol** [-'å:l] *s3* cholesterol, cholesterin
kol|filter charcoal filter **-fyndighet** coal deposit **-fält** coalfield **-förande** *a4* coal-bearing, carboniferous **-förening** *kem.* carbon compound **-gruva** coal mine (pit); (*stor*) colliery **-gruvearbetare** collier, [coal] miner **-gruveindustri** coal mining **-halt** carboncontent **-haltig** *al* carboniferous, carbonaceous, carbonic **-hydrat** carbohydrate
kolibakterie [ˣkɔ:-] coli bacillus
kolibri [ˣkåll-, *äv.* 'kåll-] *s3* hummingbird
koljk *s3* [the] colic **-smärter** *pl* colicky pains
koling *ung.* [out-of-work] longshoreman
koljt *s3* colitis
kolja *s1* haddock
koljé *s3 se collier*
kolka [ˣkåll-] ~ [*i sig*] gulp (swill) down
koll [-å-] *s3, s2, vard.* check **kolla** [-å-] *vard.* (*kontrollera*) check; (*titta [på]*) dig [in]
kollabor|atör [kåll-] collaborator **-era** collaborate
kollage *se collage*
kollagen [kålla'je:n] *s3, s4* collagen
kollager *geol.* coal seam (bed)
kollaps *s3, -a v1* collapse
kollast coal cargo, cargo of coal
kollationera [kå-] collate; (*t.ex. räkenskaper*) check (tick) [off]
kolleg|a [-'le:-, *äv.* -ˣle:-] *s3* colleague; confrère; (*tidning e.d.*) contemporary **-ial** *al* collegial, collegiate; friendly **-ialitet** friendliness; comradeship
kollegie|block student's note pad **-rum** *skol.* staff committee-room; (*lärarrum*) staff [common] room
kollegium [-'le:-] *s4* **1** (*myndighet*) corporate body, board **2** (*lärar-*) [teaching] staff **3** (*lärarsammanträde*) staff meeting **4** *univ.* course; (*anteckningar*) lecture notes (*pl*)
kollekt *s3* collection **-bössa** collection box **-håv** collection bag
kollektion [-k'ʃɔ:n] collection
kollektiv [ˣkåll-, *äv.* -'i:v] **I** *s7, s4* collective **II** *a5* collective **-ansluta** affiliate as a body **-anslutning** affiliation as a body **-avtal** collective [labour] contract, collective wage agreement **-fil** public-transport lane **-förhandlingar** *pl* collective bargaining (*sg*) **-hus** block of service-flats; *AE.* apartment hotel **-isera** collectivize **-isering** [-'se:-] collectivization **-ism** collectivism **-istisk** [-'ist-] *a5* collectivistic **-jordbruk** *abstr.*

collective farming; *konkr.* collective farm **-trafik** public transport
kollektor [-ˣlektår] *s3* collector, commutator
koller ['kåll-] *s9* [blind] staggers (*pl*)
kolli ['kålli] *s7, s6* package, parcel; (*fraktgods äv.*) piece [of goods]; (*resgods äv.*) piece [of luggage]
kolli|dera come into collision, collide; ~ *med a*) eg. *äv.* run into, *sjö.* fall foul of, *b*) *bildl.* (*om pers.*) get across, (*om förslag, plikter etc.*) clash (conflict, interfere) with, run counter to **-sion** collision; *bildl. vanl.* clash
kollisionskurs collision course; *ha råkat på* ~ *med* be on [a] collision course with
kollodium [-'lo:-] *s4* collodion, collodium
kollojd *s3* colloid, colloidal solution, suspension **-al** *a5* colloid[al]
kollokvium [ka'låkk-] *s4* colloquium
kollr|a [-å-] ~ *bort ngn* turn a p.'s head **-ig** *al* mad, crazy
kol|lämpare coal trimmer **-mila** charcoal stack
kolmonoxid carbon monoxide
kolmörk pitch-dark **-er** pitch-darkness
kolna [ˣkå:l-] get charred; ~*d* charred; *se äv. förkolna*
kolofon [-'få:n] *s3* colophon
kolofonium [-'fo:-] *s4* rosin, colophony
kolon ['kɔ:lån] *s7* colon
koloni *s3* colony; (*nybygge äv.*) settlement; (*skollovs-*) holiday camp
kolonial *a5* colonial **-ism** colonialism
kolonial|makt colonial power **-minister** (*i Storbritannien*) Colonial Secretary, Secretary of State for the Colonies **-politik** colonial policy **-varor** *pl* imported groceries **-varuhandel** (*affär*) grocer's [shop] **-välde** colonial rule
kolonis|ation colonization **-atör** colonizer **-era** colonize
koloni|st colonialist **-stuga** allotment-garden cottage **-trädgård** allotment [garden]
kolonn [-'lånn] *s3* column; *femte* ~ fifth column **-ad** *s3* colonnade
kolorado[skal]bagge [-ˣra:-] Colorado (potato) beetle
koloratur coloratura **-aria** coloratura aria **-sopran** coloratura soprano
kolorer|a colour; ~*d veckopress* illustrated weekly magazines (*pl*) **-ing** colouring, coloration
kolorimet|er [-'me:-] *s2* colorimeter, tintometer **-ri** *s3* colorimetry
kolor|ist colourist **-istisk** [-'ist-] *a5* colouristic **-jt** *s3* (*färgton*) colouring; (*färgbehandling*) colour treatment
kolos [ˣkå:lo:s] fumes (*pl*) from burned coal (coke, wood) **-förgiftning** poisoning (asphyxia resulting) from the inhalation of coal (*etc.*) fumes
koloss [-'låss] *s3* colossus; (*friare*) hulk, monster; *en* ~ *på lerfötter* a monster with feet of clay **-al** *al* colossal; (*friare*) enormous, tremendous, immense, huge **-alt** [-'a:lt] *adv* enormously *etc.*; awfully
Kolosserbrevet [-ˣlåss-] [the Epistle of Paul the Apostle to the] Colossians (*pl, behandlas som sg*)
kolostomj *s3* colostomy
koloxid carbon monoxide **-förgiftning** carbon monoxide poisoning
kolportage [kålpår'ta:ʃ] *s7* colportage, book

hawking **-roman** cheap novel

kolportör [kålpår-] book hawker; (*i sht av religiös litteratur*) colporteur; (*predikant*) lay-preacher

kol|stybb coal dust; cinders (*pl*), [charcoal] breeze **-stybbsbana** cinder track **-svart** coal (jet) black **-svavla** *s1, se koldisulfid*

kolsyra carbonic acid; ~*d* carbonated **-assimilation** carbonic-acid assimilation, photosynthesis

kolsyre|haltig *a5* aerated; *kem.* containing carbon dioxide **-snö** carbon dioxide snow

kolt [-å-] *s2* frock

kol|tablett charcoal tablet **-teckning** charcoal drawing **-tetraklorid** carbon tetrachloride **-tjära** coal tar **-trast** blackbird

kolugn [ˣkoː-] [as] cool as a cucumber

kolumbarium [-ˈbaː-] *s4* columbarium

kolumn *s3* column **-ist** columnist **-titel** *levande* ~ running head (title)

kolupplag coal depot

kolv [-å-] *s2* **1** (*på gevär*) butt **2** *tekn.* piston; (*pump-*) plunger **3** (*glas-*) flask **4** *bot.* spadix (*pl* spadices) **5** (*lås-*) bolt **-motor** piston engine **-ring** piston ring **-slag** piston stroke **-stång** piston rod

kol|väte hydrocarbon **-ångare** [steam] collier

kom [kåmm] *imperf. av 2 komma*

1 koma [ˈkåː-] *s6* (*medvetslöshet*) coma (*pl* comas)

2 koma [ˈkåː-] *s6 astr., fys.* coma (*pl* comae)

kombattant [-å-] combatant

kombi [ˈkåmbi] *s9*, **kombibil** [ˣkåmbi-] estate car; *AE.* station wagon

kombination [kåmb-] combination

kombinations|förmåga power (faculty) of combination **-lås** combination lock **-tång** combination pliers (*pl*)

kombinator|ik [kå-] *s3* combinatorial analysis **-isk** [-ˈtoː-] *a5* combining, combinatory

kombinera [-å-] combine; ~*d* combined, in one

komedj *s3* comedy; *spela* ~ (*bildl.*) act a part, put on an act **-ant** play-actor **-enn** *s3* comedienne **-författare** comedy (comic) writer

komet *s3* comet **-bana** comet's orbit **-huvud** comet's head (nucleus) **-lik** cometlike; *en* ~ *karriär* a meteoric career **-svans** comet's tail

komfort [kåmˈfårt, *äv.* ˈkåmm-] *s3* comfort **-abel** [-ˈaːbel] comfortable

komihåg [kå-] *s7, skämts.* memory

komik *s3* comic art; (*t.ex. i en situation*) comedy **-er** [ˈkoː-] comic actor, comedian

Komin|form [kåminˈfårm] [the] Cominform **-tern** [-ˈtärn] [the] Comintern (Komintern)

komisk [ˈkoː-] *a5* comic[al]; (*lustig*) funny, droll; (*löjlig*) ridiculous

komjölk cow's milk

1 komma [-å-] *s6* comma; (*decimal-*) [decimal] point

2 komm|a [-å-] *kom kommit* **I 1** come; (*ta sig fram, anlända*) arrive (*till* at, in), get; (*infinna sig äv.*) appear, *vard.* turn up; ~ *och gå* come and go; ~ *gående* come walking along (*på vägen* the road); ~ *för sent* be (come, arrive) too late; *-er strax!* coming!; *i veckan som -er* in the coming week; *inte veta vad som* ~ *skall* not know what is

[going] to come (happen); *vart vill du* ~? what are you driving at?; *ta det som det -er* take things as they come; *här -er han* here he comes (is); *här -er Eva* here comes Eva; *-er det många hit?* will there be many people [coming] here?; *vilken väg har du -it?* which way did you come?; *kom och hälsa på oss* come and see us; *påsken -er sent i år* Easter comes (is) late this year; *-er dag -er råd* tomorrow will take care of itself; *planet skulle* ~ *kl. 6* the plane was due at 6; ~ *av* (*bero på*) be due to; ~ *efter* (*efterträda*) come after, succeed; ~ *från en fin familj* come of a fine family; ~ *i* (*ur*) *balans* regain (get out of) balance; ~ *i beröring med* come in contact with; ~ *i fängelse* be put into (sent to) prison; ~ *i olag* get out of order; ~ *i ropet* become the fashion, (*om pers.*) become popular; ~ *i tid* be in time; ~ *i tidningen* get into the paper; ~ *i vägen för* get in the way of; ~ *med* (*medföra*) bring; ~ *med ursäkter* make excuses; *ha ngt att* ~ *med* have s.th. to say (*visa* show; *bjuda på* offer); *kom inte med några invändningar!* none of your objections!; ~ *på benen igen* get on one's legs again; ~ *på besök* till call at; ~ *på fest* be at a party; *det -er på räkningen* it will be put down on the bill; *jag -er sällan på teatern* I seldom go to the theatre; ~ *till ett beslut* come to a decision; ~ *till heders* come into favour; ~ *till korta, se 2 kort I*; ~ *till nytta* be of use, come in useful; ~ *till ro* settle down, get some rest; ~ *till synes* appear; ~ *till tals med ngn a*) (*få träffa*) get a word with s.b., *b*) (*komma överens med*) reach agreement with s.b.; ~ *till uttryck i* find expression in, show itself in **2** ~ *att a*) *-er att* (*uttr. framtid*) shall (*1:a pers.*), will (*1:a, 2:a o. 3:e pers.*), *b*) (*råka*) happen (come) to, *c*) (*uttr. försynens skickelse*) *han kom aldrig att återse henne* he was never to see her again; *jag kom att nämna* I happened to mention; *jag har -it att tänka på* it has occurred to me **3** (*tillkomma, tillfalla*) *det kom på min lott att* it fell to my lot to; *den gästfrihet som -it mig till del* the hospitality shown to me (I have received); *av utgifterna -er hälften på* half of the expenses refer to **4** (*betecknande tilllägg*) *härtill -er att vi måste* in addition to this we must; *till övriga kostnader -er* other costs include **5** (*lända*) ~ *ngn till godo* be of use to s.b.; ~ *väl till pass* come in handy **6** (*uppgå t.*) *det hela -er på 4 pund* it amounts altogether to £4 **7** *opers., det kom till ett uppträde* there was a scene **II** *rfl* **1** (*bero på*) come from, be due to; (*ske*) happen, come about; *det -er sig av att* it is due to the fact that; *hur -er de't sig?* how is that?, how come?; *hur kom det sig att du...?* how is it (did it come about) that you...? **2** (*tillfriskna*) recover, get better (*efter* from) **III** (*föranleda*) make (*ngn att skratta* s.b. laugh); (*förmå*) induce (*ngn att göra ngt* s.b. to do s.th.); ~ *ngn på fall* cause a p.'s downfall (ruin) **IV** (*med betonad partikel*) **1** ~ *an på, se bero*; *kom an!* come on! **2** ~ *av sig* stop [short], (*tappa tråden*) lose the thread **3** ~ *bort* (*avlägsna sig*) get away, (*försvinna*) disappear, (*gå förlorad*) get lost **4** ~ *efter* (*bakom*) come (go) behind, (*följa*) follow, (*bli efter*) get behind, (*senare*) come afterwards **5** *fingrarna kom emellan* my (etc.) fingers got caught; *det kom ngt emellan* (*bildl.*) s.th. intervened **6** ~ *emot* (*t. mötes*)

come (go) towards, (*stöta emot*) bump against (into) **7** ~ *fram a*) (*stiga fram*) come (go) up (along), (*från gömställe*) come out (*ur of*), *b*) (*förbi*) get past (*igenom* through; *vidare* on), (*på telefon*) get through, *c*) (*hinna fram, nå fram*) get there (*hit* here), (*anlända*) arrive, *d*) (*framträda*) come out, appear, *e*) (~ *t. rätta*) turn up; (*vinna framgång*) get on; *kom fram!* come here!; ~ *fram med ett förslag* make a suggestion; ~ *fram med sitt ärende* state one's business; *jag har -it fram till att* I have come to the conclusion that **8** *det kom för mig att* it occurred to me that; ~ *sig för med att* bring o.s. to **9** ~ *förbi* get round (past), *eg.* pass **10** *saken -er före i morgon* the case comes on tomorrow **11** ~ *ifrån* (*absol.*) get away, (*bli ledig*) get off; ~ *ifrån varandra* get separated; *man kan inte* ~ *ifrån att* there is no getting away from the fact that **12** *kom snart igen!* come back soon! **13** ~ *igenom* come (get) through **14** ~ *ihop sig* fall out (*om* about) **15** ~ *in i a*) (*rum etc.*) come (get) into, enter, *b*) (*skola*) be admitted to, *c*) (*tidning*) be inserted in, *d*) (*ämne e.d.*) become familiar (acquainted) with; ~ *in i bilden* come in; ~ *in med a*) (*uppgifter o.d.*) hand in, *b*) (*ansökan*) make, present, *c*) (*klagomål*) lodge; ~ *in på a*) (*sjukhus e.d.*) be admitted to, *b*) (*ämne*) get on to; ~ *in vid posten* be taken on in the Post Office **16** ~ *loss a*) (*om ngt*) come off, *b*) (*om ngn*) get away **17** ~ *med a*) (*följa med*) come along, come with (us, me *etc.*), *b*) (*deltaga*) join in (*i kriget* the war), *c*) (*hinna med*) catch (*tåget* the train), *d*) (*tas med*) be brought along; *han kom inte med på bilden* he didn't get into the picture; *han kom inte med bland vinnarna* he wasn't among the winners **18** ~ *ner på fötterna* alight (*bildl.* fall) on one's feet **19** ~ *vida omkring* travel far and wide; *när allt -er omkring* after all **20** ~ *på a*) (*stiga på*) get (come) on, *b*) (*erinra sig*) think of, recall, remember, *c*) (*upptäcka*) find out, discover, *d*) (*hitta på*) think of, hit on, (*ertappa*) come upon; *det kom hastigt på* it was sudden **21** ~ *till a*) (*anlända till*) come and see (*ngn* see s.b.), *b*) (*uppstå*) come about, arise, (*grundas*) be established, (*skrivas*) be written, (*komponeras*) be composed, *c*) (*födas*) be born, *d*) (~ *som tillägg*) be added, *e*) (*hända*) come about, happen; *frakten -er till* carriage is extra; *ytterligare kostnader har -it till* additional costs (expenses) have been incurred **22** ~ *undan* get away, escape **23** ~ *upp a*) come up, (*stiga upp*) get up, *b*) (*i nästa klass*) be moved up; *frågan kom upp* the question came (was brought) up (*till diskussion* for discussion); ~ *upp i en hastighet av* reach a speed of; ~ *sig upp* make one's way, get on **24** ~ *ut a*) *eg.* come out (*ur of*), (*lyckas* ~ *ut*) get out, (*utomlands*) get abroad, *b*) (*utges*) come out, be published, appear, *c*) (*utspridas*) get about (abroad), *d*) (*förmå betala*) afford to pay; *hans nya bok -er ut i vår* his new book will appear (come out, be published) this spring; *man vet aldrig vad som kan* ~ *ut av det* you never know what can come out of it; *det -er på ett ut* it is all one, it's as broad as it's long **25** *det -er inte mig vid* it is no business of mine **26** ~ *åt a*) (~ *över*) get hold of, secure, (*nå*) reach, *b*) (*ansätta*) get at, *c*) (*stöta emot, röra vid*) touch, come in contact with, *d*)

(*få tillfälle t.*) get an opportunity (a chance) **27** ~ *över a*) *eg.* come over, (*lyckas* ~ *över*) get over, *b*) (*få tag i*) get hold of, come by (across), *c*) (*överraska, om oväder e.d.*) overtake, *d*) (*drabba*) come upon, befall, *e*) (~ *förbi*) get past (round), (*övervinna*) get over; *han har -it över från USA* he has come over from the States; *jag -er över i morgon* I'll come round tomorrow

kommande *a4 o.* *s6* coming; (*t.ex. dagar, generationer*) ...to come; *för* ~ *behov* for future needs; ~ *släkten* (*äv.*) succeeding generations

kommanditbolag [kåmman×di:t-] limited partnership

kommando [kå'mandå] *s6* **1** command; order; *föra* ~ *över* be in command of, command; *rösta på* ~ vote to order; *stå under ngns* ~ be under a p.'s command; *ta* ~*[t] över* take command of **2** (*trupp*) body of troops

kommando|brygga [captain's (navigation)] bridge **-ord** [word of] command **-rop** shouted order (command) **-ton** tone of command; *i* ~ in a commanding (an imperious) tone **-trupp** *se commandotrupp*

kommater|a [-å-] punctuate; put the commas in **-ing** punctuation **-ingsregel** punctuation rule

kommend|ant [-å-] commandant **-antur** commandantship

kommender|a [-å-] (*föra befäl*) be in command (*över* of); (*befalla*) command, order; (*beordra*) appoint; ~ *halt* give the order 'Halt' **-ing** (*-ande*) commanding *etc.*; *få en* ~ be given a command (*sjö.* an appointment)

kommendör [-å-] **1** captain; (*i Frälsningsarmén*) commissioner; ~ *av 1. graden* commodore **2** (*ordensriddare*) knight commander **-kapten** commander

kommensurabel [-å-, -'a:bel] *a5* commensurable, commensurate

komment|ar [-å-] *s3* commentary (*till* to; *över* on); ~*er* comment (*sg*); *utan några* ~*er* without [any] comment; *kortfattad* ~ brief notes (annotations) **-ator** [-'×a:tår] *s3* commentator **-era** comment [up]on; (*förse med noter*) annotate; ~*d upplaga* annotated edition

kommers [kå'märs] *s3*, *livlig* ~ brisk trade; *sköta* ~*en* run the business (show); *hur går* ~*en?* how's business?

kommerseråd head of division of the [Swedish] national board of trade

kommersial|isera [-å-] commercialize **-isering** [-'se:-] commercialization **-ism** commercialism

kommers|iell [-å-] *a5* commercial **-kollegium** [the] [Swedish] national board of trade

komminister [-å-, -'ister] *s2* (*i Storbritannien ung.*) assistant vicar

kommiss ['kåmm-, *äv.* -'miss] *s3* (*tyg*) uniform cloth

kommissariat [-å-] *s7* commissioner's office

kommissarie [-å-, -'sa:-] *s5* **1** (*ombud*) commissary; (*polis-*) superintendent, inspector **2** (*utställnings-*) commissioner **3** (*i Sovjetunionen*) commissar

kommission [kåmmi'ʃo:n] **1** *hand.* commission; *i* ~ on commission **2** (*utskott*) commission, board, committee; *tillsätta en* ~ appoint

K

(set up) a commission **3** (*uppdrag*) commission
kommissions|arvode commission [fee] **-handel** commission business (trade)
kommissionär [kåmmiʃoˈnäːr] *s3* **1** hand. commission agent (merchant, dealer) **2** (*vid ämbetsverk e.d.*) *ung.* official agent
kommit [-å-] *sup. av 2 komma*
kommitté [-å-] *s3* committee; *sitta i en* ~ be on a committee **-betänkande** report of a committee, committee report **-ledamot** committee member
kommitt|ent [-å-] (*uppdragsgivare*) principal; ~*er* (*väljare*) constituents **-erad** [-ˈeːrad] *s9* committee member
kommod [kåˈmoːd] *s3* washstand
kommun [-å-] *s3* (*administrativ enhet*) *ung.* municipality; *AE.* township; (*stads-*) urban district, city; (*lands-*) rural district; (*myndigheterna*) municipality, local authority (*AE.* government)
kommunal [-å-] *a5* municipal, local-government; local (*utskylder* rates); ~*a myndigheter* local authorities; ~ *självstyrelse* local government **-anställd** municipal employee **-arbetare** municipal worker **-förvaltning** local government, municipal administration **-hus** city (*AE.* town) hall
kommunal|isera [-å-] municipalize **-kontor** municipal office[s] **-lagstiftning** local government legislation **-man** local politician **-nämnd** local-government committee **-politik** local-government politics (*pl*) **-politiker** local politician **-råd** municipal commissioner **-skatt** local taxes (*i Storbritannien äv.* rates) **-tjänsteman** municipal officer **-val** local-government election
kommun|block municipal union **-fullmäktige** *koll.* municipal (city) council **-förbund** *Svenska ~et* [the] Swedish Association of Local Authorities
kommuni|cera [-å-] communicate; ~*nde kärl* communicating vessels **-kation** communication
kommunikations|departement ministry (*AE.* department) of transport and communications **-medel** means (*sg o. pl*) of communications (transportation) **-minister** minister (*AE.* secretary) of transport and communications **-radio** radio; (*bärbar*) walkie-talkie **-satellit** communications satellite **-tabell** railway (steamboat and airline) timetable **-väsen** system of communications
kommuniké [-å-] *s3* communiqué, bulletin
kommunindelning division into local-government areas
kommun|ism [-å-] communism (*ofta* Communism) **-ist** communist (*ofta* Communist) **-istisk** [-ˈist-] *a5* communist[ic]
kommunist|parti Communist Party **-stat** Communist state
kommun|minister minister of local government **-styrelse** municipal executive board; city executive board
kommut|ator [kåmmuˣtaːtår] commutator **-era** commutate
komocka [ˣkoːmåcka] *s1* cowpat
Komorerna [kåˈmåː-] *pl* Comoro Islands; *eg.* the Federal and Islamic Republic of the Comoros
kompakt [-å-] *a1* compact; solid (*massa* mass);

dense (*mörker* darkness)
kompanj [-å-] *s4* company **-chef** company commander
kompanjon [-å-] *s3* partner; joint owner; *bli* ~*er* go into partnership [with each other] **-skap** *s7* partnership
kompar|abel [-å-, -ˈaːbel] *a5* (*jämförlig*) comparable **-ation** comparison **-ativ** [ˈkåmp-, *äv.* -ˈiːv] **1** *a5* comparative **2** *s3* comparative; *i* ~ in the comparative [degree] **-era** compare, form the comparative forms of
kompass [-å-] *s3* compass; *segla efter* ~ sail by the compass **-hus** compass bowl **-kurs** compass course **-nål** compass needle **-ros** compass card
kompatib|el [-å-, -ˈtiː-] *a5* compatible **-ilitet** compatibility
kompendium [-å-, -ˈpend-] *s4* compendium; summary
kompensation [-å-] compensation
kompensationsledig on compensatory leave **-het** compensatory leave
kompensera [-å-] (*gottgöra*) compensate; (*uppväga*) compensate [for], make up for
kompetens [-å-] *s3* competence; competency; qualifications (*pl*) **-bevis** certificate of qualifications (competency)
kompetent [-å-] *a1* competent (*för, till* for; *till att* to); ~ *för en plats* [fully] qualified for a post
kompil|at [-å-] *s7*, **-ation** *s3* compilation **-ator** [-ˣaːtår] *s3* compiler **-era** compile
kompis [ˈkåmp-] *s2* **1** *göra ngt i* ~ do s.th. in partnership **2** (*kamrat*) pal; *AE. äv.* buddy
komplement [-å-] *s7* complement (*till* to, of) **-färg** complementary colour **-vinkel** complementary angle **-är** *a5* complementary
komplett [-å-] **I** *a1* complete; absolute; downright **II** *adv* absolutely
kompletter|a [-å-] **1** complete; supplement; make up; ~ *varandra* complement each other; ~*nde uppgifter* supplementary details **2** ~ *i matematik* sit for a supplementary examination in mathematics **-ing 1** completing; supplementing; (*en* ~) completion; (*utvidgning*) amplification; (*av förråd äv.*) replenishment; *till* ~ *av vårt brev* to supplement our letter **2** *skol. o.d.* supplementary examination
komplex [-å-] **1** *a5* complex; ~*a tal* complex numbers **2** *s7* (*av hus o.d.*) block, group of buildings; *psykol.* complex **-itet** complexity
kompli|cera [-å-] complicate **-kation** complication
kompli|mang [-å-] compliment; *ge ngn en* ~ *för* compliment s.b. on; *säga* ~*er* pay compliments **-mentera** compliment (*ngn för* s.b. on)
komplott [kåmˈplått] *s3* plot; conspiracy
kompon|ent [kå-] component, constituent **-era** (*sammansätta*) put together; (*skapa*) create; (*balett, tavla*) design; (*maträtt*) concoct; (*tonsätta, författa*) compose **-ist** composer
komposant [kå-] *fys.* component
komposit [kå-] *s3* composite [material]
komposition [kå-] design; creation; concoction; (*tonsättning*) composition
kompositmaterial composite [material]
kompositör [kå-] composer
kompost [kåmˈpåst] *s3*, **-era** *v1* compost **-ering**

[-'e:riŋ] composting
kompott [kåm'pått] *s3* compote (*på* of); *blandad*
~ (*bildl.*) a very mixed dish
kompress [-å-] *s3* compress **-ion** [-pre'ʃɔ:n]
compression **-or** [-ˣpressår] *s3* compressor
komprimer|a [-å-] compress; ~*d luft* com-
pressed air **-ing** compressing; compression
kompromettera [kå-] compromise; ~ *sig*
compromise o.s.
kompromiss [kå-] *s3* compromise
kompromiss|a [kå-, -'missa] compromise **-för-**
slag proposed compromise **-lösning** compromise solution
kon *s3* cone; *stympad* ~ frustum of a cone
kona *s1, tekn.* cone, taper; (*på bil*) clutch
koncentrat [-å-] *s7* concentrate; *bildl.* epitome;
i ~ (*bildl.*) in a concentrated form
koncentration [-å-] concentration
koncentrations|förmåga power of concen-
tration **-läger** concentration camp
koncentrera [-å-] concentrate (*på* on); *i sht*
bildl. focus, centre (*på* on); ~ *sig* concentrate (*på*
on); ~ *sig på ngt* (*äv.*) focus (centre) one's attention on s.th.
koncentr|icitet [-å-] concentricity **-isk** [-'sent-]
a5 concentric
koncept [-å-] *s7, s4* [rough] draft (*till* of); (*kladd*)
first outline, rough copy; *tappa* ~*erna* (*bildl.*) be
disconcerted (put out)
konception [kånsep'ʃɔ:n] conception
konceptpapper scribbling-paper
koncern [kån'sä:rn, *äv.* -'sö:rn] *s3* group [of com-
panies]; concern
konces|sion [kånse'ʃɔ:n] [parliamentary] sanc-
tion (*på* for); licence; concession; *bevilja ngn* ~
grant s.b. a concession; *söka* ~ *på en järnväg* apply for powers for constructing a railway
-sionsnämnd *K~en för miljöskydd* the [Swe-
dish] national franchise board for environment
protection
koncessiv ['kånn-, *äv.* -'si:v] *a5* concessive
konciliant [-å-, -'ant, -'aŋt] *a1* conciliatory (*mot*
towards)
koncipiera [-å-] **1** (*befruktas*) conceive **2** (*göra*
utkast t.) make concepts; (*författa*) compose
koncis [-å-] *a1* concise; succinct
kondens [-å-] *s7, s3,* **-et** *s7* condensate
kondensa|tion [-å-] condensation **-tions-**
strimma vapour (condensation) trail, contrail
kondensator [-å-, -ˣa:tår] *s3, tekn.* condenser;
elektr. capacitor
kondenser|a [-å-] condense **-ing** condensation;
condensing
kondens|or [-å-, -ˣdensår] *s3* [steam] condenser
-vatten condensation [water]
kondis ['kånn-] *s7 o. s2, vard., se konditori resp.*
kondition 1
kondition [-å-] **1** (*tillstånd*) condition, state; *i ut-*
märkt ~ (*sport. äv.*) splendidly fit **2** (*tjänst*) situation **3** ~*er* (*hand.*) conditions, terms of account
kondition|al [-å-] *a5* conditional **-alis** [-ˣa:lis,
äv. -'a:lis] *r* (*i* in the) conditional [mood]
konditioner|a [-å-] condition; *väl (illa)* ~*d* in [a
state of] good (bad) repair, *se äv. beskaffad* **-ing**
conditioning
konditions|test fitness test **-träning** fitness

training
konditor [kånˣdi:tår] *s3* confectioner, pastry
cook
konditori *s4* confectioner's [shop]; (*serverings-*
ställe) coffee house (bar), café, teashop, tearoom
-varor *pl* confectionery (*sg*), cakes and pastries
kondoleans [kåndåle'ans, *äv.* -'aŋs] *s3* condolence **-brev** letter of condolence (sympathy)
kondolera [-å-å-] express one's condolence[s]
(sympathy) (*ngn med anledning av* with s.b. on)
kondom [kån'då:m] *s3* condom; *vard.* French
letter
kondominium [kåndå'mi:-] *s4* condominium
kondor [kån'då:r] *s3, zool.* condor
kondottiär [-å-å-] *s3* condottiere
kondukt|ans [-å-] *s3, elektr.* conductance **-ivi-**
tet conductivity **-or** [-ˣduktår] *s3, fys.* conductor
kondukt|ris [-å-] *se* [*kvinnlig*] *konduktör* **-ör**
(*för spårvagn e.d.*) ticket collector, conductor;
järnv. guard; *kvinnlig* ~ conductress, *vard.* clip-
pie
konfeder|ation [kå-] confederation **-erad**
[-'e:rad] *a5* confederate[d]
konfekt [-å-] *s3* assorted sweets and chocolates,
confectionery; *engelsk* ~ liquorice all-sorts; *bli*
lurad på ~*en* be thwarted; *variera* ~*en* (*bildl.*)
ring the changes **-ask** box of assorted sweets and
chocolates (confectionery)
konfektion [kånfek'ʃɔ:n] ready-made clothing
(clothes *pl*)
konfektionskläder *pl* ready-made (*AE. äv.*
ready-to-wear) clothes
konfektskål sweet-dish
konfektyr [-å-] ~*er* (*pl*) confectionery (*sg*) **-af-**
fär confectioner's [shop]
konferenc|ié [kånferaŋsi'e:] *s3,* **-ier** [-si'e:] *s3*
compere; *AE.* emcee (master of ceremonies)
konfer|ens [kånfe'rens, *äv.* -'raŋs] *s3* confer-
ence, meeting; (*större*) congress; (*rådplägning*
äv.) consultation, parley **-era** confer, consult
(*med ngn om* with s.b. about); discuss
konfession [kånfe'ʃɔ:n] confession, creed **-ell**
a5 confessional
konfessionslös (*om undervisning o.d.*) non-
confessional; (*om pers.*) adhering to no particular confession
konfetti [kån'fetti] *s9* confetti
konfidenti|ell [kånfiden(t)si'ell] *a5* confidential
-ellt *adv* confidentially, in confidence
konfigura|tion [kå-] configuration **-tiv** *a5* con-
figurational, configurative
konfirm|and [-å-] *s3* candidate for confirmation
-ation confirmation
konfirmations|kostym confirmation suit **-un-**
dervisning preparation for confirmation
konfirmera [-å-] confirm
konfiskation [-å-] confiscation
konfisker|a [-å-] confiscate **-ing** confiscation
konfityrer *se konfektyr*
konflikt [-å-] *s3* conflict; dispute; (*i roman o.d.*
äv.) problem; *komma i* ~ *med* get into conflict
with **-situation** [state of] conflict
konformad [ˣkɔ:n-] *a5* conic[al]
konform|ism [kånfår-] conformism **-ist** con-
formist

K

konfront|ation [kånfrånt- *el.* -frånt-] confrontation; *vid* ~ *med* (*vanl.*) on being confronted with **-era** confront, bring face to face (*med* with) **kon|fundera** [-å-] confuse, bewilder **-fys** *al* confused, bewildered

kongenial [kånje-] *al* congenial; *en* ~ *översättning* a translation true to the spirit of the original **-itet** congeniality; inherent affinity

kongenital [kånje-]́ *a5* congenital

konglomerat [kånglå-] *s7* conglomerate; conglomeration

Kongo ['kåŋgo] **1** *r* (*flod*) [the] Congo **2** *n* (*land*) [Republic of the] Congo

kongoles [kåŋgo-] *s3*, **-isk** *a5* Congolese

kongregation [kåŋgre-] congregation

kongress [-å-] *s3* congress; (*mindre*) conference **kongress|a** [kån'gressa] [hold a] congress **-deltagare** participant in (member of) a congress **-ledamot** *AE.* Congressman, *fem.* Congresswoman **-val** Congressional election

kongruens [-å-] *s3* congruity, congruence (*äv. mat.*); *språkv.* agreement, concord **-fall** *geom.* case of equality in all respects

kongruent [-å-] *a4* congruous, congruent (*äv. mat., geom.*); *språkv.* agreeing, concordant

kon|icitet conic[al] form **-isk** ['ko:-] *a5* conic[al]; ~ *sektion* conic [section]

konjak ['kånn-] *s3* cognac; *vanl.* brandy

konjakskupa brandy glass

konjug|ation [-å-] conjugation **-era** conjugate

konjunktion [kånjuŋ(k)'ʃo:n] conjunction

konjunktiv [ˣkånn-] *s3* (*i* in the) subjunctive [mood] **-isk** *a5* subjunctive **-it** *s3* conjunctivitis

konjunktur [kånn-] business activity, economic situation; trade (business) cycle; ~*er* business (market) conditions; *goda* ~*er* boom (*sg*), prosperity (*sg*); *dåliga* ~*er* [trade] depression (*sg*), slump (*sg*); *avmattning i* ~*en* slowdown in business activity; *uppåtgående* ~*er* business upturn (*sg*), improving markets; *vikande* ~*er* [trade] recession **-avmattning** slowdown in business activity **-betingad** *a5* cyclical (*arbetslöshet* unemployment) **-institut** *K*~*et* the [Swedish] national institute of economic research **-läge** economic situation, state of the market **-nedgång** decline in business activity **-politik** economic policy **-politisk** ~*a åtgärder* action taken to steer business activity **-svacka** slump **-uppgång** period of economic recovery, business upturn **-utveckling** business (economic) trend (development)

konkarong [kånka'råŋ] *s3, hela* ~*en* the whole lot

konkav [-å-] *a5* concave **-itet** concavity

konklav [-å-] *s3* conclave

konklu|dera [-å-] conclude, infer **-sion** conclusion, inference **-siv** *a5* conclusive

konkord|ans [kånkår'dans *el.* -'daŋs] *s3* (*bibel-*) concordance **-at** *s7* concordat

konkret *al* concrete; (*om förslag äv.*) tangible; ~ *musik* (*poesi*) concrete music (poetry) **II** *s4*, *språkv.* concrete

konkre|tion [-å-] **1** (*utan pl*) concreteness **2** *miner.* concretion **-tisera** give a concrete form to

konkubin [-å-] *s3* concubine

konkurrens [-å-, *äv.* -'ans, -'aŋs] *s3* competition (*om* for); rivalry (*om* about); *hård* (*illojal*) ~ fierce (unfair) competition; *utan* ~ (*äv.*) unchallenged; *stå sig i* ~*en* hold its (*etc.*) own in competition **-begränsning** restriction of competition; restraint-of-trade practices (*pl*) **-kraft** competitiveness, competitive strength **-kraftig** able to compete; competitive (*priser* prices)

konkurrent [-å-] *s3* competitor, rival (*om* for) **-företag** rival (competing) company, competitor

konkurrera [-å-] compete (*om* for; *med* with), enter into competition; ~ *ut* outdo, outrival; ~ *ut en firma* oust a competitor (competing firm)

konkurs [-å-] *s3* bankruptcy; failure; *begära ngn i* ~ file a bankruptcy petition against s.b.; *försätta ngn i* ~ declare s.b. bankrupt; *gå i* ~ file one's (a) petition; *göra* ~ fail, go (become) bankrupt **-ansökan** petition in bankruptcy, bankruptcy petition **-bo** bankrupt's (bankruptcy) estate **-förvaltare** (*utsedd av enskild pers. el. firma*) trustee; (*utsedd av domstol*) [official] receiver **-gäldenär** bankrupt **-lager** bankrupt's stock **-mässig** *a5* insolvent

konnot|ation [kå-] connotation **-ativ** [*äv.* 'kånn] *a5* connotative, connotive **-era** connote

konnässör [-å-] connoisseur (*av, på* of)

konossement [kånnå-] *s7* bill of lading

konsekutiv ['kånn- *el.* -'i:v] *a5* consecutive

konsekvens [-å-] *s3* (*logisk följd*) consequence; (*följdriktighet*) consistency; (*påföljd*) consequence, sequel; *det får allvarliga* ~*er* it (this) will have serious consequences **-ent I** *al* consistent **II** *adv* consistently; (*genomgående*) throughout

konselj [-å-] *s3* cabinet meeting **-president** prime minister

konsert [-'sä:r, *äv.* -'särt] *s3* concert **-era** give a concert ([a series of] concerts) **-estrad** concert platform **-flygel** concert grand **-hus** concert hall **-mästare** leader [of an orchestra]; *AE.* concertmaster **-program** *äv.* concert bill **-sal** *se* -*hus*

konserv [-å-] *s3*, ~*er* tinned (canned [*särsk. AE.*]) goods (food *sg*), preserved provisions

konservat|ism [-å-] conservatism **-iv** [*el.* 'kånn-] *al* conservative

konservator [kå-, -ˣa:tår] *s3* (*djuruppstoppare*) taxidermist; (*av tavlor e.d.*) restorer; (*vid museum*) curator, keeper

konservatorium [kå-, -'to:-] *s4* academy of music, conservatoire, conservatory

konserv|brytare tin-opener, can-opener **-burk** tin, can (*särsk. AE.*); (*av glas*) preserving-jar **konserver|a** [-å-] **1** (*bevara*) preserve **2** (*matvaror*) preserve; (*i glasflaska*) bottle; (*i burk*) can; (*i bleckburk*) tin; ~*t kött* (*vanl.*) corned (canned) beef **3** (*restaurera*) restore **-ing** preservation, bottling *etc.* **-ingsmedel** preservative **konserv|fabrik** cannery, canning (tinned--foods) factory **-öppnare** *se konservbrytare*

konsign|ation [kånsiŋna- *el.* -sinja-] consignment; ~ *on consignment* **-era** consign

konsiliant *se konciliant*

konsilium [kån'si:-] *s4* synod

konsistens [-å-] *s3* consistency; *till* ~*en* in consistency; *antaga fast* ~ (*äv.*) acquire substantial form, materialize **-fett** heavy (lubricating) grease, [cup] grease **-givare** gelling agent

konsistor|iell [kå-] a5 **1** kyrkl. consistorial **2** univ. of (pertaining to) a university court **-ium** [-'tɔ:-] s4 **1** kyrkl. consistory **2** univ. university council (court)

konsol [-'å:l el. -'såll] s3 bracket, support; byggn. console, cantilever **-hylla** bracket-shelf

konsolider|a [kå-] consolidate **-ing** consolidation

konsommé [kånn-, kåŋså'me:] s3 consommé

konson|ans [kånså'naŋs el. -'nans] s3 consonance **-ant** [-'ant] s3 o. a4 consonant **-antisk** [-'ant-] a5 consonantal

konsortium [kån'sårtsium] s4 syndicate, consortium

konspir|ation [-å-] conspiracy, plot **-atorisk** [-'tɔ:-] a5 conspiratorial **-atör** conspirator, plotter **-era** conspire, plot

konst [-å-] s3 art; (skicklighet) skill; (knep) trick, artifice; ~en fine art, the arts (pl); de sköna (fria) ~erna the fine (liberal) arts; efter alla ~ens regler according to all the recognized rules; förstå sig på ~ know about art; göra ~er do (perform) tricks; han kan ~en att he knows how to (the trick of... -ing); är det ngn ~? what's difficult about that?; det var väl ingen ~! that's easy enough!; det är ingen ~ för mig att it's easy [enough] for me to; ~en är lång, livet är kort art is long, life is short **-akademi** academy of art ([fine] arts); K~en [the] royal [Swedish] academy of fine arts **-alster** work of art

konst|ans [-å-] s3 constancy **-ant I** a1 constant; fixed, given (förhållande ratio); (oföränderlig) invariable; (beständig) permanent, perpetual **II** s3, mat. constant

konstapel [kån'sta:-] s2 **1** (polis) [police] constable **2** mil. ung. bombardier

konstart form of art, art genre

konstater|a [-å-] (fastställa) establish (att the fact that); (ådagalägga) demonstrate, prove; (betyga) certify; (påpeka) point out, draw attention to (att the fact that); (framställa som faktum) state, assert; (iaktta) notice, observe; (upptäcka, utröna) find out, discover, ascertain; ~ faktum state a fact **-ande** s6 establishment; certification; ascertainment; (påstående) statement, assertion

konst|befruktning artificial insemination **-beridare** circus-rider, equestrian **-bevattning** irrigation

konstellation [-å-] constellation

konstern|ation [-å-] consternation **-erad** [-'e:rad] a5 nonplussed, dumbfounded, taken aback

konst|fackskola college of arts, crafts and design **-fiber** synthetic (man-made) fibre **-flit** arts and crafts (pl) **-flygning** stunt flying; aerobatics (pl, behandlas som sg) **-frusen** artificial[ly frozen] (is ice) **-full** skilled; (sinnrik) ingenious **-färdig** skilful **-föremål** object of art **-förfaren** skilled; med -förfarna händer with the hands of a skilled artist **-galleri** art gallery **-gjord** a5 artificial; man-made; (falsk) imitation; ~ andning artificial respiration; ~ dimma smoke screen; på ~ väg by artificial means **-gjutning** statue-casting **-grepp 1** (yrkesgrepp) trick [of the trade] **2** (knep) [crafty] device, artifice **-gödning 1** (artificiell gödning) artificial ma-

nuring **2** (-gödsel) artificial manure, fertilizer **-hall** art gallery **-handel** (butik) art dealer's [shop] **-handlare** art dealer **-hantverk** [art] handicraft; (varor) art wares, handicraft products (pl) **-hantverkare** [arts] craftsman **-harts** artificial (synthetic) resin, plastic **-historia** history of art (äv. -historien) **-historiker** art historian **-historisk** of art history, art history **-högskola** college of fine arts

konstig [-å-] a1 **1** (besynnerlig) strange, peculiar, odd, curious, queer; en ~ kropp (vard.) an odd customer **2** (svår) intricate; (kinkig) awkward; ~are än så var det inte that is all there was to it

konst|industri art industry; arts and crafts (pl) **-industriell** of applied (industrial) art **-intresserad** a5 interested in art (etc.); den ~e allmänheten art lovers, the art-loving public

konstituera [-å-] constitute; mötet har ~t sig the meeting has appointed its executive committee; ~nde bolagsstämma statutory meeting; ~nde församling constituent assembly

konstitution [-å-] constitution **-ell** a5 constitutional; ~ monarki constitutional (limited) monarchy

konstitutionsutskott ~et [the Swedish parliamentary] standing committee on the constitution

konst|kritiker art critic **-kännare** connoisseur [of the fine arts], art expert

konstlad [-å-] a5 (tillgjord) affected (sätt manners pl); (konstgjord) artificial; (tvungen) forced; (låtsad) assumed

konst|läder artificial leather, leatherette **-lös** artless; (okonstlad) unaffected; (enkel) simple **-museum** art museum (gallery), museum of art **-mässig** a1 **1** (konstnärlig) artistic **2** (konstgjord) artificial **-njutning** artistic treat (enjoyment)

konstnär [-å-] s3 artist **-inna** [woman] artist

konstnärlig [ˣkånst-, äv. -'nä:r-] a1 artistic; det ~a i the artistry of **-het** artistry

konstnärs|ateljé artist's studio (workshop) **-bana** artistic career, career as an artist **-blick** eye of an artist

konstnärskap [-å-] s7 (det att vara konstnärlig) one's (etc.) being an artist; (konstnärlig begåvning) artistic ability

konstnärs|koloni colony of artists **-krets** i ~ar in artists' circles, among artists **-liv** ~et the (an) artist's life **-natur** artistic temperament; pers. artist; en sann ~ a true artist

konstpaus pause for [the sake of] effect

konst|ra [-å-] (krångla) be awkward; (om pers. äv.) make a fuss; (om häst) jib **-rik** (-färdig) skilful; (konstnärlig) artistic **-riktning** tendency (style) in art; school [of art]

konstruer|a [-å-] **1** (göra ritning t.) design; (uppbygga) construct **2** språkv. construe **3** mat. draw **-ad** a5 constructed; (uppdiktad) fabricated

konstruktion [kå-, -k'ʃɔ:n] **1** (konstruerande) designing etc.; construction (äv. språkv.); (uppfinning) invention; (tanke-) conception **2** konkr. construction; design

konstruktions|fel 1 tekn. constructional error (fault, defect); abstr. error in design **2** språkv. construing error **-lära** theory of constructions **-ritning** constructional drawing

konstrukt|iv [äv. 'kånn-] a5 constructive **-ör** constructor, designer; (byggmästare) constructional builder
konst|salong art gallery **-samlare** art collector **-samling** art collection **-siden, -silke** artificial silk; rayon **-skatt** art treasure **-skicklig** skilled in art (handicraft) **-skojare** art fraud **-smide** art metalwork (forging) **-stoppning** invisible mending **-stycke** (ngt svårt) feat, achievement; (trick) trick, tour de force **-ull** artificial wool **-uppfattning** conception of art **-utställning** art exhibition **-verk** work of art; (mästerverk) masterpiece **-åkare** figure skater **-åkning** figure skating **-älskare** art lover
konsul [*kånn- el. 'kånn-] s3 consul; engelsk ~ i British consul in (at) **-at** s7 consulate
konsulent [-å-] consultant, adviser
konsulinna [-å-] consul's wife; ~n X. Mrs. X.
konsult [-å-] consultant, adviser; se äv. under konsultativ **-ation** consultation **-ativ** [äv. 'kånn-] a5 consultative; ~t statsråd (ung.) minister without portfolio
konsult|era consult **-firma** firm of consultants **-uppdrag** commission for a consultant
konsulär [-å-] a5 consular
konsumbutik [-å-] cooperative shop
konsument [-å-] consumer **-förening** [consumer's] cooperative society **-kooperation** consumer's cooperation **-ombudsman** consumer ombudsman **-prisindex** consumer price index **-upplysning** consumer information **-verk** ~et [the Swedish] national board for consumer policies
konsum|era [-å-] consume **-tion** consumption
konsumtions|förening se konsumentförening **-samhälle** consumption (affluent) society **-skatt** consumption tax, excise **-varor** pl consumer goods, non-durable goods; varaktiga ~ consumer durables
kont [-å-] s2, s3 basket of birch bark carried on the back, pannier
kontakt [-å-] s3 1 abstr. contact; bildl. äv. touch; få ~ med get into touch with; förlora ~en med lose (get out of) touch with 2 konkr., elektr. contact; (strömbrytare) switch; (vägg-) socket, vard. point, plug, AE. outlet
kontakt|a [-å-] contact, get into touch with **-kopia** contact print **-lim** contact (pressure-sensitive) adhesive **-lins** contact lens **-man** contact [man]; (med allmänheten) public relations man **-mina** contact mine
kontakt|or [kån*taktår] s3 contactor **-person** se kontaktman **-svårigheter** pl difficulty (sg) in making contacts
kontamin|ation [-å-] contamination **-era** contaminate
1 kontant [-å-] a4 (sams) on good terms
2 kontant [-å-] a4 o. adv (i reda pengar) cash; ~ betalning cash payment, payment in cash; mot ~ betalning for cash, for ready money; per [extra] ~ for [prompt] cash; betala ~ pay [in] cash; köpa ~ buy for cash
kontan|affär cash transaction (deal) **-belopp** cash amount, amount in cash
kontant|er [-å-] pl cash (sg), ready money (sg) **-insats** down payment, amount [to be paid] in

cash, cash amount **-köp** cash purchase **-likvid** cash settlement
kontempla|tion [-å-] contemplation **-tiv** [äv. 'kånn-] a5 contemplative
kontenans [kånte'naŋs el. -'nans] s3, behålla ~en keep one's countenance; förlora ~en be disconcerted (put out)
kontenta [kån*tenta] s1, ~n av the gist of
konteramiral [-å-] rear admiral
konterfej [-å-] s7 portrait
kontext [-å-] s3 context **-uell** a5 contextual
kontinens [-å-] s3, med. continence
kontinent [-å-] continent; ~en (Europas fastland) the Continent
kontinental [-å-] a5 continental **-drift** continental drift **-klimat** continental climate **-sockel** continental shelf **-systemet** the Continental System
kontingent [kåntiŋ'gent el. -in'jent] s3 1 mil. contingent; (grupp) group 2 (avgift) subscription; (andel) quota
kontinu|erlig [-å-, -'e:r-] a5 continuous **-itet** continuity
konto s6 account; (löpande räkning) current account; avsluta ett ~ close an account; ha ~ i en affär have an account at a shop; insätta på ett ~ pay into an account; skriva på ngns ~ (bildl.) put down to a p.'s account **-kort** credit card **-kurant** s3 account current; (-utdrag) statement of account
kontor [kån*to:r] s7 office; (bolags, firmas äv.) offices (pl); på ~et at the office; sitta på ~ be [employed] in an office
kontoriser|a [kå-] turn residential property into offices **-ing** process of turning residential property into offices
kontorist [kå-] clerk, office employee; kvinnlig ~ lady (girl) clerk
kontors|anställd se kontorist **-arbete** office (clerical) work **-artiklar** pl office accessories (equipment sg) **-chef** office manager, head clerk **-göromål** office duties (pl) (work) **-landskap** open-plan office **-maskin** business (office) machine; (skrivmaskin) typewriter **-materiel** office supplies (pl); (pappersvaror) stationery **-personal** office (clerical) staff **-tid** office (business) hours (pl)
kontoutdrag statement of account
kontra [-å-] I prep contra; (friare) versus II v1, sport. break away **-alt** contralto **-band** contraband **-bas** double bass **-bok** se motbok **-dans** contredance, contradance; (friare) square dance **-diktion** contradiction **-diktorisk** [-'tɔ:-] a5 contradictory
kontrah|ent [-å-] [contracting] party (i, vid to) **-era 1** hand. make a contract, contract **2** språkv. contraction
kontraindikation contraindication
kontrakt [-å-] s7 contract, agreement; (hyres-) lease; enligt ~ as per contract; enligt detta ~ under this contract; avsluta ett ~ med ngn om ngt conclude (make) a contract with s.b. about s.th. **-era** contract; ~de varor goods contracted for
kontraktion [kåntrak'ʃɔ:n] contraction
kontrakts|bestämmelse provision (stipulation) of a contract (an agreement) **-bridge**

contract [bridge] **-brott** breach of contract **-enlig** [-e:n-] a5 contractual, as contracted [for] **-formulär** contract form **-prost** rural dean

kontra|mandera countermand; cancel **-märke** check **-order** counterorder, contrary order

kontrapunkt mus. counterpoint **-isk** [-'punkt-] a5 contrapuntal

kontrarevolution counter-revolution **-är** a5 o. s3 counter-revolutionary

kontrasigner|a countersign **-ing** countersign, countersignature

kontraspion counterspy **-age** counterespionage

kontrast [-å-] s3 contrast (till, mot); stå i skarp ~ till be in sharp contrast to; utgöra en ~ till form a contrast to, contrast with **-era** contrast (med, mot with)

kontrast|iv [-å-] contrastive **-medel** contrast medium **-verkan** contrast[ing effect]

kontribu|era [-å-] contribute **-tion** contribution; (skatt) tax, levy

kontring [-å-] sport. breakaway

kontroll [kån'tråll] s3 control (över over, of); check; (tillsyn) supervision, inspection; (-ställe) checkpoint, control station; ha läget under ~ control the situation **-anordning** control[ling device]

kontroll|ant [-å-å-] controller, supervisor **-besiktning** se bilbesiktning o. veterinärbesiktning **-bord** observation (control) desk (panel)

kontroller|a [-å-å-] check; verify, control; make sure (att that); (ha tillsyn över) exercise (have) control over; ~t silver hallmarked silver **-bar** a5 controllable

kontroll|grupp control group **-kommission** control commission **-lampa** (hopskr. kontrollampa) pilot lamp (light) **-läsa** (hopskr. kontrolläsa) read through for the purpose of checking **-märke** check, controlling-mark **-mäta** check the measure (ngt of s.th.), remeasure **-nummer** (-märke) check; (kodnummer) key number **-rum** control room **-räkna** re-count, check [off], verify **-siffra** check digit **-station** checkpoint, control station **-stämpel** control stamp; (för guld etc.) hallmark **-torn** flyg. control tower **-uppgift** (löneuppgift) salary (wage) statement **-åtgärd** control [measure]

kontrollör [-å-å-] controller; comptroller; checker, supervisor, inspector; (biljett-) ticket inspector; post. assistant superintendent

kontrovers [kåntro'värs] s3 controversy **-iell** a5 controversial

konträr [-å-] a5 contrary

kontur [-å-] contour [line]; (friare o. bildl.) outline **-era** contour **-fast** firmly outlined **-karta** outline map **-lös** vague[ly outlined]; undefined **-teckning** outline drawing

kontusion [-å-] contusion, bruise

konung [-å-] s2 (jfr kung) king; Gud bevare ~en! God save the King!; ~arnas ~ the King of Kings; Till K~en (i skrivelse) To His Majesty the King

Konungaböckerna [the] Kings

konungs|lig [kå'nuŋs-, äv. 'kå:-] a5 kingly (hållning deportment); regal (makt power) **-man** courtier

konvalescens [kånvale'sens el. -'ʃens] s3 convalescence

konvalescent [kånvale'sent el. -'ʃent] convalescent **-hem** convalescent home

konvalje [kån'valje] s5 lily of the valley

konvektion [kånvek'ʃo:n] convection

konvenans [kånve'naŋs, -'nans] s3 propriety, convention; (starkare) decorum; brott mot ~en breach of etiquette **-parti** marriage of convenience

konvenera [-å-] suit, be convenient (ngn to s.b., for s.b.)

konvent [-å-] convention

konventikel [kånven'tikk-] s2 conventicle **-plakatet** ung. the Conventicle Act

konvention [-å-] convention **-ell** al conventional

konverg|ens [-å-, -'gens] s3 convergence **-ent** [-'gent] a4 convergent, converging **-era** [-'ge:ra] converge (mot towards)

konversa|bel [-å-, -'a:bel] a2 conversable **-tion** conversation

konversationslexikon encyclop[a]edia

konvers|atör [-å-] conversationalist **-era** converse (om about, on)

konversion [-å-] conversion

konverter [kån'värt-] s2, tekn. converter

konverter|a [-å-] convert; (t. annan religion) become a convert **-ing** conversion **-ingsanläggning** converter plant (equipment)

konver|tibel [-å-, -'ti:-] a5 convertible **-tjt** s3 convert

konvex [-å-] a5 convex **-itet** convexity

konvoj [kån'våjj] s3, **-era** v1, **-ering** [-'e:riŋ] s2 convoy

konvojfartyg (som konvojerar) escort vessel; (som konvojeras) convoy vessel

konvolut [kånvå-] s7 envelope, wrapper, cover

konvul|sion [-å-] convulsion **-sivisk** [-'si:-] a5 convulsive

kooper|ation cooperation **-atjv** a5 cooperative; K~a förbundet [the] Swedish cooperative union and wholesale society; ~ förening cooperative [society], vard. coop, co-op **-atör** cooperator, member of a cooperative society **-era** cooperate

koordinat [koår-] coordinate **-axel** coordinate axis

koordination [koår-] coordination

koordinat|or [koårdinˣa:tår] coordinator **-system** system of coordinates

koordinera [koår-] coordinate

kopek s9 kope[c]k

kopia [-ˣpi:a] s1 copy; duplicate; (avskrift) copy, transcript; foto. print; (av konstverk o. bildl.) replica; neds. imitation; ta ~ av copy, make a copy of

kopiator [-ˣa:tår] s3, se kopieringsmaskin

kopie|bläck copying ink **-papper** copying paper; (karbon-) carbon [paper]; foto. printing paper

kopier|a copy; transcribe; foto. print **-ing** copying; foto. o. boktr. printing

kopierings|anläggning printing (processing) laboratories (pl) **-maskin** copying machine, copier

kopist copying clerk; copyist; foto. printer; (av konstverk) imitator

kopiös a5 copious; enormous

K

kopp [-å-] *s2* cup (*kaffe* of coffee); (*som mått*) cupful [of...]

koppa [-å-] *s1* pock

koppar [-å-] *s9* copper; (*-slantar*) coppers (*pl*) **-bleck** copper plate **-förande** *a4* cupriferous **-förhydning** [-y:d-] copper-sheathing **-glans** *miner.* chalcocite **-gruva** copper mine **-halt** copper content **-haltig** *a5* cupreous **-kis** *miner.* chalcopyrite, copper pyrites **-mynt** copper [coin] **-orm** *se* kopparödla **-oxid** copper oxide; (*med envärd koppar*) cuprous oxide; (*med tvåvärd koppar*) cupric oxide **-plåt** (*för taktäckning e.d.*) [plate of] copper-sheeting; (*enstaka*) copper--sheet; (*för gravyr*) copper plate **-röd** copper--coloured, [as] red as copper; (*om hår*) coppery **-slagare 1** *eg.* coppersmith **2** (*bakrus*) hangover **-stick** (*konstverk*) copperplate, print; (*konstart*) copper engraving, copper-plate engraving **-sulfat** copper (cupric) sulphate **-tryck** copperprint **-ödla** *zool.* slowworm, blindworm

koppel ['kåpp-] *s7* **1** (*hund-*) lead, leash **2** (*jakthundar*) leash **3** *tekn.* coupling **4** *mil.* shoulder belt **5** (*hop, skara*) pack

koppla [-å-] **I 1** (*hund*) put on the lead, leash **2** (*jakt. o. friare*) leash **3** *tekn.* couple up (*till* to); *elektr.* connect (*i serie* in a series); *radio., tel.* connect up (*till* to); *var vänlig ~ mig till* please put me through to **II** (*med betonad partikel*) **1** *~ av a*) järnv., radio., tel. switch off, *b*) (*vila*) relax, unwind, slack off **2** *~ ifrån* disconnect, järnv. uncouple **3** *~ ihop* (*elektr.*) connect, join up, radio., tel. connect up **4** *~ in* connect, throw in, elektr. switch in **5** *~ till* (järnv.) put on, attach **6** *~ ur* disengage, disconnect, elektr. interrupt, (*motor*) declutch

koppl|are [-å-] procurer **-eri** procuring **-erska** procuress, bawd **-ing 1** (*-ande*) tekn. connection **2** *konkr., tekn.* coupling; (*i bil*) clutch; *tel.* switch

kopplings|anordning coupling (connecting) device; *flyg. äv.* release mechanism **-dosa** elektr. coupling box **-lamell** clutch disc **-pedal** clutch pedal **-schema** elektr. wiring diagram **-ton** tel. dialling (*AE.* dial) tone

kopp|or [ˣkåppɔr] *se* koppa, smittkoppor o. vattkoppor **-ärrig** pockmarked

kopra [ˣkå:p-] *s1* copra

kopt|er ['kåpp-] Copt **-isk** *a5* Coptic; *~a kyrkan* Coptic Church **-iska** (*språk*) Coptic

kopul|ation copulation **-ativ** ['kåpp-, 'kɔ:-, -'i:v] *a5*, språkv. copulative **-era** copulate

kor *s7* choir; (*hög-*) chancel; (*där altaret står*) sanctuary; *jfr* gravkor

kora [ˣkå:-] choose, select (*till* as)

koral *s3* chorale **-bok** hymn book with tunes

korall *s3* coral **-djur** anthozoan (*pl* anthozoa) **-orm** coral snake **-rev** coral reef **-röd** coral [red] **-ö** coral island; atoll

koran *s3* [the] Koran

kord [-å:-] *s3* cord

korda [ˣkå:r-] *s1, mat.* chord

korderoj [kårde'råjj] *s3* corduroy

kordial [-å-] *a1* cordial **-itet** cordiality

kordong [kår'dåŋ] *s3* cord[on]; *bot.* cordon

kordväv cord [fabric]

Korea [-ˣre:a] *n* Korea

korean *s3,* **-sk** *a5,* **-ska** (*språk*) *s1* Korean

koreograf *s3* choreographer

koreograf|i *s3* choreography **-isk** [-'gra:-] *a5* choreographic

korg [kårj] *s2* basket; (*större*) hamper; (*i självbetjäningsbutik*) wire basket; *få ~en* (*bildl.*) be refused, get the brushoff; *ge ngn ~en* (*bildl.*) refuse s.b., give s.b. the brushoff **-arbete** wicker [work], basketwork **-blommig** *bot.* composite **-boll** basketball **-flätning** [-ä:t-] basketry **-makare** basket-maker **-möbel** [set of (*ett föremål* piece of)] wicker[work] furniture

korgosse server, acolyte; (*i kör*) choirboy

korgstol wicker[work] chair

koriander [-'ann-] *s9* coriander

korjnt *s3* currant

korint[i]er [-'int([s]i)er] Corinthian **-brev** *K~en* [the] Corinthians (*pl, behandlas som sg*); *första K~et* the First of Corinthians (*eg.* the First Epistle of Paul the Apostle to the Corinthians)

korintisk [-'rint-] *a5* Corinthian

korintkaka currant cake

korist chorister; (*opera- äv.*) member of the chorus; (*kyrko- äv.*) choir-member

kork [-å-] *s2* **1** (*ämne*) cork **2** (*propp*) cork, stopper; *dra ~en ur* uncork; *sätta ~en i* cork **3** *styv i ~en* cocky, swollen-headed **korka** cork; *~ igen* (*till*) cork; *~ upp* uncork

kork|ad [-å-] *a5* (*dum*) stupid **-bälte** cork [life] belt **-bössa** popgun **-dyna** cork pillow **-ek** cork oak **-matta** linoleum; *hand. äv.* lino **-skruv** corkscrew

korn [-ɔ:-] *s7* **1** (*frö, kornformig smådel*) grain (*äv. bildl.*); *ett ~ av sanning* a grain of truth **2** (*sädesslag*) barley **3** (*riktmedel*) bead; *mil. äv.* front sight; *få ~ på* get sight of, bildl. äv. spot, vard. äv. get wind of; *ta ~ på* draw a bead on; *ta...på ~et* get (hit off)...to the life **4** *se under skrot*

korn|a [-ɔ:-] *~* [*sig*] granulate **-ax** ear of barley **-blixt** flash of summer lightning **-blå** cornflower blue **-bod** granary

kornell *s3, bot.* cornel

kornett [-å-] *s3, mus. o. mil.* cornet **-ist** cornetist, cornet player

korn|gryn barley grain; *koll.* hulled barley **-grynsgröt** barley porridge

kornig [-ɔ:-] *a1* granular **-het** granularity; granulation; *foto.* graininess

kornisch [-å-] *s3* cornice

korn|knarr *s2* corncrake **-mjöl** barley meal (flour)

korollarium [kårå'la:-] *s4* corollary

korona [kå°rå:-] *s1, astr.* corona

korp [-å-] *s2* **1** *zool.* raven **2** (*hacka*) pickaxe, mattock

korp|a [-å-] *~ åt sig* grab [for o.s.] **-gluggar** *pl* (*ögon*) giglamps

korporation [kårpå-] corporate body, body corporate; association **korporationstävling** intercompany (interworks) tournament

korporativ *äv.* [kårpå-] *a5* corporative **-ism** corporative system of society

korpral [-å-] *s3* (*vid armén*) lance corporal; private, (*vid flottan*) ordinary rating, (*vid flyget*) leading aircraftman; *AE.* (*vid armén*) corporal, (*vid flottan*) petty officer 3. class, (*vid flyget*) sergeant

korpsvart raven [black]
korpul|ens [-å-] *s3* stoutness, corpulence **-ent** *a1* stout, corpulent
korpus ['kårr-] *s2* **1** *boktr.* long primer **2** (*kropp*) body **-kel** [-'puss-] *s3* corpuscle
korr [-å-] *s7, vard., se* korrektur
korrek|t [-å-] *a1* correct; (*felfri*) faultless, impeccable **-tion** [-k'ʃɔ:n] correction **-tjv** *s7* corrective
korrektur [-å-] *s7* proof [sheet], printer's proof; *första* ~ first proof[s], (*spalt-*) galley proof; *ombrutet* ~ page proof; *tryckfärdigt* ~ clean proof; *läsa* ~ *på* read the proofs of, proofread **-avdrag** pull[ed proof], proof leaf **-fel** error in a (the) proof **-läsa** read in proof, proofread; *dåligt -läst* badly proofread **-läsare** proofreader **-läsning** proofreading **-tecken** proofreader's mark **-ändring** alteration in [the] proof
korrel|et [-å-] *s7 o. a4* antecedent **-ation** correlation **-era** correlate
korrespondens [kårrespån'dens, -'daŋs, -åŋd-] *s3* correspondence **-institut** correspondence school **-kort** correspondence card **-kurs** correspondence course **-undervisning** postal tuition
korrespond|ent [-å-å-] correspondent; correspondence clerk **-era** correspond
korridor [kårri'då:r] *s3* corridor; *AE. äv.* hallway; (*i hus äv.*) passage; *AE. äv.* hall; *polit.* lobby **-politik** lobby politics (*pl*), lobbying
korriger|a [kårri'ʃe:-] correct; (*revidera*) revise **-ing** correction; revision
korro|dera [kårrå-] corrode **-sion** corrosion
korrosions|beständig corrosion-resistant, noncorrodible **-skyddsmedel** corrosion preventing agent
korrugera [kårru'ge:-] corrugate; ~*d plåt* corrugated sheet [metal]
korrumpera [-å-] corrupt
korryp|t [-å-] *a4* corrupt **-tion** [-p'ʃɔ:n] corruption; *AE. polit. äv.* graft
kors [-å-] **I** *s7* **1** cross; *i* ~ crosswise; *Röda K~et* the Red Cross; *krypa till* ~*et* eat humble pie; *lägga armarna i* ~ fold one's arms; *lägga benen i* ~ cross one's legs; *sitta med armarna i* ~ (*bildl.*) sit idle (doing nothing); *inte lägga två strån i* ~ not lift a finger **2** *mus.* sharp **II** *adv,* ~ *och tvärs* crisscross, in all directions **III** *interj* well, I never!, Oh, my!, bless me!
korsa [-å-] cross; (~ *varandra*) intersect; *bildl.* thwart, (*ngns planer* a p.'s plans); (*om tankar*) traverse, run counter to (*varandra* each other); ~ *sig* cross o.s.
korsar [-å-] *s3* corsair
kors|as [-å-] *dep* cross [each other], intersect; *bildl.* traverse each other, crisscross **-band** *post., skicka som* ~ send as printed matter **-befruktning** cross-fertilization **-ben** *anat.* sacrum **-blommig** cruciferous **-drag** through (cross) draught **-eld** crossfire
kor|selett [-å-] *s3* cors[e]let **-sett** *s3* corset; *åld.* stays (*pl*)
kors|farare crusader **-formig** [-å-] *a5* cross-shaped, cruciform **-fästa** crucify **-fästelse** crucifixion **-förhör** cross-examination **-förhöra** cross-examine **-förlamning** *se* korslamhet **-gång** cloister **-hänvisning** cross-reference
Korsika ['kårs-] *n* Corsica

korsika|n [-å-] *s3*, **-nsk** *a5* Corsican
kors|kyrka cruciform church **-lagd** *a5* laid crosswise; (*om ben*) crossed; (*om armar*) folded; ~*a benknotor* crossbones **-lamhet** paraplegia
korsning [-å-] **1** (*väg- e.d.*) crossing, intersection; *planskild* ~ flyover, overpass **2** *biol.* crossing, crossbreeding; *konkr.* cross
korsning|sfri without crossroads **-näbb** crossbill **-ord** crossword [puzzle]; *lösa ett* ~ do (solve) a crossword **-riddare** crusader **-rygg** ~*en* the small of the back **-spindel** diadem spider **-stygn** cross-stitch **-tecken** *göra -tecknet* cross o.s., make the sign of the Cross
korstol [ˣkɔ:r-] [choir] stall
kors|tåg crusade **-virkeshus** half-timbered (framework) house **-vis** crosswise, traversely **-väg** crossroad; *vid* ~*en* at the crossroads **-ört** groundsel
1 kort [-ɔ-] *s7* card; *klätt* ~ court (picture) card; *ett parti* ~ a game of cards; *spela* ~ play [at] cards; *blanda bort* ~*en för ngn* (*bildl.*) confuse s.b., put s.b. out; *lägga* ~*en på bordet* (*bildl.*) put (lay) all one's cards on the table; *sköta sina* ~ *väl* play one's cards well (right); *sätta allt på ett* ~ stake everything on one card, put all one's eggs in one basket; *titta i ngns* ~ peep at a p.'s cards, *bildl.* be up to a p.'s little game
2 kort [-å-] **I** *a1* short; (*tidsbet. äv.*) brief; *bildl.* short; (*avmätt äv.*) abrupt, curt; ~ *om huvudet* short-tempered; ~ *till växten* short [in stature]; ~*a varor* haberdashery (*sg*), small wares, *AE.* notions; *en* ~ *stund* a little while; *efter en* ~ *tid* in a short time, shortly afterwards; *inom* ~ before long, shortly; *göra* ~*are* (*äv.*) shorten; *göra processen* ~ *med* make short work of; *gör pinan* ~! don't prolong the agony!; *komma till* ~*a* fall short (*med* in), (*i tävling e.d.*) fail; *redogöra för ngt i* ~*a drag* give a short (brief, concise) account of s.th. **II** *adv* shortly, briefly; (*t.ex. uttala* ~, ~ *tillmätt*) short; ~ *efter* soon after; ~ *sagt* (*och gott*) in short, in so many words, (*i själva verket*) in fact, to make a long story short; *andas* ~ take short breaths; *hålla ngn* ~ keep s.b. on a tight rein
korta [-å-] *v1,* ~ [*av*] shorten
kortbrev [-ɔ:-] letter card; *AE.* double postal card
kort|byxor [-å-] *pl* shorts **-distanslöpare** sprinter
kortege [kår'te:ʃ *el.* -'tä:ʃ] *s5* cortege
kort|eligen [-å-] in short **-fattad** *a5* brief; *K~ lärobok i A* Short (Concise) Textbook of **-film** short film; short **-form** *språkv.* abbreviated form **-fristig** *a1* short-term **-het** shortness *etc.*; brevity; *i* ~ briefly; *i* ~ *redogöra för* outline, summarize **-huggen** *a5, bildl.* abrupt
kort|hus [-ɔ-] house of cards **-hög** pile of cards
kortison [kårti'så:n] *s4* cortisone
kortklippt [-å-] *a4* [cut] short; (*om hår äv.*) closely cropped, bobbed
kort|konst [kɔ-] card trick **-lek** pack [of cards]
kort|kort [-å-å-] ~ *kjol* miniskirt, *vard.* mini **-livad** *a5* short-lived
kort|oxe [-ɔ-] inveterate card player **-register** card index (file) (*över* of)
kort|sida [-å-] *n* the short side (end) **-siktig** *a5* short-range, short-term **-skallig** brachycephalic

-sluta *-slöt -slutit* short-circuit **-slutning** [-u:-] short circuit

kortspel [-ο-] **1** (*-ande*) playing cards, card-playing; *fuska i* ~ cheat at cards **2** (*ett* ~) card game **-are** card player

kortsynt [ˣkårtsy:nt] *al* short-sighted

kortsystem [-ο-] card[-index] system

korttids|anställning [-å-] short-time (temporary) employment **-minne** short-term memory

kort|tänkt [-å-] *al* short-witted, short-sighted, unthinking **-varig** *al* [of] short [duration]; short--lived, transitory (*framgång* success); *~t straff* short-term penalty **-varor** *se korta varor under 2 kort I* **-varuhandlare** haberdasher **-våg** short wave

kortvågs|behandling short-wave treatment **-radio** short-wave radio **-sändare** short-wave transmitter

kort|växt [-å-] *al* short [in stature] **-ända** *se kortsida* **-ärmad** *a5* short-sleeved

korum [ˣkο:-] *best. form o. pl =, äv. s7* [regimental] prayers (*pl*)

korund *s3* corundum

korus [ˈkο:-] *i uttr.: i* ~ in chorus

korv [-å-] *s2* sausage **korva** *rfl* (*om strumpa*) wrinkle

korvett [-å-] *s3* corvette

korvgubbe hot-dog man

korv|ig [-å-] *al* rucked-up, wrinkly **-kiosk** hot-dog stand **-skinn** sausage-skin **-spad** *klart som* ~ (*bildl.*) as plain as a pikestaff **-stoppning** sausage-making, sausage-filling; *bildl.* cramming **-stånd** hot-dog stand **-öre** *inte ett* ~ not a brass farthing

koryfé *s3* coryphaeus (*pl* coryphaei), (*friare äv.*) leader; *iron.* bigwig

kos *r, springa sin* ~ run away; *har flugit sin* ~ has disappeared (flown)

kosa *s1* course, way; *ställa ~n* steer (direct) one's course (steps) (*mot* to), make for

kosack *s3* Cossack **-dans** Cossack dance

kosing *vard.* dough (*särsk. AE.*)

kosinus *se cosinus*

ko|skälla cowbell **-skötare** cowherd, cowman

kosmet|ik *s3* **1** (*skönhetsvård*) beauty care **2** (*skönhetsmedel*) cosmetic **-iker** [-ˈme:-] cosmetician **-isk** [-ˈme:-] *a5* cosmetic; *~t medel* cosmetic [preparation] **-olog** cosmetologist; beautician

kosmisk [ˈkåss-] *a5* cosmic; ~ *strålning* cosmic rays (radiation)

kosmo|drom [kåsmåˈdrå:m] *s3* cosmodrome **-gonj** *s3* cosmogony **-log** cosmologist **-logi** *s3* cosmology **-logisk** [-ˈlå:-] *a5* cosmologic[al] **-naut** *s3* cosmonaut **-polit** *s3*, **-politisk** [-ˈli:-] *a5* cosmopolitan

kosmos [ˈkåsmås] *r, best. form =*, cosmos

kospillning cow dung

kossa [-ο-] *s1* [moo-]cow

kost [-å-] *s3* (*föda*) food, diet; (*förplägning*) fare; *blandad* ~ mixed diet; *mager* ~ poor diet, scanty fare; ~ *och logi* board and lodging, bed and board

1 kosta [-å-] *det ~r på a*) it is a trial, *b*) (*är pinsamt*) it is very painful (trying); *det ~r på krafterna* it saps one's (*etc.*) strength

2 kosta [-å-] cost; (*belöpa sig t.*) amount to; ~

ngn möda give s.b. trouble; ~ *mycket pengar* cost a great deal of money; ~ *på* pay for, meet the expenses of; ~ *på ngn en god uppfostran* [find the money to] give s.b. a good education; ~ *på sig* treat o.s. to; *kunna* ~ *på sig* be able to afford; ~ *vad det* ~ *vill* no matter what it costs, cost what it may, at all costs; *vad ~r det?* how much is it?, what is the price [of it]?, what do you want for it?; *vad får det ~?* how much are you prepared to pay for it?; *det ~r mer än det smakar* it is more trouble than it is worth; *han har ~t sina föräldrar mycket pengar* he has been a great expense to his parents

kostbar [-å-] *al* costly, precious

kost|föraktare *ingen* ~ no despiser of good food **-håll** fare, diet

kostlig [-å-] *al* **1** (*dyrbar*) precious **2** (*löjlig*) priceless

kostnad [-å-] *s3* cost (*äv. ~er*); (*utgift*) expense; (*utlägg*) outlay, expenditure; (*avgift*) charge; (*arvode*) fee; *utan* ~ free of charge; *diverse ~er* sundry expenses; *fasta ~er* overheads, fixed costs; *rörliga ~er* prime (variable) costs; *stora ~er* heavy expenses; *för en ringa* ~ at a trifling cost; *inklusive alla ~er* all costs included; *medföra ~er* involve expenditure; *stå för ~erna* pay (bear, stand) the expenses (costs); *ådraga sig ~er* incur expenses

kostnads|analys costs analysis **-beräkna** cost **-beräkning** costing, computation of costs **-fri** free [of cost (charge)] **-fråga** question of costs **-förslag** quotation, estimate [of costs], tender **-kalkyl** cost estimate, statement of costs **-krävande** costly, expensive **-skäl** financial reason; *av* ~ costwise **-ökning** increase in costs **-övervältring** transfer of costs

kostpengar *pl* food allowance (*sg*), board wages

kostsam [-å-] *al* costly, expensive

kostvanor *pl* eating habits

kostym *s3* **1** suit; *mörk* ~ dark lounge suit **2** *teat. o.d.* costume, dress **-bal** fancy-dress ball

kostymer|a dress up **-ing** (*-ande*) dressing up; (*dräkt*) dress

kostym|pjäs *teat.* costume piece **-tyg** suiting

kota *s1* vertebra (*pl äv.* vertebrae)

kotangent [ˣkο:-] *s3, mat.* cotangent

kotiljong [-ˈjåŋ] *s3* cotillion

kotknackare [ˣko:t-] *vard.* chiropractor

kotlett [-å-] *s3* cutlet; (*med ben*) chop **-fisk** catfish, wolffish **-rad** [the] ribs (*pl*)

kotpelare [ˣkο:t-] spinal (vertebral) column, spine; *vard. o. bildl.* backbone

kotte [-å-] *s2* cone

kotteri [-å-] *s3* coterie, set; (*klandrande*) clique **-väsen** cliquism

kottfjäll cone scale

kotyledon [kåtyleˈdå:n] *s3* cotyledon

kovall *s3* cow-wheat

kovänd|a veer, wear **-ning** *sjö.* veering, wearing; *en* ~ (*äv.*) a veer, a volte-face

kpist [ˣkå:-] *s2, se kulsprutepistol*

krabat fellow; young beggar, rascal

krabb *al, sjö.* choppy, short

krabba *s1* crab

krack|a *kem.* crack **-bensin** cracked petrol (*AE.* gasoline)

krackeler|a, -ing crackle
krack|er ['krakk-] cracking plant **-ning** cracking
-ningsanläggning cracking plant
krafs *s7* (*skräp*) trash
krafs|a scratch **-ning** scratching
kraft *s3* **1** force; (*förmåga, elektr.*) power;
(*styrka*) strength; (*energi*) energy; (*livaktighet*)
vigour, vitality; (*verkan*) effect; (*intensitet*) intensity; *drivande ~* driving force, prime mover; *fysisk ~* physical power (strength); *av alla ~er* with
all one's strength, (*t.ex. ropa*) with all one's
force, (*t.ex. springa*) as hard as ever one can; *i sin
fulla ~, i sin ~s dagar* in one's prime; *med ~* (*t.ex.
uttala sig, uppträda*) with vigour (energy); *ge ~ åt*
lend (give) power to, (*ngns ord*) lend (give) force
to; *hushålla med sina ~er* conserve one's strength
(energy); *pröva sina ~er* try one's strength; *samla
~er* regain (build up) one's strength; *spänna alla
sina ~er för att* strain every nerve to; *ägna hela
sin ~ åt att* apply the whole of one's energy to (+
ing-form); *hans ~er avtog* his strength was failing
2 *konkr.* (*arbetare*) worker, (*medarbetare*)
helper, cooperator; *den drivande ~en inom* the
leading force in; *duglig ~* capable man (woman);
yngre ~er younger men; *förvärva nya ~er* get new
people **3** *jur.* (*gällande ~*) force; *i ~ av* by (in)
virtue of, on the strength of; *träda i ~* come into
force, take (come into, go into) effect; *vinna laga
~* gain legal force; *äga ~* hold good, be in force;
till den ~ och verkan det hava kan for what it is
(may be) worth
kraft|ansträngning exertion, effort; *göra en ~*
make a real effort, put on a spurt **-besparing**
saving of power **-centrum** centre of force
-foder concentrated feed (fodder) **-full** powerful, forceful; (*fysiskt*) vigorous, strong; (*om t.ex.
vilja*) energetic **-fält** field of force; *elektriskt
(magnetiskt) ~* electric (magnetic) field **-för-
brukning** expenditure of energy; *elektr.* power
consumption **-förlust** *med.* loss of strength;
tekn. power loss **-försörjning** power supply
kraft|ig *a1* **1** powerful; (*livlig o. ~*) vigorous;
(*energisk*) energetic; (*verksam*) effective; (*stark*)
strong (*äv. bildl.*); (*t. hälsan*) robust; (*eftertryck-
lig*) emphatic; (*våldsam*) violent; (*intensiv*) intense, acute; *~ protest* strong protest; *~ ökning*
sharp (substantial) increase; *ett ~t slag i huvudet*
a violent (heavy) blow on the head **2** (*stor*) big,
great, considerable; (*om mat*) tremendous **3** (*om mat*)
nourishing; (*mäktig*) rich; (*bastant*) substantial
(*måltid* meal) **-kabel** power cable **-karl** strong
man **-källa** source of power (energy); *bildl. äv.*
source of strength **-ledning** power [trans-
mission] line **-lös** powerless; weak, feeble; (*orkeslös*) effete **-mätning** *bildl.* trial of strength
-nät grid **-papper** kraft [paper] **-prestation** *en
verklig ~* a really great achievement, a real feat
-prov trial of strength **-reaktor** power reactor
-station power station (plant) **-tag** *ett verkligt
~* a really strong pull (*vard.* big tug), *bildl.* a real
effort **-uttryck** oath, expletive; *använda ~* use
strong language **-utveckling** generation of
power **-verk** power station (plant) **-värmeverk**
combined power and heating plant **-åtgärd**
strong (drastic) measure **-överföring** power
transmission

krag|e *s2* collar; *ta ngn i ~n* criticize s.b. sharply;
ta sig i ~n pull o.s. together **-handske** gauntlet
-knapp collar stud **-nummer** size in collars
-snibb collar point **-stövel** top boot **-ödla**
frilled lizard
krake *s2* (*häst-*) jade, hack; (*stackare*) weakling;
(*kräk*) wretch
krakel *s7* (*gräl*) squabble, row; (*med slagsmål*)
brawl
krakmandel ['ᵏkra:k-] dessert almond
kral *s3* kraal
1 kram *s7* (*varor*) small wares (*pl*)
2 kram *a1* (*om snö*) wet, cloggy
3 kram *s2* (*-ning*) hug
krama 1 (*pressa*) squeeze (*saften ur* the juice out
of) **2** (*omfamna*) embrace, hug
kramhandel fancy-goods (small-ware) shop
kramp *s3* cramp; (*konvulsion*) convulsion,
spasm; *få ~* get (be seized with) cramp
krampa *s1* clincher, clamp, cramp [iron]
kramp|aktig *a1* spasmodic; (*konvulsivisk*) con-
vulsive (*gråt* crying); *~t försök* desperate effort
-anfall attack of cramp **-artad** [-a:r-] *a5* cramp-
like **-lösande** antispasmodic (*äv. ~ medel*)
-ryckning spasm, twitch **-stillande** *se -lösande*
-tillstånd spasmodic condition; spasticity
kramsfågel *koll.* [edible] small birds (*pl*)
kramsnö wet snow
kran *s2* **1** (*tapp-*) tap; *särsk. AE.* faucet; (*ventil-*)
stopcock **2** (*lyft-*) crane **-arm** jib **-balk** *sjö.* cat-
head **-bil** crane lorry
kranium ['kra:-] *s4* cranium
krans *s2* **1** wreath; (*blomster- äv.*) garland **2**
bildl. ring, circle **3** *kokk.* ring-shaped bunloaf
(biscuit)
krans|a *se bekransa* **-artär** coronary artery **-for-
mig** [-å-] *a5* wreath-shaped **-kärl** coronary vessel
kranskötare crane operator
krans|list cornice, ornamental moulding **-ned-
läggning** laying of wreaths
kranvagn crane truck; *AE.* derrick car
krapp *s3*, **-rot** *bot.* madder **-röd** madder red
-rött *best. form det -röda* madder [lake]
kras *s7, gå i ~* go to (fly into) pieces **krasa**
[s]crunch
krasch *s3* crash (*äv. bildl.*), smash; *bildl. äv.* collapse, failure **krascha** go crash; (*om företag,
vard.*) go smash
kraschan *s3* grand star
kraschlanda *flyg.* crash-land
krass *a1* crass; (*utpräglad äv.*) gross; (*grovkor-
nig*) coarse
krasse *s2, bot.* cress; *se äv. indian-, kryddkrasse*
krasslig *a1* ailing, seedy, poorly; *vard.* under the
weather; *AE. vard.* mean
krater ['kra:-] *s2* crater **-lik** craterous **-sjö** crater
lake
krats *s2, tekn.* scraper **kratsa** scrape; scratch
kratta I *s1* (*redskap*) rake **2** (*ynkrygg*) coward,
funk **II** *v1* rake [over]; *~ ihop* rake together
krav *s7* **1** demand (*på ngt* for s.th.; *på att* to +
inf.; *på livet* of life); (*anspråk*) claim (*på* to); requirement; *rättmätigt ~* legitimate claim; *resa ~*
bring claims, claim; *ställa höga ~* be exacting;
ställa stora ~ på a) make great (heavy) demands

upon, *b*) (*ngns förmåga*) put to a severe test **2** (*anmodan att betala*) demand (*hövligare:* request) for payment; (*skuldfordran*) monetary claim

kravall *s3, vanl. pl*, *~er* riots; (*gatu-*) street disturbances **-polis** riot police (squad) **-staket** crowd control barrier, crush barrier

kravatt *s3* necktie **-nål** tiepin

kravbrev letter requesting payment; (*påminnelse*) reminder; *AE.* collection letter

kravellbyggd [-ˣvell-] *a5* carvel-built

kravla [-a(:)v-] ~ [*sig*] crawl

krax, krax|a croak **-ande** *s6* croaking

krea|tion (*modeskapelse*) creation **-tjv** [*äv.* 'kre:a-] *a1* creative **-tivitet** creativity

kreatur [ˣkre:a-] *s7* animal; (*fä*) beast; *koll.* cattle (*pl*); *bildl.* creature, tool

kreaturs|avel cattle breeding, stockbreeding **-besättning** stock [of cattle], livestock **-foder** cattle feed (fodder) **-handlare** livestock dealer **-lös** *~t jordbruk* crop farming **-ras** breed of cattle **-skötsel** stockraising

kreatör creator, designer

1 kredit [ˈkre:-] *n* (*tillgodohavande*) credit; *debet och* ~ debits and credits

2 kredjt *s3* (*förtroende, betalningsanstånd*) credit; *på* ~ on credit; *få* (*ha*) ~ get (have) credit; *köpa på* ~ (*vard.*) buy on tick

kredit|avtal credit agreement **-behov** credit requirements (*pl*) **-bevis** *se kreditkort*

krediter|a credit; ~ *ngn för ett belopp* (*äv.*) credit an amount to a p.'s account **-ing** credit, entry on the credit side

kredit|förening credit association (society) **-givning** [-ji:v-] granting of credit[s *pl*], credit facilities (*pl*); lending **-institut** finance company (house)

kreditjv *s7* **1** *bank.* letter of credit **2** (*diplomats*) credentials (*pl*), letters of credence **-brev** *se kreditiv 2*

kredit|kort credit card **-köp** purchase on credit, credit purchase **-marknad** credit market

kreditor [ˣkre:- *el.* ˈkre:-] *s3* creditor; *~er* (*bokför.*) (*AE.*) account payable

kredit|post [ˈkre:-] credit item (entry)

kredjtrestriktioner *pl* credit restrictions

kreditsida [ˈkre:-] credit side

kredjt|stopp credit freeze **-stöd** credit aid **-upplysning** credit report **-värdighet** credit rating **-åtstramning** credit squeeze (restraint)

kreera [kreˈe:ra] create

krematorium [-ˈtɔ:-] *s4* crematorium

kremer|a cremate **-ing** cremation

Kreml *n* the Kremlin

kremla *s1, bot.* russula

kreneler|ad [-ˈle:-] *a5, arkit.* crenellated **-ing** crenellation

kreol [-ˈå:l] *s3* Creole **kreolsk** [-ˈå:lsk] *a5* creole

kreosot [-ˈså:t] *s3, s4* creosote

krepera (*krevera*) burst, explode

Kreta *n* Crete

kretens|are [-ˣtens-] *s9,* **-isk** [-ˈtens-] *a5* Cretan

kretjn *s3* cretin **-ism** cretinism

kreti och pleti [ˈkre:-, ˈple:-] Tom, Dick and Harry

kretong [-ˈtåŋ] *s3* cretonne; (*blank*) chintz

krets *s2* circle; ring; *tekn.* circuit; (*område*) district; *i ~en av sin familj* in the bosom of one's family; *i diplomatiska ~ar* in diplomatic circles; *i välunderrättade ~ar* in well-informed circles (quarters)

krets|a circle, fly (go) in circles; (*sväva äv.*) hover; (*om tankar e.d.*) revolve, circulate (*kring* round) **-gång** circle; cyclic motion **-lopp** circulation, rotation; (*jordens*) orbit; (*av nöjen e.d.*) round; (*årstidernas*) cycle

krev|ad *s3* explosion, burst **-era** explode, burst

kria [ˣkri:a] *s1* [written] composition **-bok** composition book **-rättning** correction of compositions

kricka *s1, zool.* common teal

kricket [ˈkrikk-] *s2* cricket **-grind** wicket **-plan** cricket ground **-spelare** cricketer

krig *s7* war; (*-föring*) warfare; *det kalla ~et* the cold war; *för det moderna ~et* for modern warfare; *befinna sig i* ~ be at war; *börja* ~ start a (go to) war (*mot* against); *föra* ~ make (wage) war; *förklara* ~ *mot* (*friare*) proclaim war against; *förklara ett land* (*ngn*) ~ declare war on a country (against s.b.); *vara med i* ~ see active service

kriga make war

krigar|e soldier; *poet.* warrior **-folk** nation of soldiers **-liv** military life; *~et* (*äv.*) soldiering **-yrke** *~t* the military profession

krigför|ande *a4* belligerent; *icke* ~ nonbelligerent **-ing** [form of] warfare; (*-förande*) waging of war

krigisk [ˈkri:-] *a5* warlike (*anda* spirit; *folk* nation); martial (*utseende* appearance)

krigs|arkiv [ˣkrikks-] military record office **-artiklar** *pl* articles of war **-barn** war baby **-beredskap** preparedness for war; general alert **-brand** war conflagration **-buss** *en gammal* ~ an old campaigner **-byte** war trophy; *som* ~ as booty **-dans** war dance **-domstol** military tribunal (court) **-fara** danger of war, war risk[s *pl*] **-fartyg** warship, man-of-war **-flotta** navy; battle fleet **-fot** war-footing; *komma på* ~ *med* (*bildl.*) get at loggerheads with; *stå på* ~ be on a war-footing; *sätta på* ~ mobilize **-fånge** prisoner of war **-fångeläger** prisoner-of-war camp **-fångenskap** captivity **-förbrytare** war criminal **-förbrytelse** war crime **-förklaring** declaration of war **-förnödenheter** *pl* military supplies, munitions **-handling** act of war **-herre** warlord **-hetsare** warmonger, agitator for war; jingoist **-historia** military history **-händelser** *pl* war incidents **-här** army, military force **-härjad** *a5* war-ravaged **-högskola** military academy **-industri** war (armaments) industry **-invalid** disabled soldier **-ivrare** *se -hetsare* **-konjunkturskatt** excess profits tax **-konst** art of warfare; (*ngns*) strategy **-korrespondent** war correspondent **-list** stratagem (*äv. bildl.*) **-lycka** fortune[s *pl*] of war; *med skiftande* ~ with varying success in the field **-makt** military power; *~en* the armed forces; *...vid ~en* military... **-man** member of the armed forces; *pl äv.* armed service personnel **-materiel** war material, munitions **-minister** minister of war; (*i Storbritannien*) minister of defence; *AE.* secretary of defense **-mål** war aim **-målning** war paint **-operation**

military operation **-orsak** cause of war **-placering** war posting **-plan** plan of campaign, military plan **-risk** risk of war; *försäkr.* war risk **-råd** *hålla* ~ hold a council of war **-rätt** (*domstol*) court martial; *ställa ngn inför* ~ court-martial s.b. **-sjukhus** military hospital **-skada** (*ngns*) injury sustained in war, war injury; (*materiell* ~) war damage (loss) **-skadestånd** war indemnity, reparations [for war damages] **-skola** military academy **-skådeplats** theatre of war, front; *bildl.* scene **-stig** *på* ~*en* on the warpath **-styrka** war strength **-tid** *i* (*under*) ~[*er*] in (during) wartime, in times of war **-tillstånd** state of war; *när landet befinner sig i* ~ when the country is at war **-tjänst** active service; *göra* ~ be on active service **-trött** war weary **-tåg** military expedition **-utbrott** outbreak of war **-vetenskap** military science **-veteran** ex-serviceman; *AE.* veteran **-viktig** [of] military [importance]
krikon [-ån] *s7, bot.* bullace
krill *s2, zool.* krill
Krim [-imm] *n* the Crimea
kriminal *s3 o.* a5 criminal **-fall** criminal case **-film** crime film, thriller **-inspektör** detective inspector; (*chef*) detective chief inspector
kriminaliser|a make (declare to be) criminal, outlaw **-ing** criminalization
kriminal|itet criminality **-kommissarie** detective chief inspector; (*chef*) detective superintendent **-konstapel** detective [constable] **-lagstiftning** penal legislation **-polis** ~*en* the criminal police; (*i Storbritannien*) the Criminal Investigation Department (*förk.* C.I.D.) **-politik** penal policy **-reportage** crime reporting; article[s] on criminal case[s] **-roman** detective novel **-vård** treatment of offenders **-vårdsnämnden** [the Swedish] national paroles board **-vårdsstyrelsen** [the Swedish] national prisons and probation administration
kriminell a1 criminal
krimino|log criminologist **-logi** *s3* criminology
krimskrams *s7* (*grannlåt*) knickknacks (*pl*), gewgaws (*pl*)
kring *rumsbet.* round, around; *tidsbet.* [round] about; (*friare, bildl.*) round; (*om, angående*) about, concerning **-boende** a4, de ~ those (the people) living all around **-byggd** a5 surrounded by buildings **-farande** a4 itinerant **-flackande** a4 roving; travelling about **-fluten** a5 washed, surrounded (*av by*) **-gå** *bildl.* get round, circumvent, bypass; (*undvika*) evade; *en* ~*ende rörelse* a flanking movement; *ett* ~*ende svar* an evasive answer **-gärda** [-jä:r-] fence in (*äv. bildl.*); enclose
kringla *s1, ung.* figure-of-eight biscuit, twist-biscuit
kring|liggande a4 surrounding, neighbouring **-resande** a4 travelling; (*om t.ex. predikant*) itinerant; ~ *teatersällskap* touring (itinerant) theatre company **-ränna** *mil.* surround, envelop **-ränning** surrounding, envelopment **-segla** sail round **-skuren** a5 restricted, cut down, curtailed **-skära** circumscribe, curtail, restrict, limit **-spridd** a5, *ligga* ~ be scattered about (around) **-strykande** a4 strolling; (*i smyg*) prowling **-stråla** bathe in light, shine round about **-stå-**

ende a4 the people (*etc.*) standing round, the bystanders **-synt** [-y:-] a1 broad-minded **-värva** v2 envelop; *vara* ~*värvd av* be enveloped in
krinolin *s3* crinoline; hoops (*pl*)
1 kris *s2* (*dolk*) kris, creese
2 kris *s3* crisis (*pl* crises)
kris|artad [-a:r-] a5 critical **-läge, -situation** crisis, critical situation
kristall *s3* crystal **-glas** crystal; cut glass **-klar** a5, **-isk** a5 crystalline
kristall|isation crystallization **-isera** crystallize **-isk** [-'tall-] a5 crystalline **-klar** crystal clear, crystalline **-krona** cut-glass chandelier **-kula** crystal ball **-mottagare** *radio.* crystal set (receiver)
kristall|ografi *s3* crystallography **-olja** white spirit **-socker** granulated sugar **-system** crystal system **-vas** cut-glass vase **-vatten** crystal water
kristen a5 Christian; *den kristna läran* the Christian doctrine; *den kristna världen* (*äv.*) Christendom; *vara* ~ be a Christian **-dom** [-dɔmm] *s3* **1** Christianity **2** *skol.* religion, scripture
kristendoms|fientlig Antichristian **-kunskap** *se kristendom 2* **-lärare** teacher of religious knowledge **-undervisning** religious instruction
kristenhet Christendom (*äv.* ~*en*)
kristid time of crisis; *ekon.* depression, slump; ~*en* (*äv.*) the crisis
kristids|nämnd rationing board **-vara** *s1* wartime product
Kristi himmelsfärdsdag Ascension Day
kristillstånd critical state, [state of] crisis
krist|lig a1 Christian; (*from*) pious; *ett* ~*t byte* (*vard.*) a fair exchange (swop); *K~a Föreningen av Unga Kvinnor* (*Män*) Young Women's (Men's) Christian Association (*förk. se KFUK o. KFUM*) **-ligt** adv like Christians (a Christian)
krist|na **1** (*omvända*) Christianize **2** (*döpa*) christen **-torn** *se järnek*
Kristus Christ; *efter* ~ anno Domini (*förk.* A.D.); *före* ~ before Christ (*förk. B.C.*)
kristus|barn ~*et* the Christ-child; *Madonnan med* ~*et* the Madonna with the Infant Christ **-bild** image of Christ **-gestalt** figure of Christ
krit|a *s1* chalk; (*färg.*) crayon; *ta på* ~ (*vard.*) buy on tick; *när det kommer till* ~*n* when it comes to it **ll** *v1* chalk; (*skor e.d.*) whiten, pipeclay **-avlagring** chalk bed (stratum) **-bit** piece of chalk **-brott** chalkpit
kriterium [-'te:-] *s4* criterion (*pl* criteria) (*på* of)
kritig a1 chalky
kritik *s3* **1** criticism (*över, av* on, of); *under all* ~ beneath contempt, miserable; *inbjuda till* ~ invite criticism; *läsa med* ~ read critically; *möta stark* ~ encounter severe criticism **2** (*recension*) review, notice; ~*en* (~*erna*) the critics (*pl*); *få god* ~ be favourably reviewed
kritiker ['kri:-] critic; (*recensent*) reviewer
kritik|lysten critical; fault-finding **-lös** uncritical; (*utan urskillning*) indiscriminate
krit|isera **1** (*klandra*) criticize; comment adversely on, censure, find fault with; *vard.* run down, slate **2** (*recensera*) review **-isk** ['kri:-] a5 critical; (*avgörande äv.*) crucial (*punkt* point)
krit|klippa chalk cliff **-perioden** the Creta-

ceous [period] **-pipa** clay pipe **-streck** chalk line **-strecksrandig** pinstriped **-teckning** chalk (crayon) drawing **-vit** as white as chalk, snow white; ~ *i ansiktet* as white as a sheet

kroat [kroˈaːt] *s3* Croat **Kroatien** [-ˈaːtsien] *n* Croatia **kroatisk** [-ˈaːtisk] *a5* Croatian

krock [-å-] *s2* (*bil-*) collision, crash, smash [up]; (*i krocketspel*) croquet **krocka** (*om fordon*) collide, crash, smash; *vard.* go smash; (*i krocketspel*) croquet **krockera** (*i krocketspel*) croquet **krocket** [ˈkråck-] *r* croquet **-klot** croquet ball **-klubba** croquet mallet

krog *s2* restaurant; (*värdshus*) inn **-gäst** patron **-rond** pub-crawl **-rörelse** *idka* ~ keep a restaurant (an inn) **-sväng** pub-crawl **-värd** innkeeper

krok *s2* **1** hook; (*fönster- e.d.*) catch; *få på* ~*en* (*äv. bildl.*) hook; *lägga ut sina* ~*ar för* spread a net for, try to catch; *nappa på* ~*en a*) eg. bite at the bait, *b*) bildl. swallow the bait; *sätta mask på* ~*en* bait the hook with a worm **2** (*krökning*) bend, curve; *gå en stor* ~ go a long way round; *slå sina* ~*ar kring* prowl round **3** *boxn.* hook **4** (*vrå*) nook, corner; *här i* ~*arna* in these parts, about here

kroka hook; ~ *av* unhook; ~ *fast* hook on

krokan *s3* ornamented (pagoda-shaped) cake

krokben *sätta* ~ *för ngn a*) eg. trip s.b. up, *b*) bildl. upset a p.'s plans

krokett *s3, kokk.* croquette

kroki *s3* sketch

krok|ig *a1* crooked; (*böjd*) bent; (*i båge*) curved; *gå* ~ walk with a stoop; *sitta* ~ sit hunched up **-linje** curve[d path]

krok|na [-oː-] get bent (*etc.*), bend; (*falla ihop*) collapse **-näsa** hooknose; *vard.* beak **-näst** [-ä-] *a4* hooknosed

krokodil *s3* crocodile **-skinn** crocodile skin **-tårar** *pl* crocodile tears

krok|ryggig *a1* with a crooked back, stooping, bent **-sabel** scimitar

krokus [ˈkroː-] *s2* crocus

krokväg roundabout (circuitous) way: ~*ar* (*bildl.*) devious paths, underhand methods

krollsplint [-å-] *s2* vegetable fibres (*pl*)

krom [-åː-] *s3, s4* chromium, chrome **kroma** chrome

kromatisk [-ˈmaː-] *a5, mus. o. fys.* chromatic

krom|dioxid chromium dioxide **-garva** chrome tan **-grönt** best. form det -gröna chrome green **-gult** best. form det -gula chrome yellow **-haltig** *a5* chromiferous

kromosom [-ˈsåːm] *s3* chromosome

krom|oxid chromium oxide **-stål** chrome (chromium) steel

krona *s1* **1** crown; (*adels-*) coronet; (*påve-*) tiara; *skapelsens* ~ the crowning work of creation; *en* ~ *bland städer* a pearl among cities; *nedlägga* ~*n* abdicate [the throne]; *sätta* ~*n på verket* put on the finishing touch, crown the work, *iron.* cap (beat) everything **2** ~*n* (*staten*) the State (Crown); *en* ~*ns karl* (*ung.*) a soldier of the King; *i* ~*ns tjänst* in the service of the Crown; *på* ~*ns mark* on Crown (government) land (property); *vara klädd i* ~*ns kläder* wear the King's uniform **3** (*träd-*) [tree-]top, crown; (*blom-*) corolla; *anat.* crown; (*tand-*) crown; (*ljus-*) chandelier **4** (*mynt*)

krona, [Swedish *etc.*] crown **5** ~ *eller klave?* heads or tails?; *spela* ~ *och klave* toss (*om* for)

kron|belopp kronor (crown) amount, amount in kronor (crowns) **-brud** bride who wears the parish bridal crown at her wedding **-hjort** red deer; (*hane äv.*) stag

kroniker [ˈkroː-] chronic invalid **-hem** home for chronic invalids

kron|isk [ˈkroː-] *a5* chronic **-iskt** *adv* chronically; ~ *sjuk, se* kroniker

kron|jurist law officer of the Crown; (*i Storbritannien äv.*) Attorney (Solicitor) General **-juvel** crown jewel **-koloni** crown colony

krono|assistent assistant bailiff **-direktör** director of an enforcement district **-fogde** senior enforcement officer; (*chef*) head of an enforcement district **-fogdemyndighet** enforcement service **-gods** Crown property

kronograf *s3* chronograph

krono|gård Crown farm **-häkte** local prison **-jord** Crown land **-jägare** *ung.* state forester; *AE.* forest ranger

kronolog|i *s3* chronology **-isk** [-ˈlåː-] *a5* chronologic[al]; *i* ~ *ordning* in chronological order

kronometer [-ˈmeː-] *s2* chronometer

krono|park *se* -skog **-skatt** state [income] tax; *AE.* federal (national income) tax **-skog** Crown (State) forest

kron|prins crown prince **-prinsessa** [-ˣsessa] crown princess **-vittne 1** (*huvudvittne*) principal witness **2** (*vittne mot medbrottsling*) *bli* ~ turn king's (queen's) *AE.* state's) evidence **-vrak** *vard.* army washout, reject **-ärtskocka** [-skåcka] *s1* [globe] artichoke

kropp [-å-] *s2* body; (*bål*) trunk (*och lemmar* and limbs); (*slaktad*) carcass; *flyg.* body, fuselage; *fasta och flytande* ~*ar* solid and fluid bodies; *främmande* ~*ar* foreign bodies; *en konstig* ~ (*vard.*) a rum chap (customer); *i hela* ~*en* all over; *till* ~ *och själ* in mind and body; *våt inpå bara* ~*en* wet to the skin; *bära ylle närmast* ~*en* wear wool next to one's skin; *darra i hela* ~*en* tremble all over; *inte ha en tråd på* ~*en* be without a stitch of clothing, not have a stitch on; *inte äga kläderna på* ~*en* not own the clothes on one's back

kroppkaka [-å-] potato dumpling with chopped pork filling

kropps|aga corporal punishment **-ansträngning** physical exertion **-arbetare** labourer, manual worker **-arbete** manual labour (work) **-byggare** body builder **-bygge** body building **-byggnad** bodily (physical) structure; (*fysik*) physique; (*-beskaffenhet*) constitution **-del** part of the body **-hydda** body **-konstitution** physical constitution **-krafter** *pl* physical strength (*sg*)

kropps|lig [-å-] *a5* bodily, physical; (*om t.ex.* straff) corporal **-pulsåder** *stora* ~*n* aorta **-rörelse** movement of the body; (*motion*) physical exercise **-språk** body language **-storlek** *målning i* ~ life-size painting **-straff** corporal punishment **-styrka** physical strength **-temperatur** body temperature **-tyngd, -vikt** weight of the body **-visitation** [personal] search **-visitera** search [from head to foot] **-värme** heat (temperature) of the body **-övning** ~*ar* physical

exercises
kross [-å-] *s2, tekn.* crushing mill, crusher
kross|a crush (*äv. bildl.*); (*slå sönder*) smash;
shatter, wreck (*äv. bildl.*); (*finfördela*) pound,
grind down; ~ *fienden* (*äv.*) rout the enemy; ~
ngns hjärta break a p.'s heart; ~ *allt motstånd*
crush all resistance **-skada** (*hopskr. krosskada*)
bruise, contusion **-sår** (*hopskr. krossår*) [severe]
bruise (contusion)
kroton ['krå:tån] *best. form o. pl* = croton
krubb *s7, vard.* grub, feed
1 krubba *v1, vard.* grub, feed
2 krubba *s1* manger, crib
krubbitare (*särskr. krubb-bitare*) crib-biter
krucifix [-'fiks] *s7* crucifix
kruka *s1* **1** pot; (*burk*) jar; (*med handtag*) jug,
pitcher **2** (*ynkrygg*) coward, funk
kruk|makare potter **-makeri** pottery **-skärva**
potsherd **-växt** pot plant
krull|a ~ [*sig*] curl; ~ *ihop sig* curl itself up **-hårig**
curly-haired **-ig** *a1* curly
krum [-umm] **I** *a1* curved, crooked; (*böjd*) bent,
(*i båge*) arched **II** *s2, s4, i* ~ arched
krumbukt|a [-'bukta] (*göra -er*) twist and turn;
(*slingra sig*) hem (hum) and haw; *buga och* ~ bow
and scrape **-er** *pl* **1** (*krökar*) curves, bends; (*bug-
ningar*) obeisances **2** (*omsvep*) circumlocutions;
(*undanflykter*) subterfuges, prevarication (*sg*);
(*invändningar*) humming and hawing (*sg*)
krumelur 1 (*släng*) flourish, curl; *rita ~er* doodle
2 *pers.* oddity
krum|språng caper; gambol; *göra* ~ cut capers,
gambol **-stav** crosier, crozier
krupit *sup. av krypa*
krupp *s3, med.* croup
1 krus *s7* (*dryckeskärl*) jar; (*vatten-*) pitcher
2 krus *s7* **1** (*på sömnad o.d.*) ruff[le]; *koll.* frill-
ing **2** (*-ande*) ceremony; (*fjäsk*) fuss; *utan* ~ without [any] ceremony
krusa 1 (*göra krusig*) crisp, curl; (*rynka*) ruffle;
(*vattenyta*) ripple **2** (*fjäska för*) cringe, truckle
(*för* to); stand on ceremony (*för* with); *jag ~r ingen!* I go my own way regardless of everybody!
krusbär ['kru:s-] gooseberry
krusbärs|buske gooseberry [shrub] **-kräm**
gooseberry cream (fool)
krusiduller [-'dull-] *pl, eg.* curls; *bildl.* frills; (*i
skrift*) flourishes
krus|ig *a1* curly; (*om kål e.d. äv.*) crisp; (*vågig*)
wavy; (*om t.ex. blad*) wrinkled **-kål** kale, borecole **-lockig** curly-haired **-mynta** [-ˣmynn-,
ˣkru:s-] *s1, bot.* mint
krusning [-u:-] (*på vatten*) ripple
krustad *s3* croustade
krut *s7* gunpowder; (*energi*) spunk; *han var inte
med när ~et uppfanns* he'll never set the world
(the Thames) on fire; *ont* ~ *förgås inte så lätt* ill
weeds grow apace **-durk** powder magazine (*äv.
bildl.*) **-gubbe** *vard.* tough old boy **-hus** powder
house **-laddning** powder charge
krutong [-'åŋ] *s3* crouton
krut|rök gunpowder smoke **-stänkt** *a4* powder-
stained **-torr** bone-dry **-tunna** powder barrel
krux [krukks] *s7* crux
kry *a1* well; hale [and hearty]; *pigg och* ~ fit and
well **krya** ~ *på sig* get better, recover, come [a]

round
krycka *s1* crutch; (*handtag*) handle, crook
krydd|a I *s1* spice (*äv. bildl.*); *kokk.* seasoning,
flavouring **II** *v1* season, flavour, spice (*äv. bildl.*);
starkt (*svagt*) *~d* highly (slightly) seasoned (*etc.*)
-bod (*speceriaffär*) grocer's shop **-doft** (*hopskr.
kryddoft*) smell of spice[s *pl*] **-grönt** green herbs
(*pl*) **-krasse** garden cress **-kvarn** spice mill
-nejlika clove
krydd|ning seasoning, flavouring **-ost** clove-
-spiced cheese **-peppar** allspice **-skorpa** spiced
rusk **-smak** flavour of spice **-smör** butter mixed
with herbs **-stark** highly seasoned, hot **-växt**
aromatic plant, herb
Kryddöarna *pl* [the] Spice Islands
krylla *se myllra*
krymp|a *v3* shrink (*i tvätten* in the wash); ~ *ihop*
shrink [up] **-behandlad** *a5* antishrink treated
-fri unshrinkable, preshrunk, nonshrinking; San-
forized (*varumärke*) **-ling** cripple **-mån** shrinkage [allowance] **-ning** shrinkage
kryo|kirurgi [ˣkry:ɔ-] cryosurgery **-ljt** *s3* cryo-
lite **-teknik** cryogenics (*pl, behandlas som sg*)
kryp *s7* [small] creeping (crawling) thing (creature); *vard.* creepy-crawly; *ett litet* ~ (*om barn*) a
little mite
krypa *kröp krupit* **1** creep (*äv. om växt*); (*kräla*)
crawl; ~ *på alla fyra* crawl on all fours; ~ *bakom
ngn* (*bildl.*) shield o.s. behind s.b.; *det kryper i
mig när jag ser* it gives me the creeps to see; *bilen
kröp uppför backen* the car crawled up the hill **2**
(*bege sig*) go (*till kojs* to bed; *i fängelse* to prison);
~ *i kläderna* get into one's clothes **3** (*svansa*)
cringe, grovel **4** (*med betonad partikel*) *nu kröp
sanningen fram* now the truth came out; ~ *ihop
a*) (*om en*) huddle up, (*om flera*) huddle
together, *b*) (*huka sig*) crouch (cower) down
kryp|ande *a4* (*inställsam*) servile, cringing **-by-
xor** *pl* crawlers **-eri** cringing, obsequiousness **-fil**
crawler lane **-hål** *bildl.* loophole **-in** [-'inn] *s7*
nest, hole, retreat; (*vrå*) nook, corner **-skytt**
stalker; (*tjuvskytt*) poacher; *mil.* sniper
krypta *s1* crypt
krypt|era write in cipher (code) **-isk** ['krypt-] *a5*
cryptic
krypto ['kryptɔ] *s6* cipher, code **-gam I** *s3* cryp-
togam **II** *a5* cryptogamic **-grafera** cipher, code
-grafj *s3* cryptography **-gram** [-'gramm] *s7* cipher, code, cryptograph
krypton [-'å:n] *s4, s3* krypton
kryptoteknik cryptography
krysantem|um [-ˣsann-] *s9 el. -en -er* [-'te:-]
chrysanthemum
krysoljt *s3* chrysolite
kryss 1 *s7* (*kors*) cross **2** *s2, sjö.* beating, cruising;
ligga på ~ be tacking
kryssa 1 (*korsa*) cross; ~ *för* put a cross against
2 *sjö.* beat (*mot vinden* [up] against the wind),
beat to windward, tack; (*segla fram o. tillbaka*)
cruise; ~ *över gatan* zigzag across the street
kryss|are 1 *sjö., mil.* cruiser **2** (*jakt*) cruising
vessel, yacht; *se äv. havskryssare* **-faner** plywood **-ning** cruise
kryssnings|fartyg cruise liner **-robot** cruise
missile
kryss|prick *sjö.* spar buoy **-valv** cross vault[ing]

K

kryst|a (*vid avföring*) strain [at stool]; (*vid förlossning*) bear down **-ad** *a5* strained, laboured; (*om kvickhet äv.*) forced **-ning** strain **-värkar** *pl* labour [pains]

kråk|a *s1* **1** *zool.* crow; *hoppa* ~ hop; *elda för -orna* let all the heat from the fire go up the chimney **2** (*tecken*) tick; (*utmärkande fel*) error mark **3** (*huvudbonad*) bonnet **-bo** crow's-nest **-bär** crowberry **-fötter** *pl, bildl.* pothooks; scrawl (*sg*) **-slott** *skämts.* rookery **-spark** *sömn.* featherstitch **-sång** *det fina i ~en* the beauty of it **-vinkel** *skämts.* one-horse town, hole

kråma *rfl* prance [about]; (*om pers. äv.*) strut (swagger) [about]; (*om häst äv.*) arch its neck

krångel ['kråŋel] *s7* bother, trouble; (*svårighet*) difficulty; *AE. vard.* bug[s]; *ställa till* ~ make a fuss (difficulties) **-makare** troublemaker

krångla [ˣkråŋla] **1** make a bother (a fuss, difficulties) (*med betalningen* about the payment); ~ *till ngt* get s.th. into a muddle, make a muddle of s.th. **2** (*ej fungera*) be troublesome; (*förorsaka krångel*) give (cause) trouble; *låset* ~*r* the lock has jammed **3** (*fumla med*) fiddle with **4** (*göra undanflykter*) quibble, beat about the bush; (*bruka knep*) be up to tricks **5** *rfl*, ~ *sig fram till* muddle one's way through to; ~ *sig ifrån* manage to get out of; ~ *sig igenom* get through somehow

krånglig *al* troublesome, tiresome; (*kinkig*) awkward; (*invecklad*) difficult, complicated

1 krås *s7* giblets (*pl*); *smörja* ~*et* feast, do o.s. well (*med* on)

2 krås *s7* (*hals- o.d.*) frill, ruffle

kråsnål tiepin

1 kräfta *s1* **1** *zool.* crayfish, crawfish ; *röd som en kokt* ~ as red as a boiled lobster **2** *K~n* (*astr.*) Cancer

2 kräfta *s1* (*med.*) cancer

kräft|bur crayfish pot **-djur** crustacean **-fiske** crayfishing **-gång** backward movement **-kalas** crayfish party **-pest** crayfish disease **-skiva** *se -kalas*

kräft|svulst cancerous tumour (growth) **-sår** cancerous ulcer; *bildl.* canker

kräk *s7* **1** *se kryp* **2** *se kreatur* **3** (*neds. om människa*) miserable beggar (wretch); *ett beskedligt* ~ (*äv.*) a milksop; *stackars* ~ poor thing (wretch)

kräkas *v3, dep* be sick, vomit; ~ *upp* vomit, bring up

kräkla [ˣkrä:k-, ˣkräkk-] *s1* crosier, crozier

kräk|medel emetic **-ning** [-ä:-] vomiting; *häftiga ~ar* violent attacks of vomiting **-rot** *bot.* ipecac[uanha]

kräl|a crawl; ~ *i stoftet* (*bildl.*) grovel [in the dust] (*för* to) **-djur** reptile

kräm *s3* cream; *jfr hud-, sko-*

krämaraktig *al* mercenary

krämar|e shopkeeper, tradesman; *neds.* huckster **-folk** *ett* ~ a nation of shopkeepers **-själ** *pers.* mercenary soul

krämfärgad cream-coloured

krämp|a *s1* ailment; *-or* aches and pains

kräng|a *v2* **1** (*luta åt ena sidan*) cant, list, heel (heave) [over]; roll; *flyg.* bank **2** (*lägga på sidan*) cant, heave down **3** *se vända* [*ut och in på*]; ~ *av sig en skjorta* struggle out of a shirt **-ning** canting, heel[ing]; lurch, roll; *flyg.* banking **-nings-**

hämmare stabilizer

kränk|a *v3* (*lag e.d.*) violate, infringe; (*överträda*) transgress; (*förorätta*) wrong; (*förolämpa*) insult, offend; (*såra*) hurt, outrage **-ande** *a4* insulting, offensive; ~ *tillmälen* abusive treatment **-ning** (*jfr kränka*) violation, infringement; transgression; wrong; insult, offence; outrage; ~ *av privatlivets helgd* violation of privacy

kräpp *s3, s4* crepe, crape

kräpp|a, -era crinkle; (*hår e.d.*) wave **-nylon** stretch nylon **-papper** (*hopskr.* kräppapper) crepe paper

kräs|en *a3* fastidious, particular, choosy (*på* about); *vara* ~ be hard to please **-lig** [-ä:-] *al* (*om mat*) choice, delicious; sumptuous **-magad** *a5* fussy; squeamish

1 kräva *s1* crop

2 kräva *v2* **1** (*fordra*) demand, [lay] claim [to] **2** (*erfordra*) call for; (*behöva*) require, need; (*nödvändiggöra*) necessitate; (*ta i anspråk*) take; ~ *mycket tid* take up much time **3** *olyckan krävde flera dödsoffer* the accident cost the lives of several people (claimed several victims) **4** (*anmana att betala*) apply for payment, demand payment of, (*skriftligt*) dun (*på* for); ~ *ngn på pengar* press s.b. for money, request s.b. to pay

krävande *a4* exacting; (*prövande*) trying; (*påkostande*) severe; *en* ~ *uppgift* (*äv.*) an arduous task

krögare innkeeper

krök *s2* bend; (*flod-, väg- e.d.*) curve, wind, winding

krök|a *v3* bend; (*göra krokig*) make crooked; (*armen, fingret*) crook; ~ [*på*] *läpparna* curl one's lips; ~ *rygg* (*om djur*) arch its back; *inte* ~ *ett hår på ngns huvud* not hurt a hair of a p.'s head; *det skall* ~*s i tid som krokigt skall bli* best to bend while it is a twig **-ning** [-ö:-] (*-ande*) bending *etc.*; (*en* ~) *se krök*

krön *s7* crest; (*allmännare*) top, ridge, crown; (*mur- o.d.*) coping **kröna** *v3* crown (*ngn till kung* s.b. king); ~*s med framgång* be crowned with success, be successful

krönika ['krö:-] *s1* chronicle; annals (*pl*), records (*pl*); (*tidnings- e.d.*) review, column

krönike|böcker *K~na* [the] Chronicles **-skrivare** chronicler, annalist **-spel** chronicle play; (*hist. festspel*) pageant [play]

krönikör chronicler, annalist; (*i tidning*) columnist

kröning coronation

kröningsceremoni coronation ceremony

kröp *imperf. av krypa*

krösus ['krö:-] *s2* Croesus

kub *s3* cube; *upphöja i* ~ raise to the third power, cube

Kuba *n* Cuba

kub|an *s3,* **-ansk** [-'a:nsk] *a5* Cuban

1 kubb *s2* (*hatt*) bowler [hat]; *AE. äv.* derby [hat]

2 kubb *s2* (*hugg- etc.*) block

kubbe *s2, se 2 kubb*

kubera cube

kubjk *s9* cubic **-fot** cubic foot **-innehåll** cubic contents, cubature, cubage **-meter** cubic metre **-mått** cubic measure **-rot** cube root **-tum** cubic inch

kub|isk ['ku:-] *a5* cubic **-ism** Cubism **-ist** Cubist

-istisk [-'iss-] *a5* Cubist[ic]
kuckel ['kukk-] *s7* hanky-panky; hocus-pocus
kuckeliku I *interj* cock-a-doodle-doo! **II** *s6* cock-
-a-doodle-doo call
kuckla fiddle
kudd|e *s2* cushion; (*säng-*) pillow **-krig** pillow
fight **-var** *s7* pillowcase
kuf *s2* queer (odd, rum) customer **-isk** ['ku:-] *a5*,
vard. odd, queer
kugga 1 (*underkänna*) reject, fail, plough; *hon
blev ~d* she failed (was ploughed) **2** (*lura*) take
in
kugg|bana rack (*särsk. AE.* cog) railway **-drev**
gear drive; pinion
kugge *s2* cog (*äv. bildl.*), gear tooth
kuggfråga poser, catch question
kugg|hjul gear[wheel], cogwheel (*äv. bildl.*)
-stång rack **-växel** gear, gearing
kujon *s3* coward, funk **-era** domineer, bully
kuk *s2*, *vard.* cock, prick
kukeliku *se* kuckeliku
kuku I *interj* cuckoo! **II** *s6* cuckoo call
kul *oböjligt a* funny, amusing; *ha ~* have fun; *det
var ~ att träffas* it was nice meeting you
1 kula *s1* (*håla*) cave, hole; (*lya*) lair, den; (*bostad*, *vard.*) digs (*pl*)
2 kula *s1* **1** ball; (*gevärs- äv.*) bullet; (*pappers-,
bröd- e.d.*) pellet; (*vid omröstning*) ballot; *skjuta
sig en ~ för pannan* blow one's brains out; *den ~n
visste var den tog* (*bildl.*) that shot went home **2**
sport. shot; *stöta ~* put the shot **3** (*leksak*) marble; *spela ~* play marbles **4** (*bula*) bump (*i pannan* on the forehead) **5** *börja på ny ~* start afresh
kul|bana (*projektils*) trajectory **-baneprojektil**
ballistic missile **-blixt** fireball
kulen *a3* raw [and chilly], bleak
kul|formig [-å-] *a5* ball-shaped, spherical, globu-
lar **-gevär** rifle **-hammare** ball-peen hammer
-hål bullet hole
kuli ['ku:-] *s3* coolie
kulinarisk [-'na:-] *a5* culinary
kuling half-gale; *styv* (*hård*) ~ moderate (fresh)
gale **-varning** small craft warning
kuljss *s3* coulisse; wing; *bakom ~erna* (*bildl.*) behind the scenes; *i ~erna* (*vanl.*) in the wings
kulkärve volley of bullets
1 kull *s2* (*av däggdjur*) litter; (*av fåglar*) hatch;
covey; brood; (*av grisar*) farrow; (*friare*) batch
2 kull *se* omkull
3 kull I *interj* you're "it" **II** *s7*, *leka ~* play tag
1 kulla *s1* (*dal-*) Dalecarlian woman (girl)
2 kulla *v1*, ~ *ngn* tag s.b.
kullager [ˣku:l-] ball bearing
kullbyttera 1 (*tumla överända*) topple over **2**
(*om fordon*) turn over (*i diket* into the ditch);
(*göra konkurs*) fail, come a cropper
1 kulle *s2* (*hatt-*) crown
2 kulle *s2* (*höjd*) hill; (*liten*) hillock; (*grav-*)
mound; *de sju kullarnas stad* City of the Seven
Hills
kulled [ˣku:l-] ball-and-socket joint
kullerbytta *s1* somersault; *göra en ~* eg. turn
a somersault, b) (*falla*) tumble, go tumbling over
kullersten cobble[stone]; *koll.* cobbles (*pl*)
kullerstens|gata cobbled street **-ås** cobble es-
ker

kullfallen *a5* that has fallen over (down)
1 kullig *a1* hilly; (*kuperad*) undulating
2 kullig *a5* (*om boskap*) hornless, polled
kull|kasta 1 *bli ~d* be thrown down (off one's
legs); *jfr kasta* [*omkull*] **2** *bildl.* upset (*planer*
plans), overthrow; (*upphäva*) reverse, set aside
-körning (*med cykel, på skidor*) fall, tumble
-ridning fall
kullrig *a1* (*buktig*) bulging, convex; (*rundad*)
rounded; (*om stenläggning*) cobbled
kull|slagen *a5*, *bli ~* be knocked over (down)
-stjälpt [-ʃ-] *a4*, *glaset låg ~* the glass had been
knocked over
kulmage potbelly
kulmen ['kull-] *r*, *best. form* =, culmination, climax; (*mera eg.*) summit, highest point, acme;
ekon. peak, maximum; *nå ~* reach its climax
(*etc.*)
kulmin|ation *astr.* culmination **-era** culminate,
reach its climax (*etc.*)
kul|penna *se* -spetspenna **-ram** abacus **-regn**
rain (hail) of bullets **-sinter** pellets (*pl*) **-sinter-
verk** pelletizing plant **-spel** marbles (*pl*)
-spetspenna ballpoint [pen]; (*i Storbritannien
äv.*) Biro **-spruta** machine gun
kulsprute|gevär light machine gun **-pistol** sub-
machine-gun **-skytt** machine gunner **-torn** gun
turret
kulstöt|are *sport.* shot-putter **-ning** putting the
shot
kult *s3* cult **-föremål** appurtenance of a cult
-handling cult ceremony, rite
kultiv|ator [-ˣa:tår] *s3* cultivator **-era** cultivate
-erad [-ˈe:rad] *a5* cultivated, cultured, refined
kultplats cult centre (site)
kultur 1 (*civilisation*) civilization; *västerländsk ~*
Western civilization **2** (*bildning*) culture; (*förfi-
ning*) refinement; *han saknar ~* he lacks refinement, he is a rough diamond **3** (*odlande*) cultivation **4** (*bakterie-, fisk- o.d.*) culture **-arbetare**
cultural worker **-artikel** article on a cultural subject **-arv** cultural heritage **-attaché** cultural attaché **-bygd** *en gammal ~* a district with cultural
traditions **-centrum** cultural centre **-chock** culture shock **-debatt** open debate on cultural matters
kultur|ell *a1* cultural **-epok** cultural epoch **-fara**
threat to culture **-fientlig** hostile to cultural progress **-folk** civilized people **-geografi** social and
economic geography, human geography **-gär-
ning** cultural achievement **-historia** social history **-hus** arts (cultural) centre **-insats** contribution to [the spread of] culture **-institut** cultural institution **-knutte** *s2* culture vulture
-land civilized (culturally progressive) country
-liv cultural life **-minne**, **-minnesmärke**
(*byggnad o.d.*) historical monument; relic of
ancient culture **-nation** civilized nation
-nämnd arts committee; cultural affairs committee **-personlighet** leading personality in the
world of culture; *vard.* lion **-politik** cultural policy **-reservat** reservation **-revolution** cultural
revolution **-samhälle** civilized society **-råd** (*institution*) national council for cultural affairs;
(*pers.*) counsellor for cultural affairs **-samhälle**
civilized society **-sida** arts page **-språk** *de stora*

K

~*en* the principal languages of the civilized world **-strömning** cultural influence **-tradition** cultural tradition **-utskott** ~*et* [the Swedish parliamentary] standing committee on cultural affairs **-växt** cultivated plant

kulvert ['kull-] *s2* culvert; conduit

kulör colour; *bildl. äv.* shade **kulört** [-ö:-] *a1* coloured; ~*a lyktor* Chinese lanterns

1 kummel ['kumm-] *s7* **1** (*stenrös, gravrös*) cairn; (*grav- äv.*) barrow **2** (*sjömärke*) heap of stones

2 kummel ['kumm-] *s2, zool.* [European] hake

kummin [ˣkumm-] *s9, s7* caraway; [*spis-*] cum [m]in **-ost** seed-spiced cheese

kumpan *s3* companion, crony; (*medbrottsling*) accomplice

kumul|ativ [*äv.* 'kumm-] *a5* [ac]cumulative **-era** [ac]cumulate

kund *s3* customer; client; (*på krog e.d.*) patron; *fasta* ~*er* regular customers; *gammal* ~ old customer; *vara* ~ *hos* shop at, patronize; *han är* ~ *hos oss* (*vanl.*) he is a customer of ours

kunde *imperf. av* kunna

kund|krets [regular] customers, clients, clientele **-vagn** trolley

kung *s2* (*jfr* konung) king; *gå till* ~*s* appeal to the highest authority

kunga|döme *s6* (*statsform*) monarchy; (*rike*) kingdom **-familj** ~*en* the Royal Family **-försäkran** *avge* ~ make a declaration, sign a charter **-hus** royal house (family) **-krona** king's crown **-makt** royal power **-mord** regicide **-par** King and Queen, royal couple **-rike** kingdom **-värdighet** dignity of a sovereign, royalty

kunglig *a5* royal; *Hans K*~ *Höghet* His Royal Highness; *K*~ *Majestät* (*förk. Kungl. Maj:t*) the Government, the King [in Council]; *de* ~*a* the royal personages (family *sg el. pl*); *K*~*a biblioteket* [the Swedish] Royal Library **-het** royalty

kungligt *adv* royally; *roa sig* ~ have a right royal time, enjoy o.s. immensely

kungs|blått royal blue **-fiskare** *zool.* kingfisher **-fågel** goldcrest **-gambit** king's gambit **-gård** demesne of the Crown (State) **-ljus** *bot.* (*koll.*) mullein; (*art*) common mullein, Aaron's rod **-tanke** leading (basic) idea **-tiger** Bengal tiger **-vatten** aqua regia **-väg** *bildl.* royal road **-ängslilja** snake's head **-örn** golden eagle

kungör|a [-j-] announce, make known; (*utropa*) proclaim; ~ *för allmänheten* (*äv.*) give public notice of; *härmed* -*es att* notice is hereby given that **-else** announcement, publication; (*högtidlig*) proclamation; (*förordnande e.d.*) public notice

kun|na *kunde kunnat* **I** *huvudv.* (*veta, känna t.*) know; ~ *engelska* know English; ~ *ett hantverk* know a craft (trade); ~ *sin läxa* know one's lesson; ~ *utantill* know by heart; *han kan ingenting* he knows nothing **II** *hjälpv* **1** *inf.* kunna, *sup.* kunnat (*vara i stånd att*) be (resp. been) able to (capable of), (*förstå sig på att*) know (*resp.* known) how to; *inte* ~ (*äv.*) be unable to; ~ *läsa och skriva* know how to read and write; *vilja men inte* ~ be willing but unable; *skulle* ~ (= *kunde*), *vanl.* could, might (*jfr II 2 o. 3*); *skulle ha* ~*t* (= *kunde ha*), *vanl.* could, might (*jfr II 2 o. 3*); *jag har gjort så gott jag har* ~*t* I have done as well as

I could, I have done my best; *det har inte* ~*t undvikas* it has been unavoidable **2** (*uttryckande förmåga, tillfälle, uppmaning*) *kan* can, *kunde* could; *visa vad man kan* show what one can do; *jag kan* [*göra det*] *själv* I can do it myself; *han kan sjunga* he can sing; *hon kan åka skridskor* she can (knows how to) skate; *materialet kan köpas från* the material kan (is to) be had from; *vi kan ta sextåget* we can take the six o'clock train; *det kan inte beskrivas* it cannot be described; *jag kan inte få upp dörren* I can't open the door; *han kan inte komma* he can't (*är ej i stånd att* is not able to) come; *spring så fort du kan* run as fast as you can; *hur kan du vara så lättlurad?* how can you be so easily taken in?; *kan du säga mig* can you tell me; *kan ni inte vara tysta?* can't you be quiet?; *hur -de du?* how could you?; *vi -de ju försöka* we could try; *om det bara -de sluta regna* if only it could stop raining; *hur kan det komma sig att* how is it that; *vad kan klockan vara?* I wonder what the time is?; *du kan väl komma!* (*bönfallande*) do come, please!; *nu kan det vara nog!* that's enough [from you]!; *man kan vad man vill* where there's a will there's a way **3** (*uttryckande oviss möjlighet, tillåtelse, försäkran*) *kan* may, *ibl.* can, *kunde* might, *ibl.* could; *de kan komma vilket ögonblick som helst* they may come (be here) any moment now; *det kan man lätt missförstå* that may (can) easily be misunderstood; *han kan ha misstagit sig* he may have been mistaken; *det kan så vara* maybe; *du kan gå nu* you may go now; *kan jag få litet mjölk?* may (can, might, could) I have some milk, please?; *som man kan se* as you may (can) see; *kan jag få se?* may (can) I see?; *nej, det kan du inte* no, you can't (may not); *du kan göra det om du vill* you may do it if you want; *jag kan försäkra dig att* I may (can) assure you that; *det kan du ha rätt i* you may be right there; *du kan vara säker på att* you may (can) rest assured that; *du kan lika väl göra det själv* you may as well do it yourself; *hur underligt det än kan låta* strange as it may sound; *man kan lugnt påstå att* it may (can) safely be maintained (said) that; *du -de gärna ha givit mig den* you might have given it to me; *det kan väl kosta omkring 20 kronor* I should think it costs about 20 kronor; *du kan tro att det blev bra* you bet it was good; *det kan väl inte ha hänt någonting* I hope there is nothing wrong, surely nothing has happened; *det kan vara på tiden* it's about time **4** (*brukar, har en benägenhet att*) *kan* will, can, *kunde* would, could; *sådant kan hända* such things happen; *de kan vara svåra att ha att göra med* they can be difficult to deal with; *de -de sitta där i timmar* they would sit there for hours; *på våren -de floden svämma över* in spring the river could overflow its banks **5** (*annan konstruktion*) *man kan bli galen för mindre* it's enough to drive one crazy; *det är så man kan gråta* it's enough to make one cry; *det kan göra detsamma* it doesn't matter, it makes no difference; *man kan inte förneka att* there's no denying that; *det kan man kalla tur!* that's what I call luck!; *man kan aldrig veta* om there's no knowing if; *det kan du säga!* that's easy for you to say! **6** (*med betonad partikel*) *jag kan inte med dem* I can't stand them

kun|nande *s6* skill, ability; (*kunskap*) knowledge; *tekniskt* ~ technical know-how (expertise) **-nat** *sup. av kunna* **-nig** *a1* skilful, capable, competent; (*styv*) proficient; (*som har reda på sig*) well-informed **-nighet** *se kunnande*

kunskap *s3* knowledge (*äv.* ~*er*) (*i* of, on; *om* about, of); (*vetskap äv.*) cognizance (*om* of); (*inhämtad*) information; ~*er och färdigheter* knowledge and proficiency; *K~ens träd* [*på gott och ont*] the tree of knowledge [of good and evil]; *ha goda* ~*er i* have a thorough knowledge of **kunskap|a** *mil.* reconnoitre, scout **-are** *mil.* [military] scout

kunskaps|begär craving for knowledge **-källa** *min* ~ my source of information **-nivå** educational level **-område** branch (field) of knowledge **-prov** proficiency test **-teori** theory of cognition **-test** knowledge test **-törst** thirst for knowledge

kupa I *s1* (*lamp-*) shade; (*globformig*) globe; (*glas-*) glass cover, bell jar (glass); (*bi-*) hive **II** *v1* **1** cup (*händerna* one's hands) **2** *lantbr.* earth (bank) up

kupé *s3* **1** *järnv.* compartment **2** (*vagn*) coupé

kuper|a 1 (*svans o.d.*) dock, crop **2** *kortsp.* cut **-ad** *a5* (*om landskap o.d.*) hilly; (*vågformig*) undulating

kupévärmare car heater

kupidon [-'å:n *el.* -'ɔ:n] *s3* cupid

kupig *a1* convex[ly rounded]; (*utstående*) bulging (*ögon* eyes)

kuplett *s3* music-hall (revue) song; comic song **-författare** writer of revue songs

kupol [-'å:l] *s3* cupola, dome **-formig** [-år-] *a5* dome-shaped, domed **-grav** *arkeol.* dome-crowned tomb **-tak** dome, cupola roof

kupong [-'åŋ] *s3* coupon; (*mat- äv.*) voucher; (*på postanvisning e.d.*) counterfoil, (*särsk. AE.*) stub; *klippa* ~*er* (*skämts.*) be one of the idle rich **-häfte** book of coupons **-skatt** tax on share dividends

kupp *s3* coup; *en djärv* ~ a bold stroke, a daring move; *på* ~*en* (*vard.*) as a result [of it], at it **-försök** *polit. o.d.* attempted coup; (*rån-*) attempted robbery **-makare** perpetrator of a (the) coup; (*stats-*) instigator of a coup d'état

1 kur *s2* (*skjul*) shed, hut

2 kur *s3, med.* [course of] treatment (*mot* for); cure (*mot* for) (*äv. bildl.*)

3 kur *s3, göra ngn sin* ~ court s.b., pay court to s.b.

kura *sitta och* ~ sit huddled up, (*ha tråkigt*) sit around moping

kurage [-'a:ʃ] pluck, nerve; *vard.* guts (*pl*), spunk

kuranstalt spa, hydro[pathic establishment]; *fysikalisk* ~ physical therapy clinic

kurant *a1* **1** *hand.* marketable, saleable **2** (*gångbar*) current **3** *se frisk*

kurare *se curare*

kurativ [*äv.* 'ku:r-, 'kurr—] *a5* curative

kurator [-ˣa:tår] *s3* **1** *univ.* curator, president [of a student's club] **2** (*övervakare*) curator, supervisor; (*sjukhus-*) almoner; (*social-*) [social] welfare officer

kurbits *s2, s3, bot.* pumpkin

kurchatovium [-'tå:-] *s8* kurchatovium; *AE. äv.* rutherfordium

kurd *s3,* **kurder** ['kurr-] *s9* Kurd **kurdisk** ['kurr-] *a5* Kurdish

kurera cure (*för* of)

kurfurste [ˣku:r-] elector **kurfurstendöme** *s6* electorate

kuria ['ku:-] *s1* curia

kurialstil [-iˣa:l-] official (departmental) style

kuriosakabinett [-iˣɔ:sa-] curio cupboard

kuriositet curiosity; *konkr. äv.* curio; ~*er* (*äv.*) bric-a-brac; *som en* ~ as a curious fact (coincidence) **kuriositetsintresse** *bara ha* ~ be interesting only as a curiosity

kurios|um [-iˣɔ:-] *-umet -a* curiosity; (*om pers. äv.*) odd specimen

kurir *s3* courier **-post** courier's bag (pouch); *med* ~ by diplomatic (courier's) bag (*etc.*)

kuriös *a1* curious, strange, odd

Kurland ['ku:r-] *n* Courland, Kurland

kurländsk [ˣku:r-] *a5* Courland

kurort [-ɔ:-] spa, health resort

1 kurra *v1* *det* ~*r i magen på mig* my stomach is rumbling **2** (*om duvor*) coo

2 kurra *s1* (*finka*) gaol, quod

kurragömma [-ˣjömma] *i uttr.: leka* ~ play hide-and-seek

kurre *s2* chap, fellow; *en underlig* ~ a rum chap, an odd fish

kurry *se curry*

kurs *s3* **1** (*läro- o.d.*) course [of instruction] (*i* in, on); (*skol- o.d.*) curriculum **2** *sjö.* course; (*-linje*) track; *flyg.* heading; *bildl. äv.* [line of] policy, tack; *hålla* ~ *på a*) (*hamn*) stand in for, (*udde*) stand (make, head) for, *b*) (*flyg. o. friare*) steer (head) for, bear down upon; *komma ur* ~*en* (*sjö.*) fall away out of course; *ändra* ~ veer, (*friare äv.*) change one's course **3** *hand.* (*valuta-*) rate [of exchange] (*på* for); (*på värdepapper*) quotation (*på* of); (*på aktier*) price (*på* of); *efter gällande* ~ at the current rate of exchange; *lägsta* ~ (*vanl.*) [the] bottom price; *stå högt i* ~ be at a premium, *bildl. äv.* be in great favour; *stå lågt i* ~ be at a discount

kursa *vard.* sell

kurs|avgift course fee **-bok** textbook **-deltagare** course participant; student **-fall** fall (decline, drop) in prices (rates); *starkt* ~ sharp break in prices (rates) **-förändring** change of course (policy)

kursiv I *a5* italic **II** *s3* italics (*pl*); *med* ~ in italics **-era** print in italics, italicize; (*bildl., understryka*) underline; ~*t av mig* my italics **-läsning** reading at sight **-stil** *se kursiv II*

kursivt [-'i:vt] *adv, läsa* ~ read at sight (without preparation)

kurs|kamrat fellow student [in a course] **-lista** [stock] exchange list, list of stock exchange quotations; (*över utländsk valuta*) list of exchanges rates **-litteratur** study literature [for a course] **-plan** curriculum, syllabus **-stegring** rise in prices, upward tendency; (*stark*) boom **-verksamhet** (*vid univ.*) extramural activity **-värde** market value (price, rate); (*valutas*) exchange value **-ändring** change of course; (*valuta-*) change of rate

kurtage [-'a:ʃ] *s7, hand.* brokerage, commission

kurtjs *s3* flirtation **-en** *s3* courtesan **-era** ~ *ngn* carry on a flirtation with s.b. **-ör** flirt, philanderer

kurva *s1* curve; (*krök*) bend; *i* ~*n* at the curve; *ta en* ~ *för snävt* take a curve too sharp, cut a corner **kurv|ig** *a1* curving, with many curves **-linje** curving (curved) line **-tagning** cornering, [the] rounding of curves

kuscha 1 (*om hund*) lie down **2** (*kujonera*) browbeat, cow

kusjn *s3* [first] cousin **-barn** second cousin; *ett* ~ *till mig* my first cousin once removed

kusk *s2* coachman; driver

kusk|a ~ *landet runt* tour round the country; ~ *omkring* travel about **-bock** [coachman's] box, driver's seat

kuslig [-u:-] *a1* dismal, gloomy, dreary; (*hemsk*) uncanny, gruesome; *känna sig* ~ *till mods* feel creepy, have a creepy sensation

kust *s3* coast; (*havsstrand*) shore; *vid* ~*en* on the coast, (*för semester*) at the seaside; ~*en är klar* the coast is clear **-artilleri** coast artillery **-band** *i* ~*et* on the seaboard (seacoast) **-batteri** shore battery **-befolkning** coastal population **-bevakning 1** *abstr.* coast protection **2** *konkr.*, ~*en* the coastguard **-bevakningsstation** coastguard station **-fart** coastal traffic, coasting trade **-flotta** ~*n* the Coastal (*i Storbritannien ung.* Home) Fleet **-jägare** *mil.*, *ung.* commando, commando soldier **-klimat** coastal climate **-land** coastal land **-linje** coastline **-radiostation** coastal radio station **-remsa** coastal strip (belt) **-stad** coastal (seaside) town **-sträcka** stretch of coast, littoral **-trakt** coastal region

1 kut *s2*, *zool.* seal pup

2 kut *s2* (*krökt rygg*) stoop

kut|a 1 walk with a stoop **2** *vard.* (*springa*) dart (*iväg* away) **-ig** *a1*, *se krokryggig*

kutrygg hunchback, humpback **-ig** *a1*, *se krokryggig*

1 kutter ['kutt-] *s7* (*duv-*) cooing (*äv. bildl.*)

2 kutter ['kutt-] *s2* (*båt*) cutter

kuttersmycke belle of the boat

kutterspån cutter shavings (*pl*)

kutting small keg

kuttra coo **-sju** [-'ʃu:] **I** *oböjligt s* flirting, spooning **II** *oböjligt a* intimate, thick as thieves

kutym *s3* custom, usage, practice

kuva subdue; (*under-*) subjugate; (*uppror o.d.*) suppress; (*betvinga*) check, curb; (*kujonera*) cow

Kuwait *n* Kuwait

kuwait|ier [-'vait-] *s9*, **-isk** *a5* Kuwaiti

kuvert [-'ä:r, *äv.* -'ärt] *s7* **1** (*för brev*) envelope **2** (*bords-*) cover **-avgift** cover charge **-bröd** [dinner] roll **-era** put into an envelope (*resp.* envelopes) **-väska** pochette

kuvös incubator

kvacksalv|a quack **-are** quack [doctor], charlatan **-eri** quackery, charlatanry

kvad *imperf. av kväda*

kvadda (*t.ex. bil*) smash

kvader ['kva:-] *s2* ashlar, freestone

kvadrant quadrant

kvadrat square; ~*en på* the square of; *fem i* ~ five squared (raised to the second power); *två*

tum i ~ two inches square; *dumheten i* ~ stupidity at its height **-fot** square foot

kvadratisk [-'dra:-] *a5* **1** (*geom. o. friare*) square **2** *mat.* quadratic

kvadrat|meter square metre **-rot** ~*en ur* the square root of

kvadratur quadrature; *cirkelns* ~ (*vanl.*) the squaring of the circle

kvadrera square, raise to the second power

kvadriljon *s3* quadrillion; *AE.* septillion

kval *s7* (*smärta*) pain; (*lidande*) suffering; (*plåga*) torment; (*ångest*) anguish; (*vånda*) agony; *svartsjukans* (*hungerns*) ~ (*pl*) the pangs of jealousy (hunger); *i valet och* ~*et* in two minds (*om* whether), on the horns of a dilemma **-full** agonizing, torturing; (*om död*) extremely painful; (*om smärtor.e.d.*) excruciating

kvalificer|a qualify (*för* for); ~ *sig* qualify o.s. **-ad** *a5* qualified (*till* for); *-at brott* aggravated crime; ~ *majoritet* [a] two-thirds majority **-ing** qualification **-ingsmatch** qualifying match

kvalifikation qualification

kvalitativ [*el.* 'kvall-] *a5* qualitative

kvalité *s3*, **kvalitet** *s3* quality; *hand. äv.* sort, type; grade; (*märke*) brand (line) [of goods]; *vinna* (*förlora*) ~ (*schack.*) win (lose) the exchange

kvalitets|beteckning description [of quality] **-kontroll** quality check (control) **-medveten** quality conscious **-märke** mark of quality; quality brand **-vara** superior (high-class) article; quality product

kvalm *s7* closeness, stuffy atmosphere; heavy scent **-ig** *a1* suffocating, stifling, close

kvalmatch *sport.* qualifying match

kvalster ['kvall-] *s7* mite, acarid

kvantfysik quantum physics (*pl, behandlas som sg*)

kvantifiera quantify

kvantitativ [*el.* 'kvann-] *a5* quantitative

kvantitet quantity; (*mängd äv.*) amount **kvantitetsrabatt** quantity rebate (discount)

kvant|kemi quantum chemistry **-mekanik** quantum mechanics (*pl, behandlas som sg*) **-teori** quantum theory

kvant|um *-umet el. -um, pl -um el. -a* quantum

kvar *adv, se äv. under olika verb*; (*igen, i behåll, -lämnad, -glömd*) left; (*till övers*) left over; (*efter de andra o.d.*) behind; (*bevarad*) preserved; *han stannade* ~ he stayed behind; *jag vill bo* ~ *här* I want to go on living here; *hon kan inte ha långt* ~ [*att leva*] she cannot have long left [to live]; *han var* ~ *när vi gick* he was still there when we left; *under den tid som är* ~ *till påsk* during the time remaining to Easter

kvar|blivande *a4* remaining, permanent **-bliven** *a5* left over; (*-lämnad*) left behind; *-blivna biljetter* unsold tickets **-dröjande** *s6 o. a4* lingering

kvarg *s3* curd (cottage) cheese

kvarglömd *a5*, ~*a effekter* lost property (*sg*)

kvarhåll|a keep; *-en på polisstationen* detained at the police station

kvark *s2*, *fys.* quark

kvarka *s1*, *veter.* the strangles (*pl*)

kvar|leva *s1* remnant; *bildl. äv.* relic, survival;

-levor (*äv.*) remains (*efter* of); *ngns -levor* a p.'s mortal remains **-ligga** remain, stay on; (~ *med*) retain, keep **-låtenskap** *s3, ngns* ~ property left by s.b.; (*litterär*) remains (*pl*) **-lämnad** *a5* left behind

kvarn [-a:-] *s2* mill **-damm** millpond **-hjul** millwheel **-industri** flour-mill (milling) industry **-sten** millstone **-vinge** windmill sail **-ägare** owner of a mill, miller

kvar|sittare pupil who has not been moved up; *bli* ~ *i ettan* stay down in the first form **-skatt** tax arrears (*pl*), back tax **-stad** *-en -er* sequestration (*på* of); *sjö.* embargo (*på* on); (*på tryckalster*) impoundage, (*tillfällig*) suspension; *belägga med* ~ sequester, sequestrate, *sjö.* embargo, (*tryckalster*) impound **-stå** remain

1 kvart *s2, i bet.* 2 *s9* **1** (*fjärdedel*) quarter; *med hatten på tre* ~ with one's hat cocked over one eye **2** (*fjärdedels timme*) quarter of an hour; *en* ~ *i två* a quarter to two; *en* ~ *över två* a quarter past two **3** (*format*) quarto **4** *mus.* fourth **5** (*i fäktning*) quarte, carte

2 kvart *s2* **1** (*rum*) pad (*äv. tillhåll för narkomaner*)

kvarta *vard.* (*sova över*) doss down

kvartal *s7* quarter [of a year]

kvartals|avgift quarter's fee **-hyra** quarter's rent **-skifte** beginning of the new quarter **-vis** by the quarter, quarterly

kvarter *s7* **1** block; (*distrikt*) quarter, district **2** *mil.* quarters (*pl*); billet **3** (*mån-*) quarter **-mästare** quartermaster

kvarteron *s3* quadroon

kvarters|butik neighbourhood (local) shop **-polis** local policeman

kvartett *s3* quartet

kvartil *s3* quartile

kvarting *en* ~ a small bottle

kvarto ['kvarr-] quarto **-format** quarto [size]; *i* ~ in quarto

kvarts *s3, miner.* quartz

kvarts|final *sport.* quarterfinal **-format** *se kvartoformat*

kvarts|glas quartz glass **-lampa** ultraviolet lamp

kvartssekel quarter of a century; *ett* ~ (*äv.*) twenty-five years

kvartsur quartz clock (watch)

kvartär *a5* Quaternary **-perioden** the Quaternary [period]

kvarvarande *a4* remaining

kvasar *s3* quasar

kvasi|- quasi-, pseudo-; (*låtsad*) sham- **-elegant** flashy **-filosofi** pseudo-philosophy **-litterär** pseudo-literary **-vetenskap** quasi-science

kvast *s2* broom; *nya ~ar sopar bäst* new brooms sweep clean **-bindare** broommaker **-fening** *zool.* crossopterygian **-prick** *sjö.* broom-head, perch with broom **-skaft** broomstick

kvav I *a1* close; (*instängd*) stuffy; (*tryckande*) oppressive, sultry **II** *s, i uttr. gå i* ~ founder, go down, *bildl.* be wrecked, come to nothing

kved *imperf. av kvida*

kverul|ans *s3* querulousness, grumbling **-ant** querulous person, grumbler **-antisk** [-'ant-] *a5* querulous **-era** complain, croak, grumble

kvick *al* **1** (*snabb*) quick; rapid, swift; (*rask*) ready, prompt (*svar* answer) **2** (*snabbtänkt*) clever (*äv. iron.*) **3** (*spirituell*) witty; smart (*replik* retort); *göra sig* ~ *på andras bekostnad* crack jokes at other people's expense **kvicka** ~ *på* hurry up (*äv.* ~ *sig*)

kvicke *s2* (*i horn*) [horn] core; (*i hov*) [sensitive] frog

kvick|het 1 (*snabbhet*) quickness *etc., se kvick* **2** (*spiritualitet*) wit **3** (*kvickt yttrande*) witticism, joke; *AE. vard.* [wise]crack **-huvud** wit, witty chap **-lunch** quick-lunch

kvick|na ~ *till* revive, (*efter svimning*) come round, rally, *bildl.* chirp up **-rot** *bot.* couch [grass] **-sand** quicksand

kvicksilver mercury, quicksilver **-betning** mercury disinfection **-förening** mercury compound **-förgiftning** mercurialism, mercurial poisoning **-haltig** *al* mercurial **-termometer** mercury thermometer

kvick|tänkt I *al* quick-witted, ready-witted, clever **II** *adv* with ready wit, cleverly **-ögd** *al* quick-sighted; (*om iakttagelseförmåga*) rapid, swift

kvida *kvidit* wail; (*klaga*) whine, whimper **kvidan** *r, best. form* =, wail[ing] *etc.* **kvidit** *sup. av kvida*

kvidd *s3* minnon

kvig|a *s1* heifer **-kalv** cow calf

kvillajabark [-ˣlajja-] soapbark, quillai bark

kvinn|a *s1* woman; *~ns frigörelse* the emancipation of women (woman) **-folk 1** *koll.* womankind; (*kvinnor*) women; *vard.* womenfolk **2** (*ett* ~) woman **-folksgöra** a woman's job

kvinnlig *al* **1** female (*kön* sex; *organ* organ); ~ *arbetskraft* female labour; ~ *idrott* women's athletics; ~ *läkare* woman doctor; ~ *polis* policewoman; *~a präster* women clergymen; ~ *rösträtt* woman suffrage, votes for women; *familjens ~a medlemmar* the feminine members of the family **2** (*som karakteriserar kvinnor*) womanly, feminine; (*om man*) womanish, effeminate; ~ *fägring* feminine beauty; *det evigt ~a* the eternal feminine; ~ *ungdom* young women (*pl*), girls (*pl*) **-het** womanliness, womanhood, femininity; (*veklighet*) effeminacy

kvinno|bröst female breast **-emancipation** emancipation of woman **-fråga[n]** [the] woman question **-fängelse** prison for women, women's prison **-förening** women's club (association, society) **-hatare** woman hater, misogynist **-hjärta** *~t* (*ett* ~) a woman's heart **-ideal** woman ideal, ideal of a woman **-klinik** gynaecological clinic **-kön** *~et* the female sex; (*-släktet*) womankind **-linje** *på* ~ on the distaff side **-läkare** gynaecologist **-rörelse** women's-rights (feminist) movement **-sakskvinna** [-sa:ks-] woman advocate of feminism; (*rösträtts-*) suffragette **-sjukdom** woman's disease **-tjusare** [-çu:-] ladykiller **-tycke** *ha* ~ be a lady's man, have a way with women **-överskott** excess (surplus) of women

kvinnsperson woman, female

kvint *s3* (*intervall*) fifth, quint **-essens** [-'sens *el.* -'saŋs] quintessence **-ett** *s3, mus.* quintet

kvintilera (*på fiol*) scrape; (*på flöjt*) tootle

kvissl|a *s1* pimple **-ig** *a1* pimply
kvist *s2* **1** twig, sprig; (*i sht avskuren*) spray; *på bar* ~ on a leafless (bare) twig; *komma på grön* ~ come into money **2** (*i trä*) knot, knag **1 kvista** (*avkapa*) lop the twigs off **2 kvista** *vard.*, ~ *in till stan* run into town
kvist|fri free from knots, clean **-hål** knothole **-ig** *a1* **1** twiggy, spriggy; (*om trä*) knotty, knaggy **2** (*brydsam*) awkward, puzzling; *en* ~ *fråga* a tricky question **-ning** pruning **-såg** pruning saw
kvitt *oböjligt a* **1** *bli* ~ *ngn* get rid of s.b. **2** ~ *eller dubbelt* double or nothing (quit[s]); *vara* ~ be quits **kvitta 1** offset, set off, countervail; settle **2** *det* ~*r mig lika* it is all one (makes no difference) to me
kvitten ['kvitt-] *r el. n, bot.* quince
kvittens *s3* receipt **-blankett** receipt form
kvitter ['kvitt-] *s7* chirp[ing], twitter
kvitt|era receipt; (*t.ex. belopp*) acknowledge; (*lämna kvitto på*) give a receipt for; (*återgälda*) repay; *sport.* equalize; ~*d räkning* receipted invoice; *betalt* ~*s* payment received, received with thanks **-ning** offset, setoff; *bokför.* settlement per contra
kvitto *s6* receipt (*på* for); (*spårvägs- e.d.*) ticket
kvittra chirp, twitter, chirrup
kvot *s3* (*vid division*) quotient; (*friare*) quota
kvoter|a allocate quotas **-ing** allocation of quotas
kväda *kvad kvädit* sing; (*dikta*) compose, write **kväde** *s6* lay, poem, song **kvädit** *sup. av kväda*
kväk|a *v3* croak **-ande** *a4* croaking
kväkare Quaker, member of the Society of Friends
kvälj|a *v2, det -er mig a*) absol. I feel sick, *b*) (*friare*) it makes me sick (to + *inf.*) **-ande** *a4* sickening, nauseating **-ning** *få* ~*ar a*) absol. be sick, *b*) (*av ngt*) be nauseated (*av* by)
kväll *s2* evening; (*motsats t. morgon*) night; *i* ~ this evening, tonight; *i morgon* ~ tomorrow evening (night); *på* ~*en* (~*arna*) in the evening (evenings)
kväll|as *dep, det* ~ the evening (night) is drawing (coming) on **-ningen** *i* ~ at nightfall, at eventide
kvälls|arbete evening (night) work **-bris** evening breeze **-gymnasium** *ung.* evening secondary school **-kurs** evening class (course), night school **-kvisten** *på* ~ towards evening **-mat** supper **-människa** night owl (hawk) **-nyheter** *pl* late news (*sg*) **-sömnig** *vara* ~ be sleepy in the evenings **-tidning** evening paper **-vard** [-a:-] *s3* supper, evening meal
kväsa *v3* take down, teach a thing or two; ~ *ngns högmod* humble s.b., take the wind out of s.b.'s sails; (*undertrycka*) suppress
kväv|a *v2* choke, stifle, suffocate (*äv. bildl.*); (*undertrycka o.d.*) quell, suppress; ~ *elden* smother the fire; ~ *i sin linda* (*bildl.*) nip in the bud; *han var nära att* ~*s* he was almost suffocated (*av* by); *...så att man var nära att* ~*s* ...to suffocation **-ande** *a4* choking (*känsla* sensation); (*om luft*) suffocating, stifling, *vard.* choky
kväve *s6* nitrogen **-gödsel** nitrogenous fertilizer **-haltig** *a1* nitrogenous **-oxid** nitric oxide
kvävgas nitrogen
kväv|matt *schack.* smothered mate **-ning** [-ä:-]

suffocation, choking; smothering; *bildl. äv.* quelling, suppression
kvävnings|anfall choking fit **-död** death by suffocation (asphyxiation)
kybernetik [k-] *s3* cybernetics (*pl, behandlas som sg*)
kyckling [ç-] chicken; (*nykläckt äv.*) chick **-kull** brood of chickens
kyff|e [ç-] *s6* hovel, hole **-ig** *a1* poky
1 kyl [ç-] *s2* (*lårstycke*) knuckle
2 kyl [ç-] *s2, se -rum, -skåp*
kyla [ç-] **I** *s1* cold [weather]; (*kylighet*) chilliness (*äv. bildl.*); *bildl.* coldness, coolness **II** *v2* chill, cool down (*äv. bildl.*); *tekn.* refrigerate; ~ *näsan* get one's nose frostbitten
kyl|aggregat refrigerating machine, refrigerator **-anläggning** refrigerating plant
kylar|e [ç-] cooler, chiller; (*på bil*) radiator **-grill** (*på bil*) [radiator] grille **-huv** (*på bil*) bonnet; *AE.* hood **-vätska** [motorcar] antifreeze
kyl|d [çy:-] *a5* (*förfrusen*) frostbitten **-disk** refrigerated display case **-fartyg** cold-storage ship **-hus** cold store **-ig** *a1* chilly, cold (*äv. bildl.*) **-knöl** chilblain
kyller ['kyll-] *s7* buff coat
kyl|medel cooling agent **-ning** cooling, chilling; *tekn.* refrigeration **-rum** cold-storage room **-skada** frostbite; (*kylknöl*) chilblain **-skåp** refrigerator; *vard.* fridge **-slagen** *a5* (*om dryck*) slightly warm, tepid; (*om luft*) chilly **-system** cooling system **-vatten** cooling water **-väska** cool bag (box)
kymig [k-, *äv.* ç-] *a1* nasty, mean
kymr|er ['kymm-] [the] Cymry (Kymry) **-isk** ['kymm-] *a5* Cymric, Kymric
kyndel ['çynn-] *s2, bot.* [summer] savory
kyndels|mässa [ç-] Candlemas **-mässodag** Candlemas [Day]
kyniker *se cyniker*
kynne [ç-] *s6* [natural] disposition; character, temperament
kypare [ˣçy:-] waiter
kypert ['çy:-] *s2* [cotton] twill, twilled cotton
kypra [ˣçy:-] twill
kyrass [k-] *s3* cuirass **-iär** *s3* cuirassier
kyrk|a [ç-] *s1* church; (*fri-*) chapel; *engelska* ~*n* the Church of England, the Anglican Church; *gå i* ~*n* go to (attend) church (chapel) **-backe** *på* ~*n* in the open space round the church **-bok** *se kyrkobok* **-bröllop** church wedding **-båt** church boat **-bänk** pew **-folk** churchgoers (*pl*) **-fönster** church window **-kaffe** after-church coffee **-klocka** church bell; (*tornur*) church clock
kyrklig [ç-] *a1* (*om fråga, konst, ändamål e.d.*) church; (*om t.ex. myndighet*) ecclesiastical; (*om t.ex. intressen*) churchly; (*prästerlig*) clerical; ~ *angelägenhet* ecclesiastical affair; ~ *begravning* Christian burial; ~*t intresserad* with church interests, interested in church affairs
kyrko|adjunkt curate **-besökare** churchgoer **-bok** parish register **-bokförd** ~ *i* registered in the parish of **-bokföring** parish registration **-byggnad** church building **-fader** Father of the Church; *-fäder* Fathers of the early Church, Apostolic Fathers **-fullmäktig** *ung.* vestryman, member of a select vestry **-fullmäktige** *ung.*

select vestry **-furste** prince of the Church **-gård** cemetery, burial ground; (*kring kyrka äv.*) churchyard **-handbok** service (prayer) book **-herde** *Engl. ung.* vicar; rector; parson; *kat.* parish priest; ~ *N.* (*titel*) Rev. (the reverend) **-herdeboställe** vicarage; rectory **-historia** church (ecclesiastical) history **-kör** church choir **-lag** canon law **-musik** church music **-möte** synod, council

kyrkorgel church organ

kyrko|råd parish council **-samfund** denomination **-skatt** church rate **-staten** the Papal States (*pl*), the States (*pl*) of the Church **-stämma** common vestry; (*sammanträde äv.*) parochial church meeting **-år** ecclesiastical year

kyrk|port church doorway (porch) **-rätta** church mouse **-sam** *al* regular in one's attendance at church; *vara* ~ (*äv.*) be a regular churchgoer **-silver** church plate **-socken** church parish **-torn** church tower, steeple **-tupp** church weathercock (vane) **-vaktmästare** sexton, verger **-värd** churchwarden **-ängel** cherub

kysk [ç-] *al* chaste; (*jungfrulig*) virgin; *leva ~t* lead a chaste life **-het** chastity; virginity

kyskhets|bälte girdle of virginity, virgin knot **-löfte** vow of chastity

kyss [ç-] *s2* kiss **kyssa** *v3* kiss **kyssas** *v3, dep* kiss [each other], exchange kisses **kyss|täck** kissable **-äkta** kiss-proof

kåd|a *s1* resin **-ig** *al* resinous

kåk *s2* ramshackle (tumble-down) house, shack; *skämts.* house; (*fängelse*) clink, jug **-farare** *vard.* jailbird **-stad** shanty-built (shackle) town

kål *s3* **1** *bot.* cabbage **2** *göra ~ på* make mincemeat; *ta ~ på* do for; *värmen kommer att ta ~ på mig* this heat will be the death of me **-dolma** [ˣkå:ldålma] *s5* stuffed cabbage roll **-fjäril** large white **-huvud** head of cabbage **-mask** caterpillar **-rabbi** *s3* kohlrabi, turnip cabbage **-rot** swede, Swedish turnip **-soppa** cabbage soup **-supare** *de är lika goda* ~ each is as bad as the other, they are tarred with the same brush

kånka ~ *på* struggle (toil) along with

kåpa *s1* **1** (*plagg*) gown, robe; (*munk-*) cowl; (*narr-*) [jester's] cloak; (*kor-*) cope **2** *tekn.* hood, cap, cover, mantle

kår *s3* (*sammanslutning*) body; (*förening*) union; *mil. o. dipl.* corps **-anda** esprit de corps **-chef** corps commander

kår|e *s2* **1** (*vind-*) breeze **2** *det går kalla -ar efter ryggen på mig* cold shivers go down my back

kårhus students' union building

kås|era discourse (*över* on), chat, talk (*över* about, [up]on); ~*nde föredrag* informal lecture **-eri** causerie, informal talk; (*tidnings-*) chatty (topical) article, column **-ör** writer of light (conversational) articles; (*tidnings- äv.*) columnist **-ös** (*soffa*) settee

kåt *al* randy, horny

kåta *s1* [coneshaped] hut, Laplander's tent

kåbbel [ˈçäbb-] *s7* bickering, squabble; wrangling **-la** [ˣçäbb-] bicker, squabble; wrangle; ~ *emot* answer back

käck [ç-] *al* dashing (*yngling* young man); (*oförfärad*) bold, intrepid; (*tapper*) brave, gallant, plucky, sporting; (*vågsam*) daring; (*hurtig*) spir-

ited; (*munter*) sprightly; *en ~ melodi* a sprightly tune; *det var ~t gjort av dig* it was a sporting thing of you to do, it was sporting of you; *med mössan ~t på sned* with one's cap cocked on one side **-het** dashingness *etc.*; dash; gallantry, intrepidity; daring spirit, pluck

käft [ç-] *s2* **1** jaws (*pl*); *tekn.* jaw; *dödens ~ar* the jaws of death; *ett slag på ~en* a blow on the chaps; *håll ~en!* shut up!; *vara slängd i ~en* have the gift of the gab, (*slagfärdig*) be quick at repartee; *vara stor i ~en* shoot off one's mouth **2** (*levande själ*) living soul **käfta** (*prata*) jaw; (*gräla*) wrangle; ~ *emot* answer back

kägel [ˈçä:g-] *s2, boktr.* body [size] **-bana** skittle (*särsk. AE.* ninepin) alley **-formig** [-å-] *al* conical, coneshaped **-spel** (*-spelande*) skittles, *särsk. AE.* ninepins (*pl, behandlas som sg*)

kägl|a [ˣçä:g-, ˣçägg-] *s1* **1** cone **2** (*i kägelspel*) skittle, ninepin; *slå* (*spela*) *-or* play skittles (*särsk. AE.* ninepins)

käk [ç-] *s7, vard.* grub, feed **käka** *vard.* grub, feed

käkben [ç-] jawbone; *fack.* mandible

käk|e [ç-] *s2* jaw; *fack.* mandible **-håla** maxillary sinus (antrum) **-led** maxillary joint

kälkbacke toboggan run

kälkborgare [ç-] Philistine

kälkborgerlig [ç-] Philistine **-het** Philistinism, narrow-mindedness

kälk|e [ç-] *s2* sledge; *sport. vanl.* toboggan; *åka ~* sledge, toboggan **-åkning** tobogganing

källa [ç-] *s1* spring; well, (*flods äv.*) source (*äv. bildl.*) (*till* of); *från* (*ur*) *säker ~* from a reliable source, on good authority

källar|e [ç-] **1** cellar; (*-våning*) basement **2** *se krog* **-glugg** cellar air hole **-mästare** restaurant keeper, restaurateur **-trappa** cellar stairs (*etc.*) **-valv** cellar vault **-våning** basement

käll|beskattning taxation at [the] source; pay-as-you-earn system **-flod** river source **-flöde** source-tributary **-forskning** study of original sources (manuscripts) **-förteckning** list of references, bibliography **-hänvisning** reference to sources **-kritik** criticism of the sources **-sjö** springlake; (*som källa t. flod*) source-lake **-skatt** tax at [the] source, pay-as-you-earn (P.A.Y.E.) tax **-skrift** original text, source **-språng** fountain **-vatten** spring water **-åder** vein of water

kält [ç-] *s7* nagging **kälta** nag

kämpa [ç-] (*strida*) contend, struggle (*om* for); (*slåss*) fight (*om* for); ~ *med svårigheter* contend with difficulties; ~ *mot fattigdomen* struggle against poverty; ~ *mot vinden* battle against the wind; ~ *sig fram* fight one's way (struggle) along (*till* to); ~ *sig igenom en sjukdom* (*äv.*) pull through [from] an illness **-hög** giant-size **-lek** tournament-game **-tag** gigantic effort **-visa** ballad of heroes (a hero)

kämpe [ç-] *s2* fighter; (*stridande*) combatant; (*krigare*) warrior; (*för-*) champion (*för* of)

kän|d [ç-] *a* **1** (*bekant*) known; (*väl-*) well-known; (*som man är förtrogen med*) familiar; (*ryktbar*) famous, noted; *ett ~t ansikte* a well-known (familiar) face; *en ~ sak* a well-known fact, a fact familiar to all, common knowledge; *det är allmänt -t att* it is generally known (*neds.* notorious, a no-

K

torious fact) that; *vara ~ för att vara* be known as being; *~ för prima varor* (*hand.*) noted for first--quality goods; *vara ~ under namnet* go by the name of; *vara illa ~* be of bad (evil) repute, have a bad reputation; *~a och okända* the well-known and the anonymous **2** (*förnummen*) felt; *frambära ett djupt -t tack* proffer one's heartfelt thanks **kändis** ['çänn-] *s2, vard.* celebrity; (*manlig*) lion **käng|a** [ç-] *s1* boot **-snöre** bootlace **känguru** ['çäng-, 'k-] *s5* kangaroo **känn** [ç-] *s, i uttr.: på ~* by instinct; *ha på ~ att* have a feeling (an inkling) that **1 känna** [ç-]*s, i uttr.: ge till ~, se tillkännage; ge sig till ~* make o.s. known (*för* to); (*om ngt*) manifest itself **2 känn|a** [ç-] *v2* I **1** (*förnimma*) feel; (*erfara*) experience [feelings (a feeling) of]; (*märka*) notice (*smak av* a taste of); (*pröva, smaka*) try [and see] ; *~ besvikelse* (*trötthet*) feel disappointed (tired); *~ för ngn* feel for (sympathize with) s.b. **2** (*beröra med handen*) feel **3** (*~ till*) know; *känn dig själv!* know thyself!; *på sig själv -er man andra* one judges others by o.s.; *lära ~ ngn* get to know s.b., get acquainted with s.b.; *lära ~ varandra* (*äv.*) become acquainted [with each other]; *om jag -er dig rätt* if I know you at all II (*med betonad partikel*) **1** *~ av* feel; *få ~ av* be made to feel **2** *~ efter* feel; *~ efter om dörren är låst* [try the handle to] see whether the door is locked **3** *~ igen* know (*ngn på rösten* s.b. by his voice), (*ngn el. ngt man sett förr*) recognize; *~ igen sig* know one's way about (where one is) **4** *få ~ på* have to experience, come in for; *~ på sig* have a feeling, feel instinctively (in one's bones) **5** *~ till* know, be acquainted with, (*veta av, äv.*) know of, (*vara hemma i, äv.*) be up in III *rfl* feel; *~ sig för* feel one's way [about], (*sondera äv.*) sound **kännande** [ç-] *a4* feeling; sentient (*varelse* being) **kännar|e** [ç-] connoisseur; (*sakkunnig*) expert, authority (*av, på* on, in) **-min** *med ~* with the air of a connoisseur (*etc.*) **känn|as** [ç-] *v2, dep* feel; be felt; *hur -s det?* how do you feel?, what does it feel like (*att* to)?; *det -s lugnande att veta* it is a relief to know; *det -s angenämt att* (*äv.*) it is a pleasant feeling to; *~ vid* (*tillstå*) confess, acknowledge, (*erkänna som sin tillhörighet*) acknowledge; *inte vilja ~ vid* refuse to acknowledge, disown **-bar** *a1* to be felt (*för* by); (*förnimbar*) perceptible, noticeable (*för* to); (*svår*) severe, serious (*för* for); *en ~ förlust* a heavy (severe) loss; *ett ~t straff* a punishment that hurts **kännedom** [ç-] *s2* (*vetskap*) knowledge, cognizance (*om* of); (*underrättelse*) information (*om* about, as to); (*kunskap*) knowledge; (*bekantskap*) acquaintance, familiarity (*om* with); *bringa till ngns ~* bring to a p.'s notice (attention); *få ~ om* receive information (be informed) about, get to know; *ha ~ om* be aware (cognizant) of; *för* [*er*] *~* for [your] information; *till allmänhetens ~ meddelas* for the information of the public, notice is given **-märke, -tecken 1** *konkr.* [distinctive] mark, token, sign **2** (*egenskap*) characteristic, distinctive feature, criterion (*på* of) **-teckna** characterize; be a characteristic of; (*särskilja*) distinguish **-tecknande** *a4* characteristic (*för*

of); distinguishing, distinctive **känning** [ç-] **1** (*förnimmelse*) feeling, sensation; *ha ~ av sin reumatism* be troubled by one's rheumatism **2** (*kontakt*) touch; *få ~ med fienden* get in touch with the enemy; *ha ~ av land* (*sjö.*) be within sight of land **känsel** ['çänn-] *s9* feeling; perception of touch **-nerv** sensory nerve **-organ** tactile organ **-sinne** (*för tryck*) sense of touch, tactile sense; (*för smärta, köld, värme*) sense of feeling **-spröt** feeler, palp **känsl|a** [ç-] *s1* feeling (*för* ngt for s.th.; *för* ngn towards s.b.); (*kroppslig förnimmelse*) sensation (*av* köld of cold); (*sinne, intryck, uppfattning*) sense (*för* of), sentiment (*av* tacksamhet of gratitude); (*i hjärtat*) emotion; (*med-*) sympathy; *mänskliga -or* human feelings (sentiments); *hysa varma -or för* feel affection for, be fond of; *i ~n av feeling* (*att* that) **-ig** *al* **1** sensitive (*för* to), (*för drag, smitta, smärta o.d.*) susceptible (*för* to); (*om kroppsdel o. äv. om pers.*) sensible (*för* to) **2** (*-ofull*) feeling; sympathetic; (*rörande*) feeling, moving; (*ömtålig*) delicate; (*lättretlig*) touchy; *~ för kritik* sensitive to (touchy as regards) criticism **-ighet** sensitivity, sensitiveness; susceptibility; sensibility; delicacy; touchiness **känslo|betonad** *a5* emotionally tinged (coloured) **-full** full of feeling, emotional; *se äv.* känslosam **-kall** frigid **-kyla** frigidity **-laddad** *~ stämning* explosive atmosphere **-liv** emotional life; *~et* (*äv.*) the sentient life **-läge** affect **-lös** (*kroppsligt*) insensitive, insensible, numb (*för* to); (*själsligt*) unfeeling (*för* ngn towards s.b.), unemotional, callous; (*likgiltig*) indifferent (*för* to); (*apatisk*) apathetic **-löshet** insensitiveness *etc.*; insensibility; indifference **-människa** man (*etc.*) of feeling (sentiment); emotionalist **-mässig** *al* emotional **-sak** matter of sentiment **-sam** *al* sentimental; emotional; (*överdrivet*) mawkish **-samhet** sentimentality; (*överdriven*) emotionality **-skäl** sentimental reason **-tänkande** *a4 o. s6* emotional thinking **-utbrott** outburst of feeling **käpp** [ç-] *s2* stick; (*rotting*) cane; *få smaka ~en* be given a taste of the stick (cane); *sätta en ~ i hjulet för ngn* (*bildl.*) put a spoke in a p.'s wheel **-häst** hobbyhorse (*äv. bildl.*); cockhorse **-rak** bolt upright **-rapp** blow with a stick (cane) **kär** [ç-] *al* **1** (*förälskad*) in love (*i* with); *bli ~* fall in love; *få ngn ~* become attached to (fond of) s.b.; *hålla ngn ~* hold s.b. dear **2** (*avhållen*) dear (*för* to); (*älskad*) beloved (*för* by); *en ~ gäst* a cherished (welcome) guest; *en ~ plikt* a privilege; *~a barn!* my dear[s]!, my dear child (children)!; *K~e vän!* (*i brev*) Dear (My dear) Bill (*etc.*)!; *mina ~a* my dear ones, those dear to me; *i ~t minne* in fond (cherished) remembrance; *om livet är dig ~t* if you value your life; *~t barn har många namn* we find many names for s.o. we love **kärande** [ç-] *s9* plaintiff; suer **käresta** [ç-] *s1* sweetheart; (*ngns*) darling, beloved **käring** ['çä:-, 'çärr-] old woman; *hon är en riktig ~* she is a real shrew **-aktig** *al* old womanish **-knut** granny, granny['s] knot **-tand** *bot.* birds-foot-trefoil

kärkommen *a3* welcome
kärl [çä:-] *s7* vessel; (*förvarings-*) receptacle, container; *biol.* vessel, duct
kärlek [ˣçä:r-] *s2* love (*till ngn* for s.b.; *till ngt* for *el.* of s.th.); (*kristlig äv.*) charity; (*tillgivenhet*) affection (*till* for); (*hängivenhet*) devotion (*till* to); (*passion*) passion (*till* for); *av ~ till* out of love for; *den stora ~en* the great passion; *dö av olycklig ~* die of a broken heart; *förklara ngn sin ~* make s.b. a declaration of love; *gammal ~ rostar inte* love does not tarnish with age; *gifta sig av ~* marry for love
kärleks|affär love affair **-brev** love letter **-dikt** love poem **-dryck** love potion **-full** loving, affectionate; (*öm*) tender **-förbindelse** love affair **-förklaring** declaration (confession) of love **-gud** god of love **-gudinna** goddess of love **-historia 1** (*-berättelse*) love story **2** (*-affär*) love affair **-krank** lovesick **-kval** *pl* pangs of love **-liv** love life **-lyrik** love poetry **-lös 1** (*hårdhjärtad*) uncharitable **2** (*fattig på kärlek*) loveless **-löshet** lack of love **-roman** love story, romance **-scen** love scene **-sorg** disappointment in love, a broken heart
kärl|förändring vascular change **-kramp** vascular spasm **-sammandragande** *a4, ~ medel* vasoconstrictor **-vidgande** *a4, ~ medel* vasodilator
1 kärna [ˣçä:r-] **I** *s1* (*smör-*) churn **II** *v1* churn
2 kärna [ˣçä:r-] **I** *s1.* **1** (*i frukt*) pip; (*i bär, druva, melon o.d.*) seed; (*i stenfrukt*) stone; *AE. äv.* pit; (*i nöt*) kernel **2** (*i säd*) grain **3** (*i låga*) core, body; (*jordens*) kernel; *fys. o. naturv.* nucleus (*pl äv.* nuclei); *tekn.* core; (*i träd*) heartwood **4** *bildl.* kernel, nucleus; (*det viktigaste*) core, heart, essence **II** *v1, ~ ur* seed, stone, core; *AE. äv.* pit
kärn|avfall nuclear waste **-bränsle** nuclear fuel **-energi** nuclear energy **-energianläggning** nuclear power plant **-familj** nuclear family **-forskning** nuclear research **-fri** pipless, seedless, stoneless **-frisk** sound to the core **-frukt** pome **-full** *bildl.* vigorous; (*kraftfull*) racy, pithy **-fysik** *fys.* nuclear physics **-fysiker** nuclear physicist **-hus** core **-ig** *a1* full of pips (*etc.*); stony, seedy **-kemi** nuclear chemistry **-klyvning** nuclear fission **-kraft** nuclear power **-kraftinspektion** *Statens ~* the [Swedish] nuclear-power inspectorate **-kraftverk** nuclear power station **-kraftvärmeverk** nuclear power station for production of heat and electricity **-laddning** nuclear charge **-minne** *data.* core store, memory
kärnmjölk buttermilk
kärn|partikel nuclear particle **-punkt** *~en i* the principal point (the gist) of **-reaktion** nuclear reaction **-reaktor** nucler reactor **-skugga** true shadow; umbra (*pl* umbrae) (*äv. astr.*) **-sönderfall** nuclear disintegration **-trupp** picked troops **-vapen** nuclear weapon **-vapenfri** nuclear-free **-vapenförbud** ban on nuclear weapons, nuclear ban **-vapenkrig** nuclear war[fare] **-vapenprov** nuclear test **-ved, -virke** heartwood **-värmeverk** nuclear power station for production of heat
käromål [ç-] plaintiff's case
kärr [ç-] *s7* marsh; (*sumpmark*) swamp

kärra [ç-] *s1* cart; (*drag-, skott-*) barrow
kärr|hök *brun ~* marsh harrier; *blå ~* hen harrier **-mes** marsh tit
kärv [ç-] *a1* harsh (*i smaken* in (to the) taste; *för känseln* to the feel); (*om ljud äv.*) strident, rasping; (*bitande, äv. bildl.*) acrid, pungent (*humor* humour); (*om natur*) austere; (*om pers. o. språk*) harsh, rugged
1 kärva [ç-] *v1* (*om motor o.d.*) seize, jam; *det ~r till sig* it's getting tougher
2 kärva [ç-] *v1* sheaf, sheave
kärve [ç-] *s2* sheaf (*pl* sheaves)
kärvhet harshness *etc.*; acridity, pungency; austerity
kärvänlig [-'vänn-, *äv.* ˣçä:r-] fond, affectionate
kättar|bål [ç-] heretic's pile, stake **-domstol** court of inquisition
kättare [ç-] heretic
kätte [ç-] *s2* pen, [loose] box
kätteri [ç-] heresy **kättersk** ['ätt-] *a5* heretical
kätting [ç-] chain[-cable]
kättja [ç-] *s1* lust[fulness] **kättjefull** lustful, lecherous
1 käx [k-, ç-] *s7, s9, se kex*
2 käx [ç-] *s7, se tarmkäx*
3 käx [ç-] *s7* persistent asking, nagging
käxa [ç-] nag; *~ sig till ngt* get s.th. by nagging for it
1 kö [k-] *s3* (*biljard-*) cue
2 kö [k-] *s3* queue; *AE.* line-up (*av bilar o.d. äv.*) line, file, string; *mil. o. sport.* rear; *bilda ~* form a queue; *stå bakom ngn i ~n* stand behind s.b. in the queue; *ställa sig i ~* queue up, take one's place in the queue, *AE.* line up
kö|a queue [up], *AE.* line up **-bildning** queuing-up; *om det blir ~* if there is a queue **-bricka** [queue] ticket
kök [ç-] *s7* kitchen; (*kokkonst*) cuisine; (*kokapparat*) stove; *ett rum och ~* one room and kitchen; *med tillgång till ~* with kitchen facilities **köksa** *s1* cook, kitchen-maid
köks|avfall kitchen-refuse, garbage **-bord** kitchen-table **-dörr** kitchen (back) door **-fläkt** kitchen fan **-handduk** tea towel (cloth), *AE.* dishtowel **-ingång** back door **-inredning** kitchen fittings **-latin** dog Latin **-maskin** kitchen machine **-mästare** chef, chief cook **-personal** kitchen staff **-redskap** kitchen utensils (*pl*) **-regionerna** *pl* the kitchen quarters **-rulle** kitchen roll **-spis** kitchen range; (*elektr. el. gas-*) cooker, stove **-trappa** kitchen stairs (*pl*), backstairs (*pl*) **-trädgård** kitchen (vegetable) garden **-vägen** *gå ~* go through (by way of) the kitchen **-växt** vegetable; potherb
köl [ç-] *s2* **1** keel; *sträcka ~en till ett fartyg* lay [down] the keel of a vessel; *ligga med ~en i vädret* be bottom up; *på rätt ~* (*bildl.*) straight on the right track (tack)
kölapp *se köbricka*
köld [ç-] *s3* **1** cold; cold weather; *sträng ~* a severe (keen) frost; *darra av ~* shiver with cold **2** (*kallsinnighet*) coldness; (*starkare*) frigidity **-blandning** freezing mixture **-grad** degree of frost **-härdig** winter-hardy (*växt* plant) **-knäpp** cold spell **-period** cold period **-rysning** chill
köl|fena fin of a (the) keel **-hala** careen, heave

K

down; (som straff) keelhaul **-halning** [-a:-] careening; (straff) keelhauling
Köln n Cologne
köl|sträckning laying of keel **-svin** keelson, kelson **-vatten** wake (äv. bildl.), wash, track
kön [ç-] s7 sex; av manligt ~ of the male sex **-lig** [-ö:-] a1 sexual **-lös** sexless; asexual (fortplantning reproduction)
köns|akt sexual act; coitus **-cell** sex cell, gamete **-delar** pl sexual organs, genitals **-diskriminering** discrimination on the basis of sex, sexism **-drift** sex instinct, sexual desire **-hormon** sex hormone **-kromosom** sex chromosome **-kvotering** quota allocation by sex **-körtel** gonad **-liv** sex[ual] life **-mogen** sexually mature **-mognad** sexual maturity **-organ** sexual organ **-roll** sexual role **-rollsdebatt** debate on the role of the sexes **-sjukdom** venereal disease **-umgänge** sexual intercourse, sex
könummer number in queue
köp [ç-] s7 purchase; (fördelaktigt) bargain, deal; avsluta ett ~ make a purchase; ett gott ~ a bargain; ~ i fast räkning outright purchase; på ~et into the bargain; på öppet ~ on a sale-or-return basis, with the option of returning the goods; till på ~et what's more, to boot, in addition, … at that
köp|a [ç-] v3 buy, purchase (av from); ~ billigt buy cheap[ly]; ~ kontant buy for cash; ~ kakor för ett pund buy a pound's worth of cakes; ~ in (upp) buy up; ~ upp sina pengar spend all one's money [in buying things]; ~ ut en delägare buy out a partner **-are** buyer, purchaser **-centrum** shopping centre
köpe|avtal contract of sale (purchase) **-brev** bill of sale; purchase deed **-kontrakt** se -avtal
Köpenhamn [ç-] n Copenhagen
köpenickiad [k-] s3 hoax
köpenskap [ç-] s3 trade, trading; idka ~ do business
köpeskilling [ç-] purchase-price
köping [ç-] urban district, market town; hist. borough
köp|kort credit card **-kraft** purchasing power **-kraftig** with great purchasing power, able to buy **-kurs** bid (buying) price; (för valutor) buying-rate **-man** merchant, dealer, businessman; (handlande) tradesman; (grosshandlare) wholesaler **-mannaförbund** merchants' (tradesmen's) association (union) **-motstånd** buyers' (consumers') resistance **-rush** buying rush **-slagan** r bargaining **-slå** bargain (om for); (kompromissa) compromise **-stark** with great purchasing power, with [plenty of] money to spend **-tvång** obligation to buy
1 kör [k-] s3, pers. choir; (sång) chorus (äv. bildl.); i ~ in chorus; en ~ av ogillande röster a chorus of disapproval
2 kör [ç-] i uttr.: i ett ~ unceasingly, without stopping, (stått på varandra) in a stream
kör|a [ç-] v2 **I 1** drive (bil a car; en häst a horse; ngn t. stationen s.b. to the station); (föra i sin bil e.d.) take (run) [in one's car etc.]; (åka) ride, go, (i bil äv.) motor; (motorcykel) ride; (transportera) convey, carry, take; (skjuta) push; (motor e.d.) run (med bensin on petrol); kör sakta! slow

down!, dead slow!, AE. drive slow! **2** (stöta, sticka) thrust (ngt i s.th. into); run (fingrarna genom håret one's fingers through one's hair); (film) reel, run **3** ~ med ngn worry s.b.; ~ med ngt keep on about s.th. **4** kör för det! right you are!, yes let's!; kör till (i vind)! agreed!, a bargain!, done! **5** (kuggas) fail, be ploughed **II** (med betonad partikel) **1** ~ bort drive away, (avskeda) dismiss, turn out, send packing **2** ~ emot (kollidera med) run into **3** ~ fast get stuck, (om förhandlingar o.d.) come to a deadlock **4** ~ ifatt catch up **5** ~ ihjäl ngn run over s.b. and kill him; ~ ihjäl sig be killed in a driving (car etc.) accident **6** det har -t ihop sig för mig things are getting on top of me **7** ~ in a) (hö e.d.) cart (bring) in, b) (tid) save on the schedule, make up for, c) (en ny bil) run in **8** ~ om overtake (en bil a car) **9** ~ omkull have a driving accident, have a fall [from one's bicycle] **10** ~ på a) (vidare) drive on, b) se ~ emot **11** ~ sönder drive into and smash it, (vagn e.d.) have a smash-up, (väg) damage badly by driving on it **12** ~ upp (för körkort) take one's driving test; ~ upp ngn ur sängen rout s.b. out of bed **13** ~ ut ngn turn s.b. out of the room (etc.) **14** ~ över a) (bro e.d.) cross, drive across
kör|bana roadway, carriageway **-bar** a1 (trafikduglig) roadworthy **-fil** [traffic] lane **-förbud** driving ban
körig [ç-] a1, vard. hectic
kör|karl driver **-kort** driving (driver's) licence **-kortsprov** driving test **-kunnig** able to drive
körledare choirmaster
kör|lektion driving lesson **-ning** [ˣçö:r-] driving etc.; (av varor) haulage; en ~ a drive, (taxi-) a fare **-riktning** direction of travel; förbjuden ~ no thoroughfare **-riktningsvisare** [direction] indicator
körsbär [ç-] cherry
körsbärs|brännvin kirsch[wasser] **-likör** cherry brandy **-träd** cherry
körskola driving school, school of motoring
körsnär [ç-] s3 furrier
körsven [ˣçö:r-] driver
körsång choir-singing; (komposition) chorus
körteknik [ˣçö:r-] driving technique
körtel [ç-] s2 gland **-vävnad** glandular tissue
körtid driving (running) time
körvel [ç-] s2, bot. sweet cicely
körväg roadway, carriageway; (i park e.d.) drive; (rutt) route
kösamhälle society with many queues [for housing, services etc.]
kött [ç-] s7 **1** flesh; (som födoämne) meat; (frukt-) flesh, pulp **2** mitt eget ~ och blod my own flesh and blood **-affär** butcher's [shop] **-ben** meaty bone **-bulle** [force]meat ball **-extrakt** meat extract, essence of meat **-färs** minced meat, ground beef; AE. ground meat; ~ i ugn meat loaf **-ig** a1 fleshy; (om frukt) pulpy, pulpous; ~a blad fleshy leaves **-konserv** tinned (canned) meat **-kvarn** meat-mincer; (större) minching-machine **-rätt** meat course (dish) **-saft** meat juice, gravy **-skiva** slice of meat **-sky** gravy meat **-slamsa** scrap of flesh (meat)
köttslig [ç-] a1 **1** min ~e bror my own brother, my brother-german **2** (sinnlig) fleshy

kött|soppa meat broth, beef soup **-spad** stock **-stuvning** stew, ragout **-sår** flesh wound **-varor** meat products **-yxa** butcher's axe, meat-chopper **-ätande** a4 o. s6 flesh-eating, carnivorous **-ätare** pers. vanl. meat-eater; (djur) flesh-eater, carnivore

L

la [la:] vard., imperf. av lägga
1 labb s2, vard. paw
2 labb s2, zool. skua
3 labb vard. lab[oratory]
laber ['la:-] a2, sjö. light
labial al o. s3 labial **-isering** [-'se:-] labialization **-pipa** mus. flue [pipe]
labil al unstable **-itet** instability
labor|ation laboratory experiment (work) **-atjv** al laboratory, experimental **-ator** [-ˣa:tår] s3, univ. reader; Am. associate professor
laboratorie|assistent laboratory assistant; medical technician **-försök** se laboration
labor|atorium [-'tɔ:-] s4 laboratory **-era 1** do laboratory work **2** (friare) ~ med work with; ~ med färg play about with colours
labyrint s3 labyrinth (äv. bildl.); maze **-isk** a5 labyrinthine
lack s7, s3 **1** (sigill-) sealing wax **2** (fernissa) varnish, lacquer; (färg) enamel
1 lacka svetten ~r av honom he is dripping with sweat
2 lacka (försegla) seal [with sealing wax]; ~ igen seal up
3 lacka (framskrida) approach [slowly]; det ~r mot jul Christmas is approaching
lack|arbete lacquer work **-era** lacquer, japan; (fernissa) varnish; (måla) enamel **-ering** [-'ke:-] lacquering, japanning; varnishing; (bils etc. äv.) paint **-färg** enamel [paint]; syntetisk ~ synthetic paint (enamel)
lackmus ['lakk-] s2 litmus **-papper** litmus paper
lacknafta ligroin
lack|röd vermilion **-skinn** patent leather **-sko** patent-leather shoe **-stång** stick of sealing wax **-viol** wallflower, gillyflower
lada sl barn
ladd|a load; elektr. o. bildl. charge; ~ om reload, recharge; ~ en kamera load a camera; vara ~d med energi (om pers. äv.) be a live wire; en ~d roman a novel packed with action; ~ ur discharge; ~ ur sig (om batteri) run down, bildl. get out of one's system, relieve o.s. **-ning 1** abstr. loading, charging **2** konkr. load, charge
lade [vard. la:] imperf. av lägga

ladugård ['la:gård, äv. 'lagg-] cowhouse, cow-shed; AE. äv. barn
ladugårds|förman farm foreman **-karl** cowman **-piga** dairymaid
ladusvala common (barn) swallow
lafs|a slop, shuffle **-ig** al slack, sloppy
1 lag s2 (avkok) decoction; (lösning) solution; (spad) liquor; (socker-) syrup
2 lag s7 **1** (lager) layer **2** (sällskap) company; (krets) set; (arbets-) gang, team; sport. team; i glada vänners ~ in convivial company; gå ~et runt go the round; låta gå ~et runt pass round; ge sig i ~ med ngn begin to associate with s.b.; ha ett ord med i ~et have a voice in the matter; över ~ a) (över hela linjen) all along the line, b) (över huvud taget) in general; komma ur ~ get out of order **3** göra ngn till ~s please (suit, satisfy) s.b. **4** i hetaste ~et too hot for comfort; i minsta ~et a bit on the small side; i senaste ~et at the last moment, only just in time; vid det här ~et by now, by this time, at this stage
3 lag s2 law; (av statsmakterna antagen) act; ~ar och förordningar (ung.) rules and regulations; ~ och rätt law and justice; likhet inför ~en equality before the law; ta ~en i egna händer take the law into one's own hands; upphäva en ~ repeal an act; läsa ~en för (bildl.) lay down the law to, lecture; enligt ~ by (according to) law; i ~ förbjuden prohibited by law; i ~ens hägn under the protection of the law; i ~ens namn in the name of the law
1 laga v1 **1** (till-) prepare (middagen the dinner); make; AE. äv. fix; ~ mat cook; ~ maten do the cooking; ~ god mat be an excellent cook; ~ sin mat själv do one's own cooking; ~d mat cooked food **2** (reparera) mend, fix, repair **3** (ombesörja) ~ [så] att arrange (manage) things so that, see to it that; ~ att du kommer i tid make sure you are (take care to be) there in time **4** ~ sig i ordning get [o.s.] ready (till for); ~ sig i väg get going (started); ~ dig härifrån! be off with you!
2 laga oböjl. a legal; ~ förfall lawful absence, valid excuse; vinna ~ kraft gain legal force, become legal; i ~ ordning according to the regulations prescribed by law; i ~ tid within the time prescribed [by law]; vid ~ ansvar under penalty of law
lagakraftvunnen a5 having gained (acquired) legal force
lag|anda team spirit **-arbete** teamwork
lag|beredning (delegation) law-drafting committee **-bestämmelse** legal provision **-bok** statute book, code of laws **-brott** breach (infringement, violation) of the law, offence **-brytare** lawbreaker, offender **-bunden** a5 regulated by law; (som följer vissa -ar) conformable to law **-bundenhet** conformity to law
lagd a5, vara ~ för språk have a bent for languages; romantiskt ~ romantically inclined
lagenlig [-e:-] al by (according to) law, statutory
1 lager ['la:-] s2, bot. [bay] laurel, bay; skörda -rar win laurels; vila på sina -rar rest on one's laurels
2 lager ['la:-] s7 **1** (förråd) stock, AE. inventory; (rum) store (storage) room; (magasin) ware-

L

house; *från* ~ ex stock; *förnya sitt* ~ replenish one's stock, restock; *ha på* ~ have in stock, stock, *AE. äv.* carry; *lägga på* ~ lay (put) in stock; *lägga upp ett* ~ lay in (set up) a stock **2** (*varv*) layer; *geol. äv.* stratum (*pl* strata), bed; (*avlagring*) deposit; (*färg-*) coat; *bildl.* stratum; *de breda lagren* the masses, the populace **3** *tekn.* bearing
lager|arbetare storeman **-behållning** stocks [on hand] (*pl*)
lagerblad bay leaf
lager|bokföring stock (inventory) accounting **-byggnad** storehouse, warehouse
lager|bär bay berry **-bärsblad** bay leaf
lager|chef warehouse (stores) manager **-hylla** storage rack, storing shelf **-hållning** stockkeeping **-inventering** stocktaking **-katalog** catalogue of goods stocked; (*för bokhandel*) publisher's list
lager|krans laurel wreath; *vinna ~en* win the laurel wreath **-kransa** crown with laurel (*univ.* the laurel wreath)
lager|lokal storeroom, warehouse **-minskning** stock (inventory) reduction **-utrymme** storage space
lageröl lager beer
lag|fara have legally registered (ratified) **-faren** *a5* (*om pers.*) knowledgeable in legal matters **-fart** entry into the land register, legal confirmation of one's title; *ansöka om* ~ apply for the registration of one's title to a property; *det hindrar inte ~en!* (*vard.*) that needn't stand in the way! **-fartsbevis** certificate of registration of title **-föra** sue, proceed against **-förslag** [proposed] bill; draft [law]; *framlägga ett* ~ present a bill
lagg ⚬ ⚬(*panna*) [flat] frying pan, griddle; *en* ~ *våfflor* a round of waffles **-kärl** barrel, cask
lag|kapp *s3, sport.* relay **-kapten** *sport.* captain of a (the) team
lagklok versed in the law; *en* ~ (*bibl.*) a lawyer
lagledare *sport.* manager of a team
lag|lig [ˣlaːg-] *al* lawful; (*rättmätig*) legitimate, rightful; (*-enlig*) legal; *~t betalningsmedel* legal tender, *AE.* lawful money; ~ *ägare* rightful (legal, lawful) owner; *på* ~ *väg* by legal means **-ligen** legally; lawfully; ~ *beivra* bring an action against, take legal steps against; ~ *skyddad* protected by law **-lighet** lawfulness; legitimacy; legality **-lott** lawful (legitimate) portion (share) **-lydig** law-abiding **-lydnad** obedience to the law **-lös** lawless **-löshet** lawlessness **-man** chief judge (*vid tingsrätt* of a district court, *vid länsrätt* of a county administrative court)
lagning [-aː-] repairing, mending, fixing
lagom [-åm] **I** *adv* just right (enough); (*tillräckligt*) sufficiently; (*med måtta*) moderately, in moderation; *precis* ~ exactly right (enough); ~ *stor* just large enough; *i* ~ *stora bitar* in suitably-sized pieces; *en* ~ *lång promenad* a walk of suitable length; *skryt* ~*!* stop blowing your own trumpet!; *det var så* ~ *roligt!* it was anything but fun! **II** *oböjl. a* just right; (*nog*) enough; (*tillräcklig*) sufficient, adequate; (*passande*) fitting, appropriate, suitable; *på* ~ *avstånd* at the (an) appropriate distance; *blir det här* ~*?* will this be enough (about right)?; ~ *är bäst* there is virtue in

moderation, gently does it; *det var* ~ *åt dig!* that served you right!
lagparagraf section (paragraph) of a law, enactment
lagr|a [ˣlaːg-] **1** *geol.* stratify; dispose in layers (strata) (*äv. bildl.*) **2** (*lägga på lager*) store (*äv. data.*), stock; (*spara*) put by , hoard; (*vin*) lay down **-ad** *a5* (*om ost*) ripe; (*om sprit o.d.*) matured; (*om virke*) seasoned **-ing 1** stratifying *etc.*; stratification **2** storing, storage; (*för kvalitetsförbättring*) seasoning, maturing
lag|rum *se lagparagraf* **-råd** council on legislation **-samling** body of laws, code **-språk** *på* ~ in legal language **-stadgad** *a5* statutory, laid down (prescribed) by law **-stifta** make laws (a law), legislate; ~*nde församling* legislative body, legislature; ~*nde makt* legislative power **-stiftare** legislator, lawmaker **-stiftning** *konkr.* legislation **-stridig** *al* contrary to (at a variance with) [the] law; (*olaglig*) illegal **-söka** sue, proceed against **-sökning** [legal] action (proceedings *pl*)
lagt [lakkt] *sup. av lägga*
lagtima *oböjligt a* held in the ordinary course; ~ *riksdag* ordinary parliamentary session
lagtävling *sport.* team competition
lagun *s3* lagoon
lag|utskott ~*et* [the Swedish parliamentary] standing committee on civil-law legislation **-vigd** *a5* lawfully wedded; *min* ~*a* (*vard.*) my better half **-vrängare** perverter of the law; (*neds. om advokat*) pettifogger
lagård [ˈlaː-] *se ladugård*
lag|ändring revision (amendment) of the law **-överträdelse** transgression of the law, misdemeanour; offence
laka ~ *ur* soak
lakan *s7* sheet **lakansväv** sheeting
1 lake *s2* (*salt-*) brine, pickle
2 lake *s2, zool.* burbot
lakej [-ˈkejj] *s3* [liveried] footman; lackey (*äv bildl.*); (*föraktligt*) flunk[e]y; (*ngns lydige tjänare*) henchman **-själ** servile soul
lakon|isk [-ˈkoː-] *a5* laconic **-ism** laconicism
lakrits [ˈlaː-, ˈlakk-, -ri(t)s] *s3* liquorice **-pastill** *BE. ung.* pomfret-cake, Pontefract cake **-rot** *bot.* liquorice root
lakt|at *s4, kem.* lactate **-os** [-ˈåːs] *s3, kem.* lactose
laktuk [ˈlakk, -ˈuːk] *s3, bot.* lettuce
lakun *s3* lacuna (*pl* lacunae); (*friare*) gap, pause
lalla babble; mumble
lam *al* **1** (*förlamad*) paralysed **2** *bildl.* lame, feeble
1 lama *s1, zool.* llama (*äv. tygsort*)
2 lama *s1* el. **-n** *-er* (*munk*) lama
lama|ism lamaism **-kloster** lama monastery
lam|ell *s3, naturv. o. biol.* lamella (*pl* lamellae); *geol. äv.* scale, flake; *tekn.* wafer, lamina (*pl* laminae); (*i koppling*) disc; *elektr.* segment **-artad** [-aːr-] *a5* lamellar, lamellate; scaly, flaky; disc-like **-glas** laminated glass **-koppling** [multiple] disc-clutch **-trä** laminated wood
lamhet [-aː-] **1** (*förlamning*) paralysis (*i* of, in) **2** *bildl.* lameness
laminat *s7* **laminera** *v1* laminate
lamm *s7* lamb **lamma** *v1* lamb

lamm|bringa *kokk.* breast of lamb **-kotlett** *vanl.* lamb chop **-kött** *kokk.* lamb **-stek** *kokk.* roast lamb **-ull** lamb's wool **-unge** young lamb, lambkin

lamning [ˣlamm-] lambing

lamp|a *s1* lamp; (*glöd-*) bulb **-borste** lamp-brush **-ett** *s3* bracket candlestick, sconce **-fot** lamp foot(stand) **-glas** [lamp] chimney **-hållare** electric light socket **-kupa** [lamp] globe **-skärm** lampshade

lam|slagen *a5* paralysed (*äv. bildl.*); ~ *av fasa* paralysed with terror **-slå** paralyse

land *-et länder* (*i bet. 4 o. 5 s7*) **1** (*rike*) country; *det egna ~et* one's native country; *vårt ~* (*vanl.*) this country, Sweden (*etc.*); *i hela ~et* in the whole (throughout the) country; *inne i ~et* inland; *Johan utan ~* John Lackland **2** (*mots. sjö e.d.*) land (*äv. geol. o. bildl.*); ~ *i sikte!* (*sjö.*) land ahoy (in sight)!; *se hur ~et ligger* see how the land lies (wind blows); *gå i ~* go ashore, land; *gå i ~ med* (*bildl.*) accomplish, manage, succeed in; *inåt ~et* landward[s]; *långt inåt ~et* far inland; *på ~* (*mots. t. sjöss*) on shore, ashore, (*mots. i vattnet*) on land; *till ~s* by land; *Sverige är starkt till ~s* Sweden is powerful on land **3** (*mots. stad*) country; in the country; *livet på ~et* (*äv.*) country life; *resa ut till ~et* go out to (go into) the country **4** (*odlad mark*) land **5** (*trädgårds-*) plot

land|a land; *flyg. äv.* touch down **-amären** *pl, åld., inom våra* ~ within our borders **-avträdelse** cession of territory (land) **-backen** *på* ~ ashore, on shore on dry land **-bris** land breeze **-djur** land animal **-fäste** (*bros*) abutment **-förbindelse** connection with the mainland (land) **-förvärv** acquisition of territory (land) **-gång** gangway; *flyg.* entrance ladder **-hockey** hockey, (*särsk. AE.*) field hockey **-höjning** land elevation **-krabba** *bildl.* landlubber **-känning** *få* ~ have a landfall, sight land **-mina** land mine **-märke** *sjö.* landmark **-ning** landing; *flyg. äv.* alighting

landnings|bana airstrip, landing strip, runway **-förbud** *det är* ~ *på flygplatsen* the airport is closed for landing **-ljus** landing light **-plats** landing place; *flyg. äv.* landing ground **-sträcka** landing run **-ställ** undercarriage; *AE.* landing gear **-tillstånd** permission to land

land|område territory **-permission** *sjö.* shoreleave; liberty **-remsa** strip of land

lands|arkiv county records office **-bygd** country [side]; rural area[s *pl*] **-del** part of the country; province **-fader** beloved monarch **-fiskal** *ung.* district police superintendent [and public prosecutor]; *AE.* district attorney, sheriff **-flykt** exile **-flyktig** exiled **-flykting** exile; refugee **-förrädare** traitor [to one's country] **-förräderi** treason **-förrädisk** treasonable, traitorous **-församling** rural parish **-förvisa** banish [from the country], exile, expatriate **-förvisning** banishment, exile, expatriation **-hövding** county governor **-kamp** international match

landskap *s7* **1** (*landsdel*) [geographical] province, county, shire **2** (*ur natur- o. konstsynpunkt*) landscape; (*sceneri*) scenery

landskaps|arkitekt landscape architect **-gräns** provincial (county) boundary **-målare** landscape-painter, landscapist **-vapen** coat of arms of a province

lands|kommun rural district **-lag 1** *s2, jur.* national law code **2** *s7, sport.* [inter]national team **-lagsspelare** international, member of a country's team **-man** fellow countryman, compatriot; *vad är han för* ~? what nationality is he? **-maninna** fellow countrywoman **-mål** dialect **-omfattande** nationwide **-organisation** *L~en i Sverige* [the] Swedish Trade Union Confederation; *Brittiska ~en* the Trades Union Congress (*förk.* TUC); *Amerikanska ~en* American Federation of Labor and Congress of Industrial Organizations (*förk.* AFL-CIO)

landsort *i ~en* in the provinces (*pl*)

landsorts|bo man (*etc.*) from the provinces, provincial **-stad** provincial town **-tidning** provincial newspaper

lands|plåga national scourge; *vard.* nuisance **-sorg** national mourning

landstig|a land **-ning** landing; *göra en* ~ land, effect a landing

landstigningstrupper *pl* landing forces

lands|ting *ung.* county council **-tingsman** county councillor **-tingsråd** county commissioner

land|storm *ung.* veteran reserve **-stormsman** militiaman **-stridskrafter** *pl* land forces **-strykare** tramp **-ställe** (*sommarställe*) place in the country, country house (cottage)

lands|väg [ˣlan(d)s-, ˈlan(d)s-] highway, main road; *allmän* ~ public highway **-vägsbro** road bridge **-vägsriddare** *se luffare* **-ända** part of the country; (*avlägsen*) remote district

land|sänkning subsidence [of the earth's crust] **-sätta** land, put on shore; ~ *med fallskärm* [drop by] parachute **-sättning** landing *etc.* **-tunga** tongue of land, spit **-vind** *sjö.* land wind (breeze) **-vinning** reclamation of land; *bildl.* advance, achievements; *vetenskapens ~ar* achievements in the field of science **-vägen** *fara* ~ go by land

landå [-n-, -ŋ-] *s3* landau

langa 1 pass [from hand to hand]; *vard.* shove over **2** ~ *sprit* carry on an illicit trade in liquor (*etc.*), bootleg **langare** bootlegger; *AE.* moonshiner; (*narkotika-*) dope pedlar, pusher

langett [-ŋg-] *s3* buttonhole stitching; *sy* ~ do buttonhole stitching **-era** buttonhole stitch

langning 1 (*vid brand*) bucket-passing **2** (*sprit-*) bootlegging

langobard [-ŋ(g)-] *s3* Lombard **-isk** *a5* Lombard

langust [-ŋg-] *s3, zool.* spiny lobster

lank *s3* (*tunn dryck*) wish-wash

lanka *s1, kortsp.* small (low) card

lanolin *s3, s4* lanolin[e]

lans *s2* lance; *bryta en* ~ take up the cudgels (*för* for)

lansera launch, bring out, introduce; ~ *ngt på marknaden* put s.th. on the market

lansett *s3* lancet **-fisk** lancelet **-formig** [-å-] *a1* lancet-shaped **-lik** *biol.* lanceolate

lansiär [lan-, laŋ-] *s3, mil.* lancer

lant|adel *-n* the county **-arbetare** farm worker (hand, labourer) **-befolkning** country (rural) population **-brevbärare** country (rural) postman **-bruk** agriculture, farming industry; *jfr* *jordbruk* **-brukare** *se jordbrukare*; *Lantbru-karnas Riksförbund* Federation of Swedish Farmers

lantbruks|högskola agricultural college **-maskin** agricultural (farm) machine (*pl* machinery) **-nämnd** county agricultural board **-produkt** agricultural (farm) product; ~*er* (*äv.*) agricultural (farm) produce (*sg*) **-redskap** agricultural implement, farm tool **-skola** agricultural school **-styrelse** *L~n* [the Swedish] national board of agriculture **-sällskap** agricultural society **-universitet** *Sveriges L~* [the] Swedish university of agricultural sciences **-utställning** agricultural show

lantegendom estate

lantern|a [-ˣtä:r-, ˣlann-] *s1* lantern; light; *flyg.* navigation light **-jn** *s3* lantern; skylight [turret], clerestory

lant|gård farm, [agricultural] holding **-handel** country shop, general store **-handlare** country (village) shopkeeper **-hushåll** farm (country) household **-hushållning** husbandry, agronomy **-hushållsskola** rural domestic school **-is** ['lann-] *s2, vard.* country bumpkin; *AE. äv.* hick **-junkare** country squire **-lig** *a1* rural (*behag* charm; *enkelhet* simplicity); country (*liv* life); *neds.* rustic (*sätt* manners *pl*); (*mots. stadsaktig*) provincial **-liv** country (rural) life

lant|lolla *vard.* country wench **-man** farmer **-mannaparti** agrarian (farmer's) party **-mannaskola** agricultural college (school) **-mästare** farm foreman **-mätare** [land] surveyor **-mäteri** [land] surveying **-mäteriverk** *Statens* ~ central office of the [Swedish] national land survey **-ras** *jordbr.* native breed **-vin** home-grown wine **-värn** militia

laotier [la'ɔ:t(s)i-, la'å:-] Laotian **laotisk** [-'ɔ:-] *a5* Laotian

lapa lap; lick up; *bildl.* drink in, imbibe

lapidar|isk [-'da:-] *a5* lapidary; (*kortfattad*) brief, laconic **-stil** lapidary style

lapis ['la:-] *s2* lunar caustic, silver nitrate; ~ *lazuli* lapis lazuli **-lösning** silver-nitrate solution

1 lapp *s2* (*folk*) Laplander, Lapp

2 lapp *s2* (*tyg-*) piece; (*påsydd*) patch; (*pappers-*) slip, scrap; (*remsa*) strip, slip, label

lappa patch; (*laga äv.*) mend; ~ *ihop* patch up

lapp|hund Lapland dog **-kast** *sport.* reverse (kick turn) on skis **-kåta** Laplander's hut

Lappland ['lapp-] *n* Lapland

lapplisa *s1* [woman] traffic warden; *vard.* meter maid

lapp|ländsk *a5* Lappish, Lapland **-mark 1** *L~en* Lapland **2** nomadic Laplander's territory

lappri ['lapp-] *s6, sådant* ~ such trifles (*pl*)

lappsjuka melancholia induced by isolated life

lapp|skomakare cobbler **-skräddare** repairing-tailor **-täcke** patchwork quilt **-verk** [*ett*] ~ [a piece of] patchwork

lapsk *a1* Lappish, Lapp; *se lappländsk* **lapska** *s1* **1** (*kvinna*) Laplander (Lapp) woman **2** (*språk*) Lapp, Lappish

lapskojs ['lappskåjs, ˣlapp-] *s3, kokk.* lobscouse

lapsus ['lapp-] *s9, s2* lapse, slip

larm *s7* **1** (*buller*) noise; din, row; (*oväsen*) clamour, uproar **2** (*alarm*) alarm; *slå* ~ sound the

larm|a 1 (*bullra*) clamour (*över* about), make a noise (*över* at, about) **2** alarm, sound the alarm **-ande** *a4* clamouring, clamorous; noisy **-beredskap** alert **-klocka** alarm-bell **-signal** alert

1 larv *s3* larva (*pl* larvae), caterpillar, grub

2 larv *vard.* nonsense, rubbish

1 larva (*traska*) tramp, trudge, trot

2 larva *rfl* behave flippantly; ~ *dig inte!* don't be silly!

larvfötter *pl, tekn.* caterpillars, caterpillar treads

larvig *a1* (*enfaldig*) foolish; (*dum*) silly

larvstadium larval stage

laryng|it [-ŋg-] *s3* laryngitis **-oskop** [-å:p] *s7* laryngoscope

lasarett *s7* [general] hospital

lasaretts|fartyg hospital ship **-läkare** hospital doctor; resident physician (surgeon)

lasciv [la'ʃi:v] *a1* lascivious

laser ['la:-] *s2, fys.* laser (*förk. för Light Amplification by Stimulated Emission of Radiation*)

laser|a glaze, paint over with transparent colour [s] **-ing** glazing

laserstråle [ˣla:-] laser beam

lask *s2, tekn.* scarf [joint], fish joint; (*på handske, sko*) rib **laska** scarf; rib

lass *s7* [wagon]load; (*belastning*) load; (*börda*) cartload (*med* of); *fullt* ~ a full load; *få dra det tyngsta* ~*et* (*bildl.*) do the lion's share [of the work] **lassa** load; ~ *på ngn för mycket* (*bildl.*) overload s.b.; ~ *på ngn ngt* load s.b. with s.th.

lasso ['lasso] *s3* lasso; *kasta* ~ throw a lasso **-kast** *ett* ~ a lasso cast

1 last *s3* cargo, freight; (*belastning*) load; (*börda*) burden; *med* ~ *av* carrying (with) a cargo of; *lossa* ~*en* unload, discharge one's (its) cargo; *stuva* ~*en* trim the hold, stow the cargo; *ligga ngn till* ~ be a burden to s.b.; *lägga ngn ngt till* ~ lay s.th. to a p.'s charge, blame s.b. for s.th.

2 last *s3* (*fördärvlig vana*) vice

1 lasta (*klandra*) blame; (*starkare*) censure

2 lasta load (*på* on to); *sjö. äv.* ship, take in cargo; *djupt* ~*d* deep-laden; *ett skepp kommer* ~*t* (*lek*) the mandarins

lastageplats [-ˣta:ʃ-] loading site; *sjö.* wharf

lastbar *a1* vicious, depraved **-het** viciousness, depravity

last|bil lorry, truck; *AE äv.* freight car **-bilschaufför** lorry (truck) driver, trucker (*särsk. AE.*) **-bilstrafik** road transport (haulage) **-brygga** loading ramp (gangway) **-båt** cargo ship, freighter **-djur** beast of burden **-dryghet** dead weight capacity **-fartyg** *se -båt* **-flak** platform [body] **-fordon** goods vehicle, van, truck **-förmåga** carrying (loading) capacity **-gammal** ancient, old as the hills **-kaj** loading dock, wharf **-lucka** cargo hatch; (*öppningen*) [cargo] hatchway **-märke** load (Plimsoll) line **-ning** loading; lading **-pall** *se pall* **-pråm** lighter; (*större*) lump **-rum** hold, cargo space **-ångare** cargo steamer, freighter

lasur 1 *miner.* lapis lazuli, lazurite **2** (*äv. lasyr*) painting in transparent (glazing) colour[s]

lat *a1, n sg obest. form obruklig* lazy; (*maklig*) indolent; (*sysslolös*) idle **lata** *rfl* be lazy (idle); *gå och* ~ *sig* laze, take it easy

lat|ens s3 latency **-ent** al latent
later pl, stora ~ high-and-mightiness (sg), grand
airs; ha ~ give o.s. airs
latex ['la:-] s3, s7 latex
lathund 1 (lätting) lazybones, slacker **2** (radpap-
per) lined paper; (moja) crib, cab; (för räkning)
ready reckoner
latin s7 Latin
Latinamerika n Latin America **latinameri-
kansk** Latin American
latinare [-*ti:-] **1** Latin **2** skol. ung. classical
student **latiner** [-'ti:-] Latin
latin|isera latinize **-linje** gå ~n read classics **-se-
gel** lateen sail
latinsk [-'ti:-] a5 Latin; ~a bokstäver Roman letters
latityd s3 latitude
lat|mansgöra ett ~ a soft (an easy) job **-mask**
s2 lazybones
latrin s3 **1** (avträde) latrine, privy **2** (spillning)
excrement[s pl]
latsidan i uttr.: ligga på ~ be idle (lazy), take
things easy
latta s1 (träribba) lath, slat; (i segel) batten
laudatur [-*da:-] n honours (pl)
laura s1, vard. jaywalker
lav s2, bot. lichen
lava s1 lava **-ström** stream of lava
lave s2 **1** (i bastu) bench, ledge **2** (gruv-) head
frame, pitgear head
lavemang s7 enema (pl äv. enemata) **-spruta**
rectal (enema) syringe
lavendel [-'venn-] s9 lavender **-blå** lavender
blue
laver|a konst. wash; tint **-ing** konkr. wash (tint-
ed) drawing
lavett s3 gun carriage
lavin s3 avalanche (äv. bildl.) **-artad** [-a:r-] a5
avalanche-like, like wildfire; en ~ utveckling an
explosive development
lavoar [-ɔ'a:r] s3 washstand
lavyr s3, se lavering
lax s2 salmon; en glad ~ a lively spark
laxatjv s7 purgative; laxative, aperient **laxera**
take an aperient (etc.) **laxermedel** se -ativ
lax|fiske salmon fishing **-färgad** salmon col-
oured (pink) **-stjärt** snick. dovetail **-trappa**
salmon ladder **-öring** salmon trout
layout [lej'aut] s3 layout **-man** layout man
le log lett smile (åt at); lyckan log mot dem fortune
smiled on them
lealös vard. loose-limbed, loose-jointed
lebeman ['le:-] man about town, roué
lecitin s4, kem. lecithin
1 led s3 **1** (väg o.d.) way, track; (riktning) direction **2** (far-) passage, channel; (rösad) [moun-
tain] track, trail, footpath
2 led 1 s3, anat. joint; (finger-, tå- äv.) phalanx;
darra i alla ~er tremble in every limb; dra en arm
i ~ [igen] put an arm back into joint; gå ur ~ get
dislocated; känna sig ur ~ feel out of sorts; ur ~
är tiden the time is out of joint **2** s7, s4 (länk) link
(äv bildl.); (etapp) stage; (i ekvation) term, side;
(beståndsdel) part, element; (rad av pers.) row,
line; mil. rank; ingå som ett ~ i be a component
(part) of (an element in); de djupa ~en the rank

and file of the people, the masses; en man i (ur)
~et a common soldier; stå i främsta ~et be in the
front rank (bland of) **3** s3, s7 (släkt-) generation;
degree; line; språkv. element; i rätt nedstigande
~ in a direct line (från from)
3 led al **1** (trött) tired (sick, weary) [to death]
(på, vid of); vard. fed up (på, vid with) **2** den ~e
the Evil One **3** (elak) wicked, evil
4 led imperf. av 1, 2 lida
1 leda s1 (avsmak) disgust; (motvilja) repug-
nance; (vedervilja) loathing; (trötthet) weariness;
känna ~ vid feel disgust at; få höra ända till ~
hear till one is sick to death of it
2 leda vl (böja i leden) bend [at the joint], flex; ~
mot be articulated to; ~d axel (tekn.) articulated
shaft
3 leda v2 **1** (föra) lead; (väg-) guide; fys. o. elektr.
conduct **2** (om dörr, väg o.d.) lead, go, take one;
~ till a) lead to, b) (medföra) bring about, c) (ge
upphov t.) give rise to, bring on **3** (anföra) conduct; (affärsföretag) manage, direct, be in charge
of; (anfall) lead; ~ förhandlingarna be in the
chair, preside **4** ~ sitt ursprung från trace one's
(its) origin from (back to), originate from **5** (med
betonad partikel) ~ bort lead off, (vatten, ånga
o.d.) carry off; ~ in vatten lay water on; ~ in sam-
talet på turn the conversation on to
ledad a5, se 2 leda
ledamot -en ledamöter member; (av lärt
sällskap) fellow; ständig ~ life-member
ledande a4 leading; (t.ex. princip äv.) guiding,
ruling; fys. conductive; de ~ inom the leaders of,
those in a leading position within; i ~ ställning in
a leading (key, prominent) position
ledarbegåvning gift as a leader; pers. brilliant
leader
ledar|e 1 pers. leader; (väg-) guide, conductor;
(företags-) manager, executive, director, head,
principal, AE. president; (idrotts-) manager, organizer **2** fys. conductor (för of) **3** (tidningsarti-
kel) leader, editorial **-egenskaper** pl qualities
of leadership **-gestalt** en ~ a born leader **-hund**
1 (i hundspann) leader [dog] **2** (för blinda) guide
dog **-inna** [woman etc.] leader **-plats 1** (ngns)
position as a leader **2** (i tidning) på ~ in the
leader (editorial) column **-skap** s7 leadership;
(för företag) managership **-skribent** leader writer **-spalt** leader column **-stick** ung. subsidiary
leader **-ställning** vara i ~ be in a leading position (at the head), hold the lead
ledas v2, dep (känna leda) be (feel) bored (åt by;
ihjäl to death)
ledband (koppel) leading-strings (pl); gå i ~ be
in leading-strings; gå i ngns ~ be lead by the nose
by s.b.
ledbar [-e:-] al jointed; (böjlig) flexible
led|brosk anat. articular cartilage **-bruten** stiff
in the (one's) joints **-djur** arthropod
ledfyr sjö. range (leading) light; beacon (äv.
bildl.)
ledgångsreumatism rheumatoid arthritis
ledig al **1** (lätt o. ~) easy; (om hållning, rörelse
o.d.) free, effortless, unhampered; (om sätt att
vara) free and easy; en ~ gång an agile (easy)
gait; en ~ handstil a flowing hand[writing]; ett ~t
uppträdande an easy manner, free and easy man-

ners (*pl*); *känna sig* ~ *i kläderna* feel at one's ease (feel easy) in one's clothes; *skriven i* ~ *stil* written in a natural style; ~*a!* (*mil.*) [stand] at ease! **2** (*ej upptagen om pers.*) free, at leisure; (*sysslolös*) idle, unoccupied; (*om t.ex. kapital*) idle, uninvested; (*om sittplats o.d.*) unoccupied; (*om tjänst o.d.*) vacant; (*att tillgå*) available; (*om taxi*) disengaged, (*på skylt*) vacant, (*på taxi*) for hire; *bli* ~ *a*) (*från arbetet*) get, (be let) off [work, duty], *b*) (*få semester*) get one's holiday, *c*) (*om hembiträde*) have her evening out; ~*a platser* vacancies; *på* ~*a stunder* in [one's] leisure (spare) moments (time) **-förklara** declare vacant, announce (advertise) as vacant

ledighet 1 (*i rörelser*) freedom, ease; (*i uppträdande*) easiness, ease of manner **2** (*från arbete*) time off [work, duty]; (*semester*) holiday, *AE.* vacation; (*ledig tid*) free (spare) time, leisure

ledighets|kommitté *tillhöra* ~*n* (*vard.*) be a member of the leisured classes **-tid** leisure time

ledigt *adv* **1** easily *etc.*, *se ledig*; *röra sig* ~ move with ease; *sitta* ~ (*om kläder*) fit comfortably; *tala* ~ be a fluent speaker; *du hinner* ~ you get there in time easily; *vi får* ~ *plats i bilen* we'll have an empty (a free) seat in the car **2** *få* (*ge, ha, ta*) ~ get (give, have, take) time off; *ta sig* ~ *några dagar* take a few days off

ledkapsel *anat.* joint-capsule

ledljus guiding light

ledlös jointless; (*friare*) loose-jointed

led|motiv *mus.* leitmotif, recurrent theme; *bildl.* leading (guiding) principle

ledning [ˣle:d-] (*väg-*) guidance; (*-tråd*) clue, lead (*till* to); (*skötsel*) management, conduct, direction; (*krigs-*) [war] command; *fys.* conduction; *sport.* lead; *ta* ~*en* (*äv. sport.*) take the lead; *överta* ~ *en av* take charge of; *med* ~ *av* guided by, with the aid of; *med* ~ *av dessa upplysningar* on the basis of this information; *till* ~ *för* for the guidance of; *under* ~ *av* under the guidance (*etc.*) of **2** *konkr.*, ~*en* the managers (directors) (*pl*), the management, (*för parti*) the leaders (*pl*), *mil.* the commanders (*pl*) **3** *elektr.* wire, line, cable; (*rör-*) pipe, conduit, duct; *dragning av elektriska* ~*ar* electric wiring

lednings|brott *tel.* line breakdown **-förmåga** conductivity **-motstånd** line (conductor) resistance **-nät** electric supply mains; (*högspännings-*) distribution system **-stolpe** pylon, telegraph pole **-tråd** electric wire

ledsag|a [ˣle:d-] *v1* accompany; (*beskyddande*) escort **-are** *se följeslagare*

ledsam [*vanl.* ˣlessam] *a1* **1** (*tråkig*) boring, tiresome, tedious **2** (*sorglig*) sad; *det var* ~*t!* how sad!, I am so sorry! **3** (*obehaglig*) disagreeable, unpleasant; (*förtretlig*) annoying; *en* ~ *historia* a disagreeable (sad) story **-het** boringness *etc.*; boredom; *få* ~*er för* have trouble on account of; *råka ut för* ~*er* meet with unpleasantness; *här vilar inga* ~*er!* not a dull moment here!

ledsen [ˣlessen] *a3* sorry (*för, över* about); (*bedrövad*) grieved (*för, över* at, about); (*olycklig*) unhappy (*för, över* at, about); (*sorgsen*) sad (*över* about); (*förargad*) annoyed, angry (*för, över* at; *på* with); *jag är mycket* ~ *över* I am very sorry about, I deeply regret; *var inte* ~*!* don't be sad!,

cheer up!; *han är inte* ~ *av sig* he doesn't let anything get him down

ledskena guide-rail

ledsna [ˣlessna, ˣle:ds-] get (grow) tired (*på* of); *ha* ~*t på ngn* (*ngt*) have had enough of (be fed up with) s.b. (s.th.)

ledsnad [ˣless-, ˣle:ds-] *s3* (*bedrövelse*) sorrow, distress, grief (*över* at); *med uppriktig* ~ with sincere regret

ledstjärna lodestar (*äv. bildl.*), guiding star

ledstyv stiff-jointed

led|stång handrail; banisters (*pl*) **-syn** *med.* locomotor vision; *han har* ~ he can only just see his way about **-tråd** clue

ledung *s2, hist.* maritime (predatory) raid

leende I *a4* smiling; (*om natur o.d. äv.*) pleasant; *vänligt* ~ with a kindly smile; *lev livet* ~*!* keep smiling! **II** *s6* smile

1 lega *s1* (*rävs*) lodge; (*hares*) form; (*björns*) cache

2 lega *s1, jur.* hire; (*lejning*) hiring, hire

legal *a1* legal

legaliser|a legalize **-ing** legalization

legalitet legality

1 legat *s3* (*sändebud*) legate

2 legat *s7, jur.* legacy, bequest

3 legat [ˣle:-] *sup. av ligga*

legation legation **legationssekreterare** secretary of (to) [a] legation

legend *s3* legend

legend|arisk [-'da:-] *a5* legendary **-artad** [-a:r-] *a5* like a legend **-bildning** *abstr.* legend-making, legend-creation; *konkr.* legend **-omspunnen** legendary

leger|a *v1*, **-ing** *s2* alloy

legio ['le:-] *oböjl. a pl, de är* ~ their number is legion

legion [-gi'ɔ:n] *s3* legion **legionär** *s3* legionary [soldier]

legitim *a1* legitimate

legitimation identification; (*för yrkesutövning*) authorization, certification; *mot* ~ upon identification, on proof of identity

legitimations|handling, -kort identity card

legitimera legitimate, legitim[at]ize; ~*d* legitimated *etc.*, (*om läkare*) registered, fully qualified, authorized, (*om apotekare*) certifi[cat]ed; ~ *sig* prove (establish) one's identity, identify o.s.

legitimitet legitimacy

lego|arbete piecework **-soldat** mercenary [soldier] **-tillverkning** contract manufacture **-trupper** *pl* mercenary troops

leguan *s3, zool.* iguana

legymer [-'gy:-] *pl* vegetables

leidnerflaska [ˣlejd-] Leyden jar

leja [ˣlejja] *v2* engage, hire; *sjö. äv.* charter

lejd *s3* safe-conduct

lejdare 1 *sjö.* [sea] ladder **2** *gymn.* rope-ladder

lejon [ˣlejjån] *s7* lion; *en men ett* ~*!* one, but what a one! **-gap** *bot.* snapdragon **-hjärta** *Rikard L*~ Richard Coeur de Lion ([the] Lion-Heart) **-inna** lioness **-klo** *visa* ~*n* (*bildl.*) show one's mettle **-parten** the lion's share **-tämjare** lion-tamer **-unge** lion cub

lek *s2* **1** game; (*-ande*) play (*med dockor* with dolls), playing (*med döden* with death); (*t.ex.*

kattens ~ *med råttan*) toying, dallying; ~ *och idrott* games (*pl*); *en* ~ *med ord* playing with words; *den som sig i* ~*en ger får* ~*en tåla* once you must take the consequences; *på* ~ in play; *vara ur* ~*en* be out of the game (the running) **2** (*fiskars*) spawning; (*fåglars*) pairing, mating **3** (*kort-*) pack [of cards]

lek|a *v3* **1** play (*en lek* [at] a game); (*friare o. bildl.*) *äv.* toy, dally; ~ *med döden* (*äv.*) treat death lightly; ~ *med ngns känslor* trifle with a p.'s feelings; *livet -te för henne* life was a game for her; *inte att* ~ *med* not to be trifled with; *han är inte att* ~ *med* (*äv.*) he won't stand any nonsense; *vara med och* ~ join in [the game] **2** (*om fiskar*) spawn; (*om fåglar*) pair, mate

lekam|en [-'ka:-] *r* body **-lig** *a1* bodily; corporeal; ~*en* bodily *etc.*, in the body

lek|ande *a4*, ~ *lätt* as easy as winking **-boll** *bildl.* plaything, toy **-dräkt 1** (*fisks*) spawning array **2** (*barns*) playsuit; rompers (*pl*) **-full** playful (*äv. bildl.*), full of fun **-kamrat** playmate, playfellow

lek|man layman; (*ej fackman*) nonprofessional, amateur **-mannamässig** *a1* lay; amateur

lekmogen (*om fisk*) ready to spawn, mature

lekotek *s7* toy-lending library

lek|park playground **-plats** playground

leksak toy

leksaks|affär toyshop **-bil** toy (model) car **-djur** toy animal

lek|skola nursery school, kindergarten **-stuga** play house **-terapi** play therapy **-tid** (*fisks, fågels*) spawning (*etc.*) time (season); *jfr leka 2*

lektion [-k'ʃo:n] lesson; *ge* ~*er i* give lessons in; *ta* ~*er för ngn* have lessons with (from) s.b.

lektor [*'lektår, 'lekk-*] *s3* (*vid läroverk*) senior master; *univ.* lecturer; ~ *i engelska* senior master of English **-at** *s7* (*vid läroverk*) post as senior master; *univ.* lectureship

lektris [woman] reader **lektyr** *s3* reading [matter]; things to read (*pl*) **lektör** (*manuskriptläsare*) [publisher's] reader

lekverk *det är ett* ~ *för mig* it is child's play (a simple matter) for me

lem [lemm] *s2* limb, member **-lästa** maim, mutilate; (*göra ofärdig*) cripple, disable

lemonad *s3* lemonade

len *a1* **1** (*mjuk*) soft; (*slät*) smooth **2** (*om ljud o.d.*) bland (*röst* voice) **lena** soothe (*i halsen* the throat) **lenhet** softness; smotthness; blandness

leninism Leninism

leopard [-a:-] *s3* leopard **-hona** leopardess

lepra [*'le:p-*] leprosy

ler|a *s1* clay; (*sandig*) loam; (*dy*) mud; *bränd* ~ fired clay; *eldfast* ~ fire clay; *hänga ihop som ler och långhalm* stick together through thick and thin **-botten** (*i sjö*) clayey bottom **-duva** clay pigeon **-duveskytte** clay-pigeon shooting **-fötter** *i uttr.*: *en koloss på* ~ a colossus with feet of clay **-gods** earthenware, pottery **-golv** earth (mud) floor **-gök** toy ocarina

ler|ig *a1* clayey, loamy; (*om t.ex. väg*) muddy **-jord** clay[ey] soil **-koka** *s1* clod [of clay] **-krus** stone (earthenware) jar **-kärl** earthen[ware] vessel; *koll.* earthenware, crockery, pottery **-skiffer** shale **-skärva** *arkeol.* potsherd **-välling** mass (sea) of mud

lesbisk *a5* lesbian

less *a1, vard.* fed up (*på* with)

leta search, hunt, look (*efter* for); ~ *efter ord* be at a loss for words; ~ *i minnet* cast about in (ransack) one's memory; ~ *igenom* search, ransack; ~ *reda på* try to find; ~ *upp* hunt up; ~ *ut* pick out; ~ *sig fram* find (make) one's way

letal *a1* lethal; mortal

letarg|i *s3* lethargy **-isk** [-'tarr-] *a5* lethargic

1 lett *s3* Lett, Latvian

2 lett 1 *sup. av le* **2** *sup. av leda*

lett|isk [*'lett-*] *a5* Lettish; *geogr.* Latvian **-iska** [*'lett-*] *s1* **1** (*språk*) Lettish **2** (*kvinna*) Lettish woman

Lettland [*'lett-*] *n* Latvia

leukemi [levke'mi:] *s3, med.* leukaemia

lev *s3* loaf

lev|a *v2, sup. äv. -at* **1** live; (*existera*) exist, be in existence; ([*ännu*] *vara vid liv*) be alive; (*kvar-*) survive; (*väsnas*) be noisy, make a noise; ~ *ett glatt liv* lead a gay life; *så sant jag -er!* as sure as I stand here!; *-e konungen!* long live the King!; *-e friheten!* Liberty for ever!; *den som -er får se* he who lives will see; *ja, må han* ~ (*ung.*) for he is a jolly good fellow; *om jag får* ~ *och ha hälsan* if I am spared and keep well; *om han hade fått* ~ if he had lived; ~ *högt* live sumptuously; *hur -er världen med dig?* how is the world treating you?; ~ *som man lär* practise what one preaches; ~ *som om var dag var den sista* take thought for the morrow; *låta ngn veta att han -er* give s.b. a hot time [of it]; ~ *i den tron att* be under the impression that; ~ *kvar* live on, survive, exist still; ~ *med a*) (*i skildring o.d.*) take a great interest in, *b*) (*i stora världen*) go [out] into society, be a man (*etc.*) of fashion; ~ *om a*) (*sitt liv*) live over again, relive, *b*) (*svira*) lead a fast life, be a fast liver; ~ *på* live [up]on, (*om djur*) feed on; ~ *på stor fot* live in great style; ~ *upp a*) (*förmögenhet*) run through, use up, *b*) (*på nytt*) revive; ~ *vidare* go on living **2** (*om segel*) flap, slap, shake **3** ~ *sig in i* enter into (*ngns känslor* a p.'s feelings)

levande *a4* **1** living; animate (*väsen* being); (*predik. om pers.*) alive; (*mots. död, uppstoppad, slaktad e.d.*) live; (*livfull*) lively (*hopp* hope); (*livlig*) vivid (*skildring* description); (*om t.ex. porträtt*) lifelike; *en* ~ *avbild av* the very image of; ~ *blommor* real (natural) flowers; ~ *djur* living animals; ~ *eld* burning fire; ~ *ljus* lighted candles; *teckna efter* ~ *modell* draw from life; *ett* ~ *exempel på* a living example of; *ett* ~ *intresse för* a living (live) interest in; ~ *kraft* (*fys.*) kinetic energy; *på ett* ~ *sätt* in an animated (a vivid) way; *som föder* ~ *ungar* viviparous; *inte en* ~ *själ* not a [living] soul **2** *inte veta sig ngn* ~[*s*] *råd* be at one's wits ends; *inte få ngn* ~[*s*] *ro* get no peace anywhere **-göra** make lifelike (live)

levang [*'le:-*] deck brush

Levanten [-'vann-] *r* [the] Levant

levantinsk [-i:-] *a5* Levantine

leve *s6* cheer; viva[t]; *utbringa ett fyrfaldigt* ~ *för* give four (*Storbritannien* three) cheers for

levebröd livelihood, living

lever [*'le:-*] *s2* liver

leverans [-ans, -aŋs] *s3* **1** (*tillhandahållande*) furnishing, supplying (*av* of); (*avlämnande*) delivering, delivery **2** *konkr.* delivery; goods delivered (*pl*); (*sändning*) consignment; *vid* ~ on delivery **-avtal** delivery agreement **-dag** day (date) of delivery, delivery date **-förmåga** ability to deliver **-klar** ready for delivery **-tid** time (date) of delivery **-villkor** *pl* terms (conditions) of delivery **-vägran** refusal to supply

leverantör [-an-, -aŋ-] supplier, deliverer; contractor; (*livsmedel*) purveyor

levercirrhos [-sirå:s] *s3, med.* cirrhosis of the liver

leverera (*tillhandahålla*) supply, furnish; (*avlämna*) deliver; *fritt* ~*t* carriage free

lever|fläck mole; birthmark **-korv** liver sausage, liverwurst

leve|rne *s6* **1** (*levnadssätt*) life; *hans liv och* ~ his life [and way of living] **2** (*oväsen*) hullabaloo **-rop** cheer

lever|pastej liver paste **-sjukdom** liver (hepatic) disease **-tran** cod-liver oil

levit *s3* Levite

levnad [-e:-] *s3* life

levnads|bana career **-beskrivning** biography; curriculum vitae **-förhållanden** *pl* conditions of living; circumstances **-glad** [high-]spirited, light--hearted, buoyant **-konstnär** adept in the art of living, s.b. who gets the best out of life **-kostnader** *pl* cost of living (*sg*), living costs **-kostnadsindex** cost-of-living index **-lopp** life span; *ngns* ~ [the course of] a p.'s life **-regel** rule of conduct **-standard** standard of living **-sätt** manner (way) of living (life) **-tecknare** biographer **-teckning** biography, life (*över* of) **-trött** weary of life **-vanor** *pl* habits (ways) of life (living) **-villkor** *pl* conditions of life **-år** year of life

levra [-e:-] *rfl* coagulate, clot; ~*t blod* clotted blood, blood clot, gore

lexikalisk [-'ka:-] *a5* lexical

lexiko|graf *s3* lexicographer **-grafi** *s3* lexicography **-grafisk** [-'gra:-] *a5* lexicographical

lexik|on ['leksikån] *s7, pl äv. -a* dictionary; (*för dött språk vanl.*) lexicon

lian *s3* liana, liane

libanes *s3* Libanese **-isk** *a5* Libanese

Libanon ['li:-ån] *n* Lebanon

liberal I *a1* liberal II *s3, polit.* Liberal

liberaliser|a liberalize **-ing** liberalization

liberalis|m liberalism **-tisk** *a5* liberalist[ic]

liberalitet liberality

libero ['li:-] *s5*, (*fotboll*) sweeper

librettist librettist **libretto** [-'brettɔ] *s9, s7* libretto

Libyen ['li:-] *n* Libya

libyer ['li:-] *s9* Libyan **libysk** ['li:-] *a5* Libyan

licens *s3* licence; permit **-ansökan** application for a licence **-avgift** licence fee **-era** license **-innehavare** licensee, licence-holder **-tillverkning** manufacture on licence

licentiat [-n(t)si-] licentiate; *filosofie* ~ (*ung.*) master of arts, doctor of philosophy; *medicine* ~ (*ung.*) bachelor of medicine **-avhandling** licentiat [examination] treatise **-examen** licentiate examination

1 lid|a *led -it; tiden -er* time is getting on, time is passing; *det -er mot kvällen* it is getting [on] towards evening, night is drawing on; *det -er mot*

slutet med honom his life is ebbing out, his life is drawing towards its close; *vad det -er* sooner or later, (*så småningom*) by and by

2 lid|a *led -it* **1** (*utstå*) suffer; (*uthärda*) endure; (*drabbas av*) sustain, incur; ~ *brist på* be short of; ~ *skada* (*äv.*) be injured (damaged), take harm, (*om pers.*) be hurt **2** (*pinas*) suffer (*av* from); (*ha plågor*) be in pain **3** (*tåla*) bear, stand, endure

lidande I *s6* suffering **II** *a4* suffering (*av* from); afflicted (*av* by); *bli* ~ *på* be the loser by (from), lose by

lidelse passion **-fri** dispassionate, passionless **-full** passionate; impassioned (*tal* speech) **-fullhet** passion; (*glöd*) enthusiasm, fervour, vehemence

lider ['li:-] *s7* shed

liderlig *a1* lecherous, lewd **-het** lechery, lewdness

lidit *sup. av 1, 2 lida*

lie ['li:e] *s2* scythe **-mannen** the grim reaper, Death

liera *rfl* ally o.s. (*med* to, with) **lierad** *a5* allied, connected

lift *s2* lift **lifta** hitchhike **liftare** hitchhiker

liga *s1* **1** (*förbrytarband*) gang, set **2** *sport.* league **3** *hist.* league, [con]federation **-match** *sport.* league match

ligament *s7, anat.* ligament

ligatur *boktr.* ligature

ligg|a *låg legat* **I 1** (*om levande varelser*) lie, be lying [down]; (*befinna sig, vara*) be (*på sjukhus* in hospital); *bildl.* be; ~ *och läsa* lie reading, read in bed; ~ *och sova* be asleep (sleeping); *han -er redan* he is in (has gone) to bed; ~ *länge på morgnarna* lie (stay) in bed late of a morning, get up late; ~ *i underhandlingar* be engaged in negotiations; ~ *med ngn* sleep (go to bed) with s.b.; ~ *på ägg* brood, sit on eggs; ~ *vid universitet* be at the university; ~ *lågt* (*avvakta*) lie low; wait and see; *bide one's time* **2** (*om sak o. bildl.*) lie, be; (*vara belägen, i sht geogr.*) be [situated]; *kyrkan -er vid vägen* the church stands (is) at the roadside; *var skall huset* ~? where will the house be built?; *åt vilket håll -er skolan?* in which direction is the school?; *-er alldeles härintill* is quite near (close to) here; *häri -er skillnaden* this is where the difference lies; *avgörandet -er hos mig* the decision lies (rests) with me; *det -er i sakens natur* it is in the nature of the case; *det -er i blodet* (*släkten*) it runs in the blood (family); ~ *på ngt* keep [possession of] (*vard.* sit tight on) s.th.; *det -er i luften* it is in the air **II** (*med beton. part.*) **1** ~ *av sig* get out of practise (form), *vard.* get rusty **2** ~ *bi* (*sjö.*) lie to (by) **3** ~ *efter a*) (*vara på efterkälken*) be behind (in arrears), *b*) (*ansätta*) press **4** *det -er inte för mig* it is not in my line, it does not come natural to me **5** ~ *i a*) *eg.* be in (*vattnet* the water), *b*) *bildl.* stick at it, keep on (*o. arbeta* working) **6** ~ *kvar över natten* stay the night **7** ~ *nere* be at a standstill **8** *solen -er på här hela eftermiddagen* we get the sun here the whole afternoon; *vinden -er på* the wind is driving at us (*etc.*) **9** *hur -er saken till?* how does the matter stand?; *så -er det till* those are the actual facts, that is how things are; ~ *till sig* improve by keeping **10** ~ *under* (*bildl.*) be inferior to **11** ~ *över a*) (*övernatta*) stay the night (overnight), b) (*vara överlägsen*) be [the] superior

liggande a4 lying; reclining, recumbent (*ställning* position); *en avsides ~ plats* an out-of-the--way spot (*etc.*); *den närmast till hands ~ förklaringen* the explanation nearest to hand; *djupt ~* (*äv.*) deep-lying, (*om ögon*) deep-set; *bli ~* (*bli kvar*) be left [lying]

ligg|are register; *bokför. äv.* ledger **-dags** bedtime

ligge|dagar *pl* lay days **-dagspengar** *pl* demurrage (sg)

ligg|plats berth **-sjuk** *som en ~ höna* like a broody hen **-soffa** *ung.* bed-sofa **-stol** lounge--chair; deck chair **-sår** bedsore **-vagn** (*barnvagn*) perambulator; *vard.* pram

ligist hooligan **-dåd** [act of] hooliganism; (*friare*) wanton destruction, vandalism

lignin [-ŋn-] *s4* lignin

liguster [-ˈgust-] *s2, bot.* privet **-svärmare** *zool.* privet hawk

1 lik *s7* **1** corpse; [dead] body; *blek som ett ~* deathly pale; *stå ~* lie laid out; *segla med ~ i lasten* (*bildl.*) be doomed to failure; *ett ~ i lasten* (*hand.*) a dead loss, dead weight, a dud line **2** *boktr.* out flag

2 lik *s7, sjö.* leech; (*tross*) boltrope

3 lik a5 like; (*om två el. flera*) alike; (*liknande*) similar; (*i storlek, värde e. d.*) similar; *~a* identical[ly alike]; *vi är alla ~a inför lagen* all men are equal in the eye of the law; *~a barn leka bäst* like draws to like, birds of a feather flock together; *porträttet är mycket ~t* the portrait is a very good likeness; *han är sig inte ~* he is not at all himself; *du är dig då ~!* that's just like you!

lika I oböjligt a (*i storlek, värde o.d.*) equal (*med* to); (*likvärdig*) equivalent, (*identiskt ~*) identical; *är ~ med* is equal to (the same as); *två plus tre är ~ med fem* two plus three makes five; *tillsätta ~ delar av* add in equal portions; *~ mot ~* measure for measure; *30 ~* (*tennis.*) thirty all **II** *adv* in the same way (manner) (*som* as); (*jämnt; i samma grad o.d.*) equally; *~ ... som* just as ... as, (*både ... och*) both ... and; *klockorna går inte ~* the clocks don't keep the same time; *~ bra a*) just as good (*förklaring* an explanation), b) (*sjunga* sing) as well (*som någonsin* [as ever]); *i ~* [*hög*] *grad* to the same extent, equally; *~ många som vanligt* [just] as many as usual, the usual number; *de är ~ stora* they are the same (are equal in) size, (*om abstr. förhållanden*) they are equivalent (equally great *etc.*)

lika|berättigad *vara ~* have equal rights, be of equal standing (*med* with) **-berättigande** *s6* equality of status (rights) **-dan** [ˣli:ka-, -ˈdann] *a5* of the same sort (kind); *de är precis ~a* they are exactly alike (just the same, all of a piece) **-dant** [ˣli:ka-, -ˈdant] *adv* the same **-fullt** nevertheless, all the same **-ledes** likewise, similarly **-lydande** a4 of identical (the same) wording (tenor); *i två ~ exemplar* in two identical copies **-lönsprincipen** the principle of equal pay

likare standard, gauge

likartad [-a:r-] *a5* similar in character (nature) (*med* to), similar

lika|sinnad *a5* like-minded, of the same way of

thinking **-så** also; *jfr likaledes* **-väl** just as well (*som* as)

likbegängelse [-jäŋ-] funeral [ceremony]; obsequies (*pl*)

likbent [-e:-] a4, geom. isosceles

lik|besiktning postmortem examination **-bil** motor hearse **-bjudarmin** funereal expression, gloomy mien **-blek** ghastly, deathly pale, livid **-bärare** pallbearer

lik|e *s2* equal; *söka sin ~* be without an equal, be unequalled (unmatched); *en ... utan ~* an unparalleled (unprecedented) ... **-formig** [-å-] *al* uniform; (*alltigenom ~*) homogeneous; *geom.* similar (*med* to)

lik|färd funeral procession **-förgiftning** cadaverous poisoning

likgiltig 1 indifferent (*äv. om sak*); (*betydelselös*) unimportant, insignificant, trivial; *det är mig fullständigt ~t* it is all the same (makes no difference [whatever]) to me **2** (*ointresserad*) indifferent (*för* to); (*liknöjd*) listless, apathetic; impassive **-het 1** (*saks*) unimportance, insignificance **2** (*brist på intresse*) indifference (*för* to) listlessness, apathy

likhet [-i:-] resemblance, similarity (*med* to); (*porträtt-*) likeness, (*fullständig*) identity (*med* with); *~ inför lagen* equality before the law; *äga en viss ~ med* have (bear) a certain resemblance to; *i ~ med* in conformity with, on the lines of, (*liksom*) like

likhetstecken sign of equality, equal[s] sign

lik|kista coffin; *AE. äv.* casket **-lukt** smell of death

likmätigt [-i:-] *sin plikt ~* pursuant to (in pursuance of) one's duty

likn|a [-i:-] **1** (*vara lik*) resemble, be like; look like **2** (*jämföra*) compare (*vid* to) **-ande** a4 similar; *eller* (*och*) *~* or (and) the like; *av ~ slag* [of a] similar [kind]; *eller ngt ~ namn* or some name of the sort (some such name); *på ~ sätt* in much the same (a similar) way, similarly **-else** *bibl.* parable; (*bildlig jämförelse*) simile, metaphor; *tala i ~r* speak in metaphors (*bibl.* parables)

lik|nöjd indifferent; *jfr likgiltig* **-rikta** *elektr.* rectify; (*friare*) unify; standardize; *~d opinion* regimented opinion **-riktare** *elektr.* rectifier **-riktning** *elektr.* rectification; (*friare*) regimentation, standardization **-sidig** *al* equilateral **-som** [ˈli:k-] **I** *konj* like; (*ävensom*) as well as; (*~ om*) as if **II** *adv* as if; (*så att säga*) as it were, so to say; *jag ~ kände på mig I* somehow (*vard.* sort of) felt

likstelhet *med.* rigor mortis

lik|ström direct current (*förk. D.C.*) **-ställa** place on an equal footing (a level) (*med* with) **-ställd** a5 equal, of the same standing; *vara ~* rank equal, be on a par **-ställdhet, -ställighet** equality **-stämmighet** agreement

lik|tal funeral sermon (oration) **-torn** [-ɔ:-] *s2* corn **-tornsplåster** corn-plaster

lik|tydig 1 synonymous (*med* with), equivalent in meaning (*med* to) (*friare*) tantamount (*med* to) **-tänkande** a4 of the same way of thinking

lik|vagn hearse **-vaka** vigil by a corpse before burial, wake

likvid I *s3* payment (*för* of, for); (*insänd ~*) remittance; *full ~* payment in full; *som ~ för Er fak-*

L

tura in settlement of your invoice **||** *a1*, *n sg obest.*

form undviks liquid, available; (*om ställning*) solvent; ~*a medel* ready money, cash (*sg*); liquid funds (assets)

likvida ['li:k-] *s1*, *språkv.* liquid

likvid|ation liquidation; (*bolags äv.*) winding up; *träda i* ~ go into liquidation **-era 1** (*avveckla*) liquidate, wind up **2** (*betala*) liquidate, settle, discharge **3** (*upplösa*) eliminate; (*döda*) liquidate **-itet** liquidity; (*firmas äv.*) solvency

likvinklig *al* equiangular

lik|väl ['li:k-, -'vä:l] nevertheless; all the same **-värdig** *al* equivalent (*med* to); of equal value (importance) **-värdighet** equivalence

likör liqueur; *är inte min* ~ (*vard.*) is not my cup of tea

lila ['li:-, ˣli:-] *s1 o.* oböjligt *a* lilac, mauve

lilja *s1* lily

lilje|konvalje lily of the valley **-vit** lily-white **-växt** lily

lilla *a*, *best. form sg* (*jfr liten*) small; little; *barn* ~! my dear child!; *minsta* ~ *bidrag* the smallest contribution; *det* ~ *jag äger* what little I possess; *hur mår den* ~ (*lille*)? how is the (your) little girl (boy)? **lillan** *s*, *best. form sg* the little girl in the family **lillasyster** our (*etc.*) little sister **lillebror** *jfr lillasyster* **lillen** the little boy in the family; *L*~ Tiny **lilleputt** *s2*, *s3* Lilliput, Lilliputian; dwarf, pygmy

lill|finger little finger **-gammal** precocious **-hjärnan** [the] cerebellum **-slam** *s2*, *kortsp.* little slam **-tå** little toe

lim [limm] *s7* glue, (*för papper*) size **-färg** distemper

limjt *s3*, *hand.* limit; (*högsta el. lägsta pris*) maximum (minimum) price **-era** limit

lim|ma glue; (*papper, väv o.d.*) size; (*mur*) lime **-ning** (-*mande*) gluing *etc.*; *gå upp i* ~*en* (*vard.*) fly off the handle

limno|log limnologist **-logi** *s3* limnology

limousin[e] [-mɔ'si:n] *s3* limousine

limpa *s1* **1** ryemeal bread, loaf **2** *en* ~ *cigarretter* a carton of cigarettes

lim|panna gluepot **-ämne** glue-stock; (*för papper o.d.*) sizing agent

lin *s4* flax

lin|a *s1* rope; (*smalare*) cord; (*stål-*) wire; *sjö.* line; *löpa* ~*n ut* (*bildl.*) keep on to the bitter end, go the whole hog; *visa sig på styva* ~*n* (*bildl.*) show off **-bana** [aerial] ropeway (cableway); (*för skidåkare*) ski lift

lin|beredning flax-dressing **-blå** flax-blue

lind *s2* lime[-tree]; *A E.* linden, basswood

linda I *s1* swaddling clothes (*pl*); *i sin* ~ (*bildl.*) in its infancy, in its initial stage; *kväva i sin* ~ (*bildl.*) nip in the bud **II** *v1* **1** wire, tie (*omkring* round); (*slingra*) twine; *hon kan* ~ *honom runt sitt* [*lill*]*finger* she can twist him round her [little] finger; ~ *in* wrap up (*äv. bildl.*), envelop; ~ *upp* unwind; ~ *upp på* (*t.ex rulle*) wind on to **2** *med.* bind up, bandage **3** (*barn*) wrap in swaddling clothes, swaddle

lindans|are, -erska tightrope walker (dancer)

lind|ebarn baby (infant) in arms **-ning** *tekn.* winding

lindr|a (*mildra*) mitigate, appease; (*lugna*)

soothe, mollify; (*nöd o.d.*) alleviate, relieve **-ig** *al* (*obetydlig*) slight; (*ej svår*) light; (*mild*) mild; (*human*) easy; (*om straff o.d.*) lenient **-igt** *adv* slightly *etc.*; ~*t sagt* to put it mildly; *slippa* ~*t undan* get off lightly **-ing** mitigation, appeasement; (*förbättring*) amelioration; (*av t.ex. straff*) reduction (*i* of); (*lättnad*) relief (*för* to, for)

linearritning [line*ˣa:r-] linear drawing **lineär** *al* linear

linfrö flaxseed; *kem.*, *med.* linseed

linfärja cable ferry

lingarn linen thread

lingon [-ŋån] *s7* cowberry, red whortleberry; *inte värd ett ruttet* ~ not worth a straw **-ris** cowberry (*etc.*); twigs (*pl*)

lingul flax-coloured; (*om hår*) flaxen

lingv|ist [-ŋ(g)v-] linguist **-istik** *s3* linguistics (*pl, behandlas som sg*)

linhårig flaxen-haired

liniment *s7* liniment, embrocation

linjal *s3* ruler

linje ['li:n-] *s5* line; (*buss- o.d. äv.*) route, service; *mil. äv.* rank; *skol. o.d.* side, stream; *rät* ~ straight line; *den slanka* ~*n* the slender figure; ~ *4 Nr.* 4 buses (trams *etc.*) (*pl*); *uppställa på* ~ (*mil.*) draw up in line, line up; *över hela* ~*n* (*bildl.*) all along the line **-arbetare** line[s]-man **-buss** coach **-domare** *sport.* linesman **-fart** liner traffic **-fartyg** liner **-fel** *tekn.* line disturbance

linje|ra 1 ~ [*upp*] rule; ~*t papper* ruled (lined) paper **2** (*stå på linje*) range **-rederi** shipping line, liner company **-regemente** line regiment

linje|ring [-'je:-] ruling **-sjöfart** liner shipping **-skepp** line-of-battle ship **-spel** lines (*pl*); line-pattern **-trafik** intercity (interurban) traffic **-trupper** *pl* line troops **-val** *skol.* choice of line **-väljare** *tel.* series telephone set

linjär *al* linear

linka limp, hobble

linne *s6* (*tyg*) linen; *koll.* linen; (*plagg*) vest

linnea [-ˣne:a] *s1*, *bot.* linnaea

linne|skåp linen cupboard (press) **-utstyrsel** (*bruds*) stock of household linen, *vard.* bottom drawer, *AE.* hope chest **-varor** *pl* linen goods, linens

linning band

linodling flax-growing

linoleum [-'nɔ:-] *s7*, *s9* linoleum; *hand. äv.* lino **-matta** linoleum flooring **-snitt** linoleum block, linocut

linolja linseed oil

1 lins *s3*, *bot.* lentil

2 lins *s3*, *fys.*, *anat.* lens

lintott flaxen-haired child (person)

lip *s2*, *ta till* ~*en* start crying, *vard.* turn on the waterworks **lipa** cry, sob; blubber **lipsill** crybaby

1 lir|a *-an* *-e* (*mynt*) lira (*pl* lire)

2 lira *vard.* play

lirare player

lirka work [it]; ~ *med ngt* turn s.th. this way and that; ~ *med ngn* coax (wheedle, cajole) s.b.

lisa *s1* relief; (*tröst*) comfort, solace; *en ren* ~ a real mercy

lisma fawn, wheedle **lismande** *a4* fawning,

bland; ~ *tal* bland (honeyed) speech **lismare**
fawner; (*smickrare*) flatterer; *vard.* bootlicker
lispund ['liss-] lispound; *ett* ~ (*ung.*) a stone
Lissabon ['lissabån] *n* Lisbon
1 list *s3* (-*ighet*) cunning, craft[iness]; (*knep*) artifice, stratagem; *kvinnans* ~ *övergår mannens förstånd* the female of the species is more deadly
than the male
2 list *s3* (*bård*) border, edging; (*remsa*) strip;
byggn. band, fillet; (*på fotpanel*) ledge
1 lista *s1* list (*på, över* of); *svart* ~ black list; *sätta
ngn på svarta* ~*n* blacklist s.b.; *göra upp en* ~
draw up a list
2 lista *v1, rfl,* ~ *sig in i* steal (sneak) into; ~ *sig
till ngt* get s.th. by trickery
listig *a1* cunning, artful, crafty **-het** cunningness
etc.
listverk moulding[s *pl*]
lisös bed-jacket
lit *r,* *sätta* [*sin*] ~ *till* put (place) one's confidence
in, *vard.* pin one's faith on **lita** ~ *på* have confidence in, trust [in], (*för- sig på*) depend (rely)
[up]on, trust to; *det kan du* ~ *på!* you may depend
on that!
litania [-ˣni:a] *s1* litany
Litauen [-'tau-] *n* Lithuania
litau|er [-'tau-] *s9* Lithuanian **-isk** *a5* Lithuanian
lit de parade [li: dö pa'radd] *i uttr.: ligga på* ~
lie in state
lite (*i talspråk o. ledigt skriftspråk*) *se litet*
liten *litet mindre minst* (*jfr äv. litet*) small, little;
(*ytterst* ~) minute, tiny; (*obetydlig*) slight, insignificant; ~ *till växten* small, short; *som* ~ as a
child; *när jag var* ~ when I was small (a little boy
etc.); *få en* ~ have a baby; *stackars* ~ poor child;
~ *bokstav* small letter; *boktr.* lower-case [letter]
-het smallness *etc.*
liter ['li:-] *s9* litre; *AE.* liter **-butelj** litre bottle
-mått litre measure **-vis** (*t.ex. säljas* ~) by the
litre; (~ *efter* ~) litre by litre
litet I *adv* little; (*ngt* [~]) a little, somewhat, a bit;
(*obetydligt*) slightly; *han blev inte* ~ *förvånad* he
was not a little astonished; *sova* ~ sleep [for] a
little while; *jag är* ~ *förkyld* I have got a slight
cold; *för* ~ *sedan* a little while ago; ~ *var* (*till
mans*) *har* vi pretty well every one of us has; ~
varstans here and there, (*nästan överallt*) almost
everywhere; ~ *då och då* every now and then **II**
a, n till liten a little, some; (*föga*) little; *det var
ovanligt* ~ *folk där* there were unusually few people there; *vi behöver* ~ *blommor* we need a few
flowers; *bra* ~ *intresse* very little interest **III** *oböjligt s* a little; something, a trifle; (*föga*) little; ~
men gott little but good; ~ *roar småbarn* anything
will amuse a child, little things please little minds;
det vill inte säga ~*!* that's saying a good deal!; *om
än aldrig så* ~ be it ever so little!; ~ *av varje* a little
of everything
litium ['li:t(s)-] *s8, kem.* lithium
lito|graf *s3* lithographer **-grafera** lithograph
-graf| *s3* lithography; *konkr.* lithograph **-gra-
fisk** [-'gra:-] *a5* lithographic
littera ['litt-] *s1* [capital] letter **litterat** *a1 o. s3*
literate
litteratur literature **-anmälan** review **-för-
teckning** bibliography, list of references **-his-**

toria history of literature **-historiker** literary
historian **-historisk** of the history of literature
-hänvisning recommended literature; *L~ar*
Further Reading (*sg*) **-kritiker** literary critic
-sökning literature search, information
retrieval, documentary research **-vetenskap**
comparative literature
litteratör writer, author **litterär** *a1* literary;
(*om pers. äv.*) of a literary turn; ~ *äganderätt*
copyright
liturg *s3* officiating priest (clergyman) **liturgi** *s3*
liturgy **liturgisk** *a5* liturgical
1 liv *s7* **1** (*kropp*) body; ~ *och lem* life and limb;
veka ~*et* the waist; *gå* (*komma*) *ngn inpå* ~*et* get
(come) close to s.b., get to know s.b. intimately;
med ~ *och själ* wholeheartedly; *till* ~ *och själ* to
the backbone **2** (*midja*) waist; *smal om* ~*et* slen-
der-waisted **3** (*klädesplagg*) bodice **4** *få sig ngt till
~s* have s.th. to eat (some food), *bildl.* be treated
to s.th.
2 liv *s7* **1** (*levande, levnad, leverne*) life; (*tillvaro*)
existence; *börja ett nytt* ~ turn over a new leaf;
musik är mitt ~ music is what I live for; *sådant är
~et!* such is life!; *få* ~ *i* get some life into, (*av-
svimmad*) bring round; *få nytt* ~ get a new lease
of life; *gjuta nytt* ~ *i* revive, resuscitate; *det gäller
~et* it is a matter of life and death; *hålla* ~ *i* keep
alive (going); *sätta* ~*et till* lose one's life; *ta* ~*et av
ngn* take a p.'s life, make away with s.b.; *berättelser ur levande* ~*et* stories from [real] life; *ett helt
~s arbete* the work of a lifetime; *leva* ~*ets glada
dagar* (*vard.*) be having the time of one's life; *för
hela* ~*et* for life; *frukta för sitt* ~ go in fear for
one's life; *inte för mitt* ~*!* not for the life of me!;
i hela mitt ~ all my life; *han har inte ngn släkting
i* ~*et* he has no living relatives; *det är hopp om* ~*et*
(*skämts.*) where there's life there's hope; *en strid
på* ~ *och död* a life-and-death struggle; *trött på
~et* tired of [one's] life; *väcka till* ~ wake to life,
(*friare*) awaken [to life], arouse **2** *bildl.* life, vitality; (*kläm*) spirit, mettle; (*fart*) go; *AE. vard.*
pep; *det var* ~ *och rörelse överallt* there was a
bustling throng everywhere; *med* ~ *och lust* with
enthusiasm, very heartily **3** (*oväsen*) commotion,
row; *föra ett förfärligt* ~ make (kick up) a terrible
row **4** (*levande varelse*) living being; thing; *det
lilla* ~*et!* the little darling!; *inte ett* ~ not a soul
liva 1 animate, enliven; (*muntra upp*) liven
(cheer) up **2** (*egga*) stimulate; (*öva pennalism*)
rag, bully **livad** *a5* **1** (*munter*) jolly, merry **2**
(*hågad*) inclined (*för* for)
liv|aktig *a1* lively; (-*full*) animated **-boj** life buoy
-båt lifeboat **-båtsövning** boat drill **-bälte** life
belt; cork jacket; *AE.* life preserver **-dömd** *a5*
sentenced to death **-egen I** *a3* in villeinage (serfdom) **II** *s, pl* -*egna*, villein, serf **-egenskap** *s3*
villeinage, serfdom **-full** full of life (animation),
vivid, vivacious
livförsäkr|a insure (*ngn* a p.'s life; *sig* one's life)
-ing life insurance (*BE. äv.* assurance)
livförsäkrings|agent life insurance agent
-brev life insurance policy **-premie** life insurance premium
liv|garde life-guards; (*truppförband*) Life
Guards (*pl*) **-gardist** Life-Guardsman **-gi-
vande** *a4* life-giving; vivifying; animating; *bildl.*

L

äv. heartening **-hanken** *vard. i uttr.:* rädda ~ save one's skin

Livius ['li:-] Livy

livklädnad *bibl.* tunic

livlig [*li:v-] *a1* lively; (*-full*) animated, spirited; (*rörlig*) active; (*t. temperamentet*) sprightly, vivacious; (*levande*) vivid; ~ *debatt* keen debate; *röna* ~ *efterfrågan* meet with a keen (brisk, lively) demand; ~ *fantasi* lively (vivid) imagination; ~ *trafik* heavy (busy) traffic; *~t trafikerad gata* busy (crowded) street; ~ *verksamhet* lively (intensive) activity **-het** liveliness *etc.*; animation; vivacity; activity

liv|lina lifeline **-lös** lifeless; (*död*) dead; *bildl. äv.* dull; *~a ting* inanimate things **-medikus** *s2, best. form äv.* =, *pl äv.* **-medici** physician in ordinary (*hos* to) **-moder** *anat.* uterus (*pl* uteri); womb **-moderhals** cervix **-nära** support, maintain; feed

Livorno [-'vårnå] *n* Leghorn

livré *s4* livery **-klädd** liveried

liv|rem belt **-rustkammare** *L~n* [the] Royal Armoury **-rädd** terrified, frightened to death **-räddare** life-saver, rescuer **-räddning** life-saving **-räddningsbåt** lifeboat **-ränta** [life] annuity **-rätt** favourite dish

livs [lifs] *se 1 liv 4* **-andar** *pl, ngns* ~ a p.'s spirits **-avgörande** *a4* vital, of decisive importance **-bejakande** *a4* positive **-bejakelse** positive attitude to life **-cykel** life cycle **-duglig** capable of survival; healthy **-elixir** elixir of life **-erfaren** experienced, with experience of life **-erfarenhet** experience [of life] **-fara** deadly peril, danger (peril) to life [and limb]; *sväva i* ~ be in mortal danger (peril) **-farlig** highly dangerous, perilous; (*om sjukdom*) grave; ~ *spänning!* (*elektr.*) Danger! High Voltage **-filosofi** philosophy [of life] **-form** form of life **-föring** way of life **-förnödenheter** *pl* necessaries of life **-glädje** joy of living **-gnista** spark of life, vital spark **-hotande** ~ *skador* grave injuries **-intresse** chief interest in life **-kraft** vital force (power); vitality **-kraftig** vigorous, robust **-kvalitet** quality of life **-leda** weariness of life **-ledsagare**, **-ledsagarinna** life companion **-levande** lifelike; in person (the flesh) **-lust** zest for life **-lång** lifelong **-längd** length (term) of life; (*t.ex. lampas*) life **-lögn** lifelong deception

livsmedel *pl* provisions, food[s], foodstuffs **livsmedels|butik** food shop, grocer's (grocery) [store]; (*snabbköp*) self-service shop **-försörjning** food supply [system] **-industri** food [manufacturing] industry **-teknologi** food technology **-verk** *Statens* ~ [the Swedish] national food administration

livs|mod will to life **-nerv** *bildl.* vital nerve **-oduglig** unfit to live **-rum** *polit.* lebensraum; living-space **-stil** way of life **-tecken** sign of life; *han har inte givit ngt* ~ *ifrån sig* there is no news from him, he has not written

livstid *i* (*under*) *vår* ~ in our lifetime; *på* (*för*) ~ for life; *~s straffarbete* penal servitude for life

livstids|fånge prisoner serving life sentence; *vard.* lifer **-straff** lifelong punishment; imprisonment for life

livstycke (*för barn*) under-bodice

livs|uppgift task (mission) in life **-verk** life's work, life-work **-viktig** vitally important, of vital importance **-vilja** will to life **-villkor** vital condition **-åskådning** view (conception) of life; philosophy

livtag *sport.* waist lock; *ta* ~ apply a waist lock, *bildl.* wrestle

livvakt bodyguard

ljud [ju:d] *s7* sound (*äv. ~et*); *inte ge ett* ~ *ifrån sig* a) not make a (the slightest) sound, b) (*tiga*) not say a single word **ljuda** ljöd *-it* (*språkv. v1*) sound; (*klinga*) ring; (*brusa*) peal; *det ljöd röster i trappan* voices were heard on the stairs; *ett skott ljöd* a shot rang out

ljud|arkiv sound archive **-band** recording tape; *film.* sound track **-bang** *s2* sonic bang (boom) **-boj** whistling buoy **-dämpande** *a4* sound-absorbing **-dämpare** [exhaust] silencer, *särsk. AE.* muffler **-effekt** sound effect **-film** sound-film, *AE.* talkie **-härmande** *a4* sound-imitating; onomatopoe[t]ic; ~ *ord* (*äv.*) imitative word **-isolera** soundproof **-isolering** sound insulation

ljud|it *sup. av ljuda* **-kuliss** *radio.* background sound effect **-lag** *s2* sound (phonetic) law **ljud|lig** [-u:-] *a1* loud[-sounding]; resounding (*kyss* kiss) **-lära** *fys.* acoustics (*sg*); *språkv.* phonetics (*sg*), phonology **-lös** soundless, noiseless **-nivå** sound level **-radio** sound-broadcasting **-signal** sound-signal **-skridning** [-i:d-] *språkv.* sound shift **-skrift** phonetic transcription (notation) **-spår** *film.* soundtrack **-styrka** sound; (*volym*) [sound] volume **-tät** soundproof **-upptagning** sound recording **-vall** sound (sonic) barrier **-våg** sound wave **-återgivning** sound reproduction **-överföring** sound transmission

ljug|a [*ju:-] *ljög -it* lie (*för* to); tell lies (a lie, falsehood); ~ *för ngn* tell s.b. a lie (*etc.*); ~ *ngn full* tell s.b. a tissue of lies; ~ *som en häst travar* lie like a horse-coper; ~ *ihop ngt* trump up (fabricate) s.th. **ljugit** *sup. av ljuga*

ljum [jumm] *a1* tepid, lukewarm (*äv. bildl.*); *bildl. äv.* half-hearted; (*om väder*) warm **ljumma** warm [up], take the chill off

ljumsk|brock [*jumsk-] inguinal hernia **ljumske** *s2* groin

ljung [juŋ] *s3* heather, ling

ljung|a [*juŋa] lighten; flash (*äv. bildl.*); *bildl. äv.* fulminate **-ande** *a4* flashing (*ögon* eyes); *bildl.* fulminating; (*om protest o.d.*) vehement **-eld** flash of lightning

ljung|hed [j-] heatherclad moor (heath) **-pipare** *zool.* golden plover

ljus [ju:s] **I** *s7* **1** light (*äv. ~et*); *tända ~et* switch on the light; *stå i ~et för ngn* stand in a p.'s light; *se dagens* ~ see the light of the day; *föra ngn bakom ~et* pull the wool over a p.'s eyes, take s.b in; *nu gick det upp ett* ~ *för mig* now the light has dawned on me **2** (*stearin- etc.*) candle; *bränna sitt* ~ *i båda ändar* burn the candle at both ends; *söka efter ngt med* ~ *och lykta* search high and low [for s.th.]; *han är just inte något* ~ he is no great light, he is not on the bright side **II** *a1* light; light-coloured; (*lysande*) brilliant (*idé* idea), bright (*färger* colours; *framtid* future); (*om hy, hår*) fair; *det* *är redan ~an dag* it is day[light] already; *mitt på ~a dagen* in broad daylight; *stå i ~an låga* be ablaze; *~a ögonblick* lucid moments; *i ~aste minne bevarad* cherished in happy remembrance

ljus|bild slide; *föredrag med ~er* lantern lecture **-blå** light (pale) blue **-brytning** [light] refraction **-båge** electric arc **-dunkel** *konst.* chiaroscuro **-effekt** light (lighting) effect **-flöde** luminous flux **-glimt** gleam of light, *bildl. äv.* ray of hope **-gård 1** *byggn.* well, light-court **2** *(-fenomen)* corona **3** *astr.* halo, *foto. äv.* halo **-huvud** *bildl.* bright boy **-hyllt** *al* light-complexioned, fair-complexioned **-hårig** fair[-haired] **-kopiering** light printing; *(blåkopiering)* blueprinting **-knippe** light beam **-krona** chandelier; *(kristall-)* lustre **-kägla** cone of light **-källa** source of light **-känslig** sensitive to light; *(elektriskt)* photosensitive; *~t papper* sensitized paper **-lagd** *se -hyllt* **-lockig** with fair curly hair **-låga** candle-flame **-manschett** candle-ring **-mätare** light meter, photometer

ljus|na [-u:-] get (grow) light; *(dagas äv.)* dawn; *bildl.* brighten [up], get (become) brighter **-ning 1** *se gryning* **2** *(glänta)* clearing, glade **3** *bildl.* brightening[-up], change for the better, improvement **-punkt** lighting (luminous) point; *elektr.* focus; *bildl.* bright spot, consolation **-reflex** reflected light, reflection of light **-reklam** illuminated [advertisement] sign, neon sign (light) **-sax** *en ~* a pair of snuffers **-signal** light signal, signal light **-sken** shining (bright) light **-skimmer** shimmer of light **-skygg** *med.* photophobic; *bildl.* shady **-skygghet** *med.* photophobia; *bildl.* shadiness **-skylt** electric sign **-stake** candlestick, candleholder **-stark** *(om stjärna e.d.)* of great brilliance; *(om lampa e.d.)* bright **-strimma** streak of light **-stråle** ray *(kraftigare:* beam) of light **-stump** candle-end **-styrka** intensity of light; *(i normalljus)* candle-power **-stöpning** [-ö:-] candle-making

ljuster ['just-] *s7* [fishing-]spear, [fish]gig **ljustra** spear

ljus|veke candlewick **-våg** light-wave **-år** light year **-äkta** light-proof; *~ färg* fast colour

ljut|a [*ju:-] *ljöt -it, num. end. i uttr.: ~ döden* meet one's death **ljutit** *sup. av ljuta*

ljuv [ju:v] *al* sweet; *(om doft, sömn, vila äv.)* delicious; *(behaglig)* delightful *(syn* sight); *dela ~t och lett med ngn* share the fortunes (the ups and downs) of life with s.b. **ljuvhet** sweetness *etc.*

ljuvlig *al* sweet *etc.*, *jfr ljuv*

ljöd [jö:d] *imperf. av ljuda*

ljög [jö:g] *imperf. av ljuga*

ljöt [jö:t] *imperf. av ljuta*

LO [*ällo:] *fork. för Landsorganisationen*

lo *s2, zool.* lynx *(pl äv.* lynx)

lob *s3* lobe

lobb [-å-] *s2, sport.* lob **lobba** *vl, sport.* lob

lobotomi *s3* lobotomy

1 lock [låkk] *s2, (hår-)* lock [of hair]; *(ringlad)* curl

2 lock [låkk] *s7 (på kärl o.d.)* lid; *(löst äv.)* cover; *det slog ~ för öronen på mig* I was deafened

3 lock [låkk] *s7 (-ande) med ~ och pock* by hook or [by] crook; *varken med ~ eller pock* neither by fair means nor foul

1 locka [-å-] *(göra lockig)* curl, do up in curls; *~ sig* curl

2 lock|a [-å:-] **1** *(förleda)* entice, allure *([till] att into + ing-form);* *(fresta)* tempt, entice *([till] att into + ing-form);* *(fängsla)* attract; *~ ngn i fällan* trap s.b.; *~ fram* draw out *(ur of);* *~ fram tårar* draw tears *(ur* from) **2** *jakt. o.d.* call *(äv. ~ på);* *(om höna äv.)* cluck *(på* to) **lock|ande** [-å-] *a4* enticing *etc.;* tempting, attractive **-bete** lure *(äv. bildl.);* bait; *bildl. äv.* decoy **-else** enticement, allurement; attraction; temptation **-fågel** decoy bird

lockig [-å-] *al* curly

lockout [låkk'aut] *s3* lockout; *varsla om ~* give advance notice of a lockout **lockouta** [-'au-] *vl* lock out

lock|pris price to catch customers; special offer **-rop** mating call **-sång** call **-ton** callnote; *~er (bildl.)* siren call **-vara** bait, loss leader

locktång curling irons (tongs) *(pl)*

lod *s7* weight; *(sänk-)* plummet; *sjö.* lead

1 loda *sjö.* sound; *bildl.* plumb, fathom

2 loda *(ströva)* stroll [about]; *neds.* mooch [about]

lodenrock loden coat

lodjur *se lo*

lod|lina *sjö.* lead (sounding) line **-linje** vertical line **-ning** *sjö.* sounding *(äv. bildl.)* **-rät** plumb; vertical; perpendicular; *~a ord (i korsord)* clues down; *~t 5* 5 down

loft [låft] *s7* loft

log *imperf. av le*

logaritm *s3* logarithm **-isk** *a5* logarithmic **-tabell** table of logarithms

logdans barn dance

1 loge [*lo:ge] *s2* barn

2 loge [lå:ʃ] *s5* **1** *teat.* box **2** *(ordens-)* lodge

logement [låʃe-, lo-] *s7* barrack room

logera [lå'ʃe:-] **1** *(inhysa)* put up, accomodate, lodge **2** *(vara inhyst)* put up *(hos ngn* at a p.'s house *etc.),* lodge *(hos ngn* with s.b.)

logg [lå-] *s2, sjö.* log **logga** log **loggbok** logbook

loggert ['lågg-] *s2, sjö.* lugger

loggia ['låggia, -ja, 'låddja] *s1* loggia

logg|lina log line **-ning** logging

logi [-'ʃi:] *s4, s6* accommodation, lodging; *konkr.* lodging house; *kost och ~* board and lodging, full board

log|ik *s3* logic **-iker** ['lå:-] logician **-isk** ['lå:-] *a5* logical

logistik *s3* logistics *(behandlas som sg el. pl)*

logo|ped *s3* speech therapist (pathologist) **-pedi** *s3* speech pathology **-typ** *s3* logotype

loj [låjj] *al (trög)* inert; *(slö)* slack; *(håglös)* listless; *(indolent)* indolent

lojal *al* loyal *(mot* to[wards]) **-itet** loyalty

lok *s7, se lokomotiv*

lokal I *s3* place; *(rum)* room; *(sal)* hall; *(kontors-)* premises *(pl)* **II** *al* local **-avdelning** local branch **-bedöva** give a local anaesthetic *(ngn* to s.b.) **-bedövning** local anaesthesia **-färg** local colour *(äv. bildl.)* **-hyra** rent (of premises *etc.)*

lokaliser|a localize, locate, place; *vara väl ~d* be thoroughly at home in *(äv. bildl.)* **-ing** localization, location

L

lokaliserings|politik industrial location policy **-stöd** industrial location grant
lokal|itet *s3* locality **-kännedom** local knowledge **-patriot** local patriot **-patriotism** local patriotism, regionalism **-plan** *på ~et* on the local level **-samtal** local call **-sinne** *ha* ~ have a good sense of direction **-telefon** internal (interoffice) telephone **-trafik** local traffic **-tåg** local (suburban) train **-vård** cleaning **-vårdare** cleaner; (*pl*) cleaning staff
lokatt *se* **lo**
lokbiträde engine-driver's assistant **lokförare** engine driver; (*på ellok*) motorman; (*på diesellok*) engineer **lokomotiv** *s7* engine; locomotive **lokstall** engine shed
lolla [-å-] *s1* country wench
lom [lomm] *s2*, *zool.* diver, *AE.* loon
loma *se* **lomma**
lombardlån [låm'ba:rd-, ˣlåmm-] loan against security
lomhörd [ˣlommhö:rd] *a1* hard of hearing, deaf
londonbo [ˣlånndånbo] *s5* Londoner; (*infödd, vard. äv.*) cockney
longitud [lång(g)i-] *s3* longitude **-inell** *a1* longitudinal
longör [lång'gö:r] tedious passage; (*friare*) dull period
lopp [-å-] *s7* **1** *sport.* running; (*ett ~*) run; (*tävling*) race; *dött ~* a dead heat **2** (*rörelse, gång*) course; *flodens övre ~* the upper reaches of the river; *ge fritt ~ åt* (*bildl.*) give vent to; *efter ~et av ett år* after [the lapse of] one year; *i det långa ~et* (*bildl.*) in the long run; *inom ~et av* within [the course of]; *under dagens ~* (*äv.*) during the day; *under tidernas ~* in the course of time **3** (*gevärs- o.d.*) bore
lopp|a [-å-] *s1* flea; *leva ~n* (*vard.*) have a gay time, go out on the spree **-bett** fleabite **-cirkus** flea circus **-marknad** flea (junk) market; jumble sale
lord [-å-:] *s3* lord; ~ *A.* Lord A.; ~*en* his Lordship **-kansler** *L~n* the Lord Chancellor
lornjett *s3* lorgnette
lort *s2* (*smuts*) dirt, filth, muck **lorta** ~ *ner* get all dirty (*etc.*) **lortgris** little (dirty) pig **lortig** *a1* dirty, filthy, mucky
loss [-å-] *oböjl. a o. adv* loose; off, away; *kasta ~* (*sjö.*) cast off, let go; *skruva ~* (*äv.*) unscrew **lossa** **1** (*lösa upp*) loose[n]; (*ngt hårt spänt äv.*) slack[en]; (*bildl.*) relax; (*knyta upp*) untie, unfasten, undo; (*bryta loss*) detach **2** (*urlasta*) unload, discharge; (*fartyg äv.*) unship, land; ~ *lasten* discharge one's (its) cargo **3** (*skott*) discharge, fire [off] **lossna** come loose (off, untied *etc.*); (*om t.ex. tänder*) get loose; (*om färg o.d.*) loosen **lossning** unloading, discharging, discharge; landing **lossningsplats** (*för fartyg*) discharging berth; (*lossningshamn*) place (port) of discharge
lots *s2* pilot **lotsa** pilot (*äv. bildl.*); conduct
lots|avgift pilotage **-båt** pilot-boat **-distrikt** pilotage district **-ning** pilotage, piloting **-station** pilot station **-verket** [the Swedish] pilotage service
lott [-å-] *s3* **1** lot; (*andel äv.*) share, portion; (*öde*) lot, fate, destiny; (*jord-*) lot, plot; *dra ~ om* draw

lots for; *falla på ngns ~ att* fall to a p.['s lot] to; *olika falla ödets ~er* fate apportions her favours unevenly **2** (*-sedel*) lot, lottery ticket
1 lotta [-å-] *s1* member of [the Swedish] Women's Voluntary Defence Service
2 lott|a [-å-] *v1*, *se* [*dra*] *lott*; ~ *bort* (*ut*) dispose of by lottery
lott|ad *a5*, *lyckligt* ~ well off (situated) **-dragning** drawing [of lots] (*om* for) **-eri** lottery (*äv. bildl.*); *spela på* ~ take part in a lottery; *vinna på* ~ win in a lottery **-eridragning** lottery draw **-lös** portionless; *bli* ~ be left without any share, be left out **-nummer** lot-number **-sedel** lottery ticket
lotus [ˈlo:-] *s2* lotus
1 lov [lå:v] *s7* **1** (*tillåtelse*) permission, leave; *be* [*ngn*] *om* ~ ask [a p.'s] leave; *får jag* ~ *att hjälpa till* may I ([will you] allow me to) help you (*etc.*); *får jag* ~? shall we dance?; *vad får det* ~ *att vara?* what can I show (get for) you? **2** *nu får jag* ~ *att gå* I must leave now **3** (*ferier*) holiday[s *pl*]
2 lov [lo:v] *s2* **1** *sjö.* (*göra en* make a) tack **2** *bildl.*, *slå sina ~ar kring* hover (prowl) round; *ta ~en av ngn* get the better of s.b., take the wind out of a p.'s sails
3 lov [lå:v] *s7* (*beröm*) praise; *sjunga ngns* ~ sing a p.'s praises; *Gud vare* ~! thank God!, God be praised!
1 lova [ˣlå:-] (*ge löfte* [*om*]) promise; (*högtidligt*) vow; ~ *runt och hålla tunt* promise a lot, fulfil ne'er a lot; ~ *gott* promise well, be promising; *det* ~*r gott för framtiden* it promises well for the future; *det vill jag* ~! I should say so!, rather!, *AE. vard.* I'll say!; *jag har redan* ~*t bort mig till i kväll* (*äv.*) I have got another engagement this evening
2 lova [ˣlo:-] *sjö.* luff
3 lova [ˣlå:-] (*prisa*) praise; ~*d vare Gud!* blessed be God!
lovande [ˣlå:-] *a4* (*hoppingivande*) promising; (*om sak äv.*) auspicious; *det ser inte vidare* ~ *ut* (*äv.*) it doesn't look very hopeful
lovart [ˈlo:-] *r*, *i* ~ to windward, on the windward side
lov|dag holiday; *ha en* ~ have a day's holiday **-lig** [ˣlå:v-] *a1*, *den* ~*a tiden för* (*jakt.*) the open season for; *änderna blir* ~*a snart* duck-shooting begins soon
lov|ord [word of] praise **-orda** commend, praise **-prisa** eulogize; ~ *ngn* (*äv.*) sound a p.'s praises **-sjunga** sing praises unto; (*friare*) sing the praise of **-sång** song of praise; (*jubel-*) paean **-tal** panegyric, eulogy (*över* upon); encomium **-värd** *a1* praiseworthy, commendable; (*om företag, försök o.d.*) laudable
LP-skiva [ˣellpe:-] LP (long-playing) record
lucia|dagen [-ˣsi:a-] Lucia Day (*December 13*) **-firande** [-ˣsi:a-] *s6*, ~*t* Lucia Day celebrations (*pl*)
lucka *s1* **1** (*ugns- o.d.*) door; (*fönster-*) shutter; (*damm-*) gate; (*källar-*) flap; (*titthålls-*) [spyhole] hatch; *sjö.* [hatchway] lid **2** (*öppning*) hole, aperture; *sjö.* hatch **3** (*i skrift*) lacuna (*pl äv.* lacunae); *bildl.* gap; (*i minnet*) blank
lucker [ˈlukk-] *a2* loose; light, mellow **luckra** loosen, break up, mellow; ~ *upp* loosen up
ludd *s3*, *s7* fluff; nap **ludda** ~ [*sig*] cotton, rise

with a nap **luddig** *a1* fluffy, cottony, nappy **luden** *a3* hairy; *bot. äv.* downy
luff *s2, vara på* ~*en* be tramping **luffa** tramp; lumber; (*springa*) run **luffare** tramp, vagabond **luffarschack** *ung.* noughts and crosses (*pl*)
lufsa go lumbering; walk (run) clumsily **lufsig** *a1* clumsy
1 luft *s3, en* ~ *gardiner* a pair of curtains
2 luft *s3* air; (*friare äv.*) atmosphere; *fria* ~*en* the open air; *få* [*litet*] *frisk* ~ get a breath of air; *ge* ~ *åt* (*bildl.*) give vent to, vent; *behandla ngn som* ~ treat s.b. as though he did not exist; *han var som* ~ *för henne* he was beneath her notice; *det ligger i* ~*en* it is in the air; *gripen ur* ~*en* imaginary, made up
luft|a air; ~ *på sig* go out for a breath of air; (*däck*) let down **-affär** bogus transaction; fraud **-angrepp** air attack (raid) (*mot* on) **-ballong** [air-]balloon **-bevakning** air defence warning service **-bro** airlift, air bridge **-broms** *flyg.* air brake **-bubbla** air-bubble **-buren** *a5*, *-burna trupper* airborne (parachute) troops **-buss** (*flygplan*) airbus **-bössa** air gun; (*leksak*) popgun **-cirkulation** air circulation **-drag** air current, draught; *AE.* draft **-fart** (*äv.* ~*en*) flying, aviation; (*flygtrafik*) air traffic **-fartsmyndighet** civil aviation authority **-fartsverket** *L~* [the Swedish] board of civil aviation **-fartyg** aircraft (*sg o. pl.*) **-flotta** air fleet **-fuktare** humidifier **-fuktighet** humidity of the atmosphere (air) **-färd** air (aerial) trip **-förorening** air pollution; (*ämne*) air pollutant **-försvar** air defence **-gevär** air gun (rifle) **-grop** *flyg.* air pocket **-hål** air (ventilation) hole; (*-utsläpp*) air-escape
luft|ig *a1* airy; (*om t.ex. klänning*) billowy **-intag** air-intake **-konditionerad** *a5* air-conditioned **-konditionering** air conditioning **-kudde** air cushion; (*i bil*) air bag **-kuddefarkost** cushioncraft, hovercraft **-kyld** *a5* air-cooled **-kylning** air-cooling **-lager** air stratum, layer of air **-landsättning** landing of airborne troops **-led** air corridor, airway **-ledning** overhead [power transmission] line **-madrass** air bed **-maska** chain stitch **-massa** air mass **-motstånd** air resistance (friction, drag)
luft|ning airing, ventilation **-ombyte** change of air **-pistol** air gun **-post** air mail **-pump** air pump, pneumatic pump; (*för cykeldäck o.d.*) tyre-inflator **-renare** air filter (cleaner) **-rening** air purification **-rum** airspace; *flyg.* air territory **-räd** air raid **-rör** *anat.* windpipe, *fack.* trachea **-rörskatarr** bronchitis **-skepp** airship; dirigible **-skydd** air raid precautions service **-slott** castle in the air (in Spain) **-språng** (*glädje-*) caper; *göra* ~ cut capers **-streck** climate **-strid** aerial combat **-strupe** *se -rör* **-ström** current of air, air current, airflow **-tillförsel** air supply **-tom** airless; ~*t rum* vacuum, void **-torka** airdry **-trumma** *tekn.* air shaft **-tryck** atmospheric pressure **-tät** airtight, hermetic **-täthet** air density **-vapen** *se flygvapen* **-ventil** air valve **-vägsinfektion** respiratory infection **-värn** anti-aircraft defence **-värnsartilleri** anti-aircraft artillery **-värnskanon** anti-aircraft gun **-växling** ventilation
1 lugg *s2* (*ludd*) nap, (*på sammet*) pile

2 lugg *s2* **1** (*pann-*) fringe; *titta under* ~ look furtively, keep the (one's) eyes lowered **2** (*-ning*) wigging
lugga ~ *ngn* pull a p.'s hair
luggsliten threadbare; shabby (*äv. bildl.*)
lugn [luŋn] **I** *s7* calm; (*egenskap äv.*) calmness; (*upphöjt* ~) serenity; (*stillhet*) quiet; (*ro*) tranquillity; (*sinnes-*) equanimity, composure ; *i* ~ *och ro* in peace and quiet; *återställa* ~ *och ordning* restore peace and order; ~*et före stormen* the calm before the storm **II** *a1* calm; (*jämn*) smooth (*yta* surface); (*fridfull, ej upprörd*) tranquil; (*stilla*) quiet; (*mots.* ängslig) easy (*för* about); (*med bibehållen fattning*) composed; *med* ~*t samvete* with an easy conscience; *aldrig ha en* ~ *stund* never have a moment's peace; *hålla sig* ~ (*ej bråka*) keep quiet; *var bara* ~*!* don't you worry!
lugna [*x*luŋna] calm, quiet[en]; (*farhågor, tvivel o.d.*) set at rest; ~ *sig* calm o.s. (down); ~ *dig!* don't get excited!, take it easy!; ~ *dina upprörda känslor!* calm down!; *känna sig* ~*d* feel reassured
lugnande *a4* calming *etc.*; (*om nyhet o.d.*) reassuring; *med.* sedative; ~ *medel* sedative, tranquillizer **lugnt** *adv* calmly *etc.*; *ta det* ~ take it (things) easy
luguber [-'gu:-] *a5* lugubrious, gloomy, dismal
Lukas ['lu:-] Luke; ~ *evangelium* the Gospel according to St. Luke, Luke
lukrativ [-'ti:v, 'lukk-] *a1* lucrative, profitable
lukt *s3* smell; odour; (*behaglig äv.*) scent, perfume
lukt|a smell; ~ *gott* (*illa*) smell nice (nasty); *det* ~*r vidbränt här* there's a smell of burning here; *det* ~*r tobak om honom* he smells of tobacco **-flaska** smelling-bottle **-fri** free from smell; odourless; scentless **-organ** organ of smell **-salt** smelling salts (*pl*), sal volatile **-sinne** sense of smell, olfactory sense; *ha fint* ~ (*äv.*) have a keen sense of smell **-vatten** liquid scent **-viol** sweet violet **-ärt** sweet pea
lukullisk [-'kull-] *a5* Lucullan, Lucullian; (*friare*) sumptuous, luxurious
lull *adv, vard., i uttr.: stå* ~ stand on its (*etc.*) own, stand without support
lulla *gå och* ~ shamble along
lullull *s7, koll.* gewgaws (*pl*), tinsel
lumbal|punktion [-*x*ba:l-] lumbar puncture **-vätska** cerebrospinal fluid
lumberjacka windcheater, lumberjacket
lumin|ans *s3* luminance **-iscens** [-'sens, -'ʃens] *s3* luminescence **-ös** *a1* luminous; (*snillrik*) brilliant
lummer ['lumm-] *s9, bot.* club moss
lummig *a1* thickly foliaged; spreading
lump *s1* **1** rags (*pl*) **2** *vard. göra* ~*en* do one's military service **-bod** rag-and-bone] shop, junk shop
lumpen *a3* paltry; (*småaktig*) petty, mean, shabby
lump|or *pl* rags **-papper** rag-paper **-samlare** rag-and-bone man, ragman
lunch *s3* lunch; luncheon **luncha** have [one's] lunch, lunch (*på* on)
lunch|bar *s3* lunch (snack) bar **-rast** lunch break; *skol.* lunch hour (recess) **-rum** (*i företag*) dining (lunch) room; (*självservering*) canteen

L

lund *s2, s3* grove; copse

lung|a *s1* lung; *blodpropp i* ~*n* pulmonary embolism **-blåsa** pulmonary vesicle **-blödning** haemorrhage of the lungs, pulmonary haemorrhage **-cancer** lung cancer, cancer of the lung **-fisk** lungfish - **inflammation** pneumonia; *dubbelsidig* ~ double (bilateral) pneumonia **-mos** *kokk.* hashed [calf's] lights (*pl*) **-siktig** *a1* consumptive **-sot** *s3* [pulmonary] consumption, phthisis **-säck** pleural sack **-säcksinflammation** pleurisy **-tuberkulos** pulmonary tuberculosis

lunk *s3* trot; *i sakta* ~ at a slow jog trot **lunka** jog along

lunnefågel [common] puffin

luns *s2* boor, bumpkin **lunsig** *a1* (*om pers.*) loutish, hulking; (*om plagg*) baggy, ill-fitting

lunta *s1* **1** (*bok*) tome, [big] volume; *nådiga* ~*n* the Budget Bill **2** (*för antändning*) match

lupjn *s3* lupin

lupp *s3* magnifying glass, pocket lens

1 lur *s2* (*instrument*) horn, trumpet

2 lur *s2* (*slummer*) nap, doze; *ta sig en* ~ take a nap, have forty winks

3 lur *s, i uttr.: ligga på* ~ lie in wait, *bildl.* lurk; *stå på* ~ stand in ambush

1 lura (*slumra*) drop off [to sleep], doze off

2 lura 1 (*ligga på lur*) lie in wait (*på* for), *bildl.* lurk **2** (*bedra*) take in; cheat (*på* in, over); (*dupera*) impose upon, dupe; (*övertala*) coax, wheedle, cajole (*ngn att göra* s.b. into doing); (*överlista*) get the better of; *bli* ~*d* be taken in; *mig* ~*r du inte!* you dont catch me!; ~ *av ngn ngt* wheedle (coax) s.th. out of s.b.; ~ *till sig ngt* secure s.th. [for o.s.]; *låta* ~ *sig* [allow o.s. to] be taken in (cheated *etc.*)

lurendrej|are fraud, trickster **-eri** cheating; fraud

lurifax ['lu:-, -'aks] *s2* sly dog (fox) **lurpassa 1** *kortsp.* lie low **2** *bildl.* [lie in] wait **lurt** [-u:-] *vard., ngt* ~ s.th. suspect

lurvig *a1* rough; (*rufsig*) tousled; (*om hund o.d.*) shaggy

lus *-en löss* louse (*pl* lice)

lusern [-ä:-] *s3* lucerne, purple meddick, alfalfa

lusig *a1* lousy

luska *se snoka*

luspank stony-broke

lussa *v1, vard.* celebrate Lucia Day

lust *s2* **1** (*håg*) inclination, mind; (*benägenhet, håg*) bent, disposition; (*smak*) taste, liking; *få* ~ *att* (*äv.*) take it into one's head to; *kom när du får* ~*!* come when you feel inclined [to]!; *ha* ~ *att a*) feel inclined (have a mind) to, *vard.* feel like (*sjunga* singing), *b*) (*bry sig om*) care to; *tappa* ~*en för* lose all desire for **2** (*glädje*) delight, pleasure; *i nöd och* ~ in weal and woe, (*i vigselformulär*) for better for worse **3** (*åtrå*) desire

lust|a *s5* lust; desire **-barhet** [-a:-] amusement **-betonad** pleasurable; ~*e känslor* feelings of pleasure **-eld** bonfire **-gas** laughing gas, *fack.* nitrous oxide **-gård** *Edens* ~ the garden of Eden **-hus** summerhouse

lustig *a1·* **1** (*roande*) amusing, funny; (*munter·*) merry, jolly; *göra sig* ~ *över* make fun of, poke fun at; *hastigt och* ~*t* all of a sudden, straight away **2** (*löjlig*) funny, comic[al]; (*underlig*) odd,

strange, peculiar **-het** *säga en* ~ say s.th. amusing, make an amusing remark, crack a joke **-kurre** joker, wag

lust|jakt [pleasure] yacht **-känsla** sense (*-förnimmelse*: sensation) of pleasure **-mord** sex murder **-resa** pleasure trip (excursion) **-slott** royal out-of-town residence, pleasure palace **-spel** comedy **-spelsförfattare** comedy writer **-vandra** stroll about for pleasure

1 lut *s2* (*tvätt-*) lye

2 lut *s3, s7 stå* (*ligga*) *på* ~ be aslant; *ha* [*ngt*] *på* ~ have s.th. in reserve (up one's sleeve)

1 luta *s1* lute

2 luta *v1* (*lutlägga*) soak (steep) in lye

3 luta *v1* **1** lean (*äv.* ~ *sig*); incline; (*slutta*) slope, slant; ~ *sig ner* stoop; ~ *sig ut* lean out **2** (*tendera*) incline (*åt* towards); *jag* ~*r åt den åsikten att* I am inclined to think that; *det* ~*r nog ditåt* that is what it is coming to; *se vartåt det* ~*r* see which way things are going; ~ *mot sitt fall* be on the road to ruin

lutad *a5* leaning (*mot* against); inclined, sloping (*bakåt* backwards); *gå* ~ walk with a stoop **lutande** *a4* leaning; inclined (*plan* plane); (*om bokstäver o.d.*) sloped, slanted; (*framåt-*) stooping; ~ *tornet i Pisa* the leaning tower of Pisa; ~ *stil* [a] sloping hand

luteran, luterdom, lutersk *se lutheran, lutherdom, luthersk*

lutfisk [dried] stockfish

luther|an *s3* Lutheran **lutherdom** [ˣlutt-] *s2,* ~ [*en*] Lutheranism **luthersk** ['lutt-] *a5* Lutheran

lutning [-u:-] inclination; (*sluttning*) slope

lutningsvinkel angle of inclination, pitch

lut|spelare lute player, lutenist **-sångare** singer to the lute

lutter ['lutt-] *oböjl. a* sheer, pure; downright **luttra** *bildl.* try, purify, chasten; ~*d* tried, chastened **luttring** trying *etc.*; purification

luv *s2, ligga i* ~*en på varandra* be at loggerheads [with each other]; *råka i* ~*en på varandra* fly at each other, fall foul of each other

luva *s1* [woollen] cap

luxuös *a1* luxurious, sumptuous

lya *s1* lair, hole; den *äv. bildl.*)

1 lyck|a *v3, inom* -*ta dörrar* behind closed doors

2 lyck|a *s1* (*levnads-*) happiness; (*sällhet*) bliss; (*tur*) luck, good fortune; (*framgång*) success; (*öde*) fortune; *bättre* ~ *nästa gång!* better luck next time!; ~ *till* good luck!; *du* ~*ns ost!* you lucky beggar!; *göra stor* ~ be a great success; *en stor* ~ *fyllde honom* he was filled with great joy, he was brimming over with happiness; *göra sin* ~ make one's fortune; *ha* ~ *med sig a*) (*ha framgång*) be successful (fortunate), *b*) (*medföra* ~) bring [good] luck; *ha den* ~*n att* have the good fortune to, be fortunate enough to; *pröva* ~*n* try one's fortune; *sin egen* ~*s smed* the architect of one's own fortunes

lyck|ad *a5* successful; *vara mycket* ~ be a great success; *påståendet var mindre -at* the statement was hardly a happy one **lyck|as** *dep* succeed, be successful (*göra* in doing); (*gå bra*) be (turn out) a success; (*om pers.*) manage, contrive (*hitta* to find); *det* ~*ades inte alls* (*äv.*) it proved to be a complete failure; *allt* ~ *för honom* everything he touches prospers, he is successful in everything **lycklig** *a1* (*uppfylld av lycka*) happy; (*gynnad av lycka*) fortunate; (*tursam*) lucky; ~ *resa!* a pleasant journey!, bon voyage!; *i ~aste fall* at best; *av* (*genom*) *en ~ slump* by a lucky (happy) chance; *en ~ tilldragelse* a happy event **lyckligen** safely (*anländ* arrived) **lyckliggöra** make happy **lyckligt** *adv* happily *etc.*; ~ *okunnig om* blissfully ignorant of; *komma ~ och väl hem* get home safely; *om allt går ~* if everything goes favourably (well, successfully); *leva ~* live happily **lyckligtvis** fortunately, luckily; happily

lycko|bringande *a4* lucky, bringing fortune (*etc.*) [in its train] **-dag** lucky day **-hjul** wheel of fortune **-kast** lucky throw (hit) **-klöver** four-leaf (four-leaved) clover **-moral** eudaemonism; ethics of happiness **-piller** tranquillizer **-sam** *a1* prosperous; successful **-slant** lucky coin **-stjärna** lucky star **-tal** lucky number

lycksalig supremely happy, blissful **-het** bliss, supreme happiness (felicity)

lycksök|are, -erska fortune hunter, adventurer

lyckt *se 1 lycka*

lyck|träff lucky shot, stroke of luck; *en ren ~* a mere chance **-önska** ~ *ngn* congratulate s.b. (*till ngt* on s.th.) **-önskan** congratulation **-önskningstelegram** greetings telegram

1 lyda *v2, imperf. av löd* (*åt-*) obey; (*råd äv.*) follow, take; (*lyssna t.*) listen to (*förnuftets röst* the voice of reason); *ej ~ order* (*äv.*) disobey orders; ~ *roder* answer [to] the helm; ~ *under a*) (*om land o.d.*) be subject to, *b*) (*om ämbetsverk o.d.*) be under (subordinate to), be under the jurisdiction of, *c*) (*tillhöra*) belong to

2 lyd|a *v2, imperf. av löd* **1** (*ha viss -else*) run, read; *hur -er frågan?* how does the question read?; ..., *löd svaret* ..., was the reply; *domen -er på* the sentence is **2** *en räkning ~nde på 200 pund* a bill for £200; *~nde på innehavaren* made out to bearer

lydelse wording, tenor

lydfolk tributary people **lydig** *a1* obedient; (*lag-*) loyal; (*foglig*) docile; (*snäll*) good **lydnad** [-y:-] *s3* obedience (*mot* to); loyalty **lydstat** tributary (vassal) state

lyft *s7* lift, hoist, heave **lyfta** *v3* **1** lift; (*höja*) raise (*på hatten* one's hat); (*häva*) heave; *bildl.* lift, elevate **2** (*uppbära*) draw, collect (*sin lön* one's salary); (*uttaga*) withdraw, take out (*pengar på ett konto* money from an account) **3** (*om fågel*) take wing (flight); *flyg.* take off, lift; (*om dimma o.d.*) lift

lyft|anordning hoist, gin **-kran** [hoisting] crane **-ning** lift; *bildl.* elevation, uplift

lyhörd [-ö:-] *a1* **1** (*om pers.*) with a sensitive (sharp) ear; keenly alive (*för* to) **2** (*om rum o.d.*) insufficiently soundproof **-het 1** sensitiveness of hearing (ear) (*för* for); sensitive ear (*för* to); inadequacy of soundproofing

1 lykta *v1, se sluta*

2 lykta *s1* lantern; (*gat-, bil- o.d.*) lamp

lykt|gubbe *se irrbloss* **-stolpe** lamppost **-tändare** lamplighter

lymf|a *s1* lymph **-kärl** lymphatic [vessel] **-knuta** lymph node (gland) **-körtel** *se -knuta*

lymmel *s2* blackguard; scoundrel, villain **-aktig**

a1 blackguardly; villainous

lynch|a lynch **-ning** lynching

lynne *s6* **1** (*läggning*) temperament; (*sinnelag*) disposition, temper; *ha ett häftigt ~* have a hasty temper **2** (*sinnesstämning*) humour; temper, mood; *vara vid dåligt ~* (*äv.*) be in low spirits **lynneskast** *tvära ~* temperamental ups and downs **lynnesutbrott** outburst of temper **lynnig** *a1* capricious

1 lyr|a *s1* (*kast*) throw; *ta -or* catch balls

2 lyra *s1* (*mus. o friare*) lyre

lyr|formig [-å:-] *a1* lyre-shaped **-fågel** lyrebird

lyrik *s3* lyrics (*pl*); lyric poetry **lyriker** ['ly:-] lyric poet **lyrisk** ['ly:-] *a5* lyric; *bli ~* (*vard.*) grow lyrical

lys|a *v3* **1** (*avge ljus*) shine (*klart* bright[ly]); give (shed) light; (*glänsa*) gleam, glitter; (*glöda*) glow; *det -er i köket* the light is (lights are) on in the kitchen **2** *bildl.* shine (*av* with); *ansiktet -te av lycka* his (*etc.*) face was alight with happiness; *glädjen -te i hans ögon* joy shone in his eyes; ~ *inför andra* show off before other people; ~ *med sina kunskaper* (*äv.*) make a display of one's knowledge; ~ *med sin frånvaro* be conspicuous by one's abscence; ~ *med lånta fjädrar* (*äv.*) strut in borrowed plumes; ~ *upp* light up, (*illuminera*) illuminate, (*friare äv.*) lighten, brighten [up] **3** ~ *ngn* light s.b. (*nedför en trappa* down a staircase) **4** *det -er för dem* the banns are to be published for them

lysande *a4* **1** shining *etc.*; (*klar*) bright; (*själv-*) luminous; (*strålande*) radiant; (*om t.ex. dräkter*) resplendent (*i granna färger* in gay colours) **2** *bildl.* brilliant; (*storartad*) splendid; (*bländande*) dazzling (*framgång* success); (*frejdad*) illustrious; ~ *resultat* (*äv.*) spectacular result; *ett ~ undantag* (*äv.*) an outstanding exception; *gick allt annat än* ~ was by no means a brilliant success

lys|boj light buoy **-bomb** flare

lys|e *s6* light[ing] **-färg** luminous paint **-gas** coal (town, city) gas **-kraft** luminosity **-mask** glowworm

lysning [-y:-] banns (*pl*) **lysningspresent** wedding present

lysol [-'så:l] *s3, kem.* lysol

lys|olja lamp oil **-rör** fluorescent tube **-rörsarmatur** fluorescent tube fittings, neon light fittings (*pl*)

lyssna listen (*efter* for; *på* to) **lyssnarapparat** *mil.* sound detection apparatus, sound locator **lyssnare** listener **lyssnarpost** *mil.* listening post; (*radio. etc.*) listeners' mail

lysten *a3* (*glupsk*) greedy (*efter* for); (*girig*) covetous (*efter* for); (*ivrig*) eager (*på* for)

1 lyster ['lyss-] *s3, s2* lustre

2 lyster ['lyss-] *pres. sg, imperf. lyste, vanl. opers., det ~ mig att* I have a good mind to **lystmäte** *s6, få sitt ~* have one's fill (*på* of) **lystnad** *s3* greediness *etc.*; greed

lystr|a pay attention; obey (*äv.* ~ *till*); (*spetsa öronen*) prick up one's (its) ears; ~ *till ett namn* answer to a name **-ing** response; obedience; ~*!* (*mil.*) attention! **-ingsord** word of command, call to attention

lysträd [ˣly:s-] filament

lyte *s6* defect; deformity; *bildl.* fault, vice

L

1 lytt al maimed, crippled, disabled
2 lytt a, n, se lyhörd
lyx s3 luxury; (i fråga om mat o. dryck) sumptuousness; (överdåd) extravagance **-artikel** luxury **-bil** luxury car, de luxe model **-hotell** luxury (first-class) hotel
lyx|ig al luxurious **-kryssare** luxury cruiser **-liv** life of luxury **-skatt** luxury tax **-telegram** greetings telegram **-upplaga** de luxe edition
låd|a s1 **1** box; (större äv.) case; (byrå- o.d.) drawer; (maträtt) dish cooked in a baking-dish **2** hålla ~ talk the hind leg(s) off a donkey **-kamera** box camera
1 låg imperf. av ligga
2 låg ~t lägre lägst low; bildl. low, mean, base; hysa ~a tankar om have a poor opinion of
låg|a I s1 flame (äv. bildl.); (starkare) blaze; bli -ornas rov perish in [the] flames; stå i ljusan ~ be [all] ablaze; föremålet för hans ömma ~ the object of his tender passion **II** v1 blaze; flame (äv. bildl.); (glöda) glow (av with)
lågad|el ~n the lesser nobility, (i Storbritannien ung.) the gentry **-lig** of (belonging to) the lesser nobility (etc.)
lågande a4 blazing; flaming; burning (hat hatred); med ~ kinder (äv.) with cheeks afire
låg|avlönad low-paid **-frekvens** low frequency **-halsad** a5 low-necked **-halt** vara ~ have one leg shorter than the other **-het** lowness etc. **-hus** low-rise building **-inkomsttagare** low-income earner **-klackad** a5 low-heeled **-konjunktur** depression, economic (business) recession, slump **-kyrklig** Low-Church **-land** lowland[s pl] **-länt** al low-lying **-lönegrupp** low-income category (group) **-mäld** [-ä:-] al low-voiced, low-key (äv. bildl.); bildl. quiet, unobtrusive **-mäldhet** [-ä:-] bildl. quietness etc. **-mält** [-ä:-] adv in a low voice **-nivåspråk** data. low-level language **-sinnad** a5 se -sint **-sint** al base, mean **-skor** shoes **-slätt** lowland plain **-spänning** low voltage **-stadielärare** junior level teacher **-stadium** beginning stage, junior stage; -stadiet (skol.) primary department **-säsong** off season
lågt [-å:-] lägre lägst, adv low; bildl. basely, meanly; ~ räknat at a low estimate
låg|tryck 1 meteor. depression, low **2** fys. low pressure **-trycksområde** low pressure area
lågtstående a4 (om kultur o.d.) primitive
låg|tyska Low German **-vatten** low water; (vid ebb) low tide **-vattenmärke** bildl. low-water mark **-växt** al short
lån s7 loan (mot ränta at interest; mot säkerhet on security); ordet är ett ~ från engelskan the word has been borrowed from the English; ha ngt till ~s have s.th. on loan, have borrowed s.th.
låna 1 (ut-) lend (åt to); AE. äv. loan; (förskottera) advance; ~ ut lend [out]; ~ sitt namn åt allow one's name to be used by; ~ sig till lend o.s. to **2** (få t. låns) borrow (av from); ~ upp borrow; ~ pengar på raise money on
låne|ansökan loan application **-belopp** amount of the loan, loan (credit) amount **-bibliotek** lending library; circulating library **-handling** loan (credit) document **-verksamhet** lending operations (pl) **-villkor** pl terms of a loan, loan terms

lång ~t längre längst **1** (om tid o. rum) long; (väl ~, -randig etc.) lengthy; (tämligen ~) longish; (stor) great (avstånd distance), big (steg stride); lagens arm är ~ the arm of the law is far-reaching; lika ~ of equal length; hela ~a dagen all day long; inte på ~a vägar så bra not by a long way (not anything like) so good; han blev ~ i ansiktet his face fell; det tar inte ~ tid att it won't take long to; tiden blir ~ när time seems long when; på ~ sikt in the long run, on the long term, long-range ... **2** (om pers.) tall
långa s1, zool. ling
lång|bent [-e:-] al long-legged **-bord** long table **-byxor** pl long trousers, (fritids-) slacks **-dans** long-line dance **-distanslöpning** long-distance race **-distansrobot** long-range [guided] missile **-dragen** a3, bildl. protracted (debatt debate); lengthy; (tröttsam) tedious **-film** long (full-length) film **-finger** middle finger **-fingrad** a5, bildl. light-fingered **-franska** s1, s7, ung. tin loaf **-fredag** Good Friday (äv. ~en) **-fristig** al long-term **-färd** long trip (expedition, voyage) **-färdssegling** long-distance sailing **-färdsskridsko** long-distance skate **-grund** (om strand) shelving; (om vatten) shoaling **-hårig** long-haired
långivare lender; granter of a loan
lång|kalsonger pl long underpants, vard. long johns **-kok** long, slow cooking **-körare** pjäsen har blivit en ~ the play has had a very long run **-körning** long- distance run
lång|lig al longish; på ~a tider for ever so long, for ages **-livad** a5 long-lived; inte bli ~ not last long, (om pers.) not be long for this world **-mjölk** processed sour milk **-modig** patient, forbearing, long-suffering
långods borrowed (loaned) property
lång|promenad ta sig en ~ go for a long walk **-randig** bildl. long-winded, tedious[ly long] **-resa** long journey (sjö. voyage) **-rev** long line
långsam al slow (i, med in, at, over); (trög, äv. om puls) sluggish; (maklig) leisurely; (senfärdig) tardy **långsamt** adv slowly; ~ men säkert slow [ly] but sure[ly]; ett ~ verkande gift a slow[-working] poison; det går ~ för dem att it is a slow business their (+ ing-form), they are so slow in (+ ing-form) **långsamhet** slowness etc.
lång|sida long side **-sides** alongside **-siktig** al long-range, long-term **-siktsplanering** long-range planning **-sint** al resentful **-sjal** vard. one grand (= 1 000 kronor bill) **-skallig** dolichocephalic, dolichocephalous **-skepp 1** byggn. nave **2** (drakskepp) longship **-skepps** [-ʃ-] sjö. fore--and-aft **-skjutande** a4 long-range **-skäggig** long-bearded **-sluttande** a4 gradually sloping **-smal** long and narrow **-spelande** a4 long-playing (skiva record) **-strumpa** stocking **-sträckt** al of some length, longish **-synt** [-y:-] al long-sighted **-sökt** [-ö:-] a4 far-fetched; strained
långt längre längst, adv **1** rumsbet. (härifrån [away] from here); a long way (dit there; till to); gå ~ (bildl.) go far, rise high [in life]; gå för ~ (bildl.) go too far; nu går det för ~! this is too much of a good thing!; hon hade inte ~ till tårarna her tears were not far off; man kommer inte ~ med fem shilling you don't get far with five shil-

lings; *så* ~ thus (so) far; *så* ~ *ögat når* as far as the eye can see; *resa* ~ *bort* go a long journey; *vi har* ~ *till affären* we have a long way to go to the shop; *det är* ~ *mellan bra filmer* good films are few and far between; *det är* ~ *mellan gårdarna* the farms are far apart; *det är* ~ *mellan blixtarna* the lightning flashes come at long intervals; ~ *inne i tunneln* far (well) down the tunnel **2** *tidsbet.* long (*efteråt* afterwards); far (*in på det nya året* into the new year); ~ *innan* long (a long while) before; ~ *om länge* at long last; *så* ~ *jag kan minnas tillbaka* as far back as I can remember **3** (*vida*) far (*bättre* better; *överlägsen* superior to); (*mycket äv.*) much, a great deal, a lot; ~ *ifrån* (*ingalunda*) by no means **-gående** *a4* far-reaching, extensive, considerable **-ifrån** ['lå̊n̥t-] *se långt 3*

lång|tidsprognos long-term (long-range) forecast **-tradare** transport (long- distance) lorry; *AE.* freight truck; *vard.* juggernaut **-tråkig** very tedious (*etc.*) **-varig** *al* long; of long duration; (*utdragen*) lengthy, protracted; (*om t.ex. förbindelse*) long-standing **-varighet** lengthiness, protractedness **-våg** *radio.* long wave **-vård** long- -term treatment, long-stay care **-vårdsklinik** long-stay ward **-väga** *oböjligt a o. adv* from a [long] distance; *en* ~ *gäst* a guest [who has come] from afar; ~ *ifrån* from far away **-ärmad** *a5* long- -sleeved

lån|ord loan word **-tagare** borrower

1 lår *s2* (*låda*) [large] box; (*pack*-) case, chest

2 lår *s7* thigh

lår|ben thighbone, *fack.* femur **-bensbrott** fractured thigh[bone] **-benshals** neck of the femur

låring *sjö.* quarter

lås *s7* lock; (*häng*-) padlock; (*knäppe*) clasp, catch; *inom* ~ *och bom* under lock and key; *gå i* ~ (*bildl.*) go without a hitch

lås|a *v3* lock; ~ *in* lock up; ~ *upp* unlock; ~ *sig* (*om sak*) get locked, jam, (*fastna*) get stuck; ~ *sig ute* lock o.s. out **-anordning** locking device **-bar** *al* lockable, lock-up **-kolv** spring (latch) bolt **-mekanism** lock device (mechanism) **-smed** locksmith **-vred** door handle

låt *s2* (*melodi*) melody, tune, song; (*ljud*) sound, *bildl.* tune

1 låt|a *lät* -*it* (*ljuda, lyda*) sound (*som* like); *det -er misstänkt* it sounds suspicious; *maskinen -er illa* the machine makes a row; *det -er oroväckande* the news is alarming; *jo, det -er något det!* (*iron.*) tell me another one!; *det -er som om han tänkte komma* [from what I (*etc.*) hear] it seems as if he would come; *du -er inte vidare glad* you don't sound very cheerful

2 låt|a *lät* -*it* I *hjälpv* **1** let; allow to; permit to; ~ *bli ngt* leave (let) s.th. alone; ~ *ngt ligga* (*stå*) leave s.th. alone (where it is); ~ *nyckeln sitta kvar i låset* leave the key in the lock; *ingen lät märka något* no one let on about it; ~ *saken bero* let the matter rest, drop the matter; ~ *vara* leave alone; *låt vara att* even though, although; *låt så vara, men* that may be so, but **2** (*laga att*) have (*hämta ngt* s.th. fetched); get (*göra ngt* s.th. done); (*föranstalta att*) cause (*ngn göra ngt* s.b. to do s.th.); (*förmå*) make (*ngn göra ngt* s.b. do s.th.); ~ *sömmerskan sy en klänning* get the dressmaker to

make a dress; *låt se att* see to it that; *han lät tala om sig* he gave people cause to talk [about him], he got himself talked about; ~ *ngn förstå* give s.b. to understand; ~ *ngn vänta* keep s.b. waiting, let s.b. wait **3** *det -er göra sig* it is possible, it can be done; *det -er höra sig!* that's s.th. like!; ~ *sig väl smaka* tuck in; *det -er säga sig* it can (may) be said; *inte* ~ *säga sig ngt två gånger* not need to be asked twice; ~ *övertala sig* allow o.s. to (let o.s.) be persuaded **4** ~ *sitt vatten* pass one's water

låtgåsystem [-*ˣgå:-*] laissez-faire [system]

låtit *sup. av 1, 2 låta*

låtsad [*ˣlå(t)ss-*] *a5* pretended *etc.*; (*falsk*) sham, mock, make-believe

låtsa|s [*ˣlå(t)ss-*] *dep* pretend; feign; make pretence of, simulate (*vara* being); ~ *att* (*äv.*) make believe that; *han -des att han inte såg mig* he pretended not to see me; ~ *som om det regnar* behave as if nothing were the matter; ~ *inte om det!* don't let on about it!; *skall det här* ~ *vara …?* is this supposed to be …?

låtsaslek make believe

lä *n* lee; *i* ~ to leeward, on the lee[ward] side; *komma i* ~ *för land* get under the lee of the land; *i* ~ *för vinden* sheltered from the wind, in the lee of the wind; *ligga i* ~ (*bildl.*) fall short, be behind-hand

läck *oböjligt a* leaky; *springa* ~ spring a leak; *vara* ~ leak, be a leak **läcka** I *s1* leak; *bildl.* leakage II *v3* leak (*om fartyg äv.*) make water; ~ *ut* leak out (*äv. bildl.*) **läckage** [-*ˈka:ʃ*] *s7* leakage

läcker [*läkk-*] *a2* dainty, delicious **-bit** dainty, morcel; titbit **-gom** gourmet **-het** daintiness; delicacy, dainty

läder ['lä:-] *s7* leather; *en … av* ~ (*äv.*) a leather … **-arbete** leather-work **-artad** [-a:r-] *a5* leather-like; leathery **-fåtölj** leather armchair **-hud** *anat.* leather-skin, corium, dermis **-imitation** imitation leather, leatherette **-lapp** *se fladdermus* **-rem** leather strap **-varor** *pl* leather goods **-väska** leather bag

läge *s6* situation; position; (*plats*) place; (*nivå*) level; (*belägenhet*) site, location; (*tillstånd*) state, condition; *i soliga* ~*n* (*trädg.*) in a sunny location; *hålla ngt i* ~ hold s.th. in position; *i nuvarande* ~ as things stand at present; *i rätt* ~ in place; *saken har kommit i ett nytt* ~ the matter has entered a new phase, the situation has changed; *som* ~*t nu är* as matters now stand

lägel *s2* bottle; (*fat ung.*) puncheon

lägenhet 1 *se våning 2 efter råd och* ~ according to one's means **3** (*transport- o.d., resetillfälle*) opportunity; means of transport; (*båt- äv.*) sailing, ship; *med första* ~ (*sjö.*) by the first ship [sailing]

läg|er ['lä:-] *s7* **1** (*tält- o.d.*) camp (*äv. bildl.*); *slå* ~ pitch [one's] camp, encamp; *det blev oro i -ret* (*bildl.*) everybody was upset **2** (*parti*) party; *ur olika* ~ belonging to various parties **3** (*liggplats*) bed; (*djurs äv.*) lair; *reda sig ett* ~ make a bed **-eld** camp fire **-liv** camp life **-plats** camp site, camping ground

lägervall *i uttr.: ligga i* ~ be in a state of decay, lie waste

läges|bestämning determination of position **-energi** potential energy

1 lägg *s2, anat.* shank

2 lägg *s7 (pappers-, tidnings-)* file

lägg|a *lade lagt* **I** put; (*i vågrätt ställning äv.*) lay (*äv. bildl.*); (*placera på viss plats, på visst sätt e.d.*) place; (*t. sängs*) put to bed; (*ordna sängplatser för*) put to sleep; (*anbringa*) apply (*på* to); ~ grundstenen till lay the foundation stone of; ~ håret have one's hair set; ~ ägg lay eggs **II** (*med betonad partikel*) **1** ~ *an (gevär o.d.)* level, point, aim (*på* at); ~ *an på a) (eftersträva)* aim at, *b)* (*söka vinna*) make up to, make a dead set at **2** ~ *bi (sjö.)* lay (heave) to **3** ~ *bort (upphöra med)* give up, drop, (*ovana äv.*) leave off **4** ~ *fram* put out; *jfr fram-* **5** ~ *för ngn (vid måltid)* help s.b. to **6** ~ *ifrån sig* put (lay) down **7** ~ *ihop* put (place) together **8** ~ *in (jfr in-) a)* (*ngt i*) put into, *b)* se *konservera*; ~ *in ansökan* file (submit) an application; ~ *in en brasa* lay a fire; ~ *in golv* put down a floor, floor; ~ *in hela sin själ i ngt (äv.)* do s.th. wholeheartedly **9** ~ *ner a) se ned-,* *b)* (*pengar, möda o.d.*) spend, expend (*på* in, on), *c)* (*sin röst vid omröstning*) abstain [*sin röst* from voting], *d)* (*klänning*) let down, *e)* (*teaterpjäs*) withdraw **10** ~ *om a)* (*ändra*) change, alter, *b) med.* bandage, bind up, dress; ~ *om rodret* shift the helm **11** ~ *på a)* put on, *b)* (*brev o.d.*) post; ~ *på luren* hang up [the receiver] **12** ~ *till a)* (*tillfoga*) add [on], *b) sjö.* put in (*vid* at) **13** ~ *undan* put away, put aside **14** ~ *under sig (bildl.)* subdue **15** ~ *upp a)* put up (*på* on), *b)* (*mat*) dish up, *c)* (*klänning*) shorten, put a tuck in, *d)* (*hår*) dress, *AE. äv.* fix up, *e)* (*maskor*) cast on, *f)* (*fartyg, förråd*) lay up, *g)* (*an-*) start, set up, *h)* (*upphöra med*) give up; ~ *upp håret på rullar* set one's hair on rollers **16** ~ *ut a)* lay out (*äv. pengar*), *b)* (*klädesplagg*) let out, *c) sjö.* put off (out) (*från* from), *d)* (*bli tjock*) put on weight **III** *rfl a)* (*äv.* ~ *sig ner*) lie down, (*gå t. sängs*) go to bed, (*om sjuk*) take to one's bed, *b)* (*om sak*) settle, (*sänka sig*) descend, (*isbeläggas*) freeze, get frozen over, *c) bildl.* abate, subside, (*försvagas*) lie down (away), (*om svullnad*) go down; ~ *sig i* interfere, meddle (*ngt* in s.th.); *lägg dig inte i det!* mind your own business!, (*äv.*) keep clear of that!; ~ *sig till med* (*skägg o.d.*) grow, (*glasögon*) take to, (*titel e.d.*) adopt, (*bil e.d.*) acquire, (*tillägna sig*) appropriate; ~ *sig ut för ngn* take up a p.'s cause, (*hos ngn*) intercede (put in a good word) for s.b. (*hos* with)

lägg|dags bedtime **-ning 1** *bildl.* disposition, character; (*håg*) bent, turn **2** (*hår-*) setting; *tvättning och* ~ shampoo and set **-spel** jigsaw puzzle

läglig [ˣlä:g-] *a1* opportune, timely; (*passande*) suitable, convenient; *vid första* ~*a tillfälle* at your earliest convenience

lägra [ˣlä:g-] *rfl* encamp; (*om dimma, damm o.d.*) settle

lägre [ˈlä:g-] *komp. t. låg, lågt* **I** *a* lower; (*i rang, värde o.d.*) inferior (*än* to) **II** *adv* lower **lägst** [-ä:-] *superl. t. låg, lågt* lowest; ~*a växeln (på bil)* the low gear; *till* ~*a möjliga pris* at the lowest possible price, at rock-bottom price; *i* ~*a laget* too low; *som* ~ at its (their) lowest

läk|a *v3* heal (*igen* over, up) (*äv. bildl.*); (*bota*) cure; *tider -er alla sår* time heals all wounds **läk-**

ande *a4* healing; curative

läkar|arvode medical (doctor's) fee **-behandling** medical treatment **-besök** visit to a doctor **-bok** medical book

läkar|e doctor; physician; (*kirurg*) surgeon; *praktiserande* ~ general practitioner; *kvinnlig* ~ woman doctor; *gå till* ~ see (consult) a doctor, seek medical advice; *tillkalla* ~ call in a doctor **-hus** health centre **-intyg** doctor's (medical) certificate **-kår** ~*en* the medical profession **-mottagning** surgery; consulting rooms (*pl*) **-recept** [doctor's] prescription **-sekreterare** medical secretary **-undersökning** medical examination (inspection), physical examination **-vetenskap** medical science (*äv.* ~*en*) **-vård** medical attendance (care)

läkas *v3, dep* heal [up]

läke|dom [-domm] *s3* cure **-konst** [the] art of healing; *utöva* ~*en* practise medicine **-medel** medicine; pharmaceutical preparation; drug; (*botemedel*) remedy **-medelsindustri** pharmaceutical industry **-medelsmissbruk** drug abuse

läk|kött *ha gott* ~ have flesh that heals quickly **-ning** [-ä:-] healing **-ningsprocess** process of healing

läkt *s3* (*ribba*) lath, batten

1 läktare (*åskådar-*) gallery; (*utomhus*) platform, stand; (*utan tak*) *AE. äv.* bleachers

2 läktare *sjö.* lighter

läm [lämm] *s2* (*lucka*) flap

lämmel *s2* lemming **-tåg** lemming migration

lämn|a 1 leave; (*ge sig av*) quit; (*överge äv.*) give up; (*befattning äv.*) retire from; ~ *mycket övrigt att önska* leave a great deal to be desired; ~*r mig ingen ro* gives me no peace; ~ *i arv åt ngn* leave to s.b. **2** (*över-*) hand (*ngn ngt* s.b. s.th., s.th. [over] to s.b.); leave; (*in-*) hand in; *hand äv.* render; (*ge, skänka*) give; (*hjälp äv.*) render; (*bevilja*) grant; (*avkasta*) yield **3** ~ *ifrån sig* hand over; ~ *igen* return, give back; ~ *kvar* leave [behind] **-ing** se *kvarleva*

lämp|a I *s1, -or* gentle means; *gå fram med -or* go gently, use velvet gloves; *bruka -or med ngn* coax s.b.; *ta ngn med -or* coax s.b. into [doing] s.th. **II** *v1* **1** (*anpassa*) adapt, accommodate, suit (*efter* to); (*justera*) adjust (*efter* to); ~ *sig* (*foga sig*) adapt (accommodate, suit) o.s. (*efter* to); ~ *sig för* be adapted (suited) for **2** *sjö.* trim; ~ *över bord* jettison

lämp|ad *a5* adapted (*efter* to); suited (*för* for) **-lig** *a1* suitable, fitting; (*som duger, äv.*) fit; (*om anmärkning, behandling äv.*) appropriate; (*lagom*) adequate; (*tillbörlig*) due, proper; (*rådlig*) advisable, expedient; (*läglig*) opportune, convenient; *vidtaga* ~*a åtgärder* take appropriate action; *vid* ~*t tillfälle* at a suitable (convenient) opportunity **-ligen** suitably *etc.*; *det görs* ~ it is best done **-lighet** suitability; fitness

lämpor se *lämpa I*

län *s7, ung.* county, administrative district, province

länd *s3* loin; (*på djur*) hind quarters (*pl*); *omgjorda sina* ~*er* gird up one's loins

lända *v2,* ~ *ngn till heder* redound to a p.'s honour; ~ *ngn till varning* serve as a warning to s.b.

länga [-ŋ-] *s1* (*rad*) row, range; *jfr huslänga*
längd [-ŋd] *s3* **1** (*i rum*) length; (*människas*) height, tallness, stature; *geogr.* longitude; *tre meter på ~en* three metres in length; *i hela sin ~* full length; *resa sig i hela sin ~* draw o.s. up to one's full height; *på ~en* (*äv.*) lengthways, lengthwise; *största ~* (*sjö.*) length over all **2** (*i tid*) length; *i ~en* in the end, in the long run; *dra ut på ~en* be prolonged **-axel** longitudinal axis **-grad** [degree of] longitude **-hopp** long (*AE.* broad) jump **-hoppare** long-jumper **-löpning** long-distance racing **-mått** linear (long) measure **-riktning** longitudinal direction; *i ~en* lengthwise, longitudinally; *i papperets ~* lengthways of the paper
längle [-ŋ-] *-re -st, adv* long; (*i påståendesats*) [for] a long time (while); (*lång stund äv.*) for long; *ganska ~* [for] quite a long time (while); *både ~ och väl* no end of a time; *hur ~ till?* how much longer?; *för ~ sedan* a long time (while) ago, long ago; *på ~* for a long time, for ever so long; *sitt ner så ~!* take a seat while you wait!; *så ~ som* as (*nekande:* so) long as; *så ~ jag kan minnas* ever since I can remember; *än så ~* for the present (the time being)
längesedan long (a long time) ago; *vard.* ages ago
längre ['läŋ-] *komp. t.* lång, långt, länge **I** *a* **1** longer; (*rumsbet. äv.*) farther, further; (*högre*) taller; *göra ~* (*äv.*) lengthen; *för ~ avstånd än* (*äv.*) for distances greater than **2** (*utan jämförelse*) long; (*om t.ex. tal, paus, äv.*) longish, lengthy, of some length; *någon ~ tid kan jag inte stanna* I cannot stay very long; *under en ~* tid for a considerable time, for quite a long time **II** *adv* (*om rum, tid*) further, farther; (*om tid äv.*) longer; *det går inte ~ att* it is no longer possible to; *det finns inte ~* it does not exist any longer; *~ bort* farther away; *~ fram* further on, (*senare*) later on
längs [-ŋs] *~* [*efter* (*med*)] along; (*~ sidan av*) alongside **-efter** [-'efter, 'läŋs-] along **-gående** *a4* longitudinal **-med** along
längst [-ŋst] *superl. t.* lång, långt, länge **I** *a* longest; (*högst*) tallest; *i ~a laget* too long if anything; *i det ~a* as long as possible, (*t.ex. hoppas att*) to the [very] last **II** *adv* farthest, furthest (*bort* away); *~ bak* rearmost; *~ ner* (*upp*) at the [very] bottom (top) (*i* of); *~ till vänster* (*äv.*) at the extreme left
längta [-ŋ-] long, yearn (*efter* for; *efter att* to); *~ efter att ngn skall komma* (*äv.*) be looking forward to a p.'s coming; *~ bort* long to get away; *~ hem* be homesick, long for home **längtan** *r* longing (*efter* for); *förgås av ~ att ngn skall* be dying [with longing] for s.b. to (+ *inf.*) **längtande** *a4*, **längtansfull** longing, yearning, (*om blick äv.*) wistful
länk [-ŋk] *s2* link (*äv. bildl.*); *felande ~* missing link **länka** chain (*fast vid* on to); (*foga*) join, link on (*till* to) (*äv. bildl.*); *bildl. äv.* guide
1 läns *oböjligt a, pumpa ~* pump dry, drain; *hålla en båt ~* (*äv.*) keep the water out of a boat; *ösa en båt ~* bail out a boat
2 läns *s2, sjö.* following wind
1 länsa 1 *se pumpa läns under 1 läns* **2** (*friare*) empty; *bildl.* drain (*på* of); *vard.* clear out; (*förråd äv.*) make a clean sweep of

2 länsa *sjö.* run [before the wind]
läns|arbetsnämnd county labour (employment) board **-bokstav** (*på bil*) county registration letter **-bostadsnämnd** county housing board **-herre** *hist.* feoffor, feudal lord **-man** ['länns-] *ung.* constable; head of the county constabulary **-polischef** county police commissioner
läns|pump bilge-pump **-pumpa** *se under 1 läns*
läns|råd county director **-rätt** county administrative court **-skolnämnd** county board of education **-styrelse** county administrative board
länstol [ˣlä:n-, ˣlänn-] armchair, easy chair
läns|åklagare county prosecutor **-åklagarmyndighet** county public prosecution authority
läpp *s2* lip; *falla ngn på ~en* be to (suit) a p.'s taste; *hänga ~* (*bildl.*) sulk; *melodin är på allas ~ar* the song is on everybody's lips **läppja** *~ på* sip [at], just taste, *bildl.* have a taste of **läppstift** lipstick
lär *v, end. i pres* **1** (*torde*) *han ~ nog* he is likely to; *jag ~ väl inte få se honom mer* I don't expect to see him again **2** (*påstås*) *han ~ vara* he is said (supposed) to be
lära I *s1* doctrine; (*tro*) faith; (*vetenskap*) science, theory; (*hantverks-*) apprenticeship; *gå i ~ hos* be apprenticed (an apprentice) to **II** *v2* **1** (*~ andra*) teach (*ngn franska s.b.* French); (*undervisa äv.*) instruct (*ngn engelska s.b.* in English); *~ bort till ngn* let s.b. into; *~ ut* teach (*ngt t. ngn s.th.* to s.b.) **2** (*~ sig*) learn; *ha svårt för att ~* be slow at learning **3** *rfl* learn (*att skriva* [how] to write); (*tillägna sig äv.*) acquire, pick up; *~ sig uppskatta* come (grow) to appreciate
läraktig *a1* ready (willing) to learn, docile, quick at learning; apt (*elev* pupil) **-het** readiness to learn, teachability
lärarbana teaching career
lärar|e teacher (*för* of, for; *i franska* of French); instructor; (*t. yrket äv.*) schoolmaster; (*i sht vid högre skola*) master **-fortbildning** teacher inservice training **-högskola** college of education, teacher training college
lärarinna [woman] teacher, [school]mistress; *vard.* schoolmarm **lärarinneaktig** *a1* schoolmarmish
lärar|kandidat student teacher **-kår** teaching staff **-rum** staff room **-tjänst** teaching post **-yrket** the teaching profession
lärd [-ä:-] *a1* learned; (*grundligt*) erudite; (*vetenskaplig*) scholarly; *en ~* [*man*] a learned (*etc.*) man, a man of learning; *gå den ~a vägen* go in for (take up) an academic career
lärdom [ˣlä:rdomm] *s2* **1** (*kunskaper*) learning; erudition; scholarship **2** *dra ~ av* learn from
lärdoms|grad academic degree **-historia** history of learning **-högfärd** pride of learning **-prov** test of scholarship
lärft *s4, s3* linen
lärjungle [ˣlärr-] pupil; scholar; (*friare*) disciple; *Jesu -ar* the Disciples of Christ
lärk|a *s1* [sky]lark **-falk** hobby
lärkträd larch [tree]
lärkvingle *gå som -ar* (*bildl.*) twinkle, flash
lär|ling [-ä:-] apprentice; trainee **-lingstid** ap-

prenticeship [period]

läro|anstalt educational institution **-bok** textbook; manual; (*nybörjarbok*) primer **-byggnad** (*-system*) doctrinal system **-dikt** didactic poem **-fader** *kyrkl.* father of the Church; (*friare*) master **-medel** *pl* educational (teaching) materials **-mästare** master; *ta ngn till* ~ take s.b. as one's teacher **-plan** curriculum **-rik** instructive; informative; *föga* ~ not very instructive **-sal** *univ.* lecture room, (*större*) lecture theatre **-sats** precept, thesis, doctrine **-spån** *s7*, *göra sina första* ~ make one's first tentative efforts, serve one's apprenticeship **-stol** [professor's, professorial] chair **-säte** seat of learning, educational centre **-verk** *s7* secondary [grammar] school; *AE. ung.* high school and junior college; *tekniskt* ~ technical college

läroverks|adjunkt assistant master [at a secondary (grammar) school] **-lärare** secondary school master (teacher)

lär|oår apprenticeship year, (*friare*) training year **-pengar** *betala* ~ pay for one's experience **-pojke** boy apprentice

läsa *v3* **1** read (*för ngn* to s.b.; *hos*, *i* in; *om* about; *ur* from; *på läpparna* from the lips); (*genom-*) peruse; ~ *en bön* say a prayer; ~ *korrektur* proofread; ~ *ut en bok* finish [reading] a book **2** (*studera*) read (*juridik* law; *på en examen* for an examination), study; ~ *in* learn (study up) thoroughly; ~ [*på sina*] *läxor* prepare (do) one's homework **3** (*få undervisning* [*i*]) take (have) lessons (*franska* in French from); (*för privatlärare äv.*) coach (*för* with); *gå och* ~ (*för prästen*) be prepared for one's confirmation **4** (*ge undervisning i*) teach, give lessons in; ~ *latin med en klass* take Latin with a class; ~ *läxor med ngn* help s.b. with his (*etc.*) homework

läs|are 1 reader **2** *relig.* pietist **-art** reading, version **-bar** *a1* readable **-barhet** readability **-drama** chamber drama

läse|bok reader; (*nybörjar-* *äv.*) reading-book **-cirkel** reading-circle **-krets** readers (*pl*), public; *stor* ~ wide readership **-sal** reading room

läs|glasögon reading glasses **-hunger** appetite for reading **-hungrig** eager to read; *vara* ~ (*äv.*) be an avid reader **-huvud** *ha gott* ~ have a good head for study (studying)

läsida leeward side; *på* ~*n* leewards

läsk *s2*, *vard.* soft drink, *AE.* pop

läsk|a 1 (*med -papper*) blot, dry with blotting paper **2** (*släcka törsten*) quench; (*svalka*) cool; (*uppfriska*) refresh (*äv. bildl.*); ~ *sig* refresh o.s.

läskedryck [flavoured] mineral water, lemonade, soft drink

läsklass remedial reading class (form)

läskpapper (*ett* a sheet of) blotting paper

läs|kunnig able to read **-lampa** reading lamp; (*säng-*) bedside lamp

läslig [-ä:-] *a1* legible, readable **-het** legibility, readability

läs|lust inclination for (love of) reading (study) **-ning** [-ä:-] reading; (*lektyr äv.*) reading matter **— och skrivkunnighet** literacy **— och skrivsvårigheter** *pl* problems in reading and writing **-ordning** timetable, curriculum

läsp|a lisp **-ning** lisp[ing]

läst *s3* (*sko-*) last **lästa** ~ [*ut*] last

läs|värd worth reading **-år** school year; *univ.* academic year **-ämne** (*motsats övningsämne*) theoretical subject **-övning** reading exercise (practice)

lät *imperf. av 1, 2 låta*

läte *s6* [inarticulate] sound; (*djurs*) call, cry

lätt I *a1* **1** (*motsats tung*) light (*äv. bildl.*); (*om t.ex. cigarr, öl*) mild; *med* ~ *hand* lightly, gently; ~ *om hjärtat* light of heart; *känna sig* ~ *om hjärtat* feel light-hearted; ~ *på foten* light of foot, *bildl.* of easy virtue **2** (*lindrig*) slight (*förkylning* cold); easy (*rullning* roll); gentle (*bris* breeze); (*svag*) faint; *ett* ~ *arbete* (*äv.*) a soft job **3** (*motsats svår*) easy; (*enkel*) simple; *göra det* ~ *för sig* make things easy for o.s.; *han har* ~ *för språk* languages come easy to him, he finds languages easy; *ha* ~ [*för*] *att* find it easy to **II** *adv* **1** (*motsats tungt*) light; (*ytligt, nätt o. jämnt*) lightly, gently; (*mjukt*) softly; *väga* ~ (*äv. bildl.*) weigh light; *sova* ~ sleep lightly; *ta ngt* ~ take s.th. lightly, make light of s.th. **2** (*lindrigt*) slightly; (*ngt litet*) somewhat **3** (*motsats svårt*) easily; readily; *vard.* easy; ~ *fånget*, ~ *förgånget* easy come, easy go; *man glömmer så* ~ *att* one is so apt to forget (one so easily forgets) that

lätt|a 1 (*göra -are, lyfta*) lighten; (*samvete, tryck o.d.*) ease; (*spänning*) relieve, alleviate; ~ *ankar* weigh anchor; ~ *sitt hjärta* unburden one's mind (*för ngn* to s.b.) **2** (*ge -nad*) be (give) a (some) relief; (*bli -are*) become lighter (*etc.*); (*minska i vikt*) go down in weight **3** (*om dimma o.d.*) lift, become less dense; *det börjar* ~ it is beginning to clear up **4** (*bildl., bli mindre svår*) ease; *det har* ~*t litet* things have eased a little **5** (*lyfta*) lift; *flyg. äv.* rise, take off; ~ *på förlåten* lift the smoke screen, abandon secrecy; ~ *på restriktionerna* ease the restrictions; ~ *på pungen* lighten one's purse

lätt|ad *a5, bildl.* eased, relieved **-antändlig** *a1* [highly] inflammable **-are** *komp. t. lätt* **I** a lighter *etc.*, *se lätt I*; (*utan jämförelse*) light *etc.* **II** *adv* more lightly *etc.*, *se lätt II*; ~ *sagt än gjort* easier said than done **-bearbetad** *a5* easy to work **-begriplig** easily understood; obvious **-betong** porous concrete **-fattlig** *a1* easily comprehensible, easy to understand; intelligible **-flytande** (*om vätska*) of low viscosity; (*om skrivsätt, tal*) fluent, flowing **-fotad** *a5* **1** light-footed **2** *se lättfärdig* **-framkomlig** (*om skog o.d.*) [easily] penetrable; (*om väg o.d.*) easy to go (walk *etc.*) along (on) **-funnen** *a5* easily found **-fångad** *a5* easily caught (come by) **-färdig** frivolous; (*osedlig*) of lax morals; (*lösaktig*) wanton **-färdighet** frivolousness *etc.*, (*lösaktig*) wantonness **-förklarlig** *av* ~*a skäl* for obvious reasons **-förståelig** easy to understand **-förtjänt** easily earned (*etc.*) **-hanterlig** easy to handle, easily handled; *bildl.* easily manageable

lätthet 1 lightness *etc.* **2** easiness; simplicity; (*t.ex. att lära sig*) ease; (*t.ex. att uttrycka sig*) facility; *med* ~ (*äv.*) easily

lätting idler, lazybones **lättja** *s1* laziness, idleness, indolence **lättjefull** lazy; indolent

lätt|köpt [-çö:-] *a1, bildl.* easily won, cheap **-lagad** *a5* **1** (*om mat*) easy to prepare **2** (*-reparerad*) easy to repair **-ledd** *a1* easily guided (led);

(*om pers. äv.*) tractable **-lurad** *a5* easily taken in (duped *etc.*); *han är* ~ he's a sucker (*vard.*) **-läslig** (*om handstil*) legible **-läst** [-lä:st] *a4* **1** *se lättläslig* **2** (*om bok, författare*) easy to read **-löslig** easily dissolvable **-manövrerad** *a5* manageable, handy; *flyg.* manoeuv(e)rable **-matros** ordinary seaman **-metall** light metal **-mjölk** low-fat milk

lättna become (get) lighter; *bildl.* lighten, become brighter; *det börjar* ~ (*äv.*) things are looking up **lättnad** *s3, bildl.* relief (*för* for, to), alleviation; (*i restriktioner*) relaxing (*i* of), relaxation (*i* in, of); (*förenkling*) simplification; *det känns som en* ~ it is a relief; *dra en* ~*ens suck* breathe a sigh of relief

lätt|påverkad *a5* easily influenced (affected), impressionable **-retlig** irritable; touchy **-road** *a5* easily amused **-rökt** lightly smoked **-rörd** (*bildl. om pers.*) easily moved (*etc.*); (*om sinne*) excitable; (*om hjärta*) responsive; (*känslosam*) emotional **-rörlig** mobile; *bildl.* very active **-saltad** *a5* slightly salted **-sam** *a1* easy **-sinne** (*obetänksamhet*) thoughtlessness, recklessness; (*slarv*) carelessness; (*-färdighet*) frivolousness, wantonness **-sinnig** *a1* light-hearted, happy-go-lucky, easy-going; (*om handling äv.*) thoughtless; (*-färdig*) wanton, loose **-sjungen** *a3* that sings well **-skrämd** *a5* easily frightened; fearful **-skött** [-ʃött] *a1* easy to handle, easily operated (worked) **-smält** *a1* **1** (*om födoämne*) easily digested, digestible **2** (*om bok o.d.*) *se lättläst* **-stekt** [-e:-] *a1* lightly done, underdone; *AE.* rare **-stött** *bildl.* ready to take offence, touchy **-såld** marketable, readily sold; *en* ~ *vara* (*äv.*) a product with ready sale **-sövd** *a5, vara* ~ be a light sleeper **-tillgänglig** (*hopskr. lättillgänglig*) that can easily be got at; accessible; (*om pers. äv.*) responsive, easy to get on with **-trogen** (*hopskr. lättrogen*) credulous, gullible **-vikt** *sport.* lightweight **-viktare** *sport.* lightweight **-vin** wine **-vindig** *a1* (*ej svår*) easily made, simple; (*bekväm*) handy; (*utan omsorg*) easy-going; (*slarvig*) careless **-vunnen** *a5* easily won **-åtkomlig** easy to get at, easily accessible (*vard.* get-at-able) **-öl** light lager beer

läx|a I *s1* lesson (*till* for); *ge ngn en* ~ give (*bildl.* teach) s.b. a lesson; *ha i* (*till*) ~ have as homework **II** *v1*, ~ *upp ngn* read s. b. a lesson, lecture s.b., *vard.* read the riot act to s.b. **-bok** lessonbook, textbook **-förhör** questioning on homework **-läsning** preparation (learning) of one's homework

löd *imperf av 1, 2 lyda*

löda *v2* solder; (*hård-*) braze

lödder ['lödd-] *s7* lather; (*tvål- äv.*) soapsuds (*pl*); (*fradga äv.*) foam, froth **löddra** lather (*äv.* ~ *sig*) **löddrig** *a1* lathery; (*om häst vanl.*) foaming

lödig *a1* (*om silver*) standard; *bildl.* sterling **-het** [standard of] fineness; *bildl.* sterling character (quality)

löd|kolv soldering iron **-lampa** blowlamp, soldering lamp **-ning** [-ö:-] soldering **-pasta** solder [paste] **-tenn** soldering [tin], tin solder **-vätska** soldering-fluid

löfte *s6* promise (*om* of; [*om*] *att* to + *inf.*, of + *ing-* form); (*högtidligare*) vow; *avlägga ett* ~

make a promise; *bunden av ett* ~ (*äv.*) under a vow; *ha fått* ~ *om* have had a promise of, have been promised; *ta* ~ *av ngn* exact a promise from s.b.; *hålla sitt* ~ keep one's promise; *mot* ~ *om* on the promise of **löftes|brott** breach of one's promise **-brytare** promise-breaker **-rik** promising, full of promise **löga** *rfl, åld.* bathe

lögn [löŋn] *s3,lie*; falsehood; (*liten*) fib; (*stor, vard.*) whopper; *fara med* ~ tell a lie (lies); *det var* ~ *att få ngt ur henne* (*vard.*) it was impossible to get anything out of her **-aktig** *a1* lying; (*om historia o.d.*) mendacious; (*om påstående*) untruthful **-aktighet** untruthfulness, mendacity **-are** liar **-detektor** lie detector, polygraph **-hals** liar

löja [ˣlöjja] *s1* bleak

löje [ˣlöjje] *s6* (*leende*) smile; (*åt-*) ridicule **-väckande** *a4* ridiculous; *verka* ~ have a ridiculous (comic) effect

löjlig *a1* ridiculous; (*lustig*) funny, comic[al]; (*orimlig*) absurd; *göra en* ~ *figur* cut a ridiculous (sorry) figure; *göra sig* ~ *över* make fun of **-het** ridiculousness *etc.*; absurdity

löjrom whitefish roe

löjtnant [ˣlöjj-] *s3* (*vid armén*) lieutenant, *AE.* first lieutenant; (*vid flottan*) sublieutenant, *AE.* lieutenant junior grade; (*vid flyget*) flying officer, *AE.* first lieutenant

löjtnantshjärta *bot.* bleeding heart

lök *s2* **1** (*blom-*) bulb **2** (*som maträtt*) onion **3** *lägga* ~ *på laxen* (*bildl.*) make matters worse **-formig** [-å-] *a1* onion-shaped, bulbous **-kupol** onion dome **-soppa** onion soup **-växt** bulb[ous plant]

lömsk *a1* insidious; (*bedräglig*) deceitful; (*illistig*) sly, wily; (*bakslug*) underhand; (*försåtlig*) treacherous

lön *s3* **1** (*belöning*) reward; recompense; (*ersättning*) compensation; *få* ~ *för mödan* be rewarded for one's pains; *få sina gärningars* ~ get one's deserts **2** (*arbetares*) wages (*pl*), pay, remuneration; (*tjänstemans o.d.*) salary

lön|a (*be-*) reward; (*vedergälla*) recompense; *jfr äv. avlöna*; ~ *ont med gott* return good for evil; ~ *mödan* be worth while **2** *rfl* pay; (*om företag*) be profitable (lucrative); *det* ~*r sig inte* it is no use, it is not worth while (the trouble) **-ande** *a4* (*om företag*) profitable; (*om sysselsättning äv.*) remunerative; *bli* ~ (*äv.*) become a paying proposition

löne|anspråk *pl* salary requirements; *svar med* ~ replies stating salary expected (required) **-avdrag** deduction from wages (salary), payroll deduction **-avtal** wage contract; *koll.* wages (pay) agreement **-förhandlingar** *pl* wage negotiations, pay talks; *centrala* ~ collective bargaining (*sg*) **-förhöjning** increase (rise, *AE.* raise) in salary (wages) **-förmån** emolument; ~*er* (*äv.*) payments in kind, fringe benefits **-glidning** wage drift **-grad** salary grade **-klass** subdivision of salary grade **-läge** wage situation **-nivå** wage level **-rörelse** wage negotiations (*pl*), collective bargaining **-skala** (*glidande* moving) wage (*etc.*) scale **-stegring** rise of wages (*etc.*) **-stopp** wage freeze **-sänkning** wage (*etc.*) cut **-sättning** setting of wage (etc.) rates, wage determination **-tillägg** bonus, increment **-villkor** pl salary (wage) terms, terms cf remuneration **-ökning** wage (etc.) increase

lönlös [ˣlö:n-] (gagnlös) useless, futile **1 lönn** s2, bot. maple [tree]

2 lönn r, i ~, se [i] lönndom

lönn|brännare illicit distiller **-bränning** illicit distilling **-dom** i uttr.: i ~ secretly, in secret, clandestinely **-dörr** secret door **-gång** secret (underground) passage **-krog** unlicensed gin-shop **-lig** al secret; clandestine; jfr hemlig **-mord** assassination **-mörda** assassinate **-mördare** assassin

lönsam [ˣlö:n-] al profitable, remunerative, lucrative **-het** profitability, earning capacity **-hetsberäkning** cost-benefit analysis (calculation)

lönsparande save as you earn

lönt [-ö:-] oböjligt a, det är inte ~ att du försöker it is no good (use) your trying

löntagar|e (arbetare) wage earner; (tjänsteman) salary earner; employee **-organisation** labour organization

löp|a v3 **1** run (ett lopp a race); jfr 2 springa 1; låta ~ let go; ~ fara be in danger; ~ risk att run the risk of (+ ing-form) **2** (sträcka sig) extend, run, go (längs along); en mur -er runt ... (äv.) a wall encircles ... **3** (om drivrem, kran o.d.) run, travel, go; (hastigt äv.) fly, dart; nålen -er lätt the needle goes through easily; låta fingrarna ~ över run one's fingers over **4** (om ränta o.d.) run; lånet -er med 5 % ränta (äv.) the loan carries interest at 5 % (om tik) be in heat **6** ~ till ända (om tidsfrist o.d.) run out; ~ ut (om tid) expire, run out; ~ ut ur hamnen leave (put off from) [the] harbour

löpande a4 running (äv. hand.); i sht hand. current; i ~ följd (bokför. o.d.) in consecutive order; ~ konto open (current) account; ~ order standing order; ~ rigg (sjö.) running rigging; i ~ räkning on current (running) account; ~ utgifter running (working) expenses; ~ band assembly line; (transportband) conveyor belt; producera på ~ band mass-produce

löparbana running track **löpare 1** runner **2** (bord-) table-runner **3** (schackpjäs) bishop

löpe s6 rennet

löp|eld 1 (skogseld) surface-fire **2** sprida sig som en ~ spread like wildfire **-grav** mil. sap; ~ar parallels; approaches **-knut** [running] noose

löpmage zool. abomasum, fourth stomach

löp|maska ladder, run **-meter** running-metre, linear metre **-ning 1** running; (en ~) run; (kapp-) race **2** mus. run, roulade **-sedel** placard; [news]bill **-snara** loop **-tid** (växels o.d.) currency; (låns o.d.) life; duration, [period of] validity (maturity)

lördag [ˈlö:r-] Saturday; jfr fredag

lös I al **1** loose; (rörlig) movable; (flyttbar äv.) portable; (-tagbar) detachable; (ej hårt spänd) slack; ~a blommor cut flowers; ~a delar (reservdelar) spare parts; ~ och fast egendom real and movable estate; i ~ vikt (hand.) by weight **2** (ej tät [t. konsistensen]) loose (snö snow); (mjuk) soft (blyerts lead); vara ~ i magen have loose bowels **3** (konstgjord) false (tand tooth); (mot-

sats skarp) blank (skott shot) **4** (om häst o.d.) untethered, at large; (om hund) unleashed, off the lead; (om seder) loose, lax; (om förbindelse) irregular; (om antagande, misstanke) vague; (om prat o.d.) empty, idle; ~t folk people on the loose, drifters; gå ~ be at large; ~a påståenden unfounded statements; på ~a grunder on flimsy grounds **5** bli (komma) ~ get loose; nu brakar det ~! (om oväder o.d.) now we are in for it!; slå sig ~ take a day off, (bland vänner e.d.) let o.s. go **II** adv, gå ~ på (angripa) attack, go for (ngn s.b.), go at (ngt s.th.)

lösa v3 **1** (tjudrat djur) untether, unloose; (hund) let off the leash, unleash; (friare) release, set free (från, ur from) **2** (lossa på) loose[n]; (boja, knut o.d.) undo, unfasten, untie **3** (i vätska) dissolve **4** (gåta, problem o.d.) solve **5** (ut-) redeem; (biljett e.d.) buy, take, pay for; ~ ut ngn ur (firma e.d.) buy s.b. out of **6** rfl (i vätska) dissolve, be dissolvable; (om problem o.d.) solve

lös|aktig al loose, dissolute **-ande** a4, ~ [medel] laxative

lös|as v3, se lösa 6 **-bar** al [dis]soluble **-bladsystem** loose-leaf system **-bröst** (skjortbröst) shirt front **-drivare** vagrant, vagabond **-driveri** vagrancy **-egendom** personal property (estate), movable property; chattels (pl)

lösen [ˈlö:-] r **1** (för stämpel e.d.) stamp fee (duty) **2** (för brev e.d.) surcharge **3** (igenkänningsord) password; catchword; dagens ~ the order of the day **-ord** se lösen 3

lösesumma ransom

lös|fläta false plait **-gom** dental plate **-göra 1** (djur) set free, release; (hund) let off the leash, unleash, unchain **2** (sak) detach, unfasten, unfix, disengage; (ur nät, snara e.d.) extricate **3** bildl. free, liberate; (kapital) liberate **4** rfl set o.s. free, free (release) o.s. **-hår** false hair **-häst 1** loose horse **2** bildl. gentleman without lady; (friare) gentleman at large **-kokt** lightly boiled, soft-boiled **-krage** [loose] collar **-lig** [-ö:-] al **1** (i vätska) soluble, dissolvable **2** (om problem) solvable, soluble **3** (lös) loose; (om t.ex. moral) lax, slack **-manschett** loose cuff **-mustasch** false moustache **-mynt** a4 blabbing **-ning** [-ö:-] **1** konkr. solution **2** (förklaring) solution (på of); (frågas äv.) settlement; gåtans ~ (äv.) the answer (key) to the riddle **-ningsmedel** [dis]solvent **-nummer** single copy **-nummerpris** single-copy price **-näsa** false nose **-peruk** wig, toupee **-ryckt** a4 torn loose (från off, from); (om ord, mening o.d.) disconnected, isolated

löss (pl av lus) lice

lössjord loess

lös|skägg false beard **-släppt** a4, let loose (etc); (otyglad) unbridled; (uppsluppen) wanton, unrestrained

löst [-ö:-] adv loosely etc.; (lätt) lightly; (obestämt) vaguely; sitta ~ (om plagg) fit loosely; gå ~ på 100 pund (vard.) run into £ 100

lös|tagbar [-a:g] a5 detachable **-tand** false tooth **-öre** se lösegendom

löv s7 leaf **löva** adorn with leafy branches **lövas** dep leaf, leave, burst into leaf

löv|biff leaf-thin slice[s] of beef **-fällning** [the] fall of the leaves; defoliation (äv. ~en) **-groda**

tree frog **-hyddohögtid** *relig.* Feast of Tabernacles, Sukkoth **-jord** leaf mould (soil)
lövkoja *s1, bot.* stock
löv|rik leafy, full of leaves **-ruska** leafy branch **-sal** arbour, bower **-skog** deciduous forest; *AE.* hardwood forest **-sprickning** leafing **-såg** fret saw **-sångare** willow warbler **-trä** hardwood **-träd** deciduous (*AE.* hardwood) tree **-tunn** as thin as a leaf **-verk** foliage **-äng** forest meadow

M

Maas [-a:-] *r* the Meuse
Macedonien [-ke-, -se-, -'dɔ:-] *etc., se Macedonien etc.*
machiavellisk [makia'vell-] *a5* machiavellian
machtal [ˣmakk-] Mach number, Mach
mack *s2* (*pump*) petrol pump; (*bensinstation*) filling (*AE.* gas[oline]) station; (*med service*) petrol (service) station
macka *s1, vard.* sandwich
mackab|é *s3* Maccabee **-eisk** [-'be:isk] *a5* Maccabean
mackapär *s3, vard.* gadget
mad *s3* marsh (bog) meadow
Madagaskar *n* (*ön*) Madagascar; (*republiken*) Madagascar (1958-75 Malagasy)
madagaskisk [-'gask-] *a5* Madagascan, Malagasy
madam [-'damm] *s3, åld.* woman
madonna [-ˣdånna, -'dånna] *s1* Madonna **-bild** Madonna, madonna
madrass *s3* mattress **-era** pad; quilt **-var** *s7* [bed]tick
madrigal *s3* madrigal
maffia ['maff-] *s1* Maf[f]ia
magasin *s7* **1** (*förrådshus*) storehouse; *hand.* warehouse; (*förvaringsrum*) depository; (*skjul*) shed **2** (*butik*) shop **3** (*på eldvapen*) magazine **4** (*tidskrift*) magazine **-era** store [up]; *hand.* warehouse; (*möbler äv.*) store **-ering** [-'ne:-] storing; (*möbel- äv.*) [furniture] storage
magasinshyra (*för magasin*) warehouse rent; (*för magasinering*) storage [charges *pl*]
mag|besvär stomach (digestive) trouble; upset stomach **-blödning** [an] attack of bleeding in the stomach; *med.* gastric haemorrhage **-dans** belly dance
mage *s2* stomach; (*buk*) belly; *anat. äv.* abdomen; (*matsmältning*) digestion; *vard.* tummy; *ha dålig ~* suffer from indigestion; *ha ont i ~n* have [a] stomachache (a pain in one's stomach); *vard.* have a belly ache; *vara hård i ~n* be constipated; *vara lös i ~n* have diarrhoea; *få en spark i ~n*

(*äv.*) get a kick in the guts; *min ~ tål inte* my stomach won't stand, I can't take; *ligga på ~n* lie on one's face
1 mager ['ma:-] *s9* (*österländsk vis*) magus (*pl magi*)
2 mager ['ma:-] *a2, eg. o. bildl.* lean; (*om pers., kroppsdel äv.*) thin; (*knotig*) bony; (*friare, bildl.*) meagre; (*klen*) slender; (*knapp*) scanty; *~ jord* poor (meagre, barren) soil; *~ kassa* scanty funds (*pl*); *~ ost* low-fat cheese; *~ stil* (*boktr.*) lean face; *sju magra år* seven lean years; *~ som ett skelett* a mere skeleton
mager|het leanness *etc.* **-lagd** *a5* rather thin; on the thin side
mag|grop pit of the stomach **-gördel** *med.* abdominal support; (*på cigarr*) band
magi *s3* magic **-ker** ['ma:-] magician
maginfluensa gastric flu
magisk ['ma:-] *a5* magic[al]
magister [-'jist-] *s2, filosofie ~* (*ung.*) Master of Arts (*förk. M.A.*); (*lärare*) schoolmaster; *ja ~n!* yes, Sir! **-examen** *ung.* Master-of-Arts examination
magistral [-j-] *a1* magistral; (*friare*) authoritative; (*mästerlig*) masterly
magistrat [-j-] *s3* civic (city, town) administration; municipal authorities (*pl*)
mag|katarr catarrh of the stomach, gastric catarrh **-knip** pains (*pl*) in the stomach; gripes (*pl*)
magma *s1* magma
magmun orifice of the stomach
magnat [-ŋ-] magnate; *AE. vard.* tycoon
magnesium [-ŋ'ne:-] *s8* magnesium **-blixt** magnesium flash[light]
magnet [-ŋ'ne:t] *s3* magnet (*äv. bildl.*); (*tändapparat*) magneto; *naturlig ~* (*äv.*) loadstone **-band** magnetic tape **-fält** magnetic field **-isera** magnetize **-isering** [-'se:-] magnetization **-isk** *a5* magnetic; *bildl. äv.* magnetical **-ism** magnetism **-it** *s3* magnetite **-kompass** magnetic compass **-mina** magnetic mine **-nål** magnetic needle **-ofon** [-'få:n] *s3* magnetophone, tape recorder **-pol** magnetic pole **-spole** magnetic coil **-tändning** magneto ignition
magnificus [maŋ'ni:fikus] *rector ~* vice-chancellor
magnifik [-ŋni-, -nji-] *a1* magnificent; grand, splendid
magnityd [-ŋ-] *s3* magnitude
magnumbutelj [ˣmaŋn-] magnum
mag|plask belly flop **-plågor** *pl* stomach pains **-pumpa** ~ *ngn* empty a p.'s stomach of its contents; *bli ~d* have one's stomach pumped out **-pumpning** pumping-out of the stomach
magra [-a:g-] become (get, grow) thinner, lose weight; ~ *tre kilo* lose three kilos [in weight]
mag|saft gastric juice **-sjuk** suffering from a stomach disorder **-sjukdom** disease of the stomach **-stark** *det var väl ~t!* (*vard.*) that's a bit too thick! **-stärkande** *a4* stomachic (*äv. ~ medel*) **-sur** suffering from acidity in the stomach; *bildl.* sour[-tempered], sardonic **-syra** acidity in the stomach; *bildl.* sourness of temper **-sår** gastric ulcer **-säck** stomach
magyar [-'dja:r] *s3* Magyar
magåkomma stomach complaint (trouble)

maharadja [-'radja] *s1* maharaja[h]

mahogny [-'håɲni, -y] *s9, s7* mahogany

maj [majj] *r* May; *första* ~ May Day, the first of May **-blomma** May-Day flower

majestät *s7, s4* majesty; *Hans M*~ His Majesty; *Ers M*~ Your Majesty **-isk** *a5* majestic; *(friare)* stately

majestäts|brott lese-majesty **-förbrytare** person guilty of lese-majesty

majolika [-'jɔ:-] *s1* majolica

majonnäs *s3* mayonnaise

major *s3* major; *(vid flottan)* lieutenant commander; *(vid flyget)* squadron leader; *AE.* major, *(vid flottan)* lieutenant commander

majoritet *s3* majority; *ha* ~ have (be in) a majority; *absolut (relativ, kvalificerad)* ~ absolute (relative, [a] two-thirds *etc.*) majority

majoritets|beslut majority resolution **-ställning** *vara i* ~ be in [a] majority **-val** elections conducted on the majority [voting] system

majorska [-ˣjɔ:r-] *s1* major's wife (widow)

majs *s3* maize, Indian corn; *AE.* corn **-ena** [-ˣse:-, -'se:-] *s1* cornflour; *AE.* cornstarch **-flingor** *pl* cornflakes **-kolv** ear of maize (corn), corncob **-mjöl** cornflour; *AE.* cornstarch

majsmörblomma goldilocks

majsolja maize oil

majstång maypole

majuskel [-'jusk-] *s3, boktr.* majuscule, capital letter

mak *oböjligt s i uttr.: i sakta* ~ at an easy pace, *(t.ex. arbeta)* slow but sure

1 maka *v1* move, shift *(äv.* ~ *på)*; ~ *sig* move o.s.; ~ *sig till rätta* settle o.s. comfortably; ~ *åt sig* make room, give way

2 maka I *s1* wife; *poet. äv.* spouse; *hans äkta* ~ his wedded wife **II** *oböjl. a (som bildar ett par)* that match, that are fellows (a pair)

makaber [-'ka:-] *a2* macabre

makadam [-'damm] *s3* macadam, road metal

maka|lös matchless, unmatched; incomparable; peerless **-löst** *adv* peerlessly; incomparably; *(ytterst)* exceedingly, exceptionally

makaroner [-'rɔ:-] *koll.* mac[c]aroni

mak|e *s2* **1** *(äkta* ~) husband; *poet. äv.* spouse; *(om djur)* mate; *-ar* husband and wife; *-arna A.* Mr. and Mrs. A. **2** *(en av ett par)* fellow, pair; ~*n till den här handsken* the other glove of this pair **3** *(like)* match; ~*n till honom finns inte* his match (the like of him) does not exist, you will not find his peer; *jag har då aldrig hört på* ~*n!* I never heard the like (such a thing)!, well, I never!

Makedonien [-'dɔ:-] *n* Macedonia

makedon|ier [-'dɔ:-] *s9* Macedonian **-isk** *a5* Macedonian

maklig [-a:-] *a1* easy-going; *(bekväm)* comfortable; *(loj)* indolent; *(sävlig)* leisurely

makramé *s3* macramé

makrill *s2* mackerel **-moln** mackerel sky

makro|biotik macrobiotics *(pl, behandlas som sg)* **-ekonomi** macroeconomics *(pl, behandlas som sg)* **-kosmos** [-'kåsmås] *r* macrocosm **-molekyl** macromolecule **-skopisk** [-'skå:-] *a5* macroscopic

makt *s3* power; might; *([tvingande] kraft)* force; *(herravälde)* dominion, rule; *([laglig] myndighet)*

authority; *(kontroll)* control; ~ *går före rätt* might goes before right; *vanans* ~ the force of habit; *ingen* ~ *i världen kan* no power on earth can; *sätta* ~ *bakom orden* back up one's words by force; *få* ~ *över* obtain power over, make o.s. master of; *ha (sitta vid)* ~*en* be in (hold) power; *en högre* ~ superior force; *genom omständigheternas* ~ by force of circumstances; *av (med) all* ~ with all one's might; *med all* ~ *söka att* do one's utmost to; *ha ordet i sin* ~ be eloquent, have the power of expressing o.s., *vard.* have the gift of the gab; *det står inte i min* ~ *att* it is beyond my power to; *komma till* ~*en* come into (obtain) power; *vädrets* ~*er* the weather gods

makt|balans balance of power **-befogenhet** authority; powers *(pl)* **-begär** [the] lust for power **-faktor** factor of power **-fullkomlig** despotic, dictatorial **-fördelning** distribution of power **-förskjutning** shift of power **-havande** *s9,* **-havare** *s9* ruler; *de* ~ those in power **-kamp** struggle for power **-koncentration** concentration of power **-lysten** greedy for power **-lystnad** lust for power **-lös** powerless; impotent; *(svag)* weak; *(matt)* faint **-medel** instrument of force; forcible means *(pl)* **-missbruk** abuse of power **-påliggande** *a4 (viktig)* important, urgent; *(ansvarsfull)* responsible **-sfär** sphere of influence **-spel** gamble for power; ~*et* the power game **-språk** language of force **-ställning** position of power, powerful position **-övertagande** *s6* assumption of power

makul|atur wastepaper, spoilage **-era** *(kassera)* destroy, obliterate, reject as waste[paper]; *(göra ogiltig)* cancel; ~*s!* cancelled! **-ering** [-'le:-] destruction, obliteration; cancellation

1 mal *s2 (insekt)* moth

2 mal *s2 (fisk)* European catfish, sheatfish

mala *v2* **1** grind *(till* into); *(säd äv.)* mill; *(kött äv.)* mince; ~ *på ngt (bildl.)* keep on repeating s.th.; ~ *om samma sak (bildl.)* keep harping on the same string **2** *(om tankar)* keep on revolving

Malackahalvön [-ˣlakk-] the Malay Peninsula

malaj [-'lajj] *s3* Malay[an]; *skämts. mil.* C3 (C-3) man **-isk** *a5* Malay[an]

malakit *s3* malachite

malapropå *adv* malapropos

malaria [-'la:-] *s1* malaria **-mygga** mosquito

malaw|ier [-'la:-] *s9* Malawian **-isk** *a5* Malawian

malays|ier [-'laj-] *s9* Malaysian **-isk** *a5* Malaysian

malen *perf. part. av mala* ground; *fin*~ finely ground; *grov*~ coarsely ground

malhål moth-hole

maliciös *a1* malicious; spiteful

malign [-'liɲn] *a1 med.* malignant

maljs *s3,* ~*en påstår* malicious rumour has it that

mall *s2, tekn.* mould; *(friare äv.)* pattern, model; *(rit-)* [French] curve

malla *v1,* ~ *[upp] sig, vard.* be cocky (stuck-up)

mallig *a1* cocky, stuck-up **-het** cockiness

Mallorca [maˣjårka] *n* Majorca

malm *s3* **1** *miner.* ore; *(obruten)* rock **2** *(legering)* bronze **3** *ljudande* ~ sounding brass; *han har* ~ *i stämman* his voice has got a ring in it **-berg** metalliferous rock **-brytning** ore-mining

malmedel antimoth preparation, mothproofing

agent
malm|fyndighet ore deposit **-fält** ore deposit (field) **-förande** *a4* ore-bearing, metalliferous **-förekomst** *se* -fyndighet **-gruva** ore mine **-halt** content of ore **-haltig** *al* containing ore **-klang** metallic ring **-letning** [-e:-] ore prospecting **-åder** metalliferous vein
malning [-a:-] grinding *etc.*, *se* mala
malplacerad [mallpla'se:-] *a5* misplaced, out of place; (*om anmärkning o.d.*) ill-timed
malpåse mothproof bag; *stoppa (lägga) i* ~ put in mothballs
malström [ˣma:l-] maelstrom
malsäker mothproof
malt *s4*, *s3* malt **-dryck** malt liquor
maltesare [-ˣte:-] Maltese **malteserkors** Maltese cross **malteserriddare** knight of [the Order of] Malta, knight hospitaller **maltesisk** [-'te:-] *a5* Maltese
maltos [-'tå:s] *s3* maltose, malt sugar
malträtera maltreat, ill-treat
malva *s1*, *bot.* mallow **-färgad** mauve[-coloured]
malvasir *s3* (*vinsort*) malmsey
maläten *a5* moth-eaten, mothy; (*luggsliten*) threadbare; (*om pers.*) haggard
malör mishap; (*starkare*) calamity
malört *bot.* wormwood (*äv. bildl.*); ~ *i glädjebägaren* a fly in the ointment
malörts|bägare *bildl.* cup of bitterness **-droppar** *pl* tincture (*sg*) of wormwood
mamelucker [-'lukk-] *pl* pantalet[te]s; knickers
mamma *s1* mother (*till* of); *vard.* ma, mum; *barnspr.* mummy; ~*s gosse* mother's boy; *på sin* ~*s gata* on one's native heath **-klänning** maternity dress
mammalier [-'ma:-] *pl*, *zool.* mammals
mammig *al* who clings to his (her) mother's skirts
mammografi *s3* mammography
mammon [-ån] *r* mammon; (*rikedom*) riches (*pl*); *den snöda* ~ filthy lucre **mammonsdyrkan** [the] worship of mammon
mammut ['mamm-] *s2*, *zool.* mammoth
mamsell *s3* Miss
Man [mann] *r* [*ön*] ~ the Isle of Man; *invånare på* ~ Manxman
1 man [ma:n] *s2* (*häst- o.d.*) mane
2 man [mann] *-nen män*, *mil. o.d. pl man* man (*pl men*); (*som motsats t. kvinna äv.*) male; (*arbetskarl, besättnings- e.d. äv.*) hand; (*äkta* ~) husband, man; *en styrka på fyrtio* ~ a force of forty men; *sjunka med* ~ *och allt* go down with all hands; *det skall jag bli* ~ *för!* I'll make sure that's done!; *tredje* ~ third person (party); ~ *och* ~ *emellan* from one to another; *per* ~ a head, per man, each; *på tu* ~ *hand* by ourselves, on our own (*etc.*); *som en* ~ to a man, one and all; *litet till* ~*s har vi* pretty well every one of us has; *var* ~ everybody
3 man [mann] *pron* one, you; we; (*vem som helst ibl.*) anyone; (*folk*) people, they, *vard.* folks; ~ *trodde förr* people used to think; ~ *kan aldrig veta vad som* one (you) can never know what; *det kan* ~ *aldrig veta!* one never knows!; *när* ~ *talar till dig* when people speak to you, when you are

spoken to; *om* ~ *delar linjen* if you (we) bisect the line; ~ *påstår att han är* they (people) say that he is, he is said to be; *har* ~ *hört på maken!* did you ever [hear the like]!; *eller, om* ~ *så vill* or, if you like (prefer [it]); *ser* ~ *på!* well, well!
mana (*upp-*) exhort; (*befalla*) bid; (*uppfordra*) call upon; (*driva på*) incite, urge, admonish; *exemplet* ~*r inte till efterföljd* his (*etc.*) example hardly invites imitation; ~ *till försiktighet* call for caution; *känna sig* ~*d att* feel called upon (prompted) to; ~ *fram* call forth (out); ~ *på ngn* urge on s.b.; ~ *gott för ngn* put in a good word for s.b.
manager ['männidjer, 'mann-] (*för idrottsman*) manager; (*för artist*) impresario, publicity agent
manbar [ˣmann-] *al* pubescent **-het** manhood
manbyggnad [ˣmann-] manor house
manchestersammet [ˣmannçester-, -'çest-] ribbed velvet, corduroy
manchu [-'ʃu] *s3* Manchu **Manchuriet** [-'riet] *n* Manchuria **manchu[r]isk** [-'ʃu:-] *a5* Manchurian
1 mandarin *s3* (*ämbetsman*) mandarin; (*högkinesiska*) Mandarin
2 mandarin *s3* (*frukt*) mandarin[e]
mandat *s7* **1** *jur.* authorization, authority **2** (*som riksdagsman*) mandate; commission; (*riksdagsmannaplats*) seat; *nedlägga sitt* ~ resign one's seat, *britt. parl.* accept [the Stewardship of] the Chiltern Hundreds; *få sitt* ~ *förnyat* be returned again for one's constituency **3** (*förvaltarskap*) mandate **-fördelning** distribution of seats **-tid** term of office
mandatär *s3* mandatary **-stat** trusteeship nation; (*förr*) mandatory nation (power)
mandel [ˣmann-] *s2* **1** almond; *brända mandlar* burnt almonds **2** *anat.* tonsil **-blomma** white meadow saxifrage **-formad** [-å:-] *a5* almond-shaped **-kvarn** almond grinder **-massa** almond paste, marzipan **-olja** almond oil **-träd** almond [tree]
mandolin *s3* mandolin[e]
man|dom [ˣmanndomm] *s2* (*tapperhet*) bravery, valour; (*-barhet*) manhood; (*männsklig gestalt*) human form (shape) **-domsprov** (*tapperhetsprov*) test of courage; (*vuxenhetsprov*) trial of manhood; initiation rite
mandråpare [ˣmann-] manslayer
mandsju *se* manchu
manege [-'ne:ʃ, -'nä:ʃ] *s5* manège, manege
1 maner ['ma:-] *pl* (*avlidnas andar*) manes
2 maner *s7* (*sätt*) manner; (*stil*) style; (*förkonstling*) mannerism; (*tillgjordhet*) affectation; *förfalla till* ~ become affected
manet *s3* jellyfish
man|fall [ˣmann-] *det blev stort* ~ there were a great many [men *etc.*] killed, (*i examen e.d.*) a great many failed (were rejected) **-folk** *ett* ~ a man; *koll.* men, menfolk
mangan [-ŋˈga:n] *s3*, *s4* manganese **-at** *s7*, *s4* manganate
mangel ['maŋel] *s2* mangle; *dra* ~*n* drive (*bords-*: turn) the mangle **-bod** mangle-house **-duk** mangling-sheet
mangl|a mangle; *absol. äv.* do [the] mangling **-ing** mangling; *bildl.* draw-out negotiations (*pl*)

-ingsfri noniron
mangofrukt [ˣmaŋgɔ-] mango [fruit]
mangold [ˈmaŋgåld] s2, bot. [Swiss] chard, white-beet
mangoträd [ˣmaŋgɔ-] mango [tree]
man|grann [ˣmann-] full-muster; in full force **-grant** adv, samlas ~ assemble to a man (in full force) **-gårdsbyggnad** mansion, manor house; (på bondgård) farmhouse **-haftig** a1 stouthearted; (karlaktig) manly; (om kvinna) mannish **-hål** manhole
manj s3 mania; vard. craze (på att for + ing-form)
manjck s3 gadget
manier|erad [-ˈre:-] a5 mannered, affected **-ism** mannerism
manifęst I s7 manifesto **II** a4, med. manifest **-ation** manifestation **-era** manifest; (ådagalägga äv.) display
manikyr s3 manicure **-era** manicure; absol. äv. do manicuring **-ist** manicurist
manillahampa [-ˣnilla-] Manil[l]a hemp
man|ing exhortation; (vädjan) appeal; rikta en ~ till address an appeal to **-ingsord** word of exhortation; admonitory word, word of warning
maniok [-niˈå:k, -ˈåkk] s3, bot. [bitter] cassava, manioc
manipul|ation manipulation **-era** manipulate; handle; ~ med (äv.) tamper with, (göra fuffens med) juggle with; (räkenskaper) cook
manisk [ˈma:-] a5 manic
manke s2 withers (pl); lägga ~n till (bildl.) put one's shoulder to the wheel, AE. vard. dig [in]
mank|emąng [-ŋ] s7, s4 (fel) fault, hitch, breakdown; AE. vard. bug[s] **-era** (komma för sent t.) fail [to come, to turn up]; (fattas) want, be missing
man|kön [ˣmann-] ~et the male sex; koll. äv. mankind; av ~ of the male sex **-lig a1 1** (av mankön) male; masculine **2** (som anstår en man) manly, virile **-lighet** manliness, virility **-ligt** adv like a man, manfully **-lucka** manhole [cover]
1 manna v1, sjö., ~ reling! man the bulwarks!
2 manna s1, s7 manna; som ~ i öknen like manna in the wilderness
mannagryn semolina
manna|kraft man's (manly) strength; i sin fulla ~ in the full vigour of his manhood **-minne** (i within) living memory **-mod** [manly] courage, prowess **-mån** r favouring; utan ~ (äv.) without respect of persons **-ålder** manhood
mannekąng [-ŋ] s3 [fashion] model, mannequin; (skyltdocka) [tailor's] dummy **mannekänga** [-ˈkäŋa] model **mannekänguppvisning** fashion show (parade)
manodepressjv a1 manic-depressive
manometer [-ˈme:-] s2 pressure gauge, manometer
mans se 2 man
mansardtak [-ˣsa:rd-] mansard (curb) roof
mans|bot wer[e]gild **-chauvinism** male chauvinism **-chauvinist** male chauvinist
manschętt s3 cuff; (linning äv.) wristband; tekn. sleeve; fasta (lösa) ~er attached (detachable) cuffs; darra på ~en (bildl.) shake in one's shoes **-brott** white-collar crime **-knapp** cuff link **-proletariat** white-collar workers (pl) **-yrke**

white-collar job
mans|dräkt man's (male) attire **-gris** [mullig] ~ male chauvinist pig **-göra** s7 men's ([a] man's) work **-hög** as tall as a man
manskap s7, mil. men (pl); (värvat äv.) enlisted men (pl); (servis-) [gun] personnel; sjö. crew, hands (pl)
mans|kör male (men's) choir **-lem** penis **-linje** på ~n on the spear side
manslukerska vamp
mans|namn male (man's) name **-person** man; male person
manspillan [ˣmann-] r loss of men; stor ~ heavy losses (pl)
manssamhälle male-dominated society
man|stark strong in number, numerically strong **-starkt** adv, infinna sig ~ muster strong
mansålder generation
mantal s7 assessment unit of land
mantals|blankett population census questionnaire **-längd** population register (schedule) **-skriva** register for census purposes; take a census **-skrivning** registration for census purposes **-uppgift** census registration statement
mant|el s2 **1** (plagg) cloak; (kunga- o.d. o. bildl.) mantle **2** tekn. casing, jacket; geom. o.d. mantle; (aktie-) [share] certificate **-ilj** s3 mantilla **-lad** a5, tekn. jacketed
manu|al s3, (handbok, mus.) manual **-ell** a1 manual
manufaktur|affär [-ˣtu:r-] draper's shop; AE. dry-goods store **-varor** pl (textil-) drapery [goods], AE. dry goods; (järn-) hardware
manusförfattare scriptwriter
manuskript s7 manuscript; boktr. äv. copy, matter; (film-, radio-) script; maskinskrivet ~ (äv.) typescript, typed copy
manöver s3, mil. o. bildl. manoeuvre; (knep äv.) dodge, trick; (rörelse) mil. movement, sjö. mil. exercise **-bord** console **-duglig** manoeuvrable, in working order; sjö. äv. steerable **-fel** flyg. pilot's error **-förmåga** manoeuvrability **-oduglig** unmanageable; out of control **-spak** flyg. control lever
manövrer|a manoeuvre (äv. bildl.); sjö äv. steer; (friare) handle, manage, operate **-bar** a1 manoeuvrable **-ing** manoeuvring etc.
mapp s2 file, folder
mara s1 nightmare; (plåga) bugbear; ridas av ~n be hag-ridden
marabustork [ˣma:-, -ˣbu:-] marabou
maraton|lopp [-ån-] marathon race **-löpare** marathon runner
mardröm nightmare (äv. bildl.)
mareld phosphorescence [of the sea]
margarįn s4 margarine
marginąl [-g-, -j-] s3 margin; boktr. äv. border; börs äv. difference **-anteckning** marginal note **-kostnad** marginal cost **-skatt** marginal income tax **-väljare** floating voter
marginęll [-g-, -j-] marginal
Marje bebådelsedag [-ˣbå:-] Lady (Annunciation) Day
marig a1 **1** (förkrympt) dwarfed, stunted **2** (besvärlig) vard. tricky, ticklish, knotty
marijuana [-ˣa:na] s1 marijuana, marihuana

marin I [-ˣri:-] *s3* **1** (*sjömakt*) navy; ~*en* the Marine, the Navy **2** (*-målning*) marine, seascape **II** *al* marine

marina [-ˣri:-] *s1* marina

marinad *s3*, *kokk.* marinade

marin|attaché navy attaché **-blå** navy blue

marinera marinade

marin|flyg naval air force **-lotta** (*Storbritannien*) [a] member of the Women's Royal Naval Service (*förk.* W.R.N.S.), *vard.* [a] Wren; *AE.* [a] member of the Women Accepted for Volunteer Emergency Service (*förk.* WAVES), *vard.* [a] Wave **-läkare** naval medical officer **-målare** marine painter **-målning** *se marin I 2* **-soldat** marine **-stab** naval staff

marionett *s3* marionette, puppet (*äv. bildl.*) **-regering** puppet government **-teater** (*hopskr. marionetteater*) puppet theatre (*föreställning: show*)

maritim *al* maritime

1 mark *s3* (*jordyta, jordområde o.d.*) ground (*äv. bildl.*), land; (*åker*) field; (*jordmån*) soil; *klassisk ~* classical ground; *förlora* (*vinna*) ~ lose (gain) ground; *känna ~en bränna under sina fötter* (*bildl.*) feel the place beginning to get too hot for one; *på svensk ~* on Swedish soil; *ta ~* land (alight) [on the ground]

2 mark *s9* (*mynt*) mark

3 mark *s3* [*pl* 'marr-] (*spel-*) counter, marker, fish

markant [-'kant, -'kaŋt] **I** *al* striking, marked, conspicuous; (*märklig*) remarkable **2** *adv* strikingly *etc.*

markatta 1 *zool.* guenon **2** (*vard. 'häxa'*) shrew, bitch; *jfr* ragata

markeffektfarkost (*svävare*) hovercraft

marker|a mark; (*vid spel äv.*) score; (*ange*) indicate; (*visa*) show; (*sittplats e.d.*) put s.th. in (on) to mark it; *sport.* mark; (*betona*) accentuate, emphasize **-ad** *a5* marked; (*utpräglad äv.*) pronounced **-ing** marking *etc.*

marketent|are [-ˣtent-] canteen-keeper **-eri** canteen

markförsvar land defence[s]

markgreve margrave

1 markis *s3* (*solskydd*) sun blind, awning

2 markis *s3* (*adelstitel*) Storbritannien marquess, marquis

markisinna Storbritannien marchioness

markkontroll *flyg., rymd.* ground control

marknad *s3* market; (*i samband med folknöjen*) fair; *introducera en vara på ~en* introduce (launch) an article on the market; *i ~en* on (in) the market

marknads|andel share of the market **-dag** market day **-domstol** ~*en* the [Swedish] market court **-ekonomi** market economy **-föra** market, launch, merchandise **-föring** marketing *etc.* **-läge** market situation (position), state of the market **-nöje** sideshow **-plats** (*-område*) marketplace, fairground **-pris** market price **-stånd** market stall, stand **-undersökning** market[ing] research (analysis) **-värde** market (trade) value

mark|personal *flyg.* ground personnel (staff, crew) **-robot** surface-to-surface missile **-sikt** ground visibility **-strid** ground fighting, warfare on land **-stridskrafter** *pl* ground forces

Markus ['marr-] Mark; ~ *evangelium* the Gospel according to St. Mark, Mark

mark|värdestegring rise in the value of land **-värdinna** ground stewardess **-ägare** landowner, landlord; ground owner

markör marker, scorer; *data.* cursor; *flyg.* plotter

marmelad *s3* marmelade; (*konfekt ung.*) fruit jellies **-burk** pot of marmelade

marmor *s9* marble; ... *av ~* (*äv.*) [a] marble ... **-brott** marble quarry **-era** marble; vein **-ering** [-'re:-] marbling **-kula** marble **-skiva** marble slab; (*på bord*) marble top **-stod** marble monument

marockan *s3* Moroccan **-sk** [-a:-] *a5* Moroccan, of Morocco

Marocko [-'råkkɔ] *n* Morocco

marodör marauder, exploiter

marokäng *s3* (*läder*) morocco; (*tyg*) marocain

mars *r* March

Mars *r, astr.* Mars

marsch [marʃ] **I** *s3* march; *vanlig ~* march in step; *vara på ~* be on the march (*äv. bildl.*) **II** *interj* march!; *framåt* (*helt om*) ~! forward (right about face) march!; ~ *i väg!* (*vard.*) be off with you!; *göra på stället ~* (*gymnastik o.d.*) mark time

marschall [-'ʃall] *s3* cresset

marsch|era [-'ʃe:-] march; (*skrida*) pace (*fram o. tillbaka* to and fro); *det var raskt ~t!* (*bildl.*) [jolly] quick work, that! **-fart, -hastighet** [marching] pace; *flyg.* cruising speed **-kolonn** (*trupp*) march[ing] column; (*formering*) column of route **-känga** marching-boot **-order** marching order; *ha fått ~* be under marching orders **-takt 1** *mil.* marching step; *gå i ~* walk in marching step **2** *mus.* march-time

Marseille [mar'säjj] *n* Marseilles

marseljäsen [-'jä:-] *r, best. form* the Marseillaise

Marshallplanen [the] Marshall Plan, (*officiellt*) European Recovery Programme

marsin[ne]vånare Martian

marsipan *s3* marzipan

1 marsk *s3, geogr.* marshland

2 marsk *s2, hist., rikets ~* (*Engl. ung.*) the Lord High Constable

marskalk [ˣmarrʃalk, -'ʃalk] *s2* **1** *mil.* marshal **2** (*platsvisare*) usher, *AE. äv.* floor manager; *univ. o.d.* steward; (*vid bröllop*) groomsman, (*förste ~*) best man **marskalksstav** marshal's baton

marskland marshland

marsvin *zool.* guinea pig

martall dwarfed (stunted) pine [tree]

mart|er ['ma(:)r-] *pl* torments, tortures **-era** torment, torture

martialisk [-tsi'a:-] *a5* martial

martin|process [-ˣtäŋ-] open-hearth process **-ugn** open-hearth furnace

martorn [ˣma:rtɔ:rn] *s7, s2 bot.* sea holly

martyr *s3* martyr (*för* for, to); (*offer äv.*) victim **-död** *lida ~en* suffer martyrdom (the death of a martyr) **-gloria** martyr's halo **-ium** *s4* [period of] martyrdom; *ett verkligt ~* (*friare*) a veritable affliction **-krona** martyr's crown **-skap** *s7* martyrdom

mar|ulk *s2, zool.* angler [fish] **-vatten** *ligga i ~*

M

be waterlogged **-viol** sea rocket

marxism Marxism **–leninism** Marxism-Leninism

marxist *s3*, **-isk** *a5* Marxist, Marxian

maräng *s3* meringue **-sviss** *s3* cream-filled meringue-shells

masa saunter; ~ [*sig*] *i väg* slope (shuffle) off; ~ *sig upp* [*ur sängen*] drag o.s. out of bed; *gå och* ~ be idling (lazing)

mascara [-ˣka:-] *s1* mascara

maser ['ma:-] *s3* maser (microwave amplification by stimulated emission of radiation) **-stråle** maser beam

1 mask *s2, zool.* worm; (*larv*) grub; (*kål-*) caterpillar; (*i kött, ost*) maggot; *full av -ar* alive with worms (*etc.*); *vrida sig som en* ~ wriggle like a worm

2 mask *s3*, mask (*äv. bildl.*); (*kamouflage*) screen; *bildl. äv.* guise; (-*erad pers.*) masked person; *låta ~en falla* (*bildl.*) throw off one's mask, unmask o.s.; *hålla ~en* (*spela ovetande*) not give the show away, (*hålla sig för skratt*) keep a straight face

3 mask *s3, kortsp.* finessing; (*en* ~ *äv.*) finesse

1 maska *v1* **1** *kortsp.* finesse **2** (*sänka arbetstakten*) go slow, work to rule; (*låtsas arbeta*) pretend to work; *sport.* play for time

2 maska *v1* (*sätta mask på*) bait with worms (a worm); ~ *på* bait the hooks

3 maska I *s1* mesh; (*virkad, stickad*) stitch; (*på strumpa*) ladder; *tappa en* ~ drop a stitch **II** *v1*, ~ *av* cast off; ~ *upp på en strumpa* mend a ladder

maskara *se* mascara

maskbo nest of grubs

maskera mask; (*klä ut*) dress up (*till* for); *teat. äv.* make up; (*friare o. bildl., i sht mil.*) mask, camouflage; (*dölja*) hide; (*t.ex. avsikter*) disguise; ~ *sig* mask o.s., (*friare*) dress o.s. up, make up, disguise o.s.; ~*d person* (*äv.*) masquerader; *vara ~d till* (*äv.*) impersonate

maskerad *s3* masquerade; mummery **-bal** fancy-dress ball **-dräkt** fancy dress

maskering [-ˈke:-] masking *etc.*; (*mera konkr.*) mask, screen; *i sht mil.* camouflage; (*förklädnad*) disguise; *teat.* make-up

maskerings|konst [the] art of make-up **-tejp** masking tape

mask|formig [-å-] *a1* vermiform (*äv. anat.*); worm-shaped **-gång** worm burrow (track) **-hål** wormhole

maskin [-ˈʃi:n] *s3* machine (*för, till* for); (*större*) engine; (*mera allm.*) apparatus, device; (*skriv-*) typewriter; ~*er* (*koll.*) machinery; *gjord* (*sydd*) *på* ~ done (sewn, made) on a (by) machine, machine-made; *full* ~ (*framåt*)*!* (*sjö.*) full speed [ahead]!; *för egen* ~ by its own engines, *bildl.* on one's own; *för full* ~ (*bildl.*) at full tilt (steam); *skriva* [*på*] ~ type **-bokföring** machine accounting (bookkeeping) **-driven** *a5* power-driven

maskinell *a1* mechanical; ~ *utrustning* machinery, mechanical equipment; ~*a hjälpmedel* machine aids

maskin|eri machinery (*äv. bildl.*); ~*et* (*på fartyg*) the engines (*pl*); (*på fabrik*) the plant **-fabrik** engineering (engine) works **-fel** engine trouble **-gevär** machine gun **-gjord** *a5* machine-

-made; -*gjort papper* machine paper **-industri** mechanical engineering industry **-ingenjör** mechanical engineer **-ist** engine (machine) man, mechanic; *sjö.* engineer, machinist **-mässig** *a1* mechanical **-park** machinery, machine equipment, plant **-rum** engine room **-satt** *a4, boktr.* machine-composed; linotyped, monotyped **-skada** engine trouble, breakdown **-skrift** typescript **-skrivare, -skriverska** typist **-skrivning** typing, typewriting **-skötare** [machine] operator; machine tender **-språk** *data.* machine (computer) language (code) **-stickning** machine-knitting **-sydd** *a5* machine-sewn; (*om klänning e.d.*) machine-made **-sätta** *boktr.* compose by monotype (linotype) **-sättning** *boktr.* machine composition **-söm** machined seam **-teknik** mechanical engineering **-telegraf** *sjö.* engine-room telegraph **-tvätta** wash by (in a) machine **-vara** *data.* hardware **-verkstad** machine (engineering) shop

maskning go-slow; work-to-rule; *AE.* slowdown

maskopi *s3, s4, vara i* ~ *med* be in collusion with

maskot ['maskått] *s2, s3* mascot

mask|ros dandelion **-stungen** *a5* worm-eaten

masksäker (*om strumpa*) ladder-proof, non-run

maskulin ['mask-, -'li:n] *a1* masculine; male **-um** [ˣmass-] *s4* **1** (*-t ord*) masculine [noun]; *i* ~ (*gram.*) in the masculine [gender] **2** (*karl*) male

maskäten *a5* worm-eaten, wormy

maskör *teat. o.d.* make-up man

masoch|ism masochism **-ist** masochist

masonjt *s3* masonite

mass|a *s1* **1** mass, volume; (*stort oformligt stycke*) lump **2** (*grötlik* ~) pulp; *kokk.* paste; (*deg-*) dough; *tekn.* composition; *bli till en fast* ~ become a firm mass, solidify **3** (*mängd*) mass, [large] quantity; heap, pile; lot; *en* ~ *saker* lots (heaps) of things; *prata en* ~ *dumheter* talk a lot of nonsense; *-or med folk* crowds of people; [*den stora*] ~*n* the masses (*pl*), the rank and file; (*flertalet*) the great majority; ... *i -or* (*-or med* ...) lots (heaps, quantities) of ...

massafabrik pulp mill

massage [-ˈsa:ʃ] *s5* massage

massak|er [-ˈsa:-] *s3* massacre **-rera** massacre; (*lemlästa*) mutilate; *svårt ~d i ansiktet* with his (*etc.*) face terribly mutilated

mass|arbetslöshet mass unemployment **-artikel** mass-produced article

massaved pulpwood

mass|avrättning mass-execution **-beställning** bulk bookings (orders) (*pl*) **-demonstration** mass demonstration **-död** wholesale death

massera massage; treat with massage

mass|fabrikation large-scale manufacture, mass production **-flykt** mass desertion[s *pl*] **-grav** mass (common) grave

massiv *s7* massif **II** *a1* solid; massive **-itet** solidity; massiveness

mass|kommunikation mass communication **-korsband** bulk posting (mail); *AE.* bulk third class [mail] **-media** *pl* mass media **-mord** mass murder, multicide; massacre **-mördare** mass murderer **-möte** mass meeting; *AE. äv.* rally **-producera** mass-produce **-produktion** mass production **-psykologi** mass psychology **-psy-**

kos mass psychosis **-slakt** (*hopskr. masslakt*) wholesale (mass) slaughter **-tillverkning** *se* **-produktion** **-uppbåd** *mil.* levy in mass, mass levy; (*friare*) large muster [of people] **-verkan** mass effect **-vis** in large (vast) numbers, in great quantities; *jfr massa 3*

massör masseur **massös** masseuse

mast *s3* mast; (*radio- o.d. äv.*) pylon; (*signal-*) post; (*flagg-*) pole

mastix ['mast-] *s3* mastic

mast|korg top **-kran** derrick (mast) crane

mastodont [-'dånt] *s3* mastodon (*äv. bildl.*)

masttopp masthead

masturb|ation masturbation **-era** masturbate

masugn blast furnace

masur *s9* curly-grained wood

masurka [-ˣsurr-, -'surr-] *s1* maz[o]urka

mat *s9* food; (*-varor äv.*) eatables, provisions (*pl*); *vard.* grub; *en bit ~* s.th. to eat, a bite, a snack; *~ och dryck* food and drink; *~ och husrum* board and lodging; *intages efter ~en* to be taken after meals; *vila efter ~en* rest after dinner (*etc.*); *det är ingen ~* (*eg. näring*) *i* there is no nourishment in; *~en står på bordet!* the (your) dinner (*etc.*) is on the table!; *hålla ~en varm åt ngn* keep a p.'s dinner (*etc.*) hot; *vad får vi för ~ i dag?* what are we going to have for dinner (*etc.*) today?; *dricka öl till ~en* have beer with one's dinner (*etc.*); *ha ngn i ~en* board s.b.; *vara liten i ~en* be a small eater

mata feed (*äv. bildl.*); *~ ngn med kunskaper* stuff s.b. with knowledge; *~d* (*om säd*) full[-eared]

matador [-'då:r] *s3* matador (*äv. bildl.*); *bildl. äv., vard.* big noise, bigwig; *AE.* big shot

matarbuss feeder bus

matar|e *tekn.* feeder **-ledning** feeder [cable]

mat|beredare food processor **-bestick** knife, fork and spoon set; [a set of] eating implements (*pl*); *koll.* table cutlery; *AE.* table set, flatware **-bit** [a] bite of food (s.th. to eat), snack **-bord** dining table **-bröd** [plain] bread

match [matʃ] *s3* match; *en enkel ~* (*bildl.*) child's play; *givna ~er* (*tips.*) bankers **matcha** (*låta tävla*) match **matchboll** match point

matdags *det är ~* it is time for a meal

matelass|é [mattla'se:] *s3* matelassé **-era** quilt

matemat|ik *s3, ej pl* mathematics (*pl, behandlas som sg*); *vard.* maths (*pl*) **-iker** [-'ma:-] mathematician **-ikmaskin** [electronic] computer **-isk** [-'ma:-] *a5* mathematical

materi|a [-'te:-] *s3* matter (*äv. -en*); (*ämne äv.*) substance

material *s7, pl äv. -alier* material (*till* for); (*i bok o.d. äv.*) matter **-fel** defect (fault) in material[s *pl*] **-förråd** store of materials **-förvaltare** storekeeper **-isation** materialization **-isera ~** [*sig*] materialize **-ism** materialism **-ist** materialist **-istisk** [-'ist-] *a5* materialistic **-kontroll** inventory control **-kostnad** cost of material[s] **-lära** science of engineering and building materials **-provning** materials testing **-samling** collection of material **-återvinning** material recovery, recycling

materi|e [-'te:-] *s3, se materia* **-el** *s9, ej pl* materials (*pl*); *elektr.* equipment; *mil.* munitions (*pl*); *rullande ~* rolling stock **-ell** *a1* material; *~a till-*

gångar (*äv.*) tangible assets

mat|fett cooking fat **-friare** sponger **-frisk** with a good appetite **-förgiftad** *a5* poisoned by food **-förgiftning** food poisoning **-gaffel** [table] fork **-gäst** boarder **-hållning** catering [service]

matiné *s3* matinée [performance]

mat|jord topsoil **-kniv** [table] knife **-korg** hamper **-kupong** food (dinner) check **-källare** food cellar **-lag** *s7* sitting; *mil.* mess **-lagning** cooking, cookery, preparation of food **-lust** appetite **-mor** mistress [of a (the) household]; *vard.* missis **-ning** feeding, supply **-nyttig** suitable as food, edible **-olja** cooking oil **-ordning** dietary **-os** smell of cooking (of food being cooked); cooking fumes **-pengar** *pl* housekeeping [money (*sg*)] **-pinne** chopstick **-plats** dining space **-ranson** food ration **-rast** food break; *mil. o.d.* halt for refreshment[s *pl*] **-recept** [cooking] recipe **-rester** *pl* remains [of food]; *vard.* leftovers

matriar|kalisk [-'ka:-] *a5* matriarchal **-kat** *s7* matriarchate, matriarchy

matrikel [-'trikk-] *s2* list (roll) [of members]; (*kår- äv.*) calendar, directory

matris *s3* matrix (*pl matrices*), mould

matro peace at mealtimes

matrona [-ˣtro:-] *s1* matron

matros *s3* able[-bodied] seaman; *vard.* sailor **-jacka** bluejacket, sailor's jacket **-kostym** sailor suit **-krage** sailor-suit collar

mat|rum *se matsal* **-rätt** dish

mats *r, i uttr.: ta sin ~ ur skolan* withdraw altogether, beat a retreat

mat|sal dining room **-salong** *sjö.* dining saloon **-sedel** menu, bill of fare **-servering** (*-ställe*) eating house; dining-rooms (*pl*) **-servis** dinner service **-silver** table silver **-sked** tablespoon **-skribent** cookery writer **-smältning** digestion; *ha dålig ~* suffer from indigestion (a bad digestion)

matsmältnings|apparat digestive system (tract) **-besvär** indigestion, dyspepsia **-organ** digestive organ **-process** process of digestion **-rubbning** indigestion; digestive upset

mat|strejka refuse to eat **-strupe** oesophagus, gullet **-ställe** *se matservering* **-säck** [ˣma:t-, *vard.* ˣmassäck] [bag of] provisions (*pl*), package of food, packed meal (lunch); *vard.* grub, tommy; *rätta munnen efter ~en* cut one's coat according to one's cloth **-säckskorg** provision basket; (*vid utfärd äv.*) picnic hamper

1 matt *a1* **1** (*kraftlös o.d.*) faint (*av* from, with); (*klen, svag*) weak, feeble; (*slö, slapp*) languid; (*utan kläm*) spiritless, tame; *hand.* dull; (*livlös*) lifeless; *känna sig ~* feel exhausted (washed out) (*efter after*) **2** (*färgsvag*) mat[t], dead; (*glanslös*) dull, lustreless; (*dunkel*) dim; *bli ~* (*äv.*) get tarnished, tarnish

2 matt *oböjl. a o. s3* (*i schack*) mate; *schack och ~!* checkmate!; *göra ngn ~* checkmate s.b.; *förhindra ~en* prevent [the] [check]mating

1 matta *s1* carpet; (*mindre*) rug; (*dörr-, kork- o.d.*) mat; (*grövre*) matting; *heltäckande ~* fitted carpet; *hålla sig på ~n* (*bildl.*) toe the line

2 matta *v1* weaken, enfeeble; (*trötta*) tire; weary

mattaffär rug and carpet dealer

mattas *dep* get (become, grow) weak[er]; (*om*

sken) get *(etc.)* dim[mer]; *(om pers.)* get *(etc.)* [more] tired; *(om färg)* fade; *ekon.* weaken
mattblå dull blue
1 matte *s2,* vard. mistress
2 matte *s7 (paraguayte)* maté, mate
3 matte *vard.* maths, *AE.* math
Matteus [-'te:-] Matthew; *~ evangelium* the Gospel according to St. Matthew, Matthew
mattförgylla gild with a mat[t] surface
matthandlare *se mattaffär*
matt[ig]het lassitude; faintness, feebleness *etc.*
mattpisk|are carpet-beater **-ning** carpet-beating
mattpolerad *a5* matt-finished
mattram *s3, bot.* feverfew
mattrasor *(särskr. matt-trasor) pl* rag-strips for hand-woven rugs
matt|sam *a1* fatiguing; tiresome **-skiva** *foto.* focusing screen, ground glass **-slipad** *a5* ground, frosted
mattsopare carpet sweeper
mattvarp carpet warp
mat|tvång *(på restaurang)* [the] no-drinks-without-food system **-varor** *pl* provisions, eatables, foodstuffs **-varuaffär** provision-dealer's [shop], food shop **-vrak** gormandizer, glutton **-vrå** dining recess; *AE.* dinette **-väg** *i uttr.: ngt i ~* s.th. in the way of food **-vägran** refusal to eat **-vägrare** person (child) who refuses to eat **-äpple** cooking-apple
Mauretanien [-'ta:-] *n* Mauritania
mauret|anier [-'ta:-] *s9* Mauritanian **-ansk** [-'ta:-] *a5* Mauritanian
mausergevär Mauser [rifle]
mausoleum [-ˣle:-, -'le:-] *s4* mausoleum
maxim *s3* maxim
maxim|al *a1* maximum **-era** *(göra så stor som möjligt)* maximize; *(bestämma högsta gräns för)* put an upper limit on, fix a ceiling for; *~ räntan till 5 %* set (fix) interest at a maximum of 5 % **-ering** [-'e:-] fixation of the limits; *räntans ~ till 5 %* the fixing of the interest at 5 % as a maximum
maximi|belopp maximum [amount] **-gräns** upper limit, ceiling **-hastighet** maximum speed **-pris** maximum price, ceiling price **-termometer** maximum thermometer
maximum ['maks-] *s8* maximum *(pl* maxima)
mayafolk [ˣmajja-] *~en* the Maya peoples, the Mayas
MBL *se medbestämmandelagen*
mecenat patron of the arts (sciences)
1 med *s2 (kälk- o.d.)* runner; *(gungstols- o.d.)* rocker
2 med *[vard. me:, mä:]* **I** *prep* **1** with; *~ all aktning för* with all respect to, however much one may respect; *~ eller utan* with or without; *~ nöje* with pleasure; *~ omsorg* with care, carefully; *~ rätta* rightly, with good reason; *~ säkerhet* certainly; *~ öppna armar* with open arms; *diskutera (leka) ~ ngn* discuss (play) with s.b.; *felet ~* the trouble with; *fylld ~ sand* filled with sand; *färdig ~* ready with; *jämföra ~* compare with, *(likna vid)* compare to; *kriget ~ Spanien* the war with Spain; *ned ~ ...!* down with ...!; *nöjd ~* content with; *skriva ~ en penna* write with a pencil; *tillsammans ~* together with; *tävla ~ ngn* compete

with s.b.; *vara ~ barn* be pregnant (with child); *äta ~ sked* eat with a spoon; *en man ~ långt skägg* a man with a long beard; *~ de orden lämnade han mötet* with these words he left the meeting; *ordet stavas ~ e* the word is spelt with an e; *vi bor granne ~ dem* they are our neighbours, we live next door to them; *han kom ~ ett brev* he came with a letter; *han stod där ~ hatten i hand (händerna i fickorna)* he stood there [with his] hat in [his] hand (with his hands in his pockets); *vad är det ~ dig?* what is the matter with you?; *det är samma sak ~ mig* it is the same [thing] with me **2** *([kommunikations]medel)* by;*~ tåg* by train; *betala ~ check* pay by cheque; *höja priset ~ 5 öre* raise the price by 5 öre; *skicka ~ posten* send by post; *vinna ~ 10 poäng* win by ten points; *börja ~ att förklara* begin by explaining; *vad menar du ~ det?* what do you mean by that? **3** *(släktskap, jämförelse)* to; *gift ~* married to; *lika ~* equal to; *släkt ~* related to, a relative of; *bo vägg i vägg ~* live next door to; *vara god vän ~* be good friends with (a good friend of) **4** *(innehållande)* containing, of, with; *en ask ~ choklad* a box of chocolate [s]; *massor ~ folk* lots of people; *tre säckar ~ kaffe* three bags of coffee **5** *(trots)* with, in spite of; *~ alla sina fel är hon dock* with (in spite of) all her faults she is **6** *(och)* and; *biffstek ~ lök* steak and onions; *Stockholm ~ omnejd* Stockholm and [its] environs; *herr S. ~ familj* Mr. S. and family; *det ena ~ det andra* one thing and another; *~ flera* and others; *~ mera* et cetera, and so on **7** *(inberäknat)* with, including; *~ rabatt är priset* the price less discount is **8** *(genitivförhållande)* of; with, about; *det bästa ~ boken är* the best thing about the book is; *fördelen (nackdelen) ~* the advantage (disadvantage) of; *vad är meningen ~ det?* what is the meaning of that?; *det roliga ~* the funny thing about **9** *(annan prep) ~ andra ord* in other words; *~ avsikt* on purpose; *~ en gång at* once; *~ en hastighet av* at a speed of; *~ full fart* at full speed; *~ små bokstäver* in small letters; *~ tre minuters mellanrum* at intervals of three minutes; *noga ~* particular about; *tala ~ ngn* speak to s.b.; *ha tid ~* have time for; *kapplöpning ~ tiden* a race against time; *skrivet ~ bläck* written in ink *(jfr 1)*; *det är ngt egendomligt ~ honom* there is s.th. strange about him; *hur är det ~ den saken?* what have you got to say about that?, what's the actual position?; *vad är det för roligt ~ det?* what's so funny about that?; *han har tre barn ~ henne* he has three children by her; *så var det ~ den saken* so much for that; *tillbringa kvällen ~ att sy* spend the evening sewing **10** *(annan konstr.) ~ början kl. 9* commencing at 9 o'clock; *~ eller mot min vilja* whether I like it or not; *~ åren* as the years pass[ed], over the years; *adjö ~ dig!* bye bye!; *ajöss ~ ...* there goes ...; *bort ~ tassarna!* hands off!; *fara ~ osanning* tell lies; *försök ~ bensin!* try petrol!; *jämnårig ~* of the same age as; *springa ~ skvaller* gossip, tell tales; *tyst ~ dig!* be quiet!; *ut ~ dig!* get out!; *betalning sker ~ 100 kronor i månaden* payment will be made in monthly instalments of 100 kronor; *det är ingen fara ~ pojken* the boy is all right; *jag gör det ~ glädje* I'll do it gladly; *räcker det ~ detta?* will this do (be sufficient)?; *hur står det till ~ henne?* how is she?; *tid-*

skriften utkommer ~ 10 nummer om året the journal appears 10 times a year; *~ sin artikel vill han* the purpose of his article is to **II** *adv* **1** (*också*) too; as well; *det tror jag ~* I think so too; *han är gammal han ~* he is old too **2** (*i förening med verb*) *du får inget ~ om du inte* you won't get anything (your share) unless you; *vill du följa ~?* will you come with us (me)?; *det håller jag ~ med dig om* I agree with you there; *ta ~ dig ngt att äta* bring s.th. to eat; *vara ~ a*) (*vara närvarande*) be present, *b*) (*vara medlem e.d.*) be a member; *får jag vara ~ och leka?* can I join in the game?, may I play too?; *han har varit ~ om mycket* he has seen a great deal in his days, he has been through a great deal; *jag är ~ på det* I agree to that

medalj *s3* medal (*för* for; *över* in commemoration of); *prägla en ~* strike (cast) a medal; *tilldela ngn en ~* award a medal to s.b. **-era** award a **-ong** [-'jåŋ] *s3* medallion; (*med hårlock e.d.*) locket **-utdelning** presentation of medals **-ör** medallist

medan while; (*just då äv.*) as; *sitt ner ~ du väntar* sit down while [you are] waiting; *~ ... pågår* (*äv.*) during ...

medansvarig jointly responsible (*med* with; *för* for); *vara ~* share the responsibility

medarbeta cooperate, collaborate; (*i tidning*) contribute (*i* to)

medarbetar|e fellow worker, co-worker, colleague; (*litterär o.d.*) collaborator (*i* in); (*i tidning*) staff member, contributor; (*-hjälpare*) assistant; *från vår utsände ~* from our special correspondent; *konstnärlig ~* art[istic] contributor (adviser) **-skap** *s7* collaboration **-stab** staff

medbestämmande|lagen (*MBL*) the act on employee participation in decision-making **-rätt** (*i bolag o.d.*) right of co-determination; *polit.* right of participation in decision-making

medbjuden *a5, var också ~* was also invited

medborgaranda [-årj-] civic spirit

medborgar|e citizen (*i* in, of); (*i sht i monarki*) subject; *utländsk ~* foreign national, (*ej svensk*) non-Swedish subject; *akademisk ~* member of a university **-kunskap** civics (*pl, behandlas som sg*) **-plikt** civic duty, duty as a citizen **-rätt** civil rights (*pl*); *beröva ngn ~en* (*äv.*) deprive s.b. of his franchise, disfranchise s.b. **-skap** *s7* citizenship

med|borgerlig [-årj-] civil (*rättighet* right); civic (*skyldighet* duty; *fest* festival) **-broder** companion; *relig.* brother **-brottslig** *vara ~ i* be implicated in (accessory to) **-brottsling** accomplice; accessory

meddel|a **1** (*omtala*) communicate (*ngn ngt* s.th. to s.b.), tell, let ... know, inform (notify, *i sht hand.* advise) of; *härmed ~s att* notice is hereby given that; *vi ber att få ~ att* we wish to inform you that; *vi ber Er ~ när* please let us know when **2** (*uppge*) state; (*kungöra e.d.*) announce, notify, report; (*bevilja, lämna*) give, grant, furnish; *jur. äv.* pronounce; *det ~s att* it is announced that; information has been received to the effect that **3** *~ undervisning* give tuition (*åt* to) **4** *rfl* communicate (*med* with); *~ sig med varandra* (*brevledes*) correspond [with each other] **med-delande** *s6* communication; (*budskap*) message; (*brev e.d.*) letter, note, notification; (*underrättelse*) information; (*kort skriftligt*) memorandum (*förk.* memo); *hand. äv.* advice; (*uppgift*) statement; (*officiellt*) announcement; (*anslag*) notice; *lämna ett ~* deliver a message, (*offentligt e.d.*) make a statement; *få ~ om* be notified of, receive information about; *anslå ett ~* post a notice **meddelare** informant **meddelelsemedel** means of communication **meddelsam** [-e:l-] *a1* communicative; ready to impart information

mede *s2, se 1 med*

medel ['me:-] *s7* **1** means (*sg o. pl*); (*om sak*) medium; (*utväg*) expedient; (*verktyg äv. bildl.*) instrument; (*bote-*) remedy (*mot* for, against); *lugnande ~* tranquillizer, sedative; *antiseptiskt ~* (*äv.*) antiseptic **2** (*pengar*) means, funds, resources (*pl*); *allmänna ~* public funds; *avsätta ~ till* allocate (set aside) funds for; *egna ~* private means

medel|- [ˣme:-] medium, standard; *i sht vetensk.* mean; (*genomsnittlig*) average, mean **-antal** average (mean) number **-avstånd** mean distance

medelbar *a1* indirect

medel|betyg average mark (grade) **-distans** *sport.* middle-distance **-distansrobot** intermediate-range ballistic missile **-djup** *s7* mean depth **-engelska** Middle English **-god** medium, of medium quality **-hastighet** average speed

Medelhavet *n* the Mediterranean

medel|högtyska Middle High German **-inkomst** middle (average) income **-klass** *~en* the middle classes (*pl*) **-livslängd** average [length of] life **-längd** *av* (*under, över*) ~ of (below, above) medium (average) length (height); *av ~* (*om pers.*) of medium height

medellös without means, impecunious; (*behövande*) indigent **-het** lack of means; indigence

medel|måtta *s1* average; medium; (*om pers.*) mediocrity **-måttig** *a1* medium, average; (*måttlig*) moderate; *neds.* mediocre, middling **-proportional** *mat.* mean proportional **-punkt** (*cirkels etc. o. bildl.*) centre (*av, för, till* of); (*friare äv.*) focus, central point

medelst ['me:-] (*genom*) by; (*genom förmedling av*) through, by means of

medel|stor of medium (average) size, medium--sized **-storlek** medium size; *av ~, se medelstor* **-svensson** *vard.* the average Swede **-svår** of medium (average) difficulty, moderately difficult; (*om artilleri*) of medium calibre **-tal** average (*för* for, of); *mat.* mean; *beräkna ~et* strike an average (*av* of); *i ~ on* an average; *i ~ uppgå till* (*kosta etc.*) average **-temperatur** mean temperature; *årlig ~* mean annual temperature

1 medeltid *s3* **1** *astr.* mean [solar] time **2** (*genomsnittstid*) average time

2 medeltid *s3, ~en* the Middle Ages; *Sveriges ~* Sweden's medieval period

medeltida *oböjlig a* medieval; *ibl.* Middle-Age

medel|tidskyrka medieval church **-vattenstånd** mean sea level **-väg** middle course (way) **-värde** mean value **-ålder 1** (*mellan ungdom o. ålderdom*) middle life; *en ~s man* a middle-aged

man, a man in middle life; *över ~n* past middle-
-age **2** (*genomsnitts-*) average (mean) age
med|faren *a5, illa ~ a*) (*sliten*) much the worse
for wear, in poor condition, *b*) (*bucklig e.d.*)
badly knocked about **-fånge** fellow prisoner
-född *a5* inborn, innate (*hos* in); *i sht med.*
congenital (*hos* in); (*friare*) native (*hos* to); (*livlighet*
vivacity); *det tycks vara -fött hos henne* it seems
to come natural to her **-följa** *se följa* [*med*]; (*om
bilaga*) be enclosed **-följande** *a4* accompanying;
(*bifogad*) enclosed **-föra 1** (*-bringa*) take (bring)
with one; (*ha med sig*) have (carry) with one; (*ha
på sig*) have (carry) on one; (*om tåg, buss e.d.*)
bring, take, convey **2** (*friare o. bildl.*) bring
[about] (... in its train); (*förorsaka*) cause, occasion; (*ge upphov t.*) give rise to, lead to; (*ha t.
följd*) result in, entail, involve; *~ kostnader* involve expenditure; *detta -förde att vi blev* this led
to our being **-författare** coauthor
med|giva 1 (*tillåta*) admit, permit, allow; (*be-
vilja*) grant, (*rättighet äv.*) accord; (*samtycka t.*)
consent to; *tiden -ger inte att jag* time does not allow me to; *-ger inget undantag* admits of no exception **2** (*erkänna*) admit, confess (*för ngn* to
s.b.); *det -ger jag gärna* I willingly (am quite
ready to) admit that; *det måste -ges att* it must be
confessed (admitted) that **-givande** *s6* **1** (*tillåtelse*) permission, consent; *tyst ~* tacit consent **2**
(*erkännande*) admission; (*eftergift*) concession
med|gång *s2* prosperity, good fortune; (*fram-*)
success; *i med- och motgång* for better for worse
-görlig [-jö:r-] *a1* accommodating, tractable,
complaisant (*mot* to; *i* in); amendable, easy to get
on with **-görlighet** tractability; complaisance
-havd *a5, de ~a smörgåsarna* the sandwiches
one ꞁ ꞁrought [with one] **-hjälp** *jur.* complicity
(*till* in) **-hjälpare** assistant **-håll** (*gillande*) approval; (*stöd*) support, *vard.* backing-up; (*gyn-
nande*) favour[ing]; *finna ~* meet with approval;
ha ~ hos be in favour with **-hårs** [-å:-] with the
furs; *stryka ngn ~* (*bildl.*) rub s.b. up the right
way
media ['me:-] *s1, språkv.* media (*pl mediae*)
mediaforskning media research
medial *a1* medial
median *s3* median **-värde** median value
medicin *s3* **1** (*läkarvetenskap*) medicine; *studera
~* study medicine **2** (*läkemedel*) medicine; (*preparat äv.*) drug
medicinal|styrelse [-ˣna:l-] *se socialstyrelse*
-vikt apothecaries' weight **-växt** medicinal herb
medicinare [-ˣsi:-] medical student; (*läkare*)
physician
medicine [-ˣsi:-] *~ doktor* Doctor of Medicine
(*förk. M.D. efter namnet*); *~ kandidat* graduate
in medicine; *~ licentiat* Bachelor of Medicine
(*förk. M.B. efter namnet*); *~ studerande* medical
student
medicin|era take medicine[s *pl*] **-flaska** medi-
cine bottle; (*liten*) phial **-förråd** store of medi-
cines; (*skåp*) medicine cupboard **-låda** medicine
chest **-man** medicine man
medicin|sk [-ˈsi:-] *a5* medical; *~ fakultet* faculty
of medicine **-skåp** medicine cupboard
medikament *s7, s4* medicament, medicine
med|inflytande *ha ~* have some influence (*över*

on), have a voice (say) in **-intressent** copartner
-intresserad *vara ~ i* have a part-interest in
medio ['me:-] *prep o. oböjligt s* middle, in the
middle of; *~ januari* (*äv.*) by (in) mid-January
medioker [-ˈå:-] *a1* mediocre
medit|ation meditation **-ativ** *a1* meditative,
contemplative **-era** meditate, ponder (*över*
upon, over)
mediterran *a5* Mediterranean
medi|um ['me:-] *s4* **1** (*mitt*) *se medio* **2** *fys.* me-
dium; *mat.* mean; *beräkna det aritmetiska -et av*
calculate the arithmetical mean of **3** (*medel för
spridning av ngt*) medium, agent, vehicle **4**
språkv. middle voice **5** (*spiritistiskt*) medium
med|kandidat fellow candidate **-kämpe** com-
rade-in-arms; (*friare*) fellow combatant **-kän-
nande** *a4* sympathetic **-känsla** sympathy (*för*
for; *med* with)
medl|a [-e:-] mediate; act as [a] mediator; (*vid ar-
betskonflikt o.d.*) arbitrate, negotiate; (*mellan
stridande äv.*) intervene **-are** mediator (*vid ar-
betskonflikt o.d.*) conciliator, arbitrator; *AE. äv.*
troubleshooter
medlem [-e:-] *s2* member; (*av lärt sällskap äv.*)
fellow; *icke ~* non-member; *vara ~ av* (*i*) (*kommitté e.d.*) serve (sit, be) on
medlems|antal membership, number of mem-
bers **-avgift** membership fee (subscription);
AE. dues (*pl*) **-förteckning** list of members
medlemskap [-e:d-] *s7* membership (*i* of)
medlems|kort membership card; (*i parti*) party
card **-stat** member state; (*i federation*) constituent state
medlid|ande *s6* compassion; (*medömkan*) pity;
(*deltagande*) sympathy; (*skonsamhet*) mercy; *ha
~ med* (*äv.*) pity, have (take) pity on **-sam** [-i:-]
a1 compassionate; pitying (*leende* smile); *med en
~ blick* with a look full of pity
medling [-e:-] mediation; (*uppgörelse*) settlement, arrangement; (*förlikning*) conciliation; (*i
äktenskap*) reconciliation
medlings|förslag proposal for settlement, draft
settlement **-försök** attempt at mediation **-kom-
mission** mediation (arbitration) committee
med|ljud consonant **-lut** downhill slope **-löpare**
polit. fellow traveller; opportunist **-människa**
fellow creature (being) **-mänsklighet** human
kindness **-passagerare** fellow passenger **-re-
gent** co-regent **-resenär** travelling companion
-ryckande *a4* exciting, stirring; captivating
-räkna count in, include; *ej ~d* excluded; *däri
-räknat* inclusive, inclusive of **-skyldig** accessory
(*i* in) **-sols** [-ɔ:-] clockwise, sunwise, with the
sun **-spelare** *teat. o.d.* fellow actor; *kortsp.,
film.* partner **-ströms** with the current **-syster**
sister **-sända** send along [with], enclose **-taga** *se
ta* [*med*]; *bör ~s* (*om uppgift e.d.*) should be given
(included); *hundar får ej ~s* dogs [are] not admitted **-tagen** *a5* (*utmattad*) tired out, done up (*av*
with); *känna sig ~* feel used up (run down) **-tra-
fikant** fellow passenger (road user) **-tävlare**
[fellow] competitor (*om, till* for); rival **-urs**
[-u:rs] clockwise
medusahuvud [-ˣdu:-] Medusa's (Gorgon's)
head
medverka (*samverka*) cooperate (*i, vid* in); (*vid*

fest, konsert o.d.) assist, lend one's services (*vid* at); (*deltaga*) participate, take part (*i, vid* in); (*bidraga*) contribute (*till* towards, in) **medverkan** cooperation (*i, vid* in; *till* towards); (*deltagande*) participation (*i, vid* in); (*hjälp*) assistance, support (*vid* in, at); *under ~ av* with the cooperation of, assisted by, (*i samarbete med*) in collaboration with **medverkande** *a4* cooperating *etc.*; (*bidragande*) contributory (*orsak* cause); *de ~* the performers (actors), those taking part **medvetande** *s6* consciousness (*om* of, as to); *förlora* (*återfå*) *~t* lose (regain) consciousness; *vara vid fullt ~* be fully conscious; *ingå i det allmänna ~t* be part of the public consciousness; *i ~ om* in the consciousness (aware) of **medveten** *a3* conscious (*om* of); *vara ~ om* (*inse*) be aware (sensible) of **-het** consiousness, awareness **medvetet** *adv* (*fullt* quite) consciously *etc.*; (*med vett o. vilja*) wittingly, deliberately **medvetslös** unconscious **-het** unconsciousness **medvind** tailwind, fair (following) wind; *i ~* with a favourable (*etc.*) wind; *segla i ~* sail before the wind, (*om företag*) be prospering **medvurst** *s2* German sausage **medömkan** commiseration, compassion **mefa** *s1, se markeffektfarkost* **mefistofelisk** [-'fe:-] *a5* Mephistophelean **mega|cykler** [-'sykk-] *pl* megacycles **-fon** [-'få:n] *s3* megaphone **-hertz** [-'härts] *r* megacycles per second, megahertz **megalitisk** [-'li:-] *a5* megalithic **megalomani** *s3* megalomania **megära** [-ˣgä:-, -'gä:-] *s1* shrew, termagant, vixen **mej** [mejj] *vard., se mig* **meja** [ˣmejja] (*gräs*) mow (*äv. bildl.*); (*säd, åker*) cut; *~ ner* mow down (*äv. bildl.*) **mejeri** dairy; (*butik*) creamery, dairy [shop] **mejerihantering** dairying, dairy farming **mejeriprodukt** dairy product **mejerist** dairyman **mejka** *v1, rfl, vard.* make o.s. up, make up one's face **mejning** mowing *etc.* **mejram** [ˣmejj-, 'mejj-] *s3* [sweet] marjoram **mejsel** *s2* chisel **mejsla** chisel (*äv. bildl.*), cut [with a chisel]; *~ ut* (*äv. bildl.*) chisel out; *~d* chiselled; (*om anletsdrag o.d. äv.*) clear-cut **mekanik** *s3, ej pl* **1** mechanics (*pl, behandlas som sg*) **2** *se mekanism* **mekaniker** [-'ka:-] mechanic, mechanician **mekanisera** mechanize **-ing** mechanizing, mechanization **mekan|isk** [-'ka:-] *a5* mechanical; *~ verkstad* engineering shop **-ism** *s3* mechanism; (*i ur äv.*) works (*pl*) **melanesier** [-'ne:-] Melanesian **melankol|i** *s3* melancholy; *med. äv.* melancholia **-iker** [-'kɔ:-] melancholic; melancholy person **-isk** [-'kɔ:-] *a5* melancholy; *ibl.* melancholic; (*dyster äv.*) gloomy; *vara ~* [*av sig*] (*äv.*) be of melancholy turn (temperament) **melass** *s3* molasses **melerad** [-'le:-] *a5* mixed; mottled; (*om tyg*) pepper-and-salt **mellan** (*vanl. om två*) between; (*om flera*)

among; (*mitt ibland*) in the midst of; *ibl.* inter-; *~ sina besök hos* (*äv.*) in between his (*etc.*) visits to; *titta fram ~ träden* peep out from behind (among) the trees; *~ femtio och sextio personer* some fifty or sixty persons; *det inbördes förhållandet ~* the mutual relations of; *~ fyra ögon* in private **-akt** interval [between the acts], intermission **-akts-musik** entr'acte [music], interlude **Mellanamerika** *n* Central America **mellan|blond** ashblond **-blå** medium blue **-dagarna** *pl, under ~* during the days between Christmas and New Year **-däck** *sjö.* between-decks (*pl*), *förk.* 'tween-decks (*pl*) **Mellaneuropa** *n* Central Europe **mellaneuropeisk** Central European **mellan|foder** interlining **-folklig** international **-form** intermediate (intermediary) form **-fot** metatarsus (*pl* metatarsi) **-fotsben** metatarsal [bone] **-gärde** [-j-] *s6* diaphragm **-hand 1** *anat.* metacarpus (*pl* metacarpi) **2** *kortsp.* second (third) hand; *i ~* in between, *bildl.* between two fires **3** *hand.* intermediary, middleman; *gå genom flera -händer* go via several middlemen **-handsställning** in-between position; intermediary position **-havande** *s6* (*affär*) account; (*skuld*) balance, debt; (*tvist*) dispute, difference; *ekonomiska ~n* financial transactions; *göra upp ett ~* settle a matter (an account) **-instans** intermediate authority (court of law) **-klass** *skol.* middle (intermediary) form **-klänning** semi-evening (afternoon) dress **-kommande** *a4* intervening **-komst** [-å-] *s3* intervention **-krigsgeneration** interwar generation **-krigsperiod** interwar period (years *pl*) **-landa** make an intermediate landing, touch down **-landning** intermediate landing; *flygning utan ~* nonstop flight **-led 1** *s3, anat.* intermediate (middle) joint; *bot.* internode **2** *s7* (*förmedlande led*) intermediate link, medium **-liggande** *a4* [situated] in-between, interjacent; *den ~ tiden* the time in-between, the intervening time **-läge** intermediate (middle) position **-lägg** *s7, tekn.* spacer; (*tunt*) shim, diaphragm; (*av tyg*) interlayer, interlining **-mål** snack [between meals]; *jag äter aldrig ~* I never eat between meals **-rum** *boktr. o. allm.* space; (*friare*) interval, interspace, gap; *med jämna ~* at regular intervals; *med två minuters ~* at intervals of two minutes, at two-minute intervals **-rätt** *kokk.* intermediate course; extra dish **-skikt** intermediate layer (*etc.*) **-skillnad** difference; *betala ~en* pay the extra (difference) **-skola** *ung.* middle (intermediate) school **-slag** *boktr.* space; (*mellan rader*) blank (white) line; (*mellan stycken*) space line, leads (*pl*); (*på skrivmaskin*) spacing; *utan ~* solid **-slagstangent** (*på skrivmaskin*) spacebar, spacer **-sort** *i sht hand.* medium [sort, quality] **-spel** *teat., mus.* interlude; intermezzo; *sällsamt ~* strange interlude **-stadielärare** intermediate level teacher **-stadium** intermediate (middle) stage **-station** intermediate station **-statlig** international; interstate **-stick 1** insertion **2** *se ledarstick* **-stor** medium[-sized] **-storlek** medium size **-ställning** intermediate position **-sula** mid-sole **Mellansverige** *n* Central Sweden **mellan|säsong** off-season **-tid** interval; *under*

~en in the meantime (meanwhile) **-ting** *ett* ~ *mellan* something between, a compromise between **-vikt, -viktare** *sport.* middleweight **-våg** *radio.* medium wave **-vägg** partition (division, interior) wall **-öl** medium-strong beer **-öra** middle ear

mellerst ['mell-] *adv* in the middle **mellersta** ['mell-] *a, superl.* middle; *geogr.* central, centre, middle; *M~ Östern* [the] Middle East; ~ *Wales* (*äv.*) Mid-Wales; *i* ~ *England* (*äv.*) in the Midlands

melodi *s3* melody; tune, air **-lära** melodics (*pl, behandlas som sg*)

melodi|sk [-'lɔ:-] *a5* melodious, melodic **-stämma** melody **-ös** *a1, se melodisk*

melodram *s3* melodrama **-atisk** [-'ma:-] *a5* melodramatic

melon *s3* melon

membran *s3, tekn. äv. s7* membrane, diaphragm

memoar|er [-o'a:-] *pl* memoirs **-författare** writer of memoirs

memor|andum [-ˣrann-] *s8* memorandum (*pl äv.* memoranda; *förk.* memo), note **-era** memorize, commit to memory **-ering** [-'re:-] [the] learning of ... by heart, memorization **-ial** *s7* memorandum

1 men [menn] *konj* but; only; (~ *ändå*) yet, still; ~ *så förtjänar han också bra* but then he earns a lot of money [too]; ~ *det var inte allt* (*äv.*) nor was that all; *jag vill inte höra några* ~*!* I'll have no buts!; *efter många om och* ~ after a lot of shilly-shallying

2 men [-e:-] *s7* disadvantage, detriment; (*skada*) injury; (*lyte*) disability; *vara till* ~ *för* be detrimental to; *få* ~ *för livet* be marked for life

men|a *v1, vard. o. poet. äv. v3* **1** (*tro, anse*) think, be of [the] opinion; *det* ~*r du väl inte, eller hur?* you don't think that, do you? *vad* ~*r du om ...?* what is your opinion about ...? **2** (*åsyfta*) mean; (*avse*) intend; ~ *väl med ngn* mean well by s.b.; ~ *allvar* be in earnest (*med* about); *det var inte så illa -t* (~*t*) no offence was intended; *säga ett och* ~ *ett annat* say one thing and mean another; *vad* ~*r han med ...?* what does he mean by ...?; *vad* ~*s med logik?* what is meant by logic?

menageri [-na:ʃe-] menagerie

menande I *a4* meaning, significant; knowing (*blick* look) **II** *adv* meaningly *etc.*; *blinka* ~ *åt ngn* give s.b. a knowing wink; *se* ~ *ut* look knowing

mened perjury; *begå* ~ commit perjury, perjure o.s. **-are** perjurer

menig *a1, äv. anv. som s, mil.* private, common soldier; *AE.* enlisted man; (*i flottan*) rating; ~*e man* (*allm.*) the common people **-het** the public; (*församling*) congregation

mening 1 (*uppfattning*) opinion (*om* about, of), idea, view (*om* about); *den allmänna* ~*en* public opinion; *avvikande* ~ dissenting opinion; *bilda sig en* ~ *om* form an opinion about; *inhämta ngns* ~ *om* get a p.'s opinion (hear a p.'s views) about; *säga sin* ~ give one's opinion, speak one's mind **2** (*betydelse, innebörd*) meaning, sense; (*idé, förnuft*) reason, sense; *i lagens* ~ within the meaning of the law, in the legal sense; *i viss* ~ (*äv.*) in a sense; *det vore ingen* ~ *i* (*för mig*) *att* there would be no point (sense) in (+ *ing-form*) (in my + *ing-*

form) **3** (*avsikt*) intention; (*syfte*) purpose; *det var inte min* ~ *att* I had no intention of (+ *ing-form*); *vad är* ~*en med det?* what is the sense (point) of that? **4** *språkv.* sentence; (*kort*) clause; (*längre*) period

meningit [-ŋg-] *s3* meningitis

menings|byggnad sentence structure **-byte** debate; dispute **-frände** *mina* ~*r* those who share my opinion[s] (views); *vi är* ~*r* we hold the same views **-full, -fylld** meaningful **-lös** meaningless; void of sense; senseless, useless; (*fånig*) nonsensical; *det är* ~*t att* there is no sense (point) in (+ *ing-form*); *deras* ~*a prat* (*äv.*) the nonsense they talk **-löshet** meaninglessness *etc.* **-motståndare** opponent; antagonist **-motsättning** conflict of opinion **-skiljaktighet** difference of opinion; disagreement **-utbyte** exchange of opinions **-yttring** expression of opinion

menisk *s3* meniscus

menlig [ˣme:n-] *a1* injurious, prejudicial, detrimental (*för* to) **menligt** *adv* injuriously; *inverka* ~ *på* have an injurious effect on, prejudice

menlös [ˣme:n-] *a1* innocent, harmless; (*klandrande*) puerile; *M~a barns dag* Holy Innocents' Day **-het** innocence, harmlessness

menopaus *s3* menopause

mens *s3, vard.* period; *ha* ~ have one's period

menstru|ation menstruation; menses (*pl*) **-ationsbesvär** menstrual pain **-era** menstruate

mental *a1* mental **-hygien** mental hygiene **-hygienisk** of mental hygiene **-itet** *s3* mentality **-patient** mental patient **-sjuk** mentally ill (deranged) **-sjukhus** mental hospital **-[sjuk]vård** mental care; mental health services (*pl*)

mentol [-'tå:l] *s3* menthol

mentor [-år] mentor, adviser

menuett *s3* minuet

meny *s3* menu

mer *komp. t. mycken, mycket* **1** *a* more; *mycket vill ha* ~ much will have more; *klockan är* ~ *än jag trodde* it is later than I thought; *han kommer inte någon* ~ *gång* he will not come again (any more); *vill du ha* ~ *te?* would you like some more tea?; *och, vad* ~*a är* and, what is more; *någon* ~ *gång* again some time; *med* ~*a* (*m.m.*) et cetera (etc.), and such like; *inte* ~ *än a*) (bara) no more than, *b*) (*ej över*) not more than **II** *adv* more; ~*a känd under namnet* better known as; ~ *eller mindre* more or less; *det händer* ~*a sällan* it happens [quite] rarely; *tycka* ~ *om* like ... better; ~ *än nog* (*äv.*) enough and to spare; *aldrig* ~ never again; *han förstår sig inte* ~ *på* ... *än* he has no more idea of ... than; *det är inte* ~ *än rätt att* it is only fair that; *han vet* ~ *än väl* he knows perfectly well; *det räcker* ~ *än väl* that'll be more than enough; *så mycket* ~ *som* especially (all the more) as

merarbete extra work

merceriser|a [-s-] mercerize **-ing** mercerizing; mercerization

merendels [-de:-] mostly; (*vanligtvis*) usually, generally

meridian *s3* meridian

merinkomst additional (extra) income

merinofår [-ˣri:-] merino

merit *s3* merit; (*kvalifikation*) qualification (*för* for) **-era** qualify (*för* for); ~ *sig* qualify o.s. **-för-teckning** list of qualifications, personal record **-okratj** *s3* meritocracy **-värdering** assessment of qualifications, merit rating

merkantjl *a1* commercial; mercantile **-ism** mercantilism **-systemet** the mercantile system, mercantilism

merkostnad additional (extra) cost

Merkurius [-'ku:-] Mercury

mer|part greater part **-smak** *ge* ~ whet the appetite **-värde** added value **-värde[s]skatt** value-added tax

1 mes *s2, zool.* tit[mouse]

2 mes *s2* (*ställning för ryggsäck*) rucksack frame

3 mes *s2* (*ynkrygg*) coward, funk

mesaktig *a1* faint-hearted, timorous

mesallians [-'aŋs] *s3* misalliance; *ingå en* ~ marry beneath one

mesạn *s3, sjö.* spanker, mizzen **-mast** mizzenmast

mesig *a1, se mesaktig*

meskaljn *s4* mescalin[e]

meson [-'så:n] *meson, åld.*

Mesopotamien [-'ta:-] *n* Mesopotamia **mesopotamisk** [-'ta:-] *a5* Mesopotamian; ~*a* (*abrakadabra*) double Dutch, gibberish

mesost whey-cheese

mesotron [-'trå:n] *s3, se meson*

messiạnsk *s5* Messianic

Messjas Messiah

mest *superl. t. mycken, mycket* **I** *a* most, the most; [*den, det, de*] ~*a* most, most of; *det* ~*a* most, most things; ~*a delen* most [part] of it; *det allra* ~*a* by far the greater part, the very most; *göra det* ~*a möjliga av* make the very most of; *vilken av dem gjorde* ~? which of them did [the] most? **II** *adv* most; (*för det -a o.d.*) for the most part, mostly; (*huvudsakligen*) principally, chiefly, mainly; *de* ~ *efterfrågade* ... the ... most in (in the greatest) demand; *tycka* ~ *om* like most (best); *han är som folk är* ~ he is quite an ordinary chap, he is not unusual in any way **-adels** [-de:-] mostly; for the most part; (*i de flesta fall*) in most cases; (*vanligen*) generally **-gynnadnationsklausul** most-favoured-nation clause

mestjs *s2* mestizo

meta angle, fish (*abborre* [for] perch)

meta|bolism metabolism **-don** [-'då:n] *s4* methadone **-for** [-'få:r] *s3* metaphor **-fysjk** *s3* metaphysics (*pl, behandlas som sg*) **-fysisk** [-'fy:-] metaphysical

metaldehyd [ˣme:t-] *s3* metaldehyde

metạll *s3* metal; *av* ~ (*äv.*) metal ... **-arbetare** metalworker **-glans** metallic lustre **-haltig** *a1* metalliferous **-industri** metal industry **-isk** *a5* metallic **-klang** metallic ring **-ografj** *s3* metallography **-ojd** *s3* metalloid **-skrot** [metal] scrap **-tråd** [metal] wire **-trådsnät** wire netting **-urg** *s3* metallurgist **-urgj** *s3* metallurgy

metamorfos [-mår'få:s] *s3* metamorphosis (*pl* metamorphoses)

metạn *s4* methane; marsh gas **-ol** [-'nå:l] *s3* methanol, methyl alcohol, wood alcohol

metare angler; (*med fluga*) [fly-]fisherman

metastạs *s3* metastasis

metatẹs *s3* metathesis (*pl* metatheses)

metdon fishing tackle

mete *s6* angling; [fly-]fishing

meteor [-'å:r] *s3* meteor **-jt** *s3* meteorite; (*järn-*) siderite; (*sten-*) aerolite **-liknande** meteoric **-olog** meteorologist **-ologj** *s3* meteorology **-ologisk** [-'lå:-] *a5* meteorological **-sten** meteorite

meter ['me:-] *s9, versl. s2* metre; *AE.* meter **-hög** a (one) metre high **-mått** (*redskap*) metre-measure; (*hopfällbart*) folding rule **-system** metric system **-varor** *pl, ung.* yard (piece) goods **-vis** (*per meter*) by the metre; (*meter på meter*) yards and yards, metres and metres

met|krok fish-hook **-mask** angling worm **-ning** [-e:-] *se mete*

metọd *s3* method; (*tillvägagångssätt äv.*) procedure; (*tillverknings-*) process; (*sätt*) way, manner **-jk** *s3* methodology; (*friare*) methods (*pl*), system **-isk** *a5* methodical **-iskt** *adv* methodically; *gå* ~ *till väga* proceed methodically; *gå* ~ *till väga med ngt* (*äv.*) do s.th. methodically

metod|ism Methodism **-ist** Methodist

metod|lära methodology **-studie** methods study, study of methods **-tidmätning** methods time measurement (*förk.* MTM)

metonymj *s3* metonymy

metrev [fishing] line

metr|jk *s3* prosody **-isk** ['me:-] *a5* prosodic; metrical

metronom metronome

metropol [-'på:l] *s3* metropolis **-jt** *s3, kyrkl.* metropolitan

metspö fishing rod; *med* ~ (*äv.*) with rod and line

metyl *s3* methyl **-alkohol** methyl alcohol, methanol **-enblått** [-ˣle:n-] methylene blue

Mexico ['meksikɔ] *n* Mexico

mexi|kạn *s3* Mexican **-kạnsk** [-a:-] *a5* Mexican

mezzosopran [ˣmetså-, -'pra:n] *s3* mezzo-soprano

m.fl. *förk. för med flera* and others

miạu miaow!

mickel ['mikk-] *s2* fox; *M*~ *räv* Reynard the Fox

middag ['midda:g, *vard.* 'midda] *s2* **1** (*mitt på dagen*) noon; midday; *god* ~! good afternoon!; *i går* ~ yesterday noon; *framemot* ~*en* towards midday; *på* ~*en* (~*arna*) in the middle of the day **2** (*måltid*) dinner; (*bjudning*) dinner party; *äta* ~ have dinner; *äta* ~ *kl. 7* dine at seven o'clock; ~*en är serverad* dinner is served (ready); *bjuda ngn på* ~ invite s.b. to dinner; *vad får vi till* ~? what are we going to have for dinner?; *vara borta på* ~ be out to (for) dinner; *sova* ~ have (take) an after-dinner nap

middags|bjudning dinner party; (*inbjudan*) invitation to a dinner party **-bord** dinner table; *duka* ~*et* lay the table for dinner **-gäst** dinner guest, guest for dinner **-hetta** midday heat **-höjd** meridian altitude; *bildl.* meridian **-klänning** dinner gown (dress) **-mat** dinner food **-rast** break for dinner **-sällskap** company of dinner guests **-tid** *vid* ~[*en*] at (about) noon (dinner time)

midfastosöndag [-i:-] mid-Lent Sunday; *Storbritannien* Mothering Sunday

midja [ˣmi:-] *s1* waist; *om* ~*n* round the waist

midje|kjol waist slip **-mått** waist-measurement

midnatt [-i:-] midnight
midnatts|sol midnight sun **-tid** vid ~ at midnight
midskepps [ˣmi:dʃepps] amidships
midsommar [ˣmi:d-, vanl. ˣmiss-] midsummer **-afton** Midsummer Eve **-blomster** wood cranesbill **-dag** Midsummer Day **-firande** s6 Midsummer celebration **-stång** se majstång
midströms [-i:-] in mid-current
midvinter [-i:-] midwinter
mig [mi:g, vard. mejj] pron (objektsform av jag) me; rfl myself; jag gjorde illa ~ i foten I hurt my foot; en vän till ~ a friend of mine; vad vill du ~? what do you want me for?; kom hem till ~ come round to my place; när det gäller ~ själv [speaking] for myself, as far as I am concerned; jag tror ~ veta att I think I know that
migrän s3 migraine
mikrob [-'krå:b] s3 microbe
mikro|biologi microbiology **-dator** microcomputer **-fiche** [ˣmi:kråfiʃ, -'fiʃ, -o-] s5 microfiche **-film** microfilm **-fon** [-'få:n] s3 microphone; vard. mike **-fotografering** photomicrography, micrography; (nedfotografering) microphotography **-fotografi** photomicrograph; microphotograph **-kosmos** [-'kåss-] microcosm[os] **-meter** [-'me:-] s2 micrometer
mikro|n [-'krå:n] s9, s3 micron **-organism** microorganism **-skop** [-'skå:p] s7 microscope **-skopisk** [-'skå:-] a5 microscopic[al] **-teknik** microtechnology **-våg** microwave **-vågsugn** microwave oven
mil s9 ten kilometres; eng. motsv. about six miles; engelsk ~ mile; nautisk ~ nautical mile
mila s1 (kol-) charcoal stack (kiln, pit); (atom-) atomic pile, nuclear reactor
mild a1 mild (i (till) smaken in taste); (mjuk) soft (färg colour; svar answer); (dämpad) mellow; (lugnande) soothing (röst voice); (ej sträng) lenient (dom sentence; mot to[wards]); (lindrig, saktmodig) gentle; ~a vindar gentle winds; med milt våld with gentle compulsion; ~a makter! Holy Moses!; du ~e! Good Lord!; så till den ~a grad so utterly, so awfully **-het** mildness etc.; leniency, lenience; (barmhärtighet) mercy **-ra** mitigate; temper; (lätta [på]) alleviate, relax; (dom, straff äv.) reduce **-ras** dep grow milder (etc.); soften **-väder** det är ~ a thaw has set in
miljs s3 militia **-soldat** militiaman
militant a1 militant
militariser|a militarize **-ing** militarization
militar|ism militarism **-ist** militarist **-istisk** [-'riss-] a5 militaristic
militieombudsman [-'li:tsie-, -ˣlittsie-] hist., ~en the [Swedish] Parliamentary Commissioner for Military Affairs
militär I s3 (krigsman) military man, soldier; (krigsmakt) military force[s pl]; högre ~er officers of high rank; ~en the military (pl); (hären) the army **II** a1 military **-allians** military alliance **-attaché** military (service) attaché **-befälhavare** general officer commanding [, military command area south etc.] **-diktatur** military dictatorship **-domstol** military tribunal, court martial **-flygplan** army plane **-förläggning** garrison, military camp **-högskola** M~n [the

Swedish] armed forces staff and war college **-isk** a5 military; army; (soldatmässig) soldierly; militant **-junta** military junta **-ledning** ~en the military council **-läkare** military (army, naval, air force) medical officer **-makt** military power **-marsch** military march **-musikkår** military band **-område** military command [area]; AE. military district **-polis** military police **-sjukhus** military hospital **-tjänst** military service **-utbildning** military training **-väsen** military (service) affairs (pl) **-yrket** the military profession
miljard [-'ja:rd] s3 milliard; AE. billion; en ~ (vanl.) one thousand million
miljon s3 million; fem ~er pund five million pounds **-affär** transaction involving millions [of pounds (etc.)] **-belopp** pl millions **-förlust** loss involving millions [of pounds (etc.)]; [a] loss of a million **-stad** city (town) with [over] a million inhabitants **-tals** [-a:-] millions of -te [-ˣjo:n-] (ordningstal) millionth **-är** s3 millionaire
miljö s3 environment; ibl. milieu; (omgivning) surroundings (pl); background, general setting **-förstöring** pollution [of the environment] **-påverkan** environmental influence **-skadad** a5 maladjusted **-skildring** description of social milieu **-skydd** environmental protection **-vård** control of the environment **-vådsproblem** environmental problem **-vänlig** non-polluting
milliard se miljard
milli|bar s9 millibar **-gram** [-'gramm] milligramme **-liter** [-'li:-] millilitre **-meter** [-'me:-] millimetre **-meterpapper** graph paper **-meterrättvisa** absolute fairness
millopp sport. mile race
milslång en ~ promenad a walk of a mile, mile walk; ~a köer queues miles and miles long
mil|sten, -stolpe milestone (äv. bildl.)
mils|vid stretching (extending) for miles; -vitt omkring for miles around
milt adv t. mild mildly; ~ uttryckt to put it mildly
miltals [-a:-] for miles
mim s3 mime **-jk** s3 mimicry, miming **-iker** ['mi:-] mimic **-isk** ['mi:-] a5 mimic
mimosa [-ˣmå:-, -o:-] s1 mimosa
1 min [mi:n] s3 air; mien; (ansiktsuttryck) [facial] expression; (utseende) look; göra fula ~ (en ful ~) pull an ugly (make a wry) face; inga sura ~er! no long faces!; ge sig ~ av att vara pretend to be, put on an air of [being]; hålla god ~ [i elakt spel] put a good face on it, make the best of a bad job; vad gjorde hon för ~? what was the expression on her face?; utan att förändra en ~ without moving a muscle
2 min [minn] mitt, mina, pron, fören. my; självst. mine; de ~a my people (vard. folks); denna ~ åsikt this view of mine; ~ dumbom! fool that I am!; nu har jag gjort mitt I have done my part (bit) now; skilja mellan mitt och ditt know the difference between mine and thine
min|a s1 mine; gå på en ~ hit a mine; lägga ut -or lay mines; låta -an springa (äv. bildl.) spring the mine
minaret s3 minaret
minder|värdeskomplex inferiority complex **-värdeskänsla** feeling of inferiority **-värdig** a1 inferior **-värdighet** inferiority **-årig** a1 under-

age, minor, infant; ~*a barn* minors, young children **-årighet** minority, infancy
mindetektor mine detector
mindre ['minn-] *komp. t. liten* **I** *a* **1** (*vid jämförelse*) smaller (*till* in); less[er], minor; (*kortare*) shorter (*till* in); (~ *t. antalet*) fewer; (*lägre*) lower; *bli* ~ grow (get) smaller (*etc.*); *ett* ~ *antal än tidigare* fewer (a smaller number) than before; *så mycket* ~ *orsak att* all the less reason for (+ *ingform*); *på* ~ *än en timme* in less than (in under) an hour; *ingen* ~ *än kungen själv* no less [a person] than the king himself; *ingenting* ~ *än* nothing short of **2** (*utan eg. jämförelse*) small [-sized]; (*yngre*) younger; (*obetydlig*) slight, insignificant; (*oviktig*) unimportant; (*smärre*) minor, lesser; *av* ~ *betydelse* of less importance; *i* ~ *grad* in (to) a minor degree, on a smaller scale; *man kan bli tokig för* ~ (*vard.*) it's more than enough to send one crazy; *inte* ~ *än* no fewer (less) than **3** *med* ~ [*än att*] unless; *det går inte med* ~ [*än att*] *du kommer själv* nothing less than your personal attendance will do, you must be there yourself (in person) **II** *adv* less; not very much; *mer eller* ~ more or less; *så mycket* ~ *som* the less so as; ~ *välbetänkt* ill-advised
Mindre Asien *n* Asia Minor
minera mine; lay mines; ~*t område* mined area
mineral *s7, åld. pl äv.* -*ier* mineral **-fyndighet** mineral deposit **-haltig** *a1* containing mineral[s *pl*]; mineral **-isk** *a5* mineral
minera|log mineralogist **-logi** *s3* mineralogy **-logisk** ['-lå:-] *a5* mineralogical
mineral|olja mineral oil, petroleum **-riket** the mineral kingdom **-ull** mineral wool **-vatten** mineral water **-ämne** mineral substance
min|ering [-'ne:-] mining **-fara** danger from mines **-fartyg** minelayer **-fält** minefield
miniatyr *s3* miniature **-format** *i* ~ in miniature **-golf** *se minigolf* **-isera** miniaturize **-målare** miniaturist **-målning** miniature painting; *konkr.* miniature
mini|buss minibus **-cykel** small-wheel folding bicycle **-dator** minicomputer **-golf** miniature golf **-kjol** miniskirt
minimal *a1* minimal, minimum; diminutive, infinitesimal
minimera (*göra så liten som möjligt*) minimize; (*bestämma lägsta gräns för*) fix the lower limit for
minimi|avgift minimum fee **-belopp** minimum [amount] **-gräns** lower limit, floor **-krav** minimum requirements **-lön** minimum salary (wage [s]) **-pris** minimum price, price floor
minimum ['mi:-] *s8* minimum (*pl äv.* minima)
miniräknare pocket calculator
minister [-'nist-] *s2* minister; *Storbritannien äv.* secretary of state; *svenske* ~*n i London* the Swedish ambassador in London; *brittiske* ~*n i Sverige* (*äv.*) Her Britannic Majesty's minister to Sweden **-ium** [-'te:-] *s4* ministry; *Storbritannien äv.* government department **-portfölj** *bildl.* office of minister of state, portfolio **-post** minister's appointment, ministerial duties **-president** *ung.* prime minister, premier **-råd** council of ministers; *Storbritannien* cabinet
ministär *s3* ministry, government, cabinet; *bilda*

~ form a government (*etc.*)
mink *s2* mink **-päls** mink coat
min|nas *v2, dep* remember, recollect; *om jag -ns rätt* if I remember rightly, if my memory does not fail me; *jag vill* ~ *att* I seem to remember that; *så långt tillbaka jag kan* ~ as far back as I can remember; *nu -des hon alltsammans* now it all came back to her; *han kunde inte* ~ *att han gjort det* he couldn't remember having done it; *inte på den dag jag -ns* it's so long ago I can't remember
minne *s6* **1** (*-sförmåga*) memory; mind; *tappa* ~*t* lose one's memory; *bevara* (*hålla*) *i* ~*t* keep in mind; *hålla ngt i* ~*t* bear s.th. in mind; ago *ett upp och ett i* ~ one down and one to carry; *återkalla i* ~*t* recall, recollect; *med detta i färskt* ~ with this fresh in my (*etc.*) memory; *lägga på* ~*t* commit to memory, remember; *dra sig ngt till* ~*s* remember (recollect) s.th., call s.th. to mind; *det har fallit mig ur* ~*t* it has escaped my memory (slipped my mind); *återge ur* ~*t* repeat from memory **2** *med ngns goda* ~ with a p.'s approval (consent) **3** (*hågkomst*) memory, remembrance; (*åminnelse äv.*) commemoration; (*minnesbild*) recollection; (*händelse i det förgångna*) memorable event; *ett* ~ *för livet* an unforgettable experience; *uppliva gamla* ~*n* revive old memories; *hans* ~ *skall leva* his memory will never fade; *till* ~ *av* in memory of; *vid* ~*t av* at the recollection of **4** (*memoarer o.d.*) recollections, memoirs **5** (*-sgåva, suvenir*) remembrance, souvenir, keepsake **6** *data.* store; *AE.* storage; *yttre* ~ external store (storage)
minnes|album remembrance book **-anteckning** memorandum **-beta** *s1, en* ~ s.th. not easily forgotten **-bild** picture in one's mind **-dag** memorial day **-förlust** loss of memory **-god** with a good memory **-gudstjänst** memorial service **-gåva** keepsake, souvenir **-högtid** memorial ceremony, commemoration **-lista** check list; list of engagements **-märke** memorial, monument; (*fornlämning*) relic, ancient monument **-ord** *pl* words of remembrance **-regel** mnemonic rule **-rik** rich in memories; (*oförglömlig*) unforgettable **-runa** obituary **-sak 1** (*som beror av minnet*) *en* ~ a matter of memory **2** *se suvenir* **-skrift** memorial publication **-sten** monument **-tal** commemoration speech, memorial address **-tavla** commemorative (memorial) tablet **-teckning** biography (*över* of) **-utställning** commemorative exhibition **-värd** *a1* memorable (*för* to), worth remembering
minnesång minnesong **-are** minnesinger
minoisk ['-nå:-] *a5* Minoan
minoritet *s3* minority; *vara i* ~ be in the (a) minority
minoritets|problem minority problem **-regering** minority government **-ställning** *vara i* ~ be a minority
minröjning mine clearance, removal of land mines
minsann to be sure; I can tell (assure) you; I'm blessed (blowed); *det är* ~ *inte så lätt* it is not at all that easy; ~ *om jag det begriper* I'm blessed if I understand that; *jag skall* ~ *ge dig!* my word, I'll let you have it!
minska reduce (*med* by; *till* to); diminish, decrease, lessen; (*förkorta*) shorten; (*dämpa*) abate

(*ngns iver* a p.'s zeal); (*nedskära*) cut [down] (*utgifterna* the expenses); (*lätta på*) relieve (*spänningen* the tension); ~ *hastigheten* reduce speed, slow down, decelerate; ~ *i betydelse* become less important; ~ *i vikt* go down in (lose) weight; ~ *ngt på sina anspråk* not demand quite so much, reduce one's claims **minskad** *a5* reduced *etc.*

(*med* by) **minskas** *dep* grow (become, get) less; diminish, decrease; be reduced (*i* in; *med* by); (*avtaga*) fall off; (*dämpas*) abate; (*sjunka*) fall, go down, sink; (*i värde*) depreciate **minskning** reduction, diminution, decrease; (*nedskärning*) curtailment, cut; (*i värde*) depreciation

minspel changes in facial expression; mimicry **min|spränga** blow up by mines (a mine); *bli -sprängd* be blown up by mines (a mine) **-sprängning** (-*sprängande*) [the] blowing up (*av* of) by mines; (*med pl*) mine-explosion **-spärr** mine barrage

minst *superl. t. liten* **I** *a* smallest; least; (*yngst*) youngest; (*kortast*) shortest; (*minimalast*) minimum, minutest; ~*a motståndets lag* the law of least resistance; ~*a gemensamma nämnare* [the] lowest common denominator; *utan* ~*a tvekan* without the slightest (least) hesitation; *han hade* ~ *fel* he had [the] fewest mistakes; *med* ~*a möjliga* with a (the) minimum of; *in i* ~*a detalj* [down] to the smallest (minutest) detail; *det* ~*a a*) (*som substantiv*) the least, *b*) (*som adv*) the least [*vard.* little bit]; *inte det* ~*a trött* not [in] the least tired; *inte bry sig det* ~*a om* not care twopence about **II** *adv* least; the least, at least; (~ *av allt*) least of all; *inte* ~ *viktig var frågan om* the question of … was as important as any; ~ *sagt* to say the least [of it]

minsvep|a sweep for mines **-are** minesweeper **-ning** minesweeping **minsökare** mine detector **minus** ['mi:-] **I** *s7* minus [sign]; (*friare*) minus quantity, minus; (*brist*) deficit, shortage **II** *adv* minus; ~ *10 grader* 10 degrees [Centigrade] below zero; ~ *3 %* kassarabatt less 3 % discount; *plus* ~ *noll* plus minus naught **-grad** degree of frost (below zero) **minuskel** [-'nusk-] *s3* minuscule **minustecken** minus sign **minut** *s3* **1** minute; *tio* ~*ers promenad* ten minutes' walk; *fem* ~*er över tre* five minutes past three; *en gång i* ~*en* once a minute; *på* ~*en* to the minute; *om (på) några* ~*er* in a few minutes; *i sista* ~*en* at the last minute, in the nick of time **2** *hand.* retail; *i* ~ by (*AE.* at) retail; *köpa i* ~ buy retail; *sälja i* ~ retail, sell [by] retail **-handel** retail business **-handelspris** retail price **minutiös** [-tsi'ö:s] *a1* meticulous, scrupulous; minute **minutläggare** minelayer **minut|pris** retail price **-visare** minute hand **minör** sapper **mirakel** [-'ra:-] *s7, s4* miracle **-spel** miracle play **mirakulös** *a1* miraculous **misan|trop** [-'trå:p] *s3* misanthrope **-tropi** *s3* misanthropy **-tropisk** [-'trå:-] *a5* misanthropic [al] **mischmasch** *s7* mishmash, hotchpotch, hodge-

podge **miserabel** [-'ra:-] *a2* wretched, miserable; (*ömklig*) pitiable **miss** *s2* (*misslyckande*) miss; (*felslag o.d.*) missed shot (hit, stroke) **missa** (*bomma*) miss, fail to hit (strike); (*misslyckas*) miss one's shot (hit, stroke, aim); *bildl. äv.* fail; (*om sak*) miss its mark **miss|akta** (*ringakta*) disdain; (*förakta*) despise **-aktning** disrespect, disdain; (*förakt*) contempt **-anpassad** *a5* maladjusted **-belåten** displeased (*med* at, about); dissatisfied (*med* with) **-belåtenhet** displeasure, dissatisfaction **-bildad** *a5* malformed, misshapen **-bildning** malformation; defect; deformity **missbruk** (*oriktigt bruk*) misuse; (*skadligt bruk*) abuse **missbruka** (*använda fel*) misuse; (*alkohol, förtroende, makt o.d.*) abuse; *kan lätt* ~*s* lends itself to abuse[s]; ~ *ngns godhet* take undue advantage of a p.'s kindness; ~ *Guds namn* take the name of God in vain **missbrukare** misuser; abuser **miss|dåd** misdeed; evil deed **-dådare** malefactor, evil-doer **-fall** miscarriage; *få* ~ (äv.) miscarry **-firma** *v1* insult; abuse **-firmelse** *s5* insult; abuse **-foster** abortion (*äv. bildl.*); *äv. bildl.* monstrosity **-färga** discolour, stain **-färgning** discoloration **-förhållande** disproportion, disparity (*mellan* between); (*friare*) incongruity, anomaly; *sociala* ~*n* social evils **-förstå** misunderstand; *som lätt kan* ~*s* that is liable (likely) to be misunderstood **-förstånd** misunderstanding; (*misstag*) mistake **-grepp** mistake, bad move **-gynna** treat unfairly; *exporten har* ~*ts av utvecklingen* development has been unfavourable to exports **-gärning** evil deed; (*svagare*) misdeed **-hag** *s7* displeasure (*med ngn* with s.b.; *med ngt* at s.th.); dislike (*med* of) **-haga** displease, be displeasing to; *det* ~*r mig* (äv.) I dislike it **-haglig** [-a:-] *a1* displeasing; (*starkare*) offensive, objectionable; (*förhatlig*) obnoxious; (*impopulär*) unpopular; ~ *person* (äv.) undesirable person **-handel** maltreatment (*av* of); *jur.* assault [and battery]; cruelty; *bli utsatt för* ~ be assaulted **-handla** maltreat; *jur.* assault; *bildl.* handle roughly; (*t.ex. språk*) murder **-hugg** *i* ~ by mistake **-humör** *på* ~ in a bad temper **-hushålla** ~ *med* mismanage, be uneconomical with **-hushållning** mismanagement, misuse **-hällighet** discord, dissension; ~*er* (äv.) quarrels **missjl** *s3* missile **mission** [mi'ʃo:n] **1** (*beskickning*) mission; (*kall äv.*) vocation; *ha en* ~ *att fylla* have a vocation (call) **2** *relig.* missions (*pl*); *inre (yttre)* ~ home (foreign) missions (*pl*) **-era** preach [the Gospel] **missions|förbund** *Svenska M*~*et* the Swedish Mission Covenant Church **-föreståndare** mission superintendent **-hus** mission hall, chapel **-station** mission station, mission **-sällskap** missionary society **missionär** [-ʃo-] *s3* missionary **missjv** *s7* **1** (*skrivelse*) missive; (*följebrev*) covering letter **2** *kyrkl.* ordination as a temporary curate **miss|klä[da]** be unbecoming to, not suit; *ingenting -klär en skönhet* (*ung.*) everything becomes a beauty **-klädsam** unbecoming; (*ej smickrande*) unflattering; (*-prydande*) disfiguring **-kreditera** discredit **-krediterande** *a4* discreditable (*för* to) **-kund** *r, se förbarmande; utan* ~ (*äv.*) without [any] compassion **-kunda** *rfl* have mercy (compassion) (*över* upon) **-kundsam** *a1* merciful; (*medlidsam*) compassionate, pitying **-känd** *a5* misjudged; unappreciated, underrated **-känna** misjudge, underestimate

miss|leda mislead; *jfr vilse-* **-ljud** jarring sound; *mus.* dissonance (*äv. bildl.*)

miss|lyckad (*som -ats*) unsuccessful; (*förfelad, felslagen*) abortive; *~e existenser* failures; *vara* ~ be a failure, have gone wrong **-lyckande** *s6* failure; fiasco **-lyckas** *dep* fail (*i, med* in); be (prove, turn out) unsuccessful (a failure)

miss|lynt *a4* ill-humoured; cross; *göra ngn* ~ put s.b. out [of humour], upset s.b., make s.b. cross **-lynthet** ill (bad) humour; crossness **-minna** *rfl, om jag inte -minner mig* if I remember rightly **-mod** downheartedness, depression (dejection) [of spirit[s]]; (*nedslagenhet*) discouragement **-modig** downhearted, depressed, despondent

missne *s9, s7, bot.* calla, arum lily

miss|nöjd (*i sht tillfälligt*) dissatisfied; (*i sht varaktigt*) discontented, displeased; *vara* ~ *med* (*ogilla*) disapprove of **-nöje** dissatisfaction; discontent; displeasure; (*ogillande*) disapproval (*med* of); *allmänt* ~ *råder bland* discontent is rife among; *väcka* ~ *mot en dom* give notice of appeal against a verdict **-nöjesyttring** signs (murmurs) (*pl*) of discontent **-pryda** disfigure, spoil the look of **-riktad** *a5* misdirected; (*oklok*) misguided, ill-advised

missroman sentimental novel

miss|räkna *rfl* miscalculate; *bildl.* make a miscalculation **-räkning** (*fel-*) miscalculation; *bildl.* disappointment (*för* for, to; *över* at) **-sköta** (*hopskr.* missköta) mismanage; (*försumma*) neglect; ~ *sig a*) (*sin hälsa*) neglect one's health, *b*) (*sitt arbete e.d.*) neglect one's duties (work) **-stämning** (*hopskr.* misstämning) feeling (sense) of discord (discontent, disharmony) **-sämja** (*hopskr. missämja*) dissension, discord

miss|tag mistake; (*fel*) error; (*förbiseende*) oversight, blunder, slip; *det var ett* ~ *av mig* it was a mistake on my part, it was my mistake; *göra ett svårt* ~ make a bad mistake, commit a serious blunder; *av* ~ by mistake, inadvertently **-taga** *rfl* make a mistake; be wrong; ~ *sig på* (*äv.*) misjudge, get a wrong idea of (about); *man kan ju* ~ *sig* (*äv.*) one can of course be mistaken; *man kunde inte* ~ *sig på* there was no mistaking; *om jag inte -tar mig* if I am not mistaken

miss|tanke suspicion; (*förmodan*) supposition; (*ond aning*) misgiving; *hysa -tankar* entertain suspicions (*mot ngn för ngt* about s.b. for s.th.; *om* as to); *fatta -tankar* become suspicious (*mot ngn* of s.b.; *om* about); *om* about, as to) **-tolka** misinterpret; (*ngns avsikter äv.*) misconstrue

misstro I *s9* distrust (*mot* of); (*starkare*) disbelief (*till* in) **II** *v4* distrust, mistrust, be suspicious of; (*tvivla på*) doubt

misstroende *s6, se misstro I*; lack of confidence (*mot* in) **-votum** vote of censure (*mot* on)

misstrogen distrustful, mistrustful (*mot* of); (*skeptisk*) incredulous **-het** distrustfulness *etc.*; incredulity

miss|trösta despair (*om* of); give up hope (*om* of) **-tröstan** *r* despair (*om* of)

miss|tycka take it amiss, be offended [at]; *om du inte -tycker* (*äv.*) if you don't mind **-tyda** misinterpret; misconstrue

misstänk|a suspect; ~ *ngn för ngt* (*för att ha*) suspect s.b. of s.th. (of having); be suspicious of; (*befara*) apprehend; (*svagare äv.*) fancy, guess **-liggöra** cast (throw) suspicion upon **-sam** *a1* suspicious (*mot* of); full of suspicion (*mot* against) **-samhet** suspiciousness

misstänkt *a1* suspected (*för* [*att*] of [+*ing-form*]); (*tvivelaktig*) doubtful, dubious; (*som inger misstro*) suspicious; *den ~e* the suspect; *som* ~ *för* (*äv.*) on [a] suspicion of; *vara* ~ *för* (*för att ha*) be under suspicion for (for having); *göra ngn* ~ *för* direct suspicion on s.b. for

miss|unna [be]grudge; (*avundas*) envy **-unnsam** *a1* grudging (*mot* towards); (*avundsam*) envious (*mot* of) **-uppfatta** misunderstand, misconceive; (*-tyda*) misread, put a wrong interpretation on, get a wrong idea of **-uppfattning** misunderstanding, misconception **-visande** *a4* misleading **-visning** (*kompassnålens*) deviation, variation; *ostlig* ~ easterly magnetic declination **-växt** *s3* failure of the crop[s]; [a] bad harvest **-växtår** year of crop failure **-öde** mishap, misadventure; *råka ut för ett* ~ have a slight accident; *genom ett* ~ (*äv.*) by mischance; *tekniskt* ~ technical hitch

mist *s3* mist; fog

mista *v1, v3* lose; be deprived of

miste *adv* wrong; *gå* ~ *om* miss, fail to secure; *ta* ~ *på a*) (*ngn*) mistake for s.b. else, *b*) (*ngt*) make a mistake about, misjudge; *du kan inte ta* ~ *på vägen* you cannot miss the road; *det är inte att ta* ~ *på* there is no mistaking

mistel *s2, bot.* mistletoe

mist|lur foghorn **-signal** fog signal **-signalering** fog signalling **-siren** fog siren

misär *s3* destitution; penury; (*kortspel.*) misery

mitella [-ˣtella] *s1* triangular bandage; sling

mitra [ˣmi:-] *s1* mitre

1 mitt pron, *se 2 min*

2 mitt I *s3* middle; *i* (*på*) ~*en* in the middle; *i deras* ~ in their midst; *från* ~*en av mars* (*äv.*) from mid-March **II** *adv* **1** *bryta* ~ *av* break right in two **2** ~ *emellan* midway (somewhere) between; ~ *emot* right (just, exactly) opposite, opposite; ~ *fram* right in front; ~ *framför* right (just, straight) in front of; ~ *för ögonen på ngn* right in front of a p.'s eyes; ~ *för näsan på ngn* under a p.'s very nose; ~ *i* in the [very] middle of; ~ *i ansiktet* full in the face; ~ *ibland* in the midst of, amidst; ~ *igenom* through the centre (middle) of, (*rakt igenom äv.*) right (straight) through; ~ *inne i* right in the middle (centre) of, (*landet e.d.*) in the interior of; ~ *itu* in two equal parts; *dela* ~ *itu* (*äv.*) halve; *gå* ~ *itu* break right in two; ~ *på* in the middle of; ~ *under a*) rumsbet. exactly (directly) under, *b*) tidsbet. during, just while; ~ *upp i* in the [very] middle of; *skratta ngn* ~ *upp i ansiktet* laugh in a p.'s face; ~ *uppe i* up in the

M

middle of, (*friare*) right in the midst of (*arbetet* one's work); ~ *ut i* out into the [very] middle of, right out into; ~ *ute i* out in the middle of, right out in; ~ *över* exactly above (over); *bo* ~ *över gatan* live straight across the street

mitt|bena *ha* ~ have one's hair parted in the middle **-emellan** [-ˣmell-], **-emọt** *se 2 mitt II 2*

mitten|parti centre party **-politik** centrist policies

mitterst ['mitt-] *adv* in the centre (*i* of) **mittersta** ['mitt-] *superl. a* middle, central

mitt|linje centre (central, median) line; *sport.* halfway line **-parti** central part, centre; *polit.* centre party **-punkt** centre; (*på måltavla*) bull's-eye **-remsa** (*på t.ex. motorväg*) central reserve (reservation); *A E.* median strip **-skepp** (*i kyrka*) nave **-sträng** *se mittremsa* **-söm** middle seam **-uppslag** centre spread **-ạt** *mil.* [eyes] front!

mix *s3, s2* cakemix

mixtra ~ *med* potter (meddle) with, (*göra fuffens*) juggle with **mixtur** mixture

mjau *se miau*

mjugg *i uttr.:* ~ covertly; *le i* ~ laugh up one's sleeve

mjuk *a1* soft (*till* in); (*om färgton e.d.*) softened, mellow; *bildl.* gentle (*om konturer e.d.*) sweeping, gentle; (*böjlig*) limp; (*smidig*) supple; lithe, limber; (*om rörelse o.d.*) graceful; (*eftergiven, smidig*) pliable, flexible; (*spak*) meek, mild; ~*t bröd* soft bread; *ha* ~*t anslag* (*mus.*) have a light touch; *bli* ~, *se mjukna*; *göra* ~ make soft, soften **-delar** *pl, anat.* soft parts **-glass** soft ice cream **-görare** softener, plasticizer **-het** softness *etc.*; pliancy; flexibility **-landa** softland **-landning** soft landing

mjukna [-u:-] soften, get (become) soft[er]

mjuk|ost cream cheese, cheese spread **-plast** non-rigid plastic **-porr** soft-porn **-valuta** soft currency **-vara** *data.* software

mjäkig *a1* mawkish; sloppy, sentimental

1 mjäll *s7, s9* dandruff, scurf

2 mjäll *a1* **1** (*mör*) tender **2** (*ren, vit*) transparently white

mjältbrand *veter.* anthrax

mjält|e *s2, anat.* spleen **-hugg** stitch [in the (one's) side] **-sjuk** splenetic (*äv. bildl.*); *bildl. äv.* hypochondriac **-sjuka** *bildl.* spleen; *med.* hypochondria

mjärde [ˣmjä:r-] *s2* osier basket; (*ståltråds-*) wire cage

mjöd *s7, s4* mead

mjöl *s7* flour; (*osiktat*) meal; (*pulver*) flour, powder, dust; *sammalet* ~ (*äv.*) wholemeal (*A E.* whole-wheat) flour; *inte ha rent* ~ *i påsen* (*bildl.*) not be on the level

mjöl|a flour, sprinkle over with flour **-bagge** flour-beetle **-dagg** mildew, blight **-dryga** *s1, bot.* ergot **-ig** *a1* floury, mealy

mjölk *s3* milk; *fet* (*mager*) ~ rich (thin) milk

mjölk|a **1** milk **2** (*ge mjölk*) give (yield) milk **3** (*utsuga*) milk, pump dry **-affär** dairy **-bar** *s3* milk bar; *A E.* drugstore **-bil** milk[-collecting] lorry **-bud** milkman **-choklad** milk chocolate

1 mjölke *s2, zool.* milt, soft roe

2 mjölke *s2, bot.* rosebay willowherb, fireweed

mjölk|erska milkmaid **-flaska** (*av glas*) milk-bottle; (*av bleck*) milk-can **-förpackning** milk carton **-ko** milch cow (*äv. bildl.*), milker **-körtel** lactiferous gland **-maskin** milking machine **-ning** milking **-pall** milking stool **-pulver** powdered milk **-socker** milk sugar, lactose **-syra** lactic acid **-syrabakterier** *pl* lactic-acid bacteria **-tand** milk tooth, deciduous tooth **-utkörare** milkman **-vit** milky (milk) white **-ört** *se 2 mjölke*

mjölmat farinaceous food

mjöln|ardräng [-ö:-] miller's man **-are** [-ö:-] miller

mjölon [-ån] *s7, bot.* bearberry

mjölsäck (*tom*) flour (meal) sack; (*fylld*) sack of flour

m.m. (*förk. för med mera*) etc.

mnemotekn|ik *s3* mnemonics (*sg*) **-isk** [-'tekk-] *a5* mnemonic, mnemotechnic

MO [ˣämmo] *förk. för militieombudsmannen*

mo *s2* (*sand*) fine sand; (*mark*) sandy plain, heath

moaré *s3, s4* moiré; watered silk (fabric)

moatjé [-'tçe:] *s3* partner

mobb [-å-] *s2* mob **mobba** mob **mobb[n]ing** mobbing

mobil I *a1* mobile **II** *s3* mobile **-ier** *pl, se lösegendom, bohag*

mobiliser|a mobilize; (*friare äv.*) muster **-ing** [-'se:-] mobilization

mobiltelefon [-ˣbi:l-] carphone

moçambik|ier [-'bi:k-] Mozambican **-isk** *a5* Mozambican

1 mocka [-å-] *v1* clear of dung, clean out; ~ *gräl med* (*vard.*) pick a quarrel with

2 mocka [-å-] *s9* (*kaffesort*) mocha

3 mocka [-å-] *s9* (*skinn*) suede [leather]

mockajacka suede jacket

mockakopp [small] coffee cup, demitasse

mockasjn [-å-] *s3* moccasin

mockasked [small] coffee spoon

mockaskor suede shoes

1 mod *s7* **1** (*-ighet*) courage; intrepidity; (*moraliskt äv.*) fortitude; *hans* ~ *sjönk* (*svek honom*) his courage (heart) sank (failed him); *med förtvivlans* ~ with the courage of despair; *hålla* ~*et uppe* keep up one's courage; *hämta nytt* ~ take fresh courage; *ta* ~ *till sig* pluck up courage; *tappa* ~*et* lose heart, be discouraged **2** (*sinne, humör*) spirits (*pl*); mood; *vara väl* (*illa*) *till* ~*s* be at ease (ill at ease); *vara vid gott* ~ be in good spirits; *i hastigt* ~ without premeditation; *med berått* ~ deliberately, wilfully, in cold blood

2 mod *s4* fashion; style; *bestämma* ~*et* set the fashion; *är högsta* ~ is all the fashion (rage); *läkare på* ~*et* fashionable doctor; *vara* (*komma*) *på* ~*et* be in the (come into) fashion

modal *a1* modal; ~*t hjälpverb* auxiliary of mood

modd [-å-] *s3* slush **moddig** *a1* slushy

moddlare [-å-] flat brush

mode *s6, se 2 mod* **-affär** (*hatt-*) milliner's [shop] **-docka** dressmaker's dummy (*äv. bildl.*); *bildl. äv.* fashion plate **-färg** fashionable colour **-hus** fashion house **-journal** fashion magazine **-kung** king (dictator) of fashion **-lejon** dandy, fop

modell *s3* **1** (*mönster*) model; *tekn. o. bildl. äv.* pattern; *i sht hand.* style; (*hatt-, sko-*) shape **2**

pers. [artist's] model; *sitta (stå)* ~ sit (stand) as a model *(för, åt* to); *teckna efter levande* ~ draw from living models **-bygge** *abstr.* construction of models; *konkr.* model **-era** model *(efter* from; *i* in) **-ering** [-'le:-] modelling **-flygplan** model aeroplane **-järnväg** model railway **-klänning** model gown **-lera** *(hopskr. modellera)* modelling clay, plasticine

modem *s7* modem

mode|nyck freak (whim) of fashion **-ord** vogue word

moder *-n mödrar (jfr mor)* mother; *bildl.* parent; *blivande mödrar* expectant mothers

moderat *a1 (måttfull)* moderate; *(skälig)* reasonable, fair; *~a priser* reasonable prices; *M~a samlingspartiet (i Sverige)* ~the] moderate party **-ion** moderation; restraint **-or** [-ˣra:tår] *s3, atomfys.* moderator

moderbolag parent company

moderer|a moderate **-ing** moderation

moderfartyg mother ship

mode|riktig in fashion, fashionable, trendy **-riktning** fashion trend

moder|kaka *anat.* placenta **-land** mother country **-lig** *a1* motherly; *(om t.ex. känslor, oro)* maternal **-lighet** motherliness; maternity **-liv** womb **-lös** motherless

modern [-'dä:rn] *a1 (nutida)* modern, contemporary; *(fullt ~)* [quite ~) up-to-date; *(nu på modet)* fashionable; *bli* ~ come into fashion; ~ *dans* ballroom dancing **-isera** modernize **-isering** [-'se:-] modernization **-ism** modernism **-ist** *s3* modernist **-istisk** [-'nist-] *a5* modernist **-itet** *s3* modernity; *~er* innovations, *neds.* novelties

moder|näring principal (primary) industry; *(jordbruk)* agriculture **-planta** mother plant

moders|bröst *barnet vid* ~*et* the child at its mother's breast **-bunden** *vara* ~ have a mother fixation **-famn** *i* ~*en* in the maternal (one's mother's) embrace **-glädje** maternal (a mother's) joy **-instinkt** maternal (a mother's) instinct

moderskap *s7* motherhood, maternity

moderskaps|försäkring maternity insurance **-penning** maternity allowance

moders|känsla ~*n hos henne* the mother in her **-kärlek** maternal (a mother's) love **-mjölk** *med* ~*en* with one's mother's milk, *(friare)* from earliest infancy **-mål** mother tongue, native language; *(som skolämne)* Swedish, English *etc.* **-målslärare** teacher of (in) Swedish *(etc.)*; *vår* ~ *(vanl.)* our Swedish *(etc.)* master

modersugga mother-sow

mode|sak *konkr.* fashionable (fancy) article; *abstr.* [a] matter of fashion **-skapare** fashion designer

modest *a1* modest

mode|tecknare fashion designer, stylist **-teckning** fashion drawing (design) **-tidning** *se modejournal* **-visning** fashion show

modfälld *a5* discouraged, disheartened *(över* at); *bli* ~ *(äv.)* lose courage

modifi|era modify; *(dämpa)* moderate **-kation** modification, moderation

modig *a1* **1** courageous; *(tapper)* brave, plucky; *(djärv)* bold; *(oförvägen)* gallant; *(oförskräckt)*

valiant, intrepid **2** *kosta sina ~a slantar* cost a pretty penny; *väga sina ~a 100 kilo* weigh all of 100 kilos

modist milliner, modiste

mod|lös dispirited; spiritless **-löshet** dispiritedness **-stulen** *a5* downhearted

modul *s3* module; *mat. o. fys.* modulus

modul|ation modulation **-era** modulate

modus ['mo:-] *n, r, språkv.* mood

mog|en *a3* ripe *(för, till* for; *(om frukt äv.)* mellow; *(friare o. bildl.)* mature; *bildl. äv.* ready; ~ *ålder* maturity, mature age; *efter -et övervägande* after careful consideration; *när tiden är* ~ when the time is ripe (has come)

mogen|het ripeness *etc.*; maturity **-hetsexamen** matriculation

mogn|a [-ɔ:-] ripen *(äv. bildl.)*; *eg. äv.* get ripe; *(bildl. o. friare)* mature, come to maturity **-ad** *s3* ripeness *(äv. bildl.)*; *i skt bildl.* maturity

mognads|grad degree of ripeness *(etc.)* **-process** process of maturing (growing up)

mogul ['mo:-,'må:-, *pl* -'gu:-] *s3* Mogul; *Stora* ~ the [Great] Mogul

mohair [-'hä:r] *s3* mohair

mohammedan *s3, se muhammedan*

mohikan *s3* Mohican; *den siste* ~*en* the last of the Mohicans

mojna [-å-] *sjö.* slacken, lull; ~ *av (äv. bildl.)* fall dead, die down; *när det* ~*r* when the wind slackens *(etc.)*

mojäng *s3, ~er* gear *(sg)*, gadgets

1 mol *s9 (grundenhet)* mole

2 mol *adv,* ~ *allena* entirely (all) alone, all by o.s.

mol|a ache slightly; *(friare)* chafe; *det ~r i tänderna på mig* my teeth are aching a little **-ande** *a4* aching; *(om värk)* dull; *(ihållande)* persistent

molekyl *s3* molecule **-är** *a1* molecular **-formel** molecular formula **-massa** *relativ* ~ relative molecular mass, molecular weight **-vikt** *se -massa* **-är** *a1, se -ar*

1 moll [-å-] *r, mus., gå i* ~ be in a minor key

2 moll [-å-] *s3 (tyg)* mull; light muslin

molla [-å-] *s1, bot.* goosefoot

mollskinn [-å-] moleskin

mollton *mus.* minor note **-art** *mus.* minor key

mollusk *s3, zool.* mollusc, mollusk; *(om pers.)* jellyfish

moln [-å:-] *s7* cloud *(äv. bildl.)*; *solen går i* ~ the sun is going behind a cloud; *ett* ~ *låg över hans panna* his brow was [over]clouded **-bank** *s2* cloudbank **-bildning** cloud formation *(äv. konkr.)* **-bädd** bed of clouds **-fri** cloudless, free from clouds; *bildl. äv.* unclouded **-höjd** height of cloud; *flyg.* ceiling **-höjd** *a5* cloud-enveloped **-ig** *a1* cloudy; clouded, overcast **-ighet** cloudiness; *meteor.* [amount of] cloud **-tapp** wisp of cloud **-täcke** cloud-cover **-täckt** *a4* cloud-covered, overcast **-vägg** cloud-wall

moloken [ˣmo:-] *a3* cast down, dejected; down in (at) the mouth

molotovcocktail [ˣmåll-] Molotov cocktail

mol|tiga [ˣmo:l-] not utter a sound **-tyst** absolutely silent, [as] quiet as a mouse

Moluckerna [-'lukk-] *pl* [the] Molucca *(förr* Spice) Islands, Moluccas

molvärka [ˣmo:l-] *se mola*

M

molybdęn *s3, s4, miner.* molybdenum
momang instant, moment; *på ~en* instantly, this instant
momęnt *s7* **1** (*tidpunkt*) moment, instant **2** (*beståndsdel*) moment, element; factor; (*i lagtext*) subsection, clause; (*stycke*) paragraph; (*punkt*) point; *ett störande ~* a disturbing factor **-ęn** *a1* momentary
moms [måms] *s3, se mervärdeskatt*
monąd *s2, filos.* monad
monąrk *s3* monarch **monarkį** *s3* monarchy; *inskränkt ~* constitutional (limited) monarchy **monarkism** monarchism **monarkist** *s3* monarchist **monarkistisk** [-'kist-] *a5* monarchist
mondän [-å-] *a1* fashionable, sophisticated, elegant; *~a människor* (*äv.*) the fashionable set
monegąsk *s3* Monacan, Monegasque **-isk** *a5* Monacan, Monegasque
monetär *a1* monetary
mongol [måŋ'gɔ:l] *s3* Mongol[ian]
Mongoliet [måŋgɔ'li:-] *n* Mongolia
mongol|isk [måŋ'gɔ:-] *a5* Mongolian **-[o]jd** mongoloid **-veck** epicanthus, epicanthic fold
monism [-å-] *filos.* monism
monokel [må'nåkk-] *s2, s3* monocle
mono|kotyledon [månå-, -'då:n] **I** *s3* monocotyledon **II** *a5* monocotyledonous **-krom** [-'krå:m] **I** *s3* monochrome **II** *a5* monochrome **-kromatisk** [-'ma:-] *a5* monochromatic **-kultur** monoculture **-ljt** *s3* monolith **-log** *s3* monologue; soliloquy **-man** [-'ma:n] **I** *s3* monomaniac (*på* as regards) **II** a1 monomaniac[al] **-manj** *s3* monomania **-plęn** *s7, flyg.* monoplane
monopol [-'på:l] *s7* monopoly; exclusive privilege[s *pl*]; *ha ~ på* have the monopoly of, *bildl. äv.* have the sole right to **-isera** monopolize **-isering** [-'se:-] monopolization
monoteis|m monotheism **-tisk** *a5* monotheistic [al]
mono|ton [-'tå:n] *a1* monotonous **-toni** [-'ni:] *s3* monotony
monst|er ['måns-] *s7,* **-rum** *s4* monster (*till far of* a father); monstrosity **-ruös** *a1* monstrous
monstrąns [-å-] *s3, kyrkl.* monstrance
monsųn [-å-] *s3* monsoon **-regn** monsoon rain
montage [måŋ'ta:ʃ, måŋ-] *s7, film.* montage
monter ['månn-, 'måŋ-] *s2, s3* showcase; exhibition case
montera [månn-, måŋ-] **1** (*sätta upp*) mount, fit (set) up (*på* on); (*sätta ihop*) assemble, put together; (*installera*) install; (*t.ex. hus, radiomast*) erect; *~ ner* dismantle **2** (*hatt e.d.*) trim
monter|bar [-ˣte:r-] *a1* mountable **-ing** mounting *etc.*; assembly, assemblage; installation; erection
monterings|färdig prefabricated **-hall** assembly shop
montör fitter, mechanic; *elektr.* electrician; *flyg.* rigger
monumęnt *s7* monument; *resa ett ~ över* erect (put up) a monument to
monumentąl *a1* monumental; (*friare äv.*) grand **-figur** monumental figure **-itęt** grandness **-konst** monumental art **-verk** monumental work
mopęd *s3* moped, *åld.* autocycle **-ist** mopedist,

åld. autocyclist
mopp [-å-] *s2* mop **moppa** mop, go over with a mop
1 moppe [-å-] *vard. i uttr.: ge ngn (få) på ~* give s.b. (get) a wigging
2 moppe [-å-] *vard.* moped
mops [-å-] *s2* pug[-dog] **mopsa** *rfl* be saucy (*mot* to) **mopsig** *a1, se näsvis*
1 mor [-ɔ:-, -å:-] *s3* (*folk*) Moor
2 mor [-ɔ:-] *modern mödrar* (*jfr moder*) mother; *bli ~* become a mother; *M~s dag* Mother's Day, Storbritannien *äv.* Mothering Sunday; *vara som en ~ för ngn* be like a mother to s.b., mother s.b.
morąl *s3, ej pl* (*ngns*) morals (*pl*); (*trupp- o.d.*) morale; (*-isk uppfattning*) morality; (*sedelära*) moral law, ethics (*pl, behandlas som sg o. pl*); (*sens-*) moral; *predika ~ för* preach morality to **-begrepp** moral concept **-isera** moralize (*över* [up]on) **-isk** *a5* moral; (*etisk*) ethical; *~t stöd* moral support; *M~ Upprustning* Moral Rearmament **-ist** moralist **-itęt** *s3* morality **-kaka** *se -predikan* **-lära** ethics (*pl, behandlas som sg*) **-predikan** homily, moral lecture; *hålla ~* (*äv.*) sermonize **-predikant** sermonizer, moralizer
morąs *s7* morass, swamp
morator|ium [-'tɔ:-] *s4* moratorium (*pl äv. -ia*)
morbid *a1* morbid
morbror [ˣmɔrr-, 'mɔrr-] [maternal] uncle, uncle on the (one's) mother's side
mord [-ɔ:-] *s7* murder (*på* of); *jur. äv.* homicide; *begå ~* commit murder **-brand** arson, incendiarism; *anlägga ~* commit arson **-brännare** incendiary, fire raiser **-försök** attempted murder; *~ mot ngn* attempt on a p.'s life **-isk** ['mɔ:r-] *a5* murderous, homicidal **-kommission** murder squad; *A.E.* homicide squad **-lysten** bloodthirsty **-lystnad** bloodthirstiness **-plats** scene of a murder **-redskap** murderous implement **-vapen** murder weapon; (*-iskt vapen*) deadly weapon **-ängel** destroying angel
moręll *s3, bot.* morello [cherry]
mores [ˣmå:-] *i uttr.: lära ngn ~* teach s.b. good manners
mor|far [ˣmɔrr-, 'mɔrr-] [maternal] grandfather **-farsfar** great grandfather [on the mother's side]
morfęm [-å-] *s7, språkv.* morpheme
morfin [-å-] *s4, s3* morphine, morphia **-injektion** morphia injection **-ism** morphinism, morphine addiction **-ist** morphinist, morphine (morphia) addict
morfo|logj [-å-å-å-] *s3* morphology **-logisk** [-'lå:-] *a5* morphological
morföräldrar *mina ~* my [maternal] grandparents, my mother's parents
morganatisk [-å-'na:-] *a5* morganatic
morgon [ˣmårgån, 'mårrån] (*vard. morron*) **-en** morgnar (*vard. mornar*) **1** *motsats t. kväll*) morning; *poet.* morn; *tidernas ~* (*äv.*) the beginning of time; *god ~!* good morning!; *på ~en* in the morning; *på ~en den 1 mars* on the morning of the 1st of March; *i dag på ~en* this [very] morning; *tidigt följande ~* early next morning **2** *i ~* tomorrow; *i ~ dagar* tomorrow week; *i ~ bitti[da]* tomorrow morning **-bön** morning prayers (*pl*); *skol. äv.* morning assembly **-dag** tomorrow; morrow; *uppskjuta till ~en* put off until

tomorrow **-gymnastik** early-morning exercises (*pl*) **-gåva** morning gift **-humör** [early-]morning temper **-kaffe** early-morning coffee **-kvisten** *vard. i uttr.: på* ~ early in the morning **-luft** [*börja*] *vädra* ~ begin to see one's chance **-mål** breakfast **-människa** early bird (riser) **-pigg** alert (lively) in the morning **-rock** dressing gown; *AE. äv.* bathrobe **-rodnad** ~*en* aurora, the red sky at dawn **-samling** *skol.* morning assembly **-sol** *rum med* ~ room that gets the morning sun **-stjärna** morning star **-stund** morning hour; ~ *har guld i mun* the early bird catches the worm **-sömnig** drowsy in the morning **-tidig** *vara* ~ [*av sig*] be up and about early, be an early bird **-tidning** morning paper **-toalett** morning toilet

morian *s3* blackamoor

moring (*förtöjningsring*) mooring

morisk [ˣmɔ:-, ˈmå:-] *a5* Moorish, Moresque

morkulla [-ɔ:-] *s1* woodcock

mormon *s3* Mormon **mormonsk** [-ˈmɔ:nsk] *a5* Mormon

mor|mor [ˣmɔrr-, ˈmɔrr-] maternal grandmother **-morsmor** great grandmother [on the mother's side]

morna [ˣmå:r-] *rfl* get o.s. awake, rouse o.s.; *inte riktigt* ~*d* not quite awake

morot *-en morötter* carrot

morots|färgad carrot-coloured, carroty **-saft** carrot juice

morr|a [-å-] growl, snarl (*åt* at) **-hår** *koll.* [cat's *etc.*] whiskers (*pl*) **-ning** growl, snarl

mors [-å-] *interj* hello!; *AE.* hi!

1 morsa [-å-] *v1, vard.* say hello

2 morsa [-ɔ-] *s1, vard.* mum

morse [-å-] *i uttr.: i* ~ this morning; *i går* ~ yesterday morning

morse|alfabet [ˣmårse-] [international] Morse code **-signal[ering]** Morse signal[ling] **-tecken** Morse symbol

morsgris *a1* mother's darling

morsk *a1* (*orädd*) bold, daring; (*käck*) dashing; (*karsk*) stuck-up, fierce; (*manhaftig*) stouthearted; *visa sig* ~ make the most of o.s. **morska** ~ *upp sig* pluck up courage; ~ *upp dig!* take heart! **morskhet** boldness *etc.*

mortalitet [-å-] mortality

mortel [ˣmɔ:r-] *s2* mortar; *stöta i* ~ grind (crush) in a mortar **-stöt** pestle

mortifi[c]era cancel

morän *s3* moraine **-bildning** *abstr. o. konkr.* moraine formation

mos *s4* (*massa*) pulp; *kokk.* paste, mash; *jfr äv. äppel-, potatis-*; *göra* ~ *av* make mincemeat of **mosa** reduce to pulp, pulp; (*potatis o.d.*) mash

mosaik *s3* mosaic; *lägga* ~ mosaic **-arbete** mosaic work; tesselation **-golv** mosaic (tesselated) pavement (floor) **-inläggning** inlaying with mosaic; incrustation, tesselation

mosaisk [-'sa:-] *a5* Mosaic; (*judisk äv.*) Jewish; *en* ~ *trosbekännare* a Jew

mose|bok *de fem* -*böckerna* the Pentateuch; *Första* (*Andra, Tredje, Fjärde, Femte*) ~ [the book of] Genesis (Exodus, Leviticus, Numbers, Deuteronomy)

Mosel [ˈmå:-] *r* the Moselle **moselvin** [ˣmå:-]

moselle [wine]

1 mos|ig *a1* (*-ad*) pulpy

2 mosig *a1* (*i ansiktet*) red [and bloated]; (*rusig*) fuddled, tipsy

moské *s3* mosque

moskit *s3* mosquito **-nät** mosquito net[ting]

moskovit *s3* Muscovite **-isk** *a5* Muscovite

Moskva *n* Moscow

moss|a [-å-] *s1* moss **-belupen** *a5* moss-covered, mossy **-djur** bryozoan, *vard.* sea mat

moss|e [-å-] *s2* peat moss, bog **-grön** moss green **-ig** *a1* mossy **-täcke** covering of moss

moster [ˣmoss-, ˈmoss-] *s2* [maternal] aunt

mot I *prep* **1** (*riktning*) towards (*äv. om tid*); to; *gå* ~ *staden* walk towards the town; *färden gick* ~ *söder* they (*etc.*) headed south; *hålla upp ngt* ~ *ljuset* hold s.th. up to the light; *rusa* ~ *utgången* dash to the exit; *se upp* ~ *bergen* look up to the hills; *komma springande* ~ *ngn* come running towards s.b. (in a p.'s direction); *vara vänd* ~ (*vanl.*) face; ~ *kvällen* towards the evening; ~ *slutet av året* towards (near) the end of the year **2** (*beröring*) against; *gränsen* ~ *Norge* the Norwegian border; *med ryggen* ~ *väggen* with one's back to the wall; *segla* ~ *strömmen* sail against the current; *vågorna slog* ~ *stranden* the waves lapped [on] the shore; *bilen törnade* ~ *en sten* the car bumped into a stone **3** (*uppträdande, sinnelag*) to, towards; *vänlig* ~ kind to; *hysa agg* ~ bear a grudge against; *misstänksam* ~ suspicious of; *sträng* ~ severe on, strict with; *uppriktig* ~ honest with; *i sitt uppträdande* ~ in his (*etc.*) manner (behaviour) towards **4** (*motsättning, kontrast*) against; (*jämförelse äv.*) compared to (with); *jur. o. sport. äv.* versus; *skydd* ~ protection against (from); *strida* ~ fight against; *grönt är vackert* ~ *blått* green is beautiful against blue; *väga* ~ *varandra* weigh one against the other; *det kom 10 svar* ~ *4 förra gången* there were 10 answers compared to (with) 4 last time; *brott* ~ *en förordning* breach of a regulation; *ett medel* ~ *snuva* a remedy for colds; *det hjälper* ~ *allt* it is good for everything; *det är ingenting* ~ *vad jag kan* that is nothing to what I can do; *hålla 2* ~ *1 på att* bet 2 to 1 that; *förslaget antogs med 20 röster* ~ *10* the proposal was adopted with 20 votes to 10 **5** (*i utbyte mot*) for, against; ~ *kvitto* against receipt; ~ *legitimation* on identification; ~ *skälig ersättning* for a reasonable fee (remuneration); *byta ngt* ~ *ngt* exchange s.th. for s.th.; *göra ngt* ~ *att ngn gör* do s.th. in exchange for a p.'s doing; *i utbyte* ~ in exchange for **II** *adv, se emot*

mota 1 (*hejda*) block (bar) the way for; check; head off; (*avvärja*) ward off; (*förekomma*) forestall; ~ *Olle i grind* nip s.th. in the bud, ward off impending trouble **2** (*driva*) drive; ~ *bort* drive off (away from); ~ *ihop* (*boskap*) drive (herd) together

mot|aktion counteraction, countermeasure **-angrepp** counterattack **-arbeta** (*ngn, ngt*) work against; counteract; (*söka hindra*) check; (*ngns planer*) seek to thwart (traverse); (*bekämpa*) oppose **-argument** counterargument, objection **-bevis** counterproof, counterevidence **-bevisa** refute; belie **-bjudande** *a4* repugnant, repulsive (*för* to); (*otäck*) disgusting **-bok** (*kontra-*)

[customer's] passbook; (*sparkasse-*) bankbook; (*för spritinköp*) liquor-ration book **-drag** countermove (*äv. friare*) **-eld** *mil.* counterfire, returnfire
motell *s4* motel
motett *s3, mus.* motet
mot|fordran counterclaim **-fråga** counterquestion **-förslag** counterproposal **-gift** antidote, antitoxin **-gång** *s2* (*med pl*) reverse, setback; (*utan pl*) adversity, misfortune **-hugg** counterblow, counterthrust, counterstroke; *få* ~ meet with opposition **-håll** *ha* ~ be in disfavour (*för* with) **-hårs** [-å:-] (*stryka en katt* stroke a cat) the wrong way
motig *a1* adverse, contrary; (*besvärlig*) awkward; *det har varit* ~*t* things have not been easy (*för mig* for me) **-het** reverse, setback, adversity
1 motion [måt'ʃɔ:n] (*kroppsrörelse*) exercise; *få* (*ta*) ~ get (take) exercise
2 motion [måt'ʃɔ:n] (*förslag*) motion (*i* on; *om* for); *väcka* ~ *om* submit a motion for; *väcka* ~ *i* introduce a bill in (*riksdagen* the Riksdag)
1 motionera [måtʃɔ-] (*ge motion*) give exercise, exercise; (*skaffa sig motion*) take exercise
2 motionera [måtʃɔ-] (*väcka förslag*) move (*om* for; *om att* that)
motions|cykel exercycle **-gymnastik** physical (gymnastic) exercises (*pl*), callisthenics (*pl o. sg*), keep-fit exercises (*pl*)
motionär [måtʃɔ'nä:r] *s3* mover [of a resolution]; introducer of a bill
motiv *s7* **1** motive (*för, till* for, of); (*anledning, skäl*) reason, cause (*för, till* of); *vad hade du för* ~ *till att* what was your motive for (+ *ing-form*) **2** *konst., mus. o.d.* motif (*till* for, of); (*t. tavla äv.*) subject; *mus. äv.* theme **motivation** motivation
motivera (*ange skälen för*) state [the] reasons (grounds) for, account for; (*utgöra tillräckligt skäl för*) be the motive of, motivate; (*berättiga*) warrant; (*rättfärdiga*) justify; *en föga* ~*d* ... a[n] ... for which there is little justification
motivering [-'ve:-] justification, explanation (*för* of, for); (*bevisföring*) argumentation; *psykol.* motivation; *med den* ~*en att* on the plea that
motiv|forskning motivation research **-val** choice of subject (*etc.*)
mot|kandidat rival [candidate] **-kultur** counter-culture **-ljus** *foto.* direct light **-ljusskydd** *foto.* lens hood (shade) **-lut** upgrade, ascent **-läsa** *boktr.* checkread; *bokför.* call over **-offensiv** counteroffensive **-offert** counteroffer
motor [ˣmɔ:tår] *s3* motor; engine; *stark* (*svag*) ~ high-powered (low-powered) motor **-brännolja** *se dieselolja* **-bränsle** motor fuel **-båt** motorboat; *AE. äv.* powerboat **-cykel** motorcycle; *vard.* motorbike; ~ *med sidvagn* [motorcycle] combination **-cyklist** motorcyclist **-drift** motor operation **-driven** *a5* motor-driven **-fartyg** motor ship (vessel) **-fel** engine trouble **-fordon** motor vehicle **-förare** motorist, driver **-gräsklippare** power lawnmower **-haveri** engine breakdown **-hotell** *se motell* **-huv** (*bil-*) bonnet, *AE.* hood; *flyg.* cowl[ing]
motor|ik *s3* mobility **-isera** motorize; ~*de trupper* (*biltransporterade*) lorry-borne troops, (*mekaniserade*) mechanized troops **-isk** [-'tɔ:-] *a5*

motor[y] **-ism** motorism, motoring **-ist** motorist
motor|krångel engine trouble **-man** motorist; (*-vagnsförare*) motorman **-olja** motor (engine) oil **-sport** motoring, motor sport[s] **-sprit** motor spirit **-stopp** engine (motor) failure, breakdown **-styrka** engine power **-såg** chain (power) saw **-torpedbåt** [motor] torpedoboat **-trafik** motor [ing] traffic **-tävling** motor race **-vagn** rail motorcoach, railcar; (*spårvagn*) motorcar **-vagnståg** multiple-unit train **-verkstad** motor works (*sg o. pl*); (*bil- ofta*) garage **-väg** motorway; *i sht AE.* motor highway, express highway, freeway **-värmare** engine preheater
mot|part opposite party, counterparty, opponent **-pol** antipole (*äv. bildl.*) **-prestation** service in return; (*friare*) something in return **-reformation** counter-reformation **-replik** rejoinder **-revolution** counter-revolution **-sats** contrast (*mot, till* to); opposite, contrary, antithesis (*till* of); (*i logiken*) contradictory; *bevisa* ~*en* prove the contrary; *raka* ~*en* the very (exact) opposite (*till* of); *utgöra* (*stå i*) ~ *till* be opposed to; *i* ~ *till* contrary (in contrast) to; *de är varandras* ~*er* they are absolute opposites **-satsförhållande** contrast[ing relationship]; *stå i* ~ *till* be at variance with (in opposition to) **-satt** *a4* **1** *allm. o. bildl.* opposite, contrary; opposing, conflicting; (*omvänd*) reverse; *i* ~ *fall* in the contrary case, (*i annat fall*) otherwise; *i* ~ *riktning* in the opposite direction; *på* ~*a sidan a*) on the opposite side (*av* of; *mot* to), *b*) (*i bok o.d.*) on the opposite page; *förhållandet var det rakt* ~*a* the situation was quite the opposite **2** *bot., med.* ~*a blad* oppositifolious **-se** (*se fram emot*) look forward to; (*vänta*) expect; *vi* ~*r med intresse Ert svar* (*hand.*) we look forward to your reply **-sida** opposite (other) side (*äv. bildl.*) **-skäl** counterreason; *skäl och* ~ arguments for and against, [the] pros and cons **-sols** [-sɔ:-] anticlockwise, *AE.* counterclockwise **-spelare** (*i spel*) opponent, adversary; *vara* ~ *till ngn* (*teat. o.d.*) play opposite s.b. **-spänstig** refractory; (*olydig*) insubordinate **-stridig** *a1* conflicting, contradictory **-strävig** *a1* (*-spänstig*) refractory; (*-villig*) reluctant; (*om t.ex. hår*) intractable **-ström** counter-current **-ströms** against the current, upstream **-stycke** *bildl.* counterpart; (*like*) parallel, match, equal; *sakna* ~ be unparalleled (unique) **-stå** resist, withstand; (*angrepp etc. äv.*) stand up against; *en ... som man inte kan* ~ (*äv.*) an irresistible ... **-stående** *a4* opposite; *på* ~ *sida* on the opposite page
motstånd *s7* **1** resistance (*äv. fys., elektr., mil.*); *flyg. äv.* drag; *göra* ~ *mot* resist, offer resistance to; *möta* ~ meet with resistance (*bildl.* opposition); *väpnat* ~ armed resistance **2** *konkr. elektr.* resistor, resistance box **-are** adversary; opponent; antagonist; (*fiende*) enemy; ~ *till adversary* (*etc.*) of
motstånds|ficka pocket of resistance **-kraft** [power of] resistance (*mot* to); resisting-power; (*fysisk*) resistance, staying power **-kraftig** resistant (*mot* to, against); strong **-man** member of the resistance **-rörelse** resistance movement
motstöt counterattack; *bildl. äv.* counterthrust

motsvar|a (*ha sin -ighet i, passa ihop med*) correspond (answer) to; (*vara lika mycket värd som*) be equivalent to; (*tillfredsställa*) satisfy, meet; (*uppfylla*) fulfil; *vinsten ~r inte insatsen* the profit is not in proportion to the investment; *~ ngns förväntningar* come up to a p.'s expectations **motsvarande** *a4* corresponding; (*analog*) analogous; (*liknande*) equivalent, similar; *~ värde* the equivalent; *i ~ grad* correspondingly **motsvarighet** (*överensstämmelse*) correspondence; proportionateness; (*full ~*) equivalence; (*analogi*) analogy; (*motstycke*) counterpart, opposite number; *närmaste ~ till* the closest (nearest) equivalent to (of); *sakna ~* have nothing corresponding to it (*etc.*)

motsäg|a contradict; oppose; (*bestrida*) contest; (*strida emot*) be contradictory to, conflict with; *~ sig* contradict o.s. (itself); be [self-]contradictory **-ande** *a5* contradictory; (*mot varandra stridande*) conflicting

motsägelse contradiction; (*brist på överensstämmelse*) incompatibility, discrepancy; (*inkonsekvens*) inconsistency; *inte tåla några ~r* not tolerate contradiction **-full** full of contradictions **-lusta** love of contradictions

motsätt|a *rfl* oppose, stand out against **-ning** opposition; antagonism; (*motsatsförhållande*) contrast, discrepancy, incongruity; *stå i skarp ~ till* be in striking contrast to

mott [-å-] *s9, s7, zool.* moth

mottag|a receive; (*acceptera*) accept; (*besökande*) receive, see; *alla bidrag -es med största tacksamhet* all contributions gratefully received; *vi har -it Ert brev* we have received (are in receipt of) your letter **mottagande** *s6* reception; *i sht hand.* receipt; (*accepterande*) acceptance; *betala vid ~t* pay on receipt (delivery), cash on delivery (*förk. C.O.D.*); *erkänna ~t av ett brev* acknowledge receipt of a letter **mottagarapparat** *radio.* receiving set **mottagare 1** *pers.* receiver; (*av postförsändelse*) addressee; (*av varuförsändelse*) consignee; (*betalnings-*) payee, beneficiary; (*av gåva*) donee; *sport.* striker-out **2** *konkr. radio.* receiver, receiving set **mottaglig** [-a:-] *al* susceptible (*för* to); (*känslig*) sensitive (*för* to); *~ för förkylning* (*äv.*) liable to catch cold; *~ för skäl* amenable to reason; *~ för nya idéer* receptive (open) to new ideas **mottaglighet** [-a:-] susceptibility; sensitiveness **mottagning** reception; (*läkares*) consultation rooms (*pl*), surgery; (*vid hovet äv.*) audience **mottagnings|bevis** advice of receipt (delivery); *post. äv.* post office receipt **-kommitté** reception committee **-rum** reception room; (*läkares*) consulting room **-tid** reception hours (*pl*); (*läkares*) consultation (consulting) hours (*pl*)

motto [ˣmåttɔ] *s6* motto

mot|urs [-u:-] anticlockwise, *AE.* counterclockwise **-vallskäring** cussed (contradictory) person **-veck** *sömn.* box pleat **-verka** (*~arbeta*) work against, run (go) counter to; (*upphäva verkan av*) counteract, offset, neutralize; (*söka hindra*) try to put a stop to, obstruct **-verkan** counteraction **-vikt** counterweight, counterbalance (*mot* to) **-vilja** dislike (*mot* of, to), distaste (*mot* for); (*starkare*) repugnance (*mot* against),

antipathy (*mot* for, against, to); *ha* (*hysa*) *~ mot* have a dislike (*etc.*) of, dislike **-villig** reluctant; (*starkare*) averse **-villighet** reluctance; averseness **-vind** headwind, contrary wind; *bildl.* adverse (contrary) wind; *ha ~* have the wind against one; *segla i ~* sail against the wind, *bildl.* be out of luck **-väga** [counter]balance (*äv. ~ varandra*) **-värde** equivalent; (*bank o.d. äv.*) countervalue **-värn** defence, resistance; *sätta sig till ~* offer resistance, fight back **-åtgärd** countermeasure; *vidtaga ~er* take countermeasures

moussera [mɔˈse:-] sparkle, effervesce

mu moo! **mua** moo

1 muck *n* **1** *han sade inte ett ~* he didn't say a word; *jag begriper inte ett ~* I don't understand an iota (a thing) **2** *utan ett ~* without a murmur **2 muck** oböjligt *s, vard.* demob[ilization]

1 mucka *vard. mil.* demob

2 mucka (*bråka*) growl, grumble (*över* at, about); *~ gräl* pick a quarrel

mudd *s2* wristlet, loose cuff

mudder [ˈmudd-] *s7* mud **mudderverk** dredger, dredge **muddra** dredge; *~d farled* (*sjö.*) dredged channel **muddringsarbete** dredging work

muff *s2* **1** (*klädespersedel*) muff **2** *tekn.* sleeve, socket [end]

muffin [ˈmuff-] *s7* muffin

muffkoppling sleeve (box) coupling

mugg *s2* (*liten*) mug; (*större*) jug; (*tenn- o.d.*) pot; *för fulla ~ar* (*vard.*) at top speed

Muhammed [mɔˈhamm-] Mohammed, Mahomet

muhammed|an [mɔ-] *s3* Mohammedan, Moslem, Muslim **-anism** Mohammedanism, Islam **-ansk** [-ˈda:-] *a5*, Mohammedan, Moslem, Muslim

mula *s1* mule

mulatska [-ˣlatt-] *se mulattkvinna*

mulatt *s3* mulatto (*pl* -os, -oes) **-kvinna** mulatto woman

mule *s2* muzzle; snout

mul|en *a3* overcast; clouded (*äv. bildl.*); *bildl.* gloomy; *det är -et* the sky is overcast

mulje|ra *fonet.* palatize **-ing** palatization

mull *s2* earth; mould; (*stoft*) dust (*äv. bildl.*) **-bänk** *vard.* quid (cud) of snuff

mull|bär mulberry **-bärsträd** mulberry tree

muller [ˈmull-] *s7* rumbling, rumble, rolling

mullig *al* plump

mullra rumble, roll

mulltoalett [type of] earth closet

mullvad *s2, zool.* mole

mullvads|arbete underground work **-grå** mole-coloured **-gång** mole track (run) **-hög** molehill **-skinn** (*som handelsvara*) moleskin

mulna [ˣmu:l-] cloud over, become overcast; *bildl.* darken; *det ~r* [*på*] it (the sky) is clouding over

mul- och klövsjuka foot-and-mouth (hoof--and-mout) disease

multen *se murken*

multinationell [-ˈnell, ˣmull-] multinational

multipel [-ˈtipp-] *s3, s2* multiple; *~ skleros* multiple sclerosis

multiplicera multiply (*med* by) **multiplikand**

M

s3 multiplicand **multiplikation** multiplication
multiplikations|tabell multiplication table
-tecken multiplication sign
multiplikator [-ˣka:tår] *s3* multiplier
multna moulder (rot) [away]
mulåsna mule; hinny
mumi|e ['mu:-] *s5* mummy **-fiera** mummify **-fikation** mummification
mumla (*tala otydligt*) mumble; (*knota*) mutter, murmur; ~ *i skägget* mutter under one's breath
mummel ['mumm-] *s7* mumble; mutter, murmur
mumrik ['mumrikk] *s2* odd fish, old fogey
mums I *interj* yum-yum! **II** *n, det var* ~ that was delicious (lovely) **mumsa** munch; (*knapra*) nibble
mun [munn] *s2* mouth; (*-full*) [a] mouthful (*vatten* of water); *ur hand i* ~ from hand to mouth; *i var mans* ~ the talk of the town; *med en* ~ with one voice; *med gapande* ~ open-mouthed, with a wide open mouth; *dra på* ~ smile; *gå från* ~ *till* ~ pass from mouth to mouth, be bandied about; *ha många* ~*nar att mätta* have many mouths to feed; *har du inte mål i* ~? haven't you got a tongue in your head?; *hålla* ~ keep one's mouth shut; *håll* ~*!* (*äv.*) shut up!; *hålla ngt för* ~*nen* hold s.th. to one's mouth; *prata bredvid* ~[en] let the cat out of the bag; *ta ordet ur* ~*nen på ngn* take the words out of a p.'s mouth; *ta* ~*nen full* (*bildl.*) talk big; *ta bladet från* ~*nen* speak one's mind; *alla talar i* ~[nen] *på varandra* all speak at the same time **-art** dialect
mundering [-'de:-] (*soldats*) equipment
mun|full *en* ~ a mouthful (*vatten* of water) **-giga** [-ji:ga] *s1, mus.* jew's-harp **-gipa** [-j-] *s1* corner of the (one's, its) mouth; *dra ner* -*giporna* draw down the corners of one's mouth
mungo ['muŋgo] *s3, zool.* mongoose (*pl* mongooses)
mun|harmonika mouth organ **-huggas** -*höggs* -*huggits, dep* wrangle, bicker, bandy words **-håla** oral (mouth) cavity **-häfta** *med.* trismus, *vard.* lockjaw
municipalsamhälle [-ˣpa:l-] *ung.* municipality, urban district
1 munk *s1* monk; (*tiggar-*) friar
2 munk *s2, kokk.* doughnut; (*äppel- o.d.*) fritter
munkavle muzzle, gag; *sätta* ~ *på* muzzle
munk|kloster monastery **-kåpa** monk's frock, cowl **-latin** monk's (mediaeval) Latin **-likör** Benedictine **-löfte** monk's vow **-orden** monastic order
munkorg muzzle; *förse med* ~ (*äv. bildl.*) muzzle
munkväsen ~*det* monachism
mun|läder *ha gott* ~ have a glib tongue (the gift of the gab) **--mot-mun-metoden** the mouth-to-mouth method; *vard.* kiss of life
munsbit morsel; *sluka ngt i en* ~ eat s.th. in one mouthful; *det var bara en* ~ *för honom* (*bildl.*) it was small beer for him
mun|skydd mask **-skänk** *s2* butler; cupbearer **-spel** harmonica, mouth organ **-stycke** mouthpiece; *mus. äv.* embouchure; (*cigarett-*) [cigarette] holder; (*på cigarett*) tip; *tekn.* nozzle, jet; *cigarett med* (*utan*) ~ tipped (untipped, plain) cigarette **-sår** sore on the lips

munta *s1, vard.* oral [exam], viva [voce]
munter ['munn-] *a2* merry, cheerful; (*uppsluppen*) hilarious; *vard.* chirpy; *ett* ~*t lag* a merry party; *en* ~ *melodi* a lively tune **-gök** jolly fellow **-het** merriness; gaiety; hilarity; *uppsluppen* ~ hilarious mirth (spirits *pl*)
muntlig *al* (*om översättning, prövning o.d.*) oral; (*om meddelande o.d.*) verbal; ~ *prövning* oral [examination], *univ.* viva voce [examination]; ~ *överläggning* (*vanl.*) personal conference
muntligen orally; verbally; by word of mouth
muntra ~ *upp* cheer up, exhilarate **-tion** amusement, entertainment; jollification
mun|vatten mouthwash; gargle **-vig** glib [with one's tongue]; (*slagfärdig*) quick-witted **-väder** empty (mere) talk; blether, balderdash **-öppning** orifice of the mouth
mur *s2* wall (*äv. bildl.*); *omge med* ~*ar* (*äv.*) wall in **mura** brick, build [of brick (masonry)]; ~ *igen* brick (wall) up, *bildl.* bung up (*ngns ögon* a p.'s eyes); ~ *in* build into a wall, immure; ~ *med cement* wall (line) with cement, cement **murad** *a5* walled *etc.*; bricked; *i sht bildl.* built
mur|arbas foreman bricklayer (*etc.*) **-are** bricklayer; (*sten-*) mason **-bruk** mortar **-bräcka** *s1* battering ram (*äv. bildl.*) **-gröna** *s1, bot.* ivy
murken *a3* decayed; (*starkare*) rotten
murkla *s1* morel, moril
murkna decay, get (become) rotten
murkrön coping (top) of a wall
murmeldjur *zool.* marmot; *sova som ett* ~ sleep like a log
murning [-u:-] bricklaying, masonry
murrig *al* gloomy, dull, sullen
mur|slev trowel **-tegel** [building] brick
murvel *s2, vard.* hack journalist
mur|verk masonry, brickwork, brickwall **-yta** surface [of a wall]
mus *-en möss* mouse (*pl* mice)
mus|a *s3* muse; *de nio* -*erna* the nine Muses
musch *s3* beauty spot (patch)
museal *al* museum; *har bara* ~*t intresse* is only of interest to museums
muse|föremål museum specimen, exhibit; museum piece (*äv. bildl.*) **-intendent** curator; *Storbritannien* keeper of a museum **-man** museum official, museologist **-värde** museum value
musel|man *s3* Muslim, Moslem **-mansk** [-a:-] *a5* Muslim, Moslem
museum [-'se:-] *s4* museum
musicera play (have) [some] music, make music
musjk *s9* **1** music; *sätta* ~ (*komponera* ~*en*) *till* write (compose) the music for; *det är som* ~ *för mig* it is music to my ear; *detta skall hädanefter bli min* ~ that will be my tune in the future **2** (*-kår*) band **-afton** musical evening
musik|al I *al* musical **II** *s3* musical [comedy] musical **-alisk** [-'ka:-] *a5* musical; (*om pers. äv.*) music-loving; *vara* ~ be musical, have a musical ear; *M*~*a akademien* the [Royal] academy of music **-alitet** musicality, feeling for music
musik|ant musician; fiddler **-begåvad** with a gift (talent) for music **-begåvning** gift (talent) for music; *pers.* [a] gifted musician **-direktör** graduate of the [Royal] academy of music; *mil.* bandmaster

musik|er ['mu:-] *s9* musician; *bli* ~ (*vanl.*) go in for music [as a profession] **-estrad** bandstand; (*i konserthus*) concert platform **-film** musical [film] **-förlag** music publishers (*pl*) (publishing firm) **-handel** music shop **-historia** history of music **-historiker** authority on the history of music **-högskola** school (college) of music **-instrument** musical instrument **-kapell** orchestra, band **-konservatorium** conservatory, conservatoire **-kritiker** music critic **-kår** band, orchestra; *medlem av en* ~ (*äv.*) bandsman **-liv** musical life **-lära** theory of music **-lärare** music teacher (master) **-program** musical programme **-recensent** music reviewer **-studier** *pl* musical studies; *bedriva* ~ study music **-stycke** piece of music **-teori** musical theory **-verk** musical composition, work of music **-vetenskap** musicology **-älskare** lover of music, music lover **-öra** musical ear, ear for music

musivguld [-'si:v-] mosaic gold

musjik [-'ʃi:k] *s3* m[o]ujik, muzhik

musket|druva [-a:-] muscat [grape] **-ell** *s3* muscatel [wine]

muskedunder [-'dund-] *s7, s2* blunderbuss

musk|el ['musk-] *s3* muscle; *spänna -lerna* tense one's muscles; *utan -ler* muscleless **muskel|ansträngning** muscular exertion **-arbete** work done by the muscles **-bristning** rupture of a muscle **-knippe** bundle of muscles **-knutte** *s2*, *vard.* muscleman **-spel** play of the muscles **-spänning** muscular tension **-stark** muscular, muscularly strong **-sträckning** [the] spraining of a muscle; sprain **-styrka** muscular strength **-stärkare** muscle developer **-svag** weak-muscled, myasthenic **-värk** muscular pain **-vävnad** muscular tissue

musketör musketeer

muskot [-åt] *s2* nutmeg **-blomma** (*krydda*) mace **-nöt** nutmeg

muskulatur musculature; (*ngns*) muscles (*pl*)

muskulös *a1* muscular

musköt *s3* musket

muslim *s3* Muslim, Moslem

muslin *s3, s4* (*tyg*) muslin

mussel|bank *s2* mussel-bank **-djur** lamellibranch, bivalve **-skal** mussel shell

mussera [-o-] *se moussera*

musseron *s3* tricholoma

mussla *s1* **1** (*djur*) [sea-]mussel (*äv.* kokk.), clam; bivalve; (*hjärt-*) cockle **2** (*endast skalet*) [mussel] shell

must *s3* (*dryck*) must; (*i jorden*) sap; *hand., kokk.* concentrated preparation [of ...]; *bildl.* pith; *koka* ~*en ur köttet* boil the goodness out of the meat; *arbetet tog* (*sög*) ~*en ur mig* the work took (sucked) the life out of me; *en tavla med* ~ *i färgen* a picture strong in colour

mustasch [-'ta:ʃ] *s3* moustache; *ha* ~*er* wear a moustache **-prydd** moustached

mustig *a1* juicy (*äv. bildl.*); *bildl. äv.* racy (*anekdot* anecdote), salty (*svordom* oath); *en* ~ *soppa* a tasty (nourishing) soup

mut|a I *s1* bribe; *ta -or* take (receive) bribes (a bribe); (*av* from); *-or* (*vard.*) hush money; palm oil *sg* **II** *v1* bribe (*med* with, by); *polit. äv.* corrupt **mutant** *naturv.* mutant **mutation** mutation

mutera mutate

mut|försök attempt to bribe [s.b.] **-kolv** receiver of bribes **-system** system of bribery and corruption

mutter ['mutt-] *s2, tekn.* nut **-bricka** washer

muttra mutter (*för sig själv* to o.s.); *bildl. äv.* grumble (*över* about, at)

mycelium [-'se:-] *s4* mycelium

myck|en *-et mer[a] mest* much, a great deal of; (*stor äv.*) great, big; *det -na arbetet* the great amount of work he (*etc.*) has had [to do]; *det -na regnandet* the heavy rain[s *pl*], the [great] quantity of rain [that has come down]; *det -na talet om* all the talk about

myckenhet *en* ~ *a*) a multitude of, a large (great) number of (*bilar* cars), *b*) a large (great) quantity of, plenty of (*socker* sugar)

mycket I (*subst. anv.*) much; a great (good) deal of; a great amount (quantity; *vard.* a lot) of; (*gott om*) plenty of; (*många*) a great many, many, a great (large) number of, *vard.* a lot of; (*känslobetonat*) ever so much; ~ *nöje!* enjoy yourself!; *för* ~ *möbler* too much furniture; ~ *pengar* a great deal (a lot) of money; ~ *vill ha mer* the more you have the more you want; ~ *väsen för ingenting* much ado about nothing; *ganska* ~ a good deal (*vard.* quite a lot) [of], (*före pl*) a great many; *hur* ~*?* how much?; *ha* ~ *att göra* have a great deal (a great many things) to do; *det är inte* ~ *med honom* he is not up to much; *det är inte för* ~ *att du säger tack* you might at least say thank you; *det blev för* ~ *för honom* it became too much for him; *det är väl* ~ *begärt!* that's expecting a great deal!; *hälften så* ~ half as much; *lika* ~ *som* as much as; *så* ~ *är säkert att* one thing is certain, that; *så* ~ *so much as that, that (this) much* **II** *mer[a] mest, adv* (*framför a o. adv i positiv*) very (*liten* small; *fort* fast); (*vid komp. o. vid part. som betraktas som rena verbformer*) [very] much (*mindre* smaller; *efterlängtad* longed for); (*framför afraid alike* ashamed) very much; (*djupt* deeply, greatly (*imponerad* impressed), profoundly; (*högeligen*) exceedingly, highly; (*svårt*) badly; (*synnerligen*) most; ~ *hellre* much rather; ~ *möjligt* very (quite) likely; ~ *riktigt* quite right, very true; *inte* ~ *till sångare* not much of a singer; *vara* ~ *för kläder* be a great one for (be very keen on) clothes; *hur* ~ *jag än tycker om* much as I like; *en gång för* ~ once too often; *ta 25 pence för* ~ *av ngn* charge s.b. 25 pence too much; *det gör inte så* ~ it doesn't matter [very] much; *så* ~ *bättre* so much the (all the) better; *så* ~ *mer som* all the more as; *så* ~ *very much,* (*med betonat så*) all that much; *så* ~ *du vet det!* and now you know!; *utan att säga så* ~ *som* without saying so much as **III** *a, se mycken*

mygel ['my:-] *s7* string-pulling

mygg *s9, koll.* midges, mosquitoes (*pl*); *sila* ~ *och svälja kameler* strain at a gnat and swallow a camel

mygg|a *s1* midge, gnat; mosquito **-bett** mosquito-bite **-medel** antimosquito preparation **-nät** mosquito net (netting) **-svärm** swarm of gnats (*etc.*)

mygla [-y:-] pull strings **myglare** string-puller

mykensk [-'ke:nsk] *a5* Mycenaean

mykolog mycologist

mylla I *s1* mould; (*humus*) humus; (*matjord*) top-soil **II** *v1*, ~ *ner* (*frön*) cover [up] with earth (soil); ~ *igen* fill in with earth

myller ['myll-] *s7* throng, swarm **myllra** *v1* throng, swarm

München ['mynçen] *n* Munich

myndig *a1 1 jur.* ... of age; *bli* ~ come of age, attain one's majority; *vara* ~ be of age, be legally competent **2** (*som vittnar om makt*) powerful, commanding; (*befallande*) authoritative, master-ful; *i* ~ *ton* in a peremptory tone **-het 1** (*maktbe-fogenhet*) authority **2** (*-t uppträdande*) power-fulness, authority **3** *jur.* majority, full age **4** (*samhällsorgan*) authority; *kommunala* ~*er* local government (authorities); *statliga* ~*er* central government (authorities)

myndighets|dag coming-of-age day **-förkla-ring** declaration of majority **-person** person in authority **-ålder** majority, full age

myndling ward

mynn|a (*om flod o.d.*) fall, debouch, discharge [its waters]; (*om väg, korridor etc.*) open out, emerge (*i* into); *bildl.* issue, end (*i* in) **-ing** mouth; (*flod- äv.*) estuary; (*öppning äv.*) open-ing; (*rör- o.d. äv.*) orifice; (*på vapen*) muzzle

mynnings|arm arm of an estuary **-laddare** muzzle-loader

mynt *s7* **1** coin; piece [of money]; (*valuta*) cur-rency; *slå* (*prägla*) ~ coin money; *betala i kling-ande* ~ pay in hard cash; *betala ngn med samma* ~ (*bildl.*) pay s.b. back in his own coin; *slå* ~ *av* (*bildl.*) make capital out of **2** (*institution*) mint

1 mynta *s1*, *bot.* mint

2 mynta *v1* mint, coin (*äv. bildl.*); (*prägla äv.*) stamp

mynt|enhet monetary unit, unit of currency **-fot** [monetary] standard, standard of currency **-in-kast** slot **-kunskap** numismatics (*pl, behandlas som sg*) **-ning** coinage, mintage **-samling** col-lection of coins; *konkr. äv.* numismatic collection **-slag** currency; species of coin **-stämpel** die, coin stamp **-verk** mint; *M~et* the [Swedish] Mint **-väsen** monetary system

myokardit *s3* myocarditis

myom [-'å:m] *s7* myoma

myr *s2* bog; swamp; *geol.* mire

myr|a *s1* ant; *flitig som en* ~ as busy as a bee; *sätta -or i huvudet på ngn* set s.b. puzzling, mystify s.b.

myriad *s3* myriad; ~*er* (*äv.*) countless multitude [of ...]

myr|kott [-å-] *s2, zool.* pangolin **-lejon** *zool.* antlion, *AE.* doodlebug **-lejonslända** *zool.* ant-lion

myr|malm bog ore **-mark** boggy (*etc.*) ground

myrra *s1* myrrh

myr|slok *s2, zool.* anteater **-stack** ant hill **-syra** formic acid

myrten ['myrr-] *best. f.* =, *pl myrtnar* [common] myrtle **-krona** myrtle crown

mysa *v3* (*belåtet*) smile contentedly (*mot ngn* on s.b.; *åt ngt* at s.th.); (*strålande*) beam (*mot* on)

mysig [nice and] cosy; (*om pers.*) nice

mysk *s3* musk **-djur, -hjort** musk deer **-oxe** musk ox

myst|eriespel [-'te:-] mystery play **-erium** [-'te:-] *s4* mystery **-eriös** *a1* mysterious

mysticism mysticism **mystifiera** mystify **mys-tifikation** mystification **mystik** *s3* mysticism **mystiker** ['myss-] mystic **mystisk** ['myss-] *a5* (*som rör mystik e.d.*) mystic; (*hemlighetsfull*) mysterious, mystical **mystär** *s3* mystery

myt *s3* myth (*om* of) **-bildning** creation of myths

myteri mutiny; *göra* ~ raise a mutiny, mutiny **myterist** mutineer

mytisk ['my:-] *a5* mythical; fabled, fabulous

myto|logi [-lå'gi:] *s3* mythology **-logisk** [-'lå:-] *a5* mythological **-man** *s3* compulsive liar

myxödem *s7, med.* myxoedema

1 må *v4* (*känna sig*) feel; get on, thrive; *hur ~r du?* how are you?, how are you getting on?; *jag ~r mycket bra* I am (feel) very well; *jag ~r inte så bra* I am not quite well; *jag ~r inte bra av choklad* chocolate doesn't agree with me; *du skulle* ~ *bäst av att* (*äv.*) it would be best for you to; ~ *så gott!* keep well!; ~ *som en prins* be as happy as a king; *nu ~r han!* now he is happy (enjoying himself)!

2 må *imperf. måtte* (*jfr måtte*) hjälpv may; (*uttryc-kande uppmaning*) let; (*i samband med negation*) must [not]; *jur.* may; *jag* ~ *då säga att* I must say that; *det* ~ *vara hänt* all right, then; *därom* ~ *andra döma* as to that let others judge; *några ex-empel* ~ *anföras* a few instances may be cited; *man* ~ *säga vad man vill, men* say what you like, but; *du* ~ *tro att jag var trött* you can imagine how tired I was; *ja, det* ~ *jag säga!* well, I must say!; ~ *så vara att* may be that; *vem det än* ~ *vara* who-ever it may be; *av vad slag det vara* ~ of whatever kind it is; *vad som än* ~ *hända* whatever happens (may happen)

måbär ['må:-] alpine currant

måfå *i uttr.: på* ~ at random, haphazard

måg *s2* son-in-law

måhända [-'hänn-] maybe, perhaps

1 mål *s7* **1** (*talförmåga*) speech, way of speaking; (*röst*) voice; *har du inte* ~ *i mun[nen]*? haven't you got a tongue in your head?; *sväva på* ~ *et* fal-ter, hum and haw **2** (*dial.*) dialect; tongue

2 mål *s7, jur. o.d.* case; cause, lawsuit; *fakta i ~et* case history (record); *nedlägga ~et* withdraw the case; *i oträngt* ~ without due (legal) cause

3 mål *s7* (*-tid*) meal; *ett ordentligt* ~ *mat* a square meal

4 mål *s7* **1** *sport.* goal; (*vid löpning*) winning post; (*i lek*) home; (*vid skjutning*) mark; *mil.* tar-get, objective; *från start till* ~ (*vanl.*) from start to finish; *skjuta i* ~ shoot a goal; *stå i* ~ be in goal; *vinna med två* ~ *mot ett* win [by] two [goals to] one; *kasta till* ~*s* throw at a target; *skjuta till* ~*s* practise target-shooting; *skjuta över* ~*et* (*bildl.*) overshoot the mark **2** (*friare, bildl.*) goal; (*desti-nation*) destination, end; (*syfte*) aim, object, pur-pose, end; *utan bestämt* ~ with no definite aim (object); aimlessly; *sätta sitt* ~ *högt* (*bildl.*) aim high

måla paint (*efter* from; *i* in; *med* with, in; *på* on); *bildl. äv.* depict; ~ *av* paint a portrait (picture) of; ~ *om* repaint, give a coat of paint; ~ *över* paint out (over); ~ *sig, se sminka sig* **målande** *a4* (*uttrycksfull*) graphic, vivid; (*om gest, ord o.d.*) expressive

målare|1 (*hantverkare*) painter [and decorator], house painter; (*konstnär*) painter, artist **2** *kortsp.*

court (*AE.* face) card **-färg** paint; ~*er* (*konst.*) artist's colours **-inna** [woman] artist (painter) **-konst** [art of] painting **-lärling** painter's apprentice **-mästare** master [house] painter; house-painter employer **-pensel** paintbrush **-skola** school of painting **-skrin** paintbox **-verkstad** [house-]painter's workshop

målbrott *han är i* ~*et* his voice is just breaking

mål|bur *sport.* goal **-domare** *sport.* judge; referee

måleri painting **målerisk** [-'le:-, 'må:-] *a5* picturesque

målforskning applied research

målfoto *avgörande genom* ~ photo finish

målföre *s6, förlora (återfå)* ~*et* lose (recover) one's power of speech

mål|grupp target group **-görare** [-j-] *sport.* [goal] scorer **-inriktad** targeted **-kamera** finishing-line camera **-kast** goal throw **-kvot** goal average

målla *s1* orache

mållinje (*vid löpning o.d.*) winning post, finishing line; *fotb. o.d.* goal line

1 mållös (*stum*) speechless (*av* with); *göra ngn* ~ strike s.b. dumb, dumbfound s.b.

2 mållös *sport.* goalless; *bildl.* aimless

målmedveten purposeful; (*om pers. äv.*) resolute **-het** purposefulness; (*ngns äv.*) fixity of purpose (aim)

målning [ˣmå:l-] *abstr.* painting; (*färg*) paint; (*tavla*) picture, painting

målrelaterad *a5* (*betygssättning*) criterion-referenced

målro *hålla* ~*n vid makt* keep the conversation going, keep the ball rolling

mål|siffra *fotb. o.d.* score **-skjutning** target-shooting **-skott** shot at goal

målsman ['må:ls-] **1** *jur.* next friend; (*förmyndare*) guardian; *skol.* person standing in loco parentis; (*förälder*) parent **2** (*talesman*) champion, spokesman, sponsor

mål|snöre tape **-språk** target language **-stolpe** goal post

måls|ägande *s9* [the] person injured **-ägare** plaintiff; injured party

mål|sättning objective, aim, purpose, goal **-sökande** homing **-sökningsrobot** homing missile **-tavla** target [board]

måltid meal; (*högtidligt*) repast

måltids|dryck table drink (beverage) **-kupong** luncheon voucher, *AE.* meal ticket

målvakt goalkeeper

1 mån *r* (*utsträckning*) extent; (*grad*) degree, measure; *i viss* ~ to some extent; in some degree; *i görligaste* ~ as far as possible; *i* ~ *av behov* as need arises; *i* ~ *av tillgång* as far as supplies admit, as long as supplies last

2 mån *a1* (*aktsam*) careful (*om* of); (*noga*) particular (*om sitt yttre* about one's personal appearance); (*ivrig*) eager (*om att* to); (*angelägen*) anxious (*om* about, for)

måna ~ *om* take care of; nurse; look after

månad *s3* month; *förra* ~*en* last month; [*i*] *nästa* ~ next month; *innevarande* ~ this month; *två* ~ *gånger i* ~*en* twice a month

månads|biljett monthly (season) ticket **-hyra**

monthly (month's) rent **-lång** lasting for months (a month), [a] month-long **-lön** monthly salary (pay, wages) **-skifte** *vid* ~*t* at the turn of the month **-smultron** cultivated everbearing wild strawberry **-sten** birthstone **-vis** monthly

månatlig [ˣmå:-, -'na:t-] *a1* monthly

mån|bana lunar orbit, orbit of the moon **-belyst** [-y:-] *a4* moonlit **-berg** lunar mountain

måndag ['månn-] *s2, best. form vard. äv. måndan* Monday; *jfr fredag*

månde *oböjligt v, vad* ~ *bli av det barnet?* what is to become of that child?; *vem det vara* ~ whoever it is (may be)

mån|e *s2* **1** (*himlakropp*) moon; *gubben i* ~*n* the man in the moon; *ta ner* ~*n* get hold of the moon, get blood from a stone **2** *se flintskalle* **-farkost** lunar vehicle **-färd** trip to the moon **-förmörkelse** eclipse of the moon, lunar eclipse

många *jfr mången* **1** *fören.* many; (*starkare*) a good (great) many; (*talrika*) numerous, a large number of, *vard.* lots (a lot) of; *ganska* ~ quite a number of, not so few; ~ *gånger* many times (*om* over), often; *hälften så* ~ half as many; *lika* ~ (*t.ex. vardera*) the same number of, (*t.ex. som förra gången*) just as many; *så* ~ *böcker!* what a lot of books! **2** *självst.* many; (*talrika*) numerous; (~ *människor*) many people, a great number (*vard.* lots, a lot) of people; *en bland* ~ one among many; *vi var inte* ~ there were not many of us; *enligt* ~*s åsikt är det* many people are of the opinion (many hold the view) that it is

mång|ahanda *oböjligt a* multifarious; many kinds (sorts) of; *av* ~ *slag* of many various kinds **-byggare** *bot.* polygamous [plant] **-dubbel** multifold; many times greater; *en* ~ *övermakt* an overwhelming superiority (force); ~ *verkan* multiple effect **-dubbelt** *adv* many times over; *en* ~ *överlägsen fiende* a vastly superior enemy **-dubbla** double many times over; (*friare*) multiply

mången *månget* (*äv. mångt*) *många, komp. fler* (*a*), *superl. flest*(*a*) many a[n]; *på* ~ *god dag* for many a day; *i mångt och mycket* in many respects, on very many matters **-städes** in many places

mång|fald *s3* **1** multiplicity, great variety **2** *mat.* multiple **-faldig** *al* manifold, multifold; (*varierande*) diverse; ~*a gånger* many times [over], over and over [again]; *vid* ~*a tillfällen* on numerous (frequent) occasions **-faldiga** duplicate, manifold **-faldigt**, **-falt** *adv* many times; many times over **-fasetterad** full of nuances; (*om problem*) very complex **-frestare** versatile person **-gifte** polygamy **-gudadyrkan** polytheism **-hundraårig** many centuries old; (*av* ~ *varaktighet*) for many hundreds of years **-hörning** [-ö:-] polygon **-hövdad** *a5* many-headed **-kunnig** of great and varied learning; versatile

mång|la sell from a market stall; hawk **-are** coster[monger], hawker **-erska** [woman] coster [monger]

mång|miljonär multimillionaire **-ordig** [-o:-] *a1* verbose, wordy **-ordighet** [-o:-] verbosity; wordiness **-sidig** *a1* many-sided; *bildl. äv.* diversified, varied; (*om pers.*) versatile, all-round; *geom.* polygonal **-sidighet** manysidedness *etc.*; versatility **-skiftande** *a4* diversified; variegated

M

-stavig *a1* many-syllabled; multisyllabic **-stavighet** multisyllabicity **-stämmig** *a1* many-voiced **-sysslare** versatile person; *vard.* s.b. with many irons in the fire; jack of all trades

mångt *se* mycken

mång|talig *a1* numerous **-tusende** many thousand[s of] **-tydig** *a1* of (with) many meanings; (*friare*) ambiguous, equivocal

mångård lunar halo (corona)

mångårig *a1* of many years[' duration (standing)]; *bot.* perennial

mån|landare lunar module **-landning** moon landing **-landskap** lunar landscape **-ljus** I *s7, se* månsken II *a1* moonlight, moonlit; *bildl. vard.* brilliant, just fine

månn|e, -tro I wonder; do you think?

mån|raket moon rocket **-sken** moonlight **-skifte** change of the moon **-skott** moon shot **-skugga** shadow of the moon **-skära** *s1* crescent moon; *~n (äv.)* the crescent **-sten** moonstone **-stråle** moonbeam **-varv** moon's revolution, lunation **-år** lunar year

måra *s1* bedstraw

mård [-å:-] *s2* marten **-skinn** marten [fur]; (*handelsvara*) marten [pelt]

mårtens|afton [ˣmå:r-, -ˣaff-] Martinmas Eve **-gås** Martinmas dinner (celebration)

mås *s2* [sea] gull

måste *måste måst; pres.* must; (*på grund av yttre tvång äv.*) have to; (*i samtalsspråk äv.*) have (has) got to; (*är tvungen*) am (is, are) obliged to; (*kan inte låta bli att*) cannot but; (*innebärande naturnödvändighet*) am (etc.) bound to; *imperf.* had to, was obliged to *etc.*; *om det ~ så vara* if it must be so; *han såg så rolig ut att jag ~ skratta* he looked so funny I couldn't help laughing; *vi ~ till staden* we must (*i morgon:* shall have to) go to town; *priserna ~ snart gå upp* prices are bound to rise soon; *allt vad jag har måst gå igenom* all that I have had to go through

måsunge young gull

mått *s7* **1** measure (*för* for; *på* of), gauge (*äv. konkr.*); (*abstr. äv.*) measurement[s *pl*]; (*kak-*) pastry-cutter; *ett ~ grädde* a decilitre (*Storbritannien ung.* a quarter of a pint) of cream; *ta ~ hos en skräddare till* be measured by a tailor for; *hålla ~et (om kärl e.d.)* hold the prescribed quantity, (*i längd e.d.*) be full measure (*äv. bildl.*), (*bildl. äv.* be (come) up to standard, make the grade **2** (*friare o. bildl.*) measure; (*storlek äv.*) size, dimension, proportion; (*grad*) degree; (*mängd*) amount; (*skala*) scale; (*-stock*) standard; *en diktare av stora ~* a great poet; *av internationella ~* of international standard; *efter ~et av min förmåga* as far as I am able; *efter den tidens ~* according to the standards of that time; *ett visst ~ av respekt* a certain amount (degree) of respect; *i rikt ~* in ample measure; *vidtaga ~ och steg* take measures (steps)

1 mått|a *s1* **1** moderation; mean; *hålla (med) ~* exercise (in) moderation **2** *i dubbel -o* in a double sense (degree); *i så -o* to that extent, in that degree; *i så -o som* in as (so) far as

2 måtta *v1* aim (*mot* at)

måttagning measuring

mått|angivelse [details of] measurements (*pl*)

-band tape measure, measuring tape **-beställd** *a5* made to measure; *AE.* custom[-made]

måtte *imperf. av må* **1** (*uttryckande önskan*) may; I [do] hope; *det ~ väl inte ha hänt henne något* I [do] hope nothing has happened to her; *du ~ väl förstå ...!* you will understand ..., won't you! **2** (*uttryckande visshet*) must; *jag ~ väl få göra vad jag vill!* surely I can do as I like, can't I!; *det ~ väl du veta!* you of all people must know that!; *han ~ ha gått och lagt sig* he must have gone to bed

måttenhet unit of measurement

mått|full (*återhållsam*) moderate; (*behärskad*) measured, restrained **-fullhet** moderation; moderateness; restraint; sobriety **-lig** *a1* moderate; (*i fråga om mat o. dryck äv.*) temperate; (*blygsam*) modest; *det är inte ~t vad han äter* there's no limit to what he eats **-lighet** moderation; temperance **-lös** measureless, unmeasured

måtto *se 1 måtta 2*

mått|sats set of measures (*tekn.* gauge blocks) **-stock** measure, measuring-rod; *bildl.* gauge, standard, criterion, yardstick (*på* of) **-system** system of measurement **-tagning** (*hopskr. måttagning*) measuring

Mähren ['mä:-] *n* Moravia

mähä *s6, vard.* milksop

mäkla [ˣmä(:)k-] act as a broker; (*medla*) mediate; *~ fred* negotiate (restore) peace **mäklararvode** brokerage, broker's commission **mäklare** broker; (*börs- äv.*) stockbroker; (*medlare*) mediator; *auktoriserad ~* authorized broker **mäklarfirma** brokerage (broker's) firm **mäklarrörelse** brokerage (broker's) business **mäkling** mediation, conciliation

1 mäkta *adv* tremendously, immensely; highly; *vard.* mighty, jolly

2 mäkta *v1* be capable of (*göra ngt* doing s.th.); be able to manage

mäktig *a1* **1** powerful; (*starkare*) potent; (*känslobetonat*) mighty **2** (*väldig*) immense, huge; (*storartad*) majestic, grandiose **3** (*i stånd t.*) capable of **4** (*mättande*) substantial, heavy **-het** powerfulness *etc.*

Mälaren *r* Lake Mälaren

mäld *s3* grist

män *se 2 man*

mänga mix; mingle

mängd *s3* (*stor ~*) large amount (quantity), lot; (*stort antal*) large (great) number, multitude, lot [s *pl*]; (*skara*) crowd, multitude; *en hel ~* a good deal of, a great many; *i riklig ~* in ample (abundant) quantity, in abundance; *höja sig över ~en* stand out from the crowd; *i små ~er* in small quantities **-lära** set theory, theory of sets **-rabatt** quantity discount

människ|a [-iʃa] *s1* **1** man (*äv. ~n*); (*mänsklig varelse*) human being, mortal; (*individ*) person, individual; (*varelse*) creature; *ingen ~* no one, nobody; *den moderna ~n* modern man; *bli ~ igen* (*vard.*) be o.s. again; *känna sig som en ny ~* feel like a new person; *jag är inte ~ att komma ihåg* I can't for the life of me remember; *jag är inte mer än ~* I am only human **2** *-or* men, (*folk*) people; *AE. vard.* folks; *alla -or (vanl.)* everybody, everyone (*sg*); *-or emellan* man to man

människo|ansikte *ett* ~ a man's (a human) face **-apa** anthropoid [ape] **-barn** [human] child; (*människa*) human being **-boning** human habitation **-fientlig** hostile to man **-föda** *inte lämplig som* ~ not fit for human consumption **-förakt** contempt of man[kind] **-gestalt** *en* ~ the figure of a man **-hamn** *i uttr.*: *ett odjur i* ~ a beast in human shape **-hand** *av* ~ by human hand **-hatare** manhater, misanthrope **-hjärta** human heart **-jakt** manhunting **-kropp** human body **-kännare** judge of character **-kännedom** knowledge of human nature **-kärlek** love of mankind (humanity); (*välgörenhet*) philanthropy **-lik** *al* resembling a human being; manlike **-liv** *ett* ~ a human life; *förlust av* ~ loss of life; *ett helt* ~ a whole lifetime **-massa** crowd [of people] **-natur** human nature (*äv.* ~*en*) **-offer** human sacrifice **-ras** human race **-rov** kidnapping **-skildring** character study **-skygg** shy, timid **-släktet** mankind; the human race (species) **-son** *M*~*en* the Son of Man **-spillra** wreck **-vän** humanitarian; philanthropist **-vänlig** humane; philanthropic[al] **-värde** human dignity **-värdig** fit for human beings; ~*a bostäder* (*äv.*) decent houses (*etc.*); *föra ett* ~*t liv* lead a worthwhile life **-ätare** man-eater **-öde** human destiny

mänsklig *al* human; (*rimlig*) reasonable; *förklaringen om de* ~*a rättigheterna* the Declaration of Human Rights; *allt som står i* ~ *makt* everything [that is] humanly possible; *det är inte* ~*t att* (*äv.*) it is inhuman to **-het 1** (*humanitet*) humanity, humaneness **2** *konkr.* (*människorna*) mankind (*äv.* ~*en*); *hela* ~*en* all (the whole of) mankind

märg [märj] *s3* marrow (*äv. bildl.*); *vetensk.* medulla (*pl äv.* medullae); *bot.*, *zool.* o. *bildl.* pith; *förlängda* ~*en* (*anat.*) the medulla [oblongata]; *det gick* (*skar*) *genom* ~ *och ben på mig* it pierced the very marrow of my bones; *jag frös ända in i* ~*en* I was chilled to the marrow **-ben** marrowbone

märgel [-j-] *s9* marl

märg|full full of marrow; *bildl. äv.* pithy **-lös** marrowless; pithless **-pipa** *se märgben*

märk|a *v3* **1** (*sätta -e på*) mark (*med* with; *med bläck* in ink); (*med bokstäver, namn*) letter, name; *-t av sjukdom* marked by illness; *han är -t för livet* he is marked for life; ~ *ngn* (*med slag e.d.*) scotch s.b. **2** (*lägga -e t.*) notice, observe, be (become) aware of; (*känna*) feel, perceive; (*se*) see; *låt ingen* ~ *att* don't let it be noticed (anyone notice) that; *härvid är att* ~ *att* in this connection it should be noted that; *märk väl att* [please,] observe that; *väl att* ~ observe ..., ... be it noted; *det -tes knappt* it was hardly noticeable; *bland gästerna -tes* among the guests were to be seen **-bar** *al* noticeable, perceptible, observable; (*synbar*) visible; (*iakttagbar*) appreciable; (*påtaglig*) marked, evident **-bläck** marking ink **-bok** sampler book **-duk** sampler

märke *s6* **1** (*ej avsiktligt*) mark (*efter* of); (*spår*) trace (*efter* of); (*efter tryck*) impression; (*efter slag o.d.*) dent; (*rispa*) scratch (*efter* from); *om inte gamla* ~*n slår fel* unless all the time-honoured signs play us false **2** *bot.* stigma **3** (*avsiktligt*) mark; (*idrotts-, klubb- e.d.*) badge; *hand.* brand, trademark; (*fabrikat*) make

märkes|dag red-letter day **-man** man of distinction **-vara** branded product; (*patentskyddad*) proprietary article **-år** memorable year

märkgarn marking thread

märklig *al* notable; (*beaktansvärd*) noteworthy; (*starkare*) signal; (*-värdig*) remarkable, striking; *det* ~*a* [*med saken*] *är att* the remarkable (striking) thing [about the matter] is that **märkligt** *adv* notably *etc.*; ~ *nog* remarkably enough

märkning marking

märkvärdig remarkable; (*besynnerlig*) curious, strange; (*förvånande*) astonishing, surprising; *göra sig* ~ be self-important (pompous); *det var* ~*t!* how extraordinary (odd)!; ~*are än så var det inte* it wasn't more remarkable than that, it was that simple **-het** remarkableness *etc.*; wonder; singularity; (*med pl*) marvel, remarkable feature

märla [-ä:-] *s1* staple, clincher

märlspik [-ä:-] *s1* marlinespike

märr *s2* mare; *vard.* jade

märs *s2, sjö.* top **-segel** topsail

mäsk *s3* mash

mäss *s2* (*lokal*) messroom; *sjö.* (*befäls-, officers-*) officers' mess; *abstr.* mess

mäss|a I *s1* **1** *kyrkl.* mass; *stilla* ~ low mass; *gå i* ~*n* go to (attend) mass **2** *hand.* fair **II** *v1* say (sing) mass; (*sjunga*) chant; (*läsa entonigt*) drone **-bok** missal **-fall** *det blev* ~ *i söndags* there was no service held last Sunday **-förrättare** celebrant **-hake** chasuble **-hall** exhibition hall

mässing brass

mässings|beslag brass mountings (*pl*) **-bleck** brass-sheet, plate brass **-instrument** brass (wind) instrument; ~*en* (*i orkester*) the brass (*sg*) **-musik** brass-band music **-orkester** brass band **-tråd** brass wire

mässling *s2, ej pl* [the] measles (*pl*); *få* ~[*en*] get (catch) the measles

mäss|offer [the] Eucharist Sacrifice **-skjorta** (*hopskr. mässkjorta*) alb **-skrud** (*hopskr. mässkrud*) mass vestments

mässuppassare messman

mästarbrev *ung.* mastership diploma (certificate); *Storbritannien äv.* diploma (certificate) of the freedom of a guild

mästar|e 1 (*sport. o. friare*) champion; (*sakkunnig o.d.*) expert, master-hand; ~ *på fiol* master of the violin; ~ *i tennis* champion at tennis **2** (*hantverkare, upphovsman t. konstverk o.d.*) master (*i* of); *de gamla -na* the Old Masters; *övning gör* ~*n* practise makes perfect **3** (*om Jesus*) *M*~ Master; *svära på* ~*ns ord* have blind faith in the experts **-hand** *av* (*med*) ~ by (with) a master's hand **-inna** *sport.* champion **-klass** master's (*sport.* champion) class **-prov** *bildl.* masterpiece

mäster ['mäss-] (*titel*) Master **-katten** *M*~ *i stövlar* Puss in Boots **-kock** master cook **-lig** *al* masterly; (*skickligt utförd*) brilliant[ly executed]; *vard.* champion **-lots** senior pilot **-man** (*bödel*) headsman **-skap** *s7* mastership, master's skill; (*fulländning*) perfection; *sport.* championship **-skytt** champion marksman, crack shot **-stycke** *se mästerverk o. mästarprov* **-sångare** Meistersinger **-verk** masterpiece (*av, i* of); mas-

M

terstroke

mästra (*anmärka på*) criticize; find fault with

mät *i uttr.: ta i* ~ seize, distress

mäta *v3* **1** (*eg. o. bildl.*) measure (*efter, med* by; *på millimetern* to the millimetre); (*med instrument äv.*) gauge; ~ *ngn med ögonen* look s.b. up and down, size s.b. up; ~ *djupet av* (*bildl.*) fathom; ~ *knappt* (*väl*) give short (full) measure; ~ *sig* measure o.s. (*med* with, against); ~ *sina krafter med ngn* pit one's strength against another's; *kunna ~s med ngn* come up to (match, compare with) s.b.; ~ *upp a*) take the measure[ments] (size) of, *b*) (*mjöl o.d.*) measure out (*åt* for, to) **2** (*ha en viss storlek*) measure; ~ *två meter i längd* measure two metres in length

mätavläsning meter reading

mätar|e (*el-, gas- o.d.*) meter; (*automat*) slot meter; (*instrument*) gauge, indicator **-fjäril** geometrid moth **-larv** measuring worm, geometer **-tavla** meter panel

mät|bar [-ä:-] *a1* measurable **-glas** graduated glass **-instrument** measuring instrument, gauge **-metod** method of measurement **-ning** [-ä:-] measuring *etc.*; measurement

mätress mistress; *neds.* paramour

mätsticka measuring stick; (*för vätska*) dipstick; (*med krympmått*) shrinkage rule

mätt *a1* satisfied (*äv. bildl.*) (*av* with); *vard.* full up; *bildl.* full (*av år* of years); *äta sig* ~ have enough to eat, satisfy one's hunger; *jag är* ~ I have had enough, *vard.* I am full up; ~ *på* (*äv. bildl.*) satiated with; *se sig* ~ *på* gaze one's fill at

mätt|a satisfy; appease; (*förse med mat*) fill; *kem., elektr.* saturate; *ha många munnar att* ~ have many mouths to feed; *sådan mat* ~*r inte* that kind of food is not satisfying (is not filling) **-ande** *a4* satisfying *etc.*

mätteknik measurement

mätthet *se mättnad* **mätthetskänsla** feeling of being satisfied; satisfied feeling **mättnad** *s3* (*-het*) state of being satisfied, satiation; *kem.* saturation **mättning** *kem.* saturation *a1, se mättande*

mätverktyg measuring tool

mö *s5* virgin, maid[en]; *gammal* ~ old maid

möbel ['mö:-] *s3* piece of furniture; (*möblemang*) suite of furniture (*sg*); *stoppade möbler* upholstered furniture (*sg*) **-affär** furniture shop, furnisher['s] **-arkitekt** furniture designer **-fabrik** furniture factory **-handlare** furniture dealer **-klädsel** upholstery **-magasin** furniture warehouse **-polityr** furniture polish **-snickare** cabinet-maker **-tyg** furnishing fabric **-vagn** furniture van

möblemang *s7, s4* [suite (set) of] furniture

möbler|a furnish; *AE. äv.* fix up; ~ *om* (*flytta om*) rearrange the furniture (*i* in, of) **-ing** furnishing

möd|a *s1* (*tungt arbete*) labour, toil; (*besvär*) trouble, pains (*pl*); (*svårighet*) difficulty; *lärda -or* a scholar's labour; *göra sig mycken* ~ take (give o.s.) a great deal of trouble; *det lönar inte* ~*n* it isn't worth while (the trouble); *inte lämna någon* ~ *ospard* spare no pains

möderne *s6, på* ~*t* on the (one's) mother's (the maternal) side **-släkt** mother's family

mödom *s2* virginity, maidenhood **mödomshinna** maidenhead, hymen

mödo|sam *a1* laborious, toilsome; (*om arbete o.d. äv.*) hard; (*svår*) difficult **-samt** *adv* laboriously, with difficulty; ~ *förvärvade slantar* hard-earned money

mödra|gymnastik antenatal exercises (*pl*) **-hem** home for mothers **-vård** maternity welfare **-vårdscentral** maternity clinic; (*för havande kvinnor*) prenatal clinic; (*för nyblivna mödrar*) postnatal clinic

mögel ['mö:-, 'mögg-] *s7* mould; (*på papper o.d.*) mildew-spot **mögelsvamp** mould (mildew) fungus **mögla** [ˣmö:g-, ˣmögg-] go (get) mouldy **möglig** [ˣmö:g-, ˣmögg-] *a1* mouldy, mildewy; (*förlegad*) fusty, rusty

möhippa *ung.* hen party for bride-to-be; *AE. äv.* shower

möjlig *a1* possible; (~ *att göra*) feasible, practicable; *allt ~t* all kinds of things; *det är mycket ~t* it is quite possible; *så vitt ~t* provided it is possible; *det är inte ~t annat* it simply must be so; *det är ~t att vi behöver* we may need; *skulle det vara ~t för dig att ...?* would you be able to ...?; *göra det bästa ~a av ngt* make the best (most) of s.th.; *på kortaste ~a tid* as fast as possible; *8 poäng av 10 ~a* (*sport. o.d.*) 8 points out of a possible 10; *med minsta ~a* with a minimum of **möjligast** *i ~e mån* as far as possible **möjligen** possibly; (*kanske*) perhaps; *har du ~ ...?* do you happen to have ...?, have you by any chance [got] ...?; *skulle man ~ kunna få träffa ...?* I wonder if it is possible to see (speak to) ...? **möjliggöra** make possible; (*underlätta*) facilitate; ~ *för ngn att* enable s.b. to **möjlighet** possibility; (*utsikt*) prospect, chance; (*eventualitet*) eventuality; (*tillfälle*) opportunity; (*utväg*) means (*pl*); *det finns ingen annan* ~ (*äv.*) there is no alternative **möjligtvis** *se möjligen*

mönja *i s1* red lead **II** *v1* redlead

mönster [ˣmöns-] *s7* pattern (*till* for, of) (*äv. bildl.*); *tekn.* design (*till* for, of); (*friare o. bildl.*) model (*av* of); (*urbild*) archetype, prototype; *sy efter* ~ sew from a pattern; *efter* ~ *av* on the pattern of; *ta ngn till* ~ take s.b. as one's pattern; *efter amerikanskt* ~ on the American model, as in America **-gill** model, ideal; exemplary **-gillt** [-j-] *adv* in a model way; exemplarily **-jordbruk** model farm **-skydd** protection of designs, trade mark protection **-stickning** patterned knitting **-vävd** [-ä:-] *a5* with woven patterns, figured **-vävning** patterned weaving

mönstr|a **1** (*göra mönster*) pattern **2** (*granska*) look over; scrutinize, examine closely **3** *mil.* (*hålla -ing med*) inspect, review; (*inskrivas som värnpliktig*) enlist, conscript **4** *sjö.* (*ta hyra*) sign on; ~ *av a*) (*besättningsman*) pay off, *b*) (*avgå*) sign off **-ing 1** (*granskning*) critical examination, scrutiny **2** (*inspektion av trupp*) inspection, muster; (*inskrivning av värnpliktiga*) conscription; (*på-*) signing on

mör *a1* (*om skorpa o.d.*) crisp, crumbly; (*om kött*) tender; *känna sig* ~ *i hela kroppen* ache all over (in every limb); *då blev han* ~ *i mun* that changed his tune **möra** tenderize **mörbulta** *bildl.* beat black and blue

mörda [-ö:-] murder; (*lönn-*) assassinate; *om blickar kunde* ~ if looks could kill **mördande** *a4* murdering; (*friare*) murderous; *bildl.* killing, crushing; (*om blick*) withering; ~ *konkurrens* cut-throat competition; ~ *kritik* crushing criticism; ~ *tråkig* deadly dull **mördare** murderer; (*lönn-*) assassin **mördarhand** *falla för* ~ be murdered

mördeg short crust pastry

mörderska [-ö:-] murderess

mörk *a1* dark (*till färgen* in colour); (*om färg, ton o.d.*) deep; (*något* ~) darkish; (*svagt upplyst*) dim; (*dyster*) sombre, gloomy; ~ *choklad* plain chocolate; ~ *kostym* dark lounge suit; *det ser* ~*t ut* things look bad **-blå** dark (deep) blue

mörker ['mörr-] *s7* darkness (*äv. bildl.*); dark; *bildl.* obscurity; *när mörkret faller* when darkness falls; *till mörkrets inbrott* until nightfall; *mörkrets gärningar* dark deeds **-döden** the night-driving toll

mörk|hyad *a5* dark-skinned **-hårig** dark-haired **-lockig** having dark curly hair, with dark curls **-lägga** black out (*äv. bildl.*); (*hemlighålla*) keep secret **-läggning** blackout **-man** obscurant[ist]

mörk|na get (become, grow) dark; darken; (*om blick*) grow darker; *det* ~*r fort* it gets dark quickly; *utsikterna har* ~*t* prospects are (have become) less promising **-rostad** -*rostat kaffe* dark-roasted coffee **-rum** *foto.* darkroom **-rädd** afraid of the dark **-rädsla** fear of the dark **-ögd** *a1* dark-eyed

mörsare mortar

mört *s2* roach; dace; *pigg som en* ~ [as] fit as a fiddle

möss (*pl av mus*) mice (*sg mouse*)

möss|a *s1* cap; *ta av sig* ~*n för ngn* raise one's cap to s.b.; *stå med* ~*n i hand* stand cap in hand **-märke** cap badge **-skärm** (*hopskr. mösskärm*) cap peak

möt|a *v3* **1** meet; (*råka på*) come (run) across; (*röna*) meet with, encounter, come in for; (*svårighet e.d.*) face, confront; *sport.* meet, encounter; *en hemsk syn -te oss* a terrible sight met us (our eyes); ~ *stark kritik* encounter severe criticism; *det -er inget hinder* there is no objection **2** (*invänta*) meet s.b.; *jag -er med bil* I'll meet you with the (a) car; ~ *upp* assemble, muster up **mötande** *a4* (*om t.ex. pers., fordon*) that one meets; (*som kommer emot en*) oncoming; (*som närmar sig*) approaching, coming the other way; (*som -er varandra*) that pass each other **mötas** *v3, dep* meet; encounter one another; (*gå förbi varandra*) pass one another; *våra blickar -tes* our eyes met

möte *s6* **1** (*sammanträffande*) meeting; (*tåg- etc. äv.*) crossing, passing; (*avtalat*) appointment; (*tillfälligt, fientligt*) encounter; *stämma* ~ *med* make an appointment (*AE.* a date) with; *gå (komma) ngn till* ~*s* go to meet s.b., *bildl.* meet s.b. halfway **2** (*sammankomst*) meeting; (*mera tillfälligt*) assembly, gathering; (*konferens*) conference; ~ *på högsta nivå* summit meeting **mötes** *se möte 1*

mötes|beslut resolution of (passed at) a meeting **-deltagare** participant in a meeting (conference) **-frihet** freedom of assembly **-förhandlingar** *pl* proceedings at a meeting (conference)

-lokal assembly (conference) hall **-plats** meeting place; (*för två pers.*) rendezvous; (*på väg*) passing point **-talare** speaker at a meeting (conference) **-tid** time of a meeting

N

nabb *s2* projection, stub; (*på bildäck*) tread block; (*på sko*) stud

nabo *s5* neighbour

nachspi[e]l ['na:ʃspi:l] *s7* follow-up party

nacka chop the head off, behead

nackbena back-parting

nackdel disadvantage, drawback; (*skada*) detriment; *fördelar och* ~*ar* (*äv.*) pros and cons; *till* ~ *för framåtskridandet* detrimental to progress

nack|e *s2* back of the head, nape [of the neck]; *bryta* ~*n av sig* break one's neck; *klia sig i* ~*n* scratch the back of one's head; *med mössan på* ~*n* with one's cap at the back of one's head **-grop** nape [of the neck] **-hår** back-hair **-skinn** *ta ngn i* ~*et* seize s.b. by the scruff of the neck **-skott** shot through the neck **-spegel** hand-mirror **-spärr** wryneck; *med.* torticollis **-styv** *eg.* stiff in the neck; *bildl.* stiff-necked, haughty **-stöd** headrest **-sving** (*i brottning*) headlock

nadir ['na:-] *oböjligt s, astr.* nadir

nafs *s7* **1** snap; (*hugg*) grab **2** *i ett* ~ in a flash **nafsa** snap (*efter* at); ~ *åt sig* snap up, grab hold of

nafta *s1* naphtha **naftalen, naftalin** *s4, s3* naphthalene

1 nag|el ['na:-] *s2* (*på finger*) nail; *klippa* (*peta*) *-larna* cut (clean) one's nails; *bita på -larna* bite one's nails; *vara en* ~ *i ögat på* be a thorn in the flesh to

2 nagel ['na:-] *s2* (*nit*) rivet; (*trä-*) treenail, trunnel

nagel|band cuticle **-borste** nailbrush **-bädd** nailbed

nagelfara scrutinize (scan) closely; criticize

nagel|fil nailfile **-lack** nail varnish (polish) **-petare** nail cleaner **-pinne** orange stick **-rot** root of a (the) nail **-sax** nail scissors (*pl*) **-trång** *s7* ingrowing [toe] nail

nagg *s2* (*bröd-*) [bread] pricker **nagga 1** prick **2** ~ *[i kanten*] notch; *porslinet var* ~*t i kanten* the china was chipped; ~ *sparkapitalet i kanten* nibble at one's savings **3** (*oroa*) chafe, fret **4** *se gnata* **naggande** *a4*, ~ *god* jolly good

nagla ['na:g-] nail, rivet (*vid* to)

najv *a1* naive, naïve; (*enkel*) simple; unsophisticated; (*barnslig*) childish; (*enfaldig*) silly **-ism** *se -itet*; (*konstriktn.*) naïvism **-ist** naïvist **-itet** *s3* naivety, naïveté, naiveness; simplicity; childishness

naja *sjö.*, *v1* lash

najad *s3* naiad

naken *a3* naked; *konst.* nude; (*bar*) bare (*äv. bildl.*); *bildl. äv.* hard, plain; *klä av ngn ~* strip s.b. to the skin; *med ~ överkropp* stripped to the waist; *nakna fakta* bare (hard) facts; *den nakna sanningen* the plain (naked) truth **-badare** nude swimmer, *AE. sl.* skinny-dipper **-dans** nude dancing **-dansös** nude dancer **-fröig** *a1, bot.* gymnospermous; *~ växt* gymnosperm **-het** nakedness; *konst.* nudity; *avslöjad i all sin ~* (*bildl.*) revealed in all its nakedness **-kultur** nudism **-modell** nude [life] model **-måleri** nude painting

nakterhus *s7, sjö.* binnacle

nalkas *dep* approach, draw near [to]; (*om tid äv.*) come on, be at hand

nalla *vard.* pinch, swipe, bone

nalle *s2* bruin; (*leksak*) teddy [bear]

namib|ier [-'mi:-] *s9* Namibian **-isk** *a5* Namibian

namn *s7* name; *hur var ~et?* what is your name please?; *byta ~* change one's name; *fingerat ~* assumed (false) name, pseudonym; *fullständigt ~* name in full; *ett stort ~ inom* a big name in; *ngns goda ~ och rykte* a p.'s good name; *hennes ~ som gift* (*vanl.*) her married name; *ha ~ om sig att vara* have the reputation of being; *skapa sig ett ~* make a name for o.s.; *göra skäl för sitt ~* live up to (merit) its name; *i eget ~* in one's own name; *i lagens ~* in the name of the law; *i sanningens ~* to tell the truth; *till ~et* by (in) name; *blott till ~et* in name only; *mera till ~et än till gagnet* only nominally; *under ~et ...* by the name of ...; *vid ~ A.* named A., of the name of A.; *nämna ngn vid ~* mention s.b. by name; *nämna ngt vid dess rätta ~* (*äv.*) call a spade a spade

namna name

namnam yum-yum!

namn|byte change of name **-chiffer** monogram

namn|e *s2* namesake (*till mig* of mine) **-ge** name; *en icke -given person* a person unnamed **-insamling** collection of names; petition **-kunnig** renowned, celebrated, famous **-lös** nameless (*äv. bildl.*); (*outsäglig*) unspeakable (*sorg* grief) **-plåt** nameplate **-register** index, list of names

namns|dag name day **-dagsfirande** *s6* name-day celebration

namn|sedel name slip **-skydd** protection of family (company) names **-skylt** *se namnplåt* **-stämpel** [signature] stamp, stamped signature **-teckning, -underskrift** signature **-upprop** roll call

nankin[g] ['naŋkin, -ŋ] *s2, s7* nankeen, nankin

napalm ['na:-, -'palm] *s3* napalm **-bomb** napalm bomb

1 napp *s2* (*di-*) teat, nipple; (*tröst-*) dummy [teat], comforter, *AE.* pacifier

2 napp *s7* (*fiske*) bite; *bildl.* nibble; *få ~* have a bite (*bildl.*) nibble)

1 nappa *sl* (*skinn*) nappa

2 nappa *v1* bite; *bildl.* nibble; *~ på ett erbjudande* jump at an offer; *~ åt sig* snatch, snap up

nappa|s *dep* tussle (*med* with; *om* for) **-tag** tussle (*äv. bildl.*); *ta ett ~ med* have a tussle (brush) with

nappflaska feeding (nursing) bottle, baby's bottle

naprapat *s3* naprapath

narciss *s3* narcissus

nardus ['narr-, 'na:r-] *s2* [spike]nard

nar[e] *s2* crossbar

nare *s2* (*blåst*) biting wind

narig *a1* (*om hud*) chapped, rough

narkoman *s3* drug addict (fiend); *vard.* dope fiend; *AE. sl.* junkie **narkomani** *s3* drug addiction, narcomania **narkomanvård** care (treatment) of drug addicts

narkos [-'kå:s] *s3* narcosis, anaesthesia; *ge ~* anaesthetize, administer an anaesthetic **-apparat** anaesthetic apparatus **-läkare** anaesthetist, *AE.* anesthesiologist **-medel** anaesthetic [agent]

narkotika [-'kå:-] *pl* narcotics, drugs; *vard.* dope (*sg*) **-handel** drugs traffic **-langare** drug peddler **-missbruk** abuse of narcotics

narkotisk [-'kå:-] *s5* narcotic

narr *s2* fool; (*hov- äv.*) jester; (*lättlurad pers. äv.*) dupe; *beskedlig ~* silly fool; *inbilsk ~* conceited fool, coxcomb; *spela ~* play the fool; *göra ~ av* make fun of, poke fun at **narra** (*bedraga*) deceive, take in; (*lura*) cheat; (*på skoj*) fool; (*locka*) beguile; *~ ngn att tro* delude s.b. into believing; *~ ngn att skratta* make s.b. laugh [against his (*etc.*) will]

narraktig *a1* (*löjlig*) ridiculous; (*fjollig*) foolish, silly; (*dåraktig*) vain **-het** ridiculousness *etc.*

narras *dep* tell fibs (a fib) **narri** ['narri] *s6, på ~* in jest, in (for) fun

narr|kåpa fool's cap [and bells] **-spel** [tom]foolery; buffoonery; *bildl.* farce, folly **-streck** (*spratt*) practical joke, prank

narv *s2* (*på läder*) grain

narval [ˣna:r-] *s2, zool.* narwhal[e], unicorn fish (whale)

narvsida hair side

nasal I *a1* nasal **II** *s3* nasal [sound] **-era** nasalize **-konsonant** nasal consonant **-ton** [nasal] twang **-vokal** nasalized vowel

nasare hawker, dorr-to-door salesman

nasaré *s3* Nazarene **Nasaret** *n* Nazareth

nasse *s2* porker; piggy

nasus ['na:-] *s2, vard.* beak

nate *s2, bot.* pondweed

nation [-t'ʃɔ:n] nation; *univ.* student society (association); *Förenta ~erna* the United Nations; *N~ernas förbund* the League of Nations

national|budget [-tʃɔ-] [national] budget **-dag** national holiday (commemoration day) **-dräkt** national costume **-egendom** national property **-ekonom** economist **-ekonomi** economics (*sg*), political economy **-ekonomisk** economic, of political economy; *av ~ betydelse* important to the country's economy **-epos** national epic **-flagga** national flag **-församling** *franska ~en* the French National Assembly **-hjälte** national hero **-inkomst** national income

nationaliser|a [-tʃɔ-] nationalize **-ing** nationalization

national|ism [-tʃɔ-] nationalism **-ist** nationalist

nationalitet [-tʃɔ-] *s3* nationality

nationalitets|adjektiv adjective of nationality **-beteckning** nationality mark (sign)

-principen the principle of national self-determination

nationalkaraktär [-tʃɔ-] national character **-känsla** national feeling **-monument** national monument **-museum** national museum **-park** national park; *i Storbritannien äv.* National Trust property (reserve) **-produkt** national product **-socialism** National Socialism **-socialist** *s3* National Socialist **-socialistisk** *a5* National Socialist ; *ty. äv.* Nazi **-stat** nation-state **-sång** national anthem

nationell [-tʃɔ-] *al* national

nativitet birth rate

nativitetsökning increase in the birth rate **-överskott** excess of births over deaths

natrium ['na:-] *s8* sodium **-bikarbonat** sodium bicarbonate, baking soda **-klorid** sodium chloride, salt

natron ['na:trån] *s7* [caustic] soda, sodium hydroxide **-lut** soda lye, caustic soda [solution] **natt** *-en nätter* night; *god ~!* good night!; *hela ~en* all night; *varje ~* every night, nightly; *~en till lördagen* Friday night; *i ~ a*) *(som kommer)* tonight, *b) (föregående)* last night; *om (på) ~en* at (by) night, in the night; *sent på ~en* late at night; *till ~en a*) *(t.ex. ta medicin)* for the night, *b) se följ.*; *under ~en* during (in) the night; *stanna över ~en hos (på)* stay the night at

natta *vard.* put [a child] to bed **-arbete** night work **-blind** night blind **-blindhet** night blindness **-djur** nocturnal animal **-dräkt** nightdress, nightgown; *vard.* nightie **-duksbord** bedside table

nattetid at (by) night **-fack** *bank.* night safe (depository) **-fjäril** *zool.* moth **-flygning** night flying **-frost** night frost **-gammal** *~ is* ice formed overnight **-gäst** guest for the night **-himmel** night sky **-härbärge** lodging [for the night]; *konkr.* hostel

nattiné *s3* [mid]night performance **-kafé** all-night café **-klubb** nightclub **-kräm** night cream **-kröken** *vard. i uttr. på ~* in the small hours **-kvarter** quarters (*pl*) for the night, night quarters (*pl*) **-kärl** chamber pot **-lampa** night lamp **-lig** *al* nocturnal; *(under -en)* in the night; *(som sker varje natt)* nightly *se nattdräkt* **-logi** *se -kvarter* **-mangling** all-night negotiations (*pl*) **-mara** nightmare **-mörker** night darkness **-mössa** nightcap; *prata i ~n* talk through one's hat, drivel, blether **-parkering** night parking **-pass** night duty **-permission** night leave **-portier** night porter **-ro** night's rest **-rock** dressing gown **-skift** night shift **-skjorta** nightshirt **-skärra** *zool.* nightjar; *AE.* whippoorwill **-sköterska** night nurse **-stånden** *a5 (om dryck)* flat **-sudd** *s7* night-carousing **-svart** [as] black as night, nightblack *(äv. bildl.)* **-söl** staying up late at nights **-sömn** night's sleep **-taxa** *(hopskr. nattaxa)* night rate **-trafik** *(hopskr. nattrafik)* night traffic **-tåg** *(hopskr. nattåg)* night train **-uggla** night owl *(äv. bildl.)* **-vak** *s7* nightwatching; vigils, night vigils (*pl*) *(friare)* late hours (*pl*) **-vakt** night watch; *pers.* night watchman, *mil.* night guard **-vandrare** nocturnal rambler **-vard** [-va:-] *s3* Eucharist, Holy Communion, Blessed Sacrament

nattvardsbröd sacramental bread **-gång** communion **-gäst** communicant **-vin** sacramental wine

nattviol butterfly orchis

natur nature; *(kynne äv.)* character; *(läggning)* disposition, temperament; *(beskaffenhet)* kind; *(landskap)* nature, scenery; *pers.* person[ality], character; *Guds fria ~* the open country, wide-open spaces (*pl*); *vild ~* wild nature *(på en plats: scenery)*; *~en tar ut sin rätt* nature takes its toll; *av ~en* by nature, naturally, inherently; *till sin ~ är han ...* he is ... by nature; *det ligger i sakens ~* it is quite natural; *av privat ~* of a private character (nature)

natura [-ˣtu:-] *s, i uttr.: betalning i[n] ~* payment in kind (goods, merchandise) **-förmån** payment in kind, perquisite **-hushållning** primitive (natural, barter) economy

naturallier [-'ra:-] *pl* natural-history objects **-isation** naturalization **-isera** naturalize **-ism** naturalism **-ist** naturalist **-istisk** [-'ist-] *a5* naturalistic

naturbarn child of nature **-begåvning** natural gifts (*pl*); *pers.* man *(etc.)* with great natural talent **-behov** *förrätta sina ~* relieve o.s. **-dyrkan** nature-worship **-ell** *s3* nature, disposition **ll** *al* natural **-enlig** [-e:n-] *al* natural **-fenomen** natural phenomenon **-folk** primitive people **-forskare** [natural] scientist, naturalist **-färg** natural colour **-företeelse** *se -fenomen* **-förhållanden** natural conditions (features); nature *(sg)* **-gas** natural gas **-gudomlighet** nature deity **-gummi** natural rubber **-hinder** natural obstacle **-historia** natural history **-historisk** of natural history; natural-history; *N~a riksmuseet* [the] museum of natural history **-katastrof** natural catastrophe **-kraft** natural force **-kunnighet** knowledge of nature; *skol.* nature study **-lag** law of Nature; physical law

naturlig [-'tu:r-] *al* natural; *(medfödd)* inherent, innate; *(ursprunglig)* native; *(okonstlad)* unaffected, ingenuous; *(äkta)* genuine; *dö en ~ död* die from natural causes; *~t urval* natural selection; *av ~a skäl* for natural (obvious) reasons; *i ~ storlek* full-size, *(om porträtt o.d. äv.)* life-size; *i ~t tillstånd* in a state of nature; *det är helt ~t att* it is a matter of course that **naturlighet** naturalness; unaffectedness *etc.* **naturligtvis** of course, naturally; to be sure, certainly

naturlyrik nature poetry **-läkare** nature-healer **-lära** natural science; *(som lärobok)* natural-science textbook **-makt** elemental force **-nödvändighet** physical (natural) necessity; *med ~* with absolute necessity **-park** nature-park; national park **-produkt** natural (primary) product **-reservat** nature reserve; national park; *AE.* wildlife sanctuary **-rike** *~t* the natural kingdom **-rikedom** *~ar* natural resources **-sceneri** natural scenery **-siden** real (natural) silk **-skildring** description of [natural] scenery **-skydd** protection (preservation) of nature **-skyddsområde** *se -reservat* **-skön** of great natural beauty; *en ~ plats (äv.)* a beauty spot **-skönhet** beauty of nature, natural beauty; *berömd för sin ~* noted for the beauty of its scenery **-tillgång** natural asset (source of wealth); *~ar (äv.)* natural resources

-tillstånd natural state; *i ~et* in the state of nature **-trogen** true to life; lifelike **-vetare** scientist **-vetenskap** [natural] science **-vetenskaplig** scientific **-vetenskapsman** scientist **-vidrig** contrary to (against) nature **-vård** nature conservation **-vårdsverk** *statens ~* [the Swedish] national environment protection board **-vän** nature lover **-väsen** elemental being **-älskare** *se -vän*

naur|uer [-'ɔrœr] Nauruan **-isk** *a5* Nauruan

nautisk ['nau-] *a5* nautical; *~ mil* nautical mile

nav *s7* hub; *(frihjuls-)* freewheel hub; *(propeller-)* boss

navare *s9 el. -n navrar (borr)* auger

navel *s2* navel **-binda** umbilical bandage **-sträng** umbilical cord, navel string

navigation navigation; *astronomisk ~* celestial navigation, astronavigation; *terrester ~* terrestrial navigation

navigations|hytt chart-room **-skola** school of navigation; nautical college

navigatör navigator **navigera** navigate *(efter, med* by *)* **navigering** [-'ge:-] navigation

navkapsel hub cap

naz|ism [-'sism] Nazism **-ist** Nazi **-istisk** [-'ist-] *a5* Nazi

neandertal|are, -människa [-'and-] Neanderthal man

Neapel [-'a:-] *n* Naples **neapolitansk** [-'ta:nsk] *a5* Neapolitan

nebul|osa [-ˣlɔ:-] *s1* nebula *(pl* nebulae) **-ös** *a1* nebulous

necessär *s3* dressing (toilet) case

ned down; *(-åt)* downwards; *(-för trappan)* downstairs; *(vända* turn) upside down; *uppifrån och ~* from top to bottom; *längst ~ på sidan* at the bottom of the page

nedan I *s7*, *månen är i ~* the moon is on the wane (is waning) **II** *adv* below; *här ~ (i skrift)* below; *se ~!* see below!; *jämför ~!* compare the following! **-för I** *prep* below **II** *adv* [down] below **-nämnd** *a5* mentioned (stated) below **-stående** *a4* stated (mentioned) below, following

ned|bantad *a5* reduced **-blodad** *a5* bloodstained **-bringa** reduce, lower; bring down **-brunnen** *a5* burnt down **-bruten** *a5, bildl.* broken down **-brytande** *a4* destructive *(krafter* forces); subversive *(idéer* ideas) **-brytning** breaking down; demolition; subversion **-busning** rowdyism **-bädda** put to bed; *ligga ~d (inbäddad) i* lie tucked up in **-böjd** *a5* bent down, stooping **-dekad** *a5* gone to the dogs **-dragen** *a5 (om gardin)* drawn [down], lowered

nederbörd [-ö:-] *s3* precipitation; rainfall; snowfall

nederbörds|mätare rain gauge, pluviometer, udometer **-område** *(regn- etc.)* precipitation area; *(avrinningsområde)* catchment area **-rik** with high precipitation (abundant rainfall)

neder|del lower part **-kant** lower edge (side)

1 nederlag *s7* defeat; *(förkrossande)* disaster; *lida ~* suffer defeat, be defeated

2 nederlag *s7 (magasin)* warehouse, depot, storage

nederländare Netherlander **Nederländerna** *pl* the Netherlands **nederländsk** *a5* Dutch; Netherlands

nederst ['ne:-] *adv* at the bottom *(i, på, vid* of); *allra ~* farthest *(etc.)* down [of all], at the very bottom; *~ på sidan, se under ned; ~ till höger* bottom right **nedersta** *a, superl. best. form* lowest; bottom; *~ våningen* the ground *(AE. äv.* first) floor

nedervåning ground *(AE. äv.* first) floor

ned|fall radioaktivt *~* radioactive fallout **-fart** descent; way down **-fläckad** *a5* stained all over **-frysa** freeze **-frysning** freezing; *med.* hypothermia **-fällbar** *a5* that can be let down; folding, collapsible **-färd** journey (way) down **-för** ['ne:d-] **I** *prep* down; *~ trappan* downstairs **II** *adv* downwards **-försbacke** *(en lång* a long) downhill slope; *bildl.* downhill; *vi hade ~* it was downhill [for us] **-gjord** *a5* destroyed; annihilated; *(av kritik e.d.)* picked (torn) to pieces **-gående I** *a4 (om sol o.d.)* setting; *(om pris o.d.)* declining, falling **II** *s6, vara på ~* be going down, *(om sol o.d.)* be setting **-gång 1** *konkr.* way (road, path, steps *(pl)*, stairs *(pl)*) down **2** *abstr.* descent; *(solens)* setting; *(i temperatur o.d.)* fall, drop; *(minskning)* decrease, reduction; *bildl.* decline **-gången** worn, shabby **-gångsperiod** period of decline *(ekon.* depression) **-göra** *mil.* destroy; *bildl.* annihilate; *(genom kritik)* pull (pick) to pieces; *~nde kritik* scathing criticism **-hala** haul down; *(flagga o.d.)* lower **-hopp** *sport.* landing **-hukad** *a5* crouched, crouching **-hängande** *a4* pendant, suspended; hanging down *(från* from) **-ifrån I** *prep* from down *(gatan* in the street) **II** *adv* from below (underneath); *~ och ända upp* from below upwards; *femte raden ~* fifth line from the bottom **-isad** *a5 (överisad)* covered with ice, iced up; *geol.* glaciated **-isning** [-i:s-] covering with ice; *geol.* glaciation **-kalla** invoke *(över* on), call down *(över* upon) **-kippad** [-ç-] *a5 (om sko)* down-at-heel **-kladda** smear (daub) all over **-klassa** degrade **-komma** *~ med* give birth to (be delivered of) *(en son* a son) **-komst** [-å-] *s3* delivery **-kyla** chill, refrigerate **-kylning** chilling, refrigeration **-kämpa** fight down, defeat; *(batteri)* silence, reduce **-lagd** *a5* **1** *eg.* laid down; *(om pengar o.d.)* laid out, spent **2** *(om verksamhet)* discontinued, *(om fabrik, gruva o.d.)* closed [down], shut down **-legad** *a5 (om säng o.d.)* with broken springs, sagging **-lusad** lousy; *vard. bildl., ~ med pengar* lousy *(AE. sl.* dirty) with money **-låta** *rfl* condescend *(till att* to) **-låtande** *a4* condescending **-låtenhet** condescension *(jfr lägga [ner])* **1** let down; place, deposit; *(villebråd, fiende)* kill, shoot; *~ vapnen* lay down one's arms **2** *(upphöra med)* give up, relinquish, discontinue; *(fabrik o.d.)* close [down], shut down; *~ arbetet* stop work; go on strike, strike **3** *(använda) ~ pengar i ett företag* invest (put) money into a company; *~ sin röst* abstain from voting; *~ stor omsorg på* put a lot of care (work) into **-meja** mow down *(äv. bildl.)* **-montera** dismount, dismantle **-mörk** pitch-dark **-om** below **-omkring I** *prep* round the base (foot) of **II** *adv* round the bottom **-plöja** *bildl.* plough back **-prutning** reduction, lowering

nedre ['ne:d-] *a, superl. nedersta* lower; *i ~ vänstra hörnet* in the left-hand bottom corner; *i ~*

våningen on the ground (*AE. äv.* first) floor
nedrig [ˣneːd-] *a1* (*skändlig*) heinous, mean;
(*skamlig*) infamous, shameful; *det var ~t av dig
att* it was (is) beastly of you to **nedrighet** *se ge-
menhet* **nedrigt** *adv, det gjorde ~ ont* it hurt terribly
ned|ringd *bli ~* be showered with telephone calls
-rusta disarm, cut down armaments **-rustning**
disarmament, reduction of armaments **-rust-
ningskonferens** disarmament conference
-räkna (*addera*) total, add up **-räkning** total-
ling; (*av raket o.d.*) countdown **-rökt** *a4* smoke-
laden **-rösta** vote down **-sablad** [-saː-] *a5* (*av
kritiken*) pulled (picked) to pieces **-sabling**
[-aː-] *bildl.* dressing-down, slating **-salta** *kokk.*
salt down; pickle in salt **-satt** *a4* (*minskad*) reduced, diminished; (*sänkt*) lowered; ~ *arbetsför-
måga* reduced working capacity; *till ~ pris* at a reduced (cut) price (*AE. äv.* cut rate); *få ~a betyg*
have one's marks reduced (lowered) **-sjunken**
a5, sitta ~ i be reclining in **-skjutning** shooting
down **-skriva** write down; *bokför. äv.* depreciate **-skrivning** writing down; depreciation
-skrotning [-ɔː-] scrapping **-skräpning** [-äː-]
littering up **-skuren** *a5* (*minskad*) reduced, cur-
tailed **-skälld** [-ʃ-] *a5* abused **-skärning**
(*minskning*) reduction, curtailment, cut **-slag 1**
sport. landing, alighting; (*vid kast o.d.*) pitch;
(*vid simning*) entry, dive-in **2** (*fågels*) descent;
(*flygplans*) alighting; *vid ~et* in taking ground **3**
(*projektils*) impact, percussion **4** (*på skrivmaskin*) stroke **-slagen** *a5, bildl.* downhearted,
low-spirited, dejected **-slagenhet** downheartedness; low spirits (*pl*), dejection **-slaktning**
slaughter[ing ... off] **-slående** *a4, bildl.* dis-
heartening, discouraging, depressing; (*bekläm-
mande*) distressing **-släpp** *sport.* face-off **-smit-
tad** *a5, bli ~* become infected **-smutsad** *a5* dirt-
ied, soiled; (*-smetad*) plastered [over] with dirt
-smutsning pollution; contamination; defile-
ment **-snöad** *a5* covered with snow, snowed
over **-stiga** (*se stiga* [*ner*]); *flyg.* alight; descend
(*i, till* into) **-stigning** alighting; descent
-ströms downstream **-stämd** *a1, bildl.* depressed, downhearted, dejected **-stämdhet** depression, downheartedness, dejection **-stänkt**
a4 splashed all over **-summering** adding up, addition **-sutten** *a5* with worn-out (sagging)
springs **-svärta** *bildl.* blacken the character of,
defame **-sänka** immerse **-sänkning** immersion, submergence **-sätta** (*jfr sätta* [*ner*]) (*sänka*)
put down, reduce; lower (*äv. bildl.*); ~ *straffet* reduce the sentence; ~ *priset* (*äv.*) mark down
-sättande *a4* (*förklenande*) disparaging, derogatory, depreciatory **-sättning** (*sänkning*) reduction; (*av pris äv.*) lowering; (*av hörsel o.d.*) impairment **-tagning** taking down **-teckna** write
down **-till** down in the lower part (half) (*på* of);
at the bottom (foot) **-tona** tone down **-toning**
toning down; dampening **-trampad** *a5* trampled
down **-trappa** de-escalate **-trappning** de-esca-
lation **-tryckt** *a4, bildl.* low-spiited; oppressed
-tyngd *a5* weighed (*bildl. äv.* borne) down (*av
with*) **-tysta** reduce to silence, silence **-vikbar**
[-iː-] that can be turned down; (*om krage e.d. äv.*)
... to turn down **-vikt** [-iː-] *a4* turned-down

-vissnad *a5* faded, withered **-väg** *på ~en* on the
way (road, journey) down [south] **-värdera** depreciate; *bildl.* disparage, belittle **-värdering**
depreciation; *bildl.* disparagement
nedåt [ˈneːd-] **I** *prep* down **II** *adv* downward[s], in
a downward direction; *var går gränsen ~?* what is
the bottom limit? **-böjd** *a2* that is bent downwards; down-bent **-gående I** *s6, vara i ~* be on
the down grade (the downward trend) **II** *a4*
downward[-trending]; (*om tendens o.d. äv.*) falling; ~ *konjunkturer* declining business (*sg*), falling markets **-riktad** *a5* directed downwards,
declining **-vänd** *a5* turned downwards
ned|ärvd *a5* passed on by heredity, hereditary
-över [ˈneːd-] **I** *prep* down over (across) **II** *adv,
hela vägen ~* all the way down [south]
nefrit *s3* **1** *med.* nephritis **2** *miner.* nephrite
neg *imperf. av niga*
negation negation; (*nekande ord äv.*) negative
negativ [ˈnegg-, -ˈtiːv] **I** *s7* negative **II** *a1* negative **negativism** negativism **negativist** negativist, negationist **negativistisk** [-ˈviss-] *a5*
negativist[ic] **negativt** [-iː-] *adv* negatively (*äv.
elektr.*), in a (the) negative sense
neger [ˈneː-] *s3* Negro (*pl* Negroes), black
[man]; coloured person; *neds.* darky, nigger
negera (*förneka*) deny; ~*d sats* (*vanl.*) clause
(*etc.*) containing a negative
neger|barn Negro child **-befolkning** Negro
(coloured) population **-by** Negro village, kraal
-folk Negro people **-hydda** Negro['s] hut **-höv-
ding** Negro chief **-kvarter** Negro quarter
-kvinna Negress **-slaveri** Negro slavery **-stam**
Negro tribe
neglig|é [-iˈʃeː] *s3* negligee, negligé[e], undress,
dishabille; *AE.* negligee **-era** neglect; disregard;
~ *ngn* ignore s.b.
negociera negotiate
negr|ess Negress **-ojd** *a1, n sg obest. form und-
viks* Negroid
nej [nejj] **I** *interj* no; ~, *visst inte!* oh no [certainly
not]!; ~, *nu måste jag gå!* well, I must go now!;
~, *men så roligt!* oh, what fun!, oh, how nice!; ~
~ (*vard. nänä*) män! [no], certainly not!; ~, *vad
säger du?* you don't say so?; ~, *det menar du väl
inte!* oh no, surely not! **II** *s7* no; *ibl.* nay; (*avslag
äv.*) refusal; *svara ~* answer in the negative; *säga
~ till ngt* say no to (decline) s.th.; *rösta ~* vote
against [a proposal]; *få ~* be refused; *frågan är
med ~ besvarad* (*vid sammanträde*) *o.d.* the noes
have it
nejd *s3* (*trakt*) district; (*omgivning*) surroundings
(*pl*), neighbourhood
nejlika *s1* carnation, pink; (*krydd-*) clove
nejonöga [-å-] *zool.* lamprey
nej|rop cry (shout) of 'no' **-röst** 'no'-vote, vote
against **-sägare** *en ~* one who [always] says no,
a negationist
neka 1 (*vägra*) refuse (*ngn ngt* s.b. s.th.; *att* to); ~
ngn hjälp refuse s.b. help (to help s.b.); *han ~des
tillträde* he was refused admission **2** (*förneka*)
deny (*till att ha gjort* having done); (*säga nej*) say
no; *han ~r bestämt till att ha* he definitely denies
having; *jag ~r inte till att* I won't deny that; ~ *till
en anklagelse* (*jur.*) plead not guilty **3** *rfl* deny
o.s.; *han ~r sig ingenting* he never denies himself

N

anything; *jag kunde inte* ~ *mig nöjet att* I couldn't
forgo the pleasure of (+ *ing-form*) **nekande** I *a4*
negative (*svar* answer); *ett* ~ *svar* (*äv.*) a refusal
(denial) ; *om svaret är* ~ if the answer is in the
negative **II** *adv*, *svara* ~ answer in the negative,
give a negative answer **III** *s6* denial; (*vägran*) refusal; *döma ngn mot hans* ~ condemn s.b. in spite
of his denial

nekrolog obituary [notice]

nekrọs [-å:s] *s3*, *med.* necrosis

nektar ['nekk-] *s9* nectar (*äv. bildl.*) **-jn** *s3* nectar-
ine

nematod [-'tå:d] *s3* nematode

nemesis ['ne:-] *r* nemesis; (*hämndens gudinna*)
Nemesis

neo|klassicism [-'ism, ×ne:ɔ-] neoclassicism
-kolonialism neocolonialism **-litisk** [-'li:-] *a5*
Neolithic **-logj** *s3* neologism

neon [-'å:n] *s7* neon **-ljus** neon light **-rör** neon
tube **-skylt** neon sign

nepalẹs *s3* Nepalese **-isk** *a5* Nepalese

nepotism nepotism

ner *se ned* **nere** **1** down; *längst* ~ *i* at the very bottom (end) of; *priset är* ~ *i 2 pund* the price is
down to £2; ~ *på* down on (at) **2** (*friare o. bildl.*)
low; *ligga* ~ (*om verksamhet e.d.*) be (have been)
stopped, be at a standstill **3** (*kroppsligt o. and-*
ligt) run down; (*deprimerad*) depressed, down in
the dumps

neri|um ['ne:-] *-en -er*, *bot.* oleander

nermörk pitch-dark, pitch-black

nerts [nä-] *s2* mink **-päls** mink coat

nerv [nä-] *s3* nerve (*äv. bildl.*); *bot. äv.* vein; *han*
har goda ~*er* (*äv.*) he doesn't know what nerves
are; *gå ngn på* ~*erna* get on a p.'s nerves **-bana**
anat. nerve circuit; *fysiol.* nerve path **-cell** nerve
cell, neuron **-centrum** nerve centre **-chock**
nervous shock **-feber** *se tyfoidfeber* **-gas** nerve
gas

nerv|ig *al* **1** *se nervös* **2** *bot.* veined, nerved **-im-**
puls nerve impulse **-klen** *se nervsjuk* **-knippe**
anat. nerve bundle; *bildl.* bundle of nerves **-knut**
ganglion **-krig** war of nerves **-lugnande** *a4*
nerve-soothing; ~ *medel* tranquillizer, sedative
-läkare nerve specialist, neurologist

nerv|ositet nervousness; nervous tension **-pir-**
rande *a4* thrilling, exciting **-press** nervous
strain **-påfrestande** *a4* nerve-racking, trying to
the nerves **-retning** nervous impulse; innerva-
tion **-ryckning** nervous spasm **-sammanbrott**
nervous breakdown **-sjuk** neurotic **-sjukdom**
nervous disorder, neurosis **-slitande** *a4* nerve-
-racking **-spänning** nervous strain **-stillande**
a4, *se nervlugnande* **-svag** nervous, neurasthenic
-system nervous system; *centrala* ~*et* central
nervous system (*förk.* CNS) **-träd** nerve fibre
-vrak nervous wreck **-värk** neuralgia

nervös *al* nervous; (*för tillfället*) agitated, flurried, excited; (*orolig*) uneasy, restless; (~ *av sig*)
highly-strung (*AE.* high-strung), *vard.* nervy,
jumpy **nervöst** [-ö:-] *adv* nervously *etc.*; *skruva*
sig ~ fidget uneasily

nes|a *s1* ignominy, shame, dishonour, disgrace
-lig [×ne:s-] *al* (*vanärande*) ignominious; (*skam-*
lig) shameful, disgraceful; (*nedrig*) infamous

nestor ['nestår] *s3* doyen; *vard.* grand old man

netto **I** *adv* net [cash]; (*utan emballage*) without
packing **II** *s6* [net] profit; *rent* ~ net without discount; *förtjäna i rent* ~ net, clear; *i* ~ [in] net
profit **-avkastning**, **-behållning** net proceeds
(*pl*), net yield **-belopp** net amount **-lön** net
wages (*pl*) **-pris** net price **-resultat** net result
-vikt net weight **-vinst** net gain (profit)

neural|j [nev-, neu-] *s3* neuralgia **-isk** [-'rall-] *a5*
neuralgic

neurasten|i [nev-, neu-] *s3* neurasthenia **-iker**
[-'te:-] neurasthenic [patient]

neurjt [nev-, neu-] *s3*, *med.* neuritis

neuro|kirurgi [nev-, neu-] neurosurgery; neu-
rotomy **-log** neurologist **-logj** *s3* neurology **-lo-**
gisk [-'lå:-] *a5* neurological

neuron [nev'rå:n, neu-] *s7*, *s4* neuron **neuros**
[-'rå:s] *s3* neurosis (*pl* neuroses)

neurot|isk [nev'rå:-, neu-] *a5* neurotic **-iker**
neurotic

neutral *al* neutral; *språkv.* neuter **-isera**
neutralize (*äv. bildl.*); (*motväga*) counteract
-isering [-'se:-] neutralization **-itet** neutrality
-itetspolitik policy of neutrality **-läge** neutral
position; *elektr.* neutral plane

neutrino [-'tri:-] *s5*, *pl äv. neutriner* neutrino

neutron [-'trå:n] *s3* neutron **-bestrålning** neutron radiation **-bomb** neutron bomb **-infång-**
ning neutron capture **-strålning** neutron radiation

neutrum ['neut-, 'ne:u-] *s4* (*i* in the) neuter

newfoundlandshund Newfoundland [dog]

nevö *s3* nephew

ni *pron* you; ~ *själv* [you] yourself

1 nia *v1*, *ung.* use the formal mode of address

2 nia *s1* nine

nicaragu|an *s3* Nicaraguan **-ansk** [-'a:nsk] *a5*
Nicaraguan

nick *s2* nod **nicka 1** nod (*åt* to); ~ *bifall* nod approval; ~ *till* (*somna*) drop off [to sleep] **2** *sport.*
head **nickedocka** *bildl.* yes man

nickel ['nikk-] *s9*, *s7* nickel **-gruva** nickel mine
-stål nickel steel

nickning *en* ~ *a*) a nod [of the (one's) head], *b*)
sport. a header

nidbild caricature

niding miscreant, vandal **nidingsdåd** villainy,
act of vandalism, outrage

nid|skrift lampoon, libellous pamphlet **-skri-**
vare lampooner, scurrilous pamphleteer **-visa**
rhymed lampoon

niece [ni'ä:s, -'e:s] *s5* niece

niell|a inlay with niello **-ing** niello work

niga *neg nigit* curts[e]y (*djupt* low; *för* to), drop
[s.b.] a curts[e]y

nigerer [-'ge:-] *s9* Nigerien

nigeri|an *s3* Nigerian **-ansk** [-a:-] *a5* Nigerian

nigerisk [-'ge:-] *a5* Nigerien

nig|it *sup. av niga* **-ning** [-i:g-] curts[e]y[ing]

nihil|ism nihilism **-ist** nihilist **-istisk** [-'ist-] *a5*
nihilistic

nikotin *s4*, *s3* nicotine **-förgiftning** nicotine
poisoning **-halt** nicotine content **-haltig** *al*
containing nicotine **-ism** nicotinism **-ist** nicotine
addict **-missbruk** excessive smoking

nikt *s4*, *s3* lycopodium powder

Nilen ['ni:-] *r* the Nile

nimbus ['nimm-] *s2* nimbus (*äv. bildl.*)
nio [*vard.* ˣni:e] nine; *en ~ tio stycken* some nine or ten; *jfr fem o. sms.* **niofaldig** *al* ninefold **nionde** [-å-] ninth **nion[de]del** [-å-] ninth [part] **niosvansad** *a5, den ~e katten* the cat-o'-nine-tails
nipa *s1* steep sandy river bank
nippel ['nipp-] *s2* nipple
nipper ['nipp-] *pl* trinkets; (*dyrbarare*) jewels, jewellery (*sg*) **-skrin** jewellery case
nippertippa *s1* pert miss, saucy girl
nipprig *a1, vard.* nuts, cracked
nisch *s3* niche (*äv. bildl.*)
nisse *s2* **1** *se tomte* **2** *se smörgåsnisse*
1 nit *s7* (*brinnande iver*) zeal, ardour, fervour; (*flit*) diligence, application; *ovisst ~* injudicious zeal; *för ~ och redlighet* for zealous and devoted service
2 nit *s2, s3* (*-lott*) blank [ticket]; *dra en ~* draw a blank
3 nit *s2, tekn.* rivet; *~ med försänkt huvud* flush rivet
nit|a rivet (*vid* [on] to); *~ fast* rivet [firmly]; *~ ihop* rivet together **-are** riveter **-hammare** riveting hammer **-huvud** rivet head
nitisk ['ni:-] *al* zealous, ardent, fervent; (*flitig*) diligent
nit|nagel rivet **-ning** [-i:-] riveting; *konkr. äv.* riveted joint
nitlott *se 2 nit*
nitrat *s7, s4* nitrate **nitrera** nitrify, nitrate **nitrering** [-'tre:-] nitration **nitrifikation** nitrification **nitrit** *s7, s3* nitrite
nitro|cellulosa cellulose nitrate, nitrocellulose **-glycerin** nitroglycerin[e]
nittio [*vard.* 'nitti] ninety; *jfr femtio o. sms.* **nittionde** [-å-] ninetieth **nittion[de]del** [part] **nittiotal** *på ~et* in the nineties **nittioåring** (*äv.*) nonagenarian
nitton [-ån] nineteen **nittonde** nineteenth **nittonhundratal** *på ~et* in the twentieth century
nitvinst consolation prize
nitälska be zealous (eager) (*för* for) **nitälskan** *r* zeal
niveller|a level out, equalize, reduce to one (a uniform) level; (*i lantmäteri*) level **-ing** levelling
nivå *s3* level (*äv. bildl.*); *bildl. äv.* standard; *i ~ med* on a level with; *konferens på högsta ~* (*äv.*) summit (top-level) conference **-karta** contour map **-kurva** contour line **-skillnad** difference in altitude (of level)
nix *interj* not a bit of it!, no!
Nizza [ˣnissa] *n* Nice
njugg *al* parsimonious, niggardly (*på, med* with, of; *mot* towards, to); (*på ord o.d.*) sparing (*på* of) **-het** parsimoniousness *etc.*
njurbäcken [-u:-] renal pelvis (*pl* pelves)
njur|e *s2* kidney **-formig** [-å-] *al* kidney-shaped **-sjukdom** kidney disease, disorder of the kidney[s] **-sten** kidney stone, renal calculus **-talg** suet **-transplantation** kidney transplant
njut|a *njöt -it* enjoy (*livet* life); *absol.* enjoy o.s., have a good time; *~ av* enjoy, delight (*starkare:* revel) in **njutbar** *al* (*ätbar*) eatable, edible; (*smaklig*) palatable; (*om t.ex. musik*) enjoyable **njutit** *sup. av njuta* **njutning** [-u:-] enjoyment;

pleasure, delight; feast (*för ögat:* for the eye)
njutnings|full full of enjoyment, highly (very) enjoyable **-lysten** pleasure-seeking, pleasure-loving **-lystnad** craving for (love of) pleasure **-medel** means of enjoyment (*etc.*); (*stimulerande medel*) stimulant **-människa** epicurean; hedonist **-rik** *se -full*
njöt *imperf. av njuta*
N.N. [ˣännänn] (*beteckning för obekant pers.*) so-and-so
nobb [-å-] *s2* brushoff, turndown; *få ~en* be given the brushoff, be turned down **nobba** [-å-] turn down, give the brushoff
nobel ['nå:-] *a2* noble, distinguished; (*storsint*) generous
nobelpris [noˣbell-] Nobel prize **-tagare** Nobel prize winner
nobless [nå-] nobility; *~en* (*vard.*) the upper ten [thousand]
nock [nåkk] *s2* **1** *sjö.* (*gaffel-*) [gaff] end; (*rå-*) [yard]arm **2** *byggn.* ridge **3** *tekn.* cam
nod *s3, astr., bot., fys.* node; *uppstigande ~* ascending node
nog 1 (*tillräckligt*) enough, sufficiently; *jag har fått ~* (*äv. bildl.*) I have had enough (my fill, all I want); *det är ~* that is enough (sufficient); *nära ~* almost, nearly, all but, well-nigh, practically; *mer än ~* (*äv.*) enough and to spare; *hälften kunde ha varit ~* half would have been enough; *vara sig själv ~* be sufficient unto o.s.; *nu kan det vara ~!* that'll do!, enough of that now!; *inte ~ med att han glömmer* he not only forgets; *och inte ~ med det* and that is not all; *hur skall jag ~ kunna tacka dig!* how can I thank you sufficiently!; *den kan inte ~ berömmas* it cannot be too highly praised; *förklarligt ~* as was only natural; *jag var dum ~ att* I was stupid enough to; *märkvärdigt ~* remarkably enough; *nära ~* practically; *underligt ~* strange to say; *det vore ~ så intressant att* it would be exceedingly (*vard.* ever so, jolly) interesting to **2** (*sannolikt*) probably; I expect, I dare say, I suppose; (*säkerligen*) no doubt, doubtless; (*visserligen*) I (you) [must] admit, certainly, to be sure, it is true; *du förstår mig ~* you will understand me[, I am sure (no doubt)]; *du har ~ träffat honom här* you have probably met him here; *~ vet ni att* you must know (you know of course) that; *han kommer ~* he will come all right; *jag skall ~ se till att* I'll see to it that; *det tror jag ~!* I should think so!; *det kan jag ~ tänka mig!* I can (very well) imagine that!; *det är ~ sant, men* that is probably true, but, that is true enough, but; *~ för att du har gjort dig förtjänt av det* not but what you have deserved it **3** (*tämligen*) fairly (*bra* good)
noga I *adv* (*exakt*) exactly, precisely; accurately; (*ingående*) closely, minutely, narrowly; (*omsorgsfullt*) carefully; (*uppmärksamt*) attentively; (*strängt*) strictly (*bevarad hemlighet* guarded secret); *akta dig ~ för att* take great (good) care not to; *hålla ~ reda på* keep an accurate account of; *lägga ~ märke till* note carefully; *det behöver du inte ta så ~!* you needn't be too particular about that!; *~ räknat* strictly speaking **II** *al* (*noggrann*) careful; (*precis*) exact, precise; (*nogräknad*) scrupulous; (*kinkig*) particular; (*petig*) me-

ticulous; (*fordrande*) exacting; *vara ~ med a*) be very exact in (about), *b*) be very particular about (make a point of) (*att passa tiden* being in time); *det är inte så ~ med det!* it doesn't matter very much!, it's not all that important!

nog|grann (*jfr noga II*) (*exakt*) accurate, exact; (*ingående*) close; (*detaljerad*) elaborate, minute; (*sträng*) strict; (*omsorgsfull*) careful, particular **-grannhet** accuracy, exactitude, precision; carefulness *etc.* **-räknad** [-ä:-] *a5* particular, scrupulous; (*granntyckt*) dainty **-samt** (*i högsta grad*) extremely, exceedingly; (*mycket väl*) well enough; *det är ~ känt att* it is a [perfectly] well--known fact that

nojs [nåjs] *s7, se skämt, flört* **nojsa** *se skämta, flörta*

noll [-å-] nought, naught; *vard.* aught (*på termometer etc.*) zero; *sport. äv.* none, nil; (*i tennis*) love; ~ *komma åtta* (*0,8*) nought point eight (0.8); *mitt telefonnummer är två ~ nio ~ åtta* my telephone number is two o[h] nine o[h] eight; ~ ~ (*sport.*) nil-nil, *tennis.* love all; *plus minus ~ a*) *mat.* plus minus nought, *b*) (*friare*) absolutely nothing (nil); *av ~ och intet värde* of no value what[so]ever, absolutely worthless

noll|a [-å-] *s1* nought, naught; *vard.* aught; *åld.* cipher; *vetensk.* zero; *en ~* (*om pers.*) a nobody, a nonentity **-gradig** *a1* at freezing temperature, freezing **-korrektur** *boktr.* reader's (first) proof **-läge** (*hopskr. nolläge*) *mättekn.* mechanical zero; (*friläge*) neutral [position] **-lösning** (*hopskr. nollösning*) zero option **-meridian** prime (datum) meridian **-punkt** zero; freezing point; *stå på ~en* absolute zero; *stå på ~en* be at zero (*äv. bildl.*) **-ställd 1** set to zero **2** *bildl.* expressionless, blank **-ställning** zero [position] **-taxa** free travel **-tid** *på ~* in no time **-tillväxt** zero growth

nomad *s3* nomad **-folk** nomadic people **-isera** nomadize; *~nde folk* (*äv.*) migratory people **-isk** *a5* nomad[ic] **-liv** nomadic (*friare:* roving, migratory) life

nomen ['nå:-] *s7, pl äv. nomina, språkv.* noun [and adjective] **-klatur** nomenclature

nominal|form *språkv.* noun form **-lön** nominal wage[s]

nominativ ['nomm-, 'no:-, 'nåmm-] *s3* (*i* the) nominative

nomin|ell *a1* nominal; *~t värde* (*äv.*) face value; *~t lydande på* at the face (nominal) value of **-era** nominate **-ering** [-'ne:-] nomination

nomo|grafi *s3* nomography **-gram** [-'gramm] *s7* nomogram

nonaggressionspakt nonaggression pact

nonchal|ans [nåŋʃa'laŋs, nån-, -'nans] *s3* nonchalance, carelessness; offhandedness; (*försumlighet*) negligence **-ant** [-'laŋt, '-lant] *a1* nonchalant; careless; negligent; offhand[ed] **-era** pay no attention to, neglect

nonfigurativ [-'i:v, *äv.* 'nånn-, 'nå:n-] *a1* nonfigurative

nonie ['no:-] *s5, mättekn.* vernier

non|intervention [nån-] nonintervention **-kombattant** noncombatant **-konformism** nonconformism

nonsens ['nånn-] *n* nonsense, rubbish

nopp|a [-å-] **I** *s1* burl, knot **II** *v1* **1** *tekn.* burl **2** (*om fågel*) pluck, preen; (*ögonbryn*) pluck; ~ *sig* (*om fågel*) preen its feathers **-ig** *a1* burled, knotty **nor** *s7* narrow passage, sound

noradrenalin [ˣnoːr-, -'iːn] noradrenalin[e]

nord [-oː-] **I** *s2* north; *N~en* the Nordic (Northern, Scandinavian) countries (*pl*); *i höga N~* in the Far North **II** *adv* north (*om* of); *vinden var ~ till väst* the wind was north by west

Nord|afrika *n* North Africa **-amerika** *n* North America

nordamerikansk North American

nordan [ˣnoːr-] **I** *adv, se norr II* **II** *r, se följ.* **-vind** north wind

Nordatlanten *r* the North Atlantic

nordbo northerner, inhabitant of the North

Norden [ˣnoːr-] *n el. r* the Nordic countries

Nord|england *n* Northern England, the North [of England] **-europa** *n* Northern Europe

nord|isk ['noːr-] *a5* northern; (*i etnografin*) Nordic; *de ~a länderna* the Nordic (Northern) countries; *N~a ministerrådet* [the] Nordic Council of Ministers; *N~a rådet* [the] Nordic Council; *~a språk* Scandinavian (Nordic) languages **-ism** efforts (*pl*) to promote Nordic unity **-ist** Scandinavian philologist

Nord|kalotten [ˣnoːrd-] *r* the Scandinavian (Baltic) Shield (arctic regions of Norway, Sweden, Finland and Kola Peninsula) **-kap** *n* the North Cape

nord|lig [ˣnoːrd-] *a1* (*i norr*) northern; (*från norr*) north[erly]; ~ *bredd* north latitude; *det blåser ~ vind* the wind is in (is blowing from) the north **-ligare I** *a, komp.* more northerly **II** *adv* further (more to the) north **-ligast I** *a, superl.* northernmost **II** *adv* farthest north **-man** *hist.* Norseman **-nordost** north-northeast (*förk.* NNE) **-nordväst** north-northwest (*förk.* NNW) **-ost I** *s2* (*~lig vind*) northeast wind; northeaster; (*väderstreck*) northeast (*förk.* NE) **II** *adv* northeast (*om* of) **-ostlig** [-ˣost-] *a1* northeast[ern]; *jfr nordlig* **-ostpassagen** the Northeast Passage **-pol** *~en* the North Pole **-polsexpedition** expedition to the North Pole

Nordsjön *r* the North Sea

nord|sluttning north[ern] slope **-väst I** *s2* (*~lig vind*) northwest wind; northwester; (*väderstreck*) northwest (*förk.* NW) **II** *adv* northwest (*om* of) **-västlig** [-ˣväst-] *a1* northwest[ern]; *jfr nordlig* **-västra** [-ˣväst-] northwest[ern] **-östra** [-ˣösst-] northeast[ern]

Norge ['nårje] *n* Norway

norgesalpeter Norwegian saltpetre

norm [-å-] *s3* standard (*för* of; *för ngn* for s.b.); (*måttstock äv.*) norm; (*regel*) rule; code; (*mönster*) model, type (*för* for); *gälla som ~* serve as a standard

normal [-å-] **I** *a1* normal; standard, regular; *under ~a förhållanden* (*äv.*) normally; *han är inte riktigt ~* (*äv.*) he is not quite right in his head **II** *s3* standard; type **-begåvad** *a5* normally gifted; average **-fördelning** *stat.* normal frequency distribution **-isera** normalize; standardize **-ljus** standard candle[power] **-mått** standard[ized] measure] **-pris** standard prize **-prosa** ordinary (plain) prose **-skolekompetens** diploma of

secondary education for girls **-spårig** *a1* [of]
standard gauge **-storlek** standard (normal,
regular) size **-studietid** normal length of time
needed to complete a study program[me] **-tid**
standard (mean) time **-ton** *mus.* concert pitch
-vikt regular (standard) weight **-år** mean (normal, average) year

normand [når'mand, -'maɳd] *s3* Norman

Normandie [nårman'di:, -maɳ-] *n* Normandy

normandisk [når'mandisk, -'maɳ-] *a5* Norman;
N~a öarna the Channel Islands

norm|ativ ['nårm-, -'ti:v] *a1* normative **-era**
standardize, gauge; (*reglera*) regulate **-ering**
[-'me:-] standardization **-givande** *a4* normative,
standard-forming; *vara ~ för* (*äv.*) be a rule (a
standard) for

norn|a [ˣnoː-r-] *s1* Norn; *-orna* (*vanl.*) the Weird
Sisters, the Fates (Destinies)

norpa [-å-] *v1*, *vard.* pinch, bone, swipe, snaffle

norr [-å-] **I** *n* the north; *mot ~* to the north; *rätt i
~* due north **II** *adv* [to the] north (*om* of)

norra *best. a* the north (*sidan side*); the northern
(*delarna av* parts of); *~ England* Northern England, the North [of England]; *N~ ishavet* the
Arctic Ocean

norr|gående *a4* (*om tåg o.d.*) northbound
-ifrån ['nårr-] from the north

norr|ländsk *a5* [of] Norrland **-ländska** (*språk*)
Norrland dialect **-länning** Norrlander **-man**
Norwegian **-sida** *bergets ~* the north side of the
mountain **-sken** *s7* aurora borealis; *-et* (*äv.*) the
northern lights (*pl*) **-ut** ['nårr-, -**över** ['nårr-]
northward[s], towards [the] north; (*i norr*) in (to)
the north; *längst ~* northernmost

nors [-å-] *s2, zool.* smelt; *jag vill vara skapt som
en ~ om* I'll be blowed if

norsk [-å-] *a5* Norwegian; *hist.* Norse **norska** *s1* **1**
(*språk*) Norwegian; *hist.* Norse **2** (*kvinna*) Norwegian woman

nos *s2* nose (*äv. friare*); (*hos hästar, nötkreatur*)
muzzle; (*hos fiskar, kräldjur*) snout; *blek om ~en*
green about the gills **nosa** smell, scent; *~ på* sniff
(smell) at; *~ reda på ngt* ferret s.th. out, find out
s.th.

nos|grimma muzzle **-hörning** [-ö:-] rhinoceros
noshörnings|hanne bull rhinoceros **-hona**
cow rhinoceros

nos|ig *a1* cheeky, pert (*mot* towards, to) **-kon**
nose cone **-ring** nose ring; cattle leader **-spets**
tip of the nose

nostalg|i *s3* nostalgia **-isk** [-'tall-] *a5* nostalgic

1 not *s2* (*fisk-*) [haul (drag)] seine; *dra ~* fish with
a seine

2 not *s3* **1** (*anmärkning*) note, annotation; (*fot-*)
footnote **2** *polit.* [diplomatic] note, memorandum **3** *mus.* note; (*-häfte*) music (*sg*); *spela
efter ~er* play from music; *skriva ~er* write music;
ge ngn stryk efter ~er give s.b. a good thrashing;
vara med på ~erna catch on (the drift), fall in
with the idea

nota *s1* (*räkning*) bill, account; *AE. äv.* check;
(*förteckning*) list (*på* of); *jfr tvättnota*

notab|el [-'ta:-] *a2* of note **-ilitet** *s3* notability

notariatavdelning [-ˣa:t-] trust department
notarie [-ˣta-, -'ta:-] *s5* [recording] clerk, notary; (*vid domsaga äv.*) law clerk, deputy judge

notarius publicus [noˈta:rius 'pubblikus] *r, pl
notarii publici* [-si] notary public

notblad sheet of music

noter|a 1 (*anteckna*) note (write) down, make a
note of; (*lägga på minnet*) note; (*bokföra äv.*) enter, book **2** (*fastställa pris på, äv. börs.*) quote
(*till at*) **-ing 1** noting (*etc.*) down; (*mera konkr.*)
note, notation; (*bokföringspost*) entry, item; *enligt våra ~ar* (*hand.*) according to our records **2**
hand. börs. quotation

notes|block [ˣnoː:tes-, ˣnå:ts-] [scribbling] pad
-bok notebook

not|häfte sheets (*pl*) of music; (*större*) music-
book **-ifikation** notification

notis *s3* (*underrättelse*) notice; (*tidnings-*) news-
item, paragraph; *ta ~ om* take notice of, pay attention to **-byrå** news (press) agency **-jägare**
newshawk, newshound

not|linje *boktr.* note rule

notorisk [-'to:-] *a5* notorious

not|papper music paper **-skrivare** music copy-
ist **-skrivning** copying of music **-ställ** music
stand (rack) **-system** staff **-tecken 1** *mus.* note
2 *boktr.* reference mark

notvarp *s7* seine sweep; *bildl.* crush

not|vändare person who turns pages of music
for a pianist **-växling** *dipl.* exchange of notes

nougat [noˈga:t] *s3* nougat, almond paste

nova [ˣnå:-] *s1, astr.* nova (*pl äv. novae*)

novell *s3* short story **-ist** short-story writer **-istjk**
s3 short-story writing **-samling** collection of
short stories

november [-ˈvemm-] *r* November

novis *s3* novice; (*friare*) *se nybörjare*

nu I *adv* now; *AE. äv.* presently; (*vid det här laget*)
by now (this time); *från och med ~* from now on
[wards]; (*ända*) *tills ~* up till now; *~ då* now that;
den ~ rådande (*äv.*) the present (existing); *vad ~
då?* what's up (the matter) now?; *för att ~ ta ett
exempel* just by way of example; *vad var det han
hette ~* [*igen*]? whatever was his name? **II** *s7, ~et*
the present [time]; *i detta ~* at this moment

nubb *s2* tack **nubba** tack (*vid on to*); *~ fast* tack
on, fasten with tacks

nubbe *s2* dram, schnap[p]s

Nubien ['nu:-] *n* Nubia

nubi|er ['nu:-] Nubian **-isk** *a5* Nubian

nuck|a *s1* frump **nuckig** *a1* frumpish

nudda brush; *~ vid* brush against

nudel *s2, kokk.* noodle

nud|ism nudism **-ist** nudist **-istläger** nudist
camp

nuförtiden ['nu:-] nowadays; *vard.* these days

nugat *s3, se nougat*

nuklejn *s7, s4* nuclein **-syra** nucleic acid

nukleär *a1* nuclear; *~a vapen* nuclear weapons

nu|läge present situation **-mer[a]** ['nu:-] now,
nowadays

numerisk [-ˈme:-] *a5* numeric[al] **numeriskt**
adv, en ~ överlägsen a numerically superior, a[n]
... superior in numbers **numerus** ['nu:-] *n* number **numerär** *s3* number; (*armés o.d.*) [numeri-
cal] strength **II** *a5, se numerisk*

numismat|ik *s3* numismatics (*pl, behandlas som
sg*) **-iker** [-'ma:-] numismatist **-isk** [-'ma:-] *a5* nu-
mismatic

N

nummer ['numm-] *s7* number; (*exemplar*) copy; (*tidnings-* *o.d.*) issue; (*storlek*) size; (*programpunkt* *e.d.*) item; *gammalt ~* (*av tidning o.d.*) back issue; *göra ett stort ~ av* make a great feature (fuss) of; *behandlas som ett ~* (*om pers.*) be treated as no more than a number **-byrå** *tel.* directory enquiries [office] **-följd** number sequence; *ordna i ~* arrange consecutively **-lapp** queue [number] ticket **-ordning** numerical order **-plåt** (*på motorfordon*) numberplate, *AE.* *äv.* license plate **-skiva** *tel.* dial

numrer|a number; *~de platser* numbered seats; *~d från 1 till 100* numbered 1 to 100 **-ing** numbering, numeration

numro *s, ingen böjning* number (No.)

nuna *s1, vard.* phiz, dial

nunna *s1* nun; *bli ~* (*äv.*) take the veil

nunne|dok nun's veil **-fjäril** nun moth **-kloster** nunnery, convent **-orden** order of nuns, [religious] sisterhood **-ört** corydalis

nuntie ['nuntsie] *s5* nuncio

nupit *sup. av nypa*

nusvenska present-day Swedish

nutid present times (*pl*); [the] present day; *forntid och ~* past [times] and present; *~ens människor* present-day people, people of today **nutida** *oböjligt a* present-day; modern

nutids|diktning modern poetry **-historia** contemporary (present-day) history **-människa** modern man **-orientering** knowledge of present-day (contemporary) life and events

nutria ['nu:-] *s1* nutria, coypu

nu|varande *a4* present; (*rådande*) existing; (*om pris*) ruling, current; *i ~ läge* as things stand at present, in (under) the present circumstances, as it is; *i ~ ögonblick* at the present moment **-värde** present value; *försäkr.* capitalized value

ny I *a1* new (*för* to); (*förnyad*) fresh; (*färsk*) recent (*böcker* books); (*~ o. ovanlig*) novel (*erfarenhet* experience); (*annan*) [an]other; (*ytterligare*) additional, extra (*börda* burden), further (*order* orders); *bli en ~ människa a*) (*t. hälsan*) become a new man, *b*) (*i åskådning e.d.*) become a different person; *~tt mod* fresh courage; *~tt stycke* (*boktr.*) new paragraph; *~a tiden* modern times, the modern age; *Gott ~tt år!* a Happy New Year!; *det ~a i* the novelty in (of), what is new in **II** *s6, s7* (*-tändning*) new phase of the moon; *månen är i ~* the moon is new; *jfr nymåne*

Nya Guinea [ˣny:a giˣne:a] *n* New Guinea

ny|anläggning new plant (establishment) **-anländ** *a5* newly (just) arrived; *de ~a* (*äv.*) the newcomers, the new arrivals

nyans [-'ans, -'aŋs] *s3* shade; nuance, tone; (*anstrykning*) tinge; (*om uttryck*) shade of meaning; *hans röst saknar ~er* his voice lacks modulation (variation) **nyansera** shade off; *mus.* modulate; (*variera*) vary **nyansering** [-'se:-] shading[-off] *etc.*

ny|anskaffning replacement; new acquisition [of equipment] **-anställd** new employee

nyare *a, komp.* newer *etc.*; more modern; *i ~ tid* in modern (recent) times (*pl*) **nyast** *a, superl.* newest; most modern (*etc.*); (*senast*) latest

Nya Zeeland [ˣny:a 'se:-] *n* New Zealand

ny|bakad *a5* **1** fresh from the oven, newmade,

newbaked **2** *bildl.* newly fledged **-bildad** *a5* newly (recently) formed (founded) **-bildning** new (recent) formation (creation, establishment); *språkv. äv.* neologism, coinage; *med.* new growth, neoplasm **-bliven** *a5* (*om student e.d.*) newly fledged; (*om professor e.d*) newly appointed; *hon är ~ mor* she has just become a mother **-byggare** settler, colonist; pioneer **-byggd** *a5* new[built], newly constructed (built) **-bygge** house (ship *etc.*) under construction **-byggnad** new construction (house, building *etc.*) **-börjarbok** primer (*i* of) **-börjare** beginner; novice, tyro, tiro, new hand **-börjarkurs** beginners' course

nyck *s3* whim; fancy; caprice; *genom en ödets* (*naturens*) *~* by a freak of fate (Nature)

nyckel *s2* key; *bildl.* clue; (*kod*) code, cipher; *vrida om ~n* turn the key; *~n till framgång* the key to success **-ax** key bit **-barn** latchkey child **-ben** *anat.* collarbone, clavicle **-blomster** orchis **-figur** key figure **-harpa** *mus.* keyed fiddle **-hål** keyhole **-industri** key industry **-knippa** bunch of keys **-ord** key word; (*t. korsord*) clue **-person** key person **-piga** ladybird; *AE.* ladybug **-ring** key ring **-roll** key role **-roman** roman à clef **-ställning** key position **-ämne** *tekn.* key blank

nyckfull capricious; (*om pers. äv.*) whimsical; (*om väderlek*) changeable, fickle; (*ostadig*) fitful **-het** capriciousness *etc.*; whimsicality

nydan|a fashion anew; reorganize **-are** refashioner; reorganizer, regenerator; (*pionjär*) pioneer, breaker of new ground **-ing** refashioning; reorganization, regeneration

ny|edition new edition **-emission** issue of new shares, new [share] issue **-etablering** new business starts (*pl*) **-examinerad** *a5* newly qualified **-fallen** *a5* (*om snö*) newly (fresh) fallen **-fascism** neofascism **-fascistisk** neofascist **-fiken** *a3* curious (*på* about, as to); (*alltför ~*) inquisitive, prying **-fikenhet** curiosity; inquisitiveness; *av ren ~* out of sheer curiosity; *väcka ngns ~* arouse a p.'s curiosity, make s.b. all agog **-född** newborn; *barnet är alldeles -fött* the baby has just been born **-förlovad** *hon är ~* she has just got engaged [to be married]; *de ~e* the newly engaged couple **-förvärv** *ett ~* a new (recent) acquisition **-förvärvad** *a5* newly (recently) acquired **-gift** newly married, newlywed; *de ~a* the newly-married couple **-gjord** newly made **-gotik** neo-Gothic (*äv. ~en*) **-grad** centesimal degree **-grekiska** Modern Greek **-grundad** *a5* newly founded **-gräddad** freshly-baked

nyhet (*egenskap att vara ny*) newness; (*ngt nytt*) novelty, s.th. new; (*ny sak*) novelty; (*nymodighet*) novelty, innovation; (*underrättelse*) news (*sg*); *~ens behag* the charm of novelty; *förlora ~ens behag* become stale; *en ~* (*i tidning e.d.*) a news-item, a piece of news; *en viktig ~* (*äv.*) a piece of important news; *inga ~er är goda ~er* no news is good news; *det var en ~ för mig* this is news to me; *~erna för säsongen* the novelties of the season, (*kläder*) the season's new fashions **nyhets|byrå** news (press) agency **-förmedling** news service **-utsändning** *radio.* newscast

ny|inflyttad *a5, vara ~* have just (recently)

moved in, (*i område o.d.*) be a newcomer [to the district] **-inkommen** *a5* just (recently) arrived **-inredd** *a5* recently refitted (fitted up) **-inrättad** *a5* newly established (created) **-inskriven** *a5* newly enrolled; *mil.* newly enlisted **-instudering** [preparing of a] new production; *hans ~ av Fidelio* his new characterization of Fidelio **-klassicism** neoclassicism **-klippt** *a4* newly cut; *han är ~* he has just had his hair cut **-kläckt** *a4* newly hatched **-kokt** [-ɔ:-] *a4* freshly-boiled **-kolonialism** neocolonialism **-komling** [-å-] newcomer, fresh arrival; (*i skola e.d.*) new boy (girl) **-konstruktion** new construction (design)

nykter ['nykk-] *a2* 1 sober; (*måttlig*) temperate 2 *bildl.* sober[-minded], level-headed **-het** (*äv. bildl.*) sobriety, soberness; temperance

nykterhets|organisation temperance organization **-rörelse** temperance movement **-vård** treatment of alcoholics **-vän** advocate of temperance

nykterist total abstainer, teetotaller

nyktra *~ till* become sober [again], sober up, *bildl.* sober down

ny|kärnad [-çä:r-] *a5* newly churned; fresh from the dairy **-lagd** *a5* (*om ägg*) new-laid; *håret är -lagt* my (etc.) hair has just been set

nyligen recently; lately; (*på sista tiden äv.*) latterly, of late; *helt ~* quite recently

nylon [-'lå:n] *s4, s3* nylon **-skjorta** nylon shirt **-strumpor** *pl* nylon stockings (*herr-:* socks); nylons

nymf *s3* nymph **nymfoman** *s3* nymphomaniac **nymfomani** *s3* nymphomania

ny|modig *a1* new-fashioned, modern; *neds.* newfangled **-modighet** modernity; *en ~* a newfangled thing (idea, notion) **-mornad** [-å-:] *a5* newly awakened; hardly awake **-målad** *a5* freshly painted; *är ~* has just been painted; *-målat!* wet paint! **-måne** new moon **-nazism** neonazism

nynna hum

nynorsk I *a1* Modern Norwegian **II** *s1*, *språkv.* New Norwegian

ny|odling 1 *abstr.* land reclamation 2 *konkr.* reclaimed land; (*i skog*) clearing **-omvänd** *a5* newly converted; *en ~* a new convert, a neophyte **-ordna** reorganize, reform **-ordning** reorganization, rearrangement; new order **-orientering** reorientation, readjustment

nyp *s7* pinch **nypa I** *s1* **1** (*fingrar*) fingers (*pl*); *vard.* paw **2** (*det man tar i ~n*) pinch [of ...]; *en ~ luft* a breath of air; *med en ~ salt* (*bildl.*) with a pinch (grain) of salt **II** *nöp* nupit, *äv.* *v3* pinch, nip; *det nyper i skinnet* there is a nip in the air **nypas** *nöps* nupits, *äv.* *v3*, *dep* pinch; *nyps inte!* don't pinch me!

ny|planterad *a5* newly (recently) planted; replanted **-plantering** new plantation, newly planted flowerbed (*etc.*) **-platonism** Neo-Platonism

nypon [-ån] *s7* rosehip **-blomma** dog-rose [flower] **-buske** dog-rose bush **-soppa** rosehip cream **-te** rosehip tea

ny|premiär (*på film*) rerun, revival **-pressad** *a5* newly pressed, (*om byxor äv.*) newly creased **-produktion** new production; *~ av bostäder*

newly constructed dwellings **-påstigen** *a5* who has just entered the bus (train *etc.*) **-rakad** *a5* freshly-shaved **-rekrytera** recruit new man (staff) **-reparerad** *a5* newly repaired **-rik** new--rich; *en ~* a nouveau riche; *de ~a* the new-rich

Nürnberg ['nyrn-] *n* Nuremberg **-processen** the Nuremberg trials (*pl*)

ny|romantik neoromanticism; *~en* (*äv.*) the Romantic Movement **-romantiker** neoromanticist **-rostad** [-å-] *a5* freshly-roasted

nys *s, i uttr.: få ~ om ngt* get wind of s.th.

nysa *v3, imperf. äv. nös* sneeze

ny|silver silver-plated ware; *gafflar av ~* silver-plated forks **-skapa** create anew; *~d* newly created **-skapande** *s6, ~t av* the creating of new **-skapare** innovator, creator of new; *flottans ~* the creator of the new navy **-skapelse** new creation, innovation **-slagen** *a5* (*om hö o.d.*) new-mown

nysning [ˣny:s-] sneezing; *en ~* a sneeze

ny|snö newly-fallen snow **-språklig** *a1, ~ linje* modern language side

nyspulver sneezing powder

nyss just [now], a moment ago; *en ~ inträffad olycka* a recent accident **-nämd** *a5* just mentioned (*etc.*)

nysta wind; *absol äv.* make up into balls (a ball) **nystan** *s7* ball, spool

ny|startad *a5* (*om företag*) newly established (founded *etc.*) **-stavning** new (reformed) spelling **-struken** *a5* newly ironed

nystvinda reel, hasp, spindle

ny|stärkt *a4* freshly-starched **-svenska** Modern Swedish **-teckna** *~ aktier i* subscribe to new shares in; *~de aktier* newly subscribed shares; *~de försäkringar* new insurance business (*sg*) **-teckning** (*av aktier*) new subscription

nyter ['ny:-] *a2* cheery, bright; *pigg och ~* bright and cheery

ny|tillskott new addition; new influx **-tryck** reprint

nytt *n*, *någonting ~* something new; *~ och gammalt* new things and old; *på ~* anew, once more; *börja på ~* start (begin) afresh; *försöka på ~* try again, have another try, make a new attempt

nytt|a I *s1* (*användning*) use, good; (*fördel*) advantage, benefit, profit; (*-ighet*) utility, usefulness; *förena ~ med nöje* combine business with pleasure; *~n med det* the use[fulness] (advantage) of it; *dra ~ av* benefit from, profit by, utilize, (*med orätt*) take advantage of; *göra ~* do some good, be of some use; *ha ~ av* find useful (of use); *vara till ~* be of some help, do some good; *till ~ för* of use to, serviceable for; *till ingen ~* of no use **II** *v1, se gagna*; *det ~r inte* it is no use (*att göra det* doing it) **nyttig** *a1* useful (*för* for); of use (service) (*för* to); good (*för* for); (*hälsosam*) wholesome; *det blir ~t för mig* it will do me good **nyttiggöra** utilize, use **nyttighet** (*med pl*) utility; (*utan pl äv.*) usefulness

nyttja use, employ; *jfr använda* **nyttjanderätt** usufruct, right of (to) use; *ha ~ till* hold in usufruct, have the use and enjoyment of

nytto|betonad *a5* utility; utilitarian **-föremål** useful article **-konst** applied art **-moral** utilitarian morality **-synpunkt** *ur ~* from the utility

N

(utilitarian) point of view **-trafik** commercial traffic **-varor** utility products (articles) **-växt** useful plant

ny|tvättad *a5* just washed; newly washed; (*om fönster*) newly cleaned **-tändning** appearance of a new moon **-uppfunnen** *a5* recently invented **-upptäckt** *a4* rediscovered **-utgåva** new edition **-utkommen** *a5* just (recently) published, that has just appeared **-utnämnd** *a5* newly appointed **-utslagen** *a5* (*om blomma*) that has just come out **-val** *s7* new election; *utlysa ~* appeal to the country, publish notices of a new election **-vald** *a5* newly elected **-vunnen** *a5* newly won **-värdesförsäkring** reinstatement value insurance **-zeeländare** [-ˣse:-] New Zealander **-zeeländsk** [-ˣse:-] *a5* New Zealand **-år** new year; *fira ~* celebrate New Year

nyårs|afton New Year's Eve **-dag** New Year's Day **-gåva** new-year['s] gift **-löfte** New Year resolution

nyöppnad *a5* newly started (*affär* shop); newly opened (*konto* account)

1 nå *interj* well!; (*ju*) why!; *~ då så!* oh, in that case!

2 nå *v4* (*komma fram t.*) reach (*äv. bildl.*), get (come) to, arrive at; (*upp-*) attain, achieve (*äv. bildl.*); (*räcka*) reach, attain; *~ mogen ålder* reach maturity; *enighet har ~tts om* agreement has been reached on; *jag ~ddes av nyheten* the news reached me; *han ~r mig till axeln* he comes up to my shoulder; *jag ~r inte dit* I cannot reach as far as that, it is beyond my reach; *~ fram till* reach as far as [to]; *~ ner till* reach down to; *~ upp till* reach [up to], come up to

nåd *s3* **1** (*misskund*) grace; (*barmhärtighet*) mercy; (*ynnest*) favour; *av Guds ~e* (*om kung*) by divine right, (*om t.ex. skald*) divinely gifted; *i ~ens år 1931* in the year of grace 1931; *av ~* out of mercy; *ansöka om ~* apply for a (sue for) pardon; *få ~* be pardoned; *ge sig på ~ och onåd* surrender unconditionally, make an unconditional surrender; *i ~er* graciously; *leva på ~er hos ngn* live on a p.'s charity; *låta ~ gå före rätt* temper justice with mercy; *synda på ~en* (*eg.*) presume on God's grace, *vard.* take advantage of a p.'s generosity; *finna ~ inför ngns ögon* find favour with s.b.; *ta ngn till ~er igen* take s.b. back into one's favour **2** (*höghet*) Grace; *Ers ~* Your Grace, (*Storbritannien äv.*) Your Lordship (Ladyship), my Lord (Lady); *lilla ~en* (*skämts.*) her little ladyship; *två gamla ~er* two old (elderly) ladies

nåda|skott *se -stöt* **-stöt** coupe de grâce, death-blow; *ge ~en* finish off, put out of misery **-tid** time of grace, respite

nåde I *s, se nåd I* **II** *v, i uttr. såsom: Gud ~ dig!* God have mercy upon you!; *Gud ~ om ...!* God help me if ...! **-ansökan** petition for pardon **-gåva** gift of grace; (*friare*) bounty, gratuity **-hjon** [-jo:n] *s7* receiver of charity **-medel** means of grace **-rik** abounding in grace; (*friare*) gracious, merciful **-skott, -stöt** *se nådastöt* **-vedermäle** mark of favour

nådig *a1* gracious; merciful; *Gud vare mig ~!* God be merciful to me (have mercy upon me)!; *på ~[a]ste befallning* by His (Her) Majesty's

Command; *~ frun* her (*vid tilltal:* Your) Ladyship; *min ~a* your Ladyship, my Lady, [my dear] Madam

någ|on [-ån] (*jfr något, några*) (*en viss*) some, *subst.* someone, somebody; (*en el. ett par*) a[n] ... or two (so); (*~ alls, ~ som helst*) any, *subst.* anyone, anybody; (*en, ett*) a[n]; (*en enda*) one, a single; *har du ~ bror?* have you a brother?; *-ra egna barn har de inte* they have no children of their own; *har du -ra pengar?* a) (*på dig*) have you any money?, b) (*att låna mig*) have you got some money?; *om ~ vecka* in a week or two (so); *är det ~ här?* is there anyone here?; *jag har inte berättat det för ~* I haven't told anyone; *kan ~ av er ...?* can one (any [one]) of you ...?; *~ av dem måste ha* one of them must have; *inte i ~ större utsträckning* not to any great extent; *utan ~* [*som helst*] *svårighet* without any difficulty [whatsoever]; *inte på ~ vis!* by no means!, not at all!; *på ~ -ot sätt* somehow (in some way) [or other]; *vi var -ra och trettio* we were thirty odd; *hon är -ra och trettio* she is thirty odd (something); *~ annan* someone else; *~ annan gång* some other time; *bättre än ~ annan* better than anyone else; *~ annanstans* somewhere else; *-ot eller -ra år* one year or more; *~ sådan har jag inte* I have nothing like that (of that kind); *en ... så god som ~* as good a[n] ... as any; *denne ~* this somebody; *du om ~* you if anybody; *tala svenska med ~ brytning* speak Swedish with a slight accent; *kära nån* [*då*]! goodness me!

någon|dera *fören.* one ... or the other; *självst.* one or other (*av dem* of them) **-sin** [-inn] ever; [at] any time; *~ stans, -städes* never **-stans, -städes** (*jfr någon*) somewhere; anywhere; *AE. vard.* some place, any place **-ting** (*jfr något*) something; anything

någorlunda fairly, tolerably, pretty

någ|ot [-ått] **I** *pron* (*jfr någon*) something; anything; (*-on del*) some, any; (*~ litet*) a little; *det är ~ mycket vanligt* that (it) is [a] very common [thing]; *vad för ~?* what?; *vad är det för ~?* what is that?; *det var ~ visst med honom* there was [a certain] something about him; *~ sådant har aldrig hänt förut* such a thing has never (no such thing has ever) happened before; *han är ~ av en konstnär* he is something of an artist; *vill du mig ~?* a) (*~ särskilt*) is there something you want to see me about?, b) (*~ över huvud taget*) is there anything you want to see me about? **II** *adv* somewhat; a little, a bit, rather; *~ mindre än en timme* a little less than (somewhat under) an hour; *han är ~ till fräck!* he's pretty (a bit) impudent! **någotsånär** *se någorlunda* **några** [ˣnå:g-] (*jfr någon*) some; any; *subst.* some (any) people; (*~ få*) a few [people *etc.*]; *om ~ dagar* in a few (in two or three) days

näja [ˈnä:-] oh well!

nål *s2* needle; (*hår-, knapp-*) pin; *sitta som på ~ar* (*bildl.*) be on pins and needles (on tenterhooks)

nål|a *~ fast* pin on (*på* to), fasten on (*på* to) **-brev** packet of needles **-dyna** pincushion **-pengar** *pl* pin money (*sg*) **-påträdare** needle threader **-rasp** *s7* (*på grammofon*) scratching **-spets** needle-point, pinpoint **-stick** pinprick (*äv. bildl.*)

nålsöga eye of a (the) needle
nål|vass [as] sharp as a needle **-ventil** needle
valve
nåt s2, s7, sjö. o. fack. seam
nåtla [ˣnå:t-] fack. close, bind
nåväl well; all right
näbb s2, s7 bill; (i sht rovfågels) beak; var fågel
sjunger efter sin ~ every bird pipes its own lay;
försvara sig med ~ar och klor defend o.s. tooth
and nail **-djur** zool. duckbill [platypus] **-gädda**
1 zool. garfish **2** bildl. pert (saucy) girl
näbb|ig a1, bildl. pert, saucy, impudent **-mus**
shrew[mouse]; vanlig ~ common shrew **-val** s2
bottle-nosed whale
näck s2 water-sprite; N~en Neck[an], Skottl.
Kelpie **-ros** water lily
näktergal s2 [thrush] nightingale
nämligen (framför uppräkning) namely,
skriftspr. viz.; (det vill säga) [and] that is, which
is; (emedan) for, because; ('ser ni') you see; sak
en är ~ den att the fact is, you see, that, it's like
this, you see
nämn|a v2 (om-) mention (för to); (säga) say;
(omtala) tell; (be-) name, call; ~ var sak vid dess
rätta namn call a spade a spade; ingen -d och
ingen glömd all included; under -da förutsättning
on the given assumption **-are** mat. denominator
nämnd s3 (jury) jury, panel; (utskott) committee,
board **nämndeman** juror, juryman
nämn|värd [-vä:-] a1 worth mentioning (speak-
ing of); considerable, appreciable; i ~ grad mate-
rially; ingen ~ förändring no change to speak of
nännas v2, dep have the heart to
näpen a3 engaging; sweet (dear) little (flicka
girl); i sht AE. cute
näppe s i uttr.: med nöd och ~ only just **-ligen** se
knappast
näpsa v3 (tillrättavisa) rebuke; (straffa) chastise,
punish **näpst** s3 rebuke; chastisement
1 när I konj **1** when; (just som) [just] as; (medan)
while; (-helst) whenever; ~ han kom in i rummet
såg han on entering the room he saw **2** se emedan
II adv when, at what time; ~ som helst at any time
(moment)
2 när I adv near, [near (close)] at hand; från ~
och fjärran from far and near; inte göra en fluga
för ~ not hurt a fly; det gick hans ära för ~ it hurt
his pride; jag hade så ~ sagt I [very] nearly said,
I was on the point of saying; så ~ som på except
[for], but; inte på långt ~ not by a long way; not
anything like; det var på ett hår ~ it was within an
ace of **II** prep (hos) with, near
1 nära närmare närmast o. näst **I** oböjl. a near
(äv. om tid); close; bildl. close, intimate; på ~
håll at close quarters; inom en ~ framtid in the
near future **II** adv near; (i tid äv.) at hand; close
to, nearby; bildl. closely, intimately; (nästan) almost; ~ förestående impending, imminent; vara
~ att be on the point of (falla falling), AE. äv. be
near to (+ inf.); ~ skjuter ingen hare a miss is as
good as a mile; ~ inpå near at hand; affären ligger
~ till för oss the shop is handy for us
2 när|a v2 nourish, feed (äv. bildl.); (hysa) cher-
ish, entertain; ~ en orm vid sin barm nourish a
viper in one's bosom; ett länge -t hopp a long-
-cherished hope; en länge -d misstanke a long-

boured suspicion
närande a4 nourishing; nutritious, nutritive
när|apå almost, pretty near[ly]; (så gott som)
practically **-belägen** (situated etc.) near (close)
by (at hand); adjacent, neighbouring; i sht AE.
nearby **-besläktad** closely related (akin) (med
to) **-bild** close-up [picture] **-butik** neighbourhood shop (AE. store) **-demokrati** grassroots
democracy **-gränsande** a4 adjacent, adjoining,
neighbouring **-gången** a3 intrusive; forward;
(taktlös) indiscreet; (om fråga o.d.) inquisitive;
AE. sl. fresh **-helst** whenever **-het** nearness;
(grannskap) neighbourhood, vicinity; i ~en av
(äv.) near [to]; här i ~en near (round about) here
närig a1 (snål) greedy, stingy; ('om sig') thrifty
-het greediness etc.
näring 1 (föda) nourishment (äv. bildl.); eg. äv.
nutriment; bildl. äv. fuel (åt to); ge ~ åt give (afford) nourishment to, bildl. add fuel to; ge ny ~
åt (bildl.) give new life to **2** (näringsfång industry; handel och ~ar commerce and industry
närings|behov nutritional requirement **-fattig**
of low food value; (om jord) poor **-frihet** freedom of (liberty to pursue a) trade **-frihetsom-
budsman** Competition Ombudsman **-fysio-
logi** nutritional physiology **-fång** s7, se yrke
-gren [branch of] business (industry) **-idkare**
tradesman, industrialist **-kedja** food chain **-liv**
economic (industrial) life; trade and industry
-lära nutrition **-lösning** fysiol. nutrient solution; (för bakterieodling) culture medium **-me-
del** food[stuff] **-politik** economic policy **-rik**
nutritious, of high food value **-riktig** nourishing;
of nutritional value **-ställe** restaurant; refreshment rooms (pl), eating house **-tillförsel** nutrient input (supply) **-utskott** ~et [the Swedish
parliamentary] standing committee on industry
and commerce **-värde** nutritive (food) value
-ämne nutritive (nutritious) substance
när|kamp s3, sport. infighting **-köp** se närbutik
-liggande a4, bildl. close at hand, kindred; ett ~
problem a kindred (closely allied) problem; mera
~ more immediate
närma bring (draw, push) near[er], approach; ~
sig approach, draw near[er] [to ...]; ~ sig sitt fär-
digställande near completion; klockan ~r sig 10 it
is getting on towards 10 o'clock; slutet ~de sig the
end was approaching, it was drawing near the end
närmande s6 approach, advance; renewal of
friendly relations; polit. etc. rapprochement;
otillbörliga ~n [improper] advances
närmare komp. t. nära **I** a nearer, closer; (om
väg) shorter; (ytterligare) further (detaljer particulars) **II** adv nearer, closer, more closely; in
[greater] detail; gå ~ in på frågan go into the
question in detail; bli ~ bekant med ngn become
better acquainted with s.b., get to know s.b. better; förklara ~ explain in detail, give further particulars; studera ~ examine in detail; ta ~ reda på
find out more about; jag skall tänka ~ på saken I
shall think the matter over more carefully; eller,
~ bestämt or, more exactly **III** prep nearer [to],
closer to; (nästan) nearly, close [up]on **närmast**
superl. t. nära **I** a nearest (äv. bildl.); (omedelbar)
immediate; (om vän e.d.) closest, most intimate;
(~ i ordningen) next; ~e anhörig[a] next of kin,

nearest relative[s]; *mina ~e* those nearest and dearest to me, my people, *vard.* my folks; *mina ~e planer* my plans for the immediate future; *de ~e dagarna* the next few days; *inom den ~e framtiden* in the immediate future; *var och en är sig själv ~* every man for himself; *i det ~e* [very] nearly, almost, practically, as good as **II** *adv* nearest (closest) [to]; *bildl.* most closely (intimately); immediately; next; (*främst*) in the first place; (*huvudsakligast*) principally; *de ~ sörjande* the principal (chief) mourners; *~ föregående* the immediately preceeding year; *~ på grund av* mainly because (owing to); *han ser ~ ut som en...* he looks more like a[n] ... than anything **III** *prep* nearest (next) [to]

närmevärde approximate value

närsalt nutritive salt

när|sluta *-slöt -slutit* enclose, attach **-strid** close combat, hand-to-hand fighting **-stående** *a4* close, near; (*-besläktad*) kindred; *~ företag* associated company, *AE.* affiliated corporation; *i regeringen ~ kretsar* in circles close to the Government **-synt** [-y:-] *a1* short-sighted; *med.* myopic **-synthet** short-sightedness; *med.* myopia **-vara** *-var -varit* be present (*vid* at); *~ vid* (*äv.*) attend **-varande** *a4* present (*vid* at); *de ~* those present; *för ~* for the present (time being), at present, *AE. äv.* presently **-varo** *s9* presence; (*vid möte o.d. äv.*) attendance; *i ~ av* in the presence of, before

näs *s7* (*landremsa*) isthmus, neck of land; (*landtunga*) point, headland; *se äv. udde*

näs|a *s1* nose; *peta* [*sig i*] *~n* pick one's nose; *tala i* (*genom*) *~n* talk through the nose, have a nasal twang; *dra ngn vid ~n* lead s.b. by the nose, take s.b. in; *det gick hans ~ förbi* it passed him by; *ha ~ för* have a flair for; *han låter ingen sätta sig på ~n på sig* he lets no one sit on him; *lägga ~n i vädret* (*dö*) turn up one's toes [to the daisies]; *mitt för ~ på ngn* right in front of a p.'s nose; *räcka lång ~ åt* cock a snook at, thumb one's nose at; *inte se längre än ~n räcker* not see further than the end of one's nose; *ha skinn på ~n* have a will (mind) of one's own; *stå där med lång ~* be left pulling a long face; *stå på ~n* take a header, come a cropper; *sätta ~n i vädret* toss one's head, be stuck-up (cocky) **-ben** nasal bone **-blod** nose-bleeding; *blöda ~* have an attack of nose-bleeding **-borre** [-å-] *s2* nostril **-bränna** *s1* (*tillrättavisning*) rebuke; (*minnesbeta*) lesson **-duk** handkerchief **-håla** nasal cavity **-knäpp** *s2, vard.* rebuke, snub, reprimand **-pärla** *se näbbgädda 2* **-rot** root of the nose **-rygg** bridge of the nose

nässel|djur cnidarian **-feber** nettle rash, hives, *fack.* urticaria **-fjäril** tortoiseshell [butterfly] **-kål** *kokk.* nettle soup (broth) **-utslag** nettle rash

nässla *s1* nettle

nässpets *se nästipp*

näst *superl. t. nära, adv* next (*efter, intill* to); *den ~ bästa* the second (next) best; *den ~ sista* the last but one; *~ äldste sonen* the second son

1 nästa I *s1* neighbour; *kärleken till ~n* love for one's neighbour **II** *a, superl.* next; (*påföljande*) the next, (*påföljande gång*) the next time; *den 1:a ~ månad* (*hand. äv.*) on the first prox.

2 nästa *v1, sömn.* stitch

nästan almost; *AE. äv.* (*i sht om tid*) just on; (*ej långt ifrån*) nearly; (*starkare*) all but; *~ aldrig* (*ingen*) hardly ever (anybody); *jag tror* (*tycker*) *~ att* I rather (almost) think that

näste *s6* nest; *bildl. äv.* den

näst|följande next; the immediate following **-intill I** *prep* next to **II** *adv* nearest (next) to this (it *etc.*)

nästipp tip of the nose

nästkommande *a4* next; (*nästa månad*) proximo (*förk.* prox.); *~ maj* in May next; *under ~ år* (*äv.*) during the coming year

nästla *~ sig in, se innästla*

näs|täppa *jag har ~* my nose is stopped up **-vinge** wing of the nose (nostril) **-vis** *a1* impertinent, cheeky; pert, saucy **-vishet** impertinence, cheekiness *etc.*

nät *s7* net; (*spindel- äv.*) web; (*-verk*) network (*äv. bildl.*); *tel. o.d. äv.* system **-ansluten** *a5, tel. o.d.* connected to the main system **-boll** *tennis. o.d.* net **-hinna** *anat.* retina **-hinneinflammation** inflammation of the retina **-kasse** string bag **-mage** reticulum (*pl* reticula) **-maska** [net] mesh **-planering** network planning **-spänning** mains voltage

nätt *I a1* **1** pretty; dainty; (*prydlig*) neat; *en ~ summa* a tidy (nice little) sum **2** (*knapp*) scanty, sparing **II** *adv* **1** prettily *etc.* **2** scantily *etc.*; *~ och jämnt* barely, only just **-upp** ['nätt-] just [about] **nät|verk** network; netting **-vinge** *zool.* neuropteran

näva *s1* cranesbill

näv|e *s2* fist; (*handfull*) fistful (handful) [of ...]; *slå ~n i bordet* (*bildl.*) put one's foot down; *spotta i -arna* spit on one's hands, buckle down to work

näver ['nä:-] *s2* birch bark

näv|kamp fisticuffs (*pl*) **-rätt** *hist.* fist (club) law; (*våld*) jungle law

nöd *s3* distress; trouble; (*brist*) need, want; (*trångmål*) straits (*pl*); *fartyg i ~* vessel in distress; *lida ~* be in need; *den tysta ~en* uncomplaining poverty; *~en har ingen lag* necessity knows no law; *~en är uppfinningarnas moder* necessity is the mother of invention; *när ~en är störst är hjälpen närmast* it is always darkest before dawn; *i ~en prövas vännen* a friend in need is a friend indeed; *det går ingen ~ på honom* he's well provided for; *vara av ~en* be needed (necessary); *med knapp ~* only just; *till ~s* if need be, at a pinch **-bedd** *a5, vara ~* have to be pressed **-bostad** emergency housing (flat *etc.*) **-broms** emergency brake; *dra i ~en* pull the communication cord

nödd *a5, vara ~ och tvungen* be forced [and compelled]

nöd|dop emergency baptism **-fall** *i ~* in case of need (necessity), in an emergency, (*friare*) if necessary **-fallsåtgärd** emergency measure; makeshift **-flagg** distress signal

nödga constrain; (*tvinga*) force, compel; (*truga*) press, urge **nödgas** *v1, dep* be compelled (forced) to

nöd|hamn port (harbour) of refuge **-hjälpsarbete** relief work

nödig *a1* (*nödvändig*) necessary; (*erforderlig*)

needful, requisite, required
nöd|landa forceland, be forced down **-land-ning** forced (emergency) landing **-lidande** a4 necessitous; (utarmad) needy, destitute **-läge** distress, critical position; emergency; extremity **-lögn** white lie **-lösning** makeshift (temporary) solution **-mynt** emergency coin **-raket** distress rocket **-rim** halting (makeshift) rhyme **-rop** cry (call) of distress (for help) **-saka** se nödga; bli (vara) ~d att be obliged (compelled, forced) to; se sig ~d att find o.s. compelled to **-signal** distress signal; S.O.S.; radiotel. mayday **-slakt** emergency slaughter **-ställd** a5 distressed; in distress **-tid** i ~er in times of dearth (distress, scarcity) **-torft** [-å-] s3, livets ~ the bare necessities of life **-torftig** scanty, meagre **-tvungen** a5 enforced; compulsory **-tvång** av ~ out of necessity **-utgång** emergency exit
nödvändig [ˣnö:d-, -ˈvänn-] a1 necessary **-göra** necessitate, make (render) necessary **-het** necessity; tvingande ~ imperative (urgent) necessity; med ~ (-vändigt) of necessity **-hetsartikel** necessity, necessary [of life] **-tvis** necessarily; of necessity; absolutely; måste ~ leda till is (are) bound to lead to; han ville ~ komma he would come, he insisted on coming
nöd|värn self-defence **-år** year of famine
nöj|a [ˣnöjja] v2, rfl be satisfied (content), content o.s.; ~ sig med att (inskränka sig t. att, äv.) restrict (confine) o.s. to **-aktig** a1 satisfactory **-aktigt** adv, ~ besvara give a satisfactory answer **-aktighet** satisfactoriness
nöjd a1 satisfied (äv. mätt); (för-) content[ed]; (belåten) pleased; ~ med litet satisfied with a little, easily satisfied; vara ~ på ngt (ha fått nog av ngt) have had enough of s.th.
nöje [ˣnöjje] s6 pleasure; (starkare) delight; (förströelse) amusement, entertainment; (tidsfördriv) diversion, pastime; ha ~ av, finna ~ i derive pleasure from, find (take) pleasure in, enjoy; för sitt höga ~s skull for one's own sweet pleasure, just for fun; vi har ~t att meddela we have the pleasure of informing you; det skall bli mig ett sant ~ att I shall be delighted to; jag skall med ~ göra det (äv.) I shall be glad to do it, I'll do it gladly; du får det med ~ (äv.) you are very welcome to it; mycket ~! have a good time!, enjoy yourself!; offentliga ~n public amusements
nöjes|branch entertainment industry **-establissemang** pleasure ground, amusement park **-fält** fair (pleasure) ground; AE. äv. carnival **-industri** entertainment industry **-liv** entertainments (pl) life of pleasure **-lysten** fond of amusement **-lystnad** fondness for (love of) amusement **-resa** pleasure trip **-skatt** entertainment tax
nöjsam a1, se rolig
nöp imperf. av nypa
nös imperf. av nysa
1 nöt -en nötter, bot. nut; en hård ~ att knäcka (bildl.) a hard nut to crack, a poser
2 nöt s7 **1** se nötkreatur **2** bildl. ass, blockhead; ditt ~! you silly ass (etc.)!
nöta v3 (slita) wear; (gnida) rub; ~ hål på wear through; ~ skolbänken grind away at one's classroom desk; tyget tål att ~ på the material will

wear [well] (will stand [hard] wear); du får ~ på dina gamla kläder you must wear out your old clothes [first]; ~ ut wear out; ~s get worn (rubbed)
nötboskap [neat] cattle (pl)
nöt|brun nutbrown, hazel **-frukt** nut [fruit]
nöthår cowhair
nöt|knäckare, -knäppare [[a] pair of] nutcrackers (pl)
nötkreatur pl cattle; sju ~ seven head of cattle
nöt|kråka zool. nutcracker **-kärna** kernel of a nut
nötkött beef
nötning [ˣnö:t-] wear, use; bildl. wear and tear
nöt|skal nutshell (äv. bildl.); (om båt äv.) cockleshell **-skrika** s1, zool. jay
nött a1 worn (i at); (om kläder äv.) the worse for wear, threadbare, shiny; ~a fraser hackneyed phrases
nötväcka s1, zool. nuthatch

O

o

o interj oh!; ~ ve! alas!
oaktat I prep notwithstanding; jfr trots II; det[ta] ~ for all that, all the same **II** konj [al]though, even though
o|aktsam careless (med about) **-aktsamhet** carelessness, negligence **-amerikansk** ~ verksamhet un-American activities (pl) **-anad** a5 unsuspected; unimagined; ~e möjligheter undreamed-of (undreamt-of) possibilities **-angenäm** unpleasant, disagreeable **-angripbar** [-i:p-] a1 **-angriplig** [-i:p-] a1 unassailable (äv. bildl.); (om vittnesbörd e.d.) unimpeachable; ~ bevisföring unexceptionable argumentation **-anmäld** [-ä:-] a5 unannounced **-anmärkt** a4 unchallenged; låta ngt passera ~ let s.th. pass without comment **-ansenlig** [-e:n-] insignificant; (ringa) humble; (om t.ex. lön) meagre, modest; (enkel) plain (utseende looks); (ej iögonenfallande) inconspicuous **-ansenlighet** insignificance; humbleness etc. **-anständig** indecent; (anstötlig) shocking; (slipprig) obscene; (otillbörlig) disgraceful, shameful **-anständighet** indecency; impropriety; obscenity; shockingness etc.; (i ord) indecent remark, obscenity **-ansvarig** irresponsible **-antagbar** a5, **-antaglig** a5 unacceptable, that cannot be accepted **-antastlig** a1 unassailable, inviolable; jur. unimpeachable **-anträffbar** unavailable; untraceable; not in (at home); engaged **-använd** a5 unused; (om plagg äv.) unworn; unemployed; (om kapital) idle **-användbar** unusable, useless,

of no use, unfit for use; *vard.* no good **o|aptitlig** unappetizing (*äv. bildl.*); *i sht bildl.* unsavoury; (*otäck*) disgusting **-art** bad habit **-artig** impolite, uncivil, discourteous **-artighet** impoliteness, incivility; *en* ~ a discourtesy **-artikulerad** *a5* inarticulate **oas** *s3* oasis (*pl* oases) **o|avbruten** *a5* uninterrupted; unbroken (*tystnad* silence); continuous (*verksamhet* activity); (*oupphörlig*) incessant **-avgjord** undecided; unsettled; *spel., sport.* drawn; *-avgjort lopp* dead heat; ~ *match* draw; *ärendet lämnades -avgjort* the matter was left unsettled (pending) **-avgjort** *adv, sluta* ~ end in a draw; *spela* ~ draw, tie **-avhängig** independent; (*autonom*) autonomous, self-governing **-avhängighet** independence; autonomy, self-government **-avhängighetsförklaring** declaration of independence **-avkortad** [-årt-] *a5* (*om text*) unabridged, unabbreviated; (*om t.ex. lön*) uncurtailed **-avlåtlig** [-å:-] *a1* incessant, unceasing, continuous; (*ständig*) constant **-avlönad** unpaid, unsalaried; *äv.* honorary **-avsedd** unintended; *-avsett att* irrespective of (apart from) the fact that; *-avsett hur* (*äv.*) no matter how **-avsiktlig** unintentional, unintended **-avslutad** unfinished, uncompleted; (*om räkenskaper*) not closed **-avsättbar** *a5* irremovable **-avvislig** [-i:s-] *al* not to be rejected (refused), unrejectable; imperative; *ett ~t krav* a claim that cannot be refused, an imperative demand **-avvänt** *adv* unremittingly; ~ *betrakta* watch intently **o|balans** imbalance, disequilibrium **-balanserad** unbalanced; *äv. bildl.* ill-balanced **-banad** *a5* untrodden; unbeaten; pathless; *~e vägar* unbeaten tracks **-barmhärtig** unmerciful, uncharitable; merciless **-barmhärtighet** mercilessness *etc.* **obduc|ent** [åbdu'sent] postmortem examiner **-era** perform (make) a postmortem [examination] (*ngn* on s.b.) **-ering** [-'se:-] *se obduktion* **obduktion** [-k'ʃɔ:n] *s3* postmortem [examination], autopsy **o|beaktad** *a5* unnoticed; *lämna* ~ leave unheeded, disregard, (*genom förbiseende*) overlook **-bearbetad** *a5* (*om råvara*) raw, crude; (*om metall*) unwrought; (*i maskin*) rough, unmachined **-bebodd** *a5* uninhabited; unoccupied; (*om hus*) untenanted; *~a trakter* uninhabited regions **obedd** *a5* unasked; uninvited **o|befintlig** nonexistent; that does not exist; missing **-befläckad** *a5* immaculate; (*om namn, ära o.d.*) unsullied, stainless, spotless **-befogad** unwarranted, unjustified (*anmärkning* remark) **-befolkad** [-å-] *a5* uninhabited **-befäst** unfortified; (*om stad äv.*) open; *bildl.* unstable **-begagnad** unused, unemployed; (*i reserv*) spare **-begriplig** incomprehensible; (*dunkel*) unintelligible; (*ofattlig*) inconceivable **-begriplighet** incomprehensibility *etc.* **-begränsad** unlimited; boundless (*förtroende* confidence); *jfr gränslös* **-begåvad** untalented; unintelligent **-behag** discomfort, uneasiness; (*otrevlighet*) annoyance; ('*trassel*') trouble; *få* ~ *av* have trouble from; *känna* [*ett visst*] ~ feel [slightly] ill at ease **-be-**

haglig disagreeable, unpleasant (*för* to; *mot* towards, to); *en* ~ *situation* (*äv.*) an awkward situation **-behandlad** untreated **-behindrat** *adv* smoothly, easily; unimpededly; (*fritt*) freely; *tala engelska* ~ speak English fluently **-behärskad** uncontrolled; lacking in self-control **-behörig** (*inkompetent*) incompetent; (*ej behörig, oberättigad*) unauthorized; *~a äga ej tillträde* no admittance [except on business]; (*på enskilt område*) trespassers will be prosecuted, no trespassing **-behövlig** unnecessary; not necessary (required) **-bekant I** *a* (*okänd*) unknown (*för* to); (*med ngn, ngt*) unacquainted (*med* with); (*okunnig* [*om*]) ignorant (*med* of); *det torde inte vara Er* ~ *att* you will be aware that **II** *s, pl -bekanta, mat., ekvation med flera ~a* equation with several unknowns **-bekräftad** *a5* unconfirmed; unverified **-bekväm** uncomfortable; (*ej passande*) inconvenient; unsocial (*arbetstid* working hours *pl*); (*besvärlig*) awkward **-bekymrad** unconcerned (*om, för* about, as to); heedless (*om* of) **-belevad** unmannerly, ill-mannered **obeljsk** *s3* obelisk **o|belyst** [-y:-] *a4* unlighted, unlit, not lit up **-belönad** *a5* unrewarded; unremunerated **-bemannad** *a5* unmanned **-bemedlad** without means **-bemärkt I** *a4* unobserved, unnoticed; (*anspråkslös*) humble **II** *adv* in obscurity **-bemärkthet** obscurity; *leva i* ~ live in seclusion (obscurity) **-benägen** disinclined (*för* for); unwilling, reluctant **-benägenhet** disinclination; unwillingness, reluctance **-benämnd** *a5* (*om tal*) indenominate **-beprövad** untried **-beroende I** *s6* independence **II** *a4* independent (*av* of) **-beräknelig** [-ä:-] *a1* incalculable; unpredictable; (*nyckfull*) fickle, capricious; (*ofantlig*) immense **-beräknelighet** [-ä:-] incalculability; fickleness *etc.* **-berättigad** unentitled (*till* to); (*orättvis*) unjustified, unwarranted **-berörd** [-ö:-] *a1* untouched; (*opåverkad*) unaffected; (*okänslig*) impassive, unconcerned; (*likgiltig*) indifferent **-berördhet** [-ö:-] unconcern; indifference **o|besatt** unoccupied; (*ledig*) vacant **-besedd** *a5* unseen, unexamined; uninspected **-besegrad** [-se:-] *a5* unconquered; *sport.* undefeated, unbeaten **-beskrivlig** [-i:v-] *a1* indescribable; (*outsäglig*) inexpressible **-beskuren** *a5* uncut; *bildl.* unabridged (*upplaga* edition) **-beslutsam** irresolute; undecided (*om* about); *vara* ~ (*äv.*) hesitate, waver **-beslutsamhet** irresolution; indecision; hesitation **-beslöjad** [-öjj-] *a5* unveiled; (*ohöljd*) undisguised **-besmittad** *a5* undefiled, uncontaminated, unsullied **-besticklig** incorruptible, unbribable **-bestridd** *a5* uncontested, undisputed; (*om t.ex. välde*) unchallenged **-bestridlig** [-i:d-] *al* indisputable; incontestable; (*otvivelaktig*) undoubted; (*oneklig*) undeniable **-bestridligen** [-i:d-] indisputably; unquestionably **-bestyrkt** *a4* unverified; (*om avskrift*) unattested **-beständ** insolvency; *komma på* ~ become insolvent **-beställbar** *al* undeliverable (*försändelse* item of mail) **-bestämbar** indeterminable; (*om känsla o.d.*) indefinable **-bestämd** undecided; (*om antal, tid o.d.*) indefinite; (*om känsla*) undefined; (*vag*) vague; (*oviss*) uncertain; (*otydlig*) ill-defined; *~a* *artikeln* the indefinite article; *uppskjuta på* ~ *tid* put off indefinitely **-beständig** inconstant; *(växlande)* changeable; *(ovaraktig)* impermanent, transient; *kem.* unstable **-besudlad** *se obefläckad* **-besvarad** *a5* unanswered; unreturned; *(om kärlek äv.)* unrequited **-besvärad** untroubled, undisturbed; *(otvungen)* unconstrained, [free and] easy

o|**betagen** *det är honom obetaget att* he is free (welcome, at liberty) to **-betalbar** *(komisk)* priceless, irresistible **-betald** [-a:-] *a5* unpaid; unsettled; *(om växel)* dishonoured **-betingad** *a5* unconditional; *(oinskränkt)* unrestricted, absolute; *(om förtroende, lydnad o.d.)* implicit **-betingat** unconditionally *etc.*; *(utan all fråga)* unquestionably **-betonad** unstressed, unaccented **-betvinglig** *al (okuvlig)* unsubduable; *(oövervinnelig)* invincible, inconquerable; *(oemotståndlig)* irresistible **-betydlig** insignificant; inconsiderable; *(oviktig)* unimportant; *(ringa)* slight **-betydlighet** insignificance; triviality; *(med pl)* insignificant *(etc.)* **-betydligt** *adv* slightly; a little **-betäckt** *a4* uncovered, bare **-betänksam** thoughtless; *(mot andra)* inconsiderate; *(förhastad)* rash; *(oklok)* imprudent, unadvised, ill-advised **-bevakad** unguarded; unattended; ~ *järnvägsövergång* ungated [railway] level crossing; *i ett -bevakat ögonblick* in an unguarded moment; *en* ~ *fordran* an unproved claim **-bevandrad** unfamiliar *(i* with); unversed *(i* in) **-beveklig** [-e:k-] *al* implacable, inexorable; *(om lag, logik)* inflexible **-bevittnad** *a5* unwitnessed; *(om avskrift e.d.)* unattested **-bevuxen** bare **-beväpnad** unarmed; *med -beväpnat öga* with the naked eye

o|**bildad** uneducated; *(obelevad)* rude, ill-bred **-bildbar** uneducable **-billig** *(oskälig)* unreasonable; *(orättvis)* unfair

objekt [åb'jekt] *s7* object **objektiv I** [-'ti:v] *s7, fys.* objective; *opt.* lens **II** [-'åbb-, -'ti:v] *al* objective; *(saklig)* factual **objektivism** objectivism **objektivitet** objectivity; detachment **objektsform** objective form

o|**bjuden** *a5* uninvited; *(obedd)* unasked; ~ *gäst (neds.)* intruder, gate-crasher **-blandad** unmixed, unmingled; *(ogrumlad)* unalloyed *(lycka* happiness)

oblat [sacramental] wafer **-tallrik** paten

o|**blekt** [-e:-] *a4* unbleached **-blid** unpropitious, unfavourable; *se med* ~*a ögon* regard with disapproval; *ett oblitt öde* a harsh (an adverse) fate **-blidkelig** *al* implacable, inexorable; unappeasable

obligat *a4* obbligato

obliga|tion [å-] bond **-tionslån** bond loan **obligatorisk** [-'to:-] *a5* compulsory; *(oumbärlig)* indispensable

o|**blodig** bloodless *(revolution* revolution); unbloody *(offer* sacrifice) **-blyg** unblushing, unabashed; *(skamlös)* shameless; *(fräck)* barefaced

oboe [ˣå:båe, å'bå:] *s5* oboe **-spelare** oboist

obol [å'bå:l] *s3* obol

o|**borstad** *a5* unbrushed; *(om sko)* unpolished; *(smutsig)* dirty; *(ohyfsad)* rough, rude, uncouth **-botfärdig** impenitent, unrepentant; *de* ~*as*

förhinder cooked-up excuses **-botlig** [-ɒ:t-] *al* incurable; *(om skada)* irreparable; *(ohjälplig)* incorrigible *(ungkarl* bachelor) **-botligt** [-ɒ:t-] *adv, en* ~ *sjuk* an incurable **-brottslig** unswerving *(trohet* loyalty); *(osviklig)* strict *(neutralitet* neutrality) **-brukad** *a5, se oförbrukad*; *(om jord)* uncultivated, untilled **-brukbar** unfit for use, useless **-bruklig** *al* obsolete **-bruten** unbroken, intact; *(oöppnad)* unopened; ~ *mark (äv. bildl.)* unbroken (virgin) ground; *-brutna krafter* unimpaired force

obs [åpps] *[förk. för observera] s7* [please] note, N.B. *(förk. för* nota bene)

obscen [åb'se:n, -'ʃe:n] *al* obscene **obscenitet** *s3* obscenity

observandum [åbserˣvann-] *s8* thing to be observed; *ett* ~ *(äv.)* a pointer **observans** [-'vans, -'vaŋs] *s3* observance; *(av regler)* [the] keeping *(av* of) **observation** observation **observations|förmåga** power of observation **-klass** separate class for pupils with behavioural problems **-punkt** observation spot **observator** [-ˣa:tår] *s3 (iakttagare)* observer; *(vid observatorium)* astronomer **observatorium** [-ˣto:-, -'to:-] *s4* observatory **observatör** observer **observera** observe, notice *(iakttaga äv.)* watch; *det bör* ~*s att* it should be noted that **observerbar** [-ˣve:r-] observable

obskurant obscurant[ist]

obskyr [å-] *al* obscure; *('skum')* dubious, shady **obsolet** [å-å-] *a4* obsolete

obstetr|ik [å-] *s3* obstetrics *(pl, behandlas som sg)* obstetrics **-iker** [-'te:-] obstetrician

obstinat [å-] *a4* obstinate, stubborn

obstru|ktion [-k'ʃɒ:n] obstruction *(mot* to); *AE. parl.* filibustering **-era** obstruct

o|**bunden** *eg.* unchained; *(om bok)* unbound; *(om pers.)* unfettered, unbound, free; *i* ~ *form* in prose **-bygd** undeveloped (wild) country (district); wilderness **-bäddad** *a5* unmade **-bändig** *al (svårhanterlig)* intractable; *(svår att tygla)* irrepressible; *(våldsam)* unruly **-böjlig** inflexible; *språkv.* indeclinable; *(fast)* rigid; *(orubblig)* uncompromising **-bönhörlig** [-ö:-ö:-] *al* implacable, inexorable **-bönhörligen** [-ö:-ö:-] implacably *etc.*; *(oåterkalleligen)* irrevocably

occidenten [åksi'denn-] *best. form* the Occident **ocean** *s3* ocean; *bildl. vanl.* sea **-fart** ocean trade; transoceanic traffic **-gående** *a4* ocean-going

Oceanien [-'a:-] *n* Oceania

oceano|graf *s3* oceanographer **-grafi** *s3* oceanography

oceanångare ocean liner

ocensurerad *a5* uncensored

och [åkk, *vard. å*] and; ~ *dylikt* and the like; ~ *så vidare* and so on, etc.; *ligga (sitta, stå)* ~ *läsa* lie (sit, stand) reading; *klockan tickar* ~ *tickar (äv.)* the clock keeps on ticking; *två* ~ *två* two by two; *5 pund per vecka* ~ *person* 5 pounds per week per person; *försök* ~ *låt bli att* try not to

ociviliserad *a5* uncivilized

ock [åkk] *se också, även*

ocker [ˣåkk-] *s7* usury; profiteering; *bedriva* ~ practise usury **-hyra** exorbitant rent, rack-rent **-pris** exorbitant (extortionate) price **-ränta** ex-

O

tortionate interest
1 ockra [ˣåkk-] *v1* practise usury; ~ *på ngns godhet* trade upon a p.'s goodwill
2 ockra [ˣåkk-] *s1* ochre
ockra|brun ochreous **-gul** ochre yellow
ockrare [ˣåkk-] usurer, moneylender; profiteer
också [ˈåkk-] also; as well, too; *(till och med)* even; *eller* ~ or else; *om* ~ even though; *och det gjorde (betonat) jag* ~ and so I did; *och det gjorde jag (betonat)* ~ and so did I; *det var* ~ *en fråga!* that's quite a question!, what a question!; *men så är de* ~ *vackra* but then they are beautiful
ockult [åˈkult] *a1* occult **-ism** occultism
ockupant [å-] occupier **ockupation** occupation
ockupations|armé army of occupation **-makt** occupying power **-trupper** *pl* occupation troops
ockupera [å-] occupy
o.d. *(förk för och dylikt)* and the like, and suchlike
odalbonde yeoman
odaljsk *s3* odalisque
odaterad *a5* undated
odds [å-] *s7* odds *(pl)*; ~*en stod tio mot ett* the odds were ten to one; *ha* ~*en emot sig* have the cards stacked against one
ode *s6* ode
o|deciderad undecided, wavering **-definierbar** indefinable, undefinable; *(om t.ex. charm)* subtle **-dekorerad** [-å-] *a5* undecorated; plain **-delad** undivided *(äv. bildl.)*; *(hel)* whole, entire; *(enhällig)* universal, unanimous; *-delat nöje* unalloyed pleasure; *väcka* ~ *beundran* arouse universal admiration; ~ *uppmärksamhet* undivided attention **-delbar** indivisible **-demokratisk** undemocratic
Oden [ˈoː-] *myt.* Woden
o|diplomatisk undiplomatic **-disciplinerad** [-isi-] *a5* undisciplined **-diskutabel** *a2*, **-disputabel** *a2* indisputable
odiös *a1* invidious
odjur monster; beast
odl|a [ˣoːd-] cultivate *(äv. bildl.)*; *(blommor, grönsaker)* grow; *AE. äv.* raise; *(jorden äv.)* till; ~ *sin själ* cultivate (improve) one's mind; ~ *en bekantskap* cultivate (foster) an aquaintanceship **-are** cultivator, grower; *(kaffe- o.d.)* planter **-ing** cultivation; culture; *(kaffe- o.d.)* plantation **-ingsbar** *a1* cultivable; *(om jord)* arable
odogmatisk undogmatic[al]
odon [ˣoː:dån] *s7* bog whortleberry
odonto|log [ådåntåˈlåːg] odontologist **-logj** *s3* odontology; ~*e kandidat* Bachelor of Dental Surgery; ~*e studerande* dental surgery student **-logisk** [-ˈlåː-] *a5* odontological
o|dramatisk undramatic **-drickbar** undrinkable **-dryg** uneconomical **-dräglig** unbearable; unsufferable, intolerable; *(tråkig)* boring; *en* ~ *människa (äv.)* an awful bore **-duglig** *(om pers.)* incompetent, inefficient, unqualified, unfit *(till* for), incapable *(till* of); *(om sak)* useless, of no use, worthless **-dugling** [-u:-] good-for-nothing, incompetent **-dygd** mischief; naughtiness **-dygdig** naughty; mischievous **-dygdspåse** *en riktig* ~ a real little mischief (imp)
o.dyl. *se o.d.*

odyssé *s3* Odyssey **Odysseus** [oˈdyssevs] Ulysses
o|dåga *s1* good-for-nothing, waster **-dödlig** immortal; *(oförgätlig)* imperishable *(ära* glory), deathless **-dödliggöra** immortalize **-dödlighet** immortality **-döpt** [-öː-] *a4* unchristened
odör [bad, nasty] smell
odört [ˣoː:d-] [poison] hemlock
o|eftergivlig [-ji:v-] *a1* irremissable *(krav* demand); indispensable, imperative, absolute *(villkor* condition) **-efterhärmlig** inimitable **-efterrättlig** *a1* (*oförbätterlig*) incorrigible; *(oresonlig)* unreasonable; *(olidlig)* insufferable
o|egennytta disinterestedness; altruism **-egennyttig** disinterested, altruistic **-egentlig** *(oriktig)* improper; *(bildlig)* figurative *(betydelse* sense); ~*t bråk (mat.)* improper fraction **-egentlighet** [-je-] impropriety; ~*er (i bokföring)* irregularities, *(förskingring)* embezzlement *(sg)* **-ekonomisk** uneconomic[al]; *(om pers. äv.)* unthrifty **-elastisk** inelastic **-eldad** *a5* unheated **-emballerad** *a5* unpacked
oemot|sagd *a5* uncontradicted; *(obestridd)* unchallenged **-ståndlig** *a1* irresistible **-säglig** [-äː-] *a1* irrefutable, incontestable **-taglig** [-a:-] unsusceptible, inaccessible *(för* to); ~ *för (äv.)* immune to, *(okänslig)* impervious to **-taglighet** insusceptibility; immunity
oengelsk un-English
o|enhetlig nonuniform; *(oregelbunden äv.)* irregular; *(friare)* heterogeneous **-enig** disunited; *se äv. oense* **-enighet** disagreement; dissension; discord **-ense** *vara* ~ *med* disagree with, be at variance with
o|erfaren inexperienced *(i* in); *(omogen)* callow, green **-erfarenhet** inexperience *(i* in, of) **-erhörd** [-öː-] *a1* (*exempellös*) unprecedented; *(enorm)* tremendous, enormous **-ersättlig** irreplaceable; irreparable *(skada* damage); irretrievable *(förlust* loss)
o|estetisk unaesthetic **-etisk** unethical
o|fantlig [-ˈfant-] *a1* enormous, immense, tremendous; huge: *(vidsträckt)* vast **-farbar** untrafficable, impassable; impracticable **-farlig** not dangerous, safe, involving no danger; harmless; *(oskadlig)* innocuous; *(om tumör e.d.)* benign **-fattbar** incomprehensible, unbelievable, inconceivable *(för* to) **-felbar** [-e:-] *a1* infallible; *(osviklig äv.)* unerring **-felbarhet** [-e:l-] infallibility
offensiv I [å-, -ˈiːv] *s3* offensive; *övergå till* ~*en* take the offensive **II** [ˈåff-, -ˈiːv] *a1* offensive; aggressive **-anda** aggressive spirit
offentlig [åˈfent-] *a1* public; *(officiell)* official; *det* ~*a livet* public life; ~ *hemlighet* open secret; ~*a myndigheter* public authorities; ~ *plats* public place; *den* ~*a sektorn* the public sector; ~*t uppträdande* public appearance **-göra** [-ˣfent-] announce; *(i tryck)* publish; *(förordning e.d.)* promulgate **-het** publicity; *(allmänhet)* [general] public; *framträda inför* ~*en* appear before the public **-hetsprincip** principle of public access to official records
offentlig *adv* publicly, in public
offer [ˈåff-] *s7* (*slakt- o. bildl.*) sacrifice; *(-gåva)* offering; *(-djur; byte, rov)* victim; *(i krig, olycks-*

händelse) victim, casualty; *falla* ~ *för* fall a victim to; *inte sky några* ~ shun no sacrifice **-altare** sacrificial altar **-djur** victim

offerera [å-] offer; *(lämna prisuppgift)* quote **offer|gåva** offering **-källa** holy well **-lamm** sacrificial lamb; *bildl. äv.* innocent victim

offert [å'färt] *s3* offer *(på* of, for); *(pris)* quotation *(på* for); *(anbud)* tender, *AE.* bid *(på* for); *inkomma med* ~ submit an offer; *lämna en* ~ make an offer

offer|vilja spirit of self-sacrifice **-villig** self-sacrificing

officer [å-] **-**[*e*]*n* -*are* officer *(i* in; *vid* of); *vakthavande* ~ officer of the guard; *värnpliktig* ~ conscript officer

officers|aspirant cadet, probationary officer **-grad** [officer's] rank **-kår** body of officers **-mäss** officers' mess; *sjö.* wardroom

offici|ant [å-] officiating clergyman; officiant **-ell** *al* official **-era** officiate

officin [å-] *s3 (tryckeri)* printing-office; *(i apotek)* dispensary

officiös [å-] *al* semiofficial

offra [å-] *(genom slakt)* sacrifice *(äv. bildl.*); *(bära fram offergåva)* offer [up]; *bildl. äv.* victimize; *(avstå från)* give up; ~ *livet för* give one's life for; ~ *pengar (tid) på* spend (waste) money (time) on; *inte* ~ *en tanke på* not give (pay) a thought to; ~ *åt fåfängan* pay tribute to vanity; ~ *sig* sacrifice o.s. *(för* for)

offset ['åff-] *s3* offset **-tryck** offset print[ing]

offside [åf'sajd] *s5 o. oböjl. a o. adv, sport.* offside

o|fin *(taktlös)* indelicate; *(ohyfsad)* ill-mannered, ill-bred; *(opassande)* indecorous; *(lumpen)* coarse **-finkänslig** tactless, indelicate **-fodrad** [-o:-] *a5* unlined **-fog** *s7* mischief; *göra* ~ do (be up to) mischief **-formlig** [-å-] formless, shapeless **-framkomlig** *(om väg)* impassable; impracticable *(äv. bildl.)* **-frankerad** *a5* unstamped, unpaid **-fred** *(krig)* war; *(osämja)* discord, dissension **-freda** molest **-fredstid** time of war[fare] **-fri** unfree; *(bunden)* fettered; *på* ~ *grund* on leasehold property **-frihet** lack of freedom **-frivillig** involuntary; *(oavsiktlig)* unintentional

ofrukt|bar infertile, barren; *bildl.* barren; sterile; *(om t.ex. försök, plan)* unfruitful **-barhet** infertility; barrenness *etc.* **-sam** barren, sterile **-samhet** barrenness, sterility

o|frånkomlig [-åm-] *al* inevitable, unavoidable; inescapable **-frälse I** *oböjligt s* commoner **II** *oböjligt a* untitled; *de* ~ *stånden* the commoner estates

ofta [å-] *al* often; *(upprepade gånger)* frequently; *en* ~ *återkommande* a frequent[ly recurring]; *så* ~ *jag ser* whenever I see; ~*st* in most cases, most often; *allt som* ~*st* every now and then

oftalmiatr|[k] [å-] *s3, se oftalmologi*

oftalmo|log ophthalmologist **-logi** *s3* ophthalmology **-skop** [-'å:p] *s7* ophthalmoscope

o|fullbordad [-o:-] *a5* unfinished, incomplete, uncompleted **-fullgången** abortive; *bildl.* immature **-fullkomlig** imperfect **-fullkomlighet** imperfection; ~*er (äv.)* shortcomings **-fullständig** incomplete; *(bristfällig)* defective; *(otillräcklig)* insufficient *(adress* address); imper-

fect *(kunskaper* knowledge) **-fullständighet** incompleteness; incompletion; imperfection

o|fyndig *(om bergart)* nonmetalliferous **-färd** [-ä:-] *s3* calamity; *(olycka)* misfortune; *(fördärv)* ruin; *bringa* ~ *över* bring down calamity (ruin) upon **-färdig** *(lytt)* crippled, disabled; *(halt)* lame; *(ej färdig)* unfinished **-färdstid** period of calamity; *i* ~*er* in times of stress and calamity **-färgad** *(om t.ex. glas)* uncoloured; *(om t.ex. tyg)* undyed; natural-coloured **-född** unborn

o|förarglig harmless, inoffensive **-förbehållsam** unreserved, frank; open **-förberedd** unprepared, unready **-förblommerad** unreserved; *(rättfram)* blunt; *(osminkad)* unvarnished **-förbränn[e]lig** *al, bildl.* inexhaustible; unquenchable **-förbätterlig** *al* incorrigible *(optimist* optimist); inveterate, confirmed *(ungkarl* bachelor) **-fördelaktig** disadvantageous, unfavourable; unprofitable *(investering* investment); *i en* ~ *dager* in an unflattering light; *säg inget* ~*t om honom!* don't run him down! **-fördragsam** intolerant *(mot* towards, to) **-fördragsamhet** intolerance **-fördröjligen** without delay, immediately **-fördärvad** unspoiled; *(om smak, moral o.d.)* undepraved, uncorrupted **-förenlig** incompatible, inconsistent *(med* with); irreconcilable *(åsikter* opinions)

oföretagsam unenterprising **-het** lack of enterprise (initiative)

o|förfalskad *a5 (äkta)* genuine, pure; unadulterated **-förfärad** *a5* undaunted, fearless **-förglömlig** *al* unforgettable; never-to-be-forgotten; *en för mig* ~ *... (äv.)* a[n] ... I shall never forget **-förgriplig** unassailable *(rättighet* right); *säga sin* ~*a mening* state one's definite opinion **-förgänglig** imperishable, unfading *(ära* glory); *(odödlig)* immortal **-förgätlig** [-jä:-] *al, se oförglömlig* **-förhappandes** accidentally, by chance; *(oförmodad)* unexpectedly **-förhindrad** *a5* at liberty *(att komma* to come), unprevented *(att komma* from coming) **-förklarlig** inexplicable, unexplainable; *av* ~ *anledning* for some unaccountable reason **-förkortad** [-å-] *a5, se oavkortad* **-förliknelig** [-i:k-] *al* incomparable; *(utan like)* matchless, unrivalled; *(enastående)* unique **-förlåtlig** unforgivable, inexcusable, unpardonable **-förmedlad** *a5* abrupt, sudden; unexpected **-förminskad** *a5* undiminished; unabated *(iver* eagerness) **-förmodad** *a5* unexpected; *(-förutsedd)* unforeseen; *det kom så -förmodat* it was so unexpected (sudden) **-förmåga** inability *(att* to); incapability *(att göra* to do); incompetence **-förmånlig** *se ofördelaktig* **-förmärkt I** *a4* unnoticed, unobserved; *(som sker i smyg)* stealthy **II** *adv (i smyg)* stealthily; *avlägsna sig* ~ depart unnoticed (unobserved), take French leave **-förmögen** incapable *(till* of; *att* of + *ing*-form); unable *(att göra* to do); ~ *till arbete* unable to work, unfit for work **-förneklig** [-e:-] *al* undeniable **-förnuftig** unreasonable, irrational; *(dåraktig)* foolish **-förnöjsam** hard to please (satisfy) **-förnöjsamhet** discontent[edness] **-förrätt** *s3* wrong, injury; *begå en* ~ *mot* do [an] injury to, wrong **-förrättat** *i uttr.: återvända med* ~ *ärende* return unsuccessful *(tomhänt:* empty-handed)

O

o|**försiktig** imprudent; incautious; (*obetänk-sam*) indiscreet; (*vårdslös*) careless -**försiktig-het** imprudence; incautiousness; indiscretion; carelessness -**förskräckt** *a4* undaunted, daunt-less, fearless, intrepid -**förskräckthet** un-dauntedness *etc.*; intrepidity -**förskuren** un-blended (*äv. i oförskuret skick*) -**förskylld** [-ʃ-] *a5* undeserved -**förskämd** [-ʃ-] *a1* insolent; im-pudent; *A E. sl.* fresh; (*fräck*) audacious; (*näsvis*) saucy; *en ~ lymmel* (*äv.*) a shameless rogue -**för-skämdhet** [-ʃ-] [a] piece of] insolence (impu-dence); *en ~* (*äv.*) an impertinence -**försonlig** implacable (*fiende* foe); unforgiving (*sinne* spirit) -**försonlighet** implacability -**förstådd** *a5* mis-understood; (*ej uppskattad*) unappreciated -**för-ståelig** incomprehensible; unintelligible -**för-ståelse** lack of understanding (appreciation) (*för* of) -**förstående** unsympathetic, inappre-ciative; *ställa sig ~ till* take up an unsympathetic attitude towards; *titta ~ på* look blankly at -**för-stånd** lack of judgement; imprudence -**för-ståndig** (*oklok*) imprudent, unwise, foolish; (*omdömeslös*) injudicious -**förställd** *a5* undis-guised, unfeigned; unaffected (*glädje* joy); (*upp-riktig*) sincere -**förstörbar** indestructible, un-destroyable -**försvagad** *a5* unimpaired (*kraft* force); unabated (*intresse* interest) -**försvarlig** indefensible; unwarrantable -**försynt** *se oför-skämd* -**försäkrad** [-ä:-] *a5* uninsured -**försökt** [-ö:kt] *a4* untried -**försörjd** *a5* unprovided for -**förtjänt** undeserved, unmerited; *~ värdesteg-ring* unearned increment -**förtruten** *a3*, -**för-tröttad** *a5* indefatigable; untiring, unwearied -**förtröttlig** *a1* indefatigable -**förtullad** *a5* duty unpaid, uncleared -**förtäckt** unveiled, un-disguised; *i ~a ordalag* in plain words -**förtövad** *a5* prompt, immediate -**förutsebar** *a1* unfore-seeable -**förutsedd** *a5* unforeseen; unexpected; *~a utgifter* unforeseen expenses, contingencies -**förvanskad** *a5* unadulterated; uncorrupted (*text* text) -**förvillad** *a5* unconfused, not let astray; unbiassed (*omdöme* judgement) -**förvit-lig** [-i:t-] *a1* unimpeachable, irreproachable -**förvållad** *a5* unprovoked -**förvägen** daring; undaunted; bold -**förytterlig** *a1* inalienable; *~ egendom* perpetuity -**föränderlig** unchange-able, unalterable; unvarying, invariable; (*bestå-ende*) constant -**förändrad** *a5* unchanged, unal-tered; unvaried; *på i övrigt ~e villkor* (*äv.*) all other terms and conditions remaining unaltered; *i oförändrat skick* in its original form, unchanged, unaltered

o|**gemen** (*utomordentlig*) extraordinary; (*oer-hörd*) immense -**gement** *adv*, *~ rolig* immensely funny -**generad** free [and easy], unconstrained; (*oblyg*) offhand, jaunty; (*fräck*) cool -**generat** *adv* freely *etc.*; *uppträda ~* behave naturally, be at one's ease

ogenom|förbar infeasible; (*om plan äv.*) im-practicable, unworkable -**skinlig** not transpar-ent; opaque -**släpplig** *a1* impervious; imperme-able -**tränglig** (*om skog, mörker o.d.*) impene-trable (*för* to); *~ för vatten* (*ljus*) impermeable (impervious) to water (light) -**tänkt** that has (*etc.*) not been thoroughly thought out; (*om för-slag äv.*) crude

o|**gift** unmarried, single; *~ kvinna* (*jur.*) spinster; *en ~ moster* a maiden aunt; *en ~ farbror* a bache-lor uncle; *som ~ before her* (*etc.*) marriage (get-ting married); *hennes namn som ~* (*äv.*) her maiden name -**gilla** disapprove of; dislike; (*klandra*) find fault with; *jur.* disallow, overrule; *talan ~des* the action was dismissed -**gillande I** *a4* disapproving; deprecating; *med en ~ blick* (*äv.*) with a frown **II** *s6* disapproval, disapproba-tion -**giltig** invalid, [null and] void; *göra ~* nul-lify, vitiate -**giltigförklara** declare nugatory (void); nullify; (*upphäva*) cancel, annul, invali-date -**giltigförklaring** nullification *etc.* -**gil-tighet** invalidity -**gin** [-ji:n] *a1* disobliging, unaccommodating (*mot* towards) -**gjord** un-done; *vara ute i -gjort väder* go on a fool's errand -**glättad** *a5* (*om papper*) uncalendered, antique -**graciös** ungraceful -**grannlaga** untactful, in-delicate; (*indiskret*) inconsiderate -**graverad** *a5* (*om fastighet e.d.*) unencumbered; (*orörd*) in-tact, untouched -**gripbar** *bildl.* impalpable, in-tangible; elusive -**grumlad** *a5* unpolluted (*äv. bildl.*); (*om lycka, glädje*) unclouded -**grundad** unfounded; (*oberättigad*) unjustified -**gräs** weed; *koll.* weeds (*pl*); *rensa ~* (*äv.*) weed -**gräs-bekämpning** weed control (killing) -**gräsme-del** weedkiller; herbicide -**gudaktig** *a1* ungod-ly; impious -**gudaktighet** ungodliness; impiety -**gulden** *a5* unpaid, unsettled; due -**gynnsam** unfavourable (*för* for, to); disadvantageous; un-propitious -**gärna** unwillingly; (*motvilligt*) grudgingly, reluctantly; *det gör jag högst ~* I am very much against doing it; *jag skulle ~ se att du gjorde det* I should be sorry if you did it -**gärning** misdeed -**gärningsman** malefactor, evildoer -**gästvänlig** inhospitable -**gästvänlighet** in-hospitality -**görlig** unfeasible; impracticable o|**hanterlig** (*om sak*) unwieldy, cumbersome, clumsy; (*om pers.*) unmanageable -**harmonisk** unharmonious -**hederlig** dishonest -**hejdad** *a5* unchecked, unrestrained, uncontrolled; *av ~ vana* by force of habit -**hemul** *a1* unwarranted, unjustified -**herrans** *oböjligt a* awful -**historisk** unhistorical; historically untrue -**hjälplig** hope-less; (*obotlig*) incurable; (*oförbätterlig*) incorri-gible; (*om t.ex. förlust*) irretrievable -**hjälpligt** *adv* hopelessly; *~ förlorad* irretrievably lost -**hjälpsam** unhelpful (*mot* to)

ohm [å:m] *s9* ohm

ohoj [å'håjj] *skepp ~!* ship ahoy!

o|**hyfsad** (*slarvig*) untidy, unkempt; (*plump*) ill--mannered, uncivil, rude, coarse -**hygglig** [ʾɔ:-, -'hygg-] horrible, gruesome, ghastly; (*om t.ex. brott*) atrocious, hideous; *en ~ syn* (*äv.*) a horrid (appalling, bloodcurdling) sight -**hygienisk** in-sanitary -**hyra** *s1, koll.* vermin (*pl; äv. bildl.*) -**hyvlad** [-y:-] *a5* unplaned; (*om bräda o.d. äv.*) rough -**hågad** disinclined; unwilling -**hållbar** (*om t.ex. tyg*) unserviceable, flimsy; (*om stånd-punkt, åsikt*) untenable; *mil.* indefensible; (*om situation*) precarious -**hägn** (*skada*) damage; (*åverkan*) trespass; *göra ~ på* do damage to, tres-pass on -**hälsa** ill (bad) health; (*sjukdom*) illness -**hälsosam** (*om föda*) unwholesome; (*om kli-mat o. bildl.*) unhealthy, bad for one's health -**hämmad** unchecked -**hämmat** *adv* unrestrainedly, without restraint **-hämnad** *a5* unavenged, unrevenged **-hängd** *al, vard.* unhanged, cheeky, saucy **-höljd** *al (naken)* naked; *(rättfram)* undisguised, unabashed, frank; *(öppen)* open **-hörbar** inaudible **-hörd** [-ö:-] *a5* unheard; *jur.* untried; *hans rop förklingade ~a* his cries were unheeded **-hörsam** disobedient **-hövlig** impolite, discourteous *(mot* to)

oidipuskomplex [ˣåjd-] Oedipus complex

o|**igenkännlig** unrecognizable **-igenkännlighet** unrecognizability; *intill ~* beyond recognition **-inbunden** unbound **-inskränkt** unlimited; unrestricted; *(om härskare e.d.)* absolute **-inspirerad** *a5* uninspired **-intaglig** [-a:-] *al* impregnable, inexpugnable **-intelligent** unintelligent **-intressant** uninteresting; *(tråkig)* dull **-intresse** lack of interest **-intresserad** uninterested *(av* in); *vara ~ av* not be interested in **-invigd** [-i:gd] *a5* uninitiated *(i* in[to]); *(om kyrka o.d.)* unconsecrated; *den ~e (äv.)* an outsider **-isolerad** *a5* uninsulated

oj [åjj] [oh], dear me! **oja** *rfl,* ~ *sig över* moan (complain) about

o|**just** [ˣo:ʃyst] incorrect; unfair; ~ *spel* foul play **-jämförlig** incomparable; *(makalös)* unmatched, unparalleled **-jämförligt** [-ö:-] *adv* incomparably, beyond comparison; *den ~ bästa* by far the best; ~ *mycket bättre* much better by far **-jämn** uneven *(antal* number; *kvalitet* quality); *(skrovlig)* rough, rugged; *(inte lika)* unequal; *(om klimat, lynne)* inequable; *(oregelbunden)* irregular; *(om väg)* bumpy; *kämpa en ~ strid* fight a losing battle **-jämnhet** unevenness; inequality, irregularity **-jävig** unchallengeable, competent *(vittne* witness); *(opartisk)* unbiased

ok *s7* yoke; *(trältom äv.)* bondage; *kasta av sig ~et* cast off the yoke; *bringa under ~et* put under the yoke, enslave

o|**kammad** *a5* uncombed **-kamratlig** disloyal

okapi [-ˈka:-] *s3, zool.* okapi

okarina [å-ˣri:-] *sl* ocarina

okben *anat.* zygomatic bone

o|**klanderlig** *al* irreproachable; *(felfri)* faultless; *(moralisk)* blameless, exemplary **-klar 1** *ep.* obscure, dim; *(om vätska)* turbid, muddy; *(om färg)* indistinct; *(suddig)* blurred; *(molnig)* cloudy **2** *bildl.* unclear, unlucid, vague; *(oredig)* muddled, confused; *(dunkel)* obscure *(föreställning* idea); *(otydlig)* indistinct **3** *sjö.* foul; *(tilltrasslad)* entangled **-klarhet 1** obscurity; turbidity, muddiness *etc.* **2** unclearness *etc.*; confusion; *(osäkerhet)* uncertainty **-klok** unwise, imprudent, injudicious; *(dåraktig)* foolish; *(ej tillrådlig)* inadvisable **-klokhet** unwisdom, imprudence, injudiciousness **-klädd** *(ej färdigklädd)* undressed; *(naken)* naked, without any clothes on; *(om möbel)* unupholstered **-knäppt** *a4 (om plagg)* unbuttoned; *(om knapp)* undone **-kokt** [-o:-] *a4* unboiled; *(rå)* raw **-kommenterad** [-å-] *a5 (om upplaga)* unannotated, not furnished with any commentary (notes) **-komplicerad** uncomplicated; *(om pers. äv.)* simple **-koncentrerad** unconcentrated **-konstlad** *(ej tillgjord, naturlig)* unaffected, natural **-kontrollerad** [-å-å-] uncontrolled, unchecked, unverified **-kontrollerbar** [-å-å-] *al* uncontrollable

-kontroversiell uncontroversial **-konventionell** unconventional **-krigisk** peace-loving **-kristlig** ungodly **-kristligt** *adv,* ~ *tidigt* at an ungodly hour, outrageously early **-kritisk** uncritical **-kroppslig** incorporeal, immaterial **-krossbar** [-å-] *al (om glas o.d.)* unbreakable **-kryddad** *a5* unseasoned **-kränkbar** *al* inviolable **-krönt** [-ö:-] *a4* uncrowned

oktaeder [-'e:der] *s2* octahedron

oktan [åk'ta:n] *s7, s3* octane

oktant [å-] octant

oktan|tal, -värde octane number (rating)

oktav [åk'ta:v] *s3* **1** *(format)* octavo, eightvo (8vo) **2** *mus.* octave

oktett [åk'tett] *s3, mus.* octet[te]

oktober [åk'to:-] *r* October

oktroj [åk'tråjj] *s3* charter; *(friare)* licence; *meddela ~* confer a charter

okular *s7* eyepiece, ocular

okuler|a *trädg.* bud, graft **-ing** budding, grafting

okultiverad uncultivated, uncultured; unrefined

okulärbesiktning ocular (visual) inspection

o|**kunnig** ignorant *(om* of); *absol. äv.* unlearned; ~ *om (om att) (äv.)* unaware of ([of the fact] that); ~ *i engelska* with no knowledge (ignorant) of English **-kunnighet** ignorance *(i, om* of); *lämna ngn i ~ om* leave s.b. in the dark as to; *sväva i ~ om* be unaware (ignorant) of **-kurant** unsaleable, unmarketable **-kuvlig** [-u:-] *al* indomitable; irrepressible **-kvald** [-a:-] *a5, i ~ besittning av* in undisputed possession of **-kvalificerad** unqualified **-kvinnlig** unwomanly **-kväda** abuse **-kvädin[g]sord** abusive word; ~ *(pl)* abusive language *(sg)* **-kynne** [-ç-] *s6* naughtiness, mischief; *på (av) [rent] ~* out of [pure] mischief **-kynnig** [-ç-] *al* naughty, mischievous **-kysk** unchaste **-känd** unknown *(för* to); unfamiliar; *(främmande)* strange; *av ~ anledning* for some unknown reason; *den ~e soldatens grav* the tomb of the unknown warrior; *en för mig ~ erfarenhet (äv.)* an experience new to me; *ta språnget ut i det ~a* take a leap into the unknown **-känslig** insensible, insusceptible *(för* to); *(hårdhjärtad)* unfeeling; *(utan känsel)* numb **-laddad** *a5* unloaded, uncharged

olag *i uttr.: (råka get) i ~* out of order

olag|a *oböjligt a (lagstridig)* unlawful; *(illegal)* illegal **-lig** unlawful, illegal; *(smyg-)* illicit; *förfarandet är ~t* the proceeding is contrary to [the] law

olat *s3* vice; *~er* bad habits

oldboy [ˈå:ldbåj] *s3, pl äv. -s, sport.* veteran, old boy **oldboystävling** old-boy competition

oleander [-'ann-] *s2* oleander, rosebay

oledad *anat.* inarticulate; jointless

olein [åle'i:n] *s4, s3* [tri]olein **-syra** oleic acid

olidlig [-i:d-] *al* insufferable, unbearable, intolerable

oligarkj [-å-] *s3* oligarchy **oligofrenj** *s3* mental retardation **oligopol** [-'på:l] *s7* oligopoly

olik *a5* unlike, different from (to); *vara ~a varandra* be unlike [each other], differ from one another

olika I *oböjligt a* different; *(skiftande)* varying; *(växlande)* various; *(i storlek)* unequal; *av ~ slag* of different (various) kinds; *det är så ~ hur man*

O

är (äv.) it all depends [on] how you are; *smaken är* ~ tastes differ **II** *adv* differently; unequally; ~ *långa* of different (unequal, varying) lengths; ~ *stora* unequal in size; ~ *faller ödets lotter* life is a lottery

o|likartad heterogeneous, disparate **-likformig** diversiform, nonuniform; *(heterogen)* heterogeneous; *(som växlar form)* varying, unequal; *~a* differing in shape **-likformighet** irregularity of form **-likfärgad** *(fler-)* variegated, of different colours; *(av annan färg)* differently coloured **-likhet** unlikeness *(med* to), dissimilarity *(i* in; *med* to); *(t.ex. i antal, ålder)* disparity *(i* of); *(skillnad)* difference; *(skiljaktighet)* diversity, divergence *(i smak* in tastes); *i ~ med henne* unlike (in contrast to) her **-liksidig** with unequal sides, unequal-sided; *en ~ triangel* a scalene triangle; *~t papper* duplex paper **-liktänkande** *a4, en ~* a dissident, a person holding a different opinion from one's own

olinjerad *a5* unruled

oljv *s3* olive **-grön** olive-green **-lund** olive grove **-olja** olive oil

olja [å-] **I** *s1* oil; *måla i ~* paint in oils; *sardiner i ~* sardines in oil; *byta ~* change the oil; *gjuta ~ på elden (bildl.)* add fuel to the fire; *gjuta ~ på vågorna (bildl.)* pour oil on troubled waters **II** *v1* oil, grease, lubricate

oljeaggregat oil burner

Oljeberget [å-] the Mount of Olives

olje|blandad mixed with oil **-borrning** drilling for oil **-borrtorn** derrick **-byte** change of oil **-duk** oilcloth, oilskin **-eldad** oilfired **-eldning** oil-heating, oil-burning **-fat** oil drum **-fläck** slick **-fyndighet** oil deposit **-fält** oilfield **-färg** oil paint (colour) **-förbrukning** oil consumption **-grus** oil gravel **-halt** oil content **-haltig** *a1* containing oil; *(om frö e.d.)* oleaginous **-härdad** [-ä:-] *a5* oil-hardened, oil-tempered **-kaka** oil cake **-kanna** oilcan, oiler **-kopp** oilcup, oiler **-källa** oil well **-lampa** oil lamp **-ledning** oil pipe; *(transportledning)* oil pipeline **-målning** oil painting **-mätare** oil gauge **-palm** oil palm **-plattform** oil rig **-producerande** oil-producing **-prospektering** prospecting for oil **-pump** oil pump **-raffinaderi** oil refinery **-rigg** oil rig **-rock** oilskin coat **-skiffer** oil shale **-sticka** dipstick **-ställ** set of oilskins **-tank** oil tank (cistern) **-tanker** oil tanker, oiler **-tryck 1** *konst.* oil printing, oleography; *konkr.* oleograph **2** *tekn.* oil pressure **-utsläpp** oil slick (discharge) **-växt** oil-yielding plant, oil plant

oljig [ˣåll-] *a1* oily; *bildl. äv.* unctuous

oljud noise, din, racket; *föra ~* make a noise

olle *s2* *(tröja)* sweater

ollon [ˣållån] *s7* *(ek-)* acorn; *(bok-)* beechnut, *(koll.)* beech mast; *anat.* glans *(pl* glandes) **-borre** cockchafer

o|logisk illogical **-lovandes** [-å-] without permission (leave) **-lovlig** forbidden; *(olaglig)* unlawful *(jakt* shooting; *ärende* errand); *(som sker i smyg)* illicit; *~ underrättelseverksamhet* illegal intelligence activities *(pl)* **-lust** *(obehag)* [feeling of] discomfort (uneasiness) *(över* at); *(missnöje)* dissatisfaction; *(obenägenhet)* disinclination, unwillingness, reluctance *(för* for; *för att* to) **-lust-**

betonad unpleasant **-lustig** uncomfortable, ill at ease; unpleasant **-lustkänsla** feeling of discomfort (uneasiness)

olvon [ˣålvån] *s7, bot.* guelder-rose

olycka *s1* *(ofärd)* misfortune, ill fortune, bad luck; *(bedrövelse)* unhappiness; *(ont)* adversity; *(katastrof)* disaster, calamity; *(elände)* misery; *(olyckshändelse)* accident; *(missöde)* mishap; *till all ~* as ill luck would have it; *till råga på ~n* to make matters worse; *när ~n är framme* when things go wrong; *hon har råkat i ~* she has got into trouble; *det är ingen ~ skedd* there's no harm done; *en ~ kommer sällan ensam* it never rains but it pours

o|lycklig 1 *(utsatt för -a)* unfortunate, unlucky; *(misslyckad)* unsuccessful *(försök* attempt) **2** *(om människa, liv, tid, äktenskap e.d.)* unhappy; *(eländig)* miserable, wretched **-lyckligtvis** unfortunately, unhappily **-lycksalig** [most] unhappy; *(friare)* fatal, disastrous, calamitous

olycks|barn samhällets ~ *(ung.)* the failures of society, the down and outs **-bringande** *a4* ill-fated; *(ödesdiger)* fatal, disastrous **-broder** brother in misfortune **-bådande** *a4* ill-omened, ominous, sinister **-dag** unlucky day **-fall** accident; casualty; ~ *i arbetet* industrial accident; ~ *i hemmet* accident in the home **-fallsersättning** [industrial] injury benefit, accident compensation **-fallsförsäkring** [personal] accident insurance; *AE.* casualty insurance **-fågel** *bildl., vara en* ~ be born under an unlucky star **-händelse** accident; *råka ut för en* ~ meet with an accident **-korp** *bildl.* croaker, Cassandra, *AE.* calamity-howler **-plats** scene of the accident **-profet** prophet of calamity **-risk** accident hazard, risk of accident **-tillbud** near-accident **-tillfälle** *vid ~t* at the [time of the] accident **-öde** unlucky fate

o|lydig disobedient *(mot* to) **-lydnad** disobedience *(mot* to)

olymp|iad *s3* Olympiad **-ier** [ɔ'lymm-] Olympian **-isk** [ɔ'lymm-] *a5, O~a spelen* the Olympic Games

o|låst [-å:-] *a4* unlocked **-låt** noise, din **-lägenhet** inconvenience, nuisance; *(besvär)* trouble; *(svårighet)* difficulty; *(nackdel)* drawback; *det medför stora ~er för mig* it causes me great inconvenience; *sanitär ~* public nuisance **-läglig** inopportune, inconvenient; *(illa vald)* ill-timed; *om det inte är ~t för dig* if it is not inconvenient to you **-läkt** [-ä:-] *a4, ett ~ sår* an open wound **-lämplig** unsuitable, unfit[ted], inappropriate; *(oläglig)* inconvenient; *(inkompetent)* unfit; ~ *som bostad* unfit for habitation **-lämplighet** unsuitability; unfitness; inconvenience **-ländig** *a1* rough, rugged **-läraktig** unteachable **-lärd** unlearned; unlettered **-läslig** illegible *(handstil* handwriting) **-lönsam** unprofitable **-löslig** *kem. o. bildl.* insoluble **-löst** [-ö:-] *a4 (i vätska)* undissolved; *(om problem o.d.)* unsolved

om [åmm] **I** *konj* **1** *(villkorlig)* if; ~ *du går följer jag med* if you go I will come with you; ~ *du bara vore här!* if only you were here!; *du bör* ~ *möjligt komma i väg före åtta* you should, if possible, leave before eight; ~ *vädret tillåter (äv.)* weather permitting; ~ *så är* if so, if that is the case; ~ *inget oförutsett inträffar* if nothing (unless something) unexpected happens; ~ *inte* if not, unless; ~ *inte han hade varit hade vi inte klarat det* but for him we should not have managed **2** *som* ~ as if; *även* ~, ~ *också* even though (if); *det skall bli färdigt* ~ *jag så skall göra det själv* it will be ready even if I have to do it myself; *det tycks som* ~ (*äv.*) it seems that; *som* ~ *det skulle vara så bra* as though that's any good **3** (*frågande*) if, whether; *de undrade* ~ *de fick komma* they wondered if they could come; *hade ni trevligt? - Om!* did you have a nice time? - Rather!, You bet! **4** ~ *vi skulle gå på bio?* what about going to the cinema? **II** *s* if; ~ *inte* ~ *hade varit* if ifs and ans were pots and pans; *efter många* ~ *och men* after a lot of shillyshallying **III** *prep* **1** (*omkring*) [a]round; about; *en snara* ~ *halsen* a snare round one's neck; *falla ngn* ~ *halsen* fall on a p.'s neck; *försvinna* ~ *hörnet* disappear round the corner; *hålla ngn* ~ *livet* hold s.b. by the waist **2** (*annan konstr.*) *vara kall* ~ *fötterna* have cold feet; *lätt* ~ *hjärtat* light at (of) heart; *tvätta sig* ~ *händerna* wash one's hands; *torka sig* ~ *munnen* wipe one's mouth; *ha mycket* ~ *sig* have a lot [of work] on one's hands; *låsa* ~ *sig* lock o.s. in; *vara* ~ *sig* look after number one, be a pusher **3** (*om läge*) of; *söder* ~ to the south of; *till vänster* ~ to the left of; *vid sidan* ~ *vägen* at the side of the road **4** *lova halvt* ~ *halvt* give a half-and-half promise; *par* ~ *par* two by two, in couples; *de ramlade* ~ *varandra* they tumbled over one another **5** (*om tid: under, inom*) in; ~ *dagen* (*dagarna*) in the daytime, during the day, by day; *långt* ~ *länge* at long last; ~ *lördagarna* on Saturdays; *vara ledig* ~ *lördagarna* have Saturdays off; ~ *lördag åtta dar* a week on Saturday; *vakna tidigt* ~ *mornarna* wake up early in the morning; ~ *natten* (*nätterna*) at (by) night, in the night; ~ *vintern* (*vintrarna*) in winter[time]; *två gånger* ~ *året* twice a year; *förr* ~ *åren* in former years; *året* ~ all the year round **6** (*angående*) about, of; (*över ett ämne*) on; (*beträffande*) as to; *berättelsen* (*drömmen*) ~ the story (dream) of; *fråga ngn* ~ ask s.b. about; *fråga ngn* ~ *vägen* ask s.b. the way; *förvissa sig* ~ make sure of; *boken handlar* ~ the book is about (deals with); *kännedom* ~ knowledge of; *slaget* ~ the battle of; *uppgift* ~ information about (on, as to); *en bok* (*föreläsning*) ~ a book (lecture) on; *vi var fem* ~ *lotten* five of us shared the lottery ticket; *de sade ingenting* ~ *när de skulle komma* they said nothing as to when they would come **7** (*efter adj.*) *se adjektivet* **8** (*vid begäran, tävlan*) for; *be* ~ *ursäkt* apologize; *begäran* (*önskan*) ~ request (wish) for; *förslaget* ~ the proposal for; *kämpa* ~ *segern* fight for victory; *spela* ~ *pengar* play for money; *tävlan* ~ *competition* for **9** (*innehållande, uppgående t.*) of; *ett brev* ~ *fyra sidor* a letter of four pages; a four-page letter; *en säck* ~ *50 liter* a bag holding 50 litres; *en truppstyrka* ~ *500* man a force of 500 men **IV** *adv* **1** (*omkring*) round; *en ask med papper* ~ a box wrapped in paper (with paper round it); *binda ett snöre* ~ *ngt* tie a string round s.th.; *runt* ~ *i landet* all over the country; *röra* ~ *i gröten* stir the porridge **2** (*tillbaka*) back; *se* ~ look back; *vända* ~ turn back **3** (*förbi*) past; *gå* (*köra*) ~ *ngn* walk (drive) past s.b., overtake s.b. **4** (*på nytt*) [over] again; ~ *igen* over again, once more;

~ *och* ~ *igen* over and over again, time after time, time and again; *många gånger* ~ many times over; *göra* ~ make (do) again, remake, redo; *läsa* ~ *en bok* reread a book; *måla* ~ repaint; *se* ~ *en film* see a film again

o|**magnetisk** nonmagnetic **-mak** *s7* trouble, bother **-maka** *oböjligt a* odd; *bildl.* ill-matched; *en* ~ *handske* an odd glove; *skorna är* ~ the shoes are not a pair (do not match) **-manlig** unmanly; effeminate

om|**arbeta** remodel; rework; (*plan*) revise; alter; (*bok e.d.*) revise, rewrite; (*för film e.d.*) adapt **-arbetning** [-e:-] remodelling; reworking; revision, alteration; rewriting; adaptation **-bedja** *han -bads* (*blev -bedd*) *att* he was requested (asked, called upon) to **-besörja** see (attend) to, effect **-bilda** transform (convert, turn) (*till* into); (*t.ex. ministär*) reconstruct **-bildning** transformation, conversion; reconstruction **-bonad** *a5* warm and cosy, snug

om**bord** [-'bɔ:rd] on board (*på fartyget* the ship); *fritt* ~ free on board (*förk.* f.o.b.); *gå* ~ (*äv.*) embark; *föra* ~ ship, take on board **-anställd** [person] employed on board a ship **-läggning** collision **-varande** *de* ~ those on board

om**bryt**|**a** *boktr.* make up [into pages]; *-brutet korrektur* page proof **-ning** making up, make-up

om**bud** representative; *hand. äv.* agent; (*enl. fullmakt*) proxy, authorized representative; *juridiskt* ~ solicitor, counsel, attorney, legal adviser **ombudsman** representative, commissioner; (*för bank, verk etc.*) solicitor; (*för bolag äv.*) company lawyer; (*för organisation etc.*) secretary; (*med offentligt uppdrag*) ombudsman, parliamentary commissioner

om|**bunden** *vara* ~ wear a bandage, be tied up **-byggnad** rebuilding; reconstruction; *huset är under* ~ the house is being rebuilt **-byta** *nu är det -bytta roller* now the tables are turned **-byte** change (*underkläder* of underwear); (*omväxling*) variety; ~ *förnöjer!* there's nothing like change! **-bytlig** [-y:-] *a1* changeable, variable; (*nyckfull*) inconstant, fickle; (*ostadig*) unsteady, unstable

om**dan**|**a** remodel; transform **-are** remoulder; transformer **-ing** remoulding; transformation

om|**debatterad** *a5* much discussed (debated); *en* ~ *fråga* a controversial question **-destinera** divert; reroute **-dirigera** redirect, divert **-diskuterad** *a5, se -debatterad* **-disponera** rearrange; redistribute **-disponering** rearrangement; redistribution

om**döme** *s6* (*-sförmåga*) judg[e]ment; (*urskillning*) discrimination, discernment; (*åsikt*) opinion; *visa gott* ~ show sound judgment; *bilda sig ett* ~ *om* form an opinion of

om**dömes**|**fråga** [a] question of judgment (opinion) **-gill** [-j-] *a1* discerning; judicious **-lös** undiscerning, undiscriminating; injudicious

o|**medelbar** immediate; (*naturlig*) natural; (*spontan*) spontaneous **-medelbarhet** naturalness; spontaneity **-medelbart** *adv* immediately *etc.*; directly; at once, straight off; ~ *efter mottagandet av* immediately on receipt of **-medgörlig** unaccommodating; (*oveklig*) unyielding; (*motspänstig*) intractable; (*envis*) unreasonable **-medveten** unconscious (*om* of); (*instink-*

tiv) instinctive
omelętt *s3* omelette, *särsk. AE.* omelet
omen [ˈɔː-] *s7, pl äv. omina* omen, augury; *det är ett gott ~ (äv.)* that augurs well
ometodisk unmethodical, unsystematic
om|famna *v1* embrace; *vard.* hug **-famning** embrace; *vard.* hug **-fatta 1** (*gripa om*) clasp, grasp; (*omsluta*) enclose, encircle **2** (*innefatta*) comprise, include; (*täcka*) cover, extend over; (*rymma*) contain; (*ansluta sig t.*) embrace (*en lära* a doctrine); *~ ngn med sympati* extend sympathy to s.b., regard s.b. sympathetically **-fattande** *a4* extensive; comprehensive; (*utbredd*) widespread, far-reaching; (*stor*) big, great, large **-fattning** extent, scope, compass, range; *av betydande ~ (äv.)* of considerable proportions; *i allt större ~* on an increasing scale, to an increasing extent; *i hela dess ~* to the whole of its extent, (*i stor skala*) on a large scale **-fattningsrörelse** *mil.* envelopment operation **-fluten** *a5, se kringfluten* **-flyttning** transposition; transfer, removal; *mat.* inversion **-forma** transform; *elektr.* convert **-formare** [-å-] *elektr.* converter; *AE.* generator **-formulera** redraft; (*problem e.d.*) restate
omfång *s7* extent; (*storlek*) size, bulk dimensions (*pl*); (*boktr., beräknat ~*) castoff; (*röst-*) range; *till ~et* in size (scope)
omfångs|beräkna cast off (*ett manuskript* a copy) **-rik** extensive; (*voluminös*) voluminous; (*skrymmande*) bulky
om|fördelning redistribution **-ge** *se -giva* **-gestalta** remould; transform (*ngns liv* a p.'s life) **-gift** remarried **-giv** *kortsp.* re-deal **-giva** surround; *~ ngt med en mur (ett staket) (äv.)* wall (fence) in s.th. **-givning** [-ji:v-] surroundings (*pl*); (*miljö*) environment; *han är en fara för sin ~* he is a source of danger to those around him; *i stadens ~ar (äv.)* in the environs of the town **-gjord** remade; reconstructed **-gjorda** [-jɔ:r-] *~ sina länder* gird up one's loins; *~ sig* gird o.s. **-gruppera** regroup **-gruppering** regroupment **-gående I** *a4* immediate, prompt; *~ svar (äv.)* reply by return; *per ~* by return [of post] **II** *adv* by return **-gång** *s2* **1** (*varv*) round, turn, spell **2** (*uppsättning*) set (*kläder* of clothes) **-gärda** [-jä:r-] fence round (*bildl. äv.:* about) **-hulda** cherish, foster; (*om pers. äv.*) make much of
omhänder|ha [-ˣhänd-] have charge of, supervise, manage **-taga** take charge of; *bli -tagen (av polis)* be taken in charge; *bli väl -tagen* be taken good care of
om|hölja envelop; wrap round **-hölje** envelope, cover, wrapping
omigen [ˈåmmijen] again, once more
omild ungentle, harsh (*behandling* treatment); (*om klimat o.d.*) ungenial; (*om omdöme äv.*) severe
omintetgöra [åmˣinn-] (*gäcka*) frustrate; (*korsa*) thwart
ominös *al* ominous; fatal
omiss|känn[e]lig [-ç-] *al* unmistakable; (*otvivelaktig*) undoubted; (*påtaglig*) palpable **-tänksam** unsuspicious, unsuspecting
omistlig *al* inalienable (*rättighet* right); (*oumbärlig*) indispensable; (*oskattbar*) precious; *~a*

värden priceless treasures
om|kast *sport.* re-throw **-kastare** *tekn.* [change over] switch (key) **-kastning** sudden change; (*av ordningen*) inversion; (*av bokstäver o.d.*) transposition; (*i vinden*) veer[ing]; *elektr. o. bildl.* reversal; *polit. o.d.* turnabout; (*i stämning*) veering round **-klädning** [-ä:-] changing [of clothes]; (*av möbler*) re-covering **-klädningsrum** changing-room **-komma** die; be killed; *de -komna* those who were killed (lost their lives), the victims **-koppla** *tekn.* switch over; commute **-kopplare** *se -kastare* **-koppling** changing over; reconnection; switching **-kostnad** *~er* costs, expenses, overheads; outlay, expenditure (*sg*) **-kostnadskonto** expense[s] account **-krets** circumference; *i ~* in circumference, round; *inom en ~ av fem kilometer* within a radius of five kilometres
omkring [åmˈkriŋ] round; around; (*ungefär*) about (*trettio* thirty), some (*10 shilling* 10 shillings); at about (*klockan 7* seven); *springa ~ på gatorna* run about [in] the streets; *när allt kommer ~* after all, all things considered; *vida (vitt) ~* far and wide **-liggande** *se kringliggande*
omkull (*falla* fall) down (over)
om|kväde *s6* refrain **-körning** overtaking **-körningsförbud** *ung.* overtaking prohibited, no passing **-laddning** recharge **-lasta** transship, reship; (*på järnväg*) shift, reload **-lastning** transshipment *etc.*; shifting *etc.* **-ljud** mutation, umlaut **-lokalisera** relocate
omlopp *astr.* revolution, circuit; (*rörelse*) circulation; *sätta i ~ a*) (*pengar*) put into circulation, *b*) (*blodet*) set circulating; *ett rykte kom i ~* a rumour started circulating
omlopps|bana *astr.* orbit **-hastighet** orbital velocity **-tid** period of revolution; (*pengars*) circulation period; *data.* major cycle
om|lott wrapover **-läggning** (*drift-*) rearrangement, reorganization; (*skatte-*) revision; (*förändring*) change, alteration; (*trafik-*) diversion; *~ till högertrafik* changeover (switch) to right-hand traffic **-möblera** refurnish; rearrange furniture **-möblering** refurnishing; *bildl.* reshuffle (*i regeringen* of the Cabinet) **-nejd** *se omgivning*
omnibus[s] [ˣåmm-] [omni]bus; *jfr buss*
om|nämna mention (*för* to) **-nämnande** *s6* mention
o|modern unmodern; out of date (fashion), outmoded; *bli ~* go out of fashion **-mogen** unripe (*äv. bildl.*); *bildl. äv.* immature; (*grön*) green **-mogenhet** unripeness; immaturity **-moral** (*brist på*) unmorality; (*osedlighet*) immorality **-moralisk** (*sedligt förkastlig*) unmoral; (*osedlig*) immoral
omorganis|ation reorganization **-era** reorganize; *AE. äv.* revamp
o|mornad [-å:-] *a5* drowsy, half awake, sleepy **-motiverad** *a5* unwarranted; (*oberättigad*) unfounded; (*obefogad*) uncalled-for
om|placera put in other positions, rearrange; (*ämbetsman*) transfer; (*pengar*) reinvest **-plantera** replant; transplant (*äv. bildl.*) **-pröva** reconsider; review (*äv. jur.*) **-prövning** reconsideration; review; *ta ngt under ~* reconsider s.th. **-redigera** (*bok o.d.*) revise **-registrera** re-

register **-ringa** *v1* surround; *mil. äv.* encircle
område *s6, eg.* territory; (*trakt*) district, area, region; (*gebit*) domain, sphere, department, province; (*gren*) branch; *han är expert på sitt ~* he is an expert in his field
om|räkna *se räkna* [*om*]; (*valutor*) convert (*t. svenska kronor* into Swedish kronor) **-rörning** [-ö:-] stirring **-röstning** voting, vote; *parl. äv.* division; (*med röstsedlar*) ballot voting; *anställa ~* put to the vote; *skrida till ~* take a vote; *sluten ~* secret ballot, ballot vote
oms [åms] *s3, fork.* för omsättningsskatt
omsedd *få ett sår omsett* have a wound attended to
omsider [åm'si:-] by degrees; (*till sist*) finally, at last; *sent ~* at long last
om|skaka shake up; *~s väl!* shake well before use! **-skakad** *a5* shaken (*äv. bildl.*); *bildl. äv.* shocked **-skapa** transform (*till* into) **-skiftare** [-ʃ-] (*på skrivmaskin*) shift key **-skola** *v1* re-educate, retrain; rehabilitate; (*plantor*) transplant **-skolning** re-education, retraining; rehabilitation; (*av plantor*) transplantation **-skolningskurs** retraining (rehabilitation) course **-skriva 1** *mat.* circumscribe **2** (*återge med andra ord*) paraphrase **-skriven** *a5, mycket ~* often written about, much-discussed **-skrivande** *a4* periphrastic (*verb* verb) **-skrivning 1** *mat.* circumscribing **2** (*återgivande med andra ord*) paraphrase, periphrasis, circumlocution; (*fonetisk* phonetic) transcription; *~ med 'do'* a 'do'-periphrasis **3** (*omarbetning*) rewriting **-skära** circumcise **-skärelse** [-ʃ-] circumcision
omslag *s7* **1** (*emballage*) wrapping, wrapper; (*bok-*) [dust (book)] jacket, cover **2** (*förändring*) change (*i vädret* in the weather), alteration **3** (*förband*) compress
omslags|bild cover picture (drawing, design) **-papper** wrapping (brown) paper **-revers** promissory note [with collateral security]
om|slut *bokför.* second balancing-up **-sluta** (*omge*) surround, encompass; (*innesluta*) enclose **-slutning** [-u:-] *hand.* total assets **-sorg** care (*om* for, of); (*möda*) trouble, pains (*pl*); *lägga ner ~ på* take pains (trouble) with, bestow care upon; *slösa sina ~er på* lavish one's care and attention on **-sorgsfull** careful; (*grundlig*) thorough, painstaking; (*i klädsel*) neat; (*i detalj utarbetad*) elaborate (*utförande* workmanship) **-sorgslag** *o~en* [the Swedish] act on provisions for certain mentally retarded persons **-spel** *sport.* replay; play-off **-spunnen** *a5, ~ led-ningstråd* wound (taped) wire **-spänna** *bildl.* cover, extend (stretch, range) over; embrace, span (*stora områden* vast areas) **-stigning** change **-stridd** *a5* contested, disputed, at issue; *en ~ fråga* a vexed (controversial) question **-strukturering** change in the structure; (*av industri*) [structural] reorganization **-strålad** *a5, ~ av ljus* circumfused (bathed in) light; *~ av ära* covered with glory **-styr** *se överstyr* **-stående** *oböjligt a, på ~ sida* overleaf **-ställbar** adjustable, convertible **-ställning** adjustment; (*t. ex. t. fredsförhållanden*) adaptation, changeover **-ständighet** circumstance; (*faktum*) fact; [*allt*] *efter ~erna* according to the circumstances; *de*

närmare ~erna further particulars (details), the immediate circumstances; *i knappa ~er* in reduced (straitened) circumstances; *under inga ~er* in (under) no circumstances; *under nuvarande ~er* (*äv.*) as it is, this being the case; *utan vidare ~er* without more ado (any further ceremony); *den ~en att jag har* [the fact of] my having; *befinna sig efter ~erna väl* be well considering [the circumstances] **-ständlig** *a1* circumstantial, detailed; (*långrandig*) long-winded, prolix **-störta** overthrow, upset; subvert (*ett samhälle* a society) **-störtande** *a4* subversive (*verksamhet* activity) **-störtning** overthrow, subversion **-störtningsförsök** attempt to subvert **-susa** *~s av västanfläktar* be fanned by zephyrs; *~d av sägner* wreathed in legend
om|svep *s7* circumlocution[s *pl*], roundabout way[s *pl*]; *utan ~* straight out, candidly; *komma med ~* beat about the bush **-svängning** swing (veer) round; sudden change (alteration) **-svärma** flock (swarm) around; *en ~ flicka* a favourite with the boys **-sänder** [-'sänn-] at a time **-sätta 1** (*växel o.d.*) renew, prolong **2** (*omvandla*) convert, transform (*i* into); *~ sina planer i handling* put one's plans into action; *~ i praktiken* put into practice; *~ ngt i pengar* turn s.th. into cash **3** (*avyttra*) sell, market, turn over; *aktierna -sattes till* the shares changed hands at **-sättning 1** (*av växlar, lån*) renewal, prolongation **2** (*sammanlagt försäljningsvärde*) turnover, sales; (*allm. varuutbyte*) business [volume], trade; (*av arbetskraft*) turnover (*på lärare* of teachers); *börs.* transactions (*pl*), business **3** *boktr.* recomposition
omsättnings|skatt purchase (*AE.* sales) tax **-tillgångar** *pl* current (floating) assets **-växel** renewal (continuation) bill
om|tagning repetition; *mus.* repeat; *foto.* retake **-tala 1** (*-nämna*) mention **2** (*berätta*) tell (*ngt för ngn* s.b. s.th., *s.th.* to s.b.) **-tanke** (*-tänksamhet*) consideration (*om* for); (*-sorg*) solicitude (*om* for) **-tryck** *boktr.* reprint **-tumlad** *a5* giddy, dizzy **-tvistad** *a5* disputed; *en ~ fråga* a matter of dispute (at issue), a moot question **-tyckt** *a4* popular, liked; *illa ~* disliked, unpopular **-tänksam** *a1* considerate (*om* for, of; *mot* towards), thoughtful (*om, mot* for, of); (*försiktig*) prudent **-tänksamhet** considerateness *etc.* **-töckna** darken; (*genom alkohol o.d.*) daze, muddle, fuddle; *~t tillstånd* state of confusion, daze
o|musikalisk unmusical **-mutlig** [-u:-] *a1* unbribable; incorruptible; (*friare*) inflexible, uncompromising **-mutlighet** [-u:-] incorruptibility; inflexibility
om|val *s7* re-election **-vald** re-elected **-vandla** transform, convert, change (*till* into) **-vandling** transformation, conversion, change **-vittna** give evidence of; (*betyga*) testify **-vittnad** *a5* testified to, vouched for; *ett -vittnat faktum* a certified fact **-vårdad** care; *ha ~ om* be in (have) charge of **-väg** roundabout (circuitous) way (*äv. bildl.*); *ta en ~* make a detour; *en stor ~* (*äv.*) a long way round; *få veta då ~ar* get to know in a roundabout way (indirectly) **-välja** re-elect **-välvande** *a4* revolutionary **-välvning** revolution, upheaval **-vänd** *a5* **1** reversed, turned round (upside

O

down, inside out); (*motsatt*) reverse, opposite; *mat.* inverse; ~ *ordning* reverse order; *förhållandet är det rakt ~a* the case is exactly the reverse (opposite); *han var som en ~ hand* he was a changed man **2** *relig.* converted; *en ~ a* convert **-vända** *relig.* convert; ~ *sig* be converted **-vändelse** conversion **-vänt** inversely; *och ~ and vice versa* **-värdera** revalue, reassess **-värdering** revaluation **-värld** *~en* the world around [one *etc.*] **-värva** *v2* envelop; encompass; *vara -värvd av* be enveloped in (*rök* smoke), be encompassed by (*fiender* enemies) **-växlande I** *a4* alternating; alternate; varying (*lycka* fortune); varied (*program* programme); (*olikartad*) diversified **II** *adv* alternatingly *etc.*; (*turvis*) by turns **-växling** alternation; (*förändring*) change; (*olikhet*) variety; (*motsats enformighet*) variation; *som ~* for a change; *för ~s skull* for the sake of variety

omyndig under (not of) age; *en ~ a* minor **-förklara** declare incapable of managing his (*etc.*) own affairs **-het** (*minderårighet*) minority; (*fastslagen av domstol*) legal incapacity **-hetsförklaring** declaration of [legal] incapacity **-hetstid** minority

o|**målad** *a5* unpainted **-måttlig** immoderate; (*om pris, krav äv.*) exorbitant; (*överdriven*) excessive; (*om fåfänga*) inordinate **-måttlighet** immoderation; excess[iveness]; exorbitance **-mänsklig** inhuman; (*mildare*) inhumane; (*barbarisk*) barbarous **-mänsklighet** inhumanity; barbarity **-märklig** imperceptible; (*osynlig*) indiscernible **-märkt** *a4* unmarked; *~ av åren* untouched by the passage of time **-mätbar** *a1*, **-mätlig** [ˣɔ:-, -ˈmä:t-] *a1* immeasurable; (*gränslös*) boundless **-mättad** *kem.* unsaturated **-mättlig** *a1* insatiable **-möblerad** *a5* unfurnished

o|**möjlig** [ˣɔ:-, -ˈmöjj-] impossible; (*ogörlig*) unfeasible, impracticable; *han är ~ att komma åt* there's no getting at him; *göra sig ~* make o.s. impossible **-möjligen** *se omöjligt* **-möjliggöra** make impossib.. **-möjlighet** impossibility **-möjligt** *adv, jag kan ~* I cannot possibly **omönstrad** unpatterned, plain

onanera masturbate **onani** *s3* masturbation, onanism

o|**natur** (*tillgjodhet*) affectation **-naturlig** unnatural; (*tillgjord*) affected; (*abnorm*) abnormal **ond** *ont värre värst el. al* (*i bet. 2*) **1** (*illvillig*) evil; (*elak*) wicked; (*dålig*) bad (*dröm* dream; *samvete* conscience); ~ *aning* misgiving; *i ~ avsikt* with evil intent[ion]; ~ *cirkel* vicious circle; *aldrig säga ett ont ord* never say an ill (unkind) word; *väcka ont blod* create ill feeling **2** (*förargad*) angry, vexed, annoyed, cross (*på* with; *över* at; *över att* that); *AE. äv.* mad (*på* at; *över* about); *bli ~* get angry (*etc.*) **3** (*som gör ont*) sore (*ben* leg); ~ *tand* aching tooth **4** *det onda a*) (*t.ex. som ngn gjort*) the evil, *b*) (*sjukdomen*) the malady (complaint), *c*) (*smärtorna*) the pain[s *pl*], the ache; *ta det ~a med det goda* take the good with the bad; *den ~e* the Evil One **5** *vara av ~o* be of evil; *fräls oss från ~o!* deliver us from evil!

ondgöra *rfl* take offence (*över* at); ~ *sig över att* (*äv.*) take it amiss that **ondo** *se ond 5* **ondsint**

al (*argsint*) ill-tempered; (*illvillig*) malevolent **ondska** *s1* evil; (*sedefördärv*) wickedness; (*elakhet*) malice, malignity **ondskefull** malignant, malevolent, spiteful

onduler|a [å-] wave **-ing** waving; *en ~ a* wave **oneklig** [-e:-] *a1* undeniable **onekligen** undeniably, without doubt; (*obestridligen*) indisputably **onjutbar** unenjoyable; (*oaptitlig*) unpalatable **onkel** [ˈäŋkel] *s2* uncle **onomatopoetisk** [ånɔ-, -ɔ'e:t-] onomatopoe[t]ic **onormal** abnormal **onoterad** *a5* unquoted; (*om värdepapper*) unlisted **onsdag** [ˈɔns-] *s2* Wednesday; *jfr fredag* **ont** *n* **1** evil; (*skada*) harm; (*smärtor*) pain, ache; *ett nödvändigt ~ a* necessary evil; *på gott och ~* that cuts both ways; *intet ~ anande* unsuspecting; *göra ~* (*orsaka smärta*) give pain; *det gör mig ~ att* it grieves me that; *det gör mig ~ om honom* I feel so sorry for him; *det gör ~ när du nyps* it hurts when you pinch; *ha ~ i huvudet* (*magen*) have a headache (stomachache); *ha ~ i sinnet* have evil designs; *jag har ~ i ryggen* I have a pain in my back, my back aches (hurts); *jag har inget ~ gjort* I have done no wrong (*skada:* harm); *vad har jag gjort dig för ~?* what harm have I done you?; *vi hade inget ~ av* we were not disturbed (troubled) by (*oväsendet* the noise); *det ligger ingenting ~ i det* there is nothing wrong (no harm) in that; *löna ~ med gott* return good for evil; *jag ser inget ~ i det* there is no wrong (harm) in that; *slita ~* have a rough time of it; *tro ngn om ~* believe the worst of s.b.; *det är inte ngt ~ i honom* there's no harm in him; *inget ~ som inte har ngt gott med sig* it's an ill wind that blows nobody any good **2** *ha ~ om* be short of; *ha ~ om pengar* be hard up [for money]; *ha ~ om tid* be pressed for time; *det är ~ om kaffe* coffee is scarce, there is a shortage of coffee; *det börjar bli ~ om kaffe* coffee is running short

onumrerad *a5* unnumbered; unreserved **onus** [ˈɔ:-] *s7, pl äv. onera* encumbrance, burden o|**nyanserad** without nuances; (*friare*) undifferentiated; *bildl.* oversimplified, superficial **-nykter** drunk[en], intoxicated **-nykterhet** drunkenness; insobriety **-nyttig** useless, of no use; unprofitable, futile

onyx [ˈɔ:-] *s2, miner.* onyx **onåd** disgrace; disfavour; (*misshag*) displeasure; *komma i ~ hos ngn* fall out of favour with s.b., get into a p.'s bad books **onådig** ungracious; (*ogynnsam*) unfavourable **onådigt** *adv* ungraciously, with a bad grace; *upptaga ngt ~* take umbrage (offence) at s.th.

o|**nämnbar** *a1* unmentionable **-nämnd** *a5* unmentioned; (*anonym*) anonymous **-nödan** *i uttr.: i ~* unnecessarily **-nödig** unnecessary; needless **-nödigtvis** unnecessarily; needlessly **-ombedd** [ˣɔ:åm-] *a5* unasked; uninvited **-omkullrunk[e]lig** [ˣɔ:åm-] *al* irrefutable (*åsikt* opinion); impregnable, invincible (*sanning* truth) **-omtvistlig** [ˣɔ:åm-] *al* indisputable **-ordentlig** (*om pers.*) careless, (*vårdslös*) slovenly, (*i klädsel*) untidy; (*om sak*) disorderly, (*ostädad*) untidy **-ordnad** disordered; (*om för-*

hållanden o.d.) unsettled **-ordning** [state of] disorder; (*röra*) mess, muddle; (*förvirring*) confusion; *bringa i* ~ throw into confusion, get into a mess **-organiserad** [*ˣɔːår-] *a5* unorganized; (*klandrande*) unordered; ~ *arbetare* nonunionist **-organisk** inorganic

opak *a1* opaque

opal *s3, miner.* opal **opaliserande** [-'seː-] *a4* **-skimrande** [-ˣpaːlʃim-] *a4* opalescent

o|partisk impartial, unbiassed, unprejudiced; *polit.* nonparty **-passande** (*otillbörlig*) unbecoming; (*ej på sin plats*) improper, indecorous; (*anstötlig*) objectionable **-passlig** *a1* indisposed; *vard.* out of sorts, under the weather **-pedagogisk** unpedagogic[al]

opera ['ɔː-] *s1* opera; (*-hus*) opera house **-balett** opera ballet **-föreställning** opera performance **-musik** opera music **-sångare, sångerska** opera singer

operation operation (*äv. mil.*)

operations|analys operations (operational) research (analysis) **-bas** operation base **-bord** operating table **-kniv** operating knife **-sal** operation theatre **-sköterska** theatre nurse

operativ *a1* operative **operatris** [woman, girl] operator **operatör 1** (*kirurg*) operating surgeon **2** (*maskin-*) operator **operera 1** mil. o. allm. operate **2** med. operate (*ngn för magsår* on s.b. for gastric ulcer); carry out an operation; *bli* ~*d* be operated on; *cancer kan inte alltid* ~*s* it is not always possible to operate for cancer; ~ *bort* remove, have removed by an operation

operett *s3* musical comedy; light opera, operetta

opersonlig impersonal

opiat *s7, s4* opiate

opinion *s3* opinion; *den allmänna* ~*en* public opinion; *skapa en* ~ *för* rouse public opinion in favour of

opinions|bildande *a4* that moulds public opinion **-bildare** moulder (creator) of public opinion **-bildning** moulding of public opinion **-mätning** se *-undersökning* **-möte** ung. public meeting **-undersökning** public opinion survey, [opinion] poll **-yttring** expression of opinion; manifestation, demonstration

opium ['ɔː-] *s4* opium **-droppar** *pl* laudanum, tincture of opium (*sg*) **-handel** opium traffic **-håla** opium den **-pipa** opium pipe **-rökare** opium smoker **-vallmo** opium poppy

o|placerad *a5, sport.* unplaced **-plockad** [-å-] *a5, ha en gås* ~ *med ngn* have a crow to pluck with s.b. **-plogad** *a5* uncleared by the snowplough **-plöjd** *a5* unploughed **-poetisk** unpoetical **-polerad** *a5* unpolished; *bildl. äv.* unrefined, rough **-politisk** unpolitical, nonpolitical; (*oklok*) impolitic

opossum [ɔˣpåss-] *s3, zool.* (*pungrätta*) opossum; (*pungräv*) [brush-tailed] phalanger

opp [åpp] se *upp*

opponent [å-] *s3* opponent **opponera** object (*mot* to); oppose; ~ *sig* make (raise) objections (*mot* to); ~ *sig mot* (*äv.*) object to, oppose

opportun [å-] *a1* opportune, timely; (*lämplig*) expedient **opportunist** opportunist, timeserver **opportunistisk** [-'niss-] *a5* opportunist **opportunitetsskäl** [-ˣteːts-] *av* ~ for reasons of

expediency

opposition [å-] opposition **oppositionell** *a1* oppositional (*mot* towards) **oppositions|ledare** leader of the opposition **-lust** love of opposition **-lysten** oppositional; dissentious **-parti** opposition party; ~*et* (*äv.*) the Opposition

o|praktisk unpractical; *AE.* impractical **-pressad** *a5* unpressed **-pretentiös** unpretentious **-prioriterad** *a5* unsecured, unprivileged; nonessential, nonpriority **-pris** (*det är inget* ~ it is not too expensive (quite reasonable) **-privilegierad** *a5* unprivileged **-proportionerlig** disproportionate; *vara* ~ (*äv.*) be out of [all] proportion **-prövad** untried, inexperienced; (*ej utprovad*) untested **-psykologisk** unpsychological

optik [å-] *s3* optics (*pl, behandlas som sg*) **optiker** ['åpp-] optician

optimal [å-] *a1* optimum **optimera** optimize **optimering** [-'meː-] optimization **optimism** optimism; *försiktig* ~ guarded optimism **optimist** optimist **optimistisk** [-'miss-] *a5* optimistic **optimistjolle** optimist pram **optimum** ['åpp-] *best. form optimum, äv. optimet* optimum

option [åpˈʃɔːn] option **optionstid** option period

optisk ['åpp-] *a5* optical; (*om t.ex. axel, vinkel äv.*) optic; ~ *villa* optical illusion

opublicerad *a5* unpublished

opus ['ɔː-] *s7, pl äv. opera* work, production; *mus.* opus, composition

o|putsad *a5* unpolished; (*om fönster*) uncleaned **-påkallad** *at* uncalled for **-pålitlig** unreliable; untrustworthy, not to be depended upon; (*farlig*) unsafe **-pålitlighet** unreliability; undependability **-påräknad** [-äː-] *a5* unexpected **-påtalt** [-aː-] *a4* unnoticed; without remonstrance (a protest) **-påverkad** *a5* unaffected, uninfluenced **-påverkbar** unimpressionable; immovable; unyielding

or *s7, zool.* mite

o|raffinerad unrefined, crude **-rakad** *a5* unshaved, unshaven

orakel [-ˈraː-] *s7, s4* oracle **-mässig** *a1* oracular **-svar** oracle

orange [ɔˈranʃ, -ˈraŋʃ] **I** *s5* orange **II** *a4* orange **-färgad** orange-coloured

orange|ri [-nʃ-, -ŋʃ-] orangery, hothouse **-röd** orange-red

orangutang [ɔraŋguˈtaŋ, ɔraŋu-] orang-utan, orang-outang

oransonerad *a5* unrationed

oration oration **orator** [-ˣaːtår] *s3* orator **oratorisk** [-ˈtɔː-] *a5* oratorical **oratorium** [-ˈtɔː-] *s4* oratorio

ord [ɔːrd] *s7* word; ~ *för* ~ word for word, verbatim; *ett sanningens* ~ a home truth; ~*et är fritt* (*vid möte e.d.*) the meeting is open for discussion; *det ena* ~*et gav det andra* one word led to another; *det är* ~ *och avsked med honom* he is a plain-speaking man; ~ *och inga visor* plain speaking, no beating about the bush; *använda fula* ~ use bad language; *begära* ~*et* request permission to speak; *bryta* (*hålla*) *sitt* ~ break (keep) one's word; *få* ~*et* (*äv.*) get the floor; *få ett* ~ *med i laget* get a voice in the matter; *få sista* ~*et* have the last word; *ge sitt ~ på att* give one's word that; *ha ~ om sig att vara* have the reputation of being; ... *har ~et* ... is speaking; *ha ~et i sin makt* never be at a loss for words; *i ~ och gärningar* in word and deed; *vara stor i ~en* talk big; *lägga ett gott ~ för ngn* put in a good word for s.b.; *med andra ~* in other words, *med egna ~* in one's own words; *med ett ~* [*sagt*] in a word, briefly; *märka ~* catch at words, quibble; *du sa ett ~!* you are right there!; *inte skräda ~en* not mince matters; *stå vid sitt ~* stick to one's word; *ta ngn på ~en* take s.b. at his word; *ta till ~a* begin to speak; *tala några ~ med ngn* have a word with s.b.; *tro ngn på hans ~* believe a p.'s word; *du måste tro mig på mitt ~* you must take my word for it; *vi visste inte ~et av förrän* before we knew where we were; *innan man visste ~et av* before you could say Jack Robinson; *välja sina ~* choose one's words; *överlämna ~åt* call upon s.b. to speak

orda [ˣoːr-] talk (*om* about) **-grann** literal; word for word **-lag** *pl* words, terms; *i väl valda ~* in appropriate (well-chosen) terms (phrases) **-lydelse** wording, text

ord|behandling word processing **-behandlingsmaskin** word processor **-bildning** word-formation **-blind** word-blind **-bok** dictionary **-boksförfattare** lexicographer, dictionary compiler **-byte** dispute, altercation **-böjning** word inflection

orden [ˈå:r-] *best. form* orden, *pl* ordnar order; *få en ~* have an order conferred upon one

ordens|band ribbon of an order **-behängd** *a5* covered with decorations **-brev** diploma of an order **-broder** brother of an order **-förläning** award of an order **-insignier** *pl* insignia of an order **-kapitel** chapter of an order (the Order) **-regn** shower of decorations (honours) **-sällskap** order [fraternity] **-tecken** badge of an order **-utdelning** bestowal of orders **-väsen** [the] system of orders

ordentlig [år'dent-] *a1* (*noggrann*) careful, accurate (*med* about, as to); (*ordningsam*) well-behaved, well-conducted, orderly (*ung man* young man); (*proper, städad*) tidy, neat; (*riktig*) proper, regular, real, decent; (*rejäl*) thorough, down-right, sound (*avbasning* thrashing); *ett ~t mål mat* (*äv.*) a square meal **-het** carefulness *etc.*; orderliness *etc.*; regularity *etc.*

ordentligt *adv* in a careful (*etc.*) way; properly; thoroughly; *sova ut ~* sleep one's fill

order [ˈå:r-] order (*om, på* for) (*äv. hand.*); (*uppdrag*) commission; (*instruktion*) instructions (*pl*); *mil.* order, command; *ge ~ om* (*äv.*) order; *lyda ~* obey orders; *på ~ av* by order of; *i ~* on order; *närmare ~* further instructions; *betala till herr A. eller ~* pay [to] Mr. A. or order **-bekräftelse** *se* -*erkännande* **-blankett** order form **-bok** order book **-erkännande** acknowledgement of order, confirmation of an order **-givning** [-ji:v-] *mil.* issuing of orders (an order); *flyg.* briefing **-mottagare** incoming orders clerk **-sedel** order sheet (slip) **-stock** *s2* backlog [of orders], [volume of] orders on hand

ord|fattig (*om språk*) with a small vocabulary **-fläta** *se korsord* **-flöde** flow of words **-följd** word order

ordförande *s9* (*i förening o.d.*) president; (*vid möte*) chairman (*vid* at, of); *sitta som ~* act as chairman, be in the chair, preside **-klubba** chairman's gavel **-skap** *s7* presidency; chairmanship; *under ~ av* under the presidency (*etc.*) of **-stol** president's chair; chairman's seat

ord|förklaring explanation of words (a word); *~ar* (*äv.*) explanatory notes, glossary **-förråd** vocabulary **-hållig** *a1* true (loyal) to one's word

ordinand [å-] *s3* candidate for ordination, ordinand

ordinarie [-ˈna:-] *oböjligt a* ordinary; (*regelmässig*) regular; (*om tjänst*) permanent; (*fast anställd*) on the permanent staff, (*inom förvaltn.*) established; *icke* (*extra*) *~* unestablished; *~ professor* full professor; *~ priser* usual (normal) prices

ordinata [-ˣna:-] *s1, mat.* ordinate

ordination 1 *med.* prescription **2** (*prästvigning*) ordination **ordinera 1** *med.* prescribe **2** (*prästviga*) ordain

ordinär *a1* ordinary; common, average

ord|karg of few words, sparing of words; taciturn **-klass** part of speech **-knapp** *se -karg* **-lek** pun **-lista** list of words, glossary, vocabulary (*över* of)

ordn|a [ˣå:rd-] arrange; *AE. äv.* fix; (*bringa -ing i*) put in order, tidy [up]; adjust (*sin klädsel* one's dress); (*affärer o.d.*) settle; (*reda ut*) get into order; (*reglera*) regulate, order; (*sortera*) sort; *~ efter storlek* arrange according to size; *~ med* arrange [for], provide for, attend to; *~ upp* settle, put to rights; *~ sig* arrange itself; *det ~r sig nog* things will sort themselves out, it will come out all right **ordnad** *a5* arranged *etc.*; settled; *ordnat arbete* regular work; *~e förhållanden* settled conditions

ordning [å:-] **1** order; (*ordentlighet*) orderliness, tidiness; (*metod*) method, plan; (*föreskrift*) regulations (*pl*); *i god ~* in an orderly manner; *för ~ens skull* as a matter of form, just in case; *den allmänna ~en* law and order; *få ~ på ngt* get s.th. straight; *hålla ~ i* keep in good order; *hålla ~ på* keep in order; *i ~* in order, (*färdig*) ready, all set ; *alldeles i sin ~* quite right (in order); *i vederbörlig ~* in due course; *göra i ~* get ready, prepare; *göra sig i ~* get ready (*till* for); *höra till ~en för dagen* be quite in the regular course of things; *kalla till ~en* call to order; *återgå till ~en* return to the normal [state of things] **2** (*följd*) course, order; *alfabetisk ~* alphabetical order; *i tur och ~* in turn; *den tredje i ~en* the third **3** *naturv.* order; *stjärna av första ~en* star of the first magnitude **4** (*typ, figur*) specimen

ordningsam *a1, se ordentlig*

ordnings|betyg order mark **-fråga** point of order **-följd** order, succession, sequence **-makt** police; constabulary **-man** *skol.* monitor; prefect **-människa** man (*etc.*) of method **-nummer** serial number **-polis** uniformed (*i storstad:* metropolitan) police **-regel** rule **-sinne** sense of order (method) **-stadga** regulations (*pl*) **-tal** ordinal [number] **-vakt** watchman, patrol; doorkeeper; *jfr -man*

ordonnans [årdåˈnans, -ˈnaŋs] *s3* orderly; (*motorcykel-*) dispatch rider **-officer** orderly officer;

(*adjutant*) aid[e]e-de-camp
ord|rik (*om språk*) with a large vocabulary; (*om pers.*) verbose, wordy **-rytteri** cavilling, quibbling **-slut** word-ending **-språk** proverb **-språksbok** O~en [the Book of] Proverbs **-stam** word-stem **-strid** wrangle, verbal dispute **-ström** stream of words **-stäv** *s7* saying **-svall** torrent of words **-val** choice of words **-vändning** phrase **-växling** altercation

o|**realiserbar** unrealizable, unworkable; (*friare*) utopian **-realistisk** unrealistic **-reda** disorder; (*förvirring*) [state of] confusion; (*röra*) muddle, mess; *bringa* ~ *i* throw into disorder, get into a muddle (mess); *ställa till* ~ cause confusion **-redig** confused; (*om framställning o.d.*) entangled, muddled; (*virrig*) muddleheaded; (*oklar*) vague **-redlig** dishonest **-reflekterad** *a5* unreflecting, rash, hasty

oregano [oʻre:-, -ˈga:-] *s5* oregano, origanum
o|**regelbunden** irregular; anomalous **-regelbundenhet** irregularity; anomaly **-regerlig** [-je:r-] *a1* unmanageable; *bli* ~ (*äv.*) get out of hand **-registrerad** [-j-] *a5* unregistered **-reglerad** *a5* unregulated

oren unclean; (*starkare*) filthy; (*förorenad*) impure (*äv. mus.*); *mus. äv.* false; (*grådaskig*) muddy; (*syndfull*) unchaste **orena** pollute **orenhet** impurity **orenlig** uncleanly **orenlighet** uncleanliness; *konkr.* dirt, filth

o|**rensad** (*om trädgårdsland*) unweeded; (*om bär o.d.*) unpicked; (*om fisk*) ungutted **-reparerbar** [-e:r-] *a1* irreparable (*äv. bildl.*)

orera speechify
o|**reserverad** unreserved; unqualified (*beundran* admiration) **-resonlig** unreasonable; (*halsstarrig*) stubborn, obstinate **-retuscherad** *a5* not touched-up, untouched

orfisk [ˈårf-] *a5* Orphic, Orphean
orgạn [å-] *s7* organ (*för* of); (*redskap*) instrument; (*institution e.d.*) institution, body; authority

organdi [å-] *s3* organdie, organdy
organisation [å-] organization; *facklig* ~ trade union (organization)
organisations|förmåga organizing ability **-plan** organization chart (plan) **-tvång** [the principle of the] closed shop, the obligation to join a trade union
organis|atorisk [-ˈtɔ:-] *a5* organizing, organizational **-atör** organizer **-era** organize
organ|isk [-ˈga:-] *a5* organic **-ism** *s3* organism
organist [å-] organist, organ player
orgasm [å-] *s3* orgasm
orgel [ˣårjel] *s2* organ **-harmonium** organ harmonium **-konsert** organ recital **-läktare** organ loft **-musik** organ music **-pipa** organ pipe **-register** organ stop **-spelare** organist, organ player **-trampare** organ blower
orgiastisk [årgiˈast-] *a5* orgiastic **orgie** [ˈårgie, ˈårjie] *s5* orgy; (*dryckes- äv.*) revel, carousal; ~*r* (*äv.*) revelry (*sg*), excesses; *en* ~ *av färger* a riot of colour
orientạl [å-] **I** *s3* Oriental **II** *a1* Oriental; Eastern **-isk** *a5* oriental; (*om matta äv.*) Turkish, Persian **-ist** Orientalist
Orienten [åriˈenn-] *best. form*, *r* the Orient;

Främre ~ the [Near and] Middle East
orientera [å-] **1** (*inrikta*) orient[ate] **2** (*underrätta*) inform, brief **3** *sport.* orienteer **4** *rfl* (*ta reda på var man är*) orient[ate] o.s., get one's bearings; (*göra sig bekant med*) inform o.s. (*i*, *om* about), acquaint o.s. (*i* with)
orienterad [-ˈte:-] *a5* (*inriktad*) oriented (*i norr o. söder* north and south); *polit.* sympathetic (*mot* to); (*informerad*) informed (*i*, *om* about), familiar (*i* with) **orienterande** *a4* introductory, explanatory (*redogörelse* statement) **orienterare** [-ˣte:-] *sport.* orienteer **orientering 1** (*inriktning*) orientation (*mot* towards), location; (*tendens*) trend, tendency **2** (*införande*) introduction, information; (*översikt*) survey **3** *sport.* orienteering
orienterings|förmåga sense of locality (direction) **-löpare** *se orienterare* **-punkt** checkpoint **-tavla** (*vägmärke*) advance direction sign **-tävling** orienteering race **-ämne** general subject
original [år[i]giˈna:l, -ji-] *s7* original; *pers.* eccentric [person], character; *boktr.* camera-ready copy, mechanical **-förpackning** original packing; *i* ~ as packed by the producer (*etc.*) **-handling** original [document, deed]
originalitet original originality; (*ngns äv.*) eccentricity
originalitetsjakt pursuit of originality
original|manuskript original manuscript **-språk** original language **-tappning** *vin i* ~ chateau bottled wine **-upplaga** first (original) edition
originell [år[i]giˈnell, -ji-] *a1* original; (*säregen*) eccentric, odd, peculiar
origo [-ˈri:-] *s9*, *mat.* origin; *i* ~ at the origin
o|**riktig** incorrect, erroneous, wrong **-riktighet** incorrectness, error **-rimlig** preposterous, absurd; (*obillig*) unreasonable; *det* ~*a i* the absurdity of; *begära det* ~*a* demand the impossible **-rimlighet** preposterousness; absurdity **-rimmad** *a5* unrhymed; blank
ork [å-] *s3* energy, strength, stamina **orka** [ˣårr-] have the strength (power) (*ngt* for (to do) s.th.); *jag* ~*r inte mer a*) I cannot go on any longer, I am exhausted, *b*) (*äta mer*) I cannot eat any more; *jag* ~*r inte höra på dig längre* I can't listen to you any longer; *allt vad man* ~*r a*) (*arbeta* work) one's hardest, *b*) (*skrika* shout) as loud as one can, at the top of one's voice, *c*) (*springa* run) as fast as one can, at the top of one's speed
orkad|ier [-ˈka:-] (*inv. på Orkneyöarna*) Orcadian **-isk** Orcadian
orkạn [å-] *s3* hurricane **-artad** [-a:r-] *a5* hurricane-like
orkeslös [ˣårr-] infirm; (*kraftlös*) effete, enfeebled; (*svag*) feeble **-het** infirmity; feebleness
orkester [år'kest-] *s2* orchestra; (*dans-*) band **-dike** orchestra [pit] **-dirigent** conductor; (*dans-*) bandmaster, bandleader **-ledare** *se -dirigent* **-musik** orchestral music **-verk** orchestral work
orkestr|al [å-] *a1* orchestral **-era** orchestrate **-ering** [-ˈe:r-] orchestration
orkide [årki-, -çi-] *s3* orchid
orm *s2* snake; *bibl. o. bildl.* serpent **orma** *rfl* (*ringla*) wind (*fram* along), (*om pers.*) crawl (*fram* along)

O

orm|bett snakebite **-biten** a5 snakebitten **-bo** snake's (bildl. serpent's) nest **-bunke** s2 fern **-bär** herb Paris **-gift** snake venom **-grop** snake pit **-lik** a5 snaky, serpentine **-människa** contortionist **-serum** antivenin **-skinn** (material) snakeskin; (urkrupet) slough **-slå** s5 slowworm, blindworm **-spott** cuckoo (frog) spit **-tjusare** [-ç-] snake charmer **-vråk** buzzard

ornament s7 ornament **ornamental** a1 ornamental **ornamentera** ornament **ornamentering** [-'te:-] ornamentation **ornamentik** s3 ornamental art, ornamentation

ornat official vestments (pl); (ämbetsmans) robes (pl) of office; i full ~ in full canonicals (om biskop: pontificals) (pl)

orne [ˣɔ:r-] s2 boar

orner|a ornament, decorate **-ing** ornamentation

ornito|log ornithologist **-logi** s3 ornithology **-logisk** [-'lå:-] a5 ornithological

oro s9 **1** [state of] agitation; unrest, restlessness; (sinnesrörelse) uneasiness, perturbation; (farhåga) anxiety, concern, (starkare) alarm; (nervositet) nervousness, fidgets (pl); hysa ~ för feel concern for, be anxious about; känna ~ i kroppen feel restless all over, vard. have the fidgets **2** (i ur) balance wheel **oroa** (störa) disturb, trouble, bother; ~ sig worry (för, över about) **oroande** a4 disturbing, disquieting

orolig a1 **1** (rastlös) restless; (upprörd o.d.) agitated, disturbed; troubled (sömn sleep); ~a tider unsettled (troubled) times **2** (ängslig) anxious, uneasy, worried, (starkare) alarmed; (bekymrad) concerned; vara ~ över (äv.) worry about; du behöver inte vara ~! you needn't worry! **-het** ~er disturbances, troubles, unrest (sg)

oromantisk unromantic

oros|ande restless person, rolling stone **-centrum** centre of disturbance **-element** disturbing element **-faktor** element of unrest; disturbing element **-härd** trouble spot **-moln** storm cloud **-stiftare** disturber of the peace, troublemaker; polit. agitator

oroväckande a4 alarming, disquieting

orr|e [ˣärre] s2, zool. black grouse; (orrtupp) blackcock **-höna** greyhen **-spel** blackcocks' courtship display **-tupp** blackcock

orsak [ˣɔ:r-] s3 (grund) cause (till of); (skäl) reason (till for); ~ och verkan cause and effect; av den ~en for that reason; ingen ~! don't mention it!, not at all!, AE. you're welcome! **orsaka** cause; occasion

orsaks|förhållande causal relationship, causality **-sammanhang** causal connection

ort [ɔ:rt] s3 **1** place; (trakt) locality, district; på ~ och ställe on the spot; på högre ~ in higher quarters; på högsta ~ at top level **2** (gruv.) gallery, heading **-namn** place name **-namnsforskning** place-name research, toponomy

orto|ceratit [å-] s3 orthoceratite **-donti** s3 orthodontia, orthodontics **-dox** [-'dåkks] a2 orthodox **-doxi** [-dåk'si:] s3 orthodoxy **-grafi** s1 orthography **-grafisk** [-'gra:-] a5 orthographic[al]

ortolan s3, **-sparv** ortolan

orto|ped s3 orthopaedist, orthopaedic surgeon **-pedi** s3, ej pl orthopaedics (pl, behandlas som sg) **-pedisk** [-'pe:-] a5 orthopaedic

ortoptist orthoptist **ortoptris** orthoptist

orts|avdrag basic regional tax allowance **-befolkning** ~en the local population (inhabitants) **-pressen** the local press

o|rubbad a5, sitta i -rubbat bo remain in sole possession **-rubblig** a1 immovable; bildl. unshakeable, imperturbable (lugn composure); (fast) firm, steadfast **-rutinerad** inexperienced; unskilled **-rygglig** a1 irrevocable (beslut decision); unswerving (trohet fidelity)

oråd s7, ana ~ take alarm, vard. smell a rat; utan att ana ~ unsuspectingly; ta sig det ~et före att take it into one's head to

o|rädd fearless; (djärv) intrepid, daring **-räddhet** fearlessness; intrepidity **-räknelig** [ˣɔ:-, -'rä:k-] a1 innumerable, countless, numberless **-räntabel** unprofitable, unremunerative

orätt I s3 wrong, injustice; med rätt eller ~ rightly or wrongly; göra ngn ~ wrong s.b., do s.b. an injustice; ha ~ be in the wrong **II** a4 wrong; komma i ~a händer fall into the wrong hands **-färdig** unjust; unrighteous, iniquitous **-färdighet** injustice; unrighteousness, iniquity **-mätig** unlawful, wrongful, illegitimate **-rådig** unrighteous, iniquitous **-vis** unjust (mot to, towards); unfair (mot to) **-visa** injustice; (oförrätt) wrong; de -visor som begåtts the injustices (the wrongs) of the past

o|rörd untouched; intact; (ej flyttad) unmoved; ~ natur unspoiled countryside **-rörlig** immovable; (stå stand) motionless; (om ansikte, trupper) immobile; (fast) fixed, stationary

1 os s7 mouth, estuary

2 os s7 smell [of smoke]; fumes (pl)

osa smell; det ~r there's a smell of smoke; det ~r bränt (äv.) the fat's in the fire; ~ ihjäl suffocate by smoke

o.s.a. (förk. för om svar anhålles) R.S.V.P., se under anhålla

o|sagd unsaid; det vill jag låta vara -sagt I will leave that unsaid **-sakkunnig** non-expert, incompetent **-saklig** irrelevant; not objective **-salig** (fördömd) unredeemed, damned; en ~ ande a lost soul **-saltad** a5 unsalted; fresh (smör butter) **-sammanhängande** disconnected; (lösryckt) disjointed; (förvirrad) incoherent **-sammansatt** uncompounded; (okomplicerad) uncomplicated **-sams** (jfr oense) bli ~ quarrel (med with); bli ~ ngn (äv.) fall out (get at loggerheads) with s.b. **-sann** untrue **-sannfärdig** untruthful, false **-sanning** untruth, lie; fara med ~ be untruthful, tell untruths; tala ~ tell lies (a lie), not speak the truth **-sannolik** improbable, unlikely; det är ~t att han he is unlikely to

oscill|ator [åʃiˣla:tår] s3 oscillator **-era** oscillate **oscillo|graf** [åʃilo-] s3 oscillograph **-gram** [-'gramm] s7 oscillogram **-skop** [-'skå:p] s7 oscilloscope

o|sed bad practice (hos en pers.: habit) **-sedd** a5 unseen, without being seen; unobserved **-sedlig** immoral; (stötande) indecent **-sedlighet** immorality **-sedvanlig** not customary; unusual, uncommon **-sentimental** unsentimental **-signerad** [-iŋn-, -inj-] a5 unsigned **-sinnlig** immaterial; spiritual; (okroppslig) incorporeal

osis ['ɔ:-] s3, vard. bad luck

o|självisk unselfish **-själviskhet** unselfishness **-självständig** dependent on others; (*om produkt*) imitative, unoriginal **-självständighet** lack of independence, unoriginality **-skad[a]d** *a5* unhurt, uninjured; (*om sak äv.*) undamaged; (*om pers. äv.*) safe and sound **-skadlig** harmless; innocuous (*botemedel* remedy) **-skadliggöra** render harmless (*etc.*); (*gift e.d.*) neutralize; (*kanon o.d.*) put out of action; (*bomb o.d.*) disarm **-skarp** (*slö*) blunt; (*suddig*) blurred, unsharp **-skattbar** *al* priceless, inestimable, invaluable **-skick** [ˣɔːʃikk] *s7* (*dåligt uppförande*) bad behaviour, misconduct; (*oart*) bad habit; *det är ett* ~ it is obnoxious **-skicklig** unskilful; (*fumlig*) awkward, clumsy **-skicklighet** unskilfulness; lack of skill **-skiftad** [ˣɔːʃif-] *a5* undivided (*dödsbo* estate [of a deceased person]) **-skiljaktig, -skiljbar** *al* inseparable **-skolad** *a4* untrained; untutored **-skriven** *a5* unwritten (*lag* law); (*som inget skrivits på*) blank (*äv. bildl.*); *han är ett -skrivet blad* he is an unknown quantity **-skrymtad** *a5* unfeigned, undissembled; sincere, genuine

oskuld *s3* **1** innocence; (*jungfrulighet*) virginity **2** (*orörd flicka*) virgin; innocent; *en* ~ *från landet* a country cousin **oskuldsfull** innocent; pure

o|skummad *a5*, ~ *mjölk* whole milk **-skyddad** [ˣɔːʃyd-] *a5* unprotected (*mot* against, from); (*om läge o.d.*) unsheltered; (*försvarslös*) open **-skyldig** innocent; not guilty (*till* of); (*ej stötande*) inoffensive, harmless; *förklara ngn* ~ (*jur.*) find s.b. not guilty **-skälig 1** (*orimlig*) unreasonable; excessive, exorbitant **2** (*förnuftslös*) dumb; ~*t djur* dumb animal, brute **-skära** [ˣɔːʃäː-] *vl* (*besudla*) pollute; (*vanhelga*) desecrate, profane **-skön** (*ful*) ugly; (*ej tilltalande*) unlovely; (*om ansikte o.d.*) plain; (*frånstötande*) unsightly **-slagbar** [-aːgˉ] *al*, sport. (*om pers.*) undefeatable; (*om rekord*) unbeatable **-slipad** (*om verktyg*) unground; (*om glas äv.*) uncut; (*om kniv*) dull; (*om ädelsten*) rough, uncut; *bildl.* unpolished **-släcklig** *al* inextinguishable; *bildl. äv.* unquenchable **-släckt** *a4*, ~ *kalk* quicklime, unslaked lime **-smaklig** unsavoury (*äv. bildl.*); (*obehaglig*) distasteful, disgusting (*äv. bildl.*)

osman [åsˊmaːn] *s3* Osmanli, Ottoman **osmansk** [-aː-] *a5* Osmanli, Ottoman

o|smidig unsupple; *bildl.* inelastic; clumsy; (*om pers.*) unadaptable, gauche **-sminkad** *a5* unpainted; *bildl.* unvarnished, plain (*sanning* truth) **-smord** [-ɔː-] *a5* unoiled, ungreased

osmo|s [åsˊmåːs] *s3* osmosis **-tisk** [-ˊmåː-] *a5* osmotic; ~*t tryck* osmotic pressure

o|smyckad *a5* unadorned, plain **-smält** *a4* (*om föda o. bildl.*) undigested **-smältbar** (*om föda*) indigestible; *tekn.* infusible **-snuten** *a3*, *eg.* snotty; *en* ~ *lymmel* an unlicked rascal **-snygg** unclean, slovenly, dirty **-sockrad** [ˣɔːsåkk-] *a5* unsweetened **-solidarisk** disloyal **-sorterad** un[as]sorted **-spard** [-aː-] *a5*, *ha all möda* ~ spare no pains **-specificerad** *a5* unspecified **-spelbar** [-eː-] *al* unperformable; (*om musik äv.*) unplayable; (*om pjäs äv.*) unactable **-sportslig** unsportsmanlike, unsporting

oss [åss] us; *rfl* ourselves; ~ *alla* (*andra*) all (the rest) of us; ~ *själva* ourselves

1 ost *s2* cheese; *helfet* (*mager*) ~ high-fat (low-fat) cheese; *få betalt för gammal* ~ get paid out; *en lyckans* ~ a lucky beggar

2 ost I *s2* (*väderstreck*) east, East **II** *adv* east; East; *jfr nord*

ostadig unsteady, unstable; (*om väder o.d.*) unsettled, variable; *börs.* unsettled, fluctuating; *bildl.* unstable, volatile

ostan I *r* [the, an] east wind, easterly [wind] **II** *adv* easterly; *jfr nord*

ostasiatisk Far East[ern], East Asiatic

ost|beredning cheesemaking **-bit** piece of cheese **-bricka** cheeseboard

ostentatjv *al* ostentatious

osthyvel cheese slicer (cutter)

ostindiefarare East-Indiaman **Ostindien** *n* the East Indies (*pl*) **ostindisk** East Indian; ~*t porslin* old Chinese porcelain

ost|kaka curd cake **-kant** [a piece of] cheese rind **-kniv** cheese cutter (knife) **-kupa** cheese-dish cover

ost|kust ~*en* the east coast **-lig** *al* east[erly]; *jfr nordlig*

ostmassa curd[s *pl*]

ostnordost east-northeast

ostracism ostracism

ostraffad *a5* unpunished; *vara* ~ have no police-record **ostraffat** *adv* with impunity

ostron [-ån] *s7* oyster **-bank** oyster bed (bank) **-odling** *abstr.* oyster farming; *konkr.* oyster farm

o|struken *a3* **1** (*om kläder*) unironed **2** *mus.*, *-strukna oktaven* the small octave **-strängad** *a5* unstrung

ost|skiva slice of cheese **-smörgås** cheese sandwich

ost|sydost east-southeast **-vart** eastward[s]

ostvassla whey

o|styckad *a5* (*om egendom*) undivided; (*om djurkropp*) unquartered **-styrig** *al* unruly; (*oregerlig*) unmanageable **-städad** untidy **-stämd** *al* out of tune

ostämne casein

o|stämplad *a5* unstamped; (*om frimärke*) uncancelled; (*om guld, silver*) not hallmarked **-störd** [-öː-] *al* undisturbed, untroubled; *i* ~ *ro* in unbroken peace **-stört** *adv* undisturbedly; *arbeta* ~ work in peace **-sund** unhealthy, insanitary; *bildl. äv.* unwholesome; ~*a affärsmetoder* unfair business methods

osv. (*förk. för och så vidare*) *se under* och

o|sviklig unerring (*precision* accuracy); unfailing (*punktlighet* punctuality); infallible (*botemedel* remedy) **-svuren** *a5*, *-svuret är bäst* better not swear to it **-symmetrisk** asymmetrical, unsymmetrical **-sympatisk** unattractive, disagreeable; distasteful **-synlig** invisible; *göra sig* ~ (*försvinna*) make o.s. scarce **-syrad** *a5* unleavened (*bröd* bread) **-systematisk** unsystematic; (*friare*) unmethodical **-såld** unsold **-sårbar** invulnerable **-säker** uncertain, not sure (*om* about; *på* of); (*ostadig*) unsteady, shaky (*hand* hand), faltering (*röst* voice); (*otrygg*) unsure, insecure; (*vansklig*) precarious, risky (*situation* situation); (*tvivelaktig*) doubtful; *vara* ~ *på sig själv* be unsure of o.s.; -*säkra fordringar* bad (doubt-

C

ful] debts **-säkerhet** uncertainty; unsteadiness
etc.; insecurity **-säkerhetskänsla** feeling of
uncertainty (insecurity) **-säkra** (*vapen*) cock
-säljbar unsaleable, unmarketable **-sällskaplig** unsociable **-sämja** *se oenighet* **-sänkbar** *al*
unsinkable **-sökt** unsought; (*otvungen*) natural,
spontaneous **-sötad** unsweetened

o|**tack** ingratitude; ~ *är världens lön* the world's
reward is ingratitude **-tacksam** ungrateful (*mot*
to); (*om arbete, uppgift o.d. äv.*) thankless
-tacksamhet ingratitude **-tadlig** [-a:-] *al*
blameless; (*oklanderlig*) irreproachable **-takt** *i* ~
out of time (step) **-tal** *ett* ~ [*av*] a vast (an immense) number of **-talig** [ˣoː-, -ˈtaː-] *al* innumerable, countless **-talt** [-a:-] *i uttr.: ha ngt* ~
med ngn have a bone to pick with s.b.

o|**tid** *i uttr.: i* ~ at the wrong moment; *i tid och* ~
(*eg.*) in season and out of season; *fråga inte i tid
och* ~ don't keep asking questions all the time **-tidig** *al* (*ovettig*) abusive **-tidighet** abusiveness;
~*er* abusive remarks, abuse (*sg*) **-tidsenlig** out
of fashion (date); unfashionable
otillbörlig undue; (*opassande*) improper
otillfreds|ställande unsatisfactory; unsatisfying **-ställd** unsatisfied; dissatisfied **-ställdhet**
unsatisfiedness; dissatisfaction
otill|förlitlig unreliable; undependable **-gänglig** inaccessible, remote; *vard. äv.* unget-at-able;
(*reserverad*) reserved; (*okänslig*) insusceptible,
unamenable (*för* to) **-låten** (*hopskr. otillåten*)
forbidden, not permitted; (*olovlig*) unlawful;
sport. foul **-låtlig** (*hopskr. otillåtlig*) impermissible, inadmissible **-räcklig** insufficient, inadequate **-räcklighet** insufficiency, inadequacy
-räknelig not responsible for one's actions
-räknelighet irresponsibility; insanity **-ständig** *al* unwarrantable, unjustifiable
oting *s7* nuisance, horror
otit *s3* otitis
otium [ˈoːtsi-] *s4* leisure; *njuta sitt* ~ enjoy one's
well-earned leisure (retirement)
o|**tjänlig** unserviceable; (*olämplig*) unsuitable,
unfit (*till* for) **-tjänst** disservice; *göra ngn en* ~
do s.b. a bad turn **-tjänstvillig** disobliging
-trampad *a5* untrodden **-trevlig** disagreeable,
unpleasant; (*besvärlig*) awkward, uncomfortable
-trevlighet unpleasantness **-trevnad** discomfort **-trivsam** cheerless; (*om hem o.d.*) unhomely **-trivsel** discomfort
o|**tro** disbelief, lack of faith; (*klentrogenhet*) incredulity; (*tvivel*) scepticism **-trogen** unfaithful;
(*trolös*) faithless; (*falsk*) false; (*icke rättrogen*)
unbelieving, disbelieving; ~ *mot* unfaithful (*etc.*)
to; *de -gna* the unbelievers **-trohet** unfaithfulness, infidelity (*mot* to) **-trolig** incredible, unbelievable; (*häpnadsväckande*) amazing; *det gränsar till det* ~*a* it is almost incredible; ~*t men sant*
strange but true
o|**tryckbar** *al* unprintable **-trygg** insecure, unsafe **-trygghet** insecurity, unsafeness **-tränad**
a5 untrained; (*för tillfället*) out of practice (training) **-trängd** *i -trängt mål* without due cause
-tröstlig *al* inconsolable (*över* for); disconsolate (*över* at)
otta *s1, i* ~*n* in the early morning; *vara uppe i* ~*n*
get up early; *vänta till domedags* ~ wait till

doomsday **ottesång** mat[t]ins (*sg el. pl*)
ottoman *s3* **1** (*soffa*) couch, ottoman **2** (*turk*)
Ottoman
o|**tukt** fornication, lewdness; (*med minderårig*)
child assault, *AE.* statutory rape **-tuktig** *al* indecent, obscene **-tur** bad luck; *ha* ~ be unlucky
(*i kortspel* at cards); *vilken* ~! what bad luck!
-turlig [-u:-] *al*, **-tursam** unlucky **-tursdag**
unlucky day **-tursförföljd** dogged by misfortune **-tvetydig** unmistakable; (*om uttalande
o.d.*) unambiguous, unequivocal **-tvivelaktig**
indubitable, undoubted **-tvivelaktigt** *adv*
undoubtedly; no doubt **-tvungen** unconstrained, unrestrained; (*ledig*) free and easy
-tvungenhet spontaneity, ease **-tvättad** unwashed **-tydbar** undecipherable **-tydlig** indistinct; (*om uttal äv.*) inarticulate; (*svävande*)
vague; (*om t.ex. handstil*) illegible **-tyg** *s7* (*trolltyg*) witchcraft; (*elände*) abomination, nuisance
-tyglad [-y:-] *a5* unbridled, uncurbed (*fantasi*
imagination); unrestrained (*vrede* anger); (*hejdlös*) unchecked, uncontrolled **-tymplig** *al* ungainly, clumsy **-tålig** impatient (*att göra ngt* to do
s.th.; *på ngn* with s.b.; *över* at); (*ivrig*) anxious,
eager **-tålighet** impatience **-täck** *al* nasty, horrid; *AE. vard.* mean; (*ful*) ugly; (*avskyvärd*) abominable; (*besvärlig*) awful (*hosta* cough) **-täcking** ruffian; devil **-tämd** *al* untamed **-tänkbar**
inconceivable, unimaginable; *det är* ~*t att* (*äv.*) it
is out of the question to **-tät** not [water-, air- *etc.*]
tight; (*om kärl, tak o.d.*) leaky **-täthet** leak
-törstig *dricka sig* ~ drink one's fill (*på* of)
o|**umbärlig** indispensable **-undgänglig** [-jä-]
al unavoidable; (*nödvändig*) necessary **-undviklig** [-i:k-] *al* inevitable, unavoidable **-uppfostrad** badly brought up; ill-bred **-uppfylld** *a5*
unfulfilled **-uppgjord** *a5* unsettled **-upphörlig**
[-ö:-] *al* incessant; (*idelig*) constant, continual
-upphörligen [-ö:-] *al* constantly, continually, incessantly **-uppklarad** *a5* unexplained; unsettled; ~*e mord* unsolved murder cases **-upplyst**
unlit, unilluminated; *bildl.* unenlightened, uninformed, ignorant **-upplöslig** indissoluble, insoluble **-uppmärksam** inattentive, unobservant
(*mot* to) **-uppmärksamhet** inattentiveness,
inattention; (*förbiseende*) inadvertence; (*förströddhet*) preoccupation **-uppmärksammad**
a5 unnoticed **-uppnåelig** *al* unattainable **-upptäckt** *a4* undiscovered **-uppvärmd** unheated
-ursäktlig inexcusable **-utbildad** *a5* (*outvecklad*) undeveloped; (*för yrke e.d.*) untrained **-utforskad** [-å-] *a5* unexplored **-utförbar** impracticable, unfeasible; *AE. äv.* impractical; (*om
plan o.d.*) unrealizable, unworkable **-utgrundlig** *al* unfathomable; (*outrannsaklig*) inscrutable; (*gåtfull*) enigmatic; *ett* ~*t leende* an inscrutable smile; *av ngn* ~ *orsak* for some mysterious
reason **-uthyrd** [-y:-] *a5* unlet **-uthärdlig** [-ä:-]
al unendurable; intolerable, unbearable **-utlöst**
[-ö:-] *a4* (*om pant*) unredeemed; (*om postpaket
o.d.*) undischarged; *bildl.* unreleased **-utnyttjad** *a5* unused, unemployed; ~ *kapacitet* idle capacity **-utplånlig** [-å:-] *al* ineffaceable; (*om intryck, fläck, skam*) indelible **-utrannsaklig**
[-a:k-] *al, se -utgrundlig* **-utredd** *a5, bildl.* not
cleared up; unelucidated (*orsaker* reasons); unin-

vestigated **-utrotlig** [-ɔ:-] a1 ineradicable; (om ogräs) inextirpable

outsider [ˣaɔtsajder] s9, pl äv. -s outsider

out|sinlig [-i:n-] a1 inexhaustible, unfailing **-slitlig** [-i:t-] a1 that will not wear out; hardwearing; indestructible **-spädd** undiluted **-säglig** [ˣɔ:-, -'sä:g-] a1 unspeakable **-talad** a5 unuttered, unexpressed; unspoken (tanke thought) **-tröttlig** a1 indefatigable, inexhaustible; (friare) untiring, unremitting (nit zeal) **-tömlig** a1 inexhaustible **-vecklad** a5 undeveloped; (om pers.) immature

ouvertyr [ɔv-] s3 overture

ovaksam unwatchful

oval l s3 oval ll a1 oval

1 ovan [ˣå:van] adv o. prep above; som ~ as above

2 ovan [ˣɔ:va:n] unaccustomed (vid to; (oerfaren) inexperienced (vid at); (oövad) unpractised (vid in); (ovanlig) unfamiliar (för to)

ovana 1 (bristande erfarenhet) unfamiliarity; lack of practise **2** (osed) bad habit

ovan|del upper part; top **-för** l prep above ll adv above, higher up **-ifrån** from above

ovanlig unusual, uncommon; (sällsynt) rare; (exceptionell) exceptional; det är ~t att ngn it is unusual for anyone to; det ~a i situationen the unusual feature of the situation **-het** unusualness etc.; (sällsynthet) rarity; för ~ens skull for once, by way of a change; höra till ~en be quite unusual, be out of the ordinary

ovanligt adv unusually; (friare) exceptionally, extraordinarily; ~ nog for once in a way, extraordinarily enough

ovan|läder (på sko) vamp, upper **-nämnd** a5 above-mentioned **-på** l prep on, on [the] top of ll adv on [the] top; flyta ~ (bildl.) be superior **-sida** top, upper side

ovansklig [ˣɔ:-, -'vann-] everlasting; imperishable (ära glory)

ovanstående a4 the above; av ~ framgår att (äv.) it will be seen from the foregoing that

ovarium [-'va:-] s4 ovary

ovarsam (oaktsam) heedless; (vårdslös) careless

ovation ovation, acclamation **ovationsartad** [-a:r-] a5 ovationary; ~e applåder enthusiastic applause (sg)

oveder|häftig unreliable; untrustworthy **-lägglig** a1 irrefutable **-säglig** [-ä:-] a1 incontrovertible, undeniable

overall [åver'å:l] s3 overalls (pl); (småbarns-) zip suit; (dam-) cat suit

overheadprojektor [åver'hedd-] overhead projector

o|verklig unreal; immaterial; (diktad) imaginary, fictitious **-verklighet** unreality **-verksam** inactive; inert, passive; (sysslolös) idle; (utan verkan) ineffective **-verksamhet** inactivity; inertness, passivity; idleness **-vetande** unknowing (om of; om mig how); mig ~[s] without my knowledge **-vetenskaplig** unscientific **-vetskap** i ~ om ngt (om huruvida) in ignorance of s.th. (as to whether) **-vett** (bannor) scolding; AE. vard. calling down; (skäll) abuse; ge ngn ~ give s.b. a scolding, scold s.b.; en skopa ~ a torrent of abuse; överösa ngn med ~ heap abuse on

s.b. **-vettig** scolding; abusive

o|vidkommande [-i:-å-] a4 irrelevant **-vig** (i rörelser) cumbersome; (klumpig) heavy, unwieldy, clumsy **-vigd** [-i:-] a5 unconsecrated (jord ground) **-vighet** cumbersomeness etc. **-viktig** unimportant, insignificant; inte helt ~ not altogether immaterial **-vilja** (motvilja) aversion (mot to), repugnance (mot to[wards]); (avsky) detestation (mot of); (vrede) indignation (mot with) **-villig** unwilling; (om pers. äv.) disinclined, reluctant **-villkorlig** unconditional (kapitulation surrender); unqualified, implicit (lydnad obedience) **-villkorligen** [-å:-] absolutely, positively; (obetingat) unconditionally; ~ vilja veta absolutely insist on knowing; han kommer ~ att bli he is bound to be **-vis** unwise **-viss** uncertain (om about, as to); (villrådig) doubtful, dubious (om about, of); (obestämd) indefinite, vague **-visshet** uncertainty; doubtfulness etc.; sväva i ~ om be in doubt about ; hålla ngn i ~ om keep s.b. in suspense as to **-vårdad** neglected; (om utseende äv.) untidy; (om språk) careless

oväder storm; tempest; det kommer att bli ~ we are in for a stor

oväders|centrum centre of depression; storm centre **-moln** storm cloud (äv. bildl.) **-stämning** stormy atmosphere

o|vädrad [-ä:-] a5 unaired, unventilated; (instängd) close, stuffy **-väld** s3 impartiality **-väldig** a1 impartial, unbias[s]ed, unprejudiced **-välkommen** unwelcome; (ej önskad) undesired, unwanted **-vän** enemy **-vänlig** unkind (mot to); unfriendly; (fientlig) hostile (mot to) **-vänlighet** unkindness etc. **-vänskap** enmity **-väntad** a5 unexpected; detta kom[mer] alldeles -väntat (äv.) this comes quite as a surprise **-värderlig** [-de:r-] a1 invaluable, inestimable, priceless **-värdig** unworthy (ngn of s.b.; ngt of s.th.) (oförtjänt) undeserving (ngn to s.b.); det är dig ~t it is beneath you **-världslig** unworldly **-väsen** noise, din; (bråk) row **-väsentlig** unessential, unimportant (för to); immaterial (skillnad difference) **-väsentlighet** ~er unessential things, unessentials, trifles

oxalsyra [åkˣsa:l-] oxalic acid

ox|bringa brisket of beef **-drivare** ox-driver

oxe s2 ox (pl oxen)

oxel ['ɔksel] s2, bot. whitebeam

oxeltand molar [tooth], grinder

oxfilé fillet of beef

oxfordgrupprörelsen [ˣåksfård-] the Oxford Group Movement; Moral Rearmament

oxhud oxhide

oxid [åkˣsi:d] s3 oxide **oxidation** oxidation **oxidationsmedel** oxidizer, oxidant **oxidera** oxidize **oxidering** oxidization, oxidation **oxidyl** s3 protoxide, suboxide

ox|kärra ox-cart **-kött** beef **-rulad** beef roll **-stek** joint (sirloin) of beef **-svanssoppa** oxtail soup **-tunga 1** oxtongue **2** bot. alkanet **-öga** teat. bull's eye

ozelot [ɔse'lått] s3, zool. ocelot

ozon [ɔ'så:n, å-] s3, s4, kem. ozone **-haltig** a1 ozonic **-skikt** ozone layer

oår se missväxtår, nödår

o|återhållsam incontinent; (i mat o. dryck) immoderate; (*omåttlig*) intemperate **-återkallelig** *al* irrevocable **-återkalleligen** irrevocably, beyond recall **-åtkomlig** inaccessible (*för* to); *vara ~ för* (*äv.*) be unassailable by, be out of reach of o|**ädel** ignoble, base, mean; (*om metall*) base, nonprecious **-äkta** *oböjligt a* false, not genuine; (*imiterad*) imitation, mock, artificial; (*hycklad*) spurious; (*förfalskad*) counterfeit; *~ barn* illegitimate child; *~ diamanter* imitation (false) diamonds **-ändlig** [-'änd-, *x*ɔ:-] *al* endless, interminable; (*utan gräns äv.*) boundless; (*mat. o. friare*) infinite; *i det ~a* ad infinitum, for ever and ever, indefinitely **-ändlighet** [-'änd-, *x*ɔ:-] endlessness; infinity (*äv. ~en*); *han pratade i all ~* he talked endlessly (for no end of a time) **-ändlighetstecken** infinity sign (symbol) **-ändligt** [-'änd-, *x*ɔ:-] *adv* endlessly *etc.*; *~ liten* (*äv.*) infinitesimal **-ärlig** dishonest **-ärlighet** dishonesty **-ätbar** uneatable **-ätlig** *se -ätbar*; (*om svamp*) inedible **-även** *a3*, *inte ~* not bad (amiss) (*som* as); *inte så ~* (*vard.*) not half bad o|**öm** robust, tough; (*hållbar*) durable (*tyg* cloth) **-önskad** unwanted **-öppnad** *a5* unopened **-övad** unpractised *etc.* (*jfr öva*); (*otränad*) untrained, (*för tillfället*) out of practice; (*om trupper*) undisciplined

o**över**|**komlig** insurmountable, insuperable; (*om pris*) exorbitant, prohibitive **-lagd** unpremeditated; (*-tänkt*) ill-considered; (*obetänksam*) rash, hasty **-satt** *a4* untranslated; *en ännu ~ bok* a book not yet translated (*till* into) **-skådlig** incalculable, unforeseeable (*följder* consequences); (*oredig*) badly arranged (*uppsats* essay); (*enorm*) immense, boundless **-stiglig** [-i:g-] *al* unsurmountable; *bildl. äv.* insuperable **-sättlig** untranslatable **-träffad** *a5* unsurpassed **-träffbar** *al* unsurpassable; (*fulländad*) perfect, consummate **-tänkt** *a4*, *se -lagd* **-vinn[e]lig** *al* invincible; unconquerable; (*ointaglig*) impregnable; (*om svårighet*) insuperable

P

p [pe:] *s6, s7* p; *sätta ~ för* put a stop to
pacemaker ['pejsmejker] *s2, s9, med., sport.* pacemaker, pacer
pacificer|**a** pacify **-ing** pacification
pacif|**ism** pacifism **-ist** pacifist **-istisk** [-'ist-] *a5* pacifist
1 pack *s7* (*slödder*) mob, rabble; *ett riktigt ~* a lot of riffraff, a pack of scoundrels
2 pack *se pick och pack*
packa pack; (*~ full[t]*) cram; *~ ihop a*) pack together, *b*) (*dra sig tillbaka*) shut up shop, close

down; *~ ihop sig a*) (*om pers.*) squeeze (crowd) together, *b*) (*om snö o.d.*) pack, get packed; *~ in* pack up (*i en låda* in a box); *~ ner ngt i* pack s.th. into; *~ om* repack; *~ upp* unpack; *rummet var ~t med folk* the room was packed (crammed) with people; *stå som ~de sillar* be packed like sardines; *~ sig* (*om snö*) pack; *~ sig av* (*i väg*) make (pack, bundle) off; *~ dig i väg!* be off with you!, clear out! **packad** packed; (*berusad*) tight, stoned, loaded
packdjur beast of burden, pack animal
pack|**e** *s2* package; bundle; (*hög*) pile, heap **-hus** warehouse; (*tull-*) custom-house **-huspengar** warehouse charges **-häst** packhorse **-is** pack ice **-lår** packing-case **-ning 1** (*-ande*) packing *etc.*, *se packa* **2** *mil. o.d.* pack, kit; (*bagage*) luggage; *med full ~* (*mil.*) in full marching kit **3** *tekn.* packing; gasket **-sadel** packsaddle **-sedel** packing list, delivery note **-åsna** pack-ass; *bildl.* beast of burden
padda *s1* toad
paddel ['padd-] *s2* paddle **-kanot** canoe **-åra** paddle
paddl|**a** paddle **-ing** paddling, canoeing
paff I *interj* pop!, bang!, **II** *oböjligt a*, *bli ~* be dumbfounded
page [pa:ʃ] *s5* page [boy] **-hår** page-boy coiffure
pagin|**a** ['pa:-] *s1* page **-era** paginate, page **-ering** [-'ne:-] paging, pagination
pagod [-'gå:d, -ɔ:-] *s3* pagoda
pain riche [pän'riʃ, pen-] *s9, s7* French loaf
paj [pajj] *s3* pie
paja [*x*pajja] *vard.* break down
pajas ['pajj-] *s3, s2* clown, buffoon, merry-andrew; *spela ~* play the fool **-konster** *pl* clown's tricks; buffoonery (*sg*)
paj|**botten** piecrust **-form** pie plate **-kastning** throwing pies **-skal** pie shell
paket *s7, s3* parcel, packet; package; *slå in ett ~* wrap (do) up a parcel; *slå in ngt i ~* make a parcel of s.th.; *ett ~ cigarretter* a packet (*AE.* pack) of cigarettes; *skicka som ~* send by parcel-post **-bil** delivery van **-cykel** carrier cycle **-era** pack[et], parcel up **-ering** [-'te:-] packeting, packaging **-gods** *koll.* parcel-goods (*pl*) **-hylla** luggage rack **-hållare** [luggage] carrier **-inlämning** (*post-*) parcel counter; (*för förvaring*) receiving office **-lösning** package solution **-post** parcel-post **-resa** package tour **-utlämning** delivery office
pakist|**anare** [-*x*ta:-] Pakistani **-ansk** [-a:-] *a5* Pakistani
pakt *s3* pact, treaty; covenant; *ingå en ~* conclude (make) a pact **paktum** *s8, se pakt*; (*äktenskapsförord*) marriage articles (*pl*)
paladin *s3* paladin
palankin *s3* palanquin, palankeen
palatal I *al* palatal **II** *s2* palatal **-isera** palatalize **-itisk** [-'li:-] *a5* palatal
palats *s7* palace **-liknande** palatial **-revolution** palace revolution
palaver *s3* palaver
paleo|**graf** [-å-] *s3* palaeographer **-grafi** *s3* palaeography **-litisk** [-'li:-] *a5* palaeolithic
paleonto|**log** [-åntɔ-] palaeontologist **-logi** *s3* palaeontology **-logisk** [-'lå:-] *a5* palaeontological

Palestina [-ˣsti:-] *n* Palestine
palest|inier [-'ti:-] Palestinian **-insk** [-'ti:-] *a5* Palestinian
palętt *s3* palette; pallet **-kniv** palette knife
paletå *s3* overcoat
palimpsęst *s3* palimpsest
palindrom [-'drå:m] *s3* palindrome
palissąd *s3* palisade; fencing
paljętt *s3* spangle, paillette **-era** spangle
pall *s2* stool; (*fot-*) footstool, footrest; (*last-*) pallet; (*gruv-*) stope; *stå ~* (*vard.*) stand up to, cope
palla *~ under* wedge up; *~ upp* trestle, block up
palliatįv *s7* palliative
pallra *rfl, ~ sig av* (*i väg*) toddle off; *~ sig upp ur sängen* get o.s. out of bed
palm *s3* palm **-itjnsyra** palmitic acid **-liknande** palmaceous **-olja** palm oil **-söndag** Palm Sunday (*äv. ~en*) **-vin** palm wine
palpera palpate
palsternacka *s1* parsnip
palta *~ på ngn* (*sig*) wrap s.b. (o.s.) up well
paltbröd blood bread
paltor *pl* rags
pamflętt *s3* libel[lous pamphlet], lampoon **-ist** libeller, lampoonist
pamp *s2* **1** *pers.* bigwig, tycoon, big gun (*AE.* shot) **2** (*huggvärja*) straight sword, broadsword
pampas ['pamm-] *pl* pampas (*pl*)
pampig *a1* grand, magnificent; *vard.* swell
pampusch *s3* overshoe; *~er* (*äv.*) rubbers, *AE.* galoshes
panafrikąnsk [-a:-] Pan-African
panamahatt [-ˣma:-, ˣpann-] panama [hat]
Panamakanalen [-ˣma:-, ˣpann-] the Panama Canal
panam|ęn *s3* Panamanian **-ęnsk** [-a:-] *a5* Panamanian
panamerikanįsm Pan-Americanism
panasch [-'naʃ] *s3* crest; panache
panegyr|ik *s3* panegyric **-isk** [-'gy:-] *a5* panegyric[al]
panęl *s3* **1** (*vägg- o.d.*) wainscot, panel [work]; (*golvlist*) skirting [board], *AE.* baseboard **2** (*grupp av pers.*) panel
panęl|a panel; wainscot **-debatt** panel discussion **-höna** wallflower
panera coat (dress) with egg and bread crumbs
panflöjt [ˣpa:n-] panpipe[s *pl*], syrinx
pang bang!, crack! **panga** *vard.* smash **pang- grej** *vard.* smasher **pangsuccé** smash-hit
panįk *s3* panic; *gripas av ~* be seized with panic **-artad** [-a:r-] *a5* panic[ky]; *~ flykt* (*äv.*) stampede **-känsla** sense (feeling) of panic **-slagen** panic-stricken, panic-struck **-stämning** atmosphere (feeling) of panic **-unge** minor panic
panisk ['pa:-] *a5, ~ förskräckelse för* terror of
pank *oböjligt a* broke, penniless
pankreas[körtel] [ˣpaŋk-] *s3* [*s2*] pancreas
pankromatisk [-'ma:-] panchromatic
1 panna *s1* **1** (*kokkärl*) pan **2** (*värme-*) furnace; (*ång-*) boiler
2 panna *s1, anat.* forehead; brow; *rynka ~n* knit one's brow[s *pl*]; *med rynkad ~* (*äv.*) frowning; *skjuta sig en kula för ~n* blow out one's brains; *ta sig för ~n* strike one's brow in dismay; *stöta ngn för ~n* mortally offend s.b.; *ha ~* (*fräckheten*) *att*

have the cheek to
pannben frontal bone
pannbiff *ung.* hamburger
pannbindel frontlet; (*bandage*) forehead bandage
pannkak|a pancake; *grädda -or* fry (make) pancakes; *det blev ~ av alltsammans* it all fell flat [as a pancake] **pannkakssmet** pancake batter
pann|lampa head lamp **-lob** frontal lobe **-lugg** fringe, forelock
pannrum boiler room; furnace room; *sjö.* boiler room, stokehold
pannsmycke diadem, frontlet
pannsten [boiler] scale
pannå *s3* panel
panoptikon [-'nåpp-ån] *s7* waxworks (*sg*), waxwork show
panorama [-å'ra:-, -ˣra:-, *äv.* -o-] *s7, s9* panorama
pansar *s7* **1** armour (*äv. bildl.*) **2** (*vissa djurs*) carapace **-bil** armoured car **-fartyg** armoured vessel; *hist.* ironclad **-förband** armoured unit **-hinder** dragon's teeth **-kryssare** armoured cruiser **-plåt** armour plate; *koll.* armour plating **-skepp** *se -fartyg* **-skjorta** shirt (coat) of mail **-trupper** *pl* armoured troops **-vagn** *se -bil;* (*stridsvagn*) tank **-värnskanon** antitank gun
panslavism Pan-Slavism
pansra armour[plate]
pant *s3* pledge; (*säkerhet*) security; (*under-, inteckning*) mortgage; (*i -lek*) forfeit; *lämna ~* give security; *lämna* (*ta*) *i ~* give in (take) pledge; *lösa in en ~* redeem a pledge; *sätta sin heder* (*sitt huvud*) *i ~ på* stake one's honour (head) on; *förfallna ~er* forfeited pledges; *ställda ~er* pledged securities
pantalonger [-'lån-] *pl* pantaloons, pants
pantbank pawnshop, pawnbroker's [shop]; *~en* (*vard. äv.*) uncle's
pante|ism pantheism **-ist** pantheist **-istisk** [-'ist-] *a5* pantheistic[al]
panteon ['panteån] *n* pantheon
panter ['pann-] *s2* panther **-hona** female panther
pant|förskriva mortgage, pledge **-förskrivning** mortgage deed, pledge, hypothecation **-kvitto** pawn ticket **-lek** game of forfeits **-lånare** pawnbroker; *~n* (*vard. äv.*) uncle **-lånekontor** *se pantbank*
pantomįm *s3* pantomime, dumb show **-isk** *a5* pantomimic
pant|rätt lien **-sedel** *se pantkvitto* **-sätta** pledge; give as [a] security, mortgage, hypothecate; (*i -bank*) pawn
papegoj|a [-ˣgåjja, ˣpapp-] *s1* parrot **-sjuka** parrot fever, psittacosis **-tulpan** parrot tulip
papier-maché [pap'je:ma'ʃe:] *s3* papier-mâché
papiljętt [-å-] *s3* curler; *lägga upp håret på ~er* put one's hair in curlers
papįll *s3* papilla (*pl papillae*)
pap|ism papism **-ist** papist **-istisk** [-'ist-] *a5* papistic[al]
papjemaché [papjema'ʃe:] *s3* papier-mâché
papp *s3, s7* [paste]board; (*kartong*) cardboard
pappa *s1* father (*till of*); *vard.* dad[dy], pa[pa], *AE. äv.* pop
pappask cardboard box; carton

pappenheimare [-j-] *jag känner mina ~!* I know my customers!

papper *s7* **1** paper; *ett ~* a piece of paper; *sätta på ~et (nedteckna)* put down on paper; *det finns endast på ~et* it exists only on paper **2** *(dokument, skriftlig handling)* document; *gamla ~* ancient documents; *kunna visa ~ på att* have papers to show that, be able to show documentary evidence that; *lägga ~en på bordet* put one's cards on the table; *ha klara ~* have the necessary documents [in order] **3** *(värde-)* security; *(legitimations-)* [identification] papers *(pl)* **pappers|ark** sheet of paper **-avfall** waste paper **-bruk** paper mill **-bägare** paper drinking-cup **-docka** paper doll **-exercis** paperwork, red tape **-fabrik** *se -bruk* **-handduk** paper towel **-handel** stationer's [shop] **-industri** paper industry **-kasse** paper carrier **-klämma** paperclip **-kniv** paperknife **-korg** wastepaper basket (bin); *A.E.* wastebasket; *(utomhus)* litter bin **-kvarn** *bildl.* bureaucratic machinery, red tape **-lapp** scrap (slip) of paper **-massa** [papermaking] pulp **-mugg** paper drinking-cup **-näsduk** paper handkerchief **-pengar** *pl* paper money (currency) *(sg)* **-påse** paper bag **-remsa** slip of paper **-rulle** roll (reel) of paper **-servett** paper napkin **-svala** paper dart **-tallrik** paper plate **-tiger** paper tiger **-tillverkning** papermaking, manufacture of paper **-tuss** paper pellet (ball) **-varor** *pl* paper articles (goods); *(som säljs i -handel)* stationery *(sg)*

papp|kartong cardboard box **-skiva** piece of cardboard *(etc.)* **-slöjd** cardboard modelling

paprika ['pa:-, 'papp-] *s1* paprika

papyrus [-'py:-] *best. form -en el. papyren, pl papyrer* papyrus **-rulle** papyrus roll

par *s7* **1** *(två sammanhörande)* pair; *(äkta, älskande ~ e.d.)* couple; *ett ~ skor (glasögon, byxor)* a pair of shoes (glasses, trousers); *ett äkta (nygift) ~* a married (newly-married) couple; *ett älskande ~* a pair of lovers; *ett omaka ~ a)* (*om pers.*) an ill-matched couple *b)* *(om saker)* two odd shoes (gloves *etc.*); *2 pund ~et* 2 pounds a (per the) pair, 2 pounds the two of them; *gå ~ om ~* walk in pairs (couples), walk two and two; *gå i ~* go in couples (together) **2** *(några) ett ~* a couple of, a few; *ett ~ gånger* once or twice, a couple of times; *ett ~ tre gånger* two or three times; *om ett ~ veckor* in a few (a couple of) weeks, in a week or two; *ett ~ och tjugo* twenty odd

para *biol.* mate, pair; *bildl.* unite, couple; *~ ihop* pair, mate; *avund ~d med beundran* envy coupled with admiration; *~ sig* mate, pair, copulate

parabel [-'ra:-] *s3* **1** *mat.* parabola **2** *(liknelse)* parable

parabol|antenn [-ˣbå:l-] parabolic aerial; *vard.* dish **-isk** [-'bå:-] *a5, mat.* parabolic

parad *s3* **1** *(truppmönstring)* parade; *stå på ~* be on show **2** *(-dräkt)* full dress, full-dress uniform **3** *fäktn.* parry **-era** parade; *(ståta äv.)* show off

paradigm *s7* paradigm

paradis *s7* paradise; *~et* Paradise; *~ets lustgård* the Garden of Eden; *~ på jorden* a heaven on earth **-dräkt** *i ~* in one's birthday suit **-fågel** bird of paradise **-isk** [-'di:-] *a5* paradisiac[al]; heavenly **-äpple** *bot.* crab [apple]

parad|marsch parade march **-nummer** showpiece

paradox [-'dåkks] *s3* paradox **-al** *a1* paradoxical **parad|säng** bed of state **-uniform** full-dress uniform

paraffin *s4, s3* solid paraffin, paraffin wax **-era** paraffin **-olja** liquid paraffin; *A.E.* paraffin oil

parafras *s3* paraphrase **-era** paraphrase

paragraf *s3* paragraph; *(i lagtext [o. numrerad])* section; *(i traktat o.d.)* article, clause **-ryttare** formalist; red-tapist **-tecken** section mark

paraguay|an *s3* Paraguayan **-are** [-uˣajjare] Paraguayan **-ansk** [-a:-] Paraguayan

parallaktisk [-'lakk-] *a5* parallactic **parallax** *s3* parallax

parallell I *s3* parallel ; *dra en ~ mellan* draw a parallel between **II** *a1* parallel **-epiped** *s3* parallelepiped **-fall** parallel case **-gata** parallel street **-ism** parallelism **-klass** parallel class (form) **-koppling** parallel connection **-ogram** [-'gramm] *s3* parallelogram

parallellt *adv, gå ~ med* be parallel with (to) **-trapets** trapezium, *A.E.* trapezoid

para|lysera paralyze **-lysi** *s3* paralysis **-lytiker** [-'ly:-] *s9* paralytic **-lytisk** [-'ly:-] *a5* paralytic

paramagnetism paramagnetism

parameter [-'me:-] *s2* parametr

paranoia [-ˣnåjja] *s1* paranoia **paranoid** [-å'i:d] *a5, n sg obest. form undviks* paranoiac **paranoiker** [-'nå:i-] paranoiac

parant [-'rant, -'raŋt] *a1* very elegant, striking, smart, stylish

paranöt brazil nut

paraplegiker [-'ple:-] paraplegic

paraply *s7, s3* umbrella; *spänna upp (fälla ner) ~et* put up (close) the umbrella **-fodral** umbrella cover (case) **-organisation** umbrella organization **-ställ** umbrella stand

parapsyko|logi [-'gi:, ˣpa:-] parapsychology **-logisk** [-'lå:-] *a5* parapsychological

parasit *s3* parasite **-era** live as a parasite, sponge *(på on)* **-steklar** [-e:-] *pl* ichneumon flies

parasoll [-å-] *s7, s3* parasol, sunshade

parat *a1* ready, prepared

paratyfus [ˣpa:-, -'ty:-] paratyphoid [fever]

paravan *s3 mil.* paravane

parbladig *a1, bot.* pinnate[d]

parcell *s3* *(jordområde)* site, plot

pardans couple dance; ballroom dancing

pardon *s3* *(i krig e.d.)* quarter; *(misskund)* mercy; *det ges ingen ~* no quarter is given; *utan ~* without mercy

parentation *hålla ~ över* deliver an oration to the memory of

parente|s [-en'te:s, -aŋt-] *s3* parenthesis *(pl parentheses)*; *(klammer)* bracket; *sätta ngt inom ~* put s.th. in brackets; *inom ~ sagt* incidentally, by the way **-tisk** *a5* parenthetic[al]

parer|a parry, ward off; *(besvara äv.)* retort **-ing** parrying

pares *s3* paresis

parflikig *bot.* pinnately lobed

parforcejakt [-ˣfårs-] hunt[ing]

parfym *s3* perfume; scent **-era** scent; perfume; *~d tvål* scented soap; *starkt ~d* highly scented; *~ sig* use perfume **-eri** perfumery **-flaska** perfume (scent) bottle

parhäst pair-horse (*äv. bildl.*); *köra med ~ar* drive in a carriage and pair; *de hänger ihop som ~ar* (*bildl.*) they are inseparable

pari ['pa:-] *s7* par; *i* (*till*) *~* at par; *under* (*över*) *~* below (above) par

paria ['pa:-] *s1* pariah (*äv. bildl.*); *bildl. äv.* outcast

parig *a1, zool. o.d.* paired

parikurs (*för valuta*) par of exchange, par value; (*för aktier*) face (nominal) value

Paris *n* Paris **parisare** [-ˣri:-] Parisian **pariser|hjul** [-ˣri:-] giant wheel **-smörgås** *ung.* hamburger sandwich

parisisk [-'ri:-] *a5* Parisian **parisiska** [-'ri:-] Parisian

parismod Paris fashion

paritet parity; *i ~ med* on a par with

park *s3* park; *Folkets ~* communal park; *stadens ~er* the borough parks **-anläggning** *konkr.* park

parkas *s2, s3* parka

parkera park **parkering** parking; *konkr.* car park, *AE.* parking lot; *~ förbjuden* no parking **parkerings|automat** parking meter **-avgift** parking fee **-böter** *pl* parking fines **-ficka** narrow parking space **-förbud** *det är ~* parking is prohibited **-hus** multistorey carpark **-lapp** parking ticket **-ljus** parking light **-plats** parking space; (*område*) carpark, *AE.* parking lot **-vakt** carpark attendant

parkett *s3* **1** *teat.* stalls (*pl*); *främre ~* orchestra stalls; *bakre ~* pit; *på ~* in the stalls **2** (*golvbeläggning*) parquet **-golv** parquet floor (flooring) **-läggning** parquet-floor laying **-plats** seat in the stalls, stall **-publik** stalls audience **-stav** parquet block

parksoffa park bench

parkum [ˣparr-, 'parr-] *s3, s7* (*tygsort*) fustian

parkvakt park keeper

parlament *s7* parliament; *bli medlem av ~et* (*äv.*) enter parliament; *sitta i ~et* be a member of parliament (*fork.* be an M.P.) **-ariker** [-'ta:-] parliamentarian **-arisk** [-'ta:-] *a5* parliamentary **-arism** parliamentarism **-era** negotiate, parley **-erande** [-'te:-] *s6* negotiation, parley **-ering** [-'te:-] *se -erande*

parlaments|akt act of parliament **-beslut** decision (resolution) of parliament **-byggnad** parliament building; *Storbritannien* [the] Houses of Parliament **-ledamot, -medlem** member of parliament (*fork. M.P.*) **-session** session of parliament **-val** general election

parlamentär *s3* negotiator, parleyer **-flagg** flag of truce

parlör phrase-book

parmesanost [-ˣsa:n-] Parmesan cheese

parnass *s3, P~en* Mount Parnassus; *bestiga ~en* (*bildl.*) embark on a literary career; *den svenska ~en* the Swedish Helicon

parning [ˣpa:r-] mating, pairing, copulation

parnings|akt act of mating (*etc.*) **-drift** mating instinct **-dräkt** courtship (mating) plumage **-lek** courtship **-läte** mating call **-tid** mating season

parodi *s3* parody (*på* on) **parodiera** parody **parodisk** [-'rɔ:-] *a5* parodic[al]

parodontit *s3* parodontitis

paroll [-å-] *s3* parole, password; (*parti-*) slogan

paroxysm [-å-] *s3* paroxysm

part [-a:-] *s3* **1** *se huvud-, halv-* **2** *jur.* party, side; *alla berörda ~er* all parties concerned; *~erna i målet* the parties litigant **3** *sjö.* (*kardel*) strand

partenogenes [-j-, -g-] *s3* parthenogenesis

parterr [-'tärr] *s3, trädg. o. teat.* parterre **-brottning** ground wrestling

parti *s4* **1** (*del*) part, section; (*av bok o. mus.*) passage **2** *hand.* parcel, lot, consignment; *köpa* (*sälja*) *i ~* buy (sell) wholesale; *i ~ och minut* [by] wholesale and [by] retail; *i stora ~er* in bulk **3** *polit.* party; *gå in i ett ~* join a party **4** *ta ~ för* (*emot*) take sides for (against); *ta sitt ~* make one's decision, make up one's mind **5** *spel.* game; *ett ~ schack* a game of chess **6** (*gifte*) match; *göra ett gott ~* make a good match **-anda** party spirit **-ansluten** enrolled in a party, party member **-beteckning** party label, [party] denomination **-bildning** formation of parties **-biljett** *järnv. ung.* commutation ticket

particip *s7* participle

parti|ell [-tsi'ell] *a1* partial (*solförmörkelse* eclipse [of the sun]) **-ellt** *adv* partially; *~ arbetsför* partially disabled

parti|funktionär party official **-färg** party (political) colour **-grupp** faction, section of a party **-gängare** [-jä-] partisan **-handel** wholesale trade **-kamrat** fellow partisan; *vi är ~er* (*äv.*) we belong to the same party

partikel [-'tikk-] *s2* particle **-accelerator** *kärnfys.* particle accelerator

parti|kongress party congress (*AE.* convention) **-ledare** party leader; *AE. vard.* boss **-ledning** party executive (leaders *pl*) **-lös** nonparty; independent **-medlem** party member **-ordförande** party chairman (*AE.* president) **-politik** party politics (*pl*) **-politisk** of party politics **-pris** *hand.* wholesale price **-program** party program[me] (*AE.* platform)

partisan *s3* partisan **-krig** guerilla war

partisekreterare party secretary, secretary general

partisk ['pa:r-, 'parr-] *a5* partial; bias[s]ed, prejudiced **-het** partiality; bias

parti|strid party strife (*äv. ~er*) **-styrelse** party executive **-tagande** *s6* taking of sides; showing of partiality (*för* for)

partitiv ['parr-] *a1* partitive

partitur *s7* score

parti|vis *adv, hand.* wholesale, in lots, by the lot **-vän** fellow member of a party **-väsen** party system

partner ['pa:rt-] *s9, pl äv. -s* partner

partsinlaga petition

partåig [ˣpa:r-] *a1, zool.* even-toed, artiodactylous

parvel *s2* [little] lad, youngster

parveny *s3* parvenu, upstart

par|vis [ˣpa:r-] **I** *a1, bot.* conjugate **II** *adv* in pairs (couples), two by two **-åkning** *sport.* pair-skating

pascha *s1* pasha

paskill *s3* pasquil, pasquinade

pasma *s1* lea, skein

1 pass *s7* (*bergs-*) pass, defile, gorge

2 pass *s7* (*legitimationshandling*) passport; *falskt* ~ forged passport; *utställa* (*förlänga*) *ett* ~ issue (renew) a passport

3 pass *s7* (*jakt. o. patrulleringsområde*) beat; *stå på* ~ be on guard (the lookout); *polisen på sitt* ~ the policeman on his beat

4 pass *s7* **1** *kortsp.* pass, no bid **2** *nej* ~*!* no such thing!, no thank you!

5 pass *i vissa uttr.*: *komma väl till* ~ come in handy, be serviceable; *vara till* ~ satisfy, suit; *vid* ~ *10* about 10, 10 or thereabouts (so); *hur* ~ *mycket* about how much; *kostar den så* ~ *mycket?* does it cost as much as [all] that?; *det fanns så* ~ *mycket att jag kunde* there was enough for me to be able to

6 pass *interj,* ~ *för mig!* I'm out of it!; ~ *för den!* bags I!

1 passa *kortsp.* pass

2 passa I 1 (*av-*) fit, adjust; adapt, suit (*efter* to) **2** (*stå på pass, vänta på*) wait for; ~ *tiden* be punctual (in time) **3** (*sköta*) attend to; mind, watch; look after (*barn* children); ~ *telefonen* answer the telephone **4** *sport.* pass (*äv. absol.*) **II 1** (*i storlek o.d.*) fit; (*i färg, utseende o.d.*; *vara lämplig*) suit, be suited (*till, som* as, for); (*duga*) do; *nyckeln* ~*r* the key fits (*till låset* [in] the lock); *klänningen* ~*r mig precis* the dress fits me perfectly; *grönt* ~*r honom* green suits him; *handskarna* ~*r till kappan* the gloves go well with the coat; *han* ~*r inte till lärare* he is not cut out to be a teacher; *tisdag skulle* ~ *mig bäst* Tuesday would suit me best; *kom när det* ~*r dig* come when it suits you; *de* ~*r bra för varandra* they are well suited to each other **2** (*anstå*) become, be becoming; *det* ~*r inte en dam att* it does not become (is not becoming for) a lady to **3** ~ *på tillfället* take (avail o.s. of) the opportunity **III** *rfl* **1** (*jfr II 2*) *det* ~*r sig inte* it is not proper (good form); *komma när det* ~*r sig* come when [it is] convenient **2** (*akta sig*) take care; look out (*för hunden* for the dog) **IV** (*med betonad partikel*) **1** ~ *ihop a*) (*med obj.*) fit together, *b*) (*utan obj.*) fit (go) together, *c*) (*överensstämma*) fit in; *de* ~*r bra ihop* they are well matched **2** ~ *in a*) (*med obj.*) fit [in], *b*) (*utan obj.*) fit [in]; *beskrivningen* ~*r in på honom* the description fits him **3** ~ *på* look out, be ready; ~ *på när du är i stan* take the opportunity (chance) when you are in town; *pass på!* look out! **4** ~ *upp* wait (*på ngn* on s.b.; *vid bordet* at table), attend

passabel *a2* passable, tolerable

passad[vind] *s3* [*s2*] trade wind

passage [-ˈsaːʃ] *s5* passage; (*under gata, järnväg e.d.*) subway; *astr.* transit; *hindra* ~*n* block the way; *lämna ngn fri* ~ leave (give) s.b. the right of way; *lämna fri* ~ leave the way free (*för fordon* for traffic)

passagerar|avgift [passenger] fare **-befordran** passenger transport

passagerar|e [-ˣʃeː-] passenger **-fartyg** passenger ship **-lista** passenger list **-plan** passenger airliner (plane) **-trafik** passenger traffic

passande *a4* (*lämplig*) suitable, appropriate, fit (*för* for); (*läglig*) convenient; (*anständig*) proper, decent; (*tillbörlig*) becoming; *det* ~ (*det anständiga*) decorum, good form, *allm.* the done thing

passar|e *s9* compasses (*pl*); *en* ~ a pair of compasses **-spets** *med* ~*en* with the point of the compass leg

passbyrå passport office

passbåt tender

passepartout [passarˈtɔː] *s3* passe-partout

passera 1 (*genom-, förbi- el. överfara*) pass (*äv. bildl.*); (*korsa*) cross; *ett* ~*t stadium* a passed stage; ~ *revy* pass in review **2** *kokk.* strain, pass through a sieve **3** (*gå el. komma förbi*) pass; *bussen hade redan* ~*t* the bus had already passed (gone by) **4** (*hända*) happen, take place; *det får* ~ *för den här gången* we will overlook it (let it pass) this time **5** (*förflyta*) pass, elapse **passerad** *a5* (*vissen*) faded, withered (*skönhet* beauty)

passersedel pass, permit

passform (*klädesplaggs*) fit

pass|foto passport photograph **-frihet** *inom Skandinavien råder nu* ~ no passport is now required for inter-Scandinavian travel

passgång amble **-are** ambler

passion [paˈʃoːn] passion **passionerad** [-ˈneː-] *a5* passionate; impassioned

passions|blomma passionflower **-frukt** passion fruit **-historien** the Story of the Passion **-veckan** Holy Week

passiv [ˈpass-] *a1* passive (*motstånd* resistance; *medlem* member); ~ *delägare* (*äv.*) sleeping partner; *förhålla sig* ~ remain passive **passiva** [ˈpass-] *pl, hand.* liabilities, debts; *aktiva och* ~ assets and liabilities **passivera** make passive **passivism** passivism **passivitet** passivity **passiv|um** [ˈpass-, ˣpass-] *-um -er el. s4* (*i the*) passive [voice]

pass|kontroll *abstr.* passport inspection; *konkr.* passport desk (office) **-myndighet** passport-issuing authority

pass|ning (*tillsyn*) tending, care **2** *tekn.* fit, fit-up; *dålig* ~ poor alignment **3** *sport.* pass **-opp** [-ˈåpp] *s3, s2* attendant

passpoal [-ɔˈall] *s3* piping

passtvång compulsory passport system

passus [ˈpass-] *s2* passage

pasta *s1* paste

pastej [-ˈtejj] *s3* pie; (*mindre*) pasty, patty; (*t. soppa*) pastry puff

pastell *s3* pastel **-färg** pastel colour **-krita** pastel crayon **-målare** pastel[l]ist **-målning** pastel drawing (painting)

pastill *s3* lozenge, pastille

pastisch *s3* pastiche (*på* of)

pastor [ˣpastår, ˈpast-] *s3* vicar, parson; (*frikyrklig*) minister, pastor; (*vid institution*) chaplain; (*i brevadress o.d.*) Rev. (*förk. för* [the] reverend)

pastoral I *s3* pastoral **II** *a1* pastoral **pastorat** *s7* (*befattning*) living, benefice; (*församling*) parish **pastors|adjunkt** curate **-expedition** parish [registration] office

pastorska [-ˣtɔ:r-] *s1* vicar's (*etc.*) wife

pastorsämbete parish office; *meddelanden från* ~*t* notices issued by the clergy of the parish

pastörisera pasteurize **-ing** pasteurization

paten *s3* paten

patent *s7* patent; *bevilja* (*få, söka, ta*) ~ *på* grant (obtain, apply for, take out) a patent for **-ansökan** application for a patent **-brev** letters patent

(*sg o. pl*) **-byrå** patent agency
patenter|a patent **-bar** *al* patentable
patent|innehavare holder of a patent, patentee **-kork** patent stopper **-lås** safety (Yale, snap) lock **-lösning** ready-made solution **-medicin** patent (proprietary) medicine **-rätt 1** *jur.* patent law **2** (*rätt t. patent*) patent rights (*pl*) **-skyddad** *a5* patented, protected by patent **-smörgås** *ung.* ham-and-egg sandwich **-verk** patent office
pater ['pa:-] *s2* father, pater **paternoster** [-'nåss-] *n* (*läsa ett* say a) paternoster **paternosterverk** paternoster lift, multibucket dredger; (*för vatten*) noria
patetisk [-'te:-] *a5* (*högtravande*) high-flown; (*rörande*) pathetic
patiens [passi'aŋs] *s3* [a game of] patience, *AE.* solitaire; *lägga* ~ play [at] patience **-kort** *pl* patience cards
patient [-a(t)si-] patient
patina ['pa:-] *s1* patina (*äv. bildl.*) **patinera** patinate, patine **patinering** [-'ne:-] patination, patining
pato|log pathologist **-logi** *s3* pathology **-logisk** [-'lå:-] *a5* pathological; (*sjuklig*) morbid
patos ['pa:tås] *s7* pathos
patrask *s7* rabble, mob
patriark *s3* patriarch **patriarkalisk** [-'ka:-] *a5* patriarchal **patriarkat** *s7* patriarchate **patriarkkors** patriarchal cross
patric|ier [-'tri:-] patrician **-isk** *a5* patrician
patriot *s3* patriot **-isk** *a5* patriotic **-ism** patriotism
1 patron *s3*, *best. form vard.* patron (*godsägare*) squire; (*husbonde*) master; *vard.* boss; (*skyddshelgon*) patron saint
2 patron *s3* (*gevärs-*) cartridge; (*hagel-*) shot cartridge; (*t. kulspetspenna e.d.*) refill; *lös* (*skarp*) ~ blank (ball) cartridge
patron|bälte cartridge belt **-hylsa** cartridge [case] **-väska** cartridge case (pouch)
patrull *s3* patrol; party; *stöta på* ~ (*bildl.*) meet with opposition **-båt** patrol boat
patruller|a patrol; *~nde polis* policeman on patrol duty, *AE. äv.* patrolman; *~nde polisbil* cruising car **-ing** patrolling
patrulltjänst patrol duty, patrolling
patt *oböjligt a o. r, schack.* stalemate; *ställa sig* ~ be stalemated
paulun *s3* (*säng*) four-poster bed; (*omhänge*) tester
Paulus ['pau-] *aposteln* ~ St. Paul
paus ['pa:-] *s3* pause; lull; *mus. äv.* rest; *teat.* interval, *AE.* intermission; (*i samtal o.d.*) break; *ta sig en* ~ take a rest
pauser|a pause, make a pause **-ing** pausing
paus|signal *radio.* interval (call) signal **-tecken** *mus.* rest
paviljong [-'jåŋ] *s3* pavilion; (*lusthus*) summerhouse
pax [pakks] *se 6 pass*
peang h[a]emostatic forceps
pechblände [ˣpeç-] *s6* pitchblende
pedagog [-'gå:g] *s3* education[al]ist; (*lärare*) teacher, schoolmaster **-ik** *s3* pedagogy, pedagogics (*pl, behandlas som sg*) **-isk** *a5* pedagogic[al]; educational

pedal *s3* pedal **-stämma** *mus.* pedal [point]
pedant pedant **-eri** pedantry **-isk** *a5* pedantic
pedell *s3, univ.* beadle; *vard.* proctor's dog
pediatr|ik *s3* p[a]ediatrics (*pl, behandlas som sg*) **-iker** [-i'a:-] p[a]ediatrician **-isk** [-i'a:-] *a5* p[a]ediatric
pedikyr *s3* pedicure
pegas *s3* Pegasus
pegmatit *s3, miner.* pegmatite
pejl|a (*bestämma riktning*) take a bearing on; *absol.* take bearings; ~ *land* set the land **2** (*loda*) sound (*djupet* the depth) (*äv. bildl.*) **-apparat** direction finder **-ing 1** bearing; *radio.* radio location; *ta en* ~ take a bearing **2** sounding **-signal** directional signal **-skiva** pelorus
pejorativ ['pejj-, -'ti:v] *al* pejorative
pek|a point (*på, mot* at, to); *kompassnålen ~r på norr* (*äv.*) the compass needle points north; ~ *finger åt* point one's finger at; *gå dit näsan ~r* follow one's nose; *han får allt han ~r på* he gets everything he asks for; *allting ~r på att* everything points to the fact that; ~ *ut* point out **-finger** forefinger, index finger
pekin[g]es [-ki'ne:s, -ki'ŋe:s] *s3* (*hund*) Pekin[g]ese [dog]
pekoral *s7* pompous trash, worthless literary production **-ist** writer of pompous trash
pekpinne pointer
pektin *s7, s3* pectin
pekuniär [-i-, -i'a:] *al* pecuniary, financial
pelare pillar; column
pelargon[ia] [-'gɔ:n(ia)] *s3* ([*s1, s3*]) geranium, pelargonium
pelar|gång *s2* colonnade; (*kring klostergård*) cloister; (*portik*) portico **-helgon** stylite, pillar saint **-huvud** capital **-rad** row of pillars, colonnade **-sal** pillared hall
pelerin *s3* cape, pelerine
pelikan *s3* pelican
pellejöns *s2* merry-andrew
peloponnesisk [-'ne:-] *a5* Peloponnesian
Peloponnesus [-'ne:såss] *n* the Peloponnese, Peloponnesus
pemmikan ['pemm-] *s3* pem[m]ican
penater [-'na:-] *pl* penates; household gods; *flytta sina* ~ move one's lares and penates, move house
pendang [paŋ'daŋ] companion [piece], counterpart
pendel *s2* pendulum **-rörelse** oscillation **-svängning** swing of a pendulum **-trafik** commuter service **-tåg** commuter train; shuttle service train **-ur** pendulum clock
pendla oscillate, pendulate, swing to and fro; (*åka fram o. tillbaka, t.ex. om förortsbo*) commute **pendlare** (*förortsbo som varje dag åker till o. från arbetet*) commuter **pendling** *se pendelrörelse*
pendyl [pen-, paŋ-] *s3* ornamental clock (timepiece)
penetr|ation penetration **-era** penetrate; ~ *ett problem* (*äv.*) get to the bottom of a problem
peng *s2* coin **pengar** ['peŋ-] *pl* money (*sg*); (*reda* ~ *äv.*) cash, ready money; *sl.* brass, dough; ~ *eller livet!* your money or your life!; *det kan inte fås för* ~ it is not to be had for money; *förlora* ~ *på* lose money over (by, on); *förtjäna stora* ~ make

P

big money (*på* by); *göra ngt för* ~[*s skull*] do s.th. for the money; *ha gott om* ~ have plenty of money, be well off; *ha ont om* ~ be short of money, be hard up [for money]; *det har jag inte* ~ *till* I haven't got the money (enough money) for that; *ha* ~ *som gräs* be rolling in money; *i* ~ *räknat* in terms of money; *jämna* ~ even money, the exact amount; *leva på* ~ have private means; *låna* ~ *på* raise money on; *låta* ~*na rulla* spend money like water

penibel [-'ni:-] *a2* painful, awkward

penicillin *s4* penicillin

penis ['pe:-] *s2* penis (*pl äv.* penes)

penitens *s3* penance

penjoar *s2* peignoir, dressing gown

penna *s1* **1** pen; (*blyerts-*) pencil; (*stål-*) nib; *fatta* ~*n* put pen to paper; *leva av sin* ~ live by one's pen; *en skarp* ~ (*bildl.*) a formidable pen **2** *zool.* quill

pennalism bullying **-ist** bully

penndrag stroke of the pen **-fat** pen tray **-fodral** pen[cil] case **-formerare** [-å-] pencil sharpener **-fäktare** scribbler **-förlängare** pencil holder

penning piece of money, coin; ~*ar* (*koll.*) money (*sg*); *för en ringa* ~ at a small cost **-affär** financial transaction **-angelägenhet** ~*er* money matters (affairs) **-aristokrati** plutocracy **-begär** craving for money **-behov** need for money; money requirements (*pl*) **-bekymmer** *pl* money worries **-brist** lack (shortage) of money **-fråga** matter of money **-förlust** loss of money, financial loss **-gräs** *bot.* pennycress **-gåva** money gift **-hushållning** money economy **-inrättning** finance institution **-knipa** *råka i* ~ get into money difficulties **-lotteri** lottery with money prizes **-marknad** money market **-medel** *pl* means, funds **-placering** investment of funds (money) **-politik** monetary policy **-pung** purse **-skrin** cash (money) box **-stark** financially strong; *vara* ~ (*äv.*) be in a strong financial position **-stinn** made of (rolling in) money **-summa** sum of money **-tillgång** supply of money **-transaktion** *se -affär* **-understöd** pecuniary aid, benefit payment; (*statligt*) subsidy, subvention **-värde** value of money; (*värde i pengar*) money (monetary) value; ~*ts fall* the fall in the value of money **-värdesförsämring** depreciation of money **-väsen** monetary system

pennkniv penknife **-skaft** penholder; (*kvinnlig journalist*) woman journalist, penwoman **-skrin** pen[cil] box (case) **-spets** point of a pen (*etc.*) **-stift** lead **-stump** pencil stump **-teckning** line (pencil) drawing **-torkare** [-å-] pen wiper **-väsare** *se pennformerare*

penny ['penni] *-n* pence [pens] penny (*pl* pence; *-slantar* pennies)

pensé [paŋ'se:] *s3* pansy

penséer [paŋ-] *pl, gå i sina* ~ be absorbed in thought, be in a brown study

pensel *s2* (*paint*)brush; *bot.* egret **-drag** stroke of the brush **-föring** brushwork

pension [paŋ'ʃoːn, pen-] **1** (*underhåll*) pension; *avgå med* ~ retire on a pension **2** (*skola*) boarding school; *sätta i* ~ send to a boarding school

pensionat *s7* boarding house **pensionera**

pension [... off], grant a pension to; ~*d* pensioned, retired **pensionering** [-'ne:-] pensioning, superannuation, retirement

pensionsanstalt pensions office **-avdrag, -avgift** pension contribution (charge) **-berättigad** entitled to a pension **-fond** *Allmänna* ~*en* (*AP-fonden*) the national [Swedish] pension insurance fund **-försäkring** old age pension insurance **-grundande** ~ *inkomst* income on which pension is assessed, pensionable income **-kassa** pension (benefit) society **-mässig** *a1* pensionable **-poäng** pension credits (*pl*) **-tagare** pensioner **-ålder** pensionable (retirement) age

pensionär [paŋ-, pen-] *s3* **1** (*pensionstagare*) pensioner **2** (*inackorderingsgäst*) boarder **pensionärshem** pensioners' home

pensla paint; pencil; *fint ~de ögonbryn* finely pencilled eyebrows **-ing** painting

pensum *s8* task; *AE.* assignment

pentagram [-'gramm] *s7* pentagram **-meter** [-ˣta:-] *s2* pentameter

pantry ['pentri, -y] *s6* pantry

penultima [-'nult-] *s1, best. form äv.* penultima penultimate [syllable]

pep *imperf. av 1 pipa*

peppar *s9* pepper; *spansk* ~ cayenne [pepper]; *önska ngn* (*dra*) *dit* ~*n växer* send s.b. (go) to Jericho; ~ ~! touch wood!; ~ *och salt* (*textil.*) pepper-and-salt **-kaka** gingerbread biscuit; (*mjuk*) gingerbread cake **-kakshjärta** *ung.* heart-shaped gingerbread biscuit **-korn** peppercorn **-kvarn** pepper mill **-mynta** *s1* peppermint **-myntspastill** peppermint [lozenge] **-rot** horseradish **-rotskött** boiled beef with horseradish sauce **-ströare** pepper pot

peppra ~ [*på*] pepper (*äv. bildl.*) **pepprad** *a5* peppery; *en* ~ *räkning* (*vard.*) a stiff bill

pepsin *s4, s3* pepsin

per [pärr] (~ *båt, post e.d.*) by; *bokför.* as on; ~ *person* per person, a head, each, a piece; ~ *styck* apiece, each, per unit; ~ *timme* by the hour; ~ *år* a year, yearly, annually, per annum; ~ *omgående* by return [of post]; ~ *capita* per capita; ~ *kontant* [in] cash

perborat [pärbå'ra:t] *s4, kem.* perborate

perception [-sep'ʃoːn] perception **-tiv** *a1* perceptive

perenn I *a1* perennial **II** *s3* perennial [plant]

1 perfekt [pär-] *a1* perfect

2 perfekt ['pärf-, 'pä:r-] *s7, s4, språkv.* [the] perfect [tense]; ~ *particip* past participle

perfektion [pärfek'ʃoːn] perfection **-ism** perfectionism **-ist** perfectionist

perfektum ['pärf-, 'pä:r-] *best. form -et el. -um, pl -er, språkv., se 2 perfekt*

perfid *a1, n sg obest. f. undviks* perfidious **-itet** *s3* perfidiousness, perfidy

perforera perforate; punch; *med.* pierce **-ing** perforation

pergament *s7, s4* parchment; (*t. bokband äv.*) vellum **-artad** [-a:r-] *a5* parchment-like, parchmenty **-band** parchment (vellum) binding **-handskrift** parchment [manuscript] **-rulle** roll (scroll) of parchment

pergola ['pärgå-] *s1* pergola

perifer *a1* peripheral; *bild.* outlying; *frågan var*

av ~ *art* the question was of secondary importance **periferi** *s3* periphery; (*cirkels*) circumference; (*stads*) outskirts (*pl*) **periferisk** [-'fe:-] *a5*, *se perifer* **periferivinkel** circumferential angle **perifras** *s3* periphrasis (*pl* periphrases) **perigeum** [-ˣge:-] *s4*, *astr.* perigee **perihelium** [-'he:-] *s4*, *astr.* perihelion (*pl* perihelia) **period** *s3* period **periodicitet** periodicity **periodisk** [-'ɔ:d-] *a5* periodic[al] **period|supare** dipsomaniac, periodical drinker **-tal** frequency **-vis** periodically **peri|petj** *s3* peripet[e]ia **-skop** [-'skå:p] *s7* periscope **-skopisk** [-'skå:-] *a5* periscopic **-staltjk** *s3* peristalsis (*pl* peristalses) **-staltisk** [-'stall-] *a5* peristaltic; ~*a rörelser* peristaltic movements **-styl** *s3* peristyle **-tonjt** *s3* peritonitis **perkussion** [-u'ʃɔ:n] *med.* percussion **perman|ens** *s3* permanence **-ent I** *a1* permanent **II** *s3*, *se permanentning* **permanent|a** [-'nenta] **1** (*hår*) permanent-wave; *vard.* perm; *AE. äv.* fix up; ~ *sig* have a perm **2** (*väg*) lay with a permanent surface (metalling); ~*d väg* (*äv.*) tarmac[adam] (metalled) road **-ning** permanent [wave]; *vard.* perm **permeab|el** [-e'a:-] *a2* permeable **-ilitet** permeability **permission** [-i'ʃɔ:n] leave [of absence]; (*för längre tid äv.*) furlough; *begära* (*få*) ~ ask for (get) leave (*etc.*); *ha* ~ be on (have) leave; *på* ~ on leave **permissions|ansökan** application for leave (*etc.*) **-förbud** suspension of leave; *mil.* confinement to barracks **-sedel** pass **permitt|ent** person (soldier) on leave **-era 1** (*ge permission*) grant leave to **2** (*entlediga*) lay off (*arbetare* workers), dismiss temporarily **-ering** [-'te:-] lay-off **permut|ation** *mat.* permutation **-era** permute **perniciös** *a1*, *med.* pernicious (*anemi* anaemia) **perpendik|el** [-'dikk-] *s2* perpendicular **-ulär** *a1* perpendicular **perpetuell** *a1* perpetual **perpetuum mobile** [-'pe:tuum 'må:-] *n* (*maskin*) perpetual motion machine **perplex** *a1* perplexed, taken aback **perrong** [-'råŋ] *s3* platform **-biljett** platform ticket **persed|el** [-'se:-] *s2* (*sak*) thing, article; *mil.* item of equipment; *-lar* (*mil.*) accoutrements, equipment (*sg*), kit (*sg*) **persedel|inspektion** *mil.* kit inspection **-vård** *mil.* care of kit **perser** ['pärr-] Persian **persian** *s3* Persian lamb, karakul **-päls** Persian lamb coat **Persien** ['pärr-] *n* Persia **persienn** *s3* Venetian blind **persika** *s1* peach **persikohy** peach complexion **persilja** [ˣpärr-, -'sill-] *s1* parsley; *prata* ~ talk rubbish **persimon** [pärsi'må:n] persimmon **persisk** ['pärr-] *a5* Persian; *P~a viken* the Persian Gulf **persiska** *s1* **1** (*språk*) Persian **2** (*kvinna*) Persian woman **person** *s3* person; (*i pl äv.*) people; (*i drama, roman e.d.*) character; (*betydande ~*) personage;

~*er* (*teat.*) dramatis personae, the cast (*sg*); *fysisk* ~ natural person; *juridisk* ~ artificial person; *enskild* ~ private person, individual; *offentlig* ~ person in public life, public figure; *han kom i egen hög* ~ he came in person (himself); *min ringa* ~ my humble self; *kunglig* ~ royal personage; *i första* ~ *pluralis* in the first person plural **personage** [-'na:ʃ] *s5* personage **personal** *s3* staff; personnel; employees **-administration** personnel management **-avdelning** staff (personnel) department **-brist** shortage of staff **-chef** staff (personnel) manager **personal|ier** [-'na:-] *pl* biographical data; personals **-konferens** staff committee **-politik** staffing policy **-tidning** staff magazine **-union** personal union **person|befordran** passenger service (conveyance) **-bevis** birth certificate **-bil** private (passenger) car **person|ell** *a1*, *se personlig* **-förteckning** list of persons **-galleri** collection of characters **-historia** personal history **personifiera** personify; impersonate; *den* ~*de blygsamheten* modesty personified (itself) **personifikation** personification; impersonation **person|kort** identity card **-kult** personality cult **-kännedom** knowledge of people **personlig** [-'sɔ:n-] *a1* personal; ~*t* (*på brev*) private; *för min* ~*a del* for my [own] part; *min* ~*a åsikt* my private opinion; ~*t samtal* personal talk (conversation), *tel.* personal call; *utan* ~*t ansvar* limited, without personal liability; *P~t* (*spalt i tidning*) the agony column **personligen** personally, in person; *känna ngn* ~ know s.b. personally; *inställa sig* ~ appear in person **personlighet** [-'sɔ:n-] **1** (*människans väsen*) personality **2** (*karaktär*) personality; (*framstående person äv.*) personage, person; *en historisk* ~ a historical person; *en framstående* ~ an outstanding personality (personage); *gå* (*komma*) *in på* ~*er* become personal, make personal remarks **personlighets|klyvning** *lida av* ~ have a dual personality **-typ** type of personality **person|namn** personal name **-nummer** civic registration number, personal code number **-skada** personal injury **-sökare** staff locator **-trafik** passenger traffic (service) **-tåg** (*motsats godståg*) passenger train; (*motsats snälltåg*) ordinary (slow) train **-undersökning** enquiry into personal circumstances **perspektjv** *s7* perspective; (*utsikt, framtids-*) prospect; *vidga* ~*et* (*bildl.*) broaden the outlook **-fönster** picture (vista) window **-isk** *a5* perspective **-ritning** perspective drawing **Peru** *n* Peru **peruan** *s3* Peruvian **peruansk** [-a:-] *a5* Peruvian **peruk** *s3* wig; (*enl. 1600- o. 1700-talets mod*) periwig, peruke; *vard.* mop **-makare** wig-maker; *teat. äv.* theatrical hairdresser **-stock 1** wig block **2** *bildl.* [old] fogey **pervers** [-'värs] *a1* perverted **-itet** *s3* sexual perversion **pessar** *s4* diaphragm, pessary, Dutch cap **pessim|ism** pessimism **-ist** pessimist **-istisk** [-'mist-] *a5* pessimistic **pest** *s3* plague; pestilence; *avsky ngt som* ~*en*

hate s.th. like sin; *sky ngt som ~en* shun s.th. like the plague **-artad** [-a:r-] *a5* pestilential **-böld** bubo **-härd** source of plague; *bildl.* plague-spot
pest|ilensrot [-ˣlens-] *bot.* butterbur **-smittad** *a5 (om pers.)* plague-stricken; *(om område)* plague-infested
pet *s7, se* **petgöra peta 1** poke, pick *(på* at); *~ på allt* poke one's finger[s] into everything; *~ hål i (på)* poke a hole in; *~ naglarna* clean one's nails; *~ tänderna* pick one's teeth; *sitta och ~ i maten* be pecking at one's food; *~ omkull* push over, upset **2** *vard. (tränga undan)* oust; *sport.* drop
Peterskyrkan St. Peter's Basilica
peterspenningen Peter's pence *(pl)*
petgöra finicky job
petig *a1 (noga)* finical, finicking; *(om pers. äv.)* particular, meticulous **-het** finicalness *etc.*
petimäter [-ˈmä:-] *s2* cockscomb, coxcomb, fop
petit [-ˈti:(t)] *s2, boktr.* brevier
petita [-ˣti:-] *se petitum*
petit-chou [petiˈʃɔ:] *s3* cream puff
petitess *s3* trifle
petition petition *(om* for); *inlämna en ~* hand in a petition **petitionär** *s3* petitioner
petitum [-ˣti:-] *s8* request for a [money] grant; estimate of expenditure
pet|moj [ˣpe:tmåj] *s2, vard.* telephone [dial] **-noga** *vard.* pernickety, fussy
petrifiera petrify **petrifikat** *s7* petrification, fossil
petro|grafi *s3* petrography **-kemi** petrochemistry **-kemisk** [-ˈçe:-] petrochemical
petroleum [-ˈtrɔ:-] *s3, s7* petroleum, mineral oil
Petrus [ˈpe:-] *aposteln ~* Peter the Apostle, St. Peter
petunia [-ˈtu:-] *s1, bot.* petunia
Pfalz [pfalts] *n* the Palatinate
pfalz|greve Count Palatine **-isk** [ˈpfalts-] *a5* Palatine
p.g.a. *(förk. för på grund av) se under 3 grund 3*
phon [få:n] *s3, fys.* phon
pH-värde [ˣpe:hå:-] pH value, index of pH
pi *s6, s7, mat.* pi
piaff *s3* piaffe
pianino [-ˈni:-] *s6* pianino, upright piano **pianissimo** [-ˈniss-] **I** *s6* pianissimo **II** *adv* pianissimo
pianist pianist, piano player
piano [-ˈa:nɔ] **I** *s6* piano; *spela ~* play the piano; *ackompanjera ngn på ~* accompany s.b. on the piano **II** *adv* piano; *ta det ~* take it easy **-ackompanjemang** piano accompaniment **-konsert** concert given by a pianist; *(komposition)* piano concerto
piano|la [-ˣnå:-] *s1* pianola, player piano **-lektion** piano lesson **-skola** piano conservatory; piano-playing manual **-spel** piano-playing **-stol** music stool **-stämma** piano part **-stämmare** piano tuner
piassava [-ˣsa:-] *s1* piassava, piassaba **-kvast** besom
piccola *se* **pickola piccolo** *se pickolo*
picka *(om fågel)* peck *(hål i* a hole in; *i, på* at); *(om hjärtat)* go pitapat; *~ i sig* peck up
pickelhuva spiked helmet
pickels [ˈpikk-] *s2* pickles *(pl)*
picknick [ˈpikk-] *s2, s3* picnic **picknicka** picnic,

go picnicking **picknickkorg** picnic basket
pick och pack belongings *(pl); ta sitt ~ och gå* clear out bag and baggage
pickola [ˈpikkå-] *s1*, **-flöjt** [ˣpikkå-] *s3* piccolo *(pl* piccolos)
pickolo [ˈpikk-] *s5* page [boy], buttons, footboy; *AE.* bellboy, *vard.* bellhop
pickup[p] [pikkˈapp] *s3* pick-up
piedestal [pie-, pje-] *s3* pedestal
pietet reverence *(mot* to; *för* for)
pietets|full reverential, reverent **-lös** irreverent **-löshet** lack of reverence, irreverence
piet|ism pietism **-ist** pietist **-istisk** [-ˈtist-] *a5* pietistic[al]
piff I *interj* bang! **II** *s2, sätta ~ på a)* kokk. give relish to, *b) bildl.* smarten up, put style into **piffa** *~ upp* smarten up; *AE.* revamp **piffig** *a1 (om mat)* piquant, tasty; *(stilig)* chic, smart
piga *s1* maid
1 pigg *s2 (metall-)* spike; *(tagg)* spine, quill
2 pigg *a1 (kry)* fit *(som en mört* as a fiddle); *(rask, livlig)* brisk, spry; *AE. sl* peppy; *(ˈvaken')* alert, bright, sharp; *~ och kry* bright and breezy; *känna sig ~* feel very fit; *vara ~ för sin ålder* be spry for one's years; *~ på* keen on
pigga *~ upp* cheer up; *AE. sl* pep up **piggelin** *oböjligt a* bright and cheery
pigghaj spiny dogfish
piggna *~ till* come round
pigg|svin porcupine **-svinstagg** quill **-var** *s2* turbot
pigkammare maid's room
pigment *s7* pigment **-erad** [-ˈte:-] *a5* pigmented **-ering** [-ˈte:-] pigmentation
pig|syssla servant's job **-tjusare** [-ç-] would-be ladykiller
pik *s2* **1** *(spets)* point; *(stickord)* gibe, dig *(åt* at); *jag förstod ~en* I got the message **2** *(bergstopp)* peak **3** *sjö. (akter-, för-)* peak; *~ på en gaffel* peak of a gaff **4** *mil.* pike **5** *sport., hopp med ~* jackknife dive **pika** gibe [at], taunt *(för* with)
pikador [-ˈdå:r] *s3* picador
pikant [-ˈkant, -ˈkaŋt] *a1* piquant; spicy; highly seasoned; *(om historia o.d.)* racy, spicy **-eri** piquancy
pikareskroman [-ˣresk-] picaresque novel
1 piké *s3 (tyg)* piqué
2 piké *s3 (kortspel)* piquet; *spela ~* play at piquet
pikerad [-ˈke:-] *a5 (förnärmad)* piqued *(över* at)
piket *s3* riot squad, picket **-bil** police van
pikrinsyra [-ˣkri:n-] picric acid
piktur handwriting
1 pil *s2 (träd)* willow
2 pil *s2 (vapen)* arrow; *(t. armborst)* bolt; *(att kasta)* dart; *bildl.* arrow, shaft; *kasta ~* throw darts; *snabb som en ~* [as] swift as an arrow; *Amors ~ar* Cupid's darts (shafts)
pila *~ i väg* dash away, rush off
pilaff *s3, kokk.* pilau, pilaw
pilaster [-ˈlass-] *s2* pilaster
pilbåge bow
pilfink tree sparrow
pilgift poison applied to tips of arrows
pilgrim [-imm] *s3* pilgrim
pilgrims|falk peregrine falcon **-fäderna** *pl* the Pilgrim Fathers **-färd** pilgrimage; *göra en ~ go*

on a pilgrimage **-ort** [place of] pilgrimage; *bildl. äv.* Mecca **-stav** pilgrim's staff

pilka dib (*torsk* for codfish)

pil|kastning dart-throwing; (*som spel*) darts (*pl*) **-koger** quiver

pilla pluck, pick (*på* at); ~ *på* (*äv.*) finger; *sitta och* ~ *med ngt* sit fiddling with s.th.; ~ *bort* pick off

piller ['pill-] *s7* pill; *svälja det beska -ret* (*bildl.*) swallow the bitter pill **-dosa** pillbox **-trillare** *skämts.* pillmaker

pillra *se pilla*

pilot [-'o:t] *s3* pilot

pil|regn, -skur shower (hail) of arrows **-snabb** [as] swift as an arrow

pilsner ['pils-] *s9* Pils[e]ner beer

pilspets arrowhead

pilt *s2* lad[die]

pimpelfiske jigging

pimpinell *s3, bot.* [salad] burnet

1 pimpla (*dricka*) swig; (*supa äv.*) tipple

2 pimpl|a jig (*efter abborre* for perch)

pimpling *se pimpelfiske*

pimpsten pumice [stone]

pin *på* ~ *kiv* out of sheer devilry; *det var* ~ *livat* it was hilarious; ~ *kär* desperately in love

pina I *s1* torment, pain, torture; (*kval*) agony; *död och* ~! torments everlasting!; *för själ och* ~! for mercy's sake!; *göra* ~*n kort* not prolong the agony, make short work of it **II** *v1* torment, torture; ~ *livet ur ngn* (*bildl.*) worry the life out of s.b. (s.b. to death); ~ *i sig maten* force down the food; *han hade ett* ~*t uttryck i ansiktet* his face had a pained expression; ~ *fiolen* scrape away at the violin; ~ *sig in* (*om blåst, snö o.d.*) worry [its way] through

pinal *s3* thing; *inte en* ~ nothing whatever, not an atom; *jfr grejor*

pin|ande *a4* tormenting, torturing; racking (*huvudvärk* headache); searching, piercing (*blåst* wind) **-bänk** rack

pincené [päŋs'ne:-, piŋs-]] *s3* pince-nez

pincett tweezers (*pl*); *en* ~ pair of tweezers

pinfärsk quite (absolutely) fresh

pingla I *s1* [small] bell **II** *v1* tinkle; jingle; (*telefonera*) give a ring **pinglande** *s6* tinkle, jingle

pingpong [-å-] *s2* ping pong, table tennis

pingst *s2* Whitsun[tide], Pentecost (*äv.* ~*en*); *annandag* ~ Whit Monday **-afton** Whitsun Eve, Whit Saturday (*äv.* ~*en*) **-dag** Whit Sunday, Whitsunday **-helg** Whitsuntide (*äv.* ~*en*) **-lilja** narcissus **-rörelse** ~*n* the Pentecostal Movement **-veckan** Whit[sun] week **-vän** Pentecostalist

pingvin *s3* penguin

pinje ['pinn-, 'pi:-] *s5* stonepine

pin|lig [ˣpi:n-] *a1, se pinsam*; ~*t förhör* examination under torture

pinna ~ *fast* peg (*vid* to) **pinnbult** *tekn.* stud

pinn|e *s2* (*trä-, tält-, hatt-*) peg; (*ved-*) stick; (*steg-*) rung; (*höns-*) perch; *styv som en* ~ [as] stiff as a poker; *ben smala som -ar* legs as thin as sticks; *hon är smal som en* ~ she is as thin as a rake; *rör på -arna!* stir your stumps!; *livet på en* ~ high life; *trilla av pinn* peg out **pinnhål** peghole; *komma ett par* ~ *högre* (*bildl.*) rise a step or two

pinnmo *s2* till

pinn|soffa rib-backed settee **-stol** Windsor chair **-ved** stick firewood

pino|läger *bildl.* bed of torment **-redskap** instrument of torture

pinsam [ˣpi:n-] *a1* painful; (*besvärande*) awkward, embarrassing (*situation* situation; *tystnad* silence); scrupulous (*noggrannhet* carefulness)

pinuppa [-ˣnuppa] *s1* pin-up [girl]

pion *s3* peony

pionjär *s3 1 mil.* sapper, engineer **2** (*föregångsman*) pioneer **-arbete** pioneer work **-trupp** *se ingenjörstrupper*

1 pip *s2* **1** (*på kanna*) spout **2** *bot.* tube

2 pip *interj* peep!

3 pip *s7* (*ljud*) peep; (*fågels*) chirp; (*råttas*) squeak, cheep; (*gnäll*) whine, whimper

1 pip|a *pep -it* (*om fågel*) chirp; (*om barn, mus*) squeak; (*jämra sig*) whine, whimper; (*om vind, ångvissla*) whistle; *det -er i bröstet på mig* my chest is wheezy

2 pip|a *s1* **1** (*rök-*) pipe; *röka* ~ smoke a pipe; *knacka ur* ~*n* knock the ashes out of one's pipe **2** (*att blåsa i*) pipe; (*vissel-*) whistle; *dansa efter ngns* ~ dance to a p.'s tune; *skära -or i vassen* know what tune to dance to, jump at an opportunity **3** (*rör*) pipe, tube; (*gevärs-*) barrel; (*skorstens-*) flue **4** *det här går åt* ~*n* this is all going wrong (is a mess)

pipare *zool.* plover

pipett *s3* pipette

piphuvud [pipe] bowl

1 pipig *a1* (*gäll*) squeaky (*röst* voice); (*gnällig*) whining, whimpering

2 pipig *a1* (*porös*) porous

pipit *sup. av 1 pipa*

pipkrage fluted ruff

piplera pipeclay

piplärka pipit

pip|olja tobacco juice **-orgel** pipe organ

1 pippi *s2* (*fågel*) dickybird

2 pippi *s9, ha* ~ *på* be crazy about; *det är rena* ~*n* it is pure folly

pip|rensare pipe cleaner **-rök** pipe smoke **-rökare** pipe smoker

pipsill [ˣpi:p-] *s2* crybaby

pipskaft pipe stem

pipskägg imperial, pointed beard, goatee

piptobak pipe tobacco

pir *s2, s3* pier, groyne, groin; (*mindre*) jetty; (*vågbrytare äv.*) groyne, *AE.* groin; mole

pirat pirate **-sändare** pirate transmitter **-upplaga** piratical edition

piraya [-ˣrajja] *s1* piranha, piraya

pirk *s2* jig

1 pirog [-'rå:g] *s3* (*kanot*) pirogue

2 pirog [-'rå:g] *s3, kokk.* Russian pasty

pirra tingle **pirrande I** *s6* tingling **II** *a4* tingling

piruett *s3* pirouette **-era** pirouette

pirum *oböjligt a* tipsy

pirål hagfish

pisk *s7* whipping **piska I** *s1* whip; (*hår-*) pigtail; *klatscha* (*smälla med*) ~*n* crack the (one's) whip; *låta ngn smaka* ~*n* give s.b. a taste of the whip **II** *v1* whip; flog, lash; (*mattor, kläder o.d.*) beat; *regnet* ~*de mot rutorna* the rain was beating

P

against the panes; *hunden ~de med svansen* the dog was swishing its tail; *vara ~d att göra ngt* be forced to do s.th.; ~ *på* whip [on]; ~ *upp* whip up **pisk|balkong** balcony for beating [mats *etc.*] **-käpp** carpet beater **-rapp** lash; *bildl.* whiplash **-smäll** crack of the whip **-snärt** whiplash **-ställning** carpet-beating rack

piss *s7, vard.* piss **pissa** *vard.* piss **pissoar** *s3* urinal

pist *s3, fäktn.* piste; (*cirkus-*) ring fence

pistasch [-'ta:ʃ] *s3* pistachio **-mandel** pistachio [nut]

pistill *s3* pistil; *~ens märke* the stigma [of the pistil]

pistol *s3* **1** (*vapen*) pistol **2** (*mynt*) pistole **-hot** *under* ~ at gunpoint **-hölster** [pistol] holster **-man** gunman **-mynning** pistol muzzle **-skjutning** pistol shooting **-skott** pistol shot

pistong [-'tåŋ] *s3* piston

pitprops ['pittpråps] *s2, koll.* pitprops (*pl*)

pitt *s2, vard.* cock, prick, dick

pittoresk *a1* picturesque

pivå *s3* pivot

pizz|a ['pittsa] *s1* pizza **-eria** [-ˣri:a] *s1* pizzeria, pizza parlor

pjosk [-å-] *s7* (*klemande*) coddling; (*klemighet*) mawkishness, squeamishness **pjoska** ~ *med* coddle **pjosker** ['pjåss-] *s2* milksop, mollycoddle **pjoskig** *a1* mawkish, effeminate

pjåkig *a1, inte så* ~ not half bad

pjåsk *etc., se pjosk etc.*

pjäs *s3* **1** *mil.* piece **2** (*möbel, prydnadsföremål e.d.*) piece, article **3** (*schack-*) man; (*motsats t. bonde*) piece **4** *teat.* play **-författare** playwright

pjäxa *s1* ski-boot

placenta [-ˣsenn-] *s1, anat.* placenta

placera place, put; (*skaffa anställning e.d.*) station; (*gruppera*) seat (*sina gäster* one's guests); (*pengar*) invest; (*insätta i sitt sammanhang*) place, locate; ~ *en beställning hos en firma* place an order with a firm; *jag känner igen honom men kan inte ~ honom* I know his face but cannot place him; ~ *sig a*) (*sätta sig*) seat o.s., *b*) *sport.* get a place; ~ *sig som tvåa* come second **placering** [-'se:-] placing; (*vid bord äv.*) seating; (*investering*) investment; (*läge samt sport.*) position, location **placeringskort** place card

pladask *falla* ~ fall flop down (*i smutsen* into the dirt)

pladder ['pladd-] *s7* babble, chatter **pladdra** babble, chatter **pladdrig** *a1* garrulous

plafond [-'fåŋd] *s3* plafond **-målning** *konkr.* painted ceiling

plage [pla:ʃ] *s5* beach

plagg *s7* garment; article of clothing

plagi|at *s7* plagiarism **-ator** [-ˣa:tår] *s3* plagiarist **-era** plagiarize

1 plakat *s7* (*kungörelse*) proclamation; (*affisch*) placard, poster

2 plakat *oböjligt a* (*full*) dead drunk

plakett *s3* plaquette, plaque

plan I 1 *s7* (*yta*) plane; (*nivå*) level; *ett lutande* ~ an inclined plane; *i* (*på*) *samma* ~ *som* (*äv.*) on a level with; *på ett högre* ~ on a higher level; *roll i andra ~et* second-grade part; *det ligger på ett helt annat* ~ it is on quite another plane; *på det slut-*

tande ~*et* (*bildl.*) on the down grade **2** *s7* (*flyg-*) plane **3** *s3* (*öppen plats*) open space, area, (*fyrkantig*) square; *sport.* ground; (*jfr äv.* gräs-, tennis- *etc.*) **4** *s3* (*projekt, förslag*) plan, scheme (*för, på, till* for, of); (*intrig*) plot; *göra upp ~er* make plans, plan; *ha* (*hysa*) *~er på ngt* (*på att*) have plans for s.th. (for … -ing); *det ingår inte i mina ~er* it is not part of my plans; *det finns inga ~er att hinna dit* there's not the faintest chance of getting there in time **II** *al* plane, level

plana 1 (*jämna*) level **2** (*in bil, båt*) plane

planekonomi planned economy **planenlig** [-e:-] *al* according to plan

planer|a 1 (*jämna*) level **2** (*-lägga*) plan, project; (*ha för avsikt*) intend, *AE.* äv. aim to (+ *inf.*) **-ing 1** (*jämnande*) levelling **2** (*-läggning*) planning, projection

planet *s3* **1** *astr.* planet **2** *mitt i ~en* slap in the face **planetarisk** [-'ta:-] *a5* planetary **planetarium** [-'ta:-] *s4* planetarium

planet|bana orbit of a planet **-system** planetary system

plan|geometri plane geometry **-hushållare** planner **-hushållning** economic planning, planned economy

plani|metri *s3* planimetry **-metrisk** [-'me:-] *a5* planimetric[al]

plank 1 *s9, s7, koll.* deals (*pl*), planking **2** *s7* (*stängsel*) wood[en] paling (fence); (*kring bygge e.d.*) hoarding[s *pl*]

1 planka *s1* deal; (*större*) plank

2 planka *vl, vard.* **1** (*smita in*) gate-crash **2** (*kopiera*) crib

plankorsning level (*AE.* grade) crossing

plank|strykare *skämts.* dauber **-stump** plank stump

plankton ['planktån] *s7* plankton

plan|lägga plan, make plans for, project; *-lagt mord* premeditated (wilful) murder **-läggning** planning; projection **-lös** planless; unmethodical, indiscriminate; (*utan mål*) aimless, desultory; *irra omkring ~t* wander about aimlessly **-löshet** aimlessness *etc.*, lack of plan **-lösning** *byggn.* plan[ning], design **-mässig** *al* methodical, systematical; *according to plan* **-mässighet** method[icalness] **-ritning** *konkr.* [ground] plan (*till* for, of); (*som läroämne*) plan-drawing

plansch *s3* plate, illustration; (*vägg-*) chart **-verk** volume of pictures, picture book

planskild ~ *korsning* grade-separated intersection

planslip|a grind smooth **-ning** [sur]face grinding

plant|a *s1* plant; (*uppdragen ur frö*) seedling; (*träd*) sapling; *sätta -or* set plants **plantage** [-'ta:ʃ] *s5* plantation **plantageägare** planter, plantation owner **plantera** plant; (*i rabatt äv.*) bed out; *bildl.* plant, set; ~ *om* transplant; ~ *ut* plant out **plantering** [-'te:-] *konkr.* plantation, park; *abstr.* planting **planteringsspade** planting trowel **plantskola** nursery (*för* of, for) (*äv. bildl.*)

plask *s7 o. interj* splash **plaska** splash; (*om vågor, åror*) lap (*mot stranden* on the shore; *mot båtens sidor* against the sides of the boat); (*vada*) paddle; ~ *omkring* splash about **plaskdamm** [children's] paddling-pool **plaskvåt** soaking wet

plasma *s9, s7, pl plasmer* plasma **-fysik** plasma physics (*pl, behandlas som sg*)
plast *s3* plastic; *härdad* ~ thermosetting plastic; *mjuk* ~ nonrigid plastic
plast|a, -behandla coat (spray) with plastic **-behandlad** *a5* plastic-coated **-behandling** plastic treatment **-belagd** plastic-coated **-blomma** plastic flower **-båt** plastic boat **-bägare** plastic beaker
plastellin *s3, s4,* **plastellina** [-ˣli:-] *s1* plasticine (*varumärke*)
plast|fabrik plastics plant **-flaska** plastic bottle **-folie** plastic sheeting (film) **-hink** plastic bucket
plasticitet plasticity
plastik *s3* **1** (*bildhuggarkonst*) plastic art **2** *med.* plastic surgery **3** (*konsten att föra sig väl*) deportment **-kirurgi** plastic surgery
plastisk ['plass-] *a5* plastic; (*formbar*) ductile; (*behagfull*) graceful; *~t trä* wood cement, plastic wood
plast|laminat *s7* laminated plastic sheet **-material** plastic material **-påse** plastic (polythene) bag
platan *s3* plane [tree]
platina [-ˣti:-, 'pla:-] *s9* platinum **-blond** platinum-blonde
Platon ['pla:tån] Plato
platon|iker [-'tɔ:-] *s9* Platonist **-[i]sk** [-'tɔ:-] *a5* Platonic (*kärlek* love)
plats *s3* **1** (*ställe, ort, bestämd* ~) place; (*lokalitet*) locality; (*fläck*) spot; (*öppen* ~) space, area, (*fyrkantig*) square; (*skåde-*) scene (*för* of); *veta sin* ~ know one's place; *var sak på sin* [*rätta*] ~ everything in its [right] place; *offentliga* (*allmänna*) ~*er* public places; *här på* ~*en* here, in this town, on the spot; *läkaren på* ~*en* (*äv.*) the local doctor; *vara den förste på* ~*en* be the first on the spot (to arrive); *sätta ngn på* ~ (*bildl.*) take a p. down [a peg or two]; *det vore inte på sin* ~ *att* it would be out of place (inappropriate) to **2** (*sitt-, äv. i riksdag o.d.*) seat; (*säng-*) bed; *numrerade* ~*er* numbered seats; *ta* ~ take a (one's) seat; *tag* ~*!* take your seats!; *fylld till sista* ~ packed, filled to capacity **3** (*utrymme*) room; space; (*husrum*) accommodation; *lämna* ~ *för* (*åt*) make room for; *ta liten* (*för stor*) ~ take up little (too much) room; *gott om* ~ plenty of room; *den får nätt och jämnt* ~ there is only just room for it; *ha* ~ *för 100 personer* have room (*husrum:* accommodation) for 100 persons **4** (*anställning*) place, situation, job; (*befattning*) position, post; (*ställning*) position; *fast* ~ permanent situation; *ha* ~ *hos* be in the employment of; *söka* ~ apply for a situation; *utan* ~ unemployed, out of work; *lediga* ~*er* vacancies; (*tidn.rubrik*) appointments and situations vacant; *intaga en framträdande* ~ occupy (take up) a prominent position
plats|annons ~*er* situations wanted (vacant) advertisements **-ansökan** application for a situation (*etc.*) **-beställning** seat reservation (booking) **-biljett** seat reservation [ticket] **-brist** lack of room; (*på sjukhus*) shortage of beds **-chef** local manager **-förmedling** employment bureau (agency) **-ombud** local agent **-ombyte** change of job **-siffra** *sport.* place number **-sökande** *s9*

applicant [for a situation]; (*tidn.rubrik*) appointments and situations wanted
platt I *a1* **1** flat (*tak* roof; *som en pannkaka* as a pancake); *ha* ~ *bröst* be flat-chested; ~ *fall* (*sport. o. bildl.*) flop **2** (*banal*) commonplace (*kvickhet* witticism) **II** *adv* flat; *falla* ~ *till marken* (*bildl.*) fall flat; *trycka sig* ~ *mot väggen* press one's body flat against the wall; ~ *intet* nothing at all, absolutely nothing
platta I *s1* plate; (*sten-*) slab; (*rund*) disc; (*vägg-*) tile; (*grammofon-*) record, disc **II** *v1* flatten (*till out*); ~ *till* (*bildl.*) squash
platt|fisk flatfish **-form** *s2* platform **-formsbiljett** platform ticket **-fot** flatfoot **-fotad** *a5* flatfoot[ed] **-het 1** (*utan pl*) flatness **2** *bildl.* platitude
platt|ityd *s3, se platthet 2* **-järn** flat steel (iron); *koll.* flats (*pl*) **-mask** *zool.* flatworm **-näst** [-ä:-] *a4* flat-nosed
plattsätt|are [floor-]tiler, tile-layer **-ning** tiling, tile-laying
platt|söm satin stitch **-tyska** (*hopskr. plattyska*) Low German **-tång** (*hopskr. plattång*) flat-[-nosed] pliers (*pl*)
platå *s3* plateau, tableland **-sko** platform shoe
plausibel [-'si:-] *a2* plausible; (*rimlig*) reasonable
plebej [-'bejj] *s3* plebeian **plebejisk** [-'bejj-] *a5* plebeian
plebiscit [-'si:t, -'ʃi:t] *s7* plebiscite
plejad *s3* **1** *astr., P~erna* the Pleiades **2** *litt. hist., P~en* the Pleiad[e]
plektr|on ['plektrån] *-et -er,* **plektrum** ['plekk-] *s4* plectrum (*pl* plectra), plectron
plenar|församling [-ˣna:r-], **-möte** plenary meeting
plenum [ˣple:-] *s8* plenary sitting (assembly)
pleonasm [-ˣna:sm] *s3* pleonasm **-tisk** *a5* pleonastic[al]
pleti ['ple:-] *se kreti*
pleurit *s3* pleurisy
plexiglas plexiglass
pli *s9, s7* manners (*pl*), bearing; *sätta* ~ *på ngn* (*vard.*) lick s.b. into shape
pligg *s2* peg **pligga** peg (*fast* down)
1 plikt *s3* (*skyldighet*) duty (*mot* to, towards); (*förpliktelse*) obligation; ~*en framför allt* duty first; *göra sin* ~ do one's duty; *vi har den smärtsamma* ~*en att meddela* ours is the painful duty to announce
2 plikt *s3* (*böter*) fine
plikta pay a fine (*för* for); *han fick* ~ *2 pund* he was fined 2 pounds; ~ *med livet* pay with one's life (*för* for)
plikt|förgäten [-j-] *a3* forgetful of one's duty (obligations); negligent **-förgätenhet** [-j-] dereliction (neglect) of duty **-ig** *a1* [in duty] bound, obliged **-känsla** sense of duty **-kär** devoted to duty **-människa** person with a strong sense of duty **-skyldig** dutiful; obligatory (*leende* smile) **-skyldigast** *superl. adv* dutifully, in duty bound; *skratta* ~ laugh dutifully **-trogen** faithful, dutiful **-tro[gen]het** faithfulness, dutifulness **-uppfyllelse** fulfilment of one's duty
plimsollmärke [ˣplimsåll-] *sjö.* Plimsoll mark (line), load line
plint *s2* **1** *gymn.* vaulting box (horse) **2** *byggn.* plinth; *elektr.* test terminal box

P

pliocẹn *a1, geol.* Pliocene
plira peer, screw up one's eyes (*mot* at) **plirig** *a1* peering, narrowed (*ögon* eyes)
pliss|é *s3* pleating **-era** pleat, plait **-ering** [-'se:-] pleating
plister ['pliss-] *s2, bot.* dead-nettle
plit *s7* (*knåp*) toil
1 plita (*skriva*) write busily
2 plita *s1* pimple, pustule
plock [-å-] *s7, ej pl* gleanings, odds and ends (*pl*); (*-ande*) picking **plocka 1** pick, gather (*blommor* flowers; *frukt* fruit); lift (*potatis* potatoes); ~ *av* (*bort*) pick off; ~ *fram* bring (take) out; ~ *ihop* gather together, collect; ~ *in* (*t.ex. från trädgården*) gather (pick) and bring in, (*i skåp e.d.*) put away in[to]; ~ *ner* (*t.ex. äpplen*) get (take) down; ~ *sönder* take to pieces; ~ *undan* clear away; ~ *upp* pick up; ~ *ut* take out (ur of), (*utvälja*) pick out **2** pluck (*en fågel* a fowl; *ögonbrynen* one's eyebrows) **3** *sitta och* ~ *med* sit and fiddle with; ~ *på lakanet* pluck at the sheet **plockning** picking *etc.*
plog *s2* plough; *gå bakom ~en* follow the plough; *spänna hästen för ~en* put the horse before the plough; *lägga under ~en* put under the plough
plog|a (*väg*) clear from (of) snow; (*med skidor*) stem, snowplough **-ben** *anat.* vomer **-bill** ploughshare-point **-fåra** furrow **-land** (*jordmått*) ploughland **-ning** ploughing
ploj [plåjj] *s2, s3* ploy
plomb [-å-] *s3* **1** (*blysigill*) lead [seal], seal **2** *tandläk.* filling, stopping **-era 1** (*försegla*) seal [up], lead **2** *tandläk.* fill, stop **-ering** [-'be:-] **1** sealing; *konkr.* seal **2** filling, stopping
plommon [-ån] *s7* plum **-kärna** plum stone **-stop** *s7* bowler (*AE.* derby) [hat] **-träd** plum [tree]
plotta [-å-] plot
plotter ['plått-] *s7, ej pl* (*krafs*) trifles (*pl*)
plottingbord plotting table
plottra ~ *bort* fritter (*tid äv.:* trifle) away **plottrig** *a1* jumbled, disjointed
plufsig *a1* flabby
plugg *s2* (*tapp*) plug, stopper; (*i tunna*) tap **2** *s2, vard.* (*potatis*) spud **3** *s7* (*-läsning*) swotting, cramming; (*skola*) school
plugg|a 1 (*slå in plugg i*) plug, stop up; ~ *igen* clog **2** (*läsa*) swot (*latin* Latin); *AE. sl.* dig [in]; ~ *på en examen* cram for an examination; ~ *engelska med ngn* coach s.b. in English **-häst** swot [ter] **-ning 1** plugging *etc.* **2** swotting *etc.*
1 plump *a1* coarse, rude
2 plump *s2* blot
plumpa make blots; blot (*äv.* ~ *ner*); ~ *i protokollet* (*bildl.*) make a blunder
plumphet coarseness, rudeness
plumpudding [ˣplumm-] plum pudding
plums *s2, s7, interj, adv* plop, flop **plumsa** [go] splash, flop (*i vattnet* into the water); *gå och* ~ *i leran* splash about in the mud
plundr|a rob (*ngn på* s.b. of); plunder, pillage, sack (*en stad* a town); strip (*julgranen* the Christmas tree) **-ing** robbing; plundering, pillage, sack **-ingståg** plundering expedition, raid, foray
plunta *s1* pocket flask; *vard.* pocket pistol
plural|bildning formation of the plural **-böj-**

-ning plural inflection
pluralis *s3* (*stå i* be in the) plural **pluralism** pluralism **pluralitẹt** *s3* plurality
pluraländelse plural ending
plurr *s7, ramla i ~et* fall into the water
plus [pluss] **I** *s7* (*-tecken*) plus [sign]; (*tillägg*) addition; (*överskott*) [sur]plus; (*fördel*) advantage; *termometern visar* ~ the temperature is above zero **II** *adv* plus; *2 ~ 2 är 4* two plus two make four; *det är 1 grad* ~ it is one degree above zero; ~ *minus noll* zero, nil, absolutely nothing **-fours** ['plussfårs, -'få:rs] *pl* plus fours **-grad** degree above zero **-kvamperfektum** (*i* in the) past perfect (pluperfect) [tense] **-sida** positive (credit) side
plussig *a1* bloated
plus|tecken plus [sign] **-värde** added value
pluta ~ [*med munnen*] pout
Plutarchos [-'tarkås] Plutarch
pluto|krat plutocrat **-kratj** *s3* plutocracy **-kratisk** [-'kra:-] *a5* plutocratic
plutọn *s3* platoon **-chef** platoon leader
plym *s3* plume **plymasch** [-'a:ʃ] *s3* bunch of feathers; plumage
plymå *s3* sofa cushion
plysch [-y:-] *s3* plush
plywood ['plajjvɔd] *s3* plywood
plåg|a I *s1* pain; torment; (*-oris*) plague, nuisance; *ha -or* have (be in) pain, be suffering; *vara en ~ för sin omgivning* be a plague to those around one **II** *v1* pain; torment; (*oroa*) worry; (*besvära*) bother; ~*s av gikt* (*dåligt samvete*) be tormented by gout (a bad conscience); *se ~d ut* look pained
plågo|ande tormentor **-ris** scourge; torment, plague
plågsam *a1* painful
plån *s7* (*skiva*) tablet; (*på tändsticksask*) striking surface; *tända endast mot lådans* ~ strike only on the box **-bok** wallet; *AE. äv.* billfold, pocketbook
plåster ['plåss-] *s7* plaster; *lägga* ~ *på såret* put plaster on a wound, *bildl.* pour balm into the wound **plåsterlapp** piece of plaster **plåstra** plaster; ~ *ihop* patch up; ~ *om ngn* dress a p.'s wounds, (*sköta om*) tend s.b.
plåt *s2* **1** (*metall*) sheet metal; sheet[-iron] **2** (*skiva*) plate (*äv. foto-*); *korrugerad* ~ corrugated sheeting
plåt|a *vard.* photograph **-arbete** platework, sheet-metal work **-beslag** plate covering, plating **-burk** tin, can **-rör** sheet-metal pipe (tube) **-sax** plateshears (*pl*) **-skada** sheet damage **-slagare** sheet-metal worker, plater **-slageri** *abstr.* metal-plating; (*-verkstad*) sheet-metal [work] shop, plate works **-tak** tin roof
pläd *s3, s2* [travelling] rug; (*skotsk*) plaid
pläder|a plead **-ing** (*slut-*) summing-up of the defence; *en* ~ (*äv.*) a plea
pläga *se bruka* **plägsed** custom
pläter ['plä:-] *s2* plate **plätera** plate
plätt *s2* **1** (*fläck*) spot **2** *kokk.* small pancake **-lagg** pancake iron, griddle
plöj|a [ˣplöjja] *v2* plough (*äv. bildl.*); ~ *igenom en bok* plough through a book; ~ *ner* plough in, (*vinst*) plough back; ~ *upp* (*åker o.d.*) plough up

-ning ploughing
plös s2 tongue
plötslig a1 sudden, abrupt; unexpected **plötsligen, plötsligt** adv suddenly; all of a sudden
PM, P.M. s9, s7 (förk. för promemoria) memo
pneumatisk [pnev'ma:-] a5 pneumatic **pneumoni** s3 pneumonia
pochera poach
pock [påkk] s7, se 3 lock **pocka** ~ på [urgently] insist [up]on; frågan ~r på sin lösning the problem craves (demands) a quick solution **pockande** a4 importunate, pressing, urgent (behov need); (om pers.) importune
pocketbok [ˣpåkk-] paperback; AE. äv. pocketbook
podager [-'da:-] s2 podagra, gout
podium ['po:-] s4 podium (pl äv. podia); platform
poem s7 poem **poesi** s3 poetry **poesialbum** poetry album **poet** s3 poet **poetik** s3 poetics (behandlas vanl. som sg) **poetisera** poetize **poetisk** [po'e:-] a5 poetical; poetic (frihet licence)
pogrom [-'grå:m] s3 pogrom
pointer ['påjn-] s2 pointer
pointillism [poäŋ-, äv. -ti'jism] pointillism
pojk|aktig [ˣpåjk-] a1 boyish **-aktighet** boyishness **-bok** book for boys **-byting** little chap, urchin
pojk|e [ˣpåjke, 'påjke] s2 boy; (känslobetonat) lad **-flicka 1** (-aktig flicka) tomboy **2** (omtyckt av -ar) girl for the boys **-liga** street gang **-namn** boy's name **-scout** boy scout **-spoling** young scamp (rascal), hobbledehoy **-streck** boyish prank **-vasker** s2, se -spoling **-år** under ~en during [his etc.] boyhood; alltifrån ~en ever since I (he etc.) was a boy
pokal s3 (bägare) goblet; sport. cup, trophy
poker ['på:-] s9 poker **-ansikte** poker (deadpan) face
pokulera drink, tipple, booze
pol s3 pole
polack s3 Pole
polardag [-ˣla:r-] polar day
polare vard. chum, pal, mate, AE. buddy
polar|expedition [-ˣla:r-] polar (arctic, antarctic) expedition **-forskare** polar (arctic, antarctic) explorer **-hav** polar sea **-is** polar ice
polarisation polarization **polarisator** [-ˣsa:-tår] s3 polarizer **polarisera** polarize **polaritet** polarity
polar|kalott [-ˣla:r-] polar cap **-natt** polar night
polaroid s3 polaroid (varumärke)
polarräv [-ˣla:r-] arctic fox
polcirkel polar circle; norra (södra) ~n the Arctic (Antarctic) circle
polemi|k s3, ej pl polemics (pl, behandlas som sg) **polemiker** [-'le:-] polemic, controversialist **polemisera** polemize **polemisk** [-'le:-] a5 polemic[al], controversial
Polen ['på:-] n Poland
poler|a polish (äv. bildl.); (metall) burnish; ~t ris polished rice **-ing** polishing; burnishing **-medel** polish; abrasive **-skiva** polishing wheel (disc)
polhöjd altitude of the pole
policy ['pållisi] s3 policy
poliklinik s3 outpatient department

polio ['po:-] s9 polio[myelitis] **-vaccin** antipolio vaccin **-vaccinering** polio vaccination
1 polis s3, försäk. policy
2 polis s3 **1** (ordningsmakt) police; koll. [the] police; gå in vid ~en join the police force; anmäla för ~en report to the police; efterspanad av ~en wanted by the police; göra motstånd mot ~ resist arrest; ridande ~ mounted police, AE. äv. (i lantdistrikt) ranger; ropa på ~ shout for the police; ~en har gjort chock the police have charged **2** (-man) policeman, [police] officer; constable; AE. patrolman; vard. i Storbritannien bobby; sl. cop[per]; kvinnlig ~ policewoman
polis|anmäla, -anmälan report to the police **-assistent** ung. police sergeant **-bevakning** police surveillance; huset står under ~ the house is being watched by the police **-bil** police (patrol, squad) car **-bricka** policeman's badge **-chef** police commissioner, chief constable, head of a police force; AE. chief of police, marshal **-chock** police charge **-distrikt** police district **-domare** police magistrate **-domstol** police court **-eskort** police escort **-förhör** interrogation by the police; anställa ~ med ngn hold a police interrogation with s.b. **-förordning** police regulation **-förvar** i ~ in custody; tas i ~ be taken in charge by the police **-hund** police dog **-hus** police headquarters (pl), police station **-intendent** assistant chief constable
polis|iär a1 police **-kammare** administrative police authority; Storbritannien ung. police commissioners (pl) **-kedja** police cordon **-kommissarie** police superintendent; AE. captain; biträdande ~ chief inspector **-konstapel** se 2 polis 2 **-kontor** sub-police-station **-kund** old offender; vard. jailbird **-kår, -makt** police force **-man** se 2 polis 2 **-myndigheter** police authorities **-mästare** chief constable, [police] commissioner
polisonger [-'såŋer] pl sideboards, side whiskers; AE. sideburns
polis|piket riot squad; (bil) police van **-pådrag** det var fullt ~ the police was there in full force **-rapport** police report **-razzia** police raid **-sak** police matter **-spärr** police cordon; (väg-) roadblock **-stat** police state **-station** police station **-syster** policewoman **-undersökning** police investigation **-uniform** policeman's (policewoman's) uniform **-utredning** se -undersökning **-vakt** police guard **-väsen** police [system, organization; authorities (pl)]
politbyrå [-ˣli:t-] Politburo
polit|ik s3, ej pl **1** (statsangelägenheter, statskonst) politics (sg o. pl); syssla med ~ be engaged in politics; tala ~ talk politics **2** (-isk princip, handlingssätt, slughet) policy; line of action; den öppna dörrens ~ open-door policy; föra en fast ~ take a firm line; avvaktande ~ wait-and-see policy **-iker** [-'li:-] politician **-isera** politicize **-isering** [-'se:-] politicization **-isk** [-'li:-] a5 political
politruk [-'trukk] s3 political commissar
polityr s3 [French] polish; bildl. polish
polka [ˣpåll-] s1 polka **-gris** peppermint rock **-hår** pageboy cut
pollare [ˣpåll-] sjö. bollard
pollen ['påll-] s7 pollen **-analys** pollen analysis,

P

palynology **-korn** pollen grain
pollett *s3* (*av metall*) check, counter, token; (*av papper*) ticket; (*gas-*) disc
polletter|a label, register; *AE.* check; ~ *sitt bagage* have one's luggage labelled (registered); *AE.* check one's baggage **-ing** [luggage] registration **-ingskvitto** luggage ticket; *AE.* baggage check
pollin|ation [på-] pollination **-era** pollinate
pollution pollution
polo ['pɔ:-] *s6* polo **-krage** turtleneck
polonäs *s3* polonaise
polo|spel polo **-tröja** turtleneck sweater
polsk [-å(:)-] *a5* Polish; ~*a korridoren* the Polish Corridor; ~ *riksdag* (*bildl.*) bedlam
1 polska [-å(:)-] *s1* (*språk*) Polish **2** (*kvinna*) Polish woman
2 polska [ˣpåll-] *s1* (*dans*) reel
pol|spänning terminal voltage **-stjärna** *P~n* Polaris, the North (Pole) Star
poly|amid [på-, pɔ-] *s3* polyamide **-andri** *s3* polyandry **-eder** [-'e:d-] *s2* polyhedron (*pl äv.* polyhedra) **-ester** [-'es-] polyester **-eten** polythene, polyethylene **-foni** [-få-] *s3* polyphony **-gam** *a1* polygamous **-gami** *s3* polygamy **-gamist** polygamist **-glott** [-'glått] *s3* polyglot **-gon** [-'gå:n] *s3* polygon **-krom** ['krå:m] *a1* polychrome **-mer I** *s3* polymer **II** *a5* polymeric **-merisation** polymerization **-morf** [-'mårf] *a1* polymorphous
Polynesien [-'ne:-] *n* Polynesia
polynes|ier [-'ne:-] *s9* Polynesian **-isk** *a5* Polynesian
polynom [-'nå:m] *s7, s3* polynomial
polyp *s3* **1** *zool.* polyp **2** *med.* polyp, polypus (*pl* polypi); ~*er bakom näsan* adenoids **-djur** hydrozoan
poly|teism polytheism **-teist** polytheist **-teknisk** [-'tekk-] ~ *skola* polytechnic school **-vinylklorid** [-ˣny:l-] polyvinyl chloride
polär *a1* polar
pomad|a [-ˣma:-] *s1* pomade **-era** pomade
pomerans [-'ans, -aŋs] *s3* Seville (bitter) orange **-skal** Seville-orange peel
Pommern ['påmm-] *n* Pomerania
pommersk ['påmm-] *a5* Pomeranian
pommes frites [påmm'fritt] *pl* chips, chipped potatoes; *AE.* French fried potatoes, French fries
pomo|log pomologist **-logi** *s3* pomology
pomp [-å-] *s9* pomp (*och ståt* and circumstance)
pompejansk [-å-a:-] *a5* Pompeian
Pompeji [påm'pejji] *n* Pompeii
pompös [-å-] *a1* pompous; (*högtravande*) declamatory
pondus ['pånn-] *s9* authority, impressiveness; (*eftertryck*) emphasis, weight
ponera [pɔ-, på-] suppose
ponny ['pånni] *s3* pony
pontifikat [-å-] *s7* pontificate
ponton [pån'tɔ:n, -'tå:n] *s3* pontoon **-bro** pontoon (floating) bridge
1 pop [på:p] *s3* (*grek.-kat. präst*) pope
2 pop [påpp] *s3* pop
pop|artist [ˣpåpp-] pop musician (singer) **-band** pop group **-konst** pop art

poplin [på-] *s3, s4* poplin
pop|musik pop [music] **-orkester** pop orchestra
poppel ['påpp-] *s2* poplar
popsångare pop singer
populariser|a popularize **-ing** popularization
popularitet popularity **popularitetsjakt** popularity hunting **populasen** [-'la:-] *best. form* the populace **populism** populism
populär *a1* popular (*bland* among, with) **-press** popular press **-vetenskap** popular science
por *s3* pore
porfyr [-å-] *s3* porphyry
porig *a1* porous
porla [ˣpå:r-] murmur, babble; ~*nde skratt* rippling laugh
pormask blackhead
porno|grafi *s3* pornography; *vard.* smut **-grafisk** [-'gra:-] *a5* pornographic
porositet porosity, porousness
porr *s3* porno **-tidning** porno magazine
pors [pårs] *s3* sweet gale, bog myrtle
porslin [-å-] *s4* (*ämne*) china; (*äkta*) porcelain; *koll.* china, crockery
porslins|affär china shop **-blomma** wax plant **-fabrik** porcelain (china) factory **-figur** porcelain (china) figure **-krossning** [-åss-] (*tivolinöje*) crockery shy **-lera** china clay, kaolin **-målning** porcelain (china) painting **-servis** set of china **-varor** *pl* chinaware, crockery (*sg*); (*finare*) porcelain ware (*sg*)
port [-ɔ(:)-] *s2* (*-gång*) gateway, doorway; (*ytterdörr*) [street, (front)]door; (*t. park, stad samt bildl.*) gate; *köra ngn på* ~*en* turn s.b. out [of doors]; *fienden stod framför* ~*arna* the enemy was at the gates; *stå och prata i* ~*en* stand talking in the doorway (gateway); *den trånga* ~*en* (*bildl.*) the strait gate; *Höga P~en* the Sublime Porte
portabel [-å-, -'a:bel] *a2* portable
portal *s3* portal, porch **-figur** *bildl.* outstanding (prominent) figure (personality)
portativ ['pårr-, -'ti:v] *a1* portable
porter ['på:r-] *s9* stout; (*svagare*) porter
portfölj [-å-] *s3* briefcase; (*av värdepapper*) portfolio; *minister utan* ~ minister without portfolio
port|förbjuda forbid to enter the house (country); (*utestänga*) exclude, keep out; (*bannlysa*) ban **-gång** *s2* gateway, doorway; *köra fast redan i* ~*en* (*bildl.*) get stuck at the very start (outset) **-halva** half-door, half-gate
portier [pårt'je:] *s3* hall-porter, receptionist; *AE. äv.* [room]clerk **-loge** [-lå:ʃ] *s5* reception desk
portik [-å-] *s3* portico
portion [pårt'ʃɔ:n] portion; (*mat- äv.*) helping, serving; *mil.* rations (*pl*); *i små* ~*er* in small portions (doses); *en stor* ~ *kalvstek* a large helping of veal; *en god* ~ *tur* a great deal of luck; *en viss* ~ *sunt förnuft* a certain amount of common sense; *i små* ~*er* in small doses **-era** portion (*ut* out)
portiär [pårt'jä:r] *s3* portière, curtain
portklapp knocker
portmonnä [pårtmå'nä:] *s3* purse; *AE. äv.* pocketbook
portnyckel latchkey
porto [ˣpårr-] *s6* postage; (*för postanvisning, Storbritannien*) poundage; (*för telegram*) charg-

e[s *pl*]; *gå för enkelt* ~ pass at the single[-postage] rate **-fri** free of postage, post-free **-kostnad** postage **-sats** rate of postage, postal rate

porträtt *s7* portrait; ~*et är mycket likt* the portrait is a good likeness **-album** family album **-byst** [portrait] bust **-era** portray **-ering** [-'e:r-] portrayal **-galleri** portrait gallery **-lik** like the original, lifelike **-likhet** likeness to the original **-målare** portrait painter **-måleri** portrait painting

porttelefon hall (house) telephone

Portugal ['pårr-] *n* Portugal

portugis [-å-] *s3* Portuguese (*pl* Portuguese) **-isk** *a5* Portuguese **-iska** *s1* **1** (*språk*) Portuguese **2** (*kvinna*) Portuguese woman

portvakt porter (*fem.* portress), doorkeeper, gatekeeper; (*i hyreshus*) caretaker, concierge; *AE.* janitor (*fem.* janitress)

port|vin [ˣpå:rt-] port [wine] **-vinstå** *ha* ~ have a gouty big toe

portör [-å-] botanical tin, vasculum

porös *al* porous; (*svamplik*) spongy

pose [på:s] *s5* pose, attitude, posture; *intaga en* ~ strike an attitude, adopt a pose **posera** pose (*för* to); strike an attitude; ~ *med ngt* make a show of s.th. **poserande** [-'se:-] *a4* posing, attitudinizing

position position; *bildl. äv.* status, standing; *uppge sin* ~ (*i fråga o.d.*) give up one's ground

positionsljus *sjö.* running light

1 positiv ['pɔ:s-, 'pɔss-] **I** *al* positive **II** *s3* (*i* the) positive

2 positiv *s7* (*musikinstrument*) barrel organ

positivhalare organ-grinder

positiv|ism positivism **-ist** positivist

positivspelare organ-grinder

positron [-'trå:n] *s3* positron, positive electron

possession [-e'ʃɔ:n] [landed] property (estate) **possessionat** estate owner, landed proprietor

possessiv ['påss-, -'si:v] *al* possessive (*pronomen* pronoun)

1 post [-å-] *s3* (*bokförings-*) item, entry; (*belopp*) amount, sum; (*varuparti*) lot, parcel; (*värdepapper*) block, parcel; *bokförd* ~ entry; *bokföra en* ~ make an entry, post an item

2 post [-å-] *s3* **1** *se dörr-, fönster-* **2** *se brand-, vatten-*

3 post [-å-] *s3* **1** (*-ering; plats, befattning*) post; *stå på* ~ stand sentry, be on guard; *stupa på sin* ~ be killed at one's post; *bekläda en viktig* ~ hold an important post (position) **2** (*vakt-*) sentry, sentinel

4 post [-å-] *s3* (*brev o.d.*) post, *AE.* mail; (*-anstalt*) post office; *jfr äv. postverk*; *ankommande* (*avgående*) ~ inward (outward) mail; *med dagens* (*morgonens*) ~ by today's (the morning) post; *per* ~ by post; *sortera* ~*en* sort the mail; *skicka med* ~[*en*] send by post; *lämna ett brev på* ~*en* take a letter to the post [office]

post|a post, mail, send by post (mail) **-abonnemang** postal subscription **-adress** postal (mailing) address **-al** *al* postal

postament [på-] *s7* postament, pedestal

post|anstalt post office **-anvisning** money order (*förk.* M.O.); (*på fastställt belopp*) postal order (*förk.* P.O.); *hämta ut en* ~ cash a money order **-befordran** forwarding (conveyance) by

post (mail); *avlämna till* ~ post, mail **-befordringsavgift** postage **-box** post office box (*förk.* P.O.B.) **-båt** mailboat, packet [boat]

postdater|a [-å-] postdate **-ing** postdating

post|diligens mailcoach, stagecoach, *AE.* mailcar **-distrikt** postal region (district)

postera [-å-] **1** (*ställa ut post*) station, post **2** (*gå, stå på post*) stand sentry, be on sentry duty

poste restante [påst re'staŋt, -'stant] poste restante, *AE.* general delivery

postering [-å-'te:-] picket, outpost

post|expedition [branch] post office **-expeditör** post-office clerk **-fack** *se postbox* **-förande** *a4* mail-carrying; ~ *tåg* mail train **-förskott** cash on delivery (*förk.* C.O.D.); *ett* ~ a cash-on-delivery parcel (*etc.*); *sända ngt mot* ~ send s.th. cash on delivery **-försändelse** postal article (matter, item)

postgiro postal giro service **-blankett** postal giro form **-konto** postal giro account **-nummer** postal giro account number

postgymnasial [-å-] ~ *utbildning* post-secondary [college (university)] education

postgång postal service

postiljon [på-] *s3* sorting clerk; (*förr*) mailcoach driver

postilla [-ˣtilla] *s1* collection of sermons (homilies)

postisch [pås'tiʃ] *s3* hairpiece, postiche

post|kontor post office **-kort** postcard, postal card **-kupé** mailcoach, *AE.* mailcar **-lucka** post-office counter (window)

postludium [-å-'lu:-] *s4* postlude

post|låda *se brevlåda* **-mästare** postmaster (*fem.* postmistress) **-nummer** postcode; *AE.* zip code

posto [ˣpåstɔ] *i uttr.: fatta* ~ take one's stand, post o.s.

post|order mail order **-orderfirma** mail-order company **-paket** postal parcel; *skicka som* ~ send by parcel post **-papper** notepaper, letter paper **-remissa** *se postväxel* **-röst** (*vid val*) postal vote **-rösta** vote by post **-röstning** postal voting

postskriptum [påstˣskripp-] *s8* postscript (*förk.* P.S.)

post|sparbank post-office savings bank **-sparbanksbok** post-office bankbook **-station** sub-post-office **-stämpel** postmark; ~*ns datum* date as postmark **-säck** mailbag, postbag, mailsack **-taxa** postage rates (*pl*) **-tjänsteman** post-office employee (clerk) **-tåg** mail train

postul|at [-å-] *s7* postulate **-era** postulate

postum [pås'tu:m] *al* posthumous

post|utdelning postal delivery **-vagn** mailcoach, *AE.* mailcar **-verk** ~*et* [the] Post Office **-väsen** postal services (*pl*), postal system **-växel** money order, bank[er's] draft

posör posturer *etc.*, *jfr posera*

potatis [-'ta:-] *s2* potato; *koll.* potatoes (*pl*); *färsk* (*oskalad, kokt, stekt*) ~ new (unpeeled, boiled, fried) potatoes; *skala* ~ peel (skin) potatoes; *sätta* (*ta upp*) ~ plant (lift) potatoes; *han har satt sin sista* ~ (*ung.*) he has cooked his goose **-blast** potato haulm **-bullar** *pl, kokk.* potato cakes **-kräfta** potato wart **-land** *s7* potato plot

P

(patch) **-mjöl** potato flour **-mos** mashed (creamed) potatoes (pl) **-näsa** pug nose **-odling** abstr. potato-growing; konkr. potato field **-plockning** [-å-] potato-picking **-puré** se -mos **-sallad** potato salad **-skal** potato peel (skin); (avskalat) potato peelings (pl) **-åker** potato field **potens** s3 (förmåga) potency; med. äv. sexual power, potence; mat. power **potent** a4 potent **potentat** potentate **potential** [-n(t)si'a:l] s3 potential **potentialskillnad** potential difference **potentiell** [-n(t)si'ell] a1 potential **potentiera** [-n(t)si'e:ra] intensify **potentiometer** [-n(t)siɒ'me:-] s2 potentiometer **potkes, potkäs** [påt'çe:s, 'pott-] s3 cheese creamed with spices and brandy **potpurri** [-å-] s3 potpourri; mus. äv. medley **pott** [-å-] s3, spel. pool, kitty **pott|a** [-å-] s1 chamber [pot] **-aska** potash, potassium carbonate **poäng** s3 (värdeenhet s9) point; (skol.) mark; få ~ get a point (points); få två ~ (äv.) score two; vinna (förlora) på ~ win (lose) on points; livet har sina ~er life has its points; historien saknar ~ the story lacks point (is pointless) **-bedömning** marking **-beräkning** sport. o. spel. scoring **-besegra** outpoint **-jakt** ung. collecting credits **-plats** points-winning place **-seger** victory (win) on points **-ställning** score **-summa** final (total) score **-sätta** award points to; skol. mark, assign marks to **-sättning** [the] awarding of points; skol. äv. [the] marking **-tal** [total] points (pl), score **-tera** emphasize **-tips** treble chance pool
p-piller ['pe:-] contraceptive tablet; vard. the pill
PR förk. för public relations
pracka ~ på ngn ngt foist s.th. [up]on s.b.
Prag n Prague
pragmat|iker [-'ma:-] pragmatist **-isk** a5 pragmatic[al]
prakt s3 magnificence, grandeur; splendour; visa sig i all sin ~ appear in all one's splendour; sommaren stod i sin fulla ~ summer was in all its glory **-band** de luxe binding **-exemplar** magnificent (spendid) specimen **-full** magnificent, splendid **-fullhet** se prakt **-gemak** state apartment
praktik s3 **1** practice; (övning) experience; i ~en in practice; omsätta i ~en put into practice; skaffa sig ~ get practice ([practical] experience) **2** (läkarverksamhet etc.); öppna egen ~ open one's own practice **praktikant** trainee, probationer, learner **praktikanttjänstgöring** work (etc.) as a trainee (etc.) **praktiker** ['prakk-] practician; (om läkare) practitioner **praktikfall** case study
praktisera 1 (tillämpa) put into practice; (lära sig ett yrke) get experience **2** (som läkare etc.) practise [as a doctor]; ~nde läkare general practitioner (förk. G.P.) **praktisk** ['prakk-] a5 practical; (användbar) useful, serviceable; (lätthanterlig) handy; i det ~a livet in practical life; ~ erfarenhet working experience **praktiskt** ['prakk-] adv practically, in a practical way; ~ användbar practical, useful; ~ genomförbar (utförbar) practicable; ~ taget practically, as good as
prakt|möbel magnificent piece (suite) of furniture **-pjäs** showpiece, museum piece **-verk** mag-

nificent volume (edition), de luxe edition **-älskande** fond of display, splendour-loving
pralin s3 chocolate, chocolate cream
prassel ['prass-] s7 rustle **prassla** rustle (äv. ~ med, i)
prat s7 (samspråk) talk, chat; (strunt-) nonsense; (skvaller) gossip, tittle-tattle; tomt (löst) ~ idle talk; [å] ~! rubbish!, nonsense!; vad är det för ~! what's all this rubbish!; inte bry sig om ~et take no notice of gossip
prata talk (med to, with; om about, of); chat; ~ för sig själv talk to o.s.; ~ i sömnen talk in one's sleep; ~ affärer (kläder) talk business (clothes); [vad] du ~r! nonsense!, rubbish!, fiddlesticks!; ~ strunt talk nonsense (rubbish); folk ~r så mycket people will talk; ~ omkull ngn talk s.b. down [to a standstill]; ~ på talk away, go on talking; ~s vid om saken talk it over
prat|bubbla (i serie) balloon **-ig** a1 (om pers.) talkative; (om stil) chatty; verbose **-kvarn** chatterbox **-makare** talker, chatterbox **-sam** a1 talkative, loquacious **-samhet** talkativeness, loquacity **-sjuk** fond of talking; loquacious **-stund** chat; ta sig en ~ have a chat **-tagen** best. form pl: vara i ~ be in a talkative mood
praxis ['praks-] best. f. praxis el. -en practice, custom, usage; enligt vedertagen ~ by usage; bryta mot ~ depart from practice; det är ~ att it is the custom to
prebende [-ˣbenn-, -'benn-] s6 prebendary's benefice
precedensfall [-ˣdenns-] precedent
preceptor [-ˣseptår] s3, ung. reader, associate professor
preciosa [-esiˣɒ:-] pl valuables; bric-a-brac (sg)
preciositet [-siɒsi-] preciosity, affectation
precis I a1 precise, exact; (om pers. äv.) particular; (punktlig) punctual **II** adv precisely; exactly; inte ~ not exactly; komma ~ kl 9 arrive at 9 o'clock sharp (on the dot); komma ~ [på minuten] be punctual, come on the dot; ~ som förut just as before; just ~! exactly!
preciser|a specify, define exactly; (i detalj) particularize; ~ närmare state more precisely **-ing** defining, specification
precision precision, exactitude, accuracy
precisions|arbete precision work **-instrument** precision instrument **-våg** precision balance (scales)
preciös a1 affected, precious
predestin|ation predestination **-era** predestinate
predika [-'di:-] preach (för to; om, över on); ~ bra preach a good sermon
predikament s7, s4 predicament
predik|an [-'di:-] best. form -an, pl predikningar sermon (över on); (straff-) lecture; hålla en ~ deliver a sermon (för to) **-ant** preacher; (frikyrko-) minister **-are** preacher; P~n [the Book of] Ecclesiastes
predikat s7 predicate **predikativ** [-'i:v, 'predd-] I s7, se predikatsfyllnad II a1 predicative **predikatsfyllnad** predicat[iv]e complement
predikning [-'di:k-] se predikan
prediko|samling [-ˣdi:-] book of sermons **-text** [sermon] text **-ton** sermonizing tone

predik|stol [ˣpredd-, ˣpre:-] pulpit; *bestiga ~en* go up into the pulpit; *stå i ~en* stand (be) in the pulpit **-stolspsalm** hymn just before the sermon

predispo|nera predispose (*för* to) **-sition** predisposition (*för* to)

pre|dominera predominate **-existens** preexistence **-fabricera** prefabricate **-fabrikation** prefabrication

prefekt *s3* (*fransk ämbetsman*) prefect; *univ.* head **prefektur** (*ämbete, lokal*) prefecture

preferens [-ˈraŋs, -ˈrens] *s3* preference **-aktie** preference share

prefix *s7* prefix

pregn|ans [preŋˈnans, preg-, -ˈaŋs] *s3* pregnancy **-ant** [pregˈnant, -ˈaŋt] *a1* pregnant

1 preja [ˣprejja] (*skinna*) surcharge, fleece

2 preja [ˣprejja] *sjö.* hail

prejning [ˣprejj-] *sjö.* hailing

prejudicerande [-ˈse:-] *a4* precedential; *~ rättsfall* test case **prejudikat** *s7* precedent; *skapa ett ~* create a precedent; *utan ~* (*äv.*) unprecedented

prekär *a1* precarious (*situation* situation)

prelat prelate

preliminär *a1* preliminary; provisional; *~ skatt* preliminary tax, (*källskatt*) pay-as-you-earn tax; *överskjutande ~ skatt* preliminary tax paid in excess

preludiera prelude **preludium** [-ˈlu:-] *s4* prelude

premie [ˈpre:-] *s5* **1** *försäkr. o.d.* premium (*på* on, for) **2** (*belöning*) prize, reward; (*extra utdeln. på lån e.d.*) bonus; (*export- etc.*) bounty, subsidy; *fast ~* uniform premium; *inbetalda ~r* paid-up value (*sg*) **-lån** premium bond (lottery) loan **-obligation** premium bond

premier|a (*belöna*) reward; (*boskap o.d.*) award a prize to; *~d tjur* prize bull **-ing** (*av boskap o.d.*) awarding of prizes

premiss *s3* premise

premi|um [ˈpre:-] *s4* prize, premium; *dela ut -er* give prizes

premiär *s3* first (opening) night **-biograf** first--run cinema **-dag** *på ~en* on the first night **-dansör** principal dancer **-dansös** leading ballerina **-lejon** *ung.* first-night habitué **-minister** prime minister, premier **-publik** first-night audience

prenumerant subscriber (*på* for) **prenumeration** subscription (*på* for, to) **prenumerationsavgift** subscription [fee] **prenumerera** subscribe (*på* for, to); *~ på en tidning* (*äv.*) take a paper

preparandkurs preparatory course [of study] **preparat** *s7* preparation; *mikroskopiskt ~* specimen, slide **preparation** preparation **preparator** [-ˣa:tår] *s3* preparator **preparatris** *ung.* medical technical assistant **preparera** prepare (*äv. skol.*)

preposition preposition **-ell** *a1* prepositional **prepositionsuttryck** prepositional phrase

prerafaelit *s3, konst.* Pre-Raphaelite

prerogativ *s7* prerogative

presbyter [ˈpress-] *s3* [*pl* -ˈrer] presbyter; (*lekmannaäldste*) elder **presbyterian** *s3* Presbyterian **presbyteriansk** [-a:-] *a5* Presbyterian

presenning [-ˈsenn-, ˣpress-] tarpaulin

presens [ˈpre:-] *n* (*i* in the) present [tense]; *~ particip* the present participle

1 present *a4* present

2 present *s3* present, gift; *få ngt i ~* get s.th. as (for) a present

presenta [-ˈsenta] *se skänka*

presentabel [-ˈta:-] *a2* presentable

presentartiklar *pl* gifts, souvenirs

presentation 1 (*föreställande*) introduction (*för* to); (*mer formellt*) presentation (*för* to) **2** (*uppvisande*) presentation

presentatör compere

presentbok gift-book

presentera 1 (*föreställa*) introduce (*för* to); (*mer formellt*) present (*vid hovet* at court; *för* to); *får jag ~ ...?* may I introduce ...?, meet ...; *~ sig* introduce o.s. **2** (*framvisa*) present (*äv. växel e.d.*), show

presentkort gift voucher (token)

preserv|ativ *s7* preservative **-era** preserve

preses [ˈpre:-] *r* president; moderator

president president; (*ordförande äv.*) chairman; (*hovrätts-*) Chief Justice **-kandidat** candidate for the presidency **-skap** *s7* presidency **-tid** (*ngns*) time as president, presidential term

president|ur *se presidentskap* **-val** presidential election

presidera preside (*vid* at, over) **presidium** [-ˈsi:-] *s4* presidency, chairmanship; (*i Sovjet*) presidium; (*styrelse*) presiding (administrative) officers (*pl*)

preskribera *~s* be statute-barred, be barred by the statute of limitations, lapse; *AE. äv.* outlaw; *~d fordran* (*skuld*) statute-barred claim (debt) **preskription** [-pˈʃoːn] [statutory] limitation, negative prescription **preskriptionstid** period of limitation

1 press *s3* (*om tidningarna*) press; *~ens frihet* the freedom of the press; *figurera i ~en* appear in the papers; *få god* (*dålig*) *~* get (have) a good (bad) press

2 press *s2* **1** *konkr., tekn.* press; *jfr brev-, frukt-, tryck- etc.*; *gå i ~* go to press **2** (*tryck, påtryckning*) pressure; *ligga* (*lägga*) *i ~* be pressed; *utöva* [*stark*] *~ på* exert [great] pressure [up]on; *leva under en ständig ~* be living under a constant strain **3** *det är fin ~ på byxorna* these trousers have a good crease

press|a 1 press (*kläder* clothes; *blommor* flowers); (*klämma*) squeeze (*apelsiner* oranges); (*med strykjärn äv.*) iron **2** (*tvinga, föra*) press, force; *~ ngn till* [*att göra*] *ngt* force s.b. to (into doing) s.th. **3** (*med betonad partikel*) *~ fram* press (squeeze; *bildl.* force) out (*ur, av* of); *~ sig fram* press forward, force one's way along; *~ ihop* compress; *~ in* squeeze in; *~ ner* press (force; *vard.* cut) down (*priserna* [the] prices) **-ande** *a4* oppressive (*hetta* heat); trying (*arbetsförhållanden* working conditions)

press|attaché press attaché **-byrå** press agency **-censur** censorship of the press **-debatt** debate in the press **-etik** press ethics **-fotograf** press photographer

press|gjuta die-cast **-gjutning** die-casting **-järn** flat iron **-jäst** compressed yeast

press|kampanj press (newspaper) campaign

P

-klipp press cutting **-kommentar** press comment[s *pl*] **-konferens** press conference **-lägga** send to [the] press **-läggning** going to [the] press **-läggningsögonblicket** *i* ~ at the moment of going to press **-man** pressman, journalist **-meddelande** press release **-mottagning** *hålla* ~ receive (invite) the press

pressning pressing; squeezing; *jfr pressa*

presspolemik newspaper polemics (*pl*)

press|revider press revise (proof) **-stöd** (*hopskr. presstöd*) [state] assistance to newspapers **-uttalande** announcement (statement) in the press

pressveck crease

pressylta (*särskr. press-sylta*) pork brawn

pressöversikt press review

prestanda [-'tann-, -ˣtann-] *pl* (*åligganden*) obligations; *tekn.* performance characteristics, performances **prestation** achievement; performance

prestations|förmåga performance, output [capacity], capacity **-lön** *se ackordslön* **-mätning** performance measurement

prestav *s3* (*stav*) staff at the head of a procession; (*-bärare*) staff bearer

prestera achieve, accomplish; perform

prestige [-'ti:ʃ] *s5* prestige **-fråga** matter of prestige **-förlust** loss of prestige

presumtiv *a1* presumptive; ~ *arvinge* heir presumtive

preten|dent pretender (*till* to) **-dera** (*äv.* -aŋ'de:-] pretend (*på* to) **-tion** [-taŋ'ʃɔ:n] pretension (*på* to) **-tiös** [-taŋ'ʃö:s] *a1* pretentious

preteritum [-'te:-] *s8, s4* (*i* in the) preterite

pretiosa [-(t)si ˣo:-] *se preciosa* **pretiositet** [-(t)si-] *se preciositet* **pretiös** [-(t)si'ö:s] *se preciös*

preussare [ˣpröjs-, ˣpråjs-] Prussian **Preussen** ['pröjs-, 'pråjs-] *n* Prussia **preusseri** [pröjs-, pråjs-] Prussian drill **preussisk** ['pröjs-, pråjs-] *a5* Prussian

prevalens *s3* prevalence

preventiv I *a1* preventive **II** *s7* preventive **-medel** contraceptive

prick *s2* **1** dot, spot, point; (*på måltavla*) bull's eye; (*vid förprickning*) mark, tick; *till punkt och* ~*a, på* ~*en* exactly, to a tee (T); *sätta* ~ *en över i-t* (*bildl.*) add the finishing touch; *träffa* ~ hit the mark (*äv. bildl.*); ~ *kl. 6* at six sharp **2** *sport.* penalty point **3** *sjö.* [spar] buoy, perch **4** *en trevlig* (*hygglig*) ~ a nice (decent) fellow (chap, *AE. äv.* guy)

prick|a 1 (*förse med -ar*) dot; (*skjuta prick*) hit; (*sticka hål i*) prick; ~ *av* tick [off], check off, tally; ~ *för* check (mark) off; ~ *in* dot in **2** (*brännmärka*) reprove, reprimand **3** *sjö.* buoy (*en farled* a fairway) **-fri** *sport.* without penalty points **-ig** *a1* spotted, dotted **-ning 1** dotting *etc.* **2** (*brännmärkning*) reproof, reprimand **3** *sjö.* buoyage **-skytt** sharpshooter; *mil.* sniper **-säker** *en* ~ *skytt* an expert shot

prim [-i:-] *s3, mus. o. fäkt.* prime **prima** [ˣpri:-, 'pri:-] *oböjligt a* first-rate, first-class, choice, prime; *vard.* A1, *AE.* dandy **primadonna** [-ˣdånna] *s1* prima donna; *teat.* leading lady **primadonnelater** *pl* prima donna airs

primas ['pri:-] *r* primate **primat 1** *s7* primacy **2** *s3, zool.* primate

primfaktor *mat.* aliquot part, prime factor

primitiv [-'ti:v, 'primm-, 'pri:-] *a1* primitive **-itet** primitiveness

primo ['pri:-, ˣpri:-] *pro* ~ firstly, in the first place

primtal prime number

primula ['pri:-] *s1* primula

primus ['pri:-] **I** *r, skol.* top of the class **II** *oböjl. a*, ~ *motor* the prime mover **primuskök** [ˣpri:-] primus (*varumärke*) [stove]

primär *a1* primary; (*grundläggande*) elementary; (*ursprunglig*) primordial **-lån** first mortgage loan **-val** primary [election]

primör early vegetable (fruit); firstling

princip *s3* principle; *av* (*i*) ~ on (in) principle; *det strider mot mina* ~*er* it is against my principles; *en man utan* ~*er* an unprincipled man

principal *s3* principal, proprietor, employer **principat** *s7* principate

princip|beslut decision in principle **-fast** strong-principled; *en* ~ *man* (*äv.*) a man of principle **-fråga** question (matter) of principle **-förslag** proposal on guiding principles (guidelines)

principiell *a5* founded (based) on principle; (*grundväsentlig*) fundamental; *av* ~*a skäl* on grounds of principle; ~*a hänsyn* considerations of principle **principiellt** *adv* on (as a matter of) principle

princip|lös unprincipled **-människa** person (*etc.*) of principle **-ryttare** doctrinaire **-rytteri** doctrinairism **-uttalande** declaration of principle

prins *s2* prince; *må som en* ~ feel on top of the world **-essa** [-ˣsessa] *s1* princess **-gemål** prince consort **-korv** chipolata sausage **-regent** prince regent

prior [ˣpri:år] *s3* prior (*i* of) **priorinna** prioress

prioritera give priority to **prioriterad** *a5* priority, preferential; *AE.* preferred **prioritering** *genom* ~ *av* by giving priority to **prioritet** priority **prioritetsrätt** right of priority

1 pris *s3* (*uppbringat fartyg*) prize, capture; *ta ngt som god* ~ take s.th. as lawful prize

2 pris *s2* (*nypa* [*snus*]) pinch [of snuff]

3 pris *s7, s4* (*värde, kostnad*) price (*på* of); (*begärt* ~) charge; *högt* (*lågt*) ~ high (low) price; *nedsatt* ~ reduced price, cut price (*AE.* rate); *gängse* (*gällande*) ~*er* ruling (current) prices; *höja* (*sänka*) ~*et på* raise (lower) the price of; *höja* ~*et med 6 pence* raise the price by 6 pence; ~*erna stiger* prices are rising; *stiga i* ~ advance (rise) in price, go up; *det i fakturan* (*prislistan*) *angivna* ~*et* the invoiced (listed) price; *vara värd* ~*et* be worth the price, be good value; *komma överens om* ~*et* agree on the price; *sätta stort* ~ *på att få* set great store on getting; *för gott* ~ at a moderate price; *till ett* ~ *av* at the (a) price of; *till halva* ~*et* at half-price, at half the price; *till varje* ~ (*bildl.*) at any cost, at all costs

4 pris *s7, s4* (*belöning*) prize; *få första* ~ be awarded the first prize; *tar i alla fall* ~*et* (*bildl.*) takes first prize (the cake); *sätta ett* ~ *på ngns huvud* set a price on a p.'s head

5 pris *s7* (*lov, beröm*) praise; *Gud ske* ~ glory to God; *sjunga ngns* ~ sing a p.'s praises

prisa praise, glorify; ~ *sig lycklig* consider o.s. fortunate, count o.s. lucky
prisbelöna award a prize to; *~d (vanl.*) prize *(roman* novel), prize-winning
pris|bildning fixing (determination) of prices **-billig** cheap, inexpensive
pris|boxare prizefighter **-domare** judge
pris|elasticitet price elasticity **-fall** decline (fall) in prices; *(kraftigt)* slump **-fluktuation** fluctuation in (of) prices **-fråga** matter (question) of price
pris|ge *se -giva* **-giva** give up, abandon, expose *(åt* to); *vara -en åt (äv.*) be left at the mercy of **-ning** [-i:v-] abandonment, exposure
prishoppning *ridk.* showjumping
pris|höjning rise (advance) in price[s *pl]* **-index** price index **-klass** price range **-konkurrens** price competition **-kontroll** price control **-kontrollerad** *a5* price-controlled **-krig** price war **-kurant** *s3* price list **-känslig** *~a varor* goods whose saleability is susceptible to rising prices **-lapp** price label (ticket, tag) **-lista** price list **-läge** price range (level); *i alla (olika) ~n* at all (different) prices; *i vilket ~?* at about what price?
prisma [*ˣpriss-] -t prismer el. s1* prism; *(i ljuskrona)* drop **-kikare** prism binoculars *(pl)* **-tisk** [-ˈma:-] *a5* prismatic
pris|medveten price-conscious **-märka** mark with prices, put prices on **-nedsättning** price reduction, markdown **-nivå** price level **-notering** quotation **-politik** prices policy **-reglering** price control (regulation)
prisse *s2* fellow, chap
pris|skillnad difference in price **-stegring** *se prishöjning* **-stopp** price freeze; *införa ~* freeze prices **-sänkning** price reduction (decrease) **-sätta** price, fix the price[s *pl]* of **-sättning** pricing, fixing of prices
pris|tagare prize winner **-tävlan** prize competition
prisuppgift [price] quotation *(på* for)
prisutdelning distribution of prizes
prisutveckling price trend
1 prisvärd *(värd sitt pris)* worth its price; good value [for money]
2 prisvärd *(lovvärd)* praiseworthy
privat I *a1* private, personal; *~ område* private grounds (premises) *(pl); den ~a sektorn* the private sector; *i det ~a* in private life; *jag för min ~a del* I for my part **II** *adv* privately, in private; *undervisa ~ (äv.*) give private lessons **-angelägenhet** personal matter; *mina ~er* my private affairs **-anställd** person in private employment **-bil** private car **-bilism** private motoring **-bostad** private residence **-chaufför** private chauffeur **-detektiv** private detective; *AE.* private eye **-finansierad** privately financed **-flyg** private aviation
privatim [-ˣva:-] privately, in private **privatist** external candidate
privat|kapital private capital **-lektion** private lesson **-lärare** private teacher, tutor **-lärd** *en ~* an independent scholar **-man, -person** private person ; *som ~* in private life **-praktik** private practice **-rätt** civil law **-sekreterare** private secretary **-ägd** [-ä:-] *a5* privately-owned

privilegi|ebrev [-ˈle:-] charter **-era** privilege **-um** *s4* privilege; *(monopol)* monopoly *(på* of)
PR-man [*ˣpe:ärr-] PR (public relations) officer *(förk.* P.R.O.)
pro pro; *~ forma* pro forma; *~ primo (secundo)* firstly (secondly)
prob|abel [-ˈba:-] *a2* probable **-era** try; *(guld o.d.*) assay; *tekn.* test **-ersten** [-ˣbe:r-] touchstone
problem *s7* problem; *framlägga (lösa) ett ~* pose (solve) a problem **problematik** *s3* [set of] problems *(pl)* **problematisk** [-ˈma:-] *a5* problematic [al]
problem|barn problem child **-komplex** group of problems **-lösning** solution of problems (a problem) **-ställning** problem, presentation of a problem
proboxning professional boxing
procedur procedure; process
procent *s9 (hundradel)* per cent, percent; *(-tal)* percentage; *löpa med 5 ~s ränta* run at 5 per cent interest; *hur många ~ är det?* what percentage is that?; *2-~ig lösning* a two-per-cent solution; *mot (till) hög ~* at a high percentage; *i ~ av* as a per-centage of; *ökningen i ~ räknat* the percentage increase; *vi lämnar 10 ~[s rabatt] vid kontant betalning* 10% cash discount
procent|a [-ˈsenn-] practise usury **-are** [-ˣsenn-] usurer
procent|enhet percentage point **-halt** percentage **-räkning** calculation of percentages **-sats, -tal** percentage **-uell** *a1* expressed as a percentage (in percentages)
process 1 *(rättstvist)* lawsuit, action; legal proceedings *(pl); öppna ~ med (mot)* bring an action against; *ligga i ~ med* be involved in a lawsuit with; *förlora (vinna) en ~* lose (win) a case; *göra ~en kort med* make short work of, put an end to **2** *(förlopp)* process; procedure **processa** [-ˈsessa] carry on lawsuits (a lawsuit); *~ om* litigate **processindustri** processing industry
procession [-seˈʃoːn] procession; *gå i ~* march (walk) in procession, process
processionsordning processional order
process|kontroll *tekn.* process control **-makare** litigious person **-rätt** law of [legal] procedure **-teknik** processing technique
producent producer; manufacturer; grower **-kooperation** producer's cooperation **-varor** *pl* producer[s'] goods
producera produce; manufacture; *~ sig* appear [in public]
produkt *s3* product *(äv. mat.); ~er (koll., jordbruks- e.d., äv.*) produce *(sg); inhemska ~er* domestic products, home manufacture *(sg)* **produktion** [-kˈʃoːn] production; *(framställda varor)* output; *(författares el. konstnärs)* work[s], output; *öka ~en* increase [the] production
produktions|apparat productive apparatus, machinery of production **-faktor** factor of production, productive factor **-främjande** *a4* promoting production **-förmåga** productive power (capacity), productivity **-hämmande** *a4, ~ faktorer* factors holding back production **-kostnad** cost of production **-led** stage of production **-medel** means *(sg o. pl)* of production **-metod**

method of production **-siffra** production (output) figure **-tid** production time **-utveckling** trend of production **-volym** volume of production **-ökning** increase (rise) in production **produktiv** [-'ti:v, 'prådd-, 'prɑ:-, 'prodd-] *al* productive; (*om författare*) prolific **-itet** productivity

produktutveckling product development

profan *al* profane; (*värdslig*) secular **-era** profane **-ering** [-'ne:-] profanation

profession [-e'ʃɑ:n] profession; (*näringsfång*) trade; *till ~en* by profession (trade) **-alism** professionalism **-ell** *al* professional; *bli ~* turn professional; *~ idrottsman* professional

professor [-ˣfessår] *s3* professor (*i historia* of history); *AE. äv.* full professor; *~ emeritus* professor emeritus **professorsinstallation** ceremonial installation of a professor **professorska** [-ˣsɑ:r-] professor's wife; *~n A.* Mrs. A. **professorskompetens** qualifications (*pl*) for a professorship **professur** professorship (*i historia* in history), chair (*i historia* of history); *inneha en ~* hold a professorship (chair); *inrätta en ~* found (establish) a chair

profet *s3* prophet; *de större* (*mindre*) *~erna* the major (minor) prophets; *ingen är ~ i sitt fädernesland* no one is a prophet in his own country **profetera** prophesy; (*förutsäga*) predict **profetia** [-tˣsi:a] *s1* prophecy **profetisk** [-'fe:t-] *a5* prophetic[al] **profetissa** prophetess

proffs [-å-] *s7, s9, sport.* pro (*pl* pros); *bli ~* turn pro

profil *s3* profile (*äv. tekn.*) **-era** profile **-ering** [-'le:-] profiling **-järn** section[al] (structural) iron

profit *s3* profit, gain; *för ~ens skull* for the sake of profit **-era** profit (*av* by, from) **-haj** profiteer **-hunger** thirst for gain **-ör** profiteer

pro forma [-'fårr-] pro forma **proformafaktura** pro-forma invoice

profylaktisk [-'lakk-] *a5* prophylactic **profylax** *s3* prophylaxis (*pl* prophylaxes)

progesteron [-'rå:n] *s4* progesterone

prognos [-g'nå:s] *s3, med.* prognosis (*pl* prognoses); (*väderleks- m.m.*) forecast; *ställa en ~* make a prognosis (forecast) **-karta** (*väderlek*) weather map **-ticera** prognosticate; forecast

program [-'gramm] *s7* programme; *AE.* program (*parti- äv.*) platform; (*plan, förslag*) plan; *göra upp ett ~* draw up a programme; *det hör till ~met* it is part of the programme; *stå på ~met* be on (in) the programme **-enlig** [-e:n-] *a1* according to [the] programme; scheduled **-enligt** [-e:n-] *adv* in accordance with [the] programme; as arranged **-förklaring** *polit.* [election] manifesto **-ledare** *radio.* (*vid underhållning*) compere; (*i debatt*) chairman **-matisk** *a5* [-'ma:-] programmatic **programmera** *data.* program; *AE.* program; *~d undervisning* programmed instruction **-are** [-ˣme:-] programmer **-ing** programming

program|musik programme music **-punkt** item [in (on) a programme] **-skrift** manifesto **-vara** *se mjukvara* **-värd** *s2, radio. o.d.* compere

progress|ion [-e'ʃɑ:n] progression **-iv** *al* progressive (*beskattning* taxation) **-ivitet** progressiveness

prohibitiv *al* prohibitive

projekt [-ʃ-, -j-] *s7* project; plan, scheme **-era** project; plan; *~d* projected **-ering** [-'te:-] projecting, projection; planning

projektil [-ʃ-, -j-] *s3* projectile, missile **-bana** trajectory [of a projectile]

projek|tion [-k'ʃɑ:n] projection **-tionsapparat** projector; projecting apparatus **-tionsritning** projection drawing **-tjv** *al* projective

projekt|ledare leader (head) of a project **-makare** projector; schemer

projektor [-ˣjektår] *s3* projector **projicera** project

prokansler vice chancellor

proklam|a [-'kla:-] *s1* [public] notice **-ation** proclamation **-era** proclaim

prokonsul proconsul

prokrustes|bädd, -säng [-ˣkrustes-] Procrustes' bed

prokur|a [-ˣku:-] *s1* procuration, proxy; *teckna per ~* sign per pro (by procuration) **-ator** [-ˣra:-tår] *s3* procurator **-ist** holder of procuration; managing clerk

proletariat *s7* proletariat

proletär I *s3* proletarian **II** *al* proletarian **-författare** proletarian author **-roman** proletarian novel

prolog prologue

prolong|ation [-långa-] prolongation, extension **-era** [-lånˈge:-] prolong, extend

promemoria [-'mɑ:-] *s1* memorandum (*över* on); memo

promenad *s3* **1** (*spatsertur*) walk; (*flanerande*) stroll; (*åktur*) ride; *ta* [*sig*] *en ~* take a walk; *gå på ~* go for a walk; *ta ngn med ut på en ~* take s.b. out for a walk **2** *se -plats* **-dräkt** suit **-däck** promenade deck **-konsert** promenade concert; *vard.* prom **-käpp** walking stick **-plats** promenade; esplanade **-sko** walking shoe **-väg** promenade; (*stig*) walk

promener|a walk; *gå ut och ~* go [out] for a walk **-ande** *a4, de ~* the promenaders, people out walking

promille [-ˣmille] per mil[l] (thousand) **-halt** *blodet hade en ~ av 0,5* the concentration [of alcohol] in the blood was 50 mg. per cent **-tal** per millage

prominent *al* prominent

promiskuitet promiscuity **promiskuös** *al* promiscuous

promotion conferment of doctors' degrees **promotor** [-ˣmɑ:tår] *s3, univ.* person conferring doctors' degrees; *sport.* promoter **promovend** *s3* recipient of a doctors' degree **promovera** confer a doctor's degree on

prompt [-å-] **I** *a4* prompt, immediate **II** *adv* (*genast*) promptly, immediately; (*ovillkorligen*) absolutely

promulg|ation promulgation **-era** promulgate

pronom|en [-'nå:-, -'nɑ:-] *best. form -enet, pl -en el. -ina* pronoun **-inell** *al* pronominal

prononcerad [-nånˈse:-] *a5* (*utpräglad*) decided, strong

propaganda [-ˣgann-] *s1* propaganda; *göra ~ för* make propaganda for **-avdelning** propaganda department (division, section) **-syfte** *i ~ for* propaganda purposes (*pl*) **-verksamhet** propa-

ganda activities (*pl*)
propag|andist propagandist **-era** propagate, make propaganda (*för* for)
propęn *s4, s3* propane
propedeut|ik [-ev-] *s3* propaedeutics (*pl, behandlas som sg*) **-isk** [-'devv-] *a5* propaedeutic, preparatory (*kurs* course)
propeller [-'pell-] *s2* propeller, screw; *flyg. äv.* airscrew **-axel** propeller shaft **-blad** propeller blade **-driven** *a5* propeller-driven **-plan** propeller aircraft **-turbin** turboprop
propęn *s4, s3* propene, propylene
proper ['prå:-] *a2* tidy, neat, clean
proponera propose, suggest
proportion [-rt'ʃɑːn] proportion; *stå i ~ till* be in proportion to; *i ~en 2 till 3* in the proportion of 2 to 3; *ha sinne för ~er* have a sense for (of) proportion; *står inte alls i ~ till* is out of all proportion to; *ha vackra ~er* be beautifully proportioned (well-proportioned) **proportionęl** *s3* proportional **proportionęll** *a1* proportional; *direkt* (*omvänt*) ~ directly (inversely) proportional (*mot* to) **proportionerad** [-'ne:-] *a5* proportioned (*efter* to) **proportionerlig** [-'ne:r-] *a1* (*väl avpassad*) well-proportioned; (*i visst förhållande*) proportionate (*till* to) **proportionsvis** proportionately; comparatively
proposition 1 (*förslag*) proposal, proposition; (*regerings-*) government bill; *framlägga en ~* present a bill to Parliament **2** *mat., log.* proposition
propp [-å-] *s2* stopper, plug; (*kork*) cork; *elektr.* fuse; *det har gått en ~* a fuse has blown
propp|a [-å-] cram, stuff (*med* with); ~ *igen* (*till*) plug up; ~ *i sig mat* stuff o.s. with food **-full** cram-full (*av, med* of) **-mätt** *vara ~* be full up
proprieborgen [ˣprå:-] personal surety, suretyship
props [-å-] *s9* pitprops
propsa [-å-] ~ *på ngt* (*på att få*) insist on s.th. (on getting)
propå ['prå'på:] *s3* proposal
prorektor [-ɔ:-, -å:-] prorector, pro-vice-chancellor
prosa *s1* prose; *på ~* in prose **-dikt** prose poem **-författare** prosaist, prose writer **-isk** [-'sa:-] *a5* prosaic; (*opoetisk*) unimaginative (*arbete* work) **-stil** prose style **-tör** *se -författare*
prosektor [-ˣsektär] *s3* associate professor, demonstrator [in anatomy]
proselyt *s3* proselyte, convert
proseminarium ['prɔ:-, ˣprå-] proseminar
prosit ['prɔ:-] [God] bless you!
proskri|bera proscribe **-ption** [-p'ʃɑːn] proscription
prosodj *s3* prosody **prosodisk** [-'sɔ:-] *a5* prosodic[al]
prospękt *s7* prospectus (*över* of) **-era** prospect (*efter malm* for ore) **-ering** [-'te:-] prospecting
prost *s2* [rural] dean
prostata ['pråss-, -ˣsta:-] *s9* prostate [gland]
prostinna dean's wife; *~n A.* Mrs. A.
prostitu|era prostitute; *en ~d* a prostitute **-tion** prostitution
proteg|é [-'ʃe:] *s3* protégé, *fem.* protégée **-era** (*beskydda*) patronize; (*gynna*) favour
protejn *s4* protein **-halt** protein content

protektion [-k'ʃɑːn] protection; patronage **-ism** protectionism **-ist** protectionist **-istisk** [-'niss-] *a5* protectionist
protektorąt *s7* protectorate
protęs *s3* prosthesis (*pl* prostheses); artificial limb (arm, leg); (*löständer*) denture
protęst *s3* protest; *avge* (*inlägga*) ~ *mot* make (enter, lodge) a protest against; *under ~*[er] under protest; *utan ~*[er] without a protest **-aktion** protest action
protestant Protestant **-isk** *a5* Protestant **-ism** Protestantism (*äv. ~en*)
protest|era protest (*mot* against; *en växel* a bill of exchange); *jag ~r* (*äv.*) I object **-möte** protest (indignation) meeting **-skrivelse** letter of protest **-storm** storm of protest **-sång** protest song
protokoll [-'kåll] *s7* minutes (*pl*) (*över* of); *dipl.* protocol; (*domstols- o.d.*) report of the proceedings; (*poäng-*) score, record; *föra ~et* keep (take) the minutes, keep the record; *justera ~et* verify (check) the minutes; *ta till ~et* enter in the minutes; *sätta upp ~ över* draw up a report of; *yttra ngt utom ~et* say s.th. off the record **-chef** chief of protocol **-föra** enter in the minutes, record **-förare** keeper of the minutes; recorder; (*vid domstol*) clerk [of the court]; *sport.* scorer
protokollsutdrag extract from the minutes
proton [-'tå:n] *s3* proton **-stråle** proton beam
protoplasma [-ˣplass-] *s9, s7* protoplasm
prototyp *s3* prototype **protozo** [-'så:] *s3* protozoan, protozoon; *~er* protozoa
protuberąns *s3, astr.* prominence
prov 1 *s7* (*försök, experiment*) trial, test, experiment; (*examens-*) examination; (*-skrivning*) [examination] paper; *anställa ~ med* try, test, give a trial; *efter avlagda* ~ after passing the examination[s *pl*]; *avlägga godkänt ~ i* pass the test (examination) in; *bestå ~et* stand the test; *på ~* on trial, (*om pers. äv.*) on probation, (*om varor äv.*) on approval; *sätta ngn på ~* put s.b. to the test; *sätta ngns tålamod på hårt ~* try a p.'s patience very severely; *undergå ~* undergo a test; *visa ~ på sinnesnärvaro* give proof of presence of mind **2** *s7, s4* (*varu-*) sample; (*-exemplar, exempel*) specimen; ~ *utan värde* sample of no value, trade sample; *ett fint ~ på konsthantverk* a fine specimen of handicraft
prov|a test, try [out]; (*kläder*) try on **-bit** sample, specimen **-borrning** test drilling **-docka** (*skyltdocka*) [tailor's] dummy; (*modelldocka*) lay figure
provenięns *s3* provenance; origin
provensalsk [-vaŋ'sa:lsk, -vens-] *a5* Provençal **provensalska** *s1* (*språk*) Provençal
prov|erska fitter. **-exemplar** sample, specimen **-filma** have a screen test **-filmning** screen test **-flyga** test [fly] **-flygare** test pilot **-flygning** test flight **-frukost** *med.* test meal **-föreläsning** trial lecture
provięnt *s9* provisions, supplies, victuals (*pl*); *förse med ~* provision, victual **-era** take in stores, provision **-ering** [-'te:-] provisioning, victualling **-fartyg** supply ship **-förråd** stores (*pl*)
provjns *s3* province **-ialism** *s3* provincialism **-ialläkare** [-ˣa:l-] district medical officer **-ięll** *a1* provincial

provision commission (*på* on); (*mäklarearvode*) brokerage; *fast* ~ flat (fixed) commission; ~ *på omsättningen* turnover commission

provisor|isk [-'sɔ:-] *a5* provisional; (*tillfällig*) temporary **-ium** *s4* temporary (provisional) arrangement, makeshift

prov|kandidat student teacher **-karta** *hand.* pattern (sample) card; *en* ~ *på* (*bildl.*) a variety of **-kollektion** [collection of] samples **-kropp** test piece **-kök** experimental kitchen **-köra** test **-körning** trial (test) run **-ning** [-ɔ:-] testing, checking; *konkr.* test, trial; (*av kläder*) trying on, fitting **-ningsanstalt** testing (research) station **-nummer** specimen copy

provocera provoke; incite

provoka|tion provocation **-torisk** [-'tɔ:-] *a5* provocative **-tör** [agent] provocateur

prov|predikan probationary sermon **-rum** *tekn.* test room; (*för kläder*) fitting room; (*på hotell o.d.*) showroom **-ryttare** commercial traveller; *vard.* bagman **-räkning** *skol.* arithmetic test (paper) **-rör** test tube **-rörsbarn** test-tube baby **-skjutning** artillery practice **-skrivning** written test; *konkr.* test paper **-smaka** taste **-spela** have an audition (*för ngn* before s.b.); (*pröva instrument*) try out **-stopp** *s7* (*för kärnvapen*) test ban **-stoppsavtal** test-ban treaty **-sändning** (*av varor*) trial consignment; *radio.* trial (test) transmission **-tagning** [-a:g-] sampling; taking of specimens **-tjänstgöring** probationary period (service) **-tryck** *boktr.* proof, pull **-tur** trial trip (run) **-år** year of probation; (*lärares*) student-teacher year **-årskandidat** *se provkandidat*

prudentlig [-'dent-] *al* prim, finical

prunk|a be resplendent (blazing, dazzling); make a display (*med* of) **-ande** *a4* blazing, dazzling, gaudy, showy

prut *s7*, *se -ande*; *utan* ~ without demur **pruta** bargain, haggle, beat down the price; ~ *på ngt* try to get s.th. cheaper; *få* ~ *ett pund på ngt* get a pound knocked off s.th.; ~ *av på sina fordringar* temper (moderate) one's demands; *regeringen* ~*de ner anslaget* the government reduced the subsidy **prutande** *s6* bargaining, haggling

prutgås brent [goose]

prut|mån margin for bargaining (haggling) **-ning** [-u:-] *se prutande*

pryd *al*, *n sg obest. form undviks* prim, prudish

pryd|a *v2* adorn; (*försköna*) embellish; (*dekorera*) decorate; *den -er sin plats* it is decorative where it is (stands *etc.*)

pryderi prudishness, prudery

prydlig [-y:-] *al* neat; (*om pers. äv.*) trim, smart **-het** neatness *etc.*

prydnad [-y:-] *s3* adornment, decoration, embellishment; (*-nadssak*) ornament; *vara en* ~ *för* be an ornament (credit) to (*sitt land* one's country) **prydnads|föremål** ornament; *pl äv.* fancy goods, bric-a-brac **-växt** ornamental plant

prydno [-y:-] *i uttr.*: *i sin* ~ (*i sht iron.*) in its (his *etc.*) glory

prygel ['pry:-] *s7* whipping, flogging; *vard.* hiding; *få* ~ get a whipping *etc.* **prygelstraff** flogging, corporal punishment **prygla** [-y:-] whip, flog

pryl *s2* pricker, punch, awl; ~*ar* (*vard.*) odds and ends

pryo ['pryɔ] *skol.* (*förk. för praktisk yrkesorientering*) introduction to working life

prål *s7* ostentation, parade; (*grannlåt*) finery **pråla** (*prunka*) dazzle, blaze; (*ståta*) show off (*med* with), make a show (parade) (*med* of) **prålig** *al* gaudy, showy; flaunting **prålighet** gaudiness *etc.*

pråm *s2* barge; (*hamn-*) lighter **-dragare** (*båt*) barge (lighter) tug; *pers.* barge tower **-skeppare** bargeman, bargee; lighterman

pråug *s7* [narrow] passage (space)

prångla ~ *ut* utter (*falska sedlar* counterfeit banknotes)

prägel ['*prä:-, 'prä:-] *s2* (*stämpel*) stamp; (*avtryck*) impression, impress; *bildl.* stamp, impress; *bära äkthetens* ~ bear the stamp (impress) of authenticity; *sätta sin* ~ *på ngt* leave one's stamp (mark) on s.th. **prägla** [-ä:-] strike [off] (*en medalj* a medal); (*mynta*) mint, coin (*mynt* money; *ett nytt ord* a new word); emboss; *bildl.* stamp, impress, imprint; (*karakterisera*) characterize; *personligt ~de arbeten* works with the stamp of a p.'s personality **prägling** [-ä:-] stamping; (*av mynt*) coining, coinage; (*av nya ord*) coinage

präktig *al* (*ståtlig*) splendid, magnificent; (*utmärkt, förträfflig*) excellent, good, fine

pränt *s7*, *på* ~ in print **pränta** (*texta*) print; write carefully; ~ *i ngn ngt, se inpränta*

prärie ['prä:-] *s5* prairie **-hund** prairie dog **-varg** prairie wolf, coyote

präst *s3* priest; (*i anglikanska kyrkan, prot.*) clergyman; (*frikyrklig, skotsk*) minister; *vard.* parson; *bli* ~ become a clergyman (*etc.*), take holy orders; *läsa för* ~*en* prepare for confirmation; *kvinnliga* ~*er* women clergymen; ~*en i församlingen* the parish clergyman (*etc.*) **-betyg** extract from the parish register **-dräkt** *i* ~ in canonicals (clerical attire)

präster|lig *al* clerical (*stånd* order); sacerdotal, priestly (*värdighet* dignity) **-skap** *s7* clergy; priesthood

präst|fru clergyman's (*etc.*) wife **-gård** parsonage, rectory, vicarage; *kat.* presbytery; (*frikyrklig, skotsk*) manse **-inna** priestess **-kappa** clergyman's gown **-krage 1** *eg.* clerical collar; bands (*pl*) **2** *bot.* oxeye daisy, marguerite **-man** *se präst* **-rock** cassock **-seminarium** theological seminary **-viga** ordain **-vigning** [-i:g-] ordination **-ämbete** ministry

pröjsa *vard.* fork out, foot the bill

pröva 1 (*prova, sätta på prov*) try; (*testa*) test; (*undersöka, examinera*) examine; (*överväga*) consider; ~ *lyckan* try one's luck; ~ *ett mål* (*jur.*) try a case; ~ *ett räkneexempel* check a sum; ~ *om den håller* try and see if it holds; ~ *själv!* try for yourself!; *i nöden* ~*s vännen* a friend in need is a friend indeed; ~ *sig fram* proceed by trial and error; ~ *sina krafter på* try one's strength on; ~ *en ansökan* consider an application; *vi har fått* ~ *på mycket* we have had to put up with a great deal; ~*s av ödet* be tried by Fate **2** (*underkasta sig -ning*) be examined (*i* in); ~ *in* sit for an entrance examination (*vid en skola* at a school) **3** *jur.*

(anse, finna) deem, judge *(skäligt* reasonable) **prövad** *a5 (hårt* sorely) tried (afflicted) **prövande** *a4 (besvärlig)* trying *(för ngn* to s.b.); *(granskande)* searching *(blick* look) **prövning** [-ö:-] **1** *(undersökning, förhör)* examination, test; *förnyad* ~ reconsideration, re-examination; *ta upp ett ärende till förnyad* ~ reconsider a matter **2** *(motgång, lidande)* trial, affliction **prövningsnämnd** board of examiners; *(för beskattning)* tax appeal board (committee)

prövo|sten touchstone **-tid** *(provtid)* trial (probationary) period; *(svår tid)* difficult time, time of testing

PS *förk. för postskriptum* P.S. (postscript)

psalm [s-] *s3 (kyrkosång)* hymn; *(i Psaltaren)* psalm; *Davids ~er* [the Book of] Psalms **-bok** hymn book **-diktning** hymn writing **-ist** psalmist

psalm|odikon [sal'mɔdikån] *s7, ung.* monochord **-sång** hymn singing **-vers** verse of a hymn

psaltare [s-] *(instrument)* psaltery; *P~n* [the Book of] Psalms

pseudo|händelse ['psev-] pseudo-event, pseudo-happening **-nym** *s3* pseudonym, pen name **-vetenskaplig** pseudoscientific

psoriasis [-ˣriːa-] *s3* psoriasis

pst here!

psyke *s6* psyche, mind **psykedelisk** [-'deː-] *a5* psychedelic **psykförsvar** psychological defence **psykiater** [-iˈaːt-] *s3* psychiatrist **psykiatri** *s3* psychiatry **psykiatrisk** [-kiˈaːt-] *a5* psychiatric **psykisk** ['psy:-] *a5* psychic[al]; *~a störningar* psychical (mental) disturbances **psykiskt** ['psy:-] *adv* psychically; *~ efterbliven* mentally retarded

psyko|analys psychoanalysis **-analysera** psychoanalyse **-analytiker** [-'ly:-] psychoanalyst **-analytisk** [-'ly:-] psychoanalytic[al] **-drama** psychodrama **-farmaka** [-'farr-] *pl* psychopharmacological drugs **-gen** [-'je:n] *a1* psychogenic **-log** psychologist **-logi** [-lå'gi:] *s3* psychology **-logisera** psychologize **-logisk** [-'lå:-] *a5* psychologic[al] **-pat** psychopath **-pati** *s3* psychopathy **-patisk** [-'pa:-] *a5* psychopathic

psyko|s [-'kå:s] *s3* psychosis *(pl* psychoses) **-somatisk** [-'ma:-] *a5* psychosomatic **-teknik** psychotechnology **-teknisk** [-'tekk-] psychotechnical **-terapeut** psychotherapist **-terapi** psychotherapy **-tisk** [-'kå:-] psychotic

ptro whoa!

pub [pubb] *s2* pub

pubertet puberty **pubertetsålder** [age of] puberty

public|era publish **-ering** [-'se:-] publishing, publication **-ist** publicist **-itet** publicity; *få bra ~* get good publicity

publik I *s3 (åhörare)* audience; *(åskådare)* spectators *(pl); (antal närvarande)* attendance; *(teater-)* house; *sport. äv.* fans *(pl),* crowd; *(allmänhet)* public; *den breda ~en* the public at large; *ta ~en med storm* bring down the house **II** *a1* public

publikan *s3, bibl.* publican

publik|anslutning *(stor* large) attendance, crowd **-ation** publication **-dragande** *a4* popular, attractive **-favorit** popular favourite **-framgång** success [with the public]; *(boks)* best seller

-friare *ung.* showman **-frieri** *ung.* playing to the gallery, showmanship **-rekord** attendance record **-siffra** attendance; *sport.* gate **-um** ['pubb-] *n* the audience **-undersökning** [opinion] poll

puck *s2 (ishockey-)* puck

1 puckel ['pukk-] *s7, se stryk, smörj*

2 puckel ['pukk-] *s2* hump; *(hos människa äv.)* hunch

puckel|oxe zebu **-rygg** hunchback **-ryggig** *al* hunchbacked

puckla ~ *på ngn* thrash s.b.

pudding pudding

pudel ['pu:-] *s2* poodle; *~ns kärna* the heart of the matter

puder ['pu:-] *s7* powder **-dosa** powder compact **-socker** icing *(AE.* confectioners') sugar **-underlag** foundation [cream] **-vippa** powder puff

pudr|a [ˣpu:d-] powder; ~ *sig* powder [o.s.] **-ing** powdering, dusting

pueril *al* puerile **-itet** *s3* puerility

puff *s2* **1** *(svag knall)* pop **2** *(knuff)* push **3** *(rök-)* puff **4** *(pall)* pouf[fe]; *(soffa)* box ottoman **5** *(på ärm)* puff **6** *(reklam)* puff **puffa 1** *(knalla)* pop **2** *(knuffa)* push; ~ *ngn i sidan* dig (poke) s.b. in the ribs **3** *(göra reklam)* ~ *för* puff, give a puff

puffärm puff[ed] sleeve

pugilist pugilist

puh phew!

puk|a *s1* kettledrum; *med -or och trumpeter (bildl.)* with drums beating and flags flying **-slag** beat on the kettledrum **-slagare** kettledrummer

pulka *s1* reindeer (Lapland) sleigh

pull ~ ~*!* chick chick!

1 pulla *s1 (höna)* chick, pullet; *(tös)* lass, chickabiddy

2 pulla *s1 (för spelmarker)* pool

pullover [-'å:-] *s2* pullover

pulpa *s1* pulp

pulpet *s3* desk

puls *s2* pulse; *oregelbunden (regelbunden)* ~ irregular (normal) pulse; *ta ~en på ngn* take (feel) a p.'s pulse; *känna ngn på ~en (bildl.)* sound s.b., assess a p.'s intentions

pulsa plod, plough *(i snön* through the snow)

pulsar *s3, astr.* pulsar

pulser|a *(eg. o. friare)* pulsate, throb, beat **-ing** pulsation

puls|frekvens, -hastighet pulse rate **-slag** beat of the pulse; *livets* ~ the pulse of life **-åder** artery; *stora ~n* the aorta

pultron *s3* poltroon, coward

pulver ['pull-] *s7* powder **-form** *i* ~ powdered **-isera** pulverize; ~*d (äv.)* powdered **-isering** [-'se:-] pulverization **-kaffe** instant coffee

puma *s1* puma

pump *s2* pump

1 pumpa *s1* **1** *bot.* pumpkin **2** *(kaffe-)* coffee-flask

2 pumpa *v1* pump *(äv. utfråga);* ~ *läns* pump dry, drain; ~ *upp a) (vatten)* pump up, b) *(cykelring e.d.)* pump up, inflate

pumpkolv pump piston

pumps *pl* court shoes; *AE.* pumps

pump|station pumping-station **-stång** pump handle

pund *s7* **1** *(vikt)* pound *(förk. lb.)* **2** *(myntenhet)* pound (förk. £); engelska ~ pound sterling **3** bildl. talent, pound; gräva ner sitt ~ not use one's talents; förvalta sitt ~ väl make the most of one's talents **-huvud** blockhead **-kurs** pound (sterling) rate of exchange **-sedel** pound note

pung s2 **1** (börs) purse; lossa på ~en loosen the purse strings **2** (tobaks- e.d.) pouch **3** anat. scrotum; zool. pouch, marsupium

pung|a ~ ut med fork (shell) out, part with **-björn** koala **-djur** marsupial **-råtta** opossum **-slå** fleece, bleed, skin (på of)

punisk ['pu:-] a5 Punic; ~a krigen the Punic wars

punkt s3 point (äv boktr.); (prick äv.) dot; (skiljetecken) [full] stop, AE. period; (i kontrakt, på dagordn. e.d.) item; ~ och slut! and there's an end of it!; den springande ~en the crux of the matter; en öm ~ a sore point; här sätter vi ~ we'll stop here; sätta ~ för put a stop to; tala till ~ have one's say, finish what one is saying; på alla ~er at (bildl. in) all points **-beskattning** specific taxation

punkter|a 1 (pricka) dot ; konst. stipple; ~de noter dotted notes **2** (sticka hål på) puncture **-ing 1** dotting; stipple **2** puncture; (på bilring äv.) blowout, AE. flat tyre; få ~ have a puncture

punkt|hus point (tower) block **-lig** a1 punctual, on time, on the dot; vara ~ med be punctual in **-lighet** punctuality **-strejk** selective strike, spot strike **-strejka** go on spot strike **-svetsning** spot welding **-öga** zool. ocellus (pl ocelli)

puns s2 punch **punsa** punch

punsch s3 Swedish punch

pupill s3 **1** (i ögat) pupil **2** (myndling) pupil, ward

pupp|a s1 chrysalis (pl äv. chrysalides), pupa **-skal** cocoon **-stadium** pupal stage

pur a1 pure; bildl. äv. sheer; av ~ nyfikenhet out of sheer (pure) curiosity

puré s3 purée; soup

purgatorium [-'to:-] s4 purgatory **purgera** purge **purgermedel** [-ˣge:r-] purgative [medicine]

pur|ism purism **-ist** purist **-istisk** [-'ist-] a5 puristic

puritan s3, hist. Puritan; bildl. puritan **-ism** Puritanism (äv. ~en) **puritansk** [-a:-] a5 Puritan; puritanic[al]

purjolök leek

purken a3 peevish, sulky (över about); huffy (på ngn with s.b.)

purpur s9 purple **-brämad** a5 edged with purple **-färga** colour (tekn. dye) purple **-färgad** purple [-coloured] **-röd** purple **-snäcka** purple shell

purra (väcka) call, rouse

purser ['pö:r-] s2 purser

purung [ˣpu:r-] very young

1 puss s2 (pöl) puddle, pool

2 puss s2 (kyss) kiss

pussa kiss, give a kiss **pussas** dep kiss

pussel ['puss-] s7 puzzle; (läggspel) jigsaw puzzle; lägga ~ do a puzzle, bildl. fit the pieces together **-bit** piece of a [jigsaw] puzzle

pussig a1 bloated, puffy

pussla do a puzzle; ~ ihop ngt put s.th. together

pust s2 **1** (bälg) [pair of] bellows **2** (vind-) puff, breath

1 pusta s1 (grässtäpp) ~n the Hungarian steppe

2 pusta v1 **1** (blåsa) puff **2** (flåsa) puff, wheeze; (flämta) pant; ~ och stånka puff and blow; ~ ut take a breather; låta hästarna ~ ut rest the horses

1 puta s1 pad; pillow

2 puta v1, ~ med läpparna (munnen) pout; skjortan ~de ut the shirt stuck out

1 puts s7 (upptåg) prank, trick

2 puts adv, ~ väck gone completely, vanished

3 puts s3 **1** (rappning) plaster; grout **2** (-medel) polish **3** (prydlighet) tidiness; (renlighet) cleanliness

putsa 1 (rappa) plaster **2** (fönster) clean; (skor) polish, AE. shine; (metall) polish; (häck, naglar e.d.) trim; ~t och fint neat and tidy **3** bildl. (uppfiffa) polish; (förbättra) improve, better

puts|lustig droll, comic[al] **-makare** [practical] joker

puts|medel polish, cleaning agent **-ning 1** plastering **2** cleaning; polishing; trimming **3** polishing; improvement, betterment **-trasa** polishing rag (cloth)

putt s2, golf. putt **putta** shove; ~ till ngn give s.b. a shove, (ofrivilligt) knock into s.b.; golf. putt

puttefnask s2 whippersnapper, brat, shrimp

putten ['putt-] i uttr.: gå i ~ go smash, (gå om intet) come to naught

puttra (koka) simmer, bubble [gently]; (grumsa) grumble

puzzle ['pussel] se pussel

pygmé s3 pygmy **pygmeisk** [-'me:-] a5 pygmy-ish

pyjamas [-'ja:-] s2, s9 pyjamas (pl); AE. pajamas (pl); en ~ a pair of pyjamas **-byxor** pyjama trousers (pants) **-jacka** pyjama jacket

pykn|iker ['pykk-] pyknic **-isk** ['pykk-] a5 pyknic

pynt s7 (grannlåt) finery; (julgrans- etc.) decorations, adornments (pl) **pynta** (göra fint) titivate things up; (smycka) decorate; (klä fin) smarten up; ~ sig dress o.s. up, make o.s. smart; ~d och fin smartened up

pyra v2 smoulder

pyramid s3 pyramid; (biljard-) pyramids (pl); stympad ~ truncated pyramid **-al** a1 (ofantlig) huge (succé success) **-form** pyramidal shape **-formig** [-å-] a1 pyramidal

pyre s6, ett litet ~ a tiny mite

Pyrenéerna [-'ne:-] pl the Pyrenees **pyreneisk** [-'ne:-] a5 Pyrenean; P~a halvön the Iberian Peninsula

pyrola ['py:-] s1 wintergreen

pyro|man s3 pyromaniac; incendiary; fire raiser, vard. firebug **-mani** s3 pyromania **-teknik** pyrotechnics (sg el. pl) **-tekniker** [-'tekk-] pyrotechnist **-teknisk** [-'tekk-] pyrotechnic[al]

pyrrusseger Pyrrhic victory

pys s2 little boy, youngster, brat

pysa v3 give off steam; (väsa) hiss

pyss|el ['pyss-] s7 pottering **pyssla** busy o.s. (med about); gå och ~ i trädgården potter about in the garden; ~ om look after, make comfortable

pyssling 1 pixie, manikin **2** (femmänning) de är ~ar they are fourth cousins

Pytagoras [-'ta:-] Pythagoras; ~ sats the theorem of Pythagoras **pytagoreisk** [-'re:isk] a5 Pythagorean

pyton ['py:tån] **1** *r* python **2** *adv., vard., det luktar* ~ there is a ghastly (horrible) smell; *jag mår* ~ I feel awful **-orm** python

pyts *s2* bucket **pytsa** swill, drench **pytsspruta** bucket fire-extinguisher

pytt [*jo*] ~*!* bah!, pooh!, nothing of the sort!

pyttipanna [-ˣpanna] *s1, ung.* bubble and squeak; *bildl.* hotchpotch

pyttsan ['pytt-] *se pytt*

på I *prep* **A** *rumsbet.* **1** *allm.* on; ~ *balkongen* on the balcony; ~ *bordet* (*huvudet*) on the table (head); *ärter* ~ *burk* tinned peas; ~ *golvet* on the floor; *han har fått det* ~ *hjärnan* he has got it on the brain; ~ *jorden* on the earth; ~ *kartan* on the map; *stå* ~ *knä* be on one's knees, be kneeling; ~ *land* on land; ~ *ort och ställe* on the spot; *stå* ~ *post* be on guard; *ligga* ~ *rygg* lie on one's back; *klia sig* ~ *ryggen* scratch one's back; ~ *sid. 9* on page 9 (*jfr 3*); ~ *andra sidan gatan* on the other side of the street; *inte ha någonting* ~ *sig* have nothing on; *vad hade hon* ~ *sig?* what did she wear?; *hade hon några pengar* ~ *sig?* did she have any money on (about) her?; ~ *sjön* on the lake, (~ *havet*) at sea; ~ *slagfältet* on the battlefield (*jfr 2*); *göra sig illa* ~ *en spik* hurt o.s. on a nail; ~ *svarta tavlan* on the blackboard (*jfr 2*); *gå* ~ *tå* walk on one's toes; ~ *en liten ö* on a small island; ~ *Björkö* on (at) Björkö (*jfr 2*); *behålla hatten* ~ keep one's hat on; *en kaka med grädde* ~ a cake with cream on [top] **2** (*vid gata, gård, torg, fält, land i motsats t. stad, större ö m.m.*) in; ~ *bilden* (*tavlan*) in the picture (*jfr 1*); *utan ett öre* ~ *fickan* without a penny in one's pocket; ~ *fältet* (*åkern*) in the field (*jfr 1*); ~ *gatan* in (*AE.* on) the street; ~ *High Street* in the High Street (*jfr 3*); ~ *gården* in the yard (garden, court); ~ *himlen* in the sky; ~ *Irland* in Ireland (*jfr 1*); *hon arbetar* ~ *kontor* she works in (at) an office; ~ *landet* in the country; ~ *den här platsen* in this place; ~ *sitt rum* in one's room; *ligga* ~ *sjukhus* be in hospital; *ha hål* ~ *strumpan* have a hole in one's stocking; *kaffe* ~ *sängen* coffee in bed; ~ *torget* in the [market] square (*jfr 3*); ~ *vinden* in the attic **3** (*vid hotell, restaurang, teater, möte, tillställning m.m.*) at; ~ *banken* at (in) the bank; ~ *bio* (*teater, konsert*) at the cinema (theatre, a concert); ~ *200 m djup* (*höjd*) at a depth (height) of 200 metres; *vara* ~ *fest* (*sammanträde*) be at a party (meeting); ~ *High Street 19* at 19 High Street (*jfr 2*); *bo* ~ *hotell* stay at a hotel; ~ *Hötorget* at Hötorget (*jfr 2*); *äta middag* ~ *restaurang* dine at a restaurant; *nederst* (*överst*) ~ *sidan* at the bottom (top) of the page; *slå upp böckerna* ~ *sid. 9!* open your books at page 9! (*jfr 1*); ~ *slottet* at the palace **4** (*vid sysselsättning*) for, on; *vara* ~ *besök* be on a visit; *vara ute* ~ *jakt* be out hunting; *vara ute* ~ *promenad* be out for a walk **5** (~ *en sträcka av*) for; *vi såg inte en människa* ~ *flera mil* we didn't see a soul (anybody) for several miles **6** (*uttr. riktning, rörelse*) on, on to, onto; into; to; at; *falla ner* ~ *golvet* fall on to the floor; *gå* ~ *besök till ngn* visit s.b.; *gå* ~ *styltor* walk on stilts; *kliva upp* ~ *en pall* get on a stool; *lägga ngt* ~ *bordet* put s.th. on the table; *gå upp* ~ *vinden* go up into the attic; *kasta ngt* ~ *elden* throw s.th. into the fire; *lägga ett brev* ~ *lådan* drop a letter into the box; *resa ut* ~ *landet* go out into the country; *rusa ut* ~ *gatan* rush out into the street; *stiga upp* ~ *tåget* get into (on to) the train; *bli bjuden* ~ *bröllop* be invited to a wedding; *gå* ~ *banken* (*posten*) go to the bank (post office); *gå* ~ *bio* (*teater, konsert*) go to the cinema (theatre, a concert); *lyssna* ~ listen to; *kasta ngt* ~ *ngn* throw s.th. at s.b.; *knacka* ~ *dörren* knock at the door; *ringa* ~ *klockan* ring the bell; *trycka* ~ *knappen* press the button **7** (*per*) in; *tretton* ~ *dussinet* thirteen to the dozen; *de fick en krona* ~ *man* they had one krona per man; *det går 100 pence* ~ *ett pund* there are a hundred pence in a pound; *en* ~ *tusen* one in a thousand **8** (*vid transportmedel*) by; *han kom* ~ *motorcykel* he came by motorcycle; *skicka* ~ *posten* send by post **B** *tidsbet.* **1** (*tidpunkt*) at; on; in; ~ *samma dag* [on] the same day; ~ *utsatt dag* on the appointed day; ~ *min födelsedag* on my birthday; ~ *samma gång* at the same time; ~ *kvällen den 1 maj* on the evening of the 1st of May; ~ *lördag* on Saturday; ~ *morgonen* (*kvällen, dagen*) in the morning (evening, day[time]); ~ *natten* at (in the) night; ~ *1700-talet* in the 18th century; ~ *olika tider* at different times; ~ *utsatt tid* at the appointed time; ~ *våren* (*hösten*) in [the] spring (autumn) **2** (*under*) on, during; ~ *sin fritid* in one's leisure time; *hon arbetar* ~ *jullovet* she is working during her Christmas holiday; ~ *vägen hit* on the way here **3** (*inom*) in; *det gör jag* ~ *en timme* it will take me [no more than] an hour to do it; *jag kommer* ~ *ögonblicket* I'll be with you in a moment **4** (~ *en tid av*) for; *jag har inte sett dig* ~ *evigheter* I haven't seen you for ages; *resa bort* ~ *en månad* go away for a month; *vi hyrde våningen* ~ *ett år* we rented the flat for a year; *jag har inte varit hemma* ~ *tio år* I haven't been home for ten years **5** (*efter*) after; *brev* ~ *brev* letter after (upon) letter; *den ena dagen följde* ~ *den andra* one day followed the other; *gång* ~ *gång* time after time, over and over again; *kaffe* ~ *maten* coffee after dinner **C** (*friare*) **1** (*i prep.uttr.*) of; *namnet* ~ *boken* the name of the book; *kaptenen* ~ *fartyget* the captain of the ship; *slutet* ~ *historien* the end of the story; *färgen* ~ *huset* the colour of the house; *priset* ~ *mjöl* the price of flour; *en familj* ~ *fyra personer* a family of four [persons]; *ett bevis* ~ *uppskattning* a proof of appreciation; *den regnigaste tiden* ~ *året* the rainiest time of the year; *en pojke* ~ *tre år* a boy of three **2** (*med subst.*) ~ *allvar* in earnest; *förlora* ~ *bytet* lose by the exchange; ~ *engelska* in English; *läsa* ~ *sin examen* read for one's degree; ~ *egen risk* at one's own risk; *rakt* ~ *sak* straight to the point; ~ *skämt* for a joke; ~ *sätt och vis* in a way; *komma* ~ *tal* come (crop) up; ~ *vers* (*prosa*) in poetry (prose); *det stämmer* ~ *öret* it tallies to the öre **II** *adv*; ~ *med kläderna!* on with your clothes!; *kör* ~*!* drive on!; *spring* ~ *bara!* just keep running! **III** ~ *det att* [in order] that; ~ *det att inte* lest

på|annons radio. introductory announcement **-bjuda** order; command (*tystnad* silence); impose (*skatter* taxes; *straff* a penalty) **-brå** *s6* inheritance, stock; *ha gott* (*dåligt*) ~ come of good (bad) stock **-bröd** *få ngt som* ~ get s.th. as an extra [treat] (into the bargain) **-bud** decree, edict **-budsmärke** mandatory (compulsory) sign

P

-byggnad superstructure, addition, enlargement **-bättring** touching up, improvement **-börda** [-ö:-] charge (*ngn ngt* s.b with s.th.) **-börja** begin, start, commence; *för varje ~d timme* for each hour or part of hour **-drag** *tekn.* starter; *bildl.* mobilization of effort; *ha fullt ~* (*bildl.*) be working at full speed; *värmen stod på fullt ~* the heating was full on; *polisen har fullt ~* the police are out in full force **-drivare** instigator, prompter **-dyvla** [-y:-] *se -börda* **-fallande** *a4* (*slående*) striking, remarkable **-fartssträcka** acceleration lane, slip road **-flugen** *a3* (*påträngande*) obtrusive; (*framfusig*) forward **-fordra** (*kräva*) demand; (*erfordra*) require; *om så ~s* if required **-frestande** (*mödosam*) arduous, taxing; (*besvärlig*) trying **-frestning** strain, stress **-fund** *s7* invention; (*knep*) device **-fyllning** filling-up, refilling, replenishment; *vill du ha ~?* would you like some more? **-fyllningshål** filler **-fyllningstratt** [feed] hopper

påfågel *s2* peacock

påfågels|blå peacock blue **-höna** peahen **-stjärt** peacock's train **-öga** peacock butterfly

på|följande following, next; *~ dag* [the] next (on the following) day **-följd** consequence; *jur.* sanction, punishment awarded; *vid ~ av* on pain of; *vid laga ~* under penalty of law **-föra** *~ grus på vägarna* spread gravel on the roads; *~ ngn ngt i räkning* debit (charge) s.b. with s.th. **-gå** be going on; (*fortsätta*) continue, be in progress; *~ för fullt* be in full progress; *medan programmet -gick som bäst* right in the middle of the programme **-gående** *a4* in progress; *under ~ förhandlingar* while negotiations are (were) going on; *under* [*nu*] *~ krig* during the present war; *under ~ krig* (*i krigstid*) in time of war; *den ~ högkonjunkturen* the current (present) boom **-hitt** *s7* (*-fund*) idea, invention, device; (*knep*) trick; *AE.* gimmick; (*lögn*) fabrication **-hittad** *a5* invented **-hittig** *a1* ingenious **-hittighet** ingenuity **-hopp** *bildl.* attack **-hälsning** visit, call; *få ~ av tjuvar* be visited by burglars **-häng** *s7, pers.* hanger-on, encumbrance **-hängsvagn** trailer

påk *s2* cudgel; *rör på ~arna!* get moving!; stir your stumps!

på|kalla (*tillkalla*) summon; (*kräva*) demand, call for; attract (*uppmärksamhet* attention); *av behovet ~d* essential, necessary **-klädd** dressed **-kläderska** *teat.* dresser **-klädning** [-ä:-] dressing **-kommande** occurring; *hastigt ~ illamående* a sudden indisposition **-kostad** [-ås-] *a5* expensive, lavish **-kostande** [-ås-] *a4* (*mödosam*) hard; (*prövande*) trying **-känning** stress, strain **-körd** [-çö:-] *a5* run into, knocked down **-körning** (*kollision*) smash[-up] **-körningsramp** slip road

påla pile; *absol.* drive piles

på|laga *s1* tax, duty, imposition **-landsvind** onshore wind **-lastning** loading

pålbro pile bridge **pålbyggnad** lake dwelling, pile dwelling **påle** *s2* pole, stake, post; *byggn.* pile; *en ~ i köttet* a thorn in the flesh

pålitlig [-i:t-] *a1* reliable, trustworthy **-het** reliability, trustworthiness

pålkran pile-driver

pålle *s2* gee-gee

pål|ning [ˣpå:l-] piling, pile-driving **-ningsarbete** piling-work, pilework **-stek** *sjö.* bowline [knot] **-verk** pilework, piling

på|lägg *s7* **1** (*på smörgås*) meat (cheese *etc.*) for sandwiches; (*som kan bredas*) sandwich spread **2** *hand.* extra charge (cost), increase **-läggskalv 1** *lantbr.* stock calf **2** *bildl.* up-and-coming man **påminn|na** *-de -t, v3* remind (*ngn om ngt* s.b. of s.th.); *hon -ner* [*mig*] *om sin mor* she reminds me of her mother; *det -ner mig* [*om*] *att jag måste* that reminds me, I must; *hungern började göra sig -d* hunger began to make itself felt; *~ sig* remember, recollect **-nelse** reminder (*om* of); (*anmärkning*) remark

på|mönstra (*manskap*) engage, take on; *jfr mönstra* [*på*] **-mönstring** signing on **-nyttföda** [ˣpå:-, -ˣnytt:-] regenerate; *-nyttfödd* regenerate [d], reborn **-nyttfödelse** regeneration, rebirth **-passad** *a5* watched **-passlig** *a1* (*vaken*) alert, watchful; (*uppmärksam*) attentive **-passlighet** alertness *etc.* **-peka** point out (*för* to); *det bör ~s att* it should be observed that; *jag ber att få ~* I should like to point out **-pekande** *s6* reminder; observation **-pälsad** *a5* (*väl* well) wrapped up **-ringning** call, ring **-räkna** count [up]on; expect

pås|e *s2* bag ([*med*] *skorpor* of rusks); *ha -ar under ögonen* have pouches (bags) under the (one's) eyes; *ha rent mjöl i ~n* have nothing to hide; *det har varit i säck innan det kom i ~* that's cribbed from s.b. else

på|seende *s6* inspection, examination; *vid första ~t* at the first glance, at first sight; *vid närmare ~* on closer inspection; *till ~* for inspection, on approval **-segla** run into, collide with **-segling** collision

påsig *a1* baggy; *~a kinder* drooping cheeks

påsk *s2* Easter (*äv. ~en*); (*judisk ~*) Passover; *annandag ~* Easter Monday; *glad ~!* Happy Easter!; *i ~* at Easter; *i ~as* last Easter; *när infaller ~en i år?* on what date does Easter Sunday come this year? **-afton** Holy Saturday, Easter Eve **-alamm** *~et* the paschal lamb **-dag** Easter Sunday (*äv. -en*) **-helg** *~en* Easter

påskina *end. i uttr.: låta ~* (*antyda*) intimate, hint, (*låta märka*) pretend

påsk|käring *ung.* Easter witch **-lilja** daffodil, Lent lily **-lov** Easter vacation (holidays *pl*)

påskrift (*underskrift*) signature; (*utanskrift*) address; (*inskrift*) inscription, notation

påskris twigs decorated with coloured feathers

på|skriven *a5* signed; *få -skrivet* get a reprimand (scolding) **-skruvad** *a5* screwed on; (*om kran e.d.*) [turned] on; *med ~e bajonetter* with bayonets fixed

påskveckan (*veckan före påskdagen*) Holy Week

påskynda hasten (*avfärden* the departure); quicken (*sina steg* one's steps); speed up, urge on (*arbetet* the work); hurry on (*studierna* one's studies; expedite (*saken* the matter)

påskägg Easter egg

påslag increase, rise

påslakan quilt cover (bag)

påspädning increase

pås|sjuka [the] mumps (*pl*) **-te** tea made with a

tea bag
på|stigande *a4 o. s6*, ~ [*passagerare*] passenger boarding a train (*etc.*); *tåget stannar endast för* ~ the train stops only to take up passengers **-stridig** *a1* headstrong, stubborn **-struken** *a3* (*rusig*) tipsy, merry **-strykning** application

påstå (*yttra*) declare, say, state; (~ *bestämt*) assert, maintain; (*göra gällande*) allege; *det ~s att* it is said that; ~ *motsatsen* assert the contrary; *jag vågar* ~ *att* I venture to say that; *det kan jag inte* ~ I can't say that; *ni vill väl inte* ~ *att* you don't surely mean to say that; *han ~r sig vara sjuk* he says he is ill; *han påstod sig bestämt ha sett* he insisted that he had seen; *den ~dda förlusten* the alleged loss **-ende** *s6* statement, assertion; (*förklaring*) declaration **-endesats** declarative sentence; *jakande* ~ (*äv.*) affirmative declaration

påstötning [-ö:-] reminder; *trots upprepade ~ar* despite repeated reminders

påta poke [about] (*i jorden* in the soil)

påtag|a ~ *sig* take on (*en uppgift* a task), assume (*ansvaret* the responsibility) **-lig** [-a:-] *a1* obvious, manifest; palpable; tangible **-ligen** [-a:-] obviously

på|tala comment [up]on, criticize **-tryckargrupp** pressure group **-tryckning** pressure; *utöva ~ar på* bring pressure to bear [up]on **-tryckningsmedel** means of exerting pressure **-trädning** [-ä:-] *nålens* ~ the threading of the needle **-träffa** *se* träffa på **-trängande** *a4* (*trängande*) urgent (*behov* need[s *pl*]); (*påflugen*) obtrusive, pushing **-tvinga** ~ *ngn ngt* force s.th. [up]on s.b. **-tår** second cup [of coffee *etc.*] **-tänkt** *a4* contemplated, intended, considered

påve *s2* pope; *tvista om ~ns skägg* argue about trivialities, split hairs **-döme** *s6* papacy **-krona** tiara

påver ['på:-] *a2* poor; (*om resultat o.d. äv.*) meagre

på|verka influence, affect; *låta sig ~s av* be influenced by; *~d av starka drycker* under the influence of strong drink **-verkan** influence, effect; *röna* ~ *av* be influenced by **-verkbar** *a1, lätt* ~ easily influenced, impressionable

påve|stol *~en* the Holy See, the Papal Chair **-val** papal election

påvis|a (*påpeka*) point out, indicate; (*bevisa*) prove, demonstrate **-bar** [-i:-] *a1* (*bevisbar*) demonstrable; (*påtaglig*) palpable, noticeable

påvlig ['på:v-] *a1* papal

på|yrka demand, urge **-öka** increase; *få* [*5 pund*] *-ökt* get a [five pound] rise (*på lönen* in salary) **-ökning** increase

päls *s2* (*på djur*) fur, coat; (*plagg*) fur coat; *få* [*ordentligt*] *på ~en* (*få stryk*) get a [thorough] hiding, (*få ovett*) get a [good] telling-off; *ge ngn på ~en* (*klå upp*) give s.b. a good hiding, (*läxa upp*) give s.b. a good slating

päls|a ~ *på* wrap up **-affär** fur shop, furrier's [shop] **-brämad** *a5* fur-trimmed **-djur** furred animal **-fodrad** [-o:-] *a5* fur-lined **-handlare** furrier **-jacka** fur jacket **-jägare** trapper **-kappa** fur coat **-krage** fur collar **-mössa** fur cap **-varor** *pl* furs; furriery (*sg*) **-verk** *se* -varor **-änger** *s2* carpet beetle (*AE.* bug)

pär *s3* peer; *utnämna ngn till* ~ create s.b. a peer, raise s.b. to the peerage

pärl|a [ˣpä:r-] **I** *s1* pearl; (*glas- etc.*; *svett-*) bead; (*klenod*) treasure, gem; (*sup*) drop; *äkta* (*oäkta, odlade*) *-or* real (artificial, cultured) pearls; *kasta -or för svin* cast pearls before swine; *en* ~ *bland kvinnor* a pearl among women **II** *vI* sparkle, bubble; *svetten ~de på hans panna* perspiration beaded his forehead; *~nde skratt* rippling laughter; *~nde vin* sparkling wine **-band** string of pearls (beads) **-besatt** *a4* studded with pearls **-broderad** *a5* embroidered with beads (pearls) **-broderi** beadwork; (*med äkta -or*) pearl embroidery

pärlemoknapp [ˣpä:r-] pearl button **pärlemor** *s9* mother-of-pearl **pärlemoskimrande** [-ʃ-] *a4* nacreous, iridescent

pärl|fiskare pearl fisher **-garn** pearl cotton **-grå** pearl grey **-halsband** pearl necklace **-hyacint** grape hyacinth **-höna** guinea hen **-höns** guinea fowl **-koljé** *se* -halsband **-mussla** pearl mussle (oyster) **-socker** pearl sugar **-uggla** Tengmalm's owl **-vit** pearl[y] white

pärm *s2* (*bok-*) cover; (*samlings-*) file, folder; *från* ~ *till* ~ from cover to cover

päron [-ån] *s7* pear **-blom** pear-blossom **-formig** [-å-] *a1* pear-shaped **-träd** pear tree

pärs *s3, en svår* ~ a severe test, a trying ordeal

pöbel ['pö:-] *s2* mob, riffraff, rabble **-aktig** *a1* mobbish, vulgar **-hop** *en* ~ a mob **-välde** mob rule, mobocracy

1 pöl *s2* (*vatten-*) pool, puddle

2 pöl *s2* (*kudde*) bolster

pölsa *s1, kokk.* hashed lights (*pl*), tripe

pö om pö (*så småningom*) little by little

pörte *s6* [Finland] log cabin

pös|a *v3* swell; (*om deg*) rise; ~ *över* brim (swell) over; ~ *av stolthet* be puffed up (swell) with pride **-ig** *a1* (*om kudde e.d.*) puffed; *kokk.* spongy; (*om deg*) rising; (*skrytsam*) puffed-up **-munk** *kokk.* puffed fritter, doughnut

Q

q [ku:] *s6, s7, det är* [*allt*] *fina* ~ that's A1
quatre mains [kattröˈmäŋ] *spela à* ~ play duets
quilta *se* kvilta
quisling [ˣkviss-] quisling; traitor

rabalder [-'ball-] s7 fuss, hullaballoo; (uppståndelse) commotion, stir; det blev ett väldigt ~ there was a tremendous commotion

rabarber [-'barr-] s9 rhubarb **-paj** rhubarb pie

1 rabatt s3 (blomster-) flowerbed; (kant-) [flower] border

2 rabatt s3, hand. discount; (avdrag) deduction; (nedsättning) reduction; lämna ~ allow a discount (deduction); 3% ~ på priset 3% discount off (on) the price; med 3% ~ vid kontant betalning at 3% cash discount; sälja med ~ sell at a discount

rabatt|biljett cheap-rate ticket **-era** allow a discount (deduction); reduce **-häfte** book of reduced-rate tickets **-kort** season ticket **-kupong** discount ticket; AE. äv. trade stamp **-varuhus** discount house

rabbin s3 rabbi

rabbla rattle off; ~ upp rattle (reel) off

rabiat al (ursinnig) raving; (fanatisk) fanatical, frenzied

rabies ['ra:-] r rabies; hydrophobia

rabulist rabid radical, agitator

racer ['rä:-, 'rejs-] s2, s9 racer **-bil** racer, racing car **-båt** speedboat, racer **-förare** racing driver

racing ['rejsiŋ] s2 racing

racka ~ ner på (skälla ut) fall foul of; (kritisera) run down

rackar|e (skurk) scoundrel, wretch; (kanalje) rascal; (lurifax) rogue; leva ~ kick up a row **-tyg** mischief; (starkare) devilry; hitta på ~ be up to some mischief; på rent ~ out of pure mischief **-unge** mischievous [young] imp, young rascal

racket ['rakk-] s2 racket; (bordtennis-) bat

1 rad s3 **1** row; line; file; string (pärlor of pearls); series (missöden of misfortunes); fyra i ~ four in a row; fyra gånger i ~ four times running (on end); under en ~ av år for a number of years **2** teat. o.d. circle; AE. balcony; första (andra) ~en the dress (upper) circle, AE. the first (second) balcony; översta ~en the gallery, vard. the gods **3** (skriven, tryckt ~) line; läsa mellan ~erna read between the lines; skriv ett par ~er! drop me a few lines (a line)!; ~ för ~ line by line; få betalt per ~ get paid by the line; ny ~ (anvisning) new paragraph **2 rad** (måttenhet) rad

rada place in rows (a row); ~ upp expose, display; (uppräkna) enumerate

radar ['ra:-] s9 radar **-anläggning** radar unit (installation) **-antenn** radar aerial (scanner, AE. antenna) **-fyr** radar beacon, racon **-kontroll** radar control **-navigering** radar navigation **-reflektor** radar reflector (vard. dish) **-signalist** radar operator **-skärm** radarscope, radar screen **-station** radar station **-sändare** radar transmitter **-utrustning** radar equipment **-varnare** [-va:r-] interception receiver

rad|avstånd (i skrift el. tryck) spacing, line space; dubbelt ~ double spacing **-band** rosary; [string of] beads (pl)

rader|a 1 (skrapa bort) erase, rub (med kniv: scratch) out; ~ i böckerna cook the books; ~ ut (utplåna) wipe (blot) out **2** (konst) etch **-gummi** eraser, [India] rubber **-ing 1** erasure **2** konst. etching **-kniv** erasing knife **-nål** etching needle

radhus terrace (AE. row) house

radial al radial **-däck** radial (radial-ply) tyre

radi|an s3 radian **-ator** [-ˣa:tår] s3 radiator

radi|e ['ra:-] s5 radius (pl radii, äv. radiuses) **-ell** al radial

1 radiera (utstråla) radiate, beam

2 radiera (utsända i radio) broadcast

radikal I al radical; (genomgripande äv.) thoroughgoing, sweeping **II** s3, polit. radical; kem. radical **-isera** radicalize **-ism** radicalism **-medel** radical (drastic) remedy

radio ['ra:-] s5, pl vanl. radioapparater radio, wireless; (-apparat) radio (wireless) set (receiver); i ~ on the radio (wireless, air); lyssna på ~ listen in (to the radio) **-affär** radio shop

radioaktiv [äv. 'ra:-] radioactive; ~t avfall (nedfall) radioactive waste (fallout); ~ strålning atomic (nuclear) radiation; ~t sönderfall radioactive decay, disintegration **-itet** radioactivity

radio|amatör radio amateur **-antenn** [radio] aerial (AE. antenna) **-apparat** radio (wireless) set (receiver) **-astronomi** radio astronomy **-bil** (polis-) radio patrol car; (på tivoli) bumper car, Dodgem (varumärke) **-biologi** radiobiology **-bolag** broadcasting company (corporation); Britiska ~et the British Broadcasting Corporation (förk. BBC) **-fyr** radio beacon **-fysik** radio physics (pl, behandlas som sg) **-förbindelse** radio contact **-föredrag** radio talk **-grammofon** radiogram[ophone]

radioisotop radioisotope

radio|kompass radio compass, homing device **-konsert** radio concert **-licens** radio (wireless) licence

radio|log radiologist **-logi** s3 radiology **-logisk** [-'lå:-] a5 radiological

radio|lur earphone, headphone **-lyssnare** listener **-länk** radio relay station (tower) **-mast** radio pylon (tower) **-mottagare** radio (wireless) receiver (receiving set) **-nämnd** ~en the [Swedish] broadcasting commission **-orkester** radio orchestra **-pejl** s3 direction finder **-pejling** direction finding **-pjäs** radio play **-polis** police equipped with radio **-program** radio (broadcasting) program[me] **-reparatör** radio serviceman **-reporter** radio commentator **-rör** radio valve (AE. tube) **-signal** radio signal **-sond** radiosonde **-station** radio (broadcasting) station **-stjärna** radio source (star) **-styrd** [-y:-] a5 radio-controlled, radio-guided **-styrning** radio control (guidance) **-störning** interference; (avsiktlig) jamming **-sändare** radio (wireless) transmitter **-sändning** broadcast, radio transmission **-teater** radio theatre **-teknik** radio engineering **-telefoni** radiotelephony **-telegraf** radiotelegraph **-telegrafera** wireless, radio **-telegrafi** wireless telegraphy, radiotelegraphy **-telegrafist** radio operator **-telegram**

radiogram **-teleskop** radio telescope

radioterapi radiotherapy

radio|utrustning radio (wireless) equipment **-utsändning** broadcasting, radio transmission; *en* ~ a broadcast **-våg** radio wave

radium ['ra:-] *s8* radium **-behandling** radium treatment **-strålning** radium radiation

radiär *a1* radial

radom [-'då:m] *s3* radome

radon [-'då:n] *s4, s3, kem.* radon

rad|skrivare line printer **-såningsmaskin** seed (*AE.* grain) drill **-vis** in rows

raffel ['raff-] *s7* (*rafflande innehåll*) thrills (*pl*)

raffinad *s3* refined sugar **raffinaderi** refinery

raffinemang *s7* refinement; elegance, sophistication **raffinera** refine **raffinerad** [-'ne:-] *a5, bildl.* refined; (*utsökt*) exquisite, consummate

raffinering [-'ne:-] refining

rafflande *a4* thrilling, exciting

rafräschissör scent spray, atomizer

rafs|a ~ *ihop* rake (scrape) together, (*brev. o.d.*) scribble off **-ig** *a1* (*slarvig*) slapdash

ragata [-ˣga:-] *s1* vixen, shrew

ragg *s2* goat's hair; (*friare*) shag; *resa* ~ bristle [up], get one's back up

ragga pick up casual partners **raggarbil** neckmobile, cruisemobile; (*trimmad*) hot rod **raggare** hot-rod teenager (driver)

ragg|ig *a1* shaggy; (*om hår, skägg äv.*) rough, coarse **-munk** *kokk.* potato pancake **-socka** thick sock, skiing-sock

ragla [ˣra:-, ˣragg-] stagger, reel

raglan ['ragg-] *s3, best. form o. pl äv. raglan* raglan [coat] **-ärm** raglan sleeve

ragnarök [ˣraŋŋa-] *r el. n* twilight of the gods

ragu *s3* ragout; ~ *på* … (*äv.*) stewed …

raja [ˣrajja] *s1* raja[h]

rajd *s3* reindeer drive

rajgräs [ˣrajj-] rye-grass

rak *a1* **1** straight (*linje* line; *rygg* back); (*upprätt*) erect, upright; *gå* ~ [*i ryggen*] walk erect; *gå ~a vägen hem* go straight home; *stå* ~ stand straight; *bildl.* straight[forward] **2** *sport.*, ~*a hopp* plain high-diving; *en* ~ *vänster* a straight left; *ta tre ~a set* win three straight sets **3** ~ *ordföljd* normal word order; ~*a motsatsen* exactly the reverse; *på* ~ *arm* at arm's length, *bildl.* offhand, straight off; *det enda ~a* (*vard.*) the only right thing

1 raka I *s1* rake; (*för vatten*) squeegee **II** *v1* rake

2 raka *v1* (*rusa*) dash, dart, rush (*i väg* off); ~ *i höjden* shoot up

3 raka *v1* (*barbera*) shave (*äv.* ~ *sig*); *låta* ~ *sig* get shaved (a shave); ~*s eller klippas?* a shave or a haircut?

rak|apparat safety razor; (*elektrisk*) electric shaver (razor) **-blad** razor blade **-borste** shaving brush **-don** shaving things

raket *s3* rocket; (*robot*) [guided] missile; *han for iväg som en* ~ he was off like a shot (lightning) **-bana** trajectory of a rocket **-bas** rocket (missile) base **-drift** rocket (jet) propulsion **-driven** *a5* rocket-propelled, rocket-powered **-flygplan** rocket[-propelled] aircraft **-gevär** rocket launcher, bazooka **-hylsa** rocket cylinder **-motor** rocket engine (motor) **-steg** rocket stage **-vapen** missile [weapon]

rakhyvel safety razor

rakitis [-'ki:-] *s3* rickets, rachitis

rak|kniv razor **-kräm** shaving cream

raklång (*ligga* lie) full length; *falla* ~ *på marken* fall flat on [to] the ground

rakmaskin *se rakapparat*

rakna [ˣra:k-] straighten, become (get) straight; (*om hår*) go out of (lose its) curl

rakning [ˣra:k-] shaving; *en* ~ a shave

rakryggad *a5* straight-backed; *bildl.* upright, uncompromising

rak|salong barber's [shop], barber shop **-spegel** shaving mirror **-strigel** razor strop

raksträcka straight, stretch

rakt [-a:-] *adv* **1** straight, direct; *gå* ~ *fram* walk straight on; ~ *upp och ner* straight up and down; ~ *österut* due east; *ljuga ngn* ~ *i ansiktet* tell s.b. a lie straight to his face; *det bär* ~ *åt skogen* it is going straight to the dogs; *i* ~ *nedstigande led* in a direct line; *gå* ~ *på sak* come straight to the point; *som går* ~ *på sak* straightforward **2** (*absolut*) absolutely; (*precis*) just; (*riktigt*) downright; *sälja för* ~ *ingenting* sell for next to nothing; *det gör* ~ *ingenting* it does not matter in the least; *till* ~ *ingen nytta* of absolutely no (of no earthly) use

rak|tvål shaving soap **-vatten** shaving water; (*efter -ning*) aftershave lotion

ralj|ans [-'jaŋs, -'jans] raillery, banter **-ant** [-'jaŋt, -'jant] *a1* bantering; (*spefull*) teasing **-era** banter; ~ *med ngn* chaff (tease) s.b. **-eri** raillery, banter

rall *s2, zool.* rail

rallare navvy

rally ['ralli, -y] *s6* rally **-förare** rally driver

1 ram *s2* (*tavel-, cykel-* etc.) frame (*äv. boktr.*); *bildl.* framework, setting; (*omfattning*) scope, limits (*pl*); *inom glas och* ~ framed; *inom ~en för* within the limits (scope, framework) of; *falla utom ~en för* be outside the scope of

2 ram *s2* (*björntass*) paw; *suga på* ~*arna* (*bildl.*) live on one's hump

3 ram *superl.* -*aste, oftast i best. form, på rena ~a allvaret* in dead[ly] earnest; *på rena ~a bondlandet* in the country pure and simple; *rena ~a sanningen* the plain (naked) truth

ram|a ~ *in* frame **-antenn** loope(frame) aerial

ramaskri outcry; *höja ett* ~ raise an outcry (*mot* against)

ram|avtal general (basic) agreement; *uppgöra* ~ *för* draw up the general framework for **-berättelse** frame story

ramla (*falla omkull*) fall (tumble) down; ~ *av hästen* fall off the horse; ~ *nedför trappan* fall down the stairs; *illusionerna* ~*de* my illusions were shattered

ramm *s2, sjö.* ram **ramma** ram; *bildl. äv.* strike

rammakare [ˣra:m-] frame-maker, carver and gilder

rammelbuljong *få* ~ get a thrashing

ramp *s3* **1** *teat.* footlights (*pl*) **2** (*uppfartsväg*) ramp, slope **3** *se avskjutningsramp* **-feber** stage fright **-ljus** footlights (*pl*); *bildl.*, *stå i* ~*et* be (appear) in the limelight

ramponera damage, batter

rampris bargain [price]; *till (för)* ~ at bargain prices

rams|a *s1* string; (*osammanhängande*) rigmarole; (*rimmad*) doggerel; *svära långa -or* swear like a trooper

ramsvart raven (jet) black

ram|såg frame saw **-verk** framework, framing

rand *-en ränder* **1** (*kant o.d.*) edge, verge; (*bryn*) fringe; (*brädd*) brim; *bildl.* verge, brink; *vid gravens ~* on the brink of the grave **2** (*på tyg*) stripe; (*strimma*) streak **randa** (*förse med ränder*) stripe, streak **randanmärkning** marginal note; (*friare*) comment; *förse med ~ar* annotate in the margin **randas** *dep* dawn; *när dagen ~* at daybreak; *svåra tider ~* hard times are in the offing **randhav** marginal sea **randig** *a1* striped; (*om fläsk*) streaky, *det har sina ~a skäl* there's a very good reason for it **randning** striping; stripes (*pl*)

randomisera randomize

randstat border state **randsydd** *a5* welt (*sko shoe*)

rang *s3* rank; (*social äv.*) standing, status; *företräde i ~* precedence; *ha högre ~ än* take precedence of; *ha samma ~ som* rank with; *stå över* (*under*) *ngn i ~* rank above (below) s.b.; *ambassadörs ~* ambassadorial rank; *en första ~ens* a first-rate, first-class; *en vetenskapsman av ~* an eminent scientist; *göra ngn ~en stridig* compete with s.b. for precedence, challenge a p.'s position **ranger|a** [raŋ'ʃe:ra] **1** range, rank **2** *järnv.* shunt, marshal **-ad** *a5* (*välsituerad*) well-to-do; (*stadgad*) established **-bangård** shunting (marshalling) yard

ranglig *a1* (*gänglig*) lanky; (*ostadig*) rickety, ramshackle

rang|lista ranking list **-ordna** rank **-ordning** order of precedence, ranking order; *i sträng ~* in strict [order of] precedence **-plats** leading place; *inneha en ~* hold an eminent position **-rulla** gradation list **-skala** *se -ordning*; *den sociala ~n äv.* the social ladder **-skillnad** difference in rank

1 rank *a1* (*smärt*) slim; tall and slender

2 rank *a1* (*om båt*) crank[y]

1 ranka *i uttr.: rida ~* ride a cockhorse

2 ranka *s1*, *bot.* runner, creeper; *bildl.* clinging vine

3 ranka *v1* (*rangordna*) rank

rankig *a1*, *se 2 rank*; (*skraltig*) rickety (*trilla surrey*)

rankinglista, rankningslista ranking list

rann *imperf. av rinna*

rannsak|a *jur.* try; (*förhöra*) examine, hear; (*pröva*) search, ransack (*sitt minne* one's memory); *~d och dömd* tried and found guilty; *~ hjärtan och njurar* search one's hearts **-ning** [-a:k-] *jur.* trial; (*förhör*) examination, hearing; (*prövning*) searching, ransacking; *utan dom och ~* without either judicial trial or sentence; *hålla ~ med* conduct the trial (hearing) of **-ningsdomare** judge conducting the trial **-ningsfängelse** remand prison

ranson *s3* ration; *ta ut sin ~* draw one's ration[s *pl*] **-era** ration; (*utportionera*) portion out **-ering** [-'ne:-] rationing; *~[en] av matvaror* (*äv.*) food rationing; *upphäva ~[en]* deration **-eringskort** ration card

ranta run (*i trapporna* up and down the stairs; *omkring* about)

ranunkel [-'nuŋkel] *s2, s3* ranunculus

rapa, rapning [-a:-] belch

1 rapp *s2* (*häst*) black horse

2 rapp *s7* (*slag*) blow; (*med piska o.d.*) lash

3 rapp I *s7, i ~et* in a moment, at once, in the twinkling of an eye **II** *a1* quick, swift, prompt; (*i fingrarna*) nimble; *~ i munnen* ready-tongued

1 rappa *~ till ngn* slap s.b.

2 rappa *~ på, ~ sig* be quick, get a move on

3 rappa (*kalkslå*) plaster, roughcast

rappakalja *s1* rubbish, bunkum

rapp|höna, -höns partridge

rappning plastering; *konkr.* plaster

rapport [-å-] *s3* report; account; *avlägga ~ om* report on, give a report on (of) **-era** report, make a report of **-karl** *mil.* orderly **-system** reporting system **-tjänst** *mil.* dispatch service **-ör** reporter; informant; (*angivare*) informer

raps *s3* rape, colza **-kaka** rape cake

rapsod|i *s3* rhapsody **-isk** [-'så:-] *a5* rhapsodic [al]

rapsolja rapeseed (colza) oil

rar *a1* **1** (*sällsynt*) rare, uncommon **2** (*älskvärd*) nice, kind, sweet **-ing** darling, honey **-itet** *s3* rarity; *konkr.* rare specimen; curiosity, curio

1 ras *s3* (*människo-*) race; (*djur-*) breed, stock

2 ras *s7* **1** (*skred*) [earth] slip, slide; (*jord-*) landslide; (*av byggnad*) collapse **2** (*vild lek*) romp, romping, frolic[king]

rasa 1 (*falla ner*) give way; fall down; collapse; (*om tak o.d.*) fall in; (*om jord o.d.*) slide **2** (*stoja*) romp, rampage, frolic; (*om hav, storm o. bildl.*) rage; (*vara ursinnig*) fume, rave; *ungdomen ~r* youth is having (must have) its fling; *stormen har ~t ut* the gale has spent its fury **rasande I** *a4* raging (*storm* gale; *lidelser* passions); (*ursinnig*) furious (*på* with; *över* at); *AE. äv.* mad (*på* at; *över* about); *bli ~* get into a rage (passion); *i (med) ~ fart* at a furious (breakneck) pace, at lightning speed **II** *adv* (*väldigt*) awfully (*stilig* smart); *~ hungrig* ravenously (furiously) hungry

ras|biologi human genetics (*pl, behandlas som sg*), racial biology **-blandning** miscegenation; mixture of races (*om djur:* breeds) **-diskriminering** racial discrimination, colour bar **-djur** (*häst*) thoroughbred; (*katt, hund etc.*) pedigree cat (dog) *etc.*

rasera demolish, dismantle; raze, pull down

raseri rage, fury; frenzy; *gripas av ~* be seized with frenzy; *råka i ~* fly into a rage **-anfall** fit of rage; *få ett ~* fly into a rage

rasering [-'se:-] demolition, dismantling; pulling down

ras|fördom racial prejudice **-förföljelse** racial persecution **-hat** racial hatred **-hygien** *s3, ej pl* eugenics (*pl, behandlas som sg*) **-häst** thoroughbred **-ism** racism **-ist** racist **-istisk** [-'siss-] *a5* racistic

1 rask *s7* refuse, thrash; *hela ~et* the whole lot

2 rask *a1* **1** quick, speedy, rapid, swift; (*flink*) nimble; (*fortfärdig*) prompt, expeditious; (*hurtig*) brisk; (*käck*) brave; *i ~ takt* at a rapid (brisk) pace (rate); *i ~ följd* in rapid succession **2** (*frisk*) well, healthy; *~ och kry* hale and hearty

raska *~ sig, ~ på* hurry up, make haste; *~ på ngn* hurry s.b. on

raskrig racial war

raskt adv quickly etc.; det måste gå ~ it must be done quickly; handla ~ take prompt action

ras|minoritet racial minority **-motsättning** racial antagonism

1 rasp s2 (verktyg) rasp, grater

2 rasp s7 (skrap) rasp[ing sound]; (pennas) scratching

raspa rasp, grate; pennan ~r the pen scratches

ras|problem racial problem **-ren** purebred; thoroughbred; pedigree

rassel ['rass-] s7 clatter; (av vapen) rattle, clank; (prassel) rustle; med. rale **rassla** clatter; rattle, clank; (prassla) rustle

rast s3 (vila) rest, repose; (uppehåll) pause, rest; mil. halt; skol. break, recess; utan ~ eller ro without a pause (breather), nonstop **rasta 1** (ta rast) rest, have a break; mil. halt **2** (motionera) take out for exercise

raster ['rass-] s7, boktr. screen; (TV-) raster; förse med ~ screen **-täthet** screen ruling; (i TV) scanning density

rast|lös restless; agitated, fidgety **-löshet** restlessness; agitation, fidgetiness **-ning** exercising; airing **-plats** halting place; (vid bilväg) lay-by, pull-up

rasåtskillnad se rasdiskriminering

rata (försmå) despise; (förkasta) reject

rate [rejt, rät] s5 (fraktsats) rate; (delbetalning) instalment

ratificer|a ratify **-ing** ratification

rationaliser|a [-tʃɔ-] rationalize; improve efficiency **-ing** rationalization; efficiency improvement **-ingsexpert** [business] efficiency expert

rational|ism [-tʃɔ-] rationalism **-ist** rationalist **-istisk** [-'liss-] a5 rationalist[ic]

ration|ell [-tʃɔ-] a1 rational **-ellt** adv rationally; ~ utformad scientifically outlined (designed)

ratt s2 (bil-) [steering] wheel; tekn. hand wheel; (radio-) knob **ratta** vard. drive

ratt|fylleri drunken driving **-fyllerist** drunken driver **-kälke** bobsleigh **-lås** steeringwheel lock **-onykterhet** drunken driving **-stång** steering column **-växel** steering-column gear change **-växelspak** steering-column [gear] lever

ravaillac [ˣravvajak, 'ravv-] s2 rogue; reveller

ravin s3 ravine

rayon [-'jå:n] s4 (tyg) rayon

razzia ['rattsia, 'rassia] s1 raid; roundup; göra ~ raid, round up

1 rea se jet

2 rea s1, vard., se realisation 1

reagens s7, s3 reagent, test (på for) **reagenspapper** test (indicator) paper **reagera** react (för to; mot against; på on); ~ alkaliskt give an alkaline reaction; hur ~r han inför ...? what is his reaction to ...?

reajaktplan jet fighter

reaktans s3 reactance

reaktion [-k'ʃɔ:n] reaction; response

reaktions|drift jet propulsion **-driven** a5 jet-propelled **-förmåga** reactivity **-hastighet** reaction rate (speed) **-motor** jet engine **-tid** reaction time

reaktionär [-kʃɔ-] I s3 reactionary I a1 reactionary

reaktiver|a reactivate **-ing** reactivation

reaktor [-ˣaktår] s3 reactor **-anläggning** reactor plant (installation) **-härd** s3 reactor core

reel a1 real, actual; (saklig) factual **-examen** ung. intermediate school-leaving examination; BE. motsv. General Certificate of Education, ordinary level (förk. G.C.E., O level) **-genus** common gender **-gymnasium** ung. secondary modern school

real|ia [-'a:l-] pl facts, realities; (-vetenskaper) concrete (exact) sciences **-inkomst** real income

realisation 1 hand. sale **2** (förverkligande) realization; (förvandling i reda pengar äv.) conversion

realisations|vara cut-price article **-vinst** capital gain **-värde** bargain (clearance) value, sale price

realiser|a 1 hand. sell off (out), clear stock[s] **2** (förverkliga) realize; (tillgångar äv.) convert into cash **-bar** a1 **1** (utförbar) practicable, feasible **2** (säljbar) salable, realizable

real|ism realism **-ist** realist **-istisk** [-'iss-] a5 realistic; ('nykter') matter-of-fact **-iter** [re'a:-] in reality (fact), actually **-itet** s3 reality ; i ~en in reality, practically speaking

real|kapital real capital **-linje** skol. science (modern) side **-lön** real wages (pl) **-politik** practical politics (pl) **-skola** ung. secondary modern school **-tid** data. real time **-tillgångar** pl tangible assets **-union** legislative union **-värde** real (actual) value; (mynts) intrinsic value

rea|motor jet engine **-plan** jet plane

reassur|ans [-'raŋs] s3 reinsurance **-era** reinsure

rebell s3 rebel, insurgent **-isk** a5 rebellious, insurgent

rebus ['re:-] s2 picture puzzle, rebus

recens|ent reviewer, critic **-era** review **-ion** [-n'ʃo:n] review **-ionsexemplar** review[er's] (advance) copy

recentior [-ˣsentsiår, -'sent-] s3 [pl -'å:-] univ. freshman

recept s7, med. [doctor's] prescription (på for); kokk., tekn., bildl. recipe (på for); expediera ett ~ make up a prescription; skriva ut ~ på ngt (äv.) prescribe s.th.; endast mot ~ on doctor's prescription only **receptarie** [-'ta:-] s5 dispenser

recept|belagd a5 subject to prescription; ~a läkemedel drugs sold on prescription only **-fri** sold without a doctor's prescription

reception [-p'ʃo:n] reception **-ist** receptionist

receptiv [-'i:v, 'ress-, 're:s-] a1 receptive **-itet** receptivity

receptur dispensary

recess|ion [-se'ʃo:n] recession **-iv** [-se'si:v] a1 recessive

recett s3 box-office returns (pl) **-föreställning** benefit performance

recidiv s7 relapse, return, recurrence; få ~ have a relapse

recipi|end s3 (inom orden) recipiendary **-ent** tekn. container **-era** (intas i orden) be initiated (i into); (inta i orden) conduct the initiation of

reciprocitet reciprocity **reciprok** [-å:-] a1 reciprocal

recit|ation recitation; reading **-atjv** s7 recitative **-atris, -atör** reader **-era** recite

rector ['rekk-] ~ magnificus vice-chancellor, AE.

president

red imperf. av rida

1 reda s1 **1** (ordning) order; ordning och ~ order and method; det är [ingen] ~ med honom he is [not] to be counted upon; bringa (få) ~ i bring (get) into order; hålla ~ (ordning) på keep in [good] order (jfr äv. 2) **2** få ~ på (få veta), get to know, find out, (finna) find; göra ~ för account for; ha ~ på know [about], be aware of; ha väl ~ på sig be well informed; hålla ~ (rätt) på keep count of (jfr äv. 1); ta ~ på (skaffa kännedom om) find out, (söka rätt på) find (åt ngn for s.b.) **2 reda** oböjligt a, i ~ pengar in cash, in ready money

3 red|a v2 **1** (be-) make, prepare (ett bo a nest; ett läger a bed); (~ ut) comb (ull wool); (klargöra) clear up, sort out (sina intryck one's impressions) **2** (av-) thicken (en soppa a soup) **3** rfl (om sak) det -er sig nog things will come out all right; (om pers.) get on, manage; ~ sig själv help o.s.; han -er sig nog he will manage all right **4** ~ upp settle, fix, (svårighet) clear up; ~ ut (ngt tilltrasslat) unravel, (klargöra) explain

redaktion [-k'ʃɔ:n] **1** (utgivande) editing; (utgivarskap) editorship; (avfattning) wording; under ~ av edited by **2** (personal) editorial staff; (lokal) editorial office (department) **-ell** al editorial

redaktions|chef editor-in-chief, managing editor **-kommitté** editorial committee **-sekreterare** ung. assistant editor-in-chief

redaktör editor

redan (som bestämning t. predikatsverbet) already; (i övriga fall) as early as, even, (just, själva) very; är du hemma ~? are you home already?; ~ på 1600-talet as early (long ago, far back) as the 17th century; ~ då even then, as early as that; ~ förut even before this; ~ efter tre gånger after only three times; ~ i dag this very day; ~ samma dag [on] the very same day; ~ länge [for] a long time (ever so long); ~ som barn while still (even as) a child; ~ tanken på the mere thought of

redare shipowner

redbar [ˣre:d-] al (rättrådig) honest, upright; (samvetsgrann) conscientious **-het** honesty, uprightness; conscientiousness

1 redd s3 road[stead]; ligga på ~en lie (be) in the roads

2 redd a5 thick[ened] (soppa soup)

rede s6 nest

rederi shipping company, shipowners (pl); carrier **-näring** shipping [business]

redig al **1** (ej trasslig) orderly; (om handstil) clear, legible; (lätt begriplig) intelligible, lucid; (vid full sans) in one's right senses; ett ~t huvud a clear intellect **2** en ~ portion a substantial helping; en ~ karl a reliable chap, a good sort; en ~ förkylning a severe cold

rediger|a [-'ʃe:-] edit; draft, formulate **-ing** editing

redighet clarity, lucidity

redingot ['reddiŋgåt] s3 frock coat

rediskonter|a rediscount **-ing** rediscount[ing]

redlig [ˣre:d-] al, se redbar **-en** honestly, loyally; ~ sträva make honest efforts

redlös 1 sjö. disabled **2** (drucken) blind (help-

lessly) drunk

redning [ˣre:d-] kokk. thickening (äv. konkr.)

redo oböjl. a ready, prepared; var ~! be prepared! **-bogen** a3 ready, willing **-göra** ~ för a) (redovisa) account for, report on b) (beskriva) describe, give an account of; ~ närmare för give details (a detailed description) of; i korthet ~ för outline, give a brief outline (summary) of **-görelse** [-j-] account (för of), report (för of, on)

redovis|a bokf. record; ~ för account for, give an account of; bolaget ~r vinst the company shows (reports) a profit **-ning** account; (räkenskapsbesked) statement of accounts; brista i ~ fail to render an account

redovisningsskyldig accountable, required to render accounts **-het** accountability, obligation to render accounts

redskap [ˣre:d-] s7, koll. s9 instrument (äv. bildl.); (verktyg) tool, implement (äv. bildl.); (utrustning) equipment, tackle; gymn. apparatus

redskapsbod tool shed

reducer|a reduce; cut (bring) down **-bar** al reducible **-ing** reduction **-ingsventil** reducing (back pressure) valve

reduktion [-k'ʃɔ:n] reduction **reduktionstabell** conversion table

redund|ans s3 redundancy **-ant** a5 redundant

redupli|cera reduplicate **-kation** reduplication

redutt s3, mil. redoubt

reell [re'ell] al **1** (verklig) real, actual; (påtaglig) tangible **2** se rejäl

referat s7 account, report; (sammandrag) summary

referendum [-ˣrenn-] s8 referendum (pl äv. referenda)

refer|ens s3 reference; lämna ~er give references; svar med ~er reply stating references **-bibliotek** reference library **-grupp** reference group **-ram** frame of reference

referent reporter **referera** (ge referat av) report, give an account of; ~ till refer to; ~nde till Ert brev with reference to (referring to) your letter

reflekt|ant (spekulant) prospective buyer **-era 1** (återspegla) reflect, throw back **2** (tänka) reflect, cogitate (över upon); ~ på (anbud, förslag) consider, entertain, (en vara) be open to (in the market) for, be buyer of; ~ på en plats think of applying for a post **-ion** [-k'ʃɔ:n] se reflexion **-or** [-ˣflektår] s3 reflector

reflex s3 reflex **-band** luminous tape

reflexion [-ek'ʃɔ:n] **1** fys. reflection, reflecting; (av ljud) reverberation **2** bildl. reflection, meditation; (slutsats) deduction; (uttalad) comment **reflexionsförmåga** reflective power

reflexiv ['reff-, 're:-] al reflexive

reflex|rörelse reflex movement (action) **-verkan** reflex effect

reform [-'fårm] s3 reform; införa ~er introduce reforms **-anda** reform spirit **-ation** reformation; ~en the Reformation **-ator** [-ˣa:tår] s3 reformer **-atorisk** a5 [-ˣtɔ:-] reformatory, reforming

reformert reform **reformert** [-'märt] a4, den ~a kyrkan the Reformed Church; en ~ a member of the Reformed Church, Presbyterian, Calvinist; de ~a the Reformed

reform|fiende anti-progressive **-fientlig** anti-progressive **-ism** reformism **-iver** reforming zeal **-strävande** s9, ~n reforming efforts, struggle for reform **-vänlig** favourable to reform

refraktion [-k'ʃɑːn] fys. refraction

refräng s3 refrain, chorus; *falla in i ~en* join in the chorus; *tänka på ~en* (vard.) think about leaving

refug s3 refuge, traffic island

refuser|a refuse, reject **-ing** refusal, rejection

regal s3, boktr. composing frame

regalera regale **regalier** [-'gaː-] pl regalia **regalskepp** [-ˣgaːl-] man-of-war, ship of the line

regatta [-ˣgatta] sl regatta

1 regel [ˣreː-] s2 (för dörr) bolt; *skjuta för ~n* bolt the door

2 reg|el [ˣreː-] s3 (norm etc.) rule, regulation; *-ler och anvisningar* rules and regulations; *ingen ~ utan undantag* no rule without an exception; *uppställa -er för* draw up rules for; *enligt -lerna* according to rule (the rules, the book), by the book; *mot -lerna* against the rules; *i (som) ~* as a rule, usually; *göra det till en ~* make it a rule

regel|bunden a3 regular; ~ *puls* normal pulse **-bundenhet** regularity (utan regler) lawless; (oordentlig) irregular; (tygellös) licentious **-mässig** al, se -bunden **-rätt** a4 regular; (korrekt) correct; (sannskyldig) regular, proper **-vidrig** contrary to the rule[s]

regemente [-je'mente, -g-] s6 **1** mil. regiment **2** (regering) government, rule; *föra ett strängt ~* rule with severity

regements|chef regimental commander **-kamrat** vara ~er be in the same regiment **-läkare** army (regimental) doctor **-officer** field officer **-pastor** regimental chaplain, padre

regener|ation [-j-] regeneration **-atjv** al regenerative **-ator** [-ˣaːtår] s3 regenerator **-era** regenerate

regent [-j-] ruler, sovereign; (ställföreträdare) regent **-längd** table of monarchs (rulers) **-skap** [-ˣjent-] s7 regency

reger|a [-j-] **1** (styra) govern; (härska) rule; (vara kung) reign; *medan han ~de* (äv.) during his reign **2** (behärska) rule, govern; ~s av sina lidelser be dominated by one's passions **-ing** (regeringstid) rule, reign; (-ande) rule, government; (verkställande myndighet) government; AE. vanl. administration; *tillträda ~en (om kung)* accede to the throne, (om myndighet) take office; *bilda ~* form a government; *den sittande ~en* the government in power

regerings|beslut government decision **-bildning** formation of a government **-bänken** the government (Storbritannien treasury) bench **-chef** head of the (a) government; prime minister **-fientlig** anti-government; oppositional **-form 1** (statsskick) form of government **2** (grundlag) constitution; *1809 års ~* the 1809 Constitution Act **-förslag** government proposal (proposition) **-kris** cabinet crisis **-ledamot** minister of state, cabinet minister **-organ** government organ **-parti** government party **-råd** justice of the supreme administrative court; *Storbritannien Lord Justice* **-rätt** ~en the [Swedish] supreme administrative court **-ställning** vara i ~

be in power (office) **-tid** (regents) reign; (regerings) period of office **-år** year of reign

regi [-'ʃiː] s3 management; teat. stage management; film. direction; (iscensättning) production; *i egen ~* under private management; *i statlig ~* under government auspices **-anvisning** ~ar acting (stage) directions

regim [-'ʃiːm] s3 management, administration, regime; *ny ~* (hotell- e.d.) new management **-förändring** change of management

region s3 region; district, area **-al** al regional **-al-politik** regional policy **-plan** regional plan

regissera [reʃi-] produce; (film) direct **regissör** producer; (film., radio. o. AE.) director

register [-'jiss-] s7 **1** register, roll, record; (ord-, sak-) index **2** (orgel-) [organ] stop; (tonomfång) range **-kort** index card **-ton** sjö. register ton

registrator [-ˣraːtår] s3 registrar, recorder, registry clerk **registratur** s7, s9 copies (pl) of public documents; registrar's office

registrer|a register, record **-ing** registration **registrerings|avgift** registration fee **-bokstav** (på bil) index mark **-nummer** registration number **-skylt** (på bil) numberplate, AE. license plate

regla [ˣreːg-] bolt

reglage [-'laːʃ] s7 control, lever

reglementarisk [-'taː-] a5 in conformity with regulations

reglement|e [-'mente] s6 regulations, rules (pl); ~t *föreskriver* the regulations prescribe **-era** regulate

reglements|enlig [-eːnl-] al according to regulations **-vidrig** contrary to regulations

regler|a regulate; (justera) adjust; (arbetstid, skuld etc.) settle; ~d *befordringsgång* statutory system of promotion **-bar** [-eːr-] al adjustable **-ing 1** regulation; adjustment; settlement **2** med. menstruation

reglett s3, boktr. lead; reglet

regn [reŋn] s7 rain; bildl. äv. shower, hail; *ett stritt ~* a heavy rain, a downpour; *i ~ och rusk* in chilly wet weather; *efter ~ kommer solsken* (bildl.) every cloud has a silver lining; *det ser ut att bli ~* it looks like rain

regn|a [ˣreŋna] rain; bildl. äv. shower, hail; *det ~r* it is raining; *det ~r in* it is raining in (genom fönstret at (through) the window); *det ~r småsten* it is raining cats and dogs; *låtsas som det ~r* look as if nothing were (was) the matter **-blandad** ~ *snö* rain mingled with snow **-by** rain squall **-båge** rainbow **-bågshinna** iris **-dis** rainy mist **-droppe** raindrop **-fattig** with little rain, dry **-ig** al rainy; wet **-kappa** raincoat, mackintosh, waterproof **-moln** rain cloud **-mätare** rain gauge, pluviometer **-område** area with rainfall **-rock** se -kappa **-skog** rainforest **-skur** shower [of rain] **-stänk** pl spots of rain; *det kom bara några ~* there were only a few spots of rain **-tid** rainy season; ~en (äv.) the rains (pl) **-tung** rain-laden **-vatten** rainwater **-väder** rainy weather; *vara ute i -vädret* be out in the rain

regress (återgång) retrogradation **-ion** [-e'ʃɑːn] regression **-jv** al regressive **-rätt** right of recourse

reguladetri s3 rule of three

R

regul|ator [-ˣaːtår] *s3* regulator **-jär** *al* regular
regummera retread, *AE.* recap; (*slitbana*) top-cap
rehabiliter|a rehabilitate **-ing** rehabilitation
reine claude [räːn ˈklåːd] *s5, se renklo*
reinkarn|ation [re-in-] reincarnation **-era** reincarnate
rejäl *al* (*pålitlig*) honest, reliable; (*ordentlig, bastant*) proper, jolly good; *ett ~t mål mat* a good square meal
rek *s7* registered post
rekambioräkning [-ˈkamm-] re-exchange account
rekapituler|a recapitulate **-ing** recapitulation, summing-up
reklam *s3* advertising; (*publicitet*) publicity; *konkr.* advertisement; *braskande ~* loud (showy) advertising; *göra ~ för* advertise, *vard.* boom, puff; *göra ~ för sig själv* blow one's own trumpet **-affisch** advertising poster (bill) **-anslag** publicity allocation **-artikel** publicity device; advertising gift
reklama|tion (*återfordran*) reclaim; (*klagomål*) complaint, claim; *post.* inquiry [about a missing letter (parcel)] **-tionsnämnd** *allmänna ~en* the [Swedish National] board for consumer complaints
reklam|avdelning publicity (advertising) department **-broschyr** publicity (advertising) leaflet **-byrå** advertising agency **-chef** advertising manager
1 reklamera (*klaga*) complain of; *post.* inquire for (about); *~ en leverans* reject (complain of) a delivery
2 reklamera (*göra reklam för*) advertise, *vard.* boom, puff
reklam|erbjudande bargain (special) offer **-film** advertising film, commercial **-jippo** advertising gimmick, publicity stunt **-kampanj** advertising (publicity) campaign **-konsulent** advertising consultant **-ljus** neon light **-man** publicity (advertising) expert **-material** promotion material **-pris** bargain price **-skylt** advertising sign **-tecknare** commercial artist **-teckning** *konkr.* advertisement designing; *abstr.* commercial art **-text** [advertising] copy **-tryck** advertising matter **-ändamål** *för ~* for advertising purposes
rekognos[c]er|a [-kåŋnå-, -kågnå-] reconnoitre; scout; *~ terrängen* (*bildl.*) see how the land lies **-ing** reconnaissance, reconnoitre **-ingstur** reconnoitring tour
rekommend|ation [-å-] **1** recommendation **2** *post.* registration **-ationsbrev** letter of recommendation (introduction) **-era 1** recommend (*ngn* (*ngt*) *för ngn* s.b. (s.th.) to s.b.); *~ ngn på det varmaste* heartily recommend s.b.; *som kan ~s recommendable; ~ sig* take one's leave **2** *post.* register; *~s* (*påskrift på brev*) registered (*förk.* reg[d].); *i* (*som*) *~t brev* by registered post
re|konstruera [-å-] reconstruct **-konstruktion** [-kˈʃɔːn] reconstruction
rekonvalesc|ens [-ˈsens, -ˈʃens] *s3* convalescence **-ent** [-eˈsent] convalescent
rekord [-ˈkåːrd] *s7* record; *inneha ett ~* hold a record; *slå ~[et]* break the record; *sätta ~* set up a record **-anslutning** *det blev ~* there was a rec-

ord number of participants **-artad** [-aːr-] *a5* unparalleled, unprecedented; record (*hastighet* speed) **-fart** record speed **-försök** attempt at the record **-hållare** record holder **-jakt** record-chasing **-siffra** record figure **-skörd** bumper harvest (crop) **-tid** *ny ~* new record time; *göra ngt på ~* do s.th. in record time
rekreation recreation; relaxation
rekreations|ort health resort **-resa** recreation trip
rekreera [-eˈeː-] refresh; *~ sig* refresh o.s., rest, recuperate
rekryt *s3* recruit; *göra ~en* (*vard.*) do first training period as a conscript **-era** recruit, enlist **-ering** [-ˈteː-] recruiting, recruitment **-tid** first period of compulsory military training **-utbildning** training of recruits
rektang|el [-ˈtaŋ-] *s2* rectangle **-ulär** [-ŋg-] *al* rectangular
rektascension [-asenˈʃɔːn] *astr.* right ascension
rektor [ˣrekktår, ˈrekk-] *s3* headmaster, principal; (*kvinnlig*) headmistress; (*vid univ.*) vice chancellor, *AE.* president; (*vid fackhögskola*) principal, rector, warden **rektorat** *s7* headmastership *etc.*
rektors|befattning headmastership *etc.* **-expedition** *~en* the headmaster's (*etc.*) office
rektorska [-ˈtoːrs-] *sl* headmaster's (*etc.*) wife
rekviem [ˈreː-, ˈrekk-] *s7, best. form äv.* rekviem requiem
rekvirera 1 (*beställa*) order; *kan ~s genom* obtainable through **2** *mil.* requisition
rekvisi|ta [-ˣsiː-] *pl, äv. s9* (*förnödenheter*) requisites; *teat. o.d.* properties **-tion 1** (*beställning*) order **2** *mil.* requisition **-tionsblankett** requisition form **-tör** *teat.* property man, *vard.* propman
rekyl *s3* recoil, kick **-era** recoil, kick
relatera relate, give an account of
1 relation (*berättelse*) narration; *i hans ~* in his account (version)
2 relation 1 (*förbindelse*) relation, connection; (*förhållande*) relationship; *sätta (ställa) ngt i ~ till* relate s.th. to; *stå i ~ till* be related to **2** *~er* (*inflytelserika förbindelser*) connections; *skaffa sig fina ~er* get influential connections, climb the social ladder; *sakna ~er* (*äv.*) have no friends at court
relativ [ˈreː-, ˈrell-, -ˈtiːv] **I** *al* relative (*äv. språkv.*); comparative (*lugn* quiet); *allting är ~t* everything is relative **II** *s7, s4* relative **-ism** relativism **-istisk** [-ˈviss-] *a5* relativistic **-itet** relativity **-itetsteori** theory of relativity **-sats** relative clause
releg|ation expulsion **-era** [-ˈgeː-, -ˈʃeː-] expel; *univ. äv.* send down, (*för kortare tid*) rusticate
relev|ans [-ˈans, -ˈaŋs] relevance **-ant** [-ˈant, -ˈaŋt] relevant
reliabilitet reliability
relief [reliˈeff, -j-] *s3* relief (*äv. bildl.*); *ge ~ åt* bring out in relief; *i ~* in relief **-karta** relief map **-verkan** relief effect
religion [-li(j)oːn, -gioːn] *s3* religion; (*friare*) faith, belief; (*läroämne äv.*) divinity
religions|fientlig antireligious **-filosofi** philosophy of religion **-frihet** religious freedom

-förföljelse religious persecution **-förkunnelse** preaching of a religion **-historia** religious studies (*pl*), comparative religion, history of religion[s] **-krig** religious war **-kunskap** religious education **-stiftare** founder of a religion **-undervisning** religious instruction **-utövning** religious worship (practices); *fri* ~ freedom of worship **-vetenskap** religious science; *se äv.* *-historia*

religi|ositet [-i(j)ɔ-, -ligiɔ-] religiousness, piety **-ös** [-iˈʃöːs, -giˈöːs] *al* religious; sacred (*bruk* custom)

reljk *s3* relic **-skrin** reliquary, shrine

reljkt *s3, s4* relict **-form** survival form

reling gunwale, gunnel, rail; *manna* ~ man the rail; *fritt vid* ~ (*hand.*) ex ship

relä *s4* relay **reläa** relay, pipe **relästation** relay (repeating) station

rem [remm] *s2* strap; (*smal*) thong; (*driv-*) belt; *ligga som* ~*mar efter marken* go flat out

remarkabel [-ˈkaː-] *a2* remarkable, notable

remb[o]urs [raŋˈburs] *s3* documentary credit; *A.E.* letter of credit, commercial credit

remdrift belt-drive, belt-driving

remj *s3, schack.* draw; *det blev* ~ the game was drawn; *uppnå* ~ achieve a draw

reminiscens [-iˈsens, -iˈʃens] *s3* reminiscence

remjss *s3, abstr.* commitment [for consideration]; *konkr.* [committee] report; (*läkar-*) doctor's letter of introduction, (*t. sjukhus*) admission note; *vara* (*utsända*) *på* ~ be circulated (circulate) for comment

remissa [-ˣmissa] *s1* remittance **-brev** remittance letter

remiss|debatt debate on the estimates (*i Storbritannien* Address) **-instans** body to which a proposed [legislative] measure is referred for consideration

remitt|ent I *s3* (*växel-*) payee **II** *a4, med.* remittent **-era 1** *hand.* remit **2** (*hänskjuta*) commit (refer) for a pronouncement **3** *med.* refer, send

1 remmare *sjö.* perch, stick

2 remmare (*glas*) hock-glass, rummer

remont [-ˈmånt-, -ˈmåŋt-] *s3* remount [horse] **-depå** remount depot

remontera [-månt-, -måŋt-] bloom twice in one season

remplacer|a [raŋ-, ram-] replace **-ing** replacement

remsa *s1* strip, tape; (*pappers-*) slip; (*tyg*) shred

remskiva [belt] pulley

remuladsås remoulade [sauce]

1 ren *s2* (*dikes-*) ditch-bank; (*åker-*) headland; (*landsvägs-*) verge

2 ren *s2* (*djur*) reindeer (*pl* reindeer[s])

3 ren *a1* (*ej smutsig*) clean; (*prydlig*) tidy; *bildl.* pure; (*idel*) pure, sheer, mere; (*oblandad, äkta*) pure, unadulterated; (*klar*) clear; ~*t samvete* a clear conscience; *göra* ~*t* clean (*i köket* in the kitchen); *göra* ~*t hus* (*bildl.*) make a clean sweep [of everything]; ~*a galenskapen* sheer madness; *av en* ~ *händelse* by pure (sheer) accident; *av* ~ *nyfikenhet* out of sheer curiosity; ~*t nonsens* sheer nonsense; ~ *choklad* plain chocolate; ~*a sanningen* plain truth; *säga sin mening på* ~ *svenska* speak one's mind in plain Swedish; *ett* ~*t*

hjärta a pure heart; ~*t spel* fair play; ~ *infinitiv* the simple infinitive; *en* ~ *förlust* a dead (total) loss; ~ *vinst* net (clear) profit, net proceeds; ~*t netto* net without discount, no discount

rena 1 clean; purify; (*socker*) refine **2** *bildl.* purify; cleanse, purge **renare** filter

ren|avel reindeer breeding **-bete** reindeer pasture

rendera [renˈdeː-, raŋ-] (*inbringa*) bring in, yield; (*ådraga*) bring down upon (*ngn s.b.*)

rendezvous [raŋdeˈvɔː] *s4* rendezvous (*sg o. pl*); appointment

renegat renegade; apostate

renfana [ˣreːn-] *bot.* tansy

ren|framställa produce in pure form **-göra** clean **-göring** [-j-] cleaning; (*städning äv.*) house-cleaning, cleanup **-göringskräm** cleansing cream **-göringsmedel** detergent, cleaner, cleaning-agent **-het** [ˣreːn-] cleanness *etc.* (*jfr ren*); purity (*äv. bildl.*); *hög* ~ (*kem.*) high purity **-hetsivrare** puritan

renhjord reindeer herd

renhjärtad [ˣreːnjär-] *a5* pure-hearted, pure in heart

ren|hud reindeer skin (hide) **-hudshandske** reindeer glove

ren|hållning cleaning; (*sophämtning*) refuse collection [and disposal]; (*gatu-*) scavenging, street-sweeping, street-cleaning **-hållningsverk** sanitary (scavenging) department **-hårig** *bildl.* honest, fair **-ing** cleaning, cleansing; (*kem. o.d.*) purification **-ingsverk** purifying (sewage-treatment) plant

renklo [renˈkloː, ˈreŋ-, ˈreːn-] (*plommonsort*) greengage [plum]

renko reindeer doe, doe reindeer

renkultur pure culture

ren|kött reindeer meat **-lav** reindeer moss

ren|levnad chastity, continence **-levnadsman** continent man; ascetic **-lig** [ˣreːn-] *a1* cleanly **-lighet** [ˣreːn-] cleanliness **-lärig** *a1* orthodox **-lärighet** orthodoxy **-odla** isolate, cultivate in isolation **-odlad** [-ɔː-] *a5, bildl.* absolute, downright (*egoism* egotism)

renommé [-å-] *s4* reputation, repute; *ha gott* ~ have a good name, be well reputed; *par* ~ by repute (hearsay)

renons [-ˈnåŋs, -ˈnåns] **I** *s3* void **II** *oböjligt a, vara* ~ *i spader* be without (have no) spades; *vara fullständigt* ~ *på* be absolutely devoid of, have no ... whatever

renover|a renovate; *A.E. äv.* revamp; (*byggnad, tavla o.d.*) restore; (*våning o.d.*) do up, repair **-ing** renovation; restoration; repair

ren|rakad *a5* **1** *se slätrakad* **2** (*barskrapad*) cleaned out, broke **-rasig** *a1* purebred; *se äv. rasren* **-rita** draw fair, make a fair copy of

rens *s7* trimmings (*pl*)

rens|a (*rengöra*) clean; (*bär, grönsaker*) pick over; (*fisk*) clean, gut; (*fågel*) draw; (*ogräs*) weed; (*magen*) purge; (*tömma*) evacuate; ~ *ogräs* weed **2** (*befria*) clear (*havet från ubåtar* the sea of submarines); *åskan* (*samtalet*) ~*de luften* the thunderstorm (conversation) cleared the air; ~ *bort* clear away; remove **-brunn** soakaway, sinkhole **-hacka** weeding-hoe

R

renskiljning reindeer separation (roundup)
ren|skrift *konkr.* fair (clean) copy **-skriva** make a fair (clean) copy of, write *(på maskin:* type) out **-skrivning** making a fair (clean) copy, *(på maskin)* copy-typing
renskötsel reindeer breeding (husbandry)
rens|ning cleaning *etc. (jfr rensa)* **-ningsaktion** *mil.* mopping-up operation[s *pl*]; *polit.* purge **-nål** cleaning-needle
renstek joint of reindeer; *(maträtt)* roast reindeer
rent [re:-] *adv* **1** *eg.* cleanly *etc.* **2** *sjunga* ~ sing (keep) in tune; *skriva* ~ *åt ngn* do a p.'s fair-copying [for him *etc.*]; *tala* ~ talk properly **3** ~ *omöjlig* utterly (absolutely) impossible; ~ *praktiska detaljer* purely practical details; ~ *av* simply, absolutely, downright; *jag tror* ~ *av* I really believe; ~ *ut* plainly, straight [out]; ~ *ut sagt* to put it plainly, not to mince matters; *jag sade honom* ~ *ut* I told him frankly (in so many words) **-av** ['re:nt-] *se rent 3*
rentier [raŋ'tje:] *s3* [*pl* -'e:er] gentleman of independent means
rentjur bull reindeer
rentré [raŋ-] *s3* re-entry, reappearance
ren|tryck clean proof **-två** *bildl.* clear, exonerate; ~ *sig* clear o.s. *(från misstanke* of suspicion)
rentut ['re:nt-] *se rent 3*
renässans [-'saŋs, -'sans] *s3, ~en* the Renaissance (Renascence); *uppleva en* ~ experience renaissance **-furste** Renaissance prince **-stil** Renaissance *(etc.)* style **-tiden** the Age of the Renaissance *(etc.)*
reol [re'å:l] *s3* bookcase; shelves *(pl)*
reorganis|ation [reå-] reorganization **-era** reorganize
reostat rheostat
rep *s7* rope; *(smalt)* cord; *hoppa* ~ skip; *tala inte om* ~ *i hängd mans hus* name not a rope in the house of him that was hanged, avoid painful topics
1 repa I *s1* scratch, tear **II** *v1* scratch, tear; ~ *eld på en tändsticka* strike a match; ~ *upp* unravel, *(stickning)* undo [one's knitting]; ~ *upp sig* get unravelled
2 repa *v1,* ~ *gräs* pluck handfuls of grass; ~ *vinbär* string currants; ~ *löv* strip leaves
3 repa *v1,* ~ *mod* take heart; ~ *sig* recover, improve, get better
repar|abel [-'ra:-] *a2 (-erbar)* repairable; *(möjlig att gottgöra)* reparable **-ation** repair[ing]; *vara under* ~ be under repair, be being repaired
reparations|arbete repairs *(pl)*, repair work **-kostnader** *pl* cost *(sg)* of repairs, repair costs **-utrustning** repair kit **-verkstad** repair shop, *(bil- vanl.)* garage
repar|atör repair man; *(bil-)* mechanic **-era** repair; *AE. äv.* fix; *(kläder o.d.)* mend; *våningen skall* ~*s* the flat is to be done up; *kan ej* ~*s (äv.)* is past repair
repartisera go shares *(om* for)
repatrier|a repatriate **-ing** repatriation
repe *s6, bot.* darnel
repellera repel
repertoar *s3* repertoire, repertory
repeter|a repeat; *teat., mus.* rehearse; *skol.* re-

vise **-gevär, -ur** repeater
repetition repetition; *teat., mus.* rehearsal; *skol.* revision
repetitions|kurs, -övning refresher course
repetitorium [-'tɔ:-] *s4* **1** *se repetitionskurs* **2** *(lärobok)* synopsis *(i* of)
rephoppning skipping
repig *a1* scratched, full of scratches
replik *s3* **1** *(genmäle)* rejoinder, retort, repartee; *teat.* line, speech; *vara snabb i* ~*en* have a quick tongue **2** *konst.* replica **-era** reply, retort **-föring** way of arguing **-skifte** exchange (bandying) of words
replipunkt [-ˣpli:-] *mil.* base; *bildl.* basis
report|age [-år'ta:ʃ] *s7 (nyhetsanskaffning)* reporting; *(referat o.d.)* report[age] **-er** [-'på:r-] *s2* reporter; *(radio-)* [radio] commentator
representant representative *(för* of); deputy; *(delegat)* delegate; *(handelsresande)* traveller **-huset** the House of Representatives **-skap** *s7* representation; *(representantsamling)* representative assembly
representation representation
representations|kostnader *pl* entertainment (representation[al]) expenses **-middag** official dinner **-skyldighet** *ha* ~*er* have to entertain **-våning** reception rooms *(pl)*
represent|ativ [-'i:v, 're:p-, 'repp-] *al* representative *(för* of) **-era** **1** *(företräda)* represent, act for **2** *(utöva värdskap)* entertain
repress|alier [-'sa:-] *pl* reprisals; *utöva* ~ *mot* retaliate (make reprisal) on, take reprisals against **-iv** *al* repressive
reprimand [-'mand, -'maŋd] *s3* reprimand
repris *s3* **1** *mus.* repeat; *teat.* revival; *(av film e.d.)* rerun, second presentation; *radio., TV.* repeat; *(TV i slowmotion)* action (instant) replay **2** *(omgång)* turn, bout **-era** repeat; revive; rerun **-tecken** *mus.* repeat mark
reproducera reproduce **reproduktion** [-k'ʃɔ:n] reproduction *(äv. konkr.)*
reproduktions|anstalt process-engraving establishment (laboratory) **-avdrag** reproduction proof (pull)
reproduktiv *al* reproductive
rep|slagare rope maker **-slageri** *(-slagning)* rope-making; *konkr.* rope yard, rope works **-stege** rope ladder **-stump** rope's end, short piece of rope
reptil *s3* reptile
republik *s3* republic **-an** *s3* republican **-ansk** [-a:-] *a5* republican
repulsion [-l'ʃɔ:n] repulsion
reput|ation reputation **-erlig** [-'te:r-] *al* reputable; respectable
repövning military refresher course
1 res|a *v3 (höja)* raise *(invändningar* objections); erect *(en gravsten* a gravestone); set up *(en stege* a ladder; *krav* claims); ~ *ett tält* pitch a tent; *taket är -t* the rafters are in place; ~ *talan (jur.)* lodge a complaint; ~ *sig* rise, *(stiga upp äv.)* get up; ~ *sig på bakbenen* rear [on its *(etc.)* hind legs]; ~ *sig över omgivningen* rise above its environment; *håret -te sig på mitt huvud* my hair stood on end; ~ *sig ur sin förnedring* raise o.s. from degradation

2 resa *s1, jur., första* ~*n* first offence, *tredje* ~*n stöld* third conviction for theft

3 res|a I *s1* journey (*äv. bildl.*); (*sjö-*) voyage; (*över-*) crossing, passage; (*kortare*) trip; (*rund-*) tour; (*-ande*) travel; *lycklig* ~*!* pleasant journey!; *enkel* ~ one-way trip (journey); *fri* ~ free passage; *vad kostar en enkel* ~*?* what is the single fare?; *jag har långa -or till arbetet* I have a long journey to work; *vara* [*ute*] *på* ~ be [out] travelling; *bege sig ut på* ~ start (set out) on a journey; *på* ~*n hit såg jag* coming (on my way) here I saw **II** *v3* travel, go (*med tåg* by train; *till lands* by land); (*av-*) leave, depart (*till* for); (*om handelsresande*) travel, *vard.* be on the road; *han har -t mycket* he has travelled a great deal; ~ *andra klass* travel second class; ~ *bort* go away; *han -te från London i går* he left London yesterday; ~ *för en firma* (*i affärer*) travel for a firm (on business); ~ *hem* go home; *han har -t härifrån* he has left [here] (gone away from here); ~ *igenom* pass through; ~ *in till staden* go up to town; ~ *omkring* travel round (about); ~ *ut på landet* go [out] into the country

resande I *a4* travelling; (*kring*) touring, itinerant; *ett* ~ *teatersällskap* a touring company; *vara på* ~ *fot* be travelling (on the move) **II** *s9* travelling salesman, [commercial] traveller; (*passagerare*) passenger; ~ *i tyger* traveller in fabrics; *rum för* ~ lodgings (*pl*) **-bok** hotel register, visitors' book

res|dag day of travel; (*avrese-*) day of departure **-damm** *tvätta* ~*et av sig* wash off the dust of one's journey

rese *s2* giant

rese|berättelse account of a journey; travel book **-bidrag** travelling allowance **-byrå** travel agency (bureay) **-check** traveller's cheque

reseda [-ˣse:-, -ˊse:-] *s1* mignonette

reseffekter *pl* luggage (*sg*); *AE.* baggage (*sg*); personal effects

rese|förbud injunction against leaving the jurisdiction; *åläggas* ~ be forbidden to travel **-försäkring** travel insurance **-grammofon** portable gramophone **-handbok** guide[book] **-kostnader** *pl* travel[ling] expenses **-kreditiv** traveller's (circular) letter of credit **-ledare** [tour] conductor, guide **-när** *s3* traveller; (*passagerare*) passenger **-radio** portable radio

reserv [-ä-] *s3* reserve; *pers.* extra hand (man); *mil.* reserve; *sport.* reserve, substitute; *i* ~ in reserve (store); *dolda* ~*er* hidden reserves (assets); *överföras till* ~*en* (*mil.*) be put on the reserved list **reservant** dissentient **reservare** [-ˣsärr-] *mil.* reservist **reservat** *s7* reserve; (*natur-*) national park; (*djur-*) game reserve; (*fågel-*) bird sanctuary; (*infödings-*) reservation **reservation** reservation; (*tillbakadragenhet*) reserve; *ta ngt med en viss* ~ accept s.th. with some reservation; *med* ~ *för förändringar* subject to alteration **reservationslös** unreserved; without reservation **reserv|del** spare part **-däck** spare tyre

reservera 1 reserve; set (put) aside; (*rum e.d.*) reserve, make reservations for, book [in advance] **2** ~ *sig* make a reservation (*mot* to); (*protestera*) protest (*mot* against); *vi* ~*r oss för förseningar* we make reservation for delays **reserve-**

reserve|rad [-ˊve:-] *a5* (*beställd*) reserved, booked; (*förbehållsam*) reserved, guarded **reserv|fond** reserve fund **-förråd** reserve [supply, stock] **-hjul** spare wheel **-nyckel** spare key

reservoar *s3* reservoir; cistern, tank **-penna** fountain pen

reserv|officer officer of (in) the reserve **-proviant** *s9, ej pl* emergency rations (*pl*) **-tank** reserve tank **-utgång** emergency exit, fire escape

rese|räkning travelling-expenses account **-skildring** travel book; (*föredrag e.d.*) travelogue **-skrivmaskin** portable typewriter **-stipendium** travel[ling] scholarship (grant) **-valuta** travel (tourist) allowance

res|feber (*längtan att resa*) longing to travel; *ha* ~ have the jitters before a journey **-filt** travelling rug **-färdig** ready to start (for departure)

resgods luggage; *AE.* baggage **-expedition** luggage [registration] office **-försäkring** luggage insurance **-förvaring, -inlämning** cloakroom, left-luggage office; *AE.* checkroom

residens *s7* residence **-stad** seat of provincial government; *i Storbritannien* county town

residera reside

residuum [-ˣsi:-] *s4* residue

resignation [-iŋn-, -inj-] resignation **resignera** [-ŋˊne:-, -nˊje:-] resign o.s. (*inför* to) **resignerad** *a5* resigned; *med en* ~ *min* with an air of resignation

resist|ans [-ˊans, -ˊaŋs] *s3, elektr.* resistance **-ens** *s3* resistance **-ent** *a1* resistant

res|kamrat fellow traveller; (*-sällskap*) travelling companion **-kassa** cash for a journey; travelling funds (*pl*) **-klädd** dressed for a journey

reskontra [-ˊkånn-, ˣress-] *s1* personal ledger; (*kund-*) accounts receivable ledger; (*leverantörs-*) accounts payable ledger

res|kost provisions (*pl*) for a journey **-lektyr** light reading for the journey; *skaffa sig litet* ~ get s.th. to read on the journey

reslig [ˣre:s-] *a1* tall

res|lust wanderlust **-lysten** eager to travel

resning [ˣre:s-] **1** (*uppresande*) raising, erection **2** (*höjd, ställning*) build, imposing proportions (*pl*); (*gestalt*) stature; *en man av andlig* ~ a man of great moral stature **3** (*uppror*) rising, rebellion, revolt **4** *jur.* review, new trial; *ansöka om* ~ *i målet* bring a bill of review, lodge a petition for a new hearing

resningsansökan petition for a new trial

resolu|t *a1* resolute; prompt **-tion** resolution; (*beslut äv.*) decision; *antaga en* ~ pass (adopt) a resolution; *kunglig* ~ royal ordinance, *i Storbritannien* order in council

resolutionsförslag draft resolution

resolvera [-å-] decree, decide

reson *r* reason; *ta* ~ be reasonable, listen to reason, come round **resonabel** [-ˊna:-] *a2* (*om pers.*) amenable; (*om pris, argument etc.*) reasonable

resonans [-ˊnaŋs, -ˊans] *s3* resonance **-botten** sounding board, soundboard

resonemang *s7, s4* (*diskussion*) discussion; (*samtal*) talk; (*sätt att resonera*) reasoning **resonemangsparti** marriage of convenience

R

reson|era (*jfr resonemang*) discuss; talk over; reason; ~ *bort* explain (argue) away **-erande** [-'ne:-] *a4* (*om framställning e.d.*) reasoned, discursive, argumentative **-lig** [-'so:n-] *al* reasonable; sensible

resorbera [-å-] resorb **resorption** [-p'ʃo:n] resorption

respass *bildl.*, *få* ~ get sacked, be dismissed; *ge ngn* ~ give s.b. the sack, dismiss s.b.

respekt *s3* respect; (*högaktning*) esteem; (*fruktan*) awe; *förlora* ~*en för* lose one's respect for; *ha* ~ *med sig* command respect; *sätta sig i* ~ *hos* make o.s. respected by; *visa* ~ *för* show consideration (respect) for; *med all* ~ *för* with all (due) deference to **respektabel** [-'ta:-] *a2* respectable; (*oantastlig*) irreproachable **respektabilitet** respectability

respekt|era respect, have respect for; (*åtlyda* *äv.*) adhere to **-full** respectful **-ingivande** *a4* that inspires respect **-injagande** *a4* awe-inspiring

respektive [-'ti:-, 'ress-] **I** *oböjligt a* respective **II** *adv* respectively; *de kostar 2* ~ *3 pund* they cost 2 and 3 pounds respectively

respektlös disrespectful **-het** disrespect

respengar *pl* money (*sg*) for a journey

respir|ation respiration **-ator** [-ˣa:tår] *s3* respirator **-atorisk** [-'to:-] *a5* respiratory **-era** respire

respit *s3* respite; *en månads* ~ a month's grace **-tid** respite, term of grace

res|plan itinerary, travelling plan **-pläd** travelling rug

respondent [-å-] respondent, defendant **respons** [-'åns] *s3* response **responsorium** [-'so:-] *s4* responsory

res|rutt route, itinerary **-sällskap** *abstr.* company on a journey; *konkr.* travelling companions (*pl*), (*turistgrupp*) conducted party; *få* ~ *med* ... have the company of ... on the (one's) journey

rest *s3* **1** rest, remainder; *AE. äv.* balance; (*kvarleva*) remnant (*äv. tyg-*); *mat.* remainder; *hand.* balance, remainder; ~*er* (*kvarlevor*) remains, (*matrester äv.*) leftovers, leavings; ~*en* the rest (remainder), what is left, (*de andra*) the others; *för* ~*en* (*för övrigt*) for the rest, (*dessutom*) besides, moreover, (*i själva verket*) indeed, in fact **2** *vara på* ~ *med skatterna* be in arrears with taxes; *få* ~ *på en del av ämnet* (*i tentamen*) have to sit part of an examination again

restantier [-'tantsier] *pl* arrears, outstanding debts

restaurang [-au'raŋ, -tu'raŋ] restaurant; (*hotellmatsal*) dining room **-besök** visit to a restaurant **-branschen** catering trade (business) **-chef** restaurant manager **-nota** bill; *AE.* check **-vagn** dining (restaurant) car, diner

restauration [-au-] **1** (*restaurering*) restoration **2** (*matställe*) refreshment room, dining saloon

restaurator [-ˣa:tår] *s3* restorer **restauratris** *s3* restorer **restauratör** restaurant proprietor, restaurateur, caterer

restaurer|a [-au're:-] restore **-ing** restoration

restera remain, be left; (*vara på rest med*) be in arrears (*med hyran* with the rent) **resterande** *a4* remaining, leftover; outstanding (*skulder* debts); ~ *belopp* balance, outstanding amount,

remainder; ~ *skatter* arrears of taxes; ~ *skulder* (*äv.*) arrears

restid travelling (running) time

restitu|era 1 (*återbetala*) repay, refund, pay back **2** (*återställa*) restore **-tion 1** (*återbetalning*) refund, repayment; (*tull-*) drawback **2** (*återställande*) restoration

rest|lager surplus (remainder) stock **-likvid** final payment **-längd** tax-arrears schedule; *komma på* ~ get in arrears with one's taxes **-lös** entire, absolute; unquestioning (*hängivenhet* devotion) **-par** odd pair **-parti** remnant, odd lot

restrik|tion [-k'ʃo:n] restriction; *införa* (*upphäva*) ~*er* introduce (lift) restrictions **-tiv** *al* restrictive **-tivitet** restrictivity

restrött travel-weary

rest|skatt back tax, tax arrears (*pl*) **-upplaga** remainder [of an edition]; *hela* ~*n* all the rest of the edition

resultant *fys.* resultant

resultat *s7* result; (*verkan*) effect; (*följd*) consequence; (*utgång*) issue; (*behållning*) proceeds (*pl*); *ge till* ~ result in; *utan* ~, *se resultatlös* **-lös** fruitless; *blev* ~ was without result (in vain, of no avail) **-räkning** profit and loss account

resultera result (*i* in); *det* ~*de i att* the result was that

resum|é *s3* résumé, summary, précis; *jur.* brief **-era** sum up, summarize

resurs *s3* resource; ~*er* (*äv.*) means, assets; *utnyttja sina* ~*er* make full use of (exploit) one's assets (resources)

res|van used (accustomed) to travelling **-vana** experience in travelling **-väg** route [of travel], travelling distance **-väska** suitcase; (*liten*) *AE.* *vanl.* grip

resår *s3* (*spiralfjäder*) spring; (*gummiband*) elastic **-band** elastic **-botten** springbase **-gördel** roll on [girdle] **-madrass** spring mattress **-stickning** ribbed knitting, ribbing

reta 1 (*framkalla retning*) irritate (*nerverna* the nerves); (*stimulera*) stimulate, whet (*aptiten* the appetite); (*egga*) excite (*ngns nyfikenhet* a p.'s curiosity); ~ *ngns begär* rouse a p.'s desire (passion) **2** (*förarga*) provoke, annoy, vex; (~*s med*) tease; ~ *upp sig* work o.s. up (*på* at); ~ *sig* get angry (*på, över* at)

retard|ation retardation, deceleration **-era** retard, decelerate

ret|as *dep* tease, chaff (*med ngn* s.b.; *för ngt* about s.th.) **-bar** *al* (*om organ e.d.*) reactive to stimuli; (*friare*) irritable, excitable

reten|tion retention **-tionsrätt** right of retention

ret|full irritating; (*-sam*) provoking, annoying **-hosta** hacking cough

retina [-ˣti:-, 're:-] *sl* retina

retirera retire, retreat; (*rygga tillbaka*) recoil

ret|lig [ˣre:t-] *al* (*lättretad*) irritable, fretful; (*snarstucken*) touchy; (*vresig*) irascible **-lighet** irritability; touchiness; irascibility **-medel** irritant; (*stimulerande medel*) stimulant **-ning** irritation; stimulation; (*känsel-, nerv- etc.*) stimulus, impulse **-ningströskel** stimulation (stimulus) threshold

retor [ˣre:-, 're:tår] *s3* rhetor **-ik** [-o'ri:k] *s3* rhetoric **-iker** [-'tɔ:-] rhetorician **-isk** [-'tɔ:-] *a5* rhetorical

retort [-å-] *s3* retort **-flaska** spherical flask **-kol** retort (gas) carbon

retro|aktiv [-'ti:v, 're:-, 'retrɔ-] *a1* retroactive **-grad** *a4, n sg obest.* form saknas retrograde **-spektiv** *a1* retrospective

reträtt *s3* retreat; *(tillflykt)* refuge; *slå till ~* beat a retreat; *ta till ~[en]* retreat; *ha ~en klar* keep a line of retreat open, *bildl.* have a loophole ready; *på ~* in retreat, retreating **-plats** *bildl.* a job for one's *(etc)* retirement

ret|sam [ˣre:t-] *a1* irritating, annoying, vexatious; *(förarglig)* tiresome **-sticka** *(en riktig* a regular) tease

retur return; *~er (-sändningar)* returned goods, returns; *sända varor i ~* return goods, send back; *första klass tur och ~ London* first class return London; *vad kostar tur och ~ till ...?* what is the return fare to ...?; *vara på ~* be abating (on the wane) **-biljett** return *(AE.* round-trip) ticket **-fiber** recycled fibre, secondary fibre **-glas** returnable bottle **-gods** returned goods **-match** return match (game) **-nera** return, send back **-papper** waste paper **-porto** return (reply) postage **-rätt** right of (to) return; *med ~* on sale or return

retusch *s3* retouch[ing]; *ge ngt en lätt ~ (bildl.)* touch s.th. up a little **-era** retouch, touch up **-ering** [-'ʃe:-] retouching, touching up

reumat|iker [reu'ma:-, rev-] rheumatic **-isk** *a5* rheumatic **-ism** rheumatism **-ologi** [-lå'gi:] *s3* rheumatology

1 rev *s2 (met-)* fishing line

2 rev *s7 (sand-)* sandbank, spit; *(klipp-)* reef

3 rev *s7, sjö.* reef

4 rev *imperf. av* riva

1 reva *v1, sjö.* reef, shorten; *gå för ~de segel* go under reefed sails

2 reva *s1 (rispa)* tear, rent, rip; *(skråma)* wound

3 reva *s1, bot.* runner

revalver|a revaluate **-ing** revaluation

revansch [-'vanʃ, -'vanʃ] *s3* revenge; *ta ~* take one's revenge, revenge o.s. **-era** *rfl, se [ta]* revansch **-lysten** eager for revenge; implacable, vengeful **-tanke** thought of revenge

rev|ben rib **-bensspjäll** *slaktar.* square rib[s *pl*]; *kokk.* ribs *(pl)* of pork

revel *s2, se 2 rev*

revelj *s3* reveille; *blåsa ~* sound (beat) the reveille; *~en går* the reveille is sounding

reveny *s3* profit, gain; yield

reverens *s3* reverence

revers [-ä-] *s3* **1** *(skuldebrev)* note [of hand], promissory note; IOU *(förk. av* I owe you) **2** *(på mynt)* reverse **-el** *s7 (formulär)* promissory note form; *(från ämbetsverk)* notification of the dispatch of a document (sum of money) **-lån** promissory note loan

reveter|a roughcast, lath-and-plaster **-ing** lath-and-plastering; *konkr.* roughcast coating

revid|er *s7* clean (revised) proof **-era** *(bearbeta)* revise, review; *(räkenskaper)* audit; *~d upplaga* revised edition

revir *s7* forest district; *(djurs)* territory

revision revision; *(av räkenskaper)* audit **-ism**

revisionism **-ist** revisionist

revisions|berättelse auditor's report **-firma** firm of auditors; *auktoriserad ~* firm of chartered accountants

revisor [-ˣvi:sår] *s3* auditor, accountant; *auktoriserad ~* authorized public accountant, *i Storbritannien* chartered accountant

revolt [-'vålt] *s3* revolt, insurrection **-era** revolt **-försök** attempted revolt

revolution revolution **-era** revolutionize **-erande** [-'ne:-] revolutionary; *(epokgörande)* epoch-making

revolutionskrig revolutionary war

revolutionär I *s3* revolutionary **II** *a1* revolutionary

revolver [-'våll-] *s2* revolver **-man** gunman, *AE. sl.* gunslinger **-skott** revolver shot **-svarv** capstan (turret) lathe

revorm *med.* ringworm

revy *s3, mil. o. bildl.* review; *teat.* revue, show; *passera ~* march (file) past **-artist** show artiste

revär *s3* stripe

Rhen [re:n] *r* the Rhine

rhen|sk [re:nsk] *a5* Rhine, Rhenish **-vin** Rhine wine, hock **-vinsglas** hock glass, rummer

rhesus|apa [ˣre:-] rhesus monkey **-faktor** rhesus *(förk.* Rh) factor

Rh-faktor [ˣärrhå:-] Rh factor

Rhodos ['rå:dås] *n* Rhodes

ribb|a *s1* lath, batten; *sport.* [cross]bar **-ad** *a5* ribbed *(strumpa* stocking) **-stickad** *a5, se* ribbad **-stol** wall bars *(pl)* **-verk** rails *(pl)*

ricinolja [-ˣsi:n-] castor oil

rid|a *red -it* ride *(barbacka* bareback); *han -er bra (äv.)* he is a good rider (horseman); *~ i galopp (skritt, trav)* gallop (pace, trot); *~ på ngns rygg (äv.)* be carried piggyback (pickaback); *~ in en häst* break a horse in; *~ ut stormen (bildl.)* weather the storm; *~ för ankaret* ride at anchor; *~ på ord* split hairs, quibble **-ande** *a4* riding; on horseback; *~ polis* mounted police, *AE. äv. (i lantdistrikt)* ranger **-bana** riding ground **-byxor** *pl* [riding] breeches, jodhpurs

riddar|borg feudal castle **-diktning** chivalrous poetry

riddar|e knight; *bli ~* become (be made) a knight; *vandrande ~* knight errant; *~n av den sorgliga skepnaden* the knight of the sorrowful countenance; *en damernas ~* un chevalier des dames; *fattiga ~ (kokk.)* bread fritters **-hus** *R~et* the House of the Nobility **-orden** order of knighthood (chivalry), knightly order **-sporre** *bot.* larkspur **-tiden** the age of chivalry **-väsen** chivalry

ridder|lig *a1* chivalric; *litt.* chivalric; *(chevaleresk)* gallant, courteous **-lighet** chivalry; gallantry **-skap** *s7, abstr.* chivalry, knighthood; *konkr.* Knighthood, *(under medeltiden)* Knights of the Realm; *~t och adeln* the Nobility

ridder|sman *(riddare)* chevalier, knight; *(-lig man)* man of honour

rid|dräkt riding dress; *(dams)* riding habit **-hus** riding school **-häst** saddle horse, saddler *-it sup. av rida* **-konst** horsemanship **-lärare** riding master **-ning** riding **-piska** *se -spö* **-skola** riding school **-sport** riding, equestrian sport **-spö**

F

[horse] whip; (*kort*) [riding] crop **-stövel** riding boot **-tur** ride

ridå *s3* curtain **-fall** *vid ~et* at the fall of the curtain **-slutare** curtain shutter

rigg *s2* rig[ging]; *löpande* ~ running rigging; *stående* ~ standing rigging **rigga** rig [out]; (*t.ex. metspö*) rig up; ~ *upp sig* (*vard.*) rig o.s. out

rigid *a1, n. sg obest.* form *används ej* rigid **rigiditet** rigidity **rigorös** *a1* rigorous

rik *a1* **1** (*förmögen*) rich, wealthy; *de ~a* the rich; *bli* ~ get (become) rich; *den ~e mannen* (*bibl.*) Dives **2** (*ymnig*) rich (*på* in); (*fruktbar*) fertile; (*-lig*) abundant, ample, plentiful; ~ *på minnen* full of memories; *~t urval* wide range, varied assortment; *ett ~t förråd av* a plentiful (an abundant) store (stock) of; *ett ~t liv* a full (vivid) life; *bli en erfarenhet ~are* learn by experience, be that much wiser; *i ~t mått* amply, abundantly

rike *s6* (*stat*) state, realm; (*kungadöme*) kingdom; (*kejsardöme*) empire; *bildl.* kingdom, realm, sphere; *det tusenåriga ~t* the millennium; *tredje ~t* the Third Reich; *tillkomme ditt* ~ (*bibl.*) Thy kingdom come

rikedom *s2* **1** (*förmögenhet*) wealth; riches (*pl*) **2** *bildl.* richness (*på* in); (*-lighet*) wealth, abundance (*på* of) **rikeman** rich man **rikemansbarn** *pl* children of rich parents

rik|haltig *a1* rich, plentiful, abundant **-lig** [ˣriːk-] *a1* abundant (*skörd* crop); ample, plentiful; *få* ~ *användning för* have plenty of opportunity of using; *det har fallit ~t med snö* snow has fallen in abundance; *i* ~ *mängd* in abundance, in profusion

rikoschett *s3* ricochet; (*-erande projektil*) ricochetting bullet (*etc.*) **-era** ricochet

riks|angelägenhet [ˣrikks-] national affair **-antikvarie** director-general of the central board of [the Swedish] national antiquities **-arkiv** *~et* [the Swedish] national archives (*pl*); (*i Storbritannien*) Public Record Office **-arkivarie** director-general of the [Swedish] national archives **-bank** central (national) bank; *R~en* (*Sveriges* ~) [the] Bank of Sweden **-banksdirektör** director of the Bank of Sweden **-banksfullmäktige** the board of governors of the Bank of Sweden **-bekant** known all over the country; (*ökänd*) notorious **-bibliotekarie** national librarian **-dag** [ˈrikks-] *s2, R~en* the Swedish Parliament, the Riksdag; (*i Storbritannien*) Parliament; *lagtima* ~ ordinary parliamentary session

riksdags|beslut Riksdag (parliamentary) resolution; Act of Parliament **-debatt** Riksdag (parliamentary) debate **-hus** Riksdag (Parliament) Building; (*i Storbritannien*) Houses of Parliament; *AE.* Capitol **-ledamot, -man** member of parliament (the Riksdag); (*i Storbritannien*) member of parliament (*förk.* M.P.); *AE.* Congressman, *fem.* Congresswoman **-mandat** seat in parliament (the Riksdag), (*i Storbritannien*) seat in Parliament) **-motion** bill **-ordning** Parliament (Riksdag) Act **-parti** Riksdag (parliamentary) party **-sammanträde** sitting of parliament (the Riksdag) **-val** general (parliamentary) election

riks|daler [riksˈdaː-] *s9, s2* rix-dollar **-drots** [-åˈ-]

s2, ung. Lord High Chancellor **-förening** national federation (association, union) **-föreståndare** regent **-försäkringsverket** the [Swedish] national social insurance board **-gräns** international boundary, frontier of a country **-gäldskontoret** [-jä-] the [Swedish] national debt office

riksha [ˈrikkʃa] *s1* rickshaw, jinri[c]k[i]sha **riks|idrottsförbund** *Sveriges R~* [the[Swedish Sports Confederation **-kansler** [ˣrikks-] chancellor **-likare** national standard **-marsk** constable of the realm; *i Storbritannien ung.* Lord High Constable **-marskalk** marshal of the realm; *i Storbritannien* Lord High Steward **-marskalksämbetet** office of the marshal of the realm **-museum** national museum (gallery) **-möte** parliamentary session, session of the Riksdag **-olycka** national disaster **-omfattande** nationwide **-plan** *på ~et* at a national level **-polischef** national police commissioner **-polisstyrelsen** the [Swedish] national police board **-regalier** *pl* regalia **-revisionsverket** the [Swedish] national audit bureau **-råd** (*konselj*) council of the realm; *pers.* councillor **-rätt** court of impeachment; (*BE. motsv.*) House of Lords; (*AE. motsv.*) Senate **-rös[e]** frontier cairn **-samtal** trunk call; *AE.* long-distance call **-skatteverket** the [Swedish] national tax board **-språk** standard language **-svenska** (*språk*) standard Swedish **-teater** *ung.* national touring theatre **-telefon** trunk (*AE.* toll) exchange **-vapen** national coat of arms **-viktig** of national importance; (*allmännare*) vitally important, momentous **-väg** national highway **-åklagare** prosecutor-general; *i Storbritannien* director of public prosecutions; *AE.* attorney general **-äpple** orb

rikta 1 (*vända åt visst håll*) direct (*mot* towards); aim (*ett slag mot* a blow at); (*skjutvapen*) aim, level, point (*mot* at); (*framställa*) address (*en anmärkning till* a remark to); ~ *en anklagelse mot* bring a charge (make an accusation) against; ~ *en fråga till* put a question to; ~ *misstankar mot* direct suspicion on; ~ *några ord till* say a few words to; ~ *uppmärksamheten på* draw attention to; ~ *sig till a*) (*om pers.*) address [o.s. to], *b*) (*om bok e.d.*) be intended for; ~ *sig mot* (*om tal e.d.*) be directed at **2** (*räta*) straighten; (*bräda, hjul e.d.*) true up

riktig *a1* (*rätt*) right; (*korrekt*) correct; (*verklig*) real; (*äkta*) true; (*regelrätt*) proper, regular; *det ~a* the right (proper) thing; *det var ett ~t nöje att* it was a real pleasure to; *ett ~t kräk* a poor wretch; *en* ~ *snobb* a regular snob; *han är inte* ~ he is not right in his head **riktighet** rightness; correctness; (*noggrannhet*) accuracy; (*tillbörlighet*) propriety; *det äger sin* ~ *att* it is quite true (a fact) that; *avskriftens* ~ *intygas* we (I) certify this to be a true copy

riktigt *adv* right[ly]; correctly; (*som sig bör*) properly; (*verkligen*) really; (*ganska*) quite; (*mycket*) very; *mycket* ~ quite right, sure enough; ~ *bra* really (very, quite) well, really (very) good; *jag mår* ~ *bra nu* I feel really well now; *pjäsen var* ~ *bra* the play was very good; *det anses inte* ~ *fint att* it is considered not quite the thing to; *jag mår inte* ~ *bra* I am not feeling quite well; *jag förstår inte* ~ *vad du säger* I don't quite understand what you say; *jag litar inte* ~ *på dem* I don't quite trust them; *han blev också ganska* ~ *förkyld* and sure enough he caught a cold

rikt|linje guideline; policies (*pl*); *uppdraga* ~*er för* (*bildl.*) lay down the general outline (guiding principles) for; *ge* ~ (*äv.*) outline **-märke** target **-ning 1** (*inriktande*) directing, pointing; aiming; (*uträtande*) straightening **2** (*kurs, håll*) direction, course; *bildl.* direction, (*tendens*) tendency, trend, line; (*rörelse*) movement; *i* ~ *mot* in the direction of; *i vardera* ~*en* in each (either) direction, each way; *i vilken* ~ *gick hans uttalande?* what line did he take in his remarks; *ge samtalet en annan* ~ (*äv.*) lead the conversation into another track **-nummer** *tel.* exchange code, code number **-pris** standard [retail] price, recommended retail price **-punkt** objective, aim (*för* of); *mil.* aiming point

rim *s7* [rimm] rhyme; *utan* ~ *och reson* without rhyme or reason **-flätning** [-ä:-] rhyme arrangement

rimfrost [ˣrimm-] hoarfrost, white frost

rimlexikon rhyming dictionary

rimlig *a1* (*skälig*) reasonable; (*sannolik*) likely, probable; (*måttlig*) moderate; *hålla kostnader inom* ~*a gränser* keep costs within reason (reasonable bounds); *det är inte mer än* ~*t att* it is only reasonable that **rimlighet** reasonableness *etc.*; *vad i all* ~*s namn?* what in the name of common sense? **rimligtvis** reasonably

1 rimma rhyme (*på* with; *med* to, with); *absol. äv.* make rhymes; *kan du* ~ *på tänka?* can you supply a rhyme to think?; *ha lätt för att* ~ find rhyming easy; *det* ~*r illa med* (*bildl.*) it doesn't tally (fit in) with

2 rimma *se rimsalta*

rimsalta salt slightly

rimsmidare rhymer, versifier

ring *s2* **1** ring; (*däck*) tyre, *AE.* tire **2** (*krets*) circle, ring; *meteor.* halo, (*kring solen äv.*) corona; *biol.* collar **3** (*i boxning*) boxing ring; ~*ar* (*gymn.*) rings **4** *skol.* form in the upper secondary school

1 ring|a *v2* ring; *det -er i telefonen* the telephone is ringing; ~ *av* ring off; ~ *på dörren* ring (press) the [door] bell; ~ *på betjäningen* ring for room service; ~ *till ngn* give s.b. a ring, call s.b. up, phone s.b.; ~ *ett samtal* make a phone call; *det -er och susar för mina öron* there is a ringing in my ears

2 ringa *v1* **1** *jakt., lantbr.* ring **2** (*måltavla*) draw rings on; *se äv. inringa* **3** (*klänning e.d.*) ~ *ur* cut low [at the neck]

3 ringa I *oböjl. a* **1** small, little; (*obetydlig*) insignificant (*roll* part); slight (*ansträngning* effort); *ett* ~ *bevis på* small proof (token) of; ~ *efterfrågan* little (weak) demand; ~ *tröst* poor consolation; *på* ~ *avstånd* at a short distance; *till* ~ *del* to a small extent; *ytterst* ~ infinitesimal **2** (*låg, enkel*) humble, lowly; *av* ~ *börd* of humble origin; *min* ~ *person* my humble self (person) **II** *adv* little **ringakt** (*ngt*) make light of; (*ngn*) look down upon; (*förakta*) despise **-ande** *a4* despising *etc.*; contemptuous, disdainful **-ning** disregard; (*för-*

akt) contempt, disdain; *visa* ~ *för ngt* hold s.th. in contempt

1 ringare *s9* bell-ringer

2 ringare I *a, komp. t. ringa* smaller *etc.*; (*underlägsen*) inferior (*än* to) **II** *adv* less

ringast I *a, superl. t. ringa* least *etc.*; *utan* ~*e anledning* without the slightest provocation; *inte den* ~*e aning* not the slightest idea **II** *adv* least; *inte det* ~*e* not [in] the least, not at all

ring|blomma pot marigold; (*torkad*) calendula **-brynja** ring (chain) mail **-dans** round dance; *dansa* ~ dance in a ring **-domare** *sport.* referee **-duva** wood pigeon, ringdove **-finger** ring finger **-formig** [-å-] *a1* ring-shaped, annular **-förlovad** officially engaged, betrothed

ringhet smallness, insignificance; (*låghet, enkelhet*) humbleness, lowliness

ringhörna *sport.* corner of a [boxing] ring

ringklocka bell

ringla curl; coil; (*om väg e.d.*) wind, meander; ~ *ihop sig* (*om orm*) coil itself up; ~ *sig* coil, wind, (*om lockar*) curl; *kön* ~*r sig* the queue winds **ringlar** *pl* (*av hår*) curls; (*av orm, rep*) coils

ringledning electric bell installation

ring|lek ring (round) game **-mask** annelid[an], ringed worm **-mur** encircling wall; town wall **-muskel** sphincter **-märka** ring, *AE.* band **-märkning** bird banding

ringning ringing

rink *s2* rink

rinna *rann runnit* run; (*flyta*) flow, stream; (*droppa*) drip, trickle; (*om ljus*) gutter; (*läcka*) leak; *hennes tårar rann* her tears were flowing; *det kom mina ögon att* ~ it made my eyes water; *sinnet rann på mig* I lost my temper; ~ *av* drain off; ~ *till* flow (*äv. bildl.*) begin to flow; ~ *upp* (*om flod*) rise, have its source; *saken rann ut i sanden* it came to nothing; ~ *ut* run out; ~ *över* flow over; *det kom bägaren att* ~ *över* that was the last straw **rinnande** *a4* running

ripa *s1* grouse; (*fjäll-*) ptarmigan; (*dal-*) willow grouse

ripost [-å-] *s3* ripost[e]; *bildl.* repartee, retort **-era** riposte; *bildl.* retort

rips *s3, s4* rep[p]

1 ris *s7* (*papper*) ream

2 ris *s7* (*sädesslag*) rice

3 ris *s7* **1** (*kvistar*) twigs (*pl*); (*buskvegetation*) brushwood **2** (*straffredskap*) rod, birch, birch rod; (*straff äv.*) birching; *få smaka* ~*et* have a taste of the birch (rod); *ge ngn* ~ whip (birch) s.b.; *binda* ~ *åt egen rygg* make a rod for one's own back

ris|a 1 (*ärter e.d.*) stick **2** (*ge -bastu*) birch; (*klandra*) blame, criticize **-bastu** birching

ris|fält paddy [(rice) field] **-gryn** (*ett* ~) grain of rice; (*koll.* rice **-grynsgröt** [boiled] rice pudding

rishög 1 *eg.* heap of twigs **2** *vard.* (*bil*) jalop[p]y

risig *a1* **1** (*om träd*) with dry twigs; (*-bevuxen*) scrubby **2** *vard.* (*om ting*) rotten, of low quality; (*om pers.*) in bad shape

risk *s3* risk (*för* of); *det är ingen* ~ *att* ... (*att jag* ...) there is no risk in (+ ing-form) (of my + ing-form); *löpa* ~[*en*] *att* run the risk of (+ ing-form); *med* ~ *att bli* at the risk of being; *på egen* ~ at

R

one's own risk; *ta ~er* take risks (chances); *utan ~* safely

riska *s1, bot.* edible agaric

risk|abel [-'a:bel] *a2* risky, dangerous, hazardous **-era** risk, run the risk of; hazard, (*äventyra*) jeopardize **-fri** safe **-fylld** hazardous, perilous, dangerous **-laboratorium** high-security laboratory

ris|knippa bundle of twigs, faggott **-koja** hut of twigs

riskorn grain of rice

riskvast besom

risk|tillägg danger money **-villig** *~t kapital* risk (venture) capital **-zon** danger zone; *i ~en* (*bridge.*) vulnerable

risodling *abstr.* rice cultivation; *konkr.* rice plantation, paddy [(rice) field]

risoll [-å-] *s3, kokk.* rissole **risotto** [-'åttå] *s9, kokk.* risotto

rispa I *s1* scratch; (*i tyg*) rent, rip **II** *v1* scratch; *~ upp* rip up; *~ sig* scratch o.s., (*om tyg*) fray, get frayed

rispapper rice paper

1 rista *v1* (*inskära*) cut, carve (*i* on); *bildl.* engrave, inscribe

2 rist|a *v3* (*skaka*) shake (*på huvudet* one's head); *det -er i armen* [*på mig*] I have shooting pains in my arm

rit *s3* rite

rit|a draw (*efter* from); (*göra -ning t.*) design (*ett hus* a house; *ett mönster* a pattern); *~ av* make a drawing (sketch) of, (*kopiera*) copy **-are** draughtsman, designer **-bestick** set of drawing instruments **-block** sketch block, drawing pad **-bord, -bräde** drawing board **-kontor** drawing office **-ning** [ˣri:t-] **1** *abstr.* drawing, sketching **2** *konkr.* drawing, sketch, blueprint; (*t. byggnad e.d. äv.*) design **-papper** drawing paper

rits *s2, s3* scribed line **ritsa** mark [off], scribe

rit|sal [ˣri:t-] art [class]room **-stift 1** (*-penna*) drawing pen[cil] **2** (*häftstift*) drawing pin, *AE.* thumbtack

ritt *s3* ride, riding tour

ritual *s3, s4* ritual **-mord** ritual murder (*på* of)

rituell *a1* ritualistic (*dans* dance); ritual (*ändamål* purposes)

riv *s7, bildl.* struggle, demand (*efter* for)

riv|a *rev -it* **1** (*klösa*) scratch; (*ihjäl-*) kill, tear to pieces; *~ hål på* tear a hole in; *~ sönder* tear to pieces, (*klädesplagg*) tear to rags (tatters); *~ ner* (*stöta till*) knock down; *~ upp* (*gata e.d.*) pull (take) up; *~ upp ett sår* tear open a wound; *~ ut* tear out; *~ åt sig* grab; *~ sig* (*klia sig*) scratch o.s., (*rispa sig*) get o.s. scratched **2** *kokk.* grate **3** (*rasera*) pull (*AE.* tear) down, demolish; *AE. äv.* wreck; (*kolmila*) rake out **4** (*rota*) rummage (poke) about (*bland* in) **5** (*svida i halsen*) rasp **6** *sport.,* *~* [*ribban*] knock the bar off

rival *s3* rival (*om* for; *till ngn* of s.b.); (*konkurrent*) competitor (*t. en plats* for a situation) **riva-lisera** compete (*med ngn* with s.b.; *om* for); *~ med varandra* be rivals (*om att* in + *ing- form*) **ri-valiserande** [-'se:-] *a4* rival[ling] **rivalitet** rivalry (*om* for)

rivande *a4, bildl.* tearing (*fart* pace); (*om pers.*) go-ahead, pushing **rivas** *revs rivits, dep* (*om katt*

e.d.) scratch **rivebröd** [grated] bread crumbs (*pl*)

Rivieran [-ˣä:ran] *r, best. f.* the Riviera

rivig *a1, vard.* go-ahead, pushing **rivit** *sup. av* **riva**

rivjärn grater; *bildl.* shrew **rivning** [ˣri:v-] (*av byggnad e.d.*) demolition, pulling down

rivnings|hus house to be demolished (pulled down) **-kontrakt** short-term lease [in a house which is to be demolished]

riv|start (*av motorfordon*) flying start; *han startade med en ~* he tore off **-styrka** tearing resistance

1 ro *s9* **1** (*frid*) peace; (*ostördhet*) tranquillity; (*stillhet*) quiet[ness]; *få ~* have (be left in) peace; *aldrig få ngn ~ för* get no peace from; *inte få ngn levande ~* have no peace (rest); *han har ingen ~ i kroppen* he is so restless; *i godan ~, i lugn och ~* in peace and quiet; *ta det med ~* take things (it) easy; *det tar jag med ~* that doesn't worry me; *slå sig till ~* (*slå sig ner*) make o.s. comfortable, (*dra sig tillbaka*) retire, (*bosätta sig*) settle down, (*låta sig nöja*) be satisfied (*med* with) **2** *för ~ skull* for fun; *inte för ~ skull* not for nothing

2 ro *v4* row; pull; (*med vrickåra*) scull; *~ ut och fiska* go out fishing [in a rowing boat]; *~ hit med ...!* (*vard.*) hand over ...!, out with ...!; *~ iland med ngt* bring home the bacon, succeed i doing s.th.; *~ upp sig* (*vard.*) better o.s.

roa amuse; (*underhålla*) entertain; *vara ~d av* be interested in (*politik* politics), be fond of, enjoy (*musik* music); *inte vara ~d av* not care about (for); *~ sig* amuse o.s. (*med* with), (*ha roligt*) enjoy o.s., have a good time

rob[e] [rå:b] *s3* [*s5*] robe

robot ['råbåt] *s2* robot; (*-vapen*) [guided] missile; *målsökande ~* homing missile **-bas** guided- -missile base **-vapen** [guided-]missile weapon; *koll.* missilery

robust *a1* robust

1 rock [-å-] *s2* coat; (*kavaj*) jacket; (*över-*) over-coat; (*skydds-*) overall; *för kort i ~en* be too short, not pass muster

2 rock [-å-] *s2 mus.* rock, rock-and-roll, rock-'n'- -roll

1 rocka [-å-] *s1* ray

2 rocka (*dansa*) rock, rock-and-roll, rock-'n'-roll **rock|ad** *s3, schack.* castling **-era** castle

rockhängare coat hanger

rock|musik rock [music] **-ring** hula-hoop (*varu-märke*)

rock|skört coat-tail **-uppslag** lapel **-vaktmäs-tare** cloakroom attendant

rodd *s3* rowing **roddarbänk** (*toft*) thwart **roddare** rower, sculler, oarsman; (*t. yrket*) crew

rodd|båt rowing boat; *AE.* rowboat; *sport.* crew racing boat **-sport** rowing **-tur** row, pull, boating trip **-tävling** boat race, rowing match

rodel ['rä:-] *s2* toboggan, bobsleigh

roder ['ro:-] *s7* rudder; (*ratt, rorkult*) helm (*äv. bildl.*); *flyg.* control surface; *lyda ~* obey (answer) the helm; *lägga om -ret* shift the helm; *sitta vid -ret* be at the helm **-blad** rudder blade **-skada** damage to the rudder (*etc.*)

rodna [ˣrå:d-] (*om sak*) turn red, redden; (*om*

pers.) blush (*av* for; *över* at) **rodnad** *s3* (*röd färg*) redness; flush; (*hos pers.*) blush
rododend|ron [rådå'dendrån] *-ronen -ron, pl äv. -rer* rhododendron
roff|a [ˣråffa] rob; ~ *åt sig* grab, lay hands on **-are** robber; grabber **-eri** robbery
ro|fylld peaceful; (*stilla*) serene **-givande** [-j-] *a4* soothing
rojal|ism [rå-] royalism **-ist** *s3* royalist **-istisk** [-'liss-] *a5* royalist[ic]
rokoko [råkå'kå:] *s9* rococo **-möbel** rococo furniture **-tiden** the Rococo Period
rolig *a1* (*roande*) amusing; (*underhållande*) entertaining, interesting; (*trevlig*) nice, jolly; (*lustig*) funny; ~*a historier* funny stories; *det var ~t att höra* I am glad (pleased) to hear; *det var ~t att du kunde komma* I'm so glad you could come; *så ~t!* how nice!, what fun! **-het** *säga ~er* make (crack) jokes **-hetsminister** joker, wag
roligt *adv* funnily *etc.*; *ha* ~ have a nice time, have fun, enjoy o.s.; *ha* ~ *åt* laugh at, (*på ngns bekostnad*) make fun of
1 roll [-å-] *s3* part (*äv. bildl.*); character; (*om sak*) role; *spela Romeos* ~ play the part of Romeo; *spela en viktig* ~ (*bildl.*) play an important part (role); *det spelar ingen* ~ it doesn't matter, it makes no difference; *det spelar mycket liten* ~ it matters very little; *han har spelat ut sin* ~ he is played out, he has had his day; *falla ur* ~*en* (*bildl.*) let one's mask slip; *leva sig in i* ~*en* lose o.s. in one's part; *det blev ombytta* ~*er* the tables were turned
2 roll [-å-] *s2, flyg.* roll
1 rolla [-å-] *flyg.* roll
2 rolla [-å-] (*måla*) roll on
roller ['råll-] *s2* roller
roll|fack character part **-fördelning** [role] casting **-häfte** *mitt* ~ my script **-innehavare** actor playing a (the) part, member of the cast **-lista** (*hopskr. rollista*) cast **-skapelse** creation of a character **-spel** role-playing
rolös restless
Rom [rɔmm] *n* Rome
1 rom [råmm] *s9* (*fisk-*) spawn, [hard] roe; *lägga* ~ spawn; *leka ~men av sig* (*bildl.*) sow one's wild oats
2 rom [råmm] *s9* (*dryck*) rum
roman *s3* novel **-cykel** cycle novel **-diktning** novel writing
romanesk *a5* romantic
roman|författare novelist, novel writer **-hjälte** hero of (in) a novel
romani ['råmm-, 'rɔmm-, 'rå:-] *s9* Rom[m]any
romanist Romanist, Romance philologist
romanlitteratur fiction
romans [-'mans, -'maŋs] *s3* romance (*äv. mus.*)
romansk [-a:-] *a5* (*om språk, kultur*) Romance, Romanic; (*om konst*) Romanesque, *i Storbritannien* Norman; (*om folk*) Latin
romanssångare ballad singer
romant|ik *s3* romance; (*kulturriktning*) Romanticism **-iker** [-'mann-] romantic; Romanticist **-isera** romanticize **-isk** [-'mann-] *a5* romantic
Romarbrevet [ˣrɔmm-] [the Epistle of Paul the Apostle to the] Romans
romar|e Roman **-inna** Roman woman **-riket** the

Roman Empire **-tiden** the Roman Period
romb [-å-] *s3* rhomb[us] **-isk** ['råmm-] *a5* rhombic [al] **-oid** *s3* rhomboid
romersk ['rɔmm-] *a5* Roman; ~ *rätt* Roman Law; ~*a ringar* (*gymn.*) [hand] rings **-katolsk** Roman Catholic
rom|korn roe corn **-läggning** spawning **-stinn** [hard] roed
rond [rånd, råŋd] *s3* round; (*vakts äv.*) beat; *gå* ~*en* go the rounds, (*om läkare*) do the round **-ell** *s3* (*trafik-*) [traffic] roundabout; *AE.* rotary, traffic circle
rondo ['råndå] *s6, mus.* rondo
rondskål *med.* kidney dish
rondör stoutness; plumpness
rop *s7* **1** call, cry (*av* of; *på* for); (*högt*) shout (*av* of, *for*; *på* for); (*gällt*) yell; (*-ande*) calling, clamour; *ett förtvivlans* ~ a cry of despair **2** (*vissa djurs*) call, cry **3** (*auktions-*) bid **4** *i* ~*et* fashionable, in vogue, popular
ropa call (*äv. om djur*); (*högljutt*) call out, cry, shout; *som man ~r i skogen får man svar* as the question so the answer; ~ *på* *a*) (*ngn*) call, *b*) (*ngt*) call for (*hjälp* help), cry out (*på hämnd* for vengeance), *c*) (*på auktion*) bid on; ~ *in a*) (*skådespelare*) call before the curtain, *b*) (*på auktion*) buy [at an (the) auction]; ~ *upp* call over (out) (*namnen* the names) **ropare** (*megafon*) speaking trumpet, megaphone
ror *s7*, *stå till* ~*s* be at the helm; *se äv. roder* **rorgängare** [ˣrɔ:rjäŋ-] steersman; helmsman (*äv. bildl.*) **rorkult** *s2* tiller **rorsman** *se rorgängare*
1 ros *s1, bot.* rose; *ingen* ~ *utan törnen* no rose without a thorn; *ingen dans på ~r* not all beer and skittles; *med ~or på kinderna* with rosy cheeks
2 ros *s3, med.* erysipelas
3 ros *s7* (*lovord*) praise; ~ *och ris* praise and blame
1 rosa [ˣrɔ:-] *v1* praise, sing the praises of; *den ~r inte marknaden precis* it's not exactly a dazzling success
2 rosa [ˣrå:-] **I** *n el. r* rose[-colour] **II** *oböjligt a* rose-coloured, rosy
rosafärgad *se 2 rosa II*
rosen|blad rose leaf **-bröd** *kokk.* roll **-buske** rose bush **-böna** *bot.* scarlet runner [bean] **-doft** scent of roses **-gård** rose garden **-kindad** [-ç-] *a5* rosy-cheeked **-knopp** rosebud **-krans** rose wreath; (*radband*) rosary **-kål** Brussels sprout **-odling** *abstr.* rosegrowing; *konkr.* rose plantation **-olja** oil of roses **-rasande** raging, furious **-röd** rosy, rosy red; *se allt i -rött* see everything through rose-coloured spectacles **-sten** rose diamond **-trä** rosewood **-vatten** rose-water
rosett *s3* bow; rosette; (*fluga*) bow [tie], butterfly **-fönster** rose window
rosévin rosé
rosig *a1* rosy
rosmarin [-'ri:n, ˣrɔ:s-] *s3* rosemary
rossla [ˣråss-] rattle; *det ~r i bröstet på honom* there is a rattle in his chest, he has a wheezy chest **rosslande** *a4* rattling, wheezing **rosslig** *a1* rhonch[i]al, wheezing **rossling** rattle, wheeze
1 rost [-å-] *s3* **1** (*på järn*) rust; *angripen av* ~ corroded by rust; *knacka* ~ chip the rust off **2** *bot.*

R

rust; mildew, blight

2 rost [-å-] *s2* (*galler*) grate, grid

1 rosta [ˣråss-] (*bli rostig*) rust, get rusty, oxidize; ~ *fast* rust in; *gammal kärlek ~r aldrig* an old love is hard to forget

2 rosta [ˣråss-] **1** *kokk.* roast (*kaffe* coffee); toast (*bröd* bread); ~*t bröd med smör* buttered toast; ~*t vete* puffed wheat **2** *tekn.* roast

rostbeständig rustproof, rust-resisting

rostbiff roast beef

rost|bildning formation of rust, corrosion **-brun** rusty brown

rosteri roasting house (factory), roastery

rostfläck (*på järn*) spot of rust; (*på tyg*) spot of iron-mould; (*på säd o.d.*) speck of rust **rostfri** stainless (*stål* steel); ~ *diskbänk* stainless steel sink **rostig** *al* rusty, corroded

1 rostning [-å-] (*järns*) rusting

2 rostning [-å-] *kokk.* roasting; toasting

rost|röd rust-red **-skydd** rust proofing **-skyddsmedel** anticorrosive agent **-svamp** rust fungus

rosväxter *pl* rosaceous plants

rot *-en rötter* root (*på, till* of); *språkv. äv.* base, radix; (*liten*) rootlet, radicle; ~*en till allt ont* the root of all evil; *dra ~en ur* (*mat.*) extract the square root of; ~*en och upphovet till* the root and origin of; *gå till ~en med* get to the root (bottom) of; *ha sin ~ i* (*bildl.*) have its origin in; *skog på ~* standing forest (timber); *rycka upp med ~en* pull up by the roots, *bildl.* root up, uproot; *slå ~* strike (take) root (*äv. bildl.*)

1 rota (*böka*) poke about; ~ *fram* dig up; ~ *i* rout about in, poke into

2 rota root; ~ *sig* strike (take) root; *djupt ~d* deeply rooted, deep-rooted

rotation rotation; revolution

rotations|axel axis of rotation **-hastighet** speed of rotation **-press** rotary press

rot|blad radical leaf **-blöta** *s1* soak[er], drench [er] **-borste** scrubbing brush

rote *s2, mil.* file; *gymn.* squad **rotel** *s2* (*i ämbetsverk*) department, division; *jur.* section

roter|a rotate; revolve **-ande** *a4* rotating (*hjul* wheel); revolving, rota[to]ry (*rörelse* movement; *motor* engine)

rot|fast [firmly] rooted; *bildl. äv.* securely established **-frukt** root; ~*er* (*äv.*) root crops **-fylla** fill a root cavity in **-fyllning** root filling **-fäst** *a4, bildl.* ingrained **-fästa** root; ~ *sig* (*bildl.*) establish itself (*etc.*) **-knöl** tuber, bulb **-lös** rootless **-löshet** rootlessness **-mos** mashed turnips and potatoes (*pl*) **-märke** *mat.* radical sign

rotogravyr [-ˈvyːr, ˣrɔ:-, ˣrå:-] *s3* rotogravure

rotor *s3* rotor, armature

rots [-å-] *s3* glanders

rot|saker *pl* roots **-selleri** celeriac **-skott** sucker **-stock** rhizome, rootstock **-tecken** *se rotmärke*

rotting [ˣrått-] rattan, cane **-stol** cane (rattan) chair

rottråd root fibre

rotunda [-ˣtunn-] *s1* rotunda

rotvälska [ˣrɔ:t-] *s1* double Dutch, lingo; *prata* ~ (*äv.*) talk gibberish

roué [rɔˈeː] *s3* roué, rake

rouge [rɔːʃ] *s4, s3* rouge

roulad [rɔˈlaːd] *s3, se rulad*

roulett [rɔˈlett] *s3* roulette; *spela* [*på*] ~ play roulette; *vinna på* ~ win at roulette

rov *s7* **1** (*om djur: byte*) prey; *gå på* ~ be on the prowl; *leva av* ~ live [up]on prey **2** (*om människor: röveri*) robbing, robbery; (*byte*) booty, spoil[s *pl*]; *bildl.* prey; *bli ett* ~ *för* fall a prey (victim) to; *vara ute på* ~ be out plundering; *icke akta för* ~ *att* (*bibl.*) not deem it robbery, (*friare*) think nothing of (+ *ing-form*)

rova *s1* **1** (*rotfrukt*) turnip **2** (*klocka*) turnip; *sätta en* ~ fall on one's behind

rov|djur beast of prey **-drift** ruthless exploitation, overexploitation **-fågel** bird of prey **-girig** rapacious; predatory **-girighet** rapacity **-jakt** *bedriva* ~ exhaust the stock of game **-lysten** *se -girig*

rovolja rape (colza) oil

rov|riddare robber baron **-stekel** digger wasp; mud dauber

rubank [ˈruː-] *s2, snick.* trying plane

rubb *i uttr.:* ~ *och stubb* lock, stock and barrel, the whole lot

rubba 1 (*flytta på*) dislodge, move **2** *bildl.* (*störa*) disturb, upset; (*ändra*) alter; (*bringa att vackla*) shake; *han låter inte* ~ *sig* there is no moving him; ~ *inte mina cirklar!* don't upset my calculations!

rubbad *a5* (*sinnes-*) deranged; crazy **rubbning 1** dislodging, moving **2** disturbance; alteration, change; (*nervös*) derangement; *mentala* ~*ar* mental disorders

rubel [ˈruː-] *s9, om myntstycken s3* r[o]uble

rubidium [-ˈbiː-] *s8, kem.* rubidium

rubjn *s3* ruby **-röd** ruby red

rubricer|a 1 (*förse med rubrik*) give a heading to, headline **2** (*beteckna*) classify, characterize **-ing 1** heading **2** classification, characterization

rubrjk *s3* heading, title; (*tidnings-*) headline, caption **-stil** *boktr.* display type

rucka (*rubba*) regulate, adjust; ~ *på ngns vanor* change a p.'s habits

1 ruckel [ˈrukk-] *s7* (*kyffe*) ramshackle house, hovel

2 ruck|el [ˈrukk-] *s7* (*svirande*) revelry, debauchery

ruckl|a revel, lead a dissolute life **-are** rake, fast liver

rucklig *al* (*fallfärdig*) ramshackle, tumble-down

ruckning (*klockas*) regulation, adjustment

ruda *s1* crucian

rudiment *s7* rudiment **-är** *al* rudimentary

rudis [ˈruː-] *oböjligt a, vard.* ignorant

ruelse *s5* remorse, compunction

1 ruff *s2, sjö.* deckhouse, cabin

2 ruff *s9, s7 sport.* rough play

3 ruff *s2, golf.* rough

ruffa play a rough game, foul

ruffad *a5, sjö., vara* ~ have a cabin

1 ruffig *al, sport.* rough.

2 ruffig *al* (*sjaskig*) shabby, seedy-looking; dilapidated

rufs *s7* tousle **rufsa** ~ *till* ruffle, tousle **rufsig** *al* tousled; *vara* ~ *i håret* (*äv.*) have untidy hair

rugby [ˈruggbi, -y] *s9* rugby [football]; *vard.* rugger; *AE. ung.* football

rugga 1 (*ylle e.d.*) tease[l]; ~ *upp* buff, nap **2** (*om fåglar*) moult **rugge** *s2* (*vass- o.d.*) clump; (*tuva*) tuft **ruggig** *a1* **1** (*uppruggad*) teaselled **2** (*fransig*) raw; *bok med ~t snitt* a raw-edged book **3** (*uppburrad*) ruffled (*sparv* sparrow) **4** (*sjaskig*) shabby, frowzy, frowsy; (*gråkall*) bleak, raw; (*kuslig*) gruesome **ruggning** (*fåglars*) moulting **rujn** *s3* ruin; *bildl.* äv. wreck; *det blev hans ~* it brought about his ruin; *på ~ens brant* on the verge of ruin

ruiner|a ruin (*äv. bildl.*), bring to ruin (bankruptcy); *bli ~d* be ruined, go bankrupt, *vard.* go broke; *~ sig* ruin o.s., go bankrupt **-ande** *a4* ruinous

ruin|hög heap of ruins **-stad** ruined city (town)

rulad *s3* **1** *kokk.* roll **2** *mus.* roulade, run

rulett *se* roulett

ruljangsen [-'jaŋ-] *best. form, vard., sköta* [*hela*] *~* run the [whole] show (business)

1 rull|a *s1, mil.* roll, list, register; *införa i -orna* (*äv.*) enrol; *avföra ur -orna* remove from (strike off) the list, *mil.* äv. disenrol

2 rulla *v1* **1** (*förflytta*) roll; (*linda* äv.) reel, wind; (*på hjul*) wheel; (*rep*) coil; *~ tummarna* twirl one's thumbs **2** (*förflyttas*) roll (*äv. om fartyg, dimma, åska*); *låta pengarna ~* make the money fly; *~ med ögonen* roll one's eyes **3** (*med betonad partikel*) *~ av* unroll, unwind, uncoil; *~ ihop* roll up, make a roll of; *~ ihop sig* roll up, (*om orm o.d. äv.*) coil; *~ upp* roll up, wind (coil) [up], (*gardin*) pull up, *bildl.* unfold **4** *rfl* roll [over]; *~ sig i stoftet* cringe, grovel

rullager (*särskr. rull-lager*) roller bearing

rull|ande *a4* rolling (*material* stock); *~ klinik* mobile clinic; *~ planering* ongoing planning; *~ reform* continuous reform **-bana** (*transport-*) roller conveyor; *flyg.* taxi strip, runway **-band** rolling hoop **-bord** tea (service) trolley **-bräde** skateboard **-bälte** inertia-reel seat-belt, inertia safety belt

rull|e *s2* roll; (*film-, pappers-*) reel; (*rep-*) coil; (*spole*) bobbin; (*dikterings-*) cylinder **-fåll** *sömn.* rolled hem **-gardin** [roller] blind; *AE.* shade **-lager** *se* rullager **-ning** rolling; *sjö.* äv. rolling; *sätta i ~* start rolling **-skridsko** roller skate **-sten** boulder **-stensås** boulder ridge **-stol** wheelchair, invalid chair **-sylta** collared brawn **-trappa** escalator; moving staircase **-tårta** Swiss roll

rulta I *s1* podgy woman; (*flicka*) roly-poly, dumpling **II** *v1* waddle, joggle **rultig** *a1* podgy, dumpy

1 rum [rumm] *s7* **1** (*bonings-*) room; *~ åt gatan* (*gården*) front (back) room; *beställa ~ på ett hotell* reserve a room at a hotel; *ett ~ och kök* one room and [a] kitchen **2** (*utrymme*) room; (*plats*) place; *hur många får ~ i soffan?* how many is there room for on the sofa?; *den får inte ~ här* there is no room for it here; *i främsta ~met* in the first place; *komma i första ~met* come first; *lämna ~ för* leave room for (*äv. bildl.*); *lämna* (*bereda*) *~ åt* make room for; *ta stort ~* be bulky, take up a lot of room; *äga ~* take place; (*om möte o.d.*) be held **3** (*rymd*) space; *tid*[*en*] *och ~*[*met*] time and space; *lufttomt ~* vacuum **4** *sjö.* (*last-*) hold

2 rum [rumm] *a1, i ~ sjö* in open water (the open sea)

rumba *s1* rumba

rumla go on a spree, revel **rumlare** reveller, carouser **rummel** ['rumm-] *s7* revelry

rump|a *s1* buttocks (*pl*), posterior, behind; *vard.* backside, rump **-huggen** *a3* tail-docked; *bildl.* truncated, with an abrupt end

rums|adverb adverb of place **-arrest** *mil.* open arrest **-beställning** booking of rooms (a room); (*på skylt*) receptionist **-brist** shortage of accommodation **-förmedling** room agency **-kamrat** roommate; *vara ~er* share a room **-last** hold (inboard) cargo **-lig** *a1* spatial, spacial **-ren** (*om hund o.d.*) house-trained (house-broken) **-temperatur** room temperature

rumstera rummage about (round)

rums|uppassare room attendant **-växt** indoor plant

rumän *s3* Ro[u]manian

Rumänien [-'mä:-] *n* Ro[u]mania

rumän|ier [-'mä:-] *s9* Ro[u]manian **-[i]sk** *a5* Ro[u]manian **-ska 1** (*kvinna*) Ro[u]manian woman **2** (*språk*) Ro[u]manian

run|a *s1* **1** (*skrivtecken*) rune; *rista -or* carve runes **2** (*minnes-*) obituary **-alfabet** runic alphabet

rund I *s3* circle, ring; *poet.* round **II** *a1* round; (*cirkel-*) circular; (*klot-*) spherical; (*cylindrisk*) cylindrical; (*fyllig*) plump, chubby; *en ~ summa* a round (lump) sum; *i runt tal* in round figures, roughly **rund|a I** *s1* round; *gå en ~* go for a stroll **II** *v1* **1** round (*av* off) **2** *sjö.* double

rund|abordskonferens round-table conference **-båge** round arch **-bågsstil** Romanesque (*Storbritannien:* Norman) style

rund|el *s2, trädg.* round [flower]bed; (*rund plats*) circus; (*vindling*) circle **-fil** round file **-flygning** sightseeing flight **-fråga** inquiry, questionnaire **-horisont** *teat.* cyclorama **-hult** *s7, sjö.* spar **-hänt** *a1* generous, liberal **-järn** round [bar-]-iron **-kindad** [-ç-] *a1* round-cheeked, chubby-cheeked **-kullig** *a1, ~ hatt* bowler [hat] **-kyrka** round church **-lagd** *a5* plump, rotund **-lig** *a1* ample; (*-hänt*) generous, liberal; *en ~ summa* a good round sum; *en ~ tid* a long[ish] time **-mask** roundworm **-munnar** *pl, zool.* cyclostomes **-målning** panorama (*äv. bildl.*) **-ning** (*-ande*) rounding; (*-het*) roundness, curvature; (*utbuktning*) bulge, swell **-nätt** small and plump **-radio** broadcasting **-radiostation** broadcasting station **-resa** tour, round trip **-skrivelse** circular letter, circular **-smörja** grease **-smörjning** lubrication, greasing **-stav** *pl* billets **-såg** fret saw, circular saw **-tur** sightseeing tour (trip) **-vandring** tour; *göra en ~ i* make a tour of **-ögd** *a5* round-eyed

runforsk|are runologist **-ning** runology

runga resound **rungande** *a4* resounding; *ett ~ hurra* a ringing cheer; *ett ~ skratt* a roar of laughter

runinskrift runic inscription

runka 1 (*gunga*) rock, wag; (*skaka*) shake (*på huvudet* one's head) **2** *vard.* jerk off, masturbate

runnit *sup. av* rinna

run|olog runologist **-ologi** *s3* runology **-ristare** rune cutter (carver) **-skrift** runic characters (*pl*); (*inskription*) runic inscription **-slinga** runiform ornament **-stav** rune-staff **-sten** runestone, runic stone

runt I *adv* round; ~ *om*[*kring*] round about; *det går ~ för mig* my head is in a whirl; *lova ~ och hålla tunt* promise a lot, fulfil ne'er a jot **II** *prep* round (*hörnet* the corner); ~ *om* around, all round; *resa jorden ~* travel round the world; ~ *hela jorden* the world over; *året ~* all the year round

runtecken runic character

rupie ['ru:-] *s5* rupee

ruptur rupture, breach

rus *s7* intoxication (*äv. bildl.*); *bildl.* ecstasy, transport; *ett lätt ~* a slight intoxication; *sova ~et av sig* sleep o.s. sober; *ta sig ett ~* get drunk; *under ~ets inverkan* under the influence of drink

rusa 1 (*störta fram*) rush, dash; (*flänga*) tear; ~ *fram* rush up (*framåt:* forwards); ~ *i väg* rush (dash, dart) off; ~ *i fördärvet* plunge into ruin; ~ *på dörren* rush for the door; ~ *på ngn* rush (fly) at s.b.; ~ *upp från* spring (jump) up from; *blodet ~de upp i ansiktet på honom* the blood rushed to his face; ~ *upp ur sängen* spring (dash) out of bed **2** (*om motor, ånga*) race; ~ *en motor* race (rev up, gun) an engine

rusch *s3* rush; drive **-ig** *al* energetic; go-ahead

rus|dryck intoxicating liquor, intoxicant **-drycksförbud** prohibition

rush [ruʃ] *s3, sport.* rush

rusig *al* (*berusad*) drunk; intoxicated (*av vin* with wine; *av lycka* with happiness)

rusk *s7* wet (bad) weather; *i regn och ~* in rain and storm

1 ruska *v1, det regnar och ~r* it's wet and windy

2 rusk|a *sl* tuft; (*träd-*) bunch of twigs

3 ruska *v1* (*skaka*) shake; ~ *ngn omilt* give s.b. a good shaking; ~ *liv i* shake into life, (*ngn*) rouse; ~ *på huvudet* shake one's head; ~ *om ngn* give s.b. a shaking

ruskig *al* (*om väder*) nasty, unpleasant; (*om pers.: sluskig*) disreputable, shady; (*om t.ex. kvarter*) squalid; (*otäck*) horrid; *känna sig litet ~* feel a little out of sorts (seedy) **ruskighet** (*vädrets*) nastiness *etc.*; (*otäckhet*) gruesomeness; ~*er* gruesome things, horrors **ruskigt** *adv, vard. äv.* terribly, awfully

ruskprick *sjö.* broom-beacon, broom-perch

ruskväder *se* rusk

rus|ning [ˣru:s-] rush (*efter* for); (*av motor*) racing, overspeeding **-ningstid** rush hour[s *pl*], peak period

russ *s7* Gotland pony

russifi[c]era Russify, Russianize

russin *s7* raisin **-kärna** raisin seed

rusta 1 arm (*till krig* for war); (*utrusta*) equip **2** (*göra i ordning*) prepare, make preparations (*för, till* for); ~ *upp* (*reparera*) do up, repair **3** *rfl* (*göra sig färdig*) get ready, make preparations (*till* for); (*väpna sig*) arm o.s. **rustad** *a5* (*ut-*) equipped; (*beväpnad*) armed **rusthåll** *s7, stå för ~et* (*bildl.*) be responsible for the whole affair, run the show

rustibus[s] *s2* lively child

rustik *al* rustic; (*bondaktig*) countrified; (*grov*) boorish

rust|kammare armoury **-mästare** staff ser-

geant 1st class

rustning 1 (*krigsförberedelse*) armament **2** *konkr.* armour, coat of mail; *fullständig ~* (*äv.*) panoply **rustningsindustri** armament industry

ruta I *s1* square; (*i mönster*) check; (*fönster-*) [window]pane; (*TV-*) screen **II** *v1* (*göra rutig*) check; ~*t papper* cross-ruled (squared) paper

1 ruter ['ru:-] *s9, kortsp., koll.* diamonds (*pl*); *jfr hjärter*

2 ruter ['ru:-] *r, det är ~ i henne* she has got pluck; *det är ingen ~ i honom* he has no go in him

rutformig [-å:-] *al* square-shaped **rutig** *al* check[ed]; chequered

rutin *s3* routine; (*färdighet*) professional experience, practical knowledge; ~*er* (*äv.*) procedures **-arbete** routine work **-erad** [-ˈne:-] *a5* experienced, practised, skilled **-kontroll** routine checkup **-mässig** *al* routine **-mässighet** routine **-mässigt** *adv* by routine; *neds.* mechanically

rut|mönster check (*snedvinkligt:* diamond) pattern **-papper** cross-ruled paper

rutsch|a [ˣruttʃa] slide; (*slira*) skid **-bana** chute, slide; (*vatten-*) water chute

rutt *s3* route

rutten *a3* rotten (*äv. bildl.*); putrid; (*om tänder*) decayed; (*moraliskt äv.*) corrupt, depraved **ruttenhet** rottenness *etc.*; *bildl. äv.* corruption

ruttna become (get) rotten, rot; (*om virke äv.*) decay; (*om kött äv.*) decompose

ruva sit [on eggs], brood; ~ *på* (*bildl.*) brood on; ~ *över* jealously safeguard (*sina skatter* one's treasures) **ruvning** [-u:-] sitting, brooding

1 rya [ˣry:a] *v1* shout

2 rya [ˣry:a] *s1* long-pile rug, hooked rug

ryamatta *se* 2 rya

ryck *s7* **1** (*knyck*) jerk, tug, pull **2** (*sprittning*) start; (*nervöst*) twitch, spasm; *vakna med ett ~* wake up with a start; *snabba ~* fast going, good going **3** *bildl.* (*anfall*) fit, flicker; (*nyck*) whim, freak **4** (*i tyngdlyftning*) snatch

ryck|a *v3* **I 1** (*dra*) pull, jerk; (*hastigt*) snatch; (*våldsamt*) wrench; (*slita*) tear; ~ *ngn i armen* pull s.b. by the arm **2** (*lin, hampa*) pull **3** (*ruska, dra hit o. dit*) pull, tug, jerk; ~ *i dörren* pull at the door; ~ *i klocksträngen* pull the bell[cord]; ~ *på axlarna* shrug one's shoulders (*åt* at); *det -te i mungiporna på henne* the corners of her mouth twitched **4** *mil.* march, move (*mot fienden* against the enemy; *mot målet* towards the objective); ~ *närmare* approach; ~ *ngn in på livet* press s.b. hard; ~ *till ngns undsättning* rush to a p.'s rescue **II** (*med betonad partikel*) **1** *han -tes bort vid unga år* he was snatched away in early life **2** ~ *fram* (*mil. o.d.*) push forward, advance **3** ~ *in a*) *boktr.* inset, *b*) (*om trupper*) march into, *c*) (*om värnpliktig*) join up; ~ *in i en stad* march into (enter) a town; ~ *in i ngns ställe* take a p.'s place **4** ~ *loss* wrench (jerk) loose **5** *hon -tes med av hans berättelse* she was carried along by his story; ~ *med sig* carry away **6** ~ *till* give a start, start; ~ *till sig* snatch **7** ~ *upp a*) (*ogräs*) pull up, *b*) (*dörr e.d.*) pull open; ~ *upp sig* pull o.s. together **8** ~ *ut a*) pull out, (*tand*) extract, *b*) *mil.* (*om trupp*) move out, break camp, (*om värnpliktig*) be furloughed home (released), (*om brandkår o.d.*) turn out

rycken ['rykk-] *i uttr.: stå* ~ stand it, hold one's own; *stå* ~ *för* stand up to **ryckig** *al* jerky; spasmodic; disjointed **ryckning** pull, jerk; (*nervös*) twitch, spasm; *nervösa* ~*ar* (*äv.*) a nervous tic (*sg*) **ryckvis** by jerks, by fits and starts; (*då o. då*) intermittently

rygg *s2* back; *falla ngn i* ~*en* attack s.b. from the rear; *gå bakom* ~*en på ngn* (*bildl.*) go behind a p.'s back; *ha* ~*en fri* have a line of retreat open; *hålla ngn om* ~*en* (*bildl.*) support s.b., back s.b. up; *skjuta* ~ (*om katt*) arch its back; *stå med* ~*en mot* stand with one's back to; *tala illa om ngn på hans* ~ speak ill of s.b. behind his back; *vända ngn* ~*en* (*bildl.*) turn one's back on s.b.; *så snart man vänder* ~*en till* as soon as one's back is turned

rygg|a 1 (*om häst*) back; (*om pers.*) step (*häftigt start*) back; (*dra sig tillbaka*) withdraw (*från from*); (*frukta för*) shrink, recoil (*inför at, before*) **2** *ridk.* back (*en häst a horse*) **-bedövning** spinal anaesthesia **-fena** dorsal fin **-kota** vertebra **-läge** *intaga* ~ lie down on one's back **-märg** spinal cord **-märgsprov** lumbar puncture **-rad** spine, spinal column; *bildl.* backbone **-radsdjur** vertebrate **-radslös** invertebrate; *bildl.* without backbone, spineless **-sim** backstroke **-skott** lumbago **-stöd** *eg.* support for the back; (*på stol e.d.*) back; *bildl.* backing, support **-säck** rucksack, backpack **-tavla** back **-ås** ridgepole **-åsstuga** *ung.* timber cottage open to the roof

ryk|a *imperf. rök, äv. v3* **1** smoke; reek; (*pyra*) smoulder; (*ånga*) steam; (*om damm*) fly about; *det -er in* the chimney is smoking; *rågen -er* the rye is smoking; *slåss så det -er om det* fight so the feathers fly **2** *där rök hans sista slantar* there goes the last of his money; ~ *ihop* fly at each other, (*slåss*) come to blows; ~ *på* (*anfalla*) assault, (*med fråga e.d.*) attack **-ande** *a4* smoking *etc.*; ~ *varm mat* piping hot food; *i* ~ *fart* at a tearing pace

rykt *s3* (*av häst*) dressing; grooming; *språkets* ~ *och ans* the cultivation and improvement of the language **rykta** dress; groom, curry

rykt|as *opers. dep, det* ~ *att* it is rumoured (there is a rumour) that **-bar** *al* famous, renowned; *neds.* notorious; ~ *person* (*äv.*) celebrity **-barhet** fame, renown; *neds.* notoriety; *pers.* celebrity

ryktborste grooming-brush

rykte *s6* **1** (*kringlöpande nyhet*) rumour; report; (*hörsägen*) hearsay; (*skvaller*) gossip; *det går ett* ~ *att* there is a rumour that; *lösa* ~*n* vague rumours **2** (*ryktbarhet*) fame, renown; (*allmänt omdöme om ngn*) reputation, name, repute; *bättre än sitt* ~ better than one's reputation; *upprätthålla sitt goda namn o.* ~ uphold one's fair name and fame; *åtnjuta det bästa* ~ be in the highest repute; *ha dåligt* ~ [*om sig*] have a bad reputation; *ha* ~ *om sig att vara* be reputed to be, have the reputation of being

ryktes|flora crop of rumours **-smidare** scandalmonger **-spridare** spreader of rumours **-spridning** spreading of rumours **-vis** (*som ett*

rykte) by [way of] rumour; (*genom hörsägen*) by hearsay

ryl *s2, bot.* wintergreen, shinleaf

rymd *s3* **1** (*volym*) volume, capacity **2** (*världs-*) space; *bildl.* region, sphere; *tomma* ~*en* vacancy, vacuity; *yttre* ~*en* outer space; *tavlan har* ~ the picture gives a feeling of space **-biologi** astrobiology, exobiology **-dräkt** spacesuit **-farare** spaceman (*fem.* spacewoman), astronaut **-farkost** spacecraft **-flygning** space flight **-forskare** space scientist **-forskning** space research **-färd** space trip (flight) **-färja** space shuttle **-geometri** stereometry; solid geometry **-kapsel** space capsule **-medicin** space medicine **-mått** cubic measure **-promenad** spacewalk **-raket** space rocket **-skepp** spaceship **-sond** space probe **-station** space station (platform) **-teknik** space technique (technology) **-åldern** the Space Age

rymlig *al* (*stor*) spacious, roomy; (*som rymmer mycket*) capacious; ~*t samvete* accommodating conscience

rymling fugitive, runaway; *mil.* deserter

rymma *v2* **1** (*innehålla*) contain, hold; (*ha plats för*) take, have room for, accommodate **2** (*fly*) run away; (*om fånge*) escape; (*om kvinna:* ~ *från hemmet*) elope; ~ *fältet* quit the field

rymmar|e *se* rymling; ~ *och fasttagare* (*lek*) cops and robbers **-färd, -stråt** *vara på* ~ be on the run

rymmas *v2, dep, det ryms mycket i den här lådan* this box holds a great deal; *det ryms mycket på en sida* there is room for a great deal on one page; *det ryms många i rummet* the room holds many people

rym|ning escape, flight; *mil.* desertion **-ningsförsök** attempted escape (*etc.*)

rynka I *s1* (*i huden*) wrinkle; (*på kläder*) crease, fold; *sömn.* gather **II** *v1* **1** *sömn.* gather, fold; ~ *pannan* knit one's brows; ~ *ögonbrynen* frown; ~ *på näsan* wrinkle one's nose, *bildl.* turn up one's nose (*åt* at) **2** *rfl* wrinkle, get wrinkled; (*om tyg*) crumple, crease **rynkig** *al* wrinkled, furrowed

rynktråd drawing thread

rys|a *v3, imperf. äv. rös* shiver, shake (*av köld* with cold); shudder (*av fasa* with terror); *det -er i mig när* I shudder when **-are** thriller

rysch *s7* r[o]uche, frill

rysk *al* Russian

rysk|a *s1* **1** (*språk*) Russian **2** (*kvinna*) Russian woman **-fientlig** anti-Russian **-språkig** *al* (*-talande*) Russian-speaking; (*på ryska*) in Russian **-svensk** Russo-Swedish **-vänlig** pro-Russian

ryslig [ˣry:s-] *al* terrible, dreadful; *vard.* awful **ryslighet** ~*er* horrors, (*begångna*) atrocities **rysligt** *adv* terribly *etc.*; *vard.* awfully (*snällt av dig* nice of you)

rysning [ˣry:s-] shiver; shudder

ryss *s2* Russian

ryssja [ˣryʃa] *s1* fyke (hoop) net

Ryssland ['ryss-] *n* Russia

ryssläder Russia leather

ryta *röt rutit* roar (*åt* at); (*om pers. äv.*) shout, bawl (*åt* at) **rytande** *s6* roar[ing]

rytm *s3* rhythm **rytmik** *s3, ej pl* rhythmics (*pl, behandlas som sg*) **rytmisk** ['rytt-] *a5* rhyth-

R

mic[al]

ryttar|e rider, horseman; (*i kortsystem*) tab, signal **-inna** horsewoman, woman rider **-staty** equestrian statue **-tävling** horse-riding competition

rytteri cavalry

ryttla hover

ryttmästare cavalry captain

RÅ [ärrå] *förk. för riksåklagare*

1 rå *s5, sjö.* yard

2 rå *s5, s4 (gränslinje)* boundary, borderline

3 rå *s6, s5, myt.* sprite, fairy

4 rå *a1* **1** (*okokt*) raw (*fisk* fish); fresh (*frukt* fruit) **2** (*obearbetad*) crude (*malm* ore); (*ogarvad*) raw **3** (*om klimat*) raw, damp and chilly **4** (*primitiv*) primitive; (*grov*) coarse; (*simpel*) vulgar; (*ohövlig*) rude; (*brutal*) brutal; *den ~a styrkan* brute force; *en ~ sälle* a ruffian; *ett ~tt överfall* a brutal assault

5 rå *v4* (*jfr råda*) **1** (*orka*) manage, have the strength (power) to; (*vara starkare, längre*) be the stronger (taller); *jag ~r inte med det* I cannot manage it, it is too much for me; *människan spår, men Gud ~r* man proposes, God disposes; *~ sig själv* be one's own master, have one's time to o.s. **2** (*med betonad partikel*) *jag ~r inte för att* it is not my fault that; *jag ~r inte för det* I cannot help it; *du ~r själv för att* it is your own fault that; *~ med* manage [to carry (lift *etc.*)]; *~ om* be the owner of, possess; *~ på* be stronger than, get the better of, be able to beat

råbalans *hand.* proof sheet

råbandsknop reef (square, flat) knot

rå|barkad *a5, bildl.* coarse, rough-mannered **-biff** scraped raw beef

råbock roebuck

råd *s7, i bet. 2 o. 5 äv. r* **1** (*tillrådan*) advice; (*högtidligare*) counsel; *ett* [*gott*] *~* a piece of [good] advice, *AE. äv.* a pointer; *~ och anvisningar för* hints and directions for; *be ngn om* [*ett*] *~* ask s.b. for advice; *bistå ngn med ~ o. dåd* give s.b. advice and assistance; *fråga ngn till ~s* ask a p.'s advice, consult s.b.; *få många goda ~* receive a lot of good advice; *följa* (*lyda*) *ngns ~* follow (take) a p.'s advice; *ge goda ~* give good advice; *den ~ lyder är vis* he who listens to counsel is wise **2** (*utväg*) means (*sg o. pl*), expedient, way; *finna på ~* find a way out; *veta ~ för* know a remedy for; *det blir väl ngn ~* s.th. is sure to turn up, we shall manage somehow; *det blir ingen annan ~ än att* there is no other alternative than to; *nu vet jag* [*mig*] *ingen levandes ~* now I am at my wits end (completely at a loss) **3** (*församling*) council **4** (*person*) councillor **5** (*tillgång*) means (*sg o. pl*); *ha god ~ till ngt* have ample means for s.th., be able to afford s.th.; *jag har inte ~ att* (*till det*) I haven't got the money to (for it), I cannot afford to (it); *efter ~ och lägenhet* according to one's means

råd|a *v2* **1** (*ge råd*) advise, give advice, counsel; *om jag får ~ dig* if you take my advice; *jag skulle ~ dig att låta bli* I should advise you not to do it; *jag -er dig att inte* I warn you not to **2** *~ bot för* (*på*) find a remedy (cure) for **3** (*härska*) rule; *om jag finge ~* if I had my way; *han vill alltid ~* he always wants to be master; *~ över* have control

of **4** (*förhärska*) prevail, be prevalent; be, reign; *tystnad -er överallt* (*äv.*) silence reigns everywhere; *det -er inget tvivel* there is no doubt; *det -er ett gott förhållande mellan dem* they are on good terms [with each other] **-ande** *a4* prevailing; current (*priser* prices); *under ~ förhållanden* in the circumstances, under present conditions

rådbråka 1 *hist.* break on the wheel **2** *bildl.* (*ett språk*) mangle, murder; *på ~d engelska* in broken English; *~ franska* speak broken French; *känna sig alldeles ~d* be aching in every joint, be stiff all over

råd|fråga consult; seek advice from; *~ advokat* take counsel's opinion **-frågning** [-:å-] consultation; inquiry **-givande** advisory, consulting, consultative **-givare** adviser; *jur.* counsel; (*dipl. e.d.*) counsellor **-givning** [-ji:-] guidance, counselling; advisory service **-givningsbyrå** advisory bureau, information office **-göra** *~ med* confer with; *~ med ngn om ngt* (*äv.*) discuss s.th. with s.b. **-hus** town (*AE.* city) hall **-husrätt** municipal court; (*i Storbritannien*) magistrates' court; (*för svårare brottmål*) central criminal court; *jfr tingsrätt*

rådig *a1* (*fyndig*) resourceful; resolute (*handling* act) **-het** resourcefulness; resolution; presence of mind

rådjur roe [deer]

rådjurs|blick *bildl.* fawnlike glance **-sadel** saddle of venison **-stek** [joint of] venison

råd|lig [×rå:d-] *a1* (*klok*) wise; (*till-*) advisable; *inte ~* (*äv.*) inadvisable **-lös** perplexed, at a loss; *bättre brödlös än ~* better breadless than headless **-löshet** perplexity; irresolution **-man** [borough] magistrate, alderman; (*vid tingsrätt*) judge of a district court; (*vid länsrätt*) judge of a county administrative court **-pläga** deliberate (*om* about) **-plägning** [-ä:-] deliberation, conference **-rum** respite; (*betänketid*) time for reflection (consideration)

råds [-å:-] *se råd 1*

råds|församling council, board **-herre** councillor

råd|slag *se rådplägning*; *hålla ~ se -slå* **-slå** take counsel (*med varandra* together), consult (*med ngn* with s.b.) **-snar** resourceful

råds|republik Soviet republic **-sal** council hall

råd|sturätt *se rådhusrätt* **-vill** *a1* (*villrådig*) irresolute; (*-lös*) perplexed, at a loss **-villhet** irresolution; perplexity

råg *s2* rye

råga I *s1* (*se råge*); *till ~ på allt* to crown everything; *till ~ på eländet* to make matters worse **II** *v1* heap, pile (*faten* the dishes); (*fylla t. brädden*) fill up [to the brim]; *~d* full, brimful; *en ~d sked* a heaped spoonful; *nu är måtet ~t* this is the last straw

råg|ax ear of rye **-blond** light-blond **-bröd** rye bread

råge *s2* full (good) measure

råglas crude glass

råg|mjöl rye flour **-sikt** sifted rye flour

rågummi crude rubber **-sula** crepe-rubber sole

rågåker rye field

rågång boundary [line], (*i skog äv.*) boundary clearing; *bildl.* demarcation line

råhet rawness; *bildl.* coarseness; *(brutalitet)* brutality

1 råk *s2 (is-)* crack, rift

2 råk *s7, s3, ej pl (fisk-)* guts *(pl)*

1 råka *s1, zool.* rook

2 råka *v1* **1** *(träffa rätt)* hit *(målet* the mark) **2** *(möta)* meet; encounter, come across *(äv. ~ på)* **3** *(händelsevis komma att)* happen *(göra* to do) **4** ~ *i bakhåll* fall into an ambush; ~ *i fara* get into danger, *bildl.* be endangered; ~ *i gräl* fall out, start quarreling; ~ *i händerna på* fall into the hands of; ~ *i olycka* come to grief; ~ *i raseri* fly into a rage; ~ *i slagsmål* come to blows; ~ *på avväger* go astray; ~ *ur gängorna (bildl.)* get out of gear, be upset **5** *(med betonad partikel)* ~ *fast* get caught; ~ *in i* get into, *(bli inveckladi)* be involved in; ~ *illa ut* get into trouble; ~ *på* come across; ~ *illa ut för* fall into the hands of *(en bedragare* an imposter), get caught in *(oväder a* storm), meet with *(en olycka* an accident)

råkall raw and chilly, bleak

råkas *dep* meet

rå|kopia proof **-kost** raw vegetables and fruit **-kostare** [-ås-] vegetarian **-kurr** *vard.* punch-up, brawl

råma moo; *bildl.* bellow

rå|material raw material **-mjölk** beestings *(pl), AE.* beastings *(pl)*

råmärke boundary mark; *~n (bildl.)* bounds, limits; *inom lagens ~n* within the pale of the law

1 rån *s7 (bakverk)* wafer

2 rån *s7 (brott)* robbery; *(överfall)* mugging

rån|a rob **-are** robber; mugger **-försök** attempted robbery **-kupp** *[daring]* robbery **-mord** murder with robbery **-mördare** person who has committed murder with robbery

rånock *sjö.* yardarm

rå|olja crude oil **-raka** *s1* potato pancake **-ris** brown rice **-riven** *a5* grated raw **-rörd** *a5 (sylt)* preserved by combining with sugar **-saft** raw juice

råsegel square sail

rå|siden raw silk, shantung **-skala** peel raw; *~d potatis* potatoes peeled before boiling **-skinn** [-ʃ-] *s7, bildl.* tough, brute **-skälla** *vard.* rave aginst s.b., shout at s.b. **-socker** raw (unrefined) sugar **-sop** *s2, vard.* swipe; *ge ngn en ~* swing out wildly at **-sprit** crude alcohol **-steka** *(grönsaker)* fry *[without previously boiling]; -stekt potatis* fried potatoes **-sten** raw limestone

rått|a *s1* rat; *(mus)* mouse *(pl* mice) **-bo** mouse (rat's) nest; *bildl.* rat-infested hovel **-fälla** mousetrap, rattrap **-gift** ratpoison **-hål** mouse (rat) hole **-jakt** *vara ute på ~ (om katt)* be out mouse-hunting **-lort** rat-dung **-svans** rat's tail; *(hårfläta)* pigtail **-unge** young rat (mouse) **-utrotningsmedel** rat exterminator **-äten** *a5* gnawed by rats (mice)

rå|vara raw material **-varukälla** raw-material source **-varuproduktion** primary production **-varutillgång** supply of raw materials

räck *s7, gymn.* [horizontal] bar

räck|a I *s1* row, line, range; *(serie)* series, succession II *v3* **1** *(över-)* hand, pass; ~ *ngn handen* give s.b. one's hand; ~ *en hjälpande hand* extend a helping hand; ~ *varandra handen* shake hands;

vill du ~ mig brödet? would you pass me the bread, please? **2** *(nå)* reach; *(gå ända t.)* extend, stretch; *(fortgå)* last, go on *(i evighet* for ever); *jag -er honom till axeln* I reach (come up) to his shoulder; *kön -te ut på gatan* the queue stretched out to the street; *jag -er inte dit* it is beyond my reach; *dra så långt vägen -er* go to blazes **3** *(förslå)* be enough (sufficient), suffice ; *oljan -er en vecka* there is enough oil for one week; *det -er inte långt* that won't go far; *det -er (äv.)* that will do **4** *(med betonad partikel)* ~ *till* be enough (sufficient), suffice; *få pengarna att ~ till (äv.)* make both ends meet; *tiden -er aldrig till för mig* I can never find enough time; *inte ~ till (äv.)* fall short; ~ *upp* put (stretch) up, *(nå upp)* reach up; ~ *upp handen* raise (put up) one's hand; ~ *ut handen (i trafiken)* make a hand signal; ~ *ut tungan* put out one's tongue *(åt* at)

räcke *s6* rail[ing], barrier; *(trapp-)* ba[n]nisters *(pl)*

räck|håll reach; *inom (utom)* ~ *för ngn* within (beyond) a p.'s reach **-vidd** *eg.* reach; *(skjutvapens e.d.)* range; *bildl. äv.* scope, extent

räd *s3* raid *(mot* on); *(bomb- äv.)* blitz

räd|as *-des -its, dep* fear, dread *(varken fan el. trollen* neither the devil nor his dam)

rädd *a1, n sg obest. form* undviks afraid *(för* of); *(skrämd)* frightened, scared, alarmed; *(~ av sig)* timid, timorous; *(bekymrad)* anxious *(för* about); *mycket ~* very much afraid; *vara ~ för* be afraid (frightened) of, *(sitt liv e.d.)* be in fear of; *vara ~ om* be careful with, take care of; *var ~ om dig!* take care!

rädda save; *(befria ur fara)* rescue, deliver *(från att* from + *ing-form; ur* out of); *R~a barnens riksförbund* Swedish Save the Children Federation; *den stod inte att ~* there was no saving (rescuing) it, it was beyond saving; ~ *ngt undan glömskan* rescue s.th. from oblivion; ~ *undan ngt* save (salvage) s.th.; *~nde ängel* angel of mercy **räddare** rescuer, *(ur nöd)* deliverer

rädd|hågad *a5,* **-hågsen** *a5* fearful, timid, timorous

räddning rescue; *(ur trångmål)* deliverance; *(frälsning)* salvation; *fotb.* save

räddnings|ankare *bildl.* sheet anchor **-arbete** rescue work **-båt** lifeboat **-löst** [-ö:-] *adv,* ~ *förlorad* irretrievably lost **-kryssare** rescue cruiser **-manskap** rescue party **-planka** last resort **-stege** fire escape

rädisa [ˣrädd-, ˣrä:-] *s1* radish

rädsla [ˣrädd-, ˣrä:-] *s1* fear, dread *(för* of)

räffl|a I *s1* groove; *(ränna)* channel; *(i eldvapen)* rifle II *v1* groove, channel; *(eldvapen)* rifle; *~d kant (på mynt)* milled edge

räfsa I *s1* rake II *v1* rake

räfst *s3* inquisition; *(bestraffning)* chastisement; *hålla skarp ~ med* call rigorously to account — **och rättarting** *hålla ~ med* take severely to task, call to account

räjong [-ˈjåŋ] *s3* district, area; *bildl.* range, scope

räka *s1* shrimp; *(djuphavs-)* prawn

räkel *s2, lång* ~ lanky fellow

räkenskap *s3* account; *~er* accounts, books, records; *avfordra ngn ~ för* call s.b. to account for; *avlägga ~ för ngn* render (give) an account to s.b.

R

of; ~*ens dag* the day of reckoning; *avsluta (göra upp)* ~*erna* close (settle) the accounts **räkenskapsår** financial year
räkfiske shrimp-fishing
räkna [ˊräːk-] **1** (*hop-, upp-*) count; (*göra uträkningar*) do sums (arithmetic); (*be-*) calculate, reckon; *lära sig läsa, skriva och* ~ learn reading, writing and arithmetic; ~ *till tio* count up to ten; ~ *ett tal* do a sum; ~ *i huvudet* do mental arithmetic; ~ *med bråk* do fractions; ~ *fel* miscalculate, *bildl.* be mistaken; *det* ~*s inte* that doesn't count; *hans dagar är* ~*de* his days are numbered; ~ *tvätt* count the laundry; *högt (lågt)* ~*t* at a high (low) estimate, at the most (least); *i pengar* ~*t* in terms of money; *i procent* ~*t* on a percentage basis; *förändring i procent* ~*t* percentage change; *noga* ~*t* to be exact; ~ *med* count (reckon) [up]on, (*ta med i beräkningen*) reckon with, allow for; ~ *på ngn* count (rely) on s.b. **2** (*hänföra t.*) count (*till* among); (*anse*) regard, consider, look upon; ~ *det som en ära att* count (consider) it an honour to; ~ *ngn ngt till godo (last)* put s.th. down to a p.'s credit (discredit) **3** (*uppgå till*) number; *hären* ~*de 30 000 man* the army numbered 30 000 men **4** (*med betonad partikel*) ~ *av* deduct, subtract; ~ *efter* count over; ~ *efter vad det blir* see what it makes; ~ *ihop* add (sum) up; ~ *ned* (*ange återstående tid*) count down; ~ *upp* (*pengar*) count out, (*nämna i ordning*) enumerate; ~ *ut* (*ett tal*) work out, (*fundera ut*) think (figure) out
räknare calculator
räkne|bok arithmetic book **-exempel** arithmetic example, sum [to be worked out] **-fel** mistake in calculation, arithmetical error **-färdighet** numeracy **-konst** ~*en* arithmetic **-maskin** calculating machine, calculator **-operation** calculating operation **-ord** numeral **-sticka** slide rule **-sätt** method of calculation; *de fyra* ~*en* the four rules of arithmetic **-tal** sum **-verk** counter, counting mechanism
räkning [ˊräːk-] **1** (*hop-*) counting; (*ut-*) calculation; (*upp-*) enumeration; (*skolämne*) arithmetic; *duktig i* ~ good at figures (arithmetic); *hålla* ~ *på* keep count of; *tappa* ~*en* lose count (*på* of); *gå ner för* ~ (*boxn.*) take the count **2** (*konto*) account (*hos* with); (*nota*) bill, *AE.* check; (*faktura*) invoice; ~ *på* bill (invoice) for; *kvitterad* ~ receipted invoice (bill); *löpande* ~ current account; *specificerad* ~ itemized account; *för ngns* ~ on a p.'s account (behalf); *köp i fast* ~ outright purchase; *köpa i fast* ~ buy firm (outright); *skriva ut en* ~ make out a bill (invoice); *sätt upp det på min* ~*!* put it down to my account!; *ta på* ~ take on account (credit) **3** *göra upp* ~*en utan värden* reckon without one's host; *göra upp* ~*en med livet* settle one's account with life; *hålla ngn* ~ *för ngt* put s.th. down to a p.'s credit; *ta med i* (*lämna ur*) ~*en* take into (leave out of) account; *ett streck i* ~*en för* a disappointment to; *det får stå för din* ~ that is your responsibility; *vara ur* ~*en* be out of the running
räksallad shrimp sallad
räl *s3* rail
räls *s2, s3* rail **-buss** railcar **-skarv** rail joint **-spik** rail (dog) spike
rämna I *s1* (*spricka*) fissure, crevice; (*i tyg*) rent,

slit; (*i moln*) break, rent **II** *v1* crack; (*om tyg*) rend, tear
ränk|er *pl* intrigues, machinations, plots; *smida* ~ intrigue, plot **-lysten** intriguing, scheming **-smidare** intriguer, plotter, schemer
1 ränna *s1* (*fåra*) groove, furrow; (*segel-, is-*) channel; (*flottnings-*) flume; (*transport-*) chute
2 ränna *v2* **1** (*springa*) run; ~ *i väg* run away, dash off; ~ *med skvaller* run about gossiping; ~ *i höjden* shoot up fast **2** (*stöta*) run, thrust (*kniven i ngn* one's knife into); ~ *huvudet i väggen* (*bildl.*) run one's head against the wall
rännande *s6* running; *det har varit ett förfärligt* ~ *här idag* people have been running in and out all day
rännil rill, rivulet
ränn|ing warp **-snara** running noose
ränn|sten gutter, gully **-stensunge** guttersnipe
ränsel *s2* knapsack, kitbag
1 ränta *s1* (*inälvor*) offal
2 ränt|a I *s1* interest; (*räntesats*) rate [of interest] ; ~ *på* ~ compound interest; *bunden (fast, rörlig)* ~ restricted (fixed, flexible) rate of interest; *upplupen* ~ accrued interest; *hög (låg)* ~ high (low) interest (rate); *årlig* ~ annual interest; *ge 4 %* ~ give (yield) 4 %; *löpa med 4 %* ~ carry 4 % interest; *räkna ut* ~*n* compute the interest; *leva på -or* live on the interest on one's capital; *låna* (*låna ut*) *mot* ~ borrow on (lend at) interest; *ge betalt för ngt med* ~ (*bildl.*) pay back s.th. with interest **II** *v1, rfl, se förränta sig*
räntabel [-ˊtaː-] *a2* profitable; remunerative, lucrative **räntabilitet** earning power (capacity); remunerativeness
ränte|avdrag tax relief on the interest on a loan **-avkastning** [interest] yield **-belopp** amount of interest **-beräkning** calculation (computation) of interest **-betalning** payment of interest **-bärande** interest-bearing, interest-carrying **-eftergift** interest remission **-fot** rate of interest, interest rate **-fri** free of interest **-frihet** exemption from interest **-förlust** loss of interest **-garanti** fixed interest rate **-höjning** increase in interest rate **-inkomst** income from interest **-kostnader** *pl* interest costs (charges) **-räkning** *se -beräkning* **-sats** *se -fot* **-sänkning** lowering (reduction) of interest rates **-termin** date of payment of interest
rät *a1* straight (*linje* line); right (*vinkel* angle); *bilda* ~ *vinkel med* form a right angle with, be at right angles to; ~ *maska* knit [stitch] **räta I** *s1* right side, face **II** *v1* straighten (*äv.* ~ *på*); ~ *på ryggen* straighten one's back **rätlinjig** *a1* rectilinear, straight-lined; *bildl.* straightforward
räto|roman *s3* Rhaeto-Roman **-romansk** [-aː-] *a5* Rhaetian, Rhaeto-Romanic **-romanska** [-ˊmaːn-] *s9* (*språk*) Rhaetian, Rhaeto-Romanic
rätsida right side, face; (*på mynt o.d.*) obverse; *inte få ngn* ~ *på ngt* not be able to get a proper hold (make head or tail) of s.th.
1 rätt *s3* (*mat-*) dish; (*del av måltid*) course; *en middag med tre* ~*er* a three-course dinner; *dagens* ~ today's special
2 rätt I *s3* **1** (*-ighet*) right (*till* to, of); (*-visa*) justice; ~ *till ersättning* right to compensation; ~ *till fiske* right to fish; *lag och* ~ law and justice; *få* ~

prove (be) right, (*inför domstol*) win the case; *ge ngn* ~ admit that s.b. is right; *ge ngn* ~ *till* entitle (authorize) s.b. to; *du ger mig nog* ~ *i att* I think that you will agree that; *göra* ~ *för sig* do one's full share, (*ekonomiskt*) pay one's way; *du gör* ~ *i att* you are right in (+ *ing-form*); *ha* ~ be right, (*ha* ~*en på sin sida*) be in the right; *det har du* ~ *i* you are right there; *ha* ~ *till att* have a (the) right to, be entitled to; *komma till sin* ~ (*bildl.*) do o.s. justice, show to advantage; *med* ~ *eller orätt* rightly or wrongly; *med full* ~ with perfect justice (good reason); *ta ut sin* ~ claim one's due; *vara i sin fulla* ~ be quite within one's rights **2** *få* ~ *på* find **3** (*rättsvetenskap*) law; *romersk* ~ Roman law **4** (*domstol*) court [of justice]; *inför högre* ~ before a superior court; *inställa sig inför* ~*en* appear before the court; *sittande* ~ court [in session]; *inför sittande* ~ in open court **II** *al* **1** (*riktig*) right; (*korrekt äv.*) correct; (*vederbörlig*) proper; (*sann*) true; *det* ~*a* what is right, (*vid visst tillfälle*) the right thing; *det enda* ~*a* the only right thing; ~*a ordet* the right (appropriate) word; ~*e ägaren* the rightful owner; *den* ~*e* (*i fråga om kärlek*) Mr. Right; *du är just den* ~*e att* (*iron.*) you are just the right one (person) to; *det var* ~*!* that's right!; *det är* ~ *åt dig!* it serves you right!; *det är inte mer än* ~ *och billigt* it is only fair; *komma på* ~ *bog* (*bildl.*) get on the right tack; *i ordets* ~*a* bemärkelse in the proper sense of the word; *i* ~*an tid* at the right moment; *ett ord i* ~*an tid* a word in season **2** *sticka avigt och* ~ knit purl and plain **III** *adv* **1** (*riktigt*) a) (*före verbet*) rightly, b) (*efter verbet vanl.*) right; ~ *gissat* rightly guessed; *gissa* ~ guess right; *om jag minns* ~ if I remember right [ly]; *går klockan* ~? is the clock right?; *förstå mig* ~*!* don't misunderstand me!; *när man tänker* ~ *på saken* when you come to think of it; *eller* ~*are sagt* or rather **2** ~ *och slätt förneka* simply deny; ~ *och slätt en bedragare* a swindler pure and simple **3** (*ganska*) pretty; quite, rather; *vard.* jolly; *jag tycker* ~ *bra om* (*äv.*) I quite like; ~ *många* a good number of, quite a lot **4** ~ *som det var* all at once (of a sudden) **IV** *adv* (*t. rät*) straight; right; ~ *fram* straight on (ahead); ~ *upp i ansiktet* straight to one's face; ~ *upp och ner* straight up and down

rätt|a I *oböjl. s, i vissa uttr.* **1** *dra ngn inför* ~ bring s.b. before the court; *ställa* (*stämma*) *ngn inför* ~ bring s.b. to trial, arraign s.b.; *stå inför* ~ be brought before the court; *gå till* ~ *med ngn för ngt* rebuke s.b. for s.th. **2** *finna sig till* ~ accommodate (adapt) o.s. (med to), (*trivas*) feel at home; *hjälpa ngn till* ~ set (put) s.b. right, lend s.b. a hand; *komma till* ~ be found, turn up; *komma till* ~ *med* manage, handle, (*pers. äv.*) bring round; *tala ngn till* ~ talk s.b. into being sensible, get s.b. to see reason **3** *med* ~ rightly, justly; *det som med* ~ *tillkommer mig* what right [full]y accrues to me; *och det med* ~ *and* right[ful] ly so **II** *v1* **1** (*räta upp*) straighten (*på ryggen* one's back); (*ordna till*) adjust, put straight **2** (*korrigera*) correct (*fel* mistakes); ~ *till äv.*) set right; ~ *en skrivning* mark a paper **3** (*avpassa*) adjust, accommodate (*efter* to); ~ *sig efter* a) (*om pers.*) obey (*befallningar* orders), comply with, follow (*ngns önskningar* a p.'s wishes), accommodate

(adapt) o.s. to (*omständigheterna* circumstances), conform to, observe (*reglerna* the rules), b) (*om sak*) agree with, follow; *det är ingenting att* ~ *sig efter* it is nothing to go by; *veta vad man har att* ~ *sig efter* know what one has to go by; *det -er och packer eder efter!* those are the orders you have to obey

rättare *jordbr.* [farm] foreman

rättegång *s2* action; legal proceedings (*pl*); [law] suit; (*rannsakning*) trial; (*rättsfall*) case; *anställa* ~ *mot* take legal proceedings (bring an action) against; *förlora en* ~ fail in a suit, lose a case; *ha fri* ~ be entitled to the services of a solicitor and a counsel free of charge

rättegångs|balk code of procedure, rules of court **-biträde** counsel **-fullmakt** power of attorney **-förfarande** course of law **-förhandlingar** *pl* court procedings **-handlingar** *pl* documents of a case; court records **-kostnader** *pl* court (legal) costs, legal expenses **-protokoll** minutes (*pl*) of [court] proceedings **-sak** legal matter **-sal** courtroom

rätteligen by rights, rightly **rättelse** correction, amendment, adjustment; ~*r* (*som rubrik*) errata, corrigenda **rättesnöre** *bildl.* guiding principle, guide; *ta ngt till* ~ take s.th. as a guide **rättfram** *a1* straightforward; (*ärlig*) upright; (*frispråkig*) outspoken

rätt|färdig *a1* righteous, just; *sova den* ~*es sömn* sleep the sleep of the just **-färdiga** (*urskulda*) excuse (*ngns handlingssätt* a p.'s conduct); (*fritaga*) exculpate, vindicate (*ngn från s.b.* from); (*berättiga*) justify; ~ *sig* justify (vindicate) o.s. (*inför* to) **-färdiggöra** justify, vindicate **-färdiggörelse** justification (*genom tron* by faith) **-färdighet** righteousness; justness, justice; *uppfylla all[an]* ~ fulfil all righteousness

rätthaveri *se* rättshaveri

rättighet right; privilege; *ha* ~ *till* have a (the) right to, be entitled to; *beröva ngn medborgerliga* ~*er* deprive s.b. of civil rights; *ha fullständiga* ~*er* (*om restaurang*) be fully licensed

rättika *s1* black (turnip) radish

rättmätig *a1* (*laglig*) rightful, lawful; (*befogad*) legitimate (*harm* indignation); *det* ~*a i* the legitimacy of; ~ *ägare* rightful (lawful) owner

rättning *mil.* alignment, dressing; ~ *höger!* right dress!

rättrogen (*särskr. rätt-trogen*) faithful; (*renlärig*) orthodox; *en* ~ *kristen* a true believer **-het** faithfulness; orthodoxy

rättrådig honest, upright; (*rättvis*) just **-het** honesty, uprightness; justice

rätts|anspråk legal (lawful) claim; *göra sina* ~ *gällande* assert one's legal claims **-begrepp** concept (idea) of justice; *stridande mot alla* ~ contrary to all ideas of right and justice **-fall** legal case **-filosofi** legal philosophy **-fråga** legal question **-förhållande** legal relations (*pl*) (*mellan* between); (*i stat*) judicial system (*sg*) **-handling** legal act (transaction) **-haveri** dogmatism **-haverist** litigious, dogmatic person **-historia** history of law, legal history **-hjälp** legal aid

rätt|sinnad *a5, se* rättrådig

rättsinnehavare assignee, assign

rätt|sinnig *a1* honest, upright **-skaffenhet**

honesty, uprightness **-skaffens** oböjligt a, se **-sinnig**

rätts|kapabel legally competent **-kapacitet** legal capacity (competence) **-kemi** forensic chemistry **-kemisk** of forensic chemistry; ~*t laboratorium* forensic laboratory

rättskipning [-ʃi:-] administration of justice

rättskriv|ning orthography; (*skolämne*) spelling; *ha* ~ do dictation **-ningsregler** *pl* rules for spelling

rätts|kränkning (*civilrätt*) tort, violation of a p.'s rights; (*straffrätt*) criminal offence **-känsla** sense of justice **-lig** *al* (*laglig*) legal; (*domstols-*) judicial; (*juridisk*) juridical; *på* ~ *väg* by legal means; *medföra* ~ *påföljd* involve legal consequences; *vidtaga* ~*a åtgärder* institute judicial proceedings **-läkare** medicolegal practitioner **-lärd** jurisprudent **-lös** without legal rights (protection) **-medicin** forensic medicine, medical jurisprudence **-medicinsk** medicolegal **-medvetande** legal conscience, sense of justice **-ordning** legal system **-praxis** case law, legal usage **-psykiater** forensic psychiatrist **-röta** *ung.* corrupt legal practice **-sak** case, lawsuit **-sal** courtroom **-samhälle** law-governed society **-skipning** se rättskipning **-stat** constitutional state **-stridig** unlawful, illegal, contrary to law **-säkerhet** legal security; law and order

rättstavning [correct] spelling; orthography

rätts|tjänare court usher **-tvist** legal dispute, litigation **-uppfattning** conception of justice **-vetenskap** jurisprudence, legal science **-vetenskaplig** jurisprudential, forensic **-väsen** judicial system, judiciary

rättvis *al* just (*dom* sentence; *sak* cause; *mot* to [wards]); (*opartisk*) impartial (*domare* judge; (*skälig*) fair; *det är inte mer än* ~*t* it is only fair; *hur mycket är en* ~ *klocka?* what is the right time?

rättvisa *s1* justice; (*opartiskhet*) impartiality; (*skälighet*) fairness, (*lag*) law; *för* ~*ns skull* for the sake of justice; *i* ~*ns namn* (*bildl.*) in all fairness; *låta* ~*n ha sin gång* let justice take its course; *skipa* ~ do justice; *göra [full]* ~ *åt* do ... *[full]* justice, do [full] justice to; *överlämna i* ~*ns händer* deliver into the hands of the law

rättvisande *a4* (*om klocka o.d.*) correct; *sjö.* true (*bäring* bearing) **rättvisekrav** demand for justice **rättvisligen** justly, in justice (fairness)

rättvänd *a5* turned right way round (side up)

rättänkande (*särskr. rätt-tänkande*) right-minded, fair-minded

rät|vinge *zool.* orthopteron (*pl äv.* orthoptera), orthopteran **-vinklig** *al* right-angled

räv *s2* fox; *ha en* ~ *bakom örat* always have some trick up one's sleeve; *han är en riktig* ~ he is a sly customer; *surt, sa* ~*en om rönnbären* sour grapes, said the fox; *svälta* ~ (*kortsp.*) beggar-my-neighbour **-aktig** *al* foxy, foxlike; *bildl.* cunning, sly, wily **-farm** fox farm **-gryt** fox earth (den) **-hanne** dog fox, he-fox **-hona** she-fox, vixen **-jakt** fox-hunting; (*en* ~) fox hunt **-lya** se **-gryt** **-rumpa** *bot.* common horsetail **-sax** fox trap **-skinn** fox skin **-spel** *eg.* fox-and-geese; *bildl.* jobbery, deep game; *politiskt* ~ (*äv.*) political intrigue **-svans** foxtail, foxbrush **-unge** fox cub

rö *s6, s7* reed

röd *al* red; (*hög-*) scarlet, crimson; ~ *hanen* the fire fiend; ~*a hund* (*sjukdom*) German measles, rubella; *den* ~*a tråden* the main thread, theme; *bli* ~ *i ansiktet* go red in the face; *det var som ett rött skynke* it was like a red rag to a bull; *i dag* ~ *i morgon död* here today, gone tomorrow; *inte ett rött öre* not a bean (brass farthing); *köra mot rött ljus* jump the lights; *se rött* see red; *R~a halvmånen* the Red Crescent; *R~a havet* the Red Sea; *R~a korset* the Red Cross

röd|akorssyster [-ˣkårs-] Red Cross nurse **-aktig** *al* reddish **-alg** red alga **-bena** *s1, zool.* redshank **-beta** beetroot; *AE.* red beet **-blindhet** red-blindness **-blommig** *bildl.* rosy (*kind* cheek) **-blå** reddish blue, purple **-bok** *bot.* beech **-brokig** ~ *svensk boskap* Swedish red-and-white cattle **-brun** reddish brown **-brusig** *al* red-faced **-flammig** ~ *hy* blotchy complexion **-fläckig** red-spotted **-fnasig** *al, ung.* red and chapped **-färg** red paint; red ochre **-förskjutning** red shift **-gardist** red guard **-glödga** make red-hot **-gråten** *a5* (*om pers*) red-eyed; -*gråtna ögon* eyes red with weeping **-gul** orange[-coloured] **-hake** robin [redbreast] **-hårig** redhaired; (*om pers.*) red-headed

röding char

röd|kantad *a5* red-bordered; ~*e ögon* red-rimmed eyes **-kindad** *a5* red-cheeked, rosy-cheeked **-klöver** red clover **-krita** red chalk (crayon) **-kål** red cabbage **-luva** *R~n* Little Red Riding Hood **-lätt** ruddy **-lök** red onion **-mosig** red bloated **-näst** [-ä:-] *al* red-nosed **-och vitrandig** with red-and-white stripes **-ockra** red ochre **-penna** red pencil **-prickig** dotted red **-randig** striped red, red-striped **-rutig** red-chequered, red-check **-räv** red fox **-skinn** red-skin; American (Red) Indian **-skäggig** red-bearded **-sot** dysentery **-spotta** *s1* plaice **-sprit** methylated spirit **-sprängd** *al* bloodshot (*ögon* eyes) **-spätta** *s1, se -spotta* **-stjärt** red-start **-vin** red wine; (*Bordeaux*) claret; (*Bourgogne*) burgundy **-vinge[trast]** redwing **-vinstoddy** mulled claret **-ögd** *al* red-eyed

1 röja [ˣröjja] *v2* **1** (*förråda*) betray; (*yppa*) reveal, disclose; ~ *sig* betray o.s., give o.s. away **2** (*ådagalägga*) display, show

2 röj|a [ˣröjja] *v2* (*bryta, odla upp*) clear (*mark* land); (*gallra*) thin; ~ *väg för* clear a path for, *bildl. äv.* pave the way for; ~ *undan* clear away, remove; ~ *upp* tidy up; ~ *ngn ur vägen* make away with s.b.

röjdykare frogman

röjning clearance; *konkr.* clearing **röjningsarbete** clearance work **röjningsmanskap** clearance squad

1 rök *imperf. av ryka*

2 rök *s2* smoke; (*ånga*) steam; (*i sht illaluktande*) fume[s *pl*]; *gå upp i* ~ go up (*bildl. äv.* end) in smoke; *ingen* ~ *utan eld* no smoke without fire; *vi har inte sett* ~*en av honom* we have not seen a trace of him

rök|a *v3* **1** (*om tobak*) smoke; *generar det dig om jag -er?* do you mind my smoking?; ~ *cigaretter* smoke cigarettes; ~ *in en pipa* break in a pipe **2** (*om matvaror*) smoke[-cure]; (*sill äv.*) bloat **3**

(*mot ohyra, smitta*) fumigate; ~ *ut* smoke out
rök|are smoker; *icke* ~ (*ej* -*kupé*) nonsmoker
-avvänjning antidotal treatment for smokers
-bildning smoke generation (production)
-bomb smoke bomb **-bord** smoker's table **-dy-kare** smoke-helmeted fireman
rökelse incense **-kar** censer, thurible
rök|eri smokehouse, curing house **-fri** free from
smoke; smokeless (*bränsle* fuel) **-fylld** smoke-
filled **-fång** [fume] hood, smoke bonnet **-för-bud** ban on smoking **-förgiftad** *a5* poisoned by
smoke, asphyxiated **-gas** flue gas; fumes (*pl*)
-gång *s2* [smoke] flue **-hosta** smoker's cough
(hack) **-huv** chimney cowl; smoke hood
rök|ig *a1* smoky **-kupé** smoking compartment,
smoker; (*anslag*) for smokers **-lukt** smell of
smoke **-moln** cloud of smoke
rök|ning [-ö:-] smoking; (*desinfektion*) fumiga-
tion; ~ *förbjuden* no smoking; ~ *tillåten* smoking,
for smokers **-paus** smoking break **-pelare** column of smoke **-ridå** smoke screen **-ring** smoke
ring **-rock** smoking jacket **-rum** smoking
(smoke) room **-smak** *få* ~ get a smoky taste **-su-gen** dying for a smoke **-svag** (*om krut*) smokeless **-svamp** puffball
rökt [-ö:-] *a4* smoked; (*om träslag*) fumed (*ek*
oak); ~ *sill* (*ung.*) bloater, kippered herring; ~
sidfläsk bacon
rök|topas smoky topaz **-verk** *s7, ej pl* smokes
(*pl*); *har du* ~? have you anything to smoke?
rölleka *s1* yarrow, milfoil
rön *s7* (*erfarenhet*) experience, (*pl äv.* findings);
(*iakttagelse*) observation **röna** *v3* meet with (*för-ståelse* understanding); experience (*motgång a*
setback); ~ *livlig efterfrågan* be in great demand
rönn *s2* [European] mountain ash, rowan **-bär** ro-
wanberry
röntga X-ray, take an X-ray
röntgen ['rönt-] *r* roentgen **-anläggning** X-ray
equipment (unit) **-apparat** X-ray machine (apparatus) **-avdelning** X-ray (radiotherapy) department **-behandling** X-ray treatment, radiotherapy **-bestrålning** X-raying **-bild** X-ray picture, radiograph **-diagnostik** X-ray (radio) di-
agnostics (*pl, behandlas som sg*) **-fotografe-ring** X-ray photography, radiography **-genom-lysning** fluoroscopy, radioscopy **-läkare, -olog** radiologist, roentgenologist **-plåt** X-ray
plate **-stråle** X-ray **-strålning** emission of X-
-rays, X-ray emission **-terapi** radiotherapy **-un-dersökning** X-ray (radiograph) examination
rör *s7* 1 *tekn.* tube; *koll.* tubing; (*lednings-*) pipe,
koll. piping; *elektron.* valve; *AE.* tube 2 *bot.*
reed; (*bambu-, socker-*) cane; *spanskt* ~ Spanish
reed 3 *se rörskridsko*
rör|a I *s1* mess; mishmash; (*virrvarr*) confusion,
muddle; *en enda* ~ a fine (regular) mess II *v2* 1
(*sätta i -else, rubba*) move, stir (*i gröten* the porridge; *en lem* a limb); *inte* ~ *ett finger* not lift (stir)
a finger; ~ *på sig* move, (*motionera*) get some exercise; *rör på benen!* hurry up!, get going! 2 (*be-*)
touch; *se men inte* ~! look but don't touch [any-
thing]!; *allt han rör vid tjänar han pengar på* he
makes money out of everything he touches 3
(*framkalla -else hos*) move (*till tårar* to tears) 4
(*angå*) concern, affect; *den här saken rör dig inte*

this is none of your business; *det rör mig inte i ryg-gen* it doesn't affect me (I don't care) in the least
5 (*med betonad partikel*) ~ *i* stir in, stir into; ~
ihop (*kokk. o.d.*) stir (mix) together; *han* ~
ihop alltsammans (*bildl.*) he got it all muddled
up; ~ *om i brasan* poke (rake, stir) up the fire; ~
upp damm raise (stir up) dust; ~ *upp himmel och
jord* move heaven and earth; ~ *ut med vatten* thin
down (dilute) with water 6 *rfl* move; stir; *inte* ~
sig ur fläcken not stir (budge) from the spot; ~ *sig
med grace* carry o.s. gracefully; *inte en fläkt -de
sig* not a breath of wind was stirring; *det -de sig
om stora summor* it was a question of large sums,
a lot of money was involved; *ha mycket pengar att
~ sig med* have a lot of money at one's disposal;
vad rör det sig om? what is it all about? **rörande**
I *a4* touching, moving, pathetic II *prep* concerning, regarding, as regards, as (in regard) to
rörarbetare plumber
rörd [-ö:-] *a5* moved (*äv. bildl.*); *kokk.* stirred;
(*be-, vid-*) touched; *rört smör* creamed butter;
djupt ~ deeply moved (touched)
rördrom [-åmm] *s2* bittern
rörelse 1 (*ändring av läge el. ställning*) movement; (*åtbörd äv.*) gesture, motion (*med handen*
of the hand); (*motion*) exercise; (*oro, liv*) commotion, bustle, agitation; (*gång*) motion; *mycket
folk var i* ~ a lot of people were on the move
(were about); *sätta en maskin i* ~ set a machine
in motion (moving), start a machine; *sätta sig i* ~
begin to move; *sätta fantasin i* ~ stimulate (excite) the imagination; *starka krafter är i* ~ *för att*
(*bildl.*) strong forces are at work to 2 (*affärs-*)
business, firm; (*verksamhet*) activity 3 (*ström-
ning, folk-*) movement 4 (*själs-*) emotion
-energi motive (kinetic) energy **-frihet** freedom of movement, liberty of action **-förmåga**
locomotive faculty; ability to move **-hindrad**
disabled **-idkare** owner of a firm, businessman
-kapital working capital **-riktning** direction of
movement
rörformig [-å-] *a1* tubular
rörig *a1* muddled, confused
rörled|ning piping, conduit; (*större*) pipeline
-ningsentreprenör plumbing contractor
rörlig ['rö:r-] *a1* 1 (*om sak*) movable; moving;
(*lätt-*) mobile; ~*a delar* movable (*i maskin:* moving) parts; ~*a kostnader* variable costs; ~*t kapital*
working capital 2 (*om pers.*) (*snabb*) agile, brisk;
(*livlig*) alert; (*verksam*) active; ~*t intellekt* versatile intellect; *vara på* ~ *fot* be moving about, be
on the move; *föra ett* ~*t liv* lead an active life **-het**
1 mobility; (*räntas e.d.*) flexibility; ~ *på arbets-marknaden* mobility of labour 2 agility, briskness; alertness; activity
rör|läggare pipe-layer **-läggeri** pipe-laying
-mokare plumber **-mokeri** 1 (-*installation*)
plumbing 2 *se rörledningsentreprenör* **-post**
pneumatic dispatch (tube system) **-skridsko**
tubular skate **-socker** cane sugar **-sopp** [-å-] *s2*
boletus **-tång** pipe wrench
1 rös *imperf. av rysa*
2 rös *s7, se röse*
rösa mark [with boundary-stones] **röse** *s6* cairn,
mound of stones
röst *s3* 1 (*stämma*) voice; *ha* (*sakna*) ~ have a

R

good (have no) voice; *med hög (låg)* ~ in a loud (low) voice; *känna igen ngn på* ~*en* recognize s.b. by his (*etc.*) voice; ~*- och talvård* voice and speech care **2** (*vid -ning*) vote; *avge sin* ~ cast one's vote (*för* for); *ge sin* ~ *åt* give one's vote to; *nedlägga sin* ~ abstain from voting

röst|a vote (*för, på* for); ~ *blankt* hand in a blank voting paper; ~ *ja (nej)* vote for (against); ~ *öppet (slutet)* vote by yes and no (by ballot); ~ *om ngt* put s.th. to the vote; ~ *på högern* vote Conservative

röst|ande *a4* voting; *de* ~ the voters **-berättigad** entitled to vote **-etal** number of votes; *vid lika* ~ if the votes are equal **-fiske** *polit.* angling for votes **-kort** poll card **-läge** pitch [of the voice] **-längd** electoral register **-ning** voting, vote; (*sluten*) ballot[ing] **-omfång** voice range (compass) **-plikt** voting duties (*pl*) **-resurser** *pl* vocal powers **-räkning** counting of votes **-rätt** right to vote; franchise; suffrage; *allmän (kvinlig)* ~ universal (woman's, women's) suffrage; *fråntaga ngn* ~*en* disfranchise s.b., deprive s.b. of the right to vote **-rättsreform** franchise reform **-rättsålder** voting age **-sedel** ballot (voting) paper **-siffra** number of votes, poll **-skolning** voice training **-springa** *anat.* glottis **-styrka 1** strength (power) of the (one's) voice **2** *polit.* voting strength **-värvning** canvassing [for votes] **-övervikt** majority [of votes]

röt *imperf. av ryta*

röt|a *I s1* **1** rot, decay; putrefaction **2** *vard.* luck **II** *v1, v3* **1** (*skadas av* ~) rot **2** (*lin, hampa*) ret **-månad** ~*en* the dog days (*pl*) **-månadshistoria** silly-season story **-ning** [-ö:-] rotting; retting **-skada** decay damage **-slam** sludge **-svamp** mould fungus

rött *s, best. form det röda* red; *se* ~ see red; *jfr röd*

rötägg *bildl.* bad egg, failure

röv *s2, vard.* arse, *AE.* ass

röva rob (*ngt från ngn* s.b. of s.th.); ~ *bort* abduct

rövarband gang of robbers

rövar|e robber; *leva* ~ (*leva vilt*) lead a dissolute life, (*fara vilt fram*) play havoc, raise hell; *leva* ~ *med ngn* lead s.b. a dance **-historia** cock-and-bull story **-händer** *pl, falla i* ~ be captured by bandits, *bildl.* fall among thieves **-hövding** robber chief **-näste** haunt of robbers, den of thieves **-pris** daylight robbery; *betala ett* ~ pay through the nose; *få ngt för* ~ get s.th. dirt cheap

röveri robbery, plundering

S

Saar [sa:r] *n* the Saar, Saarland **-området** the Saar territory

sabbat ['sabb-] *s3* Sabbath; *fira* ~ observe (keep) the Sabbath

sabbats|brott breach of the Sabbath **-dag** Sabbath [day] **-år** sabbatical [year]

sabel ['sa:-] *s2* sabre **-balja** scabbard, sabre sheath **-fäktning** fencing with sabre **-fäste** sabre hilt **-hugg** sabre cut **-skrammel** clank of swords; *bildl.* sabre rattling

sabin *s3* Sabine **sabinsk** [-i:-] *a5* Sabine

sabla [ˣsa:-] **I** *v1*, ~ *ner* (*bildl.*) slash, tear to pieces **II** *oböjligt a* cursed, blasted

sabotage [-'ta:ʃ] *s7* (*göra* commit) sabotage **sabotagegrupp** *mil.* sabotage unit **sabotera** sabotage **sabotör** saboteur

sachsare [ˣsaksare] Saxon **Sachsen** ['saksen] *n* Saxony **sachsisk** ['saksisk] *a5* Saxon

sacka ~ *efter* lag behind, straggle

sackarin *s4* saccharine

sadducé *s3* Sadducee

sade *vard. sa, imperf. av säga*

sadel ['sa:-] *s2* **1** saddle; *bli kastad ur* ~*n* be unseated; *sitta säkert i* ~*n* sit one's horse well, *bildl.* sit firmly in the saddle; *stiga i* ~*n* mount one's horse; *utan* ~ bareback **2** *slaktar. o. kokk.* saddle **3** (*på fiol*) nut **-bom** (*stomme*) saddletree; (*hög kant*) saddlebow **-brott** saddle-gall **-gjord** saddle-girth, bellyband **-knapp** pommel [of a saddle] **-makare** saddler, harness-maker **-makeri** saddlery **-plats** (*på kapplöpningsbana*) paddock **-täcke** saddle-blanket **-väska** saddlebag

sad|ism sadism **-ist** sadist **-istisk** [-'diss-] *a5* sadistic

sadla [ˣsa:d-] saddle, put the saddle on; ~ *av* unsaddle; ~ *om* (*byta åsikt*) change one's opinion, (*byta yrke*) change one's profession

SAF [ˣessa:eff] *förk. för Svenska Arbetsgivareföreningen* the Swedish Employers' Confederation

safari [-'fa:-] *s3* safari

saffian *s3, s4* saffian; morocco

saffran *s3, s4* saffron **saffransgul** saffron [yellow]

safir *s3* sapphire **-blå** sapphire [blue]

saft *s3, juice;* (*kokad med socker*) [fruit] syrup; (*växt-*) sap; (*kött-*) gravy; *bildl.* pith

saft|a make fruit syrup (*etc.*) out of; ~ *sig* make sap, run to juice **-flaska** bottle of juice (*etc.*) **-ig** *a1* juicy (*äv. bildl.*); (*om ört*) succulent; (*om kött*) juicy; *bildl.* highly flavoured, spicy; ~*a eder* juicy oaths **-lös** juiceless, dry **-ning** juice-making, syrup-making **-press** juice squeezer **-sås** *ung.* fruit sauce

sag|a *s1* fairy tale (story); (*nordisk*) saga; *berätta* -*or* tell fairy stories (*äv. bildl.*); *dess* ~ *är all* it is finished and done with, that's the end of it

sag|d *a5* said; *det är för mycket -t* that is saying too much; *det är inte -t* it is not so certain; *bra -t!* well put!; *nog -t* suffice it to say, *-t och gjort* no sooner said than done; *som -t var* as I said [before]

sagen ['sa:-] *i uttr.: den bär syn för* ~ it tells its own tale, it speaks for itself **sagesman** informant, spokesman, authority

sago|berättare storyteller **-bok** storybook, fairy-tale book **-djur** fabulous animal **-figur** character (figure) from a fairy tale

sagogryn *koll.* pearl sago (*sg*)

sago|kung legendary king; (*i barnsaga*) fairy-tale king **-land** wonderland, fairyland **-lik** fabulous; *en* ~ *tur* [a] fantastic [piece of] luck **-prins**

fairy[-tale] prince **-slott** fairy castle
sagt *sup. av* säga
Sahara ['sa:hara] *n* the Sahara
sak *s3* **1** *konkr.* thing; *(föremål äv.)* object, article; *~er (tillhörigheter)* belongings; *en sällsynt ~ (äv.)* a curiosity **2** *abstr. o. bildl.* thing; *(angelägenhet)* matter, affair, subject; *(uppgift)* task; *(omständighet)* circumstance; *(rättegångs-)* cause *(äv. friare)*; *~en i fråga* the matter in question; *~en är den att* the fact is that; *det är en ~ för sig* that is another story (matter); *det är en annan ~* that is quite a different matter; *det är hela ~en* there is nothing more to it, that's all there is to it; *det är min ~* it is my business; *det är inte min ~ att* it is not for me to; *det är ~ samma* it makes no difference, it doesn't matter; *för den goda ~ens skull* for the good of the cause; *göra ~ av ngt (jur.)* take s.th. to court; *hålla sig till ~en* keep (stick) to the point; *som hör till ~en* pertinent; *som inte hör till ~en* irrelevant; *i ~* essentially; *ha rätt i ~* be right in the main; *kunna sin ~* know one's job; *det är inte så farligt med den ~en* that is nothing to worry about, it is not so bad after all; *säk er på sin ~* sure of one's point; *söka ~ med ngn* try to pick a quarrel with s.b.; *till ~en!* to the point!; *han tog ~en kallt* he took it calmly, it left him cold
saka *kortsp.* discard, throw away
saker ['sa:-] *oböjligt a, jur.* guilty *(till* of) **-förklara** *~ ngn* find s.b. guilty
sak|fel factual point **-fråga** point at issue **-förare** lawyer, solicitor, attorney, counsel **-förhållande** fact, state of affairs **-granska** check facts
sak|kunnig expert; competent; *en ~* an expert (a specialist) *(på* in); *från ~t håll* in expert (authoritative) circles; *tillkalla ~a* call in experts **-kunnighet** *se* -kunskap **-kunnigutlåtande** expert opinion (report) **-kunskap** expert knowledge; *~en (de -kunniga)* the experts, competent advisers *(pl)*
saklig [-a:-] *a1 (t. saken hörande)* to the point, pertinent; *(grundad på fakta)* founded on facts; *(objektiv)* objective, unbiased; *(nykter)* matter-of-fact **-het** pertinence; objectivity
saklöst [-ö:-] *(ostraffat)* with impunity; *(utan skada)* easily, safely
sakna [ˣsa:k-] **1** *(inte äga)* lack; *(vara utan)* be devoid of *(mänskliga känslor* human feelings); be without *(mat* food); *~ humor* have no sense of humour; *~ all grund* be totally groundless; *~ ord* be at a loss for words; *det torde inte ~ intresse* it will not be without interest **2** *(märka frånvaron el. förlust av)* miss, not find, *(starkare)* feel the loss of; *~r du ngt?* do you miss anything?, *(har du förlorat ngt?)* have you lost anything?
saknad [ˣsa:k-] **I** *a5* missed; *(borta)* missing **II** *s3* **1** *(brist)* lack, want *(på* of); *(frånvaro)* absence *(av* of); *i ~ av* in want of, lacking **2** *(sorg, längtan)* regret; *känna ~ efter* miss; *~en efter henne är stor* her loss is deeply felt
sakna|s [ˣsa:k-] *dep (fattas)* be lacking; *(böra finnas)* be wanting; *(vara borta)* be missing; *tio personer -des* ten persons were missing (reported lost)
sakprosa ordinary prose
sakral *a1* sacred

sakrament *s7* sacrament **sakramental** *a1* sacramental **sakramentskad** [-'ment-] *a5, vard.* damned, confounded
sakregister subject (analytical) index
sakristia *s1* sacristy, vestry **sakrosankt** [-'saŋkt] *a1* sacrosanct
sakskäl practical reason, positive argument
sakta I *adv (långsamt)* slowly; *(tyst)* low; *(dämpat)* softly, gently; *~ men säkert* slow but sure; *~ i backarna!* gently!, take it easy!, gently does it!; *klockan går för ~* the clock is slow; *~! (sjö.)* easy ahead! **II** *al (långsam)* slow; *(tyst, svag)* low *(mumlande* murmur), soft *(musik* music), gentle *(bris* breeze); *vid ~ eld* over a slow fire **III** *v1 (minska farten [hos])* slacken; *(dämpa)* muffle, hush; *~ farten (äv.)* slow down; *~ sig (minska)* decrease, abate; *klockan ~r sig* the clock is losing [time]
sakt|eligen *se* sakta *I* **-färdig** slow, tardy **-mod** meekness **-modig** meek; *saliga äro de ~a* blessed are the meek
sak|uppgift fact **-ägare** *jur. (målsägare)* plaintiff; *(part)* party to a case
sal *s2* hall; *(på sjukhus)* ward; *allmän ~* public ward
sala *vard.* club together *(till* for)
saladjär *s3* salad bowl
salamander [-'mann-] *s2* salamander
salami [-'la:-] *s3* salami
saldera strike a balance, balance [up]
saldo ['sall-] *s6* balance; *ingående (utgående) ~* balance brought (carried) forward; *~ mig till godo* balance in my favour **-besked** advice of the balance of an account, balance certificate
salicylsyra [-ˣsy:l-] salicylic acid
salig *a1* **1** *(frälst, säll)* blessed **2** *(om avliden)* late; *~ kungen* the late [lamented] king; *i ~ åminnelse* of blessed memory; *var och en blir ~ på sin fason* everybody is happy in his own way **-en ~ avsomnad** dead and gone to glory **-förklara** beautify **-görande** [-j-] *a4* saving; *den allena ~ (vard.)* the one and only **-het** blessedness; *(stor lycka)* bliss, felicity
salin *s3* saline; saltworks *(pl, behandlas som sg)*
saliv *s3* saliva **-avsöndring** salivary secretion **-sugare** salivary extractor
sallad [ˣsall-, 'sall-] *s3, bot.* lettuce; *(maträtt)* salad
sallads|bestick salad servers *(pl)* **-huvud** lettuce **-skål** salad bowl
salmiak ['sall-] *s3* sal ammoniac
salmonella [-ˣnella] *s1* salmonella
salning [ˣsa:l-] *sjö.* crosstrees *(pl)*
Salomo Solomon; *~s Höga Visa* the Song of Solomon **salomonisk** [-'mɔ:-] *a5* Solomonic, Solomonian
salong [-'låŋ] *s3* saloon; *(i hem)* drawing room, parlour; *(teater- etc.)* auditorium; *~en (publiken)* the audience
salongs|berusad *a5* tipsy, merry **-fähig** *se* -mässig **-gevär** small-bore rifle **-kommunist** parlour communist **-lejon** society lion **-mässig** *al* fit for the drawing room; *(om pers.)* polite; *inte ~ (om pers.)* not presentable **-uppassare** *sjö.* waiter **-vagn** saloon *(AE. parlor)* car
salpeter *s2* saltpetre; nitre; *(kali-)* potassium ni-

S

trate **-syra** nitric acid
salsmöbel [-a-] dining-room furniture
salt I *s4* salt; *attiskt* ~ Attic salt (wit) **II** *a1* salt, salty; ~ *fläsk* salt[ed] pork
salt|a ~ [*på*] salt, sprinkle with salt; ~*d* salted, pickled; *en* ~*d räkning* a stiff bill; ~ *in* salt, brine **-gruva** salt mine **-gurka** pickled gherkin **-halt** salinity, salt content **-haltig** *a1* saline, briny **-kar** saltcellar **-korn** grain of salt **-kött** salt (*konserverat:* corned) beef **-lake** brine, pickle; *lägga i* ~ pickle **-lösning** saline solution **-ning** salting; pickling
saltomortal *s3* (*göra en* turn a) somersault
salt|sjö salt lake **-stod** pillar of salt **-ströare** salt shaker **-stänk** salt spray **-syra** hydrochloric acid **-vatten** salt water, brine **-vattensfisk** saltwater fish, sea fish
salu *s, endast i uttr.: till* ~ for (on) sale **-bjuda** offer for sale **-föra** *se -bjuda;* (*torgföra*) market, deal in **-hall** market hall **-stånd** booth, stand, stall
salut *s3* salute **-era** salute
salu|torg market[place] **-värde** market value
1 salva *s1* (*gevärs-* etc.) volley; salvo
2 salva *s1* ointment, salve
salvburk ointment jar
salvelse unction, pathos **-full** unctuous; *vard.* soapy
salvia ['sall-] *s1, bot.* sage
sam [samm] *imperf. av simma*
sam|arbeta [ˣsamm-] collaborate; (*samverka*) cooperate **-arbete** collaboration; cooperation
samarbets|avtal [ˣsamm-] agreement for cooperation, collaboration agreement **-man** collaborator **-nämnd** cooperation council (committee, commission) **-vilja** cooperativeness; *visa* ~ show that one is willing to cooperate **-villig** cooperative
samarit *s3* Samaritan; (*sjukvårdare*) first-aid man; *den barmhärtiga* ~*en* the good Samaritan **-kurs** first-aid course
samba *s1* samba
sam|band [ˣsamm-] connection; *ställa* (*sätta*) *ngt i* ~ *med* connect (relate, associate) s.th. with **-bandsofficer** liaison officer **-beskattning** joint taxation (assessment)
sambo [ˣsamm-] *s5, vard.* (*som jämställs med make/maka*) common law husband (wife)
same ['sa:-] *s5* Lapp, Laplander **-slöjd** Lapp handicrafts
samexistens [ˣsamm-] coexistence
sam|fund [ˣsamm-] *s7* association; (*lärt*) [learned] society, academy; (*religiöst*) denomination, communion **-fälld** *a5* **1** (*gemensam*) joint, common; (*enhällig*) unanimous **2** *jur.* joint (*egendom* property) **-fällighet** *abstr.* relationship; *konkr.* association, society **-färdsel** *s9* communication[s *pl*], intercourse; (*trafik*) traffic **-färdsled** route [of communication] **-färdsmedel** means of communication; (*transportmedel*) means of transport **-förstånd** concert, concord; (*enighet*) unity; (*hemligt* secret) understanding; (*i brottslig bemärkelse*) collusion; *komma till* [*ett*] ~ come to an understanding **-förståndspolitik** policy of compromise
samgående fusion, cooperation

samhälle [ˣsamm-] *s6* **1** society; community; ~*t* society, the community **2** (*kommun, by, tätort*) municipality, village, urban district **3** *biol.* colony **-lig** *a1* social; (*medborgerlig*) civil, civic (*rättigheter* rights)
samhälls|anda public spirit **-arbete** community work **-bevarande** *a4* conservative **-debatt** public debate on problems of modern society **-ekonomi** national economy **-ekonomisk** economic **-fara** social danger, danger to society **-farlig** dangerous to society **-fientlig** antisocial **-form** social structure (system); (*statsform*) polity **-förhållanden** *pl* social conditions **-grupp** social group **-hygien** public and environmental health **-intresse** public interest **-klass** class [of society] **-kontrakt** social contract (compact) **-kunskap** civics (*pl, behandlas som sg*) **-lära** civics (*pl, behandlas som sg*), sociology **-medicin** community and environmental health **-nytta** commonweal **-nyttig** of service to society; *ett* ~*t företag* a public utility undertaking **-omstörtande** subversive **-ordning** social order **-orienterande** ~ *ämnen* (*förk. SO-ämnen*) social subjects **-planering** national planning; planning of society **-problem** problems of society **-satir** social satire **-sektor** social sector **-skick** social order (conditions *pl*) **-skikt** *se -klass* **-struktur** social structure **-ställning** social position (status) **-tillvänd** socially aware **-vetare** sociologist, social scientist; student of sociology (social sciences) **-vetenskap** social science **-vård** social welfare
sam|hörande [ˣsamm-] *a4*, **-hörig** *a1* associated; (*inbördes förenade*) mutually connected, interlinked; (*om frågor o.d.*) pertinent, kindred **-hörighet** solidarity; (*frändskap*) affinity, kinship **-hörighetskänsla** feeling of affinity (kinship)
samisk ['sa:-] *a5* Lapp, Lappish **samiska** *s1* (*språk*) Lappish
sam|klang accord, harmony; *i* ~ *med* in harmony with **-kostnader** *pl* common costs **-kväm** *s7* social [gathering] **-könad** [-ç-] *a5* androgynous, hermaphrodite
samla **1** collect (*frimärken* stamps; *pengar* money); gather (*fakta* facts; *snäckor* seashells); (*så småningom*) amass (*en förmögenhet* a fortune); (*lagra*) store up; (*för-*) assemble, bring together; ~ *på hög* accumulate, hoard up; ~ *på sig* accumulate (*arbete* work; *en massa skräp* a lot of rubbish); ~ *sina krafter* get up one's strength (*till* for); ~ *sina tankar* collect one's thoughts, *vard.* pull o.s. together **2** *rfl* collect (gather) [together]; gather (*kring* round); (*hopas*) accumulate; *bildl.* collect o.s., *vard.* pull o.s. together
samlad *a5* collected; *ge en* ~ *bild av* give a concise picture of; ~ *skoldag* integrated schoolday; *hålla tankarna* ~*e* keep one's thoughts composed; *i* ~ *trupp* in a body; ~*e skrifter* complete works
samlag [ˣsamm-] *s7* sexual intercourse; *med.* coitus, coition
samlar|e collector **-vurm** collecting mania **-värde** value to the collector
samlas *dep* **1** (*om pers.*) collect, gather, come together; (*skockas*) congregate **2** *allm.* gather [to-

gether]

sam|lastning [ˣsamm-] groupage traffic; collective consignment **-levnad** *fredlig* ~ peaceful coexistence

samlevnads|problem *pl* problems in personal relations **-frågor** personal relationship matters **-undervisning** sex education, instruction in marital and personal relationships

samling 1 *abstr.* collection, gathering, meeting; *mil. äv.* rallying; *inre* ~ composure **2** *konkr.* collection; (*av pers.*) meeting, crowd

samlings|lins convex lens **-lokal** assembly (community) hall **-ministär** coalition ministry **-plats** meeting place **-pärm** file, binder **-regering** coalition government **-sal** *se -lokal* **-verk** compilation, collection [of articles]

samliv [ˣsamm-] life together, cohabitation; *det äktenskapliga* ~*et* married life

samma [the] same (*som* as); (*liknande*) similar (*som* to); *på* ~ *gång* at the same time, (*samtidigt*) simultaneously; *på* ~ *sätt* (*äv.*) similarly; *redan* ~ *dag* that very day; *det är en och* ~ *sak* it comes to the same thing **-ledes** likewise, in the same manner (way)

sammalen [ˣsamm-ma:-] *a5* (*om mjöl*) coarse

sammalunda *se sammaledes*

samman ['samm-, *i sms.* ˣsamm-] together; *jfr ihop, tillsammans* **-binda** join, connect **-biten** *a5, se* ~ *ut* look resolute, have a dogged expression; ~ *beslutsamhet* dogged determination **-blanda** *se blanda* [*ihop*]; (*förväxla*) confuse **-blandning** *bildl.* confusion **-bo** cohabit, live together [as husband and wife] **-boende I** *a4* cohabiting **II** *s6, ung.* common law husband (wife) **-brott** collapse, breakdown **-drabbning** *mil.* encounter, engagement; *bildl.* conflict, clash **-drag** summary, condensation, synopsis, precis; *redogörelse i* ~ abridged (concise) report **-draga 1** (*samla*) assemble; *mil.* rally, concentrate **2** (*hopdraga*) contract; *fack.* constrict; ~*nde medel* astringent **3** (*förkorta*) abridge **4** *rfl* contract; *som kan* ~ *sig* contractible **-dragning 1** concentration (*av trupper* of troops) **2** contraction (*av muskler* of muscles) **3** (*förkortning*) abridgement **-falla** (*vara samtidig*) coincide (*med* with); ~*nde* coincident, congruent; *-fallna kinder* shrunken cheeks **-fatta** sum up, summarize **-fattning** summary, summing up, recapitulation **-fattningsvis** to sum up **-flyta** flow together; (*om floder äv.*) meet; (*om färger*) run together **-fläta** interlace **-flöde** confluence, junktion **-foga** join [together]; *bildl.* unite, combine **-fogning** [-ɔ:-] **1** *konkr.* joint **2** *abstr.* joining [together] **-föra** bring together; (*förena*) combine, unite **-gadda** *rfl* conspire, plot (*mot* against)

samman|hang *s7* (*förbindelse*) connection, relation; (*följdriktighet*) coherence; (*i text*) context; *det har ett bra inre* ~ it is well integrated; *brist på* ~ incoherence; *fatta* ~*et* grasp the connection; *i ett* ~ without interruption; *ryckt ur* ~*et* detached from the context; *tala utan* ~ talk incoherently, ramble; *utan* ~ *med* independent of **-hållning** (*enighet*) unity, concord, harmony **-hänga** (*ha sambamd med*) be connected (united) (*med* with); *jfr hänga* [*ihop*] **-hängande** *a4* con-

nected, coherent (*tal* speech); (*utan avbrott*) continuous **-jämka** *se jämka* [*ihop*] **-jämkning** *bildl.* conciliation, compromise (*av åsikter* of views) **-kalla** call together; summon, convene (*ett möte* a meeting); ~ *parlamentet* convoke Parliament **-kallande 1** *s6* calling together *etc.* **2** *s9* (*person*) convener, convenor **-komst** [-å-] *s3* gathering, meeting, conference; (*av två pers.*) interview **-koppla** *se koppla* [*ihop*] **-lagd** *a5* total; *våra* ~*a inkomster* our combined income[s]; *-lagt 50 pund* a total of 50 pounds, 50 pounds in all; *utgifterna uppgår -lagt till* the expenses total **-läggningsavhandling** doctoral thesis [consisting of previously published articles by candidate, with a summary] **-länka** chain together; *bildl.* link [together] **-packa, -pressa** compress **-räkna** add (sum) up **-räkning** addition, summing up; (*av röster*) count, counting

samman|satt *a4* compound (*ord* word); (*av olika delar, äv. tekn.*) composite (*tal* number); (*invecklad*) complicated (*natur* nature); ~ *av* composed (made up) of; *vara* ~ *av* (*äv.*) consist of **-slagning** [-a:g-] (*förening*) unification, union; (*fusion*) merger, amalgamation, fusion (*av bolag* of companies) **-sluta** *-slöt -slutit, rfl, bildl.* join (*i* in), unite **-slutning** [-u:-] (*förening*) association, alliance, union; (*koalition*) coalition **-slå** (*hopslå*) nail up (together); *bildl.* turn into one, unite **-smälta 1** (*hop-*) fuse, melt together; *bildl.* amalgamate, merge **2** (*förenas, förminskas*) melt down; *bildl. äv.* coalesce; (*om färger*) blend, run together **-smältning** fusion, melting (*etc.*); (*av färger*) blending; *bildl.* coalescence, amalgamation **-snöra** *mitt hjärta -snördes av ängslan* anxiety wrung my heart; ~ *sig* compress, (*om strupe*) be constricted **-stråla** converge; *vard.* meet **-ställa** put (place) together; make up (*en tablå* a schedule); compile (*en diktsamling* a collection of poems) **-ställning** placing together *etc.*; (*förteckning*) list, specification; (*uppställning*) statement **-stötning** [-ö:-] collision; (*konflikt*) conflict; *mil.* encounter **-svetsa** weld together **-svuren** *-svurne -svurna, mest i pl* conspirator, plotter **-svärja** *rfl* conspire (*mot* against) **-svärjning** conspiracy, plot **-sätta** (*hopsätta*) join, put together, compound; (*av flera delar*) compose (*en matsedel* a menu) **-sättning** putting together, joining, composition; (*blandning*) mixture; (*struktur*) structure; (*konstitution*) constitution; *språkv.* compound **-sättningsled** element

samman|träda meet, assemble **-träde** *s6* [committee] meeting, conference; (*session*) session; *han sitter i* ~ he is at a meeting (in conference); *extra* ~ [a] called session **-trädesrum** assembly (meeting, conference) room **-trädesteknik** technique of running a meeting; conference technique **-träffa** meet; (*om omständighet*) coincide, concur **-träffande** *s6* (*möte*) meeting; *bildl.* concurrence, *ett egendomligt* ~ a curious coincidence **-trängd** *bildl.* compressed; concentrated **-vuxen** grown together, consolidated; *bot.* accrete

samme *se samma*

sammelsurium [-'su:-] *s4* conglomeration, jumble, omnium-gatherum

S

sammet *s2* velvet
sammets|band velvet ribbon **-len** as soft as velvet, velvety
samnordisk [ˣsamm-] Nordic
samojed *s3* Samoyed **-isk** *a5* Samoyedic
samordn|a [ˣsamm] coordinate; *~de satser* coordinate clauses **-ande** *a4* coordinating **-ing** coordination
samovar *s3* samovar
samp|el [ˈsaːm-] *s7* sample **-ling** [ˈsaːm-] sampling
sam|realskola [ˣsamm-] *ung.* coeducational junior secondary school **-regent** co-regent **-råd** consultation, conference; *efter ~ med* having consulted; *i ~ med* in consultation with **-råda** consult, confer **-röre** *s6* collaboration
sams *oböjligt a, bli ~* be reconciled, make it up; *bli ~ om ngt* agree upon s.th.; *vara ~* be friends; *vara ~ med ngn* be on good terms with s.b.
samsas *dep* agree (*med* with); get on well together; *~ om utrymmet* share the space
sam|segling [ˣsamm-] joint (combined) service
-sikt coarse meal **-skola** coeducational (*vard.* co-ed) school **-spel** teamwork, ensemble [playing]; *bildl.* interplay, combination (*av färger* of colours) **-spelt** [-e:-] *a1, vara ~a* play well together; *bildl.* be in accord **-språk** conversation, talk; (*förtroligt*) chat **-språka** converse, talk; *vard.* have a chat **-stämmig** *a1* in accord; unanimous **-stämmighet** accord, concordance; (*enighet*) unanimity **-sändning** radio. joint broadcast; simulcast
samt I *konj* and [also], [together] with **II** *adv, ~ och synnerligen* each and all, all and sundry; *jämnt och ~* always, constantly, (*oupphörligt*) incessantly
samtal [ˣsamm-] conversation, talk; (*småprat*) chat; (*lärt*) discourse; (*överläggning*) conference; (*telefon-*) call; *~ mellan fyra ögon* tête-a-tête, private interview; *bryta ~et* (*tel.*) interrupt the call; *~ pågår* (*tel.*) call in progress
samtala converse (*om* about), talk (*om* about, of); (*småprata*) chat; (*överlägga*) confer
samtals|avgift *tel.* call charge **-form** *i ~* in dialogue form **-rum** (*i kloster*) parlour; (*läkares*) consultation room **-räknare** [-ä:-] *tel.* telephone-call meter **-terapi** conversation therapy **-ton** *i ~* in conversational tone **-ämne** topic (subject) of conversation; *det allmänna ~et i staden* the talk of the town
samtaxer|a [ˣsamm-] assess jointly **-ing** joint taxation
sam|tid [ˣsamm-] *~en* the age in which we (*etc.*) live, our (*etc.*) age (time) **-tida** *oböjligt a* contemporary **-tidig** contemporaneous; (*sammanfallande*) coincident; (*inträffande -tidigt*) simultaneous **-tidighet** simultaneousness, contemporaneousness **-tidigt** *adv* at the same time (*med mig* as I; *som* as)
samtliga [ˣsamt-] *pl a* all; the whole body of (*lärare* teachers); *~ skulder* the total debts
samtrafik [ˣsamm-] joint (combined) service
samtyck|a [ˣsamm-] agree, give one's consent (*till att*) to; *nicka ~nde* nod assent; *den som tiger han -er* silence gives consent **samtycke** consent, assent; (*tillåtelse*) permission, leave; *ge sitt*

~, se samtycka; med hans ~ by his leave
samum *s3* simoom, simoon
samundervisning [ˣsamm-] coeducation
samuraj *s3* samurai (*pl* samurai)
sam|variera vary in correlation **-varo** *s9* being (time) together; *tack för angenäm ~!* I have enjoyed your company very much! **-verka** cooperate, work (act) together; *bildl.* concur, conspire (*till att* to) **-verkan** cooperation, united action; concurrence
samvete [ˣsamm-] *s6* conscience; *dåligt ~* a bad conscience; *~t slog honom* his conscience pricked him; *inte ha ~ att göra ngt* not have the conscience to do s.th.; *på heder och ~!* on my honour!; *det tar jag på mitt ~* I shall answer for that
samvets|agg twinge (prick) of conscience; compunction **-betänkligheter** *pl* scruples **-fråga** delicate (indiscreet) question **-förebråelse** remorse; self-reproach; *göra sig ~r* reproach o.s.
-grann conscientious; (*skrupulös*) scrupulous; (*minutiös*) meticulous **-grannhet** conscientiousness *etc.* **-kval** *pl* pangs of conscience **-lös** unscrupulous, unprincipled; (*om pers. äv.*) remorseless **-löshet** unscrupulousness *etc.* **-pengar** *pl* conscience money (*sg*) **-sak** matter of conscience **-äktenskap** *ung.* free union **-öm** overscrupulous; *en ~* (*om värnpliktsvägrare*) a conscientious objector
samvälde [ˣsamm-] *Brittiska ~t* the British Commonwealth [of Nations]
samåka car pool
sanatori|evård [-ˣtoː-] treatment at a sanatorium **-um** [-ˈtoː-] *s4* sanatorium; *AE. äv.* sanitarium
sand *s3* sand; *byggd på lösan ~* built upon the sand; *rinna ut i ~en* (*bildl.*) come to nothing
sanda sand
sandal *s3* sandal; *klädd i ~er* sandalled **-ett** *s7* sandalette
sand|bank sandbank **-blästra** sandblast **-blästring** sandblasting **-botten** sand[y] bottom **-dyn** sand dune (hill)
sandelträ sandalwood
sand|grop sandpit **-gång** gravel walk **-hög** heap (mound) of sand
sand|ig *a1* sandy **-jord** sandy soil **-kaka** (*av sand*) sand pie; (*bakverk*) sand cake **-korn** grain of sand **-låda** (*för barn*) sandpit, sandbox **-ning** sanding **-papper** sandpaper; *ett ~* a piece of sandpaper **-pappra** sandpaper **-rev[el]** shoal [of sand]; bar of sand **-slott** sand castle **-sten** sandstone **-storm** sandstorm **-strand** sandy beach (shore) **-säck** sandbag **-tag, -täkt** sandpit
sandwich [ˈsändvitʃ, ˈsand-] *ung.* canapé **-man** sandwich man
sandöken sand desert
saner|a (*göra sund*) make healthy; *mil.* degas; (*slumkvarter o.d.*) clear; (*finanser o.d.*) refinance; (*företag*) reorganize, reconstruct **-ing** sanitation; degassing; slum clearance; refinancing; reorganization, reconstruction
sanforiser|a sanforize **-ing** sanforizing
sang *s9, kortsp.* no trumps
sangvin|iker [-ˈviː-] sanguine person **-isk** *a5* sanguine

sanitets|binda [-ˣte:ts-] sanitary towel **-gods** sanitary ware **-teknik** sanitary technology

sanitär *a1* sanitary

sank I *oböjligt s, borra i* ~ sink, scuttle **II** *a1* swampy, waterlogged **-mark** marsh

sankt *mask. äv. -e, fem. -a* saint; *S~e Per* St. Peter **-bernhardshund** St. Bernard [dog]

sanktion [-k'ʃo:n] sanction; (*bifall äv.*) assent, approbation **-era** sanction, approve of

sanktpaulia [-'pau-] *s1* African violet, saintpaulia

sann *a1* true (*mot* to); (*sanningsenlig*) truthful; (*verklig*) real; (*uppriktig*) sincere; (*äkta*) genuine; *en* ~ *kristen* a true Christian; *där sa du ett sant ord!* you are right there!; *inte sant?, se [eller] hur; det var så sant!* by the way!, that reminds me!; *så sant mig Gud hjälpe!* so help me God!; *det är så sant som det är sagt* quite true, how true **sann|a** ~ *mina ord!* mark my words! **-dröm** *ha ~mar* have dreams that come true

sann|erligen indeed, really; truly; ~ *tror jag inte att de I* do not believe they; *det var* ~ *inte för tidigt* it was certainly not too soon **-färdig** truthful, veracious **-färdighet** truthfulness, veracity

sanning truth; (*-färdighet*) veracity; *tala* ~ speak the truth; *hålla sig till* ~*en* stick to the truth; *den osminkade* ~*en* plain (naked) truth; *säga ngn obehagliga* ~*ar* tell s.b. a few home truths; ~*en att säga* to tell the truth; *säga som* ~*en är* tell (speak) the truth; *komma* ~*en närmare* be nearer the truth; *i* ~ in truth, truly; *det är dagsens* ~ it is God's truth

sannings|enlig [-e:-] *a1* truthful, veracious **-enlighet** [-e:n-] truthfulness, veracity **-försäkran** statutory declaration **-halt** veracity **-kärlek** love of truth **-serum** truth drug (serum) **-sökare** seeker after truth **-vittne** witness to the truth **-älskande** veracious, truth-loving

sannolik *a1* probable, likely; *AE. äv.* apt; (*plausibel*) plausible (*version* version); *det mest ~a är* the most probable thing is; *det är ~t att de gör det* they are likely to do so **-het** probability, likelihood (*för att* that); (*rimlighet*) plausibility; *med all* ~ in all probability **-hetskalkyl** calculus of probability **-hetslära** probability theory

sann|saga true story **-skyldig** true, veritable **-spådd** *a5, bli (vara)* ~ be proved a true prophet

1 sans [saŋ] *s9, kortsp., se sang*

2 sans [sanns] *s3, ej pl* senses (*pl*); *jfr medvetande, besinning*

sansa *rfl* calm down **sansad** *a5* sober; (*modererad*) moderate; (*klok*) sensible, prudent; *lugn och* ~ calm and collected **sanslös** senseless, unconscious

sant *adv* truly, sincerely; *tala* ~ tell (speak) the truth

sapfisk ['sapp-] *a5* Sapphic

sapon|ifikation saponification **-in** *s4* saponin **-lack** [-ˣpå:n-] silver [zapon] lacquer

sappör *mil.* engineer, sapper

saprofyt *s3* saprophyte

sarac|en *s3* Saracen **-ensk** [-e:-] *a5* Saracenic[al]

sardell *s3* sardelle, anchovy **-in** *s3* sardine

sardinare [-ˣdi:-] Sardinian **Sardinien** [-'di:-] *n* Sardinia **sardinsk** [-'di:nsk] *a5* Sardinian

sardonisk [-'do:-] *a5* sardonic (*leende* smile)

sarg [-j] *s3, s2* border, edging; (*ram*) frame; (*på farkost*) coaming; (*ishockey*) boards (*pl*)

sarga [-ja] lacerate; *bildl.* harrow

sari *s3* sari

Sargassohavet [-ˣgassɔ-] the Sargasso Sea

sark|asm *s3* sarcasm; *konkr.* sarcastic remark **-tisk** *a5* sarcastic[al]

sarkofag *s3* sarcophagus (*pl äv.* sarcophagi)

sarkom [-'kå:m] *s7* sarcoma

sarong [-'råŋ] *s3* sarong

sars *s3, s4* serge

sarv *s2* (*fisk*) rudd, redeye

satan *r* Satan; *ett* ~*s oväsen* the devil (deuce) of a row **satanisk** [-'ta:-] *a5* satanic[al] **sate** *s2* devil; *stackars* ~ poor devil

satellit *s3* satellite **-bana** orbit of a satellite **-stat** satellite state **-sändning** satellite transmission **—TV** satellite TV

satin [-'täŋ] *s3, s4, se satäng* **-era** [-ti-] (*glätta*) glaze, polish

satir *s3* satire (*över* upon) **-iker** satirist **-isera** satirize **-isk** *a5* satiric[al]

satis|faktion [-k'ʃo:n] satisfaction **-fiera** satisfy

satkär[r]ing [ˣsa:t-] bitch, vixen

1 sats *s3* **1** *mat., log.* proposition; (*tes*) thesis, theme; *språkv.* clause, sentence **2** *mus.* movement

2 sats *s3* **1** (*dosis*) dose; *kokk.* batch **2** (*uppsättning*) set **3** *boktr.* type; *stående* ~ standing type **3** *sats s3, sport. o.d.* run; take off; *ta* ~ take a run, run up

1 satsa 1 (*i spel*) stake, wager, gamble; ~ *på fel häst* back the wrong horse **2** (*investera*) invest **3** ~ *på* (*inrikta sig på*) go in for, concentrate on

2 satsa *se 3 sats*

sats|accent sentence stress **-analys** parsing **-bindning** compound sentence

satsbord *koll.* nest of tables

sats|byggnad sentence structure **-del** part of [a] sentence; *ta ut* ~*ar* analyse a sentence **-fogning** [-ɔ:-] complex sentence **-förkortning** contracted sentence **-lära** syntax **-lösning** parsing

satsning (*i spel*) staking; (*investering*) investment; (*inriktning*) concentration

satsuma [-ˣsu:-] *s1 bot.* satsuma

1 satt *a1* stocky, thickset

2 satt *imperf. av sitta*

3 satt *sup. av sätta*

satte *imperf. av sätta*

sat|tyg [ˣsa:t-] *s7* devilry **-unge** imp; brat

saturera *kem.* saturate

saturnalier [-'na:-] *pl* saturnalia

Saturnus [-'turr-] *r* Saturn

satyr *s3* satyr

satäng [-'täŋ] *s3, s4* satin; (*foder*) satinet

saudi|arab Saudi **-arabisk** Saudi [Arabian]

Saudi-Arabien [ˣsau-] *n* Saudi Arabia

sauna ['sau-] *s1* sauna

sav *s3* sap (*äv. bildl.*); ~*en stiger* the sap is rising

savann *s3* savanna

savaräng *s3* savarin

savojkål [-ˣvåjj-] savoy

1 sax *s2* scissors (*pl*); (*plåt-, ull- etc.*) shears (*pl*); (*fälla*) trap; *en* ~ (*två* ~*ar*) a pair (two pairs) of scissors (*etc.*); *den här* ~*en* these scissors (*pl*), this pair of scissors

2 sax s2, vard. saxophone, sax
saxa (korsa) cross; (klippa) cut (ur en tidning out of a paper); sport. scissor; (skidor) herringbone
sax|are s9 Saxon **-isk** ['sakks-] a5 Saxon
saxofon [-'få:n] s3 saxophone **-ist** saxophonist
saxsprint split pin, cotter [pin]
scarf [ska:(r)f] s2, pl äv. scarves scarf
scen [se:n] s3 scene; (skådebana) stage; gå in vid ~en go on the stage **-anvisning** stage direction **-arbetare** stagehand
scen|ario [-'na:-] s6, pl äv. -arier scenario **-bild** set, scene **-eri** scenery **-förändring** change of scenery **-ingång** stage door **-isk** ['se:-] a5 scenic, theatrical **-konst** dramatic (scenic) art **-ograf** s3 set designer **-skola** drama school **-vana** stage experience **-öppning** proscenium opening
sch be quiet!, shush!
schaber ['ʃa:-] pl, vard. brass, dough
schablon s3, i måleri etc. stencil; gjut. template; (modell) model, pattern; bildl. cliché **-avdrag** standard deduction **-mässig** a1 stereotyped **-regel** standard rule
schabrak s7 housing
schack I 1 s7 (spel) chess; spela (ta ett parti) ~ play (have a game of) chess **2** s2, s7 (hot mot kungen i schack) check; hålla i ~ keep in check **II** interj, ~! check!; ~ och matt! checkmate!
schack|a check **-bräde** chessboard **-drag** move [in chess]; ett slugt ~ (äv. bildl.) a clever (sly) move
schakel ['ʃakk-] s2 shackle
schack|matt a4 checkmate; bildl. worn out, exhausted **-ningsperiod** sport. temporary failure of strength **-parti** game of chess **-pjäs** chessman, chess piece
schackra (driva småhandel) peddle, hawk; (friare o. bildl.) chaffer, haggle (med with); traffic (med in); (om ngt) bargain
schack|ruta square of a chessboard **-spel** abstr. chess; konkr. chessboard and [set of] men **-spelare** chessplayer
schagg s3 plush **-soffa** plush sofa
schah [ʃa:] s3 shah
schakal s3 jackal
1 schakt s7 (gruv-) shaft, pit
2 schakt s4, s3 ([jord]skärning) excavation, cutting
schakt|a excavate; ~ bort (undan) cut away, remove **-maskin** excavator **-ning** excavation
schal s2, se sjal
schalottenlök [-'lått-] shallot, scallion
schaman s3 shaman **-ism** shamanism
schampo s6, s9 shampoo **-nera** shampoo **-nering** [-'ne:-] shampoo[ing] **-neringsmedel** shampoo
schanker ['ʃann-] med. chancre; sore; mjuk ~ soft sore
schappa se sjappa
scharlakan [-'la:-, ˣʃa:r-, ˣʃarr-] s7 scarlet
scharlakans|feber scarlet fever; fack. scarlatina **-röd** scarlet
schas se sjas
schatter|a shade, shadow [out]; shade (tone) off **-ing** shading, gradation [of colours]; konkr. shade **-söm** ung. satin stitch
schatull s7 casket

schavott [-'vått] s3 scaffold; (skampåle) pillory **-era** stand in the pillory; låta ngn ~ i pressen pillory s.b. in the press
schejk s3 sheik[h] **-roman** ung. romantic novel of desert life
schellack ['ʃell-] shellac
schema ['ʃe:-, ˣʃe:-] s6 (timplan) timetable, AE. [time] schedule; (uppgjord plan) schedule, plan; (över arbetsförlopp) process chart; (formulär) form, AE. blank; filos. scheme, outline; göra upp ett ~ draw up a timetable (etc.); utanför ~t extracurricular **-lagd** a5 timetabled, scheduled **-läggning** timetabling, scheduling **-tisera** schematize; (skissera) sketch, outline **-tisk** [-'ma:-] a5 schematic; diagrammatic; ~ teckning skeleton sketch (drawing)
schersmin s3, bot. mock orange, syringa
schimpans s3 chimpanzee
schism s3 schism **-atisk** [-'ma:-] a5 schismatic [al]
schizo|fren [skitsa'fre:n] a1 schizophrenic **-freni** s3 schizophrenia
schlager ['ʃla:-] s2, s9 hit song **-musik** popular music
schlaraffenland [-'raff-] Cockaigne, Cockayne
Schleswig ['ʃle:s-] n Schleswig
schottis ['ʃått-] s2 schottische
Schwarzwald ['ʃvarts-] n the Black Forest
Schweiz [ʃvejts] n Switzerland
schweizare [ˣʃvejts-] Swiss
schweizer|franc [ˣʃvejts-] Swiss franc **-ost** Swiss cheese
schweiz|isk ['ʃvejts-] a5 Swiss, Helvetian **-iska** s1 Swiss woman
schvung s2 go, pep; verve
schäfer ['ʃä:-] s2, **-hund** Alsatian; AE. German shepherd [dog]
schäs s2 chaise **-long** [-'låŋ] s3 chaise longue
scout [skaut] s3 scout; (flick-) [girl] guide, girl scout; (pojk-) boy scout **-chef** chief scout **-förbund** scout association **-kår** scout troop **-ledare** scoutmaster **-läger** scout camp **-rörelsen** the Scout movement
screentryck [ˣskri:n-] [silk-]screen printing
scripta [ˣskripp-] s1, se skripta
se såg sett **1** see; (titta) look; (bli varse) perceive, catch sight of; (urskilja) distinguish; (betrakta) look at, regard; AE. sl. dig; (möta, träffa) meet, see; vi ses i morgon see you tomorrow; vi ses se you later; ~ bra (illa) see well (badly), have good (bad) eyesight; ~ en skymt av catch a glimpse of; jag tål inte ~ henne I cannot stand the sight of her; vi får väl ~ we shall see; få ~! let me see!; som jag ~r det as I see it; väl (illa) ~dd popular (unpopular); låt ~ att det blir gjort! see [to it] that it is done!; ... ~r du ..., you see (know); ~ där (här, hit)! look there (here)!; ~ så! now then!; ~ så där [ja]! well I never!, (gillande) that's it (the way)!; ~ gäster hos sig have guests; ~ ngn på en bit mat have s.b. to dinner (a meal) **2** (med prep.-uttr.) härav ~r man att from this it may be concluded that; ~ efter a) (ngt bortgående) gaze after, b) (leta) look for; ~ in i framtiden look into the future; ~ på look at, (noggrant) watch, observe; inte ~ på besväret not mind the trouble; ~ på slantarna take care of the pence; man ~r på

henne att you can see by her looks that; ~ *åt ett annat håll* look away; ~ *ngn över axeln* look down upon s.b. **3** (*med betonad partikel*) ~ *tiden an* wait and see, bide one's time; ~ *efter a*) (*ta reda på*) [look and] see, *b*) (*passa*) look after, take care of (*barnen* the children); ~ *efter i* look in, (*lexikon e.d.*) look up in; ~ *igenom* (*granska*) look through (over); ~ *ner på* look down upon; ~ *på* look on; ~*r man på!* just look!, why [did you ever]!; ~ *till att* see [to it] that; ~ *till att du inte* be careful not to, mind you don't; *jag har inte* ~*tt till dem* I have seen nothing of them; ~ *upp!* look sharp!; ~ *upp för* look out for, mind; ~ *upp med ...!* be on your guard against ...!; ~ *upp till* look up to, respect; ~ *ut a*) look out (*genom fönstret* of the window), *b*) (*förefalla*) look, seem; *han* ~*r bra ut* he is good-looking; *det* ~*r bra ut* it looks fine; *det* ~*r så ut* it looks like it; *det* ~*r bara så ut* it only appears so; *hur* ~*r det ut?* what does it look like?; *så du* ~*r ut!* what a fright you look!; *det* ~*r ut att bli snö* it looks like snow; ~ *över* look over, inspect, go through **4** *rfl*, ~ *sig för* be careful, look out; ~ *sig om a*) (*tillbaka*) look back, *b*) (*omkring*) look round, *c*) (*i världen*) see the world; ~ *sig om efter* (*söka*) look out for

seans [-'ans, -'aŋs] *s3* seance

seborré *s3, med.* seborrhoea

sebra [ˣse:-] *s1* zebra

sebu ['se:-] *s3* zebu

sed *s3* custom; ~*er* (*moral*) morals, habits; ~*er och bruk* manners and customs; *som* ~*en är bland* as is customary with; *ta* ~*en dit man kommer* when in Rome do as the Romans do

1 sedan [ˣse:-, 'se:-] *förk. sen* [senn] **I** *adv* **1** (*därpå*) then; (*efteråt*) afterwards; (*senare*) later **2** (*tillbaka*) *det är länge* ~ it is a long time ago; *för tio år* ~ ten years ago **3** *vard., än sen då?* what of it?, so what?; *kom sen och säg att* don't dare to say that; *och så billig sen!* and so cheap too! **II** *prep* (*från, efter*) since; ~ *dess* since then; ~ *många år tillbaka* for many years **III** *konj* since (*jag såg honom* I saw him); (*efter det att*) after (*han gått* he had gone); ~ *han gjort det gick han* when he had done that he left; *först* ~ *de gått* not until after they had left

2 sedan [-'daŋ, -'dann] *s3* sedan

sedativ I *a1* sedative **II** *s7* sedative

sede|betyg conduct mark; *få sänkt* ~ get lower marks for good conduct **-fördärv** corruption; immorality

sed|el| ['se:-] *s2* (*betalningsmedel*) bank note; *AE.* bill; *i* -*lar* in notes (paper money; *AE.* bills)

sedelag moral law, ethical code

sedel|bunt bundle of bank notes **-förfalskare** forger of bank notes **-omlopp** note circulation **-press** printing press for bank notes **-reserv** reserve of bank notes **-tryckeri** note-printing works **-utgivning** note issue, issue of bank notes

sedelär|a moral philosophy; ethics (*pl, behandlas som sg*) **-ande** *a4* moral; ~ *berättelse* story with a moral

sedermera *se sedan I 1*

sede|roman novel portraying life and manners **-sam** *a1* modest, decent; (*tillgjort*) prudish

sedeslös immoral, unprincipled **-het** immoral-

ity; (*fördärv*) depravity

sedig *a1* gentle (*häst* horse)

sediment *s7* sediment **-era** (*sjunka*) settle **-är** *a1* sedimentary

sedlig [ˣse:d-] *a1* (*moralisk*) moral; (*etisk*) ethical; *föra ett* ~*t liv* lead a virtuous life; *i* ~*t hänseende* morally, from a moral point of view **-het** morality; decency

sedlighets|brott sexual offence, indecent assault **-förbrytare** sexual offender **-polis** vice squad **-sårande** indecent, offensive

sed|vana custom, practice **-vanerätt** customary law **-vanlig** customary, usual **-vänja** *s1* custom; practice

seeda [ˣsi:da] *sport.* seed

seende *a4* seeing *etc.*; (*mots. blind*) sighted

sefardisk [-'farr-] *a5* Sephardic

sefyr [-'fy:r, 'se:-] *s3* zephyr

seg *a1* tough (*äv. bildl.*); (*om kött äv.*) leathery; (*trögflytande*) viscous; (*limaktig*) gluey, sticky; *bildl.* tenacious; ~*t motstånd* tough (stubborn) resistance **sega** *rfl,* ~ *sig upp* struggle up

segel ['se:-] *s7* sail; *hissa* (*stryka*) ~ set (strike) sail; *segla för fulla* ~ go with all sails set; *sätta till alla* ~ crowd on sail **-bar** *a1* navigable, sailable **-båt** sailing boat, *AE.* sailboat **-duk** sailcloth, canvas **-fartyg** sailing ship (vessel) **-flygare** glider [pilot] **-flygning** gliding, soaring, sailplaning **-flygplan** sailplane, soaring-plane; (*glid-*) glider **-garn** [sailmaker's] twine, packthread **-jakt** sailing yacht **-kanot** sailing canoe **-led** fairway, channel **-makare** sailmaker **-ränna** channel **-sport** yachting **-sällskap** yacht[ing] club **-yta** sail area

seger ['se:-] *s2* victory (*över* over; *vid* of, at); (*erövring*) conquest; *sport.* win; *avgå med* ~*n* come off victorious; *en lätt* ~ an easy conquest, *sport.* a walkover; *vinna* ~ win a victory **-byte** spoils of victory, booty **-herre** victor, conqueror **-hjälte** conquering hero **-huva** caul **-hymn** hymn of victory **-jubel** triumph, jubilation over a victory **-krönt** [-ö:-] *a4* crowned with victory **-rik** victorious, triumphant **-rop** triumphant shout **-rus** intoxication of victory **-tåg** triumphal progress (march) **-vilja** determination to win **-viss** sure (certain) of victory **-yra** flush of victory

seghet [ˣse:g-] toughness *etc.*; tenacity

segla [ˣse:g-] sail; make sail (*till* for); ~ *i kvav* founder, go down; ~ *i motvind* sail against the wind; ~ *omkull* capsize; ~ *på* run into, collide with; ~ *på grund* run aground; ~ *på havet* sail the sea **seglare** (*fartyg*) sailing vessel; *pers.* sailor; (*kapp-*) yachtsman

seglation sailing, navigation **seglations-period** sailing (navigation) period **segléts** *s3* sailing trip (tour); (*överfart*) crossing, voyage

segl|ing [ˣse:g-] sailing; *sport. äv.* yachting **-ingsbeskrivning** sailing directions

seglivad *a5* tough; hard to kill; *vard.* die-hard; *en* ~ *fördom* a deep-rooted prejudice

segment *s7* segment **-era** segment

segna [ˣseŋna] ~ [*ner*] sink down, collapse

segr|a [ˣse:g-] win; be victorious; *bildl.* prevail; (*i omröstning*) be carried; ~ *över, se besegra* **-ande** *a4* victorious, winning; *gå* ~ *ur striden* emerge victorious from the battle **-are** victor, conqueror; (*i tävling*) winner

segreg|ation segregation **-era** segregate **-ering** [-'ge:-] segregating; segregation

segsliten tough; *en ~ fråga* a vexed question; *en ~ tvist* a lengthy dispute

seismisk ['sejs-] *a5* seismic

seismo|graf *s3* seismograph **-log** seismologist **-logisk** [-'lå:-] *a5* seismologic[al]

sej [sejj] *s2, se gråsej*

sejdel [ˣsejj-] *s2* (*av glas*) beer mug, glass; (*av silver, tenn etc.*) tankard

sejour [se'ʃo:r] *s3* sojourn, stay

sejsning *sjö.* lanyard, seizing

sekant *mat.* secant

sekatör *s3* pruning shears, secateurs (*pl*); *en ~* a pair of pruning shears (*etc.*)

sekel ['se:-] *s7, s4* century **-gammal** centuries old; (*hundraårig*) centenary **-jubileum** centenary **-skifte** *vid ~t* at the turn of the century

sekin *s3* sequin; *-er, vard.* dough, bread

sekond [-'kånd] *s3* **1** *sjö.* second-in-command, mate **2** *boxn.* second

1 sekret *s7* secretion

2 sekret *a1* secret

sekretariat *s7* secretariat

sekreter|arbefattning [-ˣte:-] secretarial post **-are** secretary (*hos* to) **-arfågel** secretary bird

sekretess (*under* in) secrecy **-belägga** classify [as secret] **-plikt** (*läkares etc.*) [obligation to observe] professional secrecy **-skydd** (*hopskr. sekretesskydd*) secrecy safeguards (*pl*)

sekret|ion secretion **-orisk** [-'to:-] *a5* secretory

sekretär *s3* writing desk, bureau, escritoire

sekt *s3* sect **sekterism** sectarianism **sekterist** sectarian

sek|tion [-k'ʃo:n] **1** *geom.* section **2** (*avdelning*) section **3** *med.* resection **-tor** [-år] *s3* sector

sekulariser|a secularize **-ing** secularization

sekulär *a1*

sekund *s3* second; *jag kommer på ~en!* just a second!

sekunda [-ˣkunn-] *oböjl. a* second-rate; (*om virke*) seconds; *~ växel* (*hand.*) second of exchange

sekundant second

sekundchef second-in-command, colonel

sekundera second

sekund| meter metre per second **-visare** second hand

sekundär *a1* secondary **-lån** loan secured by a second mortgage **-minne** *data.* secondary storage

sekvens *s3, mus.* sequence

sel|a *~* [*på*] harness; *~ av* unharness **-bruten** galled **-don** harness

sele harness; (*barn-*) reins (*pl*); *en ~* (*barn-*) a pair of reins; *ligga i ~n* (*bildl.*) be in harness

selekt|ion [-k'ʃo:n] selection **-iv** [-'ti:v, 'sell-] *a1* selective **-ivitet** selectivity

selen *s3, s4, kem.* selenium

selkammare harness room

selleri [-'ri:, 'sell-] *s4, s3* celery **-botten** *kokk.* [filled] celeriac

selot *s3* zealot

selters|glas small tumbler **-vatten** Seltzer [water]

semafor [-'få:r] *s3* semaphore **-era** semaphore **-ering** [-ˣre:-] semaphore

semant|ik *s3, ej pl* semantics (*pl, behandlas som sg*) **-isk** [-'mann-] *a5* semantic

semester [-ˣmess-] *s2* holiday[s *pl*]; *AE.* vacation; *ha ~* be on holiday, have one's holiday[s *pl*] **-by** holiday (vacation) settlement (camp, village) **-dag** day of one's (*etc.*) holiday **-ersättning** holiday (*etc.*) compensation **-firare** holiday-maker; *AE.* vacationist, vacationer **-hem** holiday home **-lag** holidays law (act) **-lista** holiday schedule (rota) **-lön** holiday pay (*etc.*) **-månad** holiday month **-resa** holiday trip **-vikarie** holiday relief (substitute)

semestra [-ˣmess-] *se* [*ha*] *semester; ~ vid havet* spend one's holiday by the sea

semi|final [-'na:l, ˣse:-] semifinal **-kolon** [-'ko:-, 'se:-] semicolon

seminarie|uppsats [-ˣna:-] seminar essay (paper) **-övning** seminar

seminar|ist student at a training college **-ium** [-'na:-] *s4* (*lärar-*) teacher's training college; (*präst-*) [theological] seminary; *univ.* seminar

semin|ation insemination **-förening** [-ˣmi:n-] artificial insemination society (association)

semiotik *s3* semiotics (*pl, behandlas som sg*)

semit *s3* Semite **-isk** [-'mi:-] *a5* Semitic

semla *s1* cream bun eaten during Lent

1 sen [senn] *adv, se sedan*

2 sen [se:n] *a1* **1** late; *det börjar bli ~t* it is getting late; *vara ~* be late; *vid denna ~a timme* at this late (advanced) hour **2** (*långsam*) slow; tardy; *han är aldrig ~ att hjälpa* he is always ready to help; *~ till vrede* slow to anger

sena *s1* tendon, sinew

senap *s3* mustard

senaps|gas mustard gas **-korn** mustard seed

senare I *a, komp. t. 2 sen* **1** later; (*kommande*) future; (*följande*) subsequent; (*motsats förra*) latter; *de*[*n*] *~* the latter; *det blir en ~ fråga* that will be considered later; *på ~ tid* of later years, (*nyligen*) recently; *vid en ~ tidpunkt* at a future date **2** (*långsammare*) slower; (*senfärdigare*) tardier **II** *adv, komp. t. sedan* later [on] (*på dagen* in the day); *förr eller ~* sooner or later; *inte ~ än* not later than, by **-lägga** postpone; put forward **-läggning** postponement

senast I *a, superl. t. 2 sen* latest; (*sist förfluten*) last; (*nyligen inträffad*) recent; *i ~e laget* at the last moment; *på ~e tid*[*en*] lately **II** *adv, superl. t. sedan* **1** (*i tid*) latest; (*i följd*) last; *jag såg honom ~ i går* (*i lördags*) I saw him only yesterday (last Saturday); *tack för ~!* I enjoyed my stay (the evening I spent) with you very much! **2** (*ej senare än*) at the latest; *~ på lördag* by Saturday at the latest; *~ den 1:a maj* by May 1, on May 1 at the latest

senat senate **senator** [-ˣna:tår] *s3* senator

sendrag cramp

sen|färdig slow, tardy **-född** late-born **-grekisk** late Hellenic **-gångare** *zool.* sloth

senhinna sclerotic coat

senhöst late autumn; *på ~en* late in the (in the late) autumn

senig *a1* sinewy; (*om kött*) tough, stringy; (*om*

pers.) wiry

senil *a1* senile **-itet** senility

senior ['se:niår] **I** *oböjligt. a* senior, elder **II** [*sport.* -'å:r] *s3* senior member; *sport.* senior

sen|komling [-å-] latecomer **-kommen** [-å-] *a5* (*alltför sen*) tardy, belated **-latin** late Latin

sensation sensation **-ell** *al* sensational, thrilling **sensations|lysten** *vara* ~ be a sensation hunter (out after a thrill) **-makare** sensationalist **-press** yellow (sensational) press

sensib|el [-'si:-] *a2* sensitive **-ilisera** sensitize **-ilitet** sensitivity, sensitiveness

sensivitetsträning sensitivity training

sensmoral [sens-, saŋ(s)-] *s3, ~en är* the moral is

sensommar late summer; *jfr senhöst*

sensorisk [-'sɔ:-] *a5* sensory, sensorial

sensträckning strain of a tendon

sensu|alism sensualism **-alitet** sensuality **-ell** *al* sensual, sensuous

sent [-e:-] *adv* late; *bittida och* ~ early and late; *bättre* ~ *än aldrig* better late than never; *komma för* ~ be late (*till skolan* for school); *som* ~ *skall glömmas* that will not be forgotten in a hurry; ~ *omsider* at long last; *till* ~ *på natten* till far into the night

sentens *s3* maxim

sent|era [saŋ'te-, senn-] (*uppskatta*) appreciate; (*sätta värde på*) value

sentida of today, of our days

sentimental [sent-] *al* sentimental; (*gråtmild*) maudlin **-itet** sentimentality

separat I *a4* separate; (*fristående*) detached **II** *adv* separately; ~ *sänder vi* we are sending you under separate cover **-fred** separate peace

separation separation **separatist** *s3* separatist **separatistisk** [-'tiss-] *a5* separatist **separator** [-ˣra:tår] *s3* separator

separat|tryck offprint **-utställning** one-man show

separer|a separate **-ing** separation

september [-'temm-] *r* September

septett *s3* septet[te]

sept|iktank septic tank **-isk** ['sepp-] *a5* septic (*tank* tank)

septima ['sepp-] *s1, mus.* seventh

seraf *s3* seraph

serafimer|orden [-ˣfi:-] the Order of the Seraphim **-riddare** Knight of the Order of the Seraphim

serafisk [-'ra:-] *a4* seraphic

seralj *s3* seraglio

serb *s3* Serb[ian] **Serbien** ['särr-] *n* Serbia

serbisk ['särr-] *a5* Serbian **serbokroatisk** [-'krɔa:-] *a5* Serbo-Croatian

serenad *s3* serenade; *hålla* ~ [*för*] serenade

sergeant [-r'ʃant] *s3* sergeant; staff sergeant; *AE.* sergeant first class; (*vid flottan*) chief petty officer; (*vid flygvapnet*) flight sergeant, *AE.* master sergeant

serie ['se:-] *s5* **1** series; (*följd*) succession; (*om värdepapper*) issue; (*skämt-*) comic strip, cartoons (*pl*), *AE.* vard. funny; *i* ~ (*äv.*) serially **2** *sport.* division **3** *mat.* series, progression **-figur** character in a comic strip **-koppla** *elektr.* connect in series **-krock** multiple collision; *vard.*

pile-up **-magasin** comic [paper]; funny paper **-match** league match **-nummer** serial number **-tidning** comic [paper]; funny paper **-tillverkning** series (long-line) production

serigrafi *s3* serigraphy

seriös *al* serious

serologi *s3* serology

serpentin *s3* serpentine; (*pappersremsa*) streamer **-väg** serpentine road

serum ['se:-] *s8* serum

serv|a [ˣsörva] *sport.* serve; *vard.* service (*en bil* a car); (*hjälpa*) serve, back up **-boll** *s2* service **-linje** service line

serve [sörv] *s2, sport.* service, serv **-ruta** service court

server|a serve; (*passa upp vid bordet*) wait at table; ~ *ngn ngt* help s.b. to s.th.; *middagen är* ~*d!* dinner is served (ready)! **-ing 1** *abstr.* service; *sköta* ~*en vid bordet* do the waiting **2** *konkr., se matservering*

serverings|bord service table **-lucka** service hatch **-rum** pantry

servett *s3* napkin, serviette; *bryta* ~*er* fold napkins; *ta emot ngn med varma* ~*er* (*bildl.*) give s.b. a warm reception **-ring** napkin ring **-väska** napkin case

service ['sö:r-, 'sörv-] *s9* service **-hus** block of service flats; *AE.* apartment hotel **-man** (*reklamman*) agency representative; (*på -station*) petrol-station attendant **-verkstad** car service station **-yrke** service occupation

servil *al* servile; (*krypande*) cringing **-itet** servility; (*fjäsk*) cringing

servis *s3* **1** (*mat-*) service, set **2** *mil.* gun crew **-avgift** service charge; (*dricks*) tip **-ledning** service line, feeder

servitris waitress; (*på fartyg*) stewardess

servitut *s7* easement, encumbrance; *belagd med* ~ encumbered with an easement

servitutsrätt right to an easement

servitör waiter; (*på fartyg*) steward

servo|broms servo[-assisted] brake **-motor** servomotor **-styrning** power steering, servo control **-teknik** servo technique

ses *sågs setts, dep* see each other, meet; *vi* ~*!* I'll be seeing you!

1 sesam ['se:-] *s3, bot.* sesame

2 sesam ['se:-] *n, ~ öppna dig!* open sesame!

session [se'ʃɔ:n] *parl.* session, sitting; (*domstols-*) session, court; (*sammanträde*) meeting; *avsluta ~en* (*vid domstol*) close the court

sessions|dag (*vid domstol*) court day **-sal** session (assembly) room; (*vid domstol*) courtroom; *parl.* chamber

se|så now then!; (*gillande*) that's it!; (*tröstande*) come, come!

set [sett] *s7, sport. o. allm.* set **-boll** set point

sett *sup. av se*

setter *s2* setter

sevärd worth seeing, notable **-het** sight; (*byggnad e.d. äv.*) monument

1 sex [seks] *räkn* six; (*för sms. jfr fem-*)

2 sex *s7* sex

1 sexa [ˣseksa] *s1* (*måltid*) light supper

2 sexa [ˣseksa] *s1* (*siffra*) six

sex|cylindrig *al* six-cylinder (*motor* engine)

S

-dubbel sixfold

sex|dåre sex maniac **-film** sex film (movie), blue movie **-galning** sex maniac

sex|hundratalet the seventh century **-hörnig** [-ö:-] *al* hexagonal **-hörning** [-ö:-] hexagon

sexig *al* sexy **sexism** sexism

sexkant hexagon

sex|klubb sex club **-liv** sex life **-ologi** sexology

sexsiffrig *al* of six figures; *ett ~t tal* a six-figure number

sext|ant sextant **-ett** *s3* sextet[te]

sex|tio [ˣseks-, ˈseks-, *vard.* ˣseksti, ˈseksti] sixty **-tionde** sixtieth **-tioåring** sexagenarian

sex|ton [ˣsekstan] sixteen **-tonde** sixteenth **-tondelsnot** *s3* semiquaver, *AE.* sixteenth note

sexual|brott [-ˣa:l-] sex[ual] crime **-drift** sexual instinct (urge) **-förbrytare** sex criminal, sexual offender **-hygien** sexual hygiene **-itet** sexuality **-liv** sex[ual] life **-rådgivning** advisory service on sexual matters **-system** *bot.* sexual system **-undervisning** sex instruction **-upplysning** information on sexual matters

sexuell *al* sexual

sfinx [-iŋks] *s3* sphinx **-artad** [-a:r-] *a5* sphinxlike

sfär *s3* sphere; *bildl. äv.* province **-isk** [ˈsfä-] *a5* spheric[al]; *~ triangel* (*mat.*) circular triangle

shah *se* schah

shaman *se* schaman

shampoo *se* schampo

shantung [ˈʃann-] *s2* shantung

sherry [ˈʃärri, -y] *s9* sherry

shetlandsull [ˣʃett-] Shetland wool

shiamuslim [ˣʃi:a-] *s3*, **shiit** [ʃi:t] *s3* Shiit, Shiah

shilling [ˈʃill-] *s9* shilling (*förk.* s[h].); *det gick 20 ~ på ett pund* there were 20 shillings to the pound

shingla [ˣʃiŋla] shingle

shoppa [ˣʃåppa] go shopping

shopping|center shopping centre **-vagn** shopping trolley **-väska** shopping bag

show [ʃåo, ʃåvv] *s3* show

shunt [ʃunt] *s2, elektr.* shunt, bypass **-ledning** shunt lead **-ventil** shunt valve

1 si *interj* look!; (*högtidligare*) behold!

2 si *adv*, *~ och så* only so-so; *det gick ~ och så* it wasn't up to much

sia prophesy (*om of*)

siames *s3* Siamese **-isk** [-ˈme:-] *a5* Siamese

siar|e seer, prophet **-gåva** second sight

Sibirien [-ˈbi:-] *n* Siberia **sibirisk** [-ˈbi:-] *a5* Siberian

sibyll|a [-ˣbylla] *s1* sibyl **-insk** [-ˈli:nsk] *a5* sibylline

sicili|en *s3*, **-anare** [-ˣa:na-] *s9* Sicilian **-ansk** [-a:-] *a5* Sicilian

Sicilien [-ˈsi:-] Sicily

sickativ *s7* siccative

sicken *~ en!* what a character!

sickl|a *fack.* scrape **-ing** *konkr.* scraper, scraping iron

sicksack zigzag; *gå i ~* zigzag **-linje** zigzag [line]

sid *al* long [and loose]

sid|a *s1* **1** side; (*mil., byggn.*; *djurs*) flank; (*bok-*)page; *geom.* (*yta*) face; *~ upp och ~ ner* page after page; *~ vid ~* side by side; *anfalla från ~n* attack on (in) the flank; *sedd från ~n* seen side-

face; *med händerna i ~n* with arms akimbo; *på båda -or* (*äv.*) on either side (*av* of); *åt ~n* to the [one] side, (*gå step*) aside **2** *bildl.* side, part; (*synpunkt*) aspect, point of view; *visa sig från sin fördelaktigaste ~* show o.s. at one's best; *från hans ~* on (for) his part; *från regeringens ~* from (on the part of) the Government; *se saken från den ljusa ~n* look on the bright side of things; *det har sina -or att* there are drawbacks to; *hon har sina goda -or* she has her good points; *problemet har två -or* there are two sides to the problem; *stå på ngns ~* side (take sides) with s.b.; *han står på vår ~* he is on our side; *när han sätter den ~n till* when he makes up his mind to; *vid ~n av* (*bildl.*) beside, next to, (*jämte*) along with; *å ena* (*andra*) *~n* on one (the other) hand; *vi å vår ~* we for (on) our part, as far as we are concerned; *är inte hans starka ~* is not his strong point **-antal** number of pages **-bena** side parting **-byte** change of ends

siden *s7* silk **-band** silk ribbon **-glänsande** satiny, silky **-klänning** silk dress **-sko** satin shoe **-svans** *zool.* waxwing **-tyg** silk [material (cloth, fabric)] **-varor** *pl* silk goods **-väveri** silk-weaving mill

siderisk [-ˈde:-] *a5, astr.* sidereal

sid|fläsk bacon **-hänvisning** page reference **-led** *i ~* lateral[ly], sideways

sido|apparat extension [phone] **-blick** sidelong glance; *utan ~ på* (*bildl.*) without a thought for **-byggnad** annex, wing **-dörr** side door **-fönster** side window **-gata** side street, bystreet **-gren** side-branch; (*av släkt*) collateral branch **-linje** (*parallell-*) sideline; *järnv.* junction line, branch; (*släktled*) collateral line (branch); *fotb.* touchline; *barn på ~n* natural children **-replik** aside **-skepp** (*i kyrka*) lateral aisle **-spår** sidetrack (*äv. bildl.*); *järnv.* siding **-vinkel** adjacent angle **-vördnad** irreverence, disrespect

sid|roder *flyg.* rudder **-siffra** page number **-steppa** *vard.* sidestep **-söm** side seam **-vagn** (*på motorcykel*) sidecar **-vind** crosswind; *landa i ~* (*flyg.*) make a crosswind landing **-vördnad** *se* sidovördnad

sierraleonier [-leˈå:-] Sierra Leonean

sierska seeress, prophetess

siesta [-ˣess-] *s1* siesta, [after dinner] nap

siffer|beteckning number **-granskare** checking-clerk, auditor of accounts **-granskning** checking of accounts **-mässig** *al* numeral, numeric[al] **-räkning** numerical calculation **-skyddsmaskin** checkwriter **-system** numerical system **-tips** correct score forecasting **-värde** numerical value

siffr|a *s1* figure; *konkr. äv.* numeral; (*entalssiffra äv.*) digit; (*tal*) number; *romerska -or* Roman numerals; *skriva med ~or* write in figures

sifon [-ˈfå:n] *s3* siphon; soda fountain (siphon)

sig [sejj, *äv.* si:g] oneself; himself, herself, itself, themselves; *han anser* (*säger*) *~ vara frisk* he thinks (says) he is well; *tvätta ~ om händerna* wash one's hands; *man skall inte låta ~ luras* don't let yourself be deceived (led up the garden path); *det låter ~ inte göra[s]* it can't be done; *vara häftig av ~* be hot-tempered by nature; *det är en sak för ~* that's another story; *var för ~* one by one; *i och för ~* in itself; *det för med ~ … it* involves ... (brings ... in its train); *ha ögonen med* ~ keep one's eyes open; *han tog med* ~ *sin bror* he took his brother [along] with him; *ha pengar på* ~ have some money on one; *inte veta till* ~ *av glädje* be overjoyed; *han är inte längre* ~ *själv* he is no longer himself; *av* ~ *själv[t]* by itself (*etc.*); *för* ~ *själv* by o.s. (itself *etc.*); *behålla ngt för* ~ *själv* (*för egen räkning*) keep s.th. for o.s., (*hemlighålla*) keep s.th. to o.s.

sigill [-'jill] *s7* seal; *sätta sitt* ~ *under* (*på*) affix one's seal to, seal **-bevarare** (*stor-*) Keeper of the [Great] Seal; *Storbritannien* Lord Privy Seal **-lack** (*hopskr.* sigillack) sealing wax **-ring** signet (seal) ring

signa [siŋna] *se välsigna*; *den ~de dag* the blessed day

signal [siŋ'na:l] *s3* signal; *ge* ~ make a signal, (*i bil*) sound the horn; *ge* ~ *till* give the signal for **-anläggning** signalling equipment **-anordning** signalling device **-bok** code of signals, signal book

signalement [siŋna-] *s7* description **signalera** signal; (*med signalhorn äv.*) sound the horn

signal|flagga signal flag **-horn** [signal] horn; [car] horn, hooter **-ist** *mil.* signaller, signalman **-raket** signal rocket **-regemente** signal regiment **-skola** *mil.* signal[ling] school **-spaning** signal (communication) intelligence **-system** signalling system **-tjänst** communications (*pl*)

signatur [siŋn-] signature; (*författares äv.*) pen name **-melodi** signature tune, *AE.* theme song

signatärmakt [siŋnaˣtä:r-] signatory power

signer|a [siŋn-, sinj-] sign; initial, mark **-ing** signing

signetring [siŋˣne:t-] signet ring

signifik|ant [-'ant, -'aŋt] *al* significant **-atjv** [*äv.* 'siŋni-] *al* significative, significant

sik *s2*, *zool.* whitefish

1 sikt *s2* (*redskap*) sieve

2 sikt *s3* **1** visibility; view; *dålig* (*ingen*) ~ poor (zero) visibility **2** *hand.* sight, presentation **3** (*tidrymd*) term, run; *på* ~ in the long run; *on the long term*

1 sikta (*sålla*) sift, pass through a sieve; (*mjöl*) bolt

2 sikta **1** (*med vapen*) take aim, aim (*på, mot* at) (*äv. bildl.*); point (*på, mot* at); ~ *högt* (*bildl.*) aim high **2** *sjö.* sight

sikt|e *s6* **1** (*på gevär o.d.*) sight **2** (*synhåll*) sight, view; (*mål*) aim; *få ngt i* ~ get s.th. in sight, *sjö.* sight s.th.; *i* ~ in sight, *bildl.* in prospect (view); *land i* ~! land ahoy; *med* ~ *på* with a view to; *ur* ~ out of sight; *förlora ngt ur* ~ lose sight of s.th. **-punkt** point of aim (sight) **-skåra** [sighting] notch **-växel** sight draft (bill)

sil *s2* **1** strainer, sieve **2** *sl.* fix, hit, shot

sil|a **1** (*filtrera*) strain, sieve, filter; ~ *ifrån* strain off; ~ *mygg och svälja kameler* strain at a gnat and swallow a camel **2** (*sippra*) trickle; (*om ljus*) filter **-ben** *anat.* ethmoid [bone] **-duk** straining cloth, screen

sileshår *bot.* sundew

silhuett [silu'ett] *s3* silhouette

silikat *s7, s4* silicate **silikon** [-'kå:n] *s3, s4* silicone **silikos** [-'kå:s] *s3* silicosis

silke *s6* silk; *av* ~ (*äv.*) silken; *mjuk som* ~ silky

silkes|apa marmoset **-fjäril** silk[worm] moth **-len** as soft as silk; silken (*röst* voice) **-mask** silkworm **-maskodling** sericulture; *konkr.* silkworm farm **-papper** tissue paper **-snöre** silk cord; *ge ngn ~t* politely dismiss s.b. **-strumpa** silk stocking **-trikå** silk tricot **-tråd** silk thread, (*från kokong*) silk filament **-vante** använda *-vantar* (*bildl.*) use kid gloves **-vävnad** silk fabric

sill *s2* herring; *inlagd* ~ pickled herring; *salt* ~ salt [ed] herring; *som packade ~ar* packed together like sardines **-bulle** *kokk.* herring rissole **-burk** tin of herrings **-grissla** guillemot **-mjölke** *s2* milksop **-sallad** *s3* mixture of pickled herring, beetroot, cooked meat and potatoes **-stim** shoal of herring **-trut** *s2* lesser black-backed gull **-tunna** herring barrel **-val** *s2* rorqual, finback

silning [ˣsi:l-] straining; filtering

silo ['si:-] *s5, s3* silo

siluett *s3, se* silhuett

silur *s3* Silurian **-isk** *a5* Silurian

silver ['sill-] *s7* silver; *förgyllt* ~ silver-gilt **-beslag** silver-mount[ing] **-bröllop** silver wedding **-bägare** silver cup (goblet) **-fat** silver dish (plate) **-fisk** (*insekt*) silverfish **-gran** silver fir **-gruva** silver mine **-halt** silver content, fineness **-haltig** *al* argentiferous, silver-bearing **-medalj** silver medal **-mynt** silver coin; *i* ~ in silver **-penning** *sälja ngn för 30* ~*ar* betray s.b. for 30 pieces of silver **-poppel** white poplar, abele **-räv** silver fox **-sak** silver article; ~*er* (*koll.*) silverware (*sg*) **-sked** silver spoon **-skål** silver bowl **-smed** silversmith **-smide** wrought silver **-stämpel** hallmark **-te** hot water with sugar [and cream] **-tärna** arctic tern **-vit** silvery

sim|bassäng [ˣsimm-] swimming pool **-blåsa** (*hos fisk*) sound, air (swim) bladder **-byxor** *pl* swimming trunks **-dyna** swimming float **-fena** *zool.* fin **-fot** *zool.* webbed foot; *-fötter* (*för dykare*) [diving] flippers **-fågel** web-footed bird, swimmer **-hall** indoor swimming bath **-hopp** dive **-hud** web; *med* ~ *mellan tårna* with webbed feet

simili ['si:-] *s9, s7* imitation **-diamant** paste diamond **-pärla** artificial pearl

sim|kunnig [ˣsimm-] able to swim **-kunnighetsprov** swimming test **-lärare** swimming instructor

simma *vl el. sam* summit swim; *bildl. äv.* be bathed (*i* in); (*flyta*) float [on the water]; ~ *bra* be a good swimmer **simmare, simmerska** swimmer **simmig** *al* well thickened (*sås* sauce); treacly (*punsch* punch); hazy (*blick* look) **simning** swimming

simonj *s3* simony

simpa *sl* bullhead

simpel ['simm-] *a2* **1** (*enkel*) simple; plain (*arbetskläder* working clothes); common (*soldat* soldier); (*lätt*) easy **2** (*tarvlig*) common, vulgar; (*föraktlig*) low, base; (*om kläder*) mean, shabby **simpelt** *adv* **1** *helt* ~ simply **2** (*tarvligt*) low, mean[ly], shabbily; *det var* ~ *gjort* it was a mean (shabby) thing to do

simplifier|a simplify **-ing** simplification

simsalabim [-'bimm] *interj* hocus pocus

sim|skola [ˣsimm-] swimming school **-sätt** (*fritt* free) style **-tag** stroke **-tur** swim **-tävling** swimming competition

simul|ant malingerer **-ator** [-ˣla:tår] s3 simulator **-era** simulate; (om soldat) malinger

simultan a1 simultaneous **-schack** simultaneous chess-playing **-tolk** simultaneous interpreter **-tolka** interpret [speech] simultaneously

1 sin [sinn] (sitt, sina) pron one's; fören. his, her, its, their; självst. his, hers, its, theirs; ~ nästa one's neighbour; i sitt och ~ familjs intresse in his own interest and that of his family; de ~a his (etc.) relations (people), his (etc.) own family; bli ~ be[come] one's own master (boss); det kan göra sitt till that can help matters; det torra not stand to lose anything; kärleken söker inte sitt (bibl.) love seeketh not its own; vad i all ~ dar what on earth; i ~om tid in due [course of] time; på ~ tid formerly; på ~a ställen in places; hålla på sitt watch one's own interest; gå var och en till sitt all go back home

2 sin [si:n] s, i uttr.: stå (vara) i ~ be dry

sina dry; brunnen har ~t the well has dried up; ett aldrig ~nde ordflöde a never-ceasing flow of words

sinekur [-'ku:r, ˣsi:-] s3 sinecure

singalęs [siŋga-] s3 Sin[g]halese **-isk** a5 Sin[g]halese

1 singel ['siŋ-] s9 (grus) shingle

2 singel ['siŋ-] s2 **1** sport. singles (pl) **2** kortsp. singleton

singel|olycka accident involving one vehicle only **-skiva** single

singla 1 (kasta) toss [up]; ~ slant om toss for **2** (dala) float

singular [ˣsiŋgu-, 'siŋgu-] s3, se singularis **singularform** [ˣsiŋgu-] singular form **singular|is** [ˣsiŋgu-, 'siŋgu-] -en -er (stå i be in the) singular **singuljär** a1 singular

1 sinka v1 (fördröja) delay; (söla) waste time

2 sinka I s1 (metallkrampa) rivet; (hörntapp) dovetail **II** v1 (porslin) rivet; (bräder) dovetail

sinkadus s3 **1** (örfil) biff **2** (slump) toss-up, chance; en ren ~ a pure toss-up

sinnad a5 (andligt spiritually) minded; (vänskapligt amiably) inclined

sinne s6 **1** fysiol. sense; de fem ~na the five senses; ha ett sjätte ~ have a sixth sense; med alla ~n på helspänn with all one's wits about one; från sina ~n out of one's senses (mind); vid sina ~ns fulla bruk in one's right mind, in full possession of one's senses **2** (-lag) mind, temper, nature; (väsen, hjärta) soul, heart; (håg) taste, inclination, turn; ett häftigt ~ a hasty temper; ha ett vaket ~ för be alert (open) to; ~t rann på honom he lost his temper (flew into a passion); en man efter mitt ~ a man to my mind (taste); han har fått i sitt ~ att he has got it into his head to; ha ~ för humor have a sense of humour; ha ~ för språk have a talent for languages; ha i ~t contemplate; ha ont i ~t have evil intentions; i mitt stilla ~ in my own mind, inwardly; sätta sig i ~t att göra ngt set one's mind [up]on doing s.th.; till ~s in mind; sorgsen till ~s in low spirits; det gick honom djupt till ~s he felt it deeply **-bild** symbol, emblem **-bildlig** symbolical, emblematic[al] **-lag** s7 temperament, disposition; vänligt ~ friendly disposition

sinnes|frid peace of mind **-frånvaro** absence of mind **-förnimmelse** sensation **-förvirrad** a5 distracted **-förvirring** mental aberration; under tillfällig ~ while of unsound mind **-intryck** sensation, impression **-jämvikt** equanimity **-lugn** tranquillity (calmness) of mind **-närvaro** presence of mind **-organ** sense organ **-rubbad** mentally deranged **-rubbning** mental disorder, derangement **-rörelse** emotion; mental excitement **-sjuk** mentally ill, insane; en ~ a mentally ill person **-sjukdom** mental disease; insanity **-sjukhus** mental hospital; (förr) lunatic asylum **-slö** mentally deficient (retarded) **-slöhet** mental deficiency **-stämning** frame of mind **-svag** feeble-minded **-tillstånd** mental condition (state) **-undersökning** mental examination **-villa** hallucination **-ändring** change of attitude

sinnevärlden the material (external) world

sinn|lig a1 **1** (som rör sinnena) pertaining to the sense **2** (köttslig) sensual; en ~ människa a sensualist **-lighet** sensuality **-rik** ingenious (påhitt device) **-rikhet** ingenuity

sino|log Sinologue, Sinologist **-logi** s3 Sinology

1 sinom [ˣsinnåm] se 1 sin

2 sinom [ˣsinnåm] i uttr.: tusen ~ tusen thousands and thousands

sinsemellan [-ˣmell-] between (om sak: among) themselves

sintra sinter; ~de plattor sintered slabs

sinuit s3, med. sinusitis

sinus ['si:-] r **1** mat. sine **2** anat. sinus **-funktion** mat. sinusoidal function **-jt** se sinuit **-kurva** sine curve, sinusoid

sion|ism Zionism **-ist** Zionist

sipp a1 prim, prudish

sippa s1, bot. anemone, windflower

sippra trickle, drop, percolate; ~ fram ooze out; ~ ut (bildl.) transpire, leak out

sira decorate, ornament, deck

sirap s3 **1** treacle, golden syrup; AE. molasses **2** med. syrup; AE. sirup

sirąt ornament, decoration **-lig** a1 (ceremoniös) ceremonious

siręn s3 (myt. o. signalapparat) siren

sirlig [ˣsi:r-] a1 graceful, elegant; (om pers.) ceremonious, formal; (fin) dignified

sisalhampa [ˣsi:-, -ˣsa:l-] sisal hemp

siska s1, zool. siskin

sist I adv last; till ~ (som det ~a) at last, (slutligen) finally, in the end; spara det bästa till ~ save the best until last (till the end); allra ~ last of all; först och ~ from first to last; först som ~ just as well now as later; näst ~ the last but one; ~ men inte minst last but not least; den ~ anlände the last arrival (comer); han blev ~ färdig he was the last to get ready; ~ i boken at the end of the book; stå ~ på listan be the last on the list **II** konj, ~ jag såg honom var han the last time I saw him he was

sist|a -e, superl. a last; (senaste) latest; (slutlig) final; den ~ juni [on] the last of June; ~ anmälningsdag closing date for entries; ~ gången (sidan) the last time (page); ~ modet the latest fashion; ~ skriket all the rage (go); ~ smörjelsen the extreme unction; ~ vagnen (järnv.) tail (rear) wagon; hans ~ vilja his [last] will [and testament]; *den -e* (*av två*) the latter; *han var den -e som kom* he was the last to arrive; *de två ~ månaderna* the last two months; *lägga ~ handen vid* put the finishing touch to; *utandas sin ~ suck* breathe one's last; *för ~ gången* (*för all tid*) for ever (good); *i ~ instans* (*jur.*) in the court of highest instance, *bildl.* in the last resort; *in i det ~* to the very last; *på ~ tiden* lately, of late; *sjunga på ~ versen* draw to its close; *till ~ man* to a man

sist|a *s, best. form, leka ~* play tag (touchlast) **-liden** *a5* last **-nämnda** *a, best. form* [the] last- -mentioned, last-named; (*av två*) the latter **-one** [-å-] *s, i uttr.: på ~* lately

sisu ['si:-] *s9* perseverance, endurance

sisyfosarbete Sisyphean task (labour)

sits *s2 1* (*stol-, stjärt o.d.; ridk.*) seat; *ha bra ~* (*ridk.*) have a good seat *2 kortsp.* lie, lay; *dra om ~en* draw for partners; *bildl., en svår ~* a tricky situation, a sensitive position

sitt *se 1 sin*

sitt|a *satt suttit 1* (*om levande varelse*) sit; (*på -plats äv.*) be seated; (*motsats stå, ligga*) be sitting; (*om fågel*) perch; (*befinna sig*) be (*i fängelse* in prison); (*om regering*) be in office; *~ bekvämt* be comfortably seated; *sitt* [*ner*]*!* sit down, please!; *~ för en målare* sit as a model; *~ och prata* sit talking; *~ still* sit still, (*friare äv.*) keep quiet; *~ trångt* be jammed, *ekon.* be in a tight place; *få ~ a*) get (obtain) a seat, *b*) (*ej bli uppbjuden*) sit out, be a wallflower; *inte ~ i sjön* not be stranded; *~ inom lås och bom* be under lock and key; *~ med goda inkomster* have a large income; *~ vid makten* be in power; *nu -er vi där vackert!* we are in for it now!, now we are in the soup! *2* (*om sak*) be [placed]; (*hänga*) hang; (*om kläder*) sit, fit; *kjolen -er bra* the skirt is a good fit (fits well); *~ på sned* be (*hänga:* hang) askew; *mitt onda -er i* my trouble (the pain) is in; *inte veta hur korten -er* not know how the cards lie *3* (*med betonad partikel*) *~ av* dismount, alight; *~ emellan* (*få obehag*) have trouble, (*bli lidande*) be the sufferer (loser); *~ fast, se 2 fast 3*; *~ hemma* stay at home; *en färg som -er i* a fast colour; *lukten -er i* the smell clings; *nyckeln -er i* the key is in the lock; *ovanan -er i I* (*etc.*) can't free myself of the [bad] habit; *~ inne a* (*inomhus*) keep in[doors], *b*) (*i fängelse*) be in prison, do time; *bekännelsen satt långt inne* the confession was hard to get: *~ inne med upplysningar* be in possession of information; *~ kvar a*) remain sitting (seated), *b*) (*stanna*) remain, stay, *c*) (*efter skolan*) stay (be kept) in [after school]; *låt kappan ~ på!* keep your coat on!; *locket -er på* the lid is on; *~ sönder* wear out by sitting on; *jag -er inte så till att* I am not in a position to, from where I am sitting I can't; *~ illa till* (*bildl.*) be in a bad spot; *~ upp a*) (*på häst*) mount, get on, *b*) (*räta upp sig*) sit up; *~ uppe och vänta på* wait up for; *~ åt* (*om plagg*) be tight; *det -er hårt åt* (*bildl.*) it's tough; *~ över a*) (*dans e.d.; i spel*) sit out, *b*) (*arbeta över*) work overtime

sitt|ande *a4* seated; sitting (*ställning* posture); (*om regering*) in office, present; (*om domstol*) in session; *inför ~ rätt* in open court **-bad** hip (sitz) bath **-ben** *anat.* ischium **-brunn** cockpit **-bräde** seat [board] **-möbler** chairs and sofas **-ning** sit-

ting **-opp** [-'åpp] *s2* (*slag*) clout **-pinne** perch **-plats** seat **-platsbiljett** seat reservation (ticket) **-riktig** designed for comfortable sitting **-strejk** sit-down strike; shop-floor protest **-vagn** *järnv.* day-carriage; (*barnvagn*) pushchair, *AE.* stroller

situation situation; *sätta sig in i ngns ~* put o.s. in a p.'s place; *vara ~en vuxen* be equal to the occasion

situations|komik comedy; (*i film o.d.*) slapstick **-plan** byggn. layout, site plan

situerad [-u'e:-] *a5, väl* (*illa*) *~* well (badly) off

Sixtinska kapellet [-'ti:n-] the Sistine Chapel

SJ [ˣessji:] *förk. för Statens Järnvägar* the Swedish State Railways

sjabbig [ʃ-] *a1* shabby

sjabbla [ʃ-] *vard.* muff it

sjakal [ʃ-] *se schakal*

sjal [ʃ-] *s2* shawl **-ett** *s3* kerchief; head scarf

sjanghaja [ʃaŋ'hajja] shanghai

sjappa [ʃ-] *s*-bolt, scram **sjappen** ['ʃapp-] *s, i uttr.: ta till ~* take to one's heels

sjas [ʃ-] *scat!, be off!; ~ katta* shoo! **sjasa** shoo away

sjaskig [ʃ-] *a1* slovenly; mucky; shabby

sjava [ʃ-] shuffle **sjavig** *a1* slovenly, slapdash

sjok [ʃ-] *s7* lump, chunk

sju [ʃu:] seven; (*för sms. jfr fem-*) **sjua** *s1* seven

sjuarmad *a5* seven-branched (*ljusstake* candlestick)

sjubb [ʃ-] *s2* [North American] rac[c]oon

sjud|a [ʃ-] *sjöd -it* simmer; seethe (*äv. bildl.*); *~ av vrede* seethe with anger; *~nde liv* seething life **-it** *sup. av sjuda*

sju|dubbel [ˣʃu:-] sevenfold **-dundrande** [-ˣdunn-] *a4* terrific **-falt** sevenfold; seven times (*värre* worse) **-jäkla** [-ˣjä:k-] *a4, ett ~ liv* a hell of a life

sjuk [ʃ-] *a1 1* (*predikativt*) ill; (*attr. o. illamående*) sick; (*dålig*) indisposed, unwell; *den ~e* the sick person, (*på sjukhus*) the patient; *de ~a* the sick; *bli ~* get (fall, be taken) ill; *mitt ~a knä* my bad knee; *svårt ~* seriously ill; *ligga ~ i mässling* be down with the measles; *äta sig ~* eat o.s. sick; *~ av* (*i*) suffering from, *bildl.* sick with; *jag blir ~ bara jag tänker på det* the mere thought of it makes me sick *2 bildl., saken är ~* it's a shady business; *ett ~t samvete* a guilty conscience; *han ber för sin ~a mor* that's one for her and two for himself; *~ efter* (*på*) eager (*vard.* dying) for

sjuk|a [ʃ-] *s1, se sjukdom; engelska ~n* rickets; *spanska ~n* the Spanish flu; *det är hela ~n* that's the whole trouble **-anmäla** *~ ngn* (*sig*) report s.b. (report) sick (ill); *-anmäld* reported sick (ill) **-anmälan** notification of illness **-avdelning** ward, infirmary **-avdrag** deduction for sickness **-besök** visiting the sick; (*läkares*) visit to a patient, sick visit **-bädd** sickbed; *vid ~en* at the bedside **-dom** [-domm] *s2* illness, ill-health; (*speciell o. bildl.*) disease; (*ont*) complaint, disorder; *ärftlig ~* hereditary disease

sjukdoms|alstrande *a4* pathogenic **-bild** pathological picture, picture of the (a) disease **-fall** case [of illness] **-orsak** cause of a (the) disease **-sym(p)tom** sympton of a (the) disease

sjuk|ersättning sickness benefit (allowance)

-försäkring health insurance **-försäkrings-besked** health insurance card **-gymnast** physiotherapist **-gymnastik** physiotherapy, remedial exercises (pl) **-hem** nursing home **sjukhus** hospital **-direktör** hospital manager **-dräkt** hospital uniform **-läkare** hospital physician (surgeon) **-vård** hospital treatment (care) **sjuk|intyg** medical (doctor's) certificate **-journal** case record; (för en patient) case sheet **-kassa** (allmän regional) health insurance office **-kassekort** health insurance card **-ledig** vara ~ be on sick leave **-ledighet** sick leave **-lig** [-u:-] al infirm, weak in health; sickly; bildl. morbid (misstänksamhet suspiciousness) **-lighet** [-u:-] infirmity, ill-health; morbidity **-ling** [-u:-] sick person, patient; invalid **-lista** sick list **-lön** sick pay **sjuk|na** [-u:-] fall (be taken) ill (i with); sicken **-penning** sickness benefit (allowance) **-penningsklass** sickness benefit category (group) **-pension** disablement pension **-permission** sick leave **-rapport** medical report **-rum** sick room **-sal** [hospital] ward **-skriva** ~ ngn put s.b. on the sick list; ~ sig report sick (ill); -skriven sick-listed, reported sick **-skötare** [male] nurse **-sköterska** nurse; (examinerad) trained (staff, AE. graduate) nurse **sjuksköterske|elev** student nurse **-skola** nurses' training school **-uniform** nurse's uniform **-utbildning** nursing training **sjuk|stuga** cottage hospital **-syster** se sjuksköterska **-säng** se sjukbädd **-transport** conveyance of patients **-vård** medical care (attendance), nursing; care of the sick; fri ~ free medical attention (treatment) **-vårdare** male nurse; mil. medical orderly **sjukvårds|artiklar** pl sanitary (medical) articles **-biträde** assistant nurse, [hospital] orderly **-ersättning** medical expenses allowance **-kunnig** trained in nursing the sick **sjumila|steg** gå med ~ walk with seven-league strides **-stövlar** pl seven-league boots **sjunde** [ʃ-] seventh; i ~ himlen in [the] seventh heaven **-dagsadventist** Seventh-Day Adventist **-del** seventh [part], one seventh **sjunga** [ʃ-] sjöng sjungit sing; (om fågel äv.) warble; ~ falskt sing out of tune; ~ rent sing in tune; ~ ngns lov sing a p.'s praises; ~ på sista versen be on one's last legs, draw to its close; ~ in (på grammofon) record; ~ ut sing out, bildl. speak out, speak one's mind **sjungit** sup. av sjunga **sjunk|a** [ʃ-] sjönk -it sink; (om fartyg äv.) founder, go down; (falla) drop, fall (t. botten to the bottom); (minska) decrease (i antal in numbers); (i värde) depreciate, decline, sink, fall; febern ~ the fever is abating; kaffet står och -er the coffee is settling; priserna -er prices are falling (declining), prices show a downward tendency; solen -er the sun is setting; termometern -er the temperature is falling; önska att man kunde ~ genom jorden wish one could sink through the floor; känna modet ~ lose courage (heart); ~ i ngns aktning go down in a p.'s estimation; ~ i glömska sink into oblivion; ~ i vanmakt faint away; ~ ihop (bildl.) break down, collapse; ~ ner på en stol sink down on to a chair; ~ till marken

drop to the ground; ~ till ngns fötter fall at a p.'s feet; ~ undan sink, subside; han är djupt -en he has sunk very low
sjunkbomb depth charge (bomb) **sjunkit** sup. av sjunka
sju|sovare [-å-] **1** zool. dormouse **2** pers. lieabed, sluggard **-stjärnan** sg, best. form, **-stjärnorna** pl, best. form the Pleiades (pl) **-särdeles** [-ˣsä:r-] vard. terrific **-tillhållarlås** mortise (mortice) lock
sjuttio [ˣʃuttio, ʃutt-, vard. ˣʃutti, ʃutti] seventy **sjuttionde** [ˣʃuttiå-] seventieth **sjuttioåring** septuagenarian
sjutton [ˣʃuttån] seventeen; aj som ~! by Jove!, Good Lord!; det var dyrt som ~ it cost a packet; full i ~ full of mischief; för ~ gubbar for goodness sake; nej för ~! Good Lord, no!; ge ~ i att (låta bli) stop, leave off, (strunta i) not bother; ge sig ~ på att bet your life that; det vore väl ~ om it would be a wonder if **sjuttonde** seventeenth **sjuttonhundratalet** the eighteenth century
sjå [ʃ-] s7, vard. big (tough) job **-are** docker longshoreman, stevedore
sjåp [ʃ-] s7 [silly] goose, ninny **sjåpa** rfl be silly, act the ninny **sjåpig** al silly, foolish; vard. namby-pamby **sjåpighet** silliness etc.
själ [ʃ-] s2 **1** filos., psykol., rel.-hist. soul; (ande) spirit; ~ens behov spiritual needs **2** (sinne) soul, mind; det skar mig in i ~en it cut me to the heart (quick); få ro i sin ~ get peace of mind; i ~ och hjärta at heart, in one's heart of hearts; med liv och ~ body and soul; två ~ar och en tanke two minds with but a single thought; ~arnas sympati spiritual affinity; min ~ tror jag inte upon my soul if it's not **2** pers. soul; vara ~en i ngt be [the life and] soul of s.th.; där fanns inte en ~ there wasn't a soul; en glad ~ a jolly fellow; varenda ~ (vard.) every man jack
själa|glad overjoyed, delighted **-herde** pastor, shepherd of souls **-mässa** requiem **-nöd** anguish of the soul, spiritual agony **-ringning** [death] knell, passing (death) bell **-sörjare** spiritual guide **-tåget** ligga i ~ be dying, be breathing one's last **-vandring** transmigration [of souls] **-vård** cure of souls, spiritual charge of a parish
själfull soulful (ansikte face); (anderik) animated (föredrag lecture) **-het** soulfulness; animation
Själland [ˈʃäll-] n Zealand
själlös soulless; spiritless; (livlös) inanimate **-het** soullessness etc.
själs|adel nobility of mind **-dödande** soul-destroying, deadly **-egenskap** mental quality **-fin** refined, noble **-frånvarande** absent-minded **-frände** kindred spirit; vara ~r (äv.) sympathize **-frändskap** congeniality of mind, spiritual affinity **-förmögenhet** faculty, mental ability **-gåvor** pl intellectual (mental) gifts **-kval** mental suffering, agony **-lig** [-ä:-] al mental; (andlig) spiritual **-liv** intellectual (spiritual) life **-sjuk** (sinnessjuk) mentally ill; (hypokondrisk) hypochondriac[al] **-strid** mental struggle **-styrka** strength of mind
själv [ʃ-] **1** myself, yourself, himself, herself, itself, oneself; pl ourselves, yourselves, themselves; det har jag gjort ~ I did it myself; han har ~ skrivit ... he has written ... himself; ~ är bästa

dräng if you want a thing done well, do it yourself; *bli sig ~ igen* be oneself again; *komma ~* come personally (in person); *om jag får säga det ~* if I may say so myself; *tack ~!* thank you!; *vara sig ~ nog* be self-sufficient; *det kan du vara ~!* (*vard.*) so are you!; *av sig ~* of oneself, spontaneously, (*frivilligt*) voluntarily; *för sig ~* (*avsides*) aside; *tala för sig ~* talk to oneself; *i sig ~* in itself; *hon heter A. i sig ~* her maiden name is A.; *på sig ~ känner man andra* one judges others by o.s. **2** *hon är blygsamheten ~* she is modesty itself; *~e* (*~aste*) *kungen* the king himself (in person); *på ~a födelsedagen* on the very birthday; *i ~a verket* as a matter of fact; *han gör ~a grovarbetet* he does the real heavy (ground) work

själv|aktning self-respect **-antändning** spontaneous ignition, self-ignition **-bedrägeri** self--deception, self-delusion **-befruktning** self-fertilization; *bot.* self-pollination **-behärskning** self-control, self-restraint **-bekännelse** confession **-belåten** self-satisfied; complacent **-bestämmanderätt** right of self-determination, autonomy **-betjäning** self-service **-betjäningsbutik** self-service store **-betraktelse** self--contemplation, introspection **-bevarelsedrift** instinct of self-preservation **-bindare** *lantbr.* [reaper] binder **-biografi** autobiography **-biografisk** autobiographical **-deklaration** income tax return (*AE.* report) **-disciplin** self--discipline **-dö** die out of itself; *ett ~tt djur* an animal that has died from natural causes **-fallen** *a3* obvious, apparent **-fallenhet** matter of course **-förakt** self-contempt **-förbränning** spontaneous combustion **-förebräelse** self-reproach **-förgudning** self-glorification **-förhävelse** presumption **-förnekelse** self-denial **-försakelse** self-denial **-försvar** (*till* in) self-defence **-försörjande** *a4* self-supporting **-försörjning** self-sufficiency **-förtroende** self-confidence, self-reliance **-förverkligande** self-realization **-förvållad** *a5* self-inflicted

själv|gjord self-made **-god** self-righteous **-godhet** self-righteousness **-hjälp** self-help; *hjälp till ~ assistance* supplementary to one's own efforts **-hushåll** *ha ~ på* one's own housekeeping **-hushållning** economy based on domestic production [of necessities] **-häftande** *a4* [self-]adhesive **-härskare** autocrat **-hävdelse** self-assertion **-hävdelsebegär** urge to assert o.s. **-ironi** irony directed against o.s. **-ironisk** ironic at one's own expense

självisk ['ʃäll-] *a5* selfish, egoistic[al] **-het** ['ʃäll-] selfishness, egoism

själv|klar obvious; *det är ~t* it is a matter of course, it goes without saying **-kopierande** *a4* self-copying **-kostnad** prime (production) cost **-kostnadspris** cost price; *till ~* at cost [price] **-kritik** self-criticism **-kritisk** self-critical **-kännedom** self-knowledge **-känsla** self-esteem **-ljud** vowel [sound] **-lockig** naturally curly **-lysande** luminous (*färg* paint) **-länsande** *a4* self--bailing **-lärd** self-taught; *en ~* an autodidact

själv|mant [-a:-] *adv* of one's own accord, voluntarily **-medlidande** self-pity **-medvetande** self-assurance **-medveten** self-assured **-mord** (*begå* commit) suicide **-mordsförsök** at-

tempted suicide **-mordskandidat** would-be suicide **-mål** *sport.*, *göra ~* shoot the ball (*etc.*) into one's own goal **-mördare** suicide **-plågeri** self-torture **-porträtt** self-portrait **-påtagen** *a5* self-assumed **-rannsakan** self-examination **-registrerande** [-j-] *a4* self-recording **-reglerande** *a4* self-regulating, self-adjusting **-renande** self-cleaning **-risk** *försäkr.* excess, [deductible] franchise **-rådig** self-willed, wilful

själv|servering self-service [restaurant], cafeteria **-skriven** *a3*, *han är ~ som ordförande* he is just the man for chairman; *han är ~ till platsen* he is sure to get the post **-smörjande** *a4* self-lubricating (*lager* bearing) **-spelande** *~ piano* pianola (*varumärke*), *AE.* player piano **-spricka** *sl* chap; *få -sprickor på händerna* get chapped hands **-start** self-starter **-studium** self-instruction, self-tuition, private study **-styre[lse]** self-government, autonomy; *lokal ~* local [self-]government **-ständig** *al* independent; self-governed **-ständighet** independence **-ständighetsförklaring** declaration of independence **-suggestion** autosuggestion

självsvåld self-indulgence; self-will **-ig** *al* undisciplined; self-willed

själv|svängning self-oscillation **-sådd** *a5* self--sown **-säker** self-confident, self-assured **-tagen** *a5* self-assumed (*makt* power); usurped (*rätt* right) **-tillräcklig** self-satisfied; self-sufficient **-tillit** self-reliance **-tryck** gravity **-tvätt** self-service laundry, Launderette (*varumärke*), *AE.* Laundromat (*varumärke*) **-uppdragande** *a4* selfwinding **-uppfyllande** *a4* self-fulfilling **-uppoffrande** self-sacrificing **-uppoffring** self-sacrifice **-upptagen** self-centred **-utlösare** *foto.* self-timer **-utnämnd** *a5* self-styled **-utplånande** *a4* self-effacing **-vald** (*-utnämnd*) self-elected; (*frivillig*) self-chosen **-verkande** automatic, . self-acting **-verksamhet** self-activity **-ägande** *a4*, *~ bönder* owner-farmers, freeholders **-ändamål** end in itself **-övervinnelse** self-mastery; *det kostade mig verklig ~ att* it was hard to bring myself to

sjätte [ʃ-] sixth **-del** sixth [part]

sjö [ʃö:] *s2* **1** (*in-*) lake; (*hav*) sea; *gå i ~n* (*dränka sig*) drown o.s.; *~n går upp* the ice breaks up; *~n ligger* the lake is coated with ice; *på öppna ~n* on the open sea; *sätta en båt i ~n* put out a boat; *till ~ss* at sea; *gå till ~ss* (*om pers.*) become a sailor, go to sea, (*om fartyg*) put [out] to sea; *till lands och ~ss* on land and sea; *ute till ~ss* in the open sea; *kasta pengarna i ~n* throw money away; *kasta yxan i ~n* throw up the sponge; *regnet bildade ~ar på gatorna* the rain lay in great pools in the streets **2** (*-gång*; *stört-*) sea, wave; *hög ~* high (heavy) sea; *få en ~ över sig* ship a sea; *tåla ~n* stand the sea, be a good sailor

sjö|befäl ship's officers (*pl*) **-befälsskola** school of nautical studies **-björn** *bildl.*, *se sjöbuss 1* **-bod** boathouse **-borre** [-å-] *s2*, *zool.* sea urchin **-bris** sea breeze **-buss** *bildl.* sea dog, salt **2** (*farkost*) ferryboat

sjöd *imperf. av sjuda*

sjö|duglig seaworthy **-elefant** elephant seal, sea elephant **-farande** *a4* seafaring (*folk* nation); *en ~* a mariner (seafaring man, seafarer)

S

-farare seafarer **-fart** (*skeppsfart*) navigation; (*sjöhandel*) shipping [business, trade]; *handel och* ~ commerce (trade) and shipping **-fartsbok** discharge book **-fartsmuseum** maritime (nautical) museum **-fartsverket** the Swedish national administration of shipping and navigation **-flygplan** seaplane, hydroplane **-folk** *pl* (*-män*) seamen **-fågel** aquatic bird, sea bird (fowl) **-förklaring** [captain's] protest; *avge* ~ enter (make) a protest **-försvar** naval defence **-försäkring** marine insurance **-gräs** seaweed **-grön** sea-green **-gurka** sea cucumber **-gång** roll[ing], [heavy, high] sea **-hjälte** naval hero **-häst** sea horse **-jungfru** mermaid

sjö|kadett naval cadet, midshipman **-kapten** [sea] captain, master mariner **-ko** sea cow **-kort** [nautical, marine] chart **-krig** naval war[fare] **-krigshögskola** naval staff college **-krigsskola** naval college **-lag** maritime law **-ledes** by water (sea) **-lejon** sea lion **-lilja** sea lily **-lägenhet** *med första* ~ by the first boat **-lök** sea squill (onion) **-makt** sea power; (*örlogsflotta*) naval force **-malm** bog-iron ore **-man** sailor, seaman; mariner

sjömans|biff *ung.* casserole of beef, potatoes and onions **-blus** sailor's blouse **-hem** seamen's home

sjömanskap *s7* seamanship

sjömans|kista seaman's (sea) chest **-kostym** sailor suit **-krage** sailor collar **-mission** seamen's mission **-mössa** sailor's cap **-präst** seamen's chaplain **-uttryck** nautical expression **-visa** sailor's song, shanty

sjö|mil nautical mile **-militär I** *a1* naval **II** *s3* naval man **-märke** navigation mark, seamark; buoy beacon

sjönk [ʃ-] *imperf. av sjunka*

sjö|nöd distress **-odjur** sea monster **-officer** naval officer **-olycka** accident at sea **-orm** sea serpent **-penna** *zool.* sea pen **-ranunkel** great spearwort **-rapport** weather forecast for sea areas **-reglering** regulation of water level in lakes **-resa** [sea] voyage **-räddning** sea rescue; (*organisation*) lifeboat service (institution), *AE.* coastguard **-räddningsfartyg** rescue launch; lifeboat **-rätt** maritime law; (*domstol*) maritime court **-rövare** pirate **-röveri** piracy **-scout** sea scout **-seger** naval victory, victory at sea **-sidan** *från* ~ from the sea[ward side]; *åt* ~ towards the sea **-sjuk** seasick **-sjuka** seasickness **-skadad** *a5* seadamaged **-skum 1** *eg.* sea foam **2** *miner.* meerschaum **-slag** naval battle, action at sea; *bildl.* wet party **-stad** seaport [town] **-stjärna** starfish **-strid** naval encounter **-stridskrafter** *pl* naval forces **-stövel** sea boot **-säker** seaworthy **-sätta** launch **-sättning** launch[ing] **-term** nautical term **-tomt** beach lot, lakeside site **-tunga** *zool.* [European] sole **-van** used (accustomed) to the sea; *bli* ~ (*äv.*) find one's sea legs **-vana** familiarity with the sea **-vatten** lake (sea) water **-väg** sea route, seaway; *ta* ~*en* go by sea **-värdig** seaworthy **-värnskår** auxiliary naval corps

s.k. *förk. för så kallad* so-called

ska *vard. för skall, se 1 skola*

skabb *s3* [the] itch; scabies; (*hos djur*) mange **-ig**

a1 scabious, scabby; *neds.* mangy

skabrös *a1* scabrous, indecent, obscene

skad|a I *s1* injury (*på* to); *med. äv.* insult; (*förödelse*) damage; (*motsats nytta*) harm, mischief; (*förlust*) loss; ('*synd*') pity; *anställa* ~ cause (do) damage; *avhjälpa en* ~ repair an injury; *av* ~*n blir man vis* once bitten, twice shy; *bli vis av* ~*n* learn by painful experience; *det är ingen* ~ *skedd* there is no harm done; *det är ngn* ~ *på maskinen* s.th. has gone wrong (there is s.th. the matter) with the machine; *det är* ~ *att* it is a pity that; *det var* ~*!* what a pity!; *erhålla lätta* (*svåra*) -*or* be slightly (seriously) injured (hurt); *ta* ~ suffer (*av* from), (*om sak*) be damaged (*av* by); *ta* ~*n igen* make up for it; *tillfoga* ... ~ inflict damage on ... **II** *v1*, *pers.* hurt, injure; (*såra*) wound; (*sak*) damage; *abstr.* damage, injure (*ngns rykte* a p.'s reputation); *det* ~*r inte att försöka* there is no harm in trying; *det skulle inte* ~ *om* it would do no harm if; ~ *sig* be (get) hurt, hurt o.s.; ~ *sig i handen* hurt one's hand

skade|anmälan notification of damage **-djur** noxious animal; *koll.* vermin (*pl*) **-ersättning** compensation [for damage], indemnification; indemnity **-glad** spiteful, malicious **-glädje** malicious pleasure, malice **-görelse** [-j-] damage **-insekt** noxious insect **-reglering** settlement [of claims], claims adjustment

skadeslös *hålla ngn* ~ indemnify s.b.

skade|stånd *s7* damages (*pl*); *begära* ~ claim damages **-ståndsanspråk** compensation claim, claim for damages **-ståndsskyldig** liable to pay damages **-verkan** damage; deleterious effect

skad|lig [ˣska:d-] *a1* injurious, harmful (*för* to); noxious, unwholesome (*mat* food); (*menlig*) detrimental (*för* to); *ha* ~ *inverkan på* have a detrimental effect on **-skjuta** wound

skaffa 1 (*an-*) get, procure (*åt* for); (*finna*) find (*arbete* work), furnish (*bevis* proofs); (*förse med*) provide with; (*skicka efter*) send for; (~ *hit*) bring; ~ *barn till världen* bring children into the world; ~ *ngn bekymmer* cause s.b. anxiety; ~ *kunder* attract customers; ~ *sig fiender* make enemies; *jag skall* ~ *pengarna åt dig* I'll find (raise) the money for you; ~ *ur världen* do away with; ~ *fram* produce; ~ *undan* remove, get out of the way **2** (*göra*) do; *jag vill inte ha med honom att* ~ I don't want to have anything to do with him **3** *sjö.* (*äta*) eat **4** *rfl* procure (etc.) [for] o.s.; (*köpa*) buy o.s., acquire (*nya kläder* new clothes); make (*vänner* friends); obtain (*upplysningar* information), attain (*kunskaper* knowledge); (*ådraga sig*) contract (*en förkylning* a cold; *skulder* debts); (*förse sig med*) furnish (provide) o.s. with; (*finna*) find (*tillfälle* an opportunity)

skafferi larder, pantry **skaffning** *sjö.* (*måltid*) meal; food

ska[f]föttes [ˣska:-, ˣskaff-] *ligga* ~ lie head to foot

skaft *s7* **1** (*handtag*) handle (*på verktyg o.d. äv.*) shaft; (*på stövel, strumpa*) leg; *sätta* ~ *på* furnish with a handle, fix handle to **2** *bot.* stalk, stem **3** *bildl.*, *ha huvudet på* ~ have one's head screwed on the right way; *med ögonen på* ~ with one's eyes starting (popping) out of one's head

Skagen [ˈska:-] *n* the Skaw

Skagerack ['ska:-] *n* the Skagerrak
skaka 1 (*försätta i skakning*) shake; (*friare o. bildl.*) agitate (*sinnena* the senses), convulse; ~ *hand med* shake hands with; *berättelsen* ~*de henne djupt* she was deeply shaken by the story; ~ *ngt ur ärmen* (*bildl.*) do s.th. offhand (straight off) **2** (*häftigt röras*) shake (*av* with); (*darra*) shiver (*av köld* with cold); *fys.* vibrate ; (*vagga*) rock; (*om åkdon*) jog, bump (*fram* along); *samhället* ~*de i sina grundvalar* society was shaken to its [very] foundations; ~ *av skratt* shake (rock) with laughter; ~ *på huvudet* shake one's head **3** (*med betonad partikel*) ~ *av* [*sig*] shake off; ~ *om* shake up, stir **skakande** *a4* shaking; (*upp-*) harrowing (*skildring* description)
skak|el ['skakk-, 'ska:-] *s2* shaft; *hoppa över -larna* (*bildl.*) kick over the traces, run riot
skak|is ['ska:-] *oböjligt a, vard.*, *känna sig* ~ feel shaky (jittery) **-ning** [-a:-] shake (*på* of); shaking; (*darrning*) trembling; ~*ar i motorn* vibrations in the engine
skal *s7* (*hårt* ~) shell; (*skorpa äv.*) crust; (*apelsin-, äppel-* etc.) peel; (*banan-, druv-, potatis-*) skin; (*gurk-, melon-*) rind; (*på ris*) husk; (*avskalat*) peelings, parings (*pl*); *sluta sig inom sitt* ~ retire into one's shell
1 skala *v1* [un]shell; (*apelsin, potatis*) peel; (*äpple*) pare; ~ *av* peel (*etc.*) off
2 skala *s1, mat., mus.* scale; (*på radio*) dial; *i stor* (*liten*) ~ on a large (small) scale; *en karta i* ~ *1:50 000* a map on the scale of 1:50 000; *ordnad efter fallande* ~ arranged on a descending scale
skalbagge beetle; *AE. äv.* bug; *fack.* coleopteran, coleopteron
skald *s3* poet **skalda** make poetry
skalde|gåva poetic gift, poetic[al] talent **-konst** poetry, poesy **-stycke** poem, piece of poetry
skaldinna poetess
skaldjur shellfish, crustacean
skalenlig [-e:n-] *a1* made to scale
1 skalk *s2* (*brödkant*) crust; (*ostkant*) rind
2 skalk *s2* (*skälm*) rogue, wag; *ha en* ~ *i ögat* have a twinkle in one's eye
skalka *sjö.* batten down (*luckorna* the hatches) *etc.*
skalkaktig *a1* roguish, waggish **-het** roguishness
skalkas *dep* joke, jest
skalkniv skinning knife
1 skall *pres. av 1 skola*
2 skall *s7* (*hund-*) bark; (*ljud*) clang, ring, ringing; *ge* ~ bark
skalla 1 (*genljuda*) clang, ring; (*eka*) resound; *ett* ~*nde skratt* a peal of laughter **2** *sport.* head
skallbas base of the skull
skalle *s2* skull; *anat.* cranium; *tekn.* head; *vard.* pate; noddle; *dansk* ~ butt with the head
skallerorm rattlesnake
skallfraktur fracture of the skull
skall|gång *s2* chase, search; *gå* ~ *efter* search for, organize a search for **-gångskedja** searchers (*pl*); *jakt.* beaters (*pl*)
skallig *a1* bald **-het** baldness
skallra I *s1* rattle **II** *v1* rattle; (*klappra*) clatter; (*om tänder*) chatter
skallskada skull injury
skalm *s2* **1** (*skakel*) shaft **2** ~*ar* (*på glasögon*)

bows, (*på sax*) scissor-blades
skalmeja [-*mejja] *s1* shawn
skalmodell model built to scale, scale model
skalp *s3* scalp
skalpell *s3* scalpel
skalpera scalp, take s.b.'s scalp
skalv *s7* quake; (*jord-*) earthquake
skalär *a1* scalar (*storhet* quantity)
skalömsning shedding of the shell
skalövning *mus.* scale practice
skam [skamm] *s2* **1** (*blygsel*) shame; (*ngt -ligt*) dishonour; (*skändlighet*) infamy; ~ *till sägandes* to my (*etc.*) shame; *fy* ~*!* shame on you!; *det var inte fy* ~ that was not bad at all; *för* ~*s skull* for very shame; *bita huvudet av* ~*men* be past (lost to) shame; *nu går* ~[*men*] *på torra land* that's the last straw **2** (*vanära*) shame; disgrace (*för* for, to); ~ *den som ...!* shame on him that ...!; *det är ingen* ~ there is no disgrace (*att förlora* in losing); *komma på* ~ be frustrated; *få stå där med* ~*men* be put to shame **-fila 1** *möblerna var* ~*de* the furniture was the worse for wear; *med* ~*t rykte* with a tarnished reputation **2** *sjö.* chafe **-fläck** stain, taint; *vara en* ~ *för* be a disgrace to **-grepp** *eg.* grabbing of the opponent's genitals; *bildl.* hit below the belt **-känsla** sense of shame **-lig** *a1* shameful, disgraceful; (*vanhedrande*) dishonourable; *det är verkligen* ~*t att* it is really disgraceful that **-ligen, -ligt** *adv* outrageously **-lös** shameless; (*fräck*) impudent **-löshet** shamelessness; impudence **-påle** pillory; *stå vid* ~*n* (*bildl.*) be publicly disgraced **-sen** *a3* ashamed (*över* of) *AE. vard.* mean **-senhet** shame **-vrå** *stå i* ~*n* stand in the corner
skandal *s3* scandal; *ställa till* ~ cause a scandal; *vard.* kick up a row **-artad** [-a:r-] *a5* scandalous **-hungrig** fond of scandal
skandal|isera disgrace **-omsusad** *a5, ung.* scandal-prone **-tidning** scandal sheet **-unge** potential scandal
skandalös *a1* scandalous
skander|a scan **-ing** scanning, scansion
skandinav *s3* Scandinavian **Skandinavien** [-'na:-] *n* Scandinavia
skandinav|isk [-'na:-] *a5* Scandinavian **-ism** Scandinavianism
skandium ['skann-] *s8, kem.* scandium
skank *s2, s1, vard.* shank, leg
skans *s2* **1** *mil.* redoubt; (*kastell*) fortlet; *siste man på* ~*en* (*bildl.*) the last survivor, the last one out **2** *sjö.* forecastle, fo'c's'le
skapa create, make; (*alstra*) produce; (*framkalla*) cause, give rise to, engender; ~ *förutsättningar för* pave the way for; ~ *sig en förmögenhet* make a fortune; *du är som* ~*d för uppgiften* you are just the man (*etc.*) for the job; ~ *om sig* transform o.s. (*till* into) **skapande I** *a4* creative (*konstnär* artist); constructive (*sinne* mind); *inte ett* ~ *grand* not a mortal thing **II** *s6* creation, creating *etc.*
skapar|e creator **-förmåga** creative ability **-glädje** creative joy **-kraft** creative force
skapelse creation; ~*n* (*världen*) creation; ~*ns krona* the crown of creation **-berättelse** creation narrative (myth)
skap|lig [-a:-] *a1* passable, tolerable, not too bad

-ligt [-aː-] *adv*, ~ [*nog*] tolerably well, well enough **-lynne** character, disposition **-nad** *s3* shape, form, figure

skar *imperf. av 2 skära*

skar|a *s1* crowd, multitude; *mil.* troop, band (*soldater* of soldiers); *en* ~ *arbetare* a team (gang) of workmen; *en brokig* ~ a motley crowd; *en utvald* ~ a select group; *samla sig i* -*or kring* flock round

skarabé *s3* scarab

skare *s2* crust [on the snow]; ~*n bär* the snow surface is hard enough to bear

skarp I *al* (*om kniv, spets, vinkel, sluttning o.d.*) sharp; (*om egg, rakkniv, blåst o.d.*) keen; (*besk*) strong (*smak* taste); ~*t angrepp* sharp attack; ~*a hugg* (*äv. bildl.*) hard blows; *en* ~ *intelligens* a keen intelligence, *pers.* a man of keen intelligens; ~*a konturer* (*gränser*) distinct (clear-cut) outlines (limits); ~ *kritik* sharp criticism; ~ *köld* piercing cold; ~*t ljus* glaring light; ~ *ammunition* live ammunition; *en* ~ *tunga* a sharp tongue **II** *s2*, *hugga i på* ~*en* set to work with a will; *ta itu med ngn på* ~*en* take s.b. really in hand; *säga till på* ~*en* give s.b. a ticking-off

skarp|blick acute perception, penetration **-ladda** load with live cartridges **-rättare** executioner **-sill** sprat **-sinne** acumen, penetration, ingenuity; (*klarsyn*) perspicacity **-sinnig** *al* keen, acute; (*klarsynt*) perspicacious, shrewd **-skjutning** firing with live ammunition **-skuren** *a5*, ~*skurna drag* clear-cut features **-skytt** sharpshooter **-slipa** sharpen, whet; ~*d* (*äv.*) sharp-edged **-synt** [-yː-] *al* sharp-sighted **-sås** *kokk.* sauce piquante **-ögd** *al, se -synt*

skarsnö crusty snow

1 skarv *s2, zool.* cormorant

2 skarv *s2* (*fog*) joint; (*söm*) seam; (-*bit*) lengthening-piece; *bildl.* interval

skarv|a (*hopfoga*) join; *tekn.* joint, splice; (*förlänga*) lengthen; ~ *till* add, *sömn.* let in **2** (*ljuga*) stretch a point, embroider the truth **-sladd** *elektr.* extension flex (cord) **-yxa** adz[e]

skat|a *s1* magpie **-bo** magpie's nest

skatt *s3* **1** (*klenod*) treasure (*äv. bildl.*) **2** (*t. staten*) tax; (*t. kommun*) local taxes, *i Storbritannien* [town] rate, *AE.* city (municipal) taxes; (*på vissa varor*) duty; ~*er* (*allm.*) [rates and] taxes; *direkt* ~ direct tax; *indirekt* ~ indirect tax

skatta 1 (*betala skatt*) pay taxes (*etc.*); *han* ~*r för 30 000 om året* he is assessed at 30 000 a year **2** (*plundra*) plunder, rifle; ~ *en bikupa på honung* take honey from a beehive **3** (*upp-*) estimate, value; *min högt* ~*de vän* my highly esteemed friend **4** (*betala tribut*) pay tribute to; ~ *åt förgängelsen* pay the debt to nature, go the way of all flesh **5** ~ *sig lycklig* count o.s. fortunate (lucky)

skatte|avdrag tax deduction (allowance) **-belopp** amount of tax **-betalare** taxpayer **-börda** tax burden **-flykt** tax evasion **-fri** tax-free; (*om vara*) duty-free, free of duty **-frihet** exemption from taxes **-fusk** tax evasion **-fuskare** tax dodger **-förmåga** tax-paying ability **-höjning** increase in taxation **-inkomst** revenue from taxation **-krona** tax rate; *i Storbritannien ung.* rate poundage **-kvitto** (*för fordon*) motor tax disc **-lagstiftning** fiscal (tax) legislation **-lättnad** tax relief **-medel** *pl* tax revenue (*sg*)

-myndighet tax[ation] authority **-paradis** tax haven **-planering** tax avoidance **-pliktig** (*om pers.*) liable to pay tax[es]; (*om vara etc.*) taxable; ~ *inkomst* taxable (assessable) income **-politik** fiscal policy **-rätt** taxation law **-sats** tax rate **-skala** tax scale **-skolk** tax evasion **-smitare** tax dodger **-sänkning** tax reduction (relief) **-tabell** table of tax rates **-teknisk** fiscal **-termin** tax payment period **-uppbörd** tax collection, collection of taxes **-utskott** ~*et* the [Swedish Parliamentary] standing committee on taxation **-verk** tax department (division); *i Storbritannien ung.* Board of Inland Revenue, *AE. ung.* Inland Revenue Service **-återbäring** tax refund

skatt|grävare treasure hunter **-gömma** [treasure] cache **-kammare** treasury **-kammarväxel** treasury bill **-mas** tax collector **-mästare** treasurer **-ning** *fack.* approximation, estimate **-pliktig** *se skattepliktig* **-sedel** income-tax demand note; *AE.* tax-bill **-skriva** tax **-skyldig** liable to pay tax[es] **-sökare** treasure hunter

skava *v2* chafe (*äv.* ~ *på*); scrape; gall (*hål på skinnet* one's skin); ~ *hål på* rub a hole in

skavank [-'vaŋk] *s3* flaw, fault; (*krämpa*) ailment

skavsår sore

ske [ʃe:] *v4* happen, occur; (*verkställas*) be done; ~ *Guds vilja!* God's will be done!; *skall* ~*!* [all] right!; *ingen skada* ~*dd* no harm done; *allt som händer och* ~*r* all that is going on; *vad stort* ~*r det* ~*r tyst* noble deeds are done in silence

sked [ʃ-] *s2* spoon; *en* ~ ... (*som mått*) a spoonful of ...; *ta* ~*en i vacker hand* make the best of it

skeda [ʃ-] *kem.* separate, segregate

sked|and [ʃ-] *zool.* shoveller **-blad** bowl of a spoon **-drag** spoon[bait]

skede [ʃ-] *s6* phase, period; stage

sked|full [ʃ-] spoonful (*soppa* of soup) **-skaft** handle of a spoon

skedvatten [ʃ-] *kem.* aqua fortis

skedvis by the spoonful

skeende [ʃ-] *s6* course of events

skela [ʃ-] squint (*på vänster öga* in the left eye)

skelett *s7* skeleton; *bildl. äv.* framework

skel|ning [ˣʃe:l-] squint **-ögd** *al* squint-eyed, squinting; *vara* ~ (*äv.*) have a squint

skelört [ʃ-] greater celandine, swallowwort

1 sken [ʃ-] *s7* **1** (*ljus*) light; (*starkt äv.*) glare **2** (*falskt yttre*) appearance[s *pl*], semblance, guise; ~*et bedrar* appearances are deceptive; *han har* ~*et emot sig* appearances are against him; *hålla* ~*et uppe* keep up appearances; *ge sig* ~ *av att vara* make a show of being; *under* ~ *av vänskap* under the semblance (cloak) of friendship

2 sken [ʃ-] *n* (*vilt lopp*) bolting; *falla i* ~ bolt

3 sken *imperf. av skina*

1 skena [ʃ-] *v1* bolt, run away; *en* ~*nde häst* a runaway horse

2 skena [ʃ-] *s1* bar, band; (*järnvägs-*) rail; *med.* splint

sken|anfall [ʃ-] feigned attack; *mil. äv.* diversion **-bar** *al* apparent, seeming **-barligen** [-aː-] obviously **-bart** [-aː-] *adv* apparently, seemingly

skenben [ʃ-] *anat.* shinbone, tibia

sken|bild [ʃ-] phantom, distorted picture **-död I** *al* apparently dead **II** *s2* apparent death **-frukt**

pseudocarp, false fruit **-helig** hypocritical, canting **-helighet** hypocrisy, cant **-köp** sham (mock) purchase **-liv** semblance of life **-manöver** diversion, feint

skenskarv *järnv.* rail joint

skepnad [ˣʃeːp-] *s3* **1** (*gestalt*) figure; shape, guise **2** (*spöke*) phantom

skepp [ʃ-] *s7* **1** (*fartyg*) ship; vessel, craft; *bränna sina ~* (*bildl.*) burn one's boats **2** *arkit.* nave; (*sido-*) aisle **3** *boktr.* galley **skeppa** ship

skeppar|e [ʃ-] master; skipper **-brev** master's certificate **-historia** sailor's yarn **-krans** Newgate fringe (frill)

skeppning [ʃ-] shipping, shipment

skeppar|e [ʃ-] master; skipper **-brev** master's certificate **-historia** sailor's yarn **-krans** Newgate fringe (frill)

skeppning [ʃ-] shipping, shipment

skepps|brott shipwreck; *lida ~* be shipwrecked **-bruten** shipwrecked; *bildl.* derelict **-byggare** shipbuilder **-byggnad** shipbuilding **-byggnadskonst** shipbuilding engineering, naval architecture **-båt** ship's boat, launch **-dagbok** ship's log[book] **-docka** dock **-gosse** ship's boy; (*kajutvakt*) cabin boy **-handlare** ship chandler, marine-store dealer **-handlingar** ship's papers **-katt** ship's cat; (*straffredskap*) cat-o'-nine-tails **-klarerare** shipping agent, shipbroker **-klocka** ship's bell, watch bell **-kock** ship's cook **-kök** caboose **-last** cargo, shipload **-läkare** ship's doctor **-mask** shipworm **-mäklare** shipbroker **-papper** *pl* ship's papers (documents) **-präst** chaplain **-redare** shipowner **-skorpa** hardtack, ship's (sea) biscuit **-sättning** *arkeol.* ship barrow (tumulus) **-varv** shipyard, shipbuilding yard

skep|sis ['skepp-] *s2*, **-ticism** scepticism **-tiker** ['skepp-] sceptic **-tisk** ['skepp-] *a5* sceptic[al]

warp; (*vinda*) squint **2** (*ställa snett*) slope, slant; *flyg.* bank; *~ en åra* feather an oar **skevning** [-eː-] warping; *flyg.* bank[ing] **skevningsroder** aileron **skevt** [-eː-] *adv* askew

skick [ʃ-] *s7* **1** (*tillstånd*) condition, state; *i befintligt ~* with all faults, in condition as presented; *i färdigt ~* in a finished state; *i gott ~* in good condition (repair, order); *i oförändrat ~* unchanged, unaltered; *i oskadat ~* (*hand.*) intact, in good condition; *försätta ur stridbart ~* put out of action **2** *sätta ngt i ~* igen put s.th. in order again **3** *se bruk 2, sed* **4** (*uppträdande*) manners (*pl*), behaviour; *är det ~ och fason det?* do you call that good form?

skicka [ʃ-] **1** (*sända*) send (*efter* for; *med* by; *till* to); dispatch; remit (*pengar* money); *~ polisen på ngn* set the police on [to] s.b.; *vill du ~ mig brödet?* will you pass me the bread, please?; *~ bort* send away, dismiss; *~ i förväg* send on before (ahead); *~ hit* send here, send to me (us); *~ med* send [... with him (*etc.*)], (*bifoga*) enclose; *~ omkring* circulate, (*cirkulär*) circularize; *~ tillbaka* send back, return; *~ vidare* send on (forward) **2** *rfl* (*uppföra sig*) behave [o.s.] **skickad** *a5* (*lämpad*) fitted, qualified (*för* for)

skickelse [ʃ-] **1** (*bestämmelse*) decree, ordinance; *ödets ~* [the decree of] Fate, destiny; *genom en försynens ~* by an act of providence,

providentially **2** (*skepnad*) apparition **-diger** fateful, eventful

skicklig [ʃ-] *a1* skilful, clever; good (*i* at); (*duglig*) able, capable; (*händig*) dexterous; *en ~ arbetare* an able (a capable) workman **-het** skill, skilfulness, cleverness; ability, capability; dexterity

1 skida [ʃ-] *s1* **1** *bot.* siliqua **2** (*slida*) sheath, scabbard; *sticka svärdet i ~n* sheathe one's sword **2 skid|a** [ʃ-] *s1* (*snö-*) ski; *åka -or* ski, go skiing **skid|backe** ski slope **-bindning** ski binding (strap) **-byxor** ski[ing] trousers **-dräkt** ski (skiing) suit **-färd** skiing tour **-före** *bra ~* good skiing surface **-lift** ski lift **-lärare** ski instructor **-löpare** skier **-löpning** cross-country skiing **-pjäxa** ski[ing] boot **-skytte** biathlon **-spets** ski tip **-sport** skiing **-spår** ski track **-stav** ski stick (pole) **-terräng** skiing country **-tävling** skiing competition, ski race **-utrustning** skiing equipment (outfit) **-valla** ski wax **-åkare** skier **-åkning** skiing

skiffer ['ʃiff-] *s2* slate; schist; (*ler-*) shale; (*som vara*) slating; *täcka med ~* slate **-olja** shale oil **-grå** slate-gray **-tak** slate (slated) roof

skiffrig [ˣʃiff-] *a1* slaty

skift [ʃ-] *s7* (*arbetsomgång*) shift; turn; (*arbetslag*) shift, gang; *i ~* in shifts **skifta 1** (*fördela*) divide (*arv* an inheritance); *~ boet* distribute the estate **2** (*utbyta*) exchange (*hugg* blows); (*byta*) change; *~ gestalt* shift form; *~ ord med* bandy (exchange) words with **3** (*förändra sig*) shift, change; (*omväxla* [*med varandra*]) alternate; *~ i grönt* be shot (tinged) with green

skift|ande [ʃ-] *a4* changing, varied; eventful (*liv* life); *med ~ innehåll* with a varied content **-arbete** shift work

skifte [ʃ-] *s6* **1** (*fördelning*) distribution, division (*av arv* of an inheritance) **2** (*jorddelning*) parcelling[-out] (*jordområde*) parcel, field **3** (*växling*) vicissitude; (*ombyte*) change, turn; *i livets alla ~n* in the ups and downs of life

skiftes|bruk rotation farming **-rik** eventful, chequered **-vis** by turns, alternately

skift|ning [ʃ-] **1** (*förändring*) change; (*nyans*) nuance, shade, tinge; *inte en ~ i hans ansiktsuttryck* not the slightest change in his expression; *med en ~ i grönt* with a tinge of green **-nyckel** adjustable spanner; *AE.* [monkey] wrench

skikt [ʃ-] *s7* layer; (*tunt*) film; *geol.* stratum (*pl* strata); *bildl.* layer, stratum **skikta** stratify

skild [ʃ-] *a1* **1** (*olika*) separate; different, divers; *vitt ~a intressen* widely differing interests; *gå ~a vägar* (*bildl.*) go separate ways **2** (*från-*) divorced

skildr|a [ʃ-] describe, depict; (*förlopp*) relate **-ing** description; relation, account

skilj|a [ʃ-] *v2* **1** (*från-*) separate, part (*från* from); (*hugga av*) sever (*huvudet från bålen* the head from the body); (*sortera*) sort out (*renar* reindeer); *~ agnarna från vetet* sift the wheat from the chaff; *~ ngn från ett ämbete* dismiss s.b. from his office **2** (*åt-*) divide; (*ngt sammanhörande*) disunite, disconnect; *pers. äv.* separate, part; divorce (*äkta makar* married people) **3** *~ mellan* (*på*) distinguish between; *~ mellan höger och vänster* know the difference between right and left; *jag kan inte ~ dem från varandra* I cannot tell them apart **4** *rfl* part (*från* with); ~ *sig* divorce (*från sin make* one's husband); ~ *sig från mängden* stand out in a crowd; ~ *sig med heder från sin uppgift* acquit o.s. creditably of one's task

skiljaktig [ʃ-] *a1* different; ~ *mening* divergent opinion **-het** difference; disparity (*i åsikter* of opinions)

skilj|as [ʃ-] *v2, dep* part (*från* from, with); (*om äkta makar*) divorce, be divorced; *här skils våra vägar* this is where our ways part **-bar** *a1* separable

skilje|dom *s2* arbitration; award **-domare** arbitrator **-domsförfarande** arbitral (arbitration) procedure **-domstol** court of arbitration; *Internationella ~en i Haag* Permanent Court of Arbitration, the Hague Tribunal **-mur** partition [wall]; barrier (*äv. bildl.*) **-mynt** change, [small] coin **-nämnd** arbitration board **-tecken** *språkv.* punctuation mark **-väg** crossroad; *vid ~en* at the crossroads (*pl*)

skillingtryck [ʃ-] chapbook

skillnad [ʃ-] *s3* difference (*i* in; *på* between); (*avvikelse*) distinction, divergence; *det är det som gör ~en* that's what makes all the difference; *göra ~ på* make a distinction between, treat … differently; *till ~ från* in contrast to, unlike

skilsmässa [ʃ-] **1** (*äktenskapsskillnad*) divorce; *ta ut ~* sue (apply) for a divorce **2** (*uppbrott*) separation; parting (*från* with); *kyrkans ~ från staten* the disestablishment of the Church

skilsmässo|ansökan petition for divorce **-barn** child of divorced parents **-orsak** grounds (*pl*) for divorce **-process** divorce suit (proceedings *pl*)

skiltvakt [ʃ-] *s3* sentry

skimmel ['ʃimm-] *s2* roan

skimmer ['ʃimm-] *s7* shimmer, gleam; (*glans*) lustre; *sprida ett löjets ~ över* throw an air of ridicule over **skimra** shimmer, gleam

skin|a [ʃ-] *sken -it* shine; (*stråla*) beam; *solen -er* the sun is shining; ~ *av välmåga* glow with wellbeing; ~ *igenom* show through; *han sken upp* he brightened up; *han är ett klart ~nde ljus* he is a shining light

skingra [ʃ-] disperse; scatter; (*förjaga*) dispel; ~ *ngns bekymmer* banish (drive away) a p.'s cares; ~ *tankarna* divert one's mind (thoughts); ~ *ngns tvivel* dispel a p.'s doubts **skingras** *dep* disperse, be dispersed (scattered); *folkmassan ~des* the crowd dispersed **skingringsförbud** *jur.* injunction against alienation (sale) of property

skinit *sup. av skina*

skinka [ʃ-] *s1* **1** (*rimmad*) ham; (*färsk*) pork; *bräckt ~* fried ham; *kokt ~* ham **2** (*kroppsdel*) buttock

skinn [ʃ-] *s7* **1** (*hud*) skin; (*päls*) fur, pelt; (*fäll*) fell; (*läder*) leather; *hudar och ~* hides and skins; *kylan biter i ~et* the cold is biting (piercing); *inte sälja ~et förrän björnen är skjuten* don't count your chickens before they are hatched; *Gyllene ~et* the Golden Fleece; *ha ~ på näsan* (*bildl.*) have a will (mind) of one's own; *hålla sig i ~et* (*bildl.*) control o.s., keep within bounds, behave o.s.; *vara bara ~ och ben* be nothing but skin and bone **2** (*på mjölk e.d.*) film, skin

skinn|a *bildl.* skin, fleece (*ngn på* s.b. of) **-band** leather binding; [*bunden*] *i* ~ leather-bound **-beredning** dressing of fur skins **-byxor** *pl* leather breeches **-fodrad** [-ɔ:-] *a5* lined with leather **-jacka** leather jacket **-klädd** leather-covered **-knutte** *s2* rocker, leather jacket **-krage** fur collar **-mössa** leather cap **– och benfri** skinned and boned (*ansjovis* anchovy) **-rygg** *bokb.* leather back **-soffa** leather-covered sofa **-torr** skinny, dry as a bone **-varor** *pl* skins, furs, leather articles

skioptikon [ski'åp-, ʃi-] *s7* magic lantern; slide projector **-bild** slide

skipa [ʃ-] ~ *rättvisa* do justice; ~ *lag och rätt* administer justice

skippa (*slopa*) skip

skir [ʃ-] *a1* **1** (*florstunn*) gossamer; *bildl.* ethereal **2** (*klar*) clear (*honung* honey) **skira** melt (*smör* butter)

skiss *s3* sketch, outline (*till* of) **-artad** [-a:r-] *a5* sketchy **-block** sketchblock **-bok** sketchbook **-era** sketch [out], draw up outline

skit [ʃ-] *s2, vard.* shit **skita** *sket -it, vard.* shit; *det skall du ~ i* (*bildl.*) that's none of your bloody business; *det -er jag i* to hell with it **skitig** *a1, vard.* dirty **skitit** *sup. av skita* **skitsnack** *sl.* crap, bull-shit] **-viktig** uppity

skiv|a [ʃ-] **I** *s1* **1** plate, slab; (*rund*) disc, disk; (*bords-* etc.) top; (*tunt lager*) flake, lamina **2** (*grammofon-*) record; (*skuren ~*) slice; *spela in en ~* cut a record, make a gramophone recording **3** (*fest*) party **4** *klara ~n* (*bildl.*) manage it (the job), bring it off **II** *v1* slice, cut in slices **-broms** disc brake **-bytare** record changer **-formig** [-å-] *a1* disc-shaped **-ling** [-i:v-] *bot.* agaric **-minne** *data.* disk memory **-pratare** disc jockey **-rem** pulley belt **-samlare** discophil[e] **-samling** collection of records **-spelare** record-player **-stång** disc bar **-tallrik** (*på grammofon*) turntable

skjort|a [ˣʃɔ:r-, ˣʃorr-] *s1* shirt **-blus** shirt blouse **-bröst** shirt front **-linning** neckband **-ärm** shirtsleeve; *gå i ~arna* be in one's shirtsleeves; *kavla upp ~arna* roll up one's shirtsleeves

skjul [ʃu:l] *s7* shed, hovel

skjut|a [ʃ-] *sköt -it* **I 1** (*med -vapen*) shoot; (*avlossa*) fire (*ett skott* a shot); ~ *bra* shoot well, be a good shot; ~ *skarpt* shoot with live cartridges; ~ *efter* shoot at; ~ *till måls* practise target-shooting; ~ *över målet* overshoot the mark; ~ *på* (*uppskjuta*) put off, postpone; *hennes ögon sköt blixtar* her eyes flashed **2** (*förflytta*) push, shove, move (*undan* away); (*i bollspel*) shoot (*i mål* a goal); ~ *en båt i sjön* launch a boat **3** ~ *knopp* bud; ~ *skott* sprout; ~ *som svampar ur jorden* spring up like mushrooms; ~ *i höjden* a) (*växa*) shoot up, grow tall, b) (*om priser*) soar [up] **II** (*med betonad partikel*) **1** ~ *fram* push (move) forward, (*om föremål*) project, stand out, (*ila*) dash (dart) forward **2** ~ *för* push to (shoot) (*en regel* a bolt) **3** ~ *ifrån* push (shove) off; ~ *ifrån sig* push (shove) away, *bildl.* shift off **4** ~ *igen* shut, close **5** ~ *ihjäl* shoot dead **6** ~ *in sig* (*med -vapen*) find the range **7** ~ *ner* push down, lower, (*döda*) shoot down, (*flygplan*) shoot (bring) down **8** ~ *på* push **9** ~ *till a*) *se* ~ *igen*, b) (*bidraga med*) contribute **10** ~ *upp a*) (*om växter*) shoot up, *bildl.* put off, postpone, b) (*raket*) launch **11** ~ *ut* push (shove) out, (*båt*) launch, (*om föremål*) project, protrude

skjut|bana shooting range; *mil.* rifle range **-bar** *al* sliding **-dörr** sliding door **-fält** range **-fönster** sash (sliding) window **-galen** trigger-happy

skjut|it *sup. av skjuta* **-järn** gun **-järnsjournalistik** hard-hitting journalism, rapid-fire interviewing **-lucka** sliding shutter **-läge** shooting position **-mått** vernier calliper

skjutning [ˣʃuːt-] shooting, firing; *mil.* fire

skjuts [ʃuss, ʃutts] *s2* **1** (-*ning*) conveyance; *få* ~ get a lift; *ge ngn* ~ give s.b. a lift **2** (*förspänt åkdon*) [horse and] carriage

skjuts|a [ˣʃussa, ˣʃuttsa] drive, take **-håll** stage; (*-station*) relay, station **-häst** post horse

skjut|skicklighet markmanship, skill in shooting **-tävling** shooting competition (match) **-vapen** firearm **-övning** shooting practice

skjuv|a [ˣʃuː-] *tekn.* shear **-ning** shearing

sklero|s [-'råːs] *s3* sclerosis **-tisk** [-'råː-] *a5* sclerotic

sko I *s5* shoe; (*grövre*) boot; *det är där ~n klämmer* (*bildl.*) that is where the shoe pinches **II** *v4* **1** (*häst*) shoe **2** (*med beslag*) mount; (*kanta*) line **3** *rfl* line one's pocket (*på ngns bekostnad* at a p.'s expense) **-affär** shoe shop **-block** shoetree **-borste** shoebrush **-borstning** [-å-] shoecleaning; *A E.* shoeshining

skock [å-] *s2* crowd, herd **skocka** *rfl* crowd (cluster) [together]; gather together; (*om djur äv.*) flock [together]

sko|dd *a5* shod; (*kantad*) lined **-don** *pl* shoes, footwear (*sg*) **-fabrik** shoe factory

skog *s2* wood[s *pl*]; (*större*) forest; *plantera* ~ afforest; ~ *på rot* standing forest (timber); *fälla* ~ cut (fell) timber (trees); *det går åt ~en* it is all going wrong (to pieces); *i* ~ *och mark* in woods and fields, (*friare*) in the countryside, out in the country; *dra åt ~en!* go to blazes!, (*starkare*) go to hell!; *inte se ~en för bara träd* not see the wood for the trees **-bevuxen** wooded, forested, forest-clad **-fattig** poorly wooded

skogig *al* wooded, woody **skoglig** [-ɔ:-] *al* forestry, silvicultural **skogrik** well-wooded, well-forested, rich in forests (woods)

skogs|arbetare wood[s]man, lumberjack **-areal** forest[ed] area **-avverkning** felling; *A E.* logging, lumbering **-backe** wooded hillside **-brand** forest fire; *fara för* ~ danger of forest fire **-bruk** forestry, silviculture **-bruksskola** college of forestry **-bryn** edge of a (the) wood **-bygd** woodland **-bälte** forest belt **-dunge** grove; (*mindre*) copse **-duva** stock dove **-forskning** forestry research **-fågel** forest bird; *koll.* grouse, black game **-gud** silvan god, faun **-hantering** forestry, forest management **-huggare** woodcutter; *A E.* lumberman, lumberjack **-högskola** college of forestry **-industri** forest industry **-mark** wooded ground **-mus** field mouse **-mård** pine marten **-nymf** wood nymph, dryad **-plantering** afforestation **-rå** wood-spirit **-skövling** deforestation, devastation of forests **-stig** forest path **-stjärna** *bot.* chickweed win-

tergreen **-styrelse** ~*n* [the Swedish] national board of forestry **-trakt** woodland, lumberland, wooded region **-troll** woodland troll **-viol** common violet **-vård** forestry, silviculture **-väg** forest road **-äng** woodland meadow

skogvaktarboställe forester's house **skogvaktare** forester, gamekeeper, forest keeper; *A E.* [forest] ranger

sko|handlare shoe (footwear) dealer **-horn** shoehorn **-hylla** shoe-rack **-industri** footwear industry

skoj [skåjj] *s7* **1** (*skämt*) joke, jest; (*fuffens*) frolic, lark; *göra ngt för ~s skull* do s.th. for the fun of it; *på* ~ for fun; *göra* ~ *av ngn* make fun of (poke fun at) s.b. **2** (*bedrägeri*) fraud, swindle, racket **skoja 1** (*skämta*) joke, jest, lark; ~ *med ngn* pull a p.'s leg **2** (*bedraga*) swindle, cheat **skojare 1** (*skämtare*) joker, jester; (*kanalje*) scamp **2** (*bedragare*) cheat, fraud; *A E.* racketeer **skojarfirma** swindling (bogus) firm **skojfrisk** mischievous, full of fun **skojig** *al* funny; *jfr lustig*

sko|kartong shoebox **-kräm** shoe polish (cream)

1 skola *skulle -t, pres. skall* I *inf. skola*; *sup. skolat; han sade sig* ~ *bli glad om* he said that he would be glad if; *de lär* ~ *resa i morgon* they are said to be leaving tomorrow; *han lär* ~ *komma* it is thought that he will come; *han hade ~t* (*bort*) *inställa sig inför rätta i går* he should have appeared in court yesterday **II** *pres. skall, vard. ska*; *imperf. skulle* **1** (*ren framtid*) *pres.* shall (*1:a pers.*), will (*2:a o. 3:e pers.*) *imperf.*, *äv. konditionalis* should *resp.* would; *vad skall det bli av henne?* what will become of her?; *du skall få dina pengar tillbaka* you will get your money back; *jag skall aldrig glömma honom* I shall never forget him; *han och jag skall gå och bada* he and I are going swimming; *jag skall gärna hjälpa dig* I shall be pleased to help you; *han skall resa nästa vecka* he will leave (is leaving) next week; *det går nog bra skall du se* that will be all right, you'll see; *som vi snart skall få se* as we shall soon see; *vi skall träffas i morgon* we shall meet tomorrow; *jag var säker på att jag inte skulle glömma det* I was sure I should not forget it; *jag skulle gärna hjälpa dig om jag kunde* I should be pleased to help you if I could; *jag skulle ha hunnit om jag hade givit mig av genast* I should have been in time if I had started at once; *vad skulle hända om vi blev upptäckta?* what would happen if we were found out?; *han trodde inte att jag skulle lyckas* he didn't think I should succeed; *skulle han känna igen henne nu om han såg henne?* would he recognize her now if he saw her?; *i ditt ställe skulle jag ha stannat hemma* in your place I should have stayed at home; *det skulle jag inte tro* I shouldn't think so; *jag frågade om han skulle vara närvarande* I asked if he would be present; *de visste att de alltid skulle vara välkomna* they knew they would always be welcome; *skulle du vilja ha en kopp kaffe?* would you like a cup of coffee?; *jag skulle vilja visa dig* I should (would) like to show you **2** (*om ngt nära förestående el. avsett*) *pres.* am (*etc.*) going to; am (*etc.*) + *ing-form*; *imperf.* was (*etc.*) going to, was (*etc.*) + *ing-form*; *vi skall* *börja snart* we are going to start (are starting) soon; *jag skall gå och bada i eftermiddag* I am going swimming (to swim) this afternoon; *just som tåget skulle gå* just as the train was going to leave (was leaving); *han skulle just resa när jag kom* he was about to leave when I arrived; *hon sade att hon skulle resa till Paris* she said she was going to Paris; *vi skulle just sätta oss till bords* we were just going to sit down to dinner (lunch *etc.*) **3** (*egen vilja*) will *resp.* would; (*annans vilja*) shall *resp.* should; (*efter tell, want m.fl.*) *inf.-konstr.*; *jag skulle hellre dö än* I would rather die than; *vi skall väl fara, eller hur?* we will go, won't we?; *jag skulle ge vad som helst för att få se* I would give anything to see; *jag skall göra det åt dig* I will do it for you; *jag lovade ju att jag skulle göra det* I did promise that I would do it; *vad skall du med alla pennorna till?* what do you want with all those pens?; *jag skall ta med mig några skivor* I will bring some records; *jag skulle önska jag var död!* I would I were dead!; *du skall få så många du vill* you shall have as many as you want; *vad skall det här föreställa?* what is this supposed to be?; *skall vi gå på bio?* what about going (shall we go) to the cinema?; *vad vill du att jag skall göra?* what do you want me to do?; *de vill att vi skall komma* they want us to come; *de bad oss att vi skulle komma* they asked us to come; *du skall rätta dig efter vad jag säger* you are to do as I tell you; *det skall han få sota för* he shall smart (pay) for that; *du skall icke stjäla* (*bibl.*) thou shalt not steal; *han frågar om han skall ta sin bror med* he asks if he shall (should) bring his brother; *jag skulle inte få tala om det för dig* I was not supposed to tell you; *vad skall det tjäna till?* what is the use of that?; *jag vet inte vad jag skall tro* I don't know what to think; *jag lovar att det inte skall upprepas* I promise that it shall not happen again; *han gör det för att det skall så vara* he does it because that's how it is supposed to be; *skall det vara så skall det vara* one may as well do the thing properly or not at all; *skall jag öppna fönstret?* shall I open the window? **4** (*förutbestämt*) *pres.* am (*etc.*) to; *imperf.* was (*etc.*) to; *han skulle bli borta i många år* he was to be away for many years; *planet skall komma kl. 6* the plane is due at 6; *när skall jag vara tillbaka?* when am I to be back?; *de skulle aldrig återse varandra* they were never to see each other again **5** (*pres.* bör, *imperf.* borde) should, ought to; (*måste*) must, have (*imperf.* had) [got] to; *du skulle gå på den utställningen* you should go to that exhibition; *du skulle ha sett honom* you should have seen him; *jag vet inte vad jag skall ta mig till* I don't know what to do; *du skall inte tala illa om honom* you should not speak ill of him; *jag skulle ha varit försiktigare* I should (ought to) have been more careful; *vi skall alla dö* we must all die; *jag skall gå nu* (*jfr II 1, 2 o. 3*) I must go now; *du skall inte hålla boken för nära ögonen* you must not hold the book too close to your eyes; *att ni alltid skall gräla!* why must you always quarrel!; *naturligtvis skulle det hända just mig* of course it would happen to me of all people; *han skall då alltid klaga* he is always complaining, he must always complain; *det skall vara en läkare som skall kunna se det* it needs a doctor to (only

a doctor can) see that **6** (*sägs, lär*) *pres.* am (*etc.*) said to; *imperf.* was (*etc.*) said to; *skulle det verkligen förhålla sig så?* I wonder if that is really the case?; *det skall vara ett bra märke* it is said to be a good make; *han skall vara mycket rik* he is supposed to be very rich; *det sägs att han skall vara rik* they say he is rich **7** (*retoriskt*) should; *varför skulle någon frukta honom?* why should anybody be afraid of him?; *vem skulle han träffa på om inte sin egen syster* whom should he meet but his own sister?; *hur skall jag kunna veta det?* how should I know? **8** (*i vissa bisatser*) should; *att det skulle ha kommit till this!*; *om vi skulle missa tåget får vi ta taxi* if we should (were) to miss the train we must take a taxi; *om han skall kunna räddas måste något göras snart* if he is to be saved something must be done soon; *de gick närmare så att de skulle se bättre* they went closer so that they should see better; *om vi skulle ta en promenad?* what (how) about going for a walk?; *det är synd att det skall vara så kallt* it is a pity that it should be so cold; *jag är ledsen att det skall vara nödvändigt* I am sorry that this should be necessary; *hon gick tyst så att hon inte skulle väcka honom* she walked quietly so that she should (might) not wake him **9** (*annan konstr.*) *vad skall det betyda?* what is the meaning of that?; *vi väntade på att någon skulle komma* we were waiting for s.b. to come; *det är för kallt för att någon skall kunna gå ut* it is too cold for anyone to go out; *det var för dåligt väder för att tävlingen skulle kunna äga rum* the weather was too bad for the race to take place; *vad skall jag med det till?* what am I to do with that?; *det skall du säga som aldrig har försökt!* that's easy for you to say who have never tried!; *jag längtar efter att dagen skall ta slut* I am longing for the day to come to an end; *han skall naturligtvis tränga sig före!* of course, he would push in front!; *du skulle bara våga!* just you dare! **10** (*med betonad partikel*) *jag skall av här* I'm getting (*t. konduktör:* I want to get) off here; *jag skall bort* (*hem, ut*) I'm going out (home, out); *jag skall in på posten* I'm going to call in at the post office; *jag skall iväg nu* I must be off (be going) now; *det skall mycket till för att hon skall ändra på sig* it takes a lot to make her change; *det skall så litet till för att glädja henne* it takes so little to make her happy

2 skol|a l *s1* school; *~n* (*undervisningen*) school, (*-byggnaden*) the school; *gå i ~n* go to school; *vara i ~n* be in (at) school; *sluta ~n* leave school; *när ~n slutar* (*för dagen*) when school is over for the day, (*för terminen*) when school breaks up; *bilda ~* found a school; *den högre ~n* (*ridk.*) haute école; *ta sin mats ur ~n* back out **ll** *v1* **1** school, teach, train **2** (*omplantera*) transplant **skol|ad** *a5* trained, educated; cultivated (*röst* voice) **-arbete** schoolwork **skolast|ik** *s3* scholasticism **-iker** [-'lass-] scholastic **-isk** [-'lass-] *a5* scholastic **skolat** *sup. av 1 skola* **skol|atlas** school atlas **-avgift** school fees (*pl*) **-avslutning** breaking-up; *AE.* commencement **-barn** schoolchild **-bespisning** school meal service **-betyg** school report **-bildning** schooling, education **-bok** schoolbook, textbook **-bänk**

desk; *sitta på ~en (bildl.)* be at school **-dag** schoolday **-direktion** local education authority **-exempel** object lesson, typical example **-fartyg** training ship **-ferier** *pl* [school] holidays (vacation *sg*) **-flicka** schoolgirl **-flygning** training flight **-flygplan** trainer, training aircraft **-frukost** school lunch **-fröken** schoolmistress **-gång** *s2* school attendance, schooling **-gård** playground, school yard **-hem 1** boarding school **2** reform school **-inspektör** schools inspector **skolk** [-å-] *s7* truancy, nonattendance **skolka** shirk; *skol.* play truant (*vard.* hookey)

skol|kamrat schoolfellow, schoolmate; (*vän*) schoolfriend; *vi var ~er* we were at school together **-klass** [school] class **-kunskaper** *pl* knowledge (*sg*) acquired at school; schooling (*sg*) **-kurator** *BE.* educational welfare officer, *AE.* attendance officer **-kök** (*ämne*) domestic science; (*lokal*) school kitchen **-kökslärarinna** domestic science teacher; *AE.* home economics teacher

skolla [-å-] *se skålla*

skol|leda school fatigue **-ljus** shining light at school **-lov** [-å:v] *s7* holiday[s *pl*] **-lovskoloni** holiday camp **-lunch** school dinner **-läkare** school doctor **-lärare** schoolmaster, schoolteacher **-lärarinna** schoolmistress, schoolteacher **-materiel** school materials (supplies) **-matsal** [school] canteen **-mogen** ready to start school **-mognadsprov** test of readiness for school attendance **-måltid** school dinner (meal) **-mästaraktig** pedantic **-ning** [-ɔ:-] training, schooling, education **-plikt** compulsory school attendance **-pliktig** of school age **-pojke** schoolboy **-psykolog** educational (school) psychologist **-radio** school radio; broadcasting for schools **-reform** school (educational) reform **-resa** school trip; (*kortare*) outing **-ridning** manège riding, haute école **-ryttare** equestrian, manège rider **-sal** classroom **-sjuk** *vara ~* feign illness to avoid going to school **-skepp** training ship **-skjuts** school transport **-skrivning** written test **-sköterska** schoolnurse **-styrelse** local education board **-tandvård** school dental service **-television** school television **-tid** (*tid på dagen*) schoolhours (*pl*); (*period då man går i -an*) schooldays (*pl*) **-underbyggnad** [educational] grounding, [previous] schooling **-undervisning** school teaching, schooling **-ungdom** school children (*pl*) **-vaktmästare** school caretaker, *AE.* school custodian **-väg** way to school **-vägran** refusal to attend school **-värd [inna]** school help **-väsen** educational system **-väska** schoolbag; satchel **-ålder** school age **-år** school year; (*-tid*) schooldays (*pl*) **-överstyrelse** *~n* the [Swedish] national board of education

skomak|are shoemaker; shoe-repairer **-eri** shoemaker's workshop

skona spare; *~ ögonen* save one's eyes; *~ sin hälsa* take care of one's health; *~ sig* spare o.s.

skonare *s9*, **skonert** [-'närt, 'skɔ:-] *s3, pl äv. -ar* ['skɔ:-] *sjö.* schooner

skoning (*doppsko*) ferrule; (*fåll*) false hem

skon|ingslös unsparing; merciless **-sam** *a1* (*mild*) lenient; (*överseende*) indulgent; (*fördrag-*

sam) forebearing **-samhet** leniency; indulgence; forebearance

skonummer size in shoes

skopa *s1* scoop, dipper; *sjö.* bailer; (*på grävmaskin e.d.*) bucket, ladle; *en ~ ovett* a good telling-off

skopolamin *s4, kem.* scopolamine

sko|putsare bootblack, shoeblack; *AE.* shoe-shine [boy] **-putsning** cleaning (polishing) of shoes; *AE.* shoeshining **-reparation** shoe repair **-rem** shoelace

skorpa [-å-] *s1* **1** (*hårdnad yta*) crust; (*sår-*) scab **2** (*bakverk*) rusk

skorpion [-å-ɔ:n] *s3* scorpion

skorp|mjöl, -smulor *pl* golden breadcrumbs

skorr|a [-å-] **1** (*rulla på r-et*) speak with a burr, burr **2** (*låta illa*) grate, jar **-ande** *a4* burred (*r r*) **-ning** 1 burr 2 jarring sound

skorsten ['ˣskårr-] *s2* chimney; (*på fartyg, lok*) funnel; (*fabriks-*) smokestack

skorstens|eld chimney fire **-fejare** chimney sweep (sweeper) **-mur** chimney breast **-pipa** chimneypot

1 skorv [-å-] *s2* (*gammalt fartyg*) old tub

2 skorv [-å-] *s2, med., bot.* scurf

skorvig [-å-] *a1* scurfy

sko|skav *s7, ej pl* chafed feet (*pl*) **-smörja** *se skokräm* **-snöre** shoelace, shoestring **-spänne** shoe buckle **-sula** sole [of a shoe] **-svärta** shoe-blacking

skot *s7, sjö.* sheet **skota** sheet (*hem* home)

skoter ['skɔ:-] *s2* [motor] scooter

skotillverkning shoe manufacture

skotsk [-å-] *a1* Scotch; (*i Skottl.*) Scottish, Scots; *S~a högländerna* the [Scottish] Highlands **skotska** *s1* **1** (*språk*) Scotch, Scottish; (*i Skottl.*) Scots **2** (*kvinna*) Scotchwoman, Scotswoman **skott** [-å-] *s7* **1** (*gevärs- etc.; sport.*) shot; (*laddning*) charge; *ett ~ föll* a shot was fired; *jag kommer som ett ~* I'll come like a shot **2** *bot.* shoot, sprout; *skjuta ~* sprout **3** *sjö.* bulkhead; *vattentätt ~* watertight bulkhead

skotta [-å-] shovel (*snö* away the snow); *~ igen* fill in (*en grav* a grave)

skottavla (*särskr. skott-tavla*) target; *vara ~ för* (*bildl.*) be the butt of

skottdag [-å-] leap day, intercalary day

skott|e [-å-] *s2* **1** Scotchman; (*i Skottl.*) Scot, Scotsman; *-arna* (*koll.*) the Scotch (Scots) **2** (*hund*) Scottish terrier

skott|fri **1** *se skottsäker* **2** (*obeskjuten*) shot-free; *gå ~* (*bildl.*) go scot-free **-fält** field of fire **-glugg** loophole; (*för kanon*) embrasure; *komma i ~en* (*bildl.*) come under fire **-hål** bullet hole **-håll** range; *inom (utom) ~* within (out of) range (*för* of) **-kärra** wheelbarrow

Skottland ['skått-] *n* Scotland

skott|linje line of fire **-lossning** firing, discharge **-pengar** *pl* bounty (*sg*) **-rädd** gun-shy **-salva** round, volley **-skada** (*på sak*) damage caused by gunshot; *jfr -sår* **-spole** shuttle **-sår** gunshot wound **-säker** bulletproof **-tavla** *se skottavla* **-vidd** range of fire **-växling** exchange of shots; (*-lossning*) firing, shooting **-år** leap year

skovel ['skåvv-, 'skå:-] *s2* **1** (*redskap*) shovel, scoop **2** (*på vattenhjul, mudderverk etc.*) bucket;

(*på ångturbin*) blade **skovelhjul** paddle wheel; (*på ångturbin*) blade wheel **skovla** shovel
skraffera *konst.* hatch
skraj [-ajj] *a1, vard., vara* ~ have the wind up, be in a [blue] funk (*för* about), *AE.* have the jitters
skrake *s2, zool.* merganser
skral *a1* (*underhaltig*) poor, inferior; (*krasslig*) poorly, seedy; *AE. vard.* mean **2** *sjö., vinden är* ~ the wind is slight (scant) **skralt** [-a:-] *adv* badly
skraltig [ˣskrall-] *a1, se skral 1*
skramla I *s1* rattle **II** *v1* **1** rattle, clatter **2** *vard.* club together (*till* for) **skramlig** *a1* rattly
skrammel [ˈskramm-] *s7* (*-lande*) rattling *etc.*; (*ett* ~) rattle, clatter, clank
skranglig *a1* **1** (*gänglig*) lank; (*om pers. äv.*) loose-limbed **2** (*rånglig*) rickety (*stege* ladder)
skrank *s7* barrier, railing; (*domstols-*) bar **skrank|a** *s1* barrier; *-or* (*bildl.*) limits, restraints, bounds; *sociala -or* social barriers
skrap *s7, se skrapning*
skrap|a I *s1* **1** (*redskap*) scraper, rake **2** (*skråma*) scratch **3** (*tillrättavisning*) scolding; *få en ordentlig* ~ get a good rating **II** *v1* scrape; (*om katt, penna*) scratch; ~ *med fötterna* scrape one's feet; (*om häst e.d.*) paw [the ground]; ~ *ihop pengar* scrape together money; ~ *sig då knät* graze [the skin off] one's knee **-ning** [-a:-] **1** scraping *etc.*; (*en* ~) scrape **2** *med.* curettage **-nos** (*spel*) spillikins (*pl*)
skratt *s7* laughter; (*ett* ~) laugh; *brista i* ~ burst out laughing; *vara full av* (*i*) ~ be bursting (ready to burst) with laughter; *få sig ett gott* ~ have a good laugh; *ett gott* ~ *förlänger livet* mirth prolongeth life and causeth health
skratta laugh (*åt* at); *det är ingenting att* ~ *åt* it is no laughing matter; ~ *ngn rakt upp i ansiktet* laugh in a p.'s face; ~*r bäst som* ~*r sist* he laughs best who laughs longest; ~ *till* give a laugh; ~ *ut a*) (*förlöjliga*) laugh at, turn to ridicule, *b*) (~ *ordentligt*) have a good laugh; ~ *sig fördärvad åt* split one's sides laughing at
skratt|are laugher; *få -arna på sin sida* have the laugh on one's side **-grop** dimple **-muskel** risible muscle **-mås** black-headed gull **-paroxysm** fit of laughter **-retande** *a4* laughable, droll; (*löjlig*) ridiculous **-salva** burst (roar) of laughter **-spegel** distorting mirror
1 skred *imperf. av skrida*
2 skred *s7* [land]slide, [land]slip
skrek *imperf. av skrika*
1 skrev *imperf. av skriva*
2 skrev *s7* crotch, crutch
1 skreva *s1* crevice, cleft
2 skreva *v1*, ~ *med benen* straddle
skri *s6* **1** scream, yell, shriek; (*rop*) cry **2** (*djur-*) shriek; (*ugglas*) hoot **skria** scream *etc.*; cry out **skriande** *a4* crying (*nöd* need); flagrant (*orättvisa* injustice); glaring (*missbruk* abuse)
skribent writer, author
skrid|a *skred -it* (*röra sig framåt*) advance [slowly], proceed; (*med stora steg*) stride; (*glida*) glide; *arbetet -er framåt* the work advances; ~ *till huvudförhandling* (*jur.*) open the hearing; ~ *till verket* set (go) to work **skridit** *sup. av skrida*
skridsko [ˈskrissko] *s5* skate; *åka* ~*r* skate, go skating **-bana** skating-rink **-is** ice for skating

-**prinsessa** girl figure skater **-segel** skating sail, handsail **-segling** skate sailing **-tävling** skating competition **-åkare** skater **-åkning** skating
1 skrift *s3* **1** (*skrivande*) writing; (*skrivtecken*) [written] characters (*pl*); (*handstil*) handwriting; *i tal och* ~ verbally and in writing **2** (*-alster*) paper; (*broschyr*) booklet; (*tryckalster*) publication; *samlade* ~*er* collected works; *den heliga* ~ the Scriptures (*pl*), Holy Scripture (Writ)
2 skrift *s3* **1** (*förberedelse t. nattvardsgång*) shriving **2** *se bikt*
skrifta 1 shrive **2** confess **skriftermål** *s7* **1** (*nattvardsgång*) communion **2** (*bikt*) confession
skrift|expert handwriting expert **-lig** *a1* written; ~ *bekräftelse* (*äv.*) confirmation in writing **-ligt** *adv* in writing; (*genom brev*) by letter; *ha* ~ *på ngt* have s.th. in black and white **-lärd** versed in the Scriptures; *bibl.* scribe **-prov** konkr. specimen of a p.'s handwriting **-språk** written language **-ställare** writer, author **-växling** *dipl.* exchange of notes
skrik *s7* cry (*på hjälp* for help; *av förtjusning* of delight); (*gällt*) scream, shriek, yell; (*rop*) shout; (*oväsen*) clamour (*äv. bildl.*); *bildl. äv.* outcry; *sista* ~*et* all the rage, the latest craze
skrik|a I *s1* jay; *mager som en* ~ [as] thin as a rake **II** *skrek -it* cry out (*på hjälp* for help); shout, scream (*åt* at); (*om småbarn*) howl, squeal; ~ *i himlens höjd* shout to high heaven; ~ *till* cry out; ~ *sig hes* shout o.s. hoarse **-hals** screamer; (*om barn*) crybaby
skrikig *a1* screaming *etc.*; (*bjärt*) glaring (*färg* colour); (*om röst*) shrill **skrikit** *sup. av skrika*
skrin *s7* box, case, casket; (*för bröd*) bin
skrinda *s1* haycart, haywagon
skrinlägga (*inställa*) relinquish; (*uppskjuta*) postpone, shelve
skrinna skate
skripta *s1* continuity girl
skritt *s3, i* ~ at a walking pace **skritta** walk
skriv|a *skrev -it* **I 1** write; (*författa äv.*) compose; (*stava*) spell; *hur -er man ...?* how do you spell ...?; *han -er på en roman* he is writing a novel; ~ *sitt namn* sign one's name; ~ *i en tidning* write for (be a contributor to) a paper; ~ *på maskin* type; ~ *rent* make a fair copy of, copy out; *i* ~*nde stund* at the time of writing; ~ *firman på sin hustru* settle one's firm on one's wife; *får* ~ *s på hans sjukdom* must be ascribed to his illness; *han är -en i Stockholm* he is registered in Stockholm; ~ *ngn ngt på näsan* tax s.b. with s.th.; ~ *ngn ngt till godo* put s.th. down to a p.'s credit **II** (*med betonad partikel*) **1** ~ *av a*) (*kopiera*) copy, *b*) *se avskriva* **2** ~ *in* enter; ~ *in sig* (*på hotell*) register, *AE.* check in; (*i klubb o.d.*) enrol[l] o.s. **3** ~ *om* rewrite **4** ~ *på a*) (*lista*) put down one's name [on], *b*) (*växel o.d.*) stand surety **5** ~ *under* sign [one's name], *bildl.* subscribe (*på ngt* to s.th.) **6** ~ *upp* write (note, put) down, *bokför.* write up; ~ *upp ngns namn* take down a p.'s name; ~ *upp på ngns konto* charge to a p.'s account **7** ~ *ut a*) (*renskriva*) copy out, *b*) (*utfärda*) make (write) out (*en räkning* a bill), draw up (*ett kontrakt* a contract), *c*) (*skatter, trupper*) levy, *d*) (~ *t. slut*) fill up, *e*) (*läkemedel*) prescribe, *f*) (*från sjukhus*)

discharge
skriv|arbete writing, desk work **-are** writer; scribe; *data.* printer **-biträde** clerk **-block** writing pad **-bok** *skol.* exercise book; (*för välskrivning*) copybook **-bord** desk; writing table **skrivbords|lampa** desk lamp **-produkt** drawing-board product **-underlägg** *se skrivunderlägg*
skriv|byrå typewriting bureau (agency) **-don** writing materials **-else** (*brev*) letter; *jur.* writ; *polit.* address **-eri** writing; *neds.* scribbling **-fel** error (mistake) in writing; typing error; clerical error **-göromål** desk work
skriv|it *sup. av skriva* **-klåda** itch to write **-konst** art of writing; penmanship **-kramp** writer's cramp **-kunnig** able to write **-kunnighet** ability to write **-maskin** typewriter; *skriva på ~* type **-maskinsbord** typewriter (typist's) table **-maskinspapper** typing paper **-ning** [-i:v-] writing; *skol.* written examination; *rätta ~ar* mark papers, correct exercises **-papper** writing paper **-penna** [writing] pen **-pulpet** writing desk; (*hög*) writing stand **-stil** (*tryckstil*) cursive script **-ställ** writing set, inkstand **-tecken** [written] character; graphical sign **-underlägg** writing (blotting, desk) pad **-vakt** *BE.* invigilator, *AE.* proctor **-övning** writing exercise
skrock [-å-] *s7* superstition
skrocka [-å-] (*om pers.*) chuckle
skrockfull superstitious **-het** superstition, superstitiousness
skrodera swagger, bluster, brag
skrof|ler ['skråff-, 'skroff-] *pl* scrofula **-ulös** *a1* scrofulous
skrot *s7* scrap; (*järn-*) scrap [iron]; *de är av samma ~ och korn* they are birds of a feather
1 skrota *sjö., vinden ~r* [*sig*] the wind is veering
2 skrot|a (*förvandla t. skrot*) scrap, reject; (*fartyg e.d.*) break up; *gå och ~* (*vard.*) moon about
skrot|bil junk heap **-handlare** scrap [iron] merchant, junk dealer **-hög** scrapheap **-upplag** scrap yard **-värde** scrap value
skrov [-å:-] *s7* **1** (*kropp*) body; (*djurskelett*) carcass; *få litet mat i ~et* get some food inside one **2** *sjö.* hull
skrovlig [ˣskrå:v-, ˣskråvv-] *a1* rough; (*om klippa*) rugged; (*hes*) hoarse, raucous
skrovmål [-å:v-] *få sig ett ~* have a square meal
skrubb *s2* (*utrymme*) closet, cubbyhole, box-room
skrubb|a (*skura*) scrub; (*skrapa*) rub **-hyvel** rough (scrub) plane **-sår** graze, abrasion
skrud *s2* attire, garb **skruda** deck, dress
skrump|en *a3* shrunk[en], wrinkled **-lever** cirrhosis [of the liver] **-na** shrivel, shrink
skrupelfri [ˣskru:p-. ˣskrupp-] unscrupulous
skrupler *pl* scruples **skrupulös** *a1* scrupulous
skrutinium [-'ti:-] *s4* scrutiny
skrutit *sup. av skryta*
skrutt *vard.* **1** *s2* (*person*) good-for-nothing **2** *n* (*sak*) rubbish **3** *du ser ut som en ~* you look awful **-ig** *a1, vard.* wretched, miserable
skruv *s2* screw; (*på fiol*) [turning] peg; *dra åt* (*lossa på*) *en ~* tighten (slacken) a screw; *högergängad ~* right-hand screw; *ha en ~ lös* have a screw loose; *det tog ~* (*bildl.*) that did it (went home)
skruv|a screw; *~* [*på*] *sig* fidget, squirm; *~ av* (*loss*) unscrew; *~ fast* screw up (on), fasten; *~ i* screw in (on); *~ ner* lower, turn down (*gasen* the gas); *~ till* screw up (down); *~ upp* screw up, (*öppna*) unscrew, open, (*gasen*) turn up, (*priser*) push (force) up **-boll** *sport.* spin ball *helical auger* **-bult** screw bolt **-gänga** screw thread **-hål** screw hole **-is** pack ice **-lock** screw lid (cap) **-mejsel** screwdriver **-mutter** nut **-nyckel** spanner, *AE.* wrench **-stycke, -städ** vice; *AE.* vise **-tving** screw clamp
skrymm|a *v2* take up [a great deal of] space; be bulky **-ande** *a4* bulky, voluminous
skrymsla *s1*, **skrymsle** *s6* corner, nook
skrymt *s7, se skrymteri* **skrymta** be a hypocrite, dissemble **skrymtare** hypocrite, dissembler
skrymteri hypocrisy; cant[ing]
skryt *s7* boast[ing], brag[ging], swaggering; *tomt ~* [an] empty (idle) boast; *säga ngt på ~* say s.th. just to show off **skryta** *skröt skrutit* boast, brag (*med, över* of); *~ med* (*äv.*) show off
skrytsam *a1* boastful, bragging **-het** boastfulness, bragging
skrå *s6* [trade] guild; livery company; (*friare*) fraternity, corporation **-anda** *a4* guild spirit; *neds.* cliquishness
skrål *s7* bawl[ing], bellow **skråla** bawl, bellow; *make a noise* **skrålig** *a1* bawling *etc.*; noisy
skråma *s1* scratch, cut; superficial wound
skråordning guild statutes (*pl*)
skråpuk *s2* scarecrow; repulsive mask
skrå|tvång obligation to belong to a guild **-väsen** guild system
skräck *s3* terror (*för* of, to); (*fasa*) horror; (*skrämsel*) fright, dread; (*plötslig*) scare, panic; *sätta ~ i* fill (strike) ... with terror, terrify **-bild** frightful image; *bildl.* terrifying picture **-exempel** hair-raising example **-figur** fright, bugbear **-film** horror film, bloodcurdler all **-fylld** horror-filled **-injagande** *a4* horrifying, terrifying **-kabinett** chamber of horrors **-propaganda** atrocity (terror) propaganda **-regemente** reign of terror, terrorism **-slagen** panic-stricken, horror-struck **-stämning** atmosphere of terror **-välde** terrorism **-ödla** dinosaur
skräda *v2* (*malm*) pick, separate; (*mjöl*) bolt; *inte ~ orden* not mince matters (one's words)
skräddar|e tailor **-gesäll** journeyman tailor **-krita** French chalk **-mästare** master tailor **-räkning** tailor's bill **-sydd** *a5* bespoke, tailor-made, tailored; *AE.* custom-made; *bildl.* tailor-made, custom-made, custom-built
skrädderi (*yrke*) tailoring [business]; *konkr.* tailor's shop, *AE.* tailor shop
skräll *s2* crack, bang; (*åsk-*) clap of thunder; *bildl.* crash, sensation **skrälla** *v2* **1** crack *etc.* **2** score a surprise win, win against all odds **skrällande** *a4* cracking *etc.*; *~ hosta* hacking cough; *~ högtalare* blaring loudspeaker
skrälle *s6, ett gammalt ~* (*om piano*) a cracked old piano, (*om pers.*) a decrepit old body; *ett ~ till vagn* a rickety old car
skrällig *a1, se skrällande*
skräm|ma *v2* frighten; (*plötsligt*) scare, startle; *bli -d* be frightened (scared); *låta ~ sig* be intimi-

dated; ~ *upp* frighten, terrify, *(fågel)* beat up; ~
livet ur ngn scare the life out of s.b.; *ge en ~nde
bild av* give a terrifying picture of **-sel** ['skrämm-]
s9 fright, scare **-skott** warning shot; *bildl.* empty
menace

skrän *s7* yell, howl **skräna** yell, howl; *(gorma)*
bluster **skränfock** [-å-] *s2* blusterer, bawler
skränig *al* vociferous, noisy

skränka *v3, tekn.* set the teeth *(en såg* of a saw)
skräp *s7* rubbish, trash; junk; *(avskräde)* litter;
prata ~ talk nonsense; *det är bara* ~ *med honom*
he is in a bad way **skräpa** *ligga och* ~ lie about
and make the room *(etc.)* [look] untidy; ~ *ner* litter, *absol.* make a litter **skräphög** heap of rubbish **skräpig** *al* untidy, littered **skräpkam-
mare** lumber room **skräpsak** trifle, trifling
matter

skrävel ['skrä:-, 'skrävv-] *s7* bragging; *vard.*
bounce **skrävla** [ˣskrä:v-, ˣskrävv-] brag, bluster **skrävlare** [ˣskrä:v-, ˣskrävv-] braggart,
blusterer

skröna *sl* tall tale

skröplig [ˣskrö:p-, ˣskröpp-] *al* frail, fragile;
(orkeslös) decrepit **-het** frailty, fragility; de-
crepitude

skröt *imperf. av skryta*

skubba 1 *(gnugga)* rub, chafe **2** *(springa)* be off,
clear out

skudda ~ *stoftet av sina fötter* shake the dust off
one's feet

skuffa push, shove **skuffas** *dep* jostle

skugg|a 1 *s1* *(motsats ljus)* shade; *(av ngt)* shadow
(äv. bildl.); *-or och dagrar* light and shade; *ställa
i ~n (bildl.)* put in the shade; *en ~ av sitt forna
jag* a mere shadow of one's former self **II** *v1* **1**
shade **2** *(följa o. bevaka)* shadow; *vard.* tail **-bild**
(silhuett) silhouette; *bildl.* phantom, shadow
-boxning shadow-boxing **-ig** *al* shady, shadowy
-kabinett *i Storbritannien* shadow cabinet **-lik**
a5 shadowy **-liv** shadowy existence **-ning** shading; *konkr.* shade, shadow; *(övervakning)* shadow-
owing **-sida** shady *(bildl. äv.* dark, seamy) side
-spel shadow play

skuld *s3* **1** *(penning-)* debt; *ha stora ~er* be heavily in debt; *infria sina ~er* meet one's liabilities;
stå i ~ *hos* be indebted to; *sätta sig i* ~, *se skuld-
sätta; resterande ~er* arrears; *tillgångar och ~er*
assets and liabilities **2** *(förvållande)* fault, blame;
(synd) guilt; *vems är ~en?* whose fault is it?, who
is to blame?; *jag bär största ~en för detta* I am
most to blame in this matter; *fritaga ngn från* ~
exculpate s.b.; *kasta ~en för ngt på ngn* lay (put)
the blame for s.th. on s.b.; *ta hela ~en på sig* take
the entire blame [on o.s.]; *vara* ~ *till* be to blame
for; *vara utan* ~ not be responsible (to blame);
förlåt oss våra ~er (bibl.) forgive us our trespasses **-belastad** burdened with debt; guilty
(samvete conscience) **-börda** burden of debt;
guilt **-ebrev** *se skuldsedel*

skulderblad shoulder blade; *anat.* scapula

skuld|fri free from debt; *(om egendom)* unen-
cumbered; *(oskyldig)* guiltless, innocent **-för-
bindelse** *se skuldsedel* **-känsla** sense of guilt
-medveten guilty *(min* look)

skuldr|a *sl* shoulder; *vara bred över -orna* be
broad-shouldered

skuld|regleringsfond debt adjustment fund
-satt *a4* in debt, indebted; *(om egendom)* encumbered **-sedel** instrument of debt, [promis-
sory] note, note of hand, I.O.U. (= I owe you)
-sätta *(egendom)* encumber; ~ *sig* run into debt,
incur (contract) debts

skull *i uttr.: för din* ~ for your sake; *gör det för
min* ~ *(äv.)* do it to please me; *för vädrets* ~ *(t.
följd av)* because (on account) of the weather; *för
Guds* ~! for God's sake!; *för en gångs* ~ for once;
för skams (syns) ~ for the sake of appearances,
for form's sake; *för skojs* ~ for fun; *för säkerhets*
~ for safety[´s sake]

1 skulle *imperf. av 1 skola*

2 skulle *s2* *(hö-)* hayloft

skulor *pl* swill *(sg)*

skulpter|a sculpture; carve in stone *(etc.)*; *vard.*
sculp **-ing** sculpturing

skulptris sculptress **skulptur** sculpture **skulp-
tur|al** sculptural **skulptör** sculptor

1 skum [skumm] *al* dusky, dim, misty; *(beslö-
jad)* veiled *(blick* look); *(ljusskygg)* shady *(individ* individual)

2 skum [skumm] *s7* foam; *(fradga)* froth, spume;
(lödder) lather; *(på kokande vätska)* scum; *vispa
till* ~ beat (whip) to a froth

skum|bad foam bath **-bildning** frothing
-gummi foam rubber

skumma 1 *(bilda skum)* foam, spume, froth;
(om vin) sparkle; *(om öl)* foam, froth; *(om läskedryck e.d.)* fizz; ~ *av ilska* foam with rage **2** *(av-
skilja skum)* skim; ~ *grädden av mjölken* skim the
cream off the milk; ~ *en tidning* skim through a
paper **skummjölk** skim[med] milk

skumpa *v1,* ~ *[i väg]* scamper off (away); *(om
åkdon)* jog, bump **skumpig** *al* bumpy *(väg
road)

skumplast foam plastic

skumrask *s7* dusk [of the evening] **-affär** shady
business (transaction) **-figur** suspicious individual

skumsläckare foam extinguisher

skumögd *al* purblind, dim-sighted; bleary-eyed

skunk *s2* [striped] skunk

skur *s2* shower; *(regn- äv.)* downpour, drencher;
spridda ~ar scattered showers

skur|a scour, scrub; *(polera)* polish, burnish
(mässing brass) **-borste** scrubbing brush **-duk**
scouring cloth **-golv** plain deal floor **-gumma**
charwoman **-hink** bucket, pail

skurit *sup. av 2 skära*

skurk *s2* scoundrel, villain; *(skojare)* rascal,
blackguard **-aktig** *al* villainous, scoundrelly
-aktighet villainy **-streck** evil deed; dirty trick

skur|lov *skol., vi har* ~ our shcool is closed for
cleaning **-pulver** scouring powder **-trasa** scouring cloth

skut|a *sl* small cargo boat; *vard.* boat, old ship
-skeppare skipper

skutt *s7* leap, bound **skutta** leap, *etc., jfr hoppa*

skvadron *s3* squadron of cavalry

skval|a stream *(äv. bildl.)*; pour, spout **-ande** *s6*
pouring

skvaller ['skvall-] *s7* gossip; *(lösa rykten)* town-
talk; *(förtal)* slander; *skolsl.* sneaking **-aktig** *al*
gossipy; *(förtalande)* slanderous **-bytta** *sl* gos-

sip, gossipmonger, telltale; *skolsl.* sneak **-histo-ria** piece of gossip **-krönika** chronicle of scandal **-käring** [old] gossip, scandalmonger **-rör** overflow pipe **-spegel** window mirror **-tacka** *s1, vard., jfr -bytta*

skvallr|a gossip, tattle; *skolsl.* sneak; ~ *för mamma* tell mother; ~ *på ngn* report s.b.; ~ *ur skolan* tell tales out of school; *hans min ~de om his looks* betrayed **-ig** *al, se skvalleraktig*

skvalmusik nonstop popular music [on the radio]; (*bakgrundsmusik*) muzak (*varumärke*)

skvalp *s7* splash[ing], lap[ing] **skvalpa** (*om vågor*) lap, ripple; (*skvimpa*) splash to and fro; (*spilla*) spill

1 skvatt *n, inte ett* ~ not a thing (scrap)

2 skvatt *adv,* ~ *galen* clean crazy, mad as a hatter

skvattram [-amm] *s3, bot.* wild rosemary

skvimpa ~ [*över*] splash over

skvätt *s2* drop, splash (*mjölk* of milk); *gråta en* ~ shed a few tears **skvätta** *v3* splash, spill; (*småregna*) drizzle **skvättbord** *sjö.* waterboard, washboard

1 sky [ʃy:] *s2* (*moln*) cloud; (*himmel*) sky, heaven; *lätta ~ar* light clouds; *stå som fallen från ~n* (*~arna*) be struck all of a heap; *skrika i högan* (*himmelens*) ~ cry blue murder; *höja till ~arna* praise to the skies

2 sky [ʃy:] *s3* (*köttsaft*) gravy, meat juice; *AE.* pan gravy

3 sky [ʃy:] *v4* shun, avoid; (*frukta*) dread; *inte* ~ *ngn möda* spare no pains; *inte* ~ *några kostnader* spare no expense; ~ *som pesten* shun like the plague; *bränt barn ~r elden* once bitten, twice shy

skydd [ʃ-] *s7* protection (*mot* against, from); (*försvar*) defence; (*av växel*) protection, honour; (*mera konkr.*) shelter; (*tillflykt*) refuge; *i ~ av* under cover of (*mörkret* darkness); *söka ~ a*) (*mot*) take (seek) shelter (*mot vinden* from the wind); *b*) (*hos*) seek protection, take refuge (*hos* with); *till* ~ *för* for the protection of

skydda [ʃ-] protect; (*försvara*) preserve, defend (*mot* against, from); (*värna*) shield; (*trygga*) safeguard; (*mera konkr.*) cover, shelter; *~d från insyn* screened off from people's view; *lagligen ~d* protected by law; *~d verkstad* sheltered workshop

skydds|ande guardian spirit **-anordning** safety device (contrivance) **-dräkt** protective suit **-färg** protective colouring **-galler** [protective] grating **-glasögon** *pl* protective goggles **-handskar** protective gloves **-helgon** patron [saint] **-hem** reformatory [school]; *BE.* approved school; *AE.* institution for juveniles **-hjälm** hard hat, crash (protective) helmet **-häkte** preventive arrest, protective custody **-ingenjör** safety engineer **-kläder** protective clothing **-kommitté** safety committee **-konsulent** chief probation [and parole] officer **-kräm** barrier cream **-ling** ward, protegé **-lös** defenceless **-mask** *s3* respirator **-medel** protective agent; *med.* prophylactic **-märke** trademark **-nät** safety net **-ombud** safety controller (representative) **-omslag** (*på bok*) dust jacket (cover) **-område** *mil.* restricted area **-patron 1** *se -helgon* **2** (*gynnare*) patron, favourer **-rum** [air-raid] shelter; *mil. äv.* dugout

-tillsyn probation **-tull** protective duty **-uppfostran** correctional education **-vall** (*mot havet*) sea defence work **-ympning** vaccination **-åtgärd** protective measure, preventive **-ängel** guardian angel

sky|drag waterspout, tornado **-fall** cloudburst

skyffel [ˈʃyff-, ˣʃyff-] *s2* shovel; (*sop-*) dustpan **skyffla** [ˣʃyff-] shovel; ~ *ogräs* hoe weeds; (*snö*) shovel (clear) snow

skygg [ʃ-] *al* shy (*för* of); (*blyg*) timid; (*rädd*) frightened; (*tillbakadragen*) reserved; (*ängslig*) timorous; (*om häst*) skittish **skygga** start, take fright (*för* at); (*om häst*) shy (*för* at); ~ *för* (*vara rädd för*) shy of, shrink from **skygghet** shyness *etc.*; timidity, fear; reserve **skygglappar** blinkers, *AE.* blinders

skyhög towering, colossal; sky-high

skyl [ʃ-] *s2* shock, stook

1 skyla [ʃ-] *v2* (*hölja*) cover; hide (*sitt ansikte* one's face); ~ *över* cover [up], *bildl.* veil, hide

2 skyla [ʃ-] *v1* (*säd*) shock, stook

skyldig [ʃ-] *al* **1** (*betalnings-*) in debt; *vara ~ ngn ngt* owe s.b. s.th.; *vad är jag ~?* what do I owe [you]?, (*vid uppgörelse*) how much am I to pay?; *vara ngn tack* ~ be indebted to s.b.; *inte bli ngn svaret* ~ have a reply ready **2** (*som bär skulden t. ngt*) guilty (*till* of); *jur.* convicted, found guilty (*till* of); *den ~e* the culprit (offender); *erkänna sig* ~ plead guilty; *förklara ngn* ~ find s.b. guilty, convict s.b.; *göra sig* ~ *till* commit, be guilty of (*ett brott* a crime) **3** (*pliktig*) bound, obliged; *vara* ~ *att* have to; *han är inte* ~ *att* (*äv.*) he is under no obligation to **-het** duty, obligation (*mot towards*); *ikläda sig ~er* assume liabilities; *rättigheter och ~er* rights and obligations

skyldra [ʃ-] ~ *gevär* present arms

skylla [ʃ-] *v2,* ~ *ngt på ngn* blame s.b. for s.th.; ~ *på otur* plead bad luck; *du får* ~ *dig själv* you only have yourself to blame; ~ *ifrån sig* put (lay) the blame on s.b. else

skylt [ʃ-] *s2* sign[board]; (*reklam-*) advertisement board, poster **skylta** display [one's goods]; ~ *med* put on show, display, *bildl.* show off, display; ~ *om* redress a shop window

skylt|docka dummy, lay figure **-fönster** shop window; *AE.* show (store) window **-låda** showcase **-ning** (*-ande*) displaying, window-dressing; *konkr.* window-display **-ställ** display stand (rack)

skyltvakt [ʃ-] sentry

skymf [ʃ-] *s3* insult, affront, offence; (*kränkning*) outrage **skymfa** insult, affront, offend; (*kränka*) outrage **skymflig** *al* ignominious (*död* death); outrageous (*behandling* treatment) **skymford** insulting (abusive) word; *koll.* abusive language (*sg*), insults (*pl*)

skym|ma [ʃ-] *v2* **1** (*fördunkla*) stand in the way (light) of; (*dölja*) conceal, hide; *du -mer mig* you are [standing] in my light; *hennes blick -des av tårar* her eyes were dimmed (blinded) by tears **2** (*mörkna*) *det -mer* it is getting dark (dusk); *det -de för ögonen på henne* her eyes grew dim **-ning** twilight, dusk, nightfall; *hålla* (*kura*) ~ sit in the twilight

skymt [ʃ-] *s2* glimpse; (*aning*) idea, suspicion; (*spår*) trace; *fånga* (*se*) *en* ~ *av* catch a glimpse

S

of; *en ~ av hopp* a gleam of hope; *utan ~en av bevis* without a trace of evidence; *inte en ~ av intresse* not the slightest interest; *inte en ~ av tvekan* not a trace of hesitation

skymta [ʃ-] **1** (*se en skymt av*) catch a glimpse of **2** (*skönjas*) be dimly seen (visible); *~ fram* peep out; *sjön ~r* [*fram*] *mellan träden* the lake glitters through the trees; *solen ~r fram* the sun peeps out [from behind the clouds]; *~ förbi* be seen flitting past

skymundan [ʃ-, -ˣunn-] *n*, *i ~* in the background (shade); *hålla sig i ~* keep o.s. out of the way

skynd|a [ʃ-] hurry, hasten (*t. ngns hjälp* to a p.'s rescue); *~ långsamt!* hasten slowly!; more haste, less speed!; *~ ngn till mötes* hasten to meet s.b.; *~ på* hurry up (on); *~ på med* hurry on with; *~ sig* hurry [up] **-sam** *al* speedy; prompt (*hjälp* help); (*rask*) quick, hurried (*steg* steps) **-samhet** speed [iness], promptness *etc.*

skynke [ʃ-] *s6* cover[ing], cloth; ... *är för honom ett rött ~* for him ... is like a red rag to a bull

skyskrapa skyscraper

skyt [ʃ-] *s3* Scythian **-isk** [ˈʃy:-] Scythian **-iska** [ˈʃy:-] *s1* (*språk*) Scythian

skytt [ʃ-] *s2* shot, marksman; *S~en* Sagittarius, the Archer

skytte [ʃ-] *s6* shooting **-förening** rifle (shooting) club **-grav** trench

skyttel [ʃ-] *s2* shuttle

skyttelinje firing line

skytteltrafik shuttle service

skåda behold, see; (*varsebli*) perceive; *~ dagens ljus* see the light of day

skåde|bana *s1* stage; scene **-bröd** showbread **-lysten** eager to see; (*nyfiken*) curious **-penning** medal **-plats** *bildl.* scene [of action] **-spel** spectacle, sight; *teat.* play, drama **-spelare** actor; *bli ~* go on the stage **-spelarkonst** art of acting, histrionic art **-spelartrupp** theatrical company **-speleri** *se* -spelarkonst; (*förkonstling*) artificiality **-spelerska** actress **-spelsförfattare** playwright, dramatist

skål *s2* **1** (*kärl*) bowl; (*spilkum*) basin **2** (*välgångs-*) toast; *dricka ngns ~* drink [to] a p.'s health; *utbringa en ~ för ngn* propose a toast to s.b.; *~!* here's to you!, cheers! **skåla 1** *~ för* propose a toast to; *~ med* drink to (*varandra* one another) **2** (*urholka*) scoop (gouge) [out] **skålformig** [-å-] *al* cup-shaped, bowl-shaped

1 skålla *s1* (*tunn platta*) scale, lamina

2 skålla (*med hett vatten*) scald

skållhet scalding (boiling, *vard.* piping) hot

skålpund *ung.* pound

skåltal toast; after-dinner speech

Skåne *n* Scania **skånsk** *al* Scanian

skåp *s7* cupboard; *AE. äv.* closet; (*med lådor*) cabinet; (*i omklädningsrum*) locker; *bestämma var ~et skall stå* wear the breeches **-bil** [delivery] van, *AE.* panel truck **-dörr** cupboard (*etc.*) door **-mat** (*rester*) remnants (*pl*); *bildl.* stale stuff **-supa** drink in private (on the sly) **-supare** secret drinker

skåra *s1* score; (*inskärning*) notch; (*spår*) groove, slot; (*sår*) cut

skäck [ʃ-] *s2* piebald horse **-ig** *al* piebald, pied

skädda [ʃ-] *s1* (*fisk*) dab

skägg [ʃ-] *s7* **1** beard; *ha ~* have (wear) a beard; *låta ~et växa* grow a beard; *tala ur ~et* speak out; *tvista om påvens ~* split hairs **2** *biol.* barb; (*på mussla*) beard **-botten** *mörk ~* a blue chin **-dopping** great crested grebe

skägg|ig *al* bearded; (*orakad*) unshaved **-lös** beardless **-strå** [a] hair [out] of one's beard **-stubb** bristles (*pl*); (*eftermiddagsskägg*) five-o'clock shadow **-svamp** barber's itch (rash) **-töm** (*på fisk*) barbel **-växt** [growth of] beard[s *pl*]; *han har kraftig ~* his beard grows fast

skäl [ʃ-] *s7* reason (*till* of, for); (*orsak*) cause, ground; (*bevekelsegrund*) motive; (*argument*) argument (*för och emot* for and against); *så mycket större ~ att* so much more the reason to; *vägande ~* weighty arguments; *av principiella ~* on ground of principle; *göra ~ för sig* give satisfaction; *ha allt ~ att* have every reason to; *det har sina* [*randiga*] *~* there are very good reasons for it; *med* [*fullt*] *~ kan man säga* one is [fully] justified in saying; *det vore ~ att* it would be well to; *det vore ~ i att du försökte* you would do well to (you had better) try; *väga ~en för och emot* weigh the pros and cons **skälig** *al* reasonable, fair; *finna ~t* find it proper **skäligen** (*tämligen*) pretty (*enkel* simple); (*rimligtvis*) reasonably, fairly

skäll [ʃ-] *s7, se ovett*

1 skälla [ʃ-] *v2* bark; (*om räv*) yelp, cry; (*vara ovettig*) scream, bellow; *~ ngn för bracka* call s.b. a Philistine; *~ på* (*bildl.*) abuse, scold; *~ ut* blow up, tell off

2 skälla [ʃ-] *s1* bell; *nu blev det annat ljud i ~n* then things took on a new note

skällko bell-cow

skällsord word of abuse; *pl koll.* foul language (*sg*), invectives

skälm [ʃ-] *s2* rogue; (*lymmel*) rascal; (*-unge*) monkey, trot; (*spjuver*) wag; *en inpiskad ~* an arch rogue; *med ~en i ögat* with a roguish twinkle **-aktig** *al* roguish; mischievous; *~ blick* arch look **-roman** picaresque novel

skälm|sk [ʃ-] *al, se skälmaktig* **-stycke** piece of roguery; (*spratt*) practical joke

skälv|a [ʃ-] *v2* shake, quake; (*darra*) tremble, quiver (*av* with) **-ande** *a4* shaking *etc.*; tremulous **-ning** shaking *etc.*; (*en ~*) tremor; (*rysning*) thrill

skämd [ʃ-] *a5* (*om kött*) tainted; (*om frukt*) rotten; (*om luft, ägg*) bad **skämma** *v2* (*fördärva*) spoil; (*vanpryda*) mar; *för mycket och för litet skämmer allt* too much and too little spoils everything; *~ bort* spoil; *~ ut* dishonour, put to shame; *~ ut sig* disgrace o.s. **skämmas** *v2, dep* be a-shamed; *det är inget att ~ för* that is nothing to be ashamed of; *boken skäms inte för sig* the book does itself credit; *~ ögonen ur sig* die of shame; *fy -s!* shame on you!

skämt [ʃ-] *s7* joke, jest; *dåligt ~* bad (poor) joke; *grovt ~* coarse joke; *förstå ~* understand (be able to see) a joke; *säga ngt på ~* say s.th. in fun; *~ åsido!* joking apart! **skämta** joke, jest; *~ med* make fun of, poke fun at **skämtare** joker, jester, wag

skämt|artikel party novelty **-historia** funny story **-lynne** humour **-sam** *al* jocular; (*hu-*

moristisk) humorous; (*rolig*) funny, comical, droll; *ta ngt från den ~ma sidan* take s.th. as a joke **-samhet** jocularity, humour **-serie** comic strip; *AE.* funny **-tecknare** comic artist, cartoonist **-teckning** cartoon **-tidning** comic magazine (paper)

skänd|a [ʃ-] defile, pollute; desecrate (*gravar* graves) **-lig** *a1* infamous (*handling* deed); (*neslig*) nefarious, atrocious (*brott* crime) **-lighet** infamy, atrocity, outrage

1 skänk [ʃ-] *s2* (*skåp*) sideboard, buffet; cupboard

2 skänk [ʃ-] *s3* (*gåva*) gift, present; *till ~s* as a gift **skänka** [ʃ-] *v3* **1** give (*äv. bildl.*); present (*ngn ngt* s.b. with s.th.); *~ bort* give away **2** *~ i [glasen]* fill the glasses

skänkel [ʃ-] *s2* shank, leg (*äv. tekn.*)

skäppa [ʃ-] *s1* (*rymdmått*) bushel; *ge ngn ~n full* let s.b. have it; *sätta sitt ljus under en ~* hide one's light under a bushel

1 skär [ʃ-] *a1* (*ren*) pure, clean; (*obefläckad*) immaculate; *[ren och] ~ lögn* a downright lie

2 skär [ʃ-] *a1* (*ljusröd*) pink, light red

3 skär [ʃ-] *s7* (*ö*) skerry, rocky islet

4 skär [ʃ-] *s7* **1** (*egg*) [cutting] edge **2** (*skåra*) notch **3** (*med skridsko*) stride

1 skära [ʃ-] *s1* **1** sickle **2** (*mån-*) crescent

2 skära [ʃ-] *skar skurit* **1** cut (*äv. bildl.*); (*kött*) carve; *~* (*korsa*) *varandra* intersect, (*om gator*) cross; *~ halsen av sig* cut one's throat; *~ i bitar* cut up (... to pieces); *~ i remsor* shred; *~ i skivor* slice; *~ i trä* carve; *fartyget skär* [*genom*] *vågorna* the ship cleaves the waves; *~ tänder[na]* gnash (grind) one's teeth; *~ alla över en kam* treat all alike; *~ guld med täljknivar* coin money; *~ pipor i vassen* have a big income and little to do for it; *det skär i öronen* it jars (grates) upon my ears **2** (*med betonad partikel*) *~ av* (*bort*) cut off; *~ för* carve; *~ ihop* (*tekn.*) seize; *~ in* incise; *~ in i* cut into; *~ till* cut out; *~ upp* cut up, (*öppna*) cut open; *~ ut* carve **3** *rfl* cut o.s.; *kokk.* curdle; *~ sig i tummen* cut one's thumb; *det skar sig mellan dem* they clashed with one another

skär|ande *a4* cutting *etc.*; (*om ljud*) piercing, shrill **-bräde** (*chopping*) board; (*för bröd*) breadboard **-brännare** cutting blowpipe, fusing burner **-bönor** French beans

skärgård [ˣʃä:r-, ʃä:r-] archipelago, fringe of skerries; *i ~en* in the archipelago (skerries) [off Stockholm *etc.*]

skärm [ʃ-] *s2* screen; *tekn.* shield; (*på huvudbonad*) peak **skärma** *~* [*av*] screen, shield; *~ för* screen off

skärmaskin cutting machine; (*för matvaror*) slicer

skärm|bild mass radiograph, fluoroscopic image **-bilda** *v1* mass-radiograph **-bildsfotografering** mass radiography, X-ray screening **skärmmössa** peaked cap

skärmytsl|a [ˣʃä:r-] skirmish **-ing** skirmish

skär|ning [ˣʃä:r-] cutting **-ningspunkt** [point of] intersection

skärp [ʃ-] *s7* belt; (*broderat o. uniforms-*) sash

skärpa [ʃ-] **I** *s1* sharpness, keenness *etc.* (*jfr skarp*); *foto., TV* definition; (*klarhet*) exactness, stringency; (*i ton*) acerbity; *det är ~ i luften*

there's a nip in the air **II** *v3* sharpen (*äv. bildl.*); *bildl. äv.* strengthen, quicken; (*öka*) increase, heighten; *konflikten har skärpts* the conflict has deepened (been aggravated); *~ kontrollen* increase (tighten) the control; *~ sina sinnen* sharpen one's senses; *~ straffet* increase (raise) the penalty; *~ tonen* sharpen one's (*etc.*) tone; *~ uppmärksamheten* be more vigilant; *~ sig* sharpen up; *nu får du ~ dig* pull yourself together now **skärpedjup** *foto.* depth of field (definition) **skärpning** sharpening *etc.*; aggravation **skärpt** *a1, vard.* sharp, smart, bright

skärra [ʃ-] *~ upp* frighten, worry; *~ inte upp dig* don't get excited **skärrad** *a5, vard.* in a state, all of a dither

skärseld [ˣʃä:rs-] purgatory; *bildl.* ordeal

skärskåd|a [ʃ-] view, examine; scrutinize; scan **-ande** *s6* viewing, examination; *ta i ~* inspect, examine

skärslipare knife grinder

skärsår cut, gash

skärtorsdag [ʃ-] Maundy (Holy) Thursday

skärv [ʃ-] *s2, bibl.* mite; *min sista ~* my last farthing

skärva [ʃ-] *s1* (*kruk- o.d.*) sherd, shard; (*glas-, granat- o.d.*) splinter; (*friare*) fragment, bit

sköka [ʃ-] *s1* harlot

sköld [ʃ-] *s2* shield; (*vapen- äv.*) [e]scutcheon; *zool.* scutellum; (*på sköldpadda*) shell; *bildl.* shelter **-brosk** *anat.* thyroid cartilage **-emärke** [heraldic] bearing **-körtel** thyroid gland **-mö** Amazon **-padd** *s3* tortoise (turtle) shell **-padda** (*land-*) tortoise; (*vatten-*) turtle **-paddsskal** tortoise shell **-paddssoppa** turtle soup

skölj|a [ʃ-] *v2* rinse; (*spola*) wash; *vågorna -er stranden* the waves wash the shore; *~s överbord* be washed overboard; *~ av* rinse off; *~ bort* wash away; *~ sig i munnen* rinse one's mouth **-kopp** finger bowl **-ning** rinsing *etc.*; (*en ~*) rinse, wash; *med.* douche **-skål** (*på matbord*) finger bowl **-vatten** rinsing water

1 skön [ʃ-] *n* discretion; *efter eget ~* at one's own discretion

2 skön [ʃ-] *a1* beautiful; fair; (*angenäm*) nice; (*behaglig*) comfortable; *den ~a* the fair lady (one); *ha sinne för det ~a* have a sense of beauty; *~t!* that's fine!; *en ~ historia* (*iron.*) a pretty story **skön|ande** lover of the arts **-het** [-ö:-] beauty (*äv. konkr.*); *konkr. äv.* belle

skönhets|behandling beauty treatment **-drottning** beauty queen **-expert** cosmeticologist; *AE. äv.* beautician **-fel, -fläck** flaw **-ideal** idea of beauty **-medel** cosmetic, beauty preparation **-salong** beauty salon (parlour); *AE.* beauty shop (parlor) **-sinne** sense of beauty **-sömn** *vard.* beauty sleep **-tävling** beauty contest (competition) **-vård** beauty care **-värde** aesthetic value

skönj|a [ʃ-] *v2* discern; *inte ~ ngn ljusning* see no signs of improvement **-bar** *a1* discernible; (*synlig*) visible; (*tydlig*) perceptible

skön|litteratur [ʃ-] fiction, belles-lettres **-litterär** literary; *~t arbete* work of fiction **-målning** *bildl.* idealization, gilding **-skrift** calligraphy

sköns|mässig [ˣʃö:ns-] *a1* discretionary, optional **-taxering** discretionary (arbitrary) [tax] assessment

skör [ʃ-] *a1* brittle (*nagel* nail); (*spröd*) fragile, frail; *tyget är ~t* the cloth tears easily

skörbjugg [ˣʃöːr-] *s2* scurvy

skörd [ʃöːrd] *s2* harvest (*äv. bildl.*); (*gröda*) crop; *av årets ~* of this years's growth; *en rik ~ av erfarenheter* a rich store of experience **skörda** harvest; reap (*äv. bildl.*); (*bär*) pick; *som man sår får man ~* as you sow, so shall you reap

skörde|fest harvest festival (home) **-maskin** harvester, harvesting machine **-tid** harvest time **-tröska** *s1* combine [harvester] **-utsikter** *pl* harvest prospects

skörhet [ˣʃöːr-] brittleness; fragility, frailty

skörlevnad [ˣʃöːr-] loose living

skört [ʃ-] *s7* tail, flap **skörta** *~ upp a) (bedraga)* fleece, overcharge, *b) (fästa upp)* tuck up

1 sköt [ʃ-] *imperf. av skjuta*

2 sköt [ʃ-] *s2* drift net

sköt|a [ʃ-] *v3* **1** (*vårda*) nurse, tend (*sjuka* sick people); (*om läkare*) attend [to]; *~ sin hälsa* look after one's health; *~ om* take care of, attend to, nurse; *~ om ett sår* dress a wound; *sköt om dig väl!* take good care of yourself! **2** (*förestå*) manage; run (*en affär* a shop); (*ombesörja*) attend (see) to; (*se efter*) look after, take care of; *~ sitt arbete* do one's work; *~ hushållet* do the housekeeping; *~ kassan* (*räkenskaperna*) keep the cash ([the] accounts); *~ korrespondensen* handle the correspondence; *~ sina kort* (*äv. bildl.*) play one's cards well; *inte kunna ~ pengar* not be able to handle money; *~ sina plikter* discharge one's duties; *den saken -er jag* I'll attend to that; *sköt du ditt!* mind your own business! **3** *rfl* (*uppföra sig*) conduct o.s. (*bra* well); (*~ om sig*) look after o.s.; *han har måst ~ sig själv* he has had to manage by himself **-are** tender, keeper **-bord** nursing table

sköte [ʃ-] *s6* **1** lap; bosom (*äv. bildl.*) **2** vagina **3** (*moderliv*) womb **-barn** *bildl.* darling, favourite

sköterska [ʃ-] nurse

sköterske|biträde assistant nurse **-elev** pupil nurse, probationer **-uniform** nurse's uniform **-utbildning** training of nurses

skötesynd [ʃ-] besetting sin

skötsam [ˣʃöːt-] *a1* well-behaved; orderly; (*plikttrogen*) conscientious

skötsel [ˈʃött-] *s9* care, tending (*av* of); (*tillsyn*) attention, attendance; (*av maskin*) operation, running; (*förvaltning*) management; (*odling*) cultivation; *kräva ~* need (require) attendance (care) **-anvisning** operating instructions (*pl*)

skövl|a [ˣʃöːv-, ˣʃövv-] devastate; (*ödelägga*) ravage; wreck (*ngns lycka* a p.'s happiness); (*skog*) damage by reckless cutting **-ing** devastation; ravage

slabba splash about **slabbgöra** mucky job **slabbig** *a1* sloppy, splashy

slacka slacken

1 sladd *s2* **1** (*tågända*) [rope's] end **2** (*ledningstråd*) flex[ible cord]; *AE.* cord **3** *bildl., komma på ~en* bring up the rear; *komma med på ~en* slip in with the rest

2 sladd *s2* (*med fordon*) skid

sladda lurch, skid, slip sideways

sladdbarn child born several years after the other[s] [in a family]; *vard.* afterthought

sladder [ˈsladd-] *s7* chatting, babbling; gossip **-tacka** *s1* gossipmonger

sladdlampa portable worklamp

sladdra chatter, babble; gossip

sladdrig *a1* (*slapp*) flabby, limp; (*om tyg*) flimsy

slafs *s7* sloppiness **slafsa** *~ i sig* lap up, gobble up

1 slag *s7* (*art, sort*) kind, sort; (*typ*) type; *fack.* species; (*kategori*) category, class; *alla ~s* all kinds of; *böcker av alla* [*de*] *~* all sorts (kinds) of books, books of every description; *allt ~s* every kind of; *han är något ~s direktör* he is a manager of some sort (some kind of manager); *i sitt ~* of its kind, in its way; *vad för ~?* what?

2 slag *s7* **1** (*smäll*) blow (*äv. bildl.*), stroke, hit; (*lätt*) pat, dab; (*rapp*) lash, cut; (*knytnävs-; knackning*) knock; *ge ngn ett ~* deal s.b. a blow; *ett ~ för örat* (*bildl.*) a knockout blow; *ett ~ i luften* (*äv. bildl.*) a shot in the dark; *hugg och ~* biffs and blows; *~ i ~* in rapid succession; *göra ~ i saken* clinch the matter; *i* (*med*) *ett ~* all at once, straight off; *slå ett ~ för* strike a blow for **2** (*rytmiskt ~*) beat; *koll.* beating; (*hjärtats äv.*) throbbing; (*puls- äv.*) throb; (*pendel-*) oscillation **3** (*klock-*) stroke; *på ~et sex* at six o'clock sharp, on the stroke of six; *komma på ~et* arrive on the dot **4** (*-anfall*) [apoplectic] stroke; *få ~* have a stroke; *jag höll på att få ~* (*vard.*) I nearly had a fit; *skrämma ~ på ngn* frighten s.b. out of his wits **5** (*fält-*) battle (*vid* of) **6** (*varv*) turn, round; (*kolv-*) stroke; (*tag*) moment, while; *ett ~ trodde jag* at one time I thought **7** *sjö.* tack; *göra ett ~* tack, beat **8** (*fågeldrill*) warbling **9** (*på plagg*) facing; (*rock- äv.*) lapel; (*på ärm*) cuff; (*byx-*) turn-up, *AE.* cuff

slag|a *s1* flail **-anfall** apoplectic stroke **-björn** killer bear **-bom** lift gate; (*i vävstol*) batten **-bord** gate-leg[ged] table **-dänga** *s1* hit, street ballad

slag|en *a5* struck (*av förvåning* with surprise); (*besegrad*) defeated, beaten, *AE. äv.* beat; *en ~ man* a broken man **-fast** impact resistant **-fält** battlefield battleground **-färdig** *eg.* ready for battle (fight); *bildl.* quick at repartee, quick-witted **-färdighet** *eg.* readiness for battle; *bildl.* ready wit, quickness at repartee

slagg *s3, s4* slag, cinder[s *pl*], clinkers (*pl*), dross, scoria **slagga** (*avlägsna slagg*) take off the slag; (*bilda slagg*) form slag

slagg|artad [-aːr-] *a5* slaggy, cindery; scoriaceous **-bildning** slag formation; scorification **-hög** slag heap

slag|hållfasthet impact strength, shock resistance **-hök** goshawk **-instrument** percussion instrument

slag|it *sup. av 2 slå* **-kraft** striking power (*äv. bildl.*); effectiveness **-kraftig** effective **-kryssare** battle cruiser **-linje** line of battle **-längd** *tekn.* [ram] travel, [piston] stroke **-löda** braze **-man** (*i bollspel*) batsman **-nummer** hit **-ord** catchword, slogan **-ordning** battle array **-påse** punching bag; *bildl.* whipping boy **-regn** downpour, pelting rain **-ruta** *s1* divining (dowsing) rod **-sida** *sjö.* list; *bildl.* preponderance; *få ~*

heel over; *ha* ~ have a list **-skepp** battleship **-skugga** projected shadow

slags|kämpe [*slakks-] fighter; rowdy **-mål** *s7* fight; *råka i* ~ come to blows; *ställa till* ~ start a fight

slag|stift *mil.* striker; firing pin **-svärd** large [two-handed] sword **-trä** (*i bollspel*) bat **-tålig** knock resistant **-uggla** Ural owl **-vatten** *sjö.* bilge water **-verk 1** (*i ur*) striking mechanism **2** *mus.* percussion instruments (*pl*) **-växling** exchange of blows

slak *al* slack (*lina* rope), loose; (*kraftlös*) limp; ~ *i benen* wobbly at the knees **slakna** [*sla:k-] slacken, flag

slakt *s3, s7* slaughter[ing] **slakta** slaughter; (*döda*) kill; (*människor*) massacre; *bildl.*, ~ *en bil* strip down a car

slakt|arbutik butchery, butcher's shop **-are** butcher **-avfall** offals (*pl*) **-boskap** beef (slaughter) cattle **-bänk** slaughterer's block; *leda till* ~*en* (*bildl.*) be led to the slaughter **-eri**, **-hus** slaughterhouse **-mask** slaughtering mask **-offer** sacrifice, victim

slalom ['sla:låm] *s3* slalom; *åka* ~ do slalom-skiing **-backe** slalom slope **-byxor** *pl* slalom pants **-skida** slalom ski **-tävling** slalom

1 slam [slamm] *s2, kortsp.* slam

2 slam [slamm] *s4* mud, ooze; slime

slam|avlagring siltration, silt deposit **-bildning** sludge (slime) formation

slamma (*rena*) wash, purify; (*kalkstryka*) limewash; ~*d krita* precipitated chalk, whiting; ~ *igen* get filled with mud

slammer ['slamm-] *s7* rattle, clatter; (*vapen- etc.*) jangle

slam|mig *al* muddy, slimy **-ning** elutriation; desludging

slampa *sl* slut, slattern, hussy **slampig** *al* sluttish, slatternly, slipshod

slamra ~ [*med*] rattle, clatter

slams *s7* slovenliness **slamsa I 1** *sl* (*av kött*) scrap **2** (*kvinna*) *se slampa* **II** *vl* **1** (*slarva*) scamp **2** (*sladdra*) babble, chatter **slamsig** *al* **1** *se slampig* **2** (*om kött*) flabby

slana *sl* pole

1 slang *s2* tube (*äv. inner-*), hose

2 slang *s3* (*språk*) slang

3 slang *i uttr.: slå sig i* ~ *med* strike up an acquaintance with

slang|båge catapult; *AE.* slingshot **-gurka** cucumber **-klämma** hose clip (clamp) **-koppling** hose coupling (coupler) **-lös** ~*a däck* tubeless tyres

slang|ord slang word **-uttryck** slang expression

1 slank *imperf. av 2 slinka*

2 slank *al* slender, slim

slankig *al* limp, lank[y]

1 slant *imperf. av slinta*

2 slant *s2* coin; (*koppar-*) copper; *för hela* ~*en* (*bildl.*) for all one is worth; *ha en sparad* ~ have some money saved; *en vacker* ~ a nice sum; *slagen till* ~ fit for nothing; *vända på* ~*en* (*bildl.*) be economical, look at every penny

1 slapp *imperf. av slippa*

2 slapp *al* slack, loose; (*sladdrig*) flaccid; (*kraftlös*) soft, limp; (*matt*) languid; (*löslig*) lax (*moral* morals *pl*)

slappa *vard.* laze around **slapphet** slackness *etc.*; flaccidity; laxity; lack of energy **slappna** ~ [*av*] slack, slacken, relax

siarv *s7* carelessness, negligence; (*oreda*) disorder **slarva I** *sl* careless (negligent, slovenly) woman (girl) **II** *vl* be careless; ~ *med* scamp, (*klädsel o.d.*) neglect; ~ *bort* lose; ~ *ifrån sig* do by halves **slarver** ['slarr-] careless fellow; *en liten* ~ a slapdash boy **slarvfel** careless mistake **slarvig** *al* careless, negligent; (*hafsig*) slovenly; (*osnygg*) untidy **slarvsylta 1** *kokk.* minced meat **2** *bildl.* mincemeat

slashas [*sla:s-] *s2* ragamuffin, good-for-nothing

slask *s7* **1** (*-ande*) splashing; (*-väder*) slushy weather **2** (*väglag*) slush **3** *se slaskvatten* **4** *se slasktratt*

slask|a 1 splash about; ~ *ner* splash **2** *det* ~*r* it is slushy weather **-hink** slop pail **-spalt** light column **-tratt** [kitchen] sink **-vatten** slops (*pl*), dishwater

slatt *s2* drop

1 slav *s3* (*folk*) Slav

2 slav *s2* (*träl*) slave (*äv. bildl.*); *vara* ~ *under* be a slave to (the slave under)

slav|a slave; (*friare*) drudge **-arbete** slave labour **-binda** make a slave of **-drivare** slave-driver **-eri** bondage, slavery **-göra** slavery; *bildl.* drudgery **-handel** slave trade; *vit* ~ white-slave traffic **-handlare** slaver, slave-trader **-inna** [female] slave

1 slavisk ['sla:-] *a5* (*t. 1 slav*) Slav[ic], Slavonic; ~*a språk* Slav[on]ic languages

2 slavisk ['sla:-] *a5* (*t. 2 slav*) slavish; *bildl. äv.* servile

slaviskhet servility

slav|ism Slavism **-ist** Slavist

slav|kontrakt contract which binds one hand and foot (*äv. bildl.*) **-marknad** slave market **-piska** slave-driver's whip; *ha* ~*n över sig* (*bildl.*) be slave-driven **-skepp** slave ship **-ägare** slave owner

slejf *s3, s2* strap **-sko** strap-shoe

slem [slemm] *s7* slime; *fack.* mucus; (*vid hosta*) phlegm **-avsöndrande** *a4* mucus-secreting **-bildning** *abstr.* formation of mucus; *konkr.* mucus secretion **-hinna** mucous membrane **-lösande** *a4* expectorant **-mig** slimy; *fack.* mucous; (*klibbig*) viscous

slentrian *s3* routine; *fastna i* ~ get into a rut **-mässig** *al* routine; *undersökningen var* ~ the investigation was a matter of routine

slet *imperf. av slita*

slev *s2* ladle; *få en släng av* ~*en* (*bildl.*) come in for one's share **sleva** ~ *i sig* shovel into one's mouth

slick *s2* lick **slicka** lick; ~ *i sig* lap [up]; ~ *på* lick; ~ *sig om munnen* lick one's lips; ~*t hår* sleek hair **slicke|pinne** *s2* lollipop **-pott** [-å-] *s2* **1** (*pekfinger*) forefinger **2** (*hushållsskrapa*) dough-scraper

slid *s3, tekn.* slide; (*i ångmaskin*) [slide] valve **slida** *sl* sheath (*äv. bot.*); *anat.* vagina

sliddersladder ['slidd-] *s7* fiddle-faddle; ~! fiddlesticks!

slid|hornsdjur bovid animal **-kniv** sheath knife

slik *al* such like; ~*t* that sort of thing

slimmad *a5*, ~ *skjorta* slim-fit shirt
slinga *s1* coil, loop; *sjö.* sling; (*ornament*) arabesque; (*blad-*) creeper; (*rök-*) wisp
slinger|bult *s2* **1** (*undanflykt*) dodge, prevarication **2** *pers.* dodger **-växt** creeper, trailing plant
slingra 1 (*linda*) wind, twine; (*sno*) twist **2** (*om fartyg*) roll **3** *rfl* wind [in and out]; (*sno sig*) twist, twine; (*om flod äv.*) meander; (*om orm*) wriggle; (*om växt*) trail, creep; *bildl.* dodge, hedge; ~ *sig om varandra* (*äv.*) intertwine; ~ *sig från ngt* (*bildl.*) wriggle out of s.th.; ~ *sig undan* (*bildl.*) get out of **slingrande** *a4* winding; (*om flod, väg äv.*) meandering, serpentine **slingrig** *a1* sinuous, tortuous, winding **slingring** *a1* twine, wriggle; *sjö.* roll
1 slinka *s1* wench, hussy
2 slinka *slank slunkit* **1** (*smyga*) slink (*i väg, undan* away, off); ~ *om hörnet* slip round the corner; ~ *igenom* (*förbi*) slip through (past); ~ *in* (*äv.*) steal (sneak) in **2** (*hänga lös*) dangle, hang loose
slint *s, i uttr.: slå* ~ come to nothing, fail **slinta** *slant sluntit* slip; *jag slant med foten* my foot slipped; *glaset slant ur handen på mig* the glass slipped out of my hand
slip *s2* slipway; *ta upp ett fartyg på* ~ take up a vessel on to the slips
slipa (*skärpa*) grind, whet, sharpen; (*glätta*) grind; (*polera*) polish; (*glas e.d.*) cut **slipad** *a5, bildl.* smart; cunning **slipare** grinder; cutter **slipduk** abrasive cloth
sliper ['sli:-] *s2* [railway] sleeper; *AE.* [railroad] crosstie, tie
slip|eri grindery **-maskin** grinding machine **-massa** mechanical wood pulp **-ning** [-i:p-] grinding *etc., jfr slipa*
slipp|a *slapp sluppit* **1** (*undgå*) escape [from]; (*besparas*) be spared [from]; (*inte behöva*) not need [to] (have to); (*undgå*) avoid; *du -er [göra det]* you needn't [do it]; *du -er inte [ifrån det]* you cannot get out of it; *kan jag få* ~? can I be excused [let off]?; *låt mig* ~ *se det!* I don't want to see it!; *jag ser helst att jag -er* I would rather be excused (rather not); ~ *besvär* save (be spared) trouble; *han slapp göra det* he did not have to do it; *för att* ~ *straff* to avoid punishment **2** (*med betonad partikel*) ~ *ifrån* get away [from], escape; ~ *in* be admitted (let in); ~ *lös* break loose, (*bli släppt*) be set free; *elden slapp lös* a fire broke out; ~ *undan* escape, *absol.* get out of it; ~ *undan med blotta förskräckelsen* get off with a fright; ~ *upp i sömmen* come apart at the seams; *det slapp ur mig* it escaped me; ~ *ut* get (be let) out, (*sippra ut*) leak out
slipprig *a1* slippery; (*oanständig*) indecent, obscene
slips *s2* tie
slip|skiva grinding wheel **-sten** grindstone
slira slip, slide; (*om fordon*) skid; (*om hjul*) spin **slirig** *a1* slippery **slirning** [-i:r-] sliding, slide; (*fordons*) skidding; (*kopplings*) slipping
sliskig *a1* sickly sweet; *bildl.* oily
slit *s7* toil, drudgery **slita** *slet slitit* **1** (*nöta*) wear (*hål på* a hole in); *den håller att* ~ *på* it stands a great deal of wear; *slit den med hälsan!* you're

welcome to it!; ~ *ut* wear out; ~ *ut sig* wear o.s. out with [over]work **2** (*knoga*) toil, drudge; ~ *och släpa* toil and moil; ~ *ont* have a rough time of it **3** (*rycka*) pull (*i* at); tear (*av* off; *sönder* to pieces); ~ *sitt hår* tear one's hair **4** *rfl* get loose, (*om båt*) break adrift (loose) **slitage** [-'ta:ʃ] *s7* wear [and tear] **slitas** *slets slitits, dep,* ~ *mellan hopp och fruktan* be torn between hope and dread **slitbana** (*på däck*) [tyre] tread **sliten** *a3* worn [out]; (*lugg-*) threadbare, shabby, shiny; *bildl.* hackneyed (*fras* phrase) **slitit** *sup. av slita* **slitning** [-i:t-] wear; *bildl.* discord, friction
slits *s2* slit; (*på kläder*) vent **slitsa** slit
slit|sam [-i:-] *a1* strenuous, hard; *ha det ~t* have a hard time [of it] **-stark** hardwearing, durable, lasting **-styrka** durability, wearing qualities **-sula** outsole **-varg** *han är en* ~ he is hard on his clothes
slockn|a [-å-] go out; lie down; (*somna*) drop off; ~*d vulkan* extinct volcano; ~*d blick* dull (lifeless) look **-ande** *a4* expiring; dying down
slog *imperf. av 2 slå*
slogan ['slo:-, 'slå:-] *s3, äv. best. form slogan, pl slogan* slogan, catch phrase
slok|a slouch, droop; ~ *med svansen* drag one's tail **-hatt** slouch hat **-örad** *a5* lop-eared; *bildl.* crestfallen
slopa (*avskaffa*) abolish, reject; ~ *tanken på* abandon (give up) the thought of
slott [-å-] *s7* palace; (*befäst*) castle; (*herresäte*) manor [house], hall
slotts|fogde warden of a castle **-fru** chatelaine **-herre** lord of a (the) castle (manor) **-kapell** chapel of a palace, chapel royal **-lik[nande]** palatial **-park** castle (palace) park **-ruin** ruined castle **-tappning** chateau wine **-väbel** *s2* superintendent of a royal palace
slovak *s3* Slovak **-isk** *a5* Slovak
slo|ven *s3* Slovene **-vensk** [-e:-] *a5* Slovenian, Slovene
sludder ['sludd-] *s7* slurred speech **sluddra** slur one's words; (*om drucken*) talk thick **sluddrig** *a1* slurred; thick
slug *a1* shrewd; (*listig*) cunning, sly, wily; (*finurlig*) resourceful
slugga *vard.* slog, *AE.* slug **slugger** ['slugg-] *s2, vard.* slogger, *AE.* slugger
slughuvud *ett* ~ a sly dog
sluka *v1, imperf. äv. slök* swallow (*äv. bildl.*); devour (*böcker* books); ~ *maten* gobble up (bolt) one's food
slum [slumm] *s3* slum **-kvarter** slum[s *pl*], slum district
slummer ['slumm-] *s9* slumber; (*lur*) doze, nap
slump *s2* **1** (*tillfällighet*) chance; luck, hazard; *av en* ~ by chance, accidentally; *en ren* ~ a mere chance (toss-up); ~*en gjorde att jag* it so happened that I; ~*en gynnade oss* fortune favoured us **2** (*återstod*) remnant
slump|a 1 ~ [*bort*] sell off (at bargain prices; *vard.* dirt cheap) **2** *det ~de sig så att* it so happened that **-artad** [-a:r-] *a5,* **-mässig** *a1* haphazard, chance, random **-urval** random sample **-vis** *adv* (*på en slump*) at random (haphazard)
slumr|a slumber, be half-asleep; (*ta en lur*) doze, nap; ~ *in* doze off [to sleep] **-ande** *a4* slumber-

ing; *bildl.* dormant, undeveloped

slumsyster woman Salvationist working in slums

slung|a I *s1* sling **II** *v1* sling; *(honung)* extract; *(friare)* fling, hurl; ~ *ngt i ansiktet på ngn* throw s.th. in a p.'s face **-boll** sling ball

slunkit *sup. av 2 slinka*

sluntit *sup. av slinta*

slup *s2 (skeppsbåt)* launch, pinnace; *(enmastad)* sloop

sluppit *sup. av slippa*

slurk *s2* drink; swig; a few drops

slusk *s2* shabby[-looking] fellow; *(lymmel)* ruffian **sluskig** *a1* shabby

sluss *s2* lock; *(dammlucka)* sluice; *(luft-)* airlock **sluss|a** *(gå igenom sluss)* pass through a lock; *(låta gå genom sluss)* take through a lock **-avgift** lock dues *(pl)*, lockage **-bassäng** lock chamber **-ning** lockage, passing [a ship] through a lock **-port** lock gate **-trappa** flight of locks

slut I *s7* end; *(avslutning)* ending, termination, close, finish; *(utgång)* result; *när ~et är gott är allting gott* all's well that ends well; *~et blev att han the end of it* (result) was that he; *~et på visan blev* the end of the story was; *få ett ~* come to an end; *få ~ på* get to the end of, see the end of; *göra ~ med ngn* break it off with s.b.; *göra ~ på a)* *(göra av med)* use up, consume, *b)* *(stoppa)* put an end to; *i (vid) ~et* at the end; *känna ~et nalkas* feel that the end is near; *dagen lider mot sitt ~* the day is drawing to a close; *läsa ~ en bok* finish reading a book; *till ~* at last, finally; *ända till ~et (vard.)* to the bitter end; *från början till ~* from beginning to end; *låt mig tala till ~* let me finish what I was saying **II** *oböjligt predik.* at an end, [all] done (over), finished; *det måste bli ~ på* there must be an end to *(ofoget* this mischief); *är ~ a)* *(i tid)* is at an end, is over *b)* *(om vara o.d.)* is used up, *(slutsåld)* sold out, *c)* *(om krafter, tålamod e.d.)* is exhausted; *kaffet är ~* there is no more coffee; *jag är alldeles ~* I am dead beat; *det är ~ mellan oss* it is all over between us; *ta ~, se sluta II 2; ... har tagit ~ (hand.)* we are [sold] out of ..., there is no more ...; *bensinen håller på att ta ~* we are (getting) running short of petrol; *aldrig tyckas ta ~ (äv.)* seem endless (interminable)

slut|a I *slöt -it* **1** *(till-)* close, shut; ~ *leden* close the ranks; ~ *ngn i sin famn* lock s.b. in one's arms; ~ *en cirkel kring* form a circle round; ~ *ögonen för (bildl.)* shut one's eyes to; ~ *till* shut, close; ~ *upp* gather, assemble **2** *(göra upp)* conclude *(fred* peace); ~ *avtal* make (conclude, come to) an agreement **3** *(dra -sats)* conclude *(av* from) **II** *v1, imperf. äv. slöt* **1** *(av-)* end, bring to an end; *(säga t. slut)* conclude; *(göra färdig)* finish; ~ *skolan* leave school **2** *(upphöra, ta slut)* end *(med* with; *på konsonant* in a consonant); come to (be at) an end, stop, cease; *AE. äv.* quit; (~ *sin anställning)* leave, quit; ~ *gråta* stop crying; *han ~de läsa på sidan ...* he left off reading on page ...; ~ *röka* give up (stop) smoking; ~ *där man börjat* come full circle; *det kommer att ~ illa* it will end badly; *hon har ~t hos oss* she has left us; *hans liv ~de i fattigdom* he ended up in poverty; ~ *i en spets* end in a point; *han ~de med några uppskattande ord* he wound up (concluded)

with a few appreciative words; ~ *upp* stop *(med ngt* doing s.th.) **III** *slöt -it, rfl* **1** *(stänga sig)* shut, close; ~ *sig inom sig själv* retire into one's shell **2** ~ *sig till ngn (ngt)* join s.b. (s.th.); ~ *sig tillsammans (om pers.)* unite **3** ~ *sig till ngt (komma fram t.)* conclude (infer) s.th.

slut|akt *teat.* last (final) act **-anmärkning** closing remark, final observation **-are** *foto.* shutter **-avräkning** final settlement (account) **-behandla** conclude *(ett mål* a case); *saken är ~d* the matter is settled **-betalning** final payment (settlement) **-betyg** final (leaving) certificate **-betänkande** final committee report **slut|en** *a3* **1** *(till-)* closed; *(förseglad)* sealed *(försändelse* package); ~ *omröstning* secret ballot, ballot vote; *[tätt] -na led* serried ranks; *ett -et sällskap* a private company; ~ *vokal* close vowel; ~ *vård* inpatient care, institutional care; *-et TV--system* closed-circuit television **2** *(inbunden)* reserved; *vard.* buttoned-up **-examen** final (leaving) examination; *vard.* finals **-fall** *mus.* cadence **-föra** bring to an end, conclude **-försäljning** clearance sale **-förvaring** *kärntekn.* landfill [ing], deposition, controlled tipping **-giltig** definitive, final

slut|it *sup. av sluta I o.* **III -kläm** closing remark, final comment; *(sammanfattning)* summing-up **-körd** *a5, vard.* exhausted, deadbeat **-ledning** conclusion, deduction, inference; *(i logiken)* syllogism **-leverans** final delivery

slutlig [-u:-] *a1* final, ultimate; ~ *skatt* final tax **slutligen** [-u:-] finally; *(till sist)* in the end, ultimately, eventually; *(omsider)* at last

slut|likvid final (full) payment (settlement) **-lön** terminal (severance) pay **-muskel** *anat.* sphincter **-mål** ultimate objective **-omdöme** final verdict **-plädering** concluding speech **-poäng** total points *(pl)* **-produkt** end product (item), finished product **-prov** final test **-punkt** extremity; terminal point **-redovisning** final statement of account **-replik** closing rejoinder; *(i pjäs)* closing lines **-resultat** final result **-sats** conclusion, inference; *dra sina ~er* draw one's conclusions **-scen** final (closing) scene **-sedel** *hand.* contract note, bill of sale **-signal** *sport.* final whistle **-skattesedel** final [income-tax] demand note **-skede** final stage (phase) **-spel** *sport.* finals; *(i schack)* endgame **-spurt** final spurt; finish **-stadium** final stage **-station** terminus; *AE.* terminal **-steg** *(i raket)* last (final) stage **-stycke** *(på eldvapen)* bolt **-summa** total [amount], sum total **-såld** sold out, out of stock; *(om bok)* out of print

slutt|a decline, slope [downwards]; descent; ~ *brant* slope abruptly **-ande** *a4* inclined *(plan* plane); sloping *(axlar* shoulders); slanting *(tak* roof); *komma på det ~ planet (bildl.)* to be on the downgrade

sluttentamen final examination

sluttning slope, descent

slut|uppgörelse final settlement **-vinjett** *(i bok e.d.)* tailpiece; *bildl.* concluding remark, *(höjdpunkt)* peak, culmination

slyna *s1* hussy, minx

slyngel *s2* young rascal; scamp **-aktig** *a1* ill--mannered **-åldern, -åren** the awkward age

1 slå *s2* crossbar, slat, rail
2 slå *slog slagit* **I 1** (~ *till, äv. bildl.*) strike (*ett slag* a blow; *ngn med häpnad* s.b. with amazement); hit; smite, knock; (*flera slag; besegra*) beat (*ngn gul o. blå* s.b. black and blue; *på trumma* the drum; *fienden* the enemy); (*om hjärta, puls*) beat, throb; (*om segel*) flap; *han slog henne* he beat (hit, struck) her; *samvetet slog mig* my conscience smote me; *det slog mig att* it struck me that; ~ *en bonde* (*schack.*) take a pawn; ~ *broar* throw bridges (*över* across); ~ *kana* slide, go sliding; *fönstret står och* ~*r* the window keeps banging [to and fro]; *gäddan* ~*r* the pike is splashing about; *klockan* ~*r* the clock strikes; *en vara som* ~*r* a product that catches on; ~ *fel nummer* dial the wrong number; ~ *för en flicka* court (*AE. äv.* date) a girl; ~ *i dörrarna* bang the doors; ~ *en spik i väggen* knock (drive) a nail into the wall; *regnet* ~*r mot fönstret* the rain is beating against the window; *vågorna* ~*r mot stranden* the waves are beating on the shore; ~ *armarna om* put (throw) one's arms round; ~ *papper om* wrap up in paper; ~ *ett snöre om* tie up with string; ~ *en knut* make a knot; ~ *en ring omkring* form a circle round; ~ *på stort* lay it on, do the thing in style; ~ *ngn till marken* knock s.b. down **2** (*meja*) mow, cut (*hö* hay) **3** (*hälla*) pour (*i, upp out*) **4** (*om fåglar*) warble **II** (*med betonad partikel*) **1** ~ *an a*) (*en sträng*) touch, strike, *b*) (*en ton*) strike up; ~ *an på* catch on with, captivate (*åhörarna* the audience); ~ *av a*) knock off, *b*) (*koppla ifrån*) switch off, *c*) (*hälla av*) pour off **2** ~ *av på priset* reduce (knock down) the price; ~ *av sig* get flat, lose strength **3** ~ *bort* throw away, (*tankar e.d.*) chase away, drive (shake) off; ~ *bort tanken på* ... dismiss the thought of ... from one's mind; ~ *bort med ett skämt* pass off with a joke **4** ~ *emellan* (*boktr.*) lead [out], space out **5** ~ *i a*) (*spik*) knock (drive) in, *b*) (*hälla i*) pour out (in); ~ *i ngn ngt* drum s.th. into a p.'s head, (*lura*) talk s.b. into believing s.th. **6** ~ *igen a*) (*smälla igen*) slam, bang (*dörren* the door), (*stänga*) shut (*locket* the lid), close, shut down (*butiken* the shop), (*stängas*) shut [with a bang], *b*) (~ *tillbaka*) hit (strike) back **7** ~ *igenom a*) (*tränga igenom*) penetrate, soak through, *b*) (*lyckas*) succeed, make a name for o.s. **8** ~ *ihjäl* (*äv. tiden*) kill **9** ~ *ihop a*) (*händerna e.d.*) clap, (*smälla ihop*) clash together, *b*) (*fälla ihop*) fold [up], (*slå igen*) shut, *c*) (*förena*) put together, unite, combine **10** ~ *in a*) (*krossa*) smash, break, (*dörr*) force, *b*) (*paket e.d.*) wrap up (*i* in), *c*) (*besannas*) come true; ~ *in på en annan väg* turn into (take) another road, *bildl.* branch off, take another course **11** ~ *ner a*) (*t. marken*) knock down, *b*) (*driva ner*) beat (hammer) down (*en stolpe* a pole), *c*) (*fälla ner*) let down, (*ögonen*) lower, (*krage e.d.*) turn down, *d*) (*om åskan*) strike, *e*) (*om rovfågel o. bildl.*) swoop down, pounce; *röken* ~*r ner* the smoke is driving down[wards]; *nyheten slog ner som en bomb* the news broke like a bomb **12** ~ *om* (*bildl. o. om väder*) change **13** ~ *omkull* throw (knock) over (down) **14** ~ *runt* somersault, overturn, (*festa*) go on the spree; ~ *sönder* break [to pieces] **15** ~ *till a*) strike, (*ngn äv.*) hit, *b*) (*inkoppla*) switch on, turn on, *c*) (*om relä e.d.*)

pull up **16** ~ *tillbaka* hit (beat, strike) back, beat off (*ett anfall* an attack) **17** ~ *upp a*) (*öppna*) open, (*dörr e.d.*) throw (fling) open, (*ord i ordbok e.d.*) look up, *b*) (*fästa upp*) stick up, (*affisch e.d.*) post up, *c*) (*fälla upp*) turn up (*kragen* the collar), pitch (*ett tält* a tent, *d*) (*förlovning*) break off, *e*) (*om lågor*) flare up; ~ *upp sidan 5* turn to (open at) page 5; ~ *upp en artikel på första sidan* splash an article over the front page; *hon har slagit upp med honom* she has broken it off with him **18** ~ *ut a*) knock (beat) out, (*fönster*) smash, *b*) (*breda ut*) open (*vingarna* its (etc.) wings), *c*) (*om träd, växt*) burst into leaf, come out, (*om knopp*) open, *d*) (*hälla ut*) pour out, (*spilla*) spill [out], *e*) (*fördela*) spread over (*kostnaderna* the costs); *lågorna slog ut från taket* the flames burst through the roof; *försöket slog väl ut* the experiment turned out well; *många kommer att* ~*s ut i konkurrensen* many will go under in the competition **19** ~ *över* (*gå t. överdrift*) overdo it; *vågorna slog över båten* the waves washed over the boat **III** *rfl* **1** (*göra sig illa*) hurt o.s.; ~ *sig fördärvad* smash o.s. up **2** ~ *sig för sitt bröst* beat one's breast; ~ *sig för pannan* strike one's forehead; *du kan* ~ *dig i backen på att han kommer* you bet he will come **3** (*bli krokig*) warp, cast **4** (*i prep. uttryck*) ~ *sig fram* (*bildl.*) make (fight) one's way [in the world]; ~ *sig ihop* (*för att köpa*) club together; ~ *sig ihop med* (*äv.*) join [forces with]; ~ *sig lös, se* *lös*; ~ *sig ner* sit down, (*bosätta sig*) settle [down]; ~ *sig på* (*ägna sig åt*) go into (*affärer* business); *sjukdomen slog sig på lungorna* the disease went to (affected) the lungs

slående *a4* striking (*likhet* resemblance)
slån *s9, s7* blackthorn, sloe **-bär** sloe
slåss *slogs slagits, dep* fight (*om* about; *med ngn* [with] s.b.)
slåtter ['slått-] *s2* haymaking **-gille** hay-harvest festival **-karl** haymaker **-maskin** mower
1 släcka *v3, sjö.,* ~ [*på*] slacken, ease [off]
2 släcka *v3* (*få att slockna*) extinguish, put out; (*elektr. ljus*) switch off; put out; (*gaslåga*) turn out; (*kalk; törst*) slake
släckning extinction *etc.*
släcknings|arbete fire-fighting [work] **-manskap** fire-fighting squad; fire-fighters (*pl*) **-redskap** fire[-fighting] appliance
släd|e *s2* sleigh; sledge; *åka* ~ sleigh, go sleighriding **-färd** sleigh ride **-före** *bra* ~ good snow for sleighing **-parti** sleigh excursion (ride)
slägg|a *s1* sledge[hammer]; *sport.* hammer; *kasta* ~ (*sport.*) throw the hammer **-kastare** hammer-thrower **-kastning** throwing the hammer
släkt I *s3* family; (*-ingar*) relations, relatives (*pl*); *det ligger i* ~*en* it runs in the family; ~ *och vänner* friends and relatives; *tjocka* ~*en* (*vard.*) near relations **II** *oböjligt pred. a* related (*med* to), of the same family (*med* as); *jag är* ~ *med honom* I am a relative of his; ~ *till* ~*en* related to one's relations; *vara nära* ~ be closely related; ~ *på långt håll* distantly related **-drag** family trait (characteristic)
släkt|e *s6* (*-led*) generation; (*ätt, ras*) race; *biol.* genus; *det manliga* ~*t* the male species **-fejd** family feud **-forskare** genealogist **-forskning** genealogy **-ing** relative, relation (*till mig* of

mine) **-klenod** [family] heirloom **-kär** fond of (attached to) one's family **-led** generation **-möte** family gathering **-namn** family name, surname; *biol.* generic name **-skap** *s3, s4* relationship; *bildl.* affinity, kinship **-skapsförhållande** relationship **-tavla** genealogical table **-tycke** family likeness

1 **slända** *s1 (redskap)* distaff

2 **slända** *s1, zool.* dragonfly; neuropter[an]

släng *s2* 1 *(häftig rörelse)* toss, jerk *(med huvudet* of the head) 2 *(snirkel)* flourish 3 *(slag)* lash, cut 4 *(lindrigt anfall)* touch *(av influensa* of the flu); dash *(av galenskap* of madness)

slänga *v2* 1 *(kasta)* toss, jerk, fling; dash; ~ *av sig rocken* throw off one's coat; ~ *i sig maten* gulp down the food; ~ *på sig kläderna* throw one's clothes on 2 *(dingla)* dangle *(hit o. dit* to and fro); *(svänga)* swing; ~ *i dörrarna* slam the doors; ~ *med armarna* wave one's arms about

släng|d *al (skicklig)* clever, good *(i* at) **-gunga** swing **-kappa** [Spanish] cloak

släng|lig *al (ledlös)* loose-limbed; *(om handstil)* careless **-kyss** *kasta en* ~ *till ngn* blow s.b. a kiss **-kälke** merry-go-round on the ice **-polska** swinging reel **-skott** pot shot

slänt *s3* slope

släntra saunter, stroll

släp *s7* 1 *(på klädesplagg)* train 2 *(-vagn)* trailer; *ha (ta) på* ~ have (take) in tow 3 *(slit)* toil, drudgery; *slit och* ~ toil and moil

släpa I *v1* 1 *(dra efter sig)* drag, trail; *(bogsera)* tow, tug; ~ *fötterna efter sig* drag one's feet; ~ *med sig* drag about with one; ~ *sig fram* drag o.s. along, *bildl.* drag [on] 2 *(hänga ner)* drag, trail *(i golvet* on the floor) 3 *(slita)* toil, drudge II *s1* sled, sledge

släp|ig *al* trailing, shuffling *(gång* gait); drawling *(röst* voice) **-kontakt** trailing (sliding) contact **-lift** ski tow **-logg** patent log

släpp|a *v3* 1 *(låta falla)* let go; *(tappa)* drop, let slip 2 *(frige, lösa)* release, let loose; *(överge)* give up *(tanken på* the thought of); ~ *taget* release one's hold, let go 3 *(lossna)* come loose; leave hold 4 *(med betonad partikel)* ~ *efter* release one's hold, *bildl.* get lax; ~ *efter på disciplinen* relax the discipline; ~ *fram (förbi)* let pass; ~ *ifrån sig* let go, part with, *(avstå från)* give up; ~ *in* let in, admit; ~ *lös* release, let loose; ~ *ner (sänka)* let down; ~ *på vatten* turn the water on; ~ *till pengar* contribute (furnish) money; ~ *ut* let out *(äv. sömn.)*, *(fånge)* release **-hänt** *al* butterfingered; *bildl.* indulgent, easy-going *(mot ngn* towards, with) **-hänthet** indulgence; laxity

släp|räfsa hay sweep, sweeping rakc **-sko** *elektr.* trailing (sliding) contact **-skopa** drag [line] bucket **-tåg** *ha i* ~ *(bildl.)* have in tow, bring in one's (its) wake **-vagn** trailer

slät *al* 1 smooth; *(jämn)* even, level; *(om mark äv.)* flat; *(-t hår* smooth (sleek) hair 2 *(enkel)* plain; *(-struken)* mediocre; *(usel)* poor; *göra en* ~ *figur* cut a poor figure **släta** ~ *[till]* smooth [down]; *(platta till)* flatten; ~ *ut* smooth out [the creases in]; ~ *över (bildl.)* smooth over

slät|fila smooth-file **-hugga** cut smooth **-hyvla** smooth-plane **-hårig** straight-haired; *(om hund)* smooth-haired **-kamma** comb smooth; ~*d (äv.)*

sleek-haired **-löpning** flat-race **-prick** *sjö.* spar buoy, marker **-rakad** *a5* clean-shaven **-struken** *a3, bildl.* mediocre, indifferent

1 **slätt** *adv* 1 smoothly; *ligga* ~ be smooth 2 *rätt och* ~ [quite] simply; *stå sig* ~ cut a poor figure, come off badly

2 **slätt** *s3* plain; *(hög-)* plateau

slätt|bygd, -land plain, flat country

slät|var [-ä:-] *s2* brill **-välling** thin gruel

slö *al* blunt, dull *(äv. bildl.)*; *(dåsig)* inert; *(loj)* indolent, listless **slöa** idle; *sitta och* ~ sit idle, be dawdling; ~ *till* get slack; *(dåsa till)* get drowsy

slödder ['slödd-] *s7* mob, rabble

slö|fock [-å-] *s2* dullard, mope **-het** bluntness *etc.*; indolence, lethargy

slöja [*slöjja] *s1* veil

slöjd *s3* handicraft; *(skolämne)* handicraft (woodwork, carpentry; needlework) instruction **slöjda** do woodwork *(etc.)* **slöjdalster** handmade article

slöjdans dance of the veils

slöjd|lärare craft teacher **-sal** manual workshop **-skola** handicraft (arts and crafts) school

slöjmoln cirrostratus

slök *imperf. av* sluka

slör *s2, sjö.* free (large) wind **slöra** sail (go) large

slösa 1 *(använda t. övermått)* squander, be wasteful (lavish) *(med* with) 2 *(ödsla)* waste *(pengar* money), spend [lavishly], squander; *(beröm, omsorg o.d.)* lavish; ~ *bort* waste, squander **slösaktig** *al* lavish *(med* with), wasteful *(med* with, of); extravagant **slösaktighet** lavishness *etc.*; extravagance **slösande** *a4, jfr -aktig*; ~ *prakt* lavish splendour **slösare** spendthrift, squanderer **slöseri** wastefulness, extravagance; *(av tiden)* waste *(av tiden* of time)

slöt *imperf. av* sluta

smack *n, inte ett* ~ not a bit

smack|a smack; ~ *med tungan* click one's tongue; ~ *åt (häst)* gee up **-ning** smack[ing noise], click

smak *s3* taste *(av* of; *för* for) *(äv. bildl.)*; *(arom)* flavour *(av vanilj* of vanilla); ~*en är olika* tastes differ; *om tycke och* ~ *skall man inte diskutera* there is no accounting for tastes; *falla ngn i* ~*en* please s.b., strike a p.'s fancy; *få* ~ *för* take a liking to, get a taste for; *jag har förlorat* ~*en* I have lost my sense of taste; *ha god (säker)* ~ have an unerring taste; *en person med god* ~ a person of [good] taste; *äta med god* ~ eat with gusto (a relish); *i min* ~ to my taste; *den är inte i min* ~ *(äv.)* I don't fancy it; *sätta* ~ *på* give a flavour to, season; *ta* ~ *av ngt* take on the taste of s.th.

smak|a 1 *(av-, eg. o. bildl.)* taste, have a taste of *(äv. få* ~, ~ *på)*; *(erfara)* experience; ~ *av, se avsmaka*; *[få]* ~ *riset* get a taste of the rod; *han* ~*r aldrig starkt* he never touches strong drink 2 *(ha viss smak)* taste, have a taste *(tomat* of tomato); ~ *gott (illa)* taste nice (bad), have a nice (bad) taste; *hur* ~*r det? a)* what does it taste like?, *b) (tycker du om det?)* is it to your taste?; *nu skall det* ~ *med te* tea will be welcome; ~ *på* taste; *låta sig ngt väl* ~ eat s.th. heartily, help o.s. liberally to; *det kostar mer än det* ~*r* it costs more than it is worth; ~*r det så kostar det* you won't get something for nothing; *han* ~*de knappt på maten*

S

he hardly touched the food **-bit** bit to taste; (*prov*) sample **-domare** arbiter of taste **-full** tasteful; (*elegant*) stylish, elegant **-fullhet** tastefulness; style, elegance **-förbättring** improvement in taste **-försämring** impairment of taste **smak|lig** [-a:-] *al* (*aptitlig*) appetizing; (*läcker*) delicate, dainty; tasty **-lök** *anat.* taste bud **-lös** tasteless (*äv. bildl.*); *eg. äv.* flat, insipid; *bildl. äv.* in bad taste **-löshet** tastelessness *etc.*; insipidity; *bildl.* bad taste **-nerv** gustatory nerve **-prov** sample **-riktning** taste; tendency, style **-råd** advice (*pers.*: adviser) in matters of taste **-sak** matter of taste **-sensation** taste sensation **-sinne** [sense of] taste **-sätta** flavour, season **-sättning** seasoning **-ämne** flavouring

smal *al* (*motsats bred, vid*) narrow; (*motsats tjock*) thin; (*om pers. äv.*) lean; (*slank*) slender; *vara ~ om midjan* have a slender waist; *det är en ~ sak* (*bildl.*) it is a small matter (a trifle) **-axlad** *a5* narrow-shouldered **-ben** lower shin **-bent** [-e:-] *al* slender-legged, thin-legged **-film** substandard (8 (16) mm) film **-filmskamera** cine (*AE.* movie) camera

small *imperf. av* **smälla**

smal|na [-a:l-] narrow [off, down]; (*magra, bli tunnare*) grow thinner; (*t. en spets*) taper **-randig** narrow-striped **-spårig** *al* narrow-gauge; *bildl.* narrow-minded

smaragd *s3* emerald **-grön** emerald-green

smart [-a:-] *al* smart

smash smash **smasha** smash

smaska slurp **smaskens** ['smask-] (*endast pred.*) *vard.* delicious, yummy **smaskig** *al*, *vard.* delicious, yummy

smatt|er ['smatt-] *s7* clatter; patter, rattle; (*av om) trumpet*) blare **smattra** clatter; patter, rattle; (*av (om) trumpet*) blare

smed *s3* [black]smith **smedja** [-e:-] *s1* smithy, forge

smek *s7* caressing; (*kel*) fondling; (*ömhetsbetygelser*) caresses (*pl*) **smeka** *v3* caress; (*kela med*) fondle; (*klappa*) pat **smekande** *a4* caressing; gentle, soft (*toner* tones)

smek|as *v3*, *dep* caress [each other] **-månad** honeymoon **-namn** pet name **-ning** [-e:-] caress, endearment **-sam** [-e:-] *al* caressing, fondling

1 smet *imperf. av 1, 2* **smita**

2 smet *s3* (*sörja*) sludge; *kokk.* paste, [cake] mixture; (*pannkaks-*) batter

smeta daub, smear (*på* on); *~ fast* stick; *~ av sig* make smears, (*om färg*) come off; *~ ner* [be] smear, bedaub; *~ ner sig* make a mess of o.s. **smetig** *al* smeary, sticky

smicker ['smikk-] *s7* flattery; (*inställsamt*) blandishment; (*grovt*) blarney; *vard.* soft soap **smickra** flatter, cajole; *~ sig med* flatter o.s. upon (*att ha gjort ngt* having done s.th.), plume o.s. on (*att vara being*) **smickrande** *a4* flattering; *föga ~* hardly flattering **smickrare** flatterer

smida *v2* forge (*äv. bildl.*); hammer; *bildl.* devise, concoct (*planer* schemes); *~ ihop* forge together, weld; *~ medan järnet är varmt* strike while the iron is hot

smidbar [-i:-] *al* forgeable, malleable; *~t järn* malleable (wrought) iron **-het** malleability, forg-

ing quality

smidd *a5* forged; wrought, hammered **smide** *s6* forging; *~n* hardware (*sg*), iron goods, forgings **smides|järn** forging steel (iron), wrought iron **-verkstad** forge, smithy

smidig *al* (*böjlig*) ductile, flexible; pliable, supple (*äv. bildl.*); (*vig*) lithe; *~a tyger* soft materials **-het** flexibility; suppleness

smil *s7* smile; (*hångrin*) grin; (*självbelåtet*) smirk **smil|a** smile; grin; smirk **-band** *dra på ~et* smile [faintly] (*åt* at) **-fink** sycophant, toady **-grop** dimple

smink *s4* make-up; (*rött*) rouge; *teat. äv.* grease paint **sminka** make up, paint; paint o.s.; *teat.* make up

smink|loge [-lå:ʃ] *s5* dressing room **-ning** making up; (*en ~*) make-up **-stång** stick of grease paint **-ör** make-up man

smisk *s7* smack[ing] **smiska** smack

1 smita *smet smitit* make off, run away; *vard.* hook it; (*från bilolycka*) hit and run; *~ från betalningen* dodge payment

2 smita *smet smitit*, *~ åt* (*om plagg*) be tight

smitit *sup. av 1, 2* **smita**

smitta I *s1* infection, contagion (*äv. bildl.*); *överföra ~* transmit infection II *v1*, *~* [*ner*] infect (*äv. bildl.*); *bli ~d* catch the infection (*av ngn* from s.b.; *han ~de henne* (*äv.*) she caught it from him; *exemplet ~r* the example is infectious **smittande** *a4* catching, infectious; *~ skratt* infectious laughter

smitt|bärare [disease] carrier **-fara** danger of infection **-fri** noninfectious, noncontagious **-förande** *a4* (*om pers.*) infectious; infected, contaminated; disease-carrying **-härd** focus (source) of infection **-koppor** *pl* smallpox (*sg*) **-källa** source of infection **-risk** risk of infection **-sam** *al* catching; infectious; contagious (*äv. bildl.*) **-spridare** [disease] carrier **-spridning** transmission of infection **-ämne** infectious matter, contagion

smock [-å-] *s3* (*rynkning*) smocking **smock|a** [-å-] I *s1* biff II *v1*, *~ till ngn* sock s.b. **-full** crammed full (*med* of), chock-full

smoking ['små:-] dinner jacket; *AE.* tuxedo; *vara klädd i ~* (*äv.*) wear a black tie **-skjorta** evening (*vard.* boiled) shirt

smolk [-å-] *s7* mote; some dirt (*i ögat* in one's eye); *det har kommit ~ i mjölken* (*bildl.*) there is a fly in the ointment

smor|d [-o:-] *a5* greased; oiled; *Herrans ~* the Lord's anointed; *det går som -t* it goes like clockwork **smorde** *imperf. av* smörja II **smorläder** grain-leather **smort** *sup. av* smörja II

smuggel|gods smuggled goods (*pl*), contraband; *vard.* run goods (*pl*) **-trafik** smuggling **smuggl|a** smuggle **-are** smuggler; (*sprit-*) bootlegger **-ing** smuggling

smugit *sup. av* smyga

1 smul *al*, *sjö.* smooth

2 smul *r el. n, inte ett* **~** not a scrap

smul|a I *s1* **1** (*bröd- etc.*) crumb; *-or* (*äv.*) scraps; *små -or är också bröd* better half a loaf than no bread **2** *bildl.* particle, fragment, atom; *en ~* a bit (trifle, little); *den ~ franska han kan* the little French he knows II *v1*, *~* [*sönder*] crumble; *~ sig* crumble **smulig** *al* crumbly, full of crumbs **smultron** [-ån] *s7* wild strawberry **-ställe** *eg.* place where wild strawberries grow **smussel** ['smuss-] *s7, ej pl* underhand practices (*pl*); *vard.* hanky-panky **smussla** practice underhand tricks, cheat, swindle; ~ *in* smuggle (slip) in; ~ *till ngn ngt* slip s.b. s.th.; ~ *undan* smuggle out of the way **smuts** *s3* dirt, filth (*äv. bildl.*); (*gat- etc.*) mud, soil; *dra (släpa) i ~en* drag through the mire **smuts|a** ~ [*ner*] make dirty, soil; (*smeta ner*) muck up; (*fläcka*) stain; ~ *ner sig* get dirty; ~ *ner sig om händerna* get one's hands dirty **-brun** dirty brown **-fläck** blotch, smudge **-gam** Egyptian vulture **-gris** (*om barn*) dirty [little] grub **smuts|ig** *al* dirty; filthy; (*äv. bildl.*); *bildl. äv.* foul; (*om gator etc.*) muddy; *bli ~* get dirty; *vara ~ om händerna* have grubby hands **-kasta** *bildl.* throw mud at; defame **-kastning** mud-throwing; defamation **-kläder** *pl* dirty linen (*sg*) **-litteratur** gutter literature **-säck** dirty-clothes bag **-titel** *boktr.* half-title, bastard title **-tvätt** *se* -kläder **-vatten** slops (*pl*)

smutta ~ [*på*] sip

smycka adorn, ornament; (*dekorera*) decorate **smycke** *s6* piece of jewellery, trinket; *bildl.* ornament; *~n* jewellery (*sg*) **smyckeskrin** jewel box (case)

smyg 1 *s2, se fönstersmyg* **2** *i uttr.: i* ~ stealthily, furtively, on the sly **smyga** *smög smugit* **1** (*smussla*) ~ [*in*] slip (*ngt i handen på ngn* s.th. into a p.'s hand) **2** (*oförmärkt glida*) sneak (*som en indian* like an Indian); *gå och* ~ [go] sneak [ing] about; *komma ~nde* come sneaking **3** *rfl* steal, sneak (*bort* away); ~ *sig intill ngn* snuggle up to s.b.; ~ *sig på ngn* steal up to s.b.

smyg|ande *a4* sneaking; lurking (*misstanke* suspicion); insidious (*sjukdom* illness; *gift* poison) **-handel** illicit trade **-läsa** read on the sly **-premiär** *AE.* sneak preview **-propaganda** insidious propaganda **-röka** smoke on the sly **-supa** drink on the sly **-väg** secret path; *~ar* (*bildl.*) underhand means

små *smått smärre*; *i stället för felande former används* liten (*jfr* liten) little; small; *bildl. äv.* petty; ~ *barn* little (small) children; ~ *bokstäver* small letters; *de* ~ (*barnen*) the little ones; *stora och* ~ great and small, (*om pers. äv.*) old and young **-aktig** *al* petty, mean; *AE. äv.* picayune **-aktighet** pettiness, meanness **-barn** little children; infants **-barnsaktig** *al* childish **-barnsfamilj** family with small children **-barnsåldern** infancy; childhood **-belopp** *pl* small amounts (sums) **-bil** small car; (*mycket liten*) mini-car **-bildskamera** miniature camera, minicamera **-blommig** with small flowers **-bord** small tables **-borgerlig** [petit] bourgeois **-bruk** smallholding, small farm **-brukare** smallholder, small farmer **-bröd** *koll.* biscuits (*pl*); *AE.* cookies (*pl*) **-båtar** *pl* small boats **-båtshamn** harbour for small boats, marina **-delar** *pl* particles, small parts

små|fel *pl* petty faults (errors); *tekn.* small (minor) defects **-fisk** *koll.* [small] fry **-flickor** *pl* little girls **-folk** humble folk, ordinary people **-franska** French roll **-frusen** chilly **-fräck**

cheeky **-fågel** small bird[s] **-företagare** *pl* owners of small firms (businesses, companies) **-gata** bystreet **-gnola** hum **-grisar** piglets, young pigs **-gräla** bicker **-handlare** *eg.* small dealer; *bildl.* small fry **-husbebyggelse** area of one-family houses **-kaka** *se* småbröd **-klasser** first three forms in primary school **-koka** simmer **-krafs** odds and ends (*pl*) **-kryp** insect; *vard.* bug **-krämpor** *pl* aches and pains **-le** smile (*mot* at) **-leende I** *a4* smiling **II** *s6* smile **-mynt** *se* småpengar **-mönstrad** small-patterned **småningom** [-åm] [*så*] ~ (*efter hand*) gradually, little by little, (*med tiden*) by and by **små|näpen, -nätt** sweet little **-ord** *pl* small words; *språkv.* particles **-paket** *post.* small packet **-pengar** *pl* small change (*sg*) **-planet** asteroid, planetoid **-plock** *koll.* odds and ends (*pl*) **-pojkar** little boys **-potatis** *det var inte* ~ (*bildl.*) that wasn't to be sneezed at, *AE.* that wasn't small potatoes **-prat** chat, small talk **-prata** chat **-prickig** with small dots **-påve** *neds.* big noise **-randig** narrow-striped **-regna** drizzle **-rolig** [quietly] amusing, droll **-rutig** small-checked **-rätter** *pl ung.* hors d'oeuvres **små|sak** trifle, small (little) thing; *hänga upp sig på ~er* worry about small (unimportant) things; *det är inte ~er* it is no light matter **-sint** *al, se* småaktig **-skog** brushwood **-skola** junior school **-skol[e]lärare** junior school teacher **-skratta** chuckle **-skrift** pamphlet, booklet **-skulder** *pl* small (petty) debts **-skuren** *a3* fine[ly] cut; *bildl. se* småaktig **-slantar** *se* -pengar **-slug** shrewd, artful **-snål** cheeseparing **-sparare** small saver **-springa** half run, trot **-stad** small town; (*landsorts-*) country (provincial) town **-stadsaktig** *al* provincial **-stadsbo** inhabitant of a small town (*etc.*), provincial **-sten** *koll.* pebbles (*pl*) **-summor** *pl* small (petty) sums **-sur** sulky **-svära** swear under one's breath **-syskon** *pl* small (younger) sisters and brothers **-timmarna** *pl* the small hours; *fram på* ~ in the small hours of the morning **-tokig** scatty **-trevlig** cosy; (*om pers.*) pleasant **smått I** *a, jfr* små little, small; ~ *och gott* a little of everything; *ha det* ~ be badly off; *ha* ~ *om* be short of; *hacka ngt* ~ chop s.th. small **II** *adv* a little; slightly, somewhat (*förälskad* in love) **III** *s, i vissa uttr.: vänta* ~ expect a baby; *i* ~ in little [things], in a small way, on a small scale; *i stort som* ~ in great as in little things **-ing** baby, youngster, kid **småtvätt** *s2, ej pl* smalls (*pl*) **små|varmt** *best.* hot *det -varma, koll.* hot snack **-vilt** *koll.* small game **-vägar** *pl* byroads **-växt** *a4* (*om pers.*) short [of stature]; (*om djur*) small; (*om växt*) low

smäcka *vard.* **1** (*slå*) slam, hit **2** (*ljuga*) lie, brag **smäcker** ['smäkk-] *a2* slender **smäda** abuse; (*ärekränka*) defame; ~ *Gud* blaspheme **smädedikt** lampoon, libellous poem **smädelse** abuse; defamation; *~r* invectives **smädeskrift** libel[lous pamphlet], lampoon **smädlig** [-ä:-] *al* abusive **smäkt|a** languish **-ande** *a4* (*trånande*) languishing; (*ljuv*) melting **smälek** *s2* disgrace, ignominy; *lida* ~ suffer (be

put to) shame
smäll 1 *s7, få* ~ get a spanking (smacking) **2** *s2*
(*knall, skräll*) bang, crack; *dörren slog igen med
en* ~ the door shut with a bang (slammed to) **3** *s2*
(*slag*) smack, slap; (*med piska*) lash
smäll|a *v2, imperf. i intransitiv betydelse äv. small
1* (*slå*) slap; (*ge ngn smäll*) spank, smack **2** (*fram-
bringa en smäll*) crack; ~ *i dörrarna* bang (slam)
the doors; ~ *med piskan* crack the whip; *nu -er
det!* off it goes!; ~ *igen* shut [...] with a bang,
([*om*] *dörr*) bang, slam **-are** cracker **-fet** immensely fat **-kall** bitterly cold **-karamell**
cracker **-kyss** smack
smält|a I *s1, tekn.* [s]melt **II** *v3* **1** (*göra flytande*)
melt; (*metall äv.*) smelt, fuse; (*mat o.d.*; *bildl.*)
digest; *bildl. äv.* put up with, swallow (*förtreten
one's annoyance*); *smält smör* drawn butter **2**
(*övergå t. flytande form*) melt (*äv. bildl.*); (*om is,
snö äv.*) thaw; (*lösa sig*) dissolve; (*vekna*) soften;
~ *ihop* fuse (*äv. bildl.*); (*minskas*) twindle
[down]; *-er i munnen* melts in the mouth; ~ *ner*
[s]melt down; ~ *samman* fuse (*äv. bildl.*); ~ *samman med* (*äv.*) merge into **-ande** *a4* melting
(*toner* tones); *bildl. äv.* liquid **-degel** crucible,
melting pot **-hytta** smelting works **-ning** [s]
melting *etc.*; liquefaction; dissolution; fusion; (*av
mat*) digestion **-ost** processed cheese **-punkt**
melting (fusing) point **-säkring** [safety] fuse
-ugn [s]melting furnace **-vatten** melted snow
(ice) **-värme** fusion (melting) heat
smärgel [ˣsmärjel, ˈsmärr-] *s9* emery **-duk** emery cloth **-skiva** emery wheel
smärgla [-j-] emery, grind (polish) with emery
smärre *komp. t. små* smaller; minor (*fel* faults)
smärt *a1* slender, slim
smärt|a I *s1* pain; (*häftig, kort*) pang, twinge [of
pain]; (*pina*) agony, torment; (*lidande*) suffering;
(*sorg, bedrövelse*) grief, affliction, distress;
känna ~ feel (be in) pain, (*själsligt*) be grieved
(pained) (*över* at); *med* ~ *hör jag att* I am grieved
to hear that **II** *v1* pain; (*själsligt äv.*) grieve (*djupt*
deeply) **-fri** painless; (*smidig*) smooth **-förnim-
melse** sensation of pain **-gräns** pain threshold
smärting canvas
smärt|lindring pain relief **-punkt** focus of pain
-sam *a1* painful; (*själsligt äv.*) sad, grievous, distressing; *ytterst ~ma plågor* (*äv.*) extreme pain
(*sg*) **-stillande** *a4* pain-relieving, analgesic;
(*lugnande*) sedative; ~ *medel* analgesic, ano-
dyne, sedative
smög *imperf. av smyga*
smör *s7* butter; *breda* ~ *på* spread with butter,
spread butter on, butter; *gå åt som* ~ *i solsken* sell
like hot cakes; *inte för allt* ~ *i Småland* not for all
the tea in China; *se ut som om man sålt ~et och
tappat pengarna* look as though one has made a
fortune and lost it; *komma* [*sig*] *upp i ~et* be in
clover, be in high favour **smöra** *v1* butter
smör|ask butter box **-bakelse** puff-pastry cake
-blomma buttercup **-boll** *bot.* globeflower
-deg puff paste **-dosa** butter dish **-fett** butter-
fat; butyrin
smörgås [ˣsmörr-] *s2* [piece (slice) of] bread and
butter; (*med pålägg*) open sandwich; *kasta* ~
(*lek*) play ducks and drakes **-bord** smorgasbord;
hors d'oeuvres (*pl*) **-mat** sliced meats (cheese

etc.) used on open sandwiches (*pl*) **-nisse** *s2* assistant waiter; *AE.* bus boy
smörj *s7* thrashing, licking **smörja I** *s1* **1** (*-me-
del*) grease, lubricant **2** (*skräp*) rubbish, trash;
prata ~ talk nonsense (rubbish) **II** *smorde smort
1* grease, lubricate; (*med olja*) oil; (*med salva*)
salve; (*kung e.d.*) anoint; (*bestryka*) smear; ~ *in
a*) (*ett ämne*) rub in *b*) (*ngn, ngt*) dets. *som smörja
2* ~ *ngn* (*smickra*) smooth up; ~ *ngn* (*muta*) grease
(oil) a p.'s palm **smörjare** greaser, oiler **smör-
jelse 1** (*-ning*) anointing **2** (*salva*) ointment;
(*helig olja*) chrism; *sista ~n* the extreme unction
smörj|fett [lubricating] grease (fat) **-grop** greas-
ing pit **-hall** greasing bay **-hål** lubricating (oil)
hole **-ig** *a1* (*smutsig*) greasy, smeary **-kanna** oil-
can, lubricating can **-kopp** oilcup, lubricating
cup **-medel** *tekn.* lubricant **-ning** greasing *etc.*;
lubrication **-nippel** oil (grease) nipple **-olja** lubricating oil **-spruta** grease (lubricating) gun
smör|klick pat of butter **-kniv** butter knife
-kräm butter cream **-kärna** churn **-papper**
greaseproof paper **-sopp** *s2* ringed boletus **-syra**
butyric acid
snabb *a1* rapid, swift (*rörelse* motion); speedy;
fast (*löpare* runner); prompt, quick (*svar* reply);
~ *i vändningarna* nimble, alert, agile; ~*t tillfrisknande* speedy recovery
snabb|a ~ *på* hurry up **-behandla** (*hopskr.
snabbehandla*) ~ *ett ärende* take prompt action
on (deal quickly with) a matter **-eld** *mil.* rapid
firing **-fotad** *a5* fleet-footed, swift-footed **-för-
band** adhesive plaster **-gående** *a4* fast, high-
speed **-het** swiftness *etc.*; rapidity; speed **-kaffe**
instant coffee **-kurs** short (concentrated) course
-köp[sbutik] self-service shop (*AE.* store)
-läsning speed reading **-seglande** [-e:-] *a4* fast
[-sailing] **-seglare** fast[-sailing] vessel **-sim-
mare** fast (racing) swimmer **-skjutande** [-ʃ-] *a4*
quickfiring **-skrift** shorthand [writing] **-skri-
vare** data. high-speed printer **-stål** high-speed
steel **-telefon** intercom [telephone] **-tänkt** *a1*
quick-witted, ready-witted **-tänkthet** quickness
of wit **-växande** fast-growing
snabel [ˈsna:-] *s2* trunk
snack *s7, vard., se prat, strunt* **snacka** chatter,
chat **snacksalig** *vard.* garrulous
snagg *s3* crew cut **snagga** crop **snaggad** *a5*
cropped
snappa snatch, snap (*efter* at); ~ *bort* snatch
away; ~ *upp* snatch (pick) up; ~ *upp några ord*
catch a few words
snapphane *s2, hist.* pro-Danish partisan in
Scania (17th C)
snaps *s2* schnap[p]s **-visa** drinking song
snar *a1* speedy (*bättring* recovery); quick (*t. vrede*
to anger); *inom en* ~ *framtid* in the immediate
(near) future
snar|a I *s1* snare; (*fälla*) trap; (*fågel-*) springe;
(*ränn-*) noose; *lägga ut -or för* set (lay) traps for;
fastna i ~*t* fall into the trap (*äv. bildl.*) **II** *v1* snare
snar|are *adv* **1** (*hellre*) rather; ~ *kort än lång*
short rather than long; *det är* ~ *så att* ... the fact
is that ... if anything; *jag tror* ~ *att* I am more inclined to think that **2** (*snabbare*) sooner **-ast** *adv*
1 ~ [*möjligt*] as soon as possible, at one's earliest
convenience, without delay **2** (*egentligen*) if any-

thing **-fager** pretty-pretty
snark|a snore **-ning** snore; ~*ar (äv.*) snoring (*sg*)
snar|lik rather like; ~ *i form* much of the same shape; *en* ~ *historia* an analogous (similar) story **-likhet** close similarity **-stucken** *a5* quick to take offence; touchy, susceptible **-stuckenhet** touchiness
snar|t [-a:-] *adv* soon; (*inom kort*) shortly, before long; *alltför* ~ only too soon; ~ *sagt* well-nigh, not far off; *så* ~ [*som*] as soon as, directly; *så* ~ *som möjligt, se snarast 1* **-tänkt** *a1* ready-witted, quick-witted
snask *s7* sweets (*pl*); *AE.* candy **snaska 1** eat sweets; ~ *i sig* munch **2** ~ *ner* make a mess on (of); ~ *ner sig* mess o.s. up **snaskig** *a1* messy, dirty
snatta pilfer, pinch, filch
snatter ['snatt-] *s7* quack[ing]; gabble (*äv. bildl.*); *bildl. äv.* jabber
snatteri petty theft, *jur.* petit (petty) larceny; (*butiks-*) shoplifting
snattra (*om fågel*) quack; gabble (*äv. bildl.*); *bildl. äv.* jabber
snava stumble, trip (*på* over)
sned I *a1* (*om linje, vinkel e.d.*) oblique; (*lutande*) slanting, sloping, inclined; (*skev*) askew, warped; (*krokig*) crooked (*rygg* back); *kasta ~a blickar på* look askance at **II** *s i uttr.: sitta (hänga) på* ~ be (hang) askew (on one side, awry); *gå på* ~ (*bildl.*) go [all] wrong (awry); *komma på* ~ (*bildl.*) go astray; *lägga huvudet på* ~ put one's head on one side **-belastning** uneven weight distribution **-bena** side parting
snedda 1 (*gå snett* [*över*]) edge; ~ *förbi* pass by; ~ *över gatan* slant across (cross) the street **2** (*avskära på -en*) slant, slope; *tekn.* bevel **snedden** ['snedd-] *s best. form i uttr.: på* ~ obliquely, diagonally; *klippa ett tyg på* ~ cut a piece of cloth on the cross (bias)
sned|gången *a5* (*om sko*) worn down on one side **-het** [-e:d-] obliqueness, obliquity; (*krokighet*) crookedness **-hugga** bevel **-klaff** sloping top **-rekrytering** biased (unequal) recruitment **-remsa** bias strip (band) **-skuren** *a5* cut obliquely (*om tyg:* [on the] bias) **-språng** *bildl.* slip, lapse, escapade **-steg** *jfr -språng* **-streck** slanting line, oblique [stroke], solidus, *vard.* slash **-tak** sloping roof **-vinklig** *a1* oblique-angled **-vriden** distorted (*äv. bildl.*), warped **-ögd** *a1* slanteyed
snegla [ˣsne:-, ˣsnegg-] ogle; ~ *på* ogle, look askance at, (*lömskt*) leer at
snett *adv* obliquely; awry, askew; *bo* ~ *emot* live nearly opposite; *gå* ~ *över gatan* cross the street diagonally; *gå* ~ *på skorna* wear one's shoes down on one side; *hänga* ~ hang awry (crooked); *se* ~ *på ngn* look askance at s.b.
snibb *s2* corner, point; (*spets äv.*) tip; *se äv. blöjsnibb* **snibbig** *a1* pointed
snickarbänk joiner's bench
snickar|e (*möbel-*) joiner, cabinet-maker; (*byggnads-*) carpenter **-glädje** *skämts.* ornate decorative carving **-lim** joiner's glue **-verkstad** joiner's (carpenter's) workshop
snickeri 1 (*snickrande*) joinery, carpentry **2** *se snickarverkstad* **3** (*snickararbete*) piece of car-

pentry [work] **-arbete** *se snickeri 3* **-fabrik** joinery (carpentry) shop
snickra do joinery (carpentry) work, do woodwork; ~ *en möbel* make a piece of furniture
snicksnack *s7 vard.* rubbish, nonsense
snid|a carve [in wood] **-are** woodcarver **-eri** carving; *konkr. äv.* carved work
sniff|a sniff (*äv. om missbruk*) **-ning** sniffing
snigel *s2* slug; (*med hus*) snail **-fart** *med* ~ at a snail's pace
snigla [-i:-] ~ *sig fram* creep along (forward)
sniken *a3* avaricious, greedy (*efter, på* of) **-het** greed[iness]
snille *s6* genius; *han är ett* ~ he is a man of genius **-blixt** brain wave, flash of genius
snillrik *a1* brilliant (*uppfinnare* inventor); (*om pers. äv.*) of genius **-het** genius
snip|a *s1* (*båt*) gig **-ig** *a1* pointed, peaked
snirk|el *s2, byggn.* volute; (*släng*) flourish **-lad** *a5* (*krystad*) ornate
snits *s2* chic, style; *sätta* ~ *på ngt* give s.th. style
snitsel *s2* **1** (*pappersremsa*) paper strip **2** (*av sockerbetor*) beet slices (*pl*) **-jakt** paper chase
snitsig *a1* elegant, chic
snitsla mark path with paper strips
snitt *s7* **1** (*skärning*) cut, section; *kir.* incision; *gyllene ~et* (*mat.*) the golden section **2** (*preparat*) section cutting **3** (*tvär-*) section **4** (*trä-*) [wood] cut **5** (*på kläder*) cut, pattern **6** (*bok-*) edge **-blomma** cut flower **-yta** cut, section (*etc.*) surface
sno *v4* **1** (*hopvrida*) twist; (*tvinna*) twine; (*vira*) twirl (*tummarna* one's thumbs; (*linda*) turn, wind; ~ *ett rep om* wind a rope round **2** (*springa*) scamper, run; ~ *runt på klacken* turn on the heel; ~ *om hörnet* dash round the corner **3** *rfl* twist, get twisted (*hoptrasslad:* entangled); (*skynda sig*) hurry [up] **4** *vard.* steal, lift
snobb [-å-] *s2* snob; (*kläd-*) dandy, fop **snobba** ~ [*med*] show off, swank about **snobberi** snobbery, dandyism **snobbig** *a1* (*sprättaktig*) snobbish, *vard.* stuck up; (*överdrivet elegant*) foppish
snodd *s3, s2, konkr.* string, cord; (*t. garnering*) lace
snofsig [-å-] *a1, vard.* dapper, spiffing
snok *s2* grass snake
snoka spy, pry; poke, ferret; *gå och* ~ go prying about, *vard.* snoop; ~ *efter* hunt for; ~ *i* poke [one's nose] into; ~ *igenom* rummage; ~ *reda på* hunt up, ferret out
snopen *a3* baffled, crestfallen; *se* ~ *ut* (*äv.*) look blank (foolish); *han blev ngt* [*till*] ~ he was struck all of a heap
snopp [-å-] *s2* **1** (*ljus-*) snuff, trim; (*bär-*) tail **2** *vard., barnspr.* (*penis*) willy **snoppa** (*ljus*) snuff; (*bär e.d.*) top and tail; (*cigarr*) cut; ~ *av ngn* (*bildl.*) snub s.b., take s.b. down a peg or two
snor *s7, vard.* snot **snora** snivel **snorfana** *sl.* (*näsduk*) nose rag **snorgärs** [-j-] *s2* **1** *zool.* ruff [e], pope **2** *se snorunge* **snorig** *a1* snivelling, snotty
snorkel [-å-] *s2* snorkel
snorkig [-å-] *a1* snooty
snor|unge, -valp *vard.* snotty kid, whelp
snubbeltråd tripwire **snubbla** stumble [and fall]

snubbor *pl* snubbing, rating (*sg*)
snudd *s2* light touch; ~ *på skandal* little short of a scandal; ~ *på seger* on the verge of victory **snudda** ~ *vid* graze, brush against, *AE.* sideswipe, *bildl.* touch [up]on
snugga *s1* (*pipa*) cutty [pipe]
snurr *s7* (*-ande*) whirl, rotation; *rena ~en* (*galenskapen*) sheer madness **snurra I** *s1* (*leksak*) top **II** *v1* **1** (*rotera*) whirl, spin; ~ *runt* go round and round, rotate; *det ~r runt i huvudet på mig* my head is spinning **2** (*låta rotera*) spin, whirl **snurrig** *a1* dizzy; (*virrig*) confused, muddled
snus *s4* snuff; *en pris* ~ a pinch of snuff **snusa 1** (*använda snus*) take snuff **2** (*lukta*) sniff (*på* at); (*under sömnen*) breathe heavily **snusande** *a4* snuff-taking **snusdosa** snuffbox **snusen** ['snu:-] *s best. form, vard., vara på* ~ be tipsy
snusförnuft knowingness **-ig** would-be-wise; (*om barn*) precocious; *en ~ person* a wiseacre, a know-all
snusk *s7* dirt[iness]; uncleanness, squalor; obscenity **snuska** ~ *ner* mess up, soil **snuskhummer** *vard.* [old] lecher, dirty old man **snuskig** *a1* dirty, squalid; filthy, smutty (*historia* story) **snuskpelle** *s2* dirty [little] pig
snus|malen *a5*, *-malet kaffe* finely ground (pulverized) coffee **-näsduk** bandan[n]a **-torr** [as] dry as dust (*äv. bildl.*); *vard.* bone-dry
snut *s2*, *vard.* **1** (*trut*) snout **2** (*polis*) cop[per]; *~en* the fuzz, *AE.* the heat
snutit *sup. av snyta*
snutt *s2* short piece [of music *etc.*], snatch
snuva *s1* head cold; *få* ~ catch (get) a cold **snuvig** *a1*, *vara* ~ have a cold in the head
snyft|a sob (*fram* out); ~ *till* give a sob **-ning** sob
snygg *a1* tidy; (*ren*) clean; (*vacker, om man*) handsome; (*vacker, om kvinna*) pretty; *iron. äv.* fine, pretty; *det var en ~ historia!* that's a pretty story! **snygga** ~ *upp* make tidy, tidy up; ~ *till sig* make o.s. presentable **snygghet** tidiness; cleanliness **snyggt** *adv* tidily; (*prydligt*) neatly; ~ *klädd* nicely (well) dressed
snylt|a be a parasite (sponge) (*på* on) **-gäst** parasite, sponger **-rot** *bot.* broomrape
snyt|a *snöt snutit* **1** wipe a p.'s nose; (*ljus*) snuff; *det är inte snutet ur näsan* it's not just a case of pressing a button; ~ *sig* blow one's nose **2** (*snatta*) pinch, snatch; (*lura*) cheat **-ing** punch on the nose **-ning** [-y:-] blowing (wiping) of the nose
snål *a1* **1** stingy; (*knusslig*) parsimonious, mean, cheeseparing **2** (*bitande*) cutting (*blåst* wind) **snåla** be stingy *etc.*, pinch and screw; ~ *in på ngt* save on s.th.
snål|blåst bitter wind **-het** [-å:-] stinginess *etc.*; *~en bedrar visheten* penny wise pound foolish **-jåp** *s2* miser, skinflint **-skjuts** *åka* ~ get a lift, *bildl.* take advantage [of] **-varg** *se -jåp* **-vatten** *-vattnet rinner på honom* his mouth waters
snår *s7* thicket; brush **-ig** *a1* brushy **-skog** brushwood, undergrowth
snäck|a *s1* **1** *zool.* gast[e]ropod; (*trädgårds-*) helix; (*-skal*) shell; *anat.* cochlea **2** *tekn.* worm **-formig** [-å-] *a1* spiral, helical **-skal** [sea]shell **-växel** worm gear
snäll *a1* good; (*av naturen*) good-natured; (*vänlig*) kind, nice (*mot* to); *~a du!* my dear!; *vara* ~

a) (*om barn*) be good, *b*) (*om vuxen*) be kind; *var* ~ *och stäng dörren* please shut the door; *har barnen varit ~a?* have the children behaved themselves? **-het** goodness *etc.*
snäll|press high-speed (cylinder) press **-tåg** express [train], fast train
snälltågs|biljett supplementary express [train] ticket **-fart** *med* ~ at express speed
snäppa *s1*, *zool.* sandpiper
snärj *s7* (*jäkt*) hectic time **snärja** *v2* [en]snare, entangle (*i* in) (*äv. bildl.*); *bildl. äv.* catch; ~ *in sig i* get entangled in **snärjande** *a4*, *bildl.* insidious (*frågor* questions) **snärjig** *a1*, *eg.* tangled; (*jäktig*) hectic; (*jobbig*) laborious
snärt *s2* **1** (*på piska*) lash, thong **2** (*slag*) lash **3** (*stickord*) gibe, taunt **snärta I** *v1*, ~ [*till*] lash; (*pika*) gibe at, make a crack at **II** *s1*, *se flicksnärta* **snärtig** *a1* cutting (*svar* reply)
snäs|a *v3* speak harshly to, snap at **II** *s1* snub [bing], rating, rebuff **-ig** *a1* snappish, brusque **-ning** [-ä:-] *se snäsa II*
snäv *a1* **1** (*trång*) narrow; (*om plagg*) tight, close **2** (*ovänlig*) stiff, cold; curt (*svar* answer)
snö *s3* snow; *tala inte om den ~ som föll i fjol* let bygones be bygones; *det som göms i ~ kommer upp i tö* there is no secret time will not reveal **snö|a** snow; *det ~r* it is snowing; *vägen har ~t igen* the road is blocked (covered) with snow **-blandad** *-blandat regn* sleet **-blind** snow-blind **-boll** snowball **-bollskrig** snowball fight **-by** snow squall **-bär** snowberry
snöd *a1* sordid, vile
snö|driva snowdrift **-droppe** *bot.* snowdrop **-fall** snowfall, fall of snow **-fattig** with little snow **-flinga** snowflake **-fästning** snow castle **-glopp** [-å-] *s7* sleet **-grotta** igloo **-gräns** snow line **-gubbe** snowman **-hinder** snow obstruction **-ig** *a1* snowy **-kedja** tyre chain, non-skid chain **-klädd** snowclad **-kristall** snow crystal **-lykta** lantern made of snowballs **-man** abominable snowman, yeti **-mos** *bildl.* boloney
snöp|a *v3* geld **-ing** gelding
snöplig [-ö:-] *a1* ignominious, inglorious; *få ett ~t slut* come to a sad (sorry) end
snöplog snowplough **-ning** [-ɔ:-] snowploughing
snöra *v2* lace [up]; ~ *fast* fasten [with a lace]; ~ *till* lace up (*ett par skor* a pair of shoes); ~ *på sig* put on (*skridskorna* the skates); ~ *upp* unlace; ~ *åt* draw together, (*hårdare*) tighten; ~ *sig* lace o.s. up
snör|e *s6* string, cord; (*segelgarn*) twine; (*prydnads-*) braid **-hål** lace hole, eyelet
snöripa *se dalripa*
snör|liv stays (*pl*), corset; *ett* ~ a pair of stays **-makare** lacemaker **-makeri** (*hantverk*) lacemaking; (*-verkstad*) passementerie workshop; **~er** (*tränsar m.m.*) lace (*sg*), braids and trimmings **-ning** [-ö:-] lacing
snörp|a *v3* purse (*ihop* up); ~ *på* (*med*) *munnen* purse (screw up) one's mouth **-vad** *s2* purse seine (net)
snör|rem lace; (*läder-*) strap **-rät** [as] straight as an arrow **-sko** laced shoe **-stump** piece of string
snörvl|a snuffle, speak through one's (the) nose **-ing** snuffling; (*en ~*) snuffle

snö|skata *se björktrast* **-sko** snowshoe **-skoter** snowmobile, snow scooter **-skottare** [-å-] snow clearer (shoveller) **-skottning** [-å-] snow clearing **-skovel** *se -skyffel* **-skred** avalanche **-skydd** snowbreak **-skyffel** snow shovel **-slask** sleet; slush **-slunga** snow thrower **-smältning** melting (thawing) of [the] snow **-sparv** snow bunting **-storm** snowstorm; blizzard **-sväng** *s2, vard.* snow-clearance squad **-sörja** slush, melting snow
snöt *imperf. av snyta*
snö|tjocka snow fog **-täcke** covering of snow **-täckt** *a4* snow-covered **-vidd** snowfield **-vit** snowy, snow-white; *S~* Snow White **-yra** whirling snow, snowstorm
so *best. form son, som pl används suggor* sow
soaré *s3* soirée, evening entertainment; *musikalisk ~* musical evening
sobel ['så:-] *s2* sable **-päls** sable coat
sober ['så:-] *a2* sober; subdued
social *a1* social **-antropologi** cultural (social) anthropology **-arbetare** social (welfare) worker **-arbete** social (welfare) work **-assistent** social welfare officer **-bidrag** social (*AE.* public) assistance; supplementary benefit **-byrå** welfare office **-demokrat** social democrat **-demokrati** social democracy **-demokratisk** social democratic; *Sveriges ~a arbetareparti* [the] Swedish social democratic party **-departement** *~et* [the] ministry for health and social affairs, *BE. ung.* the ministry of pensions and national insurance, *AE. ung.* the department of health, education and welfare **-ekologi** human ecology **-fall** s.b. receiving social assistance **-försäkring** national (social) insurance **-försäkringsutskott** *~et* [the Swedish] [parliamentary] standing committee on social insurance **-förvaltning** *ung.* [local authority] social services department **-grupp** social group; *~ 1* [the] upper class; *~ 2* [the] middle class; *~ 3* [the] working (lower) class **-hjälp** [public] assistance allowance; *få ~* receive public assistance, be on welfare (relief) **-högskola** school of social studies
social|isera socialize; nationalize **-isering** [-'se:-] socialization; nationalization **-ism** socialism (*äv. ~en*) **-ist** socialist **-istisk** [-'liss-] *a5* socialist[ic]
social|kunskap social studies **-lagstiftning** social (*AE.* security) legislation **-liberal** liberal social reformer **-medicin** social[ized] medicine **-minister** minister of health and social affairs **-nämnd** social welfare committee **-politik** social [welfare] policy; social politics (*pl, behandlas som sg*) **-politisk** sociopolitical, of social policy **-styrelse** *~n* [the Swedish] national board of health and welfare **-utskott** *~et* the [Swedish] [parliamentary] standing committee on social questions **-vetenskap** social science[s *pl*] **-vetenskaplig** of social science[s] **-vetenskapsman** sociologist **-vård** social welfare (assistance) **-vårdare** welfare officer, social worker **-vårdsbyrå** [local] social welfare office (bureau)
societet *s3* society
societets|dam socialite **-hus** clubhouse; casino **-lejon** social lion

socio|ekonomisk socioeconomic **-gram** [-'gramm] *s7* sociogram **-log** sociologist **-logi** *s3* sociology **-logisk** [-'lå:-] *a5* sociological **-nom** graduate from a school of social studies **-pat** sociopath
socka [ˣsåkka] *s1* sock
sockel ['såkk-] *s2* (*byggn.; postament*) base, plinth; (*fattning*) holder, mounting; (*lamp-*) socket
socken ['sɔkk-] *socknen socknar* parish **-bo** parishioner; *~r* (*äv.*) the inhabitants of a parish **-dräkt** *ung.* peasant costume **-kyrka** parish church **-stämma** parish meeting
socker ['såkk-] *s7* sugar **-bagare** confectioner **-beta** sugar beet **-bit** lump of sugar **-bruk** sugar mill (refinery) **-dricka** *ung.* lemonade **-fri** sugar-free **-haltig** *a1* containing sugar **-kaka** sponge cake **-kulör** caramel **-lag** *s2* syrup [of sugar] **-lönn** sugar maple **-lösning** sugar solution **-piller** sugar-coated pill **-plantage** sugar plantation **-pulla** sugarplum **-raffinaderi** sugar refinery **-rör** sugar cane **-sjuk** diabetic **-sjuka** diabetes **-skål** sugar basin **-ströare** sugar sifter (castor) **-söt** [as] sweet as sugar; *bildl. äv.* sugary, honeyed **-topp** sugar loaf **-tång** sugar tongs (*pl*) **-vatten** sugared water **-ärtor** sugar peas
sockra [ˣsåkk-] sweeten [with sugar], sugar; *~ på* put sugar in (on); *~ sig* sugar, crystallize
soda *s9* soda **-lut** soda lye **-vatten** soda water
sodomi *s3* sodomy
soff|a [-å-] *s1* sofa; (*liten*) settee; (*trädgårds-*) seat **-bord** coffee table **-grupp** three-piece suite **-kudde** sofa cushion **-liggare** idler; (*vid val*) abstainer **-lock** sofa seat (top); *ligga på ~et* take it easy, idle
sof|ism *s3* sophism **-ist** sophist **-istikerad** [-'ke:-] *a5* sophisticated **-istisk** [-'fiss-] *a5* sophistic[al]
soignerad [sɔanˈje:-] *a5* soigné[e]; *en ~ herre* (*äv.*) a well-groomed gentleman
soja [ˣsåjja] *s1* soya; soy **-böna** soya bean; *AE.* soybean **-sås** soy (soya) sauce
sokratisk [såˈkra:-] *a5* Socratic
sol *s2* sun
sol|a expose to the sun; *~ sig* sun o.s., sunbathe, *bildl.* bask **-aktivitet** solar activity **-altan** sun balcony (terrace)
solar *a1* solar **solarium** [-ˈla:-] *s4* solarium
solarplexus [-ˣla:r-, ˈsɔ:-] *s2* solar plexus
solaväxel [ˣså:-] sole (single, only) bill [of exchange]
sol|bad sun bath **-bada** sunbathe, take a sun bath **-bana** ecliptic, solar orb **-batteri** solar battery **-belyst** [-y:-] *a4* sunlit, sunny **-blekt** [-e:-] *a4* sun-bleached **-blind** sun-blind, blinded by the sun **-blindhet** sun-blindness **-bränd** *a5* sunburnt, tanned **-bränna** *s1* sunburn, tan **-cell** solar cell
sold [-å-] *s3, mil.* pay
soldat soldier; *bli ~* enlist, join the army; *den okände ~ens grav* the tomb of the Unknown Soldier **-ed** military oath **-esk** *s3* [licentious] soldiery **-hop, -hord** rabble of soldiers **-liv** [a] soldier's (military) life **-rock** soldier's tunic **-torp** tenement soldier's smallholding
sol|dis heat haze **-dräkt** sunsuit **-dyrkan** sun

worship **-eksem** sun rash **-el[ektrisk energi]** solar electric power, solar electricity **-energi** solar energy

solenn al solemn **-itet** s3 solemnity

sol|eruption solar flare **-fattig** not very sunny; en ~ trakt a district with little sun[shine] **-fjäder** fan **-fjäderformad** [-å-] a5 fan-shaped **-fläck** sunspot **-fångare** solar collector **-följare** sun tracker **-förmörkelse** eclipse of the sun, solar eclipse **-gass** blazing (blaze of the) sun **-glasögon** sunglasses **-glimt** glimpse of the sun **-glitter** (på vatten) sparkle **-gud** sun-god **-gård** [solar] halo **-höjd** altitude of the sun

solid al solid; ekon. äv. sound, well-established, respectable; ~a kunskaper [a] thorough (sound) knowledge

solidar|isera rfl identify o.s. (med with) **-isk** [-'da:-] a5 loyal, solidary; joint; ~ med loyal to; förklara sig ~ med declare one's solidarity with **-itet** solidarity

soliditet solidity; (ekonomisk) solvency, soundness; (persons) respectability

soliditets|byrå credit information agency; AE. mercantile agency **-upplysning** credit[worthiness] report

solig al sunny (äv. bildl.)

solist soloist, solo performer

solitär s3 solitaire

solk s7 soil **solka** [-å-] ~ ner soil

solkatt reflection of the sun

solkig [-å-] a1 soiled

sol|klar clear and sunny; bildl. as clear as noonday (daylight) **-konungen** the Sun King **-korona** solar corona, corona of the sun **-kraftverk** solar power station **-kurva** en ~ hade uppstått the rails had buckled in the sun **-ljus I** s7 sunlight **II** a5, se **-klar -månad** solar month **-mättad** sun-drenched **-nedgång** sunset, sundown; i ~en at sunset

solo ['sɔ:-] **I** s6 solo (pl äv. soli) **II** oböjligt a o. adv solo

solochvåra [-ˣvå:-] obtain valuables by false promise of marriage; bli ~d be cheated by false promise of marriage **solochvårare** con man [who cheats women out of money by false promises of marriage]

solo|dansös solo dancer, prima ballerina **-flygning** solo flight

sololja suntan oil (lotion)

solo|nummer solo **-stämma** solo part **-sång** solo singing

sol|ros sunflower **-rosolja** sunflower seed oil **-rök** haze **-segel** awning **-sida** på (åt) ~n on the sunny side **-sken** sunshine; det är ~ the sun is shining **-skensdag** sunny day **-skenshistoria** charming little story **-skenshumör** sunny mood **-skiva** sun's disk **-skydd** (i bil) sun shield (screen) **-skärm** sunshade **-spektrum** solar spectrum **-sting** (få have) sunstroke **-strimma** ray of sunshine **-stråle** sunbeam **-strålning** solar radiation **-styng** se -sting **-stånd** solstice **-system** solar system **-tak** awning; (på bil) sliding roof (top) **-teknik** solar technology **-torka** dry [...] in the sun; ~d sun-dried **-tält** awning **-uppgång** sunrise; AE. äv. sunup; i ~en at sunrise **-uppvärmning** solar heating **-ur** sundial

solution rubber solution

solv [-å-] s7, väv. heddle

sol|varg han är en riktig ~ he's as happy as a sandboy **-vargsleende** dazzling smile **-varv** revolution of the sun

solv|ens [-å-] s3 solvency; reliability **-ent** al solvent; reliable **-era** [-å-] mat. solve

sol|vind solar wind **-vända** s1, bot. rockrose **-värme** heat of the sun; fack. solar heat **-värmekraftverk** solar thermal power station **-år** solar year **-år** al solar

som [såmm] **I** pron (om pers.) who (som obj. o. efter prep äv. whom); (om djur el. sak) which; (i nödvändig rel. sats om djur, sak o. ibl. pers., äv.) that; (efter such o. vanl. the same) as; pojken ~ kommer här the boy who comes here; den ~ lever får se he who lives will see; den ~ köper en bil måste anyone who buys (anyone buying) a car must; det är en dam ~ söker dig there is a lady [who wants] to see you; han frågade vem det var ~ kom he asked who came (had come); vem är det ~ du pratar med? who is that you are talking to?; det är ngn ~ gråter s.b. is crying; huset ~ de bor i the house where (in which) they live; han brukade berätta sagor, något ~ he used to tell stories, which; allt (mycket, litet) ~ all (much, little) that; det är saker ~ vi sällan talar om these are things [that] we seldom speak of; den största konstnär ~ någonsin levat the greatest artist that ever lived; mannen och hästen ~ gick förbi the man and the horse that passed; vem ~ än kommer whoever comes; vad ~ än händer whatever happens; det var på den tiden ~ it was at the time when; de var de sista ~ kom they were the last to arrive; så dum jag var ~ sålde den! what a fool I was to sell it!; jag kom samma dag ~ han reste I arrived on the [same] day [as] he left; det är samme man ~ vi såg i går that is the same man [that, whom] we saw yesterday; hon var en sådan skönhet ~ man sällan ser she had the kind of beauty one seldom sees **II** konj **1** såväl ... ~ as well ... as; unga ~ gamla young and old alike **2** (såsom, i egenskap av) as; (såsom, i likhet med) like; redan ~ pojke even as a boy; L ~ i London L as in London; säg ~ det är tell me (him etc.) exactly how things stand; kom ~ du är come as you are, don't dress up, don't bother to change; ~ vanligt as usual; han är lika lång ~ jag he is as tall as I am; ~ tur var as luck would have it, luckily; ~ läkare måste han as (being) a doctor he must; ~ sagt as I (etc.) said before; gör ~ du vill do as you like; gör ~ jag do as I do, do like me; vara ~ en mor för ngn be [like] a mother to s.b.; vara ~ förbytt be changed beyond recognition; om jag vore ~ du if I were you; det är bara ~ du tror that's only your idea **3** han lever ~ om var dag var den sista he lives as though each day was his last; det verkar ~ om it seems as if (though) **4** (när) when; just (bäst) ~ [just] as, at the very moment [when]; rätt ~ det var all of a sudden, all at once **5** (eftersom) as, since; ~ han är sjuk kan han inte komma as (since) he is ill he cannot come **III** adv, när jag ~ bäst höll på med att while I was in the midst of (+ ing-form); du kan väl titta in ~ hastigast you can surely pop in for just a moment; när solen står ~ högst when the sun is at its height;

vi skulle resa ~ *på måndag* we were to leave on Monday **IV** *interj,* ~ *vi skrattade!* how we laughed!

somatisk [-'ma:-] *a5* somatic

somlig [ˣsåmm-] some; ~*a* (*om pers.*) some [people]; ~*a andra* some other people; ~*t* some things (*pl*); *i* ~*t* in some parts (respects)

sommar [ˣsåmm-] *s2* summer; *i* ~ this (next) summer; *i somras* last summer; *om* ~*en* (*somrarna*) in the summer; *på* ~*en 1968* in the summer of 1968; *en svala gör ingen* ~ one swallow does not make a summer **-dag** summer['s] day **-gäst** summer visitor **-kappa** summer coat **-klänning** summer dress **-kostym** summer suit **-kväll** summer evening **-lov** summer vacation (holidays) (*pl*), long vacation **-nöje** *se* **-ställe** **-sjuka** summer diarrhoea **-solstånd** summer solstice **-stuga,** **-ställe** weekend cottage, summer cottage (villa); *vårt* ~ (*äv.*) the place where we spend our summers **-tid** summertime; (*framflyttning av klockan*) daylight-saving time **-värme** summer warmth; heat

somna [-å-] ~ [*in*] fall asleep, go to sleep; *vard.* drop off; ~ *från lampan* go to sleep and leave the light on; ~ *om* go to sleep again; ~ *vid ratten* fall asleep when driving; *min fot har* ~*t* my foot has gone to sleep

somnambul [-å-] **I** *s3* somnambulist **II** *a1* somnambulistic

somt [-å-] some things (*pl*); ~ *föll på hälleberget* some fell on stony ground

son [så:n] *-en söner* son (*till* of)

sona expiate; make amends for

sonant sonant

sonar ['så:-] *s3* echo sounder, sonar, asdic

sonet sonata **-form** sonata form **-in** *s3* sonatina

sond [sånd, såŋd] *s3, kir.* probe, sound; *rymd.* probe **sondera** probe, sound; ~ *terrängen* reconnoitre, see how the land lies **sondering** [-'de:-] probing, probe, sounding **sondmatning** nasogastric feeding

sondotter granddaughter; ~*s barn* great-grandchild

sonett *s3* sonnet

sonhustru daughter-in-law

sonika ['så:-] *helt* ~ [quite] simply, without ceremony

son|lig [ˣså:n-] *a1* filial (*vördnad* piety) **-namn** family name ending in -son

sonor [-'nå:r] *a1* sonorous **-itet** sonority

son|son grandson **-sonsson** great-grandson

sop|a sweep (*gatan* the street); ~ *rent* sweep [...] clean (*från* of); ~ *upp* sweep up; ~ *rent för egen dörr* put one's own house in order; ~ *igen spåren efter* (*bildl.*) cover up one's tracks after **-backe** refuse tip **-bil** refuse [collection] lorry, dustcart; *AE.* garbage truck **-borste** brush, broom **-hink** refuse bucket **-hämtare** dustman; *AE.* garbage collector **-hämtning** refuse collection; *AE.* garbage removal **-hög** rubbish heap **-kvast** broom **-kärl** dustbin **-lår** *se* soptunna **-nedkast** refuse (*AE.* garbage) chute **-ning** [-ɔ:-] sweeping **-or** *pl* sweepings; (*avfall*) refuse, waste, *AE.* garbage (*sg*)

sopp|a [-å-] *s1* soup; (*kött-*) broth; *koka* ~ *på en spik* (*bildl.*) make s.th. from nothing **-ben** *pl*

bones for soup **-kittel** soup cauldron **-rötter** *pl* vegetables for soup, potherbs **-skål** [soup] tureen **-slev** soup ladle **-tallrik** soup plate **-terrin** *se* **-skål**

sopran *s3* soprano; (*-stämma äv.*) treble

sop|skyffel dustpan **-säck** refuse sack **-tipp** refuse (*AE.* garbage) dump **-tunna** dustbin; *AE.* garbage (trash) can **-åkare** dustman

sorbet [-'be:(t)] *s3* sorbet, sherbet

sordin [-å-] *s3, mus.* sordino; *lägga* ~ *på* (*bildl.*) put a damper on

sorg [sårj] *s3* **1** sorrow (*över* at, for, over); grief (*över* for, of, at); distress; (*bedrövelse*) affliction; (*bekymmer*) trouble, care; *med* ~ *i själen* with sorrow in one's heart; *den dagen den* ~*en* cross your bridges when you come to them; *efter sju* ~*er och åtta bedrövelser* after much trial and tribulation **2** (*efter avliden*) mourning; *bära* ~ be in (wear) mourning (*efter* for); *djup* ~ full (deep) mourning; *beklaga* ~*en* express one's sympathy; *få* ~ have a bereavement, lose a relative **-band** mourning (crape) band **-dräkt** mourning

sorge|barn problem child; black sheep **-bud** sad news, news of a death **-hus** house of mourning **-högtid** funeral ceremony **-musik** funeral music **-spel** tragedy **-tåg** funeral procession

sorg|flor mourning crape **-fri** carefree, free from care **-fällig** *a1* careful; conscientious, solicitous **-fällighet** care[fulness]; solicitude **-kant** black edge (border); *kuvert med* ~ black-edged envelope **-klädd** [dressed] in mourning **-kläder** *pl* mourning [attire] (*sg*)

sorglig [ˣsårj-] *a3* sad; (*bedrövlig*) deplorable (*syn* sight); (*ömklig*) pitiful; ~*t men sant* sad but true; *en* ~ *historia* a sad (deplorable, tragic) story **sorgligt** *adv* sadly; ~ *nog* unfortunately

sorg|lustig tragicomic **-lös** **1** *se* sorgfri **2** (*obetänksam*) careless; (*lättsinnig*) happy-go-lucky, improvident; (*tanklös*) unthinking, heedless **-löshet** carelessness *etc.* **-mantel** *zool.* Camberwell beauty, *AE.* mourning cloak **-marsch** funeral march **-modig** melancholy

sorgsen [ˣsårj-] *a3* sad; (*bedrövad*) grieved (*över* at); (*nedslagen*) depressed; (*betryckt*) melancholy, gloomy **-het** sadness *etc.*; melancholy, gloom

sork [-å-] *s2* vole; (*förr*) fieldmouse

sorl [-å:-] *s7* (*vattenbrus*) ripple; (*bäcks äv.*) murmur, purl; (*av röster*) murmur, hum; *det gick ett* ~ *av bifall genom publiken* a murmur of approval went through the house (theatre, hall *etc.*) **sorla** ripple, purl; murmur, hum

sort [-å-] *s3* sort, kind; species, description; (*märke*) brand, mark; *mat.* denomination; *den* ~*ens människor* people of that kind (sort), that sort of people; *av bästa* ~ first-rate **sortera 1** (*dela upp*) [as]sort; classify, grade; (*efter storlek*) size **2** ~ *under* belong to, (*ämbetsverk*) come under the supervision of **sorterad** [-'te:-] *a5* (*välförsedd*) well-stocked (*i* in); *vara* ~ *i* (*äv.*) have a large assortment of **sortering** [-'te:-] (*-erande*) [as]sorting, assortment; (*sortiment*) selection; *första* ~ first[s *pl*] **sorteringsmaskin** sorting (grading) machine

sortj *s3* exit

sortiment *s7* (*varulager*) assortment, range;

product mix; (*uppsättning*) set; *fullständigt ~ av* full line of, complete range of

sosse *s2, vard.* social democrat

1 sot *s7* **1** soot; (*i motor*) carbon **2** (*på säd*) brand, blight

2 sot *s3* (*sjukdom*) sickness, disease

1 sota (*umgälla*) *~ för* smart (suffer) for

2 sota 1 (*befria från sot*) sweep (*en skorsten* a chimney); decarbonize (*en motor* a motor) **2** (*svärta*) *~* [*ner*] soot, cover with soot; *~ ner sig* get o.s. sooty **3** (*~ ifrån sig*) soot, give off soot

sotar|e chimney sweep[er] **-murre** *s2, vard., se* *-are* **-mästare** master sweep

sotdöd *dö ~en* die a natural death

sot|eld chimney fire **-fläck** smudge, smut **-höna** coot

sot|ig *a1* **1** sooty; (*om skorsten*) full of soot; (*fläckig*) smudgy, smutty **2** (*om säd*) smutty, blighted **-lucka** soot door **-ning** [-ɔ:-] (*av skorsten*) chimney-sweeping; (*av motor*) decarbonization **-svamp** common smut of wheat **-svart** sooty [black]

sotsäng *ligga på ~en* lie on one's deathbed

sotviska flue brush

souschef [ˣsoːʃeːf] deputy chief

souvenir [soʋe-] *s3* souvenir, keepsake

sov [-åː-] *imperf. av sova*

sov|a [-åː-] *sov -it* sleep; (*ligga o. ~*) be asleep; *lägga sig att ~* go to sleep (bed); *~ gott* sleep soundly, be fast asleep, (*som vana*) sleep well; *sov gott!* sleep well!; *har du -it gott i natt?* did you have a good night?; *~ oroligt* have a troubled sleep; *mitt ben -er* my leg has gone to sleep; *~ på saken* sleep on it; *~ ut* have enough sleep **-alkov** bed recess **-ande** *a4* sleeping; *bildl.* dormant; *en ~* a sleeper **-dags** bedtime **-dräkt** sleeping suit

sovel [ˈsåː-] *s7* meat, cheese *etc.*

sovit [-åː-] *sup. av sova*

sovjet [-åˈ-] *s3* soviet; *högsta ~* Supreme Soviet **-isk** *a5* Soviet, of the Soviet Union **-republik** Soviet Republic **-rysk** Soviet Russian

Sovjet|ryssland Soviet Russia **-unionen** the Soviet Union

sov|kupé sleeping-compartment, sleeper **-plats** sleeping-place; (*på tåg, båt*) berth **-påse** sleeping bag

sovr|a [-åː-] pick over; sift, winnow; (*malm e.d.*) dress **-ing** picking *etc.*

sov|rum bedroom **-sal** dormitory **-stad** dormitory suburb; *AE.* bedroom suburb (town) **-säck** sleeping bag **-vagn** sleeping car, sleeper **-vagnsbiljett** sleeper ticket **-vagnskonduktör** sleeping-car attendant

spackel [ˈspakk-] *s7* putty [knife] **spackla** putty **spackling** puttying

spad *s7, sg best. form vard. spat* liquid; (*kött-*) broth; (*grönsaks- äv.*) water; *trilla i spat* (*vard.*) fall into the water

spade *s2* spade

spader [ˈspaː-] *s9, kortsp., koll.* spades (*pl*); *en ~* a spade; *~ kung* the king of spades; *dra en ~* (*vard.*) have a game of cards

spadtag cut (dig) with a spade; *ta det första ~et* throw the first sod; *inte ta ett ~* (*vard.*) not lift a finger

spagat *s3, gå ner i ~* do the splits

spagetti [-ˈgetti] *s9* spaghetti **-västern** *r, vard.* spaghetti western

1 spak *s2* lever; bar; *flyg.* control stick

2 spak *al* manageable, tractable; docile; *bli ~* relent, soften

spaljé *s3* espalier, trelliswork, latticework **-träd** trained fruit tree

spalt *s3* column; *figurera i ~erna* appear in the papers

spalt|a 1 (*dela i -er*) put into columns **2** (*klyva*) split, cleave **-bredd** column width **-fyllnad** padding **-korrektur** galley proof **-vis** (*i -er*) in columns; (*spalt efter spalt*) columns of, column after column

spana watch, look out (*efter* for); scout; *mil.* reconnoitre, observe; *~ efter* (*äv.*) search (be on the lookout) for; *~ upp* spy out; *~ ut över* gaze out over (*vidderna* the expanses); *~nde blickar* searching looks **spanare** scout; *flyg.* observer

spaniel [ˈspanjel] *s2* spaniel

Spanien [ˈspannjen] *n* Spain

spaning scout; *mil.* reconnaissance; *få ~ på ngt* (*vard.*) get wind of s.th.

spanings|arbete *~t har pågått* the search has been on **-flygplan** reconnaissance aircraft scout **-ledning** search coordination headquarters **-patrull** search party; *mil.* reconnaissance [party] **-uppbåd** search party

spanjor *s3* Spaniard **-ska** [-ˣjoːr-] Spanish woman

spankulera stroll, saunter

1 spann *s7, byggn.* span

2 spann *s2, s7, pl äv. spänner* (*hink*) pail, bucket

3 spann *s9* (*mått*) span

4 spann *s7* (*av dragdjur*) team [of horses *etc.*]; *köra* (*med*) *i ~* drive a team of [horses *etc.*]

5 spann *imperf. av spinna*

spannmål *s3* grain, corn; (*brödsäd*) cereal[s *pl*]

spannmåls|förråd corn (*etc.*) store **-handel** corn (grain) trade (business) **-magasin** granary, corn (grain) store **-produkt** grain (corn) product **-skörd** grain (corn) crop

spansk *al* Spanish; *~a sjukan* the Spanish flu; *~ peppar* red pepper; *~a ryttare* (*mil.*) chevaux-de-frise

spansk|a *s1* (*språk*) Spanish **–amerikansk** Spanish-American **-fluga** *zool.* Spanish fly; (*drog*) cantharis **-gröna** *s1* verdigris **-rör** rattan [cane]

spant *s7, sjö.* frame, rib

spara save (*pengar* money; *sina krafter* one's strength; *tid* time; *arbete* work); spare (*hästarna* the horses); (*för framtiden*) reserve (*till* of); (*uppskjuta*) put off; *~ på* save, economize, use sparingly; *~ in* save; *den som spar han har* waste not want not; *snål spar och fan tar* ever spare, ever bare; *inte ~ på beröm* be lavish in praise; *det är inget att ~ på* it is not worth saving (keeping); *~ sig* spare o.s., husband one's strength; *du kunde ha ~t dig den mödan* you could have spared yourself the trouble

sparande *s6* saving; thrift; *det privata ~t* private saving[s *pl*]; *frivilligt ~* voluntary saving **sparare** saver; depositor

spar|bank *s3* savings bank **-banksbok** savings-[-bank] book **-bössa** money-box **-gris** piggy bank

spark *s2* **1** kick; *få ~en (avsked)* get the sack, be fired (sacked) **2** kick-sledge

sparka kick; *~ av sig skorna* kick off one's shoes; *~ av sig täcket* kick off one's bedclothes; *~ bakut (om häst)* kick [out behind]; *~ fram (bildl.)* thrust forward; *~ ngn [snett] uppåt (vard.)* kick s.b. upstairs; *~ till* give a kick; *~ ut ngn* kick s.b. out

sparkapital savings *(pl)*, saved capital

sparkas *dep* kick

sparkassa savings association

sparkasseräkning savings account

spark|boll football **-byxor** *pl* rompers **-cykel** scooter **-dräkt** rompers *(pl)*

spar|klubb thrift (savings) club **-konto** thrift account; *jfr äv. sparkasseräkning*

sparkstötting kick-sledge

spar|lakan bed curtain **-lakansläxa** curtain lecture

spar|låga low heat; *ställa på ~* put on a low heat, simmer gently **-medel** *pl* savings **-obligation** savings bond

sparra *sport.* spar

sparre *s2* small square timber; *(tak-)* rafter, baulk

sparris ['sparr-] *s2* asparagus **-knoppar** asparagus tips **-kål** broccoli

sparsam [ˣspa:r-] *a1 (ekonomisk)* economical *(med* with, in); thrifty: sparing *(på (med) beröm* of one's praise); *(enkel)* frugal; *(gles)* sparse, scanty; *(sällsynt)* rare *(förekomst* occurrence) **-het** economy; thrift; *(sparsam förekomst)* scantiness

sparsamhets|kampanj economy drive (campaign) **-skäl** *av ~* for reasons of economy

sparsamt *adv* economically *etc.*; *förekomma ~t* occur rarely, be scarce

sparsmakad *a5* fastidious

spart|an *s3* Spartan **-ansk** [-a:-] *a5* Spartan

sparv *s2* sparrow **-hök** sparrowhawk **-uggla** pygmy owl

spasm *s3* spasm; convulsion, cramp **spasmo-disk** [-'mɔ:-] *a5* spasmodic

spast|iker *s9* spastic **-isk** ['spass-] *a5* spastic

spat *s3, miner.* spar

spatel *s2* spatula

spatiös [-tsi'ö:s] *a1* spacious; roomy

spatser|a walk; strut **-käpp** walking stick

spatt *s3* spavin **-ig** *a1* spavined; *(om pers.)* stiff

spe *n (narr)* derision, ridicule; *(hån)* sneer[s *pl*], gibe[s *pl*]

speaker ['spi:ker] *s2 (utropare)* compere; *AE. äv.* emcee; *(hallåman)* announcer

specerjaffär grocer's [shop], grocery [store]

speceri|er [-'ri:-] *pl* groceries **-handlare** grocer

special|affär specialized shop **-arbetare** specialist worker **-arbete** *skol.* special project **-begåvning** special gift **-byggd** *a5* specially built, *AE.* custom-made **-erbjudande** *AE.* custom-made offer **-fall** special case **-intresse** special interest; hobby

special|isera *rfl* specialize *(på* in) **-isering** [-'se:-] specialization, specializing **-ist** specialist *(på* in); expert *(på* on) **-itet** *s3* special[i]ty

special|klass *skol.* remedial class **-kunskaper** *pl* specialist knowledge **-lärare** remedial teacher **-pedagogik** special education, remedial teach-

ing **-stål** special steel **-tillverkad** *a5* specially made, *AE.* custom-made **-uppdrag** special task (charge, mission) **-utbildning** special training **-utrustning** special equipment

speciell *a1* special, particular; *(konstig)* odd, peculiar

specificer|a specify, itemize, detail, particularize **-ing** specification, specifying

specifik [-'fi:k] *a1* specific *(vikt* gravity, weight) **-ation** specification, detailed description

specimen ['spe:-] *n, pl äv. specimina* [-'si:] specimen

spedi|era forward, dispatch **-tion** forwarding (dispatch) [of goods] **-tionsfirma** forwarding (shipping) agency **-tör** forwarding (shipping) agent

spe|full *(hånfull)* mocking, derisive; *(gäcksam)* quizzical; *(om pers.)* given to mockery **-fågel** wag, tease

spegel *s2* mirror, looking glass; *se sig i ~n* look into the mirror; *själens ~* the mirror of the soul; *sjön ligger som en ~* the lake is as smooth as glass **-bild** reflected image, reflection; *bildl.* image **-blank** glassy *(yta* surface); like a mirror; *(om sjö)* [as] smooth as glass **-fäktning** dissimulation, dissembling **-galleri** gallery of mirrors **-glas** mirror (plate) glass **-reflexkamera** reflex camera **-sal** hall of mirrors **-skrift** reversed (mirror) script **-teleskop** reflecting telescope **-vänd** *a5* reversed

spegl|a [ˣspe:g-] reflect, mirror; *~ sig (avspegla sig)* be reflected *(i vattnet* in the water), *(om pers.)* look at o.s. in the mirror **-ing** reflection

speglosa gibe, scoff

spej|a [ˣspejja] spy *(efter* about (round) for); *mil.* scout **-ande** *a4* spying; searching *(blick* look) **-are** spy; *mil.* [reconnaissance] scout

spektakel [-'ta:-] *s7* **1** *(oväsen)* row; *(skandal)* scandal; *(förtret)* mischief, trouble; *ställa till ~* make a scene; *ett sånt ~!* what a nuisance! **2** *(åtlöje)* ridicule; *göra ~ av ngn* make a fool of s.b.

spektakulär *a1* spectacular

spektral|analys spectrum (spectral) analysis **-färg** spectral colour **-klass** *astr.* spectral type (class)

spektro|graf *s3* spectrograph **-skop** [-'skå:p] *s7* spectroscope

spektrum ['spekk-] *s8* spectrum *(pl* spectra); *[dis]kontinuerligt ~* [dis]continuous spectrum

spekulant 1 *(reflektant)* prospective (would-be) buyer; *hugade ~er* prospective buyers; *vara ~ på* be [a] prospective buyer of **2** *(börs-)* operator, speculator **spekulation** speculation, venture; *(börs- äv.)* operation; *på ~* on speculation **spekulationsvinst** speculative profit (gain) **spekulativ** [-'ti:v, 'spekk-] speculative **spekulera 1** speculate *(på* on; *i baisse (hausse)* for a decline (rise)) **2** *(tänka)* ponder, think *(på, över* about)

1 spel *s7 (vinsch)* winch, windlass; *(gruv-)* winder; *(-rum)* clearance, play

2 spel *s7* **1** *(-ande)* play[ing]; *(musikaliskt -sätt)* execution; *teat.* acting; *(lek; idrott)* game *(äv. bildl.)*; *~ om pengar* playing for money; *~et är förlorat* the game is up; *dra sig ur ~et* quit [the game]; *övernaturliga makter driver sitt ~* supernatural powers are abroad; *förlora (vinna) på ~*

lose (win) at play (by gambling); *det är en kvinna med i ~et* there is a woman in the case; *ha ett finger med i ~et* have a finger in the pie; *otur i ~ tur i kärlek* unlucky at cards, lucky in love; *rent ~* fair play; *spela ett högt ~* play for high stakes, *bildl.* play a high game; *stå på ~* be at stake; *sätta på ~* put at stake, stake; *ta hem ~et* win; *tillfälligheternas ~* pure chance 2 (*parningslek*) courtship 3 *kortsp.* trick

spela 1 play (*fiol* the violin; *ett spel* a game; *om pengar* for money); (*musikstycke äv.*) execute, perform; *gå och ~ piano för* take piano lessons from; *~ falskt* play out of tune, *kortsp.* cheat [at cards]; *~ hasard* gamble; *~ sina kort väl* play one's cards well; *~ ngn i händerna* play into a p.'s hands 2 *teat.* act, play; *~ herre* play the gentleman; *~ sjuk* pretend to be ill; *~ teater* (*låtsas*) make pretence 3 (*med betonad partikel*) *~ av ngn ngt* win s.th. off s.b.; *~ bort* gamble away; *~ in a*) (*inöva*) rehearse, *b*) (*på grammofonskiva e.d.*) make a recording, record; *det är många faktorer som ~r in* many factors come into play; *~ upp till dans* strike up; *~ ut ett kort* play a card; *~ ut ngn mot ngn* play s.b. off against s.b.; *han har ~t ut sin roll* he is played out (finished); *~ över a*) (*öva*) practise, *b*) (*överdriva*) overdo it, overact

spelande *a4* playing; sparkling (*ögon* eyes); *de ~* the players, *mus.* the musicians, *teat.* the actors **spelarbyte** (*fotboll*) exchange of player for reserve; (*ishockey*) change of players **spel|are** player; (*hasard-*) gambler **-automat** gambling (slot) machine, fruit machine **-bank** casino **-bar** *a1*, *teat.*, *mus.* performable; *sport.* (*om spelare*) unmarked **-bord** card (gambling) table **-djävulen** *gripas av ~* be gambling-mad **-dosa** music[al] box **speleolog|** *s3* speleology **spelevink** [-'viŋk] *s2* irresponsible youngster **spel|film** feature (full-length) film **-hall** amusement arcade **-håla** gambling den **-kort** playing card **-lektion** music lesson **-lista** *teat.* list of performances, repertory **-man** musician; (*fiolspelare*) fiddler **-mark** counter; (*-penning*) jetton **spel|ning** engagement, *vard.* gig **-passion** gambling fever **-regel** rule of the game **-rum** *bildl.* scope, margin, freedom to act; *lämna fritt ~* give free scope **-skuld** gambling debt **-säsong** theatrical season **-sätt** *mus.* [way of] execution; *sport.* style of play **-teori** *företagsekon.* game theory **-tid** (*för film*) screen (running) time; (*för grammofonskiva*) playing time **-vinst** winnings (*pl*) [at cards (from gambling)] **-år** *teat.* theatrical year **-öppning** *schack. o. bildl.* gambit; *sport.* opening [of the game] **spenabarn** suckling **spenat** spinach **spender|a** spend [... liberally], bestow (*på* upon) **-byxorna** *pl*, *ha ~ på sig* be in a generous (lavish) mood **-sam** *a1* generous, liberal **-samhet** generosity, liberality **spene** *s2* teat, nipple **spenslig** *a1* [of] slender [build]; slim **spenvarm** *~ mjölk* milk warm from the cow **sperm|a** [ˣspärr-] *s9*, *s7* sperm **spermaceti** [-'se:-] *s9* spermaceti **spermatozo** [-tå'så:] *s3*, **spermie** ['spärr-] *s5* spermatozoon (*pl* sperma-

tozoa)

speta 1 (*spreta*) stick up (out) 2 (*kliva*) stalk about **spetig** *a1* 1 (*spretande*) straggly 2 (*tunn*) skinny; *~a ben* spindly legs

1 spets *s2* 1 (*udd*) point (*äv. bildl.*); (*på finger, tunga o.d.*) tip; (*berg-*) peak, top; *geom.* apex; *bildl. äv.* head; *bjuda ngn ~en* stand up to s.b., defy s.b.; *driva ngt till sin ~* carry s.th. to extremes; *gå i ~en* walk at the head, lead the way, *bildl. äv.* be the prime mover (*för* of); *stå i ~en för* be at the head of, head; *samhällets ~ar* the leaders of society (a nation) 2 (*betyg*) with distinction

2 spets *s2*, *text.* lace; (*sydd*) needlepoint

3 spets *s2* (*hund*) spitz; Pomeranian

spets|a 1 (*göra -ig*) point; sharpen (*en blyertspenna* a pencil); *~ öronen* prick up one's ears 2 (*genomborra*) pierce; (*på nål*) pin, nail; (*på spjut etc.*) spear etc. 3 (*en dryck*) lace, *vard.* spike **Spetsbergen** Spitsbergen

spets|bov arch rogue **-byxor** *pl* [riding-]breeches **-båge** pointed (Gothic, lancet) arch **-bågsstil** pointed (Gothic) style **-fundig** *a1* subtle; hairsplitting **-fundighet** subtlety; *~er* (*äv.*) sophistry, quibbling (*sg*) **-gavel** pointed gable **-glans** *s3*, *miner.* stibnite, antimony glance **-glas** tapering dram-glass **-hacka** pickaxe

spetsig *a1* pointed (*äv. bildl.*); (*avsmalnande*) tapering; pointed (*skägg* beard); *bildl. äv.* cutting, sarcastic; *~ vinkel* acute angle **-het** pointedness *etc.*; *~er* (*sarkasmer*) sneers, sarcasms **spets|krage** lace collar **-krås** lace frill **-näst** [-ä:-] *a4* sharp-nosed **-vinklig** *a1* acute-angled **spett** *s7* crowbar; pinch bar; (*stek-*) spit **-[e]kaka** cake baked on a spit **spetälsk** *a5* leprous; *en ~ a* leper **spetälska** *s9* leprosy

spex *s7* students' farce; (*friare*) farce **spexa** *ung.* rollick **spexhumör** rollicking mood **spexig** *a1* farcial; comical

spicke|n *a5* salt-cured **-sill** salt herring **spigg** *s2* stickleback

1 spik *adv*, *~ nykter* [as] sober as a judge

2 spik *s2* nail; *slå huvudet på ~en* hit the nail on the head; *den ~en drar* (*bildl.*) that strikes home **spik|a** nail; spike; (*med nubb*) tack; *bildl.* peg, fix; *~ fast* fasten with nails, nail (*ngt vid* s.th. on to); *~ igen* nail down; *~ upp* nail [... up], placard **-huvud** head of a nail, nailhead **-hål** nail hole **-klubba** *hist.* mace **-matta** bed of nails **spiknykter** *se 1 spik* **spikpiano** tinny [old] piano **spikrak** [as] straight as an arrow (a poker) **spiksko** *sport.* track shoe **spilkum** *s2* bowl, basin

spill *s7* wastage, waste; *radioaktivt ~* radioactive fallout **spilla** *v2* (*hälla ut*) spill, drop; *~ på sig* spill (drop) s.th. on one's clothes; *~ ut* spill [out], shed; *spill inte!* don't spill it! 2 (*för-*) waste, lose; *-d möda* labour thrown away, (*friare*) waste of energy; *-da människoliv* lost lives; *det var många -da människoliv* the loss of life was very great

spillkråka black woodpecker

spillning 1 (*avfall*) refuse 2 droppings (*pl*); (*gödsel*) dung

spillo *oböjligt s, ge ... till ~* give *... up* [as lost], abandon; *gå till ~* get (be) lost, go to waste
spillolja waste oil
spillr|a *s1* (*flisa*) splinter; *-or* (*bildl.*) remaining fragments, scattered remnants, wreckage (*sg*); *falla* (*gå*) *i -or* fly (break) into splinters, fall to pieces; *slå i -or* break into fragments, *bildl.* shatter
spill|tid lost (waste[d]) time **-vatten** waste water; overflow; (*avloppsvatten*) sewage **-värme** surplus heat
spillånga [ˣspi:llåŋa, ˣspill-] (*fisk*) stockfish
spilta *s1* stall; (*för obunden häst*) loose box
spinalanestesi [-ˣna:l-] *kir.* spinal anaesthesia
1 spindel *s2, tekn.* spindle
2 spindel *s2, zool.* spider
spindelben spider's leg, *bildl.* spindleleg
spindelbult steering pivot pin, kingpin, swivel pin
spindel|nät, -väv cobweb[s *pl*]; (*tunnare*) gossamer
spinętt *s3, mus.* spinet
spinkig *a1* very thin, spindly **-het** thinness
1 spinn *r, flyg.* spin; *råka i ~* get into a spin
2 spinn *s7* (*fiske*) se *-fiske*
spinna *spann spunnit* **1** spin; twist (*tobak* tobacco); (*rotera*) spin, twirl **2** (*om katt*) purr
spinnaker [ˈspinn-, ˣspinn-] *s2* spinnaker
spinnarfjäril bombycid
spinneri spinning (cotton) mill **spinnerska** [female] spinner
spinn|fiske spinning; *AE.* bait-casting **-hus** spinning-house **-maskin** spinning machine **-rock** spinning wheel **-rulle** *fisk.* casting reel **-sida** distaff side **-spö** spinning (casting) rod
spiǫn *s3* spy **spionage** [-ˈna:ʃ] *s7* espionage, spying **spionera** spy (*på* [up]on) **spioneri** se *spionage* **spionliga** spy ring
1 spira *v1, ~* [*upp*] sprout, germinate; *~nde kärlek* budding love
2 spira *s1* (*torn-*) spire; (*trä-*) spar (*äv. sjö.*); (*stång*) pole; (*värdighetstecken*) sceptre
spiręl *s3* **1** spiral, helix; (*vindling*) whorl; *gå i ~* turn spirally **2** (*livmoderinlägg*) coil, intrauterine device (*förk.* I.U.D.) **-block** spiral notebook **-fjäder** coil spring; (*plan*) spiral spring **-formig** [-å-] *a1* spiral, helical **-rörelse** spiral motion (movement) **-trappa** spiral (winding) staircase
spirant *fonet.* fricative [sound]
spirea [-ˣre:a] *s1, bot.* spiraea
spirit|ism spiritism *-ist* spiritist **-istisk** [-ˈtiss-] *a5* spiritistic
spiritu|alism spiritualism **-ist** spiritualist **-istisk** [-ˈliss-] *a5* spiritualistic **-itęt** *s3* wit, esprit
spirituęll *a1* brilliant; witty
spirituosa [-tuˣɔ:sa] *s1* spirits; spirituous liquors **spiritus** [ˈspi:-] *r* spirit, alcohol
1 spis *s2, boktr.* rising space; *AE.* work-up
2 spis *s2* (*eldstad*) fireplace; (*köks-*) stove, range; *öppen ~* [open] fireplace; *stå vid ~en* stand over the stove, be cooking
3 spis *s3* (*föda*) food (*äv. bildl.*); *bildl. äv.* nourishment
spis|a 1 eat **2** *vard.* listen intently (*jazz* to jazz); dig **-bröd** crispbread
spisel *s2, se 2* spis **-häll** hearth[stone] **-krans** mantelpiece
spis|krok poker **-kupa** [range, ventilating] hood **-vrå** chimney (fireside) corner
spjut *s7* spear; (*kort*) dart; *sport.* javelin; *kasta ~* (*sport.*) throw the javelin **-formig** [-å-] *a1* spearshaped; lanciform (*blad* leaf) **-kast** throw of a (the) spear (*etc.*) **-kastare** *sport.* javelin-thrower **-kastning** *sport.* javelin-throwing **-skaft** shaft of a (the) spear (*etc.*) **-spets** spearhead, spearpoint (*etc.*)
spjuver [ˈspju:-] *s2* rogue **-aktig** *a1* roguish
spjäl|a I *s1* lath; (*i jalusi*) rib, slat **II** *v1* splint; *med. äv.* put in splints **-förband** splint dressing
spjälk|a split **-ning** splitting; (*atom-*) fission
spjäll *s7* damper, register; (*på motor*) throttle; *öppna ~et* open the damper (*etc.*) **-snöre** cord of a (the) damper (*etc.*)
spjäl|låda [-ä:-] crate **-ning** [-ä:-] *med.* splinting **-staket** pale fence **-säng** cot with bars **-verk** trelliswork, latticework
spjärn [-ä:-] *n, ta ~* brace one's feet (*mot* against) **spjärna** *~ emot* kick against, resist
splines [splajns] *pl, tekn.* splines
splint *s3, bot.* sapwood; *koll.* (*flisor*) splinters (*pl*)
split *s7* discord, dissension; *utså ~* sow dissension **splits** *s2, sjö.* splice **splitsa** splice **splitsning** splicing; *konkr.* splice
1 splitter [ˈsplitt-] *adv, ~ ny* brand-new
2 splitt|er [ˈsplitt-] *s7, koll.* (*flisor*) splinters (*pl*); (*granat- etc.*) splinter
splitterfri *~tt glas* safety glass **splittra I** *s1* splinter, shiver **II** *v1* splinter, break into splinters; *bildl.* divide [up]; *känna sig ~d* feel at sixes and sevens; *~ sig* (*bildl.*) divide (split) one's energy **splittring** *bildl.* split, division; (*söndring*) disruption
1 spola (*skölja*) flush, rinse, wash; *vågorna ~de över däcket* the waves washed the deck; *~ av a*) wash down (*en bil* a car), *b*) rinse, swill (*disken* the dishes); *~ bort* wash away; *~ gatorna* sprinkle (water) the streets; *~ [på toaletten]* flush the toilet; *~ en skridskobana* flood a skating rink
2 spola (*garn*) spool, reel, wind [up]; (*film*) reel
spolarvätska washer fluid **spole** *s2* **1** (*garn-; på* [*sy*]*maskin*) bobbin; (*för film*) spool; *elektr.* coil, spiral **spolformig** [-år-] *a1* spool-shaped
spolier|a spoil, wreck **-ing** spoliation
spoling *vard.* stripling; whippersnapper
spolmask ascarid
1 spolning [-ɔ:-] (*t. 1* spola) flushing *etc.*
2 spolning [-ɔ:-] (*t. 2* spola) reeling, winding
spondé [-å-] *s3* spondee **spondeisk** [-ˈde:-] *a5* spondaic[al]
sponsor [ˈspånsår] *s3* sponsor, backer
spont [-å-] *s3* groove, tongue, rebate **sponta** groove, tongue, rebate; *~de bräder* match[ed] boards; *~d och notad* tongued and grooved
spontęn [-å-] *a1* spontaneous **-ism** abstract expressionism **-ist** painter of the abstract expressionist school **-itet** spontaneity
spor *s3* spore
sporadisk [-ˈra:-] *a5* sporadic; isolated
sporde [-ɔ:-] *imperf. av* spörja
sporra [-å-] spur (*hästen* one's horse); *bildl. äv.* incite (*ngn till att* s.b. into + *ing-form*), stimulate

S

sporr|e [-å-] *s2* spur (*äv. bildl.*); (*på hund äv.*) dewclaw; *bildl. äv.* incentive, stimulus; *vinna sina -ar* (*bildl.*) win one's spurs **-sträck** *i* ~ at full gallop (speed) **-trissa** rowel

1 sport [-ɔ:-] *sup. av spörja*

2 sport [-å-] *s3* sport[s *pl*]; games (*pl*) **sport|a** go in for sports (games) **-affär** sports shop (outfitter) **-artiklar** *pl* sports (sporting) equipment (*sg*) **-bil** sports car **-dräkt** sports suit (*dams* costume); tweeds (*pl*) **-dykare** skindiver, free diver **-fiskare** angler **-fiske** angling **-flygare** private pilot **-flygning** private flying **-flygplan** private (sports) plane **-journalist** sports writer

sportig [-å-] *a1* sporty; keen on sport[s]

sportler ['spårt-] *pl* perquisites

sport|lov winter sports holidays (*pl*) **-sida** (*i tidning*) sports page

sports|lig [-å-] **1** sporting (*chans* chance) **-man** sportsman **-mannaanda** sportsmanship **-mässig** *a1* sportsmanlike

sportstuga weekend cottage, log-cabin

spotmarknad [ˣspått-] spot market

spotsk [-å-] *a1* contemptuous, scornful **-het** contempt, scorn

spott [-å-] *s3*, *s7* **1** (*saliv*) spittle, saliva **2** (*hån*) scorn

spott|a [-å-] spit; ~ *i nävarna och ta nya tag* spit in one's hands and have another go [at it] **-kopp** spittoon; *AE.* cuspidor **-körtel** salivary gland **-strit** froghopper, spittle insect, spittlebug **-styver** *för en* ~ for a song, for next to nothing

spov *s2* curlew

sprack *imperf. av spricka II*

sprak|a sparkle, emit sparks **-ande I** *a4* sparkling; crackling (*ljud* sound); ~ *kvickhet* sparkling wit **II** *s6* sparkling **-fåle** frisky colt; *bildl.* scapegrace **-galler** fireguard

sprallig *a1* frisky, lively

sprang *imperf. av 2 springa*

1 spratt *s7* trick; hoax; *spela ngn ett* ~ play a trick on s.b., trick (hoax) s.b.

2 spratt *imperf. av spritta*

sprattel ['spratt-] *s7* flounder, struggle **-gubbe** jumping jack

sprattla flounder, struggle; (*om fisk*) frisk (flap) about; (*med benen*) kick about

spray [sprejj] *se sprej*

spred *imperf. av sprida*

sprej [sprejj] *s3* spray **spreja** spray **sprejflaska** spray bottle; atomizer

spret|a sprawl **-ig** *a1* sprawling, straggling

spri *s6*, *sjö.* sprit

sprick|a I *s1* crack, fissure; (*större*) crevice; (*hud-*) chap; *bildl.* breach, schism, rift **II** *sprack spruckit* **1** crack; (*brista*) break, burst; (*rämna*) split; ~ *av ilska* burst with rage; *äta tills man är färdig att* ~ eat till one is ready to burst; *spruckna läppar* chapped lips; ~ *ut* (*om knopp*) open, (*om löv*) come out **2** (*bli kuggad*) fail, be ploughed **-bildning** cracking, formation of cracks **-fri** crack-proof **-färdig** ready to burst; (*om knopp*) ready to open

sprickig *a1* cracked; chapped

sprida *v2, imperf. äv. spred* spread; distribute (*reklam* advertisements); circulate (*ett rykte* a report); (*utströ*) scatter; ~ *en doft av* give off a smell of; ~ *glädje* bring joy; ~ *ljus över* shed light on; ~ *ut* (*semestrar, arbetstid*) stagger; ~ *sig* spread, (*skingras*) be scattered, scatter, be dispersed, disperse, (*utbreda sig*) extend; *en rodnad spred sig över hennes ansikte* a blush suffused her face; *ryktet spred sig* the rumour got abroad

spridare spreader, sprayer; (*vatten-*) sprinkler

sprid|d *a5* spread; scattered; dispersed; *en allmänt* ~ *uppfattning* a widespread view (conception); ~*a fall* isolated cases; *några* ~*a hus* a few scattered houses; *i* ~ *ordning* in scattered (*mil.* extended) order; *på* ~*a ställen* here and there **-ning** [-i:d-] spreading etc.; spread (*av en växt* of a plant; (*av tidning*) circulation, distribution; *boken har vunnit stor* ~ (*äv.*) the book has become very popular

1 spring *s7* (*-ande*) running; *det är ett* ~ *dagen i ända* people are coming and going all day

2 spring *s7*, *sjö.* sheer; (*på kabel*) spring

1 springa *s1* chink, fissure; slot, slit

2 springa *sprang sprungit* **1** run (*hit o. dit* to and fro); (*fly*) make off; (*hoppa*) spring, jump (*i sadeln* into the saddle); *vi måste* ~ *vad vi orkade* we had to run for it; ~ *sin väg* run away, make off, *vard.* skedaddle; ~ *ärenden* run errands; ~ *efter flickor* run after girls; ~ *efter hjälp* run for help; ~ *hos läkare* keep running to the doctor; ~ *i affärer* go shopping; ~ *i höjden* (*om pris*) soar; ~ *på dörren* make for the door; ~ *på bio* keep going to the cinema **2** (*brista*) burst; (*om säkring e.d.*) blow; ~ *i dagen* come to light, (*om källa*) spring forth; ~ *i luften* [be] blow[n] up, explode **3** (*med betonad partikel*) ~ *av* (*brista*) burst; ~ *fram* rush out, (*om sak*) stand out, project; ~ *ifatt* overtake, catch up; ~ *ifrån* run away from, desert; ~ *om* pass [... running], run past; ~ *omkring* run around; ~ *omkull* run down; ~ *upp a*) (*rinna upp*) spring up, *b*) (*om dörr*) fly open

spring|ande *a4* running; *den* ~ *punkten* the crucial point **-are** (*häst*) courser, steed; (*i schack*) knight **-brunn** fountain **-flicka** errand girl **-flod** spring tide **-mask** pinworm, threadworm **-pojke** errand boy, messenger **-vikarie** (*lärare*) supply teacher

sprinkler ['sprinn-] *s9, pl äv. -s* sprinkler **-anläggning** sprinkler plant (installation) **-system** sprinkler system

sprint *s2* split pin, peg

sprinter ['sprinn-] *s2* sprinter **-lopp** sprint[race]

sprisegel spritsail

sprit *s3* spirits (*pl*); alcohol; liquor; *denaturerad* ~ methylated spirits; *ren* ~ pure alcohol

sprita (*ärter*) shell, hull, pod

sprit|begär craving for spirits (liquor) **-bolag** company selling alcoholic liquors **-drycker** *pl* spirits, alcoholic liquors (beverages) **-duplicering** spirit duplication **-dupliceringsapparat** spirit duplicator **-fabrik** [alcohol] distillery **-förbud** prohibition **-haltig** *a1* spirituous, alcoholic **-kök** spirit stove **-langare** bootlegger **-missbruk** abuse of alcohol **-påverkad** *a5* under the influence of drink **-rättigheter** *pl, ha* ~ be fully licensed

sprits *s2* forcing (piping) bag **spritsa** pipe

sprit|skatt duty on spirits, liquor tax **-smugg-**

lare liquor smuggler, bootlegger
spritt *adv,* ~ *galen* stark (raving) mad; ~ *naken* stark-naked
spritt|a *spratt spruttit,* ~ [*till*] give a start, start, jump (*av förskräckelse* with fright); *det -er i benen* I want to dance so much I can't keep still **-ande** *a4,* ~ *glad* ready to jump for joy; *en* ~ *melodi* a lively tune **-ning** start, jump
spritärter shelling peas
spruck|en *a5* cracked (*tallrik* plate; *röst* voice) **-it** *sup. av* spricka II
sprudl|a [-u:-] bubble, gush **-ande** *a4* bubbling over (*av* with); sparkling (*kvickhet* wit); ~ *fantasi* exuberant imagination; ~ *humör* high spirits (*pl*)
sprund *s7* (*i plagg*) slit, opening; (*på laggkärl*) bung[hole]
sprungit *sup. av 2* springa
sprut|a *s1* spray[er], squirt; (*finfördelande*) atomizer; (*brand-*) fire engine; (*injektions-*) syringe; *få en* ~ get an injection, have a shot **II** *v1* spray, squirt; (*spola*) wash, flush; ~ *eld* spit (*om vulkan* emit) fire; *hennes ögon ~de eld* her eyes flashed fire; ~ *vatten på* throw water on, hose; ~ *in* (*med.*) inject; ~ *ut* eject, spout, throw out **-lackera** spray[-paint] **-lackering** spraying, spray painting **-munstycke** spray nozzle, jet pipe **-måla** *se* -lackera **-ning** [-u:-] spraying, squirting; (*med brandspruta*) playing the hose[s] **-pistol** spray gun
spruttit *sup. av* spritta
språk *s7* language; idiom, tongue; (*tal*) speech; manner of speaking, style; *föra ett bildat* ~ speak in an educated manner; *lärare i* ~ teacher of languages; *skriva ett ledigt* ~ have an easy (natural) style of writing; *inte vilja ut med ~et* beat about the bush; *slå sig i* ~ *med* enter into conversation with **språka** talk, speak (*om* about); (*förtroligt*) chat **språkas** *dep,* ~ *vid* talk to each other; ~ *vid om* (*äv.*) discuss
språk|begåvad *vara* ~ have a gift for languages **-bruk** usage; *gällande* ~ current usage **-centrum** (*i hjärnan*) speech areas **-familj** family of languages **-fel** linguistic error **-forskare** linguist **-forskning** linguistics (*pl, behandlas som sg*), linguistic research; *jämförande* ~ (*äv.*) comparative philology **-färdighet** language proficiency **-förbistring** confusion of tongues (languages) **-geni** genius for languages **-gräns** linguistic frontier **-historia** history of languages **-kunnig** skilled in languages; *en* ~ *person* a good linguist **-kunskap** knowledge of language[s] **-kurs** language course **-känsla** feeling for language **-laboratorium** language laboratory **-lektion** language lesson
språk|lig [-å:-] *a1* linguistic (*studier* studies); philological (*problem* problem); *i ~t avseende* from a linguistic point of view **-ljud** speech sound **-låda** *slå upp ~n* start talking **-lära** grammar **-lärare, -lärarinna** teacher of languages **-man** linguist **-melodi** intonation **-nämnd** *Svenska ~en* [the] Swedish language committee **-riktighet** grammatical correctness **-rör** *bildl.* spokesman (*fem.* spokeswoman), mouthpiece **-sam** [-å:-] *a1* talkative; (*prat-*) loquacious; (*meddel-*) communicative **-samhet** [-å:-] talkativeness *etc.* **-sinne** talent for languages; *jfr äv.* språkkänsla

-studier *pl* study (*sg*) of languages, linguistic studies **-störningar** speech disabilities (defects) **-svårigheter** *pl* difficulties in speaking and/or understanding a language **-undervisning** language teaching **-vetare** linguist; student of languages **-vetenskap** linguistics (*pl, behandlas som sg*) **-vetenskaplig** philological; linguistic **-vård** preservation of terminology and usage [in a language] **-öra** *ha ett gott* ~ have an ear for languages
språng *s7* leap, spring; (*skutt*) bound, skip; *ta ett* ~ take a leap, make a jump; *i fullt* ~ at full speed; *på* ~ on the run; *ta ~et ut i det okända* take a leap in the dark **-bräda** springboard (*äv. bildl.*) **-marsch** *i* ~ [at] double quick [time], *mil.* at a run **-segel** jumping sheet, canvas **-vis** by leaps (*etc.*)
spräcka *v3* crack; break; ~ *skallen* fracture one's skull
spräcklig *a1* speckled; mottled
spräng|a *v2* burst; (*med -ämne*) blast, blow up, explode; (*skingra*) scatter, *mil.* put to the rout; ~ *banken* break the bank; ~ *en häst* break a horse's wind; *det -er i örat* my (his *etc.*) ear is throbbing; ~ *fram* gallop along (forward) **sprängas** *v2, dep* burst, break
spräng|bomb high-explosive bomb **-deg** explosive paste **-granat** high-explosive shell **-kil** wedge **-kraft** explosive force **-laddning** blasting (explosive) charge; (*i robot o.d.*) warhead **-lista** (*vid val*) splinter list **-lärd** brimful of learning, erudite **-läsa** cram, swot **-ning** bursting *etc.*; explosion; (*skingring*) dispersion **-ningsarbete** blasting work **-skiss** exploded view **-skott** blast **-sten** blast stone, broken rock **-verkan** explosive (blast) effect **-ämne** explosive **-ämnesexpert** explosives expert
sprätt *s2* **1** dandy, fop, *AE.* dude **2** *sätta* ~ *på a*) (*ngn*) ginger up, *b*) (*pengar*) throw around
1 sprätta *v1, v3* (*skära upp*) rip [open] (*en söm* a seam), unpick (*en klänning* a dress); ~ *upp* rip up; ~ *ur* rip out (*en knapp* a button)
2 sprätta *v3, bet. 1 äv. v1* **1** (*snobba*) show off, swank **2** (*om höns*) scratch **3** (*sprida*) scatter **4** (*stänka*) spatter; (*om penna*) spurt
sprättbåge *som en* ~ (*bildl.*) like a drawn bow
sprättig *a1* smart[ly dressed], dandified, foppish
spröd *a1* brittle; short; (*klen*) fragile **-het** [-ö:-] brittleness; shortness; fragility
spröjs *s2* bar
spröt *s7* **1** (*paraply-*) rib **2** *zool.* antenna, feeler
spunnit *sup. av* spinna
spurt *s3, sport.* spurt **spurta** *sport.* spurt
spy *v4* vomit (*äv. rök* smoke); (*om kanon*) belch out **spyor** [ˣspy:or] *s, pl* vomit
spydig *a1* malicious, sarcastic, ironic[al] **-het** malice, sarcasm; *AE. äv.* wisecrack
spyfluga blowfly, bluebottle; *bildl.* caustic person
spygatt [ˣspy:-, -ˈgatt] *s7, sjö.* scupper
spå *v4, absol.* tell fortunes (*i kort* by the cards); ~ *ngn* tell s.b. his (*etc.*) fortune; *jfr äv. förutsäga;* ~ *i händer* practise palmistry, read hands; *jag ~dde rätt* my prediction came true; *människan ~r och Gud rår* man proposes, God disposes **-dom** *s2*

prophecy; prediction; soothsaying **-domskonst** art of divination **-kvinna** [female] fortune--teller; sibyl **-man** fortune-teller; soothsayer

spån *s7, s1 (trä-, metall-)* chip; *(hyvel-)* shaving; *koll.* chips, shavings *(pl)*; *dum som ett ~* as stupid as they come

spånad *s3, abstr.* spinning; *konkr.* spun yarn **spånads|lin** [fibre] flax **-växt** textile plant **spån[fiber]platta** chipboard, fibreboard **spång** *s2, pl äv.* **spänger** footbridge, plank **spån|korg** chip basket **-tak** shingled roof **-täcka** shingle

spår *s7* **1** *(märke)* mark *(efter* of); *(fot-)* [foot]step *(äv. bildl.)*, footprint; *(djur-)* track, trail; *bildl. äv.* trace, vestige; *inte det minsta ~ av tvivel* not the faintest doubt; *inte ett ~ intresserad* not a bit interested; *följa i ~en* be fast on the heels of, *bildl.* follow in the footsteps of; *förlora ~et* lose the track *(om jakthund:* scent); *komma på ~en* get on the track of, *bildl. äv.* find out; *sopa igen ~en efter sig* obliterate one's tracks; *sätta djupa ~ (bildl.)* make a profound impression; *vara inne på rätt ~* be on the right track **2** *(skenor)* rails *(pl)*; *järnv.* track; *vagnen hoppade ur ~et* the carriage (wagon) ran off the track (left the rails)

spåra 1 *(söka spår av)* track, trace *(äv. bildl.)*; *jakt. äv.* scent; *~ upp* track down, *(friare o. bildl.)* hunt out, discover **2** *(gå upp ett* [skid-] *spår)* make a track **3** *~ ur a) (järnv.)* run off the rails, derail, *b) (om pers.)* go astray, *c) (om diskussion)* sidetrack, get off the track

spår|bunden trackbound **-element** trace[r] element **-hund** sleuthhound; bloodhound *(äv. bildl.)* **-korsning** *järnv.* rail crossing **-ljus** tracer **-löst** [-ö:-] *adv* leaving no trace, without leaving any tracks; *den är ~ försvunnen* it has vanished into thin air **-sinne** scent; nose **-snö** [new-fallen] snow in which tracks are visible **-vagn** tram[car]; *AE.* streetcar, trolley [car]

spårvagns|biljett tram ticket **-förare** tram driver; *AE.* motorman **-konduktör** tram conductor

spår|vidd [track] gauge **-väg** tramway **-vägslinje** tramline; *AE.* streetcar line **-vägsstall** tram depot; *AE.* carbarn **-växel** point[s *pl*]; *i sht AE.* switch[es *pl*] **-ämne** trace[r] element

späck *s7* lard; *(val-)* blubber

späck|a lard; *bildl.* interlard; *en ~d plånbok* a bulging (fat) wallet **-huggare** *zool.* killer [whale], grampus **-nål** larding needle **-strimla** lardon

späd *a1 (mycket ung)* tender *(grönska* verdure; *ålder* age); *(spenslig)* slender *(växt* growth); *bot. äv.* young *(löv* leaves); *från sin ~aste barndom* from one's earliest infancy; *~ röst* feeble (weak) voice

späda *v2, ~ [ut]* dilute, thin down; *~ på ([ut]-öka)* add, mix in

späd|barn infant, baby **-barnsdödlighet** infant mortality **-barnsvård** infant welfare **-gris** sucking pig **-het** [-ä:-] tenderness *etc.* **-kalv** sucking calf

späk|a *v3* mortify *(sitt kött* one's flesh); *(friare)* castigate; *~ sig* mortify o.s. **-ning** [-ä:-] mortification *etc.*

spän|d *a1 (jfr spänna)* tight *(rep* rope); stretched;

(styv) taut; *bildl.* tense, highly strung *(nerver* nerves), intense, intent; *(om båge)* drawn; *-t förhållande* strained relations *(pl) (till* with); *högt ~a förväntningar* eager expectations; *lyssna med ~ uppmärksamhet* listen with strained (tense) attention; *jag är ~ på hur det skall gå* I am eager to see how things go

spänn *s, sätta ngt i ~* put s.th. in a press; *sitta på ~* be on tenterhooks

spänna *v2* **1** *(sträcka)* stretch *(snören* strings); strain *(musklerna* one's muscles); tighten *(ett rep* a rope); *~ en fjäder* tighten a spring; *~ hanen på en bössa* cock a gun; *~ en båge* draw (bend) a bow; *~ bågen för högt (bildl.)* aim too high; *~ sina krafter till det yttersta* muster up all one's strength, *bildl.* strain every nerve; *~ ögonen i* fasten (rivet) one's eyes on; *~ öronen* prick up one's ears **2** *(med spänne)* clasp, buckle; *(med rem)* strap **3** *(om kläder)* be tight, pull **4** *rfl* strain (brace) o.s. **5** *(med betonad partikel) ~ av a)* unstrap, unfasten, undo, *b) vard.* relax, lean back, *~ av sig skridskorna* take off one's skates; *~ fast* fasten, buckle (strap) on *(vid* to); *~ för (ifrån) (absol.)* harness (unharness) the horse[s]; *~ på sig* put on *(skridskorna* one's skates), strap on *(ryggsäcken* one's knapsack); *~ upp* undo, unfasten, *(rem)* unstrap, *(paraply)* put up; *~ ut* stretch, *(magen)* distend, *(bröstet)* expand; *~ åt* tighten

spännande *a4, bildl.* exciting, thrilling; *en ~ bok (äv.)* a thriller **spänne** *s6* buckle, clasp, clip **spänning** tension; *tekn. äv.* strain, stress; *elektr.* voltage; *bildl.* tension, excitement, stress, strain; *livsfarlig ~ (på anslag)* live wire; *hållas i ~* be kept on tenterhooks; *vänta med ~* wait excitedly (eagerly)

spännings|fall *elektr.* voltage (potential) drop **-förande** *a4, elektr.* live, under tension **-tillstånd** state of strain

spänn|kraft tension, elasticity, resilience, *bildl.* tone **-ram** tenter **-skruv** turnbuckle **-vidd** span; *stat.* range; *bildl.* scope

spänsband waistband

spänst *s3* vigour, elasticity; *bildl.* buoyancy **spänstig** *a1* elastic, springy; *(kraftig)* vigorous; *bildl.* buoyant; *gå med ~a steg* walk with a springy gait **-het** elasticity, spring[iness]; vigour; *bildl.* buoyancy

spänt *adv (jfr spänd), iakttaga ngn ~* observe s.b. intently

spänta split *(stickor* wood)

1 spärr *i uttr.: rida ~ mot* tilt against (at); *bildl.* resist, struggle against

2 spärr *s2, boktr.* spaced-out type (letters *pl*)

3 spärr *s2, tekn.* catch, stop, barrier; *järnv.* gate, barrier; *(hinder)* block, obstacle; *(väg-)* roadblock; *skol.* restricted intake

4 spärr *s2, (i bowling)* spare

1 spärra 1 *(ut-)* spread out, stretch open; *~ upp ögonen* open one's eyes wide **2** *boktr.* space out; *~d stil* spaced-out type (letters *pl*)

2 spärra 1 *(avstänga)* bar; block [up]; obstruct *(vägen för ngn* a p.'s passage); blockade, close *(en hamn* a port) **2** *hand.* block *(ett konto* an account); *~ en check* stop [payment of] a cheque

spärr|ballong barrage balloon; *vard.* blimp **-eld**

barrage [fire] **-hake** [locking] pawl; (*på kugghjul*) click, catch **-konto** blocked (frozen) account **-ning 1** barring *etc.*; obstruction; blockade **2** (*av konto e.d.*) blocking, freezing **-vakt** järnv. ticket collector

spätta *s1, zool.* plaice **-filé** fillet of plaice

spö *s6* **1** (*kvist*) twig; (*käpp*) switch; (*ridpiska*) whip; (*met-*) rod; *regnet står som ~n i backen* it's pouring rain, *vard.* it is raining cats and dogs **2** *slita ~* be publicly flogged (whipped) **spöa** flog, whip

spök|a (*visa sig som -e*) haunt a place, walk the earth; *det ~r i huset* the house is haunted; *gå uppe och ~ om nätterna* be up and about at night; *~ ut sig* make a fright of o.s. **-aktig** *a1* ghostlike; (*hemsk*) weird, uncanny **-bild** TV ghost

spök|e *s6* ghost, spectre; *vard.* spook; *bildl.* scarecrow, *se ~n på ljusa dagen* be haunted by imaginary terrors **-eri** *~er* ghostly disturbances **-historia** ghost story **-lik** ghostlike, ghostly; (*kuslig*) uncanny, weird; *ett ~t sken* a ghostly light

spöknippe bundle of rods

spök|rädd afraid of ghosts **-skepp** phantom ship **-skrivare** ghostwriter **-slott** haunted castle **-timme** witching hour

spöregn downpour, pouring rain **spöregna** pour, pelt

spörja *sporde sport* **1** (*fråga*) ask, inquire **2** (*erfara*) learn

spörsmål *s7* question, matter, problem; *ett intrikat ~* an intricate problem

spöstraff whipping, flogging

squash [skvåʃ, skoåʃ] *s3* (*spel o. grönsak*) squash

stab *s3* staff; *tjänstgöra på ~* be on the staff

stabil *a1* stable; *en ~ firma* a sound firm; *~a priser* stable prices **-isator** [-ˣsa:tår] *s3, sjö.* stabilizer; (*flygplans-, ubåts-*) tailplane **-isera** stabilize; *förhållandena har ~t sig* conditions have stabilized (become more settled) **-isering** [-ˈseː-] stabilization **-itet** stability

stabs|chef chief of staff **-officer** staff officer

1 stack *imperf. av* sticka *II o.* stinga

2 stack *s2* stack, rick; (*myr-*) ant hill (heap); *dra sitt strå till ~en* do one's share (*vard.* bit)

stacka stack, rick

stackare [poor] wretch; (*ynkrygg*) coward, funk; *en ~ till ... * a wretch of a ...; *en fattig ~* a beggar; *den ~n!* poor thing (devil)!; *en svag ~* a weakling, a pitiable creature; *var och en är herre över sin ~* everybody is s.b.'s master **stackars** *oböjligt a* poor (*krake* wretch); *~ du* (*dig*)! poor you!; *~ liten!* poor little thing!

stackato [-ˈka:-, -ˈkattå] *s6 o. adv, mus.* staccato

stackmoln cumulus

1 stad *s3* (*på väv*) selvage, selvedge; *AE.* selvage

2 stad *r* (*ställe*) stead; abode; *var och en i sin ~* each in his own place

3 stad *-en städer, best. form vard.* stan (*samhälle*) town; (*större o. katedral-*) city; *~en* Paris the city of Paris; *den eviga ~en* the Eternal City; *land och ~ town and country*; *han har blivit en visa för hela stan* he is the talk of the town; *bo i ~en* live in [the] town; *gå ut på stan* go into town; *lämna ~en* leave town; *resa till ~en* go up to town; *springa*

stan runt efter rush round town for; *över hela ~en* all over the town

stadd *a5, ~ i fara* in [the midst of] danger; *vara ~ i upplösning* be disintegrating; *~ på resa* on the move; *~ vid kassa* in funds

stadde *imperf. av* städja

stadfäst|a confirm (*en dom* a sentence); establish (*en lag* a law); legalize, sanction (*en förordning* a decree); ratify (*ett fördrag* a treaty) **-else** confirmation; establishment; legalization, sanction; ratification

stadga I *s1, i bet. 2 äv. s5* **1** (*stadighet*) consistency; steadiness, firmness (*äv. bildl.*) **2** (*förordning*) regulation, statute; *föreningens ~r* the charter (*sg*) (rules) of the association **II** *v1* **1** (*ge fasthet*) consolidate, steady **2** (*föreskriva*) direct, prescribe, enact; (*bestämma*) decree **3** *rfl* consolidate, become firm[er] (steadier); (*om vädret*) become settled; (*om pers.*) settle down **stadg|ad** *a5* steady, staid; *en ~ herre* a staid (reliable) man; *komma till ~ ålder* arrive at a mature age; *ha -at rykte för att vara* have a well-established reputation of being

stadge|enlig [-ˈeːn-] *a1* according to regulation (rules *pl*), statutory **-ändring** alteration of [the] rules (statutes)

stadig *a1* steady; (*fast*) firm; (*stabil*) stable; (*grov o. stark*) square built, sturdy; (*tjock*) stout; (*kraftig*) substantial (*mat* food), thick (*gröt* porridge); *bildl.* (*varaktig*) permanent (*kund* customer); *~ blick* firm look; *~ hand* steady (firm) hand; *ett ~t mål mat* (*äv.*) a square meal; *ha ~t arbete* have a steady job (regular work) **stadigt** *adv* steadily *etc.*; *sitta ~* (*om sak*) be firmly fixed; *stå ~* stand steady (firm) **stadigvarande** *a4* permanent (*anställning* employment); constant; *~ inkomst* steady income

stadion [ˈsta:djån] *n* stadium

stadium [ˈsta:djum] *s4* stage; (*skede*) phase; *befinna sig på ett förberedande ~* be at a preparatory (an initial) stage

stads|antikvarie city (town) antiquarian **-arkitekt** town (city) architect **-arkiv** municipal (city, town) archives (*pl*) (records office) **-barn** town (city) child **-befolkning** urban (town) population **-bibliotek** public (town, city) library **-bo** town dweller; (*borgare*) citizen; *~r* townspeople **-bud** [town] messenger; (*bärare*) porter **-budskontor** messengers' (porters') office **-del** quarter of a city (town), district **-fiskal** public prosecutor; *AE. ung.* district attorney **-fogde** [court] bailiff; *AE.* sheriff, marshal **-fullmäktig** city (town) councillor; *~e* city (town) council (*sg*) **-förvaltning** civic (city, town) administration **-gas** town (coal) gas **-gräns** city (town) boundary **-hotell** principal hotel in a town **-hus** town (city) hall **-kärna** [the old] city centre **-lag** urban code **-liv** town (city) life **-läkare** municipal (city, town) medical officer **-mur** town (city) wall **-plan** town plan **-planerare** town planner **-planering** town (city) planning **-port** town (city) gate **-rättigheter** *pl* town charter (*sg*) **-teater** municipal theatre **-vapen** city arms (*pl*)

stafett *s3* **1** (*kurir*) courier **2** *se* -pinne; *springa ~* run in a relay race **-löpning** relay race **-pinne** [relay-race] baton

S

staffage [-'faːʃ] *s4* figures (*pl*) in a landscape **-figur** *eg*. foreground figure; *bara en* ~ (*bildl*.) just an ornament

staffli *s4, s6* easel **-målare** painter who uses an easel

stafylokock [-'kåkk] *s3* staphylococcus (*pl* staphylococci)

stag *s7, sjö*. stay; *gå över* ~ go about **staga** *sjö*. stay (tack) ship; *allm*. stay

stagn|ation [-ŋ-] stagnation; (*stopp*) stoppage, standstill **-era** stagnate

stag|ning [-aː-] staying **-vända** tack, go about

1 staka *rfl* stumble, hesitate; ~ *sig på läxan* stumble over one's lessons

2 staka 1 punt, pole ([*fram*] *en båt* a boat [along]) **2** mark (*en väg* a road); ~ *ut, se utstaka* **stake** *s2* pole, stake; (*ljus-*) candlestick

staket *s7* fence, railing[s *pl*], paling

stal *imperf. av* stjäla

sta|lagmit *s3* stalagmite **-laktit** *s3* stalactite

1 stall *s7* (*på fiol*) bridge

2 stall 1 (*för hästar*) stable; *AE. äv*. barn; (*uppsättning hästar*) stud **2** (*lok- etc*.) depot, garage

stall|a stable **-backe** stable yard **-broder** companion; *vard*. chum **-dräng** stableman, groom **-knekt** stableman **-lykta** (*hopskr. stallykta*) hurricane lamp, storm lantern **-pojke** stableboy

stam [stamm] *s2* **1** (*träd-*) stem, trunk (*äv. bildl*.); *språkv*. stem, radical **2** (*i checkbok o.d*.) counterfoil, stub **3** (*släkt[e]*) family, lineage; (*folk-*) tribe; *en man av gamla* ~*men* a man of the old stock **-aktie** ordinary (*AE*. common) share; ~*r* (*koll*.) stock (*sg*), equities; *utdelning på* ~*r* ordinary dividend **-anställd** *a o. s* regular **-bana** main line [railway]; *norra* ~*n* the main northern line **-bok** (*över djur*) pedigree book; (*över hästar*) studbook; (*över nötkreatur*) herd-book **-bord** regular table **-fader** [first] ancestor; progenitor **-form** (*med avseende på härstamning*) primitive (original) form **-gäst** regular [frequenter] (*på en restaurang* of a restaurant), habitué **-kund** regular customer

1 stamma *se härstamma*

2 stamma (*tala hackigt*) stutter; (*svårare*) stammer; ~ *fram* stammer out

stammanskap regulars (*pl*)

stammare stutterer, stammerer

stammoder [first] ancestress

stamning stuttering, stammering

stam|ord radical word **-ort** place of origin

stamp 1 *s7, se stampning 2 s2, tekn*. (*hål-*) punch; (*stämpel*) stamp

1 stampa 1 stamp (*i golvet* [on] the floor); (*om häst*) paw the ground; *stå och* ~ *på samma fläck* (*bildl*.) be still on the same old spot, be getting nowhere; ~ *takten* beat time with one's feet; ~ *av sig snön* stamp the snow off one's shoes; ~ *till jorden* trample down the earth **2** *sjö*. pitch, heave and set **3** stamp, punch (*hål i* a hole in); (*kläde*) mill, full

2 stamp|a *vard*., ~ *på* (*pantsätta*) hock, pop **stampen** ['stamm-] *endast best. form, vard*. (*pantlånekontor*) *på* ~ at uncle's, in hock

stamp|kvarn stamp[ing] mill **-maskin** stamp, stamping machine **-ning** stamping; pawing; *tekn*.

punching, pounding

stam|ros standard rose **-tavla** genealogical table; pedigree (*äv. om djur*) **-tillhåll** [favourite] haunt **-träd** genealogical (family) tree

standar *s7* standard

standard ['stann-] *s3* standard **-avvikelse** *stat*. standard deviation (error) **-brev** form letter **-format** standard size **-hus** house of standard design; (*monteringsfärdigt*) prefabricated house **-höjning** rise in the standard of living; *en allmän* ~ a general rise in the living standard **-isera** standardize **-isering** [-'seː-] standardization **-modell** standard design **-mått** standard size; (*likare*) standard measure[ment] **-prov** *skol*. standardized achievement test **-sänkning** lowering of one's standard [of living] **-utförande** standard design **-verk** standard work

standert ['stann-] *s2, sjö*. [broad] pennant

1 stank *s3* stench, stink

2 stank *imperf. av* stinka

stanna 1 (*upphöra att röra sig*) stop, stand still; (*av-*) come to a standstill; (*upphöra äv*.) cease; *hjärtat har* ~*t* the (his *etc*.) heart has stopped (ceased to beat); *klockan* ~*de* the (my *etc*.) watch stopped; ~ *i växten* stop growing; ~ *på halva vägen* stop halfway; *han lät det* ~ *vid hotelser* he went no further than threats; *reformerna* ~*de på papperet* the reforms never got past the paper stage; *det* ~*de därvid* it stopped at that **2** (*om vätska*) cease to run; (*stelna*) coagulate; *kokk*. set **3** (*dröja kvar*) stay [on], stop; (*slutgiltigt förbli*) remain; ~ *hemma* stay [at] home; ~ *hos ngn* stay with s.b.; ~ *kvar* stay [on]; remain; ~ *till middagen* stay for dinner; ~ *över natten* stay the night (*hos* with); *låt det* ~ *oss emellan!* this is between you and me! **4** (*hejda*) stop; (*fordon äv*.) bring to a standstill; (*maskin*) stop

stannfågel sedentary (nonmigratory) bird

stannförening stannic compound

stanniol [-'joːl, -'jåːl] *s3* tinfoil **-papper** tinfoil

1 stans *s3, versl*. stanza

2 stans *s2* punch

stans|a ~ [*ut*] punch **-maskin** punching machine **-ning** punching **-operatris** puncher, punching-machine operator

stapel *s2* **1** (*trave*) pile, stack **2** *skeppsb*. stocks (*pl*); *gå* (*löpa*) *av* ~*n* leave the stocks, be launched, *bildl*. take place, come off **3** (*på bokstav*) stem; *nedåtgående* (*uppåtgående*) ~ downstroke (upstroke) **-avlöpning** launch, launching **-bar** *a1*, ~*a stolar* nesting (stacking) chairs **-bädd** stocks (*pl*), slip, slipway **-diagram** histogram, bar graph **-stad** staple town (port) **-vara** staple [commodity]

stapl|a ['stɑː-] ~ [*upp*] pile [up], heap up, stack **-ingsbar** stackable

stappl|a (*gå ostadigt*) totter; (*vackla*) stagger; ~ *sig fram* stumble along; ~ *sig igenom läxan* stumble through one's lesson **-ande** *a4* tottering, staggering; *de första* ~ *stegen* the first stumbling steps

stare *s2* starling

stark *a1* strong; (*kraftfull*) powerful (*maskin* engine); (*om maskin äv*.) high-powered; (*hållbar*) solid, durable; (*fast*) firm (*karaktär* character); (*utpräglad*) pronounced, mighty; (*intensiv*) intense; ~ *blåst* high wind; ~*a drycker* strong drinks; ~ *efterfrågan på* great (strong) demand for; ~ *fart* great speed; ~ *färg* strong colour; ~*t gift* virulent poison; ~*t inflytande* powerful influence; ~ *kyla* bitter (intense) cold; ~*a misstankar* grave (strong) suspicions; ~ *motvilja* pronounced aversion; ~*a skäl* strong reasons; ~*a verb* strong verbs; *är inte min ~a sida* is not my strong point; *en sex man ~ deputation* a deputation of six men; *med den ~ares rätt* with the right of might **-sprit** spirits (*pl*); *AE.* hard liquor **-ström** high-tension current

starkt *adv* strongly *etc.*; ~ *kryddad* highly seasoned; *lukta ~ av* smell strongly of; *jag misstänker ~ att* I very much suspect that; *det var väl ~* that's a bit thick (much)

stark|varor *pl* spirits **-vin** dessert wine **-öl** strong beer

1 starr *s3, bot.* sedge

2 starr *s2* (*sjukdom*) [*grå*] ~ cataract; *grön ~* glaucoma

starrblind *bildl.* purblind

start [-a(:)-] *s3* start; *AE. vard.* kickoff; *flyg.* takeoff; (*av företag*)starting, launching

start|a [-a(:)-] start; *AE. vard.* kick off; *flyg.* take off; (*företag*) start, launch; ~ *en affär* open a business **-anording** starter **-avgift** entry fee **-bana** *flyg.* runway; tarmac (*varumärke*) **-block** starting block

start|er ['sta:r-] *s2, sport.* starter **-förbud** *flyg.*, *det råder ~* all planes are grounded **-grop** starting hole; *ligga i ~arna* (*äv. bildl.*) be waiting for the starting signal **-kablar** jump leads, *AE.* jumper cables **-kapital** initial capital **-klar** ready to start **-knapp** starter button **-kontakt** starter **-linje** starting line **-motor** starting motor **-nyckel** ignition key **-pedal** starting pedal; (*på motorcykel*) kick-starter **-pistol** starting pistol **-platta** (*för robot e.d.*) launch[ing] pad **-raket** booster, launching vehicle **-signal** starting signal **-skott** *sport.* starting shot; ~*et gick* the pistol went off **-snöre** starting strap **-vev** starting handle, crank

stas *s3, med.* stasis

stass *s3* finery

1 stat *s3* (*samhälle; rike*) state; ~*en* the State; *Förenta ~erna* the United States [of America]; ~*ens finanser* Government finance (*sg*); *S~ens Järnvägar* the Swedish State Railways; ~*ens tjänst* public (government) service; *i ~ens tjänst* in the service of the State; ~*ens verk* Government (civil service) departments; *på ~ens bekostnad* at public expense

2 stat *s3* **1** (*tjänstemannakår*) staff; (*förteckning*) list of persons belonging to the establishment **2** *föra* [*stor*] ~ live in [grand] style; *dra in på ~en* cut down expenses

3 stat *s3* **1** (*avlöningsanordning*) establishment; *officer på ~* permanent officer **2** (*budget*) estimates (*pl*), budget

statare farm labourer, cotter

statera walk on, be a super (extra)

statik *s3, ej pl* statics (*pl, behandlas som sg*)

station [-(t)'ʃo:n] station; *ta in en ~* (*radio.*) tune in a station **-era** station **-ering** [-'ne:-] stationing

stations|inspektor stationmaster **-samhälle** town (village) around a railway station **-skri-**

vare railway clerk **-vagn** (*bil*) estate car; *AE.* station wagon

stationär [-tʃo'näːr] *al* stationary

statisk ['sta:-] *a5* static; ~ *elektricitet* static electricity

statist *teat.* walker-on, supernumerary, *vard.* super; *film.* extra

statist|ik *s3, ej pl* statistics (*pl, behandlas som sg*) **-iker** [-'tiss-] statistician **-isk** [-'tiss-] *a5* statistic [al]; *S~a centralbyrån* Statistics Sweden; ~*a uppgifter* statistical data (*sg*), statistics; ~ *årsbok* statistical yearbook

stativ *s7* stand, rack; (*stöd*) support; (*trebent*) tripod

statlig [ˣsta:t-] *al* state (*egendom* property); government (*verk* office); national (*inkomstskatt* income tax); public (*institution* institution); ~*t ingripande* government (state) intervention; *i ~ regi* under government auspices, run by the State

stats|angelägenhet affair of state **-anslag** government (state, public) grant (subsidy) **-anställd** *a5* employed in government service; *en ~* a government (state) employee **-arkiv** [public] record office **-bana** state (state-owned) railway **-besök** state (official) visit **-bidrag** *se statsunderstöd* **-budget** national budget **-chef** head of a (the) state **-egendom** state (national, public) property; *göra till ~* nationalize **-fientlig** subversive (*verksamhet* activity) **-finanser** *pl* public (government) finances **-finansierad** *a5* state-financed **-form** form of government, polity **-fru** lady of the bedchamber **-fängelse** state prison **-förbrytare** political offender **-förbrytelse** political crime, high treason **-förbund** association (union, [con]federation) of states **-författning** constitution **-förvaltning** public (state) administration **-gräns** state boundary, frontier

stats|hemlighet state secret **-historia** political history **-inkomster** *pl* public (national) revenue (*sg*) **-kalender** official yearbook (directory) **-kassa** treasury, exchequer **-klok** politic, versed in state affairs **-klokhet** political wisdom **-konst** statesmanship, statecraft; diplomacy **-kontoret** [the Swedish] agency for administrative development **-kontrollerad** *a5* state (government) controlled **-kunskap** political science **-kupp** coup d'état **-kyrka** established (national, state) church; *engelska ~n* the Church of England, the Anglican Church; *svenska ~n* the Lutheran State Church of Sweden; *avskaffa ~n* disestablish the Church **-kyrklig** state-church **-lån** government (state) loan **-lära** sociology **-lös** stateless **-makt** state authority, power of the state; ~*er* (*äv.*) government authorities; *den fjärde ~en* (*pressen*) the fourth estate **-man** statesman; (*politiker*) politician **-minister** prime minister, premier; *ställföreträdande ~* deputy prime minister **-obligation** government bond; ~*er* (*äv.*) government securities, consols **-papper** *pl* government securities, treasury bills **-polis** national (state) police **-revision** auditing of public (state, national) accounts

stats|råd 1 *pers.* [cabinet] minister, councillor of state; *Storbritannien äv.* secretary of state; *konsultativt ~* minister without portfolio **2** (*ministär*) council of state cabinet **3** (*sammanträde*) cabinet council (meeting); *konungen i ~et* the king in council **-rådinna** [cabinet] minister's wife **-rådsberedning** *~en* [the] cabinet office **-rätt** constitutional law **-sekreterare** under-secretary of state **-skatt** national (state) tax **-skick** constitution **-skuld** national debt **-teater** national theatre **-tjänst** public (civil) service **-tjänsteman** civil servant, government employee **-understöd** government subsidy, state aid **-understödd** *a5* state-subsidized **-utgifter** *pl* state (government) expenditure (*sg*) **-verksproposition** budget bill (proposals *pl*) **-vetare** *vard.* political scientist, expert in (student of) political science **-vetenskap** political science **-vetenskaplig** of political science **-vetenskapsman** expert on political science **-välvning** [political] revolution **-överhuvud** *se statschef*

statt *sup. av städja*

statuera *~ ett exempel* make an example

status ['sta:-, *x*sta:-] *s2, s7* (*ställning*) status; (*affärsföretags*) standing; *~ quo* status quo; *rättslig ~ legal status* **-symbol** status symbol

statuter [-'tu:-] *pl* rules, regulations, statutes

staty *s3* statue **-ett** *s3* statuette

stav *s2* staff; *sport.* pole; (*skid-*) ski stick (pole); (*i tunna*) stave; *bryta ~en över ngn* (*bildl.*) condemn s.b. [outright]

stava spell; *hur ~s ...?* how do you spell ...?; *~ och lägga ihop* put two and two together; *~ sig igenom* spell one's way through

stavbakterie rod-shaped bacterium, bacillus

stav|else syllable **-fel** spelling mistake; orthographical error

stav|hopp pole vault; (*-hoppning*) pole-vaulting; *hoppa ~* pole-vault **-hoppare** pole-vaulter **-kyrka** stave ᴠchurch **-lampa** electric torch **-magnet** bar magnet

stavning [-a:-] spelling; (*rättskrivning*) orthography

stavrim alliteration

stearin *s4, s3* stearin[e], candle-grease **-ljus** candle **-syra** stearic acid

1 steg *imperf. av stiga*

2 steg *s7* **1** step (*äv. bildl.*); (*gång äv.*) gait, pace; *små ~* short steps; *ta stora ~* take great (long) strides; *gå framåt med stora ~* (*bildl.*) advance with rapid strides; *~ för ~* step by step, *bildl. äv.* gradually; *hålla jämna ~* keep pace (*med* with); *med långsamma ~* at a slow pace; *med spänstiga ~* with a springy gait; *följa på några ~s avstånd* follow a few paces behind; *styra (ställa) sina ~ till* direct one's steps to; *ta första ~et till försoning* make the first move towards conciliation; *ta ~et fullt ut* (*bildl.*) go the whole way (*vard.* hog); *vidtaga sina mått och ~* take measures **2** *tekn.* stage

stega 1 *~ [upp]* step out, pace **2** *~ i väg* stride out (along)

stege *s2* ladder

stegel *s7* wheel **stegla** [-e:-] break upon the wheel

steglitsa [*x*ste:-, -'litt-] *s1* goldfinch

steg|längd pace **-löst** *adv, ~ variabel* infinitely variable

stegpinne rung

1 stegra [-e:-] *rfl* rear; *bildl.* rebel; object

2 stegr|a [-e:-] raise, increase; (*förstärka*) intensify, heighten

stegring rise, increase; intensification, heightening

stegräknare pedometer

stegvagn ladder truck

stegvis step by step, by steps; (*gradvis äv.*) gradually, by stages (degrees)

1 stek *s7, sjö.* hitch; bend

2 stek *s2* joint; *kokk.* roast meat, joint [of roast meat]; *ösa en ~* baste a joint

steka *v3* **1** roast (*kött* meat; *kastanjer* chestnuts); (*i stekpanna*) fry; (*i ugn*) roast (*potatis* potatoes); (*halstra*) broil **2** *bildl., solen steker* the sun is broiling; *~ sig i solen* broil (bake) in the sun **stekande** *a4* broiling, roasting (*hett* hot; *sol* sun) **stekas** *v3* roast, be roast, broil, be broiling

stekel *s2, zool.* hymenopteran, hymenopteron

stek|fat meat dish **-fett** frying fat **-flott** dripping **-fläsk** sliced pork **-gryta** braising-pan **-het** broiling, roasting **-hus** steakhouse **-ning** [-e:-] roasting *etc.*, *jfr steka* **-nål** [meat] skewer **-os** smell of frying (*etc*) **-panna** frying pan, *AE.* frypan **-spade** slice, spatula **-spett** spit **-sås** [pan] gravy

stek|t [-e:-] *a4* roast (*kött* meat); fried (*potatis* potatoes; *ägg* eggs); baked (*äpplen* apples); *för mycket* (*litet*) *~* overdone (underdone); *lagom ~* well done **-ugn** [roasting] oven **-vändare** turnspit, roasting jack

stel *a1* stiff (*äv. bildl.*); (*styv*) rigid (*äv. bildl.*); (*av köld*) numb; *bildl.* formal, reserved (*sätt* manners *pl*); *~ av fasa* paralysed (frozen) with horror; *vara ~ i ryggen* have a stiff back; *en ~ middag* a very formal dinner **-bent** [-be:-] *a1* stiff-legged; *bildl.* stiff, formal **-frusen** (*om pers.*) stiff with cold, frozen stiff; (*om kött, mark e.d.*) [hard] frozen **-het** stiffness *etc.*; rigidity; *bildl. äv.* formality, constraint **-kramp** tetanus, *vard.* lockjaw

stellarastronomi [-*x*la:r-] stellar astronomy

stelna [-e:-] get (grow) stiff; stiffen; (*övergå i fast form*) solidify; (*om vätska*) congeal, coagulate, (*om blod äv.*) clot; *kokk. äv.; ~de metaforer* frozen metaphors; *~ till is* be congealed into ice; *man ~r till med åren* one stiffens up as one gets older; *han ~de till när han fick se oss* he froze when he caught sight of us

sten *s2* stone (*äv. i frukt o. med.*); *AE. äv.* rock; (*liten*) pebble; (*stor äv.*) boulder, rock; *bryta ~* quarry stone; *en ~ har fallit från mitt bröst* that's a load off my mind; *hugga i ~* (*bildl.*) bark up the wrong tree; *kasta ~ på* throw stones at; *lägga ~ på börda* increase the burden; *inte lämna ~ på ~* not leave one stone upon another; *det kunde röra en ~ till tårar* it is enough to melt a heart of stone

sten|a stone (*till döds* to death) **-art** variety of stone **-beläggning** paving **-bit** *zool.* lump **-block** boulder [stone], block of stone **-bock 1** *zool.* ibex; steinbok **2** *astr., S~en* Capricorn **-brott** quarry **-bräcka** *bot.* saxifrage **-bumling** boulder **-bär** stone bramble

stencil *s3* stencil; *skriva en ~* cut a stencil **-era** stencil **-ering** [-'le:-] stencil copying

sten|dammlunga silicosis **-död** stone dead;

vard. [as] dead as a doornail **-döv** stone deaf, [as] deaf as a post **-flisa** chip of stone **-fot** *byggn.* stone base **-frukt** stone fruit; *fack.* drupe **-get** chamois **-gods** stoneware **-golv** stone floor **-gärdsgård** *se stenmur* **-huggare** stonemason **-huggeri** stonemasonry **-hus** stone house; (*tegel-*) brick house **-hård** [as] hard as stone (flint); (*bildl.*) adamant **-häll** stone slab; (*platta*) flagstone; (*i öppen spis*) hearthstone

sten|ig *a1* stony; rocky (*bergsluttning* hillside); (*mödosam*) hard **-kaka** *vard.* 78 [record] **-kast** (*avståndsmått*) stone's throw **-kista** caisson **-kol** [pit] coal, mineral (hard) coal

stenkols|formation *geol.* carboniferous formation **-förande** *a4* carboniferous **-gruva** coal mine, colliery **-tjära** coal tar

sten|kross stone crusher **-kruka** stoneware (earthenware) jar **-kula** (*leksak*) [stone] marble **-kummel** cairn [of stones] **-lägga** pave **-läggning** *abstr.* paving; *konkr.* pavement **-mur** stone wall; (*tegel-*) brick wall **-murkla** turbantop

steno|graf *s3* shorthand writer, stenographer; ~ *och maskinskriverska* shorthand typist **-grafera** take down in shorthand; *absol.* write shorthand **-grafi** *s3* stenography, shorthand **-grafisk** [-'gra:-] stenographic, shorthand, in shorthand

stenogram [-'gramm] *s7* stenograph, shorthand notes; *skriva ut ett* ~ transcribe shorthand notes **-block** shorthand pad

sten|parti rock garden, rockery **-platta** stone slab, flagstone **-rik** *bildl.* rolling in money **-riket** the mineral kingdom **-rös[e]** mound (heap) of stones **-skott** flying stone [hitting a motorcar] **-skvätta** *s1* wheatear **-slipare** stone polisher, lapidary **-sliperi** stone polisher's workshop **-sopp** *s2* cep **-stil** lapidary style **-sätta** *se stenlägga* **-sättare** paver **-sättning** *arkeol.* circle (row) of stones, cromlech **-söta** *s1, bot.* polypody **-tavla** *bibl.* table of stone

stentorsröst [ˣstentårs-] stentorian voice

sten|tryck lithography, lithographic printing; *konkr.* lithograph **-ull** mineral (rock) wool **-yxa** stone axe **-åldern** the Stone Age; *yngre* (*äldre*) ~ the neolithic (palaeolithic) period **-åldersmänniska** Stone Age man **-öken** stony (rocky) desert; (*bildl. om stad*) wilderness of bricks and mortar

stepp *s3* tap dance

stepp|a tap-dance **-dansör** tap-dancer

stereo ['ste:-] *s5* stereo, stereophonic sound **-anläggning** stereo [equipment] **-foni** [-å'ni:] *s3* stereophony **-fonisk** [-'få:-] *a5* stereophonic **-fotografi** stereophotography **-metri** *s3* stereometry **-metrisk** [-'me:-] *a5* stereometric **-skop** [-'skå:p] *s7* stereoscope **-skopisk** [-'skå:-] *a5* stereoscopic **-typ I** *a5* stereotyped, set (*leende* smile) **II** *s3* stereotype, cliché **-typi** *s3* stereotyping

steril *a1* sterile; (*ofruktbar*) barren (*mark* ground) **-isera** sterilize **-isering** [-'se:-] sterilization **-itet** sterility; barrenness

sterling ['stö:r-, 'stä:r-] *pund* ~ pound sterling **-blocket** the sterling area (bloc)

stetoskop [-'skå:p] *s7* stethoscope

stia [ˣsti:a] *s1* [pig]sty, *AE.* pigpen

---

stick I *s7* **1** stick[ing]; (*nål-*) prick; (*med vapen*) stab, thrust; (*insekt-*) sting, bite **2** *lämna ngn i* ~*et* leave s.b. in the lurch **3** (*gravyr*) engraving, print **4** *kortsp.* trick **II** *adv,* ~ *i stäv* (*sjö.*) dead ahead, *bildl.* directly contrary (*mot* to)

stick|a I *s1* **1** (*flisa*) splinter, split; (*pinne*) stick; *få en* ~ *i fingret* run a splinter into one's finger; *mager som en* ~ [as] thin as a rake **2** (*strump-*) [knitting] needle **II** *stack stuckit* **1** (*med nål e.d.*) prick, stick; (*med kniv e.d.*) stab; (*slakta*) stick; (*om insekt*) sting, bite; (*stoppa*) put (*handen i fickan* one's hand into one's pocket); (*häftigare*) thrust; *bildl.* sting; ~ *kniven i* stab [... with a knife]; ~ *eld på* set fire to, set on fire; ~ *hål på* prick (make) a hole in, puncture; ~ *en nål igenom* run a pin through; ~ *in huvudet* i pop one's head into; *hans ord stack mig i själen* his words cut me to the heart **2** (*gravera*) engrave **3** (*med -or*) knit; (*på symaskin*) stitch; (*vaddera*) quilt **4** *det -er i bröstet* I have a pain in my chest; *lukten -er i näsan* the smell makes my nose itch; *ljuset stack mig i ögonen* the light dazzled me; ~ *till sjöss* put out (*om pers.* run off) to sea; *kom så -er vi!* (*vard.*) come on, let's go (get out of here)!; ~ *sin väg* clear out, hit the road **5** *rfl* prick o.s.; *jag stack mig i fingret* I pricked my finger **6** (*med betonad partikel*) ~ *av* (*kontrastera*) contrast (*mot, från* to); ~ *emellan med* fit in; ~ *fram a*) stretch (stick) out (*nosen* its etc. nose) *b*) (*skjuta fram*) project, protrude; *månen -er fram* the moon is peeping out; ~ *ner* (*ihjäl*) stab [to death]; *det stack till i foten* I had a sudden twinge in my foot; *det stack till i honom* (*bildl.*) he felt a pang; ~ *upp a*) stick up (*huvudet* one's head) *b*) (*framträda*) stick up (out), (*träda i dagen*) crop up, *c*) *vard.* be cheeky; ~ *ut* stick out; ~ *ut ögonen på ngn* put out a p.'s eyes; ~ *över a*) *kortsp.* take, *absol.* take it, *b*) (*kila över*) pop over

stickande *a4* shooting (*smärta* pain); pungent (*lukt* smell); piercing (*blickar* looks); ~ *smak* pungent (biting) taste

stick|as *stacks stuckits, dep* prick, sting (*jfr sticka II 1*) **-beskrivning** knitting instructions **-bäcken** bedpan

stickel ['stikk-] *s2, tekn.* graving tool

stickelhår (*i päls*) bristles (*pl*)

stick|garn knitting yarn (wool) **-ig** *a1* prickly **-kontakt** (*-propp*) plug; (*vägguttag*) point, wall socket

stickling cutting, slip

stick|maskin knitting machine **-ning 1** knitting (*äv. resultat.*) **2** (*-ande känsla*) pricking [sensation] **-ord 1** (*gliring*) sarcasm, taunt **2** (*uppslagsord*) entry, headword **3** *teat.* cue **-propp** plug **-prov** sample (spot) test; *ta ett* ~ take a sample **-provsförfarande** sample-test procedure **-provsundersökning** random sampling **-replik** *se -ord 1 o. 3* **-spår** *järnv.* dead-end siding (track) **-vapen** pointed (stabbing) weapon

1 stift *s7* **1** (*att fästa med*) pin, brad, tack; (*rit-*) drawing pencil, crayon; (*penn-*) pencil lead; (*grammofon-*) needle **2** *bot.* style

2 stift *s7, kyrkl.* diocese

stift|a (*in-*) found; establish (*en fond* a fund); institute (*regler* rules); form (*ett förbund* an alliance); ~ *bekantskap med ngn* make a p.'s acquaintance; ~ *fred* conclude (make) peace; ~ *lagar* institute laws, legislate **-ande** *s6* founding *etc.*; foundation; establishment **-are** founder; originator

stiftelse foundation; institution, establishment **-urkund** charter of foundation; (*bolags*) memorandum of association; *AE.* articles of incorporation, corporate charter

stiftpenna propelling (automatic) pencil

stifts|adjunkt diocesan curate **-jungfru** [secular] canoness **-stad** cathedral city, diocesan capital

stifttand pivot (pin) tooth

stig *s2* way. track

stig|a *steg -it* **1** (*kliva*) step (*fram* forward); walk (*in i rummet* into the room); *jag kan inte ~ på foten* I can't put my weight on my foot; ~ *i land* go ashore; ~ *miste* make a false step; ~ *närmare* step nearer **2** (*höja sig*) rise; (*om pris äv.*) increase, go up, (*från säljarsynpunkt*) advance, improve; *flyg.* climb, ascend; (*öka*) rise, increase; *aktierna -er* shares are going up; *barometern -er* the barometer is rising; *febern -er* his (*etc.*) temperature is going up; ~ *i ngns aktning* rise in a p.'s esteem; ~ *i pris* advance (rise) in price; ~ *i rang* acquire a higher rank, advance; ~ *i värde* rise in value; *tårarna steg henne i ögonen* tears rose to her eyes; ~ *till a*) (*nå*) rise to, attain, *b*) (*belöpa sig t.*) amount to; ~ *ur sängen* get out of bed; *framgången steg honom åt huvudet* success went to his head **3** (*med betonad partikel*) ~ *av* get off, (*häst*) dismount, (*tåg*) get off; ~ *fram* step forward, approach; ~ *in* step (walk) in; *stig in!* please come in!, (*som svar på knackning*) come in!; ~ *ner* descend; ~ *på* (*absol.*) come in; ~ *på tåget* get on the train, take the train (*vid at*); ~ *upp* rise, *vard.* get up; ~ *upp från bordet* (*äv.*) leave the table; ~ *upp i en vagn* get into a carriage; *stig upp!* get up!; *en misstanke steg upp inom henne* a suspicion arose within her; ~ *upp på* mount, ascend; ~ *ur* get (step) out (*en vagn* of a carriage); ~ *ur sängen* get out of bed; ~ *ut* step out; ~ *över* step over (across)

stigande *a4* rising; (*ökande äv.*) increasing, growing; (*om pris*) rising, advancing; ~ *konjunkturer* rising tendency; ~ *kurva* upward curve; *efter en ~ skala* on an ascending scale, progressively; *vara i ~* be on the rise

stigarledning *se* stigrör

stigbygel stirrup; (*i örat*) stirrup-bone; *fack.* stapes (*pl*)

stigfinnare pathfinder

stig|hastighet *flyg.* rate of climb **-höjd** ceiling **-it** *sup. av* stiga

stigma [*ˣstigg-*] *s6* stigma

stigman highwayman, brigand; footpad

stigmatiser|a stigmatize **-ing** stigmatization

stig|ning [-i:g-] rising, rise, ascent; (*ökning*) increase; (*i terräng*) incline, slope; *flyg.* climb **-ort** *gruv.* raise **-rör** ascending pipe, riser **-vinkel** *flyg.* angle of climb

stil *s2* **1** (*hand-*) hand[writing] **2** (*konstnärlig ~, stilart; bildl.*) style; touch, manner; *det är ~ på honom* he has style; *det är hennes vanliga ~* it is her usual way; *hålla ~en* observe good form; *i ~ med* in keeping with; *ngt i den ~en* s.th. in that

line; *i stor ~* on a large scale **3** *skol.* [written] exercise **4** (*trycktyp*) type; *spärrad ~* spaced-out letters (*pl*) **5** (*tideräkning*) style **-art** style **-bildande** style-forming **-blomma** *ung.* unsuccessful attempt at rhetorical brilliance **-brott** breach of style **-brytning** *ung.* clash of styles **-drag** characteristic of a style **-enlig** [-e:-] *a1* in keeping with the style [of the period]

stilett *s3* stiletto **-klack** stiletto (spike) heel

stil|full stylish, tasteful, in good style **-gjuteri** *boktr.* type foundry **-grad** *boktr.* type size, size of type

stilig *a1* stylish, elegant, chic, *vard.* smart; *det var ~t gjort av henne* it was a fine thing of her to do

stiliser|a (*förenkla*) stylize, conventionalize **2** (*formulera*) word, compose **-ing 1** formalizing *etc.* **2** wording

stil|ist stylist; *en god ~* a master of style **-istik** *s3* stylistics (*pl el. sg*) **-istisk** [-'liss-] *a5* stylistic; *i ~t avseende* as regards style **-känsla** feeling for style, artistic sense (taste)

still *se* stilla I

stilla I oböjligt *a o.* adv **1** (*utan rörelse, äv. bildl.*) still; (*lugn*) calm; (*svag*) soft (*bris* breeze); (*tyst*) quiet; *S~ havet* the Pacific [Ocean]; ~ *vatten* calm (unruffled) waters; *S~a veckan* Holy Week; *tyst och ~* quiet and tranquil; *föra ett ~ liv* lead a quiet life; *det gick ett ~ sus genom salen* a gentle murmur went through the room (hall); *ligga* (*sitta, stå, vara*) ~ lie (sit, stand, be) still; *vi sitter för mycket ~* we lead a too sedentary life; *smedjan stod ~* the forge was at a standstill; *stå* (*var*) ~*!* keep still (quiet)!; *luften står ~* the air is not stirring; *det står alldeles ~ för mig* just can't remember, it's gone completely out of my head; *tiga ~* be silent **II** *v1* (*dämpa*) appease; (*lugna*) quiet; (*lindra*) soothe, alleviate (*smärtan* the pain); ~ *sin hunger* appease one's hunger; ~ *sin nyfikenhet* satisfy one's curiosity; ~ *sin törst* slake (quench) one's thirst

stillahavskusten the Pacific Coast

stilla|sittande I *a4* sedentary (*arbete* work) **II** *s6* sedentary life **-stående I** *a4* stationary (*luft* air); stagnant (*vatten* water); (*utan utveckling*) unprogressive **II** *s6* standstill; stagnation **-tigande** *a4* silent; in silence; ~ *finna sig i ngt* accept s.th. in silence

stillbild still

stilleben ['still-, -'le:-] *s7* still life (*pl* still lifes)

stille|stånd *s7* **1** *mil.* armistice, truce **2** (*vid industri o.d.*) standstill **-ståndsavtal** truce

still|film film strip **-het** calm, quiet; stillness, tranquillity; *begravningen sker i ~* the funeral will be strictly private; *i all ~* quite quietly, in silence; *leva i ~* lead a quiet life

stillna quieten down; (*mojna*) abate, drop

stillsam *a1* quiet, tranquil; *vara ~ av sig* be of a quiet disposition

stil|lös without style, in bad style **-löshet** lack of style **-möbler** *pl* period furniture **-prov** (*handstils-*) specimen of a p.'s handwriting; *boktr.* type specimen **-ren** [of] pure [style] **-sort** *boktr.* kind of type; *fel ~* wrong fo[u]nt (*förk.* w.f.)

stiltje [*ˣstilltje*] *s9* calm; lull

stilvidrig at variance with the style [of the whole]

stim [stimm] *s7* **1** (*fisk-*) shoal; (*av småfisk*) fry **2**

(*stoj*) noise, din **stimma 1** (*om fisk*) shoal **2** (*stoja*) be noisy, make a noise

stimul|ans [-'lans, -'laŋs] *s3* stimulation (*till* of); stimulus; (*medel*) stimulant **-antia** [-'lantsia] *pl* stimulants, stimuli **-era** stimulate; ~*nde medel* stimulant **-ering** [-'le:-] stimulation **-us** ['sti:-] *r, pl stimuli* stimulus (*pl* stimuli)

sting *s7* (*stick*) prick, sting (*äv. bildl.*); *bildl. äv.* pang (*av svartsjuka* of jealousy); (*kraft*) bite, go; *det är inget* ~ *i det här* there is no punch in this **stinga** *stack stungit* sting; *jfr sticka* **stingslig** *al* touchy, irritable

stink|a *stank* (*sup. saknas*) stink; ~ *av ngt* smell strongly of s.th., *vard.* stink of s.th. **-djur** skunk **-näva** *s1, bot.* herb Robert

stinn *al* (*uppblåst*) inflated; (*utspänd*) distended; (*av mat*) full [up]; *en* ~ *penningpung* a bulging (fat) purse

stins *s2* stationmaster

stint *se* ~ *på ngn* look hard at s.b.; *se ngn* ~ *i ögonen* look s.b. straight in the eye

stipel ['sti:-] *s3, bot.* stipel; stipule

stipendiat holder of a scholarship

stipendie|ansökan application for a scholarship (grant) **-fond** scholarship fund **-nämnd** scholarship committee

stipendium [-'penn-] *s4* scholarship; (*bidrag*) grant, award

stipul|ation stipulation **-era** stipulate; state

stirra stare, gaze (*på* at); ~ *som förhäxad på* stare as one bewitched at; ~ *sig blind på* (*bildl.*) have eyes for nothing else but **stirrande** *a4* staring; ~ *blick* (*äv.*) fixed look **stirrig** *al* scatterbrained; nervous

stjäla [ʃ-] *stal stulit* steal (*äv. bildl.*); ~ *sig till att göra ngt* do s.th. by stealth; ~ *sig till en stunds vila* snatch a short rest

stjälk [ʃ-] *s2* stalk; stem **-blad** stem leaf **-stygn** stem stitch

stjälp|a [ʃ-] *v3* **1** (*välta*) overturn; tip; upset (*äv. bildl.*); ~ *av* (*ut*) tip out; ~ *i sig* gulp down; ~ *upp* turn out **2** (*falla över ända*) [be] upset, turn (topple, tip) over **-ning** tipping, upsetting

stjärn|a [ˣʃä:r-] *s1* star **-baneret** the Star-Spangled Banner, the Stars and Stripes **-beströdd** *a5* starred, starry **-bild** constellation **-fall 1** (*-skott*) [swarm of] shooting star[s *pl*] **2** (*ordensregn*) shower of decorations **-formig** [-å-] *al* star-shaped; *fack.* stellar, stelliform **-fysik** astrophysics (*pl, behandlas som sg*) **-himmel** starry sky **-karta** star chart **-kikare** [astronomic] telescope **-klar** starlit (*natt* night); starry (*himmel* sky); *det är* ~*t* the stars are out (shining) **-lös** starless **-skott 1** *se -fall 1* **2** (*underhållare*) shooting star **-smäll** *vard., ge ngn en* ~ make s.b. see stars, knock s.b. into the middle of next week **-system** stellar (star) system **-tydare** astrologer **-år** sidereal year

stjärt [ʃ-] *s2* tail (*äv. tekn.*); (*på pers.*) behind, bottom **-fena** tail (caudal) fin **-fjäder** tail feather **-lanterna** *flyg.* tail (rear) light **-mes** long-tailed tit

sto *s6* mare; (*ungt*) filly

stock [-å-] *s2* **1** (*stam*) log; *sova som en* ~ sleep like a log; *över* ~ *och sten* up hill and down dale, across country; *sitta i* ~*en* be (sit) in the stocks **2**

(*på gevär*) stock **3** *tryck från* ~*ar* (*boktr.*) block printing

1 stocka [-å-] (*hattar*) block

2 stocka [-å-] *rfl* clog; stagnate (*äv. om trafik*); *orden* ~*r sig i halsen* the words stick in my throat

stock|blind stone-blind **-bro** pole bridge **-eld** log fire **-fisk** stockfish

stockholmare [-å-å-] inhabitant of Stockholm, Stockholmer

stock|hus log house **-konservativ** *en* ~ a die-hard conservative

stockning [-å-] (*avbrott*) stoppage; (*försening*) delay; (*blod-*) [blood] stasis; (*trafik-*) traffic jam, block, congestion; *bildl.* deadlock

stock|ros hollyhock **-ved** logwood

1 stod *imperf. av stå*

2 stod *s3* (*bildl-*) statue

stoff [-å-] *s7, om tyger o.d. s4* stuff (*till* for) (*äv. bildl.*); material[s *pl*]; (*ämne*) [subject] matter **-era** hem

stofil *s3* odd fish; *gammal* ~ (*äv.*) old fogey

stoft [-å-] *s7* dust; (*puder*) powder; (*jordiska kvarlevor*) ashes, remains (*pl*); *kräla i* ~*et* for crawl in the dust before **-hydda** mortal clay **-korn** grain of dust

sto|icism [-å-] stoicism **-iker** ['stå:-] stoic **-isk** ['stå:-] *a5* stoic[al]

stoj [ståjj] *s7* noise, din **stoja** make a noise, be noisy; (*om barn äv.*) romp **stojig** *al* noisy, boisterous; romping

stokastisk [-'kass-] *a5* stochastic; *stat. äv.* random

stol *s2* chair; (*utan ryggstöd*) stool; *sticka under* ~ *med* hold back, conceal; *sätta sig mellan två* ~*ar* (*bildl.*) fall between two stools

stola [ˣstå:-] *s1* stole

stolgång *s2* **1** (*ändtarmsmynning*) anus **2** (*avföring*) stools (*pl*), motion

stoll [-å-] *s2, gruv.* gallery; *AE.* adit

stolle [-å-] *s2* fool, silly person

stollift chair lift

stollig [-å-] *al* cracked, crazy

stolpe [-å-] *s2* post; pole; (*stötta*) prop, stanchion; (*i virkning*) treble; (*minnesanteckning*) brief note, jotting

stolpiller suppository

stolpskor *pl* climbing irons

stols|ben chair leg, leg of a chair **-karm** arm of a chair **-rygg** back of a chair **-sits** [chair] seat

stolt [-å-] *al* proud (*över* of); (*högdragen*) haughty; *med en* ~ *gest* with a proud gesture; *vara* ~ *över* (*äv.*) pride o.s. on, take pride in **-het** pride (*över* in); (*högdragenhet*) arrogance; *berättigad* ~ legitimated pride; *sårad* ~ (*äv.*) pique, *sätta sin* ~ *i* take pride in **-sera** *absol.* swagger; (*gå o.* ~) swagger about; (*om häst*) prance; ~ *med* parade

stomatit *s3* stomatitis

stomme *s2* frame[work], shell; skeleton (*äv. bildl.*)

stomp [-å-] *s2* stump

stop *s7* **1** (*kärl*) stoup, pot **2** (*rymdmått*) quart

1 stopp [-å-] **I** *s7* (*stockning*) stoppage (*i röret* in the pipe); (*stillastående*) stop, standstill (*äv. bildl.*); *sätta* ~ *för* put an end (a stop) to; *säg* ~*!* (*vid påfyllning*) say when! **II** *interj* stop!

2 stopp [-å-] *s2* **1** (*på strumpa e.d.*) darn **2** (*pip-*) fill

1 stoppa [-å-] **1** (*hejda*) stop, bring to a standstill; stem (*blodflödet* the flow of blood) **2** (*stanna*) stop, come to a standstill **3** (*förslå*) suffice, be enough **4** (*orka*) stand the strain; *han ~r nog inte länge till* he can't stand the strain much longer

2 stoppa [-å-] **1** (*laga hål*) darn (*strumpor* socks) **2** (*fylla*) fill (*pipan* one's pipe); stuff (*korv* sausages; *med tagel* with horsehair); upholster (*möbler* furniture); (*proppa*) cram; *~ fickorna fulla med* fill one's pockets with **3** (*sticka in*) put (*ngt i fickan* s.th. into one's pocket); tuck **4** (*med betonad partikel*) *~ i ngn ngt* stuff s.b. with s.th.; *~ i sig* put away; *~ ner* put (tuck) down; *~ om ett barn* tuck a child up [in bed]; *~ om en madrass* re-stuff a mattress; *~ på sig* put into one's pocket, pocket; *~ undan* stow away

stopp|**boll** *sport.* drop shot -**förbud** (*på skylt*) No waiting; *~ gäller* waiting is prohibited
stoppgarn darning wool (cotton, worsted)
stopp|**gräns** stopping limit -**knapp** stop button -**plikt** (*hopskr. stopplikt*) obligation to stop
stoppljus stoplight
stopp|**ning** [-å-] (*jfr 2 stoppa*) darning; filling; stuffing *etc.* -**nål** darning needle
stopp|**signal** halt signal, red light -**skruv** set (stop) screw -**skylt** stop sign
stoppsvamp darning egg (mushroom)
stopp|**ur** stopwatch -**volley** *sport.* stop volley
stor -*t* större störst **1** (*i sht om ngt konkr.*) large (*hus* house; *förmögenhet* fortune); (*i sht i kroppslig bet.*) big (*näsa* nose), (*starkare*) huge; (*reslig*) tall; (*i sht om ngt abstr.*) great (*skillnad* difference); *bildl. äv.* grand; *Alexander den ~e* Alexander the Great; *Karl den ~e* Charlemagne; *dubbelt så ~ som* double the size of, twice as large (*etc.*) as; *lika ~ som* the same size as, as large (*etc.*) as; *hur ~ är han?* how big is he?; *en ~ beundrare av* a great admirer of; *~ bokstav* capital [letter]; *~ efterfrågan* great (large, heavy) demand; *ett ~t antal* a great (large) number (*barn* of children); *hon är ~a flickan nu* she is a big girl now; *den ~a hopen* the crowd; *han är ~a karlen nu* he is quite a man now; *en ~ man* a great man; *vara ~ i maten* be a big eater; *ett ~t nöje* a great pleasure; *~a ord* big words; *bruka ~a ord* talk big; *du ~e tid!* good heavens!; *i ~a drag* in broad outline; *i det ~a hela* on the whole, by and large; *till ~ del* largely, to a great extent **2** (*fullvuxen*) grown-up, adult; *de ~a* grown-up people; *när jag blir ~* when I grow up

storartad [-a:r-] *a5* grand; magnificent, splendid; *på ett storartat sätt* (*äv.*) magnificently, splendidly
storasyster big sister
stor|**belåten** highly satisfied -**blommig 1** *bot.* large-flowered **2** (*om mönster*) with a large floral pattern -**bonde** farmer with extensive lands -**boskap** cattle
Storbritannien *n* Great Britain
stor|**cirkel** great circle -**dia** *s1, s6* overhead transparency -**drift** large-scale production (*jordbr.* farming) -**dåd** great (noble) achievement -**ebror** big brother

stor|**en** ['stɔ:-] *best. form, sjö.* the main -**familj** extended family -**favorit** main favourite -**finans** high finance -**främmande** distinguished guest[s *pl*] -**furste** grand duke -**furstendöme** grand duchy -**förbrukare** bulk (big) consumer -**företag** large[-scale] enterprise (company) -**gods** large landed estate -**gråta** cry copiously -**hertig** grand duke -**het** [-ɔ:-] **1** *abstr.* greatness; *fack.* magnitude **2** *mat.* quantity **3** (*om pers.*) great man (personage); (*berömdhet*) celebrity; *en okänd ~* an unknown celebrity (quantity)
storhets|**tid** (*lands*) era of greatness -**vansinne** megalomania, illusions (*pl*) of grandeur
stor|**hjärna** *~n* [the] cerebrum -**industri** big (large[-scale]) industry
stork [-å-] *s2* stork
storkapital big capital
storkbo [-å-] stork's nest
storkna [-å-] choke, suffocate
stor|**kommun** big (large) municipal district -**konflikt** major conflict -**kornig** coarse-grained -**kors** (*av orden*) grand cross (*förk.* G.C.) -**kök** catering [service] -**lek** *s2* size; dimensions (*pl*); (*omfång*) extent, width, vastness; (*rymd*) volume; *fack.* magnitude; *av betydande ~* of large dimensions; *i ~* in size (*etc.*); *i naturlig ~* life-size; *stora ~ar* (*av plagg e.d. äv.*) outsizes; *upplagans ~* number of copies printed -**leksordning** magnitude, order; size; *av ~en* in the region of (*500 pund* 500 pounds), of the order of (*5% 5%*); *av första ~en* of the first order (magnitude); *i ~* in order of size -**ligen** [-ɔ:-] greatly; highly; very much -**ljugare** arrant liar -**lom** black-throated diver
storm [-å-] *s2* **1** (*vind*) storm (*äv. bildl.*); gale; (*oväder*) tempest; *det blåser upp till ~* a storm is brewing; *~ i ett vattenglas* a storm in a teacup; *lugn i ~en!* calm down now!; *rida ut ~en* (*äv. bildl.*) ride out the storm **2** *mil., ta med ~* (*äv. bildl.*) take by storm; *gå till ~s mot* make an assault upon **3** *se stormhatt 1*
storma [-å-] **1** (*blåsa*) storm; *det ~r* storm is raging, it is stormy, a gale is blowing **2** *bildl.* (*rasa*) storm, rage; (*rusa*) rush; *~ fram* rush forward **3** *mil.* assault, force, storm
stor|**makt** great power -**maktspolitik** [great-] power politics (*pl*) -**man** great man; magnate; (*berömdhet*) celebrity
stormande [-å-] *a4* **1** *eg., se stormig* **2** *bildl.* thunderous (*applåder* applause); tremendous, enormous (*succé* success); *göra ~ succé* (*om skådespelare äv.*) bring down the house
stor|**marknad** hypermarket, out-of-town superstore -**maskig** *a1* wide-meshed, coarse-meshed -**mast** mainmast
storm|**by** heavy squall -**centrum** storm centre -**driven** *a5* storm-tossed -**flod** flood [caused by a storm] -**fågel** fulmar -**förtjust** absolutely delighted -**gräla** quarrel furiously (*med* with); *~ på ngn* storm at s.b. -**hatt 1** (*hög hatt*) top (high) hat **2** *bot.* monkshood
storm|**ig** *a1, eg. o. bildl.* stormy; tempestuous (*känslor* emotions); *bildl. äv.* tumultuous (*uppträde* scene); *~t hav* rough sea -**klocka** alarm bell -**lykta** hurricane lamp, storm lantern

-ning *mil.* assault, storming **-plugga** swot; read hard, cram **-rik** immensely rich **-segel** storm sail **-steg** *med* ~ by leaps and bounds **-styrka** gale force **-svala** storm[y] petrel **-trupp** *mil.* storming party **-tändsticka** fusee **-varning** gale warning **-vind** gale [of wind] **-virvel** violent whirlwind, tornado

stor|märs *sjö.* maintop **-mästare** grandmaster **-mönstrad** large-patterned **-möte** general meeting **-ordig** [-ɔ:rd-] *a1* grandiloquent; (*skrytsam*) boastful **-pamp** *vard.* big noise (shot), bigwig, VIP **-politik** top-level politics (*pl*) **-politisk** ~*t möte* summit meeting **-rengöring** spring-cleaning **-rutig** large-checked **-rysk, ryss** Great Russian **-rökare** heavy smoker **-segel** mainsail **-sint** *a1* magnanimous, generous **-sinthet** magnanimity, generosity **-skarv** *zool.* cormorant **-skifte** amalgamation of smallholdings into large production units **-skog** large forest **-skojare** big swindler **-skrake** goosander; *AE.* merganser **-skratta** roar with laughter, guffaw **-skrika** yell (scream) [at the top of one's voice] **-skrävlare** swaggerer, big braggart **-slagen** *a3* magnificent, grand **-slagenhet** magnificence, grandeur **-slalom** giant slalom **-slam** *kortsp.* grand slam **-slägga** *ta till* ~*n* (*bildl.*) go at s.th. with hammer and tongs **-spov** curlew **-stad** big town, city; metropolis **-stadsaktig** *a1* metropolitan, fitting to a big town **-stadsbo** inhabitant of a big town (*etc.*), city dweller **-stilad** *a5* grand, fine

Stor-Stockholm Greater Stockholm

stor|strejk general strike **-stâtlig** majestic, grand, magnificent **-städning** *se storrengöring* **-stövlar** *pl* high boots **-säljare** best seller

stort [-ɔ:-] **I** *adv* largely *etc.*; *inte* ~ *mer än* not much more than; *det hjälper inte* ~ it won't help much; *tänka* ~ think nobly **II** *a, i* ~ on a large scale; *i* ~ *sett* on the whole; *slå på* ~ make a splash, do the thing big

stor|ting Storting, Norwegian Parliament **-tjuta** howl **-tjuv** masterthief **-tvätt** big wash **-tå** big (great) toe **-verk** *se stordåd* **-vesir** grand vizier **-vilt** big game **-vulen** *a3, se storstilad* **-vuxen** tall [of stature] **-ätare** big eater; (*frossare*) glutton **-ögd** *a1* large-eyed **-ögt** *adv, titta* ~ *på* gaze round-eyed at

straff *s7* punishment (*för* for); *jur.* penalty, *avtjäna sitt* ~ serve one's penalty; *milt* ~ light (mild) punishment; *strängt* ~ severe sentence; *lagens strängaste* ~ the maximum penalty; *ta sitt* ~ take one's punishment; *till* ~ *för* as (for) [a] punishment for **straffa** punish (*för* for); (*näpsa*) reprove; ~*s med böter eller fängelse* carries a penalty of fines or imprisonment; *synden* ~*r sig själv* sin carries its own punishment **straffad** *a5* punished; *jur.* convicted; *tidigare* ~ previously convicted

straff|arbete penal servitude; *livstids* ~ penal servitude for life; *ett års* ~ one year's hard labour **-bar** *a1* punishable; (*brottslig*) criminal; (*friare*) condemnable **-dom** *Herrens* ~ divine judgement **-eftergift** remission [of penalty] **-exercis** punishment drill **-fri** (*hopskr. straffri*) exempt from punishment **-friförklara** (*hopskr. strafffriförklara*) discharge without penalty, exempt from punishment **-frihet** (*hopskr. straffrihet*) impunity, exemption from punishment **-fånge** (*hopskr. straffånge*) convict **-fängelse** (*hopskr. straffängelse*) penitentiary, convict prison **-föreläggande** (*hopskr. straffföreläggande*) *ung.* order [of summary punishment] **-kast** *sport.* penalty [throw] **-koloni** penal settlement **-lag** criminal (penal) code (law) **-lindring** reduction [of penalty] **-område** *sport.* penalty area **-predikan** hellfire sermon; (*friare*) severe lecture **-påföljd** penalty, [punitive] sanction; *vid* ~ on penalty **-register** criminal (police) records (*pl*) **-ränta** penal interest, interest on arrears **-rätt** *jur.* penal (criminal) law **-rättslig** criminal, penal **-slag** *sport.* penalty [shot] **-spark** *sport.* penalty [kick] **-tid** term of punishment; *avtjäna sin* ~ (*äv.*) undergo one's sentence, *vard.* do one's time

stram *a1* (*spänd*) tight, strained; *bildl.* stiff (*uppträdande* bearing); (*reserverad*) distant; *en* ~ *livsföring* an austere way of life; *en* ~ *kreditpolitik* a stiff (restrictive) credit policy **strama** (*sträckas*) be tight, pull; ~ *åt* tighten, stiffen **stramalj** *s3* canvas [for needlework] **stramhet** [-a:-] tightness *etc.*; *bildl.* stiffness **stramt** [-a:-] *adv* tightly *etc.*; *sitta* ~ be (fit) tight; *hälsa* ~ give a stiff greeting

strand -*en stränder* shore; (*havs-* *äv.*) seashore; (*sand-*) beach; (*flod-*) bank **strand|a** run ashore, be stranded; strand (*äv. bildl.*); *bildl. äv.* fail, break down **-aster** sea aster **-brink** [steep river] bank **-brädd** waterside; brink of the water **-fynd** flotsam, jetsam **-hugg** *göra* ~ (*om sjörövare*) raid a coast, (*om seglare*) go ashore **-ning** stranding *etc.*; *bildl. äv.* failure **-pipare** *zool.*, *större* ~ ringed plover **-promenad** (*väg*) promenade, *AE.* boardwalk **-remsa** strip of shore, foreshore **-råg** lyme grass **-rätt** right to use the beach; (*rätt att bärga vrakgods*) salvage right **-satt** *a4, bildl.* stranded, at a loss (*på* for) **-skata** oystercatcher **-sätta** *bildl.* fail, leave in the lurch **-tomt** beach lot, lakeside site **-vallmo** yellow horned poppy **-ägare** riparian owner

strapats *s3* hardship **-rik** adventurous **strass** *s3* paste, strass; rhinestones (*pl*) **stra|teg** *s3* strategist **-tegi** [*äv.* -'ʃi] *s3* strategy **-tegisk** [-'te:-] *a5* strategic[al] **stratifier|a** stratify **-ing** stratification **stratosfär** stratosphere

strax I *adv* **1** (*om tid*) directly, immediately; (*med ens*) at once; (*om ett ögonblick*) in a moment; [*jag*] *kommer* ~*!* just a moment (minute)!; *klockan är* ~ *12* it is close on twelve o'clock; ~ *efter* just (immediately) after **2** (*om rum*) just (*utanför* outside); ~ *bredvid* close by; *följa* ~ *efter* follow close on **II** *konj*, ~ *jag såg dig* directly (the moment) I saw you

streber ['stre:-] *s2* pusher, climber, thruster; *AE. vard.* go-getter **-aktig** *a1* pushing

streck *s7* **1** (*penndrag*) stroke; (*linje*) line; (*grad-*) mark; (*kompass-*) point; *munnen smalnade till ett* ~ his (*etc.*) mouth became a thin line; *vi stryker* ~ *över det* (*bildl.*) let's forget it; *ett* ~ *i räkningen* a disappointment; *hålla* ~ (*bildl.*) hold good, be true; *artikel under* ~*et* feature article 2 *polit.* qualification 3 *(kläd-)* cord, line 4 *(spratt)* trick; *ett dumt* ~ a stupid trick

streck|a mark with lines; *(skugga)* hatch; ~ *för* check (tick) off; ~ *under* underline; *~d linje* broken line **-kliché** line block **-ning** *(i ritning e.d.)* streaking; *(skuggning)* hatching **-teckning** line drawing

stred *imperf. av strida*

strejk *s3* strike; *gå i* ~ go (come out) on strike; *vild* ~ wildcat strike

strejk|a strike, go (come out) on strike **-ande** *a4* striking; *de* ~ those (the workers *etc.*) on strike, the strikers; ~ *hamnarbetare* dock strikers **-brytare** strikebreaker, non-striker; *neds.* blackleg, *AE.* scab **-hot** strike threat **-kassa** strike fund **-rätt** right to strike **-vakt** picket **-varsel** strike notice, notice of a strike; *utfärda* ~ serve notice of strike

strepto|kock [-'kåkk] *s3* streptococcus *(pl* streptococci) **-mycjn** *s4* streptomycin

stress *s3* stress **stressa 1** put under pressure **2** *vard.,* *han* ~*de iväg till jobbet* he dashed off to work; *han* ~*de som en galning för att hinna i tid* he rushed off his feet to make it on time **stressad** *a5* under stress (tension); overstrained **stressande** *a4* stressful **stressfaktor** stress factor

streta strive, struggle *(med* with; *mot* against); ~ *emot* resist, struggle against *(äv. bildl.);* ~ *uppför backen* struggle up the hill

1 strid *a1* rapid, violent *(ström* current); torrential *(regn* rain); *gråta* ~*a tårar* weep bitterly

2 strid *s3* struggle *(för* for; *mot* against; *om* about); *(kamp, äv. mil.)* fight, combat, battle; *(dispyt)* dispute, altercation; *inre* ~ inward struggle; *livets* ~ the struggle (battle) of life; *en* ~ *på liv och död* a life and death struggle; *öppen* ~ open war; *en* ~ *om ord* a dispute about mere words; *det står* ~ *om honom* he is the subject of controversy; *i* ~*ens hetta* in the heat of the struggle *(bildl. äv.* debate); *stupa i* ~ be killed in action; *i* ~ *med (mot)* in opposition to, in contravention of; *inlåta sig i* ~ *med* get mixed up in a fight with; *råka i* ~ *med* get into conflict with; *stå i* ~ *mot* be at variance with; *göra klar[t] till* ~ prepare for action; *gå segrande ur* ~*en* emerge victorious from the battle; *ge sig utan* ~ give up without a fight

strid|a *stred -it, v2* **1** fight *(om* for); battle *(för* for); *(friare)* struggle, strive *(för* for); *(tvista)* contend *(om* about) **2** *(stå i motsats [till])* be contrary (opposed, in opposition) to; *det -er mot lagen* it is contrary to (against) the law **stridande** *a4* **1** *mil.* combatant, fighting; *(friare)* contending, opposing; *de* ~ the fighters, *mil.* the combatants **2** *(oförenlig)* adverse, opposed *(mot* to), contrary *(mot* to), incompatible *(mot* with) **stridbar** *a1* fighting *(skick* trim); *(stridslysten)* battling *(sinne* spirit **stridig** *a1* **1** *se stridslysten* **2** *(omstridd)* disputable, disputed; *göra ngn rangen* ~ contend for precedence with s.b., *bildl.* run s.b. close **3** *(motstridig)* contradictory; conflicting; *~a känslor* conflicting feelings **stridighet 1** *(motsättning)* opposition, antagonism **2** *(tvist)* dissension, dispute **stridit** *sup. av strida* **strids|anda** fighting spirit **-beredskap** readi-

ness for action **-domare** umpire **-duglig** in fighting trim; fit for fight **-duglighet** fighting efficiency **-flygare** fighter pilot **-flygplan** fighter aircraft **-fråga** controversial question (issue), point at issue **-gas** war gas **-handling** act of war [fare] **-handske** gauntlet **-häst** charger **-humör** fighting mood **-iver** *i ~n* in the heat of the battle **-krafter** *pl* military [armed] forces **-kämpe** warrior, combatant **-laddning** warhead **-ledning** supreme command **-linje** battle line, front **-lust** fighting spirit **-lycka** fortune[s *pl*] of war **-lysten** eager for battle; *(friare)* aggressive, quarrelsome; argumentative **-lystnad** pugnacity, fighting mood **-medel** weapon **-robot** guided missile with warhead **-rop** war (battle) cry **-skrift** [polemical] pamphlet **-spets** warhead **-tupp** gamecock, fighting cock **-vagn** tank, armoured car **-vagnsförband** armoured unit **-vapen** combat weapon **-vimmel** confusion of battle; *mitt i -vimlet* in the thick of the battle **-yxa** battle-axe; *(indians)* tomahawk; *gräva ner ~n* bury the hatchet *(äv. bildl.)* **-åtgärd 1** *mil.* action **2** *(på arbetsmarknaden)* industrial action **-äpple** apple of discord, bone of contention **-övning** tactical exercise, manoeuvre

strig|el *s2* strop **-la** [-i:-] strop

strike [strajk] *s2 (bowling)* strike

strikt *a1* strict; *(sträng)* severe; ~ *klädd* soberly dressed

stril *s2* spray nozzle **strila** spray; *(spruta)* sprinkle; ~ *in* filter in; ~ *ner* come down steadily

strimla I *s1* strip, shred **II** *v1* cut in strips, shred

strimm|a *s1* streak; *(rand)* stripe; *(i marmor)* vein; *bildl.* gleam **-ig** *a1* streaked, striped

string|ens [-ŋ'gens] *s3* stringency; cogency **-ent** *a1* stringent; logical

strip|a *s1* wisp of hair **II** *v1* strip **-ig** *a1* lank, straggling *(hår* hair)

strippa *vard.* **I** *v1* strip **II** *s1* stripper

strit *s2, zool.* cicada *(pl äv.* cicadae)

strof [-å:-] *s3* stanza

strong [-å-] *a1 (fin)* fine; *(stram)* strict

strontium ['stråntsium] *s8* strontium

stropp [-å-] *s2* **1** strap, strop; *sjö. äv.* sling; *(på skor)* loop **2** *pers.* snooty devil **-ig** *a1* snooty, stuck-up

strosa stroll around; mooch about

struk|en *a5, en* ~ *tesked* a level teaspoonful *(salt* of salt) **-it** *sup. av stryka*

struktur structure; *bildl. äv.* texture **-alism** structuralism **-ell** *a1* structural **-era** structure **-formel** structural formula **-omvandling** structural change (transformation) **-rationalisering** structural rationalization

struma *s1* struma, goitre

strump|a *s1* stocking; *(kort)* sock; *-or (koll.)* hose *(sg)* **-byxor** *pl* [stretch] tights

strumpe|band suspender; *(ringformigt o. AE.)* garter **-bandshållare** suspender *(AE.* garter) belt **-bandsorden** the Order of the Garter

strump|fabrik hosiery, stocking manufactures *(pl)* **-läst** *i ~en* in one's stockinged feet **-sticka** knitting needle **-stoppning** darning of stockings *(etc.)*

strunt *s3, s4* rubbish, trash; *det vore väl* ~ *om* it would be the limit if; *å ~!* bosh!, poppycock!; *~ i det!* never mind!; *prata* ~ talk nonsense (rubbish) **strunt|a** ~ *i* not care a bit about (a fig for) **-förnäm** would-be refined **-prat** nonsense, rubbish; *AE.* boloney **-sak** trifle **-summa** trifle, trifling sum

strup|e *s2* throat; (*svalg*) gorge; (*luft-*) windpipe; *anat.* trachea; (*mat-*) gullet; *få ngt i galen* ~ have s.th. go down the wrong way; *ha kniven på ~n* have no alternative, be at bay **-grepp** stranglehold **-huvud** larynx **-katarr** laryngitis **-ljud** guttural sound, guttural **-lock** epiglottis **-mikrofon** throat microphone **-tag** se *-grepp*

strut *s2* cornet, cone

struts *s2* ostrich **-fjäder** ostrich feather **-plym** ostrich plume **-politik** *bedriva* ~ be unwilling to face unpleasant facts

strutta strut, trip

stryk *s7* (*ge ngn* give s.b.) a beating (whipping); (*i slagsmål*) a thrashing; *få* ~ be beaten (*äv. bildl.*); *ett kok* ~ a good thrashing; *han tigger* ~ (*bildl.*) he is asking for a thrashing; *ful som* ~ ugly as sin

stryk|a *strök strukit* **1** (*med handen e.d.*) stroke; (*släta*) smooth **2** (*med -järn*) iron **3** (*be-, med färg e.d.*) paint, coat; ~ *salva på ett sår* smear ointment on a wound; ~ *smör på brödet* spread [a piece of] bread with butter **4** (*bryna*) whet **5** ~ *eld på en tändsticka* strike a match **6** (*utesluta*) cut out, delete (*ngt i en text* s.th. from a text); (~ *över*) cross (strike) out; *stryk det icke tillämpliga!* cross out what does not apply!; ~ *ngn ur medlemsförteckningen* strike s.b. off the list of members; ~ *ett streck över* draw a line through, *bildl. se streck 1* **7** *sjö.* strike (*flagg* one's colours; *segel* sail) **8** (*ströva*) roam, ramble (*omkring* about); *flygplanet strök över taken* the aeroplane swept over the roofs **9** ~ *askan av en cigarr* knock the ash off a cigar; ~ *handsken av handen* strip the glove off the hand; ~ *håret ur pannan* brush one's hair from one's forehead; ~ *på foten* give in (*för* to) **10** *rfl* rub (*mot* against); ~ *sig om munnen* wipe one's mouth (*med* with); ~ *sig över håret* pass one's hand over one's hair **11** (*med betonad partikel*) ~ *bort* sweep off (away); ~ *fram* pass; ~ *för* mark, check off; ~ *förbi* sweep past; ~ *in* rub in (*salvan* the ointment); ~ *med a*) (*gå åt*) go [too], (*om pengar*) be spent, *b*) (*dö*) die, perish; ~ *omkring* rove [about], (*om rovdjur*) prowl about; ~ *omkring på gatorna* wander about the streets; ~ *på* spread, lay on; ~ *tillbaka* stroke back; ~ *under* underline, *bildl.* emphasize, stress; ~ *ut* (*utplåna*) strike out, (*utradera*) scratch out, erase, (*torka bort*) rub out; ~ *över* (*med färg*) give another coat of paint

stryk|ande *a4*, ~ *aptit* ravenous appetite; *ha* ~ *åtgång* (*hand.*) have a rapid sale **-bräda** ironing board **-erska** ironing woman **-filt** ironing cloth **-fri** noniron **-inrättning** ironing workshop **-järn** [flat]iron **-mangel, -maskin** ironing machine

stryknjn *s4, s3* strychnine

stryk|ning [-y:-] **1** (*smekning*) stroke, stroking; (*gnidning*) rubbing **2** (*med -järn*) ironing **3** (*med färg e.d.*) painting, coating **4** (*uteslutning*) deletion, cancellation **5** *geol.* strike, course

stryk|pojke *bildl.* whipping boy, scapegoat **-rädd** afraid of getting thrashed

stryk|tips results pool **-torr** ready for ironing

stryk|tålig tough, durable **-täck** cheeky, impudent

stryp|a *v3, imperf. äv. ströp* strangle; throttle (*äv. bildl. o. tekn.*); (*friare o. tekn.*) choke **-ning** [-y:-] strangling *etc.*; strangulation; *bildl. äv.* constriction **-sjuka** croup; (*hos djur*) strangles (*pl*) **-ventil** throttle valve

strå *s6* straw (*äv. koll.*); (*hår-*) hair; (*gräs-*) blade; *ett* ~ *vassare* a cut above; *dra det kortaste ~et* get the worst of it, come off worst; *dra sitt* ~ *till stacken* do one's part (bit); *inte lägga två ~n i kors* not lift a finger **-hatt** straw hat

stråk *s7* (*samfärdsled*) passage, course; thoroughfare

stråk|drag stroke of the bow

stråk|e *s2* bow **-ensemble** string ensemble **-föring** bowing; *ha en bra* ~ have a good bow hand **-instrument** string[ed] (bow) instrument **-kvartett** string quartet **-orkester** string orchestra (band)

stråkväg highroad, thoroughfare; *den stora ~en* (*bildl.*) the beaten track

strål|a beam, be radiant (*av glädje* with joy); (*skina*) shine (*äv. bildl.*); (*sprida -ar*) radiate, emit rays **-ande** *a4* beaming, radiant; brilliant (*solsken* sunshine); (*lysande*) brilliant (*äv. bildl.*); ~ *glad* radiantly happy; ~ *ögon* sparkling eyes

strål|behandling radiation treatment, radiotherapy **-ben** *anat.* radius **-blomma** ray flower **-blomstrig** [-å-] *al* radiate **-brytning** refraction **-dos** radiation dose

strål|e *s2* **1** ray, beam; *bildl.* gleam (*av hopp* of hope) **2** (*vätske-*) jet, spray; (*fin*) squirt **3** *bot.* radius **-form** *i* ~ in the form of rays **-formig** [-å-] *al* radiate[d], radiating **-glans** radiance (*äv bildl.*); (*friare*) brilliance **-kamin** radiation heater **-kastare** searchlight; (*på bil*) headlight; (*för fasadbelysning*) floodlight; *teat.* spotlight **-kastarljus** searchlight; *teat.* spotlight; (*fasadbelysning*) floodlight **-kirurgi** radiation surgery **-knippe** bunch (pencil) of rays **-ning** [-å:-] beaming *etc.*; (*ut-*) radiation; (*be-*) irradiation

strålnings|biologi radiation biology **-detektor** radiation detector **-energi** radiant energy, emissive power **-kemi** radiation chemistry **-källa** source of radiation **-mätare** *kärnfys.* radiation meter, radiac dosimeter **-olycka** radiation accident **-risk** [ionizing] radiation risk **-skydd** protection against radiation **-värme** radiant heat **-värmare** radiant heater

strål|sjuka radiation sickness **-skada** radiation damage (*på pers.* injury) **-skydd** se *strålningsskydd* **-svamp** *koll.* actinomycete **-svampsjuka** *veter.* actinomycosis, *vard.* lumpy jaw

stråt *s2* path, way **-rövare** highwayman, brigand: footpad

sträck **1** *n, utan pl, i* [*ett*] ~ at a stretch, on end; *vara borta månader i* ~ be away for months on end; *läsa timmar i* ~ read for five hours without stopping; *sova hela natten i ett* ~ sleep all night through **2** *s7* (*flyttfågels-*) flight (track) of migratory birds

sträck|a I *s1* stretch; (*väg-*) length, distance, way; (*järnvägs-*) section, run **II** *v3* **1** (*räcka ut; tänja; spänna*) stretch (*händerna mot* one's hand to[wards]; *på benen* one's legs; *en lina* a rope); (*ut-*) extend; (*för-*) strain (*en sena* a tendon); ~ *på sig* straighten (pull) o.s. up, stretch **2** ~ *kölen till ett fartyg* lay [down] the keel of a vessel **3** ~ *vapen* lay down one's arms, surrender **4** (*om fåglar*) migrate **5** *rfl a*) (*ha utsträckning*) stretch, extend, *b*) (~ *ut kroppen*) stretch o.s., *c*) (*räcka*) stretch [out], reach; ~ *sig längs kusten* run along the coast; *längre än till 10 pund -er jag mig inte* I will go no farther than £ 10; ~ *sig över 10 år* extend over a period of ten years; ~ *ut sig på sängen* stretch out on the bed **6** (*med betonad partikel*) ~ *fram handen* hold out one's hand; ~ *upp sig a*) *se sträcka* [*på sig*], *b*) (*klä sig fin*) dress up; ~ *ut a*) extend, stretch out, *b*) (*förlänga*) prolong (*äv. bildl.*), *c*) (*gå fort*) stride (step) out; ~ *ut huvudet genom fönstret* put one's head out of the window; *låta hästen* ~ *ut* give one's horse its head **-bänk** rack; *ligga på ~en* be on the rack; *hålla ngn på ~en* (*bildl.*) keep s.b. on tenterhooks **-förband** traction bandage **-läsa** read without stopping **-ning** (*-ande*) stretching *etc.*; (*ut-*) extension; (*riktning*) direction; (*för-*) strain

1 sträng *a1* severe (*kyla* cold); (*ytterst noggrann*) strict (*disciplin* discipline), rigorous (*rättvisa* justice), rigid (*uppsikt* supervision); (*allvarlig*) stern (*min* look), austere (*uppsyn* countenance); ~*t arbete* exacting work; *hålla* ~ *diet* be on a strict diet; *vara* ~ *mot* be severe (*mot barn*: strict) with

2 sträng *s2* (*mus.*; *båg-*) string (*äv. bildl.*); *bildl. äv.* chord; *ha flera ~ar på sin lyra* (*båge*) (*bildl.*) have more than one string to one's bow

stränga string; ~ *sin lyra* (*bildl.*) tune one's harp (lyre)

strängaspel playing upon a stringed instrument

sträng|eligen strictly, severely; *jfr strängt* **-het** severity; strictness, rigour

stränginstrument stringed instrument

strängt *adv* **1** severely *etc.*; *arbeta* ~ work hard; ~ *förbjudet* strictly forbidden (prohibited); ~ *hållen* (*om barn*) strictly brought up; ~ *konfidentiellt* strictly confidential; ~ *upptagen* fully occupied, pressed for time **2** (*noga*) *hålla* ~ *på* observe rigorously; ~ *taget* strictly speaking

sträv *a1* rough; (*i smak o. bildl.*) harsh; (*barsk*) stern, gruff; ~ *smak* (*äv.*) acerbity; *under den ~a ytan* (*bildl.*) under the rough (rugged) surface

1 sträva *s1*, *byggn.* strut, shore; (*sned*) brace

2 sträva *v1* strive; (*knoga*) toil; ~ *att* endeavour to; ~ *efter* strive for; ~ *mot himlen* (*om torn e.d.*) soar aloft; ~ *med* work hard at, struggle with; ~ *till* aspire to; ~ *uppåt* strive upwards, *bildl.* aim high

strävan *best. form strävan, pl -den* striving, aspiration; (*ansträngning*) effort; (*möda*) labour, toiling; (*bemödande*) endeavour; *misslyckas i sin* ~ fail in one's efforts; *hela min* ~ *går ut på att* it is my greatest ambition to

strävbåge *byggn.* flying buttress

sträv|het [-ä:-] roughness, harshness *etc.* (*jfr sträv.*); (*i smak*) acerbity, asperity **-hårig** rough--haired; (*om hund*) wire-haired

strävpelare *byggn.* buttress

strävsam [-ä:-] *a1* **1** (*arbetsam*) assiduous, industrious, hard-working **2** (*mödosam*) laborious, strenuous; *föra ett ~t liv* lead a strenuous life **-het** industriousness; thrift

strävt [-ä:-] *adv, ha det* ~ have a hard time of it

strö I *s7* litter **II** *v4* strew; sprinkle (*socker på* sugar on; *över* over); ~ ... *omkring sig* scatter [... about]; ~ *pengar omkring sig* splash money around; ~ *rosor för ngn* (*bildl.*) flatter s.b.

ströare castor, dredger **ströbröd** breadcrumbs

strödd *a5*, ~*a anmärkningar* casual remarks; ~*a anteckningar* odd notes

strög *s7* main street, boulevard

strök *imperf. av stryka*

strökund odd (stray) customer

ström [-ömm] *s2* **1** (*flod*) stream; river (*äv. bildl.*); (*flöde*) flood (*av tårar* of tears), flow (*av ord* of words); (*häftig*) torrent (*äv. bildl.*); *en* ~ *av folk* a stream of people; *en* ~ *av blod* a stream of blood; *gästerna kom i en jämn* ~ the guests arrived in a steady stream; *vinet flöt i ~mar* wine flowed freely **2** (*i luft, vatten; äv. elektr.*) current; *bildl. äv.* tide; *följa med ~men* (*äv. bildl.*) follow the tide, drift with the current; *gå mot ~men* go against the current (*friare o. bildl.*: tide); *stark* ~ (*i vatten*) rapid current; *sluta* ~*men* switch on the current, close the circuit **-avbrott** power failure; (*avstängning*) power cut **-brytare** switch; (*för motor e.d. äv.*) circuit breaker **-drag** current; race **-fåra** stream (*äv. bildl.*); (*flodbädd*) bed **-förande** *a4* live, charged; *vara* ~ be alive **-förbrukning** power (current) consumption **-fördelare** (*i bil*) distributor **-försörjning** power (current) supply **-kantring** *bildl.* turn of the tide (*äv. om tidvatten*), changeover **-karlen** [-ka:ren] *se näcken* **-krets** circuit **-linje** streamline **-linjeform** streamlining, streamlined shape **-linjeformad** [-å-] *a5* streamlined **-lös** *elektr.* dead **-löshet** absence of current

strömma stream, flow; (*om regn, tårar*) [come] pour[ing]; (*häftigt*) gush, rush; *den välvilja som ~de emot mig* the goodwill that met me; ~ *fram* pour out; ~ *in* rush in, [come] pour[ing] in; *folk ~de till* people came flocking; ~ *ut* stream (*etc.*) out, (*om gas e.d.*) escape; *folk ~de ut ur teatern* people came pouring out of the theatre; ~ *över* overflow

strömming Baltic herring

ström|mätare *elektr.* amperemeter, ammeter; *se äv. elmätare* **-ning** current, flow, stream; *bildl.* current, tide **-riktning** direction of current **-skena** conductor rail **-snål** electricity-saving **-stare** dipper, water ouzel **-styrka** *elektr.* current [intensity], amperage **-stöt** current rush, impulse

ström|t *a4, end. i n,* ~ *vatten* rapid-flowing water **-virvel** whirl[pool], eddy

ströp *imperf. av strypa*

ströppla *fack.* stipple

strö|skrift pamphlet, tract **-socker** granulated (castor) sugar

strössel ['strôss-] *s9, s7, ej pl, fack.* hundreds and thousands (*pl*)

ströv|a stroll, ramble; wander; (~ *hit o. dit*) stray; ~ *omkring* range, rove; ~*nde renar* stray

reindeer **-område** rambling area **-tåg** ramble, excursion; *pl äv.* wanderings; *bildl.* excursion
1 stubb *se rubb [och stubb]*
2 stubb *s2 (av säd e.d.)* stubble; *(skägg-)* bristles *(pl)*
stubb|a crop *(håret* the hair); *dock (svansen på en hund* a dog's tail) **-brytare** *(hopskr. stubbrytare)* [stump] grubber (puller) **-brytning** *(hopskr. stubbrytning)* stump pulling
stubb|e *s2* stump, stub **-ig** *a1* stubbed, stubb[l]y **-svans** bobtail, docked tail **-åker** stubble field
stubjn *s3*, **-tråd** fuse
stuck *s3* stucco **-atur** stucco [work] **-atör** stucco worker
stuck|en *a5, bildl.* nettled, offended **-it** *sup. av sticka II*
student [university, college] student, undergraduate; *ta ~en* qualify for entrance to a university **-betyg** higher school certificate; *Storbritannien* General Certificate of Education at Advanced level (A level) **-bostad** room in [student] hall of residence, student flat **-examen** higher school examination; *Storbritannien* [examination for the] General Certificate of Education at Advanced level *(förk.* G.C.E. at A level) **-förening** student association **-hem** students' hostel; *AE.* dorm[itory] **-ikos** [-'kå:s] *a1* student-like; carefree, high-spirited **-kamrat** fellow student **-kår** students' union **-liv** university (college) life **-mössa** student's cap **-rabatt** student reduction **-rum** room in [student] hall of residence **-ska** girl student; undergraduate; *AE. vard. äv.* co-ed **-skrivning** written examination for entrance to a university
studer|a study *(språk* languages; *till läkare* to be a doctor); *~ medicin (äv.)* be a student of medicine; *~ juridik* study (read) law; *låta sina barn ~* let one's children go to college (the university); *~ vid universitetet* study (be) at the university, go to college; *en ~d karl* a scholar, a man with a university education **-ande I** *s9* student *(vid* at); *(vid univ. o. högskola)* undergraduate; *(skolelev)* pupil; *ekonomie ~* student of economics; *juris ~* law student, student of law; *medicine ~* medical student; *odontologie ~* dental surgery student; *teknologie ~* student of engineering (technology); *teologie ~* divinity student, student of theology (divinity) **II** *a4, den ~ ungdomen* schoolboys and schoolgirls, [the] young people at college (the university) **-kammare** study
studie ['stu:-] *s5* study *(över, av* of); *(konstnärs äv.)* sketch *(av* of); *(litterär)* essay *(över* on) **-begåvning** aptitude for studies; *han är en ~* he is a gifted student **-besök** educational (study) visit **-cirkel** adult education class, study circle **-dag** teachers' seminar **-finansiering** study support **-handbok** guide for students **-intyg** proof of registration **-kurs** course of studies **-ledare** leader of a study circle **-ledighet** study (educational) leave **-lån** study loan **-material** study material **-medel** study support **-objekt** object of study **-plan** plan of studies, curriculum; *(för visst ämne)* syllabus **-rektor** *ung.* director of studies **-resa** study trip **-rådgivare** educational adviser **-rådgivning** educational guidance **-skuld** study debt, debt incurred for higher edu-

cation **-stöd** study support **-stödsnämnd** *centrala ~en* [the Swedish] national board for educational assistance **-syfte** *i ~ for* purposes of study **-teknik** study technique **-år** *pl* years of study
studio ['stu:-] *s5* studio **studiosus** [-ˣɔ:-, -ˣå:-] *r* student
studi|um ['stu:-] *s4* study; *bli föremål för ett ingående ~* be the subject of close study; *bedriva -er* study; *lärda -er* advanced studies; *musikaliska -er* the study *(sg)* of music; *vetenskapliga -er* scientific research
studs *s2* rebound, bounce **studsa** rebound, bounce *(mot väggen* off the wall); *(om kula)* ricochet; *bildl.* start, be taken aback **studsare** sporting rifle
studs|matta trampoline **-ning** rebounding *etc.*; repercussion
stug|a *s1* cottage; *(vardagsrum)* living room **-by** holiday village **-knut** cottage corner **-sittare** home-body
1 stuka *s1* potato *(etc.)* clamp
2 stuka *v1* **1** *(kroppsdel)* sprain **2** *(deformera)* batter, knock out of shape; *bildl.* browbeat, crush, humiliate **3** *tekn.* upset, jump
stukning [-u:-] **1** spraining; *en ~* a sprain **2** battering *etc.*; browbeating, humiliation **3** upsetting
stul|en *perf. part. av stjäla* **-it** *sup. av stjäla*
stulta *v1 (om barn)* toddle
stum [stumm] *a1* dumb; *(mållös)* mute *(beundran* admiration); *(som inte uttalas)* silent, mute; *~ av förvåning* dumb with astonishment; *bli ~* be struck dumb *(av* with) *(ej fjädrande)* rigid **-film** silent film **-fin** *~ linje (boktr.)* obtuse (blunt) line **-het** dumbness; muteness
stump *s2* stump, end; *sjunga en ~* sing a tune **stumpa** *s1* toddler; poppet
stund *s3* while; *(ögonblick)* moment, instant, minute; *(eg. timme)* hour; *en god ~* quite a while; *det dröjde en ~ innan* it was some little time before; *en liten ~* a few minutes, a short while; *han har sina ljusa ~er* he has his bright moments; *när ~en är kommen* when one's hour has come; *min sista ~* my last hour; *från första ~[en]* from the [very] first moment; *för en ~ sedan* a [little] while (few minutes) ago; *i denna ~* [at] this [very] moment; *ännu i denna ~ vet jag inte* I don't know to this [very] moment; *i farans ~* in the hour of danger; *i samma ~* at the same moment *(som* when); *i sista ~[en]* at the [very] last moment, just in time; *om en liten ~* in a little while, presently; *på lediga ~er* in one's spare (leisure) moments; *adjö på en ~!* so long!
stund|a approach, be at hand **-ande** *a4 (nästkommande)* next; *(in-)* coming **-ligen** constantly **-om** [-åm] at times; *se äv. ibland* **-tals** [-a:-] now and then; at intervals
stungit *sup. av stinga*
stup *s7* precipice, steep **stupa 1** *(falla omkull)* fall; *hästen ~de under honom* his horse went down under him; *~ i säng* tumble into bed; *~ på en uppgift (bildl.)* fail in a task; *jag var nära att ~ av trötthet* I was ready to drop [with fatigue], was tired to death **2** *(i strid)* fall, die, be killed; *de ~de (subst.)* the killed (fallen) **3** *(brant sänka sig)* descend abruptly, incline sharply **4** *(luta)* tip *(en*

S

balja a tub)
stup|full reeling drunk **-rör** drainpipe **-stock** block
sturig *a1* sullen, sulky
stursk *a1* (*uppstudsig*) insolent, impudent; (*fräck*) brazen; (*högfärdig*) stuck-up; *vara ~* (*äv.*) give o.s. airs, show off **-het** insolence; bumptiousness
stuss *s2* seat; *vard.* bottom, behind
stut *s2* steer **-eri** stud [farm]
stuv *s2* remnant [of cloth]; *~ar* (*äv.*) oddments
1 stuva *kokk.* cook in white sauce; *~d potatis* potatoes in white sauce
2 stuva (*inlasta*) stow; (*kol, säd äv.*) trim; *~ om* shift, rearrange; *~ undan* stow away
stuvare stevedore, longshoreman
stuvbit *se stuv*
stuveri|arbetare *se stuvare* **-förman** stevedore's foreman
1 stuvning [-u:-] (*kött-*) stew; (*vit sås*) white sauce
2 stuvning [-u:-] (*inlastning*) stowage, stowing
stybb *s3, s4* coal dust; *sport.* cinders (*pl*)
styck *oböjligt s* piece; *per ~* each, a piece; *1 krona [per] ~* 1 krona each (a piece); *kostnad per ~* piece cost, cost each; *pris per ~* price each
stycka 1 *slaktar.* cut up **2** (*uppdela*) divide up; (*~ sönder*) cut into pieces; *~ till tomter* parcel out in plots
stycke *s6* **1** (*bit, del*) piece (*bröd* of bread); (*avsnitt*) part; (*lösryckt*) fragment; *ett ~ land* a piece of land; *bestå av ett enda ~* consist of one single piece; *jag har hunnit ett bra ~* I have made considerable progress (*på* with); *i ett ~* all [in] one piece, all of a piece; *slå i ~n* smash, knock to pieces **2** (*avdelning*) part, section (*av en bok* of a book); (*ställe*) passage; (*i skrift*) paragraph; (*musik-*) piece [of music]; (*teater-*) play; *tredje ~t nedifrån* third paragraph from below; *sjunga ett ~* sing a song; *valda ~n* selected pieces (passages) **3** (*hänseende*) respect, regard; *i många ~n* in many respects **4** (*exemplar*) piece; specimen, *vi var tio ~n* we were ten, there were ten of us; *kan jag få tio ~n* may I have ten; *ett par ~n* a couple of; *en tjugo, trettio ~n* twenty, thirty or so **5** (*väg*) way; (*sträcka*) distance; *det är bara ett litet ~ dit* it is only a short distance, it is not far from here; *ett gott ~ in på nästa år* well on into next year **6** (*neus. om kvinna*) *elakt ~* nasty piece of work; *lättfärdigt ~* trollop **-bruk** gun foundry (factory) **-gods** (*t. sjöss*) general (mixed) cargo; (*t. lands*) part loads; *järnv.* part-load traffic, parcels (*pl*) **-pris** price each (a piece, per unit) **-vis** (*per styck*) by the piece; (*en efter en*) piece by piece, piecemeal
styckjunkare *mil.* sergeant-major of artillery; *AE.* warrant officer
styck|mästare *slaktar.* butcher **-ning 1** cutting up **2** dividing up; partition; (*sönderdelning*) dismemberment
styckvis *se styckevis*
stygg *a1* bad, wicked; (*om barn*) naughty; (*o-täck*) nasty, ugly **-else** abomination **-het** wickedness; naughtiness **-ing** naughty (nasty) thing
stygn [-ŋn] *s7* stitch; *sy med långa ~* tack
stylt|a *s1* stilt; *gå på ~or* walk on stilts

stymp|a maim, mutilate; (*friare o. bildl.*) mangle; (*förvanska text e.d.*) mutilate; *geom.* truncate; *~d kon* (*äv.*) frustum of a cone **-are** (*klåpare*) bungler **-ning** maiming *etc.*, mutilation; truncation
1 styng *s7, sömn.*, *se stygn*
2 styng *s7, se sting*
3 styng *s7* (*insekt*) botfly
styr *r, hålla ~ på, hålla i ~* keep in order (in check); *hålla sig i ~* keep a hold on o.s., restrain o.s.; *över ~, se överstyr*
styr|a *v2* **1** (*föra*) steer (*ett fartyg* a ship; *en bil* a car), (*fartyg äv.*) navigate; (*stå vid rodret*) be at the helm; *~ i hamn* bring into port **2** (*rikta*) direct (*sina steg* one's steps); (*leda*) guide; (*behärska*) control, dominate; *~ sina begär* control one's desires; *~ sin tunga* curb one's tongue; *~ sig* control (master) o.s.; *~ allt till det bästa* arrange things for the best, see things through **3** (*bestämma över*) govern, rule (*landet* the country); *~ och ställa i huset* manage the house; *~ och ställa som man vill* have a free hand, *vard.* be cock of the roost **4** *språkv.* govern (*genitiv* the genitive) **5** (*med betonad partikel*) *~ om* (*bildl.*) see to (about); *~ om att* see to it that; *det skall jag ~ om* I will see to it that; *~ till, se ställa [till]*; *~ till sig* get [o.s.] into a mess; *vad du har -t till dig!* what a fright you look!; *~ ut från land* stand off shore; *~ ut till sjöss* make for the open sea; *~ ut sig* dress up
styr|ande *a4* governing (*myndighet* body); *de ~* those in power, *vard.* the powers that be **-bar** *a1* steerable, dirigible **-bord** ['sty:r-] *s, böjligt endast i genitiv, sjö.* starboard; *för ~s halsar* on the starboard tack **-bordslanterna** starboard light
styre *s6* **1** (*fartygs*) helm; (*-stång*) handlebar[s *pl*] **2** rule; *sitta vid ~t* be in power (at the helm)
styrelse 1 *abstr.* government; administration, regime **2** *konkr.* (*bolags-*) board [of directors]; (*förenings-*) council, committee; *sitta i ~n* be on the board **-berättelse** annual report, report of the board **-ledamot** director, member of the board (council, committee); *han är ~ i* he is on the board [of directors] of **-ordförande** chairman of the board (committee) **-sammanträde** board (committee) meeting **-sätt** system (form) of government
styrenplast polystyrene
styr|esman governor; (*föreståndare*) director **-fart** *sjö.* steerage-way **-förmåga** manoeuvrability **-hytt** pilot house, wheelhouse **-inrättning** steering gear
styrk|a I *s1* **1** strength (*hos, i* of); (*kropps- äv.*) vigour; (*kraft*) power; force; (*intensitet*) intensity; *den råa ~n* brute force; *med hela sin ~* with all one's strength; *har aldrig varit min ~* has never been my strong point; *pröva sin ~ på* try one's strength on; *vinna ~* gain strength, (*om sak*) gain [in] force **2** (*krigs-, arbetar-*) force; (*numerär*) number[s *pl*]; *väpnad ~* armed force **II** *v3* **1** (*stärka*) strengthen, confirm; (*ge ~*) fortify; *-t av mat och dryck* fortified with food and drink **2** (*bevisa*) prove, give proof of; (*med vittne*) attest, verify; (*bekräfta*) confirm; *-t avskrift* attested copy
styrke|demonstration display of [military]

power **-förhållande** *ett ojämnt* ~ uneven odds **-grad** [degree of] strength **-tår** bracer, pick-me--up

styr|man ['sty:r-] mate; *förste* ~ first mate (officer) **-medel** instrument[s] of control **-ning** [-y:-] steering; *(manövrering)* operation control; *(ledning)* management **-organ** *flyg.* controls *(pl)*; *data.* control unit **-sel** ['styrr-] *s9 (stadga)* firmness; *bildl.* stability **-skena** guide rail **-snäcka** steering box **-spak** steering lever; *flyg.* control column **-spindel** steering knuckle **-stång** *(på cykel)* handlebar **-teori** control theory **-växel** steering gear **-åra** steering oar

styv *a1* **1** *(stel)* stiff *(i lederna* in the joints); *(spänd)* tight, rigid *(fjäder* spring); ~ *bris* stiff breeze; *visa sig på ~a linan (bildl.)* show off; ~ *i korken (vard.)* cocky, snooty **2** *en* ~ *timme* a good hour; *ett ~t arbete (tungt)* a stiff (tough, hard) job **3** *(skicklig)* clever *(i* in, at), good *(i* at); capital *(simmare* swimmer); ~ *i engelska* good at English

styv|barn stepchild **-bror** stepbrother **-dotter** stepdaughter

styver ['sty:-] *s9, s2* stiver; farthing; *hålla på ~n* stick to one's cash, be tightfisted

styv|far stepfather **-förälder** step-parent

styv|hala *sjö.* haul taut **-het** [-y:-] stiffness *etc.*

styv|moderlig stepmotherly; *(friare)* grudging, unfair *(behandling* treatment) **-mor** stepmother **-morsviol** wild pansy, heartsease, *AE.* Johnny--jump-up

styv|na [-y:-] stiffen, become (get, grow) stiff **-nackad** *a5, bildl.* obstinate **-sint** *a1* obstinate, headstrong, stubborn **-sinthet** obstinacy, stubbornness

styv|son stepson **-syskon** stepbrothers and stepsisters **-syster** stepsister

styvt [-y:-] *adv* **1** stiffly *etc.*; *hålla* ~ *på a) (ngt)* insist [up]on, *b) (ngn)* se great store by, think a lot of **2** *(duktigt)* det var ~ *gjort!* well done!

stå *stod stått* **1 1** *eg.* stand [up]; *han har redan lärt sig* ~ he has already learnt to stand; *han stod hela tiden* he stood (was standing [up]) the whole time; *det ~r en stol där* there is a chair [standing] there; *få* ~ *(inte sitta)* have to stand; *låta ngn* ~ *(inte sitta)* let s.b. stand [up]; ~ *ostadigt* wobble, *(om sak äv.)* be shaky (rickety); ~ *stilla* keep still, not move; *tornet ~r ännu* the tower is still standing; *kom som du går och ~r!* come just as you are! ~ *och vänta* stand (be) waiting; ~ *inte där och se dum ut!* don't stand there looking foolish! **2** *(vara)* be, stand; *(vara placerad)* be placed; *(ha sin plats)* be kept; *(äga bestånd)* remain, last, exist; *(vara skrivet)* be written; *grinden ~r öppen* the gate is open; *maten ~r och kallnar* the food is getting cold; *hans liv stod inte att rädda* his life couldn't be saved; *låta ngt* ~ *(inte flytta)* leave, *(inte röra)* leave alone, *(om ord e.d.)* keep; *han ~r som ägare till* he is the owner of; ~ *ensam i livet* be alone in the world; *det ~r dig fritt att* you are free (at liberty) to; ~ *som objekt till* function (act) as the object of; *det kommer att* ~ *dig dyrt* you'll pay for this; *nu* ~*r vi då vackert!* now we are in a fix!; ~ *som ett levande frågetecken* look the picture of bewilderment; *hur ~r det? (sport.)* what is the score?; *det ~r 6–4* the score (it) is six

four; *var skall tallrikarna* ~*?* where do the plates go?; *så länge världen ~r* as long as the world remains (lasts); *det ~r i Biblen* it says in the Bible, the Bible says; *vad ~r det i tidningen?* what's in the paper?; *det ~r Brown på dörren* there is Brown on the door; *orten ~r inte på kartan* the place is not marked on the map; *läsa vad som ~r om* read what is written about; *var ~r den dikten?* where is that poem to be found? **3** *(inte vara i gång) klockan ~r* the clock has stopped; *klockan har ~tt sedan i morse* the clock has not been going since this morning; *maskinerna ~r stilla* the engines are (stand) idle; *hur länge ~r tåget här?* how long will the train stop (wait) here?; *affärerna (fabriken) ~r stilla* business (the factory) is at a standstill; *mitt förstånd ~r stilla* I just can't think [any more] **4** *(äga rum)* take place; *(om slag)* be fought; *när skall bröllopet* ~*?* when is the wedding to be?; *bröllopet stod i dagarna tre* the wedding went on for three days; *slaget vid Brännkyrka stod år 1518* the battle of Brännkyrka was fought in 1518 **5** ~ *sitt kast* take the consequences; ~ *risken* run the risk, chance it **II** *rfl* **1** *(hålla sig)* keep; *mjölken ~r sig inte till i morgon* the milk won't keep until tomorrow; *målningen har ~tt sig bra* the paint has worn well; *det vackra vädret ~r sig* the fine weather will last **2** *(klara sig)* manage; ~ *sig bra i konkurrensen* hold one's own in competition; *vi ~r oss på några smörgåsar* a few sandwiches will keep us going; *vi ~r oss till middagen* we can do (manage) until dinner **III** *(med obetonad prep)* **1** *det är ingenting att* ~ *efter (eftertrakta)* that is not worth while; ~ *efter ngns liv* seek a p.'s life **2** ~ *för a) (ansvara för)* be responsible (answer) for, *b) (sköta)* be in charge of, *c) (innebära)* represent, stand for; ~ *för betalningen* pay; ~ *för dörren (bildl.)* be approaching (imminent); ~ *för följderna* take the consequences; ~ *för vad man säger* stand by what one has said; *det yttrandet får* ~ *för honom* if he has said so, he'll have to stand by it **3** ~ *i affär* work in a shop; ~ *i blom* be in bloom; ~ *i förbindelse med* be in touch with; ~ *i genitiv* be in the genitive; ~ *i ljuset för ngn* be in a p.'s light; ~ *i tur* be next; ~ *i vatten till fotknölarna* be up to one's ankles in water; ~ *i vägen för ngn* be in a p.'s way; *aktierna ~r i 100 kronor* the shares are quoted at 100 kronor; *ha mycket att* ~ *i* have many things to attend to **4** *företaget ~r och faller med honom* the venture (business) stands or falls with him **5** *valet ~r mellan* the choice lies between **6** *klänningen ~r vackert mot hennes hår* the dress goes well with her hair; *uppgift ~r mot uppgift* one statement contradicts the other **7** ~ *på benen* stand on one's legs, (~ *upp)* stand [up]; ~ *på egna ben* stand on one's own feet; *det får* ~ *på framtiden* we must let the matter rest for the time being; ~ *på näsan* fall on one's face; ~ *på sin rätt* stand on one's rights; *barometern ~r på regn* the barometer is pointing to rain; *termometern ~r på noll* the thermometer is at zero **8** *hoppet ~r till* my (etc.) hope is in; ~ *till förfogande* be available (at disposal); ~ *till svars för* be held responsible for; *vattnet ~r mig till knäna* the water comes up to my knees **9** ~ *under förmyndare* be under guardianship, have a guardian **10** *det ~r mig upp*

S

i halsen I'm fed up to the teeth with it **11** ~ *vid sitt ord* stand by (stick to) one's word **IV** (*med betonad partikel*) **1** ~ *bakom* (*stödja*) be behind, support, (*ekonomiskt*) sponsor **2** ~ *bi a*) (*räcka till*) last, hold out, *b*) (*stödja*) support **3** ~ *efter a*) (*komma efter*) come after, follow, *b*) (*bli förbigången*) be passed over (*för ngn* by s.b.); *låta ngt* ~ *efter för ngt annat* let s.th. be neglected in favour of s.th. else **4** ~ *emot, se motstå* **5** ~ *fast* be firm; ~ *fast vid* stand by **6** ~ *framme* (*framtagen e.d.*) be out (ready), (*t. påseende*) be displayed, (*skräpa*) be [left] about **7** ~ *för* (*skymma*) stand in front of; *det ~r för mig att* I have an idea that **8** ~ *i* (*knoga*) work hard, keep at it; *arbeta och* ~ *i* be busy working **9** *jag lät pengarna* ~ *inne på banken* I left the money on deposit **10** ~ *kvar* (*förbli stående*) remain standing, (*stanna*) remain, stay **11** ~ *på* (*vara påkopplad*) be on; *det stod inte länge på förrän* it was not long before; *vinden stod på hela dagen* the wind blew all day; *fartyget ~r hårt på* the ship is fast aground; ~ *på sig* (*hävda sig*) hold one's own, (*inte ge vika*) be firm; ~ *på dig!* don't give in!; *vad ~r på?* what's going on? **12** *hur ~r det till?* how are you?; *hur ~r det till hemma?* how is your family?; *det ~r illa till med henne* she is in a bad way; *så ~r det till* [*med den saken*] that is how matters stand; *det här ~r inte rätt till* there is something the matter with this; *de åt så det stod härliga till* they were eating like anything **13** *han fick alltid* ~ *tillbaka för sin bror* he was always pushed into the background by his brother **14** ~ *upp, se uppstå* **15** ~ *ut a*) (*skjuta ut*) stand out, project, protrude, *b*) (*härda ut*) stand (put up with) it; ~ *ut med* stand, bear, put up with **16** ~ *över a*) (*i rang*) be above [in rank], (*vara överlägsen*) be superior (*ngn* to s.b.), *b*) (*hålla efter*) stand above, *c*) (*vänta*) wait (*till* till), *d*) (*i spel*) pass [one's turn], miss a turn
stående I *a4* standing; (*stilla-*) stationary (*bil* car); *bli* ~ *a*) (*bli kvar*) remain standing, *b*) (*stanna*) stop, come to a standstill; ~ *armé* (*skämt*) standing (army) joke; *en* ~ *rätt på matsedeln* a standing dish on the menu; *ett* ~ *uttryck* a stock phrase; *de närmast* ~ those immediately around him (*etc.*); *på* ~ *fot* offhand **II** *s6* standing position; *~t blev tröttsamt* having to stand was tiring
ståhej [-'hejj] *s7* hullabaloo, fuss
stål *s7* steel **-band** steel strip (tape) **-blank** [as] bright as steel **-borste** wire brush **-fjäder** steel spring **-grå** steel[y] grey **-hjälm** steel helmet **-kant** steel edge **-klädd** steel clad **-konstruktion** steel structure **-lina** steel rope (wire, cable) **-penna** [pen] nib **-plåt** steel plate, sheet steel **-rör** steel tube **-sätta** *bildl.* steel, brace; ~ *sig* brace (harden) o.s. **-tråd** [steel] wire **-trådsnät** wire netting **-ull** steel wool (shavings *pl*) **-verk** steelworks (*sg o. pl*)
stånd *s7, i bet. 6 -et ständer* **1** (*skick*) state, condition; (*gott* ~) repair, keeping; *få till* ~ bring about; *komma till* ~ come (be brought) about, be realized; *sätta i* ~ *a*) (*ngt*) put in order, *b*) (*ngn*) put in a position, enable; *sätta ngn ur* ~ make s.b. incapable (*att tala* of speaking), make s.b. unfit (*att arbeta* for work); *sätta ngt ur* ~ damage s.th., put s.th. out of order; *vara i* ~ *till* be able (*att ar-*

beta to work), be capable (*att arbeta* of working); *vara ur* ~ *att* be unable to **2** (*ställning*) stand; *hålla* ~ hold one's ground, hold out; *hålla* ~ *mot* resist **3** (*salubod*) stall, booth **4** (*planta*) stand **5** (*levnadsställning*) station, status; *ogift* ~ unmarried state; *äkta ~et* the married state; *inträda i det äkta ~et* enter into matrimony **6** (*samhällsklass*) rank, class; (*andligt spiritual*) estate; *gifta sig under sitt* ~ marry beneath one['s station]; *de fyra ~en* the four Estates **7** *vard.* (*erektion*) hard-on; *få* ~ (*äv.*)
stånd|a *se stå* **-aktig** *a1* steadfast, stable; *vara* ~ (*äv.*) stand firm, persevere **-aktighet** steadfastness, stability; perseverance
ståndar|e 1 (*stöd*) standard, upright **2** *bot.* stamen (*pl äv.* stamina) **-knapp** anther **-mjöl** pollen
stånd|punkt standpoint, position; *bildl.* point of view; *välja* ~ take up a position (an attitude); *ändra* ~ take up another position (attitude), revise one's opinion; *stå på en hög* ~ be at a very high level; *på sakernas nuvarande* ~ in the present state of things, as matters stand now **-rätt** *mil.* martial law
stånds|cirkulation movement of persons from one social class to another **-mässig** *a1* consistent with one's station [in life] **-person** person of rank **-riksdag** Diet of the Four Estates **-samhälle** *ung.* class society
stång *-en stänger* **1** (*tjock*) pole, staff; (*tunnare*) bar, rod; (*stift*) stick; *hålla ngn ~en* (*bildl.*) hold one's own against s.b.; *flagga på halv* ~ fly the flag [at] half-mast **2** *sjö.* pole, spar **3** (*i betsel*) bar
stånga butt; (*spetsa på hornen*) toss [on the horns] **stångas** *dep* butt; (*stånga varandra*) butt each other
stångjärn bar (rod) iron
stångjärns|hammare tilt [hammer] **-smedja** ironworks forge **-smide** hammered iron
stång|korv sausage of barley and meat **-krok** (*fiskeredskap*) ledger tackle **-piska** queue **-störtning** *sport.* tossing the
1 stånka *s1* tankard
2 stånka *v1* puff and blow; (*stöna*) groan
stånkande *a4* puffing and blowing; groaning
ståplats standing room **-läktare** stand with standing accommodation
ståt *s3* splendour, grandeur; *med stor* ~ with great pomp, in great style **ståta** parade; ~ *med* make a great display of, show off
ståthållare governor
ståtlig [-å:-] *a1* (*praktfull*) magnificent, grand; (*imponerande*) impressive (*byggnad* edifice); stately (*hållning* bearing); *en* ~ *karl* a fine-looking fellow
stått *sup. av stå*
stäcka *v3* clip; *bildl.* foil, thwart, (*ngns planer* a p.'s plans)
städ *s7* anvil (*äv. anat.*)
städa (*göra rent*) clean, *AE. vard.* fix up (*en våning* a flat); (*ställa i ordning*) put things straight (*på skrivbordet* on the desk); (*ha storstädning i*) clean out; ~ *efter* tidy up after; ~ *efter sig* leave things tidy; ~ *undan* put away (out of the way); ~ *åt ngn* clean for s.b. **städad** *a5* tidy; (*proper*) decent, proper; (*om pers. äv.*) well-behaved

städ|are cleaner **-bolag** cleaning company (agency) **-dille** cleaning mania **-erska** charwoman, cleaning-woman; (*kontors-*) cleaner **-hjälp** charwoman, daily help

städja [-ä:-] *stadde statt* engage, hire

städ|ning [-ä:-] cleaning; tidying [up] *etc.*; charring **-rock** overall; *AE.* smock

städse [-ä:-] always; constantly

städ|skrubb, -skåp broom cupboard

städsla [-ä:-] *se städja*

ställ *s7* **1** (*stöd*) rack, stand **2** (*omgång*) set

ställ|a I *v2* **1** (*placera*) put; place; set; (*~ upprätt*) place (set) upright, stand **2** (*sätta på visst sätt*) set right; (*inställa*) adjust, regulate (*instrument* instruments), set (*klockan på två* the clock at two) **3** (*rikta*) direct (*sina steg* one's steps); (*adressera*) address; *~ anspråk på* make demands on; *~ en fråga till* put a question to; *~ problem under debatt* bring problems up for discussion; *~ ngt på framtiden* let s.th. rest for the time being **4** (*lämna*) give (*borgen* security) **5** (*med prep uttryck*) *~ i ordning* put in order (to rights); *~ i skuggan* put in the shade, *bildl. äv.* obscure, overshadow; *~ ngn inför rätta* commit s.b. for trail; *~s inför frågan om* be faced with the question whether; *~ ngn mot väggen* (*bildl.*) drive s.b. into a corner; *~ stora förväntningar på* have great expectations of; *~ ngn till ansvar för* hold s.b. responsible for; *~ ngt till rätta* put (set) s.th. right **II** (*med betonad partikel*) **1** *~ bort* put aside (down) **2** *~ fram* put forward (*äv. klocka*); *~ fram stolar åt* place chairs for **3** *~ ifrån sig, se ~ bort* **4** *~ in radion* tune in (*på en annan station* another station; *på program 3* to the third program); *~ in i ett skåp* put into a cupboard; *~ in sig på att* make up one's mind to **5** *~ om a*) [re]-adjust (*sin klocka* one's watch), *b*) (*ordna*) see about (to), arrange **6** *~ till* arrange (*kalas* a party); *~ till en scen* make a scene; *vad har han nu -t till?* what has he been up to now?; *så ni har -t till!* what a mess you have made [of it (things)]! **7** *~ tillbaka* put back, replace (*i skåpet* in the cupboard) **8** *~ undan* put away **9** *~ upp a*) (*ställa högre*) put up, (*resa*) raise (*en stege mot väggen* a ladder against the wall), *b*) (*ordna*) arrange (*i en lång rad* in a long file), mil. draw up, *c*) (*deltaga*) take part, join in, (*låta deltaga*) put up; *~ upp sig* form up, get into position; *~ upp sig på linje* line up **10** *~ ut* put out; *~ ut på en mässa* exhibit goods at a fair; *~ ut en växel på* make out (draw) a draft (bill) on **III** *rfl* **1** (*placera sig*) place (station) o.s. (*i vägen för ngn* in a p.'s way); stand (*framför* in front of; *på tå* on tiptoe; *på en stol* on a chair); *~ sig i rad* line up; *~ sig in hos ngn* curry favour with s.b.; *~ sig på ngns sida* side (take sides) with s.b. **2** (*bete sig*) behave (conduct) o.s.; (*låtsas*) feign (*sjuk* illness); *~ sig avvaktande* take up a wait-and-see attitude; *inte veta hur man skall ~ sig* not know what attitude to take; *det -er sig dyrt* it is (will be) expensive; *hur -er du dig till …?* what is your attitude towards …?

ställbar *a1* adjustable

ställ|d *a5* **1** placed *etc.*; *ha det gott -t* be well off; *en växel ~ på* a bill (draft) payable to **2** (*svarslös*) nonplussed; at a loss

ställe *s6* **1** (*plats, rum*) place; (*'fläck'*) spot; (*i skrift*) passage; *på ~t a*) eg. in (at) the place, *b*) (*genast*) on the spot, there and then; *på ~t marsch!* mark time!; *på ~t vila!* stand at ease!; *på annat ~* in (at) another place, somewhere else; *på ngt ~* somewhere; *på ort och ~* on the spot; *på rätt ~* in the right place; *lägga ngt på rätt ~* put s.th. in its proper place; *på vissa (sina) ~n* in some places, here and there **2** *i ~t* instead [of it], (*i dess ~*) in place of it (that); *i ~t för* instead of (*att komma* coming); *sätta ngt i ~t för* substitute s.th. for, replace s.th. with; *om jag vore i ditt ~* if I were you; *upptaga ngn i barns ~* adopt s.b.; *vara ngn i mors ställe* be a mother to s.b.

ställföreträd|ande *a4* acting, deputy, assistant; *~ lidande* vicarious suffering **-are** deputy, proxy, substitute; *vara ~ för* deputize

ställning 1 (*sätt att stå etc.*) position (*äv. mil.*); (*läge*) situation; (*inställning*) attitude; (*social position*) status, standing; (*samlags-*) position; *sport.* core; *ekonomisk ~* financial position; *liggande ~* lying (recumbent) position; *statsrättslig ~* [constitutional] status; *underordnad ~* subordinate position; *i ledande ~* in a key (leading) position; *ta ~ till* decide on, consider, make a decision on **2** *konkr.* stand; (*byggnads-*) scaffold [ing]; (*stomme*) frame

ställnings|krig positional war[fare] **-steg** göra *~* stand at attention **-tagande** *s6* attitude (*till* to); decision; *vårt ~* our standpoint

ställverk *järnv.* signal box (cabin); *elektr.* bridge signal cabin

stämband [ˣstämm-] vocal cord

stäm|d *a5* (*vänligt favourably*) disposed (*mot* towards); *avogt ~ mot* prejudiced against **-gaffel** tuning fork

stämjärn [ˣstämm-] [wood] chisel

1 stämm|a I *s1* **1** (*röst*) voice; *mus.* part; *första ~n* the first (leading, principal) part **2** (*rösträtt*) vote; *ha säte och ~ i* have a seat and a vote in **II** *v2* **1** *mus.* tune; pitch (*högre* higher); *~ högre* (*äv.*) sharp; *~ lägre* (*äv.*) deepen; *~ upp en sång* strike up a song **2** *bildl.*, *det -er* [*sinnet*] *till eftertanke* it gives you s.th. to think about; *jfr äv.* stämd **3** (*passa ihop, överens*) agree, accord, tally; *AE. äv.* check; *~ med originalet* be in accordance with the original; *kassan -er* the cash account balances; *räkenskaperna -er inte* there are discrepancies in the accounts; *räkningen -er* the account is correct; *det -er!* quite right!, that's it!; *~ av* (*bokför.*) tick off, balance; *~ överens* agree, accord

2 stämma *v2* (*hejda*) stem, check; *~ blod* sta[u]nch blood; *det är bättre att ~ i bäcken än i ån* it is better to nip it in the bud

3 stämma I *s1* (*sammankomst*) meeting, assembly **II** *v2* **1** *jur.* bring an action against, sue; *~ ngn som vittne* summon s.b. as a witness **2** *~ möte med ngn* arrange to meet s.b.

1 stämning 1 *mus.* pitch, key, tune; *hålla ~en* keep in tune **2** (*sinnestillstånd*) mood, temper; *en festlig ~* a festive atmosphere; *~en var hög* (*tryckt*) spirits (*pl*) ran high (were depressed); *~en bland folket* (*äv.*) public sentiment; *upprörd ~* agitation, excitement; *komma (vara) i ~* get (be) in the right mood

S

2 stämning *jur.* writ, [writ of] summons; *delge ngn en* ~ serve a writ (summons) on s.b.; *ta ut* ~ *mot* cause a summons to be issued against, sue **stämningsansökan** application for a summons, plaint
stämnings|bild lyrical (sentimental) picture **-full** full of feeling; moving; solemn **-människa** spontaneous person
stämpel *s2* **1** (*verktyg*) stamp, punch; (*mynt-*) die **2** (*avtryck*) stamp (*äv. bildl.*); (*på frimärke*) postmark, cancel; (*guld-, silver-*) hallmark (*äv. bildl.*); (*på varor e.d.*) brand, mark **-avgift** stamp duty (tax) **-dyna** stamp pad **-färg** stamp [ing] (marking) ink **-klocka** time clock **-skatt** stamp duty (tax)
1 stämpla (*med stämpel*) stamp; mark, impress (*äv. bildl.*); (*guld, silver*) hallmark; (*post-*) postmark, cancel; (*skog*) blaze; (*med brännjärn*) brand (*äv. bildl.*)
2 stämpla (*konspirera*) plot, conspire
1 stämpling (*t. 1 stämpla*) stamping *etc.*
2 stämpling (*t. 2 stämpla*) ~*ar* conspiracy, plotting (*sg*), machinations
stäm|skruv [*stämm-] peg **-ton** concert pitch
ständer ['stänn-] *pl, se stånd 6*
ständig *a1* permanent (*sekreterare* secretary); constant (*oro* worry); perpetual; ~ *ledamot* life-member; ~*t utskott* standing committee
stäng|a *v2* shut (*dörren* the door); close; (*med lås*) lock; (*med regel*) bolt; (*med bom*) bar; (*hindra*) bar, obstruct (*utsikten* the view); *vi -er kl. 5* we close at five; ~ *butiken* shut up shop; ~ *dörren efter sig* shut the door behind one; ~ *sin dörr för* close one's door to; *dörren -er sig själv* the door shuts by (of) itself; ~ *en fabrik* shut down (close) a factory; ~ *av, se avstänga*; ~ *igen om sig* shut (lock) o.s. in; ~ *in* sig shut o.s. up; ~ *sig inne på sitt rum* keep (lock o.s. up in) one's room; ~ *till* close, shut [up], lock [up]; ~ *ute* keep (shut) out (*ljuset* the light); ~ *ngn ute* shut s.b. out
stängel *s2* stalk, stem; (*bladlös*) scape
stäng|ning shutting, closing *etc.* **-ningsdags, -ningstid** closing time
stängsel ['stäŋ-] *s7* fence; (*räcke*) rail[ing]; enclosure; *bildl.* bar, barrier **-tråd** fencing wire
stänk *s7* (*vatten-*) sprinkle, sprinkling, drop; (*smuts-*) splash; (*av vattenskum o.d.*) spray; *bildl.* touch, tinge (*av saknad* of regret); *få några grå* ~ *i håret* get a powdering of grey in one's hair
stänk|a *v3* sprinkle (*vatten på* water on; *tvätt* clothes); splash, sp[l]atter; (*småregna*) spit, sprinkle; (*dugga*) drizzle; ~ *ner* splash all over (*med* with); *regnet började* ~ it began to spit **-bord** *sjö.* washboard **-flaska** sprinkler bottle **-ning** sprinkle, sprinkling, splash[ing] **-skydd** (*på bil*) mudflap, splash guard **-skärm** (*på fordon*) mudguard, wing; *AE.* fender
stäpp *s3* steppe **-höns** Pallas's sandgrouse
stärbhus estate [of a deceased person] **-delägare** heir, beneficiary
stärk|a *v3* **1** (*göra stark[are]*) strengthen (*karaktären* the character); fortify (*ngn i hans tro* s.b. in his belief); (*i sht fysiskt*) invigorate; (*bekräfta*) confirm (*misstanken* the suspicion); *äv. med mat och dryck* take some refreshment[s] **2** (*styv-*) starch **-ande** *a4* strengthening *etc.*; ~ *medel*

tonic, restorative **-else** starch **-krage** starched collar **-ning** starching **-skjorta** starched shirt; (*frack-*) dress shirt
stätta *s1* stile
stäv *s2* stem
1 stäva *s1* (*mjölk-*) milk pail
2 stäva *v1, sjö.* head (*norrut* [to the] north)
stävja [-ä:-] check, put a stop to; (*tygla*) restrain; ~ *ngns iver* damp a p.'s ardour
stöd *s7, tekn.* support (*för ryggen* for one's back); prop, stay, foot; *bildl.* support; aid (*för minnet* for the memory); (*om pers.*) support[er]; *ekonomiskt* ~ economic aid (assistance); ~ *för ett påstående* support of a statement; *få* ~ *av* (*i tvist*) be backed up by; *ge* [*sitt*] ~ *åt* support; *med* ~ *av* with the support of; *som* ~ *för* (*bildl.*) in confirmation (as a proof) of; *ta* ~, *se stödja* [*sig*]
stöd|a *v2, se stödja* **-aktion** [action to] support **-de** *imperf. av stödja*
stöddig *a1* heavily built; substantial; *vard.* stuck-up
stödförband [emergency] splint
stödja [-ö:-] *stödde stött* support; (*stötta*) prop [up]; (*friare o. bildl.*) sustain; (*luta*) rest (*huvudet i handen* one's head in one's hand); (*grunda*) found, base (*sina uttalanden på* one's statements on); *inte kunna* ~ *på foten* not be able to stand on one's foot; ~ *sig* support o.s., (*luta sig*) lean, rest (*mot* against; *på* on); ~ *sig på* (*bildl.*) base one's opinion upon
stöd|jevävnad *anat.* connective tissue **-köp** supporting purchase **-lån** stand-by (emergency) loan **-mur** retaining wall **-område** development area **-punkt** point of support; *tekn.* fulcrum; *mil.* base **-trupper** *pl* supporting troops, reserves **-undervisning** remedial instruction **-åtgärder** support
stök *s7* (*städning*) cleaning; (*före helg o.d.*) preparation **stöka** clean up; potter; *gå ut och* ~ potter about; ~ *till* make a mess **stökig** *a1* untidy, messy
stöld *s3* steal; (*en* ~) theft; *jur.* larceny; *föröva en* ~ steal; *grov* ~ grand larceny **-försäkra** insure against theft **-försäkring** theft insurance; (*inbrotts-*) burglary insurance **-gods** stolen goods (*pl*) **-kupp** raid **-säker** thief-proof
stön *s7* groan **stöna** groan; (*svagare*) moan **stönande** *s6, se stön*
stöp *s7, gå i* ~*et* come to nothing **stöpa** *v3* cast, mould; ~ *bly* (*äv.*) melt lead; ~ *ljus* dip candles; *stöpt i samma form* (*bildl.*) cast in the same mould **stöpning** [-ö:-] casting *etc.* **stöpslev** *vara i* ~*en* (*bildl.*) be in the melting pot
1 stör *s2, zool.* sturgeon
2 stör *s2* pole, stake
1 störa *v1* pole (*bönor* beans); stick (*ärtor* peas)
2 störa *v2* disturb (*ngn i hans arbete* s.b. at his work); (*göra intrång på*) interfere with (*ngn i hans arbete* a p.'s work); (*oroa*) trouble; harass (*fienden* the enemy); (*avbryta*) interrupt; *förlåt att jag stör* excuse me for disturbing you; *jag hoppas att jag inte stör* I hope I am not disturbing you; *inte så det stör* (*vard.*) not so that you'd notice; ~ *en radioutsändning* jam a broadcast
stör|ande *a4* disturbing; ~ *uppträdande* disorderly conduct **-ning** [-ö:-] disturbance; *radio.*

äv. jamming, interference; (*-ande buller*) noise; (*själslig*) mental disorder; *atmosfäriska ~ar* atmospherics

störnings|skydd suppressor, interference eliminator **-sändare** radio. jamming station, jammer

störr|e ['större] *komp. t. stor* larger, bigger *etc.*, *jfr stor*; major; (*ganska stor*) large, considerable, fair-sized; *bli ~ (öka)* increase, (*växa*) grow, (*om barn*) grow up; *~ delen* the greater part, the majority; *desto ~ anledning att* all the more reason for (+ *ing- form*); *närmast ~ storlek* one size larger; *vara ~ än (i antal)* greater in number; *en ~ order* a large order

störst *superl. t. stor* largest, biggest *etc.*, *jfr stor*; (*ytterst stor*) utmost, maximum; *~a bredd (på fartyg)* overall width; *~a delen* the greatest part, (*huvuddelen*) the main (major) part, (*flertalet*) the greater number, most (*av dem* of them); *med ~a möjliga aktsamhet* with the greatest care, with all possible care; *till ~a delen* for the most part, mostly, (*huvudsakligen*) principally, mainly

stört absolutely, downright (*omöjligt* impossible)

störta 1 (*bringa att falla, äv. bildl.*) precipitate, throw (*ngn nedför trappan* s.b. down the stairs); (*stjälpa*) tip; (*avsätta*) overthrow (*en diktator* a dictator); *~ ngn i fördärvet* bring about (cause) a p.'s ruin, ruin s.b. **2** (*falla*) fall (tumble) [down] (*ner i* into); (*med flygplan*) crash; (*om häst*) fall; *~ omkull* fall (tumble) down; *~ samman* collapse, (*om byggnad*) fall in, *bildl.* break down; *~ till marken* drop to the ground **3** (*rusa*) rush, dash, dart (*fram* forward); *~ upp* spring to one's feet **4** *rfl* precipitate (throw) o.s. (*i* into); rush, dash; *~ sig på huvudet i vattnet* plunge headlong into the water; *~ sig över* fall upon (*ngn* s.b.) pitch into (*maten* the food)

stört|bombare dive bomber **-dyka** *flyg.* nosedive **-dykning** *flyg.* nose dive **-flod** torrent (*äv. bildl.*) **-hjälm** crash helmet **-lopp** (*på skidor*) downhill race **-ning** *flyg.* crash **-regn** downpour, torrential rain **-regna** pour down; *vard.* rain cats and dogs **-sjö** heavy sea; *få en ~ över sig* ship a heavy sea; *en ~ av ovett* a torrent of abuse **-skur** heavy shower; *vard.* drencher; *bildl. se -sjö*

stöt *s2* thrust (*äv. bildl.*); *fäktn. äv.* pass; (*slag*) hit; blow; (*knuff*) push, shove; (*dunk*) knock, bump (*i huvudet* on the head); (*av vapen; biljard-*) stroke; (*sammanstötning*) shock (*äv. elektr.*); *aktas för ~ar (på kolli*) handle with care, fragile; *ta emot första ~en* take the first impact

stöt|a *v3* **I 1** ('*köra*') thrust; hit, blow *etc.*; *~ foten mot en sten* hit one's foot against a stone; *~ huvudet i taket* bang one's head on the ceiling; *~ kniven i bröstet på ngn* stab s.b. in the chest; *~ käppen i golvet* strike one's stick on the floor **2** (*krossa*) pound; (*i mortel äv.*) pestle **3** (*förarga*) offend, give offence to, (*starkare*) shock; (*såra*) hurt; *det -er ögat* it is an eyesore; *det -er örat* it jars upon my ear; *~ och blöta en fråga* thrash over a problem **4** (*om åkdon*) bump, jolt; (*om skjutvapen*) kick; *fäktn.* thrust, make a pass **5** (*gränsa*) border (*till* [up]on); (*blåsa*) blow (*i trumpet* the trumpet); *~ i blått* incline to blue, have a tinge of blue in it; *~ på motstånd* meet with resistance; *det -er på bedrägeri* it verges (borders) on fraud **6**

(*med betonad partikel*) *~ bort* push away, *bildl.* repel; *~ emot* knock (bump) against; *~ fram* (*ljud*) emit, jerk out, utter; *~ ifrån sig* push back (away), (*ngn*) repel; *~ ihop a*) knock (bump) together, (*med en skräll*) clash [together], (*kollidera*) collide, *b*) (*råkas*) run into; *~ ihop med a*) (*kollidera*) collide with, run into, *b*) (*träffa*) run across each other; *~ omkull* upset, knock over; *~ på a*) *sjö.* strike, *b*) (*råka*) come across *c*) (*påminna*) jog a p.'s memory (*om ngt* about s.th.); *~ till a*) (*knuffa till*) push, bump, *b*) (*ansluta sig till*) join, *c*) (*tillkomma*) come on; *~ ut a*) (*en båt från land*) push (shove) off, *b*) (*utesluta*) expel **II** *rfl*, *~ sig på knäet* hurt (bruise) one's knee; *~ sig med ngn* fall out with s.b., offend s.b.

stöt|ande *a4* (*anstötlig*) offensive, shocking; (*obehaglig*) objectionable **-dämpare** shock absorber

stöt|esten *bildl.* stumbling block **-fångare** bumper, fender; *AE.* (*på lokomotiv*) cowcatcher **-ig** *a1* shaky; jolting **-säker** shockproof

1 stött *sup. av stödja*

2 stött *a4* **1** (*skadad*) hurt, damaged; (*om frukt*) bruised **2** (*förolämpad*) offended (*på ngn* with s.b.; *över* at, about); *bli ~* take offence

stötta I *s1* prop, support, stay; (*gruv-*) pit prop; *sjö.* stanchion, pillar **II** *v1* prop [up]; *bildl.* support, bear up **stöttepelare** *eg.* prop, support; *bildl.* mainstay; *samhällets ~* the pillars of society

stöt|trupp shock troops (*pl*) **-vapen** thrusting weapon **-vis** by jerks; (*om vind*) in gusts; (*sporadiskt*) intermittently **-våg** shock wave

stövare harrier

stövel ['stövv-, 'stö:-] *s2* high boot **-knekt** bootjack **-krage**, **-skaft** bootleg

stövl|a [ˣstövv-, ˣstö:-] stalk, stride; trudge **-ett** *s3* bootee

subaltern [-'tä:rn] *s3*, **-officer** subaltern [officer]

subba *s1, vard., neds.* cow, good-for-nothing

subjekt *s7* subject **-iv** ['subb-, -'ti:v] *a1* subjective **-ivism** subjectivism **-ivitet** subjectivity, subjectiveness

subjektskasus nominative case

sub|kultur subculture **-kutan** *a1* subcutaneous (*injektion* injection)

sublim *a1* sublime

sublimat *s4, s3* mercuric chloride, [corrosive] sublimate

sublim|era *kem. o. psyk.* sublimate, sublime **-ering** [-'me:-] sublimation **-itet** sublimity

submarin *a1* submarine

subordin|ationsbrott breach of discipline, case of insubordination **-era** (*underordna*) subordinate; (*vara underordnad*) be subordinate (*under* to)

subrett *s3, teat.* soubrette

subsidi|er [-'si:-] *pl* subsidies **-era** subsidize

subskribent subscriber **subskribera** subscribe (*på* for); *~d middag* a subscription dinner **subskription** [-p'ʃo:n] subscription

sub|stans *s3* substance; (*ämne*) agent; *ytaktiv ~* surfactant **-stantiell** [-[t]si'ell] *a1* substantial **-stantiv** *s7* noun, substantive **-stantivera** convert into a noun **-stantivisk** *a5* substantival (*användning* use); substantive (*sats* clause) **-sti-**

S

tuera substitute **-stityt** s7 substitute **-strøt** s7 substratum (pl substrata), substrate **-tjl** a1 subtle; fine-drawn **-tilitøt** s3 subtlety **-trahønd** s3 subtrahend **-trahera** subtract (från from) **-traktion** [-k'ʃo:n] subtraction **-traktionstecken** minus sign **-tropisk** [-'trå:-] a5 subtropical **-vention** [-n'ʃo:n] subvention **-ventionera** subsidize **-versjv** a1 subversive **succé** [suk'se:, syk-] s3 success; göra ~ be (score) a success, teat. äv. bring down the house **-författare** successful writer, best seller **-roman** best seller

succession [sukse'ʃo:n] [right of] succession **successionsordning** order of succession **successiv** [-'si:v, 'suks-] a1 successive; gradual **successivt** adv gradually, by gradual stages **suck** s2 sigh (av lättnad of relief); ~arnas bro the Bridge of Sighs; dra en djup ~ heave a deep sigh; utandas sin sista ~ breathe one's last **sucka** sigh (av with; efter for; över for, at) **suckøt** ²3, s4 candied peel **Sudøn** n the Sudan **sudanesisk** [-'ne:-] a5 Sudanese

sudd 1 s7 (klotter) scribbling; (med bläck o.d.) smudge **2** s2 (tuss) pad, wad **sudda 1** (plumpa) blot; (smutsa) soil, smear **2** ~ bort (ut) erase, efface, rub out, (från svarta tavlan) wipe off; ~ ner blur, smudge, blot; ~ över blot out **3** (festa) go on the spree **suddgummi** eraser, rubber **suddig** a1 blurred, blotched; (otydlig) fuzzy; (om skrift) indistinct; foto. fogged

suffjx s7 suffix
sufflé s3 soufflé
suffler|a prompt **-ing** prompting
sufflett s3 hood; hopfällbar ~ (på bil) folding top **sufflör** teat. prompter **-lucka** prompt box **sufflös** prompter
suffragøtt s3 suffragette
sug 1 s7 (-ning) suck, draw **2** s2 (-anordning) suction apparatus **3** i uttr.: tappa ~en (ge upp) lose heart, give up **suga** sög sugit suck (honung honey; på tummen one's thumb; (om pump) draw, fetch; bildl. drink in, imbibe; ~ musten ur ngn take the life out of s.b.; det suger i magen på mig my stomach is crying out for food; sjön suger the sea air takes it out of one; ~ på ramarna live on one's hump; ~ i sig suck up, absorb; ~ ut suck out, bildl. bleed, fleece; ~ ut jorden impoverish the soil; ~ sig fast adhere (vid to) **sug|ande** a4, en ~ känsla i magen a sinking feeling; en ~ uppförsbacke a gruelling climb; ~ blickar come-hither looks **-anordning** suction apparatus **-en** a3 peckish; vara ~ på be longing for **-fisk** remora, suckerfish **-fot** sucker foot **sugga** s1 sow
suggerera suggest **suggestibel** [-'ti:-] a2 suggestible **suggestion** [-e'ʃo:n] suggestion **suggestjv** a1 suggestive
sug|hävert siphon **-it** sup. av suga **-kopp** suction cup **-kraft** suction power **-mun** suctorial mouth **-ning** [-u:-] sucking etc., suction **-pump** suction pump **-rör** (för dryck) straw; tekn. suction pipe; zool. sucker **-skål** suction cup (disc) **-ventil** suction valve **-vårta** zool. sucker **sujett** [sy'ʃett, su-] s3 actor, fem. actress **sukta** ~ efter ngt sigh in vain for s.th.

1 sula I s1 sole (äv. tekn.) **II** v1 sole
2 sula s1, zool. booby
sulfa s1 sulpha; AE. äv. sulfa **-preparat** sulpha drug
sulføt s7, s4 sulphate; AE. sulfate **-fabrik** sulphate mill
sulfjd s3 sulphide; AE. sulfide **sulfjt** s7, s3 sulphite; AE. sulfite **sulfonamid** [-ˣfå:-] s3 sulphonamide; AE. sulfonamide
sulky ['sullki, -y] s3 sulky; (barnvagn) pushchair, stroller
sul|läder sole leather **-ning** [-u:-] soling **sultøn** s3 sultan **-øt** s7 sultanate
summa s1 sum; (belopp äv.) amount; (slut-) [sum] total; en stor ~ a large sum [of money]; rund ~ round (lump) sum; ~ summarum all told, altogether, in all; ~ tillgångar total assets; en nätt ~ a tidy sum, a pretty penny
summarisk [-'ma:-] a5 summary; (kortfattad) succinct, brief; ~ översikt summary
summer ['summ-] s2 buzzer
summer|a sum (add) up **-ing** summation; bildl. summing-up, summary
summerton buzzer signal (tone)
summit sup. av simma
sump s2 **1** (kaffe-) grounds (pl) **2** (-mark) fen, marsh **3** (fisk-) corf, fish chest; (i båt) well **sumpa** vard. (missa) muff, miss
sump|bäver coypu, nutria **-feber** malaria, marsh fever **-gas** marsh gas **-höna** crake **-ig** a1 (sank) swampy, marshy **-mark** s3 fen[land], marsh, marshland, swamp
1 sund s7 sound, strait[s pl]; ett smalt ~ (äv.) a narrow passage (channel)
2 sund a1 sound (äv. bildl.); (hälsosam) healthy; en ~ själ i en ~ kropp a sound mind in a sound body; sunt förnuft common sense
sund|het soundness; health **-hetsintyg** [clean] bill of health, health certificate
sunnan I adv from the south **II** r south wind **-vind** south wind
sunnjt s3 Sunnite
sup s2 dram; (brännvin) schnap[p]s
sup|a söp -it drink; (starkare) booze; han -er he is a heavy drinker, he is heavy on the booze; ~ ngn full make s.b. drunk (tipsy); ~ sig full get drunk (tipsy); ~ in (bildl.) inhale, imbibe; ~ upp sina pengar drink away one's money; ~ ur drink up **-ande** s6 drinking; boozing **-broder** drinking companion
sup|é s3 supper **-era** have supper
superb [-'ärb] a1 superb
super|fosföt superphosphate **-intendønt** superintendent **-lativ** ['su:-] I s3 superlative II a1 superlative **-makt** superpower **-oxjd** peroxide **-sonisk** [-'så:-] a5 supersonic **-stjärna** superstar **-tanker** supertanker
sup|gille drinking bout, vard. booze, spree **-ig** a1 addicted to drink[ing]
supinum [-ˣpi:-] s4, best. form äv. supinum [the] supine, (motsv. i eng.) past (perfect) participle
supit sup. av supa
supple|ant [-'ant, -'aŋ] deputy, substitute; (i styrelse äv.) deputy member
supplemønt s7 supplement **-band** supplementary volume **-vinkel** supplementary angle **-är** a5

supplementary
supplera supplement, fill up
supplik s3 supplication, petition **-ant** suppliant, petitioner
supponera suppose (att that)
supra|ledare [ˣsu:-] superconductor **-ledning** superconductivity
suprematj s3 supremacy
supyt s3, s2 tippler, boozer
sur al **1** sour; (syrlig) acid, sharp; kem. acid, acetous; bildl. sour, surly; se ~ ut look sour (surly); göra livet ~t för ngn lead s.b. a dog's life; det kommer ~t efter one will have to pay for it afterwards; bita i det ~a äpplet swallow the bitter pill; ~t sa räven om rönnbären "sour grapes", said the fox **2** (fuktig) wet, damp; ~ pipa foul pipe; ~ ved green wood; ~a ögon bleary eyes
1 sura sitta och ~ sulk
2 sura s1, relig. sura[h]
surdeg leaven
surf|a [ˣsurfa, sörfa] surf, go surfing **-ing** [ˈsurr-, ˈsörr-] surf-riding **-bräda** surfboard
sur|het [ˣsu:r-] sourness etc.; acidity **-kart** green fruit; bildl. sourpuss **-kål** kokk. sauerkraut **-mjölk** sour milk **-mulen** a3 sullen, surly **-mulenhet** sullenness, surliness
sur|na [-u:-] sour, turn (get) sour **-puppa** s1 sourpuss; grouch
surr s7 hum[ming]; (av röster äv.) buzz[ing]; (av maskin) whir[ring]
1 surra hum; buzz; whir
2 surra sjö., ~ [fast] frap, lash, make fast
surrealis|m surrealism **-tisk** a5 surrealist[ic]
surrogat s7 substitute; makeshift
sur|stek kokk. ung. marinated roast beef **-strömming** fermented Baltic herring **-söt** bittersweet
surt [-u:-] adv sourly; smaka ~ taste sour, have a sour taste; ~ förvärvade pengar hard-earned money (sg)
surven [ˈsurr-] best. form., i uttr.: hela ~ (vard.) the whole lot
surögd al bleary-eyed
sus s7 **1** (vindens etc.) sough[ing]; sigh[ing]; (friare) murmur[ing]; det gick ett ~ genom publiken a murmur went through the audience **2** leva i ~ och dus lead a wild life, go the pace **susa 1** (vina) sough; sigh; det ~r i öronen på mig my ears are buzzing **2** (ila) whizz, swish; ~ förbi sweep (om bil: flash) past
susen [ˈsu:-] best. form vard., i uttr.: göra ~ do the trick
susning [ˣsu:s-] se sus 1
suspekt al suspect
suspen|dera [susp-, sysp-, -enˈde:-, -aŋˈde] suspend **-sion** [-pen-, -paŋ-] suspension **-sjv** [-pen-, -paŋ-] al suspensive; ~t veto delaying veto
suspensoer s3 jockstrap, athletic supporter, suspensory [bandage]
sutare tench
sutenör pimp, ponce
suterrängvåning [-ˣräŋ-] basement
suttit sup. av sitta
sutur suture **-tråd** suture [thread]
suvenjr se souvenir
suverän I s3 sovereign **II** al sovereign (stat state);

(överlägsen) supreme; superb (tennisspelare tennis player); med ~t förakt with supreme contempt **-itet** sovereignty; supremacy
svabb s2 swab **svabba** swab
svacka s1 depression, hollow
svada s1 volubility, torrent of words; ha en förfärlig ~ have the gift of the gab
svag al, allm. weak (förstånd intellect; kaffe coffee; skäl argument; syn sight; verb verb); feeble (försök attempt; (kraftlös) powerless; (klen) delicate (till hälsan in health); (om ljud, färg) faint; (om ljus) weak, poor; (lätt) light (cigarr cigar); (skral) poor (hälsa health; ursäkt excuse); (sakta) soft (bris breeze); ha en ~ aning om have a faint idea of; ett ~t hopp a slight (faint) hope; det ~a könet the weaker sex; köttet är ~t the flesh is weak; den ~a punkten the weak point; i ett ~t ögonblick in a moment of weakness; bli ~ weaken; vara ~ för have a weakness for, be fond of, (ngn äv.) have a soft spot for **-dricka** small beer **-het** weakness etc.; (ålderdoms-) infirmity; (svag sida) foible; (böjelse) weakness **-hetstecken** sign of weakness **-hetstillstånd** weak condition, general debility **-presterande** low-achieving; de ~ the low achievers **-sint** al feeble-minded **-ström** light (low-power) current **-strömsledning** communication (low-voltage) line **-synt** [-y:-] al weak-sighted
svagt [-a:-] adv weakly etc.; (klent) poorly (upplyst illuminated)
svaj [svajj] s7 **1** ligga på ~ (sjö.) swing at anchor; med mössan på ~ with one's cap at a jaunty angle **2** radio. wobbling, fading; (om skivspelare) wow and flutter **svaja 1** sjö. swing **2** (vaja) float **svajig** al **1** swinging (gång gait) **2** (flott) stylish
sval al cool (äv. bildl.)
sval|a s1 swallow; en ~ gör ingen sommar one swallow does not make a summer **-bo** swallow's nest
svalde [-a:-] imperf. av svälja
svalg [svalj] s7 **1** anat. throat; fack. pharynx **2** (avgrund) abyss, gulf
svalgång gallery
svalk|a I s1 coolness, freshness **II** v1 cool; (uppfriska) refresh; ~ sig cool [o.s.] off, cool down, refresh o.s. **-ande** a4 cooling, refreshing
svall s7 surge; (våg- äv.) surging of [the] waves; (dyning) swell; bildl. flush, flow **svalla** surge; swell; (sjuda) seethe; diskussionens vågor ~de the discussion became heated; känslorna ~de feelings ran high; ~ över overflow **svallning** surging; swelling; hans blod råkade i ~ his blood began to boil **svallvåg** surge; (efter fartyg) wash
svaln|a [-a:l-] ~ [av] get cool, cool down (äv. bildl.) **-ing** cooling down
1 svalt [-a:-] sup. av svälja
2 svalt [svallt] imperf. av svälta
svalört lesser celandine, pilewort
svam|la ramble [on]; (utbreda sig) discourse (om upon) **-lig** al rambling; (oredig) vaporous (artikel article) **-mel** [ˈsvamm-] s7 rant, verbiage; (nonsens) drivel
svamp s2 **1** bot. fungus (pl fungi); (ätbar) mushroom; (ej ätbar) toadstool; med. fungoid growth; plocka ~ go mushrooming **2** (tvätt-) sponge; tvätta med ~ (äv.) sponge; dricka som en ~ drink

S

like a fish **-aktig** *al* 1 *bot.*, *med.* fungous; mushroom[-like] **2** spongy **-bildning** fungus [growth], fungosity **-dödande** ~ *medel* fungicide **-förgiftning** fungus poisoning **-ig** *al* 1 *med.* fungoid **2** spongy **-infektion** fungus infection **-karta** mushroom (fungi) chart **-kännare** mycologist, expert on fungi **-kännedom** mycology **-odling** mushroom cultivation (growing) **-plockning** mushroom gathering

svan *s2, s1* swan **-damm** swannery **-dun** swan's--down **-esång** swan song (*äv. bildl.*)

svang *s, i uttr.*: *vara* (*komma*) *i* ~ be (get) abroad

svanhopp *sport.* swallow dive, *AE.* swan dive

svank *s2, s7* hollow **svanka** be sway-backed

svankrygg sway-back **-ig** *al* sway-backed

svann *imperf. av svinna*

svans *s2* tail; *astr.* trail (*äv. bildl.*); *bildl.* following, train

svans|a ~ *för* (*bildl.*) cringe to, fawn on **-kota** caudal vertebra **-lös** tailless **-motor** rear engine **-spets** tip of a tail

svanunge cygnet

svar *s7* answer (*på* to); reply; (*motåtgärd*) reply, counter; (*reaktion*) response; *jur.* rejoinder; ~ *betalt* reply paid (*förk.* R.P.); *jakande* ~ (*äv.*) acceptance; *nekande* ~ (*äv.*) refusal; ~ *med löneanspråk* replies stating salary expected; *bli ~et skyldig* not answer (reply); *inte bli ~et skyldig* have a reply ready; *få* ~ *på en fråga* get an answer to a question; *ge ngn* ~ *på tal* answer back, give s.b. tit for tat; *om* ~ *anhålles* an answer is requested, (*på bjudningskort*) R.S.V.P.; *som* ~ *på Ert brev* in reply to your letter; *stå till* ~*s för* be held responsible for

svara answer; reply (*på* to); (*skriftligen äv.*) write back; (*reagera*) respond; *rätt ~t!* that's right!; ~ *näsvist* give an impudent reply; *han ~de ingenting* he made no reply (*på* to); ~ *för* (*ansvara för*) answer (be responsible) for, account for; *jag ~r för att* I'll see to it that; ~ *i telefonen* answer the telephone; ~ *mot* correspond (answer) to, meet, match; *vad ~de du på det?* what did you reply (say) to that?; ~ *på en fråga* (*ett brev*) answer a question (letter); *jag ~de ja på hans fråga* I answered yes to his question

svarande *s9, jur.* defendant **-sidan** the defending party, the defence

svaromål *s7, jur.* [defendant's] plea, defence; *ingå i* ~ reply to a charge

svars|kupong reply coupon **-lös** at a loss for a reply; *bli* ~ be nonplussed; *göra* ~ reduce to silence; *inte vara* ~ have an answer ready **-not** [note in] reply **-porto** return postage **-signal** *tel.* reply signal **-skrift** [written] reply

svart I *al* black (*äv. bildl.*); (*dyster*) dark; *S~a havet* the Black Sea; *~e Petter* (*kortsp.*) old maid; *~a börsen* the black market; *familjens ~a får* the black sheep of the family; *~a hål* black hole; *~a Maja* black Maria; *~a tavlan* the blackboard; *bli* ~ get (grow) black, blacken; *stå på ~a listan* be on the black list **II** *s, best. form det svarta* black (*äv. schack.*); *de ~a* the blacks; *få ~ på vitt på ngt* get s.th. in black and white; *klä sig i* ~ dress in black; *måla i* ~ paint in black colours; *se allting i* ~ look on the dark side of things

svartabörs|affär black market transaction **-haj**

black-marketer, spiv

svart|betsa ebonize **-blå** blue-black **-broder** Black Friar, Dominican **-bygge** *ung.* house built without planning permission **-fläckig** blackspotted **-fot** (*indian*) Blackfoot; (*strejkbrytare*) blackleg, scab **-hårig** black-haired **-ing** darky **-jord** black earth **-klädd** [dressed] in black **-konst** (*magi*) black magic (art), necromancy **-krut** black powder **-kråka** carrion crow **-lista** blacklist **-mes** coal tit **-muskig** *al* swarthy **-måla** paint in black colours **-målning** *bildl.* blackening **-na** blacken, get (grow, turn, go) black; *det ~de för ögonen på mig* everything went black for me **-och-vitrandig** *al* zebra striped, black-and-white striped **-peppar** black pepper **-prickig** black-dotted **-rock** (*präst*) black-coat **-rost** (*på säd*) black rust **-sjuk** jealous (*på* of) **-sjuka** jealousy **-skjorta** blackshirt, fascist **-soppa** goose-giblet soup **-syn** pessimism **-vit** black and white, monochrome (*film* film) **-ögd** *al* black-eyed, dark-eyed

svarv *s2* [turning] lathe **svarva** turn [in a lathe] **svarvad** *a5* turned; *bildl.* well-turned, elaborate [d] **svarvare** turner, lathe operator **svarveri** turning-mill **svarvstol** [turning] lathe

svass|a ~ (*omkring*) strut about **-ande** *a4* (*om gång*) strutting; grandiloquent, highfalutin[g], hi-falutin

svastika ['svass-] *s1* swastika

svavel ['sva:-] *s7* sulphur; *AE.* sulfur **-aktig** *al* sulphur[e]ous **-bad** sulphur bath **-blomma** [-ˣblomma, ˣsva:-] flowers (*pl*) of sulphur **-haltig** *al* sulphurous, sulphuric **-kis** sulphur pyrite, iron pyrites **-lukt** sulphurous smell **-predikant** fire-and-brimstone preacher **-sticka** sulphur match **-syra** sulphuric acid **-syrad** *a5*, *-syrat natron* sodium sulphate **-syrlighet** sulphurous acid **-väte** hydrogen sulphide

svavla [-a:-] *vl* sulphurate, sulphurize

Svea rike the land of Sweden **svear** *pl* Swedes

svecism *s3* Swedishism

sved *imperf. av svida*

1 sveda *s1* smart[ing pain]; ~ *och värk* physical suffering

2 sved|a *v2* singe (*om frost*) nip; (*om solen*) parch; *lukta -d* smell burnt

svedja [-e:-] burn woodland

svedje|bruk burn-beating **-land** burn-beaten land

1 svek *imperf. av svika*

2 svek *s7* treachery, perfidy; (*bakslughet*) deceit, guile; *jur.* fraud

svek|full treacherous, perfidious; deceitful, guileful; fraudulent **-fullhet** treacherousness *etc.*; guile **-lös** guileless, single-hearted

sven [svenn] *s3* swain, page; *riddare och ~ner* knights and squires **-dom** *s2* chastity **-sexa** stag party

svensk I *al* Swedish; *~a kronor* Swedish kronor (*förk.* SEK); *en* ~ *mil* a Swedish mile, 10 kilometres **II** *s2* Swede **svenska** *s1* **1** (*språk*) Swedish **2** (*kvinna*) Swedish woman

svensk|amerikan Swedish-American **-amerikansk** Swedish-American **—engelsk** Anglo--Swedish; Swedish-English (*ordbok* dictionary) **-finne** Finn living in Sweden **--fransk** Swedish-

-French, Franco-Swedish **-född** Swedish born, Swedish by birth **-het** Swedishness **-lärare** Swedish teacher, teacher of Swedish (*-talande*) Swedish-speaking **2** (*avfattad på -a*) in Swedish, Swedish **-talande** Swedish-speaking

svep *s7* sweep; *i ett* ~ at one go **svepa** *v3* **1** (*vira*) (*äv.* ~ *in*) wrap [up] (*i* in); (*lik*) shroud, lay out; ~ *om* [*kring*] *sig* wrap around one, wrap o.s. up in **2** *sjömil.* sweep for (*minor* mines) **3** (*hastigt dricka el. äta*) knock back **4** (*blåsa hårt*) sweep (*fram* along) **svepande** *a4* sweeping (*argument* argument)

svep|e *s6, bot.* involucre **-ning** [-e:-] **1** (*min-*) sweeping **2** (*av lik*) shrouding; *konkr.* shroud **-skäl** pretext, subterfuge; prevarication; *komma med* ~ make excuses

Sverige ['sverrje] *n* Sweden

svets *s2, abstr.* welding; *konkr.* weld

svets|a weld **-aggregat** welding set **-are** welder **-loppa** welding spark **-låga** welding flame **-ning** welding

svett *s3* perspiration; *vard.* sweat; *arbeta så ~en lackar* work till one is dripping with perspiration; *i sitt anletes* ~ in the sweat of one's brow **svettas** *dep* perspire; *vard.* sweat (*äv. bildl.*); *jag* ~ *om fötterna* my feet are sweaty

svett|bad (*stark -ning*) bath of perspiration; (*bad*) sweat[ing bath] **-drivande** *a4* ~ [*medel*] sudorific, sudatory **-droppe** drop of perspiration **-drypande** all in a sweat, dripping with perspiration **-ig** *a1* perspiring; *vard.* sweaty; *bli* ~ perspire **-körtel** sweat gland **-ning** sweat[ing], perspiration; *komma i* ~ start sweating **-pärla** bead of perspiration **-rem** sweatband

svib|el ['svi:-] *s2, boktr.* pie[d type] **-la** [-i:-] pie

svicka *s1* spigot, plug

svid *s2, vard.* suit, outfit

svid|a *sved -it* smart; (*friare*) ache; *såret -er* (*äv.*) the wound is very painful; *det -er i ögonen* [*på mig*] my eyes smart; *röken -er i ögonen* the smoke makes my eyes smart; *det -er i halsen* [*på mig*] my throat feels sore, I have a sore throat; *det -er i själen på mig att se* it breaks my heart to see; *det -er men det -er gott* it hurts but you feel better for it **-ande** *a4* smarting; *med* ~ *hjärta* with an aching heart **-it** *sup. av svida*

svik|a *svek -it* **1** (*överge*) fail, desert; (*i kärlek*) jilt, *vard.* chuck; ~ *en vän i nödens stund* leave a friend in the lurch; ~ *sitt löfte* break one's promise, go back on one's word; ~ *sin plikt* fail in one's duty **2** (*svikta, tryta*) fail, fall short; *krafterna svek mig* my strength gave out; *minnet* (*modet*) *-er mig* my memory (courage) fails me; *rösten svek honom* his voice failed him **-it** *sup. av svika* **-lig** [-i:k-] *a1* fraudulent (*förfarande* proceeding [*s pl*]), breach of trust

svikt *s2* **1** (*spänst*) spring[iness], elasticity; (*böjlighet*) flexibility; *ha* ~ (*äv.*) be springy (flexible) **2** (*trampolin*) springboard; diving board **svikta** **1** (*ge svikt*) be resilient; (*gunga*) shake, rock **2** (*böja sig*) bend (*under* beneath); (*ge efter*) give way, sag **3** *bildl.* flinch, give way, waver **svikt|ande** *a4, med aldrig* ~ with never-failing (unflinching) **-hopp** (*i simning*) springboard diving; *gymn.* jumping on the spot

svim|färdig ready to drop **-ma** ~ [*av*] faint

[away], swoon, fall into a swoon, *vard.* pass out; ~ *av trötthet* faint with fatigue **-ning** fainting, swoon; (*medvetslöshet*) unconsciousness **-nings- anfall** fainting-fit

svin *s7* pig; *koll. o. bildl.* swine; *bildl. äv.* hog

svin|a ~ *ner* make a dirty mess (*sig* of o.s.) **-aktig** *a1* piggish, swinish; *bildl. äv.* mean; (*oanständig*) indecent, filthy (*historia* story); beastly (*tur* luck) **-aktighet** piggishness *etc.*; meanness; ~*er* (*i ord*) foul (filthy) things **-avel** pig breeding **-borst** pig's (hog's) bristle

svindel *s9* **1** (*yrsel*) giddiness, dizziness; *med.* vertigo; *få* ~ turn giddy (dizzy) **2** (*svindleri*) swindle, humbug, trickery

svindl|a **1** *det ~r för ögonen* my head is swimming; *tanken ~r* the mind reels **2** (*bedriva -eri*) swindle, cheat **-ande** *a4* giddying, dizzying; giddy, dizzy (*höjd* height); *i* ~ *fart* at a breakneck pace; ~ *summor* prodigious sums [of money] **-are** swindler, crook, cheat, humbug **-eri** *se svindel 2*; ~*er* swindles

svineri filth, dirty habits

sving *s2, sport.* swing **svinga** swing; brandish (*svärdet* the sword); ~ *sig* swing o.s.; ~ *sig ner* swing down; ~ *sig upp a*) (*i sadeln*) vault (swing o.s. up) [into the saddle], *b*) (*om fågel*) take wing, soar, *c*) *bildl.* rise [in the world]

svin|gård piggery, pig farm **-hugg** ~ *går igen* tit for tat, the biter bit **-hus** piggery **-kall** beastly cold **-koppor** *pl* impetigo (*sg*) **-kött** pork **-läder** pigskin **-mat** pig (hog) feed; (*av avfall*) pigwash, swill **-målla** *s1* fat hen, *AE.* pigweed

svinn *s7* waste, wastage; loss **svinna** *svann svunnit* (*om tid*) pass; *svunna tider* days gone by

svin|pest swine fever, *AE.* hog cholera **-päls** *bildl.* swine, dirty beggar **-skötare** pigman, swineherd **-skötsel** pig-breeding **-stia** pigsty, pigpen; *bildl.* sty

svira be on the spree

svirvel *s2* swivel

svischa swish

sviskon [-ån] *s7* prune

svit *s3* **1** (*följe*) suite **2** (*rad*) succession, series; (*av rum*) suite; *kortsp.* sequence **3** (*påföljd*) aftereffect; *med.* sequela (*pl* sequelae)

svor *imperf. av svära* **-dom** [-domm] *s2* oath; (*förbannelse*) curse; ~*ar* swearing, bad language (*sg*)

svull|en *a3* swollen (*kind* cheek); puffed **-na** ~ [*upp*] become swollen, swell **-nad** *s3* swelling

svulst *s3* **1** (*tumör*) tumour, tumefaction **2** *bildl.* bombast, pomposity, turgidity **-ig** *a1* bombastic, inflated, turgid **-ighet** *se svulst 2*

svult|en *a5* famished **-it** *sup. av svälta*

svunn|en *a5* bygone, past (*tid* time) **-it** *sup. av svinna*

svur|en *a5* sworn **-it** *sup. av svära*

sväger ['svä:-] *s2* brother-in-law

svål *s2* (*svin-*) rind; *se äv.* huvudsvål

svångrem belt; *dra åt ~men* (*bildl.*) tighten one's belt

svår *a1* **1** (*besvärlig*) difficult (*för* for); (*mödosam*) hard (*uppgift* task; *för* for; *mot* on); (*invecklad*) complicated (*problem* problem); ~ *examen* stiff examination; *ett ~t slag* a hard blow; *en* ~ *tid* hard times (*pl*); ~ *uppgift* (*äv.*) difficult problem, arduous task; ~ *överresa* rough crossing; *ha ~t för att* find it difficult to; *ha ~t för ngt* find s.th. difficult; *ha ~t för att fatta* be slow on the uptake; *ha mycket ~t för att* have great difficulty in (+ *ing*-form); *ha det ~t a*) suffer greatly, *b*) (*ekonomiskt*) be badly off, *c*) (*slita ont*) have a rough time of it; *jag har ~t för att tro att* I find it hard to believe that; *det är ~t att* it is hard (difficult) to **2** (*allvarlig*) grave, serious, severe (*sjukdom* illness); *ett ~t fall a*) eg. a serious fall, *b*) *bildl.* a grave (difficult) case; *i ~are fall* in [more] serious cases; *~t fel a*) (*hos sak*) serious drawback, *b*) (*hos pers.*) serious fault, *c*) (*misstag*) grave error; *~ frestelse* sore (heavy) temptation; *~ förbrytelse* serious offence (*jur.* crime); *han har ~t hjärtfel* he has a serious heart condition; *~ hosta* bad cough; *~ kyla* severe cold; *~a lidanden* severe (great) suffering (*sg*); *~ olycka* great misfortune, (*enstaka olyckshändelse*) serious accident; *ha ~a plågor* be in great pain; *~ sjö*[*gång*] rough sea **3** *vara ~ på ngt* be overfond of s.th.; *du är för ~!* you are the limit!, you are too bad!

svår|anträffbar hard to contact, elusive **-artad** [-a:r-] *a5* malignant (*sjukdom* illness) **-bedömd** *a5* difficult to appraise (assess, *vard.* size up) **-begriplig** hard (difficult) to understand; (*dunkel*) abstruse **-definierbar** difficult to define **-fattlig** *a1*, *se* -begriplig **-flirtad, -flörtad** *a5*, *eg.* unapproachable; *bildl.* hard to convince **-framkomlig** ~ *väg* difficult (rough) road **-förklarlig** difficult to explain **-gripbar** hard to get hold of; *bildl.* elusive **-hanterlig** difficult to manage (handle); (*friare, om pers.*) intractable, (*om sak*) awkward

svår|ighet difficulty; (*möda*) hardship; (*besvär*) trouble; (*olägenhet*) inconvenience; (*hinder*) obstacle; *göra ~er* make difficulties; *det möter inga ~er* that's not difficult, *vard.* that's all plain sailing; *däri ligger ~en* that's the trouble; *i ~er* in trouble; *utan* ~ without any difficulty **-ighetsgrad** degree of difficulty **-ligen** [-å:-] hardly, scarcely **-läslig** *a1*, **-läst** [-ä:-] *a1* difficult to read; (*om handstil*) hardly legible **-löslig** *kem.* sparingly soluble **-löst** [-ö:-] *a4* difficult to solve; (*om gåta*) hard, intricate **-mod** melancholy; (*nedslagenhet*) low spirits (*pl*); (*dysterhet*) gloom, spleen **-modig** melancholy, sad; gloomy **-såld** difficult to sell; hard-selling

svår|t [-å:-] *adv* seriously (*sjuk* ill); badly (*sårad* wounded) **-tillgänglig** difficult of access (to get at); (*om pers. äv.*) distant, reserved **-tillgänglighet** difficulty of access; reserve **-uppnåelig** *a1* difficult (hard) to achieve **-åtkomlig** *se* -tillgänglig **-överskådlig** difficult to survey

svägerska sister-in-law

svälja *v2*, el. *svalde svalt* swallow (*äv. bildl.*); *bildl. äv.* pocket; ~ *förtreten* swallow one's annoyance; *~ ner* swallow; *~ orden* swallow one's words

sväll|a *v2* swell; (*höja sig*) rise; (*utvidga sig*) expand (*äv. bildl.*); *seglen -er* the sails are swelling (filling); *~ upp* swell up (out), become swollen; *~ ut* swell [out], (*bukta ut*) bulge out **-ande** *a4* swelling; (*uppsvälld*) turgescent; *~ barm* ample bosom

svält *s3* starvation; (*hungersnöd*) famine; *dö av ~* die of starvation

svält|a 1 *svalt svultit* starve; (*starkare*) famish; *~ ihjäl* starve to death **2** *v3* (*imperf. äv. svalt*) (*låta hungra*) starve; *~ sig* starve o.s.; *~ ut* starve out **-född** [half] starving, underfed **-gräns** *leva på ~en* live on the hunger line **-konstnär** person who needs very little food **-kost** starvation diet **-lön** starvation wages (*pl*)

svämma ~ *över* [rise and] overflow [its banks]

sväng *s2* (*rörelse*) round; (*krök*) bend, turn; (*av flod, väg e.d.*) curve, wind[ing]; *ta ut ~en* take the corner wide; *ta sig en* ~ (*dansa*) shake a leg; *vägen gör en* ~ the road bends (turns); *vara med i ~en* be in the swing **-ig** *a1* swinging

sväng|a *v2* **1** (*sätta i rörelse*) swing (*armarna* one's arms); (*vifta med*) wave; (*vapen*) brandish; (*vända*) turn (*bilen* the car) **2** (*hastigt röra sig*) swing (*fram o. tillbaka* to and fro); (*pendla*) oscillate (*äv. bildl.*); (*svaja*) sway; (*om sträng*) vibrate; (*kring en tapp*) swing, pivot; (*rotera*) turn, rotate; (*göra en sväng*) turn; *~ av* turn off; *~ in på* turn into; *~ med armarna* swing one's arms; *~ om a*) turn round, (*om vind*) veer round, *bildl.* shift, change, *b*) (*i dans*) have a dance; *~ om på klacken* turn on one's heels; *~ om hörnet* turn the corner; *~ till* (*hastigt laga till*) knock up; *bilen -de upp på gården* the car swung up into the courtyard **3** *rfl* (*kretsa*) circle, rotate; (*göra undanflykter*) prevaricate; *~ sig med* flaunt (*latin* Latin) **-bar** *a1* revolving, pivoting **-borr** breast drill **-bro** swing (pivot, swivel) bridge

sväng|d *a5* (*böjd*) bent, curved **-dörr** swing[ing] door; revolving door **-hjul** flywheel; (*i ur*) balance wheel **-ning** (*gungning*) swing; (*fram o. tillbaka*) oscillation, vibration; (*rotation*) wheeling, rotation

svängnings|radie turning radius **-rörelse** oscillatory motion, oscillation **-tal** frequency, number of oscillations

sväng|rum space to move, elbowroom (*äv. bildl.*) **-tapp** pivot, swivel

svära *svor svurit* **1** (*använda svordomar*) swear (*över* at); (*förbanna*) curse **2** (*gå ed*) swear (*på, att* that; *vid* by); (*avge löfte äv.*) vow; *~ dyrt och heligt* make a solemn vow; *~ falskt* perjure o.s., commit perjury; *jag kan ~ på att* I'll swear to it that; *det kan jag inte ~ på* (*vard.*) I won't swear to it that; *~ sig fri* swear one's way out **3** *~ mot* clash with (*äv. om färg*)

svärd [-ä:-] *s7* sword **-fisk** swordfish **-formig** [-å-] *a1, bot.* ensiform

svärdotter daughter-in-law

svärds|dans sword dance **-egg** sword edge **-fäste** sword hilt **-hugg** sword cut **-lilja** iris **-sidan** *i uttr.: på ~* on the male (spear) side **-slukare** sword swallower

svär|far father-in-law **-förälder** parent-in-law

svärm *s2* swarm (*av* of); (*flock*) flock **svärma 1** (*om bin*) swarm, cluster; (*om mygg e.d.*) flutter about **2** *~ i månskenet* spoon in the moonlight; *~ för* fancy, (*starkare*) be mad about, (*för pers. äv.*) be crazy about **svärmare 1** (*drömmare*) dreamer; fantast **2** (*fjäril*) sphinx (hawk) moth **svärmeri 1** enthusiasm (*för* for); *religiöst ~* fanaticism, religiosity **2** (*förälskelse*) infatuation; (*om pers.*) sweetheart **svärmisk** ['svärr-] *a5* dreamy;

romantic, fanciful **svärmning** swarming [of bees]; flutter

svär|mor mother-in-law **-son** son-in-law

svärta I *s1* **1** (*färg*) blackness; (*ämne*) blacking **2** *zool.* scoter **II** *v1* blacken; ~ *ner* blacken, *bildl.* *äv.* defame; *handskarna ~r av sig* the colour comes off the gloves

sväva 1 (*glida*) float, be suspended; (*om fågel*) soar; (*kretsa*) hover (*äv. bildl.*); (*hänga fritt*) hang; (*dansa fram*) flit (glide) along; ~ *genom luften* sail through the air; ~ *omkring* soar **2** ~ *i fara* be in danger; ~ *i okunnighet om* be in [a state of] ignorance about; ~ *mellan liv och död* hover between life and death; ~ *på målet* falter in one's speech **svävande** *a4* floating *etc.*; *bildl.* vague, uncertain **svävare, svävfarkost** hovercraft

sy *v4* sew (*för hand* by hand; *på maskin* on the machine); (*tillverka*) make; *absol.* do needlework; *kir.* sew up, suture; *låta ~ ngt* have s.th. made; ~ *fast* (*i*) sew on; ~ *ihop* sew up; ~ *in* (*minska*) take in; ~ *om* remake **-ask** workbox **-ateljé** dressmaker's [workshop]

sybarit *s3* sybarite

sy|behör *s7* sewing materials (*pl*), haberdashery; *AE. äv.* notions (*pl*) **-behörsaffär** haberdasher's [shop], haberdashery **-bord** worktable, sewing table

syd *s9, adv o. oböjligt a* south

Sydafrika *n* South Africa **sydafrikansk** South African **Sydamerika** *n* South America **sydamerikansk** South American **Sydeuropa** *n* Southern Europe **sydeuropeisk** South European

syd|frukt *~er* citrus and tropical fruits **-gående** *a4* southbound **-kust** south[ern] coast **-lig** [-y:-] *a1* southern (*länder* countries); south[erly] (*vind* wind); *~are* further south; ~ *bredd* south latitude **-ländsk** *a5* southern, of the South **-länning** southerner **-ost I** *s2* (*~lig vind*) southeast wind; southeaster; (*väderstreck*) southeast (*förk.* SE) **II** *adv* southeast

Sydostasien Southeast Asia

syd|ostlig [-ˈosst-] *a1* southeast[ern] **-ostpassaden** *best. form* southeast trade wind **-pol** *~en* the South Pole **-polsexpedition** Antarctic expedition **-sluttning** southfacing slope **-staterna** the Southern States; the South (*sg*) **-svensk** Southern Swedish **-sydost** south-southeast (*förk.* SSE) **-vart** southwards **-väst I** *s2* (*~lig vind*) southwest wind; southwester; (*hatt*) sou'wester **II** *adv* southwest **-västlig** [-ˈvässt-] *a1* southwest[ern] **-östlig** *a1* southeasterly

syfili|s [ˈsy:-] *s2* syphilis **-tisk** [-ˈli:-] *a5* syphilitic

syfta aim (*på* at); (*häntyda*) allude (*på* to), hint (*på* at); ~ *högt* aim high; ~ *på* (*avse*) have in view (mind); ~ *till* (*eftersträva*) aim at; ~ *tillbaka på* refer [back] to

syft|e *s6* aim, purpose, end, object [in view]; *vad är ~t med ...?* what is the object (purpose) of ...?; *i ~ att lära känna* with a view to getting to know; *i detta ~* to this (that) end (purpose); *i vilket ~?* to what end?; *med ~ på* with regard to **-emål** *se* syfte **-linje** sight line **-ning** aiming *etc.*; *tekn.* alignment

sy|förening sewing circle; *i Storbritannien äv.* Dorcas society **-junta** sewing guild

sykomor [-ˈmå:r] *s3* sycamore

sy|korg work basket **-kunnig** able to sew

syl *s2* awl; *inte få en ~ i vädret* (*vard.*) not get a word in edgeways

sylfid *s3* sylph **-isk** *a5* sylphlike

syll *s2, järnv.* sleeper, *AE.* crosstie, tie; *byggn.* [ground] sill

syllogism *s3* syllogism

sylt *s3* jam, preserve **sylta I** *s1* **1** *kokk.* brawn **2** (*krog*) third-rate eating house **II** *v1* preserve, make jam [of]; ~ *in sig* (*vard.*) get [o.s.] into a mess; ~ *in sig i* (*med*) (*vard.*) get mixed up in (with)

sylt|burk jam pot (jar); (*med sylt*) pot (jar) of jam **-gryta** preserving pan (kettle) **-lök** pearl onion; (*-ad lök*) pickled onions (*pl*) **-ning** preserving **-socker** preserving sugar

sylvass [as] sharp as an awl; *~a blickar* piercing looks

sy|lön dressmaker's (tailor's) charges (*pl*) **-maskin** sewing machine

symbios [-ˈå:s] *s3* symbiosis

symbol [-ˈbå:l] *s3* symbol; (*om pers. äv.*) figurehead **-ik** *s3* symbolism **-isera** [-ˈse:-] symbolize **-isk** *a5* symbolic[al]; (*bildlig*) figurative; ~ *betalning* token payment **-ism** symbolism

symfon|i *s3* symphony **-iker** [-ˈfå:-] **1** (*kompositör*) symphonist **2** (*orkestermedlem*) member of a symphony orchestra

symfoni|orkester symphony orchestra **-sk** [-ˈfå:-] *a5* symphonic

symmetr|i *s3* symmetry; *brist på ~* lack of symmetry, asymmetry **-isk** [-ˈme:-] *a5* symmetric[al]

sym|patetisk [-ˈte:-] *a5* sympathetic; *~t bläck* (*äv.*) invisible ink **-pati** *s3* sympathy (*för* for; *med* with); *gripas av ~ för ngn* take a liking to s.b.; *hysa ~ för* sympathize with; *~er och antipatier* likes and dislikes; *~erna var på hennes sida* she got all the sympathy **-patisera** sympathize (*med* with) **-patisk** [-ˈpa:-] *a5* nice, likeable; *äv.* sympathetic; attractive (*utseende* looks *pl*); *~a nervsystemet* the sympathetic nervous system **-patistrejk** sympathy (sympathetic) strike **-patisör** sympathizer

symposium [-ˈpå:-] *s4* symposium

sym[p]tom [-ˈtå:m] *s7* symptom (*på* of) **-atisk** [-ˈma:-] *a5* symptomatic

syn *s3* **1** (*-sinne*) [eye]sight; (*-förmåga*) vision; ~ *och hörsel* sight and hearing; *få ~ på* catch sight of; *förlora ~en* lose one's [eye]sight; *förvända ~en på ngn* throw dust in a p.'s eyes; *ha god* (*dålig*) ~ have good (poor, weak) eyesight; *komma till ~es* appear **2** (*åsikt*) view, opinion; outlook; *hans ~ på* his view of; *ha en ljus ~ på* take a bright view of **3** *bära ~ för sägen* look like it; *för ~s skull* for the look of the thing; *till ~es* apparently, seemingly, to all appearances **4** (*ansikte*) face; *bli lång i ~en* pull a long face; *ljuga ngn mitt i ~en* lie in a p.'s face **5** (*anblick*) sight; *en härlig ~* a grand spectacle; *en ~ för gudar* a sight for the gods **6** (*dröm-*) vision; *ha ~er* have visions; *se i ~e* (*se orätt*) be mistaken **7** (*besiktning*) inspection, survey

syna inspect, survey; examine; ~ *ngt i sömmarna* (*bildl.*) look thoroughly into s.th.

synagoga *s1* synagogue

synaps *s3* synapsis, synapse

syn|as *v3, dep* **1** (*ses*) be seen; (*vara -lig*) be visible (*för* to); (*visa sig*) appear (*för* to); *-s inte härifrån* cannot be seen from here; *det -s inte* it doesn't show; *fläcken -tes tydligt på* the spot could be seen clearly on; *det -tes på honom att* you could tell by looking at him that; *som -es* (*äv. bildl.*) as is evident, as you can see; *vilja ~* want to make a show; *vilja ~ vara förmer än* want to appear superior to; *~ till* appear, be seen; *ingen människa -tes till* not a soul was to be seen **2** (*tyckas*) appear, seem (*för ngn* to s.b.); *det -tes mig som om* it looked to me as if; *vägen -tes henne lång* it seemed a long way to her **-bar** *a1* visible; (*märkbar*) apparent; (*uppenbar*) obvious, evident **-barligen** [-a:-] apparently; (*tydligen*) evidently, obviously **-bild** visual picture **-centrum** visual centre

synd *s3* **1** sin; *~en straffar sig själv* sin carries its own punishment; *förlåt oss våra ~er* (*bibl.*) forgive us our trespasses; *begå en ~* commit a sin; *bekänna sin ~* confess one's guilt; *för mina ~ers skull* (*vard.*) for my sins; *hata ngn som ~en* hate s.b. like poison; *det är ingen ~ att dansa* there is no harm (sin) in dancing **2** (*skada*) pity; *så ~!* what a pity (shame)!; *det är ~ och skam att* it is really too bad that; *det är ~ att du inte kan komma* what a pity you can't come; *det är ~ om honom* one can't help feeling sorry for him; *det är ~ på så rara ärter* (*vard.*) what a waste!; *det vore ~ att påstå att* you can't really say that; *tycka ~ om* pity, feel sorry for

synda sin, commit a sin (*mot* against); (*bryta mot*) trespass (*mot* against)

synda|bekännelse confession of sin[s] **-bock** scapegoat; *vard.* whipping boy **-fall** *~et* the Fall [of man] **-flod** flood, deluge; *~en* the Flood; *före* (*efter*) *~en* antediluvian (postdiluvian) **-förlåtelse** remission of sins; *kyrkl.* absolution; *ge ngn ~* absolve s.b. of his (*etc.*) sin[s] **-pengar** (*orätt vunna*) ill-gotten gains; (*om pris*) exorbitant price (*sg*)

synda|re sinner **-register** *bildl.* list (register) of one's sins **-straff** punishment for [one's] sin[s]

synderska sinner, sinful woman

syndetikon [-'de:-, -ån] *s7* [fish] glue

synd|fri free from sin, sinless **-full** full of sin; sinful (*liv* life) **-ig** *a1* sinful; *det vore ~t att* it would be a sin to **-igt** *adv* **1** sinfully **2** *vard.* awfully

syndikal|ism syndicalism **-ist** *s3* syndicalist **-istisk** [-'liss-] *a5* syndicalist[ic]

syndikat *s7* syndicate; combine; trust

syndrom [-'å:m] *s7* syndrome

syn|eförrättning inspection, survey **-fel** visual defect **-fält** field (range) of vision (sight) **-förmåga** [faculty of] vision, [eye]sight **-håll** *inom* (*utom*) *~* within (out of) sight (view) **-intryck** visual impression

synka (*vard. för synkronisera*) sync

synkop [-'kå:p] *s3* syncope

synkop|e ['synn-] *s3, språkv. o. med.* syncope **-era** syncopate **-ering** [-'pe:-] syncopation

synkrets *se synfält; bildl.* [mental] horizon, range of vision

synkron [-'krå:n] *a1* synchronous **-isera** synchronize; *~d växellåda* synchromesh gearbox

-isering [-'se:-] synchronization **-isk** *a1* synchronic **-motor** synchronous motor **-ur** synchronous clock

syn|lig [*ˣsy:n-] *a1* visible (*för* to); (*iögonfallande*) conspicuous; (*märkbar*) discernible; *bli ~* become visible, (*komma i sikte*) come in sight, *sjö.* heave in sight; *~t bevis* physical evidence **-lighet** visibility **-minne** visual memory

synner|het *r, i ~* [more] particularly (especially); *i all ~* in particular; *i ~ som* (*äv.*) all the more [so] as **-lig** *a1* particular; (*påfallande*) pronounced **-ligen** particular; extraordinarily; *~ lämpad för* eminently suited for; *~ tacksam* extremely grateful; *samt och ~* (*allesammans*) all and sundry

synnerv optic (visual) nerve

synod [-'nå:d, -'nɔ:d] *s3* synod

synonym I *a1* synonymous **II** *s3, s7* synonym **-ordbok** dictionary of synonyms

synop|s [-å-] *s3*, **-sis** [-'nåpp-] *s3* synopsis **-tisk** [-'nåpp-] *a5* synoptic (*karta* chart)

synorgan organ of sight

syn|punkt *bildl.* point of view, viewpoint; *från medicinsk ~* from a medical point of view; *från en annan ~* from a different angle **-rand** horizon **-sinne** [faculty of] vision, [eye]sight; *med ~t* (*äv.*) visually

syn|sk [-y:-] *a5* clairvoyant **-skadad** with defective vision **-skärpa** visual acuity **-sätt** outlook, approach

syn|taktisk [-'takk-] *a5* syntactic[al] **-tax** *s3* syntax **-tes** *s3* synthesis

syntet|fiber synthetic (man-made) fibre **-isera** synthesize, synthetize **-tisk** [-'te:-] *a5* synthetic [al]

syn|vidd range of vision (sight) **-villa** optical illusion **-vinkel** visual (optic) angle; *bildl.* angle of approach

sy|nål [sewing] needle **-nålsbrev** packet of needles

syokonsulent [*ˣsy:ɔ-] *ung.* careers master (mistress, adviser)

sypåse workbag

syra I *s1* **1** *kem.* acid; *frätande ~* corrosive acid **2** (*syrlig smak*) acidity, sourness; *äpplenas friska ~* the fresh tang of the apples **3** *bot.* dock, sorrel **II** *v1* acidify, sour **-angrepp** corrosion **-bad** acid bath **-fast** acid-proof, acid-resisting **-överskott** excess of acid, hyperacidity

syre *s6* oxygen **-brist** lack of oxygen **-fattig** deficient in oxygen **-förening** oxygen compound **-haltig** *a1* containing oxygen, oxygenous

syrén *s3* lilac, syringa **-buske** lilac [bush]

syretillförsel oxygen supply (feed)

syrgas oxygen **-apparat** oxygen apparatus **-behållare** oxygen cylinder (container)

Syrien ['sy:-] *n* Syria

syr|ier ['sy:-] *s9* Syrian **-isk** ['sy:-] *a5* Syrian

syrlig [*ˣsy:r-] *a1* acid (*äv. bildl.*), sourish, somewhat sour; *göra ~* acidify **-het** [sub]acidity, sourness; *bildl.* acidity

syrsa *s1* cricket

syrsätt|a oxygenate, oxygenize **-ning** oxygenation

syrtut *s3* surtout; frock coat

sy|saker *pl, se sybehör* **-silke** sewing silk

syskon [-ån] *s7* brother[s] and sister[s]; *fack.*
sibling[s] **-barn 1** (*kusin*) *vi är* ~ we are [first]
cousins **2** (*pojke*) nephew, (*flicka*) niece **-bädd**
sova i ~ bundle **-skara** family [of brothers and
sisters]
syskrin workbox
sysselsatt *a4* occupied (*med* with; *med att* in +
ing-form); (*upptagen*) engaged (*med* in, with;
med att in + *ing-form*); (*strängt upptagen*) busy
(*med* with; *med att* + *ing-form*); (*anställd*) employed (*vid* on; *med* in)
sysselsätt|a occupy; engage; keep busy; *hur
många arbetare -er fabriken?* how many workers
does the factory employ?; ~ *sig med* occupy
(busy) o.s. with; *vad skall vi* ~ *barnen med?* what
shall we occupy the children with? **-ning** (*-ande*)
occupying; (*göromål*) occupation, employment;
konkr. äv. work, something to do; *full* ~ full employment; *utan* ~ idle, with nothing to do, (*arbetslös*) out of work, unemployed
sysselsättnings|problem employment prob-
lem **-terapi** occupational therapy
syssl|a|a *s1* **1** (*sysselsättning*) occupation *etc.*; (*gö-
romål äv.*) work, business, task; *husliga -or*
household (domestic) duties, *AE. äv.* chore;
sköta sina -or do one's work; *tillfälliga -or* odd
jobs **2** (*tjänst*) office, employment; *sköta sin* ~
discharge one's duties **II** *v1* busy o.s., be busy
(*med* with); (*göra*) do; (*plocka*) potter (*med*
over); (*yrkesmässigt ägna sig åt*) do [for a living]
syssling second cousin
sysslo|lös idle; (*arbetslös*) unemployed, out of
work; (*overksam*) inactive; *gå* ~ go idle, do nothing **-löshet** idleness, inactivity; unemployment
-man (*vid sjukhus*) manager, superintendent; (*i
konkurs*) receiver; (*domkyrko-*) deacon
systęm *s7* system; (*friare*) method, plan; *period-
iska -et* the periodic table; *enligt ett* ~ on (according to) a system; *sätta i* ~, *se systematisera*
systematįk *s3, ej pl* systematics (*pl, behandlas
som sg*), systematism; (*klassificering*) classification **-er** [-'ma:-] systematist
systematiser|a systematize, reduce to a system
-ing systematizing; (*med pl*) systematization
system|atisk [-'ma:-] *a5* systematic[al]; me-
thodical **-bolag** [state-controlled] company for
the sale of wines and spirits **-butik** [state-con-
trolled] liquor shop
system|erare [-×me:-], **-man** computer pro-
grammer **-skifte** change of system **-teori** systems theory **-vetenskap** systems analysis
syster *s2* sister; (*sjuk-*) nurse **-dotter** niece **-far-
tyg** twin ship **-företag** sister company, affiliated firm **-lig** *a1* sisterly **-skap** sisterhood **-son**
nephew
sytråd sewing cotton (thread)
syvende *till* ~ *och sist* in the final analysis
1 så *s2* tub, bucket
2 så I *adv* **1** (*på* ~ *sätt*) so, (*starkare*) thus; (*i* ~
hög grad) so, such; (*vid jämförelse*) as, (*nekande*)
so; (*hur*) how; *den* ~ *kallade* the so-called; ~ *att
säga* so to speak; *si och* ~ [rather] so-so; *än si än*
~ now this way now that; *han säger än si än* ~ he
says one thing now and s.th. else later; *hur* ~?
how then?, how do you mean?; *det förhåller sig*
~ *att* the fact is that; ~ *går det när* that is what

happens when; ~ *får man inte göra* you must not
do that; ~ *skall man inte göra* that is not the way
to do it; ~ *sade han* those were his words; *det ser
inte* ~ *ut* it doesn't look like it; *skrik inte* ~*!* don't
shout like that!; ~ *slutade hans liv* that's how his
life ended; *han var listigare än* ~ he was more
cunning than that; *även om* ~ *skulle vara* even if
that was so; ~ *är det* that's how it is; *är det inte* ~*?*
isn't that right?; *det är* ~ *att* the thing is that; *det
är nu en gång* ~ *att* it so happens that; *tack* ~
mycket! thank you so much!; ~ *dum är han inte*
he is not that stupid; *det var* ~ *dåligt väder att* it
was such bad weather that; *med* ~ *hög röst* in
such a loud voice; *det är inte* ~ *lätt* it is not so
easy; *hon blev* ~ *rädd att* she was so frightened
that; *du skrämde mig* ~ you frightened me so;
inte ~ *stor* som not so big as; *han skakade* ~ *stor
han var* he was shaking all over; ~ *snällt av dig!*
how nice of you!; ~ *stor du har blivit!* how tall you
have grown!; ~ *du säger!* whatever are you say-
ing? **2** (*i vissa uttryck*) ~ *här* (*där*) like this (that);
~ *där en 25 år* round about 25 years, (*om pers.*)
somewhere about 25; ~ *där en tio pund* a matter
of ten pounds; ~ *här kan det inte fortsätta* it
(things) can't go on like this; *rätt* ~ quite; *för* ~
vitt provided (*han kommer* that he comes) **3** ~*?*
(*verkligen*) really?; ~ [*där*] *ja!* (*lugnande*) there
you are!; *se* ~, *upp med hakan!* come now, cheer
up! **4** (*sedan*) then; *först hon* ~ *han* first she then
he **5** (*konjunktionellt*) then, and; *kom* ~ *får du se*
come here and you will see; *om du säger det* ~ *är
det* ~ if you say so, then it is so; *vill du* ~ *kommer
jag* if you wish I shall come; *vänta* ~ *kommer jag*
wait there and I shall come; *men* ~ *är jag också*
but then I am **II** *pron, i* ~ *fall* in that (such a) case,
if so; *i* ~ *måtto* to that (such an) extent (*att* that);
på ~ *sätt* in that way
3 så *v4* sow (*äv. bildl.*); (*beså äv.*) seed
sådan [×så:-, *vard.* sånn] such; like this (that); *en*
~ *a*) (*fören.*) such a[n], *b*) (*självst.*) one of those;
en ~ *som han* a man like him; ~ *där* (*här*) like
that (this); ~ *är han* that is how he is; ~*t* (*självst.*)
such a thing; *allt* ~*t* everything of the kind; *ngt
*~*t* such a thing, s.th. of the kind; ~*t händer* these
things will happen; *det är* ~*t som händer varje dag*
these are things that (such things as) happen every day; ~*t är livet* such is life; *en* ~ *vacker hatt!*
what a beautiful hat!; ~*a påhitt!* what ideas!
sådd *s3* sowing; (*utsådd säd*) seed
såd|ig *a1* branny **-or** *pl* bran (*sg*)
sådär *se 2 så I 2* **-främt** *se såvida*
1 såg *imperf. av se*
2 såg *s2* saw; (*sågverk*) sawmill
såg|a saw (*av* off); ~ *till* saw; ~ *sönder* saw up
-blad sawblade **-bock** sawhorse **-fisk** sawfish
-klinga (*cirkel-*) circular sawblade **-ning** [-å:-]
sawing **-spån** sawdust **-tandad** *a5* sawtoothed;
fack. serrate[d] **-verk** sawmill; *AE.* lumber mill
-verksindustri sawmill (*AE.* lumber) industry
så|här *se 2 så I 2* **-ja** [´så:-] *se 2 så I 3*
såld *a5* sold; *gör du det är du* ~ (*vard.*) if you do
that you are done for **sålde** *imperf. av sälja*
således 1 (*följaktligen*) consequently, accordingly **2** (*på det sättet*) thus
såll *s7* sieve, sifter, strainer; (*grovt*) riddle **sålla**
sift, sieve; riddle; *bildl.* sift, screen

S

sålt *sup. av sälja*

sålunda thus; in this way (manner)

sång *s3* song; (*sjungande*) singing (*äv. som skol-ämne*); (*kyrko-*) hymn; (*munkars*) chant, chanting; (*dikt*) poem; (*avdelning av dikt*) canto **sång|are 1** *pers.* singer; (*i kör äv.*) chorister; (*t. yrket*) professional singer; (*jazz- o.d.*) vocalist **2** *zool.* warbler **-bar** *a1* singable, melodious **-bok** song book **-erska** [female] singer *etc., jfr sångare* **-fågel** songster, singing bird, songbird **-förening** singing club; choral society, glee club **-gudinna** muse **-kör** choir **-lektion** singing lesson **-lärare** singing master **-lärarinna** singing mistress **-mö** muse **-röst** singing voice **-spel** musical; ballad opera **-stämma** vocal part **-svan** whooper [swan] **-trast** song thrush **-övning** singing exercise

sångings|man sower **-maskin** sowing machine; (*rad-*) [sowing] drill

sånär almost

såp|a I *s1* soft soap **II** *v1,* ~ [*in*] soap **-bubbla** soap bubble; *blåsa -bubblor* blow bubbles **-hal** slippery; *vägen var* ~ the road was like a skating rink **-lödder** soapsuds (*pl*), lather **-vatten** suds (*pl*), soapy water

sår *s7* wound (*äv. bildl.*); (*bränn-*) burn; (*skär-*) cut; (*var-*) sore (*äv. bildl.*); *ett gapande* ~ a gash, a deep cut

såra wound (*äv. bildl.*); *bildl. äv.* hurt **sårad** *a5* wounded (*äv. bildl.*); (*skadad*) injured; *djupt* ~ deeply hurt; ~ *fåfänga* pique; *känna sig* ~ feel hurt (offended); **-sårande** *a4* (*kränkande*) insulting, offensive

sår|bar [-å.-] *a1* vulnerable; *bildl. äv.* susceptible; *vard.* touchy **-barhet** vulnerability *etc.*; touchiness **-feber** surgical fever **-förband** bandage **-ig** *a1* covered with sores; (*inflammerad*) ulcered **-salva** ointment [for wounds] **-skorpa** scab, crust

sås *s3* sauce; (*kött-*) gravy, juice **såsa 1** (*tobak*) sauce **2** (*söla*) dawdle, loiter **såskopp 1** *se sås-skål* **2** *pers.* dawdler, slowcoach, *AE.* slowpoke **såsom** ['så:såm] **1** (*liksom*; *i egenskap av*) as; ~ *den äldste i sällskapet* as the eldest present [at the gathering] **2** (*t. exempel*) for instance; such as **sås|sked** sauce ladle, gravy spoon **-skål** gravy dish, sauce boat **-snipa** sauce boat

såt *a1, ej gärna i enstavig form,* ~*a vänner* intimate friends, great chums (pals)

så|tillvida [-ˣvi:-] ~ *som* [*in*] so far as, inasmuch as **-vida** [-ˣvi:-] provided (*inget oförutsett inträffar* [that] nothing unforeseen happens); ~ *annat ej överenskommits mellan parterna* unless the parties have agreed otherwise **-vjtt** as (so) far as (*jag vet* I know) **-väl** ['så:-, -'vä:l] ~ *stora som små* big as well as small, both big and small

säck *s2* sack; (*mindre*) bag; *en* ~ *potatis* a sack of potatoes; *köpa grisen i* ~*en* buy a pig in a poke; *i* ~ *och aska* in sackcloth and ashes; *svart som i en* ~ [as] black as ink; *det har varit i* ~ *innan det kom i påse* he (*etc.*) has picked that up from somewhere (someone) else; *bädda* ~ make an apple-pie bed **säcka** (*hänga som en säck*) be baggy; ~ *ihop* (*bildl.*) collapse

säck|hållare sack holder **-ig** *a1* baggy **-löpning** sack race **-pipa** bagpipe[s *pl*] **-pip[s]blåsare**

piper, bagpiper **-väv** sacking, sackcloth

säd *s3* **1** ([*frön av*] *sädesslag*) corn; *i sht AE.* grain; (*utsäde*) seed; (*gröda*) crop[s *pl*] **2** (*sperma*) sperm, semen; seed (*äv. bildl.*)

sädes|avgång ejaculation **-ax** ear of corn **-cell** sperm [cell] **-fält** cornfield **-korn** grain of corn **-kärve** [corn]sheaf (*pl* sheaves) **-slag** [kind (variety) of] corn (grain), cereal **-ärla** wagtail **-vätska** seminal fluid

säg|a [*vard.* ˣsäjja] *sade* (*vard. sa*) *sagt* **I 1** say (*ett ord* a word; *nej* no); (*berätta*; ~ *till, åt*) tell; ~ *ja* [*till ...*] (*äv.*) answer [...] in the affirmative, (*förslag*) agree to ...; ~ *nej* [*till ...*] (*äv.*) answer [...] in the negative; *gör som jag -er* do as I say (tell you); *vem har sagt det?* who said so?, who told you?; *-er du det?* you don't say?, really?; *det -er du bara!* you're only saying that!; *så att* ~ so to speak; *om jag så får* ~ if I may say so; *om låt oss* ~ *en vecka* in [let us] say a week; ~ *vad man vill* men say what you will, but; *inte låta* ~ *sig ngt två gånger* not need to be told twice; *sagt och gjort* no sooner said than done; *ha mycket att* ~ (*bildl.*) have a great deal to say; *det vill* ~ that is [to say]; *förstå vad det vill* ~ *att* know what it is [like] to; *vad vill detta* ~? what is the meaning of this?; *han slog näven i bordet så det sa pang* he banged his fist down on the table; *det må jag* [*då*] ~*!, jag -er då det!* I must say!, well, I never!; *vad -er du! sa!* well, I told you so!, what did I tell you?; *det -s att han är rik, han -s vara rik* he is said to be rich; *jag har hört* ~*s* I have heard [it said], I have been told **II** (*med betonad partikel*) **1** ~ *efter* repeat **2** ~ *emot* contradict **3** ~ *ifrån* speak one's mind; *säg ifrån när du är trött* let me (*etc.*) know when you are tired; ~ *ifrån på skarpen* put one's foot down **4** ~ *om* say over again, repeat; *det -er jag ingenting om* I am not surprised [to hear that], (*det har jag inget emot*) I have nothing against (no objection to) that **5** ~ *till ngn* tell s.b.; *gå utan att* ~ *till* go without leaving word; *säg till när du är färdig* let me (*etc.*) know when you are ready; ~ *till om ngt* order s.th. **6** ~ *upp en hyresgäst* give a tenant notice [to quit]; ~ *upp sin lägenhet* give notice [of removal]; ~ *upp ngn* give s.b. notice, *vard.* sack s.b.; ~ *upp sig* (*sin plats*) give notice; ~ *upp ett kontrakt* revoke (cancel) an agreement; ~ *upp bekantskapen med* break off relations with **7** ~ *åt ngn* tell s.b. (*att han skall komma to* come) **III** *rfl,* ~ *sig vara* pretend to be (*glad* happy); *han -er sig vara sjuk* he says he is ill; *det -er sig* [*av sig*] *själv* [*t*] it goes without saying

sägandes *i uttr.: skam till* ~ to my (*etc.*) shame I (*etc.*) must admit

sägen ['sä:-] *sägnen* [-ŋn-] *sägner* [-ŋn-] legend **-omspunnen** legendary

säk|er ['sä:-] *a2* (*viss*) sure (*om, på* of, about), certain (*på* of); positive (*på* about); (*som ej medför fara*) safe (*förvar* custody), secure; (*pålitlig*) safe, trustworthy, reliable; (*garanterad*) assured (*ställning* position); ~ *blick* [a] sure eye; ~*ra bevis* positive proofs; *gå en* ~ *död till mötes* [go to] meet certain death; *är det alldeles* ~*t?* is it really true?; *så mycket är* ~*t att* this much is certain that; *vara* ~ *på sin sak* (*vara viss*) be certain [that] one is right, be quite sure; *kan jag vara* ~ *på det?*

can I be sure of that?; *är du ~ på det?* are you sure (certain) [about] that?; *jag är nästan ~ på att vinna* I am almost certain to win; *du kan vara ~ på att du* you may rest assured that; *lova ~t att du gör det* be sure to do it; *det blir ~t regn* it is sure to rain; *vara ~ på handen* have a steady (sure) hand; *vara ~ i engelska* be good at English; *det är -rast att du* to make quite sure you had better; *-ra papper* good securities; *gå ~ för* be safe from, be above; *ingen går ~* no one is safe (immune); *sitta ~t i sadeln, se sadel; ta det -ra före det osäkra* better be safe than sorry; *vara på den -ra sidan* be on the safe side; *från ~ källa* from a reliable source (a trustworthy informant); *~ smak* infallible taste; *ett ~t uppträdande* assured manners (*pl*) **säkerhet 1** certainty; safety, security; (*själv-*) confidence, assurance; reliability; *för ~s skull* for safety's sake; *den allmänna ~en* public safety; *i ~* in safety, safe; *sätta sig i ~* get out of harm's way; *med* [*allt*] *~ certainly*; *med ~ komma att* be sure (certain) to; *veta med ~* (*äv.*) know for certain **2** (*borgen; garanti*) security; *ställa ~* give (provide, furnish) security; *~ i fast egendom* real security **säkerhets|anordning** safety device (appliance) **-avstånd** safe distance **-bestämmelser** *pl* security (safety) regulations **-bälte** safety (seat) belt; *ta på sig ~t, vard.* belt up **-kedja** door (safety) chain **-lina** safety harness **-lås** safety lock **-marginal** safety margin, clearance **-nål** safety pin **-polis** security police **-risk** security risk **-rådet** the Security Council **-skäl** reasons of security **-synpunkt** security (safety) point of view **-tjänst** (*mot spionage etc.*) counterintelligence, security service **-tändsticka** safety match **-ventil** safety valve **-åtgärd** precautionary measure, precaution; *vidtaga ~er* take precautions

säker|ligen certainly, no doubt, undoubtedly **-ställa** ensure, guarantee; (*ekonomiskt äv.*) provide with sufficient funds; *~ sig* protect (cover) o.s. (*för* against)

säkert ['sä:-] *adv* (*med visshet*) certainly, to be sure, no doubt; *AE. äv.* sure; (*stadigt*) securely, firmly; (*pålitligt*) steadily; *du känner dem ~* I am sure you know them; *det vet jag* [*alldeles*] *~* I know that for certain (sure); *jag vet inte ~ om* I am not quite sure (certain) whether

säkr|a [-ä:-] **1** (*skydda*) safeguard, secure; (*ekonomiskt*) secure, guarantee **2** (*vapen*) put (set) at safety (half-cock); (*göra fast*) fasten, secure **-ing** *elektr.* fuse; (*trög*) delayed-action fuse; (*på vapen*) safety catch; *en ~ har gått* a fuse has blown

säl *s2* seal **-bisam** muskrat **-fångst** sealing

sälg [-j] *s2* sallow **-pipa** willow pipe

sälj|a *sålde sålt* sell; (*marknadsföra*) market; (*handla med*) trade in; *~ ngt för 5 pund* sell s.th. for 5 pounds; *~ i parti* sell wholesale; *~ i minut* retail; *~ ngt i fast räkning* receive a firm order for s.th.; *~ slut* clear; *~ ut* sell out **-are** seller; *jur. äv.* vendor; *~s marknad* seller's market **-bar** *a1* saleable, marketable; *inte ~* unsaleable **-främjande** *a4, ~ åtgärder* sales promotion (*sg*) **-förmåga** ability to sell **-ingenjör** sales engineer **-kurs** selling rate (price); *sälj- och köpkurs* ask and bid price **-ledare** sales executive (manager)

säll *a1* blissful; (*salig*) blessed; *de ~a jaktmarkerna* the happy hunting grounds

sälla ~ sig till join, associate [o.s.] with

sällan seldom, rarely; *~ eller aldrig* hardly ever; *~ förekommande* [of] rare [occurrence]; *högst ~* very seldom, *vard.* once in a blue moon; *inte så ~* pretty frequently, quite often

sälle *s2* fellow; *en oförvägen ~* a daredevil; *en rå ~* a brute

sällhet felicity, bliss

sällsam *a1* strange; singular

sällskap *s7* **1** (*samling pers.*) party; company; *slutet (blandat) ~* private (mixed) party (company) **2** (*samfund*) society; (*församling*) assembly; (*förening äv.*) association, club **3** (*följeslagare; samvaro*) company; *får vi ~?* (*på vägen*) are you going my way?; *för ~s skull* for company; *göra ~ med ngn* go with s.b.; *gör du ~ med oss?* are you coming with us?; *hålla ngn ~* keep s.b. company; *råka i dåligt ~* get into bad company; *resa i ~ med ngn* travel together with s.b.

sällskap|a ~ med associate with **-lig** [-a:-] *a1* social; (*som trivs i sällskap*) sociable (*läggning* disposition)

sällskaps|dam [lady's] companion (*hos* to) **-dans** ballroom dance (dancing) **-hund** pet dog **-lek** party game **-liv** social life, society; *deltaga i ~et* move in society; *debutera i ~et* come out **-människa** sociable person **-resa** conducted tour **-rum** drawing room; (*på hotell e.d.*) lounge, assembly room **-sjuk** longing for company **-spel** party (parlour) game **-talang** social talent

Sällskapsöarna *pl* the Society Islands

sällspord [-ɔ:-] *a5, se -synt*

sällsynt [-y:-] *a1* rare, uncommon; unusual; *en ~ gäst* an infrequent (a rare) visitor; *en ~ varm dag* an exceptionally hot day **-het** rarity; *det hör till ~erna* it is a rare thing (is unusual); *det är ingen ~* it is by no means a rare thing

säl|skinn sealskin **-skytt** sealer **-skytte** sealing **-späck** seal blubber

sälta *s1* saltness, salinity; *mista sin ~* (*äv.*) get (become) insipid

sälunge seal calf

sämja *s1* concord, amity, harmony **sämjas** *v2, dep* agree (*i fråga om* on); *jfr samsas*

sämre ['sämm-] **I** *a, komp. t. dålig* (*vid jämförelse*) worse; (*underlägsen*) inferior (*kvalitet* quality; *än* to), poorer; (*utan eg. jämförelse*) bad, poor; *bli ~* (*äv. om sjuk*) get (grow) worse; *han är inte ~ för det* he is none the worse for that **II** *adv, komp. t. illa* worse; badly, poorly

sämsk|garva chamois **-skinn** chamois [leather]; wash-leather

sämst *a o. adv, superl. t. dålig, illa* worst; *han är ~ i klassen* he is the worst in (at the bottom of) the class; *tycka ~ om* dislike most

sända *v2* **1** send; *hand. äv.* dispatch, transmit; (*pengar*) remit; *~ med posten* post, mail; *~ vidare* forward, send (pass) on **2** *radio.* transmit, broadcast; *TV* televise, telecast

sändar|amatör radio amateur **-anläggning** transmitting equipment

sändare *radio.* transmitter **sändebud 1** envoy; (*minister*) minister; (*ambassadör*) ambassador **2** messenger, emissary

S

sänder ['sänn-] *i uttr.: i* ~ at a time; *en i* ~ (*äv.*) one by one; *litet i* ~ little by little; *en sak i* ~ one thing at a time

sänd|lista mailing list **-ning 1** sending; (*varu-*) consignment; (*med fartyg*) shipment **2** *radio.* transmission, broadcast

sändningstid *radio.* air (transmission) time; *på bästa* ~ (*i TV*) during peak viewing hours

säng *s2* **1** bed; (*själva möbeln äv.*) bedstead; *i* ~*en* in bed; *hålla sig i* ~*en* stay in bed; *skicka i* ~ send to bed; *stiga ur* ~*en* get out of bed; *ta ngn på* ~*en* catch s.b. in bed, *bildl.* catch s.b. napping; *dricka kaffe på* ~*en* have coffee in bed; *ligga till* ~*s* be in bed; *lägga till* ~*s* put to bed **2** (*träd-gårds-*) bed **-botten** bottom of a (the) bed[stead] **-dags** *det är* ~ it is time to go to bed; *vid* ~ at bedtime **-fösare** nightcap **-gavel** end of a (the) bed (bedstead) **-gående** *s6, vid* ~*t* at bedtime, on retiring **-halm** bedstraw **-himmel** canopy **-kammare** bedroom **-kant** edge of a (the) bed; *vid* ~*en* at the bedside **-kläder** bedclothes; bedding (*sg*) **-lampa** bedside lamp **-liggande** [lying] in bed; (*sjuk*) confined to [one's] bed; (*sedan länge*) bedridden; *bli* ~ (*lägga sig sjuk*) take to one's bed **-linne** bed-linen **-matta** bedside rug **-omhänge** bed-curtains, bed-hangings (*pl*) **-plats** sleeping accommodation; bed **-skåp** box bed, wardrobe bed **-stolpe** bedpost **-täcke** quilt **-värmare** warming pan; hot-water bottle **-vätare** bed-wetter **-vätning** bed-wetting **-överkast** bedspread, counterpane

sänk|a *l s1* **1** (*fördjupning*) hollow, depression [in the ground]; (*dal*) valley **2** *med., se* sänknings-reaktion **II** *v3* **1** (*få att sjunka*) sink; (*borra fartyg i sank*) scuttle; (*i vätska*) submerge **2** (*göra lägre, dämpa*) lower (*priset* the price; *sina anspråk* one's pretentions; *rösten* one's voice); ~ *blicken* drop one's eyes; ~ *fanan* dip the flag; ~ *priserna* (*äv.*) reduce the prices; ~ *vattennivån i en sjö* lower (sink) the level of a lake; ~ *skatterna* cut (lower, reduce) taxes **3** *rfl* descend; (*om sak*) sink, droop; (*om mark*) incline, slope; (*om pers.*) lower (demean) o.s.; ~ *sig till att* condescend to; *skymningen -er sig* twilight is falling; *solen -er sig i havet* the sun is sinking into the sea **-bar** *al* folding down; *höj- och* ~ vertically adjustable

sänk|e *s6* (*på metrev*) sinker, lead; (*smides-*) die, swage **-håv** scap (scoop) net **-lod** plumb [bob], plummet **-ning 1** sinking *etc.*; (*av pris*) reduction, lowering **2** (*fördjupning*) declivity, downward slope **-ningsreaktion** sedimentation rate (reaction)

Säpo ['sä:-] (*förk. för* säkerhetspolisen) the [Swedish] security police

sär|a ~ [*på*] separate, part **-art** specific nature (type) **-behandla** (*missgynna*) discriminate against, disfavour; (*gynna*) favour **-beskattning** individual (separate) taxation **-deles** extraordinarily, exceedingly **-drag** characteristic; (*egenhet*) peculiarity **-egen** *a3* peculiar, singular **-fall** special case

särk *s2, åld.* shift; *vard.* (*nattsärk*) nightshirt

sär|klass *i* ~ a class of its own **-ling** individualist, eccentric, character **-märke, -prägel** *se* särdrag **-präglad** [-ä:g-] *a5* striking, peculiar, individual, distinctive **-skild** *a5* (*bestämd, viss*) special, particular; (*avskild*) separate; (*egen*) individual, peculiar; *vid* ~*a tillfällen* on special (*olika:* several) occasions; *ingenting -skilt* nothing special (in particular); *i detta* ~*a fall* in this specific case; *måste anges -skilt* must be specified separately **-skilja** separate, keep separate; (*åt-*) distinguish; (*ur-*) discern **-skiljande** [-ʃ-] *s6* separation; distinction **-skilt** [-ʃ-] *adv* [e]specially *etc.*; (*för sig*) apart; *var och en* ~ each one separately; ~ *som* [e]specially as (since) **-skola 1** school for handicapped children **2** (*motsats* samskola) school for boys (girls) only **-skriva** write in two words **-ställning** *intaga en* ~ hold a unique (an exceptional) position **-tryck** offprint, separate impression; ~ *ur* reprinted from

säsong [-'såŋ] *s3* season; *mitt i* ~*en* in mid-season **-arbetare** seasonal worker **-arbetslöshet** seasonal unemployment **-betonad** seasonal **-biljett** season ticket

säte *s6* (*sits*) seat; (*huvudkvarter*) headquarters (*pl*); (*residens*) residence; (*bakdel*) seat, *vard.* behind; *ha sitt* ~ reside; *skillnad till säng och* ~ (*jur.*) separation from bed and board, judicial separation; *ha* ~ *och stämma* have a seat and vote

säter ['sä:-] *s2, se* fäbod

säteri *ung.* manor

sätes|bjudning *med.* breech presentation (birth) **-förlossning** breech delivery

1 sätt *s7* way, manner; fashion; (*tillvägagångs-*) method; (*umgänges-*) manners (*pl*); *ha ett vinnande* ~ have winning manners; *vad är det för ett* ~? don't you know any better?, what do you think you are doing?; *på* ~ *och vis* in a way, in certain respects; *på allt* ~ in every way; *på annat* ~ in another (a different) way; *på bästa* ~ in the best [possible] way; *på det* ~*et* in this way (manner); *på ett eller annat* ~ somehow [or other], in some way; *på mer än ett* ~ in more ways than one; *inte på minsta* ~ not by any means, in no way; *det är på samma* ~ *med* it is the same [thing] with; *på sitt* ~ in his (*etc.*) way; *på så* ~ in that way, (*som svar*) I see

2 sätt *s7* (*uppsättning*) set

sätt|a *satte* sätt **I 1** (*placera*) place, put; (*i sittande ställning*) seat (*ett barn på en stol* a child on a chair); ~ *barn till världen* bring children into the world; ~ *en fläck på* make a mark (stain) on; ~ *frukt* form fruit; *inte* ~ *sin fot på en plats vidare* not set foot in a place any more; ~ *färg på* colour, *bildl. äv.* lend (give) colour to; ~ *händerna för öronen* put one's hands over one's ears; ~ *klockan på sex* set one's watch at six; ~ *komma* (*punkt*) put a comma (full stop); ~ *ngn främst* put s.b. first; ~ *ngn högt* esteem s.b. highly, think highly of s.b.; ~ *värde på* value **2** (*plantera*) plant, set **3** *boktr.* compose, set **4** *komma* ~*ndes* come dashing (running) **II** (*med betonad partikel*) **1** ~ *av a*) ~ *av ngn någonstans* put s.b. down somewhere, *b*) (*rusa iväg*) dash off (away), *c*) (*pengar*) set apart, earmark **2** ~ *bort* put aside **3** ~ *efter* (*förfölja*) set off after; run after **4** ~ *fast a*) (*fästa*) fix (*på* to), *b*) (*ange*) report **5** ~ *fram* put (set) out, (*stolar*) draw up; ~ *fram en stol åt* bring [up] a chair for **6** ~ *för* put up (*fönster-luckor* shutters) **7** ~ *i a*) put in, *b*) (*införa*) install, *c*) (*installera*) install; ~ *i ngn ngt* (*inbilla*) put s.th.

into a p.'s head; ~ *i sig mat* (*vard.*) stow away
food **8** ~ *ihop* put together, *bildl.* (*utarbeta*) draw
up, compose (*ett telegram* a telegram), (*ljuga*) invent, make up **9** ~ *in a*) put ... in, put in ..., (*brev
e.d.*) file, *b*) (*börja*) set in, begin; ~ *in pengar i*
(*bank*) deposit money in, put (place) money into,
(*företag*) invest money in; ~ *ngn in i ngt* initiate
s.b. into s.th. **10** ~ *ner* put down, (*plantera*)
plant, set; reduce, depress **11** ~ *om* reset, replace, (*omplantera*) replant, *boktr.* reset, (*växel*)
renew, prolong **12** ~ *på sig* put on (*kläder*
clothes), take on (*en viktig min* consequential
airs) **13** ~ *till alla klutar* clap on all sail; ~ *till livet*
lose (sacrifice) one's life **14** ~ *undan* put by
(aside) **15** ~ *upp a*) put up (*ett staket* a fence),
put ... up (*på en hylla* on a shelf), *b*) (*grunda*)
found, set up (*en affär* a business), *c*) (*skriftligt
avfatta*) draw up (*ett kontrakt* a contract); ~ *upp
ett anslag* stick up a bill; ~ *upp en armé* raise an
army; ~ *upp gardiner* hang curtains; ~ *upp håret*
put up one's hair; ~ *upp ngn mot ngn* prejudice
s.b. against s.b.; ~ *upp en teaterpjäs* stage a play;
sätt upp det på mig put it down to my account **16**
~ *ut a*) put out, (*ett barn*) expose, *b*) (*skriva ut*)
put down (*datum* the date) **17** ~ *åt ngn* (*bildl.*)
clamp down on s.b. **18** ~ *över* (*forsla över*) put
across; ~ *över ett hinder* leap (jump) over a fence
III *rfl* **1** *eg.* seat o.s.; ~ *sig* [*ner*] sit down (*i soffan*
on the sofa); ~ *sig bekvämt* (*äv.*) find a comfort-
able seat; *han gick och satte sig vid* he went and
sat down by; *gå och sätt er!* go and sit down! **2**
(*placera sig*) place o.s.; put o.s. (*i spetsen för* at
the head of); *det onda har satt sig i ryggen* the
pain has settled in my (*etc.*) back; ~ *sig fast* stick;
~ *sig emot* oppose, rise (rebel) against; ~ *sig i respekt* make o.s. respected, ~ *sig in i* familiarize
o.s. with, get acquainted with, get into (*ett ämne* a
subject); ~ *sig upp i sängen* sit up in bed; ~ *sig
över* (*bildl.*) disregard, ignore, not mind **3** (*sjunka* [*ihop*]) settle; *huset har satt sig* the house has
settled **4** (*om vätska*) settle; (*om grums e.d.*) settle to the bottom

sättar|e compositor, typesetter **-lärling** com-
positor's apprentice

sätteri composing room **-faktor** composing-
-room foreman

sätt|lök (*blomlök*) bulb **-maskin** *boktr.* com-
posing (typesetting) machine, composer, type-
setter **-ning 1** setting; (*plantering*) planting **2**
boktr. composing, [type]setting **3** (*hopsjunk-
ning*) sinking, settling **4** *mus.* setting, arrangement **-potatis** seed potatoe

säv *s3* rush

sävlig [ˣsäːv-] *a1* slow, leisurely; *vara* ~ (*äv.*) be
a slowcoach, *AE.* slowpoke **-het** slowness

sävsångare sedge warbler

söcken [ˈsökk-] *s, i uttr.: i helg och* ~ [on] weekdays and Sundays **-dag** weekday, workday

söder [ˈsöː-] **I** *s9* south; *~n* the South **II** *adv* south;
~ *ifrån* from the south; ~ *ut* to the south

Söder|havet the South Pacific **-havsöarna** *pl*
the South Sea Islands

söder|sol *med* ~ facing south **-vägg** south-fac-
ing wall **-över** [ˈsöː-] in the south, southwards

södra [ˣsöːd-] *a, best. form* southern; ~ *halvklotet*
the southern hemisphere; *S~ ishavet* the Antarc-

tic Ocean

sög *imperf. av suga*

sök|a *v3* **1** seek (*lyckan* one's fortune); (*forska,
spana*) search (*efter* for); (*leta efter*) look for
(*nyckeln* the key), be on the lookout for (*arbete*
work); (*försöka träffa*) call on, want ([have]
come) to see; ~ *ngns blick* (*äv.*) try to catch a p.'s
eye; ~ *bot för* seek a remedy (cure) for; ~ *efter*
search (look) for; *han -te efter ord* he was at a loss
for words; ~ *i fickorna* search (rummage) in
one's pockets; ~ *kontakt med* try to [establish]
contact [with]; ~ *lugn och ro* try to find (be in
search of) peace and quiet; ~ *läkare* go to (consult) a doctor; ~ *sanningen* seek [the] truth; *kärleken -er icke sitt* (*bibl.*) love seeketh not its own;
vem -er ni? whom do you want to see?; *en dam
har -t er* a lady has called on (*per telefon*: rung,
called) you **2** (*för-*) try; ~ *vinna ngt* try (seek) to
win s.th. **3** (*an- om*) apply for (*plats* a post); try
(compete) for (*ett stipendium* a scholarship) **4**
(*lag-*) sue for (*skilsmässa* a divorce) **5** (*trötta*) try;
luften -er the air is very relaxing **6** *rfl*, ~ *sig bort*
try to get away; ~ *sig till* seek; ~ *sig till storstä-
derna* move to the cities; ~ *sig en annan plats* try
to find another post **7** (*med betonad partikel*) ~
fram hunt out; ~ *igenom* search (look) through;
~ *upp a*) seek out, *b*) (*be-*) go to see; ~ *ut* (*välja*)
choose, pick out

sökande I 1 *s6* search; pursuit **2** *s9, pers.* applicant, candidate (*t. en plats* for a post); (*rätts-*)
claimant, plaintiff; *anmäla sig som* ~ send (give)
in one's name as a candidate **II** *a4* searching (*blick*
look); *en* ~ *själ* a seeker, an enquirer

sökaranläggning paging equipment **sökare 1**
foto. [view]finder **2** (*-ljus*) [adjustable] spotlight

sökarljus *se sökare 2*

sökt [-öː-] *a4* (*lång-*) far-fetched; (*tillgjord*)
affected

söl *s7* (*senfärdig*) tardiness; (*dröjsmål*) delay

1 söla (*vara långsam*) loiter, lag [behind]; (*dröja*)
delay, tarry; ~ *på vägen hem* loiter on the way
home

2 söla (*smutsa*) soil (*äv.* ~ *ner*)

sölig *a1* (*långsam*) loitering, tardy, laggard

sölja *s1* buckle, clasp

sölkorv *vard.* slowcoach, dawdler; loiterer; *AE.*
slowpoke

1 söm [sömm] *s7, koll. äv. s9* (*hästsko-*) horse
nail

2 söm [sömm] *s2* seam; *med., anat.* suture; *gå
upp i ~men* come apart at the seam; *syna ngt i
~marna* scrutinize s.th.

sömlös seamless **sömma** sew, stitch

sömmersk|a seamstress; (*kläd-*) dressmaker
-etips (*ung.*) pools coupon filled in by a greenhorn (*eg.* seamstress)

sömn *s3* sleep; *falla i* ~ go to sleep, fall asleep;
gnugga ~en ur ögonen rub the sleep out of one's
eyes; *gå* (*tala*) *i ~en* walk (talk) in one's sleep; *ha
god* ~ sleep well, be a sound sleeper; *i ~en* in
one's sleep; *gråta sig till ~s* cry o.s. to sleep

sömnad *s3* sewing, needlework

sömn|drucken heavy with sleep **-givande**
soporific **-gångaraktig** *a1* somnambulistic
-gångare sleepwalker, somnambulist

sömn|ig *a1* sleepy; (*dåsig*) drowsy; *~t väder* le-

S

thargic weather **-ighet** sleepiness *etc.* **-lös** sleepless; *ha en ~ natt* have a sleepless night **-löshet** sleeplessness; *med.* insomnia; *lida av ~* be unable to sleep, suffer from insomnia **-medel** sleeping drug, soporific; hypnotic **-sjuka** *(afrikansk)* sleeping sickness **-tablett** sleeping tablet **-tuta** *sl* great sleeper; sleepyhead

sömsmån seam allowance

söndag ['sönn-] *s2* Sunday; *sön- och helgdagar* Sundays and public holidays

söndags|barn Sunday child; *han är ett ~ (äv.)* he was born under a lucky star **-bilaga** Sunday supplement **-bilist** Sunday driver **-bokstav** dominical letter **-fin** *göra sig ~* put on one's Sunday best **-frid** sabbath calm **-kläder** *pl* Sunday clothes; *vard.* Sunday best **-promenad** Sunday walk **-seglare** Sunday sailor **-skola** Sunday school

sönder ['sönn-] **I** *pred. a* broken; (*-riven*) torn; (*i bitar*) [all] in pieces **II** *adv* (*isär*) asunder; (*i flera delar*) to pieces, (*mera planmässigt*) into pieces; (*itu*) in two; *gå ~* get broken, break, smash [in two]; *krama ~* squeeze to bits; *slå ~* break, (*krossa äv.*) smash (*ett fönster* a window); *slå ngn ~ och samman* beat s.b. up **-bruten** broken [in two] **-bränd** *a5* burnt up (through); badly burnt **-dela** break up; (*stycka*) disjoint, dismember; *kem.* decompose **-delning** breaking up; disjointing *etc.*; *kem.* decomposition **-fall** disintegration, decomposition **-falla** fall to pieces; *bildl. o. fys.* disintegrate; (*kunna indelas*) be divisible (*i* into); *kem.* decompose (*i* into) **-fallshastighet** *kärnfys.* decay (disintegration) rate **-frusen** frozen to pieces **-kokt** [-ɔ:-] *a4* boiled to bits **-körd** (*om väg*) rutted **-läst** tattered **-riven** *a5* torn to pieces **-skjuten** [-ʃ-] *a5* riddled with bullets **-skuren** *a5* cut to pieces **-slagen** broken; *han var ~ i ansiktet* his face was badly knocked about **-slitande** *a4* tearing apart; *bildl.* shattering (*sorg* sorrow); excruciating (*smärta* pain) **-smula** crumble, crush **-trasad** *a5* tattered [and torn], in rags

söndr|a (*dela*) divide; (*avskilja*) sever, separate; (*göra oense*) disunite; *~ och härska* divide and rule; *~ sig i två grupper* divide (split up) into two groups **-ig** *a1, se trasig* **-ing** (*splittring*) division; (*oenighet*) discord, dissension, disagreement; (*schism*) schism

söp *imperf. av supa*

1 sörja *sl* sludge; (*smuts*) mud

2 sörj|a *v2* **1** (*i sitt sinne*) grieve (*över* at, for, over), feel grief (*över* at); *det är ingenting att ~ över* that is nothing to worry about **2** (*en avliden*) mourn; (*bära sorgdräkt efter*) be in mourning for; *~ förlusten av ngn (äv.)* grieve for (feel grief at) the loss of s.b. **3** *~ för* (*ombesörja*) attend to, see to (about); (*ha omsorg om*) provide (make provisions) for (*sina barns framtid* the future of one's children); *det är väl -t för henne* she is well provided for

sörjig *al* sludgy, slushy

sörpla drink noisily; *~ i sig* lap up

söt *al* **1** (*i smaken*) sweet (*äv. bildl.*); (*om vatten, mjölk*) fresh; *~ doft* sweet scent **2** (*vacker*) pretty, lovely; (*intagande*) charming, attractive; *AE. äv.* cute; *~a du!* my dear!

söt|a sweeten **-aktig** *al* sweetish, sickly sweet **-ebrödsdagar** *pl* halcyon days

söt|ma [*sött-] *sl* sweetness **-mandel** sweet almond **-mjölk** fresh milk; (*oskummad*) whole (full-cream) milk **-ning** [-ö:-] sweetening; sugaring **-ningsmedel** sweetening [agent], sweetener **-nos** *s2* darling, poppet; *AE.* honey, cutie **-potatis** batata; *koll.* batatas, sweet potatoes (*pl*) **-saker** *pl* sweets, sweetmeats; *AE.* candy; *vara förtjust i ~ (äv.)* have a sweet tooth **-sliskig** sickly sweet, mawkish **-sur** sour-sweet (*äv. bildl.*)

sött *adv* sweetly, in a sweet manner; *smaka ~* have a sweet taste; *sova ~* sleep peacefully

sötvatten freshwater

sötvattens|biologi limnology **-fisk** freshwater fish

söv|a *v2* **1** (*få att sova*) put to sleep; (*vagga t. sömns*) lull [to sleep]; (*göra sömnig*) make sleepy (drowsy); *bildl.* silence (*samvetet* one's conscience) **2** (*vid operation* an[a]esthetize; (*med kloroform äv.*) chloroform **-ande** *a4* soporific (*medel* drug); *~ mummel* drowsy murmur **-ning** [-ö:-] administration of an[a]esthetics **-ningsmedel** an[a]esthetic

ta *tog tagit* **I** take; (*~ fast*) catch, capture, seize; (*tillägna sig*) appropriate; (*~ med sig hit*) bring; (*~ sig*) have (*lektioner* lessons; *en cigarr* a cigar); (*göra*) make, do; *~ hand om* take charge of; *~ ngn i armen* take (seize) s.b. by the arm; *han vet hur han skall ~ henne* he knows just how to take her; *~ ledigt* take time off; *~ ngt för givet (på allvar)* take s.th. for granted (in earnest); *han tog det som ett skämt* he took it as a joke; *~ tid* take time; *~ fast tjuven* catch the thief; *han tog varenda boll* he caught every ball; *~ betalt* be paid; *~ bra betalt* know how to charge (make people pay); *vad ~r ni för ... ?* how much do you charge for ...?; *det tog honom hårt* it affected him deeply (hit him hard); *man ~r honom inte där man sätter honom* he has a will of his own; *vem ~r du mig för?* who do you think I am?; *~ fasta på* bear in mind, keep hold of; *skall vi ~ och öppna fönstret?* shall we open the window?; *kniven ~r inte* the knife does not bite; *var tog skottet?* where did it hit (go)?; *~ galoscher* put on rubbers; *var skall vi ~ pengarna ifrån?* where are we to find the money (get the money from)?; *~ det inte så noga* don't be too particular (fussy) about it; *~ pris* win a prize; *han ~r priset (bildl.)* he takes the cake; *~ tåget* take the train; *det ~r på krafterna* it tells on the (one's) strength; *han tog åt mössan* he touched his cap **II** (*med betonad partikel*) **1** ~ *av a*) take off (... off), *b*) (*vika av*) turn off; ~ *av* [*sig*] *kappan* take off one's coat **2** ~ *bort* take away (... away), remove **3** ~ *efter* imitate; copy **4** ~ *emot a*) (*mot-*) receive, (*folk äv.*) see (*gäster* guests), (*an-*) accept (*erbjudandet* the offer), take in (*tvätt* laundry), take up (*avgifter* fees), *b*) (*avvärja*) parry (*stöten* the blow), *c*) (*vara i vägen*) be in the way, offer resistance, *d*) (*vara motbjudande*) be repugnant; ~ *emot sig med händerna* put out one's hands to break one's fall; ~*r doktorn emot?* can I see the doctor? **5** ~ *fram* take out (... out) (*ur* of), produce (*biljetten* one's ticket) **6** ~ *för sig av* help o.s. to **7** ~ *hem a*) *kortsp.* take, get (*ett stick* a trick), *b*) *sjö.* reef (*seglen* the sails); ~ *hem på* shorten (*skotet* the sheet) **8** ~ *i* (*med händerna*) pull away, (*hjälpa till*) lend a hand, (*anstränga sig*) go at it [vigorously]; *det tog i att blåsa* the wind got up; *vad du* ~*r i!* you do go the whole hog, don't you? **9** ~ *ifrån* take away [from], (*ngn ngt äv.*) deprive s.b. of s.th. **10** ~ *igen* take back; (*förlorad tid äv.*) make up for; ~ *igen sig* (*vila sig*) take a rest, (*repa sig*) recover, come round **11** ~ *in a*) take in, (*bära in*) carry (bring) in, (*importera*) import, (*radiostation*) tune in to, *c*) (*förtjäna*) profit by, *d*) (*beställa*) order, *e*) (*läcka, bli överspolad*) ship (*vatten* water), *f*) (*ngn i en förening*) admit, *g*) (*slå sig ner*) put up (*hos ngn at* a p.'s house; *på hotell* at a hotel) **12** ~ *itu med* (*ngt*) set about [working at], set to work at, (*ngn*) take in hand **13** ~ *med* (*föra med sig*) bring; ~ *med ngt i räkningen* take s.th. into account **14** ~ *ner* take (fetch, bring) down, (*segel*) take in **15** ~ *om* take (read, sing, go through) again, *mus., teat., film äv.* repeat **16** ~ *på* [*sig*] *a*) (*klädesplagg o.d.*) put on, *b*) (*ansvar*) take upon o.s., (*för mycket arbete e.d.*) undertake, *c*) (*viktig min*) assume **17** ~ *till a*) take to (*vintermössan* one's winter cap), *b*) (*beräkna*) set up, charge (*för högt pris* a too high price), *c*) (*börja*) start, set about (*att + inf. el. ing-form*), *d*) (*överdriva*) overdo it, exaggerate; ~ *mod till sig* pluck up courage **18** ~ *tillbaka* take (carry, bring) back, (*ansökan, yttrande*) withdraw, (*löfte*) retract **19** ~ *undan* take away, (*för att gömma*) put out of the way **20** ~ *upp* (*jfr upp-*) *a*) take (carry, bring) up, (*från marken; passagerare*) pick up, *b*) (*öppna*) open, (*en knut*) undo, *c*) (*lån e.d.*) take up, *d*) (*order, skatter*) collect, *e*) *bildl.* bring up (*ett problem* a problem), (*en sång äv.*) strike up; ~ *upp sig, se repa sig, förkovra sig* **21** ~ *ur* take out [of], (*tömma äv.*) empty, (*fågel*) draw, (*fisk*) gut, (*fläck*) remove **22** ~ *ut a*) take (carry, bring) out, *b*) (*från bank*) withdraw, draw, *c*) (*lösa*) make out (*en rebus* a rebus), solve (*ett problem* a problem); ~ *ut en melodi på piano* pick out a tune on the piano; ~ *ut satsdelar* analyse [a sentence]; ~ *ut stegen* stride out **23** ~ *vid* (*börja, fortsätta*) step in, follow on, (*om sak*) begin, start; ~ *[illa] vid sig* be upset (put out) (*för* about) **24** ~ *åt sig a*) (*smuts e.d.*) attract, *b*) (*tillskriva sig*) take (*äran för* the credit for), *c*) (*känna sig träffad*) feel guilty; *vad* ~*r det åt dig?* what is the matter with you? **25** ~ *över* take over **III** *rfl* **1** take, have (*ett bad* a bath), (*servera sig*

äv.) help o.s. to (*en kopp te* a cup of tea); ~ *sig för pannan* put one's hand to one's forehead **2** (*växa till*) grow (come) on, (*om eld*) begin to burn; (*bli bättre*) improve **3** (*med betonad partikel*) ~ *sig an* take up; ~ *sig fram a*) (*bana sig väg*) [manage to] get, (*hitta*) find one's way, *b*) (*ekonomiskt*) make one's way, get on; ~ *sig för ngt* (*att + inf.*) set about s.th. (+ *ing- form*); *inte veta vad man skall* ~ *sig till* not know what to do; *vad* ~*r du dig till?* what are you up to?; ~ *sig ut* (*eg. bet.*) find (make) one's way out (*ur* of); ~ *sig bra ut* look well, show to great advantage

tabbe *s2* blunder, bloomer; *AE.* boner

tabell *s3* table (*över* of) **-form** *i* ~ in tabular form; *uppställning i* ~ tabular statement; *ordna i* ~ tabulate **-huvud** table heading

tabernakel [-'na:-] *s7* tabernacle

tablett *s3* **1** (*läkemedel*) tablet; (*hals- etc.*) lozenge **2** (*tallriksunderlägg*) table mat **-förgiftning** poisoning from overdose of tablets, tablet poisoning

tablå *s3* tableau (*pl* tableaux), schedule; *teat.* tableau

tabu [-'bu:, 'ta:-] **I** *s6* taboo; *belägga med* ~ taboo **II** *oböjligt a* taboo **-föreställning** taboo

tabul|ator [-ˣla:tår] *s3* tabulator [key] **-era** tabulate

taburett *s3* **1** tabo[u]ret; stool **2** (*statsrådsämbete*) ministerial office, seat in the Cabinet

tack *s7, s9* thanks (*pl*); *ja* ~*!* yes, please!; *nej* ~*!* no, thank you (thanks)!; ~ *så mycket!* many thanks!, thank you very much!; ~ *ska du ha!* thanks awfully!; ~ *för att du kom* thank you for coming; ~ *för lånet!* thank you [for the loan]!; ~ *för senast!* thank you for a lovely (nice) evening (party *etc.*)!; *hjärtligt* ~ *för ...!* most hearty thanks for ...!; *det är* ~*en för ...!* that's all the thanks you get for ...!; ~ *och lov!* thank heavens!; *vara ngn* ~ *skyldig* owe s.b. thanks; ~ *vare* thanks (owing) to

1 tacka *v1* thank (*ngn för* s.b. for); ~ *ja* (*och ta emot*) accept with many thanks; ~ *nej* [*till ...*] decline ... with thanks; *jo jag* ~*r* [*jag*]*!* well, I say!, well, well!; ~ *för det!* of course!; *det är ingenting att* ~ *för!* don't mention it!; ~ *vet jag ...* give me ... any day; *ha ngn att* ~ *för ngt* owe s.th. to s.b.

2 tacka *s1* (*fårhona*) ewe

3 tacka *s1* (*järn-, bly-*) pig; (*guld-, silver-, stål-*) ingot

tackbrev letter of thanks

tackel ['takk-] *s7* tackle [block]; ~ *och tåg* the rigging

tackjärn pig iron

tackkort thank-you card

tackl|a *sjö.* rig **2** *sport.* tackle **3** ~ *av* (*magra*) grow (get) thin, fall away **-ing 1** *sjö.* rig[ging] **2** *sport.* tackle

tacknämlig [-ä:-] *a1* (*värd tack*) praiseworthy; (*gagnelig*) worthwhile, profitable, rewarding

tack- och avskedsföreställning farewell performance

tackoffer thank-offering

tacksam *a1* grateful (*för* for; *mot* to); (*mot försynen o.d.*) thankful (*för, över* for); (*uppskattande*) appreciative (*för* of); (*förbunden*) obliged; (*givande*) rewarding, worthwhile (*uppgift*

T

task); *jag vore er mycket ~ om* I should be very much obliged to you if **-het** gratitude; thankfulness

tacksamhets|bevis token (mark) of gratitude **-skuld** debt of gratitude; *stå i ~ till* be indebted to *(ngn för* s.b. for)

tacksamt *adv* gratefully *etc.*; *vi emotser ~ Ert snara svar* we should appreciate your early reply; *vi erkänner ~ mottagandet av* we acknowledge, with thanks, [the] receipt of; *~ avböja* regretfully decline

tacksägelse *framföra sina ~r till ngn* proffer one's thanks to s.b. **-gudstjänst** thanksgiving service

tacktal speech of thanks

tadel ['ta:-] *s7* blame, censure; *utan fruktan och ~* without fear and without reproach **tadellös** blameless **tadla** [-a:-] *se* klandra

1 tafatt *s3* *(lek)* tag

2 tafatt [ˣta:-] *a1* awkward; clumsy

taffel ['taff-] *s2* **1** *hålla öppen ~* keep open house **2** *mus.* square piano **-musik** mealtime music **-täckare** footman laying the [Royal] table

tafflig *a1, vard.* awkward, clumsy

tafs *s2* **1** *(på metrev)* trace, leader, *AE.* snell **2** *få på ~en* get it hot; *ge ngn på ~en* give s.b. it hot **tafsa** fiddle, tamper; *~ på ngn* paw s.b.

taft *s3, s4* taffeta

tag *s7* **1** *(grepp)* grip, grasp *(omkring* round); hold *(i, om* of); *sport.* tackle; *fatta (gripa, hugga) ~ i* grasp (seize, catch) [hold of]; *få ~ i (på)* get hold of, *(komma över)* come across, pick up; *släppa ~et* leave hold of, let go, *(ge upp)* give in (up); *ta ett stadigt ~ i* take firm hold of **2** *(sim-, år-)* stroke; *simma med långa ~* swim with long stroke., *ta ett ~ med sopborsten* have a go with the broom; *ha ~en inne* have the knack [of the thing]; *komma (vara) i ~en* get started, be at it **3** *(gång, liten stund)* little while; *kom hit ett ~!* come here a second[, will you]!; *en i ~et* one at a time; *i första ~et* at the first try *(vard.* go); *jag ger mig inte i första ~et* I don't give up at the first try **taga** *se* ta **tagas** *se* tas

tagel ['ta:-] *s7* horsehair **-madrass** horsehair mattress **-orm** hairworm **-skjorta** hair shirt

tag|en *a5* taken *etc.*; *bli [djupt] ~ av* be deeply affected by; *han såg mycket ~ ut* he looked deeply moved *(trött:* very tired); *strängt -et* strictly speaking; *över huvud -et* on the whole

tagg *s2* prickle; *(törn-)* thorn; *naturv.* spine; *(på -tråd)* barb **-ig** *a1* prickly; thorny; spiny **-svamp** hedgehog mushroom **-tråd** barbed wire, barbwire **-trådshinder** barbed-wire entanglement **-trådsstängsel** barbed-wire fence

tagit *sup. av* ta[ga]

tagla [ˣta:-] *sjö.* serve

tagning [-a:-] *film.* take

taiwanes *s3* Taiwanese **-isk** *a5* Taiwanese

tajma *vard.* time

tajt *a1, vard.* tight

tak *s7* *(ytter-)* roof; *(inner-)* ceiling *(äv. bildl.)*; *(på bil etc.)* top; *bildl.* roof, shelter, cover, *(övre gräns)* ceiling; *brutet ~* mansard (curb) roof; *här är det högt (lågt) i ~* this room has a lofty (low) ceiling; *i ~et* on the ceiling; *grödan är under ~* the harvest is housed; *ha ~ över huvudet* have a roof

over one's head; *vara utan ~ över huvudet (äv.)* have no shelter; *ingen fara på ~et* no harm done, all's well

taka *oböjligt a, pl, ~ händer* [legal] trust; *sätta ngt i ~ händer* deposit s.th. with a trustee (on trust)

tak|belysning ceiling lighting; ceiling fitting **-bjälke** beam [of the roof] **-bjälklag** tie beams *(pl)* **-dropp** *(från yttertak)* eaves drop; *(från innertak)* dropping from the ceiling **-fönster** skylight, fanlight **-krona** chandelier **-lagsfest** [-a:gs-] party for workmen when roof framework is completed **-lampa** ceiling lamp **-list** cornice **-lucka** roof hatch **-lök** *bot.* houseleek **-målning** ceiling painting; *~ar (äv.)* painted ceilings **-nock** roof ridge **-panna** roofing tile **-papp** roofing-felt **-räcke** *(på bil)* roof rack **-ränna** gutter **-skägg** eaves *(pl)* **-stol** roof truss

takt *s3* **1** *(finkänslighet)* tact, delicacy; *(urskillning)* discretion **2** *(av musikstycke)* bar; *(versfot)* foot **3** *(tempo)* time; *mus. äv.* measure; *(friare)* pace, rate; *(vid rodd)* stroke; *ange ~en* set the time *(vid rodd:* the pace); *gå i ~* keep in step; *hålla ~en* keep time; *hålla ~ in med* keep pace with; *i ~ med musiken* in time to the music; *komma ur ~en* get out of time (step, the pace); *slå ~en* beat time; *stampa ~en* beat time with one's foot; *öka ~en* increase the speed (pace); *nu skall ni få se på andra ~er* this is where we get a move on **4** *(motors)* stroke **-art** time **-beteckning** time signature **-del** beat

tak|tegel roofing tile **-terrass** roof terrace, terrace roof

takt|fast *(om steg e.d.)* measured; *marschera ~* march in perfect time **-full** tactful; discreet **-fullhet** tactfulness; discretion

takt|ik *s3* tactics *(pl, behandlas som sg)* **-iker** ['takk-] tactician

taktil *a1* tactile

taktisk ['takk-] *a4* tactical

takt|känsla 1 *mus.* sense of rhythm **2** *(-fullhet)* sense of tact, tactfulness **-lös** tactless, indiscreet **-löshet** want of tact; tactlessness **-mässig** *a1* rhythmical **-pinne** baton **-streck** bar[line]

tak|täckare roofer; *(med -tegel)* tiler; *(med halm)* thatcher **-täckning** roofing; tiling; thatching **-ås** roof ridge

1 tal *s7, mat.* number; *(räkne-)* sum; *hela ~* integers, whole numbers; *ensiffriga ~* digits; *fyrsiffriga ~* numbers of four digits, four-figure numbers; *i runt ~* in round figures (numbers)

2 tal *s7* *(förmåga (sätt) att tala, språk)* speech; *(prat)* talk[ing]; *(sam-)* conversation; *(anförande)* speech, address; *~ets gåva* the gift of speech; *hålla ~* make a speech; *i ~ och skrift* verbally and in writing; *falla ngn i ~et* interrupt s.b., cut s.b. short; *det blev aldrig ~ om* there was never any question of; *det kan inte bli ~ om* there can be no talk (question) of; *föra på ~* bring up [for discussion]; *komma på ~* come (crop) up; *det är på ~ att* there is a talk of (+ ing-form); *på ~ om* speaking of

tala speak *(med* to; *om* about, of; *på* in); *(prata, konversera)* talk *(i telefon* on the telephone); *i sömnen* in one's sleep; *i näsan* through one's nose); *~ är silver, tiga är guld* speech is silver, silence is golden; *~ förstånd med* talk sense to; *får* *jag* ~ *ett par ord med dig?* can I have a word with you?; ~ *rent* (*om barn*) speak properly; *allvarligt* ~*t* seriously speaking; ~ *för* (*t. förmån för*) speak for (in favour of), (*tyda på*) indicate, point towards; ~ *för sig själv* (*utan åhörare*) talk to o.s., (*i egen sak*) speak for o.s.; *de* ~*de i munnen på varandra* they were all talking at the same time; ~ *om* speak (talk) about (of); ~ *illa om* speak disparagingly about; *det är ingenting att* ~ *om!* (*avböjande*) don't mention it!; *för att inte* ~ *om* to say nothing of, not to mention; *låta* ~ *om sig* give rise to a lot of talk; ~ *om* (*berätta*) tell; ~ *inte om det för ngn!* don't tell anybody!; ~ *sig hes* talk o.s. hoarse; ~ *sig varm för* warm up to one's subject; ~ *till ngn* speak to (address) s.b.; ~ *ur skägget* speak up; ~ *ut a*) (*så det hörs*) speak up (out), *b*) (~ *rent ut*) speak one's mind; *vi har* ~*t ut med varandra* we have had it out [with one another]; ~ *vid ngn att han* tell (ask, arrange with) s.b. to (+ *inf.*)

talan *r* suit; (*kärandes*) claim; (*svarandes*) plea; *föra ngns* ~ plead a p.'s cause, (*friare*) be a p.'s spokesman; *nedlägga sin* ~ withdraw one's suit; *han har ingen* ~ (*bildl.*) he has no voice in the matter **talande** *a4* speaking *etc.*; (*uttrycksfull*) expressive; (*menande*) significant (*blickar* looks); (*om siffror*) telling; *den* ~ the speaker

talang talent, gift, aptitude; *pers.* talented (gifted) person **-full** talented, gifted **-fullt** *adv* with great talent **-lös** untalented **-scout** talent scout, star spotter

talar|e speaker; (*väl-*) orator; *föregående* ~ the previous speaker; *han är ingen* ~ he's not much of a speaker **-konst** art of [public] speaking; rhetoric **-stol** platform, rostrum

tal|as *dep, höra* ~ *om* hear of; *jag har hört* ~ *om honom* I have heard of him; *vi får* ~ *vid om saken* we must have a talk about it (talk the matter over) **-bok** talking book **-esman** spokesman (*för* of); *göra sig till* ~ *för* voice the feelings of **-esätt** (*stående* current) phrase, mode of expression **-fel** speech defect **-film** sound (talking) film; *vard.* talkie **-för** *a5* talkative, loquacious **-förmåga** faculty (power) of speech; *mista* ~*n* lose one's speech

talg [-j] *s3* tallow; (*njur-*) suet **-dank** tallow dip **-ig** *a1* tallowy, greasy **-körtel** sebaceous gland **-ljus** tallow candle **-oxe** great tit

talhytt call (telephone) box

talisman *s3* talisman

talj|a *s1*, **-block** tackle [blocks *pl*]

talk *s3* talc[um] **talka** talc **talkpuder** talcum powder, talc

talkör chorus; choral speech

tall *s2* (*träd*) [common] pine, pine tree, Scots (Scotch) pine (fir); (*trä*) pinewood, redwood **-barr** pine needle[s *pl*] **-barrsolja** pine-needle oil

tallektion elocution lesson

tallium [ˈtall-] *s8* thallium

tallkott|e pine cone **-körtel** pineal gland (body); *fack.* epiphysis

tallrik *s2* plate; *djup* ~ soup plate; *flat* ~ ordinary [dinner] plate; *en* ~ *gröt* a plate of porridge **tallriksis** pancake ice

tall|ris pine twigs (*pl*) **-skog** pine forest **-tita** *s1*

willow tit

tallös innumerable, countless

talman speaker; *parl.* Speaker of Parliament (*i Sverige äv.* the Riksdag)

talmud [ˈtaːl-] Talmud

talong [-ˈlåŋ] *s3* counterfoil; *AE.* stub; *kortsp.* talon

tal|organ organ of speech; (*röst*) voice **-pedagog** speech therapist **-pjäs** *teat.* straight play **-registreringsapparat** recording machine, recorder

talrik numerous; ~*a* (*äv.*) numbers of **talrikt** [-iː-] *adv* numerously, in large numbers; ~ *besökt* well-attended

tal|roll *teat.* spoken part **-rubbning** impairment of speech **-rör** speaking tube

tal|s [-aː-] *i uttr.: komma till* ~ *med* get to speak to, talk to **-scen** dramatic theatre **-språk** spoken (colloquial) language; *engelskt* ~ spoken (*etc.*) English

talsystem number system, system of figures

talteknik elocution, speech training

talteori theory of numbers

tal|trast song thrush **-tratt** *tel.* mouthpiece **-trängd** *a1* eager to speak; (*som vana*) loquacious, garrulous **-övning** conversation exercise (practice); (*uttals-*) speech training

tam *a1* tame; (*om djur*) domestic[ated] **-boskap** domestic cattle (*pl*)

tambur hall; (*kapprum*) cloakroom

tamburin *s3* tambourin

tambur|major drum major; *vard. se följande* **-vaktmästare** cloakroom attendant

tam|djur tame (*etc.*) animal **-fågel** poultry **-får** domestic[ated] sheep **-het** tameness

tamp *s2* [rope's] end

tampas *dep* tussle

tamponera *v1*, **tampong** [-ˈpåŋ] *s3* tampon

tamsvin pig

tamtam [ˣtammtamm] (*gonggong*) gong, tam-tam; (*trumma*) tom-tom

tand *-en tänder* tooth (*pl* teeth); (*vilddjurs*) fang; *tekn.* tooth, cog; ~ *för* ~ a tooth for a tooth; *tidens* ~ the ravages (*pl*) of time; *få tänder* be teething, cut one's teeth; *försedd med tänder* toothed; *ha ont i tänderna* have toothache; *hålla* ~ *för tunga* (*bildl.*) keep one's own councel; *visa tänderna* show one's (*om hund:* bare its) teeth (*mot at*) **tanda** tooth; indent

tand|agnisslan *i uttr:* *gråt och* ~ weeping and gnashing of teeth **-ben** toothbone **-borste** toothbrush **-borstglas** tooth glass **-borstning** [-å-] brushing of teeth **-brygga** dental bridge

tandem [ˈtann-] (*hästspann*) *s7*, (*cykel*) *s2* tandem **-cykel** tandem cycle **-sadel** pillion; *AE.* buddy seat

tand|garnityr set of teeth, denture **-hals** neck of a tooth **-hygien** dental hygiene **-hygienist** dental hygienist **-kirurgi** dental surgery **-klinik** dental clinic **-krona** crown of a tooth **-kräm** toothpaste **-kött** gum; *fack.* gingiva; ~*et* the gums (*pl*) **-läkarborr** dentist's drill **-läkare** dentist, dental surgeon **-läkarexamen** dental degree **-läkarstol** dentist's (dental) chair **-lös** toothless **-ning** *konkr.* toothing; (*såg-*) serration; (*kuggar*) teeth cogs (*pl*) **-pasta** toothpaste, dentifrice **-petare** toothpick **-rad** row of teeth **-reglering** prevention and correction of irregular dentition; orthodontics (*pl*) **-röta** [dental] caries **-skydd** (*i boxning*) gumshield; mouthpiece; *sport.* chin protector **-sköterska** dental nurse **-sprickning** teething, cutting of the teeth **-sten** tartar; scale **-ställning** brace[s *pl*] **-tekniker** dental technician (mechanic) **-tråd** dental floss **-utdragning** tooth extraction **-val** toothed whale **-vall** alveolar ridge **-vård** dental care (service) **-värk** toothache **-ömsning** second dentition

tangent [-nj-, *i sht tekn. o. geom.* -ŋg-] **1** *mus., tekn.* key **2** *geom.* tangent **-bord** (*i skrivmaskin*) keyboard **-ial** [-ŋgen[t]si'a:l] *a1*, **-iell** [-ŋgen[t]si-'ell] **1** tangential

Tanger [taŋ'ʃe:] *n* Tangier

tanger|a [-ŋg-, -nj-] **1** (*gränsa t.*) touch upon, border on **2** *geom.* be a tangent to, touch **3** *sport.* equal **-ingspunkt** tangential point; *bildl.* point of contact

tango ['taŋgo] *s5* tango

tanig *al* thin **-het** thinness

tank 1 *s2* (*behållare*) tank, container **2** *s2* (*stridsvagn*) tank **tanka** fill up, refuel **tanker** ['tann-] *s2* tanker **tankbil** petrol (*AE.* gas[o-line]) truck; *Storbritannien äv.* tank (tanker) lorry

tank|e *s2* thought (*på* of); (*idé*) idea (*om, på* of); (*åsikt*) opinion (*om* about); (*avsikt*) intention; (*plan*) plan (*på* for); *blotta ~ en på* the mere thought of; *var har du dina -ar?* what are you thinking about?; *ha -arna med sig* have one's wits about one; *ha en låg ~ om* have a poor opinion of; *ha ~ på att göra ngt* have got the idea of doing s.th.; *jag har aldrig haft en ~ ditåt* such a thought has never occurred to me; *i ~ att* with the idea (intention) of (+ *ing*-form); *försänkt i -ar* lost in thought; *jag hade ngt annat i -arna* I was thinking of s.th. else; *det leder* [*osökt*] *~n till* it makes one think of; *med ~ på* bearing ... in mind; *få ngn på andra -ar* make s.b. change his mind; *komma på bättre -ar* think better of it; *utbyta -ar om* exchange ideas about

tanke|ansträngning mental exertion (effort) **-arbete** brain work **-bana** line of thought **-diger** profound **-experiment** intellectual experiment **-frihet** freedom of thought **-förmåga** capacity for thinking **-gång** *s2* train of thought **-läsare** thought-reader, mind-reader **-möda** *se* -ansträngning **-skärpa** mental acumen **-ställare** warning, food for thought; *få sig en ~ get* s.th. to think about **-utbyte** exchange of thoughts (ideas, opinions) **-verksamhet** mental activity **-väckande** *a4* thought-provoking **-värld** world of ideas **-överföring** telepathy, thought transference

tankfartyg tanker

tank|full thoughtful, contemplative **-lös** thoughtless, unreflecting; (*om pers. äv.*) scatter-brained **-löshet** thoughtlessness *etc.*; *en ~ a* thoughtless act

tankning refuelling, filling up

tank|spridd *a5* absent-minded **-spriddhet** pre-occupation (absence) of mind **-streck** dash

tankvagn tank wagon; *i sht AE.* [rail] tank car

tannin *s4, s3* tannin, tannic acid

tant *s3* aunt; (*smeksamt*) auntie; *~ Andersson* Mrs. Andersson

tantal *s3, s4, kem.* tantalum; (*malm*) tantalite

tantaluskval *pl* torments of Tantalus

tantiem [taŋt-, tant-, -i'e:m, -i'ä:m] *s7* commission on profit[s *pl*], bonus

tantig *al* old-maidish; frumpy

tanzan|ier [-'(t)sa:-] *s9*, **-isk** *a5* Tanzanian

tapet *s3* wallpaper; (*vävd*) tapestry; *sätta upp ~er* hang (put up) wallpaper; *vara på ~en* (*bildl.*) be on the tapis **-klister** paperhanger's paste **-rulle** roll of wallpaper

tapetser|a [hang] paper, decorate; *~ om* repaper **-are** [-ˣse:-] upholsterer **-arverkstad** upholstery [work]shop, upholstery **-ing** paperhanging, wallpapering

tapioka [-i'åk:a, -iˣå:ka] *s1, bot.* tapioca

tapir *s3, zool.* tapir; (*schabrak-*) Malayan tapir

tapisseri tapestry **-affär** fancywork shop **-arbete** fancywork, tapestry work

tapp *s2* **1** (*i tunna e.d.*) tap, faucet; (*i badkar, båt e.d.*) **2** (*t. hopfästning*) peg; (*trä-*) tenon; (*axel*) journal; (*sväng-*) pivot, trunnion **3** (*syn-cell*) cone **4** (*hö-*) wisp; (*ull-*) flock; (*moln-*) wisp

1 tappa (*vätska*) tap (*äv. med.*); (*av-, ~ upp*) draw [off]; *~ på buteljer* draw [... off]; pour (tap) into bottles; *~ blod av* bleed, draw blood from; *~ i vatten i badkaret* run water into the bath; *~ ur vattnet ur* let the water out of

2 tappa (*släppa*) drop, let fall; (*förlora*) lose (*äv. ~ bort*); *~ i golvet* drop (*etc.*) on (to) the floor; *~ huvudet* (*bildl.*) lose one's head; *~ bort sig* get lost, lose o.s.; *~ bort varandra* lose (get separated from) each other

tapper ['tapp-] *a2* brave; courageous; (*ridderligt ~*) gallant **-het** bravery, valour; courage **-hetsmedalj** medal for valour; distinguished service medal

tapp|hål taphole, pouring hole **-kran** drain cock **-ning** (*av vätska*) drawing, tapping; *vin av en god ~* a vintage wine; *i annan ~* (*bildl.*) formulated differently, in a different form

tappt *i uttr: ge ~* give in

tapto ['tapp-] *s6* tattoo; *blåsa ~* beat (sound) the tattoo; *AE.* taps (*pl*)

tara *s1* tare

taran|tel [-'rann-] *s2* tarantula **-tella** [-ˣtella] *s1* tarantella

tarer|a tare **-ing** taring

tariff *s3* tariff; schedule (list) [of rates]

tarm *s2* intestine; *~arna* (*äv.*) the bowels (entrails, *vard.* guts) **-flora** intestinal flora **-kanal** intestinal canal **-katarr** intestinal catarrh **-käx** [-ç-] *s7* mesentery **-ludd** intestinal villi (*pl*) **-vred** *s7* ileus, intestinal obstruction **-vägg** intestinal wall

taro *s5* taro, elephant's ear, dasheen

tars *s3* tarsus (*pl* tarsi) **-led** tarsal joint

tartar *s3* Tartar **-biff** *se råbiff* **-sås** tartar sauce

tartelett *s3* tartlet

tarv *s7, förrätta sitt ~* ease nature **tarva** require, demand, call for **tarvas** *dep, se behövas* **tarvlig** *al* (*enkel*) frugal (*måltid* meal); (*smaklös*) cheap (*klänning* dress); (*om pers. o. smak*) vulgar, common; (*lumpen*) shabby (*uppförande* behaviour)

tarvligt adv frugally etc.; bära sig ~ åt behave shabbily (mot to) **tarvlighet** frugality; cheapness; vulgarity etc.; ~er vulgarities

tas togs tagits, dep, vard., hon är inte god att ~ med she is a difficult person (child)

taskig vard. (elak) mean; (orättvis) unfair; (dålig) poor, lousy

taskspelar|e juggler, conjurer **-konst** ~er juggling (conjuring) tricks

tass s2 paw; bort med ~arna! hands off!; räcka vacker ~ put out a paw nicely; skaka ~ med shake hands with **tassa** patter, pad

tassel ['tass-] s7, tissel och ~ tittle-tattle **tassla** tittle-tattle

tatar s3 Ta[r]tar

tattar|e ung. gypsy **-unge** gypsy kid

tatuer|a tattoo **-ing** tattooing

tautologi tautology

tavel|förfalskare forger of paintings **-galleri** picture gallery **-ram** picture frame **-samling** collection of pictures **-utställning** exhibition of paintings

taverna [-ˣvärr-] s1 tavern

tavla [ˣta:v-] s1 **1** konst. picture (äv. bildl.) **2** (platta) table; (anslags-) board; svarta ~n the blackboard **3** vard., vilken ~! what a slip-up (AE. boner)!

tax s2 dachshund

1 taxa v1, flyg. taxi

2 taxa s1 (pris) rate, charge; (för personbefordran e.d.) fare; (telefon-) fee; (förteckning) list of rates, tariff; enhetlig ~ standard (flat) rate; full ~ full rate

taxameter [-ˈme:-] s2 taximeter, fare meter **-bil** se taxi

taxe|bestämmelser tariff (fare) regulations **-höjning** increase of charges (etc.); (av biljettpris) increase in fares

taxer|a assess [... for taxes] (till at), tax; (uppskatta) rate; (värdera) estimate, value; ~d inkomst assessed income; han ~r för 5 000 pund om året he is assessed at 5,000 pounds a year **-ing** [tax] assessment; för hög ~ over-valuation; ~ till kommunal (statlig) inkomstskatt assessment for local (national) income tax

taxerings|belopp sum charged, amount of assessment **-distrikt** assessment district **-kalender** taxpayers' (ratepayers') directory **-man** [tax] assessor **-myndighet** assessment authority **-nämnd** assessment board (committee) **-värde** rat[e]able value; AE. tax assessment [value] **-år** year of assessment

taxi ['taksi] s9 taxi [cab], cab **-båt** taxi boat **-chaufför** taxi driver, cab driver, cabman **-flyg** taxiplane service **-station** taxi (cab) rank; AE. taxi (cab) stand

tazett [-s-] s3 French daffodil

tbc [tebe'se:] best. form tbc-n T.B., t.b. **-sjuk** subst. TB-sufferer

T-benstek T-bone steak

Tchad n Chad **tchad|ier** ['tʃa:-] s9, -isk ['tʃa:-] a5 Chadian

TCO [tese'o:] (förk. för Tjänstemännens Centralorganisation) se under tjänsteman

1 te s4 tea; koka (dricka) ~ make (have) tea

2 te v4, rfl appear

teak [ti:k] s3 teak

teater [-e'a:-] s2 theatre; absurd ~ theatre of the absurd; spela ~ act, bildl. play-act; gå (vara) på ~n go to (be at) the theatre; gå in vid ~n go on the stage **-affisch** playbill **-besök** visit to the theatre **-besökare** theatre-goer **-biljett** theatre ticket **-chef, -direktör** theatre manager **-folk** stage people **-föreställning** theatrical performance **-historia** stage history **-kikare** opera glasses (pl) **-kritiker** dramatic critic **-pjäs** [stage] play **-publik** theatre-goers (pl); audience **-recension** theatrical review **-sällskap** theatrical company **-viskning** stage whisper

teatralisk [-ˈtra:-] a5 theatrical

te|bjudning tea party **-blad** tea leaf **-blask** vard. dishwater **-burk** tea caddy **-buske** tea plant

tecken ['tekk-] s7 sign (på, till of); (känne-) mark (på of); (symbolisk figur) symbol (äv. kem.); mat. sign; (skriv-) character, sign; (signal) signal (till for); det är ett gott ~ it is a good sign; göra ~ åt ngn make signs (a sign) to s.b.; i enighetens ~ in a spirit of unity; på givet ~ at a given sign (signal); till ~ på as a token (mark) of; visa alla ~ till att show every sign of (+ ing-form); inte ett ~ till rädsla not a vestige (trace) of fear **-förklaring** key to (the table of) signs **-ruta** (t.ex. på miniräknare) display **-språk** sign language **-tydare** auger

teckna 1 (ge tecken) sign (make signs, a sign) (till, åt to) **2** (skriva) sign; (genom namnteckning utlova) put one's name down for; ~ aktier subscribe for (to) shares; ~ firman sign for a company; ~ kontrakt make (enter) into a contract **3** (rita) draw (efter from; för for); (skildra äv.) delineate, depict; ~ av sketch [off]; ~d film [animated] cartoon; ~d serie comic strip; djuret är vackert ~t the animal is beautifully marked **4** rfl (an- sig) put one's name down (för for); (av- sig) be depicted (i ngns ansikte on a p.'s face); ~ sig för en försäkring take out an insurance; ~ sig till minnes commit to memory

teckn|are 1 drawer, artist; (illustratör) illustrator **2** (aktie-) [share] subscriber **-ing 1** drawing; konkr. äv. sketch (i ord) description **2** zool. markings, lines (pl) **3** hand. subscription (av aktier to shares)

tecknings|bevis subscription certificate (Storbritannien warrant) **-lektion** drawing lesson **-lista** subscription list **-lärare** drawing master, art teacher **-rätt** hand. subscription right **-rättsbevis** hand. participation certificate **-undervisning** teaching of drawing

tedags vid ~ at tea time

teddy|björn teddy bear **-kappa** artificial fur coat

tedeum [-ˣde:-] s7, best. form äv. tedeum Te Deum

tefat saucer; flygande ~ flying saucer

1 teg s2 strip (piece) of tilled land

2 teg imperf. av tiga

tegat sup. av tiga

tegel ['te:-] s7 [building] brick; koll. bricks (pl); (tak-) tile, koll. tiles (pl); eldfast ~ firebrick **-bruk** brickworks, brickyard; brick kiln **-bränning** brick-burning, tile-burning **-mur** brick wall

T

-panna [roofing] tile; pantile **-röd** brick-red
-rör tile (earthenware) pipe **-sten** brick
-stensroman great thick novel, tome **-tak** tile
[d] roof **-täckt** *a4* tiled
te|hus teahouse **-huv** tea cosy **-jn** *s4* theine
teis|m theism **-tisk** [-'iss-] *a5* theistic[al]
tejp *s3* tape
tek|a *sport.* face off **-ning** *sport.* face-off
te|kaka teacake **-kanna** teapot **-kittel** kettle
tekn|ik *s3* **1** (*ingenjörsvetenskap*) technics (*pl*);
engineering, technology; ~*ens framsteg* technological advances **2** (*tillvägagångssätt*) technique
-ikalitet *s3* technicality **-iker** ['tekk-] technician, engineer **-isk** ['tekk-] *a5* technical; technological; ~ *högskola* institute of technology; ~*t*
missöde technical hitch; ~*t museum* museum of
science and technology
tekno|krat technocrat **-log** technologist, tech-
nological student **-logi** *s3* technology **-logisk**
[-'lå:-] *a5* technological
tekoindustri textile and clothing industry
te|kopp teacup; (*som mått*) teacupful [of] **-kök**
tea urn
telefon [-'få:n] *s3* telephone; *vard.* phone; *det
ringer i* ~*en* the telephone is ringing; *det är* ~ *till
dig* you are wanted on the telephone; *svara i* ~
answer the telephone; *tala i* ~ talk (speak) on the
telephone; *per* ~ by (on the, over the) telephone
-abonnent telephone subscriber **-apparat**
telephone [apparatus] **-automat** slot telephone;
AE. pay [tele]phone **-avgift** telephone rental
(charge) **-avlyssning** wire-tapping **-central**
telephone exchange **-era** telephone (*efter* for; *till*
to); *vard.* phone, *AE.* call (*till ngn* s.b.) **-förbin-
delse** telephone connection **-hytt** call (telephone) box; *AE.* telephone booth
telefon|i *s3* telephony **-ist** telephone operator
-katalog telephone directory (*AE.* book)
-kiosk *se telefonhytt* **-kontakt** *stå i* ~ *med* keep
in touch by telephone with **-kö** telephone queue
[service] **-ledning** telephone circuit (wire) **-lur**
receiver **-nummer** telephone number; *hemligt* ~
unlisted telephone number **-påringning** telephone call **-reparatör** telephone mechanic
-räkning telephone bill **-samtal** telephone
conversation; (*påringning*) telephone call; *åberopande vårt* ~ referring to our telephone conversation **-station** telephone exchange (call office;
AE. office) **-stolpe** telephone pole **-svarare**
telephone answering machine; *pers.* answering-
-service operator **-terror** threatening phone calls
-tid telephone hours (*pl*) **-tråd** telephone wire
-vakt telephone answering service **-väckning**
alarm call **-väkteri** phone-in [radio programme]
-växel telephone exchange
telefoto wirephoto, telephoto
telegraf *s3* telegraph **-arbetare** telegraph-ser-
vice worker **-era** wire, telegraph; (*utom Europa
äv.*) cable **-ering** [-'fe:-] telegraphy; cabling
telegraf|i *s3* telegraphy **-isk** [-'gra:-] *a5* tele-
graphic **-iskt** [-'gra:-] *adv* telegraphically; *svara
~ wire* (cable) back **-ist** telegraph operator; *sjö.*
radio officer **-station** telegraph office **-stolpe**
telegraph pole **-verk** telegraph service
telegram [-'gramm] *s7* telegram; *vard.* wire;
(*utom Europa*) cable[gram]; ~ *med betalt svar* re-

ply-paid telegram **-adress** telegraphic (cable)
address **-avgift** telegram (*etc.*) charge **-bild**
telephoto **-blankett** telegram form (*AE.* blank)
-byrå news (press) agency; *Tidningarnas* ~ [the]
Swedish central news agency **-pojke** telegraph
boy **-remissa** telegraphic remittance (money order, transfer) **-stil** telegraphic style
tele|kinesi telekinesis **-kommunikation**
telecommunication[s *pl*] **-objektiv** telephoto
lens **-ologi** teleology **-pati** *s3* telepathy **-patisk**
[-'pa:-] *a5* telepathic **-printer** [-'prinn-] *s2* tele-
printer, *AE.* teletypewriter **-printerremsa**
ticker tape
teleskop [-'skå:p] *s7* telescope **-antenn** telescopic aerial (antenna) **-isk** [-'skå:-] *a5* telescopic
tele|station telephone and telegraph office
-teknik telecommunication [engineering] **-tek-
niker** telecommunication engineer **-teknisk**
telecommunication **-verket** [the Swedish] tele-
communications administration **-vision** televise, telecast **-vision** television (*förk.* TV); *vard.*
telly (*Storbritannien*), video (*AE.*); *intern* ~
closed-circuit television; *komma i* ~ appear on
television, be on TV; *se på* ~ watch television
(the TV); *sända per* ~, *se -visera*
televisions|apparat television (TV) [set] **-ka-
mera** television camera **-ruta** viewing screen
-sändare television transmitter **-sändning**
television transmission (broadcast)
telex ['te:-] *s2* telex; *AE.* teletype (*varumärke*)
telexa ['te:-] telex, teletype
telfer ['tell-] *s2* [electric] hoist (telpher)
tellur *s3, s4* tellurium
teln [-e:-] *s2* net-rope
telning ['te:l-] (*skott*) sapling; (*avkomma*) offspring; (*unge*) kid
tema [*x*te:-, 'te:-] *s6* **1** (*ämne*) theme (*äv. mus.*) **2**
(*skolstil*) composition; (*översättning*) translation
3 *språkv., säga* ~ *på ett verb* give the principle
parts of a verb **-tisk** [-'ma:-] *a5* thematic
temp *s2, vard., ta* ~*en* take one's temperature
tempel ['temm-] *s7* temple **-dans** temple dance
-herreorden the Order of Knights Templar[s]
-skändare [-ʃ-] desecrator of a temple **-tjänare**
temple servant; *bibl.* Levite
1 tempera ['temm-] *s9* tempera, distemper
2 tempera *v1* time, set a fuse
temperament *s7* temperament
temperaments|full temperamental **-sak** *en* ~
a matter of temperament
temperatur temperature; *absolut* ~ thermody-
namic (absolute) temperature **-fall** fall of (in
the) temperature **-förändring** change of (in
the) temperature
temperer|a **1** (*värma*) temper, warm, take the
chill off **2** *mus.* temper **-ad** *a5* (*om vin e.d.*) tem-
pered; (*om klimat e.d.*) temperate **-ing** warming,
tempering
tempo ['temm-] *s6* **1** (*hastighet*) pace, speed;
mus. tempo (*pl* tempi); *forcera* ~*t* force the pace,
speed up **2** (*handgrepp*) operation **-arbetare**
semiskilled worker **-arbete** serial production
-beteckning *mus.* expression mark **-rel** *a1*
temporal **-rär** *a1* temporary
tempus ['temm-] *n* tense **-följd** sequence of
tenses

ten *s2* [metal] rod
tendęns *s3* tendency; (*utvecklingsriktning*) trend **-fri** nontendentious **-roman** novel with a purpose
tendentiös [-n(t)si'ö:s] *a1* tendentious; (*friare*) bias[s]ed
tender ['tenn-] *s2* tender
tendera tend (*mot* towards; [*till*] *att* to)
Teneriffa [-ˣriffa] *n* Tenerife
tenn *s4* tin; *engelskt* ~ pewter **-bägare** pewter tankard **-folie** tinfoil **-gjutare** pewterer **-gjuteri** pewter foundry
tennis ['tenn-] *s2* tennis **-arm** tennis elbow (arm) **-bana** tennis court **-boll** tennis ball **-hall** covered tennis court, tennis hall **-racket** tennis racket **-sko** tennis shoe **-spelare** tennis player **-tävling** tennis tournament
tenn|kanna pewter jug **-lödning** tin (soft) soldering **-plåt** (*material*) sheet tin; *konkr.* tin sheet, tinplate **-soldat** tin soldier **-stop** pewter mug
tenǫr *s3* tenor **-klav** tenor clef **-saxofon** tenor saxophone **-stämma** tenor voice
tensįd *s3* surfactant, surface-active agent
tenta *vard., se tentamen o. tentera*
tentakel [-'takk-] *s3* tentacle, feeler
tent|amen [-'ta:-] *r, -amen -amina* examination; *muntlig* ~ oral examination, viva [voce]
tentamens|läsa revise, read (study) for an examination **-period** examination period **-skräck** horror of exams
tentąnd *s3* examinee, candidate
tentativ [-'ti:v, 'tenn-] *a1* tentative
tent|ator [-ˣa:tår] *s3* examiner **-era 1** (*prövas*) be examined (*för* by; *i* in) **2** (*pröva*) examine; *absol.* conduct an examination
teodl|are tea planter **-ing** tea growing; *konkr.* tea plantation
teodolįt *s3* theodolite, *AE.* transit
teo|log theologian **-logį** *s3* theology; (*som studieämne äv.*) divinity; *~e doktor* doctor of theology (divinity); *~e studerande* theology student, student of theology (divinity) **-logisk** [-'lå:-] *a5* theological; *~ fakultet* (*äv.*) faculty of theology
teorę|m *s7* theorem **-tiker** [-'re:-] theoretician, theorist **-tisera** theorize (*om, över* about) **-tisk** [-'re:-] *a5* theoretic[al]
teorį *s3* theory
teo|sof [-'så:f] *s3* theosophist **-sofį** [-så'fi:] *s3* theosophy **-sofisk** [-'så:-] *a5* theosophic[al]
tepåse tea bag
terapeut [-'pevt] *s3* therapist **-isk** [-'pevv-] *a5* therapeutic[al]
terapį *s3* therapy
term *s3* term
termer ['terr-] *pl* (*bad*) thermae
termįk [-'mi:k] *s3* thermal[s *pl*]
termin [-'mi:n] *s3* 1 (*del av läsår*) term; *AE.* semester 2 (*tidpunkt*) stated (fixed) time, term; (*förfallotid*) time of maturity, due date; (*betalnings-*) day (time) of payment; *betalning i ~er* payment by instalment
terminal [-'na:l] I *a1* terminal II *a1* terminal
terminologį *s3* terminology
termins|affär forward deal (transaction) **-avgift** term fee **-betyg** term report **-vis** by (in) in-

stalments
termisk *a5* thermal, thermic
termistor [-ˣmistår] *s3* thermistor
termit [-'mi:t] *s3* termite, white ant
termo|dynamik [ˣtärr-, -'i:k] thermodynamics (*pl, behandlas som sg*) **-dynamisk** [ˣtärm-, -'na:-] thermodynamic[al] **-elektrisk** [ˣtärr-, -'lekk-] thermoelectric[al] **-element** [ˣtärr-] [bimetallic] thermocouple **-grąf** *s3* thermograph **-meter** [-'me:-] *s2* thermometer; *~n visar 5 grader* the thermometer stands at 5 degrees; *~n faller* the temperature is falling **-meterskala** thermometric (thermometer) scale **-nukleär** [ˣtärr-, -'ä:r] thermonuclear **-plast** [ˣtärr-] thermoplastic
termos ['tärr-] *s2*, **-flaska** thermos [flask] (*varumärke*) **-kanna** vacuum jug
termostat *s3* thermostat **-reglerad** thermostat controlled
terpentįn *s3, s4* turpentine
terrakotta [-ˣkåtta] *s9* terra cotta
terrarium [-'ra:-] *s4* vivarium; terrarium
terrąss *s3*, **-era** *v1* terrace **-formig** [-å-] *a1* terraced
terrester [-'ress-] *a2* terrestrial
terrier ['tärr-] terrier
terrįn *s3* tureen
territorial|gräns [-ˣa:l-] limit of territorial waters **-vatten** territorial waters (*pl*)
territor|ięll *a1* territorial **-ium** [-'to:-] *s4* territory
terror ['tärrår] *s9* terror **-balans** balance of terror **-dåd** terrorist act
terror|isera terrorize **-ism** terrorism **-ist** terrorist
terror|verksamhet terrorist activity **-vapen** *pl* terror weapons
terräng *s3* terrain; ground, country; land; *kuperad* ~ hilly country; *förlora* ~ lose ground **-bil** cross-country vehicle, *AE.* all-terrain vehicle (*förk.* ATV), jeep **-förhållanden** *pl* nature (condition) (*sg*) of the ground **-gående** *a4* cross-country (*fordon* vehicle) **-löpning** cross-country running (run; *vid tävling:* racing, race) **-ritt** cross-country riding (ride)
ters *s3* tierce; *mus. äv.* third
tertiär [-tsi'ä:r] *a1* tertiary **-lån** loan secured by a third mortgage, third mortgage loan **-tiden** the Tertiary [Age]
terylen [-'le:n] *s3, s4* terylene (*urspr. varumärke*); *AE. äv.* dacron (*varumärke*)
terzin [-'tsi:n] *s3* terza rima (*pl* terze rime)
tes *s3* thesis (*pl* theses)
te|servis tea service (set) **-sil** tea strainer **-sked** teaspoon; (*som mått*) teaspoonful [of] **-sort** type (blend) of tea; *~er* (*äv.*) teas
1 test *s2* (*hår-*) wisp
2 test *s7, s9* (*prov*) test; *data.* check
testa test
testa|mentarisk [-'ta:-] *a5* testamentary **-mente** [-'menn-] *s6* 1 *jur.* [last] will [and testament]; *upprätta sitt* ~ make (draw up) one's will; *inbördes* ~ [con]joint will 2 *bibl., Gamla (Nya)* *~et* the Old (New) Testament **-mentera** ~ *ngt till ngn* bequeath s.th. to s.b., leave s.b. s.th. **-mentsexekutor** executor [of a will] **-tor**

T

[-ˣa:tår] *s3* testator; *fem.* testatrix
test|bild test pattern, test card; *AE. äv.* resolution chart **-cykel** ergometer bicycle **-flygare** test pilot
testikel [-'tikk-] *s2* testicle, testis (*pl* testes)
testning testing
testosteron [-'rå:n] *s4* testosterone
testpilot test pilot
tetanus ['te:-] *r* tetanus
tetraeder [-'e:d-] *s2* tetrahedron
te|vagn tea trolley **-vatten** water for the tea; *sätta på ~* put the kettle on; *-vattnet kokar* the kettle is boiling
teve *s2, se TV o. television*
te|veronika *s1*, **-ärenpris** *s3, bot.* germander speedwell
t.ex. (*förk. för till exempel*) e.g., for example; say
text *s3* text; (*bibelställe*) passage; (*motsats musik*) words (*pl*); (*sammanhang*) context; *sätta ~ till musik* put the words to music; *gå vidare i ~en* (*bildl.*) go on; *lägga ut ~en* (*bildl.*) embroider things
text|a 1 (*skriva*) use (write in) block letters **2** (*uttala tydligt*) articulate **-analys** textual analysis **-are** calligrapher **-författare** author of a text; (*t. film*) scriptwriter; (*t. opera*) librettist; (*reklam-*) copywriter **-förklaring** textual commentary **-häfte** book of accompanying text
text|il *al* textile **-fabrik** textile mill (factory) **-fiber** textile fibre **-ier** *pl* textiles, textile goods **-industri** textile industry **-konstnär[inna]** textile stylist, pattern designer **-lärare** teacher of textile craft **-varor** *pl, se textilier*
text|kritik textual criticism **-kritisk** critical **-ning** block writing, lettering **-reklam** editorial advertising **-sida** page of text **-ställe** passage, paragraph **--TV** teletext
textur texture
t.f. [ˣteeff] (*förk. för tillförordnad*) acting (*rektor* headmaster)
t.h. (*förk. för till höger*) to the right
thai|ländare *s9*, **-ländsk** *a5* Thai **-ländska** (*kvinna*) Thai woman **-siden** Thai silk **-språk** Thai
Themsen ['temm-] *r* the [River] Thames **-mynningen** the Thames Estuary
thinner ['tinn-] *s9* thinner **-sniffning** thinner sniffing
thoraxkirurgi [ˣtɔ:-, ˣtå:-] thoracic surgery
thriller ['trill-, *äv. eng. uttal*] *s9* thriller
thymus ['ty:-] *r* thymus (*pl äv.* thymi)
tia [ˣti:a] *s1* ten; (*sedel*) ten-kronor note
tiar[a] [-ˣa:r(a)] *s3* [*s1*] tiara
Tibet *n* Tibet
tibet|an *s3* Tibetan **-ansk** [-a:-] *a5* Tibetan **-anska** [-'ta:n-] **I** (*språk*) Tibetan **II** (*kvinna*) Tibetan woman
1 ticka *s1* polypore
2 ticka *v1* tick
ticktack (*om mindre klocka*) ticktick; (*om större klocka*) ticktock; (*om hjärta*) ticktack
tid *s3* **1** time (*och rum* and space); (*-punkt äv.*) hour, moment; (*period*) period, space; (*tidsålder*) day[s *pl*], time[s *pl*]; *beställa ~* make an appointment (*hos* with); *bestämma [en] ~* set a day (date) (*för* for); *en ~ brukade jag* at one time I

used to; *en ~s vila* a period of rest; *när jag får ~* when I get time (an opportunity) (*med, till* for; *att* to); *har du ~ ett ögonblick?* can you spare a moment?; *allt har sin ~* there's a time for everything; *kommer ~ kommer råd* don't cross your bridges until you get to them; *medan ~ är* while there is yet time; *ta ~* (*sport.*) time; *ta god ~ på sig* take one's time; *det är god ~* there is plenty of time (*med (till*) *det* for that); *det är hög ~ att* it is high time to; *~en är knapp* time is short; *den ~en den sorgen* worry about that when the time comes; *~en för avresan* the time (hour, date) for departure; *~en går* time passes; *~ens gång* the course of time; *~ens tand* the ravages of time; *ha ~en för sig* have the future before one; *hela ~en* all the time; *nya ~en* the new age; *se ~en an* bide one's time, wait and see; *öppet alla ~er på dygnet* open day and night; *alla ~ers största målare* the greatest painter ever; *alla ~ers chans* the chance of a lifetime; *det var alla ~ers!* that was simply marvellous!; *andra ~er andra seder* manners change with the times; *det var andra ~er då* times were different then; *gamla ~er* ancient times, the old days; *långa ~er kunde han* for long periods he could **2** (*med föregående prep.*) *efter en* (*ngn*) *~* after a time (while), (*om särskilt fall*) some time afterwards; *efter en månads ~* after [the lapse of] a (one) month, in a month's time; *~ efter annan* from time to time; *vara efter sin ~* be behind the times; *enligt den ~ens sed* in accordance with the custom of those times; *från vår ~* from (of) our times; *för en ~* for some time; *för en ~ av sex månader* for a period of six months; *nu för ~en* nowadays; *före sin ~* ahead of one's time; *i ~* in time (*för, till* for; *för att för* + *ing-form*); *i ~ och evighet* for all time; *i ~ och otid* at any time (all times); *i god ~* in good time; *i rätt (rättan) ~* at the right (in [due]) time; *i sinom ~* in due course; *i två års ~* for [a period of] two years; *i vår ~* in our times (age); *förr i ~en* in former times, formerly; *i alla ~er* (*hittills*) from time immemorial; *med ~en* in [course of] time, as time goes on; *på Cromwells ~* in Cromwell's day[s *pl*]; *springa på ~* (*sport.*) run against time; *på bestämd ~* at the appointed time; *på min ~* in my time (day); *på senare ~* in recent times; *på senaste (sista) ~en* latterly, recently; *fara bort på en ~* go away for a time; *det är på ~en att vi* it is about time we; *under ~en* in the meantime, meanwhile; *under ~en 1–10 maj* during the period 1–10 May; *under den närmaste ~en* during the next few days (weeks); *under en längre ~* for a long (any great length of) time; *gå ur ~en* be removed; *vid ~en för* at the time of; *vid den ~en* at (by) that time; *vid den här ~en* by now (this time); *vid den här ~en på dagen* at (by) this time of the day; *vid en ~ som denna* at a time like this; *vid sjutton* at about seven [o'clock]; *över ~en* beyond (past) the proper time **3** *~s nog* early enough
tidelag *s7* bestiality, sexual intercourse with animals
tide|räkning chronology; *gregorianska ~en* the Gregorian calendar **-varv** period, age, epoch
tidgivning [-ji:v-] time signalling; (*i radio*) time announcement
tidig *al* early **tidigare I** *a, komp. t. tidig* earlier;

(föregående äv.) previous, former, prior **ll** *adv* earlier; at an earlier hour, sooner; *(förut)* previously, formerly **tidigarelägga** advance; ~ *ett sammanträde* hold a meeting earlier **tidigast** *a, superl. t. tidig o.* adv earliest; *allra* ~ at the very earliest

tidigt *adv* early; *för* ~ too early *(för* for; *för att* to), *(i förtid)* prematurely *(född* born); *det blev* ~ *höst* autumn was early; ~ *på dagen (morgonen)* early in the day (morning); ~ *på våren (äv.)* in early spring; *vara* ~ *uppe* be up early; *vara för* ~ *ute (bildl.)* be premature

tid|kort timecard, clock card **-lön** time rate (wages); *(daglön)* day[work] rate; *ha* ~ be paid by the hour **-lös** timeless **-lösa** *s1, bot.* autumn crocus, meadow saffron **-mätare** time meter **-mätning** measurement of time, chronometry

tidning [*ti:d-] newspaper; paper; *daglig* ~ daily [paper]; *det står i ~en* it's in the paper

tidnings|anka hoax, canard **-artikel** newspaper article **-bilaga** newspaper supplement **-bud** person who delivers newspapers **-försäljare** newsagent, newsvendor; *AE.* newsdealer **-kiosk** newsstand, bookstall **-man** newspaperman, *fem.* newspaperwoman **-papper** hand. newsprint, news stock; *en bit* ~ a piece of newspaper **-press** *(samtliga ~ar)* press **-redaktion** newspaper office **-redaktör** newspaper editor **-stöd** state newspaper subsidy **-urklipp** press cutting; *AE.* clipping; *bok för* ~ scrapbook, press-cutting book **-utgivare** newspaper publisher

tid|punkt point [of time]; time; *vid ~en för* at the time of **-rymd** period, space of time

tids [-i:-] *se tid 3*

tids|adverb adverb of time **-anda** *~n* the spirit of the age **-befrakta** *v1,* **-befraktning** *s2,* time charter **-begrepp** idea of time **-begränsad** limited in time **-begränsning** time limit **-besparande** *a4* timesaving **-besparing** time saved **-beställning** appointment **-bestämma** date; *-bestämt straff* fixed term [of imprisonment] **-brist** lack of time **-bunden** dated, of its period **-enhet** unit of time **-enlig** [-e:-] *a1* in keeping with the times; up-to-date **-faktor** time factor **-frist** time limit, deadline; *(anstånd)* respite **-fråga** *en* ~ a matter of time **-följd** *i* ~ in chronological order **-fördriv** *s7, till* ~ as a pastime **-förlust** loss of time **-gräns** time limit **-inställd** timed; ~ *bomb* time bomb **-inställning** *foto.* shutter setting

tidskrift periodical [publication], publication; journal, review; *(lättare)* magazine

tidskrifts|artikel article in a periodical *(etc.)* **-nummer** issue of a periodical *(etc.)* **-stöd** state magazine subsidy

tidskrivare time recorder

tids|läge situation at the time; *nuvarande* ~ the present juncture **-nöd** lack of time **-period** period, space, time **-plan** timetable, time schedule **-signal** time signal **-skede** epoch **-skildring** picture of the time **-skillnad** difference in time **-spillan** *r* waste of time **-studie** time [and motion] study **-studieman** time-study man, timer **-trogen** true to the period; faithful **-typisk** characteristic of the time **-vinst** time-saving;

med stor ~ with a great gain of time **-ålder** age **-ödande** *a4* time-consuming, time-wasting

tid|tabell timetable; *AE. äv.* schedule **-tabellsenlig** [-e:n-] *a1* scheduled **-tagare** *sport.* timekeeper **-tagarur** stopwatch; timer **-tagning** timekeeping **-tals** [-a:-] *(stundtals)* at times; *(långa tider)* for periods together **-vatten** tide; tidal water **-vattenkraftverk** tidal power station **-vis** *(då o. då)* at times; *(med mellanrum)* intermittently, periodically

tig|a *teg tegat (äv. -it)* be (remain) silent *(med* about); ~ *med ngt (äv.)* keep s.th. to o.s.; ~ *som muren* keep silent; ~ *ihjäl* hush up; *tig!* shut up!; *han fick så han teg* it silenced him; *den som -er samtycker* silence gives consent

tiger [*ti:-] *s2* tiger **-hane** male tiger **-hjärta** *tröst för ett* ~ a poor consolation **-hona** female tiger **-lilja** tiger lily **-skinn** *(på tiger)* tiger's coat; *(avdraget)* tiger skin **-språng** tiger's leap *(äv. bildl.)* **-unge** tiger cub

tigga *v2* beg *(av* of; *om* for); *AE. sl.* panhandle; *gå omkring och* ~ go begging; ~ *och be* beg and beg; ~ *ihop* collect by begging; ~ *sig fram* beg one's way along; ~ *sig till ngt av ngn* coax s.th. out of s.b.; ~ *stryk (vard.)* ask for a thrashing

tiggarbrev begging letter

tiggar|e beggar; *AE. sl.* panhandler; *(yrkesmässig äv.)* mendicant **-munk** mendicant friar **-påse** beggar's wallet **-ranunkel** crowfoot **-stav** beggar's staff; *bringa ngn till ~en* reduce s.b. to beggary

tigger|i begging **-ska** beggar-woman

tigit *sup. av tiga*

tigr|erad [-'re:-] *a5* tigrine **-inna** tigress

tik *s2* bitch

tilj|a *s1 (planka)* board; *beträda ~n* go on the stage; *gå över ~n (om skådespel)* be performed

till l *prep* **1** rumsbet. *(äv. friare)* a) allm. to; *(in ~)* into; *(mot)* towards; *vägen* ~ *handelsboden* the road to the shop; ~ *vänster* to the left; *ända ~ stationen* as far as the station; *ha gäster* ~ *middagen* have guests to dinner; *ha fisk* ~ *middag* have fish for dinner; *dricka öl* ~ *maten* have beer with one's food, b) *(ankomst)* at *(vid orter)*, in *(vid länder, stora städer)*; *ankomsten* ~ *Arlanda (Stockholm)* the arrival at Arlanda (in Stockholm); *han anlände* ~ *stationen (Sicilien)* he arrived at the station (in Sicily); *vid deras ankomst* ~ *staden* on their arrival in the city (at the town); *komma* ~ *ett resultat* arrive at a result, c) *(avresa)* for; *bussen (tåget)* ~ *A.* the bus (train) for A.; *vid vår avresa* ~ *London* on our departure for London; *lösa biljett* ~ *A.* buy a ticket for A. **2** tidsbet. *(som svar på 'hur länge')* till, until; *(ända ~)* [up] to; *(vid tidpunkt)* at; *(ej senare än)* by; *(avsett för viss tid)* for; *jag väntade* ~ *klockan sex* I waited till six o'clock; *jag väntade från klockan fem* ~ *klockan sex* I waited from five o'clock to (till) six o'clock; ~ *långt in på natten* till far on into the night; *vi träffas* ~ *påsk* we will meet at Easter; ~ *dess* by then; *ända* ~ *dess* up to that time; *du måste vara hemma* ~ *klockan sex* you must be home by six; *natten* ~ *lördagen* Friday night; *vi har ingen mat* ~ *i morgon* we have no food for tomorrow; *jag reser hem* ~ *jul* I am going home for Christmas; *köpa en ny hatt* ~ *våren* buy a new hat

T

for the spring; *sammanträdet är bestämt ~ i mor-gon* the meeting is fixed for tomorrow; *jag har tre läxor ~ i morgon* I have three lessons for tomorrow **3** *(dativförhållande)* to; *(avsedd för)* for; *jag sade det ~ dig* I said it to you; *skriva ~ ngn* write to s.b.; *sjunga ~ gitarr* sing to [the accompaniment of] the guitar; *det finns post ~ dig* there are some letters for you; *fyra biljetter ~ söndag* four tickets for Sunday; *hans kärlek ~ pengar* his love of money; *av kärlek ~ nästan* out of love for one's neighbour; *vår tillit ~ honom* our confidence (trust) in him **4** *(genitivförhållande)* of; to; *hon är dotter till en general* she is a (the) daughter of a general; *dörren ~ huset* the door of the house; *författaren ~ pjäsen* the author of the play; *en källa ~ (bildl.)* a source of; *mor ~ två barn* the mother of two children; *nyckeln ~ garaget* the key to the garage; *en vän till mig (min syster)* a friend of mine (my sister's); *ägaren ~ bilen* the owner of the car **5** *(efter verb) se verbet* **6** *(uttr. ändamålet)* for; *(såsom)* as, by way of; *köpa gardiner ~ köket* buy curtains for the kitchen; *sakna pengar ~* lack money for; *~ metspö använde han* he used ... as a fishing rod; *ge ngn ngt ~ julklapp* give s.b. s.th. as a Christmas present; *ha ngn ~ vän* have s.b. as a friend **7** *(uttr. verkan, resultat)* to; *~ min fasa* to my horror; *vara ~ hinder för* be a hindrance to; *~ skada för* to the detriment of **8** *(uttr. förändring)* into; *omvandlingen ~* the transformation (change) into; *översättning ~ svenska* translation into Swedish; *en förändring ~ det bättre* a change for the better **9** *(vid pris o.d.)* at; *(vid måttsuppgift)* of; *jordgubbar ~ 15 kronor litern* strawberries at 15 kronor per litre; *~ en längd av sex meter* of a length of 6 metres **10** *(i fråga om)* in; *(genom)* by; *~ antalet (utseendet)* in number (looks); *~ det yttre* in external appearance; *läkare ~ yrket* doctor by profession **11** *(i egenskap av)* of; *det var en baddare ~ gädda!* that pike is a real whopper!; *ett nöt ~ karl* a fool of a man; *ett ruckel ~ hus* a ramshackle old house; *en slyngel ~ son* a rascal of a son **12** *(före inf.) ~ att börja med* to begin with; *ett gevär ~ att skjuta med* a gun for shooting (to shoot with); *~ att inte karl ~ att* he's not the man to **13** *~ och med* up to [and including], *AE.* through; *~ och med söndag (äv.)* inclusive of Sunday, *AE.* through Sunday; *jfr II 4* **14** *svag ~ måttlig vind* light to moderate winds; *det var 20 ~ 30 personer där* there were 20 or (to) 30 persons there; *1 ~ 2 tabletter* one to two tablets **II** *adv* **1** *(ytterligare)* more; *en gång ~* once more; *det kommer tre ~* three more are coming; *ta en kaka ~!* have another biscuit!; *lika mycket ~* as much again; *det gör varken ~ eller från* it makes no difference **2** *(på instrumenttavla o.d.)* on **3** *(tillhörande)* to it; *ett paraply med fodral ~* an umbrella with a case to it; *en radio med batteri ~* a radio and battery [to it] **4** *~ och med* even *(jfr I 13)*; *~ och från (då o. då)* off and on; *hon går ~ och från (om städhjälp)* she comes in; *åt skolan ~* towards the school; *vi skulle just ~ att börja* we were just about to start (on the point of starting) **III** *konj, ~ dess [att]* till, until

tillaga|a *(särskr. till-laga)* make *(soppa* soup; *te* tea); *(steka)* cook; *(göra i ordning)* get ready, prepare; *(tillblanda)* mix **-ning** *(särskr. till-lag-*

ning) making *etc.*; preparation; *~ av mat* cooking **tillbaka** [-'ba:-] back; *(bakåt)* backwards; *sedan fem år ~* for the last (past) five years; *sedan ngn tid ~* for some time [past] **-bildad** *a5, biol.* vestigial **-blick** retrospect; *(i film, bok)* flashback **-böjd** bent backwards **-dragen** *bildl.* retiring, unobtrusive, reserved **-draget** *adv, leva ~* live in retirement **-gående** *a4* retrograde; retrogressive; *bildl. äv.* declining **-gång** *(nedgång)* retrogression, decline, setback *(i of)* **-lutad** *a5* leaning backwards; *(om pers. äv.)* leaning back, reclining **-satt** *a4, känna sig ~* feel slighted (neglected) **-syftande** *a4* referring [back] to **-visa** *(förslag)* reject, refuse; *(påstående)* refute; *(beskyllning)* repudiate

till|be[dja] worship; *(friare)* adore **-bedjan** [-e:-] *best. form* -bedjan, *r* worship; adoration **-bedjansvärd** *a1* adorable **-bedjare** [-e:-] adorer; *hennes ~* her admirer **-behör** *s7, pl* accessories, fittings, appliances; *(reservdelar)* spare parts **-blivelse** coming into being; *(begynnelse)* origin, birth **-bommad** *a5* barred and bolted **-bringa** spend, pass *(med att in + ing-form)* **-bringare** jug; *AE.* pitcher **-bucklad** *a5* dented **-bud** *(olycks-)* narrow escape **-byds** [-u:-] *se bud 5* **-byggnad** extension, addition **-börlig** [-ö:-] *a1* due; proper *(aktning* respect); *(lämplig)* fitting, appropriate **-börligen** [-ö:-] duly *etc.* **-dela** allot (assign, give) [to]; award *(ngn ett pris* s.b. a prize, a prize to s.b.); confer, bestow *(ngn en utmärkelse* a distinction [up]on s.b.); *(vid ransonering)* allocate; *~ ngn ett slag* deal s.b. a blow **-delning** allotment, assignment, allocation; award; conferment, bestowal; *konkr.* allowance, ration **-dels** [-e:-] partly **-dess** *konj. ~ [att]* till, until

till|dra[ga] *rfl* **1** *(draga åt sig)* attract *(uppmärksamhet* attention) **2** *(hända)* happen, occur **-dragande** *a4* attractive **-dragelse** occurrence; *(viktig)* event **-döma** *~ ngn ngt* adjudge s.th. to s.b., award s.b. s.th.; *-dömd ersättning* award **-erkänna** *~ ngn ngt* award (grant) s.b. s.th.; *modern -erkändes vårdnaden om barnet* the mother was granted the custody of the child; *~ ngt en viss vikt* ascribe (attach) a certain importance to s.th. **-falla** go (fall) to; accrue to **-fart** [-a:-] *s3* means of access **-fartsväg** approach, access road **-flykt** refuge *(mot, undan* from); *ta sin ~ till a)* *(en pers.)* take refuge with, go to for refuge, *b)* *(stad, land etc.)* take refuge in, *c) bildl.* resort (have recourse) to, take refuge in **-flyktsort** place of refuge *(undan* from) **-flöde** *(flods etc.)* feeder stream, affluent; *bildl.* inflow, influx **-foga 1** *(-lägga)* add (affix, append) *(till* to) **2** *(förorsaka)* inflict *(ngn skada* harm on s.b.), cause *(ngn en förlust* s.b. a loss); *~ ngn ett nederlag (äv.)* defeat s.b. **-freds** [-e:-] *oböjligt a* satisfied, content; *~ med livet* at one with the world

tillfreds|ställa ['till-] satisfy, give satisfaction to, content; *(göra t. lags äv.)* please; *(begäran)* gratify; *(hunger e.d.)* appease; *~ ngns anspråk* fulfil a p.'s expectations **-ställande** *a4* satisfactory *(för* to); *(glädjande)* gratifying *(för* to) **-ställd** *a5* satisfied, content *(med* with) **-ställelse** satisfaction *(över, med* at)

till‖friskna recover (*efter, från* from); *absol. äv.* get well (*vard.* get better) again **-frisknande** s6 recovery **-frusen** frozen (iced) over; (*om farvatten*) icebound **-fråga** ask; (*rådfråga*) consult (*om* as to, about); *han ~des om sina åsikter* he was asked his opinion **-frågan** *i uttr.: på ~* when asked (*om* about) **-fullo** [-ˣfullo] *se full 3* **-fyllest** [-'fyll-] *se fyllest* **-fånga** [-ˣfåŋa] *se l fånga* **-fångataga** [-ˣfåŋa-] capture; *bli -fångatagen* be taken prisoner **-fångatagande** [-ˣfåŋa-] s6 capturing, capture

tillfälle s6 (*tidpunkt*) occasion; (*lägligt*) opportunity; (*möjlighet*) chance, possibility; *~t gör tjuven* opportunity makes the thief; *begagna ~t* take the opportunity; *bereda ngn ~ att* provide s.b. with an opportunity to (of + *ing*-form); *det finns ~n då* there are times when; *få* (*ha*) *~ att* find (get) an opportunity of (+ *ing*- form) (to); *så snart ~ ges* when an opportunity occurs (arises); *för ~t* (*för närvarande*) at present, just now, (*för ögonblicket*) for the time being; *inte vara i ~ att* be unable (in no position) to, not be in a position to; *vid ~* when opportunity occurs, when convenient; *vi ber Er meddela oss det vid ~* please let us know at your convenience; *vid detta ~* on this occasion; *vid första* [*bästa*] *~* at the first opportunity, at your earliest convenience; *vid lämpligt ~* at a suitable (convenient) opportunity; *låta ~t gå sig ur händerna* let the opportunity slip, miss the opportunity

tillfällig al (*då o. då förekommande*) occasional; (*av en händelse*) accidental, casual, incidental; (*kortvarig, provisorisk*) temporary; *~t arbete* casual work; *~a arbeten* odd jobs; *inkomst av ~ förvärvsverksamhet* income from incidental sources; *~t utskott* select committee **-het** accidental occurrence (circumstance); (*slump äv.*) chance; (*sammanträffande*) coincidence; *av en* [*ren*] *~* by pure chance **-hetsdikt** occasional poem **tillfälligt** *adv* temporarily, for the time being **-vis** accidentally, by accident; (*oförutsett*) incidentally; (*av en slump*) by chance; (*helt apropå*) casually

tillför‖a bring (*ngn ngt* s.th. to s.b.), supply, furnish (*ngn ngt* s.b. with s.th.; *-d effekt* (*fys.*) [power] input

tillförlitlig [-i:t-] al reliable, trustworthy; authentic; *ur ~ källa* (*äv.*) on good authority **-het** reliability, trustworthiness; authenticity

till‖förordna appoint temporarily; *~d* acting (*professor* professor), [appointed] pro tempore **-försel** s9 supply, delivery, provision (*av* of); *~ av nytt kapital* provision of fresh capital **-förselväg** supply route, approach **-försikt** s3 confidence (*till* in) **-försäkra** secure, ensure (*ngn ngt* s.b. s.th.); *~ sig ngt* secure (make sure of) s.th. **-gift** [-j-] s3 forgiveness; *be om ~* ask for forgiveness **-given** [-j-] a3 attached; affectionate; (*om make, hund*) devoted; *vara ngn mycket ~* be very devoted (attached) to s.b.; *Din -givne* (*i brev*) Yours sincerely (*t. nära vän:* affectionately **-givenhet** [-j-] attachment, devotion, devotedness (*för* to); (*kärlek*) affection (*för* for) **-gjord** affected; (*konstlad*) artificial **-gjordhet** [-j-] affectation; affected manners (*pl*)

tillgodo [-ˣgɔ:-] *se under godo* **-göra** rfl utilize;

avail o.s. of; *bildl.* profit by (*undervisningen* the education) **-havande** s6 balance in one's favour, balance due to one; (*i bank*) [credit] balance (*hos* with), holdings, assets (*pl*); *ha ett ~ hos* have a balance in one's favour with; *vårt ~ hos er* the amount you owe us, our account against you **-kvitto** credit note (*AE.* slip) **-räkna** rfl, *~ sig ngt* (*kreditera sig*) put s.th. to one's credit, (*rabatt*) allow o.s. s.th., *bildl.* take the credit for s.th. **-se** pay due attention to; satisfy, meet (*krav* demands); supply, provide for (*ngns behov* a p.'s needs)

till‖grepp (*ur kassa e.d.*) misappropriation (*ur* from); (*stöld*) theft **-gripa 1** take unlawfully, seize upon; (*stjäla*) thieve; (*försnilla*) misappropriate **2** *bildl.* resort (have recourse) to **-gå 1** (*försiggå*) *det brukar ~ så att* what usually happens is that, the normal procedure is that; *spelet ~r så att* the rules of the game are that **2** *finnas att ~* be obtainable, be to be had (*hos* from); *ha ngn* (*ngt*) *att ~* have s.b. (s.th.) at hand **-gång** s2 **1** (*förfogande*) access (*t.* telefon to telephone); *jag har ~ till bil i dag* I have the use of a car today **2** (*värdefull ~*) asset; (*bildl. om pers.*) asset; *~ar* means, assets, resources; *~ar och skulder* assets and liabilities; *leva över sina ~ar* live beyond one's means; *fasta* (*rörliga*) *~ar* fixed (current) assets; *han är en stor ~ för företaget* he is a great asset to the company **3** (*förråd*) supply (*på* of); *~ och efterfrågan* supply and demand; *~ på arbetskraft* supply of labour, labour supply **-gänglig** [-jäŋ-] al **1** (*som man kan nå*) accessible (*för* to); (*som finns att -gå*) available (*för* for, to), obtainable; (*öppen*) open (*för* to); *med alla ~a medel* by every available means; *parken är ~ för besökare* the park is open to visitors **2** (*om pers.*) easy to approach, approachable; (*vänlig*) affable **-gänglighet** [-jäŋ-] **1** accessibility **2** affability

tillhanda [-ˣhann-] *se hand 3* **-hålla** (*saluföra*) sell; *~ ngn ngt* supply (furnish, provide) s.b. with s.th.; *~s* (*äv.*) be on sale

till‖handla rfl buy o.s. (*av ngn* off, from s.b.) **-hands** *se hand 4* **-hjälp** *med ~ av* with the aid (assistance) of; *med din ~* by your aid (help) **-hopa** [-'hɔ:-] [al]together, in all **-hygge** weapon **-håll** haunt (*för* of); *ha sitt ~ hos ngn* have one's quarters with s.b. **-hålla** *~ ngn att* urge s.b. to; *~ ngn att inte* tell s.b. not to

tillhör‖a 1 belong to; (*vara medlem av äv.*) be a member of; (*räknas t.*) be among (one of); *jag tillhör inte dem som* I am not one of those who; *~ en förnäm släkt* (*äv.*) come of a distinguished family **2** *se tillkomma* **-ande** a4 belonging to; appurtenant; *en maskin med ~ delar* a machine complete with fittings **-ig** al, *en mig ~ a*[n] ... belonging to me **-ighet** possession; [private] property; *mina ~er* (*äv.*) my belongings; *politisk ~* political affiliation

tillika [-ˣli:-, -'li:-] also, as well, ... too; (*dessutom*) besides, moreover; *~ med* together with

tillintet‖gjord [-ˣinn-] (*nedbruten*) crushed (*av sorg* with sorrow) **-göra** (*nedgöra*) annihilate; (*besegra*) defeat completely; (*krossa*) crush (*äv. bildl.*); (*förhoppningar*) shatter; (*planer*) frustrate; *~nde blickar* withering looks **-görelse** [-j-] annihilation; demolition; ruin; shattering;

frustration
tillit confidence, trust, faith (*till* in); reliance (*till* on); *sätta sin ~ till* put one's confidence in
tillitsfull confident; confiding, trustful
till|kalla summon, call; *~ hjälp* summon assistance; *~ läkare* send for a doctor **-klippning** cutting **-klippt** *a4* cut out **-knyckla** (*skrynkla*) crumple [up]; (*hatt e.d.*) batter [about] **-knäppt** *a4* buttoned-up; (*om pers.*) reserved **-komma 1** (*komma som tillägg*) *se komma* [*till*]; *dessutom -kommer* (*äv.*) is **2** (*uppstå*) *se komma* [*till*] **3** (*vara ngns rättighet*) be (a p.'s) due; (*åligga*) be incumbent [up]on; *det -kommer inte mig att* it is not for me to **4** *-komme ditt rike!* Thy Kingdom come! **-kommande** *a4* (*framtida*) future, coming, ... to come; *hennes ~* (*som subst.*) her husband-to-be (future husband) **-komst** [-å-] *s3* coming into being (existence); (*uppkomst*) origin, rise **-koppla** attach, hook on; *järnv.* couple [up]; (*motor*) put in[to] gear **-krånglad** *a5* (*-trasslad*) entangled; (*invecklad*) complicated **-kämpa** *rfl* obtain (gain) after a struggle; *~d* hard-won
tillkännagiv|a [-ˣçänn-] notify, announce, make known (*för* to); (*röja*) disclose; *härmed -es att* notice is hereby given that **-ande** *s6* notification, announcement, declaration; (*anslag äv.*) notice
till|mäle *s6* word of abuse, epithet; *grova ~n* (*äv.*) invectives **-mäta 1** (*uppmäta*) measure out to, allot **2** (*tillräkna*) attach to; *~ ngt betydelse* attach importance to s.th.; *~ sig äran* take the credit **-mätt** *a4* measured out; apportioned
tillmötes [-ˣmö:-] *se möte 1* **-gå** (*ngn*) oblige, meet; (*begäran, önskan*) comply with **-gående I** *a4* obliging (*sätt* manners), courteous; (*om pers.*) accommodating (*mot* to[wards]) **II** *s6* obligingness, courtesy, compliance; *tack för Ert ~* thank you for your kind assistance
till|namn surname, family name **-närmelsevis** [-ˣnärr-] approximately; *icke ~* nothing like
tillopp (*särskr. till-lopp*) (*tillflöde*) influx, inflow; (*av ånga*) induction, inlet; (*av människor*) rush, run
tillopps|kanal feeder; (*t. motor*) lead **-rör** delivery (feed) tube
till|pøss *se 5 pass* **-platta** flatten, compress; *känna sig ~d* (*bildl.*) feel crushed (sat on)
till|ra roll; trickle **-reda** prepare, get ready **-reds** [-e:-] *vara* (*stå*) *~* be ready (*för, till* for; *för* (*till*) *att* to) **-rop** call, shout; *glada ~* joyous acclamations **-ropa** hail; (*om vakt*) *o.d.* challenge **-ryggalägga** [-ˣrygg-] cover
tillråd|a advise, recommend, suggest **-an** *r, på ngns ~* on the (by) advice of s.b. **-lig** *a1* advisable **-lighet** advisability
tillräck|lig *a1* sufficient, enough (*för, åt* for); *vi har ~t med* we have ... enough; *mer än ~t* more than enough, enough and to spare **-ligt** *adv* sufficiently, enough; *~ många* a sufficient number of; *~ ofta* often enough, sufficiently often
tillräkna *~ ngn ngt* put s.th. down to s.b.; *~ ngn förtjänsten av ngt* give s.b. the credit of s.th.; *~ sig* take (ascribe) to o.s.; *~ sig själv hela äran* take all the credit o.s.
tillräknelig [-ä:-] *a5* accountable (responsible) [for one's actions] **-het** accountability

tillrätta [-ˣrätta] *se rätta I 2* **-lagd** *a5, ~* [*för*] arranged (adjusted) to suit **-lägga** correct, make clear **-visa** reprove, censure; (*starkare*) reprimand, rebuke **-visning** reproof, censure; reprimand, rebuke
tills I *konj* (*t. dess att*) till, until **II** *prep* (*t. ngn tidpunkt*) up to; *~ för två år sedan* until two years ago; *~ vidare* until further notice; *~ på lördag* till (until) Saturday
till|sagd *a5* told; *han är ~* he has been told; *är det -sagt?* (*i butik*) are you being attended to [, Sir (Madam)]? **-sammans** [-ˣsamm-] together (*med* with); (*sammanlagt*) in all, altogether; (*gemensamt*) jointly; *alla ~* all together; *äta middag ~ med* dine with; *det blir 50 pund ~* it will be 50 pounds in all; *~ har vi 50 pund* we have 50 pounds between (*om fler än två:* amongst) us **-sats 1** (*-sättning*) adding, addition **2** (*ngt -satt*) added ingredient; (*liten ~*) dash; *bildl.* admixture, addition **-satsmedel** additive **-se** (*ha -syn över*) look after, superintend; (*sörja för*) see [to it] (*att ngt blir gjort* that s.th. is done) **-sinnes** [-ˣsinnes] in mind; *munter ~* in high spirits **-sjst** finally; at last **-skansa** *rfl* appropriate for o.s.; *~ sig makten* usurp power **-skjuta** contribute, pay in (*kapital* capital) **-skott** *s7* contribution; (*utökning*) addition, increase **-skottsvärme** incidental heat gain **-skriva 1** (*skriva t.*) write to **2** (*-räkna*) *~ ngn ngt* ascribe (attribute) s.th. to s.b., (*-erkänna äv.*) credit s.b. with s.th.; *~ sig, se tillräkna* [*sig*] **-skrynkla** crease (crumple) up
tillskynd|a (*tillfoga*) cause (*ngn en förlust* s.b. a loss) **-an** *r, på ngns ~* at the instigation (instance) of s.b. **-are** initiator
tillskär|a cut out **-are** cutter **-ning** cutting out
till|slag (*tennis etc.*) hit; (*fotboll*) kick **-sluta** close, shut (*för* to) (*äv. bildl.*) **-slutning** [-u:-] **1** (*-slutande*) closing [up] etc. **2** (*an-*) *mötet hölls under stor ~* the meeting was very well attended **-spetsa** *eg.* sharpen, point; *bildl.* bring to a head; *läget har ~ts* the situation has become critical **-spillo** [-ˣspillo] *se spillo* **-spillogiva** (*låta gå förlorat*) allow to run to waste; *en -spillogiven dag* a wasted day **-stampa** (*jord o.d.*) stamp **-stoppa** stop (shut) [up] **-strömning** streaming in; (*om vätska*) inflow; (*-skott utifrån*) influx; (*publik-*) stream, rush **-stymmelse** *inte en ~ till* not a trace of; *utan varje ~ till* without any semblance of **-styrka** recommend, support, be in favour of **-styrkan** *r* recommendation **-stå** (*medge*) admit; (*bekänna*) confess (*för* to; *att* to)
1 tillstånd *s7* (*tillåtelse*) permission, leave; (*av myndighet äv.*) sanction; (*-sbevis*) permit, licence; *få ~ att* receive (be granted) permission to; *ha ~ att* (*äv.*) have been authorized (licenced) to; *med benäget ~ av* by kind permission of
2 tillstånd *s7* (*beskaffenhet; skick*) state, condition; (*sinnes-*) state [of mind]; *fast* (*flytande*) *~* solid (liquid) form; *i dåligt ~* in bad condition (repair); *i naturligt ~* in the natural state; *miner.* native; *i berusat ~* in a state of intoxication; *i medtaget ~* in an exhausted condition
till|ståndsbevis permit, licence; *AE.* license, certificate **-städes** [-ˣstä:-] *vara ~* be on the spot, (*närvarande*) be present; *komma ~* arrive

to the place **-städesvarande** a4, de ~ those present **-ställa** (-sända) send (forward) to; (överlämna) hand [over] to **-ställning 1** entertainment, (fest) party (för for, in honour of); en lyckad ~ a successful party **2** det var just en skön ~ (iron.) that's a nice business **-stöta** (inträffa, tillkomma) occur, happen; (om sjukdom) set in **tillsvidare** [-ˣvi:-] se vidare II 6 **-anställning** nontenured appointment

till|syn s3, ha ~ över supervise, superintend, be in charge of; utan ~ (äv.) unattended **-synes** [-ˣsy:-] se syn 3 **-syningsman** supervisor (över of)

tillsyns|lärare deputy head teacher **-myndighet** supervising authority

till|säga se säga [till] **-sägelse** (befallning) order (om for); (uppmaning) summons; (begäran) demand (om for); (tillrättavisning) admonition, reprimand; få ~ [om] att receive orders (be told) to; utan ~ without being told **-sätta 1** (utnämna) appoint, nominate; ~ en tjänst nominate (appoint) s.b. to a post, fill a vacancy; ~ en kommitté set up a committee **2** (-lägga) add on (till to) **3** (blanda i) add (till to) **-sättande** s6 **1** ~t av tjänsten the appointment to a post **2** addition **3** adding **tillta** se tilltaga

till|tag (företag) venture; (försök) attempt; (påhitt) trick; ett sådant ~! (äv.) what a thing to do! **-taga** increase, grow **-tagande I** a4 increasing etc. **II** s6 increase, growth; vara i ~ be on the increase **-tagen** a5, knappt ~ on the small side, (om mat e.d.) scanty in quantity, (om lön) meagre; väl ~ a good (fair) size **-tagsen** [-tags-, -taks-] a3 enterprising, go-ahead; (djärv) bold, daring

till|tal address; används i ~ is used as a form of address; svara på ~ answer when [one is] spoken to **-tala 1** (tala t.) address, speak to; (ngn på gatan) accost; den ~de the person addressed (spoken to) **2** (behaga) attract, please; (i sht om sak) appeal to; det ~r mig mycket (äv.) I like it very much **-talande** a4 attractive, pleasing (för to); acceptable (förslag proposal)

tilltals|form vocative form **-namn** Christian name normally used; ~et understruket (på formulär e.d.) underline the name used **-ord** word (form) of address

till|trasslad a4 entangled; ~e affärer muddled finances **-tro I** s9 credit, credence; confidence (till in); sätta ~ till a) (ngn) place confidence in, b) (ngt) give credit (credence) to; vinna ~ gain credence (hos with) **II** v4, ~ ngn ngt believe s.b. capable of s.th., give s.b. credit for s.th. **-träda** (befattning) enter upon [the duties of]; (ta i besittning) take over (en egendom a property); ~ arv come into [possession of] an inheritance; ~ sin tjänst take up one's duties (an appointment) **-träde** s6 **1** (-trädande) entry (av into possession of); entrance (av ämbete upon office) **2** (inträde) entrance, admission; (tillstånd att inträda) admittance; luftens ~ the access of the air; bereda ~ för give access to; fritt ~ admission (entrance) free; ~ förbjudet no admittance; ha ~ till have admission to; barn äga ej ~ children [are] not admitted; obehöriga äga ej ~ no admittance except on business **-trädesdag** day of taking possession; (in-

stallationsdag) inauguration day **-tugg** s7 snack **-tvinga** rfl obtain (secure) by force **-tyga** illa ~ ngt (ngn) use (handle) s.th. (s.b.) roughly, vard. manhandle s.th. (s.b.); han var illa ~d he had been badly knocked about **-tänkt** a4 (påtänkt) contemplated, proposed; (planerad) projected, intended **-valsämne** optional (AE. elective) subject **-vand** a5 addicted (vid to)

tillvaratag|a [-ˣva:-] take charge of; (bevaka) look after; (skydda) protect, safeguard; (utnyttja) utilize (tiden time), take advantage of; ~ sina intressen look after (protect) one's interests **-ande** s6, ~t av the taking charge of (looking after)

tillvaro s9 existence; life; kampen för ~n struggle for existence

tillverk|a manufacture, make, produce **-are** manufacturer etc. **-ning** (-ande) manufacture, make, production; (det som -ats) manufacture, make, product; (-ningsmängd) output, production; ha ngt under ~ have s.th. in production

tillverknings|kostnad cost of production **-pris** factory (cost) price **-process** manufacturing process

till|vinna rfl gain, obtain, secure; (ngns respekt äv.) win **-vita** ~ ngn ngt charge s.b. with s.th. **-vitelse** charge, imputation (för of; för att of + ing-form) **-väga** [-ˣvä:-] se väg 2 **-vägagångssätt** course (line) of action, procedure **-välla** rfl usurp, arrogate to o.s. (rätten att the right of + ing-form) **-växa** grow; bildl. äv. increase (i in) **-växt** s3 growth; (ökning) increase; vara stadd i ~ be increasing (growing, on the increase) **-växttakt** rate of growth **-yxa** rough-hew, rough-cut; (friare) roughly shape

tillåt|a (särskr. till-låta) **1** allow, permit; (samtycka t.) consent to; (om sak) admit (allow) of; (finna sig i) suffer; tillåt mig fråga om ni allow me to (let me) ask if you; -er ni att jag röker? do you mind my smoking?; om ni -er if you will allow me; om vädret -er weather permitting; min ekonomi -er inte det my finances won't allow it **2** rfl (unna sig) allow (permit) o.s.; (ta sig friheten) take the liberty to (of) + ing-form **-else** permission, leave; (av myndighet e.d.) licence, authorization; be om ~ att ask [for] permission to; få ~ att be allowed (permitted) to, (be given) permission to; med er ~ with your permission **-en** a5 allowed, permitted; (laglig) lawful; är det -et att ...? may I ...?; det är inte -et att röka här smoking is not allowed here; högsta -na hastighet the maximum speed allowed, the speed limit; vara ~ (jakt.) be in season **-lig** [-å:-] a1 allowable, permissible

tillägg (särskr. till-lägg) s7 addition; (t. dokument äv.) rider, additional paragraph; (t. bok) supplement, appendix; (t. manuskript) insertion; (t. brev) postscript; (t. testamente) codicil; (löne-) rise, bonus; (anmärkning) addendum (pl addenda); rättelser och ~ corrections and additions, corrigenda and addenda; procentuellt ~ [a] percentage addition; dock med det ~et att it being understood, however, that; utan ~ without any addition

tillägga add (till to)

tilläggs|avgift extra (additional) fee, surcharge

T

-bestämmelse additional (supplementary) regulation **-biljett** supplementary ticket **-pension** supplementary pension **-pensionering** allmän ~ (förk. ATP) national supplementary pensions scheme **-plats** sjö. berth, landing (mooring) place **-porto** surcharge, additional postage **-premie** försäkr. additional (extra) premium

till|ägna [-'äŋna] **1** (dedicera) dedicate (ngn en bok a book to s.b.) **2** rfl (tillskansa sig) appropriate, seize [upon], lay hands on; (förvärva) acquire (kunskaper knowledge); (tillgodogöra sig) assimilate, profit by; orättmätigt ~ sig ngt appropriate s.th. unlawfully **-ägnan** [-äŋn-] r dedication **-ämna** intend, have in view **-ämnad** a5 intended; (påtänkt) premeditated

tillämp|a (särskr. till-lämpa) apply (på to); (metod e.d.) practise; kunna ~s på (äv.) be applicable to; ~ ngt i praktiken put s.th. into practice; ~d forskning applied research **-bar** a1 applicable **-lig** a1 applicable (på to); stryk det ej ~a strike out words not applicable; i ~a delar wherever applicable (relevant) **-ning** application (på to); äga ~ på be applicable to

tillända [-ˣänn-] se 1 ända I 1 **-lupen** a5 expired; vara ~ be at (have come to) an end

till|öka add to; (göra större) enlarge **-ökning** (-ökande) increasing, enlargement (av, i of); konkr. increase (av of); increment (på lön in one's salary); vänta ~ [i familjen] be expecting an addition to the family **-önska** wish **-önskan** wish; med ~ om best wishes for **-övers** [-'ö:-] se övers

tilta s1, lantbr. ridge

1 tima [ˣti:ma] åld. happen, occur

2 tima [ˣtajma] vard. time, coordinate

tim|antal number of hours **-arbete** work by the hour

timbal s3 **1** mus. kettledrum **2** kokk. timbale

timbre ['täŋber] s9 timbre

timer ['tajj-] s9 time switch

tim|förtjänst hourly earnings (pl) **-glas** hourglass, sandglass

timjd a1, n sg obest. form undviks timid

timing ['tajj-] timing, coordination

timjan s9 thyme

tim|lig a1 temporal; det ~a things temporal; lämna det ~a depart this life **-lärare** ung. part--time teacher **-lön** hourly wage[s pl], payment by the hour; få ~ be paid by the hour

timma s5, **timme** s2 hour; (lektion) lesson; en ~s resa an hour's journey; varannan ~ every other hour; åtta timmars arbetsdag an eight-hour day; efter en ~ an hour later; i ~n an hour; i flera timmar for [several] hours; om en ~ in an hour; per ~ per (by the) hour

timmer ['timm-] s7 timber; AE. lumber **-avverkning** logging, timber cutting (felling) **-bil** timber lorry, AE. logging truck **-bröt** log jam (blockage) **-flottare** log driver **-flotte** log raft **-flottning** timber (log) driving **-huggare** woodcutter, logger; AE. lumberjack **-koja** log cabin **-lass** load of logs (timber) **-man** carpenter **-ränna** flume **-släp** log (timber) raft (transport) **-stock** log; dra ~ar (snarka) be driving one's hogs to market

timotej [-'tejj] s3 timothy [grass], AE. herd's grass

tim|penning hourly wage **-plan** timetable

timra build with logs, construct out of timber; absol. do carpentry; ~d stuga timbered cottage

timslag på ~et on the stroke of the hour

timslång of an hour's duration, lasting an hour

tim|tals [-a:-] for hours together, for hours and hours **-vis** by the hour **-visare** hour (small) hand

1 tina s1 **1** (laggkärl) tub **2** (fiskredskap) creel

2 tina v1, ~ [upp] thaw (äv. bildl.), melt; (bildl. om pers.) become less reserved (more sociable)

tindra twinkle; (starkare) sparkle, scintillate; ~nde ögon starry-eyed

1 ting s7 (sak) thing; (ärende äv.) matter; (föremål) object; saker och ~ [a lot of] things

2 ting s7 (domstolssammanträde) district-court sessions (pl), crown courts (pl); Engl. förr assizes, quarter sessions (pl); hist. thing; sitta ~ be on duty at a district court

tinga (beställa) order [in advance], bespeak; (ngn) retain, engage; (göra avtal om) bargain for

tingeltangel [-'taŋ-, ˣtiŋ-] s7 noisy funfair, cheap entertainment

tingest ['tiŋ-] s2 thing, object; vard. contraption

tings|dag sessions day **-hus** courthouse, law courts (pl) **-meriterad** a5, ~ jurist (ung.) jurist with district-court practice **-meritering** ung. period of service in a district court **-notarie** clerk of a [district] court **-rätt** district (city) court; court of first instance **-sal** sessions hall **-tjänstgöring** court practice

tinktur tincture

tinn|e s2 pinnacle; bildl. summit; torn och -ar towers and pinnacles; försedd med -ar pinnacled

tinning temple

tio [ˣti:ɔ, vard. ˣti:e] ten; (för sms. jfr fem-); ~-i--topp top ten **-dubbel** tenfold **-dubbla** multiply by ten, increase tenfold **-falt** ten times, tenfold **tio|hörning** [-ö:-] decagon **-kamp** sport. decathlon **-kampare** sport. decathlete **-kronesedel, -kronorssedel** ten-kronor note

tion|de [-å-] **I** räkn. tenth **II** s9, s7 tithes (pl); ge ~ pay [one's] tithes **-[de]del** tenth **-[de]dels** [-de:ls] oböjligt a, en ~ sekund one (a) tenth of a second

tio|pundssedel ten-pound note; vard. tenner **-tal** ten; ett ~ (ung. tio) about (some) ten; i jämna ~ in multiples of ten; under ett ~ år for ten years [or so]; på ~et (1910-talet) in the nineteen-tens **-tiden** vid ~ [at] about ten [o'clock] **-tusental** i ~ in tens of thousands **-tusentals** [-ˣtu:-, ˣti:ɔ-, -a:-] i ~ år for tens of thousands of years **-årig** a1 ten-year-old **-åring** ten-year-old boy (etc.), boy (etc.) of ten **-årsdag** tenth anniversary (av of) **-öring** ten-öre piece

1 tipp s2 (spets) tip (av of)

2 tipp s2 (avstjälpningsplats) tip, dump; (på lastfordon) tipping device; lastbil med ~ tipper truck (lorry), AE. dump (tip) truck

1 tippa (stjälpa ur) tip, dump

2 tippa (förutsäga) spot; sport. play the pools

1 tippning (avstjälpning) tipping, dumping; ~ förbjuden! no tipping allowed!

2 tippning sport. playing the pools

tippvagn 1 (lastbil) se 2 tipp **2** järnv. tipping

truck; *AE.* dump car
tips *s7* **1** (*vink*) tip[-off], hint; *ge ngn ett* ~ give s.b. a tip **2** (*fotbolls-*) football pools; *vinna på* ~ win on the pools
tips|a tip **-kupong** [football-]pools coupon **-rad** line on a pools coupon **-vinst** [football-]pools win (dividend)
tiptop [-tåpp] *oböjligt a* tiptop, first-rate
tirad *s3* tirade
tisdag ['ti:s-] *s2* Tuesday; (*jfr fredag*)
tiss|el ['tiss-] *s7*, ~ *och tassel* tittle-tattle **-la** ~ *och tassla* tittle-tattle
tistel *s2, bot.* thistle
tistelstång shaft, pole
titan 1 *s3, myt.* Titan **2** *s3, s4, kem.* titanium **-isk** *a5* (*jättelik*) titan[ic] **-vitt** titanium white
tit|el ['titt-] *s2* **1** (*bok- etc.*) title (*på* of); *med* ~*n* entitled **2** (*persons*) title; (*benämning*) designation, denomination; *lägga bort* -*larna* drop the Mr. (*etc.*)
titel|blad title page **-match** championship (title) match **-roll** *teat. e.d.* title role **-sida** title page **-sjuka** mania for titles **-vinjett** headpiece
titrer|a titrate **-ing** titration
1 titt *adv*, ~ *och tätt* frequently, repeatedly, over and over again
2 titt *s2* **1** (*blick*) look; (*hastig*) glance; (*i smyg*) peep; *ta sig en* ~ *på* have a look at **2** (*kort besök*) call (*hos* on; *på* at); *tack för* ~*en!* kind of you to look me up!
titta 1 look (*på* at); (*hastigt*) glance (*på* at); (*kika*) peep (*på* at); ~ *efter* gaze after, (*söka*) look for; ~ *i* have a look at (in); ~ *för djupt i glaset* be too fond of the bottle; ~ *sig i spegeln* look (have a look) at o.s. in the mirror; ~ *ngn djupt in i ögonen* look deep into a p.'s eyes; ~ *på* (*äv.*) have a look at; *vi skall ut och* ~ *på möbler* we are going to the shops to look at furniture; ~ *på TV* watch TV; *jag vill inte* ~ *åt honom* I can't bear the sight of him; *titt ut!* boo!, *AE.* peekaboo! **2** (*med betonad partikel*) ~ *efter* (*undersöka*) [look and] see; ~ *fram* peep out (forth); *vill du* ~ *hit ett ögonblick* will you come over here for a minute; ~ *in a*) look in (*genom fönster* at the window), *b*) (*hälsa på* kort (drop) in (*till* to see); ~ *in hos ngn* look s.b. up; ~ *in i* look into; ~ *ner* lower one's eyes; ~ *på* look on, watch; ~ *upp* look up, raise one's eyes; ~ *ut genom fönstret* look out of the window; ~ *ut ngn* stare s.b. out of the room
tittar|e (*TV--*) **1** viewer **2** (*voyeur*) Peeping Tom, voyeur **-frekvens** television audience measurement (T.A.M.) rating **-storm** *TV-programmet utlöste en* ~ the TV switchboard was jammed with angry callers after the programme
titt|glugg spy hole **-hål** peephole **-skåp** peepshow **-ut** *s2, leka* ~ play [at] bo-peep
titul|atur title[s *pl*] **-era** style, call; ~ *ngn* (*äv.*) address s.b. as **-är** *al* titular[y]
tivoli ['ti:-] *s6* amusement park; *AE. äv.* carnival
tixotrop [-'å:-] *a1* thixotropic
tja [ça:] well!
tjafs [ç-] *s7* tommyrot **tjafsa** talk a lot of tommyrot
tjall|a [ç-] squeal **-are** informer, squealer
tjat [ç-] *s7* nagging **tjata** nag **tjatig** *al* nagging; (*långtråkig*) tedious

tjatter ['çatt-] *s7*, **tjattra** ['ˣçatt-] *v1* jabber, chatter
tjeck [çekk] *s3* Czech **-isk** ['çekk-] *a5* Czech **-oslovak** *s3* Czechoslovak
Tjeckoslovakien [çekk-, -'va:-] *n* Czechoslovakia
tjej [çejj] *s3* (*flicka*) girl, bird; (*kvinna*) woman
tjo [ço:] *s7*, ~ *och tjim* whoopee-making **tjoa** [ˣço:a] shout **tjohej** *interj* whoopee!
tjock [çåkk] *al* thick; (*om pers.*) stout, fat; (*tät*) dense, thick; ~ *grädde* thick cream; *det var* ~*t med folk på gatan* the street was packed with people
tjock|a [ˣçåkka] *s1* fog **-bottnad** [-å-] *a5* thick-bottomed **-flytande** viscous, viscid, heavy, thick **-hudad** *a5* thick-skinned (*äv. bildl.*) **-huding** *zool.* pachyderm **-is** ['çåkk-] *s2, vard.* fatty, fatso **-lek** *s2* thickness; (*dimension*) gauge; *med en* ~ *av 1 meter* 1 metre thick **-magad** *a5* big-bellied
tjock|na [ˣçåkk-] thicken; ~ *till* get (become) thicker **-olja** heavy fuel oil **-skalig** *al* (*om nöt, ägg o.d.*) thick-shelled; (*om potatis, frukt o.d.*) thick-skinned, thick-peeled **-skalle** fathead, num[b]skull **-skallig** thickheaded (*äv. bildl.*) **-tarm** large intestine, *fack.* colon **-ända, -ände** thick-end, butt-end
tjog [çå:g] *s7* score; *ett* ~ *ägg* (*vanl.*) twenty eggs; *fem* ~ five score of **-tals** [-a:-] scores; ~ *med* scores of **-vis** by the score
tjuder ['çu:-] *s7* tether **tjudra** [ˣçu:-] tether (*fast vid* up to)
tjuga [ˣçu:-] *s1* hayfork
tjugo [ˣçug:o, *vard.* -ge] (*för sms. jfr. fem-*) twenty **-en** [-'enn, -'e:n] twenty-one **-ett 1** *räkn* twenty-one **2** *kortsp.* blackjack, vingt-et-un, pontoon **-femårsjubileum** twenty-fifth anniversary **-femöring** twenty-five-öre piece **-första** [-'första] twenty-first
tjugon|de [ˣçu:gån-] twentieth **-[de]dag** ~*en* (~ *jul*) Hilarymas [Day] **-[de]del** twentieth
tjugo|tal *ett* ~ about (some) twenty; *på* ~*et* (*1920-talet*) in the [nineteen] twenties
tjur [çu:r] *s2* bull
tjura [ˣçu:-] sulk, be in a sulk
tjurfäkt|are bullfighter **-ning** bullfighting; *en* ~ a bullfight
tjurig [ˣçu:-] *al* sulky **-het** sulkiness
tjur|kalv bull calf **-skalle** stubborn (pig-headed) person **-skallig** *al* stubborn, pig-headed **-skallighet** stubbornness, pig-headedness
tjus|a [ˣçu:-] enchant, charm; (*friare*) fascinate **-arlock** kiss (*AE.* spit) curl **-ig** *al* captivating, charming **-kraft** power to charm **-ning** [-u:-] charm, enchantment; fascination; *fartens* ~ the fascination of speed
tjut [çu:t] *s7* howling; (*ett* ~) howl **tjuta** *tjöt tjutit* howl; (*skrika*) shriek, yell; (*om mistlur*) hoot; *stormen tjuter kring knutarna* the storm is howling round the house **tjutit** *sup. av tjuta*
tjuv [çu:v] *s2* thief; *ta fast* ~*en!* stop thief!; *som en* ~ *om natten* like a thief in the night **-aktig** *al* thievish **-eri** theft; *jur.* larceny **-fiska** poach fish **-fiskare** fish poacher **-fiske** fish poaching **-gods** stolen property (goods *pl*) **-godsgömma** cache **-godsgömmare** [-j-] re-

ceiver of stolen property (*etc.*); *sl.* fence **-gubbe** old rascal **-hålla** keep back [for later] **-knep** *bildl.* sharp practice; dirty trick **-koppla** (*bil*) bypass the ignition switch **-larm** burglar alarm **-liga** gang of thieves (burglars) **-lyssna** eavesdrop **-lyssnare** eavesdropper; *radio.* wireless pirate **-läsa** read on the sly **tjuv|nad** [ˣçu:-] *s3* stealing, theft; *jur.* larceny **-nadsbrott** larceny **-nyp** *ge ngn ett* ~ pinch s.b. on the sly, *bildl.* give s.b. a sly dig – **och-rackarspel** *vard.* underhand dealings, skulduggery **-pojke** young rascal **-pojksaktig** *a1* roguish **-pojksstreck** dirty trick **-skytt** poacher **-skytte** poaching **-språk** argot, thieves' slang **-stanna** (*om motor*) stall **-start** *sport.* false start; *vard.* jumping (beating) the gun **-starta** *sport.* jump (beat) the gun **-streck** dirty trick **-titta** ~ *i* take a look into on the sly **-tjockt** *jag mår* ~ I feel lousy **-tryck** pirate edition **-åka** steal a ride **-åkare** fare dodger

tjäder [ˈçä:-] *s2* capercaillie; *koll. äv.* woodgrouse **-höna** hen-capercaillie **-lek** capercaillie courtship **-tupp** cock-capercaillie

tjäle [ˣçä:-] *s2* ground (soil) frost; *när* ~*n går ur jorden* when the frost in the ground breaks up

tjäll [ç-] *s7* humble abode

tjäl|lossning thawing of frozen soil, break of the frost **-skada** frost damage **-skott** frost heave; (*hål*) pothole

tjän|a [ˣçä:-] **1** (*förtjäna*) earn (*pengar* money); gain (*på affären* by the bargain); ~ *ihop* save up; ~ *in sin pension* earn one's pension **2** (*vara anställd*) serve (*hos* in a p.'s house; *som* as a[n]); ~ *staten* serve the State; ~ *hos ngn* (*äv.*) be in a p.'s service (employ); ~ *upp sig* work one's way up; ~ *ut* (*om soldat*) serve one's time; *den har* ~*t ut* it has seen its best days **3** (*användas*) serve, do duty (*som* as); ~ *ngn till efterrättelse* serve as an example to s.b.; *det* ~*r ingenting till att* there is no use (point) in (+ *ing*-form); *vad* ~*r det till?* what is the use (good) of that?

tjän|ande [ˣçä:-] *a4* serving (*till* as); ~ *andar* ministering spirits **-are** servant; (*betjänt*) manservant; *en kyrkans* ~ a minister of the Church; *en statens* ~ a public servant; ~*!* hello!, (*vid avsked*) bye-bye! **-arinna** [maid]servant, domestic [servant] **-lig** [-ä:-] *a1* serviceable (*till* for); (*passande*) suitable (*till* for); (*ändamålsenlig*) expedient (*till* for); *vid* ~ *väderlek* when the weather is suitable

tjänst [ç-] *s3* **1** (*anställning*) service; (*befattning*) appointment, place, situation; (*högre*) office, post; (*prästerlig*) charge, ministry; *i* ~ on duty, in service; *i* ~*en* on official business, (*å ämbetets vägnar*) ex officio, officially; *i statens* ~ in the service of the State; *vara i ngns* ~ be employed by s.b., be in a p.'s service; *lämna sin* ~ resign one's appointment; *söka* ~ apply for a situation (job); *ta* ~ (*om tjänare*) go into service (*hos ngn* in a p.'s house), (*allmännare*) take a job (situation) (*som* as); *utom* ~*en* off duty **2** (*hjälp*) service (*mot* to); *be ngn om en* ~ ask a favour of s.b.; *göra ngn en* ~ do s.b. a (good turn); *gör mig den* ~*en att* oblige me by (+ *ing*-form); *göra ngn den sista* ~*en* pay one's last respects to s.b.; *varmed kan jag stå till* ~? what can I do for you?; *till er* ~*!* at

your service (command)! **3** (*nytta*) service; *göra* ~ do service (duty), serve, (*fungera*) work **-aktig** *a1* ready to render service, obliging **-duglig** fit for service; (*om sak*) serviceable **tjänste|ande** servant; *vard.* slavey **-angelägenhet** official matter **-avtal** employment contract **-betyg** certificate of service **-bil** official (company) car **-bostad** housing accommodation supplied by a company; official residence **-brev** official letter; *skicka som* ~ send as official matter **-bruk** official use **-ed** oath of office **-fel** breach of duty **-flicka** servant [girl], maid **-folk** [domestic] servants (*pl*) **-förmåner** fringe benefits **-förrättande** *a4* acting; in charge **-grad** rank **-läkare** staff medical officer **-man** employee, clerk; (*högre*) official, officer; (*stats-*) civil servant; *vard.* white-collar worker; *Tjänstemännens centralorganisation* (*förk.* TCO) [the Swedish] central organization of salaried employees **-mannabana** white-collar career **-mannakår** staff of officers and employees **-meddelande** official communication **-pension** occupational pension **-plikt 1** official duty **2** compulsory service **-resa** official journey, journey on official business; (*i privat tjänst*) business trip (journey) **-rum** office **-ställning** *mil.* official standing **-tid 1** (*anställningstid*) period of service **2** (*kontorstid*) office hours **-utövning** *under* ~ when discharging one's duties **-vikt** (*bils*) kerb weight plus driver's weight **-ålder** *gå efter* ~ go by seniority **-år** year[s *pl*] of service (in office) **-ärende** official matter

tjänstgör|a serve (*som* as; *på*, *vid* at); (*om pers. äv.*) act (*som* as); (*vara i tjänst*) be on duty, (*vid hovet o.d.*) be in attendance (waiting) (*hos* on) **-ande** *a4* on duty, in charge, (*vid hovet*) in attendance **-ing** service; duty; work; attendance; *ha* ~ be on duty

tjänstgörings|betyg testimonial, certificate of service **-reglemente** service regulations (*pl*) **-tid 1** (*daglig*) [office] hours (*pl*), hours (*pl*) of service (duty) **2** (*tid i samma tjänst*) [period of] service

tjänst|ledig *vara* ~ be on leave (off duty); ~ *för sjukdom* on sick leave; *ta* ~*t* take leave of absence **-ledighet** leave [of absence] (*för sjukdom*) sick leave **-villig** obliging, helpful, eager to help

tjär|a [ˣçä:-] **I** *s1* tar **II** *v1* tar; ~*t tak* tarred roof **-blomster** red German catchfly **-bloss** pitch torch, link **-fläck** tar stain **-ig** *a1* tarry **-kokare** tar-boiler

tjärn [çä:rn] *s2*, *s7* tarn

tjär|ning [ˣçä:r-] tarring **-papp** tarred [roofing] felt

tjöt [çö:t] *imperf. av tjuta*

toa [ˣto:a] *s9*, *vard.*, BE. loo, AE. john

toalett *s3* **1** (*WC*) toilet, lavatory; (*offentlig*) public convenience; AE. washroom, rest room; (*på restaurang o.d.*) cloakroom, men's (ladies') room; *gå på* ~ go to the toilet **2** (*klädsel*) toilet, dress; *stor* ~ full dress; *göra* ~ make one's toilet; *göra* ~ *till middagen* dress for dinner **-artiklar** toilet requisites **-bord** dressing (toilet) table; AE. *äv.* dresser **-borste** lavatory brush **-papper** toilet paper (tissue) **-rum** toilet [room], lavatory; *se äv. toalett 1* **-saker** *pl* toiletries **-tvål** (*hopskr.*

toalettvål) en ~ a bar (piece) of toilet soap
tobak ['tɔbb-, 'tɑ:b-] *s3* tobacco; *ta sig en pipa* ~ have a pipe **-ist** tobacconist
tobaks|affär tobacconist's [shop], tobacco shop **-blandning** blend of tobacco **-burk** tobacco jar, humidor **-buss** quid **-handlare** tobacconist **-märke** brand of tobacco **-planta** tobacco plant **-pung** tobacco pouch **-rök** tobacco smoke **-rökning** tobacco smoking; ~ *förbjuden* no smoking **-varor** *pl* tobacco [products]
toddy ['tåddy, -i] *s2, pl äv. toddar* toddy
toffel ['tåff-] *s1* slipper; *stå under ~n* be henpecked, be tied to s.b.'s apron strings **-djur** slipper animalcule **-hjälte** henpecked husband **-regemente** petticoat government
tofs [-å-] *s2* tuft, bunch; *(på fågel äv.)* crest; *(på möbler, mössa)* tassel **-lärka** crested lark **-mes** crested tit **-vipa** lapwing, peewit
toft [-å-] *s3* thwart
tog *imperf. av ta*
toga [*ˣtå:-] *s1* toga
togoles *s3*, **-isk** *a5* Togolese
tok 1 *s2, pers.* fool; *(obetänksam pers.)* duffer **2** *oböjligt i uttr.: gå (vara) på* ~ go (be) wrong; *jag har fått på* ~ *för mycket* I have been given far too much **toka** *s1* fool of a woman (girl); *en liten* ~ a silly little thing
tokajer [-'kajj-] Tokay
tok|er ['tɔ:-] *-ern -ar, se tok 1* **-eri** folly, nonsense; ~*er (upptåg)* foolish pranks **-ig** [ˣtɔ:-] *al* mad *(av* with; *efter* after; *i, på* on); *(oförståndig)* silly, foolish; *(löjlig)* ridiculous; *(-rolig)* comic, droll; *(mycket förtjust)* crazy *(i* about); *det låter inte så ~t* that doesn't sound too bad; *det är så man kan bli* ~ it's enough to drive one round the bend **-igt** [ˣtɔ:-] *adv* madly *etc.*; *bära sig* ~ *åt* act foolishly (like a fool) **-rolig** [extremely] funny (comic, droll) **-stolle** madcap; crazy guy
toler|abel [-'a:-] *a2* tolerable **-ans** [-'rans, -'raŋs] *s3* tolerance *(mot* towards) **-ant** [-'rant, -'raŋt] *al* tolerant, forbearing *(mot* towards); *(friare)* broadminded **-era** tolerate, put up with
tolft [-å-] *s3* dozen
tolfte [-å-] twelfth **-del** twelfth
1 tolk [-å-] *s2 (verktyg)* gauge; *AE.* gage
2 tolk [-å-] *s2 (översättare o.d.)* interpreter; *göra sig till* ~ *för (bildl.)* voice, *(åsikt)* advocate
1 tolka [ˣtåll-] *sport.* go skijoring
2 tolka [ˣtåll-] *(översätta muntligt)* interpret; *(dikt)* translate, interpret; *(handskrift)* decipher; *(återge)* render; *(uttrycka känslor)* express, give expression to; ~ *på engelska* interpret into English; *hur skall jag* ~ *detta?* what am I to understand by this?
tolk|are [-å-] *(av musik, roll o.d.)* interpreter, renderer **-ning** interpretation *(av* of); *(av handskrift)* decipherment; *(av dikt)* translation; *(muntlig)* interpretation; *felaktig* ~ misinterpretation; *fri* ~ free rendering **-ningsfråga** question of interpretation, matter of opinion
tolv [-å-] twelve; *(för sms. jfr fem-)*; *klockan* ~ *på dagen (natten)* at noon (midnight)
tolv|a [-å-] *s1* twelve **-fingertarm** duodenum *(pl duodena[s])* **-hundratalet** *på* ~ in the thirteenth century **-tiden** *vid* ~ at about twelve **-tonsmusik** twelve-tone music

Tolvöarna *pl* the Dodecanese [Islands]
t.o.m. *(förk. för till och med) se till I 13 o. II 4*
tom [tɔmm] *al* empty, void *(på* of) *(äv. bildl.)*; *(ej upptagen)* vacant; *(naken)* bare; *(oskriven)* blank; *(öde o.* ~) deserted; ~*t prat* empty words; ~*t skryt* vain boasting; *känna sig* ~ *i huvudet* feel void of all thought (unable to think); *känna sig* ~ *i magen* feel empty inside; *det känns* ~*t efter dig* it feels so empty without you
tomat tomato **-juice** tomato juice **-ketchup** tomato ketchup **-puré** tomato purée **-soppa** tomato soup
tombola ['tåmm-] *s1* tombola
tom|buteljj empty bottle **-fat** empty cask **-glas** *koll.* empty bottles *(pl)* **-gång** idling, idle running; *gå på* ~ idle, tick over **-het** emptiness, bareness *(etc.)*; vacancy; *bildl.* void **-hänt** *al* empty-handed
tomografj *s3* tomography
tomrum empty space; *(lucka)* gap; *(på blankett o.d.)* blank; *fys.* vacuum; *bildl.* void, blank; *han har lämnat ett stort* ~ *efter sig* he has left a void (great blank) behind him
tomt [-å-] *s3 (obebyggd)* [building] site, lot; *(kring villa e.d.)* garden, grounds *(pl)*; *lediga* ~*er* vacant sites
tomte [-å-] *s2* brownie; goblin **-bloss** sparkler **-bolycka** married bliss **-nisse** little brownie
tomt|gräns boundary of a building site **-hyra** ground rent **-jobbare** land speculator **-karta** land register map **-mark** land for building on **-rätt** site-leasehold right **-rättsavgäld** [-j-] *s3* rent for a leasehold site
1 ton [tånn] *s7 (viktenhet = 1 000 kg)* metric ton; *(Storbritannien, ca 1016 kg)* long ton; *(AE., ca 907 kg)* short ton
2 ton [tɔ:n] *s3 (mus.; färg-; bildl.)* tone; *(röst äv.)* tone of voice; *(på -skala)* note; *(-höjd)* pitch; *(mus. o. friare)* key[note], tune; *(umgänges-)* tone, manners *(pl)*; ~*ernas rike* the realm of music; *ange ~en a) mus.* give (strike) the note, *b) bildl.* give (set) the tone; *i befallande* ~ in a tone of command; *hålla* ~ keep in tune; *hålla ut ~en* hold the note; *stämma ner ~en (bildl.)* temper one's tone; tone down; *ta sig* ~ put on (assume) a lofty air *(mot ngn* towards s.b.); *träffa den rätta ~en* strike the right note; *takt och* ~ good manners; *det hör till god* ~ it is good form
ton|a *(ljuda)* sound; *(ge färgton åt)* tone *(äv. foto.)*; ~ *bort a) (förtona)* die away, *b) (få att upphöra, avlägsna)* fade out **-al** *al* tonal **-alitet** tonality **-anda** *a4* sounding; *fonet.* voiced *(ljud sound)* **-art** *mus.* key; *berömma ngn i alla ~er* sing a p.'s praises in every possible way **-band** recording tape **-dikt** symphonic (tone) poem **-diktare** composer **-fall** intonation; accent
tonfisk tunny [fish], tuna
ton|givande *i* ~ *kretsar* in leading quarters **-gång** ~*ar a) mus.* progressions, successions of notes, *b) bildl.* strains **-höjd** pitch **-ing** toning, tinting **-konst** [art of] music **-kontroll** tone control **-läge** *mus.* pitch; *(rösts omfång)* range, compass **-lös** *(om röst)* toneless; *(om ljud)* flat, dull **-målning** tone picture
tonnage [tå'na:ʃ] *s4* tonnage
tonomfång range, compass

tonsill [tån'sill] *s3* tonsil
ton|skala musical scale **-steg** interval **-styrka** intensity of sound
tonsur [tån'su:r] tonsure
ton|sätta set to music **-sättare** composer **-sättning** [musical] composition **-vikt** *språkv.* stress; accent; *bildl.* emphasis; *lägga ~ på a) eg.* stress, put stress on, *b) bildl.* emphasize, lay stress on
tonår|en [ˣtånn-] *pl, i ~* in one's teens **-ing** teenager
tonåtergivning tone reproduction
topas *s3* topaz
topograf|i *s3* topography **-isk** [-'gra:-] *a5* topographic[al]
1 topp [-å-] *interj* done!, agreed!, a bargain!
2 topp [-å-] **I** *s2* top; (*bergs- äv.*) summit; (*väg-*) crest; (*friare*) peak, pinnacle; *från ~ till tå* from top to toe; *i ~en* at the top (*av* of); *med flaggan i ~* with the flag flying; *hissa flaggan i ~* run up the flag; *vara på ~en av sin förmåga* be at the height of one's powers **II** *adv, bli ~ tunnor rasande* boil over with rage, blow one's top
topp|a 1 (*-hugga*) pollard; (*växt*) top **2** (*stå överst på*) top, head **-befattning** top-level position (post) **-belastning** peak (maximum) load **-dressa** *trädg.* top-dress **-dressing** *trädg.* dressing **-form** *vara i ~* be in top form **-formig** [-å-] *a1* conical **-hastighet** maximum (top) speed **-hemlig** top-secret **-ig** *a1* conical **-klass** top class **-konferens** summit conference (meeting) **-kraft** first-rate capacity **-kurs** *hand.* top (peak) rate **-lanterna** masthead light, top light **-lock** cylinder head **-luva** [pointed] knitted cap **-modern** ultramodern **-murkla** [edible] morel **-mössa** pointed (conical) cap **-möte** summit meeting **-prestation** (*hopskr.* topprestation) top performance **-punkt** (*hopskr.* toppunkt) highest point, summit **-rida** bully **-segel** topsail **-siffra** peak (record) figure **-socker** loaf sugar **-märke** topmark **-ventil** overhead valve
Tor *myt.* Thor
tordas [ˣto:r-] *vard., se töras* **tordats** *vard., sup. av töras* **torde 1** (*i uppmaning*) will, (*artigare*) will please; *ni ~ observera* you will please (*anmodas:* are requested to) observe; *ni ~ erinra er* you will remember **2** (*uttr. förmodan*) probably; *det ~ dröja innan* it will probably be a long time before; *man ~ kunna påstå att* it may (can; might, could) probably be asserted that; *ni ~ ha rätt* I dare say you are right **tordes** *imperf. av töras*
tordmule [ˣto:rd-] *s2* razorbill, razor-billed auk
tordyvel [ˣto:rd-] *s2* dor [beetle]
tordön [ˣto:r-] *s7* thunder **tordönsstämma** voice of thunder, thunderous voice
torft|ig [-å-] *a1* (*fattig*) poor; (*enkel*) plain; (*knapp*) scanty, meagre; *~a kunskaper* scanty knowledge (*sg*) **-ighet** poorness *etc.* **-igt** *adv* poorly *etc.*
torg [tårj] *s7* (*öppen plats*) square; (*salu-*) market, marketplace; *Röda ~et* the Red Square; *gå på ~et* go to the market, (*för att handla*) go marketing **-dag** market day **-föra** take (bring) to market, market, *bildl.* bring forward **-gumma** market woman **-handel** market trade, marketing

-kasse market bag **-skräck** agoraphobia **-stånd** market stall
torium ['to:-] *s8, kem.* thorium
tork [-å-] **1** *s2* drier, dryer **2** *oböjligt i uttr.: hänga på ~* hang [out] to dry; *hänga ut tvätten till ~* hang the washing out to dry
tork|a [-å-] **I** *s1* drought, dry weather; *svår ~* severe drought **II** *v1* (*göra torr*) dry, get dry; *~ tvätt* dry the washing **2** (*~ av*) wipe [dry], dry; *~ disken* dry the dishes; *~ fötterna* wipe one's feet; *~ sina tårar* wipe away (dry) one's tears **3** (*bli torr*) dry, get dry; (*vissna äv.*) dry up **4** (*med betonad partikel*) *~ bort a)* (*av-*) wipe off (up), *b)* (*~ ut*) get dried up, (*om vätska*) dry up; *~ fast* dry and get stuck; *~ ihop* dry up; *~ in* dry in, *bildl. äv.* come to nothing; *~ upp a)* (*av-*) wipe (mop) up, *b)* (*bli torr*) dry up, get dry; *~ ut* dry up, run dry **5** *rfl* dry (wipe) o.s. (*med, på* with, on); *~ sig om händerna* dry one's hands; *~ dig om munnen!* wipe your mouth! **-arblad** (*på bil*) [windscreen] wiper blade **-huv** hood hairdrier (hairdrier) **-ning** drying; (*av-*) wiping [off], mopping [up] **-skåp** drying cabinet (cupboard) **-streck** clothesline **-ställ[ning]** drying rack; (*för disk*) plate rack **-tumlare** tumbler [drier], tumble drier **-ugn** drying kiln (oven, furnace)
1 torn [-o:-] *s2, bot.* spine, thorn
2 torn [-o:-] *s7* **1** tower; (*litet ~*) turret; (*spetsigt*) steeple; (*klock-*) belfry **2** (*schackpjäs*) rook, castle
torna [-o:-] *~ upp sig* pile itself (themselves) up, *bildl.* tower aloft
tornad|o [-'na:-] *s5, s3* tornado
torner|a tourney, joust **-ing, -spel** tournament, tourney, joust
tornfalk kestrel
tornister [-'niss-] *s2* **1** (*proviantväska*) canvas field bag **2** (*foderpåse*) nosebag
torn|seglare [common] swift **-spira** spire; steeple **-svala** *se tornseglare* **-uggla** barn owl **-ur** tower clock
torp [-å-] *s7* crofter's holding; (*sommarstuga*) cottage **-are** crofter
torped [-å-] *s3* torpedo; *målsökande ~* homing torpedo; *skjuta av en ~* launch a torpedo **-båt** torpedo boat **-era** torpedo (*äv. bildl.*) **-ering** [-'de:-] torpedoing
torr [-å-] *a1* dry; (*torkad*) dried; (*uttorkad*) parched, arid (*jord* ground); (*om klimat*) torrid; *bildl.* bald (*siffror* figures), (*tråkig*) dry, dull; *jag känner mig ~ i halsen* my throat feels dry; *han är inte ~ bakom öronen* he is [still] wet behind the ears; *på ~a land* on dry land; *ha sitt på det ~a* be comfortably off **-batteri** dry[-cell] battery **-boll** *vard.* stick-in-the-mud, sobersides **-dass** dry privy **-destillation** destructive (dry) distillation **-destillera** carbonize, burn without flame **-docka** *sjö.* dry dock **-het** dryness; parchedness; aridity **-hosta I** *s1* dry cough **II** *v1* have a dry cough **-jäst** dry yeast **-klosett** earth closet **-lägga** drain; (*mosse, sjö*) reclaim **2** (*införa spritförbud*) make dry **-läggning 1** drainage; reclamation **2** making (turning) dry **-mjölk** powdered (dried) milk **-nål, -nålsgravyr** *konst.* dry point **-rolig** (*hopskr.* torrolig) droll; (*om historia e.d.*) drily amusing **-rolighet** (*hopskr. torro-*

lighet) dry wit; drily witty remark **-schamponering** dry shampoo **-sim** swimming practice on land **-skaffning** cold food; *mil.* haversack ration **-skodd** *a5* dryshod **-spricka** sun shake **-substans** dry (solid) matter **-ögd** *a1* dry-eyed

torsdag ['tɔːrs-] *s2* Thursday; (*jfr fredag*)

torsion [tår'ʃɔːn] torsion

torsionsfjäder torsion spring

1 torsk [-å-] *s2, med.* thrush

2 torsk [-å-] *s2, zool.* cod[fish]

torsk|fiske cod-fishing **-lever** cod liver **-lever-olja** cod-liver oil **-rom** cod roe

torso ['tårr-] *-n torser, s3* torso

tortera torture

torts [-ɔː-] *sup. av töras*

tortyr *s3* torture; *utsättas för* ~ be tortured (put to the torture) **-bänk** rack **-kammare** torture chamber **-redskap** instrument of torture

torv [-å-] *s3* peat; *ta upp* ~ dig [out] peat[s]

torv|a [-å-] *s1* (*gräs-*) [piece of] turf; (*jordbit*) plot [of ground]; *kärleken till den egna* ~*n* love of one's own little acre **-brikett** peat briquette **-mosse** peat bog (moor) **-mull** peat mould **-strö** peat litter **-tak** sod roof **-täcka** sod, turf

tosig *a1, se tokig*

tota ~ *ihop* (*till*) put together [some sort of] (*ett brev* a letter), get together (*en middag* a dinner)

total *a1* total; entire, complete; ~*t krig* total war (warfare) **-bild** general (overall) view (picture) **-förbud** total prohibition **-förlust** total loss **-förstöra** totally destroy (demolish) **-försvar** total (military, economic, psychological and civil) defence **-haverera** become a total loss; ~*d bil* a completely smashed up car **-haveri** total loss; total wreck

totalisator [-ˣsaːtår] *s3* totalizator; *vard.* tote; *spela på* ~ bet with the totalizator **-spel** tote-betting

total|itet totality **-itär** *a1* totalitarian **-kvadda** *vard.* wreck, smash up, *AE. sl.* total **-vägrare** conscientious objector who also refuses to do community service **-värde** aggregate (total) value

totem ['tå:-] *s9, s7* **-påle** totem [pole]

1 toto *s9, vard., se totalisator*

2 toto *barnspr.* (*häst*) gee-gee

tott [-å-] *s2* (*hår-, garn- etc.*) tuft [of ...]

tov|a I *s1* twisted (tangled) knot (bunch) **II** *v1,* ~ [*ihop*] *sig* become tangled **-ig** *a1* tangled, matted

tox|icitet [-å-] toxicity **-ikologi** *s3* toxicology **-in** *s4, s3* toxin **-isk** ['tåks-] *a5* toxic

trad *s3* [shipping, (sea)] route

tradera hand down, transmit orally [from one generation to another]

tradig *a1* (*långtråkig*) tedious

tradition tradition **-ell** *a1* traditional

traditions|bunden tradition bound; *vara* ~ be bound by (rooted in) tradition **-rik** rich in tradition

trafik *s3* **1** traffic; (*drift*) service; *genomgående* ~ through traffic; *gå i* [*regelbunden*] ~ *mellan* ply between; *visa hänsyn i* ~*en* show courtesy on the road; *sätta in en buss i* ~ put a bus into service; *vårdslöshet i* ~ careless driving; *ej i* ~ (*på skylt*) depot only **2** (*hantering*) traffic, trade; ~*en med narkotika* the traffic in narcotics **-abel** [-'kaː-] *a2*

trafficable -anhopning traffic jam **-ant** user, customer; (*landsvägs-*) road-user; (*fotgängare*) pedestrian **-belastning** traffic load **-bil** (*last-*) lorry; (*taxi*) taxi[cab] **-buller** noise from traffic **-delare** traffic pillar (island) **-döden** the traffic toll

trafiker|a (*färdas på*) use, frequent, travel by; (*ombesörja trafik på*) operate, work, ply on; *livligt* ~*d* heavily trafficked, busy; ~ *en linje* operate a route **-bar** [-ˣkeː-] *a1* trafficable

trafik|flyg air service; civil aviation **-flygare** airline (commercial) pilot **-flygplan** passenger plane **-fyr** traffic light (signal) **-fälla** road trap **-förordning** traffic regulation **-förseelse** traffic offence **-försäkring** traffic insurance **-hinder** traffic obstacle; hold-up in [the] traffic **-knut** traffic centre (junction) **-konstapel** policeman on point duty; *AE., vard.* traffic cop **-kort** heavy vehicle licence **-led** traffic route **-ledare** *flyg.* control officer **-ljus** traffic light[s] **-märke** traffic sign **-olycka** traffic (road, street) accident **-polis** (*polisman*) policeman on point duty, traffic policeman; *koll.* traffic police **-signal** traffic signal (light) **-skylt** traffic sign, signpost **-stockning** traffic jam, congestion of the traffic **-stopp** traffic hold-up **-säkerhet** road safety **-säkerhetsverk** ~*et* [the Swedish] national road safety office **-teknik** transport engineering **-utskott** ~*et* [the Swedish parliamentary] standing committee on transport and communications **-vakt** traffic warden **-vett** good traffic sense **-väsen** traffic services (*pl*) **-övervakning** traffic supervision

tragedi [-ʃe'diː] *s3* tragedy **-enn** *s3* tragedienne

traggla (*käxa*) go on (*om* about); (*knoga*) plod on (*med* with)

trag|ik *s3* tragedy; ~*en i* the tragedy of **-iker** ['tra:-] tragedian **-ikomisk** [-ˣkɔ:-] *a5* tragicomic [al] **-isk** ['tra:-] *a5* tragic[al] **-öd** *s3* tragedian

trailer ['trej-] *s2*, (*släpvagn o. film.*) trailer

trakass|era pester, badger; persecute **-eri** pestering, badgering; persecution

trakom [-'å:m] *s7* trachoma

trakt *s3* (*område*) district, parts (*pl*); region; *här i* ~*en* in this neighbourhood, hereabout[s], round about here

trakta ~ *efter* aspire to, aim at; ~ *efter ngns liv* seek a p.'s life

traktamente [-'menn-] *s6* allowance [for expenses], subsistence allowance

traktan *r, se diktan*

traktat 1 (*fördrag*) treaty; *ingå en* ~ make a treaty **2** (*småskrift*) tract

trakter|a 1 (*bjuda*) treat (*ngn med* s.b. to); (*underhålla*) regale (*ngn med* s.b. with); *inte vara vidare* ~*d av* not be flattered (particularly pleased) by **2** (*spela*) play; (*blåsa*) blow **-ing** (*förplägnad*) entertainment [provided]; *riklig* ~ sumptuous banquet, *vard.* plenty of food

traktor [-år] *s3* tractor; (*band-*) caterpillar [tractor]

traktör innkeeper; restaurateur, caterer

tralala *interj* tra-la-la!

1 trall *s2, s7* (*golv-*) duckboard; *sjö.* grating

2 trall *s2* (*låt*) melody, tune; *den gamla* ~*en* (*bildl.*) the same old routine

1 tralla *v1*, ~ [*på*] warble, troll
2 tralla *s1* (*transport*-) truck; (*dressin*) trolley
tramp *s7* tramping, tramp **trampa I** *s1* (*på cykel o.d.*) pedal; (*på maskin*) treadle **II** *v1* tramp, tread; (*cykel, symaskin etc.*) treadle, pedal; (*tungt*) trample; (*orgel*) blow the bellows of; ~ *i klaveret* drop a brick, put one's foot in it; ~ *ngt i smutsen* (*bildl.*) trample s.th. in the dirt; ~ *ihjäl* trample to death; ~ *ner a*) (*jord*) tread down, *b*) (*gräs*) trample down, *c*) (*skor*) tread down at the heels; ~ *ngn på tårna* tread on a p.'s toes; ~ *sönder* tread (trample) to pieces; ~ *ur* (*koppling*) de-clutch; ~ *ut barnskorna* grow up; ~ *vatten* tread water
tramp|bil (*för barn*) pedal car **-båt 1** (*nöjesfarkost*) pedalo **2** (*fraktfartyg*) *se* trampfartyg **-cykel** pedal cycle **-dyna** pad, matrix
tramp|fart tramping, tramp trade; *gå i* ~ run in the tramp trade **-fartyg** tramp [vessel], tramp steamer
tramp|kvarn treadmill (*äv. bildl.*) **-mina** *mil.* antipersonnel mine
trampolin *s3* [high-diving] springboard; (*vid simhopp äv.*) diving board, high-board **-hopp** high-board diving
trams *s7*, *vard.* nonsense, drivel, rubbish **tramsa** act (play) the fool, fool around **tramsig** *a1* daft; *nu är du* ~ you are being silly
tran *s3*, *s4* train (whale) oil
tran|a *s1* crane **-bär** cranberry
trancher|a [-aŋˈʃe:-, -an-] carve **-kniv** carving knife
trandans dancing of cranes
trankil [-aŋˈki:l] *a1* cool, calm
tran|kokeri tryworks (*sg o. pl*), train-oil factory **-lampa** train-oil lamp
trans *s3* trance; *vara i* ~ be in a trance
trans|aktion transaction **-alpin[sk]** [-i:-] trans-alpine **-atlantisk** [-ˈlann-] transatlantic
transcendent [-nsenˈdent, -nʃen-] *a4*, **-el** *a1* transcendent[al]
transfer [ˈtrans-] *s9* transfer **-era** transfer **-summa** transfer fee
transform|ation transformation **-ator** [-ˣaːtår] *s3* transformer **-era** transform
transfusion [blood] transfusion
transistor [-ˣsistår] *s3* transistor **-isera** transistorize **-radio** transistor radio **-teknik** transistor technology
transit [ˈtrans-, -ˈsiːt] *s3* transit **-era** pass (convey) in transit, transit **-ering** [-ˈteː-] [forwarding in] transit **-hall** transit lounge (hall)
transitiv [ˈtrann-] *a1* transitive
transito [ˈtrann-, -ˣsiː-] *s9* transit **-hall** *se* transithall **-handel** transit trade (business)
Transjordanien [-ˈdaː-] *n* Trans-Jordan
tran|skribera transcribe **-skription** [-pˈʃoːn] transcription
translator [-ˣlaːtår] *s3* translator; *auktoriserad* ~ authorized (registered) translator
trans|mission transmission; *tekn. äv.* counter-shaft transmission **-missionsväxel** transmission gear **-mittera** transmit **-mutation** transmutation **-ocean[sk]** [-aː-] *a5* transoceanic, overseas **-parang** transparency **-parent** [-ˈrent, -ˈraŋt] *a1* transparent **-piration**

(*svettning*) perspiration; *bot.* transpiration **-piramedel** deodorant **-pirera** (*svettas*) perspire; *bot.* transpire **-plantat** *s7* transplant, organ (tissue) transplanted **-plantation** transplantation, [skin] grafting **-plantera** transplant, graft **-ponera** transpose **-ponering** [-ˈne:-] transposition
transport [-å-] *s3* **1** (*forsling*) transport[ation], conveyance; (*fraktavgift*) cost of transport; *under* ~*en* in transit; *fördyra* ~*en* increase the cost of transport **2** (*överlåtelse av check etc.*) transfer; *bokför.* carried forward (*utgående saldo*), brought forward (*ingående saldo*) **3** (*förflyttning*) transfer, removal; *söka* ~ apply for transfer (*etc.*) **-abel** [-ˈaːbel] *a2* transportable **-apparat** conveyor **-arbetare** transport worker **-band** conveyor belt **-behållare** [transport] container **-chef** *mil.* transportation officer **-era** (*jfr transport*) **1** transport, carry, convey **2** (*överlåta*) transfer (*på* to); *bokför.* carry (bring) forward **3** (*förflytta*) transfer, remove **-fartyg** *mil.* transport vessel, troopship **-företag** [road] haulage (transport) business; *AE.* trucking business **-försäkring** transport (transportation) insurance **-kostnad** transport[ation] (carrying, shipping) cost **-medel** means of transport (conveyance) **-väsen** transport [service] **-ör** *tekn.* conveyor
trans|position *mus.* transposition **-sibirisk** [-ˈbiː-] trans-Siberian **-substantiation** [-(t)siaː-] transubstantiation
trans|umera copy in extract **-sumt** [-ˈsumt] *s7* extract
transuran *s4*, *s3*, *kem.* transuranic element
transvers|al [-el] *s1* transversal [line] **II** *a1* transverse, transversal **-ell** *a1*, *se* transversal II
transvestit *s3* transvestite **-ism** transvestism
trapets *s7*, *s4*, *mat.* trapezium; *AE.* trapezoid **2** *s3*, *gymn.* trapeze **-konstnär** trapeze artiste
trapp|a I *s1* (*utomhus*) stairs (*pl*), flight of stairs; (*farstu-*) doorstep[s *pl*]; (*inomhus*) stairs (*pl*), staircase, stairway, flight [of stairs]; *en* ~ *upp* on the first (*AE.* second) floor, (*i tvåvåningshus*) up-stairs; ~ *upp och* ~ *ner* up and down stairs; *i* ~*n* on the stairs; *nedför* (*uppför*) ~*n* down (up) the stairs, downstairs (upstairs) **II** *v1*, ~ *av* reduce; ~ *ned* reduce; ~ *upp* escalate, step up **-avsats** (*inomhus*) landing; (*utomhus*) platform **-gavel** stepped gable **-hus** stairwell **-ljus** staircase light **-räcke** [staircase] banisters (*pl*) **-steg** step, stair; *bildl. äv.* stage **-stege** stepladder **-uppgång** staircase; stairs (*pl*)
tras|a I *s1* **1** [piece of] rag; shred; *falla* (*slita*) *i -or* go to [tear [in]to] rags; *utan en* ~ *på kroppen* without a rag of clothing on one's body; *våt som en* ~ wringing wet; *känna sig som en* ~ feel washed out **2** *se damm-, skur-* **II** *v1*, ~ *sönder* tear [in]to rags (shreds, *äv. bildl.*) **-docka** rag doll **-grann** (*om pers.*) tawdry, shoddy; (*om sak*) gaudy **-hank** ragamuffin, tatterdemalion **-ig** *a1* ragged, tattered; (*om kläder äv.*) torn; (*i kanten*) frayed; (*sönderbruten*) broken; (*i olag*) out of order; ~*a nerver* frayed nerves
traska trudge; trot (*i väg* off; *omkring* [a]round)
tras|matta rag (rug) [mat] **-proletariat** lumpenproletariat
trassat *hand.* drawee

trassel ['trass-] *s7* **1** (*oreda*) tangle; *bildl. äv.* muddle, confusion; (*besvärligheter*) trouble; bother (*sg*), complications (*pl*); *ställa till* ~ make trouble (*för ngn* for s.b.), *vard.* kick up a fuss **2** (*textilavfall*) cotton waste, waste wool **-sudd** piece of cotton waste

trass|ent *hand.* drawer **-era** *hand.* draw

trassl|a (*krångla*) make a fuss, be troublesome; ~ *ihop* get into a tangle, entangle; ~ *in sig a*) get itself (o.s.) entangled (*i* in), *b*) (*bildl. om pers.*) entangle o.s., get o.s. involved (*i* in); ~ *med betalningen* be irregular about paying; ~ *till a*) se ~ *ihop*, *b*) *bildl.* muddle; ~ *till sina affärer* get one's finances into a muddle; ~ [*till*] *sig* get entangled; ~ *sig fram a*) make one's way along with difficulty, *b*) *bildl.* muddle along; ~ *sig ifrån* wriggle out of **-ig** *a1* tangled, entangled; (*friare*) muddled; ~*a affärer* shaky finances

trast *s2* thrush

tratt *s2* funnel; (*matar- etc.*; *stormvarningssignal*) hopper

1 tratta *s1, hand.* draft, bill [of exchange]

2 tratta *v1*, ~ *i ngn ngt* (*äv. bildl.*) stuff s.b. with s.th.; ~ *ngt i öronen på ngn* din s.th. into a p.'s ears; ~ *ngn full med lögner* stuff s.b. with a lot of lies

trattformig [-å-] *a1* funnel-shaped, funnelled

trauma ['trau-] *s6* trauma **-tisk** [-'ma:-] *a5* traumatic

trav *s4, s3* trot; *rida i* ~ ride at a trot; *sätta av i* ~ start trotting; *hjälpa ngn på* ~*en* (*bildl.*) put s.b. on the right track, give s.b. a start

1 trava (*lägga u trave*) pile, stack (*virke* wood)

2 trava trot; ~ *på* trot along

trav|are se *travhäst* **-bana** trotting course (track)

trave *s2* pile, stack (*böcker* of books; *ved* of wood)

travers [-'värs] *s3* **1** (*lyftkransanordning*) overhead [travelling] crane; (*tvärbalk*) cross member **2** *mil.* traverse

travestera *v1*, **travesti** *s3* travesty, spoof

trav|häst trotter, trotting horse **-kusk** sulky driver **-sport** trotting **-tävling** trotting race

tre three; (*för sms. jfr fem-*); ~ *och* ~ (~ *i taget*) three at a time; *ett par* ~ *stycken* two or three; *alla* ~ *böckerna* all three books; *vi gjorde det alla* ~ all [the] three of us did it; *i* ~ *exemplar* in triplicate, in three copies; *alla goda ting är* ~ all good things are three in number

tre|a *s1* three; (*lägenhet*) three-room flat, flat with two bedrooms; ~*n[s växel*] [the] third [gear]; *han kom* ~ he came in third (as number three); *han blev* ~ he was number three **-bent** [-e:-] *a4* three-legged **-dela** divide into three; *geom.* trisect **-dimensionell** *a1* three-dimensional, three-D

tredje [*'tre:d-*] third; ~ *graden* (*jur.*) third degree; ~ *klass* third class; ~ *man a*) (*jur.*) third party, *b*) *kortsp.* [the] third hand; ~ *riket* the Third Reich; ~ *världen* the Third World; ~ *statsmakten* the Press **-dag** ~ *jul* the day after Boxing Day **-del** third; *en* ~*s* a third of; *två* ~*ar* two thirds **-klassbiljett** third-class ticket

tredsk [-e:-, *vard.* tresk] *a1* refractory, defiant

tredska *s1* refractoriness, defiance; *jur.* obstinacy, contumacy **tredskas** *dep* be refractory

tredsko|dom judgement by default **-domsför-**

farande undefended proceedings (*pl*)

tredubb|el treble, threefold, triple; *det -la priset* treble (three times) the price **-la** treble, triple

treenig triune **-het** triunity, trinity; ~*en* the Trinity

trefaldig *a1* threefold, treble, triple **-het** [*'tre:-*, -'fall-] *kyrkl.* [the] Trinity **-hetssöndag** ~*en* Trinity Sunday

tre|falt threefold, trebly; thrice (*lycklig* blessed) **-fas** three-phase **-fasström** three-phase current **-fjärdedelstakt** [-*'fjä:r-*] three-four [time], *A E.* three-quarter time **-fot** tripod **-glasfönster** triple glazing (*koll.*) **-hjulig** [-j-] *a1* three-wheeled **-hjuling** [-j-] three-wheeler; (*cykel*) tricycle; (*bil*) tricar **-hundratalet** fourth century **-hundraårsjubileum** tercentenary, tercentennial **-hörning** [-ö:-] triangle **-kant** triangle **-kantig** triangular; ~ *hatt* cocked (three-cornered) hat **-klang** *mus.* triad **-klöver** *bot.* three-leaf clover; *bildl.* trio **-kropparsproblemet** the three body problem **-kvart** *på* ~ at an angle

trekvarts *i* ~ *timme* for three quarters of an hour **-lång** three-quarter length **-strumpa** knee hose (sock)

treledare three-wire, triple wire

trema *s6* di[a]eresis (*pl* di[a]ereses)

tremakts|avtal tripartite agreement **-förbund** triple alliance **-fördrag** tripartite treaty

tre|mannadelegation three-man delegation **-mastare** three-master, three-masted schooner **-milsgräns** three-mile limit **-motorig** *a1* three-engine[d]

tremul|ant *mus.* tremulant **-era** quaver, sing (play) with a tremolo **-ering** [-'le:-] tremolo

tre|månadersväxel three-month bill **-männing** second cousin

trenchcoat ['tren(t)ʃkått] *s2* trench coat

trend *s3* trend, fashion **-ig** *a1* trendy

trenne three

trepaner|a trepan, trephine **-ing** trepanation, trephining

tre|procentig *a1* three-percent **-radig** *a1* three-rowed **-rumslägenhet** three-room[ed] flat; two-bedroom flat **-sidig** *a1* trilateral **-siffrig** *a1* three-figure; three-digit **-sitsig** *a1* three-seated **-skift** three-shift **-snibb** triangular cloth **-spann** team of three horses, troika; *köra* ~ drive three in hand **-språkig** *a1* trilingual **-stavig** *a1* trisyllabic[al] **-steg** *sport.* triple jump, hop, step and jump **-stegsraket** three-stage rocket **-stjärnig** [-ʃä:-] *a1* three-star (*konjak* brandy) **-stämmig** *a1* for three voices, in three parts **-takt** *mus.* three-four time, *A E.* three-quarter time **-taktsmotor** three-stroke engine **-tal** (*antal av tre*) triad; *kortsp.*, ~ *i ess* three aces; ~*et* [the number] three **-tiden** *vid* ~ [at] about three [o'clock]

tretti|o [*'tretti*(o), 'tretti(o)] thirty; *klockan tre och* ~ at three thirty **-onde** [-å-] thirtieth **-on[de]del** thirtieth [part]

trettio|tal *ett* ~ some (about) thirty; *på* ~*et* (*1930-talet*) in the thirties **-årig** *a1* thirty-year[-old]; ~*a kriget* the Thirty Years' War

tretton [-ån] thirteen **-dagen** Twelfth Day, Epiphany **-dagsafton** Twelfth Night **-de** thir-

teenth **-hundratalet** *på* ~ in the fourteenth century **-årig** *a1* thirteen-year-old
tre|tumsspik three-inch nail **-tungad** *a5* three-tongued; three-tailed (*flagga* flag) **-udd** trident **-uddig** *a1* with three prongs
trev|a grope [about] (*efter* for); ~ *efter ord* fumble for words; ~ *i mörkret* go groping about (*bildl.* be groping) in the dark; ~ *sig fram* grope one's way along **-ande** *a4* groping, fumbling; *bildl. äv.* tentative **-are** feeler
trev|lig [ˣtreːv-] *a1* pleasant, agreeable; (*mera vard.*) nice; *AE. äv.* cute; (*rolig*) enjoyable; (*om lägenhet o.d.*) comfortable; (*sällskaplig*) sociable; ~ *resa!* a pleasant journey!, bon voyage!; *vi hade mycket* ~*t* we had a very nice time, we enjoyed ourselves very much; *vi har haft mycket* ~*t* we have had a wonderful time; *det var* ~*t att* [*få*] *höra* I am glad to hear that; *det var just* ~*t!* (*iron.*) what a pretty kettle of fish! **-ligt** *adv* pleasantly *etc.* **-nad** *s3* comfort, comfortable feeling; *sprida* ~ *omkring sig* create a cheerful atmosphere
tre|våningshus three-storeyed house **-värd** *kem.* trivalent **-årig** *a1* three-year[s']; (*om barn o. djur*) three-year-old **-åring** child of three [years of age]; (*om häst*) three-year-old
tri *s9, vard.* trichlor[o]ethylene
triangel [-ˈaŋ-] *s2* triangle **-drama** eternal-triangle drama **-formig** [-åˑ-] *a1* triangular **-mätning** triangulation **-punkt** triangulation point **triangul|ering** [-ŋguˈleː-] triangulation **-är** *a1* triangular
trias [ˈtriː-] *r* Trias **-perioden** the Triassic period
tribad *s3* tribade
1 tribun *s3* (*plattform*) platform, tribune
2 tribun *s3* (*rom. ämbetsman*) tribune
tribun|al *s3, s4* tribunal **-at** *s7* tribunate, tribuneship
tribut *s3* tribute
1 trick *s7, s2, kortsp.* trick [over book]
2 trick *s7* (*knep*) trick, dodge; (*reklam- etc.*) gimmick
trickfilmning trick filming **tricks** *s7, se 2 trick*
tricksa use tricks; ~ *med bollen* dribble
triftong [-ˈtåŋ] *s3* triphthong
trigonometr|i *s3* trigonometry **-isk** [-ˈmeː-] *a5* trigonometric[al]
trikin *s3* trichina (*pl* trichinae)
trikloretylen [-ˣklåˑr-] trichlor[o]ethylene
trikolor [-ˈlåːr] *s3, ~en* the Tricolour
trikå *s3* **1** (*tyg*) tricot, stockinet[te] **2** ~*er* tights; *hudfärgade* ~*er* fleshings **-affär** knitwear shop **-fabrik** knitwear factory **-underkläder** *pl* machine-knitted (cotton) underwear **-varor** *pl* knitwear (*sg*), knitted (hosiery) goods
triljon *s3* trillion; *AE.* quintillion
trilla I *s1* (*vagn*) surrey **II** *v1* **1** (*rulla*) roll; ~ *piller* make pills **2** (*ramla*) drop, fall, tumble; (*om tårar*) trickle; ~ *omkull* tumble over; ~ *av pinn* (*vard.*) kick the bucket
trilling triplet
tri|lobit *s3* trilobite **-logi** *s3* trilogy
trilsk *a1* (*motsträvig*) contrary; (*egensinnig*) wilful; (*omedgörlig*) intractable; (*tjurig*) mulish, pigheaded **-ska** *s1* contrariness *etc.* **trilskas** *dep* be contrary (*etc.*)
trim [trimm] *s9, s7* trim; *vara i* ~ (*sport. o. vard.*)

be in good trim
trimaran *s3* trimaran
trim|ma *sjö.* trim (*äv.* pälsen *på hund*); (*justera motor o.d.*) trim, adapt **-ning** trimming, trim
trind *a1* (*rund*) round[-shaped], roundish; (*fyllig*) plump, *vard.* tubby, chubby **-het** roundness; rotundity
trio [ˈtriːo] *s5* trio **triod** [-ˈåːd] *s3* triode **triol** [-ˈoːl, -ˈåːl] *s3* triplet
1 tripp *s3, s2* (*resa*) [short] trip (*äv. narkotikarus*); *göra* (*ta sig*) *en* ~ go for (take) a trip
2 tripp *i uttr.: ~ trapp trull a*) (*spel*) noughts and crosses, tick-tack-toe, *b*) *bild.* one, two, three [going down in height]
tripp|a (*gå på tå*) trip along; (*knarka*) trip **-ande** *a4* tripping; ~ *steg* mincing steps
trippel|allians ~*en* the Triple Alliance **-vaccinering** three-way D.P.T. (diphtheria, pertussis and tetanus) inoculation
trippmätare trip meter
triptyk *s3* triptych
triss *s3, kortsp., se tretal*
triss|a I *s1* (*small*) wheel, trundle, disc; (*i block e.d.*) pulley; (*sporr-*) rowel; *dra på -or!* (*vard.*) go to blazes! **II** *v1, ~ upp priserna* push up the prices
trist *a1* (*långtråkig*) tiresome, tedious; (*dyster*) gloomy, dismal; (*sorgsen*) sad, melancholy; (*föga uppbygglig*) depressing, dreary **-ess** tiresomeness *etc.*; melancholy
triton [-ˈtåːn, -ˈtoːn] *s3* triton
triumf *s3* triumph **-ator** [-ˣfaːtår] *s3* triumphator **-båge** triumphal arch **-era** triumph; (*jubla*) exult **-erande** [-ˈfeː-] *a4* triumphant, exultant; ~ *leende* triumphant smile **-tåg** triumphal procession (*bildl.* march, progress) **-vagn** triumphator's chariot; car of triumph
triumvir *s3* triumvir **-at** *s7* triumvirate
triv|as *v2, dep* get on well, be happy; (*frodas*) thrive; (*blomstra*) flourish, prosper; *han -s i England* he likes being (likes it) in England; ~ *med* like, (*ngn äv.*) get on [well] with
trivial *a1* trivial; commonplace **-itet** *s3* triviality
trivsam [-iː-] *a1* pleasant, comfortable, cosy, snug; (*om pers.*) easy to get on with, congenial **-het** cosiness, hominess; congeniality
trivsel [ˈtriːv-] *s9* (*välbefinnande*) wellbeing, comfort[ableness]; (*trevnad*) ease, cosiness
tro I *s9* **1** belief (*på* in); (*tillit, tilltro*) faith, trust (*till, på* in); ~, *hopp och kärlek* faith, hope, love; *den kristna* ~*n* the Christian faith; *i den* ~*n att* believing (thinking) that; *leva i den* ~*n att* believe that; *i den fasta* ~*n att* convinced that; *i god* ~ in good faith, bona fide; *sätta* ~ *till* trust, believe, (*ngn äv.*) put confidence in **2** *svära ngn* ~ *och lydnad* swear allegiance to s.b.; *uppsäga ngn* ~ *och lydnad* withdraw one's allegiance from s.b.; *på* ~ *och loven* on one's honour; *skänka ngn sin* ~ give s.b. one's plighted word **II** *v4* **1** believe, trust; (*förmoda*) think, suppose, *AE. o. vard.* guess, reckon; (*föreställa sig*) imagine, fancy; *ja, jag* ~*r det* yes, I believe so; *jag skulle* ~ *det* I should think so; ~ *det som som vill!* believe that if you like!; *du kan aldrig* ~ *hur* you can't possibly imagine how; ~ *mig*, ... take my word for it, ...; believe me, ...; ..., *må du* ~*! ...*, I can tell you!; *det* ~*r du bara!* that's only your imagination (an idea

of yours)!; *det var det jag ~dde!* [that's] just what I thought!; *det ~r jag det!* I should jolly well think so!; ~ *ngn om gott* expect well of s.b.; ~ *ngt om ngn* believe s.th. of s.b.; ~ *ngn på hans ord* take a p.'s word for it; ~ *ngn vara* believe s.b. to be; ~ *på* believe in (*äv. relig.*), (*hålla för sann*) believe **2** *rfl* think (believe) o.s. (*säker* safe); ~ *sig vara* think that one is, consider (believe) o.s. to be; ~ *sig kunna* believe o.s. (that one is) capable of (+ *ing-* form) (able to)

tro|ende *a4* believing; *en* ~ a believer; *de* ~ (*äv.*) the faithful **-fast** true, constant (*vän* friend); loyal (*vänskap* friendship); faithful (*kärlek* love); (~ *av sig*) true-hearted, trusty **-fasthet** constancy; loyalty; faithfulness

trofé *s3* trophy

trogen *a3* faithful (*intill döden* unto death; *mot* to); true (*sina ideal* to one's ideals); *sin vana* ~ true to habit

trohet faithfulness; fidelity; loyalty

trohets|brott breach of faith **-ed** (*avlägga* take the) oath of allegiance **-löfte** vow of fidelity **-plikt** allegiance

trohjärtad [-j-] *a5* true-hearted; (*ärlig*) frank; (*förtroendefull*) confiding

Troja [ˣtråjja] *n* Troy

troj|an [-å-] *s3*, **-ansk** [-a:-] *a3* Trojan

trojka [ˣtråjj-] *s1* troika

troké *s3* trochee **trokeisk** [-'ke:isk] *a5* trochaic

trolig *a1* probable, likely; *AE. äv.* apt; (*trovärdig*) credible, plausible; *det är ~t att han* he will probably (is likely to); *det är föga ~t* it is hardly likely; *hålla* [*det*] *för ~t att* think it likely that; *söka göra ngt ~t* try to make s.th. plausible **-en**, **-tvis** very (most) likely, probably; *han kommer* ~ *inte* he is not likely to come

troll [-å-] *s7* troll; (*elakt*) hobgoblin; *när man talar om* ~ *står de i farstun* talk of the devil and he'll appear; *ditt lilla* ~*!* you little witch

troll|a [-å-] (*utöva* -*dom*) conjure; (*om* -*konstnär*) perform conjuring tricks; ~ *bort* spirit (conjure) away; ~ *fram* conjure forth (up) **-bunden** spellbound **-dom** [-domm] *s2* witchcraft, sorcery; (*magi*) magic; *bruka* ~ use magic, practise witchcraft **-domskonst** ~*en* [the art of] witchcraft **-dryck** magic potion **-eri** magic, enchantment **-erikonstnär** *se* -*konstnär* **-formel** magic formula; charm, spell; (*besvärjelse*) incantation **-karl** magician, wizard; sorcerer **-konst** ~*er* (*häxas*) magic (*sg*); (-*konstnärs*) conjuring (jugglery) trick; *göra* ~*er* perform conjuring tricks **-konstnär** conjurer **-kraft** magic power **-krets** *bildl.* magic sphere **-kunnig** skilled in magic **-kvinna** *se* -*packa* **-makt** spell **-packa** *s1* witch, sorceress **-slag** *som genom ett* ~ as if by [a stroke of] magic **-slända** dragonfly **-spö**, **-stav** magic wand **-trumma** troll drum **-tyg** *s7* witchery, sorcery

trolov|ad *a5*, *hans* (*hennes*) ~*e* his (her) betrothed **-ning** betrothal **-ningsbarn** betrothal child

trolsk [-å-] *a1* magic[al]; (*tjusande*) bewitching; (*hemsk*) weird

trolös faithless, unfaithful, disloyal (*mot* to); (*förrädisk*) treacherous, perfidious (*mot* to, towards) **-het** faithlessness; breach of faith; ~

mot huvudman breach of trust committed by an agent on his principal

1 tromb [-å-] *s3* (*skydrag*) tornado

2 tromb [-å-] *s3* (*blodpropp*) thrombus (*pl* thrombi)

trombon [tråm'bå:n] *s3* trombone **-ist** trombonist

trombos [tråm'bå:s] *s3* thrombosis

tron *s3* throne; *avsäga sig* ~*en* abdicate; *bestiga* ~*en* ascend (accede to) the throne; *störta ngn från* ~*en* dethrone s.b.

tron|a be enthroned (*på* on) **-arvinge** heir to the throne **-avsägelse** abdication **-bestigning** accession to the throne **-följare** successor to the throne **-följd** succession [to the throne] **-följdsordning** act of succession; *Storbritannien* act of settlement **-himmel** canopy **-pretendent** pretender (claimant) to the throne **-sal** throne room, room of state **-skifte** accession of a new monarch **-tal** speech from the throne

trop [-å:-] *s3*, *språkv.* trope

trop|ik *s3* tropic; ~*erna* the Tropics, the torrid (tropic) zone (*sg*) **-ikhjälm** pith helmet, topee; topi **-isk** ['trå:-] *a5* tropic[al]

troposfär *s3* troposphere

tropp [-å-] *s2* troop; (*infanteri-*) section; *gymn.* squad

tropp|a [-å-] **1** *mil.* troop (*fanan* the colour) **2** ~ *av* move off **-chef** troop (section, squad) commander

tros|artikel article of faith; (*friare*) doctrine **-bekännare** *främmande* ~ adherent of an alien creed **-bekännelse** confession (declaration) of [one's] faith; (*lära*) creed; *augsburgska* ~*n* the Augsburg Confession **-frihet** religious liberty **-frände** fellow believer **-gemenskap** communion in the faith **-iver** religious zeal **-ivrare** religious zealot

troskyldig true-hearted; frank (*blick* look)

troslära doctrine of faith, dogma

trosor *pl* briefs, panties

1 tross [-å-] *s2*, *sjö.* hawser; rope

2 tross [-å-] *s2*, *mil.* baggage (train); supply vans (*pl*)

tros|sak matter of faith **-samfund** religious community **-sats** dogma

trossbotten *byggn.* double floor[ing]; *sjömil.* lower deck; (*manskapslogement*) crew's quarter

trosviss full of implicit faith **-het** certainty of belief; assured faith

trotjänar|e, **-inna** [*gammal*] ~ faithful old servant

trots [-å-] **I** *s7* defiance (*mot* of); (*motsträvighet*) obstinacy (*mot* to[wards]), scorn (*mot* of); *visa* ~ *mot ngn* bid defiance to (defy) s.b.; *i* ~ *av* in spite of; *på* ~ in (out of) defiance; *alla ansträngningar till* ~ in spite of all efforts **II** *prep* in spite of; notwithstanding, despite

trots|a [-å-] defy; (*bjuda ... trots*) bid defiance to; (*utmana*) brave, scorn, stand up to; *det ~r all beskrivning* it is beyond description **-ig** *a1* defiant (*mot* to, towards); (*uppstudsig*) refractory (*mot* towards); (*hånfull*) scornful, insolent **-ighet** refractoriness *etc.*; defiance **-ålder** ~*n* the obstinate age

trottoar *s3* pavement; *AE.* sidewalk **-kant** kerb;

AE. curb **-servering** pavement restaurant (café)

trotyl *s3* trinitrotoluene, trotyl

trovärdig credible; *(tillförlitlig)* reliable, trustworthy; *från ~t håll* from a reliable quarter **-het** credibility; reliability, trustworthiness

trubadur troubadour

trubba ~ *[av, till]* blunt, make blunt

trubbel ['trubb-] *s7, vard.* trouble

trubb|ig *a1* blunt; *(avtrubbad)* blunted; *(ej spetsig)* pointless; *(om vinkel)* obtuse **-näsa** snub nose **-vinklig** *a1* obtuse-angled

truck *s2* truck; *(med lyftanordning)* lift truck **-förare** truck driver

trudelutt *s3, vard.* ditty, little song

truga ~ *ngn att* press s.b. to, urge (importune, solicit) s.b. to; ~ *i (på) ngn ngt* press s.th. [up]on s.b.; ~ *sig på ngn* force o.s. [up]on s.b.; ~ *i sig maten* force o.s. to eat

truism *s3* truism

trum|broms drum (expanding) brake **-eld** drumfire

trumf *s7, s2* trump; *spader är* ~ spades are trumps; *sitta med alla* ~ *på hand* have all the trumps; *spela ut sin sista* ~ play one's last trump *(bildl.* card)

trumf|a trump, play trumps; ~ *i ngn ngt* drum (pound) s.th. into a p.'s head; ~ *igenom* force through, *AE. vard.* railroad; ~ *över ngn* out trump s.b. **-färg** trump suit **-kort** trump [card] **-spel** trump game **-äss** ace of trumps

trum|hinna eardrum, tympanic membrane **-ma** *I sl* **1** *mus.* drum; *slå på* ~ beat the drum *(för* for) **2** *tekn.* drum, cylinder, barrel **II** *v1* drum; *(om regn äv.)* beat; ~ *ihop (bildl.)* drum (beat) up; ~ *på piano* strum on the piano **-minne** *data.* drum store

trumpen *a3* sulky, sullen; morose

trumpet *s3* trumpet; *blåsa [i]* ~ play (sound) the trumpet

trumpet|a trumpet *(ut* forth) **-are** [-ˣpe:-] trumpeter; *mil. äv.* bugler **-fanfar** fanfare of trumpets **-signal** trumpet signal (call) **-stek** *s7, sjö.* sheepshank **-stöt** trumpet blast

trum|pinne drumstick **-skinn** drumhead **-slagare** drummer **-slagarpojke** drummer boy **-virvel** drum roll

trupial *s3, zool.* oriole

trupp *s3* troop; *(-styrka)* contingent; *(-enhet)* unit, detachment; *(idrotts-)* team; *(teater-)* troupe, company; ~*er (mil.)* troops, forces **-förband** [military] unit **-revy** review [of troops] **-rörelse** military movement **-sammandragning[ar]** concentration of troops **-slag** branch of service, arm **-styrka** military force **-transport** transport[ation] of troops **-transportfartyg** troopship, troop carrier (transport) **-transportplan** transport plane, troop carrier [plane]

trust *s3* trust **-bildning** establishment of trusts **-väsen** trust system

1 trut *s2, zool.* gull

2 trut *s2, vard.* (mun) kisser; *hålla ~en* shut up; *vara stor i ~en* blow one's own trumpet

truta ~ *med munnen* pout [one's lips]

trutit *sup. av* tryta

tryck *s7* **1** *(fys. o. friare)* pressure *(på* on); weight

(över bröstet on one's chest); *bildl.* constraint, strain; *språkv.* stress; *utöva* ~ exert pressure, *(friare)* put pressure *(på* on); *det ekonomiska ~et* the financial strain **2** *(av bok e.d.)* print; *(av-)* impression; *komma ut i* ~ appear (come out) in print; *ge ut i* ~ print, publish

tryck|a *v3* **1** *(fys. o. friare)* press *(mot* against, to); *(klämma)* squeeze; *(tynga [på])* lie heavy on, oppress; *tryck! (på dörr)* push!; *tryck på knappen!* press the button!; ~ *ngns hand* shake a p.'s hand; ~ *ngn till sitt bröst* press (clasp) a p. to one's breast; ~ *en kyss på* imprint a kiss on **2** *(med betonad partikel)* ~ *av a)* (ta avtryck av) impress, *b)* (kopiera) copy [off], *c)* (avskjuta) fire, *absol.* pull the trigger; ~ *fast* press on; ~ *ihop* press (squeeze) together; ~ *in (ut)* press (force) in (out); ~ *sig intill* press up against; ~ *ner* press down, *(friare o. bildl.)* depress; ~ *upp* press up, force open **3** *(om villebråd)* squat; *ligga o.* *(om pers.)* lie low **4** *boktr. o.d.* print; *(med stämpel)* stamp; ~ *en bok i 2 000 exemplar* print 2,000 copies of a book; ~ *om* reprint; *-es (på korrektur)* ready for press **-alster** publication; printed matter **-ande** *a4* pressing *etc.*; *(friare o. bildl.)* oppressive; *(om väder)* sultry, close; *(tung)* heavy; *värmen känns* ~ the heat is oppressive **-are** printer; *(dans)* BE. sl. smooch **-ark** printed sheet **-belastning** [compressive] load **-bokstav** *(textad)* block letter **-dräkt** pressure suit **-eri** printing works (house); *(motsats sätteri)* press room; *skicka till ~et* send to the printer[s] **-erifaktor** press-room (printer's) foreman **-fel** printer's error, misprint **-felsnisse** *s2* printer's gremlin **-frihet** freedom (liberty) of the press

tryckfrihets|brott breach of the press law **-förordning** press law **-mål** press-law suit

tryck|färdig ready for the press (for printing) **-färg** printing (printer's) ink **-godkännande** permission to print, imprimatur **-impregnera** impregnate under pressure **-kabin** *flyg.* pressure cabin **-kammare** pressure chamber **-knapp 1** *(strömbrytare)* push button **2** *(för knäppning)* press stud; *AE.* snap fastener **-kokare** pressure cooker **-kontakt** push-button switch **-luft** compressed air **-luftsborr** pneumatic drill **-luftsdriven** *a5* pneumatic, air-operated

tryck|ning 1 *(av böcker o.d.)* printing; *godkännes till* ~ ready for press; *lämna till* ~ hand in to be printed; *under* ~ in the press; *boken är under* ~ *(äv.)* the book is being printed **2** pressing *etc.*; pressure; *(med fingret)* press **-ningskostnader** printing costs **-ort** place of publication, [printer's] imprint **-penna** automatic pencil **-press** printing press **-pump** pressure pump **-punkt 1** *fysiol.* pressure spot **2** *elektr.* pressure (feeding) point **-sak** ~*er* printed matter (paper) **-sida** *boktr.* printed page **-stark** *språkv.* stressed, accented **-stil** [printing] type **-svag** *språkv.* unstressed, unaccented **-svärta** se *tryckfärg*

tryck|t 1 pressed *etc.* **2** *boktr.* printed *(hos* by); ~*a kretsar (radio.)* printed circuits **3** *(nedstämd)* oppressed, dejected **-våg** blast wave **-år** year of publication

tryff|el ['tryff-] *s2* truffle **-era** garnish with truffles; ~*d (äv.)* truffled

trygg *a1* safe, secure (*för* from); (*om pers.*) confident; (*orädd*) dauntless, assured

trygg|a make safe, secure (*för, emot* from); safeguard; ~ *framtiden* provide for the future; ~ *freden* guarantee the peace; ~*d ålderdom* a carefree (secure) old age **-het** safety, security **-hetsavtal** job security agreement **-hetskänsla** feeling (sense) of security

tryggt *adv* safely *etc.*, with safety; ~ *påstå* confidently declare

trymå *s3* pier glass

tryne *s6* snout; *ett fult* ~ (*vard.*) an ugly mug

tryta *tröt trutit* (*fattas*) be lacking; (*ta slut*) run short, be deficient; *förråden börjar* ~ supplies are getting low (running short); *krafterna börjar* ~ *his* (*etc.*) strength is beginning to ebb; *tålamodet tröt mig* my patience gave out

tråckel|stygn tacking-stitch **-tråd** tacking-thread

tråckl|a tack; ~ *fast ngt* tack s.th. on (*på, vid* to) **-ing** tacking

tråd *s2* thread; (*bomulls-*) cotton; (*metall-*) wire; (*glöd-*) filament; (*fiber*) fibre; *den röda ~en* (*i berättelse o.d.*) the main theme; *går som en röd ~ genom* runs all through, is the governing idea of; *få ngn på ~en* (*tel.*) get s.b. on the line; *hålla i ~arna* (*bildl.*) hold the reins; *hans liv hängde på en ~* his life hung by a thread; *tappa ~en* (*bildl.*) lose the thread

tråda *v2*, ~ *dansen* dance

tråd|buss trolley bus **-drageri** [wire] drawing mill, wire mill **-fin** threadlike, finespun **-gardin** net (lace) curtain **-ig** *a1* fibrous, filamentous; (*om kött e.d.*) stringy **-kors** *fys.* cross wires (hairs) (*pl*) **-liknande** threadlike; filamentous **-lös** wireless (*telegrafi* telegraphy) **-radio** wire [d] broadcasting **-rakt** *adv* the way of the thread [*s pl*] **-rulle** (*med tråd*) reel of cotton, *AE.* spool of thread; (*för tråd*) cotton reel, *AE.* spool **-sliten** threadbare **-smal** [as] thin as a thread **-spik** wire nail **-ända** end of cotton (thread)

tråg *s7* trough; (*mindre djupt*) tray

tråk|a (*driva med*) tease, (*starkare*) pester; ~ *ihjäl* (*ut*) bore to death **-ig** *a1* (*lång-*) boring, tedious; (*om pers. äv.*) dull; (*ointressant*) uninteresting; (*besvärlig*) tiresome; (*oangenäm*) unpleasant, disagreable; *en ~ historia* a nasty affair; *en ~ människa* (*äv.*) a bore; *så ~t!* (*så synd*) what a pity!, (*det gör mig ont*) oh, I'm sorry!; *det var verkligen ~t!* that was too bad!; *det var ~t för dig!* how tiresome for you!; *det vore ~t om* I (we) should be [very] sorry if **-ighet** (*utan pl*) tediousness *etc.*; (*med pl*) trouble, annoyance **-igt** *adv* tediously *etc.*; ~ *nog* unfortunately, I am sorry to say; *ha ~t* be bored, have a tedious time of it **-måns** *s2* bore

trål *s2*, **tråla** *v1* trawl **trålare** trawler **trålfiske** trawling

trån|a pine, languish (*efter* for) **-ad** *s3* pining, languishing (*efter* for)

trång *-t trängre trängst* narrow (*i halsen* in (at) the neck; *över ryggen* across the back); (*åtsittande*) tight; (*om bostad e.d.*) cramped; *det är ~t i* there is very little space in, (*det är fullt med folk*) ... is very crowded; *det är ~t om saligheten* there's not much room to move **-bodd** *a1* overcrowded;

vara ~ be cramped for space, live in overcrowded conditions **-boddhet** overcrowding, cramped housing accommodation **-bröstad** *a5* (*intolerant*) narrow-minded; (*pryd*) strait-laced **-mål** distress; (*penningknipa*) embarrassment, straits (*pl*); *råka i* ~ get into straits (*vard.* a tight corner) **-sinne** narrow-mindedness **-synt** [-y:-] *a1* narrow; *vara* ~ have a narrow outlook **-synthet** [-y:-] narrowness; narrow outlook

trångt *adv, bo* ~ live in [over]crowded conditions; *sitta* ~ *a*) sit close together, *bildl.* be hard up, be in a tight corner, *b*) (*om plagg*) fit too tight

trånsjuka pining, languishing (*efter* for)

1 trä *v4, se 2 träda*

2 trä *s6* wood; *av* ~ (*äv.*) wooden; *ta i ~!* touch wood!

trä|aktig *a1* woodlike; *bildl.* woody, wooden **-ben** wooden leg **-bit** piece (bit) of wood **-blåsare** wood[wind] player; *-blåsarna* the woodwind (*sg*) **-blåsinstrument** woodwind instrument **-bjälke** timber beam **-bock 1** (*bock av trä*) wooden trestle **2** *pers.* dry stick **-bro** wooden bridge **-byggnad** wooden building

träck *s3* excrement[*s pl*]; (*djur-*) dung

träd *s7* tree; *växer inte på* ~ (*bildl.*) don't grow on trees; *inte se skogen för bara* ~ not see the wood for the trees

1 träda *v2* (*gå, komma*) step, tread; ~ *i förbindelse med* enter into a relationship with; ~ *i kraft* come into force, take effect; ~ *i likvidation* go into liquidation; ~ *emellan* step between, *absol. äv.* intervene; ~ *fram* come (step) forward; ~ *tillbaka* retire, withdraw (*för* in favour of); ~ *ut* step (walk) out

2 träda *v2* (~ *på*) thread (*på* on to); (*halsband äv.*) string; (*friare*) pass, slip; ~ *en handske på handen* draw a glove on to the hand; ~ *på en nål* thread a needle; ~ *en nål* (*ett band*) *igenom ngt* run a needle (ribbon) through s.th.; ~ *pärlor på ett band* thread pearls on [to] a string, string pearls; ~ *upp* thread (*på* on [to])

3 träda *s1* (*trädesåker*) fallow [field], lay-land; *ligga i* ~ lie fallow

träd|bevuxen wooded, timbered **-dunge** clump of trees **-fattig** with few trees **-fällning** wood cutting (felling) **-gren** branch [of a tree] **-gräns** timber (tree) line

trädgård ['trägå:rd, ˣträgg-] *s2* garden; *AE. äv.* yard; *anlägga en* ~ lay out a garden; *botanisk* (*zoologisk*) ~ botanical (zoological) gardens (*pl*)

trädgårds|anläggning (*-anläggande*) landscape gardening; *konkr.* garden[*s pl*], grounds **-arbetare** gardener, garden hand **-arbete** gardening, garden work **-arkitekt** landscape gardener (architect) **-fest** garden party **-förening** horticultural society **-gunga** lawn swing **-gång** garden path **-land** garden plot **-mästare** gardener **-möbel** [piece of] garden furniture **-odling** *abstr.* horticulture **-produkt** garden product; ~*er* (*äv.*) garden produce (*sg*) **-redskap** garden[ing] tool **-skötsel** horticulture, gardening **-slang** garden hose **-sångare** *zool.* garden warbler **-täppa** garden plot **-utställning** horticultural show (exhibition), flower show

T

träd|krona crown of a (the) tree, tree top **-krypare** zool. tree creeper **-lös** treeless **-plantering** plantation of trees **-slag** variety of tree, tree species **-stam** tree trunk **-topp** tree top

träexport timber export[s pl]

träff s2 **1** (skott som -ar) hit; få i en ~ score a hit **2** (möte) rendezvous; AE. date; (för fler än två) meeting, get-together

träff|a 1 (vid kast, skott e.d.) hit; strike; ~ målet (sitt mål) hit the target; när ljudet ~r örat when the sound strikes the ear; inte ~ målet (äv.) miss the mark **2** (möta) meet; see; jag skall ~ dem i morgon I shall see them tomorrow; ~ ngn hemma find s.b. at home; ~s herr A.? is Mr. A. in (at home)?, (i telefon) can I speak to Mr. A.?, is Mr. A. available?; doktorn ~s mellan 8 och 9 the doctor is at home to callers between 8 and 9; ~ på [happen to] come across (come [up]on, meet with) **3** (drabba) hit, strike; ~s av solsting get sunstroke **4** (riktigt återge) hit off; catch; ~ (gissa) rätt hit on the right answer; ~ den rätta tonen (äv. bildl.) strike the right note **5** (vidtaga) make (anstalter arrangements); ~ ett val make a choice **-ad** a5 hit; känna sig ~ (bildl.) feel guilty **-ande** a4 to the point; pertinent (anmärkning remark); (välfunnen) apposite, appropriate **-as** dep meet; vi skall ~ i morgon we shall meet (be seeing each other) tomorrow

träff|punkt point of impact **-säker** sure in aim; bildl. sure (omdöme judgment); apposite (yttrande remark); en ~ skytt a good marksman, a dead shot **-säkerhet** precision (accuracy) of aim; (i omdöme) rightness (sureness) of judgment

trä|fiber wood fibre **-fiberplatta** fibreboard **-fri** wood-free **-förädling** woodworking, wood processing

trägen a3 assiduous, persevering; ~ vinner persevere and never fear **-het** assiduity, perseverance

trä|haltig a1 woody; ~t papper paper containing wood fibres **-hus** wooden (timber) house; AE. äv. frame house **-häst** wooden horse **-ig** a1 woody; (om grönsak o.d.) tough, stringy; bildl. wooden **-industri** timber industry **-karl** kortsp. dummy **-karlsbridge** dummy bridge **-kol** charcoal **-kolsframställning** charcoal-burning **-konservering** wood preservation **-konstruktion** timber (wood[en]) structure (construction) **-kärl** wooden vessel

träl s2 thrall; serf; bildl. slave, bondsman **träla** toil [like a slave], slave (med at)

trälast timber (AE. lumber) cargo

träl|bunden enslaved **-dom** [-domm] s2 bondage, thralldom; bildl. slavery, servitude **-domsok** yoke of bondage **-göra** s6 drudgery

trä|mask woodworm **-massa** wood pulp **-massefabrik** pulp mill **-mjöl** wood meal (flour, dust)

trän|a train (i in; till for); (öva sig) practise; börja ~ go into training **-ad** a5 trained; (erfaren) experienced, practised **-are** trainer; coach

träng s3 train; Storbritannien army service corps; AE. maintenance and supply troops (pl)

träng|a v2 **1 1** (vara trång) be (feel) tight **2** (driva, pressa) drive, force, push, press; fienden -er oss från alla håll the enemy presses in upon us on every side; han -de mig efter omkörningen he cut me up after he overtook me **3** (bana sig väg) force one's (its) way (österut east[wards]); inte ett ljud -de över hans läppar not a sound escaped his lips **II** (med betonad partikel) **1** ~ av force off **2** ~ fram penetrate, force one's (its) way (till to) **3** ~ igenom penetrate, (om vatten) come through; uttrycket har -t igenom i skriftspråket the expression has found its way into the written language **4** ~ ihop (ngt) compress, (människor) crowd (pack) together; ~ ihop sig crowd together **5** ~ in ... [i] press (force) ... in[to]; ~ in i (bildl.) penetrate into; kulan -de djupt in i the bullet penetrated deep into **6** ~ ner force one's (its) way down (i into), (i sht bildl.) penetrate (i into; till to) **7** ~ på push (press) on **8** ~ undan force (push) out of its (his etc.) place (out of the way) **9** ~ ut a) (ngn) force (push) out, (ngt) displace, b) (strömma ut) force one's (its) way out, (om rök, vätska o.d.) issue [forth]; ögonen -de ut ur sina hålor his (etc.) eyes were starting out of their sockets **III** rfl, ~ sig fram a) eg. push one's way forward, b) bildl. push o.s. forward; ~ sig in intrude (i upon); ~ sig på force (thrust) o.s. upon (ngn s.b.), absol. intrude, obtrude ; minnena -er sig på mig memories come thronging in upon my mind

träng|ande a4 (tvingande) pressing; (angelägen) urgent; vid ~ behov in an (a case of) emergency **-as** v2, dep push, jostle one another; (skockas) crowd [together]; man behövde inte ~ there was no crowding

träng|re ['träŋre] **I** a, komp. t. trång narrower; more limited; (om plagg äv.) tighter; i den ~ familjekretsen in the immediate family; inom en ~ krets [with]in a [strictly] limited circle **II** adv more narrowly; (tätare) closer [together] **-sel** ['träŋ-] s9 crowding; (folk-) crush (throng) [of people]; salen var fylld till ~ the hall was thronged (packed, overcrowded) (av with); det råder ~ på lärarbanan the teaching profession is overcrowded **-st** (jfr trängre) **I** a, superl. t. trång narrowest etc. **II** adv most narrowly; closest

trängta yearn, pine (efter for; efter att to) **trängtan** r yearning

träning training; (av ngn äv.) coaching; (övning) practice; ligga (lägga sig) i ~ be in (go into) training (för for)

tränings|overall tracksuit **-skola** school for severely mentally retarded children **-värk** ha ~ be stiff [after training]

träns s2 **1** (snodd) braid, cord **2** (betsel) snaffle [bit] **tränsa** (förse med träns) cord, braid

trä|panel wood panel[ling], wainscoting **-pinne** [round] piece of wood **-plugg** wooden plug (pin) **-ribba** wooden lath

träsk s7 marsh, swamp, fen; bildl. sink

träskalle bildl. blockhead, num[b]skull

träskartad [-a:r-] a5 marshy, fenny

träsked wooden spoon

träskmark marshy (fenny) ground

trä|sko wooden shoe; (med -botten) clog **-skodans** (~ande) clog dancing; (en ~) clog dance **-skruv** (av trä) wooden screw; (av metall) wood screw **-skyddsmedel** rot-proofing agent **-skål**

wooden bowl **-slag** sort (kind) of wood **-slev** wooden ladle **-sliperi** mechanical [wood-]pulp mill **-slöjd** woodwork, carpentry, joinery **-smak** vard., jag har ~ I've got a sore bottom **-snidare** woodcarver, wood engraver **-snideri** woodcarving, wood engraving **-snitt** woodcut **-sprit** wood alcohol (spirit) **-sticka** [wood] splinter **-svarv** wood lathe

trät|a I s1 quarrel; häftig ~ fierce row **II** v3 quarrel; (svagare) bicker (om about) **-girig** quarrelsome **-obroder** sparring partner, adversary

trä|tjära wood tar **-toffel** clog **-ull** wood wool, excelsior **-varor** pl timber (sg), wood products; (bearbetade) wooden goods **-varuhandel** timber (AE. lumber) trade (business) **-varuhandlare** timber merchant; AE. lumber dealer **-virke** timber, wood, (i byggnad) woodwork; AE. lumber **-vit** en ~ bokhylla a whitewood bookcase

trög al slow (i at; i att at + ing-form); (om pers. äv.) inactive, inert, languid; (senfärdig) tardy (i att in + ing-form); (slö) dull (äv. om affärer); fys. inert; (i rörelse) sluggish; låset är ~t the lock is stiff; ha ~ mage be constipated **-djur** sloth; bildl. sluggard **-flytande** viscous, viscid; (om vattendrag) slow-flowing, sluggish **-het** slowness etc.; inactivity, inertia **-hetsmoment** moment of inertia **-läst** [-ä:-] a4 heavy (dull) [to read] **-måns** s2 sluggard, slacker

trög|t [-ö:-] adv slowly etc.; affärerna går ~ business is dull; motorn går ~ the engine is sluggish; det går ~ (om arbete o.d.) it's hard-going **-tänkt** al slow-witted, slow-thinking, slow on the uptake

tröja [ˣtröjja] s1 sweater, jersey; (under-) vest, singlet, AE. undershirt

tröska I v1 thresh; ~ igenom (bildl.) plough through **II** s1 **1** se tröskverk **2** (skörde-) combine [harvester]

tröskel s2 threshold (till of); (dörr- äv.) doorstep **-värde** fys. threshold value

trösk|ning threshing **-verk** thresher, threshing machine

tröst s3 consolation; solace; (svagare) comfort; en klen ~ a poor consolation; det är en ~ i olyckan that is some consolation; hennes ålders ~ a comfort in her old age; skänka ~ afford consolation; söka [sin] ~ i seek solace in

tröst|a console; solace; comfort; Gud -e mig! God have mercy upon me!; ~ sig console o.s. (över for); hon ville inte låta ~ sig she was inconsolable **-erik** full of consolation, consoling **-lös** (som inte låter -a sig) disconsolate; (hopplös) hopeless, desperate **-napp** dummy, comforter; AE. pacifier **-pris** consolation prize

tröt imperf. av tryta

trött al tired (av with; efter after, as a result of; på of); (uttröttad) weary, fatigued; jag är ~ på (äv.) I am sick of; jag är ~ i benen my legs are tired (av att with, from + ing-form); dansa sig ~ dance till one is tired [out]

trött|a tire; weary, fatigue; det ~r att stå standing makes you tired (is tiring); ~ ut ngn tire s.b. out **-ande** a4 tiring **-as** dep get tired (etc.) (av by) **-het** tiredness; weariness, fatigue **-hetskänsla** sense of fatigue **-köra** overdrive; overwork (äv.

bildl.) **-na** tire, get tired, weary, get weary (på of; på att of + ing-form) **-sam** a1 tiring, fatiguing

tsar [(t)sa:r] s3 tsar, czar **-döme** s6 (-rike) tsar's realm; (-välde) tsardom, czardom **-inna** tsarina, czarina

tsetsefluga tsetse (tzetze) fly

T-tröja T-shirt, tee-shirt

tu two; ett ~ tre all of a sudden; de unga ~ the young couple; det är inte ~ tal om den saken there is no question about that; på ~ man hand in private

tub s3 **1** tube **2** (kikare) telescope

tuba s1 tuba **-blåsare** tuba player

tubba ~ ngn till induce s.b. to

tuberkel [-'bärr-] s3 tubercle **-bacill** tubercle bacillus

tuberkul|in s3 tuberculin **-prov** tuberculin test **-os** [-'lå:s] s3 tuberculosis (i of) (förk. T.B.) **-sjuk** suffering from tuberculosis **-undersökning** examination for tuberculosis **tuberkulös** al tuberculous, tubercular

tubformig [-å-] al tubular

tudel|a divide into two [parts]; geom. bisect **-ning** dividing into two [parts]; geom. bisection

1 tuff s3 (bergart) tuff; (kalk-) tufa

2 tuff al vard. (hård) tough (kille guy); (snygg) smart (jacka jacket)

tuffa (om tåg) puff

tuffing tough guy

tuff-tuff-tåg barnspr. puff-puff, AE. choo-choo

tugg|a I s1 bite; chew **II** v1 chew; (mat äv.) masticate; hästen ~r på betslet the horse is champing at the bit; ~ om chew [over] again, bildl. repeat, keep harping on (samma sak the same string) **-buss** quid [of tobacco] **-gummi** (hopskr. tuggummi) chewing gum **-ning** chewing; mastication **-tobak** chewing tobacco

tuja [ˣtujja] s1 arbor vitae

tukt s3 discipline; i Herrans ~ och förmaning in good order **tukta** (aga, äv. friare) chastise, (bestraffa) punish **2** (forma) [hammer] dress (sten stone); prune (träd trees) **tuktan** r chastisement, castigation; correction **tukthus** house of correction, penitentiary

1 tull se årtull

2 tull s2 **1** (avgift) [customs] duty (på on); hög ~ heavy duty; belägga med ~ impose a duty on; hur hög är ~en på ...? what is the duty on ...?; betala 2 pund i ~ pay two pounds [in] duty **2** (-verk, -hus) customs, Customs (pl); ~en (-personalen) the customs officers (pl); gå genom ~en go through customs **3** (stads-) tollgate; (infart t. stad) entrance to a town

tull|a 1 (betala tull) pay [customs] duty (för on) **2** (snatta) ~ på (av) pinch some of **-behandla** clear through the Customs, clear [in]; ~de varor goods examined and cleared **-belägga** levy duty on; -belagda varor dutiable goods **-bestämmelser** customs regulations **-bevakning** customs supervision; konkr. preventive service **-deklaration** customs declaration **-deklarera** declare at Customs **-fri** duty-free, free of duty **-frihet** exemption from duty; åtnjuta ~ be exempt from duty **-hus** custom-house, customs house **-kryssare** revenue cutter **-mur** tariff wall (barrier) **-myndighet[er]** customs authorities

-personal customs officers (*pl*) **-pliktig** dutiable, liable to duty **-sats** tariff rate, [rate of] duty **-skydd** tariff protection **-station** customs station **-sänkning** tariff reduction **-taxa** tariff **-tjänsteman** customs officer (*högre:* official) **-union** customs union **-uppsyningsman** preventive officer **-verk** customs [and excise] department **-visitation** customs examination **-visitera** examine **-väsen** customs administration

tulpan *s3* tulip

tulta I *v1* toddle **II** *s1* little girl, toddler girl

tum [tumm] *s9* inch; *en kung i varje* ~ every inch a king; *jag viker inte en* ~ I won't budge (give an inch)

tuml|a 1 (*falla*) tumble, fall (*över ända* over); ~ *om* romp around; ~ *om med varandra* have a tussle [together] **2** ~ *en häst* caracole a horse **-are 1** (*delfin*) [common] porpoise **2** (*bägare*) tumbler

tumma 1 ~ [*på*] finger; *det ~r vi på!* let's shake upon it! **2** ~ *på* (*jämka på*) compromise with (*hederskänslan* one's sense of honour), stretch (*en regel* stretch a point) **3** (*uppmäta i tum*) gauge

tumm|e *s2* thumb; *bita sig i* ~*n* (*bildl.*) get the wrong sow by the ear; *ha* ~ *med ngn* be chummy with s.b.; *hålla* ~*n på ögat på ngn* keep a tight hand on s.b.; *hålla* -*arna för ngn* keep one's fingers crossed for s.b.; *rulla* -*arna* twiddle one's thumbs; -*en upp!* thumbs up!

tummeliten [-ˣli:-] *r* Tom Thumb

tummelplats battlefield, battleground (*för* for)

tum|metott [-'tått, ˣtumme-] *s2* thumb **-nagel** thumbnail **-regel** rule of thumb

tums|bred an inch broad (wide) **-bredd** *en* ~ the breadth (width) of an inch

tum|skruv thumbscrew; *sätta* ~*ar på ngn* (*bildl.*) put the thumbscrews on s.b., squeeze s.b. **-stock** folding rule **-sugning** thumbsucking

tumult *s7* tumult; commotion; (*oväsen*) uproar; (*upplopp*) disturbance, riot **-uarisk** [-'a:risk] *a5* tumultuous

tumvante [woollen] mitten

tumör tumour

tundra *s1* tundra

tung -*t tyngre tyngst* heavy; weighty; (*betungande*) cumbersome, burdensome; (*svår*) hard, grievous; *bildl.* ponderous, cumbrous (*stil* style); ~ *industri* (*luft*) heavy industry (air); *med* ~*t hjärta* with a heavy heart; *jag känner mig* ~ *i huvudet* my head is heavy; *göra livet* ~*t för ngn* make life a burden to s.b.; *det känns* ~*t att* it feels hard to

tunga *s1* **1** tongue; (*på våg äv.*) needle, pointer; (*i musikinstrument*) reed; (*på flagga*) tail; *en elak* (*rapp*) ~ a malicious (ready) tongue; *vara* ~*n på vågen* tip the scale; *ha ett ord på* ~*n* have a word on the tip of one's tongue; *hålla tand för* ~ keep one's own counsel; *hålla* ~*n rätt i mun* mind one's p's and q's; *mind one's step*; *räcka ut* ~*n åt* poke one's tongue out at **2** (*fisk*) sole

tungarbeta|d *a5* that is heavy to work; *ett* -*t kök* an inconvenient kitchen

tung|band *anat.* ligament of the tongue **-ben** *anat.* tongue bone

tungfotad *a5* heavy-footed

tunghäfta tongue-tie; *hon lider inte av* ~ (*vard.*) her tongue is well oiled

tungmetall heavy metal

tungomål tongue **tungomålstalande** *s6* gift of tongues, speaking in tongues

tungrodd *a5, eg.* that is heavy to row; *bildl.* heavy, unwieldy; (*om arbete*) [heavy and] time-consuming

tung|rot root of the tongue **-rygg** back of the tongue

tung|sinne melancholy **-sint** *a1* melancholy, gloomy **-spat** *s3* barytes, barite, heavy spar

tung|spene *anat.* uvula (*pl äv.* uvulae) **-spets** tip of the tongue

tungsövd [-ö:-] *a5, vara* ~ be a heavy sleeper

tungt *adv* heavily; *gå* ~ *a*) (*om pers.*) have a heavy tread, *b*) (*om maskin e.d.*) run heavily (heavy); ~ *vatten* heavy water; ~ *väte* heavy hydrogen, deuterium; ~ *vägande skäl* weighty reasons; *hans åsikt väger* ~ his opinion carries a lot of weight

tungus [-ŋ'gu:s] *s3* Tungus; ~*erna* the Tungus [ians]

tungvikt heavyweight **-are** heavyweight [boxer, wrestler]

tunik [-'ni:k, -'nikk] *s3* tunic **tunika** ['tu:-] *s1* tunic

Tunisien [-'ni:-] *n* Tunisia

tunis|ier [-'ni:-] *s9* Tunisian **-isk** *a5* Tunisian

tunn *a1* thin; (*om tyg äv.*) flimsy; (*om rock o.d. äv.*) light; (*om tråd*) fine; (*om dryck*) weak, watery

1 tunna *v1,* ~ *av* (*smalna*) get (grow) thin (thinner), (*glesna*) thin

2 tunna *s1* barrel; cask; *hoppa i galen* ~ (*bildl.*) jump in the wrong box

tunn|band barrel hoop; (*leksak*) hoop **-bindare** cooper, hooper **-binderi** *abstr.* coopering; *konkr.* cooperage

tunnbröd *ung.* thin unleavened bread

tunnel *s2* tunnel; (*gång- äv.*) subway, *AE.* underpass **-bana** underground railway; *Storbritannien äv.* tube, underground; *AE. äv.* subway **-banestation** underground (tube; *AE.* subway) station

tunn|flytande *a4* thin (*vätska* liquid) **-het** thinness *etc.* **-hudad** *a5* that has a thin skin; *bildl.* thin-skinned **-hårig** thin on [the] top **-klädd** lightly clad

tunnland *n, ung.* acre

tunn|skalig *a1* thin-shelled (*etc., jfr skal*) **-sliten** threadbare **-sådd** *a1* thinly sown; *bildl.* few and far between **-tarm** small intestine

tunt *adv* thinly; (*glest*) sparsely

tupé *s3* toupee **tupera** backcomb, tease

tupp *s2* cock; rooster; *en* ~ *i halsen* a frog in one's throat

tupp|a *vard.,* ~ *av* pass out, black out **-fjät 1** *eg.* cock's stride **2** *bildl., bara ett* [*par*] ~ only a hand ['s-]breadth; *inte ett* ~ not an iota **-fäktning** cockfighting **-kam** crest, cockscomb **-kyckling** cockerel; *bildl.* coxcomb, cocky young devil **-lur** catnap; *ta sig en* ~ (*äv.*) have forty winks

1 tur *s3* (*lycka; lyckträff*) luck; *ha* ~ have luck, be lucky; *ha* ~ *med sig* (*medföra* ~) bring luck; *ha* ~ *hos damerna* have a way with the ladies; *ha* ~*en att* have the [good] luck (be lucky enough) to; ~

i oturen (ung.) a blessing in disguise; *mer ~ än skicklighet* more good luck than good management; *det var ~ att* it was (is) lucky that, how fortunate that

2 tur *s3* **1** *(resa)* tour; *(kortare äv.)* round; trip; *(bil- äv.)* drive; *(cykel- äv.)* ride; *(promenad äv.)* walk, stroll; *~ och retur[-resa]* return journey, *AE.* round trip; *reguljära ~er* regular service *(sg)* *(flyg.* flights; *sjö.* sailings); *göra en ~* take (go for) a trip **2** *(i dans)* figure **3** *(följd, ordning)* turn; *i ~ och ordning* in turn, by turns; *nu är det min ~* now it's my turn; *stå närmast i ~* be next (on the list)

tur|a *v1*, **-as** *v1 dep*, *~ om att* take [it in] turns to; *~ om med ngn* take turns with s.b.

turban *s3* turban **-klädd** turbaned

turb|in *s3* turbine **-driven** turbine-powered, turbine-driven **-hjul** turbine wheel **-motor** turbine [engine], turbomotor

turbo|jetplan turbojet [aircraft] **-propplan** turboprop [aircraft]

turbul|ens *s3* turbulence **-ent** *a1* turbulent

turism tourism **turist** tourist; sightseer **turista** [-'riss-] *vard.* travel as a tourist

turist|attraktion tourist attraction, sight **-broschyr** travel folder **-buss** touring (sightseeing) coach **-byrå** travel (tourist) agency (bureau) **-hotell** tourist hotel **-industri** tourist industry **-information** tourist information **-karta** touring map **-klass** tourist class **-land** tourist country **-ort** tourist resort **-säng** folding bed **-valuta** tourist (travel) allowance **-väsen** tourism; tourist services *(pl)*

turk *s2* **1** Turk **2** *vard.* Turkish bath **-cypriot** Turkish Cypriot

Turkiet [-'ki:-] *n* Turkey

turk|isk ['turr-] *a5* Turkish; Turkey *(matta carpet)* **-iska** *s1* **1** *(språk)* Turkish **2** *(kvinna)* Turkish woman

turkos [-'kå:s, -'ko:s] *s3* turquoise **-blå** turquoise blue

turlista timetable

turmalin *s3* tourmaline

turn|é *s3* tour; *göra en ~* tour, make a tour **-era 1** *(vara på turné)* tour **2** *(formulera)* turn, put; *väl ~d* well-turned **-ering** [-'ne:-] tournament

turnyr *s3* bustle

tur- och returbiljett return *(AE.* round-trip) ticket

tursam [ˣtu:r-] *a1* lucky, fortunate

turturduva [ˣturr-] turtledove

turvis [ˣtu:r-] by (in) turns, in turn

tusan *r, för ~!* hang it!; *det var ~!* well, I'll be blowed!; *av bara ~* like blazes (the very deuce); *en ~ till karl* a devil of a fellow

1 tusch *s2, mus. (anslag), konst., fäkt., bildl.* touch; *(fanfar)* flourish

2 tusch *s3, s4 (färg)* Indian ink

tuschteckning pen and ink drawing

tusen ['tu:-] *a* thousand; *T~ och en natt* The Arabian Nights; *~ sinom ~* thousands and (upon) thousands; *~ tack!* a thousand thanks!, *vard.* thanks awfully; *inte en på ~* not one in a thousand; *flera ~* several thousand[s of]; *jag ber ~ gånger om ursäkt!* [I beg] a thousand pardons! **-bladstårta** puff-pastry layer cake **-de I** *s6*

thousand **II** *(ordningstal)* thousandth **-[de]del** thousandth [part] **-faldig** *a1* thousandfold **-foting** myriapod; centipede, millepede **-hövdad** *a5* many-headed **-konstnär** jack of all trades, handyman **-kronorssedel**, **-lapp** thousand--kronor note **-sköna** [-ʃ-] *s1, bot.* [common] daisy **-tal 1** *ett ~* some (about a) thousand **2** *på ~et* in the eleventh century **-tals** [-a:] thousands [of]; in thousands **-årig** *a1* a thousand years old; *det ~a riket* the millennium **-årsjubileum** millennial celebration

tuskaft *väv.* two-leaved twill

tuss *s2* wad

tussa *~ hunden på ngn* set the dog on to s.b.; *~ ihop* set each other, *(friare)* set by the ears

tussilago [-'la:-] *s5, s9, bot.* coltsfoot

tut I *s7* toot[ing] **II** *interj* toot!

1 tuta *s1 (finger-)* fingerstall

2 tuta *v1* toot[le] *(i en lur* [on] a horn); *(med signalhorn)* hoot; *~ ngt i öronen på ngn (bildl.)* din s.th. into a p.'s ears

tutning [-u:-] tooting; hooting

1 tutta *s1 (liten flicka)* little girl

2 tutta *v1*, *~ [eld] på* set fire to, set on fire

tuva *s1* tussock, tuft; *(gräs- äv.)* tuft [of grass]; *liten ~ välter ofta stort lass* little strokes fell great oaks **tuvig** *a1* tufty

t.v. *förk. för a)* till *vänster* to the left, *b)* till *vidare*, *se vidare II 6*

TV [ˣte:ve:] *s2 (jfr television)* TV; *BE. vard.* telly; *AE. vard.* video

tvagning [-a:-] *åld.* washing; *(relig. el. skämts.)* ablutions

tvang *imperf. av tvinga*

TV-apparat TV [set]

tvedräkt *s3* dissension, discord

tweed [tvi:d] *s3* tweed **-dräkt** tweed suit

tve|eggad *a5* two-edged; *bildl. äv.* double-edged **-gifte** bigamy **-hågsen** *a5* in two minds

tveka hesitate *(om* about, as to); be uncertain (doubtful) *(om hur man skall* [about] how to)

tvekamp duel; *(envig)* single combat

tvek|an *r* hesitation; uncertainty, indecision; *med (utan) ~* with some (without [any]) hesitation **-ande** *a4* hesitating *etc.*; hesitant

tvekluven forked; *bot.* bipartite

tvek|lös [-e:-] *a1* unhesitating **-löst** [-ö:-] *adv* without hesitation **-sam** *a1* uncertain, doubtful *(om* about, as to; *om huruvida* whether); *(obeslutsam)* irresolute; *känna sig ~ (äv.)* feel dubious **-samhet** hesitation, hesitance; doubt[fulness]

tvekönad [-çö:-] *a5* bisexual, hermaphrodite

tve|nne two **-stjärt** [common European] earwig **-talan** *beslå ngn med ~* convict s.b. of self-contradiction **-tydig** *a1* ambiguous; double-barrelled; equivocal; *(oanständig)* indecent; *(tvivelaktig)* dubious **-tydighet** ambiguousness; ambiguity; indecency

tvi *interj* ugh!; pshaw!

tvilling twin **-bror** twin brother **-par** pair of twins **-stjärna** twin (double) star **-syskon** *de är ~* they are twins **-syster** twin sister

tvills *s3* twill

tvina languish; *~ bort, se förtvina*

tving *s2, tekn.* clamp, cramp

tvinga *tvang tvungit, v1* force *(ngn till ngt* s.b. to do s.th.); compel (*till att* to); (*friare äv.*) constrain; (*svagare*) oblige; ~ *fram* extort (*en bekännelse* a confession); ~ *i ngn ngt* force s.b. to eat (drink) s.th.; ~ *i sig ngt* force down s.th.; ~ *på ngn ngt* force s.th. on s.b.; ~ *till sig ngt* obtain s.th. by force **2** *rfl* force o.s. (*till att* to); constrain o.s.; ~ *sig fram* force one's way forward; ~ *sig på ngn* force o.s. on s.b. **tvingande** *a4* imperative (*skäl* reasons); (*trängande*) urgent; (*oemotståndlig*) irresistible; ~ *omständigheter* circumstances over which I (*etc.*) have no control; *utan* ~ *skäl* without urgent (very good) reasons

tvinna twine; twist; (*silke*) throw

tvinsot consumption

tvist *s3* strife, quarrel; (*ordstrid*) dispute, controversy; *ligga i* ~ *med* be at strife (controversy) with; *slita ~en* decide the dispute **tvista** dispute, quarrel (*om* about)

tviste|fråga question (point) at issue, matter (point) in dispute **-frö** seed of dissension, bone of contention **-mål** civil case **-ämne** subject of contention, controversial issue

tvivel ['tvi:-] *s7* doubt; (*betänkligheter*) misgivings (*pl*); *det är* (*råder*) *intet* ~ *om* there is no doubt about; *utan* ~ without any doubt, no doubt, doubtless; *utan allt* ~ beyond all doubt, beyond [all] question **-aktig** *al* doubtful; dubious, questionable (*ära* honour); *det är ~t om* it is doubtful whether

tvivelsmål doubt[s *pl*]; *draga ngt i* ~ call s.th. in question; *sväva i* ~ *om* have doubts [in one's mind] about

tvivl|a [-i:-] ~ *på* doubt, be doubtful about, (*misstro*) mistrust, have no faith in, (*ifrågasätta*) call in question **-ande** *a4* incredulous; sceptical; *ställa sig* ~ *till* doubt, feel dubious about **-are** doubter; sceptic

TV-|kamera TV camera **-mottagare** TV set **-pjäs** television play, teleplay **-program** TV programme **-ruta** TV screen **-studio** TV studio **-sändare** TV transmitter **-sändning** TV transmission (broadcast) **-tittande** viewing **-tittare** viewer

tvungen *a3* **1** (*tvingad*) forced; enforced; *vara* ~ *att* be forced (compelled) to, have to, (*i sht av inre tvång*) be obliged to; *vara så illa* ~ have no other choice, jolly well have to; *vara nödd och* ~ be compelled to **2** *det är en* ~ *sak* it (that) is a matter of necessity **3** (*tillgjord*) forced, constrained (*leende* smile) **tvungit** *sup. av tvinga*

1 två *v4* wash; *jag ~r mina händer* (*bildl.*) I wash my hands of it

2 två räkn two; ~ *och* ~ two and two; *en* ~ *tre stycken* two or three [of them]; *det skall vi bli* ~ *om!* I can put the lid on that!; *kl. halv* ~ at half past one; *jag tar båda* ~ I'll take both [of them] **två|a** *sl* two; (*i spel*) *äv.* deuce; (*lägenhet*) two--room flat, one-bedroom flat; *hon kom* ~ she came [in] second; *~n a*) skol. the second class, *b*) (*bilväxel*) [the] second [gear] **-basisk** *kem.* dibasic **-bent** [-e:-] *a4* two-legged **-bladig** *al* (*om växt*) two-leaved; (*om propeller, kniv e.d.*) two--bladed **-byggare** *bot.* di[o]ecious plant **-cylindrig** *al* twin-cylinder (*motor* engine) **-dela** halve, split; *~d* two-piece (*baddräkt* bathing suit), in two parts **-dimensionell** *al* two-dimensional

-faldig *al* twofold; double **-familjshus** two--family house; *A E.* duplex house **-fas** two-phase **-färgad** two-colour[ed] **-hjulig** [-j-] *al* two--wheel[ed] **-hjuling** [-j-] two-wheeler **-hjärtbladig** *al*, *bot.* dicotyledonous; ~ *växt* dicotyledon **-hundratalet** *på* ~ in the third century **-kammarsystem** bicameral (two-chamber) [parliamentary] system **-krona** two-kronor piece

tvål *s2* soap; *en* ~ *a bar* (cake) of soap

tvål|a ~ *in* soap; lather; ~ *till ngn* crush s.b., deal s.b. a heavy blow **-ask** soap case **-bit** piece of soap

tvåledare two-wire

tvål|fager sleek **-flingor** *pl* soap-flakes **-ig** *al* soapy **-kopp** soap dish **-lödder** soap lather **-lösning** soap solution **-opera** *A E.* soap opera **-vatten** soapy water; soapsuds (*pl*)

två|läppig *al*, *bot.* bilabiate **-mans** for two [men, persons], two-person **-manssäng** double bed **-mastare** two-master **-motorig** *al* twin--engine[d]

tvång *s7* compulsion, coercion, constraint; (*våld*) force; *jur.* duress; *psykol.* compulsion; *det är inte ngt* ~ it is not absolutely necessary; *handla under* ~ act under compulsion (constraint); *rättsstridigt* ~ duress

tvångs|arbete forced (compulsory) labour **-föreställning** obsession **-förflyttning** compulsory transfer **-försäljning** forced (compulsory) sale **-läge** *vara i* ~ be in an emergency situation **-mata** force-feed **-medel** means of coercion **-mässig** *al* compulsive **-neuros** compulsion neurosis **-permittera** lay off **-sparande** compulsory saving **-tanke** obsession **-tröja** straitjacket (*äv. bildl.*) **-uppfostran** reformatory upbringing **-uppfostringsanstalt** reformatory, approved school **-uttagning** *mil.* conscription **-åtgärd** *vidtaga ~er* use coercive measures

två|partiregering two-party government **-procentig** *al* two-percent **-radig 1** two-line[d]; two-row[ed] (*korn* barley); double-breasted (*rock* coat) **-rumslägenhet** two-room[ed] flat, one-bedroom flat **-siffrig** *al* two-figure **-sitsig** *al* two-seat[ed]; *~t flygplan* two-seater **-språkig** *al* bilingual **-stavig** *al* two-syllable[d], dis[s]yllabic **-stegsraket** two-stage rocket **-struken** *mus.* two-line, twice-marked **-stämmig** *al* for two voices, in two parts **-taktsmotor** two--stroke (*A E.* two-cycle) engine **-tiden** *vid* ~ at [about] two [o'clock] **-vingar** *pl, zool.* dipterans **-våningshus** two-storey[ed] house **-vånings-säng** bunk bed **-vägskommunikation** two--way communication **-värd** *kem.* divalent **-årig** *al* two-year-old; (*om växt*) biennial **-åring** child of two **-årsåldern** the age of two **-äggstvilling** fraternal twin **-öring** two-öre piece

tvär I *s, i uttr.: på ~en* across, crosswise; *sätta sig på ~en a*) (*om sak*) get stuck crossways, *b*) (*bildl. om pers.*) turn obstinate (awkward) **II** *al* (*plötslig*) sudden; (*abrupt*) abrupt; (*brant*) steep; (*motsträvig*) refractory; (*vresig*) sullen, blunt, brusque; *göra en* ~ *krök* make a sharp turn; *ett ~t avbrott a*) eg. a sudden break (interruption), *b*) (*skarp kontrast*) a sharp contrast (*mot* to); *ta ett ~t slut* come to a sudden end

tvär|a cross, go across **-balk** crossbeam, stretcher **-brant** precipitous **-bromsa** slam on the brakes, brake suddenly **-gata** cross-street; *ta nästa ~ till höger!* take the next turning to the right! **-gående** *a4* transverse **-hand** hand['s-]breadth **-huggen** *a5* squared; *bildl.* abrupt **-linje** transverse line, cross-line **-mätt** *bli ~* suddenly feel full **-randig** cross-striped, banded **tvärs** across; *~ [för]* (*sjö.*) abeam of; *akter (för) om ~* abaft (before) the beam; *härs och ~, se härs; ~ igenom* right (straight) through; *~ över* straight (right) across; *bo ~ över gatan* live just across the street; *gå ~ över gatan* cross the street **tvär|skepp** *byggn.* transept **-skepps** *adv* athwartships **-slå** crossbar, crosspiece **-snitt** cross section **-stanna** stop dead, come to a dead stop **-stopp** dead stop (halt) **-streck** cross-line; cross stroke (*äv. mus.*) **-säker** absolutely sure, positive; cocksure **-säkerhet** (*självsäkerhet*) cocksureness

tvärt *adv* squarely (*avskuren* cut); (*plötsligt*) abruptly; (*genast*) at once, directly; *svara ~ reply* straight off; *käppen gick ~ av* the stick broke right in two; *bryta ngt ~ av* break s.th. right off; *svara ~ nej* refuse flatly **-emot** quite contrary to; *göra ~* do exactly the opposite of **-om** on the contrary; (*svagare*) on the other hand; *och (eller) ~* and (or) contrariwise (vice versa); *alldeles ~* just the reverse; *det förhåller sig alldeles ~* it is just the other way round; *snarare ~* rather the reverse **tvär|tystna** become suddenly silent **-vetenskaplig** interdisciplinary, multidisciplinary **-vigg** *s2* contrary person; *vard.* crosspatch **-vägg** transverse wall

tvätt *s2* wash[ing]; (*kläder t. ~*) laundry; *kemisk ~* dry-cleaning, (*-inrättning*) dry-cleaners; *~ och strykning* washing and ironing; *är på ~* is in the wash (*-inrättningen:* at the laundry); *gå bort i ~en* wash out; *skicka bort ~en* send the washing to the laundry

tvätt|a wash; (*rengöra*) clean (*fönsterna* the windows); *~ kemiskt* dry-clean; *~ åt ngn* do a p.'s washing; *~ bort* wash away; *jag måste ~ upp litet kläder* I must wash out a few clothes; *~ sig* wash [o.s.], have a wash, *AE.* wash up; *~ sig om händerna* wash one's hands **-anvisningar** *pl* washing intstructions **-balja** washtub **-bar** *a1* washable **-björn** [North American[rac[c]oon **-bräde** washboard **-eri** laundry **-erska** laundress; (*förr*) washerwoman **-fat** washbasin; *AE. äv.* washbowl **-gryta** washboiler, copper **-inrättning** laundry; *kemisk ~* dry-cleaning establishment **-kläder** *pl* laundry, washing (*sg*), dirty linen **-korg** clothes basket **-lapp** [face] flannel (cloth); *AE.* washcloth, washrag **-maskin** washing machine **-medel** washing detergent (agent, powder), detergent **-ning** washing **-nota** laundry list **-omat** launderette, *AE.* laundromat (*varumärken*) **-pulver** washing powder **-rum** washroom, lavatory **-siden** washing silk **-skinnshandske** wash-leather glove **-stuga** (*rum*) laundry **-ställ** washstand, (*väggfast*) washbasin **-svamp** [bath] sponge **-säck** laundry bag **-vante** washing glove **-vatten** washing water; (*använt*) dirty water, slops (*pl*) **-äkta** washable, washproof; (*om färg*) fast; *bildl.* authentic; (*inbi-*

ten) out-and-out

TV-övervakning [closed-circuit] TV monitoring

1 ty *konj* for; because

2 ty *v4, rfl, ~ sig till* turn to

tyck|a *v3* **1** think (*om* about; *att* that); (*anse äv.*) be of the opinion (*att* that); *det -er jag (äv.)* that's what I think; *säg vad du -er!* tell us your opinion!; *han säger vad han -er (sin mening)* he says what he thinks; *jag -er nog att* I really (do) think; *vad -er du om ...?* what do you think of ...?; *han -er att han är någonting* he thinks a great deal of himself; *som du -er!* as you please!; *du -er väl inte illa vara att jag* I hope you don't mind my (+ *ing-form*); *~ sig höra* think (imagine, fancy) that one hears; *~ sig vara* think that one is, imagine o.s. to be **2** *~ om* like (*starkare:* be fond of) (*att läsa* reading); *jag -er rätt bra om* I quite like; *jag -er mycket om* I like very much; *jag -er illa om (äv.)* I dislike; *jag -er mer om ... än ...* I like ... better than ..., I prefer ... to ...

tyck|as *v3, dep* seem; *det kan ~ så* it may seem so; *det -s mig som om* it seems to me as if; *vad -s?* what do you think (say)?

tyck|e *s6* **1** (*åsikt*) opinion; *i mitt ~* to my way of thinking, in my opinion **2** (*böjelse*) inclination, fancy (*för* for); (*smak*) liking; *fatta ~ för* take a liking (fancy) to; *om ~ och smak skall man inte tvista* (*ung.*) that's a matter of taste; *efter mitt ~* according to my taste **3** (*likhet*) likeness, resemblance; *han har ~ av sin far* he bears a resemblance to his father **-mycken** *a3* fastidious; touchy

tyd|a *v3* **1** (*tolka*) interpret; (*ut-*) decipher, solve; (*förklara*) explain; *~ allt till det bästa* put the best construction on everything; *hur skall man ~ (uppfatta) detta?* how should one take this? **2** *~ på* indicate (*att* that; *gott omdöme* good judgement), point to, suggest; *allt -er på att han* everything points to his (+ *ing-form*)

tydbar [-y:-] *a1* interpretable **tydlig** *a1* (*lätt att se*) plain, clear, sharp; (*markerad*) marked, pronounced; (*distinkt*) distinct; (*påtaglig*) obvious, apparent, evident; *~a bevis på* distinct proofs of; *~ bild* sharp picture; *~ handstil* legible (fair) hand; *i ~a ordalag* in plain terms; *det är ~t att* it is obvious (evident) that; *ha ett ~t minne av* have a distinct remembrance of; *talar sitt ~a språk* speaks for itself; *undergå en ~ förbättring* improve noticeably **tydligen** evidently, obviously, apparently **tydlighet** plainness *etc.; med all önskvärd ~* leaving no room for doubt **tydligt** *adv* (*skriva, tala etc.*) plainly, distinctly; (*uttrycka sig*) clearly; *vilket ~ framgår av* as is plain from **tydligtvis** *se tydligen* **tydning** interpretation; decipherment, solution **tydningsförsök** attempt at interpretation

tyfoidfeber [-ˣi:d-] typhoid fever

tyfon [-'få:n] *s3* typhoon

tyfus ['ty:-] *s2* (*fläckfeber*) typhus [fever]

1 tyg *s7, s4* (*vävnad*) material (*till* for); cloth, stuff; *i sht hand.* fabric; *~er* textiles

2 tyg 1 *i uttr.: allt vad ~en håller* (*med all kraft*) for all one is worth, (*i full fart*) at top speed **2** *s7, mil.* ordnance

tyg|blomma cloth flower **-bredd** width of cloth **tyg|el** *s2* rein; bridle; *bildl. äv.* check; *ge hästen* *lösa -lar* give the horse a free rein; *ge sin fantasi fria (lösa) -lar* give [a free] rein to one's imagination; *med lösa -lar* with slack reins

tygellös *bildl.* (*otyglad*) unbridled; (*om liv, pers.*) dissolute, licentious; (*om levnadssätt äv.*) loose, wild **-het** unbridled behaviour; licentiousness *etc.*

tyg|förråd ordnance depot **-förvaltare** *ung.* ordnance officer **-hus** arsenal, armoury

tygknapp covered button

tygla [ˣty:g-] rein [in]; *bildl.* bridle; (*betvinga*) restrain, check; *~ sig* restrain o.s.

tyg|packe bale of cloth **-sko** cloth shoe **-stycke** piece of cloth; (*rulle äv.*) roll of cloth

tykobrahedag [-ˣbra:-] *ung.* black-letter day

tyll *s3, s4* tulle; net

tymus *se* thymus

tyna languish, pine, fade (*bort* away)

tyng|a *v2* **1** (*vara tung*) weigh (*på* [up]on); (*kännas tung*) be (feel) heavy (*på* to); (*trycka*) press (*på* [up]on **2** (*plåga*) weigh down; *det -er mitt sinne* it preys on me (on my mind) **3** (*belasta*) weight (*med* with); burden, load (*minnet med* one's memory with) **-ande** *a4* heavy; weighty; *bildl. äv.* burdensome

tyngd *a5* weighed down (*av sorg* by grief) **II** *s3* weight (*äv. konkr.*); load; *fys.* gravity; *en ~ har fallit från mitt bröst* a weight (load) has dropped off my mind; *ge ~ åt ett argument* give weight to an argument **-kraft** *~en* [the force of] gravity (gravitation) **-lagen** the law of gravitation **-lyftare** weightlifter **-lyftning** weightlifting **-lös** weightless **-löshet** weightlessness **-punkt** centre of gravity; *bildl.* main (crucial, central) point (*i* in)

tyngre [ˈtyŋ-] **I** *a, komp. t. tung.* heavier *etc.* (*jfr tung*); *~ fordon (pl)* heavy-duty vehicles **II** *adv* more heavily **tyngst I** *a, superl. t. tung* heaviest *etc.* (*jfr tung*) **II** *adv* most heavily

typ *s3* **1** *boktr.* type; *fet (halvfet) ~* boldface[d] (semibold) type **2** (*sort*) type; model; *han är en för en lärare* he's a typical teacher; *han är inte min ~* he's not my type **typa** (*fastställa typen av*) type **typ|arm** typebar **-exempel** typical example, case in point **-fall** typical case **-huvud** [type]face **-isk** [ˈty:-] *a5* typical, representative (*för* of)

typo|graf *s3* typographer **-grafi** *s3* typography **-grafisk** [-ˈgra:-] *a5* typographical **-logi** *s3* typology

typsnitt [type]face

tyrann *s3* tyrant **-i** *s4* tyranny **-isera** tyrannize over; (*friare*) domineer over **-isk** *a5* tyrannical; (*friare äv.*) domineering

tyristor [-ˣriss-] thyristor

tyrolare [-ˣrå:-] Tyrolese, Tyrolean **Tyrolen** [-ˈrå:-] the Tyrol (Tirol) **tyrolerhatt** [-ˣrå:-] Tyrolese hat **tyrolsk** [-å:-] *a5* Tyrolese, Tyrolean

tysk I *a1* German; *T~a Riket* the German Empire, (*1918-45*) the Reich **II** *s2* German **tysk|a** *s1* **1** (*språk*) German **2** (*kvinna*) German woman **-fientlig** anti-German

Tyskland [ˈtysk-] *n* Germany

tyskvänlig pro-German

tyst I *a1* silent; still; (*lugn*) quiet; (*ljudlös*) noiseless; (*outtalad*) tacit, mute; *~ förbehåll* mental reservation; *hålla sig ~* keep quiet (silent); *han är inte ~ ett ögonblick* he can't keep silent (quiet) for a moment; *var ~!* be quiet!, silence!; *i det ~a* on the quiet, in a quiet way **II** *adv* silently; quietly, in silence; *håll ~!* keep quiet!; *hålla ~ med ngt* keep s.th. quiet; *det skall vi tala ~ om (vard.)* the less said about that, the better **tysta** silence; *~ munnen på ngn* stop a p.'s mouth, make s.b. hold his tongue; *~ ner a) (ngn)* [reduce … to] silence, *b) (ngt, bildl.)* suppress, hush up; *låt maten ~ mun (munnen)* don't talk while you're eating

tyst|gående *a4* noiseless, silent[-running] **-het** silence; quietness; (*hemlighet*) secrecy; *i [all] ~* in secrecy, secretly, privately; *i största ~* in the utmost secrecy **-hetslöfte** pledge (promise) of secrecy **-låten** *a3* aciturn; silent; (*förtegen*) reticent; (*hemlighetsfull*) secretive **-låtenhet** taciturnity; silence; reticency; secretiveness

tystna become silent; (*om ljud äv.*) cease, stop **tystnad** *s3* silence; *djup (obrottslig) ~* profound (strict) silence; *bringa ngn till ~* reduce s.b. to silence, silence s.b.; *förbigå ngt med ~* pass s.th. over in silence; *under ~* in silence; *ålägga ngn ~* enjoin silence [up]on s.b. **tystnadsplikt** obligation to observe silence; (*läkares äv.*) professional secrecy; *bryta sin ~* commit a breach of professional secrecy

tyvärr unfortunately; (*som interj äv.*) alas!; *jag kan ~ inte komma* I am sorry [to say] I can't come; *~ måste vi meddela att* we regret to inform you that; *~ inte* I am afraid not

tå *s5* toe; *gå på ~* walk on one's toes (on tiptoe); *skorna är trånga i ~rna* my (*etc.*) shoes pinch at the toes; *stå på ~ för ngn (bildl.)* be at a p.'s beck and call; *trampa ngn på ~rna (äv. bildl.)* tread on a p.'s toes **-flört** *vard.* footsie **-flörta** *vard.* play footsie

1 tåg *s7* (*rep*) rope

2 tåg *s7* **1** (*marsch*) march[ing]; *mil. äv.* expedition; (*fest- o.d.*) procession **2** (*järnvägs-*) train; *~et går kl. 2* the train leaves at two o'clock; *byta ~* change trains; *när kommer ~et?* when will the train be in (is the train due)?; *med ~[et]* by train; *på ~et* on the train; *~ till London* train[s *pl*] for London; *ta ~et till* take the (go by) train to

1 tåga *s1* (*fiber*) filament, thread; *bildl.* nerve, sinew; *det är ~ i honom* he is tough

2 tåga *v1* march; walk in procession; *~ mot fienden* march against the enemy; *~ fram* march along

tåg|attentat train outrage **-biljett** railway ticket **-färja** train ferry **-förbindelse** train service (connection); *ha bra ~r med* have an excellent train service to and from **-klarerare** [train] dispatcher **-konduktör** [train] guard; *AE.* conductor **-kupé** compartment **-ledes** by train **-luffa** travel on an interrail card **-luffare** traveller with an interrail card **-olycka** railway accident **-ombyte** change of trains **-ordning** marching order; *bildl.* slow bureaucratic procedure, red tape **-personal** train staff **-resa** train journey **-sätt** *ett ~ av 10 vagnar* a train of ten carriages (coaches) **-tid** *~er* train times **-tidtabell** railway timetable (*AE.* schedule) **-trafik** train service, railway traffic **-urspåring** derailment [of a train]

tågvirke cordage; ropes (*pl*)
tål|gångare *zool.* ~ (*pl*) digitigrades **-hätta** toecap **-hävning** [-ä:-] heel-raising **-järn** (*på sko*) toe plate
tål|a *v2* bear, endure; (*stå ut med*) stand; (*lida*) suffer, put up with; *han tål inte att ngn avbryter honom* he can't stand anyone['s] interrupting him; *jag tål henne inte* I can't stand (bear) her; *han tål inte skämt* he can't take a joke; *jag tål inte jordgubbar* strawberries upset (don't agree with) me; *han har fått vad han tål a*) (*av sprit e.d.*) he has had as much as he can stand, *b*) (*av stryk e.d.*) he has had all he can bear; *det tål att tänka på* it is worth consideration; *illa -d av* in bad favour with; *bör inte ~s* should not be tolerated
tålamod *s7* patience; *ha ~* have patience, be patient; *ha ~ med* be patient with, bear with; *förlora ~et* lose [one's] patience; *mitt ~ är slut* my patience is exhausted; *sätta ngns ~ på [hårt] prov* try a p.'s patience [severely]
tålamods|prov *ett riktigt ~* a real trial to one's patience **-prövande** *a4* trying [to one's patience]
tålig *a1* patient **-het** patience
tålmodig patient; (*långmodig*) long-suffering **-het** patience; long-suffering
tåls [-å:-] *i uttr.: ge sig till ~* have patience, be patient
tånagel toenail
1 tång *s3* (*växt*) seaweed; (*blås-*) rockweed
2 tång *-en tänger* (*verktyg*) tongs (*pl*); pliers, pincers, nippers (*pl*); *kir.* forceps; *en ~* (*två tänger*) a pair (two pairs) of tongs (*etc.*); *den vill jag inte ta i med ~* I wouldn't touch it with a bargepole
tångförlossning forceps delivery
tår *s2* **1** tear; *brista i (fälla) ~ar* burst into (shed) tears; *jag fick ~ar i ögonen* tears came into my eyes **2** (*skvätt*) drop; *ta sig en ~ på tand* have a drop [of brandy (*etc.*)] **-ad** *a5* filled with tears **-as** *dep* fill with tears; (*av blåst o.d.*) water
tår|drypande *a4* maudlin, sentimental **-dränkt** *a4* tearful **-eflod** stream of tears **-flöde** flood (torrent) of tears **-fylld** filled with tears; (*om blick, röst*) tearful **-gas** tear gas **-kanal** lacrimal (tear) duct **-körtel** lacrimal (tear) gland **-pil** *bot.* weeping willow
tårt|a [*tå:r-] *s1* cake, gâteau; (*mördegs-, smördegs- äv.*) tart; *~ på ~* the same thing twice over **-bit** piece of cake **-kartong** cake carton **-papper** cake doily **-spade** cake slice
tårögd *a1* with tears in one's eyes, with eyes filled with tears
tåspets tip of a (the, one's) toe **-dans** toe dance **-dansös** toe dancer
tåt *s2* piece (bit) of string (*grövre:* cord)
täck *a1* pretty; *det ~a könet* the fair sex
täck|a *v3* cover (*med* with); *eg. bet. äv.* coat; *trädg. äv.* cover over (up); (*skydda*) protect (*äv. växel*); *~ sina behov* supply (cover) one's needs; *~ en förlust* meet (cover) a loss; *-t bil* closed car **-ande** *s6* covering *etc.*; *till ~ av kostnaderna* to cover (defray) costs
täck|as *v3, dep* (*behaga*) *ni -[t]es erinra er* please be good enough to remember
täck|blad (*på cigarr*) wrapper **-dika** drain **-dike** covered drain **-dikning** underdrainage, pipe draining
täck|e *s6* cover[ing], coating; (*säng-*) [bed] quilt, *AE. äv.* comforter; (*skynke*) cloth; *spela under ~*[*t*] *med* (*bildl.*) be in collusion with **-else** cover[ing]; *dra ett ~ över* draw a veil over; *låta ~t falla* unveil, *bildl.* reveal, disclose **-färg** finishing (top) coat
täckhet prettiness
täck|jacka quilted jacket **-mantel** *under vänskapens ~* under the cloak (guise, veil) of friendship, under cover of friendship **-namn** assumed name **-ning** covering *etc.*; *hand.* cover (*för en check* for a cheque); (*skydd*) protection; *check utan ~* uncovered cheque; *till ~ av* in cover of, covering; *till ~ av vår faktura* in payment of our invoice **-vinge** wing sheath, shard **-vitt** lithopone
tälja *v2* ([*till*]*skära*) carve, whittle, cut
täljare *mat.* numerator
tälj|kniv (*slid-*) sheath knife; (*fäll-*) jackknife **-sten** soapstone, soaprock
tält *s7* tent **tälta** (*slå upp tält*) pitch one's tent **2** (*bo i tält*) tent; camp (be camping) [out]
tält|duk canvas **-läger** camp **-makare** tentmaker **-pinne** tent peg **-stol** camp stool **-säng** camp bed
täm|ja *v2, -de -t -d* tame; domesticate; *bildl.* curb, harness
tämligen tolerably; fairly; (*vanl. gillande*) pretty; (*vanl. ogillande*) rather; *~ bra* pretty well, [fairly] tolerable, well enough; *det är ~ likgiltigt* it makes little difference; *det blev ~ sent* it was rather (pretty) late
tänd|a *v2* **1** (*få att brinna*) light (*äv. bildl.*); (*elektr. ljus*) turn (switch) on; *tekn.* ignite, fire; *bildl. äv.* kindle; *~ [belysningen]* light up; *~ [eld] på* set fire to, set … on fire; *~ i spisen* make a fire; *stå som ~a ljus* stand like statues; *hoppet -es på nytt* the spark of hope revived **2** (*fatta eld*) ignite, catch fire; light (*lätt readily*); (*om motor*) spark, fire; *bildl., vard., ~ på ngn* (*ngt*) get turned on by s.b. (s.th.); *hon -e på honom* he turned her on
tänd|ande *a4* lighting *etc.*; *den ~ gnistan* the igniting spark **-apparat** igniter, firing device; (*vid sprängning*) blasting machine **-are** (*cigarett- o.d.*) lighter **-gnista** ignition spark **-hatt** detonator, percussion (blasting) cap **-kulemotor** compression-ignition (ignition bulb) engine **-ning** lighting *etc.*; *tekn.* ignition; *hög ~* advanced spark; *justera ~en* adjust the ignition timing **-ningslås** ignition lock **-[nings]nyckel** ignition key **-ordning** (*i motor*) firing order **-sats** (*i tändmedel*) detonating composition, fuse body; (*på tändsticka*) head **-sticka** match; *tända en ~* strike a match **-sticksask** (*tom*) matchbox; (*med tändstickor i*) box of matches **-sticksfabrik** match factory **-stift** (*i motor*) sparking (*AE.* spark) plug; (*i vapen*) firing pin **-stiftskabel** ignition wire
tänj|a *v2* stretch; *~ ut* stretch; *bildl.* draw out, prolong; *~ ut sig* stretch; *~ på en princip* stretch a principle **-bar** *a1* stretchable; *tekn.* tensile, tensible; (*elastisk*) elastic
tänk|a *v3* **1** think (*högt* aloud; *på* of, about; *väl om ngn* well of s.b.); (*fundera äv.*) meditate; (*förmoda*) suppose; (*föreställa sig*) imagine; ~

olika om hold divergent opinions about; ~ *själv* think for o.s.; ~ *för sig själv* think to o.s.; *säga vad man -er (äv.)* speak one's mind; *tänk först och tala sedan!* look before you leap!; *tänk om jag skulle ...!* supposing (what if) I should ...!; *tänk ...! a) (som utrop)* to think *(att jag är färdig* [that] I am ready), *b) (betänk)* think ...!, *c) (tänk efter)* reflect ...!; *ja (nej) tänk!* [oh], I say!; *det var det jag -te!* just as I thought!; *den är dyr, kan jag ~* it is expensive, I shouldn't wonder; ~ *på att* think of, reflect upon (+ ing-form); *ha mycket att ~ på* have a great deal to think about; *jag kom att ~ på att* the thought occurred to me that; *det vore ngt att ~ på* that's [a thing] quite worth considering; *när jag -er rätt på saken* when I come to think of it; *det är inte att ~ på* there's no thinking of that, that is out of the question; *jag skall ~ på saken* I will think it (the matter) over **2** *(med betonad partikel)* ~ *efter* think, reflect, consider; *tänk noga efter!* think [it over] carefully!; *när man -er efter (äv.)* when one comes to think of it; ~ *igenom* think ... out; ~ *ut* think out, *(plan e.d.)* devise; ~ *över* think over, consider **3** *(ämna)* intend (mean, be going; *AE. äv.* aim) to; *(anse)* consider; *vad -er du om det?* what do you think (is your opinion) of that? **4** *rfl (föreställa sig)* imagine, fancy; *(ämna [begiva] sig)* think of going [to]; *jag har -t mig att* my idea is that, I have thought that; *kan du ~ dig vad som ...?* can you imagine what ...?; *det kunde jag just ~ mig!* I might have known that (as much)!; *kan man ~ sig!* well, I never!; *det låter ~ sig* that's very possible; ~ *sig för* think a (the) matter over; *du bör ~ dig för två gånger* you should think twice; ~ *sig in i* imagine ... to o.s.; *vart har du -t dig?* where have you thought of going [to]?

tänk|ande I *s6* thinking *etc.*; *(begrundan)* meditation, reflection **II** *a4* thinking, reflective; *en ~ människa* a thoughtful (reflecting) person **-are** thinker; *filos.* speculator **-bar** *a1* conceivable, thinkable; *(friare)* imaginable; *bästa ~a* the best possible; *i högsta ~a grad* to the highest degree imaginable; *den enda ~a* the only conceivable

tänke|språk adage, proverb **-sätt** way of thinking; *(friare)* turn of mind, way of looking at things

tänk|t *a4* thought *etc.*; *(ej verklig)* imagined *(situation* situation); imaginary *(linje* line); *det var inte så dumt ~ [av dig]!* that was not such a bad idea [of yours]! **-värd** *a1* worth considering (taking into consideration); *(minnesvärd)* memorable

täpp|a I *s1 (land)* garden plot (patch); *vara herre på ~n* rule (be cock of the) roost **II** *v3* ~ *[för, igen, till]* stop up, obstruct; *jag är -t i näsan* my nose feels stopped (stuffed) up; ~ *munnen på ngn (bildl.)* shut a p.'s mouth; *-t* stopped-up, choked-up

tära *v2* consume; ~ *på* waste [... away], reduce [... in bulk], *(förbruka)* use up; ~ *på reserverna* draw on the reserves; *sorgen tär på henne* sorrow is preying [up]on her **tärande** *a4* consuming, wasting *(sjukdom* illness); wearing *(bekymmer* anxiety) **tärd** [-ä:-] *a1* worn, wasted *(av* by); *se ~ ut (äv.)* look haggard; ~ *av bekymmer (äv.)* careworn

1 tärna [ˣtä:r-] *s1 (brud-)* bridesmaid; *poet.* maid

[en]

2 tärna [ˣtä:r-] *s1 (fågel)* tern, sea swallow

tärning [ˣtä:r-] **1** die *(pl* dice); *falska ~ar* loaded (weighted) dice; *~en är kastad (bildl.)* the die is cast **2** *geom.* cube

tärnings|kast throw of a die (the dice) **-spel** game of dice; dice-playing

1 tät *s3* head; *gå i ~en för* walk *(friare:* place o.s.) at the head of

2 tät *a1* **1** *(motsats gles)* close; *(svårgenomträng- lig o.d.)* thick, dense; *(kompakt)* compact, massive; *(utan springor e.d.)* tight **2** *(som ofta före- kommer)* frequent *(besök* visits), repeated **3** *(rik)* well-to-do

täta *v1* tighten, make tight; *(stoppa till)* stop [up] *(en läcka* a leak); *(hermetiskt)* seal; *sjö.* caulk; *tekn.* pack

tätatät *s3* tête-à-tête

tät|bebyggd *a5* densely built-up **-befolkad** [-å-] *a5* densely populated **-het** [-ä:-] **1** *(vävs e.d.)* closeness; *(skogs e.d.)* density, denseness; *(ogenomtränglighet)* impenetrability; *fys.* density **2** frequency

tät|na [-ä:-] become (get, grow) dense (compact); *(om rök e.d.)* thicken **-ning** [-ä:-] tightening; *(packning)* packing

tätnings|bricka grommet **-list** *(för fönster e.d.)* weather strip, strip seal; *(mot drag äv.)* draught- -excluder

tät|ort [densely] built-up area, densely populated area **-ortsbebyggelse** city (town) buildings *(pl)* **-skriven** *a3* closely written

tätt *adv* **1** closely; densely; *hålla ~* be watertight, *bildl.* keep quiet (close); *locket sluter ~* the lid fits tight; *husen ligger ~* the houses stand close together; ~ *åtsittande* tight[-fitting], skintight; ~ *ef- ter* close behind; ~ *intill a)* adv close to, *b)* prep close up to **2** frequently, repeatedly; *breven dug- gade ~* the letters came thick and fast **-be- byggd, -befolkad** se tätbebyggd, tätbefolkad

tätting passerine

tätt|skriven se tätskriven **-slutande** *a4* tight[- fitting]

tätört butterwort

tävla [ˣtä:v-] compete *(med* with; *om* for); *han har slutat* ~ he doesn't enter competitions any more; *de ~de med varandra om priset* they competed for the prize; *skall vi ~ om vem som kom- mer först?* shall we race to see who comes first?; *de ~de om att säga henne artigheter* they vied with each other in paying her compliments; *det här märket kan ~ med* this brand can stand compari- son with; ~ *om makten* strive (struggle) for [the] power **tävlan** *r, som pl används tävlingar* com- petition *(i* in; *om* for); rivalry, emulation; *ädel ~* honourable rivalry; *delta utom ~* take part with- out competing for a prize **tävlande** *s6* compet- ing *etc.* **II** *a4* competing *etc.*; *(en ~)* competitor, *(löpare)* runner, *(i bridge e.d.)* tournament player **tävling** competition; contest; *AE. äv.* bee; *sport. äv. (löpning)* race, *(match)* match

tävlings|bana tournament ground; *(löpar-)* racetrack; *(kapplöpnings-)* racecourse **-bil** racing car, racer **-bidrag** entry; answer, solution **-do- mare** adjudicator, judge **-förare** racing driver **-regler** *pl* rules of (for) the competition (game)

-**uppgift** problem (subject) for a prize competition
tö s6 thaw **töa** thaw; ~ *bort* thaw [away]; ~ *upp* thaw (*äv. bildl.*)
töcken ['tökk-] s7 haze, mist; *höljd i* ~ shrouded (veiled) in mist, misty, hazy **-gestalt** vague figure
töcknig a1 hazy, misty
töff puff **töffa** puff
töj|**a** [ˣtöjja] v2 stretch; ~ *ut* stretch out, extend; ~ *sig* stretch **-bar** a1 stretchable; extensible **-ning** stretching; extension
tölp s2 boor; (*drummel*) lout **-aktig** a1, **-ig** a1 boorish, loutish
töm [tömm] s2 rein
töm|**ma** v2 **1** (*göra tom*) empty [out] (*i* into; *på* on [to]); (*dricka ur äv.*) drain; (*brevlåda*) clear; ~ *lidandets kalk* drain the cup of suffering; *salen -des hastigt* the hall emptied (was cleared [of people]) quickly **2** (*hälla*) pour [out] (*på flaskor* into bottles) **-ning** emptying [out] *etc.*; (*av brevlåda*) collection; (*tarmens*) evacuation; (*tappning*) pouring [out] **-ningstid** *post.* time of collection
tönt s2, *sl.* jerk, dope **-ig** a1 awkward, clumsy
tör *det* ~ *dröja innan* it will probably be some time before
tör|**as** *tordes* torts (*vard. äv. inf.: tordas, sup.: tordats*) dep dare; *hon -s inte för sin mor* she doesn't dare because of her mother; *jag -s inte* säga I'm afraid to say, (*friare*) I can't tell exactly; *om jag -s fråga* if I may ask; *jag -s lova mitt liv på det* I'd stake my life on it
törhända [-ˣhänn-] *se* måhända
törn [-ö:-] s2 **1** (*stöt*) blow, bump; *bildl.* shock; *ta* ~ (*sjö.*) bear off **2** *sjö.* (*arbetsskift*) watch; *ha* ~ have the watch **törna** ~ *emot* strike, bump into, *absol.* strike, make a bump; ~ *emot ngn* come into collision with s.b.; ~ *in* (*sjö.*) turn in
törn|**beströdd** a5, *bildl.* thorny **-bevuxen** overgrown with thorns **-buske** *se* törne 1
törne s6 **1** (*buske*) thorn bush; (*vildros*) wild rose **2** (*tagg*) thorn; *ingen ros utan* ~*n* no rose without a thorn **-krona** crown of thorns **-krönt** [-ö:-] a4 crowned with thorns **-stig** *bildl.* thorny path
törn|**ig** a1 thorny (*äv. bildl.*) **-ros** rose (*jfr* törne 1)
Törnrosa [-ˣro:-] the Sleeping Beauty
törn|**rosasömn** *bildl.* slumber, trance; sleep of the ages **-rosbuske** *se* törne 1 **-skata** redbacked shrike; *koll.* butcherbird **-snår** thornbrake, briery thicket **-tagg** thorn, prickle
törst s3 thirst; (*längtan*) longing (*efter* for); *dö av* ~ die of thirst **törsta** thirst (*efter* for); ~ *efter hämnd* thirst for vengeance; ~ *ihjäl* die of thirst
törstig a1 thirsty
tös s3 girl, lass[ie]
töva *se* dröja
töväder thaw; *det är* ~ a thaw has set in

U-balk channel [iron], U-iron
ubåt submarine; (*tysk*) U-boat
ubåts|**bas** s3 submarine base **-fara** submarine menace **-fälla** decoy ship **-jagare** submarine chaser **-krig** submarine war[fare]
U.D. [ˣu:de:] *förk. för utrikesdepartementet*
udd s2 (*skarp spets*) [sharp] point; (*på gaffel o.d.*) prong; (*flik av tyg e.d.*) point, jag, (*rundad*) scallop; *bildl.* point, pungency; *satirens* ~ the sting of satire; *bryta* ~*en av* (*bildl.*) turn the edge of; *med* ~ *mot* (*bildl.*) directed against
udda *oböjligt* a **1** (*om tal*) odd, uneven; *låta* ~ *vara jämnt* let s.th. pass **2** (*omaka*) odd; ~ *varor* (*äv.*) oddments
udde s2 cape; point; (*hög*) promontory
udd|**ig** a1 pointed; (*rundad*) scalloped **-ljud** *språkv.* initial sound **-lös** pointless (*äv. bildl.*)
ufo ['u:fo] s6 UFO (*förk. för unidentified flying object*) **-log** ufologist **-logi** ufology
ugand|**ier** [-'gann-] s9, **-isk** a5 Ugandan
uggl|**a** s1 owl; *det är -or i mossen* there is mischief brewing, something is up
uggle|**skri** owl's hoot; tu-whit tu-whoo **-unge** owlet, young owl
ugn [uŋn] s2 furnace; (*bak-*) oven; (*bränn-, tork-*) kiln
ugns|**bakad** a5 baked, roasted **-eldfast** ovenproof, heat-resisting **-lackera** stove enamel **-lucka** furnace (*etc.*) door **-pannkaka** batter pudding **-raka** oven rake **-steka** roast; (*potatis o.d.*) bake; *-stekt* roast[ed], baked **-svärta** stove polish (black) **-torka** oven (kiln) dry; bake (*tegel* bricks)
u-hjälp aid to developing countries
ukas s3 ukase
Ukraina [-ˣkrajj-] *n* [the] Ukraine **ukrain**|**are** [uˣkrajj-] s9, **-sk** a5 Ukrainian
ukulele [-ˣle:-] s5 ukulele
u-land developing country
ulk s2 bullhead
ull s3 wool; (*kamel-, get- äv.*) hair; *av* ~ of wool, woollen; *ny* ~ virgin wool; *han är inte av den* ~*en* he is not that sort (kind of man) **-fett** wool fat (grease) **-garn** wool[en yarn]; (*kamgarn*) worsted yarn **-ig** a1 woolly, fleecy; ~*a moln* fleecy clouds **-karda** wool card **-marknad** wool market **-strumpa** *se* yllesstrumpa; *gå på i -strumporna* go straight ahead **-tapp, -tott** tuft (flock) of wool
ulster ['uls-] s2 ulster
ultim|**ativ** [-'ti:v, 'ult-] a1 imperative; indispensable **-atum** [-ˣma:-] s8 ultimatum; *ställa* ~ present an ultimatum
ultimo ['ull-] s6 the last day of the month
ultra ultra **-konservativ** ultraconservative **-kortvåg** ultrashort wave **-ljud** ultrasonic (supersonic) sound **-marin I** a1 ultramarine **II** s3 ultramarine **-modern** ultramodern **-radikal** ul-

U

traradical, extreme radical **-rapid** *a1, n sg obest.
form undviks* slow-motion; *i ~* in slow-motion
-röd infrared, ultrared **-violett** ultraviolet
ulv *s2* wolf; *en ~ i fårakläder* a wolf in sheep's
clothing; *man måste tjuta med ~arna* one must
cry with the pack
umbra *s9* umber
umbär|a *nästan endast i inf.* do (go) without
-ande *s6* privation, hardship; deprivation **-lig**
[-ä:-] *a1* dispensable
umgicks [-j-] *imperf. av umgås* **umgås** *umgicks
umgåtts, dep* **1** (*vara tillsammans*) associate,
keep company; (*besöka*) be a frequent (regular)
visitor (*hos* at a p.'s house); *de ~ mycket med varandra* they see a great deal of each other; *~ i de
högre kretsarna* move in exalted circles; *ha lätt att
~ med folk* (*äv.*) be a good mixer; *de ~ inte* they
have nothing to do with one another **2** *~ med
planer på att* have plans to (+ *inf*), contemplate
(+ *ing-form*) **3** (*handskas*) *~ med* handle **-gåtts**
sup. av umgås
um|gälla [-j-] *v2* pay for; *få ~* suffer (smart) for
-gänge [-jäŋe] *s6* (*samvaro*) intercourse; (*pers.
man umgås med*) company, society; *ha stort ~*
have a large circle of friends; *sexuellt ~* sexual intercourse
umgänges|former forms of [social] intercourse
-krets [circle of] friends and acquaintances **-liv**
social life **-rätt** right of parental access **-sätt**
manners (*pl*) [in company]
undan I *adv* **1** (*bort*) away; (*ur vägen*) out of the
way (*för* of); (*åt sidan*) aside (*för ngn* for s.b.);
komma ~ get off, escape; *lägga ~* put away **2**
(*fort*) fast, rapidly; *det gick ~ i backen* we (*etc.*)
whizzed down the hill; *det går ~ med arbetet* work
is getting on fine **3** *~ för ~* little by little, one by
one **II** *prep* (*bort från*) from; *fly ~ förföljarna* run
away from the persecutors; *söka skydd ~ regnet*
take shelter from the rain
undan|bad *imperf. av undanbe[dja]* **-be[dja]**
[-e:-] *-bad - bett, rfl* decline, not seek (*återval* re-
election); *jag -ber mig* kindly spare me **-bedjas**
[-e:-] *-bads -betts, dep, rökning -bedes* please refrain from smoking; *blommor -bedes* no flowers
by request **-bett** *sup. av undanbedja* **-dra[ga]**
withdraw (*ngn ngt* s.th. from s.b.); (*beröva*) deprive (*ngn ngt* s.b. of s.th.); *~ sig* shirk, elude,
evade (*ansvar* responsibility; *straff* punishment);
det -drar sig mitt bedömande it is beyond my
power to judge **-dragande** *s6* evasion, withdrawal **-dräkt** *s3, jur.* petty embezzlement
-flykt evasion; subterfuge; prevarication, excuse; *komma med ~er* make excuses, prevaricate
excuses **-gjord** *a5* done, ready; over [and done
with] **-glidande** *a4, bildl.* evasive **-gömd** [-j-]
a5 concealed, hidden away; (*om plats*) secluded,
out-of-the-way **-hålla** withhold (*ngn ngt* s.th.
from s.b.), keep back; *~ sanningen* conceal the
truth **-manöver** evasion action **-röja** remove;
(*upphäva*) set aside **-röjning** clearance, removal
-skaffa remove, get out of the way **-skymd**
[-ʃ-] *a5* hidden, concealed; remote (*vrå* corner)
-stuvad *a5* stowed away **-stökad** *a5* finished
and done with
undan|ta *se undantaga* **-tag** *s7* exception (*från
from*, to); *~et bekräftar regeln* the exception

proves the rule; *ingen regel utan ~* [there is] no
rule without an exception; *med ~ av* (*för*) with
the exception of, except for, ... excepted; *utan ~
without* [an, any] exception; *sätta på undantag* set
aside **-taga** exempt from, except; (*göra -tag*)
make an exception for; *ingen -tagen* none excepted, exclusive of none **-tagandes** except
[for], excepting, save
undantags|bestämmelse special stipulation
(provision) **-fall** exception[al case]; *i ~, se -vis*
-lös without exception **-tillstånd** (*proklamera*
proclaim) a state of emergency **-vis** in exceptional cases, by way of (as an) exception
undantränga force out of its (his *etc.*) place;
force (push, brush) aside (*äv. bildl.*); (*om idéer
o.d.*) supersede, take the place of
1 under ['unn-] *s7* wonder, marvel; (*friare*) miracle; *~ över alla ~!* wonder of wonders!; *naturens
~* the wonders of Nature; *teknikens ~* the mar-
vels of science (technology); *göra ~* work (do)
wonders; *som genom ett ~* as if by a miracle
2 under ['unn-] **I** *prep* **1** (*om rum*) under; underneath; (*på lägre nivå*) below, beneath; *långt ~* far
below; *sätta sitt namn ~ ngt* put one's name to
(sign) s.th.; *~ ytan* below the surface **2** (*om tid*)
during (*natten* the night); in the course of (*samtalets gång* the conversation); (*om, på*) in (*våren
the* spring); (*som svar på 'hur länge'*) for (*tre
veckor* three weeks); *~ hans regering* during (in)
his reign; *~ hela veckan* throughout the week, all
the week **3** *bildl.* under (*drottning Viktoria*
Queen Victoria; *befäl av* command of); below
(*inköpspris* cost price); beneath (*min värdighet*
me) **4** *~ det* [*att*] while (*han talade* he was talking)
II *adv* underneath; beneath; (*nedanför*) under;
skriva ~ sign
under|arm forearm **-avdelning** subdivision
(*äv. mil.*), subsection, branch; *naturv.* subgroup
underbalanser|a *~d budget* budget [closing]
with a deficit **-ing** *~ av budget* deficit financing
under|bar *a1* wonderful, marvellous; (*övernatur-
lig*) miraculous **-barn** infant prodigy
underbefolkad *a5* underpopulated
underbefäl *s7* noncommissioned officer (*koll.*
officers *pl*); *AE.* enlisted man **-havare** second-
-in-command
under|bemannad *a5* undermanned, short-
handed **-ben** shank, lower part of the leg **-be-
tala** underpay **-bett** underbite, protruding
lower jaw **-betyg** *få ~* fail (*i* in), be marked below standard **-binda** *kir.* ligate, ligature **-bjuda**
underbid, undercut **-blåsa** *bildl.* fan, add fuel to
-bygga support, substantiate **-byggnad 1** *eg.*
foundation, substructure **2** *bildl.* grounding,
schooling **-byxor** *pl* pants; *AE.* underpants;
(*korta*) trunks, (*dam-*) knickers, (*trosor*) panties
-bädd (*i sovkupé, hytt*) lower berth **-del** lower
(under) part, bottom **-dimensionera** give too
small dimensions, make too small; underesti-
mate the size of **-domstol** *se underrätt* **-drift**
understatement
underdånig *a1* humble, (*krypande*) obsequious;
~st Your Majesty's most obedient servant (subject) **-het** humility; (*inställsamhet*) servility, obsequiousness
underexponer|a *foto.* underexpose **-ing** *foto.*

underexposure
underfynd komma ~ med find out, get hold of,
(inse) realize, (upptäcka) discover, get to know
underfundig al cunning, artful; subtle
underförstå understand tacitly; ~dd implied,
implicit; det var ~tt dem emellan it was understood (a tacit understanding) between them; ~tt
(nämligen) that is to say
undergiven submissive; resigned (sitt öde to
one's fate) **-het** [-j-] submissiveness, submission,
resignation (under, för to)
under|gräva undermine (äv. bildl.) **-gå**
undergo, go through; ~ förändringar change; ~
examen be examined **-gång** s2 **1** (ruin) ruin, destruction; (skeppsbrott) wreck, loss; gå sin ~ till
mötes be heading for disaster; dömd till ~
doomed [to destruction] **2** (passage) subway;
AE. underpass
undergör|ande [-j-] a4 miraculous; wonder-
-working **-are** miracle worker, wonder-worker
underhaltig al below (not up to) standard; [of]
inferior [quality] **-het** inferiority, inferior (poor)
quality
underhand privately
underhandl|a negotiate (med with; om for,
about); confer (om on); ~ om (äv.) discuss,
negotiate **-are** negotiator **-ing** negotiation; mil.
äv. parley; ligga i ~ar med be negotiating with
underhands|besked confidential communi-
cation **-löfte** confidential (informal) promise
under|havande s9 dependant, dependent; (på
gods) tenant, koll. tenantry (sg) **-hud** corium
-huggare underling; sidekick **-huset** the
House of Commons (AE. Representatives)
underhåll s7 **1** (vidmakthållande) maintenance,
upkeep (av of) **2** (understöd) allowance; support;
(t. frånskild hustru) alimony
underhåll|a 1 maintain, support; (byggnad e.d.)
keep in repair; (kunskaper) keep up; väl -en well-
-kept, in good repair **2** (roa) entertain, amuse;
divert; ~ sig med talk (converse) with **-ande** a4
entertaining etc. **-are** entertainer **-ning** entertainment, amusement; diversion
underhållnings|litteratur light literature
-musik light music **-program** entertainment
program[me]
underhålls|bidrag alimony **-fri** requiring no
maintenance **-kostnad** [cost of] maintenance
(upkeep) **-skyldighet** maintenance obligation[s
pl], duty to support **-tjänst** mil. maintenance
[service]
under|ifrån from below (underneath) **-jorden**
the lower (nether) regions (pl); Hades **-jordisk**
subterranean; underground (äv. bildl.); myt. infernal; ~ järnväg underground, AE. subway; ~a
atomprov underground nuclear tests **-kant** lower
edge (side); i ~ (bildl.) [rather] on the small (low)
side
underkast|a 1 (låta -gå) subject (submit) to; ~
ngn ett förhör put s.b. through an interrogation;
bli ~d kritik be subjected to criticism; det är tvivel
~t it is open to doubt **2** rfl (kapitulera) surrender;
(finna sig i) submit [to], resign [o.s. to] **-else** (ka-
pitulation) surrender; (lydnad) submission (under to)
under|kjol underskirt **-klass** lower class; ~en

the lower classes (pl) **-klassig** lower-class **-klä-
der** pl underwear, underclothing (sg); under-
clothes, undergarments; vard. undies **-klänning**
slip, petticoat **-kropp** lower part of the body
-kunnig al aware (om of); göra sig ~ om acquaint o.s. with **-kurs** hand., till ~ at a discount,
below par **-kuva** subdue, subjugate; (besegra)
conquer **-kyla** supercool, undercool; -kylt regn
freezing (supercooled) rain **-käke** lower jaw
-känna disallow, not approve; skol. fail, reject;
bli -känd (skol.) fail, vard. plough, AE. flunk
-kännande [-ç-] s6 disallowance; skol. rejection, failure
under|lag s7 (grundval) foundation, basis (äv.
tekn.); (stöd) support; byggn. bed[ding] **-lakan**
bottom sheet **-leverantör** subcontractor
underlig al strange, curious; odd, queer (kurre
chap); ~ till mods queer; det är inte ~t om it is not
to be wondered at if; det ~a var the funny thing
about it was **-het** strangeness etc.; oddity; hans
~er his peculiarities
underligt adv strangely etc.; ~ nog strangely
(oddly) enough
under|liv lower abdomen; (kvinnliga könsorgan)
female organs of reproduction **-livssjukdomar**
disorders of the female reproductive organs **-ly-
dande I** a4 dependent, subject **II** s9 subordinate
underlåt|a (låta bli) omit; (försumma) neglect,
fail; han -lät att he failed to; jag kan inte ~ att säga
I cannot help saying **-enhet** omission; negligence **-enhetssynd** sin of omission
under|läge weak position; vara i ~ be at a disad-
vantage, (friare) fall short, get the worst of it
-lägg s7 underlay, pad, mat **-lägsen** a3 inferior
(ngn to s.b.); jag är ~ henne (äv.) I am her inferior **-lägsenhet** inferiority **-läkare** assistant
(house) physician (surgeon) **-läpp** lower lip
-lätta facilitate, make easy (easier); det kommer
att ~ saken it will simplify matters
under|medvetande subconsciousness **-med-
veten** subconscious; det -medvetna the subconscious [mind] **-mening** hidden meaning **-mi-
nera** undermine; sap **-målig** al (otillräcklig) deficient; (dålig) inferior, poor **-närd** [-ä:-] a5 un-
derfed, undernourished **-näring** undernourish-
ment, malnutrition **-officer** noncommissioned
officer **-ordna** subordinate (under to) **-ordnad**
a5 subordinate; inferior, minor; (en ~) subordinate; av ~ betydelse of minor importance, incidental; ~ sats subordinate clause **-ordnande**
[-å:-] a4 subordinating (konjunktion conjunction) **-ordning** suborder **-pant 1** par. collateral
[security] **2** bildl. token **-presterande** under-
achieving **-pris** losing price; sälja till ~ sell at a loss
-privilegierad a5 underprivileged **-rede** [base]
frame; (på bil) chassis (pl chassis) **-redsbehan-
dla** underseal, undercoat **-redsbehandling**
underseal[ing], undercoat[ing] **-representerad**
underrepresented **-rubrik** subheading **-rätt**
lower (inferior) court, court of first instance
underrätta inform, notify, tell (ngn om s.b. of);
hand. advise, give notice; göra sig ~d om inquire
(make inquiries) about; hålla sig ~d om keep o.s.
informed about (as to); ~ mig let me know; väl
~d well informed
underrättelse information; intelligence; (nyhet)

news; (*på förhand*) notice; *en* ~ a piece of information (*etc.*); *närmare* ~*r* further information (*sg*), particulars; *inhämta* ~*r hos ngn om ngt* procure information from s.b. about s.th. **-tjänst** secret service, intelligence [service] **-verksamhet** *olovlig* ~, *se olovlig*
under|sida underside, bottom (underneath) side **-skatta** underrate, underestimate **-skott** deficit (*på* of); (*förlust*) loss **-skrida** be below, fall short of; ~ *ett pris* sell below a price **-skrift** signature; (*-skrivande*) signing; *förse med sin* ~ put one's signature to, sign; *utan* ~ (*äv.*) unsigned **-skriva** sign, put one's signature to; (*godkänna*) endorse, subscribe to **-skåp** hutch
underskön exquisitely beautiful
under|sköterska staff nurse **-slev** *s7* embezzlement; fraud; *begå* ~ embezzle
underst ['unn-] *adv* at the [very] bottom (*i* of) **understa** ['unn-] *superl. a* undermost; lowermost, lowest; ~ *lådan* the bottom drawer
under|stiga be (fall) below (short of); (*om pris*) not come up to **-streckare** feature article **-stryka** underline; (*betona*) emphasize **-ström** undercurrent **-stundom** [-*stundåm*] at times **-stå** *rfl* presume, dare, make so bold as **-ställa** submit to; refer to; *-ställd* subordinate[d] to, placed under
under|stöd support; aid, assistance; (*penning-*) benefit; *periodiskt* ~ periodical allowance **-stödja** support, assist, aid; (*ekonomiskt äv.*) subsidize, sponsor; (*förslag*) second **-stödjare** [-ö:-] supporter; sponsor
understöds|fond relief fund **-tagare** person receiving public assistance (*etc.*) **-verksamhet** public assistance
under|såte *s2* subject **-såtlig** [-å:-] *a1* as a subject; civic **-säng** lower bed **-sätsig** *a1* stocky, thickset **-sätsighet** stockiness
undersök|a examine; (*sakförhållande e.d.*) investigate, look (inquire) into **-ning** examination; investigation, inquiry; *vid närmare* ~ on closer examination (investigation)
undersöknings|domare examining magistrate; (*vid dödsfall*) coroner **-kommission** commission of inquiry **-ledare** officer in charge of an investigation, investigator
underteckn|a sign, put one's name to; ~*d* (*om brevskrivare*) I, the undersigned; *mellan* ~*de* between the undersigned **-ande** *s6* signing, signature; *vid* ~*t* on signature, on signing **-are** signer; signatory
under|titel subtitle **-ton** undertone **-trycka** suppress; (*kuva*) oppress, subjugate; (*hålla tillbaka*) repress, restrain **-tråd** (*på symaskin*) underthread **-tröja** vest; *AE.* undershirt **-utvecklad** *a5* underdeveloped; ~*e länder, se utvecklingsland*
undervattens|båt submarine; (*tysk*) U-boat **-kabel** submarine cable **-klippa** sunken rock **-läge** submerged position; *intaga* ~ submerge **-mina** submarine mine **-sten** sunken rock
undervegetation underbrush, undergrowth
underverk miracle; *världens sju* ~ the seven wonders of the world; *uträtta* ~ do (work) wonders
underviktig *a1* underweight

undervis|a teach, instruct **-ning** teaching, instruction; training, education; *högre* ~ higher education, advanced instruction; *privat* ~ private tuition; *programmerad* ~ programmed instruction
undervisnings|anstalt educational institution **-börda** teaching load **-maskin** teaching machine **-material** teaching materials (*pl*) **-metod** teaching method **-plan** curriculum **-råd** head of division of the Swedish national board of education **-sal** instruction room **-sjukhus** teaching (training) hospital **-skyldighet** *med* ~ *i* with the obligation to teach **-språk** language of instruction **-vana** teaching experience **-väsen** educational system, education
under|värdera underrate, underestimate **-värdering** underestimation, underrating **-värme** heat from below **-årig** *a1* underage, minor
undfall|a escape; *uttrycket undföll mig* the expression slipped out; *låta sig* ~ *ngt* let s.th. slip out **-ande** *a4* compliant; submissive **-enhet** compliancy, complaisance; submissiveness
und|fly flee from; escape (*faran danger*) **-få** receive (*ngn med s.b.to*) **-fägna** treat (*ngn med s.b.o.*) **-fägnad** entertainment **-gå** escape; *ingen* ~*r sitt öde* there is no escaping one's fate; *jag kunde inte* ~ *att höra* I couldn't help hearing; *den kan inte* ~ *att göra intryck* it is bound to make an impression **-komma** escape; get away; ~ *sina förföljare* escape from one's pursuers
undra wonder (*över* at); *det* ~*r jag inte på* I don't wonder (am not surprised) [at that]; ~ *på att...*! no wonder ...! **undran** *r* wonder
undre ['unn-] *a, komp. t.* 2 under [the] lower; bottom; ~ *världen* the underworld
und|seende *s6* deference; *ha* ~ *med* have forbearance with **-slippa** *se undgå, undkomma*; *låta* ~ *sig* let slip, allow to escape one **-sätta** relieve (*äv. mil.*); (*friare*) succour **-sättning** relief; succour; *komma till ngns* ~ come to a p.'s rescue (succour) **-sättningsexpedition** relief expedition
undulat budgerigar; *vard.* budgie
und|vara *sup. -varit, övriga* former saknas do without, dispense with; *inte kunna* ~ (*äv.*) not be able to spare **-vika** avoid (*att: -ing-form*); keep away from, shun; (*med list*) evade, dodge; *som inte kan* ~*s* unavoidable **-vikande I** *s6* avoidance; *till* ~ *av* in order to avoid **II** *a4* evasive (*svar* reply) **III** *adv*, *svara* ~ give an evasive answer
ung *-t yngre yngst* young (*för sina år* for one's years); *de* ~*a* the young, young people; *vid* ~*a år* early in life, at an early age; *som* ~ *var han* as a young man he was; *bli* ~ *på nytt* regain one's youth; *ha ett* ~*t sinne* be young at heart **-djur** *koll.* young stock (*sg*) **-dom** [-dåmm] *s2* **1** *abstr.* youth; *i* ~*en, i sin* ~ in one's youth **2** (*ung människska*) young person (man, girl), adolescent; ~*ar* young people; *nationens* ~ the youth of the nation **-domlig** [-dåmm-] *a1* youthful; juvenile
ungdoms|avdelning youth department; (*på bibliotek*) juvenile department **-bjudning** party for young people **-brottslighet** juvenile delinquency **-brottsling** juvenile offender (delinquent) **-böcker** *pl* juvenile books **-fängelse** reformatory [school] **-förbund** youth association

(club, *polit.* league) **-gård** youth centre **-kultur** youth culture **-kärlek** youthful passion **-ledare** youth leader **-litteratur** literature for the young **-minne** memory of one's youth **-tid** youth **-vårdsskola** *BE.* community home, borstal, *AE.* reformatory **-vän** *en* ~ a friend of one's youth **-år** *pl* early years

ung|e *s2* (*av djur*) *se* fågel-, katt- *etc.*; young; (*barn-*) kid, baby; *-ar* young [ones]; *få -ar* bring forth young; *som föder levande -ar* viviparous; *våra barn och andras -ar* our children and others' brats; *din otäcka* ~ you awful child

ungefär [unj-, uŋ-] about; something like; approximately; ~ *detsamma* pretty much the same; ~ *100* (*äv.*) 100 or so, say 100; ~ *här* somewhere about here; *för* ~ *fem år sedan* some five years ago; *på ett* ~ approximately, roughly **-lig** *a1* approximate, rough (*beräkning* estimate) **-ligen** approximately; roughly

Ungern ['uŋ-] *n* Hungary

ung|ersk ['uŋ-] *a5* Hungarian **-erska** *s1* **1** (*språk*) Hungarian **2** (*kvinna*) Hungarian woman

ung|ersven [young] swain, lad **-flicksaktig** *a1* girlish **-herre** young gentleman **-häst** colt **-höns** pullet; *kokk.* spring chicken **-karl** bachelor

ungkarls|hotell hostel for single men **-tid** bachelor days **-våning** bachelor's apartment

ungmö maid[en]; *gammal* ~ old maid, spinster

ungrare [ˣuŋ-] Hungarian

ungtupp cockerel (*äv. bildl.*)

uniform [-å-] *s3* uniform; full dress; *mil. äv.* regimentals (*pl*); *i* ~ (*äv.*) uniformed **-era 1** (*göra likformig*) make uniform **2** (*förse med uniform*) uniform **-itet** uniformity

uniforms|kappa regulation greatcoat **-klädd** in uniform, uniformed **-mössa** uniform cap **-rock** tunic

unjk *a1* unique **unikum** ['u:ni-] *s8* unique [specimen]

unilateral *a1* unilateral

union *s3* union

unions|flagga union flag; ~*n* (*Storbritannien*) Union Jack **-vänlig** pro-union

unisex *s7* unisex **-mode** unisex fashion

unison *a1* unison; ~ *sång* (*äv.*) community singing **unisont** [-o-] *adv* in unison

universal *s7* universal **-arvinge** residuary (sole) heir **-geni** all-round genius **-itet** universality **-medel** panacea, cure-all

universell *a1* universal

universitet *s7* university; *ligga vid* ~ be at a university

universitets|adjunkt *ung* junior lecturer **-bibliotek** university library **-bildad** university trained **-examen** university degree **-filial** affiliated university, branch campus **-kanslern** the chancellor of the Swedish universities and colleges *AE.* **-lektor** senior [university] lecturer, reader; *AE. äv.* assistant professor **-lärare** university teacher **-rektor** rector; *Storbritannien ung.* vice chancellor; *AE. ung.* president **-studerande** university student, undergraduate **-studier** *pl* university (*Storbritannien undergraduate*) studies **-styrelse** *BE.* senate, *AE.* board of regents (directors) **-utbildning** university education

universum [-ˣvärr-] *s8* universe

unken *a3* musty; (*om lukt, smak äv.*) stale **unket** *adv, lukta* ~ smell musty (stale)

unna ~ *ngn ngt* not [be]grudge s.b. s.th.; *det är honom väl unt* he is very welcome to it; ~ *sig ngt* allow o.s. s.th.; *han ~r sig ingen ro* (*äv.*) he gives himself no rest

uns *s7* ounce (*förk. oz.*); *inte ett* ~ (*friare*) not a scrap

u.p.a. [u:pe:'a:] (*förk. för utan personligt ansvar*) Ltd., Limited; without personal liability

upp up; (*-åt äv.*) upward[s]; (*ut*) out; *knyta* (*låsa*) ~ untie (unlock); *gata* ~ *och gata ner* up one street and down another; *hit* ~ up here; *denna sida* ~! this side up!; *det är* ~ *till dig* (*vard.*) it's up to you; ~ *med huvudet!* (*bildl.*) keep your chin up; ~ *med händerna!* hands up!, stick'em up!; ~ *ur out of; gå* ~ (*ur vattnet*) get out of the water; *hälla* ~ pour out; *vända* ~ *och ner på* turn upside down; *äta* ~ eat up **-amma** nurse, foster **-arbeta** (*jord*) cultivate; (*firma e.d.*) work up, develop

uppass|are *särskr.* upp-passare waiter; *mil.* officer's [bat]man **-erska** waitress; (*på båt*) stewardess **-ning** waiting; attendance

upp|backa back up, support **-backning** backing up, backup, support **-bjuda** muster, summon (*alla sina krafter* all one's strength); exert (*energi* energy) **-bjudande** *s6, med* ~ *av alla sina krafter* exerting all one's strength **-bjudning** invitation (*till dans* to dance) **-blanda** mix [up], intermix; (*vätska*) dilute **-blomstrande** flourishing, prospering; developing (*industri* industry) **-blomstring** prosperity, rise, development **-blossande** *a4* blazing (flaring) up; ~ *vrede* (*äv.*) flash of anger **-blåsbar** [-å:-] *a1* inflatable; pneumatic **-blåst** [-å:-] *a1* inflated; puffed up; *bildl. vard.* stuck-up **-blött** *a4*, *marken var alldeles* ~ the ground was sopping wet **-bragt** *a4* indignant, irritated; (*starkare*) exasperated **-bringa 1** (*fartyg*) capture, seize **2** (*skaffa*) procure, obtain, raise **-bromsning** braking; *bildl.* slowing down **-brott** breaking-up; (*avresa*) departure, departing; *mil.* decampment; *göra* ~ a) (*från bjudning*) break up [the party], take leave, b) *mil.* break [up the] camp **-brottsorder** order[s *pl*] to march **-brottsstämning** breaking-up mood **-brusande** *a4, bildl.* hot-tempered, irascible, impetuous **-brusning** [-u:-] burst of passion **-bränd** *a5* burnt [up] **-buren** *a5, vara mycket* ~ be thought highly (*firad*) made much) of

uppbygg|a 1 *eg. bet., se bygga upp 2 bildl.* edify **-else** edification **-elselitteratur** edifying literature **-lig** *a1* edifying **-nad** building [up], construction; (*organisering*) build-up **-nadsarbete** reconstruction

upp|båd *s7, mil.* summons to arms, calling out; (*friare*) levy; *ett stort* ~ a large force **-båda** summon to arms, call out; (*trupper äv.*) levy; (*friare*) mobilize (*hjälp* help) **-bära 1** (*erhålla*) receive, collect; ~ *skatt* collect taxes **2** (*vara föremål för*) suffer; come in for (*klander* criticism) **3** (*stödja*) support

uppbörd [-ö:-] *s3* collection [of taxes]; *förrätta* ~ collect taxes, take up the collection

uppbörds|distrikt revenue district **-kontor**

[tax] collector's (revenue) office **-man** tax collector **-termin** collection period **-verk** inland revenue office; *AE.* internal revenue service

upp|daga discover; reveal **-datera** update **-dela** divide [up] **-delning** division, dividing [up] **-diktad** *a5* invented; trumped up

uppdra *se dra* [*upp*]

uppdrag commission; mission; (*uppgift*) task, *AE.* assignment; *hand.* order; *enligt* ~ by order (direction); *med* ~ *att* with orders (instructions) to; *på* ~ *av* at the request of, as instructed by, (*mer officiellt*) by order of; *få i* ~ *att göra ngt* be instructed (commissioned) to do s.th., be charged with doing s.th.; *ge ngn i* ~ *att* commission (instruct) s.b.; *skiljas från ett* ~ be removed from office; *utföra ett* ~ *åt ngn* execute a commission for s.b.

uppdrag|a 1 *se dra* [*upp*]; (*uppfostra*) bring up; (*växter*) grow, rear **2** (*rita upp*) draw, trace; ~ *en* jämförelse draw a comparison (*mellan* between); ~ gränserna för delimit, *bildl. äv.* lay down the scope of **3** ~ *åt ngn att* instruct (order, commission) s.b. to **-en** *a5, klockan är* ~ the clock is wound up **-ning** (*av klocka*) winding up

upp|dragsgivare principal; (*arbetsgivare*) employer; (*kund*) customer, client **-driva** (*öka*) raise, increase; (*skaffa*) procure, obtain; *högt -drivna förväntningar* high expectations **-dykande** *s6* emersion; *bildl.* appearance **-dämma** dam up

uppe 1 (*mots. nere*) up (*äv. uppstigen*); (*i övre våningen*) upstairs; *vara tidigt* ~ be up early, (*som vana*) be an early riser (*vard.* bird); ~ *i landet* up country; *högt* ~ *på himlen* high in the sky **2** *vard.* (*öppen*) open **3** *vara* ~ *i tentamen* take (have) an [oral] exam

uppegga incite, egg on

uppehåll *s7* **1** (*avbrott*) interruption, break; (*paus*) pause, interval; (*tågs*) stop; *göra ett* ~ (*i tal o.d.*) make a pause, break off, (*allm. o. om tåg*) stop; *utan* ~ without stopping (a stop), incessantly **2** (*vistelse*) sojourn; (*kortare*) stay, stop; *göra* ~ *i* (*under resa*) stop over at

uppehålla 1 (*hindra*) detain, delay, keep [... back] **2** (*vidmakthålla*) keep up (*skenet* appearances); support (*livet* life); maintain (*en stor familj* a large family) **3** (*tjänst*) discharge the duties of **4** *rfl* (*vistas*) stay, live, reside; (*livnära sig*) support o.s. (*med musiklektioner* by giving music lessons); *bildl.* dwell (*vid småsaker* [up]on details)

uppehålls|ort [place of] residence; (*tillfällig*) place of sojourn, whereabouts; *jur.* domicile **-tillstånd** residence permit **-väder** dry (fair) weather

uppehälle *s6* subsistence, sustenance; *fritt* ~ free board and lodging; *förtjäna sitt* ~ earn one's living; *sörja för ngns* ~ support s.b.

uppemot ['upp-, -'mɔːt] nearly, almost

uppenbar *a1* obvious, evident; distinct, apparent; *när förseelsen blir* ~ when the offence comes to light **uppenbara 1** (*avslöja*) reveal, disclose **2** *rfl* reveal o.s. (*för* to) (*äv. relig.*); (*visa sig*) appear

uppenbarelse revelation (*om* of); *konkr.* apparition, vision **-boken** *U~* the Revelation of St. John the Divine, [the Book of] Revelation[s],

Apocalypse

uppenbarligen [-a:-] obviously *etc.*

upp|fart ascent; (*väg*) approach, ramp; *under ~en* while driving up, on the way up **-fatta** apprehend; grasp; (*förstå*) comprehend, understand; (*tolka*) interpret; *jag kunde inte* ~ *vad han sa* I couldn't catch what he said; ~ *ngt såsom* take s.th. as **-fattning** apprehension; comprehension, understanding; (*föreställning*) idea, conception; *bilda sig en* ~ *om* form an opinion (idea) of **uppfinn|a** invent; devise, contrive **-are** inventor **-ing** invention; (*nyhet äv.*) innovation

uppfinnings|förmåga [power of] invention, inventiveness **-rik** inventive; (*fyndig äv.*) ingenious **-rikedom** inventiveness; ingenuity

upp|flugen *a5* perched **-flytta** (*i lönegrad*) advance, promote; *bli ~d* (*skol.*) get one's remove **-flyttning** moving up; *skol.* remove; (*i lönegrad*) advance, rise

1 uppfordra (*uppmana*) call upon, request; (*t. strid*) challenge, summon

2 uppfordra (*forsla upp*) haul, raise [... to the surface], draw up

uppfordringsverk drawing engine; *gruv.* elevator (hoist) frame

uppfostr|a bring up; *AE. äv.* raise; (*bilda*) educate; (*uppöva äv.*) train; *illa ~d* badly brought up **-an** upbringing; education; training **-are** educator; tutor

uppfostrings|anstalt reformatory [school]; *Engl.* approved school; *AE.* institution for juveniles, workhouse **-bidrag** *jur.* alimony **-syfte** *i* ~ for educational purposes

upp|friska freshen up; refresh **-friskande** *a4* refreshing **-fräta** eat away; corrode completely **-fylla 1** (*fullgöra*) fulfil; (*plikt äv.*) perform, carry out; (*ngns önskningar äv.*) meet, comply with; *få sin önskan -fylld* have one's wish **2** (*fylla*) *bildl.* fill; ~ *jorden* (*bibl.*) replenish the earth; *-fylld av* filled with, full of **-fyllelse** accomplishment; (*av profetia*) fulfilment; *gå i* ~ be fulfilled (accomplished), come true **-fånga** catch; (*signaler*) pick up; (*hindrande*) intercept **-föda** bring up; nourish; (*djur*) breed, rear; *AE. äv.* raise **-födare** breeder **-födning** [-öː-] breeding **-följa** follow up **-följning** follow-up, following-up **-följningsbrev** follow-up letter

uppför ['upp-] **I** *adv* uphill; *vägen bär* ~ it is uphill **II** *prep* up (*backen* the hill); *gå* ~ *trappan* (*äv.*) go upstairs

uppföra 1 (*bygga*) build; raise, erect (*ett monument* a monument) **2** (*anteckna*) put down, enter **3** (*teaterstycke*) give, perform, present; (*musikstycke*) perform **4** *rfl* behave [o.s.], conduct o.s., carry o.s.; ~ *sig väl* (*illa*) behave [well] (badly), (*som vana*) have good (bad) manners

uppförande *s6* **1** (*byggande*) building *etc.*; erection, construction; *är under* ~ is being built, is under construction **2** (*av teater- o. musikstycke*) performance **3** (*beteende*) behaviour, conduct; *dåligt* ~ (*äv.*) misbehaviour **-betyg** conduct marks **-rätt** performing rights (*pl*)

uppförs|backe ascent, rise **-väg** uphill road **upp|ge 1** (*meddela*) state; give (*namn o. adress* name and address); (*säga*) say; (*rapportera*) report; ~ *sig vara* state (say) that one is; ~ *namnet* *på* name, give the name of; ~ *ett pris* quote a price; *enligt vad han själv -gav* (*äv.*) on his own statement **2** (*överge, avstå från*) give up, abandon; ~ *andan* expire, breathe one's last **3** (*utstöta*) give (*ett skrik* a cry)

upp|gift [-j·] *s3* **1** (*meddelande*) statement (*om* of); (*upplysning*) information (*om* on); (*lista*) list, specification (*om* of); (*officiell*) report (*på* on); *närmare ~er* (*äv.*) further particulars; *enligt ~* from information received, according to reports; *kompletterande ~er* supplementary data (details) (*om* on); *med ~ om* stating; *statiska ~er* returns, statistics **2** (*åliggande*) task, charge; (*kall*) mission, object (*i livet* in life); *förelägga ngn en ~* set s.b. a task; *det är hans ~ att* it is his duty (business) to **3** (*i examen o.d.*) [examination *etc.*] question; *matematisk ~* [mathematical] problem; *skriftlig ~* [written] exercise **-gifts-lämnare** informant; respondent

upp|giva *se uppge* **-given** (*tillintetgjord*) overcome (*av trötthet* with fatigue); exhausted (*av sorg* with grief) **-gjord** settled, arranged; ~ *på förhand* prearranged **-gå 1** (*belöpa sig*) amount (*till* to); *i genomsnitt ~ till* average **2** (*sammansmälta*) ~ *i* be merged (*om firma e.d. äv.* incorporated) in **-gående I** *s6*, ~ *i* absorption by (*arbete* work) **II** *a4* rising; (*om himlakropp äv.*) ascending **-gång** *s2* **1** (*väg*) way up; (*trapp-*) stairs (*pl*), staircase **2** (*himlakropps*) rise **3** (*ökning*) rise, increase; upswing, upturn **-görelse** [-j-] **1** (*avtal*) agreement; (*överenskommelse äv.*) arrangement, settlement; (*affär*) transaction; ~ *i godo* amicable settlement, settlement out of court; *träffa en ~* make an agreement, come to terms **2** (*dispyt*) dispute, showdown **-handla** purchase, buy (in, up) **-handling** purchase, purchasing, buying **-haussa** force up, boost

upphets|a excite; inflame; *bli ~d* get excited **-ande** *a4* exciting; inflammatory (*tal* speech) **-ning** excitement

upp|hetta heat, make hot; ~ *för mycket* overheat **-hettning** heating **-hinna** catch up, overtake **-hitta** find **-hittare** finder **-hjälpa** (*förbättra*) improve **-hostning** expectoration

upphov *s7* origin; source; (*orsak*) cause; (*början äv.*) beginning, origination; *ge ~ till* give rise (birth) to; *ha sitt ~ i* (*äv.*) originate in; *vara ~ till* be the cause of

upphovs|man author, originator (*till* of) **-rätt** copyright **-rättslig** ~ *lagstiftning* copyright legislation

upp|hällning 1 pouring out **2** *vara på ~en* be on the decline (wane), (*om förråd*) be running short **-hänga** suspend, hang [up] **-hängning** suspension; mounting **-häva 1** (*återkalla*) revoke, withdraw; (*förklara ogiltig*) annul, declare invalid (void); (*kontrakt*) cancel; (*neutralisera*) neutralize **2** (*avbryta*) raise (*belägringen* the siege) **3** (*utstöta*) raise (*ett skri* a cry); ~ *sin röst* lift one's voice, begin to speak

upp|höja raise (*äv. mat.*); elevate; (*berömma*) extol; ~ *i kvadrat* square, raise to second power **-höjd** *a5* **1** *bildl.* elevated, exalted; *med -höjt lugn* with supreme composure **2** (*om arbete, bokstäver*) raised **-höjdhet** elevation; loftiness **-höjelse** elevation, exaltation; promotion **-höj-**

ning *konkr.* elevation (*i marken* of the ground), rise; (*kulle*) eminence

upphör|a cease, stop (*med att göra ngt* doing s.th.); (*sluta*) end, come to an end; ~ *med* (*äv.*) discontinue, (*en vana*) give up; *firman har -t* the firm has closed down **-ande** *s6* ceasing *etc.*; cessation; (*avbrott äv.*) interruption; (*tillfälligt*) suspension

uppifrån I *adv* from above; ~ *och ner* from top to bottom **II** *prep* [down] from

uppiggande (*särskr. upp-piggande*) **I** *a4* stimulating, bracing (*verkan* effect); *något ~* a pick-me-up **II** *adv, verka ~* have a reviving (bracing) effect

upp|jagad *a5* [over]excited; heated (*fantasi* imagination); overstrained (*nerver* nerves) **-kalla 1** (*benämna*) call, name; *~d efter* called (named) after **2** (*be [ngn] att komma upp*) call up **3** (*mana*) call [up]on **-kastning** vomiting; *med.* emesis; *få ~ar* vomit **-klarna** clear up **-knäppt** *a4* unbuttoned (*äv. bildl.*) **-kok** boiling, warming up; *bildl.* rehash (*på* of); *ge ngt ett ~* boil s.th. up

upp|komling [-å-] upstart, parvenu (*fem.* parvenue) **-komma** (*uppstå*) arise (*av* from), originate (*ur* in); (*börja*) begin; (*plötsligt*) start up; *de -komna skadorna* the damage (*sg*) incurred **-kommande** *a4* possible, arising; *vid ~ skada* in case of damage **-komst** [-å-] *s3* (*tillblivelse*) origin, beginning; appearance; *fack.* genesis; *ha sin ~ i* have its origin in, originate in **-konstruera** (*uppfinna*) invent; (*hitta på*) make up, create **-krupen** *a5, sitta ~* be curled up (*i soffan* on the sofa) **-käftig** [-ç-] *a4* cheeky, saucy **-käftighet** [-ç-] cheek, sauce **-köp** (*-köpande*) buying [in], purchasing; (*ett ~*) purchase; *göra ~* do one's purchasing (*vard.* shopping) **-köpa** buy [in, up], purchase **-köpare** buyer, purchaser **-körd** [-çö:-] *a5* **1** (*däst*) bloated **2** (*lurad*) fleeced

upp|laddning charge, charging (*äv. bildl.*); *bildl. äv.* build-up; *eg. äv.* electrification **-lag** *s7* store, stock, supply **-laga** *s1* edition; (*tidningsäv.*) circulation; *bildl.* version; *förkortad ~* abbreviated (abridged) edition; *~ns storlek* number of copies printed, print **-lagd** *a5* **1** (*om vara, fartyg*) laid up; *stort -lagt projekt* large-scale project **2** (*hågad*) inclined, disposed; *känna sig ~ för att* be in a mood for, feel like (+ *ing-form*) **-lage-siffra** circulation figures (*pl*) **-lagring** storing, storage **-lagsnäring** reserve nutrition **-lags-plats** depot, storing place, storage yard **-land** *s7* surrounding area; (*innanför kusten*) hinterland **-lappning** *boktr.* making ready **-leta** find, hunt up

upp|leva (*erfara*) experience, meet with (*besvikelser* disappointments); (*leva tills ngt inträffar*) live to (*år 2000* the year 2000), [live to] see; (*bevittna*) witness; *han har -levt mycket* he has been through a lot (had an eventful life) **-levelse** (*erfarenhet*) experience; (*händelse*) event; *detta blev en ~ för mig* it was quite an experience for me **-linjera** rule [lines in] **-liva** (*förnya*) renew (*bekantskapen med* the acquaintance with); (*pigga upp*) cheer [up], exhilarate; ~ *minnet* refresh (brush up) one's memory; ~ *gamla minnen* revive old memories **-livande** *a4* cheering, stimulating **-livningsförsök** [-li:v-] *pl* attempts at resusci-

U

tation
upp|lopp 1 (*tumult*) riot, tumult **2** *sport.* finish
-luckra loosen, break up; *bildl. äv.* relax (*be-stämmelserna* the regulations, *moralen* morals)
-lupen *a5*, ~ *ränta* accrued interest, interest due
-lyfta lift up; *högt.* elevate; *med -lyft huvud* head
high **-lyftande** *a4* elevating; sublime
upplys|a 1 (*göra ljus*) light [up], illuminate **2**
(*underrätta*) inform (*ngn om* s.b. of), tell (*ngn om*
s.b.); enlighten (*ngn i en fråga* s.b. on a point)
-ande *a4* informative, illustrative (*exempel* ex-ample); (*förklarande*) explanatory (*anmärkning-ar* remarks); (*lärorik*) instructive **-ning 1** (*be-lysning*) lighting, illumination **2** (*underrättelse*)
information (*om* about, of, on); (*förklaring*) ex-planation; (*kredit-*) credit[worthiness] report; *en*
~ a piece of information; ~*ar* information (*sg*);
närmare ~*ar* further particulars (details) **3** (*bi-bringande av*] *kunskaper*) enlightenment, eluci-dation; (*kultur*) civilization, culture; ~*en* (*hist.*)
the [Age of] Enlightenment
upplysnings|byrå information office (bureau)
-tiden the Age of Enlightenment **-verk-samhet** information service (activities *pl*) **-vis**
by way of information; for your information
upp|lyst [-y:-] *a1 eg.* illuminated, lighted (lit)
up **2** *bildl.* enlightened **-låna** borrow, raise **-lån-ing** borrowing [transaction[s *pl*]] **-låta** open (*för
trafik* to traffic), make available (*för* to); ~ *ett
rum åt ngn* put a room at a p.'s disposal, grant
s.b. the use of a room **-låtelse** grant, giving up;
~ *nyttjanderätt* grant of enjoyment **-läggning 1**
sömn. shortening, taking up **2** (*planering*) plan-ning, arrangement; (*disposition*) disposition; (*av
konto o.d.*) drawing up; (*av håret*) coiffure **3**
(*magasinering*) storage, storing; (*av fartyg*) lay-ing up **4** (*på fat etc.*) arrangement **-läsare**
reader, reciter **-läsning** reading; recital **-läx-ning** sermon; *vard.* telling-off
upplös|a 1 (*knyta upp*) se *lösa* [*upp*] **2** (*komma
[ngt] att upphöra*) dissolve, wind up (*ett företag* a
company); (*skingra*) dissolve, dismiss; (*möte*)
break up; (*trupper*) disband **3** (*sönderdela*) dis-solve, disintegrate; *mat.* solve **4** (*bringa oreda i*)
disorganize; *-löst i tårar* dissolved in tears **5** *rfl*
dissolve, be dissolved (*i* into); (*sönderfalla*) de-compose **-ande** *a4* dissolving etc. **-as** *v3*, *dep*, se
upplösa **-bar** *a1* dissoluble **-ning** dissolution,
winding up (*etc.*); (*samhälls-*) disintegration;
(*dramas*) unravelling, denouement **-ningstill-stånd** state of dissolution (decomposition); *vara
i* ~ (*bildl.*) be on the point of collapse
upp|mana exhort; (*hövligt*) request, invite, (*en-träget*) urge, incite; *besökare* ~*s att* visitors are
recommended (requested) to **-maning** exhor-tation; request; summons, call; *på* ~ *av* at the re-quest of, on the recommendation of **-marsch**
marching-up; *mil.* deployment, drawing-up
-maskning mending [of a ladder] **-mjuka**
make soft, soften; (*göra smidig*) limber up; (*mo-derera*) modify, moderate **-mjukning** [-u:-]
sport. limbering-up
uppmuntr|a (*jfr muntra* [*upp*]); (*inge för-hoppningar e.d.*) encourage; (*gynna*) favour,
promote; (*uppmana*) exhort **-an** *best. form -an*,
pl -ingar encouragement; favouring, patronage

-ande *a4* encouraging; *föga* ~ anything but en-couraging, discouraging
uppmärk|sam *a1* attentive (*äv. förekommande*)
(*på, mot* to); (*aktgivande*) watchful, observant
(*på* of); *göra ngn* ~ *på* draw (call) a p.'s attention
to **-samhet** attention; (*som egenskap*) attentive-ness; (*aktgivande*) watchfulness, observation;
rikta ngns ~ *på* call a p.'s attention to; *undgå ngns*
~ escape a p.'s attention; *visa ngn* ~ pay atten-tion to s.b.; *väcka* ~ attract attention; *ägna* ~ *åt*
give (pay) attention to **-samma** notice, observe;
pay attention to; *bli* ~*d* attract attention; *en
mycket* ~*d bok* a book that has created a stir
-samt *adv* attentively; (*starkare*) intently
upp|mäta measure [out] **-mätning** measuring
[up] **-nosig** *a1* impertinent, saucy, pert **-nå**
reach, attain; arrive at; (*ernå*) obtain; (*vinna*)
gain; *vid* ~*dd pensionsålder* at pensionable age
-näsa snub (turned-up) nose **-näst** [-ä:-] *a4*
snub-nosed
uppochnedvänd [-ˣne:d-] [turned] upside
down; inverted, reversed; *bildl.* topsy-turvy
upp|odla cultivate (*-odling* [-*odlande*] culti-vation; *konkr.* cleared plot [of land] **-offra** sacri-fice (*allt* everything; *sig* o.s.) **-offrande** [-å-] *a4*
self-sacrificing **-offring** [-å-] sacrifice; *det har
kostat henne stora* ~*ar* she has sacrificed a great
deal **-packning** (*hopskr. uppackning*) unpack-ing **-passare** se *uppassare* **-piggande** *a4*, se
uppiggande **-reklamera** boost, puff **-rensa**
clean (clear) out; *mil.* mop up **-rensning** clean-ing out; *mil.* mopping-up
upprep|a repeat; (*säga om o. om igen*) reiterate;
(*förnya*) renew; ~*de gånger* repeatedly, again
and again **-repning** [-e:-] repetition; reiteration;
renewal; recurrence
1 uppresa *s1* journey up; *på* ~*n* on my (*etc.*)
journey up
2 uppresa *v3* **1** (*uppföra*) raise; put up **2** *rfl* rise,
revolt
uppretad *a5* irritated; exasperated (*folkhop*
mob); enraged (*tjur* bull)
upprik|tig *a1* sincere; (*ärlig*) honest; (*öppen*)
frank, candid; ~ *vän* true friend; *säga ngn sin* ~*a
mening* tell (give) s.b. one's honest opinion
-tighet sincerity; frankness; candour; honesty
-tigt *adv* sincerely etc.; ~ *sagt* candidly [speak-ing]; *säg mig* ~ ...*!* tell me honestly ...!
upp|ringning [telephone] call **-rinnelse** origin,
source **-rivande** *a4* harrowing, shocking **-riven**
a5, bildl. (*nervös*) worked up; ~ *av sorg* broken
by sorrow **-rop** (*av namn*) roll call, call-over;
(*vädjan*) appeal; (*på auktion*) announcement
uppror *s7* insurrection, rebellion; *mil.* mutiny;
(*mindre*) revolt, uprising; (*oro*) agitation; *göra* ~
rise in rebellion, revolt; *hans känslor råkade i* ~
he flared up **-isk** *a5* rebellious; seditious, insub-ordinate
upprors|anda rebellious spirit, spirit of revolt
-fana *höja* ~*n* raise the standard of rebellion
-försök attempted (attempt at) rebellion **-ma-kare** instigator of rebellion; (*vid myteri*) ring-leader; (*svagare*) troublemaker
upp|rusta rearm **-rustning** *mil.* rearmament;
(*renovering*) restoration, reparation **-rutten** rot-ten to the core **-ryckning** *bildl.* rousing, shak-

ing-up; *ge ngn en* ~ give s.b. a shaking-up **-rymd** *a1* exhilarated, elated **-rymdhet** exhilaration, elation **-räcka** *ta emot ngt med -räckta händer* receive s.th. with open arms **-räckna** enumerate **-räkning** enumeration; *(höjning)* adjustment upwards

upprätt *a4 o. adv* upright, erect; *(helt ~ äv.)* perpendicular

upprätt|a 1 *(grunda)* found, establish, set up *(en skola* a school); create *(en befattning* a post); ~ *förbindelser med* establish relations with **2** *(avfatta)* make, draw up *(ett testamente* a will) **3** *(rehabilitera)* rehabilitate; restore *(ngns rykte* a p.'s reputation); retrieve *(sin ära* one's honour) **-ande** *s6* raising, foundation; establishment; drawing-up **-else** reparation, redress; rehabilitation; *få* ~ obtain redress; *ge ngn* ~ make amends to s.b. *(för ngt* for s.th.) **-hålla** *(vidmakthålla)* maintain, keep up, uphold *(disciplin* discipline; *(sköta)* hold *(en tjänst* a post); *(hålla i gång)* keep going **-hållande** *s6* maintenance, upholding *etc.* **-hållare** upholder *etc.*; *ordningens* ~ the upholders of law and order **-stående** *a4* upright, erect

upp|röjning clearance, clearing **-röjningsarbete** clearance work **-röra** *bildl.* stir [up], irritate, disturb, upset **-rörande** *a4* agitating *etc.*; *(starkare)* shocking **-rörd** [-ö:-] *a1* indignant, excited; upset; *bli* ~ *över* be upset about **-rördhet** indignation, irritation; excitement

upp|sagd *a5 (om hyresgäst, personal)* under notice; *(om fördrag e.d.)* denounced; *bli* ~ get notice; *vara* ~ be under notice of dismissal **-samla** gather [up], collect **-samling** gathering, collection

uppsamlings|område *(för evakuerade)* reception area **-plats** collecting centre; assembly point *(äv. mil.)*

uppsats *s3* **1** *(i bok e.d.)* essay, paper *(om* on); *(i tidning)* article *(om* on); *(skol-*) composition **2** *(uppsättning, sats)* set **-skrivning** composition--writing, essay-writing

uppsatt *a4* **1** *(om pers.)* exalted, distinguished; *en högt* ~ *person* a person of high station **2** *boktr.* in type

uppseende attention; *(starkare)* sensation; scandal; *väcka* ~ attract attention *(genom* by) **-väckande** *a4* sensational; startling

upp|segling *vara under* ~ *(bildl.)* be brewing **-sikt** control, superintendence, supervision; *ha* ~ *över* have charge of, supervise, superintend; *stå under* ~ be under supervision *(superintendence)* **-sjö** *en* ~ *på (bildl.)* an abundance (a wealth) of **-skakad** *a5* upset, shaken, shocked **-skakande** *a4* upsetting, shocking **-skatta** *(värdera)* estimate *(efter* by; *till* at), value; *(sätta värde på äv.)* appreciate *(duglighet* ability); ~*d till 1 000 pund* valued at 1,000 pounds; ~*t pris* estimated price; *kan inte* ~*s nog högt* cannot be too highly prized **-skattning** estimation, valuation; appreciation **-skattningsvis** approximately, roughly, about **-skjuta 1** *(i tiden)* put off, postpone; *(sammanträde)* adjourn; *parl.* prorogue **2** *(raket)* launch **-skjutning** launch

upp|skov *s7* postponement *(med* of), delay; *(anstånd)* respite *(med* for); *begära* ~ apply for a term of respite; *bevilja* ~ grant a respite (prolongation); *utan* ~ without delay, immediately, promptly **-skrivning** *(av valuta)* revaluation **-skruvad** *a5* **1** ~*e priser* exorbitant prices **2** wrought-up, worked-up **-skrämd** *a5* startled, frightened **-skuren** *a5 (om bok)* with the pages cut; ~ *korv* sliced sausage; ~*skuret* slices of cold meat **-skärrad** [-ʃ-] *a5* overexcited **-skörta** [-ʃ-] *bli* ~*d* be overcharged (fleeced) **-skörtning** [-ʃ-] swindle, cheating

upp|slag *s7* **1** *(idé)* idea, project, impulse; *nya* ~ fresh suggestions, new ideas; *ge* ~ *till* give rise to, start, begin **2** *(på kläder)* facing; *(rock-)* lapel; *(ärm-)* cuff; *(på byxor)* turn-up, *AE.* cuff **3** *(i bok)* opening; *(i tidning)* [double-page] spread **-slagen** *a5 (jfr slå [upp])* **1** opened *etc.*; *som en* ~ *bok (bildl.)* like an open book; *med* ~ *rockkrage* with one's collar turned up **2** *(om förlovning)* broken [off]

uppslags|bok encyclopaedia; reference book **-ord** [main] entry, headword **-rik** full of suggestions, ingenious **-verk** work of reference, reference work **-ända** *bildl.* clue

upp|slamma silt [up]; *kem. äv.* dredge; ~*d* suspended, muddy **-slitande** *a4, bildl.* heart-rending **-slitsa** split open **-sluka** devour; *bildl.* engulf, absorb; *ett allt* ~*nde intresse* an all-absorbing interest **-sluppen** *a3* **1** *(i söm)* [ripped] open **2** *bildl.* exhilarated, in high spirits, jolly **-sluppenhet** exhilaration, high spirits *(pl)* **-slutning** [-u:-] *mil.* forming *(t. höger* to the right); *(tillströmning)* rallying, assembly **-snabba** speed up **-snappa** snatch (pick) up; ~ *ett ord* catch a word; ~ *ett brev* intercept a letter **-snyggad** *a5* tidied up **-spelning** audition

upp|spelt [-e:-] *a1* exhilarated, jolly, gay **-spetad** *a5, sitta* ~ be perched *(på* on) **-sprucken** *a5* ripped (split) [up, open] **-spåra** *se spåra [upp]* **-spärrad** *a5* wide open; *(om näsborrar)* distended **-stapla** stack **-stekt** [-e:-] *a4* fried-up **-stigande** *s6,* **-stigning** *(jfr stiga [upp])* rise, rising; *(på berg)* ascent; *(på tron)* ascension *(på* to); *flyg.* takeoff, ascent **-stoppad** [-å-] *a5 (om djur)* stuffed **-stoppare** [-å-] taxidermist **-stoppning** stuffing; taxidermy **-sträckning** *bildl.* rating, telling-off, reprimand; *AE. vard.* calling down **-sträckt** *a4 (finklädd)* dressed up **-ströms** upstream **-studsig** *a1* refractory, insubordinate **-studsighet** refractoriness, insubordination **-styltad** *a5* stilted, affected; *(svulstig)* bombastic

upp|stå 1 *(-komma)* arise; come up; *(börja)* start **2** *(resa sig)* rise *(från de döda* from the dead) **-stående** *a4* stand-up *(krage* collar) **-ståndelse 1** *bildl.* commotion, excitement **2** *(från de döda)* resurrection **-ställa** *a5* risen **-ställa** *(jfr ställa [upp])*; ~ *fordringar* make stipulations; ~ *regler* lay down (establish) rules; ~ *som villkor* state as a condition, make it a condition *(att* that) **-ställning** arrangement; *mil.* formation *(på linje* in line), parade; *(i rad)* alignment; *(lista o.d.)* list, specification; ~*!* fall in!, attention!; ~ *i tabellform* tabular statement **-ställningsplats** *mil.* parade ground **-stötning** [-ö:-] belch; *med.* eructation **-suga** absorb, draw up **-sugningsförmåga** absorbency **-sving** *s7* upswing, rise,

U

upsurge; *hand. äv.* boom **-svullen** *a5*, **-svälld** *a5* swollen **-svällning** swelling **-syn 1** (*min*) look[s *pl*], countenance **2** *se uppsikt* **-synings-man** overseer, supervisor; inspector **uppsåt** *s7* intent, intention; *i ~ att* with the intention of (*skada* damaging); *med ont ~* with malicious intent; *utan ~* unintentionally, *jur.* without premeditation; *utan ont ~* without malice **-lig** [-å:-] *a1* intentional; (*överlagd*) wilful (*mord* murder) **-ligen** [-å:-] purposely, intentionally; *~ eller av vårdslöshet* (*jur.*) prepensely or negligently

uppsäg|a *se säga* [*upp*]; *~ ngn tro och lydnad* withdraw one's allegiance from s.b. **-bar** [-ä:-] *a1* subject to notice; (*om kontrakt*) terminable; (*om lån*) redeemable **-else, -ning** [-ä:-] notice; (*av kontrakt*) notice of termination, cancellation; (*av lån*) recalling; (*av fördrag e.d.*) withdrawal; (*av personal*) notice of dismissal (to quit), warning; *med 6 månaders ~* at 6 months' notice **-ningstid** [period of] notice

upp|sända (*rikta*) offer up (*böner* prayers) **-sätta** *se sätta* [*upp*] **-sättning 1** (*-sättande*) putting up (*etc., jfr sätta* [*upp*]) **2** *konkr.* set, collection; *tekn.* equipment, installation; *teat. o. film.* production, *konkr.* [stage-]setting; *full ~ av* full set of **-söka** (*leta reda på*) seek (hunt) out; (*besöka*) go to see, call on

upp|ta[ga] 1 *se ta* [*upp*] **2** (*antaga*) take up; take (*ngn som delägare* s.b. into partnership; *som ett skämt* as a joke); (*mottaga*) receive; (*i förening*) admit; *~s till behandling* come (be brought) up for discussion; *målet skall ~s på nytt* (*jur.*) the case is to be resumed (to come on again) **3** (*ta i anspråk*) take up (*tid* time; *utrymme* room); engage (*alla ens tankar* all one's thoughts) **-tagen** *a5* **1** *eg.* taken up (*etc.*) **2** (*sysselsatt*) occupied, busy; (*om pers.*) engaged, busy; *jag är ~ i morgon eftermiddag* I am (shall be) engaged tomorrow afternoon **3** (*om sittplats*) occupied, taken, reserved; (*om telefonnummer*) engaged, *AE.* busy; *platsen* (*befattningen*) *är redan ~* the post has already been filled (is no longer vacant) **4** (*på räkning e.d.*) listed **-tagetsignal** engaged tone, *AE.* busy signal **-tagning** (*grammofon-, radio-*) recording; (*film-*) filming, taking, shooting **upp|takt** *mus.* anacrusis; *bildl.* beginning, prelude, preamble **-taxera** (*höja taxering*) raise a tax assessment **-teckna** take down, make a note of; (*folkvisor e.d.*) record, chronicle **-teckning** noting down (*etc.*); *konkr.* record, chronicle **-till** at the top **-tina** thaw **-trampa** tread, beat [out]; *~d stig* beaten track **-trappa** escalate **-trapp-ning** escalation **-träda 1** (*framträda*) appear (*offentligt* in public); (*om skådespelare äv.*) perform, give performances (a performance); *~ som talare* speak; *~ som vittne* give evidence **2** (*-föra sig*) behave [o.s.]; (*ingripa*) act (*med bestämdhet* resolutely); *~ med fasthet* display firmness **-trä-dande I** *s6* (*framträdande*) appearance; (*beteende*) behaviour, conduct **II** *a4, de ~* (*artisterna*) the performers (actors) **-träde** *s6* scene, scandal; *ställa till ett ~* make a scene **-tuktelse** *ta ngn i ~* give s.b. a good talking-to, take s.b. to task **-tåg** prank; practical joke; *ha dumma ~ för sig* be up to some silly lark **-tågsmakare** practical joker,

wag
upp|täcka discover; (*avslöja*) detect, find out; (*uppspåra*) track down; *då -tes det att* (*äv.*) it then turned out that **-täckare** discoverer, finder; detector **-täckt** *s3* discovery; (*avslöjande*) revelation; *undgå ~* (*äv.*) elude detection **upptäckts|färd** expedition **-resande** explorer **upp|tända** light; *bildl.* kindle, inflame, excite; *-tänd av iver* glowing with zeal; *~ av raseri* enraged **-tänklig** *a1* conceivable, imaginable; *på alla ~a sätt* (*äv.*) in every possible way **-vak-nande** [-va:k-] *s6* awakening

uppvakt|a (*hylla*) congratulate, honour; (*göra* [*ngn*] *sin kur*) court, *AE. vard. äv.* date; (*besöka*) call on; (*tjänstgöra hos kunglig pers.*) attend **-ande** *a4* attentive (*kavaljer* admirer); *de ~* (*gratulanterna*) the congratulators; *~ kammarherre* chamberlain-in-waiting **-ning 1** (*-ande*) attendance; waiting upon; (*hövlighetsvisit*) [complimentary, congratulatory] call; *göra ngn sin ~* pay one's respects to s.b. **2** (*följe*) attendants (*pl*); gentlemen-in-waiting, ladies-in-waiting (*pl*); *tillhöra ngns ~* belong to a p.'s suite, be in attendance on

uppvigl|a [-i:-] stir up [to rebellion (revolt)] **-are** [-i:-] agitator, instigator of rebellion (*etc.*) **-ing** [-i:-] agitation; instigation **-ingsförsök** attempt to instigate rebellion; attempted mutiny **upp|vilad** *a5* rested **-vind** *flyg.* upwind **-visa** (*framvisa*) show, exhibit, display; (*förete*) present, produce (*en biljett* a ticket); (*blotta*) show up (*felaktigheter* errors) **-visande** *s6* showing *etc.*; *vid ~t* on presentation (*av* of); *mot ~ av* upon production of **-visning** show; *mil.* exhibition, review **-vuxen** grown up; *han är ~ i* he has grown up in **-väcka** raise (*från de döda* from the dead); rouse (*lidelser* passions) **-väga** *bildl.* [counter]balance, weigh against; compensate for, neutralize **-värdera** upgrade **-värma** warm (heat) [up]; *-värmd mat* warmed-up food **-värmning** heating; *sport.* warm-up **-växande** *a4* growing [up]; *det ~ släktet* the rising (coming) generation **-växt** growth; *jfr äv. följ.* **-växtmiljö** environment s.b. grew (grows) up in **-växttid** adolescence, youth; *under ~en* while growing up

uppåt ['upp-] **I** *adv* upward[s]; *stiga ~* (*äv.*) ascend **II** *prep* up to[wards]; *~ landet* (*floden*) up country (the river) **II** *oböjligt a* (glad) in high spirits **-böjd** bent upwards **-gående I** *a4* ascending; rising; upward (*tendens* tendency) **II** *s6* ascension; *hand.* rise, hausse; *vara i ~* be on the upgrade, (*om pris e.d.*) be rising **-riktad** *a5* directed upwards **-strävande** *a4* aspiring; struggling to rise [in the world]; *bildl. äv.* ambitious (*planer* plans) **-vänd** *a5* turned up[wards]

upp|äten *a5* eaten; *vara ~ av mygg* be stung all over by gnats **-öva** train, exercise **-över** ['upp-, -ö:ver] *prep* over; *~ öronen* head over heels (*förälskad* in love)

1 ur *i uttr.: i ~ och skur* in all weathers, (*friare*) through thick and thin

2 ur I *prep* out of, from (*minnet* memory); (*inifrån*) from within; *~ funktion* unserviceable **II** *adv* out

3 ur *s7* watch; (*större*) clock; *fröken Ur* speaking

clock, (*i Storbritannien äv.*) TIM
uraffär watchmaker's [shop]
uraktlåt|a neglect, omit, fail **-enhet** omission,
failure
Uralbergen [u*ra:l-] *pl* the Urals, the Ural
Mountains
uralstring spontaneous generation
uran *s4, s3* uranium **-bränsle** uranium fuel **-fyn-
dighet** uranium deposit **-haltig** *al* uranous **-jd**
s3 uranide
ur|arta degenerate; (*friare*) turn (*till* into); ~*d*
degenerate[d], depraved **-artning** [-a:-] degeneration **-arva** *oböjligt a, göra sig* ~ renounce
all claim[s] on the estate
urban *al* **1** (*belevad*) urbane, affable **2** ([*stor*]
stads) urban
urbaniser|ing [-'se:-] urbanization **-ingspro-
cess** urbanization process
ur|befolkning original population; ~*en* (*äv.*)
the aborigines (*pl*) **-berg** primary (primitive)
rock[s *pl*] **-bild** prototype, archetype, original
(*för* of)
ur|blekt [-e:-] *a4* faded, (*-tvättad äv.*) washed
out; *bli* ~ fade, discolour **-blåst** *a4* gutted (*hus
house*) **-bota** *oböjligt a* **1** *jur., ~ brott* felony,
capital offence **2** (*oförbätterlig*) hopeless, incorrigible
ur|cell, -djur primeval cell, protozoan
uremj *s3* uraemia
urfader first father, progenitor
ur|fånig idiotic **-gammal** extremely old; (*forn*)
ancient; *en ~ rättighet* a time-honoured privilege
-germansk Primitive Germanic
ur|gröpa hollow out; (*-gröpt äv.*) concave
-gröpning hollow **-holka** hollow [out]; (*gräva
ut*) excavate, dig out; *tekn.* scoop [out]; ~*d* (*äv.*)
hollow, concave **-holkning** [-å-] (*-ande*) hollow-
ing out, excavation; *konkr.* hollow, cavity
urjn *s3* urine **-blåsa** [urinary] bladder **-drivande**
a4, ~ [medel] diuretic **-era** urinate **-förgiftning**
uraemia **-glas** urinal **-ledare** ureter
urin[ne]vånare original inhabitant, aboriginal;
pl äv. aborigines
urin|oar *s3* urinal **-prov** specimen of urine **-rör**
urethra **-syra** uric acid **-vägsinfektion** inflammation of the urinary tract
ur|klipp [press] cutting; *AE.* clipping
-klippsbok scrapbook, press-cutting book
-kokt *a4* with all the flavour boiled out [of it];
(*friare*) overboiled
urkomisk irresistibly (screamingly) funny
urkoppling (*av maskin*) decoupling, declutch-
ing; *elektr.* disconnection, interruption
ur|kraft primitive force; *bildl.* immense power
-kristendom primitive Christianity
ur|kund *s3* [original] document; record
-kundsförfalskning forging (forgery) of
documents **-källa** *bildl.* fountainhead (*äv. bildl.*)
ur|ladda discharge; (*kamera*) unload; ~*d* (*om
batteri*) dead; ~ *sig* (*bildl.*) explode, burst
-laddning discharge; *bildl.* explosion, outburst
-laka soak; ~*d* (*kraftlös*) jaded, exhausted
-lasta unload **-lastning** unloading
urmak|are watchmaker; clockmaker **-eri** *abstr.*
watchmaking, clockmaking; (*verkstad*) watchmaker's [shop]

ur|minnes *oböjligt a* immemorial (*hävd* usage);
från ~ tider from times immemorial (time out of
mind) **-moder** first mother, progenitor **-modig**
al out-of-date, antiquated, outmoded **-männi-
ska** primitive man
urn|a [*ʼu:r-*] urn **-lund** *ung.* garden of rest, out-
door columbarium
urnordisk Primitive Scandinavian
urnyckel watch (clock, winding) key
uro|graf| *s3* urography **-log** urologist **-logj** *s3*
urology
ur|oxe aurochs **-plock** selection; assortment
-premiär first performance (*för Sverige* in
Sweden)
urring|a *vl* cut out; (*i halsen*) cut low; ~*d* (*om
plagg*) low-necked, (*om pers.*) wearing a low-
-necked dress **-ning** *abstr.* cutting out; *konkr.*
decolletage, neckline, low neck
ursinn|e fury, frenzy; rage **-ig** *al* furious (*på*
with; *över* at); *bli ~* (*äv.*) fly into a rage (passion)
ur|skilja discern, make out **-skiljbar** *al* discern-
ible **-skillning** discernment; discrimination;
judgement, discretion; *med ~* (*äv.*) discrimi-
nately; *utan ~* (*äv.*) indiscriminately
urskillnings|förmåga judgement **-lös** indis-
criminate
urskog primeval (virgin) forest; *AE.* backwoods
(*pl*); jungle
urskuld|a exculpate; excuse (*sig o.s.*) **-ande l** *a4*
apologetic (*min* air) **ll** *s6* excuse, exculpation
ursprung *s7* origin; (*friare*) source, root; (*härkomst*) extraction; *leda sitt ~ från* derive one's
(its) origin from, be derived from; *till sitt ~* in
(by) origin; *av engelskt ~* of English extraction
-lig *al* original; primitive; (*okonstlad*) natural,
simple **-ligen** originally; primarily **-lighet** originality, primitiveness
ursprungs|beteckning mark (indication) of
origin **-bevis** certificate of origin **-land** country
of origin
urspår|a run off the rails, derail; *bildl.* go wrong
-[n]ing derailment
urståndsatt [-ʼstånd-] *a4* incapacitated, incapable
ursäkt *s3* excuse (*för* for); apology; (*förevändning*) pretext; *anföra som ~* plead ..., give ... as
a pretext; *be om ~* apologize, make apologies; *be
ngn om ~* beg a p.'s pardon, apologize to s.b.;
framföra sina ~er make one's excuses (apologies)
ursäkt|a excuse, pardon; ~*!* excuse me!, I beg
your pardon!, [I'm] sorry!; ~ *att jag* excuse my (+
ing-form); ~ *sig* excuse o.s. (*med att* on the
grounds that) **-lig** *al* excusable, pardonable
urtag recess, notch; *elektr.* socket, *AE.* outlet
urtavla dial; clock face
ur|tida *oböjligt a* primeval, prehistoric; *geol.* pal-
[a]eontological **-tiden** prehistoric times (*pl*)
-tima *oböjligt a* extraordinary (*möte* session); ~
riksdag (*Storbritannien ung.*) autumn session
-tråkig extremely dull **-typ** prototype; archetype
uru|guayare [-*ˣajj-*] *s9,* **-guaysk** [-ʼajsk] *a5*
Uruguayan
ur|uppförande first (original) performance
-usel extremely bad; *vard.* abysmal
ur|val *s7* choice; selection; *hand. äv.* assortment;

(*stickprov*) sample; *naturligt* ~ natural selection; *representativt* (*slumpmässigt*) ~ representative (probability) sample; *rikt* ~ large (rich) assortment (selection); ... *i* ~ (*som boktitel*) selections from ... **-valsmetod** selection method **-vattna** soak; *~d* (*bildl.*) watered down, insipid
urverk works (*pl*) of a clock (watch); *som ett* ~ (*äv. bildl.*) like clockwork
urvuxen outgrown
uråldrig extremely old, ancient
USA [ˣuːessaː, -ˈaː] the U.S.[A.] (*sg*)
usans [u-, yˈsaŋs] *s3* trade (commercial) custom; *enligt* ~ according to custom
usch ugh!
usel [ˈuː-] *a2* wretched, miserable; *vard.* abysmal; (*om pers. äv.*) worthless; (*avskyvärd*) execrable; (*moraliskt*) vile, base; (*dålig*) poor, bad (*hälsa* health; *föda* food) **uselhet** wretchedness *etc.*; misery; (*moralisk*) meanness **uselt** *adv* wretchedly *etc.*; *ha det* ~ (*ekonomiskt*) be very badly off
usling [ˣuːs-] wretch; (*starkare*) villain; (*stackare*) wretch
usurp|ator [-ˣpaːtår] *s3* usurper **-era** usurp
U-sväng (*i trafik*) U-turn
ut out; *år* ~ *och år in* year in year out; *nyheten kom* ~ (*äv.*) the news got abroad; *stanna månaden* ~ stay the month out; *~!* get out!, out with you!; ~ *och in* in and out; *vända* ~ *och in på* turn inside out; *inte veta varken* ~ *eller in* not know which way to turn, be at one's wits end; *det kommer på ett* ~ it makes no difference, it is all one; *gå* ~ *i* go out into (*skogen* the woods); *han ville inte* ~ *med det* he wouldn't come out with it; *jag måste* ~ *med mycket pengar* I must pay out a lot of money; ~ *på* out into (*gatan* the street), out on (*isen* the ice); ~ *ur* out of
ut|ackordera board out, *vard.* farm out **-age-rad** *a5, saken är* ~ the matter is settled
utan I *prep* without, with no (*pengar* money); ~ *arbete* out of work; *bli* ~ (*absol.*) have to go (do) without, get nothing; *inte bli* ~ have one's share; ~ *vidare* without further notice (ado), *vard.* just like that; *prov* ~ *värde* sample of no value; *det är inte* ~ (*vard.*) it is not out of the question; *det är inte* ~ *att han har* it cannot be denied that he had; ~ *dem hade jag* but (were it not) for them I would have; ~ *att* without (*kunna* being able to); ~ *att ngn märker ngt* without anybody's noticing anything **II** *konj* but; *icke blott* ~ *även* not only ... but [also]; ~ *därför* [and] so **III** *adv* outside; *känna ngt* ~ *och innan* know s.th. inside out
utand|as *dep* breathe out; exhale, expire; ~ *sin sista suck* breathe one's last [breath] **-ning** expiration, exhalation; *in- och* ~ inhalation and expiration
utanför I *adv* outside **II** *prep* outside; in front of, before; *sjö.* off (*Godahoppsudden* the Cape of Good Hope); *en som står* ~ an outsider
utan|läsning recitation by heart **-läxa** lesson [to be] learnt by heart
utannonsera advertise
utanordn|a ~ *ett belopp* order a sum of money to be paid [out] **-ing** directions for payment of a sum of money; *konkr.* voucher
utanpå I *prep* outside, on the outside of; *gå* ~ (*vard.*) beat, surpass **II** *adv* outside **-skjorta** tu-

nic [shirt]
utan|skrift address [on the cover]; *det syns på ~en att han är lärare* you can see by his appearance that he is a teacher **-till** by heart **-tilläxa** (*särskr. utantill-läxa*) *se utanläxa* **-verk** *mil.* outwork, outer work; *bildl.* façade
ut|arbeta work out; (*förslag e.d. äv.*) draw (make) up; (*sammanställa*) compile; (*omsorgsfullt*) elaborate; (*karta, katalog e.d.*) prepare **-arbetad** *a5* **1** worked out (*etc.*) **2** (*-sliten*) overworked, worn-out **-arbetande** *s6* working out (*etc.*); preparation; *är under* ~ is being prepared, is in course of preparation **-arma** impoverish, reduce to poverty; (*starkare*) pauperize; ~ *jorden* impoverish the soil; (*äv.*) destitute **-armning** impoverishment **-arrendera** lease (let) [out] **-arrendering** leasing
utav *se av*
ut|basunera trumpet forth, blazon abroad **-bedja** *rfl* solicit, ask for, request **-bekomma** obtain (*sin lön* one's salary); obtain access to (*handlingar* documents) **-betala** pay [out, down], disburse **-betalning** payment, disbursement; *göra en* ~ make (effect) a payment
utbild|a train; (*undervisa*) instruct; (*uppfostra*) educate; *mil. äv.* drill; (*utveckla*) develop; ~ *sig till läkare* study to become a doctor; ~ *sig till sångare* train o.s. to become a singer **-ad** *a5* trained *etc.*; skilled (*arbetare* worker); (*utvecklad*) developed **-ning** training *etc.*; (*undervisning*) instruction; (*uppfostran*) education; *få sin* ~ *vid* (*äv.*) be educated (trained) at; *språklig* ~ linguistic schooling
utbildnings|anstalt educational (training) institution **-bevis** university course matriculation certificate **-bidrag** study grant; (*för doktoranden*) postgraduate grant **-departement** ministry of education; (*i Sverige*) ministry of education and cultural affairs **-linje** study programme **-minister** minister of education; (*i Sverige*) minister of education and cultural affairs **-tid** period of training; apprenticeship **-utskott** *-et* [the Swedish parliamentary] standing committee on education
ut|bjuda offer [for sale], put up for sale **-blick** view; perspective **-blommad** *a5* faded **-blottad** destitute (*på* of); *i -blottat tillstånd* in a state of destitution **-blåsningsventil** exhaust valve; (*på ångmaskin*) blow-off [valve] **-bombad** *a5* bombed out **-bordare** [-ɔ:-] outboard motor **-breda** spread [out]; expand; (*ngt hopvikt*) unfold; ~ *sig* spread (itself), extend; ~ *sig över ett ämne* expiate upon a subject **-bredd** *a5* [widely] spread, widespread; prevalent (*åsikt* opinion); *med ~a armar* with open arms **-bredning** [-e:-] **1** (*-ande*) spreading *etc.* **2** spread, extension, distribution; (*av sjukdom, bruk*) prevalence **-bringa** propose (*en skål* a toast); ~ *ett leve för* cheer for **-brista 1** (*-ropa*) exclaim **2** *se brista 1* **-brodera** *bildl.* deck out
ut|brott (*-brytande*) breaking out; (*av sinnesrörelse*) outburst (*av vrede* of rage), fit (*av dåligt humör* of temper); (*vulkan-*) eruption; (*krigs-*) outbreak; *komma till* ~ break out **-brunnen** *a5* burnt out; (*om vulkan*) extinct **-bryta 1** (*ta bort*) break out; *mat.* remove; ~ *ur sammanhanget* de-

tach from the context **2** (*om krig, farsot e.d.*) break out **-brytarkung** escapologist, escape artist **-brytning** breaking out; breakout; (*från fängelse*) escape **-bränd** *a5* burnt out **-buad** (*från scenen*) booed off the stage; *hon blev ~* she was booed, she got the bird **-bud** offer [for sale]; (*tillgång*) supply **-buktad** *a5* bent outwards **-buktning** bulge; protuberance **-byggd** *a5* built out; (*om fönster äv.*) projecting; *-byggt fönster* (*äv.*) bow window **-byggnad** *abstr.* extension, enlargement; *konkr.* annexe, addition **ut|byta** [ex]change (*mot* for); (*ömsesidigt*) interchange; *~ erfarenheter* (*äv.*) compare notes; *~ meddelanden* communicate [with each other] **-bytbar** [-y:-] *a1* replaceable; (*ömsesidigt*) interchangeable **-byte** exchange; (*ömsesidigt*) interchange; (*behållning*) gain, profit; *i ~* in exchange (*mot* for); *få ngt i ~ mot* (*äv.*) get s.th. instead of; *lämna ngt i ~* (*vid köp*) trade in s.th. (*mot* for); *ha ~ av ngt* derive benefit from s.th., profit by s.th. **-bär[n]ing** distribution; (*av post äv.*) delivery **-böling** outsider, stranger **-checka** [-çe-] check out

ut|data data. output [data] **-debitera** impose (*skatt* taxes) **-debitering** imposition **-dela** distribute; (*portion, hand*) out; deliver (*post* mail); *~ order om* give orders for; *~ slag* deal out (administer) blows **-delning** distribution; dealing out *etc.*; (*av post*) delivery; (*på aktie*) dividend; *extra ~* bonus, extra dividend; *ge 10% i ~* yield a dividend of 10%; *~en fastställdes till a* dividend of ... was declared **-dikning** drainage [by ditches] **-drag** extract, excerpt (*ur* from) **-dragbar** [-a:-] *a1* extensible **-dragen** *a5* drawn out; (*i tid*) lengthy, long [drawn-out]

utdrags|bord extension table **-skiva** sliding leaf; (*på bord*) [pull-out] slide **-soffa** sofa bed **ut|driva** drive out (*ur* from); (*fack. o. friare*) expel; (*onda andar*) exorcise **-dunsta 1** (*avgå i gasform*) evaporate **2** (*avsöndra*) transpire, perspire; (*om sak*) exhale (*fuktighet* moisture) **-dunstning** transpiration, perspiration; evaporation **-död** extinct; (*-rotad*) exterminated; (*friare*) deserted (*stad* town) **-döende I** *a4* dying, expiring **II** *s6* dying out; extinction; *är stadd i ~* is dying out **-döma 1** (*genom dom*) impose (*ett straff* a penalty); adjudge (*ett belopp* an amount) **2** (*kassera*) reject; condemn (*ett fartyg* a vessel); *-dömda bostäder* condemned houses, houses declared unfit for habitation

ute 1 rumsbet. out; (*i det fria äv.*) outdoors, out-of-doors; (*utanför*) outside; *där ~* out there; *vara ~ och* be out (*+ ing-form*); *fåren går ~ hela året* the sheep are in the open pasture the whole year round; *äta ~* (*på restaurang*) dine out, (*i det fria*) dine out-of-doors **2** (*slut*) up; *allt hopp är ~* all hope is gone, there is no hope; *tiden är ~* [the] time is up; *det är ~ med honom* it is all up with him, he is quite done for **3** (*utsatt*) *de har varit ~ för en olycka* they met with an accident; *jag har aldrig varit ~ för ngt sådant* I have never experienced anything like that; *vara illa ~* be in a spot **4** (*omodern*) out

ute|bli[va] (*ej inträffa*) not (fail to) come off, not occur (happen); (*ej infinna sig*) stay away, not turn up (appear, come); *~ inför rätta* fail to appear in court **-blivande** *s6* absence, failure to attend; *jur.* default **-bliven** *a5* that has failed to appear (*etc.*); (*frånvarande*) absent; *~ betalning* nonpayment **-bruk** *för ~* for outdoor use **-dass** *vard.* outside privy, *AE.* outhouse **utefter** ['u:t-, -'eff-] [all] along **ute|grill** outdoor grill **-gångsfår** sheep in open pasture **-gångsförbud** curfew [order] **-lek** outdoor game **-liggare** vagrant, homeless person **-liv 1** (*på restauranger e.d.*) idka *~* go out a lot **2** (*friluftsliv*) outdoor life **-lämna** leave out, omit; (*hoppa över*) pass over **-lämnande** *s6* omission **-löpande** *a4, ~ sedelmängd* volume of notes in circulation; *~ växlar* outstanding bills **utensilier** [-'si:-] *pl* (*tillbehör*) accessories; (*redskap o.d.*) utensils, appliances **uterus** ['u:-] *r* uterus (*pl* uteri) **ute|servering** open-air restaurant (cafeteria *etc.*) **-sluta** *-slöt -slutit* exclude (*ur* from); (*ur förening*) expel; *fack.* eliminate; *det -sluter inte att jag* this does not prevent my (*+ ing-form*); *det är absolut -slutet* it is absolutely out of the question **-slutande I** *a4* exclusive, sole **II** *adv* exclusively, solely **III** *s6* exclusion; expulsion (*ur* from); elimination; *med ~ av* with the exclusion (exception) of **-slutit** *sup. av* utesluta **-slutning** [-u:-] *se -slutande III* **-slöt** *imperf. av* utesluta **-spelare** (*anfallsspelare*) forward, (*försvarsspelare*) defender; *alla -spelarna* all the players except the goalkeeper **-stående** *a4* **1** *~ gröda* standing (growing) crops (*pl*) **2** (*som ej inbetalats*) outstanding; *~ fordringar* accounts receivable, outstanding claims **-stänga** shut (lock) out; keep out; (*hindra*) debar; (*-sluta*) exclude; *bli -stängd* be shut (locked) out **-stängning** shutting out *etc.*; exclusion; debarment **ut|examinera** examine for the final degree; *AE. äv.* graduate; *~d* certified, graduate; *bli ~d* pass one's final examination; *~d sjuksköterska* trained (registered, *AE.* graduate) nurse; *han är ~d från* he is a graduate of **-experimentera** discover (find out) by means of experiment **ut|fall 1** *fäkt.* lunge; *mil.* sally, sortie; *bildl.* (*attack*) attack; *göra ett ~* (*mil.*) make a sally, *fäkt.* make a lunge, *bildl.* launch an attack (*mot* against) **2** (*resultat*) result, outturn **3** (*bortfall*) disappearance, dropping out (*av en vokal* of a vowel) **4** (*radioaktivt*) fallout **-falla 1** *se falla ut* **2** (*om lott*) give (*med 100 pund* £100); *~ med vinst* (*om lott*) be a winning ticket; *~ till belåtenhet* give satisfaction; *skörden har -fallit bra* the harvest has been good; *utslaget -föll gynnsamt för oss* the verdict went in our favour **ut|fart 1** (*färd ut*) departure (*ur* from) **2** (*väg ut*) way out, exit; (*från stan*) main road [out of the town] **-fattig** miserably poor; (*utblottad*) destitute; (*utan pengar*) penniless **-fiska** overfish **-flaggning** registration of ships under a flag of convenience **-flugen** *a5, är ~* is (has) flown; *barnen är -flugna* the children have all left home **-flykt** excursion, outing; trip; (*i det gröna*) picnic; *göra en ~* make an excursion, take a trip (*till* to) **-flyktsmål** destination of an excursion; *vårt ~ var* Bristol **-flytt-ning** moving out, removal **-flöde** outflow, discharge, escape; *bildl.* emanation **-fodra** keep,

U

feed (*med* on) **-fodring** [- o:-] feed[ing], keep **-fordra** demand; challenge

ut|forma (*gestalta*) give final shape to, model; (*-arbeta*) work out; (*text e.d.*) draw up, formulate; ~ *en annons* design (lay out) an advertisement **-formning** [-å-] shaping *etc.*; working out *etc.* **-forska** find out, investigate, search into; *geogr.* explore **-forskning** investigation; exploration **-frusen** *han är* ~ he has been frozen out, he has been sent to Coventry **-frysa** freeze out, send to Coventry **-fråga** question, interrogate; (*korsförhöra*) cross-examine **-frågning** [-å:-] questioning, interrogation; cross-examination; (*av expert inför utskott o.d.*, *äv.*) hearing **-fundera** think (work, find) out **-fyllnad** (*-fyllande*) filling up (in); *konkr.* filling; *bildl.* padding **-fälla** *kem.* precipitate **-fällbar** folding out, collapsible **-fällning 1** (*-fällande*) folding out **2** *kem.* precipitation, deposit **-färd** excursion (*jfr utflykt*)

ut|färda [-ä:-] (*-ställa*) make out, draw up; issue (*fullmakt* power of attorney); (*påbjuda*) order, impose; ~ *lagar* enact legislation; *stormvarning har* ~*ts för* a gale warning has been issued for; ~ *en kommuniké* issue (publish) a communiqué **-fästa** offer (*en belöning* a reward); promise; ~ *sig* promise, engage (*att* to) **-fästelse** promise, pledge **-för** ['u:t-] **I** *prep* down **II** *adv* down [wards]; *det bär* (*sluttar*) ~ it slopes downhill; *gå* ~ descend; *det går* ~ *med dem* (*bildl.*) they are going downhill

utför|a 1 *se föra* [*ut*] *o. exportera* **2** (*uträtta*) carry out, perform, effect, execute; (*göra*) do; ~ *en plan* realize (carry out) a plan; *ett väl -t arbete* a good piece of work **3** *hand.* carry out (*en post* an item); ~ *en summa* place (put) a sum to account **-ande** *s6* **1** *eg.* (*export*) exportation **2** (*uträttande*) carrying out, performance, execution; (*utformning*) design, model **3** (*framföringssätt*) style; (*talares*) delivery **4** *hand.* carrying out **-bar** *a1* practicable, feasible; realizable, executable

utför|lig [-ö:-] *a1* detailed; (*uttömmande*) exhaustive **-lighet** fullness (completeness) [of detail] **-ligt** *adv* in detail, fully; exhaustively **utförsbacke** downhill

utförsel *s9* export[ation] **-förbud** export ban **-tillstånd** export licence (permit)

utförs|gåvor *pl* eloquence (*sg*); *han har goda* ~ he is very eloquent **-åkning** (*på skidor*) downhill [skiing]

utförsälj|a sell out (off) **-ning** clearance (closing-down) sale **-ningspris** (*detaljhandelspris*) retail price; (*realisationspris*) bargain (clearance) price

ut|gallring sorting out; (*av skog*) thinning [out]; *bildl.* elimination **-ge 1** *se ge* [*ut*] **2** *rfl*, ~ *sig för att vara* give o.s. out (pretend) to be **-gift** *s3* expense; ~*er* (*äv.*) expenditure (*sg*); *inkomster och* ~*er* income and expenditure; *stora* ~*er* heavy expenses (expenditure); *få inkomster och* ~*er att gå ihop* make [both] ends meet

utgifts|konto expense account **-post** item of expenditure **-sida** debit side; *på* ~*n* on the debit side **-stat** estimate of expenditure

utgiva *se utge*

utgivar|e 1 (*av skrift*) publisher **2** (*utfärdare*) drawer (*av en växel* of a bill) **-korsband** (*angivelse på försändelse*) Printed Matter Rate

utgiv|en published **-ning** (*av bok*) publication; *under* ~ in course of publication **-ningsår** year of publication

ut|gjuta pour out (*äv. bildl.*); shed (*tårar* tears); ~ *sig* pour out one's feelings, (*i tal*) dilate (*över* on); ~ *sig över* (*äv.*) pour o.s. out about; ~ *sin vrede över* vent one's anger upon **-gjutelse** [-j-] pouring out; shedding; *bildl.* effusion **-gjutning** *med.* extravasation, suffusion **-grena** *rfl* branch out **-gräva** *se gräva* [*ut*] **-grävning** excavation

ut|gå 1 *se gå* [*ut*] **2** (*komma*) come, issue, proceed, (*från* from); *bildl.* start (*från* from); *förslaget -gick från honom* the proposal came from him **3** ~ *från* (*förutsätta*) suppose, assume, take it, (*ta som ämne för utläggning*) start out from **4** (*betalas*) be paid (payable); *arvode* ~*r med* the fee payable (to be paid) is **5** (*utelämnas*) *denna post* ~*r* this item is to be deleted (left out, expunged) (*ur* from) **6** (*gå t. ända*) come to an end, expire **7** ~ *som segrare* come off a victor (victorious) **-gående I** *a4* outgoing; *sjö. äv.* outward-bound; ~ *balans* balance carried forward **II** *s6* going out; (*utgång*) departure; *på* ~ (*sjö.*) outward bound **-gång 1** (*väg ut*) exit; way out **2** (*slut*) end, termination; (*av tidsfrist*) expiration; *vid* ~*en av 1968* by the end of 1968 **3** (*resultat*) result, outcome, issue; *få dödlig* ~ prove fatal **4** *kortsp.* game; *få* (*göra*) ~ score game **-gången** *a5*, *han är* ~ he has gone out; (*slutsåld*) sold out, no longer in stock; (*om bok*) out of print

utgångs|hastighet initial velocity **-läge** initial position, starting point **-material** source (basic, original) material **-psalm** concluding hymn, postlude **-punkt** starting point, point of departure; (*friare äv.*) basis (*för* of)

ut|gård outlying farm **-gåva** edition **-göra** (*bilda*) constitute, form, make; (*tillsammans* ~) compose, make up; (*belöpa sig t.*) amount to, be, total; *hyran -gör 900 kronor i månaden* the rent is 900 kronor a month; ~*s av* (*vanl.*) consist (be composed) of **-hamn** outport, outer harbour **-huggning** (*skogsbruk*) clearing **-hungra** starve into surrender; ~*d* famished, starving **-hus** outhouse **-hyrning** [-y:-] letting [out], renting, hiring [out]; *till* ~ for hire; *se äv. hyra* **-hyrningsbyrå** estate agency, house-agent's office

uthållig *a1* with staying power; persevering, persistent; tough **-het** (*fysisk*) staying power, stamina, perseverance, persistence **-hetsprov** endurance test

uthärd|a endure, stand, bear **-lig** *a1* endurable, bearable

ut|i [-'i:, 'u:-] *se i* **-ifrån I** *prep* from [out in] (*gatan* the street); from [out of] (*skogen* the woods) **II** *adv* from outside; (*från utlandet*) from abroad

util|ism utilitarianism **-ist** *s3*, **-istisk** [-'liss-] *a5* utilitarian **-itarism** *se utilism*

ut|jämna level (*äv. bildl.*), even; (*-släta*) smooth [out]; (*göra lika*) equalize; *hand.* [counter]balance; ~ *ett konto* settle an account **-jämning** levelling *etc.*; equalization; *fys. o. bildl.* compensation; *till* ~ *av* (*hand.*) in settlement of; ~ *av* *motsättningar* the straightening out of differences **-kant** (*av skog e.d.*) border; *i stadens* ~*er* in the outskirts of the town **-kast 1** *bildl.* draft (*till* of); sketch; (*t. tavla e.d.*) design; *göra ett* ~ *till* (*äv.*) trace [... in outline], design **2** (*i bollspel*) throwout **-kastare 1** *tekn.* ejector **2** (*ordningsvakt*) chucker-out; *AE.* bouncer

ut|kik [-çi:k] *s2* **1** lookout station, watch tower; *hålla* ~ be on the lookout (*efter* for), watch **2** (*-kiksplats på fartyg*) lookout, crow's nest; *pers.* lookout [man] **-kikstorn** lookout [tower] **-klarera** enter (clear) outwards **-klarering** clearance outwards, outward clearance **-klassa** outclass **-klädd** dressed up (*till* as a) **-klädning** [-ä:-] dressing up **-komma** *se komma* [*ut*]; *en nyligen -kommen bok* a recently published book **-kommendera** order out **-komst** [-å-] *s3* living, livelihood **-komstmöjlighet** means of subsistence **-konkurrera** oust, outstrip; *bli* ~*d* be outclassed (crowded out)

ut|kora elect; *den* ~*de* the chosen one **-kristallisera** crystallize (*sig* o.s.) **-kräva** claim, require; ~ *hämnd* take vengeance (*på* on); ~ *skadestånd* demand damages **-kvittera** receipt [and receive]; (*pengar*) cash; ~ *en försändelse* give a receipt for a consignment **-kyld** [-çy:-] *a5* chilled down; *rummet är -kylt* (*äv.*) the room has got quite cold **-kämpa** fight [out]; *strider* ~*des* battles were fought **-körare** delivery man **-körd** [-çö:-] *a5* **1** (*-jagad*) turned out [of doors] **2** (*-tröttad*) worn out **-körning** [-çö:-] (*av varor*) delivery **-körsport** [-çö:-]

utlandet *best. form, från* (*i, till*) ~*et* abroad; *i* ~*et* (*äv.*) in foreign countries

utlands|affärer *pl* foreign business (*sg*) **-svensk** overseas (expatriate) Swede **-vistelse** sojourn (stay) abroad

ut|led[sen] thoroughly (utterly) tired; *vard.* bored to death (*på* of), fed up (*på* with) **-levad** *a5* decrepit; (*genom utsvävningar*) debauched **-ljud** *språk.* final sound **-lokalisera** relocate [outside capital] **-lokalisering** relocation [outside capital] **-lopp** outflow; outlet (*äv. bildl.*); *ge* ~ *åt* give vent to **-lotsning** piloting out **-lotta** dispose of by lottery; (*obligation e.d.*) draw **-lova** promise

ut|lysa give notice of, publish; *ett möte* convene (call) a meeting; ~ *nyval* appeal to the country; ~ *stejk* call a strike; ~ *en tävlan* announce a competition **-låna** lend; *AE.* loan; ~ *mot ränta* lend at interest; *boken är* ~*d* the book is out on loan **-låning** lending; *affärsbankernas* ~ the advances of the commercial banks **-låningsränta** lending rate, interest rate for advances (loans) **-låta** *rfl* express o.s. (*om, över* [up]on); (*yttra äv.*) state, say **-låtande** *s6* [stated] opinion, report, statement [of opinion]; verdict; (*från högre myndighet*) rescript; *avge ett* ~ deliver (give) an opinion (*om* on, about), present a report (verdict) (*om* on) **-lägg** *s7* outlay; expense[s *pl*], disbursement; *kontanta* ~ out-of-pocket expenses **-lägga** *se lägga* [*ut*]; (*förklara*) interpret, comment **-läggning** laying [out]; (*förklaring*) interpretation, comments (*pl*); ~ *av kablar* cable-laying **-lämna** give (hand) out; issue (*biljetter* tickets); (*överlämna*) give up, surrender; (*brottsling t.*

främmande land) extradite; *känna sig* ~*d* (*bildl.*) feel deserted **-lämning** giving out, distribution, issue; (*av post*) delivery; (*av brottsling*) extradition

ut|ländsk *a5* foreign **-ländska** *s1* foreign woman (lady) **-länning** foreigner **-länningskommission** aliens commission **-lärd** *vara* ~ have served one's apprenticeship **-läsa** (*sluta sig t.*) gather, understand (*av* from) **-löpa 1** (*om fartyg*) put to sea, leave port **2** (*gå t. ända*) come to an end, expire; *kontraktet -löper den* the contract expires on **-löpare 1** *bot.* runner **2** (*från bergskedja*) spur; *bildl.* offshoot **-lösa 1** redeem; (*delägare*) buy out; (*pant*) get out of pawn **2** (*frigöra*) release; (*igångsätta*) start, trigger [off] **3** (*framkalla*) bring about, produce, create **-lösning 1** redeeming *etc.*; redemption **2** release; starting *etc.* **3** orgasm **-lösningsmekanism** release

utman|a challenge; (*trotsa*) defy; ~ *ngn på duell* (*äv.*) call s.b. out **-ande** *a4* challenging; defying, defiant; (*om uppträdande*) provocative, (*i sht kvinnas*) enticing **-are** challenger **-ing** challenge (*äv. bildl.*)

ut|manövrera outmanoeuvre **-mark** outlying land

utmatt|ad *a5* exhausted; *vard.* knocked up **-ning** exhaustion

utmattnings|krig war of attrition **-tillstånd** state of exhaustion

ut|med ['ut-, -'me:d] [all] along; ~ *varandra* alongside each other, side by side **-mejsla** chisel [out] **-minutera** sell by retail, retail **-minutering** retail sale [of liquors], retailing [of spirits] **-mynna** (*om vattendrag*) discharge (*i* into); (*om gata o.d.*) open out (*i* into); ~ *i* (*bildl.*) end [up] with, result in **-måla** *bildl.* paint, depict **-märglad** [-j-] *a5* emaciate[d], haggard **-märgling** [-j-] emaciation

utmärk|a (*sätta märke vid*) mark [out]; (*beteckna*) denote; (*angiva*) indicate; (*karakterisera*) characterize, distinguish; (*hedra*) honour; ~ *med rött* indicate (mark) in red; ~ *sig* distinguish o.s. (*äv. iron.*) (*genom* by) **-ande** *a4* characteristic (*för* of); ~ *egenskap* characteristic, distinguishing quality; *det mest* ~ *draget i* (*äv.*) the outstanding feature of

utmärkelse distinction; honour **-tecken** [mark of] distinction

utmärkt I *a4* excellent, superb; *vard.* capital, splendid, first-rate, fine **II** *adv* excellently *etc.*; ~ *god* (*äv.*) excellent, delicious, exquisite; *må* ~ feel fine (first-rate)

utmät|a *jur.* levy a distress (execution); *absol.* distrain **-ning** distraint, distress; *göra* ~ *hos ngn* distrain upon s.b., levy execution on a p.'s property

utmätnings|förfarande attachment proceedings (*pl*) **-man** [court] bailiff, distrainer

utmönstr|a (*kassera*) reject, discard **-ing** rejection, discarding

utnyttj|a utilize, exploit, use; (*t. egen fördel*) take advantage of; ~ *situationen* make the most of the situation; *väl* ~*d* did time well spent **-ande** *s6* utilization, exploitation

ut|nämna appoint (*ngn t. överste* s.b. [a] colo-

nel), nominate, make **-nämning** appointment, nomination **-nötning** wearing out **-nötnings- krig** war of attrition **-nötningstaktik** wearing- -down tactics (pl) **-nött** worn out; bildl. hack- neyed, well-worn
utochinvänd inside out
utom [ˣu:tåm] **1** (med undantag av) except, save; with the exception of; alla ~ jag all except me; ingen ~ jag no one but me; vara allt ~ be anything but, be far from; ~ att except that, besides that; ~ att det är för dyrt är det också besides being too expensive it is also; ~ när except when **2** (utan- för) outside (dörren the door); out of (fara danger); beyond (allt tvivel all doubt); inom och ~ landet at home and abroad **3** vara ~ sig be be- side o.s. (av with), (starkare) go frantic, be trans- ported (av with) **-bordsmotor** outboard motor **-europeisk** non-European
utomhus outdoors, out-of-doors **-antenn** out- door (open-air) aerial (AE. antenna) **-bruk** out- door use **-grill** barbecue **-sport** outdoor sports (pl)
utom|lands abroad **-ordentlig** extraordinary; (förträfflig) excellent; av ~ betydelse of extreme importance **-ordentligt** adv extraordinarily etc. **-skärs** [-ʃä:rs] beyond (off) the skerries; in open waters **-stående** a4, en ~ an outsider, the unin- itiated **-äktenskaplig** extramarital; ~a barn il- legitimate children
utop|i s3 utopia; utopian scheme **-isk** [-ˈtå:-] a5 utopian
ut|organ data. output device **-peka** point out; ~ ngn som indicate (designate) s.b. as **-pinad** a5 harrowed, harassed; (starkare) excruciated **-pla- cera** set out **-plantera** plant out **-plundra** fleece, strip **-plåna** obliterate, efface, wipe out (minnet av the memory of); (förinta) annihilate **-plåning** obliteration; effacing etc.; annihilation **-portionera** portion out, distribute **-post** out- post, advanced post **-postera** station, post
utpress|a 1 eg. press (squeeze) out **2** ~ pengar av extort money from, blackmail **-are** black- mailer; AE. äv. racketeer **-ning** blackmail; ex- tortion; AE. äv. racket **-ningsförsök** at- tempted blackmail **-ningspolitik** policy of ex- tortion
ut|pricka mark out; ~d farled buoyed-off fair- way **-prickning** marking; sjö. beaconage, [sys- tem of] buoyage **-prova** test [out], try out; (klä- der) try on **-provning** test, (av kläder) trying on **-prångla** hawk; ~ falska mynt utter (pass) base coin **-präglad** [-ä:-] a5 pronounced, marked, de- cided **-pumpad** a5, bildl. done up, fagged out **-rangera** discard, scrap **-rannsaka** search out, fathom
utred|a 1 (bringa ordning i) disentangle; clear up; (lösa) solve; (undersöka) investigate, inquire into; (grundligt) analyse **2** jur. (avveckla) wind up; (konkurs) liquidate **-ning 1** disentangle- ment; (undersökning) investigation, inquest; analysis; vara under ~ be under consideration; för vidare ~ for further consideration; offentliga ~ar official reports **2** jur. winding up; liquidation
utrednings|arbete investigation work **-man** investigator, examiner; (i bo) executor, adminis- trator; (i konkurs) liquidator

ut|rensning bildl. purge, cleanup **-resa** outward voyage (journey) **-resetillstånd** exit permit **-riggad** a5 outrigged **-riggare** outrigger
utrikes I oböjligt a foreign; på ~ ort abroad; ~ resa journey abroad **II** adv abroad; resa ~ go abroad **-departement** ~et [the] ministry for foreign affairs, Storbritannien Foreign Office, AE. [the] State Department **-handel** foreign trade **-handelsminister** minister for foreign trade **-korrespondent** foreign correspondent **-minister** minister for foreign affairs, foreign minister (Storbritannien secretary), AE. secre- tary of state **-ministerkonferens** foreign min- ister's conference **-nämnd** ~en the advisory coun- cil on foreign affairs, AE. the foreign relations committee **-politik** foreign politics (pl) (policy) **-politisk** relating to foreign politics (etc.); det ~a läget the political situation abroad **-repre- sentation** (ett lands) foreign service; (en fir- mas) foreign representation **-råd** head of depart- ment [of the ministry for foreign affairs] **-ut- skott** ~et [the Swedish parliamentry] standing committee on foreign affairs
utrikisk [-ˈri:-] a5 foreign; tala ~a (vard.) speak a foreign lingo
ut|rop 1 exclamation; ge till ett ~ av förvåning give a cry of (cry out with) surprise **2** (på auktion) cry **-ropa 1** (ropa högt) exclaim; ejaculate **2** (of- fentligt förkunna) proclaim (ngn t. kung s.b. king) **3** (på auktion) cry; (på gatan) hawk **-ro- pare** (på auktion) crier; (härold) herald **-rops- tecken** exclamation mark **-rota** eradicate, kill off, root out; (fullständigt) extirpate; (ett folk) exterminate **-rotning** [-ɔ:-] eradication, killing off etc.; extirpation; extermination; (av folk- grupp) genocide **-rotningskrig** war of extermi- nation **-rotningsmedel** means of extermi- nation; killer **-rusande** a4, komma ~ come out with a rush
ut|rusta equip; (med vapen äv.) arm; (fartyg o.d.) fit out; (förse) furnish, supply, provide; rikt ~d (bildl.) richly endowed; vara klent ~d å huvu- dets vägnar be weak in the head **-rustning** equipment, outfit; mil. äv. kit; maskinell ~ ma- chinery, mechanical equipment **-ryckning 1** tearing (pulling) out (jfr rycka ut) **2** (uttåg) march [ing] out; (brandkårs etc.) turnout; mil. decamp- ment, departure; (hemförlovning) discharge from active service **-ryckningsfordon** rescue vehicle **-rymma** (bostad e.d.) vacate, clear out of; mil. evacuate; (överge) abandon; ~ rättssalen clear the court **-rymme** s6 space, room (äv. bildl.); bildl. äv. scope; ge ~ för provide [space, room] for; kräva mycket ~ take up room, (om sak äv.) be bulky; ett hus med många ~n a house with plenty of storage space
utrymmes|besparande a4 space-saving **-krä- vande** requiring much space; bulky **-skäl** i uttr.: av ~ from considerations of space
ut|rymning (bortflyttning) removal; (av lä- genhet) quitting; mil. evacuation, abandonment **-räkna** (beräkna) calculate; work out (kost- naden the cost) **-räkning** calculation, working out; det är ingen ~ [med det] it is no good (not worth while) **-rätta** do (en hel del a great deal); ~ ett uppdrag carry out (perform) a commission;

~ *ett ärende* go on (do) an errand; *få ngt ~t* get s.th. done **-rättning** (*ärende*) job, errand, commission **-röna** ascertain, find out; (*konstatera*) establish

utsag|a *s1* statement; saying; (*vittnesbörd*) evidence, testimony; *enligt hans -o* according to him (what he says)

ut|satt *a4* **1** *se sätta* [*ut*] *o.* utsätta **2** (*fastställd*) appointed, fixed; *på ~ tid* at the appointed time, at the time fixed **3** (*blottställd*) exposed (*läge* position; *för* to); ~ *för kritik* subject[ed] to criticism; ~ *för fara* in danger; ~ *för förkylningar* liable to catch colds **-schasad** *se utsjasad* **-se** choose, select; ~ *ngn till ordförande* appoint s.b. chairman **1 utseende** *s6* (*val*) selecting *etc.*; appointment **2 utseende** *s6* (*yttre*) appearance, look; (*persons*) looks (*pl*); *av ~t att döma* to judge by appearances, from the look of him (*etc.*); *ha ett underligt* ~ have an odd look; *känna ngn till ~t* know s.b. by sight

ut|sida outside; exterior; (*fasad*) façade, front **-sikt** *s3* **1** *eg.* view; outlook; *ha ~ över* look (open) on to, overlook; *med ~ åt norr* facing north **2** *bildl.* prospect; chance, outlook; *ha alla ~er att* have every chance of; *ställa ngt i ~* hold out the prospect of s.th.

utsikts|berg hill with a [fine] view **-lös** hopeless **-plats** outlook **-torn** outlook tower

ut|sira decorate, deck out; (*smycka*) adorn **-sirad** *a5* ornamented; ornamental (*bokstav* letter) **-sirning** [-i:r-] ornament[ation]; embellishment **-sjasad** [-ʃ-] fagged out, dog-tired **-skeppa** ship [out]; export **-skeppningshamn** port of shipment **-skjutande** *a4* projecting; (*fram-*) protruding; salient (*hörn* angle) **-skjutning** discharge, firing, shooting; launching **-skjutningsramp** launching pad

1 utskott [-å-] *s7* (*dålig vara*) rejections, throwouts (*pl*)

2 utskott [-å-] *s7* **1** (*kommitté*) committee **2** (*utväxt*) outgrowth

utskotts|behandling debate in committee **-betänkande** committee report

utskotts|bräder *pl* rejected deals, waste boards **-porslin** defective china **-varor** *pl* defective (damaged) goods; rejects **-virke** defective [sawn] goods (*pl*); *AE.* defective lumber

ut|skrattad *a5* laughed to scorn **-skrift** clean (fair) copy; transcription **-skriva** *se skriva* [*ut*] **-skrivning 1** writing out [in full]; (*ren-*) transcription, copying; (*av kontrakt e.d.*) drawing up, making out **2** (*av skatter*) levy, imposition **3** *mil.* conscription, enlistment **4** (*från sjukhus*) discharge **-skuren** *a5* cut out **-skyld** [-ʃ-] *s3* tax; (*kommunal*) rate **-skällning** rating; *vard.* blowing up; *AE. vard.* calling down **-skämd** *a5* disgraced **-skänka** serve on the premises **-skänkning** [-ʃ-] serving on the premises **-skänkningslokal** licensed house (premises *pl*), public house **-skärning** [-ʃ-] cutting [out]

ut|slag 1 (*beslut*) decision; *jur.* (*i civilmål*) judgement; (*skiljedom*) award; (*i brottmål*) sentence; (*jurys*) verdict; *fälla ~* pronounce (give a) verdict; *hans ord fällde ~et* his words decided the matter **2** *med.* rash, eruption; *få ~* break out into a rash **3** (*på våg e.d.*) turn of the scales, devi-

ation; *mätaren gör ~* the meter is registering **4** (*resultat*) result, decision; (*uttryck*) manifestation; (*yttring*) outcrop; *ett ~ av dåligt humör* a manifestation of bad temper **-slagen** *a5* (*om blomma*) in blossom; (*om träd*) in leaf; (*om hår*) brushed out; (*utspilld*) spilt; *sport.* eliminated **-slagning** [-a:-] *sport.* elimination; (*i boxning*) knockout

utslags|fråga decisive issue; (*i tävling*) elimination question **-givande** *a4* decisive; *det blev ~ för mig* that decided me **-röst** casting vote **-tävlan** elimination (*sport.* knockout) competition (match)

ut|sliten worn-out; worn-out; (*om uttryck o.d.*) hackneyed, stale; ~ *fras* (*äv.*) cliché **-slockna** go out; (*om ätt*) die out; ~*d* (*äv.*) extinct **-slunga** hurl (fling) out; throw out; ~ *hotelser* threaten **-släpad** *a5, bildl.* worn-out; *vard.* dog-tired **-släpp** *s7* discharge (*av olja* of oil) **-släppa** (*sätta i omlopp*) issue, put on the market; (*jfr släppa* [*ut*]) **-smycka** adorn, decorate; deck out; (*försköna*) embellish (*en berättelse* a story) **-smyckning** adornment, ornamentation; embellishment; *konkr. äv.* ornament **-socknes** *oböjligt a* of another parish **-spark** *sport.* goal kick **-spekulerad** *a5* studied; artful, cunning

ut|spel *kortsp.* lead; *bildl.* move, initiative **-spelad** *a5*, *-spelat kort* card played [out] **-spelas** *dep* take place; *scenen ~ i* the scene is laid in **-spinna** *rfl* (*om samtal*) be carried on **-spionera** spy out **-spisa** cater; feed **-spisning** catering, feeding **-sprida** spread out; (*friare*) spread (*ett rykte* a rumour); (*utströ äv.*) scatter about **-språng** projection; protrusion; (*klipp-*) jut; (*bergs-*) shoulder **-spy** vomit, belch forth **-späda** dilute, thin [out] **-spädning** [-ä:-] dilution, thinning out **-spänd** spread [out], stretched; (*av luft*) inflated **-spärra 1** spread out, stretch open **2** (*från utbildning*) deny admission, exclude **-spökad** *a5* rigged out, guyed-up

ut|stake stake (set, mark, peg) out; *bildl.* lay down; (*föreskriva*) determine, prescribe **-stakad** *a5* marked out; fixed **-stakning** [-a:-] staking out *etc.* **-stansa** stamp (punch) [out] **-stoffera** dress up, garnish; (*berättelse e.d.*) pad out **-stråla** (*utgå som strålar*) [ir]radiate, emit, send forth (*ljus* light); ~ *värme* radiate (emit) heat; ~ *godhet* radiate goodness **-strålning** [ir]radiation, emission, emanation

ut|sträcka stretch [out], extend; ~ *sig* extend **-sträckning 1** (*-ande*) extension; (*i tid*) prolongation **2** (*vidd*) extent; extensiveness; (*dimension*) dimensions (*pl*); *i stor ~* to a great (large) extent; *i största möjliga ~* to the fullest possible extent; *i viss ~* to a certain degree (extent); *använda i stor ~* make extensive use of, use extensively **-sträckt** *a4* outstretched; extended; *ligga ~* lie full length (*framstupa* prostrate) **-studerad** *a5* (*raffinerad*) studied, artful; (*inpiskad*) thoroughbred **-styra** fit out; (*pynta*) dress up, array; *så -styrd du är!* what a fright you look! **-styrsel** *s2* (*utrustning*) outfit; (*bruds*) trousseau; (*t.ex. boks*) get-up; (*förpackning*) package; (*tillbehör*) fittings (*pl*) **-styrselpjäs** spectacular play **-stå** suffer, endure; (*genomlida*) go through **-stående** *a4* protruding; projecting; salient (*hörn* angle); ~ *öron* protruding ears; ~ *kindknotor* (*äv.*) high (prominent) cheekbones

utställ|a 1 *se ställa* [*ut*] **2** (*t. beskådande*) show; (*på* -*ning*) exhibit, expose, display **3** (*utfärda*) draw, make out, issue (*en växel* a bill) **-are 1** (*av varor*) exhibitor **2** (*av värdehandling*) drawer, issuer **-ning** exhibition, show; display; (*av tavlor äv.*) gallery

utställnings|föremål exhibit **-kommissarie** exhibition commissioner **-lokal** showrooms (*pl*); (*med försäljning*) salesroom

ut|stöta (*utesluta*) expel, eject (*ur* from); (*ljud*) utter, emit; (*rökmoln*) puff out; (*om vulkan*) belch out (*lava* lava); (*ur kyrkan*) excommunicate; *vara -stött ur samhället* be a social outcast **-stötning** [-ö:-] ejection; expulsion **-suga** (*jord*) impoverish **-sugare** *pers.* extortioner, bloodsucker **-sugning** sucking out; (*evakuering*) evacuation; (*av jord*) impoverishment; *bildl.* extortion

utsugnings|anordning extractor **-ventil** evacuation valve

ut|svulten starved, famished **-svängd** *a5* curved (bent) outwards **-svängning** curve **-svävande** *a4* dissipated, dissolute, disorderly **-svävningar** [-ä:-] *pl* dissipation (*sg*), excesses; extravagances **-syning** rejection, discarding; (*av träd*) marking [out] **-så** sow [out] (*äv. bildl.*) **-såld** sold out; *-sålt* (*teat.*) all tickets sold, house full, *AE.* full house **-säde** *s6* [planting] seed, grain **-sända 1** send out; (*utgiva*) publish, issue; *vår -sände medarbetare* our special correspondent **2** (*alstra*) send out, emit (*värme* heat) **3** (*i radio*) transmit, broadcast **-sändning 1** sending out; publication, issue **2** emission **3** transmission, broadcasting

ut|sätta 1 (*blottställa*) expose, subject (*för* to) **2** (*fastställa*) appoint, fix (*dagen för* the day for) **3** *rfl* expose o.s., lay o.s. open (*för* to); *det vill jag inte ~ mig för* (*äv.*) I don't want to run that risk **-sökning** [-ö:-] *jur.* recovery of a debt by enforcement order **-sökt I** *a1* exquisite, choice, select **II** *adv* exquisitely; ~ *fin* (*äv.*) very choice **-söndra** secrete, excrete **-söndring** secretion, excretion **-söndringsorgan** secretory (excretive) organ **-sövd** [-ö:-] *a5* thoroughly rested

utta [ˣuː t-] *se uttaga*

uttag 1 *elektr.* socket; *AE.* outlet **2** (*av pengar*) withdrawal; *varorna skall levereras för ~ efter köparens behov* the goods are to be delivered at (on) call **uttaga** (*jfr ta* [*ut*]) take out; ~ *i förskott* draw in advance

uttag|are (*av pengar*) drawer **-bar** [-a:g-] *a1* detachable **-ning** (*av pengar*) withdrawal; *sport.* selection **-ningstävling** trial [game]; trials (*pl*)

ut|tal pronunciation; (*artikulering*) articulation; *ha ett bra engelskt ~* have a good English accent **-tala 1** (*frambringa*) pronounce; (*tydligt*) articulate **2** (*uttrycka*) express (*en önskan* a wish) **3** *rfl* speak (*om* of, about); pronounce (*för* for; *mot* against); ~ *sig om* (*äv.*) comment (express an opinion) on **-talande** *s6* pronouncement, statement; *göra ett ~* make a statement

uttals|beteckning phonetic notation **-lära** phonetics (*pl, behandlas som sg*) **-ordbok** pronouncing dictionary

uttaxer|a levy **-ing** levy; *konkr.* taxes (*pl*)

utter [ˈutt-] *s2* otter **-skinn** otter's skin, otter

ut|tittad *a5* stared at **-tjatad** [-ç-] *a5* (*om ämne*) hackneyed; *vara ~* be fed up **-tjänad** [-ç-] *a5* who (which) has served his (*etc.*) time; *en ~ soldat* a veteran **-tolka** *se 2 tolka* **-torkad** [-å-] *a5* dried up (out) **-torkning** drying up; *fack.* desiccation

uttryck expression; (*talesätt äv.*) phrase; (*tecken*) mark, token (*för* of); *stående ~* set (stock) phrase; *tekniskt ~* technical term; *ålderdomligt ~* (*äv.*) archaism; *ge ~ åt* give expression (vent) to; *ta sig ~ i* find expression in, show itself in; *välja sina ~* choose (pick) one's expressions **uttryck|a** express (*en förhoppning* a hope; *en önskan* a wish); *som han -te det* as he put it; ~ *sig* express o.s.; *om jag så får ~ mig* if I may be permitted to say so **-lig** *a1* express, explicit, definite; ~ *befallning* express (strict) order **-ligen** expressly, explicitly; strictly

uttrycks|full expressive; (*om blick, ord*) significant, eloquent **-fullhet** expressiveness **-fullt** *adv* expressively; *with expression* **-lös** expressionless; vacant, blank (*min* look) **-löshet** expressionlessness, inexpressiveness **-medel** means of expression **-sätt** way of expressing o.s., manner of speaking; style

ut|tråkad *a5* bored [to death] **-träda** *se träda* [*ut*] ; *bildl.* retire, withdraw (*ur* from); ~ *ur* (*äv.*) leave, resign one's membership of (in) **-träde** *s6* retirement, withdrawal; *anmäla sitt ~ ur* (*förening*) announce one's resignation from **-tränga** force aside; *bildl.* supersede, displace **-tröttad** *a5* tired out, weary; (*utmattad*) exhausted **-tröttning** (*uttröttande*) tiring out; (*trötthet*) weariness, exhaustion **-tyda** interpret; (*dechiffrera*) decipher

ut|tåg march (marching) out, departure; *i sht bibl.* exodus; *israeliternas ~ ur Egypten* the Exodus **-tåga** march out, depart from **-tänja** stretch, extend **-tänka** think out; (*hitta på*) devise **-tömma** empty; *bildl.* exhaust (*sina tillgångar* one's resources); *hans krafter är -tömda* he is exhausted, he has no strength left; *han har -tömt ämnet* he has exhausted the subject **-tömmande** *a4* exhaustive, comprehensive; *behandla ~* treat exhaustively, exhaust **-tömning** emptying; exhaustion, draining; *med.* excretion, evacuation; ~ *av valutareserven* exhaustion of (drain on) the foreign exchange reserves

ut|ur [ˈuːt-, -ˈuːr] out of **-vakad** *a5* tired out through lack of sleep **-vald** chosen; selected (*verk* works); select (*grupp* group); picked (*trupper* troops); (*utsökt*) choice **-valsning** rolling out; sheeting **-vandra** emigrate **-vandrare** emigrant **-vandring** emigration; (*friare*) migration

utveckla 1 *se veckla* [*ut*] **2** (*utbilda; klargöra*) develop (*sina anlag* one's talents; *två hästkrafter* two horsepower; *en plan* a plan); (*lägga i dagen*) show, display (*energi* energy); *fys.* generate (*värme* heat); ~ *sina synpunkter* (*äv.*) expound one's views; *det är ~nde att resa* travelling broadens the mind; *tidigt ~d* (*om barn*) advanced for his (her) age **3** *rfl* develop (*till* into; *från* out of); (*om blomma, fallskärm o. bildl.*) unfold ; ~ *sig till* (*äv.*) grow into, become **utveckling** devel-

opment; progress; growth; (*i sht fack.*) evolution; *vara stadd i* ~ be developing; *~en går i riktning mot* the trend is towards
utvecklings|arbete development work **-bar** *a1* capable of development (progress) **-land** developing country **-linje** trend **-lära** doctrine (theory) of evolution; evolutionism **-möjlighet** possibility of development **-stadium** stage of development **-störd** [-ö:-] *a5* [mentally] retarded **-störning** retardation
utverka obtain, bring about, procure, secure
utvidg|a 1 (*utsträcka*) expand (*ett välde* an empire); (*göra bredare*) widen, broaden; (*göra längre*) extend; (*förstora*) enlarge; *fys.* expand, dilate **2** *rfl* widen, broaden; *fys.* expand, dilate; (*friare*) extend, expand **-ning** expansion; extension; dilation
utvidgnings|förmåga expansive power, extensibility; (*metalls*) ductility **-koefficient** coefficient of expansion
utvikning [-i:-] *bildl.* deviation; digression (*från ämnet* from the subject)
utviknings|blad gatefold, foldout **-brud** centrefold girl
ut|vilad *a5* thoroughly rested **-vinna** extract, win **-visa 1** (*visa bort*) send out; (*förvisa*) banish; (*ur landet*) expel, deport; *sport.* order off **2** (*visa*) indicate, show; (*bevisa*) prove; *det får framtiden* ~ time will show **-visning** sending out; banishment; expulsion, deportation; (*ishockey.*) penalty; (*fotboll.*) ordering off
utvisnings|beslut deportation (expulsion) order **-bås** penalty box
ut|vissla *se vissla* [*ut*] **-vissling** hiss, whistle **-väg** *bildl.* expedient, resource, way out; means; *finna en* ~ find some expedient; *jag ser ingen annan* ~ I see no other way out (alternative) **-välja** choose [out], select **-väljande** *s6* choice, selection **-vändig** *a1* outward, external **-vändigt** *adv* outwardly; [on the] outside **-värdera** evaluate **-värdshus** out-of-town restaurant **-värtes I** *oböjligt a* external, outward; *för* ~ *bruk* for external use **II** *adv se -vändigt* **-växla** exchange; interchange **-växling 1** (*utbyte*) exchange; interchange **2** *tekn.* gear[ing]; *ha liten* (*stor*) ~ be low-geared (high-geared) **-växlingsanordning** transmitter, gear mechanism **-växt** outgrowth; protuberance; *bildl.* excrescence, growth
utåt ['u:t-] **I** *prep* out into (towards); *fönstret vetter* ~ *gatan* the window looks out onto the street **II** *adv* outward[s]; *gå* ~ *med fötterna* walk with one's toes turned out **-böjd** bent outwards **-riktad** *a5* turned outwards, out-turned; *bildl.* extrovert, outgoing
ut|ägor *pl* outlying fields **-öka** increase; extend, expand; enlarge; *~d upplaga* enlarged edition **-ösa** *bildl.* shower [a torrent of] (*ovett över* abuse upon); ~ *sin vrede över* vent one's anger upon
utöva (*bedriva*) carry on (*ett hantverk* a trade); practise (*ett yrke* a profession); (*verkställa*) exercise (*kontroll* control; *rättvisa* justice); exert (*tryck* pressure); ~ *befäl* hold (exercise) command; ~ *hämnd* take vengeance (*mot* upon); ~ *inflytande på* exercise (exert) influence on, influence; ~ *kritik* criticize; ~ *värdskapet* act as host
utövande I *s6* exercise, performance, execution

II *a4* executive; ~ *konstnär* creative artist **utövare** practiser, practician
utöver [-'ö:-, 'u:t-] *prep* [over and] above, beyond; *gå* ~ exceed
utövning *se utövande I*
uv *s2* [great] horned owl
uvertyr *se ouvertyr*
uvular I *a1* uvular **II** *s3* uvular

---

va *vard.* what?
vaccin [vak'si:n] *s4, s9* vaccine **-ation** vaccination **-ationstvång** compulsory vaccination **-era** vaccinate; inoculate **-ering** [-'ne:-] vaccination
vacker ['vakk-] *a2* **1** beautiful; (*i sht om man*) handsome; (*förtjusande*) lovely; (*söt*) pretty; (*storslagen*) fine; (*tilltalande*) nice; (*fager*) fair; ~ *som en dag* [as] fair as a day in June; *~t väder* beautiful (lovely) weather; *vackra lovord* high praise (*sg*); *en* ~ *dag* (*bildl.*) one fine day **2** (*ansenlig*) handsome (*summa* sum); *det är* ~*t så!* [it is] pretty good at that!, fair enough! **3** *iron.* fine, pretty
vackert *adv* **1** beautifully *etc.*; *huset ligger* ~ the house is beautifully situated; *det var* ~ *gjort av dig* it was a fine thing of you to do; *det där låter* ~ that sounds well; ~*!* (*vard.*) well done!, marvellous! **2** *iron.* nicely, prettily; *jo* ~*!* I should think so!, not likely!; *som det så* ~ *heter* as they so prettily put it **3** *det låter du* ~ *bli!* you will just not do so!; *du stannar* ~ *hemma!* you just stop at home; *sitt* ~*!* (*t. hund*) beg!
vackl|a totter; (*ragla*) stagger; *bildl.* falter, waver, vacillate; *bruket* ~*r* the usage varies; *han* ~*de fram* he staggered along; ~ *hit och dit* (*äv.*) sway to and fro **-an** *r* wavering, vacillation; (*obeslutsamhet*) irresolution, indecision **-ande** *a4* tottering *etc.*; (*om hälsa*) uncertain, failing; *hans hälsa börjar bli* ~ his health is beginning to give way
1 vad *s3, s1* (*på ben*) calf (*pl* calves) [of the leg]
2 vad *s2* (*fisknot*) seine [net]; *fiska med* ~ seine
3 vad *s7, jur.* [notice of] appeal; *anmäla* ~ give notice of (lodge an) appeal
4 vad *s7* (*avtal*) bet (*om en summa* of a sum; *om resultatet* on the result); *slå* ~ bet, make a bet; *det kan jag slå* ~ *om* I['ll] bet you; *jag slår* ~ *om ett pund* I['ll] bet you one pound
5 vad *s7, se vadställe*
6 vad I *pron* **1** *interr.* what; ~? [I beg your] pardon?, *vard.* what?; *vet du* ~*!* I'll tell you what!; *nej,* ~ *säger du!* really!, well, I never!; ~ *nytt?* any news?; ~ *för en* what; ~ *för* [*en*] *bok* what book;

~ *för slag?* what?; ~ *är det för slags bok?* what kind of a book is that?; ~ *gråter du för?* why are you crying?, what are you crying for?; ~ *har du för anledning att* what reason have you for (+ *ing-form*); *jag vet inte* ~ *jag skall göra* I don't know what to do; ~ *är det?* what is the matter?; ~ *är det för dag i dag?* what day is it today? **2** *rel.* (*det som*) what; ~ *mig beträffar* as far as I am concerned; ~ *som är viktigt är att* the important thing is that; ~ *som helst* anything [whatever]; ~ *som än händer* whatever happens; ~ *värre är* what is [even] worse; *inte* ~ *jag vet* (*vard.*) not as far as I know **II** *adv* how (*du är snäll!* kind you are!)

vada wade (*över* across); ~ *över en flod* (*äv.*) ford a river; *han ~r i pengar* he's wallowing in money
vadan *åld.*, *se varifrån, varför*
vadar|e, -fågel shore bird, wader
vadben splint bone, fibula
vadd *s2* wad[ding]; (*bomulls-*) cotton wool; *AE.* absorbent cotton; (*fönster-*) padding **-era** wad, pad; (*täcke, morgonrock etc.*) quilt **-ering** [-'de:-] wadding, padding; (*med stickningar*) quilting **-täcke** quilt
vadeinlaga [document (notice) of] appeal
vadhelst [-'helst, 'va:d-] whatever
vadhåll|are better, backer **-ning** betting, wagering
vadmal [ˣvadd-, ˣva:d-] *s3, s4* rough homespun; frieze; russet
vadslagning [-a:g-] betting
vadställe ford[able place]
vafalls [I beg your] pardon?
vag *a1* vague; indistinct, undefined, hazy
vagabond [-'bånd, -'båŋd] *s3* vagabond, tramp; *AE. äv.* hobo; *jur.* vagrant **-era** vagabondize; be (go) on the tramp **-liv** vagabond life
1 vagel ['va:-] *s2* (*i ögat*) sty[e] (*pl äv.* sties)
2 vagel ['va:-] *s2* (*sittpinne*) perch, roost
vagg|a I *s1* cradle; *från -an till graven* from the cradle to the grave **II** *v1* rock (*i sömn* to sleep); (*svänga, vicka*) swing; (*gå ~nde*) waddle; ~*nde gång* rocking (waddling) gait **-visa** lullaby
vagn [vaŋn] *s2* **1** carriage; *AE.* car (*äv. järnv. person-*) (*större, gala-*) coach; (*last-, gods-*) wag[g]on, *AE.* car; (*kärra*) cart; *häst och* ~ a horse and carriage; (*direkt genomgående*) ~ (*järnv.*) through carriage **2** *fackl.* (*på kran*) trolley **-makare** coach-maker, coach-builder; cartwright **-makeri** (*tillverkning*) carriage-making, coach--building; (*verkstad*) carriage works (*sg o. pl*) **-park** järnv. rolling stock; (*bil-, buss-*) fleet [of cars (buses)]
vagns|axel axletree **-hjul** carriage (car) wheel
vagnskadeförsäkring insurance against material damage to a motor vehicle
vagns|korg carriage (wag[g]on) body **-last** cartload, carriage load; *järnv.* wag[g]onload, truckload **-lider** coach house
vagnsätt *järnv.* train [of coaches]
vaja [ˣvajja] *v1* float, fly; (*fladdra*) flutter, stream
vajer ['vajj-] *s2* cable, wire
vak *s2* (*is-*) hole in the ice, ice hole
vaka I *s1* vigil, watch; (*lik-*) wake **II** *v1* **1** (*hålla vakt*) watch (*hos ngn* by a p.'s bedside); keep watch; (*hålla sig vaken*) stay up; ~ *över ngn* watch (keep watch) over s.b. **2** *sjö.* (*om båt*) ride

vak|ans [-'kans, -'kaŋs] *s3* vacancy **-ant** *a4* vacant, unoccupied
vakare *sjö.* buoy
vaken *a3* (*ej sovande*) predik. awake; *attr.* waking; (*uppmärksam*) observing, noticing (*barn* child); (*pigg*) wide-awake, brisk; (*mottaglig*) open (*blick* eye), alert (*sinne* mind); *i vaket tillstånd* when awake **-het** wakefulness; *bildl.* alertness
vak|na [ˣva:k-] wake [up], awake; *bildl. äv.* awaken; ~ *till besinning* come to one's senses; ~ *till medvetande* become conscious (*om* of); regain consciousness; ~ *på fel sida* get out of bed on the wrong side **-natt** wakeful night
vaksam [ˣva:k-] *a1* watchful (*blick* eye); vigilant; on the alert **-het** watchfulness; vigilance
vakt *s3* **1** (*-hållning*) watch (*äv. sjö.*); *mil.* guard, duty; *gå på* ~ mount guard, go on duty; *ha ~en* be on duty; *hålla* ~ keep watch, be on guard (duty); *slå* ~ *om* (*bildl.*) stand up for (*friheten* liberty), keep an eye on; *vara på sin* ~ be on one's guard (on the alert); *inte vara på sin* ~ be off one's guard **2** *pers.* guard, watchman; *mil.* sentry; (*-manskap*) [men (*pl*) on] guard, *sjö.* watch; *avlösa ~en* relieve the guard
vakt|a 1 (*bevaka*) guard; watch over, look after (*barn* children); ~ *får* tend (herd) sheep; ~ *på* watch **2** (*hålla vakt*) keep guard (watch) **3** *rfl, se akta 2* **-are** watcher, guardian; (*bro-, djur- e.d.*) keeper **-arrest** close arrest **-avlösning** changing of the guard
vaktel *s2* quail
vakt|havande *a4* on duty; *sjö. äv.* of the watch **-hund** watchdog **-hållning** patrol, patrolling; guard[ing] **-kur** sentry box **-manskap** [men (*pl*) on] guard **-mästare 1** (*vid ämbetsverk*) messenger; (*på museum*) attendant; (*skol-*) porter; *univ.* beadle; (*dörr-*) doorkeeper; (*platsanvisare*) usher; (*uppsyningsman*) caretaker **2** (*kypare*) waiter **-ombyte** changing of (relieving) the guard; ~[t] *sker kl.* the guard is relieved at **-parad** changing of the guard **-post** *se vakt 2* **-tjänst** guard (*sjö.* watch) duty **-torn** watchtower
vakuum ['va:kum] *s8* vacuum **-förpackad** *a5* vacuum-packed **-förpackning** vacuum pack **-torkad** [-å-] *a5* vacuum-dried (*potatis* potatoes)
1 val *s2, zool.* whale; ~*ar* (*koll.*) cetaceans
2 val *s71* (*väljande*) choice; (*ur-*) selection; *efter eget* ~ at one's own option, according to choice; *fritt* ~ option, free choice; *göra ett bra* ~ (*äv.*) choose well; *göra sitt* ~ make one's choice; *jag hade inget annat* ~ I had no alternative; *vara i ~ et och kvalet* be in two minds (*om man skall gå el. inte* whether to go or not) **2** (*offentlig förrättning*) election; *allmänna* ~ general election (*sg*); *förrätta* ~ hold an election; *gå till* ~ go to the polls; *tillsatt genom* ~ elected, elective
valack [-'lakk, 'vall-] *s3* gelding
val|affisch election poster **-agitation** electioneering; canvassing **-arbetare** electioneer
valbar [ˣva:l-] *a1* eligible (*till* for); *ej* ~ ineligible **-het** eligibility
valberättigad entitled to vote; *en* ~ an elector; *de ~e* the electorate (*sg*)
valborgsmässo|afton [-bårjs-] Walpurgis

night **-eld** bonfire on Walpurgis night
valbyrå election office
val|d [-a:-] *a5* chosen, selected; *några väl ~a ord* a few well-chosen words; *~a skrifter* selected works **-dag** polling (election) day **-de** [-a:-] *imperf. av välja* **-deltagande** poll[ing], participation in the election; *stort (litet)* ~ heavy (low) polling **-distrikt** electoral (voting) district (*AE.* precinct)
valens *s3* valency; *AE.* valence
valeriana [-ˣaːna] *s1* valerian
wales|are [ˣɔejls-] Welshman **-isk** [ˈɔejls-] **5** Welsh **-iska** [ˈɔejl-] *s1* **1** (*språk*) Welsh **2** (*kvinna*) Welshwoman
valfisk *åld.* whale
val|fiske *vard.* fishing for votes, electioneering **-fläsk** election promise[s *pl*], bid for votes **-fri** optional; discretionary; *~tt ämne* (*skol.*) optional subject, *AE.* elective **-frihet** [right of] option, freedom of choice **-fusk** electoral rigging
val|fångare whaler; (*fartyg äv.*) whaling ship **-fångst** whaling
val|förrättare election supervisor **-hemlighet** secrecy of the polls
valhänt [-a:-] *a4* numb[ed]; *bildl.* awkward, clumsy (*försök* attempt), lame (*ursäkt* excuse); *vara ~* (*eg.*) have numb hands **-het** numbness in the (one's) hands; *bildl.* clumsiness *etc.*
validitet *s2* validity
valk *s2* **1** (*förhårdnad*) callus, callosity **2** (*hår-*) pad; (*fett-*) roll of fat
valka mill, full
valkampanj election campaign
valkig *al* callous; horny
valkokeri [whale] factory ship
val|konung elective king **-krets** constituency
valkyria [-ˈky:-] *s1* Valkyr[ie], Walkyrie
1 vall *s2* (*upphöjning*) bank, embankment; (*strand-*) dike, dyke; *mil.* rampart
2 vall *s2* (*slåtter-*) ley, temporary pasture; (*betes-*) pasture [ground (land)]; *driva i ~* turn out to grass; *gå i ~* be grazing
1 valla *v1* tend (*boskap* cattle); (*vakta*) watch, guard; (*brottsling*) take to the scene of the crime
2 valla l *s1* (*skid-*) ski wax **ll 1** wax
vallag electoral (election) law; *Storbritannien* Reform (Representation of the People) Act
vallar|e herdsman, tender **-låt** *se vallvisa*
wallboard [ˈvållbåːrd, ˈɔåll-] *s3* fibreboard; (*hård*) hardboard; (*porös*) insulation fibreboard
vall|fart pilgrimage **-fartsort** resort of pilgrims, shrine; *bildl.* Mecca
vallflicka herdsmaid, shepherdess
vallfärda go on a pilgrimage
vallgrav moat, foss[e]
vall|horn herdsman's horn **-hund** shepherd's dog; (*ras*) sheepdog, collie
vallmo *s5* poppy **-frö** poppy seed
vallokal polling station (place); poll[s *pl*]
vallon *s3*, **-sk** [-ɔ:-] *a5* Walloon
vall|pojke shepherd boy **-visa** herdsman's song
vallväxter *pl* pasture (ley) plants
val|längd electoral register **-löfte** electoral promise
vallört comfrey
val|man elector; voter **-manskår** electorate

-metod voting method **-möte** election meeting
-nederlag defeat [at the polls (elections)]
-nämnd election (electoral) committee; *~ens ordförande* (*ung.*) the returning officer
valnöt walnut
valp *s2* pup[py]; (*pojk-*) cub
valp|a whelp **-aktig** *al* puppyish
valplats field [of battle]
val|program election program[me]; platform **-propaganda** election propaganda
valpsjuka canine distemper
valrav [ˣva:l-] *s3* spermaceti
valresultat election result[s *pl*] (returns *pl*)
valross [ˣva:lråss] *s2* walrus; morse
valrörelse electioneering, election campaign
1 vals *s2* (*cylinder*) roll[er]; cylinder (*äv. skrivmaskins-*)
2 vals *s3* (*dans*) waltz
1 valsa *v1* (*dansa*) waltz
2 valsa *v1* (*låta passera genom valsar*) roll; (*plåt äv.*) laminate, sheet; *~t järn* rolled (sheet) iron; *~t stål* rolled (laminated) steel
val|sedel ballot [paper], voting paper **-seger** election victory
vals|formig [-å-] *al* cylindrical **-järn** rolled iron
valskolkare [-å-] abstainer
vals|kvarn roller mill **-ning** rolling; lamination
valspråk motto, device
valstakt *i ~* in waltz-time
valsverk rolling mill
valsätt electoral system; *proportionellt ~* proportional representation
valt [-a:-] *sup. av välja*
valtal election address (speech) **-are** election speaker
valthorn French horn **-blåsare** French-horn player
valurna ballot box
valuta [-ˣlu:-] *s1* (*myntslag*) currency; *inhemsk ~* domestic currency; *utländsk ~* foreign currency (currency); *~ bekommen* value received; *få ~ för* get good value for; *få ~ för sina pengar* (*äv.*) get one's money's worth **-bestämmelser** currency (*för utländsk valuta:* foreign exchange) regulations; *brott mot ~na* exchange control offences **-fond** monetary fund **-handel** exchange dealings (*pl*), foreign exchange **-kontor** [foreign] exchange control office **-kontroll** [foreign] exchange control **-kurs** rate of exchange **-marknad** foreign exchange market **-reserv** foreign exchange reserve[s *pl*] **-restriktioner** currency (*för utländsk valuta:* [foreign] exchange) restrictions **-tilldelning** [foreign] exchange allocation **-tillgångar** foreign exchange holdings
valv *s7* vault (*äv. bank-*); arch; *skeppsb.* counter **-båge** arch **-gång** archway **-konstruktion** arch vault[ing]
valör value; (*på sedlar o.d.*) denomination
vamp *s2, s3*, **vampa** vamp **vampyr** *s3* vampire
van *a5* (*övad*) practised, experienced; (*skicklig*) skilled; *han är gammal och ~* he's an old hand [at]; *vara (bli) ~ vid* be (get) used (accustomed) to (*att + ing-form*); *bara man blir litet ~* (*äv.*) once you get into the knack of it; *med ~ hand* with a deft (skilled) hand
van|a *s1* (*sed, bruk*) custom; (*persons*) habit; (*er-*

farenhet) experience *(vid* of); *(övning)* practice; *~ns makt* the force of habit, *ha dyrbara -or* have expensive habits; *av gcmmal ~* by force of habit, from [mere] habit; *sin ~ trogen* as is one's wont; *bli en ~* become a habit *(hos ngn* with s.b.); *ha ~n inne att* be used to; *ha för ~ att* be in the habit of *(+ ing-form)*

vanadin *s4, s3* vanadium

vanart [ˣvaːn-] bad disposition; *(starkare)* depravation

vanartig *a1* depraved, demoralized; vicious **-het** depravity, depravation

vandäl *s3* vandal **-isera** vandalize **-ism** vandalism

vande [ˣvaːn-] *imperf. av vänja*

vandel ['vann-] *s9* conduct, behaviour, mode of life; *föra en hederlig ~* lead an honourable life

vandr|a walk *(äv. bildl.*); ramble, hike; *(ströva)* wander, stroll, rove, roam *(omkring* about); *(om djur, folk)* migrate **-ande** *a4* wandering; *(kring-)* itinerant, ambulatory; travelling *(gesäll* journeyman); *(flyttande)* migratory; *den ~ juden* the Wandering Jew; *~ blad (zool.)* leaf insect; *~ njure* floating kidney; *~ pinne (zool.)* stick insect, *AE.* walking stick

vandrar|e wanderer **-folk** nomadic (migratory) people **-hem** youth hostel

vandring wandering; *(kortare)* walk[ing tour]; *(genom livet)* way; *(folk-,* djur-) migration

vandrings|bibliotek travelling library **-lust** longing to travel, wanderlust **-man** *se vandrare* **-pokal** challenge cup **-pris** challenge prize **-utställning** travelling (touring) exhibition

vane|bildande *a4* habit-forming; addictive **-djur** creature of habit **-drinkare** habitual drinker **-förbrytare** habitual criminal; *vard.* jailbird **-människa** *se -djur* **-mässig** *a1* habitual, routine **-rökare** habitual smoker **-sak** matter of habit **-tänkande** *s6* thinking in grooves

van|fejd *s3* dishonour; infamy **-för** *a5* disabled, crippled, lame; *(en ~)* cripple, disabled person **-föreställning** misconception, wrong idea, false notion **-heder** dishonour, disgrace **-hedra** dishonour, disgrace; be a disgrace to **-hedrande** disgraceful, ignominious, dishonouring **-helga** profane, desecrate **-helgande** *a4* profaning, desecrating **-helgd** profanation, desecration; *(av kyrka e.d. äv.)* sacrilege **-hävd** neglect; *komma i ~* go (run) to waste; *ligga i ~* lie waste

vanilj *s3* vanilla **-glass** vanilla ice **-sås** vanilla sauce; *(tjock äv.)* custard

vanillinsocker [-ˣliːn-] vanillin sugar

vank *r, utan ~* flawless; *utan ~ och lyte* without defect or blemish

vanka *[gå och] ~* saunter (wander) *(omkring* about)

vanka|s *dep, det -des kakor* we *(etc.)* were treated to biscuits; *det ~ stryk* he *(etc.)* is in for a thrashing

vankelmod irresolution, indecision; hesitation; *(ombytlighet)* inconstancy **-ig** irresolute, inconstant; vacillating

vanlig [ˣvaːn-] *a1* **1** *(som sker efter vanan)* usual *(hos* with); habitual *(sysselsättning* occupation); *(bruklig)* customary; *det är det ~a* that's the usual thing; *på ~ tid* at the usual time; *på sin ~a plats*

in its *(etc.)* usual place; *som ~t* as usual; *bättre än ~t* better than usual **2** *(ofta förekommande)* common *(blomma* flower; *fel* mistake; *namn* name); frequent *(missuppfattning* misconception); *(allmän)* general *(uppfattning* belief); *(alldaglig, vardags-)* ordinary *(mat* food; *folk* people); *mindre ~* less (not very) common; *~t bråk* simple (vulgar, common) fraction; *vi ~a dödliga* we ordinary mortals; *den gamla ~a historien* the same old story; *~a människor (äv.)* the common run of people; *den ~a åsikten* bland the opinion generally held by; *i ~a fall* as a rule, ordinarily, in ordinary cases; *i ordets ~a bemärkelse* in the ordinary sense of the word; *på ~t sätt* in the ordinary (usual) manner (way) **vanligen** usually, generally; as a rule **vanlighet** usualness, frequency; *efter ~en* as usual; *mot ~en* contrary to the *(his etc.)* usual practice; *det hör inte till ~erna att* it is not very common that

vanligt [ˣvaːn-] *adv* usually *etc.* **-vis** *se vanligen*

van|lottad [-å-] *a5* badly off *(i fråga om* as regards) **-makt** **1** *(medvetslöshet)* unconsciousness; *falla i ~* have a fainting-fit, faint, swoon **2** *bildl.* impotence; powerlessness **-mäktig** **1** unconscious, fainting **2** impotent; powerless, vain

vann *imperf. av vinna*

vanna I *s1* **1** *(sädes-)* fan **2** *(glastillv.)* tank furnace **II** *v1 (säd)* fan, winnow

van|pryda disfigure, spoil the look of **-prydnad** disfigurement **-ryktad** *a5* notorious, ill-famed **-rykte** disrepute, bad repute; discredit

van|sinne insanity; mental disease; *(galenskap)* madness; *driva ngn till ~* drive s.b. mad (crazy); *det vore rena ~t* it would be insane (sheer madness) **-sinnig** *a1* insane; *(tokig)* crazy; *(galen)* mad; *bli ~* go mad; *det är så man kan bli ~* it is enough to drive one mad **-sinnigt** *adv* insanely; crazily; madly; *(förstärkande)* awfully, terribly; *~ roligt* awfully funny; *~ förälskad* madly in love **-skapt** [-aː-] *a4* deformed, misshapen

vansklig *a1 (osäker)* hazardous, risky *(företag* enterprise); *(tvivelaktig)* doubtful; *(brydsam)* delicate *(uppgift* task); *(svår)* awkward

van|sköta mismanage, neglect; *trädgården är -skött* the garden is not looked after properly; *~ sig* be neglectful; *~ sin hälsa* neglect one's health **-skötsel** mismanagement; negligence; *av ~* for (from) want of proper care **-släktad** *a5* degenerate[d] **-släktas** *dep* degenerate **-styre** misrule **-ställa** disfigure, deform; *(friare)* spoil [the look[s] of], *(förvrida)* distort

1 vant *s7, s4, sjö.* shroud

2 vant [-aː-] *sup. av vänja*

vant|e *s2 (finger-)* woollen (cotton) glove; *(tum-)* mitt[en]; *lägga -arna på (bildl.)* lay hands [up]on; *slå -arna i bordet (bildl.)* put the shutters up

van|tolka misinterpret; misconstrue **-trivas** *dep* feel ill at ease (uncomfortable); not feel at home; get on [very] badly *(med ngn* with s.b.); *(om djur, växter)* not thrive; *jag -trivs med mitt arbete* I am not at all happy in my work **-trivsel** discomfort, unhappiness; *(djurs, växters)* inability to thrive **-tro** false belief; disbelief **-vett** insanity; mania; *det vore rena ~et att* it would be sheer madness to **-vettig** *a1* mad; absurd, wild **-vård** neglect, negligence, mismanagement **-vårda** *se vansköta*

-vördig disrespectful (*mot* to); (*mot ngt heligt*) irreverent (*mot* to) **-vördnad** disrespect; irreverence **-ära I** *s1* dishonour, disgrace; (*skam*) shame, ignominy; *dra* ~ *över* bring shame (disgrace) upon **II** *v1* dishonour, disgrace
vapen ['va:-] *s7* **1** weapon; *koll.* arms (*pl*); *bära* (*föra*) ~ carry arms; *gripa till* ~ take up arms; *med* ~ *i hand* weapon in hand; *nedlägga vapnen* lay down [one's] arms, surrender; *slå ngn med hans egna* ~ beat s.b. at his own game **2** *her.* (*-märke*) arms (*pl*), coat of arms **-bragd** feat of arms; (*friare*) military achievement **-broder** brother-in-arms **-brödraskap** brotherhood of arms **-bärare** weapon carrier **-dragare** *hist.* armour-bearer; *bildl.* supporter **-fabrik** armament factory **-fri** ~ *tjänst* unarmed national (military) service **-för** *a5* fit for military service **-föring** handling (wielding) of a weapon **-förråd** armoury, arsenal **-gny** clash of arms, din of battle **-gren** fighting service, branch of the armed forces **-gömma** concealed store of arms (weapons) **vapen|handel** trading in arms; armaments trade **-handlare** arms dealer **-hjälp** arms assistance **-hus** [church] porch **-licens** licence for carrying arms, firearms (*AE.* gun) licence **-lös** unarmed **-makt** (*med* by) force of arms **-rock** tunic **-samling** collection of arms **-skrammel** *bildl.* show of arms **-sköld** coat of arms, escutcheon, blazon **-slag** service branch, arm **-smed** armourer; gunsmith **-smedja** armourer's workshop **-smuggling** gunrunning **-stillestånd** armistice; truce **-stilleståndsvillkor** armistice terms **-tillverkning** manufacture of arms **-tjänst** military service **-vila** *se -stillestånd* **-vägran** refusal to bear arms **-vägrare** [-ä:-] conscientious objector; *vard.* conchie, draft resister (*AE.* dodger) **-övning** training in the use of arms
1 var *s7* (*kudd-*) case, slip
2 var *s7* (*i sår*) pus; *få* ~ *i ögonen* get infected eyes
3 var (*~t*) pron *a*) (*som adj.*) (*varenda*) every, (*varje särskild*) each; *b*) (*som subst.*) *se envar*; ~ *dag* every day; ~ *gång* every (each) time; ~ *fjärde* every fourth (*timme* hour), every four (*timme* hours); ~ *och en a*) (*som subst.*) every man (person), everybody, everyone, (~ *och en särskilt*) each [one] (*av* of), *b*) (*som adj.*) each, every; *de gick* ~ *och en till sig* each [of them] went home, they went each to his (*etc.*) own house; ~*s och ens ensak* everybody's own business; *det tycker vi nog litet* ~ pretty well every one of us thinks so; ~ *för sig* each individually, separately; *de har* ~ *sin bok* each [of them] has his book, they have a book each; *göra ngt* ~ *sin gång* do s.th. by (in) turns; *på* ~ *sin sida om* on either side of; *de gick åt* ~ *sitt håll* they went their separate ways, they all went off in different directions
4 var *adv* where; (*-än, -helst äv.*) wherever; *här och* ~ here and there; ~ *som helst* anywhere; ~ *någonstans* where[abouts]; ~ *i all världen* wherever, where on earth
5 var *imperf. av* **5 vara**
1 vara *v1, rfl, med.* suppurate, fester
2 vara *oböjligt s, ta* ~ *på* (*ta reda på*) take care of, (*använda väl*) make good use of (*tiden* one's time); *ta väl* ~ *på dig!* take good care of yourself!;

ta sig till ~ be careful, mind what one is doing; *ta sig till* ~ *för* be on one's guard against
3 var|a *s1* (*artikel*) article, product; *-or* (*äv.*) goods, merchandise, (*i sms. vanl.*) ware (*sg*); *-or och tjänster* goods and services; *explosiva -or* explosives; *korta -or* haberdashery; *tala för en* ~ (*äv. bildl.*) speak (argue) in favour of s.th.
4 vara *v1* (*räcka*) last (*två timmar* [for] two hours); (*fortfara*) go on, continue; *så länge det* ~*r* as long as it lasts
5 vara *var varit, pres. är* **I** *huvudv* **1** *allm.* be; (*existera äv.*) exist; (*äga rum äv.*) take place; (*utgöra äv.*) make; *att* ~ *eller icke* ~ to be or not to be; ~ *från Sverige* (*om pers.*) be from Sweden, (*om sak*) come from Sweden; ~ *vid posten* be working at the Post Office; ~ *av den åsikten att* be of the opinion that; *vad anser du* ~ *bäst?* what do you think is best?; *för att* ~ *så liten är han* considering he is so small he is; *såsom* ~*nde den äldste* being the oldest; *vi är fyra* there are four of us; *jag är för lång, är jag inte?* I'm too tall, aren't I (am I not)?; *om så är* if that be the case, if so; *det lilla som är* what the (the) little there is; *snäll som jag är skall jag* as I am nice I will; *vad är att göra?* what is to be done?; *vad är den här knappen till?* what is this button [meant] for?; *hon är och handlar* she is out shopping; *när är premiären?* when is the opening night?; *båten är av plast* the boat is [made] of plastic; *tre och tre är sex* three and three are (is, make[s]) six; *det är att frukta att* it is to be feared that; *det är farliga saker* these are dangerous things; *det är ingenting för mig* that is not at all in my line; *det är inte mycket med den längre* it is not up to much any longer; *det är och förblir en gåta* it remains a mystery; *det är som det är* things are as they are; *det här är mina handskar* these gloves are mine; *hur är det att bo i London?* what's it like (how do you like) living in London?; *som det nu är* as things are (matters stand) now; *goddag, det är Lily* (*i telefon*) hello, [this is] Lily speaking, hello, Lily here; *det är herr A.?* (*vid tilltal*) are you Mr. A.?, (*i telefon*) is that Mr. A. speaking?; *vad är det nu då?* what is it (what is the matter) now?; *vad är det med TV:n?* what has happened to the TV; *de var två* there were two of them (*om lotten* to share the lottery ticket; *om arbetet* on the job); *jag var där en kvart* I stayed there for a quarter of an hour; *jag var och hälsade på dem* I went to see them; *de var och mötte honom* they were there to meet him; *om jag var* (*vore*) *rik* if I was (were) rich; *det var bra att du kunde komma* it's a good thing you could come; *det var det som var felet* that's what was wrong; *det var snällt av dig att komma* it's (it was) very kind of you to come; *var inte pjoskig!* don't make [such] a fuss!; *hur trevligt det än hade varit* however nice it would have been; *har du varit på teatern* (*Macbeth*)? have you been to the theatre (to see "Macbeth")?; *jag vore tacksam om ni* I should be grateful if you; *det vore roligt* that would be fun **2** (*annan konstr.*) *deras sätt att* ~ their manners; *hur därmed än må* ~ be that as it may; *vi kan* ~ *sju i båten* there is room for seven of us (we can sit seven) in the boat; *vad får det lov att* ~? (*i butik*) what can I do for you?, (*t. gäst*) what can I offer you; *för att* ~ *utlänning är han*

V

for a foreigner he is; *får det ~ en kopp kaffe?* would you like a cup of coffee; *det får ~ för mig* I would rather not, *(jag orkar inte)* I can't be bothered; *det får ~ som det är* we'll leave it at that (as it is); *det får ~ till en annan gång* it will have to wait until another time; *den dag som i dag är* this very day; *det är bara att komma* just come; *hur vore det om vi skulle gå och bada?* what about going swimming?; *under veckan som varit* during the last week **II** *hjälpv* **1** *allm.* be; *jag är född 1931* I was born in 1931; *boken är tryckt i New York* the book was printed in New York **2** *de är bortresta* they are (have gone) away; *jag är ditbjuden i morgon* I have been invited there tomorrow; *han är utgången* he has gone out, he is out **III** *(med betonad partikel)* **1** *~ av (avbruten)* be [broken] off; *~ av med ngt (ha förlorat)* have lost, *(ha sluppit ifrån)* have got (be) rid of **2** *~ borta a)* eg. be away, *b) (försvunnen)* be missing, *c) (död)* be gone, *d) bildl.* be lost **3** *~ efter a) (förfölja)* be after, *b) (ej ha hunnit med)* be behind *(i skolan* at school); *han var långt efter oss* he was far behind us; *~ efter sin tid* be behind the times, *AE.* be a back number; *~ efter med betalningen* be in arrears with payment **4** *~ emot* be against **5** *~ för (gilla)* be in favour of; *fönsterluckorna var för* the shutters were closed (to) **6** *~ före a) (ha hunnit före)* be ahead *(sin tid* of the times), *b) jur.* be on, be before the court, *c) (dryftas)* be up [for discussion], *(behandlas)* be dealt with **7** *~ ifrån sig* be beside o.s. **8** *~ kvar a) (inte ha gått)* remain, stay [on], *b) (återstå)* remain, be left [over] **9** *~ med a) (deltaga)* take part, *(närvara)* be present *(på, vid* at), *b) (vara medräknad)* be included; *är osten med? (har vi med)* have we got the cheese?; *får jag ~ med?* may I join you (join in)?; *han var inte med planet* he wasn't on the plane; *är du med? (förstår du)* do you follow me?; *~ med sin tid* keep up with the times, be up to date; *hur är det med henne?* how is she?; *vad är det med henne?* what is the matter with her?; *~ med i (på) (deltaga i)* take part in, *(bevista)* attend; *~ med om (bevittna)* see, witness, *(uppleva)* experience, *(genomgå)* go through, *(råka ut för)* meet with, *(deltaga i)* take part in; *~ med om att (medverka)* do one's share towards *(+ ing-form)*, *(hjälpa till)* help to *(+ inf.)*; *hon är med på allt som är tokigt* she is in on anything crazy (mad) **10** *~ om sig* look after one's own interests, be on the make **11** *~ på a)* *(~ påsatt)* be on, *b) (röra vid)* be at; *~ på ngn (ligga efter)* be on at s.b., *(slå ner på)* be down on s.b. **12** *~ till* exist; *den är till för det* that's what it is there for; *~ till sig* be beside o.s. **13** *~ ur, knappen är ur* the button has come off; *nyckeln är ur* the key is not in the lock **14** *~ över a) (förbi)* be over (past), *b) (kvar)* left, [left] over; *snart är fienden över oss* the enemy will be over us any minute

varaktig *a1* lasting *(lycka* happiness), *(hållbar)* durable; *(beständig)* permanent *(adress* address); *~a konsumtionsvaror* consumer durables **-het** *(i tid)* duration; *(hållbarhet)* durability; *(beständighet)* permanency; *av kort ~ (äv.)* short-lived, brief

varande I *a4* being; *(existerande)* existing; *den i bruk ~* the ... in use **II** *s6* being; *(tillvaro)* existence

var|andra [-'and-, *vard.* -'rann] *(om två vanl.)* each other; *(om flera vanl.)* one another; *bredvid ~ (äv.)* side by side; *efter ~* one after the other (another); *två dagar efter ~* two days running, two days in succession; *tätt efter ~* close upon each other; *byta frimärken med ~* exchange stamps; *de rusade om ~* they rushed round one another; *två på ~ följande* two successive **-annan** [-ˣannan] **1** every other (second); *~ dag (äv.)* every two days; *~ vecka (äv.)* every two weeks, fortnightly; *~ gång (äv.)* alternately **2** *om vartannat* indiscriminately

varav ['va:r-] *(av vilken)* from which (what); *~ följer att* and hence (so) it follows that; *~ 100 pund är* £100 of which is

var|bildning suppuration; *konkr.* abscess **-böld** boil

varda [ˣva:r-] *vart, perf. part. vorden, se bliva*; *i ~nde* in the making

vardag ['va:r-] *s2* weekday; *(arbetsdag äv.)* working day, *i sht AE.* workday; *om (på) ~arna, till ~s* on weekdays **-lig** [ˣva:r-] *a1* everyday; *(alldaglig)* commonplace **-lighet** [ˣva:r-] triviality

vardags|bestyr *pl* daily duties **-bruk** *till ~* for everyday use *(om kläder*: wear) **-klädd** dressed in everyday clothes **-kläder** *pl* everyday clothes **-kväll** weekday evening **-lag** *i uttr.*: *i ~* in everyday life, on weekdays **-liv** everyday life **-mat** everyday (ordinary) food (fare) **-middag** everyday dinner; *kom och ät ~ med oss* come and take potluck with us **-människa** ordinary (commonplace) person **-rum** living (sitting) room, lounge, parlour **-språk** colloquial language **-uttryck** everyday expression, colloquialism

vardera ['va:r-] each; *på ~ sidan* on either side; *i vardera fallet* in both cases, in each case

vare *konjunktiv av 5 vara* be; *ära ~ Gud* glory be to God; *~ därmed hur som helst* however that may be, be that as it may

varefter [-'eff-] after which; *(om tid äv.)* whereupon

varelse being; creature

varemot ['va:r-] **I** *adv* against which; *(i jämförelse med vilken)* compared to which **II** *konj* while, whereas

varenda [-ˣenn-] every; *~ en* every [single] one

vare sig *~ ... eller inte* whether ... or not; *~ du vill eller inte* whether you want to or not; *han kom inte ~ i går eller i dag* he did not come either yesterday or today

varest ['va:r-] where; and there

vareviga [-ˣe:-] every single *(dag* day)

varflytning flow[ing] of pus; pyorrhoea

varfågel [ˣva:r-] great grey shrike

varför ['varr-, 'va:r-] **1** *(av vilket skäl)* why; for what reason, on what account; *vard.* what for; *~ det?* why?; *~ inte?* why not? **2** *(och därför)* so, and therefore; wherefore **3** *(för vilken)* for which; *orsaken ~ jag slutade* the reason [why] I left

varg [-j] *s2* wolf; *hungrig som en ~* ravenous; *äta som en ~* eat voraciously; *i veum* outlaw **-avinter** bitter winter **-flock** pack of wolves **-grop** wolf pit **-hane** [he]wolf **-hona, -inna** she-wolf **-lik** *a5* wolfish **-skinnspäls** wolfskin fur[coat]

-tjut howling of wolves (a wolf) **-unge** wolf cub; *(scout)* Cub [Scout], *(förr)* Wolf Cub
varhelst [-'helst, 'va:r-] wherever
varhärd focus of suppuration
vari ['va:ri, -'i:] in which (what), wherein
varia ['va:-] *pl* various things; *(som boktitel)* miscellanies **-bel** [-'a:bel] **I** *a2* variable, changeable **II** *s3* variable
vari|ans [-'ans, -'aŋs] *s3, stat.* variance **-ant** variant; *(i textutgåva e.d.)* variant reading; *biol.* variety **-ation** variation
variations|bredd variation range; *stat.* range **-rikedom** abundance of variation
varibland ['va:r-] among which; and among them *(etc.)*, including
varier|a 1 *(skifta)* vary; *(inom vissa gränser)* range *(mellan ... och* from ... to); *(vara ostadig)* fluctuate **2** *(förändra)* vary **-ande** *a4* varying, fluctuating
varieté *s3* **1** *(-föreställning)* variety [show], music-hall performance; *AE. äv.* vaudeville [show], burlesque **2** *(lokal)* variety theatre, music hall **-artist** variety (music-hall) artist **-föreställning** *se* varieté 1
varietet *s3, biol.* variety
varifrån ['va:r-] *adv* **1** *interr.* where ... from, from where; *~ kommer han?* where does he come from? **2** *rel.* from which; *(från vilken plats)* from where; *vi kom till A., ~ vi fortsatte till* we arrived at A., from where we continued to
varig *a1* purulent; festering
varigenom ['va:r-] *adv (jfr genom)* **1** *interr.* in what way; *(genom vilka medel)* by what means **2** *rel.* through which, by means of which; *(betecknande orsak)* whereby
varit *sup. av 5* vara
varje *(jfr 3 var)* every; *(~ särskild)* each; *(vilken ... som helst)* any; *litet av ~* a little of everything; *i ~ fall* in any case, at any rate; *i ~ särskilt fall* in each [specific] case; *till ~ pris* at all costs, at any price **-handa** *oböjligt a* diverse, various, all sorts of [things]; *(som rubrik)* miscellanies
varjämte besides (in addition to) which, and besides [that]
varken neither (... eller ... nor); *han ~ ville eller kunde* he neither could nor would; *~ bättre eller sämre än* no better nor worse than; *~ det ena eller det andra (fågel eller fisk)* neither fish, flesh nor fowl
varl|ig [ˣva:r-] *a1* gentle, soft; *jfr* varsam **-igt** *adv* gently
varm *a1* warm *(rock* coat; *färg* colour; *deltagande* sympathy); *(het)* hot *(bad* bath; *mat* food; *vatten* water); *bildl. äv.* hearty, cordial *(mottagande reception)*, ardent *(beundrare* admirer), fervent; *~t hjärta* warm heart; *~ korv* hot dog; *~a källor* hot springs; *fem grader ~t* five degrees above zero (freezing point); *bli ~* get warm (hot), *(om maskin)* warm up; *jag blev ~ om hjärtat* my heart warmed; *bli ~ i kläderna (bildl.)* [begin to] find one's feet; *ge ngt med ~ hand* give s.th. gladly (readily, of one's own free will); *gå ~ (om maskin)* run hot, get overheated; *tala sig ~ för en sak* warm up to a subject; *vara ~ om händerna* have warm hands **-bad** hot bath **-blod** *(häst)* blood horse **-blodig** *(om djur)* warm-blooded; *(om*

pers.) hot-blooded
varmed ['va:r-] *adv* **1** *interr.* with (by) what; *~ kan jag stå till tjänst?* what can I do for you? **2** *rel.* with (by) which
varm|front *meteor.* warm front **-garage** heated garage **-gång** *tekn.* overheating, running hot **-hjärtad** [-j-] *a5* warm-hearted **-köra** *(motor)* warm up, run hot **-luft** hot air **-luftsridå** hot-air curtain **-rätt** hot dish **-vatten** hot water **-vattenberedare** [electric] water heater; boiler, geyser **-vattenkran** hot[-water] tap
varn|a [ˣva:r-] warn *(för ngt* of s.th.; *för ngn* against s.b.; *för att* not to); *(mana t. försiktighet äv.)* caution *(för att* against + ing-form); *ett ~nde exempel* a warning (lesson)
varnagel [ˣva:r-] *r* example; *honom till straff och andra till ~* as a punishment to himself and a warning to others
varning warning; *(varningsord äv.)* caution; *(vink)* hint; *(förmaning)* premonition; *~ för* beware of; *ett ~ens ord* a word of warning (caution)
varnings|lampa warning light **-ljus** hazard warning light (flasher) **-märke** warning sign; *(trafik-)* danger sign **-signal** warning signal **-skott** warning shot **-triangel** warning triangle
varnolen *s3* white spirit; petroleum spirits *(pl)*
varom ['va:råm] **I** *adv, rel.* about (of) which; *interr.* about (of) what; *~ mera nedan* about which more is said (written) below **II** *konj, ~ icke* and if not
1 varp *s2* *(i väv)* warp [wires *pl*]; *(handgjord)* chain; *sätta up en ~* build up a warp; *~ och inslag* warp and weft *(AE. filling)*
2 varp *s7* **1** *se notvarp* **2** *sjö.* warp, kedge
1 varpa *väv.* **I** *s1* warping machine **II** *v1* warp
2 varpa *s1* *(sten)* stone disc
varptråd warp thread
varpå ['va:r-] *adv, rel.* on which; *interr.* on what; *(om tid äv.)* whereupon, and so, after which; *~ beror misstaget?* what is the reason for the mistake?, what is the mistake due to?
1 vars *(rel. pron, genitiv av vilken)* whose, of whom (which); *för ~ skull* for whose sake, for the sake of whom (which)
2 vars *interj, ja (jo)* ~ *(någorlunda)* not too bad; *nej, ~* not really
var|sam [ˣva:r-] *a1* wary, cautious; *(aktsam)* careful **-samhet** care; caution **-samt** *adv* warily *etc.*; *behandlas ~* handle with care
varse *oböjligt a, bli ~* perceive, *(upptäcka)* discover, *(märka)* notice
varsebliv|a *se* [bli] varse **-ning** perception
varsel ['varr-] *s7* **1** *(förvarning)* premonitory sign, presage, foreboding **2** *(vid arbetstvist o.d.)* notice, warning; *utfärda ~ om strejk* give notice of a strike; *med kort ~* at short notice
varsko [ˣva:r-] *v4* warn *(ngn om* s.b. of); give notice *(om flyttning* to quit); *polisen är ~dd* the police have been notified
varsl|a 1 *(vara förebud)* forebode, augur, portend; *~ om (äv.)* be ominous of; *det ~r illa* that is no good omen, that augurs no good **2** *(varsko)* give notice *(om* of); *~ om strejk, se* varsel 2
varsna *se* [bli] varse
varstans ['va:r-] *lite ~* here, there and everywhere

Warszawa [varˣsa:va] *n* Warsaw
1 vart *r*, *inte komma ngn* ~ get nowhere, make no progress; *jag kommer ingen* ~ *med honom* I can do nothing with him
2 vart *adv* where; *vard.* where to; ~ *som helst* anywhere; *jag vet inte* ~ *jag skall ta vägen* I don't know where to go; ~ *vill du komma* (*bildl.*) what are you driving at?
3 vart *imperf. av varda*
vartannat [-ˣann-] *se varannan 2*
vart|efter [-'eft-, 'vart-] (*efter hand som*) [according] as; (*så småningom*) little by little **-hän** where
vartill ['va:r-] *adv, rel.* to (for) which; *interr.* for what [purpose]; ~ *nyttar det?* what is the good (use) of that?
vartåt [-'å:t, 'vart-] where; in what direction; *nu ser jag* ~ *det lutar* (*bildl.*) now I see which way things are going
varu|belåning loan on goods; *konkr.* pawnbroking business **-beteckning** description of goods **-bil** delivery van, *AE.* panel truck **-bud** delivery boy (messenger) **-deklaration** merchandise description; informative label **-distribution** distribution of goods **-fordringar** *pl* commercial (trade) claims **-försändelse** consignment (*med fartyg:* shipment) [of goods] **-handel** trade, commerce **-hiss** goods (freight) lift, hoist; *AE.* freight elevator **-hus** department store **-huskedja** multiple retail organization; *AE.* chain store organization **-konto** trading (trade) account **-kännedom** knowledge of merchandise **-lager** stock [of goods], goods in stock; (*magasin*) warehouse; *inneliggande* ~ stock in trade
varulv werewolf
varu|magasin warehouse, storehouse **-märke** trademark **-märkesansökan** trademark application **-märkesskydd** trademark protection **-mässa** trade fair (exhibition)
varunder [-'unn-] under (*om tid:* during) which
varuprov sample
varur ['va:r-] *adv* out of which, from which
varu|rabatt trade discount **-skatt** purchase (*AE.* sales) tax; *allmän* ~ general purchase (*etc.*) tax **-slag** line (kind) of goods **-transport** carriage (conveyance) of goods
varutöver [-'ö:-] over and above (besides, in addition to) which
varu|utbyte exchange of goods, trade **-växel** trade (commercial) bill
1 varv *s7* (*skepps-*) shipyard, shipbuilding yard; (*flottans*) [naval] dockyard; *på* ~*et* in the shipyard
2 varv *s7* **1** (*omgång*) turn; (*hjul-*) revolution; *sport.* round, lap, (*vid stickning o.d.*) row; *linda ngt tre* ~ *runt* wind s.th. three times round **2** (*lager*) layer; ~ *ner i* ~ (*bildl.*) unwind
varva 1 (*lägga i varv*) put in layers **2** *sport.* lap
varvid ['va:r-] at which; (*om tid äv.*) when; ~ *han* (*äv.*) in doing which he
varv|ig *a1* (*skiktad*) varved (*lera* clay) **-räknare** revolution counter, tachometer
varvs|arbetare shipyard worker **-chef** shipyard manager **-industri** shipbuilding industry
varvtal number of revolutions
varöver [-'ö:-] *adv, rel.* over (at) which; *interr.* over (at) what
vas *s3* vase

vasall *s3* vassal **-stat** vassal state; satellite state
vasa|loppet the Vasa ski race, the Vasa run **-riddare** Knight of the Order of Vasa
vaselin *s4, s3* petrolatum, mineral jelly; vaseline (*varumärke*)
vask *s2* (*avlopp*) sink
vask|a wash; (*guld äv.*) pan; (*bergsvetenskap äv.*) buddle **-malm** wash ore **-ning** panning; (*guld-*) placer-mining; **-tråg** washing trough; (*guld-*) cradle, rocker
vasomotorisk [-'to:-] *a5* vasomotor (*nerv* nerve)
1 vass *s2* [common] reed; *koll.* reeds (*pl*); *i* ~*en* among (on) the reeds
2 vass *a1* sharp (*kniv* knife); keen (*egg* edge) (*äv. bildl.*); sharp-edged (*verktyg* tool); (*stickande*) piercing; (*sarkastisk*) caustic (*ton* tone); ~*a blickar* keen (piercing) looks; ~ *penna* pointed (*bildl. äv.* caustic) pen; *en* ~ *tunga* a sharp (biting) tongue; *ett strå* ~*are* [än] (*vard.*) a cut above
vassbuk *zool.* sprat
vasskant *i* ~*en* at the edge of the reeds
vassla l *s1* whey **ll** *v1, rfl* turn (go, get) wheyey
vassleaktig *a1* wheyey, wheyish
vassnäst [-ä:-] *a4* sharp-nosed, with a pointed (sharp) nose
vass|rugge clump of reeds **-strå** (*hopskr. vasstrå*) reed
vassögd *a1* sharp-eyed, with piercing eyes
Vatikanen [-'ka:-] *r, best. form* the Vatican
watt [v-] *s9* watt
wattal (*särskr. watt-tal*) wattage
vatten ['vatt-] *s7* **1** water; *hårt* (*mjukt*) ~ hard (soft) water; *rinnande* ~ running water; *per forsta öppet* ~ per first open water (*förk.* f.o.w.); *leda in* ~ lay on water: *lägga* (*sätta*) *i* ~ put in water; *ta in* ~ (*om båt*) make (take in) water, water; *på* (*i*) *svenska* ~ on Swedish waters; *under* ~ under water, submerged; *simma under vattnet* swim below the surface; *sätta under* ~ flood, submerge **2** *fiska i grumligt* ~ fish in troubled waters; *få* ~ *på sin kvarn* get grist to one's mill; *det är som att hälla* ~ *på en gås* it's like pouring water on a duck's back; *kunna ngt som ett rinnande* ~ know s.th. off pat; *känna sig som fisken i vattnet* feel thoroughly at home; *ta sig* ~ *över huvudet* (*bildl.*) take on more than one can manage, bite off more than one can chew; *i de lugnaste vatten går de största fiskarna* still waters run deep **3** *med.* water (*i knäet* on the knee); ~ *i lungsäcken* wet pleurisy **4** *kasta* ~ (*urinera*) make (pass) water
vatten|avrinning drainage **-avvisande** water-repellent **-bad** water-bath **-behållare** water tank **-blandad** mixed with water **-brist** water shortage **-bryn** *i* ~*et* at the surface of the water, (*vid stranden*) at the water's edge **-buren** *a5* waterborne **-cykel** water cycle, pedalo **-delare** watershed, divide **-djup** depth of water **-djur** aquatic animal **-domstol** water rights court, riparian court **-drag** watercourse **-droppe** drop of water **-fall** waterfall; falls, rapids (*pl*), cataract; *bygga ut ett* ~ harness a waterfall **-fallsverk** *statens* v~ [the Swedish] state power board **-fast** waterproof; water-resistant **-fattig** scantily supplied with water; (*ofruktbar*) arid **-fri** free from water; *kem.* anhydrous, dehydrated **-fågel**

waterfowl (*äv. koll.*); aquatic bird **-färg** watercolour **-förande** *a4* water-bearing **-förbrukning** water consumption **-förorening** water pollution **-förråd** supply of water **-försörjning** water supply **-glas 1** drinking-glass; *en storm i ett* ~ a storm in a teacup **2** *kem.* water glass **-grav** (*sport.*) water jump; (*vallgrav*) moat **-halt** water content **-haltig** *al* watery, containing water; *kem.* hydrous; *med.* serous **-kamma** wet comb **-kanna** (*för vattning*) watering can; (*för tvättvatten*) water jug **-kanon** water cannon **-karaff** carafe, water bottle **-kastare** hydrant **-klosett** water closet (*förk.* W.C.); *AE. äv.* bathroom **-konst** [artificial] fountain **-koppor** *se vattkoppor* **-kraft** water power **-kraftverk** hydroelectric power station (plant) **-kran** water tap; *AE.* faucet **-krasse** watercress **-kvarn** water mill **-kyld** [-çy:ld] *a5* water-cooled (*motor* engine) **vatten|ledning** water main, [water] conduit; (*-ledningssystem*) system of water mains; *det finns* ~ there is water laid on (*i huset* to the house) **-ledningsrör** water pipe; (*huvudledning*) water main[s *pl*] **-ledningsvatten** tap water **-linje** water line **-lås** waterseal, clean-out trap, drain trap **-löslig** soluble in water **-massa** volume (body) of water **-melon** watermelon **-märke** watermark **-mätare** (*för flöde*) water meter; (*för innehåll*) water gauge **-möja** *sl, bot.* water crowfoot **-odling** aquaculture **-pass** spirit (bubble) level **-pelare** column of water **-pistol** water pistol (*AE.* gun), squirt **-planing** aquaplaning **-polo** water polo **-post** [fire] hydrant **-prov 1** water sample; water test **2** *hist.* ordeal by water **-pump** water pump **-pöl** pool of water, puddle **-reglering** water regulation (control) **-reningsverk** water-purifying plant, sewage disposal plant **-reservoar** water reservoir (tank) **-ridå** water seal **-rik** abounding in water; ~ *trakt* well-watered country **-rätt** *jur.* water laws (rights) (*pl*) **-rättsdomare** judge of a water rights court **-rör** water pipe **-samling** pool of water; (*pöl*) puddle **-show** aquashow, *AE.* aquacade **-sjuk** boggy, waterlogged **-skada** water damage **-skadeförsäkring** water damage insurance **-skalle** *med.* hydrocephalus; *vard.* water on the brain **-skida** water-ski; *åka -skidor* water-ski **-skidåkning** water-skiing **-skott** *bot.* water shoot (sprout) **-slang** hose **-slipning** water sanding **-snok** grass snake **-spegel** mirror (surface) of the water **-sport** aquatic sports, aquatics (*pl*) **-spridare** water sprinkler **-stråle** jet of water **-stånd** water (sea) level; *högsta* ~ high- water level **-stämpel** watermark **-stänk** splash of water **-torn** water tower; standpipe **-trampning** treading water **-tunna** water cask; (*för regnvatten*) water butt **-turbin** water (hydraulic) turbine **-täkt** *s3* water supply (resources *pl*) **-tät** (*om tyg e.d.*) waterproof; (*om fartyg, kärl*) watertight **-uppfordringsverk** water-raising plant **-uppsugande** *a4* water-absorbent, hygroscopic **-verk** waterworks (*sg o. pl*); water service **-vård** water conservation (protection) **-väg** waterway **-växt** aquatic plant, hydrophyte **-yta** surface of water **-åder** vein of water **-ånga** steam; water vapour **-ödla** newt

vattgröt porridge [made with water]

wattimme (*särskr. watt-timme*) watt-hour

vatt|koppor *pl* chickenpox (*sg*), *med.* varicella **-lägga** soak, put in water

vattna water (*äv. djur*); (*be-*) sprinkle, irrigate; ~ *ur* soak (*sill* herring) **vattnas** *dep, det* ~ *i munnen på mig* it makes my mouth water (*när jag tänker på* to think of) **vattnig** *al* watery; *bildl.* insipid **vattning** watering; sprinkling, irrigation **vattra** water, wave; *~t tyg* moire, watered silk **vattu|mannen** *V*~ Aquarius **-siktig** *al* dropsical **-skräck** rabies; (*hos människa äv.*) hydrophobia **-sot** dropsy

vattvälling water gruel; *var och en rosar sin* ~ everyone swears by his own remedy

vax *s4* wax **vaxa** wax

vax|artad [-a:r-] *a5* waxy **-böna** wax (butter) bean **-docka** wax doll **-duk** oilcloth, American cloth **-figur** wax figure, waxwork **-gul** wax-coloured, waxen **-kabinett** waxworks (*sg o. pl*) **-kaka** honeycomb **-ljus** wax candle **-papper** wax paper **-plugg** plug of earwax

WC [ˣve:se:] *s6* W.C., toilet, lavatory **-borste** lavatory brush

VD [ˣve:de:] *förk. för verkställande direktör, se under verkställande*

ve I oböjligt *s* woe; *ditt väl och* ~ your welfare (wellbeing); *svära* ~ *och förbannelse över* call down curses on **II** *interj,* ~ *dig!* woe betide ([be] to) you!; ~ *mig!* woe is me!; *o,* ~*!* alas!; ~ *och fasa!* alackaday!

veck *s7* fold; (*sytt äv.*) pleat, plait; (*invikning*) tuck; (*skrynkla; press-*) crease; (*i ansiktet*) wrinkle; *bilda* ~ fold; *lägga* ~ put in pleats (*på* on); *lägga sig i* ~ form pleats; *lägga pannan i* ~ pucker (knit) one's brow

1 vecka *v1* pleat, put pleats in; ~ *sig* fold, crease, (*om papper*) crumple

2 vecka *sl* week; [*i*] *förra* ~*n* last week; ~ *för* ~ week by week; *en gång i* ~*n* once a week, (*utkommande etc.*) weekly; *om en* ~ in a week['s time]; *i dag om en* ~ a week today, this day week; *på fredag i nästa* ~ on the Friday of next week

veckig *al* creased; (*skrynklig*) crumpled, crinkled

veckla wrap (*in i* up in); ~ *ihop* fold up; ~ *upp* (*ut*) unfold, (*flagga*) unfurl (*äv.* ~ *ut sig*)

vecko|avlönad weekly paid (*arbetare* worker); paid by the week **-avlöning** weekly wage[s *pl*] (pay, salary) **-dag** day of the week **-helg** weekend **-kort** weekly season (*AE.* commuter) ticket **-lön** *se -avlöning* **-pengar** *pl* [weekly] pocket money (allowance) (*sg*) **-press** weekly press; ~*en* the weeklies (*pl*) **-slut** weekend **-tal** *i* ~ for weeks together (on end) **-tidning** weekly [paper, magazine] **-tvätt** weekly wash

veckända weekend

ved *s3* wood; (*bränsle äv.*) firewood **-artad** [-a:r-] *a5* woody, ligneous **-bod** woodshed

vederbör *i uttr.: den det* ~ whom it may concern, the party concerned **-ande I** *a4* the proper, the ... in question; ~ *myndighet* the proper (competent) authority, the authority concerned **II** *s9* the party concerned (in question); *pl* the parties concerned, those concerned; *höga* ~ the authorities (*pl*), the person (people) in authority **-lig** [-ö:-] *al* due, proper; appropriate; *i* ~ *ordning* in due

V

course; *med ~t tillstånd* with the necessary authorization, *(friare)* with due permission; *på ~t avstånd (äv.*) at a discreet distance; *ta ~ hänsyn till* pay due regard (attention) to **-ligen** [-ö:-] duly, properly; in due course

veder|döpare anabaptist **-faras** *-fors -farits, dep (komma t. del)* fall to (*ngn* a p.'s lot); befall (happen to) (*ngn* s.b.) **-farits** *sup. av vederfaras* **-fors** [-o:-] *imperf. av vederfaras* **-gälla** [-j-] *v2* repay; return (*ont med gott* good for evil) **-gällning** [-j-] *imperf. av vederfaras (äv. relig.*); reprisal; (*lön*) requital, recompense; (*hämnd*) retaliation; *~ens stund* day of retribution; *torde mot ~ återlämnas* reward offered for the return of **-gällningsaktion** retaliatory action **-häftig 1** (*pålitlig*) reliable, trustworthy (*person* person); authentic, sure (*uppgift* statement) **2** *hand.* solvent; *icke ~* insolvent **-häftighet 1** reliability, trustworthiness; authenticity **2** solvency **-kvicka** *v3* (*uppfriska*) refresh; (*stärka*) invigorate; (*ge nya krafter*) restore **-kvickande** *a4* refreshing; recreative; restorative **-kvickelse** refreshment; recreation; comfort

veder|lag *s7* compensation; remuneration, recompense **-lägga** confute; refute (*ngn* s.b.); contradict, deny (*ett påstående* a statement); *som inte kan ~s (äv.*) irrefutable **-mäle** *s6* token, mark **-möda** hardship; travail **-sakare** adversary **-stygglig** *a1* abominable; (*ful*) hideous **-stygglighet** abomination; horror **-tagen** *a5* established (*bruk* custom); conventional (*uppfattning* idea); accepted **-vilja** antipathy (*mot* towards); loathing (*mot of*) **-värdig** repulsive, repugnant; (*avskyvärd*) disgusting **-värdighet** repulsiveness; (*motgång*) vexation, contrariety; *~er (äv.*) horrors

vedettbåt picket boat

ved|handlare firewood dealer **-huggning** woodcutting, woodchopping **-kap** circular saw **-kubbe** chopping block **-lår** firewood bin **-pinne** stick of wood **-skjul** woodshed **-spis** wood stove **-såg** wood saw **-trave** woodpile, wood stack **-trä** log, piece of wood, [split] billet

vegetabil|ier [-'bi:-] *pl* vegetables; crops **-isk** *a5* vegetable (*föda* food)

vegetar|ian *s3* vegetarian **-isk** [-'ta:-] *a4* vegetarian (*kost* food)

veget|ation vegetation **-ativ** *a1* vegetative; *~a nervsystemet* the autonomic nervous system **-era** vegetate (*äv. bildl.*); *bildl. äv.* lead an inactive life

Weichsel ['vajksel] *r* the Vistula

1 vek *imperf. av vika*

2 vek *a1* (*som lätt böjs*) pliant, pliable; (*svag*) weak; (*mjuk*) soft; (*känslig*) gentle, tender; *~a livet* the waist; *ett ~t hjärta* a soft (tender) heart; *bli ~* soften, grow soft; *bli ~ om hjärtat* feel one's heart soften

veke *s2* wick **-garn** wick yarn

vek|het [ˣve:k-] pliancy; weakness; softness; tenderness **-hjärtad** [-j-] *a5* tenderhearted, softhearted

veklagan lamentation, wailing

veklig [ˣve:k-] *a1* soft; effeminate; (*svag*) weak [ly]; *föra ett ~t liv* lead a very easy life **-het** softness *etc.*; effeminacy

vek|ling weakling; *vard.* milksop **-na** grow soft (tender), soften; (*ge vika*) relent

vektor [ˣvektår] *s3* vector **-algebra** vector algebra **-analys** vector analysis

vela *vard.* dither

velar *a1 o. s3, språkv.* velar

velat *sup. av vilja*

velig *a1* irresolute, in two minds

wellpapp [ˣvell-] corrugated cardboard

velocipped *s3* bicycle

velour[s] [-'lo:r] *s3* velour[s]

weltervikt [ˣvell-], **-are** welterweight

velur *se velour[s]*

veläng *s3* vellum [paper]

vem [vemm] *pron* **1** *interr.* who (*som obj.* who[m]; *efter prep* whom); (*vilkendera*) which [of them]; *~ av dem ...?* which of them ...?; *~ där?* who is there?; *~ som who; ~s är felet?* whose fault is it?; *~ får jag lov att hälsa ifrån?* what name shall I say? **2** *rel., ~ som helst* anybody, anyone; *det kan ~ som helst se* anybody can see that; *~ det vara må* whoever it may be

vemod *s7* [pensive] melancholy, [tender] sadness **-ig** *a1* melancholy, sad [at heart]; blue

vemodsfylld full of sadness (melancholy)

1 ven *imperf. av vina*

2 ven *s3, anat.* vein

vend *s3*, **-er** ['venn-] *s9* Wend **-isk** ['venn-] *a5* Wendish

Venedig [-'ne:-] *n* Venice

venerisk [-'ne:-] *a5* venereal (*sjukdom* disease)

veneti|an [-etsi'a:n] *s3*, **-anare** [-ˣa:na-] *s9*, **-ansk** [-a:-] *a5* Venetian

ventjl *s3* **1** (*i rörledning e.d.*) valve **2** (*för luftväxling*) ventilator, vent[hole], air regulator **3** (*i fartygssida e.d.*) porthole; *AE.* air port **4** *mus.* valve **-ation** ventilation

ventilations|ruta quarterlight, *AE.* wing **-system** ventilation system

ventil|ator [-ˣla:tår] *s3* ventilator **-basun** valve trombone **-era 1** ventilate; air **2** (*dryfta*) discuss, debate, ventilate **-gummi** valve rubber **-hatt** valve (dust) cap **-slipning** valve grinding

ventrikel ['trikk-] *s2* (*magsäck*) stomach; (*hjärn-, hjärt-*) ventricle

venös *a5* venous (*blod* blood)

veranda [-ˣrann-] *s1* veranda[h]; *AE. äv.* porch

verb *s7* verb

verbal *a1* verbal **-isera** verbalize **-substantiv** verbal noun

verbform verbal form

verifi|era verify **-kation** (-*ering*) verification; (*intyg, kvitto äv.*) voucher **-kationsnummer** voucher number

veritabel [-'ta:-] *a2* veritable, true

verk *s7* **1** (*arbete*) work; (*litt. o. konst. äv.*) production; (*gärning äv.*) deed; *samlade ~* collected works; *ett ögonblicks ~* the work of an instant; *gripa sig ~ an, gå (skrida) till ~et* set (go) to work; *sätta kronan på ~et* crown (put the seal on) the work; *sätta i ~et* carry out, put ... into practice, (*förverkliga*) realize; *i själva ~et* as a matter of fact, actually **2** (*ämbets-*) office, [civil service] department; *stadens ~* municipal authorities; *statens ~* government (civil service) departments **3** (*fabrik*) works **4** (*fästnings-, ur-*) works (*pl*); (*me-*

kanism) mechanism, apparatus

verka 1 (*ha ~n*) work; act; *medicinen ~de inte* the medicin had no effect (did not work); *vi får se hur det ~r* we shall see how it works (what effect it has); *~ lugnande* have a soothing effect **2** (*arbeta*) work; *~ för* work for (in behalf of), devote o.s. to, interest o.s. in **3** (*förefalla*) seem, appear; *han ~r sympatisk* he makes an agreeable impression [upon one]; *hon ~r äldre än hon är* she strikes one as being older than she is

verkan *r, som pl används verkningar* (*resultat*) effect, result; (*in- äv.*) action; (*verkningskraft*) effectiveness; (*medicins*) efficacy; *orsak och ~* cause and effect; *fördröjd ~* retarded action; *förtaga ~ av* take away the effect[s] of, neutralize; *göra ~* take effect, be effective; *inte göra ~* be of no effect; *ha åsyftad ~* have the desired effect; *till den ~ det hava kan* in the hope it may work **verkande** *a4* active; (*arbetande*) working; *kraftigt ~* powerful, very effective; *långsamt ~* slow[-acting]

verklig *a1* real; (*sann*) true (*vän* friend); (*äkta*) genuine, veritable; (*faktisk*) actual (*inkomst* income); *det ~a förhållandet* the actual situation, the [real] facts (*pl*), the truth of the matter; *i ~a livet* in real life **-en** really; actually, indeed; *~?* indeed?, really?, you don't say [so]?; *jag hoppas ~ att* I do hope that; *jag vet ~ inte* I really don't know **-het** reality (*äv. ~en*); fact; (*sanning*) truth; *bli ~* materialize, come true; *i ~en* in reality, in real life, (*i själva verket*) as a matter of fact; *se ngn i ~en* see s.b. in the flesh

verklighets|flykt escapism **-främmande** out of touch with realities (real life) **-sinne** sense of reality **-skildring** realistic (true) description **-trogen** realistic, true to [real] life; (*om porträtt*) lifelike **-underlag** factual basis

verkmästare [industrial] supervisor, [factory] overseer, foreman

verkning *se* verkan

verknings|full effective **-grad** [degree of] efficiency, effectiveness; *ha hög ~* be highly efficient **-kraft** efficiency **-krets** incidence **-lös** ineffective **-område** sphere of influence **-radie** radius of action, range **-sätt** [mode of] action (operation)

verksam *al* **1** (*effektiv*) effective (*medicin* medicine) **2** (*arbetsam*) industrious, busy; (*aktiv*) active; (*driftig*) energetic; *ta ~ del i* take an active part in; *vara ~ som* work as **-het** activity; (*rörelse, handling*) action; (*arbete*) work; (*handelse.d.*) business, operations (*pl*) *oamerikansk ~* un-American activities (*pl*) **-en** cease one's activities, stop work; *sätta i ~* set working; *träda i ~* come into action (operation), start work; *vara i ~* be at work, (*om sak*) be in operation (action)

verksamhets|berättelse annual report **-form** form of activity **-fält** field of action; (*persons*) sphere of activity; *hand.* line [of business] **-lust** energy, craving for action **-år** hand. financial year

verkskydd industrial civil defence [unit]

verksläkare staff medical officer

verkstad ['värk-] *-en verkstäder* workshop; [repair, machine] shop; (*bil-*) garage; *mekanisk ~*

engineering plant (workshop); *skyddad ~* sheltered workshop

verkstads|arbetare engineering worker, mechanic **-chef** works (*AE.* plant) manager **-golv** shop floor **-industri** engineering industry **-klubb** trade union branch, works committee

verkställ|a carry out (into effect), perform; (*t.ex. dom*) execute; *~ betalningar* make (effect) payments **-ande** *a4* executive (*makt* power); *~ direktör* managing director, general manager, *AE.* president; *vice ~ direktör* deputy managing director (general manager), *AE.* [executive] vice president; *~ utskott* executive committee **-are** executor **-ighet** execution; effect; *gå i ~* be put into effect, be carried out

verk|tum [Swedish] inch **-tyg** tool, instrument (*äv. bildl.*); *eg. äv.* implement

verktygs|låda tool box **-skåp** tool cupboard (locker) **-utrustning** tool kit (outfit) **-väska** tool bag

vermiceller [-'sell-] *pl, kokk.* vermicelli

verm[o]ut ['värmut] *s2* vermouth

vernissage [-'sa:ʃ] *s5* opening of an exhibition; private view

veronal *s4, s3* veronal (*varumärke*)

veronika [-'rå:-] *s1, bot.* speedwell

vers [-ä-] *s3, s2* verse (*äv. i Bibeln*); (*strof*) stanza, strophe; (*dikt*) poem; *sjunga på sista ~en* be on one's (its) last legs; *skriva ~* write poetry (poems)

versal [-ä-] *s3, boktr.* capital [letter]; cap

vers|byggnad metrical structure **-drama** verse (metrical) drama

verserad [vär'se:-] *a5* well-mannered

vers|form metrical form **-fot** metrical foot

versifier|a versify **-ing** versification

version [vär'ʃo:n] version

vers|konst metrical art **-krönika** verse drama **-lära** prosody; metrics (*pl, behandlas som sg*) **-makare** versifier **-mått** metre **-rad** line of poetry

vertebrat [vä-] vertebrate

vertikal [vä-] vertical **-plan** vertical plane

verv [-ä-] *s3* verve, animation

vesir *s3* vizier

vespa *s1* Vespa scooter

vesper ['vess-] *s2* vesper

vessla *s1* **1** weasel; ferret **2** (*fordon*) snow cat[erpillar]

vestal *s3* vestal [virgin]

Westfalen [ˣvest-] *n* Westphalia **westfalisk** [ˣvest-] *a5* Westphalian; *~a freden* the Peace of Westphalia

vestibul *s3* vestibule; entrance hall, lobby

vet|a *visste -at* **1** know; be aware of; *det är inte gott att ~* one never knows (can tell); *du vet väl att* I suppose you know (are aware of the fact) that; *inte ~ vad man vill* not know one's own mind; *vad vet jag?* how should I know?; *vet du vad, …!* tell you what, …!; *~ sin plats* know one's place; *vet skäms!* be ashamed of yourself!; *det -e fåglarna!* goodness knows!; *så mycket du vet det!* and now you know!; *så vitt jag vet* as far as (for all) I know; *inte så vitt jag vet* not that I know of; *~ att* know how to (*uppföra sig* behave); *få ~* get to know, hear, learn (*av* from), be told (*av* by); *jag fick ~ det av honom själv* I had it from his own lips; *hur*

V

fick du ~ det? how did you get to know that (of it)?; *man kan aldrig ~* you never know (can tell); *låta ngn [få] ~* let s.b. know; *det måtte väl jag ~!* I ought to know! **2** (*med betonad partikel*) *~ av* know of; *han vill inte ~ av* a) (*ngn*) he won't have anything to do with, *b*) (*ngt*) he won't hear of; *innan man vet ordet av* before you can say Jack Robinson; *~ med sig* be conscious (aware) (*att man är* of being, that one is); *~ om* know [of, about]; *inte ~ om* (*äv.*) be ignorant of; *inte ~ till sig* not know what to do; *~ varken ut eller in* not know which way to turn **3** *rfl, inte ~ sig ha sett* not know that one has seen; *hon visste sig ingen levande[s] råd* she was at her wits' end

vetande I *a4, mindre ~* not quite right in the head, feeble-minded **II** *s6* knowledge; (*kunskaper äv.*) learning; *mot bättre ~* against one's better judgement; *tro och ~* faith and knowledge

vetat *sup. av veta*

vete *s6* wheat; *rostat ~* puffed wheat **-ax** ear of wheat **-bröd** white bread **-bulle** bun **-grodd** wheat germ **-kli** bran **-korn** grain of wheat **-mjöl** wheat flour

vetenskap *s3* science; (*-sgren*) branch of science (scholarship); *de humanistiska ~erna* the humanities (arts); *det är en hel ~* (*mycket invecklat*) it's an art in itself **-lig** [-a:-] *al* scientific; (*lärd*) scholarly **-lighet** [-a:-] scholarliness; scientific character **-ligt** [-a:-] *adv* scientifically; *bevisa ~* prove scientifically

vetenskaps|akademi academy of science[s] **-gren** branch of science (scholarship) **-historia** history of science **-man** scientist; (*humanist*) scholar **-teori** epistemology, theory of science and research

veteran *s3* veteran **-bil** veteran car

veterinär *s3* veterinary surgeon, *AE.* veterinarian; *vard.* vet **-besiktning** veterinary inspection **-högskola** veterinary college

veter|lig *al* known; *göra ~t, se kungöra* **-ligen, -ligt** as far as is known; *mig ~* as far as I know, to my knowledge

vetgirig eager to learn (know), craving for knowledge, inquiring, inquisitive **-het** thirst for knowledge; inquiring mind; inquisitiveness

veto *s6* veto; *inlägga sitt ~* interpose one's veto; *inlägga sitt ~ mot* veto, put one's veto on **-rätt** [right of] veto

vetskap [ˣveːt-] *s3* knowledge; *få ~ om* get to know, learn about; *utan min ~* (*äv.*) unknown to me

vett *s7* [good] sense; wit; *med ~ och vilja* knowingly, wittingly; *ha ~ att* have the good sense to; *vara från ~et* be out of one's senses

vett|a *-e -at, ~ mot* (*åt*) face (*norr* the north)

vette *s2* stool pidgeon, decoy

vett|ig *al* sensible; (*omdömesgill*) judicious **-lös** senseless **-skrämd** *a5* frightened (scared) out of one's wits (senses) **-villing** madman

vev *s2* crank, handle

vev|a I *s1, i samma ~* just at that (the same) moment **II** *v1, ~ [på]* turn [the crank (handle) [of]]; grind (*på ett positiv* an organ); *~ på* grind away **-axel** crankshaft **-hus** crankcase **-stake** connecting rod **-tapp** crankpin

v.g.v. *förk. för var god vänd, se vända 1*

whisky [ˈviss-] *s3* whisky; (*skotsk*) Scotch [whisky]; (*AE.*) rye, bourbon **-grogg** *en ~* a whisky and soda, *AE.* a highball

vi we; *~ andra* (*äv.*) the rest of us; *~ själva* we ourselves; *~ bröder* my brother[s] and I, we brothers

via via, by way of; through

viadukt *s3* viaduct

vial *s3, bot.* vetchling

vibr|afon [-ˈfɑːn] *s3* vibraphone **-ation** vibration **-ationsfri** vibrationless, vibration-free **-ator** [-ˣbraːtår] *s3* vibrator **-era** vibrate

vice oböjligt a **1** vice[-]; deputy (*talman* speaker) **2** *~ versa* vice versa, the other way round **-amiral** vice admiral **-konsul** vice consul **-konung** viceroy **-korpral** (*vid armén*) lance corporal, *AE.* private 1st class; (*vid flyget*) aircraftman 1st class, *AE.* airman 2nd class **-president** vice president **-värd** proprietor's (landlord's) agent, caretaker; *AE.* superintendent

vichyvatten soda water

1 vicka rock, sway; *bordet ~r* the table wobbles; *~ på foten* wag one's foot; *sitta och ~ på stolen* sit and swing on (sit balancing) one's chair; *~ omkull* tip (tilt) over, upset; *~ till* tip up, (*om båt äv.*) give a lurch

2 vicka *vard. för vikariera* sub[stitute] (*för* for)

vicker [ˈvikk-] *s2* vetch; *koll.* vetches (*pl*)

1 vid *prep* **1** *rumsbet., allm.* at; (*bredvid, invid; med hjälp av*) by; (*geogr. läge*) on; (*i närheten av*) near; (*vid gata, torg; anställd vid*) in; (*i prep. attr.*) of; (*efter fästa, binda e.d.*) to; *sitta ~ ett bord* sit at (*bredvid* by) a table; *röka ~ bordet* smoke at table; *sitta och prata ~ en kopp te* have a chat over a cup of tea; *bilen stannade ~ grinden* the car stopped at the gate; *klimatet ~ kusten* the climate at the coast; *sätta ett kryss ~ ett namn* put a cross against a name; *sitta ~ ratten* be at the wheel; *tåget stannar inte ~ den stationen* the train does not stop at that station; *studera ~ universitetet* study (be) at the university; *sitta ~ brasan* sit by the fire; *steka ~ sakta eld* fry over a slow fire; *leda ngn ~ handen* lead s.b. by the hand; *vi bor ~ kusten* we live by (near) the coast; *sida ~ sida* side by side; *~ min sida* by (at) my side; *skuldra ~ skuldra* shoulder to shoulder; *stolen står ~ väggen* the chair stands by (*intill* against) the wall; *~ gränsen* on the border; *staden ligger ~ havet* the town is [situated] on the sea; *~ horisonten* on the horizon; *en gata ~ torget* a street near (off) the square; *huset ligger ~ torget* the house is in the square; *anställd ~* employed in (at); *tjänstgöra ~ flottan* serve in the Navy; *vara (gå in) ~ teatern* be (go) on the stage; *slaget ~ Waterloo* the battle of Waterloo; *binda [fast] ngt ~* tie s.th. [on] to; *fäst ~* (*äv. bildl.*) attached to **2** *tidsbet., allm.* at; (*omedelbart efter*) on; (*omkring*) about; *~ den här tiden på året* at this time of the year; *~ den här tiden i morgon* at this time tomorrow; *~ jultiden* at Christmas; *~ tiden för* at the time of; *~ midnatt* at (*omkring about*) midnight; *~ nymåne* at new moon; *~ sin död var han* at the time of his death (when he died) he was; *~ fyrtio års ålder* at the age of forty; *~ första ögonkastet* at first sight; *~ min ankomst till* on my arrival in; *~ ett tillfälle* on one occasion, *~ sextiden* about six o'clock; *~ användningen av* when using; *~ halka* when it is slippery; ~ *kaffet talade vi om* when we were having coffee we talked about; ~ *sjukdom* in case of illness **3** *oegentlig bet.*; ~ *behov* when necessary, if required; ~ *fara* in case of danger; ~ *Gud!* by God!; ~ *allt vad heligt är* by everything that is sacred; ~ *gott mod* in good heart; ~ *namn Z.* called (named) Z., by the name of Z.; *hålla* ~ *makt* maintain, keep up; *hålla fast* ~ stick to; *stå* ~ *vad man sagt* stand by (keep to) what one has said; *van* ~ used (accustomed) to; *vara* ~ *liv* be alive **II** *adv* **1** *sitta* ~ *[sitt arbete]* stick to one's work **2** ~ *pass 15 personer* about 15 people, 15 persons or so

2 vid *a1* wide; (*-sträckt*) vast, extensive; broad (*dal* valley); (*om klädesplagg*) loose[ly fitting]; *i* ~*a kretsar* (*äv.*) widely; *det öppnar* ~*a perspektiv* it opens up wide vistas; *på* ~*a havet* on the open sea; *i* ~*a världen* in the wide world

vida *adv* **1** (*långt*) ~ [*omkring*] [far and] wide; ~ *berömd* renowned **2** (*mycket*) far (*bättre* better)

vidare *a, komp. t.* **2** *vid* **1** (*med större vidd*) wider etc. (*jfr 2 vid*); *bli* (*göra*) ~ (*äv.*) widen **2** (*ytterligare*) further (*underrättelser* particulars); more; *ni får* ~ *besked* (*äv.*) you will hear more **II** *adv* **1** (*komp. t. vida 1, 2 vitt*) wider, more widely; (*längre*) farther, further (*t.ex. gå, föra, läsa* ~) on; (*i tid*) longer, more; ~*!* go on!; *den behövs inte* ~ it is no longer needed; *innan vi går* ~ before we go any further; *läsa* ~ read on, continue to read; *och så* ~ and so on (forth) **2** (*ytterligare*) further, more; ~ *meddelas att* it is further stated that; *jag har inget* ~ *att tillägga* I have nothing to add; *jag kommer inte* ~ *att* … I won't … any more; *vi talar inte* ~ *om det!* don't let us talk any more about that! **3** (*dessutom*) further[more], also; *se* ~ *sidan 5* see also page 5 **4** (*igen*) again; *låt det inte hända* ~ don't let it happen again **5** (*särskilt*) *inte* ~ not particularly (very); *det är inget* ~ *att bo här* it's not very pleasant living here; *vi hade inte* (*inget*) ~ *roligt* it wasn't much fun, we did not enjoy ourselves very much **6** *tills* ~ until further notice, for the present; *utan* ~ without further notice (any more ado), *vard.* just like that

vidare|befordra forward, send on; (*upplysningar o.d. äv.*) pass on **-befordran** forwarding; *för* ~ *till* to be forwarded to **-utbildning** further (advanced) training (education) **-utveckling** further development

vid|bränd *a5*, *är* ~ has got burnt **-bränt** *adv*, *smaka* ~ have a burnt taste; *det luktar* ~ there is a smell of [something] burning

vidbrättad *a5* wide-brimmed

vidd *s3* **1** (*omfång*) width; *fack.* amplitude; (*kläder etc.*) fullness, looseness **2** *bildl.* (*utsträckning*) extent; (*omfattning*) scope; *i hela sin* ~ to (in) its whole extent; ~*en av hans kunskaper* the scope of his knowledge **3** (*-sträckt yta*) expanse; plain

vide *s6* willow; (*korg-*) osier **-korg** wicker basket

video ['vi:-] *s5* **1** *tekn.* video **2** *se -bandspelare* **-band** video tape **-bandspelare** video [cassette] recorder **-förstärkare** video amplifier

vidertryck backing [up]

videsnår osiery

vidfilm wide-screen film; *i* ~ on wide screen

vid|foga append, affix **-fästa** attach, fix on

vidg|a (*äv. rfl*) widen (*äv. bildl.*); expand, enlarge; (*spänna ut*) dilate; ~ *sina vyer* broaden one's mind **-as** *dep, se vidga* **-ning** widening; expansion, enlargement; dilation

vid|gå own (*att man är* being), confess **-gående** *s6* owning, confession **-hålla** maintain; keep (adhere, *vard.* stick) to; insist on **-häfta 1** (*häfta fast vid*) adhere, stick **2** *se vidlåda* **-häftning** adherence, adhesion **-häftningsförmåga** adhesiveness, adhesive capacity (power) **-hängande** *a4* attached, fastened (tied) on; ~ *adresslapp* tag, tie-on label

vidimer|a attest, ~*s* signed in the presence of, witnessed **-ing** attestation

vidja [ˣvi:d-] *s1* osier switch, wicker

vid|kommande *s6, för mitt* ~ as far as I am concerned **-kännas** *v2, dep* **1** (*erkänna*) own, admit, acknowledge **2** (*lida*) suffer, bear, endure (*en förlust* a loss); ~ *kostnaderna* bear the costs

vidlyftig *a1* **1** (*omfattande*) extensive; (*omständlig*) wordy (*berättelse* narrative); ~*a resor* extensive travels **2** (*tvivelaktig*) questionable (*affär* transaction); (*utsvävande*) fast (*herre* liver); *et* ~*t fruntimmer* a woman of easy virtue **-het 1** extensiveness etc. **2** (*i seder*) dissipation; (*-a äventyr*) escapades (*pl*)

vid|låda be inherent in; *de fel som -låder* (*äv.*) the [inherent] faults of **-makthålla** maintain, keep up, preserve **-makthållande** *s6* maintenance, upholding, preservation

vidrig [ˣvi:d-] *a1* **1** (*motbjudande*) repulsive, disgusting; (*förhatlig*) odious; (*otäck*) horrid **2** (*ogynnsam*) contrary; adverse (*omständigheter circumstances*) **-het 1** repulsiveness etc. **2** contrariness; adversity

vidrigt *adv* repulsively etc.; *lukta* ~ have a terrible smell; *smaka* ~ taste abominable

vidräkning settlement of accounts; *vard.* showdown; *en skarp* ~ *med* a sharp attack on

vidskepelse [-ʃ-] superstition

vidskeplig [-ʃe:-] *a1* superstitious **-het** superstitiousness, superstition

vidsträckt *a1* extensive, wide; vast (*område* area); expansive (*utsikt* view); ~*a befogenheter* extensive powers; *göra* ~*a resor* (*äv.*) travel extensively; *i* ~ *bemärkelse* in a wide (broad) sense

vidstående *a4* adjoining (*sida* page)

vid|syn broad outlook (views *pl*) **-synt** *a1* broad-minded **-synthet** *s6* broad- mindedness

vid|ta[ga] 1 (*företaga*) take (*åtgärder* steps); make (*anstalter* arrangements) **2** (*fortsätta*) come; (*börja*) begin; *efter lunchen -tog* after the lunch followed **-tala** arrange with; *jag har* ~*t honom om saken* I have spoken to him about it

vidunder monster; (*enastående företeelse*) prodigy **-lig** [ˣvi:d-, -'lig] monstrous; (*orimlig*) preposterous **-lighet** monstrosity

vid|vinkelobjektiv *foto.* wide-angle lens **-öppen** wide-open

Wien [vi:n] *n* Vienna

wien|are [ˣvi:nare] Viennese (*pl lika*) **-erbröd** Danish pastry **-erschnitzel** [-ʃnitsel] *s2* Wiener schnitzel **-sk** [-i:-] *a5* Viennese

Vierwaldstättersjön [fi:rvaltˣʃtätter-] the Lake of Lucerne

V

vietnames *s3* Vietnamese (*pl lika*) **-isk** [-'me:-] *a5* Vietnamese

vift *s3, ute på* ~ out on the spree

vift|a I *s1* whisk **II** *v1* wave (*farväl åt ngn* s.b. farewell); ~ *bort* whisk away (*flugor* flies); ~ *med* wave; brandish; ~ *på svansen* wag its tail **-ning** waving, wave; wag

vig *a1* agile, supple, lithe

vig|a *v2* **1** (*helga; in-*) consecrate; (*präst*) ordain; (*ägna*) dedicate, devote (*sitt liv åt* one's life to); ~ *ngn till biskop* consecrate s.b. bishop; ~ *ngn till den sista vilan* commit s.b. to his (*etc.*) last resting place; **-d jord** consecrated ground **2** (*förena genom vigsel*) marry; **~s** get married (*vid* to) **1 vigg** *s2* (*fågel*) tufted duck

2 vigg *s2, vard.* touch; *slå en* ~ *hos ngn* touch s.b. for money

vigga *vard.* touch

vighet [ˣvi:g-] agility, suppleness, litheness

vigil|ans [-'lans, -'laŋs] *s3, se* 2 vigg **-era** *se* vigga

vigsel ['vi:g-, 'vikk-] *s2* marriage [ceremony], wedding; *borgerlig* ~ civil marriage; *kyrklig* ~ church (religious) marriage; *förrätta* ~ officiate at a marriage **-akt** marriage ceremony **-attest, -bevis** marriage certificate (lines *pl*) **-formulär** marriage formula **-förrättare** person officiating at a wedding **-ring** wedding ring

vigvatten holy water **-skål** holy water stoup

vigör vigour; fettle; *vid full* ~ in full vigour (capital form)

vik *s2* bay; (*mindre*) creek; (*havs-*) gulf; *ha en vän i* ~*en* (*vard.*) have a friend at court

vik|a *vek -it el. -t* **1** fold; (~ *dubbel äv.*) double; (*fåll*) turn in; *får ej* ~*s* not bend **2** (*gå undan*) yield, give in (*för* to); (*flytta sig*) budge; *mil.* retreat; ʲᵈl. waver, flinch; ~ *för övermakten* yield to [superior] numbers; *inte* ~ *en tum* not move an inch; *han vek inte från hennes sida* he did not budge from her side; ~ *om hörnet* turn [round] the corner; ~ *åt sidan* turn aside; *vik hädan!* get thee behind me! **3** *ge* ~ give way (in) (*för* to), (*böja sig*) yield (*för* to), (*falla ihop*) collapse; *inte ge* ~ (*äv.*) hold one's own, keep firm **4** *vard.* (*reservera*) set aside; *platsen är -t för honom* the post is earmarked for him **5** *rfl* double up; (*böja sig*) bend; *benen vek sig under mig* my legs gave way under me; *gå och* ~ *sig* (*vard.*) turn in **6** (*med betonad partikel*) ~ *av* turn off; ~ *ihop* fold up; ~ *in* fold in, *sömn.* turn in; ~ *in på* turn into (*en gata* a street); ~ *ner* turn down; ~ *tillbaka a*) fold back, *b*) (*dra sig undan*) fall back, (*om pers.*) retire; ~ *undan a*) fold back, *b*) (*gå åt sidan*) give way, stand aside, (*för slag e.d.*) dodge; ~ *upp a*) turn up, (*ärmar äv.*) tuck up, *b*) (*veckla upp*) unfold; ~ *ut* unfold **vikande** *a4, aldrig* ~ never yielding, (*ständig*) incessant

vikare *zool.* ringed seal

vikariat *s7* deputyship; temporary post

vikarie [-'ka:-] *s5* deputy; (*för lärare*) substitute; (*för läkare, präst*) locum [tenens]

vikarier|a ~ *för ngn* deputize for s.b., act as a p.'s substitute **-ande** *a4* deputy; acting (*professor* professor)

vik|bar [ˣvi:k-] *a1* foldable **-dörr** folding door

viking Viking

vikinga|balk law of the Vikings **-färd** Viking expedition **-skepp** Viking ship **-tiden** the Viking Age **-tåg** Viking raid

vikit *sup. av* vika

1 vikt [-i:-] *sup. o. perf. part. av* vika

2 vikt [vikkt] *s3* **1** weight (*äv. konkr.*); *fys.* gravity; *efter* ~ by weight; *i lös* ~ in bulk; *specifik* ~ specific gravity; *förlora i* ~ lose weight; *hålla* ~*en* be full weight; *watch* one's weight (diet); *inte hålla* ~*en* be (fall) short in weight **2** (*betydelse*) importance; weight; *lägga* ~ *vid* lay stress on; *av största* ~ of the utmost importance; [*inte*] *vara av* ~ be of [no] consequence (importance)

vikta *stat.* weight

vikt|enhet unit of weight **-förlust** loss of weight

viktig *a1* (*betydelsefull*) important, of importance; (*allvarlig*) serious (*problem* problem); (*angelägen*) urgent (*sak* matter); *ytterst* ~ vital[ly important], (*mest important*) of utmost importance; *det* ~*aste* the main (most important) thing, the essential point **2** (*högfärdig*) self-important, stuck-up; *göra sig* ~ put on airs **-petter** *s2* stuck-up fellow

vikt|klass *sport.* class, weight **-lös** weightless **-löshet** weightlessness **-minskning** reduction in weight **-mängd** weight

viktoriansk [-a:-] *a5* Victorian

vikt|sats set of weights **-system** system of weights

viktualiehandlare [-ˣa:li-] provision merchant

viktualier [-'a:li-] *pl* provisions, victuals

viktökning increase in (of) weight

vila I *s1* rest (*äv. om maskin e.d.*); (*ro äv.*) repose; *en stunds* ~ a little rest; *i* ~ at rest; *söka* ~ repose; *den sista (eviga)* ~*n* the final rest **II** *v1* rest (*mot* against, on); repose; *absol. äv.* be at rest; (*vara stödd äv.*) lean (*mot* on); *arbetet* ~*r* work is at a standstill; *här* ~*r* here lies; ~ *i frid!* sleep in peace!; *saken får* ~ *tills vidare* the matter must rest there [for the present]; *avgörandet* ~*r hos honom* the decision rests with him; ~ *sig* rest [o.s.], take a rest; ~ *på* rest on, (*vara grundad på*) be based (founded) on; ~ *på hanen* have one's finger on the trigger; ~ *på årorna* rest on one's oars; *det* ~*r en förbannelse över a*) (*ngn*) a curse has fallen on, *b*) (*ngt*) there is a curse upon; ~ *ut* have a good rest

vild *a1* **1** wild; (*ociviliserad, otämjd*) savage (*stammar* tribes); (*ouppodlad, ödslig*) uncultivated; (*förvildad*) feral; ~*a djur* wild (savage) animals; *V*~*a Västern* the Wild West **2** *bildl.* wild; (*otyglad äv.*) unruly (*pojke* boy); (*rasande*) furious (*fart* pace); ~*a fantasier* wild ideas; ~ *flykt* headlong flight; ~ *förtvivlan* wild despair; *föra ett vilt liv* lead a wild (dissipated) life; *vilt raseri* frenzied rage; *bli* ~ go mad (frantic) (*av glädje* with joy); *vara* ~ (*utom sig*) be beside o.s., be mad (*av* with); *vara* ~ *i* (*på, efter*) be mad for; *vara* ~ *att* be wild to **-and** wild duck **-apel** crab apple [tree] **-basare** scapegrace **-djur** wild beast; *bildl. äv.* brute

vild|e *s2* savage; *AE. polit.* maverick **-fågel** wildfowl **-gås** wild goose **-havre** wild oats (*pl*); *så sin* ~ sow one's wild oats **-het** wildness; savagery; (*sinnelag äv.*) (wild) character; (*-sinthet*) ferocity **-hjärna** madcap **-honung** wild honey **-inna** female savage, wild woman **-katt** wildcat **-mark** wilderness, wilds (*pl*) **-marksliv** life in the wilds

-ros wild rose **-sint** *al* fierce, savage, ferocious **-svin** [wild] boar **-svinshona** wild sow **-vin** Virginia creeper, *AE*. American ivy, woodbine **-vuxen** that runs wild, wild

vilja I *s1* will; (*önskan*) wish, desire; (*avsikt*) intention; *med bästa ~ i världen* with the best will in the world; *av egen fri ~* of one's own accord (free will); *med litet god ~* with a little good will; *ngns sista ~* a p.'s last will [and testament]; *driva sin ~ igenom* work one's will; *få sin ~ igenom* get (have) one's own way, have one's will; *med eller mot sin ~* whether one will (likes it) or not; *göra ngt med ~* do s.th. on purpose (deliberately, purposely) **II** *ville velat* **1** will; (*vara villig* [*att*] *äv.*) be willing [to]; (*åstunda, önska*) want, wish, desire; (*ha lust* [*till*]) like, please; (*ämna*) intend, mean; (*stå i begrepp att*) be about (going) to; *~ ngns bästa* desire a p.'s good; *~ ngn väl* wish s.b. well; *~ är ett och kunna ett annat* to be willing is one thing, to be able another; *det ena du vill, det andra du skall* what I would I cannot and what I would not I must; *det är det jag vill* that is what I want; *du kan om du vill* you can if you want to; *jag både vill och inte vill* (*äv.*) I am in two minds; *som du vill!* [just] as you like!; *låta ngn göra som han vill* let s.b. have his own way (mind); *det vill jag verkligen hoppas* I should hope so; *det vill tyckas som om* it would seem as though; *slumpen ville att vi* [as] chance would have it, we; *vad vill du ha?* what do you want?, (*om mat e.d.*) what will you have?; *vad vill du att jag skall göra?* what do you want me to do?; *vad vill du mig?* what do you want of me?; *jag vill gärna* I should like to (*gå dit* go there), I shall be glad to (*komma* come; *hjälpa dig* help you); *motorn vill gärna stanna* the engine is apt to stop; *jag skulle ~* I should like to; *jag skulle ~ ha* I should like [to have]; *nej, det vill jag inte no*, I won't; *han vill inte att hon skall a*) (*tillåter inte*) he won't have her (+ *ing-form*), *b*) (*tycker inte om*) he does not like her (+ *ing-form*), *c*) (*önskar inte*) he does not want her to (+ *inf*.); *jag vill inte gärna* I would rather not, I prefer not to; *härmed vill jag inte ha sagt* by this I don't mean; *du vill väl inte säga att ...?* you surely don't mean to say that ...?; *jag ville inte* I did not want to, (*vägrade*) I would not **2** (*med betonad partikel*) *inte ~ fram med a*) (*pengar*) not want to fork out, *b*) (*sanningen etc.*) not want to come out with; *~ hem* want to go home; *det vill till mycket pengar* it takes (requires) a lot of money; *det vill till att kunna arbeta om* it takes a lot of work if; *~ åt (ngn)* want to get at s.b., (*ngt*) want to get hold of s.th. **3** *rfl, om det vill sig väl* (*illa*) if all goes well (if things go wrong); *det vill sig inte för mig* nothing is going right for me; *det ville sig så väl att vi* (*äv.*) as [good] luck would have it, we

vilje|akt [act of] volition **-ansträngning** effort of will **-fast** firm of purpose **-kraft** willpower **-liv** volitional life **-lös** without a will of one's own, weak-minded; (*apatisk*) apathetic **vilje|s** *i uttr.: göra ngn till ~* do as s.b. wants, humour s.b. **-stark** strong-willed; (*beslutsam*) resolute, determined **-styrka** *se viljekraft* **-svag** weak-willed **-yttring** manifestation of the (one's) will

vilk|en 1 *rel. a) självst.* (*om pers.*) who, (*om sak*) which, (*i inskränkande satser äv.*) that, *b*) *fören.* which; *-a alla* all of whom, (*om saker*) all of which; *de -as namn* those whose names; *den stad i ~ jag bor* (*äv.*) the town where I live; *gör -et du vill* do as (what) you like; *om hon kommer, -et är föga troligt* if she comes, which is not very likely **2** *interr. a*) (*vid urval*) which, *b*) (*i obegränsad bet.*) (*fören. om pers. o. saker, självst. om saker*) what, (*självst. om pers.*) who, (*vid urval*) which of them; *~ bok skall jag köpa?* (*~ av dessa*) which (*~ av alla*: what) book shall I buy?; *-a av dina skäl?* what are your reasons?; *åt -et håll skall vi gå?* which way shall we go?; *~ härlig dag!* what a lovely day!; *-a vackra blommor!* what beautiful flowers! **3** *indef., ~ som helst* anyone, anybody; *får jag ta ~ som helst* [*av de här två*]? may I take either [of these two]?; *~ som helst som* whoever, whichever; *~ ... än* whichever, whatever, (*om pers.*) whoever

vilkendera which [of them (the two)]

vill *pres. av vilja*

1 vill *s1* **I** (*villfarelse*) illusion, delusion; (*förvirring*) confusion; *optisk ~* optical illusion; *då blir den sista ~n värre än den första* (*bibl.*) so the last error shall be worse than the first **II** *v1, ~ bort* confuse; *~ bort sig* lose one's way, bild. äv. go astray; *på ~nde hav* on the boundless sea

2 villa *s1* house; (*större*) villa; (*enplans-*) bungalow; (*stuga*) cottage

villa|bebyggelse *området är avsett för ~* the area is reserved for the building of one-family houses **-kvarter** *se -område* **-olja** light fuel oil **-område** residential district (neighbourhood) **-stad** residential (garden) suburb **-ägare** houseowner

ville *imperf. av vilja*

villebråd *s7* game; (*jagat el. dödat*) quarry

villervalla *s1* (*förvirring*) confusion; (*oreda*) muddle, jumble; *allmän ~* general confusion

villfara grant, comply with (*ngns önskan* a p.'s wish)

villfarelse delusion; mistake; *sväva i den ~n att* be under the delusion that; *ta ngn ur hans ~r* enlighten s.b., open a p.'s eyes

villig *al* willing; ready, prepared; *vara ~* (*äv.*) agree (*att komma* to come) **-het** willingness; readiness

villkor [-å:r] *s7* **1** condition; *pl* (*i kontrakt, fördrag e.d.*) terms; (*bestämmelser*) stipulation, (*förbehåll*) provision, reserve; *på goda ~* on favourable (fair) terms; *på inga ~* on no condition; *på ~ att* on [the] condition that, provided [that]; *på överenskomna ~* on the terms agreed upon; *ställa som ~* make ... a condition; *ställa som ~ att* make it a condition that; *uppställa som ~* state as a condition; *våra ~* är följande our terms are as follows **2** (*levnads-*) *pl* condition (*sg*), circumstances; *leva i* (*under*) *svåra ~* be badly off, live in reduced circumstances **-lig** [-å:-] *al* conditional; *~ dom* suspended (qualified, conditional) sentence; *få ~ dom* (*äv.*) be put on probation; *~ frigivning* conditional release **-ligt** [-å:-] *adv* conditionally; *~ dömd* (*person*) probationer; *~ frigiven* on parole, released conditionally

villkors|bisats conditional clause **-lös** unconditional (*kapitulation* surrender)

V

villo|lära false doctrine; (*kätteri*) heresy **-spår komma** (*vara*) *på* ~ get (be) on the wrong track; *föra ngn på* ~ (*äv.*) throw s.b. off the scent **-väg** false path, wrong way; *föra ngn på* ~*ar* lead s.b. astray

villrådig irresolute (*om* as to); *vara* ~ (*äv.*) be in two minds (*om huruvida* as to whether) **-het** irresolution; hesitation

villsam *a1, bildl.* confusing, puzzling; ~*ma vägar* devious paths

vilo|dag day of rest **-hem** nursing (convalescent) home **-läge** rest[ing] position, *i* ~ at rest **-läger** place of repose **-paus** break, pause **-rum** (*grav*) last resting place **-stund** hour of rest, leisure hour **-tid** time of rest

vilsam [ˣviːl-] *a1* restful

vilse *adv o. oböjligt a* astray; *gå* ~ go astray, lose one's way (o.s.), (*i skogen*) get lost [in the woods]; *föra ngn* ~ lead s.b. astray, *bildl. äv.* mislead s.b. **-förd** [-öː-] *a5* led astray, misguided, misled **-gången** *a5*, **-kommen** [-å-] *a5* gone astray; stray; *känna sig -kommen* feel lost **-leda** lead astray, mislead; (*leda på fel spår*) throw off the scent, lead by the nose **-ledande** *a4* misleading, deceptive; ~ *framställning* (*äv.*) misrepresentation

vilsen lost; confused

vil|soffa couch **-stol** (*fåtölj*) easy chair, armchair; (*fällstol*) folding (reclining) chair

vilt I *adv* wildly *etc.*, *jfr vild*; *växa* ~ grow wild; ~ *främmande* perfectly (quite) strange; *en* ~ *främmande människa* an absolute (perfect, complete) stranger **II** *s7* game **-bestånd** stock of game **-handel** poulterer's [shop] **-reservat** wildlife refuge **-vård** wildlife conservation, game protection **-vårdare** game warden

vimla swarm, be crowded, teem (*av* with); a-bound (*av* in); *det ~r av folk på stranden* the beach is swarming with people; *det ~r av fisk i sjön* the lake is teeming with fish

vimmel [ˈvimm-] *s7* crowd, throng **-kantig** *a1* giddy, dizzy; (*förvirrad*) bewildered; *den gjorde mig* ~ (*äv.*) it made my head swim

vimpel *s2* streamer; *sjö. o. mil.* pennant

vimsig *a1* scatterbrained, featherbrained

1 vin *s4* (*-ranka*) vine; (*dryck*) wine; ~ *av årets skörd* this year's vintage; *där ~et går in går vettet ut* when the wine is in the wit is out; *skörda ~et* gather in the vintage

2 vin *s7* (*-ande*) whine, whiz[z]; whistle; *stormens* ~ the howl of the storm

vin|a *ven -it* whine, whistle; sough; *kulorna ven* the bullets whistled (whizzed); *vinden -er* the wind is howling; *i ~nde fart* at a headlong (rattling) pace

vin|beredning wine-making **-berg** hill planted with vines **-bergssnäcka** edible snail **-bär** (*svart*) blackcurrant; (*rött*) redcurrant **-bärsbuske** currant bush **-bärssaft** *svart* ~ blackcurrant juice

1 vind *s2* (*blåst*) wind; *väder och* ~ wind and weather; *god* (*nordlig*) ~ fair (north[erly]) wind; *svag* ~ light breeze; *växlande ~ar* variable (*sjö.* baffling) winds; *vad blåser det för* ~ *i dag?* what is the wind today?, *bildl.* (*eftersom du kommer*) what wind has blown you in here?; *med ~ens has-*

tighet with lightning speed, like the wind; *borta med ~en* gone with the wind; ~*en har vänt sig* the wind has shifted (veered); *få* ~ *i seglen* catch the wind, *bildl.* get a good start; *gå upp i* ~ sail near the wind; *driva* ~ *för våg* be adrift, be drifting [at the mercy of the winds]; *låta ngt gå* ~ *för våg* let s.th. take care of itself; *lämna sina barn* ~ *för våg* leave one's children to fend for themselves; *skingras för alla ~ar* be scattered to the winds

2 vind *s2* (*i byggnad*) attic, garret; loft; *på ~en* in the attic (*etc.*)

3 vind *a1* (*skev*) warped; askew; (*sned o.* ~) twisted

1 vinda I *s1* (*nyst-*) winder, reel **II** *v1*, ~ [*upp*] wind [up]; (*ankare*) hoist, heave [up]

2 vinda *v1* (*skela*) squint, have a squint, be cross-eyed

3 vinda *s1, bot.* bindweed

vindbrygga drawbridge

vind|böjtel *s2, pers.* weathercock **-driven 1** weather-driven; *bildl.* rootless **2** (*om väderkvarn*) wind-driven

vindel *s2* whorl; spiral **-trappa** winding (spiral) staircase

vind|energi wind energy **-fläkt** breath of wind **-flöjel** weathercock, [weather] vane **-fång 1** (*förstuga*) [small] entry, porch **2** (*yta*) surface exposed to the wind; *ha stort* ~ catch a great deal of wind **-fälle** *s6* windfall[en tree] **-hastighet** velocity of wind, wind velocity

vindi|cera reclaim, vindicate **-kation** claim for restitution of property

vindil gust [of wind]

vindistrikt winegrowing district

vind|kantring change of wind **-kast** sudden shift of wind

vindkraft wind power **-anläggning, -verk** wind power station (plant)

vindkåre breeze

vindla wind, meander

vindling whorl; *fack. äv.* convolution (*i hjärnan* of the brain); ~*ar* (*i flod, väg e.d.*) windings

vind|motor wind wheel **-mätare** anemometer, wind gauge **-pinad** *a5* windswept; (*om träd o.d.*) windblown **-pust** whiff (puff) of wind **-riktning** direction of the wind **-ros** *meteor.* wind rose; (*kompass-*) compass card **-ruta** windscreen; *AE.* windshield **-rutespolare** windscreen washer **-rutetorkare** windscreen (*AE.* windshield) wiper

vindruva grape

vindruvsklase bunch of grapes

vinds|fönster attic (garret) window **-glugg** skylight

vind|sidan the windward side; *åt* ~ windward **-skala** scale of wind force

vinds|kammare attic (garret) [room] **-kontor** boxroom [in the attic (garret)] **-kupa** attic

vindskydd windshield, windbreak

vindslucka ceiling hatch

vindspel winch, windlass

vindsrum [room in the] attic, garret [room]

vindstilla I *oböjligt a* calm, becalmed **II** *s1* calm

vindstrappa staircase up to the attic

vind|strut windsock, air sock, wind cone (sleeve) **-styrka** wind force **-stöt** gust [of wind],

squall
vindsvåning attic [storey]
vind|tunnel wind tunnel (channel) **-turbin** wind
turbine **-tyg** windproof cloth **- tygsjacka** windcheater, windjammer, *AE.* windbreaker (*varumärke*) **-tät** windproof **- vridning** shift (change)
of wind
vindögd *a1* squint-eyed **-het** squint
vinerbröd *se wienerbröd*
vinflaska bottle of wine; (*tom*) wine bottle
ving|ad *s6* winged **-ben** wing bone **-bredd**
wingspread; *flyg.* [wing]span **-bruten** broken-
winged (*äv. bildl.*)
ving|e *s2* wing (*äv. bot.*); (*på fläkt*) blade; *flaxa
med -arna* flap (flutter) the wings; *flyga högre än
-arna bär* fly too high; *få luft under -arna* (*bildl.*)
get started, get going; *pröva -arna* (*bildl.*) try
paddling one's own canoe; *ta ngn under sina -ars
skugga* (*bildl.*) take s.b. under one's wing **-frukt**
key, key-fruit **-klaff** *flyg.* wing flap **-klippa** clip
the wings of; pinion
vingla (*gå ostadigt*) stagger; (*stå ostadigt*)
wobble, sway [to and fro]
vinglas wineglass
vinglig *a1* (*som rör sig ostadigt*) staggering (*gång
gait*); (*som står ostadigt*) wobbly (*stol* chair) **-het**
unsteadiness
vinglögg mulled wine
ving|lös wingless **-mutter** wing (butterfly) nut
-par pair of wings **-penna** wing quill, pinion
-skjuten *a5* winged **-slag** wing-beat **-snäcka**
pteropod, sea butterfly **-spegel** *zool.* speculum
-spets wing tip, tip of the wing; *avstånd mellan
~arna* span **-sus** swish of wings
vin|gud god of wine **-gård** vineyard **-gårdsman**
vinedresser **-handlare** wine merchant, vintner
vinit *sup. av vinna*
vinjett *s3* vignette, [printer's] flower; (*slut-*) tail-
piece
vinjäst wine yeast
vink *s2* **1** wave; (*med handen*) beck; *lyda ngns
minsta ~* obey a p.'s every sign, be at a p.'s beck
and call; *vid minsta ~ från* at a nod from **2** (*anty-
dan*) hint; *en tydlig ~* a broad hint; *en fin ~* (*äv.*)
a gentle reminder; *ge ngn en ~* give (drop) s.b. a
hint; *förstå ~en* take the hint
vinka 1 (*med handen*) wave (*åt* at; *farväl* farewell); (*göra tecken*) beckon (*åt* to; *ngn till sig* s.b.
to come up [to one]); *~ avvärjande* make a depre-
cating gesture; *~ åt ngn att* (*äv.*) sign to s.b. to **2**
vi har inte mycket tid att ~ på we have not much
time to spare
vinkel *s2* **1** *mat.* angle; (*på rör*) knee, elbow;
(*verktyg*) try square; *död ~* dead angle; *spetsig
(trubbig) ~* acute (obtuse) angle; *i ~* at an angle;
i rät ~ mot at right angles to; *i 60° ~* at an angle
of 60 degrees; *bilda ~ mot* form an angle with **2**
(*vrå*) nook; (*hörn*) corner; *i alla vinklar och vrår*
in every nook and corner **-ben** side (leg) of an
angle **-formig** [-å-] *a1* angular **-hake** set square,
triangle; *boktr.* composing stick **-järn** angle iron
(bar) **-linjal** T-square **-mått** square rule, joint
hook **-rät** perpendicular, at right angles (*mot* to);
gå ~t mot varandra be at right angles to each other **-spets** vertex [of an angle]
vinkl|a angle, slant; weight; bias **-ing** angle,

slant; weighting; bias
vinkning waving *etc.*, *se vinka*
vin|krus wine jar, tankard **-kylare** wine cooler
-källare wine cellar **-kännare** connoisseur of
wine **-lista** wine list **-löv** vine leaf **-lövsranka**
vine leaves (*pl*)
vinn *oböjligt s, lägga sig ~ om, se vinnlägga* [*sig*]
vinn|a *vann vunnit* **1** (*segra* [*i*]; *erhålla vinst*) win
(*ett krig* a war; *pris* a prize; *en process* a suit; *på
lotteri* in a lottery); *~ i bridge* (*på tips*) win at
bridge (the pools); *~ i ärlig strid* win a fair fight;
~ på poäng win by points; *~ över ngn* (*äv.*) beat
s.b. **2** (*skaffa sig*) gain; (*förvärva*) acquire;
(*uppnå*) attain, obtain; *~ avsättning för* find a
[ready] market for; *~* [*ngns*] *bifall* meet with [a
p.'s] approval; *~ erkännande* gain (receive) recognition; *~ gehör* obtain a hearing; *~ ngns
hjärta* win a p.'s heart; *~ insteg* gain (obtain) a
footing; *~ inträde* obtain admission; *~ laga kraft*
gain legal force, become legal[ly binding]; *~ ngn
för sin sak* get s.b. on one's side, win s.b. for
one's cause; *~ spridning* become popular; *~ tid*
syfte gain (attain) one's end; *~ terräng* (*tid*) gain
ground (time) **3** (*förändras t. sin fördel*) gain (*vid
jämförelse* by comparison); ([*för*]*tjäna*) profit (*på
affären* by the transaction); *du -er ingenting på att*
you'll gain nothing by (+ *ing-form*); *hon -er i
längden* (*vid närmare bekantskap*) she improves
on closer acquaintance, she grows on you; *~ på
bytet* profit by (win on) the bargain (change);
rummet kommer att ~ på ommöbleringen the
room will improve with refurnishing **4** *~ på ngn
(knappa in)* gain [ground] on s.b., *trägen -er* perseverance carries the day
vinn|ande *a4* winning; (*tilltalande äv.*) attractive
-are winner **-ing** gain; profit; *snöd ~* sordid
gain, filthy lucre
vinnings|lysten covetous, mercenary, greedy
-lystnad greed, covetousness **-syfte** *i ~* with
the intention of gain
vinnlägga *rfl, ~ sig om* take pains (*att skriva fint*
to write well; *ett gott uppförande* to behave well);
strive after
vin|odlare wine-grower; viticulturist **-odling**
wine-growing; viticulture **-press** winepress
-provare wine-taster **-ranka** [grape]vine **-rät-
tighet** licence to serve wine **-röd** wine-red
vinsch *s2, s3* winch; hoist **vinscha** hoist
vin|skörd vintage, wine harvest **-sort** sort of
wine
vinst *s3* gain; *i sht hand.* profit[s *pl*]; (*behållning*)
proceeds (*pl*), return; (*i lotteri*) prize; (*på spel*)
winnings (*pl*); *~ och förlust* profit and loss; *på ~
och förlust* (*bildl.*) at random (a venture), on
speculation; *del i ~* share in profits; *högsta ~en*
the first prize; *ren ~* net (clear) profit; *ta in 10
pund i ren ~* make a clear profit of £10; *ge ~* yield
a profit, turn out well; *gå med ~* (*om företag*) be
a paying concern; *sälja med ~* sell at a profit; *utfalla med ~* (*om lott*) be a winning ticket **-andel**
share of (in) [the] profits **-begär** greed, cupidity
-delning protif-sharing
vinsten [ˣviːn-] tartar; *kem.* potassium bitar-
trate, potassium hydrogen tartrate; *renad ~*
cream of tartar
vinst|givande profitable, remunerative, lucra-

V

tive **-kupong** dividend warrant **-lista** [lottery] prize list, lottery list **-lott** winning ticket **-marginal** profit margin **-medel** *pl* profits
vinst- och förlust|konto, -räkning profit and loss account
vinstock [grape]vine
vinstsida *på ~n* on the credit side
vin|stuga tavern, bodega **-syra** tartaric acid **-säck** wineskin
vint|er ['vinn-] *s2* winter; *i ~* this winter; *mitt i ~n* in the middle of [the] winter, in midwinter; *i -ras* last winter; *om (på) ~n (-rarna)* in winter
vinter|badare winter bather **-bona** make fit for winter habitation **-bostad** winter residence **-dag** winter['s] day **-dvala** winter (hibernal) sleep; *ligga i ~* hibernate **-däck** snow tyre **-frukt** winter fruit **-fälttåg** winter campaign **-förråd** winter stock (supply) **-gatan** the Milky Way, the Galaxy **-grön** evergreen **-gröna** *s1* (*Pyrola*) wintergreen; (*trädgårds-*) [lesser] periwinkle **-gäck** [-j-] *s2*, *bot.* winter aconite **-halvår** winter half (term) **-härdig** hardy **-idrott** winter sports (*pl*) **-kappa** winter coat **-klädd** winterclad **-kläder** *pl* winter clothes (clothing *sg*) **-kvarter** *s7* (*lägga sig i* go into) winter quarters (*pl*) **-kyla** cold of winter, winter cold **-körning** (*bil-*) winter motoring
vinter|lig *al* wintry; brumous **-olympiad** Olympic Winter Games **-rock** winter coat, greatcoat **-solstånd** winter solstice **-sport** *s3* winter sports (*pl*) **-sportort** winter sports resort **-sömn** *se vinterdvala* **-tid I** *s3* wintertime, winter season **II** *adv* in [the] winter **-trädgård** winter garden **-väg** winter road
vintrig *al* wint[e]ry, winterly, winter-like
vinthund greyhound
vintunna wine cask (barrel)
vinyl *s3* vinyl **-plast** vinyl plastic **-platta** vinyl tile
vinår (*gott* good) vintage [year]
vin|äger [-'nä:-] *s2*, **-ättika** wine vinegar
viol *s3* violet
viola ['vi:-, -'å:la] *s1* viola, tenor violin
viol|blå violet-blue **-ett** *al* violet; (*rödaktig äv.*) purple; (*blålila äv.*) mauve
violin *s3* violin **-ist** violinist; *förste ~* first violin [ist] **-klav** treble (G) clef
violoncell [-lån'sell, -lån'sell] *s3* [violon]cello
viol|doft fragrance of violets **-rot** orrisroot
VIP [vipp] *s2* VIP (*initialord för very important person*)
vipa *s1*, *zool.* lapwing, peewit
vipp *s2*, *vard.*, *vara på ~en att* be on the point of (*+ ing-form*); *det var på ~en att han föll* he was within an ace of falling; *kola ~en* (*sl.*) kick the bucket
1 vippa *s1* **1** puff; *jfr damm-, puder-* **2** *bot.* panicle
2 vipp|a *v1* tilt (tip) [up]; (*röra sig upp o. ner*) rock, bob up and down; *~ på stjärten* wag[gle] one's tail
vipp|arm rocker [arm], lever arm **-kärra** tilt cart **-port** (*hopskr. vipport*) (*garagedörr*) overhead door
vips *~ var han borta* hey presto, he was gone!
1 vira *s9* (*kortspel*) vira

2 vira *v1* wind (*med* [round] with; *om[kring]* round); (*veckla*) wrap; (*krans*) weave; *~ in* wrap up (*i* in); *~ av* unwind
viril *al* virile
virka crochet
virke *s6* wood, timber; *AE.* lumber; *färskt ~* green wood; *hyvlat ~* planed wood; *ohyvlat ~* rough sawn timber; *kvistfritt ~* clean timber; *han är av hårdare ~ än sin bror* he's of a tougher fibre than his brother
virkes|avfall wood waste **-mätning** timber scalling **-upplag** stock of timber (wood)
virk|garn crochet yarn **-ning** crocheting; *konkr.* [piece of] crochet [work] **-nål** crochet hook
viro|log virologist **-logi** virology **-logisk** [-'lå:-] *a5* virological
virrig *al* (*om pers.*) muddleheaded, scatterbrained; (*om sak*) muddled, confused (*svar* reply); (*osammanhängande*) disconnected (*tal* speech) **-het** confused state of mind, muddleheadedness *etc.*
virrvarr *s7* confusion, muddle; *vard.* mess; *ett ~ av* a confused (tangled) heap of
virtuos I *s3* virtuoso; master **II** *al* masterly **-itet** virtuosity
virul|ens *s3* virulence **-ent** *al* virulent
virus ['vi:-] *s7*, *best. form äv. virus* virus **-sjukdom** virus disease
virvel *s2* **1** whirl (*äv. bildl.*); turbulence; (*ström-*) whirlpool, (*mindre*) eddy; *fack. o. bildl.* vortex (*pl* vortexes, vortices); (*hår-*) vertex (*pl* vertexes, vertices); *en ~ av nöjen* a whirl of pleasures; *dansens virvlar* the whirls of the dance **2** (*trum-*) roll; *slå en ~* beat a roll **-rörelse** whirling motion, gyration, turbulence **-storm** cyclone **-vind** whirlwind
virvla whirl; (*om vatten*) eddy; *~ runt* whirl round; *~ upp* whirl up
1 vis *s7* (*sätt*) manner, way; *på det ~et* in that way, (*i utrop*) oh, that's how it is!, I see!; *på sätt och ~* in a way; *på intet ~* in no way; *på sitt ~ är hon snäll* she is quite nice in her own way
2 vis *al* wise; *en ~* [*man*] (*äv.*) a sage; *Greklands sju ~e* the seven sages; *de ~es sten* the philosophers' stone; *de tre ~e männen* the three wise men, the three Magi; *av skadan bli man ~* experience is the father of wisdom; *once bit, twice shy*
1 vis|a *s1* song; ballad; *Höga ~n* the Song of Songs (Solomon); *ord och inga ~or* plain words (speaking); *hon är en ~ i hela stan* she is the talk of the town; *alltid samma ~* always the same old story; *slutet på ~n blev att* the end of the story was that
2 visa *v1* **1** show (*vänlighet* kindness; *hur man skall* how to); (*peka*) point (*på* out, to); (*ut-*) indicate, show (*tiden* the time); (*förete*) present, show (*ett glatt ansikte* a happy face), produce (*biljetten* one's ticket); (*ådagalägga*) exhibit, display (*skicklighet* skill); (*be-*) prove, show; *erfarenheten ~ att* experience proves (tells us) that; *utställningen ~s kl.* the exhibition may be seen (visited) at; *~ ngn en artighet* show courtesy to s.b.; *~ med exempel* demonstrate by example; *~ ngn på dörren* show s.b. the door, turn s.b. out; *~ tänderna* (*bildl.*) show fight; *gå före och ~ vägen* lead the way; *~ ngn vägen till* show s.b. the way to, direct

s.b. to; *klockan ~r på 8* the clock says 8; *termometern ~r på 20* the thermometer says 20 **2** (*med betonad partikel*) ~ *bort* dismiss (*äv. bildl.*), send away; ~ *fram* show, (*ta fram*) produce (*biljetten* one's ticket); ~ *tillbaka* turn back, *bildl.* reject; ~ *upp* show [up], *bildl.* exhibit, produce; ~ *ut* send out **3** *rfl* show o.s. (itself); (*framträda*) appear (*av* from; *för* to; *offentligt* in public); (*bli sedd*) be seen; (*dyka upp*) turn up; *det kommer snart att ~ sig* (*bli uppenbart*) it will soon be seen; *åter ~ sig* reappear; ~ *sig från sin bästa sida* show one's best side; ~ *sig för pengar* go round in a show; ~ *sig vara* turn out (prove) [to be]; ~ *sig vänlig* be kind, show kindness (*mot* to)

visar|e (*på ur*) hand; (*på instrument*) pointer, indicator, needle **-tavla** dial

visavj I *adv o. prep* vis-à-vis, opposite **II** *s3* vis-à--vis, lady (*etc.*) opposite

visbok song book, book of ballads

vischan *s, best. form, vard.* the back of beyond; *AE.* the sticks (*pl*); *på ~* at the back of beyond, *AE.* out in the sticks

visdiktare song (ballad) writer

visdom [-dɔmm] *s2* wisdom; (*klokhet äv.*) prudence

visdoms|ord word of wisdom, maxim **-tand** wisdom tooth

vise *s2* queen [bee]

visent European bison, wisent

viser|a visa (*ett pass* a passport) **-ing** visa[ing]

vishet [ˣvi:s-] wisdom

vishets|lära philosophy **-regel** maxim

vision vision **-är** *al o. s3* visionary

1 visjr *s3* (*titel*) vizier

2 visjr *s7* (*på hjälm*) visor; *fälla upp ~et* raise the visor; *med öppet ~* (*bildl.*) straightforwardly

visirskiva *foto.* focusing screen

visjt *s3* call; visit; *avlägga ~ hos ngn* pay s.b. a visit, call on s.b.; *fransysk ~* flying call **-ation** inspection, examination; (*kropps-*) search; *jur.* revision **-ationsresa** tour of visitation **-dräkt** afternoon dress **-era** inspect; (*tull-*) examine; (*jur. o. friare*) search **-ering** [-ˈte:-] examination; search **-kort** [visiting] card

1 viska I *s1* whisk; (*borste äv.*) wisp **II** *v1* sponge (*ett eldvapen* a firearm)

2 viska *v1* whisper (*ngt t. ngn* s.th. to s.b.; ~ *ngt i ngns öra* whisper s.th. in a p.'s ear

visk|ning whisper **-ningskampanj** whispering campaign

viskos [-ˈkå:s] *s3* viscose **-itet** viscosity

visky [ˈviss-] *se whisky*

viskös *al* viscous

visligen [ˣvi:s-] wisely

vismut [ˈviss-] *s3* bismuth

visning [ˣvi:s-] show[ing]; demonstration; (*föreäv.*) exhibition; ~ *varje timme* hourly tours

visp *s2* whisk; (*grädd-, ägg-*) beater

visp|a whip (*grädde* cream); (*ägg e.d.*) beat [up] **-grädde** double cream; whipping cream; whipped cream **-ning** whipping *etc.*

viss *al* **1** (*säker*) sure, certain (*om, på* about, of); (*tvärsäker*) positive (*på* of); *det är sant och ~t* it is true [enough]; *döden är ~* death is certain **2** (*odefinierbar*) certain (*skäl* reasons); (*bestämd äv.*) given, fixed (*tid* time); *en ~ some* (*tvekan* hesita-

tion), a certain degree of (*skicklighet* skill); *en ~ herr A.* a certain Mr. A.; *hon har ngt ~t* she has a certain s.th.; *på ~a håll* in certain (some) quarters; *till ~ grad* to (in) a certain degree (extent); *ställd till ~ person* made out to a certain name, personal

vissel|konsert hissing consert **-pipa** whistle

vissen *a3* faded, wilted (*äv. bildl.*); dry, dead; *vard.* (*dålig*) off colour, rotten, (*krasslig*) under the weather

viss|erligen it is true (*är den dyr* that it is expensive), certainly; ~ ... *men* it is true [that] (certainly) ... but **-het** certainty; (*tillförsikt*) assurance; *med ~* (*äv.*) for certain; *få ~ om* find out [for certain]; *skaffa sig ~ om* ascertain, make sure about

viss|la I *s1* whistle **II** *v1* whistle; ~ *på* whistle for, (*hund*) whistle to; ~ *ut ngn* hiss s.b. [off the stage] , *vard.* give s.b. the bird **-ing** (*-ande*) whistling; (*en ~*) whistle; (*kulas*) whizz, whistle

vissna fade; wither, wilt; die down; ~ *bort* (*om pers.*) fade away

visso *s, i uttr.: till yttermera ~* to make doubly sure, what is more

visst *adv* **1** (*säkerligen*) certainly; to be sure; (*naturligtvis*) by all means; *det kan jag ~* of course I can; ~ *skall du göra det* [you should do so] by all means; *det tror jag ~ det* I most certainly think so; *helt ~* [most] certainly; ~ *inte* not at all, by no means; *ja ~!* [yes] certainly!, of course!, yes, indeed!, *AE. äv.* sure!; *ja ~ ja!* yes, of course, that's true! **2** (*nog*) probably, no doubt; *han har ~ rest* he has left, I think; *du tror ~* you seem to believe (think); *vi har ~ träffats förr* I'm sure we must have met be fore

visste *imperf. av veta*

vis|stump scrap of a song **-sångare** ballad singer

vist *s2* (*kortspel*) whist

vist|as *dep* stay; be; (*bo*) live; *hur länge har ni -ats här?* how long have you been [staying] here? **-else** stay; (*boende*) residence **-elseort** [place of] residence, dwelling place, abode; *jur.* domicile

visthus[bod] storehouse; (*matbod*) pantry

visu|alisera visualize **-ell** *al* visual

visum *s8* visa (*pl* visas) **-ansökan** application for visa **-tvång** compulsory visa system

vit *al* white; *de ~a* white people, the whites; *~a frun* the White Lady; ~ *slavhandel* white-slave traffic; *~a varor* white goods, linen drapery (*sg*); *sjön går ~* the sea is white with foam

vit|a *s1* white [of an egg] **-aktig** *al* whitish

vital *al* vital, of vital importance; (*livskraftig*) vigorous; (*mycket viktig äv.*) momentous **-isera** vitalize **-isering** vitalizing **-itet** vitality; vigour

vitamjn *s4* vitamin; *fettlösliga* (*vattenlösliga*) *~er* fat-soluble (watersoluble) vitamins **-behov** vitamin requirement[s *pl*] **-berikad** *a5* vitamin enriched **-brist** vitamin deficiency; avitaminosis **-fattig** deficient in vitamins **-halt** vitamin content **-isera** vitaminize **-isering** [-ˈse:-] vitaminization **-källa** source of vitamins **-piller** vitamin pill **-preparat** vitamin preparation **-rik** rich in vitamins

vit|beta *bot.* white beet **-bok 1** *s2, bot.* hornbeam **2** *~en -böcker, dipl.* white book

V

vite *s6* penalty, fine; *vid* ~ under penalty of a fine; *vid* ~ *av 10 pund* under [a] penalty of a £10 fine; *tillträde vid* ~ *förbjudet* trespassers will be prosecuted

vitesföreläggande order to pay a fine

vit|fläckig white-spotted **-glödande** incandescent, white-hot **-glödga** bring to a white heat **-gran** white spruce **-grå** whitish grey; hoary **-gul** pale yellow, flaxen **-het** whiteness **-hårig** white-haired; hoary **-kalka** whitewash **-klädd** dressed in white **-klöver** white clover **-kål** white cabbage **-kålshuvud** white cabbage **-limma** whitewash

vitling [ˣvitt-] *zool.* whiting

vit|lök garlic **-löksklyfta** clove of garlic **-mena** *v1* whitewash **-mening** whitewashing; *konkr.* whitewash **-metall** white metal **-mossa** peat moss **-måla** paint white; ~*d* painted white

vit|na [-i:-] whiten, grow (*hastigt*: turn) white **-peppar** white pepper **-prickig** dotted with (spotted) white **-randig** striped [with] white **-rappa** roughcast with white plaster

vitrin *s3* (*skåp*) display cabinet; (*låda*) display case

vitriol *s3* vitriol

vit|rysk *a1*, **-ryss** *s3* Byelorussian, White Russian

Vitryssland Byelorussia, White Russia

vits *s2* (*ordlek*) pun; (*kvickhet*) joke, jest, witticism; *inte förstå* ~*en med ngt* not see the point of s.th.

vits|a pun, crack jokes, joke **-are** punster, joker **-ig** *a1* full of puns (*etc.*); witty

vit|sippa wood anemone, windflower **-skäggig** with a white beard, white-bearded

vits|ord (*vittnesbörd*) testimonial; (*omdöme*) verdict; (*i betyg*) grade, mark; *få goda* ~ be highly recommended; *äga* ~ be considered lawful evidence **-orda** testify (bear testimony) to; ~ *ngn* give s.b. a good character; ~ *ngns duglighet* recommend s.b., testify to a p.'s ability

1 vitt *best. form det vita* white; *klädd i* ~ [dressed] in white; *göra svart till* ~ swear black is white

2 vitt *adv* **1** (*vida*) widely (*skild* separated); wide, far (*åtskilda* apart); ~ *och brett*, ~ *omkring* far and wide; *orda* ~ *och brett om* talk at great length on; ~ *utbredd* widespread; *vara* ~ *skild från* (*bildl. äv.*) differ greatly from **2** *så* ~ *jag vet* as far as I know; *så* ~ *möjligt* as far as possible; *för så* ~ (*ifall*) provided, if

vitt|bekant widely known, famous; (*ökänd*) notorious **-berest** *vara* ~ have travelled a great deal, be a travelled person **-berömd** renowned, farfamed, illustrious **-berömdhet** wide renown

vitten ['vitt-] *r el. n, inte vara värd en (ett)* ~ not be worth a damn

vitter ['vitt-] *a2* literary; *en* ~ *man* (*äv.*) a man of letters **-het** literature, belles-lettres (*pl, behandlas som sg*) **-hetsakademi** academy of literature (*etc.*)

vitt|förgrenad *a5* with many ramifications, widely ramified **-gående** *a4* far-reaching (*följder* consequences); extensive (*reformer* reforms)

vittja examine [and empty] (*nät* nets); ~ *ngns fickor* (*vard.*) pick a p.'s pockets

vittn|a (*inför domstol*) witness; give evidence

(*om* of); (*intyga*) testify (*om* to), (*skriftligt*) certify; ~ *om* (*bära -esbörd om*) bear witness to, (*visa äv.*) show

vittne *s6* witness (*till* of); *ha* ~*n på* have witnesses to; *i* ~*ns närvaro* before witnesses; *inkalla ngn som* ~ call s.b. as a witness; *vara* ~ *till* be [a] witness to, witness

vittnes|berättelse deposition [of a witness], evidence **-bås** witness box; *AE.* witness stand **-börd** [-ö:-] *s7* testimony; *jur.* evidence; *bära* ~ testify; *bära falskt* ~ bear false witness **-ed** [of a witness] **-ersättning** compensation to witnesses, witness's fee **-förhör** hearing of witnesses; *anställa* ~ examine a witness **-gill** competent to witness; ~ *person* competent witness **-mål** evidence; (*skriftligt*) deposition; *avlägga* ~ give evidence

vittomfattande far-reaching, extensive; comprehensive (*studier* studies)

vittra weather, decompose

1 vittring *geol.* weathering, decomposition

2 vittring *jakt.* scent; *få upp* ~ pick up the scent; *känna* ~ *efter* (*äv. bildl.*) catch the scent

vittsvävande high-aspiring, ambitious

vit|tvätt white washing **-varuaffär** linen-draper's business (shop) **-vin** white wine **-öga** white of the eye; *se döden i* ~*t* face death [bravely]

viv *s7, poet.* spouse

vivel *s2* weevil, snout beetle

vivisektion vivisection

vivre ['vi:ver, -re] *s7* board and lodging; *fritt* ~ free board and lodging, all found

vivör man about town, rake, roué

Vlissingen [ˣfliss-] *n* Flushing

voall *s3* voile

vodka [-å-] *s1* vodka

voffla [-å-] *s1, se våffla*

Vogeserna [få'ge:-] *pl* the Vosges

vokabel [-'ka:-] *s3* vocable, word **-samling** *s2* vocabulary

vokabulär *s3* vocabulary

vokal I *s3* vowel **II** *a1* vocal **-isation** vocalization **-isera** vocalize **-ist** vocalist **-musik** vocal music **-möte** hiatus

vokativ ['våkk-] *s3* vocative

volang *s3* flounce, frill

volauvent [vållå'vaŋ] *s3* vol-au-vent

volfram ['våll-] *s3, s4* tungsten, wolfram

volleyboll ['vålli-] volleyball

volm, volma *s3 vålm, vålma*

volontär [vållån'tä:r] *s3* (*på kontor*) voluntary worker, unsalaried clerk; *mil.* volunteer

1 volt [-å-] *s3* **1** (*luftsprång*) somersault; *slå en* ~ turn a somersault **2** (*på ridbana*) volt

2 volt [-å-] *s9*, *elektr.* volt

volt|astapel voltaic (galvanic) pile **-meter** coulometer, voltameter

voluminös *a1* voluminous; (*skrymmande*) bulky

volym *s3* volume **-kontroll** volume control **-procent** percentage by volume

vom [våmm] *se våm*

vomera vomit

vorden [ˣvo:r-] *perf. part. av varda, se bliva*

vore (*imperf. konj. av 5 vara*) were; (*skulle vara*) should be (*1 pers.*), would be (*2 o. 3 pers.*); *det* ~ *trevligt* it would be nice

voter|a vote **-ing** voting, vote; *begära* ~ demand a division (*om* on); *vid* ~ on a vote
votivtavla [-ˣtiːv-] votive tablet
votum *s8* vote
vov|ve *s2 vard. o. barnspr.* doggy, doggie **–vov** *interj* bow-wow
vrak *s7* wreck (*äv. bildl.*); *bli* ~ get wrecked
vraka reject
vrak|gods wreckage, stranded goods; (*flytande*) flotsam; (*kastat över bord*) jetsam **-plundrare** wrecker **-plundring** plundering of wrecks, wrecking
vrakpris bargain price, cut rate; *för* ~ dirt-cheap
vrakspillror *pl* wreckage (*sg*), pieces of wreckage
1 vred *imperf. av* vrida
2 vred *s7* handle; (*runt äv.*) knob
3 vred *a1, n sg obest. form undviks* wrathful, irate; very angry; (*starkare*) furious (*på ngn* with s.b.)
vrede *s9* wrath; (*ursinne*) fury, rage; (*ilska*) anger; *koka av* ~ foam with rage; *låta sin* ~ *gå ut över* vent one's anger on; *snar till* ~ quick to anger
vredes|mod *i uttr.: i* ~ in anger **-utbrott** outburst of anger, fit of rage
vredg|ad *a5, se* vred; *äv.* incensed, angered **-as** *dep* get angry, become incensed
vrenskas *dep* be difficult to manage; (*om häst*) be restive (balky)
vresig *a1* cross, sullen, surly
vrick|a 1 (*vrida fram o. åter*) wriggle **2** (*båt*) scull **3** (*stuka*) sprain; ~ *foten* sprain one's ankle **-ad** *a5, vard.* (*tokig*) nuts, cracked **-borr** gimlet; (*större*) auger **-ning 1** wriggling; (*en* ~) wriggle **2** sculling **3** spraining; (*en* ~) sprain; (*ur led*) dislocation **-åra** scull[ing oar]
vrid|a vred **-it 1** (*vända*) turn (*på huvudet* one's head); (*hårt*) wring (*nacken av en tupp* a cock's neck; *sina händer* one's hands) (*sno*) twist, wind; (*häftigt*) wrench; (*slita*) wrest; ~ *och vända på ett problem* turn a problem over; ~ *tvätt* wring [out] washing; ~ *ur led* put out of joint, dislocate **2** (*med betonad partikel*) ~ *av* twist (wrench) off, (*kontakt*) switch off; ~ *fram klockan* put the clock (one's watch) forward; ~ *loss* wrench (wrest) loose; ~ *om* turn (*nyckeln* the key); ~ *på* (*gasen*) turn on, (*strömmen*) switch on; ~ *runt* turn round, revolve; ~ *sönder* break [by twisting]; ~ *till* (*kran e.d.*) turn off; ~ *tillbaka klockan* put the clock (one's watch) back; ~ *upp* (*klocka*) wind up; ~ *ur* (*tvätt*) wring out **3** *rfl* turn, revolve (*runt en axel* round an axle); (*sno sig*) twist, wind; writhe (*av smärta* with pain); wriggle (*som en mask* like a worm)
vrid|bar [-iː-] *a1* revolving, rotating, turnable **-en** *a5* twisted; (*för-*) distorted, warped; *bildl.* (*rubbad*) cracked, unhinged **-hållfasthet** torsional (twisting) strength **-it** *sup. av* vrida **-kondensator** adjustable disc condenser **-maskin** (*för tvätt*) wringer, mangle **-moment** torque, torsional moment **-motstånd** rheostat **-ning** [-iːd-] turning *etc.*; (*en* ~) turn *etc.* **-ningsrörelse** rotary movement **-scen** revolving stage
vrist *s3* instep; (*ankel*) ankle; *anat.* tarsus; *smäckra* ~*er* slim ankles **-rem** shoe-strap

vrå *s5* (*hörn*) corner, nook; (*undangömt ställe*) recess, cranny; *i en undangömd* ~ *av världen* in an out-of-the-way spot
vråk *s2, zool.* buzzard
vrål *s7* roar[ing], howl[ing], bellow[ing]
vrål|a roar, howl, bellow **-apa** howler [monkey] **-åk** *vard.* flashy high-powered car
vrång *a1* **1** (*ogin*) disobliging, perverse, contrary; *vara* ~ *mot ngn* (*vard.*) make things difficult for s.b. **2** (*orätt*) wrong; ~ *dom* miscarriage of justice, wrong verdict **-bild** distorted picture, caricature **-het** contrariness **-strupe** *få ngt i* ~*n* have s.th. go down the wrong way
vräk|a *v3* **1** heave; (*kasta*) toss; (*huller om buller*) tumble; ~ *bort* toss (throw) away; ~ *i sig maten* gobble down the food; ~ *omkull* throw over; ~ *ur sig* (*bildl.*) spit out (*skällsord* invectives); ~ *ut* heave (*etc.*) out, (*pengar*) throw to the winds **2** (*avhysa*) evict, eject **3** *sjön -er* the sea is heaving; *regnet -er ner* it's pouring [rain]; *snön -er ner* the snow is falling in masses **4** *rfl* (*kasta sig*) throw (fling) o.s. down (*i in*); *bildl. vard.* play the swell; ~ *sig i en fåtölj* lounge about in an armchair; ~ *sig i lyx* roll in luxury
vräkig *a1* ostentatious, extravagant; *vard.* flashy **-het** ostentation, extravagance
vräk|ning [-äː-] (*avhysning*) eviction, ejection **-ningsbeslut** eviction order
vränga *v2* **1** (*vända ut o. in på*) turn inside out **2** (*för-*) twist (*lag* the law)
vulgari|sera vulgarize **-tet** vulgarity
vulgär *a1* vulgar, common **-latin** popular Latin
vulkan *s3* volcano
vulkaniser|a vulcanize **-ing** vulcanization
vulkan|isk [-ˈkaː-] *a5* volcanic **-kägla** volcanic cone **-utbrott** volcanic eruption **-ö** volcanic island
vulst *s3* **1** *byggn.* torus, round **2** (*plåtslageri.*) upset **3** (*på däck*) bead, heel
vunn|en *a5* gained *etc., se* vinna; *därmed är föga -et* there is little [to be] gained by that; *därmed är ändå ngt -et* that's something anyway **-it** *sup. av* vinna
vurm *s2* mania, craze, passion (*för* for) **vurma** have a craze (passion) (*för* for)
vurpa I *s1* (*kullkörning*) fall; (*kullerbytta*) somersault **II** *v1* overturn, make a somersault
vuxen *a3* **1** (*full-*) grown-up (*barn* children), adult; *barn och vuxna* children and grown-ups (adults) **2** *vara situationen* ~ be equal to the occasion; *vara* ~ *sin uppgift* be equal (up) to one's task **-gymnasium** upper secondary school for adults **-studerande** adult student **-undervisning, -utbildning** adult education
vy *s3* view; (*utsikt äv.*) sight **-kort** picture postcard
vyss hushaby! **vyss[j]a** [ˣvyssa, ˣvyʃa] lull (*i sömn, till sömns* to sleep)
våd *s3* (*kjol-*) gore; (*tapet-*) length
våda *s1* **1** *jur., av* ~ by misadventure (accident) **2** (*fara*) risk, danger **-dråp** unintentional homicide; *jur.* chance-medley **-skott** accidental shot
våd|eld accidental fire **-lig** [-åː-] *a1* **1** *se farlig* **2** *vard.* (*förfärlig*) awful **-ligt** *adv, vard.* awfully
våffel|järn waffle iron **-vävnad** honeycomb (towelling) fabric

V

våffla s1 waffle

1 våg s2 (*för vägning*) balance; (*butiks-, hushålls-e.d.*) scales (*pl*); *V~en* (*astr.*) Libra, the Scales **2 våg** s1 (*bölja, ljud-, ljus- etc.*) wave (*äv. bildl.*); (*dyning*) roller; (*störtsjö*) breaker; *poet.* billow; *gå i ~or* surge; (*friare äv.*) go in waves, undulate; *~orna går höga* the sea is running high; *diskussionens ~or gick höga* it was a very heated discussion

1 våga (*göra vågig*) ~ *håret* have one's hair waved

2 våga 1 (*tordas*) dare [to]; venture; (*djärvas*) make so bold as to; ~ *försöket* try the experiment; ~ *en gissning* hazard a guess; *friskt ~t är hälften vunnet* boldly ventured is half won; *du skulle bara ~!* you dare!; *~r jag besvära er att ...?* may (might) I trouble you to ...?; *jag ~r påstå att* I venture to say that **2** (*äventyra*) risk, jeopardize (*sitt liv* one's life); (*sätta på spel*) stake (*sitt huvud på* one's life on); *jag ~r hundra mot ett att* I'll stake a hundred to one that **3** *rfl* venture; ~ *sig dit* (*fram*) venture [to go] there (to appear); ~ *sig på a*) (*ngt*) dare to tackle, *b*) (*ngn*) venture to approach (attack); ~ *sig ut i kylan* brave (venture out in) the cold; ~ *sig ut på djupet* dare to go into deep water

vågad a5 (*djärv*) daring, bold; (*riskfylld*) risky, hazardous; (*frivol*) risqué, *vard.* near the bone; *det är litet vågat att* it's a bit risky to

våg|berg ridge of a wave **-brytare** breakwater, pier, jetty **-dal** trough between two waves; *en ~* (*bildl.*) the doldrums (*pl*)

våghals daredevil, madcap **-ig** a1 foolhardy, reckless, rash

våg|ig a1 wavy; waving, undulating **-kam** crest of a wave **-linje** wave-line; wavy (sinuous) line **-längd** wavelength

våg|mästarroll *polit.*, *spela en* ~ hold the balance of power **-rät** horizontal, level; *~a ord* (*i korsord*) clues across **-rätt** adv horizontally; ~ *5* (*i korsord*) 5 across

vågrörelse undulatory (wave) motion, undulation

vågsam [-å:-] a1 risky, hazardous

vågskvalp lapping [of waves]

vågskål scale (pan) [of a balance]; *lägga i ~en* put in (on) the scale; *väga tungt i ~en* (*bildl.*) be weighty, carry weight

våg|spel, -stycke bold venture, daring (risky) enterprise

våg|svall surging sea, surge **-topp** crest of a wave

våld s7 **1** (*makt, välde*) power; (*besittning*) possession; *få* (*ha*) *i sitt* ~ get (have) in one's power; *råka i ngns* ~ fall into a p.'s power; *ge sig i ngns* ~ deliver o.s. into a p.'s hands; *dra för fan i ~!* go to hell (the devil)! **2** (*maktmedel, tvång*) force; (*över-*) violence; (*våldsdåd*) outrage, assault (*mot* upon); *bildl.* violation (*mot den personliga friheten* of personal liberty); *med* ~ by force, forcibly; *med milt* ~ with gentle compulsion; *yttre* ~ violence; *begå* ~ resort to violence; *begå nesligt* ~ *mot, se våldtaga*; *bruka* ~ *mot* use force (violence) against; *bruka större* ~ *än nöden kräver* employ more force than the situation demands; *göra* ~ *på* violate; *göra* ~ *på sig* restrain

o.s.; *öppna med* ~ force open **-föra** ~ [*sig på*] violate **-gästa** ~ [*hos*] abuse a p.'s hospitality, descend on s.b. [for a meal] **-sam** a1 violent; (*om pers. äv.*) vehement; (*ursinnig*) furious; (*larmande*) tumultuous (*oväsen* noise); ~ *död* violent death; *göra ~t motstånd mot* violently resist **-samhet** violence; vehemence; fury; ~*er* (*äv.*) excesses **-samt** adv violently; ~ *rolig* terrifically (terribly) funny

vålds|brott crime (act) of violence **-dåd** act of violence; outrage **-härskare** tyrant **-man** se **-verkare** **-politik** policy of violence **-verkare** perpetrator of an outrage, assailant **-åtgärder** forcible means

våld|ta[ga] violate, rape; *jur.* assault **-täkt** s3 rape; *jur.* indecent assault **-täktsförsök** attempted rape **-täktsman** person guilty of rape, rapist

våll|a (*förorsaka*) cause, be the cause of; bring about; (*åsamka*) give (*ngn besvär* s.b. trouble); ~ *ngn smärta* (*äv.*) make s.b. suffer **-ande I** s6, *för* ~ *av annans död* for causing another person's death, for manslaughter **II** a4, *vara* ~ *till* be the cause of

vålm s2 haycock **vålma** cock

vålnad [ˣvå:l-] s3 ghost, phantom, apparition; *Skottl.* wraith

våm [våmm] s2 rumen, paunch, first stomach

vånda s1 agony; throes (*pl*) **våndas** *dep* suffer (be in) agony; ~ *inför ngt* dread s.th.; ~ *över ngt* go through agonies over s.th.

våning 1 (*lägenhet*) flat; *AE.* apartment; *en* ~ *på tre rum och kök* a three-room[ed] flat with a kitchen **2** (*etage*) store[y], floor; *övre ~en* the upper (top) floor; *ett tre ~ar högt hus* a three-storey [ed] house; *på första ~en* (*botten-*) on the ground (*AE.* first) floor; *på andra ~en* (*en trappa upp*) on the first (*AE.* second) floor

vånings|byte exchange of flats **-hotell** apartment hotel **-plan** floor **-säng** bunk bed

våp s7 goose, simpleton, silly **-ig** a1 soft

1 vår *pron*; *fören.* our; *självst.* ours; *de ~a* our people, (*~a trupper*) our men; *allas* ~ *vän* the friend of all of us, our mutual friend; *vi skall göra ~t* (*~t bästa*) we shall do our part (our utmost)

2 vår s2 spring; *poet.* springtime; *i livets* ~ in the prime of life; *i* ~ this spring; *i ~as* last spring; *om* (*på*) ~*en* (*~arna*) in spring

vår|as *dep, det* ~ spring is on its way **-blomma** spring flower **-bruk** spring farming **-brytning** *i* ~*en* as winter gives way to spring

1 vård [-å:-] s2 (*minnesmärke*) monument, memorial

2 vård [-å:-] s2 (*omvårdnad*) care (*om* of); (*tillsyn äv.*) charge, custody; (*sjuk- äv.*) nursing; *få god* ~ be well cared for (looked after); *ha* ~ *om* have charge (the care) of; *den som har* ~ *om* the man (etc.) in (who takes) charge of; *lämna ngt i ngns* ~ leave s.th. in a p.'s charge

vård|a 1 take care of, look after; (*sjuka*) nurse; (*ansa*) tend; (*bevara*) preserve (*minnet av* the memory of); *han ~s på sjukhus* he is [being treated] in hospital **2** *rfl*, ~ *sig om* take care of, cherish, cultivate **-ad** a5 careful; (*om klädsel, hår*) well-groomed; (*väl-*) well-kept; (*prydlig*) neat (*handstil* handwriting); *-at språk* correct language; *använd ett -at språk!* mind how you speak!; *ett -at yttre* well-groomed appearance **vårdag** spring day **-jämning** vernal equinox **vård|anstalt** nursing home (institution) **-are** caretaker; (*sjuk-*) male nurse, attendant; (*djur-*) keeper; (*bevarare*) preserver **-arinna** nurse; *jfr vårdare* **-fall** *vara ett ~* be in need of professional care **-hem** nursing home **-kas[e]** *s2* beacon **-nad** *s3* guardianship; *ha ~en om* have the custody of **-nadsbidrag** child maintenance allowance **-nadshavare** guardian, custodian; *jur.* next friend **-personal** medical (nursing) staff **vårdslös** [ˣvå:rds-, ˣvårs-] careless (*i* in; *med* with); negligent (*i* in; *med* of); (*försumlig äv.*) neglectful (*med sitt utseende* of one's appearance); (*slarvig*) slovenly (*klädsel* dress) **vårds-lösa** neglect, be careless about, be neglectful of **vårdslöshet** carelessness, negligence, neglect; *grov ~* gross negligence; *~ i trafiken* careless driving

vård|tecken token **-yrke** occupation in medical or social services
vårflod spring flood
vårfrudagen Lady (Annunciation) Day
vår|hatt spring hat **-himmel** spring sky **-känsla** *ha -känslor* have the spring feeling **-lig** [-å:-] *a1* vernal, of spring, spring **-lik** springlike **-luft** spring air **-lök** *bot.* gagea **-mode** spring fashion **-regn** spring rain **-sidan** *på ~* when spring comes (came) **-sol** spring (vernal) sun **-städa** spring-clean **-städning** spring-cleaning **-sådd** spring sowing **-säd** spring (summer) corn (grain)
vårt|a [ˣvå:r-] *s1* wart **-bitare** *zool.* long-horned grasshopper **-björk** silver birch
vår|tecken sign of spring **-termin** spring term
vårtlik wartlike, warty
vårtrötthet spring fever
vårtsvin wart hog
vår|vind spring (vernal) breeze **-vinter** late winter
våt *a1* wet (*av* with); (*fuktig*) moist, damp; (*flytande*) liquid, fluid; *bli* (*vara*) *~ om fötterna* get (have) wet feet; *hålla ihop i ~ och torrt* stick together through thick and thin **-docka** *sjö.* wet dock **-dräkt** wet suit **-mark** wetland **-stark** *~t papper* wet-strength paper **-varm** warm and wet **-varor** *pl* liquids; (*sprit-*) alcoholic beverages **-värmande** *a4, ~ omslag* fomentation **-äng** marsh meadow
väbel [ˈvä:-] *s2, mil.* regimental sergeant major
väck [*puts*] *~ gone*, lost, vanished
väcka *v3* **1** (*göra vaken*) wake [up]; rouse [from sleep]; (*på beställning*) call; *bildl.* awaken (*äv. relig.*), [a]rouse (*till to; ur* from, out of); *~ ngn till besinning* call s.b. to his (her) senses; *~ till liv* bring back to life, *bildl. äv.* arouse, revive **2** (*framkalla*) awaken (*medlidande* compassion), cause (*förvåning* astonishment); arouse (*nyfikenhet* curiosity; *misstankar* suspicion (*sg*); *sympati* sympathy); (*upp- äv.*) raise (*förhoppningar* hopes); excite (*avund* envy); *beundran* admiration), call up (*gamla minnen* old memories), call forth (*gillande* approbation), provoke (*vrede* anger); (*ge upphov t.*) create, cause (*oro* alarm); *~ intresse* awaken (arouse) an interest; *~ tanken på ngt* evoke the idea of s.th., suggest s.th.; *~ upp-*

märksamhet attract attention **3** (*framställa*) bring up, raise (*en fråga* a question); *~ förslag om* propose, suggest
väckande *s6, ~ av åtal* [the] bringing [of] an action
väckarklocka alarm clock
väckelse [religious] revival **-möte** revivalist meeting **-predikant** revivalist **-rörelse** revivalist movement, revival
väckning awakening; (*per telefon*) alarm call; *får jag be om ~ kl.* 6 I should like to be called at 6
väckt *a4* woken, awakened *etc.*; *relig.* saved
vädd *s2, bot.* scabious
väd|er [ˈvä:-] *s7* **1** weather; *-rets makter* the clerk (*sg*) of the weather; *ett sådant ~!* what weather!; *i alla ~* in all weathers, *bildl. äv.* in rain and shine; *det är fult* (*vackert*) *~* it is dirty (nice) weather; *det ser ut att bli vackert ~* the weather looks promising; *det vackra -ret fortsätter* it is keeping fine; *vad är det för ~?* what is the weather like?; *om -ret tillåter* weather permitting **2** (*luft, vind*) air, wind; *~ och vind* wind and weather; *hårt ~* stormy weather; *prata i -ret* talk rubbish through one's hat; *släppa ~* break wind; *gå till ~s* rise [in the air], *sjö.* go [up] aloft
väder|beständig weatherproof, weather-resistant **-biten** *a5* weather-beaten **-karta** weather map (chart) **-korn** scent; *gott ~* [a] keen scent, [a] sharp nose; *hunden har fått ~ på* the dog has picked up the scent of (has scented) **-kvarn** windmill **-lek** weather
väderleks|förhållanden *pl* weather conditions **-förändring** change in the weather **-karta** weather map (chart) **-prognos** weather forecast **-rapport** weather report (forecast) **-station** meteorological (weather) station **-tjänst** weather service (bureau); meteorological office **-ut-sikter** *pl* weather forecast (*sg*)
väder|rapport weather forecast **-spåman** weather prophet **-spänd** flatulent **-spänning** flatulence **-streck** quarter; point of the compass; *i vilket ~?* in what quarter?; *de fyra ~en* the four cardinal points
vädja [ˣvä:d-] *~ till* appeal to (*äv. jur.*) **vädjan** *r* appeal **vädjande** *a4* appealing (*blick* look) **väd-jobana** lists (*pl*); (*livets* life's) arena
vädr|a [ˣvä:d-] **1** (*lufta*) air; *~ kläder* (*äv.*) give the clothes an airing **2** (*få vittring av*) scent (*äv. bildl.*); sniff **-ing** airing *etc.*
vädur *s2* ram; *V~en* (*astr.*) Ram, Aries
väft *s3* weft
väg *s2* **1** *konkr.* road; (*mer abstr. o. bildl.*) way; (*bana*) path, course; (*färd-*) journey, drive, ride, walk; (*sträcka*) distance; (*rutt*) route; (*levnadsbana*) career; *~en till* the road to; *allmän* (*enskild*) *~* public (private) road; *den breda* (*smala*) *~en* (*bildl.*) the broad (narrow) path; *förbjuden ~!* no thoroughfare!; *halva ~en* halfway; *raka ~en* the straight course; *gå raka ~en hem* go straight home; *fyra timmars ~* four hours' journey (drive, walk); *bryta nya ~ar* (*bildl.*) break new ground; *det är lång ~ till* it is a long way to; *vilken ~ gick de?* which way did they go (road did they take)?; *gå ~en fram* [be] walk[ing] along the road; *gå all världens ~* go the way of all flesh; *gå sin ~* go away, *vard.* be off; *gå din ~!* go away!,

V

make yourself scarce!; *gå sin egen* ~ go one's own way; *om du har* ~*arna hitåt* if you happen to be [coming] this way; *resa sin* ~ go away, leave; *ta* ~*en* take the road (*genom* through; *över, förbi* by); *vart skall du ta* ~*en?* where are you going (off to)?; *inte veta vart man skall ta* ~*en* not know where to go; *vart har min hatt tagit* ~*en?* what has become of my hat?; *gå före och visa* ~*en* lead the way **2** (*föregånget av prep*) *i* ~ off; *gå* (*komma*) *i* ~*en för ngn* be (get) in a p.'s way; *ge sig i* ~ be off (*till* for); *ngt i den* ~*en* s.th. like that (of that sort); *lägga hinder i* ~*en för ngn* put obstacles in a p.'s way; *längs* ~*en* along the road[side]; *på* ~*en* on the way (*dit* there); *på diplomatisk* ~ through diplomatic channels, diplomatically; *på laglig* ~ by legal means, legally; *inte på långa* ~*ar* (*bildl.*) not by a long way (chalk); *ett gott stycke på* ~ well on the way; *följa ngn ett stycke på* ~ accompany s.b. part of the way; *vara på* ~ *till* be on one's way to; *vara på* ~ *att* be on the point of (+ *ing-form*); *vara på god* ~ *att* be well on the way to; *gå till* ~*a* proceed, go about it; *under* ~*en* on the (one's) road (way), en route; *ur* ~*en* out of the way; *ur* ~*en!* get out of the way!, stand aside!; *gå ur* ~*en för ngn* get out of a p.'s way; *det vore inte ur* ~*en om* (*att*) it wouldn't be a bad idea to; *vid* ~*en* near (by the side of) the road, by the roadside

väg|a *v2* weigh (*äv. bildl.*); *hur mycket -er du?* how much do you weigh?; *hon -er hälften så mycket som jag* she is half my weight; *det -er jämnt* the scales are even; *det står och -er mellan* (*bildl.*) the decision lies (*vard.* it is a toss-up) between; ~ *skälen för och emot* weigh the pros and cons; *sitta och* ~ *på stolen* sit balancing [on] one's chair; *det är väl -t* it is good weight; *hans ord -er tungt* his words carry great weight; ~ *upp a*) *eg.* weigh out, *b*) (~ *mer än*) poise up, *c*) (*upp-, bildl.*) [counter] balance **-ande** *a4* weighty; [*tungt*] ~ *skäl* weighty reasons

väg|arbetare roadworker **-arbete** roadwork; (*på skylt*) Road Up!, Men at Work!, Road under Repair! **-bana** roadway; *slirig* ~ slippery roadway (road surface) **-bank** road embankment

vägbar [-ä:-] *a1* ponderable

väg|beläggning road surface (metalling) **-bom** [road] barrier **-byggare** road builder (maker) **-bygge** road construction (work, building, making) **-farande I** *a4* travelling; *poet.* wayfaring **II** *s9* traveller; (*trafikant*) road user **-förbindelse** road communication; *det finns* ~ *till* there is a road going to **-förvaltning** road maintenance authority

vägg *s2* wall; (*tunn skilje-*) partition; *bo* ~ *i* ~ *med* live next door to; ~*arna har öron* walls have ears; *köra huvudet i* ~*en* (*bildl.*) run one's head against a wall; *ställa ngn mot* ~*en* (*bildl.*) drive s.b. into a corner, press s.b. hard; *uppåt* ~*arna* (*bildl.*) all wrong, wide of the mark; *det är som att tala till en* ~ it's like talking to a brick wall **-almanack[a]** wall calendar **-block** *byggn.* wall panel **-bonad** wall hanging, tapestry **-fast** fixed to the wall; ~*a inredningar* fixtures; ~ *skåp* wall cabinet (cupboard) **-klocka** wall clock **-kontakt** wall socket (plug) **-lus** bedbug **-målning** mural (wall) painting **-pelare** pilaster **-uttag** point, wall socket **-yta** wall space (surface)

väg|hyvel road grader (drag) **-hållning** [road making and] road maintenance; (*bils*) roadholding **-kant** roadside **-karta** road map **-korsning** [road] crossing, crossroads **-krök** curve (bend) in the road **-lag** *s7* state of the road; *halt* ~ slippery road **-leda** guide; direct; *några* ~*nde ord* a few [introductory] directions **-ledare** guide; counsellor **-ledning** guidance; *till* ~ *för* for the guidance of; *tjäna som* ~ serve as a guide **-märke** road sign **-mätare** mileometer; *AE.* odometer **-mätarställning** mileage

vägnar [˟vä̱ŋnar] *pl,* [*på*] *ngns* ~ on behalf of s.b.; *å tjänstens* (*ämbetets*) ~ by (in) virtue of one's office, ex officio; *rikt utrustad å huvudets* ~ well equipped with brains, very clever, brainy

vägning [˟vä:g-] weighing

vägnät road network

väg- och vattenbygg|are civil engineer **-nad[skonst]** civil engineering, road construction and hydraulic engineering

vägport [road] underpass, road arch

vägr|a [˟vä:g-] refuse; (*om häst äv.*) balk, jib; ~ *att mottaga* refuse [to accept], decline **-an** *r* refusal; declining

väg|ren verge, shoulder **-rätt** right of way **-skatt** road tax **-skrapa** road grader (scraper) **-skylt** road (traffic) sign **-skäl** fork [in a road]; *vid* ~*et* at the crossroads **-spärr** road block; *mil.* barricade **-sträcka** stretch [of a road], road section; (*avstånd*) distance **-styrelse** highway (road) board **-trafikförordning** highway code, road (*AE.* highway) traffic act; *överträdelse av* ~*en* (*vanl.*) motoring offence **-underhåll** road maintenance **-verk** ~*et* [the Swedish] national road administration **-vett** road sense **-visare 1** *pers.* guide **2** (*bok*) guide, guidebook, directory **3** (*skylt*) direction post (sign), signpost **-vält** [road]roller **-övergång** viaduct, flyover, overpass

väj|a [˟vä̱jja] *v2* make way (*för* for); give way, yield (*för* to); *sjö.* veer, give way; ~ *för* (*undvika*) avoid; *inte* ~ *för ngt* (*bildl.*) not mind anything, stick at nothing **-ningsplikt** *sjö.* obligation to veer (give way)

väktare custodian, watchman, guard[ian]; *ordningens* ~ the guardians of law and order

väl I *n* welfare, wellbeing; *det allmännas* ~ the common weal; *vårt* ~ *och ve beror på* our happiness is dependent upon **II** *bättre bäst, adv* **1** *beton.* [vä:l] **a**) (*bra, gott*) well; ~ *förfaren* experienced; *allt* ~*!* all's well!; *så* ~*!* what a good thing!; *befinna sig* ~ be well; *det går aldrig* ~*!* it can't turn out well!; *om allt går* ~ if nothing goes wrong; *hålla sig* ~ *med ngn* keep in with s.b.; *ligga* ~ *till* be in a favourable position; *låta sig* ~ *smaka* enjoy one's food; *stå* ~ *hos ngn* be on the right side of s.b.; *ta* ~ *upp* receive favourably; *tala* ~ *om* speak well of; *veta mycket* ~ *att* be perfectly (fully) aware that; *det var för* ~ *att* it was a blessing that, **b**) (*alltför*) rather [too], over; (*över*) over, rather more [...] than; ~ *mycket* rather too much; ~ *stor* rather (almost too) big; *gott och* ~ well over (*1 timme* one hour); *länge och* ~ for ages, no end of a time, **c**) (*omsider, en gång*) once; *det hade inte* ~ *börjat förrän* no sooner had it begun than; *när hon* ~ *hade somnat* *var hon* once asleep she was, **d)** *inte henne men* ~ *hennes syster* not her but her sister **2** *obetonat* [väll] **a)** (*uttryckande förmodan el. förhoppning*) surely; (*förmodar jag*) I suppose; (*hoppas jag*) I hope; *du kommer* ~*?* I hope you will come!; *du är* ~ *inte sjuk* you are surely not ill?, you are not ill, are you?; *han får* ~ *vänta* he will have to wait; *jag gör* ~ *det då* I suppose I had better do that then; *det kan* ~ *hända* that's possible; *det kan mycket* ~ *tänkas att hon* there is every possibility of her (+ *ing-* form); *det var* ~ *det jag trodde* that's just what I thought; *de är* ~ *framme nu* they must be there by now; *det är* ~ *inte möjligt* it can't be possible; *det hade* ~ *varit bättre att* ... wouldn't it have been better to ...?; *du vet* ~ *att* I suppose you know; you must know, **b)** (*som fyllnadsord i frågor*) *vem kunde* ~ *ha trott det?* who would have believed such a thing?; *vad är* ~ *lycka?* what is happiness [after all]? **3** *så* ~ *som* as well as **II** *interj, ja* ~*!* of course!; *nå* ~*!* well then!

väl|an well [then]! **-artad** [-a:r-] *a5* well-behaved **-avlönad** well-paid **-befinnande** wellbeing **-behag** pleasure; complacency **-behållen** safe [and sound]; (*om sak*) in good condition; *komma fram* ~ arrive safely **-behövlig** badly (much) needed **-bekant** well-known **-beställd** well-to-do, well-off **-betänkt** well-advised, judicious; *mindre* ~ ill-advised, injudicious **-boren** honourable **-borenhet** [-å:-] *Ers* ~ your Excellency **-bärgad** well-to-do; wealthy

väld|e *s6* **1** (*rike*) state, empire **2** (*makt*) domination, power; *bringa ett folk under sitt* ~ bring a people under one's domination (sway), subject a people **-ig** *a1* **1** (*stor*) huge; enormous; (*vidsträckt*) immense, vast **2** (*mäktig*) mighty **-igt** *adv, vard.* awfully, tremendously, terrifically

väl|doftande fragrant **-etablerad** well-established **-funnen** *a5* apt (*uttryck* phrase) **-fylld** well-filled **-fägnad** food and drink; good cheer **-färd** [-ä:-] *s3* welfare; wellbeing **-färdssamhälle** welfare state **-född** *a5* well-fed; plump **-förrättad** *s5, efter* -*förrättat värv gick han* having completed his job he went **-försedd** *a5* well-stocked, well-supplied **-förtjänt** well-earned; well-deserved; *få sitt* ~*a straff* get the punishment one deserves; *det var* ~*!* that served you (*etc.*) right! **-gjord** well-made **-grundad** well-founded; good (*anledning* reason) **-gräddad** well-baked **-gång** prosperity, success; *lycka och* ~*!* all good wishes for the future! **-gångsskål** toast; *dricka en* ~ *för ngn* drink [to] a p.'s health **-gångsönskningar** *pl* good wishes **-gärning** kind (charitable) deed; (*om sak*) blessing, boon; *det var då en* ~ *att* it was a real blessing (boon) that **-gödd** [-j-] *a5* well-fattened

välgör|ande [-j-] *a4* (*nyttig*) beneficial (*solsken* sunshine); (*hälsosam*) salutary (*sömn* sleep); refreshing; ~ *ändamål* charitable purposes; *vara* ~ *för ngn* (*äv.*) be good for s.b., do s.b. [a lot of] good **-are** benefactor **-enhet** charity **-enhetsinrättning** charitable institution **-enhetsmärke** charity seal (*frimärke:* stamp) **-erska** benefactress

väl|hållen well-kept **-hängd** (*mör*) tender **-informerad** [-å-] *a5* well-informed (*kretsar* circles)

välja *valde valt* **1** (*ut-*) choose (*bland* from, out of; *mellan* between; *till* as); (*noga*) select, pick (*sina ord* one's words), pick out (*äv.* ~ *ut*); *få* ~ be allowed to choose, have one's choice; *låta ngn* ~ give s.b. the choice; *inte ha mycket att* ~ *på* not have much choice; ~ *bort* (*skolämne*) drop **2** (*genom röstning*) elect (*ngn t. president* s.b. president); (*t. eng. parl.*) return; ~ *in ngn* elect s.b. [as] a member (*i* of); ~ *in ngn i styrelse* elect s.b. to a board; ~ *om* relect **väljar|e** voter, elector **-kår** electorate

välklädd well-dressed **-het** being well dressed **välkom|men** [-å-] *a5* welcome; ~*!* I am (*etc.*) glad to see you!; *hälsa ngn* ~ welcome s.b. **-na** welcome

välkomst|bägare [-å-] *tömma en* ~ drink a toast of welcome **-hälsning** [address of] welcome **-ord** *pl* word of welcome

välkänd well-known

välla *v2* **1** gush (well, spring) (*fram* forth, up; *fram ur* from); ~ *upp* ooze **2** *tekn.* weld **vällevnad** good (luxurious) living, [life of] luxury **välling** gruel **-klocka** farm[yard] bell **väl|ljud** euphony; *mus.* harmony, melody **-ljudande** [-j-] *a4* euphonious; harmonious, melodious; (*om instrument*) with a beautiful tone; (*om toner*) sweet **-lovlig** *i* ~*a ärenden* on lawful occasions **-lukt** sweet smell (scent); perfume, fragrance; *sprida* ~ fill with fragrance, smell sweet **-luktande** *a4* sweet-smelling, sweet-scented; aromatic; fragrant **-lust** voluptuousness; sensual pleasure **-lustig** *a1* voluptuous; sensual; (*liderlig*) libidinous **-lusting** voluptuary; sensualist; (*liderlig pers.*) libertine, debauchee **-läsning** elocution **-makt** prosperity **-menande** *a4* well-meaning, well-intentioned; *i bästa* ~ with the best of intentions **-ment** [-e:-] *a4* well-meant **-meriterad** *a5* highly qualified, meritorious **-motiverad** *a5* well-founded, well-justified **-mående** *a4* thriving; (*blomstrande*) flourishing, prosperous; (*-bärgad*) well-to-do; *se* ~ *ut* look prosperous (thriving) **-måga** *s1* wellbeing, good health; *i högönsklig* ~ in the best of health **-ordnad** well-arranged, well-organized; well-managed (*affärer* affairs) **-orienterad** well-informed **-pressad** *a5* well-pressed **-rakad** *a5* clean-shaved **-renommerad** [-å-] *a5* well-reputed, well-established **-riktad** *a5* well-aimed, well-directed **-sedd** *a5* acceptable; welcome (*gäst* guest) **väl|signa** [-iŋŋa] bless **-signad** *a5* blessed; (*besvärlig, vard. äv.*) confounded; *i -at tillstånd* in the family way

väsignelse [-iŋŋ-] blessing; (*bön*) benediction; *ha* ~ *med sig* bring a blessing [in its (*etc.*) train]; *det är ingen* ~ *med* no good will come of **-bringande** *a4* blessed, beneficial **-rik** full of blessings **väl|sinnad** *a5* well-disposed **-sittande** *a4* well-fitting **-situerad** *a5* well-situated, in good circumstances **-skapad** *a5* well-shaped; (*-formad* äv.) shapely; *ett -skapt gossebarn* a bonny boy **-skriven** *a5* well-written (*bok* book) **-skrivning** *skol.* writing **-skött** [-ʃ-] *a4* well-managed (*affär* business); well-kept (*trädgård* garden); well-tended (*händer* hands); well looked after (*baby* baby) **-smakande** *a4* appetizing; (*läcker*) delicious; (*svagare*) palatable **-sorterad** (*med god sortering*) well-stocked, well-assorted; *vara* ~ have a wide range (large assortment) of goods **-stånd** prosperity; wealth **-sydd** *a5* well-tailored, well-cut

vält *s2* roller; *jordbr. äv.* packer

1 välta I *s1* (*timmer-*) log pile **II** *v1* roll

2 välta *v3* **1** (*stjälpa*) upset (*äv.* ~ *omkull*) **2** (*ramla omkull*) fall over; (*köra omkull*) turn over, (*om bil*) overturn

vältalare orator

vältalig *a1* eloquent **-het** eloquence

vältra 1 (*flytta*) roll [... over], trundle; ~ *skulden på ngn* throw the blame on s.b.; ~ *bort* (*åt sidan*) roll away **2** *rfl*, ~ *sig i gräset* roll over in the grass; ~ *sig i smutsen* wallow in the mud; ~ *sig i pengar* roll in money

väl|tränad *a5* fit **-underrättad** *a5*, *se välinformerad* **-uppfostrad** *a5* well-bred, well-mannered; *deras barn är* ~*e* their children are well brought up **-utrustad** well-equipped, well-appointed

välva *v2* **1** (*förse med valv*) vault, arch **2** *rfl* form a vault (an arch), vault **3** ~ *stora planer* revolve great plans

välvil|ja benevolence; good will, kindness; *hysa* ~ *mot* be well-disposed towards; *visa ngn* ~ show s.b. kindness; *mottogs med* ~ was favourably received **-lig** benevolent; kind[ly] **-ligt** *adv* benevolently; kindly; ~ *inställd mot* favourably disposed towards

välvning vaulting, arching; *konkr.* vault, arch

väl|vårdad well-kept; (*om pers.*) groomed **-växt** *a4* shapely, well-formed

vämj|as *v2 el. vämdes vämts, dep,* ~ *vid* be disgusted (nauseated) at (by) **-elig** *a1* nauseous, disgusting; loathsome **-else** loathing, disgust; (*starkare*) nausea; *känna* ~ *vid* be revolted by

1 vän [vä:n] *a1* fair; lovely, graceful

2 vän [vänn] *s3* friend; *vard.* pal, chum; *min lilla* ~ (*i tilltal*) my dear [child]; *en* ~ *till mig* a friend of mine, one of my friends; ~ *av ordning* a lover of law and order; *släkt och* ~*ner* friends and relations; *goda* ~*ner* close friends; *ha en* ~ *i ngn* (*ngn till* ~) have a friend in s.b., have a p.'s friendship; *bli* (*vara*) ~ *med* make (be) friends with; *jag är mycket god* ~ *med honom* he is one of my greatest friends; *inte vara ngn* ~ *av* (*äv.*) not be fond of, dislike

vänd|a *v2* **1** (*ge* (*intaga*) *annat läge*) turn; (*rikta äv.*) direct; *sjö.* go about; ~ *en bil* turn a car [round]; ~ *hö* turn over hay; ~ *ngn ryggen* turn one's back upon s.b.; ~ *stegen hemåt* direct one's steps homewards; *var god vänd!* please turn over (p.t.o.), *AE. äv.* over; *vänd mot öster* facing the east; *med ansiktet vänt mot* facing; ~ *allt till det bästa* make the best of it; ~ *ngt till sin fördel* turn s.th. to one's advantage; ~ *om* (*tillbaka*) turn [back]; ~ *på turn* [over]; ~ *på huvudet* turn one's head; ~ *på sig* turn round; ~ *på slanten* look twice at one's money; *vrida och* ~ *på* turn and twist; ~ *upp och ner* (*ut och in*) *på* turn upside down (inside out); ~ *åter* return **2** *rfl* turn (*omkring about*, *round*); (*om vind*) shift, veer; (*förändras*) change; ~ *sig kring en axel* (*äv.*) revolve on an axle; ~ *sig i sängen* (*äv.*) turn over in bed; *bladet*

har vänt sig the tables are turned; *inte veta vart man skall* ~ *sig* not know which way to turn; *hans lycka* -*e sig* his luck changed; ~ *sig ifrån* turn away from; ~ *sig mot* turn towards (*fientligt*: against, upon); ~ *sig om* turn round; ~ *sig till ngn a*) eg. bet. turn to[wards] s.b., *b*) (*med fråga e.d.*) address s.b., *c*) (*för att få ngt*) apply (appeal) to s.b. (*för att få* for), see s.b. (*för att få* about)

vändbar *a1* turnable; (*omkastbar*) reversible (*kappa* coat)

vände[l]rot *bot.* valerian

vänd|kors turnstile **-krets** tropic[al circle]; *Kräftans* (*Stenbockens*) ~ the tropic of Cancer (Capricorn) **-ning 1** (-*ande*) turning *etc.* **2** ([*in*] *riktning*) turn; (*förändring*) change (*t. det bättre* for the better); (*uttryckssätt*) turn [of phrase], term; *ta en annan* ~ take a new turn; *ta en allvarlig* ~ take a serious turn; *vara kvick i* ~*arna* be alert (nimble); *vara långsam i* ~*arna* be slow on one's feet, *vard.* be a slowcoach (*AE.* slowpoke) **-punkt** turning point (*äv. bildl.*); *bildl. äv.* crisis; *utgöra en* ~ mark a turning point **-radie** turning radius **-skiva 1** *järnv.* turntable **2** (*på plog*) mouldboard **-tapp** trunnion

vän|fast constant in friendship, [loyally] attached to one's friends **-gåva** gift from a friend **-inna** girlfriend, ladyfriend

vänja *vande vant* **1** accustom (*vid* to), familiarize (*vid* with); (*härda*) inure, harden (*vid* to); ~*s vid att* be trained to the habit of (+ *ing-form*); ~ *ngn av med att* get s.b. out of [the habit of] (+ *ing-form*); ~ *ngn av med en ovana* cure s.b. of a bad habit **2** *rfl* accustom o.s. (*vid* to); (*bli van*) get accustomed (used) (*vid* to); ~ *sig av med att* get out (rid o.s.) of the habit of (+ *ing-form*)

vänkrets circle of friends

vän|lig *a1* kind (*mot* to); (*välvillig äv.*) kindly; (-*skaplig*) friendly; ~*t ansikte* (*leende*, *råd*) friendly face (smile, piece of advice); *så* ~*t av er!* how kind of you!; *ett* ~*t mottagande* a kind reception, a friendly welcome **-ligen** kindly **-lighet** kindness; kindliness; friendliness; *i all* ~ in a friendly way, as a friend **-ligt** *adv* kindly *etc.*; ~ *sinnad* friendly

vänort sister community; adopted town (city)

vänskap *s3* friendship (*för, till* for); *fatta* ~ *för* get friendly with; *hysa* ~ *för* have a friendly feeling towards (for); *för gammal* ~*s skull* for old times' (friendship's) sake **-lig** [-a:-] *a1* friendly; *leva på* ~ *fot med* be on friendly terms with **-lighet** [-a:-] friendliness, amicability; *i all* ~, *se under vänlighet* **-ligt** [-a:-] *adv* in a friendly way; amicably; ~ *sinnad* friendly

vänskaps|band tie (bond) of friendship; *knyta* ~ *med* form a friendship with **-bevis** token of friendship **-full** kind, friendly **-match** friendly [match] **-pakt** treaty of friendship, friendship pact **-pris** *till* ~ at a price as between friends

Vänskapsöarna *pl* the Friendly Islands, Tonga

vänslas *dep* bill and coo, spoon; (*om hund*) fawn

vänster ['vänn-] **I** *a, best. form vänstra* left (*jfr höger*) **II 1** *oböjligt s, till* ~ to the left (*om* of) **2** *s9, polit.*, ~*n* the Left **-extremist** *s5*, **-extremistisk** *a5* left-wing extremist **-flygel** *polit.* left wing; *tillhöra* ~*n* be a leftist **-gänga** left-hand-

[ed] thread **-hänt** *a4* left-handed **-inner** *sport.* inside left **-parti** left- wing party; *~et kommunisterna* (*vpk*) left party communists **-prassel** *vard.* extramarital relations, (*sl.*) a little bit on the side **-radikal** leftist **-sida** (*i bok*) left-hand page **-styrning** (*av bil*) left-hand drive **-sväng** left turn **-trafik** left-hand traffic **-vriden** ~ *kommentar* pro-leftist commentary **-vridning** *polit.* veering (swing) to the left; leftism **-ytter** *sport.* outside left

vänsäll popular; *vara* ~ have many friends

vänta 1 (*motse, förvänta* [*sig*]) expect (*besked* an answer; *att ngn skall komma* s.b. to come; *av* from); (*förstå*) await, be in store for; *det är att* ~ it is to be expected; *det var inte annat att* ~ what else could you expect?; *som man kunde ha ~t sig* as might have been expected; *han ~s hit i dag* he is expected to arrive here today; *döden ~r oss alla* death awaits us all; *du vet inte vad som ~r dig* you don't know what is in store for you; ~ *ut ngn* wait for s.b. to go (come) **2** (*avvakta, bida*) wait (*på* for; *på att ngn skall* for s.b. to; *och se* and see); ~ *lite!* wait a bit!; ~ *länge* wait a long time; *få* ~ have to wait; *gå och* ~ wait [and wait]; *låta ngn* ~ keep s.b. waiting; *låta* ~ *på sig a*) (*om pers.*) keep people (*etc.*) waiting, be late, *b*) (*om svar e.d.*) be long in coming; ~ *med* (*uppskjuta*) put off, (*sitt omdöme e.d.*) postpone, reserve; ~ *inte med middagen* don't wait dinner **3** *rfl* expect (*mycket av* a lot from; *ett kyligt mottagande* a cool reception); *det hade jag inte ~t mig av dig* I didn't expect that from you

väntan *r* wait, waiting; (*för-*) expectation; (*spänd* ~) suspense; *i* ~ *på* while waiting for, awaiting, pending

vänte|lista waiting list **-tid** time of waiting, wait, waiting period; *under ~en kan vi* while we are waiting we can

vänthall waiting room

väntjänst *göra ngn en* ~ do s.b. a good turn

vänt|rum, -sal waiting room

väpna [ˣvä:p-] arm **väpnare** *hist.* [e]squire

väppling trefoil, clover

1 värd [-ä:-] *s2* host; *se äv. hyres-, värdshus-; fungera som* ~ act as host, do the honours

2 vär|d [-ä:-] *a5* **1** worth (*besväret* the trouble; *att läsa*[*s*] reading); (*värdig, förtjänt av*) worthy (*all uppmuntran* of every encouragement; *beröm* of praise); *inte vara mycket* ~ (*bildl.*) be good for nothing; *arbetaren är* ~ *sin lön* the labourer is worthy of his hire; ~ *priset* worth the price, good value; *det är -t att lägga märke till* it is worth noting; *det är inte mödan -t* it is not worth while; *det är fara -t att* it is to be feared that; *det är inte -t att du gör det* you had better not do it **2** (*aktningsvärd*) esteemed; *Er ~a skrivelse* your esteemed letter

värddjur host

värde [ˣvär:-] *s6* value; (*inre* ~) worth; *det bokförda ~t* the book value; *stora ~n* (*summor*) large sums, (*föremål*) valuable property; *pengar eller pengars* ~ money or its equivalent; *av noll och intet* ~ null and void, of no value whatsoever; *av ringa* ~ of small value; *till ett* ~ *av* to a (the) value of; *prov utan* ~ sample of no value; *ha stort* ~ be of great value; *sjunka* (*stiga*) *i* ~ fall (rise) in val-

ue; *sätta* ~ *på* attach value to, lay (put, set) store by, (*uppskatta*) appreciate; *uppskatta ngt till sitt fulla* ~ appreciate s.th. fully

värdebeständig of stable value; ~ *pension* with constant purchasing power; *~a tillgångar* real-value assets **-het** stability of value

värde|full valuable (*för* to); *det skulle vara mycket ~t om* it would be very useful (helpful) if **-föremål** article (object) of value, valuable [thing] **-försändelse** registered (insured) postal matter (*brev:* letter; *paket:* parcel) **-gemenskap** community of values **-laddad** loaded with subjective judgements **-lös** worthless; of no value, valueless **-minskning** depreciation, decrease (fall) in value **-minskningskonto** depreciation account **-mässig** *a1* in terms of value; *den ~a stegringen* the rise in value **-mätare** standard of value **-papper** valuable document; security; bond; *koll.* (*aktier*) stock (*sg*); *belåning av* ~ loans on (pledging of) securities, hypothecation **-post** registered (insured) mail

värder|a (*bestämma värdet av*) value, estimate (*till* at); (*på uppdrag*) appraise; (*om myndighet*) assess; ~ *för högt* (*äv.*) overestimate **2** (*uppskatta*) value, appreciate; (*högakta*) esteem, estimate; *vår ~de medarbetare* our esteemed colleague **-ing** valuation, estimation, estimate; appraisement; assessment; *~ar* (*allm.*) set of values

värderings|grund basis of valuation **-man** valuer; (*för skada*) claims assessor

värde|sak article (object) of value; *~er* valuables **-stegring** rise in value, appreciation **-säker** *se värdebeständig* **-sätta** *se värdera o.* [*sätta*] *värde* [*på*]

värdfolk *vårt* ~ our host and hostess

värdig [ˣvä:r-] *a1* worthy (*efterträdare* successor); (*aktningsvärd*) dignified; (*passande för*) fitting, seemly (*ngn* for s.b); *på ett ~t sätt* in a dignified manner, with dignity **-as** *dep* deign (condescend) to **-het** dignity; (*som egenskap*) worthiness; (*ämbetsställning*) position; (*rang*) rank; *hålla på sin* ~ stand on one's dignity; *anse det under sin* ~ *att* consider it beneath one (one's dignity) to

värdinna hostess; lady of the house

värdinneplikter *pl* duties of a hostesss

värdshus [ˣvä:rds-, ˣvärs-] inn; tavern; (*restaurang*) restaurant **-värd** innkeeper, landlord

värdskap [ˣvä:rd-] *s7* duties (*pl*) of [a] host (*etc.*); *utöva ~et* do the honours, act as host

värdväxt host

1 värja *v2* defend (*sitt liv* one's life; *sig* o.s.); *man kan inte ~ sig från misstanken att* one cannot help suspecting that

2 värja *s1* sword; (*stick-*) rapier

värj|fäktning sword fight **-fäste** sword hilt **-stöt** sword thrust

värk *s2* ache, pain[*s pl*]; *~ar* labour pains; *reumatisk* ~ rheumatic pains

värk|a *v3* ache; *det -er i armen* my arm aches; *det -er i hela kroppen* (*äv.*) I ache all over; ~ *ut* work out **-bruten** crippled with rheumatism

värld [vä:rd] *s2* world; (*jord*) earth; *gamla* (*nya*) *~en* the Old (New) World; *en man av* ~ a man of the world; *undre ~en* the underworld; *hur i all ~en?* how on earth?; *hela ~en* the whole world, (*alla människor*) all the world, everybody; *från*

V

hela ~en from all over the world; *det är väl inte hela ~en!* it doesn't matter all that much!; *hur lever ~en med dig? (vard.)* how's the world treating you?; *inte se mycket ut för ~en* not look much; *slå sig fram i ~en* make one's way in the world; *för allt i ~en!* for goodness' sake!; *inte för allt i ~en* not for [all] the world; *förr i ~en* formerly, in former days; *så går det till här i ~en* that's the way of the world; *se sig om i ~en* see the world; *komma till ~en* come into the world; *bringa ur ~en* settle [once and for all]

världs|alltet the universe; *fack.* cosmos **-artikel** article with a worldwide market **-artist** international (world-famous) performer **-banken** the World Bank **-bekant** universally known **-berömd** world-famous **-bild** idea (conception) of the world **-brand** world conflagration **-dam** woman of the world, lady of fashion **-del** part of the world, continent **-fred** world (universal) peace **-frånvarande** who is living in a world of his own **-frånvänd** *a5* detached **-främmande** ignorant of the world; unrealistic **-förakt** contempt of the world **-föraktare** cynic **-förbättrare** reformer **-handel** world (international) trade **-hav** ocean **-herravälde** universal (world) supremacy (dominion) **-historia** world history; *-historien* the history of the world **-historisk** of the history of the world **-hushållning** world economy; universal economics (*pl*) **-händelse** event of worldwide importance, historic event **-karta** map of the world, world map **-klass** *i ~* of international caliber **-klok** worldly wise **-klokhet** worldly wisdom **-kongress** world congress **-krig** world war; *första (andra) ~et (äv.)* World War I (II); *utlösa ett ~* unleash a world war

världslig [˟vä:rds-] *a1* worldly (*ting* matter); (*av denna värld*) mundane, of the world; (*motsats helig*) profane; (*motsats kyrklig*) secular; *~ makt* temporal power; *~a ting (äv.)* temporal affairs; *~a nöjen* worldly pleasures **världsligt** *adv* worldly; *~ sinnad (äv.)* worldly-minded

världs|litteratur world literature **-läge** *~t* the world situation **-makt** world power **-man** man of the world **-marknad** world market **-medborgare** citizen of the world; cosmopolitan **-medborgarskap** world citizenship **-mästare** world champion **-mästerskap** world championship **-omfattande** worldwide; global **-omsegling** circumnavigation of the earth; sailing round the world **-opinion** world opinion **-ordning** world order; *den nuvarande ~en (äv.)* the present order of things in the world **-organisation** world organization **-politik** world politics (*pl*) **-politisk** of world politics; *en ~ händelse* a political event of world importance **-press** world press **-problem** world problem **-rekord** world record **-rykte** world[wide] fame (renown) **-rymden** best. form outer space **-språk** world language **-stad** metropolis **-stat** world state **-trött** weary of the world **-utställning** world fair **-van** experienced in the ways of the world **-välde** world empire **-åskådning** ideology; [general] view of life

värma *v2* warm; (*hetta*) heat; *~ upp* warm (heat) up

värme *s9, fackl. s7* warmth; (*hetta*) heat (*äv. fys.*); *bildl. äv.* fervour, ardour; *hålla ~n* keep warm; *stark ~* great (intense) heat; *i 60° ~ at 60°* above zero **-alstring** heat production **-anläggning** heating plant, [central] heating **-apparat** heater **-behandla** treat with heat **-behandling** *med.* thermotherapy; *tekn.* heattreatment **-beständig** heat-resistant **-bölja** heat wave **-central** district heating plant **-dyna** [electric] heating pad **-element** (*radiator*) radiator; (*elektriskt*) electric heater **-energi** thermal energy **-enhet** thermal (heat) unit **-filt** electric blanket **-flaska** hot-water bottle **-förlust** heat loss, loss of heat **-isolera** insulate against heat **-isolering** thermal insulation **-kraftverk** thermal power station **-källa** source of heat **-känslig** sensitive to heat **-lampa** infrared lamp **-ledare** heat conductor; *dålig ~* bad (poor) conductor of heat **-ledning** central heating; *fys.* heat (thermal) conduction **-ledningselement** radiator **-lära** thermology **-motor** heat engine **-mätare** heat meter, calorimeter **-panel** heating panel **-panna** heating boiler, central heater **-platta** hotplate **-pump** heat pump **-skåp** (*i kök*) warming cupboard; (*i laboratorium*) incubator **-sköld** heat shield *med.* heatstroke **-slinga** heating coil **-strålning** thermal (heat) radiation **-ugn** [re]heating furnace **-utvidgning** heat (thermal) expansion **-verk** heating plant **-värde** calorific value **-växlare** heat exchanger

värmning heating

värn [-ä:-] *7* defence, safeguard; protection; (*skytte-*) fire trench **värna** *~ [om]* defend, safeguard; protect **värnlös** defenceless; *~a barn* (*vanl.*) orphans

värnplikt *allmän ~* compulsory military service, *Storbritannien* [compulsory] national service; *AE.* universal military training; *fullgöra sin ~* do one's military service **-ig** liable for (to) military service; *en ~* a conscript (*AE.* draftee); *~ officer* conscript officer

värnplikts|tjänstgöring national service training **-vägran** refusal to do military service **-ålder** call-up (*AE.* draft) age **-skatt** national defence levy

värp|a *v3* lay [eggs] **-höna** laying hen

värre ['värre] **I** *a, komp. t. ond* worse (*jfr illa o. ond*); *bli ~ och ~* get worse and worse, go from bad to worse; *det var ~ det!* that's too bad!; *och vad ~ är* and what's worse **II** *adv, komp. t. illa* worse; (*allvarligare*) more seriously (*sjuk* ill); *dess ~* unfortunately; *så mycket ~* so much the worse; *vi hade roligt ~* we had no end of fun; *hon var fin ~* she was dressed [up] to the nines

värst I *a, superl. t. ond* worst (*jfr illa o. ond*); *släkten är ~* preserve me (us) from relatives!; *frukta det ~a* fear the worst; *det ~a återstår* the worst is yet to come; *det ~a är att* the worst of it is that; *det var ~ (det ~a)!* well, I never!; *det var det ~a jag har hört!* I never heard the like!; *du skall då alltid vara ~* you always have to go one better; *i ~a fall* at worst, if the worst comes to the worst; *mitt under ~a* in the midst of [the], at the height of; *när … var som ~* when … was at its worst (height) **II** *adv, superl. t. illa* [the] most; *när jag var som ~ sjuk* when I was at my worst; *inte så ~*

not very (*bra* good); *jag är inte så* ~ *glad åt det* it doesn't make me any too happy

värv *s7* (*sysselsättning*) work; (*uppgift*) task; (*åliggande*) function, duty; *fullgöra sitt* ~ (*äv.*) do one's part; *fredliga* (*krigiska*) ~ (*äv.*) the arts of peace (war)

värv|a secure (*kunder* customers; *röster* votes); *mil.* enlist; ~ *röster* (*äv.*) canvass [for votes], electioneer; *låta* ~ *sig* (*mil.*) enlist; ~ *trupper* raise (levy) troops **-ning** enlistment; *ta* ~ enlist [in the army]

väsa *v3* hiss; ~ *fram* hiss [out]

väsen ['vä:-] **1** *-det -den el. väsen* (*äv. väsende* [*ᵡvä:-*] *s6*) (*varelse*) being; *det högsta* ~*det* the Supreme Being; *inte ett levande* ~ not a living soul **2** *böjs enl.* *1* (*sätt att vara*) being, nature, person, character; (*innersta natur*) essence; *till sitt* ~ of disposition **3** *-det, pl väsen* (*buller*) noise; (*ståhej*) fuss, ado; *mycket* ~ *för ingenting* much ado about nothing; *göra mycket* ~ make a great fuss (*av ngn* of s.b.; *av ngt* about s.th.); *göra* ~ *av sig* make o.s. felt [in the world]; *hon gör inte mycket* ~ *av sig* (*äv.*) she is not very pushing **-de** *se väsen 1*

väsens|besläktad kindred **-främmande** alien (*för* to) **-skild** essentially different **-skillnad** essential difference

väsentlig [-'senn-] *a1* essential; principle, main; (*betydelsefull*) important; (*avsevärd*) considerable; *det* ~*a* the essentials (*pl*); *det* ~*a i* the essential part of; *en högst* ~ *skillnad* a very important difference; *mindre* ~ (*äv.*) not so important; *i* ~ *grad* essentially, to a considerable extent; *i allt* ~*t* in [all] essentials, essentially **-en** essentially; principally, mainly; (*i väsentlig grad*) substantially **-het** essential thing; ~*er* vital points, essentials

väsk|a *s1* bag; (*hand-*) handbag; (*res-*) suitcase, valise **-ryckare** bag-snatcher

väsljud [*ᵡvä:s-*] *språkv.* fricative

väsnas [*ᵡvä:s-*] *dep* be noisy, make a noise

väsning [*ᵡvä:s-*] hissing; *en* ~ a hiss

vässa sharpen; whet

1 väst *s2* (*plagg*) waistcoat; (*AE. o. dam-*) vest

2 väst *s9 o. adv* (*väderstreck*) west, West

Västafrika West Africa

västan I *adv*, ~ [*ifrån*] from the west **II** *r, se följ.* **-vind** west wind; ~*en* (*poet.*) Zephyrus

Väst|asien Western Asia **-australien** Western Australia

västblocket the Western bloc

väster ['väss-] **I** *s9* **1** (*väderstreck*) the west; (*jfr norr*) **2** ~*n* the West (Occident); *Vilda V~n* the Wild West **II** *adv* west **-landet** the West (Occident) **-ländsk** *a5* western, occidental **-länning** westerner, occidental **-ut** westward[s]

Västeuropa Western Europe

västeuropeisk West European

västficka waistcoat pocket

västficksformat vest-pocket size

väst|front ~*en* the Western front **-got** Visigoth **-gotisk** Visigothic **-götaklimax** [*ᵡvästjö:-, ᵡväʃö:-*] anticlimax

Västindien the West Indies (*pl*)

västindisk West Indian

västklänning jumper (*AE.*)

väst|kust west coast **-lig** *a1* west[erly] (*vind*

wind); western (*landskap* provinces); *den* ~*a världen* the Western World, the West; *vinden är* ~ the wind is [from the] west; ~*ast* westernmost, most westerly (western) **-makterna** the Western Powers **-maktspolitik** Western policy **-nordväst** west-northwest **-orienterad** *bildl.* Westorient[at]ed

väst|ra *a, best. form* [the] western; *i* ~ *Sverige* (*äv.*) in the west of Sweden **-romersk** Western Roman; ~*a riket* the Western [Roman] Empire **-sida** *på* ~*n* to the west **-sydväst** west-southwest **-tysk** *s2 o. a5* West German

Västtyskland West Germany; (*officiellt*) the Federal Republic of Germany

väst|vart [väst-] westward[s] **-världen** the Western world

väta I *s1* wet; moisture, damp[ness]; *aktas för* ~ to be kept dry, keep dry **II** *v3*, ~ [*ner*] wet; ~ *ner sig* get [o.s.] wet; ~ *i sängen* wet the bed

väte *s6* hydrogen **-atom** hydrogen atom **-bomb** hydrogen bomb, H-bomb **-bombskrig** thermonuclear war **-cyanid** hydrogen cyanide, hydrocyanic acid **-kraft** hydrogen power **-peroxid** hydrogen peroxide **-superoxid** *se -peroxid*

vätgas hydrogen gas

vätmedel wetting agent

vätsk|a I *s1* liquid, fluid; *vid sunda -or* in good form **II** *v1*, ~ [*sig*] run, discharge fluid

vätske|balans fluid balance **-form** liquid state **-kylning** liquid-cooling **-pelare** liquid column

vätteros *bot.* toothwort

väv *s2* (*tyg*) fabric; (*varp*) web; *sätta upp en* ~ loom a web

väv|a *v2* weave **-are** weaver **-arfågel** weaver [bird] **-bom** beam

väv|d [-ä:-] *a5* woven **-eri** weaving mill **-erska** woman weaver **-nad** [-ä:-] *s3* [woven] fabric; *biol. o. bildl.* tissue; ~*er* (*äv.*) textiles; *en* ~ *av lögner* a tissue of lies **-nadsindustri** weaving industry **-ning** [-ä:-] weaving **-plast** [plastic-]coated fabric **-sked** [weaving] reed **-stol** loom; (*hand-*) hand loom; (*maskin-*) power loom

växa *v3* **1** grow (*t. ngt* into s.th.); (*öka*) increase (*i antal* in numbers); ~ *i styrka* increase in strength; ~ *sig stor* (*stark* strong); *låta skägget* ~ grow a beard; ~ *ngn över huvudet a*) eg. *bet.* outgrow s.b., *b*) *bildl.* get beyond a p.'s control **2** (*med betonad partikel*) ~ *bort* disappear with time; ~ *fast vid* grow [on] to; ~ *fram* grow (come) up (*ur* out of), (*utvecklas*) develop; ~ *ifatt ngn* catch s.b. up in height (size); ~ *ifrån* outgrow (*ngn* s.b.), grow out of (*en vana* a habit); ~ *igen* (*om stig e.d.*) become grassed, (*om dike e.d.*) fill up [with grass]; ~ *ihop* grow together; ~ *in i a*) eg. *bet.* grow into, *b*) *bildl.* grow familiar with; ~ *om* outgrow; ~ *till sig* improve in looks; ~ *upp* grow up; ~ *upp till kvinna* grow into womanhood; ~ *ur* grow out of, outgrow; ~ *ut* grow out, (*bli utvuxen*) attain its (*etc.*) full growth; ~ *över* overgrow

växande *a4* growing, increasing; ~ *gröda* (*äv.*) standing crops (*pl*); ~ *skog* standing forest

1 väx|el ['väks-] *s2, bank.* bill [of exchange] (*förk.* B/E); (*tratta*) draft; *egen* (*främmande*) ~ bill payable (receivable); *förfallen* ~ bill due; *prima* (*sekunda*) ~ first (second) of exchange; *ac-*

ceptera en ~ accept a bill; dra en ~ för ett belopp på ngn på sex månader draw [for] an amount on s.b. at six months; dra -lar på framtiden (bildl.) count too much on the future; inlösa en ~ discharge (honour) a bill; omsätta (utställa) en ~ renew (draw) a bill

2 växel|el ['väks-] s2 **1** (-pengar) [small] change; inte ha ngn ~ på sig have no change [about one] **2** tekn. gear; järnv. points (pl), AE. switch[es pl]; fyra -lar framåt (på bil) four forward gears; lägga om ~n (järnv.) reverse the points; passera en ~ (om tåg) take a point **3** (telefon-) [telephone] exchange; (-bord) switchboard; sitta i ~n be a switchboard operator

växel|acceptant acceptor [of a bill] **-affär 1** (enskild) bill transaction **2** göra ~er do exchange business **-belopp** amount of a bill **-blankett** bill[-of-exchange] form

växel|bord switchboard **-bruk** rotation of crops, crop rotation; bedriva ~ practise rotation farming

växel|diskontering discounting of bills **-fordringar** pl, bokför. bills receivable **-förfalskning** forging (forgery) of bills

växel|kassa small-change cash **-kontor** exchange office **-kurs** rate [of exchange], exchange rate

växellag bills of exchange (negotiable instruments) act

växel|lok[omotiv] shunting engine; AE. switch engine **-låda** gearbox; (AE. transmission [case] **-pengar** pl [small] change (sg)

växel|protest protest of a bill **-rytteri** kite-flying, bill-jobbing

växel|spak (i bil) gear lever, AE. gearshift **-spel** interplay, interaction **-spår** järnv. siding (AE. switch) track **-spänning** elektr. alternating voltage **-station** tel. subexchange **-ström** alternating current (förk. A.C.) **-strömsmotor** alternating-current motor **-sång** alternating song; kyrklig ~ antiphon

växeltagare payee [of a bill]

växeltelefonist switchboard operator

växelutställare drawer [of a bill]

växel|varm ~a djur cold-blooded animals **-verkan** reciprocal action, interaction **-vis** alternately; in (by) turns

växla 1 (pengar) change; (utbyta) exchange (ringar rings); kan du ~ 5 kronor åt mig? (äv.) can you give me change for 5 kronor?; ~ en sedel break a note (i into); ~ ett par ord med have a word with; vi har aldrig ~t ett ont ord we have never had words; ~ fel give the wrong change; ~ in (pengar) change, cash **2** (tåg e.d.) shunt, switch; (i bil) change (shift) gear, AE. shift the gears **3** (skifta) vary, change; (~ om) alternate; (om priser) fluctuate

växlande a4 varying, changing; variable (vindar winds); ~ framgång varying success; ~ öden (äv.) vicissitudes

väx|ling ing **1** (-ande) changing etc. **2** (skiftning) change; variation, fluctuation; (inbördes) alternation; (regelbunden) rotation; årstidernas ~ar the rotations of the seasons; ödets ~ar the vicissitudes of fortune **3** (av tåg) shunting, switching; (av bil) gear changing (shifting) **-ingsrik** full of

changes (etc.)

växt I a4 (väl well) grown **II** s3 **1** (tillväxt) growth; hämma i ~en check the growth of; stanna i ~en stop growing **2** (kroppsbyggnad) shape, figure, build; av ståtlig ~ of a fine stature; liten (stor) till ~en short (tall) of stature **3** (planta) plant; (ört) herb; (utväxt) growth, tumour; samla ~er collect wild flowers **-art** plant species **-biologi** plant biology **-cell** plant cell **-del** part of a plant **-familj** plant family **-fett** vegetable fat **-fiber** plant (vegetable) fibre **-färg** vegetable dye **-följd** rotation (succession) of crops **-förädling** plant breeding (improvement) **-geografi** plant geography, phytogeography **-gift** vegetable poison; (bekämpningsmedel) herbicide, weedkiller **-hus** greenhouse; (uppvärmt) hothouse **-huseffekt** greenhouse effect **-kraft** growing power **-lighet** vegetation **-liv** plant life; vegetation, flora **-lära** botany **-namn** plant name **-period** period of growth **-press** botanical (plant) press **-riket** the plant (vegetable) kingdom **-saft** [vegetable] sap **-sjukdom** plant disease **-skyddsmedel** plant protectant **-släkte** plant family **-sätt** growth habit (form) **-värk** growing pains (pl) **-värld** flora; jfr äv. -riket **-ätande** a4 herbivorous

vörda [ˣvö:r-] revere, venerate; (högakta) respect **vördig** a1, se vördnadsbjudande; (i titel) reverend **vördnad** s3 reverence, veneration; sonlig ~ filial piety; betyga ngn sin ~ pay one's respects to s.b.; hysa ~ för revere, venerate, respect; inviga ~ (äv.) command respect

vördnads|betygelse mark (token) of respect (reverence) **-bjudande** venerable; (friare äv.) imposing, grand **-full** reverent[ial], respectful (mot of) **-värd** venerable

vörd|sam al respectful **-samt** adv respectfully; deferentially; (i brevslut) Yours respectfully

vört s3 wort **-bröd** bread flavoured with wort

X

x-a [ˣeksa] ~ [över] 'x' out

Xantippa [ksanˣtippa] Xant[h]ippe

xantippa sl shrew

x-axel [ˣeks-] x-axis

Xenofon ['ksenåfån] Xenophon

xenon [kseˈnå:n] s4, kem. xenon

xerografi [kse:-] s3 xerography

X-krok [ˣeks-] picture hook

x-kromosom [ˣeks-] X-chromosome

xylofon [ksyloˈfå:n] s3 xylophone

xylo|graf [ksylo-] s3 xylographer **-grafi** s3 xylography

xylol [ksyˈlå:l] s3, kem. xylene, xylol

xylos [ksyˈlå:s] s3, kem. xylose

Y

yacht [jått] *s3* yacht **-klubb** yacht[ing] club
yankee ['jänki] *s5* [*pl* -kier] Yankee; *vard.* Yank
y-axel y-axis
yemenjt *se jemenit*
Y-kromosom Y-chromosome
yla howl **ylande** *s6* howling
ylle *s6* wool; *av* ~ [made] of wool, woollen **-filt**
woollen blanket; (*material*) wool felt **-foder**
woollen lining **-fodrad** [-ɔ:-] *a5* wool-lined,
flannel-lined **-halsduk** woollen scarf **-kläder** *pl*
woollen clothing (*sg*) **-muslin** delaine **-skjorta**
flannel shirt **-strumpa** woollen stocking (*kort:*
sock) **-tröja** jersey, sweater; (*undertröja*) woollen vest **-tyg** woollen material (cloth) **-varor**
woollen goods, woollens **-väveri** woollen mill
(factory)
ymnig *al* abundant, plentiful; heavy (*regn* rain)
-het abundance, profusion **-hetshorn** horn of
plenty, cornucopia
ymnigt *adv* abundantly *etc.*; (*blöda* bleed) pro-
fusely; *förekomma* ~ abound, be plentiful
ymp *s2* graft; bud
ymp|a 1 *med.* inoculate **2** *trädg.* graft **-kniv**
grafting knife **-kvist** graft, scion **-ning 1** *med.*
inoculation **2** *trädg.* grafting **-vax** grafting wax
yngel ['yŋel] *s7, koll.* brood; (*fisk-, grod-*) fry; (*i
romkorn*) spawn (*äv. bildl. neds.*); *ett* ~ one of
the brood (*etc.*)
yngla [ˣyŋla] breed; spawn; ~ *av sig* (*eg. o. friare*) multiply
yngling youth, young man; (*skol-*) [school]boy
-aålder [years (*pl*) of] adolescence
yngre ['yŋ-] *a, komp. t. ung* **1** younger (*än* than);
(*i tjänsten*) junior; (*senare*) later, more recent;
han är 3 år ~ *än jag* (*äv.*) he is my junior by 3
years; *av* ~ *datum* of a more recent (later) date;
se ~ *ut än man är* (*äv.*) not look one's years; *den*
~ *herr A.* Mr. A. Junior; *Dumas den* ~ Dumas
the younger; *Pitt den* ~ the younger Pitt; *de* ~ the
juniors, the younger people **2** (*ganska ung*)
young[ish], fairly young (*herre* gentleman)
yngst *a, superl. t. ung* (*jfr yngre*) youngest; latest,
most recent; *den* ~*e i* the youngest [member] of;
den ~*e i tjänsten* the most recently appointed
member of the staff
ynka *se ömka* **ynkedom** [-dɔmm] *s2, det var
rena* ~*en* it was a poor show (pitiable affair (performance)) **ynklig** *al* pitiable, miserable **ynkrygg** funk; milksop
ynnest ['ynn-] *s2* (*visa ngn en* do s.b. a) favour
-bevis [mark (token) of] favour
yppa 1 reveal, disclose (*för* to); ~ *en hemlighet
för ngn* (*äv.*) let s.b. into a secret **2** *rfl* (*uppstå*)
arise, crop up; (*erbjuda sig*) offer, present itself,
turn up
ypperlig *al* excellent, splendid; superb; (*av hög
kvalitet*) superior, first-class **ypperst** ['ypp-]
superl. a best, finest, most outstanding; choicest

(*kvalitet* quality); noblest, greatest (*man* man)
yppig *al* **1** (*om växtlighet e.d.*) luxuriant; lush
(*gräs* grass); (*om figur*) full, buxom; ~ *barm*
ample bosom **2** (*luxuös*) luxurious, sumptuous
-het 1 luxuriance; lushness *etc.* **2** luxuriousness,
sumptuousness
yr *al* (*i huvudet*) dizzy, giddy; (*ostyrig*) giddy, har-
um-scarum; *bli* ~ turn (go) dizzy (*etc.*); ~ *av
glädje* giddy with joy; ~ *i mössan* flustered, flurried, all in a fluster (flurry); *som* ~*a höns* like
giddy geese **yra I** *s1* **1** *se snöyra* **2** (*under sjukdom*) delirium; (*vild* ~) frenzy; *i stridens* ~ in the
frenzy of the fray **II** *v1* **1** (*tala i yrsel*) be delirious;
~ *om ngt* rave about s.th. **2** (*virvla*) whirl; *snön
yr* the snow is whirling (driving) about, *skummet
yr om stäven* the spray is swirling round the stem;
dammet yr i luften there are clouds of dust in the
air; ~ *igen* (*om väg*) get blocked with snow; ~
omkring go whirling about **yrhätta** madcap,
tomboy
yrka (*begära*) demand; ~ *ansvar på ngn* demand
a p.'s conviction, prefer a charge against s.b.; ~
bifall (*parl.*) move that the motion be agreed to;
~ *bifall till* support; ~ *på* demand, claim (*ersättning* compensation), apply for (*uppskov* a postponement); (*ihärdigt*) insist [up]on (*att ngn gör
ngt* a p.'s doing s.th.) **yrkande** *s6* **1** (*utan pl*) de-
manding *etc.* **2** (*med pl*) demand; claim (*på ersättning* for compensation); *parl.* motion; *på* ~ *av*
at the instance of
yrke *s6* profession; (*sysselsättning*) occupation;
(*hantering*) trade; (*kall*) vocation; *lärare till* ~*t* a
teacher by profession; *fria* ~*n* [liberal] profes-
sions; *han har till* ~ *att undervisa* teaching is his
profession
yrkes|arbetande *a4* working in a profession
(*etc.*); *de* ~ the working population **-arbetare**
skilled worker **-arbete** profession, skilled work
-erfarenhet professional experience **-fiskare**
fisherman by trade **-gren** occupational branch
-grupp occupational group **-hemlighet** trade
(business) secret **-inspektion** ~*en* [the Swe-
dish] labour inspectorate **-kunnig** skilled,
trained **-kvinna** professional woman **-liv** working (professional) life **-lärare** vocational teacher
-man craftsman, skilled worker **-medicin** occupational medicine **-musiker** professional musician **-mässig** *al* professional **-område** vocational (occupational) field (sphere) **-oriente-
ring** vocational guidance **-register** trade register, (*i tel.katalog*) classified telephone directory,
AE. yellow pages **-rådgivning** *se* - orientering
-sjukdom occupational disease **-skada** industrial injury **-skadeförsäkring** industrial injury
insurance **-skicklig** skilled **-skicklighet** professional (occupational) skill, skill in one's work
-skola vocational (trade) school **-stolthet** professional pride **-titel** professional title **-trafik**
commercial traffic **-undervisning** vocational
training **-utbildad** *a5* skilled, trained **-utbild-
ning** vocational training **-val** choice of career
(vocation, occupation, profession) **-verksam-
het** economic activity, trade **-vägledning** *se*
-orientering
yrsel ['yrr-] *s2* dizziness, giddiness; (*omtöckning*)
delirium; *ligga i* ~ be delirious; *jag greps av* ~

(*äv.*) my head began to swim **-anfall** *få ett ~* have an attack of giddiness

yrsnö whirling (driving) snow

yrvaken drowsy [with sleep], startled out of [one's] sleep

yrväder snowstorm, blizzard

ysta (*en ost*) make; (*mjölk*) make into cheese; *~ sig* curdle, coagulate

yster ['yss-] *a2* frisky, lively, boisterous; *en ~ häst* a frisky (spirited) horse; *en ~ lek* a romping game

ystning cheese-making; (*löpning*) curdling [process]

yt|a *s1* **1** surface; *geom. äv.* face; *på ~n* on the (its *etc.*) surface; *endast se till ~n* take a superficial view of things, take s.th. at its face value **2** (*areal*) area **-aktiv** surface-active **-behandla** finish **-behandling** finish[ing], surface treatment **-beklädnad** facing **-beläggning** surface coating, surfacing, coating **-beräkning** area calculation **-bildning** *geogr.* configuration **-enhet** unit [of] area **-innehåll** area **-lager** surface layer (coating)

ytlig [ˣy:t-] *a1* superficial (*äv. bildl.*); skin-deep (*sår* wound); (*grund*) shallow; (*flyktig*) cursory; *en ~ kännedom om* (*äv.*) a smattering of **-het** superficiality

yt|läge *sjö.* surface position **-mått** square measure **-post** (*motsats t. flygpost*) surface mail **-spänning** surface tension

ytter ['ytt-] *s2, sport.* outside forward **-bana** *sport.* outside track **-dörr** outer (front) door **-fil** ouside lane **-kant** outer edge, fringe, verge **-kläder** *pl* outdoor clothes **-kurva** outer curve

ytterlig *a1* extreme; (*fullständig*) utter; (*överdriven*) excessive **-are I** *komp. a* further; additional; (*mera*) more **II** *adv* (*vidare*) further; (*ännu mera*) still more; *~ ett exemplar* another (one more) copy; *~ några dagar* a few days more; *har förbättrats ~* has been further improved **-het** extreme; (*-hetsåtgärd*) extremity; *~erna berör varandra* extremes meet; *gå till ~er* go to extremes; *till ~ oartig* extremely (exceedingly) impolite

ytterlighets|fall extreme case **-man** extremist **-parti** extremist party **-åtgärd** extreme measure

ytterligt *adv* extremely; exceedingly, excessively

ytter|mera *oböjligt a, till ~ visso* what is more **-mått** outer dimension; external measurements (*pl*) **-plagg** outdoor garment **-ring** tyre, tire **-rock** overcoat, greatcoat **-sida** outer side, exterior, outside **-skor** outdoor shoes **-skär** *åka ~* skate on the outside edge **-skärgård** outer isles

ytterst ['ytt-] *superl. adv* **1** (*längst ut*) farthest out (off), outermost **2** (*synnerligen*) extremely, exceedingly, most **3** (*i sista hand*) ultimately, finally

yttersta ['ytt-] *best. superl. a* **1** (*längst ut belägen*) outermost, remotest; (*friare*) utmost; *bildl.* extreme; *den ~ gränsen* the utmost limit; *~ vänstern* the extreme left **2** (*störst, högst*) utmost; extreme; *göra sitt ~* do one's utmost, make every effort; *i ~ nöd* in direst necessity; *i ~ okunnighet* in utter ignorance; *till det ~* to the utmost (limit), (*kämpa* fight) to the bitter end, (*pressa* press) to the last ounce, (*i* (*till*) *högsta grad*) to an extreme pitch **3** (*sist*) last; *~ domen* the last judgment; *på ~ dagen* on the last day; *göra ett ~ försök* make one last (a final) attempt; *ligga på sitt ~* be in ex-

tremis (at the point of death)

ytter|tak roof **-trappa** *s1* steps (*pl*), flight of steps **-vägg** outer (outside) wall **-världen** the outer (outside) world **-öra** external ear

yttra I (*uttala*) utter, say; (*ge uttryck åt*) express; *~ några ord* utter (speak) a few words **II** *rfl* **1** (*ta t. orda*) speak (*vid ett sammanträde* at a meeting); (*uttala sig*) express an (one's) opinion (*om* about, on) **2** (*visa sig*) manifest itself; *sjukdomen ~r sig i* the symptoms of the disease are

yttrande *s6* **1** (*utan pl*) uttering **2** (*med pl*) utterance; (*anmärkning*) remark, observation, statement [of opinion]; *avge sitt ~* submit one's comments **-frihet** freedom of speech (expression)

yttre ['ytt-] **I** *komp. a* (*längre ut belägen*) outer (*hamn* harbour; *skärgård* archipelago); (*utvändig*) external, exterior (*diameter* diametre), outside (*mått* measurement); *bildl.* external (*fiender* enemies; *förbindelser* relations), outward (*skönhet* beauty); extrinsic (*företräden* advantages); (*utrikes*) foreign (*mission* missions); *Y~ Mongoliet* Outer Mongolia; *~ orsak* external cause; *~ rymden* outer space; *~ skada* external (outer) damage; *i ~ måtto* (*vanl.*) outwardly, externally **II** *n* exterior, outside; [external] appearance; *till det ~* externally, outwardly

yttring manifestation, mark (*av* of)

yt|vatten surface water **-verkan** *elektr.* skin effect **-vidd** area

yvas *v2, dep, ~ över* be proud of, glory in

yverboren [ˣy:-, -å:-] *a5, bildl.* ultrapatriotic

yvig *a1* bushy (*svans* tail; *skägg* beard); thick (*hår* hair); *~a fraser* high-flown phrases

yx|a *I s1* axe; *kasta ~n i sjön* (*bildl.*) throw up (in) the sponge **II** *v1, ~ till* rough-hew **-hammare** axe-head **-hugg** cut (blow) with (of) an (the) axe **-skaft** axe handle (helve); *goddag ~!* neither rhyme nor reason!

Z

zair|ier [saˈi:-] Zaïrese **-isk** *a5* Zaïrese

zamb|ier ['samm-] Zambian **-isk** *a5* Zambian

zenit ['se:-] *oböjligt s* [the] zenith **-avstånd** zenith distance

zeppelinare [s-, -ˣli:-] zeppelin; *vard.* zep[p]

zigenarblod [siˣje:-, -ˣge:-] gypsy blood

zigenar|e [siˣje:-, -ˣge:-] gypsy, gipsy **-flicka** gypsy girl **-läger** gypsy camp (encampment) **-musik** gypsy music **-språk** gypsy language,

Rom[m]any
zigenerska [si*x*je:-, -*x*ge:-] gypsy woman (girl)
zigensk [si'je:nsk, -g-] *a5* gypsy
zimbabw|ier [sim'babb-] Zimbabwean **-isk** *a5* Zimbabwean
zink [s-] *s3* zinc **-haltig** *al* zinc-bearing, zinciferous **-legering** zinc alloy **-plåt** zinc plate (sheet) **-salva** zinc ointment **-spat** zinc spar **-vitt** *s9* zinc (Chinese) white
zinnia ['sinnia] *s1* (*växt*) zinnia
zirkonium [sir'ko:-] *s8* zirconium
zodiak|alljus [s-] zodiacal light **-en** [-'a:-] *s, best. form* the zodiac
zon [so:n] *s3* zone **-gräns** zonal boundary **-indelning** zone division **-tariff** zone tariff, zonal rate
zoofysiologi [såå:-] zoophysiology, zoophysics
zoo|log [såå'lå:g] zoologist **-logi** *s3* zoology **-logisk** [-'lå:-] *a5* zoological; ~ *trädgård* zoological gardens (*pl*), *vard.* zoo
zooma [*x*so:-] *foto.* zoom
zoo|tomi [såått?å'mi:] *s3* zootomy **-tomisk** [-'tå:-] *a5* zootomic[al]
zulu ['su:lu] *s3* Zulu **-kaffer** Zulu-Kaffir **-språket** Zulu
zygot [sy'gå:t] *s3, naturv.* zygote
Zürich ['sy:riç] *n* Zürich, Zurich

Å

1 å *s2* [small] river; stream; *AE. äv.* creek; *gå över* ~*n efter vatten* give o.s. unnecessary trouble, put o.s. to unnecessary inconvenience
2 å *prep., se på*
3 å *interj* oh!
åberopa 1 (*anföra*) adduce (*som exempel* as an example); (*hänvisa t.*) refer to, quote, cite; (*t. försvar*) plead; ~ *som ursäkt* allege as an excuse; ~*nde vårt brev* referring to our letter **2** *rfl, se 1*
åberopande *s6, under* ~ *av a*) on the plea (*att* that), *b*) *hand.* referring to (*vårt brev* our letter)
åbo *s5* farm tenant with fixity of tenure, copyholder **-rätt** copyhold right, hereditary lease
åbrodd [*x*å:-, -å-] *s2* (*växt*) southernwood, lad's love
åbäka *rfl* make ridiculous gestures; (*göra sig till*) show off **åbäke** *s6* huge and clumsy creature (*om sak:* thing); monster, monstrosity; *ett* ~ *till karl* a great lump of a fellow **åbäkig** *al* unwieldy, hulky, shapeless

ådagalägg|a [*x*å:-, -*x*da:-] (*visa*) show [o.s. to possess], manifest, display, exhibit; (*bevisa*) prove **-ande** *s6* manifestation *etc.*
åder ['å:-] *s1* vein (*äv. bildl.*); (*puls-*) artery; *geol.* vein, lode; (*i trä*) vein, grain; (*käll-*) spring **-brock, -bråck** varicose veins (*pl*), *fack.* varix (*pl* varices) **-förkalkad** *a5* suffering from arteriosclerosis; *hon börjar bli* ~ (*äv.*) she is getting senile **-förkalkning** arteriosclerosis, *vard.* hardening of the arteries **-låta** bleed (*äv. bildl.*); *bildl. äv.* drain **-låtning** [-å:-] bleeding, blood-letting; *bildl.* drain, depletion
ådra [*x*å:-] *I s1, se åder* **II** *v1* vein; (*sten, trä e.d. äv.*) grain, streak
ådraga 1 (*förorsaka*) cause (*ngn obehag s.b.* inconvenience); bring down upon **2** *rfl* bring down upon o.s.; contract (*sjukdom* an illness); catch (*förkylning* a cold); (*utsätta sig för*) incur (*kritik* criticism); ~ *sig uppmärksamhet* attract attention
ådr|ig [*x*å:-] *al* veined, veiny; (*om trä, sten e.d.*) grained, streaked; *bot.* venous **-ing** veining; *konkr. äv.* veinage, grain, streak; *bot.* venation
ådöma sentence (*ngn ngt s.b.* to s.th.); inflict (*ngn straff* a penalty upon s.b.); ~ *ngn böter* impose a fine on (fine) s.b.
åh *se 3 å*
å|hej heave-ho! **-hoj** [å'håjj] *skepp* ~*!* ship ahoy **-hå** aha!, oh!
åhöra listen to, hear
åhörar|e hearer, listener; *koll.* audience **-dag** *skol.* parents' day **-läktare** [public] gallery
å|ja ['å:-] (*tämligen*) fairly **-jo** ['å:-] (*jo då*) oh yes; (*tämligen*) fairly
åk *s7* **1** *vard.* (*bil*) car **2** *sport.* run
åk|a *v3* **1** *eg. bet.* ride (*baklänges* backwards; *karusell* on the merry-go-round); (*färdas*) go ([*med*] *tåg etc.* by train *etc.*); (*köra*) drive ([*i en*] *bil* a car); *absol.* go by car (*etc.*); ~ *cykel* ride a bicycle (*vard.* bike); ~ *framlänges* sit facing the engine; ~ *första klass* travel (go) first class; ~ *gratis* travel free; ~ *hiss* take the lift; ~ *efter häst* drive behind a horse; ~ *kana* slide; ~ *kälke* toboggan; ~ *skidor* ski; ~ *skridskor* skate; *får jag* ~ *med dig?* can you give me a lift? **2** (*glida*) slide, glide, slip; *skjortan -er jämt upp* my (*etc.*) shirt keeps riding up; *vasen -te i golvet* the vase fell on the floor **3** (*med betonad partikel*) ~ *av* slip off; ~ *bort* go away; ~ *efter* (*hämta*) fetch [by car *etc.*]; ~ *fast* get (be) caught by the police; ~ *förbi* pass, drive past; ~ *in a*) *eg.* drive in, *b*) *vard.* (*i fängelse*) land in jail; [*få*] ~ *med* get a lift; ~ *om* overtake, pass; ~ *omkull a*) fall (*på cykel* from one's bicycle; *på vägen* on the road), *b*) (*ngn, ngt*) run down; ~ *ut a*) *eg.* go for a drive, *b*) *vard.* (*kastas ut*) be turned (kicked) out
åkall|a invoke, call upon **-an** *r* invocation
åkar|brasa *ta sig* (*slå*) *en* ~ slap o.s. to keep warm **-dräng** carter
åkar|e haulage contractor, carrier **-häst** carthorse **-kamp** *vard.* [old] hack **-taxa** (*för gods*) cartage
åkdon vehicle
åker ['å:-] *s2* (*-fält*) [tilled] field; (*-jord*) arable [land]; ~ *och äng* arable and pasture land; *ute på* ~*n* out in the field[s *pl*] **-areal** area under cultivation, arable acreage **-bruk** *se jordbruk* **-bär** arctic raspberry (bramble)

åkeri haulage contractor[s], haul[i]er; *AE.* trucker

åker|jord arable (tilled) land, cultivated field **-lapp** patch of cultivated ground **-mark** *se -jord* **-ren** headland **-senap** charlock, wild mustard **-sork** field vole **-spöke** *vard.* scarecrow **-stubb** stubble **-tistel** creeping thistle, *AE.* Canada thistle **-vicker** vetch **-vinda** bindweed **-ärt** field pea

åklaga [ˣå:-] prosecute

åklagar|e [ˣå:-] prosecutor; *Skottl.* procurator fiscal; *allmän* ~ public prosecutor, *AE.* district attorney **-myndighet** public prosecution authority **-sidan** the prosecution **-vittne** witness for the prosecution

åkomma [ˣå:kå-] *s1* complaint; affection

åk|sjuka travel sickness **-tur** ride, drive; *göra* (*ta*) *en* ~ go for a ride (drive)

ål *s2* (*fisk*) eel; *hal som en* ~ [as] slippery as an eel

åla crawl

ålder [ˈåll-] *s2* age; *av* ~ traditionally, of old; *böjd av* ~ bent with age; *personer av alla åldrar* persons of all ages; *efter* ~ according to age (*i tjänsten*: seniority); *liten för sin* ~ small for one's age; *ha ~n inne* be old enough (*för* for; *för att* to); *hon är i min* ~ she is [about] my age; *i sin bästa* ~ in the prime of life; *vid 35 års* ~ at the age of thirty-five; *vid hög* ~ at an advanced (a great) age; *mogen* ~ maturity

ålderdom [-domm] *s2* old age **-lig** *a1* ancient (*sed* custom); (*gammaldags*) old-fashioned; (*föråldrad*) archaic; *~t uttryck* archaic expression **-ligt** *adv*, ~ *klädd* dressed in old-fashioned clothes

ålderdoms|hem home for the aged, old people's home **-krämpor** infirmities of old age **-svag** decrepit, senile **-svaghet** decrepitude, senility

ålderman alderman; (*i skrå*) [guild]master

ålders|betyg birth certificate **-fördelning** age structure **-grupp** age group **-gräns** age limit **-klass** age class **-pension** retirement pension; (*folkpension*) old age pension **-president** president by seniority; (*i underhuset*) Father of the House [of Commons] **-sjukdomar** *läran om ~na* geriatrics (*pl, behandlas som sg*) **-skillnad** difference of (in) age **-streck** *falla för ~et* reach retiral age **-tecken** sign of age

ålderstigen *a5* old, aged; advanced in years

ålderstillägg seniority increment

åldfru royal housekeeper

åldr|ad *a5* aged **-ande** *a4 o. s6* ag[e]ing **-as** *dep* grow old[er], age **-ig** *a1* old; aged **-ing** old man (woman *etc.*); *~ar* old people **-ingsvård** care of the aged

åligg|a be incumbent [up]on, rest [up]on (with); *det -er honom att* (*äv.*) it is his duty to; *det -er köparen att* the buyer shall **-ande** *s6* duty; obligation; (*uppgift*) task; *sköta sina ~n* discharge one's duties

ål|kista eel hatch (trap) **-ning** [ˣå:l-] *mil.* crawling **-skinn** eel skin

ålägga enjoin (*ngn att göra ngt* s.b. to do s.th.; *ngn ngt* s.th. on s.b.); order, command; (*tilldela*) impose (*ngn en uppgift* a task on s.b.); ~ *sig ngt* impose s.th. on o.s.

åma *rfl, se åbäka*

åminnelse commemoration; *till* ~ *av* in commemoration of **-gudstjänst** memorial service

ånej [ˈå:-] (*nej då*) no!; (*inte vidare*) not very

ång|a I *s1* (*vatten-*) steam; (*dunst*) vapour (*äv. fys.*); *bilda* ~ make steam; *få upp ~n* (*äv. bildl.*) get up steam; *hålla ~n uppe* (*äv. bildl.*) keep up steam; *släppa ut* ~ let off steam **II** *v1* steam (*av* with); *det ~r från lokomotivet* the engine is steaming; ~ *bort* steam off; *tåget ~de in på* the train steamed into **-are** steamer, steamship (*förk.* S/S, S.S.); *med ~n X* by the X, by S.S. X **-bad** vapour bath **-bildning** steam generation; vaporization **-båt** *se -are*

ångbåts|bolag steamship company **-brygga** landing stage, jetty, pier **-förbindelse** steamship service **-resa** steamer voyage **-trafik** steamship service (traffic) **-turer** *pl* sailings of steamers; (*förteckning*) list of sailings

ång|central steam power station **-driven** *a5* (*om maskin*) steam-operated, steam-driven; (*om båt*) steam-propelled

ånger [ˈåŋer] *s9* repentance (*över* for, of); remorse, compunction; (*ledsnad*) regret (*över* at, for) **-full** repentant (*över* of); remorseful (*över* at); regretful **-köpt** [-çö:pt] *a4, se -full*; *vara* ~ *över ngt* regret it (what one has done) **-vecka** cooling-off week

ångest [ˈåŋ-] *s2* agony; anguish; *i dödlig* ~ in deadly (mortal) fear (*för* of) **-full** filled with agony; anguished **-känsla** [feeling of] alarm (anguish) **-skrik** cry of agony, anguished cry

ång|fartyg *se ångare* **-koka** steam **-kraft** steam power **-kraftverk** steam power station (plant) **-kvarn** steam mill **-lok, -maskin** steam-engine **-panna** [steam-]boiler **-preparerad** *a5* evaporated; *~e havregryn* rolled oats

ångra regret; feel sorry for (*att man gjort* doing); repent [of] (*sina synder* one's sins); ~ *sig* regret, be sorry, repent; *det skall du inte behöva* ~ you will not have cause to regret it

ång|slup steam cutter (launch) **-spruta** steam fire engine **-strykjärn** steam iron **-stråle** jet of steam **-ström** *r, fys.* angstrom [unit] (*förk.* Å., A.U.) **-tryck** boiler (steam, vapour) pressure **-turbin** steam turbine **-vissla** steam whistle **-vält** steamroller

ånyo [åˣny:o] anew, afresh, [once] again

år *s7* year; ~ *1960 a*) *adv* in [the year] 1960, *b*) *s* the year 1960; *nådens* ~ *1960* the year of grace 1960; *1960 ~s modell* the 1960 model; *1808 ~s krig* the war of 1808; ~ *för* ~ year by year; ~ *ut och* ~ *in* year in and year out; *Gott Nytt År!* [A] Happy New Year!; *~ts skörd* this year's harvest; *två ~s fängelse* two years' imprisonment; *ett halvt* ~ six months; *ett och ett halvt* ~ eighteen months; *hela ~et* the whole year, all the year round; *under hela ~et* throughout the year, all through the year; *bära sina* ~ *med heder* carry one's years well, wear well; *när fyller du* ~? when is your birthday?; *ha ~en inne* be of the age; *med ~en* with time; *om ett* ~ in a year['s time]; *per* ~ a year, yearly, annually, per annum; *på* ~ *och dag* for years [and years]; *vi är vänner sedan många* ~ *tillbaka* we have been friends for many years; *till ~en* [*kommen*] advanced in years; *under senare* ~

in recent years; *under de senaste ~en* during the last few years

åra *s1* oar; (*mindre*) scull; (*paddel-*) paddle

åratal *i uttr.*: *i* (*under*) ~ for years [and years]

årblad oar blade

årder ['å:r-] *s4, s3* wooden plough

år|gång *s2* **1** (*av tidskrifter e.d.*) [annual] volume; *en ~* (*äv.*) a year's issue; *gamla ~ar* back-volumes, old files **2** (*av vin*) vintage **3** (*åldersklass*) *de yngre ~arna* the younger age groups; *min ~* people of my year **-hundrade** century

årklyka rowlock; *AE.* oarlock

årlig [ˣå:r-] *a1* annual, yearly **-en** annually, yearly; *~ återkommande* annual; *det inträffar ~* it happens every year

års [å:rs] *adv, så här ~* at this time of [the] year **-avgift** annual charge (fee); (*i förening e.d.*) annual subscription (*AE.* dues *pl*) **-avslutning** breaking-up; *AE.* commencement **-barn** *vi är ~* we were born in the same year **-berättelse** annual report **-bok** yearbook, annual **-bokstav** year hallmark **-dag** anniversary **-fest** annual festival (celebration) **-gammal** one-year-old; *ett ~t barn* a one-year-old child; *ett ~t djur* (*äv.*) a yearling **-hyra** annual rent **-inkomst** annual (yearly) income **-klass** age class (group); *stat.* generation **-kontingent** *mil.* annual contingent (quota) **-kontrakt** contract by the year **-kort** season ticket [for a year] **-kull** age group; (*av elever*) batch; *efterkrigstidens stora ~ar* the large number of children born after the war, *äv.* the high birth rate of the postwar period **-kurs** form; *AE.* grade; (*läroplan*) curriculum **-lång** year-long; lasting one year (many years) **-lön** annual salary; *ha 30 000 i ~* have an annual income of 30,000 **-modell** (*av senaste* of the latest) model **-möte** annual meeting **-omsättning** annual turnover (sales) **-redogörelse** annual report **-ring** annual ring **-ränta** annual interest **-skifte** turn of the year **-skrift** yearbook **-tid** season, time of the year **-vinst** annual profit **-växt** year's crop[s *pl*]

årtag stroke of the oar[s *pl*]

år|tal date, year **-tionde** decade

årtull rowlock; *AE.* oarlock

årtusende millennium (*pl äv.* millennia); *ett ~* (*vanl.*) a thousand years; *i ~n* for thousands of years

ås *s2* ridge

å|samka *se* ådraga **-se** (*se på*) watch; (*bevittna*) witness

åsido [åˣsi:do] aside, on one side; *lämna ngt ~* (*äv.*) leave s.th. out of consideration; *skämt ~* joking apart **-sätta** (*ej bry sig om*) disregard, set aside; (*försumma*) neglect, ignore; *känna sig -satt* feel slighted **-sättande** *s6* disregard, setting aside; neglect; *med ~ av alla hänsyn* having no consideration

åsikt *s3* opinion, view (*om* of, on, about); *~erna är delade* opinions differ (are divided); *egna ~er* views of one's own; *enligt min ~* in my opinion; *ha* (*hysa*) *en ~* have (hold) an opinion; *vara av den ~en att* be of the opinion that, hold the view that; *vad är din ~ i saken?* what is your view of (on) the matter?, what do you think about it

åsikts|brytning difference of opinion **-frihet**
freedom of opinion **-förtryck** suppression of free opinion **-utbyte** exchange of views

åsk|a I *s1* thunder; (*-väder*) thunderstorm; *~n går* it is thundering, there is thunder; *~n slog ner i X.* X. was struck by lightning; *det är ~ i luften* there is thunder in the air; *vara rädd för ~n* be afraid of thunder **II** *v1, det ~r* it is thundering **-by** thundershower **-front** thundery front **-knall** thunderclap **-ledare** lightning conductor (rod) **-lik** thundery **-moln** thundercloud **-nedslag** stroke of lightning **-regn** thundery rain **-skräll** thunderclap, peal of thunder **-skur** thundershower **-vigg** thunderbolt **-väder** thunderstorm

åskåda [ˣå:-] *se åse*

åskådar|e [ˣå:-] spectator; onlooker, looker-on; (*mera tillfällig*) bystander; *-na* (*på teater e.d.*) the audience, (*vid idrottstävling*) the crowd; *bli ~ till ngt* witness s.th. **-läktare** [grand]stand; (*utan tak*) bleachers (*pl*) **-platser** *pl* places [for spectators]

åskådlig [-å:d-] *a1* (*klar*) clear, lucid; (*tydlig*) perspicuous; *ett ~t exempel* an object lesson; *en ~ skildring* (*äv.*) a graphic description **-göra** make clear, visualize; illustrate (*med* by) **-het** clearness, clarity; perspicuity

åskådning [-å:d-] (*uppfattning*) opinions, views (*pl*); outlook; *vilken är hans politiska ~?* what is his political position?, where does he stand politically?

åskådnings|materiel audiovisual materials in education: *som ~* (*friare*) as an illustration **-undervisning** audiovisual education

åsna [ˣå:s-] *s1* donkey; *bildl. o. bibl.* ass; *envis som en ~* [as] stubborn as a mule

åsne|aktig *a1* asslike, asinine **-brygga** *bildl.* crib **-drivare** donkey driver **-föl** ass's (donkey's) foal **-hingst** he-ass, jackass **-skri** bray[ing] of donkeys (a donkey)

åsninna she-ass

åstad off; *bege sig ~* go away (off), set out; *gå ~ och so* [off] and

åstadkomm|a [ˣå:-] (*få t. stånd*) bring about, effect (*en förändring* a change); (*förorsaka*) cause, make (*stor skada* great damage); (*frambringa*) produce; (*göra*) do; (*prestera*) achieve; *~ ett gott arbete* do it well, (*friare*) do a good job of work; *~ förvirring* cause confusion; *~ underverk* work wonders **-ande** *s6, för ~ av* [in order] to bring about (*etc.*)

åstund|a desire, long for; (*åtrå*) covet **-an** *r* desire, longing

åsyfta (*ha t. mål*) aim at, have in view; (*avse, mena*) intend, mean (*med* by); *ha ~d verkan* have the desired effect

åsyn sight; *blotta ~en av honom* the mere (very) sight of him; *i allas ~* in public, in full view of everybody; *i broderns ~* before his (her) brother, under the very eyes of his (her) brother; *försvinna ur ngns ~* be lost to (pass out of) a p.'s sight (view); *vid ~en av* at the sight of **åsyna** *oböjligt a, ~ vittne* eyewitness (*till* of)

åsätta *~ en prislapp på ngt* put (fix) a price ticket on [to] s.th.; *~ ett pris på en vara* put a price on an article; *det åsatta priset* the price marked

1 åt *imperf. av äta*

2 åt I *prep* (*se äv. under resp. verb*) **1** *rumsbet.* to; ([*i riktning*] *mot*) towards, in the direction of; ~

vänster (norr) to the left (north); *gå ~ sidan* step aside; *jag har ngt ~ magen* there is s.th. the matter with my stomach; *han tog sig ~ hjärtat* he put his hand to his heart **2** *glad ~* happy about; *nicka (skratta) ~* nod (laugh) at; *vad går det ~ dig?* what is the matter with you?; *göra ngt ~ saken* do s.th. about it; *hon tog ~ sig* she took it personally **3** *(uttr. dativförh.)* to; *(för ngn[s räkning])* for; *ge ngt ~ ngn* give s.th. to s.b., give s.b. s.th.; *köpa ngt ~ ngn* buy s.th. for s.b., buy s.b. s.th.; *jag skall laga rocken ~ dig* I'll mend your coat [for you]; *säga ngt ~ ngn* say s.th. to s.b., tell s.b. s.th. **4** *fyra ~ gången* four at a time **II** *adv (se äv. under resp. verb)* tight; *sitta ~* be (fit) tight

åtag|a *rfl* undertake, take upon o.s.; *~ sig ansvaret för* assume (take) the responsibility for; *~ sig ngt* take s.th. on, take a matter in hand **-ande** *s6* undertaking; *(förpliktelse äv.)* obligation, commitment, engagement

åtal *s7 (av allm. åklagare)* prosecution; *(av enskild)* [legal] action; *allmänt ~* public prosecution; *enskilt ~* private action; *väcka ~ mot ngn för ngt* take proceedings against s.b. for s.th., *(om målsägare äv.)* bring an action against (sue) s.b. for s.th. **åtala** *(om allm. åklagare)* prosecute; *(om enskild)* bring an action against; *bli ~d för* be prosecuted for; *den ~de (vanl.)* the defendant; *frikänna en ~d* acquit an accused **åtalbar** *a1* actionable, indictable

åtals|eftergift nolle prosequi; *bevilja ~* refuse to prosecute a case, withdraw a charge; *han beviljades ~* the charge brought against him was withdrawn, his case was dropped **-punkt** count [of an indictment]

åtanke remembrance; *ha i ~* remember, bear in mind; *komma i ~* be remembered (thought of)

åtbörd [-ö:-] *s3* gesture, motion; *göra ~er* gesticulate

åtel *s2* carrion

åtdraga tighten *(en bult* a bolt)

åter ['å:-] **1** *(ånyo)* again, once more; *nej och ~ nej!* no, a thousand times no!, no, and no again!; *tusen och ~ tusen* thousands upon thousands; *affären öppnas ~* the shop reopens (will be reopened) **2** *(tillbaka)* back [again]; *fram och ~* there and back, *(av o. an)* to and fro **3** *(däremot)* again, on the other hand **-anpassa** readjust **-anpassning** readjustment **-anskaffa** replace **-anskaffning** replacement **-anskaffningsvärde** replacement value (cost) **-anställa** re-engage, re-employ; *AE.* rehire **-använda** recycle **-användning** recycling **-berätta** *(i ord -ge)* relate; *(berätta i andra hand)* retell **-besätta** *mil.* reoccupy *(tjänst e.d.)* refill **-besök** *(hos läkare e.d.)* next visit (appointment); *göra ett ~* make another visit **-betala** pay back, repay; *(lån e.d. äv.)* refund **-betalning** repayment, reimbursement, refund **-betalningsskyldighet** obligation to repay (refund) **-blick** retrospect *(på* of); *(i film e.d.)* flashback *(på* to); *göra (kasta) en ~ på* look back upon

åter|bud *(t. inbjudan)* excuse; *(avbeställning)* cancellation, annulment; *ge (skicka) ~* a) *(att man inte kommer)* send word [to say] that one cannot come, send an excuse, *(t. tävling)* drop out, b) *(att ngt inställs)* cancel a party (dinner etc.), *(att ngt återkallas)* send a cancellation; *ge ~ till doktorn* cancel one's appointment with the doctor; *vi har fått några ~* a few people [sent word that they] could not come **-bäring** refund; bonus; *(i detaljhandel o. försäkr.)* dividend **-börda** [-ö:-] *v1* restore; *~ ngn t. hemlandet* repatriate s.b. **-erövra** recapture, win back **-erövring** recapture, reconquest

återfall relapse *(i* into) **-falla 1** *(i brott etc.)* relapse *(i, till* into) **2** *(falla tillbaka)* recoil *(på* upon) **-fallsförbrytare** recidivist, backslider **-finna** find again; *(-få)* recover; *adresser -finns på s. 50* for addresses see p. 50; *citatet -finns på s. 50* the quotation is to be found on p. 50 **-finnande** *s6, han var vid ~t* when he was found again, he was **-fordra** demand back, reclaim; *(lån)* call in **-få** get back; recover, regain *(medvetandet* consciousness) **-färd** *se återresa* **-föra** bring back; *~ ngt till (bildl.)* trace s.th. back to **-förena** reunite, bring together again; *~ sig med* rejoin **-förening** reunion; *Tysklands ~* the reunification of Germany **-försäkra** reinsure; *~ sig (bildl.)* take measures *(mot* against) **-försäkring** reinsurance **-försälja** resell; *(i minut)* retail **-försäljare** retail dealer, retailer; *pris för ~* trade price; *sälja till ~* sell to the trade **-försäljning** resale, reselling **-förvisa** *jur.* refer back, *AE.* remand **-förvärv** recovery, retrieval

åter|ge 1 *(ge tillbaka)* give back, return; *~ ngn friheten* give s.b. his freedom **2** *(tolka)* render; *(framställa äv.)* reproduce, represent; *~ i ord* express in words; *~ i tryck* reproduce in print; *~ på engelska* render in[to] English **-givande** [-j-] *s6*, **-givning** [-ji:v-] *s2* rendering; reproduction, representation; *(-ljud)* reproduction **-glans** reflection **-gå 1** *(gå tillbaka)* go back, return; *~ till arbetet* go back to work **2** *(om köp)* be cancelled; *låta ett köp ~* cancel a purchase **-gång 1** *(-vändande)* return *(t. arbetet* to work) **2** *jur. (av egendom)* reversion; *(av köp)* cancellation, annulment; *~ av äktenskap* annulment (nullity) of marriage **3** *bildl.* retrogression **-gälda** *(-betala)* repay; *(vedergälla äv.)* return, reciprocate; *~ ont med gott* return good for evil

återhåll|a restrain, keep back *(ett leende* a smile), suppress; *(hejda)* check; *verka ~nde* have a curbing effect; *med -en andedräkt* with bated breath **-sam** *a1 (måttfull)* moderate, temperate; *(behärskad)* restrained **-samhet** moderation, temperance; restraint

åter|hämta fetch back; *bildl.* recover, regain *(sina krafter* one's strength); *~ sig* recover **-hämtning** recovery **-igen** ['å:-] again; *(däremot)* on the other hand **-införa** reintroduce **-insätta** reinstate, reinstall **-inträda** re-enter; *~ i tjänst* resume one's duties **-inträde** re-entry, re-entrance *(i* into); resumption *(i* of)

åter|kalla 1 *(ropa tillbaka)* call back; recall **2** *(ta tillbaka)* cancel *(en beställning* an order); revoke *(en befallning* an order); withdraw *(en ansökan* an application) **3** *bildl., ~ ngn till livet (verkligheten)* bring s.b. back to life (reality); *~ ngt i minnet* recall s.th., call s.th. to mind **-kallelse 1** recall **2** cancellation; revocation; withdrawal **-kasta** *(ljus)* reflect; *(ljud)* reverberate, re-echo; *ljudet ~des av bergväggen* the sound was thrown back from the cliff **-klang** reverberation; echo (*äv. bildl.*) **-klinga** echo, resound, reverberate (*av* with) **-knyta** (*på nytt uppta*) re-establish (*förbindelser* connections), renew (*vänskap* friendship); ~ *till vad man tidigare sagt* refer (go back) to what one said earlier **-komma** come back, return; *bildl.* return, revert, recur; *ett sådant tillfälle -kommer aldrig* an opportunity like this will never turn up (come) again; *vi ber att få ~ längre fram* you will be hearing from us (we will write to you) again later on **-kommande** *a4* recurrent; *ofta* ~ frequent; ~ *till vårt brev av* further (with reference) to our letter of **-komst** [-å-] *s3* return **-koppling** *radio.* feedback [coupling] **-kräva** reclaim **-köp** repurchase **-köpa** repurchase, buy back **-köpsrätt** right of repurchase (redemption); *försäljning med* ~ sale with option of repurchase

åter|lämna return, give (hand) back **-lämnande** *s6* return **-lösa** redeem **-lösning** redemption **-marsch** march back; (*-tåg*) retreat **-remiss** recommitment, return for reconsideration; *yrka* ~ move [that a (the) bill be sent back] for reconsideration; *vi har fått ... på* ~ *...* has been referred back to us **-remittera** refer back, return for reconsideration, recommit **-resa** journey back; *på ~n* on one's (the) way back **-se** see (*träffa:* meet) again; ~ *varandra* (*äv.*) meet again **-seende** meeting [again]; *på ~!* see you again (later)!, *vard.* be seeing you!; ~*ts glädje* the joy of reunion **-skaffa** recover **-skapa** re-create **-skall** echo, reverberation **-sken** reflection **-skänka** give back; ~ *ngn livet* restore s.b. to life **-spegla** reflect, mirror **-spegling** reflection **-stod** rest, remainder; *ekon.* balance; (*lämning*) remnant, remains (*pl*) **-studsa** rebound; (*om ljud*) be reflected; (*om kula*) ricochet **-studsning** rebound[ing] **-stå** remain; (*vara kvar*) be left [over]; *det ~r ännu fem lådor* there are still five cases left; *det ~r att se* it remains to be seen; *det värsta ~r ännu* the worst is yet to come, (*att göra*) the worst still remains to be done; *det ~r mig inget annat än att* I have no choice but to **-stående** *a4* remaining; ~ *delen av året* the rest (remaining part) of the year; *hans* ~ *liv* the rest of his life **-ställa 1** (*försätta i sitt förra tillstånd*) restore; ~ *ngt i dess forna skick* restore s.th. to its former state; ~ *jämvikten* restore equilibrium; ~ *ordningen* restore order **2** (*-lämna*) return, restore, give back **-ställande** *s6* restoration, repair; return **-ställare** *en* ~ a hair of the dog [that bit one last night], a pick-me-up **-ställd** *a5, han är fullt* ~ *efter sin sjukdom* he has quite recovered from his illness **-ställningstecken** *mus.* natural, AE. cancel **-sända** send back, return **-ta[ga] 1** take back; (*-erövra*) recapture; (*-vinna*) recover **2** (*-gå t.*) resume **3** (*åter ta t. orda*) resume **4** (*-kalla*) withdraw, cancel (*en beställning* an order); retract (*ett löfte* a promise) **-tåg** retreat; *anträda ~et* start retreating; *befinna sig på* ~ be in (on the) retreat

återuppbygg|a rebuild, reconstruct **-ande, -nad** rebuilding, reconstruction **-nadsarbete** reconstruction work

återupp|föra *se* återuppbygga **-liva** revive; (*drunknad*) resuscitate; (*bekantskap*) renew; ~

gamla minnen revive old memories **-livningsförsök** [-li:v-] attempt (effort) at resuscitation **-repa** repeat, reiterate **-repning** [-e:-] repetition, reiteration **-rustning** rearmament **-rätta** (*på nytt upprätta*) re-establish, restore; (*ge -rättelse åt*) rehabilitate **-rättelse** rehabilitation **-stå** rise again, arise anew; (*friare*) be revived **-ståndelse** resurrection **-ta[ga]** resume, take up again; ~ *arbetet* resume [one's] work; ~ *ngt till behandling* reconsider s.th. **-täcka** rediscover **-väcka** reawaken; revive; ~ *ngn från de döda* raise s.b. from the dead

åter|utsända *radio.* retransmit; (*program*) rebroadcast **-utsändning** *radio.* retransmission; rebroadcast **-val** re-election; *undanbe sig* ~ decline re-election **-verka** react, retroact, have repercussions (*på* on) **-verkan, -verkning** reaction, retroaction, repercussion **-vinna** win back; (*-få*) regain, recover (*fattningen* one's composure); (*-använda*) recycle **-vinning** recycling **-visit** return visit **-väg** way back; *på ~en kom vi* on our way back we came **-välja** re-elect **-vända** return, turn (go, come) back; revert (*till ett ämne* to a subject) **-vändo** *i uttr.: det finns ingen* ~ there is no turning back; *utan* ~ (*oåterkallelig*) irrevocable **-vändsgata, -vändsgränd** blind alley, cul-de-sac; *bildl. äv.* impasse, dead end **-växt** regrowth, fresh growth; *bildl.* rising (coming) generation; *sörja för ~en* (*bildl.*) ensure the continuance (continued growth)

åt|följa accompany; (*som uppvaktning*) attend; (*följa efter*) follow **-följande** *a4* accompanying *etc.*; (*bifogad*) enclosed; *med ty* ~ with the ensuing **-gång** (*förbrukning*) consumption; (*avsättning*) sale; *ha stor* ~ sell well; *ha strykande* ~ have a rapid sale **-gången** *a5, illa* ~ roughly treated (handled), badly knocked about **-gärd** [-jä:-] *s3* measure; (*mått o. steg*) step, move; *föranledde ingen* ~ could not be considered; *lämna utan* ~ not be able to consider; *vidtaga ~er* take measures (action) **-gärda** [-jä:r-] *vi måste* ~ we must do s.th. about **-görande** [-j-] *s6* action; *det skedde utan A:s* ~ A. had nothing to do with it, it was none of A.'s doing **-hutning** [-u:-] reprimand, rating **-hävor** *pl* manners; behaviour (*sg*); *utan* ~ without a lot of fuss **-komlig** [-å-] *al* within reach (*för* of); *lätt* ~ easily accessible, within easy reach

åtkomst [-å-] *s3* possession, acquisition **-handling** title deed (document) **-tid** *data.* access time

åt|lyda obey; (*föreskrift e.d.*) observe; *bli -lydd* be obeyed **-lydnad** obedience **-löje** ridicule; (*föremål för löje*) laughing stock; *göra sig till ett* ~ make a laughing stock (fool) of o.s., make o.s. ridiculous; *göra ngn till ett* ~ make s.b. a laughing stock, hold s.b. up to ridicule

åtminstone [-ˣminstå-] at least; (*minst äv.*) at the least; (*i varje fall*) at any rate

åtnjut|a enjoy (*aktning* esteem); ~ *aktning* (*äv.*) be held in esteem **-ande** *s6* enjoyment; *komma i* ~ *av* come into possession of, get the benefit of

åtra [ˣå:-] *rfl* change one's mind; (*återta sitt ord*) go back on one's word

åtrå [ˣå:-] **I** *s9* desire (*efter* for); (*sinnlig äv.*) lust (*efter* for) **II** *v4* desire; (*trakta efter*) covet **-värd** *al* desirable

Å

åt|sida (*hitre sida*) near side; (*på mynt*) obverse **-sittande** *a4* tight[-fitting], snug[-fitting] **-skild** separate[d]; *bildl. äv.* distinct; *ligga ~a* lie apart **-skilja** separate; part; (*skilja från varandra*) distinguish [between] **-skillig** [-ʃ-] *al, fören.* a great (good) deal of; *självst.* a great (good) deal; *~a (flera)* several, (*många*) quite a number of, a great (good) many, (*olika*) various; *det finns ~a som tror det* there are many who think so **-skilligt** [-ʃ-] *adv* a good deal, considerably, not a little; *~ mer än 100 personer* well over a hundred people **-skillnad** *göra ~* make a distinction (*mellan* between); *utan ~* without distinction, indifferently **-skils** [-ʃ-] apart, asunder **-smitande** *a4* tight[-fitting] **-stramning** [-a:-] *eg.* contraction; (*ekonomisk*) tightening[-up]; (*kredit- etc.*) squeeze, restraint; (*på börsen*) stiffening **åtta I** *räkn* eight; *~ dagar* (*vanl.*) a week; *~ dagar i dag* this day week **II** *s1* eight **-dubbel** eightfold; octuple **-hundratalet** the ninth century **-hörnig** [-ö:-] *al* octagonal, eight-cornered **-hörning** [-ö:-] octagon **-sidig** *al* eight-sided, octahedral **-timmarsdag** eight-hour [working] day **åttio** [ˣåtti(o), ˈåtti(o)] eighty **-nde** [-å-] eightieth **-n[de]del** eightieth [part] **-tal** *ett ~* some eighty (*personer* persons); *på ~et* in the eighties **ått|kantig** *al* octagonal **-onde** [-å-] eighth; *var ~ dag* every (once a) week **-on[de]del** eighth [part]; *fem ~ar* five eighths **-ondelsnot** *mus.* quaver; *AE.* eighth note **åverkan** damage, injury; *göra ~ på* do damage to, damage; *utsätta för ~* tamper with **åvila** rest with ([up]on), lie upon **åvägabringa** [åˣvä:-] bring about, effect

Ä

äckel [ˈäkk-] *s7* **1** nausea, sick feeling; *bildl.* disgust; *känna ~ inför ngt* feel sick at s.th.; *jag känner ~ vid blotta tanken* the mere thought [of it] makes me feel sick **2** (*-lig person*) repulsive chap **äckla** nauseate, sicken; *bildl.* disgust; *det ~r mig* it sickens me **äcklas** *dep* be disgusted (*vid* by, at) **äcklig** *al* nauseating; (*friare*) sickening; (*motbjudande*) repulsive **ädel** [ˈä:-] *a2* noble; (*om metall, stenar*) precious; (*av ~ ras*) thoroughbred; (*högsint*) noble-minded, magnanimous; *av ~ börd* of noble birth; *kroppens ädlare delar* the vital parts [of the body]; *~t vilt* big game; *~t vin* fine vintage **-boren** noble-born **-gas** inert (rare) gas **-het** nobility, nobleness **-metall** precious metal **-mod** noble-mindedness, generosity; magnanimity **-modig** noble-minded, generous; magnanimous

-ost blue cheese **-sten** precious stone; (*arbetad*) gem, jewel **-trä** (*lövträ*) hardwood **ädling** [ˣä:d-] nobleman, noble [man] **äg|a I** *s1* **1** *i sg end. i uttr.: ha i sin -o* possess; *komma i ngns -o* come into a p.'s hands; *vara i ngns -o* be in a p.'s possession; *vara i privat -o* be private property; *övergå i privat -o* pass into private ownership **2** *pl -or* grounds; property (*sg*) **II** *v2* **1** (*rå om*) own, be the owner of; (*besitta*) possess; (*ha*) have; *allt vad jag -er och har* all I possess, all my worldly possessions; *han -er en förmögenhet* he is worth a fortune; *~ giltighet* be valid; *det -er sin riktighet* it is true (a fact); *~ rum* take place; *~ rätt att* have a (the) right to **2** *~ att a)* (*ha rättighet*) have a (the) right to, be entitled to, *b)* (*vara skyldig att*) have (be required) to **ägande|rätt** right of possession; ownership, proprietorship (*till* of); (*upphovsrätt*) copyright; *jur.* title (*till* to); *~en har övergått till* the right of possession has passed to **-rättsbevis** document of title **ägar|e** owner, proprietor; *övergå till ny ~* come under new ownership **-inna** owner, proprietress **ägg** *s7* egg; *biol.* ovum (*pl* ova); *det är som Columbi ~* (*ung.*) it's as plain as a pikestaff; *där har vi ~et* (*bildl.*) there is the crux of the matter **-bildning** ovulation **-cell** ovum (*pl* ova) **-formig** [-å-] *al* egg-shaped; *fack.* oviform **-gula** (*hopskr. äggula*) yolk; *en ~* (*vanl.*) the yolk of an egg **-kläckning** hatching, incubation **-kläckningsmaskin** [chicken, poultry] incubator **-kopp** egg cup **-ledare** *anat.* Fallopian tube; *zool.* oviduct **-lossning** ovulation **-läggning** egg-laying **-läggningsrör** ovipositor **-pulver** egg powder **-rund** oval **-röra** scrambled eggs (*pl*) **-sjuk** *gå omkring som en ~ höna* be wanting to get s.th. off one's chest **-skal** eggshell **-sked** egg spoon **-stanning** baked egg **-stock** ovary **-stocksinflammation** ovaritis **-toddy** eggnog **-vita 1** (*vitan i ägg*) egg white, white of [an] egg; *en ~* (*vanl.*) the white of an egg **2** (*ämne*) albumin; (*i ägg*) albumen, white of egg **3** (*sjukdom*) albuminuria, Bright's disease **-viteämne** protein; (*enkelt*) albumin **ägna** [ˣäŋna] **I** devote; *högt.* dedicate (*sitt liv åt* one's life to); (*skänka*) bestow (*omsorg åt* care on); *~ intresse åt* take an interest in; *~ en tanke åt ... give ... a thought; *~ sin tid åt* devote one's time to; *~ ngt sin uppmärksamhet* give one's attention to s.th. **II** *opers., som det ~r och anstår* as befits (becomes) **III** *rfl* **1** *~ sig åt* devote o.s. to (*att göra ngt* doing s.th.), *högt.* dedicate o.s. to, (*utöva*) follow (*ett yrke* a trade), pursue (*ett kall* a calling), (*slå sig på*) go in for, take up (*affärer* business) **2** (*lämpa sig*) *~ sig för* be suited (adapted) for (to), (*om sak äv.*) lend itself to **ägnad** [ˣäŋnad] *a5* suited, fitted; *inte ~ att inge förtroende* not calculated (likely) to inspire confidence; *~ att väcka farhågor* likely to cause alarm **ägo** *se äga I 1* **-delar** *pl* property (*sg*), belongings, possessions; *jordiska ~* worldly goods **ägor** *pl, se äga I 2* **äh** oh!, ah!; (*avvisande äv.*) pooh! **äkta** **I** *al* (*oböjligt a*) **1** genuine, real; (*autentisk*) authentic; (*om konstverk*) original; (*om färg*) fast; (*uppriktig*) sincere; (*sann*) true (*konstnär* artist); ~ *pärlor* real (genuine) pearls; ~ *silver* sterling (pure, real) silver **2** ~ *barn* legitimate child; ~ *hälft* (*vard.*) better half; ~ *maka* (*make*) [wedded (lawful)] wife (husband); ~ *par* married couple, husband and wife **II** *s, i uttr.: ta ngn till* ~, *se följ.* **III** *v1* wed, espouse

äktenskap *s7* marriage; *jur. äv.* wedlock, matrimony; *efter fem års* ~ after five years of married life; *barn i* (*utom*) ~*et* child born in (out of) wedlock; *ingå* ~ *med* marry; *ingå nytt* ~ marry again, remarry; *leva i ett lyckligt* ~ have a happy married life; *till* ~ *ledig* unmarried, on the marriage market **-lig** *a1* matrimonial; conjugal, marital; married (*samliv* life); ~ *börd* legitimate birth; ~*a rättigheter* marital rights

äktenskaps|anbud proposal (offer) of marriage **-annons** matrimonial advertisement **-betyg** certificate of marital (matrimonial) capacity **-brott** adultery **-brytare** adulterer **-bryterska** adulteress **-byrå** matrimonial agency **-förord** marriage settlement (articles *pl*) **-hinder** impediment to marriage **-löfte** promise of marriage; *brutet* ~ breach of promise **-mäklare** matrimonial agent, *vard.* matchmaker **-rådgivning** marriage guidance **-skillnad** divorce, dissolution of marriage **-tycke** *de har* ~ they are so well matched **-ålder** marrying age

äkt|het (*jfr äkta I 1*) genuineness, reality; authenticity; originality; sincerity; (*färg-*) fastness; *bevisa* ~*en av* authenticate **-hetsbevis** proof of authenticity **-svensk** genuinely Swedish

äld|re ['äll-] *a, komp. t. gammal* older (*än* than); (*om släktskapsförh.*) elder; (*i tjänst*) senior (*än* to); (*tidigare*) earlier; (*ganska gammal*) elderly; ~ *järnåldern* the early Iron Age; ~ *människor* old (elderly) people; ~ *årgång* (*av tidskrift e.d.*) old (back) volume; *av* ~ *datum* of an earlier date; *i* ~ *tider* in older (more ancient) times; *de som är* ~ *än jag* my elders (seniors), those older than myself; *herr A. den* ~ Mr. A. Senior; *Dumas den* ~ Dumas the elder; *Pitt den* ~ the elder Pitt **-omsorg** old-age care

äldst [*vard.* älst] *a, superl. t. gammal* oldest; (*om släktskapsförh.*) eldest; (*av två äv.*) older (elder); (*i tjänst*) senior; (*tidigast*) earliest; *de* ~*a* (*i församling e.d.*) the Elders; *den* ~*e* (*i kår e.d.*) the doyen

älg [älj] *s2* elk; *AE.* moose **-antilop** eland **-gräs** *bot.* meadowsweet **-jakt** (*jagande*) elk-hunting; (*jaktparti*) elk-hunt; *vara på* ~ be out elk-hunting **-kalv** elk calf **-ko** cow (female) elk **-stek** roast elk **-tjur** bull (male) elk **-ört** *se* **-gräs**

älsk|a love; (*tycka mycket om*) like, be [very] fond of **-ad** *a5* beloved; (*predik. äv.*) loved; ~*e Tom!* Tom darling!, (*i brev*) my dear Tom; *min* ~*e* my beloved (darling) **-ande** *a4* loving (*par* couple); *de* ~ the lovers

älskar|e lover; *förste* ~ (*teat.*) juvenile lead; *inte vara ngn* ~ *av* not be fond of **-inna** mistress **-roll** *teat.* [part of the] juvenile lead

älsklig *a1* charming, sweet, lovable **-het** charm, sweetness, lovable character

älskling darling; (*i tilltal äv.*) love; *AE.* honey; (*käresta*) sweetheart

älsklings|barn favourite child **-elev** favourite (pet) pupil **-rätt** favourite dish

älsk|og *s2* love **-ogskrank** *a1* lovesick **älskvärd** amiable, kind **-het** amiability, kindness

älta knead (*deg* dough); work (*smör* butter); *bildl.* go over again and again; ~ *samma sak* go harping on the same string

ältranunkel *bot.* lesser spearwort

älv *s2* river

älv|a *s1* fairy, elf (*pl* elves); *poet.* fay **-[a]drottning** fairy queen; ~*en* (*äv.*) Queen Mab **-[a]kung** fairy king **-dans** fairy dance **-lik** fairylike

älvmynning mouth of a (the) river, river mouth **ämabel** [-'ma:-] *a2, se älskvärd*

ämbar *s7* pail, bucket

ämbete *s6* office; *bekläda* (*inneha*) *ett* ~ hold an office; *i kraft av sitt* ~, [*p*]*å* ~*ts vägnar* by (in) virtue of one's office, in one's official capacity, ex officio

ämbets|ansvar official responsibility **-broder** colleague **-brott** malpractice, misconduct [in office] **-byggnad** government office [building] **-dräkt** official dress, uniform **-ed** oath of office; *avlägga* ~*en* be sworn in **-examen** *filosofisk* ~ Master of Arts (*förk.* M.A.), Bachelor of Education (*förk.* B.Ed.); *avlägga filosofisk* ~ pass (take) one's Master's degree **-förrättning** official function **-man** official, public (Government) officer; (*i statens tjänst äv.*) civil servant

ämbetsmanna|bana official (civil service) career **-delegation** delegation of officials **-kår** body of civil servants; officials (*pl*), official class **-välde** bureaucracy

ämbets|plikt official duty **-rum** office **-tid** period of office; *under sin* ~ while in office **-verk** government office, civil service department

ämna intend (mean, plan, *AE.* aim) to; *jag* ~*de just* I was just going to; ~ *sig hem* (*ut*) intend to go home (out); *vart* ~*r du dig?* where are you going (you off to)?

ämne *s6* **1** (*material*) material; (*för bearbetning*) blank; (*arbetsstycke*) workpiece; *han har* ~ *i sig till en stor konstnär* he has the makings of a great artist **2** (*materia*) matter, substance, stuff; *fasta* ~*n* solids; *flytande* ~*n* liquids; *enkla* ~*n* elements; *sammansatta* ~*n* compounds; *organiskt* ~ organic matter **3** (*tema, samtals-, skol- etc.*) subject; matter; theme; (*samtals- äv.*) topic; *frivilligt* ~ (*skol.*) optional (*AE.* elective) subject; *obligatoriskt* ~ (*skol.*) compulsory subject; ~*t för romanen* the subject for the novel; *litteraturen i* ~*t* the literature on this subject; *byta* ~ change the subject; *hålla sig till* ~*t* keep to the subject (point); *komma till* ~*t* come to the point; ~ *till betraktelse* food for thought

ämnes|grupp group of subjects, subject group **-kombination** combination of subjects **-konferens** *skol.* staff meeting of teachers of the same subject **-lärare** teacher of a special subject **-namn** material noun **-område** subject field **-omsättning** metabolism; *fel på* ~*en* metabolic disturbance **-val** choice of subject

än [änn] **I** *adv* **1** *se ännu* **2** *hur gärna jag* ~ *ville* however much I should like to; *när* (*var*) *jag* ~ whenever (wherever) I, no matter when (where) I; *om* ~ *aldrig så litet* however small [it may be], no matter how small; *vad som* ~ *må hända* whatever happens; *vem han* ~ *må vara* whoever he may be **3** ~ ... ~ now ..., now, sometimes ..., sometimes; ~ *si* ~ *så* now this way, now that; ~ *huttra,* ~ *svettas* shiver and sweat by turns **4** ~ *sen då?* well, what of it?, *vard.* so what? **II** *konj* **1** (*i jämförelser*) than; *mindre* ~ smaller than; *inte mindre* ~ no less than; *ingen mindre* ~ no less a person than **2** *ingen annan* ~ no other than (*kungen* the king), no one but; *inget annat* ~ nothing else but; *han är allt annat* ~ *dum* he is anything but stupid

1 ända I *s5* **1** (*äv. ände*) end; (*yttersta del äv.*) extremity; (*spetsig*) tip; *nedre* (*övre*) ~*n av* the bottom (top) of; *världens* ~ the ends (*pl*) of the world; *allting har en* ~ there is an end to everything; *det är ingen* ~ *på* there is no end to; *ta en* ~ *med förskräckelse* come to a sad end; *börja i galen* ~ start at the wrong end; *stå på* ~ stand on end, (*om hår äv.*) bristle; *gå till* ~ come to an end, expire; *falla över* ~ tumble (topple) over **2** *vard.* (*stuss*) behind, bottom, posterior, rear; *en spark i* ~*n* a kick on the behind (in the pants); *sätta sig på* ~*n* (*ramla*) fall on one's behind **3** (*stump*) bit, piece; *sjö.* [bit of] rope **4** *dagen i* ~ all day long **5** (*syfte*) *till den* ~*n* to that end **II** *v1* end

2 ända *adv* right (*till* to; *hit* here); (*hela vägen*) all the way (*hem* home); ~ *fram till* right up to; ~ *från början* right from the beginning; ~ *från 1500-talet* ever since the sixteenth century; ~ *från Indien* all the way from India; ~ *in i minsta detalj* down to the very last detail; ~ *in i det sista* down (up) to the very end; ~ *till slutet* to the very end; ~ *till påsk* right up to Easter; ~ *till midnatt* [all the time] till (until) midnight; ~ *till kyrkan* as far as (all the way to) the church; ~ *till nu* until (till, [right] up to) now, (*t. våra dagar*) down to the present time

ändalykt *s3* **1** (*slut*) en sorglig ~ a tragic end **2** (*stuss*) posterior

ändamål *s7* purpose; end; (*syfte äv.*) object; (*avsikt*) aim; ~*et med* the purpose of; ~*et helgar medlen* the end justifies the means; *för detta* ~ for this purpose, to this end; *det fyller sitt* ~ it is suited to (serves) its purpose; *ha ngt till* ~ have s.th. as an end; *välgörande* ~ charitable (charity, welfare) purposes

ändamåls|enlig [-e:-] *a1* [well] adapted (suited) to its purpose, suitable; (*lämplig*) appropriate; (*praktisk*) practical; *vara mycket* ~ be very much to the purpose **-enlighet** [-e:n-] fitness, practicality, expediency **-lös** purposeless; aimless; (*gagnlös*) useless

ändas *dep* end, terminate (*på* in, with)

ände *s2, se I ända I 1*

änd|else ending **-hållplats** bus (tram) terminus **-lig** *a1* finite **-lös** endless; (*som aldrig tar slut äv.*) interminable; *mat.* infinite **-morän** end (terminal) moraine

ändock yet, still, nevertheless, for all that

ändpunkt terminal point, end

ändr|a 1 alter; (*byta*) change, shift; (*rätta*) correct; (*förbättra*) amend; (*modifiera*) modify; (*revidera*) revise; ~ *en klänning* alter a dress; ~ *mening* change one's opinion (mind) (*om* about); *inte* ~ *en min* (*vanl.*) not move a muscle; *det* ~*r*

inte mitt beslut it does not alter my decision; *det* ~*r ingenting i sak* it makes no difference in substance; *domen* ~*des till böter* the sentence was commuted into a fine; *paragraf 6 skall* ~*s* paragraph 6 shall be amended; *obs* ~*d tid!* note the alteration of time!; ~ *om* alter; ~ *om ngt till* change (transform) s.th. into; ~ *på* alter, change **2** *rfl* alter, change; (*rätta sig*) correct o.s.; (*fatta annat beslut*) change one's mind; (*byta åsikt äv.*) change one's opinion **-ing** alteration (*äv. av klädesplagg*); change; correction; amendment; *tekn. e.d.* modification; *en* ~ *till det bättre* a change for the better; *en obetydlig* ~ a slight modification **-ingsförslag** proposed alteration (amendment)

änd|station terminus (*pl äv.* termini), terminal [station] **-tarm** rectum **-tarmsöppning** anus, anal orifice

ändå [ˣänn-, -ˈdå:] **1** (*likväl*) yet, still; (*icke desto mindre*) nevertheless; (*i alla fall*) all the same; *det är* ~ *något* it's something, anyway; *om han* ~ *kunde komma!* if only (I do wish) he could come! **2** (*ännu*) still, even (*mer* more)

äng *s2* meadow; *poet.* mead

ängd *s3, se trakt*

ängel *s2* angel; *det gick en* ~ *genom rummet* there was a sudden hush in the room; *han kom som en räddande* ~ he came like an angel to the rescue

ängla|lik angelic[al]; *hon har ett* ~*t tålamod* she has the patience of an angel (of Job) **-makerska** baby-farmer **-skara** angelic host **-vakt** guardian angel **-vinge** wing of an angel

ängs|blomma meadow flower **-kavle** [-a:-] *s2, bot.* foxtail

ängsl|a alarm, cause alarm, make anxious **-an** *r* anxiety; (*oro*) alarm, uneasiness; (*starkare*) apprehension, fright **-as** *dep* be (feel) anxious (*för, över* about); (*oroa sig*) worry (*för* about) **-ig** *a1* (*rädd*) anxious, uneasy (*för* about); ~ *av sig* timid, timorous; *var inte* ~*!* don't worry (be afraid)!; *jag är* ~ *för att ngt kan ha hänt* I am afraid (fear) s.th. may have happened **2** (*ytterst noggrann*) scrupulous; *med* ~ *noggrannhet* with [over]scrupulousness

ängs|mark meadow land **-syra** sorrel **-ull** [common] cotton grass

änka *s1* widow; (*änkenåd*) dowager; *vara* ~ *efter* be [the] widow of; *hon blev tidigt* ~ she was early left a widow

änke|drottning queen dowager; (*regerande monarks mor*) queen mother **-fru** widow; ~ *A.* Mrs. A.[, widow of the late Mr. A.] **-man** widower **-nåd** *s3* dowager — **och pupillkassa** widows' and orphans' fund **-pension** widow's pension **-stånd** widowhood **-stöt** knock on the funny (*AE.* crazy) bone **-säte** dowager's residence

änkling widower

ännu [ˣännu, -ˈnu:] **1** (*fortfarande*) still; (*om ngt som ej inträffat*) yet; (*hittills*) as yet, so far; *har de kommit* ~*?* have they come yet?; *inte* ~ not yet; *medan det* ~ *är tid* while there is still time, while the going is good; *det har* ~ *aldrig hänt* it has never happened so far; *det dröjer* ~ *länge innan* it will be a long time before; *det dröjde* ~ *så länge* so far, up to now, (*för närvarande*) for the present; ~ *när han var 80* even at the age of eighty; ~ *så sent som i* *går* only (as recently as, as late as) yesterday **2** (*ytterligare*) more; ~ *en* one more, yet (still) another; ~ *en gång* once more, (*återigen*) again; *det tar* ~ *en stund* it will take a while yet **3** (*vid komp.*) still, even (*bättre* better)

änterhake *sjö.* grapnel, grappling iron (hook)

äntligen at last; (*omsider äv.*) at length

äntr|a board (*ett fartyg* a ship); (*klättra*) climb (*uppför en lina* up a rope) **-ing** boarding; climbing

äppel|blom *koll.* apple-blossom[s *pl*] **-blomma** apple-blossom **-brännvin** apple brandy; *AE.* applejack **-kaka** apple cake **-kart** green apple[s *pl*] **-klyfta** slice of [an] apple **-kompott** stewed apples **-kärna** apple pip **-mos** mashed apples (*pl*), apple sauce **-must** apple juice **-paj** apple-pie **-skal** apple-peel **-skrott** [-å-] *s2* apple-core **-sort** brand of apple **-träd** apple tree **-vecklare** *zool.* codling moth **-vin** cider **-år** *ett gott* ~ a good year for apples

äpple *s6* apple; ~*t faller inte långt från trädet* he (she) is a chip of the old block; like father, like son

är *pres. av vara*

ära I *s1* honour; (*heder*) credit; (*berömmelse*) glory, reknown; ~ *vare Gud!* Glory be to God!; ~*ns fält* military exploits (*pl*), field of glory; *en* ~*ns knöl* a downright swine; *det är en stor* ~ *för oss att* it is a great honour for us to; *få* ~*n för* get the credit for; *får jag den* ~*n att* may I have the honour of (+ *ing- form*); *ge ngn* ~*n för* give s.b. the credit for, credit s.b. with; *det gick hans* ~ *för när* that wounded (piqued) his pride; *göra ngn den* ~*n att* do s.b. the honour (favour) of (+ *ing-form*); *ha* ~*n att* have the honour of (+ *ing-form*); *har den* ~*n* [*att gratulera!*] congratulations!, (*på födelsedag*) many happy returns [of the day]!, happy birthday!; *sätta en* (*sin*) ~ *i att* make a point of (+ *ing-form*); *vinna* ~ gain honour (credit); *bortom all* ~ *och redlighet* miles from anywhere (civilization); *... i all* ~ with all deference (respect) to ...; *göra ngt med den* ~*n* do s.th. with credit; *på min* ~! upon my honour!; *dagen till* ~ in honour of the day; *till ngns* ~ in a p.'s honour; *till Guds* ~ for the glory of God **II** *v1* honour; (*vörda*) respect, revere, venerate; ~*s den som* ~*s bör* honour where (to whom) honour is due

ärad *a5* honoured; (*om kund e.d.*) esteemed; *Ert* ~*e* [*brev*] your letter, *åld.* your favour (esteemed letter)

ärbar [ˣä:r-] *a1* decent, modest **-het** decency, modesty; *i all* ~ in all decency

äre|betygelse *se hedersbetygelse* **-girig** ambitious; aspiring **-girighet** ambition[s *pl*]; aspiration[s *pl*] **-kränka** defame **-kränkande** *a4* defamatory; (*i skrift*) libellous **-kränkning** defamation; (*skriftlig*) libel **-lysten** *se -girig* **-lystnad** *se -girighet* **-lös** infamous **-minne** memorial (*över* to, in honour of)

ärende *s6* **1** (*uträttning*) errand; (*uppdrag*) commission; (*besked*) message; *framföra sitt* ~ state one's errand, give one's message; *får jag fråga vad ert* ~ *är?* what brings you here, if I may ask?; *gå* ~*n* go [on] errands, be an errand boy (girl) (*åt* for); *gå ngns* ~*n* (*bildl.*) run a p.'s errands; *göra*

sig ett ~ *till* find an excuse for going to; *boken har ett* ~ the book has a message; *ha ett* ~ *i* (*till*) *stan* have business in town; *ha ett* ~ *till ngn* have to see s.b. about; *i lovliga* ~*n* on lawful business (errands); *med oförrättat* ~ without having achieved one's object **2** (*angelägenhet*) matter; *löpande* ~*n* [the] usual routine, current matters; *utrikes* ~*n* foreign affairs; *handlägga ett* ~ deal with (handle) a matter

ärenpris *s3, bot.* [common] speedwell

äre|port triumphal arch **-rörig** *a1* slanderous, defamatory, calumnious **-varv** *sport.* lap of honour **-vördig** venerable

ärftlig *a1* hereditary (*anlag* disposition); (*om titel e.d.*) inheritable; *det är* ~*t* (*vanl.*) it runs in the family **-het** heredity; (*sjukdoms e.d.*) hereditariness

ärftlighets|forskare geneticist **-forskning** genetics (*pl, behandlas som sg*), genetic research **-lära** genetics (*pl, behandlas som sg*), science of heredity

ärftligt *adv* hereditarily; by inheritance; *vara* ~ *belastad* have a hereditary taint

ärg [-j] *s3* verdigris; patina **ärga** (*bli -ig*, ~ *sig*) become coated with verdigris; ~ *av sig* give off verdigris **-grön** verdigris green **-ig** *a1* verdigrised; *konst.* patinated

ärke|biskop archbishop **-biskopinna** archbishop's wife **-biskoplig** archiepiscopal **-biskopsdöme** *s6* archdiocese, archbishopric, archbishop's diocese **-bov** archvillain, unmitigated scoundrel **-fiende** archenemy **-hertig** archduke **-hertigdöme** archduchy **-nöt** nitwit, utter fool **-reaktionär** archreactionary; *en* ~ (*äv.*) a die-hard **-skälm** archrogue **-stift** *se -biskopsdöme* **-säte** archiepiscopal see **-ängel** archangel

ärla [ˣä:r-] *s1* wagtail

ärlig [ˣä:r-] *a1* honest; (*hederlig*) honourable (*avsikt* intention); (*rättfram*) straightforward; (*uppriktig*) sincere; *vard.* straight, on the level; ~*t spel* fair play; *om jag skall vara helt* ~ to be quite honest, honestly; *säga sin* ~*a mening* give one's honest opinion **-en** honestly *etc.*; *det har du* ~ *förtjänat* you have fairly earned it, that is no more than your due; ~ *förtjäna sitt uppehälle* make an honest living **-het** honesty, straightforwardness; ~ *varar längst* honesty is the best policy; *i* ~*ens namn måste jag* to be quite honest I must

ärligt [ˣä:r-] *adv, se -en*; ~ *talat* to be quite honest with you

ärm *s2* sleeve **-bräda** sleeve board **-hål** armhole **-hållare** armband; *AE.* arm (sleeve) garter **-lin-ning** wristband **-lös** sleeveless

ärna [ˣä:r-] *se ämna*

äro|full glorious; honourable (*återtåg* retreat) **-rik** (*-full*) glorious; (*som förvärvat stor ära*) illustrious (*krigare* warrior)

ärr *s7* scar; *fack.* cicatrice **ärra** *rfl*, **ärras** *dep* scar; *fack.* cicatrize

ärr|bildning scar formation; *fack.* cicatrization **-ig** *a1* scarred; (*kopp-*) pockmarked

ärt *s3*, **ärta** *s1* pea

ärt|balja, **-skida** pea pod; (*tom*) pea shell **-soppa** pea soup **-törne** *bot.* gorse **-växt** leguminous plant

ärva *v2* [*få*] ~ inherit (*av, efter* from); ~ *ngn* be a

p.'s heir; ~ *en tron* succeed to a throne; *jag har fått* ~ I have come into money **ärvd** *a5* inherited; (*medfödd*) hereditary **ärvdabalk** laws (*pl*) of inheritance, inheritance code

äsch ah!, oh!; (*besviket*) dash it!; ~, *det gör ingenting!* oh, never mind!, oh, it doesn't matter!

äsk|a demand, ask for; ~ *tystnad* call for silence **-ande** *s6* demand, claim, request

äsping (*orm*) [young female] viper

äss *s7* ace

ässja [ˣäʃa] *s1* forge

ät|a *åt -it* **1** eat; (*frukost etc.*) have; *har du -it ännu?* have you had [your] dinner (*etc.*) yet?; *vi sitter och -er* we are at (are having [our]) dinner (*etc.*); ~ *frukost* have breakfast; ~ *middag* have dinner, dine; ~ *gott* get good food; *tycka om att* ~ *gott* be fond of good food; ~ *litet* (*mycket*) be a poor (big) eater; ~ *på ngt* eat (munch) s.th.; ~ *ngn ur huset* eat s.b. out of house and home **2** *rfl*, ~ *sig mätt* have enough to eat; ~ *sig sjuk* eat o.s. sick; ~ (*nöta*) *sig igenom* wear its way through; ~ *sig in i* (*om djur*) eat into **3** (*med betonad partikel*) ~ *upp* eat [up], consume; *jag har -it upp* I have finished [my food]; *det skall du få* ~ *upp!* (*bildl.*) you'll have that back [with interest]!; ~ *upp sig* put on weight, fatten [up]; ~ *ut ngn* (*bildl.*) cut s.b. out

ät|bar [ˣä:t-] *a1* eatable (*mat* food) **-it** *sup. av äta* **-lig** [ˣä:t-] *a1* edible (*svamp* mushroom)

ätt *s3* family; (*furstlig*) dynasty; *den siste av sin* ~ the last of his (*etc.*) line; ~*en utslocknade år* the family died out in **ättartavla** genealogy, genealogical table

ätte|fader [first] ancestor **-hög** barrow **-lägg** *s2* scion

ättestupa *s1, ung.* [suicidal] precipice

ättika *s1* vinegar; *kem.* acetum; *lägga in i* ~ pickle

ättiksgurka pickled cucumber, gherkin

ättik|sprit vinegar essence **-sur** [as] sour as vinegar; *bildl.* vinegary **-syra** acetic acid

ättling descendant, offspring

även also, ... too; (*likaledes*) ... as well; (*till och med*) even (*om* if, though); *icke blott ... utan* ~ not only ... but also **-ledes** also, likewise **-som** as well as **-så** also, likewise

äventyr *s7* **1** adventure; (*missöde*) misadventure **2** (*vågstycke*) hazardous venture (enterprise) **3** *jur., vid* ~ *att* at the risk of; *vid* ~ *av böter* on pain (under penalty) of fines (a fine) **4** *till* ~*s* perchance, peradventure

äventyr|a risk, hazard, jeopardize; imperil, endanger **-are** adventurer **-erska** adventuress **-lig** [-y:-] *a1* adventurous; (*riskabel*) venturesome, risky, hazardous **-lighet** [-y:-] adventurousness *etc.*

äventyrs|lust love of adventure **-lysten** adventure-loving, fond of adventure **-roman** adventure story, story of adventure; romance

ävlan [ˣä:v-] *r* striving[s *pl*] **ävlas** *dep* strive (*efter* for, after)

ö *s2* island; (*i vissa geogr. namn*) isle; *bo på en* ~ live on (*om stor ö:* in) an island

ÖB [ˣö:be:] *förk. för överbefälhavaren*

öbo *s5* islander

öda *v2,* ~ [*bort*] waste

1 öde *s6* fate; (*bestämmelse*) destiny; ~*t* Fate; Destiny; ~*n* destinies, (*levnads-*) fortunes; *skiftande* ~*n* changing fortunes, vicissitudes [of fortune]; *ett sorgligt* ~ a tragic fate; ~*ts skickelse* the decree of fate, Fate; *efter många* ~*n och äventyr* after many adventures; *hans* ~ *är beseglat* his fate is sealed; *dela ngns* ~ share a p.'s fate (lot); *finna sig i sitt* ~ submit (resign o.s.) to one's fate; *förena sina* ~*n med ngn* cast in one's lot with s.b.

2 öde *oböjligt a* desert, waste; (*övergiven*) deserted; (*enslig*) lonely; (*ödslig*) desolate; (*obebodd*) uninhabited; *ligga* ~ *a*) (*folktom*) be deserted, *b*) (*om åkerjord*) lie waste

öde|bygd depopulated (deserted) area **-gård** deserted (derelict) farm **-kyrka** abandoned church **-lägga** lay waste; (*skövla*) ravage, devastate; (*förstöra*) ruin, destroy **-läggelse** (*-läggning*) laying waste; (*om resultatet*) devastation, ruin, destruction

ödem *s7, med.* oedema (*pl* oedemata)

ödemark waste, desert; (*vildmark*) wilderness; (*obygd*) wilds (*pl*), *AE.* backwoods (*pl*)

ödes|bestämd fated **-diger** (*skickelsediger*) fateful; (*avgörande äv.*) decisive; (*olycksbringande*) fatal, disastrous, ill-fated **-gudinnor** *pl* Fates **-mättad** fateful, fatal **-timma** fateful (fatal) hour, hour of destiny

ödla [ˣö:d-] *s1* lizard; (*vatten-*) newt, eft

öd|mjuk [ˣö:d-] *a1* humble; (*undergiven*) submissive **-mjuka** *rfl* humble o.s. (*inför* before) **-mjukhet** humility, humbleness; submission; *i all* ~ in all humility

ödsla [ˣö:d-, ˣödd-] ~ [*med*] be wasteful with (of); ~ *bort* waste, squander

ödslig [ˣö:d-, ˣödd-] *a1* desolate, deserted; (*dyster*) dreary **-het** desolateness *etc.*; desolation

ödsligt *adv, ligga* ~ be lonely; *en* ~ *belägen* a desolate

öfolk (*öbor*) islanders (*pl*); (*nation*) insular nation

ög|a *-at -on* **1** eye; ~ *för* ~ an eye for an eye; *stå* ~ *mot* ~ stand face to face with; *anstränga -onen* strain one's eyes; *falla i -onen* catch (strike) the eye; *få ett blått* ~ get a black eye; *göra stora -on* open one's eyes wide, stare; *ha -onen med sig* keep one's eyes open, be observant; *inte ha -on för ngn annan än* have eyes for nobody but; *ha ett gott* ~ *till* have one's eyes on; *jag har ljuset i -onen* the light is in my eyes; *ha ngt för -onen* keep s.th. before one['s sight]; *ha svaga -on* have a poor eyesight; *hålla ett* ~ *på* keep an eye on; *i mina* (*folks*) *-on* in my (people's) eyes (opinion); *inför* *allas -on* in sight (before the eyes) of everybody; *finna nåd inför ngns -on* find favour with s.b.; *kasta ett ~ på* have a look at, glance at; *med blotta ~t* with the naked eye; *mellan fyra -on* in private, privately; *samtal mellan fyra -on* private talk, tête-à-tête; *mitt för -onen på* before the very eyes of, in full view of; *det var nära ~t* that was a narrow escape (close shave); *jag ser dåligt på vänstra (högra) ~t* the sight is poor in my left (right) eye; *se ngn rakt i -onen* look s.b. straight in the face; *skämmas -onen ur sig* be thoroughly ashamed of o.s.; *slå ner -onen* cast down one's eyes; *så långt ~t når* as far as the eye can reach **2** *(på tärning)* pip **3** *(på potatis)* eye

ögla [ˣöːg-, ˣögg-] *s1* loop, eye; *göra en ~ på* loop

ögna [ˣöŋna] *~ i* have a glance (look) at, glance at; *~ igenom* glance through, scan

ögon|blick *s7* moment; instant; *ett ~!* one moment, please!, just a moment (minute)!; *ett ~s verk* the work of a moment (an instant); *ett obevakat ~* an unguarded moment; *har du tid ett ~?* can you spare [me] a moment?; *det tror jag inte ett ~* I don't believe that for a moment; *för ~et* at the moment, at present, just now; *i nästa ~* [the] next moment; *i samma ~ jag såg det* the moment I saw it; *om ett ~* in a moment (an instant); *på ett ~* in a moment (an instant), in the twinkling of an eye **-blicklig** *a1* instantaneous; immediate, instant **-blickligen** instantly, immediately; *(genast)* at once **-blicksbild** snapshot

ögon|bryn eyebrow; *höja (rynka) ~en* raise (knit) one's eyebrows **-droppar** *pl* eye drops (lotion *sg*) **-frans** eyelash **-fröjd, -fägnad** feast for the eye, delightful sight **-färg** colour of the (one's) eyes **-glob** eyeball **-håla** eye socket, *fack.* orbit **-hår** eyelash **-inflammation** ophthalmia **-kast** glance; *vid första ~et* at first sight, at the first glance **-klinik** eye hospital (clinic) **-lock** eyelid **-läkare** eye specialist; ophthalmologist, oculist **-mått** *ha gott ~* have a sure eye; *efter ~* by [the] eye **-märke** sighting (aiming) point **-sikte** *förlora ur ~* lose sight of **-sjukdom** eye (ophthalmic) disease **-skenlig** [-ˈʃeːn-] *al* apparent; *(påtaglig)* [self-]evident; *(tydlig)* obvious **-skugga** eye shadow **-specialist** *se -läkare* **-sten** *bildl.*, *ngns ~* the apple of a p.'s eye **-tjänare** timeserver, fawner **-tröst** *bot.* eyebright **-vita** the white of the eye **-vittne** eyewitness **-vrå** corner of the (one's) eye

ögrupp group (cluster) of islands

ök *s7 (lastdjur)* beast of burden; *(dragdjur)* beast of draught; *(häst)* jade

öka 1 *(göra större)* increase *(med* by); *(ut-, till-)* add to; *(utvidga)* enlarge; *(förhöja)* enhance *(värdet av* the value of); *~ farten (äv.)* speed up, accelerate; *~ kapitalet med 1 miljon* add 1 million to the capital; *~ kraftigt* increase rapidly, undergo a rapid growth; *~ priset på* raise (increase, put up) the price of; *~ till det dubbla (tredubbla)* double (treble); *~ på* increase; *~ ut a)* *(dryga ut)* eke out, *b)* *(utvidga)* enlarge *(lokalerna* the premises), increase *(sitt vetande* one's knowledge) **2** *(tilltaga)* increase; *(om vind äv.)* rise; *~ i vikt* put on weight **ökad** *a5* increased *etc.*; *(ytterligare)* added; additional *(utgifter* expenditure *sg*); *ge ~ glans åt* lend additional lustre to **ökas**

dep se öka 2

öken [ˈöː-, ˈökk-] *s2* desert; *bibl.* wilderness; *öknens skepp (kamelen)* the ship of the desert **-artad** [-aːr-] *a5* desertlike **-folk** desert people **-kängor** desert boots **-område** desert region **-råtta** *mil. vard.* desert rat **-räv** fennec **-vandring** wandering[s *pl*] in the wilderness **-vind** desert wind; *(samum)* simoom, simoon

öklimat insular climate

öknamn nickname; *ge [ett] ~* nickname

ökning [ˣöːk-] increase *(i* of); addition; enlargement; enhancement; *~ av farten* acceleration of [the] speed

ökänd [ˣöːçänd] notorious

öl *s7* beer; *ljust ~* light beer, pale ale; *mörkt ~* dark beer, stout **-back** case of beer; *(tom)* beer case **-bryggeri** brewery **-burk** beer can **-butelj, -flaska** bottle of beer; *(tom)* beer bottle **-glas** beer glass; *(glas öl)* glass of beer **-kafé** beerhouse, public house, pub **-sejdel** beer mug; *(med lock)* tankard **-sinne** *ha gott (dåligt) ~* carry one's liquor well (badly) **-stuga** *åld.* alehouse; *AE. äv.* beer parlor **-utkörare** [brewer's] drayman **-öppnare** bottle (beer-can) opener

ölandstok shrubby cinquefoil

öm [ömm] *a1* **1** *(ömtålig)* tender, sore *(fötter* feet); *en ~ punkt (bildl.)* a tender spot, a sore point; *vara ~ i hela kroppen* be (feel) sore (aching) all over **2** *(kärleksfull)* tender, loving, fond; *~ omtanke* solicitude; *hysa ~ma känslor för ngn* have tender feelings for s.b. **-fotad** *a5*, *vara ~* have tender (sore) feet, be footsore **-het** *s1 (smärta)* tenderness, soreness **2** *(kärleksfullhet)* tenderness, [tender] affection, love **-hetsbehov** need for affection **-hetsbetygelse** proof (token) of affection, endearment **-hjärtad** [-j-] *a5* tenderhearted

ömk|a commiserate, pity; *~ sig över ngt* complain about s.th.; *~ sig över ngn* feel sorry for (pity) s.b. **-an** *r* compassion, pity **-ansvärd** [-äː-] *al* pitiable; *(stackars)* poor, wretched **-lig** *al* pitiful, miserable; deplorable, lamentable; *en ~ min* a piteous air; *en ~ syn* a pitiful (sad) sight; *ett ~t tillstånd* a piteous state

ömm|a 1 *(vara öm)* be tender (sore); *~ för tryck* ache at pressure **2** *(hysa medkänsla)* feel [compassion] *(för* for), sympathize *(för* with) **-ande** *a4 1 se öm 2 (ömkansvärd)* distressing *(omständigheter* circumstances); *i ~ fall* in deserving cases

ömsa change; *~ skinn (om orm äv.)* cast (slough) its skin

ömse *oböjligt a*, *på ~ håll (sidor)* on both sides (each side) **-sidig** *al* mutual, reciprocal; *~a anklagelser* cross accusations; *~t beroende* interdependence; *~t försäkringsbolag* mutual insurance company; *kontraktet gäller med 6 månaders ~ uppsägning* the contract is subject to 6 months' notice by either party; *till ~ belåtenhet* to our mutual satisfaction **-sidighet** reciprocity, mutuality **-vis** alternately; *(i tur o. ordning)* by turns

ömsint *a4* tender[hearted] **-het** tenderness of heart

ömsom [ˣömmsåm] *~ ... ~ ...* sometimes ..., sometimes ..., ... and ... alternately

ömtålig *al* **1** *(som lätt skadas)* damageable, easily damaged; (*om matvara*) perishable; (*om tyg*) flimsy; (*bräcklig*) frail, fragile **2** (*om hälsa*) delicate; (*känslig*) sensitive; (*mottaglig*) susceptible (*för* to) **3** (*lättsårad*) touchy; (*grannlaga*) delicate (*fråga* question) **-het** liability to damage; perishableness *etc.*; fragility; delicacy; sensitiveness; susceptibility; touchiness

önsk|a 1 wish; (*åstunda*) desire; (*vilja ha*) want; *jag ~r att han ville komma* I [do] wish he would come; *vad ~s?* (*i butik*) what can I do for you[, Madam (Sir)]?; *om så ~s* if desired, if you wish; *stryk det som ej ~s* delete as required; *lämna mycket övrigt att ~* leave a great deal to be desired; *~de upplysningar* information desired; *icke ~d* unwanted, undesirable **2** *rfl* wish for, desire; *~ sig ngt i julklapp* want (wish for) s.th. for Christmas; *~ sig bort* wish o.s. (wish one were) far away; *~ sig tillbaka till* wish one were back in **-an** *r, som pl används pl av* önskning wish, desire; *enligt ~* as desired, according to your (his *etc.*) wishes; *uttrycka en ~ att* express a wish to; *med ~ om* with best wishes for

önske|dröm [cherished] dream; pipe dream **-lista** want list; (*t. jul e.d.*) list of presents one would like **-mål** wish, desire; object desired, desideratum (*pl* desiderata); *ett länge närt ~* a long-felt want **-program** request programme **-tänkande** *s6* wishful thinking **-väder** ideal weather

önsk|ning *se* önskan **-värd** [-ä:-] *a1* desirable, to be desired; *icke ~* undesirable **-värdhet** [-ä:-] desirability, desirableness

öpp|en *a3* open; aboveboard; (*uppriktig*) frank, candid; (*mottaglig*) susceptible (*för* to); *~ båt* (*äv.*) undecked boat; *~ eld* open fire; *-et förvar* (*i bank*) safe custody; *-et köp* purchase on approval; *på -et köp* on a sale-or-return basis; *~ spis* fireplace; *frågan får stå ~* the matter must be left open; *platsen står ~ för hans räkning* the post is reserved for him; *vara ~, hålla -et* keep open; *för ~ ridå* with the curtain up, *bildl.* in public; *i ~ räkning* in open account; *i ~ sjö* on the open sea; *på -na fältet* in the open field; *vid (per) första (sista) - et vatten* at (per) first (last) open water (*förk.* f.o.w. *resp.* l.o.w.)

öppen|het openness; frankness, candour; sincerity; susceptibility **-hjärtig** [-j-] *a1* open-hearted, frank, unreserved **-hjärtighet** [-j-] open-heartedness

öppet *adv* openly *etc.*; *~ och ärligt* squarely and fairly; *förklara ~* declare freely; *ligga ~* have an exposed situation **-hållande** *s6* business (service, opening and closing) hours (*pl*)

öppn|a 1 open; (*låsa upp*) unlock; *~ för ngn* open the door for s.b., let s.b. in; *~ affär* open (start) a shop (business); *affären ~r (~s) kl. 9* the shop opens at nine [o'clock]; *~ kredit* open a credit; *~ vägen för* (*bildl.*) pave the way for; *~ ngns ögon för* open a p.'s eyes to; *vi såg dörren ~s* we saw the door open[ing]; *~!* open up!; *~s här* open here; *~s för trafik i mars* will be open to traffic in March; *dörren ~s utåt* the door opens outwards **2** *rfl* open; (*vidga sig*) open out **-ing 1** opening (*äv. i schack*); (*hål*) aperture, hole; (*mynning*) orifice; (*springa*) chink; (*för mynt*) slot; (*i mur e.d.*) gap, break; (*glänta*) glade, clearing **2** (*avföring*) motion, defecation

öppnings|anförande opening (introductory) address **-bud** opening bid **-ceremoni** opening ceremony, inauguration (ceremony)

ör|a *-at -on* **1** ear (*äv. bildl.*); *dra -onen åt sig* become wary, take alarm; *gå in genom ena ~t och ut genom det andra* go in at one ear and out at the other; *ha ~ för musik* have an ear for music; *få det hett om -onen* be in for it, get into hot water; *höra dåligt (vara döv) på ena ~t* hear badly with (be deaf in) one ear; *mycket skall man höra innan -onen faller av!* I've never heard such a thing!, well, I never!, what next!; *han ville inte höra på det ~t* (*bildl.*) he wouldn't listen at all; *vara idel ~* be all ears; *klia sig bakom ~t* scratch one's head; *det har kommit till mina -on* it has come to my ears; *som ett slag för ~t* like a [shattering] blow; *det susar (ringer) i -onen* my ears are buzzing (singing); *tala för döva -on* talk to deaf ears; *inte vara torr bakom -onen* be very green; *små grytor har också -on* little pitchers have long ears; *upp över -onen förälskad* head over heels in love **2** (*handtag*) handle; (*på tillbringare*) ear **-clips** *pl* ear clips

öre *s6* öre; *inte ha ett ~* not have [got] a penny, be penniless; *inte ett rött ~* not a bean; *inte värd ett rött (ruttet) ~* not worth a brass farthing; *inte för fem ~* not a bit; *räkna ut priset på ~t* work out the price to the last penny; *jag kan inte säga på ~t vad det kostar* I cannot tell you the exact price; *till sista ~t* to the last farthing

Öresund *n* the Sound

ör|fil [ˣö:r-] *s2* box on the ear **-fila** *~ [upp] ngn* box a p.'s ears, cuff s.b. **-hänge** (*smycke*) earring; (*långt*) eardrop; (*schlager*) hit

örike island state (country)

öring salmon trout

örlig [ˣö:r-] *s*, **örlog** [-å-] *s* [naval] war

örlogs|fartyg warship, man-of-war (*pl* men-of-war) **-flagg[a]** naval (man-of-war) flag **-flotta** navy, naval force **-hamn** naval port **-kapten** lieutenant commander **-man** man-of-war **-varv** naval dockyard (*AE.* shipyard)

örn [ö:rn] *s2* eagle **-blick** eagle eye **-bo** eyrie, aerie, eagle's nest **-bräken** *s2* bracken, brake

örngott [-å-] *s7* pillowcase, pillowslip

örn|näbb eagle's beak **-näsa** aquiline nose **-näste** *se* örnbo **-unge** eaglet, young eagle

öron|bedövande *a4* deafening **-clips** *se* örclips **-inflammation** inflammation of (in) the ear[s]; *med.* otitis **-lappsfåtölj** wing chair **-klinik** ear clinic **-läkare** ear specialist, aurist, otologist; *öron-, näs- och halsläkare* ear, nose and throat specialist, otorhinolaryngologist, *vard.* E.N.T. specialist **-lös** *en ~ kopp* a cup without a handle **-mussla** [ear] concha; (*hörpropp*) earphone **-märkning** earmarking **-propp** (*vaxpropp*) plug of wax; (*mot ljud*) earplugg **-sjukdom** disease of the ear, aural disease **-skydd** earflap; earmuff **-susning** singing (buzzing) in one's ears **-trumpet** auditory (Eustachian) tube

ör|snibb ear lobe, lobe of the ear **-språng** earache; *med.* otalgia

ört *s3* herb, plant; *~er* (*äv.*) herbaceous plants **örtagård** garden

örvax earwax; *fack.* cerumen

ös|a *v3* **1** scoop; (*sleva*) ladle (*upp* out); (*hälla*) pour; ~ *en båt* bale (bail) a boat; ~ *en stek* baste a joint; ~ *presenter över ngn* shower s.b. with gifts; ~ *på ngn arbete* overburden s.b. with work; ~ *ur sig otidigheter över* shower abuse on; ~ *ut pengar* throw one's money around, waste (squander) one's money **2** *det (regnet) -er ner* it is pouring down, *vard.* it is raining cats and dogs **-kar** bailer, dipper **-regn** pouring rain, downpour **-regna** pour

öst *r* east; *jfr nord*

Östafrika East Africa

östan *r*, **-vind** *s2* east[erly] wind

östasiatisk East Asiatic **Östasien** Eastern Asia

Östberlin East Berlin

östblocket the Eastern bloc

öster ['öss-] **I** *oböjligt s o. s9* the east; *Ö~n* the East (Orient) **II** *adv* [to the] east (*om* of) **-ifrån** from the east

Österlandet *n* the East (Orient) **öster|ländsk** *a5* oriental, eastern **-länning** Oriental

österrikare Austrian **Österrike** *n* Austria **österrikisk** *a5* Austrian

Östersjön the Baltic [Sea]

Östeuropa Eastern Europe **östeuropeisk** East European

öst|front ~*en* the Eastern front **-got** Ostrogoth **-gotisk** Ostrogothic **-kust** east coast

östlig *a1* easterly; east[ern]; *jfr nordlig* **östra** *best. a* the east; the eastern; *jfr norra*

östrogen [-'je:n] *s7, med.* [o]estrogen

östromersk *Ö~a riket* the Eastern Roman Empire; the Byzantine Empire

östron [-'å:n] *s7, med.* [o]estrone

öst|stat eastern state, East European state **-tysk** East German

Östtyskland East Germany; (*officiellt*) the German Democratic Republic, the GDR

öva 1 (*träna*) train (*ngn i ngt* s.b. in s.th.; *ngn i att* s.b. to); *mil.* drill, exercise; ~ *in* practise, (*roll e.d.*) rehearse; ~ *upp* train, exercise, (*utveckla*) develop; ~ *upp sig i engelska* brush up one's English **2** (*ut-*) exercise (*inflytande* influence); ~ *kritik* [*mot*] criticize; ~ *rättvisa* do justice; ~ *våld* use (make use of) violence **3** *rfl* practise; ~ *sig i att* practise (+ *ing*-form); ~ *sig i pianospelning* (*skjutning*) practise on the piano (with the rifle); ~ *sig i tålamod* learn to be patient **övad** *a5* practised; trained; (*erfaren*) experienced; (*skicklig*) skilled

över ['ö:-] **I** *prep* **1** over; (*högre än, ovanför*) above; (*tvärs-*) across; (*i tidsangivelse*) past, *AE. äv.* after; *bron* ~ *floden* the bridge across the river; *gå* ~ *gatan* walk across the street, *vanl.* cross the street; *bo* ~ *gården* live across the [court] yard; *500 meter* ~ *havet* 500 metres above sea level; ~ *hela kroppen* all over the body; ~ *hela landet* throughout (all over) the country; ~ *hela linjen* all along the line; ~ *hela vintern* throughout (all through) the winter; *tak* ~ *huvudet* a roof over one's head; *högt* ~ *våra huvuden* high above our heads; *bred* ~ *höfterna* broad across the hips; *höjd* ~ *alla misstankar* above (beyond) suspicion; *plötsligt var stormen* ~ *oss* suddenly the storm came upon us; *leva* ~ *sina tillgångar* live beyond one's means; *klockan är* [*fem*] ~ *sex* it is [five]

past (*AE. äv.* after) six; ~ *veckoslutet* over the weekend; *det är inte så* ~ *sig* (*inget vidare*) it's not all that good **2** (*via*) via, by [way of] **3** (*mer än*) over, more than, above; ~ *hälften* over (more than) half; *dra* [*tio minuter*] ~ *tiden* run over the time [by ten minutes] **4** (*uttr. makt, -höghet o.d.*) over; (*i fråga om rang*) above; *löjtnant är* ~ *sergeant* a lieutenant ranks (is) above a sergeant; *makt* ~ power over; *överlägsenhet* ~ supremacy to **5** (*uttr. genitivförh.*) of; (*om, angående*) [up]on; *essä* ~ essay on; *karta* ~ map of; *föreläsa* ~ lecture on **6** (*med anledning av*) at; of; *glad* (*förvånad*) ~ glad (surprised) at; *lycklig* ~ happy about; *rörd* ~ touched by; *undra* ~ wonder at **II** *adv* **1** over; above; across; *jfr över I; resa* ~ *till Finland* go over to Finland; *gå* ~ *till grannen* walk round (pop over) to the neighbour's; *arbeta* ~ work overtime; *50 pund och* ~ *på det* 50 pounds and more **2** (*kvar*) left, [left] over; *det som blir* ~ what is left, the remainder; *det blev pengar* ~ I have (he has *etc.*) some money left **3** (*slut*) over, at an end; (*förbi äv.*) past; *nu är sommaren* ~ summer is over now; *smärtan har gått* ~ the pain has passed

överaktiv [ˣö:-] hyperactive

överallt ['ö:-, -'allt] everywhere; *AE. vard.* every place; ~ *där* wherever; *han är smutsig* ~ he is dirty all over

över|ambitiös overambitious **-anstränga 1** overstrain, overexert (*hjärtat* one's heart); ~ *ekonomin* overstrain the economy **2** *rfl* overstrain o.s.; (*arbeta för mycket*) overwork o.s., work too hard **-ansträngd** overworked; (*rent fysiskt*) overstrained **-ansträngning** overwork; (*av hjärtat* of the (one's) heart) **-antvarda** [-a:r-] deliver up, entrust (*åt* to); ~ *ngn i rättvisans händer* deliver s.b. into the hands of justice **-arbeta 1** (*bearbeta för mycket*) overelaborate **2** (*omarbeta*) revise **-arm** upper arm; *anat.* brachium (*pl* brachia) **-armsben** humerus

över|balans *ta* ~*en* lose one's balance, overbalance, topple over **-balansera** ~*d budget* budget that shows a surplus **-befolkad** [-å-] *a5* overpopulated **-befolkning** overpopulation **-befäl** *abstr.* supreme command (*över* of); *konkr. koll.* [commissioned] officers (*pl*) **-befälhavare** commander in chief, supreme commander; ~*n* [the] supreme commander of the armed forces **-begåvad** hyperintelligent **-belasta** overload (*äv. elektr.*); *bildl.* overstrain, overtax **-belastning** overloading; *bildl.* overtaxing **-beskydda** overprotect **-beskyddande** overprotective **-betala** overpay **-betona** overemphasize, lay too much stress on **-bett** overbite **-betyg** honours (*pl*), mark above the pass standard **-bevisa** convict (*ngn om* s.b. of); (*-tyga*) convince (*ngn om* s.b. of) **-bevisning** conviction **-bibliotekarie** chief (head) librarian **-bjuda** outbid, overbid; *bildl.* [try to] outdo, rival; *de -bjöd varandra i artighet* they tried to outdo one another in courtesy

över|blick survey, general view (*över* of); *ta en* ~ *över* (*äv.*) survey **-blicka** survey; *bildl.* take in (*situationen* the situation); *följder som inte kan* ~*s* consequences that cannot be foreseen **-bli-**

Ö

ven *a5* remaining, left over; *komma på -blivna kartan* remain on the shelf **-boka** overbook **-bord** [-ɔ:-] *falla* (*spolas*) ~ fall (be washed) overboard; *man ~!* man overboard!; *kasta ~* (*äv.*) jettison **- bringa** deliver, convey; hand in **-bringare** bearer (*av ett budskap* of a message) **- brygga** *vl* bridge [over]; ~ *motsättningar* reconcile differences **-bud** higher bid, overbid **-byggnad** superstructure (*äv. bildl.*) **-bädd** upper bed (*i hytt e.d.* berth)

över|del top (*av plagg*), upper part **-dimensionera** oversize, overdimension; ~*d* (*äv.*) oversize[d] **-direktör** (*i statligt verk*) deputy director-general **-domare** (*i tennis*) referee **-dos, -dosera** overdose **-drag** cover[ing]; (*på möbel*) cover; (*på kudde*) [pillow]case; (*av fernissa e.d.*) coat[ing]; (*tids-*) running over the time **-dragning** (*av konto*) overdraft **-dragskläder** *pl* overalls, coveralls **-dramatisera** exaggerate; *sl.* pile on the agony

överdrift exaggeration; (*i tal äv.*) overstatement; (*ytterlighet*) excess; *gå till* ~ go too far, go to extremes, (*om pers. äv.*) carry things too far; *man kan utan* ~ *säga att* it is no exaggeration to say that

över|driva exaggerate, overstate; overact, overdo (*en roll* a part); (*gå för långt*) overdo it; *-driver du inte nu?* aren't you piling it on a bit? **-driven** *a5* exaggerated; excessive, exorbitant; *-drivet bruk av* excessive use of; *-drivet nit* overzealousness; *hon är så -driven* she overdoes it **-drivet** *adv* exaggeratedly *etc.*; ~ *noga* too careful, overcareful, overscrupulous; ~ *känslig* (*äv*) hypersensitive; ~ *sparsam* overeconomical, (*i småsaker*) cheeseparing, (*gnidig*) stingy, niggardly

över|dåd (*slösaktighet*) extravagance; (*lyx*) luxury; (*dumdristighet*) foolhardiness, rashness **-dådig** *al* **1** (*slösaktig*) extravagant; (*lyxig*) luxurious, sumptuous **2** (*utmärkt*) excellent, superb, first-rate **3** (*dumdristig*) foolhardy, rash **-dängare** past master (*i* in, at); *vara en* ~ *i* (*äv.*) be terrifically good at; *han är en* ~ *i skjutning* he is a crack shot

överens *vara* ~ be agreed (*om* on; *om att* that); *komma* ~ *om* agree (come to an agreement, *AE.* äv. get together) on (about); *komma* ~ *om att träffas* agree to meet, arrange a meeting; *komma bra* ~ *med ngn* get on well with s.b.; *de kommer bra* (*dåligt*) ~ they get on (don't get on) well [together] **-komma** [ˣö:-, -ˣens-] agree (*om* on, about); (*göra upp*) arrange, settle; *den -komna tiden* the time agreed [up]on (fixed); *som -kommet* as agreed **-kommelse** [-å-] agreement; arrangement; *enligt* ~ by (according to) agreement, as agreed [upon]; *gällande* ~*r* existing (current) agreements; *träffa en* ~ make (come to) an agreement, come to terms; *tyst* ~ tacit understanding, gentlemen's agreement **-stämma** [ˣö:-, -ˣens-] agree, be in accordance, accord; (*passa ihop äv.*) correspond, tally; *inte* ~ (*äv.*) disagree **-stämmelse** agreement; accord[ance]; conformity; (*motsvarighet*) correspondence; *bristande* ~ incongruity, discrepancy; *i* ~ *med* (*enligt*) in accordance (conformity) with, according to; *bringa* (*stå*) *i* ~ *med* bring into (be in) agreement (line)

with

över|exekutor chief executory authority (officer) **-exponera** overexpose **-exponering** overexposure **-fall, -falla** assault, attack; (*från bakhåll*) ambush **-fart** crossing; (*-resa äv.*) voyage, passage **-fettad** *a5* superfatted **-flyga** fly over **-flygla** [-y:-] *mil.* outflank; (*-träffa*) surpass, exceed; (*-lista*) outmanoeuvre, outdo **-flygning** flight over, overflight; (*vid flygparad*) fly-past **-flytta** move over (across); (*friare*) transfer **-flyttning** moving [over] *etc.*; transport; (*friare*) transfer

över|flöd *s7* (*ymnighet*) abundance, profusion, plenty (*av, på* of); (*materiellt*) affluence; (*övermått*) superfluity, superabundance; (*på arbetskraft, information*) redundance; (*lyx*) luxury; *ha* ~ *på, ha ... i* ~ have an abundance of, have ... in plenty, have plenty of; *finnas i* ~ be abundant **-flöda** abound (*av, på* in, with); ~*nde* abundant, profuse **-flödig** *al* superfluous; (*onödig äv.*) unnecessary; *känna sig* ~ feel unwanted (in the way) **-flödighet** superfluousness **-flödssamhälle** affluent society

över|full overfull, too full; (*om lokal e.d.*) overcrowded, crammed; ~ *sysselsättning* overfull employment, overemployment **-furir** (*vid armén*) sergeant, *AE.* staff sergeant; (*vid marinen*) petty officer, *AE.* petty oficer 1. class; (*vid flyget*) sergeant, *AE.* technical sergeant **-fyllnad** repletion; (*på marknaden*) glut **-färd** *se -fart* **-föra 1** *se föra* [*över*] **2** (*-flytta*) transfer, transmit; *bokför.* carry over (forward); ~ *blod* transfuse blood; ~ *smitta* transmit infection (contagion); *i -förd bemärkelse* in a figurative (transferred) sense **3** (*-sätta*) translate, turn (*till* into) **-förenkla** oversimplify **-förfinad** *a5* overrefined **-förfriskad** *a5* tipsy, intoxicated **-föring** transfer[ence] (*äv. tekn.*); conveyance, transport[ation] (*av trupper* of troops); (*av blod*) transfusion; (*av smitta*) transmission (*äv. radio.*); ~ *av pengar* transfer of money **-förmyndare** chief guardian **-förtjust** overjoyed, delighted

över|ge, -giva abandon; desert; (*lämna äv.*) leave; (*ge upp äv.*) give up; ~ *ett fartyg* abandon a ship; ~ *en plan* abandon (give up) a plan **-given** [-j-] *a5* abandoned *etc.*; *ensam och* ~ forlorn **-givenhet** [-j-] abandonment; forlornness **-glänsa** outshine, eclipse **-grepp** (*inkräktande*) encroachment (*mot* on); (*-våld*) outrage; ~ (*pl*) excesses (*mot* against) **-gripande** *a4* overarching

över|gå 1 *eg., se gå* [*över*] **2** (*-träffa*) [sur]pass (*ngns förväntningar* a p.'s expectations) **3** (*-stiga*) exceed, be beyond (above); *det ~r mitt förstånd* it is above my comprehension (beyond me) **4** (*drabba*) overtake, befall **5** (*-flyttas*) change hands, be transferred; *färger som* ~*r i varandra* colours that merge (melt) into each other; *sommaren -gick i höst* summer turned into autumn; ~ *till annat parti* go over to another party; ~ *till dagordningen* proceed (pass) to the business of the day; ~ *till katolicismen* embrace (be converted to) Catholicism, become a Catholic; ~ *till professionalism* turn professional; ~ *till annan verksamhet* pass on to other activities; *äganderätten har -gått till* the title has been transferred to

-gående *a4* passing; (*kortvarig äv.*) transient, transitory, of short duration; *av* ~ *natur* of a temporary (transitory) nature **-gång** *s2* **1** *abstr.* crossing (*över* of); (*omställning*) changeover; (*utveckling*) transition; (*mellantillstånd*) intermediate stage; (*omvändelse*) conversion; ~ *förbjuden!* do not cross! **2** (*-gångsställe*) (*vid järnväg e.d.*) crossing; (*fotgängar-, se övergångsställe*) **3** *se övergångsbiljett*; *ta* ~ *till tunnelbana* change to the underground

övergångs|bestämmelse provisional (transitional, temporary) regulation **-biljett** transfer [ticket] **-form** transitional (intermediate) form **-stadium** transitory (transition[al]) stage **-ställe** (*för fotgängare*) [pedestrian, zebra] crossing, *AE.* crosswalk **-summa** transfer fee **-tid** transition[al] period, period (time) of transition **-tillstånd** transition[al] state, state of transition **-ålder** (*klimakterium*) change of life, climacteric [age, period]; (*pubertet*) [years (*pl*) of] puberty

över|göda overfeed, surfeit **-gödsling** top dressing **-halning** [-a:-] **1** (*fartygs slingring*) lurch; *göra en* ~ (*äv. bildl.*) lurch **2** (*utskällning*) *ge ngn en* ~ give s.b. a good rating **-hand** *få* (*ta*) ~ get the upper hand (*över* of), prevail (*över* over), (*om tankar, växter e.d.*) be[come] rampant; *hungern tog ~en* hunger got the better of them (us *etc.*) **-handsknop** ~ *i åtta* figure eight knot **-het** ~*en* the authorities, the powers that be (*pl*) **-hetsperson** person in authority; (*ämbetsman*) public officer **-hetta** overheat, superheat **-hettning** overheating, superheating

över|hopa ~ *ngn med ngt* heap (shower) s.th. upon s.b., heap (shower) s.b. with; ~*d med arbete* overburdened with work; ~*d med skulder* loaded with debts, *vard.* up to one's neck in debt **-hoppad** [-å -] *a5, bli* ~ (*om text e.d.*) be omitted (left out), (*om pers.*) be passed over **-hovmästarinna** mistress of the robes **-hud** epidermis **-hus** *parl.* upper house (chamber); ~*et* the House of Lords (*Storbritannien*), the Senate (*AE.*)

överhuvud [ˣö:-] *s7, s6* head; (*ledare*) chief **över huvud** [-ˣhu:-] *adv* (*i jakande sats*) on the whole; (*i nekande, frågande, villkorlig sats*) at all; *det är* ~ [*taget*] *svårt att* on the whole it is difficult to; *han vet* ~ *taget ingenting* he knows nothing at all

över|hängande *a4* (*nära förestående, hotande*) impending; (*om fara äv.*) imminent; (*brådskande*) urgent; *det är ingen* ~ *fara* there is no immediate danger **-höghet** supremacy, sovereignty **-hölja** *bildl.*, ~ *ngn med ngt* heap s.th. upon s.b., heap s.b. with s.th. **-hövan** [-ˣhö:-] *se* [*över*] *hövan*

över|ila *rfl* be rash (hasty), act rashly; (*förgå sig*) lose one's head **-ilad** *a5* rash, hasty; *gör ingenting -ilat!* don't do anything rash! **-ilning** rashness, precipitation; *handla i* ~ act rashly **-ingenjör** chief engineer **-inseende** supervision **-isad** *a5* covered with ice, iced up **-jaget** *psykol.* the superego **-jordisk** (*himmelsk*) unearthly, celestial; (*eterisk*) ethereal, divine (*skönhet* beauty) **-jägmästare** chief forest officer

över|kant upper edge (side); *i* ~ (*bildl.*) rather

on the large (big, long *etc.*) side, too large (*etc.*) if anything **-kapacitet** surplus capacity **-kast** (*säng-*) bedspread, counterpane **-klaga** appeal against, lodge (enter) an appeal against; *beslutet kan ej* ~*s* the decision is final **-klagande** *s6* appeal (*av* against) **-klass** upper class; ~*en* the upper classes (*pl*) **-klasskvinna** upper-class woman **-klädd** covered; (*om möbel*) upholstered **-komlig** [-å-] *a1* surmountable (*hinder* obstacle); *till ~t pris* at a reasonable (moderate) price **-kommando** supreme (high) command **-kompensation** overcompensation **-konstapel** (*polis-*) [police] sergeant; (*kriminal-*) detective sergeant **-korsad** [-å-] *a5* crossed-out

över|kropp upper part of the body; *med naken* ~ stripped to the waist **-kucku** *s2, vard.* top dog **-kultiverad** overrefined **-kurs** *hand.* premium [rate]; *till* ~ at a premium **-kvalificerad** overqualified , too highly qualified **-käke** upper jaw; *anat.* maxilla **-käksben** upper jawbone; *anat.* maxillary [bone] **-känslig** hypersensitive, oversensitive; (*allergisk*) allergic (*för* to) **-känslighet** hypersensitiveness *etc.*; allergy (*för* to) **-körd** [-çö:rd] *a5, bli* ~ be (get) run over (knocked down)

överlag *adv* generally

över|lagd *a5* (*noga* well) considered; (*uppsåtlig*) premeditated; *-lagt mord* premeditated (wilful) murder, criminal homicide **-lakan** top sheet **-lappa** overlap **-lappning** overlapping **-lasta** overload, overburden; (*fartyg*) overfreight; ~ *minnet* overburden (encumber) one's memory; ~ (*berusa*) *sig* get intoxicated, intoxicate o.s. **-lastad** *a5* **1** (*berusad*) intoxicated, the worse for liquor **2** (*alltför utsmyckad*) overburdened with ornaments **-leva** survive; ~ *ngn* (*äv.*) outlive s.b.; ~ *sig själv* (*om sak*) outlive its day, become out of date; *det kommer han aldrig att* ~ he will never get over it, it will be the death of him **-levande** *a4* surviving; *de* ~ the survivors (*från* of) **-leverans** excess delivery **-levnad** survival **-liggare** *univ.* "perpetual student" **-lista** outwit; *han* ~*de mig* (*äv.*) he was too sharp for me **-ljudsbang** supersonic bang **-ljudshastighet** supersonic speed **-ljudsplan** supersonic aircraft (aeroplane)

överlopps [-å-] *i uttr.: till* ~ to spare **-energi** surplus energy **-gärning** *teol.* work of supererogation; *det vore en* ~ *att* it would be quite superfluous to

över|lupen *a5* **1** (*-vuxen*) overgrown (*med, av* with) **2** (*-hopad*) overburdened (*med arbete* with work); (*hemsökt*) overrun (*av besökare* with visitors); deluged (*av förfrågningar* with inquiries) **-lycklig** overjoyed **-låta 1** (*avhända sig*) transfer, make over (*ngt t. ngn* s.th. to s.b.); *jur. äv.* convey, assign; *biljetten får ej* ~*s* the ticket is not transferable **2** (*hänskjuta*) leave (*ngt i ngns hand* s.th. in a p.'s hands); *jag -låter åt dig att* I leave it to you to **-låtelse** transfer; *jur. äv.* conveyance, assignment **-låtelsehandling** deed (instrument) of conveyance (transfer, assignment) **-läge** *bildl.* advantage, superior position

över|lägga confer, deliberate (*om* on, about); ~ *om* (*äv.*) discuss **-läggning** deliberation; (*övervägande äv.*) consideration; (*diskussion äv.*) dis-

Ö

cussion **-lägsen** *a3* superior (*ngn* to s.b.); (*stor-artad*) excellent; (*högdragen*) supercilious; *han är mig ~ (äv.)* he is my superior; *~ seger* signal (easy) victory **-lägsenhet** superiority (*över* to); (*högdragenhet*) superciliousness **-lägset** *adv* in a superior manner; excellently; superciliously **-läkare** consultant; chief (senior, head) physician (*kirurg* surgeon)

överlämn|a 1 deliver [up, over]; (*framlämna*) hand over; (*skänka*) present, give; (*anförtro*) entrust, leave; (*uppge*) surrender (*ett fort* a fort); *~ ett meddelande* deliver a message; *~ blommor till ngn* present flowers to s.b., present s.b. with flowers; *~ i ngns vård* leave in a p.'s care, entrust to s.b.; *jag ~r åt dig att* I leave it to you to; *~d åt sig själv* left to o.s. **2** *rfl* surrender (*åt fienden* to the enemy); *~ sig åt sorgen* surrender [o.s.] (give way) to grief **-ande** *s6* delivery, handing over; presentation; surrender

över|läpp upper lip **-lärare** headmaster **-löpare** deserter; *polit.* defector, renegade

över|maga oböjligt *a* (*-modig*) presumptuous, overweening **-makt** (*i styrka*) superior force; (*i antal*) superior numbers (*pl*); *ha ~en* be superior in numbers (*över* over); *kämpa mot ~en* fight against odds; *vika för ~en* yield to superior force (numbers) **-man** superior; *finna sin ~* meet (find) one's match; *ej ha sin ~* have no superior; *vara ngns ~ (äv.)* be more than a match for s.b. **-manna** overpower **-mod** (*förmätenhet*) presumption, overweening confidence (pride); (*våghalsighet*) recklessness; *ungdomligt ~* youthful recklessness **-modig** (*förmäten*) presumptuous, overweening; (*våghalsig*) reckless **-mogen** over-ripe **-mognad** overripeness **-morgon** *i ~* the day after tomorrow **-mått** *bildl.* excess; (*-flöd äv.*) exuberance; *ett ~ av* an excess of; *till ~ to* excess **-måttan** [-ˣmått-] *adv* extremely, beyond measure; *roa sig ~* have no end of fun **-mäktig** superior (*fiende* enemy); *sorgen blev mig ~* I was overcome by grief; *smärtan blev honom ~* the pain became too much for him **-människa** superman **-mänsklig** superhuman **-mätt** surfeited, satiated (*på* with) **-mätta** surfeit, satiate; *kem.* supersaturate **-mättnad** surfeit; (*leda*) satiety **-mättning** *kem.* supersaturation

över|nationell supranational **-natta** stay the night, stay overnight; (*på hotell e.d. äv.*) spend the night **-nattning** *~ i Hamburg* stop overnight in Hamburg **-naturlig** supernatural **-nervös** very nervous, highly strung **-nog** more than enough; *nog och ~* enough and to spare **-ord** *pl* (*skryt*) boasting (*sg*); (*överdrift*) exaggeration (*sg*); *det är inga ~* that is no exaggeration **-ordna** *~ ngn över* place s.b. above **-ordnad** [-å:-] *a5* superior; *~ sats* principle clause; *~ ställning* responsible position; *han är min ~e* he is above me, he is my chief; *mina närmaste ~e* my immediate superiors

över|plats (*i hytt e.d.*) upper berth **-prestation** overachievement **-presterande** overachieving **-pris** excessive price; *betala ~ för ngt* be overcharged for s.th.; *sälja ngt till ~* overcharge for s.th.; sell s.th. at too high a price **-produktion** overproduction

överrask|a surprise; (*överrumpla äv.*) take by surprise; (*obehagligt*) startle; *~ ngn med att stjäla* catch (surprise) s.b. in the act of stealing; *~ ngn med en present* surprise s.b. with a gift, give s.b. a gift as a surprise; *glatt ~d* pleasantly surprised; *~d över* surprised at; *~d av regnet* caught in the rain **-ning** surprise; *glad ~* pleasant surprise; *det kom som en ~ för mig (äv.)* it took me by surprise; *till min stora ~ (äv.)* much to my surprise

över|rede (*av vagn e.d.*) body **-reklamerad** *a5* overrated **-resa** crossing, passage; voyage **-retad** *a5* overexcited; *i -retat tillstånd* in a state of overexcitement **-retning** overexcitation **-rock** overcoat; (*vinter-*) greatcoat **-rumpla** surprise, take unawares; *låta sig ~s* let o.s. be caught napping, be off one's guard **-rumpling** surprise **-rumplingstaktik** surprise tactics (*pl, behandlas som sg*) **-räcka** hand [over]; (*skänka*) present **-rösta 1** (*ropa högre än*) shout (cry) louder than; *larmet ~de dem* the din drowned their voices; *han ~de* he made himself (his voice was) heard above **2** (*i omröstning*) outvote

övers ['ö:-] *i uttr.: ha tid till ~* have spare time; *har du en tia till ~?* have you [got] ten kronor to spare?; *inte ha mycket (ngt) till ~ för* have no time for, not think much of

över|se *~ med ngt* overlook s.th.; *~ med ngn* excuse a p.'s behaviour **-seende I** *a4* indulgent (*mot* towards) **II** *s6* indulgence; *ha ~ med* be indulgent towards, make allowance[s] for; *jag ber om ~ med* I hope you will overlook **-sida** top [side], upper side **-siggiven** [-ˣji:-] in despair (*över, för* about, at) **-sikt** *s3* survey (*över, av* of); (*sammanfattning*) summary, synopsis (*över, av* of) **-siktlig** *a1, se* överskådlig **-siktskarta** key map **-sinnlig** supersensual; (*andlig*) spiritual **-sittare** bully; *spela ~* play the bully; *spela ~ mot ngn* bully (browbeat) s.b. **-sittaraktig** *a1* bullying **-sittarfasoner**, **-sitteri** bullying [manner]

över|skatta overrate, overestimate **-skattning** overrating, overestimation **-skeppa** ship across **-skjutande** [-ʃ-] *a4* **1** additional (*dag* day); surplus, excess (*belopp* amount); *~ skatt* surplus tax **2** (*framskjutande*) projecting (*klippa* rock) **-skott** surplus; excess; (*nettoförtjänst äv.*) profit **-skottslager** surplus stock **-skrida** cross (*gränsen* the frontier); *bildl.* exceed, overstep (*sina befogenheter* one's authority); *~ sitt konto* overdraw one's account; *~ sina tillgångar* exceed one's means **-skrift** heading; title **-skugga** overshadow (*äv. bildl.*); *det allt ~nde problemet* the all-pervading problem **-skyla** cover [up]; (*dölja*) disguise; (*släta över*) gloss over, palliate **-skådlig** [-å:-] *a1* (*klar, redig*) clear, lucid; (*-siktlig*) perspicuous; *inom en ~ framtid* in the foreseeable future **-skådlighet** [-å:-] clearness, lucidity; perspicuity **-sköljning** wash, washing **-sköterska** head nurse, sister

över|slag 1 (*förhandsberäkning*) [rough] estimate (calculation) (*över* of); *göra ett ~ över (äv.)* estimate, calculate ... [roughly] **2** (*volt*) somersault **3** *elektr.* flashover **-slagsberäkning** rough estimate **-snöad** *a5* covered with snow **-spel 1** *kortsp.* extra trick **2** *teat.* overacting **-spela** overact **-spelad** *det är -spelat nu* it's not relevant any longer, it's a thing of the past now **-spelning** [-e:l-] practising [on the piano *etc.*] **-spänd** (*hypernervös*) overstrung, highly strung, *AE.* high-strung; (*svärmisk*) romantic **-spänd-het** overstrung state; romanticism **-spänning** *elektr.* overvoltage

överst ['ö:-] *adv* uppermost, on top; ~ *på sidan* at the top of the page; *stå* ~ *på listan* head the list **översta** ['ö:-] *best. superl. a, [den]* ~ the top (*lådan* drawer); (*av två*) the upper; *den allra* ~ the topmost (*grenen* branch)

överstatlig supranational

överste ['ö:-] *s2* (*vid armén*) colonel; (*vid flyget*) group captain, *AE.* colonel; ~ *av 1.graden* (*vid armén*) brigadier, *AE.* brigadier general; (*vid flyget*) air commodore, *AE.* brigadier general **-löjt-nant** [-ˣlöjt-] (*vid armén*) lieutenant colonel; (*vid flyget*) wing commander, *AE.* lieutenant colonel **-präst** high priest

överstig|a *bildl.* exceed, be beyond (above); *ett pris ej* ~*nde* a price not exceeding; *det -er mina krafter* it is beyond my powers, it is too much for me

överstimulera overstimulate

överstinna colonel's wife; ~*n A.* Mrs. A.

över|strykning crossing-out, deletion **-strö** sprinkle, powder, dust **-stycke** top [piece, part] ; (*dörr-*) lintel **-styr** *i uttr.: gå* ~ (*om företag o.d.*) fail, go to rack and ruin, (*om plan e.d.*) come to nothing, (*välta*) topple over **-styrd** [-y:-] *a5, tekn.* oversteered; *radio.* overmodulated **-sty-relse** central (national) board **-styrning** *tekn.* oversteering; *radio.* overload, overmodulation **-stånden** *a5, vara* ~ be over (surmounted); *nu är det värsta -ståndet* the worst is over now; *ett -ståndet stadium* a thing of the past; *en* ~ *operation* a completed operation; *-ståndna faror* surmounted dangers **-ståthållare** governor [general] **-ståthållarämbetet** (*i Stockholm*) the office of the governor of Stockholm **-stämma** *mus.* upper part **-stämpla** overprint (*ett frimärke* a stamp) **-stökad** *a5* over [and done with] **-svallande** *a4* overflowing (*vänlighet* kindness); (*om pers.*) effusive, gushing; ~ *glädje* exuberant joy, rapture, excess of joy

över|svämma (*strömma ut över*) flood, inundate (*äv. bildl.*); *stora områden är* ~*de* large areas are flooded; ~ *marknaden* flood (glut) the market **-svämning** flood; (*-svämmande*) flooding, inundation **-syn** inspection, overhaul; *ge motorn en* ~ give the engine an overhaul, overhaul the engine **-synt** [-y:-] *a4* long-sighted; *fack.* hypermetropic **-synthet** [-y:-] long-sightedness; *fack.* hypermetropia **-sålla** strew, cover; ~*d med blommor* (*äv.*) starred with flowers **-sända** send; forward; (*pengar*) remit **-säng** upper bed **-sätta** translate (*från* from; *till* into); (*återge*) render; ~ *till engelska* (*äv.*) turn into English **-sättare** translator **-sättning** translation (*till* into); (*version*) version; (*återgivning*) rendering; *trogen* ~ true (faithful) translation; *i* ~ *av* translated by **-sättningsfel** mistranslation, translation error **-sättningsrätt** right of translation; translation rights (*pl*)

över|ta *se* övertaga **-tag** *bildl.* advantage (*över* over); *få* ~*et över* get the better of; *ha* ~*et* (*äv.*)

have the best of it **-taga** take over; ~ *ansvaret* take [over] the responsibility; ~ *ledningen av* take charge of, assume the management of; ~ *makten* come into power, take over (control) **-tagande** *s6* taking over **-tala** persuade; *vard.* get round; (*förmå äv.*) induce; ~ *ngn att* persuade s.b. to (*komma* come), coax s.b. into (*komma* coming); *låta* ~ *sig att* [let o.s.] be talked into, be persuaded into (*komma* coming) **-talig** *al* supernumerary **-talning** [-a:-] persuasion; *efter många* ~*ar* after much persuasion **-talningsför-måga** persuasive powers (*pl*), powers (*pl*) of persuasion **-talningsförsök** attempt at persuasion **-teckna** oversubscribe (*ett lån* a loan) **-teckning** oversubscription

över|tid overtime; *arbeta på* ~ work overtime **-tidsarbete** overtime [work] **-tidsblockad** overtime ban **-tidsersättning** overtime pay [ment] (compensation) **-tolka** overinterprete **-ton** overtone (*äv. bildl.*) **-tramp** *sport.* failure; *göra* ~ overstep the mark (*äv. bildl.*) **-trassera** overdraw **-trassering** overdraft **-tro** (*vidskepelse*) superstition; (*blind tro*) blind faith (*på* in) **-trumfa** *bildl.* go one better than, outdo **-tryck** **1** *fys.* overpressure; (*över atmosfärtrycket*) pressure exceeding atmospheric pressure **2** (*påtryck*) overprint **-trycksventil** pressure relief valve **-träda** transgress; (*förbud*) infringe, break; (*kränka*) violate **-trädelse** transgression; infringement, breach; violation; trespass; ~ *beivras* trespassers will be prosecuted **-träffa** surpass, exceed; (*besegra*) outdo, *vard.* beat; ~ *ngn i ngt* be better than s.b. in (at) s.th.; ~ *sig själv* surpass (excel) o.s. **-tydlig** overexplicit

över|tyga convince (*om* of; *om att* that); *du kan vara* ~*d om att* you may rest assured that; ~ *sig om ngt* make sure of (ascertain) s.th. **-tygande** *a4* convincing; (*i ord äv.*) persuasive; (*bindande äv.*) cogent, conclusive **-tygelse** conviction; (*tro*) belief; *i den fasta* ~*n att* in the firm conviction that, being firmly convinced that; *handla mot sin* ~ act against one's convictions **-täcka** cover **-tänd** *a5, byggnaden var helt* ~ the building was all in flames **-tänkt** *a4, ett väl* ~ *svar* a well-considered answer

över|upplaga *boktr.* [over]plus; over copies (*pl*) **-uppseende, -uppsikt** superintendence, supervision **-uppsyningsman** [chief] supervisor (overseer, inspector) **-utbilda** overeducate

över|vaka superintend, supervise; ~ (*tillse*) *att* see [to it] that **-vakare** supervisor; (*av villkorligt dömd*) probation officer **-vakning** [-a:-] supervision, superintendence; (*av villkorligt dömd*) probation; *stå under* ~ be on probation **-vara** *-var -varit* (*pres. saknas*) attend, be present at; *festen -vars av Mr. S.* Mr. S. was present at the party **-vattensläge** surface position **-vikt** **1** *eg.* overweight, excess (surplus) weight; (*bagage-äv.*) excess luggage (*AE.* baggage); *betala* ~ pay [an] excess luggage charge **2** *bildl.* predominance, preponderance, advantage; *få* (*ha*) ~*en* (*äv.*) predominate, preponderate **-viktig** *al* overweight, too heavy **-vinna** overcome; (*besegra äv.*) vanquish, conquer, defeat; ~ *en fiende* overcome an enemy; ~ *sina betänkligheter* overcome one's scruples; ~ *sig själv* get the better of

Ö

o.s. **-vintra** pass the winter, winter; (*ligga i ide*) hibernate **-vintring** wintering; (*i ide*) hibernation **-vunnen** *a5, det är ett -vunnet stadium* that is a thing of the past, I have got over that stage **-vuxen** overgrown; ~ *med ogräs* (*äv.*) overrun with weeds **-våld** outrage; *jur.* assault **-våning** upper floor (storey)

1 övervägla (*noga genomtänka*) reflect [up]on, ponder over; (*betänka*) consider; (*överlägga med sig själv*) deliberate; (*planera*) contemplate, plan; *i väl -da ordalag* in well-considered words; *när man -er vad* considering what; *jag skall ~ saken* I will consider the matter (think the matter over); *ett väl -t beslut* a well-considered decision **2 övervägla** (*väga mer än*) outweigh; (*överstiga i antal*) be in majority; *fördelarna -er olägenheterna* the advantages outweigh the disadvantages

1 övervägande *s6* consideration; deliberation; *ta ngt i* (*under*) ~ take s.th. into consideration; *efter moget* ~ after careful consideration; *vid närmare* ~ on [further] consideration, on second thoughts

2 övervägande I *a4* predominant, preponderating; *den ~ delen* the greater part, the majority; *frågan är med ~ ja besvarad* the great majority is in favour, the ayes have it; *till ~ del* mainly, chiefly; **II** *adv* (*t. största delen*) mainly, chiefly; ~ *vackert väder* mainly fair

över|väldiga overpower, overwhelm (*äv. bildl.*); *~d av trötthet* overcome by fatigue **-väldigande** *a4* overpowering, overwhelming; *en ~ majoritet* an overwhelming (a crushing) majority **-vältra** ~ *ansvaret på* shift the responsibility on **-värdera** overestimate, overrate, overvalue

-värme (*t.ex. i ugn*) heat from above, top heat **-växel** (*i bil*) overdrive **-årig** *a1* (*över viss ålder*) overage, above the prescribed age; (*över pensionsålder*) superannuated **-ösa** ~ *ngn med ngt* shower (heap) s.th. upon s.b.

övlig [ˣöːv-] usual, customary; *på ~t sätt* in the usual manner

övning [ˣöːv-] **1** (*övande*) practice; (*träning*) training; ~ *ger färdighet* practice makes perfect; *sakna ~ i* have no (be out of) practice in (*att teckna* drawing) **2** (*utövning*) exercise; ~*ar* (*äv.*) practice (*sg*); *andliga* (*gymnastiska*) ~*ar* religious (physical) exercises

övnings|bil driving-school car; learner's car **-exempel** exercise; *mat. o.d.* problem **-flygning** training (practice) flight **-fält** *mil.* training (drill) ground **-häfte** exercise book, notebook **-köra** learn how to drive; get driving practice **-körning** practice driving **-lärare** teacher in a practical subject **-område** *mil.* military training (manoeuvres) area **-uppgift** exercise **-ämne** *skol.* practical subject

övre [ˈöːv-] *komp. a* upper; (*översta äv.*) top

övrig [ˣöːv-] *a1* (*återstående*) remaining; (*annan*) other; *det ~a* the rest (remainder); *de ~a* the others, the rest (*sg*); *lämna mycket ~t att önska* leave a great deal to be desired; *det ~a Sverige* the rest of Sweden; *för ~t a*) (*annars*) otherwise, in other respects, for (as to) the rest, b) (*dessutom*) besides, moreover, c) (*i förbigående sagt*) by the way, incidentally

övärld archipelago (*pl* archipelagos)

ÖÄ *förk. för överståthållarämbetet*